The Rev'd Dr. Graeme Smith

1997

To Graeme

with lots of love and

pride

from Mum.

A HISTORY OF
THE ECUMENICAL MOVEMENT
1517–1948

A HISTORY OF
THE ECUMENICAL
MOVEMENT
1517 – 1948

EDITED BY

RUTH ROUSE

AND

STEPHEN CHARLES NEILL

FOURTH EDITION

WORLD COUNCIL OF CHURCHES
GENEVA

First published in 1954 by SPCK, London,
and The Westminster Press, Philadelphia
Second edition, 1967
Third edition, 1986
Fourth edition, 1993

ISBN 2-8254-1110-8

TO

THE DISCIPLES OF CHRIST

Whose untiring ecumenical spirit

has once again been manifest

in the generous provision of the funds

which have made possible the writing and publication

of this

HISTORY OF THE ECUMENICAL MOVEMENT

CONTENTS

CONTENTS

2. ECUMENICAL ACTIVITY ON THE CONTINENT OF EUROPE IN THE SEVENTEENTH AND EIGHTEENTH CENTURIES

by Martin Schmidt

7. VOLUNTARY MOVEMENTS AND THE CHANGING
ECUMENICAL CLIMATE
by Ruth Rouse

8. ECUMENICAL BEARINGS OF THE MISSIONARY MOVEMENT
AND THE INTERNATIONAL MISSIONARY COUNCIL
by Kenneth Scott Latourette

9. THE WORLD CONFERENCE ON FAITH AND ORDER
by Tissington Tatlow

10. PLANS OF UNION AND REUNION, 1910–1948
by Stephen Charles Neill

11. MOVEMENTS FOR INTERNATIONAL FRIENDSHIP AND LIFE AND WORK, 1910–1925
by Nils Karlström

CONTENTS

12. MOVEMENTS FOR INTERNATIONAL FRIENDSHIP AND LIFE AND WORK, 1925–1948
by Nils Ehrenström

13. OTHER ASPECTS OF THE ECUMENICAL MOVEMENT, 1910–1948
by Ruth Rouse
(based on memoranda by Dr H. Paul Douglass and Dr R. H. Edwin Espy)

14. THE EASTERN CHURCHES AND THE ECUMENICAL MOVEMENT IN THE TWENTIETH CENTURY
by Nicolas Zernov

CONTENTS

ABBREVIATIONS

Amsterdam 1948	The First Assembly of the World Council of Churches held at Amsterdam, 22 August to 4 September 1948
A.P.U.C.	Association for the Promotion of the Unity of Christendom
C.C.I.A.	Commission of the Churches on International Affairs
C.I.C.C.U.	Cambridge Inter-Collegiate Christian Union
C.I.M.A.D.E., or Cimade	*Comité Inter-Mouvements auprès des Evacués*
C.M.S.	Church Missionary Society
C.O.P.E.C., or Copec	Conference on Christian Politics, Economics, and Citizenship at Birmingham, 5–12 April 1924
C.R.	Community of the Resurrection, Mirfield
D. Th. C.	*Dictionnaire de théologie catholique*
E.C.A.	Eastern Church Association
E.C.C.O.	Emergency Committee of Christian Organizations
E.C.Q.	*Eastern Churches Quarterly*
ed.	Edited by; or editor
Edinburgh 1910	World Missionary Conference held at Edinburgh, 14–23 June 1910
Edinburgh 1937	The Second World Conference on Faith and Order held at Edinburgh, 3–18 August 1937
Eng. tr.	English translation
F. and O., or Faith and Order	The World Conference on Faith and Order
Federal Council	The Federal Council of the Churches of Christ in America
Fr. tr.	French translation
Ger. tr.	German translation
ibid.	*ibidem*, the same author in the same context
I.C.R.E.	International Council of Religious Education
id.	*idem*, the same author
I.F.O.R.	International Fellowship of Reconciliation
I.K.Z.	*Internationale Kirchliche Zeitschrift*
I.L.O.	International Labour Office, Geneva
I.M.C.	International Missionary Council
I.R.M.	*International Review of Missions*
I.T.Z.	*Internationale Theologische Zeitschrift*
I.V.F.	Inter-Varsity Fellowship
Jerusalem 1928	Meeting of the International Missionary Council, Jerusalem, 24 March–8 April 1928
Lausanne 1927	The World Conference on Faith and Order, Lausanne, 3–21 August 1927
Life and Work	The Universal Christian Council for Life and Work
L.M.S.	London Missionary Society
L.W.F.	Lutheran World Federation
Madras 1938	Meeting of the International Missionary Council, Tambaram, Madras, India, 12–29 December 1938
M.P.	Member of Parliament (in Britain)
N.C.C.	National Christian Council
n.d.	Undated; no date
nem. con.	*Nemine contradicente*, without opposition

n.p.	No place of publication shown
O.G.S.	Oratory of the Good Shepherd
O.P.	Order of Preachers (Dominican)
op. cit.	*opus citatum*, the work already quoted
O.S.B.	Order of St Benedict
Oxford 1937	The Conference at Oxford, July 1937, on Church, Community, and State
S.C.M.	Student Christian Movement
S.I.U.C.	South India United Church
S.J.	The Society of Jesus
S.P.C.K.	Society for Promoting Christian Knowledge
S.P.G.	Society for the Propagation of the Gospel in Foreign Parts
S.S.J.E.	Society of St John the Evangelist, Cowley
Stockholm 1925	The Universal Christian Conference on Life and Work held in Stockholm, 19–30 August 1925
S.V.M.	Student Volunteer Movement
S.V.M.U.	Student Volunteer Missionary Union
Tambaram	See Madras 1938
Th. Lit. Z.	*Theologische Literaturzeitung*
W.C.C.	The World Council of Churches
W.C.C.E.	The World Council of Christian Education
Whitby 1947	The Enlarged Meeting of the International Missionary Council and of the Committee of the Council, Whitby, Ontario, Canada, 5–24 July 1947
World Alliance	The World Alliance for Promoting International Friendship through the Churches
W.S.C.F.	The World's Student Christian Federation
Y.M.C.A.	The Young Men's Christian Association, or The World's Alliance of Young Men's Christian Associations
Y.W.C.A.	The Young Women's Christian Association, or The World's Young Women's Christian Association

CONTRIBUTORS

BRANDRETH, Henry Renaud Turner. Priest of the Oratory of the Good Shepherd. Vicar of St Saviour's Church, Highbury, London, N.5. Author of *Unity and Reunion: a Bibliography*, 1945; *The Oecumenical Ideals of the Oxford Movement*, 1947, etc.

EHRENSTRÖM, Nils, Th.D., Professor of Ecumenics, Boston, University School of Theology. Formerly Director of the Study Department of the World Council of Churches and Assistant Editor of *The Ecumenical Review*. Author of *Christian Faith and the Modern State*, 1937, etc.

FLOROVSKY, Georges, D.D. Formerly Professor of Eastern Church History, Harvard Divinity School, and Dean of the Orthodox Theological Seminary of St Vladimir, New York City. Author of *Eastern Fathers of the Fourth Century*; *The Ways of Russian Theology* (in Russian), 1937, etc.

KARLSTRÖM, Dean Nils, Th.D., Dean of Skara, Sweden. Author of *Kristna Samförstandssträyanden under Världskriget*, 1914–1918, 1947, etc.; and Editor of *Kristen Gemenskap* since 1928.

LATOURETTE, Kenneth Scott, Ph.D., D.D., S.T.D., D.Sc.Rel., Litt.D., L.H.D., LL.D. Sterling Professor of Missions and Oriental History, Emeritus, and Associate Fellow of Berkeley College in Yale University. Author of *A History of Christian Missions in China*, 1929; *A History of the Expansion of Christianity*, 1937–45; *A History of Christianity*, 1953, etc.

McNEILL, John Thomas, Ph.D., D.D., LL.D. Auburn Professor Emeritus at Union Theological Seminary, New York City. Author of *Unitive Protestantism*, 1930; *Modern Christian Movements*, 1954, etc.

NEILL, Bishop Stephen Charles, D.D. Visiting Professor of Missions, University of Hamburg. Formerly Fellow of Trinity College, Cambridge. Bishop of Tinnevelly, 1939–45. Author of *Christ, his Church, and his World*, 1948; *The Christian Society*, 1952; *Towards Church Union*, 1937–52, 1952; *Christian Holiness*, 1960; *The Unfinished Task*, 1957, etc.

ROUSE, Ruth, D.Litt. *Died* 1956. Formerly a secretary of the World's Student Christian Federation, 1905–24. Editorial and Education Secretary to the Missionary Council of the Church Assembly, 1925–38. President of the World's Young Women's Christian Association, 1938–46. Editorial Secretary to the Committee on the History of the Ecumenical Movement, 1948–54. Author of *Rebuilding Europe*, 1925; *The World's Student Christian Federation*, 1948, etc.

SCHMIDT, Martin, Th.D. Professor of Church History, University of Mainz. Formerly Professor at the Kirchliche Hochschule, Berlin. Author of *John Wesley*, 1953; *Geschichte der evangelischen Theologie seit dem deutschen Idealismus*, 1959, etc.

SYKES, Norman, D.D., D.Litt. *Died* 1961. Formerly Dean of Winchester, England, and Dixie Professor of Ecclesiastical History, University of Cambridge. Author of *Church and State in England in the Eighteenth Century*, 1934; *Man as Churchman*, 1960, etc.

TATLOW, Tissington, D.D. *Died* 1957. Formerly Secretary of the Student Christian Movement of Great Britain and Ireland, 1903–29; Hon. Canon of

Canterbury Cathedral. Secretary of the Institute of Christian Education. Author of *The Story of the Student Christian Movement*, 1932, etc.

TOMKINS, *Bishop* Oliver Stratford, D.D. Bishop of Bristol, England. Chairman of the Working Committee of the Faith and Order Commission of the World Council of Churches. Author of *The Wholeness of the Church*, 1950; *A Time for Unity*, 1964, etc.

VISSER 'T HOOFT, Willem Adolf, Th.D., D.D. General Secretary of the World Council of Churches until December, 1966. Editor of *The Ecumenical Review*. Author of *The Pressure of our Common Calling*, 1959; *The Renewal of the Church*, 1956; *No Other Name*, 1963.

YODER, Don Herbert, Ph.D. Assistant Professor of Religious Thought, University of Pennsylvania. Co-founder and Director of Pennsylvania Dutch Folklore Centre. Writer on the ecumenical movement in the U.S.A.

ZERNOV, Nicolas, D.Phil. Spalding Lecturer in Eastern Orthodox Culture, University of Oxford. Formerly Principal of the Catholicate College of Pathanamthitta, South India. Author of *The Russians and their Church*, 1945; *The Reintegration of the Church*, 1952; *The Christian East*, 1956, etc.

PREFACE TO THE FOURTH EDITION

The two titles included in this volume — *A History of the Ecumenical Movement 1517-1948* and *The Ecumenical Advance 1948-1968* — were originally published jointly by SPCK and Westminster Press and reprinted in 1986 by WCC Publications. Although there are other histories of the ecumenical movement, they still represent the only "official" literature on the subject.

The World Council of Churches itself was involved in the choice of writers and editors and in the final production of the titles. The aim was to present a detailed and impartial account of the many ecumenical impulses, initiatives and activities during these centuries, and to make a systematic survey of the ecumenical history of the churches.

Taking the Reformation as its starting point, the first title covers four centuries of varied endeavours towards church unity in Europe and North America. In particular it deals with the Faith and Order, World Mission and Evangelism, and Life and Work movements in the twentieth century, which led to the formation of the World Council of Churches.

The second title is mainly concerned with developments within the World Council, its programmes and activities, from 1948 through the Fourth Assembly at Uppsala in 1968. It also includes chapters on the Orthodox and Roman Catholic involvement in the ecumenical movement, on the origin and growth of national and regional councils of churches, and on the part played by confessional families in the ecumenical movement from 1948 onwards.

It has often been pointed out that as the ecumenical pioneers of the twentieth century pass from the scene, we suffer from a loss of "ecumenical memory". Even those committed to the ecumenical cause often work with only limited knowledge of past ecumenical efforts and of the continuity in the programmes, concerns and activities of the World Council of Churches and other ecumenical bodies since 1948. These volumes continue to refresh our memory and can broaden our perspective. For, when the past is forgotten, the present loses perspective and the future lacks direction. More recent trends and developments, which have become increasingly complex and controversial, can be recorded and evaluated only if the challenge, the vision and the enthusiasm of earlier decades are newly experienced.

These two titles have been out of print for some time. It is our hope that their re-publication now, in one volume, will be of help to both individuals and institutions.

Konrad Raiser
General Secretary
World Council of Churches

Geneva

FOREWORD

The production of *A History of the Ecumenical Movement* has been an enterprise sponsored by the Ecumenical Institute at Bossey near Geneva, Switzerland. The work was made possible through the generous financial support of the Disciples of Christ in America, who first made a large initial grant to the funds of the Institute for this purpose, and, when it became apparent that through lapse of time this would not be sufficient to carry the enterprise to completion, made further considerable allocations of funds.

Naturally, the World Council of Churches has been much concerned in the work. The Council, even while it was still "in process of formation", had taken steps to promote the writing of such a History; and reports on the progress of this volume have regularly been presented at meetings of its Central and Executive Committees. But this History is in no sense an official publication of the World Council of Churches; the Council is not responsible for anything contained in the volume except the quotations from its official publications, and is not bound by any of the opinions expressed by the authors in the exercise of their individual liberty. Exactly the same is, of course, true of the Ecumenical Institute, which, in sponsoring the writing of the History, has not accepted responsibility for all or any of the statements contained in it.

The History, while not in the strictest sense of the term a pioneer work, has attempted something which has previously been only rarely attempted in Christian historiography.

Divisions have existed in the Christian society since the period of the New Testament. Church History has often been written in terms of those divisions. It had long been felt that the time had come when the history of the Church should be treated from the opposite point of view, in the light of the earnest unitive efforts by which almost every century has been marked. The suggestion for the writing of an ecumenical history was made a quarter of a century ago. Then the times were not propitious; but perhaps this was no disadvantage, since these twenty-five years have contributed so rich a harvest of ecumenical material. The terms of reference of this History were that it should treat of the efforts made across the centuries to secure (1) co-operation between Christians belonging to different confessions and Churches, (2) co-operation between the several Churches and confessions, (3) union or reunion of separated Churches, (4) the full and final restoration of the unity of all Christendom. It is probable that most readers will be astonished to learn how deep, widespread, and unfailing the longing for Christian unity has been in the Churches.

By 1946 general plans for the writing of an ecumenical history had been developed by a Committee earlier formed under the chairmanship of a veteran of the ecumenical cause, Professor Adolph Keller of Zurich. Much attention was devoted to the choice of authors for the several chapters, and all those who were invited to contribute were invited also to join the Committee. The Ecumenical Institute was represented on the Committee by its Director, Professor Hendrik Kraemer. Other members were Professor Jaques Courvoisier, Dean of the Faculty of Theology in the University of Geneva; Curé L. Gauthier of the Old Catholic Church in Geneva (from 1951); and Pastor Henry Louis Henriod,

xxiii

formerly General Secretary of the World Alliance for Promoting International Friendship through the Churches and of the Universal Christian Council for Life and Work. Professor Keller served as Chairman through the whole period of the production of the History. In 1946 Miss Ruth Rouse was invited to help in the work; in 1948 she became Editorial Secretary, and was responsible for the direction and for the detailed planning of the work, as well as for the writing of two chapters. The Executive Vice-Chairman, Bishop Stephen Neill, in addition to his written contributions, devoted much time from 1947 onwards, and from October 1951 to December 1953 almost the whole of his time, to comprehensive editorial work.

The Committee had first to decide where the History should begin and where it should end. The Reformation was chosen as the starting-point. Certainly ecumenical effort did not begin in 1517. Some day a comparable study should be made of the unitive efforts of the Churches in earlier centuries. But this seemed too large a task to be undertaken all at once, and no more was found possible in this History than a very brief survey, in the Introduction, of those earlier ecumenical movements. The History was planned to end with the First Assembly of the World Council of Churches in 1948. The ecumenical movement is not to be identified with the formation of the World Council; but that event was something so new in the history of the Churches, and summed up so much that had gone before, that it seemed to mark a reasonable conclusion for this study. There are, however, no real ends in history. Amsterdam 1948, as seen in the perspective of 1954, is already part of ecumenical history; and the editorial guillotine has not fallen too rigidly on 6 September 1948.

A further problem was that of scale. At an early meeting of the Committee, it was decided that the aim was not to produce an encyclopedia of ecumenism, but to set forth a plain and readable narrative of ecumenical happenings and developments over four centuries. It was suggested that a volume of roughly 400,000 words represented the limits within which this could be done—a remarkably prophetic estimate of the size of the present volume. But this has meant that much has had to be omitted which might have been included, and that only an outline has been given of much that might better have been treated on an ampler scale. It is hoped that the fairly full Bibliography which has been provided may be sufficient to guide students who wish to undertake further investigations in any particular direction. It has been found, in the course of the preparation of the History, that on many ecumenical subjects no full and reliable study has yet been published. A list of such subjects is being prepared, and will be available at World Council headquarters, in the hope that some students of this volume may be encouraged to undertake some of the research which will be needed before a definitive ecumenical history can be written.

The reader will notice a difference of scale between the earlier and the later chapters. Events up to 1910 have been treated in outline; those after 1910 in considerable detail. The year 1910 saw the holding of the World Missionary Conference at Edinburgh, the importance of which as an ecumenical watershed, and as in many respects the starting-point of the modern ecumenical movement, has been emphasized in many contexts in the History. Since that date, ecumenical progress has been so varied and so rapid as to appear to justify that fuller treatment without which the significance of the events of 1948 could not be made clear.

By October 1947 sixteen authors, representing many different countries and confessions, had been chosen and invited to contribute chapters. All accepted the invitation. Three, however, were unable to bring to completion the work that they had undertaken, and were replaced by others. Otherwise the list of contributors, as printed in this volume, is that of those who originally received the invitation.

It was made plain to the authors that the aim was the production of a History and not of a series of detached essays, and that therefore considerably more co-operation would be required than would have been necessary if a mere symposium had been the object. A special debt of gratitude is owed to the authors for their willing acceptance of this principle, and for their gracious readiness to revise and rewrite in the light of the development of the work as a whole. As soon as each chapter was ready in first draft, it was sent out to a large number of consultants for frank comment and criticism. Altogether about two hundred consultants, in every part of the world and representing all the larger branches of the Christian Church, made their contribution in this way. Several conferences of authors were held, and helped to produce a common mind. Friends of the movement contributed memoranda, which are listed in the Bibliography. Experts were consulted on a large number of particular points. All these methods helped to make the production of the History what it was always intended that it should be—a genuinely ecumenical effort.

The aim which the Committee and the authors set before themselves was the production of a straightforward History which could be read with profit, and even with pleasure, by any serious friend of the ecumenical movement. But inevitably the History traverses fields which are unfamiliar even to professed students of ecclesiastical history, and a complete avoidance of technical terms has been impossible. It is hoped that the full Table of Contents, the captions to the pages, cross-references in the text, the Glossary and Explanatory Notes, and the Index will enable the reader to understand what he reads, and to find his way without difficulty about the History.

For the moment the History is published only in English; but tentative plans have already been set in motion for French and German translations, and it seems evident that there will be a demand for versions, complete or abridged, in a number of other languages.

To thank all who have contributed to the production of the History would extend this Foreword beyond all reasonable limits. But there are a few to whom, even in a brief Foreword, gratitude must formally be expressed: to Dr W. A. Visser 't Hooft, General Secretary of the World Council of Churches, for constant encouragement and advice; to Mr John Mackintosh for the preparation of the Index; to Professor Claire Éliane Engel of the University of Geneva for help in reading the proofs; to Miss H. Leckie, Librarian of the World Council; and not least to the two office secretaries, Miss Nancy Tredgold (1949–51) and Miss Hilary Geddie (1951–54), who endured patiently and efficiently the handling of masses of intractable and not infrequently illegible material. The Committee has been well served by the publishers and printers of this volume.

The reader may feel that there is an evident timeliness in the publication of this work. It is obvious that there are strong powers at work in our world to-day, reactionary powers of introverted self-sufficiency, producing stagnation in the Churches and preventing them from answering the call of the Master of the Church as expressed in his missionary command. A Church, however, which is content with the stage of progress attained, and does not realize that every

Church lives by continuous revival through the Spirit of the Lord, will perish, or at least will become as salt which has lost its savour.

Church History also proves that an alliance of well-organized and well-administered Churches may sometimes be of little significance, unless it is embedded in the living action of God and in the living witness of the disciples of Jesus Christ who, through faith and loyalty, through obedience, through service and sacrifice, fulfil the commission of the Church in this world. A movement is not the Church, and the Church is much more than a sum total of movements. Yet movements must not be lacking, lest the message and the witness of the Church should become unworthy of credence, and its claim to be the shining light on the path of the world should lose its validity.

It is for this reason that every Christian ought to be familiar with ecumenism; for the whole Christian Church is involved in the solution of the problems which are presented to our generation by the striving for oneness in Jesus Christ.

This History is not a work of propaganda. It attempts to set forth soberly and impartially what has happened over more than four centuries in one important field of Christian endeavour. But it will be strange if the reader does not discover that those who have been concerned in this work are men and women committed to a cause. They have undertaken this labour because they believe that the ecumenical movement has come into being through the movement of the Spirit of God in the Churches, that it is only in its beginnings, and that the further development of it is one of the most exacting tasks laid upon the Churches in the 20th century. They will be well satisfied if the study of this record of service and devotion to a cause leads the reader to a like dedication, and to a sense of responsibility to pray and work for the restoration of the visible unity of all Christian people.

January 1954   REINOLD VON THADDEN-TRIEGLAFF,
Chairman of the Board of the Ecumenical Institute,
Château de Bossey, Switzerland.

FOREWORD TO THE SECOND EDITION

A History of the Ecumenical Movement, 1517–1948 has been out of print for a number of years. So many requests have been received by the World Council of Churches for the volume to be reprinted that it has been decided to make it available once more to those who wish to be informed about the history and development of the ecumenical movement since the Reformation.

As, however, it is only ten years since this book was first published and a basic revision would delay the publication of this edition for a long time, it has been thought unnecessary to engage in any substantial re-editing or rewriting of the text at the present time; but the opportunity has been taken to correct errors of fact.

The increasing interest that is being taken in ecumenical studies has resulted in a wealth of material becoming available to the scholar, but it is still too soon to recognize clearly whether our understanding of early phases of the movement calls for any significant change or reassessment. Consequently, although the bibliography has been carefully checked, corrected, and augmented by approximately two hundred important titles of books dealing with the ecumenical history until 1948, it remains essentially a selective, and not a comprehensive, list of works and frequently refers the reader to other sources where more detailed bibliographical information may be found.

The World Council of Churches recently set up a new Committee on the History of the Ecumenical Movement. This Committee is preparing a second, shorter volume which will cover the main ecumenical developments since 1948, including the Fourth Assembly of the World Council of Churches in 1968. It is hoped that this companion volume will be ready for publication in the latter part of 1969.

THE COMMITTEE ON THE HISTORY
OF THE ECUMENICAL MOVEMENT

Geneva
September 1965.

DIVISION AND THE SEARCH FOR UNITY PRIOR TO THE REFORMATION

1. THE COMMUNITY OF CHRISTIANS

By the middle of the first century, the Roman world was becoming aware of a new community which had grown up in its midst, a community the members of which were known, at first apparently by their enemies and with somewhat contemptuous implications, as Christians. This name was attached to them because of their relationship to one Jesus of Nazareth, called Christ, who had been crucified in Judaea in the days when Pontius Pilate was procurator. The community included both Jews and non-Jews. From the Jews it was distinguished by its affirmation that Jesus was the Messiah, the expected King of Israel; from the Gentiles by the fact that its members no longer worshipped idols. From both sides it had to endure persecution; from the Jews because they had rightly understood that, if the beliefs of the Christians came to be accepted, the venerable Jewish ordinances of the temple, the law, and the sacrifices would be superseded and vanish away; from the Gentiles because they had understood, also rightly, that the Christians were proclaiming an authority higher than that of the Emperor, and were thereby undermining the foundations on which the Roman Empire rested.

Such was the Christian community, the "third race",[1] as seen from the outside. But a community can live and grow only if it has not merely a negative principle of separation from that which surrounds it, but also a strong inner principle of unity to hold it together. The Christians professed to be one people. In what did the inner unity of the fellowship consist?

It was a fellowship of love. It was understood that this special character had been appointed for it by its Founder: "By this shall all men know that ye are my disciples, if ye have love one to another" (John 13.35). St Paul recognizes that among Christians, even with all their imperfections, love of the brethren is the natural state of affairs: "Concerning love of the brethren ye have no need that one write unto you: for ye yourselves are taught of God to love one another" (1 Thess. 4.9). This love was so strong that it could treat as of no account the natural divisions of race and class—Jew and Gentile, Greek and barbarian, master and slave, were all at one within it. It found its expression in such remarkable manifestations as the sharing of goods in the earliest church at Jerusalem, and the great collection on behalf of the poor saints in Jerusalem organized by St Paul among the churches of the Gentiles. Even outsiders recognized that the distinguishing mark of the Christians was that they loved one another.

It was a fellowship of faith. The earliest confession of faith may have been no more than the affirmation "Jesus is Lord". Yet much was implied in that brief phrase: it involved the acceptance of Jesus as the promised Messiah, and therefore an attitude to the past, and in particular to the Old Testament Scriptures;

---

[1] The unsocial Jews being known in the Greco-Roman world as "the second race", this title was scornfully applied to the Christians by their enemies.

it involved the belief that Jesus was coming again with power to judge and to establish the reign of God, and therefore an attitude of expectancy towards the future.

The working out of the implications of this faith followed three main lines. There was first the steady development of Christian exegesis of the Old Testament, and in particular of what were recognized as messianic prophecies. There was the recalling of the words of Jesus and their application to present circumstances, that process of the building up of an oral tradition which lies behind the first written Gospel. There was the interpretation of the living experience of the Church through the teaching of inspired apostles and prophets. Such theological developments obviously held out the possibility of wide divergences, and such in fact existed; the interpretations of Jesus given by Paul, by John, in the Epistle to the Hebrews, and in the Apocalypse, are strikingly original and different. Yet more impressive than the diversity is the underlying unity, which makes of the New Testament as a whole a single united witness to the work of God in Jesus Christ.

It was a unity of worship. In the early days, Christians were faithful worshippers in temple and synagogue; and, even after the break with Judaism had become decisive, they followed in many things the ancient Jewish traditions. But from the beginning there had been two specifically Christian elements in worship. St Paul, enumerating the factors of unity in the Church, includes "one Lord, one faith, one *baptism*" (Eph. 4.5). The author of the Acts, depicting the unity of spirit of the earliest believers, states that "they continued stedfastly in the apostles' teaching and fellowship, in the breaking of bread and the prayers" (Acts 2.42). The breaking of bread can hardly be other than the first simple beginnings of what in course of time became the splendid elaboration of the Christian Eucharist. The exact relationship between the teaching of Jesus and these two sacramental ordinances is a matter of theological discussion; there is no doubt that the early Christians, in observing them from the beginning, believed that they were acting according to the mind of their Lord.

The problem of the relation of faith to baptism is not raised in the New Testament, the correspondence of one to the other as inward and outward being assumed. Baptism was "eschatological" in reference. One who was baptized was delivered from the old world-order, which is passing away to destruction, and made partaker of the new world-order, which is already present and operative in the resurrection of Christ, though hidden from the eyes of men. And this new world-order is that in which God is gathering all things together into unity in Jesus Christ.

Equally it was taken for granted that every baptized person would partake of the Table of the Lord. To be separated from it was the gravest judgement that could fall upon the Christian. The Eucharist, like baptism, was "eschatological" in reference; it is a sign, a proclaiming of the Lord's death till he come (1 Cor. 11.26). But it is also the sacrament of unity: "We, who are many, are one bread, one body: for we all partake of the one bread" (1 Cor. 10.17).

The fellowship was beginning to express itself in outward organization. The small Christian groups were scattered far and wide throughout the Roman world. Doubtless each enjoyed much independence in its local life. Yet it is a mistake to exaggerate their separateness. Travel in the first century was safe and rapid. The New Testament itself gives much evidence of coming and going among Christians, such as is confirmed also by later documents.

What later became the regular practice of letters of commendation from one church to another seems already to have taken its rise in the days of the New Testament (2 Cor. 3.1,2). In times of persecution, when an unknown visitor might well be a spy, it was necessary to inquire rather closely into his credentials; but once his *bona fides* was established, he became at once and fully a member of the Christian community in the place where he was.

We have much more information about the Pauline churches than about any others. It is evident that in them the Apostle played a most important rôle as the representative and guardian of unity. Each local church might have much independence; the Apostle might be a helper of their joy and not a lord over their faith (2 Cor. 1.24). Yet he did exercise an authority given him by Christ himself, to build up and not to destroy; he had and exercised the right to appoint elders, to send his deputies, to instruct, to exhort, to rebuke; and by his visits and his letters to bind the separate churches together in a sense of living unity.

Until the fall of Jerusalem in A.D. 70, the church of Jerusalem exercised a powerful influence as a centre of unity for the whole Church. To it St Paul went up to report on the success of his apostolic tours. Though not admitting any decisive authority of those "who were reputed to be pillars" (Gal. 2.9) over his own apostleship, he yet regarded it as essential to remain in fellowship with them. He taught regularly that support of the saints at Jerusalem was a spiritual duty incumbent on the churches of the Gentiles. It is not possible to define exactly the position of James, the brother of the Lord, in the church of Jerusalem; yet it is evident that, remaining always at Jerusalem, while other apostles travelled, he came to exercise great influence and authority, as the head of what all recognized to be the mother church of all the churches.

Experience comes before theology. The unity of the Christian fellowship was experienced in life before it was defined or explained. So far we have endeavoured to set forth some of the ways in which it was felt and manifested; but even in the period of the New Testament a large element of theological thought and interpretation about the Church is already present.

From an early date the new community began to think and speak of itself as the *Ekklesia*. The process by which this name came to be adopted, its relation to earlier Greek usage, to Aramaic equivalents, to Hebrew words and the rendering of them in the Septuagint, are subjects on which there is still more confident assertion than clear proof. It is evident, however, that there is a twofold use of the term in the New Testament. It may be used, in the singular, to denote the whole fellowship of Christ's people in all its scattered parts. But also in the singular, it may be used of a single Christian group in one local area; also (if, as seems probable, the singular is the correct reading in Acts 9.31: "the church throughout all Judaea and Galilee and Samaria") of the collectivity of such groups over a considerable area; and correspondingly in the plural of a number of Christian groups considered each in its separate existence.

Which came first, the whole or the part? The view has been maintained that the great *Ekklesia* came into being through the unification or coalescence of the separate parts: under the pressure of persecution and the need of fellowship, the local churches gradually formed themselves into a single whole, a kind of spiritual parallel to the Roman Empire. Such a view is not likely to find much support to-day, and the contrary interpretation is seen to be much more probable. Christ is one. From the start his people were felt to be one in him, sharing in a life derived from him. This view is confirmed by the real continuity of the people of God under the New Covenant with the people of God in the Old Testament. New Testament writers, with the utmost boldness, take over the Old Testament promises to Israel as being now applicable to the Church; the Church, as the new Israel, is the *Laos*, the People of God. Every Jewish synagogue in the Roman Empire was a part of the one people of Israel, its local manifestation; in the same way all the local churches, with the rich diversity of their life, were the local manifestations of a single redeemed people. The essential unity of the believers in Jesus was a part of the precious heritage which was transmitted from the old Israel to the new.

More than any other New Testament writer, St Paul is the theologian of the unity of the Church. His thought is developed mainly under the three images of the New Man, the Building, and the Body.

Christ is the last Adam (1 Cor. 15.45). In the first Adam, who sinned, the whole human race is a unity; in the last Adam, the whole redeemed race is equally a unity. Christ is himself the New Man, whom the believer is to put on through faith, in whom he is to be incorporated. And Christians, though many, are "one man in Christ Jesus" (Gal. 3.28; the true reading is not the uninteresting neuter, but the masculine, which gives a far more vivid, though perplexing, sense). Similarly, in Ephesians 4.13, "till we all attain unto the unity of the faith, and of the knowledge of the Son of God, unto a fullgrown man, unto the measure of the stature of the fulness of Christ", the better interpretation is not that any individual Christian as such will grow up into perfection (though it is true that it is only within the fellowship of the redeemed race that the individual will grow up into such perfection as he is capable of), but that the whole fellowship, indwelt by the Spirit of God and enriched by the gifts of each individual, will as a whole grow up to be the Christ, to realize in its own life what is already present in him, the one New Man.

For the metaphor of the Building, we may turn to Ephesians 2.19–22. By contrast with 1 Corinthians 3.11, where Jesus Christ is the foundation, here Jesus Christ is the chief corner-stone, whereas it is the apostles and prophets who are the foundation. This change may represent a certain shift of emphasis from an organic to an institutional point of view concerning the Church. Yet in the same passage the statement that the Building "groweth into a holy temple in the Lord" warns us that metaphors must not be pressed too far in theological interpretation, and that in the New Testament there is no sharp distinction between the Church as an organism and the Church as an institution.

The most characteristic of all Paul's images is that of the Church as the Body of Christ. Where this first appears, in 1 Corinthians 12, it is in connection with the doctrine of the Spirit, the diversity of whose operations within the Christian fellowship is compared to the different functions of the limbs in the human body. "Ye are the body of Christ, and severally members thereof." Diversity of operations should no more cause schism in the body of the Church than different physical functions cause schism in the natural body. Almost the same thought is expressed in Romans 12.5, except that here "we, who are many, are one body in Christ".

A deeper level of understanding is reached in the Epistle to the Ephesians. Here the starting-point is the purpose of God to "gather together in one all things in Christ" (1.10), to sum up, or to recapitulate, all things in him. The life of the Church is shown in a cosmic setting, as a crucial and central part of a universal purpose of God, a redemption wrought in Christ, through which in due course the whole wisdom of God is to be revealed. God "gave him to be head over all things to the church, which is his body, the fulness of him that filleth all in all" (1.22,23), or perhaps rather "of him who in every way in all things is being fulfilled". For the expression of Paul's thought at this point the word body is specially appropriate, since in his usage it always approaches near to the modern idea of organism. Body is that organic whole in which spirit clothes itself in order to become visible, and through which it works. God has been pleased to make his mysterious purpose manifest both to men and to principalities and powers, by working through a visible entity, the Church. But that Body has reality only in relation to its Head, on whom it entirely depends for life and for direction. Its unity within itself depends on its oneness with him. Its glory consists only in its total identification with him in his humiliation, in his sufferings, and in his triumph.[1]

It is typical of the paradox of the life of the Church, in its double character as the divinely constituted Body of Christ, and at the same time a human assemblage of very imperfect men and women, that the writer to the Ephesians, having, in the first part of his Epistle, in passage after passage of profound theology, laid the doctrinal foundation of the Church's unity, proceeds in the second part to recognize the possibility of division within that Body. He warns his readers (4.31) against bitterness, wrath, anger, clamour, railing, and malice—the characteristic causes and expressions of division. The unity of the Church is indeed divinely given, but it is a gift which must never be taken for granted. It must be striven for and enthusiastically safeguarded; otherwise it may be lost. The Epistle thus expresses in advance the apparent contradiction which runs through all Christian history and is the connecting thread in this History of the Ecumenical Movement—a recognition of that essential unity of all Christ's people, which though often obscured is never wholly lost; and the ever-repeated development of misunderstanding, contention, and division within the one fellowship. From this contradiction the Church was not free even in the period of the New Testament.

Some divisions, such as those which arose between Euodias and Syntyche at Philippi, seem to have been no more than the result of personal incompatibility between otherwise devout members of the Church. Faction at Corinth between the supporters of Paul and Cephas and Apollos seems to have arisen partly from personal loyalties to outstanding leaders, partly from differing emphases in doctrinal interpretation of the one Faith—both fruitful sources of later division in the Church. The unpleasant figure of Diotrephes in 3 John, who "loveth to have the preeminence among them" and claims the right to expel brethren from the Church, seems to represent that intolerant and censorious spirit which underlay many of the later disputes concerning problems of discipline in the Church.

All these were local problems. Far more serious was the first great controversy, that concerning the admission of the Gentiles without circumcision, which threatened to rend the young Church in pieces. The storm centre was Antioch. When emissaries from James came down and persuaded even Peter to separate

---

[1] The question of the Pauline authorship of the Epistle to the Ephesians does not affect the argument, since the Epistle can be accepted as an expression of Pauline theology, even though the hand that wrote it may not have been that of the Apostle himself.

himself from table-fellowship with the Gentiles (Gal. 2.11–14), Paul recognized that a crisis had arisen in which the unity of the Church might be finally lost. According to the most probable interpretation, arrangements were being accepted for two separate Eucharists, for the circumcised and the uncircumcised respectively. Since the fellowship of the Eucharist was the very heart of Christian unity, acquiescence in division at this point on racial or ceremonial grounds would in fact have meant the end of the unity of the Body, as the Church was coming to understand it. This has been a recurrent danger all through the history of the Church, whenever divisions based on race, caste, or colour have been allowed to break the unity of believers at the Table of the Lord. For the moment a mediating policy, as set forth in Acts 15 in the account of the Council at Jerusalem, averted this great peril. Fellowship on the basis of grace received through faith and expressed in baptism was proclaimed as the foundation of the Church, and from that foundation the Church has never since in principle departed. Yet many allusions in the Epistles show that to the end of his life Paul was followed by the embittered and relentless hostility of a party within the Church which regarded him as a traitor and a destroyer.

This continuing hostility may serve to remind us that, in the opinion of many Christians, far more serious than any division within the Church was the original schism within the People of God, as a result of which Church and synagogue have gone separate ways. This History deals only with Christian history. But a Biblical theology of redintegration, as outlined by St Paul in the 9th, 10th, and 11th chapters of the Epistle to the Romans, does not regard the restoration as complete until the old Israel and the new are reconciled and united in the adoration and service of the one Messiah.

The strained and twisted style of the Epistle to the Galatians reveals to us something of the intensity of the conflicts of long ago. Yet these tensions were still felt to be in the nature of family quarrels; they were divisions of view and practice within the Church, they were not yet divisions *of* the Church or schisms *from* it. Paul in prison at Rome can rejoice over the preaching of his opponents, since, even though their motives may be questionable, in one way or another Christ is being preached and that is the principal thing (Phil. 1.15–18). Fellowship may have been strained, but it has not wholly been destroyed.

Before the end of the New Testament period, however, darker shadows had begun to close in upon the Church. The writer of the Johannine Epistles, for example, has to warn his readers against false teachers who deny both the Father and the Son. The spirit of antichrist is that which denies that Jesus the Messiah is come in the flesh. From those who so radically change the original Gospel, there must be complete separation: "If any one cometh unto you, and bringeth not this teaching, receive him not into your house, and give him no greeting: for he that giveth him greeting partaketh in his evil works" (2 John 10,11).

The Church was face to face with the Docetists, who, in favour of a supposedly more spiritual view of the divine nature, denied the incarnation and the passion of the Son of God. This was perhaps the first form in which Gnosticism made its entry into the Church. This movement, which seems to have had a strange attraction for the speculative temperament of the Levant, existed in so many and bewildering forms that it is difficult to define it briefly. It may, however, be said that Gnosticism in all its forms involved a view of matter as in itself inherently evil, which would make impossible any contact of the divine nature with it, either in creation or in redemption; and a denial of the significance of history, which would make it impossible that history should ever be the scene of a divine act of salvation. Since Christianity is the most material and the most historical of all religions, the fight with Gnosticism had to be fought out to the death. The Gnostics claimed to be Christians, indeed to be the only true and fully developed Christians; and certainly the systems of Valentinus and Basilides contained elements of genuine Christianity. Yet, for all these Christian elements and the place accorded in most Gnostic schemes of salvation to Jesus the Christ, the heirs of the apostolic preaching came to the conviction that this was no question of alternative views within a common Christian faith, but of a system which, if accepted, would destroy the whole basis on which up till that time the society of the friends of Jesus had lived. Separation seemed to have become an inescapable duty.

Conflict led to the consolidation of the Church. It was compelled to think out its doctrine more accurately, to define the sources of its faith, and to reconsider the nature of its unity. It became aware of the threefold cord of the apostolic word, the apostolic faith, and the apostolic tradition.

In controversy with the Gnostics, the developing Catholic Church was compelled to take the first steps towards the definition of its own canon of Scripture; the process was not completed for another two hundred years; but it is remarkable that Irenaeus (before 190) quotes from every book of the New Testament except the Epistle to Philemon.

The first beginnings of formal Creeds can be traced back to this period, first in the form of baptismal confessions, later gaining in amplitude, as the definition of the Faith against heresy was felt to be an increasingly urgent duty.

As against the Gnostic claim to a secret inner tradition, the Church learned to appeal to the public proclamation of its doctrine from the time of the apostles, the authenticity of that tradition being guaranteed by its continuous history in the great centres of Christian life, and that continuous history being guaranteed by the unbroken succession of bishops from the apostolic days. At the end of the 2nd century there was no mechanical doctrine of apostolic succession; there was already a clear recognition of the place of the bishop in the Church, as the continuing witness to and guardian of its unity in time and space. Dependence on Scriptures, Creeds, and ministerial office, as the marks of the unity of the Church, continued until the tumults of the 16th century introduced a radical reconsideration of much that for centuries had been tacitly assumed.

2. THE CHURCH AFTER CONSTANTINE

During the first three centuries of its existence, the Christian Church had never been quite free from peril. Persecution varied greatly in intensity and severity; persecution of Christians by pagans never attained to the relentless efficiency of the later persecutions of Christians by Christians. Nevertheless, in spite of long periods of quiet and prosperity, persecution was always an uncomfortable reality, the advantages of which tend to be over-estimated by those who have not endured it. Still more perilous were the inner conflicts, to which we have briefly referred in the last section; at times there had seemed to be a danger lest the Faith itself might be lost in the storms of controversy. The Church had survived both these perils. In three centuries, it had grown, it had taken deep root, it had learned to express itself, and it had developed certain principles and methods by which its own inner unity might be maintained.

Then, almost without warning, it entered on a new period of security and imperial favour. At a time when the Christians were still a small minority, probably not more than ten per cent. at most of the population, Constantine realized, with the intuition of genius, that they were the people of the future, and that they alone had the creative power to infuse life into the new Empire which it was his purpose to create. As events turned out, Constantine was mistaken in his calculations. Not even the Christians could check the decay of civic life in the West. Instead, the Church was there to hold the Faith and the classical tradition in trust for the new nations that were eventually to come to birth in western Europe, and to create in Byzantium the most stable and long-lived Christian civilization that the world has yet seen.

The Church was not slow to take advantage of its new liberty. Growth, geographical and numerical, was very rapid. Great churches were built; the great liturgies came into being. The Church launched out on that wonderful century of literary production which began with the *De Incarnatione* of Athanasius, and ended with the *De Civitate Dei* of Augustine. All this was accompanied, doubtless, by some dilution of faith and a lowering of the spiritual temperature. Opinions will vary to the end of time as to the good and evil brought about in the life of the Church by "the Constantinian situation".

More important than anything else, for our present study, were certain changes in men's views as to the unity of the Church. Until the time of Constantine that unity had been in the main a unity of faith, worship, and inner spirit. From now on there was a new emphasis on the Church as an organization, and on unity in organization as the outward expression of its inner oneness.

To say, as some historians have said, that the Church simply modelled itself on the Roman Empire is an exaggeration. Yet it was inevitable that, when the relationship between Church and State had become so close, the civil and ecclesiastical organizations should influence one another. Dioceses, each under its own independent bishop, came to be grouped in provinces; the metropolitan of the province was almost always the bishop of the civil capital, and political and ecclesiastical boundaries in most cases followed the same lines. Above the metropolitans stood the patriarchs, the bishops of the great sees of Antioch, Alexandria, and Rome, to which were later added Jerusalem and Constantinople. The powers of metropolitans and patriarchs were not at the start precisely defined, but a hierarchical ladder was beginning to be clearly developed. It was the view of the Bishop of Rome that this hierarchical order was to find its highest and unifying point in the successor of Peter as the supreme ruler and guide of the Church. Considerably earlier, before the end of the 2nd century, Pope Victor had considered himself entitled to excommunicate all who did not agree with the Roman view as to the date on which Easter should be celebrated. This autocratic action met with immediate opposition. But similar claims continued to be made, and what is generally accepted as the earliest unmistakably genuine Decretal, the letter of Pope Siricius to Bishop Himerius of Tarragona in 385, already contains a highly developed doctrine of the authority to be exercised by Peter, dwelling in his successor, over the whole Church.

The Roman Catholic view is that the 4th-century Popes were simply laying claim to a papal authority which had been present in the Church from the beginning. This was not the view of contemporaries. The see of Rome had always been regarded with great veneration, as being the joint foundation of the Apostles Peter and Paul (a tradition hardly questioned in the ancient world), and as the bishopric of the capital city of the Empire. But the Roman claim to supremacy was never admitted by the great Churches of the East.

It might have been expected that the Church, living in such close amity with the Empire, would find the natural culmination of its organization in one single head, who would play in the Church the same rôle as that played in the State by the Emperor. In fact this step was never taken. The periods during which the Empire itself was under the control of one single ruler were few and brief. What the world was accustomed to was a college of several rulers, usually three or four, one among them naturally taking the lead as first among equals. On the evidence, it seems probable that the Church in the 4th century thought in similar terms of its own unity; it would have been content, within a system of patriarchal control, to accord to the Bishop of Rome a position of permanent primacy among his equals; but the Eastern Churches were never willing to contemplate such a surrender of their traditional rights as was from the beginning involved in the Roman claims. The assertion of these claims, regarded by all the other Churches as unfounded and excessive, so far from promoting the unity of the Church, has always proved irremediably divisive.

There is a tendency among Christians to idealize the Church of the earliest days, and to regard it in all things as the pattern. Certainly the pre-Constantinian Church manifested a passion, a faith, and a simplicity of devotion which have rarely been matched in later generations. Its achievements are unrivalled. Yet the post-Constantinian Church also had its glory. There are grounds for the view maintained by some historians that the Church was more effectively and fully one during the period between 313 and 451 than at any time before or since.

Yet even in this period, and with all the influences of imperial favour and pressure to secure it, the unity of the Church was never more than very imperfect. This was Constantine's great disappointment. He had selected the Christians as the objects of his favour in order that they might be the cement, the great factor making for unity, in his varied and unwieldy Empire. Almost immediately he found his purpose frustrated by the sharp and irreconcilable conflicts of the Donatist schism in North Africa. Worse was to come. Hardly had the external peace of the Church begun, before the Arian controversy threatened to destroy for ever its internal peace. This was followed in succession by the other great controversies which were to torment the minds of men and vex the life of the Church for the next five centuries.

In view of the common misunderstanding that division in the Church became a serious problem only after the Reformation, it is important to bear in mind both the number of the 4th-century divisions, many of which had their origins in the earlier centuries, and the extraordinary variety of the causes which led to them.

Some schisms, like that which followed on the election of Callistus as Bishop of Rome in 218 and which did not last very long, were due to little more than the rivalry between two powerful leaders in the Church. One at least, Montanism, was the protest of the prophetic element in the Church against the increasing weight of organization and the dullness of official routine. Differing views as to Church discipline were the origin of many divisions, such as that of the Novatianists, who took a strict view regarding the readmission to the Church of those who had lapsed in time of persecution, as against the milder policy followed by other Christian leaders. Rivalry between great sees certainly helped to inflame divisions. Antioch and Alexandria represented markedly different traditions in Biblical exegesis, which inevitably tended to develop into differing views of Christian doctrine. No one loved Constantinople, the city which had been raised to patriarchal status only because it was New Rome, the new residence of the Emperor. Differences of language and cultural background created misunderstanding, which might lead to mutual accusations of heresy. Where, as in the Donatist controversy in North Africa, differences of language, race, culture, and even social class were added to controversies over discipline and ultimately over doctrine, division tended to become so hard and bitter as to be almost beyond the possibility of cure.

Finally there were the divisions which really arose from differences in doctrine. The Arians were prepared to recognize the Son only as the highest of all created beings. The Macedonians denied the deity of the Holy Spirit. The Apollinarians affirmed that in Jesus the divine Logos had taken the place of the human spirit, and thereby seemed to impair the full and real humanity of the Mediator. The Monophysites were accused of so identifying the two natures in Christ as to obliterate the real distinction between the divine and the human. The Nestorians were accused of so emphasizing the distinction as to produce two Christs instead of one.

The early Church had no clear doctrine of heresy and schism. It was agreed that all who had separated themselves from the unity of the Church were outside the Church and the realm of grace. But in practice differences of degrees of separation from the Church were recognized. It can hardly be doubted that "Catholics" felt more kindly towards Novatianists than they did towards Arians, and different methods were actually followed in the reconciliation of penitents from various forms of heresy or schism. A doctrine of "schism within the Church" and of "heresy outside the Church" was never developed. Yet on the whole the contending parties did not set up bishop against bishop within the same see. (The Donatist habit of doing so was one of the aggravations that made the Donatist situation so difficult to deal with.) And bishops who were in communion with one another might each be in communion with bishops whom the other had anathematized; though some puritans, such as Lucifer of Cagliari, developed the view that anyone who communicated, or ever had communicated, with a tainted sheep thereby became tainted himself and unfit for the fellowship of virtuous Christians.

From the vantage-ground of history, it is possible to see that a central line of Christian tradition was gradually developing out of these clashing interpretations. But at the time this was not so. A shifting terminology, not yet scientifically determined, often made it difficult to see what the question at issue really was. It is now possible to affirm that the Council of Nicaea was right, and that, if the Church had adopted Arianism as its creed, it would have abandoned one of the central tenets by which the Church must live. But this was not evident at the time, and many of the more conservative Eastern bishops hesitated to accept what seemed to them the newfangled phraseology of the Nicene definition. Further, it is to be remembered that none of the "heretics" ever regarded himself as unorthodox. Those whom later times have stigmatized as heretics, partly at least because their cause failed, were no less passionately convinced than Athanasius that they were defending the true and only faith of the Church.

On one point, "orthodox" and "heretics" were fully agreed: the Church, to be the Church of Jesus Christ, must be one and must be world-wide; the thing that mattered more than anything else was that its unity should be safeguarded. Basil the Great affirmed that "our faith is not one thing at Seleucia, another at Constantinople, another at Zela, another at Lampsacus, and another at Rome . . . but one and the same everywhere". The heretics would cordially have agreed with him, except that they would have differed from him as to the interpretation of the words *our faith*.

If this great age of the Church was marked by endless division, it was marked also by endless efforts for the restoration of unity. Most of the familiar methods of the contemporary ecumenical movement were in operation in those early days. Meetings of leaders were held to try to discover peaceful solutions for thorny problems. An immense controversial literature was produced, often with the aim of finding a formula of accommodation in which the contending parties could find agreement. Irenic spirits tried to devise means which would make it easy for schismatics and heretics to return to the fold of the Church without undue humiliation. But above all others, the means by which the Church in the Roman Empire sought to recover its own lost unity was the Ecumenical Council.[1]

It is to be remembered that this instrument was an invention not of the Church but of the State. There had been indeed, from time immemorial, local church councils and meetings of bishops; but it was Constantine, deeply concerned about the threatened rôle of the Christians as the unifiers of his Empire, who gave orders that the episcopate of the whole of Christendom should come together at Nicaea. The Council was a Council of the Church, but it was also the Emperor's Council.

Later ages were right in attributing to Nicaea an almost fabulous importance. For the first time the Church was able visibly to present to the eyes of men that inward unity of which it had itself been conscious from the beginning. From Spain to the slopes of the Hindu Kush, the Church was present in the persons of its bishops.[2] This was the assembly of the confessors; all the bishops had lived through the days of persecution, and some of them bore in their bodies the marks of what they had endured. The presence of Constantine, still venerated by the Eastern Church under the title *isapostolos*, "equal to the apostles", lent splendour to the deliberations. The subsequently universal acceptance by the Churches of the decisions of Nicaea gives it a unique place in Christian history.

It cannot be pretended that the proceedings of the Councils were always marked by harmony, charity, or even an elementary regard for dignity. The Church is at all times very human, and theological debate rarely brings out the best in human nature. And yet the Councils were assemblies of Christian men, passionately in earnest about the truth; the best of them were sober, learned,

[1] See Appendix on the use of the word "Ecumenical". There is disagreement as to the number of the Councils which can be reckoned fully ecumenical. Roman Catholic, Orthodox, and Protestant agree in attaching special importance to the decision of the first four Councils:

Nicaea	.	.	. 325
Constantinople	.	.	. 381
Ephesus	.	.	. 431
Chalcedon	.	.	. 451

The "monophysite" Churches accept the first three, but not Chalcedon.

[2] It is to be remembered, however, that Nicaea was mainly an Eastern Council, only four bishops having been present from the West.

temperate in judgement, and charitable towards opponents. To one thing the whole wearisome series bears eloquent witness—that all the best men of the time were actuated by an unswerving and unyielding will to unity. Their failure to attain all that they desired in no way detracts from the nobility of their aims.

The gravest weakness of the Church Council as an instrument of church policy was its dependence on the State. Once it was admitted that the Emperor could take a hand in enforcing the decisions of a purely ecclesiastical assembly, the spiritual independence of the Church was gravely compromised. For, if the deep doctrines of the Christian Church depend in any degree at all on human powers for their establishment, the Faith may become a matter of party politics, and a change of government may result in a change of faith, an absurdity seen many times in the Christian world since the 4th century.

The success of the State in securing Christian unity was never more than partial.

To later ages, the triumph of the Catholic cause was the great achievement of the Age of the Councils. Almost all later Church history has been written from the Catholic standpoint, and there has therefore been a tendency to overlook or to minimize the continuance and the obstinacy of the divisions within the Church. But in fact there were considerable periods and large areas in which the "Catholics" were in a minority. In spite of imperial disfavour, heresies continued to exist and to flourish. It appears that at one moment in the 4th century there were no fewer than six bishops in Antioch, each claiming to be the sole representative of the authoritative and valid succession from the days of the apostles. It is to be noted that in 367 there were still four Novatianist churches in Constantinople itself, and that their bishop was held in universal respect. Montanism maintained itself in the uplands of Asia Minor until finally stamped out in the 6th century through the persecution under Justinian. After Arianism had ceased to exist within the Roman Empire, it took on a new lease of life among the barbarians, and continued for centuries as the religion of the Visigothic kingdoms.

Almost all these heretical Churches claimed the Christian name, read and cited the same Scriptures as the Catholics, maintained a regular episcopal succession, engaged in heroic missionary enterprise, and held on as non-conformists alongside the great Church patronized by the State. If the Church is defined in terms of specific doctrinal orthodoxy, still more if it is defined in terms of communion with one particular see, then all these heretics were outside the Church, and the problem of Christian unity does not arise. But if it is admitted that, in some sense of the term, the heretics were still Christians, the problem returns; the unity of *the Church* as an organization was secured; the People of Christ was and remained divided.

Earlier heresies disappeared or were suppressed; those of the 5th century remain to the present day as a source of unhealed division in the Christian world. The ancient "Lesser" Churches of the East—Coptic, Ethiopian, Syrian, Armenian, Assyrian—are all to this day either "monophysite" [1] or Nestorian.

To account for the permanence of these divisions, we must take account of one

---

[1] The "monophysite" Churches claim that they represent the ancient faith of the Church, and that, while they do not accept the definitions of the Council of Chalcedon in 451, they do not teach the heresy technically known as Eutychianism.

special factor by which other causes of division were reinforced—the spirit of nationalism.

The attempt of the Roman Emperors to enforce conformity in religion by means of persecution, together with their generally oppressive policy, provoked violent reactions among the non-Greek populations of the East. It is unlikely that the common people understood the delicate doctrinal issues involved. If the Melkites, the Emperor's party, was "Catholic", by reaction Copts, Armenians, and Syrians would tend to be in opposition, and would therefore be monophysites. Nationalism, political feeling, and difference of language combined to produce divisions in the Christian world that fifteen centuries have not availed to heal.

It was in Armenia that the process was carried farthest. The Church in Armenia well repays careful study, as the clearest example in the world of the way in which race, language, a distinct liturgical rite, and divergence in doctrine can work together to maintain over the centuries an independent form of the Christian faith.

Armenia can claim to be the oldest Christian kingdom in the world. Before the middle of the 4th century, the whole country was Christian at least in name, and the Faith prospered under the care of Christian kings and Christian leaders, most of whom belonged to the family of the great Apostle St Gregory the Enlightener. Under the leadership of Sahag (Isaac), who ruled as Catholicos during the first forty years of the 5th century, the Armenian language was reduced to writing by Mesrob; the Scriptures were translated, the work being completed in 434; and the Armenian liturgy began to take shape.[1] The Christianity of the country was taking on an indelibly Armenian imprint. Even earlier than this, Greek- and Syriac-speaking Christians living in Armenia had found it difficult to be at home in the Armenian Church, and had been provided with bishops of their own, a curious example of parallel episcopates in the same area based on linguistic differences.

In 506, at a Council held at Dvin, the Armenian Church, partly at least in reaction against the Nestorian Christians of Persia, who claimed that the Council of Chalcedon had vindicated their position, anathematized that Council and the Tome of Leo,[2] and reaffirmed the doctrine which it had held before the Council of Chalcedon met. Thus doctrinal difference was added to all the other causes of separation. But it was long before this division was acquiesced in or regarded as permanent by the upholders of Chalcedon. The confused history of the next two centuries is intimately involved with the changing fortunes of the Byzantine Empire in its conflicts with enemies on its eastern frontier.

When Armenian influence was strong in Constantinople, the Byzantine Church weakened in its strict adherence to Chalcedonian doctrine. When Byzantine Orthodoxy was strong, attempts were made to impose Orthodox formulations on the Armenian Church. For instance, in 633 the warrior Emperor Heraclius was successful in uniting the two Churches on the basis of a modified form of Chalcedonian doctrine; but the union lasted just as long as the life of the Emperor. The last great effort to restore unity resulted from negotiations between the Armenian Catholicos Nerses the Graceful (1166–73), the

---

[1] The Armenian liturgy, in its main features, belongs to the classical type of Eastern liturgy, but underwent a long process of development through the centuries before reaching its present form.

[2] The famous letter in which Pope Leo the Great set forth the Catholic faith as it was understood at Rome.

Emperor Manuel, and the Byzantine Patriarchs Lukas and Michael; but at the very moment when it seemed that informal agreements might develop into formal union, the Emperor Manuel, the chief promoter of unity, died (1180), and the plans for union were lost sight of in the further political confusions which ensued.

What was true of Armenia was also true, with variations, of Egypt, Syria, Mesopotamia, and Persia. The Coptic Churches of Egypt and Ethiopia adhered to monophysitism. The Church in Syria (with its great extension in South India), which confusingly styles itself the Syrian Orthodox Church, is technically monophysite. The majority of Christians in Mesopotamia and Persia became Nestorian. Thus the Church of the Roman Empire was ringed round, on its eastern frontier, by great Churches which through dissidence in doctrine, added to differences in language and culture, came to assert their complete independence of it, and have remained permanently separate from the rest of the Christian world.

The Nestorian Churches manifested immense missionary energy. They spread over the steppes of Central Asia, and by the 8th century were established in China. The collapse of these Churches was due not so much to any inner weakness as to the almost accidental conversion of the Tatar hordes to Islam. Cut off from all contact with the great centres of Christian thought in the West, living for centuries under the grave disadvantages of Moslem rule, these Churches could do little more than maintain their Christian tradition and their liturgy. Only tiny fragments of their past greatness remain to-day. Yet, through their work of introducing their Moslem masters to the masterpieces of Greek thought in Syriac and Arabic dress, these Christians were able incidentally to render an outstanding service to Western Christendom. As the Dark Ages passed away, one of the channels through which the West recovered a knowledge of Greek thought was the wealth of Latin translations from the Arabic; new processes of thought were set in motion, which reached their splendid conclusion in the *Summa* of St Thomas Aquinas.

3. THE GREAT SCHISM

Tensions between the Greek- and Latin-speaking sections of the Church began early and multiplied rapidly. Of the bishops who attended ecumenical councils, the vast majority were Greeks; but the Church of Rome claimed increasingly the right to determine and to declare the faith of the Church. The Greeks claimed to be the theologians *par excellence*, but were despised and disliked by both Latins and Syrians as logic-choppers and "disputers". Differences of terminology obscured the issues in many matters of the Faith, and embittered the controversies that raged about them.

As controversy developed, it tended to revolve around certain constantly recurring points: in dogmatics, the gradual introduction in the West of the *Filioque* clause in the Nicene Creed; in worship, the use of leavened or unleavened bread in the Eucharist; in discipline, certain rules concerning fasting, the celibacy or marriage of the clergy, and so forth. Doubtless these problems were acutely felt by some of the leaders, but behind them lay other grounds of difference: the perpetual rivalries between patriarchates; disputes as to boundaries, particularly over the dioceses of Illyricum and over ecclesiastical control of Bulgaria; rivalry in Slavonic lands between Latin missionaries entering from the West and

Byzantine missionaries coming in from the East—a rivalry which still exists in the 20th century. Politics constantly played in with ecclesiastical affairs. The coronation of Charlemagne in 800 and the establishment of what came to be called the Holy Roman Empire added a new element of chance to the game of high politics and diplomacy.

It often came about that for considerable periods two or more patriarchates were out of communion with one another; but this was not taken as a final breach, and time and again quarrels were patched up and communion, albeit on somewhat uneasy terms, was restored. It was only very gradually that the breach between East and West became irremediable, and it is not possible to determine any particular moment at which temporary estrangement passed over into permanent alienation.

Paradoxically some of the sharpest periods of hostility were brought about by well-meant attempts at conciliation. The 5th-century controversies about the Person of Christ dragged on through the 6th and 7th centuries, in a succession of complex heresies and wearisome disputes. In 482 the Emperor Zeno put out the document known as the *Henoticon*, the aim of which was to restore communion between the Patriarch of Constantinople and the Patriarch of Alexandria. Unexpectedly this irenic gesture turned itself into a controversy over the prestige and authority of the Bishop of Rome. The Pope excommunicated the Patriarch of Constantinople, and the breach, the first of its kind, lasted for nearly forty years. In 518 a change of government at Constantinople made possible a reconciliation, and the schism came to an end. But, with a sudden transformation of the scene such as was characteristic of the time, whereas before 518 the four Eastern patriarchates had been in communion with one another and none of them with Rome, after 518 Rome, Constantinople, Jerusalem, and Antioch were in communion with one another, but Alexandria was excluded from the fellowship.

The 7th century has been aptly described, using a term derived from an almost contemporary writer, as the period of the "Watery Unions". Conciliatory formulas were put forth one after the other—the *Tome of Union* of 633; the *Ekthesis* of 638; the *Type* of 648, in which the Emperor Constans forbade all disputation among his subjects on "one will or operation, or two wills or two operations". Pope Martin I convened the first Council of the Lateran, in which five hundred bishops assembled on 5 October 649 and condemned "the most impious *Ekthesis* and the abominable *Type*". The result was another period of schism between Rome and New Rome. Yet once again men grew weary of strife; in 657 a way to reconciliation was found and concord was restored.

For more than a hundred years, from about 716 to 845, the East was riven by its own peculiar conflict, over the use of and reverence due to holy images, and the resultant strife of the Iconoclasts and their opponents. Yet this strife, though incredibly bitter, was always a strife between parties within the Church as to which was to exercise control, and did not lead ultimately to the setting up of Church against Church. The end of this period was marked by the beginning of a new phase in the tension between East and West.

From the time of the publication of the *Annals* of Cardinal Baronius at the end of the 16th century, two dates have been generally accepted as marking the great crises in the relationship between the Western and the Eastern Churches: the affair of the Patriarch Photius in 867, and the affair of the Patriarch Michael Cerularius in 1054. But modern research has led to a radical revision of this judgement, and to the view that these events, though undoubtedly serious, were much less lasting and decisive in their consequences than had been traditionally supposed.

Certainly there was acute tension between Photius, the most learned man of his age, and Pope Nicholas I. Certainly at a Council held in 867, Photius joined with representatives of the other Eastern patriarchates [1] in excommunicating and deposing the Pope, a decision which could be regarded by the whole of the West only as a grave act of aggression. Yet it seems certain that when, after a period of deposition, Photius resumed the patriarchate in 877, Pope John VIII absolved and restored him, and that that Pope and his successors entered into and remained in communion both with Constantinople and with the Eastern patriarchates as a whole.

Certainly in 1054 a violent quarrel broke out between the Patriarch Michael Cerularius and the envoys of Pope Leo IX. On 17 July of that year the three legates laid on the altar of Santa Sophia a Bull excommunicating the Patriarch. Michael at once responded by summoning a Synod, in which the Roman Bull was condemned, an anathema pronounced against the Pope, and the Bull ordered to be burned. Yet this Bull was never confirmed by the authorities in Rome, and it seems that, when Michael fell from power in 1059, the Pope restored the Emperor to communion. And no formal act of separation from the West was carried out by any of the other Eastern patriarchates, which, though shorn of much of their glory by the advance of the Moslems, still retained their independence and their authority over large sections of the East.

The year 1054 can no longer be regarded as the date of the decisive breach between East and West. Much still remains obscure in the confused history of the time, yet it is evident that there was far more fellowship and communion between Eastern and Western Christians than was at one time supposed. The decisive evidence is derived from the history of the period of the Crusades. When the first Crusaders arrived at Constantinople in 1096, they were received as fellow-Christians by the Emperor Alexius; and, though the Crusaders came increasingly to dislike and distrust the Emperor and to regard him as the cause of all their misfortunes, there is nothing to show that either side regarded a decisive breach as having taken place between the Churches from which they came. On the contrary, it may be argued that it was the Crusades themselves which turned strained relations into a final and irreparable breach.

When the Crusaders captured Antioch and then Jerusalem, they accepted the Patriarchs of those cities not as schismatics but as the legitimate rulers of the Churches. There was, however, from an early date a tendency to introduce a Latin hierarchy; and, though the Latin bishops regarded themselves as the successors of the Eastern bishops and not as the founders of a new line, the election in 1099 of the papal legate Daimbert as Patriarch of Jerusalem implied an authority of the Bishop of Rome in the East such as had never been previously recognized, and was bound to lead to difficulties with the leaders of the Eastern Churches. For, however carefully concealed under the courteous language of diplomacy, the major tension all the time was that between the claim of the Pope to be the universal Head and Ruler of the Church and the unyielding firmness of the Eastern Churches in refusing to accord to him any prerogatives higher than those of the Patriarch of the West, *primus inter pares*, in the traditional great Patriarchal Five.

[1] Whose action was afterwards disowned by their Patriarchs.

It was, however, not so much the difficulties of ecclesiastical adjustment as the events of the Fourth Crusade which led to intense and undying hostility between East and West. In 1204 the Crusade, which had set out to fight the enemies of the Cross, was diverted to the capture and sack of Constantinople. The greatest Christian city in the world became the victim of Christian swords; the Eastern Christian Empire was permanently and fatally weakened in its struggle against Islam. The ephemeral Latin Empire of Constantinople came to an inglorious end in 1261; but the hatred of all things Western, for which the Crusaders were responsible, long survived its fall, and is still one of the psychological factors which make difficult any *rapprochement* between the East and the West. Seen from the East, the permanent embitterment of the relations between Christians and Moslems and between Eastern and Western Christians appears as the main fruit of those Crusades, which from another angle may be considered as part of the spiritual renaissance of western Europe.

The separation which over eight earlier centuries had grown more definite and intractable has never in eight later centuries been satisfactorily healed. And yet the sense of the *corpus christianum* never completely disappeared in either East or West. The Latin heretics, the Eastern schismatics, though no communion between them might be possible, were still in some sense fellow-Christians. That oneness of the Church which men knew to have existed in earlier days still presented itself as an ideal which Christians should earnestly seek and ensue.

This continuing ecumenical sense is manifest in various great attempts made in the Middle Ages to heal the breach between East and West, among which two stand out as having come nearer than the others to success.

The first of these was made at the second Council of Lyons, which assembled on 7 May 1274. With what appeared to be astonishing ease the great question of union was dealt with, and on 6 July of that year the Byzantine delegation declared the union of the two Churches, through the necessary submission of the Byzantines to the Pope, to have been achieved. Underneath this apparent reconciliation lay many sinister motives of political intrigue. In 1261 Michael VIII Palaeologus had succeeded in recapturing Constantinople and bringing to an end the brief and shameful episode of the Latin Empire in that city. But his power was gravely jeopardized by the menace of a fresh Crusade of the West against the East, and by the intrigues of Charles of Anjou, at that time the most powerful sovereign in western Europe. Michael decided that the only way to safety was to submit to the Pope, and thus to secure his aid against the threats of Charles; as he frankly explained to the Byzantine clergy in 1279: "As the captain of a vessel in peril, I judged it best to throw part of the goods into the sea in order to save the rest of the cargo." The Emperor's remark makes it clear that the approach to Rome was a political manoeuvre of his own, and not a serious theological approach of one Church to another.

Michael encountered unexpected opposition in the Eastern Church. He had his own party; but neither exile, bonds, nor torture could secure the submission of those who were opposed to the union, and among these were included even members of the Emperor's family. The hollowness of the agreement was revealed when, in 1280, Martin IV, a pledged friend of Charles of Anjou, succeeded to the papal throne. Michael immediately became less enthusiastic about the union; on 18 November 1281 he was excommunicated and threatened with deposition by the Pope; the Byzantine Church resumed its age-long policy of going on its own way and taking no notice of the anathemas of Rome.

The second attempt was more determined and more carefully thought out. By the beginning of the 15th century, the Eastern Roman Empire had been reduced by the assaults of the Turks to a shadow of its former greatness; it was clear to all who could read the signs of the times that Constantinople could survive only with the help of the West, and that that help would be given only on condition of the submission of the Eastern Church to the Church of Rome. For a number of years desultory negotiations had been going on. The Emperor John Palaeologus, a shrewd realist, was quite prepared to treat with the West. In 1438–9 the long *pourparlers* reached their climax in the Council of Florence, at which once again union was achieved.

The Council opened at Ferrara on 9 April 1438 in a scene of unexampled magnificence. Both the Pope and the Emperor of the East were present, each accompanied by a dazzling array of grandees in both Church and State.[1] But if those who saw the spectacle imagined that outward amity would lead on quickly to union, they were destined to be greatly disappointed. It soon became evident that the Greeks were gravely divided among themselves. The Emperor would have liked a pact of union to be signed at once, without the tedium of theological dispute, and wished to get back as quickly as possible to his proper work of defending the Empire. His son Demetrius, who accompanied him, was resolutely opposed to union. The champions of union among the churchmen were Bessarion, Archbishop of Nicaea and later Cardinal of the Roman Church, and Isidore, the Greek Archbishop of Kiev, specially brought in to secure the adhesion of Russia to the union; the chief opponent was Mark, Bishop of Ephesus.

It is unnecessary to follow all the intricacies of the theological debate. Naturally a great part of it turned on the classic question of the *Filioque* in the Nicene Creed. This was developed under two aspects. Had one part of the Church any right to make an addition to a Creed which had been accepted by the whole world-wide Church? And was the *Filioque* itself theologically tenable or heretical? The doctrine of purgatory claimed some attention. But from the start it was obvious that the point on which everything must turn was the willingness or unwillingness of the Byzantines to accept the papal claims in the fullness which they had developed during the medieval period.

Plague broke out at Ferrara, and the Council was transferred to Florence. On 10 June 1439 the Patriarch of Constantinople died; this was not allowed to interrupt the proceedings. The Emperor chafed; the theologians raged and grew weary. At last a kind of agreement was reached. On 26 June Bessarion managed to produce a formula which both parties were prepared to accept; the Easterns were willing to recognize the Pope "as the Vicar of Christ, the pastor and teacher of all Christians, having the right to guide and govern the Church, without prejudice to the privileges and rights of the Eastern patriarchs". As the nature and extent of these privileges and rights was the very subject under dispute, it might seem that this statement settled much less than it left open. Nevertheless, it was accepted by both parties. On 6 July the decree of union was solemnly read by the Pope during High Mass; it begins with the hopeful words *Let the heavens rejoice and let the earth be glad*. Then the Greeks went home,

---

[1] The Emperor and the Patriarch of Constantinople can still be seen, playing the part of two of the Magi, in the glorious fresco of Benozzo Gozzoli at Florence.

to persuade their countrymen, if they could, that the Church of Byzantium had not been utterly betrayed.

They met with little to cheer them. The entrance of John Palaeologus into Constantinople aroused the population to recrimination and insult. Russia repudiated the action of Isidore of Kiev, who was even for a time imprisoned.[1] The three other Eastern patriarchs refused their assent to the declaration of the Council of Florence. It is true that (in the last agony of Constantinople before its capture by the Turks) on 12 December 1452 the union was solemnly proclaimed in Santa Sophia. But this proclamation was formal rather than effective; though a small number of Greeks remained in communion with Rome, the Council of Florence exercised little permanent influence on the life of the Church in either East or West.

The fair hopes of union faded away, and have never again appeared above the horizon. Certain lessons can be learned from the attempts and the failures. First, ecumenical relationships can never prosper if political considerations are allowed to interfere in what is properly the sphere of the Church alone. Secondly, no true union of hearts can be attained through compromise and the evasion of difficulties. Thirdly, it is unlikely that lasting union can be achieved, unless there is some flexibility on both sides, and a preliminary agreement that certain things may be treated as unessential, disagreements regarding them being no barrier to spiritual union. Fourthly, the solemn decisions of ecclesiastical authorities will always prove ineffective unless they have roots in the life and conviction of ordinary churchmen, who are often more open to the influence of non-theological than of theological factors in the life of the Church.

The hindrances to union in the Middle Ages went deeper than ecclesiastical rivalry or theological debate. They took their origin in two divergent views of the nature of the Christian world. Most men, then as now, acquiesced in division, and, if they were aware of it at all, were not gravely troubled by it. Only the few whose vision surpassed the narrow boundaries of territory and local church— such men as Popes Gregory VII and Innocent III, and some among the wisest of the Byzantine Emperors—were able to realize that, if the Church was to fulfil its mission in the world, its need for unity was greater than any other need. But this vision led these great men to opposite and irreconcilable conclusions. To the Byzantine, unity meant the recovery by the Christian Empire of its unique position and the extension of its power in the West; to the Pope, it meant the universal recognition of the position of the Vicar of Christ as supreme over every king and ruler in the world, no less than over every churchman. Times and situations have changed. Yet the ghost of vanished imperialisms still remains to perplex and embarrass the ecumenical efforts of the 20th century.

4. THE WEST IN THE MIDDLE AGES

Efforts for the recovery of the primitive unity of the Church had failed. But the West at least might boast of the gigantic and well-articulated structure of unity which held together the countries and Churches from Iceland to Sicily, and from Spain to the farther frontiers of Poland. Never has there been a closer inte-

---

[1] Isidore, "a maleficent, crafty and mercenary man", was the last Greek Archbishop of Kiev. The Russian rejection of the Council of Florence was one manifestation of that Russian reaction against dependence on Constantinople which led to the establishment in 1589 of the independent Patriarchate of Moscow.

gration of thought, art, and Christian living than in that great century when the Gothic cathedrals were rising from the soil, Thomas Aquinas was perfecting the instruments of scholastic thought, Dante was learning to write Italian, and Francis was recovering the joy and *élan* of the original Gospel. Yet any careful study of the history shows that, impressive as was this unity, the appearance was more impressive than the reality, and that divisive forces were in operation in that period as much as in any other of the Church's history.

Most history, as we have already seen, is written from the orthodox standpoint, and by classifying divergent movements as heresies excludes them automatically from the main stream of Christian development. This has been more true of the Middle Ages in the West than of any other time and place in Christian history. Variety of thought within a fixed framework was permitted. Any divergence beyond that limit brought into play the coercive powers of both Church and State; and, since heresy was regarded as more dangerous to the individual and to the State than any natural plague, all methods were deemed legitimate for its extirpation. Yet coercive methods can never be wholly successful; there are always men who will cling more passionately to their freedom of thought than to life itself. Coercion may drive "heresy" underground; only a policy of complete extermination can ensure its disappearance, and no policy can make sure that the disappearance of one heresy will not be followed by the appearance of another. Church history is, in fact, the story of the constant tension between "orthodoxy" and "heresy"; a tension which sometimes at least takes the form of the opposition between those who, when a choice has to be made, prefer unity to truth and those who prefer truth to unity.

Those who speak warmly of the unity of Western Christendom before the Reformation sometimes forget that the price for this coercive unity was paid in a gigantic movement of dissidence from the formally established Church. Much research will yet be needed before the full history of heresy in the West can be written. It has long been clear, however, that in some of the richest provinces of the south of France, and even in parts of Italy itself, heresy had for generations the upper hand, and the Catholic Church was almost at the point of disappearance.

The true picture of the Cathari, or Albigenses, has been blurred by the perversity of tradition. Contemporary report, almost all of it bitterly hostile, represents them as monsters of indescribable wickedness; the hagiographical fancy of Protestant writers tends to depict them as pre-Reformation saints and martyrs of the Reformation. In reality there seem to have been two distinct and separable strains in the movement. There was, on the one hand, a natural reaction, such as has been seen many times in the history of the Church, against the luxury and worldliness of the contemporary Church and in favour of a return to the simpler pattern of earlier days. One part of this movement, which the Church managed to retain within the fold of orthodoxy, owed its inspiration to Francis of Assisi; another was the tradition of the Waldensians, which, in spite of relentless persecution, was able to maintain itself unimpaired until the 16th century.[1] But, on the other hand, there was undoubtedly an infiltration of dualistic and Manichean ideas, drawn from the strange sects of the Bogomils, which periodically migrated westwards from the Balkans. If this element had prevailed, the Christian faith as we know it would have disappeared; indeed, the whole future of Europe might have been endangered, since the Cathar hostility

[1] In the 16th century, the Waldensians "accepted the Reformation", though maintaining a good deal of the distinctive tradition which had come down to them from earlier centuries.

to marriage, carried to its logical conclusion, would seem to involve the final extinction of the human race.

Faced by this great peril, the forces of orthodoxy rallied to the assault. The Western world was already familiar with the idea of holy wars against the infidels; the infamous sack of Constantinople during the Fourth Crusade had shown how fatally easy it was for Christian arms to be turned against Christian brethren. In 1208 Innocent III opened a new chapter in the history of persecution by proclaiming a Crusade against the heretics of the south of France and the rich lords who supported them, bribing the northern nobles to take up arms in defence of the Church by promising them the lands of all the southern nobles whom they might reduce to ruin. The war thus launched lasted intermittently for 120 years; its principal achievement was the repeated devastation of some of the fairest provinces of Europe. But in the end the unity of the Church was after a fashion restored.

Fire and sword were not the only instruments used by the medieval Church in its zeal for the restoration of unity. The Albigensian heresy led directly to the formation of the Dominican order. Dominic saw plainly that, in face of the Albigensian emphasis on poverty, the preachers of the Catholic faith would have no chance of being heard unless they at least equalled the best of the heretics in the austerity of their lives. He saw, too, that in a time when knowledge was spreading rapidly in all classes of society, the defence of the Faith must be placed on a new footing of intellectual power. Public debates between preachers and heretics became the order of the day, and anticipated by three centuries the similar debates which convulsed the Swiss cities in the first days of the Reformation. But the Dominicans, no less than Innocent III, were men of their day. Where reason failed, they were prepared to fall back on force. The Inquisition was set up in the cities of southern France, and the work of reconciliation proceeded as much by the ruthless burning of heretics as by the proclamation of the Gospel of love.

By 1320 ecclesiastical authority reckoned that the victory over heresy had been won, and that unity had been restored to the Church. But it was not long before other divisive forces began to appear. John Wyclif was born about 1330 and died in 1384. John Hus was born about 1370, and was burned alive by order of the Council of Constance in 1415. The influence of Wyclif and the Lollards never quite died out in England; the influence of John Hus is alive in Bohemia to-day. Intermittent burnings of heretics continued all through the later Middle Ages, as evidence that the enforcement of unity from above was balanced by strivings after independence from beneath.

And yet, for all this restlessness and protest, the unity of Western Christendom in the high Middle Age was an impressive achievement. Through the slow, patient, penetrative policy of successive Popes, almost the whole of the West had been brought together in a single liturgical use—the Roman; in the use of one common language for all educated men—Latin; in one vast ecclesiastical order—the papal; in one system and method of thought—the scholastic. This overarching unity of thought, belief, expression, and worship was not felt by the men of the time as a burden imposed from without. The unity of the Western world, in spite of wars and intrigues between rulers, was the very atmosphere which they breathed. Western Europe was once again aware of its spiritual oneness; the *corpus christianum* was a felt reality, expressed in such enterprises as the Crusades at their best, or in such great Christian institutions as the Truce of God.[1] It was made a visible reality in the ease and frequency of pilgrimages.

This outward unity found its crowning manifestation in the Pope, the successor of Peter, ruling from Rome over all true Christian people in the world.

At one time it had seemed by no means certain that the Middle Ages would end with the Pope in this position of unassailed authority. Towards the end of the 14th century, a new form of division became manifest in the Christian world and gravely weakened the prestige of the papacy; with rival Popes reigning in Rome and Avignon and anathematizing one another, no one knew for certain which of the two was the legitimate successor of Peter. This shameful "Babylonish Captivity" lasted from 1378 till 1417. To bring it to an end was one of the great aims and tasks of the Conciliar movement; men looked with new hope to the great series of Councils which began with Constance in 1415.

For a time it seemed that reform might come from within, and that the Councils might be successful both in driving out scandal and in re-establishing the Church on a constitutional and conciliar basis. The opportunity was given and was lost, partly at least because the men who sat in the Councils were neither virtuous enough nor brave enough to bring about a real reformation. In the end the Popes were the chief beneficiaries of the reforming movements of a century.

The Popes had been successful in reasserting their own position as the centre of unity for the Christian world. The attempt to limit the autocracy of the Pope by constitutional arrangements had been frustrated. The great Church of the West, which since the fall of Constantinople in 1453 had tended to identify itself with the *Una Sancta*, remained centralized, monolithic, apparently unshakable. It seemed that Rome had successfully gathered within itself all ecclesiastical authority, all that was most vital in the life of the Church; that there alone the unity of the Church was to be sought, and that that unity, now newly re-established, could never again be successfully challenged.

Yet, once again as often before, it is necessary to insist that that unity was neither complete nor secure nor permanent.

Church history, as written in the West, not infrequently gives the impression that the whole Church had lived for centuries in blissful unity, until that unity was roughly shattered by the wickedness of Martin Luther. It is well to remember that, at the beginning of the 16th century, as at other times, that unity was more a myth than a reality. At the end of the Middle Ages the world-wide body of Christian people was divided between three great and almost wholly unrelated blocs.

The Western bloc, with its centre in Rome, was by far the largest of the three. Western Europe, alert with the new life and enterprise of the Renaissance, was destined for four centuries to take the lead in learning, in the art of government, and in man's mastery over his environment.

But the Eastern Churches, though pillaged and despoiled by the Moslems, were by no means a negligible factor in the Christian world. With the loss of Constantinople in 1453, leadership tended to pass from the Greek to the Slavonic world, and in 1589 Moscow was successful in securing from the Patriarch of Constantinople recognition as an independent patriarchate, "Moscow, the third Rome". The Russian Christian was proudly convinced that,

---

[1] The great attempt made by the Church to ban all fighting at certain seasons of the year; most successful in the 12th century.

now that Old Rome had become irretrievably heretical, and New Rome on the Bosporus had been paralysed by Moslem domination, God had called into existence the third Rome in the north, to be the guide and rallying-point of all Christians, and at last to bring in the true Kingdom of the Holy Spirit.

The plight of the Lesser Eastern Churches was the worst of all. They had no great centres of learning, and only intermittent and partial contacts, not always friendly, with the Churches of the West. Under the *Millet* system of the Turkish Empire,[1] they enjoyed a limited and precarious freedom. But throughout the centuries they suffered from the relentless pressure of a contemptuously hostile majority, and were weakened by the loss of many of their most promising young men to Islam. The most they could do was to hold on, with admirable faithfulness, to their ancient traditions, until at last political changes in the 19th and 20th centuries brought them greater liberty and a measure of renewal.

The Reformation of the 16th century did, however, shatter such unity as Western Christendom had enjoyed, and did introduce divisions graver and more intractable than any which had entered in since the early days of the Church. No one at the time set out with the idea of producing divisions; all the Reformers proclaimed their desire only for a sincere and thoroughgoing inward reformation of the Church. Nor did it seem likely at the start that they would succeed in producing any permanent divisions; everything suggested that these "heresies", like others in the past, would be crushed by the combined weight of Church and State, and that outward unity would be re-established, as it had been in the 14th century. It was not very long, however, before it became evident that what would satisfy the Reformers could not be carried out within the framework of the existing Church, and that, in the peculiar political conjuncture of the 16th century, strong forces would be available to protect the reforming movements from the destruction with which they seemed to be threatened.

Without Luther there would have been no Reformation, at least not in the divisive form which it actually assumed. Doubtless there were tendencies favourable to his enterprise. But unless a man had arisen, with a new and commanding message in which he whole-heartedly believed and which he could make convincing to ordinary men, with considerable gifts as a publicist and with powerful friends, it is unlikely that the 16th-century movements would have proved more effective than those of Wyclif and of Hus. At the same time, it must be recognized that the course taken by the 16th-century Reformation was partly determined by other movements which had preceded it, and had already in part undermined the structure and the unity of the Western Church.

Some of these movements were political. The rise of nations and of national feeling was beginning to pull in pieces the medieval fabric of Europe. Perhaps it was in Germany that national resentment against the corruptions and oppressions of a mainly Italian Curia was most strongly felt, but certainly Germany was not alone. If Rome had responded to this new spirit by a measure of decentralization and some recognition of national independence, unity might have been less seriously threatened; instead, centralization was increased, until Rome became not the final court of appeal but a court of first instance for innumerable legal pleas from all over the western world.

The critical temper of the Renaissance led men to question much that had been

---

[1] Each non-Moslem community was recognized as having a certain independence under the leadership of its spiritual head. The system was abolished in Turkey as recently as 1923.

taken for granted for centuries. Scholarship had demonstrated the unauthenticity of the False Decretals and the Donation of Constantine; in so far as the Roman claims to supremacy and to universal jurisdiction were based on these forged documents, men were less ready to accept those claims as valid. The recovery of Greek had made the New Testament Scriptures available in the original; the appeal beyond the medieval world to Christian antiquity became a regular feature in Christian controversy. The Churches of the Reformation claimed, and claim, that so far from being innovators they had done no more than to understand the past, and to restore the Church to what it had been in that past, when it was true to itself.

Social and economic changes were bringing to an end the feudal organization of society, within which the hierarchically organized medieval Church had been perfectly at home, and were putting increasing power into the hands of that active, thrusting burgher class, which was to find Protestantism congenial to its way of life and thought.

In many countries, Christians had become dissatisfied with the traditional forms of piety and were seeking a deeper satisfaction of their spiritual needs. The Reformation cannot be understood at all, except in the light of the immense new spiritual forces which it released, especially through putting the Bible in the hands of ordinary men in a language that they could understand. The great outburst of new devotion which accompanied the Counter-Reformation, especially in Spain, came too late to meet the need; it served to strengthen the papal cause in the lands which had in the main remained faithful to the papacy, but not to avert division or to restore unity.

The Reformation, like all human history, is a mixed record of good and evil. Members of different confessions will differ in their historical and critical judgements on it, some finding that on the whole the good greatly outweighed the evil, and others the reverse. But, whatever be the judgement on the history as a whole, it can hardly be denied that the divisions in the life of the Church which resulted from it were deeper and more serious than any inherited from the past. All earlier divisions had taken place within a common framework of tradition and worship. Even the more conservative forms of Protestantism represented a more radical breach with the past than anything since the Gnostic heresies. The most serious factor of all was the acquiescence in division, which became the basis of all post-Reformation settlements of religion. By 1555 it had become clear that the Reformation was not going to capture the whole Church. By the Peace of Westphalia in 1648, the boundaries between the Roman and non-Roman Churches were drawn almost exactly as they have remained to the present day. Men continued to express their faith in the one holy, catholic, and apostolic Church, but seem hardly to have realized that the outward expression of that unity upon earth should be the immediate object of the prayers and efforts of Christians.

The ecumenical vision was never entirely lost. But most of those who saw and proclaimed it were individuals, contending with formidable, indeed insuperable, difficulties. Centuries were to pass before the Churches as such became seriously concerned about the sinfulness of division and before the ecumenical vision became again the possession of ordinary men. The vision of Christian unity, and the slow and late repentance of the Churches, are the subject of all the chapters that follow in this History.

CHAPTER 1

THE ECUMENICAL IDEA AND EFFORTS TO
REALIZE IT, 1517–1618

by

JOHN THOMAS MCNEILL

1. THE PROBLEM OF DISUNITY IN THE REFORMATION ERA

The history of the Christian Church from the first century to the 20th might be written in terms of its struggle to realize ecumenical unity. That Christians are "all one in Christ Jesus" is a principle never surrendered, yet the world has beheld them worshipping in separated and mutually exclusive communions. The ancient and the medieval Church were alike familiar with the phenomena of schism.

In the Middle Ages the dominant Churches, allied with State power and employing both force and persuasion, sought to restrain the separatist movements that from time to time emerged. Despite all measures taken against them, non-conformist elements survived. When some of the groups were extinguished, others replaced them; when their members were scattered, they propagated their views in new areas. The grave administrative division in the West (1378–1417), when Popes of Avignon challenged those of Rome, lent encouragement to sects and heresies and to abuses that provoked criticism and discord. The Conciliar movement arose in an attempt to meet this condition. From the beginning of the 14th century able writers had been advocating a revolution in the government of the Church that would rest authority in a representative council. During the Papal Schism this teaching was revived and became the basis of a serious project. Among the objectives of the Conciliarists was what one of them called "a reincorporation and reintegration of the universal Church".[1] Their efforts were largely nullified. The Council of Constance achieved indeed the restoration of papal unity (1417), but failed to carry through a programme of reform, or to secure "the reintegration of the universal Church". The inquisitorial repression of heretics continued, though with limited success. Advocates of Conciliarism were denounced as heretics (1460), and the wounds of the Church were not healed. At the end of the 15th century, dissentients and protesters were abroad in every land.

Yet these sectarian and reforming elements were not very influential or formidable. The medieval sects, unlike the Churches of the Reformation, did not enlist reliable political support. Nor did they find adequate intellectual leadership. Some of their founders in a measure anticipated the Reformers; but they did not create the Reformation. None of the leading Reformers had a background of medieval sectarianism. They were men trained in monasteries and universities, and nursed on the bosom of the medieval Church.

The rising strength of national and territorial governments was one of the most embarrassing elements with which any universal church order would have to contend. Centuries earlier the forces of national sentiment had helped to sever large elements from the main body of Eastern Orthodoxy. The 15th-century papacy felt compelled to negotiate concordats with the national states and the smaller principalities. The rival powers were frequently at war, and in these struggles the Church was deeply involved and unable to play a reconciling rôle. Before the Reformation began, France, England, Switzerland, and Spain had

[1] Dietrich of Niem, *De modis uniendi ac reformandi ecclesiam*, Chap. xxx. (The ascription of this tract to Dietrich (d. 1418) has been questioned by some scholars.)

become autonomous nations, and many of the principalities within Germany were able to conduct themselves largely as independent states. A politically divided Europe constituted the environment of the Reformation, conditioned its development and determined its territorial and national organization.

Luther's vigorous thought pervaded Europe, but it was in Germany alone that he was the directing leader of reform. The Swiss movement led by Zwingli was never a part of the Lutheran movement. Between 1520 and 1555 Germany and Switzerland alike were in inner conflict over the issues of the Reformation, yet in both the general political structure continued almost unchanged. The Reformation gained recognition in numerous German states and in the more urbanized Swiss cantons; it failed to form a Protestant communion extending across the German-Swiss boundary. Most of the priests readily acquiesced in the profound religious change that took place in the Protestant areas, and parish life continued to function. In Geneva, before any Protestant organization arose, the old order collapsed and the bishop was expelled; the Reformed Church was almost immediately that of the community as a whole. Political concepts of unity were no longer imperial but national, and correspondingly the unity of the Church tended to be conceived in national terms. Confessions of faith affirmed the Church's universality—but they were national confessions. The modern reader should bear in mind that the persons whom we meet in this chapter had in general no thought of detaching the Church from the political order. The Church-State relationship had been close for many centuries, and responsible leaders, Roman Catholic and Protestant alike, expected this to continue.[1]

The first whole nation to adopt the Reformation was Sweden; Denmark (with Norway), England, Scotland, and the Dutch Republic followed. The Lutheranizing of the Scandinavian lands tended to the internationalizing of Lutheranism. Calvinism won territory from Lutheranism as well as from Roman Catholicism in Germany, and entered Bohemia, Hungary, and Poland with considerable force, replacing an earlier Lutheran influence. But it was checked in these areas and, except in Hungary, almost extinguished by the forces of the Counter-Reformation and the results of the Thirty Years War. Lutheran, Zwinglian, and Calvinist elements in Italy and Spain early succumbed to persecution. In France the Reformed Church entered on a struggle for existence. The Edict of Nantes (1598), which accorded to it a large measure of toleration, was to prove only a stage in the development of this struggle. The Anglican and Scottish Churches, divergent in polity and worship, criticized and attempted to reform each other.

Such, in brief, was the political geography of the Reformation. Its success was both aided and hindered by the attitudes of political rulers. Bounds were set to Protestant expansion by rival dynasties, the Habsburgs and the Valois, who between them dominated the greater part of Europe, maintaining their ties with the papacy.

Fresh manifestations of separation soon appeared on Protestant soil. The word "Anabaptist" is made to do duty for a wide variety of tenuously related movements of which the common marks were the adoption of believers' as distinct from infant baptism, and the affirmation of the authority of the "inner

---

[1] This was not true of the extreme left wing of the Reformation, in which the idea of the total separation of Church and State was already present.

light" against ecclesiastical dogma and State compulsion. Pre-Reformation parallels to most of the teachings stressed by the Anabaptists are abundant. But these movements seem to have sprung up anew in the 1520's through causes connected with the Reformation. The widespread circulation of vernacular Bibles and the new emphasis on Scripture called forth among some a reaction against the reconstituted Churches and their new ecclesiasticism. The great Reformers were not a little alarmed by these movements, which seemed to threaten all ordered life of Church and society. The modern indiscriminate toleration of religious varieties would have appalled Luther and Calvin, and the members of the sects themselves were not always more tolerant in principle. Some Anabaptists were, however, among the earliest advocates of toleration, a natural result of their tragic experience of the intolerance of others.

On the fringe of the Anabaptist type of dissent were a number of independent mystical and spiritual thinkers. The followers of one of these, Caspar Schwenckfeld, formed a "spiritual" sect that has survived in Silesia and America. Socinianism, an important anti-trinitarian movement, took on permanent organization in Poland and Transylvania.[1] Lutheranism in Germany was shaken by numerous internal theological controversies, eventually allayed by the adoption of the Formula of Concord in 1580. In Sweden, threats of division were raised by the entrance of Calvinism and the attempts of partisans of Roman Catholicism; but in 1593 the Swedish national Church became securely and unitedly attached to the Lutheran family. In the same period Brownists and Barrowists and other separatist groups of Puritans arose in England. At the beginning of the 17th century Jacob Arminius in the Netherlands introduced the first considerable modification of Calvinism, and the ensuing controversy led to the Synod of Dort (1618–19).

The facts here rapidly surveyed indicate the main elements in the problem of disunity as it was encountered in the era of the Reformation. It was already a multiple problem, and it was recognized as such. Part of the problem lay in the field of nationality and the deep loyalties to politico-social units that had been engendered. The more distinctly ecclesiastical aspects of the problem were not less grave. The Reformation had rejected with deep conviction the Roman claim stated by Pope Boniface VIII in the words: "We therefore declare, say, define, and pronounce that it is altogether necessary to salvation for every human creature to be subject to the Roman pontiff." Even when these words were uttered (1302), many millions of Christians were indifferent to the papal claim. Now it was more than ever impossible to gather the whole Christian flock into the Roman fold. To unite those outside it was also a discouragingly difficult task. Nevertheless, notable efforts were made to bring unity where it seemed possible, and testimony to the ecumenical principle was a constant emphasis on the part of many responsible leaders.

2. THE ECUMENICAL IDEAL IN REFORMATION DOCTRINES OF THE CHURCH[2]

Schism and disruption followed in the wake of the Reformation and the process has multiplied the number of autonomous units in non-Roman Christianity.

[1] See further on these movements, Chap. ii, pp. 78, 80 ff.
[2] A study of special value related to this topic, and supplying references to sources and modern Continental literature, is that of E. Wolf, "Die Einheit der Kirche im Zeugnis der Reformation", *Evangelische Theologie*, July 1938, pp. 124–58.

Critical observers of this trend have often drawn the conclusion that Protestantism has at its heart a divisive principle by which it is irresistibly driven to complete disintegration. Many Protestants have acquiesced in this view, justifying it on the ground of an unqualified religious individualism, which, with more rhetoric than research, they have professed to derive from the teaching of the Reformers. On the other hand, those who have really studied Reformation sources have found in them a consistent affirmation of the reality of the one Holy Catholic Church and a clear avowal of the principle of ecumenical unity. Those Protestants who recognize the validity of the latter judgement are, nevertheless, embarrassed by the historical record of failure to embody the principles espoused; while those who regard Protestantism as historically bound for chaos are challenged by its impressive contemporary upsurge of ecumenical interest and unitive effort.

This revival of ecumenical concern accords with the spirit of the Reformers. They sought the renovation, not the disruption, of the Church, and hoped for its reunion. They unhesitatingly accepted the ecumenical Creeds, and regarded themselves as standing within the tradition of the ancient Church in which these venerable symbols were formulated. No point of doctrine affirmed in these documents was in debate between the major Reformers and their Roman Catholic opponents. Protestant official documents, expressly or by implication, accorded full recognition to the Creeds as authentic summaries of the doctrines of Scripture. The Lutheran *Book of Concord* opens with the text of the Apostles', Nicene, and Athanasian Creeds under the title: "Three catholic or ecumenical Creeds." It is believed that this is the earliest application of the word "ecumenical" to creeds as distinct from councils. In the Preface to this Lutheran standard it is stated that the doctrine of the Augsburg Confession is "supported by firm testimonies of Scripture" and "approved by the ancient and received symbols".

The Reformers made much use of the Apostles' Creed as a basis of popular instruction. Calvin speaks of it in his Catechism as the sum of Christian doctrine and "the formula of confession which all Christians have in common". Luther and Calvin understood "Catholic Church" and "Communion of Saints" in the Apostles' Creed as referring to the same thing. The second phrase is an explanatory expansion of the first. In his interpretation of "Communion of Saints", Luther lays primary stress on the idea of the congregation or assembly (*Gemeine*, modern *Gemeinde*) of Christians. He rejects the translation of *communio* by *Gemeinschaft*, which in 16th-century German meant "participation" or "communication". Yet, as Paul Althaus has shown,[1] the implications of this word are attached by Luther to the meaning of *Gemeinde*. The members of the Church as a communion of saints (Christians advancing in holiness), share in all holy gifts, and bear one another's burdens and sins: "all things are the common possession of all". In accord with this is Luther's doctrine of the priesthood of lay Christians, which is not the individualism of an exclusive relation of God and the soul, but the communion-building principle of the mutual exercise of priesthood.[2] Calvin rests his conception of the Church's unity upon this article of the Creed:

---

[1] *Communio sanctorum, Die Gemeinde im Lutherischen Kirchengedanken, I, Luther*, Munich, 1929, pp. 38 ff., 54 ff.

[2] F. Kattenbusch, *Die Doppelschichtigkeit in Luthers Kirchenbegriff*, Leipzig, 1928, pp. 67 ff., 78 ff.; Althaus, op. cit., pp. 68 ff.

"Therefore it is called 'catholic' or universal since we are not to think of two or three Churches, lest Christ be divided—which cannot happen. . . . Therefore 'communion of saints' is added . . . because it perfectly expresses the quality of the Church, as if it were said that the saints are gathered to the fellowship of Christ by the rule that whatever benefits God confers upon them they should mutually communicate to one another" (*Institutes*, IV, i, 2-3).

The phrase "One Holy Catholic Church" in the Nicene Creed is similarly treated.[1] Luther's Larger Catechism contains a brief statement of the meaning of "One Holy Catholic Church":

"I believe that there is upon earth a holy congregation and communion of pure saints ruled under one Head, Christ, called together by the Holy Spirit in one faith, in the same mind and understanding, furnished with multiple gifts yet one in love and in all respects harmonious, without sects or schisms."

The leaders of the Reformed Churches similarly expounded from the Creeds their doctrine of the "True Church". Zwingli affirms that those who live in Christ, "the Head of all believers", constitute "the Church or communion of saints, the bride of Christ, the Catholic Church".[2]

Both Calvin and Bullinger would prefer to say with Augustine, "I believe the Catholic Church" rather than "in the Catholic Church"; yet Calvin acknowledges the Church to be "an object of faith", especially in the sense that we believe in its existence even when it lacks outward manifestation (*Institutes*, IV, i, 2–3). These Reformers apply the word "Catholic" to the Church visible as well as to the Church invisible. This distinction was not new. It is discoverable in Augustine and was stressed by Wyclif and Hus. Luther in *The Papacy at Rome* (1520) contrasted the "visible (or external) community" with the "spiritual inner Christendom (*Christenheit*)". The former contains Christians and non-Christians; the latter is the Church of the Creed, and is "not bound to Rome but is as wide as the world". The visible and invisible are not for Luther separate entities. They interpenetrate one another, and, in part, his aim as a Reformer was to give visibility to the spiritual Church of God. For Calvin the Church is invisible in two senses: (*a*) the extent of the membership of the true Church is concealed from human eyes and known to God alone; and (*b*) when evil conditions seem to proclaim that nothing of the Church is left, we are to "remember that the death of Christ is fruitful, and that God wonderfully preserves his Church, as it were, in hiding-places, according to what he said to Elijah" (1 Kings 19.18; *Institutes*, IV, i, 2).

Calvin states with emphasis that "this article of the Creed relates in some measure to the external Church", and in that connection refers to brotherly

---

[1] Luther, *Werke*, Weimar Edition, XXX (1), p. 130; editor's footnote on *Eine heilige Christliche Kirche* in the Nicene Creed. Luther's German renderings of these Creeds have *Christliche* for *Catholica*, a usage favoured by German writers prior to the Reformation, and which he preferred as suggesting the universal unity of the Christian people. "*Catholic*", he wrote in 1538, "we cannot, indeed, better turn into German than by *Christlich*", in view of the fact that "Christians are in all the world".

[2] *First Zurich Disputation*, vii, viii. In his *Reply to Emser* (1524), which was incorporated in his *Treatise on True and False Religion* (1525), he says: "The Church that with firm faith rests upon Christ, the Son of God, is the Catholic Church, the communion of saints, which we confess in the Creed."

conduct and "deference to the authority of the Church". Under the influence of Cyprian and Augustine, Calvin writes:

> "But since it is now our intention to discuss the visible Church, we may learn from her title of Mother how useful, even necessary, to us is the knowledge of her; for there is no other entrance into life unless she conceives us in her womb, gives us birth, nourishes us at her breast and still preserves us under her care and government until we cast off our mortal flesh and 'become like the angels'."

There is, he continues, no remission of sins to those in alienation from this visible Catholic Church: to be separated from it is "fatally dangerous" (*Institutes*, IV, i, 4).

In the Geneva Catechism the Holy Catholic Church is defined as "the body and society of believers whom God has predestined to eternal life". It is "holy" in the sense that in it God is forming those whom he justifies to holiness and innocence of life. The word "Catholic", or universal, means "that as there is but one Head of all believers, so they must all be united into one body, that the Church diffused through the whole world may be one and not more".

The visible Church is indicated by certain signs and marks, but the invisible Church of the elect is not always discernible by these signs. Calvin finds no entrance into spiritual life outside the visible Church, yet sees spread abroad through the world a Church of the elect not always visible. In his thought the concepts of the visible and the invisible Church are in tension but never in contradiction. We are to believe the true invisible Church of God, and to honour the visible Church and cultivate its communion (*Institutes*, IV, i, 7). Where the Word is purely preached and reverently heard, and the Sacraments are "administered according to the institution of Christ", we are to recognize the Church and not to contend against it or separate ourselves from it. To depart from the Church is to deny God and Christ (*Institutes*, IV, i, 10). Diversity on non-essential matters ought not to be an occasion of disunion. Calvin also assails those who would renounce communion through a haughty assumption of superior sanctity. The visible Church is daily advancing towards a holiness not yet attained. Its members are not without blemish; but they ardently aspire towards "perfect holiness and purity". While we ought faithfully to urge men to perfection, we ought not to desert our fellow-Christians because of their imperfections (*Institutes*, IV, i, 13–20).

Thus on the basis of the ecumenical Creeds the Reformers outline a doctrine of the ecumenical Church, laying stress on the avoidance of schism where the Word and scriptural Sacraments are honoured. In all this they were profoundly indebted to the Church Fathers. They were also in a large sense the heirs of the Conciliarists, who demanded that ecclesiastical authority be representative. Conciliarism was a frustrated revolution; but its principle remained in many minds, both as a potential danger to papal claims and as a potential influence in doctrine and polity in an age of reform.

The Conciliarist emphasis upon the Headship of Christ was renewed in the Reformation. It was, of course, a doctrine derived from Scripture and employed by the Fathers.[1] But the doctrine is rather assumed than strongly emphasized by

---

[1] *Tota ecclesia ejus, quae ubique diffusa est, cujus est ipse caput.* Augustine, *Enarratio in Psalmos*, lii, Sermo 2. Cf. lxv, Sermo 1.

the Fathers, while it is frequently stressed by the Conciliarists, and constantly affirmed in Reformation statements. It was a doctrinal basis of attack upon the headship claimed by the Pope. The world-wide Church of which Christ is Head could, said the Conciliarists, through its representatives in a council, restrain or depose a Pope. No human monarch of the Church, said the Reformers, was either necessary for government or authorized in Scripture.

The Conciliarists, with few exceptions, while affirming the authority of councils, recognized their fallibility. They provided for the correction of the decisions of councils by the action of later ones. They also regarded the council as asserting rather than supplanting the authority of Scripture. Luther was in agreement with these positions; his insistence upon the authority of the Word, and his denial of the infallibility of councils, in no sense constituted departures from essential Conciliarism, though he affirmed these positions with new emphasis.

Luther's first formal appeal for a general council was made on 28 November 1518. Here he employs phrases from the Constance decree *Sacrosancta* (1415). Since "a sacred council lawfully assembled in the Holy Spirit, representing the holy Catholic Church, is superior to the Pope in matters that concern the faith", he solemnly appeals for "a free general council". In his *Address to the German Nobility* (1520) he urges his readers as faithful Christians to do what they can "to procure a truly free council". This treatise contains elaborate proposals for reforms to be brought about by a council or series of councils free from papal control. Luther promptly followed this by a repetition (17 November 1520) of his appeal of 1518 for a free council representative of the whole Catholic Church.[1]

Kolde's view that Luther ceased to advocate the conciliar method of reform after 1521[2] is wholly erroneous. The demand for a free council was put forward by the Lutheran side with vigour in the imperial diets of the 1520's, notably the important diets held at Speyer in 1526 and 1529. In the Lutheran Protest of 1529 complaint is made of the failure to assemble "a free general Christian council", which "has been considered in all diets a suitable means" of dealing with matters in dispute. A new demand for a free general council was issued by the Protestant Princes after this diet (14 October 1529). Luther himself continued to advocate a council, either general or national, provided that it could be truly representative and free from papal dictation. He expresses a desire for it in the Schmalkald Articles adopted in February 1537. To this document Melanchthon added an appendix which contains vigorous objection to the papal domination of councils: "The judgements of synods are rightly the judgements of the Church, not of the pontiffs."

Calvin frequently affirmed the ideals of the Conciliarists and criticized with the greatest severity the papal domination of councils. In a memorandum written probably in December 1560, after the treaty of Cateau-Cambrésis between France and the Empire had renewed the issue of a council for pacification, he described the "free and universal council" that was needed "to put an end to the existing divisions in Christianity". It must be free with respect to place of meeting, personnel, and procedure, and bound only by Scripture. The location should be central to the attending nations. This interesting document offers what is virtually an agenda for the council, listing numerous points

[1] *Werke*, Weimar edition, II, pp. 36 f., 413, 415, 427; VII, pp. 75 f. Cf. Th. Kolde, *Luthers Stellung zu Conzil und Kirche bis zum wormser Reichstag, 1521.*
[2] Kolde, op. cit., p. 113.

in dispute in the realms of doctrine, worship, and polity. Calvin's council was to be a conference on Faith and Order—with power. The Pope is not excluded, but he must submit to the council's decisions and swear to abide by them. Calvin insists that, while a national synod may undertake internal reform, only a genuinely universal council can allay the troubles of Christendom.[1]

The brief statements of the doctrine of the Church contained in the Lutheran and Reformed confessions of faith strongly affirm its ecumenical nature. The Augsburg Confession (1530) teaches:

> ". . . that one Holy Church is to continue for ever. Moreover, the Church is the congregation of saints in which the Gospel is rightly taught and the Sacraments are rightly administered. And unto the true unity of the Church, it is sufficient to agree concerning the doctrine of the Gospel and the administration of the Sacraments." (vii)

In this life, however, hypocrites are mingled with the Church, hence it is "lawful to use the sacraments administered by evil men".

Melanchthon's *Apology for the Confession* (1532), expounding these articles, states that:

> ". . . the Church is not only an external society . . . but principally a society of faith and of the Holy Spirit in the heart, which however has external signs (*notas*) by which it may be recognized, namely the pure doctrine of the Gospel and the administration of the Sacraments in accordance with the Gospel of Christ."

This Church is not a "Platonic society",[2] but one that actually exists, formed of "those who truly believe and are justified, dispersed through all the world". The notion that it is an external monarchy under the Roman pontiff is repudiated. The teaching on unity in doctrine is explained with reference to a justifiable variety in ceremonies. The emphasis in these passages is manifestly on the spirituality and universality of the Church. There is also, however, a concern for the actual visible Church as a unity. This is evident, for example, from the condemnation of sectarians who, because of the Church's imperfections, would lightly break its unity.

The Reformed confessions are equally explicit. A good example is the Second Helvetic (1566), the mature statement of the mind of Henry Bullinger and everywhere honoured in the Reformed Churches. Chapter xvii is entitled: "Of the Catholic and Holy Church of God, and of the Only Head of the Church." It is here taught "that there is but one Church which we call Catholic, for the reason that it is universal and is spread out through all parts of the world, and extends to all times".

The Gallican Confession (1559), the Scots Confession (1560), the Belgic Confession (1561), the Heidelberg Catechism (1562), and the Bohemian Confession of 1575, show similar insistence on the doctrines we have noted.

Not only through their appropriation of the ancient ecumenical Creeds, but also in the assertion of universal collective authority under Christ's Headship,

---

[1] *Opera, Corpus Reformatorum*, xviii, pp. 285 ff.
[2] I.e. one which, like Plato's Republic, exists only in an ideal world.

the Reformers affirmed an ecumenical Church. The One Holy Catholic Church consists of all the faithful in all the world and through all time, and is ruled without a human monarch through representative assemblies under the Word of God. Their doctrine always stressed the concept of the invisible or spiritual Church, but related with this a more or less visible Church which is also Catholic. The conception of church reform was largely that of bringing the qualities of the invisible Church to visible expression.

The one true Catholic or universal Church, as they understood it, was not in their time to attain to convincing visibility. The leaders themselves came to sharp disagreement, especially on the doctrine of the Eucharist. Even where theology offered no barrier, national and linguistic boundaries limited fellowship. The conciliar or synodical organization of Lutheranism was seriously impaired through the control exercised by the territorial governments. The Reformed Churches from the first adopted conciliar polities. Although they enjoyed much reciprocity, as organizations they were autonomous and never achieved international integration. Yet through the dark age of its progressive fissiparation Protestantism continued to crave an existential ecumenicity.

3. EARLY ROMAN CATHOLIC REACTIONS TO PROTESTANTISM

The rigid and intractable opposition between the Roman Catholic and the Protestant Churches that has been for four centuries a central fact in the situation of the Churches makes it easy to forget that this opposition only gradually hardened and that the first generation after the outbreak of the Reformation was marked by a considerable number of irenical approaches from the Roman Catholic side.

Among the Roman Catholics of the period, the first and greatest irenical figure was Desiderius Erasmus of Rotterdam (1469–1536), the founder of a great irenical tradition which lasted on both in the Roman Catholic and Protestant Churches for many generations after his death.

The *Compactata*, articles of agreement between the Bohemians and the Council of Basle (1433), though approved by Pope Eugenius IV, were repudiated by Pius II (1462), and the Utraquists[1] remained in secession from Rome. Erasmus in correspondence (1519–21) with a Bohemian gentleman, John Slechta, made interesting suggestions for pacification. He advised the Utraquists to give up their sacramental peculiarity in the interests of unity, though he could not condemn it as an error. His comments on the customs of the Brethren were, in contrast to Slechta's, mainly favourable, and he suggests that the Pope may be persuaded to permit their rites. In 1520 two learned emissaries of the Brethren visited Erasmus at Antwerp. A friend of Erasmus states that he confessed himself in substantial agreement with them, but declined his public support on the ground that it would only harm their cause. In the same year he was urged, in a letter from Artlebus, a Moravian nobleman, to frame from a certain book of the Brethren a manual of piety which all might follow. He replied (28 January 1521) that the true guide to the Christian life was the life of Christ, and now advised the Brethren to seek unity with the papal Church. Two months earlier there had been published a project that is credited to Erasmus along with

---

[1] The more moderate party among the followers of John Hus, who maintained the right of the laity to receive the Holy Communion in both kinds.

Johann Faber, for settlement of the Luther controversy through a board of arbitration consisting of the Emperor Charles V, Henry VIII of England, and Louis II of Hungary.[1] In a Colloquy "An Enquiry Concerning Faith" (1524), Erasmus has a character, Barbatius, answer the question, "Do you believe in Holy Church?" with a negative, explaining:

> "I believe in a Holy Church which is the Body of Christ, that is, a congregation of all men throughout the world who agree in the faith of the Gospel; to sever oneself from this is a mortal crime. Cyprian teaches us to believe only in God. The Church is a body of men who, however good they may be, are not infallible."

In a late work, *On Restoring Concord in the Church* (1533), he somewhat disconsolately pleads for the spirit of conciliation and mutual toleration in disputed matters of belief and worship. In the latter he would permit a wide range of variation.

> "We have had enough of quarrels: perhaps sheer weariness may bring us together to concord, to dwell in the house of the Lord. How amiable are thy dwellings, O Lord of Hosts."[2]

Concord to Erasmus was as dear as truth; but it was not to be attained through "sheer weariness" or compromise.

After the Edict of Worms (1521), which severely condemned Luther, defenders of the papacy hoped that his movement would collapse. But imperial diets held at Nuremberg in 1522 and 1524 declined to enforce the Edict and demanded "a free general Christian council" to deal with the controverted issues. The Emperor Charles V[3] sought Pope Clement VII's consent to this, but in vain. Instead, the papal legate, Campeggio, instructed to treat separately with princes favourable to the papacy, held a meeting at Ratisbon in June 1524 with the Emperor's brother Ferdinand, the dukes of Bavaria, and certain bishops. This was the beginning of the politically divisive phase of the Reformation controversy. The League of Dessau followed in 1525; it called forth in response the Lutheran League of Torgau (1526). The reiterated Lutheran demand for a free council was unavailing. Clement would have nothing to do with a council, and Charles would not have one held without the Pope.

The great Augsburg Diet of 1530 rejected the Lutheran Confession,[4] and

---

[1] This document has been edited with introduction and notes by K. Ferguson in *Erasmi opuscula: A Supplement to the opera omnia*, The Hague, 1933, pp. 352–61. It is entitled: *Consilium cuiusdam ex animo cupientis esse consultum et Romani pontificis dignitati et Christianae religionis tranquillitati.*

[2] P. S. Allen, *Erasmus: Lectures and Wayfaring Sketches*, Oxford, 1934, Chap. iv, "Erasmus on Church Unity".

[3] The following brief table should be borne in mind:

Emperors		Popes	
Charles V	1520–56	Clement VII	1523–34
Ferdinand I	1556–64	Paul III	1534–49
Maximilian II	1564–76	Julius III	1550–55
Rudolf II	1576–1612	Paul IV	1555–59
		Pius IV	1559–65
		Pius V	1565–72
		Gregory XIII	1572–85

[4] This was the Confession of Augsburg (the *Confessio Augustana*) which is still the classic Reformation confession of all the Lutheran Churches.

adopted a refutation of it drawn up by a large committee of theologians. While the Diet continued, efforts to obtain agreement were made in a series of conferences between groups of theologians and laymen on either side, with John Eck and Philip Melanchthon (1497–1560) as the principal spokesmen. Concessions by both parties brought the differences to a minimum on the doctrine of the Eucharist, the confession of sins, the episcopate, and marriage of the clergy. But these approaches were tentative and Campeggio discouraged the effort. Luther on his part viewed the concessions of Melanchthon with alarm. Agreement, he wrote, "is impossible unless the Pope will simply abolish the papacy". The Diet by a majority resolved to enforce the Edict of Worms, and gave the Lutherans six months in which to submit (22 September). In February 1531 the Protestant estates formed the League of Schmalkald to resist the enforcement of these measures. The Turks were now menacing the Empire and Charles found himself in no position to fight an internal war.

With Pope Paul III (1534–49) Roman Catholicism began to regain religious and political strength. Yet the tide of Lutheran advance was not stemmed. The policies of Pope and Emperor were at variance, and Charles began to seek terms with the Protestants. He brought about new colloquies of the theologians during meetings of the imperial diet at Hagenau (June 1540), at Worms (November 1540), and at Ratisbon (April to July 1541). The first of these conferences considered the doctrine of justification; the second was concerned with original sin. The Ratisbon colloquy resumed these discussions and presented to the diet the so-called Ratisbon Book which contained twenty-three articles of tentative agreement. No common ground was found on the important questions of the papacy and transubstantiation, although these were discussed and, according to Calvin, who was present, Melanchthon and Bucer had "drawn up ambiguous and insincere formulas" on the latter point in the hope of an interim agreement.

During the early stages of the Counter-Reformation various proposals for compromise with the Protestants were presented by individual Roman Catholic seekers after reunion, chiefly men who were in some sense Erasmians. Ludwig Cardauns has edited, with introductions, reunion proposals by John Cochlaeus, Friedrich Nausea, and Albert of Mainz at the time of the conference at Hagenau and Worms.[1] But none of these is a unitive document in any sense of the word "union" other than that of the full recovery of the sway of the medieval Church. If Nausea treats some of the articles of the Augsburg Confession with guarded approval, he is uncompromising and militant towards its adherents. All these writers, however, seek to meet the crisis by an active programme of disciplinary reform. The humanist and Erasmian motivation of the efforts towards reunion of 1540–41 is exhibited by Robert Stupperich, who stresses the influence on the theologians in both camps (Witzel and Gropper, Melanchthon and Bucer) of the concept of "double justification" held by Erasmus.[2] The Ratisbon statement on this doctrine closely approaches the Lutheran teaching, since here the papal nuncio, Gasparo Contarini, was in virtual accord with Melanchthon. The gracious personality of this gifted Venetian, whom Paul III had raised to the cardinalate, won the goodwill of the Lutherans. But he died in August 1542, leaving no comparable representative of the desire within his communion for

---

[1] *Zur Geschichte der kirchlichen Unions- und Reformsbestrebungen von 1538 bis 1542*, Rome, 1910.
[2] *Der Humanismus und die Wiedervereinigung der Konfessionen, Schriften des Vereins für Reformationsgeschichte*, No. 160, Leipzig, 1936, pp. 30–37, 68–131.

accord with the Protestants. The Ratisbon articles were hopefully welcomed by a few liberal spirits at Rome, such as Reginald Pole (Archbishop of Canterbury 1556–58), but were wholly unacceptable to the Pope. Luther regarded them as patchwork, and the Lutheran princes were in no mood for compromise.

Reference has been made to Georg Witzel (Wicelius), a Hessian, who had briefly aligned himself with Luther but returned to the Roman communion. Witzel published at Leipzig his *Methodus concordiae ecclesiae* (1539). His other notable irenical treatise, *Via regia* (1564), was written at the behest of the Emperor Ferdinand I, whose favour he enjoyed. In these works he appears a sincere and eager advocate of reunion and reform. In the first he urges princes, Pope, bishops, doctors, and laymen to seek peace by means of a council. Witzel would abandon the scholastic formulations in favour of the doctrines of the Fathers, but he gives prior authority to Scripture. He desires that scholarly translations of the Bible and the Liturgy be prepared and authorized, and calls for the suppression of superstitions and abuses. In the *Via regia* these ideas are further developed. He would accept the first four only of the Ecumenical Councils. He treats the Lutheran doctrines with discriminating criticism and dwells upon the abuses prevalent in the hierarchical Church.[1]

Another irenical writer of the Erasmian school who won the favour of the Emperors was George Cassander (1513–66), a Flemish scholar who spent his later years in Cologne. Cassander's proposals for unity are developed in two works, *De officio pii ac publicae tranquillitatis* (1561) and *Consultatio de articulis fidei inter Catholicos et Protestantes* (1565). Cassander became celebrated for his conception of Christian reunion on the basis of "fundamental articles" of faith. These were ascertainable in Scripture and the Fathers, and were essentially comprised in the Apostles' Creed. As with Witzel, authority for what is requisite for unity stops with the Fathers ("the first six centuries"). Cassander adopts as his own the formula of Vincent of Lerins (d. 450): "What has been believed always, everywhere, and by all." He also devotes a detailed examination to the Augsburg Confession, interpreting its articles as agreeably to Roman Catholic teaching as possible.

These notions of "fundamental articles" and "the first six (or five) centuries" were to recur with great frequency in 17th-century discussions of reunion. Cassander had, however, merely brought to focus presuppositions that underlie the common appeal to the Fathers and the Creeds. The formulation of a short creed in itself assumes that there are "fundamental" articles that deserve acceptance prior to others. Calvin, Bucer, and Cranmer, not less than Erasmus, had distinguished essential from non-essential beliefs in relation to the problem of unity and separation. Calvin cites as "essential points of true doctrine" the points "that God is one, that Christ is God and the Son of God, that our salvation lies in God's mercy, and the like". As an example of non-essentials, he mentions views held of the state of the soul between death and judgement. Calvin, however, sharply attacked Cassander's *De officio*, supposing that its real

---

[1] The Oratorian, M. Tabaraud, notes the praise bestowed on him by Hugo Grotius and Richard Simon, but thinks him "too bitter and declamatory" in his reproaches against bishops and Popes: *Histoire critique des projets formés depuis trois cents ans pour la réunion des communions chrétiennes*, Paris, 1824, pp. 295 ff. The text of the *Via regia* is contained in *Georgii Cassandri et Georgii Wicelii: De Sacris nostri temporis controversiis libri duo*, edited by the statesman Hermann Conring, Helmstedt, 1649; G. L. Schmid's *Georg Witzel, ein Altkatholik des xvi Jahrhunderts*, Vienna, 1876, contains an analysis of the book, pp. 96–137.

author was François Baudouin, whose "flightiness and inconstancy" were noted by Cassander himself.[1]

The futility of the Ratisbon conversations left Charles V at a disadvantage from which he was to extricate himself by adroit diplomacy and a bold stroke of war against the League. Having defeated the Lutherans in the first Schmalkaldic War (1547), he attempted, in disregard of the Pope, a new measure of pacification pending final decision by a council. A subservient Diet of Augsburg in 1548 adopted the intended basis for this, the Augsburg Interim. It was the work of Julius von Pflug, an Erasmian, soon to be Bishop of Naumburg, with the co-operation of John Agricola, Lutheran court preacher of Brandenburg. The Protestant element in it consisted chiefly in permission of clerical marriage and of communion in both kinds, and in an ambiguous statement on justification.

The Augsburg Interim brought only dissatisfaction and confusion. Maurice, now Elector of Saxony, set forth a variant scheme prepared by Melanchthon's pliant hand though never signed by him, the Leipzig Interim (24 December 1548), which in the main upheld Lutheran doctrines but yielded much on rites and ceremonies. Other territorial governments proposed their own adjustments. But the whole effort collapsed amid a chorus of derision.

The second Schmalkaldic War, the Truce of Passau (1552), and the Peace of Augsburg (1555) left Germany divided between Roman Catholicism and Lutheranism. Calvinism, then beginning to enter the Rhine towns, went unrecognized in the settlement. The policy of Ferdinand I, like that of Charles V, constantly diverged from that of the papacy. He embarrassed the Council of Trent by his pressure for reforming action. He favoured a conciliar settlement of the religious issues, and would willingly have made such concessions to Protestantism as communion in both kinds and clerical marriage. His son, Maximilian II, personally leaned strongly to Lutheranism, but political interests prevented his adopting a bold pro-Lutheran policy. His toleration of Lutheran nobles and knights, and his refusal to consent to the decrees of Trent, were not in themselves measures conducive to Church unity.

The project of a general council had never been out of men's minds. Following an election promise, Paul III, in contrast with his predecessor, favoured a council provided he could secure control of its procedures and prevent its becoming another Constance. Not only the designs of Charles but the surviving Conciliarism within the Church endangered the papal supremacy. Charles hoped to utilize a council to restrain the Pope, bring about the submission of the Lutherans, and secure his position in Germany. The Ratisbon Conference was intended by him as preparatory to a council, and the Augsburg Interim was put forward with the same expectation. The Lutherans, however, were aware that the council now proposed would not be anything like the "free general Christian council" they had advocated.

Numerous proposals were entertained in the counter-diplomacy of Paul and Charles before the summoning of the Council to Trent; and for this meeting

[1] E. Doumergue, *Jean Calvin, les hommes et les choses de son temps*, II, p. 763, quoting Charles Drelincourt. Cf. A. Fritzen, *De Cassandri ejusque sociorum studiis irenicis*, Munich, 1865, pp. 20 ff. On Cassander see also M. Birck, *Georg Cassander's Ideen ueber die Wiedervereinigung der christlichen Confessionen in Deutschland*, Cologne, 1876; O. W. Hering, *Geschichte der kirchlichen Unionsversuchen seit der Reformation*, I, pp. 289 ff., 297, 427–41; "Fundamental Articles", by G. H. Joyce, in *Catholic Encyclopedia*; "Articles fondamentaux", by A. Tanquery, in *Dictionnaire de théologie catholique*. Conring, op. cit., has the text of the *Consultatio*. There are numerous editions of the *De officio*.

Rome made the most careful preparations.[1] It is significant that the title adopted in the decrees of Trent reads: "The sacred, holy, ecumenical Synod of Trent lawfully assembled in the Holy Ghost, the legates of the Apostolic See presiding therein." This novel style was proposed by the papal legates, after they had rejected the conciliar formula, "representing the universal Church". Thus the conciliar principle, that a council's authority must be associated with its universally representative character, was excluded. The brilliant General of the Jesuits, Diego Laynez, with other Jesuit theologians, in the later sessions lent effective support to the papal cause. The Council was suspended for ten years (1552–62) and finally closed in December 1563. It had set the form and mapped the programme of the Roman Catholic revival, upheld the papal supremacy, and pronounced anathemas on those holding the salient doctrines of Protestantism. Its decisions were ratified by Pius IV in a Bull of 26 January 1564. Another Bull followed (13 November) which made obligatory upon priests and teachers a statement in twelve articles, the Profession of Faith of the Council of Trent. The tenth article contains an uncompromising pledge of "obedience to the Roman pontiff, successor to the Blessed Peter, Prince of the Apostles, and Vicar of Jesus Christ".

The Valois kings of France, no less than the Habsburg emperors, desired a peaceable settlement of religion within their own domains, but were inclined to encourage any who offered embarrassment to their rivals. In 1534 Francis I sent William du Bellay, a brother of the Bishop of Paris, to consult with the Lutherans and Zwinglians. Philip of Hesse, Bucer, Melanchthon, Bullinger, Myconius, and others were approached, while John Sturm of Strasburg, then in Paris, and du Bellay's brother, the Bishop, supported the mission by letters. Melanchthon sent a highly conciliatory memorandum to Francis (1 August 1534).[2] He would have gone to Paris, except for his prince's opposition. His final refusal (28 August 1535) preceded by two days the condemnation of the proposal by the Sorbonne theologians. The incident thus ended in futility.

The reign of Henry II (1547–59) was marked by very severe measures against Protestantism and at the same time by its growth and organization. During the minority of Charles IX (1560–74), Catherine de Medici, as regent, under the influence of Michel de l'Hôpital, whose wife was a Calvinist, at first sought an amicable toleration leading to unity by means of a council. In September 1561, at her bidding, representatives of the Reformed Church were present at a meeting of the French clergy at Poissy. Theodore Beza of Geneva and the Italian theologian Peter Martyr Vermigli, then a teacher at Zurich, with other Reformed ministers and laymen, confronted six cardinals and other dignitaries of Church and State. Charles de Guise, Cardinal of Lorraine, and Beza were the chief spokesmen for their respective sides. L'Hôpital's opening address, urging charity and moderation, did not prevent Beza from presenting the Reformed doctrines in a forthright manner or the Cardinal from an equally uncompromising reply a week later. But the conference was resumed without great bitterness. Then came a deputation from Pius IV, led by a cardinal and, more important, including Diego Laynez. At Rome the Colloquy of Poissy was viewed as a danger to the

[1] K. D. Schmidt, *Studien zur Geschichte des Konzils von Trient*, Tübingen, 1925, pp. 13–37. The background of the Council of Trent has been amply treated by H. Jedin, *Geschichte des Konzils von Trient*. I. *Der Kampf um das Konzil*, Freiburg, 1949.
[2] A. L. Herminjard, *Correspondance des Réformateurs*, Geneva, 1866–97, III, pp. 266 ff.; J. T. McNeill, *Unitive Protestantism*, pp. 162–68.

decisions of Trent, and the Jesuit leader was the disputant chosen to bring it to naught. Having listened to a debate on the Eucharist, Laynez arose and urged the Regent to "direct those gentlemen to Trent", where, under "the infallible guidance of the Holy Spirit", the Protestants would receive, or more probably refuse, instruction. The Colloquy ended on 14 October without any result beyond the impression that such an approach was unprofitable.[1] Catherine's resolve to follow a policy of toleration was implemented by an edict of 17 January 1562, which allowed Protestant worship under restrictions; but peace was broken by the Duke of Guise (1 March) and France was torn by religious war. The principles of the *Politiques*, a party which followed the tolerant ideas of l'Hôpital, were more political than religious. The Edict of Nantes (1598) marks their late and incomplete vindication. But mere political toleration is not Church unity, and there is little that savours of unity or even of mutual understanding between the faiths in France during the period assigned to this chapter.

The Counter-Reformation reached Sweden in the reign of John III (1568–92), whose queen was an earnest Roman Catholic. John's complicated foreign relations, including an interest in a rich Naples territory, affected his religious policy. John had read the *Consultatio* of Cassander, and had as his adviser Peter Fecht, a pupil of Melanchthon who leaned towards Rome. After the death of the able Lutheran Archbishop, Laurentius Petri, in 1573, a new policy emerged. In February 1575 a set of twenty "New Ordinances" prepared by Fecht was promulgated, which introduced medieval usages; and this was followed by the "Red Book" (*Liturgia suecanae ecclesiae catholicae et orthodoxae conformis*, 1576), which mingled Roman Catholic and Lutheran services. Meanwhile Pope Gregory XIII had appointed a Congregation for the Northern Countries, and now, with John's consent or at his invitation, Jesuits entered and became active. John submitted the Red Book to Rome, and the Pope sent the able Antonio Possevino with assistants and literature to Sweden. In the negotiations that followed, John offered terms of an alliance with the Pope (March 1578), but finding Possevino unable to secure the fulfilment of an earlier promise of the Naples inheritance, he reacted against the papal diplomacy. Possevino departed and returned (1579); but Swedish resistance was now aroused under the leadership of the King's brother Charles, and the envoy withdrew in defeat (1580). After a period in which he hankered after union with the Greeks, John died a professed Lutheran.[2] Sweden was confirmed in resolute Lutheranism by the Uppsala Mote of 1593.

The projects of the theologians and the diplomacy of princes failed in every instance to produce reunion between Roman Catholics and Protestants in 16th-century Europe. It would appear that, at least after 1530, there was something unrealistic in every attempt to negotiate such a reunion. The appropriation of church property by the princes was no doubt an issue of more importance than

[1] J. Brodrick, S.J., *The Progress of the Jesuits 1556–79*, London and New York, 1947, pp. 90 ff., reports the part of Laynez. In the ample account given by Paul F. Geisendorf, *Théodore de Bèze*, Geneva, 1949, pp. 125–66, Laynez is treated incidentally, but this writer remarks that at the end of his speech, "Tears sprang to the eyes of the Queen; all her efforts had been brought to naught". See also B. F. Paist, "Peter Martyr and the Colloquy of Poissy", reprinted from the *Princeton Theological Review*, 1922.

[2] This account is based upon that given in H. Holmquist's *Reformationstidevarvet*, Vol. III of *Svenska Kyrkans Historia*, Stockholm, 1933. I have also consulted J. Wordsworth, *The National Church of Sweden*, London, 1911, and *The History of the Swedes* (1832) by E. G. Geijer, translated by J. H. Turner, London, n.d.

is apparent in the discussions. But there were areas of fundamental divergence in doctrine and usages where conviction ran deep and strong. Highly important was the unqualified Protestant repudiation not only of papal policies and papal councils but of the papacy itself—"which", says H. Eells, "the Protestants would never accept and the Catholics would never abandon".[1]

4. LUTHERANISM AND THE PROBLEM OF UNITY

In Luther's view, the Church of Christ was both holier and wider than the Roman Communion, and it was uncatholic to equate obedience to Christ with obedience to Rome. He recognized as Christians many members of the universal *Christenheit* who were out of communion with Rome. It was through reading the Fathers and ancient councils in preparation for the Leipzig Disputation (June–July 1519) that he first vividly realized this, and the point was brought to the foreground in that debate. Countering Eck's high view of papal authority, Luther referred to the "many thousands of saints" of the Greek Church who were not under the Pope. Eck also drew from him the admission that Hus had been unfairly condemned. Certain Bohemians then in Leipzig made contact with Luther and furnished him with some of Hus's books. Luther thus found himself pleading for groups regarded by Rome as schismatic or heretical. He had no doubt that his own position was more Christian, ecumenical, and truly Catholic than Eck's argument for *Romana obedientia*.[2]

More than once in 1520 Luther complained that the Romanists were in effect demanding an alteration in the Creed to make it read, "I believe in the Church of Rome". In his reply to the Bull *Exsurge Domine* which attacked him for his sympathy with the Hussites, he marvels that his opponents condemn "what is true, Catholic, and edifying".[3] In his *Letter to the Christian Nobility* he takes up the cause of the Hussites, beginning on the ground of the wrong done to Hus in the violation of his safe-conduct at Constance. Luther would give them a voice in their church affairs, and permit them to retain communion in both kinds. With the Utraquists he would tolerate the Brethren, until they should agree together.

Luther's writings and adherents began to appear in Prague as early as 1519. J. Th. Müller recites the story of no less than five deputations sent by the Bohemian Brethren to the Reformer in the years 1522–24. They had earlier sought, in travels extending to Greece and Asia Minor, some Christian body with which they might fraternize (1492). Now they looked upon Luther as in some sense the reviver of the doctrines of Hus. However, their ablest leader, Lucas of Prague, after a period of warm admiration, recoiled from agreement with Luther. Luther and Lucas found themselves at variance on the number of the sacraments and on the doctrine of the Eucharist. The adherence of the Brethren to celibacy and their practice of rebaptizing converts to their communion were also points of unresolved difference.

After the death of Lucas (1528), intercourse with the Brethren was resumed. In 1532 they framed a confession of faith to be presented in German to Margrave George of Brandenburg, and to the Western theologians. John Augusta

---

[1] "The Failure of Church Unification Efforts during the German Reformation", *Archiv für Reformationsgeschichte*, Jahrg. 42, 1951, pp. 160–73 (p. 172).
[2] Luther, *Werke*, Weimar edition, II, pp. 258, 262, 266, 269, 272, 276.
[3] Id., VI, pp. 300, 602.

(d. 1572), the irenical leader of the Brethren, invited Luther's comment, and Luther had the confession published with an introduction by him at Wittenberg (1533). A less exact version had appeared in Zurich (1532). Luther does not approve it at all points—for example, on the value of good works; but he is glad to publish it in order to promote unity among all Christians. Mutual understanding increased through the presence of many Czech students in Wittenberg, and of numerous Lutherans in Bohemia. The Brethren now determined to seek toleration from the Habsburg who had become their King, Ferdinand of Austria (later the Emperor Ferdinand I). Augusta and his colleagues prepared a new confession in Latin. Bohemian nobles attached to the Brethren undertook, and were finally permitted, to lay the statement in the King's hands (14 November 1535). His promised answer was delayed and unfavourable. Though the seven sacraments and rebaptism were excluded from this confession, Luther and Melanchthon still felt some objections. Augusta visited them three times (1536–38), and after considerable alteration of the document, Luther had it published with the Brethren's earlier address to the Margrave and a warmly commendatory preface by himself.[1]

Luther always regarded the discipline of the Brethren as too legalistic. But his attitude to their emissaries was throughout remarkably cordial. On 5 October 1542, he wrote to Augusta, who had recently been again in Wittenberg, a brief, brotherly letter:

"I admonish you in the Lord, that even as you began you may continue with us to the end, in the fellowship of the Spirit and of doctrine. . . . May the Lord strengthen, protect, keep, and establish us and you, so that we may together grow into the same image, to the glory of his mercy."

Luther would gladly have seen the Brethren and Utraquists united, and Augusta was already looking in this direction. The Utraquist approach to Luther was principally made by a rather unstable leader, Gallus Cahera, a priest of Prague, who appeared at Wittenberg in May 1523. He made a favourable impression upon Luther and, with his approval, a few months later returned to Prague. He became administrator of the consistory of Prague, and for a short time in 1524 laboured to Lutheranize the Utraquist Church. At his request, Luther wrote his tract *On the Appointment of the Ministers of the Church* (1523),[2] a plea for the election of ministers by congregations. Cahera promulgated twenty articles on the ministry, sacraments, holy days, etc.; but his abrupt reform met with resistance, to which he readily bowed in order to retain his office. By the summer of 1524 the Lutheran stage was over and Cahera was supporting a reaction favourable to Rome. An infiltration of Lutheran ideas among the Utraquists continued through later decades, and individuals among them became definitely Lutheran; but the Church as a whole was inclining in the opposite direction.

[1] J. Th. Müller, *Geschichte der böhmischen Brüder*, 3 vols., Herrnhut, 1931, I, pp. 396–417; II, pp. 40–77; E. de Schweinitz, *The History of the Unitas Fratrum*, Bethlehem, Pa., 1885, pp. 223–54. On the question of the Eucharist in the relations of Luther and Lucas, see the detailed study of E. Paschke, *Die Theologie der böhmischen Brüder in ihrer Frühzeit*, I, Stuttgart, 1935. The Confession of 1538 is given in H. A. Niemeyer, *Collectio confessionum in ecclesiis reformatis publicatarum*, Leipzig, 1840, pp. 771–817. For the *Von Anbeten des Sacraments*, a reply to Lucas' *Faith Victorious*, see Luther's *Werke*, Weimar edition, XI, pp. 417 ff.

[2] *Werke*, Weimar edition, XII, pp. 160 ff.

The Strasburg Reformer, Martin Bucer (1491–1551), was the most constant promoter of Church unity among all the 16th-century leaders. His vital conception of the Church as a society "gathered out of the world" by Christ, each of whose members "has an office and work for the common edification of the whole body and of all the members", underlies all his endeavours. His efforts began with the beginning of the controversies over the Lord's Supper. In 1521 Hinne Rode, a disciple of Wessel Gansfort, brought to Wittenberg, and later to Basle, Strasburg, and Zurich, an *Epistle on the Eucharist* written by Cornelis Henrix Hoen, which embodied Wessel's teaching. Luther could not accept it, but it was welcomed by Bucer and published by Zwingli (1521),[1] who was in full accord with its teaching and by it also confirmed in his own view.

The Colloquy held at Marburg early in October 1529 takes an important place in the history of the Reformation. The meeting was convened by Philip of Hesse, a Lutheran prince in whom Luther had lost confidence. The Emperor and the Pope had settled their quarrel, and the Diet of Speyer had added to the perils of Lutheranism. Luther and Melanchthon believed that these perils would be enhanced by an alliance of their party with the Reformed sections of Switzerland. They still hoped for a settlement in which reform would be assured in the territories of the Empire, and were in no mood to defy the Emperor by an alliance with the Swiss. Melanchthon had returned from Speyer greatly disquieted and anxious to prevent Swiss opinions from affecting future negotiations with the Emperor. Bucer, after Marburg, wrote to Ambrose Blaurer that the failure of agreement there was due to Melanchthon's devotion to the Habsburg princes.

The cleavage in theology was thus accompanied by a basic difference in ecclesiastical strategy. But apart from this, it was a serious clash of convictions. At Marburg these convictions held: neither party yielded a point of doctrine. Zwingli, however, was willing to ally himself with the Lutherans in order to form a united front of the Reformation forces and obtain political security for the movement; while Luther was inclined to press the differences harshly in order to prevent such an alignment, which he thought likely to intensify the internal problem of Germany and produce war rather than peace.

In these circumstances, what is surprising is not the disagreement on one point of doctrine, but the fact of agreement at most points. Of the statement in fifteen articles drawn up by Luther at the end of the hot encounter (3 October), Zwingli and Oecolampadius, the Reformer of Basle (1482–1531), readily accepted fourteen and a part of the fifteenth. It was, of course, on the remaining part of Article 15 that the whole argument had turned. Luther insisted on the corporeal presence, taking literally "This is my body". Zwingli held that these words can only mean, "This signifies my body". Oecolampadius held Luther's view to be "opinion, not faith". The article records assent on the spiritual reception, but admits a lack of agreement on the corporeal presence, and closes with a pledge to exercise mutual Christian charity "so far as conscience permits". The Marburg Articles had an important influence upon later Lutheran formulas, but they did not constitute a basis for the political co-operation that Zwingli sought.[2]

---

[1] Zwingli, *Opera, Corpus Reformatorum*, IV, pp. 505 ff.

[2] On the issues involved in the Marburg Colloquy the reader may consult W. Koehler, *Das Religionsgespräch zu Marburg, 1529*, Tübingen, 1929; H. von Schubert, *Bekenntnisbildung und Religionspolitik, 1529–30 (1524–34)*, Gotha, 1910; J. T. McNeill, *Unitive Protestantism*, New York, 1930, pp. 139–44; M. van Rhijn, "Die Schweiz und die niederländische Kirchengeschichte," *Theologische Zeitschrift*, VI, 1950, pp. 411–33.

At Marburg Bucer had stood with Zwingli and suffered Luther's displeasure, yet remained conciliatory. At the Augsburg Diet (1530) he presented a confession, of which representatives of Strasburg, Constance, Memmingen, and Lindau were signatories. This "Tetrapolitan" Confession states that:

> "In the Sacrament his true Body and Blood are given to eat and to drink as the food and drink of souls, by which they are nourished unto eternal life."

But it fails to indicate the manner of the presence. The document was not given a hearing by the Diet. Bucer, having first interviewed Melanchthon on 25 September 1530, visited Luther at the Coburg. Encouraged by his reception, he hastened to Zurich in the hope of finding a formula to which both parties would consent. He followed these interviews with numerous letters, but Luther's distrust of the Zwinglians remained. Later, as the prospect of any wider unity through action by a "free Christian council" receded, Bucer resumed his hitherto unfruitful efforts to promote union among Protestants. He attempted to explain the Eucharist in a manner acceptable both to Lutherans and to Zwinglians. On 1 August 1534, shortly before the death of Clement VII, Melanchthon wrote to Bucer: "I agree with you that accord with the Roman pontiff is hopeless." Melanchthon had been sounding out John of Saxony and Philip of Hesse on Bucer's proposal for agreement. At Philip's request, Bucer braved a winter storm to meet Melanchthon at Cassel on 27 December 1534.

This meeting was the first substantial step towards the Wittenberg Concord of 1536. Luther had provided Melanchthon with an uncompromising *Instruction*, in which, while affirming his willingness to lose his life on behalf of unity, he also stated that "the Body of Christ is truly broken, eaten, and torn with teeth". In the conference Bucer, as always, minimized the differences and stressed the common ground, a sacramental union of the Body and the bread. A document was drawn up by Melanchthon in the spirit of Bucer's approach. "The bread and wine are signs (*signa exhibitiva*) which, being given and received, the Body of Christ is at the same time given and received." Philip sent this formula to Luther, who now responded in a favourable way, and himself undertook an irenical correspondence with ministers in the Swiss cities. A convention of delegates was arranged which, after some delay, met at Wittenberg on 22 May 1536.

Meanwhile Luther's old suspicions had been renewed by fresh evidence of Bucer's association with the Swiss. Luther at first required of Bucer that he recant his errors and accept the manducation of the Body in the Sacrament by the ungodly as well as the good. Bucer evaded recantation and approached Luther's position by admitting that the unworthy, but not the unbelieving, receive the Body. Luther listened and yielded, saying: "Upon this point we will not quarrel." Emotional expressions of brotherhood followed. Melanchthon was commissioned to draw up a statement embodying the results of the conference. Luther encouraged Bucer and his Strasburg colleague, Wolfgang Capito (1478–1541), to seek the assent of the Swiss to the new statement. After sermons on 28 May (Sunday), the delegates took communion together.

The Wittenberg Concord teaches that "the Body and Blood of Christ are truly and substantially present, offered, and received with the bread and wine". They are offered to the unworthy, and received by them, to their judgement. A "sacramental union" is affirmed, but transubstantiation and "local inclusion" are repudiated. The agreement stands as a diplomatic rather than a theological achievement. But who shall say that it is not a Christian diplomacy that searches for the language of agreement where exactness of definition escapes us? It was heartily entered into, and all parties, including Luther, share with Bucer responsibility for its terms. Luther's "We shall not quarrel" shows that he had caught the spirit of Bucer. For years thereafter he graciously cultivated the goodwill of Bullinger and the Swiss, while Bucer urged the now wary Zwinglians to accept the terms of the Concord. But neither party advanced a specific consensus proposal, and fresh discords followed. Within Germany, however, the Concord was an instrument of unity. Some vigorous Lutherans opposed it. But Melanchthon continued to regard it as an expression of "the doctrine of the Catholic Church of Christ" (1539). Through the Concord, says G. Anrich, "German Protestantism was for the first time drawn into unity".[1]

At an early stage in the preparations for the council projected by Pope Paul III, the Italian bishop Pietro Paolo Vergerio, as papal nuncio, visited the states of Germany. He found among the Protestants considerable enthusiasm for a general council. In November 1535 he interviewed Luther at Wittenberg and was told: "We have no need for any council, but Christendom has need of one." Luther said he would appear at the council and defend his views. A few days later (1 December) Vergerio met the princes of the Schmalkald League. They demanded a free council, representative of all parts and of all ranks and restricted only by the Word of God. This was the old demand and a contradiction of the papal policy. After Luther and Paul III had died and Vergerio had become a Protestant, the issue of Protestant attendance came up again. Maurice of Saxony now demanded that the Council alter its whole procedure and reconsider its former decisions. Some Protestant states and cities actually sent envoys to Trent in 1551–52. Leopold Badhorn, representing Saxony, there denounced the papal control of the Council and appealed to the Emperor's ambassadors to bring about "a free general Christian council"—needless to say, without effect (January 1552).

The Peace of Augsburg (1555) brought a general stabilization of territorial Churches. The period that followed was not, however, one of theological peace within the Lutheran movement. Melanchthon was now the most eminent of the Lutheran theologians, but he was distrusted both for his tolerance of Calvinist views on the Eucharist and for his concessions to Romanism on various points of doctrine and worship. His connection with the Leipzig Interim (1548) called forth sharp attacks and produced the controversy over *adiaphora*, things indifferent, in which Flacius Illyricus (1520–75) was his most constant assailant. At the Conference of Worms (August 1557) the opposing Lutheran parties were

---

[1] See G. Anrich, *Martin Bucer*, Strasburg, 1914, pp. 45–63; J. T. McNeill, *Unitive Protestantism*, pp. 139–44; H. Eells, *Martin Bucer*, New Haven, 1931, Chaps. viii–x, xiv, xviii, xx, xxi; E. G. Schwiebert, *Luther and His Times*, St Louis, 1950, pp. 736–39; J. Koestlin has viewed the Concord from the side of Luther: *Theology of Luther*, English edition, II, pp. 154–96. G. Ellinger, *Philipp Melanchthon*, Berlin, 1902, pp. 530 ff., and J. W. Richard, *Philip Melanchthon*, New York, 1898, pp. 250 ff., have treated it from the side of Melanchthon. Scholars who seek more technical and detailed theological treatment of the topics discussed in this section are referred to H. Gollwitzer, *Coena Domini, die altlutherische Abendmahlslehre in ihrer Auseinandersetzung mit dem Calvinismus*, Munich, 1937, and Ernst Bizer, *Studien zur Geschichte des Abendmahlsstreits in 16. Jahrhunderts*, Gütersloh, 1940. Professor Bizer's shorter study, "The Problem of Intercommunion in the Reformation", in *Intercommunion*, London 1952, pp. 58–83, has a valuable interpretation of the theological terminology of the discussions.

unable to agree on a basis for discussion with the Roman Catholics. While Roman Catholicism was taking on new strength in Germany and Calvinism was gaining the adherence of the Rhine districts, a series of embittered controversies weakened the Lutheran cause.[1]

After the expulsion of the "Crypto-Calvinists" from Electoral Saxony (1574) and the death of Flacius, the will to peace within Lutheranism asserted itself. The Formula of Concord (1577, adopted 1580), while it did not silence all critics, essentially marks the end of this era of controversy.[2] But the effect was to preclude any fresh outreach of Lutheranism towards either of the communions to which Melanchthon had been hospitable, and to fix Lutheran doctrine in a rigid mould. The Book of Concord, in which the Formula and the earlier Lutheran statements were now assembled, opens, as noted above, with the texts of the ecumenical Creeds. But certain phrases in the document indicate that its adoption in its entirety becomes in effect the basis of communion.[3]

Luther and the other Reformers were inclined to take a favourable view of the Orthodox Eastern Churches, and to hope for their support in the increasingly exhausting conflict with Rome; but during the 16th century contacts were few and spasmodic. The translation of the Augsburg Confession into Greek in 1559 (sometimes attributed to Paul Dolscius of Plauen, but more probably the work of Melanchthon, who was an excellent Greek scholar) indicates an interest in this direction. The remarkable correspondence between the Tübingen theologians and the Patriarch Jeremiah II in the years 1574–81, though it led to no immediate result, is of importance as a first post-Reformation instance of an irenical approach by the West to the East.[4]

We have seen something of the element of ecumenicity in 16th-century Lutheranism. Throughout its evolution in that period, an ecumenical concept of the Church was constantly professed. This profession, however, was, especially in the later stage, associated rather with Scripture and the ancient Church and Creeds than with a fraternal approach to contemporary communions. Luther's early writing had promised more generous relations with non-Lutherans, but in the struggle for the recognition of Lutheranism within the Empire his outlook grew somewhat more restricted. After the favourable relations with the Swiss, noted above, he resumed his unqualified denunciation of their opinions (1544). The sacrament of communion, as Cranmer and Melanchthon both remarked, became indeed "the apple of discord" in Protestantism. Bucer lived, struggled, and died in full commitment to the principle of unity, but lost the confidence of many of those whom he sought to influence. Melanchthon reached out for fellowship with non-Lutherans, but was worsted by those who interpreted narrowly the documents he had himself compiled. In the test of events, an anxious loyalty to the Lutheran definitions overcame the desire for unity and reciprocity. For Flacius there were no *adiaphora* in the realm of doctrine; and the doctrines of the Formula of Concord constituted for its signatories an exclusive and irreformable system. In the 17th century and after, Lutheranism pre-

[1] A useful summary of these controversies is given in P. Schaff's *Creeds of Christendom*, I, pp. 258–91. F. Hildebrandt, in *Melanchthon, Alien or Ally?*, Cambridge, 1946, has an acute discussion of the *adiaphora*, with some allusions to Hitler's Germany.

[2] P. Schaff, *Creeds of Christendom*, III, pp. 93–184; *Die Bekenntnisschriften der evangelisch-lutherischen Kirche*, published by the Deutsche Evangelische Kirchenausschuss, Göttingen, 1930, pp. 739–1100.

[3] Cf. X, 5, "all the articles thereof".

[4] For a full account of these proceedings, see Chap. iv, pp. 177 ff.

vailingly regarded itself as self-sufficient, and shrank from the perils of a two-way spiritual commerce with other Christian communions.

5. ECUMENICAL OUTLOOK AND UNITIVE EFFORT IN THE CALVINIST REFORMATION

After the Conference of Marburg, the position of the men of Zurich deteriorated, and on 11 October 1531 Zwingli fell in a lost battle. The leadership of the Reformation in Zurich devolved upon Henry Bullinger (1504–75). About the same time there began an expansion of the Reformation promoted by the Church of Berne westward into the French-speaking areas then becoming attached to the Swiss Confederation. William Farel (1489–1565) was the ardent evangelist of this movement. Farel had been in contact with both Bucer and the Zwinglians, and was a consistent advocate of Protestant union.

The first contact of the Reformed Churches with the Waldensians of the Piedmontese valleys and Provence was made at a meeting of two of their emissaries, George Morel and Pierre Masson, with Farel at Neuchâtel in 1530. The Waldensians, like the Bohemian Brethren, early sought knowledge of the Reformation movements. They had already sent missions of inquiry to Germany, but of these nothing specific is known. The two Waldensian ministers (*barbes*) just mentioned also talked at Basle with Oecolampadius, explained their faith and life, and sought his counsel. The Reformation doctrines of justification and predestination were strange to them, although their view of Scripture and detachment from Rome disposed them favourably to the Reformers. Oecolampadius sent by them a long letter (13 October 1530) to the Waldensian leaders, "beloved brothers in Christ", urging a firm behaviour under persecution, and giving advice on doctrinal and practical matters, such as the careful study of the Scriptures and the abandonment of the rule of celibacy for preachers. The envoys next visited Bucer and Capito in Strasburg, bearing a recommendation from Oecolampadius, whose advice was confirmed by the Strasburg leaders. Masson was killed at Dijon; Morel returned to Merindol in Provence, whence they had set out, bearing the statements of the Reformers.

A synod of all the Waldensian communities was now called: it met (12–18 September 1532) at Chanforan on the Angrogna River in Piedmont, and was largely attended. Farel, his co-labourer Antoine Saunier, and possibly Pierre Olivétan (d. 1538), scholar of Paris and cousin of Calvin, were present. The synod adopted the teachings of the Reformed Churches on predestination and various other doctrines. It voted a generous fund for a new (French) translation of the Bible. The task of preparing this was later laid upon Olivétan, who brought the new version to publication in 1535. Calvin's first published writing as a Protestant consists of the two prefaces he provided for the Old and the New Testaments in his cousin's Bible. Despite the objections of a minority to the Chanforan decisions, the body of western Waldensians confirmed these in a second synod (1535) and remained in fellowship with the Reformed. Saunier and Olivétan returned more than once to the valleys, and Geneva sent numerous helpers, some of whom in their journeys lost their lives at the hands of enemies. At the time of the massacre of the Waldensians by Francis I (1545), Calvin did his utmost to arouse German and Swiss protests to the French government and to bring relief to the survivors. In a letter to Bullinger (24 May 1561) he praised the heroic zeal of young volunteers in ministering to their partially restored communities.[1]

John Calvin's outlook was ecumenical from the outset, but his interest in Church unity was probably quickened by his contacts with Bucer in Strasburg (1538–41). He worked in close harmony with Bucer and formed a friendship with Melanchthon, whom he met first at Frankfort in 1539. He took a minor part with these men at the Colloquies of Worms, Hagenau, and Ratisbon (1540–41).

Calvin had already, during his first period in Geneva, sought a unification of the Swiss Protestants, and had criticized Bucer for his over-zealous insistence on the Wittenberg Concord when this was resented in Berne. In February 1537 he proposed to Gaspar Megander of Berne a Swiss convention to settle the issues raised by Bucer, and in February 1538 made a similar proposal to Bullinger. The evidence of his concern for a general Protestant union belongs, however, to the period beginning with his association with Bucer and Melanchthon. In March 1540, in a letter to Bullinger, he appealed for the latter's "brotherly friendship", since

> "It concerns not our Church alone, but all Christianity, that all to whom the Lord has entrusted any charge in his Church should agree in true concord; we must therefore purposefully and carefully cherish association and friendship with all ministers of Christ. . . . As for me, as far as in me lies, I shall always labour to this end."

To this pledge he would be true.

In July 1540 Calvin met at a dinner Matěj Cervenka, a youthful minister of the Bohemian Brethren then sojourning in Strasburg. Červenka reported that Calvin asked him many questions on the ideas, rules, and history of the Brethren. They had further conferences, and Calvin wrote to John Augusta criticizing the Brethren's high esteem of celibacy. Augusta's reply of 29 June 1541 defends in the light of Scripture the position then held in his Church on this point, while expressing for himself and his associates a deep regard for Calvin. At this period the Brethren were beginning to turn from Wittenberg to Strasburg and Geneva in their contacts with the Reformation.[2] Bucer was engaged (1540–42) in friendly ecclesiastical correspondence with Augusta and other Czech Brethren.[3]

On the controverted issue of the Eucharist, Calvin held middle ground between Zwingli and Luther, and, like Bucer, sought a mediating rôle. He was firm in repudiating the "bare signs" or "mere memorial" concepts which the Lutherans ascribed to the Zwinglians. He was equally dissatisfied with the corporeal presence as affirmed by Luther, in terms of oral manducation and the literal interpretation of the words, "This is my Body". His *Little Treatise on the Holy Supper of Our Lord* is at once an irenical document and a theological

[1] I am indebted to a seminar paper by Alfred Janavel for some of the above data. Jean Leger's extensive *Histoire générale des églises évangéliques des Vallées du Piémont ou Vaudoises*, Leiden, 1669, supplies many details.

[2] E. Doumergue, *Jean Calvin, les hommes et les choses de son temps*, II, pp. 405 ff. The letter of Augusta is in Calvin's *Opera*, XI, pp. 244–48.

[3] "La correspondance entre les Frères Tchèques et Bucer, 1540-1542", *Revue d'histoire et de philosophie religieuses*, xxxi, 1951, pp. 102–56. This has been edited in French by Amadeo Molnar.

exposition. It appeared in 1540· in French: Luther knew it only in the Latin edition of 1545, and his commendation of this work thus came too late to undo the bitterness already engendered. Christ, says Calvin, is truly present in the Supper. The elements are named Body and Blood because they are instruments by which the Lord distributes the Body and Blood to us. "Christ gives us in the Supper the proper substance of the Body and Blood" (17). "We are truly made partakers of the proper substance of the Body and Blood of Jesus Christ" (60). But our participation is spiritual. We must "raise our thoughts on high and there seek our Redeemer" (42). "The Spirit of God is the bond of our participation" (60). In the *Institutes* (IV, xviii) we have a similar argument. The Holy Spirit mysteriously makes Christ's Body our food.

Calvin's doctrine was shaped independently, and he had no thought of sacrificing truth to peace. In the *Little Treatise* he refers to Luther's own use of "harsh and rude similitudes" to explain his doctrine, and to the failure of Zwingli and Oecolampadius to show "what presence" is in the Sacrament. Both parties had failed in patience to listen to each other. He hopes for a settlement of the differences when God is pleased to bring it about.

When Luther, to Melanchthon's shocked amazement, assailed the Swiss afresh in 1544, Calvin sought to calm the indignation of Bullinger. In a letter of 25 November 1544, he combines a plea for aid to the Waldensians with advice to bear with Luther who in his petulance "attacks us all together". Thus associating himself with the victims of Luther's anger, he asks Bullinger to consider how great Luther is and how mightily he has assaulted the kingdom of antichrist :

> "I have already often said that even if he should call me a devil I should still hold him in honour and acknowledge him a distinguished servant of God."

Two months later he found occasion to write to Melanchthon deploring the destructive quarrels that afford sport to the papists: "Let us mourn together ... the misfortunes of the Church"—yet rejoice that we cannot be utterly overwhelmed (21 January 1545). By the same messenger Calvin sent his only letter to Luther. He writes with warm respect to his "honoured father": "Would to God that I might take flight to you, were it but to enjoy a few hours of your conversation." The reply Calvin received was from Melanchthon who had timidly withheld the communication from Luther, and reported him to be in a suspicious and unapproachable mood. About this time an unnamed (French?) correspondent, concerned over the forthcoming papal council, urged Calvin to go to Wittenberg. Calvin replied that the cost and length of the journey, and Luther's anger, made this impracticable; he had sent his books, letters, and messengers.

To all appearance, Luther remained unfriendly. From Melanchthon's circle, however, come early anecdotes of Luther's words of admiration for Calvin's *Treatise on the Supper*, and of his remark to Melanchthon before setting out on his last journey: "In this matter of the Sacrament we have gone much too far. . . . I will commend the thing to the Lord. Do something after my death."

The death of Luther (18 February 1546) left Calvin the most effective leader of the Reformation. He and Bullinger in Switzerland were freer to act than Melanchthon and Bucer in Germany's atmosphere of strife. Calvin sought to bring Bucer and Bullinger together; but Bucer was forced out of Strasburg in

May 1549, to spend his remaining days in England. For years Calvin had made efforts to reach full agreement with Bullinger. Differences between them on the doctrine of the Eucharist remained. In the letter cited above he said: "If we could only talk together for half a day, we would agree without difficulty." Bullinger was cautious, but his writings of the time indicate that he had, as A. Bouvier remarks, "developed and deepened the objective element" in Zwingli's view of the Supper, while he still rejected the Lutheran conception of corporeal presence. Late in 1545, Bullinger published his reply to Luther's hostile treatise of 1544 and sent a copy to Calvin for his judgement. Calvin, "as a friend", criticized it for its inadequate stress on the spiritual presence. Having had no reply, more than half a year later he wrote (19 September 1547) to renew the discussion in view of common dangers. Bullinger was a little piqued by Calvin's comments, but Calvin still wooed him graciously and suggested that some day they would reach a "fuller harmony". In November 1548 he sent twenty-four propositions on the sacraments. Bullinger promptly commented on these with general approval. The accord was almost complete; it remained to express it in a formal agreement.

Calvin now attempted to obtain a similar understanding with the ministers of Berne. In anticipation of a synod held there on 17 March, he sent John Haller a set of twenty articles on the sacraments, with a fraternal letter. From Haller he received, however, only an equally friendly but discouraging criticism. Calvin's wife died on 29 March, and his letters of April show him almost "overwhelmed with grief". It was Farel, so often his monitor, who aroused him to fresh action. Geneva desired a renewal of an expiring Swiss alliance with France, and this matter was now, with the religious problem, entrusted to Calvin. On 20 May he set out for Zurich. A letter from Bullinger advising only a continuance of the correspondence reached Geneva after his departure. Joined by Farel at Neuchâtel, he hastened to Zurich, conferred unsuccessfully with the magistrates on the political alliance, but in a two-hour session with Bullinger agreed upon the terms of the historic Consensus of Zurich (in Latin, *Consensus Tigurinus*).

The whole document, in twenty-six articles, treats of the sacraments. These are described as "marks and badges of Christian profession and fellowship . . . incitements to gratitude and exercises of faith and a godly life"(7). The Lord "truly performs inwardly by his Spirit that which the sacraments figure to our senses"(8). Only the elect "partake of the reality of the sacraments" (16); "each receives according to the measure of his faith" (18). No idea of a local presence is acknowledged (21). The words "This is my Body" are to be taken figuratively, and involve no transfusion of substance (23). Transubstantiation is a gross and absurd fiction (24). The body of Christ is in heaven; though philosophically speaking this is not a place "above the skies", it is "distant from us" (25).

The Consensus was joyfully welcomed by Bucer, John Hooper, and à Lasco in England. It was promptly adopted by the Swiss Churches except Basle and Berne. Two years later they too assented, Berne reluctantly and conditionally. Doumergue observes that through Calvin's effort there were now two Protestantisms instead of three. Calvin generously gave the credit to Farel.

It was too much to hope, as Calvin did, that the Lutherans, led by Melanchthon, would be attracted by the Consensus. Some of its language was distinctly anti-Lutheran, though it was not out of agreement with the Revised Augsburg Confession of 1540. In Germany the trend in favour of the Lutheran rigorists was already setting in and would soon become dominant. Joachim Westphal of Hamburg (d. 1574) led a pamphlet attack on Calvin and the Consensus. Calvin appealed in vain to the harassed Melanchthon for his frank support, and challenged Westphal to "extract one word from Philip" (Melanchthon) on his side. The attempt to Lutheranize the French Church in Strasburg, to which Calvin had once ministered, called forth from him an appeal to the memory of Bucer and Capito, and the statement that if "that excellent servant of the Lord and faithful doctor of the Church, Martin Luther" were living, he would readily assent to the terms of the Consensus (26 August 1554).[1]

Calvin never for a moment ceased to view the Church in its totality and, as Karl Holl has noted, his ecumenicity took root in the Churches organized under his influence, resulting in a strong feeling of unity and an active intercourse between them. In conflicts within Calvinism, national difference has never played a part. In this ecumenical consciousness he sought, in fact, a "syncretism" (a word employed in his Catechism) among Protestants.[2] Calvin never drew the bounds of communion in terms of assent to one confession of faith. At the height of his conflict with Westphal he urged the English refugees at Wesel not to desert the Lutheran services there (March 1554), and he similarly advised the Puritan objectors to the Prayer Book among the refugees at Frankfort (1555). His correspondence with Poles and Englishmen shows that he had no fundamental objection to episcopacy where bishops were evangelical. He freely admits that "some churches" and persons within the Roman Communion are within the true Church. He sought to lay the foundation of a Europe-wide communion, with a doctrinal basis clearly but not narrowly defined. He hoped to obtain this by mutual deliberation and conciliar action. Had his aims been achieved, Protestantism would have taken the outlines of a Church ecumenical and conciliar, autonomous vis-à-vis the State though protected by it. The design of Calvin has the grandeur of a world-embracing Christian order, and is the more striking from the fact that he is celebrated for his stress on the sinfulness of men and of governments. He was battling for what could not be attained or maintained—an ecclesiastical utopia. Yet his basic concern was for the effectual realization of the communion of saints as a supernatural spiritual fraternity; and this, apart from structures and governments, is a perpetual concern of Christian souls.

The three Protestantisms had become two,[3] and Calvin never lost hope that the two would become one. But in his latter years he deputed much of the effort to his stalwart lieutenant, Theodore Beza (1519–1605). In 1557 Beza and Farel, sent on a mission in behalf of the persecuted Waldensians of Savoy, took the opportunity to propose a consensus with the Lutherans, and addressed a statement on the Eucharist framed by Beza to the Duke of Württemberg (10 May 1557), of which Calvin learned only later. Though it contained phrases unsatisfactory to him, Calvin did not reject it, but wrote to Bullinger to quiet the latter's

[1] The documents connected with the *Consensus Tigurinus* are in Calvin's *Opera, Corpus Reformatorum*, VII, pp. 694–744; the letters referred to, in this series Vol. XIII. For Calvin's concern for and effort towards Church unity, see also: W. Kolfhaus, *Der Verkehr Calvins mit Bullinger*, Leipzig, 1909; G. Reichel, *Calvin als Unionsmann*, Tübingen, 1909; E. Doumergue, *Jean Calvin, les hommes et les choses de son temps*, V, pp. 354–76; VI, pp. 503–26; A. Lecerf, "La Doctrine de l'Église dans Calvin", in *Études Calvinistes*, Neuchâtel and Paris, 1949, pp. 55–68; J. T. McNeill, *Unitive Protestantism*, Chap. v; A. Bouvier, *Henri Bullinger, réformateur et conseiller oecuménique*, Neuchâtel and Paris, 1940, Partie I, Chap. iv.
[2] K. Holl, *Johannes Calvin*, Tübingen, 1909, pp. 22, 54.
[3] Though still three if one includes the "sectaries" of the left wing of the Reformation.

alarm and to commend Beza. He repeatedly proposed a convention of theologians, hoping that Melanchthon would come to it and declare himself. But he had no thought of weakening the accord with Bullinger. Calvin long continued to regard Melanchthon as the spokesman of Lutheranism (if he could be induced to speak), while Bullinger saw Westphal as its authentic interpreter.

Stirred up by fresh persecution in France, Beza and Farel renewed their efforts. They secured a meeting with Melanchthon and other Lutherans at Worms, where Beza (8 October 1557) presented a new formula, in the name of the French Reformed, and only as preparatory to a projected later conference. This statement maintains scriptural language on the Eucharist and affirms: "We hold that we and you are one true Church of the Son of God." But the Germans responded only by promises to send emissaries to France, and a third visit of Beza to Germany a year later was required to bring this about. The strongly worded remonstrance to Henry II then sent (19 March 1558) marks a momentary co-operation between Lutherans and Reformed: it was unavailing.[1] Still seeking a consensus with the Lutherans, Beza went again to German cities in 1559, but Strasburg alone responded favourably.

Bullinger remained unwilling to consider union with the Lutherans, and must take his share with Westphal and the Flacian party for the failure of Calvin's hopes. Bouvier refers to his extreme caution and seems to admit R. Staehelin's charge of "confessional intolerance". He justly points, however, to the Zurich leader's great charity in personal relations. The Marian Exiles from England and other refugees in Zurich were not, assuredly, treated by Bullinger with confessional intolerance; and his wide contacts and influence as a writer make of him an ecumenical figure of high importance. His great personal loyalty to Zwingli doubtless conditioned his attitude to the Lutherans, and, although he wrote nobly of the Holy Catholic Church, like Zwingli he saw its visible organization as primarily local, and was less concerned than Calvin for its co-ordination across national lines.

We have seen that Beza represented the Protestant cause at the Colloquy of Poissy in 1561. After Calvin's death, he and his Geneva associates continued to seek unity with the Lutherans. The cause was taken up by Ambrose Wolf, known as Cristoph Hardesianus, a Palatine Calvinist who wrote irenical works. Of these the *Acta concordiae* (1575) reviews the eucharistic controversy, stressing Luther's friendly correspondence with Bullinger in 1537. Between the massacre of St Bartholomew (1572) and the Formula of Concord (1580), Beza was engaged in fresh efforts towards Reformed-Lutheran agreement. He was associated with the arrangements for the conference held in Frankfort-on-Main (27–28 September 1577) to prepare the way for a Protestant consensus and to forestall the exclusive Formula of Concord. The French Reformed Church, in national synods of 1578 and 1579, took action favourable to this project.

The celebrated *Harmony of the Confessions of Faith of the Orthodox Reformed Churches*, published in Geneva in August 1581, came out of this background; P. F. Geisendorf has shown that it was prepared under the guidance of Beza. It was attributed, through an editor's blunder, to "Monsieur Salnar", a mis-

---

[1] A. Bouvier presents (*Henri Bullinger*, pp. 160 ff.) in facsimile and in French translation, an undated document (1558?) found in Bullinger's papers bearing the title, stricken through by a line, *Conciliatio Calvinica*, but believed to be drawn up by Beza. It is in ten articles, of which the tenth sets forth five points of a basis of concord. It is addressed to the Lutherans, though perhaps used only for consultation with Bullinger. It acknowledges sin on both sides and requires each party to regard the other as sincere members of the Church.

spelling of (Jean François) Salvart (or Salvard) (d. 1585), one of his collaborators, then a Geneva minister. The *Harmony* utilizes twelve confessions,
Lutheran, Reformed, and Anglican, in order to exhibit the substantial unity of
Protestant doctrine. It was approved by the French Reformed Synod of Vitré in
1583 and appeared in English in 1586, with "A Preface in the name of the
Churches of France and Belgia"—evidently written by the compilers, though not
included in A. Ebrard's edition of the 1581 text. This preface is a Protestant
irenicon with some emphasis on the fact that "they of our side [i.e. the Re-
formed] were always desirous of peace and agreement". The variety of confessions is excused on the ground that conditions have prevented a general council
of Protestants.

In his ecumenical churchmanship, Beza remained a true disciple of Calvin. In
March 1585 he conferred with Jakob Andreae and other Lutherans at Mont-
béliard, where, under a Lutheran prince, French Protestants had been denied
communion. The futility of his effort was dramatized by the fact that at the end
Andreae refused him the "hand of fraternity", and Beza declined his offer of
"the hand of benevolence and humanity". The incident is symbolic of the failure
of Geneva's repeated attempts to overcome the cleavage that had arisen in
Protestantism almost at its beginning.[1]

6. THE ECUMENICAL INTERESTS OF EARLY ANGLICANISM

More than a decade before Henry VIII's legislation severed England from the
papacy, Tyndale, Bilney, Latimer, Frith, and the other founders of the movement were indebted alike to Erasmus and Luther. The English Reformation continued to feed upon the literary fruits of Continental Protestantism, though it was
not identified with any branch of the latter. It remained, however, favourable to
Erasmus and retained a tincture of Erasmian liberalism, but assumed a distinctively national character.

The conservative ecclesiastical policy of Henry VIII's later years accorded
with the temper of the people. The episcopal line of continuity was maintained,
and episcopacy as an institution, while not yet supported by high church interpretations, was not seriously imperilled in the 16th century. The abolition of
monasticism was the only radical change in the internal ecclesiastical polity.
The reforms of worship were abrupt only in the use of the vernacular. Even
where the changes in the meaning and structure of the liturgy were considerable,
the new forms were looked upon as essentially continuous with the old. Thus
the reformed Church of England held a strategic position in ecumenical matters.
It carried forward more that was medieval than the Continental Churches, while
it acknowledged a fraternity with both Lutheran and Reformed Protestantism.
In these respects, Thomas Cranmer (Archbishop of Canterbury 1533, martyred
1556) is the most characteristic representative of 16th-century Anglicanism.

Cranmer's reading of Erasmus and Lefèvre had early turned him to the study
of the Bible and the literature of theology, and at Cambridge he came in touch

---

[1] J. W. Baum, *Theodor Beza*, I, 1843, pp. 275 ff., 280 f., 409 ff.; H. Heppe, *Geschichte des
deutschen Protestantismus*, IV, Marburg, 1859, pp. 1–22; E. Choisy, *L'État chrétien calviniste
à Genève au temps de Théodore de Bèze*, Geneva, 1902, Partie I, Chap. xiv; J. T. McNeill, *Unitive
Protestantism*, pp. 204–20; P. F. Geisendorf, *Théodore de Bèze*, Geneva, 1949, Chaps. xi, xii;
A. Ebrard, *Salnar's Harmonia confessionum fidei*, Barmen, 1887; P. Hall, *The Harmony of
Protestant Confessions*, translated from the Latin. A new edition, London, 1842.

with men strongly influenced by Luther. In 1532, at the conclusion of his work on the Continent in behalf of Henry's matrimonial cause, he was entertained at the house of Osiander, the Nuremberg Reformer, formed a friendship with him, discussed with him liturgical reforms, and married his niece. He was not, and never became, a Lutheran, but he genuinely desired good relations between the Lutheran and the English Churches.

The actual relations, however, were more affected by Henry's political policy than by Cranmer's sentiments. Anxious to secure himself against a combination of Continental enemies, Henry sent clerical emissaries to the princes of the Schmalkald League (1535–36). Protracted discussions followed, but Henry did not finally permit the conclusion of an agreement. A month after the talks ended, Queen Anne Boleyn, who had favoured Lutherans, was executed on unproved charges (19 May 1536). Although the Ten Articles authorized by Henry in July used Lutheran phraseology, they were regarded by Melanchthon as confused and ambiguous. A century later Thomas Fuller described them as "twilight religion".

A set of thirteen articles found in Cranmer's papers in 1833 apparently served some purpose either in the negotiations of this time or in those of 1538. In that year, fearing the effects of a papal council, Henry again opened talks with the Lutherans, and they sent delegates to England. Again there were extended conversations without decision. Some of the bishops were opposed to any pact with the Lutherans, and Henry cooled towards them. He took exception to the sections on abuses in the Augsburg Confession. Although it would appear that essential agreement was reached between their leader, Frederick Myconius, and Cranmer, it was evident that the King was temporizing. Cranmer had to complain that the Germans were inhospitably housed in vermin-ridden lodgings. Henry's courtesy revived to the point of dismissing his guests with honourable gifts, and they returned in September 1538. New apprehensions led to a feeble renewal of the approaches by Henry in 1539. But by July 1540 he had turned from vacillation to hostility, forced through Parliament the reactionary Statute of Six Articles, married, dismissed, and divorced Anne of Cleves, a niece of the wife of John Frederick of Saxony, beheaded Cromwell, and burned the English Lutheran, Barnes.[1]

It was in Edward VI's reign (1547–53) that Cranmer had his opportunity. In 1546 he had read, at the suggestion of Nicholas Ridley, the treatise *De corpore et sanguine Domini* of the 9th-century monk Ratramnus of Corbie, and had been led by it to a position on the Lord's Supper closely similar to that of the Swiss theologians. C. C. Richardson has shown his accord with Zwingli with respect to the presence of Christ by his divine nature and not by his risen humanity. It is evident, too, that in his controversy with Gardiner, Cranmer was disposed to assert agreement between Bucer and Zwingli. He admits no divergence from Bucer on his own part. His ecumenical attitude is close to that of Bucer, while in his combination of unqualified antagonism to Rome with an irenic view of Protestantism, he is no less similar to Calvin. He takes Augustine and other

[1] H. Jenkyns, *The Remains of Thomas Cranmer*, Oxford, 1833, I; H. E. Jacobs, *The Lutheran Movement in England during the Reigns of Henry VIII and Edward VI*, Philadelphia, 1894, Chaps. iv, v; F. Prüser, *England und die Schmalkaldener*, Leipzig, 1929 (*Quellen und Forschungen zur Reformationsgeschichte*, 11); J. T. McNeill, *Unitive Protestantism*, New York, 1930, pp. 168–74; C. S. Carter, *The Reformation and Reunion*, London, 1938, Chap. ii; H. M. Smith, *Henry VIII and the Reformation*, London, 1948, Part I, Chap. v; E. G. Rupp, *Studies in the Making of the English Protestant Tradition*, Cambridge, 1947, Chap. vi.

Church Fathers, Ratramnus and Wyclif, Peter Martyr and John à Lasco, as his allies, and, while he condemns the doctrine of oral manducation, he shows nothing but goodwill towards Luther and Melanchthon. He sincerely sought a unification of Reformation forces.

Cranmer was a Conciliarist in his view of the Catholic Church. Late in 1534, after Henry's assertion of his headship of the national Church, he had quoted Gerson and the decrees of Constance on the authority of general councils. While Henry always feared that a general council would mean Continental solidarity against England, Cranmer would stipulate only, as he then and later stated, that it be called not by the Pope or by one prince, but with the general consent of Christian princes. At the time of his degradation from office under Mary, he presented a carefully framed appeal from the authority of the Pope to that of "a free general Christian council". Such a council, he states in language long familiar, "lawfully gathered together in the Holy Ghost, and representing the Holy Catholic Church, is above the Pope", and the Pope may not prevent appeals to it. His Conciliarism is one aspect of his ecumenical outlook. For him the Church was one, Christendom was *respublica Christiana*, and England and the Church of England were not to be severed from this unity. His support of the nationalizing policy may have involved some inconsistency here. But it was entirely consistent with his basic conviction that in Edward's reign, when he had some freedom of initiative, he should undertake to assemble a conference of representative leaders of the Reformation Churches with a view to a general consensus.

Melanchthon had remarked in a letter to Cranmer (1535) that if there were bishops like him elsewhere, concord and reform would be attained without difficulty, and had proposed to Henry the formation of a consensus. Cranmer now turned to Melanchthon for co-operation and invited him to England. The initial correspondence is not preserved, but John à Lasco, by 11 October 1547, had written to Melanchthon about "the call to England", and on 26 October Melanchthon refers to his own invitation. Apparently he did not reply to Cranmer until the following 28 January, and then it was not to accept the invitation but to commend the project for "a sum of necessary doctrine" as one that he had always entertained. He urges, too, doubtless with memories of his own experiences, that no ambiguities should be admitted to prove "an apple of contention" to posterity. His longer letter of 1 May 1548 to the Archbishop shows careful consideration of the proposal. The consensus to be written will not, he thinks, differ greatly from the Confession of Augsburg.

Cranmer pressed the invitation by numerous letters to Melanchthon, and sought to win his consent through mutual friends. John à Lasco and Albert Hardenberg of Bremen were among those enlisted in the effort to prevail upon Melanchthon. On 26 May, having received letters from "many" on the matter, Melanchthon wrote to Camerarius: "I will not yet leave Germany."

It may not have been clear to Melanchthon that what Cranmer had in mind was much more than a basis for the Church of England. This certainly became unmistakable in Cranmer's fourth letter of 10 February 1549. Here he prays God, who has "rescued our Island from the waves" of trouble that Churches elsewhere suffer, that he will gather a permanent Church not only there but in all nations. From Italy and Germany many pious and learned men have come to England and others are expected. Will not Melanchthon consent to adorn their society with his presence? The statement to be prepared by wise men taking counsel together would be the fulfilment of Melanchthon's own oft affirmed desire. He warns him against inconsistency and resistance to the manifest calling of God. There is no certainty that this letter was delivered, though it was personally entrusted to à Lasco. Three weeks later Melanchthon wrote to Cranmer without even referring to the project (1 March). In a letter of 15 April 1550 he alluded to a new invitation from England, whether from Cranmer or another. There is no evidence in all this that his prince, as in former instances, interfered to prevent Melanchthon's departure. His apparent indifference to the campaign of persuasion may be partly explained by his preoccupation with the mounting disorders of Germany.

Meanwhile England was a land of refuge and opportunity for Continental Protestant scholars. The Italians Peter Martyr Vermigli and Bernardino Ochino had arrived in December 1547; Peter Alexander of Arles, Jan Utenhove of Amsterdam, John ab Ulmis from Zurich, and many others had followed by the end of 1548. John à Lasco reached England in September 1548; Bucer, with his companion Paul Fagius, in April 1549. It was this company that Melanchthon was invited to "adorn" by his presence. His failure to co-operate seems to have halted the project. Attention was directed to the Prayer Book of 1549, and Bucer, à Lasco, and Peter Martyr were consulted with a view to its revision. Bucer praised the Zurich Consensus and à Lasco published the text of it in London in 1552. There had been much criticism of Bucer by the adherents of Bullinger in England: if Calvin could agree with Bullinger, why not Bucer and à Lasco with Bullinger's disciples? John Hooper's brief rebellion on the Vestment issue ended amicably, and this staunch English friend of Bullinger was now Cranmer's friend too. The royal Council sent Christopher Mount, then at Strasburg, to the Swiss Cantons to persuade them to form an *entente* with England. In October 1549 he was instructed to proceed further and to pledge participation in a "general or national council", if it should take the Scriptures as its standard. In this instruction, sent in the name of the boy King, the Zurich Consensus is favourably referred to. R. W. Dixon connects these fresh proposals with Cranmer's earlier project.

The reopening of the Council of Trent (May 1551), the failure of the Augsburg Interim, and the later stage of the Schmalkaldic War were watched from England with close interest. Cranmer's chief writings on the Eucharist are of this period. Bucer's death occurred on 1 March 1551. On 20 March 1552 Cranmer wrote to Bullinger recommending that a synod of learned and excellent men be convoked "in England or elsewhere", stating that the King approved it as of the utmost service to the Christian Commonwealth. On the same date he wrote to Calvin, and a week later to Melanchthon. His letter to Calvin refers to the necessity for a definition of the Eucharist in answer to that made at Trent, to which Melanchthon had recently called his attention. To each of the three Cranmer indicates that he is communicating with the others, and he suggests to Calvin that they deliberate together on the assembling of the synod.

Thus, in changed circumstances, Cranmer renews his project. Calvin's reply was prompt and enthusiastic. "I know that your purpose is not confined to England alone, but together with her you take consideration for the whole world." He deplores the lack of intercourse and of holy communion between Churches. He would not shrink from crossing ten seas to serve this end. It may be that the absence of a specific personal invitation to England in Cranmer's letter led him to suggest that his own slightness of capacity (*tenuitatem*) will excuse his absence from the conference. He will pray earnestly for its success. "I wish that my ability were equal to my zeal." He implores Cranmer to go forward until something at least is accomplished. Cranmer replied only on 4 October. Bullinger, he says, has indicated to him that it is vain to discuss a "council" while he and Melanchthon, in the disturbed state of affairs, cannot leave their own Churches. From Melanchthon no reply has come. For this and many other reasons the project must be relinquished or postponed. In May 1553 Melanchthon was again invited to England, as he notes in a letter of 10 August, with the remark that meanwhile the pious king has died. Cranmer's "many" reasons for abandoning the scheme probably included King Edward's failing health and the prospect of Mary's succession. Whatever Melanchthon's undeclared motives, personal ease was not one of them. "I am living in a wasps' nest", he wrote to Calvin on 1 October 1552; if exile comes, he added, "I am determined to turn to you". It would have been of little advantage to Cranmer's plan if he had gone to England as a refugee and not as a representative of Lutheranism.

With the death of Edward VI on 6 July 1553, Cranmer's hopes of a consensus with foreign Protestants were finally snuffed out. The project rightly deserves a notable place in the history of the Reformation. The frustration of magnificent hopes does not necessarily brand them as fatuous. Calvin, Bullinger, and Melanchthon had never been all together: if they could have met with Cranmer and others of the "learned and pious" in unhurried conference, a consensus on the Eucharist and other doctrines might readily have been reached. It would, of course, have been resisted by many in England and in Germany; but it might have proved a turning-point in Reformation history and introduced an era of intercourse and communion between Churches politically separated. A conciliar organization of the Reformation Churches might have been erected, though for this much international suspicion would have had to be overcome. Cranmer is not to be judged merely on his record as the chief of English Reformers. His espousal of a cause far wider than national reform—the integration of the severed Reformation Churches of Europe—is evidence of a sincere ecumenicity and of a certain noble grandeur of design challenging to later generations.[1]

Shortly after Matthew Parker (1504–75) was raised to the See of Canterbury, he received a letter from John Calvin rejoicing in England's happiness under Elizabeth and urging the Archbishop to induce the Queen to convoke a general

---

[1] On Cranmer's consensus project I have followed chiefly the ampler treatment in my *Unitive Protestantism*, Chap. vi, where sources and literature are noted. For the principal sources see *The Works of Thomas Cranmer*, edited for the Parker Society by J. E. Cox, Vol. I, *Writings and Disputations on the Eucharist*, Vol. II, *Miscellaneous Writings and Letters*, Cambridge, 1844–46; J. Strype, *Memorials of Thomas Cranmer* (1694), 4 vols., Oxford, 1848–54; *The Remains of Thomas Cranmer*, collected and arranged by Henry Jenkyns, 4 vols., Oxford, 1833; the *Corpus Reformatorum* edition of Melanchthon's *Opera*, II, pp. 92–95, VI, pp. 790 f., 801, 894, 918, VII, p. 573, XIII, pp. 64 f., 531 f., XIV, p. 437; *Original Letters Relative to the English Reformation*, 2 vols. (Parker Society), Cambridge, 1846–47; *Epistolae Tigurinae* (Parker Society), Cambridge, 1848. C. H. Smyth, *Cranmer and the Reformation under Edward VI*, Cambridge, 1926, and F. J. Smithen, *Continental Protestantism and the English Reformation*, London, 1927, are useful, and for Cranmer's relations with Bucer, C. Hopf, *Martin Bucer in England*, Oxford, 1946. O. S. Carter, *The Reformation and Reunion*, London, 1947, Chap. iii, treats Cranmer's association and correspondence with Reformed churchmen. C. C. Richardson's *Zwingli and Cranmer on the Eucharist*, Evanston, Ill., 1949, is illuminating. R. W. Dixon, *History of the Church of England from the Abolition of the Roman Jurisdiction*, 6 vols., Oxford, 1891–1902, Vol. III, may be profitably consulted.

assembly of Protestant ministers to frame a plan of worship and government not only for her dominions but for all the Reformed and Evangelical Churches (1560). Parker—who, it may be noted, had been ten years earlier a close friend of Bucer—brought the matter before the Queen's Council. He was instructed by it to thank Calvin and to say that, while they liked his proposal, it must be understood that the Church of England would retain its episcopate. This was alleged, in accordance with Parker's view of its history, to be derived not from Rome but from Joseph of Arimathea.[1]

During Elizabeth's reign various projects were entertained for a political common front of Protestant states, and approaches were made through ambassadors to foreign powers. Elizabeth was on good terms with the Emperor Maximilian II. His death in October 1576, with that of Frederick III of the Palatinate in the same month, led her to send ambassadors to the Continent to explore the possibilities of an alliance. The struggle in the Netherlands was turning against Spain, but the outcome of it was still in doubt. The notion of a Protestant federation was attractive to many Protestant leaders. At the beginning of 1577 Sir Philip Sidney (only twenty-three but already celebrated) was dispatched to the Palatinate and to the court of the new Emperor, Rudolf II. In August Secretary Walsingham's brother-in-law, Robert Beale, was sent to Germany to urge Lutherans and Calvinists to lay aside all contention "until the calling of a general synod", and to form a Protestant league against Spain. Going beyond his instructions, Sidney delivered a bold and eloquent speech before Rudolf, urging him to break with the Spaniards and assume the protection of religion and liberty. Under the influence of the Huguenot scholar Hubert Languet, Sidney had become an ardent Protestant with a European outlook. Both he and Beale encountered, however, the mutual suspicions and hostilities of Protestant princes. Of German states, only Hesse and the Palatinate made any response, and the latter was soon to expel the Calvinists.

The attitude of Anglicanism remained one of goodwill towards both Lutheran and Reformed Churches, but there was little thought of seeking firmer bonds with either. Archbishop Edmund Grindal (1576–83), a Calvinist with Continental Calvinist friends, took no serious step towards ecclesiastical agreement with the Reformed. Nor did his successor, John Whitgift, whose Lambeth Articles express a rigorous Calvinism, and who authorized Bullinger's *Decades* as sermon material for the clergy. John Jewel (Bishop of Salisbury 1560–71) expresses the greatest esteem for the Reformed leaders, and substantial agreement with them, yet makes no fresh proposal for closer association of Anglican and Reformed Churches. Richard Hooker (1553–1600), while he often claims (as does Whitgift) Calvin's support against the Puritans, does not seem much concerned with the practical implementation of his ecumenical conception of the Church. Both Jewel and Hooker were primarily defenders of the Church of England as a part of the Holy Catholic Church, the former against Roman Catholicism, the latter against both Rome and the Puritans of his time. Hooker, by criticizing Calvin at some points, begins the detachment of Anglican from Calvinist theology. On the doctrine of the Eucharist he stresses essential agreement with the Churches of the Continental Reformation.

[1] J. Strype, *The Life and Acts of Matthew Parker*, Vol. I, Oxford, 1821, pp. 55 f., 138 ff.; J. Collier, *An Ecclesiastical History of Great Britain*, London, 1846, VI, p. 33. The letter from Calvin outlined by Collier is undoubtedly that included in Calvin's *Consilia*, *Opera*, X, i, pp. 213 f., under the title *De quibusdam ecclesiae ritibus*.

"Take therefore that wherein we all agree, and then consider by itself what cause why the rest in question should not rather be left as superfluous than urged as necessary."[1]

In this period political dangers, especially from Spain, conditioned the Anglican interest in Continental ecclesiastical affairs. Yet the sense of the universality of the Church, and of Anglicanism as an integral part of the Holy Catholic Church, was maintained and frequently expressed.

7. RELIGIOUS DISCORDS AND UNITIVE EFFORTS IN EASTERN EUROPE

We have noted in preceding pages the contacts of Luther and Calvin with the Bohemian Utraquists and Brethren. The subsequent growth of Calvinism in Bohemia and Poland was attended by good relations between the Calvinist and Brethren Churches.

Many of the Brethren, because of their Protestant sympathies during the first Schmalkaldic War, were obliged to seek safety in Greater Poland (1548). Those who remained in Bohemia fell under severe treatment by the King, Ferdinand of Austria. John Augusta (d. 1572) lay in prison for seventeen years. Another able leader, John Blahoslav (d. 1571), corresponded with the Wittenberg crypto-Calvinist, Caspar Peucer, Melanchthon's son-in-law. Maximilian II succeeded Ferdinand in 1564: his policy brought some relief to the Protestant communions.

A new confession was drawn up, approved by the Bohemian estates at Prague, and presented to Maximilian on 17 May 1575. It is remarkable that Utraquists of Protestant beliefs, Lutherans, Calvinists, and Brethren subscribed to this confession. It is based on the Augsburg Confession, but follows the Melanchthonian view of the Lord's Supper. Thus, so far as a confession of faith could effect it, the Protestants of Bohemia were united. Maximilian refrained from persecution of its adherents, and in 1609 they secured from the Emperor Rudolf II a charter (*Maiestätsbrief*) guaranteeing to them freedom of worship on about 1,400 estates of the nobility.

In Lesser Poland (a southern section of the country) Calvin's influence grew. He wrote letters of advice to King Sigismund and to the Calvinist Chancellor, Nicholas Raziwill. Many Poles, the King included, were reading the *Institutes*. Sharing an insecure position, the Brethren in Greater Poland and the Calvinists in Lesser Poland made common cause. In a joint synod at Kozminek (1555) they adopted the Brethren's Confession of 1535 and projected a gradual amalgamation under an episcopal form of government. The agreement was solemnized by the celebration of Communion together. Calvin wrote with enthusiasm of the event: "God blesses every act of holy union of the members of Christ."

John à Lasco (Jan Laski, 1499–1560), the most widely known and influential of Polish Protestants, was an irenical theologian and a promoter of Protestant unity. He was the nephew of an archbishop of Gnesen and had high political connections. He owed his religious awakening to Erasmus, with whom he lived in Basle in 1524. Having returned to Poland, he turned to the West again in

---

[1] *Laws of Ecclesiastical Polity*, V, lxvii, 7.

1538, a declared Protestant. Remaining in western Europe until 1556, he made important contributions to the Reformed Churches.

À Lasco's friend Andreas Fricius Modrevius (Modrzewski, d. 1572) studied for some years at Wittenberg, where he lived in Melanchthon's house. He was an interested observer of the formation of the Wittenberg Concord (1536) and a warm admirer of Bucer. On his return to Poland in 1541, he entered the service of King Sigismund. With other humanists he desired a reform of the Polish Church without complete separation from Rome. After the opening of the Council of Trent he sprang into prominence with a proposal addressed to Sigismund "on the sending of delegates to a Christian council".[1] He here severely criticizes the clergy and proposes reform by means of a free general council. He writes like a 14th-century Conciliarist. Delegates elected by the people of each diocese should choose those to be sent by each nation. Popes should be elected by the whole Church, and biennial councils should nominate the Pope's ministers. Neither Pope nor council is inerrant; infallibility rests in the Scriptures alone. It is noteworthy that Modrevius' conception of the Church is at once ecumenical and democratic, and that he declaims not only against the exclusion in Poland of all but scions of the nobility from high Church offices, but also against the nomination of bishops by kings.

Modrevius remained in good standing as confidential secretary of the liberal King Sigismund. The King's service took him in the late 1540's to various parts of Europe. At Prague he was favourably impressed by the Bohemian Brethren. His proposals in writings of 1551 and 1556 for political and ecclesiastical reform show increasing evidence of Protestant opinions. Modrevius never became, however, a convinced disciple of the Reformers. He remained an irenical humanist, or, as Völker says, a Utopian.

The struggle for the religious allegiance of Poland became intense in the 1550's. There now existed in the country, chiefly in Lesser Poland, a Reformed Church of some strength, practising intercommunion with the Brethren on the basis of the Synod of Kozminek. In 1556 the Diet of Piotrków, on Protestant demand, adopted a nine-point policy in religious matters that embraced liberty of worship, permission for priests to marry, and the rejection of the judicial authority of the bishops. King Sigismund sent Paul IV proposals for reform; these included the calling of a national synod. The Pope rebuked the King severely for this, and for allowing à Lasco to re-enter Poland. A distinguished bishop was sent as legate to restore the fealty of the Polish Church.

In January of that year the Kozminek Confession and the Brethren's ritual had been approved in a synod of the Reformed. This synod also invited à Lasco to return. In April a combined synod of Calvinists and Brethren took steps towards the adjustment of certain issues between the two on worship and discipline. À Lasco reached Poland in December 1556, determined to work for the unification of Protestantism. A national diet then in session at Warsaw induced Sigismund to assent to the decisions of the recent Diet of Piotrków. Vergerio, the former papal legate, now an ardent Protestant, was present at this diet. He, too, was intent upon Protestant union, but on a Lutheran basis and with intemperate zeal. À Lasco's aim was to unite the growing Protestant forces and create a national Church in fraternal relations with Protestant Churches of the

[1] *Oratio de legatis ad concilium Christianum mittendis.* Th. Wotchke and K. E. J. Jørgensen connect this address with events in 1546; V. Krasinski and H. Dalton are apparently in error in associating it with a diet of 1552.

West. As soon as possible, he consulted with Raziwill, and was probably received by the King. In June 1557 he presided in a Reformed synod in which the union with the Brethren was reaffirmed, but with the qualification: "saving, however, Christian liberty according to God's Word, and without prejudice towards other Churches of Christ". The phrase suggests à Lasco's design to draw the Lutherans into the union. As strategic preparation for this, he wished to alter certain ceremonies and ordination requirements in the Brethren-Calvinist agreement and to revise the confession of faith. He now approached the Polish Lutheran leaders. His plan, which he confided to Melanchthon, was to obtain the favour of Duke Albert of East Prussia and the Königsberg theologians for a doctrinal agreement with the Polish Lutherans, who were in good relations with Albert's Lutheran subjects. À Lasco later visited Prussia and addressed himself to Duke Albert. The Königsbergers, however, crushed his hopes by demanding assent to the unaltered Augsburg Confession of 1530 as the basis of discussion. The Polish Lutherans likewise remained aloof.

During the last year of his life, while he kept up his unrewarded efforts to win the Lutherans, he was engaged in Christological debates with Francesco Stancaro and Georgio Biandrata. These heterodox teachers found him as unyielding as he found the Lutherans. The circle of his outlook for Church unity was drawn to exclude them, along with the Roman Catholics, and to include the Brethren, Reformed, and Lutherans of Poland, and all their fellow believers abroad. To win the Lutherans would mean to win the struggle for a Protestant Church of Poland. With indomitable patience and persistence he wooed them for three years. "Pray God", he wrote to the Prussian ministers (15 April 1558), "that sometime we may think and speak as one about everything; meanwhile let us comport ourselves towards each other with charity and Christian brotherliness." The Reformed Churches of Poland were strengthened by his labours, but his hopes of unity were unfulfilled when he died on 8 January 1560.

"Meanwhile . . . mutual charity and brotherliness." This advice was not wholly lost. The Consensus of Sendomir (1570) was primarily a pledge of mutual forbearance and charity. Roman Catholicism was now being revived in Poland. The canons of Trent had been reluctantly accepted by the clergy, and numerous Jesuits were making their influence felt. An attempt in 1564 to have foreign Protestants, including the Brethren, expelled, had been checked by the King. The bishops now offered an agreement with the Protestants on the basis of Scripture as expounded by the Fathers Augustine, Chrysostom, Ambrose, and Jerome, but on discussion qualified this so as to require that the Bible be taken as interpreted by Rome. The anti-trinitarians, too, were active and were regarded by other Protestants as extremely dangerous. Modrevius had some sympathy for the left-wing movements. In various later writings he expressed a wide tolerance for heretical and divergent elements. He likened an ecumenical council to the "harvest" in the Parable of the Tares: it alone can determine good and evil growths. Especially he stressed the avoidance of uprooting the good grain on premature judgement—a quite unusual conception in his time. Jørgensen contrasts the theological and churchly interests of à Lasco with the humanistic and political point of view of Modrevius, whose ecumenical view he describes as a popular conception of Church unity with a minimum of doctrinal requirement. There seems no evidence either of co-operation or of conflict between Modrevius and à Lasco after the latter's return to Poland. Nor is it clear that Modrevius had any part in setting the stage for the Consensus of Sendomir, although some historians see his hand in that agreement.

The pacification of 1570 was reached only after a severe clash between the Lutherans and the Brethren. The disputants agreed, however, to submit the Brethren's Confession to the Wittenberg theologians. Happily the (crypto-Calvinist) Wittenbergers pronounced the Confession sound and its adherents "our brethren deserving of Christian goodwill". The Polish Lutherans acted in accordance with this decision, and the way was suddenly opened up for a consensus of the three Protestant communions. Their representatives met at Sendomir (Sendomierz) and conferred for six days (9–14 April 1570). The Lutherans at first pressed for the adoption of the Augsburg Confession, but were persuaded, in view of the perils of the situation, to yield on this issue, and all other difficulties were at length amicably resolved.

It can hardly be doubted that à Lasco would have fully approved the terms of the Consensus. It declares that all the parties will avoid dissension, maintain peace and tranquillity, and in mutual charity labour for the upbuilding of the Church. On the one controverted doctrine of the Eucharist, it is stated that the elements in the sacraments are not bare and empty signs: they impart to believers what they signify. Not only is the substantial presence of Christ signified, but in truth the Lord's Body and Blood are distributed and shown to the partakers. In support of this interpretation the memorandum drawn up by Melanchthon for the Council of Trent (the so-called "Repetition of the Augsburg Confession", 1551) is incorporated in the document. The Consensus was warmly acclaimed by the three Churches, and although tensions arose regarding its interpretation, it was reaffirmed by various Polish synods of the later 16th century.

The Consensus came too late to bring victory to the declining cause of Protestantism in Poland. When Sigismund Augustus died in July 1572, the Roman Catholics proposed Henry of Anjou for the throne. The massacre of St Bartholomew (24 August) made it necessary for Henry to declare his innocence of persecution in order to win the Polish nobles. A pledge of mutual toleration previously adopted by the nobles was approved in the "election diet" at Warsaw in January 1573. Henry was invited on condition of his solemn acceptance of this formula, and at his coronation in Notre Dame on 10 September 1573, he took an oath to maintain it. The agreement of 1573 is known as the *Pax dissidentium*. Although most of the bishops did not concur in it, forty-one of the ninety-eight signatories were Roman Catholics. All promised to uphold "full and complete liberty of belief, that neither Catholics nor any other dissidents shall shed blood over diversity of cult", and "that they shall not mutually punish or injure or imprison or exile any for religion".

Thus the ecumenical ideals of à Lasco and of Modrevius came to fruition in a fraternal agreement (1570) and a political pact of toleration (1573), not in a united Church. The brief and feeble reign of Henry of Valois ended with his flight in April 1574. His successor was the able Transylvanian prince Stephen Batory, who brought needed strength to the nation and allowed the Churches liberty, but favoured the Jesuits. In February 1578 the Protestants, at a diet held in Warsaw, proposed the extension through Europe of agreements corresponding to the Consensus of Sendomir, and projected a general synod of the Evangelical Churches of Europe to this end. This was, however, a few months after the appearance of the Lutheran Formula of Concord, and the ill-timed Polish proposal brought no response. It stands only as evidence of Europe-wide interest in religious peace and unity on the part of Polish Protestants.[1]

Perhaps the earliest teacher of Reformation doctrines in Hungary was Simon Grynaeus, later host to Calvin in Basle and a friend of Oecolampadius and Bucer. In the early 1520's, as a professor at Buda, he was thrust into prison for his "evangelical profession" and released through pressure from the nobility, after which he escaped to Basle (1523). A few years later the versatile and energetic John Honter (d. 1549) brought Lutheranism to Transylvania, which, after 1526, was politically separated from Hungary. Honter's contemporary in Hungary, Mathias Bíro Dévay (d. 1545) may have come under Grynaeus at Buda. Studies in Wittenberg and Switzerland led him to adopt a doctrine of the sacraments described as *media sententia*, that is, half-way between the Lutheran and the Swiss position. Other Hungarians visiting in the West fell under the influence of Bucer and of Bullinger.

The first Protestant confession of the Hungarians, adopted in 1545 at the Synod of Erdöd, contains an article on the sacraments (vi) that is probably to be taken in a Lutheran sense. Thereafter the doctrines of Calvin, preached widely by Martin Kalmancsehi, made a rapid advance in both kingdoms, and conflicts between Lutherans and Reformed flared up in Transylvania and in northeastern Hungary. Various efforts were made to settle the disputes. The diet meeting at Torda in 1564 confirmed an earlier decision, that had been freely violated, giving toleration to Calvinists along with Lutherans and Roman Catholics. Peter Melius (Johasz), pastor of Debreczen (1558–72), had now become the most effective leader of the Reformed. His many writings include the *Confessio Catholica*, or Confession of Debreczen, 1562. The Confession claims the concurrence of "all the Fathers" in a doctrine of the Lord's Supper that is typically Calvinist ("a spiritual communication of Christ's real Body").

Various synods of the 1560's mark the spread of the Reformed doctrines. The Second Helvetic Confession, with its strongly ecumenical paragraphs on the Church, was adopted in 1567. In the later decades of the century, under Rudolf II, toleration was withdrawn; many Protestants suffered and many were intimidated. But no co-operation of Lutherans and Calvinists came out of this situation. A Lutheran bishop, Stephen Beythe, was favourable to the Calvinist view of the Supper, and his temporal lord, Francis Nadasdy, called a conference for pacification at Csepreg (1591). It proved unavailing, and Beythe resigned his office. In 1598 the Hungarian Lutherans adopted the Formula of Concord. A

---

[1] The work of greatest value for the Polish phase of our subject is K. E. J. Jørgensen's *Ökumenische Bestrebungen unter den polnischen Protestanten bis zum Jahre 1645*, Copenhagen, 1942. Other works consulted for this section include H. Dalton, *Johannes à Lasco*, Gotha, 1881; H. Dalton, *Lasciana nebst den ältesten evang. Synodalprotokollen Polens, 1555–61*, Berlin, 1898; H. A. Niemeyer, *Collectio confessionum in ecclesiis reformatis publicatarum*, Leipzig, 1840 (*Consensus Sendomiriensis*, pp. 551–65); A. Kuyper, *Joannis à Lasco Opera*, 2 vols., Amsterdam, 1886; D. E. Jablonski, *Historia consensus Sendomiriensis*, Berlin, 1731; P. Fox, *The Reformation in Poland: Some Social and Economic Aspects*, Baltimore, 1924; K. Völker, *Der Protestantismus in Polen*, Leipzig, 1910; "Der Unionsgedanke des *Consensus Sendomiriensis*," *Zeitschrift f. Osteuropäische Geschichte*, VII, 1933, pp. 508–25; Th. Wotsche, *Geschichte der Reformation in Polen*, Leipzig, 1911; P. Schaff, *Creeds of Christendom*, 3 vols., 4th edition, New York, 1919; V. Krasinski, *Historical Sketch of . . . the Reformation in Poland*, London, 1839–40; E. M. Wilbur, *A History of Unitarianism: Socinianism and its Antecedents*, Cambridge, Mass., 1947.

brief attempt by Stephen Bocskay to bring peace with toleration to Hungary ended with his death by poison in December 1606.[1]

8. FRESH PROJECTS FOR CONCILIATION AND UNION

Peace within the Empire was unstable, but it was substantially maintained from 1555 to 1618. In Germany, as in eastern Europe, Calvinism was advancing. Between 1578 and 1614, Nassau, Anhalt, Hesse-Cassel, and the Elector of Brandenburg adopted Reformed confessions and practices. J. L. Neve remarks that the Lutherans "felt their territory had been invaded".[2] The tension between the two main branches of Protestantism increased. Only at Helmstedt, in Brunswick, was there a Lutheran faculty favourable to Melanchthonian opinions; here George Calixtus studied and, from 1614, taught his irenical doctrines. The Formula of Concord, the defensive confession of the Lutherans, was assailed by some of the Reformed, e.g. by Zacharias Ursinus in *A Christian Admonition on the Book of Concord* (1581) and by Rudolf Hospinian of Zurich in *Concordia Discors* (1607).

Nevertheless, from the Reformed side suggestions towards conciliation with the Lutherans were repeatedly put forward, especially by national synods of the French Reformed Church. At the Synod of Sainte-Foy in 1578 a commission of four was appointed to open the question with the Lutherans. The Synods of La Rochelle (1581) and Vitré (1583) considered means towards union: the latter Synod adopted the *Harmony of Confessions*. Emissaries were sent to England, the Netherlands, Denmark, Germany, and Switzerland for discussions on Protestant union. The distinguished layman Philippe du Plessis-Mornay,[3] Governor of Saumur, was one of the chief inspirers of efforts to forge "a confederation of Protestants", or indeed of all Christians, by the method of synods and conferences. Mornay, earlier a friend of Sir Philip Sidney, kept up a wide correspondence with this end in view. The Synods of Gap (1603) and La Rochelle (1607) exhibit the French Church's continued interest in reunion. The former Synod wrote to the universities of Germany, England, and Scotland, and sent emissaries to England to propose agreement. At the latter assembly favourable communications were received from the Elector Palatine, the University of Heidelberg, synods of Holland and Zealand, and classes of the Pays de Vaud and Geneva.

The Synod of Tonneins (May–June 1614) brought the Huguenot project to full expression. King James I of England sent to this Synod, by the hand of David Hume, a Scot who was pastor at Duras in France, a letter of advice expressing his "very ardent desire to see flourish a good peace and union among all who sincerely profess the Christian faith". The Synod adopted a document of twenty-one articles setting forth a plan for procedure towards a federal union with the

---

[1] The following works have been consulted for Hungary and Transylvania: F. Balogh, "History of the Reformed Church in Hungary", *Reformed Church Review*, X, 1906, pp. 297–331; W. Toth, "Highlights of the Hungarian Reformation", *Church History*, IX, 1940, pp. 141–56; G. Banhoffer, *History of the Protestant Church in Hungary*, Introduction by M. d'Aubigné, translated by J. Craig, Boston, 1854; E. Revesz et al., *Hungarian Protestantism*, Budapest, 1927; A. Lampe, *Historia ecclesiae reformatae in Hungaria et Transylvania,* Utrecht, 1728; J. Rubini, *Memorabilia Augustanae Confessionis in regno Hungariae*, I, Poszony, 1787; G. Lencz, *Der Aufstand Bocskays und der Wiener Friede*, Debreczen, 1917; R. S. Law, *Development of the Reformed Church in Hungary during the Sixteenth Century*, B.D. dissertation, Union Theological Seminary, New York, 1948; E. Doumergue, *La Hongrie calviniste*, Toulouse, n.d. The confessions considered are in E. F. K. Müller, *Die Bekenntnisschriften der reformierten Kirche*, Leipzig, 1903, pp. 298 f., 426 ff.

[2] J. L. Neve, *Lutheranism and Movements for Church Unity*, Philadelphia, 1921, p. 51.

[3] See also Chap. ii, pp. 85, 88.

Lutheran Churches and with those of England and Scotland. First a synod, or colloquy, of representatives from King James, the Netherlands, Switzerland, the German princes, and the French Church, was to meet in a place of safety, preferably in Zealand, to frame a confession. This statement would be based on the confessions in use in the various Churches represented, but would omit "numerous points not necessary to our salvation", including the controversial issues of free will, perseverance, and predestination (i–iv). It was to be expected that those conferring would agree on the remaining "fundamental articles" (vi). The second stage would involve the meeting of another assembly to which the Lutheran princes would be induced to send representatives. An irenic general statement on the Eucharist is embodied in the document. If anyone dissents from it, let him tolerate, not persecute, his brethren. "On matters of accord let us clasp hands, and together sincerely and gladly take our way towards heaven" (xv, xvi). A copy of the Consensus of Sendomir is to be put on exhibit as a commendable example of Lutheran and non-Lutheran understanding. The resulting union would constitute "the Christian Reformed Church", in which such party names as "Lutheran", "Calvinist", "Sacramentarian" would cease to be used. The continued refusal of the French Reformed to regard Lutherans as alien is seen in the declaration of the Synod of Charenton (1631), which adopted a "decree in favour of our brothers the Lutherans". Adherents of the Augsburg Confession are to be freely received to communion since they hold, with the Reformed, "the fundamental points of true religion" and have neither superstition nor idolatry in their worship.[1]

It is to be observed that the irenical efforts of the French Reformed of this period were based upon old principles. They believed, like Calvin, in the value of colloquies as a means towards agreement, and, like the framers of the *Harmony of Confessions* (1581), looked for the meeting of a free Christian council that would adopt a consensus. They held, too, like Erasmus and Cassander, that the doctrinal terms of communion could be simplified to a few "fundamental articles". The firm Protestantism of England and Scotland and the favourable interest of King James in the union of the non-Roman Churches led the Huguenots to look to the British King as patron of the union cause. They hopefully endeavoured to awaken a response in Lutheranism. But before the Thirty Years War Lutheranism produced few writings suggesting any commerce with the Reformed.

It was not from the French Reformed alone that such proposals came. In the Netherlands, Francis Junius (1545–1602) wrote about 1590 his *Advice on Promoting Peace and Concord*,[2] and his correspondent and opponent Jacob Arminius, in February 1606, delivered an oration *On Composing the Disagreements among Christians*.[3] Arminius gives a masterly analysis of the causes of dissension, rejects the remedies proposed by Rome, presents a project for a free general

---

[1] L. Aymon, *Tous les synodes nationaux des églises réformées de France*, 2 vols., The Hague, 1710· (text of Tonneins project, II, pp. 57 ff., of Charenton decree, II, p. 500); G. de Félice, *Histoire des synodes nationaux des églises réformées de France*, Paris, 1864, pp. 160 ff.; R. Patry, *Philippe du Plessis-Mornay, un huguenot homme d'état (1549–1623)*, Paris, 1933, pp. 205 ff.; J. L. Neve, *The Lutherans and Movements for Church Union*, Philadelphia, 1921, pp. 19 ff. The articles of the Synod of Tonneins are substantially the same as those presented in the following year by du Moulin and agreed upon between him and King James I.

[2] *Consilium de pace et concordia in ecclesia Dei colenda*, published with a preface by L. Crocius, *Paraneticus de theologia cryptica*, Bremen, 1615, pp. 117–80.

[3] *Jacobi Arminii Orationes itemque tractatus*, 2nd edition, Leyden, 1613, pp. 114–50.

council whose members should be "men of wisdom and holy life . . . inflamed with the love of truth and peace", and closes with a passionate appeal. Isaac Casaubon could write in 1610 that Arminius was held by the Huguenots to be "an infamous heretic". Yet his proposals for unification were similar to those of Mornay and the French synods.

In this period David Pareus (1548–1622) of Heidelberg, pupil of Ursinus and teacher of John Amos Comenius, earlier an opponent of the Lutheran doctrine of ubiquity, wrote a weighty treatise on the union of Protestants.[1] With much learning, Pareus presents his own version of the familiar proposal for a synod of all Evangelical Churches, which he essays to prove both necessary and possible. Like Arminius, he wants a synod of "lovers of truth and peace", "not proud, contentious men . . . who seek victory rather than truth, and glory rather than peace" (iii). He thinks a free city of the Empire should be the place of meeting. He contrasts a rightly formed, free Protestant council with the Council of Trent. "The best and weightiest men would be chosen from every province and nation of the Christian world", and "the council would be ecumenical and universal". The assembly will have the task of determining what articles are fundamental; the test of faith will be the Word of God (iv, x). Pareus explains and interprets the principal earlier Protestant agreements, such as the Marburg Articles, the Wittenberg Concord, and the Consensus of Sendomir. The points of difference and of harmony of Reformed with Lutherans and of Roman Catholics with both are examined in detail. On the whole, this book is the most valuable item in the literature of the period for its revelation of the nature of the problem of disunity and the aspiration towards unity. It is significant that in his Preface to the Reader Pareus refers to the need of "a syncretism or amicable agreement against the papacy".

The proposals of Pareus and of the Synod of Tonneins were put forth in an increasingly anxious Europe. The Bohemian Charter of 1609 was soon infringed. The formation of the "Evangelical Union" (1608) was followed by that of the "Catholic League", and a cold war began in Germany which was destined to give place in March 1618 to a conflagration. Eight months later, representatives of many Reformed Churches met in the Synod of Dort to deal with the Arminian controversy in Dutch Calvinism. Its definitions of election and grace, rigidly excluding the doctrines of Arminius, won either formal or informal assent from the Reformed Churches generally. The Synod did little, however, to consolidate these Churches, while it tended to sharpen the issues between them and the Lutheran and Anglican Communions.

9. CONCLUSION

During the hundred years from Luther's Theses to the opening of the Thirty Years War, the desire for Christian reconciliation and unity found utterance in many voices and within all sections of the disrupted Church. Nor were the advocates of reunion entirely disappointed. The Wittenberg Concord, the Zurich Consensus, the Bohemian Confession, and the Consensus of Sendomir mark notable achievements. These agreements, national in scope, were all the work of theologians who were also Church leaders, and were not the result of political initiatives. Such limited unions, however, did not solve the general problem of disunity or permanently check the schismatic trend.

[1] *Irenicum, sive de unione et synodo evangelicorum concilianda*, Heidelberg, 1614.

The devisers of plans of unification, such men as Erasmus, Cassander, Bucer, Cranmer, Calvin, à Lasco, Mornay, Pareus, are not to be thought of as starry-eyed utopian idealists. In other phases of their work they all showed capacity for practical achievement. Yet on the whole they were defeated in their aims of reunion. The disruptive forces were too strong for them.

It would not be profitable to deal elaborately with the reasons for this ill success. But it may be useful to bring to notice some of the unfavourable conditions. Protestantism grew up in a series of local situations and formed territorial Churches whose local activities and problems were such as to exhaust the available energy. International or ecumenical churchmanship found little stimulus in day-to-day necessities. The various confessions of faith were themselves bases of union, and the unions they supported were wide enough to satisfy the desire of most for corporate fellowship. The craving for a larger unity was ardently felt in all communions, but by a small minority only. In the French Reformed Church alone was the union project an enduring phase of church policy. It must be recognized that, even though from 1598 this Church held the position of a tolerated minority, it lacked the security of a territorial establishment and felt the need of foreign support. The unity envisaged in its proposals, while sometimes thought of as leading to ultimate universal unity, was meanwhile to be a consolidation of Protestant forces for resistance to Rome. The motive of Protestant self-preservation, while understandable and justifiable in itself, is an inadequate motive for the promotion of a truly ecumenical reform of the Church.

Political factors were of necessity involved. Rulers who favoured and defended the Reformation were naturally looked to for support and leadership by those seeking evangelical union. Princes adhering to the Roman Church, especially where some of their subjects were resolutely Protestant, were likewise concerned with reunion projects. King Francis I's invitation to Melanchthon, Charles V's promotion of the Colloquy of Ratisbon, Queen Elizabeth's embassy to Rudolf II and to the Palatinate, and the advice of King James to the Huguenots, are instances in which eminent rulers took the initiative in efforts towards pacification or union. One point of contrast between that age and ours lies in the fact that some of the ecumenical efforts of the period had internationally powerful sponsors, while to-day reunion is proposed without political patronage. The close relationship of Church and secular government assumed as normal in the 16th century, generally speaking, no longer obtains. It was probably not conducive to unity then, since it exposed the Churches to the shifting secular diplomacy. The development of Erastianism in later generations proved injurious to the vitality and solidarity of the Churches.

Nor should we minimize the loyalties and antagonisms that hindered and still hinder reunion. Each communion cherishes its own *esprit de corps* and instinctively shrinks from any surrender of its uniqueness. Herein, says André Paul, is "the great obstacle". "Too many memories, clear or subconscious, mount guard"—memories of massacres, burnings, and embittered controversies.[1] To a great degree this situation had been reached by 1618. Each of the confessions had been fortified by scholastic defences, and each of them had been sanctified by the blood of martyrs. The feeling of solidarity within the group commanded the activity of most Christians and tended to obscure the vital loyalty to the Church that is One, Holy, and Catholic. The majority preferred a comfortable confessional immobility to the pains of ecclesiastical reconstruction, while

[1] A. Paul, *L'unité chrétienne: schismes et rapprochements*, Paris, 1930, Chap. vii.

many of the theologians felt an obligation to assail vehemently those who ventured to suggest irenical restatements of doctrine. Ecumenical projects perished in the prevailing atmosphere of scholastic polemics, inertia, and bigotry.

While we draw disquieting lessons from the futility of many of the union projects here reported, we may also find inspiration in the 16th-century ecumenical utterances we have reviewed. The leaders of the Reformation presented, in treatises and confessions, a body of teaching on the One, Holy, Catholic Church that offers a perpetual challenge to the divisive ecclesiasticism of many modern Christians in Churches great and small. Moreover, their positions were in a measure shared by their opponents prior to the Council of Trent.

The non-Roman Western Churches are to-day seeking to recover the values of realized membership in the Universal Church of the Apostles and Martyrs. They will not attain this end without attention to the thoughts and labours of 16th-century prophets of reform who confidently affirmed that "One Holy Church is to continue forever . . . the congregation of saints" (Augsburg Confession, vii), and that "the Catholic and Holy Church of God is spread out through all parts of the world, and extends to all times" (Second Helvetic Confession, xvii). The task to which they devoted themselves was the restoration of the true Catholic Church of the Creed and of the Word in unity as well as purity. Often they planned and held conferences; they sought to discover "fundamental articles"; they looked for help to general or national councils. These were not despicable and not censurable methods; but they proved inadequate to match the zeal and passion of special loyalties or to call forth a profound and general commitment to ecumenical unity.

The European scene was shifting ominously. A long and devastating war was in prospect. The drift towards religious disintegration was too strong to be reversed. The ecumenical spirit never altogether failed. But the opportunities which had been lost or rejected in the first century of the Reformation could never be recovered, and it was long before the climate again became so favourable to ecumenical enterprise and achievement.

CHAPTER 2

ECUMENICAL ACTIVITY
ON THE CONTINENT OF EUROPE IN THE
SEVENTEENTH AND EIGHTEENTH CENTURIES

by

MARTIN SCHMIDT

1. INTRODUCTION[1]

The 16th century was the century of the Reformation. The Reformation was, in essence, a vigorous and comprehensive attempt to rediscover the original content and outlook of the Gospel. Therein lies its unity. But, though all the Reformers were more or less deeply under the influence of Luther, many thinkers developed their own ideas independently, and in the variety of their understanding of the Gospel are to be discovered certain influences deriving from humanism, from the "spiritualism"[2] of the late Middle Ages, and from the scholastic tradition. By the end of the century it had become clear that the Continental Reformation had settled down in three main types. On the left were the diverse groups of the Anabaptists, with a "free Church" tradition. Scandinavia was Lutheran and Germany mainly so. France, Switzerland, Holland, Scotland, and some other countries had Churches of the Reformed type. All these stood in sharp contrast to the Roman Catholic Church, and in a less degree to the Anglican Reformation.

The 17th century was dominated by the Counter-Reformation, directed principally by the Jesuits. The consciousness of this threat in the practical world of politics, and the Jesuit challenge in the realms of theology and church life, created among Protestant churchmen the first though largely unexpressed common presupposition of Christian thought. Nowhere is this clearer than in the common front of theological discussion and defence against Robert Bellarmine (1542–1621), which, originating in France, extended through England and the Netherlands to Germany and finally to Switzerland.

On the continent of Europe the ecumenical movement entered a new phase in the 17th and 18th centuries. It manifests itself in two distinct forms, first in inward or intellectual preparation, secondly in attempts at practical achievement; or, to put it otherwise, through ecumenical thinking and through ecumenical activity. The two movements partly, though not entirely, overlap. There were spiritual movements which, without clear intention and by their very existence, expressed the ecumenical character of Christian faith, but never developed into specific plans for the unification of the Churches. On the other hand, there were proposals for the union of the Churches without any deep basis in piety or in theological conviction. There was a certain "ecumenical consciousness" that, fixed in its own self-sufficiency, took little account of the existing Churches. There were also proposals for union which grasped the practical questions involved and made earnest efforts to find a right solution for them.

Each of the two centuries is distinguished by its own special character. In the 17th century ecumenism is almost exclusively a question of unity in *doctrine*, and therefore questions of confession and dogma are in the foreground. In the 18th century the predominant concern is with unity in *life*, in piety, in the

[1] Professor F. Blanke, of the University of Zurich, who had originally undertaken the writing of this chapter, was prevented from doing so, but generously made his extensive notes and material available to Professor Schmidt. Professor Schmidt's text had unfortunately to be shortened by one-third; the shortening was carried out by the editorial staff in close consultation with Professor Schmidt.

[2] In German, *Spiritualismus* and its cognates are general terms for that form of religion which so emphasizes Christianity as an inner experience as to tend to sit loose to, to depreciate or even to condemn, all outward organization in the form of visible and local churches.

Christian moral life, in the organization of Christian life in community. In contrast to the 16th century, one aspect of the approach to unity receives little attention—that which was the special concern of the Anglican Churches and of leaders like Thomas Cranmer—unity in worship, in adoration, in prayer. Mystical "spiritualism" still tended to take this approach seriously, and therefore through that movement, and especially through the works of Pierre Poiret (1646–1719), the Latin tradition of mysticism was widely diffused. In circles influenced by it, opposition to Roman Catholicism was weakened.

Among intellectual and theological factors in ecumenical thinking, the most important was the conviction of the Churches of the Reformation that they alone constituted the true Church, the *Oikumene*. Since the Roman Catholic Church, identifying itself with the One, Holy, Catholic Church, also claimed this position, all the great Reformers felt it necessary to refute the Roman claim. For this reason, even in the 17th century, the Protestant Churches, both Lutheran and Reformed, laid claim to the title Catholic. The first writer to use the word Catholic (instead of Papist, which until then had been commonly used) in the sense of Roman Catholic, was Nicolaus Hunnius (1585–1643). As late as 1712, August Hermann Francke used the expression Catholic in the sense of "that which concerns the universal Church".[1] One of the great services rendered by the Huguenot Church in France was that it gave expression to this claim to catholicity, in the sense of ecumenicity, with notable clarity, penetration, and comprehensive learning. This point of view found its chief expression in a gigantic monument of polemical scholarship, *Panstratia Catholica* (1626), a posthumously published work of Daniel Chamier (1575–1621), professor at Montauban. It was only natural that Chamier should be a champion, in policy as well as in theory, of the unity of all the Protestant Churches of Europe.

With the abandonment of the word Catholic went acceptance of the designations Lutheran and Calvinist which had first been used by the enemies of Protestantism. The leading historian among the adversaries of the Protestant Churches was the Jesuit Louis Maimbourg (1610–86), who had Gallican tendencies, and for that reason was later expelled from the Society of Jesus. This scholar produced, in 1680, *The History of Lutheranism* and, in 1682, *The History of Calvinism*. The principal answer to him from the Lutheran side was Veit Ludwig von Seckendorf's *Historical and Apologetic Commentary on Lutheranism* (1692)[2]; on behalf of the French Reformed Churches, Pierre Jurieu wrote *The History of Calvinism and that of Popery, Set Forth in Parallel, or An Apology for the Reformers, for the Reformation and for the Reformed Churches, in Answer to a Book called The History of Calvinism by M. Maimbourg* (1682).[3] Seckendorf and Jurieu were ecumenical in their thinking; yet, under the influence of the book which they were answering, both adopted the terms Lutheranism and Calvinism without serious reflection on what they were doing. The consequences of this departure from tradition were serious. Till this time these personal appellations had been used only of the individual adherents of the various Churches; from this time on they came to be generally used of the Churches as a whole and of their systems of doctrine.

[1] In a letter to the S.P.C.K. of London, dated 26 February 1712, and preserved in the Francke Archives at Halle, A. 134 e.
[2] See Ernst Walter Zeeden in *Festschrift für Gerhard Ritter*, 1950. pp. 256–72.
[3] On Maimbourg, see article in *Dictionnaire de théologie catholique*, s.v.

2. CHRISTIAN HUMANISM

The humanism of the 16th century passed on to the succeeding generation two traditions of ecumenical thinking as determined by two sharply contrasted thinkers—Erasmus of Rotterdam and Jacob Acontius.

Acontius (d. 1566), in his own independent fashion, maintained the Erasmian tradition of Biblical orthodoxy, but under the influence of Luther gave the Bible a far more central place in his thought than Erasmus had done. Acontius was a humanist from Trent who found his second home in England. In his chief work, entitled *The Stratagems of Satan*[1] (1564), dedicated to Queen Elizabeth of England, he identified as the peculiar subtlety of the devil his skill in using differences of belief to create dissensions in the Kingdom of Christ, and in taking earthly rulers as his ministers for the condemnation of heretics and the erection of scaffolds. His earnest plea is that men should be willing to listen patiently to one another and to give up dogmatic self-assurance, since it is possible for a man unconsciously to fall into error, and while in error to be absolutely convinced of his own orthodoxy. If we seek the truth, we must seek it, not as philosophers, but as disciples of Christ, and therefore we must take Scripture alone as our guide. Every Christian affirmation must be tested in the light of its relationship to eternal life; only if a direct relationship is established can it be considered as a central truth of redemption. This general understanding of the Gospel in the light of Johannine teaching constitutes an early form of existentialism.

This desire for a radical simplification of thought leads Acontius to formulate definitively an idea which had earlier been expressed by Erasmus and his pupil John à Lasco—that of the distinction between articles of the faith which are necessary to salvation, and those which are of secondary importance. This formula is the key to his whole theology. There seems to be a slight element of scepticism in his thought, a doubt as to the existence of absolute truth, when he affirms that none other than Jesus Christ has ever been able perfectly to preserve pure doctrine, and when with penetrating acumen he shows how departures from pure doctrine have come about unnoticed and in spite of the most careful efforts of the responsible authorities to prevent them. But this scepticism is derived from the doctrine of original sin. We are all inclined by nature, according to Acontius, to presumption and to frivolity. For this reason he cannot accept the view that the truth can be mediated by Church councils. Pure doctrine can be most securely maintained when, in the formulation of dogmatic statements, Scripture is verbally followed. Since "heretics" still firmly believe in the authority of Scripture, they are greatly to be preferred to atheists and apostates. They are still fruitful branches in the Church, since the power of the Word is stronger than the errors of men. Life, according to Acontius, must correspond to doctrine, yet he never over-emphasizes the first to the detriment of the second. Above all else, with unusual penetration, he defines the nature of Christian ethics as depending on the fact that its very heart is the readiness to forgive, and that its most loathsome deformation is pharisaism. Both consequences follow necessarily from the doctrine of the forgiveness of sins through grace alone. Christian gentleness and love are the only attitudes which the believer may take up. 1 Corinthians 13 is an unconditional commandment. It is only through such love that peace can be restored in the Church.

[1] Jacobus Acontius, *Stratagemata Satanae*, ed. Gualtherus Koehler, 1927.

This Biblical humanism which reduces Christian ethics to the forgiveness of sins and mercy, and for that reason, like Sebastian Castellio, objects to the prosecution of heretics, and which, with careful minuteness, questions Church history as to the preservation or abandonment of pure doctrine and of the original life of the Church, manifests one of the most important springs of ecumenical thinking in that it rests on the central truth of redemption and, without becoming indifferent to truth, regards heretics as still fruitful branches in the Church because of their acceptance of the authority of the Scriptures. We shall constantly meet the influence of Acontius in later periods, even outside the sphere of Christian humanism.

Hugo Grotius (1583–1645) is spiritually more directly descended from his fellow-countryman Erasmus than from Acontius, though it is not to be forgotten that he spent the formative years of his youth in the family of Francis Junius.[1] Another great scholar with whom Grotius lived on terms of intimate and reverent friendship was that determined champion of the humanistic view of tradition, the Genevese Calvinist Isaac Casaubon (1559–1614),[2] who in 1610 transferred himself to England and there found the Church of his dreams. Casaubon was one of the greatest scholars of his time, with an incomparable knowledge of antiquity, but also with deep theological interest. In a speech of greeting pronounced before James I of England, the Archbishop of Sens, David du Perron, had referred to the King as lacking in one thing only—that he could not be truly described as a Catholic king. Casaubon, defending James I against this reproach, set forth his own understanding of the inner nature of catholicity in a manner which suggests an independent development of the ideas of Acontius.

With the same trenchancy as Acontius, Casaubon poses the question of the doctrines which are indispensable for the attainment of salvation. Only a few basic principles deserve this title, those in fact that are set forth plainly in the Word of God, or were accepted by the ancient Church as necessary deductions from the Word of God. On this basis Casaubon develops a comprehensive historical refutation of the assertion of Bellarmine that the Christianity of the Reformation is an innovation, setting forth point by point the undistorted testimony of the Fathers of the Church in contrast to the contemporary use made of them by Roman Catholic theologians. The Churches which have issued from the Reformation did not deliberately aim at agreement with the ancient Church, but without intention and without constraint they have reached that agreement. Their faith is that which was established by Jesus Christ himself, proclaimed by the Apostles, and witnessed to and defended in the ancient Church. That which is old is true. In the early days, when Christians daily gave evidence of brotherly charity and died for their faith in time of persecution, the Churches had made progress in the right way, inasmuch as they had grasped that Christian truth is truth manifest in action; but they reached their zenith in the age of Constantine, the Golden Century, and in the following two centuries, when Church and State constituted a unity, and in consequence a Christian culture was developed which was able to influence the whole life of mankind. Degeneracy set in only after the 6th century. Thus the ancient Church, in its whole extent and range, is canonized. Casaubon has combined the thought of Erasmus with that of Acontius.

[1] See later, pp. 86 f.
[2] On the relations between Grotius and Casaubon, see Henri Meylan, "Grotius théologien" in *Hommage à Grotius*, Lausanne, 1946, pp. 19–41.

This synthesis of humanism and Biblical orthodoxy finds its fullest development in the concept introduced by George Calixtus of the *consensus quinquesaecularis*, the agreement of the Church in the first five centuries. Calixtus (1586–1656) was born in Schleswig and was educated in Helmstedt by disciples of Melanchthon. His teacher, the Dutchman Johannes Caselius (1533–1613), a much-admired humanist of European reputation, had had friendly relationships with Casaubon. The attention of the young Calixtus had been directed towards this great man long before 1612, when he was able to meet him personally in London. This meeting was of enduring significance in the later development of Calixtus, since it was at this time that his thought took on its own special and individual character.

The traditions of the ancient Church, falsely condemned by opponents as syncretism, are his guiding principle. He too starts by accepting the Holy Scriptures as the highest authority; but tradition is also necessary, if not for the clear exposition of the Scriptures, at least for the defence of Christian truth against heretics. The traditions of the first five centuries, as found in the Fathers of the Church and the great Councils, contain the true explication of the Biblical faith, and therefore the testimony of the ancient Church is to be preferred to the confessional documents of the epoch of the Reformation. The heart of Christianity, the fundamental articles of faith, have been passed on unaltered by a process of quiet transmission through all epochs and changes up to the present time. These constitute the normative forms of Christian thought. In contrast to his opponent, Johann Konrad Dannhauer (1603–66), the theologian of Strasburg, who spoke of the *lex extensibilitatis*, the law of development in doctrine, Calixtus regards the essence of Christianity as unalterable.

The thought of Calixtus includes with the doctrine of tradition the idea of the central importance of synods. The restoration of the unity of the divided Church is to be sought through theological discussions and by joint formulation of the articles of belief—just as much later, in the early years of Pietism, Philipp Jakob Spener (1675) hoped to renew the life and practice of the Church by means of synods and the exchange of ideas. This idea found practical expression in formal meetings for the discussion of theological problems.

In comparison with Acontius and Grotius, indeed even with Erasmus and Melanchthon, with his lamentations over the *rabies theologorum*, the wild strivings of the theologians, Calixtus gives the impression of a lack of warmth. His *consensus quinquesaecularis* is a product of the study table, a homunculus produced in the retort of the scientist. It is a programme of practical action, not a fruit of spiritual conviction or of the desires of the heart. As Erich Seeberg has aptly said, its real aim is the unhistorical re-creation of an ideal period dogmatically defined. This impression is confirmed by the plain fact that the idea of missions to the heathen, which for Grotius had decisive importance, is in Calixtus completely lacking. Nevertheless, his view of tradition, as extended to the end of the first five centuries, made such an impression in his time that it made its way even into Grimmelshausen's *Adventures of Simplizissimus*.[1]

In Calixtus that second characteristic of humanism, its ethical emphasis, comes out during the course of his development more clearly than in any other writer of his type. Just as the immediate disciples of Erasmus had endeavoured to produce a valid new formulation of the doctrine of justification, with strong emphasis on man's responsibility to co-operate with God, so Calixtus lays in-

---

[1] *Der abenteuerliche Simplizissimus*, 1949, ed. III, pp. 215 ff.

creasing stress on Christian living, since the diversity of dogmas seems to him an irremovable obstacle to union. This displacement of dogma, as having only relative validity, in favour of an ethical emphasis threatened the central place of the doctrine of justification as the basis of evangelical Christendom. This threat immediately called into the field Calixtus' orthodox opponents, the theologians of Wittenberg. Nevertheless, emphasis on the Christian ethical standard as the bond of unity between the different confessions was an ecumenical contribution which looked forward to the future and to the modern world, and beyond Pietism to the period of the Enlightenment.

Calixtus was a humanist to the core. This Christian humanism, developed to its furthest consequences in a highly individual, indeed heretical, form, is to be found among the Socinians.

Fausto Sozzini (1539–1604) was a product of the same spiritual climate in 16th-century Italy as his fellow-countryman Acontius. He also found a temporary home in Basle and there fell under the spell of Castellio. It is clear, however, that, unlike Acontius, he was not deeply influenced by the thought of Luther. For Sozzini, as for Michael Servetus, the person of Jesus is the centre of theological thought. In Jesus, and particularly in his historical, earthly life, he saw God himself at work. So starting from the idea of the imitation of Christ, regarded as manifesting the highest possibilities of human life, in a profoundly ethical understanding of the Gospel which somehow anticipated the teaching of Albrecht Ritschl, he set forth exclusive devotion to Jesus as containing the whole meaning of Christianity. But one consequence of this Christocentric outlook was Unitarianism, the violent repudiation of the doctrine of the Trinity. This brought back problems of doctrine into the centre of the picture. The living Word of God, which for Acontius was central, is now of secondary importance. The place of the Church is taken by the school. The outward sign of the community of the saints is no longer the proclamation of the divine Word, but the recognition of the "saving doctrine". This "reasonable Biblical doctrine" found support in the strong emphasis laid by Sozzini on the voice of the early Church. The simple statements of doctrine, concerning which all teachers of the ancient Church are in agreement, provide the right clue to the understanding of Scripture. These teachers are, in point of fact, the Fathers of the ante-Nicene period, and the chief among them is Arius. Here again we meet the concept of "doctrine necessary for salvation", which overleaps the limits of the Churches, historically and legally constituted as separate Churches, and so makes them of no importance. There is real significance in the naughty tale directed against the Socinians, that the Dutch humanist Justus Lipsius found it possible to be a Lutheran in Jena, a Calvinist in Leiden, and a Roman Catholic in Louvain without any strain upon his conscience. Following the line of Sozzini, Daniel Zwicker (1612–78) of Danzig endeavoured, in his anonymous book *Irenicum Irenicorum*, which attracted much attention, to reconcile all parties in the Churches on the basis of the ante-Nicene tradition to which he gives the title Apostolic.

The original Biblical humanism also extended its influence in a direction precisely opposite to that of the Socinians—the world of Lutheran orthodoxy. Here again it took the form of the doctrine of the Fundamental Articles of faith. The first writer in whom it is found explicitly expressed is Matthias Hafenreffer (1561–1619). In the second edition of his *Loci Theologici* he distinguishes between two forms of theological error: that which denies fundamental articles of the Christian faith, and that which affects only secondary truths. Among the fundamental articles he includes the doctrine of God, that is to say, the Trinity and the Incarnation. He was followed by the Wittenberg theologians, Leonhard Hütter (1563–1616), Balthasar Meisner (1587–1626), and Nicolaus Hunnius, who progressively developed the concept in relation to the details of the Faith. Hütter, who wrote against Junius, affirms that the statement "Christ is our redeemer" is not by itself a sufficient expression of the Faith. Everything depends on the sense in which he is understood to be our redeemer. The Socinians would say that he is our redeemer as our example. The Lutherans, on the contrary, would say that it was through the sacrificial satisfaction made by him on our behalf. It is necessary, therefore, to define more exactly the content of the fundamental articles. If we begin not merely to list them, but also to elucidate them as integral parts of the total corpus of Christian doctrine, we at once fall into difficulties. Hütter believed that the difficulty could be met by recognizing the existence of social and educational distinctions among the hearers of the Gospel. The learned must know all the truths of the Faith, whereas the simpler may limit themselves to the fundamental truths.

Meisner accepts as fundamental articles those which concern salvation, and thus prepares the way for that limitation of the Christian confession to the contents of the second and third articles[1] in the Creed, which becomes dominant in Pietism. Hunnius works out in detail Meisner's suggestions, and abandons as unnecessary all later developments of the main doctrines of the Person of Christ and of redemption, e.g. the *communicatio idiomatum*,[2] the nature of the presence of Christ in the Holy Communion, and the ubiquity of Christ's body. From his point of view, only the doctrine of predestination, and in connection with it the question whether one who has received the grace of God can lose it, remains as an impassable barrier between Lutherans and Reformed. At this point the farthest limit of the efforts towards reconciliation has been reached.

In Hunnius we notice again the tendency towards an ethical emphasis, when, for instance, he asserts that deadly sin is as offensive to God as dogmatic error. On the other hand, in reaction against the Synod of Dort with its stern doctrine of predestination, he uses the idea of the fundamental articles to demonstrate the impossibility of union between the two great Protestant Churches. Johannes Hülsemann (1602–61) turns back to the doctrine of justification by faith. For him this is the focal-point to which all other articles of the Creed stand in an indissoluble relationship.[3] The view of Christian doctrine as a totality has prevailed against the idea of the possibility of distinctions between levels of Christian truth.

Let us take a look backward. Christian humanism has spread itself over a wide field geographically, historically, and in the history of thought. It has also developed a considerable number of directive ecumenical ideas. Of these there are, in fact, seven. The first, most general and most difficult to define precisely, is that indicated by the word *peace*; on this follows the central thought of the possibility of identifying a minimum of Christian dogma as necessary to salvation; the combination of these two principles results in the theoretical and practical demand for toleration; the idea of that central part of Christian faith which

---

[1] I.e. the doctrines respectively of redemption and sanctification.

[2] The view that, in the divine-human Person of Christ, each of the natures "communicates" its qualities and operations to the other.

[3] See Max Keller-Hüschemenger, *Das Problem der Fundamentalartikel bei Johannes Hülsemann*, 1939.

is necessary for salvation results in the ascription of a high value to tradition; emphasis on practical Christian activities leads to a corresponding emphasis on Christian ethics; and finally, this is followed by attention to the practical and technical possibilities of action through synods, and of actual Church union. It is easily seen that this wealth of thought and ideas plays a dominant part in ecumenical discussion in subsequent periods, sometimes taken over as it stood by later thinkers, sometimes combined in new patterns, and sometimes only partially accepted.

3. THE MYSTICAL OR "SPIRITUALIST" TRADITION

Even in the Middle Ages there was a continuous tradition concerning the "spiritual Church".[1] This came to expression in the Anabaptist movement as a "Biblical protest against the Reformation". For the German-speaking lands the most important figure was the Silesian nobleman, Caspar Schwenckfeld of Ossig (1489–1561), who, in contrast to many of his contemporaries, refrained from controversy and retained in particular an unfailing admiration for Luther. The mystics of the "spiritualist" movement of the 17th and 18th centuries constantly appealed to him, and the Formula of Concord was in part directed against him. In the succeeding period his influence was surpassed only by that of Johann Arndt (1555–1621). Arndt was a convinced Lutheran and a pastor of the Lutheran Church, so much so that when the Church of Anhalt came under Calvinistic influence, he gave up his office rather than submit to this ecclesiastical change. For all that, his chief concern was with the true worship of God which is bound by no external ceremonies, with an inner Church of the New Testament, which has risen above the level of the Old Testament, bound as that was to the law and to a form of worship prescribed in ritual ordinances. The obverse of his criticism of the existing Churches is a fresh emphasis on Christ in us, on the new birth, on renewal of the image of God as it was given to man in the original creation.

Contemporaneously with Arndt, Jacob Boehme (1575–1624) was setting forth similar teaching, with a sharper polemical accent due to his own painful experiences. Each of the existing Churches is only a church of stones—"blocks of stone produce no new men". The true Church is in the heart of the believer, and this he must bring with him to the worship of God in order profitably to take part in it. Such true believers constitute a universal Church of the Spirit. Boehme applied to the history of the Church the two trees in the portrayal of Paradise in the Biblical narrative. They stand in opposition to one another as the good and evil principles. The Church of Abel is persecuted and destroyed by the Church of Cain, but the true Church of Abel lives on as a hidden reality within the Church of Cain. That Church is a Christianity "free from parties"[2] and, as such, a miracle of God. This solution of the problem of the Church was adopted by Christian Hoburg (1607–75), Joachim Betke (1601–63), Friedrich Breckling (1629–1711), and later and above all by Gottfried Arnold (1666–1715). In 1698 Arnold, basing himself on Jeremiah 51.9,[3] composed the pitiless *Dirge over*

---

[1] For which see Ernst Benz, *Ecclesia Spiritualis*, 1934.

[2] Here the concrete, historical Churches are the "parties", and adherence to any one of them is adherence to a party. True Christianity stands above and is independent of them all.

[3] "We would have healed Babylon, but she is not healed: forsake her, and let us go every one into his own country: for her judgement reacheth unto heaven, and is lifted up even to the skies." *Babels Grablied* is printed in Erich Seeberg, *Gottfried Arnold* (*Mystiker des Abendlandes*), 1934, pp. 276 ff.

Babylon, which not merely foretold the disappearance of the visible Church which is now incurably sick, but called for determined efforts to hasten its disappearance. Yet when the matter is more carefully considered, it is evident that it is above all the Babylon within ourselves which has to be destroyed.

Not all went so far as this: there were those who, like Gerhard Tersteegen (1697–1769), maintained a moderate position. Different estimates of the Church underlie the variations in "spiritualist" thought. Consideration of the nourishment needed by "the new man" led Boehme to attach special importance to the Sacrament of the Holy Communion. Christian Hoburg, whose way led him from the office of a Lutheran village pastor to that of a Mennonite preacher in Altona, combined the thought of Boehme with that of Johann Arndt, as did his friend Betke, who remained within the official Church, and also Friedrich Breckling, a disciple of them both, who, as Lutheran pastor in Amsterdam, carried on an extensive and genuinely ecumenical activity. These all gave individual variation to the common melody of the "spiritualist" outlook. Hoburg lays special emphasis on Christ and his life in us as the Crucified, which has remained unknown in the concrete, historical Churches. Betke goes a step further towards recognition of the Church as an organization. For him the all-important thing is the restoration of the priesthood of all believers through the new birth and sanctification. Johann Georg Gichtel (1638–1710) gives central importance to the joy which is already attainable on earth in fellowship with the heavenly *Sophia,* wisdom. Balthasar Köpke (1646–1711), the friend of Spener, following the traditions of Roman Catholic mystical theology, describes the different levels of sanctification and perfection which a Christian is called upon to attain, and indeed can attain on earth.

Apart from the Protestant mysticism of Germany, we have to reckon also with the Latin tradition of mysticism in Spanish and French Roman Catholicism. The writings of the Spanish mystics of the 16th century, such as St Teresa and St John of the Cross, were widely read throughout our period. Even more influential was Quietism as developed by St François de Sales (1567–1622), by Mme Guyon (d. 1717), Antoinette Bourignon (d. 1680), and other writers of their type. The ideal of pure, disinterested love towards God as set out by these mystics was experienced by Christians of the most diverse communions as a point of living fellowship; the saintliness of character so glowingly set forth overleaped all confessional barriers and served in many quarters as an inspiration to practical and moral achievement in Christian living.

A peculiar combination of Christian humanism and mystical "spiritualism" is found in the *Paraenesis votiva pro pace ecclesiastica* (1626) of Peter Meiderlin (1582–1651), minister of the Church of St Anna in Augsburg. Meiderlin regrets that after the death of Arndt the old controversial spirit of the theologians has broken bounds again. His desire is for a theology of the Spirit and of love, through which God may dwell in the hearts of believers as the living Word. For him works of love, as fruits of the Spirit, are decisive. A theology without love, without the Holy Spirit, is only talk about God and not God's own Word. The question of the articles of faith necessary to salvation dominates his thought. He accepts as necessary to salvation and basic to faith only such doctrines as are included in the Creed or in the Catechism, or can claim for themselves clear testimony in Scripture. There is nothing new in this definition, but Meiderlin adds such doctrines as the Church has approved through decisions of valid synods, or through publicly accepted confessional books, and also those which are recognized by all theologians as necessary. This positive affirmation of the Church is in sharper contradiction to the tradition of "spiritualism" than it is to Lutheran orthodoxy. It is closely related to the doctrine of tradition as set forth by Calixtus, and can cite with approval the formula of Vincent of Lerins: "That which everywhere, always, and by all has been believed." Meiderlin appears to have been the author of the then constantly quoted irenical expression: "In essentials, unity; in non-essentials, liberty; in all things, charity." This catchword is found shortly afterwards in the irenical work published by the Calvinistic theologian Gregor Francke of Frankfort-on-Oder, *A Theological Consideration of the Degrees of Necessity of Christian Dogmas*.[1]

4. VARIETIES OF ECUMENICAL APPROACH

In many respects Pietism took over the heritage of mystical "spiritualism" in Germany, where it developed, to use its own phrase concerning itself, as a second Reformation. But Pietism spread far beyond the German-speaking countries, and became a movement embracing the whole of Christendom and specially concerned with the ecumenical exchange of fellowship. The field of its influence spread from Puritanism in England to the theology of "Precisianism" in the Netherlands; from the Latin mysticism of France, through the longings and proposals for reform within Lutheran late orthodoxy, to the Philadelphian movement and religious societies in England, and finally to the Methodist and Revival movements.

Lutheran late orthodoxy had already in many respects prepared the way for Pietism. In the person of such leaders as Johann Gerhard in Jena (1582–1637) and Wolfgang Franz in Wittenberg (1564–1628), it had laid itself open to the influence of the practical and personal understanding of Christianity set forth by the "spiritualist" leader Johann Arndt. In the 17th century the Universities of Rostock and Strasburg had developed a strong tradition of earnest efforts to reform the Church, in the promotion of which such men as Heinrich Müller (1631–75) and Johann Konrad Dannhauer were outstanding. In earnest self-criticism, one of the signs of which was a return from Lutheranism to Luther himself, men like Johann Tarnow (1586–1629) had appealed to the Bible against the polemical complacency and thoughtless acceptance of authority that were all too manifest in the contemporary Church. Johann Valentin Andreae (1586–1654) was the grandson of Jakob Andreae, the moving spirit and chief compiler of the Lutheran Formula of Concord of 1577. The grandson, on his journey to Geneva as a student, accepted the Calvinistic form of church discipline, and, when he himself reached a position of authority, carried out a reorganization of the regional Church of Swabia on the lines of Geneva, which is still effective at the present time. But he was not concerned only to imitate a foreign example. He desired to see, here anticipating Pietism and the Enlightenment, a true union in Christ through fellowship in Christian living, by means of which divergences in theology should be resolved. This end was to be served by the formation of a *fraternitas Christi*, a loose organization of Christian brotherhood.

Thus variously Lutheran late orthodoxy was preparing the way for Pietism;

---

[1] See Ludwig Bauer, *M. Peter Meiderlin*, Augsburg, 1906; and, for important considerations relative to Meiderlin's connection with the irenical expression, A. Eekhof, *De zinspreuk In necessariis unitas*, etc., Leiden, 1931.

but Pietism in its depths reached far beyond the prudent and practical purposes of this orthodoxy. At the very centre of Pietism is the doctrine of "the new birth". Originally, and especially in the teaching of Philipp Jakob Spener, stress is laid equally on the hidden source, the divine secret, and on the visible result, the new man in Christ. The believer is directly begotten of God. He not only bears the image of his Creator as an unseen inner force, but also by steady progress brings that inner secret to light in visible representation. His aim is perfection.[1] Later, the emphasis passes to the second factor in the new birth, man as regenerate. Only through the rebirth of individual Christians, first the clergy, and thereafter the ordinary members of the Church, can the renewal of the whole life of the Church be hoped for. For rebirth creates a new fellowship. It brings into being an invisible, "spiritual" Church, which, as the true Church, reaches far beyond all the limits of all the historical and concrete Churches. The true believers who lead a truly Christian life know in the depths of their experience that they are one both in fact and also in personal experience. Spener forcefully brings back into currency the picture of the Body of Christ, which though sick yet actually exists. Half a century later Zinzendorf expressed the matter in plain terms: "The invisible Church can become visible in the eyes of the world through the fellowship of the members."

But rebirth, though it starts as an individual experience, has a social function to perform beyond the gathering together of like-minded individuals. Rebirth involves the recovery of the realities of the early Church, that apostolic life which the first Christians lived in meekness, love, and peace, and which is still an obligation and a possibility. Exemplary lives can defend the value and truth of Christian faith against developing atheism. Pietism resulted in a flowering both of autobiography and of biography. Characteristic manifestations are the great collections of Lives of the Saints—Gottfried Arnold's *Lives of the Believers*, Johann Heinrich Reitz' *History of the Reborn*, Christian Gerber's *History of the Reborn in Saxony*, and finally Gerhard Tersteegen's *Selected Biographies of Holy Souls*. These biographies sometimes naïvely, sometimes deliberately, break through all confessional limits. Roman Catholics are found in strange fellowship, cheek by jowl with men and women of the Evangelical Churches. But we find records not only of individuals, but also of fellowships or centres of Christian life which may serve as examples to others: above all, August Hermann Francke's Orphan Asylum[2] at Halle with his plan to make it the nucleus of a Universal Seminary; the *Friedensburg*[3] of Hochmann von Hochenau in Schwarzenau; the Philadelphian Society[4] of Jane Leade and Francis Lee in London; the Unity of the Brethren[5] reconstituted by Count Zinzendorf at Herrnhut, with its various colonies; the German Christian Fellowship[6] at Basle; finally the institutions founded by Swabian Pietists at Kornthal and Beugen, which fall within the 19th century and point the way to the Lutheran centres of Neuendettelsau and Hermannsburg.

The expectation of perfection led to the development in Pietism of the millennial hope, the "hope for better times" for the Church, which Spener obstinately defended against all attacks from the side of orthodoxy. One of the blessings to be expected in the Messianic Age is the restoration of the unity of the Church. In the fostering of this hope, Pietism did not stand alone, and did not

---

[1] See Martin Schmidt, "Speners Wiedergeburtslehre", *Theol. Lit. Zeit.*, 1951, pp. 23 ff.
[2] See pp. 100 f.   [3] See pp. 103 ff.   [4] See p. 105.
[5] See pp. 101 ff.   [6] See pp. 117 ff.

simply follow the traditions of Anabaptist "spiritualism". Such hopes are also found over wide areas within orthodox Christian traditions. The attempt to take eschatology seriously, down to the details of concrete prophecy, leads to a curious but inevitable reversal of the points of view; eschatology becomes transformed into history, and through this transformation it ceases to be genuinely a doctrine of "the last things".

If, in conclusion, we ask what are the contributions of mystical "spiritualism" and Pietism to ecumenical thinking, the following are the essential points:

1. The new birth, which is a comprehensive new creation wrought by Christ living and working in us;
2. The goal of perfection for the individual believer and eschatological hope for the Church as a whole, if not for the whole world, both flowing from a serious consideration of the present and concrete situation as the sphere of God's redemptive activity;
3. The new significance attached to history, as the sphere in which God is contemporarily at work;
4. The biographical interest which derives from the central importance ascribed to rebirth; and
5. The idea of the Christian society or fellowship, which takes the place of the organized state Church and proclaims the free union of all living Christians above and beyond the limits of the historic and legally determined Confessions.

The Church of Jesus Christ must be defined in terms of its responsibility to proclaim universally the sovereignty of God and his redemptive activity in Jesus Christ. The Church is a missionary body or it is nothing at all. In the period of the Reformation the missionary impulse seems in a measure to have failed. Yet the outward appearance is deceptive. None of the great Reformers—Luther, Melanchthon, Bucer, or Calvin—ever forgets the Turks and the world of Islam. Nevertheless, it was only on the Roman Catholic side that the dawning colonial epoch, in particular the discovery of America, provoked serious attempts to develop missionary work and released new missionary forces. It is only in the 17th century that the idea of missions begins gradually to become effective in the Protestant Churches. Almost all the champions of ecumenical activity in the 17th and 18th centuries are at the same time defenders, inspirers, and organizers of missions to the heathen or to the Jews.

Of all the movements of that period this is more true of Pietism than of any other, though the "spiritualist" movement had prepared the way for it. The connection between ecumenism and missions is already recognizable in Hugo Grotius, who desired to see the Christian religion spread through the witness of sailors and merchants, and at the same time inspired Peter Heyling to undertake his missionary enterprise in Abyssinia. Justinian von Weltz (1621–68) stood in close relationship to the tradition of mystical "spiritualism". In the framework of the efforts for the renewal of the Church after the Thirty Years War, he is concerned with the restoration of Christian devotion, with the life of true godliness and Christian morality. The second of his classic writings on the subject of missions reveals in the title the definite eschatological expectation of "spiritualism". It is called *An Invitation to the Approaching Great Supper, and Proposals for a Christian Fellowship of Jesus, in which are set forth Means for the Improve-*

ment of Christendom and for the Conversion of the Heathen (1664). He is thinking now in quite definite terms of a union of Lutherans and Reformed. Though at first he addresses himself exclusively to Christians of the Augsburg Confession, his last great missionary document of the year 1664 is addressed to "all hearts that love Jesus".[1] The peculiar quality of his thought reveals a combination of Lutheran late orthodoxy, humanism, and "spiritualism", which is impressive and very characteristic of the 17th century. This brings him into close relationship with Gottfried Wilhelm von Leibniz, who likewise actively concerned himself both with missionary work and with ecumenical attempts to reunite Christians.

Of all the motives which in the 17th and 18th centuries tended to promote the union of Christendom, the least effectively developed was the political.

This motive meets us first and predominantly, as is easily understood, in France, where militant Roman Catholicism under Richelieu and Louis XIV was aiming at the total suppression and extirpation of Protestantism in its Huguenot form, and in the Netherlands, where the same process was going forward under Spanish rule. The father and chief representative of ecumenical thought in French Protestantism was Philippe de Mornay, Lord of Plessis-Marly (1549–1623),[2] but even in him theological judgement and political activity were evenly balanced. His journeys to Geneva, to Italy, to the England of Elizabeth, and to the Netherlands, his activity as adviser to Henry of Navarre, had broadened his outlook. From early years the idea of the reconciliation of the two confessions had been constantly in his mind. As early as 1581 he had written a work, repeatedly printed and translated, in defence of Christianity against atheists, heathen, and Jews. When, through the accession of Henry of Navarre to the throne, he became the recognized leader of the Huguenots, he used his influence in favour of definite plans for unity, both diplomatic and theological. His aim was the union of the two Protestant confessions; his hope was that the King of England would convene an ecumenical council. Another aspect of his work was the foundation of the theological Academy of Saumur, which was developed as an effective nursery of ecumenical theology.[3]

The theologians of the Palatinate put forth in 1606 an irenical document in which the political emphasis is stronger than in du Plessis-Mornay. Faced by the threat of the growing power of the Counter-Reformation, they called Christians to unite; but they let it be understood that in their opinion Calvinistic teaching was alone truly Christian, both on the main points of controversy—Christology, the Lord's Supper, and predestination—and in the realm of Christian worship.

In the early years of the 18th century, the political motive for Christian unity meets us again in an anonymous work, entitled *The Necessity of a Protestant and Catholic League for the Maintenance of Common Liberty*, published at Cologne in 1702. Taking as his starting-point the inhuman oppression which the Huguenots had suffered under Louis XIV, the writer warns his readers against the threat of the total enslavement of Europe by Roman Catholic France. He is concerned not only with the fate of the Calvinists, but also with that of the Lutherans, indeed with the whole of Christian Europe, which can be irreparably ruined by such religious persecutions. French imperialism will destroy every form of

---

[1] Reprinted by Paul Grössel, *Der Missionsweckruf des Barons Justinian von Weltz*, 1890.
[2] Commonly known as du Plessis-Mornay.   [3] See p. 88.

religion other than that which it professes itself. It will gradually bring under its power little Switzerland, then Germany, the Netherlands, and England. There is only one possibility of escape : political alliance with the Tsar and a closer fellowship, or even union, with the Eastern Orthodox Church, the anti-Roman convictions of which must be taken advantage of by the Western powers. The writer even goes into details of military affairs, proposing that foreign officers shall be sent to Russia to help in the training of the ill-trained Russian army. He speaks as a politician and no more when he predicts that such a league would exercise an irresistible power of attraction on other states of Europe, and bases this conviction on the fact that they could not wish to see France attain a position of political supremacy. Protestants, in defence of their faith, must make use of the purely political methods of diplomacy, political combinations, and military alliances, as Philip of Hesse and Zwingli had done in the century of the Reformation.

The ecclesiastical tone, or perhaps only undertone, is not entirely lacking. The writer emphasizes the fact that the Church is one, and one only. Christian moral principle that is common to all Christians is more important than the dogmatic divisions which keep Lutherans and Calvinists apart; these have no importance for the attainment of salvation, and are rather controversies about words. The writer makes it clear, however, that he regards Calvinism as preferable to any other form of doctrine. Tolerance, religious freedom, the sense of responsibility for the oppressed and injured, which are common human duties and common Christian responsibilities, form the positive counterpart to the negative idea of fellowship in opposition to Rome. Even the deep differences between the faith of the Eastern Orthodox Church and that of the Protestant Churches cannot be allowed to stand in the way of this indispensable co-operation.

It is only in Reformed writers that such political arguments are found. The Lutherans, following the example of their great Reformer, reject the idea of political intervention, and instead watch over purity of doctrine with almost suicidal integrity. It is only with the development of the doctrine of the State in the period of the Enlightenment that this attitude changes, as is manifest in Leibniz. His thought was determined by a comprehensive political concept which, unlike that of his predecessors, did not spring from the necessities of a situation of crisis, but looked forward positively and constructively to a new Europe, conceived as the medieval *corpus Christianum* brought up to date.

All the movements of which we have spoken are marked by their comprehensive character. The idea of Christian union was not in them a single special concern, but the consequence of their general outlook and of the structure of their thought. It was one feature of their physiognomy, perhaps the most important, but it was not the whole.

In Reformed irenical writing the situation is different. Here we are concerned with a literary tradition, with a group and a succession of writings, which set before themselves the restoration of the peace and the unity of the Church, deliberately, emphatically, exclusively, and definitely as their single purpose.

Francis Junius in Holland wrote, about 1590, the first Reformed irenical book, an earnest plea for fellowship, based on the Bible, Biblically developed, and pointing forward to the leading ideas of Pietism.[1] With this book he gave the first

[1] See also Chap. i, pp. 66 f.

impulse to what became in Heidelberg a local ecumenical tradition. The *Irenicum* of his successor, David Pareus (1548–1622), which appeared in 1614–15, was the most influential specimen of this class of writing, and its author was one of the most highly respected theologians of his time. He had been a leader in anti-Lutheran polemics. This work of his old age must therefore have come as a considerable surprise to his contemporaries.[1]

Lutherans naturally remained suspicious of these invitations to peace from the Calvinistic side—naturally, because of the reckless extirpation of Lutheran usages in worship which had taken place wherever the doctrines of Melanchthon, crypto-Calvinism, or genuine Calvinism had become the dominant force in the Church. Answers to these Calvinistic irenical writings of the School of Heidelberg were produced in the main by the theologians of the University of Wittenberg. After Frederick Balduin, Leonhard Hütter raised his voice, and drew attention to seven principal differences in doctrine which made it impossible that agreement between the two main Protestant confessions should be more than outward appearance. Shortly afterwards Paul Stein of Cassel for the Calvinists and Balthasar Mentzer for the Lutherans crossed swords. But, as Hans Emil Weber has rightly emphasized, underlying all these controversies was the sense of a common concern, a common search for mutual understanding in the field of dogma. In 1619 Balthasar Mentzer could end his reply to Stein's appeal for peace with the following words:

> "Therefore will we hold fast to peace and unity, indeed to fellowship in outward things, with one another. We will pray for one another. We will serve one another in an attempt to reach a better understanding, and do and contribute everything that can, should, or may be demanded of us, done or contributed by us, provided only that there be no infringement or minimizing of the heavenly and saving Truth, as true Christian love itself demands."[2]

The Synod of Dort (1618–19), with its definition of the doctrine of predestination, appeared to involve the rejection of all irenical approaches. The Lutherans felt that the condemnation of the Arminians was directed also against themselves. Nicolaus Hunnius expressly makes the criticism that, in the discussions at the Synod, the way indicated by Pareus was not followed, and expressed himself as thankful that God had revealed the true face of the Calvinists before all had been ensnared by the asseverations of their desire for peace. After Dort, approaches to union could not but involve departures from the position taken up by the Synod. Particularly is this true of Hugo Grotius.

The decisions of the Synod of Dort had constituted a victory for the doctrine of predestination. A rational system of thought which went beyond Calvin had tried to impose the doctrine of limited atonement as binding on all Calvinistic Churches. It is God's purpose to save a limited number of men only. This statement, although in fact a popular and inexact representation of the doctrines of Dort, must be accepted as a generally fair statement of the results of the discussions.

In the Reformed Churches the opposite view could no longer be maintained in the radical form of Arminianism, since this had been condemned as heretical.

---

[1] See also Chap. i, p. 67, and p. 89.
[2] Quoted by Otto Ritschl, *Dogmengeschichte des Protestantismus*, IV, 1927, p. 259.

In the working out of the problem of predestination a new theological school developed, with its headquarters at Saumur, in the Academy founded by du Plessis-Mornay. Moses Amyraut (1596–1664) was its principal figure. He taught the doctrine known as "hypothetical universalism". In contradistinction to Calvinistic orthodoxy, he deduced from Gen. 3.15 that God's purpose of redemption was directed towards all men; but the fulfilment of God's purpose clearly depends on man's believing. But man cannot believe in his own strength. He needs the illumination of the Holy Spirit. This takes place through a second divine election, and this is limited. The grounds for this limitation—and here Amyraut follows the stricter doctrine of predestination—lie in the secret counsel of God. Amyraut believed it possible with this formulation to do justice both to theological orthodoxy and to the desire of the godly for the assurance of salvation. The fact that his theory could fairly easily be torn to pieces by logical demonstration by no means robbed it of its influence. Its depth and its importance lay in the fact that in the doctrine of God it gave a place to love, and in its concept of faith made effective the analogy between the knowledge attainable through faith and other forms of apprehension. Amyraut, as is natural in view of the universalist tendency of his thought, repeatedly entered the field with practical and ecclesiastical writings in favour of the union of Lutherans and Calvinists, as resolved upon in France by the Synod of Charenton in 1631.[1]

The theological school of Saumur succeeded in holding its own against all attacks and suspicions. It maintained friendly contact with the Jesuits in Saumur. Also, through Amyraut, it exercised an influence on the development of William Penn and thereby on the early history of the Quaker settlement of Pennsylvania. This, if nothing else, would ensure for it an important place in the ecumenical story. In indirect connection with it stood David Blondel (1590–1655), the historian of dogma and author of polemical works against the papal primacy. In recognition of his important literary achievements he had been chosen as a professor at Saumur, but was not set free by his church of Roucy. In his book called *Authentic Accounts of the Reformed Churches of France, Germany, and Great Britain, Concerning the Peace and Brotherly Charity which all the Servants of God should Maintain among Protestants* (1655), he gives evidence of ecumenical sense directed to immediately practical aims. He was deeply concerned for the unity of all the Churches which had issued from the Reformation, and watched with the closest sympathy the historical vicissitudes through which they passed.

Jean Daillé (1594–1670), professor at Sedan, though a humanist, returned to the Biblical foundation, and so far from treating tradition, especially that of the Fathers of the Church, as a basis for faith and a common meeting-point for the fellowship of all the Churches, showed up, with comprehensive erudition and penetrating acumen, the defectiveness of this tradition. Like Acontius, he stood for the unique and exclusive authority of the canon of the Bible. Thereby he gave back to ecumenical thinking its connection with the insights of the Reformation and with the power from which the Reformation sprang.

John Amos Comenius (1592–1670),[2] known to the world chiefly for his educational reforms, but also one of the early prophets of Christian ecumenicity,

[1] See later, p. 98, also Chap. i, p. 66. On Amyraut, see Max Geiger, *Die Basler Kirche und Theologie im Zeitalter der Hochorthodoxie*, Zurich, 1952, pp. 101–18.
[2] The section on Comenius has been contributed by Professor Matthew Spinka, Waldo Professor of Church History, Hartford Seminary Foundation, Connecticut.

received his spiritual nurture in a Communion which exhibited an irenic spirit throughout its history. For the Unity of Brethren strove consistently after unity in the essentials of Christianity. This body never looked upon itself as a sect, for it had never consciously cut itself off from the Church universal but only from what it regarded as the corruption therein. Thus in 1534 it officially stated that in relation to the Roman Church "the Brethren gathered themselves into the Unity for the purpose of using in holy fellowship those good things of the old Church which they in no wise rejected, and those formerly mixed of evil and good which they purged, having rejected only all those doctrines which they knew to be evil".[1]

During his formative years, while studying at Herborn and Heidelberg, Comenius came under the influence of teachers who strengthened his ecumenical predisposition. This is particularly true of the period of study at Heidelberg, where he became acquainted with David Pareus, whose house, "Pareanum", served as the centre for those who worked for Protestant union.

Two years after his return to his native land, Comenius was ordained priest of the Unity, and became pastor at Fulnek in Moravia. But with the outbreak of the Thirty Years War, Fulnek fell a prey to the fury of the Imperial armies. Comenius was compelled to take refuge on the Bohemian estates of one of the most important members of the Unity, Count Charles of Žerotín, at Brandýs nad Orlici. There he wrote his celebrated *Labyrinth of the World*, a book in which the ecumenical theme found expression in condemnation of the fanaticism and bigotry of the confessional groups:

> "There I saw how two or three of these chapels adjacent to each other were considering joining themselves into one. But they could find no means of attaining harmony among themselves. . . . This miserable confusion and mutation of these fine Christian folk filled me with great indignation."[2]

In his *Haggaeus Redivivus* (1632), Comenius suggested a basis of union for the Protestants. He affirmed, in the first place, the essential doctrinal unity of the Evangelicals, by which term he designated besides his own Communion the Lutherans and the Reformed. He even advocated giving up these party names. The differences among them he termed non-essential, "mere misunderstanding". He advocated, in general, the adoption of a Scriptural basis for all doctrine and polity, to be interpreted in the light of the patristic Church and the early Councils:

> "As for ourselves, let us learn not to dogmatize beyond what is written, but rather to stand in the holy commandment given us. I say, let the Holy Bible alone be our canon, our faith, our standard, our rule."

Comenius' educational reforms brought him to the attention of Samuel Hartlib (1595–1662), a London gentleman of leisure[3] who was deeply interested in the plight of the Moravian scholar-bishop. Under Hartlib's auspices, an influential group of members of the Long Parliament invited him, in the spring of 1641, to England. It appears that the "pious theologians and bishops" who

---

[1] A. Gindely, *Dekrety Jednoty Bratrské*, Prague, 1865, p. 150.
[2] Matthew Spinka, tr., *The Labyrinth of the World*, Chicago, 1942, p. 74.
[3] See Matthew Spinka, *John Amos Comenius*, Chicago, 1943, pp. 63 ff., and particularly G. H. Turnbull, *Hartlib, Dury and Comenius*, London, 1947, for a fuller treatment of the subject. Turnbull's book is based on newly discovered papers of Hartlib, 1933.

were responsible for the invitation had in mind a "plan for the propagation of the gospel among the heathen" of New England, as Comenius himself reported later.[1]

The English episode, which at first promised fair success, proved in the end disappointing. Nevertheless, he at least described his grandiose scheme in great detail in his *Via Lucis*. This important work (first published in 1668) develops Comenius' ideas of a centre of world learning (to be located in England) where a group of learned men of all nations would engage in the stupendous task of gathering and systematizing universal knowledge and integrating it on the basis of principles derived from the Christian religion. Next they were to prepare textbooks in a universal language which would be used throughout the world. Thus all mankind would become one family, "for, if all men understand each other, they will become as it were one race, one people, one household, one School of God".

Comenius was active not only theoretically on behalf of Christian unity, but practically as well. This bishop of desperately poor and widely scattered exiles engaged in direct unionist efforts whenever he could. The most important of such instances was the so-called *Colloquium Caritativum* held in the Polish city of Toruń (Thorn) in 1645.[2] This represented an ambitious yet honest effort of King Wladislaw IV of Poland to bring about a union of the various religious communions, the Roman Catholics, Lutherans, and Reformed (with whom the Unity of Brethren was affiliated). But it was doomed to failure from the very beginning. Strife broke out at the start over the opening prayer, which was assigned to a Roman Catholic bishop. The Reformed and the Brethren accepted this arrangement, but the Lutherans rejected it. In the end the Lutherans held their opening service separately. Further controversy broke out even over the reading of the three confessions of faith. After fruitless harangues which lasted three months, the Colloquy was finally terminated on 21 November. Comenius, "disgusted with the haggling", had left more than a month before. Although he had anticipated such a failure, he still felt deeply disappointed. Nevertheless, with his characteristic deep-seated faith in the ultimate victory of the spirit of Christ over all sectarian divisions, Comenius wrote a treatise on Christian unity[3] which he dedicated to King Wladislaw.

English friends never ceased to hope that the "pansophic project" to be centred in England would ultimately be realized. Comenius, for his part, likewise never lost interest in English affairs. When the second Civil War broke out in 1648, he wrote an irenic appeal, *Independentia, aeternarum confusionum origo*. Another such appeal to the English Churches Comenius dedicated in 1660 to Charles II on the occasion of the King's return to England. The Latin treatise was entitled *De Bono Unitatis*, but in its English translation it bore the title *An Exhortation of the Churches of Bohemia to the Church of England*. After recommending a form of polity to the English Church, he appealed to all Christendom for unity:

"O, you Christian people, dispersed throughout Europe, Asia, Africa, America, and the Islands of the Sea, into so many Religions, Sects, Opinions,

---

[1] Spinka, *Comenius*, p. 74. See also R. F. Young, *Comenius in England*, London, 1932; but this author follows the researches of O. Odložilík "Komenský a anglický parlament" in *Českou minulosti*, Prague, 1939.

[2] See also pp. 96 f.

[3] *Christianismus reconciliabilis reconciliatore Christo*. It is hitherto unpublished. The present writer (Dr Spinka) has a copy of it.

and multiplyed into different Ceremonies, what else I pray are you now become, but as those bones of Israel in Ezekiel, scattered abroad in the field of the world! O, that it would please God to bring on that day, wherein he will put forth his omnipotent power among you; to command that there be a noise and a shaking, that so the bones may draw near one to another, and come together . . . and then the breath come from the four winds, to inspire all that are spiritually dead, that they may live . . . the life of Christ."

The great life-work, *De rerum humanarum emendatione Consultatio Catholica*, in which the matured plans of Comenius were to be fully worked out in seven volumes, was (with the exception of two volumes) believed to have been altogether lost. But in 1935 all seven volumes (in MS.) were found. In one of these, *Panorthosia* (Universal Reform), Comenius presents his mature concept of ecumenical Christendom. Since he had been a lifelong adherent of the millennial doctrine, he believed that "the new age" was about to dawn. Therein he expected that the world would be organized in a single federation, in which three governing bodies would share the supreme rule: the College of Light, a sort of academy of learned men, would form a universal educational Council; the World Peace Court would represent the political organization; and the Ecumenical Ecclesiastical Council would have supervision over the religious life of mankind. But each individual country or nation would possess its own regional organization as well.[1]

The last of Comenius' exhortations towards unity was penned by him when he was seventy-five years old. In his *Unum Necessarium* he reviewed and elaborated the principal labours of his long and sad life. Of his endeavours in behalf of Christian ecumenicity he wrote:

"The second long and difficult labyrinth were my irenic labours, i.e. my wish to reconcile Christians (if it should please God), who in various ways to their own hurt and near ruin wrangle concerning the faith. I expended much labour in this matter. So far, almost nothing has been accomplished, but perhaps my labours shall succeed yet. . . . There are but a few who hope for results. In vain, perhaps? God knows! I neither say that there is hope, nor that there is none—although the grave is opening before me."[2]

It was with these words that Comenius closed his exhortation. But if his efforts were less than successful, he nevertheless dreamed great dreams and saw glorious visions of Christian unity in the future.

The transition from Pietism to the Enlightenment at the end of the 17th and the beginning of the 18th centuries marked the beginning of a new, and in many ways most fruitful, period of efforts to promote the union of Christendom. The Thirty Years War had produced a comprehensive change in men's attitude towards life. They were weary of confessional disputations. Mystical "spiritualism" and practical Christian activity had become a power. Pietism had brought together earnest Christians in all Churches, or at least made them aware of one another. The Counter-Reformation had exhausted its strength; it no longer wielded power in the fields of politics and ecclesiastical diplomacy, but exer-

[1] J. Hendřich, tr., *J. A. Komenkého Všenáprava*, Prague, 1950, Chaps. xviii and xxvi.
[2] J. Ludvíkovský, tr., *Jednoho jest potřebí*, Prague, 1920, pp. 180–82.

cised its influence through that mystical piety which, from Spain and France, spread through the whole world. The expulsion of Protestant Christians from Salzburg carried out by Archbishop Firmian in 1731 was a belated straggler of the Counter-Reformation, and was held by all contemporaries to be an anachronism. It called out a spontaneous effort of ecumenical help and service parallel to that produced in 1685 by the revocation of the Edict of Nantes.

From another quarter, namely from England and France, a new enemy of Christian faith was threatening. This was atheism, nurtured by the intellectual despair which was a consequence of the wars of the 17th century. This menace, like the menace of the Counter-Reformation in earlier years, was favourable to a closer alliance among Christians, and made Protestants more clearly aware of what they held in common with Roman Catholics. Humanism, which since the time of the Reformation had released the greatest energies for ecumenical thought and action, for a time fell into the background; but in the Enlightenment in Germany, with its Christian characteristics, it underwent a revival in the giant figure of the politician and thinker Leibniz.

The new doctrine of the State contributed a fresh element to the 18th-century picture. The philosophers and historians of the Renaissance (Nicolo Machiavelli more clearly and decisively than any other) had worked out the idea of the *raison d'état* in terms of the self-realization of the State and its purposes. This concept was now thought out afresh, and much more deeply, by the German thinker Samuel Pufendorf (1632–94) and by Leibniz, and expressed in terms of "service to life". The concept of the State as the bearer and guardian of culture (*Kulturstaat*) was coming into being. The optimism characteristic of the Enlightenment regarded its ideals as attainable, and spared no efforts to realize them; this also was bound to be of service to all practical attempts to realize the unity of the Churches.

A typical writer of this period of transition is Pierre Jurieu (1637–1713). Jurieu had studied philosophy at Saumur and philology at Sedan; then, after travels in the Netherlands and England, he became professor of Hebrew at Sedan, and finally was pastor and professor at Rotterdam. In the course of his life, Jurieu several times modified his views. Originally he had defended the definitions of the Synod of Dort, though not in their extreme form; but gradually his central interest became the refutation of Roman Catholic claims to infallibility. In his *Treatise on the Unity of the Church and the Fundamental Articles* (1688), he defended the view that the true universal Church lies beyond all the particular historic Churches, and is not to be identified with any of them. In controversy with the Jansenist Pierre Nicole, he corrects the latter's interpretation of Noah's ark: the ark is not the Roman Catholic Church, but the universal Church of Christ, and the chambers constructed by Noah with their dividing walls symbolize the particular Churches. This is not mere exegetical fancy; Jurieu the Hebraist takes very seriously the promise made to Abraham and the prophecies of the second Isaiah regarding the universal extension of the Church; the fact that the Roman Church is only a Western Church of itself refutes its claim to be the sole and universal Church.

The unity of the Church is to be found in its Fundamental Articles. But this conclusion is reached by Jurieu on rational rather than on Biblical grounds. Only three religious systems have to be taken seriously—natural religion, and the Mosaic and Christian systems. The fundamental truths are, in the first place, those in which all these systems are agreed, particularly monotheism; and secondly, those which are peculiar to Christianity, such as belief in Jesus as Messiah and in reconciliation with God through the satisfaction of his death. Among communions which destroy this unity through fundamental errors, Jurieu assigns first place to the Socinians, and then, at some distance, second to the Roman Catholics, especially on the good Reformation ground of their deification of created beings. Jurieu could not go so far as to accept the unrestricted toleration of all forms of religion demanded by such representatives of the Enlightenment as d'Huisseau in his *Reunion of Christendom*, and Pierre Bayle (1647–1706) in his *Philosophical Commentary*.

Jurieu's writings did not have wide influence. This was partly because the methods of attaining union set forth by him in his *Consultation concerning the Establishment of Peace among Protestants* (1688) seemed to a man like Samuel Pufendorf over-hasty. That prudent lawyer preferred to believe that all things could be accomplished by time. Still more was it due to the fact that the Enlightenment was already spreading outwards from France like a flood. The point of view of Jurieu was that of an age which was already passing away.

The Enlightenment in its origins was by no means a theoretical and critical movement. It set before itself practical and positive aims. Its purpose was a comprehensive reform of human life. One thing, however, was lacking to that age, and as a consequence of this lack all attempts at Christian union under its aegis were condemned in advance to failure: this was a clear understanding of the centre of Christian faith, an apprehension of the essential content and directive purpose of the Gospel. Consequently, the ecumenical activity which took place under the new auspices was marked by immense practical activity, but solid theological substance was lacking.

5. ATTEMPTS AT UNIFICATION ON THE BASIS OF HUMANISM

Theorists are not always equally effective in practical affairs, but the greatest among them are successful in combining both gifts. The energy of such men manifests itself in attempts to bring into immediate effect the conclusions to which their thought has led them.

This is specially true of Hugo Grotius (1583–1645).[1] In early years Grotius had come under the influence of Pierre du Moulin, a pillar of rigid orthodoxy; but he had also lived as a student in the family of Francis Junius, and from him had received the inspiration for his life of ecumenical thought and action. In part his attitude was determined by his reaction against the controversial passions of the Dutch theologians, who from 1604 onwards were bitterly divided on the interpretation of the doctrine of predestination. Grotius always ranged himself on the side of the Arminians.

How early his ecumenical ideas had begun to take shape is shown by a letter of 1 November 1601, when Grotius was eighteen, addressed to Justus Lipsius, in which he sets forth as the principle of his activity as a writer that he will be on his guard not to write anything "which is not catholic and ecumenical in the sense in which those words were used by the Fathers of antiquity".[2]

[1] For Grotius, see especially an article by Fritz Blanke, "Hugo Grotius und die Einigung der christlichen Kirchen", *Reformatio*, 1953.
[2] *Briefwisseling van Hugo Grotius I*, 's Gravenhage, 1928, p. 20.

It is in line with this early conviction that he always refuses to admit the claim of any one Church—whether it be the Calvinistic Church of his own Holland, or the Lutheran Churches of Germany, or the Roman Catholic, or any of the Eastern Churches—to be the whole Church, or even to have within it the capacity to develop into a full expression of the universality of the Church. To him the Roman Church is no more than one among many; its exclusive claim to the title Catholic is unwarranted; the primacy of the Pope is no part of the Faith. When Grotius contrasts the partial or particular Churches with the Church as a whole, the universal body of Christians, it is easy to see in which direction his affections lie. The recovery of unity, both in doctrinal convictions and in outward order, appears to him as the task specially laid on his generation; to the realization of this ideal he is prepared to devote his life.

For Grotius the centre of theological thought, and therefore the centre of his thought on the unity of the Church, is the apostolic tradition as maintained in the ancient Church. The "Golden Centuries" are the three centuries leading up to the age of Gregory the Great. The principle of continuity in development is so determinative of his concept of the Church that little scope is left for the alternative principle of degeneracy or decay: so much so that when he considers the partnership of Church and State, Grotius is able to ascribe pre-eminence to the latter, and, so far from considering the establishment of a State Church as the great apostasy, he can praise Constantine and Theodosius as great Christian emperors.

Grotius was inclined to regard the particular Churches as standing all roughly on an equality. But this does not mean that he regarded the relation between them as like that of parts to a whole, since the unification of the Churches involves more than a sum in addition. The facts compel him to take seriously the question propounded by Acontius concerning the truths necessary to salvation. Among these Grotius includes the unique authority of the Holy Scriptures and redemption through Jesus Christ. He regards the doctrine of predestination as a peculiar Calvinistic addition which cannot be imposed upon the Church as a whole. Grotius wished to see the common evangelical convictions of all the Churches, other than the Roman Catholic Church, expressed through an ecumenical synod. He is thinking first of an assembly of representatives of the Lutheran, Reformed, and Anglican Churches, but regards it as possible to draw in also the Eastern Orthodox Churches and the Lesser Churches of the East. This synod should draw up a confession of unity which, however, should not be allowed to suppress the traditional confessional statements of individual Churches. Grotius was a lawyer and is here imagining not so much a union of the Churches as a federation in which all the participating Churches would retain their individuality. He develops his thought to the point of practical steps to be taken. His desire was that James I of England should take the responsibility of convening such a synod. James I himself had for a number of years been occupied with similar plans.[1] But neither his efforts nor those of Grotius were destined to meet with any concrete success. The Synod of Dort, the Thirty Years War, the condemnation of Grotius and the years of exile which he spent in France, a predominantly Roman Catholic country, made progress for the time being impossible.

On the Roman Catholic side, information had been received of Grotius' darling project. He had scarcely arrived in France when William du Vais, Keeper of

---

[1] See Jaques Courvoisier in *Ecumenical Review*, Vol. I, 1948, pp. 76–9.

the Seals and Bishop of Lisieux, greeted him with the expression of the hope that it might be possible for him to continue his work for the peace of the Church, but now, of course, in a Roman Catholic direction. Naturally enough, this was immediately followed by determined efforts to win Grotius for the Roman Catholic Church, all of which he resisted most firmly.

Grotius was much interested in the plans for union put forward by that controversial figure, the Huguenot lawyer Théophile Brachet, Lord of La Milletière from Rochelle. La Milletière was attacked from all sides simultaneously. The Sorbonne condemned his writings because of his defence of Richelieu. The leading Reformed pastors of Paris, with Pierre du Moulin at their head, were hostile to him. He was undoubtedly a secret agent of Richelieu, working to promote the plans of Louis XIII and Louis XIV for the reunion of Roman Catholics and Protestants at least in France. He ended by joining the Roman Catholic Church, and this brought upon him the suspicion of Grotius who, up to that point, had felt great sympathy with him because of his inner independence and his condemnation of all secular ambition on the part of the Church. Yet Grotius could write that the spirit of the antichrist had appeared not only on the Tiber but also by the Lake of Geneva, and he, this watchful observer of all events in all the Churches, could pour out his mockery on the Jansenists of Port-Royal.

At no time in his life did Grotius give up his plans for union. When the time was not ripe, he let them sink into the background and remain dormant. But at every opportunity he was prepared to take them up again. When he was in England in 1612, he had tried to win the support of James I and had reached a measure of understanding with a number of English ecclesiastics. When, in 1635, he became Swedish ambassador in Paris, he gave his support to the activities of John Dury.

Initially, Grotius may have been governed by no more than an emotional yearning for the peace of the Church. As time went on, the dominant note of his efforts was the increasing importance attached to tradition. He desired that men should no longer speak of Luther and Calvin, but rather of Erasmus and Melanchthon, or, better still, of the witness of the ancient Church. Instead of Calvin's *Institutes*, let men direct their attention to the *Commonitorium* of Vincent of Lerins; instead of the Acts of the Synod of Dort, let them study the declarations of the Ecumenical Councils. In 1640 Grotius emphatically rejected that identification of the Roman papacy with the antichrist, which had been common form among the Reformers. The passages in the Apocalypse which refer to antichrist are to be historically interpreted and applied to the Roman Emperor Caligula. The way for an increasingly complete acceptance of Roman Catholic tradition is unmistakably being prepared. Grotius came to defend the Roman Catholic doctrine of apostolic succession and of the sacraments; he made out a case for fasting, celibacy of the clergy, and transubstantiation. He even went so far as to put in a plea for the Roman Catholic doctrine of justification and the hierarchical organization of the Church. In his opinion, the Reformation was unnecessary. An inner reform of the Roman Catholic Church, proceeding from within itself, would better have achieved the same results. All this helps to explain the astonishing fact that Hugo Grotius, like George Cassander before him, believed that reconciliation between the Augsburg Confession and the Canons of the Council of Trent was possible. In this he was a follower of his fellow-countryman Erasmus, who, in the work of his old age, *On Restoring*

Concord in the Church, went so far as to use the expression "accommodation" (συγκατάβασις), which really involves total surrender on the part of Protestantism.

It is a tragic picture. The closer Grotius comes in spiritual experience and theological thought to the Roman Catholic Church, the claims of which he had in earlier years so energetically refuted, the lonelier he becomes, both outwardly and inwardly. He no longer really belongs to any Church. It is symbolic that he died in distant Rostock as an unknown foreigner rescued from shipwreck, and that in his last hours he received the ministrations of a pastor of that Church, the Lutheran, with which during his life he had had the least sympathetic contact.

Grotius left no immediate disciple or successor, but George Calixtus belonged to that same spiritual region in which, in addition to the traditions of Erasmus, the influence of Melanchthon lived on. Already Grotius had set the two, the Christian humanist and the humanistic Reformer, side by side as exemplary figures. The legacy of Melanchthon to his disciples was, on the one side, that high esteem for the traditions of the ancient Church which he had firmly established in the school of Wittenberg, and on the other, strong emphasis on the practical consequences for daily life which flow from the person and work of Jesus. His view of tradition, which was not Biblical but humanistic in origin, was a link beyond the range of dogmatic differences between Protestant and Roman Catholic theology. The peculiarity of Calixtus, in contrast to the general stream of humanistic tradition, is to be found not in any new thoughts, but in the special emphasis laid on two elements which are constantly present in Christian humanism—belief in the value of Christian synods, and emphasis on Christian moral standards.

Both of these principles achieved practical results in Poland. The first was the Consensus of Sendomir in 1570.[1] A whole succession of other synods and agreements followed, such as the Confederation of Warsaw in 1573, which laid the legal foundation for religious peace in Poland, the General Synod of Cracow in the same year, the Synods of Piotrków and Wilna, the General Synod of Thorn in 1595, and the General Confederation of Wilna in 1599. Finally, a new and energetic step in advance was taken in the *Brotherly Exhortation* of Bartholomew Bythner in 1607. Bythner, a Silesian by birth, took up his pen because his teacher, the Heidelberg theologian Pareus, had asked him, a Reformed pastor from Little Poland, to do something for the unity of the Church. The *Brotherly Exhortation* takes up again the cause of doctrinal reconciliation. Bythner hopes that this may be brought about along the lines of the doctrine of Acontius, in that he expressly holds fast to the Bible and makes a clear distinction between doctrines which are and those which are not necessary to salvation. In his detailed attempts to apply this principle to individual articles of the Faith, we find, as everywhere in irenic writings from the Calvinistic side, that the Calvinistic understanding of Christian dogma is regarded as superior to all others.

The close approach of the three Evangelical confessions of Poland—Lutheran, Reformed, and Bohemian Brethren—which had been brought about at Thorn in 1595, was relaxed in the course of the next fifty years. When in 1645 a new attempt was made in the same city, the initiative came from the Roman Catholic clergy, who had, in advance, reached an understanding with King Wladislaw of Poland down to the last detail. To this Colloquy came, among others, George

---

[1] See Chap. i, pp. 62 ff.

Calixtus. It is easy to understand that he had the highest expectations from the results of this meeting; but these high expectations were not fulfilled. Since the unity for which all were striving had been rendered impossible except through the unqualified victory of the Roman Catholics, the discussions ended in failure.[1]

But Calixtus carried away with him a sense of responsibility to try once more to bring the evangelical forces together, before turning again in the direction of union with the Roman Catholics. He set himself to this task by means of a book on behalf of union. Just at this period the influence of Calixtus was of considerable extent. In Helmstedt he had as a colleague from 1632 onwards the young lawyer Hermann Conring (1606–81), the founder of the history of law in Germany. This leading scholar, a prodigy who combined great gifts as a lawyer with others as an original worker in medical science and as an historian, became so absorbed in the plans for the union of the Church that in 1659 he republished Georg Witzel's book, *The Way to Godly Concord*, which had first appeared in 1537. The Lutheran University of Rinteln filled its theological chairs with disciples of Calixtus: first Johannes Henich(en), the godson of Johann Arndt, in whom, alongside the humanistic tradition, the influence of the mystical and "spiritualist" movements was manifest; later, Heinrich Martin Eccard and Peter Musäus; and finally Gerhard Walter Molanus. In 1661 these men conducted a series of discussions on religious problems with the theologians of Marburg at Cassel. But the spirit of the age had moved forward from the old adherence to tradition. Here, for the first time, it was emphatically affirmed that differences in matters of doctrine need not lead to separation between the Churches. The distinctions between fundamental articles and those which are not fundamental was given up, and doctrine as a whole was treated as a matter of minor importance. Scholars had reached the conclusion that union of the Churches on the basis of doctrinal agreement was impossible, and were now content to aim at mutual toleration. The idea of toleration, now as at the end of the creative period of the Reformation in the Diet of Ratisbon (1541), is substituted for the hope of union, and this meets with contemporary approval, especially in Reformed circles interested in ecumenism.

John Dury (1595–1680)[2] presents a remarkable example of a life which was wholly devoted to the service of ecumenical reconciliation and unity. Even external factors directed him towards this career. He was born in Edinburgh, the son of a Presbyterian minister who was later to be active abroad. He studied in Sedan, Leiden, and Oxford, and in 1625 became minister of the English congregation in Elbing. In 1626 this town passed from Polish to Swedish hands. Thereupon the Polish Diet dissolved the English company of merchants in order to direct trade through the port of Danzig. Many members of the English colony left the town of Elbing, and those who remained joined either German Lutheran or Reformed congregations. In this way a kind of practical union came into being. This led the Swedish professor of law Kaspar Godemann to write a brief discourse on unity in the doctrine of the Holy Communion. When he submitted his essay to John Dury for his judgement upon it, he had no idea that he was giving his friend the impulse which led to fifty years of activity in the service of the union of the Church.

Dury now occupied himself with Cassander's *Consultatio*, the book which had earlier made so deep an impression on Grotius. The English envoy in Elbing,

[1] See also p. 90.   [2] On other aspects of Dury's career, see Chap. iii, pp. 134 ff.

Sir Thomas Roe, lent support to his plans, put him in touch with the Swedish Chancellor Oxenstierna, and in 1636 arranged for him to visit England, where the Leipzig discussions of 1631 had attracted close attention.

During the first years of Dury's activity the general situation was extraordinarily propitious. Gustavus Adolphus, King of Sweden, and his Chancellor Oxenstierna were in favour of Christian unity. In France the Synod of Charenton had decided, in 1631, in favour of intercommunion between Lutherans and Reformed. In Poland the Count of Leszno, Rafael Leszczynski, a member of the Church of the Bohemian Brethren, had drawn up a model code of minority rights for the German Lutherans who, under the pressure of war, had migrated from Silesia. Then followed the Leipzig discussions. Under the influence of the menacing political situation which, in the first half of the Thirty Years War, had almost given victory to the Roman Catholic party, Lutherans and Calvinists in 1631 drew together in a kind of defensive alliance. The discussion on religious problems was a kind of theological pendant to this political alliance. Closer understanding was reached than ever before, though the doctrine of predestination remained as an insuperable obstacle to union. But Dury did not know how to make use of his opportunities. Gustavus Adolphus had advised him to win the approval of leading churchmen in Sweden for his plans. He limited himself, however, to obtaining the support of a military chaplain in Germany, Johannes Matthiae, later Bishop of Strängnäs, who became his lifelong friend.

The situation of nations and Churches changed suddenly with the death of Gustavus Adolphus in 1632 and, shortly after, with the Peace of Prague in 1635, which resulted in the withdrawal of Electoral Saxony from the war and from its alliance with Sweden. Dury remained for a considerable time in Sweden without obtaining any marked success. Matthiae stood alone. With the change of government in England, Dury fell under the suspicion of the new rulers; but when he came out decidedly on the side of Cromwell, he lost all his earlier friends and was by them regarded as untrustworthy. Samuel Hartlib alone remained faithful to him.

Cromwell desired to unite the Protestant world under the leadership of England. As he was negotiating with the Swiss cantons, he sent Dury with his envoy John Pell, but this promising beginning led to no result. Dury's close relationship with Cromwell did him serious harm in Germany, especially in Brandenburg-Prussia and Hesse-Cassel. When the Protector died and the Commonwealth government was overthrown, the newly-restored monarchy naturally offered no hopes to Dury, since it regarded him as a partisan of the usurper. In 1661 Dury returned to Germany, seeking everywhere for possible points of contact with the Churches. He found himself specially at home with the forerunners of Pietism, Caspar Hermann Sandhagen, the friend of August Hermann Francke's father, and Christian Scriver in Magdeburg. In 1677 William Penn came to visit him in Cassel, and each learned to value the other's friendship. The young Quaker who had once sat at the feet of Amyraut in Saumur now took over the heritage of the aged Dury. John Amos Comenius stood by him, and his foster-son Peter Figulus, the father of Daniel Ernst Jablonski, was for seven years (1636–43) Dury's personal companion and colleague; so that here also his inheritance was handed on to a later generation.

All this was a work of sowing for a distant future. For the moment confessional obstinacy once more won the day, not least in Brandenburg. There, in 1652, the Great Elector Frederick William endeavoured through a conference on the methods of preaching, teaching, and discussion, to make possible the peaceful co-existence of the rival Churches. But the plans of the Great Elector collapsed before the resistance of the nobles of his territory. This body demanded a complete restoration of the Lutheran character of the two centres of education —the University of Frankfort-on-Oder and the Joachimsthal High School in Berlin. The bitterness of this controversy dominated the Berlin discussions of religious issues in 1662–63. Once again the evil spirit of ecclesiastical ambition won the day. The great hymn-writer of the Evangelical Churches, Paul Gerhardt, who through his hymns had exercised more influence on the world-wide Church than all the ecclesiastical statesmen, was driven into exile because of his "tender conscience".

The basic principle which Dury followed, though with some inconsistency, in all his efforts for peace, was that favourite concept of the humanist and Anglican tradition, the simplicity of the early Christians and of the ancient Church, which found its classic expression, apart from the Bible, in the Apostles' Creed and in those theological principles which are common to the Fathers of the Church. From it Dury took over the catchword of "the harmony of the confessions" [1] which had been devised in 1581 by Salvart, a theologian of Geneva. But Dury went beyond it in the direction of "spiritualism" and Pietism. He accepted Johann Arndt's *True Christianity* and Lewis Bayly's *Practice of Piety* as contemporary expressions of those articles of Christian faith which are necessary to salvation, next to the Apostles' Creed, the Lord's Prayer, and the Decalogue, and desired to make use of them in promoting the unity of the Church. Like the Pietists, he kept steadily in view an existing empirical reality. This reality is the fellowship of the saints who live in indissoluble unity with one another as members of the mystical Body of Christ, strive together to attain godliness and true holiness, and help one another in this attempt. This New Testament concept of the Church underlies all the labours of Dury the Scot, and explains how it came about that, in spite of continuous disappointments, throughout his long life he never abandoned them. It is this that gives to his letters, his journals, his conversations, and his writings, the last of which was a study of the Book of Revelation, a weight that more than compensates for all adverse chances and lack of diplomatic skill, and confers on them an incontestable greatness.

6. THE ECUMENICAL ACTIVITY OF GERMAN PIETISM AND ITS OFFSHOOTS

Pietism made visible the ecumenical reality of the Church in a manner entirely different from that of all its predecessors, and so introduced a new epoch in the history of the ecumenical movement. Its appeal was made, not to doctrine, nor to the more or less skilful diplomacy of ecclesiastical politicians. Here there were no public discussions of theological problems, no synods; detailed plans for union of the Churches are regarded as of secondary importance. All the leading ideas and views of earlier ecumenical activity are, for the Pietist, unusable and worthless. He rejects the idea that doctrine is the heart of Christian faith; he rejects the idea of the state Church; he rejects the institutional incorporation of the Church in liturgy, sacrament, and Church polity—or at least without any great difficulty finds it possible to do without them all.

The decisive thing for him is that consciousness of spiritual fellowship

---

[1] See Chap. i, pp. 53 f.

which Pietism has taken over from the mystical traditions of "spiritualism", but which, with incomparable energy, power of conviction, and vigour, it sets in the centre of the stage. Pietism regards itself as a manifestation of ecumenical reality, or rather as the actual incorporation of the ecumenical idea. For this reason its ecumenical activity always gives the impression of spontaneous recognition of an already existing reality, even when its plans of action are carefully and deliberately matured.

The academic journeys of the theologians of the 17th century are transformed into the itinerant apostleship of the Separatist and Pietist preachers concerned about the situation of Christians scattered in the world.

A forerunner of Pietism is the Separatism of Jean de Labadie (1610–74) who, in his own life's journey from the Jesuit Order in France, by way of the Huguenot Churches in France and Geneva, to the "Precisianist" theology in the Netherlands, from there to German Lutheranism in Herford in Westphalia, and finally to Mennonite Altona, set forth symbolically his conviction that the true Church can be found in any existing Church, but cannot be identified with any of them. His "congregation of the twice-born", which knows itself to have been separated from the world and from Babylon, regards itself as the one true Evangelical Church, which belongs to the millennial reign of Jesus Christ.

In 1675 Philipp Jakob Spener (1635–1705) translated his book *Pia Desideria* into Latin, with the express intention of making it available to foreigners. He took careful note of the movements towards a new life of faith in England, Scotland, and Flanders, and entered into relationship with the Philadelphian Society of Jane Leade. His inheritance was taken over by August Hermann Francke (1663–1727), and was developed with Francke's own peculiar vigour. From the year 1700 Francke was in regular contact with the English Society for Promoting Christian Knowledge, and deliberately built up his Orphanage at Halle as an ecumenical foundation. He took boys from all parts of Germany and from foreign countries. These young men, after the conclusion of their studies and a period as tutors in the Orphanage, were to go back to their homes as ambassadors of Halle. With the help of the English S.P.C.K., he set the Danish-Halle mission to work in South India. His son and a friend from his youth, Samuel Urlsperger of Augsburg, took the initiative in providing pastoral care for the German immigrants in North America: this began in 1734 with the settlement of refugees from Salzburg and led, in 1742, to the foundation of the Lutheran Church in Pennsylvania. Francke arranged for his writings, and particularly the reports of his Orphanage and of the India mission, to be translated into English by his pupil, Anton Wilhelm Böhme (1673–1722). These were followed shortly after by other edifying writings—Arndt's *True Christianity*, Köpke's *Temple of Solomon*, and others composed in the same "spiritualist" and pietistic vein.

But Francke looked far beyond the Western world. In Heinrich Milde he found a young translator who took the principal share in rendering the Bible into Russian, Czech, and Polish, and also in the translation of Arndt's *True Christianity* into Russian. With the help of Count von Wreech, Francke started work at Tobolsk in Siberia among the German prisoners captured in the Northern War,[1] and thereafter in German Lutheran congregations in Russia. In every possible way, but particularly through travellers, ambassadors, officers, mer-

---

[1] The war between Sweden and Russia (1701–12), in which a number of other countries became involved.

chants, and scholars, he propagated the Pietism of Halle, which in this way spread to south-east Europe and Scandinavia, to Russia and Central Asia, to England and North America. All this was carefully planned and deliberately undertaken. Yet it all seemed to happen with the inevitability of a dynamic movement, living by its claim to be the bearer of true Christianity in the contemporary world. The work was carried on by means of a widely extended network of correspondence, carefully developed and skilfully organized, which in its purpose and its range recalls the great period of ecumenical activity in the hands of such men as Luther, Bucer, and Calvin.

The great inspirer of contact with the Eastern world was the traveller Wilhelm Heinrich Ludolf, a nephew of the famous orientalist Job Ludolf who had made the Ethiopic language and literature known in Europe. Unlike his uncle, Ludolf made his journeys not in a scientific but in an ecclesiastical interest. Deeply influenced by the mystical tradition of "spiritualism", he desired to make himself acquainted with the inner condition of all Christian Churches and groups in the world in order to form an opinion as to their readiness for reunion. This reunion was to be brought about through seeking again and bringing into consciousness the deep fellowship of apostolic simplicity. The means to this end was that awakened souls should come to know one another personally as members enjoying fellowship in the one Body of Christ. This was the purpose that Zinzendorf was later to formulate in express terms—to make the unity of the Church visible in its members.

The deepest purpose of A. H. Francke comes to expression more clearly than anywhere else in his plan for a Universal Seminary, for which the Orphanage was to be no more than a starting-point. In accordance with Lutheran tradition, he is convinced that renewal in the Church can come about only through the rebirth of the ordained ministry. Accordingly, Francke desires to bring up a new generation of young preachers who will spread abroad through the world the true and living knowledge of God. Here his ideas coincide with those of Ludolf, since the latter also wished to see the creation of an Ecumenical Seminary in Halle, which should unite German Pietists and the awakened in the Orthodox Churches of the East in preparation for missionary work.

It was only natural that Count Nicolaus Ludwig von Zinzendorf (1700–60), while living as a pupil in the Orphanage of A. H. Francke at Halle, received his initial ecumenical inspiration and the idea of his ecumenical foundation, the "Order of the Mustard Seed", which was to promote the extension of the Kingdom of God. While, however, Spener and Francke found the starting-point for their ecumenical activity subjectively in the rebirth of the individual Christian, Zinzendorf found it objectively in the Cross of Christ. He regarded the Augsburg Confession as the ecumenical confession *par excellence*, but he can on occasion say that it is the duty of the true Christian to learn something from every Church. It is right to learn from the Roman Catholics poverty of spirit, "the equality of the name of God and the name of Jesus", and a deep regard for the Church in Paradise; to learn from the Calvinists the doctrine of that election through which the heritage of the Lamb is called out; from the Lutherans, the universal mercy of God and the true consolation which comes from the Sacrament; from the Quakers, freedom for every individual conscience; and from the Mennonites, strict standards of Christian moral life. But his main concern is with practical and personal matters, with taking seriously the concrete historical situation in which

Christians find themselves. He regards the different formulations of Christian dogma as *Tropen*, means of education or edification, through which God has preserved the life of the Spirit. As such they are to be regarded as evidences of the divine patience, and must continue in existence until the time of the return of the children of God to unity. In consequence, he insists that they must be taken seriously and rejects the "latitudinarian confusion".

It is evident from what has already been said that Zinzendorf's ecumenical concern and sense of responsibility find their expression more readily in action than in thought. Like Francke, he cherished the idea of a seminary and constantly sought to realize it, beginning with a small student fellowship in Jena, and going on to the great plan for an ecumenical and basically Christian Academy of Sciences at Marienborn in Hesse. At the Danish court in 1731, ". . . I broke out and informed the King that I would produce for him a university which could fill the whole world with the Gospel". All these high-flying plans collapsed; all that remained was the theological seminary of the Moravian Brethren, which was first established in Wetterau, and then was moved to Barby on the Elbe as a disciplinary measure against the "enthusiasm" which had broken out in it. The theological education which was imparted in this seminary attached greater importance to practical piety and the childlike spirit than to technical scholarship.

In his extensive activities Zinzendorf did not limit himself to the Moravian foundation of Herrnhut and similar institutions in Germany, Holland, England, North America, Sweden, and the Baltic countries. He reached out beyond such activities to relationships with foreign Churches. From 1719 to 1738 he was in contact, personally and through letters, with Louis Antoine, Cardinal de Noailles (1651–1729), the friend of the Jansenists in Paris, and sought to prepare the soil for the true Evangelical faith by supplying him with Arndt's *True Christianity* and Johann Scheffler's hymns. This beginning led to no result. No more successful was his other undertaking to bring together the various Churches and groups in Quaker Pennsylvania through his own personal authority, in a Lutheranism understood in a Moravian sense. Here he was defeated after fierce battles by the much simpler but more realistic Heinrich Melchior Mühlenberg (1711–87).[1] A last grandiose, but not widely influential, attempt at ecumenical action was the publication in 1753 of the *London Hymn Book*, followed by the *Liturgical Booklet* in 1755 and the *Book of Litanies* in 1757. In the *London Hymn Book* Zinzendorf printed hymns from Roman Catholic sources and from the Eastern Liturgies. In the Great Intercession of the *Book of Litanies*, for the first time in an evangelical setting, all the Churches of the world were mentioned by name, and the union of the scattered children of God specified as the object of intercession. In all these documents, and especially in the *London Hymn Book*, Zinzendorf wished to demonstrate to those Christians who remained firmly set in their confessional limitations the holy harmony of all times and regions in the adoration of the Lamb.

Ecumenical activity was for Zinzendorf a necessary consequence of his faith: to be a Christian on any other terms was for him impossible. Like Francke, he carried on extensive correspondence; but, unlike Francke, he engaged also in frequent and extensive journeys, and in any place in the world where the conditions seemed to him favourable and the way prepared, he founded colonies of Herrnhut. The ecumenical activities which grew up upon the foundations which

[1] See also Chap. v, pp. 229 f.

he had laid were important and fruitful. The greatest example of all is in the beginning of the Methodist Church, since it was through their contact with the Brethren, through admiration of the childlike simplicity of their manner of life, and above all through contact with Spangenberg and Peter Böhler, that John and Charles Wesley found the decisive inspiration for their own lives. John Wesley especially, in the summer of 1738, found in Herrnhut that which he had been seeking—an early Christian congregation in contemporary existence.

Pietism in its "separatist" form was not equal to that of Halle in the importance and extent of its ecumenical work. Yet here too there was an active desire for positive ecumenical service. The founder of the "spiritualist" and Separatist centre of Berleburg on the frontier between Hesse and Westphalia was Ernst Christoph Hochmann von Hochenau (1670–1721). He desired a new Church of the Spirit which, as the virgin community, should prepare itself for the coming of the Bridegroom. He endeavoured to bring such communities into existence in various places in the German-speaking countries, and to constitute a small *élite* in Schwarzenau near Berleburg. Johann Konrad Dippel (1673–1734)—who passed through the Pietism of Halle to the Separatists, resisted all attempts to persuade him to join the Moravian Brotherhood, and chose rather to live an isolated life at Berleburg—renewed the spirit of Jacob Boehme, of Hoburg, and Betke in laying stress on a return to the Biblical demand for "a new creature" as the infallible method for bringing about reunion of the Churches. The same view was expressed by the Pietist churchman Johann Joseph Winckler in Magdeburg in 1703, when he affirmed that the doctrine of true godliness must be asserted as the one basis for union. The ruler himself must promote this by every method and means. He must appoint to vacant places only preachers who love God from the heart. He must rejoice if there are even a hundred pious hearts in his territory, since these can be the holy seed through which the union of the Churches can come to its desired fulfilment.

The last word of all these Separatists to the Babylon of distinctly organized and historically developed Churches was a final and decisive "No!" But the most important representative of sectarian Pietism in Germany, Gerhard Tersteegen of Mülheim on the Ruhr, passed beyond this mere negation. He had been awakened by Wilhelm Hoffmann, a disciple of Pierre Poiret, who had been at least temporarily influenced also by Hochmann. He was therefore familiar with the "spiritualist" climate of indifference to the Church. It is the Separatist note which is heard when he writes: "I believe and am certain that, among the Roman Catholics, as well as among the Lutherans, Reformed, Mennonites, and so forth, and indeed in all the various opinions and usages of these parties, no less than among the Separatists, souls can attain to the highest level of holiness and union with God." For himself he emphasizes that he "does not belong in the sectarian fashion to any party" but equally he has not separated himself from any.[1] But although the expression that to him "it is indifferent whether a man puts on this or that kind of religious clothing" implies a very low evaluation of the historic Churches, he never makes use of the abusive term Babylon, and never contemplates the foundation of a counter-Church of the type originated by Hochmann. It is enough for him to win souls for the Saviour, without systematically gathering them together; the invisible Church of the Spirit corresponds to the intangible character of personal encounter.

[1] Tersteegen, *Gesammelte Schriften*, VIII, pp. 173 ff.

From Separatist circles arose a number of projects for the peace of the Church which, from 1703 onwards, were published as from Friedens-Burg—the City of Peace. Friedensburg is the name of Hochmann's house in Schwarzenau, but as he built this only in 1709, the name which appears on the title-page of these publications must refer, not to the dwelling, but to the aims of Separatism as a whole. The spirit of the first tract[1] appears on the first glance to be entirely different from that of "spiritualism". The compiler, who uses the pseudonym Menander, addresses his work to a high ruling prince, evidently Frederick I, King of Prussia. This is surprising; but, more surprising still, in this book sober and intelligent exposition of concrete plans for the unification of the Churches is developed, and these, even if they do not bring into the foreground considerations of Church polity and of the legal constitution of Churches, at least direct to these subjects an attention most unusual among the Separatists. The author regards the authority of the Pope as the most important problem of all, and considers that a plan which does not find a solution of this question is bound to fail. He proposes first a plan of decentralization under which each province shall have its own bishop, and Italy the Bishop of Rome. The latter, however, is to be a general bishop of the whole Church, his authority being limited by the presence of a standing Consistory in Rome itself. In matters of worship, the author gives a sketch of an order in which only verses of the Bible should be used as versicles and responses, but which allows for the possibility of consecration and the idea of sacrifice in the Mass. Communion must be administered in both kinds. His doctrine of justification is a kind of compromise between the Reformation principle of "by grace alone" and the Roman Catholic concept of "faith formed by charity". In true pietistic vein, the author desires that the demand for a living faith, active in good works, should be expressly taken up into the dogmatic definitions of the Church. The process of unification should be initiated by a ruler who has all three Churches in his territory. He should arrange for public discussion of theological problems by the leading theologians, and the author at this point thoughtfully mentions that, in the choice of the place for the meeting, the need for a good library should be taken into consideration. He thinks that twelve scholars would be sufficient, so that each Church could be represented by four, of whose competence there could be no doubt.[2]

This project having been favourably received by the King of Prussia, the same author was encouraged to follow it up with a second, the subject of which is the unification of the two Evangelical Churches. This is set forth in the form of a discussion between Menander, Psychander, Logander, and Polander, while Nomander adds a conclusion which in part confirms and in part corrects what has gone before. Emphasis here is placed on worship. This reveals the "spiritualist" character of the whole proposal, since the decisive starting-point is the inward worship of the heart. The other participants in the conversation later introduce some modifications of this extreme "spiritualist" point of view, so that some validity is allowed to the Lutheran as well as to the Reformed element. But in order that there may be no rivalry in the future, the rites of the Church should not be derived from those of either of the existing Churches, but should be created afresh, in connection with the reform of the calendar and the

[1] See Bibliography, s.v.: *Neues und sonderbares Friedensproject.*

[2] The frontispiece of this work is remarkable. Three men are depicted sitting together at a round table: they are identifiable as the Pope, Luther, and Calvin. Before them lies an open Bible on which each places his right hand, and a stream of light descends from a cloud bearing the inscription, "Peace be with you".

preparation of a new lectionary, which should do greater justice to the riches of the Bible. In all questions of doctrine recourse should be had to that now familiar principle of Biblical simplicity. Here one sees most plainly how the times have changed. That which the 16th and 17th centuries regarded as of the utmost importance, pure doctrine, has now become peripheral. Both writings, in spite of their amateurish handling of the questions at issue, show in illuminating fashion that even "spiritualism" can give its attention to questions of Church polity and Church law.

England contributed another important manifestation of mystical "spiritualism" through the work of Jane Leade (1623–1704), with her helpers, Francis Lee and Richard Roach—the Philadelphian Society. This came into existence in the years 1694–97 and had its greatest influence in Germany. An unknown man of means had come across Jane Leade's book, *The Heavenly Cloud now Breaking*, published in 1681, and had been delighted with it. He urged on the writer the publication and translation of all her books. This encouraged her to found her spiritual Society. At first only a few faithful friends gathered around her. Among them a German living in England, Baron Georg Wilhelm von Knyphausen, was prominent. Gradually the number increased..The Society found in Johann Dittmar of Salzungen, who came to England towards the end of 1702, a tireless advocate in Germany. In 1697 the Society gave itself a kind of constitution, the Philadelphian Constitutions, in which its essential characteristics are set forth. Great importance is attached to two things: the first is the personal illumination of the individual members and their exchange of spiritual experiences with one another; the second, as the name derived from the Apocalypse suggests, is the all-embracing love which was the peculiar characteristic of the early Christian Church.[1] This overleaps the frontiers of countries and Churches, and forbids that pharisaic type of Separatism which leads each community to proclaim itself as the one and only way of salvation. The final goal is the reunion of all separated members of Christendom, the restoration of general peace among the brethren now engaged in conflict, and beyond that the conversion of the Jews and the Turks.

The idea of the "spiritual society", a small circle from which the concentrated energy of personal piety might spread abroad in the wider world of the Church and of society, had been made fashionable by the religious societies in England. One founder of many such societies, a German, Anton Horneck (1640–97), had probably, in his youth on the lower Rhine, come under the secondary influence of Labadie and of his pupil Anna Maria von Schurman.[2] Here again we find the indirect influence of mystical "spiritualism". The idea of the spiritual society maintained itself throughout the 18th century. It was to find its most influential expression in the German Christian Fellowship of Basle at the end of the 18th and the beginning of the 19th centuries.

7. ECUMENISM AND "REASONABLE ORTHODOXY"[3]

In the late summer of 1708 three men met in Geneva in the house of Jean Alphonse Turrettini (1671–1737), professor of Church history. The others were

---

[1] The anonymous work, *The State of the Philadelphian Society*, London, 1697, is cited in Nils Thune, *The Behmenists and the Philadelphians*, 1948, especially pp. 98 ff.

[2] For Anna Maria von Schurman (1607–78), "one of the rare women ecumenists", see A. Ritschl, *Geschichte des Pietismus*, I, Bonn, 1880, pp. 206 ff.

[3] The section on the Swiss Triumvirate has been contributed by Max Geiger, Doctor in Theology of the University of Basle.

Samuel Werenfels (1657–1740), professor of theology at Basle (who was accompanied by the sons of Gilbert Burnet, Bishop of Salisbury), and Jean Frédéric Ostervald (1663–1747), pastor and professor at Neuchâtel. The three men were distinguished by different gifts and interests. The brilliant Turrettini, a friend of many leading figures in the political and intellectual life of the age, stands in contrast to the more cautious Werenfels. The gifts of both these scientific theologians differed from the strongly practical talents of Ostervald as an ecclesiastical statesman. But stronger than all these differences was the common concern which bound the three men together, and justified the title of the "Swiss Triumvirate" by which they were commonly known.

The three were representatives of what is known as "reasonable orthodoxy". Our concern here is not to give a general account of this theological tendency, but to indicate those aspects of it which resulted in an interest in the unification of the Churches. "Reasonable orthodoxy" was something new in the history of Swiss Reformed theology. Its aim was to break free from the limited outlook of earlier orthodoxy and to enter into closer contact with the general intellectual movements of the age. That earlier orthodoxy had lived within the walls of the Churches. The champions of "reasonable orthodoxy" found themselves at home in an inter-confessional and extra-confessional "republic of letters" which included such men as Descartes, Bayle, Leibniz, Locke, and many others.

These wider contacts led to something like a revolution in theology. Men turned away from the familiar and accepted doctrines in search of new authorities in politics and law, in logic and metaphysics, in philosophy and theology. Leibniz had said that "variety delights us, but variety brought together in unity". These words might almost be taken as a programme for the epoch. Theologians took over the idea and applied it to the life of the Churches. They desired to see conflicting tendencies brought together through the demonstration of a Biblical basis of unity which deeply underlay them all. The clearest expression is given to this point of view by Samuel Werenfels in his *Dissertation concerning the Strife of Words of the Learned*. In these endless contentions over fruitless and subtle minutiae concerning the Trinity, the two natures in Christ, etc., is there anything beyond strife of words? Should not theology, like other sciences, return to a greater simplicity and unity? In the light of the simple Biblical message of Jesus Christ, the Son of God and Redeemer, and the equally simple demand that men should strive after virtue and true piety, the opposition between schools and confessions becomes insignificant. In this approach to theology the ecumenical thought of the Swiss Triumvirate finds its foundation.

This being so, it is not surprising that the three diligently worked for an actual union of the Churches. They were by no means the first to do so; but with the acceptance of "reasonable orthodoxy", the idea of a union of the Protestant Churches, which had so far been under suspicion as a project introduced by foreigners, for the first time became deeply rooted in the life and thought of the Swiss Churches themselves. Again and again in correspondence between Werenfels and Turrettini one finds the words "peace", "moderation", "equity", and "gentleness", and the first qualification for genuine theological thought is held to be an earnest desire for peace. The project of the three was set forth by Samuel Werenfels in his *General Discussion as to Means of Uniting the Protestant Churches which are Commonly Distinguished by the Names Lutheran and Reformed* and *Dissertation on the Manner of Uniting the Protestant Churches*; by Turrettini in his *Oration on the Reconciliation of the Differences between Protes-*

tants and his work *The Cloud of Witnesses on behalf of Moderate and Peaceful Judgement in Theological Affairs and on behalf of Reconciliation among Protestants.*[1]

Division among Protestants is a catastrophe, yet reconciliation between the Churches is no easy task. Even if it is achieved, it should not mean total uniformity. Men are too different from one another. On many points the Holy Scriptures give no precise direction. The Protestant principle of individual judgement is opposed to too rigid definition. Freedom in unessential matters must be granted. Men must recognize and love one another as brothers. This obligation to maintain tolerance and charity, peace and concord, is not a matter of individual preference, it is a duty laid by God on the conscience of every man.

In accordance with these principles, the Swiss Triumvirate developed in detail the idea of the Fundamental Articles of Christian belief. Yet they do not attempt to draw up too rigid a panel of these articles, since the situation of the Church varies from generation to generation. Scripture does not lend itself to such detailed definition. As in other sciences, a place must be left for reasonable agnosticism. Anything accepted as a fundamental belief must have been clearly revealed, and God must have given to man the necessary powers for believing it. Such fundamental beliefs must be clear and popular and free from all difference of interpretation. The theologians of this school again and again emphasized that the Fundamental Articles must be useful and necessary to the development of piety. The sole aim of religion is our sanctification. The new creation that lives in subjection to God's commandments is the end and goal of the whole Gospel. Between the Protestant Churches and the Roman Catholic Church no unity is possible, since there is no agreement on the Fundamental Articles; between Lutheran and Reformed, Church fellowship is possible and mutual tolerance is obligatory.

In earlier generations such an approach would have been impossible. It was only possible in the age of the Swiss Triumvirate through the abandonment of the ideal of pure doctrines and an inclination towards a theology based on the practice of piety. The three did not imagine that confessional differences could just be put on one side, but they tried always to emphasize that which was held in common and to minimize the points of division. In the doctrine of the Lord's Supper, both parties agreed that Christ was truly present, and disagreed only as to the exact character and nature of his presence in the bread and wine. Controversy as to the Person of Christ could not weigh against the fact that both parties firmly agreed in confessing Christ as omniscient, almighty, and omnipresent. As regards the doctrine of predestination, it was more difficult to find common ground. It must not be forgotten, however, that Paul teaches in the Epistle to the Romans that the judgements of God are incomprehensible and his ways past searching out—a warning to both sides not to indulge in undisciplined speculation.

The theoretical declarations of the Swiss Triumvirate are clear enough. To what extent are they prepared to give their principles practical effect in the life of the Churches? In this period many external circumstances had remarkably combined to prepare the way for a union of the Churches. One aspect of this preparation was the long-continued effort to secure freedom from the tyranny of the Helvetic Consensus. This document had been drawn up in 1675 by the

[1] See Bibliography (Werenfels, Turrettini) for the original titles of these works.

champions of the rigid orthodoxy of that date, as a defence against the "here-sies" of Saumur, and against other innovations. Those who accepted "reason-able orthodoxy" found the weight of it increasingly intolerable, and desired that acceptance of it should not be required of ordained ministers of the Church. In Neuchâtel personal subscription to it had never been required of the clergy. Basle had played a leading part in the adoption of this Confession; yet in 1686, under the influence of a letter from the Great Elector Frederick William, point-ing out the great dangers to Protestantism resulting from the revocation of the Edict of Nantes, ministers of the Gospel were exempted from the obligation personally to subscribe to it. Geneva was about twenty years behind the other two centres; but eventually Turrettini persuaded the Venerable Company[1] to abandon this narrow and divisive formula. The formula again became a subject of lively discussion in the year 1722. Frederick William I of Prussia and George I of England twice intervened in order to prevent the re-establishment of what could only be a source of division and conflict in the Church. It is almost certain that the influence of Ostervald and Turrettini lay behind their action.

In practical schemes for the union of the Churches, Turrettini took the lead. In 1707 the Prussian statesman Count von Metternich was sent to Geneva by Frederick I in order to ascertain the opinion of the Church of Geneva on Church union. In the name of the Venerable Company, Turrettini informed the King that "the constant and unanimous opinion of our Church has been that the Protestants of both communions are in agreement on every important and essential point concerning religion". Such differences as exist should not hinder us from "regarding one another as brothers and of joining together in one single ecclesiastical communion". The result of this gratifying answer was that Turret-tini was elected a member of the Prussian Academy, and that shortly afterwards permission was given for the formation in Geneva of an independent Lutheran congregation. The death of Frederick I in 1713, and of Queen Anne of England in 1714, was a serious blow to all projects of union. These were taken up again under Frederick William I of Prussia and George I of England, but the death of Leibniz and Molanus followed shortly after. The activity of the Swiss Trium-virate fell within a period when the best prospects for the realization of Church union were already past.

" Reasonable orthodoxy" turned also in the direction of a closer relationship with Roman Catholics. Samuel Werenfels undertook a journey to Paris in 1701 to make himself better acquainted with Roman Catholic theology, and spent three months there. In his letters to Turrettini he informed him that he found himself completely at home in the city of "le Roi Soleil",[2] sixteen years after the revocation of the Edict of Nantes. Ostervald's books were to be found in the royal library in Paris, and even in the house of Fénelon. It is recorded that at his funeral a Capuchin monk was among those standing by the grave to shed their tears over the deceased leader.

Their attitude towards the Pietists was also in process of transformation. As a strict ecclesiastical statesman Ostervald in later years came out strongly against toleration for Separatists; yet it became ever clearer that in his battles for the purity of Christian life, in the high value he set on spiritual retreats, and in his foundation of a school for poor children, he had taken over elements of Pietist devotion. At the age of sixty, Samuel Werenfels withdrew from public

---

[1] The official title, retained to the present day, of the body of ordained pastors of the Church of Geneva.   [2] Louis XIV.

life and ministerial authority in order to devote himself in Pietist fashion to the salvation of his own soul. Shortly before his death he was appointed by Zinzendorf as head of a Society of Brethren which had recently been founded in Basle.

Among the external Church relations of the Swiss Triumvirate the most important were those they entertained with the Church of England. The teaching of the Church of England was generally acceptable to the Reformed. Its outward form and constitution, its consciousness of unbroken continuity with the ancient Church, and the latitudinarianism of many of its theologians, were naturally appealing to the supporters of "reasonable orthodoxy". The Church of England was considered by the Swiss Triumvirate to be better fitted to be a mediator among the confessions than any other, since in it all the conditions which Protestants could reasonably demand had already been fulfilled. Werenfels had early made the acquaintance of Gilbert Burnet, later Bishop of Salisbury, and had dedicated one of his books to him. Turrettini had spent some time in England and became a friend of many leading churchmen. Ostervald was well known in England through his books, some of which had been translated into English. In planning the reform of the liturgy of the Church of Neuchâtel he had occupied himself with the study of Anglican models. Clear evidence of the close connection between Switzerland and England was afforded by the nomination of the three Swiss scholars as members of the English S.P.C.K. and S.P.G. The spirit and work of these two Societies appeared to the Swiss Triumvirate to be an expression in practical activity of their own deepest concerns, a worthy continuance and completion of the great work of the Reformation. In 1709, when Werenfels published his *Collection of Theological Dissertations* and dedicated it to the "illustrious Society for the Propagation of the Gospel", he expressed with the utmost clarity and emphasis his own inmost and most earnest aspirations, "that the Universal Church of Christ may reign throughout the world, and that in this Church the highest honour be ascribed to those things which are the very centre of our holy religion, the nucleus and marrow of Christian faith; in which all those who are to be saved, learned and unlearned, ought to agree; and in which all Christians of past times, who now enjoy the bliss of heaven, have agreed".

8. PLANS FOR UNION UNDER FREDERICK I, KING OF PRUSSIA, AND ERNEST AUGUSTUS, ELECTOR OF HANOVER

In the diplomatic moves under royal patronage which we have now to consider, the two principal figures are Daniel Ernst Jablonski (1660–1741) and Gottfried Wilhelm von Leibniz (1646–1716). The secondary figures are Jacques Bénigne Bossuet (1627-1704), Christoph Royas de Spinola (1626–95), and Gerhard Walter Molanus (1633–1722). Behind all discussions and efforts stood as patrons the rulers of the two related courts, Frederick I, King of Prussia, and Ernest Augustus, Elector of Hanover; the whole movement was calculated to result in an increase of prestige for these two rulers in Germany and in the whole of Europe.

Jablonski,[1] more than any other man of his epoch, seemed predestined by birth, by circumstances, and by education to ecumenical thought and activity. He was born at Nassenhuben, south-east of Danzig, in the fiercely contested

[1] On Jablonski, see also Chap. iii, pp. 153 f.

borderland between Germany, Poland, and Sweden. He was mainly of Polish race; but as his surroundings were completely German, German was in fact his mother-tongue, since in the places where he spent his youth the bitter warfare waged by the Counter-Reformation against Slav culture in Poland and Bohemia had increasingly resulted in the suppression of the Polish language. Poland was that land above all others in which, for the first time in Europe, freedom of belief and efforts to promote union had been in existence since the century of the Reformation. Jablonski's family belonged to the Church of the Bohemian Brethren. Thus he inherited the tradition of the Hussites, which combined the Reformed understanding of Christianity with a consciousness of its own individual value. The Unity of Brethren, since the meeting of its preacher Matěj Červenka with Bucer and Calvin in Strasburg in 1540, had attached itself to the Reformed Churches, especially in Poland, where in the middle of the 17th century it had about eighty congregations. Jablonski's father, who is known also by the Latinized name Peter Figulus, was not only the foster-son of John Amos Comenius, but also his son-in-law. It was even more significant that for seven years he had served as secretary to John Dury. In Leszno, John Bythner, the son of Bartholomew Bythner, was his Senior.[1]

Jablonski studied not only in the neighbouring University of Frankfort-on-Oder,[2] but also from 1680 to 1683 in Oxford, where Charles II of England had founded two scholarships for members of the Church of the Brethren. Probably he entered Christ Church, the same college which, about forty years later, received John Wesley. Here he was in a stronghold of Anglican conviction, entirely loyal to the Established Church; but since the time of Brian Walton there had also been a great tradition of philological study of the Bible which culminated in 1657 in the publication of the *Polyglott*. In 1682, during the period of Jablonski's study, the Dean of Christ Church, John Fell,[3] published the works of Cyprian. Jablonski, in earlier years, had been much in contact with English Presbyterians who, as exiles, had prejudiced him against the Church of England. All the stronger must have been the immediate impression when he encountered the Anglican Church under its most favourable aspect. He became a close friend of a man who in after years was to attain to the highest position of authority in the Church, William Wake.[4] From that time onward Jablonski's mind was entirely occupied with the plan of a great union of all Evangelical Churches, of which the corner-stones were to be the Biblical orthodoxy of the Bohemian Brethren and the Anglican tradition continuous with that of the early Church. Episcopacy, which was a common possession of both Churches, he regarded as a most precious survival from the days of the early Church. Consistently with this view, as an old man in the year 1735, he conferred the episcopate on David Nitschmann of Herrnhut, and in 1737 on Count Zinzendorf, thereby manifesting the close connection which existed between the Moravian Brethren and those of Herrnhut.

After completing his studies, Jablonski became military chaplain in Magdeburg (1683–86); then from 1686 to 1691 he was pastor and principal of the school in Leszno, the headquarters of the Polish Church of the Brethren. From 1691 to 1693, he was the Reformed court chaplain of the King of Prussia in Königsberg.

---

[1] The technical term for a superintendent (who was sometimes also a bishop) of the Church of the *Unitas Fratrum*. For Bartholomew Bythner, see p. 96.
[2] Here Jablonski came under the influence of Samuel Strimesius (1648–1730), who later collaborated with him in working out the theological foundation of his unitive ideas.
[3] Dr Fell was consecrated Bishop of Oxford in 1676, but retained the Deanery *in commendam*.
[4] In 1716 Wake became Archbishop of Canterbury. See Chap. iii, pp. 154.

In 1693 he moved to the capital, Berlin, and there began a residence of almost fifty years. Here he was in the immediate neighbourhood of the Lutheran Pietist leader, Philipp Jakob Spener, whose intimate friend he became, though he was never able to win his support for his plans for union.

This was the man who was to find, in the project of Church union, the culmination of his life's work. Like John Dury, however, he took up the task not on his own initiative but as the result of an impulse from without. Paul von Fuchs, statesman and President of the Consistory, invited him in 1697 to write a memorandum on the problems and possibilities of union. Jablonski, in preparing his statement, deliberately tried to face all the possible difficulties. He not merely looked back to the history of union and confederation in Poland, and particularly to the Consensus of Sendomir of 1570, but also took questions of doctrine very seriously. He first rejected Calixtus' idea of the *consensus quinquesaecularis*, and then, like Zinzendorf, proceeded to affirm the Augsburg Confession, the classical confession of the Reformation, as the point of departure. He carefully compared the edition of 1530 with that of 1540, which had been tacitly approved by Luther and accepted by Calvin. Like a polemical writer of the 17th century, he develops point by point the differences between the two Churches of the Reformation, especially on the subject of the Person of Christ, baptism, the Lord's Supper, and auricular confession. He makes plain that even concerning the first article of the Creed on the doctrine of God, there is no real agreement, since the doctrine of predestination is the expression of a different idea of God from that of the Lutherans. But in spite of this careful doctrinal analysis, Jablonski does not really regard doctrinal agreement as the basis of union. This he finds in the Christian way of life. He demands toleration, and asks for continuing discussions as to the content of the Faith, and hopes that from these unity will grow by the way of organic development.

Molanus opposed these proposals, on the one hand as a supporter of the *consensus quinquesaecularis*, and on the other under the influence of the painful experiences of his University of Rinteln, where the Calvinists had taken advantage of the decree of toleration to carry through a rough Calvinization of the Church. Molanus, more truly a son of the 17th century than Jablonski, demanded genuine doctrinal union as the basis of Church union, and was grateful to Leibniz for undertaking to mitigate dogmatic differences through philosophic considerations.

Nothing was achieved by these preliminary discussions. Even less favourable was the star which watched over the *Collegium Caritativum*, a theological discussion at Berlin, undertaken at the command of Frederick I in 1703. Here Molanus strove to attain genuine unity in doctrine. His desire was that a beginning should be made with the fundamental articles of the Faith. But the whole enterprise collapsed, owing to the fact that the Pietist Johann Joseph Winckler, Inspector of Magdeburg, had secretly laid before the King a plan for bringing about compulsory union through an authoritative royal declaration. This proposal of Winckler's was prematurely published by the opposition under the title *Arcanum Regium*. The whole time of the conference was taken up by violent disputes about it; the author of it was paralysed by this disclosure, and all further discussion was fatally impeded.

In the meantime Jablonski took action on behalf of the Protestant victims of the Counter-Reformation in Poland, Lithuania, Hungary, Transylvania, and Bohemia; maintained close relationships with Zinzendorf; refuted the accusations made by the Russian theologian Stefan Javorski [1] against the Churches of the Reformation; and entered into negotiations with Switzerland and England. Behind all these activities lay the idea of comprehensive organic union, not as an immediate purpose, but as a distant goal. In 1710 he went a step further than in his memorandum of 1697. In an opinion on church discipline which he put out in that year, a large part is played by a new and explicitly Anglican point of view, which had been sadly lacking in this whole century, indeed in both the 17th and 18th centuries. It is now his aim to bring about the union of the Churches through fellowship in worship and in adoration. At this point Jablonski shows himself a sharp critic of his own Reformed Church. He reproaches it for its over-emphasis on preaching, and its cold, dull worship. He finds lacking the element of awe, and affirms that there are nine necessary elements of worship, apart from the sermon. They are: (1) the confession of sin; (2) adoration on bended knee; (3) praise and thanksgiving; (4) self-dedication to God, with the promise to live only in his service and for his glory; (5) intercession; (6) reading of the Scriptures; (7) administration of the Sacrament; (8) the giving of alms; and (9) fasting. He does not regard preaching as an indispensable element in worship. Already in 1699 he had asked his friend Johann Ernst Grabe, a German who was at that time living in England, for a translation of the Book of Common Prayer. This was published in 1704 at Frankfort-on-Oder. Frederick I of Prussia had planned to accept this with some small alterations as the basic order for divine service at the chapel in the palace at Berlin and in the Cathedral.

Jablonski was prepared to go even further than this. In his book *Unprejudiced Thoughts on the Subject of Union*, published in 1716, he declared that the differences in doctrine between the Churches of the Reformation do not touch the essentials of Christianity. He was prepared to leave to each the free practice of its own form of worship, but he desired to see certain improvements in order to remove some things which were an offence to some Christians and to introduce new and edifying elements. But this programme is less far-reaching than that of his earliest writing. It fails to make a deep impression. How weak and artificial appear all these well-intentioned and carefully developed proposals for union as contrasted with the original and almost brutal self-confidence of Pietism that it, and it alone, represents the *Oikumene*, the true Church. And yet how much ripe experience purified by disappointments, how much learning which is prepared to renounce all expectations of immediate success, lie behind this book of Jablonski.

Leibniz is one of those grandiose figures which defy analogies and tidy classifications, and by the universal range of their interests and their power leave their impress on every movement of their age. The course of his life provided him with ample starting-points for ecumenical activity. In the first enthusiasm of early manhood he had, though a Lutheran, been active at the court of the Prince Bishop of Mainz; there he was ceaselessly exposed to the solicitations of Roman Catholics eager for his conversion. Thence he transferred himself to Hanover, where dynastic and cultural connections with England inevitably directed his attention to a wider world. He was in sympathy with Peter the Great in Russia; devoted to the Egyptian plan and the China mission; and even, at the beginning of his activity, concerned with the difficult problems of politics in Poland. Leib-

[1] See Ludolf Müller, *Die Kritik des Protestantismus in der russischen Theologie vom 16.–18. Jahrhundert*, 1951, pp. 68 ff., 79 ff.

niz was a man who leaped from task to task, from plan to plan, dowered as he was with towering genius and an unwearied capacity for work. Yet he did not dissipate his energies, since the whole was constantly present in his mind. His philosophy is a curious combination of contrasts: rational causality and the theological concept of creation; rational teleology and theological eschatology; the Hellenic doctrine of evil as defect and the Christian conviction of sin as the basic evil of the world; the Christian assurance of redemption and a this-worldly optimism; all these are compounded with yet other elements in one great amalgam. In the same way, his political views are a strange combination of Christian universalism with modern secular nationalism. Yet all these contrasts and apparent contradictions are held together in his powerful mind as a totality, bound up into unity by a single regulative idea.

This idea can be summed up in a phrase—belief in Europe as the spiritual centre and home of mankind. Europe as a cultural, political, and religious unity must be restored. This restoration is to be regarded not as a visionary dream, but as an immediate practical task to which the minds of thinkers and the activities of diplomats are to be directed in the confident expectation of its achievement. There can be no mere turning back to the Middle Ages, though the medieval *corpus Christianum* supplies the framework for some of Leibniz' ideas. The deeper origin of those ideas lies further back in Augustine's doctrine of the *City*, or *Citizenship, of God*, as the expression in history of the universal order of the world. In the mind of Leibniz this basic concept takes shape in the vision of a Christian civilization of unlimited extension, developed under the direction of a body which is at the same time Church and State and bearer of culture. In that body a great rôle is naturally reserved for the Christian emperor whose special task it is to maintain peace and to care for the Church, for its unity in faith and life; but with the medieval tradition of the Holy Roman Empire are combined Teutonic elements, in the ideal of the religious king, which are to be found already set forth in *Beowulf*. The great Councils of the earlier epochs find their counterpart in the international conferences of statesmen, which serve as an instrument of agreement and order among the conflicting political powers.

It is evident that this is a political rather than a religious concept. Yet it is important not to underestimate the part played by the Church in the thought of Leibniz. The Church for which he longs, and for the actualization of which he strives, must as a universal Church include within itself all the expressions of Christian life and faith. It cannot therefore be identified with any of the existing Churches; but this statement must not be regarded as involving the contrary error of the "spiritualists", that the empirical Churches can be treated with indifference. One of the aims of Leibniz is to rescue the term "the Catholic Church" from the discredit into which it has fallen. If there is to be a universal Church, he is willing to admit the primacy of the Pope within it; he is prepared to defend the Roman dogma of transubstantiation; he even throws off the outlines of a *System of Theology*. As we shall see, Leibniz later found it necessary to change his favourable opinion of the Roman Church—perhaps because that Church in the 18th century obstinately refused to become that which Leibniz had fancied it might be.

It is in the light of this Christian universalism that all the excursions of Leibniz into ecumenical realms, whether more deeply marked by the political or by the religious colouring, are to be understood.

The first of his constructive writings dealt with an issue of burning contemporary interest—the forthcoming election to the Polish crown, and the special function of this kingdom in the general scheme of European life. The well-being of Poland, as indeed of every kingdom, must be considered from the standpoint of the well-being of the Christian world as a whole. Poland occupies a peculiar situation between Christendom and the realms of the barbarians. For this reason it is its responsibility to maintain a Crusade on behalf of the rest of Europe, its duty to do everything in its power to keep alive the will to maintain this Crusade. The future King of Poland must be already a Roman Catholic by conviction; he must, however, be just and tolerant towards non-Roman Christians in his country, as indeed the traditions of that country demand. He must avoid civil war, in order to keep himself available for wars against the external foe.

The almost medieval idea of a common Crusade against the unbelievers recurs several times in Leibniz' writings. He pictures it as a great Christian enterprise in which the civil power, the Empire, should co-operate with the Pope, and the Emperor should make plain that his title *Advocatus Ecclesiae Universalis* is something more than a mere title. By this means Leibniz hopes to put an end to the unprofitable religious wars among Christians and to guarantee the peace of the world through the restoration of the might of the Empire. For this reason Germany is all-important in his thought, from the point of view both of history and of geopolitics. Germany is the central country. Germany is the bearer and the sponsor of the tradition of that Holy Roman Empire which brought forth Christian Europe. Therefore Germany must be strengthened in every possible way and brought to the highest attainable level of prosperity.

Other countries, however, also engage his attention. For years France had been playing a destructive rôle in Christian Europe. The Egyptian plan, developed by Leibniz in the years 1671–72, is an attempt to turn French power into channels where it can do less harm, and to divert its desire for imperialistic expansion in the direction of Moslem Egypt. In 1668, when the book *Lithuanus* was written, Russia is still to Leibniz a part of the barbarian world; later, under Peter the Great, it had come to appear as a manifest instrument for the diffusion of Western culture.

These wide-ranging views are balanced by a second leading idea of Leibniz—his belief in the efficacy of a *society*, that typical 18th-century idea, a society of the *élite*. In his book, written in 1671, *Thoughts on the Establishment of a Society*, he bases his society firmly on faith, hope, and charity, through the recognition of God's omnipotence; he ascribes to it the apprehension of God's divine nature; he describes its members as *Oratores* and *Sacerdotes*. In all this it is plain that a new doctrine of the Church, based on the idea of creation rather than that of redemption, is being built up; under indirect influences of "spiritualism" the philosophical society is taking the place of the historic Church. In 1669 he sets before his Philadelphian Society, in the realms of theology and philosophy, of the sacred and of the profane, a comprehensive task of surpassing grandeur. This is nothing less than the perfection of the world as a whole, *perfectio universi*. The society of Leibniz' imagination is on the one hand to be a power destined to conquer the world and to bring in the sovereignty of God; on the other, it in part resembles the Christian Church, through the strong emphasis which is laid on the spirit of service. One of the tasks assigned to this society is that of reconciling the conflicting confessions. Yet the definition of such a specific task within the comprehensive scheme of the society is hardly necessary. The society in itself is all-sufficient. It comprises in a single unit Church, State, and institution for the promotion of culture.

If Leibniz' thought is followed to its logical conclusion, it results in a complete breaking up of the traditional structure of the Church in favour of a new philosophic universalism. This is the beginning of the epoch of the great, bold invasions of the territory of theology by philosophy, which was to continue through the later 18th and the 19th centuries. Yet, by a paradox of the kind with which we are becoming familiar in the work of this extraordinary man, when it comes to practical questions affecting the unity of the Church, it is natural to him to turn back to tradition and to express new thoughts in ancient forms and formulas. It is not simply that in all his efforts for the union of the Churches, Hugo Grotius is ever present to his mind as his great example. He took seriously the traditional categories of Christian thinking. As early as his sixteenth year he had plunged himself in the study of dogmatic writings, Roman Catholic, Lutheran, and Reformed, in order to acquaint himself precisely with the tenets of the various confessions and the points of difference between them. His kinship with the humanistic tradition is seen in his acceptance of the distinction between fundamental and secondary articles of the Christian faith. Like Grotius, he believed that only the great universal Church of the future will possess the whole truth of the Gospel; no single Church can now boast of its possession.

Leibniz looked far and wide in the service of this universal Church. He hoped that decisive steps in favour of union would be taken by Peter the Great, though, unlike the more sanguine of his contemporaries, he did not put much confidence in the extension of Protestant influence in the dominions of the Tsar. In this connection, as well as in that of the extension of Christian culture, he attached the greatest importance, both from political and religious considerations, to Christian missions in non-Christian lands. But naturally the heart and centre of the unitive efforts of Leibniz was his concern for reunion between the Church of Rome and the Protestant Churches of the continent of Europe.

From 1691 onwards Leibniz was in regular correspondence with Bossuet, Bishop of Meaux and tutor to the Dauphin. The noble irenical temper of the great Christian orator seemed to mark him out as the ideal partner for Leibniz in such an amicable discussion. Yet in fact, if Leibniz was one of the first voices of the modern world, Bossuet was one of the last voices of a medieval period which had not yet quite disappeared, and no close intellectual contact between them was ever possible.

Leibniz had by this time withdrawn to some extent from his favourable attitude towards the Roman Church. If that Church, in idle and unprofitable self-complacency, takes its stand on the definitions of the Council of Trent and claims the right to persecute heretics, it disqualifies itself from being considered genuinely Catholic. For the Council of Trent was not truly ecumenical: the French Church had not accepted it; and, by refusing to hear the Protestants, it had revealed its partisan character. Now the conciliar principle is the alpha and omega of Leibniz' plans for union. He is able to assure Bossuet that the Protestants are prepared to submit to the authority of a universal council, only of course on the understanding that such a council bears upon it the unmistakable marks of ecumenicity. As a ground for common understanding, Leibniz offers to Bossuet the idea of the indefectibility of the Church, maintained through the hierarchy and the general assemblies of the Church, but not guaranteed by the Pope alone.

To this approach it was not possible for the Roman Catholic Bossuet, for all his irenic temper, to make any very encouraging answer. For him, the visible Church, centred in the papacy and its hierarchical organization, is the great reality, and to this principle he holds with unshakable firmness. He defends the validity of all the decisions made by the Church, since the repudiation of any of them, or even a doubt concerning it, must be considered as undermining the very principle of tradition. To make any concession in matters of dogma would involve a denial of the special character of revealed truth. Concerning the great truths of salvation, compromises cannot be effected, as they can in merely human affairs. This was the last word from the Roman Catholic side. This being said, there was nothing for Leibniz to do but to announce his final rejection of that Church and to break off the negotiations.

Leibniz met with no success in his unitive efforts; and yet his great ideas were not without their value. We should not allow ourselves to be blinded to this value by the political wrappings in which these ideas were presented and the opportunism from which they were not exempt. Leibniz deliberately directed his efforts towards the French Church with its Gallican traditions and its sometimes more intimate loyalty to secular rulers than to the Pope. But his real concern was throughout with the universal Church; it was for the coming of that Church that he desired to prepare the way.

The practical efforts made in this period to establish Christian unity leave on the mind an impression of feebleness and artificiality when compared with the elemental force of the new world of ideas and of the energy with which Leibniz strove to realize them. Certainly much goodwill and much acumen were expended on them. The General of the Franciscan Order (later Bishop of Wiener-Neustadt), Christoph de Spinola, who in 1683 spent more than five months in Hanover in ceaseless contact with Protestant theologians, in drawing up his document in preparation for the great assembly for the promotion of the unity of the Church, *Rules to Govern the Reunion of all Christian Churches*, endeavoured to go as far as possible in tolerance towards Lutherans and Reformed, even to the point of treating certain Roman Catholic dogmas as matters of indifference. But the articles for discussion, as drawn up by him, in reality represent only the Roman Catholic attitude. Only Molanus, the Abbot of Lokkum and pupil of Calixtus, and his friend Barckhaus, regarded them as a valid basis for discussion. The purely theological discussion carried on between Molanus and Bossuet from 1691 onwards seemed to open up hopeful prospects, because of the strongly syncretistic tendency of the theologian of Hanover, which went even beyond the broad ideas of his teacher Calixtus. The negotiations, however, collapsed over the obstacles of the infallibility of the Church and the papacy. Even the attempts to reach union between the Protestant Churches, which led in 1703 to the *Collegium Caritativum* of Berlin, were not seriously renewed after the failure of the Berlin discussions. The charitable polemics of Valentin Ernst Löscher and the bitter polemics of Erdmann Neumeister expressed once again with strong conviction the Lutheran protest against every tendency towards treating doctrinal differences lightly.

After the collapse of these efforts, the bicentenary of the Reformation produced yet one more attempt to bring the Protestant Churches together in unity.

The *Corpus Evangelicorum* at Ratisbon, the official body representing the Protestant Princes of Germany, and King Frederick William I of Prussia were united in desiring this. Among the theologians the lead was taken by Christoph Matthäus Pfaff (1686–1760), Chancellor of the University of Tübingen. Pfaff bases his appeal in part on reactions against the Bull *Unigenitus* of 1713, which he regards as marking a yet further departure on the part of the Roman Church from the true doctrine of *sola gratia*, which therefore makes all the more urgently necessary a reconciliation between those who hold to the Scriptural doctrine. Thus once again, as at the beginning of the 17th century, we find attempts to promote Christian unity called into being by a sense of need for common defence against the perils of the Counter-Reformation.

Pfaff follows the well-worn path of minimizing doctrinal differences. In all essentials Lutherans and Reformed are already one; even on the three most contested points—Christology, predestination, and the Lord's Supper—the differences are due more to differences in terminology and in underlying philosophical concepts than to anything else. Naturally this somewhat cavalier attitude to doctrine exposed the author of these plans to vigorous controversial attack. But such attacks fell short of the heart and centre of Pfaff's views. Unlike Leibniz, Pfaff is not concerned with new ideas of Europe, ecclesiastical diplomacy, cultural tasks, vast programmes, and so forth. In essence the Professor of Tübingen desires to take up again in its simplest form the original task of the Reformation —the proclamation of the all-sufficient and saving grace of God.[1]

All these attempts to promote union leave on the mind a mixed impression. On the one hand, in spite of their openness towards the other participants in the discussion, in spite of the practical experience and energy, the acumen and the careful attention expended on them, theologians like Molanus and even Jablonski were working with ideas that were already out of date. Over against them the supra-dimensional philosophy of Leibniz stands as a young and unexhausted power. Men reach the point of close contact and fellowship in common work and in technical organization, but never that of the genuine confrontation of one by another.

9. BETWEEN THE 18TH AND 19TH CENTURIES

The latest expression of ecumenical activity in the 18th century was the German Christian Fellowship (*Deutsche Christentumsgesellschaft*), a development of the idea of the "spiritual society". The way for it was prepared by Hieronymus Annoni (1697–1770), pastor of Wallenburg and Muttenz near Basle. Annoni in his early years had spent some time in Berleburg and later in Herrnhut. He had been inclined to radical Pietism and to Separatism, but had found his way back to the official ministry of the Church. As a result, however, of his association with Separatism, he came to understand as his life-work the gathering together and care of individual souls. His intense activity as preacher and "awakener of souls" brought such numbers of visitors to his house that it came to look more like an inn than a parsonage. In 1746 he composed a form of intercession in verse for the scattered children of God throughout the world. "A Christian often and with pleasure seeks Zion's children far and near" is its striking beginning.

In 1756 he formed the Fellowship of Good Friends (*Gesellschaft guter*

---

[1] See Christoph Matthäus Pfaff, *Gesammelte Schriften*, Halle, 1723, II, pp. 48 ff.; and Paul Schreyer, *Valentin Ernst Löscher und die Unionsversuche seiner Zeit*, 1938, pp. 87 ff.

Freunde), in Basle to promote the honour of God and the salvation of men. The programme of the Good Friends foreshadows that of the German Christian Fellowship. Members are to practise brotherly love, to gather news from the Churches, especially from the mission-fields, and to hold themselves ready to meet any urgent practical needs.

Twenty-four years later Johann August Urlsperger (1728–1806), again in Basle, developed the possibilities of this earlier plan and founded the German Christian Fellowship. The ancestry of the Fellowship can be traced through J. A. Urlsperger and his father Samuel Urlsperger (1685–1772) to Halle and to Francke, who exercised a powerful influence on the older Urlsperger and his whole life-work.

Towards 1780 J. A. Urlsperger began in Basle to gather together and bring into intimate relationship active promoters of pure doctrine and true godliness. His own first concern in so doing and in promoting the German Christian Fellowship was the development of apologetic literature, in particular the working out of a new Biblical and rational basis for the doctrine of the Trinity, as a defence against the attacks of modernist theologians. The emphasis of the members, however, was rather on practical Christian service. Their duty to the pure truth which they believed themselves to possess must be fulfilled in "active piety". They were more interested in edification than in apologetic.

Meetings were held monthly and careful minutes were kept. After prayer and reading of the Scriptures, letters from friends of the cause were read and plans were made for activities to be undertaken for the glory of God. At their second meeting on 27 September 1780 the decision was taken to publish a magazine for which, following the Pietist tradition, edifying biographies should be prepared. Emphasis was laid on the provision of literature which would be helpful in the cure of souls. The first desire of the Society was "that the Kingdom of God should come, and the Kingdom of Satan be destroyed". Contemporary records of the battle for the Kingdom of God were sought—examples of answers to prayer, "manifestations of the righteous judgements of God". This made possible a Christian interpretation of recent history.

All this was in line with the theology and activities of earlier spiritual societies. But the German Christian Fellowship had a new ethos of its own and a special contribution to give to the growth of the ecumenical idea. It was the first society definitely founded on an international and an inter-Church basis, and it demonstrated that such a society was possible, necessary, and welcome.

It was international. Once established in Basle, the Fellowship spread with astonishing rapidity. Urlsperger on his travels to promote the cause had immediate success with the German congregation in London—not unnaturally, since England had already for a century been the home of the idea of the "spiritual society". The Fellowship spread rapidly in German cities—Nuremberg, Stuttgart, Frankfort-on-Main, Tübingen, Flensburg, Halberstadt, and Dresden—and by 1784 was established in Amsterdam. The spirit of Christian fellowship manifestly corresponded closely to the sense of need experienced by those circles which had remained definitely Christian in the epoch of the Enlightenment. Its international aspect presented little difficulty in that age, when barriers between the nations were lower. No better illustration could be found of the changed relations between the nations in the 20th century than the fact that in the early 19th a society bearing the name of one nation—German—could influence a wide international constituency.

But the spirit of unity in the German Christian Fellowship survived also the far more difficult testing of inter-Church relationships. It was consciously ecumenical in its aim. Urlsperger, himself a Lutheran, believed that all differences of teaching between Lutherans and Reformed should give way before the unity of all true believers. The membership of the Fellowship extended beyond the official Churches. It included Moravians and Mennonites in Germany and Holland, other smaller Continental sects, Anglicans in England, and even Roman Catholics. Socially as well as ecclesiastically, it was catholic: it touched all ranks of society and included judges, statesmen, generals, men of business, and artisans.

It gave birth to all manner of united enterprises which were carried on on the same principles—the Basle Mission House, the Basle Missionary Society, Bible and Tract Societies; and through the personality of Steinkopf, its first Secretary,[1] exercised influence on the development of such interdenominational societies in Britain as the Bible Society, the Religious Tract Society, and others.

The main significance of the German Christian Fellowship is that it successfully experimented with and demonstrated the possibilities of an international inter-Church society. It thus paved the way for those many voluntary societies which were the characteristic product of the Evangelical Awakening in the 19th century on both sides of the Atlantic, and were so powerful a preparation for the ecumenical movement as we know it to-day.[2]

10. CONCLUSION

The 17th and 18th centuries, as compared with the century of the Reformation, brought about many great changes in ecumenical thought. The most striking of all these differences is the following: in the 16th century, through the recovery of the proclamation of the Gospel, the Churches which issued from the Reformation on the Continent were convinced that they were the Church, the *Oikumene*. The true succession of the pure Church which lived by evangelic truth was to them all-important. They made the same claim to the traditions of the past as the early Christians had made in relation to the Old Testament. They felt it possible to abandon a formal and legally established apostolic succession, because they were assured that, in fact, they had it in their purity of doctrine. They were the Church: the Roman Catholics, or as they called them, the Papists, were the heretics.

In the 17th and 18th centuries, on the contrary, under the influence of "spiritualism" men became accustomed to speak of the three "parts" of the divided Church (*Kirchenparteien*) which stood over against one another.[3] The idea of the Church was pluralized into that of Churches. The Church became again, as it had been in the medieval world, a body the nature of which is determined rather by its law and by its organization than by the faith which it professes. The restoration of the unity of the Church was no longer regarded as the task of the Word of God alone. And so attempts were made by way of agreement, discussion, formulas, tradition, or alternatively through the manifestations of Christian life, individual Christian personality and Christian life in community, to bring about the unity of the Church. This resulted in a serious

[1] See Chap. vii, p. 312.   [2] See Chap. vii, pp. 310–15.
[3] I.e. Lutheran, Reformed, and Roman Catholic.

danger of forgetting the Reformation principle of justification by grace alone, received through faith alone.

The history of the ecumenical movement in these two centuries presents great examples of conscious ecumenical thought and ecumenical activity, of mutual understanding, sympathy, and willingness to serve. Apart from planned and conscious attempts at union, it offered also examples of undesigned but deeply significant encounters. It gives evidence of ceaseless striving which never allowed itself to become embittered by any ill-success or disappointment. It remains the history of a yearning, but also of a promise.

CHAPTER 3

ECUMENICAL MOVEMENTS IN GREAT BRITAIN
IN THE SEVENTEENTH AND EIGHTEENTH CENTURIES

by

NORMAN SYKES

1. INTRODUCTION[1]

"For my part, Sir," observed Dr Samuel Johnson, "I think all Christians, whether Papists or Protestants, agree in the essential articles; and that their differences are trivial; and rather political than religious." The good Doctor's opinion may seem as unrealistic as superficial in retrospect of the melancholy history of controversy and strife between Christians of the several Churches. But his words have the merit of expressing a salient characteristic of the many discussions of ecclesiastical union during the 17th and 18th centuries: namely, the recognition and acceptance of a distinction between the essential and non-essential articles in Christian faith and confessional standards, and the important part played by political or social factors in ecclesiastical divisions. For these two centuries, despite their experience of religious wars and civil conflicts of essentially religious basis, were fruitful in discussions and projects of ecclesiastical union; and the principle of differentiation between fundamentals and non-essentials was ubiquitously stated and iterated, alike within the British Isles and on the European continent.

2. FROM THE ACCESSION OF JAMES I TO THE LONG PARLIAMENT

By the time of the accession of James I to the throne of England (1603), the religious situation in both his kingdoms was becoming stabilized. In England, thanks pre-eminently to the apologetic work of Jewel and Hooker, and to the administrative coercion of Archbishop Whitgift, on the one hand the *Ecclesia Anglicana* had stated its position as standing firmly in the *via media* between Rome and Geneva, and on the other the frontal assault of the Presbyterian and classical movement had at least been driven underground. From the standpoint of apologetic, what had seemed at first sight a compromise dictated by mere political expediency was now realized to embrace a positive theological principle, and the Church of England, though as yet but a little city of Zoar compared with the forces of the Counter-Reformation and of militant Calvinism, was beginning to serve alike as a refuge and a rallying-ground for those to whom the strait-waistcoats whether of Trent or of Geneva proved too narrow for comfort.

In Scotland, the Reformation, which at first had been by no means unequivocally Presbyterian, since it had left the government of the Church "in a moderate imparity" with "tulchan" bishops who might develop into Protestant prelates, had been firmly riveted to the Reformed pattern by Andrew Melville; and James VI of Scotland had had personal experience—which he was not to forget when he became also James I of England—of the uncertain authority and prestige of a monarch under Presbyterian ecclesiastical surveillance.

If the 17th century opened with the apparent victory of Episcopacy in England and of Presbyterianism in Scotland, the way might seem open for attempts to conciliate the defeated parties, as a first step towards that union of Protestants in the face of a renovated Church of Rome, which was the aspiration of the new

[1] Some shortening of Professor Sykes' text and some co-ordination of his material with that of Professor Schmidt having been found necessary, the final redaction of this chapter was carried out by the editorial staff, who accept responsibility for the final form of the chapter as here printed.

epoch. If such a union could be effected in Great Britain, the example might spread and the pattern be copied by Protestants of the European continent, whose position was even more seriously challenged by the Counter-Reformation.

Accordingly, during James I's progress from Scotland to London, the Millenary Petition, bearing the date of April 1603, was presented to him by a number of signatories who desired modestly and moderately to lay before him the points at which the episcopal system pressed sorely upon tender Presbyterian consciences. Indeed the contrast between the sweeping demands and aggressive temper of the Elizabethan *Admonitions to Parliament* (1572) and the deferential tone and limited objectives of the Millenary Petition, was itself a measure of the changed circumstances. The Jacobean petitioners were at pains to insist that they were "neither as factious men affecting a popular parity in the Church, nor as schismatics aiming at the dissolution of the state ecclesiastical, but as the faithful servants of Christ and loyal subjects to your majesty, desiring and longing for the redress of divers abuses of the Church". Nor were their detailed requests such as to deny this initial moderation. They reminded their new sovereign that they had "in respect of the times, subscribed to the Book [of Common Prayer] —some upon protestation, some upon exposition given them, some with condition rather than the Church should have been deprived of their labour and ministry"; and that their present demands were simply "to be eased and relieved" of the "burden of human rites and ceremonies" in four specific articles.

The first article demanded the removal from the Book of Common Prayer of unnecessary or harmful rites and ceremonies; attention to "the longsomeness of service"; insistence on uniformity in doctrine, with the suppression of survivals of popish opinion and practice.

The second required stricter admission of fit persons only to the ministry, with removal of those that were already entered but could not preach; the renewal of the statutes permitting clerical marriage; and more lenient terms of clerical subscription.

The third article desired the abolition of pluralities—the holding of a number of parishes by one incumbent—and better provision for the preaching ministry.

The fourth was directed against excommunications, especially those issued on trivial grounds, by lay ecclesiastical officials; against the delays and irritations of ecclesiastical suits; and the too ready issuing of special licences for marriage.

These abuses the petitioners professed themselves ready to prove "not to be agreeable to the Scriptures", if the King would grant them audience; and they concluded with an iterated assurance that they desired "not a disorderly innovation, but a due and godly reformation".[1]

The petition obviously embraced both matters which a sober and impartial judgement would agree to be abuses in need of reform, and others of more disputable character, such as the demand for the abolition of Confirmation and of the terms "priest" and "absolution". It is arguable, moreover, that the supplicants fell into the mistake which their successors at the Restoration were to imitate, of enumerating too many and too various grievances. But, as has been already observed, compared with the demand in the *Admonitions to Parliament* for root-and-branch extirpation of episcopacy, and for the supplanting of the Book of

---

[1] H. Gee and W. J. Hardy, *Documents illustrative of English Church History*, No. LXXXVIII, pp. 508–11.

Common Prayer by the Genevan service book or some variant thereof, the Millenary Petition was both modest and moderate in its programme. Apart from the reform of financial, administrative, and judicial abuses, the desires of its signatories would have been satisfied with a permissive omission of the "nocent ceremonies".

But if the Presbyterian demands were now for toleration and comprehension rather than for the supersession of the episcopalian system and the Prayer Book by Presbyterianism, the classical régime, and a Scottish or Genevan liturgy, it should not be forgotten that the Elizabethan age had seen the rise of Independency, the principles of which were untouched by the Millenary Petition, and the professors of which opinions would have remained an intractable problem even if a *modus vivendi* were reached with the petitioners. Though the career of Robert Browne may present still unsolved problems to the historian (particularly the long period of outward conformity to the Established Church and of silence upon controverted matters of Church polity which followed his turbulent youth), it can hardly be denied that he had enunciated the principles of Independency. These principles had been clarified and expounded by Henry Barrow, John Greenwood, and John Penry, who had, moreover, sealed their testimony with their blood; and side by side with Presbyterian criticism of the Church of England there stood the conception of the Church as a Gathered Church, composed of the elect whom God in each village and age called out of the midst of a naughty world to be his witness and faithful remnant, in which each local church was completely sovereign and autonomous, where there was no distinction of clergy and laity but all Church members were churchmen, the office of pastor being a distinction of function rather than of order, and in which the civil magistrate from the Justice of the Peace to the King had no authority or jurisdiction, save in so far as individual magistrates might be churchmen. Evidently even the full realization of the Millenary Petition would not reconcile Independency to the Established Church.

Furthermore, the beginning of the 17th century saw the domestication on English soil of another offshoot of Independency, the Church of the Baptists, the pioneers of which were John Smythe and Thomas Helwys, and the principal ground of whose divergence from the Independents was their conviction "that infant baptism was no baptism at all in the New Testament sense, but that baptism was commanded by Christ and was the basis of Church fellowship".[1]

The immediate outcome of the Millenary Petition was the summoning by royal authority of the Hampton Court Conference, at which episcopalians and petitioners were to examine the possibility of reconciliation between the *status quo* and the demands for reform and modification. Neither the course of that Conference nor the methods adopted by the King as moderator held out much promise of agreement. On 14 January 1604 there assembled on the Anglican side Archbishop Whitgift, eight bishops, six deans, the dean of the chapels royal, and two doctors of divinity; and on the Puritan side, four divines only, Drs Rainolds and Sparkes with Mr Knewstubbs and the Master of Emmanuel College, Cambridge (Laurence Chaderton).

Three sessions were held: at the first the King conferred with the conformists only; at the second he heard the objections of the Puritans, but in the presence

[1] E. A. Payne, *The Free Church Tradition in the Life of England*, pp. 34 f. (1944 edition).

of the Anglicans also; and finally at the third he informed the petitioners of the alterations in the Book of Common Prayer which the bishops by his command had made. There was evident point in the complaint of the Puritans that "the King sent for their divines, not to have their scruples satisfied, but his pleasure propounded; not that he might know what they would say, but they what he would do in the matter".[1] The consequential changes in the liturgy and government of the Church, even together with the order for the preparation of a new translation of the whole Bible, fell far short of the hopes and requests of the Millenary Petitioners; and thus the gulf between conformist and nonconformist was unbridged. This was an unhopeful beginning to a century of projects for "comprehension".

Meantime James was showing a like determination in the ecclesiastical affairs of his northern kingdom, which he sought to bring into line with the pattern of what he held to be the better established Church in England. Before his accession to the English crown he had appointed in 1600 three titular bishops in Scotland; but after his accession he was anxious to convert the titular into a real episcopate; and to this end in 1606 he summoned eight of the principal Presbyterian ministers to London to confer with him. The deputation was led by Andrew Melville, than whom episcopacy and James had no stouter adversary, whilst the episcopalian party in England was led by the equally redoubtable Archbishop Richard Bancroft, with whom Melville had crossed literary swords before. The various conferences produced no agreement; and resort was had to royal diplomacy in Scotland.

An assembly at Linlithgow in 1606, which claimed to be a lawful General Assembly, provided for a "constant moderator" in every presbytery, that existing bishops should be such moderators in their own presbyteries, and that moderators should be elected where they did not yet exist. Thus the bishops were integrated into the government of the Church, since they were also to be moderators of the provincial synods. In 1609 Parliament restored them to their former authority, dignity, prerogative, privileges, and jurisdiction; in 1610 a High Commission was set up in Scotland on the English model; and in the same year the General Assembly at St Andrews assented on behalf of the Church to the new episcopal powers.

There remained only the conversion of these superintendent-moderators into bishops by the bestowal on them in England of the *munus consecrationis*. When a query was raised by Bishop Lancelot Andrewes as to whether they should not first be ordained to the presbyterate according to the English Ordinal, Bancroft successfully resisted the suggestion, and it was decided that, to avoid reviving objections to the former claims of the subordination of the Scottish to the English Church, the Archbishops of Canterbury and York should not participate in the rite. Accordingly, on 21 October 1610 the three Scottish divines were consecrated privately in the Bishop of London's chapel by the Bishop of London and three other bishops. Thus the union of the two crowns had been followed by the union of Churches under episcopal government; and the problems of domestic union seemed to promise a solution by the enforcement of conformity in England and the imposition of episcopacy in Scotland. Moreover, the consecration to the episcopate *per saltum* of Scottish presbyters had set an important precedent for future reference.

[1] Thomas Fuller, *The Church History of Britain*, Book X, ed. J. S. Brewer, IV, pp. 303 f.

But James I was anxious to assert his ecclesiastical authority outside the boundaries of his two kingdoms; and to this end he welcomed the opportunity of ensuring that the Churches of England and Scotland were represented at the Synod of Dort.[1] To this quasi-ecumenical council of the Protestant Churches of the Continent, James dispatched delegates: Bishop George Carleton of Llandaff; Dr Joseph Hall, Dean of Exeter; Dr John Davenant, Lady Margaret Professor of Divinity at Cambridge; and Dr Samuel Ward, Master of Sidney Sussex College, Cambridge, as representing the Church of England; to whom was later added, as representing the Church of Scotland, Mr Walter Balcanquall, Fellow of Pembroke College, Cambridge.

The instructions given by their royal master embraced injunctions to "inure themselves to the practice of the Latin tongue" in order to increase their facility of speaking therein; to debate privately and agree upon all points at issue, and in case of any new matter arising in debate, to go apart in order to reach the like unanimity, "and this to be done agreeable to the Scriptures and the doctrine of the Church of England"; to advise the Churches represented at the Synod to exclude from the pulpit matters "which are the highest points of schools and not fit for vulgar capacity", to introduce no innovations in doctrine, but to hold fast to their formal Confessions, to preserve good correspondency with the other Reformed Churches by respecting their public Confessions; in case of "main opposition", to exercise their influence in favour of "positions moderately laid down which may tend to the mitigation of heat on both sides"; to maintain frequent correspondence with the King's ambassador through whom the King's further pleasure would be made known; and finally to conduct themselves according to "advice, moderation, and discretion".[2]

With private admonitions to the space of two hours from James, and with these formal instructions, the delegates reached Dort for the opening of proceedings on 3 November. Dr Hall retired during the course of the sessions owing to indisposition, and was replaced on 7 January 1619 by Dr Thomas Goad, one of the Archbishop of Canterbury's chaplains; and when on 20 April the Belgic Confession was introduced to determine the issues before the Synod, the Bishop of Llandaff in the name of the English delegates gave their approval to the doctrinal decrees, but protested formally against those concerning discipline, forasmuch as they asserted the principle of parity of ministers, which the Church of England did not accept and which, as Carleton contended, was neither according to the institution of Christ himself nor after the practice of the Apostolic Age. Notwithstanding, the British delegation signed the doctrinal decrees next after the President, the two Assessors of the President, and the two synodal Scribes. On their return home they were cordially received by the King, to whom also the States-General addressed a formal and fulsome letter of thanks for his condescension in sending representatives.

To Richard Baxter it appeared to be the case that "so far as I am able to judge . . . the Christian world since the days of the Apostles, had never a Synod of more excellent divines than the Westminster Assembly and the Synod of Dort". Thus to outward appearance James I had emphasized the complete agreement of the Churches of England and Scotland in the highest points of Calvinist doctrine with the foreign Reformed Churches, whilst stoutly maintaining episcopacy and repudiating the Presbyterian principle of parity of ministers. But James was already witnessing the influx of a new tide of theological opinion in England;

[1] See Chap. ii, p. 87.   [2] Thomas Fuller, op. cit., V, pp. 462 f.

and the Arminian tenets anathematized at Dort were to become the dominant tradition of the Laudian school of churchmanship, whose influence was waxing as the years of James I waned.

The reign of his son and successor, Charles I, indeed was to mark the watershed in the history of ecumenical relations during the 17th century; alike in respect of the domestic controversies between Episcopalian and Presbyterian in England and Scotland, and of the attitude of Anglicans towards the Protestant Churches of the Continent. In the British Isles, the increasing emphasis on episcopacy as of the *bene esse*, if not strictly of the *esse*, of the Church tended to drive a wedge between the established Churches at home and their Lutheran and Reformed allies abroad; whilst the political identification of the cause of episcopacy with that of monarchy led to the fall of the former with the defeat of the Crown in the first Civil War.

Even before the decisive events and influence of the civil wars, the ecclesiastical climate had begun to change. The Arminian school, by its emphasis upon the ministry of the Sacraments rather than upon that of the Word, and its eulogy of the Church of England as having preserved through its retention of episcopacy an uninterrupted succession from the ancient and the medieval Church, tended to raise barriers between itself and those churchmen, both at home and abroad, who held fast to Calvin's theology and Church order.

In Scotland in 1637 a revision of the Book of Common Prayer was published, whose general object was "the restoration to the Order for the Administration of Holy Communion of portions of the office which had been lost to the Church of England since the first Liturgy of King Edward VI".[1] Its Communion Office therefore bore "the marks of the patristic and liturgical study of Andrewes and his school, and also of their practical interest in the decent performance of divine worship". The determination of Charles I and his advisers to enforce the use of this book instead of Knox's book, and its consequent introduction into St Giles' Cathedral, Edinburgh, fired the train which led to the Bishops' War, and thence at short intervals to the quarrels between Charles I and the Long Parliament and to the beginning of civil war. Henceforth the cause of Episcopacy was lost in Scotland until the Restoration of Charles II, and Presbyterianism came back into possession of the field.

Within the Church of England itself the contest between the Laudian and the Puritan traditions found expression chiefly in the observance or non-observance of the "nocent ceremonies", since there could be no question of any serious modifications of liturgy or Church order. But the growing emphasis upon episcopacy had important repercussions. Even Joseph Hall, one of the delegates to the Synod of Dort, wrote in *Episcopacy by Divine Right*, of that form of Church polity that

> "for the main substance, it is now utterly indispensable, and must so continue to the world's end. Indispensable by any voluntary act; what inevitable necessity may do in such a case, we now dispute not; necessity hath dispensed with some immediately divine laws. Where that may be justly pleaded, we shall not be wanting both in our pity and our prayers."

[1] E. C. Ratcliff, "Christian Worship and Liturgy" in *The Study of Theology*, ed. K. E. Kirk, 1939, pp. 462 f.

This was a strong and positive doctrine of episcopacy; but it left a loophole for the foreign Reformed Churches by allowing that

> "they were forced to discard the office as well as the men; but yet the office because of the men; as popish, not as bishops; and to put themselves for the present into such a form of government, at a venture, as under which they might be sure without violent interruption to sow the seeds of the Gospel."[1]

Of much greater weight and influence was the attitude of Bishop Lancelot Andrewes towards the Presbyterian order of the Reformed Churches of the Continent. In his Letters to Molinaeus (Pierre du Moulin) he drew the same distinction as Hall between what was essential to the being and to the completeness of a Church:

> "But even if our order be admitted to be of divine authority, it does not follow that without it there can be no salvation, or that without it a Church cannot stand. Only a blind man could fail to see Churches standing without it. Only a man of iron could deny that salvation is to be found within them. We are not men of iron of that type; we set a wide distinction between the two things. Something which possesses divine authority may be lacking, at least in matters of outward governance, and yet salvation may remain unimpaired. .... Condemnation of one thing is not involved in preferring to it another thing which is better. We do not condemn your Church, if we recall it to another form of government, which was preferred by the whole of antiquity, to that form of government, in fact, which we enjoy."

This opinion, expressed in his *Responsio ad secundam Epistolam Molinaei*, was iterated in his *Answer to the Third Epistle*:

> "You ask whether your Churches have sinned against the divine authority. That I did not say. I said only that your Churches lacked something which has divine authority; but the fault is to be attributed not to you but to the evil of the times. For your France did not find kings so favourable as ours in Britain to the work of the reformation of the Church. But one day, when God grants better times, even that which is lacking can by God's grace be supplied. In the meantime, however, it was not right to abolish the name of bishop, which has been so regularly used in divine things. What advantage is there in abolishing the name, when the thing is retained? And the thing itself you have retained."[2]

Because of the prestige attaching to Andrewes' name, his judgement on the Reformed Churches was quoted frequently throughout his century, as indicating the Anglican insistence on episcopacy where it could be had, whilst allowing the *esse* of a Church to be present where historical necessity had prevented the maintenance of the episcopal order. The distinction between the name and thing (*nomen* and *res*) of episcopacy, with the suggestion that the Protestant Churches of the Continent had preserved the latter whilst relinquishing the former, was allowed even by William Laud in respect of the Lutherans, whom he differen-

---

[1] Joseph Hall, *Works*, X, pp. 152 f.
[2] L. Andrewes, *Opuscula*, pp. 191, 211 (tr. from the Latin).

tiated from the Reformed precisely in this point. For he rebutted the assertion that "all the reformed kirks" were Presbyterian in polity and order by asking whether the asserters

> "be so strait-laced as not to admit the Churches of Sweden and Denmark, and indeed all or most of the Lutherans, to be reformed Churches? For in Sweden they retain both the thing and name; and the governors of their churches are, and are called, bishops. And among other Lutherans the thing is retained, though not the name. For instead of bishops they are called superintendents, and instead of archbishops general superintendents. And yet even here too these names differ more in sound than in sense. For bishop is the same in Greek that superintendent is in Latin. Nor is this change very well liked by the learned. Howsoever, Luther since he would change the name, did yet very wisely, that he would leave the thing, and make choice of such a name as was not altogether unknown to the ancient church."[1]

Much discussion has been evoked by the question as to whether the Church of England before the Act of Uniformity of 1662 admitted ministers of the foreign Reformed Churches, ordained according to the Presbyterian manner, to hold benefices in England without reordination. In regard to benefices without cure of souls, a category including cathedral dignities such as deaneries and prebends, it is probable that instances of such tenure can be established. For these dignities could be held by laymen, and *a fortiori* by persons ordained in the foreign Reformed Churches; and not until the Act of Uniformity of 1662 was the possession of priest's orders required for cathedral dignities. Moreover, it must be remembered that such dignitaries were not required to celebrate the Holy Communion; or, if they did so, like William Whittingham, Dean of Durham, were liable to ecclesiastical process; and Archbishop Whitgift affirmed that Whittingham would have been deprived, had he not died *pendente lite*, unless he had procured a royal dispensation to the contrary. In like manner Whitgift refused to recognize the orders received abroad by Walter Travers, one of the leading Presbyterians of Elizabeth's time, and finally prohibited him from preaching, though his office of Reader at the Temple Church was in the gift of the benchers.

On the other hand, Whitgift's predecessor, Archbishop Grindal, through his vicar-general granted a licence to a Scottish Presbyterian minister, Mr John Morison, to preach and administer the sacraments throughout the province of Canterbury. The only authenticated case of a person in foreign Presbyterian orders having been instituted without episcopal ordination to a benefice with cure of souls is that of Peter De Laune, *ordinatus presbyter per doctores et professores Collegii de Leyden*, 26 June 1599. De Laune subsequently became minister of the Walloon congregation in Norwich. In 1628 Archbishop Abbot claimed the rectory of Redenhall as his Option on the consecration of Bishop Francis White to the See of Norwich; and upon its vacancy in 1629 he nominated De Laune to the Earl of Arundel, in whose presentation it lay. Accordingly, De Laune received institution on 12 November 1629 from the same bishop; and he remained there during the episcopates of White, Corbet, Wren, and Montagu, nor was his possession disturbed by Archbishop Laud's metropolitical visitation in 1635. But although this case is authenticated by Bishop Wren's Consignation

---

[1] W. Laud, *Works*, III, p. 386.

Book at his visitation of 1636, it would be temerarious to lay too much stress upon an isolated example. The paucity of such cases illustrates the insistence of the Church of England upon episcopal ordination as the indispensable qualification for ministry in its service.

With the Bishops' War which resulted from the ill-starred attempt to introduce the Scottish Prayer Book, Charles I was driven to call a Parliament; and, after the failure of the Short Parliament, the famous Long Parliament assembled in 1640 to reform what it deemed amiss in the royal administration of Church and State. Inevitably the issue of episcopacy was to the fore; but the rising temper of the time was too strong to allow of an impartial and dispassionate consideration of the claims of the bishops, apart from their fatal association with the Crown. Two schemes for the reduction, yet retention, of episcopacy were debated in the House of Lords in 1641; and their terms are interesting as being indicative of the possible lines of compromise between bishops and presbyters.

Bishop John Williams of Lincoln produced a project of church discipline in ten articles, of which the most important provided

> "that every bishop shall have twelve assistants besides the dean and chapter; four to be chosen by the king, four by the Lords, and four by the Commons, for jurisdiction and ordination; and that in all vacancies, these assistants, with the dean and chapter, shall present to the king three of the ablest divines in the diocese, who shall choose one to be bishop."

Archbishop Ussher's device "for the reduction of episcopacy into the form of synodical government, received in the ancient Church" proposed to limit the powers of diocesan episcopacy by its compulsory association with suffragan bishops and synods of presbyters. Particularly he wished to authorize the rector and churchwardens of every parish to admonish and reprove evil-livers, with power, if they would not amend, to suspend them from the Lord's Supper and to present them to the next monthly synod. This synod was to be constituted by the appointment of a suffragan bishop for each rural deanery who should convoke a monthly assembly of all the incumbents of the deanery, at which decisions should be made by a majority of votes. Similarly, diocesan synods should be held once or twice a year, for revision of the transactions of the monthly synods and for the consideration of other matters; in which the diocesan bishop (or one of his suffragans appointed by him in his absence) should preside; and which should embrace all the suffragan bishops and at least some representatives of the incumbents of each deanery. Finally, there should be a provincial synod composed of all diocesan and suffragan bishops with representatives of the clergy of every diocese, and presided over by the Primate of the province or a diocesan bishop of his appointment. It should be held triennially; and Ussher was anxious, if Parliament were in session, to combine the two provincial synods into one national council to receive appeals from inferior synods, to examine their acts, and to consider "all ecclesiastical constitutions which concern the state of the Church out of the whole nation".[1]

In calmer times, when king and bishops were less suspect, these or similar proposals might have been accepted and tried; but they had little chance of success in 1641; instead, the extremer counsels which favoured a root-and-branch extirpation of episcopacy, followed by proscription of the Book of Com-

[1] Daniel Neal, *History of the Puritans*, ed. J. Toulmin, II, pp. 400 f.

mon Prayer, prevailed. Moreover, the comparative ill-success of the parliament-
ary forces in the early stages of the first Civil War compelled an alliance with the
Scots; as the price of which the northern allies demanded the supersession of
Episcopacy by Presbyterianism.

At long last, therefore, the day of which Elizabethan presbyterianly-minded
ministers of the Church of England had dreamed was come; and to the Westminster Assembly in July 1643 "from every county came grave, elderly, learned
men, episcopally ordained under Elizabeth or James, beneficed clergy who
had conformed for years to the Prayer Book and worn their surplice. . . . These
divines, now that they were free to mould the Church after their will, showed
that their bent was Presbyterian."[1] With the exception of the Scottish commissioners (and even of these, three of the four ministerial members had been
episcopally ordained), all the members had received episcopal ordination, and
almost all had been conformists. Their number of 121 divines even included
four bishops and five doctors of divinity (though only one or two of these
attended in defiance of the King's prohibition); and they were reinforced by
thirty lay assessors—ten peers and twenty commoners.

Now the policy of "tarrying for the magistrate" promised to bear refreshing,
if tardy, fruit; and the aspirations of the authors of the Elizabethan *Admonitions
to Parliament* seemed on the verge of realization. The positive work done by the
Assembly was important on any reckoning. Its sessions lasted from the summer
of 1643 to the autumn of 1647; its *Confession of Faith*, and its *Larger* and *Shorter
Catechisms*, have established their position on their own merits; and its *Directory
for the Public Worship of God* has been described as "the first comprehensive
attempt to find an order of worship which would prove acceptable to the whole
body of Puritans, Presbyterian and Independent".[2] Negatively, its enemies were
dispossessed by the abolition of episcopacy and by the prohibition of the Book
of Common Prayer in January 1645. Here we may appropriately cite Richard
Baxter's eulogy on the Assembly:

> "The divines there congregate were men of eminent learning and godli-
> ness, and ministerial abilities and fidelity; and being not worthy to be one
> of them myself, I may the more freely speak that truth which I know, even
> in the face of malice and envy, that, as far as I am able to judge by the
> information of all history of that kind, and by any other evidences left us,
> the Christian world since the days of the Apostles, had never a synod of
> more excellent divines (taking one thing with another) than this Synod and
> the Synod of Dort were."[3]

But by a singular irony of history the Presbyterian triumph was destined to be
short-lived. From the outset the House of Commons refused to entrust the
"power of the keys" to spiritual authority alone, but insisted on allowing an
appeal from the decisions of ecclesiastical tribunals to the High Court of Parliament. Nor did the Scottish-Parliamentary military alliance work out as had been
intended by the Scots. For if a major part of the victory at Marston Moor (1644)
rested with the Scottish soldiers, at Naseby (1645) it was Cromwell's New Model

---

[1] E. W. Watson, *The Church of England*, pp. 165 f.
[2] Horton Davies, *The Worship of the English Puritans*, p. 141.
[3] M. Sylvester, *Reliquiae Baxterianae*, I, p. 73.

Army which won the success; and the first principle of this army was liberty of conscience and the toleration of Independency.

During the Commonwealth and Protectorate the framework of a national establishment of Christianity was maintained: the parochial system being preserved, the ministry supported by the traditional compulsory payment of tithe, private patronage being respected, and Cromwell himself administering the former Crown patronage. The purging of the existing ministry was undertaken by local Committees of Ejectors, and the modern editor of Walker's *Sufferings of the Clergy* has estimated that the number of benefices under sequestration between 1634 and 1660 totalled 2,425.[1] The vacancies thus created were filled principally by "three godly sorts of men", Presbyterian, Independent, and Baptist ministers, who carried the certificate of a national Committee of Triers, which judged not by academic learning, nor by any particular standard of theological confession, nor by form of ordination, but by godly life and conversation. Baxter held that these Committees

> "did abundance of good to the Church. They saved many a congregation from ignorant, ungodly, drunken teachers. That sort of men that intended no more in the ministry than to say a sermon as readers say their common prayers, and so patch up a few good words together to talk the people asleep with on Sunday, and all the rest of the week go with them to the alehouse and harden them in their sin; and that sort of ministers that either preached against a holy life, or preached as men that were never acquainted with it; all those that used the ministry but as a common trade to live by, and were never likely to convert a soul; all these they usually rejected, and in their stead admitted of any that were able, serious preachers, and lived a godly life, of what tolerable opinion soever they were. So that though they were many of them somewhat partial for the Independents, Separatists, Fifth-Monarchy-men, and Anabaptists, and against the Prelatists and Arminians, yet so great was the benefit above the hurt which they brought to the Church, that many thousands of souls blessed God for the faithful ministers whom they let in."[2]

The result was certainly a remarkable experiment in comprehension, and in this it reflected faithfully the sentiments of Cromwell himself, who was distinguished beyond the great majority of his contemporaries by his toleration of diversity of opinion. His principle was expressed in a speech to the second Protectorate Parliament:

> "If men will profess—be they those under Baptism, be they those of the Independent judgement simply, or of the Presbyterian judgement—in the name of God, encourage them, countenance them; so long as they do plainly continue to be thankful to God, and to make use of the liberty given them to enjoy their own consciences. For, as it was said to-day, this is the peculiar Interest all this while contended for."[3]

Not content with such a latitude within the official ministry of the Church, he extended by executive action practical toleration to those too extreme even

---

[1] A. G. Matthews, *Walker Revised*, London, 1948, pp. xiv f.
[2] M. Sylvester, *Reliquiae Baxterianae*, I, p. 72.
[3] Oliver Cromwell, *Letters and Speeches*, ed. Thomas Carlyle, Speech V.

to be included within his settlement, and particularly to the Quakers and the Jews. If his religious establishment lacked unity in doctrine, ordination, and liturgy, it was designed to express a unity of spirit in the bond of peace between all sorts of godly ministers and people. Moreover, it had one all-important consequence for the future history of England. The circumstance that it was "not so much a Church as a confederation of Christian sects working together for righteousness" enabled it to provide such a seed-ground and protection for nonconformity "that the storm which followed the Restoration had no power to root it up".[1] When the problem of ecclesiastical reconstruction came to be examined after the Restoration, it was apparent that, in addition to the old issue of the possibility of "comprehension" of Presbyterian and Anglican within one national Church, there was the new problem of the necessity of a parallel "indulgence" or toleration for the various Protestant sects.

3. ECUMENISM AT HOME AND ABROAD

Ecumenical sentiment during the first half of the 17th century did not find expression only in projects for home reunion; and no apostle of Protestant unity was more indefatigable or resourceful than John Dury.[2] His career indeed was so ecumenical, or cosmopolitan, that it is difficult to decide to which Church and country his religious biography properly belongs, whilst his ecclesiastical allegiance defies definition; for he received first Presbyterian ordination by the Presbytery at Dort; then Anglican ordination at the hands of Bishop Hall of Exeter, one of the English delegates to the Synod of Dort, and presentation to a benefice in England; later he was a member of the Westminster Assembly and took the Solemn League and Covenant; and again with the triumph of Independency he took the Engagement also.

This comprehensive confessional charity was illustrative of the weakness no less than the strength of his ecclesiastical position and policy; for whilst testifying his zeal to become all things to all men, if by any means he might gain some for his schemes of unity, it brought suspicion on his motives, so that he could secure no countenance whatever in England after the Restoration.

Dury believed himself to be "a peacemaker without partiality", and in many important respects his work was an anticipation of later 17th-century attempts at union. "My aim shall be none other", he averred, "but to stir up . . . thoughts of brotherly kindnesse, of meekness, and of peace; to the end that some wayes may be taken up, which will help to reconcile the Affections of many divided about Circumstantials; to preserve and keep entire the Unity which remains about Fundamentals; and to prevent or cure the manifold Misprisions, which increase our confusions, and obstruct the Remedies of our diseases."[3]

Here may be caught the authentic note of distinguishing between fundamentals and non-essentials which was the root-principle of the ecumenical minds of his age. Parallel therewith was his emphasis on practical divinity as more important than academic theology:

"From all of which we shall inferre this Conclusion: That the studie of Practical Divinitie, is of far greater concernment unto all, and far more to

[1] C. H. Firth, *Oliver Cromwell*, pp. 368 f.   [2] See also Chap. ii, pp. 97 ff.
[3] J. M. Batten, *John Dury: Advocate of Christian Reunion*, p. 105.

[be] heeded, esteemed, and entertained in the Schools of the Prophets, then the studie of contemplative mysteries and notions of Divinitie; whereupon Controversial matters are ordinarily attendants. . . . This then is the compleat end of Practical Divinitie, to teach men the wisdom which is profitable unto the salvation of their souls, and the direction of the whole conversation to God's will; that they may be enabled whatever they do, to do all in God by walking in his light."[1]

Similarly, he was emphatic in his conviction of the close connection between the co-operation of the Churches in Christian missions amongst infidels and the growth of a spirit of unity amongst themselves. The practical applications of his principles were equally interesting, if somewhat disconcerting to many of his contemporaries. Thus he described his decision to receive episcopal ordination in England as follows:

"As for the Church of England . . . I did look upon it as a Church of Christ, true in respect of the doctrine professed therein, and eminent for all spiritual gifts bestowed upon it; that I judged the government thereof by bishops with indifference, and that I took them as men commissioned by the king to be his delegates. . . . I did not think that the Ordination which I had to a particular place beyond the Seas, by men who were under another kind of Church-Government could sufficiently authorize me to administer a public charge in this place, and under this Government, where the Law of the Land had provided another way of authorizing men to their places."[2]

Again, whilst acting as Anglican chaplain at Rotterdam, in order to unite the diverse elements in his congregation, he made use of a Dutch translation of the Book of Common Prayer, though he did not think himself bound to a strict compliance with its forms of divine service:

"I therefore intending to unite them in the substance of their Gospell worship, followed a middle way, neither strictly formal, nor altogether informall; which did not offend the discreet and sober; but did not answer the expectation of the fiercer sort of either side, who were neither fully displeased nor well pleased with my moderation. . . . And by this rule I made use of the Leiturgie at Rotterdam, neither laying it wholly aside in respect of the substance of the prayers; nor binding myself to the whole formality of it."[3]

It is worthy of passing notice that Dury's ordination at Exeter seems to have been to the priesthood, without mention of his prior admission to the diaconate. For it is stated that he was ordained by Bishop Hall in his cathedral on 24 February 1634 "with the imposition of the hands of several presbyters together with himself", which establishes that he received the order of priesthood.[4]

Notwithstanding the failure of his efforts to persuade all Protestant Churches to adopt a common confession of faith and to devise a form of polity combining

---

[1] J. M. Batten, *John Dury: Advocate of Christian Reunion*, p. 132.
[2] Ibid., pp. 47 f.   [3] Ibid., p. 99.
[4] In the Anglican Churches, at the Ordering of Deacons the bishop alone lays hands on the candidate. At the Ordering of Priests the Rubric lays it down that "The Bishop with the Priests present shall lay their hands severally upon the head of every one that receiveth the Order of Priesthood".

Episcopal, Presbyterian, and Independent elements, tribute cannot be withheld from his self-denying devotion and "vow of perseverance in the worke" to which his life was dedicated. Nor can it be doubted that, though born out of due time, he expressed the principles of true ecumenicity in his affirmation:

> "One position is laid as the ground-worke of all this negotiation, which is that the onely Meanes to reunite devided Protestants, and knit their Churches together in a bond of brotherly love, is to bring them to make a publick profession of one and the same Confession of Faith in respect to Fundamentalls. For I find it to be agreed upon, and yielded on all sides, that if the Fundamentall Truthes of Faith and Practice be acknowledged and professed by two Churches, that those Churches ought for this cause to profess sisterly love one towards another, and they ought not for some differences in things not fundamentall, to break the unitie of the spirit through unprofitable debatements."[1]

The period of the Interregnum, which had seen such novel experiments in ecclesiastical government and in education, had also witnessed other developments in the relationship of Anglican churchmen with other Churches. Trading relations with the Middle East, of which the foundation in 1579 of the Levant Company was a symbol and agent, had already led to the appointment of Anglican chaplains to minister to the needs of merchants and traders, and therewith also to a cultivation of interest in and sympathy with the Eastern Orthodox Churches. The *rapprochement* with the Eastern Churches which had begun by chaplains to trading stations received a further impetus through the wanderings of individual eminent Anglicans on the continent of Europe and beyond, during their exile in the period of the Interregnum. Amongst the most influential and important of these exiles was Isaac Basire, chaplain at Smyrna, whose travels took him from France to Italy, Greece, Aleppo, and Jerusalem; whilst the duties of chaplain at Aleppo were discharged from 1655 to 1670 by Robert Frampton, a future Bishop of Gloucester and one of the Non-jurors. There was little exaggeration in John Evelyn's tribute to Basire as "that great traveller, or rather, French Apostle, who had been planting the Church of England in divers parts of the Levant and Asia".[2]

Basire's letters cast occasional revealing light on his own indefatigable endeavours to propagate an understanding of Anglicanism amongst the Orthodox Churches, and also on the measure of success which could attend such an individual venture, and on his own impressions of these Churches. His methods were as interesting as individual. At Zante he disseminated a Greek translation of the Catechism of the Book of Common Prayer, "the product whereof was so notable that it drew envy and consequently persecution upon me from the Latins". When the Metropolitan of Achaia invited him "to preach twice in Greek at a meeting of some of his bishops and clergy, and it was well taken", Basire likewise left a copy of the Anglican Catechism with his host. At Aleppo he "had frequent conversation with the Patriarch of Antioch", with whom he left "a copy of our Catechism translated into Arabic"! In Jerusalem he enjoyed such friendly personal relations with the Greek Patriarch, that the latter "(the better to express his desire of communion with our old Church of England by

[1] J. M. Batten, *John Dury: Advocate of Christian Reunion*, p. 74.
[2] John Evelyn, *Diary* (10 July 1661).

me declared unto him) gave me his Bull of patriarchal seal in a blank (which is their way of credence) besides many other respects".

With the Latins also he enjoyed friendly discourse about "the validity of our ordination"; they "received him most courteously into their own convent, though he did openly profess himself a priest of the Church of England"; and at his parting "the pope's own vicar . . . gave him his diploma in parchment under his own hand and public seal, in it styling him Sacerdotem Ecclesiae Anglicanae and S. Theologiae Doctorem". After a visit to Mesopotamia, Basire procured a Turkish translation of the Catechism for transmission there!

As a further proof of the catholicity of Basire's sympathies, in Constantinople he wished that he might receive instructions from the exiled Charles II to discuss with the Patriarch "proposal of communion with the Greek Church (*salva conscientia et honore*)"; adding that "to such a communion, together with a convenient reformation of some grosser errors, it hath been my constant design to dispose and incline them". After this it was still more remarkable that he should have settled for a few years at the invitation of the Prince of Transylvania as professor of theology in the Protestant faculty of the University of Alba Julia (Weissembourg).[1]

> "All this is outwardly very little. But apart from the demonstration of the divine power, in uplifting means in themselves so frail and feeble, especially among a people like this, which still walks in darkness and dwells in the shadow of death, our English Martyrology makes me hope that something will come of it, since indeed the English Reformation began with a simple catechism."[2]

Notwithstanding the small scale of such individual ventures, cumulatively they exercised a considerable influence, thanks largely to the presence at Constantinople after the Restoration of a series of eminent Anglican chaplains, Drs Thomas Smith and John Covel and Mr Edward Brown, and to the interest of Sir Paul Ricaut, secretary to the Ambassador to the Porte and afterwards Consul at Smyrna. At any rate this influence was considerable in England, where the books of Smith and Covel on the Eastern Orthodox Church aroused a wide interest.

Particularly, this revived knowledge of the East helped to bring about a perceptible shift of emphasis in Anglican tradition on the importance of episcopacy. The chaplains brought home tidings of a venerable and ancient Church which, whilst determinedly hostile to Rome, had preserved its immemorial doctrine and worship, and had known nothing of the storms of the Western Reformation. In their turn, like Basire, they had propagated the idea of the orthodoxy of the Church of England, and had sought for points of contact between their several traditions. Naturally these were most readily found in the Book of Common Prayer and the Ordinal; and especially in the retention in both communions of episcopacy and their common repudiation of the papacy. There resulted an appreciable heightening in Anglican apologetic of the value of episcopacy, and an increased emphasis on the continuity of doctrine and polity which it represented.

[1] W. N. Darnell, *The Correspondence of Isaac Basire, with a Memoir of his Life*, London, 1831, pp. 115–20.
[2] Ibid., p. 124. Tr. from the French.

This tendency was reinforced by other experiences of Anglican exiles during the Interregnum, particularly on the part of those divines who followed the fugitive Stuart court in France; and it exercised an important influence on their relations both with Roman Catholics and with the foreign Reformed Churches. On the one hand, the Anglican exiles, from Charles II downwards, and especially his clergy who were impoverished and driven almost to begging their bread, were subjected to constant pressure of proselytism from the Papists. On the other, the Huguenots expected them to signify their sense of the common front of Protestants against Rome by joining with them in divine worship and in the Sacrament of the Lord's Supper. Moreover, Charles II himself was similarly placed in a strait betwixt two painful alternatives: his hopes of a return to England seemed dependent on a revulsion of royalist feeling on the part of Presbyterians in Britain; yet at the same time he was dependent on the alms of Roman Catholic sovereigns abroad. There was a constant danger, as there were ubiquitous temptations, to opt for one or other of these practical supports, at the expense of the poor Anglican Church, which was anathema to both. Hence his faithful clergy were imbued with a new sense of the urgency and imperative necessity of upholding the *via media* as their only anchor and hope of survival; and therewith of refusing the overtures of Papists and Huguenots alike.

The relations between Canterbury and Rome were naturally the chief point in which the Laudian school differed from its Elizabethan predecessors. Hooker indeed had refused to accept the Puritan contention that whatever had been used by Rome was forbidden to Churches of the Reformation:

"To say that in nothing they may be followed which are of the Church of Rome were violent and extreme. Some things they do in that they are men, in that they are wise men and Christian men some things, some things in that they are men misled and blinded with error. As far as they follow reason and truth, we fear not to tread the selfsame steps wherein they have gone, and to be their followers. Where Rome keepeth that which is ancienter and better, others whom we much more affect leaving it for newer and changing it for worse; we had rather follow the perfections of them whom we like not, than in defects resemble them whom we love."[1]

Similarly, he held that

". . . touching those main parts of Christian truth wherein they constantly still persist, we gladly acknowledge them to be of the family of Jesus Christ; and our hearty prayer unto God Almighty is, that they may at length (if it be his will) so yield to frame and reform themselves, that no distraction remain in anything, but that we all may with one heart and one mouth glorify God the Father of our Lord and Saviour, whose Church we are."[2]

During Hooker's lifetime, indeed, political conditions made almost impossible any impartial and dispassionate survey of the questions dividing Roman and Anglican; but with the accession of the Stuart house, new ecclesiastical and political tendencies brought them to the fore.

It would be an exaggeration to describe the polemical interchanges of James I

[1] R. Hooker, *Of the Laws of Ecclesiastical Polity*, V, xxviii, 1.   [2] Ibid., III, i, 10.

and Bellarmine, or of Laud and Fisher, as *prolegomena* to reunion; but during the reign of Charles I, Christopher Davenport, a convert from Anglicanism who in religion assumed the name of Franciscus a Sancta Clara, published in 1634 a treatise on some of the principal theological issues dividing Rome and Protestants, *Deus, Natura, Gratia*; in which he examined the teaching of the Anglican formularies, and appended a summary of Anglican teaching on other points. In this examination he approved nineteen of the Thirty-nine Articles and parts of five others as Catholic, and consonant with Scripture and with the tradition of the Fathers and Councils; to nine Articles and halves of two others he allowed a favourable interpretation; whilst six Articles and parts of three others seemed to him beyond his capacity to construe favourably. The treatise was at most an individual *ballon d'essai*, which might enlighten Roman circles on the differences between the Church of England and the Protestant dissenters, and thus begin a long process of education.

Some attention may here be given to those Articles which even the patience of Davenport could not reconcile with Roman Catholic teaching.

Article VI, "Of the Sufficiency of the Holy Scriptures for Salvation", with its distinction of authority between the Canonical Books and the Apocrypha, seemed to him to approximate to heresy. Article XIX, "Of the Church", he held to be inadequate, though true so far as it went, since it did not exclude a more precise definition of the Church. To Article XX, "Of the Authority of the Church", he appended an interpretation that the Church might exercise its authority so to interpret Holy Scripture as to make explicit what was implicit in its text.

On General Councils (Article XXI), he asserted that their decrees in matters of faith, forasmuch as they did not create but only declared belief, were inerrant in so far as they made explicit what had hitherto been only implicit in the deposit of faith. Article XXII, "Of Purgatory", was yet more difficult, but Davenport's ingenuity was not to be defeated; the "Romish doctrine" condemned by the Article was identified with unofficial interpretations as distinct from the official interpretations of the Roman Church.

On the Sacraments (Article XXV), the first two paragraphs were held to be acceptable; whilst the third, differentiating "those five commonly called Sacraments" from the two Gospel Sacraments, was not unacceptable, in so far as it did no more than make a distinction in the authority and importance of the various ordinances. It was not heretical to question whether Confirmation and Unction were of dominical institution. The condemnation of Transubstantiation in Article XXVIII might seem wholly incompatible with the doctrine of Trent; but Anglican Eucharistic doctrine, as expounded by Andrewes and Montagu, is found to be reconcilable with it. Article XXXI, "Of the one Oblation of Christ finished upon the Cross", again presented great difficulties: but Davenport argued that the Article condemned only distortions of Catholic doctrine and adduced Andrewes and Montagu as witnesses to an Anglican doctrine of the Eucharistic sacrifice.

Perhaps the most important of all Davenport's admissions were those which related to Article XXXVI, "Of the Consecration of Bishops and Ministers". The Ordinal of Edward VI was accepted as sufficient for the validity of Holy Orders; and since the Form for the Ordaining of Priests conveys authority to dispense all the sacraments, the power to offer sacrifice is implied therein. Nevertheless, the Orders thus conveyed were irregular, since they diverged from the Pontifical of the Roman Church.

On Article XXXVII it was observed that the "power of the keys" could in no circumstances be committed to laymen, though the authority of jurisdiction might well be granted to them by the Pope; and the powers claimed for the King of England were no greater than those possessed by the sovereigns of France. The denial by the Article of papal jurisdiction in England might be interpreted as relating to the temporal power, extending to ecclesiastical power only during the period of schism between Rome and England.

Davenport's detailed examination of the Articles of Religion, though of course only the work of a private theologian, is of considerable interest as marking the first attempt from the side of Rome towards a theological reconciliation of the Anglican Articles with the Council of Trent. Although the reader may agree with the comments of a recent writer that Davenport's exegesis *a vraiment été laborieuse, et peu naturelle en certain cas*,[1] his bold essay was notable in its own day, and interesting as an anticipation of the later parallel commentary of the Gallican theologian, Dr Du Pin, in his correspondence with Archbishop Wake.[2] Even two such swallows do not make a summer; but they may presage the coming of a gentler climate in the relations between the separated traditions of Rome and Canterbury.

The arrival in England of a Roman agent, the Oratorian Gregorio Panzani,[3] gave an adventitious importance to the publication of Davenport's book. But Panzani was authorized to report, not to negotiate; and Rome was interested only in the possibility of concessions in matters of discipline, not in jurisdiction or doctrine. Moreover, Laud was opposed almost as much to Rome as to Geneva; and though Panzani showed considerable insight and ingenuity in the reports which he sent to Rome of the theological sympathies of the several English bishops, not even the foundation of a formal negotiation was established. The subsequent experiences of Anglican exiles during the Interregnum sharpened rather than softened their antipathies to Rome; though the Royal Martyr's two sons, Charles II and James II, were to add to the complexities of the post-Restoration religious position in Great Britain, the one by his crypto-conversion and the other by his open espousal of Roman Catholicism.

4. RESTORATION TO REVOLUTION

With the restoration of the Stuart line in the person of Charles II in 1660, the first ecclesiastical problem awaiting solution was that of the possibility of "comprehending" Presbyterian and Episcopalian in the Church settlement. At first prospect, the position of the Presbyterians seemed strong; they had a majority in the Convention Parliament, and they were supposed to have the support of General Monk, the principal agent in England of the Restoration. Moreover, they had had time during the Commonwealth to repent of their overthrow of Episcopacy and the Book of Common Prayer, since their own substitution therefor of the Presbyterian order and the liturgical and confessional standards of the Westminster Assembly had been sadly short-lived. To many leading Pres-

---

[1] "Was indeed laborious, and in certain cases forced": Maurice Nédoncelle, *Trois aspects du problème anglo-catholique au XVIIème siècle*, Paris, 1951, p. 95.
[2] See later, pp. 154 ff.
[3] See H. R. T. Brandreth, "Grégoire Panzani et l'idéal de la réunion sous le règne de Charles Ier d'Angleterre", *Irénikon*, Tome XXI, 1948, pp. 32–47, 179–92.

byterians, Independency seemed a greater enemy than Anglicanism; nor was the principle of toleration generally accepted by either Episcopalian or Presbyterian.

It is still a moot question whether the Presbyterian party might not have succeeded if they had insisted on extracting their own religious conditions from Charles II as a precondition of his restoration. What is certain is that the Declaration of Breda (with its general promise of "a liberty to tender consciences, and that no man shall be disquieted or called in question for differences of opinion in matters of religion, which do not disturb the peace of the kingdom; and that we shall be ready to consent to such an Act of Parliament as, upon mature deliberation, shall be offered to us, for the full granting that indulgence") was too imprecise to guarantee anything, especially when the Parliament which regulated the ecclesiastical settlement proved to be the ultra-Royalist and Anglican Cavalier Parliament.

More promising seemed to be the King's Declaration concerning Ecclesiastical Affairs on 25 October 1660; in which Charles professed his satisfaction to find "the most able and principal asserters of the presbyterian opinions" to be "neither enemies . . . to episcopacy or liturgy, but modestly to desire such alterations in either as, without shaking foundations, might best allay the present distempers". Accordingly, having judged that "they all approve episcopacy, they all approve a set form of liturgy, and they all disapprove and dislike the sin of sacrilege and the alienation of the revenue of the church", the Declaration adumbrated a series of concessions which might prove effectual to the healing of the schism; including the nomination to the episcopate of "men of learning, virtue, and piety" (bishoprics being actually offered to Baxter, Calamy, and Reynolds), who would "be frequent preachers . . . and preach very often in some church of their diocese"; the appointment of suffragan bishops to assist the diocesan bishops in their administration; the compulsory association of presbyters with bishops in the offices of ordination and jurisdiction, such presbyters being drawn in equal numbers from the cathedral chapters and by election of the diocesan clergy; the performance of Confirmation "rightly and solemnly, by the information and with the consent of the minister of the place"; the constitution of a commission, composed of "an equal number of learned divines of both persuasions" to revise the Liturgy and Canons; and finally the permission to disuse the "nocent ceremonies" during the interim period before the report of the commission.[1]

From such a programme much might be expected; but the result belied hope. Side by side with the political restoration went the restoration of episcopacy in the Church and of the Bench in the House of Lords, the summoning of Convocation, and the appointment of bishops to vacant sees (only Reynolds of the Presbyterian party accepting a bishopric, and on the terms of the Declaration); so that when the Convention Parliament gave place to the Cavalier without any statutory safeguards having been enacted for the Presbyterian position, it was plain that the Anglicans had won hands down. In point of fact, the Savoy Conference met too late to affect the ecclesiastical settlement.

"A meeting at the Savoy between divines of the two schools in the spring of 1660 would have been different from such a meeting in the spring of 1661. Something at least like equal terms might have been secured at the

[1] E. Cardwell, *Documentary Annals of the Reformed Church of England*, II, pp. 285–301.

former date, but it is plain that afterwards the men of Geneva stood no chance with those of Canterbury. Episcopacy and the Liturgy were in possession."[1]

Some responsibility for the failure of the Savoy Conference may be laid at the door of Richard Baxter, who allowed Gilbert Sheldon to manoeuvre him into a disadvantageous tactical position by consenting to marshal every conceivable objection and amendment to the Book of Common Prayer, instead of concentrating on the few essential changes and leaving unessentials aside; thereby giving plausible ground for the allegation that he sought not compromise but complete victory. But there can be little doubt that the issue of the Church settlement at the Restoration was predetermined by agreement between the returned Anglican exiles and Clarendon. The form and content of the religious settlement was decided, not by those Anglicans who had stayed at home and some of whom had conformed during the Commonwealth, but by the exiled divines, whose experiences abroad had sharpened their antipathy to both Rome and Geneva, and whose resolve was to tread straitly the *via media*, be it never so narrow and arduous a path. The revision of the Liturgy was therefore undertaken by Convocation, and accepted without change by Parliament: from the standpoint of the Presbyterians its two chief obstacles were the requirement of episcopal ordination on the one hand and a strict and unvarying conformity to the Book of Common Prayer on the other.

On St Bartholomew's Day 1662, therefore, the exodus took place; and some 1,760 incumbents were deprived of their benefices for non-conformity to the requirements of Prayer Book and Ordinal.[2] This decisive event had one consequence of the utmost importance. The Presbyterians now found themselves, willy-nilly, in the same position as the Sects; and their religious future was bound up indissolubly with that of Independents and Baptists. Henceforth, though ideas of "comprehension" lingered for a generation, and several projects to that end were discussed, the Presbyterians were committed also to obtaining an "indulgence" or toleration for their fellow-dissenters. Moreover, the problem of Presbyterian ordinations became a new and intractable element in all discussions concerning the healing of internal divisions.

A further influential consequence of the Restoration settlement and of the virtual exclusion of dissenters from the Universities of Oxford and Cambridge was the provision of new means of education for the sons of dissenters and for the ministry of the dissenting Churches. In part this was discharged by the Dissenting Academies, which have an honourable and distinguished place in the history of English education, since they introduced the teaching of what might be called "modern subjects" in history, philosophy, languages, and science. But in part the need was met by the migration of intending pastors to Continental universities (as well as to those of Scotland) for their theological education, particularly to the United Provinces. By this means contact and correspondence were maintained between English dissenters and their European brethren, and English philosophy and theology were fructified by their Continental counterparts.

[1] John Stoughton, *The Church of the Restoration*, p. 160. (Vol. III of *A History of Religion in England*.)
[2] A. G. Matthews, *Calamy Revised*, p. xiii.

If the Presbyterians were dissatisfied with the settlement of the Church of England, they had as little cause for satisfaction in the progress of events in Scotland. Charles II, indeed, in his days of adversity had taken the Covenants; and there were other and stronger political reasons against the attempt to restore Episcopacy and overthrow Presbyterianism in his northern kingdom. But the fervour of royalism prevailed over caution, and it was decided that bishops should be reintroduced into the Church of Scotland. Moreover, the precedent of James I's reign, when bishops had been consecrated for Scotland without their previous ordination to the diaconate and priesthood, was not now to be followed; for Sharp and Leighton, not having been ordained deacon and presbyter, were required first to receive such ordination before being consecrated to the episcopate. Thus in Scotland an episcopate was superimposed upon a Presbyterian clergy; yet "no attempt was made to impose the condition of episcopal ordination upon the existing clergy in general".[1] Indeed, when the Scottish bishops returned home, "soon after their arrival, six other bishops were consecrated; but not ordained priests and deacons". The result was a somewhat uncertain amalgam of episcopacy and presbytery; for "so the whole church had a face of unity, while all sat together in the same judicatories, though upon different principles".[2]

Notwithstanding the rigour of the ecclesiastical settlement and the persecuting character of the so-called "Clarendon Code", leading divines of both the Episcopalian and Presbyterian persuasions in north and south Britain cherished the hope of the prevalence of more irenic sentiments; and during the generation between the restoration and the final expulsion of the Stuart dynasty, various endeavours to resuscitate the ideal of "comprehension" were made.

In Scotland Archbishop Robert Leighton was both by temper and policy a convinced champion of such projects; and in 1670 he made a resolute attempt to bring them to a successful issue. As bases of an accommodation between Episcopalians and Presbyterians, he proposed: that the Church should be governed by the bishops and their presbyters conjointly in their synods; that bishops should merely act as presidents and in matters both of jurisdiction and of ordination should be guided by the majority of their presbyters; that the presbyters should be allowed to make a declaration that they submitted to the bishops only for the sake of peace; that the bishops should not claim a negative vote over the decisions of their presbyters in synods; and that provincial synods should sit triennially, or oftener if the king should summon them, with power to receive complaints against the bishops and to censure them. This scheme, whilst departing from the principle of parity of ministers, reduced the authority of bishops so greatly that it provoked from Sharp the protest "that episcopacy was to be undermined, since the negative vote was to be let go"; and, on the other hand, it seemed to the Presbyterians only the thin end of the wedge.

Accordingly, Leighton offered still further concessions: that the dissenting brethren attending presbyteries and synods "shall not only not be obliged to renounce their own private opinion concerning church government, or swear or subscribe anything contrary thereto, but shall have liberty at their entry to the said meetings to declare it and enter it in what form they please"; that "all church affairs shall be managed and concluded in Presbyteries and Synods by

[1] A. J. Mason, *The Church of England and Episcopacy*, p. 275.
[2] Gilbert Burnet, *History of My Own Time*, I, pp. 139 f.

the free vote of the Presbyters or the major part of them"; that "if any difference fall out in the Diocesan Synod betwixt any of the members thereof, it shall be lawful to appeal to a Provincial Synod"; that Intrants lawfully presented by the patron and duly tried by the presbytery "shall be ordained on a day agreed by the Bishop and Presbytery, with a sermon and if possible in the parish church"; and that no such Intrant "be obliged to any Canonical Oath or Subscription to the Bishop"; and that freedom of speech in presbyteries and synods should be guaranteed. Despite these additional safeguards, the Presbyterians would not accept Leighton's mediation, and his essay in peace-making, though well intended, was a complete failure.

In the Church of Scotland, therefore, Episcopacy and Presbyterianism lay side by side without agreement; and the struggle between the two forms and principles of Church government was protracted and intense; until the Revolution settlement of 1689 brought the sympathies and political influence of the new sovereign on the side of the Presbyterians, and finally determined the conflict in their favour, so that the lot of Episcopalians in Scotland was worse than that of Protestant dissenters in England after the passing of the Toleration Act.

It is in the light of this failure to achieve peace in Scotland that the parallel projects in England for the comprehension of Presbyterians in the Church of England may be considered. With the elevation of John Wilkins, brother-in-law of Oliver Cromwell, to the bishopric of Chester in 1667, a champion of reconciliation now sat on the Bench. Moreover, with the fall of Clarendon and the succession of the Cabal, the tortuous policy of Charles II was inclining to mitigate the severities of the persecuting code and to inaugurate a régime of toleration of dissenters from the Established Church. Accordingly, statesmen and divines (including the Lord Keeper Bridgeman, Lord Chief Justice Hales, Bishops Wilkins and Reynolds, Drs Burton, Tillotson, and Stillingfleet, together with Baxter, Bates, and Manton) co-operated to produce a scheme of "comprehension" for the Presbyterians and of "indulgence" or toleration for the Sects. The proposals put forward by the Anglicans included, first and foremost,

> "that such persons as in the late times of disorder had been ordained by presbyters, shall be admitted to the exercise of the Ministerial Function by the imposition of the hands of the bishop, with this or the like form of words: Take thou authority to preach the Word of God, and administer the Sacraments in any congregation of the Church of England, where thou shalt be lawfully appointed thereunto."

The second item suggested a new form of subscription:

> "I, A.B., do hereby profess and declare, that I do approve the doctrines, worship, and government established in the Church of England, as containing all things necessary to salvation; and that I will not endeavour by myself, or any other, directly or indirectly, to bring in any doctrine contrary to that which is so established. And I do hereby promise that I will continue in the communion of the Church of England, and will not do anything to disturb the peace thereof."

A further clause proposed the making optional of the "nocent ceremonies", and a considerable list of alterations in the Book of Common Prayer was appended.

With regard to the Sects, it was proposed that they "may have liberty for the exercise of their religion in public, and . . . to build or procure places for their public worship . . . either in or near towns"; provided that the preachers and buildings should be registered, and that persons presenting a certificate of attendance should be exempted from the legal penalties for non-conformity; that this "indulgence" should not carry any relief from civil disabilities or obligations to pay parish rates, and that it should be limited at first to three years.

The crux of the "comprehension" was soon perceived to lie in the problem of ordination. "The grand stop in our treaty", as Baxter truly observed, "was about Reordination; and Dr Wilkins still insisted on this, that those consciences must be accommodated who took them for no Ministers who were ordained without Bishops"; whilst Baxter replied that the Presbyterians could not consent to anything which seemed to signify reordination. Finally, a compromise was agreed upon, in Baxter's words:

> "Instead of the liberty to declare the validity of our ordination, which would not be endured, it was agreed that the terms of collation should be these: Take thou Legal Authority to preach the Word of God and administer the Holy Sacraments in any Congregation of England, where thou shalt be lawfully appointed thereunto: that so the word *Legal* might shew that it was only a general Licence from the King that we received, by what Minister soever he pleased to deliver it. And if it were by a Bishop, we declared that we should take it from him but as from the King's Minister."

The attempt to introduce a Bill to this effect into Parliament was frustrated, and the matter went no further.

With the further development of the events of Charles II's reign, at home in the form of the Popish Plot and abroad in the rise of France to a position of hegemony in Europe, the fear of popery led to a renewal of the ideas of comprehension and indulgence in order to strengthen the Protestant interest against its common enemy. Accordingly, in 1680 further talk was heard of a Bill for uniting His Majesty's Protestant subjects; and Drs Tillotson and Stillingfleet, with the approval of Bishops Morley and Ward, made another approach to Baxter and his friends, "to treat of an act of comprehension and union". Baxter produced the draft of an Act for the Healing and Concord of His Majesty's Subjects in Matters of Religion, and conferences followed at which an agreement was reached. But when the Anglican Deans reported the terms of their agreement to Bishop Ward of Salisbury, "there was a full end of all the treaty; the Bishops had no further to go; we had already carried it too far".[1] So the project of union was not revived, until the pressing menace of popery during the reign of James II once more awakened the fears of Protestants and their desire for unity and security.

Notwithstanding the failure of these efforts and the tactical mistakes of Baxter as a negotiator, his name remains in the first rank of 17th-century divines who were inspired by a truly ecumenical temper and whose genius was fertile in projects of union. Both in his voluminous writings and in his organization of

[1] M. Sylvester, *Reliquiae Baxterianae*, Part III, pp. 23 f. and 156 f.; D. Neal, *History of the Puritans*, ed. J. Toulmin, IV, pp. 433 f. and 580 f.

such practical ventures as the Worcestershire Association, Baxter strove with zeal equal to that of Dury for ecclesiastical unity. He emphasized holiness as the indispensable mark of the Church, and desired to concentrate on the fundamental articles of faith, and to allow difference of opinion and practice in nonessentials. In the dedication to his *Saint's Everlasting Rest* he wrote:

> "Will God never put it into the hearts of Rulers to call together some of the most godly, learned, moderate, and peaceable of all four opinions, not too many, to agree upon a way of union and accommodation, and not to cease till they have brought it to this issue: [to come as near together as they can possibly in their principles; and where they cannot, yet to unite as far as may be in their practice, though on different principles; and, where that cannot be, yet to agree on the most loving, peaceable course in the way of carrying on our different practices]; that so as Rup[ertus] Meldenius saith, we may have Unity in things necessary, Liberty in things unnecessary, and Charity in all?"[1]

Baxter maintained a friendly relationship with "divers foreign divines", though somewhat chary to enter into correspondence with them for fear of detection; observing that he "knew so well what eyes were upon him, and how others had been used in some such accounts, that he durst not write one letter to any beyond the seas", and contenting himself therefore with sending answers to their letters "by word of mouth only".[2] At home he co-operated with John Dury in an abortive attempt to find a common platform of agreement between Presbyterian and Independent divines during the period between the victory of Cromwell over Charles II at Worcester in 1651 and the institution of the Committee of Triers in 1654.[3]

Baxter's own position is best described in his own words: "You could not (except a Catholick Christian) have trulier called me, than an Episcopal-Presbyterian-Independent."[4] Accordingly, he was ready to accept Ussher's reduction of episcopacy to a constitutional form; and his Worcestershire Association, embracing Episcopalian, Presbyterian, and Independent ministers, was designed as a practical example of mutual co-operation and toleration. His aim alike in his writings and in his conferences was to lay down the principles of union amongst those who might be described in another of his pregnant phrases as "meer Catholicksmen of no faction, nor siding with any party". His importance and influence have been aptly summarized by a recent writer:

> "The first exponent of Ecumenism in England, he claimed that all who accepted the Apostles' Creed as a summary of belief, the Lord's Prayer as a summary of devotion, and the Decalogue as a summary of duty, were truly Christians and members of the Catholic or Universal Church of Christ."[5]

---

[1] R. Baxter, *The Saint's Everlasting Rest*, 3rd edition, 1652, Dedication. Rupertus Meldenius is now generally believed to have been the pseudonym of Peter Meiderlin of Augsburg, on whom see Chap. ii, pp. 81 f.

[2] M. Sylvester, *Reliquiae Baxterianae*, II, pp. 441–44.

[3] See G. F. Nuttall, "Presbyterians and Independents: Some Movements for Unity 300 Years ago", in *The Journal of the Presbyterian Historical Society of England*, Vol. X, No. 1, 1952, pp. 4–15.

[4] Baxter, as quoted by Dr Nuttall in op. cit.

[5] Horton Davies, *The English Free Churches*, London, 1952, p. 79.

As the struggle for the survival of Protestantism against the policy of James II advanced, Archbishop Sancroft laid seriously to heart the dangers springing from division; and in a series of Articles issued to all bishops of his Province on 27 July 1688, admonished them to exhort their clergy

> "more especially that they have a very tender regard to our brethren, the protestant dissenters, that upon occasion offered they visit them at their own houses, and receive them kindly at their own . . . persuading them (if it may be) to a full compliance with our church, or at least, that whereto we have already attained, we may all walk by the same rule, and mind the same thing. And in order hereunto, that they take all opportunities of assuring and convincing them, that the bishops of this church are really and sincerely irreconcilable enemies to the errors, superstitions, idolatries, and tyrannies of the church of Rome. . . . And in the last place, that they warmly and most affectionately exhort them to join with us in daily fervent prayer to the God of peace, for an universal blessed union of all reformed churches, both at home and abroad, against our common enemies; that all they that do confess the holy name of our dear Lord, and do agree in the truth of his holy word, may also meet in one holy communion, and live in perfect unity and godly love."

But Sancroft went further than this; and, according to the account given by Bishop Wake of Lincoln in his speech in the House of Lords at the trial of Dr Sacheverell in 1710, the Primate

> "foreseeing some such revolution as soon after was happily brought about, began to consider how utterly unprepared they had been at the restoration of king Charles II to settle many things to the advantage of the church; and what a happy opportunity had been lost, for want of such a previous care for its more perfect establishment. It was visible to all the nation, that the more moderate dissenters were generally so well satisfied with that stand which our divines had made against popery . . . as to express an unusual readiness to come in to us. And it was therefore thought worth while, when they were deliberating about those other matters, to consider at the same time what might be done to gain them without doing any prejudice to ourselves. The scheme was laid out, and the several parts of it were committed, not only with the approbation, but by the direction of that great prelate, to such of our divines as were thought most worthy to be intrusted with it. . . . The design was in short, this: to improve, and if possible, amend our discipline; to review and enlarge our Liturgy by correcting some things, by adding others and, if it should be thought advisable by authority, when this matter should be legally considered, first in Convocation, then in Parliament, by omitting some few ceremonies which are allowed to be indifferent in their usage, so as not to make them of necessity binding on those who had conscientious scruples respecting them, till they should be able to overcome either their weaknesses or their prejudices respecting them, and be willing to comply."[1]

Unfortunately, details of this "comprehension" scheme have been lost, and the course of political events frustrated its fulfilment. For the substitution of

[1] E. Cardwell, *Documentary Annals*, II, pp. 375 f.; G. D'Oyly, *Life of Sancroft*, I, pp. 327 f.

William and Mary as King and Queen for James II involved the Archbishop and others of his brethren in the delicate conflict of conscience, which forbade them to take an oath of allegiance to the new Sovereigns. When, therefore, the ecclesiastical aspects of the Revolution settlement came under consideration and the question of "comprehension" was again raised, the secession of the Non-juring prelates and clergy fatally weakened the Church at a moment when authoritative and firm leadership was essential.

In 1689 a Bill for Comprehension was presented to the House of Lords, the main provisions of which were to substitute for the Declaration required by the Act of Uniformity of 1662 a form expressing simple approval "of the doctrine and worship of the Church of England as containing all things necessary to salvation" and submission "to the government thereof as by law established"; and to require conditional ordination of ministers in Presbyterian orders with the form "Take thou authority to preach the Word of God and administer the Sacraments, and to perform all other ministerial offices in this Church of England"; together with regulations in respect of the "nocent ceremonies". When the Bill was received in the House of Commons, that House addressed the Crown to issue a summons for the meeting of Convocation in order that the question might first be debated there.

In preparation for this consideration by Convocation, a royal commission was issued to ten bishops and twenty priests of the Church of England to prepare a project for submission to Convocation and Parliament. But the meetings of this commission were characterized by considerable abstention on the part of some members; and, though the majority persevered in their task and produced a scheme, it never came to debate in the Convocation of Canterbury. For the first business of the Lower House of Convocation being, on the direction of the Archbishop, to elect a Prolocutor, the decisive victory in this election of Dr Jane, who had withdrawn from the meetings of the commission, over Tillotson, indicated the temper of the lower clergy, and in fact the project was never discussed. The significance of the episode is that it marked the end of schemes of "comprehension" as serious attempts to heal the breach between the Church and dissenters. Whilst the Anglicans were willing to offer concessions concerning "nocent ceremonies" and other matters of secondary importance relating to the Book of Common Prayer, the obstacle to agreement lay in their requirement of episcopal ordination as indispensable to ministry.

In place of comprehension a Toleration Act was passed which provided relief for loyal, orthodox Protestant ministers and congregations. All Trinitarian dissenters were to be allowed freedom for the public exercise of their religion, by the registration of their meeting-houses in the Court of the Bishop, or the Archdeacon, or at the general or quarter sessions of the Justices of the Peace, by the holding of all meetings for public worship with unlocked doors, and with due evidence of doctrinal orthodoxy on the part of the ministers. The importance of this Act was that it established a legal, if limited, toleration by parliamentary statute, not by royal dispensing power; but its weakness lay in the circumstance that it said nothing about the provision of education for a dissenting ministry. "Indulgence" had triumphed over "comprehension"; and the few remaining advocates of the latter were soon to be submerged in the new theological controversies and interests of the 18th century. During the course of that century, indeed, the religious balance of forces in England was completely changed by the virtual landslide of the Presbyterians into Arianism and Unitarianism; so that the problems of reunion did not arise again until the Methodist separation from the Established Church raised at any rate new forms of an ancient question.

The problems and varying fortunes which befell the Protestant dissenters during the changes of the 17th century raised issues of importance concerning the principles and methods of their own relationship to each other. The principal questions centred in terms of communion, that is, the conditions of admission to the Holy Communion, which varied from Church to Church and from time to time. The tradition of the 16th-century Separatists had been to restrict communion to persons who were members of a local "gathered church"; but in the following century advocates of "mixed communion" were found, including John Bunyan, Walter Cradock, Vavasour Powell, and Morgan Llwyd. The Savoy Declaration of 1658, representing the position of 120 Congregational churches, laid down, on the one hand, that ministers were "not obliged to dispense the Seals to any other than such as (being saints by calling, and gathered according to the order of the Gospel) they stand related to, as pastors and teachers"; whilst allowing, on the other hand, that "churches gathered and walking according to the mind of Christ, judging other churches (though less pure) to be true churches, may receive unto occasional communion with them, such members of those churches as are credibly testified to be godly, and to live without offence". Isaac Watts, in the 18th century, admitted as occasional communicants at his church any members of "the three denominations of Dissenters, viz. Presbyterian, Independent or Baptist". Among the Baptists customs differed, the General or Arminian Baptists, after a strict beginning which confined the Communion to their own members, broadened their practice during the 17th century; whilst within the Particular or Calvinistic Baptists, Bunyan led the movement for a "mixed Communion"; and a General Assembly of "Pastors, Messengers, and Ministering Brethren" in London in 1689 allowed to each church liberty in this matter.[1]

Both during the Protectorate and after the ejection of 1662, the Presbyterians had to determine their attitude in this respect towards their other dissenting brethren. Despite the efforts of Baxter and Dury to effect an agreement between these several parties, no practical results ensued; and only the strong arm of the Lord Protector enabled them to live side by side within the same national establishment of Christianity. When the Restoration settlement left them all equally outside the Church of England, a long-term policy had to be found; and when the last hope of "comprehension" for the Presbyterians disappeared in 1688–89, steps were taken to draw together the several communions. In 1690 "Heads of Agreement", drawn up mainly by John Howe, were widely accepted amongst London ministers, and led to the "Happy Union" of 1691. Their principal points were that congregations, in choosing their pastors, should consult neighbouring ministers whose concurrence in ordinations was "ordinarily requisite"; that "in order to concord" and in difficult cases, synods should be held as consultative bodies, to whose advice the several churches should attach weight; and that the confessional orthodoxy of the churches should be testified by adherence to the doctrinal articles of the Thirty-nine Articles, or of the Westminster Confession, or its Larger or Shorter Catechism, or of the Savoy Confession, as being agree-

[1] E. A. Payne, "Intercommunion from the 17th to the 19th Centuries", pp. 96 ff. in *Intercommunion*, edited by D. M. Baillie and J. Marsh, London, 1952.

able to the Scriptures, "the only Rule of Faith and Practice". Upon this basis some advance between Presbyterians and Independents towards "mutual open Communion" was achieved.[1] Unhappily, theological controversy effected early breaches in the agreement, so that by the end of 1694 the "Happy Union" was virtually dissolved so far as London was concerned.

A generation later, the foundation in 1727 of the "General Body of Protestant Dissenting Ministers of the Three Denominations residing in and about the cities of London and Westminster" proved more successful, for these "Dissenting Deputies" still continue and enjoy the right on ceremonial occasions of direct access to the Sovereign.[2] They provided a practical means of mutual consultation and action, which was serviceable, if not successful, in the efforts to secure amelioration of the dissenters' position by agitation for the repeal of the Test and Corporation Acts. However, controversy concerning the doctrine of the Trinity and the *vis inertiae* of the century combined to weaken the effects of this promising overture; the former by evoking new divisive influences, the latter by stifling adventurous policies.

Towards the end of the 18th century the spirit of co-operation found new expression in the foundation of the London Missionary Society by some Anglican clergymen and dissenting ministers, with the express purpose "not to send Presbyterianism, Independency, Episcopacy, or any other form of Church Order and Government . . . but the glorious Gospel of the blessed God" to the mission-field. Similarly, the British and Foreign Bible Society and the Religious Tract Society were founded each with a dual secretariat of one Anglican and one dissenting minister, together with one "foreign" secretary, and have continued as models of ecumenical co-operation till the present day.

One healing practice survived the collapse of projects of "comprehension"— the occasional communion of dissenters with the Church of England. After the ejection of 1662, some of the leading Presbyterian divines maintained the custom of occasional (that is, regular but infrequent) communion with the Established Church as a testimony to their acceptance of its reformed character, though they felt bound in conscience to decline complete conformity. The practice was "fairly general in the early years of the eighteenth century, particularly among Presbyterians and Baptists", and "as late as 1818 Dr Olinthus Gregory and Robert Hall, the noted Baptist preacher, corresponded about 'Occasional Conformity' as practised by Baxter and Howe, and showed their approval of it".[3]

The purely religious origin of this practice, entirely dissociated from all political requirement as a qualification for office under the Crown, was expounded by Edmund Calamy to Gilbert Burnet during the debates on the Occasional Conformity Bill in the reign of Anne, as follows:

> "That the communicating with the Church of England was no new practice among the Dissenters, nor of a late date, but had been used by some of the most eminent of our ministers ever since 1662, with a design to shew their charity towards that church, notwithstanding they apprehended

---

[1] A. Gordon, *Freedom After Ejection*, London, 1917, pp. 152–57; E. A. Payne in *Intercommunion*, as above.

[2] B. L. Manning, *The Protestant Dissenting Deputies*, ed. B. Greenwood, London, 1952, was published after the revision of this chapter had been completed and therefore could not be utilized.

[3] E. A. Payne, in *Intercommunion*, p. 94.

themselves bound in conscience ordinarily to separate from it; and that it had long been also practised by a number of the most understanding people among them, before the doing so was necessary to qualify for a place. We reminded him that Mr. Baxter and Dr. Bates had done it all along, and been much reflected on by several of their own friends on that account; and added that, should the bill then depending pass into a law, it . . . would bid fair for destroying that little charity yet remaining among us, and make the breach between the two parties wider than ever."[1]

John Howe also approved of the custom, having not only "openly declared for this occasional conformity" but defending its continuance after the super-imposition of a political relation, on the ground that "no man can allow himself to think, that what he before counted as lawful is by this supervening consideration become unlawful".[2] Moreover, he believed this to be generally true of his brethren:

> "In 1662 most of the considerable ejected London ministers met, and agreed to hold occasional communion with the now re-established church—not quitting their own ministry, or declining the exercise of it as they could have opportunity. And as far as I could by enquiry learn, I can little doubt this to have been the judgement of their fellow-sufferers through the nation in great part ever since."[3]

If this healing custom was desired and practised on the part of those ejected in 1662, it seems also to have been allowed by the generality of Anglican church-men. The correspondence interchanged between Archbishop John Sharp of York and Ralph Thoresby, the eminent dissenter of Leeds, on this point illustrates the Primate's approval of the practice, though it should be observed that his encouragement was partly motivated by the hope (realized in Thoresby's case) that occasional communion would develop into full conformity.

The Revolution of 1689 affected profoundly not only the internal constitutional development of Great Britain but also its relations with foreign powers; since this country was drawn shortly into a European coalition to resist the hegemony of France. Through this the Church of England was brought into closer relations with foreign Protestants than had been the case since the end of the Commonwealth. There was a tradition of the reception of foreign Protestants visiting England to communion with the Established Church, which was stated in some detail by the chaplain of Bishop Peter Gunning of Ely, in defence of his master against the criticism of Baxter:

> "First, does not his highness the Prince of Orange and his noble and honourable retinue join in communion with us, as often as they have occasion to come over hither; and are not any of their ministers and others of the Dutch churches publicly permitted to come to our communion? And do we not thereby own them for Christians and fellow-members of the same catholick church? And do they not thereby own us for the like? . . .

---

[1] E. Calamy, *A Historical Account of my own Life*, I, p. 473.
[2] E. Calamy, *Life of John Howe*, I, pp. 68, 70.
[3] R. F. Horton, *John Howe*, p. 83.

If at any time any of the French Protestants come over to our country, do we not likewise profess our concord with them in the substantial principles of the Christian religion? Come we likewise to consider the remains of the ancient Bohemians, do we not hold all friendly communion with them? . . . The same charity and concord is always shewn to the Lutheran churches, some of whom have often communicated with the lord bishop of Ely. . . . The like concord I can show with the Helvetian, Hungarian, and Transilvanian churches, and all that profess the catholick faith."[1]

Anglican divines ministering abroad welcomed foreign Protestants to communicate with them, as did John Cosin at Charenton during the Interregnum and William Wake during his chaplaincy at Paris; though whilst the former approved of reciprocity in this respect, the latter at that time did not. On this matter there was no uniformity of practice amongst Anglicans, some of whom were willing to communicate with foreign Protestants when abroad, whilst others were not. During the period of their exile, Bishops Sysderf and Bramhall, together with George Morley and Richard Steward, refused to communicate with the Huguenots of Paris; whilst Cosin and, at a later date when in exile with the Non-jurors, Denis Granville, formerly Dean of Durham, counselled and approved of the reception by Anglicans of Holy Communion at the hands of the foreign Reformed. Gilbert Burnet was himself "an occasional conformist in Geneva and Holland" and declared himself ready to be so again[2]; Archbishop Ussher stated that "with like affection I should receive the Blessed Sacrament at the hands of Dutch ministers if I were in Holland as I should do at the hands of the French ministers if I were in Charenton"[3]; and even Archbishop Sharp publicly declared that "if he were abroad, he would willingly communicate with the Protestant churches, where he should happen to be".[4]

The tradition of the reception of foreign Protestants to communion in England was so firm that, when in 1709 a Bill for naturalizing foreign Protestants was debated in Parliament, the Tory high churchmen wished to require as a condition of such naturalization that they should "receive the Sacrament according to the usage of the Church of England", whilst Whig low churchmen desired that permission should be given for reception "in any Protestant church"; and the line of division amongst bishops and laity lay in this point.

5. THE EIGHTEENTH CENTURY AND ECUMENICAL EFFORT

The Revolution settlement brought to the English throne the Calvinist William of Orange, himself an occasional conformist; and when he was succeeded by Queen Anne, who was zealously and entirely Anglican, her husband Prince George of Denmark, a Lutheran, was likewise an occasional communicant with the Church of England. Indeed, the Act of Settlement of 1701, which provided for the perpetuation of the Protestant succession in the house of Hanover, required all future sovereigns to "join in communion with the Church of England", as the two first Hanoverian sovereigns, George I and II, and their families did. A practical precedent and example, therefore, seemed to have

---

[1] W. Saywell, *Evangelical and Catholic Unity: A Vindication of Peter, Lord Bishop of Ely*, pp. 302 ff.

[2] Cobbett, *Parliamentary History*, VI, col. 164.

[3] A. J. Mason, *The Church of England and Episcopacy*, p. 122, citing Elrington's *Life of Ussher*.

[4] T. Sharp, *Life of Archbishop John Sharp*, I, pp. 377 f.

been provided for a basis of union between the Church of England and the Lutheran and Reformed Churches of the European continent, which union was pressed forward by the close association of the principal Protestant powers in the coalition against Louis XIV. Accordingly, there developed protracted and interesting negotiations, the object of which was the union of the Lutheran and Reformed Churches in the dominions of the King of Prussia on the basis of their acceptance of episcopacy and of a Liturgy modelled closely on the Book of Common Prayer, and thereafter of a union of both with the Church of England.

The moving spirit in this irenic project, Daniel Ernst Jablonski, had lived in England, and studied at Oxford, from 1680 to 1683, during which time he had shed his prejudices against the Established Church to such an extent as to become enthusiastically devoted to its form of public worship and government, and he had also become acquainted with some of its leading bishops and clergy.[1]

The two principal Protestant powers in the Empire at this time were Brandenburg (Prussia) and Hanover. Jablonski first engaged himself in the results of a correspondence initiated between Leibniz and Ezekiel von Spanheim *De pace ecclesiastica*. In following up this initiative, he sought to achieve an organic ecclesiastical union of the Lutheran and Reformed Churches, on the basis of agreement on the fundamentals of the Christian faith and an agreement to differ on non-fundamentals, and in regard to rites and ceremonies by an appeal to the Church of the 3rd and 4th centuries, of which he saw the contemporary interpreter and mirror in the Church of England.

Meantime Jablonski himself was consecrated to the episcopate of the *Unitas Fratrum* in 1699; and having won over to his ideals the Elector Frederick III of Brandenburg (who was anxious, in view of his recognition by the members of the Grand Alliance as Frederick I, King of Prussia, to dignify his coronation by the establishment of a titular episcopate), he set to work to contrive an official approach from Berlin to London. Two copies of a recently published German translation of the Book of Common Prayer were sent respectively in 1704 to Queen Anne and to Archbishop Thomas Tenison of Canterbury. Unfortunately, Tenison never sent a formal acknowledgement of the gift; and the omission, whether designed as an intentional slight or the result of oversight, almost made an end of the overture before it had been launched. Not until the Tory victory at the general election of 1710 in Great Britain brought a new administration to power was the climate favourable to a renewal of the experiment.

During the next three years, 1710–13, a considerable volume of memoranda and correspondence passed between the ecclesiastical and political leaders, which might have furnished a practical programme for action, if the quarrels amongst the allies in the negotiations leading to the Treaty of Utrecht in 1713 had not thwarted the high hopes entertained in earlier years. The affair was reopened by a letter from Jablonski to Archbishop Sharp of York in the autumn of 1710, to which the northern Primate replied in cordial terms, welcoming both Jablonski's project for the establishment in Prussia of episcopacy and a liturgy according to the Anglican pattern, and his suggestion of an interchange of letters in support of the project. The Secretary of State, Henry St John, instructed Lord Raby at Berlin to express to the Prussian authorities in State and Church

---

[1] The following account of Jablonski is taken from my Albrecht Stumpff Memorial Lecture, 1950, published by S.P.C.K. under the title *Daniel Ernst Jablonski and the Church of England*. See also Chap. ii, pp. 109–12.

"that Her Majesty is ready to give all possible encouragement to that excellent work", and also had a formal interview about it with the Prussian Minister in London. Jablonski therefore set to work to popularize a knowledge of the Anglican Liturgy and to prepare the way for a restoration of episcopacy. Since the Prussian King was especially jealous of the "rights of the ruling Prince in ecclesiastical affairs", it was even more necessary to persuade him that episcopacy would not entrench upon his authority as *summus episcopus* than to convince him of its descent from the apostolic age; and here the Anglican example of the royal supremacy was an invaluable aid.

But the schemes of churchmen were shipwrecked on the rocks of political dissension, arising out of the protracted peace preliminaries at the end of the War of the Spanish Succession. Moreover, during the years 1713–14 the principal actors were removed by death, in the persons of the King of Prussia, Queen Anne, and Archbishop Sharp. Jablonski had therefore to wait until the internal confusion and foreign reactions consequent on the accession to the British Crown of the house of Hanover had become sufficiently clarified, before embarking on any attempt to renew old measures with new men in authority in Church and State.

It was singularly fortunate for the irenic churchmen of that century that, in December 1716, William Wake was nominated to succeed Thomas Tenison in the primacy of all England, for he was a firm friend and indefatigable champion of the ecumenical movement of his age. His own interest in reunion had been kindled by his youthful experiences in Paris as chaplain to the British Ambassador, Lord Preston, from 1683 to 1685, where he used his time to good advantage to cultivate acquaintance with some of the Gallican theologians of the Sorbonne, and to familiarize himself with the standpoints of the principal Protestant Churches represented in the French capital. Between 1685 and 1716 almost a generation of foreign war had intervened; but in 1716 he set to work with avidity to restore broken correspondence and to begin new efforts towards the desired goal. In the course of the next decade he maintained long and learned correspondence in Latin with the chief leaders of European Protestantism and with some French divines of the Sorbonne, in which the principles of union were fully debated.

From the outset Wake's first principle was that of distinguishing between fundamentals and non-fundamentals in matters of faith no less than of rites and ceremonies.

"In the meantime", he observed to his Gallican friends, Dr L. E. Du Pin and Dr Piers Girardin,

> "so far are they right to distinguish matters of doctrine from matters of order and discipline; in which last national churches may vary without breaking the unity of the catholic church. But then they should in points of doctrine too, distinguish fundamentals, in which all ought to agree, from others of lesser moment, in which error or difference may be tolerated. And I am much mistaken if they must not at the last, come to the Creeds of the first four General Councils, if ever they mean to restore peace to the Church."[1]

[1] J. H. Lupton, *Archbishop Wake and the Project of Union between the Gallican and Anglican Churches*, describes part of Wake's work, though his account is incomplete. The rest is taken from Wake's MSS., on which I am working extensively.

From this basis he never strayed; but insisted throughout, alike to Roman Catholic correspondents and to foreign Protestants, that a wide latitude of opinion on secondary issues must be allowed, and amongst such secondary points he included the doctrines of the Eucharist, predestination, and election. To him unity did not imply uniformity:

> "I make no doubt that a plan might be framed to bring the Gallican church to such a state that we might each hold a true catholic unity and communion with one another, and yet each continue in many things to differ, as we see the Protestant churches do . . . To frame a common confession of faith, or liturgy, or discipline for both churches is a project never to be accomplished. But to settle each so that the other shall declare it to be a sound part of the catholic church and communicate with one another as such—this may easily be done without much difficulty."

Accordingly, he sent to his friends of the Sorbonne the Anglican Book of Common Prayer, the Ordinal, and the Thirty-nine Articles of Religion. In regard to the first, he was ready to meet their susceptibilities, as later he was in respect also of the Lutherans, by consenting to omit the Black Rubric; in regard to the Ordinal, he wrote long and learned letters to insist on the unbroken maintenance by the Church of England of its episcopal succession and on the validity of its consecrations; and he commended the Articles of Religion to their study. In reply, the doctors of the Sorbonne approved six points, submitted to them by Dr Girardin as a basis of agreement and union between the two Churches: first that in non-essentials differences of usage should constitute no barrier to union but should be allowed; secondly, that worship could be offered to God without the use of images; thirdly, that the invocation of the saints was not essential to Christian prayer, but that every Christian should be free to pray directly and immediately to God; fourthly, that the communion of the laity in both kinds should be permitted; fifthly, that the authority of the bishops proceeded from God alone, but that subordination within the episcopate was allowable; and sixthly, that the Eucharist could be celebrated without elevation. Wake was so pleased with this programme that he held the way to be open for further steps to effect an actual union:

> ". . . to agree to own each other as true brethren and members of the catholic Christian church; to agree to communicate in everything with one another; which on their side is very easy, there being nothing in our Offices in any degree contrary to their own principles; and would they purge out of theirs what is contrary to ours, we might join in the public services with them; and yet leave one another in the free liberty of believing transubstantiation or not; so long as we do not require anything to be done by either in pursuance of that opinion. The Lutherans do this very thing. Many of them communicate not only in prayers, but in the communion with us; and we never enquire whether they believe consubstantiation, or even pay any worship to Christ as present with the elements, so long as their outward actions are the same with our own, and they give no offence to any with their opinions."

There remained of course the problem of the papacy; and here Wake was eager that the Gallican Church should throw off the papal yoke, as his own

Church had done, and should establish itself as an autonomous national Church, leaving the question of recognition of a primacy of honour to Rome for future determination by a general council. His aim was defined as:

> "to convince them of the necessity of embracing the present opportunity of breaking off from the pope, and going one step farther than they have yet done in their opinion of his authority, so as to leave him only a primacy of place and honour, and that merely by ecclesiastical authority, as he was once bishop of the imperial city."

This was a strong demand to make even of divines bred in the tradition of the Gallican Liberties; but Wake would have nothing of the papal headship *divino jure*, but only of a primacy of honour and that by ecclesiastical authority. In reply Du Pin and Girardin took up a position of minimizing the authority of the papacy over the Gallican Church in actual practice; whilst in theory the former preferred a definition of the papal primacy which made it little more than that of *primus inter pares*. The Pope was simply *inter episcopos primus*. There was some justification for the mordancy of Wake's comment in a private letter to the English chaplain in Paris concerning this statement:

> "As to the pope's authority, I take the difference to be only this: that we may all agree, without troubling ourselves with the reason, to allow him a primacy of order in the episcopal college. They would have it thought necessary to hold communion with him, and allow him a little canonical authority over them, as long as he will leave them to prescribe the bounds of it. We say fairly, we know of no authority he has in our realm."

From the Gallican side, perhaps the most interesting item was the *Commonitorium* of Du Pin on the Thirty-nine Articles, which bears notable affinities with the essay of Christopher Davenport. Unfortunately, the *Commonitorium*, after being rediscovered during the present century, has since disappeared; and our knowledge of its contents must still derive from the summary printed by Dr Archibald Maclaine as an appendix to his edition of Mosheim's *Ecclesiastical History*.[1] Its preface examined the English Reformation, and the author then proceeded to a particular consideration of the Articles of Religion, in relation to the differences between the two Churches in matters of faith, rites and ceremonies, and moral doctrine. From considerations of space, it is possible to refer here only to some of the more important of his comments.

The first five of the Articles Du Pin approved; whilst the VIth, concerning the sufficiency of Scripture for all things necessary to salvation, he would

> "readily grant, provided that you do not entirely exclude Tradition, which doth not exhibit new articles of faith, but confirms and illustrates those which are contained in the Sacred Writings, and places about them new guards to defend them against gainsayers".

In respect of Article XIV, he commented that works of supererogation are

> "works conducive to salvation, which are not a matter of strict precept but of counsel only; that the word, being new, may be rejected, provided it be owned that the faithful do some such works".

[1] J. L. Mosheim, *An Ecclesiastical History*, ed. Archibald Maclaine, London, 1768, Vol. V, Appendix III.

In Article XIX he desired that, to the definition of the Church there given, there should be added the words "under lawful pastors", and that the reference to the errors of particular Churches might be omitted. Similarly, with regard to Article XX, "Of the Authority of the Church", he agreed that the Church has not the power to ordain anything contrary to the word of God; but observed that it must be taken for granted that the Church would never do this in matters which overturn the substance of faith. In respect of General Councils, as mentioned in Article XXI, he held that Councils received as such by the universal Church cannot err; even though particular councils not so received may err, yet it was not the province of every private individual to reject anything in their decisions which he thought to be contrary to Scripture.

In relation to the number of the Sacraments, he insisted that the "five commonly called Sacraments" be acknowledged as such, according to the Roman tradition, but this did not involve any opinion as to whether they were instituted immediately by Christ or not.

So far as the practice of communicating the people in one or both kinds was concerned, he was willing for the matter to be left to each Church for regulation according to its own custom.

Clerical marriage he was prepared to allow where the laws of the Church did not prohibit it. He would not have the English ordinations, as described in Article XXXVI, pronounced to be null (though admitting that some of them might be), but in case of union, desired the English clergy to be continued in their offices "either as of right, or through the indulgence of the Church". In regard to Article XXXVII, he allowed its definition of the royal supremacy, and agreed with its denial of the temporal and immediate spiritual jurisdiction of the papacy; but affirmed that moderate members of the Church of England would be prepared to acknowledge the responsibility of the See of Rome, in virtue of its primacy, to preserve the true faith and canonical discipline of the universal Church, and to correct breaches of both, provided the liberties and privileges of particular Churches were respected.

More generally, he deprecated attempts to assign responsibility for the schism effected at the Reformation, and approved the discipline and Liturgy of the Church of England. Perhaps the most striking of his general observations was that

> "an union between the English and French bishops and clergy may be completed, or at least advanced, without consulting the Roman Pontiff, who may be informed of the union as soon as it is accomplished, and may be desired to consent to it; that, if he consents to it, the affair will then be finished; and that, even without his consent, the union shall be valid; that, in case he attempts to terrify by his threats, it will then be expedient to appeal to a general council".

This was strong meat, even from a Gallican theologian; and the success of such a bold venture would depend on the support of the civil power. Accordingly, it is not surprising that the correspondence of Wake and the Gallican divines was necessarily inconclusive and indeterminate. For the doctors of the Sorbonne were a dissident and unrepresentative minority of their Church, exacerbated by the attitude of Rome in the Bull *Unigenitus* and its consequences, but unsure of the support even of the Cardinal Archbishop of Paris, and with little hope of effective backing from the Regent Orleans. Moreover, Wake was not writing on behalf of, nor even with the cognizance of, his fellow-bishops of the Church of England. But the episode has an interest as showing the points of agreement and conciliation which could be discussed between learned and moderate churchmen on both sides of the channel.

In his correspondence with foreign Protestants, Wake had the advantage of a firmer starting-point in the traditional friendly relations of the Church of England with the Continental Churches, both Lutheran and Reformed. To Jean Le Clerc of Amsterdam he expressed his fervent wish that the foreign Reformed Churches would restore episcopacy in their constitution, and meantime (echoing not only the sentiment but the very words of Lancelot Andrewes) declared that he was not of such iron breast as to deny the validity of their ministries and sacraments because of their lack of bishops. To the Antistes of Zurich, Peter Zeller, he emphasized his desire for the restoration of bishops in the Swiss Reformed Churches, and his authorization of intercommunion for members of those Churches sojourning in England and for Anglicans resident in Switzerland. Similarly, to the Church at Basle he affirmed the unity of the Church of England and that of Basle in the fundamentals of faith, and his conviction that divergences upon secondary points did not involve breach of communion; in support of which he appealed to current practice in regard to intercommunion as known to both parties; and particularly to the circumstance of the ruling sovereigns in England, who had become Anglican communicants here without renouncing their Lutheran churchmanship in Hanover.

Nor did Wake shrink from the practical responsibilities of his counsel. If the Church of England advocated the restoration of episcopacy in the foreign Reformed Churches, it must enable this to be realized. Accordingly, he suggested to J. F. Ostervald of Neuchâtel that the services of Anglican bishops and presbyters might be a means of securing episcopal ordination for future ministers of that Church. To one of the foreign Churches, indeed, the Moravian *Unitas Fratrum*, he was able to make more cordial advances, and to Jablonski of Berlin he wrote a letter of emphatic recognition of the episcopal succession of that Church. At that time, indeed, it seemed as if ecclesiastical and political circumstances combined to point the way to formal negotiations for union of the Lutheran and Reformed Churches under the aegis of the Church of England.

But the irenical labours of Wake, in his extensive and protracted correspondence with foreign Protestants, likewise failed of practical effect. In great part this was due to the outbreak in the leading Swiss Reformed Churches of an acute and prolonged controversy concerning the subscription required of ministers to the Helvetic Consensus.[1] Further, this dispute had unfortunate repercussions on other Reformed Churches of the Continent, and on their relations with the Churches of the Augsburg Confession. In a series of lengthy Latin letters, the Archbishop iterated to all parties to the dispute not only his personal conviction but also the historic Anglican tradition of "comprehensiveness": that is, of the official allowance of a wide variety of opinion on matters not fundamental to faith or essential to salvation:

"The moderation of the Church of England in this respect has been very exemplary; and we have felt the good effect of it in that peace we enjoy

[1] See Chap. ii, pp. 107 f.

among our ministers, notwithstanding their known difference of opinion in many considerable articles of Christian doctrine. The XXXIX Articles ... have been subscribed more than once in our public synods, indifferently, by bishops and clergy of different persuasions. We have left everyone to interpret them in his own sense; and they are indeed so generally framed that they may, without any equivocation, have more senses than one fairly put upon them."

But though these learned historical expositions served to set forth the Anglican theory and practice, they were less successful in composing the problems at issue in the Swiss Churches, or between the Reformed and Lutheran Confessions; and there can be no doubt that these controversies were a grave hindrance to the Archbishop's hopes and schemes for corporate Protestant unity. Nor were political difficulties lacking, or without their own share of responsibility for the paucity of practical results of such an intense ecumenical correspondence. The long correspondence of Wake and Jablonski is full of examples and reminders of the intractable nature of political problems. The fair prospects which seemed to have been presented by the Hanoverian succession in England faded into the prosaic reality of inertia and decline.

Soon political obstacles multiplied. The temporal rivalries between the two German Electorates of Brandenburg and Brunswick introduced a new element of complication into the ecclesiastical problems. Even in practical matters, the conducting of delicate negotiations in three places, London, Berlin, and Hanover, was a sufficient complication in itself; and in the background of German affairs stood the *Corpus Evangelicorum* at Ratisbon, where the jealousies of thirty-nine sovereign states had to be composed before a common policy could be achieved. Moreover, when the statesmen seemed on the point of action, the suspicions and opposition of the rigid theologians had to be overcome; and between these two stools the hopes of the leaders, Wake and Jablonski, fell finally. It has to be admitted that the greater part of the responsibility for the failure lay with the Hanoverian entourage of George I; and the Prussian King justly tired of the tedium and protraction of the negotiation. Thus the hope of Protestant union within the territories of the King of Prussia, and the participation of the Church of England as a first step towards the restoration of episcopacy to the foreign Protestants, faded.

Faced by these setbacks, Wake could achieve little of a practical character. He encouraged both theological students and presbyters of the Protestant Churches of the Continent to visit the English universities for the furtherance of their studies and, wherever possible, to receive Anglican episcopal ordination before returning to the public ministry of their own Churches. He warmly counselled this step both to ministers intending to serve the congregations of foreign Protestants settled in England and to students whose ultimate objective was to serve in the ministry of their home Churches. But this, though productive of closer personal relations, did not affect the wider problem of ecclesiastical union.

Nor were the official replies of the several Swiss Churches to Wake's overtures concerning the restoration of episcopacy such as to support high hopes. They were complimentary and cordial in tone, but showed no readiness to undertake so bold a venture. They praised the episcopate of the Church of England, and assured its Primate that they would not quarrel about forms and names of ministry; but they evinced no intention of taking practical steps to restore episcopacy amongst their own Churches. Accordingly, Wake fell back upon the suggestion of an agreed confession of faith and liturgy, as a means both of inducing a sense of common purpose and of fostering a conviction of practical unity.

> "We shall never become a compact body, nor make any great figure in the world, while we continue a disjointed people, and have everyone his separate confession and form of worship; so I could wish that there might be an agreement in some common form of both; which would make us all appear one reformed Church in the several countries in which we are dispersed."

But even J. A. Turrettini in Geneva poured cold water on this project; pointing out that in nothing was ecclesiastical opinion more tenacious and conservative than in liturgies; and illustrating his argument by pointed reference to the Scottish Prayer Book of 1637. Similarly with regard to theological confessions, it would be impossible to construct a new form on which all would agree, and it must be sufficient if the various Churches could be content to accept each other as orthodox in fundamentals and to agree to differ in non-essentials.

Throughout the 18th century, the Society for Promoting Christian Knowledge, founded in 1698, maintained a close connection and co-operation with Continental Churches, Lutheran and Reformed, and with their leading clergy. By its custom of offering the status of Corresponding Member to foreign divines, it contrived a means of associating many such in its work.[1] In the institution of Corresponding Members, it was followed by its sister Society for the Propagation of the Gospel, founded in 1701. The privilege of election to Corresponding Membership was highly valued by foreign divines, who recorded this honour along with their academic degrees on the title-pages of their published works.

The S.P.C.K. secured the translation of some of its publications into foreign tongues and of important foreign books into English. Among the volumes translated into English were Ostervald's *Grounds and Principles of the Christian Religion*, Johann Arndt's *True Christianity*, Grotius' *The Truth of the Christian Religion*, A. H. Francke's *Short Introduction to the Practice of the Christian Religion* and his *Pietas Hallensis*. Amongst English works translated into foreign languages may be mentioned Jablonski's translation of Josiah Woodward's *Account of the Rise of the Religious Societies in London*, writings on the same subject by Anton Horneck, and tracts by Robert Nelson.

In another field the S.P.C.K. was a pioneer, namely in its support of German Lutheran missionaries in South India. For a short early period from 1710 to 1728 it contributed financial help to missionaries sent out by the Danish-Halle Mission to work in the Danish territory of Tranquebar. But from 1728 it employed them in "the English Mission" in English or independent territory and as agents for the propagation of the Anglican tradition, in the continued default of English volunteers for this work. The Danish-Halle Mission was a joint enterprise of the Danish King who desired Christian missions in his territories and of A. H. Francke, who, since Danish missionaries were not forthcoming in adequate numbers, secured Lutheran volunteers from amongst German students, for the most part studying in the Pietist University of Halle. The task of providing the human personnel for the English Mission also was com-

[1] See Chap. ii, p. 109.

mitted successively to the two Franckes, father and son, while that of provision for their maintenance was undertaken by the S.P.C.K. Indeed, a formal letter from Archbishop Wake to A. H. Francke explicitly acknowledged this division of responsibility. In all, the S.P.C.K., between 1728 and 1825, employed in its service, or partly supported, some sixty missionaries, all of whom had received Lutheran ordination.

Some of these Lutheran missionaries were employed as salaried chaplains by the East India Company to minister the Word and Sacraments to members of English communities; others, under the aegis of the S.P.C.K., ministered to scattered congregations of English people, and to congregations of Indians or Eurasians. Annual reports of their work and progress were sent by the missionaries to the Society, which included them regularly in its own annual report. These missionaries (some of whom had been ordained by Danish Lutheran bishops) used the Book of Common Prayer, administered the two dominical Sacraments, and instructed children according to the Anglican Catechism. The first translation of the Book of Common Prayer into Tamil was made by the Lutheran missionaries.

The S.P.C.K. very early set up a special committee on Protestant Missions in the East Indies, which included amongst its members such prominent churchmen as Robert Nelson and Thomas Bray. The formal approval accorded by the S.P.C.K. to these agents may be illustrated by a Minute of 1758 in relation to the missionaries in Cuddalore, commending their zeal and diligence "in training up children in the nurture and admonition of the Lord, in preparing adults for Christian baptism, in preaching the Word . . . and in rightly and duly administering the Sacrament of the Lord's Supper". Upon occasion some of these Lutheran missionaries also conferred ordination, according to the Order of their Church, upon Indians as "country priests" to minister to the scattered Indian congregations. There is no evidence that any of these "country priests" in South India was reordained according to the Anglican rite. The most notable among them was Satthianadan, whose sermon on the occasion of his ordination (1790) was published in English by the S.P.C.K. to emphasize the need for and the possibilities of an Indian ministry.

The support of foreign ministers in Lutheran Orders during the first century of S.P.C.K. history was generally unchallenged. With the coming of the 19th century, however, the position was changed; first by the success of William Wilberforce and others in securing the establishment of an Anglican bishopric in India, and later by the Tractarian emphasis upon episcopacy and apostolic succession. The Church Missionary Society, founded 1799, at first followed the example and precedent of the S.P.C.K. in employing Lutheran (and also Reformed) missionaries trained in the Basle Mission House, but after the arrival of an Anglican Bishop of Calcutta, it was expected that all future missionaries, whatever their nationality, and all Indian ministers, would receive episcopal ordination. In 1825, moreover, the S.P.C.K. formally transferred the missions under its direction to the S.P.G. Thereafter, episcopal ordination became the rule for all ministers serving under Anglican auspices in India.

A consequence of the ecclesiastical changes of the English Revolution of 1688 was the resumption of relations with the Eastern Orthodox Churches on the part of the Non-jurors. A body of Anglican bishops, priests, and laymen, not inconsiderable in weight of learning and piety though small in numbers, seceded from the Established Church because they could not in conscience take the required oaths of allegiance to William III and Mary, having already taken similar oaths to James II, whom they regarded as still King *divino jure*. Consequently they suffered deprivation of their benefices, and organized themselves into a Non-juring Church, which maintained a vigorous and aggressive polemic against their juring brethren, whom they aspersed as schismatic. The paucity of their numbers and their comparative lack of influence led the Non-jurors to seek support and alliance from the Eastern Orthodox Churches. Their overtures to the Church of Jerusalem, however, met with a rigid demand for complete submission to Eastern Orthodox standards of belief, and the suggestion of an alliance of equals was rejected.

The *coup de grâce* was administered to the venture when Wake himself wrote in September 1725 to the Patriarch of Jerusalem, exposing the schismatic character of the Non-juring communion, "who, having neither place nor church in these realms, have bent their efforts to deceive you, who are ignorant of their schism".[1] Thus ended this episode which indeed was in its nature rather romantic than realistic; and there remained only individual and personal contacts between the Church of England and the Eastern Orthodox Churches. Not the least interesting of these was the conversion, about 1694, of Gloucester Hall at Oxford into a college for the education of youths of the Greek Church under the energetic principalship of Dr Woodroff, who had been in communication with various Eastern prelates, and particularly with the Patriarch Callinicus of Constantinople, to this end. The venture unfortunately came to an end after only a decade's history; and the remaining personal contacts were chiefly occasioned by such episodes as the visit to Great Britain of the Metropolitan Arsenius of Thebais towards the end of Queen Anne's reign, and the conferment of honorary degrees by Oxford and Cambridge on other distinguished visitors. Such contacts, however, were those of academic and ecclesiastical courtesy, and could contribute little to the work of organic union beyond the cultivation of better personal relations, and therewith of mutual understanding of the theological positions of their respective Churches.

During the 18th century individual approaches between leading Protestant dissenters and Anglican bishops continued to be made concerning the possibilities of union. These were facilitated on the one hand by the temper of the age, which was averse from dogmatism and sympathetic towards a latitudinarian interpretation of formularies; and also by the circumstance that two of the most eminent prelates of the Georgian Church, Joseph Butler and Thomas Secker, had received their early education in the Dissenting Academies. On the side of the dissenters, Philip Doddridge inherited many of the ideals and much of the irenic temper of Richard Baxter, and initiated discussions with influential churchmen. In a letter of 29 September 1743, Bishop Secker, then occupying the See of Oxford, complimented Doddridge on the fact that he himself in particular and, more generally, the dissenters "have done excellently of late years in the service of Christianity", and expressed the pious hope that "our common warfare will make us chiefly attentive to our common interest and unite us in a closer alliance".[2]

---

[1] G. Williams, *The Orthodox Church of the East in the Eighteenth Century*, 1868, p. lvii.
[2] *The Correspondence and Diary of Philip Doddridge*, ed. J. D. Humphreys, London, 1830, IV, p. 272.

Two years later, on 21 February 1745, Secker wrote further:

> "Your favourable opinion of the Church of England gives me no surprise, but much pleasure. And as I agree with you heartily in wishing that such things as we think indifferent and you cannot be brought to think lawful, were altered or left free, in such a manner as that we might all unite, so I have no reason to believe that any one of the bishops wishes otherwise; and I know some that wish it strongly, . . . nor perhaps were the body of the clergy ever so well disposed to it as now. But still I see not the least prospect of it."[1]

Despite this discouraging attitude, Doddridge persisted in his hopes; and in 1748 Dr Chandler, the eminent Presbyterian divine, discussed the prospect of union with Bishops Gooch and Sherlock. The latter prelate observed that the system of the Established Church

> "consists of three parts, Doctrine, Discipline, and Ceremonies; as to the last, they should be left indifferent, as they are agreed on all hands to be; as to the second, our Discipline is so bad that no one knows how or where to mend it; and as to the first, what is your objection?"

Chandler replied that the Articles must be expressed in Scriptural language and the Athanasian Creed be discarded; to neither of which did the Bishops offer any objection in principle. When the question of reordination was raised, Chandler insisted that none of his brethren would renounce his Presbyterian ordination, but "if their lordships meant only to impose their hands on us, and by that rite recommend us to public service in their society or constitution, that perhaps might be submitted to". The interview closed with a recommendation of the Bishops that Chandler should wait on Archbishop Herring at Lambeth; which accordingly was done.

> "The Archbishop received him well, and being told by Gooch what Chandler and he had been talking on, viz. a Comprehension, said, A very good thing; he wished it with all his heart; and the rather because this was a time which called upon all good men to unite against infidelity and immorality which threatened universal ruin; and added, he was encouraged to hope from the piety, learning, and moderation of many Dissenters, that this was a proper time to make the attempt."[2]

Later in the same year Doddridge also had an interview with Herring,

> "and had as free a conversation with him as I could have desired. It turned . . . especially on the affair of a Comprehension; concerning which I very evidently perceived that though his grace has most candid sentiments of his Dissenting brethren yet he has no great zeal for attempting anything in order to introduce them into the church, wisely seeing the difficulties with which it might be attended; but when I mentioned to him in the freedom of our discourse, a sort of medium between the present state and that of a

---

[1] *The Correspondence and Diary of Philip Doddridge*, ed. J. D. Humphreys, London, 1830, IV, pp. 381 f. [2] Ibid., V, pp. 42 ff.

perfect coalition, which was that of acknowledging our churches as un-schismatical, by permitting the clergy to officiate among us, if desired, which he must see had a counterpart of permitting Dissenting ministers occasionally to officiate in churches, it struck him much, as a new and very important thought; and he told me more than once, I had suggested what he should lay up in his mind for further consideration."[1]

Doddridge indeed had rightly judged that Archbishop Herring was of too timorous a nature to attempt anything positive either towards a "comprehension" or an interchange of pulpits, and his primacy was characterized by an unswerving determination *quieta non movere*. Moreover, when Secker himself succeeded to Canterbury in 1758, it does not appear that he initiated any practical measures towards "comprehension". Indeed, his biographer, Beilby Porteus, observed that

> "with the Dissenters his grace was sincerely desirous of cultivating a good understanding. . . . He considered the Protestant Dissenters in general as a conscientious and valuable class of men, and was far from taking the spirit of certain writings to be the spirit of the whole body. With some of the most eminent of them, Watts, Doddridge, Leland, Chandler, Lardner, he maintained an intercourse of friendship or civility, by the most candid and considerate part of them he was highly reverenced and esteemed; and to such amongst them as needed help, he shewed no less kindness and liberality than to those of his own communion."[2]

Notwithstanding the initiative of Doddridge and Chandler, therefore, and even granted the irenic spirit of Herring and Secker, nothing practical emerged from their abundance of goodwill.

It is more difficult to ascertain the place of the greatest figure of 18th-century religion in England, John Wesley, in a history of ecumenical tendencies. For although he touched religious life at many points, both in this country and in the New World, and although it was his proud claim that the world was his parish, yet the principal result of his missionary labours was the foundation of a new Society, and the addition thereby of another to the divided members of Christ's Catholic Church.

It is important, therefore, to observe that as early as 1746 he had become convinced by his reading of Stillingfleet's *Irenicum* and of Lord Chancellor King's *Enquiry into the Constitution, Discipline, Unity, and Worship of the Primitive Church* that he had "as good a right to ordain as to administer the Lord's Supper"; and "that bishops and presbyters are the same order, and consequently have the same right to ordain". Accordingly, it was only by the exercise of a considerable self-denial that he refrained so long from expressing this conviction in action. "For many years", he wrote in 1784, "I have been importuned from time to time to exercise this right by ordaining part of our travelling preachers. But I have still refused, not only for peace' sake, but because I was determined as little as possible to violate the established order of the National

---

[1] *The Correspondence and Diary of Philip Doddridge*, ed. J. D. Humphreys, London, 1830, V, pp. 75 f.
[2] Beilby Porteus, *A Review of the Life and Character of Archbishop Secker*, prefixed to Vol. I of *The Works of Thomas Secker*, London, 1811, pp. xlii f.

Church to which I belonged."[1] It is true that in 1747 he had commissioned Joseph Cownley as a preacher by placing the New Testament in his hands with the injunction, pronounced over the kneeling aspirant, "Take thou authority to preach the Gospel". But not until 1784 did he formally ordain ministers, and at first only for the American colonies; claiming that there were no bishops there to discharge this duty, and consequently

". . . my scruples are at an end; and I conceive myself at full liberty, as I violate no order and invade no man's right by appointing and sending labourers into the harvest."

Later he was driven by the logic of events to ordain also for Scotland, and finally for England, though he admitted to the presbyterate only three men for service in England. The fundamental cause of these actions lay in the constant pressure from his converts that they might receive the Sacrament of the Lord's Supper from the hands of their own preachers, upon whom they attended for the preaching of the Word, instead of having recourse monthly to their parish churches which they did not otherwise frequent.

In his conviction of the identity of the New Testament bishop and presbyter, John Wesley was in accord with a considerable volume of opinion in his own century; but his action in ordaining ministers, instead of breaking down the barriers between his Societies and the Established Church, served rather to increase their number and height. Thus the greatest religious figure of his age contributed more perhaps to the accentuating than to the healing of the divisions of the universal Church.

Notwithstanding, the Methodist revival was fruitful in kindling corresponding movements and itself drew inspiration from a variety of sources. It had evident affinities with the German Pietist movement, and Wesley himself visited Herrnhut. Similarly, it was closely related to the Great Awakening in the American colonies, though in this connection it was Whitefield rather than Wesley who made the greater impact upon the Evangelical Revival beyond the Atlantic. It was Whitefield's Calvinistic Methodism, too, which had most in common with the Evangelical Revival in the Church of England, and led for a period to close co-operation amongst all Calvinistic evangelicals, irrespective of differences of Church order. Examples of this have already been mentioned in relation to the London Missionary Society and the British and Foreign Bible Society; whilst the Countess of Huntingdon's college, founded at Trevecca in 1768, trained ministers indifferently for episcopal and non-episcopal Churches.

In the earlier stages of the Anglican Evangelical Revival, moreover, many of its leaders, such as Grimshaw, Berridge, and Simeon himself, practised an itinerant ministry; whilst co-operation found expression in such curious ways as the subscriptions given by Grimshaw and Henry Venn to the erection of independent chapels within Anglican parishes, in order to ensure continuity of evangelical teaching when a change in the incumbency was followed by deviations from this tradition. This co-operation, however, did not endure; for, on the one hand, the Calvinistic dissenters found themselves driven into the position of licensing their chapels as dissenting meeting-houses; and, on the other hand, Charles Simeon abandoned the itinerant ministry, and earned the reproach of being "more of a Church-man than a Gospel-man" by his part in the foundation of the

[1] *The Letters of John Wesley*, ed. John Telford, Standard Edition, VII, pp. 21, 238.

Church Missionary Society contemporary with the gradual withdrawal of the Evangelicals from the London Missionary Society and some other forms of co-operation with dissenters.

The Methodist revivals, both in their Arminian and Calvinistic forms, there-fore combined an ecumenical spirit and ideal with an actual result in the founda-tion of new denominations.

6. THE REASONS FOR FAILURE TO ATTAIN ORGANIC UNION

The reasons for the failure of the multifarious efforts which have been briefly surveyed to attain the objective of organic union are not far to seek. In the first place, little practical progress could be made without the active support of the civil power. Alike in Wake's correspondence with his Gallican friends of the Sorbonne, and in his negotiations with Jablonski at Berlin, the sympathy and practical help of the temporal authorities were necessary to success; and this ancillary prop was lacking for a variety of reasons. Throughout his voluminous correspondence there run two threnodic refrains: those of the indifference of the ministers of state and of the opposition of the rigid theologians, which together frustrated all his hopes and schemes. The champions and protagonists of union realized clearly that it could be achieved only on the basis of agreement in those fundamental articles of faith which are essential to salvation, and of agreement to differ on the wide range of non-essentials. Yet this principle was hard of acceptance by divines who esteemed every point of their confessional statements incapable of difference of interpretation. In vain did Wake point to the actual practice of the Church of England in the original framing of its Thirty-nine Articles and in the subsequent history of their interpretation as a pattern and model for the foreign Churches. The theological controversies in the Swiss Churches, centring in the Helvetic Consensus, were evidence of the little disposi-tion of many theologians to compromise even on non-essentials; whilst within the Empire the same differences divided Lutheran from Reformed.

Nor were the obstacles confined to matters of faith. The problems of Church order were equally intractable. On the Roman side, Wake's correspondence with Drs Du Pin and Girardin was followed by a protracted literary controversy in which Père Le Courayer defended the validity of Anglican Orders, supported by lengthy extracts sent by Wake with explanatory comments from the Lam-beth Registers and other ecclesiastical archives. This exposition of the Anglican position led to no practical result; but it was probably of considerable service in familiarizing educated French opinion with the facts of the Anglican episcopal succession. In his relations with foreign Protestants, Wake was insistent on the necessity for their restoration of episcopacy; and this was the chief stumbling-block likewise to all schemes of "comprehension" at home of Protestant dis-senters within the Church of England. Much play was made with the precedent of Archbishop John Bramhall, who, in ordaining some Scottish presbyters, gave to Edward Parkinson Letters of Orders containing this clause:

"Not annulling the former orders (if he had received any such) nor decid-ing as to their invalidity, much less passing judgement of condemnation on all the sacred orders in the foreign Churches—that we leave to the One who alone can judge—but only supplying whatever may previously have been lacking that is required by the canons of the Anglican Church and caring for the future peace of the Church, that all occasion of schism may be taken away and that the consciences of the faithful may be satisfied in such a way that none may have cause to be doubtful concerning his ordination or reject as invalid his priestly acts." [1]

How far this form of conditional ordination would have been satisfactory to English Presbyterians or foreign Reformed Churches, it is impossible to say. But the same problems remain to-day. Agreement in the fundamentals of the Faith is still not universally accepted as sufficient for mutual recognition and union; and the question of episcopacy remains the chief stumbling-block to unity. In some respects Wake was in advance not only of his own but of our generation; for he recognized the validity of the ministries and sacraments of the foreign Reformed Churches, and authorized members of those Churches resident in or visiting England to communicate with the Church of England, and Anglicans sojourning abroad to communicate with the Protestant Church of the territories of their residence. Perhaps the best epitaph upon the irenical movement of the 17th and 18th centuries, and on the individuals who sponsored it, is that written by Wake to one of his friends in relation to his own work:

"And when that day shall come, in which I stand before the judgement-seat of Jesus Christ, this will be not the least part of my confidence and hope: that though I may have been otherwise an unprofitable servant, nevertheless I have ever sought, counselled, and with all my zeal and effort pursued those things which belong to the peace of Jerusalem."

[1] J. Bramhall, *Works*, I, p. xxxvii. Tr. from the Latin.

CHAPTER 4

THE ORTHODOX CHURCHES AND THE
ECUMENICAL MOVEMENT PRIOR TO 1910

by

GEORGES FLOROVSKY

1. INTRODUCTION[1]

For many centuries, the Eastern and Western Churches lived in almost complete separation from one another. Yet this separateness is always to be understood in the light of the complementary truth that these differing blocks of insights and convictions grew out of what was originally a common mind. The East and the West can meet and find one another only if they remember their original kinship and the unity of their common past.

Christian unity was not long maintained, or rather has never been fully realized. Yet there is justification for speaking of the undivided Church of the first millennium. Throughout that period, there was a wide consensus of belief, a common mind such as has not existed at any later date. Men were convinced that the conflicting groups still belonged to the same Church, and that conflict was no more than estrangement caused by some grievous misunderstanding. The disruption of the Church was abhorred by all concerned, and division, when it came, was accepted with grief and reluctance.

Permanent separation between East and West was preceded by the decay of the common mind and of the sense of mutual responsibility within the one Body. When unity was finally broken, this was not so much because agreement could not be reached on certain doctrinal issues, as because the universe of discourse had already been disrupted. The East and the West had always been different, but the differences had prevented neither Jerome from being at home in Palestine nor Athanasius in his western exile. But gradually the point was reached at which the memories of the common past were obliterated and faded away, and Christians came to live contentedly in their own particular and partial worlds, mistaking them for the Catholic whole.

This separation was partly geographical, a matter literally of east and west. It was also in part a matter of language. Greek had been the universal language of the Mediterranean world, the common tongue of civilization, as of Christian thought and expression. But this factor of unity grew weaker, as Greek came to be generally forgotten in the west. Even Augustine knew it only imperfectly. Translations of Greek Christian classics into Latin were rare, of Latin classics into Greek even rarer. When the new barbarian nations came on the scene, they were unable to assimilate more than a small part of the traditions of the classical past. When the cultural recovery of the West at last arrived, very little of the Greek heritage was saved, and living continuity with the common past of the Church universal was broken. There were now two worlds, almost closed to one another.

The division also involved a conflict between the old and the new. Byzantium continued in the old ways. The West, as it recovered its intellectual vigour, developed a new method and a new technique of thought; under the influence of the great philosophical development of the 13th century, Western Christian doctrine took its definitive shape. Between the old patristic and the new scholastic approach there is a great gulf fixed. To the Eastern, union presented itself

[1] Unfortunately Professor Florovsky's text has had to be shortened, with his approval, to less than half its original length. Professor Florovsky hopes shortly to publish a book on the subject of this chapter, which will include in greater detail the material set forth in this chapter, as well as the material here necessarily excised.

as the imposition of Byzantinism on the West; to the Western, as the Latinization of the East. Each world chose to go on in its own way; the Westerns neglecting the Greek patristic tradition, which came more and more to be forgotten; the Greeks taking no account of anything that had happened in the West since the separation. In all ecumenical conversations to-day, the greatest difficulty of all is the recovery of the common universe of discourse.

The papal claims appear to be the main cause of the separation, and indeed present a continual obstacle to any *rapprochement*. But these claims should not be considered out of relationship to political factors. All Christians were agreed that there must be one universal Christian commonwealth. It was natural to identify that spiritual body with the one existing "world-wide" commonwealth, the Roman Empire. The only question was where the centre of direction of this commonwealth was to be found. Constantine had transferred the centre to Byzantium; the West maintained that in A.D. 800, with the coronation of Charlemagne, there had been a new *translatio imperii*,[1] and that now once again the whole of Christendom must be ruled from Rome. It was this extension of the schism from the theological to the social and political realm which made it clear how deep and irrevocable it had become.

The Byzantine Empire grew weaker and finally disappeared; the West flourished and grew increasingly strong. Because of its strength, the West has tended to regard its Christianity as normal Christianity, and to look upon the classical, patristic tradition of the East as an exotic or aberrant growth. Byzantium has been either tacitly ignored or disapproved. This judgement has not been without its plausibility. The centuries of Turkish bondage have grievously thwarted the development of Eastern Christendom. Regard for tradition may easily develop into a supine archaism. Byzantium has sometimes slept. But Byzantium is still alive in the things of the spirit, the representative of an authentic Christian tradition, linked by unbroken continuity with the thought of the apostolic age. Recovery of a genuine ecumenical unity will be possible only through mutual rediscovery of East and West and a wider synthesis, such as has sometimes been attempted but never yet achieved.

Even after the Reformation, the political factor played a large and unhelpful part. The point of departure was still the centrality of the West. Participants thought in terms of two opposing blocs; there was still too much of the spirit of "conversion", and of the imposition of one system of thought on the other world. Discussions were usually on particular points, and not on the basic issues. It was only in the 19th century that better understanding of history made possible more sympathetic *rapprochement*. The genuine theological issues have been brought into the foreground, and it has been realized that the problem of Christian unity is primarily a problem of the doctrine of the Church. Even though no practical ways to a solution have been found, at least the lines have been set in such a way as to make meeting fruitful and ecumenical discussion a promise of ecumenical fulfilment.

2. BOHEMIANS AND BYZANTINES

There was hardly any period at which negotiations of one kind or another were not in progress between the Orthodox and the Churches of the West, but over almost all these negotiations hung the heavy shadow of political opportunism.

---

[1] Transference of the seat of empire.

The complete failure of the union patched up between the East and the West at Florence (1439)[1] showed that along this path there was no true way out from division, that true solutions could be found only through unfettered theological understanding, and that this could be achieved only through a general council of the Church.

Throughout the 15th century the idea of a general council was constantly before the eyes of men. The Fathers at the Council of Basle had desired the participation of the Greeks, and had even sent a special message to Constantinople to invite the presence of a delegation—unsuccessfully, since Pope Eugenius IV was able to divert the Greeks to his own Council of Ferrara, later of Florence. But the clearest appeal to the whole of Christendom was made by a Western group which anticipated the Reformers of the 16th century, not only in a number of their convictions, but also in the hope that allies might be found among the Greeks against the nearer power of Rome. At Basle in 1434 the Hussites demanded that their cause should be submitted to a plenary council, at which the Greeks, including the Patriarch of Constantinople, and the Armenians should be present.[2]

The extent to which John Hus himself was influenced by the Eastern tradition is still an open question. There is obvious exaggeration and bias in the contention of some early historians,[3] that the whole Hussite movement was a deliberate return to the Eastern tradition, which had once been established in Moravia by St Cyril and St Methodius. Hus himself can hardly have been well acquainted with the Orthodox Church, and derived his teaching mainly from Wyclif. On the other hand, it is interesting to note that Wyclif did on occasion invoke the authority of the Greeks, if only because they were opposed to Rome. It is certain that not all memories of the Slavonic rite had been obliterated in Bohemia. We may with confidence go so far as to say that some of the Hussites were interested in the Greek Church chiefly as an example of what might be termed non-Roman Catholicism, but also because in the teaching and practice of the Eastern Church they could find an extra argument in favour of Communion in both kinds[4] which to them was as the Ark of the Covenant. At a later stage of development, when it had become clear that there was no further possibility of reconciliation with Rome, there was a specially strong reason for an appeal to the East, in the hope of securing recognition from the Patriarchs, and so of dealing with the problem of a regular succession in the ordained ministry.

It is probably in this context that we are to understand the remarkable attempt made shortly before the fall of Constantinople to establish communion between the Utraquist branch of the Hussite movement and the Church of Constantinople. Although a number of official documents and the testimonies of some contemporary writers have survived, it is impossible to draw up a clear narrative of what happened. In particular, it is not clear by which side the initiative was taken. A Czech source, the Historia Persecutionum Ecclesiae Bohemicae,[5] states plainly that the initiative was taken by Rokyzana, the Calixtine Archbishop-elect of Prague, that an appeal was made to the Greek Church in 1450, and that a satisfactory reply was received. Some scholars doubt whether this evidence is reliable, and a rather different account is given in the Greek sources. The main facts, however, seem to be well established.

[1] See Introduction, pp. 18 f.   [2] Mansi, Concilia, XXVII, pp. 857f.
[3] E.g. P. Stransky, in his Respublica Bohemiae, Lugd. Batav., 1634.
[4] Sub utraque, hence the title Utraquists by which some of the Hussites were known.
[5] Ed. of 1648, Chap. xviii, p. 60.

In 1452 one Constantine Platris Anglikos, "a humble priest of Christ", arrived in Constantinople and presented on behalf of the Czechs a "book of faith", i.e. a confession, on the strength of which he was favourably received by the Greeks. In this confession Constantine refers to the change of faith at a recent council, obviously the Council of Florence. He declares that he himself had been persecuted by the Papists, and had had to wander from city to city, until finally he arrived at the city "of true priesthood". He utterly repudiates the claims of the Pope. In order to test the extent of his agreement with Orthodox doctrine, the Greeks required him to answer a number of questions; these were drawn up by Gennadius Scholarius, the future Patriarch of Constantinople, one of the best Greek scholars of the day, who was also well acquainted with Western doctrine. The Greeks seem to have been satisfied that Constantine held the true faith and expressed right ideas on all points of doctrine, sacraments, and orders. Upon his departure he was given an *ekthesis* (statement) of the Faith, signed by a number of Greek bishops and theologians. Both documents still exist in Greek.[1]

Who was this Constantine Anglikos? He calls himself "Constantine Platris, and otherwise Czech Anglikos, a humble and unworthy priest of Christ". No person of this name is known from any other document. Clearly he was a foreigner—otherwise there would have been no point in examining him as to his beliefs. Why was he called Anglikos? Was he an Englishman, or at least in some way connected with England? In that case, what had he to do with the Czechs? It has been suggested that he was in fact no other than the famous Peter Payne, at one time Master of St Edmund Hall, Oxford, a fervent Wyclifite, who was deeply involved in the Hussite movement. This identification must be judged highly improbable. All that we know of Peter Payne suggests that his associations were with the Taborites, the more radical among the Hussites, and it is hard to imagine a more unsuitable emissary from the Calixtine, or more conservative, party to the Church of Greece. Peter Payne was known in Bohemia as "Peter Anglikos", or simply as "Anglikos", but it is not necessary to conclude that he had a monopoly of this title.

In the reply of the Greeks to "the confessors of the true faith of Jesus Christ", it is stated, on the evidence of "Anglikos", that there were many people of the same conviction in various countries—Moldavia, Bohemia, and within the Teutonic and Hungarian borders—and that even in England, among emigrants from these countries, there was a considerable group of Christians inclined to the Orthodox faith. A brief exposition of Orthodoxy follows. In conclusion, it is plainly stated that a profession of true faith is not of itself sufficient, and that it is necessary to be in communion with the true Church, i.e. with the four Eastern patriarchates. The Czechs are invited to join the Greeks. Priests will be sent to instruct them, and some adjustments in matters of ritual are not impossible. As far as we can judge from the reply sent by the Czechs to the Greeks, this message was favourably received by the Prague Consistory of Hussites of the Calixtine section.[2]

Who were the Greeks with whom Constantine was negotiating? The signatures to the Greek document are revealing. Every single one of the signatories, including Gennadius, belongs to the group of irreconcilable opponents of the

---

[1] They were published by the Patriarch Dositheos, in his *Tomos Agapes*, Jassy, 1698. A copy of this work was sent in 1725 by the Patriarch Chrysanthos of Jerusalem to Archbishop Wake, who deposited it in the Bodleian Library at Oxford.

[2] In Freher, *Rerum bohemicarum Scriptores*, Hanoviae, 1602.

agreement of union made at the Council of Florence. The intransigent enemies of the union had a special interest in negotiation with the Czechs, who were also bitterly opposed to Rome, and had been excommunicated by that same Council which had succeeded in annexing the East. We have already indicated the motives which may have led the Utraquists to seek a *rapprochement* with the Greeks. It was a case of two minority groups reaching out to one another in order to overcome the isolation from which each was suffering.

Confusion is thrown into this picture by the only Greek source in which the episode is mentioned—the well-known *Chronicon Ecclesiae Graecae* of Philip Cyprius.[1] Here it is suggested that the first step in the negotiations was taken in Constantinople. When word reached the Greeks of the noble effort of the Bohemians to reform the Church, they were filled with hope and confidence that communion could be established with them, and this they greatly preferred to communion with the Italians, of whom they had learned more than enough at the Council of Florence. They therefore sent a priest, Constantine Anglikos, to Prague to inquire into the matter. The report of this Greek delegate being satisfactory, he was sent again to Bohemia with a formal proposal. But in the following year, 1453, negotiations were terminated by the fall of Constantinople.

It is difficult to reconcile the two versions of the story; yet the episode is deeply revealing. It shows that already at that date the East had become involved in the actions and reactions of west European ecclesiastical policy. While standing firm in its own tradition, it could readily find points of contact with those in the West who were in opposition to Rome. Conversely, the East presented itself as a welcome ally to all non-Roman Christians in the West.

The episode of Constantine Anglikos as such had no results. The Calixtine party grew weaker rather than stronger and the further development of the Hussite movement took other directions. Yet it is interesting to note that again in 1491 delegates of the Czech Brethren were sent to the East in search of a living faith and a pure tradition. Unfortunately, very little is known of the results of this mission, though it seems probable that one of the delegates at least reached Moscow. Even more remarkable is the fact that in 1599, at the meeting with the Orthodox at Wilna with a view to the reopening of negotiations, Simon Turnovsky, one of the prominent Brethren leaders in Lithuania, referred in his proposals to the negotiations undertaken by Constantine Anglikos nearly one hundred and fifty years before.[2]

3. EAST AND WEST RELATIONSHIPS FROM THE REFORMATION UNTIL THE 19TH CENTURY

The Reformation was a crisis of the Western Church and did not directly affect the Church in the East. But before long the Reformation spread to some countries with a large Orthodox population, and the Orthodox were thereby compelled to face the implications of the new religious situation in the West. Poland was specially important in this respect.

The Orthodox, and especially the Greeks, were vitally interested in the political changes brought about by the religious strife in the West. They still cherished the hope of liberation, and still hoped that some help might come from

[1] Latin trans. by Blancardus, Leipzig and Frankfort, 1687. It must be said that the statements of Philip Cyprius give a far weaker impression of reliability than the Czech sources.

[2] Regenvolscius, *Systema Historico-chronologicum Ecclesiarum Slavonicarum*, Trajecti ad Rhenum, 1652, p. 495.

the Western powers. But now the situation was markedly changed. The West itself was divided. The main political consequence of the Reformation was that Europe was split into two hostile camps; religious divisions gradually hardened into the two great political alliances which were to struggle for victory in the Thirty Years War (1618–48). The Greeks had now to decide with which of the two power blocs it was wisest to associate their hope of freedom.

These Western powers themselves were interested in the moral support of the Orthodox, at that time under Turkish domination. We can trace through the centuries the close interest taken by foreign embassies at Constantinople in all discussions between the Ecumenical Patriarchate and the various European Churches. All ecumenical conversations unfortunately came to be complicated by diplomatic intrigues and political calculations. The inescapable fact was that at that period no political alliance with any European power—whether Roman Catholic or Protestant—was possible without some regulation of relationships in the religious as well as in the political field. Thus many of these ecumenical conversations were initiated, not so much because of any immediate theological concern, as from heavy diplomatic pressure arising from the general international situation.

There was another aspect of this general situation which should not be overlooked. Both religious groups in the West were interested in the witness of the Orthodox Church, which was regarded by all as a faithful representative of an ancient tradition. One of the matters of debate between Rome and the Reformers was precisely this: had Rome been loyal to the ancient tradition, or was it guilty of many unwarranted innovations and accretions? Conversely, was the Reformation really a return to the doctrine and practice of the primitive Church, or was it a deviation from it? In this debate the witness of the Eastern Church was of primary importance. Like the great reforming Councils and Wyclif before him, Luther would on occasion invoke the Greek testimony to the fact of Roman departures from the tradition of the Faith. In the 16th and 17th centuries we find the witness of the Eastern Church quoted constantly by both parties in the Roman-Protestant controversy. Roman apologists would insist on the complete agreement between Rome and the East, recently consolidated by the Union of Florence. They would insist on the unbroken unity of doctrine between the two Catholic communions through the ages, in spite of the "schism". On the other hand, various Protestant writers, and especially German Lutherans, would try to prove that the East was basically irreconcilable with Rome. They would point out that the very fact of the separation was proof that the two Churches were not in agreement.

The Protestants were always interested in the life and destiny of the Christian East. On the one hand, they were interested in securing exact and first-hand knowledge of the Turkish Empire, and especially of the Christian population in these conquered areas, for whom Western Christians could not fail to feel sympathy. On the other, Russia was becoming an increasingly decisive factor in the general shaping of European policy, especially in the East. Many books, of various types and of different degrees of competence, were written in the period after the Reformation on the life, doctrine, and ethos of the Eastern Churches, partly by travellers, partly by foreign chaplains and diplomats resident in the East, partly by scholars who could use not only written or printed material, but also information obtained from Greek exiles or from occasional visitors. No comprehensive survey of this literature exists; it was, nevertheless, of decisive importance in shaping European public opinion on oriental affairs. It is difficult to summarize the impressions which Western readers might gather from these various sources. There was usually a tension between two general impressions. On the one hand, Western visitors were often bewildered by the low standards of life prevailing among the Orthodox, in the main the consequence of centuries of bondage; and by the unfamiliar character of life in the Near East and even in Russia. Some concluded that this East did not really belong to Europe, but was another and an alien world, more closely linked with Asia. The Protestants tended to be unfavourably impressed by the ritualistic character of the Church, which they would describe as superstitious and even idolatrous. Some Roman Catholics shared this opinion, if for different reasons, and wished to plan a fresh evangelization of the barbarian and schismatic East.

On the other hand, true scholars could easily detect, beneath this unappealing surface, a deep spiritual life and the glorious heritage of the early Church. They were inclined to suggest that this heritage should be disentangled from its barbaric and superstitious setting, that is to say, that the Eastern Church should experience its own Reformation, and free itself from the embarrassing legacies of its own Middle Ages. In this way it might come very close to the Protestant world. Few Continental Protestants felt that there was anything they themselves could learn from the East. Anglicans, on the contrary, were inclined to believe that the prospective contribution of the Eastern Church might be considerable, simply because in the Greek Church continuity with the undivided Church of the first centuries had never been broken.

It is against this complicated background that we have to consider the various ecumenical contacts between the East and the West.

In 1557 a special Swedish delegation visited Moscow. Two prominent Church leaders were among the delegates—Laurentius Petri, the first Lutheran Archbishop of Uppsala, and Michael Agricola, the Finnish Reformer. The delegates met with the Metropolitan of Moscow (Macarius), obviously on the initiative of the Tsar Ivan the Terrible. The main topics for discussion were the veneration of icons and fasting. Greek was the language of the conversation, but Russian interpreters were very poor. The episode is interesting as a proof of interest on both sides in the religious aspect of relationship between the two nations.[1]

In the year 1573 a new Imperial Ambassador was appointed to Constantinople, Baron David Ungnad von Sonnegk. He took with him a Lutheran chaplain, Stephen Gerlach, a graduate of Tübingen University and subsequently professor at the same, who carried private letters for the Ecumenical Patriarch from Martin Crusius, a prominent Hellenic scholar of the time, and Jakob Andreae, Chancellor of the University. It might seem that Crusius had originally no ecclesiastical concern; he was interested rather in getting first-hand information on the contemporary state of the Greek nation under Turkish rule. Yet even in these first letters unity and fellowship in the Faith had been emphatically mentioned. A few months later a further letter was dispatched from Tübingen under the joint signature of Crusius and Andreae, to which a copy of the Augsburg Confession in Greek had been appended. Gerlach was directed to submit

---

[1] A very picturesque description of the meeting is given in the old biography of Olaus and Laurentius Petri: Johan Göstuf Hallman, *The Twenne Bröder och neriksboer, som then Evangeliska Läran Införde uti Nordlander, then Äldre Mest. Olaff Petri Phase, Första Evangeliska Kyrrioherde Öswer Stockholms Stad, then Yngre Mest. Lars Petri hin Gamle, Första Evangeliska Erkiebishop uti Uppsala, Til Lefwerne och Wandel*, Stockholm, 1726, pp. 118–21.

it to the Patriarch, and to obtain from him a reply and comments. It was suggested that the Patriarch might see that there was basic agreement in doctrine between the Orthodox and the Lutherans, in spite of an obvious divergence in ritual practice between the two Churches.

The reply of the Patriarch, Jeremiah II, was friendly, but disappointing from the Lutheran point of view. The Patriarch suggested that the Lutherans should join the Orthodox Church and accept its traditional teaching. He wrote in his own name, as an individual and not with synodical authority, but naturally he had the advice and co-operation of other Greek hierarchs and scholars. It seems that Theodosius Zygomalas was the main contributor, but the final draft was carefully revised by Jeremiah himself. The document was by no means an original composition, nor did it claim originality. It was deliberately compiled from traditional sources. The main authorities were Nicolas Cabasilas, Symeon of Thessalonica, and Joseph Bryennios, all renowned Byzantine theologians of the 14th and 15th centuries, and, among the early Fathers, especially St Basil and St John Chrysostom. Great emphasis was laid on loyalty to tradition. This constituted probably the greatest difficulty for the Lutherans, with their emphasis on "Scripture only".

There were some special points on which the Patriarch could not agree with Lutheran teaching. He agreed, in general, with the Lutheran view of original sin, but wished to stress human freedom as well. Nothing can be done without the divine initiative, yet the grace of God is freely received, and therefore faith and good works cannot be separated, nor should they be opposed to each other or sharply contrasted. In the chapter on the sacraments, the Patriarch insisted that there are seven sacraments. He could not accept the doctrine of the Holy Eucharist, as expounded in the Augsburg Confession; the Eucharist is not only a sacrament, but also a sacrifice. The Patriarch stressed the importance of the Sacrament of Penance, from both the theological and the moral points of view. He disavowed all abuses which had crept into penitential practice, but strongly insisted on penitential exercises as a helpful medicine for sinners. In conclusion, the Patriarch dwelt at length on some controversial points of practice—the invocation of saints and monastic vows.

Strangely enough, the Patriarch said hardly anything on the doctrine of the Church, and nothing at all about eschatology. He seemed to be satisfied with the statement on Holy Orders in the Augsburg Confession, that no man can administer the sacraments and preach the Word of God, "unless he has been duly called and ordained to this function". This was a vague statement and could be variously interpreted. Clearly the Orthodox interpretation was not the same as the Lutheran. The Patriarch concluded his message with a concrete proposal. If the Lutherans were prepared whole-heartedly to adhere to the Orthodox doctrine as expounded in his reply, he was prepared to receive them into communion, and in this way the two Churches could be made one.

The whole document is irenical in tone, and perhaps for that very reason it failed to carry conviction. It was not so much an analysis or criticism of the Augsburg Confession as a parallel exposition of Orthodox doctrine. It is the last doctrinal statement set forth in the East, in which little or no influence of Western tradition can be detected. It was, in some sense, an epitome of and an epilogue to Byzantine theology. It is clear that the Patriarch was interested in the new move in the West away from Rome, and he was probably asking himself to what extent it was possible to expect the Western dissenters to join the

Eastern Church. For him, this was the only natural approach to the problem of unity, and possibly it was the only approach which in the 16th century could have been considered. The East had been for centuries estranged from the West, and the crux of the separation was the papal claim to supremacy. Now there was a new anti-Roman movement in the West. Might this develop as a return to that earlier tradition, which the East had for ages steadfastly maintained?

The Lutherans at Tübingen were interested in exactly the same problem, but from an opposite point of view. Was the Orthodox East prepared to accept that sound doctrine which, as they held, had been formulated in the Confession of Augsburg? The Patriarch's comments were a disappointment. The Tübingen theologians felt themselves obliged to offer explanations, and supplied the Patriarch with some fresh material. The correspondence went on for several years, but was at last terminated by the Patriarch's refusal to enter into any further discussions on doctrine. He was prepared to continue friendly contacts, and in fact some years later another series of letters was exchanged between Jeremiah and his Tübingen correspondents; in these doctrinal topics were not handled.

Two points remain for consideration. First, the Greek translation of the Augsburg Confession which was sent to Constantinople was itself a remarkable document. The translation was first published in Basle in 1559 under the name of Paul Dolscius, and was reprinted in Wittenberg in 1584. There seems to be little doubt that the translation was in reality made by Melanchthon himself, with the help of a certain Demetrios, a deacon of the Greek Church, who was on mission in Germany and was staying with Melanchthon at the very time at which the translation was being made. The text used was not the official version, but a special version of the Variata of 1531; the translation was a free interpretation of the text, rather than a literal rendering. There is no doubt that this Greek translation was intended primarily for the Greeks and not for domestic circulation: Melanchthon was much annoyed by its publication, as he alleged, without his knowledge and consent. Was this just a diplomatic disguise or an adaptation to Greek usage? Or was the whole venture inspired by a deep conviction that basically and essentially Lutheran doctrine was in agreement with the patristic tradition? Melanchthon was a good patristic scholar and his respect for the Greek Fathers was genuine. He could sincerely believe that the Lutheran Confession might be acceptable to the Greeks. In 1559 he had sent a copy, with a personal letter, to the Patriarch Joasaph. His letter, however, probably never reached the Patriarch.

It does not seem that the Tübingen theologians intended their correspondence with the Patriarch Jeremiah for publication. They were compelled to publish by an unfortunate breach of confidence on the part of the Greeks. A copy of the Patriarch's first reply, by inadvertence or by a deliberate indiscretion, came into the hands of a Polish priest, Stanislaus Socolovius, who was chaplain to the King of Poland, Stephen Batory, and he published it in Latin, with some comments of his own, under an offensive title: *The Judgement of the Eastern Church: on the main doctrines of the heretics of our century* (1582). The book immediately obtained wide currency and was translated into German. Pope Gregory XIII himself, through a special messenger, congratulated the Patriarch upon his noble rejoinder to the "schismatics". This unexpected and premature publicity compelled the Lutherans to publish all the documents (1584). This publication at once provoked a rejoinder by the Roman Catholics. An irenical approach had proved to be a call to battle.

This intervention by a Polish priest becomes immediately intelligible in the light of the religious situation in Poland at the time.[1] The Reformation had quickly spread to Poland, and at first had great success. Numerous Lutheran and Calvinistic communities were established, especially in Lithuania. The attitude of the Roman Catholic episcopate and clergy was hesitant and passive. The Reformation had the support of the royal court. Poland, in the first half of the 16th century, could be described by a contemporary as a "paradise for heretics". It took a long time before the Roman Church could mobilize its forces. The invitation issued to the Jesuits (upon the initiative of Cardinal Stanislaus Hosius, one of the leaders at the Council of Trent) decided the struggle. At the same time there was a change of dynasty in Poland, and the new king was whole-heartedly on the Roman Catholic side. But there was also a large Orthodox population in the country. Roman propaganda was concerned not only with the suppression of the "Protestant heresy", but also with the abolition of the "Eastern schism". In the resulting conflicts, it was of importance whether the Orthodox attached themselves to the Roman or to the Protestant side.

Ultimately there was a split among the Orthodox themselves. Some of the higher clergy were in favour of Rome, and in the end almost all the bishops, repudiating the authority of Constantinople, went over to Rome; thus a Uniate Church was inaugurated in Poland by the so-called Union of Brest (1596).[2]

This secession of the Orthodox bishops created a strained and difficult situation for the Orthodox. The Polish Government, now avowedly pro-Roman, contended that the action of the bishops was binding on the people, that, from the legal point of view, the Orthodox Church no longer existed in Poland, and that those Orthodox who refused to follow their bishops were nothing but schismatics and rebels, and as such outlaws. Very few, however, among the clergy and laity were ready to follow the bishops. For many years a vigorous struggle raged between the Orthodox and the Uniates, not without bloodshed and the use of violence. There was also a continuous effort, in the name of religious freedom, to secure legal recognition for the Orthodox Church. It was natural for the Orthodox to seek the aid of their Protestant brethren, who were, at least from the legal point of view, in the same situation.

In 1577 a book was published by a Polish Jesuit, Peter Skarga, on *The Unity of the Church and the Greek Apostasy*, and this was followed later by another book in defence of the Uniate Church in Poland (1596). The Orthodox published a rejoinder—the *Apokrisis* (1597)—under the pseudonym of Christopher Philalethes. This was the chief apology from the Orthodox side. It was widely distributed, and reissued even in the 19th century, as a genuine statement of Orthodox belief. But in reality it was compiled by a Protestant. A Calvinist layman, Martin Bronsky, a distinguished Polish diplomat, was the author of this pro-Orthodox volume. It was based mainly on Calvin's *Institutes* and on the Calvinist anti-Roman polemical literature, a fact which could not escape detection by the Jesuits.

More important than theological controversy was the close co-operation between Orthodox and Protestants in the common fight for freedom. The Council convened at Brest in 1596 for the official promulgation of the union with Rome was broken up by the Orthodox laity. They were aided by the delegates of the Ecumenical Patriarch, one of whom, Nicephorus, was arrested and

---

[1] On earlier ecumenical activities in Poland, see Chap. i, pp. 60 ff.
[2] See Chap. xv, pp. 678 ff.

executed by the Polish Government as a political spy and rebel. The Council was split into two separate meetings—the Uniate minority with all the bishops, and an overwhelming majority of clergy and laity. The latter drafted a vigorous protest against the violation of their faith and religious freedom. The antipathy of the Orthodox to the Union was obvious, but their problem remained unsolved. The Orthodox had no legal status in Poland and no bishops. Canonically the Orthodox Church in Poland and Lithuania was under the jurisdiction of Constantinople, and thus Constantinople became vitally interested in the result of the struggle.

Politically much depended on the side taken by Poland in the general European conflict, by the result of which the solution of the Eastern question would be determined. Poland was already at loggerheads with Hungary and Sweden, which were associated with the Protestant cause. Again, the attitude of Moscow was of grave importance. Since the end of the 15th century, the Holy See had been deeply interested in the attitude of Moscow, and had made various attempts to secure its political support. In these attempts political and ecclesiastical problems were always intermingled. In the latter part of the 16th century, Rome was desperately interested in the question of the relations between Poland and Moscow. One of the greatest of Roman diplomats, who was also an expert theologian, Antonio Possevino, was sent to Moscow in the days of the Tsar Ivan IV (the Terrible). His political mission was to secure the adhesion of Moscow to the pro-Roman European league, and also its participation in the projected offensive against the Turks, in which the Orthodox living under Turkish rule were naturally vitally concerned. At the same time, Possevino was one of the promoters of the Uniate Church in Poland. At one time Ivan IV was regarded as a candidate for the Polish throne, and in the electoral campaign he had the support of both the Orthodox and the Protestants, but was strongly opposed by the Roman Catholics.

It is in this confused perspective that we have to interpret the unexpected visit of the Ecumenical Patriarch (the same Jeremiah II who had corresponded with Crusius and his friends at Tübingen) to Moscow, a few years before the Council of Brest. Certainly he had reasons of his own for making this difficult and dangerous journey. The Emperor at Moscow was at that time the only Orthodox ruler of international importance. The result of the Patriarch's visit was also unexpected. The Church of Russia was raised to the status of a new Patriarchate (1589); in the following year this was officially recognized by all the Patriarchs in the East, but was bitterly resented in Poland. As leader of the Greeks in Turkey, the Patriarch was interested both in the support of the Orthodox ruler of Russia and in the sympathy of the Protestant nations. For this reason he wished to continue friendly contacts with Protestant theologians. He wrote to Tübingen again during his stay in Moscow. All these non-theological factors weighed heavily on the ecumenical deliberations of that time.

Two special episodes must be recorded at this point. The first was more curious than important. In 1570 a Polish diplomatic mission went to Moscow. One of the delegates, John Krotovsky, was a member of the Church of the Czech Brethren and a convinced Protestant. He was accompanied by a theologian of that Church, John Rokyta, a prominent Senior of the community in Lytomysl. They had hoped to convert the Tsar to their faith. This was of importance, inasmuch as they were prepared to support Ivan as a candidate for the throne of Poland and Lithuania. The Tsar himself was interested in theology and was well read in patristic writings. He arranged for a public disputation about the Faith to be held. The Tsar imagined Rokyta to be a Lutheran, and dealt with Protestantism in general in his replies. Rokyta presented his statement, and Ivan answered with a lengthy theological treatise repudiating Lutheran heresies, a copy of which was handed to Rokyta.[1] This was in no sense an original work, but the argument was conducted on a genuinely theological level. The documents were published in Latin shortly after the meeting took place.

In the meantime, the legal position of the Orthodox in Poland remained unsatisfactory. Constantinople was interested in the situation. It is of interest to record that for several years an official representative of the Patriarchate was in Poland, helping the Orthodox resistance. This was Cyril Loukaris, the future Patriarch of Alexandria and Constantinople and author of the famous pro-Calvinist Confession. It seems that he made his first contacts with Protestants during his stay in Poland, and that his experience there to a great extent determined his later position in the interconfessional situation.

In 1599 an important conference met in Wilna. A small group of Protestant ministers, including Lutherans, Calvinists, and Brethren, met with the representatives of the Orthodox clergy and laity. The Orthodox leader was Prince Constantine Ostrogsky, one of the greatest magnates under the Polish Crown and a prominent leader in the field of education and literature. It was on his initiative and with his help that the first Slavonic Bible was printed, in his city Ostrog in Volhynia, in 1580. In a sense, he can be described as one of the first supporters in the Orthodox Church of the ecumenical idea. He was deeply concerned for Christian unity, and, above all, he desired that Christians in Poland should be united. For that reason he was interested at the same time in a *rapprochement* between the Orthodox and the Roman Catholics, and in a confederation of the Orthodox with the Protestants. He was more of a statesman than a churchman, and there was some ambiguity in his vision of Christian unity. Yet he did much to strengthen his own Church.

The immediate purpose of the Wilna meeting in 1599 was to agree on the policy to be followed in the struggle for religious freedom. A kind of confederation for that purpose was established, and then the further question of union was raised. The initiative was taken by the President of the Brethren Church in Poland, Simon Turnovsky, who suggested that an attempt to achieve complete religious unity should be made. The Orthodox representatives at the meeting were evasive, not to say openly hostile. Some questions for further discussion were drafted and sent to Constantinople, under the joint signature of the Protestant leaders. The letter was acknowledged by the Locum Tenens of the Patriarchate, the future Patriarch of Alexandria, Meletios Pigas. The reply was non-committal, as Meletios was anxious to avoid at that moment an open conflict with the Polish Government. No further action was taken. The initiative taken by the Brethren Church was indicative of a sincere desire for unity. Yet there was a utopian flavour about the whole enterprise, since the authors of the proposal were unaware of the depth of the differences between themselves and the Greek Church.

Since the fall of Constantinople, the Greek Church had had to face a very grave problem. An increasing number of Greeks was going to study in western

---

[1] It seems that this very copy is now in private hands in the United States—a photostat copy is available in the New York Public Library.

universities, especially in Italy. Even those who kept the faith of their fathers were in danger of being inwardly Westernized or Latinized. In 1577 the famous College of St Athanasius had been established at Rome, specially for Greek students. Roman propaganda among the Greeks was steadily growing, and was usually supported by some among the Western powers. The only alternative available was to send students to Protestant universities in Germany, Holland, or Switzerland. The real harm done by this Western education was not so much that some unorthodox ideas were adopted by the Orthodox, as that they were in danger of losing their Eastern or Orthodox mentality, and of thereby becoming estranged from the living tradition. At the same time the Orthodox Church was compelled to clarify its position in the raging conflict between Rome and the Reformation. It became usual at that time to use Protestant arguments against Rome and Roman arguments against Protestants, without checking either carefully in the light of Eastern tradition.

This was the root of a "pseudomorphosis" of Orthodox thought. This term was used by Oswald Spengler "to designate those cases in which an older alien culture lies so massively over the land that a young culture, born in this land, cannot get its breath and fails not only to achieve pure and specific expression-forms, but even to develop fully its own self-consciousness". We may use the term also in a wider sense. "Pseudomorphosis" may become a kind of schism in the soul, in cases where an alien language or symbolism, for some imperative reason, is adopted as a means of self-expression. "Thus", to continue the quotation from Spengler, "there arise distorted forms, crystals whose inner structure contradicts their external shape, stones of one kind presenting the appearance of stones of another kind."

Many reasons led Orthodox theology in those ages to speak in the idiom of the Roman or Protestant worlds. At first the influence was confined to theological vocabulary and method. The term "transubstantiation", unknown in patristic Greek, was first adopted without any desire to innovate in doctrine. The next step was to borrow the full scholastic terminology to express the doctrine of the sacraments. On the other hand, it was tempting to use Protestant terminology, e.g. on the doctrine of original sin, which had never been adequately formulated in the age of the Fathers or in Byzantine theology.

Further, we must not forget the continued pressure of non-theological factors. The Turkish Government used frequently to intervene in the election of Patriarchs, and paid special attention to the political orientation of the candidates. Patriarchs, especially in Constantinople, were often deposed, sometimes again re-elected. The long list of Patriarchs in the late 16th and 17th centuries gives the impression that usually a pro-Roman candidate was followed by a pro-Protestant, and vice versa.

It is in this connection that we must understand the strange and tragic career of Cyril Loukaris.

This remarkable man was born in Crete in 1572, and, after a period of study in Italy, was sent to Poland to serve as a champion of the Orthodox faith. In 1602, at the early age of thirty, he became Patriarch of Alexandria, and held this position for nearly twenty years. He was then transferred to Constantinople as Ecumenical Patriarch. His eighteen years' tenure of the patriarchal throne was marked by endless trials and reversals of fortune. From the time of his service in Poland, he had been a strenuous opponent of the Roman Catholic Church, which, supported by France, was bending all its energies towards making its position dominant in the Turkish Empire. The Roman Catholics retaliated by using against Loukaris every possible weapon of calumny, intrigue, and even violence. Four times he was deposed from his office, and four times reinstated. At last his enemies were successful in compassing his destruction: on 7 July 1638 he was.executed by orders of the Sultan Murad, and his body thrown into the Sea of Marmora.

Loukaris was a high-minded man, with a profound desire to bring about a reformation in the life of the Orthodox Churches and a restoration of the life of the sorely-oppressed Greek people. But the political complexities of his time often drew him away from his religious duties on to the slippery paths of politics, and his career was marked by uncertainty of principle and inconsistency of action. He "failed to reconcile his duty as the Primate of the Orthodox Church with the exigencies of high politics and with his aims as spiritual leader of his Nation".[1] Yet he stands out as the most remarkable figure in the history of the Orthodox Churches since the capture of Constantinople by the Turks (1453), and he is still widely venerated in Greece, and in Crete, his native island, as a great national leader and martyr.

The Greek Churches, under Turkish domination, were desperately in need of Western help. From an early date Loukaris was convinced that the Roman Catholics were wholly unreliable, and that such help as was desired could be obtained only from the Protestant powers. At Constantinople he was in touch with the embassies of all the Protestant nations, and corresponded with King Gustavus Adolphus of Sweden and his famous Chancellor Axel Oxenstierna, and the Transylvanian prince Bethlen Gabor, the champion of Protestantism in Hungary.

As early as 1602, Loukaris had become acquainted with the Dutch diplomat Cornelius Haga, who was later Dutch Minister at Constantinople, and with the Calvinistic theologian Uytenbogaert. The exact nature of Loukaris' relations with Protestants and Protestantism has been and is still a matter of controversy; but it seems clear that from this time on he became deeply interested in the study of Protestant theology, and tended to combine certain Calvinistic elements with his Orthodox convictions.

Later on Loukaris entered into relations with the Anglicans through the mediation of the British Ambassador at Constantinople, Sir Thomas Roe, a man of wide ecumenical vision and a friend and adviser of John Dury. Through Roe, he made contact with Archbishop Abbot of Canterbury, to whom he presented an ancient codex of the Pentateuch in Arabic. He also presented to King James I the famous *Codex Alexandrinus* of the Bible.[2] The Anglicans reciprocated with the gift of a printing-press with new typography, on which a number of theological works were printed before it fell victim to the fury of the Jesuits. According to one witness,[3] Loukaris had intended to dedicate his *Confession of Faith* to Charles I of England.

Even during his days at Alexandria Loukaris had begun to enter into contact with the Church of England. It was no accident that in 1617 he sent his Protosynkellos, Metrophanes Kritopoulos, to study theology at Oxford. We do not know exactly what instructions were given to Kritopoulos; but, on his way back

---

[1] The judgement is that of the late Archbishop Germanos of Thyateira, *Kyrillos Loukaris*, p. 31.

[2] This precious gift arrived in England after the death of James I.

[3] Thomas Smith, in his *Narratio*.

to Greece after the completion of his studies at Oxford and Helmstedt, he stopped at Geneva, and certainly entered into discussion with the pastors and professors there as to the possibility of closer relations between the Orthodox and Protestant Churches. It was as a result of these discussions that the Geneva Church dispatched a representative to Constantinople, the Piedmontese Antoine Leger, a convinced Calvinist, who was to play a most important part in the subsequent history of Loukaris.

In 1629 Leger published at Geneva, in Latin, a work entitled *The Confession of Faith of the Most Reverend Lord Cyril, Patriarch of Constantinople, set forth in the name and with the consent of the Patriarchs of Alexandria and Jerusalem and other heads of the Eastern Churches.* French, English, and German translations followed almost immediately, though it appears that the complete Greek text was not printed until 1633.

The sensation was immense. Here was one of the greatest Patriarchs of the Orthodox Churches of the East setting forth his faith in the authentic terms of Calvinism. The experts could recognize in the eighteen articles of the Confession the influence of the writings of Calvin himself, and of the *Confessio Belgica.* Immediate use was made of the Confession by both sides in the Roman Catholic-Protestant controversy—by the Protestants to prove the essential oneness of their faith with that of the Eastern Churches, by the Roman Catholics to prove the apostasy of the Greeks.

It was not long before efforts were made to prove that the Confession was a forgery. These, however, cannot be sustained. The original of the Confession is preserved in the Public Library at Geneva. The manuscripts, allusions in the letters of Loukaris, and the testimonies of contemporaries combine to prove beyond a shadow of doubt that the Confession really was his work. Nor can this be regarded as really surprising. It is probable that the emotional and political pressure exercised by Leger strengthened the Calvinistic impress on the Confession; but Loukaris had been deeply influenced by his contacts with the West, and there is no doubt that he had come to accept certain identifiably Calvinistic tenets. As Hugo Grotius commented, in this matter Loukaris was actuated by political rather than by theological motives. The setting forth of the Confession was an ecumenical gesture, intended to facilitate the *rapprochement* between the Orthodox and the Protestants which Loukaris judged to be necessary, and to secure the support of the Protestants in the conflicts which he saw to be inevitable. Yet this procedure was highly dangerous. An element of falsity was introduced into inter-ecclesiastical relationships, and reactions within the Orthodox Church were such as to make impossible the very thing that Loukaris had desired.

Loukaris was without doubt an outstanding personality. Yet his following within his own Church was comparatively small, and his position as Patriarch gave him no right to speak on behalf of the whole Church. Shortly after his death, the Confession was condemned by two synods, and this not only because the successor of Loukaris, Cyril of Beroea, was inclined to support the Roman Catholic cause; the condemnations represented fairly the Orthodox reactions to the situation. But it was not enough to condemn Loukaris; the harm, from the Orthodox point of view, could be undone only by the official substitution for the unorthodox Confession of another Confession, genuinely Eastern and Orthodox. The violence of the controversies which raged in the 17th century, and the repeated efforts to refute Loukaris, testify to the gravity of the situation.

The first theological refutation of Loukaris came from Kiev. This was the famous Orthodox Confession, commonly known by the name of its author or editor, Peter Mogila, a Moldavian by birth, of Polish education and training, and Metropolitan of Kiev. The work was a kind of catechism, and the name of Loukaris was not even mentioned. But contemporary writers unanimously regarded the document as a reply or rejoinder to the heretical Confession of Loukaris. It is difficult to say to what extent Mogila himself was the author of this catechism; probably it was a collective work. Originally it was written in Latin, and the original text has recently been discovered and published. There is no doubt that the book was written not only under Latin influences but also on the basis of Roman sources, e.g. the Catechism of Peter Canisius. Serious objections were raised against the original draft by Greek theologians, especially Meletios Syrigos I, during the consultation on the document at Jassy in 1642, and certain changes were made in the text. Meletios translated the document into Greek, and this edited and amended text received the approval of the Ecumenical Patriarch Parthenios in 1643. It was first printed in Holland in 1667, and was immediately used by the Roman Catholics for polemical purposes.

Peter Mogila may be regarded as almost an extreme case of the pseudomorphosis of which we have already spoken. It was he who organized in Kiev the first theological school for the Church of that region. For a variety of reasons, this school was organized on a Roman Catholic pattern. It was a Latin school, in the sense that all subjects, including theology, were taught in Latin. In Kiev in the early 17th century, this method might be considered normal, since in Poland Latin was the official language of education and even of the courts. When, however, the system was extended to Great Russia, the situation became abnormal. And this is what happened. All the theological schools were established on the Kiev model, and until the early 19th century all theological education was given in Latin, which was neither the language of public worship nor the spoken language of the worshippers. Thus theology became detached from the ordinary life of the Church, while the Orthodox schools became closely linked to the theological schools of the West, in which, whether Protestant or Roman Catholic, Latin was the language of instruction. In Kiev in the 17th century, the identification went so far that Roman Catholic text-books were actually used in the theological school.

In the 18th century, the contrary pseudomorphosis occurred. Theophanes Prokopovich (1681–1736) had studied in the Jesuit College in Rome, and had actually become a Roman Catholic. However, on returning to Kiev in 1704, he resumed his Orthodox faith, and became professor of theology and later rector of the theological academy in that place. In 1718 he was appointed Bishop of Pskov by Peter the Great. By reaction against Roman Catholicism, he introduced a number of Protestant theological text-books into the course of studies, and his own System of Theology, written in Latin, was in the main based on the *Syntagma* of Amand Polanus, a Reformed theologian of Basle. The successors of Prokopovich followed his lead.[1]

It is important not to exaggerate the effects of these contacts in either direction. Certain scholars were influenced by Western theological ideas, and this influence made easier a number of genuinely ecumenical contacts. But, although it took a long time for Orthodox theology to recover its native independence, those who had undergone these external influences were never truly representa-

[1] See later, pp. 189, 195.

tive of the Orthodox tradition, and there was always an element of illusion in hopeful contacts based on their presentation of the Eastern faith.

An interesting exchange of views between Russian theologians and Lutherans took place in Moscow in the early 17th century. The new Tsar of Russia, Michael Romanoff, planned to marry his daughter to a Danish prince, Valdemar, who was a Lutheran. There were difficulties in the way. The Russians would not agree to the marriage of the princess to a prince who was not Orthodox. Matters were not helped on by the decision of a Church Council held in Moscow in 1620 not to recognize any baptisms other than those of the Orthodox Church. Prince Valdemar naturally refused to be "rebaptized" and was deaf to all the attempts of the Russians to persuade him. For a considerable time discussion continued between the prince's chaplain, Pastor Faulhaber, and a group of Orthodox clergy. This was not so much an ecumenical exchange of ideas as a confessional dispute; yet it gave an opportunity for frank discussion of agreements and disagreements between the two Churches, Orthodox and Lutheran. In the end, however, the marriage proposals broke down, and Prince Valdemar went home.

The Roman Catholics had long been accustomed to invoke the witness of the Greek Church. The most interesting example of this use of the Eastern witness is to be found in the negotiations between the French Ambassador at Constantinople, the Marquis de Nointel, and the Greek bishops in the last quarter of the 17th century. These were connected with the famous French controversy on the Eucharist between the group of Port-Royal, Arnauld, Nicole, and others, including Renaudot the liturgiologist, and the Calvinist theologians, especially Claude, the Huguenot minister of Charenton.[1] One of the main questions discussed by the controversialists was the Eucharistic faith and doctrine of the ancient Church, and in this connection the testimony of the Eastern Church was sought and scrutinized. A careful study of the ancient liturgies of the East became necessary, and the great liturgiological publications of E. Renaudot were directly connected with the dispute. Reference to Eastern belief and practice was one of the main arguments on both sides, but the Eastern witness was differently interpreted.

The Western controversy naturally centred on the term "transubstantiation", the shibboleth of the Roman party, and it was essential to determine the meaning attached by the Orthodox to this particular terminology. The inquiry was pursued along two lines. First, the testimonies of the Greek Fathers, including the early liturgical texts, were scrutinized; secondly, an authoritative statement and interpretation was sought from the contemporary Eastern Church. The Calvinists used regularly to invoke the Confession of Loukaris, while the Romans were anxious to discredit and to discard this document; but nothing would serve to discredit Loukaris, who after all had held for many years two great patriarchal sees in the East, except an official document of authority at least equal to his.

The Roman Catholics were searching for witnesses everywhere, using the help of French diplomatic and consular officials in the various Orthodox centres. De Nointel was able to obtain a series of statements from individuals and from hierarchical groups; but the greatest reward of his zeal was that he succeeded in securing a "conciliar" statement, signed by all the Eastern Patriarchs and by

---

[1] The Roman Catholic documents and treatises related to this controversy were collected in the great book: *Perpetuité de la foi de l'Église catholique sur l'Eucharistie* (new edition by Migne, in four volumes, Paris, 1841).

other prelates, the famous Decree of the Council of Jerusalem of 1672. It is certain that a copy of the Decree was communicated to de Nointel officially and directly by the Patriarch Dionysius of Constantinople himself, and that the Ambassador was asked to produce an official acknowledgement of its receipt. It is difficult to say to what extent he had exercised any direct pressure. It seems, however, that he was urging the Orthodox to dissociate themselves, as clearly as possible, from the pro-Protestant tendency exhibited in the Confession of Loukaris.

We must not identify the "Romanizing" tendency in the Orthodox theology of the 17th century with a leaning towards union with Rome. Strangely enough, in most cases these "Romanizing" theologians were openly "anti-Roman". Peter Mogila himself, in spite of his close dependence upon Roman sources in his theological and liturgical publications, was the head of the Orthodox Church in Poland, whose very purpose and aim was to defy the Uniate Church of that country. Dositheos, the Patriarch of Jerusalem, who was chiefly responsible for the Council of 1672, was also a staunch "anti-Roman" (or "anti-Latin", as he would have been described in his own time), an ardent defender of tradition, a vigorous fighter against Roman propaganda and proselytism in the East. Later on, it was he who was persistently to dissuade Peter the Great from using in Russia any of the graduates of the Kiev college, or any "foreigners", meaning probably Greeks educated in Italy, whom he suspected of a "Latinizing" tendency.

The whole situation had a definite ecumenical significance. For historical reasons, the Orthodox had to restate their tradition with direct reference to the Roman-Protestant conflict and tension. At that time, the main problem was that of faith and doctrine, with a special emphasis on sacramental theology. The problem of Orders was touched upon but slightly and occasionally. The most interesting feature in this early phase of Orthodox ecumenical contacts was that it was recognized, in practice and implicitly, that the Christian East belonged organically to the Christian world, and that its witness and attitude were highly relevant to the life and destiny of Christendom at large. This was in itself an ecumenical achievement: it was no longer possible for the East and the West to ignore each other.

Peter the Great (1672–1725) was seriously concerned with ecclesiastical affairs. During his first visit to Holland, England, and other countries in 1699, he was interested not only in west European techniques, but in questions of ecclesiastical organization. In London he had conversations with Archbishop Tenison of Canterbury and with Bishop Burnet of Salisbury, who wrote of him: "I have been oft with him. On Monday last I was four hours there. . . . He hearkened to no part of what I told him more attentively than when I explained the authority that the Christian Emperors assumed in matters of Religion and the Supremacy of our Kings. I convinced him that the question of the Procession of the H. Ghost was a subtlety that ought not to make a schism in the Church. He yielded that Saints ought not to be praied to and was only for keeping the image of Christ, but that it ought only to be a Remembrance and not an object of worship. I insisted much to show him the great designs of Christianity in the Reforming men's hearts and lives which he assured me he would apply himself to."[1]

[1] Unpublished letter to Dr Fall, Precentor of York Cathedral, in Bodleian Library, MS. Add. D.23.

The interest displayed by Peter was in line with what is known of his outlook at that time. It seems that he was already fairly well acquainted with the problems of the Reformation, especially in its political aspect. He may well have been introduced to the subject by those foreigners in the "German Settlement" in Moscow, with whom he was very intimate. In London he had contacts with the Quakers. Apparently his interest in ecclesiastical problems was widely known; if so, we can understand why, as early as 1708, Leibniz should select Peter as the most suitable person for convening a new Ecumenical Council.

There was a general feeling among German Protestants at that time that a *rapprochement* between them and the Church of Russia was quite feasible. It was felt that the necessary adjustments in faith and doctrine could easily be made. Only the Church in Russia had to be somehow "reformed". What is usually called "the ecclesiastical reform" of Peter was in fact a sort of political Reformation, with an open proclamation of the Emperor's ultimate authority both in spiritual and in temporal affairs, a complete disregard of the traditional Canon Law of the East. The fact that the Eastern Patriarchs agreed to the change and recognized the new arrangement does not obscure the true meaning of the reform.

What was even more important was that, in the newly organized theological schools, a kind of Lutheran Orthodoxy was established as normal teaching. The greatest representative of this "Lutheranized Orthodoxy" was Theophanes Prokopovich, a very learned man, the chief ecclesiastical adviser of Peter.[1] Prokopovich was in constant intercourse with foreign scholars. There was a group of foreign scholars in the new Academy of Science at St Petersburg, and one of its members published in 1723 an interesting booklet under the provocative title: *Ecclesia Graeca Lutheranizans*.[2]

Some special links existed between Russia and the famous Pietist centre in Halle. The ecumenical interests of the Halle circle had always a missionary as well as an ecumenical connotation. Slavonic publications of the Halle centre show that there was an attempt to propagate Lutheran ideas in Russia.[3] In connection with the marriage of Peter's son Alexius to a German princess, the Berlin Academy, upon the proposal of Heineccius, the author of an interesting book on the Eastern Church,[4] was considering a plan for the "evangelization" of Russia, and sought the advice of Leibniz.

There was one Russian (or Ukrainian) student at Halle, Simon Todorsky, a brilliant student of Oriental languages, who was later Bishop of Pskov and instructed Catherine II in religion. Catherine II says of him that, in his opinion, there was no real difference between Lutheran doctrine and that of the Eastern Church. Under these presuppositions, a *rapprochement* between the two Churches could easily be achieved. No practical proposal to that effect, however, was ever brought forward on the Orthodox side. The only result was that the concept of the Church became increasingly vague in Russian theology.

Two episodes of the early 18th century call for special attention: the attempt by the doctors of the Sorbonne to negotiate a reunion with the Church of Russia, and the proposal of a concordat made by British Non-juring bishops to the Orthodox Churches in Russia and in the Near East. These proposals were very

---

[1] See above, p. 186.　　[2] See Bibliography (Kohlius).　　[3] See Chap. ii, pp. 100 f.
[4] John Michael Heineccius (1674–1722), *Eigentliche und wahrhafftige Abbildung der alten und neuen Griechischen Kirche*, Leipzig, 1711.

different in scope and nature, yet in both cases the initiative was taken by a minority group which desired to escape from its historical isolation.

During his stay in Paris in 1717, Peter the Great was received in a solemn session at the Sorbonne, and the question of the restoration of unity between the Churches of the East and of the West was raised. The French Church at that time was sorely agitated by debates on the famous Bull *Unigenitus*, which had been promulgated by Pope Clement XI in 1713.[1] Immediately upon the publication of the Bull, the Sorbonne had accepted it, but reluctantly, under the threats and pressure of the State. But after the death of Louis XIV the doctors reversed their decision, and voted almost unanimously in favour of an appeal to a future general council.

The Appellants, as they were then labelled, wished to strengthen their position by an alliance with other Churches. They had, as it seems, no special interest in the Eastern tradition, of which probably they had only vague notions, and no particular sympathy for the Eastern ethos. What they were interested in was prospective allies against the papacy, and doubtless they had been impressed by the growing prestige and influence of Peter the Great in the international field. Peter declined to take any action himself, but suggested that a direct approach might be made to the Russian bishops. A memorandum was drafted, signed by eighteen doctors, and registered at the Archbishop's office. It was a typical "uniate" proposal, except that the position of the Pope was explained in the Gallican spirit. The difference in rite and doctrines was admitted. On the *Filioque* clause it was said that both interpretations, Western and Eastern, were essentially to the same effect. The memorandum ended with a pathetic appeal to the Tsar, who, as a new Cyrus, could achieve the peace and unity of the separated Churches.

The document was sent to Russia, and a non-committal reply was communicated to the Appellants through official channels. It was pointed out that the Church of Russia was not competent to act on its own authority, being but a part of the Orthodox Communion. It was suggested, however, that correspondence might be opened between theologians of the two groups. This reply was drafted by Prokopovich, who had no sympathy with the Roman Catholic Church, even in a Gallican disguise. Another reply, compiled by Stefan Javorski (d. 1722), was in the meantime published in Germany, with the signatures of several bishops. It was to the same effect, though drafted by a man of "Romanizing" tendencies. The Sorbonne proposal was at the same time attacked from the Protestant side by Johann Franz Buddeus, in his interesting pamphlet *Reconciliation between the Roman and Russian Churches impossible*.[2] Buddeus was an intimate correspondent of Prokopovich, from whom he had obtained full information.

The second approach to Peter the Great was made by British Non-jurors.[3] The canonical position of the Non-juring group was precarious; its bishops had no recognized titles and but a scattered flock. Some leaders of the group took up the idea that they might regularize their position by a concordat with the Churches of the East. Non-jurors maintained in theology the tradition of the

---

[1] *Unigenitus* condemned 101 propositions alleged to have been found in the writings of the Jansenists. The Bull was not officially received until 1720, owing to the strength of the opposition it aroused in the French Church.

[2] *Ecclesia Romana cum Ruthenica irreconciliabilis*, Jena, 1719.

[3] See also Chap. iii. pp. 147 f.

great Caroline divines, who had always been interested in the Eastern tradition and in the early Greek Fathers. The Greek Church had remonstrated strongly against the execution of Charles I; the Russian Government had acted to the same effect, cancelling on that occasion the privileges of English merchants in Russia. Among the original Non-jurors was Bishop Frampton, who had spent many years in the East and had a high regard for the Eastern Church. Archbishop Sancroft himself had been in close contact with the Eastern Church a long time before. Thus there were many reasons why Non-jurors should look to the East.

In 1712 an opportunity was given them to establish contact with the Eastern Churches through a travelling Greek bishop, Arsenius, Metropolitan of Thebais in the Patriarchate of Alexandria, who came to England with a letter from the newly elected Patriarch Symeon Capsoules to Queen Anne. Some of the Non-jurors seized this opportunity to make inquiry on certain points of doctrine, especially on Eucharistic doctrine, so loudly discussed in connection with the controversy between Claude and Arnauld. Finally they commissioned Arsenius, who was going to Russia, to present their memorandum to Peter the Great. Another copy was simultaneously dispatched to the East, through Arsenius' Protosynkellos, the Archimandrite Joseph. The signatories regarded themselves as "the Catholick Remnant" in Britain, and applied for recognition and intercommunion. Their intention was to revive the "ancient godly' discipline of the Church", and they contended that they had already begun to do this.

This phrase probably referred to that liturgical reform or revision on which the same group was engaged at that time. A new "Communion Office taken partly from Primitive Liturgies and partly from the first English Reformed Common Prayer Book", was published in 1718. It was at once translated into Greek and Latin, and copies were forwarded to the Orthodox. The compilers probably thought that this new Office, deliberately shaped on an ancient and Eastern pattern (and especially on the "Clementine" Liturgy, i.e. that of the *Apostolic Constitutions*), would be the best proof and recommendation of their doctrinal orthodoxy in the eyes of Eastern people. The Greeks, however, were unfavourably impressed by the idea of composing a new Communion rite, and insisted on the exclusive use of the traditional Eastern Liturgy. Certain doctrinal points called, in the opinion of the applicants, for careful reserve. The *Filioque* clause was explained as referring only to the temporal mission of the Son; the writers were prepared to omit it, if reunion were likely to be hindered by its retention. Purgatory should be rejected, but a "certain inferior mansion" is to be admitted as a dwelling-place of the departed. Canons of the ancient Councils must be respected, but cannot be regarded as being of the same authority as "the Sacred Text", and therefore can be dispensed with if need be. No invocation of saints should be permitted, but communion with them in their perfect charity should be maintained. Concerning the Eucharist, it was stated that no "explanation" of the Mystery can be made obligatory, so that everyone may freely receive the Sacrament in faith, and worship Christ in spirit, "without being obliged to worship the sacred Symbols of His presence". Finally, serious misgivings were recorded concerning the use of pictures in worship. Strangely enough, the question of Orders was not even mentioned. The signatories expressed the hope that a concordat could be agreed on, and that a church might be built in London or elsewhere to commemorate the achievement, "to be called Concordia", under the jurisdiction of Alexandria, in which services might be conducted according to the Eastern rite and according to the rite of "the united British Catholicks".

The Non-jurors' document was signed in London on 18 August 1716. The application was favourably received by the Tsar and forwarded to the Eastern Patriarchs. Two years passed before a synodal reply, dated 12 April 1718, was ready. The reply was drafted chiefly by Chrysanthos Notaras, the Patriarch of Jerusalem, but signed by other hierarchs as well. It proved to be wholly discouraging. It was plainly stated that "our Oriental Faith is the only true Faith". The attempt of "the Luthero-Calvinists" to misrepresent it by publication of an heretical Confession, under the name of the learned Loukaris the Patriarch, was strongly disavowed. Then followed a detailed analysis of the proposal itself. There is no room for adjustment or dispensation in matters of doctrine—complete agreement with the Orthodox faith is absolutely indispensable. Besides this, the Canons of the seven Ecumenical Councils ought to be accepted even "as the Holy Scriptures" are accepted.

On all points raised by the Non-jurors, explanation was offered. A clear distinction was made between *latreia, doulia,* and *hyperdoulia*,[1] in order to make plain the doctrinal implications of the invocation of saints. Icons are a silent history, while Scripture is a speaking picture. The Eucharistic doctrine, professed by the Non-jurors, was sharply rejected as "blasphemy"; it is not enough to believe that "some grace" is united with the Sacrament—otherwise there would be a communion in grace and not in the Body of Christ—the elements are truly transformed, converted, and transubstantiated, or "changed" to become one with Christ's Body in heaven. Dispensations are available "in all temporary decrees", but only after exact scrutiny and by a synodal authority. Instead of permitting liturgical innovations, the writers look forward to the day when the Liturgy of St John Chrysostom will be sung in St Paul's Cathedral. All practical problems can be settled later; unity in faith must be the beginning of everything. Again no mention is made of the problem of Orders.

It is difficult to say to what extent the Eastern hierarchs understood the real position of their British correspondents, of the "pious remnant of the primitive faith" in Britain. No word was said of the Established Church, and no explanation of the historical situation was given. It is hard to imagine that the Eastern hierarchs did not ask themselves who those people in Britain might be. In any case, they were under deep suspicion; "for being born and educated in the principles of the Luthero-Calvinists and possess'd with their prejudices, they tenaciously adhere to them like ivy to a tree".

Two further documents were appended to the Eastern reply: (1) a synodal answer (especially on sacraments), "sent to the lovers of the Greek Church in Britain" in 1672, and (2) another synodal statement on the Holy Eucharist, dated 1691. It was obvious that the two partners in the conversation spoke different idioms. Nevertheless, the conversation was not yet terminated. In 1723 the Non-jurors sent to the East their second memorandum. They had not lost hope, probably because of "the generous encouragement" given by Peter the Great. In fact, the Russian Synod, established in 1721, was prepared to discuss the proposal, without committing itself in advance to any statement, and suggested that for this purpose two British delegates might be sent to Russia, for "a friendly conference in the name and spirit of Christ" with two delegates of the Russian Church. The delegates were designated, but their departure was delayed. The

[1] Three different degrees of worship or veneration.

negotiations with the Russian Church were terminated by the death of Peter the Great in 1725.

In the meantime the Greeks sent in reply to the Non-jurors' rejoinder a copy of the decrees of the Jerusalem Council of 1672. The different attitude of the Greek and Russian Churches to the Non-jurors' proposal can easily be explained, if we remember that at that time Theophanes Prokopovich was dominant in the newly formed Russian Synod, whereas the Greeks held strictly to the rigid line taken at Jerusalem under the guidance of Dositheos. It may be added that Peter the Great, for political reasons, was inclined to sympathy with the Jacobite cause. The whole enterprise was terminated by the intervention of Archbishop Wake, who wrote in September 1725 to the Patriarch Chrysanthos of Jerusalem to make clear the schismatic character of the alleged "Catholick remnant in Britain", probably in reply to the inquiries made by the Orthodox through the Anglican chaplain in Constantinople.

On the whole, the comment made by William Palmer on the negotiations is valid: "Both the Russian Synod and the British bishops seemed to treat of a peace to be made by way of mutual concession without clearly laying down first the unity and continuity of the true Faith in the true Church." He adds that the Greeks were free from this charge, since they spoke openly of "conversion". In other words, the whole ecumenical endeavour was vitiated by a lack of clear understanding about the doctrine of the Church. This was not an accidental omission. We meet with the same omission time and again, from Jeremiah's correspondence with the Lutherans up to the middle of the 19th century, when for the first time the doctrine of the Church was brought to the fore in all ecumenical negotiations. It is remarkable that in the time of the Non-jurors the question of Anglican Orders was not raised by the Orthodox correspondents.

4. THE EARLY 19TH CENTURY

The early decades of the 19th century were marked by unusual spiritual unrest in Europe. In the turbulent atmosphere of those stormy years, many were led to the conviction that the whole political and social life of the nations needed to be radically rebuilt on a strictly Christian foundation. Many utopian plans were formed, of which the most conspicuous was the famous Holy Alliance (1815).

Contracted by three monarchs, of whom one was Roman Catholic (Austria), another Reformed (Prussia), and the third Eastern Orthodox (Russia), this was an act of utopian ecumenism, in which political scheming and apocalyptic dreams were ominously mingled. It was an attempt to recreate the unity of Christendom. There is but one Christian Nation, of which the nations are the branches, and the true Sovereign of all Christian people is Jesus Christ himself, "no other than he to whom belongeth might". As a political venture, the Holy Alliance was a complete failure, a dreamy fiction, or even a fraud. Yet it was a symptomatic venture. It was a scheme of Christian unity. But it was to be a "unity without union", not a reunion of Churches so much as a federation of all Christians into one "holy nation", across the denominational boundaries, regardless of all confessional allegiances.

The initiative in the Holy Alliance was taken by the Russian Emperor, Alexander I, who was Orthodox but lived under the inspiration of German pietistic and mystical circles (Jung-Stilling, Baader, Madame de Krudener). A special Ministry was created in 1817, the Ministry of Spiritual Affairs and National Instruction, and, under the leadership of Prince Alexander N. Galitzin, became at once the central office of the utopian propaganda.

Another centre of this utopian ecumenism was the Russian Bible Society, inaugurated by an imperial rescript in December 1812, and finally reorganized on a national scale in 1814. The Russian Society was in regular co-operation with the British and Foreign Bible Society, and some representatives of the British Society were always on the Russian committee. The immediate objective of the Society was to publish and to distribute Bible translations in all languages spoken in the Russian Empire, including modern Russian. In the first ten years over 700,000 copies were distributed in forty-three languages or dialects. Along with the distribution of the Scriptures a mystical ideology was also propagated, an ecumenism of the heart. Positive results of this endeavour should not be overlooked; specially important was the translation of the Bible in modern Russian, undertaken by the Society with the formal consent of the Holy Synod. Unfortunately the new ideology was often enforced on the faithful by administrative pressure, and no criticism of the doctrines of "Inner Christianity" was permitted. This policy could not fail to provoke vigorous resistance. Many felt that the Bible Society was propagating a new faith, and tending to become a "new Church", above and across the lines of the existing Churches. Ultimately, the Russian Society was disbanded by order of the Government in 1826 and its activities were brought to an end. The Russian translation of the Bible was completed only fifty years later, and this time by the authority of the Church itself.

The whole episode was an important essay in ecumenism. Unfortunately, the problem was badly presented. Instead of facing existing differences and discussing controversial points, people were invited to disregard them altogether and to seek communion directly in mystical exercises. There was an obvious "awakening of the heart" at that time, but no "awakening of the mind".

In the *Conversation of a seeker and a believer concerning the truth of the Eastern Greco-Russian Church* (1832), by Philaret, Metropolitan of Moscow, we find the considered opinion on the basic ecumenical question of one who had been through the experiences of the age of revival, and yet was deeply rooted in the Catholic tradition. The immediate purpose of this dialogue was to give guidance to those Russians who were at that time troubled by Roman Catholic propaganda. But Philaret sets forth the problem of Church unity in all its width. He begins with the definition of the Church as the Body of Christ. The full measure and inner composition of the Body is known to Christ alone, who is its Head. The visible Church, the Church in history, is but an external manifestation of the glorious Church invisible, which cannot be "seen" distinctly, but only discerned and apprehended by faith. The visible Church includes weak members also. The main criterion here is that of Christological belief: "Mark you, I do not presume to call false any Church which believes that Jesus is Christ. The Christian Church can only be either purely true, confessing the true and saving divine teaching without the false admixtures and pernicious opinions of men, or not purely true, mixing with the true and saving teaching of faith in Christ the false and pernicious opinions of men." Christendom is visibly divided. Authority in the Church belongs to the common consent of the Church Universal, based on the Word of God. Ultimately separated from the Church are only those who do not confess that Jesus is Son of God, God Incarnate, and

Redeemer. The Eastern Church has ever been faithful to the original deposit of faith, it has kept the pure doctrine. In this sense it is the only true Church. But Philaret would not "judge" or condemn the other Christian bodies. Even the "impure" Churches somehow belong to the mystery of Christian unity. The ultimate judgement belongs to the Head of the Church. The destiny of Christendom is one, and in the history of schisms and divisions one may recognize a secret action of the divine Providence, which heals the wounds and chastises the deviations, that ultimately it may bring the glorious Body of Christ to unity and perfection.

Philaret was much ahead of his time, not only in the East, though to some extent his ideas served as the basis for the return to Orthodoxy of the Uniates in western Russia (1839). Yet his outline of the problem was clearly incomplete. He spoke of one aspect of unity only, namely unity in doctrine. He did not say much about Church order. Probably Vladimir Soloviev was right in his critical remarks: "The breadth and conciliatory nature of this view cannot conceal its essential defects. The principle of unity and universality in the Church only extends, it would seem, to the common ground of Christian faith, namely the dogma of the Incarnation. . . . The Universal Church is reduced to a logical concept. Its parts are real, but the whole is nothing but a subjective abstraction." This is an exaggeration. The Church Universal was for Philaret not a logical concept, but a mystery, the Body of Christ in its historical manifestation. It is true, however, that the sacramental aspect of the Church was not sufficiently emphasized, and for that reason the relation between the invisible unity of the Church and its historical state at present, "the Church in its divided and fragmentary condition", was not clearly explained.

Philaret was probably the greatest theologian of the Russian Church in modern times. He was a living link between several generations: born in 1782, he became Metropolitan of Moscow in 1821, and died in 1867, vigorous and active till the day of his death. He was widely read in the mystical literature of all ages and of all confessions, and he was always impressed by "warm piety" wherever he might find it. Philaret had been a student at a time when Russian theological schools were dominated by Protestant text-books, and the influence of Protestant theology can easily be recognized in his writings. All these influences enlarged his theological vision. He was aware of the existing unity of Christendom and of its destiny. Yet at the same time he was deeply rooted in the great traditions of the Orthodox Churches, and the true masters of his thought were the Fathers of the Church.[1]

The second quarter of the 19th century was a time of theological revival in many countries. There was a rediscovery of the Church as an organic and concrete reality, with special stress on her historic continuity, perpetuity, and essential unity. The famous book of Johann Adam Moehler (1796–1838), Professor of Church History in the Catholic Faculty of Tübingen (and later at Munich), *Unity in the Church, or the Principle of Catholicism* (1825), must be mentioned in this connection. Moehler's conception of Church unity meant a move from a static to a dynamic, or even prophetic, interpretation. The Church was shown to be not so much an institution as a living organism, and its institutional aspect was described as a spontaneous manifestation of its inner being.

---

[1] On Philaret, see Bibliography (Stourdza and esp. Florovsky, *The Ways*, etc., pp. 166–84). Also A. P. Stanley, *Lectures on the History of the Eastern Church* (Everyman ed.), p. 377; and for a personal impression *Memoirs of Stephen Grellet*, I, pp. 395 f., 414, 421.

Tradition itself was interpreted as a factor of growth and life, and Moehler's appeal to Christian antiquity was by no means just an archaeological concern. The past was still alive, as the vital power and spiritual leaven, as "the depth of the present".[1]

In Russia, Alexis S. Khomiakov (1804–60) was very close to Moehler in his doctrine of the Church, and probably was well acquainted with his writings, though he arrived at his conclusions by an independent study of the Fathers.[2] In all these cases there was a renewed interest in Christian antiquity, regarded rather as a source of inspiration than as a ready pattern to which the Church must be conformed. Identity of Christian belief must be warranted by universal consent through the ages. But this was no longer considered simply as a formal identity of doctrine, taken as a set of propositions, but rather as a perpetually renewed experience of the living Church, which professes beliefs and teaches doctrines out of its unchangeable vision and experience. The Church itself now becomes the main subject of theological study.

5. BETWEEN THE CHURCHES

One of the most remarkable aspects of this general revival of interest in the Church was the Oxford Movement in England and in the Anglican Churches. The Church of England, it was and is maintained by Anglican authorities, *is* the Catholic Church in England. But if so, what is the relation of this Catholic body to other Catholic Churches elsewhere? The first answer was given in the "Branch" theory of the Church. As J. H. Newman succinctly expressed it: "We are the English Catholics; abroad are the Roman Catholics, some of whom are also among ourselves; elsewhere are the Greek Catholics."[3] But since the co-existence of more than one form of the Catholic Church in one place involves schism, "Catholics" when in England should be Anglican, when in Rome Roman, and when in Moscow Orthodox.[4]

This theory amounted to the contention that, strictly speaking, the Church was not divided at all, and that only visible communication or communion had been broken; the problem of reunion therefore consisted in the restoration of the suspended intercommunion, or in the mutual recognition of the separated branches of the Catholic Church. This view was pressed strongly and persistently by William Palmer, of Worcester College, Oxford,[5] in the book which can be regarded as the first systematic presentation of the Tractarian doctrine of the Church: *A Treatise on the Church of Christ: designed chiefly for the use of students of Theology* (1838). In the author's opinion, external communion did not belong to the essence of the Church, and consequently the Church was still one, although the visible unity of the body had been lost. It should be noted again that, according to this theory or interpretation, a very wide variety of doctrinal views and practices was compatible with essential unity. Or, in other words, the

---

[1] On Moehler, see further Bibliography.

[2] For recent studies in the thought of Khomiakov, see Bibliography.

[3] Sermon on "Submission to Church Authority", 29 November 1829, in *Parochial and Plain Sermons*, III, ed. of 1885, pp. 191 f. Where and when the "Branch" theory was first worked out is uncertain, but something very like it is already found in the prayer of Bishop Lancelot Andrewes for "the Catholic Church—Eastern, Western, British".

[4] See J. H. Newman, "Prefatory Notice" to W. Palmer, *Notes on a Visit to the Russian Church*, pp. v–vii.

[5] W. Palmer of Worcester College is to be clearly distinguished from "Deacon" W. Palmer of Magdalen College, whose visits to Russia will be described later in this chapter.

main emphasis was on the reality of the Church, and not so much on doctrine as such.

It was precisely at this point that a major misunderstanding between the Anglican and Orthodox Churches was bound to arise. Even though the Orthodox did not on all occasions openly and formally question the initial assumption of the Anglicans, it was inevitable that they should always insist on identity in doctrine, and make the reality of the Church itself dependent upon the purity and completeness of the Faith. The basic obstacle to *rapprochement* between Anglicans and the Churches of the East lay precisely here. Eastern theologians were bound to insist that the Orthodox Church is the only true Church, and all other Christian bodies are but schisms, i.e. that the essential unity of Christendom has been broken. This claim could be variously phrased and qualified, but, in one form or another, it would unfailingly be made.

The early Tractarians were not deeply interested in the Eastern Churches or in the possibility of contact with them. A world of ignorance, prejudices, and misunderstanding still existed between the Churches. But gradually a change took place. As early as 1841, we find E. B. Pusey writing: "Why should we . . . direct our eyes to the Western Church alone, which, even if united in itself would yet remain sadly maimed, and sadly short of the Oneness she had in her best days, if she continued severed from the Eastern?" [1] There can be little doubt that Pusey had been stirred and interested by the new contacts which had begun to take effect shortly before he wrote these words.

In 1839 the Rev. George Tomlinson, at that time Secretary of the S.P.C.K., and later first Bishop of Gibraltar (1842), was sent to the East, primarily in order to ascertain the needs of the Greek Church in the field of religious literature. He was given commendatory letters, written in classical Greek and addressed to "the Bishops of the Holy Eastern Church", by the Archbishop of Canterbury and the Bishop of London. He called on the Patriarch of Constantinople and explained to him the character of the English Church, stressing its Catholic character and its friendly disposition "toward the Mother Church of the East". He explained that the Church of England had no missionary objectives in the Levant, but was interested only in fraternal intercourse with the Eastern Church.[2]

The same attitude was also taken by the American Episcopal representative at Constantinople, the Rev. Horatio (later Bishop) Southgate, the acting head of the "mission" of the Protestant Episcopal Church to the East. He was following closely the official instruction given to him by the Presiding Bishop, Alexander V. Griswold: "Our great desire is to commence and to promote a friendly intercourse between the two branches of the One Catholic and Apostolic Church." Bishop Griswold was himself a man of strong Evangelical convictions, but his directives were coloured by a characteristically Anglican conception of ecumenical relationships.[3]

Pusey seemed to be justified in his conclusions. "This reopened intercourse with the East", he wrote to the Archbishop, "is a crisis in the history of our Church. It is a wave which may carry us onward, or, if we miss it, it may bruise us sorely and fall on us, instead of landing us on the shore. The union or dis-

---

[1] *A Letter to the Rev. R. M. Jelf, D.D.*, Oxford, 1841, pp. 184 f.

[2] George Tomlinson, *Report of a Journey to the Levant.*

[3] See P. E. Shaw, *American Contacts*, pp. 35 ff.; and for the earlier American "mission" of Dr Hill, see S. D. Denison, *A History of the Foreign Missionary Work of the Protestant Episcopal Church*, I, New York, 1871, pp. 142 ff.

union of the Church for centuries may depend on the wisdom with which this providential opening is employed."[1] In this perspective, "the Palmer episode" appears as much more than an eccentric personal venture, deeply as it was coloured by the individual character of the man and his private convictions and manners.

William Palmer (1811–79) was described by one of his friends as an "ecclesiastical Don Quixote". He was a man of unusual abilities: wide learning, powerful intellect, steadfastness of purpose, unbending sincerity; but rather inflexible and obstinate. His main weakness was "his inability to reconcile himself to the conditions of imperfect humanity and human institutions". In 1840 Palmer decided to visit Russia. He went, fortified by a Latin letter from the President of Magdalen College, the venerable Dr Routh. The letter stated that Palmer was going to Russia in order to study the doctrines and rites of the Church, and to learn Russian. Then followed an unexpected sentence: "Further, I ask, and even adjure in the name of Christ, all the most holy Archbishops and Bishops, and especially the Synod itself, that they will examine him as to the orthodoxy of his faith with a charitable mind, and, if they find in him all that is necessary to the integrity of the true and saving faith, then that they will also admit him to communion in the Sacraments."

As was to be expected, Palmer's hope was frustrated. His claim to be a member of the Catholic Church was met with astonishment. Was not the Church of England, after all, a Protestant body? In 1838 and 1839 Palmer had written in Latin an Introduction to the Thirty-nine Articles, which he endeavoured to interpret in a "Catholic" sense. This he now offered to the Russian authorities as a basis for doctrinal discussion. Not everything in Palmer's explanations was satisfactory to the Russians. They insisted on complete conformity in all doctrines, and would not consent to confine agreement to those doctrines which had been formally stated in the period before the separation of East and West. The main interlocutor of Palmer was the Archpriest Basil Koutnevich, who was a member of the Holy Synod. He was ready to admit that doctrinal differences between the Orthodox and Anglican Churches, if properly interpreted, were inconsiderable. Nevertheless, in his opinion, the Anglican Church was a separate communion. The Eastern Church was the only true and orthodox Church, and all other communions had deviated from the truth. Yet, since "Christ is the centre of all", some Christian life was possible in the separated bodies also. Naturally the Russians were staggered, as Palmer himself stated, "at the idea of one visible Church being made up of three communions, differing in doctrine and rites, and two of them at least condemning and anathematizing the others". In Palmer's opinion, Russian theologians and prelates were not at all clear on the definition of the visible Catholic Church, "but were either vaguely liberal, or narrowly Greek".

Palmer met many people with whom he could discuss problems as he could have done at home, at Oxford or elsewhere. Finally, he had an interview with the Metropolitan Philaret. The latter could not accept Palmer's initial assumption that the unity of the Church could be preserved when there was no longer unity in doctrine. "The Church should be perfectly one in belief", Philaret contended. The distinction between essential dogmas and secondary opinions

[1] E. B. Pusey, *A Letter to His Grace the Archbishop of Canterbury, on some Circumstances connected with the Present Crisis in the English Church*, Oxford, 1842, p. 118.

seemed to him precarious and difficult to draw. "Your language", Philaret told Palmer, "suits well enough for the 4th century, but is out of place in the present state of the world . . . now at any rate there is division." And therefore it was impossible to act in an individual case before the question of relationship between the two Churches, the Anglican and Orthodox, had been settled in general terms. Moreover, it was by no means clear to what extent Palmer could be regarded as an authentic interpreter of the official teaching and standing of the Anglican Church.

In brief, the Russian authorities refused to regard Palmer's membership in the Church of England as a sufficient reason for claiming communicant status in the Orthodox Church, and could not negotiate reunion with a private individual. Yet there was readiness from the Russian side to inaugurate some sort of negotiations. Palmer returned to Russia in 1842, with slightly strengthened credentials. The Russian Synod once more refused to negotiate on his terms, but welcomed his desire to enter into communion with the Orthodox Church. Identity of belief was stressed as an indispensable prerequisite of communion, and reference was made to the answer given by the Eastern Patriarchs to the Non-jurors in 1723. Palmer persisted and presented a new petition to the Synod, asking that a confessor should be appointed to examine his beliefs and to show his errors. Fr Koutnevich was appointed and made it clear that, in his opinion, certain of the Thirty-nine Articles were obviously not in agreement with Orthodox doctrine. Palmer, in reply, offered his own conciliatory explanation of the Articles in question. But could he prove that his contentions would be endorsed by responsible authorities of the Church to which he belonged?

Palmer's next task, therefore, was to defend his views as being not merely personal to himself, but a legitimate exposition of Anglican doctrine, and to secure some kind of official approbation. His method was to republish in English Philaret's *Longer Russian Catechism*, together with a long Appendix, consisting mainly of excerpts from Anglican official documents and from the works of leading divines, aimed at demonstrating the existence within Anglicanism of a tradition of doctrine capable of being reconciled with the demands of the Orthodox. The whole was published anonymously at Aberdeen in 1846 under the title *A Harmony of Anglican Doctrine with the Doctrine of the Catholic and Apostolic Church of the East*.[1] Palmer, who was by now somewhat doubtful as to how far the State-ridden Church of England was likely to be attracted to his ideas, turned to the Scottish Episcopal Church, in the hope that it might synodically assert such doctrine as he had commended to the Russians. Palmer's book and his appeal did meet with some response among Scottish Episcopalians, but it was wholly unrealistic to suppose that that Church would endanger its relations with the whole of the rest of the Anglican Communion by coming out boldly in favour of doctrines which the majority of its bishops and faithful members did not hold.[2]

The negative attitude of the Scottish bishops came as a great shock to Palmer; after a time of grave indecision, he decided to seek admission to the Orthodox Church. An unexpected difficulty confused his plans. The validity of his bap-

---

[1] A Greek translation of this book was published at Athens in 1851.

[2] Bishop Torry of St Andrews, Dunkeld, and Dunblane did consent to write an "advertisement" to Palmer's appeal. J. M. Neale, regretting that more attention was not paid to Palmer's book, expressed the judgement that "it will probably stand, in the further history of our Churches, as the most remarkable event that had occurred since the disruption of the Nonjurors". *Life and Times of Patrick Torry, D.D.*, 1856, p. 224.

tism was questioned by the Greeks, whereas in Russia it had been formally recognized. He could not reconcile himself with such a flagrant dissension within the same communion on a matter of primary importance. On the other hand, he could not continue outside what he had come to regard as the visible communion of the Catholic Church. Finally, he joined the Church of Rome.[1] In his conversations with the Russian ecclesiastical authorities Palmer was concerned mainly with those particular points of doctrine on which disagreement was alleged to exist between the two Churches. The ultimate question, however, concerned the nature and character of the Anglican Communion itself. For Palmer it was a "branch" of the Church Catholic. For the Orthodox this claim was unacceptable for two reasons. First, Palmer could prove that some individuals in the Anglican Churches did hold "Orthodox beliefs", but not that this was the faith of the whole Communion. Secondly, the Orthodox were not themselves in agreement as to the status of non-Orthodox communions. Discussion centred on this very point in the correspondence of Palmer with Khomiakov in the years 1844–54.

Khomiakov was a layman and had no official position in the Church. Yet his influence was to grow. His aim was to bring back Orthodox teaching to the standard of the Fathers and the experience of the living Church. The unity of the Church was the source of his theological vision. The Church is itself unity, "a unity of the grace of God, living in a multitude of rational creatures, submitting willingly to grace". This is a mystery. But the mystery is fully embodied in the visible, i.e. historical, Church. Khomiakov's conception was much more sacramental than mystical. The reality of the sacraments, in his conception, depended upon the purity of the Faith, and he hesitated therefore to admit the validity or reality of sacraments in those Christian bodies which were in schism or error. The "One Church" was for Khomiakov essentially identical with the Orthodox Church of the East. Just because the unity of the Church was created by the Spirit and not by organization, a schism, in Khomiakov's opinion, would inevitably cut the separated off from the inner unity of the Church. The "Western communions", in his view, were outside the Church. Some links obviously still did exist, but they were of such a character that no theological formulation was possible: "united to her by ties which God has not willed to reveal to her". The Church on earth cannot pass an ultimate judgement on those who do not belong to its fold. It is impossible to state to what extent errors may deprive individuals of salvation.

The real question is, however, about the identity of the Church itself. What is essential here is, first of all, "a complete harmony, or a perfect unity of doctrine". For Khomiakov, this was not merely an intellectual agreement, but rather an inner unanimity, a "common life" in Catholic truth. "Unions" are impossible in the Orthodox Church—there can be but "unity". This "unity" has been actually broken: the West separated itself from the unity. Unity can be restored only by a return of those who went their own way, instead of abiding in unity. "The Church cannot be a harmony of discords; it cannot be a numerical sum of Orthodox, Latins, and Protestants. It is nothing if it is not perfect inward harmony of creed and outward harmony of expression."

Khomiakov believed that "sacraments were performed only in the bosom of the true Church", and could not be separated from that unity in faith and grace which was, on his interpretation, the very being of the Church. Variations in

[1] On the Palmer episode see Bibliography, especially under Palmer, Shaw.

the manner in which the Orthodox Church received those who decided to join it made no real difference. The rites may vary, but in any case some "renovation" of the rites conferred outside the Orthodox Church "was virtually contained in the rite or fact of reconciliation". This was written before Palmer had to face the fact of divergent practice in the matter of reconciliation in his own case. When this happened, Khomiakov expressed his disagreement with the Greek practice, but refused to attach great importance to the difference. In any case, there had to be some act of first incorporation into the Church. For Khomiakov the Church was real precisely as an actual communion in truth and in grace, both inseparably belonging together. Those who do not share in this communion are not in the Church. The reality of the Church is indivisible.

It was at this point that the first editor of Khomiakov's letters to Palmer (in Russian), Fr Alexander M. Ivantzov-Platonov, Professor of Church History at the University of Moscow, found it necessary to add a critical footnote. On the whole, he shared Khomiakov's interpretation of the Church, but was not prepared to deny the presence of sacramental grace in the separated communions. Ivantzov had studied at the Moscow Academy, and was probably influenced by the ideas of Philaret. There was an obvious difference between the two interpretations: Philaret's conception was wider and more comprehensive; Khomiakov was more cautious and reserved. Both interpretations still co-exist in the Orthodox Church, with resulting differences of approach to the main ecumenical problem.[1]

Palmer's approach to the Russian Church was a private and personal move. Yet it did not fail to arouse interest in the Anglican Church among the Russians. At his first departure from Russia in 1842 he was told by the Chief Procurator of the Holy Synod, Count Pratassov, that a new chaplain was to be appointed to the Russian Church in London, who might be able to learn the language and study Anglican divinity. In 1843 the Rev. Eugene Popov, a graduate of the St Petersburg Theological Academy, was transferred from Copenhagen to London, and continued to serve there until his death in 1875. Fr Popov used to send periodical reports to the Holy Synod concerning ecclesiastical affairs in England, and established close links with some leading churchmen, including Pusey and Newman. Unfortunately, these reports were published only in part, many years after the author's death, and only in Russian. Fr Popov at first had hopes of union, but changed his attitude in later years.[2] Certain links were established between Oxford and Moscow, and theological professors and students in Moscow used to collate Greek manuscripts of the Fathers for the *Library of the Fathers*. Nor were books on Anglicanism, brought by Palmer to Russia and presented by him to the Academy in St Petersburg, left without use. One of the students was advised to write his thesis on Anglicanism compared with Orthodoxy, apparently on the basis of materials supplied by Palmer.[3] In both countries there were groups earnestly interested in *rapprochement* between the respective

[1] Khomiakov's letters to Palmer were first published in Russian, in *Pravoslavnoe Obozrenie* ("The Orthodox Review"), 1869, with notes by Fr A. M. Ivantzov-Platonov. The full text in English appears in Birkbeck, *Russia and the English Church*, and see further Bibliography.

[2] "Letters of the Very Rev. E. J. Popov on Religious Movements in England" were published by L. Brodsky in *Khristianskoe Chtenie* ("Christian Reading"), April, May, June 1904, and June, July, September 1905 (they cover the period from 1842 to 1862); cf. also "Materials concerning the question of the Anglican Church", consisting of notes and letters of Fr Popov and Fr Joseph Vassiliev (Russian chaplain in Paris), in 1863–65, in the same magazine, July and August 1897.

[3] This student was later Russian chaplain in Stuttgart, Fr J. J. Bazarov.

Churches. John Mason Neale, by his historical studies and translations of Eastern liturgical texts, did more than anyone else to further this idea.

In 1851, when the repercussions of the famous Gorham case were at their height, an attempt was made to approach the Church of Russia in order to secure recognition of a group of Anglicans which was contemplating secession from the Established Church. Although this was not in any sense an ecumenical move, some points in the project were of interest. The proposed basis of reunion was to include recognition of the seven Ecumenical Councils, the Russian Catechism as an outline of doctrine, and repudiation of Lutheran or Calvinist leanings. Connection with the Russian Church was expected to be only temporary. Anglican rites and devotional forms were to be kept, and the English language to be used. The Synod was asked to investigate the problem of Anglican Orders, and, in the event of a favourable decision, which was expected, to confirm the clergy in their pastoral commission. The scheme led to nothing; but it affords some evidence of increasing concern in certain quarters for more intimate connection with the Orthodox East.[1]

The Association for the Promotion of the Unity of Christendom was founded in 1857, with the intention to unite "in a bond of intercessory prayer" Roman Catholics, Greeks, and Anglicans.[2] The Eastern Church Association was created in 1863, on the initiative of John Mason Neale, and two Orthodox priests were on its standing committee from the beginning—Fr Popov and the Greek Archimandrite, Constantine Stratoulias. The leading Anglican members were Neale, George Williams, and H. P. Liddon. Williams had spent several years in Jerusalem as chaplain to the Anglican bishop there. His well-known book on the Non-jurors in their relations with the East, in which all the relevant documents were published in English for the first time, was undoubtedly related to the new ecumenical endeavour. Neale never had an opportunity of visiting the Eastern countries. But Liddon went to Russia in 1867, had an interview with Philaret shortly before his death in the same year, and was deeply impressed by all he saw in Russia. "Sense of God's presence—of the supernatural—seems to me to penetrate Russian life more completely than that of any of the Western nations."[3]

The Primus of the Episcopal Church in Scotland, Robert Eden, Bishop of Moray, Ross, and Caithness, visited Russia in 1866, and also had a talk with the Metropolitan Philaret. His concern was solely with intercommunion, as distinguished from, or even opposed to, reunion. That intercommunion should be restored which existed "between members of independent Churches in the early days of Christianity". Prejudices should be removed, and some mutual understanding between bishops of the different Churches established. Nothing else was envisaged.[4]

The purchase of Alaska and the Aleutian Islands from Russia in 1867 by the United States, and the transfer of the Russian episcopal see from Sitka to San

[1] Fr Eugene Popov to the Chief Procurator, Count Pratassov, *Khristianskoe Chtenie*, May and June 1904.

[2] See further Chap. vi, pp. 278 f.

[3] John Octavius Johnson, *Life and Letters of Henry Parry Liddon*, London, 1904, pp. 100 f. To W. Bright he wrote about the services: "there was an aroma of the fourth century about the whole".

[4] See Bishop Eden's preface to the English translation of D. A. Tolstoy, *Romanism in Russia: an Historical Study*, London, 1874, I, pp. viii f., and R. Eden, *Impressions of a recent Visit to Russia. A Letter . . . on Intercommunion with the Eastern Orthodox Church*, London, 1867.

Francisco, brought the Episcopal Church in the United States into direct contact with the Church of Russia. It is curious to find that when, in the middle of the century, in connection with the gold rush in California, a considerable number of Anglicans established themselves there, the question could be raised whether they might not appeal to the Russian bishop on the spot, rather than to the remote Anglican bishops in the eastern states, for aid and authority, and call themselves the Church of California. At the General Convention of the Episcopal Church in 1862, one of the deputies, Dr Thrall, raised this question. It was, he affirmed, desirable to nominate a special committee of inquiry and correspondence, which should present to the Orthodox authorities the claims of the Protestant Episcopal Church as a part of the Church Catholic, and as such qualified to assume care of Russians in the Pacific area. A commission, the "Russo-Greek Committee", was appointed with limited authority, "to consider the expediency of communication with the Russo-Greek Church, to collect information on the subject", and to report to the next General Convention.[1]

The American delegates stopped in England on their way to the East, and conferred with the British. Some consultations were held also with the Russian experts, Fr Popov and Fr Joseph Vassiliev, the Russian chaplain in Paris, who was invited specially for this purpose. The problem under discussion was intercommunion, i.e. mutual recognition of the Churches, including the recognition of Anglican Orders by the Orthodox. It was made clear that the Eastern Church would not enter into any formal communion with Anglican Churches, unless certain changes were made in Anglican formularies. The Church of England was hardly in a position to make any changes. It was hoped that the Americans, less tied by tradition and free from the State connection, would go ahead and create a precedent.

One of the American delegation, Dr Young, visited Russia in 1864, and was received by the Metropolitans of St Petersburg (Isidor) and Moscow. The Russian Synod was not prepared to take any formal steps, but recommended further study of a rather informal character. Philaret was favourably disposed, but anticipated misunderstandings among the laity; bishops and the learned would understand the problem, but, as Young recorded his words, "the difficulty will be with the people". It was a pertinent remark; in Philaret's opinion, obviously, reunion or *rapprochement* could not be brought about simply by an act of the hierarchy, but presupposed some participation of the general body of believers. He had some difficulties concerning the validity of Anglican Orders. Finally, he suggested five points for further study: (1) the Thirty-nine Articles and their doctrinal position; (2) the *Filioque* clause and its place in the Creed; (3) Apostolic Succession; (4) Holy Tradition; (5) the doctrine of Sacraments, especially Eucharistic doctrine. It was decided that an interchange of theological memoranda should be arranged for between the Russian and Anglican commissions. At the same time, the common interests of Russia and America in the Pacific area were stressed, including the missionary endeavour of both nations. The American delegates favoured the plan of establishing a Russian bishopric at San Francisco, and also of a Russian parish in New York.[2]

A long report on these negotiations was presented by the Russo-Greek Committee to the General Convention in 1865. It was decided to extend its

---

[1] On similar and in part parallel action in England, see Chap. vi, pp. 280 f.
[2] The latter was established in 1870, but closed down in 1883.

commission, and to empower it to correspond with the authorities of all the Eastern Churches and to secure further information. It was made clear, however, that the Church was not prepared for any other type of negotiations.[1]

During the next three years, various questions, especially that of the *Filioque* clause in the Nicene Creed, were widely discussed. A comprehensive report on the negotiations was presented to the General Convention of the Episcopal Church in 1868. The prospects seemed to be favourable, and no insuperable barriers had been discovered. The main problem was that of Orders. It was suggested that the Russian Synod might be willing to send delegates to investigate the problem. Intercommunion must be interpreted, as it had been stated by the theological commission of the Canterbury Convocation in 1867, as "mutual acknowledgement that all Churches which are one in the possession of a true episcopate, one in sacraments, and one in their creed, are, by this union in their common Lord, bound to receive one another to full communion in prayers and sacraments as members of the same household of Faith".[2] A year later the Archbishop of Canterbury (Tait) approached the Ecumenical Patriarch, requesting him, in compliance with the recommendation of the Committee on Intercommunion of the Canterbury Convocation, to allow Anglicans dying in the East to be buried in Orthodox cemeteries and to be given Christian burial by Orthodox clergy. A copy of the Book of Common Prayer in Greek was appended to the letter. The Archbishop's request was granted by the Patriarch, Gregory VI, who at the same time raised certain difficulties about the Thirty-nine Articles.[3]

The most interesting episode in the negotiations at that time was the visit of the Archbishop of the Cyclades, Alexander Lykurgos, to England in 1869 and 1870. He came to England in order to consecrate the new Greek Church at Liverpool. George Williams acted as his guide and interpreter. Archbishop Lykurgos' personal theological position was widely tolerant, his scholarly background being German, and in his early years as Professor at the University of Athens he had encountered some difficulties because of his broad opinions. During his stay in England a conference was organized at Ely, at which all points of agreement and disagreement between the two communions were systematically surveyed. The only point at which no reconciliation between the two positions could be reached was precisely the *Filioque* clause. The Archbishop insisted on its unconditional removal. Then followed some other controversial topics—the number and form of the sacraments, the doctrine of the Eucharist, the position of the priesthood and second marriages of bishops, the invocation of saints and prayers for the departed, the use of icons and the related question of the authority of the Seventh Ecumenical Council. A certain measure of understanding was reached, but the Archbishop staunchly defended the Orthodox point of view. He concluded, however, that in his opinion the Church of England was "a sound Catholic Church, very like our own", and that "by friendly discussion, union between the two Churches may

---

[1] Russian material on this episode: letters of various persons to Philaret, in *Letters of clerical and lay persons to the Metropolitan Philaret of Moscow 1812–67*, ed. A. N. Lvov, St Petersburg, 1908, pp. 192 f., 342 f., 349 f., 623 f.; Philaret's Memorandum in the *Collection of Comments and Replies*, V, pp. 537 ff.; his statement on Anglican Orders in *Pravoslavnoe Obozrenie*, 1866.

[2] *Journal of the Proceedings in 1868*, pp. 148, 169, 256, 258 f., 276, 421 f., 484 f.

[3] *Journal*, etc., *1871*, Report of the Joint Committee, pp. 564 ff. Cf. Karmiris, *Orthodoxy*, etc., pp. 332 f. The late Archbishop Germanos regarded this action as "the first step towards the *rapprochement* of the Churches in a purely ecclesiastical matter". See *The Christian East*, Vol. X, No. 1, 1929, p. 23.

be brought about". There was no discussion of the doctrine of the Church or Orders, and no attempt was made to define the prospective union or mutual recognition. The Archbishop reported favourably to the Synod of Greece on his visit and negotiations.[1] The American General Convention in 1871 took cognizance of these new developments and decided to continue the activities of the Russo-Greek Committee.

The secession of a considerable Old Catholic group from Rome in protest against the decrees of the Vatican Council challenged the Orthodox Churches to form an opinion as to the nature and ecclesiastical status of the new body, and as to the attitude to be taken with regard to this non-conforming Catholic minority in the West.

In this connection the name of Franz Baader must be mentioned once more. His interest in the Eastern Church dated from earlier times. In the 1830's he had had to consider the whole problem afresh, in the context of a growing resistance to the Ultramontane trend of thought and practice. "Catholicism" has been disrupted since the split between the East and the West, and it is in the East that the true Catholic position has been kept and continued. The Eastern Church has therefore much to contribute to the prospective redintegration of the life of the Church. Baader summarized his ideas in the book *Eastern and Western Catholicism*, published in 1841.[2] This book has been recently described (by Dr Ernst Benz) as "the greatest ecumenical writing of the 19th century". It would be difficult, however, to find out to what extent it exercised direct influence on wider circles.

In the years immediately preceding the Vatican Council there had been increasing unrest among the Roman Catholic clergy, especially in France. In 1861 a learned French priest, the Abbé Guettée, whose *History of the Church in France* had been put on the Index, joined the Orthodox Church in Paris and was attached to the Russian Embassy chapel. In co-operation with the Russian chaplain, Fr Joseph Vassiliev, Guettée founded a magazine dedicated to the cause of reform and reunion, *L'Union Chrétienne*, which had for many years a wide circulation in the West. At first Guettée was interested in co-operation with Anglicans, but later became bitterly hostile to them. He regarded a return to the faith and practice of the early Church and reunion with the East as the only way out of the Roman impasse. In a sense, this view was an anticipation of the later Old Catholic movement.

Another name to be mentioned in this connection is that of Joseph J. Overbeck, who published in the 1860's a number of booklets and pamphlets, in German, Latin, and English, advocating not only a return to Orthodoxy, but also a re-establishment of the Orthodox Church in the West. Overbeck (1821–1905) was originally a Roman Catholic priest and for a time on the Theological Faculty at Bonn. He left the Roman Catholic Church and migrated to England, where he remained till the end of his days. In 1865 he joined the Russian community in London as a layman. But he had a larger plan in his mind. He expected to see the secession of a considerable group of priests and laymen from the Roman

[1] G. Williams, *A Collection of Documents relating chiefly to the Visit of Alexander, Archbishop of Syros and Tenos, to England in 1870*, London, 1876; D. Balanos, "Archbishop A. Lykourgos", in *Theologia*, Vol. I, 1923, pp. 180–94 (in Greek); cf. Karmiris, op. cit., pp. 337 f. There seems, however, to have been a darker side to the visit of Alexander. He was closely in touch with the group of Timothy Hatherly (see p. 206), for whom he carried out ordinations; and there is reason to believe that he went so far as to "reordain" one who was already an Anglican priest.

[2] For the full German title of this book, and for other material on Baader, see Bibliography.

obedience in the near future, and was eagerly concerned with the problem of restoring an Orthodox Catholicism in the West. Reunion with the East he regarded as the only practical solution, but he desired to preserve the Western rite and all those Western habits and traditions which might be compatible with the faith and canons of the Orthodox East. He had in fact formed an ambitious project for an Orthodoxy of the Western rite, somehow parallel to the Catholicism (Uniate) of the Eastern rite.

A formal appeal was presented to the Russian Synod (and probably to the Ecumenical Patriarchate) in 1869, and in 1870 and 1871 Overbeck visited Russia. A provisional draft of the proposed rite was prepared by Overbeck, based mainly on the Roman Missal, with certain insertions from the Mozarabic rite. In principle, the Holy Synod was prepared to approve the scheme, but the final decision was postponed in connection with the further development of the Old Catholic movement. The Synod was anxious to ascertain whether there was a sufficient number of people in the West prepared to join the project in question. The scheme was forwarded to the Ecumenical Patriarch in the same year (or in 1872), but it was only in 1881 (and after Overbeck's personal visit to the Phanar) that action was taken. A committee was appointed to examine the project. It reported favourably in 1882, and the Patriarch gave his provisional approval, provided that the other Churches concurred. It seems that a protest was made by the Synod of the Church of Greece. The whole scheme came to nothing and was formally abandoned in 1884 by the Russian Synod, on the advice of the new Russian chaplain in London, Fr Eugene Smirnov.

There was an obviously utopian element in the scheme, and it failed to rally any considerable number of adherents. And yet it was not just a fantastic dream. The question raised by Overbeck was pertinent, even if his own answer to it was confused. His vision was of an original primitive Catholicism, restored in the West with the help of and in communion with the Orthodox Churches of the East, which had never been involved in the variations of the West. Overbeck's project was strongly resented by Anglican partisans of intercommunion with the East. It was denounced as "a schismatic proceeding, and a mere copying of the uncatholic and uncanonical aggressions of the Church of Rome". It was described as an attempt to set up "a new Church", with the express object of proselytizing, "within the jurisdiction of the Anglican Episcopate".

On the other hand, Overbeck was suspected by those who could not imagine Catholic Orthodoxy in company with a Western rite. This was the attitude of a small group of English Orthodox, led by Fr Timothy Hatherly. This man had been received into the Orthodox Church in London in 1856 by "rebaptism" and ordained to the Orthodox priesthood at Constantinople in 1871. He had a small community at Wolverhampton. His missionary zeal was denounced to the Patriarch of Constantinople, and he was formally forbidden by the Patriarchate "to proselytize a single member of the Anglican Church", as such action would undermine a wider scheme of ecclesiastical reunion. It seems that this disavowal of Hatherly's intentions was the cause of his joining the Russian Church. He had no sympathy for Overbeck's plan. He wanted simply Eastern Orthodoxy, probably with the use of English as the liturgical language.

In Russia Overbeck's project was heartily supported by the Chief Procurator of the Holy Synod, Count Dmitry A. Tolstoy, a staunch opponent of all Roman claims and the author of a book on *Romanism in Russia*.[1] Tolstoy's interest and

---

[1] English edition, with preface by the Bishop of Moray, etc., 2 vols., London, 1874.

sympathy were probably determined by non-theological considerations. The whole scheme can be fully understood only in the context of the intricate historical situation in Europe in the years preceding and following the Vatican Council. Ecclesiastical questions could not be separated from political, and the Vatican dogma itself had obvious "political" implications.[1]

The hope of reunion was clearly expressed in the Munich Manifesto of the German Old Catholic group in June 1871, and reunion with the Greek-Oriental and Russian Church was mentioned in the Programme of the first Old Catholic Congress, held at Munich in September of the same year. The purpose and the guiding principle of the new movement was to reform the Church in the spirit of the early Church. An Orthodox visitor was present at the Congress, Professor J. Ossinin of the Theological Academy at St Petersburg, who was to play a prominent rôle in the later negotiations between Orthodox and Old Catholics. Orthodox visitors also attended later Congresses, among them Fr John Janyshev, at that time Rector of the Theological Academy at St Petersburg, Colonel (later General) Alexander Kireev, and from Greece Professor Zikos Rhossis of Athens, as a semi-official representative of the Holy Synod of the Greek Church.

In Russia the cause of the Old Catholics was sponsored and promoted by a group of clergy and intellectuals, united in the Society of the Friends of Religious Instruction. Russian visitors to Old Catholic conferences were members and delegates of this Society, and not official representatives of the Church. A special Commission to carry on negotiations with the Orthodox was appointed at the Old Catholic Congress at Constance, under the chairmanship of Professor J. Langen. This Commission at once established very close contact with the Russian group. The main problem under discussion was that of doctrinal agreement. An "Exposition of the principal differences in dogmas and liturgy which distinguish the Western Church from the Eastern Orthodox" was prepared by the Russian Society and submitted to the Old Catholic Commission early in 1874. It was actively discussed by correspondence.

Finally, a Reunion Conference was convened at Bonn in September 1874. This was an informal conference of theologians, not a formal meeting of official delegates. Its historical significance was that for the first time theologians of the two traditions met for frank and impartial conference on the basic tenets of the Catholic faith. The first point of divergence was the *Filioque* clause. After a long debate it was agreed that the clause had been inserted irregularly, and that it was highly desirable to find a way by which the original form of the Creed could be restored, without compromising the essential truth expressed in the article.

The second Conference met, again at Bonn, in 1875. Membership was larger. The Orthodox group also was much larger and more representative, including delegates officially appointed by the Ecumenical Patriarch, the Church of Rumania, the Church of Greece, the Metropolitan of Belgrade, and others. The main problem was that of reconciliation between the Western and the Eastern doctrines of the Holy Spirit. After a protracted and rather strained debate, the Conference finally agreed on a common statement, based on the teaching of St John of Damascus, which could be regarded as a fair summary of the doctrine held in common by the East and the West in the age of the Ecumenical Councils. Orthodox delegates hesitated to commit themselves to any statement on the validity of Anglican Orders. On the other hand, they could not agree that invocation of the saints should be regarded as an optional practice and left to the

[1] For literature on Overbeck, see Bibliography.

private discretion of individual believers or communities. The general feeling was that the Conference had succeeded in providing a basis for agreement on the doctrine of the Holy Ghost, a feeling which unfortunately proved to be based on unwarranted optimism.[1]

Some Orthodox were prepared to favour immediate recognition of, and inter-communion with, the Old Catholics, as constituting, as it were, a faithful Ortho-dox remnant in the West, even though it had been temporarily involved in the Roman schism. All that was needed was that the existing unity should be acknowledged and attested without any special act of union. This point of view was represented, among the Russians, by A. A. Kireev, Fr Janyshev, and Pro-fessor Ossinin. On the other side, it could be argued that, even after their seces-sion from the Vatican, the Old Catholics were still in schism, since Rome had been in schism for centuries, and separation from Rome in the 19th century did not necessarily mean a true return to the undivided Church of the early centuries. Unfortunately, the doctrine of the Church was never discussed at this period of the negotiations, and the meaning of reunion was not adequately defined.[2]

Contacts between the Orthodox and Old Catholics ceased for a period, and were renewed only after the formation of the Old Catholic Union (1889) and the second International Old Catholic Congress at Lucerne (1892). In 1892 the Russian Synod appointed a special Committee under the chairmanship of Anthony (Vadkovsky), at that time Archbishop of Finland (later Metropolitan of St Petersburg and Presiding Member of the Synod). By the end of the year this Committee was ready with its report, which was approved by the Synod and communicated to the Eastern Patriarchs. Conclusions were generally in favour of recognition. This was also the tenor of the book *Old Catholicism*, published in 1894 by V. Kerensky, later Professor at the Theological Academy of Kazan. In Greece there was a sharp division of opinion; Archbishop Nice-phoras Kalogeras of Patras and Professor Diomedes Kyriakos of the University of Athens defended the Old Catholic cause, whereas two other Professors, Zikos Rhossis and Mesoloras, opposed it violently. The Patriarch Anthimos of Con-stantinople, replying to the Reunion Encyclical of Leo XIII, *Praeclarae gratula-tionis*, in 1895, cited the Old Catholics as defenders of the true Faith in the West.

In the meantime, the third International Congress of Old Catholics at Rotter-dam in 1894 appointed its own Commission to examine the Russian report. Three points were singled out for further study: the *Filioque* clause; the doc-trine of Transubstantiation; and the validity of the Dutch Orders. This time there was division among the Russian theologians: two Kazan Professors, Gusew and Kerensky, found the Old Catholic interpretation of the points under discussion evasive and discordant with the Orthodox position; Janyshev and Kireev, on the contrary, were perfectly satisfied with them. A vigorous contro-versy ensued. The most important contribution to the discussions was an essay by Professor V. V. Bolotov, of the Academy of St Petersburg, *Thesen über das*

---

[1] Professor Langen summarized the whole discussion in his book *Die Trinitarische Lehr-differenz zwischen der abendländischen und der morgenländischen Kirche*, Bonn, 1876. On the Russian side, similar statements were made by S. Kokhomsky, *The Teaching of the Early Church on the Procession of the Holy Ghost*, St Petersburg, 1875, and N. M. Bogorodsky, *The Teaching of St John of Damascus on the Procession of the Holy Ghost*, St Petersburg, 1879.

[2] Brief survey and analysis: Dr Otto Steinwachs, "Die Unionsbestrebungen im Altkatholiz-ismus", in the *Internationale Kirchliche Zeitschrift*, 1911, pp. 169–86, 471–99. For the early period of the movement consult the minutes of the Congresses, and *Bericht über die Unions-Konferenzen*, ed. Dr H. Reusch, Bonn, 1874, 1875; English translation—*Reunion Conference at Bonn, 1874*, London, 1874; *Report of the Union Conferences . . .*, New York, 1876.

"*Filioque*".[1] Bolotov suggested a strict distinction between (1) dogmas, (2) *theologoumena*, and (3) theological opinions. He defined a *theologoumenon* as a theological opinion held by those ancient teachers who had recognized authority in the undivided Church and are regarded as Doctors of the Church. All *theologoumena* should be regarded as permissible, so long as no binding dogmatic authority is claimed for them. Consequently, the *Filioque*, for which the authority of St. Augustine can be quoted, is a permissible theological opinion, provided it is not regarded as expressing a doctrine which must be believed as a necessary article of the Faith. On the other hand, Bolotov contended that the *Filioque* was not the main reason for the split between the East and the West. He concluded that the *Filioque*, as a private theological opinion, should not be regarded as an *impedimentum dirimens* to the restoration of intercommunion between the Orthodox and Old Catholic Churches. It should be added that the clause was omitted by the Old Catholics in Holland and Switzerland, and put in parentheses in the liturgical books in Germany and Austria, to be ultimately omitted also. That is to say that it was excluded from the formal profession of the Faith.

At this point in the negotiations the doctrine of the Church was mentioned for the first time, to the effect that the Old Catholic movement should be regarded as a schism, and could be received into communion with the Orthodox Church only on the basis of a formal acceptance of the full theological system of the contemporary Church. This thesis was first maintained by Fr Alexis Maltzev, the Russian chaplain at Berlin and a distinguished liturgiologist, in 1898, and then developed by Bishop Sergius (Stragorodsky), at that time Rector of the Theological Academy of St Petersburg (later the second Patriarch of Moscow after the Revolution). This contention was strongly opposed by another Russian theologian, Fr Paul Svetlov, Professor of Religion in the University of Kiev. In Svetlov's opinion, the Church was "an invisible or spiritual unity of the believers, scattered in all Christian Churches", ultimately embracing all who could describe themselves as Christians. The Orthodox Church is no more than a part of the Church Universal, of which the Old Catholic Church in its own right is another part. This radicalism could not commend itself to the ecclesiastical authorities. Nevertheless, theological conversation was continued till the outbreak of the first world war, and Orthodox visitors and observers attended all Old Catholic Congresses. But no official action has yet been taken.[2]

6. TOWARDS THE TWENTIETH CENTURY

Friendly contacts between Anglican and Eastern Orthodox hierarchs and individuals, especially in the East, were numerous in the 1870's and 1880's, but usually they were acts of ecclesiastical courtesy, and did not perceptibly promote the cause of reunion or *rapprochement*.

In 1888 the third Lambeth Conference adopted an important resolution:

[1] Published in German translation by Kireev, without the name of the author, in the *Revue Internationale*, 1898, pp. 681–712.

[2] Brief survey in the articles of Steinwachs (see previous note). The course of negotiations and discussions can be followed in the articles and chronicle of the *Revue Internationale* (1893–1910) and *Internationale Kirchliche Zeitschrift* (since 1911). Summary of Kerensky by Kireev, III, 1895, 2. Bishop Sergius, "Qu'est-ce qui nous sépare des anciens-catholiques," ibid., XII, I, 1904, pp. 159–90. Extracts from the articles by Svetlov: "Zur Frage der Wiedervereinigung der Kirchen und zur Lehre von der Kirche", ibid., XIII, 2, 3, 1905; cf. his Russian book, *Christian Doctrine*, I, Kiev, 1910, pp. 208 ff. On Kireev, Olga Novikoff, *Le Général Alexandre Kiréeff et l'ancien-catholicisme*, Berne, 1911.

"This Conference, rejoicing in the friendly communications which have passed between the Archbishop of Canterbury and other Anglican Bishops, and the Patriarchs of Constantinople and other Eastern Patriarchs and Bishops, desires to express its hope that the barriers to fuller communion may be, in course of time, removed by further intercourse and extended enlightenment." It seems, however, that the "barriers" were felt to be formidable, if not insuperable. "It would be difficult for us to enter into more intimate relations with that Church so long as it retains the use of icons, the invocation of the Saints, and the cultus of the Blessed Virgin", even if the Greeks disclaim the sin of idolatry.

In the same year, in connection with the celebration of the 900th anniversary of the Conversion of Russia, the Archbishop of Canterbury (Benson) decided to send an official letter of congratulations and good wishes to the Metropolitan of Kiev. In the letter he referred to common foes of the Russian and Anglican Churches, meaning obviously Rome, and to their unity in the faith of the Gospel as expounded by the Ecumenical Councils of the undivided Church. In his reply, the Metropolitan Platon unexpectedly raised the question of formal reunion. "If you also, as appears from your letter, desire that we may be one with you in the bonds of the Gospel, I beg you to communicate to me distinctly and definitely upon what conditions you consider the union of your and our Churches would be possible." Archbishop Benson replied in the name of the bishops of England and made two points: "First and above all, the drawing together of the hearts of the individuals composing the two Churches which would fain 'be at one together'. Secondly, a more or less formal acceptance of each other's position with toleration for any points of difference: non-interference with each other upon any such points." The first point amounted to the authorization of inter-communion, which Benson regarded as a preliminary to reunion rather than as its goal; and in the second the recognition of Anglican Orders was implied. No action was taken by the Russian Church on this proposal.[1]

Nevertheless, in the next decade official contacts between the Church of England and the Church of Russia were strengthened and multiplied. Bishop Creighton of Peterborough (later of London) attended the Coronation of the Emperor Nicholas II in 1896, as an official envoy of the Church of England, and Archbishop Maclagan of York visited Russia in the following year. In 1897 Archbishop Anthony (Vadkovsky) of Finland went to England to represent the Russian Church at the Diamond Jubilee of Queen Victoria. These visits belong rather to the history of attempts to promote friendship between nations through Churches than to the history of Christian reunion.[2]

There was, however, one feature in the general situation which could not fail to draw the Church of England and the Orthodox Churches together. Discussion of Anglican Orders in Rome in the middle 1890's and the final repudiation of their validity by the Pope in 1896 were followed in Russia with a keen interest, and the *Responsio* of the English Archbishops was accepted with satisfaction. Copies of this document were officially communicated to all Russian bishops, and probably to all Orthodox bishops in various countries of the East. It is interesting to observe that the reply of the Roman Catholic bishops in England to

[1] The whole story is told by W. J. Birkbeck, *Birkbeck and the Russian Church*, London and New York, 1917, pp. 1–16. See also *The Life of Edward White Benson, sometime Archbishop of Canterbury*, by his son, A. C. Benson, II, London, 1899, pp. 155 ff.

[2] See *Birkbeck and the Russian Church*, and *Life and Letters of Mandell Creighton*, by his wife, 2 vols., London, 1905.

the epistle of the Anglican Archbishops was also forwarded officially to all Orthodox bishops by Cardinal Vaughan, with a covering letter, in which the Cardinal expressed his awareness that the Orthodox were as solicitous in guarding the true doctrine of priesthood and sacraments as the Church of Rome.

It was natural that at this moment an inquiry into the validity of Anglican Orders should be initiated in Russia, albeit in an unofficial way. *An Enquiry into the Hierarchy of the Anglican Episcopal Church* was published in Russian by Professor V. A. Sokolov of Moscow Theological Academy. It included a critical analysis of the papal Bull, and the author concluded with the suggestion that Anglican Orders could be recognized by the Orthodox. To the same conclusion came another Russian scholar, Professor Athanasius Bulgakov of Kiev Theological Academy. Both tracts were translated into English and published by the Church Historical Society.[1]

In 1898 Bishop John Wordsworth of Salisbury paid a visit to the East and visited the Ecumenical Patriarch (Constantine V). A "friendly relationship" between the two Communions was initiated, and direct correspondence between the Phanar and Lambeth Palace established. A special Commission was created at Constantinople in order to survey the doctrinal position of the Anglican Church, and an Anglican representative, Archdeacon Dowling, was invited to participate. An explanatory pamphlet was published in 1900 by Bishop Wordsworth, with the approval of the Archbishop of Canterbury, and immediately translated into Russian and Greek: *Some points in the Teaching of the Church of England, set forth for the information of Orthodox Christians of the East in the form of an answer to questions*.[2] This was a semi-official statement.

In 1902 the new Ecumenical Patriarch, Joachim III, formally invited all autocephalous Orthodox Churches to express their opinion on relations with other Christian bodies. The Russian Synod replied by an elaborate epistle. The Synod was inclined to consider baptism conferred outside the Orthodox Church as valid, respecting the sincerity of belief in the Holy Trinity; and apostolic succession in the Latin Church as regularly preserved. With regard to the Anglican Churches, the Synod felt that, first of all, "it was indispensable that the desire for union with the Eastern Orthodox Church should become the sincere desire not only of a certain section of Anglicanism, but of the whole Anglican community, that the other . . . Calvinistic current . . . should be absorbed in the above-mentioned pure current, and should lose its perceptible, if we may not say exclusive, influence . . . upon the whole Church life of this Confession which, in the main, is exempt from enmity towards us". All charity should be extended to the Anglicans, "but at the same time a firm profession of the truth of our Ecumenical Church as the one guardian of the inheritance of Christ and the one saving ark of divine grace" must be maintained.

In the same year Chrestos Androutsos, Professor of Dogmatics in the University of Athens, published his great essay on *The Validity of English Ordinations, from an Orthodox-Catholic point of view*. He made two preliminary points. First, intercommunion cannot be separated from dogmatic union.

---

[1] English titles: *One Chapter from an Enquiry into the Hierarchy of the Anglican Episcopa Church*, by Sokolov; *The Question of Anglican Orders, in respect of the "Vindication" of the Papal Decision*, by A. Bulgakoff, London, 1899.

[2] London, 1900; 2nd edition, in Greek and English, 1901; and see also E. W. Watson, *Life of Bishop John Wordsworth*, London, 1915, pp. 217 ff., 339 ff., and W. C. Emhardt, *Historical Contacts of the Eastern-Orthodox and the Anglican Church*, New York, 1920.

Secondly, it was impossible to discuss the validity of the Orders of any body separated from the true Church, and no statement can be made on them. Consequently the only question that could profitably be discussed by Orthodox theologians was a practical one—what attitude should the Orthodox Church adopt in the case of reception of individual Anglican clerics into the Church? The external, i.e. ritual, aspect of Anglican ordinations could be regarded as adequate. There was, however, some uncertainty as to the purpose of these rites, as the Anglican doctrine of the ministry seemed to be ambiguous if judged by Orthodox standards. Yet, provided that this ambiguity had been removed by a formal declaration of the Church, it would be possible to accept as valid the Orders of those Anglican priests who desired to join the Orthodox Church. This was a document of momentous importance. It became at once, and still is, the basis of the ecumenical policy of the Greek Church.[1]

The problem was shifted from the realm of theology to that of canon law or pastoral discretion. For the first time the concept of "Economy" was applied to ecumenical relations. This concept has never been clearly defined or elaborated. Its meaning was nevertheless intelligible: for a solution based on theological principles some occasional practical arrangements were substituted. It was assumed that the Orthodox Church could not say anything at all about the ecclesiastical status of the separated bodies, as they had none. At this point there was an obvious difference between the Greek approach and that of the Russian Church. Russian theologians would not dispense with the theological, i.e. ecclesiological, problem as such, difficult and, in the last resort, "antinomical" as it might be. The problem of unity was for them essentially a theological, and not primarily a canonical, problem.

In 1904 Archbishop Tikhon of North America, later the first Patriarch of Moscow after the restoration in 1917, formally requested the Holy Synod to make an official statement on the procedure to be used in the case of reception of Anglican clerics into the Orthodox Church. In particular, he wished to know whether it was permissible to allow them to continue the use of the Book of Common Prayer for services. A special Commission was appointed by the Holy Synod and presented a detailed report, analysing the offices of the Prayer Book. The conclusion was that the offices were rather "colourless and indefinite" with regard to their doctrinal content, and therefore, if they were to be used "in Orthodox parishes, composed of former Anglicans", certain corrections and additions must be made in the text, in order to bring it into agreement with Orthodox doctrine. Concerning the reception of Anglican clergy, the Commission recommended, "pending a final judgement" of the Church, "a new conditional ordination".[2]

The fifth Lambeth Conference (1908) requested the Archbishop of Canterbury to appoint a permanent Committee to deal with the relations of the Anglican Communion with the Orthodox East, and suggested that certain forms of intercommunion could be brought into effect at once (e.g. in cases of emergency). In 1912 a Russian Society of the Friends of the Anglican Church was inaugurated in St Petersburg. The first President was Eulogius, at that time Arch-

---

[1] J. A. Douglas, *The Relations of the Anglican Churches with the Eastern Orthodox, especially in regard to Anglican Orders*, London, 1921, p. 17.

[2] The "Report" was published in the Alcuin Club Tracts, by W. J. Barnes and W. H. Frere, with valuable notes by the latter, London, 1917, and again in *The Orthodox Catholic Review*, Vol. I, No. 6, June 1927.

bishop of Volhynia and Member of the Governmental Duma, later Metropolitan of the Russian Church in Western Europe and Exarch of the Ecumenical Patriarch. He was succeeded by Sergius, Archbishop of Finland, later Patriarch of Moscow. The Statutes of the Society were approved by the Holy Synod. A branch of the Society was organized in the United States. On the invitation of this Society a group of Anglican bishops and clergy joined the parliamentary delegation of Great Britain to Russia in 1912. Series of lectures were organized at St Petersburg and Moscow, delivered by Dr Walter H. Frere, C.R., on the Life of the Anglican Church, and by Fr F. W. Puller, S.S.J.E. Fr Puller's lectures were published (in English and in Russian) as *The Continuity of the Church of England*.[1] They formed an impressive vindication of the Catholic claims of the Anglican Communion. During his visit, Fr Puller had several theological conversations with the Orthodox, of which he speaks in the Preface to his book. The question of the *Filioque* was surveyed once more, to the effect that on this point there was in principle no disagreement between the two Churches. Puller attributed this "change of attitude" on the Russian side "to the influence of the great Russian theologian, Bolotov". The world war interrupted the work of the Society.

It must be added that the great All-Russian Church Council of 1917–18, at its very last meeting (on 20 September 1918), passed the following resolution, upon the proposal of the Section on the Union of the Christian Churches: "The Sacred Council of the Orthodox Russian Church, gladly seeing the sincere efforts of the Old Catholics and Anglicans towards union with the Orthodox Church on the foundation of the doctrine and tradition of the ancient Catholic Church, bestows its benediction on the labours and efforts of those who are seeking the way towards union with the above-named friendly Churches. The Council authorizes the Sacred Synod to organize a Permanent Commission with departments in Russia and abroad for the further study of Old Catholic and Anglican difficulties in the way of union, and for the furtherance as much as possible of the speedy attainment of the final aim." No commission could be organized in Russia at that time, but the work of Russian theologians in western Europe in the ecumenical field was in line with the desire and commendation of the Council.[2]

Negotiations with the Old Catholics and Anglicans revealed a serious divergence of opinions among the Orthodox theologians themselves, and these internal polemics were sometimes very heated. Christian unity implies two things: unity in faith or doctrine, and unity in the life of the Church, i.e. in sacraments and worship. In the first period of the ecumenical conversation between the East and the West the main attention was given to the first aspect. The first discovery was disappointing: there was a difference indeed, and a difference of such character as to make agreement hardly possible. The *Filioque*, the doctrine of the Eucharist, the invocation of saints, Mariology, prayers for the departed—on all these points no concession could be made by the Orthodox, though a clear distinction could be made between a binding doctrine and theological interpretation.

In the later period of discussion, the whole problem of the doctrine of the

[1] London, 1912.
[2] *The Anglican and Eastern Churches. A Historical Record, 1914–1921*, London, 1921, especially pp. 27 ff.

Church was brought to the fore. The main issue was: what is the Church Universal? and in what sense do schismatic bodies still belong to the Church? Some Orthodox theologians held that the separated bodies did not belong to the Church at all, and therefore were not only historically but also spiritually outside it; others that they were still, in a certain sense and under special conditions, related to the Church existentially. On the latter view, the sacraments of the non-Orthodox were not necessarily repeated on their becoming Orthodox, it being understood that they had some real charismatic significance even outside the strict canonical boundaries of the Church. This has determined the common practice of the Russian Church in the 19th and 20th centuries.

On the other hand, this practice could be interpreted in the light of the theory of Economy, which is characteristic of modern Greek theology; in this case, the fact of non-repetition of sacraments would not imply any recognition of these non-Orthodox ministrations, and should be interpreted simply as a pastoral dispensation. This point of view was represented in Russia by Khomiakov, and in recent times was elaborated with daring radicalism by the late Metropolitan Anthony (Khrapovitski).

Anthony, at that time Archbishop of Kharkov and a permanent Member of the Holy Synod, replied to an invitation to participate in the Conference on Faith and Order by a long letter, in which he frankly stated his point of view. There was no spiritual reality, "no grace", outside the Orthodox Church. All talk about "validity" is just "talmudic sophistries". What is outside the Orthodox Church is just "this world, foreign to Christ's redemption and possessed by the devil". It makes no difference, Anthony argued, whether the non-Orthodox have or have not "right beliefs". Purity of doctrine would not incorporate them in the Church. What is of importance is actual membership in the Orthodox Church, which is not compromised by doctrinal ignorance or moral frailty. But, in spite of this categorical exclusion of all non-Orthodox from Christendom, Anthony was wholeheartedly in favour of Orthodox participation in the proposed Conference on Faith and Order. "Indeed, we are not going to concelebrate there, but shall have to search together for a true teaching on the controversial points of faith."[1]

This survey would be incomplete if we omitted the name of Vladimir Soloviev (1853–1900). Soloviev was never interested in the ecumenical problem, in so far as it concerned the search for unity between the Orthodox and the world of the Reformation. His attitude towards the Reformation and Protestantism always tended to be negative, though in his later years he did speak occasionally of a "super-confessional" Christianity, and even of a "religion of the Holy Spirit". Nevertheless, his contribution to the discussion on Christian unity was momentous. "The broken unity" of Christendom, "the Great Controversy", i.e. the "Separation of the Churches", were in his opinion the main fact and the main tragedy of the Christian world. The reunion of Christendom was for him, therefore, not merely one special and particular problem of theology and of Christian action, but the central problem of Christian life and history. Soloviev was mainly concerned with the question of reconciliation between the East and Rome, and in a sense he was pleading for a very particular kind of *Unia*. In fact,

---

[1] "Correspondence of Archbishop Anthony with the representatives of the Episcopal Church in America", in *Vera i Razoum* ("Faith and Reason"), 1915 and 1916, in Russian translation from the French.

he simply did not believe that Churches were separated. There was an historical estrangement, an external break, but, in an ultimate sense, there was still one (mystically) undivided Catholic Church.

He was right in his basic vision: the Church is essentially one, and therefore cannot be divided. Either Rome is no Church at all, or Rome and the East are somehow but one Church, and separation exists only on the historical surface. This thesis can be interpreted in a limited sense, i.e. as including only Rome and Eastern Orthodoxy. But it could be reinterpreted in a wider sense, and in that case an important and truly ecumenical plea would be presented. The merit of Soloviev was that he tried to clarify the presuppositions that underlie the Catholic doctrine of the Church. His ultimate ecumenical vision, so vividly presented in his *Story of the Antichrist*, included the whole of Christendom and the fullness of Christian tradition—the spiritual insight of the Orthodox East, the authority of Rome, and the intellectual honesty of Protestantism. But this unity transcends history.[1]

The true legacy of Soloviev is neither his "Romanism" nor his utopian theocratic dream, but his acute sense of Christian unity, of the common history and destiny of Christendom, his firm conviction that Christianity is the Church.

This was his challenge. An earnest attempt at an inclusive Catholic redintegration would be the answer. It would take us beyond all schemes of agreement. The issues, discussed time and again in the abortive ecumenical negotiations in previous centuries, are still burning. It is necessary to realize the nature and the scope of those questions which the Orthodox were bound to ask, and will ask again and again, in order to understand and interpret the meaning of the ecumenical encounter between the Orthodox East and the West at large.

[1] Soloviev, *La Russie et l'Église universelle*, Paris, 1889; English translation, *Russia and the Universal Church*, London, 1948. For other works by and on Soloviev, see Bibliography.

INTRODUCTORY NOTE TO THE CHAPTERS ON THE NINETEENTH CENTURY

With the 19th century, the development of ecumenical thought and life becomes much more complex than in the 18th. It seems therefore wise to preface the three following chapters with an introductory statement, indicating the principles which have been followed in assigning subjects to the three authors; some of the main points at which the 19th century differed from those which preceded and followed it; and the convergence of 19th-century trends on those ecumenical developments which will be the subject of the chapters on the 20th century.

Chapter 5 is concerned with all ecumenical developments in the United States of America in the 19th century, giving a backward glance at American ecumenical activity in the 17th and 18th centuries. Other parts of the world, including Canada, are dealt with in Chapters 6 and 7.

Chapter 6 is concerned with movements of approach between the Churches as such, and with the development of ecumenical ideas and ideals in the Churches.

Chapter 7 takes up the ecumenical significance of voluntary movements and societies, especially those which arose out of the Evangelical Awakening. It also indicates from point to point the changing ecumenical climate, as the century advances, as seen in all types of unitive effort.

Nineteenth-century progress in "the mission-field" and the ecumenical attitudes of the Roman Catholic Church are dealt with in these three chapters, which also contain material supplementary to that given in Chapter 4 on the Orthodox Churches in the 19th century.

Many 19th-century events and tendencies will be seen to converge on the Edinburgh Missionary Conference of 1910, as the watershed between miscellaneous ecumenical strivings and the integrated ecumenical movement of more recent times.[1] Earlier ecumenical activities were spasmodic, isolated, and lacked continuity. Individuals, groups, movements, and Churches contributed ideas concerning the Church or concerning unity, taking action on them often in a regrettable separation. Yet they builded better than they knew towards the time when they would begin to build together. Each movement contributed something to the growth of the ecumenical idea, and was associated with the emergence of some emphasis which later became formative in the ecumenical movement.

Ecumenical movements should never be considered, and cannot be understood, apart from the social, economic, and intellectual background of their times. Changes in these fields, in part at least, account for the differences in ecumenical possibilities and ecumenical achievements between the 18th and 19th centuries. The following are among the new factors, which together form the common background of these three chapters. The 19th century was:

An era of western political expansion. The nations of Europe and America were rapidly extending their influence in Africa, Asia, and other parts of the world. With this imperial expansion went ecclesiastical enlargement. All the problems

---

[1] For the purpose of these chapters, the 19th-century period is treated as continuing until 1910, the point from which succeeding chapters take up the narrative.

of Christian unity were posed in a new key, and solutions were to be sought in hitherto untried contexts.

An era of international action and reaction. This was largely brought about by improved communications—the steamship, the railway, and the telegraph—which made possible a much speedier exchange of religious contact and inspiration. It was the age of conferences. From the middle of the century, the national and international religious conference, on a scale unknown since the dissolution of the Council of Trent in 1563, became a regular feature of Christian life and the most potent instrument of ecumenical development.

An era of societies. Chapter 2 has shown the importance of the "spiritual society" in the thought both of Pietism and of the Enlightenment. But the 18th-century society developments were small in comparison with those of the 19th, when much of the active life of the Churches found expression in societies organized for the most varied purposes, religious, missionary, and philanthropic.

An era of emigration and immigration, involving vast movements of population. These movements carried with them their Church traditions and problems, and introduced them into their new environment. Every *diaspora*, small and great, throughout the centuries has tended on the one hand to create ecumenical problems and on the other to be a vehicle of ecumenical advance; this is true whether the *diaspora* in question is one of political or religious exiles, foreign students or foreign commercial communities, or a migration due to the pressure of economic necessity. Throughout the 19th century we shall meet instances of the importance of the *diaspora* in promoting ecumenical advance.

An era of revolutions. Although, by contrast with the stormy 20th century, the 19th must be considered the century of the long peace, it was a century of revolutionary change. It opened with the French Revolution and its aftermath, and closed amid the first rumblings of the Balkan Wars. It saw the Napoleonic Wars and the defeat of Napoleon, resulting in the Holy Alliance aiming at "one Christian Europe"; the rise of united Italy and of the German Empire; the liberation of Greece and of the Balkan States. The defeat of Russia by Japan in 1905–06 made plain to those with eyes to see that the old colonialism was dying.

An era of industrial upheaval. In 1848 Karl Marx published the Communist Manifesto. In the next hundred years, the uprising of the industrial working class was far more important than any other phenomenon. It was followed, rather at a distance, by a quickened social conscience in all the Churches, expressed in the great papal Encyclicals, the *Innere Mission* in Germany, the Christian social movement in England, and the American Social Gospel.

Though the history of nations, countries, and Churches continued to follow separate lines and to be marked by many local peculiarities, it is evident that all these background factors were international in their incidence, and could not but prepare the way for a continual, though fitful, growth of the ecumenical attitude. It is the fascinating task of these three chapters to seek to trace through this shifting scene the working out of God's unitive purpose for his Church.

CHAPTER 5

CHRISTIAN UNITY
IN NINETEENTH-CENTURY AMERICA

by

DON HERBERT YODER

1. DIVISIVE FORCES IN AMERICAN CHURCH LIFE

At the close of the 19th century, William Reed Huntington, one of the chief advocates of Christian unity in the United States, wrote that in America the sectarian principle had reached the *reductio ad absurdum*: "Almost all are ready to admit that we have had disintegration enough, and that what we want now is construction. The thing that takes the heart out of us is the immensity of the undertaking. We feel as a tribe of savages might feel if shown the *Teutonic* or the *Campania*, and told to substitute that type of boat for their dug-outs and canoes. And yet the ocean liner is but the final term in a long process of evolution from the dug-out. With God all things are possible; and with man, God helping him, more things are possible than we dare dream."[1]

During the 19th century the Churches had kept pace with the expansion of the nation, but at the price of increased disunity. Scattered over the ecclesiastical map of the United States was an amazing variety of church groups. There were Episcopalians and Congregationalists; German, Swedish, Danish, Norwegian, Finnish, and Icelandic Lutherans; New School and Old School Presbyterians; Arminian Baptists, Calvinistic Baptists, and Two-Seed-in-the-Spirit Predestinarian Baptists; Methodist Episcopalians, Free Methodists, Republican Methodists, Wesleyan Methodists, and African Methodists—and so on up to a grand total, in 1890, of 143 several denominations.

Before taking up the story of the attempts made prior to 1910 to fit into some sort of unity the shattered pieces of American Protestantism, it will be rewarding to look briefly at the reasons why the American church pattern is so much like one of the old patchwork "crazy quilts" that American grandmothers used to prize so highly—a coverlet of disparate patches, put together without regard for an over-all pattern, but aesthetic according to Grandmother's ways of thinking. The American ecclesiastical map had its reasons for being what it was, and it is our task first of all to determine what were the divisive factors in American church life which caused this denominational fragmentation. For it has been this extremely complex division of American Christianity into several hundred denominational, sociological, national, and racial groups which has led to the typically American answers to the problem of Christian unity.

The major reason for the fragmentation of American Christianity is that all the European schisms have been transplanted to American soil. The very heterogeneity of the American population—stemming as it does from every country and class and church group in Britain and the Continent—has ensured a varied religious pattern in the New World. While America has been a sociological melting-pot in which transplanted European traditions and cultures have for the most part coalesced into something new and American, religion has been, denominationally speaking, the conspicuous exception to this general levelling process. For the conservatism of religion is such that most of the transplanted European schisms have refused to be healed on American soil, even though the causes of the original division have long since subsided.

For an excellent example we may consider the Presbyterians. By the middle of

[1] *A National Church*, p. 45.

the 19th century there were in America, in full bloom as separate denominations, not only the American counterpart of the Church of Scotland, but all the major Scottish schisms from the mother Church.

The other great denominations of Europe were represented as well. All the groups which trace their origin to the Anabaptist and Puritan movements found their way to America and have maintained their separate existence ever since. The Continental contingent began arriving in the late 17th century, and has kept coming ever since—first the Germans and the Swiss, with their several varieties of national Church as well as the sectarian expressions of their religious culture; later the Roman Catholics of southern and central Europe, the Uniates, and the various Eastern Orthodox and Lesser Eastern Churches. This, then, is the obvious primary cause of the fragmentation of American Christianity into now more than 250 varieties of denominational life.[1]

This picture might have been somewhat relieved had the European family groups of Churches done more uniting in the New World. But with few exceptions the "family reunions" of sister denominations have had to wait until the 20th century. The main exception was the union of several of the Presbyterian Churches, which in 1858, following the Scottish example, merged to form the United Presbyterian Church. But for most Churches the nationalist ties were stronger than the religious. The bonds of language and custom continued in America to draw the emigrants from one European nation apart from those of another, even though they shared the same general type of Christianity.

In this wrestling with transplanted nationalism the Lutherans provide the principal object lesson. Even they, with almost complete confessional agreement on the fundamentals of Lutheranism, could not form one united Church in the United States, for most of the national varieties of European Lutherans preferred to remain separate from one another. Even within the same national group, there were sociological and other non-theological factors which thwarted an all-Lutheran union. The different varieties of German Lutherans refused to co-operate with each other. The western Lutherans, stemming from the conservative "Old Lutheran" emigration of the 19th century, remained aloof from the Pennsylvania German Lutherans of the 18th-century emigration, who represented a marriage of German Pietism with American Puritanism and Revivalism.[2]

But the effects of immigration and transplanted nationalism upon the pattern of American denominationalism do not exhaust the factors that caused division. Fragmentation continued on American soil. The frontier experience, which the majority of Americans shared as they moved westward in the 18th and early 19th centuries, was another great divisive factor. The individualism of the frontiersman, who depended upon himself alone to carve a home out of the wilderness, found intellectual and emotional expression in the various new types of religious life that grew up on the frontier. This individualism, combined with

[1] See especially William Warren Sweet, "Cultural Pluralism in the American Tradition", *Christendom*, 1946, pp. 316–26, 501–08, and Carl Wittke, *We who Built America—the Saga of the Immigrant*, New York, 1946.

[2] See H. Richard Niebuhr, *The Social Sources of Denominationalism*, and "Some Sociological Factors in Lutheran Disunity", *Lutheran Church Quarterly*, Oct. 1946, pp. 337–47; Abdel Ross Wentz, *The Lutheran Church in American History*, Philadelphia, 1923, pp. 295–343; Carl E. Schneider, *The German Church on the American Frontier*, St Louis, 1939, pp. 27 f.

the revivalism which developed in America as a response to the challenge of the frontier, produced several native frontier Churches and schismatic groups.

Native Churches, such as the Disciples of Christ and "Christians" and Cumberland Presbyterians, grew up on the western frontier, chiefly because the conservative Presbyterians of Kentucky and Tennessee refused to modify the "orderly ways of the fathers" into the type of revivalistic religion which the frontier needed if it was to be won for the Church. The same problem among the American-German Churches of Pennsylvania and Maryland—the refusal of the majority of the Lutheran, Reformed, and Mennonite Churches to adopt the revivalist system—led to the formation, in the period 1789–1810, of the German Methodist groups: the Church of the United Brethren in Christ, the Evangelical Association, and other related denominations.

Not only did these new groups arise, but the older denominations quarrelled internally over revivalism, producing further schisms. During long decades of the 19th century, the Lutherans, German Reformed, Episcopalians, and Presbyterians fought the battle of "New Measures" (revivalist techniques) versus the catechetical method of the fathers. Not only did they react in favour of or against the revivalist methods of camp meetings and lay ministry, but especially against the "low churchism" which had come to be distinctive of frontier worship. For the frontier was a levelling influence in worship. American Methodists like to recall how Bishop Coke, on his first visit to the infant American Churches in 1784–85, came into the pulpit a few times wearing clerical gown and bands, but soon discarded them as incompatible with the frontier worship service. Besides, such things could not be fitted into the limited confines of a circuit-rider's saddle-bags![1]

Not only were the European schisms transplanted and modified by the adoption of revivalism and other frontier techniques of church work, but the transplanted theological systems were modified in the new environment. Partly as a reflection of the American pioneer spirit of optimism and activism, partly through such varied impulses as Deism and Methodism and, after the Civil War, Biblical criticism and the Social Gospel, various leading spirits of the Calvinistic denominations, in particular the Presbyterians and the Congregationalists, were led generation after generation to question the main tenets of the Calvinist doctrinal system.

This Great Rebellion against Calvinism went on for decades, resulting in several important theological schisms. In the period up to the Civil War, the extreme liberals formed the Unitarian and Universalist Churches, while the middle-of-the-roaders, who attacked Calvinism from the Arminian side of the theological fence, founded such groups as the Disciples of Christ and the Cumberland Presbyterians. With the withdrawal of the schismatics, the main citadels of Calvinist orthodoxy in Congregationalism and Presbyterianism remained intact until modified from within, after the Civil War, through the joint impulse of Biblical criticism and the Social Gospel.[2]

There were sectional and racial schisms also. By 1850, the Southern statesman John C. Calhoun had begun to fear an inevitable civil war, since, as he pointed

---

[1] See Bibliography (Peter G. Mode, William Warren Sweet).
[2] See Sweet, *Religion in the Development of American Culture*, chapter on "Revolt Against Calvinism"; and Herbert W. Schneider, *A History of American Philosophy*, New York, 1940.

out in the Halls of Congress, the strongest ties that had bound the North and South together into a nation, the ties between Christians in the same Church, had been snapped over the question of slavery.[1]

It was the "national" Churches, that is, those which, having best adapted their methods to the needs of the expanding frontier, had spread themselves most evenly over the length and breadth of the country, which suffered most from regional schism. These were the Methodist, Baptist, and Presbyterian Churches. "Sectional" Churches, like the Congregationalists, which were confined to New England and the northern Middle-West, escaped schism over the slavery question, though not without deep internal agitation. Several temporary schisms, such as that in the Episcopal Church, caused by the Civil War, were healed without permanent scars soon after the close of hostilities in 1865. But from 1845 on it was impossible in the United States to be simply a Methodist or a Presbyterian or a Baptist. One had to take sides and be either Methodist Episcopal (Northern Methodist) or Methodist Episcopal Church, South; Northern or Southern Baptist; or Northern Presbyterian ("Old School" or "New School") or Southern Presbyterian ("Old School" or "New School"). To this day the only one of these three major schisms to be bridged has been the Methodist division of 1845.[2]

While the white Churches were dividing over the question of slavery and the rights of their coloured brethren, the Churches of the American Negro were contributing their own distinctive problems in the ecumenical sphere. The problem of racial schisms, i.e. separate Negro denominations, while not limited to the United States, at least is not one of the ecumenical problems faced by the European lands. The history of the church relations of the American Negro begins in the colonial period with his inclusion in the white Churches of the South, always however in an inferior position. Among the freed Negroes of the North there soon developed all-Negro Churches under Negro leadership, such as the African Methodist Episcopal Church (1816) and the African Methodist Episcopal Zion Church (1821). After the Civil War, many of the Southern Negroes withdrew from the white denominations, mostly of their own volition, and organized denominations which could spread through the South under Negro leadership. The ecumenical picture of the 20th century is still complicated racially in the United States by the division of the American Negroes between all-Negro independent denominations, the largest of which are the various Negro Methodist and Baptist groups, and inter-racial denominations such as the Methodist, the Episcopal, the Northern Presbyterian, the Congregational Christian, the Lutheran, and the Roman Catholic Churches.[3]

Among the reasons for the multiplicity of denominations in the United States, the separation of Church and State, which came in the period immediately following the American Revolution, holds a prominent place. America was one of the first countries where denominations could divide into smaller groups, each independent, without calling down upon the perpetrators of the schism the police power of the State. Undoubtedly the psychological climate of free America has tended to increase divisions. An increased impetus to sectarianism was thus a direct result of complete religious liberty.

[1] See also Chap. x, pp. 451 f..
[2] See Chap. x, pp. 451–54.
[3] See Niebuhr, *Social Sources*, Chaps. vi, vii, and ix; and Sperry, *Religion in America*. Chap. x and Appendix E.

But perhaps, too, as Vincent L. Milner pointed out in the preface to his *Religious Denominations of the World*,[1] "perfect religious freedom is the primary condition of Christian Unity". Although the first effect of religious freedom "may be to multiply religious divisions, its final effect is to heal them". And he thought that eventually "sects will disappear in the overflowing fullness of faith and love".[2]

A last disunitive force in American Church history, which has grown since the Civil War with the increasing Roman Catholic emigration from Ireland, Germany, and Southern Europe, is the tension between Roman Catholics and the Protestant Churches. In the Colonial period the relations between the two groups festered from the political and economic rivalry between Protestant England and Roman Catholic Spain and France. But while Roman Catholics were officially outlawed, in what Roman Catholic historians refer to as "the Penal Age of American Catholicism", the local scene was not without many evidences of friendship and co-operation. The picture is brightened considerably by the inclusion of the colonies of Maryland (1634), Rhode Island (1636), and Pennsylvania (1682), those pioneer civil expressions of religious liberty, based on the varying toleration policies of the liberal Roman Catholic Baltimore family on the one side and of the Puritan-Baptist-Seeker Roger Williams and the Quaker William Penn on the other.

The 19th century opened, *malis avibus*, with a volley by "Oliver Oldschool, Esq.", the editor of *The Portfolio*, Philadelphia's choicest literary magazine, who in 1801 doubted whether any "compromise, union, or agreement between papists and protestants can ever take place, except upon the broad bottom of atheism and infidelity".[3] The tension between the two types of Christianity increased as Roman Catholic emigration grew in mid-century. In the 1840's and 1850's the movement known as "Native Americanism" or "Nativism", basically aimed against all recent emigrants, for sociological and economic reasons channelled itself into anti-Catholicism with attacks on churches, convent-burnings, impassioned tracts and "exposés" of convent and clerical life. This Protestant crusade, which made its way into several political campaigns, although interrupted by the slavery controversy and the Civil War, broke out again in the latter half of the 19th century with the infamous American Protective Association, founded 1887, as well as with the Ku Klux Klan. Fortunately, these latter movements included only a minority of rabid Protestants. In the higher reaches of American Protestantism, the Evangelical Alliance (1846) was not without an anti-Catholic emphasis.[4]

Of eventual Protestant and Roman Catholic union the American proponents have been few and far between. With the exception of a few men like Philip Schaff, whose conception of Church history as development of Church forms from earlier ages pictured an eventual merging of "Catholic" and "Evangelical"

---

[1] Philadelphia, 1873.

[2] See especially H. K. Rowe, *History of Religion*, Chap. iv, "The Consequences of Freedom".

[3] *The Portfolio*, Vol. I, No. 28. Reprinting Jonathan Boucher's "Sermon on Schisms and Sects", the Editor affirmed that "the dream of the union of all sects seems to be a proper object of poetry or religious enthusiasm, but will not be expected by the experienced politician, any more than the cessation of war, which our philosophers would have us to expect from the establishment of republics, and the slaughter of kings".

[4] See especially Ray A. Billington, *The Protestant Crusade, 1800–1860—A Study of the Origins of American Nativism*, New York, 1938; and Gustavus Myers, *History of Bigotry in the United States*, New York, 1943.

emphases in Christianity, and Professor C. A. Briggs of Union Theological Seminary, New York, who expressed his hopes for a union of Protestant and Catholic "Modernists", we look in vain. There were no Malines Conversations in America. And appeals to union or even co-operation from the Roman Catholic side of the controversy are also hard to find, with the exception of such militant ex-Protestants as Orestes Brownson and Isaac Hecker. The invitation of Pius IX to the Protestant world in 1870 to return to "Catholic Unity" was ignored by most American Protestant church bodies, except the General Assembly of the Presbyterian Church, U.S.A., which, an early historian of American Presbyterianism tells us, "sent a courteous but decided refusal".[1]

Relations of the Eastern Churches in the United States with Protestantism have been consistently better than those of Rome. With their married clergy and their insistence upon lay organizations within individual congregations, the Churches of the East have seemed to the Protestant majority in America to be more "Americanized" than their Roman Catholic brethren, who have done little to democratize their polity by giving to the laity such a share in local control as is common in most of the Protestant denominations. And whereas Rome, with the exception of the separated Old Catholic and Polish National Catholic Churches, has maintained her unity in America, the Churches of the Eastern tradition have even paralleled the divisiveness of American Protestantism, in setting up separate American organizations based on national origins. The first-generation problems of adjustment to a new culture have kept the scattered Orthodox groups apart in America, although with the passage of time and increased Americanization the picture may be altered. From the Protestant side of the picture it has been principally the Protestant Episcopal Church which has been concerned with *rapprochement* between the ecclesiastical East and West. And after 1910 any historian of ecumenical relations must take into account the co-operation of some of the Eastern Churches with the Federal and National Councils of Churches.[2]

2. THE SEVENTEENTH- AND EIGHTEENTH-CENTURY BACKGROUND

Although throughout the 17th and 18th centuries the American religious scene was crystallizing into its familiar pattern of denominationalism, there were certain factors, both external and internal to church life, which attempted to dissolve away some of the individual segments of the pattern and melt them into some semblance of Christian co-operation and unity. To these some attention must be successively directed.

New England Puritanism, one of the great moulding forces in American religion, has not usually been thought of as ecumenically-oriented or for that matter as irenic. Clarke's epigram that "while Old England is becoming new [i.e. tolerant], New England is become old [intolerant]" was all too true in the 17th century, when any stray Quaker or Baptist was likely to be whipped right out of the self-righteous Puritan commonwealth of Massachusetts. As a Puritan state Connecticut was set upon a broader foundation than Massachusetts, and it was there with the Saybrook Platform of 1708 that Connecticut Congregationalism

[1] For Schaff and Briggs, see Bibliography; and Robert Ellis Thompson, *A History of the Presbyterian Churches in the United States*, New York, 1895, p. 205.
[2] See P. E. Shaw, "The Greek Mission of the Episcopal Church, 1828–99", in *The Historical Magazine of the Protestant Episcopal Church*, Sept. 1941; and Bibliography.

began officially to modify its strict congregational polity in the direction of Presbyterianism. This step led later to extremely close co-operation between the two denominations. Yet the more conservative and less irenic colony of Massachusetts produced in the 17th and 18th centuries at least three prophets of Christian unity—John Eliot, Cotton Mather, and Jonathan Edwards.

John Eliot (1604–90), one of America's pioneer Protestant missionaries among the Indians, was concerned with the reunion of the Presbyterian and Congregational "parties", as he called them. In his missionary work among the American Indians, he developed a combined Presbyterian-Congregationalist polity, providing the churches with "ruling elders" and with synods or councils. In his irenic correspondence with Richard Baxter, as well as in his printed writings, Eliot urged co-operation among Churches to carry on missionary work both in heathen lands and in "professing nations where there is darkness", to send the Church into the newer settlements, to deal with questions of "Faith and Order", with controversies and strife, to root out heresy and destroy schism, to appoint feasts and fasts, to manage "the great Wheel of publick Prayer", and to bring the Churches into the "Communions of Councils". In a most original way Eliot sketched out a union plan involving four orders of Councils: District (Monthly) Councils, Provincial (Quarterly) Councils, National (Yearly) Councils, and to top his structure, an "Oecumenical Council", which was to be in continuous session at Jerusalem, and was to make use of the Hebrew language. Suspicious of "the vast revenues which the Anti-christian Hierarchy have fatted and enriched themselves withall", Eliot went on record as being "religiously opposed" to endowments to the Councils. "The particular duties of the Oecumenical Council" Eliot passed over, perhaps wisely, in silence. "I leave them", he concludes, "to their consideration, whose happy position it shall be to see those glorious times, when such Councils shall be called."[1]

New England's second contribution to the gallery of ecumenical pathfinders was Cotton Mather (1663–1728). This many-sided pastor of Boston, who is unfortunately best remembered for his witch-hunting activities, wrote a life of John Eliot in which he comments favourably upon Eliot's plan to unite Presbyterians and Congregationalists, "tho' a Congregational" himself. To accomplish "the noble design of evangelising the world" he advocated the formation of interdenominational and international missionary societies of "great, wise, rich, learned and godly men in the three kingdoms". And in his correspondence with August Hermann Francke, a recent trove of primary significance in ecumenical history, Mather reveals his aim as the union of all the Christian Churches (excluding Rome alone) in America and all over the world, under the sign of the Eternal Gospel. As the "angels of the Eternal Gospel", he praises by name Boehme, Arndt, Spener, and Francke, and in a lengthy letter outlines a fourteen-point basis of union upon which the scattered Churches must, he feels, unite.[2]

Revivalism, that typically though not uniquely American phenomenon, has had both unitive and divisive effects upon American Christianity. This has been true of all the great revivals. Even the first, the Colonial or Great Awakening,

---

[1] In addition to Bibliography, see "Some unpublished correspondence of the Rev. Richard Baxter, and the Rev. John Eliot, the Apostle of the American Indians, 1656–1682", edited by F. J. Powicke, M.A., in *The Bulletin of the John Rylands Library*, Vol. 15, No. 2, July 1931.

[2] See Mather, *Life of the Rev. John Eliot*, pp. 108 ff; and especially Ernst Benz, "Pietist and Puritan Sources of Early Protestant World Missions (Cotton Mather and A. H. Francke)", *Church History*, Vol. XX, 1951, pp. 28–55.

which involved large colonial areas from Georgia to Nova Scotia, began the process. Not only were the competing Churches temporarily welded into co-operation in the great evangelistic work of the revival, but the Awakening, giving to the colonies their first intercolonial leaders such as Jonathan Edwards and George Whitefield, was one of the religious factors helping to gird the colonies into the secular unity which was later called into action in the American Revolution.

Jonathan Edwards (1703–58), the leader of the New England phase of the Awakening, illustrates in his thinking the unitive influence of revivalism. For Edwards, the first step towards closer unity was praying together. In his *Thoughts on the Revival of Religion in New England* (1740), Edwards first expresses his desire, following the Scottish plan for a "Concert" of praying-groups for evangelism, for "an agreement of all God's people in America, that are well affected to this work, to keep a day of fasting and prayer to God; wherein we should all unite on the same day" to pray for a more glorious revival, and hopes that God "would bow the heavens and come down, and erect his glorious kingdom through the earth".

In a later work, Edwards writes that union is "one of the most amiable things, that pertains to human society". Since God has made of one blood all nations, "it becomes mankind all to be united as one family". Not only does he find civil union "amiable"—"but more a pious union and sweet agreement in the great business for which man was created, and had powers given him beyond the brutes; even the business of religion; the life and soul of which is love". And he proves from scattered Biblical verses from the Song of Songs, the Psalms, and Ephesians, that since the Church "in all her members, however dispersed, is thus one holy society, one city, one family, one body", so it is very desirable "that this union should be manifested, and become visible".

Although these ideas had little effect on 18th-century America, from Edwards' frequently republished writings there spread through 19th-century America the practice of the "concert of prayer" for revival, which was used in connection with foreign and home missionary work, and has had some unitive effect on American Christianity. The Revival of 1857–58 sprang out of such united prayer-groups.[1]

William Penn's generous promise of religious liberty had channelled the flood-tides of the late colonial emigration Pennsylvania-wards. Not only did his English and Welsh Quaker compatriots set sail for Penn's Woods, but with them, and included in Penn's patent of toleration, came Anglicans, Roman Catholics, Baptists, and other British church groups. From the green hills of Ulster came the hardy Scottish-Irish Presbyterians, who scattered Presbyterian churches and schools all along the forested ridges of the Alleghenies. And, following Penn's own visit to the Rhine country in 1677, there came to his American colony thousands of German-speaking emigrants from the Rhineland and Switzerland. These included the so-called "Church People" (Lutherans and Reformed), the "Plain People" (Mennonites, Amish, and Brethren), and the Moravians. Because of this diversified colonial emigration, Pennsylvania, of all the states with a colonial foundation, still has the largest number of religious groups among its population.

[1] In addition to Bibliography, see especially John Foster, "The Bicentenary of Jonathan Edwards' 'Humble Attempt' ", in *International Review of Missions*, Oct. 1948, pp. 375–81.

Where but in heterogeneous Pennsylvania, that Babel of the persecuted sects and Churches of Europe, was it more natural for the actual reunion of American Christendom to begin? With so much diversity and individualism, it was natural for the next step to be some sort of consolidation. The bond which already pointed them to closer unity was the fact that all the Churches of German Pennsylvania had shared in the awakening brought to the German and Swiss Churches by the Pietist movement. Just as the main stream of New England religious influence can be understood only in reference to Puritanism, so the Pennsylvania German groups can be understood only by an analysis of their common framework of Pietism. The unitive bond was Pietism; the agent who attempted, unsuccessfully, to boil down into something consistent the rich brew that seethed in Pennsylvania's religious cauldron, was Count Zinzendorf.

Fresh from Herrnhut, that throbbing heart of the Moravian missionary impulse, Zinzendorf had come to Pennsylvania in 1741 to head the Moravian missions among the Indians and the Germans. Upon his arrival he found that for five years (1736–41) the Pietists of the Perkiomen Valley north of Philadelphia had been meeting every four weeks for devotions, prayer, and mutual edification, in a group calling itself the Associated Brethren of the Skippack; this under the impulse of Johann Adam Gruber's *Gründliche An- und Aufforderung an die ehemaligen erweckten Seelen in Pennsylvanien* (1736). Zinzendorf visited this group, and in 1741 Henrich Antes, one of its leaders, sent out a *Call* to Pennsylvania's religious leaders to unite in "The Pennsylvania Congregation of God in the Spirit", to "remedy the frightful evil wrought in the church of Christ . . . through mistrust and suspicion". Antes, the "pious layman of the Skippack", voiced his concern as to "whether it would not be possible to appoint a general assembly, not to wrangle about opinions, but to treat with each other in love on the most important articles of faith, in order to ascertain how closely we can approach each other fundamentally, and, as for the rest, bear with each other in love on opinions which do not subvert the ground of salvation".

And so, in 1742–48, a series of Pennsylvania Synods was held, the fame of which reached the ears of the Pietist leaders in Europe. These Synods were attended by Lutherans, Reformed, Presbyterians, Episcopalians, Quakers, Mennonites, Brethren, Sabbatarians, Inspired, and Individual Separatists. The union they symbolized was a spiritual one—the Congregation of God in the Spirit. Although, according to the *Trope* principle of Zinzendorf,[1] the participating members were to retain their denominational membership, the Synods urged co-operation in the practical work of evangelizing the Indians, and asked for an interchange of ministers and devotional literature, as well as intercommunion.

Unfortunately, this Congregation of God in the Spirit only drew the lines of denominational division more sharply. The participating Churches renewed their denominational consciousness, and one by one they withdrew, until in 1748 the Moravians, like the Farmer in the Dell in the nursery game, were left standing alone. One outcome of the Synods was the sending of Henry Melchior Muhlenberg (1711–87) to America in 1742, to organize the scattered Lutheran churches into a Lutheran Synod, thus counteracting Zinzendorf's activities among the Lutherans; and of Michael Schlatter (1716–90) to do likewise for the embryonic Reformed congregations in Pennsylvania. Even the Mennonites had their denominational spirit sharpened, and began to republish in America the

[1] See Chap. ii, p. 102.

martyr books of their Anabaptist ancestors, to point their children to the past rather than to the ecumenical future.

Why did Zinzendorf's beautiful ideal fail of realization? The principal reason was that the various church and sectarian groups of Pennsylvania failed to comprehend just what Zinzendorf meant by a "Church in the Spirit". Most of the leaders feared that the Count was really trying to make Moravians out of all who joined the Synods. They were unable to understand that the Moravian goal in the 1740's was only to "awaken" the members of the "sleeping" Churches to a sound religious experience, on the Moravian Pietist plan, to be sure, but allowing them to retain their denominational connections.. Undoubtedly the Count's personality was another serious hindrance to the union. His over-humble renunciation of the titles of Count and Moravian Bishop upon arrival in Pennsylvania, and his insistence on being known simply as the "Lutheran" clergyman "Ludwig de Thurnstein", appeared to many to conceal an ulterior motive.

But as we look back on those far-off days, the figure of the warm-hearted unionist Zinzendorf, the man who dared to attempt what the boldest ecumenical minds of the 19th century only ventured to pen, stands head and shoulders above most of his contemporaries. Zinzendorf failed to unite the Churches of Pennsylvania into even a spiritual unity, but his ideals are bearing fruit in the more hospitable soil of the 20th century.[1]

America's colonial period was characterized by a psychological dependence upon Europe. And to the European Churches, up to the period of the American Revolution, America was a mission-field. Not only was the bond of mother-daughter love close between American and British Episcopalians, Congregationalists, Baptists, Quakers, and Presbyterians, but scholarly epistles in Latin, German, and Dutch flew back and forth across the Atlantic from the Dutch and German Churches of the Middle Colonies to the mother Churches of the Continent.[2] For instance, both the Dutch Reformed Churches of the Hudson Valley and the German Reformed Churches of Pennsylvania and the South were under the maternal wing of the Reformed Church of Holland until 1791–93, when the ecclesiastical apron-strings were severed. Gradually these transatlantic ties were renewed in the 19th century, so that by the period of the world wars of the 20th century, it was often these American Churches of German background which were in the best position to act as go-betweens in the great problem of European relief. And so the seed sown two centuries ago has borne ecumenical fruit at last.

The Lutheran churches in the colonial period enjoyed particularly close relations not only with the Reformed congregations, with whom they frequently shared a "union church" building, but also with the Anglicans. There are on record several cases of ordination of Lutheran clergymen by the Church of England for service in the colonies, and the Court Chaplain of the House of Hanover in London, Pastor Ziegenhagen, promoted good relations between the two groups at the top. The relations of Domine Charles Magnus von Wrangel,

---

[1] In addition to Bibliography (Blanke), see Jacob John Sessler, *Communal Pietism Among Early American Moravians*, New York, 1933; and John Joseph Stoudt, "Pennsylvania and the Oecumenical Ideal", *Bulletin Theological Seminary of the Reformed Church in the United States*, Lancaster, Pa., Vol. XII, No. 4, October 1941, pp. 171–97.

[2] For this transatlantic correspondence, see the various editions of the *Hallesche Nachrichten*, for the Lutherans; and for the Reformed, William J. Hinke (editor), *Minutes and Letters of the Coetus of the German Reformed Congregations in Pennsylvania, 1747–1792*, Philadelphia, 1903.

Provost of the Swedish Lutheran churches on the Delaware, with the Anglicans were also particularly cordial. So close was this Lutheran-Anglican relation that Pennsylvania's S.P.G. missionary, Thomas Barton, could write back to his superiors in England in 1776 that "the German Lutherans have frequently in their Coetus's propos'd a union with the Church of England, and several of their clergy, with whom I have convers'd, are desirous of addressing . . . my Lord Archbishop of Canterbury and the Bishop of London upon this subject". With the merger of the Lutherans as well as the "Dutch Calvinists" of Pennsylvania into the "National Church", it was evident to Barton that "the Church of England must then certainly prevail at last". His sanguine hopes came to naught, but later generations have not been without those Lutherans and Episcopalians who feel that their Churches should wed.[1]

If reaching the thousands of unchurched people in the colonies was the first great problem that faced the colonial Churches, resulting in the Great Awakening, the second great crisis of the 18th century was the American Revolution. It, too, divided and united the American Churches into curious new patterns, according to which side they favoured.

One of the principal religious problems agitating the American mind in the years leading up to the American Revolution was the attempt to secure for the colonies an Anglican episcopate. Installing bishops in America should have been an easy matter, for until the Revolution the Church of England was the established Church, with varying degrees of privilege, in every colony south of the Mason and Dixon Line. But despite the attractiveness of the ideal and the privileged position of the Church, each proposal to carry out the plan was met by violent opposition. And not only did this opposition come from the American representatives of Britain's dissenting Churches, but Southern Anglicans themselves, who were accustomed to running parish affairs to their own lay tastes, helped to thwart every attempt of the British authorities to bestow an episcopate upon their Church establishments.

Presbyterians and Congregationalists, who had unpleasant memories of skirmishes with episcopal authority in the British Isles, opposed Anglican bishops for the colonies, because they feared that their Lordships would come endowed, as in England, with political as well as spiritual authority. New Englanders lost valuable sleep envisioning bishops' palaces rising on the sacred Yankee soil, Church courts to try Congregational "heretics" (thus reversing an old New England custom), a greedy clergy with control over marriages and wills, and even mitred bishops dominating the colonial assemblies.

To frustrate any possible plans to secure bishops for America, the Presbyterians of the Middle Colonies joined with the Connecticut Congregationalists in a series of anti-episcopal conventions (1766–75). These conventions corresponded with the English "Committee of Dissenters" in London, whom they stirred up to oppose the introduction of bishops into the colonies. This kept Parliament from going ahead with the plan, since it needed the support of the English dissenters. In addition to forestalling any parliamentary action in favour of a colonial episcopate, these joint Presbyterian-Congregationalist conventions prepared the way for the frontier Plan of Union of 1801.

[1] In addition to Bibliography (H. M. Muhlenberg), see Pascoe's *Two Hundred Years of the S.P.G.*, London, 1901, p. 37; and "Colonial Anglo-Lutheran Relations", *The Historical Magazine of the Protestant Episcopal Church*, June 1947.

As a direct result of the Revolution came a heightened sense of "Americanism" or American national spirit, of being different at last from the European motherlands. This new psychological orientation brought the Churches of America closer to each other than they had been in the colonial period. After the war, America faced, psychologically as well as geographically, westward across the rich and untilled lands of the west, rather than eastward across the Atlantic to England and Europe. Her psychology became imperial and expansive rather than colonial and dependent.

In destroying the State-Church systems in most of the colonies, the Revolution also opened the floodgates for the last advance of the sectarian spirit. With no restraints or compulsion on the part of the State to support any one brand of religion, experimentation in religion became freer than ever. In this complete freedom to be different, Americans pulled sectarianism to the end of its rope somewhere in the second half of the 19th century. But since that time the centrifugal force has been expended, and a centripetal counter-force is at last taking its place.[1]

3. THE CHALLENGE OF THE FRONTIER

Vastly more important than the American Revolution in Americanizing religion was the frontier challenge which faced all the American Churches from the close of the Revolution to the Civil War (1783–1865). The extent and areas of the influence of the frontier will continue to be debated as one of the main questions in American historiography, but the groundwork laid by the "Frontier School" of American historians shows beyond a doubt that the key to at least some political, social, and religious attitudes in the United States can be found in the frontier experience which generation after generation of the pioneers shared.[2]

Following the Revolution, all America seemed to be on the move westward. A folk movement of such proportions naturally affected the organized church life of the United States. The unchurched character of western society was a challenge to the Churches. The West was a home mission-field for a century. For the rough-and-ready life in the backwoods, with its ceaseless back-breaking toil to make the barest physical existence possible, left little time for the immediate planting of Churches by the pioneers themselves. The psychology of the frontier left its own peculiar stamp upon American worship and polity and theology.

The problem faced by all the Churches of the frontier was how to retain the frontiersmen in the Church, or, if they were without visible means of spiritual support, to win them for the Church. In most cases it was a free-for-all—there were no ethics in the battle for the souls of the pioneers. Baptists were obliging enough to immerse any stray Methodists they could find, mounted Methodist circuit-riders were glad to rope and brand Calvinistic sheep with the marks of Arminius and Wesley.

Not all the Churches, however, rode into the frontier to compete. Two of the leading denominations decided to join hands for western mission work. The

[1] See especially Edward F. Humphrey, *Nationalism and Religion in America*, Boston, 1924; John W. Thornton, *The Pulpit of the American Revolution*, Boston, 1876; Arthur L. Cross, *The Anglican Episcopate and the American Colonies*, New York, 1902.

[2] Frederick J. Turner, *The Frontier in American History*, New York, 1920; Bibliography (Peter G. Mode) and Sweet, "The Frontier in American Christianity", in *Environmental Factors in Christian History*, Chicago, pp. 390–8.

most heartening evidence of union in answer to the challenge of the frontier was the Plan of Union (1801–52), which for over half a century united, for the purpose of evangelism, the Presbyterians and the Congregationalists.

With their record of *rapprochement* and co-operation during the colonial period, the two Churches were prepared psychologically for a union. The polity of the two denominations was not so disparate as the terms Congregational and Presbyterian suggest. Connecticut Congregationalism, with its system of "consociations", was quite similar to the Presbyterianism of the Middle Colonies. In fact, as one learns from the autobiographical novels of Harriet Beecher Stowe which picture 19th-century life in the Congregational villages of Connecticut, the Congregationalists were so aware of this relationship that they commonly referred to themselves as Presbyterians.[1]

As the two Churches began to mingle on the western New York frontier, the leaders of both groups began to manifest a concern for co-operation. As early as 1787 Timothy Dwight, the grandson of Jonathan Edwards and his successor as the acknowledged leader of New England Congregationalism—who after the turn of the century was to lead the great New England revival emanating from Yale College—began working on plans to draw the General Association of Connecticut into closer union with the Presbyterian General Assembly. Negotiations in the closing years of the 18th century led in the spring of 1801 to the adoption by the two Church bodies of a four-point Plan of Union. Later the Congregational Associations of Vermont, New Hampshire, and Massachusetts also ratified and supported the Plan.

Provision was made, where desired, to settle Presbyterian ministers in Congregational churches, and Congregationalists in Presbyterian churches, each congregation to discipline itself according to its own time-honoured disciplinary system. If trouble arose between minister and congregation, the case could be appealed to the presbytery or association to which he belonged. Provision was also made for "union congregations" made up of both Presbyterians and Congregationalists.

In other words, the denominations were to move westward hand in hand, setting up their own overlapping associations and presbyteries, but each allowing the local churches to accommodate themselves to either party. At first in central and western New York both associations and presbyteries were established, with the associations in the majority. But, owing to the more effective organization of the presbyteries, the New York associations were by the year 1822 all absorbed into the presbyteries, through a corollary of the Plan of Union which became known as the Accommodation Plan. By this Plan, adopted in New York State in 1808 and applied also in Ohio, Indiana, Illinois, Michigan, and Wisconsin, Congregational churches and ministers could become members of the Presbyterian presbyteries, but retain certain Congregational rights, so that absorption was not complete.

"Such is the famous 'Plan of Union'," wrote a Presbyterian historian in 1856, "and perhaps never was article framed in a more catholic spirit, or more perfectly adapted to promote Christian charity, and union, between the people of God who happen to be thrown together in a forming society, and yet differ in their views of what is the best method of conducting church order and discipline."

[1] See especially Sweet, *Religion on the American Frontier*, II and III; Robert H. Nichols, "The Plan of Union in New York", *Church History*, March 1936; C. L. Zorbaugh, "The Plan of Union in Ohio", *Church History*, June 1937.

This Plan, he continues, "met the approbation of the missionaries and of the people, and soon went into practical and successful operation. Under it all antagonisms seemed to be harmonized; Presbyterian and Congregationalist, each found the essentials of his favourite polity combined with some of the better features of the other; and they two becoming one, united heart, hand, and resources, in building up Christ's Kingdom".[1]

But by 1852, when increased denominational consciousness led the Congregationalists to abrogate the Plan of Union, certain leaders of the Church had begun to look back upon this presbyterianizing of the Congregationalists of western New York and other areas where originally they had been in the majority, as a distinct loss to the denomination. As one Yankee wit put it at the time, "the Presbyterians milked Congregationalist cows, only to make Presbyterian butter and cheese". But the consensus of modern students of the Plan is that this later generation seems to have mistaken the spirit of the fathers of the Plan. From the documents of the time we gain no impression of unwilling absorption —if the Congregationalists were absorbed, it was because they desired it at the time. Actually there was a two-way accommodation. Judging the frontier churches from the way the whole church membership ran the internal affairs of the congregation, they were Congregational; judging them from their fellowship with other churches in a presbytery, they were Presbyterian. For these "accommodated" churches the people coined the good-natured nicknames of "Congreterial" or "Presbygational" churches.

Despite its rejection in 1837 by the Old School Presbyterians and in 1852 by the Congregationalists, the Plan of Union accomplished much good on the frontier. For half a century it united at least partially the national evangelistic forces of two of the major Churches in the United States, providing an object-lesson as to what could be done through concerted action. It led to the further co-operation of the two groups, and others, in the great missionary and benevolent societies. And if the Congregationalists lost out in some areas to their Presbyterian brethren, they did it willingly, preferring a more closely integrated system of church polity than their own body afforded.

In the case of the Presbyterians also the Plan of Union was a mixed blessing. Certainly the New England element, which came into the service of the Presbyterian Church in the areas where the Plan of Union was in operation, liberalized it to an extent unknown in areas where no Congregational influences penetrated. The historic position of Union Theological Seminary in New York City, as over against conservative Princeton, is a good case in point. There are still churches in the Middle States which express written preference for a Princeton graduate; a "Union man" will not do. This liberalizing of part of the Presbyterian General Assembly led in 1837–38 to the splitting of the Assembly into the "Old School" and "New School" branches of Presbyterianism. There were many causes at work, but it is significant that the areas where the Plan of Union had operated became for the most part "New School". Fortunately, this schism was only temporary, the two northern and southern branches coming together in the North and in the South in the "Great Reunions" of the 1860's.

The historians of American Congregationalism affirm that "for a time the possibilities of united religious action were better illustrated by this movement, centrally and marginally, than by anything else up to the inception of the Federal Council of Churches". It had in it the making, "not indeed of an

[1] William S. Kennedy, *The Plan of Union*, pp. 151 f.

American Church, but of a United Church in New England and the North, which, combining the best qualities of Congregationalism and Presbyterianism, would have had a corporate power and distinction neither communion now alone possesses".[1]

The first half of the 19th century witnessed in the United States the founding and successful operation of a whole series of interdenominational societies, fruits of the "Second Awakening". Responding to the challenge of the frontier, the Churches saw a wave of revival sweep over the country for a second time in American history. Beginning in the South, the revivals spread to the West, while a concomitant awakening began at Yale College under the ministrations of Timothy Dwight, and spread from New Haven throughout New England. This Second Awakening changed the cultural tone of America. In the years following the Revolution, Deism and liberal theology had begun to make inroads against the citadels of orthodoxy. But the revival, sweeping over the entire country, fastened upon the Churches the familiar pattern of evangelical Protestant orthodoxy, which was to hold its own until after the Civil War, when the winds of liberalism again agitated the waters of theology.[2]

These interdenominational societies that grew out of the Second Awakening can be divided into two classes, according to purpose. The first classification includes those with an evangelistic or missionary motive. Among these societies, most of them with earlier British parallels, were the American Board of Commissioners for Foreign Missions (1810); the American Home Missionary Society (1826); the American Education Society (1815), formed to provide education for prospective ministers; the American Bible Society (1816), whose mission was to spread the Bible through the "destitute" settlements of the West and among the foreign-language groups thronging America's shores from Europe; the American Sunday-School Union (1824), which organized myriads of Sunday Schools and stocked countless Sunday School libraries on the frontier; and the American Tract Society (1825), which published literally millions of copies of religious and devotional volumes, moral tracts, hymnals, and periodicals. The purpose of every one of these was evangelism.[3]

But not only did American Protestants unite in extra-ecclesiastical bonds to form missionary societies—they also joined to form similar societies to reform American society in the image of American Protestantism, with its Puritan and revivalist undertones. Among these organizations were the American Society for the Promotion of Temperance (1826), the American Peace Society (1828), and the American Antislavery Society (1833). There was a society for almost every reform, in those stirring days when first the evils of slavery and war and intemperance were exposed to the burning light of the American Christian conscience.

The significance of these societies in the total history of the ecumenical movement is manifold. In them, for the first time in American history, members of more than two denominations co-operated, in an outward, visible organization,

---

[1] Gaius Glenn Atkins and Frederick L. Fagley, *History of American Congregationalism*, Boston, 1942, pp. 147 f.

[2] See especially Charles R. Keller, *The Second Great Awakening in Connecticut*, New Haven, 1942; Catharine C. Cleveland, *The Great Revival in the West, 1797–1805*, Chicago, 1916.

[3] See Oliver Wendell Elsbree, *The Rise of the Missionary Spirit in America*, Williamsport, Pa., 1928; Colin B. Goodykoontz, *Home Missions on the American Frontier*, Caldwell, Idaho, 1939; Edwin Wilbur Rice, *The Sunday-School Movement, 1780–1917, and the American Sunday-School Union, 1817–1917*, Philadelphia, 1917; and Bibliography (Baird).

in what we should now class as movements in the field of Life and Work. Secondly, these societies were national, with a nation-wide conception of their missionary task. This helped to give some of the more provincial denominations, those formerly limited to specific geographical areas in the East—as, for instance, the German groups—a broader outlook.

A main drawback was the way in which the denominations were related to the societies. With the exception of one or two of the missionary societies, they were all voluntary societies, made up not of official representatives from the denominations, but of those individually concerned over the prospect of the missionary impulse. This had its weak points, but was the best the times could afford. So delicate was the relation between the co-operating groups that the American Bible Society was forced to publish the Bible "without comment" so as not to offend any of the supporting groups. There was thus no attempt at doctrinal compromise, but simply outward co-operation. At the board meetings of the American Bible Society, when prayer was offered, whether liturgical or free, "there were always some present who were not able to say 'Amen' ". It was soon decided to "discontinue the exercises of prayer[1] and preaching" and "thereby avoid all interference with the various opinions of members regarding the forms of religious worship". The strongest point in favour of the voluntary system was the large participation of Christian laymen which these societies enjoyed.

A second drawback was that these societies were supported by only a few of the major denominations. The principal supporters of the system were the Congregationalists and Presbyterians, Dutch and German Reformed, and General Synod Lutherans. Even among these, the Presbyterians maintained their own denominational missionary society, thus dividing their attention between denominational and interdenominational interests. And some of the most significant of the American denominations maintained an aloofness from most of these societies which dulled the impact they might otherwise have had. The Methodists, for instance, supported their own missionary societies exclusively. Several of the frontier groups, notably the Baptists and Disciples, at least for a time, reacted against "organized missions", and refused to set up "unbiblical"[2] missionary societies or support those already in operation. And most of the Episcopalians, despite their interest in Church unity from other directions, maintained isolation from these significant interdenominational movements. Hence the interdenominational societies, while drawing their membership from several major groups, never became representative of the great body of American Christianity as a whole. But in a sense they were the 19th-century forerunners of the various missionary and benevolent groups which finally, in 1950, united in the National Council of the Churches of Christ in the United States of America.

4. THE UNITIVE CONTRIBUTION OF THE DISCIPLES OF CHRIST

On the western Pennsylvania frontier, in the opening years of the 19th century, there lived two Scottish-Irish preachers of the "Seceder" variety of Presbyterianism—Thomas Campbell (1763–1854) and his son Alexander Campbell (1788–1866). These men developed an approach to Christian unity which was not only

[1] See Chap. vii, p. 315, for the similar restriction in the British and Foreign Bible Society.
[2] Termed "unbiblical" because no precedent could be found in the New Testament for "missionary societies".

peculiarly American, but which has provided a continued impulse to unity into the present century.[1]

Thomas Campbell had been concerned over Christian divisions in Northern Ireland. By 1804 there were flourishing in Ulster four separate species of "Seceder" Presbyterians, all stemming from the Secession Church of 1733, a schism from the Church of Scotland. Unsuccessfully, he laboured to reconcile these small divisions of Zion in Northern Ireland, and, when he came to the Presbyterian region of western Pennsylvania in 1807, he began his irenic approach to the sister denominations there. "Rebuked and admonished" by his tiny presbytery for admitting non-Seceders to the Lord's Table in the Communion season, he finally withdrew from his Church in 1808. The following year he gathered to himself a little group of like-minded people which called itself the Christian Association of Washington, Pennsylvania.

To explain his position, he published in 1809 a now famous apologia for Christian unity, the so-called *Declaration and Address*. This document, one of the great milestones on the path of Christian unity in America, was a Declaration of Independence to all those on the frontier who desired to transcend the sectarian spirit. His message to the liberated souls is—push through the tangled underbrush of the Protestant creeds, which are for the most part human opinions only, to the pure spring of Bible truth. Unite in Christian Associations, rejecting human creeds and rallying around the Bible alone. "Sick and tired of the bitter jarrings and janglings of a party spirit"—so Campbell describes himself, after his tilt with conservative Presbyterianism on the frontier. "We would desire to be at rest," he writes, "and, were it possible, we would also desire to adopt and recommend such measures as would give rest to our brethren throughout all the Churches: as would restore unity, peace, and purity to the whole Church of God."

What was Campbell's plan for the promotion of Christian unity? His cry was, "Back to the primitive Church!" "Restore" the Church to its "primitive unity, purity, and prosperity"—that is the task for all of us. Already we agree on the fundamentals of the Christian faith, so that where we differ, "our differences, at most, are about the things in which the kingdom of God does not consist, that is, about matters of private opinion or human invention".

The only way we can be one is to unite on the fundamentals, requiring as articles of faith nothing but what the Bible expressly teaches, nothing but what Christ and the apostles enjoined upon the New Testament Church. Though the Bible in its entirety is to be used, the New Testament alone is to provide the constitution for the worship, discipline, and government of Campbell's Church of the Restoration. Even inferential truths from the Scriptures cannot be made binding, only the express commands. In other words, the now familiar Disciples' motto is here implied: "Where the Scriptures speak, we speak; where they are silent, we are silent." In other words, "Back to the New Testament Church!" Clear away "the stumbling-blocks—the rubbish of ages", as Campbell calls the creeds and doctrines of the post-apostolic Church, for like barnacles on the hull of a ship they impede the progress of Christianity.

In their attempt to be strictly "New Testament", the Disciples celebrated the Lord's Day rather than the Sabbath, they called themselves Disciples or Christians—refreshing improvements on Lutheran, Reformed, Methodist, and the rest. Ministers they called elders or evangelists, or by other New Testament

[1] See Bibliography (Thomas Campbell, Alexander Campbell).

terms. So insistent were they on these "Biblical terms for Biblical things" that their critics on the frontier came to speak of the "dialect of Campbellism". But this emphasis on the Bible and on the simplicity of the Christian faith appealed to the frontier mind, so that in the West the Disciples ran a close third to the Methodists and the Baptists as the great popular Church. And, true to their democratic emphasis, they refused to make a sharp distinction between clergy and laity. Unordained laymen can do anything ordained elders do—preach, conduct public worship—if they actually *can*, as Professor Garrison once put it. And in their zeal for liberty, they have retained a strict congregational polity, always reacting against "overhead organizations". In their national conventions even to-day there are no official delegates—anyone can come and anyone can be heard. With typical frontier informality, they still combine the atmosphere of an ecclesiastical body with that of a midwestern "Old Home Week".

Although it is now an antiquated term in the Disciples' fellowship, early Disciples preachers spoke frequently of "The Plea", by which they meant the Campbells' plea for Christian union. As the son, Alexander Campbell, worked out his full rationale of the Plea in *Christianity Restored* (1835), later reworked into his *Christian System*, the ultimate principle of his "Current Reformation", as Disciples called their movement, was the conversion of the world. For the conversion of the world nothing is essential but the union and co-operation of Christians, and "nothing is essential to the union of Christians but the Apostles' teaching and testimony". "Neither truth nor union alone", he wrote, "is sufficient to subdue the unbelieving nations, but truth and union combined are omnipotent." The "material principle" of this new Reformation was the Union of All Christians, while the "formal principle" was the restoration of Primitive Christianity.[1]

Later Disciples have not held these three principles in the same balance as the founding fathers. They have tended to emphasize one or the other in a way that often overshadows the rest. In fact, Alexander Campbell himself, while emphasizing union, began a period in Disciples history which stressed first and foremost "Restoration" principles. But the post-Civil War leaders, among them Isaac Errett, editor of *The Christian Standard*, and J. H. Garrison, editor of *The Christian-Evangelist*, again called for missions and union. In the 20th century there has arisen a younger generation of liberal Disciples leaders, who have exalted Church union as the greatest of Disciples contributions to American Church life. A conservative wing, emphasizing the Restoration principle, has since 1906 been separate. These Churches of Christ, as they call themselves, are popularly known as "the Antis", from the fact that they oppose the use of musical instruments in worship, evidently not on Old Testament but on New Testament grounds. These conservative sons of the founding fathers oppose existing agencies for union, such as the National Council, with the same vehemence as do Southern Baptists.[2]

There is something deeply and uniquely American about the Disciples movement. Its simplicity, its warm-hearted informality in worship, its suspicion of any lurking seeds of clericalism, its vocal insistence upon congregational indepen-

[1] See especially Hiram Van Kirk, *A History of the Theology of the Disciples of Christ*, St Louis, 1907.
[2] For the later history of the Disciples, see Bibliography (Ainslie); Winfred Ernest Garrison and Alfred T. DeGroot, *The Disciples of Christ, A History*, St Louis, 1949; and Garrison, *Whence and Whither—Disciples of Christ*, St Louis, 1948.

dence, all bear the mark of the American frontier. Thomas Campbell's impatience with credal "roots of bitterness and apples of discord", while growing out of his experience with the divided Churches of Ulster, found ready root among the frontier people of the Ohio and Mississippi Valleys. Most American is Campbell's appeal to all "Bible Christians" to leave "human creeds" behind and march forward with him into the new day of organic Christian union.

For Campbell's plan was a plan of organic Christian union of the sort that threw tradition to the winds. His new Christian Association marked a complete break with the denominational past, which was more possible in the mobile and fluid society of 19th-century America than it was in tradition-rooted Europe. When later on in the century William Reed Huntington of the Protestant Episcopal Church offered his plan of organic union, the spirit of it was different from Campbell's. For Huntington based his union plan upon Catholic tradition rather than upon cutting away all the post-Biblical "underbrush", as the Campbells advised. But both of these plans were bolder and more original than either Schmucker's plan or the federal union plan which eventuated in the Federal Council of Churches in 1908.

The paradox in the Campbellite position, as viewed from the standpoint of 20th-century union efforts, is that his organic union was to be accomplished through voluntary associations of individuals, who were to "come out" from their denominations and unite on the Bible. The Campbells placed the problem of Church union on the individual personal level, forcing those who felt as they did to break with their old denominations, rather than building a new Christian Church out of the co-ordinated denominational machinery of several merging Churches. At least the Campbells, in announcing their own positive programme for union, saved themselves the ecclesiastical carpentry which the 20th-century organic mergers between denominations have so often involved.

In the 19th century[1] the Disciples' contribution to ecumenical thought consisted principally of polemics and dogmatic pronouncements concerning the requisites for Christian unity. The 20th century brought with it a fresh awakening based on serious re-examination of the Disciples' position and ways of communicating it to other Churches. At the time of the Disciples' Convention in 1910, the President, Dr Peter Ainslie, called a mass meeting to consider problems of Christian unity. Out of this meeting was created a Commission on Christian Union, which began its work by calling a conference of Baptist, Disciples, Episcopalian, and Presbyterian leaders at New York on 28 February 1911.

In 1914 the Commission was incorporated and became the Association for the Promotion of Christian Unity. Under Ainslie's leadership the Association published literature, held conferences, and presented the general theme of Christian unity wherever possible. It continues to serve as the active agent of the Disciples for promoting unity both among Disciples and in relation to other Churches.

In 1911 Ainslie had initiated the publication of *The Christian Union Quarterly* as an organ of the Association. In 1934 the *Quarterly* became the quarterly *Christendom*, first owned and edited by C. C. Morrison, and later edited by H. Paul Douglass for the American section of Faith and Order and Life and Work.

[1] It is convenient at this point to give brief indications of later contributions of the Disciples to the ecumenical cause, though this involves a departure from the general chronological scheme of the History.

Peter Ainslie, who perhaps more than any other single man was responsible for recalling the Disciples to a sense of ecumenical mission, was President of the Association until 1925. At that time, because he increasingly advocated acceptance by the Church of those whom Christ had obviously accepted, whether they had been baptized by immersion or not, Ainslie came under strong criticism. Shrinking from the possibility of harmful controversy, he declined re-election as President. His long-time associate, H. C. Armstrong, continued to serve the Association devotedly as Executive Secretary until 1941.

While some Disciples regarded Ainslie as no longer a true representative of their position, others honoured him as their foremost advocate of Christian union since Thomas Campbell. That this latter appraisal has steadily gained ground is shown in the benefactions which founded the Peter Ainslie Memorial Lecture, to be given annually at Rhodes University College, Grahamstown, South Africa, on the theme of Christian unity,[1] and the William Henry Hoover Lectureship in Christian Unity at the Disciples Divinity House, Chicago University.

In addition to a continuing interest in the possibilities of organic union,[2] Disciples have taken an active, indeed a leading, part in every movement for Christian understanding and co-operative action—in the International Sunday-School Association, in the International Council of Religious Education, in the Federal Council of Churches, in co-operative educational work in the mission-field, and in each of the World Conferences which led up to the formation of the World Council of Churches in 1948. In their programme of inter-Church aid Disciples have contributed far more largely to the needs of other communions than to those of churches of their own fellowship.

At their best, Disciples have thought of themselves as a movement within the Church seeking after the unity of the Church.[3] While sometimes uncomfortably aware of tensions within their own body, they insist that their fundamental aim is still the same, namely to unite Christians and to make Christianity more effective and more universal by strengthening loyalty to Christ combined with liberty in theological opinions.

The question of the originality of the message of the Campbells has been carefully worked out by Disciples historians. There was nothing particularly new in Campbell's plea to restore the apostolic ordinances, for that has been attempted in all Christian generations and by many denominations. The Glasites or Sandemanians and the Haldane brothers of Scotland also held the same principles, and their influence upon the Campbells is well known. What was new in the Campbells' teaching was their unitive motive, whereby they sought to promote the unity of the Church through the restoration of primitive Christianity. And this was new only as compared with the Scottish developments, for it was not unique in America.

At the time of the Second Awakening, when the Campbells were beginning their reforming labours, there appeared in isolated sections of the United States several movements parallel to the Disciples. These took the Bible alone for their creed, called themselves simply "Christians", and hoped on that basis to unite a

---

[1] The first lecture was given in 1949 by Dr G. H. Clayton, Anglican Archbishop of Capetown, and the second by Dr Sidney M. Berry, Minister and Secretary of the International Congregational Council.
[2] See Table of Unions, Appendix to Chap. x.
[3] See George Walker Buckner, Jr., *Winds of God*.

divided American Protestantism. Elias Smith (1769–1840) of New England, James O'Kelly (1735–1826), the ex-Methodist circuit-rider who founded the Republican Methodist Church in Virginia and North Carolina, and Barton W. Stone (1772–1844) of Kentucky, all contributed "Christian" movements to the American denominational map. Some of these later merged with the Disciples of Campbell; others joined in 1931 with the Congregational Churches to form the Congregational Christian Churches; and still others remain separate as the "Churches of Christ". Even in the German-speaking areas of Pennsylvania there was a "Christian" movement, led by an ex-Reformed minister named John Winebrenner (1797–1870), who founded the "Church of God". Like the Campbells and these other "Christian" prophets, Winebrenner felt "it is contrary to scripture to divide the church of God into different sects and denominations".[1]

It is one of the ironies of history that all these movements, starting on the premise of restoring the unity of a divided Christendom, crystallized into denominations. On the frontier, the ecclesiastical competitors of the Disciples did not refrain from calling attention to this gaping hiatus between principle and practice. A Methodist from Iowa, in a red-hot anti-Campbellite tirade, himself forgetting how the Wesleyan movement had also crystallized into a Church, called the Disciples "a very denominational Ishmael among the Churches, waging a perpetual war of denunciation and proselytism against them", and spoke sneeringly of their "self-deception" in claiming not to be a denomination.[2] And even in the 20th century a former President of the International Convention of the Disciples pointed out that "in a Disciple convention the word 'denomination' is rarely heard and a visiting speaker from another group is well advised if he speaks of 'your communion' rather than 'your denomination'".[3] So strong is the feeling that the Disciples are not "just another denomination" that in the early years of this century, when it was proposed to federate the Churches of America into the Federal Council, many Disciples opposed the movement on the ground that their joining such a movement would be a tacit admission of their denominational status.

5. THE ECUMENICAL IMPACT OF THE AMERICAN-GERMAN CHURCHES

From an obscure part of the American Zion—the Churches of the Lutheran and Reformed traditions—there came not only the first American plan for organic union based on doctrinal compromise, but two of the principal ecumenical leaders of 19th-century American Protestantism, Samuel Simon Schmucker (1799–1873) and Philip Schaff (1819–93). In the early 19th century the American-German Churches, Lutheran and Reformed, were among the least of the ecclesiastical tribes. Handicapped as they were by the problem of adjustment to the English language, and facing the task of ministering to the waves of 19th-century migration west of the Alleghenies, they for the most part turned inward rather than outward, and did not make any profound impression upon American culture. But in one area of Christian life, namely in the drive towards

[1] See Bibliography (O'Kelly, Stone); and John Winebrenner, *A Brief View of the Formation, Government, and Discipline of the Church of God*, Harrisburg, 1829.
[2] T. McK. Stuart, *Errors of Campbellism, Being a Review of All the Fundamental Errors of the System of Faith and Church Polity of the Denomination Founded by Alexander Campbell*, Cincinnati, 1890.
[3] Clarence E. Lemmon, "A Step Toward Organic Union—A Disciples View of Church Federal Union", *Christian Century*, 9 June 1943.

Christian unity, they had a message for their sister Churches of the Anglo-American tradition.

It was partly the challenge of the frontier, partly the example of the Union of Lutherans and Reformed in Prussia,[1] which prompted the leaders of the Lutheran and German Reformed Churches of the middle and southern states to closer co-operation and union proposals in the two decades following the Lutheran Tercentenary of 1817. This movement affected all the German Lutherans and Reformed of colonial stock, including those in Pennsylvania, New York, Maryland, Virginia, North Carolina, and Ohio. Had it succeeded, Calixtus' dream would have seen fulfilment and a new American-German Church would have resulted.[2]

So companionable were the spiritual descendants of Luther, Calvin, and Zwingli in early America on the local and lay level that thoughts of a wedding were seriously entertained. The common German cultural background of both groups, and their common pietistic heritage, led in America to the development of a peculiarly Pennsylvania German religious institution, the "union church". By the term "union church" was meant a co-operative affiliation in the local community between the Lutheran and the Reformed congregations, who owned and used a common church property and building, where they worshipped on alternate Sundays. The degree of co-operation ranged from joint ownership of the property, with separate services, consistories, and Sunday Schools, to churches with a common consistory, Sunday School, treasury, and even union services. Hundreds of these union or community churches were founded until about 1900, when the respective synods began to discourage any new unions. There are still in eastern Pennsylvania over 175 of these historic union churches in operation.[3]

In some cases the Lutheran and Reformed country parishes were so constituted that both of them embraced the same five or six union churches, each served in circuit by a Lutheran and a Reformed pastor. Intercommunion and intermarriage further strengthened the bond. For the union church a whole literature issued from the German presses of eastern Pennsylvania, including religious periodicals, prayer-books, liturgies, catechisms, and the ever-present *Gemeinschaftliches Gesangbuch* of 1817, which reached its twenty-second edition in 1884. So close and congenial was the relation among the laymen of a union church that it used to be proverbial among the farmers of German Pennsylvania that the only difference between the Lutherans and Reformed was that the Reformed began the Lord's Prayer with *Unser Vater*, the Lutherans with *Vater Unser*.

The Lutheran Tercentenary of 1817 and the Prussian Plan of Union kindled the flame of interest in union. In the enthusiasms aroused in that memorable year, Pastor Gottlieb Schober (1756–1838), an ex-Moravian Lutheran pastor in North Carolina, in his Reformation sermon, voiced the hope that "the spirit of love and Union" might be awakened "among all who believe the divinity of Jesus Christ, the sole mediator between God and man, so that we might come to

[1] See Chap. vi, pp. 286 ff.
[2] See Don Yoder, "Lutheran-Reformed Union Proposals, 1800–1850; An American Experiment in Ecumenics", *Bulletin Theological Seminary of the Evangelical and Reformed Church in the United States*, Vol. VII, No. 1, Lancaster, Pa, pp. 39–77.
[3] See Mark O. Heller, "The Union Church Problem in Eastern Pennsylvania", *Lutheran Church Quarterly*, Vol. XIV, 1941; and *Study and Survey of the Union and Rural Congregations of the Evangelical Lutheran Ministerium of Pennsylvania*, 1944.

the blessed time foretold of old when we will live in peace as one flock under one shepherd". He even envisioned a "general assembly of all denominations", in which all Churches could unite and to which all might send official delegates. In the same year Schober wrote to the Ministerium of Pennsylvania, expressing the idea "that it would be good if the Lutherans and Reformed were to unite with each other", and "founded his wish on the European example".[1]

Discussions pro and con appeared in the church periodicals of the early 1830's. The principal apologist for union was Johann Augustus Probst (1792–1844), Lutheran minister of Pennyslvania, who in 1826 issued his important tract *Die Wiedervereinigung der Lutheraner und Reformirten*, urging the establishment of a union "Evangelical Church", based on the levelling of doctrine which had already occurred. In 1836-37 the Synods debated the question a final time, but the movement came to naught.

What conclusions can be drawn as to the reasons for the failure of this once promising unitive movement in American Christianity? Several factors entered into the change of sentiment from pro-union to vigorously anti-union. While the laymen in the union churches were ready for union, the ministers, educated as they were in separate seminaries, began to emphasize the "distinctive" Lutheran heritage and the "distinctive" Reformed heritage. The confessional reaction within Lutheranism was prompted partly by native American Lutherans, partly by immigrant Germans, principally "Old Lutherans", who took over much of the Lutheran leadership in East and West. The Reformed Church also became interested in her own background and separate future, and looked to the sister Churches of the Reformed tradition for a new union partner.[2] And among the practical deterrents to union plans was the all too obvious time of troubles which made rough sailing for the Prussian Union in Germany. This was pointed out as an object lesson of what would happen in America were the two groups to merge, and negotiations came to a close.

The flavour of the unionist spirit which was spread abroad in the Lutheran and Reformed Churches of America in the earlier years of the 19th century is evident in George Lochman's final thoughts in his Lutheran History of 1818. They sound almost modern. "In concluding", he writes,

"I cannot help expressing my pleasure, in observing that the different denominations are drawing nearer to each other, and that bigotry is rapidly declining. In some parts of Germany and in Prussia, the distinction of Lutheran and Reformed is already done away, and both churches consider themselves as one body. And God grant! that this spirit of union and brotherly love may continue to spread! God grant, that all who profess and call themselves Christians may be led into the way of truth, and hold the faith in unity of spirit, in the bond of peace, and in righteousness of life!"

The influence of Samuel Simon Schmucker upon the Lutheran Church has been bitterly debated by Lutheran historians in many volumes since his death in 1873. For he represented the tendency towards an "Americanized" Lutheranism, using the English language, winning converts by the revivalistic methods of the larger denominations. For many years his ideas were dominant in the Lutheran

---

[1] See A. L. Graebner, *Geschichte der Lutherischen Kirche in America*, St Louis, 1892, I, p. 682.

[2] See Bibliography (Ferm and Good).

General Synod and in the Lutheran Seminary at Gettysburg, Pennsylvania, which Schmucker headed for the first forty years of its existence.[1]

Schmucker was largely rejected by his own people. A generation arising after the Civil War swung back to a strictly confessional position. Yet for a generation, under his irenic example, a large part of the Lutherans in America, those known as the General Synod Lutherans, entered into American church life as an equal among equals. In the 1830's and 1840's, the General Synod Lutherans even supported several of the interdenominational societies, principally the American Home Missionary Society. Such co-operation would have been unheard of among the General Council Lutherans, who in 1872 passed their "Galesburg Rule" which proclaimed "Lutheran pulpits for Lutheran ministers only, Lutheran altars for Lutheran communicants". Although the General Council Lutherans have since 1918 been merged with the General Synod Lutherans in the United Lutheran Church, there is still some difference of spirit between Gettysburg Theological Seminary, which has lingering traces of Schmucker's influence, and the former General Council Seminary, Mount Airy.

It is always interesting to trace the way in which the leaders of great movements have been prepared for receiving the mantle of leadership. Schmucker's preparation for ecumenical leadership involved a wider acquaintance with American church problems than that possessed by any other Lutheran leader of his generation. Born in 1799 at Hagerstown, Maryland, and serving a pastorate in Virginia, he came to understand the peculiar problems of the Churches of the South. In 1817 he travelled through the Ohio Valley, and became acquainted with frontier problems of evangelization. His theological education he gained at Calvinistic Princeton, and while there he was the room-mate of a young man who became one of the outstanding Presbyterian ecumenical leaders in that century—Dr Robert Baird, the first American scholar to trace American religious history not in patriotic denominational terms but in terms of the contributions of all the Churches.[2] And lastly, Schmucker's Pietist upbringing and his own conversion led him to understand the basic Puritanism and revivalism of the major American denominations, so that all his life he worked with rather than against the Anglo-American Churches.

Following his work in consolidating the Lutheran General Synod in the 1820's, Schmucker devoted his talents to the question of Christian unity in America. In 1838, from his busy study at the Seminary at Gettysburg, he was able at last to issue his first work on Christian unity, the *Fraternal Appeal to the American Churches. With a Plan for Catholic Union, on Apostolic Principles.* The *Appeal* was reprinted in 1839, and went through various later editions. The final one came out as Schmucker's parting shot at the "red banner of sectarianism"— that rare volume with the title *The True Unity of Christ's Church: Being a Renewed Appeal to the Friends of the Redeemer, On Primitive Christian Union, And the History of its Corruption.*[3]

Schmucker's plan for Christian union involved the foundation of what he called the Apostolic Protestant Church. As the doctrinal *sine qua non* upon which the constituent denominations were to unite, Schmucker worked out a United

[1] In addition to Bibliography (Anstadt and Ferm), see Abdel Ross Wentz, *History of the Gettysburg Theological Seminary*, Philadelphia, 1926; Bente's *American Lutheranism*, 2 vols., St Louis, 1919, gives the "Missouri" anti-unionist view.

[2] See Bibliography (Baird). Baird edited *The Christian Union and Religious Memorial* (1847–50), the pioneer unionist periodical in America, a fruit of American interest in the Evangelical Alliance of 1846.   [3] See Bibliography (Schmucker).

Confession based on the doctrines in Protestantism which were common to all Protestant creeds and therefore "fundamental". This consensus of all the main Protestant creeds of the Reformation era embraced twelve articles. These were phrased, not in original formulations by Schmucker, but in the very words of the older creeds themselves. Thus Article I, "Of the Scriptures", was drawn from the Thirty-nine Articles of the Church of England and from its daughter-creed in the Methodist *Discipline*, while Article II, "Of God and the Trinity", used the Lutheran and Moravian wording. After subscribing to the United Confession, the various denominations were to give up their "party" names and become simply branches of the Apostolic Protestant Church. Enough of "sectarian idolatry" or "man-worship"! The inordinate veneration of Luther, Zwingli, Calvin, and Wesley was to him just as evil as splintering the Corinthian churches into the factions of Paul, Apollos, and Cephas.

Although the local churches were to be left much as before, retaining their larger creeds, their own way of worship, their ministry and discipline, such a union would have certain advantages over the present chaos of sectarianism. For there would be free interchange of ministry, and most certainly open communion. Schmucker's united Church was thus a federation—for he would keep the denominational machines intact, but bundle them together vertically, like sticks in a faggot. His was the first of a long line of American plans for federative union; its family resemblance to the Philadelphia Plan of 1918–20,[1] and E. Stanley Jones' Plan of Federal Union, is more than superficial.

In several ways, however, Schmucker seems to have yearned for a union that would go deeper than federation. Although he more than once expressed his fear of the "one big church", which smacked of Rome's monolithic ecclesiastical machine, he hoped that his confederated union would be simply a station on the road to even closer unity. Its primary goal was to remove the competition and jealousies that rend the seamless robe of Christ. Making careful provision for the retention of diversity along with unity, he yet gives the impression that, perhaps as the years pass, the individual shibboleths will disappear.

Another point in Schmucker's plan, familiar also in 20th-century discussions on union, is his emphasis on the value, if not of union, at least of co-operation at the "grass roots" level. Schmucker's confederated churches in one local area, for instance, were urged to hold joint annual Communion services. The "Monthly Concert" (the famous 19th-century prayer-meeting for missions) could also be held by rotation in the local confederated churches. Even the Sunday Schools could share in the unity by learning to know each other in joint exercises and celebrations. And, most basic of all, there should be mutual recognition of each other's ministry and exchange of pulpits.

Schmucker's Apostolic Protestant Church of America never came into being. But his thorough exposition of the necessity of Church union, his candid facing of the evils of the denominational spirit—more exhaustive even than Campbell's —provided the arguments for the 20th-century ecumenical movement. He did work that did not need to be done again. The main area where his ideas were brought at least to partial fruition was in the formation of the Evangelical Alliance in 1846, the American Branch of the Alliance in 1867, and the Federal Council of the Churches of Christ in America in 1908.[2]

---

[1] See also Chap. x, pp. 445 f.
[2] See Bibliography (Hutchison, pp. 10 f., and Macfarland, *Christian Unity*, pp. 52 f.) and General Bibliography (Slosser, pp. 178–83).

Thirty miles across the mountains from Gettysburg, in the Allegheny Mountains, was another little town and another infant theological seminary from which came flashes of ecumenical lightning. From 1836 to 1871 little Mercersburg, the German Reformed School of the Prophets in Pennsylvania, contributed more than its share of original ideas and creative Church leaders to the American religious scene. The wider impact of Mercersburg came through the co-operative labours of its two principal professors, John Williamson Nevin (1803–86), a Scottish-Irish Presbyterian in background, and Philip Schaff (1819–93), the great Swiss-American theologian. The historical and doctrinal works of these men, in tractate, book, and periodical form, led to a theological and liturgical emphasis in American Church history generally referred to as the Mercersburg Movement.[1]

Philip Schaff was born at Chur in the Grisons. His early education bridged the gap between Germanic and Romance Switzerland. After studying in Lutheran Germany, the young Swiss Reformed theologian was called in 1844 to the theological seminary of the German Reformed Church in the United States. There in Mercersburg he conceived and began his great history of the Christian Church, the first volume of which was published in 1851 as the *Geschichte der Apostolischen Kirche*.

Finding a wider area of activity in the Presbyterian Church, Schaff in 1863 became Professor of Church History at Union Theological Seminary in New York City. It was there that he published his *Creeds of Christendom* and edited his commentaries and encyclopedia, all of which have ecumenical significance. In 1888 he organized the American Society of Church History, and in 1893, shortly before his death, delivered the great irenic address on the Churches of Christendom before the World's Parliament of Religions, meeting in connection with the Columbian Exposition at Chicago. It was through Church history and symbolics that Schaff had his greatest influence upon the ecumenical movement. His many visits to Europe and his books on America and Germany helped to give him the well-deserved title of "Pontifex", as Professor Bahrdt once called him—a "bridge-builder" between the Churches of the Old World and the New.

The influence of Schaff upon the German Reformed Church comes in connection with that of Nevin in the "Mercersburg Theology". Nevin's emphasis lay in the direction of a theological basis for Church unity—unity being the expression of the very nature of the Christian Church. Schaff's theory of historical development, which predicted a future merging of Protestantism and Catholicism into an Evangelical Catholicism, and his irenic treatment of medieval Church history, met with a varied reception in his own and the sister Churches of the Reformed-Presbyterian family. In his own German Reformed Church the extreme High Church party, over a dozen of them, packed their theological bags for Canterbury or Rome, while the extreme anti-Mercersburgers, preferring the modified revivalism and Puritanism of the Presbyterian and Dutch Reformed Churches, found spiritual rest in those havens. The Mercersburg insistence upon churchliness and liturgical worship almost sundered the German Reformed Church in the years 1867-78; but fortunately the dispute was amicably settled,

---

[1] In addition to Bibliography (Richards, Schaff, and Nevin), see George W. Richards, "Philip Schaff—Prophet of Church Union", *Christendom*, 1945, pp. 463–71; Scott Francis Brenner, "Philip Schaff the Liturgist", *Christendom*, 1946, pp. 443–56; and the "Schaff Memorial Number" of *Bulletin Theological Seminary of the Evangelical and Reformed Church in the United States*, Vol. XV, No. 4, Oct. 1944.

although a rival theological seminary and rival periodicals, expressive of the "Old Reformed" position, continued to exist for years.[1]

The continuing influence of Mercersburg had led the Reformed Church in the United States to seek to express the basic unity of the Christian Church by merging with sister denominations. Until 1934 this urge had been unsatisfied, despite several attempts at union with Churches within the Reformed-Presbyterian family. For instance, as early as 1838 and as late as 1920, and at several intervening dates, the German Reformed Churches of Pennsylvania have attempted to merge their denomination with their full-blooded sister, the Reformed Protestant Dutch Church (now the Reformed Church in America) of New York and New Jersey. But the plans to merge these two American representatives of the Continental Reformed tradition have come to naught. In each case it was theological differences which broke up the union conventions, the Dutch representing a more conservative Calvinistic position than the Germans. The interesting attempt at the organic merger of the Reformed Church in the United States with the Northern Presbyterians (1908–12) was shelved, when it was pointed out that the Reformed delegates would represent only a small proportion of the total delegation of the new "union" General Assembly, and that such a union would be more an absorption of a small body by a larger than a wedding of equals.

In the 20th century the ecumenical mantle of Schaff passed to George Warren Richards (b. 1869), the principal intermediary between the Reformed Churches of America and the mother Churches of the European homeland. Professor Richards, who for many years headed the Lancaster Theological Seminary, Mercersburg's successor, expressed the Mercersburg enthusiasm for Christian unity by spearheading the movement which led to the formation of the Evangelical and Reformed Church in 1934. After a long series of unsuccessful union attempts with the Lutherans (1817–37), the Dutch Reformed (1838–1920), and the Presbyterians (1908–12), the Reformed Church finally found a congenial partner in the Evangelical Synod of North America, the small American counterpart of the German Prussian Union.[2] Such a consistent and recurring strain of ecumenical interest would seem to give historical backing to H. Paul Douglass' contention that among the American denominations the one with the most favourable 20th-century attitude towards practicable Church union was the Reformed Church in the United States.[3]

6. EPISCOPALIAN VARIATIONS ON THE THEME

At the close of the American Revolution, in which their pastors and people had been torn between conflicting loyalties to king and to adopted country, the Episcopalians went through a critical period of reorganization. Their former organic connection with the mother Church of England broken, they were faced with the problem of organizing an independent American branch of their Church. The first step in clearing the ecclesiastical decks for action was the setting up of an American episcopate, which was accomplished with no opposition now that the Revolution was over. Led by a generation of far-seeing leaders,

[1] See Bibliography (Good), and especially Luther J. Binkley, *The Mercersburg Theology*, Lancaster, Pa., 1953.
[2] Full details in Don Yoder, *Church Union Efforts of the Reformed Church in the United States*, 1947 (unpublished Ph.D. thesis, Divinity School, The University of Chicago).
[3] *Church Unity Movements*, p. 465.

including Bishop William White of Pennsylvania, they weathered the storm successfully, organizing the Protestant Episcopal Church of the United States in the year 1789.

From 1789 on, their growth has been more rapid than in the colonial period, when, with the support of the Crown and of the Society for the Propagation of the Gospel, they were able to become the established Church in at least six of the thirteen colonies. One of the sources of their new strength was the invasion of "missionary territory" such as New England, that ancient stronghold of Congregationalism. From the flourishing missionary areas in New England came some of the most creative leadership of the Episcopalians in the 19th century.

In face of the prejudice of New Englanders (who looked upon "Churchmen" as unwelcome dissenters from the Congregational State-Church), of the revivalists (who thought "Churchmen" cold and unevangelistic), and of the other non-liturgical groups (who thought the Episcopal Church a stepping-stone in the direction of Rome), the Protestant Episcopal Church forged ahead in the 19th century. An aggressive home missionary policy planted Episcopal churches in the Middle and Far West, so that by 1900, while still small in numbers, they had spread over the whole country and were one of the leading denominations in point of influence. Furthermore, they had found a great mission for their Church—to lead the movement towards Christian unity.

In the first half of the 19th century, when certain brave souls were crusading for a united Church of America, the Episcopalians developed their own variation on the theme. As the Reverend Thomas Hubbard Vail (1812–89) of Hartford, Connecticut, expressed it in 1841, the drive towards Christian unity in America had hitherto gone off in the wrong direction. In his opinion, "Instead of endeavouring to strike out an entirely new system of ecclesiastical unity, the proper and only feasible course is to select, for the purpose of uniting within it, some system already established, and which realizes most nearly the idea of a Comprehensive Church, and if it be not in every respect perfect, to improve it, if it will allow improvement, into perfection". "It may be", he felt, "there is such a system amongst us—a system whose structure is capable of any modification, and in whose organization are instrumentalities by which it may be shaped into any form which the majority of the Christians in our country may desire. We believe there is such a system among us." Naturally the existing system was his own Protestant Episcopal Church, which, in the course of 302 pages, he attempts to prove to be the Comprehensive Church.

Vail realized that, at least for the purpose of discussion, a plan for ecclesiastical union must be offered. The fault of earlier works on the subject lay in just this lack of a concrete plan. To talk of Christian union without an outward, visible, ecclesiastical unity is impossible. "We do not think", he says, "that any progress can be made towards Christian Union except upon the basis of an United Church." The Episcopal Church offers the comprehensive programme for unity, writes Vail, for it includes within itself all the points of Church life which the other denominations hold essential, as well as its own individual excellences, e.g. the threefold ministry.

"Cast in your lot with us", calls Vail to other sister denominations. If the Protestant Episcopal Church be the Comprehensive Church, it is the "bounden duty of all Christians to unite themselves with it at once . . . even if it be at some personal sacrifice". "You may outnumber us in a year; you may have the control in our parishes, in our Diocesan Conventions, in our General Convention", he generously admits. "You may revise and rearrange our laws. Be it so! We are willing to be melted down with you, in our own crucible, into one mass of Christian love and fellowship." Come yourselves, and bring others, he calls —"Come in your strength—whole Associations and Consociations, whole Presbyteries and Conferences."

He closes with words that must have awakened interest even among those who opposed his denominational approach to Christian unity: "We call for a true Christian unity, which shall expand itself through the land; which shall go into all the little villages, and all the private dwellings, over the whole length and breadth of our long and our broad country, and unite hearts, and unite voices, and unite labour, and strength, and wealth, that have always before been separated—which shall bring into one Comprehensive Church all the disciples of Christ."[1]

While the Vail approach, addressed to the Christian public, was reprinted at least twice during the century, its proposals proved too vague for application, and it was left to other minds to work in more specific and practical ways to awaken the Church to its newly-conceived mission. At the General Convention of 1853, Dr William Augustus Muhlenberg (1796–1877) led a group of presbyters in addressing to the House of Bishops the now famous "Muhlenberg Memorial". The proposals outlined in the Memorial, to use its own words, sprang from "the divided and distracted state of our American Protestant Christianity", the new forms of 19th-century "unbelief", the renewed activity of "Romanism", and "the utter ignorance of the Gospel among so large a portion of the lower classes of our population". These needs of American society led the petitioners to express their desire to see the Protestant Episcopal Church gird herself for action by broadening her appeal to the American public.[2]

The Memorial appeals to the assembled bishops to set up "some ecclesiastical system, broader and more comprehensive than that which you now administer, surrounding and including the Protestant Episcopal Church as it now is, leaving that Church untouched, identical with that Church in all its great principles, yet providing for as much freedom in opinion, discipline, and worship as is compatible with the essential Faith and Order of the Gospel".

The practical side of the Memorial, which must be considered in connection with the tracts and additional proposals inspired by it, was that it sought the extension of episcopal authority so as to provide for the ordination of men "among the other bodies of Christians around us", who would gladly receive episcopal ordination, "could they obtain it, without that entire surrender which would now be required of them of all the liberty in public worship to which they have been accustomed". These "able ministers of the New Testament" would not have to "bring themselves to conform in all particulars to our prescriptions and customs". If they expressed belief in the Holy Scriptures as the Word of God, the Apostles' and Nicene Creeds, the two Sacraments, and the "doctrines of grace" as expounded by the Thirty-nine Articles, these men were to be free to conduct their worship services with minimal reference to the Prayer Book forms, except in the case of the Eucharist, and were to report to the ordaining bishop every three years.

[1] See Bibliography (Vail).
[2] For the similar ideas of William H. Lewis, see Bibliography (Lewis).

The Memorial, as well as Muhlenberg's "Evangelical Catholic" movement, had a profound though not immediate effect upon the Church. The Broad Church emphasis, to which Muhlenberg's irenic position was one of the contributing historical strands, helped eventually to serve as a bridge of conciliation between the conflicting High and Low Church parties in his Church. The principal immediate result of the Memorial was the appointment in 1856 of a committee to renew the correspondence with the Church of Sweden, which had lapsed since colonial days. Unfortunately for Muhlenberg's plans for wider Christian union around an Episcopalian nucleus, churchmen of all opinions became absorbed in the national problems leading up to the Civil War, so that it was not until 1870 that another important voice was heard calling the Protestant Episcopal Church to lead the movement towards American Christian unity.[1]

The most influential of the Episcopalian advocates of Christian unity in the 19th century was William Reed Huntington (1838–1918), another of New England's contributions to Episcopalianism, who, like Vail and Muhlenberg, conceived the new mission for the Protestant Episcopal Church—to lead the drive towards Christian unity in America. In 1870 Huntington's first volume, entitled *The Church Idea—An Essay Toward Unity*, was launched on the waves of public opinion. Thoroughly in favour of Christian unity, he simply proclaimed the existence of a "Church of the Reconciliation"—his own Protestant Episcopal Church—which should invite all the Christian groups to join it, to form the "Catholic Church of America".[2]

What Huntington's little volume did that was new was to set forth a minimum list of "essentials" of Anglicanism upon which other groups could unite. Here he went further than Vail and was more specific than Muhlenberg. When Huntington had boiled Anglicanism down to its irreducible minimum, there remained his basis for a united Church—a platform later to be known as the "Chicago-Lambeth Quadrilateral". As first formulated in 1870, this pioneer union proposal included: (1) the Holy Scriptures as the Word of God; (2) the primitive Creeds as the rule of faith; (3) the two Sacraments ordained by Christ himself; and (4) the historic episcopate as the keystone of governmental unity.[3]

Like many other 19th-century Church unionists, including Campbell and Schmucker, Huntington wanted to simplify the Faith. To him as to them, the Reformation confessions—the basis of so many of our divisions—were too long and involved. Using familiar Civil War terms, he likens them to an "old battleship". We need instead a "modern ironclad", with "heavy guns and few", and these "heavy guns and few" the Apostles' and Nicene Creeds supply. The advantage of his plan was, he thought, that it admitted of including the "Catholic" groups as well as the Protestants in a general invitation to Christian reunion. For these were the less hopeless days before Leo XIII, in his Bull *Apostolicae Curae* (1896), finally condemned Anglican Orders.

Huntington's challenge stirred up a wide, though again not immediate, response in his own Church. The House of Bishops at the General Convention of 1886 finally adopted his "Quadrilateral" as the four-point basis to be used in

[1] See Bibliography (Muhlenberg); and E. R. Hardy, Jr., "Evangelical Catholicism, W. A. Muhlenberg and his Memorial Movement", in *Historical Magazine of the Protestant Episcopal Church*, Vol. XII, 1944, pp. 155–92.

[2] See Bibliography (Huntington and Suter); and Don Yoder, "Preview of a United Church", *Christian Century*, 28 February 1951.

[3] See also Chap. vi, pp. 264 f., and Chap. x, pp. 446 ff.

future Episcopalian proposals of unity, and it was reaffirmed in slightly modified form by the Lambeth Conference of 1888. And in the wake of Huntington's book there sprang up Church unity societies and circles in various Episcopal dioceses; in their discussions and reports the student will find the first glimmerings of interest in Presbyterian-Episcopalian union.[1]

Not all the contemporary criticisms of Huntington's work are favourable. When it was reduced to its essence, the Episcopalian plan was actually denominational. It involved consolidation by rallying around the Episcopalian banner. Although it was a union in which variety was to be preserved, Dr Charles W. Shields of Princeton, Huntington's chief non-Episcopalian supporter and critic, wrote that such a union would be like Aaron's rod swallowing up the rods of Pharaoh's magicians, or like gaining immortality at the loss of personal identity. "Moreover," he writes, "should the invitation be heeded, the little consolidating body, with all its conservative vigour, would soon be resisting the intrusion of so much foreign and uncongenial material, or find it not very easy of assimilation."[2] And Robert Ellis Thompson, a Presbyterian historian writing in 1895, turned the tables on the Episcopalians by suggesting his own Presbyterian Church as the much needed "central and moderating influence between opposed extremes". "She has more affinity with all the diverse elements of our ecclesiastical life than has any other Church. She has been a Puritan church in the Puritan age, and a Methodist church in the age of the Awakening; and she is returning to what she was before the Puritan influence touched her, in adapting herself to the churchly tendencies of the present age."[3]

But Huntington had not yet spoken his last word. That came in 1898, when he published *A National Church*. With a last longing glance backward, he here gives up his earlier insistence on making Anglicanism the basis of a united American Church. The American Catholic Church should be thoroughly American, he writes. It should express the heart and soul of this people, just as the historic Church of England expresses its national character. "The English ivy is a beautiful plant," he admits, "and nothing is one-half so becoming to church walls; but unfortunately the English ivy does not flourish in all climates, and to insist that it shall be 'ivy or nothing' in a land where the woodbine and other fairly presentable vines are indigenous is a mistake."

In *A National Church* he further enlightens us on how a united Church could come about, presenting the "geographical" or "territorial" approach to Christian unity. Since obviously the three territorial units of most importance in America are the nation, the state, and the county, in a national united Church the unit would be the nation, with states and counties as its smaller component units. How would this national Church work? Beginning on the county level, there would be individual, local churches. These would be independent, except that they look for advice and aid to their "chief pastor", whose residence and centre of administration is the county-town. This chief pastor or "overseer" (how carefully Huntington avoids the word bishop!) "oversees" the missionary work of the area. From time to time, clerical and lay counsellors gather around this leader, consulting together for the good of religion in the county, talking over

---

[1] See *Annual Reports of the Church Unity Society of the Diocese of Pennsylvania*, 1888 ff.; and Samuel G. Inman, "The Christian Union Foundation", *The Christian Union Quarterly*, Vol. XIII, 1923–24, pp. 47–59.

[2] *The United Church of the United States*, pp. 95–98.

[3] *A History of the Presbyterian Churches in the United States*, New York, 1895, p. 313.

the religious needs of the towns and villages, and planning their united campaigns.

Here we have, then, a microcosm of the united Church. In it justice is done to the "home-rule" or congregational principle, for the local churches manage their own affairs and finances and choose their own pastors. The presbyterial principle is present also, in the yearly (or more frequent) meetings of representatives, lay and clerical, from the local churches. The principle of leadership, the modified episcopal principle, is likewise in evidence, for each county group of churches has its head.

On the state level, the "overseers" of the various counties, with representative pastors and laymen from each county, meet together once every three years or oftener. The larger questions with which the state council was to deal were Church-State relations, religious education, marriage and divorce, church property, and so on. The presidency of the state council would naturally fall to one of the "county overseers". On the national level, Huntington pictures for us a bicameral assembly convened once a decade or oftener, representing all the states of the union. The smaller of the two Houses is made up of representative "chief pastors", one or two from each state; the larger, of pastors and laymen in numbers proportionate to the population of the states they represent. All of which has a realistic and American ring and is certainly a most original approach.

On the question of worship, Huntington again admits the need of compromise. Obviously the several types of Protestant worship cannot be merged into one. "But what is there foolish", he writes, "in the suggestion that a single building, by the simple device of a greater frequency in the hours of service than is common among Protestants, might be made to meet the devotional needs alike of those who love a formal and those who prefer, I will not say an informal, but a less formal method of publicly worshipping Almighty God?"

Thus Huntington's second plan involved a national Church made up of local union churches, where all varieties of Christians could worship at different times in the same building. There is much in this plan that bears a close resemblance to Charles Clayton Morrison's plan of organic union outlined at the Greenwich Conference in 1949. Huntington, like Morrison, would dissolve the denominational superstructures, allowing each individual church to retain its own system of worship, but merging presbyteries, synods, and conferences horizontally, on three different geographical levels. Thus, despite its imperfections, Huntington's plan is nearer to the present movements towards organic union than was Schmucker's plan of "confederation" (1838). Despite the neglect of his work at the hands of historians, William Reed Huntington can be called the John the Baptist of the 20th-century movement towards organic rather than federal union of the American Churches.

7. THE TRIUMPH OF FEDERAL UNION

One of the keys to ecumenical progress in the latter half of the 19th century lies in the decline of revivalism in the major Churches and its rechannelling into other groups, with the development out of it of new co-operative movements of ecumenical significance. In the first half of the century the spirit of revivalism had drawn the major denominations into common evangelistic work. But after 1865 many Church leaders, faced with new needs and challenges, began to re-examine both revivalism and the theology that underlay its methods. The changed conditions in American society led to the development of the religious education method to replace revivalism among the major Churches, and the rise of American liberal theology, especially in its social outreach phase as seen in the Social Gospel, to replace the individualistic, pietistic type of revival theology.[1]

Critics and opponents of the revivalist system felt that its work was done. To continue the method indefinitely would exhaust the spiritual soil of America as one-crop farming had exhausted the rich soil of the South. Instead of forcing all Church members, including children, through a sudden climactic conversion experience, the critics of revivalism pointed the way to the modern religious education movement, which has encouraged a gradual growth into grace and a growing up within the Church. As the leaders of the Churches came to see the necessity for co-operating in this new movement, it bore ecumenical fruit in the form of the International Sunday-School Lessons (1872) and the International Council of Religious Education (1922).[2]

The new problems that faced the Churches in the post-Civil War era grew for the most part out of the rise of the industrial city. If the earlier revivalism had sprung up to meet the challenge of the movement of rural people westward on to new frontiers, the new Social Gospel arose to meet the challenge of the industrial city. The teeming slums and patent inequalities of the city posed a double problem to the American Churches. Not only did they wish to "church" the new areas and keep their members who moved to the city from the country, but they saw the necessity for remoulding and refining the society of the industrial city in the Christian image. Ecumenically speaking, these two aims led to the formation of local church federations, the earliest of which was the Federation of Churches and Christian Workers of New York City (1895); and the rise of the "Settlement House" and the "Institutional Church".[3]

As revivalism spread into new areas of Church life in the second half of the 19th century, several new movements of world-wide ecumenical significance emerged out of it. Out of the "city" revival of 1857–58 had grown the American Y.M.C.A. and Y.W.C.A. The widespread revival campaigns of Dwight L. Moody (1837–99), the American layman with an ecumenical concern that reached across the Atlantic, resulted in an interest in world evangelism, especially among students, which led in 1887 to the formation of the Student Volunteer Movement. Moody's influence upon the British and Continental student groups and the formation of the World's Student Christian Federation (1895) have been described elsewhere.[4] But it is to be noted that this was largely a case of *lux ex occidente*. The ecumenical star had arisen on the American horizon. Also important is the fact that the movements inspired by Moody's apostolic vision were movements of laymen with a concern for missions and Christian unity.

Revivalism in its period of rechannelling after the Civil War produced the first really ecumenical hymnals in America—the "gospel song" books of Ira D. Sankey, P. P. Bliss, and others, whose pens were as prolific as their outlook was evangelistic. Like the earlier camp-meeting and revival hymns of the frontier, indeed like the hymns of 18th-century German Pietism, these "gospel songs"

[1] See Bibliography (Garrison, *The March of Faith*; Cavert and Van Dusen; Atkins).
[2] See further Chap. xiii, p. 612.
[3] See Charles Howard Hopkins, *The Rise of the Social Gospel in American Protestantism, 1865–1915*, New Haven, 1940; James Dombrowski, *The Early Days of Christian Socialism in America*, New York, 1936; W. A. Visser 't Hooft, *The Background of the Social Gospel in America*, Haarlem, 1928.
[4] See Chap. vii, pp. 341 f., and Bibliography to that chapter.

were intensely evangelistic and aimed the arrows of God at the heart of the singer. These simple and informal hymns, with their choruses and rousing popular tunes, completely captured the less formal of the American Protestant Churches. The standard denominational hymnals also became ecumenical in the post-Civil War period, in that they began to draw from the writers of all Church groups. No longer were Presbyterian hymnals limited to metrical versions of the Psalms, or Methodist hymnals confined to the Wesleys' hymns. The fact that in America the major Church groups all sing the same hymns in worship has been a strong factor in preparing American Christendom psychologically for the 20th-century emphasis on organic Church union.

But the "old-time religion", which was "good enough for Paul and Silas", as the revival song carols it, was far from dead. As the Methodist, Presbyterian, Congregational, and other Churches that had shaped American religion more than any others in the early 19th century became less and less revivalistic, the revivalist mantle fell upon a rising group of "Holiness" and "Pentecostal" Churches, mostly patterned after the old-time Methodist type of religion. These Churches embalmed the revivalist system so successfully that it has kept its outward form until the present day, without however striking off any original by-products. These "Holiness" denominations, as well as the "Holiness" wings within the larger denominations, led indirectly into the Fundamentalist movement of the 20th century, which has been one of the principal stumbling-blocks to wider Church union in America. The fundamentalist Churches, often revivalist in practice, ultra-conservative in theology, and utterly opposed to anything that smacks of the Social Gospel, thus came to form a wing of American Protestantism standing in open opposition to the major Churches, which since 1890 have had a strong intinction of Biblical criticism and the Social Gospel. The out-and-out break between the two did not come, however, until after 1940, with the formation of a rival ecumenical machine made up of an American Council of Christian Churches (1944) and an International Council of Christian Churches (1948), both in open and violent opposition to the National and World Councils.[1] There is also a National Association of Evangelicals, "a voluntary association of Bible-believing Christians from various denominations, who wish to bear positive and united witness to the Christian faith once delivered as it is revealed in the New Testament".[2] Thirty-five of the smaller denominations are affiliated to this Association which, though it takes no part in the wider ecumenical movement, is less hostile to it than the two other organizations named above.

A growing world-consciousness on the part of the major American Churches led in the 1860's and 1870's to American participation in the confessional world alliances, the impulse to which came partly from Europe, partly from America.[3]
   All of them have made negative as well as positive contributions to the general ecumenical movement. Positively, they have in their American branches tended to draw together Churches of the same tradition. In this respect the American branch of the World Presbyterian Alliance has been most fruitful, having included cousins as well as sisters in the family reunions it has held. The several movements for pan-Presbyterian union in America in the 20th century have all come out of the co-operation of the separate Churches in this type of

---

[1] See Bibliography (Clark and Cole).
[2] *Yearbook of American Churches*, ed. Benson Y. Landis, New York, 1952, p. 10.
[3] See further Chap. vi, pp. 263–68, and Chap. xiii, pp. 613–19.

denominational federation. Negatively, these movements sometimes, and not entirely unconsciously, become channels for a greater denominational spirit, in that they over-emphasize the contributions of only one type of Protestant heritage. In this sense they are denominational substitutes for the authentic ecumenical movement.

In addition to the denominational world alliances, American Churches participated in the Evangelical Alliance. Although the Alliance was organized in 1846, the constant irritant of the slavery question—i.e. could the Alliance admit members who owned slaves?—made it impossible to organize a branch Alliance in the United States until 1867. But after the close of the Civil War the chief obstacle to organization was removed, and the American Evangelical Alliance was formally organized. The purposes of the American Branch, as outlined at the first meeting, were "co-operation with other national Branches of the Alliance; the promotion of religious liberty; the counteraction of infidelity and superstition; and the strengthening of union and fellowship amongst Protestant Evangelicals". These purposes were carried out specifically through the holding of biennial meetings and the formation of state and city alliances as auxiliaries; correspondence with the other national and auxiliary branches; the annual Week of Prayer, participated in by from twenty to fifty thousand churches annually; and co-operation with the other Alliances in promoting religious liberty throughout the world.[1]

Basically, the story of the Alliance, being a voluntary organization of individual Christians rather than an integral federation of Churches appointing their official delegates, is the history of its chief leaders. A series of capable laymen, notably William E. Dodge, who was President from 1867 to 1893, and such ecclesiastical wheelhorses as Philip Schaff, Irenaeus Prime, and Josiah Strong, directed the destinies of the Alliance throughout the remainder of the century.

Josiah Strong (1847–1916) succeeded Schaff as the principal leader of the Alliance. Symbolic of the earlier and later approaches to ecumenical unity were Schaff and Strong—Schaff the irenic scholar who laid the groundwork for better understanding between the various groups, theologically and historically; Strong the activist, who helped to kindle the fires of the Social Gospel. General Secretary from 1885 to 1898, Strong toured the country organizing branch alliances to make the union more effective, and conducting religious censuses to reach the unchurched. Strong's programme for building up the social service interest of the Alliance included a General Christian Conference in Washington, D.C., in 1887, to consider "the present perils and opportunities of the Christian churches of the country" and the best means of awakening them to their responsibility. His great contribution to the movement was his emphasis upon federation in the local communities. "If now the churches of each city and town were organized for co-operation, constituting what might be called the *collective church* of the community, and these collective churches were knit together into county and state organizations—all of which is entirely practicable—the Christian public opinion of the state could quickly and emphatically utter itself."

Strong's approach to union, as outlined in his volume *The New Era or The Coming Kingdom*, was practical rather than theological. Big "business, open-eyed, has seen and seized the immense advantage which lies in consolidation,

[1] See Slosser, *Christian Unity*, pp. 187 ff.; and especially Wallace N. Jamison, *A History of the Evangelical Alliance for the United States of America*, 1946, unpublished, available at Brown Ecumenical Library of Union Theological Seminary, New York City.

organization," he notes, "but the Protestant churches do not yet appreciate this advantage". He thunders like a 19th-century Amos against those churches which, through the "competitive struggle" growing out of the over-churching of the small towns, are "led to cater to the rich". And the smug isolation of Protestant pastors from others working in the same city filled him with scorn. "Imagine two military captains or colonels, set for the defence of the same city, fighting a common enemy for twenty-five years, before holding a council of war or even having met!"

Although the Alliance continued to exist on paper until 1944, when the corporation was dissolved and the funds were transferred to the Federal Council, it was largely a dead letter after 1900. Strong resigned in 1898, his activist policy opposed by the conservative directors, who were more interested in the theological *status quo* than in the invigorating winds of the Social Gospel. Schaff had died in 1893; the organization of the Federal Council in 1908, going several steps further than the Alliance in the direction of closer unity, made the latter a back number. As the early leaders died, little remained for the Alliance to manage other than the Annual Week of Prayer, and even this was finally taken over by the Federal Council.

Shortly before his death, Philip Schaff made a now famous address on "The Reunion of Christendom" before the World's Parliament of Religions, in connection with the Chicago World's Fair of 1893. In this address Schaff urged a "federal or confederate union" resembling the "political confederation of Switzerland, the United States, and the modern German Empire". This federation would be a "voluntary association of different Churches in their official capacity, each retaining its freedom and independence in the management of its internal affairs, but all recognizing one another as sisters with equal rights, and co-operating in general enterprises, such as the spread of the gospel at home and abroad, the defence of the faith against infidelity, the elevation of the poor and neglected classes of society, works of philanthropy and charity, and moral reform". This farewell address of the aged ecumenical leader was thus prophetic of the Federal Council of the 20th century, and even more so of its successor, the National Council.[1]

It was Elias B. Sanford (1843–1932), a New England Congregationalist with a strong admixture of Methodism, who formulated the plans and held the preliminary meetings which resulted in the Federal Council.[2] While his New England brother, William Reed Huntington, had urged an organic union of the American Churches, no federal unionist was more outspoken against organic union than Sanford. Organic union was to him "an iridescent dream that is not in accord with New Testament authority and the leadership of our Lord and Saviour Jesus Christ the head of the Church". He could "see no signs that Protestantism is an effete and dying phase of Christianity". Indeed, he thought "the bringing of Roman, Greek and Reformed Churches into one great Catholic body" a goal that "aside from the impossibility of its achievement is by no means desirable". "There is indeed but *one flock*," he suggests, "but there is room in the pastures of Divine love and service for many folds."

[1] See Bibliography (Schaff, Hutchison, Macfarland).

[2] For Sanford, see Bibliography. For his earlier writings on Christian unity, see his articles in *The Union Advocate*, Pittsburgh, Pa., 1871–72. In 1873 Sanford was Editor of *Church Union*, a New York paper which was taken over by Mrs Elizabeth B. Grannis, a Disciple advocate of Christian unity (1873–93).

Drawing together the earlier strands of ecumenical thought, he helped to combine the ideas of Schmucker and Strong into the Federal Council, rejecting those of Campbell and Huntington. By November 1905 his ideas had so captured the American Protestant world that he was able to arrange for the great Inter-Church Conference on Federation, in Carnegie Hall, New York City, which drew up the constitution for the Federal Council. This Carnegie Hall meeting of 1905 represented an advance over the Evangelical Alliance in that at last a meeting of Church groups was held with official Church sanction, rather than a scattered convention of interested individuals from various denominations. By 1908 the national assemblies of the constituent bodies had adopted the constitution, and the Federal Council came into being.

The object of the newly formed Council, which has enabled a large portion of American Christendom to speak with a united voice during the period of the two world wars, as set forth in its constitution, was: (1) to express the fellowship and catholic unity of the Christian Church; (2) to bring the Christian bodies of America into united service for Christ and the world; (3) to encourage devotional fellowship and mutual counsel concerning the spiritual life and religious activities of the Churches; (4) to secure a larger combined influence for the Churches of Christ in all matters affecting the moral and social condition of the people, so as to promote the application of the law of Christ in every relation of human life; and (5) to assist in the organization of local branches of the Federal Council to promote its aim in their communities.

Although the constitution urged the formation of local councils of Churches, it was not these local councils of Churches which sent representatives to the Federal Council, but rather the denominations themselves. Thus the problem of local and national federation, of federation at the top and federation at the bottom, was not successfully solved. Strong, the most vocal advocate of federation at the bottom, made the point at the 1905 assembly that the churches of the same community "have much more in common with each other than with Churches hundreds or thousands of miles away, with which the only distinctive bond is a denominational name, a non-essential doctrine, a common form of government or of ritual".

This is the principal difference between the Federal Council and its embryonic predecessor, the American Evangelical Alliance. With the exception of a few officially elected delegates, the Alliance was a voluntary convention of individuals. The Alliance was also often "evangelical" in the low church and anti-Catholic sense, whereas the Federal Council has sought the co-operation of the high church Protestant and Orthodox bodies. The third difference between the 19th- and 20th-century approaches to federal union lies in the increased social interest shown by the Federal Council, which was in a sense a product of the awakened social conscience represented in the Social Gospel movement.

With the foundation of the Federal Council in 1908, the federal principle of Church union had, at least for the time being, triumphed. The constitution of the Council, as indeed its very name implies, provided only for federal union rather than the organic union urged by Huntington. It was to have "no authority over the constituent bodies adhering to it; but its province shall be limited to the expression of its counsel and the recommending of a course of action in matters of common interest to the churches, local councils and individual Christians". Nor did the Council have any "authority to draw up a common creed or form of government or of worship, or in any way to limit the full autonomy of the

Christian bodies adhering to it". Thus the entire question of organic union, into a new and native American United Church rather than a loose Federation of American Churches, was deferred until the post-1910 era, when with such plans as the Greenwich Plan of 1949–50, renewed interest in general organic union blossomed forth on American soil.

But although federal union triumphed in the post-Civil War era, there have been heartening instances of interest in organic union. Several family reunions took place, including that of the Cumberland Presbyterians and the Northern Presbyterians in 1906. And before 1910, much spadework was done to lay the foundations for organic unions which were to take place after 1910. For example, the tripartite Lutheran union which resulted in the formation of the United Lutheran Church in 1918 was prepared for by the Lutheran "Diets" of 1877–78, and the adoption of a Common Service Book in 1888. Negotiations for a Methodist "family reunion" involving the Northern and Southern sister Churches, which had been separated since 1845, began in 1876, and the Methodist Protestants were invited to participate in 1908—thirty years before the union was actually consummated in 1939. In the 1880's came the first suggestion of the Christian and Congregational union which took place finally in 1931. Exactly parallel has run the course of ecumenical history in the United States to that of her neighbour to the north. In Canada, the organic union of Congregationalists, Methodists, and Presbyterians into the United Church of Canada (1925) was preceded and prepared for by a lengthy series of unions whose genealogical trees reach far back into the 19th century.[1]

As the 19th century drew to a close, the American Churches were nearer to a solution of their peculiar ecumenical problem than they had been when the Campbells began their reforming labours on the western frontier. Schmucker could write in 1870, when he published the third edition of his *Fraternal Appeal*, that though American Christendom was still divided, it was much more imbued with the spirit of love and union than thirty-two years before, when the first edition of his book issued from the press. And Huntington wrote in 1898, "It demands less courage to reprint this little book to-day than it did to print it thirty years ago. . . . Acquiescence in sectarianism, as being presumably the ordinance of God, has ceased to be the almost universal state of mind it was in the United States of 1869. Doubtless it is a widespread temper still, but it is not what it was then."

As we look back upon these early ecumenical beginnings in America, it is the books and tracts on Christian unity by Campbell, Schmucker, Huntington, Sanford, and others which can be spotlighted as the greatest contribution made to the ecumenical movement by 19th-century America. These theorists of Church unity discussed the question from most angles, making it unnecessary in this 20th century to repeat their fundamental labours. They laid the groundwork of theory for the practical superstructure of Christian unity in America. They prepared the climate of Church opinion in favour of closer union. They cleared the sectarian skies for the ecumenical day which was to dawn with the Federal Council in 1908, and brighten with the founding of the National Council in 1950.

If the 19th century had contributed nothing but the theory, its work would have been worth while. But actually America went further than the point of

[1] See Chap. vi, pp. 301, 304 f., and Chap. x, p. 454.

theory in that several actual unions took place and others were attempted. The loose and unsatisfactory Evangelical Alliance gave way to the Federal Council; and towards the end of the period, several organic unions within denominational families helped to unite and strengthen these denominations for unions which they would later make with less closely related Churches. With the exception of the latter, it was the federal type of union, as proposed by Schmucker and Sanford, which triumphed, over against the closer type of organic union urged by Campbell and Huntington.

In estimating the contribution of the United States to the ecumenical movement, an unexpected phenomenon is observable, viz. that the plans for the union of Churches, whether on a federal or an organic basis, which in a sense led up to the Faith and Order movement,[1] developed in what we usually think of as activist and non-theological America, while Europe, with its greater preoccupation in theological matters, contributed more than its share to the background of the Life and Work movement.

By 1910 America was nearer, but not much nearer, to the fulfilment of the ideal of Christian unity as presented by Campbell, Schmucker, Huntington, and other 19th-century ecumenical prophets. The movement was marching forward, if somewhat unevenly, and at least the ecclesiastical air was cleared for the future. The story of the post-1910 developments in America, with their resounding successes in the field of organic mergers between denominations, and their equally disheartening setbacks to the whole movement, will be told elsewhere. It is enough, in closing, to draw one more word of wisdom from William Reed Huntington:

> "We are tempted to grow hard, we are tempted to grow bitter, we are tempted to grow cynical; for human life, as we see it, has much that is repellent to show, much that is despicable, much that is sordid. Is there, we ask, can there be any hope for such a world as this? The vision of the city that is at unity with itself is God's reply. For that it is worth one's while to live. For that some, peradventure, might even dare to die."

[1] See Chap. ix, pp. 407–10.

CHAPTER 6

APPROACHES OF THE CHURCHES TOWARDS EACH OTHER IN THE NINETEENTH CENTURY

by

HENRY RENAUD TURNER BRANDRETH, O.G.S.

1. INTRODUCTION

The ecumenical activities of Christians cannot remain unaffected by the general situation of the Churches and by the changing climate of social, political, and international affairs.

The great new fact of the 19th century was that astonishing expansion of the Christian world which has led eminent historians to call that century the greatest of all the Christian centuries since the first. Churches which had long lived in geographical or denominational isolation found themselves changed almost unawares into world-wide fellowships with new responsibilities, and had to find a fresh type of organization to match a situation previously unknown.

The formation of World Denominational Fellowships, their growth, and their ecumenical service, are therefore the subject of the first part of this chapter.

This outward expansion was paralleled by a widespread recovery of the sense of the Church and a new theological understanding of its nature as a spiritual society. Conspicuous among these movements of theological recovery was the so-called Oxford Movement in the Church of England. But the process was not confined by geographical or party and confessional limitations. Evangelicals and Broad Churchmen among Anglicans, Free Churchmen, especially towards the end of the century, Orthodox like Khomiakov and Soloviev, and leaders in Continental Protestantism, were finding themselves driven to ask new questions, or to ask again old questions, about the nature of the Church. The centre of ecumenical interest was slowly shifting to the area of "ecclesiology", the doctrine of the Church. It is easy to see how this came about. To find the Church is to find its unity; both that essential unity which belongs to it in the purpose of God, and that unity which still somehow exists in the midst of division and is in some way already a part of Christian experience. To become aware of the unity of the Church in the purpose of God is to realize the obligation resting on all Christians to seek by all worthy means the recovery or manifestation of that unity upon earth.

The development of ecumenical ideals in different areas and traditions is the subject of the second part of our chapter.

Some groups and Churches tried to give effect to their ecumenical ideals by seeking visible unity. Many of these efforts came to nothing at the time. Some must be judged to have been mistaken, though some contained germs of promise that were to fructify only in a later century. But there is also a record of solid achievement—of unions of Churches which were made and proved durable, and of a growing tendency towards union to offset that continuing fragmentation which added diversity to the Christian map of the world but gravely hindered the effectiveness of the witness of the separated fragments.

Plans of union in Europe and in the British Commonwealth, projected or accomplished, are described in the final part of our chapter.

2. WORLD DENOMINATIONAL FELLOWSHIPS

Six World Denominational Fellowships were founded in the 19th century. Their developments up to 1910 are recorded here in the order of their foundation.[1]

[1] For their later developments, and for other similar fellowships founded in the 20th century see Chap. xiii, pp. 613–20.

The Anglican Communion, in its world-wide expansion, has grown into a fellowship of independent provinces which constitutes a unique contribution to the reconciliation of unity with diversity, of liberty with loyalty. Among the forces which keep the two tendencies in balance none is more important than the decennial Conference of Anglican bishops held at Lambeth Palace, the London home of the Archbishop of Canterbury.

The immense ecumenical significance which the Lambeth Conference has to-day could hardly have been predicted from its somewhat inauspicious beginnings in 1867, in the painful dispute over the doctrines and status of Bishop Colenso of Natal. The process which led to the holding of the first Conference was initiated by a resolution of the Church of England in Canada in 1865, which was blessed by the Convocation of Canterbury. Archbishop Longley summoned the Conference to meet in 1867 and, though there was some opposition in powerful quarters, seventy-six bishops, nineteen of them from the United States, accepted his invitation.[1]

From the beginning, the Lambeth Conference has disclaimed any intention of turning itself into a Synod. It has no right to pass decrees which will be binding on any Church; its resolutions carry no more than the weight of their own spiritual authority. This prudence has served to dissipate the original anxieties, and no Anglican bishop now hesitates to accept the invitation. In 1867 it was not certain whether another such Conference would ever be held; it was not till 1888 that it came to be taken for granted that Conferences would be held at ten-year intervals. The Consultative Body, which continues in existence after the dissolution of a Conference, was not finally organized until 1930.

The first Lambeth Conference had been called to discuss domestic concerns of the Anglican Communion. It was only in 1888 that the ecumenical possibilities of such a gathering first began clearly to emerge. True, the Conference of 1878 had had before it the question of Moravian Orders. It had discussed relationships with Old Catholics "and other persons in the Continent of Europe who have renounced their allegiance to the Church of Rome and are desirous of forming some connection with the Anglican Church, either English or American". By 1888 the increasing momentum of ecumenical events had affected those attending the Conference. Committees were appointed to consider Anglican relations with large sections of Christendom—with the Scandinavian Lutherans, with the Reformed Churches, the Old Catholics, the Eastern Churches, and with Free Churchmen in England. The Report of the Committee on "Home Reunion" was the most important and proved a landmark in ecumenical history. The bishops had before them a report adopted by the General Convention of the Protestant Episcopal Church in the United States, meeting in Chicago in 1886. This report contained the original form of what came to be known as the "Chicago-Lambeth Quadrilateral" and, in view of the subsequent history and influence of that formula in ecumenical negotiations, it must be quoted at length.

> "We do hereby affirm that the Christian unity now so earnestly desired . . . can be restored only by the return of all Christian Communions to the principles of unity exemplified by the undivided Catholic Church during the first ages of its existence; which principles we believe to be the substantial deposit of Christian Faith and Order committed by Christ and His

[1] At the 1948 Lambeth Conference 326 bishops were present, 196 from outside the British Isles.

Apostles to the Church unto the end of the world, and therefore incapable of compromise or surrender by those who have been ordained to be its stewards and trustees for the common and equal benefit of all men.

"As inherent parts of this sacred deposit, and therefore as essential to the restoration of unity among the divided branches of Christendom, we account the following, to wit:

"1. The Holy Scriptures of the Old and New Testament as the revealed Word of God.

"2. The Nicene Creed as the sufficient statement of the Christian Faith.

"3. The two Sacraments—Baptism and the Supper of the Lord—ministered with unfailing use of Christ's words of institution and of the elements ordained by Him.

"4. The Historic Episcopate, locally adapted in the methods of its administration to the varying needs of the nations and peoples called of God into the unity of His Church."[1]

This Chicago Quadrilateral was, with some modifications, accepted by the 1888 Lambeth Conference Committee on Home Reunion as supplying "a basis on which approach may be, under God's blessing, made towards Home Reunion". The Committee changed the form of the first three points to read as follows:

"(a) The Holy Scriptures of the Old and New Testaments, as 'containing all things necessary to salvation', and as being the rule and ultimate standard of faith.

"(b) The Apostles' Creed, as the Baptismal Symbol; and the Nicene Creed, as the sufficient statement of the Christian Faith.

"(c) The two Sacraments ordained by Christ Himself—Baptism and the Supper of the Lord—ministered, etc."

The fourth point, which has subsequently proved the most controversial, was left unaltered.

This Quadrilateral, reaffirmed by subsequent Conferences,[2] has been the basis of all Anglican negotiations with non-episcopal Churches, and in a wider ecumenical setting has come to be accepted as a reasonable basis on which to build. Originally, as the above quotations show, the four points were regarded, in America as at Lambeth, as a *terminus a quo* from which there could be no dispensation, but from which, when accepted, one might proceed to the discussion of other matters in dispute. Considerable controversy has been engendered within the Anglican Communion by an interpretation of the Quadrilateral which would make it a *terminus ad quem*, that is to say, would regard it as constituting in itself a sufficient basis for *reunion* rather than, as originally intended, as a basis for *discussion* with a view to reunion.

Since 1888 the Lambeth Conferences have steadily enlarged the scope of their deliberations. As they have done so, the Anglican Communion has come to occupy, in some ways, a central position in ecumenical developments and to exercise greater influence than its comparatively small numbers might seem

---

[1] *Journal of the General Convention, 1886*, p. 80.
[2] The form was modified by the 1920 Conference in its famous "Appeal to all Christian People", though it may be argued that its substance was unaltered.

to entitle it to claim. In the same way the Archbishop of Canterbury has come to carry a unique ecumenical responsibility.

In July 1875 three leading Presbyterians, two from America and one from Scotland, organized the first meeting of the Alliance of Reformed Churches throughout the World holding the Presbyterian System. At this meeting sixty-four delegates, representing twenty-one independent Churches, were present. The basis on which they met was the supremacy of Holy Scripture, adherence to the Consensus of Reformed Confessions, and a general acknowledgement of Presbyterian principles. Two years later, in 1877, the first general Conference of the World Presbyterian Alliance was held in Edinburgh and was widely representative of Reformed Christianity. The most notable event at this meeting was a paper read by Philip Schaff [1] on *The Harmony of the Reformed Confessions.* Schaff hoped that the Alliance might produce a doctrinal statement which all its constituent Churches would be able to subscribe. A continuing committee was appointed to investigate this proposal, but it was abandoned by the time of the third meeting of the Alliance at Belfast in 1884.

The Alliance, as its name suggests, is not primarily concerned with reunion, and, indeed, between 1884 and 1925 the subject of organic union entered little into its discussions. [2] This is not to say that Churches holding the Presbyterian system have been indifferent to the question of reunion; they have, in fact, been leaders in the promotion of the cause in many parts of the world. But these efforts have been carried out by individual Churches and not as enterprises of the World Alliance as such. The Alliance has provided a central rallying-point, in which the Reformed Churches have met for discussion of world-wide concerns important to them all, and has served as an instrument for co-operation in many and varied forms of Christian activity.

In 1876 the General Conference of the Methodist Episcopal Church in the United States, meeting in Baltimore, passed a resolution empowering its bishops to appoint a committee to correspond with the other Methodist bodies in America with a view to convening a conference representative of them all. The negotiations were sufficiently successful to justify an approach to British Methodism two years later; a delegate attended the Wesleyan Conference at Bradford and presented the scheme for consideration and approval. Approval was given and a committee appointed, all agreeing that the conference should be held in the City Road Chapel in London, in the graveyard of which John Wesley lies buried. Some passages from the declaration of aims put forward by this committee indicate the scope of what came to be called the Methodist Ecumenical Conferences:

"The conference is not for legislative purposes, for it will have no authority to legislate. It is not for doctrinal controversies, for Methodism has no doctrinal differences. It is not for an attempt to harmonize the various polities and usages of the several branches of the one great Methodist family, for Methodism has always striven for unity rather than uniformity. It is not, in a word, for consolidation but for co-operation. It is to devise

On Schaff, see Chap. v, pp. 246 f.
[2] At the Jubilee meeting of the Alliance at Cardiff in 1925 a number of important papers on religious unity were read.

such means for prosecuting our home and foreign work as will result in the greatest economy and efficiency, to promote fraternity, to increase the moral and evangelical power of a common Methodism, and to secure the speedy conversion of the world.

"A Methodist Ecumenical Conference might properly consider such topics as these: the duty of Methodism in respect of popery, paganism, scepticism, intemperance and kindred vices. . . . Methodism as a missionary movement, the relation of the home to the foreign work, and the best mode of avoiding waste and rivalries, and the securing instead thereof sympathy and co-operation between different Methodist bodies occupying the same or contiguous mission fields."[1]

This statement was accepted by the Wesleyan Conference at Birmingham in 1879. Two years later, in September 1881, the first Methodist Ecumenical Conference met in London, and to it came delegates representing twenty-eight Methodist bodies in twenty countries. Since then the Conference has met approximately once in ten years, the number of constituent Churches being gradually reduced as Methodism has secured unity within itself.

In 1889 the Old Catholic Churches of the world joined in the Union of Utrecht. This to-day is made up of the Old Catholic Churches in the Netherlands, Germany, Switzerland, Austria, and Czechoslovakia, and the Polish National Catholic Church in the United States and in Poland, each Church being represented by its bishops. The Conference of Old Catholic Bishops is recognized as the highest authority in the Churches, and as such set forth in 1889 the fundamental principles of Old Catholic doctrine in the "Declaration of Utrecht", a document of clearly marked ecumenical tendency. Among other duties, the Conference of Bishops is charged with the responsibility for determining the relation of the Old Catholic Churches to other Christian communions. In consequence, it was this body which in 1931 decided on the establishment of intercommunion between the Old Catholic and the Anglican Churches; in 1948 affirmed the adherence of the Old Catholic Churches to the World Council of Churches; and in 1950 defined the attitude of those Churches to the new Roman Catholic definition of the dogma of the Assumption of the Blessed Virgin Mary.

In the 1870's there had been various moves for an international organ of Congregationalism. Most of these moves had come from America and Canada, though an article had appeared in the British Congregationalist in England in 1874 suggesting a world Congregational conference. In 1885 the initiative was taken by the Congregational Union of Ontario and Quebec, which passed a resolution asking the Congregational Union of England and Wales to consider the possibility of such a world meeting, and to canvass opinion in other parts of the world. Australia at once reacted favourably as, later, did the Congregationalists of the United States. The first International Congregational Council was called in London in 1891, a second was held in 1899, and a third in 1908. Ecumenical questions as such have not figured largely in their programmes, though inevitably they have been the background of much discussion.

The idea of a Baptist World Congress had actually been suggested several times during the later years of the 18th century. Dr A. C. Underwood sees the

[1] W. J. Townsend, The Story of Methodist Union, pp. 121 f.

idea foreshadowed in John Rippon's dedication of the first number of the *Baptist Annual Register* in 1790 to "all the baptized ministers and people in America, England, Ireland, Scotland, Wales, the United Netherlands, France, Switzerland, Poland, Russia, Prussia, and elsewhere . . . with a desire of promoting an universal interchange of kind offices among them and in serious expectation that before many years elapse . . . a deputation from all these climes will meet probably in London to consult the ecclesiastical good of the whole".[1]

However, effect was not given to these words for more than a hundred years; at last, in 1905, largely through the efforts of J. H. Shakespeare, one of the most notable Baptist ecumenists of his day,[2] arrangements were made for the first Baptist World Congress to meet in London. The most remarkable fact revealed by the Congress was the spread of the Baptist movement throughout the world, and particularly on the continent of Europe. "In the year of Waterloo (1815) there was no Baptist Church on the mainland of Europe and in the year 1850 there were only about 4,000 Church members."[3] Yet twenty-three nations responded to the invitation to the Congress and nearly every European country was represented.

The important outcome of this Congress was the foundation of the Baptist World Alliance which, in the words of Dr J. H. Rushbrooke, one of its pioneers, is "the instrument of all Baptists throughout the world for three great purposes: (1) to express and promote unity and fellowship among them; (2) to secure and defend religious freedom; (3) to proclaim the great principles of our common faith".[4] The Congress meets normally every five years, and anyone appointed by a regular Baptist organization may become a member.

3. ECUMENICAL IDEALS OF VARIOUS CHURCHES AND PARTIES

Ecumenical Ideals on the Continent of Europe. Europe in the 19th century breathed an air remarkably different from that of the 18th. A quarter of a century of the Napoleonic wars had swept away innumerable landmarks; and, though the Holy Alliance[5] attempted to put things back, it was attempting the impossible—much had been destroyed which could never by any possible means be restored. The century was one of motion, revolution, and change. New ideas were emerging, especially from the German mind, in literature, in historical criticism, and in philosophy. Though few of these new movements of thought were specifically religious, it was impossible for faith and theology to remain unaffected by them; it took time for the Christian Churches to determine the relationship between the old faith and the new ideas. Even in the mid-20th century the process has not been altogether completed.

There was, however, a real continuity to balance the discontinuity. Though in Germany Pietism had lost a good deal of its original impetus and power, its extensions in such great movements as the Evangelical Revival in Britain and elsewhere reached their highest point of effectiveness in the 19th century, and carried forward much of the ecumenical tradition of Pietism. The Basle Missionary

---

[1] A. C. Underwood, *A History of the English Baptists*, London, 1947, pp. 178 f.
[2] The most important memorial of his ecumenical work is his book *The Churches at the Crossroads*, published in 1918.
[3] J. H. Rushbrooke, *The Baptists of Europe*, p. 6.
[4] *Baptist Quarterly*, Vol. IX, p. 69, quoted by Underwood, op. cit., p. 250.
[5] Between the Emperors of Russia and Austria and the King of Prussia. See also Chap. iv, pp. 193 f.

Society, for instance, supplied many recruits to the Church Missionary Society of London; the joint work of Lutheran, Reformed, and Anglican in the mission-field was a genuine example of ecumenical co-operation;[1] although it also drew attention to the difficulties of such co-operation, especially in such matters as the principles and practice of ordination. From Basle also emanated the strong Protestant support for the evangelical movement among Roman Catholics in Bavaria, associated with such leaders as Bishop Sailer of Ratisbon (1751–1832).[2]

Another manifestation of Pietism in its 19th-century form was the support given by many Lutheran and Reformed Christians in Europe, who had been touched by the Evangelical Awakening, to the Evangelical Alliance. The international Conferences of the Alliance held in Paris, Geneva, Amsterdam, Copenhagen, and Basle were attended by theologians and Church leaders not themselves members of the Alliance; this helped to spread awareness of ecumenical problems and ideals among the Churches of the Continent.

Those forces, however, which determined the life of the Churches in the 19th century must be sought elsewhere as well as in Pietism. The 18th century had been the period of the Enlightenment, of a cool rationalism, which frowned on "enthusiasm" and took little account of the emotional and intuitive aspects of man's being. By reaction, the 19th century was the age of the Romantic movement and of idealism. Experience, emotion, sentiment were now to be valued above pure reason; it is possible that what the age lost in clarity it gained in depth. The influence of Romanticism was to be felt in various directions in the life of the Churches.

On one side, it manifested itself as concentration on the depth of inner experience—experience of the reality of the transcendent by way of feeling. When divorced from strong Christian conviction, this feeling might lose itself in a vague pantheism, a natural religion, which would find expression in a rather sentimental yearning for the religious unity of all mankind.

Under another aspect, Romanticism looked back to the past—not to the sober, well-proportioned 18th century, but to the mysteries of Gothic architecture and the glories of a rather idealized Middle Age. In the mind of a man like Novalis, the yearning for the restoration of the ancient political unity of the *corpus christianum* was accompanied by a desire for the renewal of the "catholicity" of the Church, sentimentally rather than theologically conceived. It is easy to understand how a ruler like Frederick William III of Prussia could imagine it to be his vocation to restore in the 19th century the religious and cultural unity of the medieval synthesis.[3]

Finally, as far as Germany was concerned, the renewed national feeling which developed during the wars against Napoleon found expression in that desire for a united national Church which, already found in Herder (1744–1803), was more fully developed by Fichte (1762–1814). The way for this idea had been prepared by the Enlightenment, with its tendency to treat doctrinal and confessional differences as of minor significance; but its growth depended on that particular form of nationalism which was characteristic of the post-Napoleonic period; and the stronger the emphasis on the national idea, the less recognizably Christian became the concept of the national Church.

It is in the light of all these tendencies that it is possible to estimate the ecumenical importance of Friedrich Schleiermacher (1768–1834), the father of

[1] See Chap. vii, p. 311.   [2] See Chap. vii, p. 313.   [3] See pp. 286 ff.

modern theology. Schleiermacher was well fitted both by temperament and training for the irenic task. He had been brought up in an intellectual Reformed orthodoxy tempered by education in the Pietistic atmosphere of a Moravian school. For him religion could never be exhausted in purely intellectual formulations; it included the contemplation of the universe, but it must also be based upon the deep inner piety of absolute dependence upon God. Dogmatic formulations thus became of secondary importance:

> "The Protestant Church is not well adapted to present a complete agreement throughout the whole range of doctrine and practice—an agreement which has not as a matter of fact been realized in either of the great Confessions—but rather a variety in doctrine and practice, which yet is not allowed to break up the fellowship of the Church."[1]

But, on the other hand, the Christocentric character of the thought of Schleiermacher and his pupils was a bulwark against the dissolution of genuinely Christian ideas in a haze of mystical and pantheistic sentiment.

The promotion of the unity of the Church was, in Schleiermacher's view, one of the tasks to which serious Christian theology was by its very nature committed. In 1804 he published an important irenical tract, under the cumbrous title, *Two impartial verdicts in the matter of Protestant Church organization especially in relation to the Prussian State*, followed in 1811 by *A critical exposition of the study of theology*, in which was developed the idea that one of the practical tasks of theology is to make possible "joint leadership of the Christian Churches by mutual consent".

Apart from the Prussian Union of 1817, a number of attempts were made in the 19th century to bring the Churches in Germany into closer fellowship with one another. From 1653 till 1806 the Protestant Princes had been held together by the *Corpus Evangelicorum*, an authoritative body recognized by the law of the Holy Roman Empire. When the Empire came to an end in 1806, the *Corpus* ended with it. The reconstruction of the age of Napoleon left the Churches in a chaotic condition; the old 16th-century principle *cuius regio eius religio* no longer had any meaning, since almost all the reconstructed principalities included both Protestants and Roman Catholics. The disunion of the Protestants was all the more felt as a weakness because of the firm hierarchical order by which the Roman Catholics were held together in unity.

The first attempts to create some kind of unity were made in 1846. After two years of confused negotiations a "Diet of the Churches" (*Kirchentag*) was held at Wittenberg in 1848. The Diet was successful in bringing into existence a League of German Evangelical Churches; but this was something very far short of a German Evangelical Church. Only one permanent organization was set up —the Central Committee of the Home Missions of the German Evangelical Churches[2]—a child of the brain of Johann Hinrich Wichern,[3] which has continued to operate until the present day. Nevertheless, the Diet continued to meet at regular intervals until 1872, and served as a valuable ecumenical focus, though opposition from various quarters prevented its ever attaining to the status of a General Synod of the German Churches.

---

[1] *Über die . . . einzurichtende Synodalfassung*, 1817, p. 7.
[2] *Centralausschus für die Innere Mission der Deutschen Evangelischen Kirchen*. For the significance of *Innere Mission*, see Chap. xi, p. 509 and footnotes.
[3] On Wichern, see Chap. vii, p. 314.

One of the chief hindrances lay in the attitude of the Princes. Plans had been put forward for the separation of Church and State, but these had not been carried to the point of giving the Churches genuine independence under synodical government; and, though the newly constituted Church Councils were no longer organs of the State, they continued to be under the control of the rulers. In 1852 steps were taken to secure a measure of common action among the Churches through recourse to an older plan, and the Eisenach Conference of German Evangelical Church Governments (*Eisenacher Konferenz deutscher evangelischer Kirchenregierungen*) came into being. By degrees almost all the regional Churches entered into relationship with it. Although the Conference was only a loose confederation with no authority over any of the Churches which joined it, its meetings, which continued at regular intervals until 1903, were of great significance in the life of the Churches as a symbol of the desire for unity and of the need for a closer unity than had yet been achieved. Among its practical successes were the revision of the lectionary, plans for a common hymnal, and the revision of Luther's translation of the Bible. In 1903 the Committee of the German Evangelical Churches was formed as the permanent organ of the Conference. This may be regarded as a direct forerunner of the Federation of 1922 and of the Evangelical Church in Germany (1948).[1]

It was from Britain and mainly from the Church of England that many of the ecumenical activities and forward movements of the 19th century on the European side of the Atlantic originated.

Each of the three parties[2] which moulded the destinies and thought of the Church of England in the 19th century made a distinctive contribution to preparation for the new ecumenical age of the 20th. In the late 18th century the development of any distinctive attitude towards other Churches was hindered by the isolation of the Church of England. At the turn of the century external factors broke down this isolation and encouraged Anglican relations with other Churches. One factor was the missionary activity of the Church of England, transforming it into a world-wide fellowship with new ecclesiastical contacts in many lands. A second, bringing in particular a new spirit into relations with Roman Catholics, was the phenomenon of French refugee clergy in England.

In the year 1792 some 8,000 French bishops and priests found refuge in England from the anti-clerical furies of the French Revolution. The country as a whole, and the Church in particular, rose to the occasion with real Christian charity. A committee of relief was formed, of which the Bishops of London (Beilby Porteus) and Durham (Shute Barrington) were members. The influence of these exiles was considerable in giving Anglican clergy and laity of different schools of thought a very different view of the Roman Catholic character from that which they had formerly held.

"Their presence in various parts of England, their high bearing, sound principles and religious demeanour, tended largely to soften British prejudices against the Faith of their forefathers. The strong language of the Edwardian *Homilies*, the Armada, Guy Fawkes' conspiracy, the policy of

---

[1] See Chap. x, pp. 466 ff. Much of the material for this section has been drawn from memoranda by Dr Wolfgang Schweitzer, *Privatdozent* in the University of Heidelberg, and by Dr F. Siegmund-Schultze.

[2] See note on Party Terminology in the Church of England, p. 306.

James II, all more or less began to be looked at from a somewhat different point of view."[1]

Ecumenical Ideals of the Evangelical Party in England. Church of England Evangelicals produced no specific schemes for reunion; none the less they played their part in preparing for the ecumenical movement of the 20th century, particularly in the attitude they displayed to Churches other than their own, and their conviction that co-operation between Christians of different denominations in Christian witness and service is a normal and natural part of the Christian life. Their main emphasis was on personal religion and salvation. The proclamation of the Gospel of redemption to all mankind at home and abroad was their passion; in this mission of redemption they associated themselves with all those whom they believed to share with them the gift of life in Christ. This association took shape in a number of societies, missionary, evangelistic, and concerned with social reform, which created amongst Christians of various Churches a sense of fellowship transcending national and ecclesiastical boundaries.

The general Evangelical line with regard to unity with Nonconformists was well expressed by the Rev. the Hon. Baptist Noel:

> "He [the Evangelical] would hold brotherly communion with those who, after examination of the Scriptures, with prayer and reflection, believe that it is the will of the great Head of the Church that they should, on various particulars, dissent from us, allowing us, at the same time, the liberty which they claim for themselves. . . . To deny them to be members of the Body of Christ, to be alienated from them and to treat them with coldness or with jealousy, while they bear on their character and conduct all the great scriptural marks which prove them to be the children of God, is to do them wrong, and to manifest a spiritual blindness, a want of power to discern Christian character, affording a fearful sign that we have never been taught of God ourselves."[2]

This pronouncement, though written by one who twelve years later became a Baptist, is an accurate picture of the general Evangelical attitude.

The formation of the Evangelical Alliance[3] owed much to Church of England Evangelicals. Some held aloof from the Alliance for various reasons, but rarely because they hesitated to be brought into co-operation and fellowship with those of other denominations.

In Britain the co-operation of the Evangelicals was naturally confined to relationships with Scottish Presbyterians and English Nonconformists, Unitarians excepted. Their missionary activities brought them into touch not only with Continental Protestant Churches but with almost all the ancient Eastern Churches in Russia, the Near East, and India.[4]

Even with Roman Catholics there was much Evangelical co-operation, especially in the circulation of the Bible. Relations between Roman Catholics and Protestants were more friendly in this period than later. There is actually one instance of suggestions for reunion with Rome, remarkable as coming from a bishop who was known as a "Low Churchman". The Hon. Shute Barrington,

---

[1] *The National Review*, November 1888. The best account of the French exiles is F.-X. Plasse, *Le Clergé français réfugié en Angleterre*, 2 vols., Brussels and Paris, 1886.
[2] *The Unity of the Church*, pp. 13 f. See Bibliography (Noel).
[3] See Chap. vii, pp. 318–24.   [4] Ibid., pp. 312 f.

Bishop of Durham in 1806, and again in 1810, devoted Charges to the subject of Rome. In both these Charges he was vigorously anti-papal, but in the second, after stating that "fidelity to our own principles compels us to regard some of the doctrines of the Romish Church as involving habits of Sacrilege, Blasphemy and Idolatry", he nevertheless went on to say:

> "If by persevering in a spirit of truth and charity, we could bring the Roman Catholics to see these most important subjects in the same light that the Catholics of the Church of England do, a very auspicious opening would be made for the long desired measure of Catholic Union. . . . And what public duty of greater magnitude can present itself to us, than the restoration of peace and union to the Church by the reconciliation of two so large portions of it, as the Churches of England and Rome? If I should live to see a foundation for such a union well laid and happily begun . . . with what consolation and joy would it illumine the last hours of a long life."[1]

The attitude of many Evangelicals was vigorously anti-Roman Catholic and became increasingly so as the century advanced. It is well, however, to remember that a number of leading Evangelicals, including William Wilberforce and Daniel Wilson,[2] with the approbation of the aged Simeon, wrote in support of, and in 1829 voted for, Roman Catholic emancipation. A number of High Churchmen of the day were less liberal in their views.

The Evangelicals produced no special doctrine of the Church, but they did much to renew devotion to the Church's Liturgy and Sacraments. They restored Confirmation to its proper place in the Church's life. In regard to Church Order, there were many grades of approach to the problem. Men like Charles Simeon, while emphasizing to the full the Evangelical message of personal salvation, yet held deeply to the notions of Church Order. Others, like Berridge of Everton, saw the need "of preaching the Gospel to men who were perishing: there was no time for scruples about Church Order".[3] It is interesting to note that when *The Record*, the organ of the party, in reviewing the *Tracts for the Times*, appeared to belittle the doctrine of Apostolic Succession, it created such opposition among its readers that the editor had to modify his statement.[4]

There are certain indications of a conscious ecumenical interest amongst Evangelicals. In the many volumes of sermons produced by Evangelical clergy in the early 19th century a surprising number of sermons are on Unity.

As regards intercommunion and open communion, Charles Simeon both communicated and administered Communion in the Church of Scotland. Dean Alford and other prominent Evangelicals took the same line concerning communicating in other Churches. When the question of Communion services at interdenominational conferences came up, it was usually Evangelical clergy who were ready to arrange services according to the Anglican rite, to which all members of the conference were invited.[5]

Ecumenical Ideals of Broad Churchmen. The contribution of Broad Churchmen to ecumenical thought has been too little recognized. Their minds were much occupied with the nature of the Church and they undoubtedly developed a dis-

---

[1] *Charges to the Clergy of Durham* (ed. of 1813), pp. 88, 98 ff.
[2] Bishop of Calcutta, 1832–58.
[3] Charles Smyth, *Simeon and Church Order*, Cambridge, 1940, p. 256.
[4] *The Record*, 12 December 1833, quoted by Balleine, *History of the Evangelical Party in the Church of England*, p. 216.   [5] See Chap. vii, p. 337.

tinctive doctrine concerning it. Prominent members of this group were Thomas Arnold of Rugby, Charles Kingsley, Augustus and Julius Hare, Frederick Denison Maurice, and Arthur Penrhyn Stanley. With them may be associated theologically the Scots, McLeod Campbell of Row and Erskine of Linlathen. For what they held in common, we must class these men together as "Broad Churchmen", though they emphatically repudiated party names, and Maurice expressly dissociated himself from "liberals" and "Broad Churchmen".

Frederick Denison Maurice (1805–72) made an outstanding contribution to ecumenical thought.[1] His views were largely a result of his own experience: "there was . . . no considerable body of English dissenters, or of English parties, which he had not known from within".[2] Maurice emphasized "the idea of a Church Universal not built upon human inventions or human thought, but upon the very nature of God himself and upon the union which he has formed with his creature". According to Maurice, Christ is the head of the whole human race (and not only of a portion of it), since all men are created in Christ and have been redeemed by him, and by virtue of their creation and redemption are in some sense in the Church, whether or no they recognize themselves to be so.

Such an idea of the Church is by its very nature inclusive, and gave the men who held it a concern for reunion in the form of a comprehensive Church. They desired to see a comprehensive national Church—the Church of England enlarged to include all Nonconformists, except Roman Catholics and Unitarians. Their very ideal of the Church and its unity, however, militated against their making a strong mark on ecumenical history. They not only indignantly rejected party names, but their inclusive idea of the Church forbade them to join parties, even a " 'no party' party", or to form organizations to promote reunion or, indeed, anything else. Their attitude has sometimes led to their being accused of regarding religious affiliation as more or less a matter of indifference. This was certainly not the case with Maurice, who, in *The Kingdom of Christ*,[3] develops not only his conception of the Church Universal, but shows how that conception bears on the part which the Church of England is called upon to play within the Church Universal, and on the relationships which should obtain between the Church of England and other Christian bodies. The book is instinct with irenic ideas.

Charles Kingsley (1819–75) had a yearning for reunion amounting sometimes almost to agony. Writing to Maurice in 1864, he declares: "It is the aspiration which is working in all thinking hearts: which one thrusts away fiercely at times as impossible and as a phantom, and finds oneself so much meaner, more worldly, more careless of everything worth having, that one has to go back to the old dream."[4]

It is remarkable that, despite the Broad Church aversion to planning, it was Thomas Arnold of Rugby (1795–1842) who put forward the most definite, perhaps the only definite, scheme for home reunion that appeared during the 19th century. In 1833 he published a pamphlet, *Principles of Church Reform*, in which he set forth the appalling state of religion in England. He was pessimistic as to the state of organized religion in general, and of the Church of England in particular. In 1832 he had written: "The Church as she now stands, no human power

---

[1] See Alec R. Vidler, *Witness to the Light*, New York, 1947 (English ed., *The Theology of F. D. Maurice*, London, 1948), Chap. viii, "United Confession of the Name" and *passim*.
[2] *Life of Frederick Denison Maurice*, edited by his son, 3rd ed., I, p. 337.
[3] See Bibliography (Maurice).
[4] Quoted in *Review of the Churches*, 15 October 1892, p. 50.

can save." [1] His pamphlet proposed as a remedy that the Church of England should make itself in a very real sense national, by so reorganizing its constitution as to include all the Protestant denominations. This he desired should be done by Act of Parliament, for in general the Broad Churchmen were strongly Erastian. Arnold put forward various suggestions—that the size of dioceses should be reduced; that each bishop should govern through an elected council of clergy and laity; that those too poor to receive a university education should not be excluded from the ministry; that parishes should be allowed some say in the appointment of their clergy. He was clear that government should be by what is now known as "constitutional episcopacy", and that all should be episcopally ordained, though he seems not to have contemplated the reordination of Protestant ministers. All services should be held in the parish church—a liturgical service in the morning and on Saints' Days, and non-liturgical services in the evening or on weekdays.

Arnold's proposals roused great opposition; the Church of his day would have none of his ideas, though some of his recommendations have since become commonplaces of Anglican practice and strategy. The Nonconformists showed no enthusiasm, perhaps not unnaturally, seeing that their comprehension in the Church of England was proposed as "a means of modifying their fanaticism and dissociating them from the utter coarseness and deformity of their chapels". [2]

Few of the Broad Churchmen made efforts to cultivate friendship or to develop contacts with men of other Churches. The outstanding exception was Arthur Penrhyn Stanley (1815–81), Dean of Westminster, who throughout his life bent his energies to breaking down barriers between members of different Churches. "Our need for some larger framework for the Church of Christ haunted him in youth and was to his last consciousness the cherished and dominating idea of his life." [3] One passage perhaps as well as any other sums up his thought:

> " 'I die in the faith of the Catholic Church, before the disunion of East and West.' Such was the dying hope of good Bishop Ken. It was an aspiration which probably no one but an English Churchman would have uttered. We may not be able to go along with the whole of the feeling involved in the thought. But it expresses a true belief that in the Church of England there is a ground of antiquity, of freedom and of common sense, on which we may calmly and humbly confront both of the great divisions of Christendom, without laying ourselves open to the charge of ignorant presumption, or of learned trifling, or of visions that can never be realized. We know, and it is enough to know, that the Gospel, the original Gospel which came from the East and now rules the West, is large enough to comprehend them both." [4]

Stanley persistently sought the acquaintance of leading Nonconformists, and invited to the pulpit of Westminster Abbey every type of Anglican and some from other folds. His most fiercely contested action was the invitation given, as the result of a suggestion from Bishop Westcott, to all the members of the Revision Committee of the New Testament to begin their labours by partaking of

---

[1] A. P. Stanley, *Life and Letters of Dr Arnold*, I, p. 326.
[2] *Principles of Church Reform*, 4th ed., pp. 75 and 99.
[3] R. E. Prothero, *Life and Letters of Dean Stanley*, London, 1909, II, p. 114.
[4] *Lectures on the History of the Eastern Church*, 5th ed., p. 52.

Holy Communion in Westminster Abbey. All were invited and all but one partook. But one of those who partook was the Rev. G. Vance Smith, a Unitarian, who added fuel to the flames of controversy when, just after the event, he wrote a letter to *The Times* declaring his rejection of the Nicene Creed. Stanley stood firm as to the rightness of his action, though regretting the pain it had caused.[1]

His belief deepened that "A movement immeasurable, irresistible, is mysteriously drawing all the Churches towards each other . . . forced out of their isolation and exclusiveness . . . realizing their imperfections and their need of each other to rise towards the perfect Church".[2] Yet, despite this belief, Stanley never proposed any definite plan of reunion. He held that "true union is union of better knowledge and mutual appreciation, and frank recognition of the different vocation of various Churches, and that it is the duty of Churches to build each other up".[3]

A rather different contribution was made by the great group of Cambridge New Testament scholars—Joseph Barber Lightfoot (1828–89, Bishop of Durham 1879–89), Brooke Foss Westcott (1825–1901, Bishop of Durham 1889–1901), and Fenton John Anthony Hort (1828–92). All three were members of Trinity College, and throughout their lives were associated in innumerable projects of scholarship and Christian service. Early correspondence reveals them as deeply concerned about the nature of the Church. Hort's lectures on *The Christian Ecclesia*, published posthumously in 1897, are a penetrating study of the New Testament evidence, though not all his conclusions have commended themselves to later scholars. Lightfoot's *Dissertation on the Christian Ministry*, appended to his commentary on Philippians (1868), still ranks high as an interpretation and exposition of the early evidence on this complex theme. Westcott and Hort especially were disciples of F. D. Maurice and shared his passion for the application of Christian principles to social problems. Their engagement in the Christian Social movement [4] brought them into friendly contact and co-operation with Christians of many schools of thought and diverse communions.

From Oxford, Edwin Hatch (1835–89) produced in 1881 his book *The Organisation of the Early Church*, which had the unusual distinction of being translated into German only two years later by no less a person than Adolf von Harnack. Although Hatch's conclusions,·even more than those of Hort, have failed to establish themselves in general acceptance, his book did good service in forcing on the attention of scholars and churchmen the fundamental ecumenical questions about the nature and character of the Church.

Ecumenical Ideals of the Oxford Movement. The Oxford Movement was the flowering into life and activity of the old High Church party which had persisted within the Anglican Communion since the break with Rome in the 16th century. It was not, in that sense, a new movement, and its early protagonists constantly asserted that they were but reaffirming old and tried truths of Anglicanism. The central contribution of Tractarianism was a recovery of the doctrine of the Church. In the late 18th and early 19th centuries, various external factors influenced the development of the recovery of that doctrine and influenced it in a specifically ecumenical direction, particularly in the direction of reunion with the Roman Catholic Church. Amongst these was the presence, already referred to,

[1] See also Chap. vii, p. 337.
[2] Quoted from the Appendix to Père Hyacinthe's *Catholic Reform*, London, 1874, with Preface by Dean Stanley.
[3] Prothero, op. cit., p. 456.   [4] See Chap. vii, pp. 331 f.

of the French refugee clergy in England. There were, however, other factors. Some stir was caused in 1818 when a learned Anglican clergyman, the Rev. Samuel Wix, published his *Reflections concerning the Expediency of a Council of the Church of England and the Church of Rome being holden, with a view to accommodate Religious Differences.* This book gave rise to several pamphlets, and led men to think seriously of the question.[1]

In the main, the early Tractarians were so occupied with the internal state of the Church of England that they found little time to look outwards. The *Tracts for the Times* were "to combat Popery and Dissent", and few would describe that as an ecumenical platform.

> "What had we at this time to oppose to the triumph of the Papacy, and the fury of political dissent, which in every street issued its proclamations calling on the people to rise and destroy that 'black and infernal hag', the Church of England? We had a weak and divided Church . . . from this disorganization of thought and action in England sprang 'the third Oxford Movement' of 1833 and all it involves of good and evil."[2]

The Tractarians soon discovered, however, that one cannot set out to revive a "catholic" doctrine of the Church without, at the same time, giving close consideration to the doctrine of its unity and thus, inevitably, looking outwards. For the early Tractarians, looking outwards almost inevitably meant looking towards Rome, whether in friendship or in hostility.

In 1841 appeared the famous *Tract XC, Remarks on certain Passages in the Thirty-nine Articles.* This was written, but not signed, by J. H. Newman (1802–91), later Cardinal. The Tract was introduced with these words, which sufficiently explain its writer's intentions:

> "It is often urged, and sometimes felt and granted, that there are in the Articles propositions or terms inconsistent with the Catholic faith. . . . That there are real difficulties to a Catholic Christian in the Ecclesiastical position of our Church at this day, no one can deny; but the statements in the Articles are not in the number; and it may be right at the present moment to insist upon this."[3]

The storm broke. Part of the trouble was certainly caused by Newman's use of the word "catholic". It is not clear, on reading the Tract, when he is using it to refer to his own Anglo-Catholicism, to the Catholicism of the undivided Church, or to Roman Catholicism. In some places, however, he was unequivocal. For example, in dealing with Article XVI, on the Sacrifice of Masses (*Sacrificia Missarum*):

> "Nothing can show more clearly than this passage that the Articles are not written against the Creed of the Roman Church, but against actual existing errors in it, whether taken into its system or not."[4]

The more conservative Tractarians were alarmed. Newman, however, did not lack powerful support, and the conservative John Keble could write:

> "Until English Churchmen, generally, sympathise with him so far, I see no chance of our Church assuming her true position in Christendom, or of

[1] See Brandreth, *The Oecumenical Ideals of the Oxford Movement,* pp. 9 f.
[2] W. Palmer, *Narrative of Events connected with the Tracts for the Times,* 2nd ed., pp. 28 ff.
[3] 1st ed., p. 2.　　　　　　　　[4] Ibid., p. 59.

the mitigation of our present unhappy divisions. . . . I found hardly anything in it which had not been before avowed and explained and vindicated."[1]

The younger men of the Oxford school were neither alarmed nor always prudent. One of the most brilliant and erratic of them, William George Ward, in a pamphlet in defence of *Tract XC*, asked:

"May we not by the way allude to this as one of the numberless marks we have on us of being a living branch of Christ's Church, that the Roman Church and ours *together* make up so far more adequate a representation of the early Church (our several defects and practical corruptions as it were protesting against each other) than either separately?"[2]

In a second pamphlet he went further and described the Roman Church as

"having held up for imitation certainly more than any other Church of modern times patterns for evangelical sanctity and having been even in her worst times, on most points, a firm and consistent witness in act and word for orthodox doctrine, whom in that respect it rather becomes us to imitate than to criticise".[3]

Alarm was increased by Roman Catholic reactions in England. Bishop (later Cardinal) Wiseman published *A Letter on Catholic Unity addressed to the Right Hon. the Earl of Shrewsbury*, in which he said:

"That the feelings that have been expressed in favour of a return to unity by the Anglican Church are every day widely spreading and deeply sinking, no one who has means of judging, I think, can doubt. . . . Such interpretation can be given to the most difficult Articles as will strip them of all contradiction to the decrees of the Tridentine Synod."[4]

Another Roman Catholic who wrote a widely-read pamphlet on the subject, and who for the next thirty-five years was to take an increasingly prominent part in Anglican-Roman relations, was the layman Ambrose Lisle Phillipps (later known as Ambrose Phillipps de Lisle), an Anglican who had joined the Church of Rome before the beginning of the Oxford Movement.

The storm of protest caused by *Tract XC* and the other Romeward advances, the affair of the Jerusalem Bishopric,[5] and the inner working of his own mind and temperament, caused Newman to secede to Rome in 1845. With him went several of the more extreme men; those Tractarians who remained in the Church of England took up an attitude of even greater caution than before.

The next definite advance with regard to the Church of Rome was made in 1857. In the spring of that year Phillipps published a pamphlet, *On the future Unity of Christendom*, which was, perhaps, the most conciliatory statement that had come from a Roman Catholic source up to that time. This paved the way for the foundation, in September 1857, of the Association for the Promotion of the Unity of Christendom, founded on the Anglican side by Bishop Forbes

[1] *The Case of Catholic Subscription to the Thirty-Nine Articles Considered*, pp. 10 f.
[2] *A Few Words in support of Number 90 of the Tracts for the Times*, p. 33.
[3] *A Few More Words in support of Number 90* . . . , p. 80.
[4] *Letter on Catholic Unity*, pp. 21, 38.   [5] See pp. 288 ff.

of Brechin and Dr F. G. Lee, and on the Roman Catholic side by Lisle Phillipps and A. W. Pugin. Its purpose, as stated at the meeting at which it was launched, was "for united prayer that visible unity may be restored to Christendom".[1] Prominent Roman Catholics and leaders of the second generation of the Oxford Movement (the older men, on the whole, stood aloof) rapidly showed their sympathy by joining the Association. Cardinal Wiseman had been friendly to the project, but by 1864 he had virtually become incapable of directing affairs, and more and more had passed into the unyielding hands of Dr Manning, a former Anglican, but now a bitter enemy of the Church of England. In April 1864 Manning persuaded the English Roman Catholic bishops to address a letter to the Holy See on the subject, while at the same time making clear at Rome what the reply should be. It was as he desired. The A.P.U.C. was condemned in principle, and Roman Catholics were forbidden to have any part in it.

In spite of this grave check, there appeared later in the same year one of the greatest examples of Anglican irenic writing. In November Manning wrote an Open Letter to Dr Pusey on *The Workings of the Holy Spirit in the Church of England*. He summed up his conclusions thus:

> "I am afraid, then, that the Church of England, so far from being a barrier against infidelity, must be recognized as the mother of all the intellectual and spiritual aberrations which now cover the face of England."[2]

Pusey started to reply in the old, weary form of religious controversy, and then suddenly changed his plan and decided to make his answer a plea for reunion. The result was the first *Eirenicon*.[3] The book was partly a vindication of the "catholic" character of the Church of England, but nearly ninety pages were devoted to a vigorous denunciation of certain excessive devotions to the Blessed Virgin Mary which, while not being *de fide*, were permitted by authority. "I doubt not", said Pusey, "that the Roman Church and ourselves are kept apart much more by that vast practical system which lies beyond the letter of the Council of Trent, things which are taught with a quasi-authority in the Roman Church, than by what is actually defined."[4]

Pusey was here enunciating a principle, dear to the Tractarians, of the "two Romes" existing side by side in the same system; on the one hand the Rome of the Councils and official definitions, which could be shown to be not too remote from official Anglicanism, and on the other the popular Romanism which went far beyond those official decrees and with which Anglicanism could not find peace. But Pusey was quite clear that, although the Thirty-nine Articles might need explaining to Roman Catholics, the Council of Trent also needed explaining to Anglicans.[5]

We have no space to deal with the reactions to the book.[6] In the years that followed, Pusey published two further parts, spurred on by the Pope's summons to the Vatican Council in June 1868. By the time the third part appeared early in

---

[1] For a full account of the A.P.U.C., see Brandreth, *Dr. Lee of Lambeth: A Chapter in Parenthesis in the History of the Oxford Movement*, Chap. v, p. 30.

[2] Op. cit., p. 30.

[3] For full title, see Bibliography (Pusey).

[4] *Eirenicon*, 1st ed., p. 98.

[5] See, e.g., his speech to the English Church Union in *English Church Union Monthly Circular*, Vol. II, p. 197.

[6] For a fuller treatment see Brandreth, *Oecumenical Ideals of the Oxford Movement*, Chap. iv.

1870 Pusey was discouraged by the intransigent attitude adopted by the Ultramontane party. The third *Eirenicon* is significantly entitled *Is Healthful Reunion Impossible?* Then came the Vatican Council, with its definition of Papal Infallibility which Pusey had been dreading, and the title of the third *Eirenicon* was altered, in all subsequent issues, to *Healthful Reunion as conceived possible before the Vatican Council.* "I have done what I could", he wrote to Newman later that year, "and now have done with controversy and Eirenica." [1]

The early Tractarians had little contact with the Eastern Churches, and in many cases showed extraordinary ignorance of them. On the other hand, Professor P. E. Shaw has clearly demonstrated that Tractarian theory made an important contribution to

> "that theological approximation to the East which has been associated with the modern Anglican movement towards reunion. The notes of the Church upon which the Tractarians insisted were those also emphasized by the Orthodox. There was, further, the aim to prove that notwithstanding expressions to the contrary, variations in practice, and non-adherence to the letter of certain canons, the faith of the Anglican Church agreed with that of the Eastern." [2]

The first of the great friends of the Orthodox in England was John Mason Neale, a man of vast learning in many subjects. In 1847 Neale published the first part of his monumental *History of the Holy Eastern Church*, dealing with the history of the Patriarchate of Antioch, and in 1850 he published the general introduction to the work in a volume of more than 1,200 pages. This work was, of course, for scholars and specialists; but Neale introduced the Eastern Churches to the Churches of the West in a much more popular manner by his translations of Eastern hymns and liturgies. These include such well-known hymns as "Christian, dost thou see them" and "The day is past and over".

Neale was also largely instrumental in the founding of the Eastern Church Association in 1863. This was a year of activity in Eastern questions. In July Bishop Samuel Wilberforce of Oxford moved in the Upper House of the Convocation of Canterbury that:

> "His Grace the President be requested to direct the Lower House to appoint a Committee to communicate with the Committee appointed at a recent Synod of the Bishops and clergy of the United States of America as to Intercommunion with the Russo-Greek Church, and to communicate the result to Convocation at a future Session." [3]

The Committee was appointed and published some extremely interesting and valuable reports. The E.C.A. was soon given an important task. Neale wrote to a friend in November 1864:

> "The American Church has had a semi-official request from the Holy Governing Synod, through Philaret of Moscow, for information on five points: 1. Our Succession; 2. Tradition; 3. The Articles; 4. *Filioque*; 5. The

[1] H. P. Liddon, *Life of E. B. Pusey*, London, 1893–99, IV, p. 193.
[2] *The Early Tractarians and the Eastern Church*, p. 45.
[3] *Reports made to the Convocation of the Province of Canterbury by the Committee on Intercommunion with the Eastern Orthodox Churches, 1865–69*, ed. Fraser, p. 3.

Seven Sacraments. In the Eastern Association we have divided these among ourselves for a short plain treatise. . . . I have to draw up a series of propositions about the insertion of the clause (not the doctrine) *Filioque*, which Archdeacon Randall is to get through Committee, if he can, and then through the Lower House, and S. O. [Wilberforce] will fight it through the Upper. It ends with our deep sorrow for the insertion. Is not this like business?"[1]

In 1868 the E.C.A. addressed a Memorial to the General Convention of the Protestant Episcopal Church in America, in which it asserted that for various reasons the American Church was better qualified than the English for working towards reunion with the East.[2] Unhappily, the E.C.A. appears to have thought that it had thus passed over its responsibility, and it rapidly declined in importance. In the 1890's, through the efforts of Bishop John Wordsworth of Salisbury and Dr A. C. Headlam, it began a short period of useful work and sent one or two students to reside in Orthodox countries in order to study the life of their Churches. It was made clear that "its representatives in the East must always go, not as representatives of a society, but directly or indirectly as representatives of the Church".[3] In 1906 the more progressive Anglican and Eastern Orthodox Churches Union was founded; the E.C.A. amalgamated with this body in 1914.

While the E.C.A. was declining, however, there was passing through Oxford a young man who was destined to be one of the greatest influences on Anglican-Orthodox *rapprochement* for many years to come—W. J. Birkbeck, a layman, who became deeply immersed in Russian ecclesiastical affairs. He published occasional works on the Russian Church, the most notable being his edition (1895) of Deacon Palmer's correspondence with Khomiakov under the title *Russia and the English Church during the last Fifty Years*. But Birkbeck's importance was not in what he wrote, but in what he was, one who enthusiastically introduced the two Churches to one another in his own person. He was an expert in Russian affairs and, until his death in 1916, was the trusted adviser on all such matters of the Anglican episcopate and, on more than one occasion, of the British Government.[4] Birkbeck's torch was handed on to a number of men, one of the most notable being Canon J. A. Douglas, for nearly half a century the living symbol of the increasing understanding between the two Churches.

The attitude of the Tractarians towards the Protestant Churches was, from an ecumenical point of view, negative. Reunion with Dissent could only come by way of submission, since on the Tractarian view of the Church all Protestant bodies were outside it. "There is not a dissenter living", said Newman, "but inasmuch, and so far as he dissents, he is in sin."[5] Not all expressed themselves so forthrightly, but the result was the same.

Gradually this attitude changed and, although the Oxford Movement continued to look primarily towards Rome and the East, in the latter half of the century some leading Anglo-Catholics were prepared to co-operate in attempts to bring the Nonconformist bodies in England into the picture. In 1873 an

---

[1] *Letters of John Mason Neale*, London and New York, 1910, pp. 344 f.
[2] The Memorial is printed in *Journal of the General Convention, 1868*, pp. 480–87.
[3] *E.C.A. Report for 1894*, p. 10.
[4] See *Birkbeck and the Russian Church*, edited by Athelstan Riley, and *Life and Letters of W. J. Birkbeck*, by his wife.
[5] *Parochial and Plain Sermons*, III, p. 220.

Anglican layman, A. T. Mowbray, founded the Home Reunion Society, of which, in 1875, Bishop Harold Browne of Winchester became President, and Horatio, third Earl Nelson (1823–1913), Chairman. The aims of the Society were clearly set forth in the second article of its constitution:

> "The purpose of the Society shall be to present the Church of England in a conciliatory attitude towards those who regard themselves as outside her pale, so as to lead to the corporate reunion of all Christians holding the doctrines of the Ever-Blessed Trinity and the Incarnation and Atonement of our Lord Jesus Christ. The Society, though it cannot support any scheme of comprehension compromising the three Creeds, or the Episcopal constitution of the Church, will be prepared to advocate all reasonable liberty in matters not contravening the Church's Faith, Order, or Discipline."

This Society continued to work in a quiet way for the next forty years, publishing a long and useful series of essays and papers, and holding meetings for discussion with Nonconformists. The greater part of its organization was carried on by Lord Nelson, who made it his life's work. When he died in 1913, the Home Reunion Society ceased to exist. Though it did not lead to any visible result, the irenic work of the Society, and especially of Lord Nelson, did not fail to meet with friendly response in Free Church circles in England.

Ecumenical Ideals of English Nonconformists. In the divided state of English Nonconformity, it was hardly to be expected that any distinctive Nonconformist ecumenical ideal would emerge: nor does the 19th century show any plan for reunion (outside their own particular denominations, Methodist and Baptist) [1] proposed by Nonconformist bodies or groups. Certain factors continuously militated against the development of an ecumenical spirit amongst them—in particular their struggle for civil rights and the closely connected campaign for disestablishment. [2]

There were, however, occasions when Nonconformist groups or bodies espoused ecumenical action. The foundation of the Evangelical Alliance owed much to the initiative of Nonconformists. Congregationalists took the lead, and such an alliance was suggested by the Rev. J. Angell James at a meeting of the Congregational Union in 1842. The idea appears to have been stirring for some time among Independents. In 1834, in connection with the founding of the Congregational Union in 1831, two English Congregationalists visited the United States, and amongst other things propounded the idea of an alliance between "kindred Churches of whatever name" and of a "triennial or quinquennial convention by delegates of the leading religious bodies in America and of reformed Churches in England, Holland, France, and Germany for the purpose of promoting a community of faith, harmony, and love, and energetic and combined service for the redemption of the world . . . the times call for movements of this comprehensive order". [3]

Nothing like a common Nonconformist attitude towards an ecumenical question appeared again until 1888—this time of a negative character. When the Archbishop of Canterbury (Benson) forwarded the Chicago-Lambeth Resolu-

---

[1] See pp. 263–68.   [2] See Chap. vii, p. 334.
[3] *Narrative of Visit to the American Churches by the Deputation from the Congregationalist Union of England and Wales*, 1835, II, pp. 286 ff.

tions to the heads of the leading Free Churches in England, answers were sent by the Congregational Union, the Baptist Union, the Wesleyan Methodist Conference, and the Presbyterian Synod. There was apparently no concerted action, but each body treated the fourth clause concerning the historic episcopate as barring the way to further consideration.[1] Many Nonconformists would have approved the attitude expressed by one of their distinguished leaders, Dr R. F. Horton:

> "To come forward and invite Nonconformists to reunion on the bland terms that they should incontinently surrender the very point for which they had striven, the very point in which their conviction had been established in their favour, first by experience, and latterly by impartial scholarship, was not, when one comes to reflect, a probable way of securing the object. Confusion of thought could hardly go further; it raised a previous question, whether Episcopal intelligence could justify the surrender, which Episcopal charity demanded."[2]

Though in the latter half of the century Nonconformists initiated no moves towards union, certain lines of interest and thought were developing amongst their leaders, which prepared the way for more directly ecumenical action at a later stage.

Much Nonconformist thinking centred on the nature and function of the Church. This is markedly shown in the two volumes of *Ecclesia*, a symposium of essays by Free Church leaders, for the most part Congregationalists.[3] More than half the essays are concerned with the nature and functions of the Church, and in general a high doctrine is enunciated.

In certain quarters interest was manifested in liturgical improvements. A Congregationalist minister of great influence in this direction was the Rev. John Hunter (1848–1917),[4] who insisted on the need for the Nonconformist Churches to use in their services the best elements of worship from all Churches. His compilation of *Devotional Services for Public Worship* is widely used in the English Free Churches and in Scotland up to the present day.

There is little record of Free Church thought on reunion. The writers in *Ecclesia* displayed interest in (though scarcely approving) Tractarian moves towards union with Rome and the East, but felt that there was an absence of interest amongst Anglicans in general in union with Nonconformists. But, if Free Churchmen did not initiate moves towards reunion, they always responded cordially to invitations for conferences on unity, e.g. from Canon Fremantle for the Sion College Conferences in the 1890's, and from Dr W. Sanday to the remarkable Conference in Oxford in 1901 on Differing Conceptions of Priesthood and Sacrifice.

At the beginning of the 1890's, however, serious interest in reunion questions was roused amongst many of the most responsible Free Church leaders, and expressed by the share which they took in Henry Lunn's *Review of the Churches*,

---

[1] See an article contributed to the *United Presbyterian Magazine* in 1894 by Alexander Mackennal, and quoted in his *Life and Letters* (by Dugald Macfadyen, London, 1905), p. 233.
[2] *The Reunion of English Christendom*, pp. 143 f.
[3] See Chap. vii, p. 335, and Bibliography (Reynolds).
[4] Leslie S. Hunter, *John Hunter, D.D.*, London, 1921. Also John Hunter, *The Coming Church, A Plea for a Church Simply Christian*, London, 1905; *A Plea for a Worshipful Church*, London, 1903; *Devotional Services for Public Worship*, London, 1900.

founded in 1891, and the Grindelwald Conferences on Home Reunion, 1892–96.[1] Such men as Hugh Price Hughes and Percy Bunting (Wesleyan), Donald Fraser (Presbyterian), Alexander Mackennal (Congregational), John Clifford (Baptist), and others took part in the most serious spirit in the incisive discussions in the *Review* and at the Conferences. Their attitude roused interest in reunion amongst their denominations. In spite, or perhaps because, of the utmost freedom of speech, intransigence on the most controversial issues was less and less in evidence; and Hugh Price Hughes declared at Grindelwald that Episcopacy had been a fact, not a dogma, since the days of St John. Why then shudder at it as a *sine qua non* of anything approaching reunion? [2]

The Free Church leaders who took part at Grindelwald were the men mainly responsible for the founding of the Free Church Congress in 1892 and the National Council of the Evangelical Free Churches in 1896; this, though definitely a federation of Nonconformist Churches, was regarded by Charles Berry, Hugh Price Hughes, and others as a necessary first step towards a general union of the Churches.

Through the century, there were irenic spirits amongst Free Churchmen who prayed and witnessed for the ideal of Christian unity. R. W. Dale of Birmingham, the Nonconformist friend of Bishop Gore, was eager for reunion, though extremely pessimistic as to any early possibilities even amongst Free Churches.[3] Henry Robert Reynolds, editor of *Ecclesia* and co-editor of the *British Quarterly Review*, saw in the Chicago-Lambeth Quadrilateral "obviously a very strong and Godly feeling arising in favour of some close union with all Christians". Reynolds was an appreciative and much appreciated member of the Langham Street Conferences (1887–89), at which, under the presidency of Lord Nelson, six Church of England clergymen and six Congregational ministers met frequently in quiet conference. According to Reynolds, these Conferences "brought to light how much more they had in common than the things on which they differed". "Societies of men might as well monopolise gravitation as grace."

But the prophet of ecumenism amongst Free Churchmen was Dean Stanley's opposite number, Dr John Stoughton,[4] Professor of Church History at Hackney College. The two men were close friends and fellow-labourers for Christian unity from their first meeting in 1864 till Stanley's death in 1881. Stoughton's great literary work was his eight-volume *History of Religion in England*. It is his speciality to describe the relations between denominations, and, if at any time a move of any kind was made by anyone or any group towards Christian unity, Stoughton never fails to record it. He is the ecumenical peacemaker amongst British Church historians.

Ecumenical Ideals in Scotland. In Scotland, as in England, clergy and laity touched by the Evangelical Awakening took an active share in promoting the Evangelical Alliance. It was in Scotland that *Essays on Christian Reunion* (1845), by far the most important literary preparation for the Alliance, was published. In this book and elsewhere leaders showed concern for union amongst the Churches as such, over and beyond union amongst Christian individuals. They wanted, in the words of Thomas Chalmers, "co-operation with a view to incorporation". Chalmers and others of the Free Church of Scotland leaders,

[1] See Chap. vii, pp. 338–41.
[2] *Life of Hugh Price Hughes*, by his daughter, London, 1904, p. 391.
[3] See Chap. vii, p. 334.   [4] See Bibliography (Stoughton).

perhaps conscious of the division it had created, after the Disruption of 1843 as before it, gave very much attention to questions of Christian unity.[1]

Leaders in all the Presbyterian Churches showed a steady concern for Christian unity. Dr John Tulloch, Dr Robert Lee, and Dr William Milligan of the Church of Scotland joined with Bishop Wilkinson of St Andrews in founding the Christian Unity Association of Scotland, to promote unity between various Churches. In 1901 deputations from the Christian Unity Association to the General Assemblies of the Church of Scotland, the United Free Church, and the Episcopal Church in Scotland, secured the setting aside of 13 October as a special day of prayer for union amongst the Churches in Scotland.[2] For the first time a Scottish bishop (Wilkinson) appeared on the floor of a Presbyterian General Assembly.

The main ecumenical developments in the last half of the 19th century in Scotland[3] were naturally concerned with union amongst the different varieties of Presbyterians. This movement for union had by 1900 reduced the major Presbyterian bodies to two, the Church of Scotland and the United Free Church. Many Presbyterian leaders, absorbed in these great questions of Presbyterian reunion, did not suffer themselves to be diverted to consider their relations with other Churches.

Within the Church of Scotland two societies were organized with the primary object of improving the Church's liturgy and worship—the Church Service Society, founded in 1865 and led by Drs Tulloch, Caird, and Macleod; and the later Scottish Church Society, founded by Dr Milligan in 1892. All of them were outspoken advocates of Church unity. Dr Milligan in his Croall lectures (1879–80) declares:

> "To speak of making the world believe in a risen Lord by mere Bible circulation or missionary exertion is to waste time and strength unless it is attended by the spectacle of unity";

while amongst the aims of the Scottish Church Society was

> "the deepening of a penitential sense of the sin and peril of schism and the furtherance of Catholic unity in every way consistent with true loyalty to the Church of Scotland."

On the United Free Church side, Dr Alexander Whyte was a determined champion of union. On the Whitsunday of Prayer for Unity called for by the leaders of almost all the Churches in England and Scotland in 1906, he preached on the text "That they may all be one", and like Chalmers before him looked beyond the ranks of Protestantism to a union of Christendom which would embrace the Greek Church, "the mother of us all", and the Latin Church, "her first child".[4]

Outside Presbyterianism, there were certain 19th-century movements towards reunion in Scotland. In 1897 the coming together of the Congregationalists and the Evangelical Union (a secession from the Secession Church which took place in 1843 as a protest against extreme Calvinism) blended two important minor elements amongst non-Presbyterians in Scotland.

Two men laboured incessantly and with conviction for *rapprochement* between the Church of Scotland and the Episcopal Church in Scotland (and ultimately

[1] See Chap. vii, pp. 318 ff.   [2] See Chap. vii, pp. 347 f.   [3] See pp. 303 f.
[4] G. F. Barbour, *The Life of Alexander Whyte, D.D.*, New York, 1925, Chap. xxvi, p. 512.

with the Church of England). Charles Wordsworth, Bishop of St Andrews (1853–92), though an Englishman, was firmly attached to the principles of the Episcopal Church in Scotland; nevertheless a constant aim of his life was *rapprochement* with Presbyterians.[1] His ideal was a united Church comprising both Presbyterians and Anglicans. He put forth a plan for concomitant ordination by the presbyterate of both Churches together with the bishop. He held that Presbyterian Orders were irregular but perfectly valid. He was in close and friendly touch with the leading Presbyterian divines of his day, William Milligan and others, but received little encouragement for his union plans either from them or from his Episcopal brethren. Dr James Cooper of the Church of Scotland was devoted to the cause of reunion between Presbyterians and Anglicans and "an undiscouraged advocate of Christian unity" generally.[2] His special efforts to promote Presbyterian and Anglican reunion met with little sympathy from Church of Scotland leaders, but the Lambeth Conference of 1908 took note of his emphasis on the precedent of the settlement of 1610 in Scotland [3] as combining Presbyterianism and Episcopacy in a way which might provide lines of guidance for reunion.[4]

4. TOWARDS THE UNION OF THE CHURCHES

In the 18th century concern with the possible reunion of the Churches was in the main limited to a number of enlightened individuals. The first half of the 20th century was to be the great epoch of the reunion of separated Church bodies and denominations. The 19th century stands midway between the two. The Churches themselves began to move and to negotiate directly with one another. The tide seemed to be setting away from the divisiveness which had marked the history of almost all the great Protestant denominations and in favour of a renewal of fellowship. Nothing was achieved comparable to the great reunions of the 20th century; yet the 19th century, especially in its second half, was able to show ecumenical developments which were often far from insignificant.

The Prussian Plan of Union, 1817. One of the largest and most interesting unions of the 19th century was that achieved by the King of Prussia between the Lutheran and Reformed Churches in his dominions in 1817 and the following years.

The ruling family of Prussia belonged to the Reformed Church. In the east, centre, and north ninety-eight per cent of the population was Lutheran; in the Rhineland and Westphalia, where the Roman Catholics were stronger, the majority of the Protestants were Reformed. There were also some forty parishes of Huguenots, who had been welcomed by the Elector Frederick William after the revocation of the Edict of Nantes. At the end of the 18th century, rationalism was at its height, and there was not much exaggeration in the remark: "Taking it all round, the Church had become a department of State, intended to make the people moral and obedient."[5]

[1] See Bibliography (Wordsworth).
[2] H. J. Wotherspoon, *James Cooper, A Memoir*, London, 1926, pp. 249–65.
[3] See Chap. iii, p. 126.
[4] James Cooper, *Reunion: A Voice from Scotland. Addresses in London at King's College*, London, 1918.
[5] Louis Noir, *L'Union des églises protestantes en Prusse sous Frédéric-Guillaume III*, p. 31. For the general spiritual climate in Germany, see pp. 268 ff.

Although the different confessions maintained their separate existence in Prussia as in other states, the ruler exercised his control over them through a single ministry for spiritual affairs, with one minister at its head.

General considerations in favour of unity might have led to nothing practical had it not been for the influence exercised on the mind of Frederick William III by F. S. Sack, from whom he had received his religious education. In 1798 Sack addressed a letter to the Minister of State, Baron Thulemeyer, in which he said:

"The two Churches are sisters, and united by the tolerance of their sovereign: the difference between the two ecclesiastical systems has lost its former importance, and no longer warrants any real separation between them. Why should this separation, which has lasted until now, be perpetuated by a double ritual, or even in a reinstituted ritual? In any case, the two rituals are very much alike, and their differences are in words rather than in reality."

This idea remained for some time a shadow without form. But it was taking hold. The disasters of the renewed Napoleonic wars had brought about something of a revival of religion as well as of national spirit, and the King, now under the influence of D. E. Borowski, a Reformed pastor who had drunk deeply of Lutheran teaching, was taking his religion even more seriously than before.

To other forces making for union was now added the powerful voice of Schleiermacher.[1] Schleiermacher was prepared to recognize that, in the conditions then prevailing in Germany, the initiative in promoting movements for the union of the Churches could be taken only by the rulers of the various German territories; he was, however, implacably opposed to such exercise of coercive authority as would involve the violation of the liberty of the individual conscience. Unity might be directed from above; but it could be developed and maintained only as a natural growth from the inner piety of the Churches, finding its readiest expression in the fellowship of worship.

In 1817 the King of Prussia took decisive action and himself drew up the main outlines of a proclamation in popular style, requiring the unification of the various confessions within his dominions. The Church authorities were authorized to treat the differences between Lutheran and Reformed as non-existent for the purposes of admission to the Holy Communion, appointment to vacant parishes, and so forth. But such deep and long-continuing divisions do not readily lend themselves to being treated as non-existent; in actual fact some parishes remained Lutheran, others Reformed, others united on the basis of loyalty to the Scriptures and the early Creeds of the Church alone. When the King tried to draw the bonds of his federation tighter, he ran into opposition.

The great bone of contention was the liturgy which the King tried to introduce in 1822, though only one-sixteenth of the clergy had approved it. With this further development of royal autocracy in the affairs of the Church, Schleiermacher's support weakened. Others went further. The clergy of Breslau refused *en masse* to use the new liturgy. They were followed by other Old Lutherans. Many of the recalcitrants were suspended from their office as pastors. Finally, at a General Synod held in Breslau in 1841, they founded the Evangelical Lutheran Church in Prussia. Thousands of orthodox Lutherans left Germany for the freer air of America, and carried with them not merely their own rigidly

[1] On Schleiermacher's ecumenical views, see pp. 269 f.

Lutheran ideas, but also a deep suspicion of other Churches, so that an effort at reunion in Europe produced by reaction a new spirit of particularism in America.[1]

The Prussian Union continued to develop slowly in the face of continuing controversies about liturgies, creeds, and confessions. The rationalists disliked it as being still too dogmatic; the orthodox because it failed to safeguard the distinctive dogmatic traditions of each Church. It was able to survive at all only because the pressure of the State continued for more than a century to keep it in being, and because there was a strong centre party which genuinely believed in union and held that it could be maintained without such compromises as would involve disloyalty to truth. But,

> "the 'Prussian Evangelical Union', which produced a church without a general polity, a common worship, or a common statement of belief, and without any adequate sense of religious unity, can obviously be called a union only with reservations."[2]

Schleiermacher was right; the Union became effective only so far as it grew out of and was supported by the inner piety of the Christian congregations.

Prussia was not the only area in which movements for union coincided with the tercentenary of the Reformation (1817). But the only regions in which the Churches were able to achieve a genuinely organic union, resulting in the foundation of one Protestant Christian Church, were Nassau and Baden. There the Churches possessed or created for themselves corporate bodies having legal personality, which could act on behalf of the Churches as a whole. Where such organs for corporate action were lacking, the most that could be achieved was a rather ill-defined federal union.

The Jerusalem Bishopric. Some years after the Prussian Union, Frederick William IV of Prussia attempted to introduce episcopacy into the Prussian Church, with the intention, apparently, of promoting some kind of union with the episcopal Churches. The means by which this was to be accomplished was the foundation of a joint Anglican-Prussian bishopric in Jerusalem, and in 1841 C. C. J. Bunsen was sent to England by the King of Prussia to carry on the necessary negotiations. Bunsen (he became Baron in 1857) was the best agent the King could have had; he was a great admirer of the Church of England and had produced a Prayer Book on Anglican lines for the use of the German Church. He was of irenic mind, and the scheme was, in Archbishop Brilioth's words, "as it were a child of his own heart".[3] In essence the scheme was simple. The bishop was to be nominated by England and Prussia in turn; he was to ordain German clergy on their subscription to the Confession of Augsburg, and Anglican clergy on their subscription to the Thirty-nine Articles. The bishop would have jurisdiction over the Anglicans in those parts, of whom there were few at the time, as well as over such Protestant congregations as would accept him. It seems clear that there was a political factor in the plan—an attempt, by an Anglo-German protectorate over Protestants in the Levant, to balance the traditional protectorate over Latin Christians, which had long given France a dominant political influence in that area. In 1841 an Act was passed by Parliament to make

---

[1] See Chap. vii, p. 325.   [2] J. T. McNeill, *Unitive Protestantism*, p. 306.
[3] *The Anglican Revival*, p. 161.

possible the consecration of an Anglican bishop for work in territories not under the British Crown.

The scheme received considerable support in England, including that of the Archbishop of Canterbury (Howley) and of the Bishop of Oxford (Wilberforce). In 1835 the Church Missions to Jews[1] had succeeded in establishing itself in Jerusalem and was carrying on a promising work. To Evangelicals the time seemed ripe for the formation of a Hebrew Christian Church in Palestine under a Jewish Christian "successor of St James".

From the Tractarian side the whole scheme roused the fiercest opposition. Fuel was added to the fires of opposition by J. R. Hope (later Hope-Scott), who had originally been favourable to the scheme, but had changed his mind after a long talk with Baron Bunsen. He wrote of him:

> "That gentleman, while professing Catholic principles, disparaged the primitive Church as a witness to those points on which he had formed his own theory. He maintained that any father of a family might consecrate the Eucharist, and in speaking of the proposed Bishopric, he described it, as far as I remember, to be the foundation of a new body which was to supplant eventually all other portions of the Church."[2]

The first Bishop appointed for Jerusalem under this Act was a converted Jewish Rabbi, the Rev. Michael Alexander. On his death, after an episcopate of only four years, it was the turn of the King of Prussia to appoint; his choice fell upon the Rev. Samuel Gobat, a Swiss from the Bernese Jura trained in the Basle Mission House, who had worked for a number of years as a missionary of the Church Missionary Society in Abyssinia and the Near East. He was a fine scholar, a master of many languages, and was already in deacon's Orders. In 1846 he was ordained priest in London and five days later consecrated bishop.

Gobat's work was heavily criticized in certain quarters. The main charge against him was that he sought to make proselytes from the Eastern Churches. This was contrary to Anglican policy, which was to assist and bring new life into Churches weakened by centuries of Moslem oppression. Some members of these Churches had been influenced by Western reforming movements and incurred ecclesiastical censure or excommunication from their own communions. Gobat's problem was what to do with them if they desired to join the Anglican Church. After a number of painful experiences, he decided he could not for ever refuse to accept them:

> "And now what am I to do? I have never wished to make Converts from the old Churches, but only to lead to the Lord and to the knowledge of His truth as many as possible. From henceforth I shall be obliged to receive into our communion such as are excluded for Bible-truth's sake from other Churches, and I trust that in doing so, even though men should blame me for it, the Lord will grant His blessing."[3]

Looking back after more than a century, one can appreciate his motives while at the same time understanding the Orthodox and High Church opposition to his action.

[1] The official title of this Society is The London Society for the Promotion of Christianity among the Jews.
[2] Robert Ornsby, *Memoirs of J. R. Hope-Scott*, London, 1884, I, pp. 29–78.
[3] *Memoirs of Bishop Gobat*, p. 265.

But this was not the basic weakness of the Jerusalem scheme. A union based on Acts of Parliament without serious theological thought and without careful consideration of all that is involved in it can hardly fail to end as a union of foolscap and blotting-paper—and this is just what the Jerusalem union proved to be. As a means of restoring the historic episcopate to the Prussian Church, it miserably failed. Only two German pastors were ordained by Gobat, and these on their return to Germany failed to obtain recognition as ministers from their own Church. In 1886 the original agreement between England and Prussia was dissolved.

After an interval, the bishopric in Jerusalem was revived by Archbishop Benson on a strictly Anglican basis; it has since admirably served an ecumenical purpose as a neutral and friendly place of meeting for all the not always harmonious Churches represented in Jerusalem, and has carefully avoided ecumenical adventures and short-cuts.

Unitive Movements in the Netherlands. In the Netherlands the 19th century was an era of divisions rather than of their removal; yet there were also encouraging signs of the existence of ecumenical conviction.

A movement in the direction of unity appeared at the end of the 18th century and continued through the first three decades of the 19th. The initiative was taken by the Remonstrant (Arminian) Church, the Synod of which in 1796, and again at a later date, addressed letters to all the Protestant Churches asking for their co-operation in plans for the reunion of the Churches sprung from the Reformation. No actual union was achieved (except one or two instances of reunion between local churches, e.g. the Remonstrants and the Mennonites at Dokkum), but there was a marked and widespread interest in questions of unity, which expressed itself in exchange of pulpits and of visits between synods. Intercommunion was advocated; in 1817 the General Synod of the Reformed Church in the Netherlands resolved that members of other Protestant bodies might be admitted to Communion in that Church.

Several societies were established for promoting union amongst Protestants. The most important of these, *Christo Sacrum* (1797–1830), was originally founded in Delft, and did much to bring members of different Churches into contact with each other. It was hoped that such a bond of concord might at last lead to the uniting of denominations. Unfortunately, the members of *Christo Sacrum* were ejected from the Netherlands Reformed Church as being heretical; against its will the Society was obliged to become an independent Church and was recognized as such by the State. A similar influence in the direction of unity was exercised from 1845 onwards by a society called the "Christian Friends", under the leadership of Pastor O. G. Heldring, and its publication *The Society: Christian Voices.*

Throughout the 19th century leaders in various Churches in Holland appeared who were devoted to the cause of union—such men as Canzius, the founder of the *Christo Sacrum*, and at a later date Dr J. H. Gunning (1858–1940), who, through his writings, communicated his deep longing for the *Una Sancta* to a wide circle of Christian people.

Two major secessions from the Dutch Reformed Church took place in the course of the century. In 1834 the Christian Reformed Church came into being. In 1886 the eminent theologian Abraham Kuyper led out a much greater number in a secession which led to the formation of the strictly Calvinistic *Gereform-*

eerde Kerken. In 1892 about half the members of the Christian Reformed Church joined the *Gereformeerde Kerken* in a minor reunion by which the number of Churches existing in Holland was not reduced.[1]

Lutheran and Reformed in Hungary. A notable attempt was made in Hungary in the 1840's to overcome the age-long division between the two great Protestant Communions. On 24 February 1841 an appeal for the union of the Hungarian Churches was published in the Press. In answer, the Chief Inspector of the Lutheran Church proposed the union of the two Confessions; but the terms in which he did so indicated that this was a specimen of ecclesiastical diplomacy rather than the expression of a deep spiritual concern:

> "The abolition of our differences we regard as being in harmony with our age of enlightenment, this age of the dominance of humanism."

For the moment it looked as though something might come of these proposals; a *Protestant Magazine for Church and School* was founded on an interdenominational basis, and the official courts of the two Churches nominated a committee of sixty members to work out a scheme of union.

The movement was temporarily submerged in the Hungarian national uprising of 1848–49, but came to life again briefly in 1855, in connection with the formation of a joint theological faculty in Budapest. But the forces making for division were stronger than those making for union. By degrees the union movement died away, and, except for happier personal relationships, nothing of permanent significance had been achieved.

Lutheran and Reformed in Austria. The long-repressed Protestants of Austria obtained their first relief with the promulgation on 13 October 1781, by the liberal-minded Emperor Joseph II, of the Patent of Toleration. But toleration is not the same as equality before the law, and the Protestants had to wait almost eighty years before the Emperor Francis Joseph, Joseph II *redivivus*, gave them this second boon in the Protestant Patent, issued on 8 April 1861.

On 15 December 1891 the Protestants of the two main confessions set out the constitution of what in some ways is a unique union, the Evangelical Church of the Augsburgian and Helvetic Confessions. For all purposes of dealing with the Government, the Church acts as a unity; as a unity it has become a member Church of the World Council of Churches. In all other respects the liberty of each Confession is maintained and is expressed in its doctrine, worship, and organization. For the Lutherans, the Augsburg Confession (in the form of 1530 or that of 1540) is authoritative; for the Reformed, the main confessional documents are the Heidelberg Catechism and the Second Helvetic Confession.

Regard for the traditions of each confession is carried to such a point that in the schools children learn the catechism of the Church to which they belong, without separation and in the same class—a happier state of affairs than is to be found in many other areas.

The Old Catholic Churches and Ecumenical Relations. Old Catholics of the continent of Europe and North America claim that theirs is *par excellence* the ecumenical Church, since from the beginning of their separate existence the

---

[1] For later developments, see Chap. xiii, pp. 627 f.

union of all Christians on the basis of the ancient Faith of the Church has been their principal concern.

In 1870 the Vatican Council proclaimed the new dogma of the Infallibility of the Pope. In Germany, Austria, and Switzerland, groups of Roman Catholic priests and laymen refused to accept this dogma and were excommunicated.

Leading members of the groups met in a Congress at Munich in 1871 to work out for themselves a provisional organization. The purpose of this Congress was not to precipitate a schism, but to provide for the spiritual needs of those who had refused to submit to the Vatican Council. This proved impossible without forming a separate body, but the Old Catholics did not leave the Roman Communion until they were sure that their needs could not be met in any other way.

> "The Old Catholic movement, as we understand it, is not simply a protest against the new dogmatic definitions of the Vatican Council, but it is a return to the true catholicism of the one and undivided Church, and a challenge to all Christian confessions to unite on the basis of the original Christian Faith."[1]

The very first Old Catholic Congress, that of 1871—at which an Anglican priest was present bearing letters of greeting from the Bishops of Ely (Harold Browne) and Lincoln (Christopher Wordsworth)—formulated the directive which has determined Old Catholic ecumenical activity ever since:

> "We hope for reunion with the Greek-Oriental and Russian Churches, the separation of which was not brought about by any decisive causes, and which is not based on any irreconcilable doctrinal difference. We hope for a gradual *rapprochement* with the Protestant and with the Episcopal Churches."

Old Catholic ecumenical endeavours met with a warm response in England in the Anglo-Continental Society, and in St Petersburg in the Society of Friends of Spiritual Enlightenment. It was on the basis of these approaches that Reunion Conferences were held at Bonn in 1874 and 1875.[2]

The necessary sacramental basis for the new body was at hand in the ancient Church of Utrecht. This Church had been isolated from Rome since the time of the Jansenist controversy in the 17th century, but had retained the ancient Catholic order and life.[3] The Church of Utrecht had naturally taken a close interest in the new movement, and the Archbishop (Loos) had been present at the second Old Catholic Congress at Cologne in 1872, where he had advised against separation from Rome. In 1873 he promised to consecrate a bishop for the German Old Catholics and, although he died before he could do so, the promise was redeemed by the only surviving Dutch bishop, Hermann Heykamp, Bishop of Deventer.

In March 1872 Ignaz von Döllinger (1799–1890) delivered his famous lectures on *The Reunion of the Churches*,[4] at the conclusion of which he said:

---

[1] From a memorandum supplied by Mgr E. Lagerwey, Bishop of Deventer (available at W.C.C. office, Geneva).

[2] See *Report of the Proceedings of the Reunion Conference held at Bonn, 1874*; *Report of the Reunion Conference held at Bonn, 1875*; and F. Meyrick, *Correspondence between members of the Anglo-Continental Society and Old Catholic and Oriental Churchmen*, London, 1874, 1875.

[3] For a modern account of the Church of Utrecht see Bibliography (Moss). An earlier account which Moss has not entirely superseded is Neale, *History of the So-called Jansenist Church of Holland*, London, 1851.   [4] See Bibliography (Döllinger).

"What can, what ought to be done? . . . The right instruments would be found in men, both of the clergy and laity, who would unite for common action, first in Germany, untrammelled by instructions, and simply following their own mind and judgement. They would soon draw others to them in rapidly increasing numbers, by the magic power of a work so pure and pleasing to God, and would thus be brought into communication with like-minded men in other countries. The basis of their consultations would be Holy Scripture, with the three œcumenical Creeds, interpreted by the still undivided Church of the early centuries. Thus would an international society of the noblest and most beneficial kind be formed, and what began as a snowball might well become an irresistible avalanche."[1]

Döllinger's was by far the most powerful mind among the Old Catholics; agreement with his passion for union combined with the fact of their isolated position to set them along that path. This desire took concrete shape in 1874 when the first Reunion Conference of Old Catholic, Orthodox, Anglican, and Danish theologians met for three days at Bonn. On this occasion quite remarkable agreements were achieved. A second Conference was held in 1875 at which some agreement was reached with the Orthodox on the subject of the *Filioque* clause.

Throughout this period the main ecumenical preoccupation of the Old Catholics was with the Eastern Churches.[2] Protestantism was largely outside their purview, though friendly contacts were maintained with the Churches of Scandinavia. Contacts with Anglicanism were numerous, and fostered in England by the Anglican and Continental Churches Society, which, in a series of brochures, published much correspondence between Anglican and Old Catholic scholars. There were, too, various instances of intercommunion between Anglicans and Old Catholics.

In all this the Church of Utrecht stood markedly aloof—it was unrepresented even at the Bonn Conferences—and its attitude in general had been unfriendly towards such advances. As late as 1904 the Dutch position *vis-à-vis* Anglicanism was substantially unaltered. This is made clear in a letter from Bishop van Thiel of Haarlem to the Russian theologian General Kireev, concerning the giving of Communion in the Old Catholic Church at Olten to the American Episcopalian Bishop Brent. Van Thiel affirmed that both he and the Archbishop of Utrecht (Gul) were agreed that "this kind of thing should not occur again".[3]

This cautious attitude of the Church in Holland was not, however, typical of the Old Catholics as a whole. They were ready to reach out in all directions towards fellowship with Christians of other Churches. Though naturally they were more at home with episcopal bodies, their answer to an invitation to be present at the sixth General Conference of the Evangelical Alliance, a body composed of Christians of both episcopal and non-episcopal Churches, in 1873 is sufficiently remarkable:

"At the same time we were to express our sincere pleasure at the testimony this invitation renders to our unchanging purpose and endeavour, expressed by us from the very first, to reunite all Christian confessions into one great Church of Christ, in which any particular Church though united

[1] *The Reunion of the Churches*, pp. 162 f.
[2] See Chap. iv, pp. 207 ff., and Chap. x, p. 468.
[3] *The Old Catholic Church of Holland in relation to the Orthodox and Anglican Churches*, privately printed, 1908, p. 8.

as far as essential doctrines are concerned may still preserve all other peculiarities corresponding to its national character, its historical antecedents and training, and its political and social condition."[1]

The second international Old Catholic Conference held at Lucerne in 1892 was attended by representatives of many Churches. One of the most fruitful decisions of the Conference was that which called for the foundation of an international theological review and an international theological faculty.[2] The Old Catholic faculty at Berne has always retained its international character, especially through its training of students from Orthodox countries. Under various titles the *Internationale Theologische Zeitschrift* has continued to the present day to render notable ecumenical service.[3]

Gradually the attitude of the Church in Holland softened. Other Churches also showed themselves desirous of relations with the Old Catholics. In 1908 was founded the Society of St Willibrord, the specific aim of which was to promote union between the Anglican and Old Catholic Churches, and which had a president and secretary in each Church. So far as the Church of England was concerned, the movement continued to gain strength until, in 1931, it led to the establishment of formal intercommunion between the two Churches.[4]

The Unitas Fratrum and the Ecumenical Cause. Like the Old Catholic Churches, the *Unitas Fratrum*, better known in the English-speaking world as the Moravian Church, has been deeply committed to the ecumenical cause, in both its missionary and its unitive aspects. In general, its activity has been guided by Zinzendorf's *Tropenidee*, the belief that each particular Church has its own distinctive contribution to make to the Church universal, and that it is the duty of each Church to share its own special gift with all the other Churches.[5] This being so, it was contrary to the Moravian ethos to enter into negotiations for union as an ecclesiastical body with another Church. Their most fruitful contribution in the 19th century was through their "*diaspora* work" of spiritual ministry to isolated groups of Christians, and still more through their "preachers' conferences". In the latter they brought together, for spiritual help in gatherings not unlike retreats, ministers of the Lutheran, Reformed, and other Churches in Germany. Ministers rejoiced in the atmosphere of unity in these conferences, contrasting it with the factions and difficulties of their local situations.

There was, however, one exception to the Moravian attitude of reserve towards negotiations for Church union in their relations with the Anglican Churches from 1875 onwards. The initiative here was from the Anglican side, and it may be wondered whether either side really understood the ecumenical ideals of the other.

The first step was taken by the Lambeth Conference of 1878, when a series of problems in Anglican-Moravian relations, propounded by the Bishop of Barbados (Mitchinson), was discussed. Nothing, however, was really done until 1906, when a committee was formed to consider the question. This committee issued a most competent report in 1907, dealing extensively with the subject of the validity from the Anglican standpoint of Moravian Orders, the case for which it found non-proven on historical grounds.[6] The Lambeth Conference of

[1] *History of the Sixth General Conference*, pp. 477 f.
[2] See Otto Gilg, *Christkatholizismus in Luzern*, Lucerne, 1946, *passim*.
[3] See Chap. xiii, p. 635.   [4] See Chap. x, pp. 468–71.
[5] See Chap. ii, p. 102.   [6] For a more favourable opinion, see Chap. iii, p. 158.

1908 passed resolutions on the strength of this report. Doctrinal agreement in essentials appeared to present no difficulty, and it was suggested that three Anglican bishops should take part in Moravian consecrations.

Within a few weeks of the close of the Lambeth Conference, a session of the Synod of the Moravian Church was held at Dukinfield at which were present Bishop Ethelbert Talbot of Central Pennsylvania (since 1909 Bethlehem) and Bishop Hamilton Baynes, Assistant Bishop of Southwell. This was the first occasion on which Anglican bishops had been present at a Moravian Synod. Bishop Talbot was the bearer of a letter of goodwill from the Archbishop of Canterbury (Davidson),[1] and in the warmth of his own greetings went far beyond the Lambeth Conference in saying:

> "Your bishops have come down in historical continuity through the first of the bishops, through Christ and the holy Apostles down to the present time. That is what we call the historical succession or historic episcopacy, and something which you hold as precious and as very sacred. We recognize that, and that is a very strong point of kinship and alliance already between you and us." [2]

Bishop Talbot also recorded the interesting fact that in Bethlehem, Pennsylvania, an early Moravian settlement where he lived, a measure of free intercommunion existed between the two Churches.

The Moravian General Synod at Herrnhut in 1909 welcomed the Lambeth proposals with some reservations, but definite action has not resulted from them. Official conversations were not resumed until 1920, and, although these fall outside the limits of this chapter, it may be convenient here to summarize them. In an exchange of letters[3] it was made clear that, to the Moravians, the Anglican proposals implied absorption, and also that they were unwilling to abandon intercommunion with other Churches for the sake of fuller relations with Anglicans. Yet, in its final letter, the Moravian Committee expressed the hope that intercommunion might yet come to pass.

The Lambeth Conferences have shown a steadily increasing range of ecumenical interest, but the great Anglican record of specific approaches to unity belongs almost wholly to the 20th century. In the 19th, relations with the Old Catholics did not go beyond general interest and friendliness. Approaches to the Moravians were marked by long hesitations and uncertainties. Of the negotiations yet to be chronicled, two led on to no definite result, and the third was no more than a preparation for the achievement which was to follow in the succeeding century.

The Church of Sweden and the Anglican Church. The Church of Sweden has a long history of friendly relations with the Anglican Communion, with from time to time at least partial intercommunion and recognition of ministries.

The first Swedish settlement in America was founded on the banks of the Delaware in 1637. When the Swedes were left without a pastor they gladly accepted the services of Anglican priests; and there is evidence that, conversely, Anglicans had no hesitation about accepting the ministry of Swedish clergy. The second wave of Swedish immigration began in 1841. Gustaf Unonius was

---

[1] See *Verbatim Report of a Closed Session of the Synod of the Moravian Church, Dukinfield,* p. 7, and W. G. Addison, *The Renewed Church of the United Brethren, 1722–1930,* London, 1932, pp. 146–70. [2] *Verbatim Report,* p. 9. [3] Printed in full in Bell, *Documents,* II, pp. 117–42.

invited to become pastor to the immigrants and, there being no Swedish bishop in America, was advised by the Swedish Church to seek ordination from the Episcopal Church.[1] In 1861 Bishop Whitehouse of Illinois received Pastor Bredberg "on his letters of orders from the Bishop of Skara".[2] In 1874 the same Bishop Whitehouse proposed the union of the (Swedish) Augustana Synod with the Protestant Episcopal Church. After 1866 "Swedish emigrants to the United States were recommended to the Protestant Episcopal Church in such places where there was no access to a Swedish Evangelical Lutheran community".[3]

In 1829 the Church Missionary Society in London accepted as a candidate the Rev. Peter Fjellstedt, the first foreign missionary of the Church of Sweden, who had been trained at the Mission House in Basle. Fjellstedt had been ordained in 1825 by Bishop Bjurback of Karlstad, and no question was raised as to the adequacy of his episcopal ordination to qualify him for work under an Anglican missionary society.[4]

In 1837, at the request of the Bishop of London (C. J. Blomfield), and with the authority of the King of Sweden, Swedish bishops confirmed the children of English residents in that country.

It may be said that these interchanges had been sporadic, and lacked synodical authority; yet they had high official sanction on both sides, and were far more than the unchecked adventures of individuals. It was on such long-continued friendly contacts that the Lambeth Conference was prepared to build when in 1888 one of its committees declared of the Swedish Church that:

> "as its standards of doctrine are to a great extent in accord with our own and its continuity as a national Church has never been broken, any approaches on its part should be most gladly welcomed with a view to mutual explanation of differences, and the ultimate establishment, if possible, of permanent intercommunion on sound principles of Ecclesiastical polity."

Later Lambeth Conferences proceeded slowly but surely, and after that of 1908 something was done. Commissions were appointed in Sweden and England. Bishop John Wordsworth of Salisbury learned Swedish and wrote his classic book *The National Church of Sweden*. The stage was set for the happy progress which will be recorded elsewhere in this History.[5]

Bishop Gray and the Dutch Reformed Church in South Africa. Robert Gray, the first Bishop of Capetown (1847-74), was not the type of prelate whom one would normally associate with ecumenical activity. He was, in fact, a narrow 19th-century High Churchman. Yet throughout his life the subject of Christian unity, and particularly as it affected South Africa, was one of his major concerns. One of his Charges was devoted mainly to the subject, and in it he said:

> "I have ever looked with interest upon the proceedings of the Evangelical Alliance, though based, as I think, upon an essentially wrong principle, because I have regarded its formation as the expression of a conviction that our present state is a wrong one, and ought not to be persevered in."[6]

[1] John Wordsworth, *The National Church of Sweden*, pp. 400 f.
[2] J. H. Swinstead, *Relations between the Anglican and Swedish Churches*, London, 1920, p. 6.
[3] Bell, *Documents*, I, pp. 186 f., and especially p. 187, n. 1.
[4] Carl Anshelm, *Peter Fjellstedt*, Stockholm, 1930, I, pp. 80–83, 139–49.
[5] See Chap. x, pp. 471 ff.
[6] Printed in *Sermons on the Reunion of Christendom*, ed. F. G. Lee.

In view of this, it is not so surprising as might at first sight appear to find Bishop Gray urging his Synod in 1870 to pass resolutions deploring schism and asking for expressions of opinion on the matter from other communions. These resolutions were forwarded to the Synod of the Dutch Reformed Church, which suggested the formation of a joint committee to investigate the matter. Bishop Gray replied cordially, accepting the suggestion but laying down certain principles on which he desired agreement before any meeting took place. These demands showed, in fact, considerable failure to understand the Dutch Reformed position, and they were rejected in a lengthy reply from the Dutch Synod. Bishop Gray answered this, but the affair proceeded no further.[1]

Canterbury and Rome: the Question of Anglican Orders. The modern Church has never been without its great ecumenical figures. One of these, who devoted his life with singular tenacity to the cause of Catholic reunion, was the Hon. Charles Wood, later the second Viscount Halifax.[2]

Halifax's name is connected primarily with two major events in the history of Anglican-Roman Catholic relations: the papal inquiry into Anglican ordinations in the 1890's, and the Malines Conversations of the 1920's.

The first of these events dated from 1890 when Halifax imparted some of his enthusiasm to a young French priest, Fernand Portal, who commenced to study Anglicanism. The two exchanged a number of visits, and there was born the idea of a direct approach to Rome on the subject of Anglican Orders. Halifax saw Cardinal Vaughan, the Roman Catholic Archbishop of Westminster, who wished to begin with the question of Rome itself. Perhaps part of his subsequent hostility was due to the small attention which Halifax paid to his wishes.

The affair began to take shape. Halifax bombarded people on all sides, and "even Archbishop Benson and Cardinal Vaughan exchanged a few desultory shots at long range". In December 1893 the first *ballon d'essai* appeared in the shape of an article by Portal (writing under the name of Fernand Dalbus) in *La Science catholique*, and entitled *Les Ordinations anglicanes*. Portal's final judgement was that the ordinations were not of certain validity. In 1894 several works appeared on the subject, notably by Abbé Duchesne, who was in favour of validity, and by Mgr Gasparri, who was against it. In the following year *La Revue Anglo-Romaine* was founded and edited by Portal.

By this time the affair was front-page ecclesiastical news, and representations had been made to Rome at the highest level to open an inquiry. In April 1895 Leo XIII issued his Apostolic Letter *Ad Anglos*, which clearly failed to understand the English mind, and simply appealed to the English people to return to its true home in the Church of Rome; it indicated little hope of imaginative advance.

In September 1895 it became known that a full inquiry was to be made and a Commission set up This Commission assembled in March 1896 and consisted of Dom (later Cardinal) Aidan Gasquet, Mgr (later Cardinal) Gasparri, Canon Moyes, the Abbé Duchesne, a Franciscan Fr David Fleming, and a Spanish Jesuit Fr de Augustinis. Of these Duchesne was the only one known to be definitely in favour of the validity of Anglican ordinations; Gasquet and Gasparri were more or less definitely opposed, and the others doubtful. Two

---

[1] See *Life of Bishop Gray*, edited by his son, London, 1875; see also *A Correspondence Relative to Proposals for Union between the English and Dutch Reformed Churches in South Africa*, Capetown, 1871.
[2] See J. G. Lockhart, *Charles Lindley, Viscount Halifax* (*passim*).

Anglicans, Fr F. W. Puller, S.S.J.E., and Canon T. A. Lacey, went to Rome to give unofficial help if required.[1]

The result is well known: in September 1896 appeared the Bull *Apostolicae Curae*, which declared Anglican Orders absolutely null and void. Halifax, ever an optimist, refused to believe that the door had been finally closed, and held that the advantages of the reopening of negotiations between the two Churches outweighed the temporary setbacks.

He found further consolation in the official reply of the two English Archbishops—Frederick Temple and W. D. Maclagan—to the Bull. This *Responsio* was mainly the work of Bishops Wordsworth, Stubbs, and Creighton, though Archbishop Temple took great personal pains, as he expressed it, to "cut out all the thunder".[2] This document set forth, in terms more explicit than have been used by such authority before or since, the High Anglican doctrine of the priesthood and sacraments.

Canterbury and Rome: the Malines Conversations.[3] For the next quarter of a century Halifax continued quietly to prepare men's minds for that union in the eventual consummation of which he never lost faith. In 1920 the Lambeth Conference issued its "Appeal to All Christian People", to which Cardinal Mercier, Archbishop of Malines, sent a cordial reply. The way was open for Halifax's second major ecumenical adventure.

Portal took the initiative by suggesting that he and Halifax, then eighty-two, should visit Cardinal Mercier. Halifax, who had thought his life over, jumped at the opportunity. Portal's proposal was for informal joint conferences, and the Cardinal had received the idea sympathetically. Halifax, characteristically, had visions of going to Malines armed with a dossier furnished by Archbishop Davidson of Canterbury. He, of course, received nothing of the kind, but Davidson did give him a private letter of introduction, making clear that he was acting in an individual capacity only. Cardinal Mercier saw the two friends and agreed to sponsor the desired Conversations, which were arranged to take place from 6–8 December 1921.

On the Anglican side Halifax secured the attendance of Dr Armitage Robinson, Dean of Wells, one of the most learned clergymen of his day, and of Fr W. H. Frere of Mirfield, subsequently Bishop of Truro. On the Roman Catholic side the Cardinal summoned his Vicar-General, Mgr van Roey (later Archbishop of Malines and Cardinal) to sit with himself and Portal. Detailed reports of the Conversations have been published and are readily accessible.[4] To the Anglicans were later added Bishop Gore, a scholar of immense prestige but the author of more than one avowedly anti-papal book, and Dr B. J. Kidd, a man of vast patristic learning, but liable to be obstructive in argument. On the Roman side the new members were the Abbé Hippolyte Hemmer, a learned historian, and Mgr Batiffol, a patristic scholar of international repute, who, in a Memorandum written in 1923, had stated his own view of the matter thus:

[1] Lacey subsequently published a more or less day-to-day record of events, under the title *A Roman Diary*, London, 1910.
[2] *Memoirs of Archbishop Temple*, by Seven Friends, II, p. 261.
[3] The Malines Conversations are so closely connected through the personalities of Lord Halifax and the Abbé Portal with that which precedes that it has been felt best to include the account of them in this chapter, rather than in Chap. x, to which chronologically they belong.
[4] See Halifax, *The Conversations at Malines: Original Documents*, and Bivort de la Saudée, *Documents sur le problème de l'union anglo-romaine (1921–27)*. See also G. K. A. Bell, *Randall Davidson*, Chap. lxxxix; and Bibliography (Halifax, Portal).

"It is no use thinking of a reconciliation of the Anglican Church; that would be utopian; but we can draw nearer to the Anglo-Catholic movement, encourage and enlighten it, perhaps help to detach it from the political or modernistic elements in Anglicanism. That is the perspective in which we must direct our work; conversations without any immediate aim, but helping to make Anglo-Catholic opinion advance in a Catholic direction."[1]

Such ideas could not commend themselves to the Anglicans involved nor, indeed, to the Abbé Portal, while it is not clear that even Cardinal Mercier himself held such views. It is true that his knowledge of Anglicanism was extremely limited, but at the fourth Conversation in 1925 he read out with apparent approval the famous paper "by an anonymous scholar" on "The Church of England United, not Absorbed", which was a plea for an Anglican Uniatism with a Patriarchate, having considerable autonomy, at Canterbury.[2]

The Malines Conversations were, in one sense, private meetings between eminent individuals on both sides. On the other hand, an official character was imparted to them when Mercier sought, and received, a letter from Cardinal Gasparri stating that "the Holy See approves and encourages your conversation".[3] On the strength of this Archbishop Davidson was prevailed upon to give carefully qualified recognition, though not authorization, to the discussions. The Anglican bishops, however, when consulted, were less favourable than the Primate.

The Conversations proceeded calmly in the great salon of the Palace at Malines. Cardinal Mercier was an old and frail man when Halifax and Portal first approached him, and as the years wore on the malignant disease of which he was a victim restricted him more and more. In 1925, after the fourth Conversation, he died; and during the following year Portal died of a stroke. In October 1926 the fifth and last Conversation took place at Malines, under the presidency of the new Archbishop, Mgr van Roey. All present realized that this would be the end of the venture. All that was discussed was the publication of the Report and Memoranda. In January 1928 Pope Pius XI issued his Encyclical *Mortalium Animos* which, though it did not mention them by name, was taken as condemning the Malines Conversations. Colour was given to this supposition when, two weeks later, the *Osservatore Romano* announced baldly that there would be no more Conversations.

It is not easy to assess the value of the Malines Conversations. To-day, both on the Anglican and the Roman side, there is a clear conviction that they must not be repeated. But that is not necessarily to label them a failure, for, indeed, the spirit of Malines has informed many small and informal meetings between members of the Roman and other Churches, and has shown itself as a torch whose light has waxed rather than waned.

In one sense Malines fittingly sums up nearly a century of endeavour to put into practice the ecumenical ideals of the Oxford Movement. The Tractarians and their successors always saw their task primarily in terms of Rome and the East. Inevitably, therefore, their endeavour and their influence have tended to appear one-sided. For them the Catholic Church—outwardly divided yet inwardly one through the sharing of a common sacramental life—was the basic

[1] Bivort de la Saudée, *Documents*, pp. 81 f.
[2] It subsequently became known that the author was Dom Lambert Beauduin, a liturgist and canonist of eminence, and founder of the "Monks of Unity".
[3] Lockhart, op. cit., II, p. 283.

reality. On their view the Catholic Church was limited to those communions which have preserved intact a ministry in apostolic succession and the Faith of the undivided Church. If Anglicans ever came to accept a view of reunion which, while embracing the Protestant Churches, excluded the ancient Churches of Rome and the East, the work of the Tractarians would have been in vain. If, however, as is increasingly the case, the ecumenical movement accepts the view that reunion can mean only the gathering into one of all the separated and divided people of God, then the labours and witness of the Tractarians are seen to have made a valuable contribution to the development of the movement as a whole.

Reunion amongst Methodist Churches. The story of Methodism in the 19th century was largely one of schisms and *rapprochements.* The divisions in Methodism mainly took their rise in England, but the first successful attempts to heal them are to be found among the Methodist Churches overseas.

Townsend justly calls Canada "the proto-leader of union".[1] The first Methodist sermon was preached in Canada in 1782; by 1832 there were five distinct Methodist Churches there, all owing their origin to divisions in British Methodism, with one exception—the Methodist Episcopal Church, which had come from the United States. But the work of union began even before the process of fissiparation had ended. To resolve serious difficulties between Wesleyans and members of the Methodist Episcopal Church, a partial union was formed in 1833, though with a continuing remnant on the Methodist Episcopal side. A schism of only twelve years' duration was healed in 1841 when the followers of Henry Ryan, who had formed themselves into an independent Canadian Wesleyan Methodist Church, united with the Methodist New Connexion which had opened a mission in Canada in 1837. Two years later the New Connexion united with the Protestant Methodists in eastern Canada.

It was the Methodist New Connexion which continued to press for a more comprehensive and general Methodist union, and to ask for a quadrennial general conference, but with little tangible result. About 1870, however, the pace quickened, following an editorial in the *Toronto Methodist Recorder* which demanded that the difficulties in the way of union be looked in the face as soon as possible. In March 1871 reunion committees met to discuss terms of union, and a basis was drafted and submitted to the Conferences of the four Churches which were prepared to consider union. This was acceptable to the Wesleyans and the New Connexion alone, and in 1873 these two agreed upon a basis. Then, however, the Methodist New Connexion Conference in England raised objections in a turgid and wordy resolution in which they spoke of hearing "with equal surprise and regret" of the proposed amalgamation, and raised various obstacles.

Further negotiations followed, in which the Wesleyans made concessions and the New Connexion none; and in 1874 the British Conference gave a grudging assent to the union, which was consummated later in the year. Thus was taken the first step towards complete Methodist union in Canada.

Townsend is probably right in believing that it was the Methodist Ecumenical Conference of 1881[2] which gave the necessary stimulus to this more complete union. All the four Methodist bodies in Canada were represented at it, and the desire for union "did not so much follow from anything that was said or done at the London Conference as from the association and Christian intercourse

---

[1] W. J. Townsend, *The Story of Methodist Union*, p. 63.   [2] See p. 267.

that took place during the sessions of the Conference".[1] To-day it may seem strange that before 1881 one kind of Methodist should have regarded another kind of Methodist as a strange being, but this was certainly the case, and not only in Canada.

Discussions followed the London Conference until, in 1883, a reunion conference of the four bodies was held at Belleville, Ontario; there, after five days of protracted debate, union was agreed upon, following the *volte face* of one of its most vigorous opponents. Formal union was delayed until 1 July 1884, on which day, in law and in fact, Canadian Methodism became one.

We have dwelt on the story of Methodist union in Canada because that story is typical of Methodist union in other parts of the world.[2] The story repeats itself in Australia, where, up to 1892, there were four Methodist Churches. Here again, it was the Ecumenical Conference of 1881 which gave the impetus to union. There were more difficulties and checks here, owing to the fact that negotiations were carried on separately in the different Australian provinces. It was not until 1 January 1902 that Methodism became one throughout the Commonwealth of Australia.

Ireland in the 19th century produced a Methodist denomination of its own, which before the end of the century had become reunited with the Wesleyans. Methodists in Ireland had usually received sacramental ministrations from the Church of Ireland. In 1814 strong demands began to be made that Methodists should receive Communion from the hands of their own preachers. This was opposed by Adam Averell, one of the foremost Irish Methodists of his time. In 1816 the Irish Conference authorized ministers to baptize and celebrate Holy Communion, and Averell at once became the centre of opposition. In one year 7,500 members joined him, and thus was formed a body which took the title of Primitive Wesleyan Methodists. In 1861 they had over 14,000 members with 85 ministers. In 1871 the Anglican Church of Ireland was disestablished, and the Primitive Wesleyans, enmeshed in their trust deeds and constitutions which could be modified only by an Act of the British Parliament, were in a difficult position. An Act of Parliament was passed allowing them to co-operate with any religious body or society in Ireland on which their Conference might decide. This opened the possibility of union among Irish Methodists; in 1878 the "Primitives" consummated their union with the Wesleyan Methodist Church of Ireland.

Negotiations were soon undertaken for a wider union of Irish Methodists, in effect for union between the Wesleyans and the New Connexion. After long negotiations this was effected in 1905.

It would be unfair to leave the subject of Methodist union with, perhaps, the impression of an almost reckless dividing and uniting. The other side is well expressed by a notable Methodist scholar, Dr H. B. Workman:

"The divisions of Methodism have not been founded upon reasons that will commend themselves without reserve at the bar of history. Too often they have been the results of misunderstanding or of tactless administration; above all, they have been the outcome of the 'settling down' process through which every great movement and institution must pass. Nor must

[1] Townsend, op. cit., p. 71.
[2] For Methodist union in the United States, see Chap. x, pp. 451–54.

we overlook the influence of the strong democratic wave which characterized the century after Waterloo, in producing friction in a body so conservatively organized as was Wesley's Methodism.

"In defence of Methodism we might plead that the divisions which attended this 'settling down' have not been more marked or numerous than those which have accompanied every other great religious awakening. The dynamic forces which underlie a great revolt are never at first static, whatever they may become in process of time."[1]

Presbyterian Reunion. Another group of Churches which has shown a remarkable faculty for division and reunion is the Presbyterian.

A strong tendency to divide, arising out of a combination of deep religious conviction and stubborn individualism, had been manifest in parts of Scotland from the middle of the 17th century, but the first great division within Presbyterianism belongs to the first half of the 18th. This was the movement known as the Secession, which received its impetus from two causes—the belief of the seceders that the faith of the Church was being whittled away by the dominant party; and, the actual occasion of it, the virtual acceptance by the General Assembly, in 1732 and 1733, of the Act of Patronage which, passed in 1712, gave the Crown or private patrons the right of presentation to vacant benefices and, in effect, deprived the laity of their voice in the matter. Various other reasons were given to justify the schism, one of which was the repeal of the Act against Witchcraft, "thus dethroning the word of God". So the Seceders formed the Associate Presbytery, which grew rapidly and refused all overtures from the Scottish Church to return to its fold. The secession was basically an assertion of the spiritual independence of the Church, with opposition to civil interference and official legalistic methods, as well as to the type of "moderate" minister usually appointed by patrons.

By 1761 the Seceders had split into two bodies, and again into four bodies, over points which to-day seem trivial as a justification for schism, but which seemed vital at the time to men who were deeply in earnest about their faith.[2]

In 1761 another separation took place with the formation of the Presbytery of Relief. Again the issue was the operation of patronage, though the spirit of dissent was less bitter than in the case of the Seceders.

The next great division in Scotland, the Disruption, took place in 1843: it tore the great Church of Scotland in twain. The cause of division was, once again, patronage. The moderate party in the Church of Scotland, which deemed the advantages of the Establishment sufficient to outweigh the disadvantages of the Patronage Acts, was on the wane, and the General Assembly of 1832 was the last in which it had a decided majority. In 1833 Dr Thomas Chalmers proposed a principle of veto upon private nominees:

"That no minister be intruded into any pastoral charge contrary to the will of the congregation, and that the dissent of a majority of the male heads of families resident within the parish ought to be of conclusive effect in setting aside the nominee of the patron."[3]

[1] *Methodism*, Cambridge, 1912, p. 89.
[2] See for a good account of these C. G. McCrie, *The Church of Scotland: Her Divisions and Unions.*
[3] J. R. Fleming, *A History of the Church in Scotland, 1843-1874*, p. 20.

In 1834 this was passed into an Act, but litigation followed and the Court of Session declared that the Act of Veto was illegal. Uneasy unity was maintained until the meeting of the Assembly at Edinburgh in 1843. Here it became clear that a majority would not vote contrary to the principle of State control, and 474 ministers left the Church of Scotland. Thus was started the Free Church of Scotland.

> "This was the classic victory of the Free Church principle over that of State control in the spiritual sphere, rich and wonderful in its consequences, but nevertheless making a lamentable breach in the religious unity of Scotland."[1]

Although in one sense the battle appears to have been fought on material grounds, it was, in fact, profoundly spiritual, and was an assertion of the supremacy of the spiritual within its own sphere. Its results, too, were as beneficial as those of schism can ever be, for it forced the Scottish Churches back to their deeper foundations and to a seeking of unity on the highest levels. The story of Presbyterianism in Scotland in the latter half of the 19th century is largely the story of that search.[2]

A partial reward of this search was the coming together in 1847 of the Secession and Relief traditions in the United Presbyterian Church, numbering 518 congregations and at once rising to a position of great influence. Smaller unions followed. The majority of the Original Seceders ("Auld Licht") joined the Free Church in 1852; and the Reformed Presbyterian Synod united with the Free Church in 1876.[3]

Throughout the last half of the century, the Free Church of Scotland and the United Presbyterian Church explored the possibilities of union. Negotiations were pursued with vigour, especially in the decade from 1863 onwards, but led to no result. They were resumed in the 1890's. By 1893 "there was really no reason left for continued separation except the dread of division in the Free Church ranks, and that had nearly ceased to count as an argument when the minority in the Assembly sank to the low figure of twenty-seven. The United Presbyterian Synod was entirely unanimous for going forward".[4]

On 31 October 1900 two great Scottish Churches, all negotiations over, met together as one United Free Church of Scotland. In all, the Free Church brought 1,068 congregations into the union, and the United Presbyterian Church 593, the two together including nearly half a million communicants. At the end of the 19th century there remained only one major division between Scottish Presbyterians. The healing of that remaining division was to be the task of the 20th century.[5]

Unhappily, union was not achieved without new division. In 1893 a small group calling themselves the Free Presbyterians seceded from the Free Church. In 1900 a more serious split took place. Twenty-five ministers and sixty-three congregations of the Free Church (mainly in the Highlands) refused to enter the Union, declaring that the Free Church, by uniting with the United Presbyterians, had so far departed from its own faith and order that it was no longer the Free Church; and, affirming that they alone were truly the Free Church, they claimed

---

[1] J. R. Fleming, *The Story of Church Union in Scotland*, London, 1929, pp. 25 f.
[2] For good accounts, see the two books by J. R. Fleming quoted above.
[3] In the same year the two sections of Presbyterianism in England became one.
[4] Fleming, *The Story of Church Union in Scotland*, p. 42.
[5] See Chap. x, pp. 449 ff.

the entire property of the Church in Scotland and in the great missions overseas. Tedious litigation crawled up from court to court. On 1 August 1904 a full bench of the House of Lords, by five votes to two, declared in favour of the "Wee Frees". An impossible situation was created. The continuing Free Church could not make use of even a quarter of the churches, manses, and colleges thus legally assigned to it. British common sense came to the rescue; under an Act of Parliament, the Churches (Scotland) Act, passed on 11 August 1905, commissioners were appointed to divide the property equitably between the Churches. This was in the end achieved, but not without heartburning and bitterness.

The "Wee Free" case is among the most famous ecclesiastical cases in the whole history of the Church. It is a reminder that even Churches which insist most strongly on complete freedom from the State are, in respect of the property which they hold, subject like any other corporation to the law of the land; and may serve as a warning to those who engage in negotiations for the unity of the Churches that they do well to look ahead to the possible legal consequences of their actions, as well as to their spiritual benefits.

The story of Presbyterian division in Scotland is largely mirrored in Canada:

"At the outset we find the course of Canadian Presbyterianism affected by the importation from the motherland of differences which had arisen in Scotland and had no real pertinence to colonial life. The history of Canadian Presbyterianism is, therefore, in large measure, the story of the transplantation of these differences, and their subsequent fusion in Canada not only anticipated similar Presbyterian unions in Scotland and the United States, but may even have contributed to the drawing together of the reformed churches holding the Presbyterian system, in a World's Alliance."[1]

Apart from isolated chaplains to Scottish troops, Presbyterianism was not represented in Canada until 1764, after which date the various divisions followed one another very rapidly. But here, too, men quickly realized that the disunions were meaningless when transported across the Atlantic, and turned their thoughts to union. Even so, it took more than twenty years to come to the point where they would and did unite.

The first Canadian union took place in 1817 when a Burgher and anti-Burgher Presbytery united, together with three ministers of the Established Church of Scotland and two Congregational ministers, to form the United Presbyterian Synod in Nova Scotia. The ice thus broken, unions followed in a steady stream. In 1818 there was a union with the Dutch Reformed, and further unions followed in 1840, 1850, 1860, 1861, 1866, 1868, and 1875.[2]

The Union of 1840, which brought into being the Synod of the Presbyterian Church of Canada in Connection with the Church of Scotland, with seventy-six settled ministers, was of special importance. Unfortunately the Synod was subjected almost immediately to all the strains of the Disruption in Scotland. The Presbyterian Church in Canada was not established, and there was no reason at all for the Disruption to travel overseas. Unhappily, the divisive spirit reasserted itself with results that are summarized by Dr Silcox as follows:

"The majority of the synod remained loyal and voted sixty-eight ministers to twenty-three, but the non-concurring minority went out in 1844 and

[1] C. E. Silcox, *Church Union in Canada*, p. 57.
[2] Ibid., p. 469.

formed a Free Church synod. . . . The Disruption is also responsible for the fact that in many of the larger towns and smaller cities of Canada one might still find, as late as 1925, two Presbyterian churches usually within a short distance of each other—sometimes across the corner—but, generally speaking, appealing to a different clientele. . . . Those who continued to belong to the Auld Kirk tended to be Conservative in politics . . . those who attended the lineal descendant of the Free Church were Liberal in politics, a trifle warmer in their religious enthusiasms and not infrequently drawn from the middle classes."[1]

The greatest of the Presbyterian unions was that of 1875. In that year all the four main streams of Presbyterianism in Canada decided to come together and to form the Presbyterian Church in Canada. Some small groups, a few of which continue in isolation to the present day, refused to join the united Church; but the vast majority of Presbyterians in Canada found a home in that great Church which, as is recorded elsewhere in this History, sought in the 20th century to enter into yet wider union with Christians of other denominations.[2]

5. CONCLUSION

The 19th century in Europe was a period of immense, indeed explosive, vigour and creative power. Some of its achievements in science and philosophy, just because of their vigour, tended to have divisive force; and the Churches could not remain unaffected by what was passing around them.

The century saw the appearance of a number of new divisions. A secession from the Roman Catholic Church brought into existence the Old Catholic Churches, a movement pledged from the start to ecumenical service. The Presbyterians and Methodists experienced repeated fragmentation in many countries. A number of new bodies grew up, such as the "Plymouth Brethren",[3] which nurtured an intensive piety within themselves, but had no interest at all in ecumenical questions or movements. Even more important than these ecclesiastical divisions were those brought about by the impact of science and historical criticism. The old tensions between orthodox and liberal took on new forms, and the lines were being laid down for those continuing tensions between conservative and liberal, fundamentalist and critical, "catholic" and "protestant", which constitute horizontal divisions in the Church, and are a continuing problem to the ecumenical movement.

But these divisive factors were offset by powerful currents making for unity.

In the political sphere, the unification of Germany and Italy were among the greatest achievements of the century. The first day of the 20th century was marked by the coming into existence of the Commonwealth of Australia through the union of separate colonies and provinces. In the Church, these movements were paralleled by certain unitive tendencies not unaffected by political considerations.

Some of the greatest achievements were within the various confessions, as

---

[1] Silcox, op. cit., pp. 65 f.

[2] See Chap. x, pp. 454–58. Space forbids more than a reference here to the Presbyterian unions which were achieved in Australia in 1900, in New Zealand in 1901, in India in 1904, in China in 1905, and in Korea in 1907—a list which helps to justify the view that the 20th century so far has been the great century of Christian union.

[3] See Chap. vii, p. 317.

these came to feel their unity across national frontiers, and reorganized themselves on a world-wide basis. Almost all the actual unions of Churches achieved were intra-confessional, the Methodists and Presbyterians in many countries taking the lead in this movement for union.

Interconfessional movements for the unity of the Churches led to little result, though in certain cases they helped forward mutual understanding and fellowship.

During the century, every confession and almost every country was in some way affected by ecumenical movements or tendencies. But it must be admitted that the volume of actual achievement was disappointing; the 19th century remains the century of promise, pointing to an inheritance into which the 20th was at least to begin to enter.

NOTE

Party Terminology in the Church of England

Much misunderstanding of Anglican positions is due to confusion in the use of terms, for which Anglican inconsistency is at least in part responsible.

In the 18th century it was customary to speak of three groups within the Church of England: the High, the Low, and the Latitudinarian (the term Broad Church seems to have come into current use only in 1854). The High Church party maintained firmly the connection between the Crown and the Church and believed that there should be only one Church in England. The Low Church party was liberal in politics, entirely loyal to the Hanoverian succession, and less rigid than the High Church party in its attitude to dissenters. The Latitudinarian group, weary of controversy about dogma, influenced by Deism and "the religion of all reasonable men", was loyal to the National Church as an institution, but in many cases sat remarkably loose to its dogmatic traditions.

All these traditions survived into the 19th century; but the old names are frequently applied to new groupings and movements, to which they do not properly apply. The Evangelicals ("Low") came into existence through the revivals and awakenings of the 18th century. The Anglo-Catholics or Tractarians ("High") rediscovered the nature of the Church as a spiritual society, and reasserted the continuity of the Church of England with its pre-Reformation past. Modernists ("Broad") affirmed the right and the duty of the Church to re-state its doctrine, when necessary, in the light of modern knowledge and criticism. The old terminology had thus only a limited relevance to the 19th-century situation, and further developments in the 20th century have rendered it even less relevant today.

CHAPTER 7

VOLUNTARY MOVEMENTS
AND THE CHANGING ECUMENICAL CLIMATE

by

RUTH ROUSE

1. INTRODUCTION

This third chapter on the 19th century has a double objective. Its first aim, following on that of the preceding chapter on movements of approach between the Churches as such, is to show the part played in 19th-century preparation for the modern ecumenical movement by voluntary movements, especially those which arose out of the Evangelical Awakening.[1]

Its second aim is to show the variation of ecumenical climate in the 19th century. We shall pause at intervals to take barometric and thermometric readings of the ecumenical weather, to register the changes in ecumenical climate which they record, and to indicate in particular the tendencies amongst Churches and church parties and in different lands which favoured progress towards Christian union or which held back such progress. Throughout we shall bear in mind that the last years of the 19th century bring us to the verge of a new epoch in ecumenical Church history; and that at the close of this chapter we shall find ourselves facing that crucial event in the history of the ecumenical movement, the Edinburgh World Missionary Conference in 1910, which was in a real sense the dividing line between one ecumenical era and another.

The voluntary movements with which we are concerned here are inextricably connected with the Evangelical Awakening, the outstanding religious movement of the late 18th and early 19th centuries. The history of this great spiritual awakening cannot be written here; our task is to indicate its fundamental motives and to show in what way they promoted unity and union amongst Christians and amongst Churches.

2. THE EVANGELICAL AWAKENING: ITS ECUMENICAL RESULTS

The origins of the Evangelical Awakening differed in different countries and Churches. In Germany, the Evangelical Revival can be traced to the Pietist movement in the 18th century and its successors in the 19th.[2] In Britain its impulse came largely, though not wholly, from the evangelistic efforts of the Wesleys and Whitefield and the rise of Methodism. In America it arose from the Great Awakening of the 18th century and the 19th-century response of the Churches to the spiritual needs of the frontier.[3]

But whatever its origins, its spirit and its underlying motives were always the same. Its passion was evangelism—evangelism at home and to the ends of the earth. One result of this passion was in evidence everywhere—the coming into being of societies, voluntary movements, or organizations, in which Christians of different Churches and different nations banded themselves together to win the world for Christ. The compelling impulse which drew them together was the sense, born of their personal experience of salvation, that all men everywhere have need of Christ. As redeemed, they had a mission to proclaim redemption.

These societies and movements were pioneers, albeit unconscious pioneers, of the movement for Christian unity which was to come. They were not ecumenical in objective. Each had some specific aim of its own—missionary work or social

[1] By voluntary movements are understood movements or organizations initiated not by a Church as such but by a group of Christians or by some Christian individual.
[2] See Chap. ii, pp. 99–101, 103, 105.   [3] See Chap. v, pp. 222 f., 227 f.

reform—but, though not ecumenical in aim, they were ecumenical in result. They were not called into existence to promote Christian unity as such; they were built on no theory of Christian unity; but they created a consciousness of that unity, a "sense of togetherness" amongst Christians of different Churches. Though rarely formulated, the fundamental conception of Christian unity which lay beneath their common striving was that all true Christians share the life in Christ, that they are one by virtue of that sharing, and that this oneness is the essential Christian unity.

Three features appeared wherever the Evangelical Awakening spread: international Christian intercourse and action; a missionary awakening showing itself in the formation of missionary societies; efforts directed to social reform.

The Evangelical Awakening knew no national boundaries: it crossed the Atlantic Ocean; it spread from country to country. The flame of the remarkable Awakening which took place in Geneva early in the century was kindled from many sources: from Germany through the Moravian groups founded by Zinzendorf and his friends; from Russia through Madame de Krudener, the friend of the Emperor Alexander I; from the teaching of evangelically-minded pastors in Geneva itself; from Scotland through Robert Haldane, the evangelist, whose Bible study meetings in 1816 won converts to an evangelical faith amongst theological students, later themselves to become leaders in the Awakening. The flame spread to Montpellier and Montauban, centres of Protestantism in the south of France, touching and awakening future evangelical leaders—members, for example, of the Monod family, so influential in French Protestant history. From Switzerland and France the spark passed to Holland and Belgium. In the Netherlands a spiritual awakening took place, led by two converted Jews, Capadose and Da Costa, which did much to forward the cause of Christian unity in Holland by bringing members of different Churches to work together. In all these countries and others, Evangelical Societies were founded and were fostered by visits and gifts from other lands. Christians of different nations as well as of different Churches found fellowship with each other in the service of Christ and became conscious of their oneness in him.

Missions and ecumenism are inseparable. Revival, missions, Christian unity, is an inevitable series. No outburst of missionary zeal, unless it be the Jesuit Mission of the 16th century, has ever paralleled the missionary developments resulting from the Evangelical Awakening between 1790 and 1820. Their ecumenical results were outstanding.

In Germany, wherever the Awakening (*Erweckung*) spread, from Württemberg to Prussia, from Prussia to Saxony, though the revival took different and characteristic shapes in each area, three results were sure to appear—a missionary movement, a softening of barriers between the Churches, and an eagerness for international co-operation. It is the peculiar distinction of Germany that, twenty years before the founding of any German missionary societies, German effort had already concentrated on the training of missionaries for their task, no matter where it might lie. Jänicke, minister to a Bohemian church in Berlin, who in 1800 started a Missionary Training Institute, had no idea of how his missionaries could reach the field. No less than thirty of those whom he had trained went out under the English Church Missionary Society between 1800 and 1810, while others joined the London Missionary Society or the Netherlands Missionary Society.

The Basle Mission House, a missionary training school, was founded in 1815 by leaders of the German Christian Fellowship,[1] some years before the Basle Missionary Society began to send out missionaries. From the first it was both international and inter-Church—it trained both German Lutherans and Swiss Reformed, with a sprinkling of other nations, French and Russian. During the 19th century, Basle supplied the C.M.S. with no less than 152 missionaries, including men of outstanding quality—Rhenius, Krapf, Weitbrecht, and many more. Jänicke's Institute and the Basle Mission House resulted in interesting examples of Lutheran, Reformed, and Anglican missionary co-operation and united effort.

In Britain, between 1792 and 1813, every great denomination had developed a missionary organization: the Baptist Missionary Society; the London Missionary Society; the Church Missionary Society (in addition to the two-hundred-year-old Anglican missionary societies—the Society for Promoting Christian Knowledge and the Society for the Propagation of the Gospel); the Church Missions to Jews; Presbyterian Societies in Edinburgh and Glasgow; the Wesleyan Methodist Missionary Society. All these were denominational organizations with the exception of the L.M.S., which was started as a union effort of Congregationalists, Presbyterians, Methodists, and Anglicans. Its foundation was hailed as "the funeral of bigotry", and it has never changed its interdenominational basis, though it early became very largely Congregational, as one after another the other denominations formed their own societies. Besides the L.M.S., the two great auxiliaries of missions—the Religious Tract Society (1799) and the British and Foreign Bible Society (1804)—were founded on an inter-Church basis; each had a committee half Anglican and half Nonconformist, and each had three co-secretaries, one Anglican, one Nonconformist, and one, be it noted, "foreign" secretary, i.e. a Continental. In America, a few years later, there was a similar outburst of missionary zeal, expressing itself in similar societies.[2] Ecumenical results from these missionary movements were quick to appear.

Missionaries of different Churches realized their fellowship and interdependence. In Calcutta, Baptist and Congregational missionaries and Anglican chaplains met frequently for united prayer in Henry Martyn's pagoda on the Hooghly: "As the shadow of bigotry never falls upon us here, we take sweet counsel and go together to God's House as friends."[3] "The utmost harmony prevails and a union of hearts unknown between persons of different denominations in England."[4]

The new missionary enterprise gave rise at once to co-operation and unity amongst Christians of different Churches. When the first Baptist missionaries, Carey and his colleagues, were beginning their work in Bengal in the late 1790's, they were eager to make contact with the German missionaries of the Danish-Halle Mission in South India, in order to learn from their ninety years of missionary experience.

William Carey (1761–1834) himself, before going to India, had been of opinion that each denomination should work separately in the mission-field—"if . . . intermingled . . . their private discords might throw a damp upon their spirits, and

---

[1] *Deutsche Christentumsgesellschaft*. See Chap. ii, pp. 117 ff.
[2] See Chap. v, pp. 235 f.
[3] S. Pearce Carey, *William Carey*, London, 1923, p. 253.
[4] Letter from Carey to Dr Ryland, 20 January 1807, quoted in George Smith, *William Carey*, p. 190.

much retard their public usefulness".[1] A dozen years of missionary experience modified his views, and he developed such an ecumenical attitude towards other Churches that, in 1805, he proposed and urged the calling of a missionary conference "of Christians of all denominations" in 1810 at Capetown for the pooling of missionary experience on the problems common to them all. The Capetown gathering was to be succeeded by other such conferences every ten years.[2]

At the home base as well as in the field, the same unifying effect of missions was manifest. Records exist of monthly meetings for prayer and conference of the secretaries of the missionary societies in London, which began in 1819 and continued for over a hundred years. Such union meetings were then a unique phenomenon, as united prayer and conferences between Christians of different denominations were at that time deemed impossible. The impossible became the possible and natural amongst the missionary-minded.[3]

Missionary enterprise promoted contact and understanding between the Churches. The British and Foreign Bible Society, in the first ten years of its existence (1804–14), established branch societies in many European countries and supplied Bibles not only to the Lutheran and Reformed Churches, but to the Orthodox Churches in Russia and Greece, to Copts, Armenians, Abyssinians, Jacobites, and to the Syrian Church in Malabar; it had friendly relations with many Patriarchs and ecclesiastics in all these ancient Eastern Churches. The Society co-operated also with Roman Catholics, employed them as agents, and circulated their versions of Scripture.

A missionary statesman, the John R. Mott of that day, was the medium of much of this ecumenical advance, a German, C. F. A. Steinkopf (1773–1859). After studying at Tübingen, he first became Secretary of the German Christian Fellowship[4] at Basle, then in 1801 chaplain of the German Savoy Chapel in London. He was the foreign Secretary of the Bible Society, as well as of the Religious Tract Society.[5] He travelled repeatedly all over Europe, establishing Bible Societies and recruiting young men for all existing missionary societies; he was an influential liaison officer between all European and British missionary interests. He had friends in every Church, including many Roman Catholics.

The attitude of the Protestant missionary societies towards the Orthodox and other Eastern Churches was at this period unanimously friendly and marked by an ecumenical spirit. Contact with them was eagerly sought as being the main hope for the evangelization of Moslems, Hindus, and other non-Christians. Missions should be planted among them, the Scriptures should be circulated, schools should be established, not to convert them to Protestantism (this was deliberately discountenanced),[6] but to help to purify and strengthen their faith and life, so that they might witness to Christ amongst the non-Christians.

In 1806 Claudius Buchanan (1766–1815), Anglican chaplain in Calcutta, an Evangelical of Evangelicals, visited Travancore to investigate the state of religion, and to promote the circulation of the Scriptures amongst Hindus, Jews, Roman Catholics, and Syrian Christians. He conferred with the Metropolitan of the Syrian Church, Mar Dionysius, and his clergy, on the translation of the

---

[1] William Carey, *An Enquiry into the Obligation of Christians to Use Means for the Conversion of the Heathens. In which the Religious State of the World, the Success of the Former Undertakings, and the Practicability of Further Undertakings are Considered*, Leicester, 1792, p. 84.   [2] See Chap. viii, p. 355.

[3] For later ecumenical results of missionary work, see Chap. viii, *passim*.

[4] See Chap. ii, pp. 117 ff.   [5] See p. 311.

[6] It must be noted that in the mid-century, some of these missions, chiefly American, adopted a different policy and began to build up Protestant Churches in the areas concerned.

Bible into Malayalam, on the establishment of Christian schools in every parish, and on "their disposition to a union with the English Church", though he found that such a union was not within the range of practical possibilities at that time. He believed that "Providence was about to unfold itself by dispensing the Bible throughout the East by means of this people . . . a Church possessing the Bible, and abjuring Roman corruption . . . possessing, too, an ordination with which ours is scarcely to be compared . . . what more required to make them a useful people in evangelising that dark region?"[1] Others amongst the Evangelical chaplains held the same views.

As regards the Roman Catholic Church, the Protestant missionaries of that era cultivated friendly relations with Roman Catholic missionaries and sought to learn from their experience.

The early years of the 19th century were days of *rapprochement* between the Churches to a degree that is little realized to-day. Even between Protestants and Roman Catholics the *rapprochement* was closer than it has ever been since that time. In Europe the German Christian Fellowship not only had Roman Catholics amongst its members, but one of them, a priest, Johannes Gossner, for some months acted as its secretary at Basle, many years before he left the Roman Catholic Church. In the early years of the 19th century there was a remarkable evangelical awakening amongst Roman Catholic priests in Bavaria. This was fostered in every way by the Protestant missionary group at Basle; the priests concerned were urged on no account to leave their Church but to give their message within it. In France, after Napoleon's Concordat of 1801/2, a quite new interest in union between Roman Catholics and Protestants was manifest. A number of books on union possibilities were produced: the Roman Catholic Matthieu Tabaraud in 1808 published a masterly history of reunion efforts in the previous three hundred years; Rabaut le Jeune, a French Protestant, produced a similar volume.[2]

In Ireland in 1824 the Roman Catholic Bishop of Kildare and Leighlin, Dr James Doyle, wrote a remarkable letter to the Chancellor of the Exchequer on "The Union of the Churches", which appeared in the *Dublin Evening Post*, in which he offered to resign every office he held if by so doing he could "in any way contribute to the union of my brethren and the happiness of my country". The letter created some sensation at the time, but produced no practical effort towards the union of the Churches, such as the Bishop desired. Charles Butler, a Roman Catholic lawyer in London, in 1816 published a comparative study on the various confessions, Catholic, Orthodox, and Protestant, ending with "An Essay on Reunion," in which he shows an amazingly broad-minded desire for Christian unity. He takes his stand with Nicholas Vansittart, Chancellor of the Exchequer and President of the Bible Society, in saying, "If we cannot reconcile all opinions, let us reconcile all hearts".[3]

Attack on social evils—concern in the Lord's name for the bodies as well as the souls of men—was no less characteristic of the early leaders of the Evangelical Awakening than their missionary zeal, and like that zeal it brought Christians of different Churches and nations together.

Jean Frédéric Oberlin (1740–1826)[4] is a classic instance of a Christian social

---

[1] Hugh Pearson, *Memoirs of the Rev. Claudius Buchanan*, II, *passim*.
[2] See General Bibliography (Tabaraud and Rabaut le Jeune).
[3] Charles Butler, *Confessions of Faith*, London, 1816.
[4] D. E. Stoeber, *La Vie de J.-F. Oberlin*, Paris, 1911.

reformer who promoted Christian unity. A pastor in Alsace at the time of the French Revolution, through his social and educational work and his zeal for the spread of the Scriptures (he was an ardent supporter of the British and Foreign Bible Society), he changed the barbaric conditions existing in the Ban de la Roche, and attracted wide attention. His parish was a Protestant island in the midst of Roman Catholic communes. His work and his personality succeeded in dissipating the aversion of his neighbours for "Huguenots, Lutherans, and Protestants". They came to hear him preach and to ask for Bibles: he called himself a *"catholique évangélique"*. The friendly relations which he established between Roman Catholics and Protestants have left their imprint on inter-confessional relationships in Alsace, where it is to this day not uncommon for Protestant and Roman Catholic services to be held in the same church building.

In Germany it was the children of the Awakening who initiated sorely-needed social reforms: Theodor Fliedner (1800–64), through his training of deaconesses and nurses at Kaiserswerth; J. H. Wichern (1808–81), through his work for juvenile delinquents (*Das Rauhe Haus*) at Hamburg, for combating epidemics, and for other health schemes, for prison reform; F. von Bodelschwingh (1831–1910), at a later date, through his Bielefeld institutions (Bethel). These men were internationally-minded; they visited England to study social religious work there. Wichern and others freely recognized their debt to John Howard and Elizabeth Fry. They were also ecumenically-minded. Wichern in particular was a pioneer of Christian unity and contributed to the growth of the ecumenical idea. He called to his aid men and women of goodwill in all Churches—Lutheran, Reformed, and United—and was closely connected with the two most ecumenical of Christian institutions in Germany—the *Kirchentag* (the "Diet" of the German Churches) and the *Innere Mission*. Both came into existence in the revolutionary period around 1848; both were, and were intended to be, a Christian bulwark "against atheistic Communism". Wichern appreciated fully the ecumenical significance of the *Kirchentag*, which was, to quote his words, "Not a union but a confederation of . . . the Lutheran and the Reformed confessions . . . and the United type".

The *Innere Mission*,[1] which was supported by all three confessions, sprang directly from Wichern's efforts. Appealing in 1847 to the *Kirchentag* for the foundation of the *Innere Mission*, Wichern foreshadowed the ideals of Life and Work. He was not merely concerned with helping the young, the poor, and the suffering, but with the spiritual reformation of the whole land. "The preaching of salvation to a nation which lacks it" was his famous definition of the *Innere Mission*: it became a slogan. "We need a regeneration of our fundamental conditions in State, Church, and community."[2] This is Wichern's verdict in 1847, not, as might be thought, the verdict of J. H. Oldham in 1937 at the Oxford Conference on Church, Community, and State.

The long uphill campaign, first against the slave trade and then against slavery as an institution on British territory, waged for thirty years by William Wilberforce (1759–1833), Charles Grant, Zachary Macaulay, and their friends, owed much to the group of Church of England Evangelicals, christened from its habitat "the Clapham Sect"; but "those remarkable men" of Clapham could never have attained their goal without the help and support of Methodists,

---

[1] "Home Missions" is an inadequate translation for *Innere Mission*. For its significance and for Wichern himself, see Chap. vi, p. 270, and Chap. xi, p. 509.
[2] Friedrich Oldenberg, *Johann Hinrich Wichern*, II, p. 49 and *passim*.

Quakers, and other Evangelical dissenters, "my staunchest allies", as Wilberforce called them. Quakers and other Nonconformists were already campaigning against the slave trade in the 17th century. Movements for prison reform began in England largely amongst the Quakers. John Howard (1726–90), a Congregationalist, as he travelled to investigate Continental prison conditions, found support for his ideas amongst Reformed, Lutherans, Orthodox, and Roman Catholics. So did Elizabeth Fry (1780–1845) on her visits to the Continent, while in England Evangelical clergy and laity, both men and women, rallied to her aid in her schemes for the reform of prisons.

National and international temperance and purity movements and peace societies at a somewhat later date also played their part in bringing Christians of different nations and Churches together.[1]

Were there no difficulties and hindrances to all this progress in Christian unity? Was this banding together of Christians through the Evangelical Awakening to win the world for Christ no more than the inevitable result of their personal loyalty to their common Lord? Did it come easily? A clear answer is hard to give. In Britain, for example, in the late 18th century and the early 19th, the lines between Church and Dissent were not so sharply drawn as later. "Borderland" churches existed, where it was hard to tell whether they were or were not Church of England; churchmen and dissenters frequently attended each other's services and listened to each other's preachers. Charles Simeon, though he did not love Dissent in his parish, felt no difficulty either in receiving or administering Communion in the Church of Scotland as the Established Church of that country. John Newton, after a meeting of the Baptist Association in Olney, records:

> "Yesterday ministers remaining in town breakfasted with me. We seemed all mutually pleased. I thank Thee, my Lord, that Thou hast given me a heart to love Thy People of every name: and I am willing to discover Thine image without respect of parties."[2]

This attitude persisted amongst Evangelicals, both Nonconformist and Anglican, throughout the 19th century.

On the other hand, the organization of societies was made difficult by rooted ideas and prejudices which have long since disappeared. The various Protestant denominations were convinced that they could not pray together. The Bible Society was organized in 1804 on an interdenominational basis,[3] but, incredible as it may seem, not till 1859 did the Society have prayer at its committee meetings or at its Annual Meetings. The Society wished to have Quakers on its committees, and these could not, without in their view dishonouring the Holy Spirit, be present at prearranged prayer.

It was a universally held assumption that Christians of different denominations could not meet in conference without quarrelling and intensifying their differences. When William Carey proposed the holding of a World Missionary Conference,[4] the Secretary of the Baptist Missionary Society, Andrew Fuller, turned the project down, declaring that "in a meeting of all denominations, there would be no unity, without which we had better stay at home".[5]

[1] See pp. 331 f.
[2] *Newton's Diary*, 1776, quoted in William Addison, *The English Country Parson*, London, 1947, p. 118.   [3] See p. 311.   [4] See p. 312.
[5] Letter of Andrew Fuller to William Ward, Serampore, 2 December 1806.

Unanimity in sentiment and opinion amongst delegates was regarded as a necessary prerequisite to conference. It is interesting to speculate whether this rooted opposition to interdenominational conferences was due to the fact that almost all conferences between different Churches held since the Reformation had been on questions relating to reunion, and that few if any had led to any practical result.

The unpalatable conclusion must be accepted that one feature of the Evangelical Awakening, as of other dynamic spiritual awakenings, was a tendency to create divisions or new denominations. Those to whom certain truths had become infinitely precious felt that these truths could only be defended and nurtured through separàtion. Methodism, the earliest form of the Evangelical Awakening, produced a mighty division in Protestant Christendom. The *Réveil* in Switzerland and France played its part in leading to the formation of Free Churches in several Swiss cantons and in France. It was the Evangelical ministers in the Church of Scotland whose conscience in the matter of the spiritual freedom of the Church drove them to the Disruption in 1843 and to the foundation of the Free Church of Scotland.[1]

Yet it was from these very divisions that the later leaders of the ecumenical movement emerged, such men as Merle d'Aubigné (1794–1872) in Switzerland and Adolphe Monod (1802–56) in France. New College, the Free Church College in Edinburgh, from its beginning after the Disruption, has been a centre for theological students from Hungary, Czechoslovakia, Italy, America, and all parts of the world; many of these have become leaders of ecumenical efforts in their own Churches.

Despite all these hindrances, as we look over the first quarter of the century, encouragements outweigh the difficulties. In the united missionary and social reform efforts which were the fruit of the Evangelical Awakening, there were abundant signs in many lands that the active co-operation between the members of Protestant Churches had led to the development of an ecumenical spirit. Friendly relations between Protestants and Roman Catholics had reached a more advanced stage than they ever did again within our period. But the forces making for Christian unity were scattered and lacked cohesion and self-consciousness. No movement arose to direct these forces into conscious and coherent ecumenical endeavour, and a time of reaction was at hand. The friendly 1820's were succeeded by a period of intensified denominational strife.

German Lutheranism revived its vigorous opposition to Reformed Church doctrines and practice, and attacked the "syncretism of Basle", including all Basle missionary and union activities. Instead of one united international and inter-Church effort for missions—the Basle Missionary Society—new regional societies on definitely Lutheran lines appeared all over Germany—the Hermannsburg, the Berlin, the Leipzig Missionary Societies, and so forth. There was a strong reaction against the Union introduced by the King of Prussia in 1817.[2]

The formation of the Free Churches in Switzerland and France was the source of much bitterness between them and the National Churches. In France, Protestant Church historians record "a wave of dissidence" in the 1840's, when Methodists, Baptists, Plymouth Brethren, and Congregationalists withdrew from the thin ranks of French Protestantism and formed denominations of their own.

[1] See Chap. vi, pp. 302 f.   [2] See p. 325 and Chap. vi, pp. 286 ff.

A denominational stiffening manifested itself in all quarters. *Rapprochement* between Roman Catholics and Protestants became more and more difficult. Bible Society and other forms of co-operation in Europe were suppressed by Roman Catholic authorities. This change corresponded in time with the re-establishment of the Jesuit Order in 1814 and was certainly not unconnected with it. In England agitation for Roman Catholic emancipation and what were believed to be signs of Roman Catholic aggression reawakened the English fear of popery.

In England, the reaction against unity movements showed itself in the heightening of barriers between Anglicans and Nonconformists, resulting from a vigorous campaign on the part of Nonconformists for the disestablishment of the Church of England. Thomas Binney (1798–1874), the well-known Congregational minister, in spite of his recorded conviction on the need "to seek a clear approximation of church to church, and the ultimate recognition and reunion of all", nevertheless could proclaim in a sermon:

> "It is with me . . . a matter of deep, serious, religious conviction, that the Established Church is a great national evil; that it is an obstacle to the progress of truth and godliness in the land; that it destroys more souls than it saves: and that therefore its end is to be devoutly wished by every lover of God and man."

Controversy was conducted with gloves off. The Church of England was thought of before everything else as the Establishment. The phrase was in everyone's mouth. Anglicans were known as Establishmentarians. Anglicans of all types, Evangelicals, old-fashioned High Churchmen, and Tractarians, believed firmly that Church establishment was for the welfare of the nation. The day was far distant when disestablishment would be advocated by certain Anglicans in the interests of spiritual freedom. The British Anti-State Church Association (in 1853 renamed the Liberation Society) was founded in 1844, and waged war with vigour under the able leadership of Edward Miall, editor of *The Nonconformist*. Its activities created distrust of Nonconformists, even amongst friendly and co-operative Anglicans. Bitterness increased on both sides.[1]

New denominational societies were formed as opposed to united efforts. New denominations appeared. In Scotland the evangelistic activities of the Haldane brothers resulted in the emergence of Scottish Congregationalists and Scottish Baptists. In England the "Plymouth Brethren" appeared. They were convinced that the existing Churches were useless, and wherever Brethrenism spread it roused anti-Church feeling, as well as prolific division between Open Brethren and Close Brethren. Their first leader, John Darby (1800–82), travelled widely on the Continent; division followed in his trail, and his followers are known as *les Darbistes* and *die Darbisten*. Edward Irving (1792–1834) founded the Catholic Apostolic Church. Irvingism, like Brethrenism, spread to the Continent with divisive effects, and ultimately absorbed many of those Bavarian Roman Catholic priests who had been affected by the Evangelical Awakening.[2]

Horizontal divisions, stretching across the vertical divisions of Protestantism, appeared. In England, Scotland, and wherever the Bible Society had spread in

---

[1] G. Kitson Clark, *The English Inheritance*, London, 1950, pp. 125 f., and specially Chap. viii.
[2] See p. 313. It is to be noted, however, that the aims of Edward Irving, though not the consequences of his work, were consciously ecumenical and inclusive.

Europe, its activities were hindered by violent controversy as to whether it should or should not circulate the Apocrypha. Varied theories on the interpretation of prophecy had a markedly divisive effect.

All this reaction against Christian unity led to a counter-reaction in its favour.

3. THE EVANGELICAL ALLIANCE

Signs of this new demand for unitive action appeared on all sides, in many quarters, and in many lands. Numerous books on the subject of Christian union appeared in the 1830's and 1840's both in America and Britain. Typical was *Essays on Christian Union*, produced in Scotland in 1845, definitely in connection with the demand for an "evangelical alliance" of some sort, and in preparation for it. All these books show serious and earnest study on questions of unity and reunion. Earlier plans for reunion are analysed to discover why they failed. New plans are suggested. Some of these have a very modern sound. Is not the World Conference on Faith and Order foreshadowed by the man who writes: "The plan for friendly conferences on points which have divided the friends of religion holds out the nearer prospect of healing breaches, and restoring unity to . . . a divided Church" ?[1]

The continent of Europe, the United States, Scotland, and England, all claim that the idea of an evangelical alliance originated in their area. All can make out a good case.

From Germany, Dean Kniewel of Danzig in 1842 made extensive tours in England, France, Belgium, and Switzerland to get into touch with the leaders of the Churches and to propose to them "the foundation of a spiritual union amongst all those who in all lands are fighting for God's holy cause and for the pure Gospel". This union was to take the shape of a "Christian federative state, in a form similar to the North American States or the Union of German States", in which no one confession was to be dominant but each was to be free to develop and grow in its own territory.[2]

In the mid 1830's Dr Merle d'Aubigné and others at Geneva tried to institute a fraternal confederation amongst the Swiss Churches; while in France, at Lyons, what would now be called a "union church" was formed, embracing French Reformed Protestants, Methodists, Baptists, and others.

From America came a vigorous and strongly Protestant impetus which helped to precipitate the calling of the first conference of the Evangelical Alliance. Dr Patton, a Presbyterian minister, in 1845 wrote, with the backing of other leaders, to John Angell James (1785–1859), the well-known Congregational leader in England, proposing a convention of delegates from all Evangelical Churches of the Continent, of America, of Scotland, Ireland, etc., to meet in London, to "lift up a standard against papal and prelatical arrogance and assumption, and to embody the great essential doctrines which are held in common by all Protestants".

Scotland played a weighty part. Thomas Chalmers (1780–1847) and certain other leaders amongst the men of the Disruption made common cause in the interests of Christian unity with other Presbyterian bodies in Scotland. They did not a little to bring about the Evangelical Alliance through a letter to evangelical Christians in England, urging that in October 1845 a conference of representa-

---

[1] *Essays on Christian Union*, London and Edinburgh, 1845, p. 509.
[2] *Reiseskizzen von Dr T. F. Kniewel*, Leipzig, 1843, *passim*.

tives of Evangelical Churches should be held at Liverpool to prepare for a larger conference, where some sort of definite union amongst Evangelical Churches might be founded. This letter had much influence, but in honesty it should be recorded that they had been requested to send it by brethren from various Churches in England who thought that a proposal from Scottish Churches would be more likely to have effect than an appeal from any one Church in England.

In England a number of meetings with the object of promoting an alliance were held. Congregationalists took a lead in this matter, and such an alliance was first suggested by Angell James at a meeting of the Congregational Union in 1842. The idea discussed at that time was that a union should be formed amongst Churches "holding the voluntary system" (i.e. Nonconformist Churches), with the object of combating Infidelity and (three interesting "Ps") Popery, Puseyism, and Plymouth Brethrenism. Wiser counsels prevailed, and a meeting of people of many denominations, including the Church of England, was convened on 1 June 1843 at Exeter Hall; such was the enthusiasm that 12,000 tickets were issued and thousands who had secured them were turned away.

Two very different ideals of the kind of union to be aimed at had appeared amongst those who were advocating some sort of evangelical alliance. The one was a union of individual Christians belonging to different Churches. The other, to use the phraseology of the time, was "co-operation immediately, with a view to incorporation afterwards". This was the ideal of Thomas Chalmers, and meant a *rapprochement* amongst the Churches as such. Chalmers indeed went far and confessed himself "sanguine of union even still more comprehensive than that which we are immediately aiming at, and by which not only the smaller but the larger differences of the Christian world will at length be harmonised". In other words, he envisaged ultimate union with Rome and the East.[1]

It seems evident from the above account that the weight of opinion amongst those seriously considering the question was in favour of some kind of union or at least federation between the Churches as such. It was, however, the idea of a union amongst Christian individuals of different Churches that was actually embodied in the constitution of the Evangelical Alliance. The decision for an individual Christian membership as opposed to a federation or union of Churches was taken at the preparatory conference in Liverpool (1–3 October 1845).[2]

At length, August 1846 saw the remarkable gathering which founded the Evangelical Alliance. Though held in London, it was both international and inter-Church; 800 Christian leaders assembled from the United States and Canada, England, Scotland, Ireland, Wales, France, Switzerland, Holland, Germany, and Sweden. Ten per cent of the delegates came from America, surely an amazing number, considering the travel conditions of the time. Six per cent came from the Continent. The delegates belonged to no less than fifty-two different branches of the Church of Christ. It was a meeting of remarkable enthusiasm, hailed as if it were the beginning of the Millennium, spoken of by delegates as the crowning moment of their lives. In contrast it is somewhat of a shock to read the severely measured terms of the actual resolution passed when the Alliance was founded:

[1] *Essays on Christian Union*, p. 17.
[2] *Brief Statement of the Procedure of the Conference in Liverpool for Promoting Christian Union and of the Object of the Proposed Evangelical Alliance*, Liverpool, 1845.

"That members of this Conference are deeply convinced of the desirableness of forming a Confederation, on the basis [1] of great evangelical principles held in common by them, which may afford opportunity to members of the Church of Christ of cultivating brotherly love, enjoying Christian intercourse, and promoting such other objects as they may hereafter agree to prosecute together; and they hereby proceed to form such a Confederation, under the name of 'THE EVANGELICAL ALLIANCE'."

That this was all may be taken as a measure of the real difficulties which had been faced and overcome, of the real triumph achieved. Dr Edward Steane, the first Secretary of the Alliance (an honorary office), a Baptist minister, wrote of the Conference:

"It has required incessant thoughtfulness and the most watchful care lest an indiscreet word spoken or sentence written should wound the sensitiveness or offend the prejudices of the curiously mixed and balanced ideas of which our association is composed—Churchmen and Dissenters, Presbyterians and Methodists, Establishmentarians and Voluntaries."

National susceptibilities demanded no less consideration than denominational. The Americans complained that the British had settled important questions in advance before the Conference, without waiting to know American opinion, for example concerning the basis to be adopted. The American delegation, moreover, nearly left the Conference when the British brought up the question of whether slave-holders could be admitted to membership of the Alliance. The Germans felt they had occasion to complain,[2] as indeed they have often done since after later ecumenical gatherings, that owing to their lack of fluency in English the German point of view was ignored and never effectively presented; moreover, that all the proceedings and decisions were dominated by American and British methods and points of view.

But despite all difficulties and obstacles, the reality of Christian unity had at last found a corporate expression. The Evangelical Alliance was there. It was the one and only definitely ecumenical organization (its founders, it should be noted, not seldom employed the term "ecumenical") which arose out of the Evangelical Awakening in the 19th century. As such it is of great significance. Both its

[1] The Basis of the Evangelical Alliance adopted in 1846 was as follows: "That the parties composing the Alliance shall be such persons only as hold and maintain what are usually understood to be Evangelical views, in regard to the matters of Doctrine understated, namely: (1) The Divine Inspiration, Authority, and Sufficiency of the Holy Scriptures. (2) The Right and Duty of Private Judgement in the Interpretation of the Holy Scriptures. (3) The Unity of the Godhead, and the Trinity of Persons therein. (4) The utter Depravity of Human Nature, in consequence of the Fall. (5) The Incarnation of the Son of God, His work of Atonement for sinners of mankind, and His Mediatorial Intercession and Reign. (6) The Justification of the sinner by Faith alone. (7) The work of the Holy Spirit in the Conversion and Sanctification of the sinner. (8) The Immortality of the Soul, the Resurrection of the Body, the Judgement of the World by our Lord Jesus Christ, with the Eternal Blessedness of the Righteous, and the Eternal Punishment of the Wicked. (9) The Divine institution of the Christian Ministry, and the obligation and perpetuity of the ordinances of Baptism and the Lord's Supper.

"It is, however, distinctly declared: First, that this brief Summary is not to be regarded, in any formal or Ecclesiastical sense, as a Creed or Confession, nor the adoption of it as involving an assumption of the right authoritatively to define the limits of Christian Brotherhood; but simply as an indication of the class of persons whom it is desirable to embrace within the Alliance: Second, that the selection of certain tenets, with the omission of others, is not to be held as implying, that the former constitute the whole body of important Truth, or that the latter are unimportant."

[2] J. W. Massie, *The Evangelical Alliance*, London, 1847, p. 416; see also Chap. ix, p. 417.

strength and its weakness deserve careful study in their relation to the growth of the ecumenical idea.

The Alliance, from the first, produced certain remarkable and far-reaching results.

It stimulated united prayer. Its most characteristic achievement is the setting aside each year of a week for united prayer, beginning on the first Sunday in the year. For a hundred years it has issued a "call to prayer to Christians over all the world", with the backing of many leaders of the Churches. Without question, the week of prayer has caused Christians of different Churches all over the world to realize that they are one in Christ, and has stimulated their sense of unity. In many a Swiss village, for example, this was the one time in the year when members of the National Church, the Free Church, the *Darbistes* (Plymouth Brethren), and other sects, realized that although they were divided, sometimes bitterly, over certain questions, they were nevertheless one in a common Lord.

The annual celebration of this week of prayer once and for all disposed of the widely-held belief that even evangelical Christians belonging to different Churches could not conscientiously pray together. The Alliance laid the greatest stress on united prayer. When it was pointed out to the leaders that Clause 9 in their Basis excluded Quakers and Plymouth Brethren from membership in the Alliance, the leaders replied that they realized this, but that they were not prepared to pay the same price as the Bible Society had done in order to secure Quakers as members:[1] they were determined to be free to have "social prayer".

Its international conferences were something new in Church history. The Alliance was an international organization from the day of its foundation, though the title "*World's* Evangelical Alliance" was not adopted until the 20th century. The Alliance was not indeed the first organization to hold international conferences. That honour must go to the Peace and Anti-Slavery Societies. The first General Peace Convention was held in London in June 1843, and brought together 150 delegates from America, Britain, and the Continent.[2] It was immediately preceded by a conference of the British and Foreign Anti-Slavery Society. But the international conferences of the Evangelical Alliance, through their size, character, and representative nature, were of the greatest importance in stimulating a sense of unity amongst Christians of different nations and Churches. These conferences were held every few years at strategic points and for strategic reasons—in London, 1851, for example, on the occasion of the Great Exhibition; in New York, 1873, after the end of the Civil War. All these conferences brought together speakers of different Churches on a Christian international platform and often on a platform that was wider than that of the Alliance itself. They were always the occasion for an elaborate and careful survey of the religious life of the world—surveys which are of great historical value.

It was a powerful instrument of international Christian education through its journals in different countries. *Evangelical Christendom*, the magazine of the British organization, was the Ecumenical Press Service of its day. Though its information was often given with a certain bias, for many years it provided more and wider information about the Churches and religious conditions in different countries than can be found in any ecumenical journal to-day. For

[1] See p. 315.
[2] *The Proceedings of the First General Peace Convention*, London Peace Society's Office, 1843.

example, its files for two or three years in the 1860's contain important series of articles—on the Mennonites; on the Lutheran Churches of Scandinavia; on the Universities of Germany, religiously considered; on the Armenian Church; on the Waldensians; on the Churches in Holland; and a long series on South America: besides individual articles on the Maronites; on Johann Arndt; on the Abbey of Lokkum; and on the Jerusalem Bishopric.

It was a powerful advocate of Missions. It would be difficult to exaggerate the services of the Alliance to the cause of world-wide Missions; it was, for example, at the Annual Meeting of the British Alliance that the plan for the first International Missionary Conference in 1854 was mooted at a meeting presided over by Alexander Duff (1806–78), the pioneer in India of Christian educational work at the university level.

At successive Alliance conferences, a session or more was always given to the subject of Missions. A thorough survey of the missionary position in the world was usually a feature—that given by Professor Christlieb of Bonn at the Basle Conference of 1879 occupies 164 pages in the Report, and is quite masterly. Such surveys anticipate those in the *International Review of Missions*. An advanced and forward-looking policy is often advocated on questions of self-support, the indigenous Church, and, in general, on missionary comity, despite a tendency to support and encourage missions in Europe and the Near East which had for their object the conversion of Christians from one form of the Christian faith to another.[1]

It had one distinctive, strong, and continuous practical activity—the defence of religious liberty. Again and again it successfully defended oppressed religious groups and persons, and secured government action in their favour, including, be it noted, non-Protestant groups—Roman Catholics, for instance, in Russia or in Sweden, or the Nestorian Church under Moslem rule in Turkey.

There were other points, however, at which the Alliance disappointed the hopes of many of its early friends.

It ignored the relations of the Churches with each other. It was an organization of individual Christians, not of Churches. It aimed at making the "Invisible Church visible", "that the world may know", but the truth that the Invisible Church is one lacks missionary power so long as the members of the Invisible Church remain in visibly separate and competing folds. At conference after conference, the Moravians faithfully pointed to their *Tropenidee*[2] of the relation of the Churches to each other as being a higher ideal of Christian unity than that of the Alliance. Aloofness from plans for reunion might almost be said to have become an Alliance article of faith. At the greatest Conference it ever held, in New York, 1873, though it recorded Dr Samuel Schmucker's plan[3] in its report, the Alliance refused to discuss his appeal for an official confederation of the Protestant denominations, as being alien to the objects of the Alliance as "a voluntary union of individual Christians of different Churches".[4]

Its basis, or rather its doctrinal requirements for membership, were rigid. The branches of the Alliance in some countries, notably in France, reacted against these requirements from the first, and insisted on adopting a basis more like that of the "Paris Basis" of the Y.M.C.A.[5] The narrowness of its basis was one cause of the practical disappearance of its American branch in the 1890's.

[1] See p. 312, footnote 6.   [3] See Chap. ii, pp. 101 f., and Chap. vi, pp. 294 ff.
[2] See Chap. v, pp. 244 f.   [4] *Report of the E.A. Conference, 1873*, p. 742.
[5] See p. 327.

It lacked central leadership and organization. Spiritual and intellectual leaders in the Churches approved it and spoke on its platforms; strong men presided at its conferences, Sir Culling Eardley in Britain, William Dodge in America; but no John R. Mott arose to devote himself to its cause. It had no central organization whatever. Its conferences were arranged for as and when proposals were made by one or other of the national organizations. Most of the national branches of the Alliance looked to the British Alliance to take the lead in organizing the conferences; this it usually did, though not without exciting criticism from other nations. Not until the 1890's did it develop even the simplest form of central committee for arranging conferences, and then, rather curiously, on the demand not of activist America or Britain, but of Switzerland and Germany. Its secretaries were usually busy ministers. The day of full-time salaried secretaries was still far away in the 20th century.

It lacked a forward-looking programme. At its Jubilee Conference (1896) at Mildmay, London, it surveyed the accomplishments of the past half-century, but proposed no programme for the next fifty years, to the outspoken disappointment of its warm friend, Professor Lucien Gautier of Geneva. Its lack of programme lost it important support. Thomas Chalmers, in his pamphlet on its foundation in 1846, put his finger on this as its weak point and urged the Alliance to undertake a vigorous, united programme of home missions. Its lack of programme was partly due to the late date at which it appeared in the field of united endeavour, when there were already in existence interdenominational societies for promoting almost every form of Christian service—foreign missions, city missions, Bible and Tract societies, and so forth.

It gained little support from the great Protestant Churches of Germany and Scandinavia. This had something to do with its activities in the defence of religious liberty. Ecumenically considered, these had their weak side. The Alliance was always prone, sometimes perhaps uncritically, to defend the small body or sect against the national Church. Thus it tended to alienate from itself the great Protestant Churches of Europe: in 1884, for example, when it was proposed to hold the Alliance Conference in Sweden, most of the bishops of the Swedish Lutheran Church took measures to prevent the holding of the Conference in their country, on the ground of its close connection with "the sects which were hostile to them". It was held in Copenhagen instead.

It pursued incompatible objectives. From its beginning it combined the aim of uniting Christians in the bonds of brotherly love with the aim of combating popery and Puseyism. Throughout its history it has been outspokenly anti-Roman Catholic. Its ardent friend in the Church of Scotland, Norman Macleod, felt obliged at the London Conference in 1851 to enter a plea that "even Roman Catholics should be addressed in a spirit of kindness and love". It was strongly hostile in its attitude to certain groups. This made for its success with other groups, for it is an unfortunate trait in human psychology, even amongst Christians, that in propaganda attack makes a stronger appeal than constructive proposals. It is interesting to note that this negative tendency was deplored by some speakers in the initial debates on the objects of the Alliance during the preparatory conference at Liverpool.[1]

With all its strength and weakness, the Alliance holds a unique place in the history of 19th-century ecumenism, for with the exception of the Association for the Promotion of the Unity of Christendom,[2] no other society of Christians

[1] J. W. Massie, *The Evangelical Alliance*, p. 117.   [2] See p. 347, and Chap. vi, pp. 278 f.

belonging to different Churches was founded for the express purpose of working towards Christian unity, until the idea of the World Conference on Faith and Order was first mooted in 1910.

Here let us pause to register the evidences which can be traced during these fifty years of the growth of the ecumenical idea and of progress made towards Christian union. We have seen thrown on the screen of Church history:

First, the development of one of the most powerful and dynamic missionary movements the world has ever seen—a movement which early proved itself a force making for co-operation and unity between Christians of different Churches.

Secondly, the coming into being of a new thing in Church history—a definite organization for the expression of unity amongst Christian individuals belonging to different Churches, namely the Evangelical Alliance.

Thirdly, the development of a sense of "togetherness" amongst a large body of Christian people of many different nationalities and Churches. They had learnt to feel themselves one in Christ, across national and ecclesiastical boundaries, had banded themselves together in voluntary societies, and had come to look upon co-operation with each other in the service of their Lord as a normal and joyful part of the Christian life. Christians conscious of this "togetherness" became the volunteer reserve force of ecumenism. When the call came at length in 1910 to spend and be spent in the ecumenical movement, such men and women were a prepared group. As Eugene Stock, editor and historian of the C.M.S., speaking for Church of England Evangelicals, reminded the Anglo-Catholics at the World Missionary Conference in Edinburgh, 1910: "We have been accustomed all along to enter into common conference and co-operation with our separated brethren."

Fourthly, an increasing demand for a drawing together of the Churches as such. In the latter half of the century, this movement of *rapprochement* between the Churches had an increasing record of accomplishment.

4. VOLUNTARY MOVEMENTS IN THE SECOND HALF-CENTURY: TENSIONS AND TENDENCIES

The second half of the 19th century was marked by many changes in the ecumenical climate. The growth of the ecumenical idea and the progress made towards Christian union were conditioned by, and can only be understood in their relation to, several factors which we shall study successively:

(1) Tensions between differing ideals of Christian unity.

(2) Continued ecumenical results from the voluntary movements associated with the Evangelical Awakening.

(3) The gradual infiltration of the ecumenical idea into wider circles in the Churches and in the nations.

(4) The appearance towards the end of the period of certain new conceptions of Christian unity and of the means by which it may be attained. These new conceptions created the atmosphere which made possible the Edinburgh World Missionary Conference of 1910, and the emergence therefrom of the International Missionary Council, Faith and Order, Life and Work, and of the ecumenical movement as we know it to-day.

Throughout this period progress towards Christian union was conditioned and hindered by theological differences amongst those who with equal sincerity were aiming at union amongst Christians. Different conceptions of the nature of Christian unity and of the paths by which it might be reached came unfortunately to be associated with different schools of theological thought, and became involved in their disagreements, to the great detriment of ecumenical advance. As we have seen, in the 17th and 18th centuries[1] there was a constant tension between two ideals of the path to Christian union which may be roughly described as "Unity in truth" and "Unity in Christian fellowship". These ideals need not be contrary the one to the other, but as emphasis is laid on one or the other, different types of approach inevitably develop.

Protestantism in the 19th century in the Lutheran and in the Reformed Churches of the continent of Europe was profoundly affected by the spirit of the Enlightenment. Similar tendencies appeared in Britain and in America. On the one hand, in many quarters influenced by the rational or rationalistic canons of the Enlightenment, the ideas of the supernatural, of grace and redemption, were almost wholly eliminated from Christian preaching and thought. On the other hand, this produced in certain quarters in the Churches a strong reaction against the influence of the Enlightenment, a stiffening of confessional consciousness, and an insistence on rigid orthodoxy.

In the matter of Christian union, these strong confessional movements naturally regarded emphasis on a certain understanding of truth or on the acceptance of certain sharply defined confessional systems as the indispensable basis of any approach to unity. This brought them into collision with the type of approach which had developed in those voluntary movements which we have been studying, in which disagreement in matters of doctrine was not allowed to impede co-operative action or fellowship, and in which the bond of unity was the common sharing of a certain type of Christian experience.

Those who insisted on unity in truth as the only path to Christian union could not but oppose what they regarded as the compromising disloyalty to truth and the woolly-headed or sentimental character of the type of ecumenism based on unity in fellowship and on a common Christian experience. The way in which the convictions of the unity-in-truth school of thought affected ecumenical progress may be seen in different areas.

The attempt to force through the Prussian Union of 1817 led to a strong reaction amongst conservative Lutherans and to the formation of the Evangelical Lutheran Church, and impeded certain promising moves towards Christian unity through voluntary organizations.[2] This Lutheran reaction in Prussia had marked results in the United States. A number of conservative Lutherans left Prussia for the freer air of America, and there organized in 1847 the German Evangelical Synod of Missouri, Ohio, and Other States. This body under its later name—the Lutheran Church (Missouri Synod)—is one of the largest and strongest Lutheran bodies in America, and has proved a serious obstacle to union even amongst Lutherans. It has taken up a rigidly confessional and unco-operative position on the basis of all the Lutheran symbolic books, and refuses to enter into any kind of co-operation or union with the World Council or any other body, such as would in its view compromise the revelation of truth which it has received through the Holy Scriptures in their Lutheran interpretation.

[1] See Chap. ii, *passim*, and Chap. v, pp. 228 ff.
[2] See Chap. vi, pp. 287 f.

In the Netherlands the Dutch Reformed Church had suffered almost more than any other under the influence of the rationalist tradition and had lost much of its Calvinistic and confessional character. This led to the withdrawal from the Church of various bodies which laid stress on unity in truth. In 1886, under the leadership of Abraham Kuyper (1837–1920), a large number left the Dutch Reformed Church to form the Reformed Churches (*Gereformeerde Kerken*), based on a rigid and Calvinistic understanding of the Scriptures. This body of orthodox Reformed Churches, which has now a membership of 700,000, refuses all co-operation with the Ecumenical Council of the Netherlands and other unitive movements and organizations.[1]

In Britain sharp tension developed between the Anglo-Catholic party in the Church of England and Evangelicals of all types in the matter of ideals of Christian unity. The Anglo-Catholic school in all matters connected with reunion insisted on unity in truth. Truth meant for them firm adherence to Anglican doctrine as they understood it, including a determined insistence on their own view of the ministry and the sacraments, and in particular on a rigid and exclusive theory of apostolic succession. They regarded all Protestants and Nonconformists as in the ranks of heretics, and saw possibilities for reunion only in the opposite direction—with the Church of Rome and with the Orthodox Churches of the East. They looked with grave suspicion on all interdenominational movements towards unity. They had a rooted idea (a groundless assumption so far as Evangelical movements were concerned) that movements uniting members of different Churches must inevitably be based on indifference to or surrender of truth, on "doctrines on which all could agree", on a Highest Common Factor which must inevitably lead to liberalism or unbelief.

The Evangelical school of thought, on the other hand, while laying emphasis on the need for unity on great Christian fundamentals (their orthodoxy was as rigid as that of the Anglo-Catholics), stood for the ideal of unity in Christian fellowship, and, on the basis of a conviction that they shared the life in Christ, found it possible to work with those with whom they were not in complete doctrinal agreement. The Evangelicals as a whole were profoundly suspicious of the motives and actions of Anglo-Catholics. They tended to condemn Anglo-Catholic moves in any direction as "Romanizing", and the interest of the Anglo-Catholic party in reunion with Rome roused in them the Englishman's easily awakened fear of popery.

This tension between Anglo-Catholic and Evangelical ideals of Christian unity had far-reaching consequences; although it had its rise in England, it was felt throughout the English-speaking world and also in the Christian communities founded by British and American missionary societies in Africa and the East, with results in slowing down ecumenical action in the mission-field.

Looking back from the standpoint of 1948 and the Amsterdam Assembly of the World Council of Churches, it is easy to see that the ideals of Christian unity so long associated with warring parties and schools of thought are not hostile but complementary ideals. Unity in truth and unity in Christian fellowship are both necessary constituents in any true Christian unity. If ever real Christian union is to be attained, it must be sought along both paths of approach —*rapprochement* between Churches as such, and movements of co-operation and fellowship between individual Christians of different confessions. But these lessons learned from forty years of united ecumenical endeavour were hidden

[1] See Chap. xiii, pp. 627 f.

from the gaze of sincere lovers of unity in the 19th century who, with equal sincerity, pursued unity along different paths.

In the 1840's and 1850's arose two movements which were destined perhaps more than any other results of the Evangelical Awakening to prepare for and affect the course of the modern ecumenical movement. The two great Christian youth movements, the Young Men's Christian Association and the Young Women's Christian Association, were founded in England in 1844 and 1854 respectively. Both movements spread quickly to America, where they underwent enormous developments, and soon extended all over the world. Leap over a hundred years and study the World Council of Churches' platform at Amsterdam and other such ecumenical assemblies; four-fifths of those assembled on these platforms probably owed their ecumenical inspiration to some connection with the Y.M.C.A., with the Y.W.C.A., or with the closely-connected Student Christian Movement. John R. Mott began his ecumenical career as a Y.M.C.A. secretary, as did W. A. Visser 't Hooft. None of these three organizations originally registered amongst its specific aims the bringing together of Christians of different Churches or the promoting of *rapprochement* between the Churches as such, though it is recorded of young George Williams that when he was discussing the foundation of the Y.M.C.A. with three other young men in the drapery business, he exclaimed, "Here we are, an Episcopalian, a Methodist, a Baptist, and a Congregationalist—four believers but a single faith in Christ. Forward together!"

Certain Y.M.C.A. pioneers undoubtedly perceived the ecumenical possibilities of the Association; above all Henri Dunant of Geneva, Switzerland, founder of the Red Cross, and intimately connected with the founding of the Y.M.C.A. In March 1855, before the first international Y.M.C.A. conference in Paris, Dunant wrote to the Associations of the whole world in the name of the Geneva Association, that their aim must be "to spread abroad that ecumenical spirit which transcends nationalities, languages, denominations, ecclesiastical problems, ranks, and occupations: to realize in a word, and as far as possible, that article in the Creed which we all of us adhere to: 'I believe in the Communion of Saints and in the Holy Catholic Church'." Not a few of the early leaders were deeply concerned about the unity of the world Christian community, and sought to create among laymen and clergy a sense of Christian community through the experience of thinking and working together on common Christian tasks. But for the most part the early leaders of the Y.M.C.A. and Y.W.C.A. were indifferent to ecclesiastical questions and to the relations of Churches. Neither the Y.M.C.A. nor the Y.W.C.A. before 1910 displayed that overwhelming interest in ecumenical questions and activities that has characterized them later.[1] Wherein, then, has lain the peculiar power of these movements to produce ecumenical leadership?

Like earlier evangelical movements, they were wholeheartedly evangelistic and missionary. The so-called Paris Basis of the Y.M.C.A., adopted in 1855, expresses their attitude:

> "The Young Men's Christian Association seeks to unite those young men who, regarding Jesus Christ as their God and Saviour, according to the Holy Scriptures, desire to be His disciples in their faith and in their life, and to associate their efforts for the extension of His Kingdom amongst young men."

[1] See Chap. xiii, pp. 599–612.

They were consciously and convincedly international. No officer's or merchant's wife abroad, if she had been a member of the Y.W.C.A. at home, was content till she had brought into existence a Y.W.C.A. in the land where her lot was cast. Both organizations developed into world movements. Contact with every nation meant contact with every Church. Their pioneer secretaries in every land sought allies in the cause of youth amongst the leaders of the Churches; in this way knowledge of the various Churches began to seep through from one land to another. They specialized in international conferences and worked out a technique for their success and efficiency. This technique is one of their great gifts to the Church and to the ecumenical cause.

They early and persistently turned their faces towards the East and Africa. American and European secretaries gloried in finding and training Oriental leaders, and in working with them and under them. Perhaps more than any other movement they have been used to reveal the significance of the younger Churches to the older. V. S. Azariah (1874–1945), the first Indian Anglican bishop, went almost *per saltum* from the Y.M.C.A. secretariat to the episcopate.

They realized the strategic importance of the student world. The Y.M.C.A. and the Y.W.C.A. in North America early entered the universities and colleges and organized the Student Departments of the Y.M.C.A. and Y.W.C.A. The leaders of these Student Departments, John R. Mott and others, had a large share in bringing into being student Christian movements in many lands, sometimes as student departments of the two Associations, sometimes under other names. But whatever their origin and under whatever name they function, the membership of the student Christian movements has produced a remarkably high proportion of the leaders of the ecumenical movement.

Other world youth movements, or movements on behalf of youth, developed later—for example, the young people's society known as Christian Endeavour, the World's Sunday School Association (known since 1947 as the World Council of Christian Education)[1]—and in their international conferences brought Christians of different denominations together. But as their activities were centred in the local church they afforded less opportunity for ecumenical education than the two earlier movements.

Three features in the missionary history of this period deserve detailed notice because of their close relation to the growth of the ecumenical idea.

No voluntary movement has been more powerful in its effects in drawing the Churches together than the Student Volunteer Movement for Foreign Missions.[2] Beginning at the first student Christian conference in 1886 at Mount Hermon, Massachusetts, when a hundred students banded themselves together by a pledge to become missionaries overseas,[3] the movement spread rapidly through North America, Britain, and the Dominions, and through the universities of Europe. By 1945, at the most conservative estimate, 20,500 students from so-called Christian lands, who had signed the declaration, reached the field, for the most part under the missionary societies and boards of the Churches.

The Student Volunteer Movement, the missionary wing of the Student

[1] See Chap. xiii, p. 612.
[2] Ruth Rouse, *World's Student Christian Federation*, Chap. viii, "The Federation and the World-Wide Mission of the Church".
[3] At Mount Hermon the students declared themselves "Willing and desirous, God permitting, to become foreign missionaries". This was later modified to "It is my purpose, if God permit, to become a foreign missionary".

Christian Movement, had a peculiar power to knit together its members in the close fellowship of their common and mighty adventure. This fellowship soon came to have results in Christian unity. A. T. Polhill-Turner, one of the Cambridge Seven,[1] the first Secretary of the British Student Volunteer Missionary Union, in 1893 records his vision of its ecumenical future:

> "It aims at banding together all students whose hearts are stirred up by the Holy Spirit to obey our Master's parting command to take the Gospel to every creature. . . . Feeling the pulse of Christian students where I have visited, I have found that they seem just ripe for such a movement, welding into one Union our students—Episcopalian, Presbyterian, Wesleyan, Baptist and Methodist alike—united into a brotherhood hitherto thought impossible, all one in Christ Jesus."[2]

The inspiration of the S.V.M. was powerful in the Church at large, especially through the influence of its great quadrennial conferences in America, Britain, and Germany. It produced a number of kindred movements at the home base which have united men and women of different Churches in a close bond—such as volunteer movements amongst teachers, nurses, etc., the Missionary Study Movements in America and Britain, the Laymen's Missionary Movement, and so forth.

Dr Mott, speaking in 1911 at the twenty-fifth anniversary of the founding of the S.V.M. at Mount Hermon, traced the way in which this movement had taught the Church a new attitude and had led up to and made possible the Edinburgh World Missionary Conference of 1910:

> "The Edinburgh Conference has familiarized Christians of our day with this idea of looking steadily at the world as a whole, of confronting the world as a unit by the Christian Church as a unit. It was not so twenty-five years ago."[3]

To one missionary leader at the home base, a new vision of missionary unity to come was granted in this period. Here, as not seldom, the prophet came from Germany. Gustav Warneck (1834–1910) of Halle, one of the greatest authorities on missions in his own day, laid before the third International Missionary Conference, meeting in London in 1888, proposals which were a veritable blue print for the International Missionary Council.[4] His proposals included a Standing Central International Committee with its headquarters in London, to consist of the representatives of Protestant missionary societies elected by National Missionary Conferences which were to be established in every land. (A Conference of German Missionary Societies had already been established in 1885.) Amongst its functions were to be the regular publication of general missionary statements, the holding of regular decennial missionary conferences, the putting forward of proposals for united action by missionary societies at home or abroad, and the settlement of questions in dispute between missions. It was presented to an unheeding Church. Warneck could not be present at the Conference himself. The plan was printed in the report, but was not discussed at the Conference. Twenty-two years were to pass before Warneck's plan began to be realized at the Edinburgh Conference of 1910.

[1] See p. 331.   [2] Tatlow, *The Story of the Student Christian Movement*, pp. 37 f.
[3] Rouse, *W.S.C.F.*, p. 97.
[4] *Report of the Missionary Conference, London, 1888*, II, p. 437.

During this period two new groups of missionary societies appeared, both of which presented certain difficulties to the growth of ecumenism.

The Anglo-Catholic awakening in this period produced a new and vigorous group of societies—the Universities' Mission to Central Africa, the Oxford Mission to Calcutta, the Cambridge Mission to Delhi, and others—besides bringing new strength to the oldest Anglican missionary societies, the S.P.C.K. and the S.P.G. Certain Anglo-Catholic leaders, after contact in the mission-field with men of other Churches and other societies, developed strong ecumenical sympathies and became leaders in union efforts (Henry Whitehead, Bishop of Madras 1899–1923, was an outstanding example); but as a whole these societies held aloof from co-operative effort. It was not until the Edinburgh Conference of 1910 that this group of societies, by deciding to take part in that gathering, began to play a rôle in the ecumenical movement.[1]

Another feature of this period was the formation of a number of undenominational societies, usually founded to reach some great unevangelized area: examples are the China Inland Mission, the South Africa General Mission, the North Africa Mission; in the United States, the Christian and Missionary Alliance; in Germany, the Neukirchen China Allianz, the Liebenzell Mission, and others. Such missions present ecumenical opportunities and problems. They bring the members of different denominations into fellowship and common endeavour; their success in evangelism is undoubted. But they are often unwilling, usually on theological grounds, to enter National Missionary or Christian Councils; and so soon as the time comes when the Church must be built up from converts they have won, they are confronted with questions of order, difficult of solution where the missionaries are drawn from many different Churches.

In the Evangelical Awakening in the second half of the 19th century, as in the first, there was concern for evangelism at home as well as overseas. Prayer for the Holy Spirit was answered by times of revival, and men were raised up who had a message of converting power. Revival is an international phenomenon; it is rarely confined to one nation. The revival which came to Scotland in the late 1850's spread to England, Wales, and Ireland. It was fostered by visits from American evangelists, Charles Finney and D. L. Moody. It had repercussions across Europe from France to Finland, and was carried by Lord Radstock into Russia. It has been christened the Second Evangelical Awakening.[2] In Britain clergy and laity from all the Churches and from most parties within the Churches joined hands in these revival efforts. (Anglo-Catholics and the more radical elements in Nonconformity for divers reasons stood aloof.) Their objective was not conversion only, but membership in the Churches, and tens of thousands of new members were gathered in: this had the ecumenical effect of strengthening the confidence of Church leaders in united work. In happy contrast to certain earlier revivals, this second great awakening produced no new sects or schisms.

The classic instance of an international revival with marked ecumenical consequences is a Student Christian Movement saga, the story of revival passing backwards and forwards across the Atlantic as a result of the work of the great evangelist Dwight L. Moody. With his companion Ira D. Sankey, the American

[1] See Chap. viii, pp. 357, 360.
[2] J. Edwin Orr, *The Second Evangelical Awakening*, London, 1949.

evangelist came to Britain in 1873 and again in 1882; on both visits his most distinctive work was done amongst students. On his first visit he roused the University of Edinburgh, and discovered and called to his aid a young theological student, Henry Drummond, destined to become the most powerful student evangelist yet seen and to touch the students of many lands. In Moody's meetings at Cambridge in 1882 leading oarsmen and cricketers were profoundly influenced —the Studds and Stanley Smith. Their group became known as the Cambridge Seven. They went out under the China Inland Mission, but before their going they gave the call to Christ and to the mission-field in the universities of Britain and America. J. E. K. Studd, while holding evangelistic meetings at Cornell University in the United States, was the means of bringing one student in particular to decision for the Christian life. That man was John R. Mott, the inspirer and founder of the World's Student Christian Federation, who carried the message of Christ back again across the Atlantic to students of Europe and throughout the world—the man who, if any deserves the title, may be called the pioneer of the modern ecumenical movement.

Social reform movements developed in many countries of Europe during this period. These movements, and their unitive influence in Germany, France, Switzerland, Sweden, and America, are dealt with elsewhere in this History.[1]

In Britain, as an accompaniment of the second Evangelical Awakening, important welfare societies came into existence, such as Dr Barnardo's Homes and Sir Wilfred Grenfell's Mission to Labrador. This is the period of the rise of the Salvation Army through the insight and genius of Catherine and William Booth —that international movement at once profoundly and fundamentally evangelistic and at the same time practically concerned with the physical and social needs of men and women. Some deplore the fact that instead of working out its ideals in co-operation with all the Churches the Salvation Army has itself become a denomination.

This, too, was the era of the first great attack on *laisser-faire* economic doctrines and on their ghastly fruit in the exploitation of women and children in factories and mines. Lord Shaftesbury was upheld in his long and weary struggle in Parliament by a simple evangelical faith; his was, however, an individual effort, not supported to the extent he could have wished by his fellow Evangelicals or by the Churches as such.

A strong impetus to social reform and at the same time to Christian unity came from the Broad Churchmen. Maurice and Kingsley translated their faith into terms of social reform in "the Christian Socialists", Working Men's Colleges, and Co-operative Movements. Later on, the Cambridge group of scholars, Westcott and others, combined with certain Anglo-Catholic leaders— Canon (later Bishop) Gore and Canon H. Scott Holland—to found the Christian Social Union and the Industrial Christian Fellowship, both Anglican organizations. But these leaders were not content without the fellowship of other Christians; they desired and sought Free Church and Roman Catholic co-operation, and did much to bring into being the Interdenominational Social Service Council with its epoch-making interdenominational conferences at Swanwick.[2] Gore was foreshadowing Life and Work when he wrote:

"Some of us . . . felt that, while denominational societies must convert their own bodies, there was needed a fellowship of all the religious bodies

[1] See Chap. xi, pp. 510 f.   [2] See Chap. xi, p. 510.

which name the name of Christ. . . . The 'Christian Social Crusade' seeks
to form and affiliate to one another interdenominational agencies, whereby
the sundered portions of the Christian Church may learn to act as one body
in the task of public social and moral witness."

There was a deep concern that Christians should glorify God in practical,
everyday life. Faith must sanctify as well as justify. In Germany this concern
found expression for the most part in the *Gemeinschaftsbewegung* (Fellowship
Movement), a 19th-century successor and heir of 18th-century Pietism. Throughout Germany within the existing Churches informal groups of men and women
met to seek a deeper spiritual life through prayer and Bible study. They were not
separatists; they looked upon their groups as *ecclesiolae in ecclesia*. The movement was in no way organized or centralized, but formed a natural network of
communication through which spiritual inspiration passed from group to group
and from land to land.

In Britain and America, satisfaction of the same yearning was sought in conventions such as those of Keswick and Mildmay. These conventions gathered
together without distinction speakers and hearers from all Churches. This again
was an international movement. The inspiration of "Keswick", founded in the
1870's, spread to other lands: Germany had its Blankenburg, Switzerland its
Morges. The platform, too, was international; the South African Dutch Reformed minister Andrew Murray, the German Dr Baedeker, were everywhere
welcome. The motto over the Keswick platform is "All One in Christ Jesus":
something of the meaning of that unity should have come home to Anglicans
who received a message of transforming power in their lives from the Baptist
F. B. Meyer, or the Presbyterian George MacGregor; or to Baptists or Plymouth
Brethren who learned some secret of victory over sin from the Anglican Handley
Moule. No direct move, however, towards the union of the Churches has resulted
from Keswick.

The Mildmay Conference was founded by the Rev. William Pennefather in the
1850's. Its inspiration was more specifically ecumenical than that of Keswick.
Behind Pennefather's first conference lay his "thought of attempting some
practical recognition amongst the Churches . . . on a platform of spiritual
fellowship, which while firm in its bases of truth should be high enough to rise
above the hedgerows of denomination". But Mildmay, like Keswick, has produced no direct moves for reunion. In marked and interesting contrast are the
manifold ecumenical results in movements of Christian unity resulting from the
American conferences at Northfield, started by D. L. Moody.

It is somewhat surprising that Mildmay, Keswick, and other such phenomena,
e.g. the movement for Retreats, as a whole have produced so little direct ecumenical result. Aid to personal devotion, to prayer and meditation, to learning
the secret of God's power in the life of the Christian, reach the longing heart
from no one special communion. Thomas à Kempis, Brother Lawrence,
Madame Guyon have a message for Protestants of every kind. The Baptist
John Bunyan, the Quaker John Woolman, the Dutch Reformed Andrew Murray, speak to Catholics of every type. Why does the inspiration they give so
rarely seem to rouse in those they help a desire to know more of the Churches to
which their spiritual teachers belong?

A study of Christian hymnology and of the authors represented in official
denominational hymn-books in the English language provokes the same ques-

tion. Every Church has provided itself with an ecumenical hymn-book. Anglican hymnaries draw on Luther, on the rich treasures of the Wesleys, on Moravian hymnology, on Isaac Watts and Philip Doddridge amongst Independents, on Samuel Rutherford, Horatio Bonar, and George Matheson amongst Presbyterians. Free Church and Presbyterian congregations express their penitence, thanksgiving, and aspiration in the words of the Roman Catholics Faber and Newman, or of the great Orthodox hymns brought into the ken of Western Christians by the translations of J. M. Neale. But the ecumenical implications of our hymn-books are realized by few Christians. Hymnology and ecumenism is an almost unexplored area.

5. THE GROWTH OF THE ECUMENICAL IDEA IN THE CHURCHES

The second half-century [1] saw the gradual infiltration of the ecumenical idea into many lands and into many Churches. This growth of the ecumenical idea was intermittent, frequently interrupted, partial, one-sided in its range of interests and manifested irregularly in different areas; but with all these qualifications the period was one of ecumenical education in which preparation for the modern ecumenical movement can be traced.

In France and Switzerland this was a barren period—the ecumenical doldrums. There was an almost complete absence of interest; according to one Church historian there was considerable ecclesiastical activity but not a shadow of ecumenism. There were, however, one or two exceptions. In both France and Switzerland, here and there, there were prophets of the ecumenical idea. Outstanding amongst them is Tommy Fallot (1844–1904), a French Reformed pastor, equally remarkable for his influence in promoting social reform and for his far-reaching ecumenical ideas. His interest in both derived partly from his connections with Oberlin and the Ban de la Roche.[2] He was the grandson of Daniel Le Grand, one of Oberlin's close friends. The inspirer of the Christian social movement in France, he helped to found the "Association Protestante pour l'Étude pratique des questions sociales" which, with its organ Le Christianisme Social, exercised great influence. He was a prophet of union amongst the Churches; what he desired to see, as he set it forth in his paper at the Basle Conference of the Evangelical Alliance in 1879, was not a "union of uniformity" but a "multiform union" in which the Churches could share their treasures. His vision came to embrace the Roman Catholic Church. Both his social and his ecumenical ideals profoundly influenced his disciples Wilfred Monod, Élie Gounelle, and Marc Boegner, his nephew and biographer.[3] It is remarkable how often Continental social reformers identified themselves with movements for Christian unity. In Switzerland another prophet of unity throughout his life was Ernest Naville, the friend of Fallot.[4]

An important contribution to our knowledge of the ecumenical situation in this period comes from Switzerland through Armand de Mestral, a pastor in the Canton of Vaud. On a visit to England as a young man he was much influenced by Pusey. He hoped that in the Vatican Council Rome might be offering an instrument for healing the divisions of Christendom (how deep must have been his disappointment), and in 1869, by way of preparing men's minds for the

---

[1] See Chaps. v and vi, *passim*. [2] See pp. 313 f.
[3] Marc Boegner, *La vie et la pensée de T. Fallot*, 2 vols., 1914, 1926.
[4] Ernest Naville, *L'Unité du monde chrétien*, 1893; and Hélène Naville, *Ernest Naville, sa vie et sa pensée*, Geneva, 2 vols., 1913, 1917.

Council, he published his *Tableau de l'Église chrétienne*, a comprehensive survey of all the Christian Churches of the world, the only available cross-section picture of conditions at that time in the various Churches and of their relation to each other. He was amazed at Protestant ignorance of and indifference to the ancient Churches of the East.

In Britain in this period the ecumenical outlook was in many ways dark. Even amongst those who yearned for Christian unity hopelessness prevailed. Archbishop Benson, writing to Randall Davidson, Dean of Windsor, in the 1880's, says, "The dream of union is simply inappreciably and infinitely far off". R. W. Dale of Birmingham, who recognized "the spiritual unity of Nonconformists with those from whom we are most widely separated, Catholics and Anglicans amongst them", saw no hope even for possible federation amongst Nonconformists. When approached on this subject he pointed to Baptists, Congregationalists, Wesleyans, and Presbyterians, all holding competing services in one small summer seaside resort:

> "No use saying such a policy is hateful. I could swear when I think of it. It exists . . . far too strong to be suppressed. Even different Methodist communities cannot combine. How can we dream of a more general confederation?"

It was an era of separation between the Churches. Some almost consecrated the principle of separation. Even so good a Christian as Dean Hook of Chichester declares: "As religious persons, we must not seek to act in common. Where religion is not concerned, there let us meet with neighbourly feeling and endeavour to promote the comfort of our fellow-creatures." He would act together with Nonconformists in a literary club, not in a Bible society.

There was an almost complete absence of co-operation. The period provides but one example of joint action. On 4 July 1871 the Archbishop of Canterbury (Tait) invited a group of Free Churchmen and Anglicans to meet at the House of Lords to discuss how to combat the prevailing infidelity. This mid-century Life and Work conference lasted but one day and was not repeated.

Sectarian bitterness was as rife as ever between Anglicans and Nonconformists. The reason is not far to seek. It was a period of continuous struggle on the part of the Free Churches for the removal of their civil disabilities in relation to religious tests for admission to Oxford and Cambridge, church rates, burial rights in Church of England churchyards, religious education in elementary schools (the 1870 Education Act was the occasion of bitter strife). The lesson is clear—no question of the union of Churches can be profitably discussed except on the basis of complete equality of civil rights between the religious bodies concerned.

On the other hand, the continuous efforts of the Nonconformists to bring about disestablishment caused chronic anxiety amongst Anglicans. Friction was acute in the 1860's over the disestablishment of the (Anglican) Church of Ireland, and in the 1890's over threatened disestablishment in Wales.

But this dark picture is not the whole truth: there is much evidence in the various Churches of the growth of the ecumenical idea. The 1880's saw a change for the better in relationships between the Church of England and the Free Churches. Tension lessened, barriers were lowered. A number of Nonconformist grievances had been removed. Disestablishment was still in the air, but there was a disposition on the part of both Anglicans and Free Churchmen to consider how the Church of England might be reformed, and to suggest such plans as might make comprehension within the Church more acceptable to Nonconformists. Addresses signed by large bodies of clergy and laity advocating changes —the relaxing of the Act of Uniformity, more variety in services, more power to the congregations and to the laity, especially in the choice of incumbents—were presented to the Archbishops or to the Houses of Convocation. Many meetings were held between Anglicans and Free Churchmen to advocate that the basis of the Church should in some way be widened so as to include the entire Christian thought and life of the nation.[1] But these were plans for reform and comprehension, not for reunion. The Churches as such took no official action, and no new conception of Church unity was brought to light.

Some of the best brains in the Churches were occupied with ecumenical and cognate questions. In 1870 a group of Anglicans was preparing a symposium on *The Church and the Age*, edited by their chairman, the Rev. W. D. Maclagan (Archbishop of York 1891–1909).[2] A group of prominent Nonconformists was discovered to be preparing a Nonconformist symposium of a similar kind, to be entitled *Ecclesia*.[3] The two groups dined together and drank to the health of their respective enterprises. Both symposia treat of relations between the Churches and of possible reunion.

The reports of the Church Congresses provide remarkable evidence of the extent to which the minds of Anglicans of all types were exercised on questions of Christian unity. Church Congresses were held regularly, each year in a different diocese, from 1861 till 1938. They were unofficial gatherings, but they brought together all parties in the Church of England, and the subjects chosen for discussion are a clear indication of the subjects which were interesting clergy and laity.

Each year, almost without exception, under different aspects, the questions of reunion with English Nonconformity, or with Continental Protestantism, or with the Eastern Churches, or of relations with the Roman Catholic Church, were taken up, the discussions being usually of a high and well-informed order. The diverse views of all parties in the Church were freely expressed. A number of suggestions for reunion were made on these occasions. At Wolverhampton in 1867 it was suggested that "amongst the Wesleyans (presuming them willing) two or three of their ministers should receive episcopal orders and be consecrated bishops, and that these should confer Holy Orders on their ministers"— a suggestion not unlike that put forward by the Archbishop of Canterbury (Fisher) in a sermon before the University of Cambridge in 1946.[4] This is but one of many instances in which proposals for Christian union have been suggested and then forgotten, only to be acclaimed as completely new ideas when they reappeared many years later. The possibility of mutual ordination or commissioning was suggested at least once in the 18th century.[5]

Certain Anglican bishops, most of them strong churchmen, deliberately cultivated friendly relations with Nonconformists. Bishop Fraser of Manchester (1870–86) was called by a Nonconformist mayor "the Bishop of all denominations", though he made no secret of his desire to see the Nonconformists return to the Church.[6]

---

[1] See *Church Reform*, ed. Albert Gray and Canon Fremantle, London, 1888, *passim*.
[2] *The Church and the Age, Essays on the Principles and Present Position of the Anglican Church*, London, 1870.
[3] *Ecclesia*, 2 vols., London, 1870, 1872.
[4] See Chap. x, pp. 484 ff.   [5] See Chap. iii, p. 163.
[6] J. W. Diggle, *The Lancashire Life of Bishop Fraser*, p. 170.

There were men, all too few, who dedicated themselves to bringing opposing elements together—John Stoughton (1806–97) amongst Free Churchmen, and Arthur Penrhyn Stanley (Dean of Westminster 1864–81).[1] In estimating Stanley's contribution to Christian unity, it should be realized that his irenic approaches went far beyond England. He travelled widely and made contacts with the leaders of the Churches: in Russia, Greece, Mount Athos, Syria, Palestine, Egypt, and Constantinople with the ancient Eastern Churches; in Sweden and Denmark with Lutherans; in Herrnhut with Moravians; in Hungary and France with Reformed; in the United States with many Churches. He was the friend of Döllinger, of Père Hyacinthe, and of Baron Bunsen. He attended the Old Catholic Congresses in 1871 and 1872. He was in Rome just before the Vatican Council, and deeply regretted that he could not remain, as Archbishop Tait had recalled him for the Ritual Commission. His books did much for ecumenical education, e.g. his *Eastern Church* and his *Lectures on the Church of Scotland* (though some Scots would say that here his zeal was not according to knowledge).

On the continent of Europe, and especially in Germany, a cloud on the international political horizon brought about a united effort in the realm of the future concerns of Life and Work. Christians in various lands began to concern themselves about peace and disarmament. In Britain in 1889 Canon Westcott (later Bishop of Durham) called together a conference of Christians representing the various Churches to consider the excessive armaments of Europe. All the major denominations were represented by leading ecclesiastics of all schools of thought. They brought resolutions calling for prayer and common action before their respective Churches, and Westcott became Chairman of the Provisional Committee of the Christian Union for Promoting International Concord,[2] a foreshadowing of the World Alliance for Promoting International Friendship through the Churches, formed just a quarter of a century later on the threshold of the first world war.

More directly related to the founding of the World Alliance and of great importance ecumenically was the exchange of visits between the German and the English Churches in 1908 and 1909, and the organization of the Associated Councils of Churches in the British and German Empires for Fostering Friendly Relations between the Two Peoples.[3]

In the realm of thought a valuable ecumenical contribution was made by clubs and societies of learned men belonging to various Churches and religions. These played a special part in promoting religious understanding among scientists, university professors, philosophers, statesmen, literati, as well as ecclesiastics—the Metaphysical Society (1869–80), the Synthetic Society (1896–1908), the London Society for the Study of Religion (1903–26). In all of these that most catholic of Romans, Baron Friedrich von Hügel (1852–1925), took a leading part.

The united work of Christian scholars of different nations and Churches on religious encyclopaedias, dictionaries, histories, and series of commentaries was an area in which the Churches actually served each other through sharing their riches of knowledge and research, sometimes internationally, sometimes within the bounds of one language or country, in such enterprises as the *Realencyklopädie für protestantische Theologie und Kirche*, *Die Religion in Geschichte und Gegenwart*, Kittel's *Wörterbuch zum Neuen Testament*, the *International Critical*

[1] See Chap vi, pp. 275 f.
[2] Arthur Westcott, *Life and Letters of Brooke Foss Westcott, Bishop of Durham*, II, pp. 16–24.
[3] For the history of these Councils, see Chap. xi, pp. 511–15.

Commentary, the *International Theological Library*, the *Expositor's Bible*, Hastings' *Encyclopædia of Religion and Ethics*, and many others.

The supreme instance of the ecumenical effect of the common labour of Christian scholars is seen in the Companies who, in correspondence with similar groups of Americans, worked together for years, first on the revision of the English New Testament and then of the Old. Their repeated meetings in the Jerusalem Chamber in Westminster Abbey, their intimate conference, the wonderful harmony which prevailed among them, their appreciation of each other's scholarship and still more of each other's religious quality, made their work together a deep spiritual and ecumenical experience. To all the New Testament revisers the greatest spiritual experience of their fellowship came through the inaugural Communion Service proposed by Canon Westcott and arranged for by Dean Stanley. To quote Hort, "What one goes back to is that marvellous Communion in Henry VII's Chapel. Its quiet and solemnity . . . is never to be forgotten. It is, one can hardly doubt, the beginning of a new period in Church history."[1]

It was in the second half-century that the intercommunion issue became prominent. The earlier question of whether Christians of different denominations could pray together had been in general happily solved, but a new question became crucial: could they meet together at the Lord's Table? Controversy on this subject laid an even more serious burden on sensitive minds and consciences. In all its different aspects—intercommunion between Churches, open communion, joint Communion services, occasional communion—the issue was to become central in all reunion discussions, and was at times the cause of bitter strife.[2] Here we would note only two points.

With the exception of the controversy stirred up by the Revisers' Communion Service in Westminster Abbey, questions about united communion invariably arose in connection with *conferences*, that special feature of Church life in the 19th century which played so great a part in ecumenical developments. Criticism was directed against Anglican clergy who took part in joint Communion services at Evangelical Alliance Conferences in Berlin (1857) and New York (1873); against Bishop Tait's action in administering communion to all the members of an international Y.M.C.A. Conference in London in 1857; against the open Communion services arranged in connection with the Grindelwald Conference (1892); in the violent Kikuyu controversy in 1913.[3] Again there was recurring shock and disappointment amongst students and other young people at Christian conferences to find there was difficulty in the way of their receiving communion with their friends belonging to other Churches. Wherever Christians assemble themselves together in the name of their common Lord, the intercommunion issue appears.

Towards the end of our period the intercommunion question began to be discussed from a particular angle, namely, whether intercommunion should be regarded as a means towards reunion or whether it should be regarded as its goal, and in most discussions on intercommunion this question takes a prominent place.

[1] A. F. Hort, *Life and Letters of Fenton John Anthony Hort*, I, p. 139; and see Chap. vi, pp. 275 f.

[2] For other periods and other occasions when intercommunion has been of importance in the history of ecumenism, see Appendix on Intercommunion, pp. 741–44.

[3] See Chap. x, p. 447.

6. THE EMERGENCE OF NEW FACTORS DETERMINING MODERN
ECUMENICAL DEVELOPMENT

At the opening of the last decade of the century no signs are to be seen of the modern ecumenical movement, though there are many evidences of preparation. The shame of division had begun to penetrate the consciousness of the Church. The missionary enterprise was supplying the sense of urgency. Union plans were multiplying in the mission-field; the younger Churches were beginning to realize that for them union was an imperative necessity.

Movements of the Churches as such towards each other had an increasing record of accomplishment. Voluntary movements bringing together Christians of many Churches and nations had induced in them a consciousness of their "togetherness".

But there was no sign as yet that the various Churches and parties would join in a united ecumenical movement. Pietist and theologically orthodox groups on the Continent, Evangelicals and Anglo-Catholics in Britain, remained in their separate camps, regarding each other with suspicion and distrust. These different elements were in solution in the waters of Christendom. What reagents would cause the crystallization of these elements into some new united combination? What was to secure that these conceptions of Christian unity and the way to attain it should come to be regarded not as hostile and divergent, but as complementary and convergent?

In the early 1890's factors appeared which contributed two new thoughts to the growth of the ecumenical idea. These two thoughts, by their reaction on each other and by their reception in the Churches, changed the course of Church history and made possible the modern ecumenical movement.

The first of these new ideas was that the Churches as such must face their differences together through their official representatives. This conception of the line of approach to union was largely developed and fostered through a new series of conferences and a new ecumenical periodical—the Grindelwald Conferences and the *Review of the Churches*. A leader at length appeared conscious of a mission to take vigorous action about reunion. Henry Lunn, a young Methodist of catholic outlook, ordained minister, medical doctor, missionary, journalist, and tourist agent, from early youth had a passion for bringing hostile elements, whether political or religious, face to face with each other in friendly discussion. Hitherto Anglo-Catholics and Evangelicals, and their counterparts in other countries, had acted through the creation of societies of like-minded people. Henry Lunn made it his purpose to bring together the unlike-minded, and to challenge them to face together the question of reunion.

Lunn could do nothing to persuade the Churches as such to take unitive action. He did the next best thing: he brought together men, who, if not the representatives of their Churches, were at least representative churchmen, and representative of as many denominations, points of view, and schools of thought as possible.

He first provided them with a meeting-ground in the printed page. In the *Review of the Churches*, published monthly 1891–95, and quarterly 1895–96, the Churches were brought face to face by Henry Lunn, journalist. As contrasted with organs of single denominations, groups, or parties, the *Review* was unique. Its five sub-editors were prominent ecclesiastical leaders—Frederick William Farrar, Anglican; Percy Bunting, Methodist layman; Donald Fraser,

Presbyterian; Alexander Mackennal, Congregationalist; John Clifford, Baptist; amongst its contributors were Roman Catholics, Old Catholics, and Unitarians. It presented symposia on all the most contentious points at issue between the Churches—the Nature of the Church, Episcopacy, Apostolic Succession, Clerical Celibacy, Biblical Criticism, Disestablishment, Religious Teaching in Elementary Schools; all these were discussed with the utmost frankness. It recorded every kind of effort in any country towards Christian unity or re-union; it gave regular news of the Churches all over the world; it described every great religious and social movement or personality. The conditions prevailing in Christendom in the five years during which the first series[1] of the *Review* appeared live again for the student as during no other lustrum between 1800 and 1910.

But Lunn was not content that the Churches should tilt with the printed word; they must meet face to face. As Christian tourist agent he offered the double lure of winter or summer sport and reunion discussion. Six times between 1892 and 1895 did he bring together at Grindelwald (once at Lucerne) Home Reunion Conferences,[2] gatherings of churchmen such as had never met since the Reformation—Anglicans, Baptists, Congregationalists, Presbyterians, Quakers, with an occasional French or Swiss Reformed or Old Catholic. For the most part they were British, for Lunn's primary aim was home reunion. They were invited as representatives of elements as diverse as possible—Free Churchmen and Presbyterians of every type; amongst Anglicans, Evangelicals, and Broad Churchmen, with always a certain number from the High Church party, though these were harder to secure. Athelstan Riley, lay leader amongst Anglo-Catholics, and John Clifford, militant Baptist minister—such were the extremes which met at Grindelwald.

The results were immediate. Enormous and quite new interest in reunion was aroused all over the world and in many Churches; and it was discussed in countless papers, secular or religious. The Grindelwald Conferences were news; not for nothing was Lunn a journalist.

In the calm atmosphere of the Swiss valleys men met together, and lasting and significant friendships were formed. Amazing prejudices and ignorances were revealed and dissipated. Free Churchmen confessed themselves astonished to meet Anglicans who were both deeply spiritual and reasonable in debate. An Anglican theological professor told the Secretary of the Congregational Union that he had thought that all Nonconformists were Unitarians, that they had no sacraments, that they were all individualists and had no regular ministry.

Speaking and discussion were as unfettered as in the *Review*, and on the same controversial subjects. No one was inhibited, not even the Anglican professor who made it quite clear that what he wished to see was not reunion but absorption into his own Church. The real stumbling-blocks to reunion were uncovered. Anglicans explained why many of them considered episcopacy a *sine qua non* of reunion, and why they felt that reunion efforts must include Rome and the East as well as Protestant Churches. Nonconformists were challenged to explain why

[1] The second series of the *Review* appeared from January 1924 to July 1930. Another valuable source of ecclesiastical information for the period is the *Religious Review of Reviews*, modelled on W. T. Stead's *Review of Reviews*, and appearing monthly from 1890 to 1896. Unlike Lunn's *Review of the Churches*, it gave no special attention to the question of unity and reunion, except as they were mentioned in current religious periodicals.

[2] Full reports of the speeches and discussions at each Conference were given in the *Review of the Churches*.

their Churches had responded so grudgingly, if at all, to the Lambeth Quadrilateral of 1888; their complete distrust of Anglican motives was revealed.

Prayer for reunion was emphasized throughout as the essential preliminary to any true union. In 1892 a letter in *The Times*, signed by prominent representatives of the larger denominations, appealed for prayer for the coming Grindelwald Conference on the first Sunday mornings in June, July, August, and September. In appeals issued after the 1894 and 1895 Conferences, and signed by the representatives of the different Churches, a Reunion Sunday, if possible Whitsunday, was proposed. In response to an approach made to him from the Grindelwald Conference, in 1894 the Archbishop of Canterbury (Benson) asked all bishops and clergy on Whitsunday to use the Prayer for Unity from the Accession Service in the Book of Common Prayer, and expressed the hope that other religious bodies would do the same. On that Whitsunday sermons on unity were preached by many Anglican and Free Church clergy. In 1895 the Archbishop repeated his appeal, and once more there was a wide response; this time, in obedience to the command of the Pope, the Roman Catholic Church in England offered special prayers for unity.

Impetus was given to movements of unity. Plans for the National Council of the Evangelical Free Churches were maturing; its chief promoters were Grindelwald men. The Council was formed in 1896, and, although its membership was composed not of official representatives of Churches but of individual church members, it could in a real sense voice Free Church opinion. It was suggested that little progress could be made in reunion negotiations until the Church of England could speak with a united voice. To this end a number of ideas were put forward, including some which reappeared in the Enabling Act of 1920 and the coming into being of the Church Assembly. Many practical plans were suggested looking towards reunion. Indeed the student of modern plans for reunion misses but one suggestion—anything like the idea of mutual ordination or commissioning.

As the Conferences progressed, a conviction emerged that no further progress was likely to be made until the Churches as such should decide to meet to discuss reunion through their officially appointed delegates. Not until after Edinburgh 1910 was this idea, propounded at Grindelwald, realized in practical action through the launching of the Faith and Order movement. The Grindelwald Conferences must not, of course, be given the sole credit for the idea of this new type of reunion conference. The Lambeth Conference with its commissions on the relations of the Church of England with the Church of Sweden, or with the Moravian Church, was already experimenting with official negotiations between Churches. Nor can any direct connection be traced between the idea of official conferences between the Churches as propounded at Grindelwald and the genesis of the same idea in the mind of Bishop Brent and others at Edinburgh 1910.[1] But it was at Grindelwald that the idea was first propounded.

It may fairly be claimed that the *Review of the Churches* and the Grindelwald Conferences began a new phase in the growth of the ecumenical idea. These Conferences had, of course, their limitations. The horizon of the Conferences, though not of the *Review*, was limited to reunion in Britain. This was not the case in the second series of Conferences which Lunn (now Sir Henry Lunn) started at Mürren in Switzerland in the 1920's, at which both the Continental and the American Churches were represented.

[1] See Chap. viii, pp. 360 f.; and Chap. ix, p. 407.

The Grindelwald Conferences ignored almost entirely the great reunion possibilities and significance of the missionary enterprise of the Church, in spite of valiant protests entered by Professor T. M. Lindsay of Glasgow, the Convener of the Free Church of Scotland Board of Foreign Missions.

The Conferences took no account of the mind of youth, especially of student youth. At Grindelwald in 1895 no prophet called attention to the founding of the World's Student Christian Federation a month earlier. But student youth was beginning to grapple with the problem of a divided Christendom, and it was from the Christian student world that the second new idea was to emerge, out of which the modern ecumenical movement was born.

By 1895 the Student Christian Movements of many lands had already coalesced in the World's Student Christian Federation.[1]

This was the movement which was destined to produce the great bulk of the leadership of the modern ecumenical movement, the men and women who were to bring about its most characteristic developments—the International Missionary Council, and the Faith and Order and Life and Work movements. If this should seem too great a claim for the Student Christian Movement—often by no means impressive in its local university manifestations—glance at the following names: John R. Mott, Robert Wilder, Nathan Söderblom, W. A. Visser 't Hooft, Valdemar Ammundsen, J. H. Oldham, Tissington Tatlow, Zoë Fairfield, William Temple, William Paton, Henry Louis Henriod, Marc Boegner, Suzanne de Diétrich, Friedrich Wilhelm Siegmund-Schultze, Hanns Lilje, V. S. Azariah, David Yui, T. Z. Koo, Michi Kawai, Germanos Strenopoulos, and Stefan Zankov. All these and hundreds more began their ecumenical career as members or officers in some S.C.M., or were won for ecumenism by some contact with the movement.

The pioneering rôle of the S.C.M. in the ecumenical movement can be clearly discerned if the career of John R. Mott is studied. Led to decision for the Christian life by J. E. K. Studd at Cornell University, as soon as he graduated in 1888 he became General Secretary of the Student Y.M.C.A. and Chairman of the Student Volunteer Movement for Foreign Missions. From his student days onwards he perceived the connection between the S.C.M. and the drawing together of the Churches; at Cornell he brought men from every Church, including the Roman Catholic, into the Student Y.M.C.A. He took the lead in founding the W.S.C.F. at Vadstena, Sweden, in 1895, when setting out on a two years' tour (the first of many) amongst the universities and colleges around the world. Even then he saw in the Federation an ecumenical force, and but a few days after its foundation wrote:

" The Federation will . . . unite in spirit the students of the world . . . in doing this it will be achieving a yet more significant result—the hastening of the answer to our Lord's prayer, 'that they all may be one'. We read and hear much about Christian union.[2] Surely there has been recently no more hopeful development towards the real spiritual union of Christendom than the World's Student Christian Federation which unites in common purpose and work the coming leaders of Church and State in all lands."

It was due to Mott's insight and persistence that only sixteen years later the Constantinople Conference of the Federation was held, with its epoch-

[1] Rouse, *W.S.C.F.*, *passim*, and in particular Chap. xiv, "The Dawn of Ecumenism".
[2] This was the time of the Grindelwald Conferences.

making representation of the Eastern Churches.[1] He steadily cultivated relationships not only with all Protestant Churches but also with the ancient Churches of the East, and did much to draw them into the ecumenical movement. A remarkable incident in this phase of his activities was when in 1913 he, an American Methodist layman, chaired the first conference on reunion amongst the different branches of the Syrian Church in India.[2]

The successive phases of his life work all developed from his activities in the Student Christian Movement, and were all of ecumenical import. His evangelistic work amongst students brought to Christ and into his service many hundreds of those who were to be leaders of Life and Work and Faith and Order. From the day he joined the Student Volunteer Movement at the Mount Hermon Student Conference in 1886,[3] missions were his passion. His world-wide travels brought him into contact with the missionary expansion of the Church throughout the world. It was natural that he should be chosen Chairman of the Edinburgh World Missionary Conference, 1910,[4] and Chairman of the International Missionary Council, when formed in 1921, and of its international meetings at Jerusalem and Tambaram. He took a leading part in the other ecumenical movements which developed from Edinburgh 1910. He chaired the Oxford Conference on Church, Community, and State in 1937, and the Westfield Conference in the same year, which did so much to determine the development of the World Council,[5] of which he became, in 1948, the Honorary President. The striking ecumenical implications of his life-long work for the Y.M.C.A. and of his work during two world wars are treated in a later chapter.[6]

What was the new ecumenical idea which the Student Christian Movement was destined to introduce to the Church? From their beginnings in the 1880's and 1890's the leaders of the older student movements in America and Europe had been evolving, often unconsciously enough, the idea of a new type of Christian organization, a new conception of the basis on which Christians belonging to different Churches might unite to win the world for Christ—"on an 'interdenominational' rather than an 'undenominational' basis".[7] Behind this ugly and clumsy terminology lay a creative idea. Let the Secretary of the Student Christian Movement of Great Britain and Ireland define the term as worked out in his own movement:

. "The Student Christian Movement is interdenominational, in that while it unites persons of different religious denominations in a single organization for certain definite aims and activities, it recognizes their allegiance to any of the various Christian Bodies into which the Body of Christ is divided. It believes that loyalty to their own denomination is the first duty of Christian students and welcomes them into the fellowship of the Movement as those whose privilege it is to bring into it, as their contribution, all

[1] See Chap. xiii, pp. 602 ff., and Chap. xiv, pp. 650 f.
[2] See Rouse, W.S.C.F., p. 158, and Chap. xiv, p. 653.
[3] See p. 328.   [4] See Chap. viii, p. 356.
[5] See Chap. xvi, pp. 702 f.   [6] See Chap. xiii, pp. 601–04.
[7] The terminology shifted from "interdenominational" to "interconfessional" and later to "ecumenical", but the meaning of the three terms was constant as used in the Student Christian Movement. "Interdenominational" included Protestant, Anglican, Orthodox, and the Church of Rome. The opinion that "interdenominational" as opposed to "interconfessional" was used in the S.C.M. to include Protestant and Anglican Churches only is erroneous.

that they as members of their own religious body have discovered or will discover of Christian truth."[1]

This was the conception which was ultimately to bring into fruitful conjunction the two ideals of Christian unity and the way to attain it, which we have watched developing in Church movements and in voluntary associations throughout the 19th century; the idea which was to win the confidence of certain Churches or Church parties which had hitherto held aloof from co-operation, and to make possible for them the share which they are now taking in the modern ecumenical movement. In essence it was the idea of a movement in which the Churches would give their riches, not give them up; would share their heritage, not surrender it.

What features made this particular Christian youth organization the medium by which a new ecumenical idea was introduced to the Church, and gave it also its power to produce ecumenical leaders?

These were student movements, of students, by students, and for students. Almost until the end of the 19th century, the eternal tendency of Christian students to organize had, broadly speaking, been frowned on by their Christian elders and by university authorities. The Company of Pastors in Geneva refused to recommend for ordination in the National Church certain theological students, partly because they had been identified with the groups which met for Bible study and prayer under the influence of Robert Haldane in 1816. They had to seek ordination in England or Scotland. When, in 1806, undergraduates at Cambridge planned to promote a university branch of the recently founded Bible Society, they were compelled to leave the matter to their elders, and the great Evangelical Isaac Milner, President of Queens' College, declared that "if undergraduates were permitted to organize for the purpose of diffusing a knowledge of the Bible, it would not be long before they were banding together to spread subversive political ideas".

Now at length, in the last quarter of the 19th century, students could organize freely, and with common sense and divine recklessness combined, they dared ecumenical experiments undreamed of by the official Churches.

Their primary aim was missionary and evangelistic. It was their desire to win for Christ and for the service of his Kingdom students from all Churches, a desire which forced them to take the divisions of Christendom seriously and to initiate ecumenical action.[2]

The Student Christian Movements started with a working nucleus of men and women strongly evangelical in the best sense of that word, but ready to work with other types of Christian. The founders of these movements in America and Europe were for the most part children of evangelical families, but they escaped the dangers of evangelical narrowness. They started with the belief that they shared the life in Christ with fellow-believers, and they therefore felt no personal difficulty about associating in a movement with those of other Churches, parties, or schools of thought. Their evangelistic and missionary zeal made them seek association, e.g. in Britain, with the most advanced of Anglo-Catholics, the most radical of Free Churchmen, and with scholars and students holding widely differing views on the inspiration of the Scriptures.

The Movement provided experimental laboratories in which new ecumenical

---

[1] See Chap. ix, pp. 405 f., and for further details, Tatlow, *The Story of the Student Christian Movement*, pp. 389–412.　　　　[2] See for illustrations Chap. xiii, pp. 602 ff.

attitudes, individual and corporate, were produced. These laboratories were the Student Movement conferences. To them came students to find themselves living in the closest fellowship with members of many Churches other than their own. Siegmund-Schultze records the impression made on German students by the presence of foreign students at their conferences, and the part this played in their ecumenical education.

When leaders of the Churches were invited to the conferences, they found themselves in the midst of an ecumenical fellowship in actual operation; they were profoundly moved by the "Federation meeting" at which foreign visitors spoke and which was always a central feature of S.C.M. conferences; they learned spiritual riches in types of worship to which they were unaccustomed; they learned new depths of the riches of God in Christ from the lips of those whose Church traditions were other than their own, and who came from nations and communions which they had never met, and never could meet in any denominational conference or fellowship. Above all, they had time and opportunity to form lasting friendships with men and women of other nations and Churches and schools of thought with whom they experienced a living and actual spiritual unity.

Illustrations abound. It was on his visit during his student days to the Northfield Student Conference in America in 1891, and through meeting students of many denominations, that the young Swedish Lutheran Nathan Söderblom wrote in his diary, "Lord, give me humility and wisdom to serve the great cause of the free unity of Thy Church".[1]

In 1907 Dr V. S. Stuckey Coles, the head of Pusey House, Oxford, came to a Student Movement conference to find out why and how this movement had been the means of the conversion of an Oxford undergraduate whom he had entirely failed to help. The author has a vivid memory of seeing this stalwart Anglo-Catholic seated at the foot of a staircase in earnest talk with Mary Hodgkin, a Quaker, finding spiritual fellowship in unexpected quarters. Friendship with her brother, Henry Hodgkin, followed. From that time on he supported the Student Movement.

It was through some such experience of Christian unity that at the end of the 19th century and in the first decade of the 20th leaders of many Churches, Reformed, Lutheran and Methodist, Presbyterian and Orthodox, Baptist and Anglican, Congregationalist and Quaker, all over Europe and America, throughout the British Commonwealth and amongst the younger Churches of Africa and the East, were led to abandon an attitude of aloofness and were prepared to play their part in the modern ecumenical movement.

The impasse of four centuries was beginning to break down under the influence of the two new ecumenical ideas which had begun to stir in the consciousness of the Churches. The Grindelwald Conferences had stressed the need that the Churches as such should meet through their official representatives, to face both their agreements and their differences and to work towards union. The Student Christian Movement had removed the great psychological obstacle which stood in the way of such meetings between the Churches, by demonstrating the possibility of a new type of Christian organization within which loyal members of the different Churches could come together without sacrifice of truth or honesty and in full loyalty to what they believed to be their God-given heritage.

[1] Rouse, *W.S.C.F.*, p. 157.

The day of the modern ecumenical movement was dawning. Already its great features—the International Missionary Council, the World Alliance for Promoting International Friendship through the Churches, Faith and Order and Life and Work—can be discerned on the horizon. The focusing point of the ideas and inspiration which made the new ecumenical movement possible was the Edinburgh World Missionary Conference, 1910. It was a watershed between two eras of Church history. Before 1910 ecumenical movements were like rays of light struggling through a closed shutter into a dark room. Since 1910 the shutters have been flung back and light pours into all the corners of the room. There is "a thousand times more aspiration, a thousand times more accomplishment".

7. THE MAINSPRING OF ECUMENICAL ADVANCE

In the foregoing chapters of this History the ecumenical movement stands revealed as a movement of the Spirit of God; but its mainspring has scarcely been touched on—those movements of prayer without which ecumenical activities would be useless if not dangerous.

Prayer for unity has always been enjoined by the Churches. Wherever the Roman rite is used, prayer is made daily that our Lord will grant to his Church "that peace and unity which is according to his will". The liturgies of the East all contain moving and beautiful prayers to the same end. So also do the liturgies of the Churches of the Reformation, and specially of the *Unitas Fratrum*. In the Anglican Communion hundreds of thousands of communicants week by week beseech God "to inspire continually the universal Church with the spirit of truth, unity, and concord".

But besides such liturgical prayer, organized movements of prayer have sprung up which have given focus and direction to prayer for unity.

A movement of united prayer for the Holy Spirit and Revival originated in Scotland in the 1740's and passed from Scotland to America. It was closely connected with revivals on both sides of the Atlantic and found prophetic voice in Jonathan Edwards' *Humble Attempt*.[1] It swept back from America to England and passed on to Holland, Switzerland, and Germany. In the last decades of the 18th century the call to united prayer was taken up by various Churches in the Midlands, especially by Baptists and Independents, and to it can be directly traced the great outburst of missionary activity in Britain and America in the early 19th century, with its outstanding results in drawing Christians of different Churches together in that fellowship in evangelism which was the seed-bed of ecumenism. In this movement Christians of different denominations did not as yet pray together, but prayed in groups within the boundaries of their own Churches. Meetings of Christians of different Churches for united prayer were to come in the 19th century.

The mantle of Jonathan Edwards fell on James Haldane Stewart,[2] the pioneer in the 1820's and 1830's of a widespread movement for prayer for the Holy Spirit. He began life as a lawyer, but was later ordained in the Church of England. He travelled much on the Continent for his health, and came into close touch with the revival in Geneva which owed so much to his kinsman Robert

---

[1] See Chap. v, p. 228; John Foster, "Jonathan Edwards' 'Humble Attempt' ", *I.R.M.*, October 1948, pp. 373–81; Ernest A. Payne, *The Prayer Call of 1784*, Baptist Laymen's Missionary Movement, 1941; and, by the same author, *Before the Start—Steps towards the Founding of the L.M.S.*, London, 1942.

[2] See Bibliography (Haldane Stewart).

Haldane.[1] In 1821 he published *Hints for a General Union of Christians for Prayer for the Outpouring of the Holy Spirit*. By 1855 the Religious Tract Society had circulated 332,137 copies of this work.

Haldane Stewart went further than Jonathan Edwards in that he organized a regular Union for Prayer; he also laid greater stress on the bringing together of Christians of various denominations. It was a memorable day when he assembled in his rectory in Liverpool to discuss his plan such leaders of the Churches as Daniel Wilson, later Bishop of Calcutta; George Burder, Congregationalist, Secretary of the London Missionary Society; Edward Irving, founder of the Catholic Apostolic Church[2] but at this time still amongst the Presbyterians; Jabez Bunting, the leading Methodist; and the German Dr Steinkopf.[3] He preached widely all over Britain, and in Scotland enlisted the support of Thomas Chalmers. Like Jonathan Edwards, he laid stress on special Days of Prayer, and in 1837 was advocating the setting aside of the first Monday of the year. He endeavoured, unsuccessfully, to secure Dr Pusey's support for this idea.[4] Once more inspiration to united prayer crossed the Atlantic. In 1837 Haldane Stewart heard from a Mrs Sweet that an *Invitation to United Prayer for the Outpouring of the Holy Spirit* had been published in America and that a Concert of Prayer had begun there.

Although Haldane Stewart never identified himself to any extent with the Evangelical Alliance, it always regarded his Union for Prayer as a primary cause leading to its foundation. His Day of Prayer on the first Monday of the year possibly suggested to the Alliance its New Year Week of Prayer, its most significant achievement.[5]

In addition to the Alliance Week, a number of special days or weeks were adopted by various organizations in the interests of united prayer for their special objectives. St Andrew's Day is now widely observed in many denominations as a Day of Prayer for Missions; the W.S.C.F. issues an Annual Call to the Day of Prayer for Students on the third Sunday in February;[6] the World's Y.M.C.A. and the World's Y.W.C.A. jointly sponsor a Week of Prayer and World Fellowship in November. This Week and the Students' Day are observed in almost every country and in every Church, as is also the Women's Day of Prayer for Missions on the first Friday in Lent, promoted by the United Council of Church Women in the United States.

These movements amongst Christians in separated Churches for united prayer for revival have not developed into definite movements of prayer for union amongst the Churches; none the less they have laid trails in the direction of unity. The Calls to Prayer of the Federation and of the World's Y.M.C.A. and Y.W.C.A. lay increasing stress on prayer for unity.

The impulse to prayer for the reunion of Christendom was to come largely, though not entirely, from the Anglican Communion or from the initiative of individual Roman Catholics or Anglo-Catholics.[7]

In 1840 the first proposal for a union for prayer for unity came from a Roman Catholic, Fr Ignatius Spencer, a convert to Rome, who, when on a

[1] See p. 310.

[2] The Catholic Apostolic Church gives a larger place to prayers for unity than almost any other body, and especially to prayers of penitence for indifference to the sin of "endless divisions and mutual hatred". See *Liturgy and other Divine Offices of the Church*, London, 1880.

[3] See p. 312.   [4] Henry Parry Liddon, *Life of E. B. Pusey*, II, pp. 33 f.

[5] See p. 321.   [6] Rouse, *W.S.C.F.*, p. 89.

[7] From this point on much of the information given is based on a memorandum prepared for this History by the Rev. H. R. T. Brandreth, O.G.S.

visit to Oxford, proposed a union for prayer for unity to Newman and Pusey. Pusey saw difficulties; [1] amongst others, that he had rejected such an approach from the Low Church side, i.e. from Haldane Stewart. Newman thought that such a union might be possible within the Church of England, and he and Pusey sought to find a plan for a prayer union which might meet with the approval of the bishops. Newman issued a Plan of Prayer for Union, but the idea met with little episcopal encouragement.

Anglican and Roman initiative lay behind the Association for the Promotion of the Unity of Christendom, the first society actually formed to pray for unity.[2] This Association, which united in its membership Anglicans, Roman Catholics, and Orthodox, had for its sole object daily intercession for unity through the use of this petition, followed by the Lord's Prayer:

> "O Lord Jesus Christ, who saidst unto Thine Apostles, Peace I leave with you: My Peace I give unto you; regard not my sins, but the faith of Thy Church; and grant her that Peace and Unity which is agreeable to Thy Will, who livest and reignest for ever and ever. Amen."

Founded in 1857, it had by 1864 enrolled over 5,000 Anglicans, 1,000 Latins, and 300 Greeks. The Association, although it had received papal blessing at its inception, was condemned in principle by the Pope in 1864, and its Roman Catholic members were forced to withdraw. The papal seal was thus put on the idea that united prayer between Roman Catholics and other Christians was impossible—a strange fate for a union for prayer for unity with no other purpose.

The Lambeth Conferences have never met without pressing on the Anglican Communion concern for a divided Christendom and the need for prayer for reunion. The action of the bishops at the Second Conference in 1878 was typical, when they record:

> "Believing that [united] intercession ever tends to deepen and strengthen that unity of His Church for which our Lord earnestly pleaded . . . your Committee trusts that this Conference will recommend the observance throughout the Churches of the Communion of a season of prayer for the unity of Christendom . . . they venture to suggest that . . . the time should be the Tuesday before Ascension Day . . . or any of the seven days after."[3]

As decade after decade the Lambeth Conference gave closer attention to problems of reunion, the bishops continued to emphasize that Anglicans within their own Communion, and in united intercession with others, should be constantly in prayer for unity. The Grindelwald Conference on Home Reunion took up the idea of the observance of Whitsunday as a Day of United Prayer for Reunion.[4]

In the first decade of the 20th century there is evidence of growing conviction amongst the Churches that reunion will come only as Christians unite in prayer for it. In 1901 deputations from the Christian Unity Association of Scotland addressed the General Assemblies of the Church of Scotland, the United Free

[1] Liddon, *Life of E. B. Pusey*, II, p. 127–34.
[2] Gaius Jackson Slosser, *Christian Unity*, pp. 213–16; Chap. vi, pp. 278 f.; H. R. T. Brandreth, *Dr Lee of Lambeth*, London, 1951, pp. 76–117.
[3] *The Five Lambeth Conferences*, London, 1920, pp. 53, 86, 205.
[4] See p. 340.

Church, and the Episcopal Church in Scotland, urging the setting aside of 13 October as a special day of prayer for union amongst the Churches of Scotland. Five years later another and urgent united call to prayer for unity on Whitsunday was issued in a letter to the London *Times* of 25 April 1906: it was signed by the Archbishops of Canterbury and York, the Primus of the Episcopal Church in Scotland, the Moderators of the Church of Scotland and the United Free Church, and the heads of most of the Free Churches in England; they appealed to every congregation within their jurisdictions for prayer for unity at their morning service on Whitsunday. Profoundly alarmed at the intense bitterness engendered between Nonconformists and Anglicans over Augustine Birrell's Education Bill then before Parliament, their united purpose in issuing the letter was to rouse Christians in all the Churches to the sin and danger of their divisions, and to prayer for unity.

The Octave of Prayer for Unity, 18–25 January, now so widely observed throughout Christendom, has a curious history. On St Peter's Day, 1900, the Rev. Spencer Jones, an Anglican country clergyman, preached a sermon in a series organized by the A.P.U.C. It grew into a book entitled *England and the Holy See: An Essay towards Reunion*.[1] This book was a lucid expression of the mind of the advanced Anglican papalist school; it created a minor sensation and was translated into several European languages. This led to a correspondence between Spencer Jones and the Rev. Paul James Wattson, editor of a paper called *The Lamp*, who was at that time a priest of the Protestant Episcopal Church in the United States, but later joined the Church of Rome.

In 1907 Spencer Jones urged that St Peter's Day each year might be observed by pro-papal Anglicans as a day for preaching sermons on the prerogatives of St Peter, and on Rome as the centre of unity. Watson considered that an even better idea would be an Octave to be observed annually from the Feast of St Peter's Chair (18 January) to the Feast of the Conversion of St Paul (25 January). The purpose of this Octave was, primarily, eight days of prayer for the reunion of Christendom on a papal basis. In December 1909 the observance received the official blessing of Pope Pius X, and later Pope Benedict XV extended its observance to the whole Roman Catholic Church. It was also observed by a certain number of Anglican congregations, as well as by Orthodox, who, while in most cases they presumably sat lightly to its doctrinal presuppositions, yet welcomed the opportunity of joining in a concerted effort of prayer for unity. But the vast majority found the papal basis an insuperable obstacle to participation.

In the early 1930's, however, there came into prominence one of those great ecumenical figures who from time to time emerge in the Roman Catholic Church—the Abbé (later Mgr) Paul Couturier, a priest of the Archdiocese of Lyons. Couturier saw the dilemma which the Octave, as then observed, created for non-Roman Christians. He sought a formula of prayer in which all might join without any wounding of denominational loyalties, and he found it in the Roman Missal. With the encouragement of the Archbishop of Lyons, he advocated the Octave of Prayer on the inclusive basis that "our Lord would grant to His Church on earth that peace and unity which were in His mind and purpose when, on the eve of His Passion, He prayed that all might be one". The success

[1] Not to be confused with the book published in France in 1941 by the same author, entitled *L'Église d'Angleterre et le Saint-Siège*, an entirely different work specially written for the French public.

of this was immediate; it was a basis on which all could unite, and on it in increasing numbers Protestants, Orthodox, Anglicans, and Roman Catholics have united in prayer. The movement was greatly helped by the "Calls to Prayer" issued annually by the Abbé Couturier, until his death on 24 March 1953.

Faith and Order also fostered an Octave of Prayer for Unity. From its earliest days it laid stress on such prayer: in 1913 the Faith and Order Commission of the Protestant Episcopal Church issued a leaflet pleading for widespread Whitsunday prayer for unity,[1] and in 1915 published a Manual of Prayer for Unity. The preparatory Conference of Faith and Order at Geneva in 1920 resolved to appeal for a special Week of Prayer for the Unity of the Church, ending with Whitsunday. From then on, "Suggestions for an Octave of Prayer for Christian Unity" were issued annually until, in 1941, Faith and Order changed its dates to those of the January Octave, thus ensuring that during that week throughout Christendom there should ascend to the Father a united cry for that which is the very meaning of ecumenism. There are, of course, many who at that time unite in meetings for prayer; but this January week means that those who, for reasons of conscience, feel unable to join in such meetings, can yet take part in united prayer, though its unity be that of time rather than of place.

We have traced the history of two movements for united prayer, the earlier for the Holy Spirit and for revival, the later for unity. We see an abundant answer to both in continuous spiritual awakening, and in all the events which led to Edinburgh 1910, and to the modern ecumenical movement. The whole story should teach us something of the way in which God moves the world through the Church by leading his faithful people to pray for those things which it is his will to grant.

[1] Faith and Order Pamphlet 15, *Prayer and Unity*, by a layman.

CHAPTER 8

ECUMENICAL BEARINGS
OF THE MISSIONARY MOVEMENT
AND THE INTERNATIONAL MISSIONARY COUNCIL

by

KENNETH SCOTT LATOURETTE

1. INTRODUCTION

The ecumenical movement was in large part the outgrowth of the missionary movement. Throughout its course it has been closely related to the world mission of Christianity, both in continuous service in countries in which Christianity has long been potent, and in countries where it has been recently introduced; it belongs, exclusively, neither to the older nor to the younger Churches.

That the ecumenical movement should have been so intimately connected with the missionary outreach of Christianity is not surprising. The strong current which in the 19th and 20th centuries drew Christians of many communions together in a unity more inclusive than had ever before been known paralleled the greatest geographic expansion of the Faith that had yet been seen. In the 19th and 20th centuries this extension became for the first time literally world-wide. In western Europe it endeavoured to reach the populations of the industrial and commercial cities whose rapid growth was one of the most marked features of the period. In the Americas, Australasia, and South Africa it sought, with amazing success, to hold to the Faith the vast immigration which poured into these regions from Europe and the British Isles. It also won a large proportion of the non-Aryan peoples of these lands—the Indians and Negroes in the Americas, the Aborigines in Australia, the Maoris in New Zealand, and the Bantus in South Africa. Through student Christian movements it reached out to the intellectuals. It also touched, in many places with striking results in the emergence of younger Churches, almost every country and tribe in what are commonly called the non-Christian countries of the world.

The Protestant phases of this expansion were closely connected with the great revivals which swept across Europe and North America in the 18th and 19th centuries. These revivals largely disregarded denominational and confessional lines. They had much in common in their theology and especially in their religious experience. Those moved by them felt a kinship which transcended inherited ecclesiastical barriers. By them they were impelled to spread their faith. They dreamed of reaching all mankind. The slogan "The Evangelization of the World in this Generation", which in the last decade of the 19th century became the watchword of the Student Volunteer Movement for Foreign Missions, was implicit in the motive which stirred them all. In countless missionary and other organizations Christians of more than one denomination, bound together by the faith which characterized the revivals, worked hand in hand for the spread of the Gospel. They did so chiefly as individuals and not as official representatives of their respective Churches. Yet in these associations they found and developed a fellowship which transcended denominational divisions.

Moreover, as the Faith spread throughout the inhabited world, largely through those who had been roused by these religious awakenings, co-operation across confessional boundaries multiplied. Indeed, it was here, in missions overseas, that the movement towards unity was most marked. Missions and ecumenism is precisely the subject of this chapter.

At first the initiative of missionaries was dominant in this growing movement towards unity. Eventually, however, nationals, members of the younger Churches, joined in it or led it. To prevent duplication and overlapping of effort, arrangements of "comity" were entered into, by which a town or an area was assigned exclusively to one denomination. Societies and committees were instituted for joint action in special phases of missionary effort—education, Bible translation, literature, medicine, and famine relief. Joint planning for approach to particular areas was devised. Nation-wide and regional conferences of missionaries were convened, notably in Japan, China, India, and Africa. In a few places, as in the Province of Fukien in China, at an early date denominations which were closely akin shared in bringing into being younger Churches which from the beginning constituted a single ecclesiastical unit.

Missionaries were the first to feel the tragedy of divisions among the Churches. Not that all missionaries shared that conviction. Many, perhaps the majority, held firmly to their inherited denominational patterns. Some, indeed, stimulated by contact with representatives of other denominations, felt strong advocacy of their confessional convictions to be a solemn duty, and on occasion and in some regions keen interdenominational rivalries were witnessed. Many from sincere conviction refused to join in co-operative enterprises. Yet in time the challenge of the common task tended to draw denominations together. Once transported from the setting in which the inherited confessional loyalties seemed an accepted and immutable part of the religious landscape, more and more missionaries came to believe that divisions among Christians were a scandal, a denial of the Faith. As they joined in travel, in summer resorts, and in the growing co-operative enterprises, they found joint worship possible, even imperative, and grew in sympathetic understanding of one another and in appreciation of the convictions and practices of confessions other than their own. In many aspects missionary conferences proved to be pioneers in methods which later have become classical in all ecumenical work.

Inevitably, many Christian nationals became impatient with imported divisions, based, they believed, upon an alien history which was irrelevant to the situation in their own land. Some nationals, of course, became more ardently and persistently denominational than the missionaries. In several areas fresh divisions multiplied at the instance of younger churchmen. Actually, more separatist movements sprang up in the lands of the younger than of the older Churches. Yet a large proportion of the leaders of the younger Churches became unhappy over Christian disunion and laboured to end it.

In the West, as the 19th century advanced, national organizations were formed to bring together the official representatives of the various missionary societies, irrespective of denomination.

International gatherings for the furtherance of missions were held, those in London in 1878 and 1888 and in New York in 1900 being especially notable. The last gathering was called, significantly, the Ecumenical Missionary Conference "because the plan of campaign which it proposes covers the whole area of the inhabited world". Attendance at these international gatherings was progressively larger.

The segment of the story which is covered in the present chapter is only part of a larger whole. It must be seen merely as a part, although a highly significant part, of a total, world-wide movement. On every continent and in almost every land there was a growing movement towards Christian unity. If it stemmed primarily from what, in the most inclusive sense of that term, is called Protestantism, it reached out also towards all other branches of the Church. This chapter is concerned only with the missionary movement and with developments in co-operation among Christians in connection with it. We must, however, never forget that at the same time co-operation was developing rapidly in the lands of the older Churches, and that numbers of the older as well as of the younger Churches, not content with a co-operation which preserved existing ecclesiastical divisions, were coming together in actual unions of Churches.

Our detailed study begins with the year 1910, a year which was crucial both for the ecumenical movement as a whole and for the missionary movement in particular. Like the year 1948, it was signalized by an event which ushered in a fresh era of ecumenical adventure. That event was the World Missionary Conference held at Edinburgh. In it countless earlier efforts culminated and were given a fresh impetus. From it many new movements towards Christian unity took their origin. Edinburgh 1910 was one of the great landmarks in the history of the Church.

2. THE WORLD MISSIONARY CONFERENCE, EDINBURGH 1910

The World Missionary Conference which met in Edinburgh in the quiet summer of 1910 was one of those events the significance of which is more clearly seen as it recedes into the distance. Even at the time it was hailed as a major occurrence. Succeeding developments more than confirmed the contemporary estimate.

Edinburgh 1910 was the outgrowth and climax of earlier gatherings through which Protestants had been drawing together in their purpose to give the Gospel to the world. As its organizers rightly pointed out,[1] it was in a succession which began with meetings held in New York and London in 1854, continued in Liverpool in 1860, in London in 1878, in London again in 1888, and especially in New York in 1900. Indeed, the idea of such gatherings dates back to William Carey, who had suggested decennial interdenominational world conferences, and had concretely proposed the year 1810 and the place, Capetown, for the first of the series. This seemed impracticable to his friends in England. Indeed, their leader believed that real unity would be impossible in such an assembly, and the gathering was never held.[2] There is no evidence that the memory of Carey's proposal survived in such fashion as to contribute to Edinburgh 1910. National and regional conferences of missionaries from 1854 onwards made more direct contributions to the ideas from which the Edinburgh Conference developed, and some of them did more to suggest patterns and methods of work than the series of conferences held in the West.

Edinburgh 1910 summed up and focused much of the previous century's movement for uniting Christians in giving the Gospel to the world. Its membership and leadership were predominantly from the societies which had arisen from the religious awakenings within Protestantism in the preceding century and a quarter.

[1] *World Missionary Conference 1910*, IX, pp. 3 ff.

[2] See Ruth Rouse, "William Carey's 'Pleasing Dream' ", in *I.R.M.*, April 1949, pp. 181–92.
The full text of Carey's suggestion to Andrew Fuller, Secretary of the Baptist Missionary Society, written from Calcutta, 15 May 1806, is as follows:
"The Cape of Good Hope is now in the hands of the English; should it continue so, would it not be possible to have a general association of all denominations of Christians, from the four quarters of the world, kept there once in about ten years? I earnestly recommend this plan, let the first meeting be in the Year 1810, or 1812 at furthest. I have no doubt but it would be attended with very important effects; we could understand one another better, and more entirely enter into one another's views by two hours conversation than by two or three years epistolary correspondence."
The original letter is preserved in the vestry of St Mary's Baptist Church, Norwich, England.

John R. Mott, who headed the first of the preparatory commissions, who presided at most of the sessions, who became Chairman of the Continuation Committee and of its outgrowth, the International Missionary Council, and who was in many ways the master mind of the gathering, was a spiritual child of the revival movement.[1] In an unusual degree he combined a dignified, commanding presence, deep religious faith, evangelistic zeal, the capacity to discern ability and promise in youth and to inspire it, wide-ranging vision, courage, tact, administrative ability, power over public assemblies as a presiding officer, and compelling, convincing speech. A Methodist, a layman, not theologically trained, not using for conversation or public address any other language than his native English, he won the respect and co-operation of thousands of men and women of many races, nations, tongues, and ecclesiastical connections. A prodigious and seemingly indefatigable worker, he found time for an enormous amount of solid and diversified reading. An incessant traveller, there were few phases of the ecumenical movement in which he did not play an outstanding part. In his earlier years he engaged in world-wide journeys as an evangelist to students—the future leaders of their peoples. He sought to win them not only to Christian faith but also to the service of interdenominational student Christian movements. After 1910 he increasingly devoted his time to organizations which would bring Christians together in service and in giving the Gospel to the world. He dreamed and acted in terms both of individuals and of movements which would influence nations and mankind as a whole. He had a rare power of enlisting outstanding men for the enterprises with which he was concerned.

The Executive Secretary, Joseph H. Oldham, who shared with Mott the major creative thinking of the Conference and who became the Secretary of the Continuation Committee and the first Secretary of the I.M.C., had been a secretary of the Student Christian Movement of Great Britain and Ireland and of the Y.M.C.A. in India. A Scot, a student of Edinburgh and Oxford, quiet, profoundly religious (his *Devotional Diary* had a wide circulation), scholarly, deeply read, seeking by a sure instinct what he called "first-class minds", Oldham gave himself with great ability and concentration to any task which claimed his attention. Having devoted himself to one project and carried it to a point where he felt that it could go on without him, he would move to another. The Edinburgh Conference and its implementation in the life of the world-wide Christian fellowship were his main interest for twenty-six years, from 1908, when he was appointed Secretary for the Conference, until 1934, when he was made chairman of the Preparatory Committee for the Life and Work Conference of 1937. After his return in 1900 from service in India, he spent a short period of study at Halle (1905), and thus became acquainted with the German mind. He continued his contacts with Christian thought in Germany and, commanding as he did the confidence of German leaders, helped to draw the Continental missionary forces into a structure which was predominantly Anglo-American.

In Mott and Oldham a younger generation came to the fore, a generation which, passionately committed to the world mission, had also grown up in the student Christian movements with their interdenominational outlook and training. They and others like them were henceforth to have an increasing share in moulding the ecumenical movement.

Edinburgh 1910 did more than build on past achievements in evangelism and unity: it prepared for the turbulent years which lay ahead, blazed new trails in

[1] See Chap. vii, p. 331.

Christian fellowship and co-operation, and enlisted and inspired men who were to become outstanding in the ecumenical movement in later years.

Only four years after the gathering, the first of the great 20th-century storms broke over the world. Yet during the period of preparation and throughout the meetings, to all except a few far-seeing spirits, the world appeared relatively peaceful. In the Conference addresses one searches in vain for any hint of the wars which were so soon to convulse mankind. Some recognition was given to the rising tide of nationalism in the East and to the problems which this presented to the Christian forces. But there was no prophetic sense of what was coming upon the world. And yet the Conference did help to give to the Christian forces a sense of unity and a continuing organizational structure which enabled them to meet the storm and to build successfully in its midst.

Although Edinburgh 1910 stood in the succession of earlier conferences, in many ways it marked a distinct advance over its predecessors.

The Conference was composed of official delegates from missionary societies. To at least two of the earlier conferences, those of 1888 and 1900, representatives had been appointed by various missionary organizations, but they were also open to any who might care to come. Indeed, the sponsors of the Ecumenical Missionary Conference of 1900 had rejoiced that thousands had been in attendance. By contrast, the membership of the Edinburgh Conference was limited to those delegated by their respective organizations (except for some places reserved for special nominations by the Executive Committee). Only societies which actually had missionaries at work abroad were eligible, and representation was in proportion to the share of each in the missionary enterprise, as measured in financial giving. Since many of the societies were the official agencies of their respective denominations, the Conference was more nearly a body authorized to speak for the Churches than any of the gatherings which had preceded it. It included many who were church-minded. Yet it was still a conference of societies and not a council of Churches.

Not all missionary societies were invited. Only those were included which were operating among non-Christian peoples. Efforts to win Christians from one form of the Faith to another—as by some American denominations on the continent of Europe, or among the ancient Churches in the Near East, or among the Roman Catholics of Latin America—were not to be in the purview of the gathering. Missions whose purpose it was to hold to the Faith emigrants from Europe to other lands were not included. These limitations seemed to be advisable, if the Conference was to be sharply focused and not widely scattered in its objectives. They made it possible for the German societies, sensitive about Methodist and Baptist missions in Germany, to send representatives; and for Anglo-Catholics, who looked askance at missions by Protestants among peoples of other Christian traditions than their own, to come to the Conference. The narrowing of the scope of the Conference to missions among non-Christian peoples made it possible to bring in a larger number of societies and a greater variety of ecclesiastical and theological convictions than had been represented in any previous gathering. Largely because of the influences which issued from Edinburgh 1910, the ecumenical movement became widely inclusive.

Edinburgh 1910 was primarily a consultative assembly. The purpose of earlier missionary gatherings had been largely to educate, inform, and impress the

general public, to bring home to Western peoples and especially to the membership of the Churches the urgency, the achievements, and the possibilities of the
missionary enterprise. They had heartened missionaries and had been demonstrations of progress towards unity of purpose. The Edinburgh Conference, while
not underrating the importance of these objectives, made possible consultation
through which the missionary agencies could plan together the next steps in
giving the Gospel to the world. It was not authorized to legislate for the missionary societies, but it could enable them to form a common mind and prepare for
joint action.

To forward these great objectives, extended preliminary studies were undertaken on a scale unknown in the earlier gatherings. Such studies had been a
feature of a few missionary conferences, notably that held in Madras in 1900,[1]
but in none of them was the coverage so extensive nor had so many been enlisted in their preparation. In 1908 an international committee was chosen,
of which Oldham was made the Executive Secretary. By it eight subjects were
selected as the major topics of the Conference, and a commission was appointed to prepare material for the Conference under each several head. This
procedure proved to be a precedent for later gatherings of the ecumenical movement, including the enlarged Meetings of the I.M.C. in 1928, 1938, and 1947, the
Conference on Life and Work held at Oxford in 1937, and the first Assembly of
the World Council of Churches in 1948.

The work of the commissions extended over many months. The membership
was drawn from scores of countries and denominations, and opinions and
information were elicited from hundreds of correspondents of every shade of
theological conviction and ecclesiastical connection. As chairman of the first
commission, Mott sent personal letters to about six hundred people all over the
world, asking their attention to the questions which he put to them. This assembling of material and thought in itself promoted an ecumenical atmosphere. It
brought into ecumenical currents hundreds who until then had been unaffected
by them. It set a precedent for what later came to be called "ecumenical conversations" through which the mind of the world-wide Church was ascertained, and
the thinking of its various branches was enriched by cross-fertilization.

The topics of the eight commissions may serve as a summary of the work of
the Conference and of its reports. They were (1) Carrying the Gospel to all the
Non-Christian World, (2) the Church in the Mission Field, (3) Education in relation to the Christianization of National Life, (4) the Missionary Message in relation to Non-Christian Religions, (5) the Preparation of Missionaries, (6) the
Home Base of Missions, (7) Missions and Governments, and (8) Co-operation
and the Promotion of Unity.

Three of these topics had especial bearing upon the growth of the ecumenical
movement. The first report emphasized the world-wide mission of the Church.
The second stressed the development of what later were called the younger
Churches, and made abundantly clear that a leading purpose of the missionary
enterprise was, as indeed it had long been, to bring into being self-governing,
self-supporting, and self-propagating Churches in every field. The eighth was
ecumenical in both title and intention. It was significant of continuous progress
in this area that Edinburgh 1910 paid more attention to this subject than its predecessors of 1888 and 1900. This was partly because it had more achievement to
report, partly because of increasing intensity of interest. Although one of its

[1] See especially Hogg, *Ecumenical Foundations*, pp. 21 ff.

basic principles was that "no expression of opinion should be sought from the Conference on any matter involving any ecclesiastical or doctrinal questions on which those taking part in the Conference differed among themselves", the issue of co-operation and unity was given extensive attention. It was reported without evident disagreement that "the ideal which is present to the minds of the great majority of missionaries is" that it is "the aim of all missionary work to plant in each non-Christian nation one undivided Church of Christ". It was also declared that in "some mission fields at any rate, the problem of unity may, before long, be settled, or at any rate taken in hand, by the indigenous Churches independently of the views and wishes of western missionaries".[1]

At Edinburgh 1910 a far more important part was played by members of the younger Churches. Some had been present at earlier gatherings. Their potential importance had been recognized in the attention paid to training leaders from among them. An Indian had taken part in the discussions at Liverpool in 1860; significantly he had declared that more nationals must share in the work of Bible translation. At least six had spoken at one or other of the meetings of the Ecumenical Missionary Conference in New York in 1900. But the younger Churches seem to have been entirely unrepresented at the Centenary Conference of the Protestant Missions of the World held in London in 1888. Only six or seven Chinese were amongst the 1,170 who were present at the China Centenary Missionary Conference in Shanghai in 1907, and those only as visitors. There had been few Indian members of the Decennial Missionary Conferences in their country; out of 118 persons present at the great Bangalore Conference in 1879 only fourteen had been Indian.

At Edinburgh 1910 members of the younger Churches were still few. They came, not as representatives of these Churches, for Churches as such were not represented. They were seventeen in number, of whom fourteen were appointed by the missionary societies with which they were connected, and three specially chosen by the Executive Committees in Britain and America. There was opposition in some quarters even to the appointment of these few.

Few though they were, these seventeen were accorded positions on the programme quite out of proportion to their number. Of the forty-seven public addresses given at noon and in the evenings, they were responsible for no less than six, and all took an active part in the discussions. One spoke on "The Contribution of Non-Christian Races to the Body of Christ", and two others on "The Problem of Co-operation between Foreign and Native Workers". Especially memorable was the address of V. S. Azariah, later to be the first Indian bishop of the Anglican Communion, who, speaking on the latter topic, described the barrier which often separated missionaries from their Indian co-workers, and concluded: "Through all the ages to come the Indian Church will rise up in gratitude to attest the heroism and self-denying labour of the missionary body. You have given your goods to feed the poor. You have given your bodies to be burned. We also ask for *love*. Give us FRIENDS."[2] Three members of the younger Churches were appointed to the all-important Continuation Committee of the Conference.[3] This advance was prophetic of the growing place which the younger Churches were to have in the ecumenical movement in the years ahead.

---

[1] *World Missionary Conference, 1910*, VIII, pp. 83, 86.
[2] *World Missionary Conference, 1910*, IX, p. 315.
[3] Bishop Y. Honda of Japan, the Rev. Chêng Ching-yi of China, and the Rev. Dr K. S. Chatterjee of India.

That movement was to embrace younger and older Churches on terms of equality.

The Edinburgh gathering was much more comprehensive ecclesiastically than its predecessors. The earlier meetings had been made up mainly of those who came out of the Evangelical Awakenings. They were emphatically Protestant and did not look with a friendly eye upon the "Catholic" tradition. At Edinburgh Anglo-Catholics came and took an active part. Their considerable hesitations were overcome only by the assurance that questions of faith and order would not be brought before the Conference for discussion or resolution.[1] They had felt that they could come only if it was recognized that they must not be asked to compromise convictions which to them were of major importance. Their presence added to the inclusiveness of the gathering, and foreshadowed an early expansion of the ecumenical movement to take in elements which had thus far not been drawn into it. Anglo-Catholics frankly stated their position in the discussions on co-operation and unity. At Edinburgh Christians of very different allegiances found that uninhibited discussions could be carried on in an atmosphere of common worship, that in a fellowship knit together and deepened by prayer conscientiously-held differences could be clearly stated and transcended without surrender, and that the unity of Christ's Church in the midst of differences could be clearly felt.

Edinburgh 1910 was in a remarkable way a training-ground for those who were later to be leaders of the ecumenical movement. Three of these, John R. Mott, Joseph H. Oldham, and V. S. Azariah, have already been mentioned. Of a fourth, Charles H. Brent, more will be said in many parts of this History. A fifth, Chêng Ching-yi, became outstanding in the I.M.C., the National Christian Council of China, and the Church of Christ in China. The list could be greatly extended, for few if any of the members of the Conference escaped the contagion of its spirit. Their appreciation of the ecumenical movement was either strengthened or awakened for the first time. Especially notable was the use as stewards or ushers of a number of younger men, almost all former members of the Student Christian Movement of Great Britain and Ireland. Some of these were later to play a conspicuous part in the ecumenical movement, and owed much of their interest in it to their Edinburgh experience. Outstanding among them was William Temple, without whom it would be impossible to think of the ecumenical movement in its contemporary form.[2]

Edinburgh 1910 gave the impulse which issued in the World Conference on Faith and Order. It was as a delegate to the Edinburgh Conference that Bishop Charles H. Brent saw the vision which led him to initiate that movement. At that time missionary Bishop for the Philippines of the Protestant Episcopal Church in the United States, Bishop Brent felt that by its self-denying ordinance, which forbade discussion of differences of opinion in doctrine and ecclesiastical structure and practice, the gathering was failing to face some of the basic issues confronting Christians. Speaking from the floor, he declared that he entirely

---

[1] See Chap. ix, p. 406.

[2] Among the others were, to give them their later and better-known titles: the Very Reverend John Baillie, D.D., D.Litt., S.T.D., Professor of Divinity in the University of Edinburgh from 1934; the Reverend Canon John McLeod Campbell, M.C., D.D., Principal of Trinity College, Kandy, Ceylon, 1924–35, Secretary of the Overseas Council of the Church Assembly, 1935–53; the Right Reverend Kenneth Escott Kirk, D.D., Bishop of Oxford from 1937; Sir Walter Moberly, D.S.O., K.C.B., D.Litt., Vice-Chancellor of the University of Manchester 1926–34; the Right Reverend Neville Stuart Talbot, D.D., Bishop of Pretoria 1920–33; Herbert George Wood, D.D., Professor of Theology in the University of Birmingham 1940–46.

accepted the wisdom of the decision that questions of faith and order should not be included in the programme of the Conference, since that body was primarily concerned with practical co-operation. Yet, he went on to say, Christians could not rest content with co-operation between separated bodies, and the causes of division must be examined with a view to their removal. Characteristically, he expressed his intention to do something about it. What he did is recorded in the history of the genesis of the Faith and Order movement.[1]

It is less easy to trace a direct connection between Edinburgh 1910 and the genesis of Life and Work. But Nathan Söderblom moved readily in the atmosphere of fellowship created by the Student Christian Movement, the importance of which in the planning of the Edinburgh Conference we have already indicated; he had early come under the influence of John R. Mott, and had been impressed by the ecumenical outreach of his work. As Life and Work developed, J. H. Oldham was to create yet another of those personal links, on which the growth of the ecumenical movement has so much depended, and to bring into Life and Work the fruits of the experience which he had gained in the preparation of the earlier Conference.[2]

Edinburgh 1910 marked a new sense of fellowship among Christians. In his address which closed the Conference, Mott declared that "gathered together from different nations and races and communions" the delegates had come to realize their "oneness in Christ".[3] None of its predecessors had been as widely representative of world-wide Christendom or had included so many nations, races, and shades of ecclesiastical conviction. Yet a fellowship had been discovered in Christ which transcended all the barriers. The growing realization of this fellowship was to be one of the most significant characteristics of the ecumenical movement.

As a qualification of these claims, however, it must be noted that the Conference was overwhelmingly Anglo-American. Not only were younger churchmen very few, but representatives from the continent of Europe were a small minority. In consequence, the Conference did not immediately do as much to spread the ecumenical spirit among the Churches of the Continent as it did in the British Isles and the United States and among British and American missionaries. This was due not only to the fact that representatives from the Continent were in a minority, but also, and even more, to the almost total separation between the Churches on the continent of Europe and the missionary societies. Influences bearing on the missionary societies were, therefore, in that region much slower in affecting the Churches than they were in the Anglo-American world.

Edinburgh 1910 was prophetic of a new movement towards the unity of the Churches. Although the question of Church union was not, and could not be, on its agenda, the potential significance of the Conference for Christian unity was not lost either on those who attended it or on outside observers. During the discussion of the Report of the Commission on Co-operation and the Promotion of Unity, the problem of wider unity was referred to by many speakers. Silas McBee, the editor of *The Churchman* (New York), read a letter received by him from Mgr Bonomelli, Bishop of Cremona, in which the Bishop wrote that he

[1] Bishop Brent's memorable speech at Edinburgh in which he declared his purpose to undertake such a movement is noted in a letter of J. H. Oldham to the author of 5 May 1949. See also Chap. ix, p. 407.

[2] Note also the speech by Dr G. K. A. Bell at Stockholm 1925 on "The Continuation of the Conference" in *The Stockholm Conference 1925*, ed. G. K. A. Bell, p. 684.

[3] *World Missionary Conference, 1910*, IX, p. 347.

recognized amongst the delegates to Edinburgh elements of faith "more than sufficient to constitute a common ground of agreement, and to afford a sound basis for further discussion, tending to promote the union of all believers in Christ".[1]

Though representatives of the Roman Catholic Church and the Orthodox Churches were not present at the Conference, and indeed had not been invited, Anglican speakers, Bishop Brent among them, reminded the Conference that it was essential not to forget the importance of these two great bodies of Christians. The Bishop of Southwark (E. S. Talbot) expressed the hope that "perhaps when next some Conference like this shall gather, the spirit of unity may have brought it to pass that some representatives of that [the Roman Catholic] Church may be able to enter into personal conference with their separated brethren". But the strongest expression of all came from a Free Churchman, Dr R. Wardlaw Thompson of the London Missionary Society, who said: "I long for the time when we shall see another Conference, and when men of the Greek Church and the Roman Church shall talk things over with us in the service of Christ."[2]

Edinburgh 1910 created a Continuation Committee to carry on its work. This was the great achievement of the Commission on Co-operation and the Promotion of Unity. Dr Mott began his closing address on 23 June with the words: "The end of the Conference is the beginning of the conquest. The end of the planning is the beginning of the doing."[3] Yet even two days before it had not been certain that there would be any "doing". The idea of a permanent organ of international co-operation, to carry on the work which had been begun at Edinburgh, was still so new as to arouse deep anxieties and hesitations in the minds of many members of the Conference. But at the end of a long discussion, marked by deep feeling, in which every aspect of the question was canvassed, the vote was declared to be unanimous in favour of the acceptance of the plan. On this declaration the Conference rose to its feet and sang the Doxology. The step was indeed momentous, since the formation of this Committee was the outstanding precedent for the organization of the ecumenical movement as it was later to develop.[4]

3. FROM EDINBURGH 1910 TO AMSTERDAM 1948

The World Missionary Conference, Edinburgh 1910, was the birthplace of the modern ecumenical movement. This was seen especially in relation to worldwide evangelism—the proclamation of the Gospel—and the planting of the Church throughout the world. While through the prosecution of missions Protestants had been coming together as never before, the Edinburgh gathering accelerated the pace. It cannot be said too often or too emphatically that the ecumenical movement arose from the missionary movement and continues to have at its heart world-wide evangelism.

Parallel developments were seen in several aspects of the missionary enterprise—in its international organization and in many regions and nations. These

[1] *World Missionary Conference, 1910*, VIII, pp. 220–23.
[2] Ibid., pp. 198 f., 234, 216. It is interesting to note that a small monthly, *Reunion,* issued during this period by a group of papally-minded Anglo-Catholics, devoted much attention to the phenomena of "Edinburghism" and its implications for reunion.
[3] *World Missionary Conference, 1910*, IX, p. 347.
[4] The whole discussion in *World Missionary Conference, 1910*, VIII, pp. 187–218, is deserving of careful study.

developments of various kinds interacted on one another. They contributed to other phases of the ecumenical movement and were also affected by them. For convenience it is necessary to describe them in various categories, according to geographical areas and to type; but it must be remembered that many of them went forward concurrently, and that each has to be fitted into a general world picture. The strands of connection with one another cross and recross in inextricable fashion.

Ecumenical developments were more rapid in the lands of the younger Churches than in the West. This was to be expected. Churches and institutions in their formative stages are naturally more flexible than those which have been long established. Moreover, traditions and institutions which had arisen to meet particular situations confronting the older Churches might in other lands prove to be entirely irrelevant, and might even constitute a handicap to the progress of the Gospel. They therefore were more easily transcended or abolished than would have been possible in the countries of their origin. Then, too, the urgency of carrying the Gospel to peoples hitherto untouched by it, and of planting and nourishing Churches in fresh surroundings, made for co-operation and unity across inherited denominational and confessional barriers.

We shall first describe co-operation on an international scale. Next, we shall consider developments in the older or sending Churches in furtherance of the world mission. Then we shall sketch the achievements, some of them breathtaking, in the lands of the younger Churches. Finally, we shall point out the fashion in which the missionary movement was generally integrated into other phases of the ecumenical movement.

4. THE GROWTH OF CO-OPERATION IN THE INTERNATIONAL SCENE

Enlarged co-operation on an international scale, as envisaged at Edinburgh 1910, was achieved beyond the fondest dreams of those who had dared to propose it. The initial instrument was found in the Continuation Committee set up by the Edinburgh gathering.

The ideas underlying the Continuation Committee and the I.M.C. were not new. At the Centenary Conference in London in 1888, Gustav Warneck, the outstanding scholar of his day on missions, pleaded for a single organization, representative of all missionary societies. His suggestions were, in almost every detail, those which were put into effect a generation later.[1] It appears that Warneck's proposals had been entirely forgotten; yet the Continuation Committee of the Edinburgh Conference was to create a structure which was to be almost an exact embodiment of his plans.

The Continuation Committee set vigorously about its labours. Its membership, drawn from many countries and denominations and including some from the younger Churches, was witness to the new inclusiveness which had come out of Edinburgh 1910. Almost inevitably Mott was chosen as Chairman and Oldham as Secretary. Under the able editorship of Oldham and his co-editor Georgina Gollock, a notable quarterly journal, *The International Review of Missions*, was inaugurated for the discussion on a high intellectual level of problems and issues which concerned the entire world mission of the Church. Its first number appeared in January 1912. The *Review* immediately took its place as the outstanding supra-confessional international journal in the field of

---

[1] See Chap. vii, p. 329.

missions. Its wide range of contributors and reviewers, from many lands and differing ecclesiastical and theological traditions, its extensive bibliographies, and its annual surveys of the world mission, covering as they did Roman Catholic as well as Protestant developments, contributed notably to the nourishment of the ecumenical spirit.

From October 1912 to May 1913, Mott held a series of eighteen regional and three national conferences in Asia—in Ceylon, India, Burma, Malaya, China, Korea, and Japan. These were prepared in the thorough manner characteristic of him, and embraced both missionaries and nationals from the various missions and Churches of their respective areas. They dealt with the problems confronting the Christian forces and paid especial attention to the progressive assumption by nationals of responsibility for Christian witness and organization, and to comity, co-operation, and unity.[1]

The India National Conference recommended a plan for the formation of provincial representative councils of missions and of a national missionary council made up of delegates from the provincial bodies. To make the project a reality, an Interim Committee was appointed.

The China National Conference made specific proposals for greater co-operation in higher education, in theological instruction, in literature, and in the reciprocal recognition of Church discipline, and it adopted a constitution for the China Continuation Committee.

In Korea a Field Advisory Committee was recommended. In Japan the conferences did not go as far as the parallel gatherings in India and China, but declared that the tendency in that country was towards several independent Churches. However, they came out in favour of the formation of a Christian university for the entire country and a first-class Christian college for women. They also expressed the hope that all Churches might eventually come together, approved the organization of a Christian Literature Society, and recommended the establishment of a Continuation Committee for Japan.

The coming of the first world war interrupted the prosecution of the plans for a comprehensive international missionary council. Indeed, for a time the conflict seemed to shatter hopes that such a body would ever come into being. However, the co-operation that had already begun made possible major achievements during the war years. Through the efforts of Oldham, a proposal of the British Government to require a licence of all non-British missionaries within the Empire was withdrawn. Virtual assurance was obtained that no action would be taken without consulting the missionary societies.

Early in 1918, after the entry of the United States into the war, a conference of British and North American missionary agencies formed what was called the Emergency Committee of Co-operating Missions. It was composed of eight representatives of North American societies, eight from British societies, and one each from such other countries as might wish to join. Mott was Chairman and Oldham Secretary. Its purpose was to deal with relations between missions and governments, to safeguard the interests of the missions of countries which had suffered from the war, and to further the correlation of the plans of missionary agencies. This arrangement was made because of an unfortunate division between the German missionary leaders and their constituency on the one hand and the Anglo-American wing of the missionary movement on the other.

[1] For the main ecumenical results of these conferences, see pp. 379 f., 388, and 392.

This was the most serious breach which had thus far occurred in the ecumenical spirit and structure as expressed at Edinburgh 1910 and developed from it.

Until the 1880's the outstanding men in German missions had insisted upon the supra-national character of missions. However, when Germany became a colonial power and German nationalism was intensified, there was a tendency to ally German missions with German overseas political and commercial interests. This helped to reinforce the suspicion with which the British and French colonial authorities regarded German missionaries, and heightened the resentment felt by German missionary leaders at the Allied denunciations of Germany for its alleged responsibility for the outbreak of the war. So long as the United States was officially neutral, Mott had been able to hold the confidence of the German missionary forces. When, however, after the entry of the United States into the war, Mott served on an official American mission which visited Russia in June 1917, the Germans felt that he had betrayed them. They also deeply resented accusations in Anglo-American quarters that German missionaries in Allied territories had served as enemy agents. The Germans did not resign from the Continuation Committee but were unable to attend its meetings; some of the societies in neutral countries on the Continent were unwilling that the Committee should attempt to function in the absence of the Germans. Action, however, was imperative to deal with war and post-war conditions; it was to meet these urgent needs that the Emergency Committee was set up. It was in effect composed of the members of the Continuation Committee who were in a position to carry on business without compromising the Germans; and the Continuation Committee remained in a state of suspended animation, awaiting the time when the Germans would again be able to take part in its affairs.

The feelings of the German leaders were again inflamed by Clause 438 of the Treaty of Versailles. It had originally been proposed that German missionary property, like other German property, should be appropriated by the Allied governments towards the payment of German debts. Through the good offices of Oldham, the possessions of the German missions were saved from this wholesale liquidation, and, in accordance with Clause 438, were placed in the hands of "boards of trustees appointed by or approved by the Governments and composed of persons holding the faith [sic] [1] of the mission whose property is involved". The German missionary leaders, instead of rejoicing that property worth between three and four million pounds had been saved for the missionary cause, persisted in regarding this as a dark design to bring German missions under Allied control, and in suspecting their best friends of having betrayed them—a remarkable example of the extent to which the judgement of even Christian men can be distorted by feelings in a time of deep distress.

Only slowly were the Germans reassured and brought back into the missionary phases of the ecumenical movement. Archbishop Söderblom played a large part in effecting the reconciliation; at a meeting of the World Alliance in Oud Wassenaar, Holland (30 September–3 October 1919) he and German churchmen and missionary leaders were present and discussed the problem of German missions. In a visit to Germany in 1920 Mott-did much to remove German resentment. Yet many years were to pass before the old fellowship in co-operation was fully restored.[2]

Oldham almost single-handed had saved German mission properties from confiscation. He, moreover, did more than any other man to ensure religious

[1] The French text reads *"ayant les croyances religieuses"*.   [2] See Chap. xii, pp. 565 f.

liberty and freedom for missionary operations in the territories which the Paris settlement assigned as mandates.[1] It was largely through his efforts that in September 1919 a convention was signed by the representatives of the leading powers which, in the spirit of the Berlin Act of 1885 (which had guaranteed missionary freedom in much of Africa), assured religious liberty in Africa and the right of missionaries to undertake work in it.

Through the structure for co-operation substantial financial help was given to the German missions which had suffered grievously in the war and post-war years. In 1920 the Foreign Missions Conference of North America voted to recommend to its constituent bodies that they make provision for $2,000,000 to assist the missionary societies of continental Europe. This was a foreshadowing of the still larger aid which two decades later was to be given through the International Missionary Council. The gifts did not reach the total of $2,000,000, but, thanks largely to the generosity of some of the Lutheran Churches in the United States, they attained substantial dimensions. In 1922 more than $258,000 was provided for German missions alone.

In spite of the breach with the Germans, happily only temporary, the newly emerging international structure for co-operation in missions, as yet only in its tentative stages, had come just in the nick of time and had proved its worth and the reality of the growing world-wide unity in Christ.

5. THE INTERNATIONAL MISSIONARY COUNCIL

As soon as possible after the war, plans were resumed for bringing into being the permanent international organization contemplated by the Edinburgh Conference and its Continuation Committee. Progress had been slow. Two years after Edinburgh 1910 and two years before war broke out, a meeting of the Continuation Committee had reluctantly decided that the time had not yet arrived for constituting what was then described as the International Committee. In June 1920 an international missionary conference was convened at Crans in Switzerland. The gathering was not large, but it included some representative Germans—the first time since the war that it had been found possible to draw them into such a meeting. Mott was Chairman of the Business Committee and Oldham was Secretary. Plans were drawn up for what was still called the International Missionary Committee and were submitted to the respective national bodies.

The meeting at which the International Missionary Council was finally constituted was held in October 1921, at Lake Mohonk in New York State. In that pleasant mountain resort, which has often been the scene of international and inter-racial gatherings, when the autumn foliage was at the height of its brilliant colouring, the dream of Edinburgh, indeed of Warneck a generation earlier, was brought to fulfilment.

Sixty-one representatives were present from fourteen different countries. They were overwhelmingly from the West. Only seven members of the younger Churches were present. The Germans were, unfortunately, conspicuous by their absence, for the *Ausschuss*,[2] speaking for the German societies, had voted that so

---

[1] See the declaration of the German leaders in *Allgemeine Missionszeitschrift*, 1917, pp. 205 ff.; Heinrich Frick, *Die evangelische Mission*, 1922, pp. 390–402; E. Lehmann, N. Söderblom, K. B. Westman, *Enig Kristendom*, Stockholm, 1919; manuscript memorandum by J. H. Oldham, 22 May 1950, available at W.C.C. office, Geneva.

[2] On the *Ausschuss*, formed in 1885, see p. 373.

long as German missions were excluded from the territories of the late enemies of the Fatherland they could not participate in an international conference. The missionary section of the ecumenical movement was not as yet truly world-wide, nor had it succeeded in bridging the gulf between Christians of warring nations as effectively as it was to do two decades later. Yet at Lake Mohonk a declaration was adopted to the effect that available information did not substantiate the charges of seditious action made against German missionaries in the colonies of the Allies, and this action did much to reassure the Germans. German delegates were present at a meeting of the International Missionary Council at Oxford in 1923, and from that time onward Germany played its full part in the deliberations and activities of that body.

The constitution adopted at Lake Mohonk was based upon the plan formulated at Crans, which in the interval had been endorsed by the responsible national organizations. In turn, it was submitted to these same bodies for final approval. To guard against the idea that the body was to have executive functions, the name was changed from the earlier "International Missionary Committee" to "The International Missionary Council". It was expressly declared that "the only bodies entitled to determine missionary policy are the missionary societies and boards, or the churches which they represent, and the churches in the mission field".[1] Members were to be the national missionary organizations, not, as in the later World Council of Churches, individual Churches. At the outset these national organizations were seventeen in number. All but four were in the lands of the older Churches. The functions of the International Missionary Council were defined as being

> to stimulate thinking and investigation on missionary questions,
>
> to make the results available for all missionary societies and missions,
>
> to help to co-ordinate the activities of the national missionary organizations of the different countries and of the societies they represent,
>
> to bring about united action where necessary in missionary matters,
>
> to help unite Christian public opinion in support of freedom of conscience and religion and of missionary liberty,
>
> to help unite the Christian forces of the world in seeking justice in international and inter-racial relations,
>
> to be responsible for the publication of *The International Review of Missions* and such other publications as in the judgement of the Council may contribute to the study of missionary questions,
>
> to call a world missionary conference if and when this should be deemed desirable.

It was proposed that normally the Council should assemble every two years, and provision was made for a Committee of the Council to act for the latter between the meetings.[2]

The success of the Council was assured by the choice as its first officers of John R. Mott as Chairman and J. H. Oldham and A. L. Warnshuis as Secretaries. The main office was in London, in the building appropriately called Edinburgh House, the centre also for the Conference of British Missionary Societies. Before long a second office was opened in New York, and Warnshuis,

[1] *Minutes of the International Missionary Council, Lake Mohonk, New York, U.S.A., October 1–6, 1921*, p. 34.   [2] *Minutes, Lake Mohonk*, p. 36.

an American who had seen missionary service in China, was placed in charge. Mott gave a large proportion of his time to the Council, and was actually as well as titularly its chief executive officer. Within a few years (1927) William Paton, an Oxford graduate, became Oldham's associate in London. Quiet, thoughtful, scholarly, feeling deeply but not readily showing his feelings, with considerable contempt for shoddiness in thought and execution, Paton had given evidence of his qualities as a secretary of the British Student Christian Movement, and in books, of which the most widely known is *Jesus Christ and the World's Religions*. His appointment as the first Secretary of the National Christian Council of India in 1922 had ensured the success of that pioneer body. With wider responsibilities, he quickly acquired the stateman's gift of holding many things in his mind at once, of taking long views while at the same time shrewdly judging the possibilities of immediate action, and remaining sensitive to the new demands made by a ceaselessly changing situation; he was soon recognized as an outstanding leader in the ecumenical movement, and his vision and energies ranged even beyond the wide boundaries of the missionary enterprise.

Under the broad charter of its expressed purposes and directed by its extraordinarily able corps of officers, the I.M.C. extended its activities in many directions as a co-ordinating and central planning agency for the large majority of the Protestant missions. Through their extensive travels and wide contacts the officers helped to knit together in growing understanding and fellowship Christians of many lands and confessions. By 1948 the membership of the Council had increased from the initial seventeen to thirty national or regional co-operative bodies. The growth in strength and maturity of the younger Churches was vividly demonstrated by the fact that, whereas of the original seventeen members only four were in the lands of these Churches, in 1948 eighteen, or more than half, were in that category, and four others were on the way towards making application for membership.

The progress of the I.M.C. in fostering world-wide fellowship among Christians and in furthering united planning and action in presenting the Gospel to all men is seen vividly through the enlarged Meetings of the Council which were held on the Mount of Olives in the spring of 1928, at Tambaram, on the outskirts of Madras, in December 1938, and at Whitby, Ontario, in July 1947. In unconscious implementation of the dream of William Carey, such meetings have been held roughly every decade. Unlike the pre-1910 gatherings, but in the tradition of Edinburgh 1910, they were primarily for joint consultation and comprehensive planning by official representatives of national or interdenominational bodies.

The Jerusalem Meeting marked noteworthy advances. Partly as an unhappy legacy of the first world war and partly from distrust of the social emphasis of the programme, no Germans were present. As for Edinburgh 1910, preparation for Jerusalem 1928 was developed through careful, comprehensive studies, which were issued in a series of volumes. The scope was broadened to include religious education, missions and race conflict, missions and industrialism, and missions and rural problems. Missions were thus seeking to touch life comprehensively from more angles than in earlier years. Recognition of the fact that the overwhelming majority of men live in rural communities led further, as a sequel of the Jerusalem Meeting, to the extensive journeys of Kenyon L. Butterfield, an American expert on rural problems. He gave counsel to missions and

Churches in many countries and helped to stimulate and guide a rising interest in reaching adequately the rural communities of Asia, Africa, and the Philippines.

In part to follow up the concerns of the problems of industrialization, authorization was given for the creation of what eventually came to be known as the Department of Social and Economic Research and Counsel. For its first head the choice fell on J. Merle Davis, the son of a missionary to Japan and himself for some years a missionary in that country. In the course of the next two decades Davis conducted important studies in Africa and Latin America, and on the problem of obtaining an adequate economic basis for the support of the younger Churches.

From Jerusalem, too, came the impetus for the creation of the International Committee on the Christian Approach to the Jews, which acted in close cooperation with the I.M.C.

One of the prominent issues at Jerusalem was the relation of the younger and the older Churches. The younger Churches were much more largely represented at Jerusalem than they had been at Edinburgh 1910. At Edinburgh, as we have seen, technically they were not represented, for the younger churchmen who were present came as representatives of British and American missionary societies. The increased place of the younger Churches at Jerusalem was partly due to their rapid growth in numbers and in competent leaders. It was also a reflection of the rising tide of resentment throughout the non-Western world against domination by the West.

At Jerusalem the world-wide threat of secularism to Christianity was recognized. It was, indeed, given major attention.

The outstanding place in the preparation was given to the Christian message, and of the documents issuing from the Meeting that which attracted the most widespread attention was a brief statement of the Christian message, which was chiefly the work of William Temple.[1] Jerusalem 1928 gave a fresh impetus to evangelism: it helped to stimulate the Kingdom of God Movement in Japan and the Five Year Forward Movement in China.

The Meeting at Tambaram in December 1938 marked a further advance in the ecumenical movement. It was larger than the Jerusalem gathering. Moreover, more countries were represented than at Jerusalem; more, indeed, than were to be seen at Amsterdam 1948. Even more striking was the place of the younger Churches. Their representatives constituted slightly more than half the body of official delegates. In ability and devotion many were the equals of those from the older Churches. Indeed, it was a matter of common comment that the outstanding delegation was not from one of the lands of the West but from China, and some others of the non-Occidental countries were not far behind. It was also significant that, although the two countries were in effect at war, China and Japan were both represented. Strained relations were felt between the delegations, but both joined in the worship and discussions of the Conference.

One major emphasis of the Tambaram Meeting was on the Church. This, too, was significant, especially when taken together with the large place held by the younger Churches. It was evidence that these Churches, while mostly small

[1] Part of the Message of Lausanne 1927 was incorporated into this document—a good example of ecumenical "cross-fertilization". See *Jerusalem Meeting Report*, I, pp. 481 ff. ("There is a draught in the hut this evening for some reason so my own candle is hopeless on the table. I have had to put it on the floor and write lying on the boards on my tummy." F. A. Iremonger, *William Temple, Archbishop of Canterbury, his Life and Letters*, p. 396.)

minorities in their respective peoples, were now strong enough to assume much of the burden not only of their own support and direction, but also of the evangelization of their respective lands. The Church was becoming world-wide. Missionaries from the older Churches would still be needed and would be welcomed, but they must increasingly work in association with and under the direction of the younger Churches.

As was fitting, the initial volume of the series which recorded the Meeting bore the title *The Authority of the Faith*. Even greater emphasis was placed upon this subject than at the two predecessors of Tambaram. This was reinforced by a preliminary book written at the request of the I.M.C. by Dr H. Kraemer, later Professor of the University of Leiden, on *The Christian Message in a Non-Christian World*, and by the discussions which arose out of the volume.

Significant, too, was the large volume, edited by J. Merle Davis, on *The Economic Basis of the Church*. This gave recognition to a fundamental problem: if the younger Churches were really to be rooted in the life of their respective nations, they must be able eventually to maintain themselves financially without assistance from the older Churches; to do so might result in a structure quite different from that imported from the older Churches and more nearly in accord with the economic position of the younger Churches.

Much interest was voiced in the achievement of unity among Christians. Both older and younger churchmen expressed themselves on the urgency of the issue.

The storm of the second world war was already lowering when the Tambaram Meeting assembled. One of the major contributions of Tambaram was the added sense of Christian unity which it brought on the eve of the severe strain to which that unity was to be subjected by the tempest so soon to break. The first phase of that war, the invasion of China by Japan, had already made necessary a change in the place of the gathering from Hangchow, as originally planned, to Tambaram.

The onset of the war immediately brought a major crisis to German missions. The British command of the seas at once cut off reinforcements and financial aid from their supporting constituencies at home. Moreover, most of the German missions, with China, Japan, and Sumatra as major exceptions, were in areas governed by Great Britain or the British Dominions. In such areas German missionaries along with other German nationals faced internment.

In this emergency the I.M.C. and its constituent bodies and associated societies came to the rescue. Influenced by representations from William Paton, the Secretary of State for the Colonies expressed his hope that as many "enemy alien missionaries" as possible might maintain their customary activities in Africa. This was actually made possible for all but a few. In India the National Christian Council helped to obtain release for a considerable period for numbers of interned German missionaries. Fully as important was provision for the continuation of financial support. Already crippled by exchange regulations which had been instituted by the Hitler régime and had been in force for several years, German missions now faced even more straitened days. In October 1939, only a few weeks after the outbreak of the war, an unsolicited gift of £250 ($1,000) came from Scotland for their relief. Thus the ecumenical tie transcended both national and denominational barriers, for Scotland was at war with Germany, and the contribution from a Presbyterian would be used chiefly for Lutheran missions.

Assistance was given also by Swedish and American Lutherans and, in the Netherlands Indies, by Dutch missionaries.

When in 1940 German armies overran the Netherlands, Denmark, Norway, and France, the world mission was abruptly confronted with an even graver emergency. The Churches in these lands were severed from their missions, and reinforcements and funds could no longer be sent. To meet this need, the I.M.C., especially through its New York Office, took steps to aid what were strikingly and appropriately denominated "orphaned missions". Acting in close co-operation with the I.M.C., the United States Committee of the Lutheran World Federation enlarged the support which it had undertaken for German missions to embrace other Continental Lutheran missions. Money flowed in from additional sources. Some of it was sent through the I.M.C. and some directly through denominational channels. Substantial assistance went from the United States and Canada to British missions, but aid was also given from Great Britain to Continental missions. Australia helped generously. Gifts small in money but entailing sacrifice and indicative of the reality of the ecumenical tie were received from Christians of the younger Churches. Although the totals did not equal the pre-war budgets of the "orphaned missions", the money contributed kept these enterprises alive. So far as can be ascertained, no unit of missionary effort was forced to discontinue for lack of funds. The achievement, much larger than that of the first war period and to meet a far larger need, witnessed to the striking growth of the ecumenical fellowship in the interval between the two wars.

No sooner had the war ended than the I.M.C. brought together representatives of its constituent bodies which had been physically separated by the fighting. At a meeting of the Ad Interim Committee, held in Geneva, Switzerland, in February 1946, it was quickly discovered that, in contrast with the first world war, the disruption had been only physical and not both physical and spiritual. Without any sense of strain, but only with thanksgiving that now it was possible for fellowship to be visibly renewed, Germans met with Englishmen, Scots, Canadians, and Americans, with whom their country had been at war, and with French and Dutch whose lands had been occupied by German armies.

The strength and viability of the I.M.C. were also demonstrated by its ability to survive the loss of men who had led in creating it, and that in the time of severe testing resulting from the war. Oldham had ceased to be active as early as 1934, having undertaken other work in connection with the Life and Work movement. Mott retired from his position as chairman in 1941. He had been far more than Chairman, for he had contributed a large part of his time without salary or charges for the expenses of his extensive journeys on behalf of the Council. Because of age, Warnshuis retired in 1942, and Merle Davis not long thereafter. Paton died in 1943. Yet able successors were found and the work of the Council continued with undiminished vigour.

At the earliest possible moment an enlarged Meeting was held in succession to Edinburgh 1910, Jerusalem 1928, and Tambaram 1938, to plan for the expansion of the world mission of the Church. It met in the quiet town of Whitby, Ontario, in July 1947. Because of the expense involved, the Whitby gathering was not as large as its three predecessors. However, its spirit was as courageous and its hopes as high as were those of the earlier Meetings. Its main theme was what it eventually termed "expectant evangelism", and it thought and planned in terms of the entire human race. Moreover, as at no earlier gathering, a sense of intimacy was felt between the representatives of the younger and the older Churches. All were declared to be "partners in obedience" to the Great Commission. Indeed, when representatives of the older and the younger Churches met separately to discuss issues on which they had been at variance in earlier sessions, it was discovered when they came together in joint session that complete unanimity had been reached. The ecumenical movement had taken another stride forward.

Increasingly, co-operation was achieved between the International Missionary Council and the World Council of Churches. From the very inception of the latter in 1938 as a body "in process of formation", the two worked very closely together. Two of the officers of the I.M.C., Mott and Paton, also became officers of the Provisional Committee of the World Council of Churches, and numbers of other individuals served on the committees of both. By action of each body, taken in 1948, the International Missionary Council was officially described as being "in association with" the World Council of Churches, and the World Council of Churches as "in association with" the International Missionary Council. To make the connection clear, that designation was placed on the letter-heads of both organizations. The two co-operated in the Commission of the Churches on International Affairs and in the *Ecumenical Press Service*, and a Joint Committee was set up to facilitate the collaboration of the two bodies. The two shared in a Joint Commission on East Asia, which met in Manila in February 1948 with the purpose of making the ecumenical movement more real to the younger Churches in Asia, and prepared the way for the first common meeting of the East Asia Churches in Bangkok in 1949.

In the twenty-seven years between its organization and the first Assembly of the World Council of Churches, the I.M.C. had made notable contributions to the emergence of a world Christian community. It had brought together a large proportion of the missionary forces of the Churches in joint planning and action for the evangelization of the world; it had contributed to the growth of the younger Churches and had knit them into fellowship with the older Churches on a basis of full equality; it had provided a channel for saving the missions of the Churches of continental Europe from the disasters threatened by the second world war; it had conducted *The International Review of Missions*; it had aided studies of Christian education in more than one land; it had furthered important research in a number of directions; it had been instrumental in obtaining a thorough study of the urgent problem of religious liberty[1] and in furthering religious liberty on a world-wide basis; it had promoted Christian literature, notably in Africa; and through the International Committee on the Christian Approach to the Jews it had become a channel for co-operation in evangelism among the Jews. Most notably, the Council had nourished a growing sense of the unity in fellowship and worship of Christians the world around. Its genius was that of bringing Christians of many nations and confessions to plan, work, and pray together in witnessing to the Gospel to all men.

In doing this it had concentrated on the obligation resting on Christians to seek to win all men to Christ. To be sure, it had not been able fully to ignore questions of faith and order. At some of its Meetings it had arranged Commun-

[1] M. S. Bates, *Religious Liberty: An Inquiry*, New York, 1945.

ion services to which all in attendance were welcomed.[1] At Jerusalem and Tambaram it had given much attention to the Christian message, an endeavour which inevitably involved discussion on the essence of the Christian faith. Yet the stress was upon bearing witness to the Gospel.

Not all Protestant agencies joined in the I.M.C. Substantial groups, among them some of the most actively missionary, held aloof for fear of compromising their faith. Yet through the I.M.C. the missionary forces of a large majority of the older Protestant Churches joined with the overwhelming majority of the younger Protestant Churches in "expectant evangelism". They did this in spite of diverse theological and ecclesiastical views. Anglo-Catholics and Quakers, high Lutherans and Baptists, came together in amicable fellowship. At Tambaram widely differing theologies found vigorous advocates in the discussion of the provocative volume by Kraemer, and no agreement was reached except that of mutual trust and common loyalty to Christ. In spite of the absence of important Protestant bodies, the I.M.C. was demonstrating that when Christians made evangelism their object, even when they could not entirely agree as to what was involved in that term, Christians of many traditions could work together and in working together could grow in mutual understanding, love, and enlarging and deepening faith.

6. GROWING CO-OPERATION IN THE LANDS OF THE OLDER CHURCHES

The years which followed Edinburgh 1910 witnessed a development of the regional missionary bodies which had been in existence before it and a rapid multiplication of additional organizations for collective planning and action. The I.M.C. was deliberately built on these national and regional bodies and in turn encouraged their formation.

The oldest of these national bodies was the Committee of the German Evangelical Missions (*Ausschuss der deutschen evangelischen Missionen*). This was formed in 1885 of representatives of twelve German societies. Originally its chief function was co-operative approach on behalf of the German societies to the German Colonial Office. In 1922 the Federation of German Evangelical Missions (*Deutscher evangelischer Missionsbund*) was constituted and the *Ausschuss* continued as its standing committee. In 1933, because of the new internal political situation in Germany due to the coming to power of Hitler and the National Socialists, the Federation gave way to the Assembly of German Evangelical Missions (*Deutscher evangelischer Missionstag*) representing thirty-three societies. A smaller inner group, the Council of German Evangelical Missions (*Deutscher evangelischer Missionsrat*), served as a continuous executive committee.

Many years earlier the Continental Missionary Conference of Europe had come into existence. From time to time it brought together representatives of the missionary societies of Germany, Denmark, Finland, France, the Netherlands, Norway, Sweden, and Switzerland. From 1886 onwards it met in Bremen, usually every fourth year. It was led by the confessionally moderate groups rather than by the strict Lutherans. It welcomed contacts with Anglo-American missions, and at its last meeting in 1935 Paton and Mott were present.

---

[1] At Tambaram there were two Communion services—one Anglican and one Free Church; at Whitby, there were three—one Anglican, one Lutheran (Swedish and Finnish), and one of the United Church of Canada.

The largest of the member bodies of the I.M.C., the Foreign Missions Conference of North America, also antedated Edinburgh 1910. It was constituted in January 1893 by representatives of twenty-three organizations in Canada and the United States. Its annual meetings were attended predominantly by administrators of mission boards and were primarily for consultation on subjects of common interest. The Conference contributed substantially to the Ecumenical Missionary Conference held in New York in 1900. Gradually its scope and functions were enlarged. In 1907 a permanent standing committee known as the Committee of Reference and Counsel was constituted. Edinburgh 1910, in the preparation for which the Foreign Missions Conference of North America had an important share, gave a further impetus. Special attention was directed to the recruiting and adequate preparation of missionary personnel. In 1914 the Missionary Research Library was founded and shortly became one of the two largest collections of missionary literature in the world.[1] The Missionary Research Library provided facilities for research in connection with the world mission, which were open to every denomination and to qualified students from all Churches. In 1925 a convention was assembled by the Conference for the purpose of deepening the commitment to the world mission of the constituency of the Churches of Canada and the United States, and was attended by nearly 3,500 delegates. In 1933 meetings for the same purpose were held in thirty-four separate centres. In 1934 the Federation of Women's Boards of North America, which had been formed in 1913, fused with the Foreign Missions Conference. Commencing in 1926, conferences on medical missions were held biennially through 1932, and in 1938 the Christian Medical Council of Overseas Work was set up with a full-time director. In 1933 a Rural Missions Co-operating Committee was inaugurated, in which several bodies, including the International Missionary Council and the Agricultural Missions Foundation, were represented.

By 1948 the membership of the Foreign Missions Conference had grown from twenty-three societies to 107. These represented many different shades of theological opinion and widely varying ecclesiastical traditions. Its annual meetings, largely attended as they were by the full-time secretaries of the missionary societies, were occasions for intimate fellowship, joint worship, and frank discussion of common problems. The Conference could not legislate for its member boards, but its recommendations frequently led to joint action by the boards and, above all, it engendered a spirit of unity.

Increasingly the mission boards were planning and working together through the committees of the Foreign Missions Conference which dealt with different areas—Africa, China, India, Japan, Korea, South-east Asia, and Latin America. Simply to name the other committees is to show the ever-widening scope of co-operation—Christian Literature for Africa, Associated Mission Medical Office (caring for the health of missionaries), Christian Religious Education, Co-operation with the Churches of Europe, Work among Moslems, Radio, Visual Education and Mass Education, World Literacy and Christian Literature, Audio-Visual Aid Overseas, Interchange of Christian Literature, Research, Public Presentation, Christian Ministry to the Blind Overseas, the Christian Approach to Communism, Interchange of Christian Leadership, International Relations and World Peace, and English-speaking Union Churches Overseas.

Edinburgh 1910 contributed to the formation in June 1912 of another highly

[1] The second is the Day Missions Library at Yale University.

important regional body, the Conference of Missionary Societies of Great Britain and Ireland. The Conference had annual meetings and a Standing Committee to act for it between the yearly gatherings. It made possible a co-operative approach to governments, a function which early assumed major dimensions as a result of the first world war. Through the Conference Oldham rendered much of his notable service during the struggle, and he and Kenneth Maclennan proved an effective team in protecting the property of German missions and in obtaining permission for non-British missionary societies to serve in British possessions. The British Government laid down the condition that only those societies would be admitted which were "recognized" by the Conference of Missionary Societies of Great Britain and Ireland or the Foreign Missions Conference of North America. The existence of a co-operative structure at this point served the world mission well and saved for the younger Churches a richer Protestant contribution than would otherwise have been permitted.

The British Conference of Missionary Societies formed a Missionary Press Bureau, and worked with the United Council for Missionary Education (organized in 1907 as the United Council for Missionary Study) and with the British Board of Study for the Preparation of Missionaries, a body which came into being in 1911 as an outgrowth of Edinburgh 1910. The Conference also addressed itself to the joint production of Christian literature for China, India, Africa, and Moslem lands, to the opium question in collaboration with the League of Nations, to the protection of labour in British and other colonial territories, and to the maintenance of religious liberty. The British Advisory Board of Medical Missions was formed for the study of medical education, at first chiefly in China. Regional committees were appointed for co-operative planning and action for such areas as Africa, India, the West Indies, and the Far East. As in America, one of the major phases of the Conference's programme was the common approach to "the cultivation of the home base"—the deepening of the interest of the Churches of Great Britain and Ireland in the foreign missionary enterprise.

The United Missionary Council of Australia was constituted in 1920, but as a result of a visit by Mott in 1927 this gave way to the National Missionary Council of Australia. In 1926, also as an outcome of a visit by Mott, the National Missionary Council of New Zealand was created. As was natural, the Australian and New Zealand Churches, while having small missions elsewhere, regarded the South-west Pacific as their chief field. This, with its vast distances, its small populations on widely scattered island groups, and its many languages, was both challenging and difficult. In 1937 and again in 1945 conferences were held for joint planning for the South-west Pacific. In February 1948, a large conference on that area was convened by the National Missionary Councils of Australia and New Zealand to devise a comprehensive programme for the whole of that vast region.

In 1912 the Swedish Committee of Co-operation of the Missionary Societies (from 1922 onwards the Swedish Missionary Council—*Svenska Missionsrådet*) came into being, and had as its first Secretary Karl Fries who, typical of the contribution to the ecumenical movement of those who had caught the vision in student Christian circles, had been a co-founder, with Mott, of the World's Student Christian Federation.[1]

Similar national missionary councils were formed successively in Denmark (1912), Finland (1918), Norway (1922), Switzerland (1923), and the Netherlands

[1] Manuscript memorandum of Professor K. B. Westman, 19 June 1950.

(1929). The Northern Missionary Council (*Nördiska Missionsrådet*), with representatives from Sweden, Norway, and Finland, was constituted in 1923.

In many another way in the lands of the West, Christians were being drawn together in seeking to spread the Gospel in the lands of the younger Churches.

The most important of all to the missionary cause was the Student Volunteer Movement for Foreign Missions, which long antedated the Edinburgh Conference, but which in the post-Edinburgh period both in the United States and Europe, under slightly varying names, continued to recruit for the service of the younger Churches men and women of high qualifications and deep devotion.

The Missionary Education Movement of the United States and Canada acted officially for many mission boards and prepared and published a large amount of literature for the promotion and study of missions in the Churches.

The Laymen's Missionary Movement, another pre-Edinburgh organization inspired by the Student Volunteer Movement, lived on though with decreasing impetus. Also of major importance in this period was the Laymen's Foreign Mission Inquiry, which in 1930-32 made a careful study of some of the missions in India, Burma, China, and Japan. Its findings proved provocative, since its "liberal" view of the nature and the tasks of the Christian mission was not everywhere acceptable; but of the value of the factual survey there could be no doubt, and the resultant discussions led to a deepened understanding of the missionary motive.

In the United States co-operative bodies were formed for the support of the Christian colleges maintained either entirely or chiefly through American funds. These were the Near East College Association, formed in 1927, and the Associated Boards for Christian Colleges in China, organized in 1932 and succeeded by the more centralized United Board for Christian Colleges in China.

In Toronto there came into being in 1927 the Canadian School of Missions, which represented a number of theological colleges and missionary societies of several denominations, and which served as a teaching institution and a club for missionaries and missionary candidates. It was a miniature ecumenical movement.

Special attention must be directed to the United Bible Societies, organized in 1947 by Dr Herman Rutgers of Holland, which brought together co-operatively sixteen national Bible Societies. Bible Societies were one of the early forms of ecumenical co-operation. Beginning with the oldest, the British and Foreign Bible Society, founded in 1804, they were maintained by men and women of many different denominations. Their supporters, indeed, worked as individuals, and not as official representatives of the Churches. Yet these societies were a means of co-operation among those of diverse views on faith and order. In some mission-fields, long before the creation of National Christian Councils, they provided the one focal point of continuous inter-Church co-operation.

For the most part they were organized nationally, the largest being the British and American Societies. Since they sought not only to spread the Scriptures in their own lands but also in other countries, often there was duplication of effort, overlapping of fields, and even competition. To avoid these, some adjustments in territory were made. For instance, the British Society assumed responsibility for Persia and the American society for Mexico and Central America. In 1932 a conference of the British, Scottish, and American Societies in London prepared the way for the unification of the work of the three in China. In the ensuing years joint agencies of the British and American Societies were set up in the Near East, Latin America, China, and Japan. In the Netherlands Indies, the British, Dutch, and Scottish Societies consolidated their operations under the administration of the Netherlands Society. In the 1930's and 1940's, as a result of the vision of the 1932 meeting, national Bible Societies came into being in Japan, Brazil, India and Ceylon, Korea, and, in a preliminary fashion, in China.

At last, in May 1946, at a meeting in London in which thirteen national societies in Britain, Europe, and the United States were represented, a constitution was drafted for the United Bible Societies. In the following year sixteen societies joined the new body, and by June 1949 the membership had risen to twenty-four. The purpose was not only fellowship and consultation, but also the safeguarding of freedom for the circulation and use of the Scriptures, encouraging the formation of national societies and, especially, the wider dissemination of the Bible as a means towards winning the world for Christ and forming and maintaining the Church.[1]

7. GROWING CO-OPERATION IN THE LANDS OF THE YOUNGER CHURCHES: CO-OPERATION IN CHINA

It was not only in the lands of the sending or older Churches that the impulse to give the Gospel to the world progressively drew Christians together. Even more in the lands of the receiving or younger Churches Christians were coming together. This was to be expected. In them ecclesiastical traditions were still in their beginning. Christians were small minorities, at times almost infinitesimal, set in a non-Christian environment and entrusted with the divine commission to bear witness to their faith and to seek to win all to it. Transplanted from the countries in which they had originated and from the historical settings in which they had arisen, the denominations and confessions often seemed to have little reason for continued existence, to be almost anachronisms.

It would be giving a distorted view to represent the younger Churches as universally concerned with problems of Christian union. We have earlier stated, · as a plain if sorrowful fact, that in at least one area—South Africa—younger Churches showed even more divisions than could be found anywhere in the lands of the older Churches.[2] China saw a multiplication of movements and groups through the initiative of Chinese Christians, independently of co-operative agencies. Somewhat similar reports, although none so striking, came from other lands of the younger Churches. Nevertheless, as from the very first days of the Church, there was a longing for unity, a longing inspired by the very nature of the Gospel, which again and again found expression among younger churchmen.

In the light of such conditions and longings it is not surprising that in the lands of the younger Churches in a great variety of ways—through conferences, committees, councils, and institutions—and in almost countless instances, planning and action were achieved across imported ecclesiastical barriers. Here were to be found the most comprehensive among organic unions of Churches. Here, too, were innumerable co-operative activities which dealt with almost every aspect of the life of missions and Churches. Often this was on a local or a provincial scale. In many instances it had a national or a regional scope.

[1] Manuscript memorandum of Eric M. North, Chairman of the Council of the United Bible Societies, 12 August 1949.
[2] B. G. M. Sundkler, *Bantu Prophets in South Africa*, London, 1948, *passim*.

So multiform is the story that simply to list all co-operative undertakings would prolong this chapter far beyond its proper dimensions and, while impressive, would prove arid for all but those technically concerned. Here we can merely describe briefly some of the outstanding examples of co-operation. We shall do this first by taking one major land, China, and sketching the course of co-operative action. We shall, then, more briefly, consider other nations and regions, pointing out resemblances and unique features in each. Finally we shall attempt to indicate the main features common to most of the lands of the younger Churches. It will be strange if the total cumulative impression is not one of mounting unity, a unity far greater than that as yet attained in the lands of the older Churches. On the great frontiers of the Faith, witnessing to the Gospel among peoples who previously had had little or no opportunity to learn of it, Christians were being constrained to work together. In doing so, they were realizing the unity that was theirs in Christ and were in the very vanguard of the ecumenical movement.

China has been chosen for extensive study primarily because it has a larger population than any other country and therefore constitutes the greatest mass challenge to the Gospel. Here, too, the variety of the missionary forces was as marked, and therefore the difficulty of comprehensive co-operation as great, as in any other country. Missionaries came to China from the British Isles, from the United States and Canada, and from many European countries. While after 1910 missionaries from the United States slightly outnumbered those from any other land, they were not a majority of the whole missionary body. The many scores of missionary societies represented almost all denominations, shades of theological opinion, and convictions about faith and order. Here, on the one hand, co-operation developed very far and in a multiplicity of forms; here, on the other hand, strong and important elements, relatively as numerous as in any major field except South Africa, declined to be drawn into the ecumenical movement. Here, too, because of political vicissitudes Christianity, and with it the ecumenical movement, met a larger number of severe storms than in any other great non-Christian country.

Long before 1910 a large measure of co-operation, fellowship, and unity had been achieved in a wide variety of ways. Missionaries of several denominations had joined in translating the Bible. National conferences of Protestant missionaries had been held in 1877, 1890, and 1907, with an increasing attendance and mounting results. Evangelism was central—the 1890 conference issued an appeal for one thousand new missionaries in five years, an appeal which seems to have been met. The Centenary Conference of 1907, celebrating the first hundred years of Protestant missions in China, projected a continuing organization to bring about "the formation of a Federal Union under the title, the Christian Federation of China". At least two of the provincial councils which were envisaged as part of this structure were created and survived for several years.

There were also regional Christian educational associations. *The Chinese Recorder*, founded in 1867 as *The Missionary Recorder*, was designed to serve the entire missionary body. The Christian Literature Society, earlier the Society for the Diffusion of Christian and General Knowledge, under its great Secretary Timothy Richard (1845–1919), who was zealous for the union of Christians and eager and sanguine for the early winning of all China to the Christian faith, was in part an outgrowth of the 1877 Conference and was not limited to any one denomination. The Educational Association of China and the China Medical Missionary Association brought together missionaries from several denominations. Here and there, as in the University of Nanking, the North China Union College, the North China Union College for Women, the Shantung Christian University, and other institutions, several denominations co-operated in higher and professional education.

The China Inland Mission, with the largest number of missionaries in the Empire, while of one theological complexion, drew its personnel from several denominations and countries. As elsewhere, the Young Men's and the Young Women's Christian Associations, the former especially prominent in China, had a membership which came from many different denominations and made for an inclusive fellowship. At summer resorts missionaries were finding fellowship across denominational lines. In some cities they were coming together for union services in English. A few beginnings were being made in Church union, but almost always of branches of the same or similar confessions.

Nearly all this co-operation and union was initiated and carried through by missionaries; Chinese were only beginning to share in the direction of Churches and other Christian institutions.

Had there been no Edinburgh 1910, co-operation and unity would undoubtedly have grown, together with the growth of Chinese leadership. But that gathering and the international developments which followed it modified processes which were already under way, gave additional impetus, and drew China into the world-wide ecumenical movement.

In 1913, under the chairmanship of Mott acting for the Continuation Committee of the Edinburgh Conference, five delegated conferences were held in as many sections of China, followed by a national conference, two-thirds of the members of which had been chosen by the sectional gatherings. The time was ripe for the comprehensive planning which marked these gatherings, for China had recently passed through that stage of her prolonged revolution in which the Confucian monarchy had given way to a republic, and the Chinese were declared to be more open to the Christian message than at any previous period.

Both Chinese and missionaries shared in the deliberations, and the spirit of unity and brotherhood was marked. Evangelism was stressed. Desire was expressed for "the unity of the whole Church of Christ in China", and it was suggested that in place of the various denominational designations one name be given to all, *Chung-Hua Chi-Tu Chiao-Hui* ("The Church of Christ in China"), that Churches of similar ecclesiastical order unite, that there be organic union of Churches already enjoying intercommunion, and that there be local and provincial federations. The Conference recommended uniform Christian terms for use by the Churches and the preparation of a common hymn-book and of a book of prayers for public worship in those Churches which desired it. It made specific proposals for close co-operation in higher education, in theological instruction, in the production of literature, and in the reciprocal recognition of Church discipline.

Provision was made for a China Continuation Committee to carry out the recommendations of the conferences and to maintain contacts with the Continuation Committee of the Edinburgh Conference and mission boards in the Occident. At least one-third of the members of the Committee were to be Chinese. At the outset a Chinese, Chêng Ching-yi, and an American, E. C.

Lobenstine, were appointed Secretaries. A Secretary for Evangelism was soon added, A. L. Warnshuis, later to become a secretary of the I.M.C.

Chêng Ching-yi became one of the most prominent leaders in the ecumenical movement. Of Manchu stock, the son of a Congregational pastor, he had himself been pastor of an independent congregation in Peking, formerly connected with the London Missionary Society. He was not yet thirty years old when he rose to international prominence at the Edinburgh Conference. He was later to be Chairman of the National Christian Conference of 1922, Secretary of the National Christian Council, the first Moderator of the Church of Christ in China, and the first Chairman of the undenominational Chinese Home Missionary Society. As a vice-chairman of the I.M.C., he travelled widely and was a familiar figure in ecumenical gatherings and in church circles in the West. Easily at home in English, he had no difficulty in making his convictions known in the Anglo-American world. Dignified, poised, possessed of a deep faith, his best-remembered words were characteristic of him: "O Lord, revive thy Church, beginning with me."[1]

In 1917 the China Continuation Committee achieved one of its initial successes in drawing up a comity agreement, setting forth principles to guide any mission proposing to open work in an area in which another Protestant society was already established. In the next two years the agreement was officially approved by most of the missions. Its outstanding achievements were the National Christian Conference held in Shanghai in May 1922, and the formation of the National Christian Council.

For the National Christian Conference elaborate preparations were made. It was hoped that the gathering would not only issue in a National Christian Council but that it would prepare for marked advance in evangelism and the building of the Church in China. To this end, somewhat after the pattern of Edinburgh 1910, five study commissions were appointed. The most comprehensive and detailed survey made of the missionary enterprise in any country was carried through, and its findings were published in a massive volume, *The Christian Occupation of China.*[2] In striking contrast with the Centenary Missionary Conference, held only fifteen years earlier, which was overwhelmingly missionary in its personnel, half the delegates to the 1922 Conference were Chinese, and the Chairman was Chêng Ching-yi. A large proportion of those in attendance represented the Chinese Churches, and the general theme was "The Chinese Church". The Church in China was coming of age.

In many ways that Church was still divided, for it had been planted by more than a hundred different societies representing scores of denominations from many different lands. Church consciousness was either non-existent or weak. By tradition Chinese Christians were not church-minded and, as a reflection of that attitude, the favourite expression was not "the Church in China" but "the Christian Movement in China". Yet in those very words there was a sense of unity and a longing to express it in terms which, by avoiding traditional language fraught with ancient and imported controversies, might serve to make it real.

At the time of the Conference, the division in the Protestant forces was accentuated by rising tension between "conservatives" and "liberals". The breach was chiefly in the missionary body and overpassed denominational lines. Many missionaries were fearful of the "modernist" views, which they believed to be domi-

---

[1] Nelson Bitton in *The International Review of Missions*, October 1941, XXX, pp. 513–20.
[2] Chinese and English editions were published in Shanghai in 1922.

nant in the China Continuation Committee. In 1920 the conservatives organized the Bible Union, through which to establish fellowship among themselves and to combat what they regarded as the tendencies among the liberals towards weakening confidence in the inspiration and authority of the Scriptures and permeating the Chinese Churches with their views. One fundamentalist declared that of the thirteen theological seminaries in China only four were "safe", and that of the forty-eight Bible schools only nine or ten could be "depended upon".[1] By 1921 the Bible Union had enrolled 1,700 members, and on the eve of the National Christian Conference it held a national convention in Shanghai. This was not a passing phenomenon. The division between conservatives and liberals was a continuing obstacle to unity among Protestant forces in many lands, and nowhere more strikingly than in China. Increasingly the separation, originally mainly in the ranks of the missionaries, spread among the Chinese and was fostered by indigenous movements in which missionaries had no share.

Many members of the Bible Union and many sympathizers were members also of the National Christian Conference, and, owing to the tension between them and the more liberal members, it seemed for a time that that body might not be able to reach agreement on any important matter. Memorable was the mingled assertion and appeal of one of the Chinese delegates, T. T. Lew, that "the Chinese Church shall teach her members to agree to differ and resolve to love". In his own person Lew combined both sides of the controversy. Physically so frail that his friends wondered how he kept alive, brilliant, highly-strung, he was reared in a conservative *milieu*, had his advanced education in liberal institutions in China and the United States, and was to teach in the "liberal" theological faculty of Yenching University. His appeal and the quiet behind-the-scenes labours of those who longed for unity were crowned by temporary triumph. The seemingly impossible was achieved, and the Conference authorized the formation of the National Christian Council. Some of the theologically most conservative missions supported it, including the Christian and Missionary Alliance and the China Inland Mission.

A successful effort was made to keep the National Christian Conference and the National Christian Council from being purely nationalistic and isolated from the world-wide ecumenical movement. Both Mott and Oldham were prominent at the Conference, and the National Christian Council became a member of the I.M.C.

The National Christian Council was, however, unable to bring to full realization the dream of achieving "the unity of the whole Church of Christ in China". The Roman Catholics were not included in it, nor was any effort made to bring them in. They accounted for more than three-fourths of the baptized Christians in China, a much larger proportion than in any other land in Asia except Ceylon. They had been continuously represented in China nearly three times as long as Protestants. Like Protestants, but quite independently of them, they had been stressing the development of a national organization and Chinese leadership. In the very year of the (Protestant) National Christian Conference, Rome had created an Apostolic Delegation for China, and in 1924 a general synod, the first of its kind, was held in Shanghai. Emphasis was increasingly placed on the creation of a Chinese body of clergy. In 1926 six Chinese were consecrated bishops in St Peter's in Rome by the Pope himself, the first Chinese to be elevated to the episcopate since one lone instance in the 17th century.

[1] C. H. Coates, *The Red Theology in the Far East*, London, 1926, p. 142.

Not even all Protestants joined in supporting the National Christian Council. Most of the Lutherans and all the missions of the Southern Baptists of the United States and the Churches associated with them held aloof. In the fourth year of the Council's existence the China Inland Mission and the Christian and Missionary Alliance withdrew, for they felt that they could not assent to what they deemed the modernist trends due to its prevailingly liberal membership. A mounting number of independent Chinese Christian groups sprang up, largely conservative and ardently evangelistic, which did not associate themselves with it. They were evidence that Christianity was becoming more deeply rooted in China. Not all of them were divisive, but most of them were highly critical of existing Churches.[1] The League of Evangelical Churches, largely Chinese in leadership, while not as militant as the Bible Union, was to some degree a rival of the N.C.C.

To difficulties arising within the Christian forces were added others in the political environment. In 1922, even before the N.C.C. was formed, an anti-religious, predominantly anti-Christian movement began and lasted until 1926. It was compounded of many elements, but was mainly nationalist, anti-imperialist, anti-British, and was furthered by the Communism which then won its first great success in China. It brought difficulties to missions and Churches and placed a heavy burden of leadership upon the Council. To this storm were added chronic civil war and banditry. These made travel and communication difficult on a national scale and proved a grave handicap to the nation-wide operations of the Council. In September 1931 came the Japanese action which separated Manchuria from the rest of China. The Japanese-created State of Manchukuo, which comprised all of Manchuria and part of Inner Mongolia, tended to cut off the missions and Churches in its territories from those in the rest of China. In July 1937, what proved to be large-scale Japanese operations broke out and led to the Japanese occupation of almost all the eastern and coastal regions, to the accompaniment of bitter and prolonged warfare. Thousands of Chinese, including many Christians, migrated from Japanese-occupied regions to unoccupied China. The fighting and the political division rendered the maintenance of national unity in the Church all but impossible, and curtailed the activities of Christian organizations which sought to operate on a nation-wide scale.

Even before the defeat of the Japanese in 1945 and their repatriation, the rising Communist power in the North created what was in effect a distinct State and so impeded efforts at unity, whether in Christian or non-Christian circles. The continued growth of Communist might brought additional problems, for Communism was frankly anti-religious. While in theory it tolerated religion, including Christianity, it insisted upon curtailing some of the operations of the Churches and demanded that Christians cut themselves loose from what it regarded as imperialistic missions. It also placed obstacles in the way of continuing contacts with the ecumenical movement. These were all the greater because of the Communist conviction that so important a phase of the ecumenical movement as the World Council of Churches was the religious front of the capitalist West, and because of the antagonism of Communism in general, and especially Chinese Communism, to the United States, the country from which so many missionaries had come and with which so many Chinese Christians had close ties.

[1] For a description of some of these movements, see *China Christian Year Book*, 1932–33, pp. 175-92, and 1934–35, pp. 97–110.

In spite of these various handicaps, Christianity persisted, Christians grew in numbers, and co-operation on a national scale increased.

The N.C.C. drew into its fellowship the majority of the Protestant Christians in China, and endeavoured to plan comprehensively for reaching the entire nation. The revised Constitution adopted in 1929 based the Council solidly upon the Chinese Churches by providing that 65 per cent of its members must be elected directly by the co-operating Churches and 20 per cent by national Christian organizations, leaving 15 per cent to be co-opted. In 1932 the member Churches contained about 70 per cent of the Protestant strength in China.

In 1932 the Council inaugurated a Five Year Movement to advance the Christian forces afresh after the destructive anti-foreign and anti-Christian tide of the 1920's. The Five Year Movement sought to deepen the life of Christians. Remembering the slogan given by Chêng Ching-yi, "Go forward", it also had as its aim the doubling of the number of Christians in the five years.

The N.C.C. embraced in its programme a wide diversity of projects—the Christianization of the home, Christian religious education, Christianizing economic relations, literature, rural work, international relations, relief, and health promotion. A National Commission on Religious Education was created in 1931 to co-ordinate and promote religious education under the control of the Church. The physical centre of the N.C.C., the Missions Building in Shanghai, furthered a sense of the nation-wide unity of the Protestant forces by being the headquarters for other organizations which were channels of co-operation.

When the full-scale Japanese invasion which began in 1937 forced so many of the Chinese to the West and divided the country between occupied and un-occupied China, the N.C.C. continued to operate. For a time it remained at its traditional seat in Shanghai. As always since its creation, it stressed evangelism. It called for a "Forward Movement". It joined in the work of relief to refugees, the wounded, and orphaned missions. It helped to keep Christians in various parts of the country in touch with one another, and sponsored a Youth and Religion campaign in which several national Christian co-operative agencies joined in presenting the Gospel, especially to students. It opened an office in Chungking, the capital of unoccupied or free China, there to aid in Christian enterprises among both the local and the immigrant population. By 1942 Chung-king was the seat of the main office, though a local office was maintained in Shanghai. After the expulsion of the Japanese in 1945, the N.C.C. once more made Shanghai its sole centre. From there, in the optimism which characterized the first months after the defeat of Japan, it projected another Forward Move-ment, and planned for the training of Chinese to enter the various fields in which a Christian approach was to be attempted.

It was not through the N.C.C. alone that progress towards Christian unity was effected. The Anglicans originating from the missions of several branches of that communion joined in forming a Chinese national body, the *Chung Hua Sheng Kung Hui* ("The Holy Catholic Church in China"), the first General Synod of which met in 1913. Lutherans of many shades of confessionalism and of several nations joined in forming one Lutheran Church in China. A beginning had been made in 1913 in the founding of a Lutheran theological seminary at Shekow which served more than one mission. It was in 1920 that a group of mis-sions in Central China founded this new national unit in the Lutheran brother-hood, and other missions eventually joined it.[1] Similarly there came into being a

[1] Letter of Professor K. B. Westman (MS.), 19 June 1950.

Presbyterian Church of China, and this later constituted the nucleus of a much more comprehensive union, the Church of Christ in China, which embraced not only Presbyterians, but also the Reformed, the United Evangelicals, the United Brethren, and some of the Congregationalists, Baptists, and Methodists.[1]

Several of the enterprises which had been begun before 1910, and which were either interdenominational or enlisted individuals from several denominations, continued to operate. The *Chinese Recorder* served all the Protestant interests until its discontinuance in 1941 after the United States and Britain were drawn into the war with Japan. The Christian Literature Society survived the shock of the revolutions and wars. The Y.M.C.A. and the Y.W.C.A. grew. Especially did the former multiply its units and add to its membership. The China Medical Missionary Association became the China Medical Association, and in that form merged (1932) with the National Medical Association, which was made up of Chinese regardless of their religious faith. The missionary element became the Council on Medical Missions in that more inclusive body.

To these means of co-operation and fellowship among Christians others were added after 1910. In them, as was natural, Chinese initiative played an increasing part. Some, too, were in part the product of the growing spirit of co-operation which was to be seen throughout the Protestant world, stimulated by Edinburgh 1910 and the I.M.C. Thus the Chinese Home Missionary Society, an undenominational, purely Chinese organization, with Chêng Ching-yi as its first Chairman, was formed at Kuling in the summer of 1918. It sprang out of a small group that had been called to meet Frank Buchman, an independent evangelist, the leader of the movement which for a time was called the Oxford Groups and later Moral Rearmament. The mission was, however, quite independent of Buchman, grew rapidly, and within a few years had expanding enterprises in the South-west and Manchuria. Kenyon L. Butterfield, an expert in rural problems, made extended journeys in China, as an outgrowth of which there came into being the North China Rural Service Union, composed for the most part of missionaries who were devoting themselves to rural communities. This body and the N.C.C. inspired the creation in 1932 of the North China Industrial Service Union, only partly Christian in membership, to aid farmers in making better use of their time in the winter months when, in the traditional cycle of the agricultural year, they were idle for a number of weeks, unproductive and subject to moral disintegration.

In cities inter-church councils or committees and pastors' unions were steadily increasing in numbers. They paralleled the increase in Chinese leadership and Chinese initiative, and were an indication of the direction in which the younger Churches in China were moving.

When, during the Japanese invasion, several of the Christian publishing agencies migrated to the wartime capital of free China, Chungking, they found it wise to associate in what was called the United Christian Publishers. This joint effort proved so satisfactory that after the expulsion of the Japanese seven of the agencies organized the Council of Christian Publishers. One of the constituents of these two co-ordinating bodies, the Literature Production Programme, outlined a project for translating into Chinese an extensive selection from the Christian classics of all the ages, regardless of the ecclesiastical allegiance of the authors. It hoped thus to do for Christianity in China what, many centuries earlier, had proved of substantial aid in rooting Buddhism in China—making accessible

[1] See Chap. x, pp. 458 ff.

in Chinese the most notable expositions of the Faith. In this they enlisted not only Protestant scholars of several denominations but also Roman Catholics.

In two other ways the spirit of unity inherent in the Gospel rose to meet the tragedy of the Japanese invasion and found in it fresh opportunities for expression. One of these was the foundation of many *ad hoc* relief committees, in which Roman Catholics and Protestants of diverse complexions joined to alleviate the physical distress of the non-combatant sufferers from the fighting, floods, and droughts which unhappily punctuated these years. In a quite different fashion, in the enforced close associations of some of the internment camps, notably in Weihsien in Shantung, intimate friendships were formed not only between Protestants of several denominations but also between Roman Catholic and Protestant missionaries. Most of these friendships could not be maintained after the internees were repatriated, but none who had experienced them could forget them.

Especially marked in China was co-operation in education, notably in institutions on the university level and for preparation for the ministry. This was significant, because in their formative years Christian youths of different denominations were living, studying, and worshipping together and were thus gaining some feeling, perhaps vague and slight but still significant, for the Church which transcends denominational barriers. It also meant that hundreds of youths who became Christians and were baptized while in these union institutions had very little sense of denominational attachment, even though baptism took place in one or another of the Churches in the community.

Indeed, here lurked a grave danger; church-consciousness, at best weak among Chinese Christians, was almost entirely absent in a large proportion of the Christian students. They had little or no sense of the historical continuity of the Church, and corporate loyalty to it was weak. It followed that a large proportion of the students, out of whom should have come the leadership of the Church, were lost to it. This was strikingly true of former students and graduates of the union universities. They found adjustment to the local congregations, usually small, without much vision, and with poorly-trained pastors, so difficult that either they formed no connection with them or, if they did so, tended to be inactive or to drift away. Again and again this was remarked of Christians, the product of union Christian schools, who served as government officials. It was also a matter of comment that a declining proportion of the graduates of union Christian universities went into the full-time service of the Church. Fortunately this was not universally true, and outstanding examples could be cited of men and women trained in the union Christian middle schools and universities who became staunch supporters of the local churches. Among these the ecumenical spirit was either already strong or was readily cultivated.

Interdenominational co-operation in educational institutions, and especially in colleges and universities, had begun before 1910. After that year it mounted steadily. A memorable milestone was the China Educational Commission, which was headed by Professor, later President, E. D. Burton of the University of Chicago. It was in China from September 1921 till January 1922. It came at the instance of the China Christian Educational Association, the China Continuation Committee, the Committee of Reference and Counsel of the Foreign Missions Conference of North America, and the Conference of British Missionary Societies. It was, therefore, pre-eminently a co-operative study. It surveyed the entire scope of Christian education in China. Among its recommendations was the organization of all the Protestant educational institutions of China into one structure, stressing middle schools and Chinese leadership, and working in association and not in competition with the government system of education. This thorough-going co-ordination of Christian education was never carried through, partly because of the anti-Christian nationalist storms which broke only a few weeks after the Commission had made its report. Yet either before or after the Commission's work the majority of the Christian colleges and universities and several of the middle schools became union institutions in whose support two or more denominations joined.

Fully as important, perhaps even more so, for the achievement of Christian unity, was the growing co-operation in theological education. By the mid-1930's the only graduate schools of theology, Nanking Theological Seminary and that attached to Yenching University on the outskirts of Peking, were union institutions; the four outstanding theological colleges were also in that category. All were international and interdenominational in their support and staff. Some of the institutions of lower grade, including Bible schools for women, were interdenominational. A study of theological education, made in 1934 and 1935 under the National Committee for Christian Religious Education in China, with Dean Luther A. Weigle of the Yale University Divinity School as its special counsellor, gave further impetus towards comprehensive interdenominational planning for the training of the professional leadership of the Church in China.

It was significant for the unity of the Christian forces in China that missionaries of several denominations received their introduction to the language in Peiping (Peking) in what was eventually known as the College of Chinese Studies. In the close fellowship of that school they made approaches to reciprocal understanding and a sense of underlying unity at the very beginning of their service in China.

This survey of co-operation among the Protestants in China as a phase of the movement towards Christian unity is by no means exhaustive. It remains to sum up the achievements of this period and also the limitations to which the achievements were subject. In China Christianity was being planted by all of its three largest branches—the Roman Catholic Church, the Orthodox Church (through comparatively small Russian missions), and Protestantism. To the divisions of Protestantism imported from without others were being added in increasing number by Chinese initiative. It is no wonder that a Roman Catholic description of Christianity in China scornfully headed its chapter on Protestantism "From Confucius to Confusion". Could the Church in China attain unity? Since here, as in the rest of the world, there was no prospect of a unity which would embrace both Roman Catholics and Protestants, and but remote likelihood of one which would bring Russian Orthodox and Protestants together, could Protestants achieve it among themselves?

The obstacles in the way of unity even among Protestants were very great. While some Chinese deplored the divisions in the Church, few of them were really church-conscious or prepared by tradition or training to wrestle with the problems of faith and order which lay at the very foundations of most of the divisions. In general, they were inclined to dismiss them somewhat impatiently as irrelevant. As yet Chinese Christianity had produced no first-class theologian. Historic Chinese culture made for individualism and small groups with no common cohesion. This was reflected in the many new movements, Chinese-led and bearing the Christian name, which added to the confusion.

Yet the years after 1910 saw striking progress towards unity. The world-wide ecumenical movement made itself felt with outstanding results. Increasingly the movement towards unity, like the Churches themselves, was on Chinese initiative and under Chinese leadership. By long tradition the Chinese were practical, interested in morals and in the improvement of society. It may have been because of these inherited Chinese traits that the movement took the form of co-operation in doing rather than that of organic union, and that the largest of the organic unions, the Church of Christ in China, owed more in its pioneering stages to missionaries than to Chinese. By 1948 unity, even in co-operation, was by no means fully attained. Yet great strides had been made towards it, and more and more the Chinese leaders themselves had been penetrated by the spirit of union.

In the 20th century the Chinese Church began to produce leadership for the universal Church. Repeatedly we have had occasion to mention the contribution of Chêng Ching-yi. We have also noted the name of T. T. Lew. The list of those known in ecumenical circles the world around might be almost indefinitely prolonged. At once there springs to mind T. Z. Koo, a railway official, who first became prominent in the meeting of the W.S.C.F. in Peking in 1922 and then served for many years as a secretary of the Federation. With his clarity of mind and speech and his deep spiritual insight he became a familiar and welcome visitor in student Christian circles in many lands. T. C. Chao, enthusiastic, keen, with philosophical and theological interests, Professor at Yenching University, from 1935 onwards increasingly Pauline in his understanding of the Gospel, was one of the members of the first Presidium of the World Council of Churches. Miss Wu I-fang, clear-headed, poised, President of Ginling College, was prominent in the National Christian Council and in the International Missionary Council. The ecumenical movement was infinitely richer for these and others like them.[1]

8. CO-OPERATION IN THE LANDS OF OTHER YOUNGER CHURCHES

This rapid sketch of the progress towards Christian union in China, and the even more rapid sketch of the parallel developments elsewhere which follows it, make plain certain patterns which tended to develop themselves in almost every country.

Certain outstanding Church unions have to be recorded, but in the main the story is rather that of co-operation in practical affairs than of steady progress towards ecclesiastical unity. In almost every country, co-operation found its over-all expression in a national Christian council; and these bodies, which might so easily have become the expression of a national separatism in religion, were saved from this danger by the membership of almost all of them in the International Missionary Council, and by the participation of many younger Churches in the World Council of Churches. Within the national framework were many regional bodies, and organizations for co-operation in education, in theological training, in Bible translation, and in almost every other form of Christian work. Everywhere the sense of evangelistic urgency reinforced powerfully the movement towards fellowship. Much of the development took place

[1] It will be evident to the reader that this account of progress towards union in China refers only to the period before the Communist victory in 1949, which has created many new difficulties for the Chinese Churches and for the moment rendered impossible their participation in the world-wide ecumenical movement.

informally, through meetings of missionaries in the hill-stations where they gathered for their holidays, and in personal friendships across national and racial frontiers.

Everywhere the principle of comity, already established before 1910, came to be more fully accepted, as missions and Churches became more deeply involved in the areas for the evangelization of which they had accepted responsibility. But always there were certain groups which for conscientious reasons found themselves unable to accept any limitation on their freedom of action. The tension between "liberal" and "conservative" was everywhere felt. Independent younger Church groups added to the confusion of tongues which the missionaries had introduced.

And everywhere there was the change of emphasis, as the younger Churches asserted their independence and developed their own leadership. Not all this new leadership was ecumenically minded; but there was a steadily increasing undercurrent of demand that new forms of unity should be sought out and put into effect. This demand was so all-important that it is dealt with again at length at the conclusion of this chapter.

Japan. Although Protestant Christianity in Japan was nearly a generation younger than in China, in 1948 Protestant Christians constituted proportionately a slightly larger fraction of the population. Moreover, indigenous leadership had come earlier to the fore, and the Churches acquired independence from control by missionaries sooner than in China. Here, during the second world war and the years immediately preceding that conflict, the Government exerted much more pressure on the Churches than did the Government of China.

In Japan a Federation of Churches was formed in 1911, and worked in close co-operation with the Conference of Federated Missions which had come into being in 1902. The Continuation Committee which arose out of Mott's post-Edinburgh tour included members of both these bodies and of Churches and missions not related to either. In 1922, largely at the instance of the newly formed I.M.C., there was held a National Christian Conference. The major achievement of that gathering was the constituting of the National Christian Council which became a member of the I.M.C. The National Christian Council was predominantly Japanese in leadership. To it the Conference of Federated Missions transferred many of its functions, and the Christian Literature Society came partly under its control. While it did not become as prominent as the corresponding bodies in China and India, in 1928 it inaugurated a nation-wide evangelistic campaign, thus carrying out the primary purpose of co-operation in the lands of the younger Churches. This campaign coalesced with one led by Toyohiko Kagawa, and the two together, under the designation of the Kingdom of God campaign, sought to win a million adherents for the Christian faith.

After December 1941 and the entry of Japan into the war, the National Christian Council was altered under pressure from the Government; it became the liaison body between the latter and all Christian organizations, was re-organized as the Christian Commission on Co-operation with a Roman Catholic Archbishop as Chairman, and in it there were included Protestants, Roman Catholics, and Orthodox. This enforced co-operation could not endure and lapsed after the defeat of Japan in 1945. The Church of Christ in Japan also came into being early in 1941 in anticipation of pressure from the State.[1]

[1] See Chap. x, pp. 460–63.

In 1948 the N.C.C. was reconstituted, but its loss of vigour in the war period handicapped it, and the Church of Christ in Japan, embracing as it did the majority of Protestant Christians, seemed to make it less necessary than formerly. After 1945 eight of the larger North American missionary societies instituted a united approach to Japan. They sought through one joint agency in that country to meet the requests of the Church of Christ in Japan for personnel and funds. This agency, the Interboard Committee for Christian Work in Japan, represented the North American boards which joined in it, the Church of Christ in Japan, and the National Christian Education Association.

Japan did not produce as many indigenous Christian sects as China, but the lack of a sense of church-consciousness was nearly as great. A movement which influenced many of the intellectuals was led by Kanzo Uchimura. Through lecturing, writing, and teaching the Bible he gained a wide hearing. He did not associate himself with any Church and discouraged those influenced by him from doing so.[1]

Japan has made notable contributions in personnel to the ecumenical movement. Outstanding was Toyohiko Kagawa. While his effect was not great on the organization of the Church, he was essentially interdenominational in his outlook and his practice. Although he was something of an individualist and often went on his way without much regard for the Churches, unlike Uchimura he did not oppose them, often worked through them, and in his extensive missions in Britain and America was sponsored by congregations of many denominations and by interdenominational bodies. Highly sensitive, he came from an unhappy childhood and youth in a non-Christian home, and was won to the Christian faith through the love of a missionary. For a time he lived a life of devoted self-giving in one of Japan's worst slums, then became an evangelist at large to his country, stressing co-operatives and other measures of help for the under-privileged. In spite of imperfect eyesight and other physical disabilities, he accomplished a prodigious amount of work, writing and lecturing at a pace which few men in good health could have stood.[2]

Korea. In Korea, much smaller than Japan and from 1904 to 1945 ruled by that country, the Protestant forces learned less of co-operation and were more deeply divided than in Japan. There were indeed some educational institutions in which two or more denominations joined; early in the history of Protestant missions a comity arrangement had been entered into by the major missions, and there was a Federal Council of Protestant Evangelical Missions in Korea which in 1924 changed its title to the National Christian Council of Korea.

However, in the 1930's and 1940's political conditions were very adverse. The Japanese rulers feared Korean nationalism and sought to crush it. To that end they forced upon Korea State Shinto, the official patriotic cult of Japan. They attempted to compel Christian Churches and educational institutions to conform. This led to divisions in the Churches between those who complied and those who refused to do so. In an effort to amalgamate the Churches of Korea with those of Japan, the Japanese authorities required the dissolution of the N.C.C. and insisted upon co-operation through the N.C.C. of Japan. They also sought to merge the Korean Churches with the corresponding denominations

---

[1] Kanzo Uchimura, *The Diary of a Japanese Convert*, Chicago, 1912.
[2] See his autobiographical book, *Before the Dawn*, New York, 1924 (tr. from the Japanese of *Across the Death Line*), and the life by William Axling, *Kagawa*, New York and London, 1932.

in Japan. After the defeat of Japan in 1945 the partition of Korea into the Russian and American zones, separated by the 38th parallel of latitude, followed by the setting up of rival governments, made collaboration between the Churches of the North and the South impossible. In the South divisions going back to the degree of co-operation and non-co-operation with the Japanese, and also stemming from personal rivalries, dogged the course of post-1945 co-operation. However, in 1946 the National Christian Council was reconstituted, and in other ways many Protestants worked together across denominational lines.

Indonesia. Indonesia presented a unique situation. Here was a huge archipelago comprising hundreds of islands, large and small. In 1910 the Dutch controlled almost the whole area, exceptions being the Portuguese possessions in Timor and the British in north-western Borneo. Here there were more Protestant baptized Christians than in all the rest of the Far East put together. Here, unlike Asia, the islands of the Pacific, Latin America, and most of Africa, where the missionaries were predominantly from the British Isles, the Dominions, and the United States, the younger Churches were overwhelmingly the fruit of Dutch and German initiative.

At first sight, this would have seemed to facilitate co-operation and even union, for the majority of the Dutch missionaries were of the Reformed tradition and the largest German missions combined the Reformed and Lutheran backgrounds. However, the situation was by no means simple, and presented serious obstacles to inclusive co-operation.

Distances were great, and there were many peoples and languages. One of the largest of the younger Churches, that of the Bataks, the product of the (German) Rhenish Missionary Society, was essentially a racial Church. Some others of the younger Churches were also racial. A large proportion of the Protestants were members of the Protestant Church in the Netherlands Indies, earlier called the East Indian Church. This was mainly the outgrowth of pre-19th-century conversions, but it also contained a substantial European membership, most of it Dutch. In addition, it included many members of mixed racial origin, and some Indonesians from 19th- and 20th-century missions. Until 1935 its clergy were appointed and paid by the State. In that year, as a result of nationalist pressure from the Indonesians, administrative separation between the Church and the State was effected, but until the Japanese occupation in 1942 some financial assistance was given by the State. The Protestant Church of the Netherlands Indies was itself a kind of federation of regional Churches. Restive under the control of Dutch clergy and of the alien colonial Government, several of its units attained a high degree of autonomy.

From the same desire for independence from Western dominance, a growing number of small bodies arose, some of which wished to hold no fellowship with white Christians. Marked theological differences in the Reformed Churches in the Netherlands were reflected in the existence of a variety of missionary societies and their resultant younger Churches, and among these co-operation could not always be achieved. There were also missions of bodies such as the Christian and Missionary Alliance which were not of the Reformed tradition, and some of these found collaboration and fellowship difficult.

In spite of these obstacles, some degree of co-operation was attained. The most distinctive of its expressions was the Missions Consulate. This was established in 1906 to represent all the missions in the Netherlands Indies in their relations with the State. The Consulate proved invaluable in a great many matters of common interest to all the Churches and missions. All the Protestant missionary bodies of the islands joined in supporting it. In 1931 the Netherlands Indies Mission Council was formed, a stage in a development which dated back to the middle of the 19th century. It did not include, however, all the missions and Churches. The Batavia headquarters of the Netherlands Bible Society was also a unifying influence. In partial succession to a central training-school for pastors and teachers which had been in existence near Batavia from 1878 to 1926, in 1934 a union theological college was opened at Buitenzorg, and in 1936 was moved to Batavia (Djakarta).

The Japanese conquest in 1942 and the defeat of the Japanese in 1945 opened new chapters in the history of Indonesia and of Christianity in the islands. In general, the movement, already well under way, for the independence of the Churches from European control was greatly accelerated. Efforts towards co-operation were confused, but contacts were maintained, even though imperfectly, with various world-wide aspects of the ecumenical movement; Indonesians were present at some of the world conferences, including that of the I.M.C. at Whitby in 1947 and the World Conference of Christian Youth at Oslo in the same year. It was not until 1950 that a National Christian Council came into being; this was remarkable in approximating more closely to a National Council of Churches than most of the National Christian Councils in other lands.

South-east Asia. We must pass rapidly over the lands of South-east Asia which lie between Indonesia and India.

There were so few Protestants in *French Indo-China*, and they mostly the fruits of one missionary society—the Christian and Missionary Alliance—that special measures to promote union among them were scarcely called for. In all the other major political units co-operation made progress.

In 1929 the National Christian Council of *Thailand* (*Siam*) was organized, largely at the instance of the I.M.C., and embraced bodies which had a wide range ecclesiastically, from the Society for the Propagation of the Gospel (Anglican), through the American Presbyterian Mission, the largest in the country, to a Chinese Baptist Church, the Christian and Missionary Alliance, and the Seventh Day Adventists.

In the British portion of the *Malay Peninsula* and the associated *Singapore*, the Christian Council of Malaya was launched in January 1948. Before the Japanese occupation there had been the Malayan Committee of Reference and Counsel in which the several Protestant bodies had joined. The further development of 1948 had been hastened by plans projected by Christians while in a Japanese internment camp. Moreover, in 1948 Trinity College was constituted by Anglicans, Presbyterians, and Methodists for the joint training of clergy.

Because of the inclusive British political tie, until after the second world war the missions and Churches in *Burma* and *Ceylon* were grouped administratively and for fellowship in the National Missionary Council of India, Burma, and Ceylon, a product of the Continuation Committee of the Edinburgh Conference, and in its successor, the National Christian Council of India, Burma, and Ceylon, organized in 1922 and a constituent member of the I.M.C. Within that inclusive structure there were regional councils. Among these were the Burma Christian Council and the Ceylon Christian Council. The second world war, with the Japanese occupation and the confusion which followed the expulsion of the Japanese, partly dislocated the pre-war development in Burma. The political independence of Burma was followed, in 1949, by the full autonomy of the Burma Christian Council and its direct affiliation with the I.M.C. Similarly, but earlier (1947), the Ceylon Christian Council became independent and had direct membership in the I.M.C. In Ceylon co-operation developed into a most interesting movement towards the union of all the larger Protestant bodies in the island.[1]

India. India shared with China the distinction of having the largest population of any country on the globe. Even more than China it presented a challenge and a problem to those who dreamed of Christian unity on a nation-wide scale as an accompaniment of unity on a world scale. Unlike China, it had no long tradition or experience of an inclusive political unity to facilitate Christian unity. Great Britain had brought more of it under one rule than had any other power, either foreign or Indian, but even the British *Raj* did not embrace quite all the country, France and Portugal still retaining small colonial possessions. Moreover, deep religious and social cleavages existed. There were gulfs between religious communities, notably between Moslems and Hindus, and also between castes. Great linguistic diversity was an added obstacle. It was the imported English which was most nearly common to the entire land, and that was used only by the educated minority. However, a kind of cultural tie reinforced by a rising tide of nationalism gave cohesion and made of India far more than a geographical expression.

The obstacle presented to Christian unity by the great variety of forms in which the Faith was presented to India was fully as great as in China or any other land outside the United States. Here were Roman Catholics, nearly half the total of those bearing the Christian name. The ancient Syrian Church in Southwest India, itself divided, constituted another large segment. The Mar Thoma Church, a development from the Syrian Church through contact with Anglicans, was an important element. Proportionately Protestants were increasing more rapidly than any of the other main branches of the Church and were far more numerous than in China. British, American, and Continental Protestant agencies were extensively represented. Anglicans, Lutherans, Reformed, Presbyterians, Congregationalists, Methodists, Baptists, and many others of diverse theological and national backgrounds were all there. The fundamentalist-modernist cleavage was also present, though not so fully organized and sharply self-conscious as in China.

Formidable though the obstacles to unity were, before 1910 co-operation among Protestants had already proceeded fully as far as in China. Interdenominational regional conferences of missionaries had been convened and, as in China, decennial missionary conferences had been held for the entire country. The pattern of the preparation for one of these had substantially influenced that of Edinburgh 1910. In 1908 the South India United Church, one of the bodies which later entered into the Church of South India, was formed, mainly from Presbyterian and Congregational elements.

To this trend towards unity the influences stemming from Edinburgh 1910 gave an added impulse. In 1912, out of Mott's post-Edinburgh tour, came the National Missionary Council of India, Burma, and Ceylon. In January 1922,

[1]See Chap. x, pp. 476-79.

largely through the wise counsel of the first Secretary of the I.M.C., J. H. Old-ham, the National Missionary Council became the National Christian Council of India, Burma, and Ceylon. The change from the designation "Missionary" to "Christian" symbolized the increased share of Indians, and it was expressly stipulated that at least half the members of the new Council must be nationals. The N.C.C. was based, not as in China upon the direct membership of Churches and missions, but upon the delegates from regional councils which in turn were representative of the Churches and missions. A later constitution, however, gave direct representation to some of the larger Churches and missions. The two first Secretaries were an Indian, K. T. Paul, and an Englishman, William Paton. Both were extremely able and gave the new body an impetus which was to make it one of the most effective members of the I.M.C.

As the years passed, the N.C.C. added to the number of its regional councils and broadened its activities. It aided in famine relief, promoted literature, agricultural education and village improvement, set up a Youth Committee, and inaugurated a Christian Home Movement. Always it stressed evangelism, especially through the mass movements from which came so large a percentage of the accessions to the Churches. The proportion of Indians in the secretariat increased. During the second world war valuable aid was accorded to interned German missionaries, and after the war the return of German missionaries was facilitated. When, in 1947, the creation of the two separate States of India and Pakistan led to vast shifts of population, accompanied by acute distress among millions of refugees, the Council, helped by funds contributed co-operatively by American Churches through Church World Service and by Churches and individual Christians of many denominations in many lands, gave extensive relief. The formation of Pakistan led in 1950 to the creation of a National Christian Council for that country.

In India as in China there was a Medical Missionary Association, later, as the indigenous element increased, to be called the Christian Medical Association of India. There were also literature societies, including a Christian Literature Society for India. As in China, co-operation was outstanding in the field of education, and especially in higher education. Many Christian colleges were supported by the joint enterprise of several denominations. In 1919 there was a survey of Christian village schools in which mission boards of Britain and North America joined. In 1930–31 an international, interdenominational commission of the I.M.C., headed by Dr A. D. (later Lord) Lindsay, Master of Balliol College, Oxford, made a comprehensive study of Christian higher education.

As in China, theological education displayed a striking measure of co-operation. While there were many denominational institutions, interdenominational colleges and seminaries provided much of the leadership. Serampore College was the centre of the theological enterprise for the whole of India. Founded by that great pioneer of modern Protestant missions, William Carey, through a charter from the Danish Government later confirmed by the Governments of Great Britain and Bengal, it had authority to grant degrees, including those in divinity. It was, indeed, the only institution in India which possessed the latter privilege. In 1910 the theological department became interdenominational.

From the beginning of the century, Indians increasingly played a leading part in the world-wide ecumenical movement. The list is long and includes both men and women. If one name is to be singled out, it must be that of V. S. Azariah.

We have already met him as one of the most striking members of the Edinburgh Conference. Of humble Tamil stock, he was born and reared in a Christian family and from childhood was dedicated to the service of God. For a time he was a secretary of the Y.M.C.A. with work primarily among students. He was the chief organizer and became the first Secretary of the undenominational National Missionary Society of India, which had been formed in 1905 and twenty years later had a staff of ninety-seven, working in five different parts of India. In 1912 he was consecrated as Bishop of Dornakal, the first Indian to be raised to the Anglican episcopate. Under his leadership that diocese became noted for successful evangelism through Indian clergy and laity. He was Chairman of the National Christian Council of India and one of the leaders in the movement which issued in the Church of South India. He was active and influential in the I.M.C. An able administrator, a man of prayer, a born teacher, warm in his evangelistic zeal, Bishop Azariah was a major gift of Indian Christianity to the universal Church.

The Near East. What is sometimes called the Near East presented a more difficult problem in the development of Christian co-operation than any other portion of the globe. It is a huge area, including Iran, Iraq, Turkey, Syria, Lebanon, Palestine, Jordan, the various divisions of Arabia, Egypt, and Ethiopia. The chief unifying factor is Islam, for here that faith is dominant. For our purposes North Africa is reckoned a part of the Near East. In all this vast region Christians were minorities, in most of its units small minorities. Moreover, they were deeply divided. Here were the ancient Eastern Churches—Orthodox, Copts, Nestorians, Armenians, Jacobites—by long history regarding one another with suspicion and even hostility. Here Roman Catholics were active. Protestant bodies were numerous, and on strongly held doctrinal grounds some of them were unwilling to work together.

In spite of the difficulties, some degree of comprehensive co-operation and a consequent approach to unity were realized. To this a formative stimulus was given by Edinburgh 1910 and the I.M.C. In 1911 a conference on missions to Moslems met in Lucknow. The Continuation Committee of that gathering merged its plans with those of the I.M.C. In 1924 regional conferences led by Dr Mott were held at the instance of the latter body and culminated in a general conference in Jerusalem. Out of these gatherings came a Christian Literature Committee for Moslems, and what eventually was called the Near East Christian Council. The two worked closely together.

Unique in the Christian world was a body in Egypt called the Committee of Liaison. On it were represented Roman Catholics, Maronites, Greek Orthodox, Greek Catholics, Copts, Anglicans, and more than one variety of Protestants. Its primary purpose was a joint approach to the Government in matters of common interest, but it also worked on an agreed syllabus for religious education. This Committee justified the claim that Cairo was the most ecumenical city in the world.[1] Over the whole area, a most valuable unitive work was done by Robert P. Wilder; the last phase of his long life of service to the missionary cause was his work as the first Secretary of the Near East Christian Council.

Africa. Africa south of the Sahara was another extensive area in which comprehensive Christian unity was extremely difficult to attain. The obstacles were

[1] Maurice Richmond, *Memorandum on the Committee of Liaison*, supplied as a preparatory document for this History; and Chap. xiv, p. 652.

in part the great distances, in part the many political divisions, and in part the lack of any sense of cultural unity such as existed in most other countries and regions.

Yet here, after 1910, Christianity made more rapid and striking numerical advance, both Roman Catholic and Protestant, than in any other major area. Comprehensive planning and action seemed to be called for, both because the area had a measure of geographic cohesion, and even more because of its common problem of primitive cultures undergoing the revolutionary impact of European civilization.

Through the initiative of its first Secretary, the I.M.C. early turned its attention to Africa. For several years Oldham made Africa his special concern. In 1926, largely at his instance, an international missionary conference for planning for Africa was held at Le Zoute, Belgium. The designation deliberately chosen for the gathering was "the Christian mission in Africa" rather than "Christian missions in Africa", for the purpose was to cover unitedly the Christian approach to all ranges of African life. The conference was a landmark in Protestant effort for Africa. Out of it came the International Committee on Christian Literature for Africa, a sub-committee of the I.M.C. In this about two score British and American societies joined with the purpose of producing a wide range of sound Christian reading matter for the whole of Africa.

As Chairman of the I.M.C., Mott visited Africa in 1934 and held conferences in South Africa and the Congo, which greatly promoted co-operation among Protestant forces in these lands. Through its Department of Social and Industrial Research the I.M.C. made detailed studies of particular problems affecting the African.

A result of one of these studies was a unique co-operative effort, the United Missions in the Copper Belt, in the southern part of the Belgian Congo and in Northern Rhodesia, in which Anglicans, Baptists, Congregationalists, Methodists, and Presbyterians collaborated in meeting the needs of the workers in the mines. In the fields of education and social welfare all five denominations worked as a single team. Roman Catholic missions co-operated in the staffing and control of African schools. In Church work collaboration was flexible. In this Anglicans remained independent, while the other members of the United Missions co-operated closely, some even moving towards Church union. This freedom for missions to work together in certain spheres and elsewhere to go their own ways in friendship was the essence of the project.[1]

Bodies, sometimes called Missionary Councils and sometimes Christian Councils, came into being in various political divisions of Africa. Here there is space to call attention to only two of them, those in Northern and Southern Rhodesia. They are singled out because in each of them, quite contrary to usual experience elsewhere in the world, Roman Catholics participated.[2]

South Africa. The situation in South Africa was even more baffling and complex than elsewhere. Here the strong Dutch Reformed Churches, the symbol and tie of Boer or Afrikaner nationalism, are extremely conservative both in theology and on the race issue, and found fellowship difficult with those Churches, also strong, which had Anglo-Saxon connections or were purely African. Race tensions were as multiform and acute as anywhere on the globe. Moreover, the proliferation of Bantu sects seemed to make impossible any structure of fellowship inclusive of all Protestant Christians.

[1] Memorandum of Miss D. B. Gibson, July 1950.   [2]Ibid.

Yet even in South Africa efforts were made at co-operation, and with some success, although never fully comprehensive of all Protestant forces. There were several regional missionary conferences, and a Ciskeian Missionary Council was inaugurated in 1925. Conferences held under the chairmanship of Mott in 1934 were comprehensive in their membership, with Dutch, Anglo-Saxons, and Africans in attendance. Out of them came a Continuation Committee, to which was assigned the task of creating a Christian Council of South Africa. The Council was formed, and during the second world war it held two important conferences. Yet the Dutch Reformed Churches found association with it embarrassing and formed a Federal Council of their own. Unity in the Protestant forces, even in fellowship, was far from being an accomplished fact.

Latin America. It will be recalled that, as a corollary of restricting the scope of Edinburgh 1910 to non-Christian peoples, missions among Roman Catholics in Latin America had been excluded from the purview of that gathering (although the South American Missionary Society—Anglican—working among pagan Indians had been included). However, some of the delegates who were concerned with Latin America met informally at Edinburgh to consider the needs of that area. Partly as a consequence of this, in 1913 a conference on missions in Latin America was held under the auspices of the Foreign Missions Conference of North America. From this came the Committee on Co-operation in Latin America. One of the earliest achievements of the Committee was the calling, in 1914, in Cincinnati, of a conference of missionaries and secretaries of boards represented in Mexico, through which, to avoid overlapping and duplication of effort, extensive readjustments were made of territories in which the different denominations were working, and other co-operative measures were adopted.

In 1916 a Congress on Christian Work in Latin America was convened in Panama. This was by far the largest and most widely representative gathering of the Evangelical forces in Latin America which had thus far been held. The preparation, like that for Edinburgh 1910, included preliminary studies by eight commissions. The Committee on Co-operation in Latin America was authorized to carry out the recommendations of the Congress. Again following the precedent of Edinburgh 1910, regional conferences, seven in number, were convened in the months following the Panama Congress, and by the beginning of 1919 regional committees had been constituted in eight centres.

In 1925, in conscious succession to the Panama gathering, a Congress on Christian Work in South America assembled in Montevideo. This recorded a striking advance in Evangelical Christianity in Latin America in the intervening nine years—to no small degree the outcome of united study, a united programme, and the presentation of a common front. In 1929 an Hispanic American Evangelical Congress was held in Havana.

Latin America was brought into the fellowship of the I.M.C., and its representatives were present at the enlarged Meetings of that body in Jerusalem in 1928, at Tambaram in 1938, and at Whitby in 1947. The Committee on Co-operation in Latin America continued, with headquarters in New York City; but increasingly Latin Americans came to the fore in the ecumenical movement. Outstanding among them was the Mexican G. Baez Camargo; author, editor, teacher, scholar, cultured, highly intelligent, deeply Christian, he was a familiar and welcome figure at many ecumenical gatherings.

In every country in Latin America Protestants continued to multiply. The growth was especially spectacular in Brazil. Here strong and large Churches came into being and were active and successful in spreading their faith. In other Latin American republics, notably Chile and the Argentine, the younger Churches displayed marked vitality. Although Protestantism was not indigenous to the region, but had been imported, partly by immigrants from Europe and the United States and partly through missions from Britain and North America, by 1948 it had become deeply rooted and was self-propagating.

Not only was co-operation developing on a continental scale; it was also growing in particular countries and regions. Some of this was the work of missions. Increasingly it represented the initiative of Latin American Christians. To mention a few concrete examples, we find: a Committee on Co-operation in Brazil, formed in 1916 and succeeded by a federation of Evangelical Churches (the Evangelical Confederation of Brazil);[1] the National Christian Council of Mexico, formed in 1927, and soon followed by the National Evangelical Council of Mexico; a Board of Christian Work in Santo Domingo in which Methodists, Presbyterians, and United Brethren joined, and which nourished congregations that bore the common name of the Dominican Evangelical Churches; the United Andean Mission, begun in the 1940's, in which several denominations shared and which had as its object the nurturing of a Christian culture based upon the land and centring in the Church of Christ.[2] Here, as in so many other parts of the world, there were theological seminaries in which two or more denominations joined.

Co-operation among the Protestant forces in Latin America was by no means complete. Many missions, some of them of the "faith" type drawing support from more than one denomination, held theological convictions which kept them aloof from the bodies associated with the Committee on Co-operation in Latin America and the I.M.C. Yet here as elsewhere co-operation has made steady progress.

The Philippines. Although, because of geography and language, the Philippines were not included in the Latin American co-operative structure, religiously they had so much in common with that region that it is natural to think of the two areas as belonging together. Here was a country in which Roman Catholic Christianity, planted and nourished by Spaniards, was dominant. Here Protestantism had been introduced from the United States and had won most of its converts from the nominally Roman Catholic constituency. In 1948 it completed its first half-century of life. Here from the very outset there was much co-operation. In 1898 plans were made to divide the territory among the several societies to prevent overlapping and to ensure complete coverage. In Manila the Union Theological Seminary, inaugurated in 1907, drew its support from several denominations. There was a national body, founded in 1939, called the Philippine Federation of Evangelical Churches, which had membership in the I.M.C. There were unions of Churches. The Japanese occupation (1942–45) brought complications and was the occasion of fresh divisions. These were not completely resolved by the expulsion of the Japanese, but extensive co-operation persists.

[1] E. Braga and K. G. Grubb, *The Republic of Brazil*, London, 1932, p. 92.
[2] W. S. Rycroft, *Indians of the High Andes*, New York, 1946, pp. v–viii, 315–20.

9. THE YOUNGER CHURCHES AND ECUMENISM

Increasing participation by the younger Churches and their leaders in the movement for Christian co-operation has been a recurring feature in the brief surveys, country by country, included in this chapter; but the growth of a sense of ecumenical responsibility in those Churches had been very gradual, and full participation of the younger Churches in the ecumenical movement belonged to a very recent phase of Church history.

Four stages may, perhaps, be distinguished in this development.

There was, first, the rediscovery of one another by younger churchmen across the confessional barriers introduced from the West. In the vast territories of Africa and Asia and Latin America, distances are great and, until recently, modern means of travel were few; the small new Churches lived in isolation from one another. The 19th-century principle of comity did good by removing or preventing much harmful overlapping and competition; but it also introduced many absurd divisions. Most of the leading Christian families in South India, the descendants of the great converts of the 19th century, were spread out all the way from Cape Comorin to Madras and beyond; each branch naturally tended to be active in the area where it lived, and dutifully became "Danish Lutheran" or "American Dutch Reformed" or whatever it might be; but when the members of these families met, they were bound to note that, loyal as they might be to the Church of their immediate allegiance, the divisions between them were caused originally by no more than accidents of geography. Part of the violent reaction against the West was visible in a tendency to treat these ecclesiastical divisions lightly, or to regard them as having no validity in an Oriental setting.

The second phase was the recognition by younger Church leaders that these divisions existed and were to be taken seriously, combined with a steady determination that denominational differences must be overcome and the way to full and stable Church unity discovered. Out of many impressive younger Church statements on this theme, a few may be cited here.

The Indian ministers, assembled in the Tranquebar Conference (1–2 May 1919), which was the genesis of the Church of South India, declared:

> "We believe that the challenge of the present hour . . . and the present critical situation in India itself, call us to mourn our past divisions and turn to our Lord Jesus Christ to seek in Him the unity of the body expressed in one visible Church. We face together the titanic task of the winning of India for Christ—one-fifth of the human race. Yet, confronted by such an overwhelming responsibility, we find ourselves rendered weak and relatively impotent by our unhappy divisions—divisions for which we were not responsible, and which have been, as it were, imposed upon us from without, divisions which we did not create, and which we do not desire to perpetuate."[1]

The China National Conference, held at Shanghai (11–14 March 1913), which included thirty-five leading Chinese Christians, spoke strongly on the subject of the unity of the Church in China:

> "*Manifesting the Unity Which Exists*—In order to do all that is possible to manifest the unity which already exists among all faithful Christians in

[1] G. K. A. Bell, *Documents*, I, pp. 278 f.

China and to present ourselves, in the face of the great mass of Chinese non-Christian people, as one brotherhood with one common name, this conference suggests as the most suitable name for this purpose 'The Christian Church in China'.

"*Steps Towards a Larger Unity*—As steps towards unity, this conference urges upon the Churches:

"1. The uniting of Churches of similar ecclesiastical order planted in China by different missions.

"2. The organic union of Churches which already enjoy intercommunion in any particular area, large or small.

"3. Federation, local and provincial, of all Churches willing to co-operate in the extension of the Kingdom of God."[1]

In 1931 a Conference on Church Union was held by the representatives of most of the non-Roman missions working in Eastern Nigeria. At that meeting the African delegates, sitting separately, passed the following resolution:

"In view of the great Commission we have received from our Lord, of His express desire that His people should be one, and of the desirability of presenting a united front to the world in the evangelisation of our people, we, the African delegates representing the Churches of the Eastern Regional Committee of the Christian Council of Nigeria, deprecate the existence of divisions among us as a source of weakness and strongly urge that steps be taken to the consolidation of Union among Churches."

The best known of these statements was that put forth at Tambaram in 1938 by the younger Church members of the Section on Co-operation and Unity:

"During the discussions it became abundantly clear that the divisions of Christendom were seen in their worst light in the mission field. Instances were cited by the representatives of the younger churches of disgraceful competition, wasteful overlapping, and of groups and individuals turned away from the Church because of the divisions within. Disunion is both a stumbling block to the faithful and a mockery to those without. We confess with shame that we ourselves have often been the cause of thus bringing dishonour to the religion of our Master. The representatives of the younger churches in this Section, one and all gave expression to the passionate longing that exists in all countries for visible union of the churches. They are aware of the fact of spiritual unity; they record with great thankfulness all the signs of co-operation and understanding that are increasingly seen in various directions; but they realize that this is not enough. Visible and organic union must be our goal. This, however, will require an honest study of those things in which the churches have differences, a widespread teaching of the common church membership in things that make for union and venturesome sacrifice on the part of all. Such a union alone will remove the evils arising out of our divisions. Union proposals have been put forward in different parts of the world. Loyalty, however, will forbid the younger churches going forward to consummate any union unless it receives the wholehearted support and blessing of those through whom these churches

[1] *Addresses and Papers of John R. Mott*, V, p. 117.

have been planted. We are thus often torn between loyalty to our mother churches and loyalty to our ideal of union. We, therefore, appeal with all the fervour we possess, to the missionary societies and boards and the responsible authorities of the older churches, to take this matter seriously to heart, to labour with the churches in the mission field to achieve this union, to support and encourage us in all our efforts to put an end to the scandalous effects of our divisions, and to lead us in the path of union—the union for which our Lord prayed, through which the world would indeed believe in the Divine Mission of the Son, our Lord Jesus Christ."[1]

It is in accord with the tenor of such statements that, of thirty-four united Churches that came into existence in the period under review, sixteen were in the lands of the younger Churches, and of fifteen sets of negotiations for corporate union in progress at the time of writing eight were in those same regions.

The third phase of younger Church ecumenism was the mutual discovery of younger Churches across the barriers of race and country. The younger Churches had been far more closely linked to the sending countries than to one another; connected with centres in the West like the spokes of a wheel, they had had hardly any contact with one another round the rim. Christians in India and China were far better informed respectively about Britain and the United States than they were about one another. Indonesia almost touches Australia; but, though hundreds of Indonesian students had sailed half round the world to study in Holland, few, if any, had studied at an Australian university: the mutual discovery of Indonesia and Australia had to wait for the period of reconstruction after the second world war.

This mutual discovery led to some sharp surprises. Younger churchmen were not a natural species; it was at first disturbing to Indians and Chinese to discover that the psychological differences between them were at least as great as those between Asians and Europeans. But repeated meetings at ecumenical conferences helped their Christian leaders to see that they had a rich and diverse contribution to make to the treasures of the universal Church.

This was the special significance of the East Asia Consultation held at Manila in 1948. With only two Westerners present, leaders of the East Asian Churches met for the first time as such, for unrestricted discussion of their own problems. At the start they were suspicious of the proposal to treat East Asia as a region: might not the establishment of an East Asia Secretariat of the World Council of Churches and the International Missionary Council result in the production of an East Asian ecumenism, a spurious and second-rate article in contrast to the genuine thing? It was only when they were assured that there was no conflict between this proposal and their full participation in the world-wide Christian movement that they were willing to accept this strategic forward move.

Finally, the eagerness of the younger Churches to become member Churches of the World Council of Churches set the seal on this development of ecumenical participation. The smaller the Church, the greater seemed to be its desire to have membership in the great world-wide fellowship; local weakness seemed a strong argument in favour of sharing directly in the strength of the world-wide Church. The fact that the World Council's definition of autonomy excluded great self-governing African Churches, while admitting tiny Churches in other parts of the

[1] *The Madras Series*, IV, *The Life of the Church*, pp. 376 ff.

world, was a matter of deep regret to Christians in tropical Africa.[1] Each year saw some additions to the list of younger Churches which were full members of the World Council; that body showed its sense of the importance of their contribution when it elected a Chinese, Dr T. C. Chao, as one of its first Presidents; and on his resignation replaced him by Miss Sarah Chakko, a member of the ancient Syrian Church of India.

10. SUMMARY

As we come to the end of this chapter, let us seek to sum up in a few generalizations the main characteristics of the development which we have been sketching.

First of all, there was a movement which was almost world-wide in its scope and which was rapidly growing. Significantly and tragically, it did not include Russia, nor, with a few exceptions, did it embrace Roman Catholics. It was a phase and a stage in an even larger and more inclusive movement which is the subject of this History, and must always be viewed in relation to it. Even if our concern were only with the co-operative features of the ecumenical movement in foreign missions and the lands of the younger Churches, these must be seen in conjunction with the co-operative undertakings in the lands of the older Churches, the Federal Council of the Churches of Christ in America, the British Council of Churches, and the World Council of Churches. This chapter tells only a portion of the story of the amazing fashion in which, with accelerated pace since 1910, Christians of the world were drawing together, largely in quite new ways.

The ecumenical movement as we here know it had its main impulse and its main achievements in what has organizationally been the most divided branch of the Church, Protestantism, but in one fashion or another it reached out to other forms of the Faith, notably to the Roman Catholic Church and the Orthodox Churches, and drew into its fellowship many, even though a small minority, from these bodies. Very significantly, moreover, the ecumenical movement, particularly in the aspects which are the subject of this chapter, embraced both older and younger Churches.

The younger Churches, still minorities in their respective countries, but most of them rapidly growing in numbers and in competent leadership, had a mounting share in the ecumenical movement and in some respects were in the vanguard. Fresh divisions there were. They were more numerous in the lands of the younger than of the older Churches, alarmingly so in some countries. Yet, because of their greater flexibility, the anachronism of the imported divisions, and the challenge which they faced, the younger Churches experimented more boldly than the older in co-operative and union enterprises.

In the second place we must note that the most numerous forms of ecumenical experiment in the lands of the younger Churches, as of the older Churches, were co-operative undertakings. They did not erase historic confessional and denominational divisions. Instead, frankly recognizing and respecting them, they brought together either individuals who were members of different Churches or the official representatives of the Churches and of the societies which were the

---

[1] The definition of autonomy, for which see *The First Assembly of the World Council of Churches*, pp. 202 f., had made difficult the admission of a number of large Churches, particularly of the Methodist and Anglican types, which, though possessing full local autonomy, remained more closely integrated with older Churches than, for example, those of the Presbyterian or Reformed type.

organs of the Churches. The purpose was to accomplish what could better be done together than separately. This might be in the distribution of the Bible, in the production and circulation of other forms of Christian literature, in joint approaches to the rural problem, in educational institutions, including theological schools and colleges, or in nation-wide programmes of evangelism. Questions of faith and order were not disregarded. That would have been impossible. Indeed, because of them some Churches and societies either did not join at all in co-operative ventures or did so on expressly limited conditions. Yet in general these issues did not come to the fore and, while not ignored, were not allowed to become obstacles in the way to co-operative action.

A third important generalization is that co-operation was largely by national and regional units, but national and regional units drawn into a global structure. Had the units been purely national or regional, a new and dangerous set of divisions might have been added to the old, and the emerging world-wide fellowship might have been obscured or stifled by them. That danger was especially acute in a day of intense and rising nationalism. Happily, through the International Missionary Council the regional and national bodies have been brought into global co-operation. Moreover, an increasing number of the younger Churches have joined the World Council of Churches, and this fellowship and the International Missionary Council have entered into intimate association with each other.

As the final and highly significant generalization we must stress the fact that the compelling motive in all the co-operation which we have been describing has been evangelism. The missionary enterprise arises from the divine commission to bear witness to the Gospel throughout the world and to win all men to discipleship to Christ. From this came the ecumenical movement, and the growth of that movement was due primarily to it. Unity was sought not as an end in itself but as a means to evangelism. Whether or not in its precise words, the injunction kept ringing in the ears of the leaders of both older and younger Churches: "By this shall all men know that ye are my disciples, if ye have love one to another." Especially did that petition from the high-priestly prayer of their Lord keep spurring them on: "that they may all be one; even as thou, Father, art in me, and I in thee, that they also may be in us: that the world may believe that thou didst send me". As they sought to fulfil the command by planning, working, and praying together, Christians found that in them the apparently impossible was being realized; underneath the barriers which had long divided them they were finding an inclusive unity in Christ.

CHAPTER 9

THE WORLD CONFERENCE ON FAITH AND ORDER
by
TISSINGTON TATLOW

1. TOWARDS EDINBURGH 1910

The origin of the proposal to hold a World Conference on Faith and Order is always and rightly associated with the World Missionary Conference, Edinburgh 1910, although the reasons for this are little understood. This Edinburgh Conference was preceded by the Ecumenical Missionary Conference, New York 1900, which before it disbanded decided that a decade later another conference in the international decennial series should take place, and on this occasion at Edinburgh. A committee representing British missionary societies with a strong Scottish element was appointed to bring it about. In 1906 this committee began to make plans for the next World Conference. It was aware that the missionary societies prepared to take part did not include any society connected with the Church of England except those known as Evangelical.[1] Some important and representative Church of England missionary societies, and notably the Society for the Propagation of the Gospel, had not taken part in the previous world conferences.

The Student Christian Movement of Great Britain and Ireland, however, had established a relationship with the Church of England that no other organization which included members of Nonconformist Churches or their representative societies had achieved.[2] The Executive Committee preparing for the Edinburgh Conference therefore invited the General Secretary of the Student Christian Movement, himself a clergyman of the Church of England, to join it, expressing in their letter of invitation their hope that he would bring the Church of England into the coming Conference.

To explain in full how it came about that the S.C.M. had established a relationship with the Church of England which was unique would be to tell the story of ten years' discussion between the leaders of the S.C.M. and a number of influential groups and individuals in the Church of England.[3] What was important in relation to the preparations for Edinburgh 1910 was that the S.C.M. had won a number of influential Anglicans to its support as a result of their belief that a new basis had been established by the Movement on which Christians of all denominations could come together without compromise of principles held by any one group to be of fundamental importance; this basis, established as the result of a decade of thought and conference, was designated "interdenominational".

The Edinburgh Conference Committee was planning the Conference on such an interdenominational basis as had been worked out by the S.C.M. The result was that it was able to secure the co-operation of some of the most representative Anglican churchmen in England on one or other of its eight preparatory commissions, and the acceptance by the S.P.G. of an invitation to be officially represented at Edinburgh 1910.

In the course of setting up the eight preparatory commissions to prepare reports on the main subjects for the consideration of the Conference, the Com-

[1] For definition of terms, see Note on p. 306. [2] See Chap. vii, pp. 343 f.
[3] Tatlow, *The Story of the Student Christian Movement*, Chaps. ix and xxi.

mittee asked J. H. Oldham and Tissington Tatlow to present personally its invitation to the first few members of the Church of England to be invited, thinking, as proved to be the case, that they would be responsive to invitations handed to them by leaders in the Student Movement, since they had already taken part in S.C.M. conferences. Two of the first Anglicans to be approached, the Bishops of Southwark (Edward Stuart Talbot, later Bishop of Winchester) and Birmingham (Charles Gore, later Bishop of Oxford), not only accepted the invitation to share in the work of the commissions, but a little later, on 3 November 1908, addressed a joint letter on the subject of the Edinburgh Conference to the Standing Committee of the S.P.G., which had already declined an invitation to take part, in which they said:

> "We think that it would be widely harmful, and a great loss to ourselves, if the Anglican Church were left outside it. We have had some dealings with its executive officers and have satisfied ourselves that it is not at all what would be understood by the word "undenominational", but: (1) it proceeds upon the principle of entire mutual respect between Christian denominations, and (2) it has definitely pledged itself that questions affecting the differences of Doctrine and Order between the Christian bodies shall not be brought before the Conference for discussion or resolution."[1]

The writers then went on to say that they had become members of the commissions preparing the subjects for the Conference, and concluded, "We desire to express our very earnest hopes that the S.P.G. will be strongly and powerfully represented".

Later, Bishop H. H. Montgomery, Secretary of the S.P.G., reported to the monthly meeting of the Society that the Standing Committee had appointed to represent it at Edinburgh 1910 thirty-four persons, the full delegation assigned to the Society by the rules of the Conference. In making this announcement Bishop Montgomery said, "For the first time, so far as I am aware, the undenominational platform has been forsaken, showing an immense advance toward the yet far distant reunion of the future. . . . There is no doubt that the Student Volunteer Movement has been the pioneer in this new direction". That the decision was not without its difficulties for the S.P.G. is shown by the very large correspondence in which Bishop Montgomery was involved and by the formal Remonstrance addressed to the Standing Committee by 900 incorporated members of the Society.

The decision of the S.P.G. to share in the Edinburgh Conference and the acceptance by many representative Anglicans of places on the eight preparatory commissions marked an important new phase in the ecumenical movement. For more than half a century Anglicans had shared in international missionary conferences, but almost all of those who had done so had been Evangelicals. When the World Missionary Conference assembled at Edinburgh in 1910, its Anglican members of all parties were numbered by the score and took a leading part in all its deliberations. From that time onwards no important ecumenical conference has been held at which Anglo-Catholics have not been represented. This has had important results beyond the ranks of Anglicanism.

The next link in the chain was Bishop Brent of the Protestant Episcopal

[1] Standing Committee Minutes, S.P.G.

Church in the United States, then Bishop of the Philippine Islands. Addressing the Edinburgh Conference towards its close, he said, "We are sons of God, and being sons of God, it is not fitting that we should have anything less than a task which will bring out all the capacity of God's children. During these past days a new vision has been unfolded to us. But whenever God gives a vision He also points to some new responsibility, and you and I, when we leave this assembly, will go away with some fresh duties to perform".[1] The new vision was the vision of a united Church. Bishop Brent was one of many who received that vision at Edinburgh, and it laid upon him the responsibility of leadership. Before he left Edinburgh he told friends that he had made the resolve to call his own Church to take the lead in preparing another world conference, this conference to deal with those matters of faith and order which had been excluded from the Edinburgh programme.

In October 1910, the day before the General Convention of the Protestant Episcopal Church met at Cincinnati, Bishop Brent addressed a mass meeting attended by both Houses of Convention, the delegates of the Women's Auxiliary, and scores of visitors. He spoke of the Edinburgh Conference, of the need for unity there revealed, and of his own conviction that the time had come to examine differences frankly in a world conference on faith and order. Robert Gardiner, an influential layman, suggested that steps should be taken to secure some definite action by the Convention. Accordingly the Rev. W. T. Manning, later Bishop of New York, on 19 October proposed a resolution which was passed unanimously, first by the House of Deputies and then by the House of Bishops:

> "That a Joint Commission be appointed to bring about a Conference for the consideration of questions touching Faith and Order, and that all Christian Communions throughout the world which confess Our Lord Jesus Christ as God and Saviour be asked to unite with us in arranging for and conducting such a Conference."

The Commission was duly appointed, and elected the Bishop of Chicago (C. P. Anderson) as President and Robert Gardiner as Secretary. While it was Brent who had conceived the idea of a world conference on faith and order, it was upon Gardiner that most of the work fell. Brent was a missionary bishop and his duties kept him in the Philippine Islands, though as President of the International Opium Commission he was already an international figure. Throughout the rest of his life he exercised a profound influence on the Faith and Order movement. But it was to Gardiner that clergy and laity looked as their leader in this new enterprise; and not men of his own Church only—within a very short time he had correspondents all over the world. Mr J. Pierpont Morgan was so moved by the prospect of action on a world scale that he at once gave $100,000 to assist the movement.

2. THE BEGINNINGS OF FAITH AND ORDER

A new movement was afoot. Peter Ainslie of the Disciples of Christ, addressing as President their Annual Convention on 18 October 1910, the day before the Protestant Episcopal Church had passed its resolution, dealt candidly with the

[1] *World Missionary Conference, 1910*, IX, p. 330.

uncharitableness of many among the Disciples in their attitude towards Christians of other denominations, and spoke of the grave disloyalty to Christ and to the early traditions of their Church displayed in their lack of activity on behalf of Christian union. Following his address, he took steps to create the Commission on Christian Union (which some years later was styled the Association for the Promotion of Christian Unity) of which he was elected President. His first act in this capacity was to send a telegram of greeting to the Commission of the Episcopal Church appointed to promote a World Conference on Faith and Order. Dr Ainslie also launched in 1911 the *Christian Union Quarterly*, which he carried on until his death in 1934.[1]

The National Council of Congregational Churches in the United States, on the very same day and quite independently, appointed a special commission to consider any overture which might be made "in view of the possibility of fraternal discussion of Church unity suggested by the Lambeth Conference of Bishops in 1908". The men concerned recognized these happenings as a movement of the Spirit of God, whereat they rejoiced.

The Commission of the Episcopal Church appointed a Committee on Plan and Scope, which held frequent meetings and examined large numbers of suggestions before it was ready to suggest to the Commission what its general plan of action should be. Subsequently it advised the Commission to ask the prayers of all Christian people for the movement; to secure the appointment of independent but co-operating Commissions of all the Churches of the world; to bring such Commissions into conference, and through an Executive appointed by them to work out plans for a World Conference on Faith and Order.

There was no doubt in the minds of those responsible from the start for the leadership of the movement that participation in the Conference by representatives of the whole Christian world, Roman Catholic, Orthodox, and Protestant, should be sought. It was made clear

> "that all Christian Communions throughout the world which confess our Lord Jesus Christ as God and Saviour should be asked to unite with the Protestant Episcopal Church in arranging for and conducting a conference based on a clear statement and full consideration of those things in which we differ, as well as of those things in which we are one".

A conference was envisaged, the purpose of which would be study and discussion without power to legislate or to adopt resolutions:

> "the conference is for the definite purpose of considering those things in which we differ, in the hope that a better understanding of divergent views of faith and order will result in a deepened desire for reunion and in official action on the part of the separated Communions themselves. It is the business of the conference not to take such official action, but to inspire it and to prepare the way for it."[2]

The response throughout the United States was immediate, and a large number of Churches began the appointment of co-operating Commissions. Mr Gardiner was active in the preparation and widespread dissemination of litera-

---

[1] See Chap. v, pp. 239 f.
[2] *Report of Committee on Plan and Scope, adopted April 20, 1911.* No. 1 in the series of Faith and Order pamphlets.

ture descriptive of what was proposed. The result was that when the Episcopal Church Commission met in April 1911, not only had eighteen American Protestant Churches, including all the major denominations, Presbyterian, Congregationalist, Methodist, and so forth, appointed representative Commissions, but plans had been made to enter into communication with the Church of England, the Roman Catholic Church, the Old Catholic Churches, and the Orthodox Churches.

There was a good deal of discussion both in the Commission of the Episcopal Church and in its Committee on Plan and Scope as to the order in which invitations to share in the movement for a World Conference should be issued, and also by whom. Although the importance of this may not be apparent to a later generation, consultation on these points occupied more than a year, and the advice of a considerable number of persons in various Churches and countries was taken. The care that was expended on this subject was largely due to the intensity of feeling between different sections of the same denomination in the United States, a problem which did not present itself in other parts of the world. Those divisions of Methodists, Presbyterians, and Baptists which had their roots in the period of the Civil War were unknown in other countries. Dr Newman Smyth, a Congregational leader, was a valued adviser of the Episcopal Church Commission, for although leadership in the movement was vested exclusively in that Commission, there was no lack of friendly conference with leading men in a number of different Churches, and numerous meetings of Congregational, Baptist, and Presbyterian ministers were addressed by the President of the Commission.

In June 1912 a deputation was sent to the Anglican Churches of Great Britain and Ireland, consisting of the Bishop of Chicago (C. P. Anderson), the Bishop of Southern Ohio (Boyd Vincent), the Bishop of Vermont (A. C. A. Hall), and the Rev. William T. Manning, Rector of Trinity Church, New York. On 25 June a conference took place at Lambeth Palace between this deputation and a representative Church of England group. The way had been prepared by correspondence with the Archbishop of Canterbury (Davidson), and he called to Lambeth Palace to receive the delegation the Archbishop of York (Lang), the Bishops of London (Winnington Ingram), Bath and Wells (Kennion), and Gloucester (E. C. S. Gibson), the Deans of Westminster, St Paul's, Wells, and Ely, Bishop Tucker, and Bishop Walsham How. As a result, the two Archbishops agreed to appoint a representative committee whose work should be "to watch the progress of the arrangements for the proposed conference, organize support and help in England for these endeavours and especially to stimulate general interest and regular and widespread prayer".

The deputation then went north and discussed the proposed Conference with the Primus of the Episcopal Church in Scotland (Robberds of Brechin), who had with him the Bishops of Glasgow (Campbell), Moray (A. J. Maclean), and St Andrews (Plumb). They referred the question of the Conference sympathetically to the autumn meeting of the bishops, who agreed to appoint a Commission, at the same time stressing their sense of the importance of ensuring that as far as possible the projected Conference should be representative of all the Christian Churches of the world.

In Ireland they conferred with the Primate of the Church of Ireland (J. B. Crozier), together with the Bishop of Meath (Keene), and the Bishop of Down,

Connor and Dromore (D'Arcy), who undertook to bring the matter before the next meeting of the bishops of the Church of Ireland; subsequently this Church appointed a Commission.

The American delegation took the opportunity of discussing with the Church leaders whom they met in the British Isles a question which had given rise to a considerable amount of discussion in the United States—what should be the actual subjects to be discussed by the World Conference? They were clear themselves that points of agreement ought to be stated and that there should be a full discussion of differences. But they were troubled by the fact that

> "very few of the writers of the 40,000 to 50,000 letters which have been received, have noted that the chief object of the Conference is the discussion of differences. Very many of them propose one concordat or another, and not a few of them are content to demand, or at best to rejoice at what they suppose to be the prospect of, a surrender by the Episcopal Church of most of its distinctive tenets."[1]

Such suggestions of correspondents invariably arose from their assumption that the World Conference was to be concerned with the creation of a united Church out of existing denominations. Even at the Lausanne Conference in 1927 there were some present who to the end thought that that was the aim of the Conference.

Many have asked how it was that the Anglican Communion bulked so large at the start of the movement. The answer is simple. The idea of the Faith and Order Conference, the promotion of the idea on a world scale, and the money that made it possible, all came from members of the Protestant Episcopal Church, and it was not until ten years had gone by that the Anglicans in America found it possible to transfer their leadership to a body representative of the Anglican, Lutheran, Orthodox, Reformed, and other Churches of Europe and America.

The first occasion on which representatives of Commissions appointed by the Churches came together was on 8 May 1913, at the Hotel Astor, New York. The Commissions of fifteen Churches were represented. All these were Commissions of Churches in the United States, except the Church of England Co-operating Committee which was represented by its Secretary (Tissington Tatlow) who was visiting theological colleges of the Episcopal Church in the United States at the invitation of the Student Department of the Y.M.C.A. There was also present a member of the Holy Orthodox Church of Russia, Dean Hotovitsky, who attended as the representative of Archbishop Platon, head of the Russian Orthodox Church in the United States. The meeting had been convened by the Commission of the Protestant Episcopal Church. Gardiner reported that in the United States, Canada, and England twenty-two Commissions had been appointed; many more Churches were represented among the 7,580 persons who had asked that their names be entered on a mailing list to receive future publications. It was already a remarkable list, including names in the United States and Canada, in all the countries of Europe, and in Arabia, Ceylon, China, India, Japan, Korea, Palestine, Persia, Syria, and Turkey in Asia.

[1] *F. and O. Pamphlet No. 30*, p. 17.

The first matter which engaged the attention of the conference was how to secure the appointment of Commissions representative of the Presbyterian and Free Churches throughout the British Isles, to which written invitations had been sent, but with few results. Mr Tatlow's suggestion that a deputation should be sent to the Free Churches, similar to that sent the previous year to the Church of England, was adopted.

The conference then proceeded to consider the kind of World Conference for which it was working. The interest of their conclusions lies in the fact that even at this early date principles were laid down from which the movement never departed:

"1. That the true ideal of the World Conference is of a great meeting participated in by men of all Christian Churches within the scope of the call, at which there shall be consideration not only of points of difference and agreement between Christians, but of the values of the various approximations to belief characteristic of the several Churches.

"2. That while organic unity is the ideal which all Christians should have in their thoughts and prayers, yet the business of the Commissions is not to force any particular scheme of unity, but to promote the holding of such a Conference as is above described.

"3. That in order that the World Conference may have a maximum value, the questions there to be considered shall be formulated in advance by committees of competent men representative of various schools of thought, these committees to be appointed at as early a date as is consistent with assurance that their truly representative character cannot be successfully challenged."[1]

Before the meeting closed, the Chairman called on Dean Hotovitsky, as the one visitor present, to speak. Several people had said that the meeting had been in itself a kind of ecumenical conference. The Russian made a very friendly speech and promised to seek support for the World Conference when he returned to Russia, saying that he was sailing for his home country in a week. He remarked, however, that "one of your distinguished bishops today likened this council to a sort of ecumenical council. I do not feel that it is much of an ecumenical council". The first step should be to bring the Protestant Churches together; if they were able to do that, they might go on to consider how to "reconcile such differences as exist with the Eastern Orthodox Church or with the Roman Catholic Church".[2] If he was candid in indicating the long road to be travelled, there was on the other hand no doubt about his sympathy for the movement.

The deputation to the Free Churches of the British Isles, of which Dr Peter Ainslie of Baltimore (Disciples), Dr Newman Smyth of New Haven (Congregational), and Dr H. W. Roberts of Philadelphia (Presbyterian) were members, visited Great Britain the following spring, and was successful in securing the appointment of commissions or co-operating committees from all the Free Churches, and in Scotland from the Presbyterian Churches. There was a cordial meeting between the Archbishops' Committee and the American visitors, and it was the statement of the latter group to the Archbishops' Committee that a number of Free Church leaders had expressed a desire to enter into relationships

[1] *F. and O. Pamphlet No. 24*, p. 46.   [2] Ibid., p. 48.

with the Church of England which paved the way for the first meeting (April 1914) between the Church of England and the Free Churches. At this meeting a representative group of men was appointed by the Archbishops' Committee and by representatives of the English Free Church Commissions in connection with the proposed World Conference. Two interim reports resulted, entitled *Towards Christian Unity*, the first in February 1916 and the second in March 1918.[1] When the Lambeth Conference of 1920 issued "An Appeal to All Christian People", this was recognized as having its roots in the two interim reports. All this work done in England was warmly welcomed by the Commission of the Protestant Episcopal Church, since its members felt that Church leaders in England understood the kind of world conference for which they were trying to prepare. The Joint Committee of Anglicans and Free Churchmen continued to meet until its place was taken, some years later, by formal conversations between the Church of England and the Free Churches.[2]

To return to the year 1914: discussions which had been proceeding for some time concerning an approach to the Roman Catholic Church, the Orthodox Churches, and the Protestant Churches of the Continent had not ceased; and the fact that all the Churches of Europe had their counterparts in North America as the result of immigration[3] led to consultations as to how best to approach the mother Churches in Europe. This intercourse was acclerated when the Episcopal Church Commission decided to send yet another deputation to Europe in 1914. This deputation was to visit "the Churches of the Continent of Europe and of the Near East and also the Roman Catholic Church"; but the first world war broke out, and at the last minute the visit had to be postponed.

Both Cardinal Gibbons and Cardinal Farley of the Roman Catholic Church in the United States had friends in the Episcopal Church who had told them of the projected Conference and of their desire to bring into it the Church of Rome. Both promised to speak favourably at Rome about the proposed World Conference. In the same way contact was made with Archbishop Platon of the Russian Orthodox Church, and he promised to prepare the way for the deputation when it went to Moscow.

By 1911 the proposed World Conference had been put before the leaders of Churches of every type all over the world. A letter about it had been addressed not only to all the bishops and clergy of the Protestant Episcopal Church in the United States, but also to all the bishops of the Anglican Communion, and to all the Cardinals and bishops of the Roman Catholic Church throughout the world. By this date 100,000 copies of the proposals relating to the Conference had been posted to individuals and large numbers of replies received. Mr Gardiner described these as almost all sympathetic and reported to his committee that "certainly not more than ten were of a hostile character". While letters were sent out at first in English, within little more than a year after the inception of the movement the Secretary had secured help which enabled him to issue letters also in Latin, French, and Italian, and he indicated that replies would be welcome not only in these languages but in modern Greek, Russian, or German.

In the summer of 1914 Mr Gardiner wrote in Latin to Cardinal Gasparri, informing him of the proposed World Conference; a translation of the Cardinal's reply reads as follows:

---

[1] G. K. A Bell, *Documents Bearing on the Problem of Christian Unity and Fellowship, 1916–1920*, pp. 3–14.

[2] See Chap. x, pp. 484 ff.   [3] See Chap. v, pp. 221 f.

From the Vatican, December 18, 1914.

"Your project of an international convention of all who believe in Jesus Christ as God and Saviour to accomplish the speedy fulfilment of the final prayer of the Lord, that all may be one, I have, in obedience to your request, submitted to the Most Blessed Father.[1] I need not here describe the affection with which I saw the August Pontiff kindled for you. For you well know that the plans of the Roman Pontiffs, their cares and their labours have always been specially directed to the end that the sole and unique Church which Jesus Christ ordained and sanctified with His divine Blood should be most zealously guarded and maintained, whole, pure and ever abounding in love, and that it should both let its light shine and open wide its door for all who rejoice in the name of man and who desire to gain holiness upon earth and eternal happiness in heaven.

"The August Pontiff, therefore, was pleased with your project of examining in a sincere spirit and without prejudice the essential form of the Church [*intimam Ecclesiae formam*] . . . and He earnestly hopes that under the spell of its native beauty you may settle all disputes and work with prosperous issue to the end that the mystical body of Christ be no longer suffered to be rent and torn, but that by harmony and co-operation of men's minds and likewise by the concord of their wills, unity of faith and communion may at last prevail throughout the world of men.

"Thanking you, then, that you have thought well to request the aid and support of the Roman Pontiff in expediting your worthy project, His Holiness expresses His earnest desire that the end may answer your expectation, and He asks the same of Christ Jesus with fervent prayers, all the more because, with the voice of Christ Himself sounding before and bidding Him, He knows that He Himself, as the one to whom all men have been given over to be fed, is the source and cause of the unity of the Church."[2]

Mr Gardiner asked and received permission from the Cardinal to give this letter some publicity.

As a result of the widespread dissemination of letters about the World Conference many articles appeared on the subject in the Protestant religious Press of Europe, in the organ of the governing Holy Synod of the Russian Orthodox Church, *Tserkovnyia Viedomosti*, and in *La Ciencia Tomista*, the organ of the Spanish Dominicans. All wrote sympathetically of the proposed Conference, the two last, however, maintaining the exclusive position of their respective communions.

It was at this point that the first world war broke upon the world. The disastrous consequences of this event for the world and for the Churches have been indicated in many connections in this History.[3] For Faith and Order the blow was in some respects specially severe. Just at the time when a new movement to promote the unity of the Churches was being launched, the Churches found themselves ranged along wholly new lines of division. For now to the age-long causes of separation were added the new bitternesses of a conflict in which both sides believed themselves to be in the right and felt free to call down the blessing of God upon their arms. Long years were to pass before the Anglo-American

[1] Pope Benedict XV.   [2] *F. and O. Pamphlet No. 30*, pp. 12 f.
[3] See especially Chap. viii, pp. 364 ff.

world was able to co-operate on terms of easy equality, free from suspicion, with the defeated nations of the continent of Europe.

Inevitably Faith and Order work in Europe and other parts of the world came almost completely to an end. Travel became impossible; contacts were broken; international life was for the time being at an end. It was only in North America that further progress was possible.

The Protestant Episcopal Commission rose to the occasion. The idea of sending a deputation to Europe had naturally been abandoned, but several lines of local activity were still open to the Commission. It decided to assemble a North American Preparatory Conference, and this met at Garden City, Long Island, 4–6 January 1916. Sixty-three men attended, representing fifteen Churches. They showed remarkable insight into what subjects would actually engage the attention of more than one world conference, when they decided that the subjects to be considered should be:

  I. The Church, its nature and functions;
 II. The Catholic Creeds, as the safeguards of the faith of the Church;
III. Grace and the Sacraments in general;
 IV. The Ministry, its nature and functions;
  V. Practical questions connected with the missionary and other administrative functions of the Church.

When the war ended, the Episcopal Church Commission lost no time in dispatching a deputation to visit Europe and the Near East. The Bishops of Chicago (C. P. Anderson), Southern Ohio (Boyd Vincent), and Fond du Lac (R. H. Weller), the Rev. Dr E. L. Parsons (later Bishop of San Francisco) and Dr B. T. Rogers sailed from New York on 6 March 1919.[1]

The deputation planned first of all to visit Greece, but it took much longer to get there than they expected, owing to delays consequent upon the war. A French cruiser and military motor-cars, an American submarine and private cars took them on a zig-zag route to Athens, where they spent nine days. They were given every opportunity of presenting the plan of the World Conference, including a visit to the Holy Synod. They met representatives of the Church, the State, and the University, and before they left received the following letter addressed to the Bishop of Chicago as Chairman of the delegation:

“We are very well disposed toward the proposal for the summoning of a world-wide Ecclesiastical Conference, which the American Episcopal Church is addressing to the Churches through you and your fellow bishops. From the letter which you have placed in our hands, and from the oral explanation which you have added to it, we are convinced that the purpose of the Conference is indeed holy, in accordance with the prayer of our Lord ‘That all’ those who believe on Him ‘may be one’. We heartily congratulate the Episcopal Church in America which has undertaken this noble effort, from which we rightfully expect progress for the better in the relations between the Churches ‘until we all come together into the unity of the faith and of the knowledge of the Son of God’. . . . Accepting with readiness the invitation addressed to us, and embracing your Holiness and

[1] F. and O. Pamphlet No. 32, Report of the Deputation to Europe and the East.

your companions with much love, we pray our Saviour Christ to direct your steps unto every good work.

"In Athens, March 29, 1919.

(*Signed*) Meletios of Athens,
Evthymios of Phanarion and Thessaliotis,
Germanos of Demetrias,
Ambrosios of Navpaktia and Evritania,
Dionysios of Gythion and Oetylos."

The visitors expressed great gratitude to Professor H. S. Alivisatos who, as friend, guide, and interpreter, had given them much help.

The deputation then proceeded to Constantinople, stopping on the way to explain the plan and purpose of the Conference to the Metropolitan of Smyrna. At Constantinople they were received by the Holy Synod, to which they presented a formal address: a reply signed by the Locum Tenens, Nicolaus, Metropolitan of Cesaria, said:

"We assure you that the Church of Constantinople, when the time and place of the conference are fixed, will send in time competent delegates."

In Constantinople the deputation made several contacts with the Armenian Church, the clergy assuring them that the invitation would be referred to the Catholicos of all the Armenians and his Synod at Etchmiadzin, and that they might be sure of the acceptance of the invitation. The deputation then set sail for the island of Halki in the Sea of Marmora, where they met the President of the Orthodox Theological College, Dr Germanos Strenopoulos, later Archbishop of Thyateira and a President of the World Council of Churches. Here they met also Archbishop Platon, Metropolitan of Odessa, with whom the Episcopal Church Commission had had contact a few years before when he was head of the Russian Orthodox Church in the United States. He was at Halki as a result of having been driven from Russia into exile. Archbishop Platon said to them:

"The Church of Russia is now sick in body, mind and soul, but when she gets well again she will doubtless be represented at the conference."

He was the only bishop of the Russian Church whom they were able to meet, since at that time Russia was entirely inaccessible. Their next port of call was Sofia. They found that the Exarch of Sofia had recently died and that there, as in a number of other bishoprics, a locum tenens was in charge. The men they met were friendly, but decided that the invitation could not be dealt with until the Holy Synod had filled several vacancies. Their experience in Rumania was much the same. In Serbia, where they spent a fortnight, their reception was cordial and the Archbishop of Belgrade and Metropolitan of Serbia warmly accepted the invitation to be represented at the Conference.

From Belgrade the deputation proceeded to Rome in order to present the invitation to Pope Benedict XV. Archbishop Cerretti, an official at the Vatican, undertook to arrange an audience with the Pope and a meeting with Cardinal Gasparri. The formal invitation of the Commission, written in Latin, and a statement in English of the proposal for a World Conference on Faith and

Order were presented to His Holiness in advance of the visit. The deputation, on arriving at the Vatican on the appointed day, 16 May, were received by Cardinal Gasparri who gave them a cordial welcome, expressing his own desire for the visible unity of the Church. The Americans reported that they sought some expression of opinion from the Cardinal as to the attitude of the Roman Catholic Church towards the World Conference, and his reply was that they would be received cordially by the Pope. The deputation subsequently reported that the Pope's personal attitude was most cordial, but

> ". . . the contrast between the Pope's personal attitude towards us and his official attitude towards the Conference was very sharp. One was irresistibly benevolent, the other irresistibly rigid. The genuineness of the Pope's personal friendliness towards us was as outstanding as the positiveness of his official declination of our invitation. His Holiness himself emphasised the distinction."

The deputation made an attempt to state the case for a World Conference on Faith and Order, but the official response to their invitation had been decided in advance of this visit, and as they left the audience-room the following written statement was handed to them:

> "The Holy Father, after having thanked them for their visit, stated that as successor of St Peter and Vicar of Christ he had no greater desire than that there should be one fold and one shepherd. His Holiness added that the teaching and practice of the Roman Catholic Church regarding the unity of the visible Church of Christ was well known to everybody and therefore it would not be possible for the Catholic Church to take part in such a Congress as the one proposed. His Holiness, however, by no means wishes to disapprove of the Congress in question for those who are not in union with the Chair of Peter, on the contrary, he earnestly desires and prays that, if the Congress is practicable, those who take part in it may, by the Grace of God, see the light and become reunited to the visible Head of the Church, by whom they will be received with open arms."

Some of the deputation had hoped for another result, and it is reported that when they were returning from their visit the Anglo-Catholic member of it, the Bishop of Fond du Lac, after remaining silent for some time, raised his fist to heaven and expressed his judgement on the Bishop of Rome in terms more forceful than complimentary.[1]

The deputation divided at Rome. The Bishop of Fond du Lac and Dr Rogers sailed for Alexandria and met the Patriarch, who accepted the invitation and decided to appoint a Commission. They then went to Cairo and saw the Coptic Patriarch, who also accepted the invitation and agreed to appoint a Commission. They had a similar experience at Jerusalem with the Patriarch Damianos, and at Damascus with the Patriarch of Antioch.

The other members of the deputation went straight to Paris, where they consulted Professor Wilfred Monod as to which of the French Protestant Churches should be invited. They then passed on to Bergen and Oslo, preparing the way

[1] William Adams Brown, *Toward a United Church*, p. 60.

with Church leaders for a later visit, and came to Uppsala where they were received with great cordiality by the Archbishop, Dr Söderblom. The Archbishop took much pains to explain fully the nature and position of the Church of Sweden, and subsequently a Commission with Professor Edgar Reutersköld as its Chairman was appointed. When they returned to Norway it was to find all ready for the appointment of a Commission by the Norwegian Church. They were not able to visit all the countries where they had planned to meet Church leaders, especially regretting their inability to go to Finland, Denmark, and Holland, though these countries were open to them. The only closed countries were Russia and Germany, which they reported "were inaccessible on account of internal conditions".

It was to prove far more serious than the Episcopal Church Commission realized that their deputation was unable to gain access to Germany and to hold discussions with the leaders of the German Churches. The Americans took great pains to secure the interest of the Roman Catholic and Orthodox Churches, but assumed on quite insufficient grounds that the Protestant Churches of the continent of Europe would readily take part in the Conference then being planned. The German Churches were certainly interested in the unity of the Church of Christ. From the first they were ready to take part with conviction in the Life and Work movement, and in the preparation for its Stockholm Conference in 1925, but the whole development of the Faith and Order movement roused their suspicions. It was on lines unfamiliar to them; the terms in which invitations and correspondence were couched were Anglo-American. There was a strong feeling on the Continent as a whole, not only in Germany, that the Faith and Order movement was an Anglican imperialist move, entirely ignoring Continental circumstances and the Continental point of view. The German Churches at this stage refused all invitations to take part in the World Conference.

3. PREPARING FOR LAUSANNE 1927

The Commission of the Protestant Episcopal Church, having presented the invitation to a World Conference for the consideration of questions touching faith and order through letters and personal deputations to all the Churches of Europe, as well as to the Churches of the Middle East and of North America, decided to invite all co-operating Committees and Commissions to send three delegates each to Geneva "to decide what subjects should be prepared for the World Conference".[1] In response there assembled at the Athénée in Geneva, from 12–20 August 1920, Church leaders from "about forty nations representing seventy autonomous Churches, including all the great families or groups of Trinitarian Churches, except the Church of Rome, which had declined to participate". The Conference achieved three things:

(1) It appointed a Continuation Committee, a decision of immense importance for the future. To this Continuation Committee were elected fifty-one persons who came from many countries in Europe, from the United States of America, Australia, India, China, and Japan, and included Anglicans, Armenians, Baptists, Congregationalists, Czech Brethren, Disciples, Eastern Orthodox, members of the Society of Friends and of the German Evangelical Church, Lutherans, Methodists, Old Catholics, Presbyterians, and Reformed. Bishop Brent was elected Chairman, Dr George Zabriskie, Treasurer, and Mr Robert

[1] *F. and O. Pamphlet No. 33: Report of the preliminary meeting at Geneva, Switzerland, August 12–20, 1920.*

H. Gardiner, Secretary. Responsibility for the leadership of the movement was transferred from the Protestant Episcopal Church of the United States to this international and inter-Church Committee, thus bringing about what that Church had long desired. The Continuation Committee was charged with the duty of carrying on the work of preparing a World Conference on Faith and Order, fixing its date, and choosing a place for it to meet.

(2) It brought the Orthodox Church into the movement. Earlier the same year the Patriarchate of Constantinople had addressed its famous Encyclical letter "unto all the Churches of Christ wherever they be", stressing the desirability of promoting understanding and practical co-operation between all Christian Churches in both East and West. The Encyclical asked that a response be made to its suggestions.[1] The Metropolitan of Seleukia (Germanos) told the Geneva Conference that, just when the Ecumenical Patriarchate had decided to issue its Encyclical, the invitation came to join the movement to promote a World Conference on Faith and Order, and that they had accepted the invitation with great joy.

Eighteen men from the Orthodox Churches were present in Geneva, among them Professors Alivisatos and Papadopoulos, Church of Greece; Archbishop Eulogius of Volhynia, Church of Russia, who was in exile; Archimandrite Stephan and Professor Zankov, Church of Bulgaria; and representatives of the Orthodox Churches of Rumania and Serbia, and of the Patriarchates of Constantinople and Alexandria.

The Orthodox nevertheless were doubtful about the movement. The question of proselytizing was causing them anxiety, and the two Church of England delegates, Bishop Gore and Mr Tatlow, found much of their time occupied with this issue behind the scenes, the Orthodox present being emphatic that if they were to take part in the movement they must be assured that proselytizing activities amongst them by the missionaries of non-Orthodox Churches would cease. The two Church of England delegates had, again behind the scenes, some candid discussions on the subject with the American and British Free Church representatives.

(3) Some German Church leaders were present, and a beginning was made towards securing German co-operation. The Germans who came to Geneva, though not official representatives of the Churches, took part cordially in the discussions, and among those appointed to the Continuation Commitee were Dr Siegmund-Schultze and Dr A. W. Schreiber (United Church), Dr A. Lang (Reformed), and Dr Ihmels (Lutheran). Throughout all the negotiations with the German Churches much was owed to Dr Siegmund-Schultze, who had met Mr Gardiner at Constance at the first meeting of the World Alliance held just before the outbreak of the first world war. Their friendship had led to continual exchange of ideas which, together with Siegmund-Schultze's steady presentation, in his quarterly *Die Eiche*, of the progress of the Faith and Order movement, made friends for it in Germany.

The experience of the Geneva Conference was a great spiritual event in the lives of all present. Bishop Brent, speaking of the movement as a pilgrimage in search of unity, said at the close:

"The Spirit of God was the strength of the pilgrims. He made us one in our fellowship. The Conference was a living body. Life touched life, nation

[1] See Chap. x, p. 446.

touched nation, the spirit of the East held communion with the spirit of the West as perhaps never before. By invitation on the last day of the Conference we gathered together . . . in the Russian Orthodox Church in Geneva for the solemn worship of the Divine Liturgy. Anglican, Baptist, Old Catholic, Presbyterian, Wesleyan, Lutheran, Quaker, were all there, and all there to worship. The Metropolitan of Seleukia [Germanos] in a spiritual address spoke to the pilgrims of his own joy in the vision of unity, and told how, out of the transfigured troubles and pains of the present would rise the glory of the future."[1]

The first meeting of the Continuation Committee took place the day before the Geneva Conference ended, and appointed a Subjects Committee which issued a series of questions for discussion by the Commissions of the Churches, as follows:

(1) What degree of unity in faith will be necessary in a reunited Church?

(2) Is a statement of this one faith in the form of a Creed necessary or desirable?

(3) If so, what Creed should be used or what other formulary would be desirable?

(4) What are the proper uses of a Creed and of a Confession of Faith?

The Subjects Committee continued to issue series of questions to the Commissions and studied with care the answers received.

The Continuation Committee held its second meeting at Stockholm in 1925, and decided to call the World Conference on Faith and Order for 1927. It was agreed that the meeting should last for about three weeks, number 500 persons, and be held at Lausanne. The Subjects Committee continued to work at the programme for the World Conference; but when the Continuation Committee met at Berne in 1926 a rumour had gained wide currency to the effect that a programme had been decided upon which would restrict the freedom of the Conference, in that decisions were being made for it in advance. The Continuation Committee therefore declared, "The draft Agenda prepared at Stockholm is now obsolete". This referred to the programme the Subjects Committee had worked out. It was then decided that the official programme should contain no more than the actual subjects to be discussed.

The Subjects Committee had been appointed because some of those who had long been associated with the movement were convinced that some attempt must be made in advance of the Conference to find out the range of agreement and disagreement between the Churches. This had been the actual objective of the work done by the committees which the Churches had been asked to set up in connection with the World Conference. They had done it sometimes alone and sometimes in co-operation with other Churches. They had also done it with very different degrees of thoroughness. In order that this preliminary work should be put to its proper use Canon H. N. Bate of Carlisle (Dean of York 1932–41) was asked by Bishop Brent at the first session of the Lausanne Conference to make a statement relative to the work done by the Subjects Committee.[2] It was ultimately decided that the World Conference should consider:

[1] *F. and O. Pamphlet No. 33: Report of the preliminary meeting at Geneva, Switzerland, August 12–20, 1920,* p. 92.
[2] *Faith and Order: Proceedings of the World Conference, Lausanne, August 3–21, 1927,* ed. H. N. Bate, pp. 36–40; *F. and O. Pamphlets No. 46 and No. 52.*

(1) The call to unity
(2) The Church's message to the world—the Gospel
(3) The nature of the Church
(4) The Church's common confession of faith
(5) The Church's ministry
(6) The Sacraments
(7) The unity of Christendom and the place of the different Churches in it.
The main body of work in preparing the agenda for the Conference was done by
three men: the Bishop of Bombay (E. J. Palmer), Canon H. N. Bate, and Mr
Ralph Brown.

To the deep sorrow of the Churches in all lands, Robert Gardiner died on
15 June 1924.
"The profound impression", wrote Bishop Brent, "made upon the Christian
world by what he was and did baffles description. It is not too much to say that
there is not a Church in Christendom, great or little, ancient or new, that does
not know his name and feel kinship with his lofty soul."
Robert Hallowell Gardiner was fifty-five years old when he was asked to
become Secretary of the Episcopal Church Commission on its constitution in
1910. He carried on his own work as a lawyer while at the same time acting as
the leader of the ever-increasing work involved in assembling the World Conference. He never received any payment for his services, indeed the movement
was often financially in his debt, and the provision made for an office and staff
seems to have been very meagre in view of the huge correspondence and the
amount of literature prepared and circulated. Gardiner possessed a combination
of qualities which made him an ideal man for the position he held. A quiet,
steady man of first-class judgement and an easy approach to the great variety
of men with whom he had contact, he knew when to act and how to act, handling a variety of ecclesiastical affairs with confidence. How he came to know as
much as he did about the Churches of the world, no one knew. He never talked
about himself. A member of the Protestant Episcopal Church of the United
States, he was an understanding friend of all the Churches. His contacts with
the Protestant Churches of Europe were specially appreciated, and Continentals
spoke of him as "the noblest figure that American Christianity has produced".
It was due to his insight, faith and courage, patience and unceasing industry
that the movement was established on a solid foundation.[1]
The man who bore some of the heaviest burdens in the years after Gardiner
died, up to and including the Lausanne Conference, was Canon Bate. All his
gifts as a scholar, linguist, and administrator were used to the full. He was an
unassuming man, and probably only those closely associated with the final
stages of preparation and the actual work of the Lausanne Conference knew
how much its successful issue had depended upon his work.

4. THE FIRST WORLD CONFERENCE

When the Lausanne Conference[2] assembled in the handsome buildings of the
University on 3 August 1927, there were present 385 men and nine women,
together with a staff of twelve. They came from 108 Churches—Lutheran and

[1] See Hermann Sasse, *Die Weltkonferenz für Glauben und Kirchenverfassung*, Berlin, 1929, pp.
26–29.   [2] See Bibliography, p. 749.

Reformed, Old Catholic, Orthodox, Anglican, Methodist, Congregational, Baptist, and Disciples. The majority were officially appointed representatives of their Churches. Africa, America, and Europe were well represented, but from Asia unfortunately there came only two nationals and some missionaries. For most it was a new experience to find themselves in an international gathering. The majority of those who already had such experience had received it when as students they had attended conferences of the World's Student Christian Federation. In all the delegations from the Churches, except probably that from the Old Catholic Church, were some who had been leaders of the S.C.M. in their university days and thus had learned something of denominations and countries other than their own. Those to whom an international conference was a novel experience often confessed themselves bewildered; but this was a stage which passed quickly, for the atmosphere generated was both friendly and inspiring.

After the opening service in the Cathedral, the Conference began its work by electing Bishop Brent as President. He was in poor health and asked that Dr A. E. Garvie be appointed deputy Chairman.

The method followed was to devote four successive days to hearing representative men in seven or eight confessions expound from the point of view of their Church the first half of the agenda. Following each speech there was general discussion. After four days the Conference divided into four sections of about equal size for three days of simultaneous discussion of the first four subjects. The Conference then came together again to discuss the first draft of the report prepared by each section. A similar plan was followed with the second half of the agenda, and by 20 August six reports had been accepted for transmission to the Churches.

The report of Section VII dealing with "The Unity of Christendom and the relation thereto of existing Churches", however, met with difficulties. The first draft of its report was presented to the Conference by its Chairmen, the Archbishop of Uppsala (Söderblom), the Archbishop of Armagh (D'Arcy), and General Superintendent Otto Dibelius of Berlin.

The draft began with a strong appeal to the Churches to collaborate in the field of applied Christianity, and referred especially to Life and Work and the World Alliance as bodies out of which a Council of Churches for purposes of practical collaboration might be developed. The discussion in the plenary meeting did not concentrate on this part of the report but on other sections; in consequence the Archbishops of Uppsala and Armagh who revised the report did not make any considerable change in this statement concerning practical collaboration. Unfortunately, Söderblom had to leave the Conference before the second draft was presented to the whole gathering. This much-discussed departure had nothing to do with the report. It was due simply, to quote his own words, "to pressing engagements connected with my office". He also records that "had I the faintest idea . . . that new difficulties would be made, I would have done my utmost to stay through the last day".[1]

[1] *Pater Max Pribilla und die Oekumenische Erweckung; Einige Randbemerkungen von Nathan Söderblom*, Uppsala, 1931, p. 18. The *Randbemerkungen* were comments by Söderblom on *Um kirchliche Einheit, Stockholm—Lausanne—Rom. Geschichtlich-theologische Darstellung der neueren Einigungsbestrebungen*, Freiburg, 1929, by the Jesuit Fr Max Pribilla. Söderblom recognizes the importance of the book as being the only study of the modern ecumenical movement undertaken by a Roman Catholic at that time: and, moreover, a careful study made in a friendly spirit. Söderblom's comments and corrections on Pribilla's statements throw many interesting sidelights on what actually occurred at Stockholm and Lausanne.

The revised draft was presented by the Archbishop of Armagh. But this time some delegates voiced strong objections against the wording of the paragraph concerning practical collaboration. Those delegates whose standpoint was Anglo-Catholic felt that by accepting this report the Conference would commit itself to a conception of ecumenical relations in which inter-Church collaboration would be emphasized at the expense of unity in faith and order. They proposed, therefore, that the report should be sent back to the Continuation Committee. On the other hand, there were many delegates who felt that this report was an essential part of the total achievement of the Conference. Dr T. T. Lew of China protested vigorously against the proposal that the report should not be accepted in the same way as the others: if it were not so accepted, he would feel obliged to withdraw his vote for the other six reports which he had supported as seen in the light of the Report on Unity. The Chairman explained the impossibility of withdrawing a vote already cast.

In the end, the Conference agreed to the suggestion of the President that the report should be received on the understanding that it be referred to the Continuation Committee for further consideration. Bishop Brent paid a tribute to the skill, experience, and learning which had been given to the compilation of the report under the guidance of Archbishop Söderblom, but added that probably the Conference was not ready for the discussion of so difficult a problem; nevertheless the report would prove valuable for future study. The report was referred to the Continuation Committee: the final revision appeared as an appendix to the Lausanne Report.[1]

It was in the simultaneous meetings of the four sections and their drafting committees that the more important discussions and final formulations took place. A brief description of what happened in one may be taken as typical of all.

Section IV dealt with "The Church's Common Confession of Faith". There were 115 members—Americans and Europeans, drawn from countries as different as Ireland, Russia, Sweden, Portugal, and France. There was one Oriental—a Japanese. A few members—for example, Bishop Brent and Dr Peter Ainslie—had long taken a lead in the movement. Some, especially Archbishop Germanos and Bishop Gore, had been well known in the movement since the Geneva Conference 1920, but the majority were strangers to each other. Some vigorously-worded opinions were heard during the first meeting and a good deal of heat was generated. "We must declare our loyalty to the Nicene Creed", said an Orthodox, to which a Congregationalist replied, "Well, I think we should clear all that old lumber out of the way". The section seemed to be divided into two main groups, one protesting loyalty to the Scriptures and the other to the Creeds. But even within these groups there was division, for by the Scriptures some meant the Bible alone, while others held with fervour to tradition as being a part of Scripture. Others thought that the Nicene Creed should stand alone, while German members declared their loyalty to several different confessions of faith. The atmosphere was tense when the time came to separate for luncheon, and a good many were seeking light on the subjects discussed: one man came up to a member with whom he had made friends and asked, "Can you tell me of any volume in which I could read one of these old creeds they have been talking about?" He was delighted at the immediate loan of a Book of Common Prayer, in which the Apostles' and Nicene Creeds were pointed out to him.

[1] *Faith and Order, Lausanne, 1927*, pp. 435 ff.

But confusion and misunderstanding began steadily to be dissipated; men who had valued the historic Creeds all their lives came to understand men who did not use them, but who nevertheless had learned to base their Christian doctrine on serious study of the New Testament. It should be remembered that every section had to cope not only with misunderstandings arising from different approaches but also with the difficulties caused by language. Each section, as indeed the whole Conference, worked in English, French, and German, but the greater part of the discussion was in English, and those delegates whose knowledge of English was imperfect were at a constant disadvantage and under a heavy strain.

In the background there was always lurking the question of the aim of the Conference. At no time had this become clear to everybody. Some of the Americans thought that the Conference aimed at achieving a plan for a united Church before it dispersed, and some of the Orthodox were never disabused of the same idea. In vain did the President, Bishop Brent, again and again restate the purpose of the Conference as being an occasion on which "both agreements and disagreements were to be carefully noted". "It is not", he said, "a conference that aims at complete agreement; still less at a united Church." These misconceptions of the aim were at least partly responsible for a marked feature of the latter part of the Conference—a series of declarations on their position by the members of different communions.

On behalf of the Evangelical Lutherans, on the morning of 17 August, a declaration was read in German, French, and English, signed by Lutheran leaders from France, Norway, Latvia, the United States, Germany, and Sweden (Archbishop Söderblom himself).[1] It set forth their profound conviction of the need for unity, and their whole-hearted sympathy with the aims and spirit of the Conference, but also their desire that no final vote should be taken on propositions formulated at the Conference, and that all such material and reports should be worked over by a representative Commission and passed on for study to the various communions. The proposals of the Evangelical Lutherans were not unlike the procedure with regard to the future of the reports, to which leaders of the Conference had been led: this procedure is explained in a Preamble to all the reports prepared by Bishop Brent with the help of Dr Francis Hall, Bishop Palmer of Bombay, and the members who had signed the Lutheran declaration.[2]

There can be little doubt that behind this cautious attitude towards pronouncements lay the feeling among the Lutherans and other Continentals that difficulties of language and the use of Anglo-Saxon methods of procedure unfamiliar to them had prevented them from making their due contribution to the discussions, and made them hesitate to assume responsibility for the decisions reached. The difficulty is a very real one, and has been expressed by German delegates at many ecumenical gatherings from the foundation Conference of the Evangelical Alliance in 1846 onwards.

The next morning, 18 August, Archbishop Germanos asked permission to read a declaration on behalf of the Orthodox.[3] The Orthodox present represented the Ecumenical Patriarchate, the Patriarchates of Alexandria, Jerusalem, Serbia, and Rumania, and the Orthodox Churches of Greece, Cyprus, Bulgaria, and Poland, together with a bishop and a priest of the Russian Ortho-

---

[1] *Faith and Order, Lausanne, 1927*, pp. 373 ff. 　　　[2] Ibid., pp. 375 and 459 f.
[3] Ibid., pp. 383–86.

dox Church in exile. Continuous meetings took place among them, and as the time drew near when the reports of the sections would be presented to the Conference for acceptance, they realized that they could not present a united front, partly owing to there being both conservative and progressive groups among them.

Their declaration stated that they had welcomed an invitation to the Conference and had "taken part in every meeting held here for the purpose of promoting closer brotherhood and fellowship between the representatives of the different Churches and for the general good and welfare of the whole body of Christians". It went on to regret "that the bases assumed for the foundation of the Reports which are to be submitted to the vote of the Conference, are inconsistent with the principles of the Orthodox Church". They would vote for the report of Section II, "The Church's Message to the World—the Gospel", but would abstain from voting on the other reports. Their declaration went on to elaborate their position; its frequent references to reunion and a united Church suggested that they thought the object of the Conference was to achieve at once a united Church. The tension among the Orthodox was considerable, and Archbishop Germanos, after he had read the declaration, returned to his seat with the tears pouring down his face. Their declaration did not make any difference to their practical participation in the Conference, as they continued to take a full share in all the discussions.

These two statements gave rise to other statements by groups and individuals expounding the position for which they stood, in particular by a group of Reformed Churches in Europe, and by the Society of Friends.[1] The Conference had, however, become a spiritual fellowship, manifestly the work of the Spirit of God; how to express that fellowship in a united Church was the great question still without solution, a question to which the Conference had deliberately refrained from attempting to give an immediate answer.

It was a shock to many to find that no provision had been made for a united celebration of the Holy Communion to which the whole Conference could be invited. The authorities of the Cathedral invited all the members to a celebration of the Holy Communion according to the Reformed rite of the National Church of the Canton of Vaud. Many members availed themselves of this opportunity. But this did not satisfy the desire of many for a Conference Celebration. In speaking on the seventh report on "The Unity of Christendom", Dr Peter Ainslie called on the leaders to arrange for a Conference Celebration at the concluding service on the last Sunday, as the finest expression of the equality of all Christians before God. His plea was earnestly supported by the Bishop of Bergen, Dr Peter Hognestad, but no action was taken.[2]

When the Lausanne Conference came to review its work at the close, the full Conference had unanimously adopted a statement on "The Call to Unity"[3] prepared by the officers of the Conference and the chairmen and secretaries of the six sections.

The full Conference had received, nem. con., "The Church's Message to the World—the Gospel". This report, which was mainly the work of Professor Adolf Deissmann, was accepted by the members of the Orthodox Churches as

---

[1] Faith and Order, Lausanne, 1927, pp. 395 and 409–13.
[2] Ibid., pp. 346 and 366; and F. Siegmund-Schultze, "Rückblick auf Lausanne", Die Eiche, 1927, pp. 366 ff.
[3] Faith and Order, Lausanne, 1927, pp. 460 f.

well as by the rest of the Conference. It was destined to play an important part in the whole ecumenical movement. Part of it was incorporated into its own Message by the Jerusalem Meeting of the International Missionary Council in 1928,[1] and it was used by the Church of Christ in China in its Constitution as its statement of faith.

The Conference had accepted, *nem. con.*, the reports of Sections III, IV, V, and VI, on "The Nature of the Church", "The Church's Common Confession of Faith", "The Ministry of the Church", and "The Sacraments". It had referred the report of Section VII to the Continuation Committee.

5. LAUSANNE 1927 TO EDINBURGH 1937

Before the Lausanne Conference dispersed, a Continuation Committee of ninety-two men and three women was appointed, with Bishop Brent as Chairman, Dr A. E. Garvie as Vice-Chairman, George Zabriskie as Treasurer, and Ralph W. Brown, General Secretary. The importance of the rôle played by the Continuation Committees appointed at Geneva 1920, Lausanne 1927, and Edinburgh 1937 is realized by few. The meetings of these Continuation Committees which took place annually were Lausanne and Edinburgh Conferences in miniature, drawing leaders of different Churches into fellowship and understanding, carrying on a steady process of education in each other's tenets, constantly discussing major issues and making decisions which greatly increased the value of the World Conference. A Business Committee composed of leaders of denominations in the United States was charged with the duty of carrying on the work of the Continuation Committee between its annual meetings.

On 21 March 1928 the Continuation Committee submitted to the Churches which had taken part in the Lausanne Conference the reports of the seven sections into which it had been divided, six reports having been received by the Lausanne Conference, and the seventh, after some revision, by the Continuation Committee, as the Lausanne Conference had directed.[2] The Continuation Committee asked the Churches "not only for an examination of the substance of the Lausanne Reports but also for a considered judgement upon the steps which should now be taken in furtherance of the work of the Conference, and, if possible, for an assurance that the Churches are prepared to continue their co-operation". The letter closed by saying that

"The Lausanne Conference has been a real venture of faith. That faith was sustained by the manifest tokens of the divine presence in our worship, our deliberations and our whole fellowship. In the same faith, and with humble prayer for continued guidance, help and inspiration, we submit the present results of our work to the Churches upon whose co-operation the future of this movement towards Christian unity depends."

When the Continuation Committee met at Prague in 1928, Archbishop Germanos, Dr Adolf Deissmann, Pastor Charles Merle d'Aubigné, and Archbishop Söderblom were appointed Associate Vice-Chairmen. In anticipation of replies from the Churches to the reports of the Lausanne Conference, a Reference

---

[1] See *Jerusalem Meeting Report*, I, pp. 481 ff., and Chap. viii, p. 369.
[2] *F. and O. Pamphlet No. 55.*

Committee, with Canon Bate as convener, was chosen. These replies soon began to come in, and varied in length from a short memorandum to a printed volume of considerable size. It was realized that intensive study was needed of those subjects disagreement on which prevented unity, and the whole matter was referred back for further consideration in 1929.

There was a growing feeling that the Universal Christian Council on Life and Work and the World Conference on Faith and Order tended increasingly to cover the same ground. Consequently Faith and Order appointed a small committee to confer with a similar committee of Life and Work on the subject of their mutual relationship. This was the first hint of the movement which was to grow until it brought the two bodies together in the World Council of Churches.[1] The report of the joint sub-committee, while favourable to friendly contact between the officers of the two movements, made no suggestion at this date of any formal relationship.

On 27 March 1929 Bishop Brent, who had been seriously ill for some time, died at Lausanne, and with his passing the movement lost the man who had been its leader for nineteen years.

When Brent went to the World Missionary Conference, Edinburgh 1910, Christian unity was already a central interest in his life: "I cannot", he said, "understand people who are indifferent to or idle in the cause. It stands as the background of all Christian life and thought." His experiences as a missionary had constantly kept the unity of the Christian Church uppermost in his mind, for

> "we missionaries have moments of deep depression when the consciousness sweeps over us that it is little short of absurd to try to bring into the Church of Christ the great nations of the Far East unless we can present an undivided front."

He was a man well practised in leadership, for in 1903 the Governor of the Philippines (W. H. Taft) had made him a member of a Commission sent to visit Japan, Formosa, China, Saigon, Java, and Burma to report on the use of opium and on the traffic in the drug. The Commission elected him its President, and from that date to his death he was intimately connected with successive attempts to control the traffic in opium.

Charles Henry Brent was a Canadian by birth. Ordained in 1886 in the diocese of Toronto, he went soon after to the United States, where he eventually became a citizen, working first in a parish in Buffalo, and then in Boston, where he remained until he became Bishop of the Philippines. He was elected on three occasions to other bishoprics, but only consented to become Bishop of Western New York in 1918, when it became clear that his health would no longer stand the strain of life in the Philippines. After he had taken the action which made the Protestant Episcopal Church the leader of a movement for a World Conference on Faith and Order, he was prepared at once to undertake further work in the cause, but the first world war intervened; it took him to France, where ultimately he became Senior Chaplain of the American Expeditionary Force. At the end of the war he again became active on behalf of Faith and Order, and in 1920 presided at the preliminary Conference of the movement

[1] See Chap. xvi, *passim.*

at Geneva. From that time onwards he worked prodigiously to ensure the success of the Lausanne Conference. William Temple wrote of him that

> "his position as the pivotal person of the conference was plain, and his quiet, firm and often humorous control of the discussions was most effective."[1]

Brent understood the subject of unity—unity in diversity. He had a deep trust in truth, which explained his readiness to scrutinize impartially the most loved practices and formularies, and his willingness to sacrifice everything except essential principles. He was not like the distinguished cleric of whom he wrote in his diary, "The only kind of unity he can grasp is where everyone agrees with him". His appreciation of traditions other than his own opened many doors of friendship to him, and when he died it was said of him that he had more friends than any man of his time, "warriors and ecclesiastics, pagans and Christians, lovers and little children". The secret was his unique capacity for giving himself to all kinds of people and for loving them all. Above all, he was a man of prayer; frequent in his warning that the life of prayer was difficult, he declared, "those alone labour effectively among men who impetuously fling themselves upward towards God". Charles Brent was such a man. No wonder that when he died messages poured in to the Faith and Order office from the leaders of the Churches of Europe and America expressing deep sorrow at the loss of one acclaimed by all as a beloved leader and friend, one who through prayer, as Professor Wilfred Monod of Paris wrote, "had acquired the triple secret of wisdom, enthusiasm and serenity".

The Continuation Committee met in August 1929 at Maloja, Switzerland, when those attending were the guests of that pioneer in reunion, Sir Henry Lunn, himself a member of the Continuation Committee.[2] The first act of the Committee was to elect the Archbishop of York (William Temple) as Chairman in place of Bishop Brent. In Dr Temple's absence the chair was occupied by Dr A. E. Garvie.

Replies from the Churches to the findings of the Lausanne Conference soon began to come in.[3] To secure intensive study of them, it was decided to appoint a Theological Committee. Its purpose was to provide a representative body of experts to whom such subjects as the meaning of Grace, Ordination, and Episcopacy might be referred with a view to their preparing material for a further world conference. The Theological Committee was placed under the care of the Bishop of Gloucester (A. C. Headlam) and took as its first subject the doctrine of Grace. In point of fact, he did far more than chair the Committee, having the major responsibility for selecting and inviting scholars from a number of Churches and countries, who both wrote and exchanged documents and met to discuss the points of theology before them. Dr Headlam rendered immense service to the Faith and Order movement. He was a man of great learning and of clear and strong convictions, but had the defects of his qualities, and this gave rise to certain criticisms of the movement. He was liable to try to fit others to his own pattern by devising formulas to which all could assent, though giving

---

[1] Alexander C. Zabriskie, *Bishop Brent, Crusader for Christian Unity*, p. 189.
[2] See Chap. vii, pp. 338 ff.
[3] *Convictions: A Selection from the Responses of the Churches to the Report of the World Conference on Faith and Order held at Lausanne in 1927*, ed. Leonard Hodgson.

different interpretations to the words which embodied Headlam's own convictions.

Already the possible date of the next world conference was being canvassed, and the Continuation Committee on 27 August 1930 decided that a second World Conference on Faith and Order should be convened not later than 1937.

It was at the Maloja meeting that Canon Tatlow was first asked to select a group of young men and women to attend the meetings of the Continuation Committee as visitors. It was hoped that thus a number of younger people would be drawn into the work of the movement and would later become its leaders. The following year a youth group of eleven men, from France, England, Ireland, Germany, Holland, Sweden, Russia, the United States, and China attended the Continuation Committee. A youth group became a regular feature of the annual meetings and in time supplied many valued leaders.

It was in 1930, in consequence of the removal of the office of the movement from Boston to Geneva, that Dr Floyd Tomkins became Assistant Secretary in New York. It was hoped that he would also conserve the movement's finances, as Mr George Zabriskie was no longer available as Treasurer; his health had begun to fail and he died in 1931. The movement owed Zabriskie a lasting debt: he was no figure-head treasurer, but from the first a leader; a man of good judgement and wide understanding, he gave valuable support to Brent and Gardiner, taking a full share in all departments of the work. Dr Tomkins carried on much of the work of Gardiner and Zabriskie, and became one of the small group of men on whom the leadership of the movement rested.

When the Continuation Committee met in August 1931 at High Leigh, Hoddesdon, England, much interest centred in the work of the Theological Committee appointed two years previously. It had begun with the consideration of the doctrine of Grace. Different sections of the subject had been allotted to various members who spent a year preparing papers. These were circulated in English, French, and German to all members, and ultimately a meeting lasting for thirteen days was held at Gloucester, when the whole subject was discussed. The result was an agreed report which all the members of the Theological Committee signed; later a large volume, *The Doctrine of Grace*,[1] was published, containing a series of studies on such subjects as Grace in the New Testament; Grace in the Greek Fathers; Grace in St Augustine; the Medieval and Modern Roman Conception of Grace; the Reformation Theology of Grace—Luther, Melanchthon, Zwingli, Calvin; Grace in the Mystical Writers; and a number of related topics. These studies, the work of individual members of the Committee, were the basis of the agreed report.

It was at this meeting that the death of Nathan Söderblom, Archbishop of Uppsala and Primate of the Church of Sweden, was reported. Although his name is known above all as the creator of the Life and Work movement, his services to Faith and Order had been constant and of the greatest value.

The financial slump after the boom which followed the first world war, the effect of which was felt especially in the United States, necessitated drastic retrenchment on the part of the Continuation Committee. It held no meetings in 1932 and 1933, its Geneva office was closed, and Mr Brown offered his resignation, which was accepted with regret, for his services had proved of considerable value.

Somewhat earlier, the Executive Committee had appointed Canon Leonard

[1] *The Doctrine of Grace*, ed. W. T. Whitley, D.D., London, 1932.

Hodgson of Winchester as Theological Secretary; when the retrenchments of 1932 were made, it asked him as a temporary measure to become responsible for the work of General Secretary. To this Canon Hodgson agreed, and took the movement's office into his house at Winchester; when in 1938 he became Regius Professor of Moral and Pastoral Theology at Oxford, the office went with him to Christ Church, Oxford, the temporary measure of 1932 still being in operation. It was a piece of good fortune for the movement that Canon Hodgson was not only a distinguished theologian but also a first-class man of business. He carried on the work of General Secretary right up to the Edinburgh Conference 1937, the organization of which was his responsibility. The "temporary" arrangement continued until the World Conference on Faith and Order became part of the World Council of Churches at its first Assembly, Amsterdam 1948. Canon Hodgson was so good an administrator that the arrangement worked smoothly, and the Continuation Committee hardly noticed that they were allowing a plan intended only to be temporary to continue year after year.

The recasting of the plans of the Continuation Committee made it necessary to reconsider the use to be made of the replies of the Churches to the reports of Lausanne 1927. The Secretariat had already communicated to the members of the Continuation Committee summaries of many of the documents received, containing the views expressed by a large number of Churches after their examination of the reports of the seven sections of the Lausanne Conference. A certain number of these documents had been circulated *in extenso*. The first answer was received in 1927, in the form of a sympathetic message from the bishops of the Old Catholic Churches; for the next seven years a steady stream of documents came from Churches all over the world. The Committee had hoped to publish all replies in full, but before long the volume of material had become so great, while financial resources remained strictly limited, that this was seen to be impossible. The Continuation Committee had, however, to keep in mind not only the duty of informing its own members as to the course of the Faith and Order movement, but also the importance of the education of the Churches generally in the subject. Accordingly, the Executive Committee drafted a series of questions formulated as a result of the experience gained by the study of the memoranda from the Churches, which it hoped would result in study by ever-widening circles. These questionnaires dealt with the Doctrine of Grace, the Sacraments, and the Nature and Purpose of the Church.

The promotion of study groups was successful; they met in France, Germany, England, Scotland, Norway, Sweden, South Africa, New Zealand, and the United States, were representative of many Churches, and in many cases were composed of leaders in the respective Churches. In Berlin, for example, the German Evangelical Church, the Evangelical Lutheran Church, the Evangelical Church of the Old Prussian Union, the Greek Orthodox Church, and the Rumanian Orthodox Church were all represented in the group. In France a group whose members came from Paris, St Étienne, Montpellier, Strasburg, and Tours was representative of the Reformed Church, the Evangelical Reformed Church, the Evangelical Free Churches, the Lutheran Church, and the Lutheran Church of Alsace and Lorraine. In other countries the groups were equally varied in composition. Looking through the reports of their work one finds many well-known names: the Dean of York (H. N. Bate), Professor Martin Dibelius, Professor Henri Clavier, Professor Hermelink, Professor Siegmund-Schultze, Professor Wobbermin, General Superintendent W. Zoellner, Privatdozent D. Bonhoeffer, Dr (later Bishop) Hanns Lilje, Dr W. Freytag, Professor Karl Ludwig Schmidt, Professor Dietrich Schmidt, Professor (later Bishop) W. Stählin, the Rev. Arnold Werner, and the Rev. Gustaf Ankar.

The Continuation Committee resumed its interrupted sessions in 1934 with a meeting from 3–6 September at Hertenstein, Switzerland. The Churches were beginning to look forward with expectation to the second World Conference, and the Committee spent some time in discussing the programme for it. Fifty-two Churches had already appointed 173 delegates. The Continuation Committee, instead of reappointing the Theological Committee, formed three Commissions on: The Church and the Word, with Dr Zoellner as Chairman and Professor Sasse as Secretary; the Ministry and the Sacraments, with the Bishop of Gloucester (A. C. Headlam), Chairman, and Dr Dunkerley, Secretary; and the Church's Unity in Life and Worship, Dean Willard Sperry, Chairman—soon succeeded by the Rev. (later Bishop) Angus Dun—and Dr Floyd Tomkins, Secretary. Apart from business, half the time of the meeting was devoted to papers and discussions on The Church and the World and The Church and the Word in preparation for the next World Conference.

The following year, 1935, Hindsgaul, Middelfart, Denmark, was the place of meeting; it was decided to hold the World Conference in Edinburgh, and a programme was agreed upon. An important step was the appointment of Professor Henri Clavier of Montpellier as Travelling Secretary for the movement in preparation for the Edinburgh Conference. In the autumn of 1936 Clavier visited Germany, Czechoslovakia, Hungary, Yugoslavia, Rumania, Bulgaria, Turkey, Syria, Palestine, and Egypt. The following April and May he went to Italy, Albania, Greece, Egypt, Palestine, Syria, Turkey, Rumania, Poland, Lithuania, Latvia, Estonia, Finland, and Austria. In these journeys he was also working on behalf of the Life and Work Conference at Oxford which preceded Edinburgh. Clavier prepared carefully beforehand by correspondence for his visits. Largely as a result, he was able to see the more important Church leaders in the countries visited and to address gatherings of people called to meet him. It was a strenuous programme carried out in the face of some serious difficulties, and it was due to his devoted work that many Churches in Europe and in the Middle East were represented, which apart from his efforts would not have had anyone at Edinburgh. Dr Tomkins was equally untiring in his efforts to see that Churches on the American continent were all represented.

It was unfortunate that financial difficulties had interfered with the regular meetings of the Continuation Committee, as this delayed the appointment of the three Theological Commissions until 1934; too little time remained for their work, and for the publication of their results; the most important of these, the volume on *The Ministry and the Sacraments*,[1] did not appear until May 1937. The financial situation, indeed, embarrassed the whole preparation for Edinburgh. The American Committee had found the entire sum needed to pay for the Lausanne Conference in 1927, and Archbishop Temple and Dr Garvie felt strongly that the money for the forthcoming Conference in Edinburgh should be provided in Great Britain. In the upshot, the American Committee provided $35,000, which was used for preparations in America and for the expenses of American delegates; while the sum necessary for the expenses of the Conference in Edinburgh was raised in Great Britain by Canon Tatlow appealing in the

[1] *The Ministry and the Sacraments*, ed. R. Dunkerley and A. C. Headlam, London, 1937.

name of Archbishop Temple. The sum subscribed was not only sufficient for the expenses of the Conference, but left a balance which, together with subsequent contributions from the Churches in various countries, covered the whole cost of the Faith and Order movement until it became part of the World Council in 1948, and enabled the Continuation Committee to hand over £4,000 to the Commission on Faith and Order of the World Council for the initiation of its work.

6. THE SECOND WORLD CONFERENCE, AND AFTER

When the second World Conference on Faith and Order assembled on 3 August 1937 at Edinburgh, it was composed of the representatives of 123 Churches; there were 344 delegates with 84 alternates and 15 Continuation Committee members. These 443 persons were appointed by the Churches to which they belonged. Delegates, or in their absence their alternates, alone had the right to vote. In addition there were eight guests of the Conference and 53 members of the Youth Group, a total of 504 persons. These alone had admission to all sessions of the Conference whether sectional or full; the public and Press were admitted only to the full sessions. The Conference had behind it the work done at the Lausanne Conference and some years of preparatory work by the Theological Commissions, and the meetings of the Continuation Committee. Looking back, however, it is clear that the preparatory bodies had had too little time for their work; the Conference itself was too short, though it worked hard during the sixteen days of its sessions.

Its first act was to appoint officers, since the term of office of those previously appointed comes to an end the moment that a World Conference on Faith and Order convenes. The Archbishop of York (Temple) was elected as President of the Conference, the Archbishop of Thyateira (Germanos), the Bishop of Sträng-näs (Aulén), Pastor Marc Boegner, Dr A. E. Garvie, and the Rev. J. Ross Stevenson as Vice-Presidents; Canon Hodgson as General Secretary, Dr Floyd Tomkins and Professor Clavier, Associate Secretaries; Canon Tatlow, Financial Secretary. There were gaps in the ranks, and none were missed more than Charles Brent, Peter Ainslie, Nathan Söderblom, Charles Gore, Adolf Deissmann, and Wilhelm Zoellner, who had all died since the Lausanne Conference, the last two in 1937.

The Conference began with a service in the High Kirk of St Giles at 10 a.m. on 3 August, conducted by the Very Rev. Charles L. Warr, Dean of the Thistle; lessons from the Bible were read by Archbishop Germanos and Dr Y. Brilioth, Dean of Lund. Dr J. Ross Stevenson read "The Church's Message to the World—the Gospel", the second report of the Lausanne Conference, and the Archbishop of York preached the sermon.

The Conference met without a delegation from the German Evangelical Church, passports having been refused by the German Government—a sign of the growing strength and intolerance of the National Socialist movement. The Conference suffered not a little from the absence of the Germans. It lacked the distinctive German Lutheran contribution to the theological discussions; in consequence heavy responsibility rested on the representatives of the Scandinavian Churches. There was lacking also the spiritual contribution which the experience of the German "Confessing Church" under the Hitler régime could have made to other Churches. But the loss was great to the German Churches also; they suffered both spiritually and intellectually through their isolation from the Edinburgh Conference and from the marked developments which took place in the whole Faith and Order movement.

The Continuation Committee had prepared a programme at its meeting at Hindsgaul; this was approved, and chairmen of sections and several committees were appointed. The method of the Conference was to divide into four sections and discuss simultaneously the reports of the Commissions which had been engaged for several years in their preparation. The subjects of the sections were:

I. The Grace of our Lord Jesus Christ
II. The Church of Christ and the Word of God
III. The Church of Christ: Ministry and Sacraments
IV. The Church's Unity in Life and Worship.

In practice each of the four sections carried on its work by further grouping of its members. This sectional work began the day after the Conference assembled and continued for ten days, when the whole Conference met in full session to receive and discuss *seriatim* the section reports. These by this time had become five in number, as Section IV had asked that the Communion of Saints, a subject upon which it had worked, be given a place of its own in the report of the Conference.

Before the second revision of the reports began, the delegates from the Orthodox Churches made a united statement which was read by Archbishop Germanos. The statement expressed their satisfaction and joy in sharing in the Conference, pointed out that members of the Orthodox Churches had taken their full share in the discussions, but wished to mention that often the form in which statements came to be cast was not congenial to them. Generalizations in abstract language did not appeal to the Orthodox mind. The statement proceeded to review each section and to state the difference of outlook of the Orthodox. They reiterated the view expressed by the Orthodox Churches' delegates at the time of the Lausanne Conference and elsewhere

"that the general reunion of Christian Churches may possibly be hastened if union is first achieved between those Churches which present features of great similarity with one another."

They stressed the great spiritual profit derived from daily intercourse with the representatives of other Christian Churches during the Conference. The statement was signed by the seventeen Orthodox who represented at Edinburgh the Ecumenical Patriarchate, the Patriarchates of Jerusalem, of Alexandria, and of Antioch, the Churches of Cyprus, Bulgaria, and Greece, the Orthodox Church of Latvia, and the Russians in exile—these last numbering seven, led by the Metropolitan Eulogius from Paris.

A Memorial was also presented to the Conference, approved by the Congregationalists present from all parts of the world, petitioning the World Conference to call on all the Churches of Christendom to unite in steadfast witness to Christ and his teaching.

The second revision of the several sections of the report lasted from 16–18 August, when it was accepted, *nem. con.*, for transmission to the Churches.

The Edinburgh Conference marked a definite advance upon that held ten years earlier at Lausanne. The report was fuller and richer; it is a document of some 14,000 words.[1] A full account of the discussions that led to its making and final adoption will be found in the official Report of the Conference. The advance was due chiefly to two things. There were present ninety-five persons who had been at Lausanne in 1927. This meant that many of different countries and Churches met as old friends who through their contact and friendship had grown in understanding of confessions other than their own. The other change was due to the theological preparation, a new development in the life of the movement since Lausanne.

It was a help to the spirit of the Conference that it began with ten days' work in groups. This gave members a further chance of learning to know one another. When the whole Conference assembled and received the report of Section I, "The Grace of our Lord Jesus Christ", it was an immense encouragement to all, and in a very special way to the Continental Churches, that they found the report, as presented to them, prefaced with the statement that, "There is in connection with this subject no ground for maintaining division between Churches". The Conference concurred with the judgement of the section and accepted the report. Cheered by this, it proceeded to discuss "The Church of Christ and the Word of God" and "The Communion of Saints", suggesting some changes in each; and then passed on to "The Ministry and Sacraments", the most thorny of all the subjects discussed. As Professor D. M. Baillie said in presenting it, the report revealed deep differences but was

> "far ahead of anything the Churches are likely to have reached at present. Is not this the value of these œcumenical gatherings? We have come to discover our nearness to one another, and agreements were reached, not by compromise, but by genuine rapprochement which could not have come about otherwise. If it can happen on this ground of Ministry and Sacraments, it can happen on any ground; and if it can happen in a Conference such as this, it can happen also in the churches themselves. . . . Something is here happening which is most significant."[2]

The last section dealt with the Church's Unity in Life and Worship, and presented the one report over which some heat was generated in an otherwise harmonious atmosphere. This friction arose solely on one point—the proposal for the formation of a World Council of Churches. By 18 August the whole report had been completed and was accepted for presentation to the Churches.

On 11 August the Conference interrupted its main work to consider a proposal which the Life and Work movement had put before the Clarens meeting of the Continuation Committee the previous year. It was that a special committee of both movements and other ecumenical organizations should be asked to review "the whole ecumenical movement and lay the results before the two conferences at Oxford and Edinburgh". The Clarens meeting concurred, and ultimately a body which came to be known as the Committee of Thirty-five was appointed and met at Westfield College in London from 8–10 July 1937. The Edinburgh Conference appointed a committee of sixty persons to examine and report to it on the proposals of the Committee of Thirty-five. After a long and at times heated debate, the recommendation to approve a World Council of Churches was carried. The Bishop of Gloucester made two attempts to secure rejection

[1] *F. and O. Pamphlet No. 90: Report of the Second World Conference on Faith and Order.*
[2] *The Second World Conference on Faith and Order, Edinburgh, August 3–18, 1937,* ed. Leonard Hodgson, p. 136.

of the proposal, and later, when the chapter on "The Church's Unity in Life and Worship" was being considered, he insisted that a paragraph approving in principle the formation of a World Council of Churches should have added to it the words "Some members of this Conference desire to place on record their opposition to this proposal". Only when this addition was made was it possible to secure that the report be accepted *nem. con.*[1]

The Continuation Committee in preparing the programme had put down for the last morning "Question of Affirmation of union in allegiance to our Lord Jesus Christ in view of the world-situation". The Conference at its very beginning had appointed a Committee to watch the proceedings and to draft the proposed Affirmation. The Chairman of the Committee entrusted with this most important task was the Rev. Dr Robert Ashworth of the Northern Baptist Convention, U.S.A. The draft affirmation represented the unanimous mind of the Committee; it was approved by the Conference *nem. con.*, and perhaps the most solemn moment of the whole gathering was the adoption of the Affirmation by a standing vote. This memorable Affirmation is as follows:

"We are one in faith in our Lord Jesus Christ, the incarnate Word of God. We are one in allegiance to Him as Head of the Church, and as King of kings and Lord of lords. We are one in acknowledging that this allegiance takes precedence of any other allegiance that may make claims upon us.

"This unity does not consist in the agreement of our minds or the consent of our wills. It is founded in Jesus Christ Himself, Who lived, died and rose again to bring us to the Father, and Who through the Holy Spirit dwells in His Church. We are one because we are all the objects of the love and grace of God, and called by Him to witness in all the world to His glorious gospel.

"Our unity is of heart and spirit. We are divided in the outward forms of our life in Christ, because we understand differently His will for His Church. We believe, however, that a deeper understanding will lead us towards a united apprehension of the truth as it is in Jesus.

"We humbly acknowledge that our divisions are contrary to the will of Christ, and we pray God in His mercy to shorten the days of our separation and to guide us by His Spirit into fullness of unity.

"We are thankful that during recent years we have been drawn together; prejudices have been overcome, misunderstandings removed, and real, if limited, progress has been made towards our goal of a common mind.

"In this Conference we may gratefully claim that the Spirit of God has made us willing to learn from one another, and has given us a fuller vision of the truth and enriched our spiritual experience.

"We have lifted up our hearts together in prayer; we have sung the same hymns; together we have read the same Holy Scriptures. We recognise in one another, across the barriers of our separation, a common Christian outlook and a common standard of values. We are therefore assured of a unity deeper than our divisions.

"We are convinced that our unity of spirit and aim must be embodied in a way that will make it manifest to the world, though we do not yet clearly see what outward form it should take.

[1] For later developments, see Chap. xvi, *passim.*

"We believe that every sincere attempt to co-operate in the concerns of the kingdom of God draws the severed communions together in increased mutual understanding and goodwill. We call upon our fellow-Christians of all communions to practise such co-operation; to consider patiently occasions of disunion that they may be overcome; to be ready to learn from those who differ from them; to seek to remove those obstacles to the furtherance of the gospel in the non-Christian world which arise from our divisions; and constantly to pray for that unity which we believe to be our Lord's will for His Church.

"We desire also to declare to all men everywhere our assurance that Christ is the one hope of unity for the world in face of the distractions and dissensions of this present time. We know that our witness is weakened by our divisions. Yet we are one in Christ and in the fellowship of His Spirit. We pray that everywhere, in a world divided and perplexed, men may turn to Jesus Christ our Lord, Who makes us one in spite of our divisions; that He may bind in one those who by many worldly claims are set at variance; and that the world may at last find peace and unity in Him; to Whom be glory for ever."

It was upon this note that the Conference was brought to a close. It had owed much to the Archbishop of York. Humour, quick insight, skill, and impartiality made him an ideal Chairman, and the applause as the Conference stood to acclaim him made their appreciation plain. It was a remarkable Conference chiefly in that, as Canon Hodgson said as it closed, it had been what those who had planned it hoped it might be—"a genuine *Conference*" where there had been "a genuine interchange of thought". "You have", he said, ". . . taken hold of the material provided in advance and written your own Report." The spirit in which it was all done was reflected in a closing and characteristic remark by the President: "I am profoundly grateful to be able to say that you have been a very easy team to drive." A Continuation Committee was appointed, and the Conference adjourned to St Giles' Cathedral to close with an Act of Thanksgiving.

The Report, the composition of which constituted the work of the Edinburgh Conference, was printed in the autumn of 1937, and sent at once to the Churches which had been represented at it. The following September the full record of the Conference was published under the title *The Second World Conference on Faith and Order*.

In the meantime, the Faith and Order movement shared in a further step towards a World Council of Churches; it participated in a meeting of fourteen persons appointed by the Edinburgh and Oxford Conferences to plan a constitution for such a Council. These persons called a conference at Utrecht in May 1938 to assist in this work. When the Continuation Committee of the Faith and Order movement met at Clarens later in the year, it spent much time discussing the draft constitution of the World Council of Churches, and after some amendments decided that it satisfied the conditions on which the Edinburgh Conference had agreed that the World Conference on Faith and Order should become part of the World Council of Churches when its first Assembly was held.

The Clarens meeting also made plans for setting up a Commission on the Church, appointing Dr R. Newton Flew as its Chairman, together with a co-operating American Theological Committee on the same subject under the chairmanship of Dr G. W. Richards.

The Continuation Committee met in 1939, again at Clarens, when it decided that a Commission should be appointed on Ways of Worship, under the chairmanship of Professor G. van der Leeuw of Groningen, Holland, and a Commission on Intercommunion under the chairmanship of Professor D. M. Baillie of St Andrews. The Committee decided to give time for the three Commissions to be constituted and to carry out their work: accordingly, the next Continuation Committee was not to be held till the summer of 1941. The 1939 meeting, however, was cut short as a result of the European situation, which was so serious that it became desirable to enable members living in distant countries to start for home. The second world war intervened and the next meeting held in connection with the movement was the Executive Committee held on 20 February 1946 at Geneva.

The ecumenical movement suffered a grievous loss by the unexpected death of William Temple. He had so established his position in ecumenical affairs that whenever a chairman was wanted his was the name that instinctively leaped to everyone's mind. He had all the qualities needed in the great leader: ability of a high order, quickness in understanding, remarkable clarity in statement, width of sympathy and unfailing patience, and a fund of humour. He became Archbishop of Canterbury in 1942 and died in 1944, leaving the whole Christian world mourning the loss of one who had become known and loved in all the Churches.

Dr A. E. Garvie also died during the war. He had long been relied on not only as Vice-Chairman of Faith and Order but as a wise adviser; Bishop Brent at Lausanne and Archbishop Temple at Edinburgh both turned to him for help. Whether in the field of social service or in the work for Christian unity, he had long been a leader. Dr Garvie was a Congregationalist; an accomplished theologian; Principal of New College, London (1914–22), and of the combined New and Hackney Colleges (1922–33). Scottish by birth, but brought up in Poland till the age of eleven, he spoke German fluently and knew European Church life intimately. A deeply spiritual man of sympathetic temperament, he had friends in all the Churches.

When the Continuation Committee met after a lapse of eight years at Clarens on 28 August 1947, its first act was unanimously to invite the Rt Rev. Yngve T. Brilioth, at that time Bishop of Växjö, Sweden, to become Chairman in succession to Archbishop Temple; it appointed Dr Newton Flew as Vice-Chairman in place of Dr A. E. Garvie, considered a number of practical issues relating to the integration of the movement into the World Council of Churches, and received reports relating to its Commissions on the Church, Ways of Worship, and Intercommunion.

Speaking for the Commission on the Church, Dr Flew said that it had only been possible before the outbreak of war to hold a brief meeting, when outline plans had been made for four volumes: (1) Biblical, (2) historical, (3) confessional, and (4) an attempt at synthesis. The American Theological Committee had been able to do a great deal of work, but otherwise the Commission had its work before it. The work of the Commission on Ways of Worship had only just begun; it had held its first meeting at Oxford in January 1947. The Commission on Intercommunion on its European side had not met before the 1947 Clarens meeting, but the American section had already produced a report.

The final meeting of the Continuation Committee of the World Conference on Faith and Order was held (21 August 1948) at Amsterdam, when it gave consideration to a constitution for the Faith and Order Commission of the World Council of Churches, which was ultimately submitted for final adoption to the Central Committee of the World Council of Churches. The members of the Continuation Committee appointed at Edinburgh in 1937 became the Commission on Faith and Order of the World Council of Churches, all being planned on lines which maintained the principles for which Faith and Order had stood for nearly forty years.

7. THE ACHIEVEMENTS OF FAITH AND ORDER

The reader has the right to ask what results, if any, practical and effective, have emerged from the forty years of effort and service recorded in this chapter. The reserve with which an attempt at answering this question must be made is indicated by something that is often forgotten; it is not uncommon to speak of the Faith and Order *movement*, indeed the expression has frequently been used for convenience in this chapter, but its theme and scope are accurately stated in the official title of the "movement" and in the heading of this chapter—The World Conference on Faith and Order. By this its aims, its possibilities, and its limitations are succinctly defined. Before attempting to assess the contribution of Faith and Order, it is necessary to have some answer to the prior questions as to what such a Christian Conference is for and what it may reasonably be expected to achieve.

It may be worth while to recall words written in 1915 by Father H. H. Kelly of the Society of the Sacred Mission:

> "The purpose of Conference is a better understanding of the convictions of other people. . . . The method of Conference is inquiry. Our search should be directed not so much to the discovery of agreements, as to an appreciation of differences. . . . New agreements may arise if it develop that common convictions are embodied in divergent expressions; but we must not be disappointed if we are unable to perceive changes of really opposing convictions. On the contrary, we should be well satisfied if all parties, or even some parties, come to understand better than before what their essential differences are, and what new aspects of the truth they represent. . . . Lastly, and most important, if Conferences are to be effective in preparing the way for the reunion of Christendom, we must recognize that we ourselves are powerless, and that God alone can give us grace to find and accept that unity which He desires." [1]

It may be that the warning in the last sentence has sometimes been ignored, and that churchmen in conference have been tempted to think that they could achieve more than is really possible for human wit and resources. On the whole, however, the tendency has been in the opposite direction. It has not always been easy to remember that in any true Biblical theology faith and works are always conjoined, and that, wherever unity has come, it has come only through the faith, the labours, and the courage of men who, fired by the vision of unity, have been willing to make costly acts of obedience to what they firmly believed to be the will of God.

[1] *F. and O. Pamphlet No. 28*, pp. 9 f. and 33.

If acts are less the concern of conferences than discussions, and the direct promotion of union movements has been excluded from the purview of Faith and Order, it can nevertheless be maintained that Faith and Order has been one of the main instruments in bringing about a revolution in Church relationships.

(1) If churchmen of the most diverse confessions to-day regard it as natural to meet in conference, that in itself is a measure of the success which Faith and Order has achieved. Younger men in the middle of the 20th century can hardly have any idea of how difficult, even impossible, it was, even a generation earlier, to get their fathers to meet at all, or of what mountains of prejudice, suspicion, and hesitation had to be overcome before the first World Conference became feasible. There had indeed been interconfessional meetings before, but never before over such a wide range of divisions, never before on such a world-wide scale, never before with such utter frankness in speech commingled with unfailing charity. It was for these reasons that Lausanne 1927 presented itself to the conscience of churchmen as something new in the history of the Churches.

(2) Participation in World Conferences has been for almost all the participants a profound spiritual experience. Most of the time has been spent in discussion—intellectual, sometimes heated, occasionally arid. That is daily work. But, as conferences have come to an end, most of the delegates have been able to say, "We have dwelt in the presence of God; we have felt the Holy Spirit moving among us". To some, service of the ecumenical cause in Faith and Order has come as a spiritual and life-long vocation. Many others have found themselves permanently enriched, across the barriers of race, language, and confession, by deep and lasting friendships in Christ.

Put in another way, this means that the *Una Sancta*, the true and undivided Body of Christ, has become for many a felt and experienced reality. Men and women have attended the conferences as *Christians*, and have recognized as Christians those still divided from them in many ways. This means that the *Una Sancta* is already, albeit faintly and dimly, descried. No thoughtful man would commit the absurdity of identifying the ecumenical movement or Faith and Order with the *Una Sancta*. But, if we so earnestly desire unity, it is because we already have it in Christ who is not divided. If we can discern the likeness of Christ in separated fellow-Christians, it is because we and they alike are already in some sense in the Body of Christ, and therefore already members one of another.

(3) With this has come a steadily deepening sense of the wrongness of division. A true theology of the Church can deal only with a Church which is one as Christ is one. We are all in an abnormal situation. Even for those who, like the Orthodox, simply identify the Church with their own Church, the fact that so many baptized and believing Christians are outside their fellowship is a fact of which, in the ecumenical encounter, serious account is to be taken. To attempt to distribute blame for our divisions is a futile endeavour. But there are few among the delegates to a World Conference who would claim to be wholly free from the sin of fostering or maintaining the spirit of division by impenetrability to new truth, by confessional arrogance, by misrepresentation of the convictions of others and contempt for their ideals, by criticism not wholly motivated by charity and the desire for the elucidation of truth. The work of Faith and Order has gone forward in a spirit of simple and unforced penitence. All we like sheep have gone astray.

(4) Contact in Faith and Order has meant a real discovery or rediscovery of

one another by the Churches. Forty years ago, those who met were often shamefully ignorant of one another's deepest convictions; forty years of Faith and Order publications have made it inexcusable (though unfortunately not impossible) for serious students to harbour wild delusions about the beliefs of others.[1] It was the shock of discovery, the sense that hidden things were being revealed, the feeling that a new age was about to begin, which gave to Lausanne 1927 something of the atmosphere of apocalypse. If there seems at times to have been recession in ecumenical conviction, that is because, paradoxically, ecumenical discovery of the faith of others has driven almost all the confessions back on a fuller understanding of the faith by which they themselves profess to have lived. Between 1927 and 1948 "confessionalism", a new sharpening of confessional self-consciousness and expression, was widely observable. This is not necessarily anti-ecumenical, though it can become so. It has come to be widely recognized that, if a united Church ever comes, it must be a Church into which every Church can bring not a dull and minimal residuum of faith, but the fullness of the experience of Christ which it has had in separation. A Confession can hardly communicate the fullness of its experience to others unless it knows itself exactly what that experience is.

(5) These confessional emphases should not be allowed to obscure the range of agreement that has become manifest. The Lausanne "Call to Unity", the Edinburgh "Affirmation of Allegiance", and the Report on the Doctrine of Grace, indicate areas of doctrinal consensus which can now be taken for granted, but which would have astonished the early pioneers of the movement. Spiritual agreements cannot be expressed in mathematical terms; but few perhaps would dispute the affirmation that, in the doctrinal realm, the agreements between the Churches cover eighty-five per cent of the ground.

(6) These agreements have not been reached by any subtle process of compromise, or the adoption of ambiguous formulas under which deep differences of conviction might lie concealed. As has been noted earlier, there was a time in the history of Faith and Order when such formulas represented a real danger; but that is long in the past, and the reaction against any such paltering with the truth has been very strong. It is recognized that progress towards the truth can be maintained only by frank, even on occasion brutal, expression of differences. If anything, later Faith and Order reports have erred in the other direction, stating apparently irreconcilable views and recording impasses, and giving, perhaps unintentionally, the impression that all the possibilities of reconciliation have already been exhausted. But even the impasse is not felt as a ground for despair, since it lies between those who are ever more conscious of their fundamental unity in Christ and of the working of the Holy Spirit in their discussions.

(7) Paradoxically, though the Churches have made good progress in stating their agreements, they have been extraordinarily unsuccessful in locating their differences. Many attempts have been made to define them, but none has yet proved satisfactory. The Churches are aware that profound differences still exist between them; but whenever any Church, in addition to defining its own position, has attempted to set forth what it understood to be the position of another Church, it has always been met by the indignant rebuttal, "That is not in the least what we believe". Discussion has circled round the obvious points of difference—the ministry, the sacraments, the doctrine of grace, the nature of the Church—and still the discussion continues, without a finally satisfactory defini-

[1] For the parallel contributions of Life and Work in this field, see Chap. xii, pp. 593 f.

tion of exactly what the discussion is about. This is not to say that no progress has been made; even the Roman Catholic Church, which has stood outside the Faith and Order movement, and the Orthodox Churches, which have only to a limited extent been drawn into it, have made real advances towards an understanding of the position of Christians from whom they are separated. Naturally this progress has been more marked in those Churches which have been more fully committed to the ecumenical cause.

(8) At two points discussion has helped to make clear the nature of these inevitable differences and the difficulty of defining them. It has become increasingly clear that the experience of each Christian body is a totality, in which doctrine, worship, organization, and practical activity are inseparably joined together:

> "Each of these views sees every part of the Church's life in the setting of the whole, so that even where the parts seem to be similar they are set in a context which, as yet, we find irreconcilable with the whole context of the other. As so often in the past, we have not been able to present to each other the *wholeness* of our belief in ways that are mutually acceptable."[1]

The totality of a Church's experience is as indefinable as life itself. That, in consequence, the communication of this experience is impossible except through the sharing of a common life in a united Church, has been the conviction of those communions which have made the courageous leap forward into actual unity: it has not been a conviction to which the Faith and Order movement as a whole has been committed.

(9) There has been increasing awareness that divisions have been created and are maintained by many factors other than those of difference in theological convictions and their expression. Theological differences have always been related to a context of historical, social, economic, racial, and other forces, which have sometimes played a greater part in precipitating division than the purely theological factors. Before Edinburgh 1937, an American Committee produced a report entitled "The Non-theological Factors in the Making and Unmaking of Church Union". The matter was not fully discussed, and it was agreed that it should appear on the agenda of the next World Conference on Faith and Order. The widespread interest in the subject aroused in connection with the Lund Conference of 1952 falls outside the limits of this History, but will be a continuing concern of the ecumenical movement for many years to come.[2]

(10) It is in part the prevalence of these non-theological factors which make it difficult to assess the exact contribution of Faith and Order to "objective progress towards Christian union". Other sections of this History make it clear that the movement towards the union of separated Christian bodies was in existence long before the birth of Faith and Order, and that its tempo and impetus were rapidly increasing in the half-century prior to Lausanne 1927. Of the many unions which have taken place in the last forty years[3] only one—that between the Protestant Churches in France—can be attributed in any marked degree to the direct influence of the Faith and Order movement. Nevertheless, Faith and Order, though it observed most scrupulously its own rule not to engage in any move-

[1] *The Universal Church in God's Design*, pp. 212 f.
[2] See especially the impressive article by Dr C. H. Dodd: "A Letter Concerning Unavowed Motives in Ecumenical Discussions", *The Ecumenical Review*, Vol. II, No. 1, pp. 52–56.
[3] See the whole of Chap. x, and the Table of Plans of Union and Reunion, pp. 496–505.

ment for the union of the Churches, and not to commend any particular scheme of union, did help to create the atmosphere in which the problems of disunity were constantly kept before the Churches. It was significant that such great architects of actual unions as Bishop E. J. Palmer of Bombay in India and Dr G. W. Richards in the United States were at the same time closely associated with the development of the Faith and Order movement.

(11) Faith and Order has helped to create, or at least to make permanent and normal, a new type of relationship between Christian scholars and leaders in the Church. This new relationship has been well expressed by Dr Yngve Brilioth (at that time Bishop of Växjö) in his address to the first Assembly of the World Council of Churches at Amsterdam in 1948:

> "It may be described as a sincere willingness to speak the truth in love— to take differences seriously, but at the same time to see to the motives rather than to their expression, to look for the hidden unity in the apparent diversity, to honour all genuine forms of Christian thought and practice. It has been the conviction of the leaders of the Movement that theological work is certainly worth while although the practical results may be slow to emerge. This peculiar temperament has been in a certain sense academic, but the scholars' task has been illumined by the vision of the one Church, holy, catholic and apostolic, a vision that has convinced us of its eternal reality although its external realisation may recede into a distant future."

(12) Finally, Faith and Order has revealed the fluidity of the situation in which the separated Churches find themselves. Although the ultimate union of Christendom may seem as remote now as when the Faith and Order discussions began, it is clear that the divisions of theological conviction to-day do not in the least tidily coincide with the divisions into denominations. Although there is undoubtedly a tough resilience in the corporate, denominational distinctions, both doctrinal and non-doctrinal, it is also true that on no major theological question do the dividing lines exactly correspond with denominational allegiance. Allies on one question may be opponents upon another, but in either case they may be drawn from different confessions. This fluidity might betoken the dawn of a much wider unity or of a different pattern of schism. It is needless to be anxious as to which, for the Faith and Order movement at its best is solely concerned with truth. As we come to be "sanctified in the truth", unity will come.

CHAPTER 10

PLANS OF UNION AND REUNION
1910–1948

by

STEPHEN CHARLES NEILL

1. INTRODUCTION

The forty years between 1910 and 1950 have achieved more towards the overcoming of differences between Christians, and towards the recovery of the lost unity of the Body of Christ, than any period of equal length in the previous history of the Christian Churches.

From the heights of 1950, it is possible to discern that the Edinburgh Missionary Conference of 1910 had much to do with this great achievement. It was one of the first manifestations of that new ecumenism, in which Christians have learned to accept with equal sincerity both the underlying unity of faith in Christ which has never been lost and the seriousness of the differences by which the Christian communions are kept in separation.

At the time this was by no means evident. Edinburgh 1910 was a gathering of Christian leaders concerned with the problems of the missionary expansion of the Church. As a result of the almost complete separation between "mission" and "Church" in the countries of the continent of Europe, although Continental friends of missions came and poured the peculiar treasures of their experience into the common stock of Edinburgh, hardly a ripple stirred in the Continental Churches. It was only with the slow emergence of the Faith and Order movement, the rise to independence of the younger Churches, and the creative work of the International Missionary Council that the full ecumenical significance of Edinburgh 1910 became apparent.

The great Conference was held at the end of an epoch. The atmosphere was still that of 19th-century expansion, of the growth of European and American power in the world, and of an optimistic liberal theology. Most of the harvest of its sowing was to be gathered in a changed world of apocalyptic disasters and despairs.

This, too, was not immediately apparent. Much of the optimism survived the first world war. It was widely hoped that that war was the last manifestation of the bestial element in human nature, and that, now that these noxious humours had been cleared away, mankind might at last emerge from the jungle on to the sunlit heights of peaceful civilization. From these generous aspirations was born the League of Nations. That League, "the high that proved too high, the heroic for earth too hard", disappointed the hopes of its friends and withered away in futility. But it must never be forgotten that at the time it was judged, and rightly judged, the noblest effort yet made in the history of man to resolve the differences between the nations by peaceful deliberation and not by war.

It was impossible that the Churches should remain unaffected by these aspirations, and by the readiness for common action which was manifesting itself among the nations. The Churches in a new way became aware of one another, and began to prepare the way for their own closer union. Three remarkable illustrations will suffice to indicate the nature of these new thoughts and hopes.

In America much interest was for a time aroused by the so-called Philadelphia Plan. In 1918 a Conference on Organic Union had been attended by representatives of nineteen Christian communions; the Continuation Committee of the Conference had been authorized to draw up a Plan of Union. The Plan was ready in 1920. It looked towards a federal union, "The United Churches of Christ in America", which should be rather more than a federation and rather less than a union, but always with the view that this should be a stage on the way to full organic union of all those denominations which should be willing to accept the Plan. It was not expected that the Plan would prove attractive to Churches other than those which were already united in a common "evangelical faith", and which were willing to accept or recognize one another's sacraments, and therefore the more difficult questions of faith and order played no part in the discussions.

For a time, fortune seemed to favour the Plan. But the first official body which voted on it, the General Assembly of the Presbyterian Church in the United States, rejected it; and thereafter, though the Continuation Committee remained in being, the Plan had no further effective history.

The second move came from the Orthodox world. In January 1920 an Encyclical Letter was addressed by the Ecumenical Patriarchate of Constantinople "to all the Churches of Christ, wheresoever they be". It is now known that almost the whole of this epoch-making document was the work of Archbishop Germanos, later Metropolitan of Thyateira and Exarch of the West, and one of the first Presidents of the World Council of Churches.[1] The form of address is remarkable. The Orthodox Churches of the East maintain that they are the Church of Christ, and that *Church* is an appellation which no other Christian body in the world has a right to claim. Yet here in a document which, though not fully synodical and canonical, was intended to carry, and has carried, great weight in all the Christian Churches, other Christian bodies are courteously and frankly addressed as Churches.

The letter opens in strains of mingled charity and prophecy:

> "Our Church is of the opinion that a closer intercourse with each other and a mutual understanding between the several Christian Churches is not prevented by the doctrinal differences existing between them and that such an understanding is highly desirable and necessary, and in many ways useful in the well-conceived interest of each one of the Churches taken apart and as a whole Christian body, as also for preparing and facilitating the complete and blessed union, which may some day be attained with God's help."[2]

The practical proposals of the letter include much that has since become current practice in the ecumenical movement. First, it was requested that the Churches, in spite of their dogmatic differences, should come closer to one another in a spirit of frank interchange of thought and Christian love. Secondly, it was indicated that the Churches must have some organ of common expression and action which could play, in the world of the Churches, somewhat the same part as the League of Nations, with happy auspices unhappily unfulfilled, was just beginning to play in the world of politics. Thirdly, the letter called the Churches to remember that they must aim at nothing less than the consummation of unity in one great Church of all the followers of Jesus Christ.

The third great event was the publication, by the Lambeth Conference of 252

---

[1] At that time, the Ecumenical Patriarchate was vacant; the letter was signed by Dorotheus, Metropolitan of Brussa, Locum Tenens of the Patriarchal Ecumenical Throne, and by eleven other Metropolitans.

[2] See Bell, *Documents*, I, pp. 44–48.

Anglican bishops assembled in July 1920, of an "Appeal to All Christian People".

The Conference met in some apprehension, since the Anglican Communion had recently been troubled by the Kikuyu Controversy,[1] the echoes of which had not yet died away. There was a danger that, on the subject of Christian union, the Conference might agree on nothing, or might agree only on such platitudes as are better not expressed. One man more than any other delivered the Conference from this possible frustration—Cosmo Gordon Lang, at that time Archbishop of York and later Archbishop of Canterbury. He helped his fellow-bishops to think in larger terms of the kind of unity which the Church of Christ ought to desire, and to produce, not a flat ecclesiastical statement, but a passionate appeal to Christian people all over the world to think again of the evils of disunion and to seek the will of God for the healing of a divided Church. The Encyclical Letter opened up the theme, as follows:

"The weakness of the Church in the world of to-day is not surprising when we consider how the bands of its own fellowship are loosened and broken. . . . But the war and its horrors, waged as it was between so-called Christian nations, drove home the truth with the shock of a sudden awakening. Men in all Communions begin to think of the reunion of Christendom, not as a laudable ambition or a beautiful dream, but as an imperative necessity."

The "Appeal" reinforced this statement in formulations which have become classical expressions of ecumenical desire:

"We acknowledge all those who believe in our Lord Jesus Christ, and have been baptized into the name of the Holy Trinity, as sharing in the universal Church of Christ which is His Body. We believe that the Holy Spirit has called us in a very solemn and special manner to associate ourselves in penitence and prayer with all those who deplore the divisions of Christian people, and are inspired by the vision and hope of a visible unity of the whole Church. . . .

"This means an adventure of goodwill and still more of faith, for nothing less is required than a new discovery of the creative resources of God. To this adventure we are convinced that God is now calling all the members of His Church."

After quoting the "Lambeth Quadrilateral",[2] though not quite in its original form, the bishops went on to indicate the part that they believed might be played by the historic episcopate in a united Church and ministry:

"May we not reasonably claim that the Episcopate is the one means of providing such a ministry? It is not that we call in question for a moment the spiritual reality of the ministries of those Communions which do not possess the Episcopate. On the contrary, we thankfully acknowledge that these ministries have been manifestly blessed and owned by the Holy Spirit as effective means of grace. . . . If the authorities of other Communions

[1] See *Towards a United Church*, London, 1947, pp. 15–74.
[2] See Chap. vi, pp. 264 f.

should so desire, we are persuaded that, terms of union having been otherwise satisfactorily adjusted, Bishops and clergy of our Communion would willingly accept from these authorities a form of commission or recognition which would commend our ministry to their congregations, as having its place in the one family life."

It cannot be said that all the high hopes raised by these and other ecumenical ventures were fulfilled. Use and wont have immense power. Differences of conviction are deep and real. Suspicion, prejudice, and rivalry are not exorcized by a word. Yet, on the whole, during this period the Churches had far less reason to be ashamed of themselves than the nations and the states. The growth towards mutual confidence and unity, though not sensational, was steady. When the storms of the second world war beat upon the Churches, the value of what had been gained became evident; during the first world war, the links of Christian fellowship had been almost wholly severed; during the second, though strained to the uttermost, they held. The post-war period revealed the inner spiritual development which had quietly been going forward all the time.

As we have seen, the Philadelphia Plan found little immediate response. But when, in 1949, eight of the largest denominations in the United States met in the Greenwich Convention to plan what may prove to be the largest union of Protestant Churches ever to have taken place, it was taken for granted that the Philadelphia Plan would be the starting-point for their deliberations.

The Orthodox Churches did not rapidly follow up the proposals of the Encyclical of 1920; yet those Churches, in spite of hesitations, were represented at all the great ecumenical conferences held in Europe in this period; and, at the first Assembly of the World Council of Churches in 1948, made their distinctive and indispensable contribution to the growth of ecumenical thought and understanding.

In England, discussions between the Church of England and the Free Churches, arising out of the "Appeal to All Christian People", petered out gradually with nothing tangible accomplished. Yet, when discussions were renewed in 1947, though difficulties remained formidable, the change in the ecumenical climate was apparent.

And all the time, in all the continents, in all the great confessions, with a persistence and passion perhaps unknown in any previous epoch, the search for closer outward fellowship and corporate unity was going on.[1] Only a full-scale survey could give an idea of the range of problems that have had to be faced, the variety and ingenuity of the solutions that have been tried, and the resolution and self-sacrifice with which schemes of union have been carried through. Since such a survey could not be attempted within the narrow limits of this chapter, it has seemed best to select a small number of negotiations, differing in geographical area, in confessional approach, and in the type of union aimed at, in the hope that imagination, working on this limited range of facts, may be able to produce a not too seriously distorted picture of the whole field. What is here set forth should serve as a warning to those who think that Church unions can be brought forth quickly, as an encouragement to those engaged in the endless labour of unity negotiations, and as a challenge to those who think that the corporate union of all Christ's people is an empty dream without reality or content.

[1] See Table, pp. 496–505, for justification of this statement.

2. CORPORATE UNIONS—INTRA-CONFESSIONAL

Presbyterian Union in Scotland. Among the forms of Church polity accepted in the Christian world, few, if any, have tended more than Presbyterianism to the multiplication of divisions. Since the Reformation, Scotland has been an overwhelmingly Presbyterian country: yet the bond of a common confession of faith and a common Church order has not kept Scottish Christians within the limits of a single Church, and it might tax even the wisdom of the learned to state exactly the nature of the Original Secession and the Relief, of the "Auld Licht" and the Free Presbyterians, and the differences in faith and practice that have so long held them in separation.

But, if Presbyterianism is fruitful in divisions, it is fertile also in the resource and patience through which divisions are brought to an end. Scotland in the 19th century had a notable record in the field of Church union. When at last, on 31 October 1900, the Free Church of Scotland and the United Presbyterians became one in the United Free Church, only one major separation remained to be overcome. Fully ninety per cent of the Presbyterians in Scotland were now to be found either in the Church of Scotland or in the United Free Church. Large-hearted Christians soon began to look to the possibility of a further great act of union, in which these two should become one.

The difficulties in the way were certainly formidable. Churches which live in separation develop a difference of ethos, which is sometimes more potent to maintain division than the legal or theological formulations in which it is rationalized. The Church of Scotland was somewhat stiff in its orthodoxy, attached to ancient traditions, and not readily amenable to change. The United Free Church was more flexible in its liturgical practice and in its attitude to the historic Confessions, and had recently had experience of all the many adjustments that any Church union must involve. But deeper than any differences of tradition and temper was the sharp cleavage of conviction on the relationship between Church and State. The Church of Scotland was established and clung tenaciously to establishment; as late as 21 May 1908 the General Assembly of the United Free Church passed, by 380 votes to 167, a resolution that "the disestablishment and disendowment of the State Church in Scotland is necessary in the interest both of the State and of the Church".

Those who voted for this resolution must have been astonished and cheered when the very next day the General Assembly of the Church of Scotland, sitting just over the way in Edinburgh, sent a formal message to its separated brethren, asking them

> "to confer in a friendly and generous spirit on the present ecclesiastical situation in Scotland; and especially in the meantime with a view to discover in what manner a larger measure of Christian fellowship and co-operation than now exists may be secured and the way further prepared for that closer union for which many hearts long and pray."

On 29 May, the General Assembly of the United Free Church, with only two dissentient votes, appointed a large committee to study the whole question and to report the following year.

Agreement was reached at the start that the establishment of the Church by the State was not to be regarded as involving any right on the part of the State to control the Church, but only as the continuance of that national and public recognition of the Christian religion which the old Free Church itself had always recognized as proper and desirable. This thorny question so readily settled, it might have been thought that there was nothing further to keep the Churches apart, and that union might immediately follow. As Professor James Denney expressed it in 1914, all that had to be done was "to secure at once spiritual freedom and the national recognition of religion, without prejudice to the interest or conscience of anyone". Yet twenty years were to intervene between the first approach from the Church of Scotland and the achievement of union.

It may seem in retrospect that some of the objections raised from one side or another were trivial. But, if there is one thing more than any other which is made plain by this ecumenical History, it is that no conviction sincerely held by any Christian man may be treated as trivial, and that no progress towards union is possible unless due respect is paid to the beliefs and even to the prejudices of those who sincerely desire to come together in Christ.

It had been the custom for the Sovereign to send a Lord High Commissioner to represent him at the General Assembly of the Church of Scotland. Was not this an infringement of the rights of Jesus Christ, the sole Head of the Church?

A part of the stipends of ministers was drawn from a charge, legally enforceable, on the property of landowners. To one party in the United Free Church it was a matter of principle that the ministers should depend on the free gifts of Christ's people, and on nothing else.

Slowly and patiently the negotiators tried to meet these and other objections, and to prepare the way for a union which could honestly be accepted by all. Since the Church of Scotland was an established Church, the first action had to be taken by Parliament. In 1921 a Bill was introduced, by which the right of the Church to legislate for itself in all matters of doctrine and practice, without interference by the State or the civil courts, was secured; but at the same time regard was paid to the duty of the nation in its corporate capacity to render homage to God in Christ and to seek to promote the Kingdom of God. There was little opposition in Parliament, and on 25 July 1921 the Bill received the royal assent.

On this basis the Churches set to work to complete the process of unification. On both sides there were strong minorities which found the plan of union unsatisfactory at one point or another; but it became steadily clearer that the heart of the great majority was set upon union. By 1928 the final proposals were before the Churches. All through the later months of 1928 and the early months of 1929 the slow process of voting went on in Presbyteries, in Kirk Sessions, and in congregations. In both Churches, every Presbytery without exception, and in many cases unanimously, approved of the union. In Kirk Sessions and congregations there was an unreconciled minority of nearly ten per cent. Until the last moment it was hoped that the difficulties of this minority might be met, but in the end this hope was frustrated. A small number of United Free Church ministers, with some supporters, declared that their objections of principle had not been met, and that, even at the cost of continuing in disunion, they must stand firm on the ground that they had taken up.[1]

Union was consummated on 2 October 1929. On that day, the General Assemblies of the two Churches met for the last time in separation. Two

---

[1] In 1949 the continuing United Free Church of Scotland had 24,338 members.

processions set out for St Giles' Cathedral. As they met and merged, they burst into praise in the words of Psalm 133 (metrical version):

> Behold how good a thing it is
> And how becoming well
> Together such as brethren are
> In unity to dwell.

After worship together in St Giles', all went together to the Industrial Hall for their first General Assembly. A resolution was unanimously passed, declaring that the two Churches "do and henceforth shall constitute one Church, and that the name of the Church shall be The Church of Scotland". Those present felt that this was a true union in the Spirit, and not merely an adjustment of ecclesiastical machinery.

To create a union is easier than to live it out. Both Churches were represented in almost every parish in Scotland, and amalgamation presented many delicate problems of adjustment in which susceptibilities played a greater part than principles. But, though many must have felt passing irritations and inconveniences, there are few of either tradition who would desire to go back to the days of division. Presbyterianism in Scotland is more united than it has been for centuries. Ninety per cent of the Presbyterians in the country and more than seventy per cent of the total population are, at least in virtue of their baptism, members of a great national Church, which claims, not without reason, to be the visible expression of the duty of the nation in its corporate capacity to render homage to God in Christ and to promote his Kingdom.

Making American Methodists One People. Methodism in America was first organized in 1784, when John Wesley himself sent out Thomas Coke as the first Superintendent for the Methodists in that continent.[1]

The system bequeathed by Wesley to his followers was highly centralized and authoritarian. The feeling that evangelistic zeal was being stifled under organization, and restiveness under such ministerial control as gave no scope to lay leadership, eventually led to division; between 1828 and 1832, a considerable body of the faithful left the Methodist Episcopal Church to found, on a more democratic basis, the Methodist Protestant Church.

The gravest division, however, in American Methodism arose, not from differences about theology or organization, but as a result of that grave social tension which for more than a generation threatened to divide the United States into two hostile nations. In 1844 the General Conference took note of the case of Bishop James O. Andrew, who by his second marriage had become the owner of a number of slaves. After a long debate, the majority passed a resolution "that it is the sense of this General Conference that he desist from the exercise of his office so long as this impediment remains". It was carefully explained that this was not a sentence of deposition; but the implied condemnation of slavery was too much for the feelings of the Southerners. A separation was arranged, and the Methodist Episcopal Church, South, came into being.

The Southerners always maintained that the result was the co-existence of two parallel Churches, with equal rights and independence, a view in which they

---

[1] The first Conference elected Francis Asbury to serve with Coke as Superintendent. Within a few years, the Superintendents came to be generally known as Bishops.

were supported by a decision of the Supreme Court of the United States handed down on 25 April 1854. Many among the Northerners, however, took the view that those who had separated themselves were schismatics. After the victory of the North in the Civil War, the attitude of the conquerors, not excepting church-men, was gravely lacking in tact and generosity; feelings between the two Churches were so seriously inflamed that a resumption of Christian relationships between them seemed hardly possible.

A change for the better came about in 1874. Fraternal relations were resumed, though with an explicit reservation on the part of the South that "organic unity is not involved in fraternity". But experience ere long showed that "fraternity" was not able to deal with the problems of overlapping, and even of harmful competition and rivalry, as both Northerners and Southerners migrated into the newly opened territories of the West, or crossed the old lines of geographi-cal division. The feeling that some form of closer fellowship was the only possi-ble solution was growing steadily in both the Churches.

In 1910 a Joint Commission faced the issue of union squarely and in the following year produced its first "tentative suggestions for union". These met with considerable approval, and in 1916 the General Conference of the Method-ist Episcopal Church "hailed with joy the prospect of an early reunion". But criticisms of these proposals proved more damaging than had been expected, and the General Conference of 1920 could go no further than to ask its com-missioners to continue their work in the hope that a more satisfactory plan might be evolved.

The Joint Commission set to work afresh, and by July 1923 had worked out what came to be generally known as the Partnership Plan. This was a plan not so much for organic union as for close federal union between two still almost wholly independent Church organizations. Once again the prospects of success were good. The General Conferences accepted the scheme by large majorities. But in the Southern Annual Conferences, where there were fears of Northern domination and of the subjection of white congregations to Negro bishops, there was considerable opposition; and though a majority of favourable votes was recorded, this was less than the three-quarters majority required for imple-mentation of the Plan.

In 1934 negotiations were resumed, this time with the participation of the Methodist Protestant Church. By this time it had become clear that nothing less than full organic union would solve all problems and meet all needs.

The resolution of theological tensions (except for some difficulties between the more liberal and the more conservative elements in the Churches) played no part in the negotiations. All were agreed in accepting the Bible as the sole rule of Christian faith and conduct. All accepted the classical formularies of Methodism. All were able to agree that to those desiring to enter the member-ship of the Methodist Church, two questions only should be put:

(1) Do you confess Jesus Christ as your Saviour and Lord and pledge your allegiance to His Kingdom?
(2) Do you receive and profess the Christian faith as contained in the New Testament of our Lord Jesus Christ?

It was in the realm of organization that the greatest difficulties had to be over-come. The Methodist Protestant Church had never had bishops. Now, for the sake of union, it was prepared to accept episcopacy, being assured that the development of a more democratic polity in all the Churches was a sufficient safeguard against such episcopal autocracy or tyranny as the founders of the Church had feared a century before.

In 1935 the Joint Commission was ready with a plan, which involved a considerable measure of decentralization and divided authority in the Church between six separate bodies and groups.

As before, the Church was to be governed by a *General Conference*, half clerical and half lay, which, meeting quadrennially, was to exercise "full legislative power over all matters distinctively confessional", and also to have extensive control in such matters as the conditions of Church membership, the qualification and duties of ministers, and the powers, duties, and privileges of bishops.

Under the General Conference, there were to be six *Jurisdictional Conferences*, also meeting quadrennially, to which were to be assigned heavy responsibilities for promoting evangelistic, educational, missionary, and benevolent interests; and in particular the duty of electing bishops, who, though elected to serve in one jurisdictional area, were yet to be regarded as bishops of the whole Church. Precedents for such Jurisdictional Conferences were not to be found in the organization of any of the uniting Churches. Five of these Conferences were to be regional, one racial. It was proposed that the Negro annual conferences, mission conferences, and missions should be grouped together in one Central Conference. To some even this appearance of racial discrimination was distasteful; but many of the truest friends of the Negro felt that the development of fully independent Negro leadership would best be promoted if the Churches of that race were gathered in a single Jurisdiction rather than scattered geographically among the other five.

Churches overseas, brought into existence by the missions of the Methodist Churches, were to be organized in *Central Conferences*, charged with much the same responsibilities as the Jurisdictional Conferences in the United States, and equally with the duty of choosing the bishops for those Churches. In the past, centralization had perhaps hindered the growth of these younger Churches to full adult stature; now the aim was to give "the largest possible self-determination and self-control without an estranging autonomy and separating independence".

The Judicial Council, a feature taken over from the practice of the Methodist Episcopal Church, South, was to play, in relation to the Church, much the same part as in secular affairs is played by the Supreme Court of the United States. Its task should be to pronounce on the constitutionality of all acts of all authorities within the Church, if invited in regular form to do so; not to make the law of the Church, but to declare what the law and constitution are and mean, especially in relation to acts which might seem to contravene them.

The Annual Conferences, as before, were to be those local bodies, representative of both ministers and laity, which were to carry responsibility for the affairs of the Church in each constituted local area.

The plan proposed to continue the *Council of Bishops*, the historic itinerant General Superintendency instituted by Wesley himself, charged with the specific duties of placing the ministry, presiding over the Annual Conferences, and supervising and promoting the spiritual interests and affairs of the entire Church.

During the years 1936, 1937, and 1938, this Plan received general approval

from the responsible bodies in all the three Churches. In the Methodist Protestant General Council, "the result of the vote was received in silence; the importance of the act was too great for applause".

The uniting Conference of fifty bishops and 900 delegates met at Kansas City
in April and May 1939. The work of the Joint Commission had been so well
done that the final work of drafting involved no major changes in the plan, and
took only thirteen days. On 10 May the famous phrase "the Methodists are one
people" acquired a new significance. In the uniting session, five formal declarations of unification were read, and assented to with the words "We do so
declare". Then followed the pledge of loyalty, repeated by all the delegates
together: "To the Methodist Church thus established we do solemnly declare
our allegiance, and upon all its life and service we do reverently invoke the
blessing of Almighty God." The formal vote of union was then taken, and
found to be unanimous; whereupon the choir raised the strains of the Hallelujah
Chorus from Handel's *Messiah*.

Thus was achieved, without leaving behind any large dissenting minority,
the largest organic union yet recorded among the Protestant Churches.[1] When
the Methodist Church, first but not alone among the Churches, divided on the
issue of slavery, it was remarked that one of the strongest ties that made for the
unity of the nation in a time of bitter strain was giving way. After the Civil War,
the political unity of the United States was restored, though the wounds of that
dreadful period were slow to heal; but still the Churches held apart. With the
union of the Methodists and their rededication of themselves as "one people"
to the promotion of Scriptural holiness throughout the whole of the United
States, almost a century of division was wiped out and a striking answer given
to the criticisms of those who maintain that Protestantism in America is always
divisive and never unitive in its effects.

3. CORPORATE UNIONS—TRANS-CONFESSIONAL

The United Church of Canada. On 10 June 1925, through the amalgamation of
four groups of Canadian Churches, the United Church of Canada was born.
This in itself was a memorable event in the history of Christendom. But it was
only the last stage in a long process of unification, which has been one of the
most remarkable features in Canadian Church history. The experts have com-
puted that the United Church has gathered into itself forty distinct Christian
bodies, made one through nineteen distinct acts of Church union.[2]

In Canada, with its vast areas and scattered population, the evils of overlapping and rivalry have been more evident than elsewhere. Immigrants brought
their own denominations with them, and most of the divisions known in Europe
quickly reproduced themselves in Canada, until it was no unusual thing to find
six struggling churches in a township with no more than 500 inhabitants. But
from an early date the contrary tendency began to take effect, and Canadian
Christians were learning to discover one another across the barriers of distance
and denominational loyalty. The 19th century was the great period of unification within the confessions. By the end of the century that work had been

---

[1] The Methodist Church had in 1950 a membership of almost nine million. There are more
Baptists than Methodists in the United States, but the Methodist Church is considerably
larger than the largest Baptist body, the Southern Baptist Convention, which in 1950 had
6,761,265 full members.

[2] For earlier history, see Chap. vi, pp. 300 f., 304 f.

almost accomplished; with the dawn of the new century the stage was set for a far wider trans-confessional union.

The first definite proposal came, on 18 September 1902, from the General Conference of the Methodist Church assembled at Winnipeg. Among the speeches made before the Conference by fraternal delegates of the Presbyterian and Congregational Churches, there was one which attracted far more than ordinary attention. Principal William Patrick of Manitoba College spoke emphatically of the growing spiritual needs of the Canadian West, and asked if the time had not come for a definite step towards closer union between Churches which had so much in common and were facing together so great a spiritual need. In response to this direct challenge, the Conference decided to invite those Churches to appoint committees to confer with a committee of Methodists on the feasibility of organic union. The other denominations agreed and appointed their committees. The "preliminary parley" of the three committees together was held at Toronto on 21 April 1904, and a resolution was passed declaring that organic union was both desirable and practicable.

The complex story of the progress of the movement towards union may conveniently be divided into four periods:

The preparation of the Basis	1904–1910
The commitment of the negotiating denominations to the Basis	1910–1917
The truce	1917–1921
The struggle to secure enabling legislation	1921–1925

The doctrinal basis of union, in its first form, was arrived at in the course of the year 1905. The members of the committee and most members of the negotiating Churches were convinced that in the essentials of the Christian faith the Churches were already one, and no need was felt at the time for lengthy theological argument or elaborate theological statement. After a brief preamble, in which the Churches declared their intention to maintain "our allegiance to the evangelical doctrines of the Reformation", the main principles of the Faith were set out in twenty articles. Neither the Westminster Confession nor the classic expressions of the Methodist faith exercised a determining influence on the phrasing of these articles. One, a mediating statement between the Arminian and Calvinistic views on the doctrine of election, was original:

"We believe that God, out of His great love for the world, has given His only begotten Son to be the Saviour of sinners, and in the Gospel freely offers His all-sufficient salvation to all men. We believe also that God, from the beginning, in His own good pleasure, gave to His Son a people, an innumerable multitude, chosen in Christ unto holiness, service and salvation."

For the rest the main sources were the Brief Statement of the Reformed Faith, prepared by the Presbyterian Church in the U.S.A. in 1905, and the Articles of the Faith of the Presbyterian Church in England, prepared in 1890.

By 1908, questions of doctrine having been provisionally settled, the negotiators believed that the greater part of their work was done. They did not then realize that the waters would get deeper, as the negotiations moved on from doctrine to the training of the ministry; from the ministry to polity; from polity to administration; and from administration to law.

On the ministry, no serious doctrinal divisions came to light. Each of the three bodies was willing to recognize the ministries of the others as valid and regular, and no attempt was made until after the consummation of union to go into the deeper theological questions involved in the nature of the ministry of the Church.[1]

In the field of administration, there were practical problems that called for solution. The Methodists held to the tradition of an itinerant ministry, located by the central Conference, and largely independent of the congregations which it was appointed to serve. Both Presbyterians and Congregationalists held that a minister should be called by the church in which he was to exercise his ministry, and that once called he should not be separated from that church by any external ecclesiastical authority. Compromise was clearly necessary. It was proposed that the right of appointment should be vested in the Settlement Committee of the Conference, each individual congregation having the right to call a minister, if it desired to exercise that prerogative. Difficulties which arose after union suggest that the negotiators would have been wise at this stage to go more deeply into the difficulties which were certain to arise in the application of their suggested compromise.

All the uniting Churches were familiar with synodical or conciliar forms of Church government. But whereas the presiding officers of the other two Churches held office for one year only, the General Superintendent of the Canadian Methodist Church was elected for eight years, and in fact between 1884 and 1925 that Church had had only two General Superintendents. A serious attempt was made to combine the merits of the two systems; in the final result perhaps rather more was adopted of the Presbyterian system than of the other two, and the Moderator of the United Church of Canada holds office only for a single year.

In 1910 the three Churches gave provisional assent to the Basis of Union as it was at that time before them. It was at this point that the voice of discontent and opposition first began seriously to be heard. Of the presbyteries of the Presbyterian Church, twenty out of seventy voted against union. It was felt necessary to send the question down to Kirk Sessions and congregations. When the vote was taken, it was found that almost a third of those voting were hostile both to the idea of union and to the proposed Basis of Union. By 1916 the opposition had increased to forty per cent. Feeling in favour of union was strongest in the west. Opposition was centred in the east, and it was in the east that the strongest and best-organized Presbyterian churches were to be found.

From 1917 to 1921, by mutual agreement between the Churches, a truce was observed during which attempts were made to bring the minorities, and especially the strong Presbyterian minority, into line.

The opponents of union took the view that the majority, having voted in favour of the extinction of the Presbyterian Church in Canada, were no longer of it: the faithful minority in the General Assembly was alone competent to handle the affairs of the Church, and the others henceforth had neither part nor lot in it. The majority took its stand on the 122nd rule of the Church, which stated that "the General Assembly being the supreme court of the Church, its decisions are final". Since by the rule no right was accorded to a minority to block the decisions of a majority, there can be hardly any doubt that the General Assembly was constitutionally correct in its action, and this view was later taken by the Canadian Parliament. But never in the history of negotiations for Church

---

[1] In 1926 a long and scholarly statement on the nature of the ministry was issued by a committee under the chairmanship of Dr John T. McNeill.

union has the question of the moral, as against the legal, rights of a majority been more acutely raised.

There is no doubt that theological and religious factors were at work in the Presbyterian opposition, and in particular the fear that the grand old tradition of Presbyterian faith and witness was jeopardized by the Basis of Union. But there were as well other and less admirable motives: some disliked the more emotional forms of Methodist worship; others objected to the part played by Methodists in the campaign for prohibiting alcoholic liquor; and some were simply opposed to any change from the well-worn and the familiar. All attempts at reconciliation proved unavailing; and the proportions of supporters and opponents of the Scheme remained in 1921 almost exactly what it had been in 1910.

The Presbyterian majority having decided to go forward into union, the next step was to ask both the Dominion Parliament and the Provincial Parliaments for enabling legislation to ensure the legal validity of the actions of the Churches, and to avoid the danger of extensive litigation later on—a danger which the Free Church case in Scotland had made real to all the participants, and especially to the Presbyterians. Once again the whole bitter quarrel between the supporters and the opponents of the Scheme had to be fought out before a parliamentary committee, not all the members of which belonged to the negotiating Churches. Then a doubt was raised whether the Canadian Parliament itself, under the British North America Act of 1867, had the necessary powers to legislate. In the end, the risk was taken, and the legality of the decisions then made has never since been challenged. Finally, when it became clear that a division within the Presbyterian Church could not be avoided, congregations and Kirk Sessions had to be called upon to vote yet once more, in order that a fair distribution of the property might be made. Even now, the interpretation of the figures is difficult; but it appears that 784 congregations, among them many of the strongest in Canada, voted against union, and 4,512 in favour; and that of the individual members, slightly more than a third desired to remain in the Presbyterian Church and outside the Union. Then the sword of division penetrated to the breaking up of Christian charity even within families. Time has healed many of the wounds; but there are still those who cannot speak without pain of that time of bitterness and estrangement.

On 19 July 1924, the Enabling Bill received the royal assent, and became part of the law of Canada. On 10 June 1925, the United Church of Canada (the name had been determined in 1914) was solemnly inaugurated in the Mutual Street Arena in Toronto. In the course of the service, representatives of the uniting Churches expressed as follows the gifts which they hoped to bring into the common treasury of the new fellowship:

Presbyterian: In vigilance for Christ's kirk and covenant, in care for the spread of education and devotion to sacred learning.

Congregational: In the liberty of prophesying, the love of spiritual freedom and the enforcement of civic justice.

Methodism: In evangelical zeal and human redemption, the testimony of spiritual experience, and the ministry of sacred song.

Local Union: In the furtherance of community-life within the Kingdom of God.[1]

[1] In a large number of centres, union on the national scale had been preceded by the formation of Local Union Churches.

The Union was an accomplished fact. Its integrity has been tested by a quarter of a century of common life, and the workmanship in the main pronounced good.

Adjustments led inevitably to strains and friction. Some churches became superfluous through the Union; it was not easy in any place for the adherents of one particular tradition to see it yield and disappear. The constitution had not made it clear, in cases of tension, whether the right of a congregation to call its own minister or the injunctions of more central authorities were to prevail. It is greatly to the credit of all concerned that, though tensions were many, they never became so strong as to jeopardize the Union.

This stability makes it clear that, though the Union may have been achieved by compromise and the evasion of difficulty, there were also strong forces making for and maintaining unity.

In the first place, what had seemed only evil had within it a seed of good. The remorseless opposition of the Presbyterian minority had compelled the friends of union to fight shoulder to shoulder in a long and exhausting campaign, and thus to attain, even before union, a common outlook and a sense of brotherhood far more intimate than at the start had seemed possible.

Theological renewal has played its part in promoting unity. The United Church has been compelled, partly by criticism from outside, to think out more clearly its own theological position. The rather negative liberalism, which was one of its dangers in the early days, has given place to a more positive presentation of the Christian faith.

In worship, great liberty has been allowed for the retention of all forms and methods which were in use before union: but the United Church has shown itself truly catholic in drawing on all the great liturgical traditions of the Church of Christ. Its suggested order for the Holy Communion has been acclaimed by experts as one of the best in the world.

The United Church is developing into what it desires to be, a great national Church. Geographically the most widely distributed of all the Churches in Canada, it is in a better position than any other to make the ministrations of religion available to all classes of people. Not content with the unity already attained, it stretches out its hands to the other communions which have still remained separate, in the hope that, whereas this Union is a great achievement in itself, to later ages it may present itself as only one step forward in the development of a great and truly catholic Church of Canada.[1]

The Church of Christ in China. In no country in the world has the desirability of Christian union been more self-evident than in China. In 1938, 123 separate non-Roman missionary organizations were at work in China; all the main denominations were represented, as well as many others not so well known in the annals of Christendom.

The formation in 1922 of the National Christian Council of China[2] was a great step forward in Christian co-operation; but Chinese Christians rightly regarded this as the beginning and not the end of the process. In the year of its formation, the Council passed the following resolution:

"We believe that there is an essential unity among all Chinese Christians and that we are voicing the sentiment of the whole Chinese Christian body

[1] See Neill, *Towards Church Union, 1937–1952*, pp. 76–9.   [2] See Chap. viii, p. 381.

in claiming that we have the desire and the possibility to effect a speedy realisation of corporate unity, and in calling upon missionaries and representatives of the Church in the West, through self-sacrificial devotion to our Lord, to remove all obstacles in order that Christ's prayer for unity may be fulfilled in China."

A beginning had already been made in 1918, when the Synods of the Presbyterian and Congregational Churches had appointed a committee to prepare plans for corporate union. After 1922 the plan was enlarged, and a call to union sent out very widely to Churches and missions in every part of China. The response was widespread and rapid. Within five years, Churches in connection with the Baptists, Congregationalists, Methodists, Presbyterians, Reformed, United Brethren in Christ, United Church of Canada, and independent Chinese Churches agreed to join the Union. Sixteen missionary societies gave their cordial support. It was possible to hold the first Synod of the Church of Christ in China in 1927.

The extent of the union movement must not be exaggerated. Neither the Chinese province of the Anglican Communion nor the Lutherans were willing to join. Thus in planning for union some of the more difficult questions of doctrinal statement and Church polity, such as episcopacy, were never even raised. All the Churches which joined the Union were able to accept one another, without further delay, as holding the essentials of the Christian faith; all were able mutually to accept one another's ministries and sacraments. Yet the range and variety of the bodies represented makes the attainment of unity a remarkable achievement. Presbyterians have always stood for a strict confessional orthodoxy and a regional organization of churches. Congregationalists and Baptists, with their dislike of credal formulations and their insistence on the autonomy of the local congregation, stand on the left of the Free Church tradition; yet some of the independent Chinese Churches were considerably further to the left than they.

Part of the success of the movement must be attributed to the extreme simplicity of the "bond of union" which is the one essential in the structure of the Union:

> "Based on the principle of the freedom of formulating her own faith, the bond of union shall consist:
> "(1) In our faith in Jesus Christ as our Redeemer and Lord, on whom the Christian Church is founded: and in our earnest desire for the establishment of His Kingdom throughout the whole earth.
> "(2) In our acceptance of the Scriptures of the Old and New Testaments as the divinely inspired Word of God, and the supreme authority in matters of faith and duty.
> "(3) In our acknowledgement of the Apostles' Creed as expressing the fundamental doctrines of our common evangelical faith."

In the next article of the constitution it is laid down that "any constituent Church, in addition to the acceptance of the bond of union, may retain its original standards of faith".

The very simplicity of these statements raises the question whether the Church of Christ in China should not be regarded as a federation rather than as a

Church. The full liberty of faith and practice accorded to each existing denomination must result in far greater variety than is normally to be found within a Church. Those who planned the Union were clear in their own minds that what they desired was a Church, but they would have added that in so vast a country as China, with little more than a million non-Roman Christians, and where the rules of mission comity have been fairly well observed, any attempt to produce at once uniformity of profession and practice would be self-defeating; growth in unity must be the fruit of union, and not the pre-condition of it.

The organization of the Church is well calculated to promote growth in fellowship. There is a General Assembly which meets every four years, and a General Council which meets every other year. Local bodies meet more frequently. The General Secretary and the Executive Secretary are elected for a period of eight years, and thus contribute an element of stability in a Church, the constituent parts of which are so widely separated, and the other officers of which change so frequently. In 1949 an observer wrote: "The volume of work which is given to the General Assembly Office by all parts of the Church, and the sense of Christian solidarity and of national Church consciousness evident at the 1948 General Assembly meeting, show that the Church is in reality a working organic union."

The united Church has three mission-fields of its own, one of them among the aboriginal tribes in the far south-west. Increased evangelistic activity is always a sign of reality in the life of a united Church.

Since 1927 there have been no new accessions to the Church of Christ in China. It is probable that further progress towards union must be preceded by deeper theological thought, and a growth of church-consciousness both in the Church of Christ in China and in the other Churches with which it has fellowship in the National Christian Council. The tribulations of the post-war period have driven Chinese Christians back on the foundations of their faith; this period of difficulty and suffering may lead them to bring to birth in their country a greater and more perfect union than they have yet ventured to imagine or to devise.

The Church of Christ in Japan. Modern missionary work in Japan began only in 1858. Yet, in 1938, apart from the Roman Catholic and Orthodox Churches, a Christian community of little more than 200,000 members was divided among many Churches, and was receiving the ministrations of no less than sixty-eight organizations. Japanese Christianity has tended not to be greatly interested in Western denominational divisions; but, although various attempts to break away from the denominational pattern had been made, great success had not been achieved, and the divisions continued. The impulse to a great step forward in Church union came not from the Churches themselves but from the Government.

On 1 April 1940 the Government passed the Religious Bodies Law. In some ways this was of great advantage to the Churches, since for the first time Christianity was recognized, along with Shintoism and Buddhism, as one of the religions of Japan. On the other hand, the Law made possible minute and harassing official control of a faith the tenets of which were suspected of being incompatible with the imperial ambitions of Japan. The Law as such did not enforce the unification of the Protestant Churches. But the Minister of Education let it be known that any body with less than 5,000 members was unlikely to secure registration under the Law. This indirect pressure, combined with the already existing sentiment in favour of union, and the feeling that one united Protestant Church was much more likely to obtain favourable treatment from the Government than many small ones, was enough to bring almost all the Churches into line. Forty-two denominational groups agreed to form the Nippon Kirisuto Kyodan, the Church of Christ in Japan.

The Seventh Day Adventists from the start refused to join. Their organization was broken up, though single congregations could continue to exist as voluntary associations, without the measure of protection afforded by the Religious Bodies Law.

The Nippon Sei Ko Kwai, the Anglican province in Japan, sought separate recognition, but was refused it. Sixty-eight of its 229 congregations, with three bishops, agreed to enter the Kyodan, the rest of the Church remaining aloof. In March 1942 the Sei Ko Kwai was legally dissolved. On 24 August 1943 the three bishops who had joined the Kyodan consecrated seven others, in order to ensure the episcopal succession in a time of danger and difficulty.

The Holiness Church had joined the Kyodan. But its strong eschatological emphasis, and its proclamation of Jesus Christ as the coming King, brought it into disfavour with authorities who recognized no royalty other than that of the Emperor of Japan. On 26 June 1942 most of the leaders of that Church were arrested, and endured various degrees of harshness in prison. On 7 April 1943 the dissolution of the Holiness Church was decreed, and its name was expunged from the list of bodies adhering to the Kyodan.

The Kyodan, as it eventually took shape, included Presbyterians, Methodists, Congregationalists, Baptists, Lutherans, Disciples, and a number of smaller bodies. Its Constitution was accepted in November 1941.

There is no doubt that those who brought the Kyodan into existence intended that it should be a fully orthodox Christian body. Its first declaration states as essential articles of faith that

"the triune God, Father, Son and Holy Spirit, as revealed in the Holy Bible, forgives sin, justifies, sanctifies and endows with eternal life those who believe through the atonement of Jesus Christ, who died for the sins of the world and rose again."

But in the next four years the Kyodan was never able to set forth a full declaration of faith, since no form of words proposed satisfied the exacting demands of the all-powerful Minister of Education. The statement in the Constitution as one of "the life principles of this Kyodan" that the Japanese Christian should

"make your Christian faith stronger by following closely the way of traditional Japanese moral teaching, and thus contribute your share to the future of the Japanese empire"

could hardly be held to satisfy the claims of Christian orthodoxy.

Church order, under the Constitution, was highly centralized and autocratic. At the start the Church was organized in eleven blocs of related denominations; the denominations retained some liberty, and their heads acted in some sense as a privy council to the head of the Church. But in 1942 this arrangement was

given up, and centralization became complete. The law of 1940 had laid it down
that

> "each sect and denomination shall have a head who shall manage and
> represent the sect or denomination. . . . The recognition of the competent
> minister is necessary for [his] appointment to become effective."

The Constitution of the Kyodan stated that

> "a man who is elected by the general assembly and is approved by the
> Minister of Education will become the Kyodan *torisha*."

Within the strict limits of government supervision, the *torisha* was to have extensive, indeed almost unlimited, power. He was to have authority to appoint,
discipline, and dismiss pastors, to levy assessments on the Churches for the
conduct of affairs, and to manage the estates and properties of the Church.
Church affairs were to be conducted by eight departments; but, as the heads of
these departments were to be appointed by the *torisha*, and to be removable at
his pleasure, they constituted no effective check on his dictatorship.

The record of Japanese Christians during the war years is a mixture of heroism
and subservience, of perplexed loyalties and sorely tested fidelity. The wonder is
not that the Kyodan accomplished little, but that under the conditions of its
existence it was able to accomplish so much.

In 1945 the war ended. One of the first acts of the occupying powers was to
cancel the Religious Bodies Law. The Churches were free. The existence of the
Kyodan hung in the balance.

Some of the confessionally stricter bodies, such as the Church of the Nazarene, immediately withdrew.

The Lutherans would gladly have stayed in, if the Kyodan could have been
declared to be a federation; when the leaders affirmed that the Kyodan must be
considered a Church, the Lutherans, in loyalty to their own confessional traditions, regretfully gave up their membership.

Within three years of the end of the war, the Nippon Sei Ko Kwai had been
reunited as an independent Church. Difficulty was caused by the ambiguous
status of the six survivors among the bishops consecrated in August 1943; but
when the Sei Ko Kwai, following the recommendation of the Lambeth Conference of 1948, agreed to accept these men back as bishops, validly but irregularly
consecrated and without jurisdiction, the last difficulty was removed and reconciliation was complete.

In spite of these and other smaller defections, the Kyodan managed to hold
together, retaining the same groups as the United Church of Canada—the
Presbyterians, Methodists, and Congregationalists. But the inner tensions continued to be severe. There was a strong feeling that all the war-time leaders
should resign, since none of them could claim a record free from over-zealous co-
operation with the Government to the detriment of the true Christian interests
of the Church. All wished to see much decentralization, and the restoration of
a more democratic polity. Some felt that the recognition of denominations, as
such, within the Church was necessary.

To some extent these various desires have been met. At the first post-war
General Assembly of the Church, in November 1946, the war-time *torisha* was

replaced. Every trace of the former government control was removed. The authoritarian structure of the Church was modified. But no step was taken to recognize the denominations, or to give them scope for independent witness within the Church. This is a problem of which it is certain that the last has not been heard.

The most serious problem of all remains. The Kyodan claims to be a Church. But if it is a Church, on what confessional basis does it take its stand? The Presbyterian elements, familiar with clearly defined dogmatic formulations, claim that a Church cannot exist for ever without defining the terms of its belief. To some among the Congregationalists, with their traditional dislike of creeds and formulations of faith, even the acceptance of the Apostles' Creed seems to endanger the liberty of the Christian conscience. This continuing tension is as yet far from being resolved.

It is not yet certain that the Kyodan will be able to resist the disruptive tendencies by which it is assailed and to hold together. But to most observers it seems probable that it will stand the strain, and will emerge successfully, though perhaps somewhat reduced in size, from its trials. If so, as the largest Christian body in Japan, it should have great gifts to contribute to the development of Japanese Christianity in the new day of opportunity.

The Protestant Churches in France. The Protestants in France had been for more than a hundred years a despised and persecuted sect, when, by the law of "the 18 Germinal, Year X" (7 April 1802), Napoleon I gave legal recognition to the Protestants, and brought their Churches under the protection and the control of the State. Napoleon gave much, but he withheld one essential thing, without which Presbyterian Church order is fatally incomplete—authority to convene a national synod. At last, in 1872, the Third Republic gave permission to hold the desired synod. The 30th Synod was held after an interval of 213 years since the 29th. But in seventy years of comparative freedom the Church had lost that unity which it had maintained through centuries of danger and oppression.

The first division took place in 1849, when a number of pastors who had come under the influence of the Revival Movement, especially in Geneva, feeling themselves thwarted by what they regarded as the unspiritual condition of the Church and by its connection with the State, separated themselves from it, and constituted the Union of Evangelical Free Churches. In 1851 the Evangelical Methodist Church of France came into being.

Forces making for division were at work also within the Reformed Church itself. With the holding of the Synod of 1872, it became clear that the tensions had already become too strong for the unity of the Church to be maintained. The burning issue was the adoption of a Confession of Faith. Liberalism in France had developed in an extreme form; its attitude towards confessions of faith was pungently expressed by one member, who is reported to have said, "If you ask us to sign a declaration that two and two make four, we will not sign it". The more orthodox party was determined to have a Confession. That which was finally adopted was brief and moderate in tone; but even this was too much for the liberal wing. The State connection maintained a semblance of unity; but in reality from 1872 on there were two Churches—the National Union of Evangelical Reformed Churches, including nearly seventy per cent of all the Protestant Churches in France; and the more liberal National Union of Reformed Churches. In 1905 separation between Church and State was brought

into effect in France; with this new liberation the uneasy partnership was dissolved, and the two groups became in organization what they had long been in
fact—separate and independent Churches.

Even then, separation was far from complete. Protestants of all groups
worked with one another in the Federation of French Protestant Churches, the
first steps towards the formation of which had been taken in the very year of the
separation, 1905. Pastors of different tendencies met for joint study and prayer.
And scarcely had the separation taken place when new forces making for union
began to make themselves felt. The searching experiences of the first world war
(as set forth in the so-called "Petition of the Chaplains"), the rediscovery of
Biblical theology, in part under the influence of Karl Barth, and in particular
the development of the Faith and Order movement, and its great World Conference at Lausanne in 1927, made former causes of division seem antiquated,
and led men to a wholly new consideration of ancient problems. The Church had
been split by disagreement as to the very basis of the Christian faith; and honest
union could come about only as the result of a new-found fellowship in faith.

The first definite proposal for union seems to have been set forth, at the
Assembly of French Protestantism held in Marseilles in 1929, by Pastor H.
Roux, in an allocution under the title "The Desire of the Young":

> "When we think of unity, our idea of it is of a substantial and real unity,
> the unity which comes from on high, the unity of the Body of Christ. We
> believe that it is through unity in faith, and by a common confession of
> Christian truth, that unity can be attained."[1]

Widespread discussion followed in local Church bodies and regional synods.
In 1933 the Regional Synod of the Drôme (Evangelical) and the Regional
Synod of the 9th Region of the Reformed Church both sent forward resolutions
in favour of a movement towards unity. These resolutions were considered by
the Synods of the two Churches, which happened to meet almost simultaneously
in Paris in June of the same year. The Synod of the Reformed Church, which met
first, took the initiative in approaching the Evangelical Synod; the approach
was welcomed. Joint Committees were set up; by the end of 1933 the representatives of the two Churches were ready to begin their work.

The first problem, inevitably, was that of a Confession of Faith, and on this
rock the negotiations almost foundered. It seemed impossible to find a formulation which could satisfy the orthodoxy of the more conservative, without in-
fringing what the more liberal regarded as essential liberties of belief and interpretation. At last, in January 1935, the Joint Commission had before it a draft
which seemed to offer hope of reconciliation without mere compromise; this
was many times revised in detail, and was finally adopted by the Synods of the
Churches in 1936 and 1937.

The Church first affirms its continuity with the historic faith of the whole
Church, and its expression of that faith in its formulas and in its worship:

> "In the Communion of the universal Church, [it] affirms the continuity
> of the Christian faith, through the successive affirmations in the Apostles'
> Creed, the Ecumenical Creeds, and the Confessions of Faith of the period
> of the Reformation, especially the Confession of Rochelle."

[1] Published in *Foi et Vie*, 15 December 1929, pp. 131–41.

But it ends by stating that:

> "Impelled by the action of the Holy Spirit, it shows forth its faith by its works; it labours in prayer for the awakening of souls, for the manifestation of the unity of the Body of Christ, and for peace among men. Through evangelization, missionary work. and the fight against social ills, it prepares the way of the Lord, until the Kingdom of God and his righteousness are brought in in the coming of its Head."

Clearly this is as much a programme of action as a Confession of Faith; but the two elements were needed to meet the desires both of those to whom Christianity was primarily adhesion to the Faith once delivered to the saints, and of those who experienced it most deeply as a life to be lived and a witness to be borne.

The next major difficulty concerned the terms of subscription to the Confession of Faith to be required of the pastors of the Church. Traditionally, affirmation of faithfulness to the Confession had been part of the solemnity of ordination. Liberals feared that strict interpretation of the pledge might deny to the pastor the needed liberty of interpretation; conservatives feared that liberty of interpretation might be held to justify the pastor in denying the very essentials of the Faith. Eventually a compromise not wholly satisfactory to either party was reached. The affirmation of faith during the ordination service was retained, but it was to be introduced by a preamble explaining that

> "[the Church] recalls to you the facts and the truths on which the Church of God is founded, as well as the permanent principles of the Reformation. You will proclaim your adherence joyfully, as a free and personal affirmation of your faith. Without committing yourself to the letter of the formulas, you will proclaim the message of salvation which they express."

In 1935 the decision of a number of the Free Churches and of the Methodist Church to join in the movement for unity raised a third major problem—the status and qualifications of a member of the Church. It was necessary to reconcile the "multitudinist" tradition of the larger Churches with the Free Church insistence on the need for a personal experience of the grace of Christ. A solution of this apparently insoluble contradiction was found by making a distinction between *membership* and *responsible membership* in the Church. "The Reformed Church of France recognizes as its own all those whom it has baptized, or in accordance with the terms of its discipline admitted to its fellowship." But those who desire it may, at the age of twenty-one and on approval by the Church, become *responsible members*, and thus acquire the right to take part also in the government of the Church. The Church does not claim to judge the consciences of individuals, but expects of those who apply for responsible membership a living faith in God, the determination to pray and work in the fellowship of the Church, and conformity to the rules of the Church for life and discipline.

The Constituent Assembly of the united Church was held at Lyons in April 1938. The title "The Reformed Church of France" was chosen for the new fellowship. The 31st National Synod of the Church was held in Paris in December of the same year.

It has to be recorded with regret that unity was not perfectly achieved. A group of pastors, mostly in the South of France, feeling that the purity of the

Faith was not sufficiently guaranteed by the formulas of the united Church, refused to join it, and formed the Union of Reformed Evangelical Independent Churches. But the great majority of Protestants in France (exclusive of Alsace and Lorraine) have found a home in the Reformed Church. The union has been tested by the strains of the war and the post-war period, and has held firm. The resources of the Church are far from equal to the immense tasks and opportunities that lie before it; but it is already clear that new spiritual riches and a new spirit of adventure have been discovered within the reunited Church.

4. TRANS-CONFESSIONAL FELLOWSHIP

The Evangelical Church in Germany. Since the Reformation, Protestants in Germany had been divided among many wholly autonomous regional Churches. Of the twenty-eight which existed in 1933, twenty were Lutheran in confession; two were Reformed; the remaining six were United, among them the Old Prussian Union of 1817, by far the largest of German Evangelical Churches.[1]

In 1922 the Federation of German Evangelical Churches had been formed as an instrument of common action, but without infringement of the autonomy of the regional Churches.

When Adolf Hitler came to power in 1933, one of his aims was the unification of the Protestant Churches in Germany. Many leading churchmen shared the view that the time had come when closer fellowship would be of advantage to the Churches. On 11 July 1933 the Constitution of the German Evangelical Church was accepted by the Government and three days later incorporated in a law.

It was not long before opposition began to manifest itself, as churchmen came to realize that the new Church might come into the hands of those who would subvert the Gospel and make it subservient to nationalistic and non-Christian aims. In 1933 the Emergency League of Pastors was formed. In May 1934 the "Confessing Synod" of the German Evangelical Church was held at Barmen, and sent out its famous Declaration in which is found the statement that

> "Jesus Christ, as witness is borne to us concerning him in the Holy Scriptures, is the sole Word of God to which we must hearken, and which we must trust and obey, whether in life or in death.
>
> "We reject as false the doctrine that the Church can and should recognize, as sources for its proclamation, besides and apart from this sole Word of God, other events and powers, forms and truths as a revelation from God."

Unfortunately, there were differences of opinion even among those present as to the force of this Declaration. Some hoped that it might prove to be a Confession of Faith, on which a united Church faithful to the word of God could be built; others did not accept it as in any way absolving the Churches from loyalty to their own historic confessions.[2]

The next eleven years were a time of conflict, oppression, and martyrdom, during which experience of spiritual fellowship strengthened the will to outward

---

[1] See Chap. vi, pp. 268 ff. and 286 ff. It must be borne in mind that there are also Free Churches, with which this section is not concerned.

[2] Not without reason, since the Confessing Synod in its "Explanations" affirmed that "the German Evangelical Church can attain to true ecclesiastical unity only by the method of preserving the Confessions of the Reformation epoch, and promoting an organic union of the regional Churches and congregations on the basis of their own confessional positions".

unity. As soon as the war ended, the question as to what form that outward unity should take could be faced.

On 31 August 1945 an Assembly of the Churches was held at Treysa. This, although it lacked precise ecclesiastical status, appointed the interim Council of the Evangelical Church in Germany. A second more official Assembly was held, also at Treysa, in June 1947, and appointed a Committee to produce a draft Basic Order for the Evangelical Church in Germany. The draft was ready by November 1947. It was considerably amended at the Assembly held at Eisenach in July 1948, and was finally accepted and signed on 3 December 1948.

The Basic Order provides for a Synod of 120 members, a Church Conference consisting of the directing authorities of the regional Churches, and a Council of eleven members, chosen jointly by the Synod and the Church Conference. The Council has as its instruments the "Chancery" and the "Foreign Office" of the Church.

In 1948 the United Evangelical Lutheran Church of Germany came into being. Its Constitution came into force on 31 December of that year, less than a month after the acceptance of the Constitution of the Evangelical Church in Germany. Most of the Lutheran Churches in Germany joined it, not as a rival to the Evangelical Church in Germany, but as the expression of a confessional loyalty by which they felt themselves bound.

The Evangelical Church in Germany was accepted by the World Council of Churches as a member Church; but, on the insistence of the Lutherans, it was agreed that, under the heading "Evangelical Church in Germany", the names of the twenty-seven[1] regional Churches adhering to it should be printed, and that after the name of each Church adhering to the United Evangelical Lutheran Church of Germany, the word "Lutheran" should be added.

Within the Evangelical Church in Germany, each regional Church retains much autonomy and full liberty to maintain its own confessional standards. Yet the Church is more than a federation; a Church which has once joined the Evangelical Church and agreed to determine its relations to the other uniting Churches on the basis of brotherliness has surrendered its right to withdraw by unilateral action. The character of this Church, as it has so far developed, is described in its (unofficial) Church Year Book in the following terms:

> "The Evangelical Church in Germany is a federation [*Bund*] and a unity. It is not a Church in the full sense of the term. But it is more than a mere confederation of independent Churches, come together just for the dispatch of certain business. It is a Church in process of coming into existence."[2]

But some leaders in the Church would regard even this cautious statement as going further than the facts warrant, and would insist that no more can be affirmed than the official wording of the first two articles of its Basic Order:

> "(1) The Evangelical Church in Germany is a union [*Bund*][3] of Lutheran, Reformed, and United Churches. It respects the confessional

[1] The Church of Bremen had not at that time joined the Evangelical Church in Germany.
[2] *Kirchliches Jahrbuch 1945–1948*, Gütersloh, 1950, p. 453.
[3] It will be evident to the reader that the difficulty of understanding and presentation in this section resides largely in the word *Bund*. The title of the Church is unmistakably "The Evangelical *Church*" (*Kirche*), not *Churches*. How, then, is the word *Bund* to be interpreted? Is it *union, federation, confederation*, or *fellowship*? It is precisely on this point that different views are held in the Church itself; and any account of it which goes beyond citing, *in German*, its official documents is exposed to criticism from one side or another.

basis of the member Churches, and presupposes that they make their Confession effective in the teaching, life, and order of the Church.

" (2) In the Evangelical Church in Germany the existing fellowship of German Evangelical Christendom is made visible."

5. INTERCOMMUNION BETWEEN EPISCOPAL CHURCHES

The Old Catholic Churches and Christian Union.[1] The Old Catholic Churches have never ceased to work for Christian union, in accordance with what they believe to be the situation providentially given to them among all the Churches of the world.

References have been made earlier to relationships between the Old Catholic Churches and the Orthodox Churches of the East.[2] The tragic events of the first world war and the Russian revolution brought to an end the promising negotiations of which General Kireev had been one of the chief inspirers. After the war it fell to the Ecumenical Patriarchate to take the initiative in seeking the renewal of contact.

The preliminary Conference held at Geneva in 1920 in preparation for the World Conference on Faith and Order gave the desired opportunity. On 19 August a special meeting was held, with Archbishop Germanos in the chair, between the delegates of the Orthodox Churches and representatives of the Old Catholic Churches in Switzerland. Dr Germanos, in his official report on this meeting, wrote most warmly on the possibilities of union and recommended that the Patriarchate should communicate to Bishop Herzog, the Swiss Old Catholic Bishop, its hope that the unity of the two Churches, so deeply longed for, might soon be brought to pass. This advice was followed, and in an official letter of 18 November 1920 (old style) to Bishop Herzog, the hope of unity was clearly and warmly expressed.[3]

The World Conference on Faith and Order, held at Lausanne in 1927, gave a similar opportunity for meetings between the representatives of the two groups of Churches. At a private meeting, convened by Archbishop Germanos, the differences between the Churches were further discussed; and the suggestion was made by the Archbishop that two Commissions should be appointed to prepare a formal statement on the basis of which an Orthodox Synod could decide on the question of intercommunion with the Old Catholics, since the discussions had shown that such a degree of unity already existed as might suitably be expressed by a further advance towards intercommunion.

The two Commissions met at Bonn on 27 and 28 October 1931. The proceedings were limited to the exchange of information. Yet to the direct question "What do the Orthodox think of the Old Catholic Churches?", Archbishop Germanos replied that it was the deep wish of the Orthodox that the union existing between Orthodox and Old Catholics should find its expression in intercommunion.[4]

The difficulty on the Orthodox side has been that such proposals for unity can be dealt with, in a fully official manner, only by a Synod or Pro-Synod of all the Orthodox Churches of the East. Disturbed political conditions have made im-

---

[1] This section owes much to information supplied by Dr A. Küry, Old Catholic Bishop in Switzerland.
[2] See Chap. iv, pp. 205 ff., and Chap. vi, pp. 291 ff.
[3] E. Herzog, "Wiederbeginn der Unionsverhandlungen mit der Orientalischen Kirche" in *Inter. Kirch. Zeitschrift*, 1920, pp. 225–28.   [4] Ibid., 1932, pp. 18 ff.

possible the holding of such a Synod, and it has not therefore been possible to follow up officially this promising beginning. Of a direct or formal approach to unity there is as yet nothing further to record.

With another great group of Churches, Old Catholic approaches to union have reached a happier conclusion. From the time of the Bonn Conference of 1874 onwards, mutual interest between the Old Catholic and Anglican Churches had been continuous and lively; but, largely owing to the extremely cautious attitude of the Church in Holland, little if any definite progress had been made in fifty years. A new period opened with the Lambeth Conference of 1920, which reiterated "the desire expressed at previous Conferences to maintain and strengthen the friendly relations which exist between the Churches of the Anglican Communion and the ancient Church of Holland and the Old Catholic Churches, especially in Germany, Switzerland and Austria".

In response to this expression of friendship, Mgr Francis Kenninck, then recently consecrated Archbishop of Utrecht, appointed a Commission to consider the question of Anglican Orders. The Old Catholic Conference, which assembled at Bonn in 1925, requested the Conference of Old Catholic Bishops to make a formal decision on this subject. After the necessary consultations had been held, Mgr Kenninck was able to write to Archbishop Davidson of Canterbury informing him that the Old Catholic Churches had formally accepted Anglican Orders as valid and regular.

The next step was taken in 1930, when the three bishops of the Old Catholic Church in Holland visited England during the Lambeth Conference, and conferred with Anglican bishops from various areas of the world, including America. The outcome of this discussion was the appointment by the Church of England, and by the Old Catholic Churches of Holland, Germany, and Switzerland, of Commissions authorized to enter into formal negotiations with a view to intercommunion.

The Commissions met at Bonn, that city of many memories, on 2 July 1931. Perhaps never in the history of the Christian Church has business of such importance been transacted with such speed. The meetings lasted only for a single day.

Naturally there was some divergence between the interests and preoccupations of the negotiating parties. The Old Catholics, who found and find themselves more at home with Anglo-Catholics than with other groups in the Church of England, asked somewhat apprehensive questions as to the strength of "the Protestant party" in the English Church, and as to the extent to which they would be expected to unite with it. A statement made by the Bishop of Gloucester (A. C. Headlam) seems to have allayed their anxieties. The Anglicans wished to know whether Old Catholics could accept the Anglican doctrine of the supremacy of Holy Scripture, as set forth in the VIth Article of Religion:

> "Holy Scripture containeth all things necessary to salvation, so that whatsoever is not read therein, nor may be proved thereby, is not to be required of any man, that it should be believed as an article of the Faith, or be thought requisite or necessary to salvation."

When these words were read out, the Bishop of Deventer declared that they exactly represented Old Catholic teaching on the subject.

The conclusions of the Commissions were then drawn up in what has come to be known as the Agreement of Bonn:

"1. Each Communion recognizes the catholicity and independence of the other, and maintains its own.

"2. Each Communion agrees to permit members of the other Communion to participate in the Sacraments.

"3. Intercommunion does not require from either Communion the acceptance of all doctrinal opinion, sacramental devotion, or liturgical practice characteristic of the other, but implies that each believes the other to hold all the essentials of the Christian Faith."

This agreement, in its brevity and clarity, is a model which might have been followed to their advantage by many other negotiators in the cause of union. The principle set forth is unambiguous. If two Churches are in agreement on the essentials of doctrine and Church order, even wide divergences in interpretation and practice ought not to hold them apart; full agreement in every detail is not to be required as a precondition of intercommunion.

The Bonn Agreement was accepted by the Episcopal Synod of the Old Catholic Churches meeting at Vienna on 7 September 1931; by the Convocations of the Provinces of Canterbury and York in January 1932. In the course of the next few years it was formally accepted by almost all the provinces of the Anglican Communion. In 1946 the Bonn Agreement served as the basis on which intercommunion was established between the Polish National Catholic Church, which is in communion with the Old Catholic Churches in Europe and the Protestant Episcopal Church in the United States, an action which was noted "with satisfaction and approval" by the Lambeth Conference of 1948.

The Bonn Agreement laid down the terms for full intercommunion between the Churches concerned. This is far less than organic union. There has been no fusion of organization. There is no joint and authoritative Synod. Bishops of the Old Catholic Churches are not members of the Lambeth Conference. But the Agreement provides for far more than that limited and temporary intercommunion which has been found possible in some other parts of the Church on the basis of "economy". Old Catholics and Anglicans have gone far together on the road of joint action. Old Catholic bishops have taken part in the consecration of Anglican bishops, Anglican bishops in the consecration of Old Catholics.[1] During the second world war the Old Catholic Bishop in Switzerland confirmed Anglican candidates whom no Anglican bishop could reach. For some years the Old Catholic priest in Djakarta (Batavia) conducted services for the Anglicans resident in that city, in English and according to the Anglican rite.

The present relationship between the Old Catholic Churches and the Anglican Communion is the one example in the West of intercommunion between a

---

[1] These joint consecrations raise some interesting possibilities. In 1896, by the Bull *Apostolicae Curae*, Pope Leo XIII condemned Anglican Orders as absolutely null and void; but the Church of Rome has always recognized the consecrations and ordinations of the Old Catholic Churches. At least fifty Anglican bishops now have directly or indirectly the Old Catholic as well as the Anglican succession, and are therefore recognized by many Roman Catholic authorities as validly consecrated bishops. A time is likely to arrive at which the entire Anglican episcopate will have this double succession. From the Anglican point of view this adds nothing whatsoever to the authority or regularity of Anglican consecrations; but if ever the Roman Catholic Church desired closer relations with the Anglican Communion, this fusion of the successions might serve as a means by which one of the great existing barriers could be removed.

Church which passed through the crisis of the Reformation in the 16th century and another which, though in a sense it has had its own reformation, escaped the perturbations of that difficult time. To both the Churches concerned, this is only one part of their many-sided outreach; both claim, each in its own special way, a central standing within the Christian body, able to reach out with equal understanding towards Roman Catholic, Orthodox, and Protestant, and therefore charged by God with a special responsibility to work tirelessly for the final and total reunion of all Christians in one single Body of Christ.

The Church of England and the Church of Sweden. An earlier chapter[1] has recorded leisurely discussions between the Church of England and the Church of Sweden from 1888 to 1908; in the following twenty years the fruits of these discussions became manifest.

In 1911 the Anglican Commission set forth in its report the following opinions:

"1. That the succession of bishops has been maintained unbroken by the Church of Sweden, and that it has a true conception of the episcopal office.

"2. That the office of priest is also rightly conceived as a divinely instituted instrument for the ministry of Word and Sacraments, and that it has been in intention handed on throughout the whole history of the Church of Sweden."

On the basis of this report, the Lambeth Conference of 1920 passed two resolutions:

· "24. The Conference . . . recommends that members of that Church, qualified to receive the Sacrament in their own Church, should be admitted to Holy Communion in ours. It also recommends that on suitable occasions permission should be given to Swedish ecclesiastics to give addresses in our Church.

"25. We recommend further that, in the event of an invitation being extended to an Anglican Bishop or Bishops to take part in the consecration of a Swedish Bishop, the invitation should, if possible, be accepted, subject to the approval of the Metropolitan."

In 1922 the Swedish bishops addressed a lengthy and dignified reply to the bishops of the Anglican Communion.[2] In this document a difference between the interests of the negotiating parties is clearly evident. The Anglicans, with their traditional dislike of detailed definition in matters of dogma, were quickly satisfied that the Church of Sweden holds all the essentials of the Christian faith, and directed most of their attention to questions of ministry and Church order. The Swedes made it clear that they did not consider any system of Church order as having exclusive divine authority, though they were glad to "regard the peculiar forms and traditions of our Church with the reverence due to a venerable legacy from the past". They were much more concerned to know whether the Church of England was sound on the doctrine of Scripture as supreme over every other

[1] Chap. vi, pp. 295 f. The Anglican Commission there referred to was appointed by Archbishop Davidson of Canterbury in 1909, under the chairmanship of Dr H. E. Ryle, Bishop of Winchester (1903–11).   [2] Reprinted in Bell, *Documents*, I, pp. 185–95.

expression of the Faith, and on the all-sufficiency of the grace of God as set forth in the doctrine of justification by faith alone. It was only when they were able to convince themselves that "there is an essential unity in that fundamental conception, which we have now briefly indicated" that they were willing to accept the Lambeth proposals for the mutual reception of communicants, for the interchange of pulpits on suitable occasions, and for fellowship in the consecration of bishops.

The Anglican Commission had noticed with mild regret that episcopal Confirmation was not part of the regular practice of the Swedish Church. It must have given the Swedish bishops considerable pleasure to reply, drawing attention to

> "the very great importance that our Church attaches to the thorough instruction of the first communicants in the fundamentals of the Christian faith, as being an indispensable condition for Confirmation—a requirement that does not seem to be paid the same attention in the Anglican practice of Confirmation. Against the admission to the Lord's Supper of persons confirmed in the Anglican Church, hesitation has earlier been expressed among us because of the duty of instruction laid on the Church in Matt. xxviii. 20."

No resolution on the Lambeth proposals has been passed by the English Convocations;[1] and the practice of fraternal relations must therefore be held to have a somewhat unofficial character. There has been, however, a great deal of fellowship along the lines of the Lambeth proposals. Already on 19 September 1920, before the reply of the Swedish bishops had been received, two English bishops had taken part in the consecration of two Swedish bishops at Uppsala.[2] Since then there have been at least six occasions on which bishops of one Church have taken part in the consecration of bishops of the other.[3] In 1935 the Bishop of Strängnäs ordained a deacon for the Protestant Episcopal Church in the United States, using the American rite. Exchange of pulpits has been frequent.

These negotiations and agreements have brought to light several points of general ecumenical significance.

First, the Lambeth Conference took the view, which is not acceptable to all Anglicans, that two Churches may enter into a measure of fellowship without either involving the other in all its own ecclesiastical relationships. Thus the Church of Sweden remains in full communion with the Churches of Norway, Denmark, Iceland, and Finland, all of which at one time or another have lost the continuity of their episcopal succession, whereas the Anglican Communion, while accepting limited intercommunion with the Church of Sweden, has no similar relations with Norway, Denmark, or Iceland, and is only gradually entering into fellowship with the Church of Finland, as that Church recovers the historic succession which was lost in 1884.

Secondly, it was made clear that the existence in one Church of what another Church must regard as irregularities or abnormalities need not be regarded as rendering impossible a measure of fellowship between them, though it may delay

---

[1] In 1935 the Convocations of Canterbury and York did express themselves in favour of rather similar relationships between the Church of England and the Church of Finland.

[2] A highly entertaining account of this event and of the steps that led up to it has been left on record by one of the participants, Bishop H. Hensley Henson, in *Retrospect of an Unimportant Life*, I, pp. 319 ff., and II, pp. 34–52.

[3] One of them being the episcopal consecration of the writer of this chapter.

the development of full intercommunion. Part of the resolution adopted by the Lambeth Conference of 1920 reads as follows:

> "If the authorities of any province of the Anglican Communion find local irregularities in the order or practice of the Church of Sweden outside that country, they may legitimately, within their own region, postpone any such action as is recommended in this resolution until they are satisfied that these irregularities have been removed."

There was, from the Anglican point of view, very good reason for the inclusion of this politely-worded note. The bishops were well aware that the Church of Sweden had extensive missionary work in China, India, and South Africa, and that these missions, like the earlier missions of the Anglican Communion itself, had grown up without any direct episcopal supervision. In the Swedish Church this presented no serious difficulties: pastors were ordained, as required, by missionaries who were not bishops, and in South India the closest fellowship was maintained with the German (Leipzig) mission, which was non-episcopal. A Swedish bishop was provided for India in 1921, and for South Africa in 1949; and this element of irregularity is therefore passing away. But the Anglican bishops, though they recognized its existence, did not feel themselves debarred thereby from recommending a considerable degree of fellowship between the Swedish and the English Churches.

The Anglican Churches have continued to work steadily towards closer relationships with all the Scandinavian Churches; but, except in the cases of Sweden and Finland, the problem of the historic episcopate remains unsolved; the Churches have not yet found it possible to enter into any relationship of intercommunion, and fellowship exists only in terms of friendship and goodwill.

6. UNION BETWEEN EPISCOPAL AND NON-EPISCOPAL CHURCHES

The Church of South India. In May 1919 a Conference of thirty-three men, all but two of whom were Indians, met at Tranquebar, the little town on the south-east coast of India rendered for ever holy by the arrival in July 1706 of the first missionaries to reach India from the non-Roman Churches of the world. A memorable Statement was issued by the Conference; it included the words:

> "We believe that the challenge of the present hour . . . calls us to mourn our past divisions and turn to our Lord Jesus Christ to seek in Him the unity of the body expressed in one visible Church. We face together the titanic task of the winning of India for Christ—one-fifth of the human race. Yet, confronted by such an overwhelming responsibility, we find ourselves rendered weak and relatively impotent by our unhappy divisions—divisions for which we were not responsible, and which have been, as it were, imposed upon us from without."[1]

The idea of Church union in India was not new. Some of those who signed this Statement were ministers of the South India United Church, a body which had come into existence in 1908, through the union of nearly all the Presbyterian and Congregational missions in South India in a Church with certain federal

[1] The Statement is reprinted in full in Bell, *Documents*, I, pp. 278–81.

characteristics, allowing much independence to the eight regional Councils of which it was composed. But the men of Tranquebar were inspired by a new vision of a great Church of South India in which all those Churches which accept the supremacy of Holy Scripture might find their unity.

Their enthusiasm found immediate response in the Churches. In September 1919 the General Assembly of the South India United Church appointed a Committee "to confer with the representatives of the Anglican and Mar Thoma[1] Churches; and such other bodies as they may deem wise, with a view to the possibility of union". In February 1920 the Episcopal Synod of the Anglican province in India (from 1930 onwards to be known as the Church of India, Burma, and Ceylon) appointed a similar Committee. Five years later, the Methodist Church of South India came into the negotiations.

The Church of South India is unique in that for the first time in history a Church which has maintained the historic succession of the episcopate has succeeded in entering into full corporate union with non-episcopal Churches. The achievement was not easy; nine years passed before the first edition of the *Scheme of Church Union in South India* was published, another eighteen before the new Church was inaugurated.

Questions of faith caused no prolonged difficulties. Within somewhat wide limits of interpretation, the three Churches found themselves in agreement on the Scriptures as the supreme authority in faith and life, on the Nicene Creed as the authorized summary of Biblical doctrine, and on Baptism and the Holy Communion as sacraments of the Gospel. It was otherwise when the Joint Committee came to consider the question of the ministry.

A Church must have a single ministry, everywhere equally recognized. But how were the two disparate traditions to be reconciled? Many would have been happy if the Churches had been content, without further definition, to accept one another's ministries as true ministries within the Church of God. This was unacceptable to Anglicans, who do not accept non-episcopal ministries as possessing equal authority and validity with their own. Anglicans would have been happy if the ministers of other Churches could have seen their way to accept episcopal ordination. Non-Anglicans were unwilling to do anything that might seem to cast doubt on the ministry that they had previously exercised. Various schemes of conditional ordination and supplemental ordination were carefully considered, and rejected.

In the end, it was decided to allow for a period of at least thirty years, during which the Churches would be growing together, and the process of unification would be coming to completion. It was agreed that, from the time of union, all ordinations should be carried out by bishops with the assistance of presbyters, but that all who were ministers at the time of union should be accepted with equal rights and status, except that congregations should be safeguarded against having thrust on them a ministry which they were not able conscientiously to accept. This meant that, during the period of unification, there would be three types of minister in the Church—those ordained after the union, those episcopally ordained before union, and those non-episcopally ordained before union. This was bound to involve certain inconveniences and abnormalities. But the plan was perfectly honest, in recognizing both the consequences of four

---

[1] The reformed section of the ancient Syrian Orthodox Church of South India; see Table, p. 499. This Church, though deeply interested in the plans for union, did not take part in the negotiations.

centuries of division and the desire for union, and in pointing forward to a time in which that union could be perfectly attained.

From 1929 onwards progress was very slow. The Scheme was amended and re-amended, grew in size and became ever more complex. Anglicans were anxious lest the statement of the Faith might leave the door open to syncretism. Congregationalists feared that episcopacy, with whatever safeguards, might take away their Congregational liberties. The Methodists insisted on the addition of a long homiletic chapter on the duties of the laity. Everywhere there was a tendency to expatiate, to explain, and to safeguard. But at last the long process of preparation was over, and the time came when the Churches must record their decisive votes on the Seventh Edition of the Scheme.

The Methodists, who had felt less difficulties than the other negotiating Churches, were the first to take action. On 28 and 29 January 1943, by an almost unanimous vote, the Synod recorded its judgement that the Methodist Church in South India should enter into union with the other two Churches.

For Anglicans the situation was more difficult. In many parts of the world, Anglican opposition to the Scheme was steadily hardening, and the charge was freely made that, under the Scheme, essentials of both faith and order were being jettisoned. The Church of India was pressed to delay its vote until after the meeting of the Lambeth Conference, which, owing to the outbreak of war, had been postponed from 1940. In the end, that Church decided that further delay would be harmful, and in January 1945 passed a timid and oddly-worded resolution finally adopting "the Scheme of Church Union in South India . . . in order to permit the dioceses of Madras, Travancore and Cochin, Tinnevelly, and Dornakal to carry out their practically unanimous desire to enter into union with the Methodist and South India United Churches".

The S.I.U.C. was perhaps more afflicted by inner tensions than either of the other Churches. At times it seemed that the largest of the eight Councils, that in South Travancore, would never accede to the terms of union. When, however, the final vote was taken, the patience of the supporters of the Scheme was justified. In September 1946 the General Assembly accepted it by a more than ninety per cent majority.

A year was spent in the final preparations for union. On 27 September 1947, the Church of South India was inaugurated in the Cathedral of St George at Madras. The area covered by the Church had been divided into fourteen dioceses. The five Anglican bishops were re-elected to continue their functions; nine new bishops, Indian and European, chosen from among the clergy of all the uniting Churches, were consecrated on the day of the inauguration. Episcopal and non-episcopal had at last come together in a single Church. A million Indian Christians, formerly separated by Western denominational allegiances, had been brought together in one Church, wholly independent and rooted in the soil of India.

Unhappily, union was not achieved without producing new division. The North Tamil Council of the S.I.U.C., in which the extreme Congregational influence had been strongest, was allowed to remain outside the union, on the understanding that it could vote itself into it, if and when it so desired.[1] Thirty thousand Anglicans in the Nandyal area of the diocese of Dornakal, not animated solely by religious reasons, refused to enter the union; what might have

---

[1] It did so desire in 1950, and entered the Church of South India as part of the new diocese of Coimbatore, which was constituted in that year.

been only a temporary disagreement has hardened into what seems likely to be a long-lasting division.

Many questions of detail were left unsettled at the time of union. The new Church is occupied in developing its own liturgy and completing its local and diocesan organization. In many areas the passage from division to unity has been far from smooth, and the process is far from complete. But visitors to the Church have been impressed by the strength and the reality of the unity already attained, by the mutual enrichment of the various traditions which have been brought together, and by the new confidence in evangelistic witness which unity has brought with it.[1]

The non-episcopal Churches concerned have found no difficulty in declaring themselves in full communion with the Church of South India. As was to be expected, the Anglican attitude has been more reserved. The Lambeth Conference of 1948 found it possible to

> "(b) give thanks to God for the measure of unity locally achieved by the inauguration of the Church of South India, and we pledge ourselves to pray and work for its development into an ever more perfect fulfilment of the will of God for His Church; and we
> "(c) look forward hopefully and with longing to the day when there shall be full communion between the Church of South India and the Churches of the Anglican Communion;"[2]

but found itself unable to make one agreed recommendation "in regard to the bishops, presbyters, and deacons consecrated or ordained at or after the inauguration of that Church". The Convocations of the Church of England in 1951 postponed for five years decision as to the relations which should exist between the Church of England and the Church of South India.

The measure of unity achieved in 1947 was regarded by churchmen in South India as only a beginning. Ere long, their Church was engaged in conversations with the Lutherans and the Baptists, without any immediate practical results. The significance of the South India Scheme of Union beyond South India is shown in the immense influence it has exercised on the text of the Schemes of Union that have been prepared in Ceylon, in North India, in Iran, and in Nigeria. The Church of South India consciously regards itself as a challenge to the divided Churches of the West. Union in India has certainly resulted in some abnormalities both within the South India Church and in its relations with other Churches. But churchmen in South India regard their state of union as normal. The gravest abnormality is just that state of disunion in which the Churches in the West have so long acquiesced; and that abnormality must continue, until the Churches in the West also find their way to full corporate unity in one great Church of Jesus Christ.

7. PLANS FOR UNION STILL UNDER CONSIDERATION IN 1948

Ceylon and Northern India. Ceylon is so near to India that there is always a tendency for the outside world to regard it as part of the larger country. This it is not, and never has been. Closely allied to India in race, language, and com-

---

[1] See, for example, G. K. A. Bell (Bishop of Chichester) in *The Ecumenical Review*, Vol. II, No. 3, pp. 150–54.　　　　[2] *The Lambeth Conference 1948*, pp. 38 f.

merce, Ceylon has always maintained its own ways and traditions and has developed a character of its own. In 1947 Ceylon, with fewer reserves than India and Pakistan, freely chose to remain within the British Commonwealth of Nations as an independent and self-governing dominion.

Buddhism, which disappeared from India, the country of its origin, a thousand years ago, is still the religion of the majority of the inhabitants of Ceylon. At the beginning of this century Buddhism underwent a remarkable revival; the work of the Christian missions became more difficult and, though conversions continued to occur and the number of Christians to increase, the proportion of Christians to the total population remained stationary, or even showed a slight tendency to decrease. In recent years attempts have been made to identify the profession of Buddhism with Ceylonese patriotism and to secure for Buddhism a privileged position as the national religion. Though the Christian Churches have not yet encountered serious difficulties, it is natural that the purely spiritual arguments in favour of unity should be reinforced by a sense of the need to stand together in face of the new opportunities and the new problems which have accompanied political independence.

Christians in Ceylon form about ten per cent of the population, but the great majority of them are Roman Catholics, descendants of the converts born in the days of Portuguese political supremacy. Christians of other Churches amount only to about 100,000 in a population of more than seven million, though their influence on the life of the country is much greater than their numbers might suggest.

Ceylon had been closely involved in the plans for Church union in South India. The Anglican diocese of Colombo, as part of the Church of India, Burma, and Ceylon, had had to vote formally on the South India Scheme. The Congregational Churches in the north of Ceylon had been part of the South India United Church, and became in 1947 the Jaffna diocese of the Church of South India. Inevitably, the minds of churchmen were directed towards the possibilities of Christian union in Ceylon.

The first meeting to discuss the problem appears to have been held in 1934. The first invitation to the Churches to enter into negotiations was issued by the Ceylon Provincial Synod of the Methodist Church in February 1940. The invitation was accepted by all the constituent Churches of the National Christian Council of Ceylon—the Anglican, Methodist, Presbyterian, Baptist, and Congregational Communions, in their local manifestations. The Joint Committee on Church Union was formed in November 1940, and after a year of work reported to the Churches that, in its judgement, there was sufficient basis of agreement between the Churches to justify the opening of formal negotiations. A Negotiating Committee was then formed, and issued an interim report in 1946. On 5 July 1949 the Secretary signed the completed Scheme of Church Union in Ceylon.

The influence of the South India Scheme can be recognized on almost every page, and many paragraphs are almost verbatim quotations from the earlier Scheme. Where the situations were so closely parallel, nothing was to be gained by doing over again what South India had satisfactorily done. At two points, however, there are notable variations in the Ceylon Scheme.

In South India none of the Baptist bodies had accepted the invitation to take part in the union negotiations: in Ceylon the Baptists had been from the beginning one of the negotiating Churches, and, perhaps for the first time in history, Baptists and Episcopalians found themselves advancing together in the search for a union which could include them both.

The dilemma has been met by provision in the Scheme both for the baptism of infants, here called "sponsored baptism", and for the baptism of older persons on the public profession of faith, here called "believer's baptism". It is proposed that "where parents do not wish their children to receive sponsored baptism they shall bring them to a service of dedication", and it is provided that, if a minister has conscientious scruples about administering baptism in infancy, he may arrange for some other minister of the Church to perform the rite. "But both those who have received sponsored baptism in infancy and those who have received believer's baptism shall become communicant members of the Church of Lanka through receiving confirmation."[1]

This compromise must seem indefensible to those Baptists who regard infant baptism (even when supplemented by Confirmation) as no true baptism, and to those of other Churches who hold that the Church has no right to withhold the benefits of baptism from children born to Christian parents. To others it may commend itself as a reasonable and realistic way of dealing with a difference in practice which, though serious, ought not in itself to stand as a barrier to fellowship within one Church.

The Ceylon negotiators, well aware of the difficulties that had arisen in South India through the continuance of a divided ministry in the Church, and of the many criticisms that on that ground had been levelled at the South India Scheme, proposed a plan for the unification of all ministries from the start.

It is suggested that, on the consummation of union, the first bishops of the Church of Lanka (Ceylon) [2] shall receive, through prayer and the laying on of hands of ministers of all the uniting Churches, a wider commission to exercise their ministry in the Church of Lanka. Thereafter the bishops may receive such presbyters of the uniting Churches as may desire it into the presbyterate of the new Church of Lanka, with the laying on of hands and a formula which shall include the words:

> "Forasmuch as you were called and ordained to the ministry of the Church of God in the . . . Church, and are now called to the ministry of the Church of God as Presbyter within this Church of Lanka; receive from God the power and grace of the Holy Spirit to exercise the wider ministry of this office."

The Preface to this Order of Commissioning states clearly that

> "the use of this rite does not imply a denial of the reality of any commission or ordination previously received by those now seeking to become Presbyters in this United Church; nor is it presumed to bestow again or renew any grace, gifts, character or authority that have already been bestowed upon them by God through whatever means;"

but it also declares that

> "In so doing, it is the intention of this Church to continue and reverently to use and esteem the threefold ministry of Bishop, Presbyter and Deacon which existed in the undivided Church."

[1] *Proposed Scheme of Church Union in Ceylon*, Madras, 1949, pp. 13 f.
[2] The Proposed Scheme provides (p. 20) that those "who have not already received episcopal consecration shall be consecrated by three duly authorized Bishops, if possible from outside Ceylon, representing different Church traditions and acceptable to all the uniting Churches".

The Lambeth Conference of 1948 declared that it recognized "the proposed scheme for Church Union in Ceylon . . . as being, in many respects, among the most promising of the various schemes of its type in different parts of the world", and, in generally welcoming the negotiations informally begun in North India, expressed "the hope that in the working out of the proposed scheme account may be taken of the lessons to be derived from South India and of the proposals made in Ceylon".[1]

Discussions on Church union in North India began in 1929. In 1937 a proposed Basis of Negotiation was prepared, and from that time on discussions with increasing official recognition were carried on between the United Church of Northern India (Congregationalist and Presbyterian), the Anglicans, the Baptists, and the Methodists—Churches with about a million members scattered over the vast areas of India and Pakistan northwards from the Deccan. The Scheme of Union, as it took shape, included the same characteristic features as the Ceylon Scheme in provision both for sponsored and for believer's baptism, and proposals for the unification of all ministries by the mutual laying on of hands with prayer at the inauguration of union.

Undoubtedly it would be a great advantage to a united Church to have from the start a fully unified ministry. Those planning for Church union in Ceylon and in North India believe that this can be done without prejudice to existing ministries, without defining too closely what is believed to be effected by the act, and leaving it to God to supply whatever is deficient in the ministries of the uniting Churches. The difficulties are likely to be felt more acutely outside the united Church than within it. In deciding its relationship to those new Churches, the Church of England, for example, would have to decide whether it could recognize this supplemental ordination as equivalent to episcopal ordination. If it decided that it could, this would seem to conflict with the statements of the preface to the service, as printed in the Scheme; if it decided that it could not, the relationship between the Church of England and these new Churches would be complicated by as many difficulties as its relationship with the Church of South India. To some these difficulties seem so great that they prefer a scheme like that of South India, free from ambiguity and any appearance of subterfuge. To others it appears that the Ceylon and North India Schemes offer a way out of grave and acutely-felt difficulties, and are therefore to be welcomed as a constructive contribution to the work of bringing together episcopal and non-episcopal Churches. No decision can immediately be taken by the Churches which are seeking to enter into union; there will be time for all the arguments on both sides to be fully canvassed, and for the Churches to convince themselves whether this solution leads to another impasse, or whether it is a genuine thoroughfare to Christian union.

Christian Union and the Law. In the United States of America the principle of the separation of Church and State has been carried further than perhaps in any other country in the world; yet even there Christian bodies which hold most firmly to this principle have found themselves entangled in proceedings in the secular law courts, and faced by claims on the part of the State to adjudicate in what they had considered purely spiritual concerns.

The first edition of the Basis of Union between the Congregational Christian Churches and the Evangelical and Reformed Church was published in March

---

[1] *Lambeth Conference 1948*, pp. 41 f.

1943. Both the negotiating Churches had come into existence as the result of successful mergers. Both these mergers had been regarded by those who entered into them as one step forward on the way to wider organic union.

In 1931 the Congregational Churches and the Christian Church had come together on the basis that "this union shall be conditioned upon the acceptance of Christianity primarily as a way of life, and not upon uniformity of theological opinion or any uniform practice of ordinances". The unification of the two bodies in states and districts was completed by 1936.

The Evangelical and Reformed Church came into existence at Cleveland, Ohio, on 26 June 1934, through union between the Evangelical Synod of North America and the Reformed Church in the United States, two bodies which have been described as "of Swiss and German background with basic agreements in doctrine, polity and culture".[1] This union was remarkable in that it was consummated before constitutional organization for the united Church had been worked out. The Constitution was not finally adopted till June 1940, and the unification of organizations became finally effective only on 1 February 1941. Before this date the Evangelical and Reformed Church had committed itself to negotiations with a view to corporate union with the Congregational Christian Churches.

This venture was more difficult than those in which the Churches had previously been engaged, since the unification of Congregational and Presbyterian systems of church government has never proved easy. But progress was rapid. The Basis of Union was six times revised and, having been accepted by the Joint Committee of the Churches in its final form on 22 January 1947, was sent down to the Churches for their consideration, This brief document, setting forth a Scheme of Union in which it was hoped that justice had been done to the special contributions of each tradition in faith, polity, and organization, proposed for the new Church the name "The United Church of Christ". Lest such a name might seem presumptuous, it was explained that it "expresses a fact: it stands for the accomplished union of two church bodies each of which has arisen from a similar union of two church bodies. It also expresses a hope: that in time soon to come, by further union between this Church and other bodies, there shall arise a more inclusive United Church".[2]

Procedure with regard to this Basis differed in the two Churches. The Evangelical and Reformed decided that, if the plan obtained a two-thirds majority in the General Synod, and approval by two-thirds of the thirty-four local Synods, it should be deemed accepted by the Church. In due course all these things came to pass, and the Evangelical and Reformed Church declared itself committed to the union.

The General Council of the Congregational Christian Churches decided to send the plan to the local councils and churches for advisory action, and it was added that if seventy-five per cent of the conferences, councils, churches, and members voting had already approved the Basis of Union, this might be deemed a sufficient majority to justify the General Council in going forward into union. Although the favourable votes of churches and members were less than seventy-five per cent, the General Council held, at its meeting at Cleveland, Ohio, on 5 February 1949, that the union had been approved by a vote "sufficient to warrant the consummation of the union", and declared itself ready to go ahead as soon as the Evangelical and Reformed were ready.

[1] F. S. Mead, *Handbook*, p. 81.   [2] *The Basis of Union*, etc., 1947, pp. 4 f.

For some time rumblings of discontent had been heard from the minority. These now swelled and increased in violence. It was maintained that the proposed merger with a Presbyterian Church would fatally compromise Congregational principles, especially the autonomy of the local congregation, and that the General Council had no constitutional authority to commit the whole denomination to a merger of this kind. One opposed group took the decisive step of appealing to the secular law courts to determine an issue on which the Church had failed to reach agreement within itself; the Cadman Memorial Congregational Society of Brooklyn and the Cadman Memorial Church sued Helen Kenyon, as Moderator of the General Council of the Congregational Christian Churches of the United States, in the Supreme Court of New York State.

The case was heard in November and December 1949 and January 1950. It was debated in the largest possible fashion, and behind all the legal technicalities arose continually the question of the nature of the Congregational Churches and of the authority that could be exercised by a central body among them. Mr. Justice Meier Steinbrink took the view that

> "the General Council has not now, and never has had, power or authority to make any contract or commitment binding upon the plaintiff Church, or any of the Congregational Christian churches, which would in any measure affect the status of any of the Congregational Christian churches as independent or autonomous".

He therefore entered a sweeping judgement on behalf of the plaintiffs:

> "That defendant The General Council of the Congregational Christian Churches of the United States, its members, present and future, officers, attorneys, employees, agents and instrumentalities be and hereby are permanently enjoined and restrained from carrying out or consummating, either in the name of or on behalf of defendant The General Council of the Congregational Christian Churches or on behalf of any or all of the several Congregational Christian Churches, The Basis of Union of The Congregational Christian Churches and The Evangelical and Reformed Church, with or without the Interpretations thereof or any provisions, revisions or amendments thereof."

By other clauses in the judgement, the General Council was restrained from merging or uniting itself with "any other body or organization whatsoever", and also from attempting to make such changes in its organization or constitution as would enable it "to do or perform any of the acts or things herein prohibited".[1]

This judgement affected many other Churches besides those directly concerned. Other great bodies, such as the Baptists and the Disciples of Christ, are organized on the basis of the autonomy of the local congregation. The search for Christian unity is the very *raison d'être* of the Disciples as a separate communion. Recently they had reopened conversations with the American (Northern) Baptist Convention. Is the law really such that these and other Christian bodies are for ever frozen within themselves? Can a conscientious minority hold up for ever a merger on which an equally conscientious majority is agreed? The issue could not be left undecided. The case went up on appeal; in April 1952 the original judgement was reversed.

[1] Oral judgement, handed down on 26 January 1950, p. 3. Written judgement, handed down on 20 February 1950, pp. 4 ff.

The legal issue was only the superficial focus of a genuinely theological problem regarding the nature of the Church. In the original Congregationalism, "the local churches are the only ultimate existences: all else is the shadow of the local churches". Later Congregationalism has developed central organs, through which it is possible for the local churches, if they so desire, to act together as a denomination. One of the leaders of the movement for unity, Dr Douglas Horton,[1] argues that this developed Congregationalism alone is adequate to the needs of the present day. The older type "may have been effectual in the days of an agrarian economy, when the village was the pivotal point of the nation's life. . . . Now, however, in order to out-guess and out-manoeuvre anti-Christian forces which are organized at higher levels than that of the village or local district, it is necessary to have a flexible church unit with sufficient authority over itself to be able to act unrestrictedly at those levels".

To those who are not Congregationalists it may seem that the original independency has proved unworkable, not because an agrarian has changed into an industrial economy, but because at the start it was based on a misreading of the New Testament; and in practice, in negotiations between Congregationalists and those of other religious traditions, the relationship between independence and interdependence is one of the first problems which is likely to be raised.

All the frustrations and agonies of the long-protracted litigation may have been worth while if they have driven Christians, Congregationalists and others alike, back to a reconsideration of the bases of their doctrine of the Church, without clearer understanding of which genuine ecumenical progress is likely to remain impossible.

8. PLANS FOR CLOSER FELLOWSHIP WITHOUT CORPORATE UNION

The Australian Proposals. Corporate union is the ultimate aim of almost all plans for promoting closer fellowship between the Churches; but corporate union takes a long time to arrive, and pastoral situations may arise which cannot wait for the slow movement of ecclesiastical machinery. In vast and sparsely-populated countries, such as Australia and Canada, many Churches are trying to care for small and scattered groups of their own people, who desire to obtain the ministrations to which they have been accustomed but are quite unable to support as many ministers as would be required to meet all their needs. If it were possible to find means through which every minister of a group of Churches could be authorized to minister to members of all those Churches, wherever he might find them, and every member of those Churches could accept without scruple the ministry of every minister, an urgent pastoral need would have been met, and one step would have been taken on the way to fuller unity.

In 1937 the National Missionary Conference of Australia found itself faced by a pastoral problem of this kind. In Papua (New Guinea) the spheres of the various missionary societies had early been fixed by the Government, and comity between the Churches had been carefully observed. But as Papuan Christians moved from one area to another, Anglican missionaries had begun to follow their people into the territory assigned to the Congregationalists. In the attempt to meet this and similar situations, leaders among the Anglicans, Methodists, Presbyterians, and Congregationalists found themselves led to develop what have come to be known as the Australian Proposals for Intercommunion.

[1] In a pamphlet entitled *Of Equability and Perseverance in Well Doing*, published in 1950. The title was originally that of an essay by the Rev. John Robinson (1575–1625).

The aim of these proposals was not to unite Churches, not even to unite ministries, but so to extend the authority of existing ministries as to ensure that a ministry which is accepted in one Church is accepted also in others, which still retain their own separate identity. If the aim is thus strictly limited, the Churches are under no compulsion at this stage to work out all the difficult problems of faith and order, the settlement of which is the indispensable preliminary to corporate union.

Extension of authority to minister involves some new form of ministerial commission. The Australian proposal is that ministers of Churches which are prepared to work together on this basis should receive from the ordaining authorities of the Churches other than their own an extended authorization, accompanied by the laying on of hands, and that this authorization should be in every case the same. The Proposals, as finally formulated on 29 October 1943, include a Declaration, a Formula, and a number of Rubrics.

The Declaration, to be made by any minister desiring extension of ministerial commission, is as follows:

"(a) I, believing myself to have been duly called and ordained to the ministry of the Word and Sacraments in the Church of God, am yet conscious of a desire for a wider exercise of the office in a reunited Fellowship.

"(b) I, also believing that God wills one Communion and Fellowship for the building of His Kingdom, and that there should, therefore, be an interchange of commissions between all who have been regularly called and lawfully set apart for the Ministry of His Holy Word and Sacraments, am humbly prepared by the mutual laying-on-of-hands with Prayer, freely and willingly, to give and to receive, to bestow and to share, so far as lies within my power, such further authority as shall seem 'good to the Holy Ghost and to us'."

The Mutual Formula reads:

"Receive the Holy Ghost for the wider exercise of thy ministry in the Church, take thou authority to preach the Word of God and to minister Christ's Sacraments, in fulfilment of the ministry of reconciliation in the congregations whereunto thou shalt be further called or regularly appointed; and see that thou stir up the grace bestowed upon thee in the Call of God and by the laying-on-of-hands."

This method is open to the objection that, even though the formula be the same, there would, as a matter of fact, be difference of conviction in the Churches as to what was being given and received in the mutual laying on of hands.

The Lambeth Conference of 1948 gave these proposals a much less enthusiastic approval than had been hoped by the promoters. The fear was expressed that such a half-way house as the Australian Proposals might be accepted as supplying all that was needed, and that the further objective of corporate union might be lost sight of:

"In spite of the disadvantages attaching to such schemes, which are noted in the Report of the Committee on Unity, the Conference is not prepared to discourage further explorations along this line, if they are linked with provisions for the growing together of the Churches concerned and with the definite acceptance of organic union as their final goal."[1]

[1] *Lambeth Conference 1948*, p. 41.

Supporters of the plan would maintain both that the goal of organic union had never been lost sight of, and that such fuller fellowship as is contemplated would certainly result in the growing together of the Churches. No one at present can say whether they are right or wrong. Just evaluation of such schemes of extension of ministerial commission must wait until one of them has been brought into effect, and until its results in the life of the Churches has been observed over a number of years.

Anglicans and Free Churchmen in England. The Lambeth Conference of 1920 had aroused great hopes in England, as in other parts of the Christian world. The Lambeth Conference of 1930 appeared to be much more cautious in its approach to Christian union, and there was widespread disappointment at what was taken to be a withdrawal from the courageous spirit of the "Appeal to All Christian People".

Official negotiations between the Church of England and the Free Churches had petered out; but in 1931 a strong unofficial group was convened by Canon T. Tatlow. This group had before it the first edition of the *Scheme of Church Union in South India*; and after several years' work produced, in 1936, a remarkable document, *Outline of a Reunion Scheme for the Church of England and the Evangelical Free Churches of England*, in which were set forth the possible implications of South India principles for the British situation. In 1933 official discussions were resumed; and in 1938 the official group took over the *Outline of a Reunion Scheme*, edited it with the minimum of changes, and published it on its own authority with prefaces by Archbishop Lang of Canterbury and Dr A. E. Garvie.

The year 1938 was not a favourable time for the appearance of such a document. Men's minds were preoccupied with the explosive international situation. First reactions from the Methodist Church were somewhat encouraging; but in 1941 the Free Church Federal Council published an unfavourable reply to the proposals, and thereafter little was heard of them.

In many ways relations between the Church of England and the Free Churches had improved. Most of the grievances of Free Churchmen against the special privileges of the Established Church had been met. Co-operation in many Christian enterprises, and particularly in the British Council of Churches,[1] had led to personal friendships among the leaders in all the Churches and to a release of tensions. But Church relations in England seemed to have settled down to a stalemate, when the Archbishop of Canterbury (Fisher), preaching before the University of Cambridge on 3 November 1946, gave a new turn to the discussions. It seemed to him that the fact of the Establishment set grave difficulties in the way of corporate union. Would it be possible to proceed one step at a time? Could the Free Churches take episcopacy into their own systems, as a means towards establishing common sacraments and a commonly accepted ministry? "The Church of England has not yet found the finally satisfying use of episcopacy in practice: nor certainly has the Church of Rome. If non-episcopal Churches agree that it must come into the picture, could they not take it and try it out on their own ground first? ... As it seems to me, it is an easier step for them to contemplate than those involved in a union of Churches; and, if achieved, it would immensely carry us forward towards full communion, without the fearful complexities and upheavals of a constitutional union."[2]

[1] See Chap. xiii, pp. 624 f.
[2] The sermon was reprinted in *Church Relations in England*, pp. 5–12.

The interest aroused by this sermon was sufficient to encourage the hope that discussion of it might be fruitful. The Archbishop of Canterbury personally appointed a group of Anglicans, who were in no sense official delegates of their Church, to meet the Free Churches; the Free Churches in England all appointed official delegates to take part in joint conversations. The first meeting was held in 1947, the last in 1950; in November of the latter year a report appeared under the title *Church Relations in England*.

The Joint Conference had not been asked to draw up a constitution for a united Church, nor to formulate proposals for union. Its task was simply to draw out the implications of the Cambridge sermon, and to indicate what, in its opinion, would be the consequences if any one of the Free Churches desired to treat with the Church of England on the basis of taking episcopacy into its own system. The conditions of advance were drawn up under six heads. The first deals with mutual recognition of faith; the fourth with the use of Confirmation; the sixth with organic union as the goal of all discussions of Church union. The three more controversial articles must be cited in full:

"2. The Free Church would 'take episcopacy into its system' by the acceptance of an episcopate consecrated in the first instance through Bishops of one or more of the historic episcopal Churches, and thus linked with the episcopate of the past, and would adopt episcopal ordination as its rule for the future. The Church of England would acknowledge that the Bishops and episcopally ordained Presbyters were from the outset duly commissioned and authorized for the same offices in the Church of God as its own Bishops and Priests.

"3. The Church of England would agree to admit to communion baptized and duly commended communicant members of the Free Church in good standing, and would officially authorize duly commended communicant members of the Church of England in good standing to receive the sacrament of Holy Communion at the hands of such Ministers of the Free Church as had been either consecrated to the episcopate or episcopally ordained or further commissioned to the Presbyterate.

"5. It would be recognized that the Free Church, though itself episcopal, or in process of becoming episcopal, would yet continue to maintain the relations of fellowship and intercommunion which it at present enjoys with non-episcopal Churches; and the Church of England, though not able to adopt the like policy for itself, would yet not regard the matter as one which should stand in the way of the achievement of intercommunion between itself and the Free Church." [1]

The Conference declared itself "satisfied that only on such terms as these could the Archbishop's proposals be implemented". But there was less than unanimity as to the acceptability of the proposals themselves:

"Although not all members of the Joint Conference would, as at present advised, be prepared as individuals to commend the suggested policy to their Churches, many on both sides would be ready to do so. All the members of the Conference would plead that no Communion should refuse this way towards closer unity except under an inescapable sense of obligation." [2]

[1] *Church Relations in England*, pp. 44 ff.   [2] Ibid., p. 46.

Three points are noted as likely to create special difficulty:

Some in the Free Churches find the acceptance of episcopacy in any form impossible; they judge it to be without warrant of Holy Scripture, and contrary to what they believe to be the true order of the Church.

If episcopacy were accepted by a Free Church, it would be faced by the problem of two classes of ministers within its ranks, one acceptable, the other unacceptable to Anglicans. This would present an intolerable obstacle, unless it could be removed by some satisfactory form of supplemental commissioning.

Some Anglicans find it impossible to accept the view that the Church of England could be in communion with an episcopal Church, which itself was in communion with non-episcopal Churches. To them this would involve illegitimate compromise on an essential Anglican principle.

No official action had at the time of writing been taken by any Church on the Archbishop's proposals, or on the development of them in the report of the Joint Conference. It is too early to say whether this new approach will prove useful as a means of solving long-standing and almost intractable problems.

9. THE ORTHODOX CHURCHES AND OTHER EPISCOPAL CHURCHES

Orthodox Christians have never left their fellow-Christians in any doubt as to their views. To them the Holy Orthodox Church *is* the Church, and there is no other. They, alone among the Churches of Christendom, have retained the apostolic faith in its purity; they alone have valid and unquestionable sacraments; they and they alone have the plenitude of divine grace. But the Orthodox have never treated other Christians as being simply heathen (though they have sometimes presumed to baptize again those who had already been baptized in other communions); and among the Churches they have made a distinction between those which claim to have retained the historic succession and the episcopal ministry, and those which make no such claim.

Throughout the centuries many attempts have been made by Orthodox Churches to bring into fellowship the Lesser Eastern Churches of Armenia, Egypt, and beyond; but the memories of ancient conflicts are still so bitter as to make almost impossible any *rapprochement* between the Churches as Churches, even were the difficulties presented by doctrinal differences less than they actually are. But some progress is to be noted in personal approaches and friendly relationships. The Catholicos Patriarch of all the Armenians, George VI, was present as an honorary guest at the Conference of Heads and Representatives of Autocephalous Orthodox Churches held at Moscow in July 1948, and spoke a number of times during the proceedings, though apparently the question of Church relationships was not raised. A friendly approach by the Church of Greece to the (Monophysite) Church of Ethiopia is something new in ecumenical relationships.[1]

Of relationships between the Orthodox Churches and the Roman Catholic Church there is nothing to record, other than increasing interest on the Roman side in all the problems of the Eastern Churches, and a certain lessening of the traditional tensions. The continuing mutual interest of the Orthodox and Old Catholic Churches is dealt with elsewhere. It remains to consider Orthodox-Anglican relations in the period under review.

[1] At the time of writing, a number of Ethiopian students were receiving theological training in the seminaries of Greek-speaking Orthodox Churches.

Of friendly relationships there had been a great deal, and at times these had extended as far as a measure of intercommunion "by economy". Thus the delegation sent by the Patriarchate of Constantinople to London in 1920 mentioned in its report

"as a certain fact, and well evidenced, that during the duration at least of the period of war, Englishmen in Macedonia received the Sacrament from Serbian priests, who had permission for the purpose from the competent Church authorities, that the Serbian students staying in England received from Anglican priests. . . . It was also told us that the Patriarch Tikhon permitted such Intercommunion, which, as is known, the previous Russian Metropolitans by no means permitted."[1]

The year 1920 marked a quickening of Orthodox relationships with the Western world. In that year an Orthodox delegation had been present at the Lambeth Conference and had attended some of the sessions of the Committee on Unity. Two years later the Ecumenical Patriarch and the Holy Synod of Constantinople put forth a memorable statement on the validity of Anglican Orders:

"As before the Orthodox Church, the Ordinations of the Anglican Episcopal Confession of bishops, priests, and deacons, possess the same validity as those of the Roman, Old Catholic, and Armenian Churches possess, in as much as all essentials are found in them which are held indispensable from the Orthodox point of view for the recognition of the 'Charisma' of the priesthood derived from Apostolic Succession."[2]

In the course of the next ten years the Churches of Alexandria, Jerusalem, and Cyprus, followed in 1935 by that of Rumania, agreed to recognize the validity of Anglican ordinations.

The limitations of this decision must be recognized. Only a General Council of all the Orthodox Churches could pronounce definitively on such a question; the opinion even of the Ecumenical Patriarch, though weighty, is not authoritative; and, on Orthodox principles, even the acceptance of the Orders of another Church need not lead on to any measure of intercommunion. Yet even such qualified recognition has its importance. No Anglican imagines that Orthodox recognition could add anything to Orders which he himself regards as wholly valid and regular; but almost all would be happy to see cleared out of the way one of the many obstacles to the expression of full fellowship between the Churches.

In 1925 the 1,600th anniversary of the Council of Nicaea was celebrated in Westminster Abbey, in the presence of the Patriarchs of Alexandria and Jerusalem, two Russian Metropolitans, and representatives of the Churches of Greece and Rumania. The Creed, commonly but incorrectly called the Nicene Creed, was solemnly recited, first in its Western form, and then in the shorter form in use in the Orthodox Churches.[3]

In 1939 the question of Anglican Orders was taken up by the theological faculty of the University of Athens, which, after careful consideration, reached a generally favourable conclusion; but no action on this report has yet been taken by the Church of Greece.

[1] Bell, *Documents*, I, p. 61.   [2] Ibid., pp. 93 f.
[3] Without the words "and the Son" after "proceeding from the Father".

In this field, as in so many others, ecumenical progress was interrupted by the disasters of the second world war. When the return of peace made possible the renewal of relations, the Orthodox Churches were more concerned with the question of participation in the ecumenical movement as a whole than with specific questions of Christian unity. To this generalization there is, however, one exception.

In 1948 the Patriarch Alexis of Moscow invited the heads of Orthodox autocephalous Churches to a Conference in Moscow. The right of the Patriarch of Moscow to convene such a Conference was sharply contested from Constantinople; and though Archbishop Germanos, the Exarch of Constantinople in the West, was present at the Conference, it is clear that it cannot be taken either as representative of the whole Orthodox world or as authoritative throughout it.

Among the subjects discussed was the validity of Anglican ordinations. This was treated at great length and with considerable learning in a number of papers; but the basic misunderstandings of Anglican theology and of the Anglican position generally betrayed by every one of the speakers, show what a long distance has still to be travelled along the road of mutual illumination. The gist of the debate was a return to the well-known Orthodox position that complete unity in faith and doctrine must precede intercommunion, and that, until that is attained, judgements on ordinations and Orders cannot be more than conditional. A long resolution passed at the end of the Conference contains the following principal points:

"1. . . . If the Orthodox Church cannot agree to recognize the correctness of Anglican teaching on the sacraments generally, and on the Sacrament of Orders in particular, neither can she recognize the validity of Anglican ordinations which have actually taken place.

"2. . . . We express the desire that the Anglican Church should alter her doctrinal teaching from the dogmatic, as well as from the canonical and ecclesiastical, points of view.

"3. . . . We declare that the present Anglican hierarchy could receive from the Orthodox Church recognition of the validity of its priesthood, if, as a preliminary, there had been established between the Orthodox and the Anglican Churches a formally expressed unity of faith and confession as indicated above. When once such longed-for unity is established, recognition of the validity of Anglican Orders can be accomplished in accordance with the principle of Economy by the only authoritative decision which we recognize—a conciliar decision of the whole of the Holy Orthodox Church."[1]

To some this decision was disappointing, since it seemed to withdraw, and perhaps did in reality in a measure withdraw, from the position taken up by a number of Orthodox Churches between 1920 and 1940. But in principle the resolutions contain nothing new. The Orthodox Churches have always held the view that intercommunion has significance only as the expression of full dogmatic union; and, since they believe themselves to be in possession of all the truth, any doctrinal disagreements can be resolved only by the total surrender of any Church which wishes to enter into fellowship with them. Ecumenical progress depends upon frank statement in the spirit of charity: it is universally

---

[1] *Conférence Orthodoxe de Moscou*, II, pp. 445 f.

recognized that no true unity can come about through the concealment or the underestimating of differences. The Orthodox serve the whole ecumenical cause by the firmness with which they take their stand on positions from which they are not prepared to depart.

For many reasons, not least among them the serious differences between the Greek- and Arabic-speaking Orthodox Churches and those in the Slavonic world, the holding of a Pan-Orthodox Conference or Synod must be judged extremely unlikely. Progress in fellowship must therefore, in the meantime, be sought by other means than through official ecclesiastical declarations.

10. CHURCH UNION—DIFFICULTIES AND ENCOURAGEMENTS

The average friend of the ecumenical movement, inexpert in ecclesiastical affairs, tends to be so much disturbed by the evident divisions among Christians as to do less than justice to the valiant efforts of the Churches to set their house in order. The brief sketch of some movements given in this chapter, and still more the summary statement in the Appendix, afford convincing evidence of the range, persistence, and ingenuity of the attempts made by Christians of many confessions to do away with the scandal of division, and of the solid character of their achievements. In the forty years under review, more unions between Churches have been accomplished than in any earlier period of equal length. At the time of writing, more plans for union were under serious consideration by the Churches than at any single moment in the past history of the Church.

The achievement becomes even more remarkable when full account is taken of the difficulties, doctrinal, administrative, and psychological, that stand in the way of all Church unions—difficulties greater than can be apprehended except by those who have themselves taken a hand in the work of trying to unify the Churches. The wonder is not so much that failures and disappointments have been many, as that any united Churches at all have come into existence.

There are, first, the difficulties in the realm of faith. Some Churches are wedded to long and elaborate confessions of faith, and demand as a condition of union acceptance of the totality of these dogmatic formulations. Others, while insisting on certain traditional expressions of the Faith, such as the Nicene Creed, are prepared to admit considerable differences on matters which are not precisely set forth in Scripture or in the Creeds; and, where agreement has been reached on these necessary articles, do not regard the existence of variations as necessarily a barrier to intercommunion or even to full organic union. Yet others, holding that loyalty to Jesus Christ and to his Spirit is the one essential in the life of the Church, are averse to all dogmatic formulations. Adherents of this view tend to hold that, since spiritual unity already exists among all faithful Christians, no other unity need be sought; or, being themselves willing to unite with others on very simple terms, are irritated by what seem to them the unreasonable demands of Churches which are not content with so flexible a definition of their faith.

It is evident that union of Churches within the second or within the third category presents no special difficulties. The difficulties are immensely increased when Churches in the second group desire to enter into fellowship with Churches in the third. To the one side, dogmatic formulation presents itself merely as the delimitation of the field within which the liberty of Christian thinking is to be enjoyed; to the other it may appear as an intolerable restriction on the freedom of Christian experience and expression. Our survey has shown that such unions are not impossible; but they demand on both sides great humility and teachableness, and a delicate mutual respect for spiritual needs and convictions.

The aim of Christian union cannot rest content with the exclusion of any Christian body. But when consideration is extended to the group of Churches first indicated above, the difficulties in the way are felt in their full intensity. All the recent pronouncements of the Roman Catholic Church make it quite clear that possible terms of union would involve for all other Christian communions the repudiation of their own past history, and total acceptance in every detail of Roman Catholic dogma, as it now is, or as it may come in any future age to be determined. Individuals and groups have acceded to these terms. No single Christian communion has ever been prepared to purchase unity at this price; [1] and there seems no likelihood that the Roman Catholic Church, now or in the future, will consider the modification of the terms of union that it offers.

Difficulties of faith are closely paralleled by difficulties of order.

Some Churches regard a particular form of Church order and of the ministry as a part of the Faith, divinely given and indefectible; and cannot admit the validity of the orders and sacraments of Christian communions which have departed from this divinely-given structure. Others, while holding that there is one form of the ministry (usually the episcopal) which is according to the mind of Christ and without which the Church cannot realize the fullness of its being, are prepared to recognize, at least in some degree, the spiritual reality and effectiveness of the ministries of other Churches. Yet others hold that, while order is necessary in the Church, no particular form can claim divine sanction as against any other, and have no difficulty in accepting as valid any regularly constituted ministry.

In this field, also, special interest attaches to the efforts of the second and third groups of Churches to enter into fellowship. True agreement without dishonesty and subterfuge is not easily come by. Those who believe in the equality of ministries tend to demand that those with whom they are negotiating should also admit this equality—the very thing which in honesty it is impossible for them to do. Those who honestly hold that their ministry has a fullness and a validity that others do not possess tend for the sake of agreement to suppress their own views and to claim less than they really believe. One of the chief criticisms of the Church of South India has been that union was reached, not by the resolution of differences, but by the refusal to state exactly where the differences lay.

There is a general impression that, once the covenant of union has been signed, uniting Churches live happily ever after. If this were true, Church history would be a less exciting study than it is. In reality just the fact of coming together makes tensions more severely felt than they were in separation; and every serious attempt to live together in Christian fellowship demands adjustments, patience, and the continuous exercise of forgiveness. Only if these are fully given by all can a union reach such stability as entitles it to be judged successful.

Difficulties may arise over things that in themselves are trivial. The vesture used by the ministers of one uniting tradition is unfamiliar to those of another. One group is familiar with individual communion cups at the Holy Communion, another holds firmly to the use of the common cup. Every congregation is unwilling to change familiar hymn tunes for others less well known. When Churches live in separation these things do not matter; when they live together they may come to matter very much indeed.

[1] For a partial exception, see Introduction, pp. 18 f.

The unification of worshipping groups may prove more difficult than the unification of confessions. In many places union has meant that two churches have found themselves brought into forced fellowship; but old traditions and attachments die hard; neither has been willing to give way to the other, and the two continue in practical separation long after the union has been achieved on a higher level. Almost all unions have meant that hundreds of such problems have had to be solved, not without dust and heat.

In nothing do the existing Christian confessions differ more from one another than in the share which they assign to lay folk in the administration of the Church. All unions are based on the principle of maintaining all existing freedoms and privileges. But it may well happen that a minister accustomed to much freedom of action may, after union, find himself much more closely watched over and controlled by a lay council than he desires; or conversely a lay council accustomed to exercising almost unlimited control over its minister may find that, after union, the minister has become responsible to some central body of the Church, and so has acquired far greater local freedom than he had ever enjoyed before.

In practice it is far more in such fields than in the area of dogmatic definition and expression that the strains and tensions of life in union are felt, and by a far greater number of people. Given goodwill and a patient resolve to find a way through, a Christian solution can always be found, and in the process of finding it the bonds of fellowship may even be strengthened.

But there is always the possibility that a union which has been achieved may not stand the test of time. Strains may prove stronger than had been expected; agreement may turn out to have been hasty and superficial, or based on expediency rather than on principle. If strains reach a certain point of intensity, there is no solution other than separation; marriage may after all end in divorce. The great and glorious fact on which this survey must end is that, of all the united Churches which have come into existence in the 20th century, hardly one has shown any signs of falling apart in dissolution. Time has shown many imperfections in the work, and much revision of the original ideas of union has had to be carried through. But those who have had experience of life in these united Churches are almost unanimous in affirming that, though union may have brought loss in certain directions and though some hopes may have been unfulfilled, it is impossible that they should ever consider going back to their earlier state of division. To do so would seem too manifest a betrayal of the cause of Christ.

It is true that less than a generation has passed since the achievement of these unions, and a generation is a very short time in the life of the Church. But the first ten years are the most difficult time of testing. If these united Churches have stood the test, have grown steadily into closer unity than was experienced in their beginnings, have begun to show signs of maturity and permanence, it is permissible to infer that there is more in them than human contrivance, and that they have so far stood the test because their unity is rooted in the will of Christ for his Church, and not in the wit or wisdom of men.

11. TO WHAT DOES IT ALL LEAD?

This chapter has described a number of efforts to promote the unity of Christ's Church. These are marked by great diversity of approach, and great variety in the solutions of ancient problems which have proved acceptable. But all are attempts to attain organic or corporate union, to bring into existence one Church where two or more Churches have previously existed. All such efforts spring from the conviction that the unity among Christians for which Christ prayed was intended to be a unity of faith, of worship, of administration, and of witness; that it should be, in fact, a unity which is not merely spiritually experienced by believers, but a manifest reality, apprehensible even by those who are not Christians at all.

Such convictions are widely, and perhaps increasingly, held in the Christian world. But it is well to recall that they have by no means found universal acceptance.

Some hold that the divisions within the Christian world community have on the whole been of advantage to it. The factor of competition between co-existent Churches has helped to preserve them all from the lethargy which is the besetting peril of monopoly. Elements of truth latent in the Gospel from the beginning have been fully worked out, when one among the Churches has accepted witness to one truth or one aspect of truth as its special responsibility in the Christian world. If all were to be amalgamated in a single Church, variety would be replaced by a monotonous uniformity, and adventurous seeking after truth would be at a discount.

An historian might reply that, in the high Middle Age, when the Church in Western Europe had reached its highest point of effective unity, its life was marked by an extraordinarily rich diversity in thought, devotion, and action, and that it was the divisions of the 16th century which led to confessional rigidity in both the Roman Catholic and the Protestant worlds. Yet the critic of union movements has a valid point to make. As we have seen, every movement for Church union is faced with the problem of ensuring that all the riches of each of the uniting confessions is genuinely brought into the common life, and that legitimate variety is not stifled under the desire for uniformity. All these experiments are as yet too young for it to be possible to determine whether they have been successful in bringing the contrasting factors of order and spontaneity, of unity and variety, into a stable equilibrium.

Others would maintain that all these laborious efforts at outward union are beside the point, since the unity which is given to Christians in Christ is spiritual, and as such can neither be diminished by the variety of outward fellowships, nor promoted by organizational readjustments.

To these critics it must be conceded that, unless there were a sense of already existing spiritual unity underlying all the divisions in the Christian world, there would be no reason for Christians to seek for visible unity; and also that no movement for corporate union is likely to come to fruition, unless it is accompanied by a steadily deepening experience of inner fellowship in Christ. But to admit this is by no means to admit that Christians can be content with this inner fellowship, as though this were all that is to be desired. The New Testament concept of unity is expressed in the words *There is one body and one spirit.* In Pauline language, *body* is that which serves as the outward expression of *spirit*, and *spirit* is that which needs a *body* as its visible expression. If there is true unity in spirit, that unity must necessarily express itself in the unity of the organism through which the spirit acts in the visible world.

One alternative to corporate union, which finds eloquent champions in the Christian world to-day, is federal union. Why should not the Churches, while continuing to exist as independent units, enter into such a compact with one another that ordination to the ministry in one body should convey the right of ministry in all, and that membership in one Church should convey with it the privileges and responsibilities of membership in all the rest? Why should not the Churches develop organs for common action, when common action is desired, without infringement of their right to act independently when they feel it right to do so?

This solution makes a strong appeal to laymen, who tend to be impatient of the subtleties of theological debate, and to be more concerned with the practical work and witness of the Church in the world than with the exact definition of its faith and order. But it is precisely on practical grounds that this solution is open to the gravest objections. If the Churches were all able mutually to recognize one another's standing as Churches and the validity of one another's ministries and sacraments, federal union might seem to be an immediately available cure for division. But at least three-quarters of the Christians in the world are to be found in the Roman Catholic, Orthodox, Old Catholic, Anglican, and Lutheran Communions, which on one ground or another do not recognize the equal standing of Churches and the equal validity of ministries. Such Churches may readily agree that there are wide areas of Christian co-operation in which the Churches may work together without raising ultimate questions of faith and order; they cannot agree that these questions are never to be raised, or that an acceptable solution can be reached merely by the evasion of difficulties.

One of the happiest signs of progress in the Christian world in recent years has been the widespread development of international and interconfessional Christian co-operation. But the expectation that this might satisfy the desire for unity has not been fulfilled. The slogan "service unites, doctrine divides" has been seen to represent a superficial understanding of the situation. In point of fact, those who have learned to co-operate most closely in practical tasks have found themselves restive under the remaining hindrances to full Christian fellowship; and those who have started in the field of common Christian action have found themselves driven back from practical problems to theological foundations, to the consideration of those deeper convictions that make men Christians, but in the variety of their expressions hold them back from a fully unified Christian witness.

It must be admitted that, apart from these divergent and sincerely held convictions with regard to Christian unity, there are other less admirable motives, which make work for Church union difficult.

There is, first, the cheerful acquiescence of the majority of Christians in the fact of division. From our infancy we have known nothing but a divided Christendom, and denominational divisions are so familiar as to be taken for granted. The suggestion that things might be otherwise and that there might be another way for Christians is not always either intelligible or welcome.

There are the non-theological factors which help to make division permanent —conservatism, the fear of change, devotion to old traditions, a sense of responsibility to truth as it has been received and held, prejudice against others, and unwillingness to learn. Some of these motives are admirable, representing that faithfulness and steadiness of conviction without which the stability of the Church would be imperilled. Others are all too evidently rationalizations of human laziness, timidity, and selfishness, by which the operation of the divine Spirit within the human spirit is impeded or rendered impossible.

Then there is a specious form of devotion to truth, the besetting danger of theologians, which masks a perhaps unconscious inner determination that nothing shall ever be done. Without true agreement, no union can have such life in it as will enable it to survive; but, if it is necessary to wait until everyone is agreed on every single item of debate, the King's government cannot be carried on, and no union can ever be achieved.

In every age of Christian history, the visible unity of the Church has been the concern of many faithful Christians. The great renewal of concern in this matter by which the 20th century has so far been marked appears to be associated, in part at least, with the recovery of the Biblical doctrine of the Church as the People of God. An individualistic concept of salvation has increasingly given way before a recognition that the doctrine of the Church is not an optional addition to theology, but an essential part of the Gospel. With this has come an increasing conviction that the Church must be one, as God is one, and as Christ is one. But the convictions of the theologians have been reinforced empirically by the experiences of many who in one way or another have been led to walk in new ways of Christian fellowship; they have been driven, sometimes against their will, to realize that their longing for oneness with their separated brethren cannot be satisfied by anything less than full corporate unity in a single Church, and that that unity can be achieved not superficially, but only by a renewed understanding of the basic convictions of Christian faith. At the same time, the desire for union is strengthened by the purely practical recognition that the witness of the Church, surrounded by an increasingly hostile world, is gravely weakened by its divisions, and that no Church, unaided by the resources of all the others, is adequate to manifest the fullness of the truth as it is in Jesus Christ, as against the false gospels by which mankind is in danger of being led astray.

Certain conclusions seem to follow from the survey which has here been made of certain plans of union, and from others for which it has been impossible to find space in this chapter:

(1) The making of divisions in the Church is easy; the repairing of them is far more difficult.

(2) The work of planning Church union cannot be hurried; even when division is comparatively recent and does not touch fundamental issues, a whole generation may elapse before the difficulties can be honestly and satisfactorily dealt with.

(3) Union must always involve some loss; but union can never come if those who are seeking it are asking themselves all the time "How much do we stand to lose as the price of union with these people?" instead of asking "How much shall we gain through accepting their treasures as our own?"

(4) The difficulties that have had to be faced are strangely varied; but, where the will to unity has been strong and honest, there is hardly any difficulty that has not yielded to treatment.

(5) It may be well worth while to wait many years in order to reconcile a conscientious minority which is unable to accept a plan of union; but such a minority cannot claim the right to frustrate for ever the will of the majority. The most agonizing problem in the search for unity is the decision as to the circumstances, if any, in which unity may rightly be purchased at the price of fresh divisions.

(6) Almost every united Church will suffer, after union, the severe testing of a long period of unification. This cannot be avoided, however careful the

preparation for union may have been; but, faced with patience and humility, it can be a period of great value, provided that every possible step is taken to ensure that nothing is lost of the heritage of any of the uniting Churches.

(7) In spite of the difficulties and frustrations that union may involve, in the period under review no united Church has been dissolved, and the vast majority of those who have entered into union would affirm that it is unthinkable that they should ever go back to their previous state of division.

(8) The final and terrible difficulty is that Churches cannot unite, unless they are willing to die. In a truly united Church, there would be no more Anglicans or Lutherans or Presbyterians or Methodists. But the disappearance from the world of those great and honoured names is the very thing that many loyal churchmen are not prepared to face. Much has already been achieved. But until Church union clearly takes shape as a better resurrection on the other side of death, the impulse towards it is likely to be weak and half-hearted; and such weak impulses are not strong enough to overcome the tremendous difficulties in the way.

(9) The attitude of the Churches should therefore be neither one of timid resignation, as though nothing could be done, nor of adolescent optimism, as though the problem was already nearly solved. What is needed is a sober realism, that takes account of all the obstacles, but also recognizes that to faith and obedience, in response to the clearly declared will of God, the word "impossible" does not exist.

APPENDIX TO CHAPTER 10

TABLE OF
PLANS OF UNION AND REUNION
1910–1952

I. MERGERS INVOLVING FULL ORGANIC UNION

A. INTRA-CONFESSIONAL (the dates given are those of the attainment of organic union)

1. *The United States of America*   1911
   i. The Northern Baptist Convention
   ii. The Free Baptist Churches
   The name THE NORTHERN BAPTIST CONVENTION was retained. (Since 1950 THE AMERICAN BAPTIST CONVENTION)

2. *The United States of America*   1917
   i. Hauge's Norwegian Evangelical Lutheran Synod
   ii. The Synod of the Norwegian Evangelical Church of America
   iii. The United Norwegian Lutheran Church in America
   To form THE NORWEGIAN CHURCH OF AMERICA. (Since 1946 THE EVANGELICAL LUTHERAN CHURCH)

3. *The United States of America*   1918
   i. The General Synod of the Lutheran Church in the United States
   ii. The General Council of the Lutheran Church in the United States
   iii. The United Synod of the South
   To form THE UNITED LUTHERAN CHURCH

4. *The United States of America*   1920
   i. The Presbyterian Church in the United States of America
   ii. The Welsh Calvinistic Methodist Church

   The name THE PRESBYTERIAN CHURCH IN THE UNITED STATES OF AMERICA was retained

5. *The United States of America*   1922
   i. The Evangelical Association
   ii. The United Evangelical Church
   To form THE EVANGELICAL CHURCH

6. *The United States of America*   1924
   i. The Reformed Church in the United States
   ii. The Hungarian Reformed Church in America
   The name THE REFORMED CHURCH IN THE UNITED STATES was retained

7. *Central Africa* (*Nyasaland*)   1924
   i. The Presbytery of Blantyre (Church of Scotland Mission)
   ii. The Presbytery of Livingstonia (United Free Church of Scotland Mission)
   To form THE CHURCH OF CENTRAL AFRICA, PRESBYTERIAN; joined, in 1926, by
   iii. The Presbytery of Mkhoma (Mission of the Dutch Reformed Church in South Africa)

8. *The United States of America*   1925
   i. The Congregational Churches
   ii. The Evangelical Protestant Churches of North America
   The name THE CONGREGATIONAL CHURCHES was retained

9. *Korea*   1926
- i. The Korean Methodist Episcopal Church
- ii. The Korean Methodist Episcopal Church, South

To form THE KOREAN METHODIST CHURCH

10. *Scotland*   1929
- i. The Church of Scotland
- ii. The United Free Church of Scotland

The name THE CHURCH OF SCOTLAND was retained

11. *The United States of America*   1930
- i. The Lutheran Synod of Buffalo
- ii. The Evangelical Lutheran Synod of Iowa and Other States
- iii. The Evangelical Lutheran Joint Synod of Ohio and Other States

To form THE AMERICAN LUTHERAN CHURCH

12. *Mexico*   1930
- i. The Mexican Methodist Episcopal Church
- ii. The Mexican Methodist Episcopal Church, South

To form THE UNITED METHODIST CHURCH OF MEXICO

13. *England*   1931
- i. The Wesleyan Methodist Church
- ii. The United Methodist Church
- iii. The Primitive Methodist Church

To form THE METHODIST CHURCH

14. *The United States of America*   1939
- i. The Methodist Episcopal Church
- ii. The Methodist Episcopal Church, South
- iii. The Methodist Protestant Church

To form THE METHODIST CHURCH

15. *Switzerland*   1943
- i. The National Church of Neuchâtel
- ii. The Evangelical Church of Neuchâtel, independent of the State

To form THE REFORMED EVANGELICAL CHURCH OF NEUCHÂTEL

16. *Holland*   1946
- i. The Dutch Reformed Church
- ii. The Reformed Churches in the Netherlands in Restored Connection

The name THE DUTCH REFORMED CHURCH was retained

17. *Brazil*   1949
- i. The Evangelical Church of Rio Grande do Sul
- ii. The Lutheran Church in Brazil
- iii. The Evangelical Synod of Santa Catarina and Paranà
- iv. The Synod of Central Brazil

To form THE SYNODAL FEDERATION OF LUTHERAN CHURCHES IN BRAZIL
In spite of its title, this body claims to be and to act as a Church

18. *Madagascar*   1950
- i. The Norwegian Mission
- ii. The Mission of the Evangelical Lutheran Church in America
- iii. The Mission of the Lutheran Free Church in America

To form THE MALAGASY LUTHERAN CHURCH

19. *Holland*   1951
- i. The Evangelical Lutheran Church in the Netherlands
- ii. The Restored Evangelical Lutheran Church in the Netherlands

The name THE EVANGELICAL LUTHERAN CHURCH IN THE NETHERLANDS was retained

B. TRANS-CONFESSIONAL (the dates given are those of the attainment of organic union)

20. *India*   1924
Missions and Churches, founded by
  i. The American Evangelical Mission of the Evangelical and Reformed Church
  ii. The American Marathi Mission of the American Board of Commissioners for Foreign Missions
  iii. The American Presbyterian Mission
  iv. The Canadian Presbyterian Mission
  v. The Church of Scotland Mission
  vi. The Irish Presbyterian Mission
  vii. The London Missionary Society
  viii. The English Presbyterian Mission
  ix. The New Zealand Presbyterian Mission
  x. The United Church of Canada Mission
  xi. The Welsh Presbyterian Mission

To form THE UNITED CHURCH OF NORTHERN INDIA

21. *Canada*   1925
  i. The Presbyterian Church in Canada
  ii. The Methodist Church of Canada
  iii. The Congregational Churches in Canada
  iv. Local Union Churches

To form THE UNITED CHURCH OF CANADA

22. *The Philippine Republic*   1929
  i. The Presbyterian Church
  ii. The Congregational Churches
  iii. The Church of the United Brethren in Christ

To form THE UNITED EVANGELICAL CHURCH OF THE PHILIPPINES

23. *Puerto Rico*   1931
  i. The Congregational Churches
  ii. The Christian Churches
  iii. The Church of the United Brethren in Christ

To form THE UNITED EVANGELICAL CHURCH OF PUERTO RICO

24. *The United States of America*   1931
  i. The Christian Churches
  ii. The Congregational Churches

To form THE CONGREGATIONAL CHRISTIAN CHURCHES

25. *Siam (Thailand)*   1934
  i. The Siamese Presbyterian Church
  ii. The Chinese Presbyterian Churches in Siam
  iii. The Chinese Baptist Churches in Siam

To form THE CHURCH OF CHRIST IN SIAM

26. *The United States of America*   1934
  i. The Evangelical Synod of North America
  ii. The Reformed Church in the United States

To form THE EVANGELICAL AND REFORMED CHURCH

27. *Guatemala*   1936
  i. The Presbyterian Church
  ii. The Central American Mission

To form THE EVANGELICAL CHURCH IN GUATEMALA

28. *France*   1938
  i. The Union of Reformed Churches of France
  ii. The Union of Reformed Evangelical Churches of France
  iii. The Evangelical Methodist Church of France

To form THE REFORMED CHURCH OF FRANCE

29. *Japan*   1941
  i. The Japanese Presbyterian and Reformed Church
  ii. The Japan Methodist Church

iii. The Japan Congregational Churches
and other denominations

To form THE CHURCH OF CHRIST IN JAPAN (NIPPON KIRISUTO KYODAN)

Many denominations and groups separated themselves from the Kyodan in and after 1945

30. *The Philippine Republic*   1944
   i. The Disciples of Christ
   ii. The United Church of Christ
   iii. The United Evangelical Church of the Philippines
   iv. The Methodist Church
   v. The Independent Methodist Church
   and other denominations

   To form THE EVANGELICAL CHURCH OF THE PHILIPPINES

After 1946 only the Disciples of Christ, the United Brethren, and one or two smaller denominations remained in the Evangelical Church

31. *Central Africa (Rhodesia)*   1945
   i. The Presbytery of North-eastern Rhodesia
   ii. The London Missionary Society
   iii. The Union Church of the Copper Belt

To form THE CHURCH OF CENTRAL AFRICA IN RHODESIA
joined in 1951 by

   iv. La Société des Missions Évangéliques de Paris (Barotseland Church)

32. *The United States of America*   1946
   i. The Evangelical Church
   ii. The Church of the United Brethren in Christ

   To form THE EVANGELICAL UNITED BRETHREN CHURCH

33. *India*   1947
   i. The Church of India, Burma, and Ceylon (dioceses of Madras, Travancore and Cochin, Tinnevelly, and Dornakal)
   ii. The South India United Church
   iii. The Methodist Church of South India

   To form THE CHURCH OF SOUTH INDIA

34. *The Philippine Republic*   1948
   i. The United Evangelical Church of the Philippines
   ii. The Philippine Methodist Church
   iii. The Evangelical Church of the Philippines

   To form THE UNITED CHURCH OF CHRIST IN THE PHILIPPINES

II. FULL INTERCOMMUNION ACHIEVED

35. *Europe*   1931
   i. The Old Catholic Churches
   ii. The Church of England and other Anglican Churches

36. *The United States of America*   1946
   i. The Protestant Episcopal Church (and other Anglican Churches)
   ii. The Polish National Catholic Church

III. LIMITED INTERCOMMUNION ACHIEVED

37. *Europe*   1930
   i. The Church of England
   ii. The Church of Sweden

38. *Europe*   1935
   i. The Church of England
   ii. The Church of Finland

39. *India*   1936–37
   i. The Mar Thoma Syrian Church of Malabar

   ii. The Church of India, Burma, and Ceylon

40. *The Philippine Republic*   1948
   i. The Philippine Episcopal Church (A missionary district of the Protestant Episcopal Church in the U.S.A.)
   ii. The Philippine Independent Church (The Aglipayan Church)

IV. FEDERAL UNIONS INVOLVING LESS THAN FULL ORGANIC UNION

41. *Switzerland*   1920
  i. Cantonal Reformed Churches in Switzerland
  ii. The Federated Reformed Churches of Central Switzerland
  iii. The Free Church of the Canton of Geneva
  iv. The Free Church of the Canton of Vaud
  v. The Methodist Church in Switzerland
  vi. Some congregations outside Switzerland

  To form THE FEDERATION OF SWISS PROTESTANT CHURCHES

42. *Germany*   1922
  Twenty-eight autonomous regional Churches

  To form THE FEDERATION OF GERMAN EVANGELICAL CHURCHES

43. *Spain*   1923
  i. The Spanish Evangelical Church
  ii. The Spanish Reformed Church (Episcopal)
  iii. The Methodist Church of Ceyana

  To form THE FEDERATION OF EVANGELICAL CHURCHES IN SPAIN

44. *China*   1927
Missions and Churches founded by or in connection with
  i. The Baptist Churches
  ii. The Congregational Churches
  iii. The Methodist Churches
  iv. The Presbyterian Churches

  v. The Reformed Churches
  vi. The United Brethren in Christ
  vii. The United Church of Canada
  viii. Independent Chinese Churches

  To form THE CHURCH OF CHRIST IN CHINA (CHUNG HUA CHI TU CHIAO HUI)

45. *Great Britain*   1944–51
  i. The Congregational Union of England and Wales
  ii. The Presbyterian Church of England

In 1951 these Churches resolved to "enter into a new and solemn relationship with one another, covenanting together to take counsel with one another, etc."

46. *Germany*   1948
  Twenty-seven autonomous regional Churches, Lutheran, Reformed, and United

  To form THE EVANGELICAL CHURCH IN GERMANY;
joined in 1951 by the Church of Bremen

47. *Germany*   1948
  Ten autonomous regional Evangelical Lutheran Churches

  To form THE UNITED EVANGELICAL LUTHERAN CHURCH IN GERMANY

Each constituent Church retains much independence, and each adheres as an independent member Church also to the Evangelical Church in Germany

V. NEGOTIATIONS WITH A VIEW TO ORGANIC UNION STILL IN PROGRESS IN 1952

(The dates in Sections V–VIII indicate in each case the date at which the negotiations began)

48. *The Union of South Africa*   1907
  i. The Congregational Union of South Africa
  ii. The Methodist Church of South Africa

  iii. The Presbyterian Church of South Africa

A Preliminary Basis of Union was drawn up in 1935

49. *The Union of South Africa*   1911
   i. The Church of Sweden Mission
   ii. The Norwegian Mission
   iii. The Berlin Mission
   iv. The Mission of the Evangelical Lutheran Church of America (Schreuder Mission)
   v. The Hermannsburg Mission

   With a view to forming THE AFRICAN LUTHERAN CHURCH OF SOUTH AFRICA

   In 1949 an Advisory Synod of the Co-operating Lutheran Missions was formed and a draft Plan of Union prepared

50. *Iran (Persia)*   1927
   i. The Evangelical Church of Iran (Presbyterian)
   ii. The Episcopal Church in Iran (Anglican)

   A new draft Basis was prepared in 1945

51. *The United States of America*   1925
   i. The American Baptist Convention (till 1950 the Northern Baptist Convention)
   ii. The Disciples of Christ

   A proposal for functional union was rejected in 1929 by the Baptists. Negotiations were hopefully resumed in 1946

52. *India*   1929
   i. The Church of India, Pakistan, Burma and Ceylon
   ii. The Methodist Church (British and Australasian Conferences)
   iii. The United Church of Northern India
   iv. The Methodist Church in Southern Asia
   v. Churches Associated with the Baptist Missionary Society in India and Pakistan

   With a view to organic union

   An almost complete *Plan of Church Union in North India and Pakistan* was published in 1951

53. *Australia*   1933
   i. The Methodist Church of Australia
   ii. The Congregational Churches in Australia

   Suspended from 1935–48, when the Presbyterians joined in tripartite negotiations, and renewed when the Presbyterians withdrew from the discussions

54. *Nigeria*   1934
   i. The Dioceses of Lagos and of the Niger (Anglican Province of West Africa)
   ii. The Methodist Church of Nigeria
   iii. The Church of Biafra (Presbyterian)

   Originally the negotiations affected only Eastern Nigeria; in 1947 a Church Union Conference for the whole country was set up

55. *The United States of America*   1936
   i. The Congregational Christian Churches
   ii. The Evangelical and Reformed Church

   With a view to forming THE UNITED CHURCH OF CHRIST

56. *Ceylon (Lanka)*   1940
   i. The Church of India, Pakistan, Burma, and Ceylon (Dioceses of Colombo and Kurunagala)
   ii. The Methodist Church in Ceylon
   iii. The Presbyterian Churches in Ceylon
   iv. The Baptist Churches in Ceylon
   v. The Jaffna Diocese of the Church of South India

   With a view to forming THE CHURCH OF LANKA

   A complete Scheme of Union was set forth in 1947

57. *The United States of America*   1949
   i. The Congregational Christian Churches
   ii. The Disciples of Christ
   iii. The Evangelical and Reformed Church

iv. The International Council of Community Churches
v. The Methodist Church
vi. The African Methodist Episcopal Church
vii. The African Methodist Episcopal Zion Church
viii. The Coloured Methodist Episcopal Church
ix. The Presbyterian Church in the United States of America
x. The Presbyterian Church in the United States
xi. The Protestant Episcopal Church (observing)

What began as the "Greenwich Conversations" has developed so far in the direction of a plan for organic union as to deserve inclusion in this list, rather than in list VI.

58. *The United States of America*   1949
i. The Evangelical Lutheran Church of America
ii. The American Lutheran Church
iii. The United Evangelical Lutheran Church
iv. The Augustana Evangelical Lutheran Church
v. The Lutheran Free Church
With a view to organic union

59. *Madagascar*   1949
i. The London Missionary Society
ii. La Société des Missions Évangéliques de Paris
iii. The Friends Foreign Missionary Association
With a view to organic union

60. *The United States of America*   1949
i. The Methodist Church
ii. The Protestant Episcopal Church
With a view to intercommunion and possibly organic union

The first report of the Commissions on Unity of the two Churches was issued in April 1952.

61. *Pakistan*   1950
i. The Church of India, Pakistan, Burma, and Ceylon (Diocese of Lahore)
ii. The Methodist Church in Southern Asia
iii. The United Church of Northern India (Lahore and Sialkot Councils)
iv. The United Presbyterian Church
v. The Associate Reformed Presbyterian Church

Owing to the political difficulties between India and Pakistan, separate negotiations have been initiated

62. *The United States of America*   1950
i. The American Lutheran Church
ii. The Lutheran Church—Missouri Synod

A "Common Confession of Faith" was submitted to the Churches in 1950

63. *The United States of America*   1952
i. The Presbyterian Church in the United States of America
ii. The Presbyterian Church in the United States
iii. The United Presbyterian Church of North America
With a view to organic union

64. *The United States of America*   1952
i. The United Lutheran Church in America
ii. The Danish Evangelical Lutheran Church of America
With a view to "affiliation"

VI. NEGOTIATIONS FOR CLOSER FELLOWSHIP NOT INVOLVING ORGANIC UNION

65. *Australia*   1937
i. The Church of England in Australia and Tasmania
ii. The Congregational Union of Australia

iii. The Methodist Church in Australia
iv. The Presbyterian Church of Australia

Plan for a unification of ministries without corporate union

66. *Canada*   1946
   i. The United Church of Canada
   ii. The Church of England in Canada

A scheme proposing measures for the unification of the ministries of the two Churches was issued in 1946

VII. CONVERSATIONS BETWEEN REPRESENTATIVES OF CHURCHES, WITH A VIEW TO BETTER UNDERSTANDING OR MUTUAL RECOGNITION

67. *Orthodox Relationships*   1920
   i. The Holy Orthodox Churches
   ii. The Church of England and other Anglican Churches
   iii. The Old Catholic Churches

68. *The Malines Conversations*   1921
   i. Members of the Church of Rome
   ii. Members of the Church of England

Conversations abandoned in 1925

69. *Great Britain*   1930
   i. The Church of England
   ii. The Moravian Church in England

In 1937 it was decided by representatives of both Churches that the conversations should be discontinued

70. *Australia*   1931
   i. Anglicans
   ii. Methodists

   With a view to fuller understanding and agreement

A report was published in 1947, but no formal plan of union between the Churches was proposed

71. *Ireland*   1937
   i. The Presbyterian Church in Ireland
   ii. The Methodist Church in Ireland

   With a view to better mutual understanding and possibly to organic union

Conversations have revealed a wide range of agreement, but no plan for organic union is yet before the Churches

72. *Great Britain*   1947
   i. Members of the Church of England appointed by the Archbishop of Canterbury
   ii. Representatives of the Free Churches in England

A joint report, *Church Relations in England*, published 1950

73. *Great Britain*   1947
   i. Members of the Church of England appointed by the Archbishop of Canterbury
   ii. Representatives of the Church of Scotland
   iii. The Episcopal Church in Scotland (observing)
   iv. The Presbyterian Church of England (observing)

A joint report, *Relations between the Church of England and the Church of Scotland*, published 1951

74. *Australia*   1950
   i. The United Evangelical Lutheran Church of Australia
   ii. The Evangelical Lutheran Church of Australia

   With a view to altar and pulpit fellowship, and possibly to organic union

VIII. NEGOTIATIONS TEMPORARILY OR PERMANENTLY ABANDONED

75. *The United States of America*   1907
   i. The Presbyterian Church in the United States of America

   ii. The United Presbyterian Church of North America

1931, Proposed Basis of Union; abandoned in 1935

76. *East Africa (The Kikuyu Proposals)*
                                1910
    i. The Church of England (Dioceses of Uganda and Mombasa)
   ii. The Church of Scotland Mission
  iii. The United Methodist Mission
   iv. The Africa Inland Mission (interdenominational)

1932, Proposed Basis for Church Union in East Africa ; 1943, the Christian Council of Kenya was formed, without a plan for Church union

77. *The United States of America*   1917
    i. The Congregational Churches
   ii. The Disciples of Christ

No action taken by the Churches

78. *The United States of America*   1918
    "The Philadelphia Plan"
Nineteen denominations launched ·the plan for formation of the "United Churches of Christ in America"; but, after promising beginnings, the plan was abandoned in the early 1920's.

79. *The United States of America*   1919
    i. The Congregational Churches
   ii. The Protestant Episcopal Church

A Canon was adopted under which a minister of a non-episcopal Church might receive episcopal ordination and continue to serve as a minister in his own Church. Two cases of episcopal ordination under the terms of this Canon are on record.

80. *Australia*   1920
    i. The Presbyterian Church of Australia
   ii. The Methodist Church of Australia
  iii. The Congregational Union of Australia
   iv. The Church of England in Australia and Tasmania

1927, Anglicans withdrew
1951, Presbyterians rejected the proposed Scheme of Union; negotiations between the Methodists and the Congregationalists alone continue

81. *The United States of America*   1925
    i. The Methodist Episcopal Church
   ii. The Presbyterian Church in the United States of America

Negotiations were given up in 1930 since both Churches were fully occupied in intra-confessional negotiations for union

82. *The United States of America*   1925
    i. The Presbyterian Church in the United States of America
   ii. The Reformed Church in America

Direct negotiations were brought to an end by a vote of the General Synod of the Reformed Church in 1931

83. *The United States of America*   1926
    i. The Presbyterian Church in the United States
   ii. The Associate Reformed Presbyterian Synod

Negotiations were brought to an end in 1934 by an adverse vote of the Associate Reformed Synod

84. *The United States of America*   1927
    i. The African Methodist Episcopal Church
   ii. The African Methodist Episcopal Zion Church

Negotiations were abandoned in 1931 owing to a lack of real readiness on either side for union

85. *The United States of America*   1928
    i. The Evangelical Synod of North America
   ii. The Church of the United Brethren in Christ
  iii. The Reformed Church in the United States

Negotiations were abandoned in 1931 because of other negotiations for union in which these Churches were engaged

86. *The United States of America*   1929
    i. The Presbyterian Church in the United States of America
   ii. The Presbyterian Church in the United States

iii. The United Presbyterian Church of North America

iv. The Reformed Church in America (Dutch)

v. The Reformed Church in the United States (observing)

1931, Plan of Union rejected by the Presbyterian Church in the U.S.; the Plan was not followed up by the other bodies

87. *Ireland* 1931

i. The Church of Ireland

ii. The Presbyterian Church in Ireland

Negotiations were abandoned by mutual consent in 1934, as no agreement was in sight

88. *The United States of America* 1937

i. The Protestant Episcopal Church

ii. The Presbyterian Church in the United States of America

1946, action by the Protestant Episcopal Church led to a suspension of the negotiations which have not been re-opened

89. *The United States of America* 1937

i. The Protestant Episcopal Church

ii. The Reformed Episcopal Church

Negotiations suspended in 1943

90. *Australia* 1941

i. The Baptist Churches

ii. The Churches of Christ

91. *New Zealand* 1941

i. The Presbyterian Church of New Zealand

ii. The Methodist Church of New Zealand

iii. The Congregational Union of New Zealand

Negotiations temporarily suspended in 1949

CHAPTER 11

MOVEMENTS FOR INTERNATIONAL FRIENDSHIP AND LIFE AND WORK
1910–1925

by

NILS KARLSTRÖM

1. INTRODUCTION[1]

When the first world war broke out in 1914, international co-operation among Christians had already made considerable progress. A measure of world-wide fellowship had been achieved between groups belonging to different countries and confessions, and several international organizations with varied aims had come into existence. Our special interest lies in those efforts towards co-operation, international and interdenominational, in the fields of Christian social action and international problems, which prepared the way for the World Alliance for Promoting International Friendship through the Churches, and later for the Life and Work movement.

The Christian social action which developed in the 19th century—e.g. ministries of service, the "Home Missions",[2] and Settlements—broke through both denominational and national barriers. In 1861 an international organization for Evangelical Deaconess Training Institutions, both Lutheran and Reformed, grew out of Theodor Fliedner's Institute at Kaiserswerth. The Bethel Institutions at Bielefeld founded by Friedrich von Bodelschwingh—homes for epileptics, work colonies for the unemployed, etc.—inspired similar organizations in other countries. J. H. Wichern, the founder of the *Innere Mission* and of ministries of service for men, believed that such Christian and charitable activities provided "one of the most powerful evidences for the true catholicity of the Church", and was therefore one of the spheres in which the unity of the Church should first be achieved.[3] The Settlement movement, started in England in the 1880's, spread to other lands. Deeply impressed by the Toynbee Hall Settlement in Whitechapel, the young German pastor Friedrich Siegmund-Schultze started a Settlement in East Berlin in 1911. This became a centre for social and international co-operation, of the highest importance in relation to the efforts towards mutual understanding during the first world war.[4]

Gradually, however, it came to be realized that social problems could never be solved through charitable activities alone, however necessary and efficient these might be. The root causes of social evils must be discovered and dealt with. Force was lent to these ideas by contemporary socialist criticism of existing society. Many Christians, though rejecting the Marxist world-view and its hostility to Christianity, nevertheless recognized that much of the socialist criticism was justified, and sought to awaken public opinion in favour of social reform carried out in a Christian spirit. Such efforts were stimulated by similar endeavours in the Roman Catholic Church.

In England the efforts initiated in the 1840's by the Christian Socialists took form in 1889 in the Christian Social Union, an association of Anglicans which

---

[1] Dean Karlström's Swedish text had unfortunately to be reduced by about one-third in length. Owing to ill-health, Dean Karlström was unable to revise the English text in detail, and for this in its final form the editorial staff is responsible.

[2] The German term *Innere Mission* covers a greater range of charitable, social, and evangelistic activities than is generally covered by the English term "Home Missions". See Chap. vii, p. 314, and Glossary.

[3] Address on the *Innere Mission* at the Church Assembly at Stuttgart, 1857, in which Wichern referred to an earlier discussion on "*Evangelische Katholicität*". See M. Gerhardt, *Johann Hinrich Wichern*, 1932, p. 23.

[4] F. Siegmund-Schultze, "Toynbee Hall", in *Die Eiche*, 1914, p. 85.

aimed at examining Christian principles in their application to modern social and economic conditions, and at demonstrating that Christianity is a power for social righteousness. Later, Social Service Unions were started by the English Free Churches. In 1911 representatives of these different unions founded the Interdenominational Social Service Council,[1] the bodies represented ranging from Roman Catholics to Unitarians. The Council held a remarkable series of annual conferences at Swanwick where, though their services of worship were held separately, men and women of different Churches were brought into the closest Christian fellowship and co-operation. The Council drew up a common Christian social programme, "A Statement of Social Principles".[2] Such efforts, renewed after the first world war, resulted in the so-called Copec Conference (Conference on Christian Politics, Economics, and Citizenship) in 1924, the importance of which for Life and Work will be considered later in this chapter.

In Germany Adolf Stoecker, Adolf von Harnack, and others, uniting various ecclesiastical and theological tendencies, founded in 1890 the *Evangelisch-Sozialer Kongress* with a programme resembling that of the Christian Social Union in England. When, however, the younger party in the *Kongress*, led by Friedrich Naumann, took an increasingly radical direction both politically and theologically, Stoecker in 1896 withdrew and founded the *Freie Kirchlich-Soziale Konferenz*. In 1896, at a conference in Erfurt, Naumann founded a new political party, the *National-Sozialer Verein*, intended to promote both national strength and social reform. Naumann exercised a widespread influence outside Germany. Nathan Söderblom, then a young Swedish pastor in Paris, was present at the Erfurt Conference. In his articles on the Conference, Söderblom described Christian social movements as a powerful factor making for unity amongst the Protestant Churches, and thus prophetically connected Christian social endeavour with the idea of Christian unity.[3]

In France Tommy Fallot is regarded by the Christian social movement as its real founder. Two of his disciples, Élie Gounelle and Wilfred Monod, were destined to become leading personalities in Life and Work. In many Protestant parishes, fellowships pledged to unselfish service were joined by both orthodox and liberals. Champions of social Christianity declared that where unity in the will to do good was already present, dogmatic differences had little significance. The *Association protestante pour l'étude pratique des questions sociales*, founded in 1887 and finding expression in the review later to be known as *Le Christianisme Social*, became the focus of the Christian concern for social righteousness.

In Switzerland the Christian social movement was characterized by serious efforts to make contacts with the socialist movement. According to its spokesmen, Hermann Kutter and Leonhard Ragaz, the labour movement's demand for a reconstruction of the economic order was essentially a Christian demand. They sharply criticized the Churches for neglecting the social principles of the Gospel.

In the United States a similar movement began to attract notice at the turn of the century. "The Social Gospel" became the commonly accepted name for an important trend in American church life, associated with such names as Walter Rauschenbusch, Francis G. Peabody, and Shailer Mathews. Starting from the view that the Kingdom of God is something to be realized in this world order,

---

[1] See Chap. vii, pp. 331 f.
[2] Lucy Gardner, "The Origin of the Conference", in *C.O.P.E.C. Conference Handbook, Birmingham, 1924*, pp. 109 f.
[3] From 1887 onwards, Christian social activity in Germany was able to express itself regularly in the columns of a periodical, *Die Christliche Welt*, with Professor Martin Rade as editor.

these men insisted that the whole life of society must be leavened by the spirit of Christianity. The most significant of an "epidemic" of American church pronouncements on Christian social principles was the declaration adopted by the Federal Council of the Churches of Christ in America at its constituent meeting in 1908, "The Social Creed of the Churches". The minimum programme laid down in this "credo" did much to form American church opinion on social matters.

In the years before the war international Christian co-operation on social questions was already under way, France taking the lead. Representatives from Christian social movements were invited by the French Association to a conference held at Besançon in 1910. There La Fédération Internationale des Chrétiens Sociaux[1] was launched by delegates from France, Switzerland, England, Germany, Belgium, and Italy. The new association adopted a programme taking a definite stand on a number of social questions. This was criticized, especially by the Germans, who considered it a mistake at the same time to lay down Christian principles and to tie the movement to a particular programme of action.[2]

The Fédération Internationale planned another conference to be held in September 1914 in Basle with wider international representation. Christianity and world peace was one subject proposed for discussion. But by September 1914 world peace had already been shattered. The conference was never held.

The sense of the responsibility of Christians for world peace had led also to more direct attempts to unite Christians in service to the cause of peace. Those efforts were intensified in the last decade before the first world war. It was increasingly felt that this was a task which could not be the concern only of men active in political life. The Churches and their leaders also were called to work for the application of Christian principles to international relations, for the promotion of mutual understanding between nations, for the development and the strengthening of international law. In this undertaking Christians of different countries and confessions ought to advance on a common front.

Such ideas resulted in a united Christian approach to the second Hague Conference in 1907. On the initiative of British Christian friends of peace, a memorandum was drawn up giving expression to the Christian conviction that arbitration should be used as the means of settling conflicts between the nations. Among those who signed the memorandum were Church leaders both in Europe and in America, and a special deputation presented it to the Hague Conference.[3]

The Chairman of this deputation was J. Allen Baker, M.P.[4] Himself a Quaker of strong convictions, Baker worked zealously for a stronger Christian contribution to peace and international collaboration. In the first place he regarded it as essential to persuade the English and German Churches to use their weight to bring about better relationships between England and Germany. From the beginning of the 20th century tension between the two countries had been growing. Lovers of peace worked hard to reconcile differences and to overcome difficulties. For instance, in 1905, at the World Peace Conference at Lucerne, steps were taken which led to the formation of committees of conciliation both in England and Germany.

[1] G. Kopp, "Der erste Internationale Evangelisch-Soziale Kongress in Besançon," in Die Christliche Welt, 1910, pp. 679 ff.

[2] R. Liechtenhan, "Der Internationale Kongress für soziales Christentum in Basel, 27–30 September 1914", in Die Christliche Welt, 1914, p. 723.

[3] The Churches and International Friendship, Movements Leading up to Conferences at Constance and Liége, August 1914.

[4] Elizabeth B. Baker and P. J. Noel Baker, J. Allen Baker, London, 1927.

Baker had for a long time pondered the possibility of the exchange of visits on a large scale between English and German churchmen. At the Hague Conference he was able to arouse the interest of one of the German leaders, Baron Eduard de Neufville. After their return to their own countries, both these peacemakers succeeded in securing the support of leading men in both Church and State. On the invitation of an English interconfessional committee, which included Roman Catholic members, about 130 German churchmen visited England in the summer of 1908.[1] These represented all the main confessions—the Evangelical State Churches, the Free Churches, and the Roman Catholic Church; among them were a number of the official leaders of these Churches. The programme included fellowship in worship, Protestants and Roman Catholics holding their services separately, and visits to religious, cultural, and civic institutions, as well as various social engagements. During the following summer more than a hundred English churchmen were invited to pay a similar visit to Germany.[2]

As a result of the success of these visits, in April 1910 an organization was created with the somewhat cumbrous title The Associated Councils of Churches in the British and German Empires for Fostering Friendly Relations between the Two Peoples. These Councils were organized as national associations with individual membership, and developed a widely representative character with a number of official Church leaders at their head. In England the work was directed by an executive committee with J. Allen Baker as Chairman, and Willoughby Dickinson, a lawyer who was also a Member of Parliament, as Secretary. In July 1911 a quarterly, *The Peacemaker*, was started with J. H. Rushbrooke, a Baptist, as editor. Director F. A. Spiecker, a much trusted layman with wide experience in the *Innere Mission* and in support of missions overseas, was appointed President of the German Council and Chairman of its executive committee. Friedrich Siegmund-Schultze became Secretary both of the Council and the executive committee, and was also editor of the German Council's quarterly *Die Eiche*, founded in 1913. Both Councils regarded it as their task—to quote Archbishop Davidson of Canterbury, speaking at the British Council's annual meeting in May 1914—to create "the right atmosphere" for dealing with the relations between the two great powers.[3]

In the spring of 1914 a hopeful atmosphere still prevailed in circles interested in the Anglo-German Church movement. In the address already quoted Archbishop Davidson declared himself convinced that in the situation then obtaining the existence of the two Councils was no longer absolutely necessary; they stood for something which had already been practically secured.[4] It is significant that a man holding such high office should have been so decidedly optimistic only a few months before the outbreak of war. It is evident—and other declarations made by leading churchmen bear this out—that the prevailing atmosphere even in Christian circles was one of evolutionary optimism.

Before the catastrophe of August 1914, however, the Anglo-German Church Councils had succeeded in making contact with peace-loving groups in a number of other countries, and in starting with them an international Christian organization. Allen Baker had already in 1908 suggested the holding of a world

---

[1] See report of the British Council in German and English, *Der Friede und die Kirchen—Peace and the Churches*, 1909, and Chap. vii, p. 336.

[2] See report of the German Committee, *Friendly Relations between Great Britain and Germany*, 1910.

[3] *The Peacemaker*, Vol. II, June 1914, p. 5.   [4] Ibid., pp. 5 f.

conference of the Churches on the question of peace. He claimed that the time was ripe for the creation, at such a conference, of a world association for international co-operation through the Churches.[1] During a journey to the United States in the spring of 1909 Baker tried to interest American friends of peace in his project. A united Christian contribution to efforts on behalf of peace had been one of the items on the programme when the Federal Council was founded in 1908.[2] The leaders of the Council were now won over to the European churchmen's plans for international action. On behalf of the Federal Council Dr Charles S. Macfarland visited both London and Berlin in the summer of 1911 and had consultations there with the leaders of the Anglo-German Councils. In the following year he was called to the general secretaryship of the Federal Council, and played, in the following decades, an important rôle in work for closer understanding between the Churches. In February 1914 the industrial magnate Andrew Carnegie offered a gift of two million dollars for the peace work of the Churches, to be administered by a foundation, the Church Peace Union, specially created for the purpose and comprising representatives of the Protestant, Roman Catholic, and Jewish bodies. The Secretary of the new foundation was one of the leaders of the Federal Council, Dr Frederick Lynch, a prominent figure in the ecumenical movement during the war years.[3]

From yet another quarter came the idea of an international peace congress. In January 1914, on the suggestion of the National Evangelical Reformed Church of the Canton of Vaud, the Conference of the Swiss Reformed Churches invited the European Churches to be represented at a conference to be held during the course of the year in Berne. The purpose of the conference was a discussion on ways and means by which the Churches could contribute more effectively to the promotion of righteousness and peace among the nations, to the reduction of armaments, and consequently of the danger of war.[4] The driving force in this undertaking was Professor Louis Emery of Lausanne. But, as the majority of answers were negative, the proposed conference was postponed.

The action of the Swiss Churches had, however, awakened the interest both of the Anglo-German Councils and of church circles in the United States interested in the problem of peace. The various groups entered into contact with one another, and in London, in 1914, in connection with the annual meeting of the British Associated Council, they decided to take united action; a number of representatives of the more important Protestant Churches in Europe and America were to be invited to a conference to be held at Constance on 3 and 4 August 1914, in order to examine the contribution which the Churches could make to friendly relationships among the nations. Contact had been made with a Roman Catholic peace organization founded in June 1911, *La Ligue internationale des Catholiques pour la Paix*, which had decided to convene a conference at Liége, to be presided over by Cardinal Mercier, on 10 and 11 August 1914. A grant from the Church Peace Union was to make these conferences financially possible.

[1] *Der Friede und die Kirchen*, 1909, p. 9.
[2] See C. S. Macfarland, *The Churches of Christ in America and International Peace*, 1914, and *The Churches and International Relations*, 1917, i–iv.
[3] Frederick Lynch, *Personal Recollections of Andrew Carnegie*, 1920, pp. 154 ff.
[4] See the appeal, *An die führenden Vertreter der Kirchen*, sent out in December 1914 with a view to the formation of a Swiss National Council of the World Alliance, published in *Die Eiche*, 1916, pp. 71 ff.

In general, invitations to the Constance Conference were directed to individuals,[1] as the experience of the Swiss had shown that the sending of invitations to official Church bodies involved endless delays, and that it was to be feared that many denominations would decline the invitation. It was only in the United States that official representatives of the Churches were appointed by the Federal Council. Thus the new international movement for mutual understanding lacked the semi-official character of the Anglo-German Church Councils. The German Church authorities on the whole took a critical attitude towards the Constance Conference. As long as nothing more was involved than specialized undertakings with limited horizons, such as the Anglo-German Church movement for mutual understanding, these authorities had been favourably disposed. But they feared that at an international Christian peace conference attention might be focused on awkward problems in a manner the consequences of which could not be readily foreseen, and that the German delegates might find themselves in embarrassing situations.

About 150 delegates, representing thirteen countries, were expected. But at the end of July the political situation in Europe reached a point of disastrous tension. Some countries were already mobilizing; railway traffic was disorganized by movements of troops; in some cases frontiers were already closed. Only half the expected delegates reached Constance after more or less adventurous journeys.[2]

The Conference was due to open on Monday, 3 August. But catastrophe was rapidly approaching. On 1 August Germany declared war on Russia; France fulfilled her treaty obligations by mobilizing in turn. As the majority of the delegates who were likely to reach Constance had already arrived, the Conference opened on Sunday morning, 2 August, with J. Allen Baker as Chairman. It was not a time for debates and deliberations. After a few short reports the delegates united in prayer for Europe in the terrible situation by which it was confronted. An American, a German, an Englishman, a Frenchman, and a Swiss prayed in turn, each using his own language but all in one and the same spirit. The Conference then decided to send a telegraphic appeal to the heads of States and the prime ministers of all the European countries, and also to the President of the United States "to avert a war between millions of men, among whom friendship and common interests had been steadily growing, and thereby to save Christian civilization from disaster and to assert the power of the Christian spirit in human affairs".

In the course of Sunday two more sessions were held. But at the evening meeting a message was received from the German authorities to the effect that the last opportunity for a safe and unbroken journey through Germany would be provided by a train leaving on Monday morning. As hotels and banks were already closing, it was a case of yielding to *force majeure*.

Before the delegates parted, they adopted four resolutions directed towards continued activity in the spirit of the Conference. It was affirmed that it was the collective and inescapable duty of the Churches to use their influence with the nations, their representatives, and their governments, to bring about friendly international relationships. National committees should be established in order to enlist the Churches "in their corporate capacity" in the cause of mutual understanding. A central body to maintain co-operation between the national committees must be established. To carry out these resolutions the Conference elected

---

[1] *The Churches and International Friendship, Report of Conference held at Constance, 1914.*
[2] Frederick Lynch, *Through Europe on the Eve of War*, 1914.

a Committee of fifteen members with power to co-opt others. The choice of a name for the new organization and certain technical problems were referred to this International Committee. The Conference itself adjourned, intending to meet later in London or wherever it might prove possible to gather the largest number of delegates.

On Monday morning, 3 August, the delegates left Constance. Most of them had to travel via Cologne to the Dutch frontier, through swarming masses of German troops in movement—it was the very day on which Germany declared war on France. "A peace congress athwart a war-front on the very day on which war breaks out . . . is in truth something unique!" [1] All went well. The passengers were under the special protection of the German authorities, and Siegmund-Schultze accompanied them as far as Cologne. On 5 August the Constance delegates who had reached London met for a short final gathering. The question of a message from the Conference was left to the International Committee. In the discussion it was emphasized that it was not the Christian idea of peace and reconciliation which had broken down, but the whole system which had tried to build security on an ever-intensified race of armaments. But there was a conviction that after the war a time would come when men would realize with increasing clearness the significance of moral forces even in international relationships. It was on this note of hope that the Constance Conference ended.

At the meeting in London those members of the International Committee who were present took some necessary decisions regarding the future of the organization. Allen Baker was chosen as Chairman, W. P. Merrill, an American, as Vice-Chairman, and Dickinson, Emery, Lynch, Siegmund-Schultze, and Jacques Dumas, a Frenchman, as co-ordinate Secretaries, Dickinson and Lynch serving also as executive secretaries. The International Committee was enlarged to sixty members, the new members to be nominated by the national committees which, it was hoped, would be established in various countries. The name of the association was now settled: The World Alliance of Churches for Promoting International Friendship. Only in a few countries did the association secure such recognition by the Churches as could justify such a title, and at the Berne Conference of 1915 the name of the Alliance was changed to correspond more exactly with its character—the World Alliance for Promoting International Friendship through the Churches.

The outbreak of war wrecked the Constance Conference; the Roman Catholic conference was never held at all. Nevertheless, at the eleventh hour Christians had formed an international association for peace which was to be a pioneer in modern ecumenical efforts to solve international problems.

2. CHRISTIAN EFFORTS TOWARDS INTERNATIONAL UNDERSTANDING

The outbreak of the world war was a disaster to the cause of Christian co-operation in international affairs. The war made communication between the various Christian countries difficult, if not impossible; far worse, it destroyed to a large extent their inner spiritual fellowship. On both sides Churches and their leaders threw themselves into the conflict. The manifestos exchanged at the beginning of the war by leading churchmen of the chief belligerent powers[2]

---

[1] Statement by Eivind Berggrav, later Bishop of Oslo.

[2] (1) *An die evangelischen Christen im Auslande;* (2) *The European War: Reply to the Appeal of German Theologians;* (3) *Réponse à l'appel allemand aux chrétiens évangéliques de l'étranger.*

are evidence of the extent to which distrust and disunion had sprung up even among those who in pre-war years had been active in Christian work for mutual understanding. In both warring camps men were firmly convinced that they were fighting in a just cause. The growing unity of Christendom was rent asunder. Yet fellowship was not wholly destroyed. Some points of contact still remained; these became growing points for new co-operative activities, some of which were of cardinal importance in the development of the movement later to be known as Life and Work.

The World Alliance could not well have been started under more unfavourable auspices. But its leaders did not allow themselves to be disheartened; the war had made mutual understanding among Christians even more necessary than before. In spite of the difficulties caused by the war, the International Committee succeeded in bringing the Alliance into existence in several countries, even if only in a small way, and in maintaining contact between the several national groups. Such progress as was made was due in the first place to the efforts of Dr Benjamin F. Battin, Professor of German at Swarthmore College, Pennsylvania, who was the Alliance's international organizer during the war and carried out a most important work of liaison. Baker also, up to the time of his death in July 1918, undertook numerous journeys on behalf of the World Alliance, both to European countries and to the United States, even after the intensification of submarine warfare had made journeys by sea extremely perilous.[1]

It is remarkable that national committees of the World Alliance were formed even in belligerent countries, and first of all in England and Germany. In these cases the World Alliance was heir to the Anglo-German Church Councils, although the new groups never received such semi-official recognition as had been accorded to their predecessors.

Periodicals preserved their continuity. The British review, *The Peacemaker*, was replaced at the beginning of 1915 by *Goodwill*, Rushbrooke continuing to serve as editor. In Germany Siegmund-Schultze continued to produce *Die Eiche*, which during the war published mainly documents dealing with mutual understanding through the Churches. The task was arduous. A number of blanks in *Die Eiche* for July 1915 are evidence of the difficulties caused by the German censorship; part of Siegmund-Schultze's comments on material dealing with the treatment of prisoners of war and interned civilians in England and Germany had simply been suppressed. In December 1914 Professor Adolf Deissmann issued the first of his *Evangelische Wochenbriefe*. These letters, which were sent to addressees in the United States, Britain, and other European countries, were intended primarily as a means of breaking through the spiritual isolation with which Germany was threatened in consequence of the blockade. Deissmann's aim was to keep neutral countries informed of the German standpoint on current questions, above all on the question of the Churches and the war. But his letters had also an ecumenical purpose—to strengthen the gravely imperilled sense of Christian fellowship.

All these periodicals pleaded for sobriety, justice, and Christian service as against the hysterical passions of war. They were also significant factors in the development of Life and Work, and have proved invaluable as source material concerning Christian work for mutual understanding and unity both during and after the war.

[1] *Annual Report of the Federal Council*, 1914, pp. 35 ff.

When the International Committee of the World Alliance assembled in August 1915 at Berne, the Alliance could reckon on more or less firmly organized national groups in eight countries, in addition to Britain and Germany, viz. France, Italy, the United States, Holland, Switzerland, Denmark, Norway, and Sweden. At the Berne Conference, held in the midst of the storms of war, representatives met not only from a number of neutral states but also from three of the belligerent countries—Britain, Germany, and Italy. This was the only Protestant Christian conference during the war which was attended by delegates from both the warring camps. Discussions were carried on in a spirit of mutual trust and fellowship. "The impression made by the Christian consideration and tact with which 'enemies' met, bore themselves, and talked, can never be forgotten by a neutral delegate", wrote one of the Swedish participants, Knut B. Westman [1] some years later.

At Berne the name of the World Alliance and its constitution were definitely determined. It had become clear that the name chosen in August 1914 did not closely correspond to the character of the Alliance. Its national committees had in most cases been built up by individuals interested in the aim of the association, who formed themselves into a committee and gradually co-opted new members. The Alliance represented not so much Churches as individual churchmen. On the other hand, the Alliance was most anxious that the Churches themselves should share in the work of promoting mutual understanding. Therefore the new name chosen by the International Committee was The World Alliance for Promoting International Friendship through the Churches.[2] In accordance with the resolutions of the Constance Conference, a constitution was drawn up and later approved by the national committees.

Relief for war victims was one of the first tasks of the World Alliance. *Caritas inter arma* became the motto of an extensive service of aid to interned civilians and to prisoners of war. Such assistance given to citizens of enemy countries was unpopular in the countries at war and at first met with a good deal of opposition. But later on it won the confidence of ever wider circles, and was instrumental in the establishment of friendly relations between individuals in the countries estranged from one another. This service kept the idea of Christian unity alive, and paved the way for direct co-operative action.

One of the main concerns of the World Alliance committees was the stabilization and development of international law after the war. An effective organization for the settlement of international disputes was indispensable, if similar disasters were to be avoided in the future. The ancient idea of a league of nations, as the safeguard and instrument of international justice, was being revived during the war years. Appeals made by a number of the national committees of the World Alliance bear witness to a rising tide of Christian public opinion in favour of such a league.

In December 1914 the Fellowship of Reconciliation was founded in Britain by a group who saw in a pacifist direction the solution of problems raised for Christians by the war. It spread to other lands, and in October 1919 the International Fellowship of Reconciliation was organized. The I.F.O.R. has branches in twenty different countries: it has always been ecumenical in its effects, and

---

[1] Later Professor of Church History and Missions at the University of Uppsala, and Vice-Chairman of the International Missionary Council.
[2] In German, *Weltbund für internationale Freundschaftsarbeit der Kirchen*; in French, *Alliance universelle pour l'amitié internationale par les Églises.*

very successful in bringing Roman Catholics into co-operation with the members of other Churches.[1]

Till the spring of 1917 the United States succeeded in remaining neutral, but the problems arising from the war situation engaged the close attention of American churchmen, particularly of the leaders in the Federal Council of Churches.

Until the entry of the United States into the war the Federal Council stood firmly for strict American neutrality, supported all plans for American mediation between the warring powers and for the establishment of firmer principles of international justice after the war, and set in motion an extensive programme for the relief of those who had suffered. Proposals for a visit to Europe by an American delegation were dropped, as it was felt that in the then prevailing atmosphere such a visit would serve no useful purpose, but part of the aim in view was effected through a personal visit of Dr Macfarland, then General Secretary of the Federal Council, to Europe in December 1915.

One of the problems discussed by Macfarland with European churchmen was that of an international Christian conference in connection with the negotiations for peace at the conclusion of the war; Macfarland held that, when the political powers met to settle the terms of peace and to lay the foundations for a new international order, the Churches also should meet and should make their voice heard on the moral aspects of the political problem. He won for his project the support of many of the groups with which he came into touch during his European tour. Some were prepared to support another of Macfarland's plans—that even before the war ended a representative conference of Church leaders, with participants from both belligerent and neutral countries, might be convened. The first project was later approved both by the American World Alliance Committee at its first national conference in April 1916, and by the Federal Council's Quadrennial Meeting in December of the same year. The second idea, that of an international Christian conference during the war, attracted wide attention, as a result of initiatives with which we shall later be concerned.

In December 1916 came the first official moves in favour of peace; on the one hand the overtures made by the Central Powers on 12 December concerning negotiations with a view to peace; on the other, President Wilson's Note of 18 December inviting the belligerents to declare their views as to terms of peace, and as to measures to be taken in order to prevent future armed conflicts.

Macfarland, who had been in touch through the German Ambassador in Washington with political leaders in Germany, notified Deissmann and Siegmund-Schultze of his efforts, and urged them to make contact with the German Ministry of Foreign Affairs and the official leadership of the Churches.[2] No answer to these approaches was ever received. After the war it became known that Macfarland's cables had never reached those to whom they were addressed. Both messages had been lying in the Foreign Office in Berlin; the German Ministry for Foreign Affairs had apparently thought it inadvisable to let

---

[1] See Lilian Stevenson, *Towards a Christian International: the Story of the International Fellowship of Reconciliation*, London, 1941.

[2] See the appeal which about seventy American churchmen sent out on 1 January 1917, *A Plea for a Lasting Peace*, which in its turn called forth a message from about 700 churchmen representing the Federal Council, World Alliance, and Church Peace Union: *The Peace Negotiations of the Nations—Suggestions for Adequate Guarantees for Lasting Peace*.

leading German churchmen hear of the indirect criticism of German policy implied in Macfarland's appeal.

In the American Churches, President Wilson's policy met with a mixed reception. It was strongly supported by leading men within such national organizations as the Federal Council, the Church Peace Union, and the World Alliance. But there were also influential Christian circles which insistently issued warnings as to the danger of promoting "a premature peace in Europe"; peace must imply victory for the principles of truth and righteousness—otherwise it could only sow the seeds of new catastrophes.[1]

Tension between the United States and Germany continually increased. When, on 1 February 1917, the German Government proclaimed unlimited submarine warfare, even President Wilson felt that the limit of patience had been reached. On 3 February diplomatic relationships were broken off and, on 6 April, the United States declared war on Germany. Almost all American churchmen, even those who had earlier insisted on strict neutrality, now felt that their Government had taken the only course consistent with honour and Christian principle.

Further contacts between the American Churches and the Churches of the Central Powers, even for purposes of relief, became impossible. Christian work for mutual understanding thus became the responsibility of the countries which still remained neutral, and in particular of the Scandinavian nations.[2]

Even during the first years of the war significant contributions had been made by the Scandinavian countries to the cause of mutual understanding. In May 1914 Nathan Söderblom had been elected Archbishop of Uppsala. Immediately after the outbreak of war he had endeavoured to persuade Church leaders in various countries to join in an appeal "for peace and Christian fellowship". Söderblom felt keenly the responsibility laid on the Churches, especially in countries which had been spared the catastrophe of war. The Church had been unable to prevail against the spirit of hate and division. Söderblom's action was prompted by his anguish at the weakness of the Church and at the devastation caused by the war.

The appeal was in the nature of a confession of faith in the universal supranational Church. It began with words which later became classic in the ecumenical movement: "The war is causing untold distress. Christ's body, the Church, suffers and mourns. Mankind in its need cries out: O Lord, how long?" All political considerations must be excluded. Judgement on the causes of war must be left to a later verdict of history. Two things, however, must, in the circumstances of the day, be proclaimed by the Church; it must call "for peace and for Christian fellowship"—the phrase used in the title of the appeal.[3]

Söderblom did not expect that a Christian appeal for peace, even if it were supported by leading churchmen of different nations, would have discernible effects on the progress of the war: he had far too clear a sense of political realities. But he was convinced that it was nevertheless the urgent duty of the Church's servants to keep the idea of peace alive among the nations and their

[1] R. H. Abrams, *Preachers Present Arms*, 1933, is a well-documented, but strongly pacifist, statement concerning American ecclesiastical opinion during the first years of the world war.

[2] See especially *The Churches Allied for Common Tasks*, ed. S. McCrea Cavert, pp. 201 ff., on the help rendered by the American Churches to the countries at war.

[3] Printed in full in Swedish, German, English, and French in Karlström, *Kristna samförståndssträvanden*, pp. 578–80.

leaders. Faced by the challenge of the war, the Church's leaders simply could not keep silence. The essential thing was to assert and to make manifest Christian supranational unity as against the disruptive forces of war. On the one hand the appeal recognized all the obligations laid upon the Christian by loyalty to his own country and its vocation; on the other hand it proclaimed the Christian's faith in God's sovereignty, in which alone the destiny of all peoples can be fulfilled and in which the unity of all Christians is implied.

The leading churchmen of the countries at war were unwilling to sign the appeal. The answers received reflect the conflict of ideas which was going on behind the conflicts of the armed fronts.

For the German Church leaders, the principal representatives on the one side, the issue was clear. The war was a just and defensive war; peace could come only when the war had reached such an end as would secure for Germany an honourable peace. They could not take action which might weaken the hands of their leaders and their people.

To the British the issue presented itself in terms of moral principles infringed in the most brutal manner by the German violation of Belgian neutrality. In order that these principles might be vindicated, the war must go forward to an Allied victory.

For the French the dominating fact was that a large part of France had been occupied by the invader; the total evacuation of France must precede any discussion of the possibility of peace. At such a time of national crisis French Protestant leaders could not take any action which might suggest lack of solidarity with their fellow-countrymen.

Among neutrals, Söderblom was more successful. Leaders in Denmark, Norway, Holland, Switzerland, the United States, and two churchmen representing minorities within the warring countries—Finland and Transylvania—signed the appeal. Towards the end of November 1914 it appeared in the Press of various countries, and also as a four-page leaflet with the text in seven languages.

The attempt to secure a united Christian appeal for peace and a declaration of unity had failed. The refusals received from the belligerent countries showed how deep the cleavage went even within the Christian Church. For all that, it was significant that some authoritative voices had been raised on behalf of the supranational Christian fellowship. In the very midst of the din of war the Church, the one universal Church, had made its voice heard; with the publication of the appeal, the Swedish Archbishop came to the fore as a leader in international Christian efforts to promote mutual understanding. "From this time on", wrote Macfarland in a later book,[1] "Nathan Söderblom gradually became a personal symbol of what was to be undertaken."

The peace appeal of November 1914, as Söderblom himself declared later on, was "the beginning of more than we surmised at that time".[2] It marks the starting-point of what later developed into the Life and Work movement.

It was clear in Söderblom's mind that the appeal of 1914 was only the beginning of the mission he felt called upon to accomplish for the cause of peace and Christian fellowship. During the war he went on working for the unity of the Church along various lines. As far as possible he maintained relationships with leading churchmen in belligerent as well as in neutral countries; and he served as a link between individuals and church organizations in the countries

[1] C. S. Macfarland, *Steps Toward the World Council*, 1938, p. 42.
[2] N. Söderblom, *Kristenhetens möte i Stockholm*, Uppsala, 1926, p. 13.

at war, which at that time could not make direct contact with one another. Aid to prisoners and other war victims was one of the principal branches of his international activity. His correspondence as intermediary between the war-stricken countries often concerned investigations about prisoners of war or missing persons, and the help which he was able in many cases to render won him new friends and increased his authority.

The world war drew the Scandinavian peoples ever closer together and made them keenly conscious of their inner oneness and fellowship in a common destiny. The Churches, too, learned to co-operate. From this point of view Söderblom's contribution was of decisive significance. "Söderblom was the Archbishop of the North", wrote Hans Ostenfeld, Bishop of Copenhagen, "not as though he claimed so to be, but just because of his spiritual approach and power of leadership." Under his guidance co-operation between the Northern Churches came to be ever more closely linked with that work for the unity of the Church universal, of which the Swedish Archbishop became the centre. The fellowship amongst the Scandinavian Churches constitutes the starting-point of those attempts to make the idea of Christian unity a reality, which, in the later years of the war, flowed out from Uppsala.

3. THE IDEA OF AN INTERNATIONAL CHRISTIAN CONFERENCE DURING THE WAR

In the spring of 1917 an intensification of efforts for conciliation was evident, both in the political and in the religious worlds. War-weariness began to be insistently felt. The enormous loss of human life, the ever-increasing lack of food, the uncertain prospects of a peace based on victory appeared to some to lend support to the idea of peace by conciliation. In the world of political discussion, the most prominent advocates of this view were to be found in the labour movement and in the Vatican.

At the outbreak of war, contrary to the expectations of many, national feeling had proved stronger than the international solidarity of the working class, and the labour movement had been as ineffective as the Churches in the cause of peace. But in the summer of 1917, when the Russian revolution was opening out new hopes to the world of labour, it was found possible to hold at Stockholm not, as had been proposed, an international conference, but separate deliberation between a Dutch-Swedish committee of labour leaders and representatives of the labour movement in some of the belligerent countries. Through these deliberations, which came to be known as the Stockholm Conference, the main terms of a peace of conciliation were blocked out—no annexations, no war indemnities, and the right of peoples to self-determination. In those dark days "the Stockholm idea" presented itself at least as the beginning of light, though the practical consequences, outside the realm of ideas, were small. Almost at the same time, on 11 August 1917, Pope Benedict XV addressed a Note to the heads of states in which he urged, in terms not very different from those suggested by the labour leaders, the need for a peace of conciliation. This action was seriously resented by many devout Roman Catholics, especially in France, but the Pope's intervention encouraged endeavours for peace in other circles.

Under the hard pressure of the war situation, and stimulated by these efforts of others, Protestant Christian work for mutual understanding also quickened its tempo in 1917. In country after country questions were asked as to what, if anything, Protestant Christians were doing for peace, and many felt that the time had come when the Churches should express themselves plainly in favour of a peace by conciliation and not by conquest.

The first task was to manifest that fellowship of Christians which transcends national frontiers. From various quarters came suggestions for an international Christian conference to be held even before peace was restored, the aim of which should be both to manifest and to strengthen the inner unity of Christians and to develop the Christian contribution to peace and reconciliation among the nations. The idea appeared spontaneously and almost simultaneously in different places within the Protestant world. Gradually circles which were occupied with such plans made contact with one another and began to work together. The threads came together in the hands of the Swedish Archbishop, who became the driving force in all attempts in the course of the next few years to bring about the assembling of an international Christian conference.

In the spring of 1917 Söderblom launched a new effort in the interests of peace and Christian fellowship, which was avowedly a follow-up of the peace appeal of November 1914. This took the form of a Manifesto from Evangelical Churches in Neutral Countries, signed by Söderblom and by leading churchmen in Denmark, Norway, Holland, and Switzerland.[1] The appeal argued that the war amounted to the "self-destruction" of the whole of European culture. Therefore the signatories wished to "keep the hope of peace living", and declared themselves in favour of every effort to bring about a "righteous and durable peace". The last words, according to Söderblom's own explanation, were intended as support for the efforts at that time being made by the labour movement. Söderblom was among those who set great hopes on those efforts and, through this passage in the Manifesto, he wished to make clear that the Churches stood by the Stockholm Conference of the socialist parties. The appeal concluded with the declaration of the signatories that they had always been and that they remained ready to serve as agents for the renewal of the ties that war had severed, specially those of a religious and ecclesiastical character, so as, if possible, to be of service to their brethren in the countries at war. Advantage was later to be taken of this invitation; during the last years of the war it led on to significant events on the Christian front for unity.[2]

During the spring and summer of 1917 still other voices were raised in neutral countries, advocating a stronger Christian contribution to the building up of public opinion in favour of peace. Of even greater importance, however, was the fact that in some of the belligerent nations also feelings in favour of peace by negotiation and of more vigorous activity on the part of the Churches in the cause of peace were developing among Christians.

In Germany most of the leaders still clung to the idea of peace by conquest; but a growing minority believed that it was the duty of Christians in Germany to work for peace by conciliation, and to welcome the proposals for peace which were coming in from neutral countries. "The socialists are already at Stockholm: when shall we get as far as that?" was the question asked in one of the articles that called for more vigorous Protestant activity on behalf of peace.[3] In the Reichstag a majority in favour of peace by conciliation secured in July 1917 the adoption of the so-called Peace Resolution, a success which was not without

[1] The appeal in question, as well as the second Manifesto of 1917, is reproduced *in extenso* in the documents appended to Karlström, op. cit., pp. 626 ff., in which a detailed analysis of it is to be found.
[2] See later, pp. 526–30.   [3] *Die Christliche Welt*, 1917, p. 561.

its repercussions in Evangelical circles. The leading organ of liberal churchmanship in Germany, *Die Christliche Welt*, warmly took up the cause; Adolf Deissmann in his *Evangelische Wochenbriefe* hailed with joy every endeavour to manifest Christian unity in time of war.

In England, too, from the spring of 1917 onward, the desire of certain groups for more active participation in Christian work for peace found expression in various plans for an international Christian conference. In response to an appeal from the Friends' Yearly Meeting in May 1917,[1] the British Council for Promoting an International Christian Meeting was formed at the end of July 1917, with a membership drawn from most of the larger Church bodies in Britain. The Council's task was to endeavour to arrange an international conference at which Christians from both belligerent and neutral countries could meet for meditation and prayer; such a conference would, or might, help to create such spiritual conditions as would make possible lasting peace.

At the beginning of August 1917 this new Council heard of the Manifesto which neutral Church leaders, on Archbishop Söderblom's initiative, had sent out at the end of May. In the middle of August the Council directed to the Archbishop a request that he would arrange for an international Christian conference to be held even before the war ended. The Council expressed the wish that Söderblom should approach the Orthodox and Roman Catholic Churches as well as others. In Christian work for unity, the British have always insisted on full ecumenicity—a principle consonant with Söderblom's intentions and his doctrine of the Church.

At that time the question of an international Christian conference was becoming a live issue also among other groups in the English Churches, and found expression in *The Challenge*, the Anglican weekly of which William Temple, then Rector of St James's Church, Piccadilly, was editor. It was the failure of the attempt to convene a genuinely international labour conference at Stockholm which led Temple to take up the matter. He believed that it was now the duty of the Churches to come forward and try to bring about an international Christian conference in the service of peace and reconciliation—"a Christian Stockholm", as it was then called in England and in Germany. Temple contended that moderate public opinion in various countries had reached agreement as to certain essential principles to be observed in any future peace settlement; it was the Churches' concern to encourage the growth of such opinions and to promote these new tendencies among the nations.

When Archbishop Söderblom heard of what was happening in England, he decided to go ahead. The Scandinavian committees of the World Alliance were planning a conference for the autumn of 1917.[2] Söderblom's project was now to bring about an international Christian conference in connection with this meeting, a conference in which representatives from the belligerent countries as well as from others should take part. With this in view he approached the other Scandinavian Primates, Bishop Ostenfeld of Copenhagen and Bishop Tandberg

---

[1] Karlström, op cit., pp. 638 f.
[2] In July 1917 the Secretary of the British national committee of the Alliance, Willoughby Dickinson, had proposed the holding of two separated World Alliance conferences, the one for the "Entente" states, the other in the region of the Central Powers. Members from neutral countries were to take part in both conferences, so that common action could be prepared for, if and when it should prove desirable and possible to bring it about. But it had not been possible to carry Dickinson's proposal into effect.

of Christiania (now Oslo), and they agreed to join with him in sending out invitations for such a conference to be held at Uppsala in December 1917.

In the middle of October invitations were sent out. The Primates referred to the fact that among Christians on both sides of the battle-front there was evident a strong desire for some manifestation of the Church's unity; the world situation seemed to call with special force for such a testimony to the unity of Christians in Christ. They recalled that leading statesmen in different countries had agreed to advocate the establishment of an instrument of international law, including mutual agreement with regard to arbitration and disarmament, and they declared themselves in general agreement with the principles set forth in the Pope's peace appeal of August 1917. But if those principles were to become effective they must have the support of a stronger sentiment of Christian brotherhood transcending national frontiers. The projected conference was intended to deepen the unity of Christians among themselves, as well as to emphasize the Church's duty to resist the evil passions of war and to encourage a spirit of justice and goodwill among the nations. The invitation also stated that the presence of representatives from both belligerent groups was desired, on the understanding that, if one party refused, the invitation to the other might be revoked.

No detailed programme was drawn up. It was agreed, however, to follow the method which had been found useful in a number of Red Cross conferences, attended by both Germans and Russians: the representatives from neutral countries were first to hold discussions with those from the belligerent nations separately, and meetings of delegates from countries at war with one another should be held only if both parties desired it, and if the spiritual conditions were such as to hold out hopes that meetings between them would be profitable.

Invitations to the Uppsala Conference were addressed to three different groups: official Church bodies, or official representatives of Churches; World Alliance leaders in different countries; and a number of individual churchmen.

In Germany the official Committee of the German Evangelical Churches[1] declined the invitation. It was feared that an international conference, in the then existing circumstances, would involve the German delegates in painful and difficult situations, and also that their willingness to meet Christians from enemy countries might be misinterpreted to the prejudice of their reputation for loyalty to Germany and its cause. Certain individual German churchmen, on the other hand, took a favourable attitude to the Conference. Government circles proved helpful and anxious to go as far as possible to meet the desires of the Swedish Archbishop, in view of his "honest friendship towards Germany"[2] and his leading position in the Protestant world. Consultations in Berlin resulted in the formation of an unofficial German delegation comprising, among others, General Superintendent Lahusen, Professor Deissmann, and Dr Siegmund-Schultze; the Ministry for Foreign Affairs undertook to provide passports and travelling expenses for delegates.

The Austrian Evangelical Church Executive[3] in Vienna took the same uncompromising attitude as the German Church Committee. The Hungarian Churches, on the contrary, took in principle a favourable attitude, and

---

[1] *Deutscher Evangelischer Kirchenausschuss.*   [2] *Ehrliche Deutschfreundlichkeit.*
[3] *Evangelischer Oberkirchenrat.*

the Evangelical Lutheran Church of Hungary even appointed an official delegation.

Efforts to secure representation of the Churches in the countries of the "Entente" were unsuccessful.

Leaders of the Church of England, represented by the Archbishops of Canterbury and York, declined the Scandinavian invitation, arguing that in the existing delicate situation they could not send representatives to a conference where questions of a political or semi-political character would be discussed. Discussion of political problems with citizens of enemy nations was the sole responsibility of the British Government, which was unlikely to grant passports to churchmen to attend the conference in question. The British Committee of the World Alliance declared that it could not undertake to send delegates to a meeting attended by churchmen from both neutral and belligerent countries, at which questions of a political nature would be on the agenda. It was well known that the Government was wholly averse to British participation in such a conference; it was committed to the total defeat of Germany, and was not prepared to encourage any movement in favour of a peace by negotiation. Later, in the House of Commons, Lord Robert Cecil, at that time Minister for Blockade, revealed that it was with his approval that the Archbishop of Canterbury had declined the invitation to the Uppsala Conference, and that the Government had refused to issue passports.

But official disapproval accounted only in part for British reluctance to join in the proposed conference. In view of William Temple's earlier interest in the project, his objections are of special interest. Time being so short, it was impossible that representative delegations could be got together, at least from the American Churches, and Temple regarded American participation in the conference as indispensable. Further, he considered that the linking of the conference with the World Alliance was a mistake. To allow something as important as an international Christian conference to be nothing more than an appendage to a sectional meeting of the World Alliance, which itself was no more than a private fellowship of individual Christians, was to throw the conference out of balance and to endanger its success. Temple hoped that Archbishop Söderblom would again take the initiative, but this time for a conference standing on its own feet, and so timed as to make possible genuinely representative attendance.

The invitation sent to the French Church leaders was three months on the way and reached them only in the middle of January 1918. But the answer, when at last it was received, showed that no French delegation could have been expected, even if the invitation had arrived in time. It would be an illusion, said the French answer, to imagine that Frenchmen and Germans could be brought together to talk of peace and brotherhood while large parts of France were still occupied by German troops, and Christians in Germany had shown no sign of penitence for the crimes committed by their country.

Even with the United States, postal communications were so slow that the invitation arrived only after the date fixed for the conference. But there again leading churchmen would in any case have declined the invitation. After the American declaration of war, American Christians had come to believe that such meetings of Christians of different countries with a view to reconciliation and co-operative reconstruction must be postponed until after the war.

The Archbishop of Finland, Gustaf Johansson, declined the invitation, pointing to the critical situation Finland was in, and expressing his doubts as to whether the conference could bring any great influence to bear on the warring countries. A Polish churchman, who at the time happened to be on a visit to Sweden, General Superintendent Bursche, declared himself willing to take part in the meeting.

From neutral countries, representatives of the World Alliance committees in Holland, Switzerland, and the Scandinavian countries were invited, and all of them accepted. After the plan for the conference had had to be altered because of the abstention of those invited from the "Entente" countries, the Scandinavian delegation was greatly enlarged through invitations to individual churchmen.

As regards the Roman Catholic Church, the Vatican was not invited to be represented at the Uppsala Conference, 1917. Some individual Roman Catholic churchmen were invited, but only two answers were received. The Archbishop of Cologne, Cardinal von Hartmann, referred to the peace efforts made by the Vatican; the Pope having taken action in the matter, Roman Catholics could identify themselves with his action and no other. Some time after the Uppsala meeting an answer was received from the Archbishop of Warsaw, Alexander Kakowski. He expressed his great joy that a conference inspired by a true love of peace should have been convened "by those who believe in our Lord Jesus Christ and recognize in Him their Saviour and Master"; he recommended universal Christian co-operation in order to express in deeds the Christian message of love, without making the recognition of papal supremacy a necessary condition for such collaboration. This unmistakable recognition of a fellowship in faith between Roman Catholic and Evangelical Christians is impressive; although the Vatican later on refused to be represented at an international conference, Söderblom considered himself, in the light of Kakowski's letter, entitled to hope for the co-operation of individual Roman Catholic priests.

Neither the Patriarchate of Constantinople nor the Greek Church was invited to the Uppsala Conference of 1917. On the other hand, an attempt was made to secure representation from the Russian Church, but no answer to the invitation was ever received.

By the end of November 1917 it had become clear that the Conference would not be attended by churchmen from both the belligerent groups. It was therefore resolved, in accordance with the proviso set forth in the invitation, that the membership should be limited to churchmen from neutral countries.

The Neutral Church Conference at Uppsala took place from 14 to 16 December 1917, and included about thirty-five participants from Holland, Switzerland, Denmark, Norway, and Sweden.

Its main concern was preparation for the proposed international conference. In spite of the difficulties involved, Archbishop Söderblom insisted that a new attempt must be made to hold a general Christian conference in wartime. Though doubts were raised as to the possibility of carrying out the Archbishop's plan, the Uppsala meeting followed his advice and commissioned the three northern Primates to renew the invitation to an international Christian conference to be held probably in April 1918. It was further resolved that the new conference should not be associated with the World Alliance. This met the objections of William Temple and *The Challenge*. By way of agenda, the questions discussed at the Uppsala meeting were regarded as a sufficient outline. Deliberations on these themes had resulted in certain common expressions of opinion, and these might serve as a basis for discussion at the later international conference.

The findings of the Uppsala meeting were summed up under three main headings: (1) The unity of Christians; (2) Christians and the life of Society; (3) Christians and international law. Moreover, the Conference adopted a resolution, passed in 1916 at a conference of missionary leaders, on the supranational character of missions.

The findings on the unity of Christians manifest the essential features of that concept of unity which later found expression in the Life and Work movement. First, the Conference defines the unity of Christians as a unity which is basically religious. Unity is not to be sought for in anything external, anything we human beings can create. It is wholly and completely God's own act in and through Christ. The Cross of Christ is the very centre of unity, a power able to unite men in spite of all earthly differences. Secondly, the meeting characterized Christian unity as a unity in diversity. The new movement towards unity, for which the meeting stands, does not intend to encroach on the independence of various Church bodies, each historically conditioned in regard to its nature and its own special tasks. It seeks not uniformity but free co-operation between the Churches. Thirdly, Christian unity is considered as a unity in life and proclamation. Unity does not exist for its own sake. It must be transformed into Christian action in the various domains of human life.

The Conference deliberately made no attempt to reach a doctrinal formulation of Christian unity: unity is not to be sought in the acceptance of one doctrinal system or another. Behind the different interpretations of faith, *fides quae creditur*, stands faith itself, *fides qua creditur*, the human heart apprehended by Christ and trusting in him. Unity in faith can therefore exist even where confessions of faith are different. This type of interpretation was current in much of the theology and church life of the time. In seeking, later on, to characterize the fellowship in faith on which Life and Work is founded, Söderblom made use of the same categories of thought.[1]

In its second resolution, the Uppsala Conference dealt with the principles underlying the Church's attitude to social and international problems. It insists on the Church's right and duty to consider every sphere of human life in the light of the Gospel, and with the Gospel as judge; all theories of the autonomy [2] of social and political life are rejected. The meeting devoted special attention to the problem of the Church and war. There was sharp division of opinion on some points, especially on absolute pacifism and on the rights of conscientious objectors. But first and foremost the Conference emphasized "the profound contradiction between war and the Spirit of Christ" and insisted on the Church's duty "to work with all its might for the removal of the causes of war, whether social, economic, or political".

The third finding commends the solution of international conflicts through the development of international law. Just as the Church in ancient times considered the State, and lawful order within the State—well-established order instead of chaos—as an expression of God's will, so now it is the duty of the Churches to make their influence felt in the building up of a lawful order as between states, in order that their common life may be founded "on the principles of truth, justice, and love". The practical implications of these principles can be worked

---

[1] See especially N. Söderblom, *Pater Max Pribilla und die ökumenische Erweckung*, 1931.
[2] *Eigengesetzlichkeit*.

out only in concrete situations, but it is the task of the Church to "evoke and foster a spirit of Christian brotherhood and love, self-discipline and mutual justice".

The Conference had received assurances from various quarters that many Christians, even in belligerent countries, were favourable to it and to its purposes. There was a steady increase in the number of those who insisted that the Churches must more and more act as a force striving for peace among the nations. To all such groups, the Uppsala Conference presented itself as a rallying-point and a symbol of hope.

During the year 1918 the northern Primates made two further attempts to convene an international Christian conference. In accordance with the commission they had received from the Neutral Conference, they first sent out an invitation for 14 April. But it soon became evident that the time allowed for preparation was too short, particularly for the representatives who might be expected to come from America and from the Eastern Churches. In February, therefore, it was decided to postpone the conference, and a new invitation was sent out, this time for 8 September. For the third time, however, nothing came of it. The refusals were so numerous that Söderblom and his colleagues thought it best to postpone the meeting *sine die*.

The official leaders in different countries took a negative or at any rate noncommittal attitude towards the plan. Moreover, men's attitude towards the conference was deeply affected by their views on the political situation. When in May some English papers published the news that the Unitarian Church had declared itself in favour of the conference, the caption was: "To pray with the Huns?"

On the other hand, some change of feeling may be noted in regard to the conference and the aims for which it stood. In England especially, in spite of much opposition, such ideas were winning ground in certain circles. The British Committee of the World Alliance was prepared to accept the Scandinavian invitation if it proved possible to obtain passports. The strongest support for the conference idea came from the British Council for Promoting an International Christian Meeting. The leading personalities—first and foremost the Secretary, Miss Marian Ellis, later Lady Parmoor—worked indefatigably to influence English public opinion. Public meetings were arranged over the whole country, with talks and resolutions in favour of the proposed conference. A conference at Oxford in July 1918 specially deserves mention. Deliberations at this Oxford meeting led to the acceptance of the resolutions passed by the Neutral Conference.

Otherwise the situation was largely unchanged. It was still possible to reckon on delegations of individual churchmen from Germany and Hungary. On the other hand, leaders in France and in the United States once more declined the invitation, partly on the ground that in their opinion the chief architect of the plan, Archbishop Söderblom, was decidedly "pro-German"—an interpretation of his attitude which Söderblom himself was never willing to accept.

In 1918 invitations were extended to the Roman Catholic and Orthodox Churches. In addition to the Vatican, the Ecumenical Patriarchate at Constantinople and the Greek and Russian Churches were now invited.

The Cardinal Secretary of State declined the invitation on behalf of Pope Benedict XV. Rome's conception of unity was firmly stated in the document: the only way to unity is the turning to Rome of all non-Roman Churches.

The Orthodox Churches took a friendly attitude towards the project. Foundations were thus laid for that co-operation of Orthodox and Western Christianity which is one of the most notable results of present-day ecumenism. The agonizing experiences of the Orthodox Churches during the war forced them out of their former isolation, and gradually a new orientation, even in religious and theological concerns, began to become apparent. Some in Orthodox Church circles, while still holding fast to that understanding of the Faith which constitutes the unity of the Orthodox Churches among themselves, were beginning to move towards a wider concept of unity, comprehending all those who recognize Jesus Christ "as God and Saviour". Orthodox churchmen insisted, however, with particular earnestness on the dogma of Christ's divinity as being the cornerstone of everything that could properly be regarded as Christian faith.

For his negotiations with the Ecumenical Patriarchate, Söderblom had an invaluable intermediary in Dr Johannes Kolmodin, then attaché at the Swedish Embassy in Constantinople. Kolmodin succeeded in arousing the interest of the Orthodox Church leaders in Söderblom's project, and as early as February 1918 the Holy Synod declared itself in favour of participation in the April conference. When the conference had to be postponed, the Patriarchate appointed two Orthodox leaders as lecturers in the series of addresses on the unity of the Church which the Olaus Petri Foundation,[1] on Söderblom's initiative, arranged at Uppsala in the autumn of 1918. The negotiations conducted by Kolmodin may have played some part as a preparation for the remarkable letter sent out by the Ecumenical Patriarchate in January 1920.[2] In this document some of the ideas of Söderblom can be recognized. The letters of Kolmodin to Söderblom made it plain that the Orthodox leaders had become acquainted with these ideas during their discussions with him.

In the course of 1918 Söderblom also succeeded in getting into touch with a number of other Orthodox Churches. The Metropolitan Basileios (later the Patriarch Basileios III) sent a message to the conference planned for September 1918, in which he expressed his whole-hearted agreement with the aims of the conference. But he declared it impossible to include in the ecumenical fellowship those who denied Christ's divinity.[3] The Metropolitan Meletios of Athens announced his willingness to appoint delegates to the conference, but passports were refused by the Western Powers. In a personal letter to the Scandinavian leaders Meletios expressed his joy at their proposal. Söderblom used the services of a Swedish traveller to convey invitations also to some Russian Church leaders, among others the Patriarch Tikhon and Archbishop Benjamin, who, in principle, seem to have taken a favourable attitude towards the conference. Through Professor Nikolai Glubokovski (who, at Söderblom's invitation, gave a series of Olaus Petri lectures at Uppsala in September–October 1918 on the Russian Church and its work for unity) a valuable personal connection was formed between Söderblom and the Russian Church.

On 8 September 1918, the date for which, for the third time, the international

---

[1] The Olaus Petri Foundation is a lectureship foundation, called after the Swedish 16th-century Reformer and translator of the Bible (d. 1552); not to be confused with his brother, Laurentius Petri, who in 1531 was consecrated the first Lutheran Archbishop of Uppsala: see Chap. iv, p. 177. The Foundation invites outstanding religious personalities and scholars to lecture at the University of Uppsala.

[2] See Chap. x, p. 446.

[3] A Swedish translation of this message, as well as of a number of other documents and articles, has been published in the volume *Den ortodoxa kristenheten och kyrkans enhet*, Uppsala, 1921, pp. 111–32.

conference had been convened in vain, the Scandinavians wired to their colleagues in different countries: "Our prayers are holding an ecumenical conference." Answers in the same words were sent from both sides of the front.

"Our prayers are holding an ecumenical conference." This, then, was the result
of the three invitations—when looked at from without, a failure, but inwardly
a victory. For it implied that the plan now had advocates for whom its realization had become, as for Nathan Söderblom himself, "a holy and imperative
duty".

4. "A SPIRITUAL PEACE CONFERENCE"

The world war had come to an end and no international Christian conference
had met. But the war itself had given vividness to the ideas of which the conference plan was an expression. With appalling clearness it had demonstrated
the need of Christian intervention in the international sphere. Christian efforts
for reconciliation and union appeared more than ever urgent.

The first thing to be done was to bring about those consultations between
Church representatives which had proved impossible as long as the war continued.
Söderblom's first idea was for a conference to take place between the signing of
the armistice on 11 November 1918 and the assembling of the Peace Conference,
so that the Church could raise its voice in favour of conciliation before the peace
negotiations began. Such a meeting would prepare for a conference on a large
scale to be held later on. Towards the end of November 1918 Söderblom communicated his proposal to the Archbishop of Canterbury, Randall Davidson.
But Davidson took a negative attitude:

> "A conference held during the diplomatic and international negotiations
> would undoubtedly be regarded, however mistakenly, as an attempt to
> intervene in the negotiations themselves. To this I could not be party. . . .
> Christian Churches and communities will be able to speak both more freely
> and with greater weight after the conclusion of peace, when the process of
> reconstruction under new conditions is going on."[1]

The same point of view was expressed by Church bodies in other victorious
countries.

As indicated above, during the early war years the World Alliance had dis-
cussed the question of a Christian conference to be held immediately after the
war, between the armistice and the conclusion of peace, in order that the
Church might work effectively for a peace of conciliation. But even within the
World Alliance such plans had been given up in the latter part of the war.
Efforts were now directed towards bringing about a meeting of the International
Committee of the World Alliance itself immediately after the conclusion of
peace. These efforts were crowned with success. This was the first Christian conference after the war, and it proved of decisive significance for the growth of
mutual understanding among Christians in post-war years.

The Conference was held at Oud Wassenaar near The Hague, from 30 September to 3 October 1919, with about sixty participants. Most of these were members of the World Alliance International Committee, but various National

---

[1] G. K. A. Bell, *Randall Davidson*, p. 941. The student should not miss the incomparable
account of the first personal meeting between Randall Davidson and Nathan Söderblom provided by Dr Bell from his own recollections on pp. 1048–51.

Committees had in some cases sent substitutes for regular members who were prevented from attending. Fourteen countries in all were represented. The American, British, and German delegations were the largest. France was represented only by two Methodists. The leaders of the French Reformed Churches, as before, declared that they could not meet German churchmen so long as the German Church leaders failed to acknowledge the wrongs done by Germany, particularly in the violation of Belgian neutrality. To a large extent the delegations were made up of men who, during the war, had been carrying on the Christian work of mutual understanding between the different countries. But, even among them, the war and the isolation in which it had resulted had bred a measure of misunderstanding and suspicion. The Oud Wassenaar Conference made it possible for churchmen of different countries to discuss controversial questions together. On some points it yielded results which justified the characterization of Oud Wassenaar by some delegates as a "spiritual peace conference".[1]

The question of war guilt, the central and most burning of all the problems debated in post-war years, was taken up at Oud Wassenaar. Separate negotiations between the Belgian, French, Italian, and German delegations showed the impossibility of agreement in the political realm. The French and Belgians demanded that the German delegates should recognize the affirmation of Germany's war guilt as well-founded and the severities of the Treaty of Versailles as justified. The Germans argued that the French and Belgian delegates should endeavour to secure a revision of those clauses in the Treaty which they regarded as unfair. Yet, in spite of national divergences, a real depth of religious fellowship was reached during those separate deliberations. A unity binding all participants together as disciples of one Master was experienced. All united in condemning war in itself as a manifestation of the spirit of vengeance and hate, and promised each other that in future they would faithfully work together on a basis of Christian conviction.

The value of the spiritual understanding reached during those separate deliberations was seen when a declaration made by the President of the French World Alliance Committee, Professor Wilfred Monod, produced acute tension. In a written document addressed to the Oud Wassenaar Conference, Monod laid it down as a condition for a renewal of fellowship within the World Alliance that the German delegates should at least condemn the violation of Belgian neutrality as morally wrong and indefensible.[2]

The German delegates to Oud Wassenaar were themselves ready to make such a declaration, since it concurred with their own convictions. (As soon as the censorship ended in November 1918, one of the German representatives, Professor Deissmann, had branded the infringement of Belgian neutrality as an appalling and fateful iniquity.[3]) On the other hand, the Germans were anxious that no political conditions should be laid down for the renewal of fellowship within the World Alliance. They emphasized that no such conditions had been attached to the invitation to the Oud Wassenaar Conference. Others, including

---

[1] Lynch and Deissmann in *Evangelischer Wochenbrief*, Nr. 137/41, 1919, p. 7.

[2] As the discussions in connection with Monod's document were considered as unofficial, no account of them is to be found in the minutes of the Oud Wassenaar Conference. See, however, *Evangelischer Wochenbrief*, Nr. 137/41, 1919, pp. 8 ff., and *Die Eiche*, 1919, pp. 138–51 (by F. Siegmund-Schultze; a full and most important article).

[3] *Evangelischer Wochenbrief*, Nr. 91/92, 1918, pp. 3 f.

the British representatives, concurred in this point of view, and explicitly affirmed that the Germans should not feel themselves under constraint in the matter.

The German delegates, however, decided to make a declaration to the effect that they personally considered Germany's violation of Belgian neutrality an act of moral transgression. They also referred to the separate consultations which they had had with the French, Belgian, and Italian delegations, and stated that, from the religious point of view, understanding and unity had been reached and that all were ready for co-operation.

The German declaration at Oud Wassenaar produced a profound impression and made trustful co-operation within the World Alliance possible for the French, Belgian, and Italian Committees. The French Committee declared itself ready to co-operate in the World Alliance with all Christians in Germany who could subscribe to the German declaration at Oud Wassenaar. Outside World Alliance circles, however, the declaration occasioned lively discussions. In some quarters in Germany a decidedly critical attitude was taken towards a confession which was described as a national self-abasement. Again, for instance among French Protestants, there was a demand that the German Churches should officially make a similar declaration. The question of war guilt was by no means removed from the realm of debate between the Churches.

The question of the supranationality of missions was also to the fore at the Oud Wassenaar Conference. After a thorough discussion, the delegates agreed on certain resolutions which even representatives from the nations recently at war were willing to endorse. It was proclaimed that liberty to carry Christ's Gospel to all nations was essential to the life of the Christian Church, and one of the fundamentals of religious freedom.[1] The session at which these resolutions were passed was one of the most solemn moments of the Oud Wassenaar Conference. After their adoption, Archbishop Söderblom spontaneously started the German hymn *Nun danket alle Gott*.

The World Alliance and its leaders aimed at finding a solution to international problems through the strengthening of international law. It was therefore only natural that they should hail with joy the decision made at Versailles concerning the establishment of a League of Nations. In a document addressed to the new League, they expressed both their agreement with the principles on which it was based and their desire for the wider development of those principles. The League of Nations, if it were adequately to fulfil its task, should include all countries. Every country which sought for admission and declared itself willing to comply with the League's statutes should be admitted. Clearly it was the admission of Germany to the League for which the World Alliance International Committee was pleading; under the Treaty, Germany was not to be admitted to the League immediately on its formation.

The Peace Treaty had brought into existence religious and cultural minorities in a number of countries. The International Committee called on the League to see to it that the cultural and religious rights of those minorities should in the future be respected. The protection of religious minorities was always a primary interest of the World Alliance.

In a separate document addressed to the League of Nations, the International

[1] See Chap. viii, pp. 365 f.

Committee gave a specific instance of its desire to secure protection for religious minorities. This concerned certain sections of the Hungarian Evangelical Churches. Owing to the dismemberment of Hungary decided upon at Versailles, there would be considerable Protestant minorities in Rumania, Czechoslovakia, and Yugoslavia with their predominantly Orthodox and Roman Catholic populations. The Hungarian delegates at the Oud Wassenaar Conference appealed to the World Alliance to take up the cause of those minorities. The Committee responded and appealed to the League of Nations to ensure that Hungarian Protestant Christians could maintain their connection and fellowship with the central administration of the Hungarian Evangelical Churches. These appeals were ineffectual owing to the powerful political forces at work; the division of Hungary was carried through by the Trianon Treaty in 1920, and the problem of religious minorities in those regions became, and long remained, a burning question.

With regard to the future work of the World Alliance, the Oud Wassenaar Conference passed some resolutions in which international law was indicated as the sphere in which the Alliance could best develop its work for peace. The consciousness of right and wrong, and the human laws and governments based thereon, are to be considered as gifts of God to man. As Christians we must proclaim the sanctity of law and must resist any glorification of power and violence, whether in the international or in the social realm. But every existing juridical order is imperfect and in need of constant improvement, as moral consciousness develops. It is therefore the duty of Christians to promote new developments in social and international relationships. All this is typical of Söderblom's way of thinking, and some of the wording may have been taken over from the resolutions passed at the Uppsala Conference in December 1917.

The question of an international Christian conference was introduced at Oud Wassenaar by Archbishop Söderblom, who gave an account of what had been done in the matter during the war and, in the name of the northern Primates, presented an invitation to an international conference intended to deal with the attitude of the Church on social and international problems. Söderblom's ecumenical plans had ripened during the war, and now took shape in the proposal for an Ecumenical Council of the Churches which should be able to speak on behalf of Christendom on the religious, moral, and social concerns of men. During the spring and summer of 1919 Söderblom had enlarged in a number of articles[1] on the necessity of such a common mouthpiece of the Churches. His conclusion was that it was impossible to wait until unity should be achieved in matters of faith and order before moving towards closer co-operation between the Churches. Above all else, the powerlessness of the Churches in the crisis of war had shown the imperative need of a united front for action by them in the international sphere. Reconciliation and brotherhood amongst the peoples must find a place in the creed no less than other articles of faith. Equally necessary was a united effort of the Churches for the solution of social problems. Such an Ecumenical Council would not encroach on the independence of the individual Churches. The Council would possess influence only by virtue of the spiritual

[1] Intended for an international reading public, especially "Die Aufgabe der Kirche: Internationale Freundschaft durch Evangelische Katholizität" in Die Eiche, September 1919, and "The Church and International Goodwill" in The Contemporary Review, September 1919. See also N. Karlström, "Ein ökumenischer Kirchenrat" in Oekumenische Einheit, Vol. III, No. 2, 1953, pp. 93–102.

authority it might attain through judgements passed on important questions affecting the nations. Here we can descry one of the principles now accepted as the policy of the World Council of Churches.

In view of the Roman Catholic attitude of exclusiveness, Söderblom gave up as hopeless the idea of co-operation with Rome. On the other hand, he thought that the Ecumenical Council should be built around two of the oldest of the great offices of the Church: the Patriarch of Constantinople and the Archbishop of Canterbury should be *ex officio* members of the Council. Further, the other branches of "Evangelical-Catholic" Christendom in Europe and America should be represented through elected members proportionately to their importance and to the special contribution which each could make. Söderblom recommended that, in the formation of the Council, *ex officio* membership should be combined with election on a broad democratic basis; just how this was to be achieved he did not indicate in detail. He was prepared also to find room in the Council for a number of independent Christian organizations other than Churches.

Söderblom outlined these plans at Oud Wassenaar, and at the same time extended an invitation to the international conference which it was proposed to hold in one of the Scandinavian countries. If Uppsala were chosen, the expenses of the conference were already guaranteed.

Sympathy with this project was expressed in various quarters. It was particularly supported by the representatives of the American Federal Council. In a special declaration the Swiss delegates, headed by their leader President Herold, insisted on the need for common action to "unite Protestants". At an earlier period, when Söderblom's war-time plans were under discussion, the Swiss had desired to limit the conference to Protestant Churches. All were agreed that nothing was to be gained by inviting the Vatican to such a meeting.

As the result of the deliberations at Oud Wassenaar, the International Committee of the World Alliance expressed its full sympathy with the plan. It considered, however, that the organizing of such an official Church conference lay beyond the competence of the World Alliance. It was decided to pass on this decision to the national committees of the World Alliance to be communicated by them to the ecclesiastical authorities in the various countries.

The plan for an international Christian conference was thus taken out of the hands of the World Alliance, and the new endeavours appear as an independent undertaking; they developed into the Life and Work movement. During the meeting at Oud Wassenaar unofficial action was taken to further the plan: a committee with full powers to act was set up; its members were Archbishop Söderblom, Dr Macfarland, and President Herold. Before leaving The Hague, these three decided that a meeting in Paris in November 1919 should make plans for a larger preparatory conference. Invitations to attend this meeting were addressed to the countries in which the idea of an international Christian conference had been kept alive during the war, that is to say, in addition to the Scandinavian countries, the United States, Great Britain, Switzerland, and Hungary.

The Paris meeting on 17 November 1919 took the form of a small committee meeting with only about ten participants from the United States, Switzerland, and Sweden. Among the American representatives prominent figures were Dr Lynch, and Dr Henry A. Atkinson, one of the leaders in the Church Peace Union, who later became General Secretary both of the organizing committee for the Stockholm Conference, 1925, and of the Conference itself. Switzerland was represented by President Herold and Professor Choisy. As representatives of Sweden, Söderblom had sent the Swedish pastor in London, A. O. T. Hellerström (who, during the war, had been Söderblom's intermediary in dealings with the British church leaders and was well acquainted with his ecumenical plans) and Yngve Brilioth, then a university lecturer, who happened to be in England engaged in research and was at the last moment called in as a member of the Swedish delegation.

But no British representatives were present in Paris. Archbishop Davidson had fully set forth his views in writing; he considered the sending of a delegation to Paris superfluous. He gave general approval to the conference plan, but laid down certain conditions for the co-operation of the Church of England. He emphasized the necessity of thorough preparation, recalling that it had taken two years to prepare for the Edinburgh Conference of 1910; and recommended caution, where the matter in question was the stand which the Church was to take on problems which touched even lightly on the political sphere. Again, Davidson was insistent that the conference must be genuinely ecumenical; this involved sending invitations to both the Roman Catholic and the Orthodox Churches. If this was not done, the Church of England might find itself unable to participate either in the preparatory work or in the conference itself. The same insistence on full ecumenicity had come from Britain during the war, having been expressed also by the British Free Churches. This was entirely in accordance with Archbishop Söderblom's ideas and aims, but not with those of the Swiss representatives who, as we have seen, wished to limit the proposed conference to the Protestant Churches. Lastly, Archbishop Davidson insisted on the need to set up a representative committee with Church leaders from different countries to do the preliminary work, and to appoint a man who could devote his whole time to it.

The main result of the Paris deliberations was that general approval was given to the idea of holding an international Christian conference. It was agreed that a larger preparatory conference should be convened for the summer of 1920, and Dr Lynch was commissioned to take the steps necessary to implement this decision. Responsibility for the preparatory conference was thus entrusted to the Federal Council in America.

5. THE FOUNDING OF LIFE AND WORK

The Conference, from 9 to 12 August 1920,[1] assembled about ninety delegates from fifteen countries. The invitations sent out by the Federal Council had been addressed only to the Protestant communions. It is not known whether this limitation was based on principle or whether it was due to the fact that the Geneva Conference was only to be in the nature of a preliminary meeting. It is certain that within the Federal Council there were some who opposed the sending of invitations to the Roman Catholic and Orthodox Churches. According to the invitation, delegations might consist either of official or of unofficial representatives of the Churches.

The American delegation, which was the largest and was officially nominated by the Federal Council, included a number of leading men from that Council,

---

[1] It is to be borne in mind that the preparatory meeting of Faith and Order took place also at Geneva in the same month, directly after that of Life and Work. See Chap. ix, pp. 417 ff.

among others Macfarland, Lynch, and A. J. Brown, and also some of the most notable figures in other ecumenical organizations, such as C. H. Brent, R. H. Gardiner, W. P. Merrill, and J. A. Morehead.

The next in size was the Swedish group, an official delegation headed by Archbishop Söderblom. Söderblom had wished that the Swedish Free Churches also should be represented at the Geneva Conference. The Free Church Joint Committee affirmed its sympathy with the proposed conference, on the understanding that it would comprise only Protestant Church bodies and that the programme would include only such questions as could be considered of common interest to all Protestant Churches. On the other hand, since the Geneva Conference was limited to Protestant communions, the Church of England took no part in it, in accordance with the principle laid down by Archbishop Davidson.[1] The National Council of Evangelical Free Churches in England was officially represented by its General Secretary, the Rev. Thomas Nightingale. The Scottish Churches were represented, among others, by the Moderator of the Church of Scotland, Dr James Cooper, who even during the war had been a supporter of Archbishop Söderblom's ecumenical plans.

The German Evangelical Church Committee[2] did not receive an invitation to the Geneva Conference. The Federal Council no doubt applied the principle that, where difficulties concerning representation might arise, it was better not to approach official Church bodies but to turn to individuals or to unofficial organizations. In the case of Germany, the invitation had been addressed to Professor Julius Richter, who was known to the Federal Council as a member of the Edinburgh Continuation Committee and as one of the delegates to the Oud Wassenaar Conference. Richter never discussed the invitation with the German Evangelical Church Committee, which in consequence had no occasion to express an opinion as to German representation at the Life and Work Conference, though it had refused to take part in the Faith and Order Conference convened at the same time.

Although official German representation at an international Christian conference was not at that time practicable, it proved possible to secure the presence of some unofficial German representatives. In reply to Söderblom's invitation, Siegmund-Schultze declared himself willing to participate in the Conference, and even succeeded in persuading two German churchmen, Professor A. Lang and Missionsdirektor A. W. Schreiber, who were attending the Faith and Order Conference in a private capacity, to be available also for the sessions of the preparatory conference for Life and Work. The Methodist Pastor (later Bishop) A. Melle, and Deaconess Emma von Bunsen also took part as representatives from Germany. The former had been appointed by the German Free Church Joint Committee, the latter had been personally invited by Archbishop Söderblom.

The Federation of French Protestant Churches was represented, among others, by Professor Raoul Allier, Dean of the Protestant Faculty in Paris. The Belgian and the Italian Protestant Churches were also represented, the latter by the Moderator of the Waldensian Church, Pastor Ernesto Giampiccoli. Among neutrals, the Danish, Norwegian, and Swiss Churches were represented. Dr Adolph Keller, at that time Secretary of the Swiss Federation of Protestant

---

[1] But no official decision had at this time been reached on the question of whether invitations should be sent to the Roman Catholic and Orthodox Churches, or not.

[2] *Deutscher Evangelischer Kirchenausschuss.*

Churches and later one of the Secretaries of the Stockholm Conference, 1925, was present as a member of the Swiss delegation.

The outstanding figure at the Geneva Conference was undoubtedly Archbishop Söderblom. He had a definite ecumenical programme, with which we are already acquainted, and which Life and Work was to be called into existence to carry into effect. At the first plenary session he set forth this programme explicitly under the title "Idea and Need of an Ecumenical Conference", leading up to the proposal for an ecumenical conference which, in its turn, should set up the Ecumenical Council of Churches which was an essential part of his plan. These plans received support from various sides, and Dr Lynch brought forward a definite proposal for the holding of an international Christian conference some time during the next two or three years. However, before a decision could be taken, the French introduced another issue which threatened to wreck the Conference—the question of war guilt.

An official document, emanating from the Federation of French Protestant Churches, was presented to the Conference. The French churchmen declared themselves convinced that the unity, of which the Geneva Conference was an expression, was a necessity; for that reason they had not declined the invitation. But an unresolved moral problem still stood as a barrier between the Churches of the former belligerent countries. All Christian Churches indeed shared in a common guilt as having failed so to imbue the nations with the spirit of the Gospel as to make a world war impossible. But the Churches of the Central Powers were specially guilty. Individual Germans had, no doubt, recognized the wrongs which had been done, and the German representatives at the Oud Wassenaar Conference had condemned the violation of Belgian neutrality by Germany. But the German and Austro-Hungarian Churches as such had never made a similar admission. As long as they kept silence, it was hardly possible to think of any co-operation between the Evangelical Churches in the sphere of Life and Work.

The French point of view was supported by the Belgians, whereas the Moderator of the Waldensian Church, Pastor Giampiccoli, who had lost a son in the war (as had also Professor Allier), spoke most moving words of reconciliation.[1]

Siegmund-Schultze laid stress on the fact that the Germans present were not official delegates, and that a discussion of political issues had not been included in the invitation which they had accepted. Missionsdirektor Schreiber went one step further. He expressed his disagreement with the pronouncement made at Oud Wassenaar by the German representatives, and pointed out that it had been condemned by many in Christian circles in Germany.

The fact that the German representatives were not official delegates, but had been invited in a private capacity, offered a way of escape from what threatened to become an intolerable situation. It was impossible to demand that those present should speak in the name of the German Churches. In the end it was decided that no action should be taken on the document presented by the French.

The question of war guilt was one of the two issues which threatened to nullify the progress made at the Geneva Conference. The other was the problem of the scope of an international Christian conference.

---

[1] He invited the Conference to repeat together the Lord's Prayer; in the circumstances the words "as we forgive them that trespass against us" came home to the delegates with more than ordinary force.

Catholicity was an integral part of Söderblom's doctrine of the Church. What the northern Primates had proposed during the war was a genuinely ecumenical Christian conference; invitations had been addressed to representatives of the Roman Catholic and Orthodox Churches as well as to the Anglican and Protestant Communions. At Geneva, Söderblom strongly insisted that invitations should be sent to all Christian Churches. He pointed out that to convene an *ecumenical* conference of *Protestant* Churches involved a contradiction in terms. The Swiss contended that the point of view of the Roman Catholic Church was such as to make co-operation with it impossible. Söderblom replied that he himself did not entertain hopes of Roman Catholic co-operation, but that the decision to reject an invitation was one that must be made by Rome herself. If any communion were to be excluded *a priori* from the coming conference, those responsible for it would themselves from the start have taken up a sectarian attitude. The debate led to the decision that all Christian Churches should be invited to the international conference. This decision, made on 11 August 1920, marks one of the great victories in the history of the ecumenical movement.

The question of a confession of faith as a basis for the coming conference was hardly discussed at Geneva. No definition of what was meant by the term "Christian Churches" was arrived at, and the Committee on Arrangements which was set up was instructed to decide which Churches should be invited. Here Life and Work sharply diverged from Faith and Order, which, from the outset, laid down as the basis of the movement the confession of faith in Jesus Christ "as God and Saviour".

At the Geneva Conference important contacts were made between Life and Work and Orthodox Christendom. Some Orthodox churchmen had come to Geneva in connection with the preparatory Conference of Faith and Order, among them the Metropolitan Germanos of Seleukia. Archbishop Söderblom invited this Greek Orthodox delegation to attend the Life and Work Conference as visitors, and called on one of the Swedish delegates, Pastor Herman Neander, to greet the Orthodox in modern Greek. Dr Germanos replied to this greeting, and expressed the joy with which Orthodox Church leaders welcomed the idea of an international Christian conference. He also pointed out that these plans were closely in line with the Encyclical which the Ecumenical Patriarchate had sent out in January 1920,[1] and which recommended the establishing of a League of Churches for the fulfilment of certain common tasks. It was undoubtedly a bold stroke on Söderblom's part to invite the Orthodox churchmen to the Life and Work Conference without previous discussion or authorization. It was a step taken in faith, and later developments have fully confirmed the wisdom of what was then done. Protestant and Orthodox churchmen entered into such a realistic experience of fellowship in the Faith as is the mainstay of Life and Work.

Further preparations for the coming ecumenical conference were entrusted to a Committee on Arrangements consisting of twenty-five persons, with Söderblom as Chairman and Macfarland and Lynch as General Secretaries. It was decided that the conference itself should, if possible, take place in 1922 or 1923, and the programme as drawn up included the attitude of the Churches both to social and to international problems, in accordance with the programme

[1] See Chap. x, p. 446.

of the Uppsala Conference of 1917 and with the resolutions which had there been accepted.

The Committee on Arrangements was later replaced by a committee of official representatives. But, through the establishment of this provisional committee, Life and Work had obtained a working instrument, and the Geneva meeting of 1920 can therefore rightly be described as the constituent conference of the Life and Work movement. The Committee on Arrangements held two meetings at Geneva, immediately after the preparatory Conference. It was decided to form three sections of the Committee—for America, the European Continent, and the British Empire respectively—to serve as the nuclei for the development of the conference plans. The words Universal Conference of the Church of Christ on Life and Work—modified in the following year to Universal Christian Conference on Life and Work—were there adopted as the title for the conference. The term Life and Work thus goes back to the Geneva Conference of 1920.

6. FROM GENEVA 1920 TO STOCKHOLM 1925

It had been decided that a Universal Conference should be held; a provisional instrument had been created to bring the Conference into being. It was not long before the promoters of the plans realized the difficulties involved in bringing the Churches to co-operate on a scale much greater, as Professor Deissmann claimed, than that of the Council of Nicaea, to which Stockholm 1925 has sometimes been compared.

The first meeting of the Provisional Committee, held at Peterborough, England, in April 1921, made one important decision—to add to the three sections already constituted a fourth, for the representation of the Orthodox Churches.

Much more critical was the meeting held the following year at Hälsingborg. Here the organization of the movement was completely recast. The place of the Provisional Committee was taken by an International Committee of thirty-eight members (which it was planned later to increase to not more than fifty),[1] and an Executive Committee of twenty with wide powers. In view of the time required for the preparation of an ecumenical conference, the date was wisely postponed till August 1925. Stockholm was selected as the meeting-place, in response to the exceedingly generous invitation extended by the Swedish Churches and people.

It had been decided in 1920 to invite the Roman Catholic Church to be represented at the Universal Conference. Archbishop Söderblom accordingly decided to make a preliminary approach to the Vatican in concert with the other northern Primates. In their letter to the Pope in February 1921, they emphasized that the co-operation between the Churches for which they were striving did not aim at any interference with the faith, ritual, or dogma of any Church body; they desired only to appeal to all Christ's disciples, whatever their confession, to follow the Master in deeds of love, in a common endeavour and with one mind, since the suffering of the world cried out for Christian love and for common Christian action, as far as that might prove to be possible.

The reply from Cardinal Gasparri on behalf of the Pope, dated April 1921, was, like an earlier communication to the northern Primates, addressed to

[1] An interesting ecumenical touch is that "the Canadian Churches were given liberty to add two members either to the American or to the British group".

Perillustres Viri,[1] and only expressed the Pope's gratitude for the communication received and for the minutes of the Geneva meeting which had been enclosed. The silence on the central point of the letter, the invitation to the Stockholm Conference, could only be taken to mean that the Vatican declined to co-operate with the Life and Work movement. At the meeting in Peterborough it was decided to take no further steps in relation to the Roman Catholic Church. The Vatican therefore received no formal invitation to the Stockholm Conference of 1925.

Contacts with the Orthodox Churches at Geneva in 1920 have already been referred to. In 1924 the Executive Committee resolved that a delegation should be sent to visit the Eastern Churches. In accordance with this decision, two visits were paid by Dr Atkinson, Dr Alexander Ramsay, the Organizing Secretary of the World Alliance, and Pastor Herman Neander to a number of Orthodox Churches, and promises of co-operation in the movement were received from several of the leaders of these Churches.

At Hälsingborg, the International Committee had before it the suggestion, made by the General Secretary of Faith and Order, that Life and Work might be interested in holding its Conference in Washington in 1925, just after the first World Conference which Faith and Order was planning to hold in that city in May of that year. After thorough consideration, the International Committee arrived at the conclusion that it would be better to keep the two conferences separate. The goal of the Faith and Order movement was relatively distant, whereas the Christian Churches should be able "without difficulty" to unite at once in an effort to apply Christian principles to burning social and international problems. The answer of the Committee quoted Dr Kapler: "Doctrine divides, but service unites." The Life and Work movement, it said, was aiming at common service; such common service in the field of practical problems might well help to break down walls and prejudices between Church bodies, and create a spirit of brotherhood which would make it easier to realize also the aims of the Faith and Order movement.

The Committee's answer is typical of one of the streams of thought which met in the Life and Work movement of that time. Subsequent developments involved some revision of the belief that the Churches could "without difficulty" unite at once for common action in the field of social and international problems.

After the first world war, the Christian social movement in England had taken on a development closely parallel to Life and Work—the Conference on Christian Politics, Economics, and Citizenship, commonly called Copec for short.[2] The Conference was held in Birmingham in April 1924, but preparations had been begun in 1921. Chaired by William Temple, and owing much to such leaders as Dr Hugh Martin and Canon C. E. Raven, Copec was the most considerable effort made up to that date anywhere in the world to focus Christian thought and action on the urgent problems of the day.

All the subjects scheduled for discussion at Stockholm 1925, and a good many others as well, were handled in the twelve volumes of the Copec reports,

[1] "Highly illustrious men"—a form of address at least equivocal in addressing Bishops and Primates of great Christian Churches.

[2] Among those present at Copec were Ruth Rouse, as Member of Commission, and Stephen Charles Neill, representing the Ely Diocesan Conference.

on the basis of wide and intensive preparation, in which Roman Catholics had participated. The Executive Secretary, Miss Lucy Gardner, later a leader in many activities of Life and Work, early established personal contacts with the leaders in that movement. Defining the relationship between the two, Dr Temple said succinctly at the opening session of the Conference: "Our Conference is itself the British preparation for the Universal Conference on the Life and Work of the Church."[1] The Copec reports were, in fact, submitted in abridged form as the British contribution to Stockholm 1925; no preparation of equal thoroughness had been carried out anywhere else in the world.[2]

As early as the Hälsingborg meeting the subjects with which the Stockholm Conference was to deal had taken shape under the following six headings:
(1) The general obligation of the Church in the light of God's plan for the world—the basic and fundamental questions
(2) The Church and economic and industrial problems
(3) The Church and social and moral problems
(4) The Church and international relations
(5) The Church and education
(6) Ways and means for promoting co-operation between the Churches, and for their closer association on federal lines. It was intended to discuss under this heading the continuance of the work of the Conference as a common enterprise.

These subjects were discussed by the sections into which the International Committee had been divided, and preliminary reports were prepared in advance of the date of the Conference.

These brief summary statements convey no impression of the spiritual travail and adventure through which Stockholm was born. In the annual meetings of the International and Executive Committees, in the sections, in the preparatory meetings for discussion in many countries, leaders in the Churches were beginning to meet one another across the frontiers of nations and confessions. Those personal friendships, which are the very stuff of creative ecumenical development, were becoming firmly established, and were creating in advance the atmosphere of fellowship in which the great Conference was to do its work. Since Anglican objections to a purely Protestant Conference had been met, the Church of England joined warmly in the preparations. From 1922 onwards the German Churches were officially represented. Among the first Germans to be present was Dr Kapler, at that time President of the Federation of German Evangelical Churches, and later to become one of the most distinguished figures in the Life and Work movement.

That these preparations were to those who took part in them neither a dry administrative routine nor a genial philanthropic crusade, but a deeply spiritual pilgrimage, is made clear by the terms of the official invitation which was sent out in April 1924:

"No Christian can doubt that the world's greatest need is the Christian way of Life not merely in personal and social behaviour but in public opinion and its outcome in public action. . . . In short, we hope under the guidance of the Spirit of God, through the counsel of all, to be able to formulate programmes and devise means for making them effective, whereby

[1] *The Proceedings of C.O.P.E.C.*, p. 20.
[2] It is to be noted that Archbishop Söderblom was present at the Copec Conference, and addressed it on the subject of the Universal Conference. See *Proceedings*, p. 261.

the *fatherhood of God and the brotherhood of all peoples* will become more completely realized through the Church of Christ. . . . We depend for success from first to last upon the guidance of the Holy Spirit."[1]

The final stages of preparation were carried through in Stockholm itself. Just ten days before the Conference opened, the International Committee met, and appointed five Commissions and eleven Sub-Committees to work on the many reports and studies which had come in from the sections and national groups. After a week of strenuous labour, these working parties had reduced chaos to some kind of order, and were able to present their reports to the International Committee at its last pre-Conference session, only two days before the Conference opened. These reports were then printed, and distributed to the members of the Conference as the raw material for their study and discussions. Nothing now remained but for the Conference to begin its work.

To record the Conference and all that flowed from it will be the task of another chapter. We may conclude this introductory survey with a backward glance from the standpoint of Nathan Söderblom and his colleagues. They could look back on many years of hope, frustration, effort, and delay, now at last rewarded with memorable success. It may well have seemed to them the crowning moment of a lifetime.

[1] *The Stockholm Conference 1925*, ed. G. K. A. Bell, pp. 17, 18, 20.

CHAPTER 12

MOVEMENTS FOR INTERNATIONAL FRIENDSHIP
AND LIFE AND WORK
1925–1948

by

Nils Ehrenström

1. STOCKHOLM 1925

The Universal Christian Conference on Life and Work which met in the capital of Sweden in August 1925 was the fruit of a vision earlier seen by men agonized by the distress of a war-torn humanity and the lamentable weakness of a divided Christendom. That vision was solemnly accepted and proclaimed as an impelling call to the Churches everywhere. It released a movement of inspiration, of thought, and of action, which has become a lasting ferment in world Christianity.

On 19 August 1925 more than 600 delegates from thirty-seven countries assembled in the Cathedral at Stockholm for the opening service of the Conference. Immediately after the service the delegates repaired in procession to the Royal Palace to be received by the King and Queen of Sweden. In inviting the King formally to open the Conference, the Archbishop of Uppsala said:

> "When the Spirit of God visits humanity, it is the same flame that is kindled in human hearts, although land and water separate them. . . . God grant that the flames kindled in our hearts may be purified and united here into a fire of love and justice that shall enlighten Christendom with a new clearness of the eternal and Divine truth and that shall warm the souls and the Church with the ardent compassion of Christ."

The King, in his reply, pointed out that, though statesmen and rulers

> "may succeed in passing good laws and in effecting well-advised measures, that does not mean that the end in view is gained; because laws and statutes are more or less ineffective as long as they are not founded on goodwill in the hearts of men and on a mind which puts love and justice above and before selfishness. It is therefore in the hearts of men that we must lay the foundation for peace and for mutual trust within the community as well as between the peoples."[1]

It was a remarkable assemblage of men and women from many lands and many Churches. But on that first day all eyes were turned towards one single figure; for Stockholm 1925 more than any other great Christian conference was the child of one heart and one brain; in a most unusual way Nathan Söderblom, Archbishop of Uppsala, *was* Stockholm 1925.

Many factors had combined to prepare Söderblom for ecumenical leadership. A childhood and youth spent in a poor Swedish parsonage brought him early into close touch with the way in which ordinary men and women really live. In his parental home reigned a profound evangelical piety and a missionary interest which marked his whole life. The Student Christian Movement gave decisive ecumenical impulses. His periods of work as pastor of the Swedish Church in Paris and as Professor in Germany made him comprehensively European in outlook. His Lutheranism was irenic and generous in acknowledging the treasures bestowed on other traditions—though perhaps sometimes underestimating the stubborn realities of doctrinal and ecclesiastical divergences.

[1] *The Stockholm Conference 1925*, ed. G. K. A. Bell, pp. 45 ff.

Years of intensive study in the history of religions enabled him to see the Christian faith in the widest context of the spiritual adventures and strivings of men. His unexpected elevation to the See of Uppsala, when his name was only third on the list of the three presented to the King, brought to him new opportunities which he was quick to grasp. A country such as Sweden, neutral by tradition and conviction, could serve, as no other, as a reconciling factor in a world so bitterly torn by the passions of war and their slow and discouraging aftermath. Now in his sixtieth year, he could see the fruit of many years of vision, imagination, and practical effort; the Universal Conference on Life and Work was an accomplished fact.

To an unusually wide acquaintance with the life of Churches in many centuries and countries, Söderblom added deep and genuine indignation at the failure of those Churches to live up to the height of their vocation, and in particular at the spiritual treacheries and disasters involved in a war between professedly Christian nations. He had the imagination to conceive largely, administrative ability adequate to the realization of his ideas, contagious enthusiasm, diplomatic tact, and patience unwearied and undiscouraged by the many rebuffs and set-backs that accompany any attempt to get the Churches to do anything together. Unlike many ecumenical leaders, Söderblom was a master of languages; perfectly at home in Swedish, French, and German, he had also a wide command of English. An authentic and indispensable touch was his great sense of humour and his amazing faculty of creating around him an atmosphere of joyous festivity. But it was a humour glittering over mysterious depths; it is suggestive that his sympathetic study of Luther carries the title *Humour and Melancholy*.

No man is wholly adequate to the ecumenical enterprise. Yet, even if there were limitations and imperfections, no one who knew him could doubt that Söderblom was a great man, fit for a time of spiritual adventure. The Bishop of Chichester (Bell), whose association with him dates from before the Stockholm Conference, has asserted that during the first half of the 20th century Söderblom stands out as the man "who did more than any other Christian leader or teacher to unite Orthodox and Evangelical Churches of all nations and communions in a common fellowship, for the sake of Christ, and His truth and justice and peace".[1] His efforts opened up to the Churches new fields and new possibilities of common action; if there had been no Söderblom, there would have been no Stockholm 1925; if there had been no Stockholm 1925, the World Council of Churches, at least in its present form, would not exist.

The aim of the Conference was well expressed in the sub-title of its multilingual hymn-book: *Communio in adorando et serviendo oecumenica*. Reverent worship was its very heart. On the first Sunday the Church of Sweden had invited all delegates to participate in a service of Holy Communion according to the Swedish rite. The American Dr A. J. Brown, in his sermon, called upon his fellow delegates to "testify anew to our utter need of divine forgiveness, and our sole dependence upon Christ's atoning sacrifice, our reverent sense of His presence in this place, our fellowship with one another in the Gospel, and our full purpose for the coming days to walk more worthily as His disciples". To many, this service was the highest point of the Conference. But a deep impression was made also by the memorial service for the Patriarch Tikhon of Russia, conducted by the Patriarch of Alexandria; and by the concluding service in Uppsala Cathedral,

[1] In his Introduction to Peter Katz, *Nathan Söderblom: A Prophet of Christian Unity*, p. 10.

at which the Archbishop of Uppsala preached and the Patriarch of Alexandria, Photius, recited the Nicene Creed in Greek. There was a deep sense of spiritual fellowship, a realization of the already existing unity in the Church of Christ.

Under the six main headings decided on in 1922,[1] the Conference surveyed the whole range of Christian social concern. The members had in their hands the reports prepared just before the Conference met. The all too numerous topics and set speeches prevented any extensive plenary discussion; as often, the inner life of the Conference, with its growth of mutual understanding and fellowship, developed more in personal encounters and informal groups in between meetings rather than in the formal sessions. Nor did time permit the drafting of fresh reports to be issued on the authority of the Conference.

One unforeseen feature of the Conference was what Archbishop Söderblom, with a twinkle in his eye, referred to as the "chief issue of the Conference, not printed in the programme". The plans had involved a careful elimination of questions of faith and order, not merely because these were the concern of another branch of the developing ecumenical movement, but because it was believed that theological debate would mar the practical and realistic quality of the Conference. Thus the first subject, the Purpose of God for Humanity and the Duty of the Church, was merely treated in a series of addresses, but no opportunity was offered for its discussion. But problems of ultimate faith, even when most carefully expelled from the front door with a pitchfork, have a tendency to get in again by the back. It soon became evident that, running like a thread through all the deliberations, was one major and inescapable problem of theology.

Two of the key-note addresses on the first day brought out the matter in dramatic fashion. The Bishop of Winchester (F. T. Woods), in his opening sermon, had referred to "the establishment of the sovereignty of Jesus Christ", and to the setting up of "the Kingdom of God on earth". Almost immediately afterwards, Bishop Ihmels of Saxony sounded a different note: "Nothing could be more mistaken or more disastrous than to suppose that we mortal men have to build up God's kingdom in the world." The tension between these different conceptions of the Kingdom of God came to dominate much of the discussion and, because not squarely faced, led to continual misunderstanding. This misunderstanding was not eased when the theological issue was confused with national and confessional categories—such as American activism versus German other-worldliness, or Calvinism against Lutheranism. Here an antithesis was revealed—partly theological, partly geographical and cultural—which in changing manifestations was to preoccupy the movement for many years to come.

The "Message of the Universal Christian Conference on Life and Work" was the only official utterance of the meeting. Carefully prepared and moderately phrased, this document, in spite of some inevitable allusions to the first world war and its consequences, is much less dated than might have been expected, and in its enunciation of central ecumenical themes is a worthy prelude to the many similar ecumenical documents which have followed it. It contains expressions of penitence for the failure of the Churches to do their duty, affirms the obligation resting on the Churches to apply the Gospel "in all realms of human life—industrial, social, political and international", but limits "the mission of the Church", which "is above all to state principles, and to assert the ideal, while

[1] See Chap. xi, p. 541.

leaving to individual consciences and to communities the duty of applying them with charity, wisdom and courage". It looks beyond the Churches, since "we gratefully recognize that now we have many allies in this holy cause"—the young of all countries; those who are seeking after truth by whatever way; the workers of the world, many of whom "are acting in accordance with these principles".

The Message ends on a deeper note, in which some phrases are curiously prophetic of later experiences and other responses to the ecumenical challenge:

> "Only as we become inwardly one shall we attain real unity of mind and spirit. The nearer we draw to the Crucified, the nearer we come to one another, in however varied colours the Light of the World may be reflected in our faith. Under the Cross of Jesus Christ we reach out hands to one another. The Good Shepherd had to die in order that He might gather together the scattered children of God. In the Crucified and Risen Lord alone lies the world's hope."

In all the records of the Conference, nothing is more striking than the way in which speaker after speaker reverts to the Cross of Christ as that centre of unity in which the Churches experience already the fact and the promise of Christian unity.

The Conference had met, listened, debated, discussed, and dispersed. To what had all the labour, effort, and devotion poured into Stockholm 1925 amounted?

> "Much human weakness, some mixed and ambiguous motives, dissensions and human and all too human pettiness, vanity and egotism have been evident in the preparations for and during the progress of the Conference. Once more have we witnessed how God can use us, in spite of our sins and miserable incapacity, for accomplishing His will. And now, at the end of this meeting, we ask Him to forgive us. We ask each other for forgiveness. And we join in adoration of His will and holiness. . . . Now that the Conference is over everybody will see how natural it was, how it came as a necessary result of the actions and reactions and conditions of our time. It was an expression of a general longing."[1]

So, in humility, at its close spoke its chief architect. The delegates knew that something great had happened; they were willing to leave it to history to determine how important these happenings might be for the world-wide Church.

We may select for special mention some of the points which marked an advance on anything that had gone before.

(1) Earlier world conferences had been assemblages of interested individuals or spokesmen of particular Christian interests; at Stockholm, with the exception of a small number of representatives of international Christian organizations, all the delegates had been appointed by their respective communions. It is true that they were not plenipotentiaries, and that it was most carefully laid down in the letter of invitation that the Churches would not be bound by any of the findings of the Conference "unless and until they are presented to and accepted by the authorities of each communion"; but this is a limitation which must be attendant on all ecumenical activity, as long as the Churches remain in separation.

The presence of a strong delegation from the Orthodox Churches, led by the

[1] Söderblom in *The Stockholm Conference 1925*, p. 728.

Patriarchs of Alexandria and Jerusalem, was of immeasurable significance. As has been noted earlier, authorities of the Church of England were resolutely set against the participation of that Church in any conference to which the ancient Churches of the East and West had not been invited. The absence of the Church of Rome, except for a few individual observers, was inevitable and regrettable. The presence of the Orthodox stamped the movement as genuinely ecumenical, and made easier the whole-hearted self-committal of the Anglican and Old Catholic Communions to its development. Their contribution was notable, and was prophetic of the gifts that the Orthodox were to bring to the later conferences in the great ecumenical series. On the other hand, the absence of the Church of Russia meant that that historic Church was not among the founding Churches of the modern ecumenical movement.

The greatest weakness in the membership was on the side of the younger Churches. Only six nationals were present from India, China, and Japan. The difficulties of finance and travel were considerable, and the view still prevailed that these Churches were the province of the International Missionary Council. But this weakness did not characterize Stockholm 1925 alone; it is only in more recent years that the ecumenical movement has ceased to be an essentially Western phenomenon.

Nevertheless, with all its limitations, the Conference was ecumenical in aim and intention. It was the considered opinion of more than one well-qualified observer that it "justified its ambitious title of œcumenical or universal in motive and operation. It envisaged the whole Church".[1]

(2) In the minds of many, perhaps the greatest achievement of the Conference was the new spiritual and psychological climate, the fresh discoveries of Christian fellowship, transcending denominational oppositions and national antagonisms, which it brought about. The strains and stresses within the Conference sometimes nearly led to explosions. It is almost impossible for those who did not live through the period to realize the intensity of the bitterness between nations which lasted for many years after the signing of the Armistice in 1918. Even in 1925 "all wise people thought it impossible" that such a conference could be held. Perhaps the most dramatic moment of the deliberations was when Superintendent Klingemann of Germany challenged, both for theological and political reasons, the almost religious fervour with which some delegates had spoken of the League of Nations; and Pastor Élie Gounelle implored the Germans not to stand aside from the League, saying, "We await you, we stretch out our hands to you". As a later section will show, the controversy of which this was a poignant expression was to go on for many years.

No less deep was the confessional cleavage, not to speak of the abysmal ignorance about one another which existed among the Churches at that time. Great care had been taken not to offend the susceptibilities of the Churches by precipitating confessional issues. But experience showed once again that members of different confessions cannot meet in frank intercourse without becoming more vividly aware of the particularities and distinctive positions of other traditions, and at the same time by reaction becoming more conscious of the spiritual riches of their own. As a Danish bishop remarked: "I for my part have become a better Lutheran through Anglo-Saxon influence, deeper convinced of the central truth of our tradition, but also recognizing that in the course of time we had lost something of the original riches, which we will have to take up again."

[1] Charles H. Brent, *Understanding*, p. 7.

It was therefore a real spiritual triumph, that, in spite of all the difficulties, on the whole harmony and fellowship prevailed. As the Bishop of Saxony expressed it: "What seemed impossible has come to pass. We have met together, and not merely in a formal way. We have really tried to work together in the unity of the Spirit. Above all, those of us who collaborated in the various commissions have been privileged to look into each others' hearts, and I am sure that we shall not forget that."[1]

(3) Stockholm 1925 affirmed in unmistakable terms the responsibility of the Churches for the whole life of man. In doing so, it brought to focus the manifold and scattered endeavours of generations. The Conference was sometimes called the "Nicaea of ethics". The King of Sweden, in opening the Conference, referred to the great assembly which had met 1,600 years before in A.D. 325. But such a parallel is misleading. Stockholm 1925 did not produce any ecumenical social creed or solve any controversial problems of Christian action. In the brief span of its twelve days it made a rapid survey of the needs of contemporary society; it appealed to the conscience of the Christian world and indicated possible lines of advance. The moderation with which its claims were expressed constituted no small part of the effectiveness of its appeal. Its distinction lay in the universality of its outlook and the sincerity of its concern. Yet it did give the Churches something to live up to; in its bold affirmation of the universal sovereignty of Christ, it demanded unconditional acceptance of principles which even Churches that nominally accepted them had too often allowed to remain a dormant part of their creed.

The echoes of the Conference throughout the world were truly remarkable. It had been, so its Message asserted, "the most signal instance of fellowship and co-operation, across the boundaries of nations and confessions, which the world has yet seen".[2] And the various reactions did indeed reveal the powerful impact of a great event.

Acclaimed by some as the most important ecclesiastical happening of the century, inaugurating a new epoch in Christian history, the Conference was condemned by other contemporaries as a dismal failure or, even worse, as a device of the devil. The verdicts passed followed no distinct national or denominational party lines. Stockholm 1925, like every great ecumenical event before or since, proved to be an unexpected divider of spirits and, not infrequently, brought together unexpected allies.

More than anywhere else the Conference found a resounding echo in Sweden, Germany, and Switzerland, where vigorous efforts were made to bring home its message to the Churches, and where the problems it had thrown up roused intensive discussion. In Germany especially the resultant controversies were lively. Many of the German delegates had arrived hesitant, sceptical, and weighed down by the burdens of a defeated nation. They went back heartened by the brotherly reception they had received, and made courageous endeavours to interpret and defend the ideas of Life and Work. It was an arduous campaign; comparatively few Christians as yet realized the need for and the potentialities of such a Christian International for common service. Opposition was raised on both religious and political grounds. In some circles the Conference was assailed as a move of Allied imperialism under the disguise of religion. The theo-

[1] *The Stockholm Conference 1925*, pp. 731 f.
[2] Ibid., p. 710.

logical criticism was equally severe and serious. Spokesmen of Pietism, of rigid Lutheran orthodoxy, and of the nascent dialectical theology for once made common cause, denouncing the meddling of the Church in worldly affairs and the naïve optimism displayed in certain Anglo-Saxon utterances.

In England, reactions to Stockholm 1925 were in part conditioned by the continuing effects of the Conference on Christian Politics, Economics, and Citizenship, which had been held in Birmingham in 1924. Copec produced no continuing organization and therefore remained an isolated event, but it had occupied the time and thought of many leaders in the Churches. People in England were surprised to hear Stockholm 1925 described as a pioneer enterprise; in their view, as regards boldness of thought and practical realism, Copec had, if anything, the advantage.[1] Yet even in England the importance of the Stockholm Conference was recognized, as an international endorsement of the concern for the social responsibility of the Churches which had been steadily growing in England for three-quarters of a century, and as a revelation to the English Churches of their own middle position between the "activism" of the Americans and the "other-worldliness" of the Germans.

The Conference was more keenly appreciated by the Scottish Churches as a stirring novelty. This was not surprising, as Scotland has traditionally paid greater attention to religious developments on the Continent, and was, moreover, less concerned than England in Copec.

In the United States, to a higher degree even than in England, it was felt that Stockholm 1925—apart from its symbolic nature as the first ecumenical gathering of its kind—chiefly afforded a new impetus and outreach to social ideals already firmly rooted in American Protestantism. In order to avoid duplication of machinery, the American members of the Stockholm Continuation Committee sought the co-operation of the Federal Council of Churches in promoting its aims. This association ensured the invaluable support of a large interdenominational body. Between 1925 and 1930, Life and Work in America owed much to the continuing support of such ecumenical leaders as Dr William Adams Brown and Dr C. S. Macfarland, General Secretary of the Federal Council, and to their continuing work as interpreters of the movement to the American Churches. But the association had also certain drawbacks. The Federal Council was widely suspected, especially in conservative circles, for its alleged liberalism and promotion of the Social Gospel. In so far as Life and Work appeared to be an activity of the Federal Council, acceptance of it was made difficult in those same conservative circles. When, in 1930, an American Section of the Universal Christian Council was formed with Dr Henry Smith Leiper as Secretary, the Stockholm movement was able to stand on its own feet, and to make its own individual impact on the life of the American Churches.

The participation of a strong group of Eastern Orthodox leaders had been one of the highlights of the gathering. They had been received with all due honour and undisguised interest. Several of them on their return paid high tribute to this new venture, which was so evidently in line with the famous Encyclical Letter issued by the Ecumenical Patriarchate of Constantinople in 1920.[2] On the other hand, they could not fail to report the overwhelmingly Protestant charac-

---

[1] It is to be noted that Roman Catholics served as full members of almost all the commissions which prepared for Copec. Some of the Reports had the distinction, rare for ecumenical literature, of running rapidly into a third edition.

[2] See Chap. x, p. 446.

ter of the gathering, manifest in its membership, its worship, and its discussions. It is therefore no wonder that in Orthodox countries interest in ecumenical developments, then as later, hardly went beyond a small circle of broad-minded leaders.

The reactions in Roman Catholic quarters were interesting. On well-known grounds the Vatican had declined the invitation to send representatives. But this did not prevent many Roman Catholics, notably in countries with confessionally mixed populations, from showing a sympathetic understanding of the aims of Life and Work, both in articles in the Press and, more outspokenly, in correspondence with Conference leaders. Not a few regretted the absence of their Church at a gathering convened for the purpose of marshalling the Christian forces for practical social tasks. But, as was to be expected, the predominant opinion was critical, if not frankly hostile. Stockholm 1925, it was averred, lacked a definite basis of faith, and was therefore to be regarded as a dangerous and unfruitful enterprise.

Both as a "mount of transfiguration" and as a "rock of offence", the Conference was a landmark in ecumenical history. In many minds it kindled great hopes of a new departure. It left to the future a striking challenge in fertile ideas and initiatives, and problems awaiting solution. It is in terms of those ideas and those problems that the history of Life and Work has to be written.

2. THE GROWTH OF LIFE AND WORK

The members of the Stockholm Conference were agreed that the work so auspiciously begun must be carried forward boldly, and that this could not be done without some form of continuing organization. As one speaker remarked, ".Disembodied spirits do not saw much wood". On the other hand, they were mindful of the limitations of their mandate. They had no authority to set up any kind of international church council or federation, or even to commit their Churches to the purpose and findings of the Conference.[1] While some, like Dr G. K. A. Bell (from 1929 Bishop of Chichester), envisaged the formation of an International Christian Council on Life and Work, others, more cautious, regarded such plans as premature and visionary.

The gathering unanimously decided to appoint a Continuation Committee, among the duties of which would be:

"(1) To perpetuate and strengthen the spirit of fellowship which this Conference so happily exemplifies. . . .

"(3) To carry on the work of the Conference and to consider how far and in what ways its practical suggestions may be made operative.

"(4) To gather information regarding the methods of co-operation among the churches in the various countries for the objects which are the concern of the Conference, to take counsel with them as to methods of closer international co-operation, to do what may be found wise to facilitate the formation of such agencies in countries where they do not now exist. . . .

"(5) To consider the practicability of holding another Universal Christian Conference on Life and Work at some future date."[2]

---

[1] The same wise caution in the statement of ecumenical possibilities is found again and again expressed in the records of the first Assembly of the World Council of Churches, Amsterdam 1948.   [2] *The Stockholm Conference 1925*, pp. 707 f.

It was expressly declared that the Committee should "have no power to speak in the name or on behalf of the churches or to take any action that shall commit any church, its deliverances being simply its own opinion, unless any particular deliverance or deliverances shall be expressly approved by the church or churches concerned".[1] The members of the Continuation Committee were instructed to maintain "close and official" connection with their Churches. In most cases their appointment was subsequently approved or sanctioned by the communions to which they belonged. This was the case with all the Orthodox members. Thus, although the Committee did not constitute a joint agency of the Churches, it was to a large degree composed of their officially recognized representatives. In a number of countries, however, the relationship was deliberately left more informal. The pattern, adopted in the preparatory stage, of operating in Sections was maintained. To the four earlier Sections— American, British, European Continental, and Eastern Orthodox—there was now added a fifth embracing "Churches in other lands", the representatives of which were to be elected later.

A Movement takes Shape. In 1930 the Continuation Committee was reconstituted as a permanent body, the Universal Christian Council for Life and Work. This change marked the official acceptance of a principle which had already become evident in the five years' work of the Continuation Committee—that, whereas the holding of periodical conferences is a useful part of ecumenical activity, concerns such as those of Stockholm 1925 can be adequately dealt with only by a permanent body, officially recognized, through which the work of one conference can be linked to that of another, and the Churches continuously kept in touch with one another and with the progressive development of ecumenical thought and activity. The principal objective of the Council, according to its Constitution, was "to perpetuate and strengthen the fellowship between the churches in the application of Christian ethics to the social problems of modern life".[2] Noteworthy is the stipulation concerning the five Sections: "The Sections shall be the constituent bodies of the Council, and shall be in each case responsible for their own organisation. The Sections shall be composed of representatives of the Churches."

The setting-up of the projected fifth Section, including the younger Churches, proved impracticable and this Section never came into being. As a substitute solution, it was decided in 1934 that the National Christian Councils in Asia and Africa should be recognized as doing the work of the fifth Section, and that representation of the younger Churches at ecumenical gatherings should be ensured through the International Missionary Council.[3] To obviate, at least in some measure, the markedly Western orientation of the movement, close personal contacts were maintained with the Department of Social and Economic Research of the I.M.C., established in Geneva after the Jerusalem Meeting of 1928. This collaboration was later strengthened when I.M.C. leaders like J. H. Oldham and W. Paton became associated with the preparations for the Oxford Conference of 1937.[4] It is indicative of the growing convergence of

---

[1] *The Stockholm Conference 1925*, p. 707.

[2] *Minutes . . . Continuation Committee of Life and Work, Chexbres, Switzerland, September 1930*, pp. 16 ff.

[3] *Minutes of the Meeting of the Universal Christian Council, Fanø, Denmark, 1934*, p. 61.

[4] See p. 584. These two leaders also strengthened the association between Life and Work and the ecumenical traditions of the World's Student Christian Federation.

interest and outlook that when the I.M.C. planned its Meeting at Tambaram in 1938, it definitely built on the results of Oxford 1937. Yet even at Oxford the younger Churches were represented by only twenty-nine delegates out of 425, and of these only sixteen were nationals of the countries which they represented.

The Life and Work leaders started forth, actuated by the conviction that they were "preachers of a new message to Christians, to be known in future as 'Stockholm' ".[1] With silvery oratory Wilfred Monod, a noble mystic and sufferer under the evils of the world, founder of a Protestant Franciscan lay order and passionate supporter of every movement for social reform, used to proclaim the "prophetic thought and missionary testimony" of the Stockholm message.[2] Fraternities of "Companions of Stockholm" were set up to work for "the carrying through of urgent reforms in conformity with the ideal of Stockholm".[3]

The movement became a laboratory of fertile ideas and projects. Many of the activities, later more fully developed by the World Council of Churches, had their prophetic beginnings in the early stages of the movement, or were at least recognized as a necessary expression of the ecumenical impulse—interdenominational inter-Church aid, an ecumenical training institute, the introduction of an ecumenical approach in the study of Church history and in theological education generally, and even the project of writing an Ecumenical History.

The Continuation Committee took up its responsibilities with vigour and vision. Archbishop Söderblom was appropriately chosen as its first President, to be followed in turn by the Presidents of the other Sections—Bishop Theodore Woods of Winchester, Archbishop Germanos of Thyateira, and the American Dr A. J. Brown. At first one name only was proposed for the office of General Secretary, that of Dr Henry A. Atkinson, Secretary of the (American) Church Peace Union; but this did not meet with the approval of the Continental representatives, already alarmed by the non-theological and activist emphasis from the Anglo-Saxon world by which it seemed that Life and Work might be overwhelmed. On strong representations made by them and on the motion of Professor Deissmann on behalf of the German delegation, it was arranged that Professor Adolph Keller of Switzerland should serve with Dr Atkinson as Co-ordinate General Secretary, Dr Atkinson to carry executive responsibility for the work of the Continuation Committee and its Commissions and Dr Keller for the International Christian Social Institute and, after 1930, for ecumenical "education and extension". In 1928, Life and Work set up its headquarters in Geneva, thus establishing contact both with other international Christian organizations and with the League of Nations and the International Labour Office.

The appointment of Dr Atkinson and Dr Keller was in a way symbolic of a dialectical though sometimes exhausting tension, which persisted through many years of work, between what may be called roughly the American and the European points of view; the American, more concerned with immediate practical applications, and thinking of research in terms of the collection of factual data which could be applied in urgent reforms, the European deeply interested in principles, and looking to research for the elucidation of the ways in which

---

[1] Archbishop Germanos in his presidential address at the *Meeting of the Continuation Committee of Life and Work, Prague, 1928*, p. 24.
[2] *Minutes . . . Continuation Committee of Life and Work, Chexbres, Switzerland, September 1930*, p. 63.
[3] *Minutes . . . Continuation Committee of Life and Work, Prague, 1928*, p. 19.

Christian principles can be applied to complex modern problems; the American sitting somewhat loose to the existing Churches, the European deeply aware from the start of the problem of the Churches with their varying confessions and widely differing approach to social problems; the American more empirical, the European more theoretical, or, as the Europeans perhaps would have said, more thorough, in its approach.

Archbishop Söderblom remained the revered inspirer and counsellor of the movement until his death in 1931. The Stockholm Conference had been the crowning point of his life-long ecumenical efforts; soon afterwards increasing ill-health and heavy primatial duties forced him to transfer the burden of the day to other shoulders. The chairmanship of the Continental Section passed to Dr Kapler, President of the Federation of Evangelical Churches in Germany. New leaders came to the fore. With rare distinction and gentle firmness, the Bishop of Chichester (Bell) guided the Council as its Chairman during some of its most critical years. His handling of the relations with the German Churches, in a time of fierce struggle which placed before the ecumenical movement perplexing and difficult choices, was a masterpiece of pastoral statecraft. Another great leader during this period was Professor William Adams Brown, the Nestor among American theologians and an ecumenical veteran. Moving with equal ease in Faith and Order, Life and Work, and the World Alliance, he took a prominent part in the efforts to draw these movements closely together.

Unfolding Activities. One of the first tasks of the movement was to bring into existence the International Christian Social Institute, which had been proposed at Stockholm by Bishop Einar Billing of Västerås and Pastor Élie Gounelle. This process revealed much diversity of view as to what the Institute should be and do. Some felt that it should reflect the larger ecumenical inspiration of Stockholm, rather than restrict itself to the single field of social justice. The majority felt that at the start it would be wiser to accept the limitation to social and industrial concerns. Some thought that it should serve as a centre of co-ordination for Christian social work, and a clearing-house of factual information. Others felt that it should offer to the Churches, whenever desired, practical guidance "based on the knowledge already gained regarding the social obligations of the Churches". Yet others felt that the first task was precisely the laying of the foundations of a knowledge of the Christian bases of social action.

The Charter of the Institute, as drawn up by Dr Keller and Dr W. M. Tippy, and accepted by the Continuation Committee in 1927, set forth in detail the programme of the Institute, in the light of its threefold task:

> "(a) It should be a centre for mutual knowledge, correlation and co-operation of all socially active Christian organizations in the different religious communions and countries. . . .
> "(b) It should study in the light of Christian ethics by strictly scientific methods the social and industrial facts and problems in the widest sense. . . .
> "(c) It should be a centre of information, by which the exchange will be facilitated of knowledge, experience and methods which can be serviceable to the Church in its social-ethical tasks."[1]

It is difficult for the student, looking back from a later date, to realize the pioneer character of almost everything that Life and Work had to undertake.

[1] *Minutes . . . Continuation Committee of Life and Work, Winchester, 1927*, pp. 10–13.

The Churches were extraordinarily ignorant of one other's life, suspicious, much given to darkening counsel by the use of labels—Anglo-Saxon, activist, liberal, and the like—without thought, unwilling to learn from one another, almost wholly unversed in any kind of international co-operation. The leaders realized from the start that if the movement were to make any headway, there must be a sustained effort of education, study, and practical activity; education both in expounding the ecumenical idea and in interpreting the Churches to one another; study of the manifold areas of *malaise* in the field of social and industrial life; practical activity in the application of Stockholm principles to the life and witness of the Churches.

The International Institute was hampered throughout its life by inadequate financial support, especially after the economic depression burst upon the world in 1929. It was not always able to put its purposes into effect. But it was successful in laying down almost all the principles, lines of activity, and methods (many of them already familiar in missionary and student circles), which have since become normal parts of the ecumenical enterprise.[1]

To explain the Churches to one another, it launched the almost new science of "comparative ecclesiology".[2] Apart from the books produced by its Director, Professor Keller,[3] one of the most remarkable manifestations of this approach was the invaluable series *Ekklesia*, in which, under the editorship of Professor Siegmund-Schultze, experts in many countries co-operated to produce volume after volume on the Churches in the different countries of Europe.[4] It was recognized that most of the teaching of Church history in universities was narrowly confessional in outlook. A successful attempt was made to secure both the reconsideration of Church history teaching from an ecumenical point of view, and the introduction of specific courses on ecumenical subjects in the theological curriculum. To this end Dr Keller visited more than a hundred universities and theological schools, in both Europe and America, to lecture and to discuss with the faculties the problem of ecumenical teaching.

From 1929-31, the Institute produced a tri-lingual quarterly, *Stockholm*, the first official ecumenical periodical, in which Dr A. E. Garvie, Pastor Élie Gounelle, Professor D. A. Titius, and Dr W. M. Tippy co-operated, with Dr Keller as editor. Unhappily this, like so much else in the ecumenical programme, fell a victim to the financial stringency resulting from the world economic crisis.

The first steps were taken towards the formation of a graduate school of ecumenical studies in connection with the theological faculty of the University of Geneva. When this proved at the time impossible of realization[5] its place was taken by an annual "Ecumenical Seminar" in Geneva, sponsored by the Universal Christian Council. After three years of preliminary study, the first Seminar was held in 1933, and was followed by others in each of the three succeeding years. In the four years, it was attended by nearly three hundred students from many countries, who through lectures, discussions, and personal contacts, were led into the heart of the ecumenical situation and its problems. Its truly ecumenical

---

[1] See especially A. Keller in *The Ecumenical Review*, Vol. II, No. 4, pp. 346–75.

[2] There is no satisfactory English equivalent for the convenient German term *Ökumenische Kirchenkunde*.

[3] See especially *Protestant Europe: its Crisis and Outlook*, London, 1927.

[4] In all, fifteen volumes were published. The first and one of the best was that by Dr G. K. A. Bell on *Die Kirche von England* (1934).

[5] The plan was destined to be realized, under the auspices of the World Council of Churches. in 1952.

character may be indicated by a short selection from the list of the lecturers who took part—Karl Barth, William Adams Brown, Emil Brunner, Fr (later Bishop) Cassian, Eugène Choisy, Martin Dibelius, Toyohiko Kagawa, Nicol MacNicol, Reinhold Niebuhr, William Pauck, George W. Richards, Arvid Runestam, Paul Tillich, G. van der Leeuw, Stefan Zankov.

With the approach of the second world war, the activities of the Seminar were interrupted. But for a number of years, similar Seminars were conducted in some of the larger cities of the United States; here should be noted also the ecumenical activities of Dr Jesse M. Bader, the founder of the National Preaching Mission in the United States.

Like the World Council after it, Life and Work planned to do much of its work through commissions, covering a remarkably wide range of subjects. Some of the Commissions developed ambitious plans of work which for one reason or another they were not able to carry out; but they proved their value as the instrument through which Life and Work was able to keep in touch with and to influence the social activities of the Churches, and with the great secular international organizations. Space forbids the mention of more than four of these Commissions and their work.

To bridge the gulf between the Churches and the working classes had from the outset been one of the preoccupations of the movement. With passionate eloquence men like Élie Gounelle, the inspirer of the French *Christianisme Social*, urged Life and Work to lead the Churches out of their middle-class isolationism. It must demonstrate, more by pioneer deeds of social justice than by pious words, that it followed the Carpenter of Nazareth in his compassion for the multitudes, toiling, hungry, and without security. Under the chairmanship of Gounelle, a Commission on Church and Labour evolved ambitious plans to establish contacts with the various labour organizations, employers, and workers.

The need for a firm theological grounding of the movement had already made itself felt at Stockholm in 1925. There were also among its leaders some who held the view that interchange of theological thought, regardless of its results for social action, performed an essential function in strengthening ecumenical fellowship. To meet this need, a Commission was set up "for co-operation among theologians", with two German New Testament scholars of international repute, Adolf Deissmann and Martin Dibelius, as its leaders. It arranged study conferences on such subjects as "The Kingdom of God", "*Mysterium Christi*", and "The Church". Professor Deissmann, one of the writers of the Stockholm Message and of the Lausanne 1927 Declaration on "The Gospel", and many of his colleagues on the Commission, were equally active in Faith and Order, thus anticipating the later unification of the two movements.

If the movement, as its champions hoped, was to serve as a ferment of rejuvenation within the Churches, it must pay special attention to the rising generation and enlist their enthusiasm. A Youth Commission was created which, in conjunction with other Christian world youth organizations located at Geneva, arranged over a period of years a series of extremely lively study weeks, which showed a refreshing disrespect for ecclesiastical prudence. This Commission later merged with a similar World Alliance agency of remarkable vigour in an Ecumenical Youth Commission, one of the sponsoring bodies of the World Conference of Christian Youth which was held in Amsterdam in August 1939.[1]

[1] See Chap. xvi, p. 708.

The International Christian Press Commission undertook to disseminate information in the world Press on the Stockholm movement and on the life of the Churches. It issued frequent "ecumenical letters", arranged exhibitions of ecumenical literature and regional conferences of journalists and editors, promoted religious broadcasting, and exercised a noticeable influence, especially on the Continent, in bringing home the ecumenical idea to a wider public. Out of this grew, in 1933, the weekly *International Christian Press and Information Service* (later the *Ecumenical Press Service*), which over the years has gained steadily increasing recognition as a purveyor of ecumenical world news.

One ecumenical activity of this time, though not strictly a responsibility of Life and Work, was so closely connected with it that it may appropriately be described in connection with the developing enterprise of Life and Work—the European Central Bureau for Inter-Church Aid.[1] A pioneer venture in ecumenical relief, it began its work under the patronage of the Federal Council of the Churches of Christ in America and the Federation of Swiss Protestant Churches, later joined by other European Churches. At a conference in Copenhagen in 1922, the Bureau was officially established with offices in New York and Geneva and with Professor Keller as Director.

The first task of the Bureau was to help Churches, Christian institutions, and ministers in distress. This task it fulfilled without partiality and in the widest spirit of brotherhood. Christians in sixteen countries—Orthodox, Armenians, Assyrians, and Chinese in time of famine, no less than European Protestants— were the recipients of timely help. The International Protestant Loan Association,[2] a non-profit-making mutual aid society, was established in order to enable the Churches to help themselves through the accomplishment of tasks for which their own unaided resources were inadequate. This ecumenical service continues to be rendered. In part with the help of a Rockefeller grant, a leadership programme was developed and scholarships provided in order to enable students of theology to pursue their studies in their own country or abroad.

Often referred to as the "relief arm" of the ecumenical movement, or the "Red Cross of the Churches", the Bureau continued its beneficent work until 1945, expending over the years about 12 million Swiss francs, and a much larger sum in dollars. In that year, by its own wish, it merged with the Department of Reconstruction and Relief of the World Council of Churches (in process of formation) and transferred its assets to the Department, and to Church World Service in New York.

In 1933 the plight of non-Aryan refugees from the Nazi régime faced the Churches with a new challenge. The European Central Bureau, Life and Work, and the World Alliance joined in setting up an International Christian Commission for Refugees, with the Bishop of Chichester (Bell) as Chairman. Stimulating the Churches to face up to their responsibilities, and engaging in practical assistance and resettlement programmes, this too was a significant manifestation of ecumenical fellowship. Among the refugee pastors and theologians from Germany, not a few became notable ecumenical bridge-builders in their new homes —thus demonstrating again the truth that the Christian refugee is a natural carrier of ecumenical germs.

[1] See Adolf Keller, *Zur Lage des europäischen Protestantismus*, 1922, and also his article in *Die Eiche*, 1933, No. 1, pp. 28–40.
[2] *Association Protestante Internationale de Prêts* (APIDEP).

A Time of Heart-searching. The reorganization of the movement and the formation of the Universal Christian Council in 1930 did not mean that all was peaceful in the Life and Work garden, or that a permanent resting-place had been discovered. On the contrary, the records of the immediately succeeding years are marked by a sense of crisis, of heart-searching, and of uncertainty.

This was in part due to the financial crisis of those years; the situation was indeed so critical that at one time some leaders in the movement thought that it might be necessary to close down the work altogether. But the real crisis was interior and independent of any adverse outward circumstances.

Life and Work was facing the same difficulty as arises in every movement which starts with an outburst of enthusiasm. The initial impulse is inevitably followed by months and years of steady humdrum work, in which it is difficult for enthusiasm to be maintained, and easy for the sense of direction to be lost. Some of the pioneers had already passed away; their place had been taken by younger men to whom the visions and aspirations of Stockholm were known only at second-hand.

But deepest of all was the unresolved tension which, as we have seen, existed already at the Stockholm Conference itself, between those who held diverse views as to the Kingdom of God—between those to whom Stockholm 1925 was primarily a movement for the renewal of the life of the Churches, and those to whom it was primarily a practical expression of the life already existing in the Churches and a means of closer co-operation.

Archbishop Söderblom had often spoken of Life and Work as a movement of revival. Did the movement still deserve that title in 1932? Most of its supporters would confidently have affirmed that it did; yet that there was anxiety on the subject is shown by the presidential address of the Bishop of Chichester in that year. The Bishop called for "a deeper spiritual experience", and an effort to bring together "the keen minds in the different churches . . . to interpret to the present generation in terms it will understand the necessity of God in Christ" and to work out "the fundamental principles for which the Christian religion stands in a material or secular age".[1] On the same occasion Professor (later Bishop) Runestam, a son-in-law of Archbishop Söderblom, pleaded for a radical re-examination of the purpose of the whole movement. "The original idea and the inspiring power in the hearts of the founders", he declared, was a shared life in the given unity, a fellowship in worship and in witnessing to God's wondrous acts in Christ. But had this original purpose been maintained, or had the emphasis on the practical in certain areas of the Life and Work constituency resulted in a subtle reversal of values, putting first things second and second things first?

The annual meeting in 1933 was held at the residence of Bishop Irenei of Novi Sad, while singing groups of "bogomoltsi"[2] passed by, day after day, on a pilgrimage to the famous monastery of Kovil. William Adams Brown, Chairman of the Administrative Committee, pointed to two tasks as being of major importance—"The need of fixing some comprehensive goal which the ecumenical movement as a whole may take as its ultimate objective, and the need for reinforcing the motives which furnish the movement with its driving power".[3] An incident occurred during that meeting which dramatically lighted up cer-

---

[1] *Minutes . . . Universal Christian Council for Life and Work, Geneva, 1932,* pp. 1 ff.
[2] " Those who pray to God"—a lay movement of renewal in the Serbian Orthodox Church.
[3] *Minutes . . . Executive Committee of the Universal Christian Council, Novi Sad, Yugoslavia, 1933,* p. 6.

tain new forces that had come into operation since the Stockholm Conference in 1925. The Committee met in a tense atmosphere; it had to deal with profoundly disturbing happenings in Germany. In the opening session the members had listened, in a spirit of solemn rededication, to the reading of the Stockholm Message. Then, in the course of the discussion, a spokesman of the new Church government in Nazi Germany shocked the audience by launching a frontal attack on the very basis of Stockholm 1925. "Its message is obsolete . . . the off-spring of the humanitarian ideals of the Enlightenment and the French Revolution. . . . The rising Reformation theology to-day would put a critical question-mark at almost every sentence in it."[1] Evidently these words expressed only one German point of view and would have been met by the flat disagreement of the great German leaders who from the beginning had supported the Stockholm movement. Nevertheless, they disclosed grave tensions and new trends of thought in Europe, with which increasingly Life and Work would have to deal.

3. INTERNATIONAL FRIENDSHIP THROUGH THE CHURCHES

The preceding chapter has shown the part played by the World Alliance in preparing the way for the Stockholm Conference of 1925. Its activities had produced a far-flung network of personal contacts and an expanding atmosphere of friendship and mutual confidence among religious leaders, which greatly helped the new movement in its beginnings. Stockholm 1925 in its turn, by dramatically focusing world attention on the ecumenical cause, gave a new impetus to the efforts of the World Alliance for peace. From the outset there was a considerable overlapping of personnel in the governing bodies. To prevent wasteful duplication, it was agreed in 1926 that "matters relating to the study and promoting of international fellowship through the Churches should, for the present, be regarded as the province of the World Alliance".[2]

Yet such division of the field could not be absolute. Similarity of concern and purpose—notwithstanding distinct dissimilarities in temper and method—resulted over the years in close relationships in various areas, culminating in the establishment of a joint General Secretariat and a variety of common undertakings.[3]

Developments in the World Alliance. The structure of the Alliance had been firmly developed before 1925, and remained unaltered through the years. The meetings of its supreme body, the International Council, composed of some 145 members appointed by the various National Councils, were sufficiently rare occurrences to stand out as memorable landmarks: 1928 in Prague, 1931 in Cambridge, 1935 in Chamby (Switzerland), and 1938 in Larvik (Norway). In their different moods and concerns, these gatherings mirrored the changing phases of advance and, disconcertingly soon, the disillusioning breakdown of international co-operation.

This structure was marked by one feature, which guaranteed great freedom and flexibility in national activities, but which later blocked the way to union with other ecumenical movements. It was based on constituent National

---

[1] To Wilfred Monod, who had taken a prominent part in the drafting of the 1925 Message, this attack involved an unconscionable betrayal of a sacred trust. He recalls the incident in his autobiography, *Après la journée*, Paris, 1938, p. 302.

[2] *Minutes . . . Continuation Committee of Life and Work, Berne, 1926*, p. 12.

[3] See p. 566.

Councils, each free to determine conditions of membership in its own body. As originally phrased at the Constance Conference, the objective of the National Councils should be "to enlist the Churches, in their corporate capacity, in a joint endeavour to achieve the promotion of international friendship and the avoidance of war".[1] But this objective was in practice implemented in diverse ways. In some countries, especially on the continent of Europe, the National Councils worked in close relation with ecclesiastical authorities; in most areas, however, they remained entirely independent agencies, based on the personal adhesion of their members. The American Council, the most powerful and vigorous of all, working closely with the Church Peace Union, presented an exceptional pattern in that it included on equal terms Protestants, Roman Catholics, and Jews. Some of its most influential members were, moreover, keenly interested in enlarging the movement into a united peace front of Christian and non-Christian faiths. The comprehensive membership and the unofficial status of the World Alliance enabled it to pursue its course relatively unhampered by the misapprehensions, hesitations, and prejudices still prevalent in many ecclesiastical quarters.

The evolution of the international situation and of its own work led the World Alliance to repeated re-appraisals of its message and function. One of its main statements of policy, adopted at the Conference at Prague in 1928, may be cited as indicating how it conceived its ecumenical mandate:

"The work of the World Alliance for International Friendship through the Churches rests upon the readiness of its National Councils and of the Churches working together in them to use their influence with the peoples, parliaments and governments of their own countries to bring about good and friendly relations between the nations. . . .

"Among the international questions which affect moral-religious or Church interests, the following are the most important:

(a) The securing of religious freedom and of the rights of Churches, groups or sections of people in any country.

(b) The prevention of every oppression, injury or obstruction of any Churches, congregations, schools, institutes and other works in any sphere of religious activity.

(c) The elucidation of other political or church events which are calculated to endanger good relations between the Churches.

(d) The promotion of positive relations between Christians, congregations and Churches of the different lands.

(e) Endeavours towards the conciliation of class and race antagonisms which become of international importance.

(f) Support of proposals and measures calculated to promote justice in the relations between the peoples."[2]

Within this vast range there were certain issues which claimed the particular attention of the Alliance. Its resolutions and actions continued to show constant preoccupation with disarmament, religious and national minorities, religious liberty, refugees, the strengthening of the League of Nations, and mitigation of tensions between particular nations.

[1] See Constitution, reprinted in the *World Alliance Handbook, 1938*, pp. 18 f.
[2] *World Alliance Handbook, 1938*, pp. 24 f.

In tackling such problems the Alliance manifested its belief in the primary importance of creating "atmosphere" and "climate", of cultivating mutual friendship and confidence among religious leaders of different countries. Its numerous regional conferences, particularly those in the Balkans and in the Baltic countries, were among the most successful ventures of the World Alliance, and at times had remarkable effects in the life of the nations. Here Church representatives were brought together, suspicious of one another's designs, intensely loyal to their own denominational or national group, and under the gentle coaching of impartial ecumenical friends they learned to precede their nations on the narrow path of reconciliation.

An outstanding instance concerns the strained relations between Bulgaria and Yugoslavia in the 1920's. At the World Alliance meeting held in Avignon in 1929, the problem was discussed with the Orthodox Church leaders present, the leading figures being Archbishop Stefan of Sofia on one side, and Bishop Irenei of Novi Sad on the other. This discussion was followed by an exchange of visits of official delegations of the two Churches, which not only proved effective in making public opinion aware of the need for better relationships, but paved the way for *rapprochement* at the political level. The visits of ecclesiastical dignitaries led on to similar exchanges of visits by kings and government leaders. This happy *rapprochement* was a direct result of World Alliance activity in the Balkans. More than any other part of the ecumenical movement, the World Alliance was successful in that period in securing the support both of Church authorities and youth leaders in the Orthodox Churches.

As seen from the declaration quoted above, the interests of the Alliance ranged far beyond international affairs in the strict sense. This broader view of its objectives was particularly noticeable in the German branch, which in fact was the recognized agency for ecumenical education and promotion in general in that country, until the Nazi régime made it inoperative.[1] Professor Siegmund-Schultze, one of the founders and foremost leaders of the World Alliance, rendered a signal service to the German-reading public by making his quarterly, *Die Eiche* (1912–33), a sounding-board for the entire ecumenical cause.[2]

The deterioration of the international situation in the 1930's threw new obstacles in the path of the World Alliance, blocking its advance at many points, particularly on the Continent. The discussions of these years abound with reaffirmations of its basic principles and with exhortations to a more concentrated campaign for peace. But while for some—especially in the United States, less touched by the international earthquake—this meant a call to pursue more vigorously the course already set, others felt that the time had come for a radical re-examination of principles. Was the Alliance's concept of peace, was its work for peace, based firmly enough on the very rock of the Christian religion? Had it perhaps over-estimated the power of friendship and goodwill to overcome the stubborn forces of conflict operating in society?

At a meeting of the International Council in 1936, Bishop Ammundsen delivered a presidential address on "The Present World Situation", memorable for its depth of religious discernment and its judicious statesmanship. "Our social and international work shall neither be isolated from the regular activity of the Church, nor try to replace it. . . . Our endeavours must be rooted in personal faith and in the whole doctrinal, educational and sacramental life of the

---

[1] Cf. F. Siegmund-Schultze in *Oekumenische Einheit*, I, Heft 2, 1950, p. 170.
[2] On the series *Ekklesia* edited by him, see above, p. 556, n. 4.

Church." In co-operating with workers for peace holding other beliefs, we must "always accentuate our definite Christian motive and message, which will also determine the methods".[1]

Efforts at International Reconciliation. It is the outstanding merit of the World Alliance—seconded by Life and Work at critical moments and particularly in the deeper theological elucidation of the problems—that it created a new international outlook in leading circles in the Protestant and Orthodox Churches. Moreover, in its manifold activities it offered object-lessons of considerable consequence for the future—how to translate the broadened sense of social responsibility into terms of practical action, how to inform Christian public opinion, how to bring Christian conviction to bear on governments, and so forth. This was in many respects a new and startling experience, especially for the Churches on the European continent, less accustomed than religious bodies in the Anglo-Saxon countries to exercising the democratic right of criticism and constructive co-operation in the shaping of national and foreign policies. And still more, in the ecumenical movement they slowly learned to speak and act, not as a religious minority group within the national community, but as joint-members of the one truly universal community. Non-Roman Christendom found a living voice in matters of international morality; and, on occasions when its warnings and counsels concurred with those of the Roman Catholic Church, something like a Christian world conscience began to manifest itself.

An historian has observed that the attitude of American Protestantism to international affairs in the period between the two world wars was marked by a constant tension and at best an unstable equilibrium between "internationalist" and "pacifist" elements, i.e. between those who stood for an international order of justice, dependent upon economic and military sanctions as a last resort, and those whose basic impulse was goodwill and amity, avoidance of war in any circumstances, and constant pressure for disarmament and neutrality.[2] The same tension can be traced in the ecumenical movement at large, though immensely complicated by the explosive problems of the European continent. As an ecumenical body, the World Alliance sought with considerable success to maintain a broad basis of fellowship between Christians holding divergent views on international affairs, by stressing elements of common conviction. Thus there emerged over the years at least the outline of a distinct code of international morality, which enabled the ecumenical leaders to speak out in unmistakable terms on critical occasions, and to denounce acts of aggression and international injustice.[3]

Sympathetic support was given to the endeavours of the League of Nations as an attempt to replace international anarchy by the universal reign of law; but, as its failure to master the situation became increasingly manifest, the support became more critical. Continued advocacy of the principles of the League of Nations was linked up with denunciation of the unwillingness of governments—for reasons of selfish national interests—to make it a workable instrument. In the middle 1930's the conviction began to gain ground in Christian quarters that the paralysis of the League of Nations sprang from a congenital defect—its

[1] Address reprinted in *In Memoriam, Bishop Valdemar Ammundsen*, 1937, pp. 35 ff.
[2] John A. Hutchison, *We are not Divided*, pp. 205 ff.
[3] Cf. the long list of "Principal Resolutions passed by the World Alliance" recorded in the *Handbook, 1938*.

retention of the concept of unlimited national sovereignty. But the constructive idea of a supranational authority was too controversial and revolutionary and too remote from the dismal realities to receive more than scanty attention at the time.

A wave of revulsion, on humanitarian and religious grounds, against the evils of war and against the humiliating identification of many religious bodies with the cause of their respective nations in the first world war, remained one of the strongest emotional forces in the growing peace movement, which was such a signal feature in the history of the inter-war period. The signing of the Kellogg-Briand Pact for the outlawing of war in 1928 was regarded by many religious bodies as a decisive step towards a warless world. The World Alliance meeting at Prague in 1928, which coincided with the signing of the Pact, concentrated on the disarmament question. It called upon the Churches to urge the League, and their respective governments, to "complete with all despatch the international arrangements" for "a universal system of settling disputes by peaceful judicial methods".

The exasperating slowness of most of the major powers in implementing the pledge of general disarmament, provided for in the League Covenant, led to one of the most courageous and far-sighted actions that the ecumenical movement has ever taken—the adoption of the so-called Eisenach-Avignon Resolution. Endorsing the Kellogg Pact, it urged the Churches to draw the logical conclusion for their own attitude from the pact's renunciation of war as an instrument of national policy. The Resolution, initiated and presented by the Bishop of Chichester (Bell) and supported by Wilfred Monod and Walter Simons, a former President of the Supreme Court of the German Reich, was accepted by Life and Work at Eisenach in 1928 and transmitted to the World Alliance "with the Committee's approval of its spirit and purpose". The following year, at Avignon, the World Alliance approved the declaration with slight changes and decided to pass it on to the Churches and religious agencies all over the world, urging "its serious consideration and most effective possible action". The main sentences read:

"(2) We believe that war considered as an institution for the settlement of international disputes is incompatible with the mind and method of Christ, and therefore incompatible with the mind and method of His Church.

"(3) While convinced that the time must come for the revision of existing treaties in the interests of peace, we maintain that all disputes and conflicts between nations, for which no solution can be found through diplomacy or conciliation, ought to be settled or solved through arbitration, whether by the World Court or by some other tribunal mutually agreed. . . .

"(4) We earnestly appeal to the respective authorities of all Christian communions to declare in unmistakable terms that they will not countenance, nor assist in any way in, any war with regard to which the Government of their country has refused a bona fide offer to submit the dispute to arbitration."[1]

The last paragraph is obviously the crucial one. Here loyalty to the nascent international order is definitely set above loyalty to national states. The statement

[1] Quoted in *World Alliance Handbook, 1938*, p. 52.

received unusual publicity. The response of the Churches was encouraging, considering their traditional propensity to support, with good or bad conscience, their governments in any war. It was endorsed in substance by the Lambeth Conference of 1930, by the General Conference of the Church of Sweden, and by other religious bodies.

Alongside of undaunted efforts to plead the cause of arbitration and the reduction of armaments, the World Alliance joined with other like-minded groups in urging governments to establish alternative civilian service for conscientious objectors. Here again the leaders went far ahead of the prevailing opinion in the Churches. The Oxford Conference in 1937 codified the advance in its declaration that the Churches should respect the conscientious decisions of their members "whether they are led to participate in, or to abstain from, war, and maintain with both alike the full fellowship of the Body of Christ".[1]

The ecumenical peace front, the reality of which these few examples may serve to indicate, was no facile accomplishment. It represented a hard-won victory of the ecumenical spirit over conflicting convictions and fractional loyalties. Time and again the experience of these years demonstrated that the united efforts of the Churches in promoting peace and justice involved a prior task of reconciliation among Christians—a spiritual act of a deeper order than merely agreeing on resolutions and interventions.

A notable instance was the handling of the war guilt issue, which for long remained a festering sore in the relations between the Churches of the formerly warring nations. Seven years passed before the Churches were able to tackle this issue squarely. By common consent, the matter of war guilt was not discussed officially at the Stockholm Conference, though it was brought up by the German delegation in informal conversations.[2] Before leaving Stockholm, the German delegation sent a letter to the Continuation Committee stating that, as long as the question remained unsolved, it "must ever weigh heavily on our souls", and pleading "that an elucidation of the War Guilt Question is morally a task of paramount importance . . . in consideration of the future ecumenical co-operative work of the Churches".[3]

The point at issue was the interpretation of Article 231 of the Versailles Treaty, which the Germans felt to be an intolerable imputation to Germany alone of responsibility for the war. The confidential negotiations on this most difficult question during the year 1925–26—abounding in dramatic scenes and exchanges— are an instructive object-lesson in the carrying out of the ecumenical ministry of reconciliation, with its victories and its frailties. A small committee, with Principal A. E. Garvie, "that canny and Christian Scot", as impartial Chairman, had been entrusted with the delicate mission of preparing a reply to the German letter, for consideration at the Life and Work Continuation Committee at Berne in August 1926. Repeated attempts to reach agreement failed. The outcome was in doubt up to the very last minute. But finally the differences were resolved in a joint declaration, mainly drafted by Wilfred Monod, which brought the fellowship out of an apparently hopeless impasse. The Declaration confines itself to moral and religious considerations, and repudiates in advance any attempt to exploit it for political ends. Addressing itself first to the German

---

[1] *The Churches Survey Their Task*, p. 182.
[2] See Chap. xi, p. 537. William Adams Brown records such a meeting of German and American delegates in *Toward a United Church*, pp. 84 f.
[3] *Minutes   Continuation Committee of Life and Work, Berne, 1926*, p. 21.

brethren, it affirms the supranational unity "in the communion of Jesus Christ" as the reason why Christians "do not make their mutual attitude dependent upon official declarations recorded in diplomatic documents. . . . The cause of the Church of Jesus Christ, one and indivisible, becomes our common cause, a cause which cannot be interpreted by any particular State". The Declaration goes on to urge an unbiased investigation of "all the responsibilities concerning the outbreak and the conduct of the war", and appeals to the Churches to proclaim "the magnanimity of God in the forgiveness of sin" as the reconciling power in international relations.[1]

"The corpse overboard!" With these words one of the delegates gave vent to the sentiment of immense relief and gratitude evoked by the settlement of this explosive issue. But the corpse was still to reappear in different disguises as a vexatious attendant at ecumenical gatherings for many years to come. The whole story serves to illustrate the unending difficulties and stresses involved in the incarnation of the ecumenical spirit, but no less its very real power to transcend conflicts, and even transmute them into a more precious fellowship.

Later History of the World Alliance. Many changes had occurred in the leadership of the Alliance. Lord Dickinson remained Honorary Secretary until 1931, when he was elected President and Chairman of the International Council, on the death of Randall Davidson (Archbishop of Canterbury till 1928). He was succeeded in 1935 by Bishop Ammundsen of Haderslev, Denmark, who had already served as Chairman of the Minorities Commission from its inception in 1930, and later as Chairman of the Management Committee. The untimely death of Bishop Ammundsen in 1936 deprived the Alliance of one of its wisest and most devoted leaders. Dickinson and Ammundsen were both men who, by virtue of their intense passion for peace, their Christian statesmanship, and their gift for friendship, in different ways personified the genius of the Alliance.

Dr Atkinson resigned from the general secretaryship in 1932, but as one of the four international Secretaries till 1946 he remained one of the leading executive officers. Receiving but slight financial support from the National Councils, the World Alliance would have been unable to carry out its extensive international programme without the continued aid of the Church Peace Union, which supplied almost the whole of its funds. Yet this financial dependence on another organization was a weakness, and the temporary advantage was later seen to have been all too dearly bought.

The appointment of H. L. Henriod as joint General Secretary of the World Alliance and Life and Work from 1933 to 1938 symbolized and reinforced the liaison between the two movements. They issued a common bulletin, *The Churches in Action*, and co-operated in the *International Christian Press and Information Service*, in arranging regional conferences, and in other activities. Their youth commissions were merged into one. A consultative group was set up to confer on matters of common interest. In his annual report in 1934, the joint General Secretary felt justified in stating that this group "could without revolution become the joint Administrative Committee of both movements, pending their full amalgamation".[2] Some, impatient of the confusing and wasteful dispersion of ecumenical effort, went ahead and elaborated detailed proposals

---

[1] *Minutes . . . Continuation Committee of Life and Work, Berne, 1926*, pp. 21 ff., 31 ff.
[2] *World Alliance Annual Report, 1933–34*, pp. 44 f.

for a merger.[1] Meanwhile, plans were being made for a still more comprehensive integration of the entire movement. When these discussions matured in the plans for a World Council of Churches, in which Life and Work and Faith and Order should be united, many leaders—notably in Scandinavia, Holland, and Great Britain—favoured the inclusion of the World Alliance as well.

To understand why this more comprehensive union did not take place, it is necessary to recall the opposing currents and changing patterns within the ecumenical movement since 1925. The catholicity and timeliness of the programme of Life and Work during the years preceding the Oxford Conference had placed it in a pivotal position. Its evolution towards a more theological and church-centred outlook resulted in a growing affinity with Faith and Order, while on the other hand it retained a broad community of interests with the World Alliance. Many in Life and Work and in the World Alliance were in favour of a *mariage à trois*. But the incompatibility of temper between Faith and Order and the World Alliance was too great for this to be possible. The leaders in Faith and Order, while willing, albeit somewhat hesitantly, to join with Life and Work on certain conditions, were firmly opposed to the inclusion of the World Alliance with its even greater "worldliness" and theological indefiniteness. A similar resistance was manifest in certain World Alliance quarters for exactly opposite reasons; viewing with misgivings the ascendancy of "ecclesiasticism", they feared that it would quench the spirit of prophecy. The crux of the matter was the position of the American World Alliance Council, with its inter-faith membership and the unwillingness of its leadership to accept constitutional and temperamental readjustments which they felt would be a betrayal of the genius of the movement.

It may be convenient at this point to desert strict chronology, and to indicate the ways in which, though the World Alliance as such ceased to exist, the post-war world found other forms and new methods for the expression of the ideals for which the Alliance had stood.

In 1938 the World Alliance reaffirmed its traditional policy of being "a free organisation working primarily in and through the Churches for the cause of peace, and in association with the other branches of the ecumenical movement".[2] In the same year, consultations with the Provisional Committee of the World Council of Churches led to the declaration that "the two movements are distinct in that the World Council of Churches desires to represent the Churches direct and that the World Alliance desires to be and to remain an autonomous and independent movement which serves the Churches", but provided for the closest co-operation between the two movements in many fields. H. L. Henriod continued his work as General Secretary of the Alliance, and was appointed liaison officer between the two movements.

In August 1939 the Management Committee of the Alliance met at Geneva to celebrate the twenty-fifth anniversary of its formation. The Alliance had been founded in the very week in which the first world war had broken out; its silver jubilee was observed under the shadow of another approaching conflict. At the meeting, Dr Atkinson quoted a letter which he had received in February 1914 from Andrew Carnegie, the donor of the Church Peace Union Fund: "Peace is about a reality now; and before you have gone very long, permanent peace will be established in the world, and then you will find yourselves trustees of a fund

---

[1] Cf. *Record of Proceedings of the Ninth International Conference of the World Alliance, Chamby, Switzerland, 1935*, pp. 34 ff.

[2] *Minutes of Business Sessions of the International Council of the World Alliance, Larvik (Norway), 1938*, p. 23.

and will not know what to do with it." The illusions of a generation were to be shattered by the disasters of an even more universal conflict, and the Alliance was to be subjected to strains from which in fact it never recovered.

Even before the war started, it had become evident that the World Council, though only in process of formation, was increasingly drawing to itself the support of leaders in almost all the Churches. Unlike the Council, the Alliance had not an adequate staff, strategically located in different countries, and so able to continue operations in spite of all the difficulties created by the war. The General Secretary, H. L. Henriod, valiantly attempted to carry on. But growing disagreements as to the policy of the Alliance, and the cessation of financial support from the Church Peace Union, led to the closing down of the Geneva Office in March 1944.

After the war, attempts were made to re-establish the Alliance on an international basis; but ere long it became clear that the fissiparous tendencies had reached a point at which it was no longer possible to restore the old organization. In 1944 Dr Robert Dexter, a Unitarian, was sent over from the United States to explore the possibilities of creating the Alliance afresh, but this time on a definitely inter-faith basis, "bringing together in each country groups of religious-minded individuals", and without involving itself "in questions of faith, order, and other ecclesiastical or credal issues". The crisis was reached at a meeting of the Management Committee of the Alliance, held at Tring, England, in July 1946. Most of the European representatives felt that, if the Alliance was to continue at all, it must be on the old unmistakably Christian basis. The Church Peace Union, on the other hand, pursued its efforts in favour of an inter-faith organization to work for peace, and this was in due course set up under the name The World Alliance for International Friendship through Religion. In the meantime the World Council of Churches and the International Missionary Council working together had set up the Commission of the Churches on International Affairs, a body which was charged with many of the interests that had earlier been the concern of the Alliance. It was impossible that the Alliance could continue to exist in its old shape.

The authorities of the Alliance bowed to the inevitable. On 30 June 1948, the old World Alliance for International Friendship through the Churches was formally dissolved. It had lived and done its work through a period of intense and growing strain. Now its concerns were to be in the hands of others, and it was to live on, not as itself, but through those who had breathed deeply of its spirit, and were able to carry forward something of its achievements into an ecumenical movement which was developing new forms to meet new needs in a world radically changed by the upheavals of the second world war.

4. BATTLEFIELDS OF ECUMENICITY

The spiritual travail of the two movements with which we are dealing in this chapter, and especially of Life and Work, crystallized over the years in a distinctive body of ecumenical insights and ideas. It deserves a special analysis, since it offers a significant contribution to the nascent doctrine of ecumenicity. But let us first briefly consider the historical and religious background.

A Period of Religious and International Turmoil. To those caught in its whirlpools, the period with which we are dealing appeared as an abrupt turning-point in Christian history. It was, at the least, a stormy decade, providing a rough passage with many perilous moments for the ecumenical barque and its inexperienced crew, as it proceeded on its uncharted course. The European continent was the storm-centre.

The earthquake of the first world war and its consequences had shaken the foundations of Western society, with its widespread belief in the divinity of man and in limitless progress. Events seemed to justify the position of those who had maintained their foothold on the rock of the Reformation, distrusting all human efforts and proclaiming the "otherness" of God. Theological liberalism had no adequate answer to give to agonized souls lost in the wilderness of fear and insecurity. Luther and Calvin, long wrapped in the cerements of distorting traditions, rose again and found devoted and vocal followers. Their resurrection, one of the most significant factors in recent religious history, was paralleled by a renewal of denominational self-consciousness. Among the uncertainties and convulsions of a passing age, preachers and theologians began to set their eyes on the certainties of "the last things". Karl Barth, and others in different ways, went forth announcing Christianity as the mystery of the "Word of God", not as the projection or confirmation of man's highest aspirations and ideals, but as the judgement of God upon them.

These movements, seeking fresh inspiration and strength in the great doctrines of the Reformation and its interpretation of the Bible, by no means captured the Continental Churches as a whole. The Christian social movement, though chastened by events, continued to exert a notable influence far beyond the diminishing group of its faithful adherents. Some of its noblest exponents, such as Wilfred Monod and Élie Gounelle in France, F. Siegmund-Schultze in Germany, Bishop Ammundsen in Denmark, were among the great leaders of the ecumenical movement. At the other extreme, Pietism of different shades still held its ground, fortified by the work of conservative theologians and in uneasy partnership with confessional neo-orthodoxy.

These trends had their counterparts in the Anglo-Saxon world, though in characteristically Anglo-Saxon forms. The victorious nations were slower than the defeated to lose their belief in progress, with its expression in a liberal and optimistic theology. Christians bent their efforts to "hastening" the coming of the Kingdom of God. Some hailed the nascent world community, organized in the League of Nations, as a new manifestation of its glorious advance. Theological liberalism and social gospels of various brands remained strongly influential till well into the 1930's, when they began to lose power; and as the climate of world affairs deteriorated, powerful critics, both from the right and from the left, launched damaging attacks. The newest of these movements, the dialectical theology, in contrast to its rapid expansion on the European continent, was too uncongenial to the prevailing mood in Anglo-Saxon Protestantism to make much headway during this period.

It is useful thus to recall, however briefly, some of the shifting religious moods and movements which exercised their sway over Western Christianity during these years, for they profoundly affected the ideological evolution of the ecumenical movement. The same was true of world events in general. Movements concerned with the relationship of Christianity to the social and international order could not but be highly sensitive to the cataclysmic changes which took place in world society during the latter part of "the long armistice".

In view of all that happened in the years that followed, it may seem to a later generation almost incredible that the war should have been followed in large parts of the western world by a period of optimism and confidence. Yet there was for a time a collective feeling of exaltation, for which contemporary events appeared to afford a justification. But this period was short. There came in rapid succession an uninterrupted series of shattering blows: the Wall Street crash of 1929, the Manchuria incident, the disastrous failure of the Disarmament Conference at Geneva in 1932, the sinister growth of totalitarian tyrannies. The League of Nations crumbled, whilst the nations frantically sought an illusory security in economic and political autarky. The spectre of another world conflagration and its attendant horrors haunted the minds of peoples and statesmen. In the short span of a few years Western civilization seemed to have reverted to a barbarian jungle—a highly technicized jungle, equipped with terrifying powers for the annihilation of mankind.

It was in this period of revolutionary changes—in mind and in society—that the modern ecumenical movement went onward to discover its own identity. Assailed from right and left, by friends and foes alike, battered by the storms of events, it was a miracle that, unlike so many noble ecumenical argosies of other days, it did not founder in its course. Embracing, or at least seeking to embrace, an immense range of ecclesiastical traditions and religious groups, it ran the danger of becoming a neutral point of meeting for disparate elements and not a rallying-point for advance. If, on the other hand, endeavouring to express a growing unity of mind and purpose, it were to allow itself to become dominated by the convictions of a few dynamic groups, it would fall into the opposite danger of becoming a new factor not of fellowship but of discord. This dilemma of chaotic inclusiveness or one-sided definiteness has accompanied the movement all along. It is not surprising that now and then it was caught on both horns of its dilemma. More amazing is the extent to which, over the years, often in painful but fruitful conflict, it reached beyond this dilemma to a united and unifying testimony.

"*Communio in adorando et serviendo oecumenica.*" The history of Life and Work and of the World Alliance can, in one sense, be treated as the history of the shifting interpretations of this motto of the Stockholm Conference. The movements did not set out with a fixed and rigid notion of the united experience aspired to; they embraced many diverse interests and religious outlooks, and their progress on the road to clarity is therefore characterized by the interplay of fluid and often inchoate impulses and ideas, never systematized into a "theology of ecumenicity".

What was the nature of this ecumenical fellowship in worship and service? What different meanings of unity did it connote? Were the movements animated by a concern for unity in a deeper sense, or were they merely functional agencies for the attainment of certain practical ends?

Many did indeed look upon them primarily as service agencies. A purely pragmatic and instrumental ecumenicity presented certain attractive qualities which won it numerous adherents. It chimed admirably with a certain Protestant temper, which, professing the simple undogmatic faith of the liberal interpretation of Jesus, was loath to let divisive theories of sacrament and creed obstruct its service to suffering humanity. For a different reason it also suited well those who, while firmly holding to the truth of their historical traditions, and opposed to any semblance of interdenominational syncretism in matters of faith, yet were anxious to join with Christian brethren, without prejudice to principles, in efforts for human welfare and social amelioration.

At first sight it might appear as if this were the whole story. In the French and German languages, the title "Life and Work" was significantly rendered "The Ecumenical Council for Practical Christianity"[1]—a welcome target for the gibes of some theological critics. And the existence of Faith and Order, specializing in problems of doctrinal and ecclesiastical unity, by inference tended to strengthen the impression that the two other movements were concerned only with practical co-operation for common ends. It is none the less evident that their motives and aspirations were more complex and possessed a firmer spiritual anchorage. Basically there was an awareness, sometimes clearer, sometimes more faint, that they also were rooted in the paradox of unity amid disunity—a unity not to be created, but accepted and testified to in the fellowship of believers, and radiating through it into the world.

How, then, did Life and Work and the World Alliance conceive their particular function within the wider movement? More specifically, how did they come to grips with the divided state of the Churches which they desired to stir to a common witness? Four approaches can be distinguished in the ecumenical discussions of those years.

(a) In Hälsingborg in 1922 the principle was established, and later reaffirmed at Stockholm 1925, that the scope of Life and Work should be limited to "united practical action . . . leaving for the time our differences in Faith and Order". For many of the supporters of the movement, this represented no more than a temporary and pragmatic separation, with a view to practical effectiveness, of two things which inherently belong together. But others were prepared to develop from this principle a whole system of the relationship between doctrine and action, theory and practice, and of the relative merits of different roads to unity.

Archbishop Söderblom developed and expounded the latter position, on practical grounds, more persuasively than anyone else. A prophet in the guise of an Archbishop, he was more strongly impelled by the urgency and the overriding power of the call he had received than repelled by the obstacles and perils he encountered. The mission had to be performed at all costs. "We cannot afford to remain separated and in a state of unnecessary impotence caused by our separation, up to the time when we shall be truly united in faith and church organization".[2] And here "the path of love", so he was convinced, offered a "more excellent way" for a common crusade against the evils of society than did the Roman method of absorption or even the Wittenberg insistence on unity in matters of faith. Using his favourite metaphor of the soul and the body, he asserted that the disciples of Christ are already at one in the soul of the Church, a God-given unity "at the bottom of our Christian trust and experience",[3] which immediately offers adequate ground for common service, but which also must eventually receive appropriate embodiment in doctrines and institutions and forms of worship.

Söderblom was too firmly rooted in the Lutheran tradition not to insist that

---

[1] *Oekumenischer Rat für praktisches Christentum* and *Conseil oecuménique du Christianisme pratique.*

[2] Söderblom, *Christian Fellowship, or the United Life and Work of Christendom*, New York, 1923.

[3] From his address at the Lausanne Conference, in *Faith and Order: Proceedings of the World Conference, Lausanne, August 3–21, 1927*, ed. H. N. Bate, p. 330.

"no unity can be achieved by ignoring the existence of the confessions, disregarding their sacred experiences and their indigenous customs and constitutions. Only by understanding our own confession more deeply can we learn mutual respect and come nearer to unity". [1] Yet it was the genius of the Life and Work approach that, by bringing Christians and Churches together in works of love and mercy and in a developing atmosphere of mutual understanding and trust, it at the same time furthered the cause of full organic unity.

Other authoritative spokesmen—such as Archbishop Germanos, Bishop Bell of Chichester, William Adams Brown, Wilfred Monod, Adolf Deissmann—frequently expressed themselves in similar vein. There exists a remarkable sequence of Greek Orthodox statements along these lines, from the Encyclical of 1920 onwards. By an intriguing coincidence, similar ideas were developed in almost identical terms in important Anglican documents of the same period. The following statement offers a classical formulation of this attitude: "We say deliberately that in the region of moral or social questions we desire all Christians to begin at once to act together as if they were one body, in one visible fellowship. This could be done by all alike without any injury to theological principles. And to bring all Christians together to act in this one department of life as one visible body would involve no loss and manifold gain. We should get to know and trust one another: we should learn to act together: we should thus prepare the way for fuller unity."[2]

Such a concept of socio-moral ecumenicity belongs to a long and broad stream of Christian thought with many tributaries: the emphasis of Pietism on life as against dead doctrine; the belief held by generations of apologists that, while people were turning away from controversies about dogma, the precepts of Christian morality retained their undisputed sway, being self-evident and self-authenticating; the tradition of symbolo-fideist theology; and, last but not least, the tested everyday experience of actual co-operation in many fields between people holding the most diverse religious tenets.

(b) A small group, mainly to be found among American supporters of the World Alliance, sympathized with the idea of a wider ecumenical fellowship in which sincere men of many religions might join. The desperate struggle against injustice and oppression, against hatred and war, is an undertaking in which all men, of whatever religious persuasion, are involved. Moreover, when it comes to the broad outlines of the better world to be built, a remarkable measure of agreement can be observed among all people of goodwill, stretching far beyond the boundaries of the Christian religion.

This universalist or humanistic ecumenicity, again, conspicuously demonstrates the influx of another stream of thought into the modern ecumenical movement—the long tradition of doctrines of Natural Law and allied notions of "the moral conscience of mankind" or "a moral world order". Yet the sway of this complex of ideas extended further than one particular group; it was and still is an accepted element in the social and international outlook of large parts of Protestantism (notably in the Anglo-Saxon world) as of Roman Catholicism.

(c) The positions thus far described, as could be expected, came under violent fire from schools of thought which held more firmly to confessional orthodoxies.

[1] Söderblom, *Christliche Einheit*, Berlin, 1928, p. 98.
[2] *Christianity and Industrial Problems. Report of the Archbishops' Committee*, 1918, p. 3. See also the Report of the Committee on "The Church and Industrial Problems" of the Lambeth Conference, 1920 (*The Lambeth Conferences, 1867–1948*, pp. 74 f.).

Both in the United States and in Europe important groups stood aloof, denouncing the syncretistic dangers of a venture which, in their view, discounted ultimate truth and betrayed the treasures of particular traditions. The disjunction of religious creed from social action was declared to be inconsistent and illegitimate. On the contrary—so it was contended, not only by doctrinaire confessionalists—it must be recognized that the faith professed by a Church works itself out in a distinctive way of life, a distinctive attitude to society, as for instance in the Lutheran doctrine of the Two Realms. It would therefore be a fallacy to believe that it would be easier to achieve unity on matters of social change than on central issues of the Faith. Any large-scale scheme to move the Churches to join forces would be doomed to failure, unless preceded by careful examination of the particular approaches characteristic of individual Church traditions, and elucidation of the conditions of co-operation.

Already the discussions at and after the Stockholm Conference had revealed the sharp dialectic of differing convictions, and pointed to a problem which demanded closer scrutiny. With the strengthening of confessional consciousness in the early 1930's, these schools of confessional or even confessionalist ecumenism gained momentum and forced Life and Work to reconsider its whole position. This was in a lesser degree true of the World Alliance, which largely remained faithful to its more pragmatic and interdenominational approach.

(d) Under the impulse of its own initial convictions, and of keen criticism from some of its supporters, Life and Work increasingly recognized the importance of theological factors, and thus steered a course which gradually brought it into convergence with Faith and Order. It was an evolution not without its stresses and strains. Many of those who from the outset had been fervent supporters of the Stockholm idea now felt compelled to raise a warning voice, or lost interest in the movement. In the high-minded resolve of the founders to go ahead in unity, in spite of unresolved doctrinal differences, they had seen a great hope for a new advance of prophetic Christianity. And now they felt that the ecumenical movement was degenerating into a seminar on social theology and comparative ecclesiology, in which the atmosphere of barren controversies was being recreated.

The charge was misleading. What had happened was that the leaders, accepting the fact that the original Stockholm foundations offered no permanent solutions, were beginning to explore new pathways in the field of social thought and action leading beyond pragmatic undenominationalism and doctrinaire confessionalism alike. This approach was experimental, worked out by the circuitous process of trial and error, but its rationale can easily be stated.

The real problem is not the common formulation of social programmes, but the rebirth of faith and a revitalized sense of social concern, quickening the whole Christian body. The missionary dogmas of secular movements can only be met on their own level, that is, by a reaffirmation of the Christian message for man and for society. But since the Churches proclaim this message in different, even contradictory, ways, the attainment of the objective involves several complementary tasks.

It will be necessary to show why and how each Church, to be true to its own heritage and genius, should be more vigorously concerned with the problems of society. It will further be necessary to foster in the Churches a new readiness for exchange and mutual consultation; a readiness to learn from one another's convictions and experiences, victories and failures, and to define the broad areas of agreement and disagreement in the realm of social policy. Yet even a cross-fertilization of this kind does not by itself lead beyond the *status quo* of existing Church traditions; it may merely result in a brittle front of *ad hoc* co-operation at points where their divergent lines happen to intersect. A third step or task is therefore imperative if this venture is to be truly ecumenical. Those associated with the ecumenical movement affirm their belief in the *Una Sancta*, a reality which operates in and through the diverse Churches, and which is the unifying centre of their life and witness before the world. Consequently the goal of their aspirations must be not simply broader co-operation for social ends, but that the Churches in so co-operating may manifest and carry towards its fullness their common life in the one Body of Christ.

But, because of its particular focus, Life and Work deals with the diversities of Christendom primarily in so far as they affect life in society; and here the issue of unity and disunity takes on a new complexion, different from that of Faith and Order, for the reason that social decisions are conditioned, not only by basic religious and moral attitudes, but by a multitude of sociological and technical factors. As a result, the lines of agreement and disagreement on social and political matters often cut across the lines of confessional allegiance. Thus, if Life and Work is to be realistic, it can follow neither the road of undenominational pragmatism nor that of doctrinaire confessionalism. It must indeed take serious account of doctrinal and other differences that keep Christendom divided; but its task is to concentrate attention on those complexes of beliefs by which social judgement and conduct are actually determined, and to stimulate the Churches to concerted advance.

Considerations of this kind were a recurrent feature in the discussions in the 1930's, especially in the Life and Work study programme. A conference held in Geneva in 1932 on this very problem of "Church, Creed, and Social Ethics" was an important milestone in these endeavours to elucidate the complex relationship between denominational patterns and social attitudes.

Towards the Church in the Churches. The idea of the Church as the great ecumenical reality has always been a part of ecumenical thinking; yet the renewed emphasis on the idea, which appeared almost simultaneously in the missionary world and in Life and Work in the 1930's, came to a number of supporters of the movements almost with the shock of a new discovery. This, of course, it was not. Söderblom had significantly claimed that "at Stockholm we made the first attempt to hear the Church as such, and to set it in motion".[1] Yet at that time a Church-centred outlook was to be found only in certain parts of the ecumenical constituency—mainly in Eastern Orthodoxy, in Anglicanism, and in parts of the Lutheran world. Large Protestant groups still centred their belief on individual salvation or on the immanent Kingdom of God. But by 1937 it had become clear that the Church and its nature was one of the central problems, perhaps the central problem, to which at that date ecumenical thinking must be directed.

Many factors, theological and non-theological, combined to bring about this change in ecumenical climate, which without doubt greatly helped forward the consolidation of the ecumenical movement in a World Council of Churches.

Biblical and theological researches reaffirmed the centrality of the Church in the divine economy, as the appointed herald and incipient embodiment of the Kingdom that is nigh. This weight of scholarship naturally gave added impetus

[1] *Pater Max Pribilla und die ökumenische Erweckung*, p. 40.

to the convictions of those who from the beginning had stood for a Church-centred understanding of the movement. New spiritual horizons were, moreover, discovered in contacts with Orthodox piety and worship.

Another most powerful challenge was the German Church struggle. The fight of the "Confessing Church" and its claim to be the true Church of Jesus Christ in Germany presented a challenge which over the years profoundly affected the ecumenical movement, by raising critical questions about the nature of the true Church and the requirements of ecumenical solidarity. And many, both Christians and non-Christians, who had thought little about the Church, were brought to a new realization of its significance when it emerged as the impregnable bulwark against the onslaughts of a totalitarian pseudo-church, and as a witness to the meaning of true community. For various reasons it devolved upon the Universal Christian Council to act as the chief spokesman of the ecumenical conscience in the negotiations with religious and political leaders in Germany which ensued after 1933.[1] Here it was forced, step by step, to grapple at the existential level with ultimate issues of the faith and order of the Church—a situation which became a major motive in its preoccupation with the problems of Church, Community, and State, and further demonstrated the impossibility of keeping Life and Work and Faith and Order apart.

This evolution towards a more definitely Church-centred outlook was most pronounced in Europe, where church traditions were stronger and the factors just mentioned were more strongly operative. The decision taken by the Universal Christian Council in 1934 to plan a world conference on "Church, Community, and State" found universal assent. No doubt, at that time many still regarded the use of the term "Church" in the title as a conventional formula; what they were really interested in was the contribution of religion in fighting the mounting political and economic crisis. But the following year, 1935, brought further significant indications of the direction in which the wind was blowing. This was the year in which Karl Barth was invited to give his challenging lectures at the Ecumenical Seminar in Geneva on "The Church and the Churches", indicating his conversion from a critical spectator to a—no less critical—supporter of the ecumenical cause; William Adams Brown published his book, *The Church: Catholic and Protestant*, advocating "that the church deserves a greater place in the loyalty and affection of Christians than is given it by many American Protestants today", and admitting that this claim "runs counter to the prevailing trend of popular opinion"; the President of the World Alliance, Bishop Ammundsen, affirmed that "our endeavours must be rooted ... in the whole doctrinal, educational and sacramental life of the Church"; and J. H. Oldham, the directing genius of the Oxford Conference, expounded the thesis "that in the question of the Church are centred many of the major problems that concern mankind—not Christians alone but modern man".[2]

The mounting trend did not remain unchallenged. The opposition came from several quarters, and was actuated by different motives. Exponents of social and liberal Christianity, mindful of their battles with the inertia and conservatism of ecclesiastical bodies, feared that the movement would lose its pioneering and

---

[1] The dramatic and highly instructive story of the interrelation of the ecumenical movement and the German Church struggle, and the lessons it offers regarding the duty and limitations of ecumenical interventions in domestic church affairs, is still unwritten. The official actions of the Universal Christian Council are documented in its Minutes from 1933 onwards.

[2] See his article in *The Student World*, October 1935; and his pamphlet, *The Question of the Church in the World of Today*, London, 1936.

progressive impulse. Many lay people viewed with dismay the new pre-occupation with theological and ecclesiastical matters. "Enthusiasts" and believers in the Inner Light failed to see why the invisible fellowship of believers should be encumbered by so much attention to doctrinal and institutional paraphernalia.

Those who held such views believed that the great movement initiated by Stockholm 1925 would be safer in the hands of an independent minority within the Churches than in the constricting limits of official inter-Church co-operation. These critics did not win the day, and the ecumenical movement continued to develop as a fellowship of the Churches. Nevertheless their criticisms served a useful purpose in reminding the leaders of the movement that the official often tends to be the static, and that a movement soon ceases to move unless it is quickened by the inspiration which comes rather from groups and individuals than from the main body.

Two French leaders may be chosen to illustrate this counter-movement of dissent. In a remarkable letter to Söderblom on the forthcoming Faith and Order Conference at Lausanne,[1] Wilfred Monod expressed his conviction that the Conference would be successful in the measure that it proclaimed the *non possumus* opposed by all prophetic religion to all clerical and sacramentarian religion. Reproaching the promoters of Faith and Order for confusing "faith as trust (the sole faith announced in the Gospel) and faith as credal belief (required by the Church)", he went on to intimate in a picturesque anecdote his misgivings about the appearance of similar tendencies in the Life and Work movement: "Last night I dreamed that I was making a heated speech about the programme which we set before the Christian world in 1925. I cried out, 'We have tried to change the course of a certain type of Christianity. But we keep falling back into the old rut. The Stockholm Continuation Committee is now harking back to questions of dogma and ritual!' I was indignant, horrified! To-night I hope I shall dream of the mystic ladder with the angels ascending and descending. That will be pleasanter and healthier."

Monod kept loyally to his ideal of true ecumenicity. In a speech in 1932 he complains, contrasting the foolishness of the Gospel with the cautious wisdom of the Churches, that the Universal Christian Council, "far from being revolutionary, is now hardly even reformist". He sums up the temptations of the contemporary world in a striking triad: "Misconception of the problem of *property*, which engenders class-war; misconception of the problem of *patriotism*, which fosters international war; and misconception of the problem of the *Sacrament*, which gives rise to strife between the Churches."[2]

Similarly, his friend, Élie Gounelle, in a nostalgic comparison between 1925 and 1937, expressed his uneasiness, avowing that he felt like a complete stranger in the new ecumenical climate.[3] "At Stockholm and Lausanne the idea of the Kingdom of God was right in the foreground . . . the prophetic and missionary spirit definitely prevailed over the spirit of sacerdotalism and ecclesiasticism . . . But at Oxford and Edinburgh the Church placed itself in the foreground . . . and the higher clergy directed the game." To him, and to many others, the crusading watchword of the Oxford Conference, "Let the Church be the Church", signal-

---

[1] Letter of 2 January 1927, filed in the Söderblom archives at Uppsala.
[2] *À la Croisée des Chemins*, Geneva, 1932, p. 19.
[3] "Les Grandes Conférences Œcuméniques d'Oxford et d'Edimbourg" in *Le Christianisme Social*, Sept.-Dec. 1937, pp. 173 ff.

ized the triumph of ecclesiastical introversion. Looking to the future, Gounelle felt that the only hope for the ecumenical movement was "the alliance of the priestly and the prophetic functions within the Church". It was precisely because they believed in the possibility of such an alliance that other supporters of the movement favoured that development which led in the end to the formation of the World Council of Churches.

The Supranationality of the Church. There is another aspect of the emphasis on the Church which deserves special mention—the affirmation that the Church Universal is not only trans-confessional but also supranational. After the first world war the missionary enterprise translated this into practical policy, when it successfully advocated the return of German missionaries to their fields.[1] In a joint declaration of 1926, Life and Work and the World Alliance solemnly declared "that it is the duty of every Communion . . . to emphasize the supernational character of the Church, and therefore to do all in its power to cultivate international fellowship on a Christian basis".[2] It was a bold affirmation of faith, a banner held ever higher and with unflinching fortitude, as the international barometer set towards "stormy" in the 1930's. The tested experience of a wider Christian fellowship transcending barriers of nation and race, the coincident growth of international confessional organizations, the advance in theological thought about the nature of the Church, and paradoxically the adverse influence of resurgent nationalism—all these combined to bring this article of ecumenical faith increasingly to the fore. Like other ecumenical ideas, this too was wrought out step by step in wrestling with concrete circumstances, eventually developing into a body of common sentiment and conviction—a body which yet comprehended persistent differences of view and many problems still unsolved or not even perceived.

The supranationality of the Church was a concept in which various motives and ideas intermingled. Fundamentally it expressed the recovered vision of the unity and universality of the Body of Christ, divine in its origin and essence, a fellowship of faith and love where there is neither Jew nor Greek, coloured nor white, but where "Christ is all, and in all". As in earlier periods of history, the revolutionary implications of this affirmation were soon to become manifest. It was put to the test, to mention a few examples only, in the successful resistance of religious leaders in Germany to the project of establishing a segregated non-Aryan Church, on the ground that Hebrew Christians by their baptism had been incorporated into the one Church; and in the persistent efforts of the Churches associated with the ecumenical movement to maintain and strengthen their fellowship across the political and ideological "Iron Curtains" of the time.

But does this fellowship in the *Una Sancta*, professed as an object of faith, and experienced as a fact, have any bearing on the shaping of international relations? Or do international Church relationships and international political affairs move on two disparate and never intersecting planes? As usual, the problem became acute when it moved on to the level of a practical challenge. All the Churches believed in peace and fervently expressed their desire for it; but what could or should the Churches do about it? This was no theoretical problem. From 1933 onwards, a second world war seemed ever more inevitable; this was a grave challenge to individual Churches, and still more to bodies like the Univer-

[1] See Chap. viii, pp. 367, 375, and Chap. xi, p. 532.
[2] *Minutes . . . Continuation Committee of Life and Work, Berne, 1926*, p. 12.

sal Christian Council for Life and Work and the World Alliance, which by their very nature were pledged to supranational thought and action.

There are comparatively few traces before the 1930's of any serious attempt to elucidate this problem. But once the significance of the proposition had been fully recognized, it led off into new fertile lines of thought, and to the elucidation of the relations, both of contact and of contrast, between ecumenicity and internationalism. Some identified the one with the other. Others, holding a docetic view of the Church Universal, or wishing to stress the non-political nature of the movement in order to secure it against the claims of such governments as the Nazi régime to be sole arbiters in international affairs, contended that they belonged to entirely separate spheres of life. But the main stream of thought took a different course. As the Body of Christ, embracing people "of all nations, and kindreds, and peoples and tongues", the Universal Church is committed to serve as an exemplar, a pattern, and a leaven of true world community. By its very existence, and in the measure that it realizes its own unity, it is the strongest potential factor for international and inter-racial peace. As illustrations of the movement of thought in these years, three ecumenical thinkers of different national backgrounds may be cited.

Wilfred Monod called upon the world-wide Church to give a soul to the League of Nations.[1] Already, on his initiative, the French Council of the World Alliance had adopted as a guiding principle that "the political League of Nations, in order to become workable, must be inspired by a moral league of peoples, and the soul of that must be a spiritual league of the Churches".

In 1934, a Swedish theologian, Arvid Runestam, asserted: "The supernational Church must act. . . . Only as united in the great supernational Church can we speak with authority and do we find courage to challenge the political powers. Christianity must speak to the State and to the authorities of this world, out of the very centre of the one Church. But the supernational Church must also speak for its own sake: in order to be brought to a stronger realisation of its own existence. . . . We do not belong only to an earthly nation. We are members of another and greater people. And we must learn to love this people as dearly as our own, and to make as great sacrifices for it as for our own country. . . . We need both a radical Christian revival all over the world, and a growing consciousness and more adequately organised forms of the supernational Church, which can thus become a better instrument in the hand of God for conquering the powers of evil."

Max Huber, former President of the World Court at The Hague and of the International Red Cross Committee, developed the idea of the supranational ethos of the Universal Church as a source of international law. "Only Christians, as members of the *Una Sancta*, understand the deep foundations of a legal order, which can extend beyond the limits of the national communities. Only on the basis of the *Una Sancta* can a supranational ethos be built up. Without such an ethos, all law, especially international law, which has behind it no power or compulsion or only limited and insecure forces, remains a fragile structure."[2]

By 1937 what had been implicit at Stockholm 1925 had become explicit in the minds and utterances of leaders in the Churches and in the ecumenical movement, as a result of this long travail of thought in a darkening world. The Oxford

---

[1] In *L'Église peut-elle donner une âme à la Société des Nations?* Geneva, 1932.
[2] See his articles in *The Universal Church and The World of Nations*, 1938, and in *The Student World*, 1st Quarter, 1939.

Conference, in its Message to the Churches, gave forceful expression to the point of common agreement which at that date had been reached: "If war breaks out, then pre-eminently the Church must manifestly be the Church, still united as the one Body of Christ, though the nations wherein it is planted fight each other, consciously offering the same prayers that God's Name may be hallowed, His Kingdom come, and His Will be done, in both, or all, the warring nations."[1]

This was more than a rhetorical expression of pious hope. It bore testimony to a conviction which had become almost self-evident to Christian leaders. And it stood the test of fire in the terrible strains and temptations resulting from a new world war.

5. ECUMENICAL THOUGHT ON SOCIETY AND THE STATE

In 1930 the place of the Stockholm Continuation Committee had been taken by the Universal Christian Council for Life and Work. This change afforded the opportunity for a reconstruction of the movement's centre in Geneva. As has already been shown, the International Christian Social Institute, with a small staff and a limited budget, had developed an extensive and ever-growing programme of ecumenical study and education. In 1929 it was able to appoint its first Secretary for Research, Dr Hans Schönfeld, a trained economist and ordained pastor delegated to the Council by the Federation of German Evangelical Churches, who showed a special aptitude for drawing into the research fellowship an efficient group of co-workers. In 1930 the Church of Sweden made available a second permanent worker, the Rev. Nils Ehrenström. Appeals to the Churches for further help were not successful, in so far as no other permanent workers could be appointed, though valuable help was given by temporary colleagues who were spared by their Churches for longer or shorter periods of service. In 1931 the Institute was reorganized, and a Research Department set up, of which Dr Schönfeld became Director.

The research work of the 1930's was firmly based on the work which had earlier been accomplished by the Institute. Before research, in the proper sense of the term, could begin, a survey of the available material and of already existing social activities of the Churches had to be made. Masses of material were accumulated, and made readily accessible to the Churches in non-technical form in the occasional bulletin *Life and Work* (1927–30). The subjects dealt with included the activities of the League of Nations and the International Labour Office, and other developments in international social work, relations of religion and labour, and social endeavours within the Churches. A network of correspondents in various countries was established; their first assignment was to supply data for an international survey on the social work of the Churches.[2] Over the years a number of similar surveys were produced for the stimulation and guidance of the constituency, on such subjects as *Social Programmes of the Churches and Voluntary Religious Organisations, The Churches and the Godless Movement, The Conscientious Objectors before the Law.*

Following a pattern developed by the Federal Council of Churches of Christ in America, the Institute undertook experiments in influencing international social legislation. This was felt to be a field of strategic importance which the non-Roman communions thus far had not occupied, for lack of an appropriate

[1] *The Churches Survey Their Task*, 1937, p. 59.
[2] Adolf Keller, *Die Kirche und die soziale Arbeit*, Zurich, 1927.

agency to express their common concerns. The International Labour Office for many years had an official in charge of relations with Protestant bodies, Dr Georges Thélin, who took an active part in developing these relations, served on several Life and Work committees, and reported regularly and officially to the Council. The League of Nations similarly maintained a liaison officer with the Life and Work and World Alliance headquarters in Geneva. Thus the ecumenical leaders gained access both to personal and to official channels—a facility frequently used over the years in relation to a variety of concerns. In such inquiries as those on the Welfare of Seamen and on Child Labour in Non-industrial Occupations, the Institute drew the attention of the Churches to the moral implications of draft conventions of the I.L.O., urging them to intervene with their governments in order to secure proper consideration of desirable amendments. These actions were paralleled by direct representations to the I.L.O. and to government delegates on the basis of the material received from Churches and religious organizations. To obtain the strongest possible impact, these official approaches were undertaken jointly with the other Christian world organizations located in Geneva.[1]

In 1929 the Institute was ready to undertake its first major project of research, a study of the problem of unemployment. Since this was the gravest social and human problem of the time—with the number of unemployed in Western lands alone amounting to the incredible figure of some twenty millions—it was natural that such a project should find ready response in many Churches. A series of national study conferences and inquiries was arranged, leading up to an international conference of economists, industrialists, and churchmen in Basle in 1932. The report of the Conference, *The Churches and the World Economic Crisis*, attracted widespread attention. The Universal Christian Council took it as a basis for a pressing appeal to the Churches to combat unemployment and to alleviate the distress of those most deeply afflicted.

Along with this inquiry, another field of research was opened up. The theological basis of social action had increasingly been claiming overt recognition. Significantly enough, the demand came with particular insistence from the lay experts. From 1930 onwards the Institute entered squarely into the debate on the foundations of Christian sociology, natural law, and "the orders of creation" —incidentally a term and a problem which during the whole of the 1930's (owing to its misuse as a religious sanction for the Nazi revolution) became the focus of one of the fiercest controversies ever waged in Continental theology.

In a series of international study conferences, devotees of the social gospel, Anglo-Catholic advocates of a Christian sociology, Barthians, Lutherans, and Orthodox, were brought together to discuss the bases for social action. Initially these meetings resulted in confusion. To sift the problems, to discern the authentic religious motives behind unfamiliar formulations, to locate the points of genuine conflict, to search for reconciling affirmations without violating consciences, proved to be a much harder task than many participants had expected. But the discussions offered constant opportunities to cultivate ecumenical virtues: trust in advance of understanding, patience and humour, loyalty to given truth, and humble readiness to receive new truth. Conflicts of opinion rarely led to a break; sometimes, indeed, they led to a new awareness of an encompassing truth beyond the established and divisive categories of intellectual understanding. At one of these conferences, a round-table discussion on the Christian

[1] Especially the World's Y.M.C.A. and the World's Y.W.C.A.

conception of man turned into a spirited debate between Peter Barth (a noted Calvin scholar, brother of Karl Barth) and an Anglo-Catholic sociologist, the Rev. V. A. Demant. Every new argument made the gulf more evident. Suddenly in a spontaneous gesture Peter Barth grasped his opponent's hand across the table and said in French with his quaint Swiss-German accent, "*Quand même, we are brothers in Christ!*" This *quand même* points to the mysterious well-spring of ecumenical creativity.

As an illustration of the wide range of subjects covered, brief mention may be made of an inquiry into Calendar Reform and a fixed date for Easter, a matter which was occupying the League of Nations in the 1930's. Undeterred by the remark of a member of its Committee that "Calendar Reform . . . would be a good intelligence test for a well-trained monkey", the Research Department gave a limited amount of time to an inquiry that was felt by a number of religious bodies to be important; and received its reward in the Council's recognition for the first time by the League of Nations, which had asked it to report on the subject, as the representative organ of non-Roman Christendom.[1]

A basic problem underlying these ecumenical studies was the reintegration of two great movements of thought and experience which for centuries had been allowed to drift apart—the theological, and the economic and sociological. A conference organized by the Research Department at Rengsdorf in 1933 on the Church and Contemporary Social Systems illustrates the attempt to advance the exploration of ecumenical social thought by means of the combined efforts of theology and sociology. During the first part of the week the theological members, drawn from a great variety of religious traditions, discussed basic Christian assumptions and criteria, whilst the social and political scientists acted as *advocati diaboli*, pressing the theologians to re-examine the relevance for social action of their divergent denominational convictions. The findings provided the framework for the second part of the Conference, in which the social experts held the stage, seeking to measure the concepts of society implied in socialism and capitalism, in Communism and Fascism, by common Christian yardsticks. The experiment proved unsatisfactory; the two partners were still too far apart in assumptions and language to achieve in a few days a real meeting of minds.

During 1933 steps were taken to enlarge the forum of ecumenical group thinking and to transform it into a more permanent enterprise.[2] Distinguished thinkers, at first in Europe, were invited to join international teams for the purpose of sustained co-operative study by means of written exchange and occasional meetings. As they developed, these teams proved an invaluable method of ecumenical cross-fertilization. The subjects chosen—The Kingdom of God and History, Natural Law and Orders of Creation, The Christian Understanding of Man, The Teaching Office of the Church in Social Matters—reflect the increasingly felt need to work out the premises of Christian action in society; they also indicate nodal points in the dialogue between Christianity and secular culture at the time.

The Rengsdorf Conference deserves notice also for another reason. It met in March 1933, just after a newly-elected Reichstag had given the Nazi Government free rein. It was symptomatic of the tense atmosphere of general insecurity

---

[1] See the Research Department's report, *The Churches and the Reform of the Calendar*, 1935, pp. 30 ff.

[2] See *Minutes of the Meeting of the Advisory Committee on Research, Geneva, June 1933*; and *Minutes of the Meeting of the Executive Committee of the Universal Christian Council, Novi Sad, Yugoslavia, 1933*, p. 30.

that the German hosts secretly feared an inquisitive irruption by the local Gestapo. It was, therefore, against a background of pressing actualities that the Conference unanimously asserted its conviction that "the State must not arbitrarily violate the legal rights of the individual, nor of associations in society, nor may it destroy the institutions of the family nor of the Church, which exist alongside of it, but it should respect them in their own right and also for the sake of its own well-being. Consequently the Christian must reject the all-inclusive and completely authoritarian State". The gauntlet had been thrown down.

In the Life and Work and World Alliance discussions on social and international affairs, the expanding rôle and claims of the modern State had inevitably attracted growing attention. But it took the advent of the Nazi régime with its ideology of "blood and soil", and the shock of the incipient Church struggle in Germany, to compel a wider recognition of the gravity of the new issues that were emerging in the relations between Church and State. Faced by this fresh challenge, the Universal Christian Council, in the summer of 1933, authorized its Research Department to invite the Churches to join in a comprehensive study of the authority and function of the State in its relation to the individual, the community, world order, and the Church. Unwittingly, a chain-reaction was thus started which eventually changed the course of Life and Work, and became a major factor in making it a spearhead in the Christian battle during the 1930's. The response was immediate and heartening. The results of intense preparations in a score of countries were gathered up in an international conference in Paris, in April 1934, on The Church and the State of To-day. The discussions were dominated by the conviction that the Christian Church must tackle the new political situation on a far broader basis than the institutional relationships of Church and State, or the defence of religious liberty. This situation indicated a profound cultural change, "a manifestation of a shift in man's total understanding of life", demanding the response of a total faith.[1]

The Conference proved a remarkable success, on account both of the quality of its discussions and of the range of its membership. It was presided over by Dr Marc Boegner, President of the Protestant Federation of France. The attendance of the General Secretaries of the World Alliance, Faith and Order, the I.M.C., and the W.S.C.F. conspicuously demonstrated both increasing co-ordination in the realm of ecumenical study and widespread concern with the subject. The Conference for the first time brought into association with the study programme of Life and Work such eminent thinkers as Nicolas Berdyaev, Emil Brunner, Max Huber, and J. H. Oldham, who were here won to its cause. Professor Max Huber, the Swiss statesman and jurist, wrote: "For more than twenty-seven years I have been taking part in many conferences and commissions of international character—diplomatic, judicial, and scientific—but I believe that the commission which has just met is the first that I have left without a feeling of having been disillusioned. On the contrary, I have left this conference with a new confidence in the possibilities of international co-operation. Furthermore, your commission is the first with which I have had to do that has commenced and ended its work with genuine worship and prayer. It is thanks to that common ground of spiritual prayer-life that the members of the commission never allowed themselves to depart from their main task."

[1] See Preface to the Conference Report, *Die Kirche und das Staatsproblem in der Gegenwart*, Geneva, 1934; 2nd enlarged edition, Geneva ,1935.

Towards a Second World Conference. Meanwhile, for some years, the Universal Christian Council had been considering the convening of a second world conference. It was originally to have been held in 1935, ten years after Stockholm. But in 1932 the Council felt constrained to postpone it to 1937, "in view especially of the new situation created by the economic crisis and also of the need of deeper and fuller preparation".

The biennial meeting of the Council at Fanø, Denmark, during the last week of August 1934, stands out as perhaps the most critical and decisive meeting in its history. Here the Council solemnly resolved to throw its weight on the side of the Confessing Church in Germany against the so-called "German Christians" and by implication against the Nazi régime.

The Minutes of the meeting reveal the explosive nature of this decision. After the Council had heard a speech from a delegate specially sent by the Nazi Reichsbischof Müller, and had passed a resolution including the affirmation that:

> "The Council declares its conviction that autocratic Church rule, especially when imposed upon the conscience in solemn oath; the use of methods of force; and the suppression of free discussion are incompatible with the true nature of the Christian Church."

Bishop Heckel, on behalf of the German delegation, read a long protest, which among many other objections stated that

> "The German Delegation rejects the one-sided stress on a particular group in the German Church and the approval given by the Council to the special theological view of that group. The Delegation find in this an attitude to the internal situation of the German Church which transgresses the limits of the task of the Universal Christian Council in a very questionable way."

Here, also, the Council formally approved the proposal to focus the world conference of 1937 on the theme of Church, Community, and State, and to seek to mobilize the forces of the Churches for a combined thrust.[1] In part a joint meeting of the governing bodies of Life and Work and the World Alliance, it also demonstrated the progressive *rapprochement* of these two movements. The plenary sessions were appropriately devoted to the Church and the State of To-day (a discussion based on the findings of the Paris Conference), and the Church and the World of Nations. A conference held at the same time by the Ecumenical Youth Commission went even further than its elders in bluntly urging the Churches "to dissociate themselves from every Church that does not affirm this universalism [of the Word of God], on the ground that it is not Christian".

In announcing the programme of the World Conference, the Council issued an Explanation to the Churches, which in apt terms stated the new setting and urgency of the problem:

> "The great extension of the functions of the State everywhere in recent times and the emergence in some countries of the authoritarian or totalitarian State raise in a new and often an acute form the age-long question of

[1] The formulation of the theme offers an interesting illustration of the difficulties of ecumenical semasiology. As nearest equivalents to "Community" the German, French, and American titles used the terms "*Volk*", "*Nation*", and "Society", thus revealing distinct approaches to a common problem or rather a common area of concern.

the relation between the Church and the State. The gravity of the modern problem lies in the fact that the increasing organisation of the life of the community, which is made possible by modern science and technique and which is required for the control and direction of economic forces, coincides with a growing secularisation of the thought and life of mankind. . . . No question, therefore, more urgently demands the grave and earnest consideration of Christian people than the relation between the Church, the State and the Community, since on these practical issues is focused the great and critical debate between the Christian faith and the secular tendencies of our time. In this struggle the very existence of the Christian Church is at stake."[1]

Fanø 1934 was of decisive importance as the central connecting link between Stockholm 1925 and Oxford 1937. The action there taken inaugurated a new phase in ecumenical thinking. It brought the expanding programme on which the Council had been engaged over several years to a definite point of decision, and compelled the Churches, as perhaps nothing else could have done, to recognize the Council as an indispensable instrument of their common life.

Realizing that the plans sanctioned at Fanø would require the sustained attention of an executive staff, the Council instructed its Research Department to devote itself entirely to these preparations, and strengthened its Advisory Commission on Research. Among its members were men who for many years (and indeed up to the time of writing) were intimately associated with the development of ecumenical thought—John Baillie, Emil Brunner, V. A. Demant, Leonard Hodgson, Wilhelm Menn, W. A. Visser 't Hooft, H. P. Van Dusen, and others. One of the new members added was at once appointed Chairman—an unusual procedure befitting an unusual man—Dr J. H. Oldham, who became the chief architect and outstanding exponent of the Oxford project. The Paris Conference had disclosed to him the developing possibilities of the Research Department as an instrument for focusing the mind of the Churches on vital tasks of common concern. As Chairman of the Research Committee till 1938, he now unreservedly invested all his wisdom and experience, his rare knowledge of men and world affairs, his gift of imparting his own missionary zeal to others, in this new venture. His introductory pamphlet, Church, Community, and State: A World Issue, with its provocative presentation of the questions to be tackled, became a classic of its kind.

The preparatory programme covered a formidable range of interests—no less than nine separate though interlocking subjects. The central subjects were those named in the title of the Conference: The Church and its Function in Society; Church and Community; Church and State. A second group comprised three further areas, closely related to the Conference theme: Church, Community, and State in relation to Education; Church, Community, and State in relation to the Economic Order; The Universal Church and the World of Nations. Lastly, in accord with the general trend of thought in the Life and Work movement, provision was made for a continued study of theological foundations: The Christian Understanding of Man; The Kingdom of God and History; The Christian Faith and the Common Life.

The choice was not an arbitrary or a hasty one. The subjects represented the

[1] Minutes of the Meeting of the Universal Christian Council for Life and Work, Fanø, 1934, pp. 47 ff.

natural outgrowth of the activities of the preceding years, and accentuated major concerns in the contemporary Christian outlook. The inclusion of a special study of the Church in relation to Society is noteworthy—not least for the reason that it, like the other theological inquiries, had the by-product of contributing to the spiritual amalgamation of Life and Work and Faith and Order.

To measure the significance of the Oxford undertaking within the Christian movement of the time, as well as its own spiritual climate and strategic approach, it is essential to note the objective to which it was directed. Its purpose was something far larger and more important than the preparation and holding of a conference, or adding to the proliferation of ecumenical documents. What it had in view was an historical situation in which the perennial conflict between the Church and the world was again reaching a new pitch of terrible intensity, due to the onslaught of militant secular and neo-pagan forces; and the need for arousing the whole Christian community to face the gravity of the situation, the magnitude of the task, and its own pitiful inadequacy. The Conference—as was frequently stated—must not be regarded as an "isolated and unrelated event" but merely as incidental to a concerted long-range effort to think out afresh the Christian witness concerning man's life in society. It was an effort to aid the Churches, through mutual counsel and help, to wage their battle with greater energy and a clearer sense of direction.

The preparatory studies developed into a venture of ecumenical thinking, which in thoroughness and range of co-operation has perhaps never been equalled by any previous Christian world gathering. By giving definiteness to the Christian mind in face of the perils and opportunities of a changing world situation, it exercised a potent, though largely intangible, influence on the thought and polity of the Churches. Not least important among its results was the fact that, by enlisting leading Christians from different walks of life in an enriching fellowship of thought and study, it won many new adherents to the ecumenical cause.

But gain was to some extent balanced by loss. The progressive concentration of the Life and Work movement on preparing its forthcoming world conference tended to overshadow, and to some extent to push aside, other aspects of its many-sided programme. There were complaints that the initial concern of Life and Work with measures of social welfare was now being shelved. In part this was an optical illusion; in part it was true. It was one of those situations where a major strategic choice inevitably entails a reconsideration of priorities along the whole line. In retrospect, however, it would seem that the course adopted by the Council in planning for the Oxford Conference was a deeply discerning interpretation of the needs of the time. The trend of events made the theme not less but more timely and opportune as the year 1937 drew closer.

The discussion of the subjects was carried out by means of an intricate network of interacting groups, held together by the central staff through personal correspondence and visits. For each subject a small team of writers of basic papers and editorial consultants was formed, each team surrounded by a larger circle of some thirty to forty persons engaged in commenting—often at considerable length—on successive drafts of the papers circulated. Altogether about 250 papers were produced and circulated with discrimination to different kinds of groups—thus fortunately causing intellectual indigestion only to the staff. The written interchange was interspersed with a series of about twenty small planning meetings and study conferences. These, by bringing together for informal and lively consultation thoughtful Christians from many lands—theologians, philosophers, historians, educationists, social-scientists, people engaged in politics and industry—became the sounding-board and testing-ground for many of the ideas and convictions which eventually moulded the Oxford gathering.

The participation extended far beyond the 300 to 400 contributors with whom the staff was able to maintain personal contact. The Oxford theme was discussed in all manner of groups and gatherings. It gave rise to a whole literature on the Church's relation to the State and to Society. In the United States preparations were taken in hand by the American section of the Universal Christian Council, whose Secretary, Dr H. S. Leiper, carried out an extensive work of education. The study programme was directed by a special Advisory Council, with Dr John R. Mott as Chairman and Dean H. P. Van Dusen and Professor John C. Bennett as Secretaries. Besides religious leaders, it included a host of prominent lay people from various walks of life. Somewhat earlier, a similar Advisory Council had been formed in Great Britain, presided over by Sir Walter Moberly, a prominent figure in British university life, and likewise composed of distinguished churchmen and women. The Continental Churches, more immediately affected by the totalitarian revolution, naturally showed particular eagerness to share in this venture. Their leaders, profoundly perturbed by the happenings in Germany, realized that the issues of Nation and State were becoming a matter of life or death to the Churches. A notable feature was the keen interest displayed among the Eastern Orthodox Churches. A representative group of Russian religious thinkers in Paris contributed a symposium on *Church, State, and Man*, which still ranks among the weightiest Orthodox utterances on these problems.[1]

It was of considerable ecumenical significance that a number of Roman Catholic thinkers on the Continent and in Britain readily agreed to participate, on a private and informal basis, in various aspects of the programme. Sharing the same perils and tribulations under the pressures of the totalitarian State, Christians were driven closer together on common ground. Cardinal Faulhaber of Munich, a famed Roman Catholic leader under the Nazi régime, voiced this sentiment when he said to an ecumenical visitor: "Catholic and Protestant are separated by many important matters of dogma, but there are great central convictions common to both and now subject to the sharpest attack. What we face to-day is a conflict not between two halves of Christianity, but between Christianity and the world."[2] This co-operation did not remain without visible fruits. As a contribution to an endeavour which they regarded as a common Christian cause, some of these Continental Roman Catholics took the step, probably unprecedented in ecumenical history, of publishing a companion volume to the Oxford literature.[3]

The wide interchange preceding the Oxford gathering, with its elaborate process of authorship and critical editing, was distilled into an imposing array of volumes. These constitute a treasure-house for the student of ecumenical Christianity in the middle 1930's; more than that, their exposition of the Christian Gospel in its encounter with the strange gospels of the time contains a host

---

[1] On the Athens Conference of Orthodox Theologians, see Chap. xiv, pp. 657 f.
[2] Reported by Dr Samuel McCrea Cavert in an article in *The Christian Century* of 23 October 1935. It was Cardinal Faulhaber who said "we are not redeemed by German blood, but by the precious blood of our Lord Jesus Christ".
[3] *Die Kirche Christi: Grundfragen der Menschenbildung und Weltgestaltung.* Ed. Otto Iserland.

of penetrating insights, which have grown in relevance with the passing of time. Here a preliminary clarification was effected, which furnished invaluable background material for the World Conference itself. The project was too ambitious to allow for publication of the volumes, with one exception, before the Conference convened, but the main essays were widely distributed in advance. During the second world war the remaining stock of the English edition was burnt out in the bombardment of London. Yet the ideas gathered up in the Oxford volumes began new growth among the ashes. They are still exercising a pervasive influence on Christian thought.

6. OXFORD 1937

"*Dominus illuminatio mea.*" This inscription in the coat-of-arms of the University of Oxford aptly symbolizes the spirit of the gathering which took place in that ancient home of learning from 12 to 26 July 1937.

The world scene had undergone almost incredible changes since Life and Work had held its first great gathering at Stockholm in 1925. It was one of those periods when the majestic flow of history seems to be precipitated into a turbulent cataract, tossing events around in vertiginous swirls. In the middle 1920's it was commonly believed, at least in the West, that the world was steadily moving forward to "peace on earth among men of goodwill". During the intervening years these optimistic expectations had been rudely shattered. The Oxford Conference met—as the opening sentences of its Message pointedly state—"at a time when mankind is oppressed with perplexity and fear. Men are burdened with evils almost insupportable and with problems apparently insoluble". There was a widespread, chilly feeling that a new world war was imminent; in fact the dress rehearsal had already begun in China and in Spain. A Chinese delegate, Timothy Tingfang Lew, in a rousing speech imploring the assembly to pay serious attention to the tragic situation in Asia, spoke of the one and a half million Christians in his home country "facing a threat of a titanic struggle which may determine their entire history, their freedom and even their existence".

And beneath all else lay the central question of all, which from the outset had been the dominant concern of the Oxford undertaking, imparting to it a sense of urgent mission. Open persecution or more subtle attempts to make religion subservient to the new Caesarisms were in evidence everywhere. To quote J. H. Oldham in his authoritative introduction to the official Conference Report: "The fundamental religious problem of to-day ... is ... the problem of the relation of the Church to the all-embracing claims of a communal life. It is the problem 'how religion is to survive in a single community which is neither Church nor State, which recognizes no formal limits, but which covers the whole of life and claims to be the source and goal of every human activity'.... The question which ... meets us again to-day is ... the question of the relation between the Church as owning allegiance to a supramundane authority and the integrated body which is community-state or state-community. The essential theme of the Oxford Conference ... was the life and death struggle between Christian faith and the secular and pagan tendencies of our time."[1]

Oxford became, for a fortnight, a presentation in miniature of the human pandemonium. And no less of that of the Churches—with their discordant

---

[1] *The Churches Survey Their Task*, pp. 9 f. Dr Oldham was himself quoting from an article by Mr Christopher Dawson (*The Tablet*, 26 June 1937).

voices, their vested spiritual and national interests, their unfaithfulness and self-satisfaction. "We do not call the world to be like ourselves, for we are already too like the world."[1] But this very situation tended to create an atmosphere of honest realism in analysing the ills of society and of the Church, an expectancy subdued but trustful, a common hearkening after the guiding voice of the Spirit, which marked both the deliberations and the services of worship.

Stockholm 1925 was a living presence at Oxford. There were not a few personal links; but those who had been at Stockholm felt the loss of the magnetic leadership of the man who by force of his vision and personality had been the heart and soul of that earlier gathering. Archbishop Söderblom had died six years to the day before the Conference convened; a reverent tribute was paid to his memory at the opening session, when the Archbishop of Canterbury (Lang) spoke of his "versatility of mind, his vitality of spirit, his insights into the needs of his times, his foresight of the needs of the future, and the unquenchable optimism of his faith".

The 425 regular members of the Conference included 300 delegates officially appointed by the Churches, representing 120 communions in forty countries. One hundred co-opted delegates were appointed by the Universal Christian Council in order to ensure the assistance of eminent experts in various fields—a galaxy of scholars and men and women of practical affairs. The remaining twenty-five comprised fraternal delegates and ecumenical officers. There was in addition an almost equal number of visitors or associate delegates and youth representatives. The membership constituted a cross-section of Christendom, with the exception of the Roman Catholic Church; only some personal observers from that Communion were present by invitation.[2] The absence of Rome was accepted as a fact, deeply regrettable, yet perfectly comprehensible in view of Rome's dogmatic position.

But there was another notable absence, which caused considerable stir, and perhaps more dramatically than anything else brought home the grim immediacy of the theme of the Conference. German Church leaders had taken a prominent part in the preparations for the Conference. But the Nazi Government had barred the attendance of the official delegation from the German Evangelical Church; indeed, Pastor Niemöller and several others among the expected delegates were under guard or languishing in prison. The Conference, therefore, felt moved to send a special message of sympathy and solidarity to "their brethren in the Evangelical Church in Germany". It mentioned especially the afflictions and the steadfast witness of the Confessing Church, but also made an explicit reference to the struggle of the Roman Catholic Church. This led to a painful incident. Three Germans were present at the Conference, a Methodist and two Baptists, from small Free Churches which had kept aloof from the struggle in the Evangelical Church. In a public protest against the message, the Methodist claimed that "the Federation of Evangelical Free Churches in Germany are grateful for the full liberty of proclaiming the Gospel of Jesus Christ". He went on to express their "gratitude that God in His providence has sent a leader who was able to banish the danger of Bolshevism in Germany . . . and to give it a new faith in its mission and future".[3] It was a telling testimony—but in quite a different sense from that which the speaker had intended.

---

[1] From the Message, ibid., p. 57.
[2] One Roman Catholic was present throughout as a co-opted delegate.
[3] From the record of the proceedings.

The weakness of the Continental delegations accentuated the preponderance of Anglo-Saxon ways of thought, manifest already in the fact that not less than 300 of the 425 delegates came from the United States and the British Commonwealth. The Orthodox Churches and the Lesser Eastern Churches were represented by some two score dignitaries and scholars.[1] Again there was a disproportionately small participation from younger Church areas, both in the preparatory stages and in the Conference itself—only thirty, though this was an advance on the six at Stockholm. But among the thirty were some, such as Dr V. S. Azariah, first Indian bishop of the Anglican Communion, who made a deep impression by their spiritual and intellectual stature.

The Oxford Conference, like Stockholm 1925, was a worshipping community. The most abiding impression retained by the delegates was neither its world-embracing company of communions and nations, nor the quality of its thought, but its interweaving of devotion and deliberation. In a remarkable way, it spelled out the root connection of cultus and culture. A Congregationalist participant well recaptured the atmosphere in these words: "In Saint Mary's in Oxford and later in St Giles' in Edinburgh, where we met daily for intercession, there came to us such a sense of spiritual oneness about the altar of God as to make all who partook of the experience mystically aware of the presence of the Church. That Church, one, holy, catholic, appeared then in its beauty to eyes no longer holden; and all responded to the impulse of the same Spirit. There the richness which is in Christ was poured in lavish abundance and in its many forms of beauty . . . into the souls of worshippers."[2] "In the periods of silence", so testifies another member, "there was often an overpowering sense that things were happening in the spiritual world, and that in the coming years one might expect to see in the breaking out of new life in countless directions an answer to the prayers that were being offered together to God."[3]

Nevertheless the tragic depth of disunity amid unity was manifested in the fact that no services of Holy Communion were included in the official programme. On the closing Sunday the authorities of the Church of England took the exceptional step of inviting baptized communicant members of the Conference to receive the Holy Gifts at two simultaneous services, celebrated by the Archbishop of Canterbury, among whose assistants was Bishop Azariah of Dornakal, and by the Bishop of Chichester (Bell). It was a moment of heavenly vision for those who felt in their conscience free to kneel at the communion rail. But those services, as arranged for the whole Conference, caused great pain to the Orthodox delegates who, unable to participate, felt that they were thus inadvertently set apart.[4]

Oxford 1937 can be characterized as an ecumenical study conference on a world scale. It was designed to be a culminating point in a continuing process of clarifying and crystallizing Christian thought and strategy in regard to burning issues of human society. The programme was shaped accordingly. The plenary sessions in the first week were devoted to a series of addresses, rivalling one another in penetrating insight, which sketched a suggestive panorama of the

[1] This delegation, though small, represented the Ecumenical Patriarchate, the Patriarchates of Alexandria and Antioch, the Churches of Cyprus, Greece, Rumania, Yugoslavia, Bulgaria, Poland, the Russian Church in Exile, the Coptic Orthodox Church, the Armenian Church, and the Church of the Assyrians.
[2] Dr Douglas Horton in an article on "Oxford and Edinburgh, 1937" in *World Christianity*, Fourth Quarter, 1937.
[3] J. H. Oldham in *The Churches Survey Their Task*, pp. 18 f.
[4] See L. A. Zander's critical article in *Irénikon*, Nov.–Dec. 1937, pp. 505–35.

world situation and of the task of the Church. For the purpose of constructive discussion, the delegates were assigned to five Sections, which dealt with five themes: Church and Community; Church and State; Church, Community, and State in relation to the Economic Order; Church, Community, and State in relation to Education; The Universal Church and the World of Nations. The latter had a subsection on the controversial issue of the Christian Attitude to War. No praise could be too high for the work carried out by the Sections under their respective Chairmen—Sir Walter Moberly, Professor Max Huber, Mr John Maud, President H. S. Coffin, President J. A. Mackay, and Dr W. A. Visser 't Hooft. The theological studies included in the preparatory programme served as a general frame of reference. The deliberations of the Conference were guided by Dr John R. Mott. A committee under the chairmanship of the Archbishop of York (Temple)—a man whose unique gift for irenic formulation here as elsewhere proved of the greatest service—drafted a general Conference Message, which was unanimously adopted before the close.

The method of working out the documents of the Conference was that which is usual in such ecumenical gatherings. Yet it deserves notice, since it well demonstrates the fascinating maieutic art by which so-called "ecumenical ideas" are brought to birth. Well in advance, a draft report was elaborated on the subject of each section, intended "to focus attention on those aspects of the subject which, in the light of the preparatory work and discussions, seem to be the most central, the most vital, the most appropriate for consideration by the Conference, and the most urgently calling for action. The memoranda should attempt to state clearly both the measure of common Christian conviction which the preparatory work has shown to exist, and also the major divergences of view which have manifested themselves".[1] In addition, the Churches were invited to express their opinion as to the questions requiring primary attention at the gathering.

The prefabricated reports did not, however, find favour with the Sections, and were soon discarded after having served as useful stimulants—or irritants. After the usual period of abortive starts and of anguished frustration, new designs of thought then began to take shape in the travail of the fertile, though sometimes chaotic, discussions of the Sections. The main creative work of synthesis and writing, however, rested with small drafting committees, which in their nightly labours had to sift and digest, besides the discussions, piles of written suggestions and amendments. The resultant drafts were then corrected and amplified in successive stages of scrutiny. The wealth of material and the shortness of time did not permit a detailed examination in the plenary sessions during the second week. The reports were therefore not submitted to the whole Conference for formal adoption, but referred back to the Sections for revision and approval, and commended by the Conference "to the serious and favourable consideration of the Churches".

The final documents were thus the outcome of an immense effort of genuine group thinking; it would require a source-criticism, as refined as that applied to the Biblical writings, to identify the origin and the successive mutations and amalgamations of the convictions here set forth. Compared with the preliminary reports, they exhibit a remarkable advance in registering both the actual growth of common belief and the measure of still unresolved conflict, and also in many

[1] *Minutes of the Meeting of the Universal Christian Council, Chamby, Switzerland, August 1936*, p. 48.

instances a distinct shift of emphasis and perspective. This achievement goes to show once more that there is no soil more propitious for the advancement of truth than the prayerful and receptive atmosphere of personal encounter.

It has been stated by a sober historian that "the authority of the Oxford reports was unprecedented, at least in Protestant social ethics, and their competence enabled them to rank with the best of secular thought, a phenomenon scarcely seen since the seventeenth century".[1] A detailed analysis of their contents would lead beyond the scope of this narrative. It will be appropriate, however, to indicate some outstanding features of the gathering.

(1) "Let the Church be the Church!" This crusading motto has re-echoed around the Christian world as the quintessence of the Oxford venture.[2] Indeed, the Conference gathered up and reinforced a multiple movement of concentration on the Church—not as an end in itself, but for the sake of a more authentic and forceful Christian expansion into the world. Its concern was with the problem of community—the function of the redeemed and redemptive community in serving the communities of men.

Oxford 1937 did not develop any coherent and unified conception of the Church; this was obviously outside its purpose and competence. The emphasis on the Church provided rather, as it were, the common universe of discourse, encompassing a maze of varieties and contradictions of belief. Yet certain controlling insights can be discerned.

The Conference brought a fresh, invigorating experience of the universality of the Church, witnessed to in the discoveries of personal fellowship, in the sense of solidarity with suffering and struggling brethren all over the world, in the common stand against monolithic idolatrous societies of creed and nation, race and class. The cause of "the Churches under the Cross" was solemnly espoused as a common cause; and it began to dawn upon the ecumenical mind that persecution and martyrdom, as in ages past, might be not so much a catastrophe as the harbinger of a Church reborn.

Moreover, while the assumptions of Western and especially of Anglo-Saxon Christianity still played a predominant rôle, the Conference earnestly strove to transcend this limitation in seeking a larger vision of the world-wide missionary Church. In this respect, the stirring contributions of spokesmen of the younger Churches were of the highest significance.

The most distinctive feature of the Oxford ecclesiology, however, was its bold declaration of the independence of the Church over against mundane counter-churches of any and every kind. This conviction was spelled out in all the reports: "The primary duty of the Church to the State is to be the Church, namely, to witness for God, to preach His Word, to confess the faith before men, to teach both young and old to observe the divine commandments, and to serve the nation and the State by proclaiming the Will of God as the supreme standard to which all human wills must be subject and all human conduct must conform. These functions of worship, preaching, teaching, and ministry the Church cannot renounce whether the State consent or not."[3]

[1] J. H. Nichols, *Democracy and the Churches*, Philadelphia, 1951, p. 235.
[2] It is interesting to note that this famous phrase does not appear in the printed Conference material. It occurred in the first draft of the Report on "The Universal Church and the World of Nations", written by its Chairman, Dr John A. Mackay, and it reappears in the Message of the Conference in the following form: "The first duty of the Church, and its greatest service to the world, is that it be in very deed the Church."
[3] *The Churches Survey Their Task*, p. 82.

(2) Another distinguishing mark was the organic blending of theological reflection with the everyday experiences and problems of the lay mind. Reaping the fruits of the theological development of Life and Work, the Oxford Conference took for granted that social and political questions are basically religious questions, and therefore a legitimate and necessary province of theological investigation. But perhaps of even greater consequence for the future was the emphasis placed on the responsibility of the laity for shaping the social thought and performing the social task of the Church. Here again, Oxford 1937 acted as a loud-speaker for convictions which had gradually emerged in the preparatory process. If a change had at least begun to take place in the Protestant outlook on this vital matter, this was due not least to the persistence and forcefulness with which J. H. Oldham had articulated the doctrine that "if the Christian witness is to be borne in social and political life it must be through the action of the multitude of Christian men and women who are actively engaged from day to day in the conduct of administration, industry, and the affairs of the public and common life".[1]

(3) At a memorable service in St Paul's Cathedral, London, arranged jointly for the delegates to the Oxford and Edinburgh Conferences, the Archbishop of Canterbury preached on the text, "Speak unto the children of Israel, that they go forward". To those who at Oxford had wrestled together to discern the Word of God for a time of confusion and despair, this came as a fitting climax. The fellowship, worship, and deliberations of the Conference had a cumulative impact, generating a clearer sense of direction and a firmer determination among those who came within the range of their influence.

An immense effort was made, notably in the Anglo-Saxon world, to bring home the message of the Conference to the rank and file of the Churches. The violent reactions in Germany made it evident that the Nazis were more perspicacious than many churchmen in assessing the gathering strength of Christian conviction which the Conference symbolized. In Britain it became a major incentive in the efforts which eventually led to the creation of the British Council of Churches in 1942.

Oxford sounded no clarion call of prophecy. Nevertheless it is true to say that many of its affirmations concerning the indispensable freedoms of the Church, the Christian attitude to war, and the cardinal tests of a responsible economic order, at least set up helpful signposts to guide the wayfarer on an ever-darkening road. The influence of the Oxford Conference is evident in numerous declarations and interventions of religious bodies in war-time, as, for instance, in the famous Ten Peace Points, jointly propounded in December 1940 by Church leaders in Britain, including the Roman Catholic Archbishop of Westminster (Cardinal Hinsley).

We have noted more than once the growing convergence of Life and Work and Faith and Order. Before dispersing, the Conference approved, with only two dissenting votes, the proposal for a World Council of Churches in which the two movements should become one. As a consequence, the Universal Christian Council for Life and Work, on 13 May 1938, at Utrecht, transferred its responsibilities and functions to the new Provisional Committee of the World Council of Churches in Process of Formation.[2]

[1] *The Churches Survey Their Task*, p. 44.
[2] See Chap. xvi, p. 704.

7. CONCLUSIONS

This chapter and that which precedes it cover between them barely a single generation of human life. Some readers may be inclined to wonder why the events of this period have been recorded in such detail, and treated as having so much importance in the general ecumenical picture. If any reader asks such a question, he is paying unconscious tribute to the greatness of the achievements of the ecumenical movement in the 20th century.

It is hard for anyone born after the beginning of the century to realize the extent to which in 1914 the Churches still lived in separation from one another. There were of course certain points of connection, and a good deal of exchange of knowledge and friendship, often on the initiative of individuals; other chapters have shown how the Churches were gradually being brought into greater awareness of one another. But for the most part, each went its own way, concentrating on its own tasks and its own immediate responsibilities. Most of the great leaders were still personally unknown to one another.

In 1914 there was no clear or generally accepted view of the social responsibility of the Church. Some Churches were prepared to surrender to the State the whole responsibility for the political, international, and social realms, regarding the task of the Church as purely "other-worldly". Others, while not accepting this dichotomy, were uncertain as to how the responsibility of the Church was to be defined or carried out. There had never been lacking enterprises of Christian charity in response to special need, but these were often unco-ordinated and unrelated to clear principles of action. In many of the fields touched by their work, Life and Work and the World Alliance were pioneers.

When the Stockholm Conference met in 1925, there were few precedents to guide it. Edinburgh 1910 had in some respects shown the way. But that was a gathering of Christian groups and societies bound together by a special concern. Stockholm 1925 was a meeting of Churches, many of which, such as the Orthodox, had hardly any previous experience of participation in international religious discussion, to consider together problems which had been the subject of lively controversy almost from the beginning of the Christian era. Inevitably Stockholm 1925 raised a great many more questions than it could answer, questions to some of which the Oxford Conference twelve years later was to give an answer. Oxford 1937 in its turn raised other great questions, to which the ecumenical answer is slowly being worked out.

Stockholm 1925 set up an organization for the continuance of its work. It was agreed that the Churches must have and must express a mind on social questions. But where was that mind to be found? The Roman Catholic Church had made a beginning, with the great Encyclicals from *Rerum Novarum* (1891) onwards, in the formulation of Christian social doctrine; the non-Roman Churches had no corresponding authorities. If they pronounced on specific questions, they were liable to be convicted of presumptuous ignorance by the experts; if they limited themselves to generalities, no one would very much wish to listen to pious platitudes. It was evident that hard and continuous study would be needed, if the witness of the Churches was to be worthy and effective.

There was a continuous and fruitful tension between study of immediate situations and study directed towards a deeper understanding of the Gospel truths in their application to social conditions. Both were necessary, since abstract study, unchecked by reference to immediate needs, may lose itself in a cloud of theoretical generalities, and study of specific problems unrelated to principles may tend to tie the Churches down to partial and empirical solutions.

An even more urgent task was the education of the Churches. It is impossible to exaggerate the part played by small conferences, meetings of councils and committees which gave opportunity for the expression of clashing points of view without the infringement of Christian charity, by seminars and lecture tours, and by the steady stream of publications directed towards making the Churches aware of one another and of their common responsibilities. In this field no ground can permanently be won; the task has to be begun over again almost from the start with the emergence of each new generation.

The passage of the years overthrew many of the early presuppositions of ecumenical thinking. Up till 1914 the climate of thought was generally favourable to optimism; that optimism survived in some quarters, though with increasing difficulty, for about ten years after the end of the first world war. As the skies darkened, the Churches were compelled to be more than ever aware of the world in both its Biblical senses, as the world which God loved and in which he is perpetually at work, and as the world which has organized itself apart from God, and therefore devises continually new forms of rebellion against him. The world changes more rapidly than the Church, and the Church is always slow to apprehend the changed situation. Yet if the Church or the ecumenical movement speaks to a situation that is already past, its words are spurned as irrelevant, if not worse. Only slowly did Christians come to perceive that the rise of totalitarian systems had introduced a new era for the world and for the Church. It was the genius of Oxford 1937 that it seized on the central issue of the times, the emergence of the new State which is a parody of the divine society, the Church, and yet spoke to the new situation in terms of the unchanging assurances of the Faith.

The preparations for Oxford 1937 did much to bring to a head a tendency (already implicit in Stockholm 1925), which had been slowly growing within the movement, to recognize on the one hand the importance of theology, and on the other the centrality of the Church. It was at this point that divergences between Life and Work and the World Alliance began to be plainly evident. The World Alliance largely continued to hold to the pragmatic view that the raising of questions of dogma is likely to have a paralysing effect on the practical activities of Christians, and that its own best service could be rendered as a free association, untrammelled by the slowness and conservatism of the ecclesiastical mind. Life and Work gradually took the narrower and, as many friends of the movement would feel, the more central path of finding a new freedom in closer association with the Churches and their life, and thus prepared the way for that union out of which the World Council of Churches was born.

The theological emphasis had never been wholly lacking in the movement; even at Stockholm 1925 voices had been raised to insist that practical action without a serious theological basis is futile. As the work developed, the need for theological understanding came to be ever more strongly felt; indeed one of the causes for certain tensions between Life and Work and Faith and Order during a considerable part of the period under review was the tendency for Life and Work to trespass on what Faith and Order regarded as its own special field. Could there be a clearer proof of the artificiality of the separation between the two movements? Any serious attempt to find a Christian solution for even a small problem (as St Paul discovered in dealing with the Sunday collection at

Corinth) leads back step by step to the deepest mysteries of the Faith; and conversely any attempt to understand fully any of the great Christian doctrines leads on to the discovery of its applications in unsuspected realms. The formation of the World Council of Churches was only the expression of an underlying unity which had existed from the beginning.

Although it was only with the formation of the World Council in 1948 that the Churches, as such and officially, engaged themselves in the ecumenical movement, Life and Work had aimed from the beginning at being a movement of the Churches. Most of those who came to Stockholm 1925 were not simply interested individuals but delegates officially or quasi-officially appointed by their Churches. The purpose of the movement had been to challenge and to educate the Churches in the field of social and international responsibility. But what is a Church, and by what does it live? The German Church struggle, and the emergence of the Churches as the only powers able to exert an effective resistance, even to the point of martyrdom, to totalitarian aggression, brought the idea and the doctrine of the Church again into the centre of the picture. It had become evident to many that a day had arrived in which the loosely organized efforts of men of good-will were no longer adequate, and that nothing less than the intense and corporate loyalty of the Churches as such to Jesus Christ could stand against the ruthless enemies of the mid-20th century.

The record of these years is marked by increasing depth of understanding, and a steady and almost inevitable convergence of Life and Work and Faith and Order towards a central point. At the same time, the movement was characterized by certain weaknesses, which have not yet been fully overcome.

Life and Work and the World Alliance were both almost exclusively Western in outlook and range of operations. Life and Work had indeed planned to develop a fifth section embracing the younger Church areas ; its failure ever to bring this fifth section into being is a clear indication of where the centre of its interests really lay. This was a grave defect. The revolutions of the Western world presented painfully urgent problems, but an even greater revolution was already on the way, and of this the ecumenical movement of the time seems hardly to have been aware. In 1905 the Japanese victory over the Russians heralded the end of the late 19th-century form of colonialism. The nations of the East began to rouse themselves from their complacent acquiescence under Western control, political or economic; the unchanging East became that part of the world where the greatest changes followed one another with the most breathless rapidity, and half the population of the world broke loose from its ancestral moorings. The Churches in Asia and Africa began to be faced by problems more difficult and urgent than any that had confronted the Churches since Augustine wrote his great book on *The City of God*. The ecumenical movement has not yet fully shaken itself free from its Western origins to become genuinely the expression of the concerns of a world-wide Church.

From its beginnings, Life and Work lived in a dialectical tension between emphases which, though in fact complementary, have sometimes been presented in an almost contradictory form. At times large sections of its supporters seemed to proclaim the view that social and political reform would prove the panacea for all human ills. The constant and necessary preoccupation of the movement with social and political questions sometimes gave the impression that the movement was committed to the view that a change in conditions would result in a change in hearts; the constant and growing protest against this view on theological grounds was not always heard. This tension is part of the legacy which Life and Work has passed on to the continuing ecumenical movement, except that the liberal optimism, which outlived the first world war, disappeared with the second.

It has been perhaps inevitable, but none the less a grave disadvantage to the ecumenical movement, that the various aspects of ecumenical concern—the unity and renewal of the Church, the evangelistic task among peoples who have never known Christ or have rejected him in the dim and distorted form in which he has been presented by the Churches, the social and political witness of the Churches—have been developed in separation from one another. Progress towards integration has been made, but the process is as yet very far from complete. Life and Work brought into the larger fellowship the rich experiences of a period of varied experimentation and solid achievement. To say that Life and Work died in 1938 would be to give a wholly false impression of what happened ; the movement merely changed its name, to continue its work and witness with undiminished vitality within the wider embrace of the World Council of Churches.[1]

[1] The continuance of the traditions of the World Alliance in the Commission of the Churches on International Affairs has already been set forth on p. 568.

CHAPTER 13

OTHER ASPECTS OF
THE ECUMENICAL MOVEMENT
1910–1948

by

RUTH ROUSE

1. INTRODUCTION[1]

Every chapter of this History has borne witness to the range and variety of the efforts to which the desire for Christian unity has given rise in different centuries and countries. Much space has of necessity been given in the five preceding chapters to the convergence of a number of originally separate streams in the formation of the World Council of Churches. But this is not the whole story. The World Council neither is nor claims to be the entire ecumenical movement. It is a significant current in the whole advancing process of unity, but there are many other manifestations of the ecumenical spirit which contribute to the forward sweep of the whole.

Along with the convergent movements there are others which are parallel and do not meet, and yet others which may be described as divergent since they seek unity on principles different from those which have brought the World Council into being. It has been comparatively easy to deal with the convergent movements since they can be subsumed under certain unifying principles and tend towards a point of meeting. But for these other movements there are no such unifying principles. Their significance lies in their very divergence and variety.

The chapter which follows might well be called Varieties of Ecumenical Experience, and is therefore bound to be fragmentary rather than organic in structure. An attempt will be made, however, to indicate the nature of each of these various aspects of the ecumenical movement, its connections with movements described in other chapters, and the part which it plays in the general picture of the Christian movement towards unity.[2]

2. THE WORLD CHRISTIAN LAY MOVEMENTS

There are three movements which have played such a rôle in the history of the World Council as to justify those who call them its "Major Allies". These are the Young Men's Christian Association, the Young Women's Christian Association, and the Student Christian Movement, known in their world forms as the World's Alliance of Young Men's Christian Associations, the World's Young Women's Christian Association, and the World's Student Christian Federation.[3]

All were in their origin youth movements, or movements on behalf of youth. The Federation remains so by virtue of its student objective. The Y.M.C.A. and the Y.W.C.A. have so extended their services to all classes and ages of the community as to make "lay movements" a more correct title.

[1] This chapter is partly based on extensive memoranda by Dr H. Paul Douglass, and Dr R. H. Edwin Espy, Executive Secretary, National Student Council of the Y.M.C.A., New York, and has been brought to its present form, with much additional material, by Miss Ruth Rouse, Editorial Secretary of the Committee on the History of the Ecumenical Movement. Dr Douglass had originally been selected as the author for this chapter. He was prevented by illness from completing his work, and died on 14 April 1953.

[2] Certain special aspects of ecumenical thought and activity, in Eastern Orthodoxy, in the Roman Catholic Church, and in the lands of the younger Churches, receive separate treatment in Chaps. iv, viii, xiv, and xv.

[3] For a survey of the ecumenical aspects of these three movements in the 19th century, see Chap. vii, pp. 327 ff.

Their rôle in the ecumenical movement has been and is to-day pre-eminently that of pioneers; this is to such an extent the case that considerable parts of the earlier history of the modern ecumenical movement, the problems with which it has wrestled, the gradual emergence of its principles, can best be learned from the records of these lay movements. The three movements have certain common characteristics which fit them for their pioneering rôle.

The first is that they are not Churches. They are voluntary movements made up of individual members and independent of the Churches as ecclesiastically organized. All three are primarily associations of lay Christians led by lay men and women. They are free, ready to adventure, experiment, and make mistakes. They push out to the ends of the earth. They have a gift for evoking the qualities of leadership, and it is a commonplace that the majority of leaders of the ecumenical movement have been trained in their ranks.

Although autonomous, they are deeply interdependent. The Y.M.C.A. and the Y.W.C.A., with a century of history behind them, have run largely on parallel lines, the Y.W.C.A., the younger by ten years, "greatly influenced by . . . its older, larger, and more experienced brother organization".[1]

The basis of all three movements is evangelical in the essential meaning of that word. The so-called Paris Basis of the Y.M.C.A. adopted in 1855 reads:

> "The Young Men's Christian Association seeks to unite those young men who, regarding Jesus Christ as their God and Saviour[2] according to the Holy Scriptures, desire to be His disciples."

The bases of the World's Y.W.C.A. and of the W.S.C.F. at the time of their foundation, 1894 and 1895 respectively, were expressed in practically the same terms as that of the World's Y.M.C.A. Although in 1913 and 1914 the Y.W.C.A. and the Federation adopted formulas differing considerably in wording from the original, the essential meaning was in no way altered.[3]

Moreover, the basic aims of all three are the same. These aims are essentially evangelistic and missionary; and it is the constant endeavour to fulfil these aims which has made the lay movements pioneers of ecumenism. The actual process of pioneering varies according to the relation between the lay movements and the Churches in the area concerned—a relationship far from uniform. In North America and certain Oriental lands the basis of full Association membership was, both in City and Student Associations, until a process of change to a personal basis began in the 1920's, membership "in an evangelical Church", i.e. a Protestant Church other than Unitarian; Christians belonging to other Churches could be admitted only as "associate members". Student Christian Movements, on the other hand, have had as a rule a personal basis—usually a statement of adherence to a particular aim—and their membership is open to all who accept their basis. In Germany, Norway, and Denmark the Y.M.C.A. and the Y.W.C.A. are for the most part[4] parish organizations fulfilling the function performed by young people's societies in the local church in other lands, and are

---

[1] Anna V. Rice, *A History of the World's Y.W.C.A.*, New York, 1947, p. 142.
[2] It is striking that the wording "Jesus Christ as God and Saviour" is the same as the basis of the Faith and Order movement, adopted in 1910, and of the World Council itself, adopted in 1938, though there is no evidence that knowledge of the Y.M.C.A. basis in any way influenced the choice made by Faith and Order.
[3] See Note on Bases of World's Y.W.C.A. and W.S.C.F., p. 641.
[4] In great cities, Associations of a more institutional kind are found.

thus closely associated with the official Church, Lutheran or Reformed, though not an organic part of its machinery.

The relationship of Student Christian Movements to the Y.M.C.A. and Y.W.C.A. also varies in different countries. Certain Student Movements affiliated to the W.S.C.F., e.g. in the United States, China, and Japan, are integral parts, Student Departments, of the Y.M.C.A. and the Y.W.C.A. respectively. In the large majority of countries, however, the national Student Christian Movement is an organization not organically connected with the Y.M.C.A. and Y.W.C.A. Secretaries of all three world movements play into each others' hands, exchange information, and, when travelling, forward each others' interests. Each sends fraternal delegates to the committees and conferences of the other two, and they have many joint commissions and training schemes. All have their world headquarters in Geneva.

There is a certain difference between the ecumenical history of the two senior movements, founded in 1844 and 1855 respectively, and the Student Christian Movements [1] which, for the most part, came into existence between 1890 and 1910. The two senior movements were in the 19th century, broadly speaking, comparatively little concerned with their relation to the Churches.[2] After the first world war a notable change took place; the greatness of the Y.M.C.A. and the Y.W.C.A. contribution to the ecumenical movement is evident, but it is largely a post-1920 phenomenon.

The Student Christian Movements, on the other hand, almost from the first were conscious of the vital importance of their relations with the Churches and early took up the cause of Christian unity. Their success in ecumenical pioneering was due to their character as a movement of students. In the first place they were groups of men and women of university age or just beyond it; they were led by students on behalf of students; they were movements rather than organizations, less responsible than their seniors, freer to try experiments and to take risks.[3] The very insignificance of the S.C.M.s was an advantage: if their experiments succeeded, the Churches could profit by their success; the failures of these foolish young things the Churches could disclaim. In the second place, the committees of the Federation and of the national S.C.M.s contributed to the ecumenical movement not only future leaders with an ecumenical attitude but also the stuff of ecumenical ideas. Secretaries and committee members spent many days thinking together on all manner of Christian problems. J. H. Oldham once told the author that it was on S.C.M. committees that he first "learned to think"; and many other ecumenical leaders could give the same testimony. Ideas hammered out in such groups later passed into the armoury of the Churches' thought.

Let us trace the pioneering process at work. The lay movements, impelled not by the logic of abstract argument but by opportunity for expansion in new directions, advance into a new area; they find it impossible to render to youth the spiritual and social service they desire without the co-operation of the Churches of the country; they enter, in every way open to them, into friendly relations

---

[1] It is important to note that when the general term "Student Movements" or "Student Christian Movement" is used in this chapter, it is always understood to cover all the movements within the W.S.C.F., including the Student Departments of the Y.M.C.A. and the Y.W.C.A. If in ecumenical pioneering the junior movement is in advance of its seniors, it must be remembered that the S.C.M.s were in many cases brought into existence by student leaders of the senior Associations, from whom they derived certain of their ideals.

[2] See Chap. vii, pp. 327 ff.　　　　　　　　[3] See Chap. vii, p. 343.

with these Churches and secure wherever possible their help in their work for youth. The lay movements, by such interaction with the Churches, develop church-consciousness and conscience and increasingly seek to promote ecumenical relations between the Churches.

The Student Christian Movements in differing countries have held steadily before them the aim of bringing students of every denomination into their membership. The Student Department of the Y.M.C.A. in North America, under the leadership of John R. Mott, was determined to bring into the movement universities, colleges, and theological schools of every non-Roman denomination. Lutheran and Episcopalian institutions for various reasons proved somewhat difficult. German, Scandinavian, and English religious leaders likely to have influence with Lutherans and Episcopalians were invited to America to travel amongst the colleges concerned, with good results. By 1910 the inclusive aim was largely attained: colleges of every denomination had been entered.

In Britain an early effort of the S.C.M. was a conference of theological students convened in April 1898 in Birmingham in the hope of bringing into a movement generally accounted "evangelical" the Anglo-Catholic theological colleges of the Church of England and the more radical Free Church colleges. This hope was largely realized, and the good results of the entrance of the Student Movement into their colleges won for it the confidence of all types of Free Churchmen and of not a few Anglo-Catholic leaders. It was this trust in Student Movement methods which finally inclined certain Anglican societies which might otherwise have stood aloof to send delegates to the Edinburgh World Missionary Conference 1910—an apparently small step which ushered in a new ecumenical era.[1] Similar stories might be told of the way in which, in country after country, Student Movement ecumenism led on to ecumenism in the Churches.

The Conference of the W.S.C.F. in Constantinople in 1911 was chiefly significant in that it drew the ancient Eastern Churches, for centuries largely isolated from Western Christendom, for the first time into touch with the emerging ecumenical movement. It touched the Balkans, and the whole Near East from Turkey to Egypt.

"When since the early Councils . . .", wrote Dr Mott, "has there come together a gathering representing so nearly the entire Christian Church?"

"Although not designed in advance, its distinctive note might be characterized as Christian unity . . . the very fact that such a gathering could be held made incarnate and vivid this great idea. . . . There sat together in common counsel and fellowship day after day members of the Greek Orthodox, Syrian, Armenian, Coptic, Protestant, and Roman Catholic communions."[2]

The Conference had the blessing of the Ecumenical Patriarch and other leaders of the ancient Eastern Churches. Its aim was to extend the S.C.M. throughout the Near East, but before this could be done it was necessary to make clear to the leaders of the Eastern Churches that the movement would be

---

[1] For details see Chap. vii, p. 343; Chap. viii, pp. 357, 360; and Chap. ix, pp. 405 f.

[2] *Report of the Conference of the W.S.C.F., Constantinople, 1911*, p. 19; *Addresses and Papers of John R. Mott*, Vol. VI, p. 393; Rouse, *World's Student Christian Federation*, pp. 149–64. See also Chap. xiv, pp. 650 f.

open to student members of these Churches. To secure this end the W.S.C.F. Committee passed a resolution:

"The General Committee puts on record its opinion that no student, to whatever branch of the Christian Church he may belong, should be excluded from full membership in any national movement within the Federation if he is prepared to accept the basis of the Federation."[1]

The Committee requested all national movements affected by this resolution to consider making their bases conform to this principle. Sooner or later they all did so. Though the vast majority of the members of the movements affiliated to the Federation were Protestants, the Federation as a central movement had nothing in its basis which excluded Roman Catholics or Orthodox from full membership, and it is interesting to note that there was already on the Executive Committee, as it met at Constantinople, a non-Protestant member—K. C. Chacko of the Malankara Syrian Church in India. The resolution was designed to secure the removal of all possible difficulties in the way of the policy of a door open to members of all Churches.

After the Conference, Student Christian Movements were organized by John R. Mott, Ruth Rouse, and others, in Rumania, Serbia, Bulgaria, and Greece; while a joint Y.M.C.A. and Y.W.C.A. was formed for the Turkish Empire. Led by D. A. Davis and E. O. Jacobs, two American Y.M.C.A. secretaries, both to play prominent parts in the ecumenical pioneering of the Y.M.C.A., and two American women—Frances Gage and Anna Welles—this joint movement entered almost every college and school in the area. This promising joint Y.M.C.A.-Y.W.C.A. movement was brought to an end by the outbreak of war in 1914, but the struggling Student Christian Movements in the Balkans all survived.

Moreover, the Constantinople Conference had still wider ecumenical consequences. Through it the way began to open for the entrance of Orthodoxy into the stream of the ecumenical movement. Contact with the Conference brought certain Orthodox ecclesiastics, destined themselves to become leaders in the ecumenical movement, into touch for the first time with leaders of Western Churches—Dr (later Archbishop) Germanos, at that time President of the Orthodox Theological School at Halki, Nicolai Velimirovic, later Bishop of Ochrida in Serbia, Archimandrite Scriban of Rumania, and others. Conversely, contact with these men and others introduced Western leaders, notably Nathan Söderblom, to the thought and life of the Eastern Churches. The future Archbishop of Uppsala had long since dedicated himself to the cause of unifying the Protestant Churches.[2] He learned at Constantinople to take the Eastern Churches into his ecumenical vision.

The Constantinople Conference was a spearhead thrust of the Federation into the Orthodox world. There was, however, represented at the Conference, one existing student fellowship from an Orthodox land. For some years there had existed in Russia an S.C.M. with branches in St Petersburg, Moscow, and Kiev. Its membership included both Orthodox and non-Orthodox; it entered the Federation at its subsequent conference at Lake Mohonk in 1913. Baron Nicolay, its founder and leader, and certain Russian students were delegates to Constantinople, and did much to help in pioneering the S.C.M. in the Balkans.

---

[1] *W.S.C.F. General Committee Minutes*, 1911, pp. 7–10.
[2] See Chap. vii, p. 344.

Entirely apart from the S.C.M. there was a city Y.M.C.A. in St Petersburg, promoted by the American Y.M.C.A. and run on strictly Orthodox lines. When the Russian revolution came, the Y.M.C.A. was suppressed; the S.C.M. survived, though forced underground.

Both world wars provided opportunities for the ecumenical pioneering activities of the lay movements. The extension of the Y.M.C.A. after the first world war into the Balkans and Asia Minor, as well as into Czechoslovakia and Poland, was directly an outcome of the Y.M.C.A. war work amongst men in the forces. As the Eastern European sections of Allied armies returned home in 1919, the Y.M.C.A. went with them, and in most cases a new national Y.M.C.A. movement developed. The Y.M.C.A. became established in ten countries which had large Orthodox populations, and speedily developed friendly relations with the Orthodox Church. Of equal significance was the remarkable post-war development of Y.M.C.A. work in Roman Catholic countries such as Poland and Italy.

The war years, naturally, provided less opportunity for ecumenical pioneering on the part of the S.C.M. than for the two senior movements, so many of its leaders being actually in the armed forces. But no sooner was the first world war over than the W.S.C.F. was called into its largest enterprise—that of European Student Relief. During four years the students of forty-two nations contributed well over £500,000 for the relief of their starving fellow students in nineteen lands.[1] Close fellowship developed between the Federation and the world student organization of the Roman Catholic Church, *Pax Romana*, and has continued to this day.

No sooner had the second world war broken out than the leaders of the three lay movements, together with the Provisional Committee of the World Council, established for consultation an informal Emergency Committee of Christian Organizations, which paved the way for more official association of the four bodies after the war.

In both world wars not only the work of the Y.M.C.A. amongst men in the armed forces, but its vast enterprise in co-operation with the Red Cross on behalf of prisoners of war, had marked ecumenical results, through the bringing together of men across all the usual barriers of life. It brought them together under Christ in circumstances where the elemental unity of his Church manifestly transcended all lesser differences. It broke down the opposition of the indifferent, and won remarkable co-operation in camp service from Roman Catholics, an ecumenical result obtained through the characteristic Y.M.C.A. medium of practical helpfulness. The same was true of the work of both the Y.M.C.A. and the Y.W.C.A. in camps for refugees.

Wartime provided pioneering opportunity also for the Y.W.C.A. During the first world war the American Y.W.C.A. sent secretaries to France to work amongst the women in the armed forces. In co-operation with the French Y.W.C.A., the American secretaries developed clubs and hostels for the benefit of young women in munition factories. This led to calls to establish similar work in Belgium, Czechoslovakia, Poland, Latvia, Estonia, Rumania, Greece, and other lands. As a result, a national Y.W.C.A. was developed in each of these lands, and this led to ecumenical relations with and between the Churches

---

[1] Rouse, *Rebuilding Europe*, London, 1925, *passim*. European Student Relief continues today under the title of World Student Service.

of these countries. These Y.W.C.A.s, except in Poland, continued at work until, in the case of those which passed behind the Iron Curtain, they were for the most part suppressed. The work of the British Y.W.C.A. for women in the forces in both world wars, but especially in the second, was carried on wherever British forces were to be found, from Morocco to Japan, from Germany to Ceylon. "In Great Britain the multiplication of its [the Y.W.C.A.'s] services to women in the forces in far distant parts of the world . . . forged new links in its relation with the Church."[1]

Women leaders in the S.C.M. and the Y.W.C.A. took a major share in creating and working through C.I.M.A.D.E. (*Comité Inter-Mouvements auprès des Évacués*), the organization brought into being during the second world war by the Protestant Churches and the lay youth movements in France. Its ecumenical influence has been considerable. Throughout their history the Y.W.C.A. and the Federation have provided an invaluable training-ground for women leaders in the ecumenical movement. To take but a few examples, we may name Una Saunders, Cornelia van Asch van Wijck, Suzanne de Diétrich, Sarah Chakko, Ruth Woodsmall, and Charlotte Adams.

With the end of the second world war, work for prisoners of war was succeeded by the programme of help to displaced persons and refugees, in which again the Y.M.C.A. and the Y.W.C.A. assumed large responsibility. Work in camps or amongst groups of displaced persons proved of special significance to the ecumenical relations of the two organizations with the clergy of different confessions, Protestant, Orthodox, and Roman Catholic. There was constant and extensive co-operation, especially in arranging services of worship. In many places, joint Y.M.C.A. and Y.W.C.A. organizations have been set up amongst groups of displaced persons belonging to different Churches, and there are few efforts of the two Associations which have engendered a more ecumenical spirit. Displaced persons readily grasped the ideal of the Associations as having a world-wide international and interconfessional outlook, and carried this ideal with them as they made contacts with the Associations in the new lands where hundreds of thousands of them settled. These developments are examples of a phenomenon frequently encountered in our studies, namely that groups of exiles provide a soil in which ecumenical ideas and movements take root and flourish.

Another ecumenically important development fostered in the early 1920's by both the S.C.M. and the Y.M.C.A. was the Russian Student Christian Movement in Exile. With the migration or expulsion of at least a million White Russians into Europe, this movement came into being in most European countries, and ever since has carried on its service to Russian youth and Russian Christian culture. It did not arise out of the earlier movement in Russia but developed as a practically confessional Orthodox movement. It was fostered and helped by the American Y.M.C.A., as also by Anglicans in England. Its headquarters are in Paris. In the same headquarters are to be found a group of Russian Orthodox institutions, the most important of which is the Theological Academy of St Sergius, which has done an outstanding work in training Russian Christian leaders.[2] The Y.M.C.A. Press, which has published nearly 400 books or pamphlets by Professor Berdyaev and other leading Russian thinkers of the 20th century, has made a significant contribution to the Christian culture of the world.

[1] Rice, *World's Y.W.C.A.*, p. 252.   [2] See further Chap. xiv, pp. 661 ff.

The American Y.M.C.A. supplied this Russian Student Christian Movement in exile with strategic workers—Paul B. Anderson and Donald Lowrie, both remarkable for their life-long service to and their vast knowledge of the Russian people. From contacts between the Russian Movement in Exile and Anglican members of the S.C.M. sprang the Fellowship of S. Alban and S. Sergius. There also exist an Orthodox and Scottish Presbyterian Fellowship, and an Orthodox and Lutheran Fellowship.[1] Eastern Orthodoxy is now studied in the West: there are seminars on Orthodoxy in German and American universities.

The period between the two world wars was a time of change and development in the ecumenical position of all three lay movements, as they were led to restate their position and principles in the light of new calls and opportunities. The three movements were fully conscious of their common responsibility in this matter. "Our three organizations are part of a wider movement in the churches, which has set itself to find a solution for the divided church of Christ."[2] They collaborated in a Joint Commission on Ecumenical Questions, and in co-operation with Life and Work established in Geneva a Joint Ecumenical Centre, the *Cercle Söderblom*. But in each movement there have been special problems and developments arising out of the needs of their particular constituencies.

Certain questions which arose about the Lutheran confessional character of S.C.M.s in Denmark and Norway; further advance into the lands of the ancient Eastern Churches; and the Orthodox character of the Russian Student Movement in Exile, all brought up the question of whether it was permissible to admit to the Federation groups of students organized on a confessional basis. The Federation General Committee, after discussion at successive meetings, finally in 1932 formulated the following principles as guiding thoughts for the policy of national movements:

"We believe that the inherent character of the Federation . . . makes it desirable as the general practice of our movements, to encourage groups who accept students who belong to any branch of the Christian Church or to no Church, if they are prepared to accept the basis of the Federation or whatever equivalent test is approved by the Federation.

"We regard as consistent with Federation policy the formation of confessional groups in local centres, and even on a national scale. But we can admit such groups in the Federation only if they are willing to enter into fellowship with other groups of an interconfessional or confessional nature, and to share effectively in the life, both of the national movement which they jointly compose, and of the Federation as a whole."[3]

These decisions were of the utmost importance in determining the attitude of the Federation to extensive changes in the position of two of its oldest movements which were reported to the Committee in 1938.[4]

The more drastic was the dissolution of the German S.C.M. by decree of the Head of the Police. The outcome was that the S.C.M. was incorporated into the

[1] See Chap. xiv, pp. 662 ff.
[2] Report by Miss Charlotte Adams to the World's Y.W.C.A. Commission on Ecumenical Questions, 1931, pp. 3 ff.
[3] *General Committee Minutes*, 1932, pp. 24 f.   [4] Ibid., 1938, pp. 15 f.

Studentengemeinden, student congregations in the universities under the aegis of the official Church, and with a student pastor appointed and supported by the Church. This form of organization the Federation was able to accept, and it continued to operate after the end of the Nazi régime.

The other development affected student Christian movements in America. Whereas the Student Y.M.C.A., the Student Y.W.C.A., the Student Volunteer Movement, and the Inter-Seminary Missionary Alliance had up to that time together constituted the representation of the Federation in the United States, the increase and growth of student organizations of several denominations in the universities had made this an anachronism. The Federation Committee took official account of the changed situation, and, as the Church organizations had expressed desire for connection with the Federation, agreed to recognize as its affiliated representative in the United States a committee which would include the former member movements of the Federation, as well as certain denominational student movements which desired to affiliate. This is known as the United Student Christian Council.

Many developments took place during the second world war, and the 1946 meeting of the Federation records:

> "The church-consciousness of National Movements and members has increased greatly since 1938. . . . Present statements of ecumenical policy and . . . the whole question of worship within the Federation should be the subject of fresh examination."[1]

One question relating to worship which has continuously agitated the Federation is that of intercommunion at conferences,[2] raised by one generation of students after another. The Federation has given considerable attention to the subject in *The Student World*.[3]

The 1946 meeting passed a strong resolution in support of the World Council of Churches, citing the Youth Department and the Ecumenical Institute as special opportunities for close co-operation.

The World's Y.W.C.A.,[4] from its inception in 1894, held its doors open to the members of all Churches. In its first annual report, 1895, its President stated: "We emphasize the interdenominational as well as the international character of the World's Y.W.C.A. Every member of every outward and visible church is welcome to join our ranks, provided she can subscribe to our basis."

As in the case of the Federation, the Associations in Denmark and Norway were practically confined to members of the Lutheran Church, and the World's Y.W.C.A. was forced to consider its attitude towards confessional groups within the Association.

Since the Berlin Conference in 1910, when for the first time Orthodox delegates were present from Russia and Bulgaria, every conference has registered some new step taken in relationship to the Churches. The Stockholm Conference in 1914 took the important step of altering the Basis,[5] hitherto practically identical with that of the World's Y.M.C.A., to a form of wording which it was hoped would make it easier to secure the co-operation of Orthodox and possibly

[1] *General Committee Minutes*, 1946, pp. 22 f.   [2] See Chap. vii, p. 337.
[3] *The Student World*, First Quarter, 1950.
[4] Rice, *World's Y.W.C.A.*, pp. 129–33 and 200–07.
[5] See Note on Basis of World's Y.W.C.A., p. 641.

of Roman Catholic authorities. To this Basis was added a statement of Aim and Principles, amongst other things on its relation to the Church:

> "The World's Y.W.C.A. desires to be representative of all sections of the Christian Church in so far as they accept the basis. It . . . desires to enlist the service of young women for young women in their spiritual, intellectual, social, and physical advancement, and to encourage their fellowship and activity in the Christian Church."

This idea of making the Association an ecumenical fellowship was not, however, universally acceptable in the Y.W.C.A. constituency; there was persistent uneasiness, especially in the northern countries, about the possible consequences to the spiritual work of the Y.W.C.A. of the admission of Roman Catholics to active membership. This culminated in 1928 at the World's Y.W.C.A. Conference in Budapest in sharp divergences of opinion about the constitutional changes adopted at Stockholm in 1914. The World's Y.W.C.A. maintained its position but paid the price in the withdrawal of the National Committee of Finland in 1930 and of South Africa in 1931. Finland re-entered the World's Association in 1946, but South Africa remained outside. The Roman Catholic question, however, was not the sole cause of these withdrawals. There were also differences on the question of amusements, and on emphasis on social and industrial problems.

The World's Y.W.C.A. has given continuous study to its ecumenical relationships. From 1928 to 1931 a survey of the whole field was undertaken by a Commission on Ecumenical Questions, with a special worker, Miss Charlotte Adams of the United States.

An important Conference of the World's Council of the Y.W.C.A. was held at Beirut, Lebanon, in 1951. The Near East was chosen as giving the World's Council opportunity for direct acquaintance with the realities of its ecumenical problems through contact with the ancient Eastern Churches and the Roman Catholic Church. The ecumenical principles of the World's Y.W.C.A. were prominent in the discussions. It was freely recognized that the Y.W.C.A. had its origin in Protestantism and that the majority of its members are and are likely to remain Protestants. The following resolutions were passed on its ecumenical position:

> "Although, in some countries, the Y.W.C.A. is, and may remain, a Protestant movement, the World's Y.W.C.A. cannot be a Protestant movement. In order that the World's Y.W.C.A. may grow more truly an ecumenical movement . . . it is recommended:
>
> "That members be brought to realize the tension that is involved in maintaining loyalty to a church in which one is deeply rooted while, at the same time, following a vision of Christian unity;
>
> "That a clear statement be prepared, explaining what it means to be an ecumenical movement."[1]

Elected at Beirut to serve on the Executive Committee were one member of the Maronite Church from the Lebanon and two Roman Catholics from Latin America. Already in the 1930's there had been an Orthodox member from Rumania on the Committee.

[1] *Minutes . . . Beirut, October 14–24, 1951*, p. 21.

In the Y.M.C.A. also, advance into new spheres produced an increased con-
sciousness of ecumenical responsibility, first and continuously in relation to
Protestant Churches; next in relation to Orthodoxy; and lastly in relation to
Roman Catholics.

The World's Y.M.C.A. has specialized in relations with Orthodoxy, and has
endeavoured at every point to work out its policies in Orthodox lands in consultation with the leaders of the Orthodox Churches. Notable instances were
three consultations of leaders from Orthodox Churches with Y.M.C.A. leaders
under the chairmanship of Dr John R. Mott, held at Sofia, Bulgaria, 1928;
Kephissia, Greece, 1930; and Bucharest, Rumania, 1933. Resolutions were
passed declaring:

> "It is understood that in predominantly Orthodox countries the work of
> the Y.M.C.A. should be conducted in harmony with the principles of the
> Orthodox Church and in consultation with its leaders. . . . The form of
> organization [of a national Y.M.C.A.] should be one which grows out of
> the life and needs, particularly the Church life, of the nation."[1]

> "The Y.M.C.A. in Orthodox countries . . . affords an opportunity for
> Orthodox youth and its spiritual leaders to experience fellowship with
> Christians of the Western Churches for deeper understanding and enrich-
> ment, and thus to share, with the Y.W.C.A. and the W.S.C.F., in the work
> of movements of œcumenic purpose."[2]

At its Conference at Nyborg Strand in 1950, it reaffirmed its ecumenical vocation in the resolution:

> "The World's Committee notes with deep satisfaction that the Y.M.C.A.,
> by virtue of its lay character . . . is successfully enlisting in its membership
> . . . young men and boys of all the Christian confessions . . . the Y.M.C.A.,
> with the Y.W.C.A., has opportunities for pioneering in work toward the
> fulfilment of our Lord's Prayer 'that they all may be one', which may be
> open to few if any other organizations."

An acid test of the ecumenical ideals of the lay movements was provided
between the two world wars by the awakening of the Churches to the importance
of work amongst young people and their entrance into what had been peculiarly
the field of the lay movements, through the formation of Church youth movements in several of the large Protestant denominations. The lay movements
dealt with the new situation in a Christian and statesmanlike fashion, best
illustrated by the way they joined forces with the new Church youth movements
at the Amsterdam World Conference of Christian Youth in 1939. This Conference was "of unique significance because it was the first great co-operative
effort to bring together a world-wide gathering of Christian youth".[3]

The Amsterdam Conference was sponsored by the three lay youth organiza-
tions and the Ecumenical Youth Commission. Collaborating bodies were the
International Missionary Council, the World's Sunday School Association, the
International Society of Christian Endeavour, and the Continuation Committee

[1] World's Committee of Y.M.C.A.s, *Objectives, Principles, and Programme of Y.M.C.A.s
in Orthodox Countries*, Geneva, 1933, pp. 16–20.
[2] Ibid., pp. 6 f. and 12.   [3] Rice, *World's Y.W.C.A.*, p. 228.

which had been appointed by the second World Conference on Faith and Order in 1937. All these bodies contributed to the planning, but the major responsibility was carried by the lay movements. The officials of the Conference included W. A. Visser 't Hooft as Chairman, H. L. Henriod, earlier a secretary of the W.S.C.F. for fourteen years, Tracy Strong of the World's Y.M.C.A., Marianne Mills of the World's Y.W.C.A., and Edwin Espy, of the Student Department of the American Y.M.C.A. The lay organizations represented more countries than any Church organization and could secure delegates from lands where little or no Church youth work existed. Members of the staff and young workers specially appointed by the three bodies gave months of time and travel in preparing for the meeting.

The Conference was clear evidence of the progressing interpenetration of the ecumenical interests of the lay organizations and of the Churches. According to the official Conference report:

> "They [the lay Christian bodies] have helped to bring the vision of the Universal Church to many generations of young people. In sharing the direct responsibility for preparing the Amsterdam Conference, they have felt this work to be . . . the direct and natural outgrowth of certain continuing elements in their own heritage and purpose. . . . The whole Christian world has become deeply convinced of the necessity for a more united Church . . . and it is clear to many that the three Oecumenical Youth Movements have been closely interwoven with this advance."[1]

Plans were laid for a permanent body to conserve and extend the values of the meeting. After temporary suspension due to the war, these plans were resumed in 1945, and the second World Conference of Christian Youth was held in Oslo in 1947, the first major post-war gathering of Christians from all parts of the world. The World Christian Youth Commission, representing the lay movements, the World Council of Churches, and the World Council of Christian Education,[2] was constituted in 1948, as an organ of collaboration between the Movements.

The relationship between the world youth movements and the central ecumenical movement has always been close. The lay movements, since they are not Churches, are not members of the World Council, but the constitution of the Council provides for "a consultative relationship" with the three lay movements and other non-Church world organizations. This consultative relationship is a close one; fraternal representatives of the lay movements are always present at World Council conferences and Central Committee meetings and take a leading part on its commissions. They co-operate with the World Council's Youth Department and with the Ecumenical Institute. The relationship in general works smoothly and well.

Yet the fact must be faced that there exists in some quarters in the Y.M.C.A. and Y.W.C.A. a certain uneasiness about their relations with the World Council and the effect that these may have on their work in the future. When living and growing movements are in question, it is not surprising that tensions should arise. Such tensions are both a problem and a challenge.

In the first place, the Associations fear that, with the increasing activity of the

---

[1] *Christus Victor*, Geneva, n.d., p. 7.   [2] See p. 612.

World Council as well as of the Churches themselves in the realm of youth work, the primary rôle of the Y.M.C.A. and Y.W.C.A.—spiritual and social service to young men and women and boys and girls—may be seriously curtailed; any such limitations of the essential vocation of the lay movements would be a disaster both to them and to the Churches. As early as 1938 the Executive Committee of the World's Y.M.C.A. reported:

> "The Church's rediscovery of its larger place and function in the community has placed our own and related Christian Youth Movements before new problems in a number of areas. . . . One of the most important problems which confronts our Christian Youth Movements *and* the Churches at this time is the working out of a formula and plan of collaboration which is based on a thorough understanding of the distinctive functions of each, and which recognizes the interdependence of the Church and its lay instruments."

This resolution reflected the concern of the Y.M.C.A. both to serve the Churches and "to insure the Y.M.C.A. under present changing conditions the possibility of adhering to its traditional policy of working with boys and young men whether within the Church or not reached by the Churches".

In the second place, some leaders of the Y.M.C.A. see in the present situation danger to what they believe to be the highest interests of the general ecumenical movement. They contrast the ecclesiastically-constituted World Council of Churches with the ideal of a universal Christian council in which the lay and non-ecclesiastical Christian organizations would be included as participants on equal terms with the Churches. They fear that, in the new emphasis upon the importance of the Church and the Churches as such, the full contribution of the non-ecclesiastical Christian organizations and institutions may not be realized within the evolving organization of the Church.[1]

Certain leaders raise the further question whether the lay organizations are not actually more ecumenical than the World Council of Churches, on the ground that while actual membership of the World Council has so far been entered only by Protestant, Anglican, Old Catholic, and some Orthodox and Lesser Eastern Churches, many branches of the Y.M.C.A. and Y.W.C.A., e.g. in Latin America and the United States, include in their individual membership large numbers of Roman Catholics, in certain Latin American countries amounting to ninety-five per cent. They regard the lay Associations as having a peculiar mission to pioneer ecumenical advance in Roman Catholic lands, though they do not underestimate the difficulties, especially of faithful adherence to the fundamental religious aims of the Associations in Roman Catholic areas or where there is a predominantly Roman Catholic membership.

However, despite the misgivings of some Association leaders, there has been general acceptance and welcome by the lay movements of the World Council and the other ecclesiastically-constituted bodies. The lay movements are convinced of the continuing contribution they have to bring to general ecumenical movements, and they seek to make this contribution in harmony with the desires of the Churches. The ecclesiastically-constituted bodies have high regard for the ecumenical achievements of the lay movements. The first published statement of

[1] S. Wirt Wiley, *History of Y.M.C.A.-Church Relations in the United States*, New York, pp. 203 f.

the World Council plans after the Oxford and Edinburgh Conferences in 1937 indicated that one of its functions could be "to establish communication with Christian movements on a world-wide scale", especially with the lay youth movements. The Churches on the whole—certainly as they are represented in the ecumenical world organizations—welcome with gratitude the help of lay movements. The World Council continues to regard the three lay movements as its "major allies", and to look to them for their characteristic contributions in pioneering entrance for the ecumenical movements into new groups and areas.

A world-wide organization to promote Christian education arose out of the Sunday School movement begun in 1780 in England by Robert Raikes. Sunday Schools spread rapidly, and in the next hundred years national Sunday School associations were formed in many countries. A World Sunday School Convention in 1889 in London was a natural development. This Convention was the first of thirteen. These have been of ever-increasing size and representative character. They bring together church men and women of many countries and of almost all non-Roman denominations. They have registered a constant improvement in lesson material, in schemes for training Sunday School teachers, and in ever wider Christian educational impact on different age groups and classes of society.

The World's Sunday School Association was founded at the Convention in Rome in 1907; in 1924 it became a federation on a world basis of national and interdenominational bodies directed towards the interests of Christian education, and especially towards drawing the Churches together in that interest. It was only in 1947 that it adopted the title World Council of Christian Education as indicative of the vast scope of its work for Christian education.[1]

Both its world organization and the national organizations give sympathy and support to work for ecumenical advance. Its largest association, the International Council of Religious Education (I.C.R.E.; "international" as embracing the United States and Canada), was one of the eight Inter-Church Councils which entered the National Council of Churches in the United States.[2]

To the World Council of Churches it has the same advisory relationship as the three "major allies". It co-operated with these three movements in the World Conferences of Christian Youth in Amsterdam in 1939 and Oslo in 1947. It is a member of the World Christian Youth Commission. Through its Youth Department it collaborates closely with the Youth Department of the W.C.C. The success of the W.C.C.E. in drawing the Churches into co-operation with each other may be judged from the fact that the member denominations of its branch in North America, the I.C.R.E., number no less than forty; they embrace the Boards of Christian Education of all the great Protestant Churches and denominations in the United States and Canada. Under the auspices of the I.C.R.E., the Protestant Churches of America co-operated through the labours of their most distinguished scholars to produce in 1946 the Revised Standard Version of the New Testament, followed in 1952 by the Revised Standard Version of the Old Testament.

[1] In 1950 the words "and Sunday School Association" were added to this title.
[2] See p. 623.

3. WORLD DENOMINATIONAL FELLOWSHIPS

Fellowships within ecclesiastical families, the redintegration of separate Churches which share the same central history and tradition, was a process which began in the 19th century amongst Presbyterians, Old Catholics, Congregationalists, Baptists, and Methodists: [1] it has been vigorously carried on in the 20th century by these and other confessions.

Though greatly varying in outward organization and methods, the main denominational fellowships have certain common characteristics. All have arisen out of and are built up around a series of international conferences held at intervals varying from four to ten years; all seek to strengthen the weak Churches within their confession; all endeavour to heal the divisions within the confession —theological divisions, as found amongst Baptists and amongst Presbyterians; racial divisions, such as exist between White and Negro churches amongst Baptists and Methodists in the United States. Our aim here is to study the objectives and achievements of the world fellowships and their effectiveness in bringing about co-operation or reunion between the Churches within the family concerned; and also to investigate the attitude of each towards the ecumenical movement in general and the World Council of Churches in particular.

The Alliance of Reformed Churches throughout the World holding the Presbyterian System. Organized in 1875, the Alliance has proved to be chiefly a fraternal gathering of Reformed and Presbyterian Churches. It operates in two sections, Eastern and Western, with joint sessions or "General Councils" held at intervals, the fifteenth in Montreal in 1937 and the sixteenth in Geneva in 1948. The Churches of the Western section did much to encourage their brethren under Nazi oppression and contributed emergency funds through the European Central Bureau for Inter-Church Aid. It has always given large attention to questions of religious liberty. The General Council scheduled to meet in Geneva in 1941 was deferred on account of the war until 1948, in which year, with a view to the prospective organization of the World Council, the Alliance created a special committee on the ecumenical movement. The Geneva session discussed the "distinctively doctrinal standards" that unite Churches of the Presbyterian order—always one of the major interests of the Alliance.

The Churches within the Alliance cover a wide range of national and linguistic differences, with considerable actual doctrinal variation. The entire group has consistently shown great loyalty to the ecumenical ideal. It co-operates freely and closely with World Council activities. The Executive Committee of the Alliance, at its meeting in Cambridge, England, in 1949, affirmed that its supreme purpose is not to promote world Presbyterianism as an end in itself, but to make the Reformed tradition the servant of God's redemptive purposes through the wider agency of the Church Universal.

The International Congregational Council. Founded in London in 1891, the Council has met intermittently. The session held in Boston in 1920 brought together 3,000 delegates from thirteen countries. The session in Wellesley, Mass., in 1949 established the Council as a continuing organization with headquarters both in Great Britain and in America.

Among the Council's objects, as formally stated, is that of strengthening the

[1] See Chap. vi, pp. 263 ff.

Congregational contribution to the World Council of Churches and the ecumenical movement generally. Congregationalists as a body have tended to welcome, promote, and initiate unitive movements.[1] It was the desire of the Congregational Christian Churches to unite with the Evangelical and Reformed which provided a test case in the United States as to the legal right of such religious bodies to unite.[2]

The General Council of the Congregational Christian Churches in the United States has included a special Service for Ecumenical Worship in its Book of Worship for Free Churches.[3]

The Old Catholic Union of Utrecht. This Union, founded in 1889, is otherwise known as the Conference of Old Catholic Bishops: its nature and activities are described in an earlier chapter.[4]

The World Methodist Council. This Council was founded in 1881 and is composed of representatives from twenty-four areas of Methodism in the five continents. Until the Conference held at Oxford in 1951 it operated under the title of the Ecumenical Methodist Conference; there, to avoid confusion of terms, it changed its name to the World Methodist Council, its conferences being known as World Methodist Conferences. In recent reorganization the number of its sections was significantly reduced from twenty-eight to twenty-four as the result of unions between separated Churches within Methodism. The fellowship has been influential in promoting such unions.[5]

The Council's aim and motivation were most definitely expressed in the foreword to the conference at Springfield, Mass., in 1947: "The mission of Methodism . . . can best be carried on with the closest integration of the Methodist Church throughout the world, in prayer, thought, purpose, and service."

The prospectus of the 1951 Conference explained the Council's attitude towards the ecumenical movement:

> "We welcome with deep gratitude the inauguration of the World Council of Churches and the steps which are being taken towards reunion in different parts of the world. It is because our loyalty is pledged to the World Council that we would reconsider our own tradition and its place in the Universal Church. We dare not contemplate a reunited church in which the characteristic emphases of Methodism are obscured."

Bishop Ivan Lee Holt, when President of the Ecumenical Methodist Conference, referring to the fear that strong denominational organizations might militate against the World Council of Churches, asserted:

> "The World Council will never be stronger than the Churches which compose it, and it will therefore be to the advantage of the interdenominational agency if such a group as Methodism perfects its world-wide contacts and swings its full power behind the World Council."

The Baptist World Alliance. This Alliance was founded in 1905. It includes Baptist unions, conventions, and missionary societies throughout the world, with a communicant membership of approximately 13,500,000, eighty-five per cent of

---

[1] See Chap. vi, p. 267; Chap. vii, p. 319; and Chap. ix, p. 408.
[2] See Chap. x, pp. 479 ff.   [3] New York, 1948.
[4] See Chap. vi, p. 267.   [5] See Chap. vi, pp. 300 ff.

whom are found in the United States. It is explicitly a voluntary and fraternal organization without ecclesiastical authority, seeking "to express and promote unity and fellowship among the Baptists of the world; to proclaim the principles of their common faith; and to defend and enlarge religious freedom".

Baptist World Congresses devoted serious attention to questions of Christian unity and reunion at successive meetings at Stockholm in 1923, Berlin in 1934, Atlanta, Georgia, in 1939, and Copenhagen in 1947.[1] At Atlanta reports carefully prepared by Commissions were presented and discussed, on "The Baptist Contribution to Christian Unity" and on "The Reports and Findings of the Oxford and Edinburgh Conferences". The Baptist attitude as expressed at these Congresses would seem to be:

That Baptists believe themselves called to witness to certain truths—that the Church is composed only of believers and founded on personal faith in Christ, the necessity for personal conversion, and believer's baptism on confession of faith.

That their primary responsibility is to give this witness, and they can only consider either union or co-operation with other Christian bodies, if this witness is not thereby compromised. On the whole, Baptist opinion would seem to be that, in the present circumstances, they must continue their separate witness.

That before considering their relations with other Christian bodies, Baptist churches must first seek union amongst themselves.

No common agreement has been reached amongst Baptist bodies as to participation in the World Council. Some have declined to join. Despite the somewhat tentative attitude of the Alliance towards the ecumenical movement and the hesitation of certain Baptist churches about the Council, the Baptist denomination in different countries has supplied a number of leaders who have played and are playing a distinguished part in ecumenical affairs in their own countries and in the World Council; by 1953 no less than eleven Baptist bodies had become members of the Council.

American Baptists have taken a large part in relief schemes in Europe, and different Baptist bodies, including the Southern Baptists, are doing much to help the Baptist churches in Europe, for example through generous support given to the Baptist Theological Seminary at Rüschlikon near Zurich, both in funds and personnel.

The Lutheran World Federation. This Federation came late on the scene, but has developed strongly and rapidly. The way for it was prepared by the General Evangelical Lutheran Conference which, although at first confined to Germany, was even before 1900 extended to Scandinavia. In 1923 at Eisenach an organization was effected under the name of the Lutheran World Convention, uniting Lutherans on the doctrinal basis of the Holy Scriptures, the unaltered Augsburg Confession, and Luther's Shorter Catechism. World Assemblies were held in Copenhagen in 1929 and in Paris in 1935. In 1936 the Executive Committee of the World Convention took important action on ecumenical relations. It declared that Lutherans were perplexed by ecumenical movements, international and local. Lutheran solidarity was shown to be both doctrinal and practical: the churches should multiply efforts to establish a Lutheran consciousness in their members.

[1] *Report of Stockholm Congress*, p. 224; *Report of Berlin Congress*, pp. 172–76; *Report of Atlanta Congress*, pp. 115–38; *Report of Copenhagen Congress*, p. 56.

In 1947 a proposal to transform the Lutheran World Convention into a Lutheran World Federation was adopted. The Constitution thus defines its nature:

"The Lutheran World Federation shall be a free association of Lutheran Churches. It shall have no power to legislate for the Churches belonging to it but shall act as their agent in such matters as they assign to it."

Amongst the Federation's purposes are:

"To bear united witness unto the Gospel of Jesus Christ as the power of God for salvation;
"To cultivate unity of faith and confession among the Lutheran Churches of the world;
"To foster Lutheran participation in ecumenical movements;
"To support Lutheran groups in need of spiritual or material aid."

One effect of the development of a strong Lutheran consciousness has been the continued emphasis by Lutherans on the important principle of confessional representation in the World Council of Churches. In explanation of this position Dr Franklin Clark Fry has declared: "For us the strongest existing realities outside of our individual churches are the ties which unite us with our fellow confessors of the Augsburg Confession. All over the world our primary Christian loyalties are not geographical but confessional."

The constitutional amendment adopted by the first Assembly of the World Council of Churches in 1948 satisfied the desires of the L.W.F. It reads:

"Seats in the Assembly shall be allocated to the member churches by the Central Committee, due regard being given to such factors as numerical size, adequate confessional representation and adequate geographical distribution."[1]

The confessional tendency of the L.W.F. has produced reactions both within and outside Lutheranism. In the United States it has caused some Lutheran bodies to take a cautious attitude towards co-operative movements and the World Council. In Europe this revival of specifically Lutheran consciousness has caused considerable concern lest strongly confessional world denominational fellowships should conflict with the work of the World Council. Recent conferences would seem to supply strong evidence of the desire of the L.W.F. to take an active part in the affairs of the World Council, and to stand behind its work.

From the beginning relief activities on a large scale were a prominent feature of the work of the L.W.F. A striking feature was the success of the Federation in developing a united direction for Lutheran missionary work throughout the world.

The World Convention of the Churches of Christ. Church bodies bearing this designation (but known as Disciples of Christ in the United States, where in

---

[1] *The First Assembly of the World Council of Churches*, p. 113. See also *The Lutheran Churches of the World, 1952*, ed. Abdel Ross Wentz, L.W.F., Geneva, p. 77.

1952 they numbered 1,815,627 adults and were rapidly growing) are somewhat thinly dispersed in thirty-five countries outside America. In 1930 an organization for fellowship, without ecclesiastical authority and undertaking no administrative functions, was created at Washington, D.C. The second meeting was held in Leicester, England, in 1935, the third in Buffalo, N.Y., in 1947, and the fourth in Melbourne, Australia, in 1952. The extreme independency of the congregations of the Disciples' tradition is likely to ensure that the Convention is limited to fellowship and mutual discussion.

In general, the traditional position of the Disciples towards Christian union makes a large section of their people sympathetic to all ecumenical effort, and many well-known ecumenical leaders have come from their ranks. The Disciples co-operate freely in and give generously to World Council enterprises, e.g. the Ecumenical Institute at Bossey.[1] Their contributions to Inter-Church Aid have been given almost entirely to other communions, and in Europe especially to needy Orthodox Churches.

The Friends' World Committee for Consultation. The life of the Society of Friends (Quakers) finds its most natural expression in the small local groups rather than in any centralization of responsibility. There is, however, a growing corporate sense throughout the Society, and in 1920 an All Friends' Conference was held in London. Smaller international conferences with American participation were held regularly in Europe from 1931 onwards.

The second Friends' World Conference at Swarthmore, Pa., in 1937, encouraged the creation of an international organ—the Friends' World Committee for Consultation. It consists of representatives of forty-five independent Quaker groups in twenty-four countries. It has no authority to commit any of its constituent bodies without their express consent, but seeks to develop a common life through better understanding among Friends throughout the world.

Friends are widely known through the Quaker relief and reconstruction service in East and West, a marked feature of which is the co-operation, through personal service and finance, of many members of other Churches. This co-operation is due to sympathy with the spirit of the Friends' work. The effort is made not only to relieve material need but to express fellowship with the sufferers and to contribute towards peace and international reconciliation on a religious basis.

Friends were actively interested from the beginning in the various movements which led to the formation of the World Council. The independent groups (Yearly Meetings) of Friends in different countries varied in their attitude towards membership in the World Council, but were in general fully sympathetic to its main purpose.

The Lambeth Conference of Anglican Bishops. The Lambeth Conference, convened for the first time in 1867, was the earliest of the "world denominational fellowships".[2] But the term is not a very happy one as applied to the Lambeth Conference, since the Conference expresses, not the fellowship of independent Churches within a denomination, but of independent provinces within a Church, a distinction in very much more than words. Moreover, there are developments

[1] For one notable contribution, see Foreword.
[2] For its increasing interest in relations with other confessions and in plans for reunion or *rapprochement*, see Chap. vi, pp. 264 ff.; and Chap. x, pp. 446 ff.

which may make the term inapplicable to the Anglican Communion in any sense at all.

The Lambeth Conference continued to meet roughly every ten years, always devoting great attention to unity. The Conferences of 1930 and 1948 had to take note of a remarkable change in the situation. The Anglican Churches had reached out in every direction in search of closer fellowship or unity; some among them had relations, more or less intimate, of intercommunion with the Old Catholic Churches, the Church of Sweden, the Church of Finland, the Mar Thoma Syrian Church in India, the Church of South India, and the Philippine Independent Church. The Anglican Communion was beginning to overflow its bounds. Taking note of this, the Conference of 1948 passed a prophetic resolution on "A Larger Episcopal Unity":

> "The Conference, welcoming the fact that some of the Churches of the Anglican Communion are already in intercommunion with the Old Catholic Churches, looking forward to the time when they will enter into communion with other parts of the Catholic Church not definable as Anglican, and desiring that Churches thus linked together should express their common relationship in common counsel and mutual aid, recommends that bishops of the Anglican Communion and bishops of other Churches which are, or may be, in communion with them should meet together from time to time as an episcopal conference, advisory in character, for brotherly counsel and encouragement."[1]

In their Encyclical Letter, the bishops went further and showed themselves ready to recognize that progress towards Church union might involve in the end the disappearance of their own Church as a separate denomination:

> "Reunion of any part of our Communion with other denominations in its own area must make the resulting Church no longer simply Anglican, but something more comprehensive. There would be, in every country where there now exist the Anglican Church and others separated from it, a united Church, Catholic and Evangelical, but no longer in the limiting sense of the word Anglican. The Anglican Communion would be merged in a much larger Communion of National or Regional Churches, in full communion with one another, united in all the terms of what is known as the Lambeth Quadrilateral. . . . We look to, and work for, the larger family, and we are thankful that in so many parts of the world other Churches are joined with us in working for it."

With characteristic Anglican caution, however, the bishops warned against "a betrayal of our trust before God if the Anglican Communion were to allow itself to be dispersed before its particular work was done".[2]

It is a fact that the variety of tendencies within the Anglican Communion makes unified Anglican action difficult, and nowhere more than in the field of Church union. Some look to Rome and to the Orthodox, others to the Protestant Churches of the continent of Europe, others to the non-Anglican Churches in the British Commonwealth and the United States. These tendencies act as a check on one another. Anglicans, moreover, are alive to the danger that a small

---

[1] *Lambeth Conference 1948*, Part I, p. 45.
[2] Ibid., pp. 22 f.

union quickly achieved in one area may hinder or prevent the achievement of a larger unity elsewhere. Such caution at times presents an appearance of inconsistency or even of duplicity, and not infrequently perplexes those in other Churches who are unfamiliar with the inner life of the Anglican Communion. In so far, however, as the Anglican Communion as a whole can be said to have an official attitude towards schemes of reunion or towards its own future, it is that set forth by the bishops in 1948.

The International Association for Liberal Christianity and Religious Freedom. International congresses of "liberal" Churches originated in 1900, and four were held before 1910. The International Association was founded in 1930 as a continuing body to function between congresses. It represents twenty-three member groups in seventeen countries and individual members in all parts of the world.

The member groups are of three types: those of ancient origin within the Protestant Reformation, such as the Magyar Unitarian Churches in Hungary and Rumania and the Remonstrant Church in Holland; those which have recently revolted from the Roman Catholic Church, though retaining many of its rites and customs; modern Unitarian and other "liberal" Churches. Despite their wide divergences, the various member groups have been able to agree on a united statement of purpose:

> "To maintain communications with free Christian groups in all lands, who are striving to unite religion and liberty and to increase fellowship and co-operation among them.
> "To bring into closer union the historic liberal Churches, the liberal elements in all churches and isolated congregations, and workers for religious freedom.
> "To draw into the same fellowship other religious groups throughout the world which are in essential agreement with our ways of thinking."[1]

This group shows a desire for contacts with the organized ecumenical movement. In 1938 a publication of the Secretariat[2] exhorted the friends of liberal Christianity to active participation in the ecumenical movement whenever it is permitted them. As this Association does not and cannot accept the basis of the World Council of Churches, it has no official relations with the Council. In the United States Universalist churches were denied admission to the Federal Council of the Churches; on the other hand, many individual "liberal" churches are included in State and Local Councils, especially in the northern and eastern states.[3]

The crucial question in regard to all these Fellowships is their effect on the progress of the general ecumenical movement. Almost all have declared their purpose to support the World Council; and seven of the largest—Baptists, Congregationalists, Disciples, Friends, Lutherans, Methodists, and Presbyterians—have the same consultative relationship to the World Council as the world lay movements, and are invited to send fraternal delegates to the meetings of the Central Committee.

It seems clear from our study that ecumenical attitudes within denominational

[1] Secretariat of the International Association, 1938.
[2] Becker, *Liberal Christianity and the Ecumenical Movement*, 1938.
[3] For the attitude of the British Council of Churches, see p. 625.

families exercise considerable influence on the general ecumenical climate. Membership in these Fellowships often provides a step towards definite unions between the Churches within the Fellowship. As a whole, the integration of denominational families must be reckoned as a stage in the movement towards the ultimate unification of the Church. Temporarily, however, and perhaps for long periods, they may prove instruments for delay and the sharpening of differences, or even result in holding back the more ecumenically-minded Churches and compelling them to take the slower pace of their confessional group. Unless the ecumenical vision is kept in the forefront, they may create the impression that the limited ecumenism of the confessional group is sufficient, and so hold back the movement towards wider unity.

It has been made clear elsewhere in this History[1] that, while the 19th century was fruitful in unions within denominations, trans-confessional unions of Churches are in the main a 20th-century phenomenon. Such united Churches exist in Japan, China, South India, Canada, and other countries. All express their firm intention of retaining the closest relationships with those Churches or fellowships with which their constituent members were earlier in communion. But how those relationships are to be maintained presents some interesting new problems.

A united Church cannot be fully a member of a denominational fellowship. For it to accept that status would be to repudiate its own repudiation of denominationalism. Yet to separate itself entirely from such fellowships would be to deny one of the basic principles on which the union was formed. At the same time, the united Churches feel a very strong sense of kinship with one another, though probably no one would go so far as to suggest the formation of a world denominational fellowship of interdenominational Churches. No doubt some form of continuing relationship between the old Churches and the new will in the course of time be worked out.

This is no more than to say that every genuine step towards Church union cuts across all existing situations, and presents questions which cannot be answered in terms of any of the existing categories of ecclesiological thought.

4. MOVEMENTS OF FORMAL ECCLESIASTICAL CO-OPERATION

The 20th century has produced a large number of movements which bring together representatives of the Churches as such for purposes of co-operation. In many countries these take the form and name of National Councils of Churches. These organizations vary considerably in constitution and method according to the history and genius of the Churches and the country concerned. Councils in certain European countries where there is one dominant or State Church differ in type from those in countries like Britain and America where there are numerous denominations.

The common and distinctive characteristic of these Councils is that they are ecclesiastical alliances, in which the several Churches are officially represented much as they are in the World Council. Whether they came into existence before it or after it, their pattern resembles that of the World Council, and in every case they work in the closest sympathy and co-operation with it. The connection is indeed often so close as to give rise to the idea that they are national

[1] See Chap. x, p. 445 and *passim*.

branches of the World Council. This is not so. Whatever may ultimately be the result of the approximation of their work to that of the Council, no one of these National Councils as such is to-day constitutionally a part of the World Council, with the exception of the Federation of Protestant Churches in Switzerland.[1] They differ from it at various points in organization; for example, in many cases they comprise not only Churches but also voluntary organizations, such as the lay youth movements.

An important feature of the Councils in the United States and Britain is a network of Local Councils of Churches. These Local Councils are of the utmost ecumenical importance, as the more "local" they are the greater power they have to implant Christian ideals of unity in the minds of individual members of local congregations.

The sections which follow describe some of the existing National Councils of Churches of differing types, always with particular reference to their ecumenical significance and relationships and their place in the general ecumenical movement.

The Federal Council of the Churches of Christ in America. This Council is of special importance in ecumenical history as being a pioneer amongst National Councils.[2] It made experiments and sometimes mistakes; it led to the formation of other Councils and passed on the results of its experience to them; it finally initiated the greatest experiment yet made in co-operation between the Churches.

The Council's main objects, as set forth when it was founded in 1908,[3] were: "(*a*) to express the fellowship and Catholic unity of the Christian Church; (*b*) to bring the Christian body of America into united service for Christ and the world". It had "no authority to draw up a common creed or form of government or worship or in any way to limit the full autonomy of the Christian bodies adhering to it". As to its basis, the Constitution contained the clear requirement that the member denominations were to be those which recognize Jesus Christ as "Divine Lord and Saviour".

The Council was an almost new departure in ecumenical history, an organization constituted by the definitely ecclesiastical action of the Churches through their highest authorities. By 1910 thirty-one denominations had joined, including the great majority of American Protestants, exceptions at that time being the Southern Baptists, the Lutherans, and the Protestant Episcopal Church. The United Lutheran and Protestant Episcopal Churches early accepted limited membership, and the latter came into full membership in 1940, at the same time as four Eastern Orthodox bodies. In spite of these additions, the number of Churches within the Council in 1948 was twenty-nine in contrast to thirty-one in 1910, a reduction due to unions which had taken place between member Churches.

At the time of the merger of the Federal Council with other bodies to form the National Council of Churches,[4] the number of local congregations within the federated Churches was 143,959, with a total membership in the neighbourhood of 32 millions.

In 1910 the young Council published its first report. Its major activities were in the areas of social service and temperance. It participated with the equally youthful Home Missions Council in a programme of co-operative advance in

[1] See p. 629.
[2] It was not the first of such Councils: that honour goes to France (see p. 629).
[3] For the steps which led to its formation, see Chap. v, pp. 256 ff.   [4] See pp. 623 f.

home missions,[1] advocating that denominational mission boards should decline to aid Churches flagrantly duplicating Christian effort. There was a specially close relation between the Home Missions Council and the Federal Council. In 1910 the Federal Council spent $16,000.

Its report in 1948 presents an amazing advance. The Council had expanded so as to cover by Departments, Commissions, or Committees virtually the whole range of Christian concerns, except those which, like foreign missions and Christian education, had already been undertaken by specialized Councils.[2] Its major units of organization were Field Administration, Evangelism, International Justice and Goodwill, Race Relations, Religious Radio, Christian Social and Industrial Relations, Marriage and the Home, Just and Durable Peace, the Ministry, Religion and Health, and Worship. In 1945 the Council expended no less than $642,000.

The remarkable scope and magnitude of the Council's work were reached, writes Dr Macfarland, "not by the promulgation of clear-cut plans and schemes but by the attempt to meet needs and opportunities as they arose and to gather the forces which the hour demanded".[3] Permanent structure and function evolved gradually through a process of trial and error. "Unstable equilibrium, made safe by continuous forward movement, was the Council's most firmly established characteristic during its formative period."[4]

The ultimate success of the Council was due in large measure to the distinguished leadership of its first General Secretary, Dr Charles S. Macfarland. He was indefatigable in personal contacts with officials of Churches and of nations and in service to the world-wide ecumenical movement. His audacity, aggressiveness, tenacity, and willingness to take risks went far towards making the Council what it became.

During twenty-five years of experiment and constant re-appraisal, a more definite sense of central direction steadily developed within the Council; the formative period as a whole established the Council as the fellowship and the voice of the Churches, and gave it a dawning consciousness of that ecumenical stream of movement to which it belonged and to which it significantly contributed. In 1932 a reorganization and a revision of the Constitution took place. Directive and pervasive leadership for the new stage of more regular and constructive work was found in the personality and administrative skill of Dr Samuel McCrea Cavert. First as its associate Executive and from 1921 as its General Secretary, Dr Cavert's winsome friendliness and conciliatory spirit kept the movement on an even keel through two strenuous decades (including the crisis of the second world war); personally unassuming, he not only occupied the throne but was often the power behind it. Graciously and practically wise, but without obstinately espoused personal policies, he led the Council into a greatly widened range of work and expanded membership.[5]

---

[1] In the American sense of the term, "home missions" cover all kinds of missionary work carried on amongst communities outside the range of normal parish life: work amongst non-Christian immigrants—Japanese, Chinese, or Indians; amongst North American Indians; amongst Eskimos in Alaska; and amongst remote groups of immigrants or special classes like "share-croppers"—landless families in the southern and south-western states who farm small acreages for a share in the crops.   [2] See p. 623.

[3] For the history of the Federal Council see Charles S. Macfarland, *Christian Unity in the Making*, New York, 1948, and *Across the Years, an Autobiography*, New York, 1936. See also *Twenty Years of Church Federation*, ed. Samuel McCrea Cavert, New York, 1929.

[4] See Douglass Memorandum (available at W.C.C. Offices, Geneva).

[5] Ibid.

The final phase of the Council's evolution was growing participation in the general ecumenical movement. After Edinburgh 1937 the Council recognized this concern by establishing a Standing Committee for the Study of Christian Unity. The Council gave its hearty support to the World Council at every stage of its "process of formation". Like his predecessor, Dr Cavert also served the world-wide movement for Christian unity. He received leave of absence to go to Geneva in 1942 and again in 1947–48, to share in the organizing of the World Council, and contributed greatly to its final shaping.

Local Councils of Churches have had a somewhat chequered history in relation to the Federal Council. Some Local Councils are older than the Federal Council itself. The Federal Council's early attempt to organize Local Councils all over the country failed. Success attended the Local Council movement only when promoted from the bottom upwards, through a widespread system of locally initiated Councils, each officially representative of the local churches of various denominations, in the same way that the Federal Council is representative of the Churches of the nation.

Nevertheless, the total movement of Local Councils grew conspicuously and effectively. In 1949 City and Local Councils with paid leadership numbered 181; in addition there were 666 Councils under voluntary leadership, and forty State Councils. The Local Councils are jealously independent, but a central directive force has been found in the Association of Council Secretaries. A growing ecumenical consciousness within the Local Councils was convincingly expressed in recent constitutions, which have tended to include the original phrase of the Federal Council to the effect that Councils represent the essential unity of the Churches of Christ.

It remains to record the last and most significant stage of the Federal Council's history—its euthanasia, in other words its leadership in the consolidation of practically all phases of co-operative activity between the Churches in a National Council. This story involves an explanation of a system of specialized national Councils which had been developing in America during many decades. Side by side with the Federal Council as a formal alliance of the denominations as such, there came into existence numerous national inter-Church organizations federating denominational mission boards or other administrative agencies of the Churches for some special aim. In their constitutions they were officially representative of the Churches. The national Councils with specialized aims included with the Federal Council in the National Council of the Churches of Christ in the United States of America were the following:

The Foreign Missions Conference of North America[1]
The Home Missions Council of North America[2]
The International Council of Religious Education[3]
The National Protestant Council of Higher Education[4]
The Missionary Education Movement of the United States and Canada[5]
The United Stewardship Council
The United Council of Church Women, representing approximately ten million Protestant women.

[1] See Chap. viii, p. 374.   [2] See pp. 621 f.   [3] See p. 612.
[4] See p. 607 on the Student Christian Movement and Church Boards, and Clarence Shedd, *The Church Follows Its Students*, New Haven, 1938; also *United States Student Christian Movement*, Information Service, Federal Council of Churches, December 1948.
[5] See Chap. viii, p. 376.

This epoch-making union of eight national Councils had long been under discussion, having been formally proposed by the Federal Council in the early 1930's. The specific plan of merger was accepted at a conference held in Atlantic City in 1941. It was formally approved by twenty out of its constituent denominations. Its consummation with a membership of 32 millions in December 1950 united practically all organized aspects of the Churches' common life in an ecclesiastically-constituted organ of common action. This is a long step towards a practically united Church in the United States. It is the longest step, short of organic union, as yet taken in any country towards union amongst the Churches.

The Canadian Council of Churches. The organization of this Council was consummated in 1944. For many years previously the United Church of Canada had been a member of the Federal Council of Churches in America. When the proposal was made to merge the existing Councils in the United States into a National Council of Churches, vigorous Canadian national sentiment, combined with the growth of the ecumenical spirit in Canada, strongly suggested that the time was ripe for the formation of a Canadian Council of Churches. Canadian groups whose interests would naturally be combined in a Council already existed, for example, the Joint Committee on Evangelization, the Committee for the World Council of Churches, and the Religious Education Council of Canada. These were merged in the Canadian Council of Churches, of which Dr W. J. Gallagher became the first Secretary. The Council entered into close co-operation with the Christian Social Council of Canada.

The member Churches are the Church of England in Canada, the Baptists, Disciples, Evangelical United Brethren, Friends, Presbyterians, Reformed Episcopal, Ukrainian Orthodox, the United Church of Canada, and the Salvation Army. The Y.M.C.A., the Y.W.C.A., and the S.C.M. are affiliated organizations. The Departments of the Council are those for Ecumenical Affairs, Evangelism, Social Relations, and Christian Education.

As regards ecumenical affairs, the most important actions and activities of the Council have been its acting as host in 1950 to the Central Committee of the World Council of Churches and to the World Convention on Christian Education; the recommendation in 1948 that Faith and Order should be given an increasing place in the Council's educational processes; the inclusion of the Foreign Missions group, previously within the Foreign Missions Conference of North America; and the regular broadcasting of ecumenical news every Saturday over the whole Canadian radio system. The Council looks forward to the formation of Local Councils of Churches all over the Dominion, and maintains close relations with the World Council of Churches.

The British Council of Churches. In contrast to the pioneering character of the Federal Council in America, the British Council of Churches was a product of the ecumenical movement in its later phase. It entered a more limited field within which it has been less opportunistic and has experienced fewer tensions.

After Oxford 1937, steps were taken to bring into existence two organizations officially representative of the Churches. The Council on the Christian Faith and the Common Life was a small body, composed of a few ecclesiastical leaders and an equal number of co-opted laymen. The Commission of Churches for International Friendship and Social Responsibility was a larger and more representative body. Both used as their organ the influential *Christian News*

Letter, edited by J. H. Oldham, and conducted "Religion and Life" weeks in numerous communities. Four years later it was decided to unite the two bodies in the British Council of Churches. In 1942, by the action of sixteen denominations and several interdenominational organizations, the British Council was constituted. Its doctrinal basis was the same as that of the World Council, but it provided that two bodies which had been represented in its predecessor agencies might continue as members of the national body or of the Local Councils associated with it without accepting that basis.

In 1950 the British Council consisted of 119 members officially appointed to represent the member Churches in England, Scotland, Ireland, and Wales—Anglican, Baptist, Congregationalist, Friends, Methodist, Moravian, Presbyterian, Salvation Army; and the affiliated lay youth agencies—the Y.M.C.A., the Y.W.C.A., and the S.C.M. The Council is "in association with" the Conference of British Missionary Societies; there is a strong sense that the Church is called both "to Mission and to Unity".

The Council is the official instrument of the Churches "to facilitate common action"—in Christian Education, Evangelism, Inter-Church Aid, International Affairs, Social Responsibility, Rural Questions, and Youth Work; "to promote co-operation in study and to further the cause of Christian Unity"; and "to act for the Churches in Britain in all matters of common concern relating to their participation in the world-wide activities of the World Council", with which it maintains the closest possible connection.[1] Unlike the Federal Council in America, the British Council maintains a department directly concerned with Faith and Order. One of its strongest lines of work is its Youth Department, which carries on extensive activities, including conferences, both national and local; it issues a series of original and attractive youth pamphlets. The Youth Department has received grants-in-aid from the Ministry of Education in recognition of the educational value of its work. The Publication Department of the British Council is active and efficient: it was a Commission of the Council which produced the widely-read report *The Era of Atomic Power*. In Scotland there came into existence two organizations working regionally on behalf of the British Council and the World Council—the Scottish Churches Ecumenical Committee, officially representative of the Churches in Scotland, and an unofficial body, the Scottish Churches Ecumenical Association.

Local Councils of Churches play a considerable rôle in Britain. In 1949 there were in existence 175 such Local Councils and they are increasing in numbers: seventy-five per cent of them are associated with the British Council as autonomous bodies, such association being entirely voluntary. The Council seeks to help and guide Local Councils but does not organize them. Some Local Councils are extremely active and are usually successful in securing the participation of a large proportion of the local churches. They thus can carry on the inter-Church education of the man in the pew, that ecumenically strategic personality. Some have considerable influence with the municipal authorities.

The Australian Council for the World Council of Churches.[2] The circumstances of Australia, a continent the size of the United States but with a population of

---

[1] See *The British Council of Churches, a process, a prophecy, a power*, a publicity leaflet; and *The Church in the World*, the Council's bi-monthly bulletin.
[2] See memorandum (available at W.C.C. Office, Geneva) by Dr John Mackenzie and the Right Rev. G. H. Cranswick, who also contributed material for the statement which follows.

barely 9,000,000; its lack of national and social unity; its isolation in the far South; the immense distances between the various state centres; and its political responsibilities for vast areas in the South Pacific, all combine to make understanding and co-operation between the Churches at once difficult and imperatively necessary.

From 1910 onwards there were many conferences on Christian unity, and several unsuccessful attempts were made to secure the union of non-episcopal Churches; but for many years it was only in the State of Victoria that practical steps were taken to give effect to the recommendations of Lausanne 1927. In 1942 a representative Committee, afterwards known as the Victoria Regional Committee of the World Council of Churches, was appointed. This Committee was for several years the sole official representative of the ecumenical movement in Australia. It prompted the formation of similar committees in neighbouring states, and was largely responsible for the steps which led to the organization in 1946 of the Australian Council for the World Council of Churches.

Thus there came into being a genuine Council of Australian Churches, with a section in each state and with Commissions on Faith and Order, Life and Work, Evangelism, Education, etc. Australia was strongly represented at Amsterdam in 1948 and, in spite of the time and expense involved, has been well represented at other ecumenical gatherings in Europe and America. In co-operation with the National Missionary Council, it is giving consideration to the situation of the Australian aborigines, and to the promotion of more earnest missionary efforts in New Guinea and the South Sea islands where Australia has special responsibilities. It is also aiming at closer and more helpful relationships with the Churches of South-East Asia. Its Commission on Evangelism plans to enlist the co-operation of parishes in efforts to reach the unchurched masses at their doors; while the Commission on Education aims to secure a larger place for Christian teaching over the whole educational field from the primary school to the university. In this sphere encouraging results have already been achieved. Effective nation-wide machinery has been set up to give substantial assistance to the world-wide Inter-Church Aid movement.

The National Council of Churches in New Zealand.[1] For the first hundred years of European settlement, New Zealand was in the pioneer stage of development, and the Churches had little leisure for ecumenical activities. The last twenty-five years, however, have seen a striking growth of the desire for unity, and its expression in organization.

Among the leaders of this movement, New Zealand owes much to Dr Campbell West-Watson, Bishop of Christchurch (1926–51) and Archbishop of New Zealand (1940–51). It was he who in 1921 founded the Council of Religious Education, in which six Churches joined. The Bible Class movement had been for a number of years the characteristic youth activity of all the Churches; the Council co-ordinated these activities, and most Churches co-operated in issuing an annual Bible Class syllabus, in camps, and in other gatherings for youth. The most important unitive action taken by the Council of Religious Education was its initiation of an annual conference, in which the leaders of all the youth movements met to share their plans and difficulties, to pool ideas, and to worship together. In this way a whole generation of youth

[1] See memorandum (available at W.C.C. Office, Geneva) by the Rev. H. W. Newell, formerly Secretary of the National Council of Churches in New Zealand.

leaders were bound together in friendship and understanding. It was the Council of Religious Education which promoted the use of the studies issued by Faith and Order, and sent delegates to Oxford and Edinburgh in 1937.

Following on such preparatory efforts, the formation in 1941 of the National Council of Churches, again on Dr West-Watson's initiative, was an almost inevitable step. The aim of the Council is "to examine existing differences between the Churches in order to bring out the underlying unity; to facilitate common action by the Churches on all matters where there is agreement or the possibility of agreement". The eight denominations which became members of this National Council include ninety per cent of the church people of the Dominion, other than Roman Catholics who form slightly over ten per cent of the population.

In relation to religious education, the New Zealand Council has taken a part (as successor to an organization called the Bible-in-Schools League) in leading the education authorities to consider afresh the completely secular character of the national system of education. The University of New Zealand, hitherto strictly secular, has instituted divinity degrees of a high standard. The Council has also set up a Maori section, which is becoming an important instrument of Christian co-ordination among that growing community.

In 1945, for the first time, these eight New Zealand Churches met in conference at Christchurch. The two hundred delegates considered such subjects as Evangelism under present-day conditions; the future of the Maori people; New Zealand's responsibilities in the South Pacific; Christian order in the use of land, industry, and commerce; and Education. The message issued spoke of "the sheer joy of fellowship, a deep sense of unity in diversity, a growing sense of the guidance of the Holy Spirit and a wonderful measure of agreement".

The National Council has done great service to the somewhat isolated Churches of the Dominion by giving them a sense of growing fellowship with the World Council, with other Churches, and with other National Councils in many countries. It has brought the New Zealand Churches consciously into the family of Christian people throughout the world.

The Ecumenical Council of Churches in the Netherlands.[1] The conferences and local organizations of the World Alliance for Promoting International Friendship through the Churches played a considerable part in ecumenical developments in Holland. In 1935 an Ecumenical Council, combining the Life and Work and Faith and Order interests represented by the earlier Stockholm and Lausanne Committees, was established. In 1946 its basis, both of organization and doctrine, was brought into conformity with that of the World Council of Churches. A Youth Commission was organized later. The member Churches are the Netherland Reformed Church, which, with its almost three million members, includes over three-quarters of the membership of Protestant Churches in the Netherlands; the Remonstrant Brotherhood (Arminian); the Evangelical Lutheran Church; the Old Catholic Church; the General Mennonite Society; the Union of Baptist Communities; and the *Unitas Fratrum* (the Moravian Community).

The Restored Evangelical Lutheran Church was formerly listed as a member, but in 1951 united with the Evangelical Lutheran Church. The League of Free Evangelical Communities in the Netherlands sends a representative to meetings of the Council, but is not actually a member.

[1] *Oecumenische Raad van Kerken in Nederland.*

Of the Churches which hold aloof from the Ecumenical Council, by far the largest and most important is the *Gereformeerde Kerken* (the "Reformed Churches") with, in 1952, 674,688 members.[1]

The work of the Ecumenical Council is carried on by various departments: propaganda for awakening ecumenical consciousness in the congregations; youth work; relations with government; Inter-Church Aid; study and research; together with departments for the investigation of social questions, international questions, and questions relating to Faith and Order.

An ecumenical influence is exercised by the Netherlands Missionary Council. It was reorganized in 1946 and is the only place where Churches within the Ecumenical Council meet with the more conservative bodies, for example the "Reformed Churches". A Missionary Congress organized by the Missionary Council in 1949 on future missionary policy in Indonesia was the first broadly ecumenical national conference held in Holland. At it all non-Roman groups and Churches were officially represented. The formation of the Council of Churches in Indonesia[2] has had ecumenical repercussions at the home base amongst Churches of all types, including some that do not belong to the Ecumenical Council.

The development of a comprehensive Council in the Netherlands owes not a little to the fact that the decision to establish a World Council was made on Dutch soil at Utrecht in 1938; and that subsequently the first World Conference of Christian Youth in 1939 and the first Assembly of the World Council in 1948 were held at Amsterdam.

The Co-operative Fellowship of Christian Churches in Germany.[3] A Federation of German Evangelical Churches was organized at Stuttgart in 1922 and included twenty-eight territorial Churches, at that time State-supported. Of the twenty-eight, the majority were Lutheran in confession, two were Reformed, and six were "United", i.e. were a union of Lutheran and Reformed.[4] The *Unitas Fratrum* was also included, but the Free Churches were not. Under the National Socialist régime the independent functioning of the Federation ceased. Whatever action was taken in its name was under totalitarian duress.

Between 1945 and 1948, the Churches which had been represented in the Federation took steps towards a much closer union; and in December 1948 the Evangelical Church in Germany was formally constituted.[5] The Free Churches in Germany did not enter that Church, but in 1948 a Federation amongst Churches in Germany with a wider range than the original Federation of 1922 came into existence.

This Co-operative Fellowship of Christian Churches was created at Cassel in March 1948, and brings together the Evangelical Church and the Free Churches, including the Baptists, Methodists, Evangelicals, United Brethren, and Mennonites. Those Free Churches together constitute about one and a half per cent of German Protestantism.[6] The Old Catholics are also in the Fellowship.

The Fellowship declares that its organization does not affect the autonomy of the individual Churches. It hopes to secure better relations between member

[1] See Chap. vi, pp. 290 f.   [2] See Chap. viii, p. 391.
[3] *Arbeitsgemeinschaft Christlicher Kirchen in Deutschland.*
[4] See Chap. vi, p. 271, and Chap. x, pp. 466 ff.
[5] See Chap. x, p. 467.
[6] This statement is based on the figures given for the Churches in Germany in the *World Christian Handbook*, London, 1949.

bodies "through theological conversations", and by mediation in cases of difficulties which might arise between them. The association in the Fellowship of State-supported Churches with Free Churches and of Lutherans and Reformed with Christians of other ecclesiastical types is something new in Germany, and may lead to interesting ecumenical developments when its organization and functioning have been submitted to the test of time. Its chief activity has been the maintenance of the Ecumenical Centre in Frankfort-on-Main.

The Federation of Protestant Churches in Switzerland.[1] All the official Protestant Churches in Switzerland belong to the Reformed family, with minor variations—Calvinistic, Zwinglian, and others. The influence of the Swiss Reformers of the 16th century has been as deep and abiding as that of the Lutheran Reformation in Germany.

The Federation of Protestant Churches has a lengthy ancestry. Soon after the Reformation the representatives of the Protestant cantons created an Evangelical Diet to promote their common interests. This union lasted for three centuries. From 1858 onwards a Conference of Swiss Churches brought together representatives of the Cantonal Churches, and out of this grew the Federation of Protestant Churches in Switzerland. It was founded in 1920, partly through the example and inspiration of the Federal Council in America. The chief function of the Federation is to represent the Swiss Churches in relation to the federal Government, to other Christian Churches, and to the World Council.

The member Churches are the Cantonal Churches recognized by the State, the Cantonal Free Churches, the Methodist Church, the federated evangelical parishes in the Roman Catholic cantons, and Swiss parishes abroad. The Swiss Federation is a member of the World Council, as being entrusted with the representation of the Swiss Churches in relation to the Council.

The Swiss Federation is strategically situated for carrying out its ecumenical responsibilities. It has counted amongst its officers and collaborators many distinguished leaders of the World Alliance, Faith and Order, Life and Work, and of the World Council—Adolph Keller, Eugène Choisy, Alphons Koechlin, Max Huber, Karl Barth, and Emil Brunner. The location in Geneva of the headquarters of the World Council, and at Bossey of the Ecumenical Institute, gives the Swiss Federation constant opportunities of contact with the central ecumenical movement.

The Protestant Federation of France.[2] The Protestant Federation of France was founded in 1905. It is, so far as can be ascertained, the earliest example of anything like a national Council of Churches, having come into existence three years before the Federal Council of Churches in America. Its aims were and are:

> "To demonstrate the essential unity of Protestantism in France;
> "To forward campaigns in favour of moral, social, and religious progress;
> "To safeguard freedom for Protestant worship, and to uphold with public authorities, where necessary, the rights of the Churches in the Federation."

[1] *La Fédération des Églises Protestantes de la Suisse; Schweizer Evangelischer Kirchenbund.* See memorandum by Pastor Arnold Mobbs (available at W.C.C. Office, Geneva).
[2] *Fédération Protestante de France.*

Its most important function through the years has been to represent the federated Churches in their relations with the State, in order to secure their corporate liberties, and to defend the personal liberty of the individual, whether Protestant or otherwise. Scarcely had the Federation been founded when it was called upon to defend the cause of religious liberty for Protestants in Madagascar against the attacks of anti-clericalism. Since then it has, at different times, taken action with governments to secure legal status for the conscientious objector; to combat the traffic in alcohol in Africa; and, under the Vichy régime, to resist anti-Semitism.

The Federation comprises seven Churches or unions of Churches: the Reformed Church of France; the Reformed Church of Alsace and Lorraine; the Union of Independent Reformed Evangelical Churches;[1] the Church of the Augsburg Confession in Alsace and Lorraine; the Evangelical Lutheran Church of France; and the Federation of Evangelical Baptist Churches in France. The Methodist churches belonged as such to the Federation until 1938, when they united with others to form the Reformed Church of France.

Almost all the Protestants of France are included in the Federation. One small group of Methodist churches has remained outside, as have also the Pentecostal churches, the Adventists, and the Brethren (known in France as *Darbistes*).

As the Federation includes non-Presbyterian denominations, it is not a member of the World Presbyterian Alliance. Four of the federated Churches belong to the World Council of Churches, with which the Federation has the friendliest relations.

Other national councils or federations of Churches in Europe are the Federal Council of the Protestant Churches in Italy, and a similar organization in Hungary, both of which include Baptists and Methodists as well as the older Protestant Churches of the land. There are beginnings also of such federations of Protestant Churches in Portugal and in Spain.

In the northern countries—Sweden, Denmark, and Finland—there exist National Ecumenical Councils in part composed of official representatives of the Churches. These Councils deal with relationships with the World Council and cognate bodies, and with approaches to governments on matters of common concern to the Churches.

In South Africa alone amongst the Dominions of the British Commonwealth of Nations nothing like a truly national Council of Churches has yet come into existence. The Christian Council of South Africa, founded after Dr Mott's visit in 1934, has not functioned as was hoped.[2]

Only brief reference can be made here to the extremely important group of National Christian Councils in the lands of the younger Churches, which have been treated in greater detail elsewhere.[3] They have developed out of the work of the International Missionary Council and are in many cases unions of indigenous Churches and missionary agencies. They fulfil in the lands concerned the same function as similar Councils in the West. The latest of them—the Council of Churches in Indonesia—more than any of its predecessors is definitely a Council of Churches, and does not include either missionary agencies or the youth movements.

[1] This Union entered the Federation in 1949.   [2] See Chap. viii, p. 396.
[3] See Chap. viii, pp. 377–97.

5. MOVEMENTS OF DIFFUSED ECUMENICITY

"Diffused ecumenicity" is here used to denote the spread amongst lay folk of the consciousness of the sin of division and of the duty of getting together with other Christians; in other words, the development of the ecumenical spirit at "grass roots". Until this spirit triumphs there, and the man and woman in the pew desire to understand the Church to which their neighbour belongs and his beliefs and ways of worship, ecumenical movements at higher levels will prove barren of permanent result.

Diffused ecumenicity—partial, insufficient, and limited—is to be found in every country and in every Church and confession, and is manifested increasingly in a thousand varied forms. We can give but a few typical instances of such ecumenicity, and of the instruments which are used to diffuse it.

A Lutheran pastor in the Eastern Zone of Germany has prepared an attractive series of *Ecumenical Profiles*, pamphlets with wood-cut portraits and brief biographies of ecumenical leaders—John R. Mott, Adoph Keller, Tissington Tatlow, and others—specially designed to catch the attention of men and women in the local churches.

Thousands of ecumenical study circles are being carried on in various countries, either in individual parishes or amongst local groups composed of members of different Churches. Excellent study material is available to the leaders of these circles, designed to bring the ecumenical message into the heart of the local church and directing attention to the actual problems of the contemporary ecumenical situation.

Transatlantic steamers and aircraft are busy transporting scores of groups of members of some one Church in America to Europe to study the life and work of Churches other than their own—perhaps a Baptist or Methodist group from one city intent on visiting Lutheran or Reformed congregations in Scandinavia, Germany, or Switzerland. A west-bound stream is carrying Europeans to America with a similar purpose.

Fruitful contacts between local congregations in different countries and continents have been established through the Interchange of Preachers scheme which now works regularly between Britain and North America, and is promoted by the British Council of Churches, the National Council of Churches in the United States, and the Canadian Council of Churches. In connection with Inter-Church Aid, "church to church" links are formed between individual congregations in different countries.

Women, with their genius for detail, play a major part in diffusing ecumenicity. The Council of Church Women in Rochester, N.Y., has for years arranged a system of visitation to the services of worship of different Churches, and issued a service of united worship "in the spirit of the Lord's Supper". The Women's Committee of the National Council of Churches in New Zealand has prepared *Ecumenical Prayers* for use in local churches. Women of the Presbyterian Church in the United States raised a fund of $70,000 towards the work of their denomination amongst students; they decided to devote a considerable part of it to helping students to attend ecumenical conferences.

Attendance at or study of the ways of worship of other Churches is a fruitful means of promoting ecumenical understanding. *Venite Adoremus*, published by the World's Student Christian Federation, is a collection of services of worship used in a number of communions; it is widely used and greatly appreciated.[1]

In many lands broadcasting is playing a great and increasing rôle in diffusing ecumenical understanding. In many countries, Sunday after Sunday, and on weekdays also, clergy and laity of various Churches have the opportunity given them in broadcast sermons and addresses to learn something of each others' doctrines and teaching. Through broadcast services of worship, moreover, clergy who could never attend the services of other Churches, and lay folk who rarely do so, can join in and learn to understand each others' ways of worship. Through television they can share in each others' most solemn acts of worship not only through the ear but through the eye. The British Broadcasting Corporation, through the services of worship arranged by its Religious Department, and through its Hymn-book and Service Book,[2] definitely aims at the promotion of ecumenical understanding amongst listeners-in.

The practice of the Agape[3] has been revived in a Norfolk village in England as an expression of Christian unity between the members of Anglican and Methodist Churches. This sharing of worship has meant ecumenical fellowship at a deep level of spiritual experience.[4]

Nothing can do more to awaken an ecumenical spirit in parish life than the worship of God through the hymns of other nations and Churches.[5] This stands out in the story of the influence of *Cantate Domino*, the multi-lingual hymnal originally compiled by Suzanne Bidgrain when a secretary of the Federation, and issued by the W.S.C.F. in 1924. *Cantate Domino* has been used at all the great ecumenical conferences held since its publication. At the Amsterdam Conference of Christian Youth in 1939 it so inspired the Czech delegates that, in their isolation during the second world war, they produced a Czech version with words and music, and so felt themselves in spiritual touch with their Amsterdam friends on the other side of the line. The sixth edition of *Cantate Domino*[6] was a truly ecumenical production. Its editor was an American woman member of the Protestant Episcopal Church; its two musical editors were an American Lutheran and a Swiss Reformed; a Swiss woman transcribed the whole, music and all, for the printer; the far-seeing and ecumenically-minded Hazen Foundation in the United States gave a grant of money; the S.C.M. in Finland gave the paper; the book was printed in Switzerland, and the Swiss Government admitted the paper without duty.

Other multi-lingual hymn-books are *Communio*,[7] issued for Stockholm 1925, and *Laudemus*,[8] issued by the World's Y.M.C.A. The pioneer in multi-lingual hymn-books was a collection of twenty-nine *Psaumes et Cantiques*, prepared by the Evangelical Alliance for its Conference in Geneva in 1861.

Music has its own power to convey the ecumenical message. In the 1930's a choir of Russian refugees gave liturgical concerts in Reformed churches in 179 Swiss towns; they were everywhere entertained in Swiss homes. The Protestants, living in a religious world poles apart from Orthodoxy, learned its spirit as they

---

[1] *Venite Adoremus*, Second Edition, W.S.C.F., 1951.
[2] *The B.B.C. Hymnbook*, published for B.B.C. by Oxford University Press, 1950; *New Every Morning*, the Service Book published by B.B.C., revised 1948.
[3] The "love feast" (as distinct from the Holy Communion), which was a characteristic feature of early Christian worship.
[4] *Intercommunion*, ed. Donald Baillie and John Marsh, pp. 388–96.
[5] See Chap. vii, pp. 332 f.   [6] *Cantate Domino*, W.S.C.F., 1951.
[7] *Communio in Adorando et Serviendo Oecumenica*, Stockholm, 1925.
[8] *Laudemus*, World's Y.M.C.A., Geneva, 1923.

joined, through music, in the living prayers of the Orthodox Church. "One such concert does more for ecumenism than any conference", said a woman in Geneva. Music and Christian hospitality interpreted what books and words could never express.[1]

In prisoners-of-war camps and in camps for refugees and displaced persons, united services and plans for worship have done much to rouse an ecumenical spirit. The pamphlet used in November 1952 in the joint Y.M.C.A. and Y.W.C.A. Week of Prayer was prepared by an interconfessional group of displaced persons—Roman Catholic, Orthodox, and Protestant.

Movements of united prayer[2] do much at the local level to diffuse the ecumenical spirit. During the Y.M.C.A. and Y.W.C.A. Week of Prayer in Jerusalem in November 1951 seven services were held according to various rites—of the Syrian Orthodox, the Armenian, the Coptic Orthodox, the Greek Orthodox, the Abyssinian, and the Anglican Churches, as well as a service in the Y.M.C.A.— surely a wonderful contribution to the ecumenical education of the membership of the local churches concerned.

There is no end to the range of these widely-diffused ecumenical activities, nor to the creative imagination which inspires them. Therein lies one great hope of the ecumenical movement. But there lie also some of its problems. There is no end to the variety of questions which may arise between churches in the same small area—questions which can be solved only as the growth of the ecumenical spirit generates the determination in the local churches "to behave Christianly towards each other". Two notable movements have in diverse ways arisen from the problems of Christian unity in small localities.

The term "comity" was first used in connection with a problem which arose long ago in the foreign mission-field when missions of different denominations entered the same field and their work overlapped. Similar problems arise in Western lands when, as too often happens, several weak congregations of different denominations are in struggling competition in a small town of a few hundred people. In the new housing areas in Britain and elsewhere, an acute post-war problem has been the provision of adequate Christian ministration by the different Churches without overlapping or rivalry.

In the United States successive attempts have been made to solve this class of problem through national Church comity conferences or councils, usually under the joint auspices of the Federal Council of Churches and the Home Missions Council. The Home Missions Council of North America, which was formed in 1908, has been throughout its history the chief exponent of comity between the denominations in providing churches for rural America, and has been a pioneer in many other comity efforts.[3] Such efforts in America have concentrated, not on mere correction of maladjustments, but on a policy of promoting positive methods of church planning or strategy such as may best secure spiritual provision and ministry for the needs of the locality concerned. Much has been accomplished to reduce overlapping.

It has, however, to be recognized that comity presents perhaps the thorniest problem in relation to co-operative action. It assumes the essential interchangeability of denominations; here a Methodist church is to disappear, there a Presbyterian. In this sense denominational sovereignty is diminished, and in the last analysis this poses an issue ultimately of faith and order for Churches which feel

---

[1] For details see Chap. xiv, p. 662; and L. A. Zander, *Vision and Action*, London, 1952, pp. 212 ff.   [2] See Chap. vii, pp. 345 ff.   [3] See pp. 621 f.

that they must assert their confessional distinctiveness. Accommodation at this point differs from accommodation in the general range of co-operation, where no issue of ecclesiastical principle is involved. Thus comity, while it is going forward with increasing strength, confronts definite limitations.[1]

"Union churches", organized to provide spiritual ministry for scattered people belonging to different Churches in foreign cities or in small frontier towns, or for other local reasons, are met with in many lands. In the United States they are very numerous, and to a large number of them a special name has come to be applied—the community church. These churches are now organized as a distinct movement which was incorporated in the early 1940's as the National Council of Community Churches. This movement is peculiar to the United States. It shows signs of considerable growth, and in 1947 claimed to include 3,600 churches.

Many delicate questions arise as to the place and effect on ecumenical relationships of the Community Church movement. All these churches are non-denominational, many are strongly anti-denominational—"a definite protest of plain people against the invasion of their communities by outside ecclesiastics. . . . Nothing has happened in one hundred years so disconcerting to sectarian leaders as this movement".[2] It is not surprising, in view of such pronouncements, that the Community Church movement is regarded with disapproval and hostility in some denominational headquarters. On the other hand, the Home Missions Council and the Federal Council have in general fostered the movement as tending to overcome the religious maladjustment caused by multiple denominational organizations in small localities, and also as helping to meet the needs caused by vast housing developments in the war and post-war years.

The Community Church movement itself professes an ecumenical purpose. With its possibilities for good and its achievements, the movement cannot be ignored. But there would seem to be a danger, though the movement disclaims the idea, that it might develop into a separate denomination, or that it might become so militantly critical of the whole denominational system as to separate itself from the general movement for Church co-operation. The future of the Community Church movement is uncertain, and against it a question mark must for the present be appended.

6. ECUMENICAL JOURNALISM AND ECUMENICAL THINKING

The ecumenical movement has naturally sought intellectual as well as spiritual and organic expression. Men have tried to discover what the ecumenical movement is, what lies behind it, and what may be learned from it for the guidance of the Church in the light of past experience of success and failure. They have tried to work out a theory or theology of ecumenism on which its practical activities may be based.

Many valuable books have appeared on various phases of the ecumenical movement. The Study Department of the World Council was called into exist-

[1] See Douglass Memorandum; also Douglass, *Church Comity: A Study of Co-operative Church Extension in American Cities*, 1929; and also *Report of the Joint Committee to Restudy Comity*, Federal Council and Home Missions Council, 1942.
[2] Piper, *When Christians Unite*, Butler, Indiana, n.d.

ence to harvest the results of the ecumenical hard labour of the best brains in the Churches, and has done so in many reports of ecumenical conferences and commissions. Commissions are the modern instrument which facilitates and promotes the ecumenical thinking of the Church. Ecumenical thinkers have at their disposal valuable bibliographies,[1] though in the field of ecumenical bibliography much remains to be done.

But the most valuable historical record of ecumenical thinking in all its changing phases and emphases is to be found in Christian journalism. Many students may be surprised to learn that for over a century the Church has always had available some periodical record, even if partial, of the changes and chances of ecumenical history. This continuous record owes much to two very different bodies—the Evangelical Alliance and the Old Catholic Church.

From 1847 onwards the British branch of the Evangelical Alliance has published *Evangelical Christendom*, usually as a monthly. Although in the 20th century it has confined itself more closely to the affairs of the Evangelical Alliance, for many years in the 19th century it steadily provided a real instrument of ecumenical education by making available information about the Churches and religious conditions in many countries, as well as about movements of co-operation or reunion between Churches.[2]

The Old Catholic Church, as one fruit of its second International Conference held at Lucerne in 1892,[3] launched in 1893 an international theological monthly, first in German, as the *Internationale Theologische Zeitschrift*, then in 1895 in French as the *Revue Internationale de Théologie*, and from 1911 onwards in German as the *Internationale Kirchliche Zeitschrift*. This review is one index of the ecumenical purpose of the Old Catholic Church; the whole ecumenical cause owes much to its editors, from Professor Michaud to Bishop Küry. It is a uniquely valuable storehouse of information about the ecumenical movement, especially in relation to matters of Faith and Order.

The 1890's saw the beginning of a remarkable and almost continuous series of periodicals, for the most part quarterlies, avowedly and specifically devoted to the cause of Christian unity. These had four early but short-lived forerunners in ecumenical journalism—*The Christian Union and Religious Memorial*, 1847–50, issued by the Presbyterian Dr Robert Baird;[4] *The Evangelical Catholic*, issued, 1851–53, by William August Muhlenberg of the Protestant Episcopal Church to implement his eager "desire to promote union with the Protestant bodies of Christendom";[5] in Britain *The Reunion Magazine*, 1877–79, edited by F. G. Lee, which ran to only four numbers; and, more circumscribed in its aims, *La Revue Anglo-Romaine*, edited by Abbé Portal, which appeared weekly from November 1895 to December 1896 and recorded, in addition to much valuable material on other subjects, the earlier efforts of its editor and Lord Halifax to promote reunion between the Church of England and the Church of Rome.[6]

Ecumenical journalism is a modern Christian vocation to which a remarkable series of editors have, from 1891 onwards, dedicated themselves. Conspicuous amongst them were Henry Lunn, English Methodist; Silas McBee, American Episcopalian; Peter Ainslie, American Disciple; and Friedrich Siegmund-Schultze, German Evangelical.

[1] See Bibliography, p. 747.　　　　　　　[2] See Chap. vii, pp. 321 f.
[3] See Chap. vi, p. 294.　　　　　　　　[4] See Chap. v, p. 244.
[5] James Thayer Addison, *The Episcopal Church in the United States 1789–1931*, New York, 1951, p. 168.
[6] See Chap. vi, p. 297.

In 1891 Henry Lunn provided the Churches with an ecumenical forum—*The Review of the Churches*, published monthly till 1895 and quarterly till 1896.[1] Stimulated by the Edinburgh World Missionary Conference and its outcome in Faith and Order, and by the "irenic itinerary"[2] which he made through the Near East with Dr Mott in 1911, Silas McBee, the editor of the publications of the Protestant Episcopal Church, produced *The Constructive Quarterly* (March 1913 to June 1922). Following in like manner on the events of Edinburgh, the apostle of ecumenism among the Disciples, Peter Ainslie, in 1911 launched *The Christian Union Quarterly*, which he carried on until his death in 1934. Both these American quarterlies sought to cover the whole range of Christian Churches, but of the two Silas McBee devoted more attention to Roman Catholic and Orthodox questions.

From 1910 onwards there was no break in quarterly ecumenical journalism. Soon after *The Constructive Quarterly* had ceased to appear, Henry Lunn in 1924 began to issue the second series of *The Review of the Churches*, at the time when he re-started his reunion conferences in Switzerland. This second series continued until 1930. After Ainslie's death, *The Christian Union Quarterly* was enlarged and transformed in *Christendom*, first owned and edited by Dr Charles Clayton Morrison, and later edited by Dr Paul Douglass on behalf of the American section of Faith and Order and Life and Work. *The Ecumenical Review*, begun in 1948 as the organ of the World Council, was the direct successor of *Christendom*. The Disciples of Christ have played an outstanding part in ecumenical journalism. "The Disciples", it has been said, "do not have bishops, they have editors" —amongst them Ainslie, the Garrisons, father and son, and Charles Clayton Morrison.

These ecumenical quarterlies vary to some extent in the amount of space they devote to actual ecumenical news and to editorial comment, and in the place they give to the theological aspects of ecumenism. But otherwise, most fortunately for the research student, they are curiously similar in method and range. The editor is always assisted by an editorial board of leaders from several Churches. All these quarterlies provide exciting reading: they show the varying or contradictory states of ecumenical thought and opinion through symposia on great questions and events, sometimes occupying the greater part of two or three issues; e.g. on the 1920 Lambeth "Appeal to All Christian People" (*The Constructive Quarterly*, December 1920 to December 1921); on the proposed Church of South India (*The Review of the Churches*, January to April 1930); on the conception of the Church held by different communions (*Christendom*, Summer and Autumn 1944); on all the great ecumenical conferences—Copec 1924, Stockholm 1925, Lausanne 1927, and the rest.

Their contributors are drawn from every Christian community and are given the greatest freedom of expression. *The Constructive Quarterly* opens with an article by the Roman Catholic Wilfrid Ward on "Union Amongst Christians", attacking the whole idea as chimerical and undesirable. Their biographical articles sometimes provide the only life-history available of certain ecumenical leaders. They rescue from oblivion episodes in past ecumenical history, which would otherwise have been forgotten. They are invaluable to the historian. In them can be seen the actual processes of ecumenical thinking—the best brains

[1] See Chap. vii, pp. 338 f., and 339, n. 1, on the *Religious Review of Reviews*.
[2] Silas McBee, *An Irenic Itinerary*, New York, 1911.

of the Churches hammering out ecumenical theories and convictions on the anvil of contemporary events and experience.

Germany, through Friedrich Siegmund-Schultze, from 1913 to 1933 rendered special service to ecumenical thinking. In 1913, through the ever ecumenically-inclined *Furche Verlag*, Siegmund-Schultze began to issue the quarterly *Die Eiche*.[1] Through periods of the utmost tension during the first world war and the beginning of the National Socialist régime, he never ceased to publish records of all important ecumenical documents on relations between the Churches, accounts of all important ecumenical conferences, and every kind of information which might break down the barriers of ignorance and prejudice between the Churches. The files of *Die Eiche*, over a period of twenty years, fill what would otherwise have been serious gaps in ecumenical history, as does also its successor, the annual *Ökumenisches Jahrbuch*, published by Siegmund-Schultze, 1934 to 1937. In 1950 Siegmund-Schultze, in conjunction with Professor F. Heiler, once more entered the field of ecumenical journalism with the annual *Die Oekumenische Einheit*.

In English there are three periodicals, each of which, though not primarily devoted to questions of unity, renders outstanding service to the ecumenical movement. *The International Review of Missions* was a product of the Edinburgh Conference of 1910, and has always followed with sympathetic understanding all the ecumenical movements which sprang from that gathering. It is the Churches' special source of knowledge concerning the younger Churches which have sprung from missionary effort. Its files have for forty years supplied a continuous and invaluable survey of ecumenical literature in that section of its bibliography devoted each quarter to "Comity Co-operation and Unity". *The Christian Century*, founded in 1884 under the name of *The Christian Oracle* as the organ of a group of the Disciples of Christ specially concerned with Christian unity, in the second decade of this century, under the ownership and editorship of Charles Clayton Morrison, cut loose from any denominational connection. It takes its own critical line on ecumenical questions, but perhaps more than any other periodical can be depended on to supply current impressions of what is going on in the sphere of Christian union. *The Student World*, the quarterly organ of the W.S.C.F., from 1908 onwards, has steadily aimed at keeping the members of Student Christian Movements abreast of the ecumenical thought of the day, and not infrequently devotes an entire issue to some ecumenical question, for example, intercommunion.

Important are various magazines issued by communities or societies devoted to ecumenism: *Irénikon*, in French, the organ of the Prieuré d'Amay in Belgium, 1926 onwards; *Vers l'Unité Chrétienne, Bulletin Catholique d'Information Mensuel*, published by the Centre "Istina" in Paris; and *Unitas*, in Italian, French, and English editions, the organ of the Association *Unitas* and the League of Prayer for the Return of the Separated to the Unity of the Church. The Scandinavian countries, since 1928, have had their own ecumenical quarterly, *Kristen Gemenskap* (Christian Fellowship), edited by Dean Nils Karlström.

Magazines issued by societies which, because of their main objective, are interested in some one phase of reunion, provide valuable source material on that phase, e.g. *The Christian East*, issued by the Anglican and Eastern Churches Association, and *Sobornost*, the organ of the Fellowship of S. Alban and S. Sergius.

[1] See Chap. xi, p. 512.

General religious periodicals, besides those already quoted—weeklies, month-lies, and quarterlies—have come to devote an ever-increasing amount of space to ecumenical questions and to reports of ecumenical events. To mention but a few, in France *Le Christianisme Social* and *Foi et Vie*, in Switzerland *La Vie Protestante*, in America *Christianity and Crisis*, in England *The Frontier*, successor of *The Christian News Letter*, and *Theology*. The same increasing attention to the ecumenical movement is found in practically all denominational or party periodicals in many countries and in many languages. A parallel increase in attention can be noted in the secular Press. Ecumenical conferences are news and demand comment in leaders. All this reveals an awakening within the Churches, and outside, to the fact that the ecumenical movement is the out-standing religious phenomenon of our day.

The place of journalism in the ecumenical movement is an almost unexplored field; this brief survey is cursory and incomplete; but it will at least suffice to show that research into the course of ecumenical thinking will certainly not suffer from lack of source material.

7. STILL OTHER ASPECTS OF THE ECUMENICAL MOVEMENT

Besides the aspects of the ecumenical movement classified under the foregoing headings, there are still others which must be touched on before the picture of the 20th-century ecumenical situation can be in any way complete.

There are the 19th-century organizations—missionary, evangelistic, and re-form societies, each with a definite objective, Bible societies, Christian literature societies, anti-slavery societies, conferences for the deepening of spiritual life, etc.[1]—which, decade after decade, steadily forwarded their specific aims and at the same time brought Christians of various Churches into understanding touch with each other. This great service to Christian unity they continue to render as they carry on their work in the 20th century.

In addition, there are certain 20th-century movements with specific aims which, in pursuing their objectives, incidentally bring together Christians of many different Churches. Among them are the Fellowship of Reconcilia-tion, which is peculiarly successful in uniting members of different com-munions, including the Roman Catholic, in work for peace; and the Oxford Group movement or, as it is now called, Moral Rearmament, which, with no idea of promoting ecclesiastical unity as such, is continuously introducing to each other thousands of Christians of every nationality and of every Church and confession.

In a class by itself must be placed the continuous work of the World's Evangelical Alliance, which for more than a hundred years has based its mem-bership and its activities on the central conviction of the unity of individual Christians who, though belonging to many Churches, hold the same faith.[2] During the 20th century the Alliance has pursued its traditional unitive activi-ties in stimulating missionary activity, in rousing a consciousness of unity amongst "Evangelicals", and above all in the Universal Week of Prayer. In recent years it is more and more realizing itself as a *World* Alliance, is initiating new methods of drawing Evangelicals of all nations together, and seeking new ways of promoting evangelism and missions.

[1] See Chap. vii, pp. 310–15; and also Chap. viii, p. 353.
[2] See Chap. vii, pp. 323 f.

There is another set of movements with common characteristics which, although they cannot be classed amongst ecumenical movements in the sense used in this History, are an undoubted factor in the general ecumenical situation. Together they constitute one of the many instances in Church life of horizontal or trans-confessional movements, which express some spirit or tendency that transcends denominational boundaries and affects groups in many denominations. This group of movements and societies is part of a general movement throughout the world; they are all manifestations of an "evangelical" faith, as that faith is in general expressed by the Evangelical Alliance.[1] Each of these movements endeavours to spread this faith in various age-groups or classes or professions: the Inter-Varsity Fellowship among students, the Crusaders' Union among boys and girls in secondary schools, Youth for Christ among young people in general; there are fellowships also among officers in the armed services, doctors, bankers, and lawyers. Some exist only nationally, others are international.

In so far as it is possible to generalize about so varied a group of societies and tendencies over nearly half a century, it can be said that all of them lay great stress on personal conversion, and accept into their membership those who share the same spiritual experience and hold the same evangelical beliefs. They lay much emphasis on Bible study of a conservative type. They accomplish much in evangelism among young men and women, and have a fine record in securing recruits for foreign missionary work. In so far as they bring Christians belonging to different Churches together in fellowship and aim at world-wide evangelization, they are in harmony with and serve the aims of the general ecumenical movement.

There are, however, certain features in these movements which have a divisive rather than a unitive tendency. They take in general a somewhat negative attitude towards the World Council of Churches and kindred ecumenical movements. They fail to realize that evangelism and Bible study can be integral in the aims of movements not wholly based on the same theological concepts as their own. They tend to create divisions in the Christian front against the world, the flesh, and the devil. Not a few of them have their origins in secessions from existing movements. Typical is the Inter-Varsity Fellowship, which had its origin in the withdrawal in 1910 from the British Student Christian Movement of the Cambridge Inter-Collegiate Christian Union, one of the several older university Christian organizations which in 1893 had combined to form the S.C.M. The withdrawal of the C.I.C.C.U. was due mainly to increasingly divergent views on the inspiration of the Bible and to a new emphasis on social and international problems in the study programme of the S.C.M. The I.V.F. is in general uncooperative in relation to other Christian movements, and has caused a division on the Christian front in many universities as it has spread from country to country. In 1947 it assumed an international form with the title of the International Fellowship of Evangelical Students.

Similar withdrawals have taken place from the Y.W.C.A. The Christian Association of Women and Girls is the outcome of a secession from the Y.W.C.A. in England in the late 1920's. A division had taken place earlier in Scotland. In the early 1930's the National Y.W.C.A.s of South Africa and of Finland seceded from the World's Y.W.C.A.[2] It must be recognized, in relation

---

[1] They have no organic connection with the Evangelical Alliance, nor indeed with each other.   [2] See p. 608.

to all these organizations, that both their divisiveness and their unco-operative-ness are due to their conception of what is involved in loyalty to "evangelical" truth.

It is on an ecumenical question that some of them take definite issue with the World Council and its kindred movements. They do not aim at and are not interested in efforts to bring Churches as such into co-operation or union, and they are in particular opposed to the idea of a membership open to Roman Catholics, such as is found in the S.C.M., the Y.M.C.A., and the Y.W.C.A., and to any co-operation with Roman Catholics or with the Orthodox or other Eastern Churches as such. But in spite of certain ways in which these move-ments stand in the way of ecumenical advance, it can gladly be recognized that they serve many of the same essential ideals and aims as those of the World Council.

8. CONCLUSION

In view of the constant shifting of the current scene, it is the more necessary to try to see ecumenicity steadily and to see it whole. We have attempted in this chapter a task hitherto unessayed, a review of the varied manifestations of ecumenicity outside the series of movements which led up to the World Council of Churches. What is the effect of our study of the ecumenical movement in its wholeness on our conception of the present and future of that movement? We see:

A movement which cannot be suppressed, making for Christian unity, with sufficient force to rise above exclusive confessional loyalties; with sufficient dynamic to counteract the inherent tendency of human nature—even redeemed human nature—to schism and division; with sufficient power to overcome in tens of thousands of Christians their inherent prejudices and inertia and to command in them the devotion of their best powers of thought and will to the cause of unity.

A movement showing itself everywhere. No continent or country, no Church or Church party, no religious group or society remains wholly un-affected. It appears amongst youth, in journalism, in the ecclesiastical assem-blies of the Churches, and at the grass roots of local church life; in unitive movements in each great confession, including the Roman Catholic and the Orthodox; in impulses to prayer; in emphasis now on the Kingdom and now on the Church, now on Faith and Order and now on Life and Work.

A movement beset with difficulties. Within this movement for unity there are contradictions and tensions between the lay and the ecclesiastical groups, between movements from the top downwards and from the bottom upwards, between "catholic" and "protestant" tendencies, between con-fessional and non-Church trends. The mixture in the bowl of the Church's life is bubbling, churning, changing—what will emerge?

We cannot yet see whither all this is leading and what will be the shape of the ecumenical movement to come. We can only rejoice in the manifold tokens of God's unitive purpose in the Church, certain of one thing, that the length and breadth and depth and height of the ultimate ecumenical movement will be some-thing far beyond what the boldest ecumenist amongst us now dares to ask or think. But it is incumbent upon all of us to be sensitive and open to new light.

In the phenomena which we have been considering, we may expect to discover tokens of God's guidance and to discern indications of the pattern which will emerge for the *Una Sancta*, the pattern which we must humbly seek to find and to follow.

NOTE ON THE BASES OF THE WORLD'S STUDENT CHRISTIAN FEDERATION AND THE WORLD'S YOUNG WOMEN'S CHRISTIAN ASSOCIATION

Extracts from the

Constitution of the World's Student Christian Federation
(A) *as adopted at Vadstena, Sweden, 1895*[1]

Article II. Objects

The objects shall be: . . .

3. To promote the following lines of activity:

   (*a*) To lead students to become disciples of Jesus Christ as only Saviour and as God. . . .

(B) *as amended at Princeton, N.J., in* 1913

Article II. Objects

The objects shall be: . . .

3. To promote the following lines of activity:

   (*a*) To lead students to accept the Christian faith in God—Father, Son, and Holy Spirit—according to the Scriptures and to live as true disciples of Jesus Christ. . . .

[Strictly speaking, the Federation has no basis, but it expresses the beliefs which are the foundation of its work when it states in its objects the kind of Christian faith into which it desires to lead students.—ED.]

Extracts from the

Constitution of the World's Young Women's Christian Association
(A) *as adopted at the first World's Conference, London, 1898*[2]

Article III. Basis

The World's Young Women's Christian Association seeks to unite those young women who, regarding the Lord Jesus Christ as their God and Saviour, according to the Holy Scriptures, are vitally united to Him through the love of God shed abroad in their hearts by the Holy Spirit, and desire to associate their efforts for the extension of His Kingdom among all young women by such means as are in accordance with the Word of God.

(B) *as amended at the Stockholm Conference in* 1914

Article II. Basis

Faith in God the Father as Creator and in Jesus Christ His only Son as Lord and Saviour, and in the Holy Spirit as Revealer of Truth and Source of Power for life and service, according to the teachings of Holy Scripture.

[1] Rouse, *World's Student Christian Federation*, pp. 314–17.
[2] Rice, *World's Y.W.C.A.*, pp. 271 and 276.

CHAPTER 14

THE EASTERN CHURCHES AND THE
ECUMENICAL MOVEMENT IN THE TWENTIETH CENTURY

by

NICOLAS ZERNOV

1. THE EASTERN CHURCHES IN THE FIRST QUARTER OF THE 20TH CENTURY[1]

The end of the first world war and the collapse of three Empires, those of Russia, of Austria, and of Turkey, which followed it, form a turning-point in the history of the Eastern Christians. A comparison between their status in 1910 and in 1925 reveals far-reaching changes in their life and organization, and even in the tasks which confronted them. Without some knowledge of this revolution it is difficult to understand the part played by them in the ecumenical movement during the period now under study.

In 1910 the Eastern Churches, Orthodox and "Lesser",[2] belonged to five distinct groups.

The largest among them was that of the Russian Empire. It comprised some hundred million Christians of diverse nationalities and races. These were divided among sixty-three dioceses, some of which were so large as to contain four million members. The Russian Church had 150,000 parochial clergy, educated in four theological academies and in fifty-nine secondary theological schools called seminaries. Many of its members responded to the appeal of the "religious life". There were in Russia some 700 monasteries and convents, with 40,000 inmates. In spite of its numerical strength and the outstanding quality of some of its leaders, the Church suffered under the bureaucratic control of the Empire. The chief administrative organ was the Holy Governing Synod created by the State and directed by a lay official, the Chief Procurator, who was appointed personally by the Emperor. The bishops and parochial clergy had little freedom of action, and the lay people were deprived of any responsible participation in the government of the Church, even on the parochial level.

Among the educated classes of Russia, many looked upon the Church as an indispensable part of national life, but treated it as a body which could satisfy only the spiritual needs of the peasant community and was too old-fashioned in its outlook to meet their own requirements. This, however, was not the whole story. The great revival of Russian theology in the 19th century, partly among the ecclesiastics, partly under the leadership of a remarkable series of lay theologians, was spreading its influence ever more widely. In the early years of the 20th century a group of former Marxists, including Professors S. Bulgakov and Nicolas Berdyaev, directed special attention to the intelligentsia, in an attempt to persuade the educated class to give up its disregard of religion and to resume active participation in the life of the Church. This movement was paralleled by the revival among the leaders of the Orthodox Church of a sense of responsibility for the spiritual welfare of the intellectuals, and for their recovery for the Church.

[1] Professor Stefan Zankov of Sofia had been invited by the Committee to contribute this chapter. When it became clear that Professor Zankov would not be able to write the chapter which he had planned, the Committee turned to Dr Zernov, who undertook to fill the gap, in spite of the short time which was all that could be allowed him for the writing of his chapter.

[2] It is difficult to find a satisfactory term for the various Eastern Churches which are not in communion with either Constantinople or Rome, especially as a number of them officially refer to themselves as "Orthodox". If they are here referred to as the Lesser Eastern Churches, this is only because most of them are numerically smaller than the great Orthodox Churches, and is not to be taken as in any way passing judgement on their significance in Christian history. See p. 647.

A number of bishops and lay theologians started to clamour for the convocation of the Church Council which had not been able to meet since the end of the 17th century. Their efforts met with partial success. The project received the support of Count Witte, the President of the Council of Ministers; the Holy Synod approved it, and a preparatory commission was authorized to start work. Meanwhile the grant of religious freedom in 1905–06 released the members of the Church from their compulsory silence, and a number of periodicals appeared, in which all the most controversial religious matters were discussed. The war of 1914 occurred at a time when new movements and new tensions were becoming evident in all spheres of Russian Christian life.

The second group of Eastern Christians comprised the Churches within the Ottoman State. These were divided among the four ancient patriarchates—Constantinople, Alexandria, Antioch, and Jerusalem, which dated from the time of the Byzantine Empire, and had in the 20th century some 8,500,000 members. Christians under the Turks enjoyed a certain amount of civic self-government. They were treated as a community distinct from the Islamic overlords. But centuries of Moslem oppression had left their mark; the Christian communities had few educated leaders, and consisted mostly of enterprising merchants in the cities and hard-working peasants in the villages. New currents of life, however, were beginning to flow in the primeval channels of the Middle East. National minorities in Turkey were turning with longing eyes to hopes of independence or of reunion with their liberated fellow-countrymen beyond the borders. The Greek monopoly of Orthodox Christian education was beginning to be challenged, largely through the work of Western missions, and a new middle class was growing up, Orthodox in faith (except for a few who joined Roman Catholic or Evangelical Churches), nationalist in sentiment, and English or French by adopted speech.

The third group was that of the Orthodox Churches within the Austro-Hungarian Empire. The Government was suspicious of the Eastern Christians and favoured the Uniate Churches, which were predominant in Galicia and Transylvania.[1] The Orthodox Christians were divided into three unconnected bodies: the Serbian Church of the Karlovits (800,000), the Church of Bukovina and Dalmatia, composed of Rumanians, Russians, and Dalmatians (550,000), and the Church of Hermannstadt for the Rumanians in Hungary (220,000). All the bishops in these Churches were appointed by the Austrian Emperor, and though a theological faculty existed in Cernovits there was little intellectual vigour among the leaders of these Churches, handicapped as they were by the animosity of the Austro-Hungarian bureaucracy, which looked upon them as potential allies of the neighbouring Orthodox countries.

The fourth group included the national Churches of the Balkans: Greece (2,000,000), Rumania (5,000,000), Serbia (2,500,000), Bulgaria (3,500,000), and Montenegro (150,000), which had obtained political and ecclesiastical independence as the result of a bitter and prolonged struggle against the Ottoman Empire in the course of the 19th century. These Churches were full of vitality and ambition, and one of their main preoccupations was the liberation of the rest of their co-religionists from the foreign yoke. They still enjoyed the faithful

[1] The Uniate Churches represented those Eastern Christians who accepted the primacy of Rome but retained their Oriental ritual. Most of them came into existence in the 17th century, in many cases as the result of direct political pressure. There are at present about five million Uniates of different nationalities and rites. The best book on these Churches is D. Attwater, *The Christian Churches of the East*, 2 vols., Milwaukee, 1946–47. See Chap. xv, p. 679.

adherence of their peasant members, who owed them their very survival, but they were beginning to be deserted by the newly-created intellectual class. The members of this class thought that repudiation of religion formed an indispensable condition of admission to the superior civilization of the West. These Churches suffered also from the militant nationalism of their peoples, who, having gained their freedom from the Turk, entered into fierce competition with one another for the division of the spoils.

The fifth group was composed of the Lesser Eastern Churches, all of which, being traditionally either Monophysite or Nestorian, separated from the main body in the course of the 5th and 6th centuries, and, though retaining many characteristics in common with the Orthodox Churches, have remained in separation from them until the present day. These Lesser Eastern Churches were closely identified with their respective nations, and with the exception of the Armenian Church showed little interest in the world outside their own region. They consisted of the Armenians (4,000,000), the Copts (800,000), the Abyssinians (3,500,000), the Jacobites (100,000), the Assyrians (80,000), and the Syrian Orthodox Church in South India (450,000).[1]

The situation of the Eastern Christians on the eve of the first world war was determined by the following factors:

They lived in most cases under political systems which were either hostile to them or opposed to their freedom and self-government. The same political forces were determined to prevent closer contacts, whether among the different branches of the Eastern Church, or between them and Western Christians.

The bulk of Eastern Christians were peasants, little affected by the secularism of the modern world, who continued therefore to live in an atmosphere of deep attachment to their Church.

The leadership of the Church was in the hands of clergy and conservative-minded laity who tried, not always successfully, to reconcile the traditional outlook of the Eastern Christians with new ideas borrowed from the contemporary thought of the West.

The intellectuals of the Eastern nations were in most cases either indifferent to or critical of their Churches, and considered them fit only for simple-minded rustics.

Contacts with the Christian West were few and mostly unfriendly. Both Roman Catholics and Protestants maintained proselytizing missions in the East, and these attempts, at times supported by political pressure, made the whole Christian West appear to members of the Eastern Churches as a determined enemy.

If we turn a leaf of history and meet once more the same Eastern Christians, but this time after the storm caused by the first world war, we shall see a strikingly altered picture.

Not only had three great Empires, which had controlled the life of the vast majority of the Eastern Christians for several centuries, disappeared overnight; but, even more unexpected, the mightiest of them, Russia, had been replaced by the dictatorship of Communists, bent on a radical reconstruction of the entire political, social, and economic order. Moreover, the latter were determined

---

[1] A section of the Syrian Church is in communion with the Jacobite (Monophysite) Patriarch of Antioch, but at least an equal number of "Syrians" in South India are "Romo-Syrians", i.e. Uniates of the Syriac rite.

to replace the Christian outlook of their subjects by a new philosophy openly antagonistic to all religions. Thus the first and largest group of the Eastern Christians, that of Russia, was by 1925 engaged in a grim struggle for survival in conditions which had no exact precedent in the experience of mankind.

Though cut off from the rest of the world and deprived of all its material resources, the Russian Church met the greatest trial of its history as a self-governing body, since the All Russian Council of 1917–18 had restored canonical order in the Russian Church and placed at the head of it an elected Patriarch. The anti-religious policy of the Government drove many nominal Christians from the Church, but it brought back into the fold others who had remained aloof or critical of it under the Empire. This return to the Church was particularly noticeable among the intellectual *élite* and provided the Russian Church, especially in exile, with many outstanding leaders. It was one of the paradoxes of the Russian situation that, whilst the majority of its members were completely isolated from the rest of Christendom, a section almost a million strong found itself in the midst of Western peoples and free to organize its life according to its own convictions. Some of these Christians became active participants in the ecumenical movement, whilst others among them manifested a strong opposition to it.

The situation of the second group had also undergone important changes. After the restoration of the Turkish government in Constantinople in 1922 and the exchange of population with the kingdom of Greece, the Ecumenical Patriarchate lost the civil and political authority which it had enjoyed since the 15th century, and its activities were limited to purely spiritual functions. Its flock was also considerably reduced, for no Greek population remained in Turkey except in Constantinople and its suburbs. Its jurisdiction, however, still extended over the monastic republic of Mount Athos, Crete, the Dodekanese, some northern dioceses of the Greek kingdom, and over the Greek *diaspora*, with the exception of Africa, where the Orthodox recognize the Patriarch of Alexandria as their spiritual head.

The other ancient patriarchates were caught equally in the turmoil of the political reshaping of the Middle East, and suffered the loss of prestige and power. The revival of nationalism, closely linked with the religion of Islam in those parts of the world, adversely affected the life and security of the Christian minority, a considerable proportion of which were members of the Orthodox Churches.

With the dismemberment of the Austro-Hungarian Empire, almost the whole of the Orthodox population found itself in the territory of one or another of the greatly enlarged Balkan States; thus the third group disappeared, being absorbed in the fourth, which correspondingly gained in strength.

The Churches belonging to the fourth group were the chief beneficiaries in the changed world order. The Churches of Rumania and Yugoslavia were able for the first time in their history to reunite in one national organization the main bulk of their previously divided members. The Patriarchate of Rumania came to include 13,000,000 adherents, that of Yugoslavia 7,000,000. The Church of Greece was also considerably enlarged and became 6,000,000 strong. The Church of Bulgaria counted some 5,000,000, but received no addition to its territory. Moreover, since 1872 it had been separated from the Church of Constantinople, though it remained in communion with some of its non-Greek ecclesiastical neighbours.[1] Several new autonomous Churches came into existence as the result of the reshaping of North-eastern and Central Europe; among these were the Orthodox Church of Poland (4,500,000 members), the Church of Czechoslovakia (200,000), those of Albania (220,000), of Latvia (160,000), of Estonia (250,000), of Lithuania (50,000), and of Finland (73,600). The Orthodox Church of Japan (40,000), the fruit of the missionary work of the Russians, maintained its existence. Russian exiles built their communities in western Europe and in China. Emigrants from Europe and Asia formed a number of Orthodox dioceses in the United States and Canada, with two to three million members. The problem of their adaptation to a wholly strange environment, and their growing sense of a need for union, form a fascinating but still inchoate chapter in ecumenical relationships.

The fifth group, the Lesser Eastern Churches, had sustained two grievous losses. The Assyrians were expelled by their Moslem neighbours from their ancient home in Iraq, and partly annihilated. The same disaster befell the Armenians in Turkey, only a remnant surviving in Constantinople, in Syria and Lebanon, and in western Europe, Britain, and America.

These far-reaching changes not only profoundly affected all aspects of Church life among the Eastern Christians, but had also a considerable bearing upon their relations with the Christian West.

2. THE PART PLAYED BY EASTERN CHRISTIANS IN WORK FOR REUNION, 1910–1939

There has for centuries been a striking difference between the attitude of Eastern and Western Christians towards one another. The West was active and at times even aggressive. It tried to convert Eastern Christians to its creed, and Roman Catholics and Protestants vied with one another in making proselytes among the members of the Oriental Churches. The latter treated these missionary efforts as acts of unprovoked hostility, for, especially in countries such as Palestine, Syria, and Egypt, the Western agents disrupted the peace and unity of the local Christian communities by multiplying rival groups and sects in their midst.[2] The Western policy created among the Eastern Churches a widespread impression that both Rome and Protestantism were bent on their subjugation and destruction, and were ready to spend limitless energy and money in order to achieve this aim. Such a conviction was still prevalent among Eastern Christians on the eve of the first world war.

At that time the initiative in making contacts, both friendly and hostile, was entirely on the Western side. The spearhead of friendly penetration into the life of the Eastern Christians consisted of two main groups.

First, there was a small but very active body of Anglo-Catholics in England, led by the Rev. H. J. Fynes-Clinton, Canon J. A. Douglas, and the Rev. R. F. Borough, who founded in 1906 the Anglican and Eastern Orthodox Churches

---

[1] The Bulgarian schism was caused by the demand for parallel national hierarchies, Bulgarian and Greek, in Turkey in Europe; the Ecumenical Patriarch was prepared to recognize the Bulgarian autocephalous Church as responsible only for those provinces where the Orthodox population was indisputably Bulgarian in character.

[2] It may help to remind the reader of the complexities of Eastern Christendom, if it is mentioned that there are no less than six Patriarchs of Antioch, of whom four represent the Latin and Uniate Churches and are in communion with Rome.

Union, with the expressed object of restoring communion between these two Churches.

Secondly, there were the pioneers of the World's Student Christian Federation, who under the leadership of John R. Mott started the exploration of the hitherto unknown field of the Russian and Balkan universities, and began to make contacts with the clergy and intellectual leaders of these nations. Invaluable as was the work of the Federation, that body, as "a fellowship of students", recognized its own limitations, and never entered the field of Church relations or concerned itself directly with Christian reunion.

Both these efforts met with a mixed reception. Some Orthodox treated the newcomers as dangerous emissaries of the hostile West, others welcomed them as friends who shared the same Christian convictions and with whom co-operation could only be beneficial to both sides.

The Anglican and Eastern Orthodox Churches Union, in contrast to the scholarly but less active older society, the Eastern Church Association (founded in 1863 and revived by the Rev. A. C. Headlam, later Bishop of Gloucester, in 1893),[1] displayed great vigour. In 1910 its Secretary, the Rev. H. J. Fynes-Clinton, paid a visit to Russia, where he was warmly received. In 1912 an Anglican monk, Fr F. W. Puller of the Society of St John the Evangelist, also went to Russia and there gave a number of lectures.[2] In 1914 another distinguished "religious" of the Anglican Church, Fr Walter Frere of the Community of the Resurrection and later Bishop of Truro (1923–35), spent three months in Russia.[3] As a result of these efforts, a Russian branch of the Society was formed under the presidency of Bishop Eulogius of Kholm, later Metropolitan of the Russian Church in Western Europe (1920–46). In 1913, owing to the pressure of his diocesan work, he resigned his presidency of the Russian branch, and was replaced by Sergius, Archbishop of Finland, the future Patriarch of the Russian Church (1943–44). These activities were brought to an abrupt end by the breaking out of the first world war and the Russian revolution, but the seeds sown by the Union bore fruit in the post-war period amongst the Russians in exile.

No less valuable, though quite different in character, were the pioneering efforts in Orthodox university centres of Dr John R. Mott and his colleague Miss Ruth Rouse. In 1899 Mott paid a first brief visit to Russia, and was much impressed by that vast and neglected field for Christian evangelism. In 1909 he revisited Russia, and made a deep impact upon the Russian students who crowded the largest halls in St Petersburg and Moscow to hear an outstanding American Christian. Dr Mott's reports speak of the distinct turning from exclusively political interests towards religion, noticed by him among the Russian students on the eve of the first world war.[4] From about 1903 there gradually came into existence a Russian Student Christian Movement, under the leadership of the Lutheran Baron Nicolay, and including in its ranks both Orthodox and non-Orthodox students.[5]

In April 1911 the W.S.C.F. held its Conference in Constantinople. This was an event which brought into its orbit both Orthodox and Lesser Eastern Churches. Greeks, Russians, Rumanians, Bulgarians, Serbians, Armenians,

[1] See Chap. vi, pp. 280 f.
[2] Fourth Report of the Anglican and Eastern Churches Union, 1910–1912, p. 41.
[3] Fifth Report of the Anglican and Eastern Churches Union, 1912–1914, p. 37.
[4] Addresses and Papers of John R. Mott, II, p. 451.
[5] See Chap. xiii, p. 603.

Syrians, Maronites,[1] and Copts took part in this student gathering.[2] In connection with this Conference Mott visited universities and colleges both in the Near East and in the Balkans. He addressed student meetings in Athens, Sofia, and Belgrade. In the last-named city a hostile demonstration against him organized by the Socialists ended in a free fight between the demonstrators and the rest of the audience.[3] Mott became convinced that co-operation with the leaders of the Eastern Churches was possible and quoted in support of his optimism the words of the Principal of the Seminary at Halki near Constantinople, the Rev. Germanos Strenopoulos, later Metropolitan of Thyateira and Exarch of the Ecumenical Patriarchate for Western and Northern Europe (1922–51): "Where hearts are united, the resistance of the head will diminish. It was the looseness of the bonds of love which brought the divisions of Christianity."[4]

The first world war brought to an end this happily initiated co-operation, but its calamities produced new opportunities. The war-time service of the Y.M.C.A. among soldiers and prisoners of war created many personal friendships between Eastern and Western Christians. A significant contact was established also between a group of Serbian theological students, brought to England in 1915 to continue their interrupted studies, and the Anglican Church. There were about sixty of them, and they were placed at Dorchester and other theological colleges in and near Oxford. At the end of the war fifteen of them remained in England in order to obtain the degree of Bachelor of Letters at Oxford. There was a hope at that time that a permanent college for Eastern Orthodox students might be established in Oxford, but through lack of adequate support this plan had to be abandoned.

The inspiring leader of the Serbians was Fr Nicolai Velimirovic, later Bishop of Ochrida. He preached fiery sermons in many churches in England and left everywhere a deep impression of his remarkable personality. The Serbian clergy in exile received permission to celebrate the Orthodox Eucharist in Anglican churches, and this forged a new link between Eastern and Western Christians.[5] Work on behalf of Serbian refugee students in France, Switzerland, and other countries was carried on also by the W.S.C.F. and the Y.M.C.A.

There were similar contacts in America between Orthodox and Episcopalians. For instance, a conference was held in the General Seminary in New York, which included among its members Meletios Metaxakis, Archbishop of Athens, later Patriarch of Constantinople (1921–23) and of Alexandria (1927–35), and Dr Chrysostom Papadopoulos, later Archbishop of Athens (1923–41). Dr A. C. Headlam was in the chair. A number of leading Episcopalians, including the Bishops of Delaware and Harrisburg and Bishop Courtenay, took part.[6] This conference had its continuation in Oxford, where several similar meetings were organized for Orthodox and Armenian theologians.[7]

In the post-war years, independently of the movements described above, new and more friendly relations were also established between Eastern and Western Christians in two other parts of the world—Egypt and South India.

[1] The Maronites are the largest single Christian community in the Lebanon. They separated from the Eastern Orthodox Church on account of their monothelete heresy in the 7th century and submitted to Rome in 1182. They are about 350,000 in number.
[2] Mott, op. cit., p. 512; and Ruth Rouse, *The World's Student Christian Federation*, pp. 152 ff. See also Chap. xiii, pp. 602 ff.   [3] Mott, op. cit., p. 285.   [4] Ibid., p. 288.
[5] See *Sixth Report of the Anglican and Eastern Churches Union, 1914–21*, pp. 38 ff.
[6] See H. Alivisatos, "Aspirations Towards Unity" in *The Christian East*, Vol. I, No. 1, pp. 125 f.   [7] Ibid., pp. 81 f.

Thanks to the remarkable personality of the Rev. W. H. Temple Gairdner (1873–1928), an Anglican who dedicated his life to missionary work in Egypt, and to the no less outstanding pastoral zeal of Llewellyn Henry Gwynne (Bishop of Khartoum 1908–20, in Egypt 1920–45), the high wall of partition which in the past had separated the confessional groups in the Nile valley was broken through. The Fellowship of Unity started by Gairdner in 1921 comprised not only Anglicans, Presbyterians, Greek Orthodox, Copts, Armenians, and Syrians, but even some of those Egyptians who had become Protestants under the influence of missionaries from the West. Some of these converts had been members of the Eastern Churches; the relations of such with their former co-religionists were not at all friendly, and it was a real achievement to bring all these groups together into one society. The Fellowship of Unity organized meetings and discussions, but it also gathered its members in acts of corporate worship. As the result of its activities, the atmosphere of suspicion and even hostility existing among the Christian minorities in Egypt was to a large extent transformed into a spirit of trust and co-operation.

The ancient Syrian Church of South India had suffered bitterly through the centuries from aggression from the West. Large sections of it had been absorbed into the Roman Catholic Church, and smaller groups had become Nestorian or Anglican. On the eve of the first world war the independent Syrians were divided into two groups, the Mar Thoma Syrian Church of Malabar, which had undergone an extensive reformation, and the more conservative Malankara Church, which maintained its relations, not always on easy terms, with the Monophysite Patriarch of Antioch.

The Mar Thoma Church, which, until the formation of the Church of South India in 1947, claimed to be the only wholly autonomous Church in India, established friendly contacts with Christians of all Churches which professed faith in the one Gospel of Jesus Christ. At its annual Convention at Maramannu, often attended by not less than 50,000 people, it welcomed speakers of many Churches—Anglican, Lutheran, Presbyterian, and others. The first Indian Principal of Serampore, the great college founded by the Baptist Carey, was a priest of this Church.

The Malankara Church, suspicious of "Protestant" elements in the Anglican Church, was less accessible to influences from outside. It suffered from an internal schism between the Catholicos party[1] and the Patriarchal party, caused by disagreements as to the proper order of ecclesiastical administration. Nevertheless, even this section of Indian Christians was gradually drawn into the orbit of the ecumenical movement. From the end of the 19th century it had received much help from the Fathers of the Oxford Mission to Calcutta. Its members found themselves completely at home with these representatives of a devout and learned Anglo-Catholicism. The fruits of their work were seen in a quickened devotional life, in higher standards in the training of the clergy, and in the renewal of missionary work among non-Christians.

A new window opened on the world for this ancient Church when Syrian students in considerable numbers began to attend the Madras Christian College, a great institution supported by many Churches, but mainly under Scottish and Presbyterian leadership. The most remarkable of these students and young teachers was K. C. Chacko (d. 1947), who in his year was reckoned the intellectual

---

[1] The Catholicos is the local head of the Church, and the head of that party which desires to set constitutional limits to the authority of the Patriarch of Antioch over the Church.

equal of Sarvapalli Radhakrishnan, later Professor at Calcutta and Oxford, Indian Ambassador to Moscow, and Vice-President of the Indian Republic. Although an invalid for almost the whole of his adult life, Chacko exercised an ecumenical influence without parallel in the Lesser Eastern Churches. In 1911 he had attended the meeting of the W.S.C.F. in Constantinople; this experience was to lead on to greater things.

It was as a result of the prayers and efforts of Chacko that in January 1913 leaders of the Malankara, Mar Thoma, and Anglican Churches were induced to meet at Serampore, under the chairmanship of Dr Mott, to discuss their common problems. The atmosphere was far more friendly than anyone had imagined possible, and this conference marked a turning-point in inter-Church relationships in Travancore. A member of the Malankara Church joined the staff of the Baptist Theological College at Serampore, and from that time on an increasing number of Syrian students came either to Serampore or to the (Anglican) Bishop's College, Calcutta, for their theological training.

Ten years later, Chacko gathered round him a group of like-minded young men of the three Churches to found the Union Christian College at Alwaye in North Travancore. In view of the strained relations between the Churches in Travancore, it is a remarkable thing that members of all the Churches, as professors or students, have found at Alwaye a place where they could live and work together in peace, in loyalty both to their own Churches and to their colleagues of other confessions. There is hardly any other place in Travancore of which this can be said. Over a whole generation, Alwaye has exercised a healing ecumenical influence in an area in which the Christian situation is perhaps more complicated than in any other part of the world.

The fruits of these wider contacts were seen when both these branches of the ancient Indian Church became member Churches of the World Council of Churches, and were represented at the Amsterdam Assembly by their Metropolitans. In these wider ecumenical contacts, they came to realize how much they had in common, not only with the other Lesser Eastern Churches, but also with the Churches of the great Orthodox tradition.

The end of the first world war was followed by a universally-felt desire for closer fellowship among the Christians of all nations and of diverse traditions. The idea of a world conference of Churches made a strong appeal to many influential leaders, and a delegation consisting of the leading Episcopalians from the United States visited Europe in 1919, in order to prepare the convocation of a conference on Faith and Order. They were enthusiastically received by the bishops of the Orthodox Churches in Constantinople and in the Balkans, who assured them of their keen interest in the project.[1]

The year 1920 is a decisive date in the history of the ecumenical movement, and also in the relations between the Eastern Churches and the West. From that year till the outbreak of the second world war in 1939, there were three distinct channels for those increasingly closer contacts which culminated in the formation of the World Council of Churches with the participation of several Eastern Churches. The first channel included official negotiations between the Orthodox and the Anglicans with a view to their reunion. The recognition of the validity of Anglican ordinations occupied the central point in these discus-

---

[1] See *F. and O. Pamphlet, No. 32: Report of the Deputation to Europe and the East*; and Chap. ix, pp. 414 f.

sions.[1] The second was provided by the part played by Eastern Christians in various manifestations of the ecumenical movement such as Faith and Order, Life and Work, and the World Alliance for Promoting International Friendship through the Churches. The third consisted of diverse activities among students and young people, in part sponsored by the W.S.C.F., the Y.M.C.A., Y.W.C.A., and the World Alliance, in part independent of them. This chapter deals with the ecumenical contacts provided by the second and the third channels.

The entry of the Orthodox Church into ecumenical relationships was preceded by the issue of a moving letter addressed in January 1920 "unto all the Churches of Christ wheresoever they be" and signed by the Locum Tenens of the Patriarchal Ecumenical throne and eleven Metropolitans.[2] This epistle invited the Churches to renounce proselytism and to form a league of the Churches for mutual assistance. It suggested various practical ways of promoting goodwill, and declared that doctrinal disagreements ought not to stand in the way of joint action.[3] This epistle signified a departure from the usual cautious attitude of the Orthodox towards the West, and showed the desire of some at least among their hierarchs to take the lead in the movement towards closer fellowship.

As an outcome of this remarkable change of mind, a large delegation—eighteen in number, representing seven Eastern Churches—came to Geneva (12–20 August 1920) to the preparatory Conference of the Faith and Order movement.[4] Three of these delegates were also present at the preparatory meeting of the Life and Work movement which took place in Geneva at the same time. For many of the Orthodox delegates, this was the first occasion of meeting with representatives of non-Orthodox Churches, and the initial contacts were not always easy. Some of the Orthodox were particularly troubled by the proselytizing missions supported by some American and British groups, and made the cessation of all such activities the condition of their further co-operation.[5] In spite of these tensions, the impression produced upon the Orthodox by the leaders in Faith and Order, especially by Bishop Brent, was highly favourable, and convinced a number of them of the sincerity and genuine desire for unity animating many representatives of these new endeavours towards reconciliation.

The coming of the Orthodox to Geneva brought their Churches into the ecumenical movement, and both at Stockholm in 1925 and at Lausanne in 1927 Orthodox Christianity was well represented. The latter Conference was particularly significant, for it included some twenty-two delegates from both the Orthodox and Lesser Eastern Churches, among them Arabs, Armenians, Bulgarians, Georgians, Greeks, Rumanians, Russians, and Serbians. The Eastern Christians took an active part in the work of the Conference, by reading papers and by their participation in the commissions. The Metropolitan Germanos of Thyateira (since 1922 Exarch for Western Europe) spoke in moving words at the opening session on the urgent need for Christian unity.[6] He emphasized, however, that from the point of view of Orthodox theology "unity in faith constitutes a primary condition of reunion of the Churches". This note rang through all other Orthodox contributions, which included papers from a prominent Russian

[1] See Chrysostom Papadopoulos, *The Validity of Anglican Ordinations*, London, 1931; also Chap. x, p. 487.
[2] See *The Christian East*, Vol. I, No. 1, p. 52; also Bell, *Documents*, I, pp. 44 ff.
[3] See Chap. x, p. 446.
[4] See Chap. ix, pp. 417 f.   [5] See Chap. ix, p. 418.
[6] *Faith and Order, Lausanne 1927*, ed. H. N. Bate, New York, 1928, pp. 18 ff.

Biblical scholar, Professor N. Glubokovski, on "The Church's Message", from Chrysostom, Archbishop of Athens, and Stefan, Metropolitan of Sofia, on "The Nature of the Church", from Professor Stefan Zankov, the leading Bulgarian theologian, and Professor Sergius Bulgakov, Dean of the Orthodox Theological Institute in Paris, on "The Church's Ministry", and lastly from Nicolai Velimirovic, Bishop of Ochrida, on "The Sacraments".

The last contribution was particularly striking, for the great preacher and leader of the Serbian Christians at the end of his paper asked Protestants to trust the experience of the saints in the settlement of the controversy as to the number of the sacred mysteries:

> "If anyone should think that perhaps Baptism and the Eucharist (or other two or three of the seven Mysteries) are the only Mysteries, the only Sacraments, well—let him ask God about it; by fasting and praying tears let him ask God, and He will reveal to him the truth as He has always revealed it to the saints . . . all that we have said about the great Christian Mysteries is not an opinion of our own (if it were an opinion of our own, it would be worth nothing), but it is the repeated experience of the Apostles in the ancient days and of the saints up to our own days. For the Church of God lives not on opinion, but on the experience of the saints, as in the beginning so in our days. The opinions of intellectual persons may be wonderfully clever and yet be false, whereas the experience of the saints is always true. It is God the Lord who is true to Himself in His saints."[1]

When the time came for acceptance of the reports of the various commissions, the Metropolitan of Thyateira read a declaration in the name of the Orthodox delegates, in which they expressed their decision to abstain from voting on the reports, with the exception of that of Section II on "The Church's Message to the World". The following quotations from his speech make clear the standpoint of the Orthodox theologians at that ecumenical gathering in the work of which they so fully shared:

> "The Orthodox Church adheres fixedly to the principle that the limits of individual liberty of belief are determined by the definitions made by the whole Church, which definitions we maintain to be obligatory on each individual. . . . Therefore the mind of the Orthodox Church is that reunion can take place only on the basis of the common faith and confession of the ancient, undivided Church of the seven Ecumenical Councils and of the first eight centuries. . . . This being so, we cannot entertain the idea of a reunion which is confined to a few common points of verbal statement; for according to the Orthodox Church, where the totality of the faith is absent there can be no *communio in sacris*. . . . In consequence, while we, the undersigned Orthodox representatives, must refrain from agreeing to any reports other than that upon the Message of the Church, which we accept and are ready to vote upon, we desire to declare that in our judgment the most which we can now do is to enter into co-operation with other Churches in the social and moral sphere on a basis of Christian love . . . in making it plain that we have arrived at our decision only in obedience to the dictates of our conscience, we beg to assure the Conference that we have derived

[1] *Lausanne 1927*, p. 290.

much comfort here from the experience that, although divided by dogmatic differences, we are one with our brethren here in faith in our Lord and Saviour Jesus Christ. Declaring that in the future we shall not cease to devote ourselves to labour for the closer approach of the Churches, we add that we shall pray to God without ceasing that by the operation of His Holy Spirit He will take away all existing hindrances and will guide us to that unity for which the Founder and Ruler of the Church prayed."[1]

The Orthodox delegates met together on several occasions during the Conference, and it was a welcome opportunity for them to discuss theological problems with the members of other national Orthodox Churches. Their agreement on fundamentals did not exclude differences, and sometimes even sharp divisions, on points of policy. There were also temperamental clashes between those who favoured a more scholastic, and those who were inclined towards a more mystical, approach to religion. The Russians and the Bulgarians were more interested in dogmatic discussions. The Greeks were more concerned with practical co-operation with the West, being less optimistic in regard to the chances of agreement in dogma. It was a paradox that Professor Bulgakov (1871–1944), who was the keenest supporter of endeavours towards doctrinal understanding with the West,[2] caused the greatest stir at the Conference by introducing into its discussions the question of the significance of the Blessed Virgin Mary in the reunion of Christians. Professor Bulgakov said:

> "Holiness is the goal and essence of the Church's life: the holiness of the manhood of Christ, actualised in the communion of saints. But we cannot separate the humanity of our Lord from that of His mother, the unspotted *Theotokos*. She is the head of mankind in the Church; Mother and Bride of the Lamb, she is joined with all saints and angels in the worship and life of the Church. Others may not yet feel drawn, as I do, to name her name in prayer. Yet, as we draw together towards doctrinal reunion, it may be that we are coming potentially nearer even in this regard."[3]

The suggestion of devotion in prayer to the Virgin Mary provoked sharp opposition from the Protestant wing of the Conference, and Dr A. E. Garvie (a Congregationalist), the chairman of the meeting, stopped the speaker and called his attention to his departure from the subject of the Conference.[4] Professor Bulgakov refused to accept this ruling and renewed his plea for the recognition of Mariology as a doctrinal problem of vital importance to the ecumenical

---

[1] *Lausanne 1927*, pp. 384 f. See also Chap. ix, p. 424.

[2] Professor Bulgakov, in August 1928, gave the following list of doctrinal problems, the study of which he believed to be essential for the progress of the ecumenical movement: "First of all the questions of ecclesiology: the nature of the Church, of the ministry, and of the sacraments, especially the Eucharist. The question of redemption must be added also. But primarily the question of the meaning and importance of the veneration of the Mother of God ought to be raised, for it arises directly out of the acceptance of the Nicene Creed. This last question more than any other divides the Christian world to-day, and the attitude to it must therefore be defined with complete clarity. All these talks presuppose a long and arduous road of studies, discussions, and debates. But the disputing parties are no longer enemies, they are friends, who are seeking mutual understanding; more than that, they are brothers in Christ, though still divided brothers." *Put*, No. 13, October 1928, p. 82.

[3] *Lausanne 1927*, p. 208.

[4] N. Arseniev, "The Lausanne Conference", *Put*, No. 10, April 1928, p. 106; M. Eulogius, *The Way of My Life*, p. 588; S. Bulgakov, "The Lausanne Conference and the Encyclical *Mortalium Animos*", *Put*, No. 13, October 1928, p. 71.

movement. His persistence was crowned with some success, for the Communion of Saints was included in the programme of the second Faith and Order Conference at Edinburgh.[1] The incident was significant, for it showed how wide was the gap separating the leaders of the ecumenical movement from each other at the beginning of their work. These suspicions and misunderstandings were to a large extent removed as the result of the work of the Continuation Committees of Faith and Order and Life and Work, which met at regular intervals between 1928 and 1937. Equally important were the conferences and study groups organized by the World Alliance, the W.S.C.F., the Y.M.C.A., and other similar bodies.

Especially valuable was the work of preparation for the Oxford Conference of 1937, which brought Orthodox theologians of different nationalities into close contact with one another. Its indefatigable promoter was Dr Stefan Zankov of Sofia, who was a joint regional secretary for the Balkans of the Life and Work movement and the World Alliance. Thanks to his initiative and labours, three regional conferences were held in the Balkans: Bucharest (14–19 May 1933), Herzeg Novi (1–5 July 1935), and Novi Sad (11–16 May 1936), at which representatives of all the four main Balkan countries took part. Some Russians from Paris and some Western theologians were also invited to these gatherings. These frequent contacts among the Orthodox were a stimulating experience for them, an unexpected fruit of the ecumenical movement. The culminating point of this inter-Orthodox co-operation was reached at the Pan-Orthodox Congress of Theologians, which was held in Athens (29 November–4 December 1936). Here were gathered representatives from the theological faculties of Bucharest, Kisenau, Sofia, Belgrade, Warsaw, Paris, and Athens. There were altogether about thirty participants, including some guests from the Christian West. It was a successful gathering, for it showed a much greater agreement among Orthodox theologians than had been expected on the controversial problem of the mission of the Orthodox Church to the modern world. Professor Zankov summarized the task of the Congress in the following words:

"The Orthodox Christians await from their theologians an indication of new ways of service and leadership which they, as members of the Church, have to offer to their people."[2]

Several speeches at this Conference dealt with the Orthodox attitude to the ecumenical movement. In his opening allocution, Professor Alivisatos devoted more than a third of his time to this theme:

"The end of the world war has brought about a new and vigorous effort on the part of ecclesiastical and theological authorities and organizations in different countries with a view to the throwing down of those Chinese walls that have separated the nations and the Churches—those walls that were built as the result of the great schisms within the Churches, and of that great and laborious effort of theology which was indeed necessary but which I

[1] In the volume on *Ways of Worship*, London, 1951, printed in preparation for the third World Conference on Faith and Order in Lund, a special section on Mariology was added, a posthumous recognition of the importance to the Orthodox of Bulgakov's contention.

[2] F. Lieb, *Der erste Kongress der orthodoxen Theologie in Athen*, Oekumenischer Rat für Praktisches Christentum, p. 14.

may also describe as scholastic and fanatical, carried out with a view to the justification and the firmer establishment of the conflicting points of view. A great work for the promotion of unity has in fact been carried out by what is known as the ecumenical movement, the aim of which is the renewing of those bonds of fellowship which in earlier days were broken; with a view to the gathering together in one of all the spiritual Christian forces that exist anywhere in the world and the establishment of a single Christian front against the moral evil which threatens the destruction of every established form of worship, morals, and political organization."[1]

After outlining the threefold organization of the ecumenical movement as World Alliance, Faith and Order, and Life and Work, Professor Alivisatos pointed out that the invitation to participate in this movement had been joyfully welcomed by almost all Churches, including the Orthodox. Orthodox delegations had been present at every one of the international councils and meetings. Those who had been separated by the difficulties of political circumstances had been able to meet and come to know one another, and the Orthodox theologians had been able to present to these international gatherings the Orthodox point of view in theology, and to remind Christendom of the existence of a living contemporary Orthodoxy which some of the Westerners had imagined to be almost dead.

At the end of the Conference the following resolution was passed:

"The first Orthodox Congress of Theology, regarding the ecumenical movement for the union of the Church as a happy manifestation of the present general renewal of interest in the Church and in theology, welcomes this movement and is prepared to collaborate with it in an Orthodox spirit."

Besides Professor Zankov and Professor Alivisatos, who took a leading part in the organization and the conduct of the Congress in Athens, Professor P. Bratsiotis of Athens and Professor V. Ispir of Bucharest were the most prominent supporters of the ecumenical movement in the Balkans, and regular participants in all the international conferences and commissions.

The training of younger Orthodox men and women for ecumenical work also occupied the attention of the promoters of the movement. Many students showed great interest in it, but owing to political and financial difficulties the plans for the extension of this work could not be put into effect, and the congress of Orthodox youth leaders, scheduled for 1938, was never convoked. Nevertheless a certain number were introduced to ecumenical work through the W.S.C.F., Y.M.C.A., and Y.W.C.A., and other similar organizations. Dr Nicolas Zernov was appointed an honorary area secretary of the Youth Commission of the World Alliance and Life and Work, with the Orthodox countries as his special field (1934–39).

A number of Eastern Orthodox students were present both in Oxford and Edinburgh in 1937 among the members of youth groups invited to these ecumenical gatherings.

These two great Conferences once more brought many Eastern Christian leaders together. There were twenty-four Orthodox delegates at Oxford, as well

[1] *Procès-verbaux du Premier Congrès de Théologie Orthodoxe*, Athens, 1939, pp. 56 f.

as several from the Lesser Eastern Churches, the total membership of the Conference being about 400. Among Orthodox spokesmen was George Fedotov (1886–1951), the leading historian of the Russian Church, who formulated his impressions in the following terms:

> "A social nature of Christianity is fully accepted by the Orthodox Church. But the Orthodox peoples, due to their unfortunate history, have lost the habit of interpreting Christianity in this spirit. Religious individualism became even traditional among recent generations. The social problems, however, cannot be excluded altogether, and when they press upon the Orthodox they nowadays take a form of aggressive paganism. The Balkan Churches suffer from their destructive nationalism. The Russian Church is silent and is in chains. . . . It is a hard soil for the seeds of social Christianity and a difficult task awaits all its workers."[1]

The second Faith and Order Conference at Edinburgh gathered a widely representative group of Eastern Christians; twenty-seven of them belonged to the Orthodox Churches, the rest, ten in all, were Armenians, Copts, Abyssinians, and Syrian Indians. Thirteen Eastern Churches appointed delegates, among them the Patriarchates of Constantinople, of Alexandria, and of Antioch, the Churches of Greece, Bulgaria, Poland, Albania, and Latvia. Russian Christianity was represented by the leaders of the exiled community. Two other Orthodox Churches, those of Rumania and of Yugoslavia, accepted the invitation but were unable to send delegates to the Conference.

The Orthodox were again led by Dr Germanos, the Metropolitan of Thyateira, who read a declaration of their special standpoint similar to that of Lausanne.[2] He made it clear, however, that the Orthodox delegates had noted with great satisfaction the progress achieved during the Conference. His speech included the following statements:

> "A careful study of the Reports which are now before the Conference will show that they express many fundamental agreements which exist between us and our Christian brethren on many important points . . . we recognize that in the discussion of the veneration of the Holy Virgin, the Theotokos, and of the saints, a very valuable advance has been achieved. None the less essential differences remain, and we Orthodox have felt obliged to mention our divergent points of view in separate footnotes. . . . Brethren! After having made this declaration in order to satisfy our consciences, we are constrained and rejoice to utter a few words by which to emphasise the great spiritual profit which we have drawn from our daily intercourse with you, the representatives of other Christian Churches. With you we bewail the rending asunder of the seamless robe of Christ. We desire, as you, that the members of the one Body of Christ may again be reunited, and we pray, as you, day by day in our congregations for the union of all mankind."[3]

The Edinburgh Conference marked considerable progress in the relations between Orthodox and Lesser Eastern Churches and the Western confessions.

---

[1] G. Fedotov, "Oxford", *Put*, No. 54, December 1937, p. 61.
[2] See Chap. ix, pp. 431 ff.
[3] *The Second World Conference on Faith and Order*, ed. L. Hodgson, pp. 155 ff.

But it made also more evident than before certain discomforts and disagreements felt by the Orthodox in their participation in ecumenical work. Apart from some important but secondary questions, such as the measure of recognition, if any, to be accorded to non-Orthodox Orders, the main problem was that of the point at which Orthodox participation in the ecumenical movement might best be concentrated. This question provoked a particularly heated discussion among the theologians of the Greek-speaking Churches. There were those among them who felt that the Orthodox should share only in such common Christian efforts as were devoted to the social and political welfare of mankind; to engage in any sort of theological discussion with Protestants could only be frustrating; it would be far better to let Protestants fight out their differences with Protestants, the Orthodox standing by until there was a more united Christian West with which they might enter into relations. Others felt that to follow this policy would mean the loss of a great opportunity; the task of the Orthodox at Faith and Order conferences was indeed no more than to state clearly and uncompromisingly the Orthodox view; but was it not both a great service to the common Christian movement, and a great advantage to the Orthodox, to show themselves as a great united Christian force in such international Christian gatherings? Lastly there were also Greek theologians who advocated yet fuller participation in the ecumenical movement. Believing themselves to be the exponents of the teaching of the undivided Church, they insisted that they had nothing to fear but much to gain by entering into discussions with Western theologians, for they had the responsibility of explaining and propagating the Orthodox tradition. This controversy can be followed year by year in the columns of the Greek ecclesiastical periodicals, especially in *Ekklesia* before and after the second world war.

At Edinburgh 1937, as at later conferences, the Orthodox found themselves subject also to other difficulties of a non-theological kind. In part, they were represented by scholars, who had studied at universities in the West, and were at home both in Western categories of thought and in Western languages: such men as Archbishop Germanos, Archimandrite (later Bishop) Cassian Bezobrazov, Professor S. Bulgakov and Professor N. Arseniev, Dr (later Dean) Georges Florovsky and Professor Alivisatos. But others, including a number of the bishops, were not at home outside the world of traditional Orthodox theology. Unfamiliar with the three main languages of discussion and dependent on translation, they found it almost impossible to follow what was happening, and difficult to make an effective contribution in an assembly in which hardly anyone could understand the language in which they spoke. No one engaged in ecumenical affairs can forget for long the curse of Babel.

A separate page in the relations between the Christian East and the West during the same period was filled by the meetings between Roman Catholic and Orthodox theologians. No official negotiations were conducted between them, and in some parts of the world, such as Greece, Yugoslavia, and Eastern Poland, sharp clashes took place between these two Churches. France, however, provided the opportunity for contacts of another kind. Friendly, informal discussions and even small conferences were held in and near Paris, in which sometimes French Protestants also took part. These meetings did not aim at any formal decision; their sole object was exchange of knowledge and information, but the results achieved were often highly satisfactory. Both sides were stimulated, fresh ideas were introduced, a number of misunderstandings removed, and some personal friendship started. These informal discussions with the Orthodox, especially with the Russians, were fruitful; but their scope was limited, and a general atmosphere of mistrust and even hostility still prevailed in the wider circles of these two Churches, which could not be dispelled by the efforts of a small group of theologians free from the animosity inherited from the past.[1]

Germany was another part of the world in which Eastern and Western Christians encountered one another between the two wars. A wide gap separated the Orthodox and the German Protestants as far as teaching and worship were concerned, but these two communions seldom clashed openly and their relations in the past might be described as tolerance mixed with a sense of the superiority of one's own position. The Orthodox looked down on the German Protestants on account of the poverty of their liturgical life; the latter considered the Eastern Christians lacking in sound scholarship and infected by corrupt practices and traditions. This mutual disdain did not prevent a number of Orthodox theologians from seeking the completion of their studies in German universities, and before the first world war the best students from the Balkan countries were usually sent there to obtain higher academic distinctions.

A new page in the relations between Protestants and Orthodox was opened with the arrival of the refugees from Russia in the early 1920's. Between 1922 and 1926 Berlin was the main centre of their ecclesiastical and cultural life, and many contacts were established there between Russians and Germans. But even when Paris replaced Berlin as the capital of the Russian *diaspora*, the close relations between some German Christians and the Russians were maintained. Professor S. Frank (1877–1951), Professor F. Stepun, and Archimandrite (later Bishop) John (Schakhovskoy) were the best-known spokesmen of the Orthodox Church in Germany. On the Protestant side Dr C. G. Schweitzer and Dr H. Koch were the most active leaders.

Equally important were the relations between Ukrainian Orthodox circles and German Protestants, which culminated in the publication of a valuable book by F. Heyer on the Ukrainian Church.[2] The victory of National Socialism in 1933 loosened many of these links but was not able to break them altogether. A magazine, *Kyrios*, devoted to the study of church life in Eastern Europe, was started in 1936 and until 1943 gathered round it people interested in the Orthodox Churches.

Reunion efforts owed much to the Russian Institute of Orthodox Theology founded in Paris in 1925, the year in which the Nicene celebration took place in England, and the Life and Work Conference met at Stockholm. This centre of Orthodox learning and devotional life was founded in this Western capital by Russians in exile, with the generous help of Western Christians, mostly Anglicans. It became a lively point of Eastern and Western contacts. The professors and students of the college took an active part in all the ecumenical conferences. They were the authors of the majority of the Orthodox contributions to reunion literature.[3] The same professors, assisted by their students, participated in the work of the W.S.C.F. and the Y.M.C.A., and of the Fellowship of S. Alban and S. Sergius. Several important theological encounters took place between the teaching staff of the Institute and Western theologians, such as the

[1] N. Zernov, "From the Secretary's Diary", *Sobornost*, September 1938, p. 43.
[2] *Über die Ucrainische Kirche, 1917–1945.*
[3] L. A. Zander, *List of the Writings of Professors of the Russian Orthodox Theological Institute in Paris (1932–1936)*, Paris, 1936.

Mirfield Conference with Anglicans (1936).[1] A constant stream of Western visitors to the Orthodox Institute, some of whom stayed for lengthy periods, was also an important factor in the development of ecumenical understanding.

Another contribution to this work was made by the concerts in various countries given by the Russian student choir. The choir consisted of the theological students, and was led by a distinguished musician, I. Denisov. In the course of the years 1933 to 1939 the choir visited Switzerland, England, Scotland, Holland, Sweden, Denmark, and Norway, spending usually several weeks in each country. It sang also at the Life and Work Conference at Oxford in 1937, and at the Orthodox Eucharist at the Amsterdam Youth Conference in 1939. The wide extent of these tours, and the large congregations which flocked to hear Orthodox music, made the visits of the Orthodox choir an event in the annals of ecumenical history, for they familiarized Christians who could not easily be reached by books and learned discourses with a tradition different from their own.[2]

The diverse youth organizations which, under the auspices of the W.S.C.F., the Y.M.C.A., the Y.W.C.A., the World Alliance, and similar bodies, brought together the younger generation of Eastern and Western Christians, provided also an important channel of contacts between the Orthodox and the ecumenical movement. These youth movements did most valuable work, for they operated among men and women who were able more easily than the older leaders to appreciate new ideas, and were more ready to co-operate with people of another background and outlook. At first the Western societies made no serious attempt to adapt their work to the spirit of Eastern Christianity, and were therefore the object of criticism by the more conservative section of the Orthodox Churches. Gradually, however, the leaders of these international movements realized that the Christian East had its own contribution to make, and they began not only to teach Eastern Christians, but also to learn from them.

This change of mind was to a large extent due to the work of the Russian Student Christian Movement in exile, which originated among scattered Russian students in Europe. This movement in exile was inaugurated in 1923 after the conference held in Přerov in Czechoslovakia, and from its start it enjoyed close fellowship with the W.S.C.F. and the Y.M.C.A., the two organizations which came to its assistance. The newly-born movement included many convinced members of the Orthodox Church, who made the Eucharist the centre of all their activities, and thus introduced an element which to most youth organizations was new and unfamiliar. It was in part under their influence that the Student Federation altered the basis of its membership at the general committee meeting at Nyborg Strand in 1926. The Y.M.C.A. and Y.W.C.A. also revised their programmes of work in Orthodox countries.[3]

One of the fruits of this collaboration on the basis of equality between the East and West was the convocation in January 1927 of the Anglo-Russian Student Conference at St Albans, England, jointly sponsored by the British and Russian Student Christian Movements. Its distinctive feature was the daily celebration of the Eucharist, which was offered on the same altar, on alternate days, by the Anglicans and the Orthodox. This innovation created such close

[1] *Sobornost*, No. 7, September 1936, p. 42. [2] See Chap. xiii, pp. 632 ff.
[3] See Chap. xiii, pp. 604 ff.; *The Christian East*, Vol. XI, No. 1, p. 31; *Consultation in Bucharest*, Paris, 1933.

bonds among the participants of the Conference that an Anglo-Orthodox Fellowship of S. Alban and S. Sergius was founded at the second Conference, held once more at St Albans in 1928. Bishop Walter Frere, the well-known Anglican liturgiologist, was elected as its first President.

The Fellowship soon became a centre of various ecumenical experiments. Besides its annual general conferences, it organized a number of local conferences, which usually began with an Orthodox Eucharist celebrated in English, with a choir drawn from among Anglicans and Free Churchmen. The service was followed as a rule by papers and discussions introducing the Eastern tradition of Christianity to the members of the local congregation, which had otherwise few opportunities to meet representatives of the Orthodox Churches.

Another of the Fellowship's activities was the organization of short courses of lectures on the Eastern tradition in theological colleges in Great Britain. Both Anglican and Free Church colleges welcomed these courses. Dr Florovsky, Archimandrite Lev Gillet, and Dr N. Zernov did considerable work in this field. The Fellowship was also responsible for the exchange of students and professors, and for the organization of visits of English Christians to Orthodox centres. In 1936 an Anglo-Orthodox Conference was held in Paris.[1] In 1938 a group of English Christians visited the Orthodox Church in Estonia. English theological students went to Rumania; Rumanian, Serbian, Russian, and Bulgarian students stayed for longer or shorter periods in England.

Finally, the Fellowship started to publish a special form of reunion literature, which aimed at comparing the diverse traditions of Christianity and was written by authors who were familiar with both the Eastern and the Western outlook.

Professor Bulgakov, one of the leaders of the Eucharistic movement, deeply stirred the members of the Fellowship in 1932 by his proposal for intercommunion between those Anglican and Orthodox who reached doctrinal agreement, and who were willing to receive a sacramental blessing from the bishops of the other confession as a sign of their repentance and as the means of their incorporation into the life of the reintegrated Church. Although Professor Bulgakov's scheme was not realized, the heated discussion it provoked helped the members of the Fellowship to a deeper grasp of the problems underlying the redintegration of the Church and of the cardinal importance of the Eucharist for Christian reconciliation.[2]

During the World Conferences held in Oxford and Edinburgh in 1937 the absence of Eucharistic worship as an integral part of the programme was keenly felt by a number of participants. A letter advocating its inclusion in the programme of the next gathering was sent to the officers of the ecumenical movement. The initiative was taken by some members of the Fellowship of S. Alban and S. Sergius who had taken part in these two gatherings, and among the signatories there were no less than ten Orthodox and Anglican bishops.[3]

This suggestion found practical application in 1939 when, at the World Conference of Christian Youth in Amsterdam, the Eucharist was celebrated according to the Anglican, Reformed, Lutheran, and Orthodox rites,[4] and thus all the

[1] *Sobornost*, No. 5, March 1936, p. 239.
[2] See *Journal of the Fellowship of S. Alban and S. Sergius*, Nos. 22, 23, 25, 26; *Sobornost*, No. 4, pp. 2, 3, 12, 22 and 23; N. Zernov, *The Reintegration of the Church*, London, 1952, Appendix II; C. Phillips, *W. H. Frere*, 1947, pp. 185 ff.
[3] *Sobornost*, No. 11, September 1937, p. 38.
[4] *Christus Victor, The Report of Amsterdam 1939*, Geneva, 1939, pp. 18 and 59.

delegates had an opportunity to share, spiritually if not sacramentally, in the most sacred act of worship of those Christians who were separated from them.[1]

This contribution to ecumenical work, which arose in part out of the experience gained by the members of the Fellowship of S. Alban and S. Sergius, met with opposition from two different quarters. It was objected to by some Protestants, who desired to have an open Communion at which all members of the Conference could communicate together; it was also criticized by a minority of the Orthodox, who feared that in the circumstances a celebration of the Liturgy might take on the aspect of a theatrical spectacle rather than of a solemn act of Christian worship. Nevertheless, the Eastern clergy who were in favour of the celebration received whole-hearted support from the majority of the Orthodox delegates, more than a hundred in number and including Russians, Serbians, Rumanians, Bulgarians, Finns, Estonians, and Letts. The Orthodox were better represented numerically at Amsterdam in 1939 than at any other ecumenical gathering, and were able to play a more active rôle in it, especially in view of the keen interest in the Church which was so prominently displayed. Almost half the delegates chose "The Church" for their special studies, though six other subjects for discussion were offered to them.

This channel of contacts provided by the youth organizations, in spite of its informal nature, was one of the most fruitful in the period under observation. This was due to its comparative freedom from the political entanglements which so adversely affected the official contacts between the Orthodox Churches and the ecumenical movement. The mentality of the youth leaders also contributed to its success. Most of them had been born and brought up in the 20th century with its new sense of history, and they built their hope for Christian redintegration not on a return to the past, as advocated by the older generation of Orthodox theologians, but on the movement forward. These men and women believed in the possibility of reconciliation, not as the result of theological debate but as a gift from above which Christians can receive when, in humility and obedience to the will of God, they ask for the help and guidance of the Holy Spirit.

The Amsterdam Conference was the last ecumenical gathering before the outbreak of the second world war. The new armed conflict for six years convulsed the body of mankind, and once more radically altered the position of the Eastern Churches, thus affecting the participation of their members in work for Christian reunion.

Before describing the next period in the relations between the Eastern Churches and the West, it may be useful to enumerate briefly the main factors which affected their position in this field between the two world wars.

(a) The Russian Church was able to participate in the work for reunion only through its exiled members. (b) The Patriarchate of Constantinople was greatly hampered by the unfriendly policy of the Turkish Government.[2] (c) The other ancient patriarchates were also seriously handicapped by internal conflicts and the political pressure of the states newly created in their territories. (d) The leading rôle among the Orthodox was, therefore, assumed by the

---

[1] *Sobornost*, No. 18, p. 36; No. 20, p. 36.
[2] It was able, however, to exercise a great and indirect spiritual influence, largely through the outstanding work of its Exarch in the West, the Metropolitan of Thyateira, Dr Germanos (1922–51).

Churches of the Balkans, Rumania, Yugoslavia, Greece, and Bulgaria, and the ecumenical policy of the Orthodox depended to a large extent on their attitude.

Unfortunately, however, even these Churches were far from being well placed for the development of co-operation with the West. The two largest of them, those of Rumania and of Yugoslavia, had to face at first the difficult task of consolidating their newly-achieved national unity. Their members had lived for centuries under different political and ecclesiastical systems, and it was not by any means easy to reconcile diverse habits and tendencies and to prevent rivalries and misunderstandings. Political life in all these countries was also full of tensions, and often disturbed by revolutionary changes and bitter internal struggles. When in the early 1930's a certain stability was at last achieved, a new danger, arising from the aggressive policy pursued by Germany and Italy, told heavily on the Balkan countries. It is impossible to follow the ecclesiastical events in the last years before the outbreak of the second world war without taking into account the close interdependence of religion and politics in those countries. Friendship with the Anglican Communion and participation in the ecumenical movement became associated in the minds of their peoples with pro-Allied policy. Every move in that direction was interpreted as an act of defiance against the Axis powers. Many leaders of these Churches were in favour of the ecumenical movement, but the increasing political difficulties restricted their activities in work for reunion.

As in many Western Churches, ecumenical progress in the East in these years depended largely on the vision and efforts of individuals—some of them holders of high ecclesiastical office, others well-known theologians, some no more than leaders of youth movements. Some of them were able to gather around them a certain following, mostly among the younger generation; but even when interest was aroused it was confined to a small section of the intellectual *élite*, and had nowhere penetrated into the wider circles of Church members. Official support for the ecumenical movement was lukewarm and hesitant, and not one of the Orthodox Churches, as an organized body, gave to it serious consideration or generous financial backing.

3. THE EASTERN CHURCHES AND THE ECUMENICAL MOVEMENT DURING AND AFTER THE SECOND WORLD WAR

The second world war engulfed one after another the Churches of the East, and by June 1941 almost all their territories had been invaded and had become the battlefields of the conflicting Western powers.

As a result of this world-wide upheaval, dramatic changes took place in most of them. These were brought about not only by the reshaping of the frontiers in Eastern Europe but also by the far-reaching political and social changes which affected the life of their peoples. The most significant new factors were:

the re-emergence of the Orthodox Church in Russia, and its appearance as an organized and articulate body on the scene of ecumenical relations;

the setting up of Communist rule in Rumania, Bulgaria, Yugoslavia, Albania, Poland, and Czechoslovakia;

the disappearance of the autonomous Churches of Latvia, Lithuania, and Estonia;

the healing, in 1946, of the schism between the Bulgarians and the Church of Constantinople which dated from 1872;

finally, the coming to the West of a large new contingent of refugees from Eastern and Central Europe, among whom were many Eastern Christians.

The changes, accentuated by the tension between the bloc of Communist-controlled states and the Western nations, deeply affected relations between Eastern and Western Christians, and modified the part played by the Orthodox Churches in the ecumenical movement.

The decisive year of that period was 1948, which witnessed the seventh Lambeth Conference of Anglican bishops, the Consultation of the representatives of the autocephalous Orthodox Churches held in Moscow from 8 to 18 July, and the Assembly in Amsterdam which inaugurated the World Council of Churches.

The Moscow Consultation was convened in connection with the commemoration of 500 years of the autocephalous existence[1] of the Church of Russia, and assembled representatives of all the Orthodox Churches, with the exception of the Patriarchate of Jerusalem and the Churches of Cyprus and Finland. Three Patriarchs, those of Russia, of Rumania, and of Yugoslavia, and the Catholicos of the Georgian Church took personal part in its deliberations.[2] The Conference did not claim the authority of a Council of the Church. It was a meeting of Orthodox leaders, clerical and lay, who wished to arrive at a common policy in regard to a number of urgent problems, mostly connected with their relations with the West. Besides the Orthodox, the representatives of the Armenian Church also participated in the consultations.

The main points discussed in Moscow were the Orthodox attitude to the Vatican, the recognition of Anglican Orders, participation in the ecumenical movement, and the adoption of the Gregorian calendar. The Minutes of the Conference, published in Moscow in 1949,[3] reveal lively discussions and even disagreements among the members of the various commissions among which its members were divided. Nevertheless, all the resolutions when presented for signature were passed unanimously, and thus do not reflect the existence of different opinions among the participants in the Conference.

The decisions taken in Moscow can be described as a halt in the movement of *rapprochement* which began in 1920. The contemporary policy of Rome was condemned as "anti-Christian, anti-democratic, and anti-national".[4] Anglican Orders were not recognized, though revision of this decision was declared possible on condition of the Anglican Churches producing a satisfactory statement of their teaching on the Sacraments.[5] Further participation of the Orthodox in the ecumenical movement was discouraged on the grounds of its departure from the search for dogmatic unity and its concentration on social and political questions. The resolution embodying this decision contained the following arguments:

[1] It is to be noted that the autocephalous status of the Church of Moscow was formally accepted by four Eastern patriarchates only in 1598.

[2] Representatives of the Churches of Constantinople and of Greece were present at the celebrations, but abstained from participating in the work of the Conference.

[3] *The Acts of the Consultation of the Heads and Representatives of the Autocephalous Orthodox Churches*, 2 vols., Moscow, 1949 (in Russian).

[4] *The Acts of the Consultation*, etc., II, p. 429 (p. 443, Fr. tr.).

[5] Ibid., p. 431 (p. 446, Fr. tr.); and see Chap. x, pp. 488 f.

"The direction of the efforts of the ecumenical movement into the channels of social and political life, and towards the creation of an 'Ecumenical Church' as an influential international force, appears to us to be a falling into the temptation rejected by Christ in the wilderness. For the Church to accept it would involve departure from its own true path through attempting to catch souls for Christ by using non-Christian means.

"During the last ten years (1937–48) the question of the reunion of the Churches on a basis of dogma and doctrine has no longer been discussed.[1] This has been put back to a secondary and educational rôle, directed to the use of future generations. This being so, the contemporary ecumenical movement no longer attempts to secure the reunion of the Churches by spiritual ways and means."

It was on the strength of these conclusions that the Moscow Consultation decided to refrain from participation in the ecumenical movement as at present constituted.[2] These decisions prevented the majority of the Orthodox Churches from sending delegates to Amsterdam in 1948. The Greek-speaking Churches, the Orthodox in the United States, and the Russian Exarchate in Western Europe under the jurisdiction of the Ecumenical Patriarch, were however represented at the Assembly and welcomed the formation of the World Council of Churches. At Amsterdam there were altogether only forty representatives of the Orthodox and Lesser Eastern Churches, a small minority among the 589 official participants in this gathering. Of these forty, twenty were regularly appointed delegates; the rest were either "observers" or youth delegates, or members of the staff.

The Orthodox, in spite of their small numbers, were active in all the discussions, and the Orthodox Eucharist was celebrated during the Assembly, following the example of the two ecumenical Youth Conferences held at Amsterdam in 1939 and at Oslo in 1947.

Such were the mixed results of 1948. Its ecclesiastical conferences broke some of the links forged in the previous period, but strengthened some others. They also made it clear that many obstacles still stood in the way of fruitful co-operation between Eastern and Western Christians; the same year, however, revealed the determination of at least a minority of the Orthodox to continue their active part in the ecumenical movement and to contribute to its further development.

This desire was most clearly manifested among those Eastern Christians who were not official spokesmen of their Churches and therefore remained uninvolved in the political tensions in which the second world war had plunged the main body of the Orthodox. Among such agencies an important rôle was played by the various missionary and youth organizations in Greece, which developed manifold activities in their own country, and showed a keen interest

---

[1] It is significant that whilst a number of the Greek theologians welcome the idea of co-operation with the ecumenical movement on the basis of joint action in the field of practical Christianity and are reluctant to embark on doctrinal discussions, the Moscow Conference took the opposite view, and considered that doctrinal differences must be solved first and that practical collaboration has to follow the accomplishment of this most important task.

[2] *The Acts of the Consultation*, etc., II, pp. 435 f. (pp. 451 f., Fr. tr.). It is to be noted that these decisions are considered by the leaders of the World Council of Churches to have been based on very imperfect acquaintance with ecumenical documents, and wholly to misrepresent and misinterpret the history of the ecumenical movement in the period under discussion.

in the ecumenical movement. The miraculous survival of the Greek people after the calamities of foreign invasions followed by civil war gave to its Christian leaders a sense of universal mission, which was expressed in several manifestos and publications addressed to the Christians of the West.[1]

This movement, which compensated to some extent for the extinction of Christian youth work in other Balkan countries, was paralleled by an unexpected revival of spiritual activities among the Orthodox Arabs in Lebanon and Syria, who also had become interested in the ecumenical movement and sent their delegates, together with those of the Russians in exile and the Greeks, to the Oslo Conference in 1947 and to Amsterdam in 1948.

The impact of the second world war and its political repercussions also profoundly affected the position of the religious minorities in Egypt. In December 1944 the Committee of Liaison between the non-Moslem communities in Egypt was set up, and included Orthodox, Copts, Anglicans, Roman Catholics, Uniates, various Protestants, and even Jews. Its main purpose was to defend the legal rights of the minorities against the rising tide of Islamic nationalism, but the appointed representatives of all these Churches learned gradually to trust one another and began to co-operate in such matters as a joint campaign against illiteracy and aid to the blind.[2]

The Ecumenical Institute at Bossey, founded by the World Council of Churches in 1946, became a fruitful meeting-ground for the leaders of Eastern and Western Christendom. A similar function was performed by St Basil's House, founded in London in 1944 by the members of the Fellowship of S. Alban and S. Sergius. This centre of ecumenical work has a unique chapel containing both Orthodox and Anglican altars, at which the Eucharist is celebrated and prayers are offered for the reunion of Christendom. The summer camps of the Fellowship, held yearly in England from 1940 onwards, were also an expression of Orthodox participation in reunion work. They usually gathered some two or three hundred people of various nationalities and traditions, and were centred in the Eucharist celebrated on alternate days according to the Orthodox and Anglican rites.

The ecumenical movement found a new field of activity also among displaced persons, many of whom had been brought up in Communist schools. Some of these young people were not only converted to Christianity but even became interested in work for reunion. The generous help offered by the World Council to those people who were stranded in devastated Europe far from their homes forged new and powerful links between the Orthodox and Western Christians. The same sentiments of trust and gratitude were fostered by the assistance which Greek Christians received from the West in the reconstruction of their Church life. The great movements of population occasioned by the war caused suffering and privations to many millions, but they also provided opportunities for contacts, and taught Christians that in spite of their divisions they share the same life and faith. This discovery of the reality of Christian unity was the unexpected fruit of a disastrous war.

This last period in the history of the relations between the Eastern Christians and the ecumenical movement is still in the process of its making; in ending this short survey it may be permissible to express the hope that East and West alike

---

[1] E.g. *Towards a Christian Civilization*, Athens, 1950.

[2] See S. A. Morrison, "The Churches of the Near East and the World Council of Churches" *Ecumenical Review*, Vol. I, 1949, p. 277.

may build on the foundations laid in the years between the two world wars, and that closer co-operation and greater friendship between Eastern and Western Christians may develop with ever-increasing momentum.

4. THE SCOPE AND SIGNIFICANCE OF EASTERN PARTICIPATION IN THE ECUMENICAL MOVEMENT

A survey of the period between 1910 and 1948 indicates that the Eastern Christians' participation in ecumenical work should be treated as a preliminary and experimental stage of their partnership. Throughout these years the majority of Eastern Christians were passing through difficult times of far-reaching social and political reconstruction. These troubles cut them off from the rest of the world and made it impossible for them to take a full share in the movement for reconciliation. These unfavourable conditions did not affect only those Eastern Churches which were subjected to Communist rule. Even those among them which formed new reunited national Churches in the Balkans were, as we have seen, at the mercy of manifold political tensions, and were constantly disturbed by the intervention of political agencies. Paradoxically, the only section of the Eastern community which was free from any external pressure was that of the exiled Russian Christians who, deprived of political prestige and material resources, having lost their right to speak officially in the name of their Church, recovered their inner freedom and were able to decide on their policy in regard to the Christian West unaffected by State interference.

Orthodox co-operation with the ecumenical movement, in spite of its tentative character, has left a distinctive mark on the constitution of the World Council of Churches, and had also important repercussions within the communities of Eastern Christians. The study of this period is instructive, as providing valuable material for the better understanding of the whole problem of Christian reunion and of the rôle which the Orthodox are likely to play in it in the future.

One of the facts emerging from this survey is the great variety of opinions among Eastern Christians in regard to co-operation with the West. The existence of several schools of thought on this subject is due not only to the divergence between those who favour and those who are opposed to it, but also to the diverse motives, religious, political, and even personal, which influence those who take negative or positive attitudes in this matter. Detailed analysis of these conflicting tendencies cannot be undertaken in this chapter, and only their broad outlines are traced here.

Let us start with the arguments used by those Orthodox who oppose the ecumenical movement. These can be grouped under three main headings: political; moral; and doctrinal.

Political. The history of the Eastern Churches has always been closely linked with the destiny of their nations and states, and the majority of their members find it hard to draw a line between the religious and national communities to which they belong. It is equally difficult for them to visualize any Western ecclesiastical body independent of the interests of one or another of the Great Powers. Bitter and long experience has taught Eastern Christians, especially in the Near East, to look upon Roman Catholics as agents of France, upon Anglicans as spokesmen of Great Britain, upon Protestants as emissaries of Germany and, more recently, of the United States. It is only natural, therefore, that when representatives of the ecumenical movement approached the Eastern Churches, the latter identified them with the supposed imperialistic schemes of the Anglo-Saxon democracies, and welcomed or refused co-operation with them according to their own political sympathies.

Moral. Eastern Christians have for many centuries been exposed to the hostile attacks of the West. The zealous propagandists of various Western creeds spared no efforts in their proselytizing campaigns and thus broke the unity of Eastern homes, created aggressive minorities, and fostered anti-national feelings among Oriental Christians. This unfortunate experience accustomed the latter to look upon the Western emissaries with deep suspicion, not easily dispelled even by the assurance of friendship and of disinterested service. It was inevitable, therefore, that the activities of such organizations as the Y.M.C.A., the Y.W.C.A., and the W.S.C.F. should be disapproved of by a section of the Eastern Churches which treated them as movements aimed at undermining the allegiance of youth to their Church and nation. The fact that these international bodies publicly denied any intention of proselytism, and conducted their work in the spirit of respect for Eastern traditions, only increased the apprehensions of conservative-minded Christians who suspected some particularly sinister and secret designs behind the friendliness displayed by the Western leaders of the movements. Many of these critics insisted that the Y.M.C.A. was a branch of Freemasonry, and as such bent on working for the destruction of the Church and of her faith in the Incarnation. Those Eastern Christians who joined these organizations were regarded either as dupes, unable to understand the real designs of their masters, or as paid agents who sold themselves to the enemies of their own tradition.

This incrimination of the supporters of work for Christian reunion is most difficult to refute, for it is based not on facts but on anticipation of events yet to come.[1] Their unproved character makes them not less but often even more dangerous. These views received ecclesiastical confirmation at the Church Council of the Karlovtsy section of the Russian Church in exile, held in Yugoslavia in June 1926. The Y.M.C.A. and the Y.W.C.A. were condemned as organizations led by Freemasons and subversive of the Orthodox Church.[2]

Doctrinal. Apart from political and moral objections, some Eastern Christians based their opposition to the ecumenical movement on doctrinal grounds. They criticized it for its refusal to accept as revealed truth the teaching of the Church of the first eight centuries and to build all its activities on this traditional foundation. The representatives of this school of thought accuse the leaders of the movement of opportunism, and believe that their aim is to dispense with doctrine altogether and thus incorporate into a loose federation all the existing confessions, including the most extravagant heretical sects. These Eastern Christians consider any discussion of doctrine within the framework of the ecumenical movement as not merely unprofitable, but positively dangerous, for they fear that it can lead only to the undermining of the authority of the Orthodox Church and of the revealed truth entrusted to it for safe keeping.

A closer examination of the position taken by some critics reveals, however, that their objections are not exclusively doctrinal, for they arise also out of the

---

[1] A. Schleglov, *Beware of the Wolves in Sheep's Clothing*, Paris, 1928.
[2] *Vestnik* of the Russian Student Movement, No. 9, August 1926, pp. 11 ff. The Synod of the Bulgarian Church supported the same view in its publication entitled *The Truth about the Christian Youth Movement*, Sofia, 1926.

conviction that the possession of the fullness of Christian truth is a prerogative of some specially chosen Eastern nations, and that all the Western peoples, by their very origin, are likely to remain in heresy and cannot be delivered from this affliction. This deeply-rooted prejudice against the West is seldom formulated in words, but exercises a powerful control over the thought, feelings, and actions of many Eastern Christians, who believe that by resisting all efforts towards reconciliation they are manifesting an uncompromising loyalty to the true Church and faithful adherence to its orthodoxy in worship and teaching.

Such are the main arguments against the ecumenical movement as voiced by individuals and groups among Eastern Christians. No less diverse are the reasons for a positive attitude towards it. These can be classified also as: personal; national; and doctrinal.

Personal. Many Eastern Christians are greatly attracted to Western culture, manners, and outlook. They are fascinated by the Western way of life and thought, and some of them, as the result of this, become converts to Roman or Protestant forms of the Christian faith. Others, however, find an outlet for the same feelings in participation in the ecumenical movement, which offers them an opportunity of visiting Western countries and brings them into close contact with the leading personalities of Western Christendom. These Eastern enthusiasts for ecumenism often and rightly acquire a high reputation among their Western friends; the danger in their position is that so close an identification with the West may undermine the confidence with which they are regarded in the East, and so render them less effective ambassadors of the ecumenical movement to the Eastern Churches than they might otherwise be.

National. Some Eastern hierarchs take interest in the ecumenical movement because they hope to find in it help for their national aspirations. They consider their Western contacts as useful means for voicing their grievances and for securing the redress of the injustices done to their people. Such Christians have usually been more interested in the work of the World Alliance than in the Faith and Order movement, and they are more concerned with political and social questions than with the doctrine and liturgy of the Church. The same tendency exists also among those Orthodox who are convinced of the need of a more active social policy for Eastern Churches in their own countries, and for this reason are keen supporters of closer co-operation with Western Christians who are more experienced in this field.

Doctrinal. Equally divided are Eastern supporters of the ecumenical movement who favour it on doctrinal grounds. Some of them do so because they believe in the universal mission of Orthodoxy and wish to propagate it among Western peoples; others because they are conscious of limitations in the present-day life of their Church, including a certain doctrinal sterility in its theology, and hope to find help and inspiration in the West. There are also those among them who see the whole of Christendom as a victim of the hostility, suspicion, and misunderstandings of its divided members, and who consider that the sacred duty of each Christian is to work and pray for the redintegration of the Church.

The diverse motives which attract some Eastern Christians to the work of reconciliation, and the varied arguments used by those who abstain from it, the contradictory statements made from time to time by their leaders in regard to Christian reunion—all these factors raise the general question of the doctrinal position occupied by the Orthodox in this vital field.

It is important to bear in mind that Eastern Christians believe firmly that there can be only one Holy, Catholic, and Apostolic Church on earth, and that the Orthodox Churches of the East together are its authentic representatives. This conviction, often emphatically expressed, creates the impression that Orthodox theologians are even more exclusive than Roman Catholic, for they refuse even to treat as Christians those who are not within the fold of what they believe to be the one true Church of Christ.

The question arises as to where Eastern theologians trace the limits of the Church, and whether those who are not in communion with one of the autocephalous Churches of the East are, according to this judgement, outside or within the realm of grace.

The easiest solution of this thorny problem would be to treat the Western Christians as outsiders who only delude themselves by claiming to possess the sacraments and to have a share in the redeeming life of the Christian community. Some Orthodox theologians accept this logical conclusion, and a well-known bishop of the Russian Church, the Metropolitan Anthony Khrapovitski (1865–1936) inserted into his Catechism the following question and answer:

Q. Is it possible to admit that a split within the Church or among the Churches could ever take place?

A. Never. Heretics and schismatics have from time to time fallen away from the one indivisible Church, and, by so doing, they ceased to be members of the Church, but the Church itself can never lose its unity according to Christ's promise.[1]

This categorical statement creates an unbridgeable gulf separating those who belong to the Church from those who are outside it. It admits of no compromise or gradual transition from one state to another, and makes meaningless any participation of the Orthodox in the World Council of Churches.

It stands, however, in open contradiction with equally authoritative pronouncements and actions of other Orthodox leaders, which imply a recognition of a bond of unity between them and the separated Christians of the West. So, for instance, Alexis the Patriarch of Russia, in his opening speech at the Moscow Consultation in July 1948, called the Roman Catholic Church "the Sister Church".[2] One could multiply indefinitely quotations from the writings of Orthodox authors which either support the Metropolitan Anthony's view, or are sharply opposed to it, or try to take a middle course by explaining away the practical difficulties involved in his statements, and by accepting the fact that the word "heretic" or "schismatic" can be applied only to those who are in the orbit of the Church, for Buddhists and heathen are neither in heresy nor in schism.

Acquaintance with controversial literature on this subject proves beyond any doubt that Orthodox theologians have not yet arrived at any common mind in regard to the position of those Christians who are not in communion with their Church. It is essential to remember this, for sometimes the opinion of one school of thought among them is presented and accepted as the authoritative pronouncement of the whole Orthodox Church.

But, if Eastern theologians are still disputing among themselves on this important issue, the general behaviour of the Orthodox in regard to separated

[1] *Sremski Karlovci*, 1924, p. 58.   [2] *The Acts of the Consultation*, etc., I, p. 90.

Christians follows a distinct line which adheres faithfully to the practice of the undivided Church. According to this, Christians who have left the communion of the one Church are treated in various ways, for their alienation is not of the same degree of gravity. Some of these dissenters, if they desire to be reconciled, are received simply through the sacrament of penance; others are chrismated (confirmed), and if clergy, re-ordained; others are baptized. These diverse ways of incorporation indicate that the Orthodox Church tacitly recognizes some separated Christians as having a share in all the sacraments of the Church, others only in some of these sacraments (for usually these Christians themselves have repudiated the fullness and variety of the sacramental life, reducing it to a bare minimum), and finally the same Orthodox Church treats as outsiders some of those who call themselves Christians. These last are received through the sacraments of initiation—baptism and chrismation.

Orthodox theologians are still in search of doctrinal formulas which will solve the contradiction between the belief in one Catholic Church and the existence of schisms, heresies, and animosity among its members;[1] but the fact of their Church's recognition of some schismatic sacraments is a clear indication that the sacramental limits of the Church do not coincide with its canonical boundaries, and that therefore the work of reconciliation among those who are baptized in the Name of the Holy Trinity and who believe in the Incarnation is real and urgent, and that participation of Eastern Christians in the ecumenical movement is consonant with the true tradition of their Church.

The variety of reasons which bring Eastern Christians within the fold of the ecumenical movement explains the rifts and tensions which were manifested at most of the ecumenical gatherings. Yet in spite of these drawbacks, the rôle of the Orthodox in the development of the ecumenical movement was considerable and at times even decisive. The Orthodox were able to strengthen the desire of this new movement to find a firm foundation in sound doctrine, and they presented a view which could often reconcile the extreme wings of the Western interpretations of Christianity. They were also able to help towards satisfactory conclusions of theological debates by approaching controversial points from an angle unfamiliar to the Western spokesmen and yet consonant with the great traditions of the Church. Their presence made the ecumenical movement genuinely catholic in its scope and spirit and helped to guard against the danger of its becoming a merely pan-Protestant organization. Their chief contribution, however, was in those spheres of Christian life and worship where the Protestant West had been in the past particularly suspicious of the East; for example, in the emphasis on the Eucharist, and on veneration of the saints, and in insistence on the necessity of recognizing the significance of the Blessed Virgin Mary in the work of reconciliation. The creation of special sub-committees on the question of the veneration of the saints at Edinburgh in 1937, and support for the inclusion of the Eucharist in the programme of the conferences, were valuable gifts brought by the Orthodox into this movement for redintegration. The very opposition which they provoked and are still provoking is an indication that

[1] See *Christian Reunion* (the Ecumenical Problem and the Orthodox Church), a collection of essays written by leading theologians of the Orthodox Church, Paris, 1933, p. 156; L. A. Zander, *Vision and Action*, London, 1952, p. 224; Nicolas Zernov, *The Reintegration of the Church*, London, 1952, p. 128; S. Bulgakov, "By Jacob's Well" (John 4.23), a challenging article on the actual unity of the divided Church in faith, prayer, and sacrament, in *The Journal of the Fellowship of S. Alban and S. Sergius*, No. 22, December 1933.

they have something to give which may supplement the life of the Protestant communities at the very points where they are weakest.

But the benefit of the participation of Eastern Christians in the ecumenical movement was far from being one-sided. Eastern Christians were stimulated and enriched by these contacts. Their theologians embarked on the study of the doctrine of the Church, a subject treated almost exclusively in an arid and controversial spirit by earlier doctors of the Orthodox Church. The pastoral activities of Eastern Christians, especially in the field of youth and student work, received a powerful impetus from contact with the ecumenical movement. Eastern Christians met not only the West but also each other through the same channel, and learned both the essential unity of their experience and the existence of considerable differences among themselves, often inadequately realized by them in the past.

Finally, the ecumenical movement has revived among them the sense of their catholic vocation, obscured at times by preoccupation with their national problems and by rivalry with their neighbours. Leaders of the Eastern Churches were strengthened in their pastoral work and in their theological thinking as the result of meeting the Christian West, as a friend and not as a foe, within the framework of the World Council of Churches.

5. CONCLUSION

The life of mankind is centred in the Incarnation. The rejection or acceptance of this cardinal event constitutes the main theme of history. The Christian East and West have always had two distinct and yet complementary approaches to the Incarnation, for they have conceived the relation between matter and spirit and between an individual and a community in terms peculiar to themselves. It is only in their harmonious co-operation that a balanced presentation of Christianity can be secured.

The present political and social crisis is caused by persistent attempts to reject the truth of the Incarnation and to build the social and political order on the basis of such a denial. As at the time of the Islamic onslaught on Christianity, the members of the Eastern Churches find themselves to-day in the front line of the struggle, and thus they shield the Christian West from the full weight of this new attack. Divided Christendom in the past was not able to secure the moral victory over Islam, and compromised its position by the disastrous appeal to force. It will be fatal if the same mistake is committed again, for only the red-integrated Church can bring back into its fold the adherents of the new social and economic creeds, and convert to Christianity those non-European nations which, having become part of Western technical civilization, still reject faith in the God-Man Jesus Christ.

The future of mankind depends on the restoration of Christian unity, and the reconciliation of Eastern and Western Christians is the pivot on which the success of this task depends.[1] The ecumenical movement has made possible their friendly encounter, and this is one of its most important achievements. The goal of reconciliation still appears remote, but the gift of unity is in God's keeping, and it can be received by those who ask for it with faith and love and are prepared to do all in their power for the restoration of oneness among the followers of Christ.

[1] N. Zernov, "The Reintegration of the Christian Community and the Ecumenical Movement", *Pro Regno—Pro Sanctuario*, Nijkerk, Holland, 1950, p. 541.

CHAPTER 15

THE ROMAN CATHOLIC CHURCH AND THE ECUMENICAL MOVEMENT 1910–1948

by

OLIVER STRATFORD TOMKINS

1. GENERAL PRINCIPLES

The relationship of the Roman Catholic Church to all other Christians is regulated by the belief that it alone is the One, Holy, Catholic, and Apostolic Church founded by Jesus Christ and witnessed to in the Creeds. For centuries there was little attempt by theologians to define the nature of the Church, since its character was assumed rather than debated. The division between East and West, and the later divisions in the West which followed the Reformation, have led to various statements of the distinctively Roman Catholic position.

The most recent authoritative statements are the Encyclicals of Pope Pius XII, *Mystici Corporis Christi* (1943), and *Humani Generis* (1950), in which the central teaching is reaffirmed. Both contain an exposition of the Roman Catholic interpretation of the doctrine of the Mystical Body, to which the Pope was moved by the perils and stresses of the times. The former Encyclical speaks of the "true Church of Christ—which is the Holy, Catholic, Apostolic, Roman Church" (§ 13) of which "only those are to be accounted really members . . . who have been regenerated in the waters of Baptism and profess the true faith, and have not cut themselves off from the structure of the Body by their own unhappy act or been severed therefrom, for very grave crimes, by the legitimate authority" (§ 21). "Schism, heresy or apostasy are such of their very nature that they sever a man from the Body of the Church" (§ 22). The necessity of the papal supremacy for the true life cf the Church lies in that "Christ, the Head of the Body", rules the Church not only by "invisible and extraordinary government" but also by "visible and ordinary government, in the Universal Church through the Roman Pontiff". Christ is the principal Head of the Church, but rules the Church on earth through his Vicar, and if this visible Head is eliminated "and the visible bonds of unity broken, the mystical Body of the Redeemer is so obscured and disfigured that it becomes impossible for those who are seeking the harbour of eternal salvation to see or discover it" (§ 39).

Within this clear doctrine of the identity of the Church with the Roman Communion there are some important qualifications governing the status of "separated brethren".

It is generally taught that baptism with water in the Triune Name and with a true intention makes the baptized, in some sense, a member of the Church. There remains a vital distinction between those whose baptism is and those whose baptism is not followed by adherence to the Roman Communion. If "conditional baptism" is often administered to those who enter the Roman Communion after baptism in other communions, the fact of its being "conditional" implies that the first may have been valid; for the validity of heretical baptism, properly administered, has been accepted in the Catholic West at least since the 4th century. For example, the Encyclical *Sempiternus Rex* (September 1951, addressed primarily to the Monophysite Churches to mark the fifteenth centenary of the Council of Chalcedon) contains the phrase "all those specially marked by baptism . . . cannot continue to remain divided and separated". But the distinction remains between those who live after baptism in the Roman Church and those who do not. One writer distinguishes, in the case of a Protestant child having received valid baptism, between "the baptismal character, sanctifying grace, infused faith and charity", giving an "interior disposition" towards the full flowering of Christian life in the Church, and the "objective Christian milieu which is impoverished and distorted, a confessional or ecclesiastical order which is not the full and true life of the Church of Christ".[1] The attempt to define the distinction by suggesting that Roman Catholics belong to the body of the Church, whilst other validly baptized Christians belong only to its soul, though sometimes found, is not encouraged by modern Roman Catholic theologians, since it easily gives rise to misunderstandings and a false division.

Further, the position of the unbaptized is qualified by the doctrine of "the baptism of desire", whereby in certain circumstances some of the effects of baptism may be achieved without the rite.

It follows that, where such baptism is effected, the recipients do not come under the condemnation entailed in the principle "outside the Church no salvation". They are in some real sense within the Church. Any man may be saved who persistently submits himself to the working out, through loving obedience to God, of that grace which is already his by baptism. Even those who have never been baptized, and yet live and die faithful to the God they know, may be saved if their misconceptions about baptism and the nature of the Church were due to their "invincible ignorance".

These exceptions, though they amplify the teaching of the Roman Catholic Church as to who may be saved, in no way modify the doctrine that that Church alone is the true Church and that all Church unity depends upon the recognition of its claim to be such. This recognition might be either by individual adhesion or by the corporate reconciliation of whole groups or "Churches". The latter is best considered separately, since a widespread and long-established tradition of dealing with the Eastern Churches makes the principles clear.

2. THE ATTITUDE OF ROME TOWARDS THE EASTERN CHURCHES

Rome does not regard the Orthodox Churches as being heretical. It is not that the doctrinal differences between East and West are treated lightly, but in so far as they have not been the object of a fully authoritative definition from the Orthodox side, they are generally considered as not having a properly dogmatic value. Because of the validity of their sacraments and of their hierarchy, the Orthodox Churches are even sometimes referred to in Roman Catholic writings as "Churches",[2] but they are looked upon as dissident Churches of the Byzantine rite. The main issue at stake between them is the recognition of the Bishop of Rome as Supreme Pontiff.

For there are other Churches, also "of the Byzantine rite", which are in full communion with the papacy, acknowledged parts of the Roman Catholic Church, though retaining their own Eastern liturgical traditions and indeed such other Eastern traditions as a married priesthood. "Churches of the Byzantine rite" are those stemming from the traditions of Orthodoxy continued by the Ecumenical Patriarchate of Constantinople (Byzantium) and the autocephalous Churches in communion with it. "The Catholic Church" is not, in Roman teaching, confined to Latin Christendom. The Bishop of Rome claims jurisdiction not only

---

[1] M. J. Congar, *Divided Christendom*, London, 1939 (Eng. tr. of *Chrétiens désunis*), pp. 230–33 and note on p. 230.

[2] See Appendix IV of Congar's *Divided Christendom*, pp. 294–5, for instances in papal utterances.

over all Latin Christians as Patriarch of the West, but also over all Eastern Christians as Supreme Pontiff.

Scattered throughout the East are other Churches which are not technically Orthodox and are generally referred to as the Lesser Eastern Churches. They not merely repudiate the claim of the Bishop of Rome to be head and father of all Christians in the world, but cling to doctrines which, since the 5th century, have been declared by the rest of Christendom to be heretical. All over the East missionaries of the Roman Catholic Church are at work with sedulous devotion to win the Christians of these Churches away from their ancient allegiance; when they are successful, such Christians both accept the supreme headship of the Pope and give up the "heresies" to which they were attached.[1] Such "Uniate" Christians become in the fullest sense "Roman Catholics", but they do not become *Latins*; in many respects the traditions and customs of the ancient Eastern Churches have been preserved by them.

None of the Orthodox or Lesser Eastern Churches admits the claim of the Bishop of Rome, the Patriarch of the West, to have any standing or jurisdiction in the ancient patriarchates of the East. The attempt to assert this claim has led to serious ill-feeling and sometimes to extreme bitterness and violence. The feeling of these Churches against "Uniates" is much stronger than against Latin Catholics dwelling in their midst.

Nevertheless, the principle involved is of central importance for an understanding of the Roman Catholic conception of Church unity. It implies far less liturgical uniformity than is usually supposed, though, of course, no concessions are made regarding *dogmatic* uniformity. Many Roman Catholic writers on union with Eastern Christians lay great stress upon the capacity of the papacy to embrace a wide range of rite, practice, and tradition wholly strange to the Latin West.

Dr Adrian Fortescue collected a catena of papal pronouncements and documents from the Fourth Lateran Council (1215) to the time of Pius XI[2] to show the concern of the papacy to safeguard Eastern rites whilst seeking to establish its universal rule over all Christians. The Pontifical Greek College at Rome was founded by Gregory XIII as early as 1577. With Benedict XIV (1740–58) began a steady and consistent policy "to make it clear to the Church that to be a Catholic does not mean to be a member of the Roman rite".[3] Leo XIII founded colleges for Oriental Catholic students (1886, the Armenian College in Rome; 1896, the Melkite College in Jerusalem; 1897, the Catholic Coptic College in Cairo). In 1917 Benedict XV founded the Oriental Institute in Rome, reorganized in 1928 as part of the Gregorian University by Pius XI, who also founded the "Russicum" in 1929. As against some 370 million Latin Catholics, some ten million use Eastern rites—a small proportion of the whole, but they illustrate an important principle. Roman Catholic missionary writers often suggest that the same principle is being increasingly adapted to the development of Asian and African missionary dioceses, hitherto somewhat rigorously based

[1] The following "Catholic Eastern Churches", each with its own traditional rite and customs, have come into existence at various periods: the Armenian Catholic, Chaldean, Maronite, Melkite, Ruthenian, and Syrian (all in Eastern Europe, the Near East, or Asia Minor), Coptic (in Egypt), and Syro-Malabar and Syro-Malankara (in South India). These Oriental Rites are organized under six patriarchal and fifteen other sees, and directed under the Pope through the Sacred Congregation for the Eastern Church.

[2] Adrian Fortescue, *The Uniate Eastern Churches*, 1923.

[3] See Dom Bede Winslow, "Byzantine Catholics", *Eastern Churches Quarterly*, Vol. 5, No. 11.

{upon Latin traditions. But its operation seems to be chiefly in such spheres as indigenous art, as a legitimate expression of Roman Catholic dogma. No modification has been made, for instance, in the rule that Latin is the sole liturgical language of the missionary dioceses.

It is significant that with this developing papal policy has gone a developing papal attitude of spirit. Pius IX spoke only of the valid title, of the doctrinal and canonical rectitude, of the Catholic Church; Leo XIII added to these claims the duty of Roman Catholics to "know well" the separated Eastern Churches and hence to study them. Later Popes, especially Benedict XV and Pius XI, have given greater recognition to the need of taking into account the psychological elements involved and of rectifying, with much delicacy, the relationship between Latin Catholics and their separated Eastern brethren.

Although the final goal remains as clearly defined as ever, the approaches to it are various; the flexibility and variety within the Roman obedience mean that reunion with Rome is not necessarily to be conceived in terms so rigid and so uniform as are often supposed. A corporate reconciliation of the Church of England, with a right to maintain some of its own distinctive traditions, was in some minds at the time of the Malines Conversations.[1] That proposal did not meet with a favourable reception at the Vatican; it is, however, still possible, at least in theory, that such an approach might be made to a Church at present outside the Roman obedience but possessing valid orders as defined by Rome. Such a reconciliation would still involve an acceptance of the Catholic faith as held by all those who are in communion with the successors of Peter. In all matters of dogma, whatever the ritual or canonical variations, the Papal See claims final authority.

3. ROME AND THE ECUMENICAL MOVEMENT

Thus far we have been concerned with the relation of Rome to other Churches severally. Now we are to consider the relation of Rome to a different phenomenon—that whole complex of relationships between the non-Roman Churches known as the ecumenical movement. In this case, the attitude of Rome has been based partly upon the general principles, already noted, governing relations with non-Roman Christians at all times, partly upon a gradual formulation of attitude to what Rome increasingly recognizes as a new and important development within the field of non-Roman Christianity. This twofold response is best revealed by examining the attitude of Rome at successive stages of the history of the ecumenical movement, before attempting to summarize the present position.

Among the organizers of the Edinburgh Missionary Conference 1910 were some who would have been glad to see the Roman Catholic and Orthodox Churches represented at it. In fact only Anglican and Protestant missionary boards were invited to send representatives. But among the letters read to the Conference was one from Mgr Bonomelli, Bishop of Cremona, a personal friend of one of the leading American Episcopal delegates, Silas McBee. It is a cordial letter, applauding the idea of the Conference and asserting the need for spreading Christianity as the universal religion. The Bishop acknowledges an existing

[1] See Chap. vi, pp. 298 f., and documents 149 and 150 in Bell's *Documents*, III, pp. 21–33.

unity "great enough to warrant continuing further discussion, tending to promote the union of all believers in Christ".[1]

While the first world war was still in progress, various attempts were made by Christian leaders, especially in the neutral countries, to bring together representatives of the belligerent countries and to work for peace. In the course of these efforts, contacts had been made with individual Roman Catholics. It appears that the first direct approach to the Pope was made in a Latin letter dispatched by the three northern Primates (Seeland, Christiania, and Uppsala) on 11 March 1918, informing him of the proposal to hold a conference at Uppsala on 8 September of that year, and inviting him to send representatives to it. On 19 June 1918 Cardinal Gasparri, as Cardinal Secretary of State, dispatched a friendly and courteous reply to this letter, in which it was affirmed that such efforts as were being made by "these illustrious men" were pleasing and desirable in the eyes of the August Pontiff, especially as preparing the way to the fulfilment of the prayer contained in the words of the Gospel "that there may be one fold and one shepherd", but nothing was said as to representation of the Pope at the proposed conference.[2]

Other attempts to hold an "Ecumenical Conference" of Christians to bring Christian principles to bear upon the life of the nations were converging upon what eventually took shape as the Life and Work Conference in Stockholm in 1925. The Encyclical Letter of the Ecumenical Patriarchate in 1920, calling for a League of Christian Communions, encouraged hopes that such an event need not be purely Protestant in its range. The Universal Christian Conference on Life and Work, to which all Christian Churches were to be invited, was agreed upon at a special Conference at Geneva in August 1920; but the International Committee appointed to arrange it reported at its 1922 meeting "that steps had been taken by the Bishops of Seeland and Christiania and Uppsala, on their own responsibility, to ascertain the attitude of [the Roman Catholic] Church toward co-operation with the Conference, and that the answers received do not warrant further action. Documents and statements presented by others confirmed this judgment. No further action was deemed necessary".[3]

Parallel developments in the field of Faith and Order produced similar results. In his detailed introduction to the German edition of the Lausanne Conference Report, Professor Hermann Sasse has recorded the action taken in relation to Rome.[4] He gives the text of the Latin correspondence exchanged between Robert Gardiner and Cardinal Gasparri.[5] At that time the American promoters of the Conference had every confidence that the Roman Catholic Church would take part. This confidence had been encouraged by the participation of American Roman Catholic theologians in the committee for the theological preparation of the Conference.[6] In the spring and summer of 1919 a delegation from the Protestant Episcopal Church in the U.S.A., one of several paving the way for the preparatory Conference at Geneva in 1920, visited Europe, including Rome,

[1] For further details see Chap. viii, pp. 361 f., and Hogg, *Ecumenical Foundations*, p. 133, and note on p. 397.
[2] N. Karlström, *Rom und die Stockholmer Bewegung*, Uppsala, 1931, pp. 4–9, and Chap. xi, p. 528.
[3] *The Stockholm Conference 1925*, ed. Bell, pp. 4, 9.
[4] *Die Weltkonferenz für Glauben und Kirchenverfassung*, pp. 30–38.
[5] E.g. 2 November 1914, letter from Gardiner to Gasparri; 18 Dec. 1914, Gasparri to Gardiner on the attitude of the Pope; similarly, on 7 April 1915. The text of these letters is also given in Pribilla, *Um Kirchliche Einheit* (Appendix).   [6] Sasse, op. cit., p. 35.

and the Near East.[1] The Report of the Lausanne Conference[2] simply records that "in Rome, through the great courtesy of Archbishop Cerretti, a formal invitation and statement about the Conference were presented to his Holiness the Pope through Cardinal Gasparri: and the official refusal of the invitation was balanced by the personal friendliness and benevolence of the Pope".

The attitude of the papacy was made unmistakably clear by a decree of the Holy Office of 8 July 1927 forbidding Roman Catholics to attend the Lausanne Conference; and by the publication, after the Conference, of the Encyclical *Mortalium Animos*, 1928.

Before considering that document, we must note in passing one exception during this period to the apparently negative attitude of Roman Catholic authorities, since implicit in it was a principle later to be made more explicit.

In Great Britain a number of bodies known as Social Service Unions had been developed to carry Christian principles into practice in local civic life.[3] Between 1911 and 1914 annual summer schools were held at the Christian conference centre at Swanwick as "the Interdenominational Conference of Social Service Unions". The Bishop of Oxford (Gore) was chairman of the committee which planned the conference, whilst the chairman of the conference varied yearly. In these conferences and in the preparations for them, English Roman Catholics participated as fully as any other Christians, for it was clearly understood that the purpose of the conference was purely consultative.

After the break caused by the war, the conference committee met again in 1920. At the next meeting Malcolm Spencer moved, and William Temple (then Bishop of Manchester) seconded, the proposal to hold a larger conference —that which eventually became known as Copec (Conference on Christian Politics, Economics, and Citizenship). The proposal was accepted by the Roman Catholics present; the Copec committee and all the preparatory commissions included Roman Catholic members. From 1922–24 reports destined to become the agenda for the full conference were being drafted. At a later stage Roman Catholics withdrew from participation, since, although they remained in sympathy with the purposes of the conference, they felt unable to acquiesce in the actual formulation of the problems, e.g. presuppositions of the Commission on Marriage and the Family. We shall return to the readiness of Roman Catholics to act jointly with other Christians on social, as distinct from dogmatic, questions as well as to the difficulties encountered in so doing.

On the Feast of the Epiphany 1928 Pope Pius XI issued the Encyclical *Mortalium Animos* on "Fostering true religious union". Its attitude was uncompromising. It speaks of those who would overcome the perils and divisions of the time by seeking a "fraternal agreement on certain points of doctrine which will form a common basis of the spiritual life. With this object congresses, meetings, and addresses are arranged, attended by a large concourse of hearers, where all without distinction, unbelievers of every kind as well as Christians, even those who unhappily have rejected Christ and denied His divine nature or mission, are invited to join in the discussion. Now, such efforts can meet with no kind of approval among Catholics. They presuppose the erroneous view that all religions are more or less good and praiseworthy, inasmuch as all give expression, under various forms, to that innate sense which leads men to God and to the obedient

---

[1] See Chap. ix, pp. 415 f.   [2] *Faith and Order: Lausanne 1927*, pp. ix f.
[3] See Chap. xi, pp. 509 f.

acknowledgement of His rule. Those who hold such a view are not only in error; they distort the true idea of religion, and thus reject it, falling gradually into naturalism and atheism. To favour this opinion, therefore, and to encourage such undertakings is tantamount to abandoning the religion revealed by God".[1]

The next paragraph reads: "Nevertheless, when there is a question of fostering unity among Christians, it is easy for many to be misled by the apparent excellence of the object to be achieved. Is it not right, they ask, is it not the obvious duty of all who invoke the name of Christ to refrain from mutual reproaches and at last to be united in charity?" And it concludes: "In reality, however, these fair and alluring words cloak a most grave error, subversive of the foundations of the Catholic faith." The following pages go on to assert again the Roman Catholic claim to be the one true Church as against the desire of non-Roman Catholic Christians to treat it as one Church among many: "This being so, it is clear that the Apostolic See can by no means take part in these assemblies, nor is it in any way lawful for Catholics to give to such enterprises their encouragement or support. If they did so, they would be giving countenance to a false Christianity quite alien to the one Church of Christ."[2] It stresses the obligation to hold equally all dogma defined by Rome, since all points alike are based upon the authority of Christ, mediated by his Vicar on earth:

> "All true followers of Christ, therefore, will believe the dogma of the Immaculate Conception of the Mother of God with the same faith as they believe the mystery of the august Trinity, the infallibility of the Roman Pontiff in the sense defined by the Oecumenical Vatican Council with the same faith as they believe the Incarnation of Our Lord."[3]

It concludes with an appeal for a return to the Mother Church:

> "Thus, Venerable Brethren, it is clear why this Apostolic See has never allowed its subjects to take part in the assemblies of non-Catholics. There is but one way in which the unity of Christians may be fostered, and that is by furthering the return to the one true Church of Christ of those who are separated from it; for from that one true Church they have in the past fallen away;"[4]

and with an earnest call to prayer and to invocation of the Blessed Virgin Mary for "the speedy coming of that longed-for day when all men shall . . . be 'careful to keep the unity of the Spirit in the bond of peace'".

Among Christians outside the Roman Catholic Church, there was a general reaction of disappointment and bitterness, though, in view of earlier disappointments, many felt that nothing else could have been expected. The question of an official reply in the name of either Life and Work or Faith and Order was considered, but the conclusion was that such an official answer would be neither wise nor desirable. Many Church leaders, however, felt it necessary personally and

[1] English edition, pp. 9 f. Conferences such as Lausanne and Stockholm were, of course, attended only by Christians. There were, however, in the same period many "inter-faith" and "inter-religious" conferences, to which the strictures of the Pope might seem to apply. To many of its non-Roman readers the papal pronouncement appears to confuse two different and indeed irreconcilable movements.

[2] Ibid., p. 16.   [3] Ibid., p. 19.   [4] Ibid., pp. 20 f.

individually to reply.[1] The most striking of these individual replies came from the pen of Archbishop Nathan Söderblom.

The Archbishop opens by contrasting *Mortalium Animos* very unfavourably with the elegance and skill of the great Encyclicals of Leo XIII, and the force and adroitness of the anti-modernist *Pascendi Dominici Gregis* of Pius X, and registers strong protest against what he deemed to be the caricature of the ecumenical movement, to which reference has already been made. His main gravamen, however, is against the total failure of the Encyclical to distinguish between faith as intellectual assent and faith as the trustful submission of the soul to God, and to establish correctly the relationship between faith and love. He contrasts the attitude of the Encyclical unfavourably with that of the Orthodox leaders at Stockholm 1925, who, while insisting as strongly as ever Rome could do on the necessity of agreement in matters of dogma as the true basis of union, were yet prepared to recognize that they were already at one with brethren of the Protestant Churches in faith in our Lord and Saviour Jesus Christ, and to co-operate with them in the fields of social and ethical activity on the basis of Christian love.[2]

Voices were audible also from the Roman Catholic side which, without attempting to repudiate the basic affirmations of *Mortalium Animos*, sought to explain irenically the attitude of Rome, and seriously to understand the ecumenical movement. In 1929 Max Pribilla, S.J., published *Um Kirchliche Einheit*; this was symptomatic of a quickened interest in the theology of reunion. A variety of periodicals devoted to reunion, primarily looking towards the Eastern Churches, began to take serious note of the ecumenical movement, the *Eastern Churches Quarterly* (English Benedictines), *Irénikon* (Benedictines of Amay, later Chevetogne, in Belgium), *Vers l'Unité Chrétienne* (Istina, Paris), and, most recently, *Unitas* (founded in 1945 and edited by Fr Boyer of the Gregorian University in Rome).

The fullest, most careful, and best informed of the writings in this period was by a French Dominican, Fr M. J. Congar, at that time a friar of Le Saulchoir in Belgium. *Chrétiens désunis: Principes d'un 'oecuménisme' catholique* was published in 1937. Thus it was written before the two great ecumenical Conferences of Oxford and Edinburgh. Unfortunately, the English edition, published in 1939, obscures this fact by simply transferring Congar's surmises into the past tense.[3] Fr Congar saw in Life and Work the resultant of certain movements of the modern mind having little connection with Christian faith: chiefly nominalism (and the Lutheran disjunctions which derive from nominalism), philosophic rationalism, and pragmatic positivism. Doctrinally it subordinated the Christian outlook in practice to a philosophy of religion, and "failed to understand the true nature and role of faith". Lausanne 1927 he characterizes as a "characteristic product of the Anglican outlook". Consequently at Lausanne there were not the same "antinomies" as in Stockholm "between the visible and the invisible, Churches and Christianity, Beliefs and Faith, but on the contrary, the idea that the unity of Christians must be looked for in a creed and an ecclesiastical constitution". In summary, he concludes that Rome was right to abstain from participating in the movement both on grounds of incompatibility of doc-

---

[1] For example, four participants in Life and Work published a pamphlet, *Kritische Stimmen zum päpstlichen Rundschreiben über Einigungsfragen der Kirche*, Berlin, 1928.

[2] Swedish original in *Stockholms Tidningen*; German translation by Emil Ohly in *Die Eiche*, 1928, pp. 137–53. For his fuller reply to the criticisms of Fr Pribilla, see Bibliography.

[3] See especially pp. 117, 133, and 134 of the English edition.

trine and on grounds of prudence; for, the ecumenical movement itself being new and inchoate, the Catholic claim to uniqueness might be obscured if Rome were publicly involved in its debates. He acknowledges that, as the movement develops, it is becoming free from many of the errors present in its origins, and admits that in consequence "it is not impossible that a measure of Catholic participation may be given to some part of the work of the ecumenical movement".[1]

The main substance of this important book, however, is a restatement of the Roman Catholic position, in conscious awareness of a new and significant phenomenon, the ecumenical movement which believes "that others are Christian not in spite of their particular confession but in it and by it".[2] In that light, his final chapter adumbrates a basis for "Catholic ecumenism" to which we shall return in a final summary of present Roman Catholic thought on the ecumenical movement.[3]

By 1937 the attitude of Rome towards invitations to join in ecumenical conferences had become clear. Ecumenical leaders contented themselves with seeking co-operation in areas where experience had shown that it was likely to be given, and with sending information, as a courtesy, to Roman Catholic leaders upon all fresh developments in those fields in which Roman Catholic participation could not be expected.

A few Roman Catholic scholars collaborated personally in the widespread preparations for the Oxford Conference on Church, Community, and State, and among the essays published in the preparatory volumes was a contribution by Christopher Dawson on "The Kingdom of God and History". The Conference Report[4] simply records this "valuable, though unofficial, collaboration", and that "the authorities of the Church [of Rome] were averse to any official participation".

In preparation for Edinburgh 1937, the Chairman went so far as to repeat the explicit invitation which had earlier been refused. The Archbishop of York (Temple) wrote on 11 September 1936 to the Most Rev. Andrew MacDonald, O.S.B., Roman Catholic Archbishop of St Andrews and Edinburgh, announcing the holding of the second World Conference on Faith and Order. Dr Temple recalled in his letter that an invitation had been extended to the Church of Rome to take part in the first World Conference in 1927, and that while it was courteously acknowledged it was not accepted. He continued, "the invitation still stands as part of the whole programme and intention of our Movement. Nothing would delight us more than to hear from your Grace that the Roman Catholic Church would on this occasion be officially represented. If your Grace thinks well to convey this intimation to the Holy See, we should be most happy for this to take place". In February 1937 Dr Temple sent a reminder, and Archbishop MacDonald then wrote, saying, "I have considered the position very carefully and have come to the conclusion that it will be better for me not to co-operate actively in the Conference which is to take place in Edinburgh next August".

This negative attitude was later modified to the extent that four priests and one layman of the Roman Catholic Church were allowed to ask for admission

---

[1] Op. cit., pp. 121; 127–30; 131 f.; 140–44.
[2] Ibid., pp. xiii and 135.
[3] It must be borne in mind that Fr Congar's book was the expression of his own ideas and convictions, not all of which have commended themselves within his own Church.
[4] The Churches Survey Their Task, p. 10. See also Chap. xii, pp. 586, 588.

to the Edinburgh Conference as unofficial observers. They applied individually and were given every facility to see and hear all that happened at the Conference. They were most anxious not to be regarded as in any sense members of the Conference. In view of their desire to remain anonymous, the official report refers to the fact that there were Roman Catholic observers without official status, but gives no names.[1]

During the course of the Conference a fraternal message of fellowship and prayer and desire for Christian unity was read from the Prior of the Benedictine Priory of Amay-sur-Meuse, Belgium,[2] and a letter from Archbishop MacDonald expressing his regret that the fullness of the Conference programme would prevent the delegates from accepting an invitation to meet him, which he would gladly have given and which would have provided him with an opportunity "to explain to them personally the position of the Church of Rome and why it had not participated in this Conference".

Both Conferences approved the proposal to set up a World Council of Churches. Subsequently, when the Provisional Committee was established, Dr Temple, as its Chairman, wrote on 10 February 1939 to the Cardinal Secretary of State. The letter understands "from previous communications . . . that the Church of Rome would not desire to be formally associated with the Council", but that courtesy requires that the Holy See be informed of what is proposed, and suggests "that it may be permissible to exchange information with agencies of the Church of Rome on matters of common interest and that we should have the help from time to time of unofficial consultation with Roman Catholic theologians and scholars".[3] The Secretary of State replied to the Apostolic Delegate in Britain, who wrote, on 21 July 1939, to the Archbishop of York (Temple), informing him, on the authority of the Cardinal Secretary of State, that there would be no obstacle to his consulting confidentially English Roman Catholic bishops and the Apostolic Delegate, or to exchange of confidential information and opinion with Roman Catholic theologians.

When the Provisional Committee of the World Council of Churches held its first post-war meeting at Geneva in February 1946, a letter was sent by Mgr François Charrière, Roman Catholic Bishop of Lausanne, Geneva, and Fribourg, through Dr Brilioth, then Bishop of Växjö in Sweden. It included the sentence: "While you are met together at Geneva to concern yourselves with this essential problem [of unity] my prayer goes up with yours, in union with the prayer which Jesus made on the eve of his Passion."[4]

It must not be supposed that these approaches to the Roman Catholic Church by ecumenical bodies met with universal approval. Some Churches hold that the Church of Rome has so far departed from the truth of the Gospel that no other attitude can be taken up towards it than that of resolute and uncompromising opposition. Such contacts as the ecumenical movement has had with

[1] *The Second World Conference on Faith and Order, Edinburgh 1937*, p. 76. To the third World Conference in 1952 four observers were nominated, from amongst Roman Catholics residing in Scandinavia, by the Vicar Apostolic in Scandinavia (Mgr J. E. Mueller) on the authorization of the Holy Office, and after the Faith and Order Commission had published in its Minutes "that, if some Roman Catholic representatives request the privilege of attending the Conference as observers, the officers be authorized to welcome them". See *F. and O. Pamphlet No. 8* (new series): *Meetings . . . Clarens, Switzerland, August 13–17, 1951*, p. 51.

[2] The replies to the Prior of Amay and to Archbishop MacDonald are printed in *The Second World Conference*, p. 40.

[3] See Bell, *Documents*, III, pp. 298 f., for the text of the letters of the Archbishop of York and the Cardinal Secretary of State.

[4] *Minutes of Provisional Committee, Geneva 1946*, pp. 141 f.

the Roman Catholic Church have exposed it to criticism from some of the more strongly Evangelical bodies, and have been among the reasons advanced by them for not joining the World Council of Churches. Other Churches and groups within the ecumenical movement which take a less extreme view yet feel grave difficulty in any close contact with the Church of Rome as it is now. While recognizing as friends and partners in spirit many individual Roman Catholics, they feel that until Rome is other than she is her co-operation in the ecumenical movement would represent a danger rather than an advantage. Yet others, while not debating the matter fully on theoretical grounds, would argue that in the face of repeated refusals on the part of Rome to participate in the ecumenical movement as such or in any of its activities, it would be far better that the ecumenical movement should make up its mind not to expose itself to any more of the humiliating rebuffs, a considerable number of which have been recorded in this History.

There are, however, many in the constituency of the World Council of Churches who would agree with the line taken by such ecclesiastical statesmen as Archbishop Davidson and Archbishop Söderblom—that the very life-blood of the modern ecumenical movement is the search for fellowship with all those who name the name of Christ in sincerity; that therefore the door to co-operation with Rome must at all times and in every possible way be kept open; that rebuffs must not be taken too seriously; and that every approach towards fellowship from the Roman Catholic side must be warmly welcomed as a genuine manifestation of the ecumenical spirit. It is to be noted, however, that, since the World Council of Churches was constituted in 1948, no official approaches have been made by it to the Vatican or to any other Roman Catholic authority.

One of the subjects to which the World Council of Churches has directed special attention, and which it has specially charged the Commission of the Churches on International Affairs to watch, is the maintenance of religious liberty in all parts of the world. Unhappily, the Commission has found it necessary to devote special attention to "the nature and extent of restriction upon religious freedom in areas where Roman Catholicism or Islam is dominant".[1] It is not suggested that the Roman Catholic Church is always intolerant or that in every country where it is dominant restrictions are placed on religious liberty, or indeed that all Roman Catholics endorse all the actions of their fellow-Churchmen, or that all the non-Roman Churches have a clear conscience in this matter. Yet reports of restrictions on Protestant liberty, or even persecution, in Italy, Spain, Colombia, and other countries have roused strong feelings of disapproval and disgust in Protestant countries, and have made many Protestant churchmen feel that, until the Vatican utterly disavows some of the methods which have been followed and sets itself firmly on the side of religious liberty for all, no kind of negotiations with it should be entered into by the World Council or any of its constituent members.[2]

---

[1] *Minutes . . . Central Committee, Toronto 1950*, p. 73.

[2] See the whole Report "Religious Freedom in Face of Dominant Forces", *Minutes . . . Central Committee, Toronto 1950*, pp. 72–84, and the Resolution of the Central Committee of the World Council on this subject passed at the same meeting, ibid., pp. 12 f. The World Council of Churches has adopted as its own the Declaration on Human Rights accepted by the United Nations in 1948 in the following terms:

" Everyone has the right to freedom of thought, conscience and religion; this right includes freedom to change his religion or belief, and freedom, either alone or in community with others and in public or private, to manifest his religion or belief in teaching, practice, worship and observance."

In the period between the two world wars and after, the sense of a common heritage in peril gave to Roman Catholic-Protestant relations in many countries a depth of fellowship in Christian witness which had never before existed. In Germany, Roman Catholics and Protestants suffered and died together in prisons and concentration camps; together they sometimes served the suffering Jews or refugees; friendships were made which only death could unbind. The *Una Sancta* movement among German Roman Catholics became a means of close devotional contact with Protestants,[1] and the Roman Catholic Liturgical Movement had an influence welcomed by many Lutherans. In France, similar suffering and similar friendships led to new depths of mutual understanding and respect; Roman Catholics and Protestants wrote together in the hazardous publications of the Resistance. In Holland, during the Nazi occupation, pastoral letters were signed jointly by Roman Catholic bishops and leaders of the Reformed Churches. Thus the co-operation was often public and official to a degree unknown before or since.

In Britain, spared both the horrors and the stimulus of enemy occupation, a comparable spirit was yet to be found. The Roman Catholic Archbishop of Westminster, Cardinal Hinsley, was ready to co-operate in unprecedented ways with the Anglican Archbishops and the leaders of the Free Churches. On 21 December 1940 a Ten-Point Letter to *The Times* was signed by the Archbishops of Canterbury and York (Lang and Temple), Cardinal Hinsley, and the Moderator of the Free Church Federal Council (W. H. Armstrong). It set out the Five Peace Points from the 1939 Christmas Eve Allocution of Pope Pius XII and the five standards for a just economic order emanating from the Oxford Conference of 1937, as together to be "regarded as the true basis on which a lasting peace could be established". The Letter both expressed and stimulated a spontaneous and nation-wide impulse of common Christian witness. The British Council of Churches (formed in 1942) promoted a movement of evangelistic and social witness known as Religion and Life. A similar Roman Catholic movement, the Sword of the Spirit, was encouraged by Cardinal Hinsley to co-operate with it upon certain terms. These were set forth in a Joint Statement agreed by both bodies. It stressed the common peril, the degree of common ground, and the need for a common defence of "certain essential freedoms"; it testified to the spontaneity and power which each movement had exhibited in local life and public meetings, and expressed the intention to go forward to "work through parallel action in the religious, and joint action in the social and international, field".[2]

In all countries, in the preoccupations of peace, something of this mood passed. Old suspicions reasserted themselves; tired men reverted to narrower paths; death removed some of the greatest leaders. Truth demands that we should note with regret that the loss of the fine freshness was in some cases due to a hardening of the official Roman Catholic attitude, and that, in some countries at least, the relations between the Roman and other Churches became even worse than they were before the war. Yet, though it would be hard to define how, the moment left its imprint. Post-war relations between Roman Catholics and Protestants in many countries could never quite ignore, even if they could never quite recapture, a quality they had known in that hour.

[1] The character of its saintly founder, who was executed by the Nazis in 1944, is well portrayed in Lilian Stevenson, *Max Josef Metzger, Priest and Martyr*, London, 1952.
[2] The hope that the Sword of the Spirit might grow into a genuinely interconfessional movement was frustrated when it was made clear that only Roman Catholics would be eligible to serve on its committee.

There is also another aspect. It must not be assumed that to fasten attention on these official acts is to tell the whole story. In the life of all Christian communions, below the voice of official pronouncements is the murmur of unofficial and largely unknown voices; in the Roman Communion there is the constant dialogue between the centre and the periphery, between the *Urbs* and the *Orbis*. Part of this widespread life in the body is made up of innumerable friendships and contacts between Roman Catholics and Christians of other communions. Sometimes, as in the *Oekumenische Arbeitsgemeinschaft* in Germany,[1] it is accorded official recognition; more often it may be little more than a friendship between the local priest and the local pastor; in between, it may take the form of semi-official discussions. A considerable traffic in articles for one another's reviews and periodicals takes place, especially in French; increasingly, spreading from France, the Week of Prayer (18–25 January) is becoming a spiritual focal point each year.[2] These things are not easily defined or measured, but they become, in their sum total, as real a part of the attitude of Rome to other Christians as are the more easily described pronouncements; as a lived, felt, actual movement they are as much a matter of fact as the Encyclicals, and a fact also to be weighed against the discrimination, denunciation, and even persecution of Protestants by Roman Catholics which are also part of the life of the *Orbis*.

At the last full meeting, in America in 1947, of the Provisional Committee preparing the Assembly which was to inaugurate the World Council of Churches, Resolution 23 of the Committee on Arrangements for the Assembly reads: "that the Presidents and the General Secretary be given authority to invite a few individual Roman Catholics to attend the Assembly as unofficial observers". Subsequently "a few" was defined as "ten". Many letters were received by the General Secretary from individual Roman Catholics desirous of attending, in many cases indicating that the application had the approval of their immediate ecclesiastical superiors. Many other names were collected from the advice both of Roman Catholics and of others, and early in 1948 invitations were sent to ten persons who, whilst being prominent Roman Catholics in various countries, had shown a real understanding of the aims of the ecumenical movement and of the World Council. In April 1948 evidence came indirectly to the General Secretary that the Roman Catholic hierarchy in the Netherlands expected to make the choice of the observers; he thereupon let it be known that those invited were expected to make their own arrangements to secure canonical permission to attend the Assembly, and advised those already invited that Cardinal de Jong, Roman Catholic Archbishop of Utrecht, desired to reserve his right to give or withhold such permission. The Secretariat in Geneva expected to receive from Cardinal de Jong names of those whom he would approve. But neither then nor later did any such proposals come from the Cardinal. On 5 June 1948 the Holy Office issued a Monitum *Cum Compertum* drawing attention to Canon 1325 (iii) prohibiting "mixed meetings" without previous permission of the Holy See, and Canons 1258 and 731 (ii) prohibiting *communio in sacris*. Official permission to attend the Assembly was not accorded by the Holy See to any Roman Catholic. Consequently the only Roman Catholics present at the Assembly were journalists representing the Roman Catholic press, though Fr Boyer, the Director of *Unitas*, was in

---

[1] The fellowship for discussion between Roman Catholics and Protestants officially recognized by the Roman Catholic Archbishop of Paderborn and the Lutheran Bishop of Oldenburg. [2] See Chap. vii, pp. 348 f.

Amsterdam at the time and had personal talks with many of the delegates.

On Sunday, 22 August, while the Assembly was in progress, a pastoral letter from the Roman Catholic bishops of Holland was read in all their churches. It explained carefully the reason why the Roman Catholic Church could not take part in such an Assembly. "This aloofness is not based on any fear of losing prestige", said the pastoral letter, and concluded with an urgent call to all the priests and people to join during those days in prayer for all those taking part in the Assembly and for the many other non-Catholic Christians "who lovingly seek for unity, who truly follow Christ and live in His love and who, although they are separated from Christ's flock, yet look to the Church, be it often unconsciously, as the only haven of salvation".[1]

The Winter 1948-49 issue of the *Ecumenical Review* devoted eleven pages to reprinting extracts from some of the more striking articles about Amsterdam 1948 from the Roman Catholic press all over the world.[2] The comments range from barely concealed scorn to deeply perceptive and sympathetic judgements, and were reproduced to show that the Assembly had at least aroused considerable interest in the Roman Catholic world. Later and more mature thought produced notable comment in such Roman Catholic periodicals as *Unitas* (Fr Boyer, November and December, 1948, French edition, and No. 1, English edition), *Irénikon* (1er Trimestre, 1949), and *Études* (Père Rouquette, S.J., April 1949). It is in these writings, and in their successors, a scattered but considerable volume, that we must look for what can fairly be described as Roman Catholic ecumenism.

It should be clear from what has already been said that it is in terms of communion with, and canonical dependence upon, the Holy See that Roman Catholicism is defined. Around the acceptance of the papal claims revolve all other matters of faith and order. All Churches would agree that somewhere there is a *depositum fidei* which is given by God, and that no desire for unity would justify compromising upon it; Rome differs from all others in making the Papal Supremacy part of the *depositum*. Once this is understood, all the negations, as well as the affirmations, of Roman pronouncements to and concerning other Christians fall into perspective.

The Roman Catholic Church has always been ready to co-operate in matters concerning social and economic justice with any who accept the general principles which it defines in terms of the Natural Law. But when the content of the Faith comes under discussion, Rome is intransigent. The promulgation in November 1950 of the dogma of the Assumption of the Blessed Virgin served to underline the Roman claim to total obedience in matters of faith. Many commentators upon it in other communions deplored the way in which this decree erected one more barrier between Roman Catholic and other Christians.[3]

The Encyclical *Humani Generis* of 12 August 1950 was to deepen the impression of intransigence and opposition to all expressions of opinion which even appeared to deviate from the most rigid and exclusive papal orthodoxy. It warned against those who desire "a return, in our exposition of Catholic doctrine, to the language of Scripture and of the Fathers. Privately they cherish the hope that

---

[1] "Owing to a regrettable misunderstanding", the pastoral letter was not transmitted officially to the officers of the World Council till 31 August. See "The Roman Catholic Church and the First Assembly", in *Ecumenical Review*, Vol. I, No. 2, pp. 197–201.

[2] "Some Roman Catholic Voices about the First Assembly", ibid., pp. 202–12.

[3] See, e.g., an Orthodox statement by Professor Alivisatos, and a memorandum by a group of German Protestant theologians reported in the *Ecumenical Review*, Vol. III, No. 2, pp. 151–63.

dogma, when thus stripped of the elements which they regard as external to divine revelation, may be usefully compared with the theological opinion of other bodies, separated from the unity of the Church; this might lead, by degrees, to a levelling-up between Catholic doctrine and the views of those who disagree with us".[1]

It is therefore misleading to suggest, as some have done, that there have been any signs of a modification in Rome's traditional claims, or in the terms upon which she could recognize other Christians as full members of the Catholic Church. Indeed, there are many signs that the dogmatic claims of Rome are pressed with an increasing intransigence. But it is also misleading to ignore the existence of a quite new body of Roman Catholic thought and practice which has grown up as a result of the development of the ecumenical movement. This does not imply any new doctrine but the application of the old doctrine in a new field and in a new temper. Many articles and books could now be listed which have, as their primary purpose, exposition of the Roman Catholic view, and show evidence of equally careful attention to all the main writings and meetings connected with the ecumenical movement.

Some Roman Catholics writers (e.g. contributors to the pages of *Irénikon*) employ traditional Roman Catholic language to distinguish between an *essential* (or *substantial*) Catholicity and *accidental* Catholicity, the latter being the degree to which the Church, in particular times and places, manifests that fullness which is hers by nature of her being. Other writers, who gladly use of themselves the adjective "ecumenical", could be quoted by way of further example.

Fr Congar[2] speaks of a Catholicity which already substantially exists but is only imperfectly actualized and not fully explicit. For the Catholic this involves a serious and sustained attempt to actualize in the empirical Church a Catholicity which is already substantially hers; in relation to non-Catholics it involves not only seeking to enable them to see their own apprehensions of truth in the setting of full Catholicity, and so to renounce the errors in their own positions; but also a recognition that Roman Catholics may well have much to learn from their separated brethren in the exemplification of Christian ideas and values which they have perhaps neglected.

A similar idea was expressed by Dom Bede Winslow, primarily but not only in relation to the Eastern Churches. "We have to be prepared to learn from these dissident Eastern Churches (and from all our separated brethren, for that matter), for they have retained much that we had failed to realize for a while, of whose value we are now only beginning to be conscious. . . . The reunion then of the Orthodox Church with the Church of Rome would be the reintegration, the deepening of Rome's own inherent Catholicity. And this applies in varying degrees in the case of other Christian bodies being brought into communion with Rome. This is, of course, true . . . in considering any . . . cultural group. . . . This, however, has a far truer signification when it is a question of other Christian traditions and especially of the venerable Eastern Churches."[3]

The Toronto statement of the World Council's Central Committee in 1950 on "The Church, the Churches, and the World Council of Churches", and the plans and publications of the Faith and Order Commissions before and after the Lund

---

[1] From the English translation by Mgr Ronald Knox in *The Tablet*, 2 September 1950.
[2] Congar, *Divided Christendom*, pp. 253 ff.
[3] "Integral Catholicism and the Eastern Churches", *E.C.Q.*, April–June 1945; pp. 1–11. Official approval does not cover such expressions of personal opinion.

Conference of 1952, occupy pride of place in most of the issues in *Irénikon* and *Vers l'Unité Chrétienne* for the years 1950–53. The articles show a scrupulous desire to understand the intention of ecumenical writings, and indeed they sometimes exhibit an ingenuity of deep interpretation which credits the ecumenical committees or authors with subtleties never intended by them. The ecumenical writings are assessed and evaluated in terms of the orthodox Roman Catholic position, with courtesy and charity where agreement is impossible.

In this sense Roman Catholicism is a participant in the ecumenical conversation. Although never officially taking part in ecumenical conferences, Rome has realized that the ecumenical movement has become a phenomenon of sufficient importance in the world of religion to demand a definition of her attitude towards it. The events already recorded, leading up to the Amsterdam Assembly, lay behind the Instruction to Local Ordinaries, *Ecclesia Catholica*, issued on 20 December 1949.[1] The instruction, in effect, acknowledges that discussions between Roman Catholics and other Christians do, and will, take place on "matters of faith and morals" and lays down the conditions for them. "Mixed gatherings are not then forbidden outright, but they are not to be held without the previous sanction of the competent ecclesiastical authority." The document then goes on to say who these authorities are—local ordinaries (normally bishops) for local conferences, the Holy See itself for inter-diocesan or international conferences: "all communication in sacred rites" is forbidden, but "it is not discountenanced to open and close the meetings with a common recitation of the Lord's Prayer or some other prayer approved by the Catholic Church".

From the side of the ecumenical movement it was generally regretted that a new element of "officialness" must now always attend any converse with Roman Catholics.[2] For instance, the Executive Committee of the World Council of Churches, at its first meeting after the publication of the Instruction, took note of it and in general terms expressed regret at the narrow view of Christian unity on which the Instruction was based. It noted the loss of spontaneity which would result from the Instruction. "According to the new Instruction, all such meetings will henceforth have to be directed and supervised by the hierarchy. Thus they will lose that informal and spontaneous character on which much of their value depended. There will be less room for the pioneers." At the same time it welcomed the fact that explicit permission was given, though with certain restrictions, for Roman Catholics and Christians of other confessions to pray together, and also for the holding of interconfessional meetings on social questions.[3]

But the "ecumenical" Roman Catholics themselves welcomed it: "it does not introduce something very new; rather it ratifies a former policy", it sets the seal of official approval upon a "movement which the Holy Office recognizes explicitly to be a movement of the Holy Spirit". For the first time official Roman Catholicism considers that Christian thought has developed far enough for the Church to be able to depart from the negative and defensive position (of the last 400 years), and to "envisage positively what she may undertake in common with the Churches that she considers heretical and schismatic".[4] Another wrote that

---

[1] Signed by Cardinal Marchetti-Selvagiani as Secretary and Mgr Alfredo Ottaviani as Assessor of the Congregation of the Holy Office. See *Ecumenical Review*, Vol. II, No. 3, pp. 296 ff.

[2] But for a Roman Catholic comment upon this judgement see M. Bévenot, S.J., in *E.C.Q.*, Vol. VIII, pp. 357–64.

[3] *Minutes . . . Central Committee, Toronto 1950*, pp. 62 f.

[4] R. Rouquette, S.J., in *Études*, May 1950, pp. 240 ff.

Roman Catholics in favour of Christian unity, who had been seeking direct contact with non-Catholics, find themselves here positively encouraged, and, since this was only the beginning of a long, long road, pleaded for "patience, patience, patience".[1] The President of *Unitas* described it, for Roman Catholics, as "the great charter of unionist activity".[2]

The Instruction *Ecclesia Catholica* aptly illustrates the whole situation: on the one hand, the clear, persistent, and reiterated claim of the Roman Church to be the Catholic Church and to offer no terms for reunion but submission and return; on the other hand it gives formal and official recognition, slowly conceded as the ecumenical movement has gradually taken shape, to the fact that fellow-Christians care deeply for unity in the Church of Christ, and that they must be taken seriously, in charity and in prayer.

On these terms there is a wide territory within which it is possible to point to fruitful exchange. Protestants would instance the way in which Roman Catholics show a renewed seriousness of attention to the Bible,[3] officially encouraged in the Encyclical *Divino Afflante* of 1943; and the way in which some Roman Catholic theologians pay attention to leading non-Roman theologians. The Roman Catholic liturgical movements reaffirm many primitive Catholic beliefs and practices which had, in fact, sometimes been better exemplified in Protestant worship. Equally, Roman Catholics may claim that their contribution to the ecumenical movement has been, by their abstention, to compel non-Romans to reconsider the meaning of authority, ministry, sacraments, and dogma. And over all a totally new spirit moves, most perfectly expressed in a deeper devotion to common prayer for unity. In the Octave 18–25 January,[4] largely through the zeal of a French Roman Catholic, the late Abbé Couturier, Roman Catholics and Protestants, Orthodox and Anglicans, simultaneously and sometimes in common assembly, pray together "for the unity of the Church of Jesus Christ as He wills and when He wills". Even in face of the deep divisions here recorded, many Christian hearts find their deepest reassurance that the path towards unity will not be for ever barred in the fact that earnest prayer in this spirit already unites a growing army in all confessions. Other weapons may grow blunt, but no one can doubt, even though we cannot measure, the effectiveness of this weapon of self-negating prayer.

This brief survey suggests that the Roman Catholic authorities have recognized, in the rise of the organized ecumenical movement, a religious phenomenon worthy of careful scrutiny. As the movement has changed and developed, the emphasis of Roman Catholic pronouncement upon it has also varied. One aspect has never changed in the period between Edinburgh 1910 and the Instruction of 1950, the claim of Rome to be the Holy Catholic Church, and the corollary that unity can lie only in the submission of all "separated Christians" to the papal obedience. The changes which are discernible are rather in the terms in which the separated brethren are spoken of and spoken to, and in the growth of evident prayer for unity. What no historian can estimate is that which principally matters: how far, on both sides of this deep division between Christians, this is a story of a growth in that charity, without which all that has been recorded profiteth nothing.

[1] C. Dumont, O.P., in *Vers l'Unité Chrétienne*, No. 22, April 1950.
[2] C. Boyer, S.J., *Unus Pastor*, p. 48.
[3] See Suzanne de Diétrich, *Renouveau Biblique*, Éditions Oikumene, 1945.
[4] For further details, see Chap. vii, pp. 348 f.

CHAPTER 16

THE GENESIS OF
THE WORLD COUNCIL OF CHURCHES

by

WILLEM ADOLF VISSER 'T HOOFT

1. THE PRE-WAR YEARS, 1918–1939

The story of the origins of the World Council of Churches reminds one of the development of a theme in a symphony. At first one or two instruments introduce the new melody and one expects that the other instruments will take it up. But no, the theme disappears in the mass of sound. Here and there it tries to disengage itself, but its time is not yet. Suddenly it comes out clearly and dominates all other sounds.

In the years immediately following the first world war the desire for the formation of a "League of Churches" arose in several minds and in various places. During the spring and summer of 1919 Archbishop Söderblom gave shape to his proposal concerning an ecumenical council. The Ecumenical Patriarchate began in January 1919 to prepare its Encyclical on the *Koinonia*[1] of Churches, which was sent out in January 1920. In June 1920 Dr J. H. Oldham presented a memorandum to the international missionary Conference in Crans in which he made proposals for the formation of an international missionary council, which "will probably have before long to give way to something that may represent the beginnings of a world league of Churches". It is not clear whether these three proposals are in any way related to each other or whether they arose independently.[2] But it is clear that the fact of the emergence of a League of Nations had a very real bearing on these plans. In all three proposals that League is specifically mentioned. The argument is not that, since the nations are getting together, the Churches should also get together, but rather that the League of Nations may remain an empty shell unless the Churches join together in creating a new spirit of justice and peace. Dr Oldham's thinking about international Christian organization was also deeply influenced by his contact with the "Round Table Group" in England, several members of which played a considerable rôle in the formation of the League of Nations.[3]

The main purpose of these proposals was to set up a representative body to be controlled by the Churches as such, which would serve as a permanent link between them and enable them to bear a common witness to society and especially to international society. It is not surprising that at that time and for many years afterwards there was little response to these new ideas. The Churches had not yet been sufficiently drawn out of their isolation for the idea of a permanent link between them to seem other than utopian. It was a sufficiently difficult task to hold world conferences, such as those of Stockholm and Lausanne, and to create continuation committees of these conferences to carry out their specific decisions. The advantage of this form of ecumenical organization was its modesty; its weakness, that it left unanswered the question of the precise relation of the new bodies to the Churches. Faith and Order and Life and Work were in

---

[1] The Greek word in the New Testament and elsewhere for *fellowship*, commonly used in modern Greek for the *League* of Nations.

[2] It is possible, but not certain, that the Ecumenical Patriarchate was aware of Söderblom's plan. The Patriarchate had already decided to issue an encyclical on the subject before the printed statements of Söderblom appeared. But Dr Oldham does not believe that his own reference to a "League of Churches" grew out of the plans born in Uppsala and Constantinople.

[3] "The Round Table Group", under the leadership of Lionel Curtis, launched in 1911 *The Round Table, A Quarterly Review of British Commonwealth Affairs*, which continues to provide first-rate material on almost all international questions since its foundation.

one sense ecclesiastical movements, for they had grown out of conferences which were wholly or largely composed of Church representatives. But in their activities between the conferences they were not directly dependent upon the Churches, for the Churches had not undertaken responsibility for these movements and had not decided to accept permanent membership in them.

There were some, however, who had not forgotten the proposals emanating from Constantinople and Uppsala and who continued to believe that a council of the Churches was the true goal of effort. Thus at the preliminary meeting of Faith and Order in Geneva (1920), Professor Alivisatos repeated on behalf of the Orthodox the proposal of the Patriarchate of Constantinople to form a League (*Koinonia*) of Churches.[1] But in the 1920's these far-reaching plans did not meet with much response. At Stockholm 1925 Dr G. K. A. Bell (then Dean of Canterbury) spoke of the formation of an "International Christian Council" as desirable but not yet feasible.[2] At Lausanne 1927, the seventh section under the chairmanship of Archbishop Söderblom brought in a draft report which referred to the Constantinople proposal, and stated that a council of the Churches for practical purposes might well be evolved from the already existing organizations.[3] But this draft was severely criticized and the final report on this subject adopted by the Business Committee after the Conference state only that "it has been suggested that such a council [of Churches] might be evolved from already existing organisations".[4]

In 1930 at its meeting in Chexbres the Continuation Committee of the Stockholm Conference became the Universal Christian Council for Life and Work.[5] But this was a change in name rather than in structure. In the following years the demand for a council for which the Churches would be directly responsible grew in substance. It was voiced by both individuals and groups, such as Adolf Deissmann,[6] Henry Louis Henriod,[7] the Youth Group at the Hertenstein meeting of Faith and Order,[8] Canon Leonard Hodgson,[9] and the *Amis du Mouvement de Lausanne* in France.[10]

The idea of a World Council of Churches was in the air, but so long as there were in existence several different and independent ecumenical bodies it seemed impossible of realization. The two organizations most directly concerned were Faith and Order and Life and Work, for these had (at least in many countries) the closest relationship to the Churches. Could these two be brought together? The story of the many attempts to unite them shows that on both sides there was considerable fear lest the loss of independence might mean danger to the cause for which each stood. The meeting of Life and Work at Hälsingborg in 1922 had

---

[1] *Report of Preliminary Meeting*, pp. 75 and 80. Full text of address in *Internationale Kirchliche Zeitschrift*, 1921, p. 93 ff. See also *F. and O. Pamphlet No. 34: A Compilation of Proposals for Christian Unity.*
[2] *The Stockholm Conference, 1925*, ed. G. K. A. Bell, p. 682.
[3] *Faith and Order, Lausanne, 1927*, ed. H. N. Bate, 2nd ed., pp. 397 f.
[4] Ibid., p. 538. See also Chap. ix, pp. 421 f.
[5] The proposal to change the name was made in 1929 at Eisenach, but the new name was actually introduced a year later when the new Constitution was adopted (in French *Conseil oecuménique*, and in German *Oekumenischer Rat*).
[6] See his theses of 1930 presented at the Faith and Order meeting, Mürren, and printed in *Una Sancta*, Gütersloh, 1936.
[7] Memoranda circulated, 1932 and 1936.
[8] "A World Council for Ecumenical Christianity", *Minutes of F. and O., 1934*, p. 34.
[9] *Minutes of Ecumenical Consultative Group, London, October 1936.*
[10] *Minutes of F. and O., Clarens 1936*, p. 16. Cf. Floyd Tomkins in *News Letter*, October 1936, p. 9.

already insisted that the Life and Work and Faith and Order Conferences should not be held at the same place and about the same time, because the two movements "had better be kept distinct".[1] Equally, the reaction against the draft report brought in by Archbishop Söderblom at Lausanne showed that there were some delegates to the Faith and Order Conference who believed that their cause would not be served by closer alliance with Life and Work.[2]

Attempts made between 1928 and 1932 to arrive at closer co-ordination produced no results. Nevertheless the conviction that the two movements ought somehow to arrive at closer understanding was spreading. When in 1932 the Bishop of Chichester (Bell), on behalf of Life and Work, asked a large number of Church leaders whether in their view the 1937 Conferences of Life and Work and Faith and Order should meet separately or at the same place and about the same time, the majority of answers was definitely in favour of the second plan. Among those who desired the closest possible co-ordination were some of the leading figures in Faith and Order (William Temple, Garvie, Zoellner) and in Life and Work (W. Monod, Gounelle), as well as those connected with both (Swedish Ecumenical Committee, Deissmann, Alivisatos).[3]

But the practical problem remained to be solved. A new approach was made by a meeting of representatives of the main ecumenical bodies at York in May 1933, first proposed by Dr William Adams Brown. Dr Brown had for long felt that "we cannot permanently keep the two [Faith and Order and Life and Work] apart";[4] and when in 1933, as Chairman of the Administrative Committee of Life and Work, he spent a considerable time in Europe, he made ecumenical co-ordination one of his main concerns. Those who met at York represented Faith and Order, Life and Work, the World Alliance, I.M.C., W.S.C.F., and the World's Y.M.C.A. The meeting did not produce immediate practical results, but in the perspective of later developments it is seen to have been a turning-point, for from that moment onwards there was in existence a group of people who had confidence in each other and who were determined to find a solution to this problem of ecumenical organization.[5]

A few months later in Paris (August 1934) this unofficial consultative group met again. Dr Brown had prepared a detailed memorandum on the various ways in which the movements might collaborate. This time the problem of organization was considered in the wider context of the total task of the Church in the modern world—a subject introduced by Dr J. H. Oldham.

It is unnecessary to record in detail all the consultations and meetings during the next years at which further progress towards co-ordination was made. But, before we describe the final stage of the process of preparation, let us ask why in the mid-1930's there was a new readiness for a concentration of the ecumenical forces, and how the ground was prepared for the emergence of the World Council of Churches.

---

[1] *Minutes*, p. 37.

[2] Others at Lausanne, notably the Orthodox delegation and Dr Peter Ainslie, spoke in favour of the creation of a council of Churches. The final statement on the subject mentions the two positions: that of those who look for one council of Churches and that of those who believe that for the present Life and Work and Faith and Order should develop in independence, each following its own way. See final draft of Report of Section VII in *Lausanne 1927*, pp. 536–41.

[3] The answers are in the archives of the World Council in Geneva.

[4] "Next Steps", *Christian Union Quarterly*, July 1928, p. 23.

[5] See *Minutes, Life and Work, Novi Sad, 1933*, p. 16. For a fuller description of the meeting at York, see William Adams Brown, *Toward a United Church*, pp. 134–37.

The most obvious factor was the practical impossibility of maintaining two independent movements, both appealing for spiritual and material support to the same Churches and both making claims on the time of the same Church leaders. The financial crisis through which both movements had passed had made this very clear.[1]

But there were more compelling reasons. During the 1920's the separate existence of a movement concerned with "practical" Christianity and another movement concerned with doctrine and Church order had not been seriously challenged. In the 1930's it was increasingly felt that this separation could not be justified. The slogan "Doctrine divides but service unites", used so often as an argument for the separate existence of Life and Work, seemed misleading and inadequate in the new situation in which it was generally realized that the profoundest differences between the Churches in their attitude to society were in the realm of theological thought. Just as Life and Work, in preparing for the Oxford Conference (1937) was forced to face the doctrinal issues, so Faith and Order had to consider the "non-theological factors", e.g. the sociological realities, which constitute obstacles to unity. It is significant that at the meeting of Faith and Order in 1934 the main subject of discussion was "The Church and the World". The old distinctions were gradually breaking down.

The new situation which arose for the Church as a result of the emergence of totalitarian doctrines reinforced the conclusion that the ecumenical task must be conceived as a single whole. This total challenge could be answered only by a total response. False ideology could be met only by sound doctrine combined with practical decisions in the social and political realm. The new and violent nationalism, with its demand for a nationalized Church wholly subservient to the State, brought out more clearly than ever before the great spiritual dangers inherent in the idea of purely national Churches without any sense of cohesion or solidarity with each other. In Dr Arnold Toynbee's caustic words:

> "In the freest flight of imagination it would be difficult to conceive of a sharper contradiction of the essence of Christianity . . . than is embodied in this monstrous product of the impact of Parochialism upon the Western Christian Church in the Modern Age of our Western history."[2]

In the years of the emergence of the new totalitarianism many discovered that truth. Obviously the only remedy was a new affirmation and manifestation of universality as an essential characteristic of the Church.

All this leads on to the less tangible, but in the long run most decisive, factor—the "rediscovery of the Church" which took place in so many different circles at about the same time. This new conviction about the Church was partly based on the theological development which had taken place in the 1920's and the 1930's. The thesis that the Church was not rooted in the original Gospel, but had been added on to it, was increasingly repudiated, and both Biblical and systematic theologians were teaching with conviction that the Church is an essential element of the primitive *kerygma*, and therefore also of the Christian faith. This new consensus about the Church was reinforced by the influence of the movements for Church renewal in various countries and by the new encounter between Eastern Orthodoxy and Western Christianity. It is significant that the words which were generally picked out as the key phrase of the Oxford Conference of 1937 were—

[1] See Chap. ix, pp. 430 f.
[2] Arnold Toynbee, *A Study of History*, IV, pp. 221 f.

"Let the Church be the Church".[1] Now, in the light of that rediscovery, it became increasingly clear that the primary motive in the ecumenical movement must not be to create a sense of spiritual unity between Christians or to facilitate co-operation between Churches, however important these objectives may be, but rather to demonstrate the true nature of the Church in its oneness, its universality, and its apostolic and prophetic witness in the world.

"The more deeply the present situation in the world is studied, the clearer becomes the necessity for a deepened understanding of the ecumenical nature of the Church", wrote J. H. Oldham in 1936. The primary question before the Churches was whether they were, as separate bodies and in their totality, living and acting as the Church of Christ. This question could not be answered by a demonstration of social activity or by the presentation of the historic confessions and creeds. It cut deeper than either. It transcended the problems on which Life and Work and Faith and Order had mainly concentrated. The Churches themselves had become deeply secularized and, unless they could learn again to "be the Church" in its total consecration to God and cease to conform to the world, their message to society would be unconvincing and their efforts for greater unity meaningless. As Archbishop Temple said at Edinburgh 1937, what was needed was that the *Una Sancta* should declare itself; but this meant that the Churches should seek to help each other in all aspects of their common task and enter into full spiritual fellowship with each other.[2]

To resume the narrative of the main events leading up to the formation of the World Council: at the end of 1935 Archbishop Temple visited the United States, and the American sections of Faith and Order and Life and Work arranged for an informal consultation at the home of Dr J. Ross Stevenson at Princeton. A number of persons connected with the I.M.C., the World Alliance, and the W.S.C.F. were also invited. The Archbishop suggested that "the time had come for an interdenominational, international council representing all the Churches, with committees to carry on various projects now forming the objectives of the distinct world movements". In the discussions which followed many strong reasons were given for closer co-ordination—the complexity of the existing situation; the need to present the ecumenical task to the Churches as one single common task; the demand for a body through which the Churches would be able to speak together to the world; the more effective relating of the younger Churches to the ecumenical movement; and, last but not least, the urgency of united witness in a world in which "nationalism robs us of our spiritual inheritance—the ideal of Christendom". The consultation recommended accordingly that the informal consultative group which had been in existence for some time should be given regular status, and that the ecumenical Christian organizations at their next meetings should take suitable action to make the existing co-operation more effective. This consultation created new opportunities.

The man who translated those opportunities into specific and concrete proposals was Dr J. H. Oldham. In a memorandum prepared for the summer (1936) meeting of Life and Work, he expressed the conviction that it was now or never. "The holding of the ecumenical conferences in 1937 provides an opportunity which will not recur for many years, of having the whole question of the future

[1] See Chap. xii, pp. 574 ff.
[2] Opening Sermon, *The Second World Conference on Faith and Order*, ed. Leonard Hodgson, pp. 20 f.

of the ecumenical movement examined afresh. . . . In the historical crisis in which the Church finds itself there is need of facing these questions with the greatest deliberation and of bringing to bear upon them the best statesmanship that the Church can command. The best means of doing this would seem to be the appointment in consultation with the other ecumenical movements of a committee which would meet prior to the conferences at Oxford and Edinburgh and present a report to the conferences." This proposal was approved by the summer (1936) meetings of Life and Work and Faith and Order. The Committees of the World Alliance and of the I.M.C. also authorized their officers to participate in the work of this new committee.

The choice of the thirty-five members of the body which was to work out the new plan was left to the Ecumenical Consultative Group. This group consulted many Churches and drew up its list at a meeting held in London in October 1936.

The mandate of "the Thirty-five" was "to review the work of the ecumenical movement since the Stockholm and Lausanne Conferences and to report to the Oxford and Edinburgh Conferences regarding the future of the ecumenical movement". In starting its work on this formidable task the committee could count on the willingness of many to arrive at new solutions, but it had as yet little ground under its feet.

The Committee of Thirty-five met at Westfield College, London, 8–10 July 1937. The members present represented the main streams of the ecumenical movement, including the Y.M.C.A., the Y.W.C.A., and the W.S.C.F. No specific plan was before the meeting. But with remarkable rapidity and unanimity the thoughts of the whole group converged on one and the same conviction—that the time had come to form a World Council of Churches as a permanent organ of the Churches for the accomplishment of their common ecumenical task. The Council was defined as "a body representative of the Churches and caring for the interests of Life and Work and Faith and Order respectively".[1] The main architects of the plan were William Temple, J. H. Oldham, William Adams Brown, and Samuel McCrea Cavert, General Secretary of the Federal Council in America. It was Dr Cavert who first suggested the name "World Council of Churches".

How did it come about that a meeting of men and women of such diverse backgrounds arrived in so short a time at a common mind concerning a most intricate problem unsolved in twenty years? And how did these men and women, on the very eve of the two world conferences, dare to propose such a radically new departure? The answer is contained in the story of the preceding years. A glance at the list of those who attended this meeting shows that the majority had been engaged for many years in one or several of the ecumenical movements and had learned to co-operate closely with one another. To such men and women it seemed most natural to give organizational expression to their consciousness of one common ecumenical task. As we have seen, the idea of a World Council of Churches had come alive in the hearts and minds of many. It was realized that the theme had been present all the time, half heard and waiting for the appointed moment, which had now arrived, to dominate the symphony.

It is interesting to observe which of the main emphases in the first draft of the plan were finally taken over into the structure of the World Council of Churches

---

[1] The report of the Committee appears in the Official Reports of the Oxford and Edinburgh Conferences: *The Churches Survey Their Task*, pp. 276–81; *The Second World Conference on Faith and Order, Edinburgh 1937*, pp. 270–74.

as established in 1948. The Westfield meeting emphasized the principle, later adopted in the Constitution, that the Council should have no power to legislate for the Churches or to commit them to action without their consent. It proposed, moreover, for its structure a General Assembly to meet once in five years, and a Central Council (later called the Central Committee) to meet annually. On the other hand, the Amsterdam Assembly made considerable changes in the West-field plan with regard to the manner of representation. The Westfield meeting proposed a system of regional representation. In America delegates were to be appointed through the Federal Council. This was challenged by some at the Utrecht Conference.[1] The Amsterdam Assembly adopted a system in which equal emphasis is given to the confessional and regional principles.[2]

The plan provided for the integration in the World Council of Life and Work and Faith and Order only, and not of the other ecumenical bodies. This was because the other movements did not feel in the same way as Faith and Order and Life and Work that direct and official dependence upon the Churches as such was desirable or necessary.[3]

The World Council idea had been launched. But would the Life and Work and Faith and Order Conferences accept it? The proposals of the Committee of Thirty-five were submitted to the Oxford Conference (12–26 July 1937). Arch-bishop Temple and several other members of the Committee recommended the adoption of the new plan. The Archbishop stressed the need for a body which would provide "a voice for non-Roman Christendom", and the desirability of basing the whole ecumenical movement more directly on the Churches them-selves. The proposal was adopted with only two dissentient voices.

The common service of worship held at St Paul's Cathedral, London, for delegates to the two Conferences helped to show that Life and Work and Faith and Order were closely related to each other. The Edinburgh Conference on Faith and Order followed almost immediately (3–18 August). Since it was known that some members of the Conference were suspicious of the new proposal, the Report of the Committee was at once referred to a special committee under the chairmanship of Dr J. Ross Stevenson. This reported to the Conference as a whole on 11 August.[4] Its recommendation was to commend the plan to the favourable consideration of the Churches, but to instruct the Continuation Committee of Faith and Order to give approval to the plan only if certain guarantees could be incorporated.

The discussion was lively. Most speakers were strongly in favour of the plan, but it was clear that some members had misgivings. There was criticism of the phrase "the voice of non-Roman Christendom", which seemed to suggest some-thing akin to a Super-Church. Strong emphasis was laid on the guarantee con-cerning the basis, and it was urged that the Trinitarian basis should be maintained as the basis for all work in the field of Faith and Order. Unfortunately, the hour was late and the debate was not carried to a conclusion. A motion to adjourn was defeated by a narrow margin. When the motion to approve the report was put, it was carried with one dissentient. The matter came up again in connection with the report of the section on the Church's Unity in Life and Worship, when the Bishop of Gloucester (A. C. Headlam) expressed his fear that the new Council would pass resolutions on public affairs and so do a great deal of harm. It was

---

[1] See p. 705.   [2] For further developments in the matter of representation, see p. 720.
[3] William Pierson Merrill in *World Alliance News Letter*, April 1950.
[4] *The Second World Conference*, pp. 196–204.

decided to record that some members desired to place on record their opposition to the proposal, and with this addition the relevant paragraph was finally approved *nem. con.*[1]

The Oxford and Edinburgh Conferences had each appointed seven members and seven alternates (called the Committee of Fourteen) to put the plan into execution. But although these representatives had full authority to go forward, it was clear that in order to secure the full co-operation of the Churches themselves, it would be necessary to consult the Churches about the nature and structure of the new World Council which it was proposed to set up. Accordingly, at the first meeting of the Committee of Fourteen held in London in August 1937, it was decided to call together a special advisory Conference to aid the Committee of Fourteen in the discharge of its responsibilities, especially in drawing up the Constitution of the World Council. This Conference met at Utrecht, 9–12 May 1938. In size and composition it corresponded as nearly as possible to the Central Council proposed in the report of the Committee of Thirty-five. But there was this difference, that in the United States the delegates were not chosen by the Federal Council but by a special electoral conference held in Washington.

The Utrecht Conference laid the solid foundation on which the provisonal structure and later the permanent structure were built. No one expected that this provisional structure would have to last for ten years.

The most important constitutional questions concerned the authority and the Basis of the Council.

With regard to its authority, full agreement was reached without difficulty; it was made very clear that the World Council was in no sense a Super-Church. It was not to legislate for the Churches. As Archbishop Temple put it in his Explanatory Memorandum:

> "It is not a federation as commonly understood, and its Assembly and Central Committee will have no constitutional authority whatever over its constituent churches. Any authority that it may have will consist in the weight it carries with the churches by its wisdom."

It is interesting to note that, though certainly without intention, Archbishop Temple used almost the same words as Archbishop Söderblom, who, at Oud Wassenaar in 1919, had said, "This ecumenical council would not be invested with exterior authority, but would have to gain influence in proportion to the spiritual authority with which it would speak".[2]

The question of the Basis could not be settled so rapidly. Should the theological basis on which the Faith and Order Conference had been convened—confession of faith in our Lord Jesus Christ as God and Saviour[3]—become the basis for the World Council as a whole, or should another be formulated? The Chairman, Archbishop Temple, informed the Conference that, while the proposal to adopt the Faith and Order basis had come from many sides, some Churches had issued warnings against its adoption, since they could not conscientiously accept it. He expressed the opinion that, whether the World Council adopted this or any other basis, it could not act as an ecclesiastical court with power to decide whether a

---

[1] See Chap. ix, pp. 433 f., and *The Second World Conference*, pp. 268 f.
[2] *Ecumenical Review*, Vol. I, No. 1, p. 86; and Chap. xi, pp. 533 f.
[3] See Chap. ix, p. 435.

Church could be regarded as coming within the terms of its invitation. Each Church must decide whether it was ready and able to collaborate on this basis. Canon Hodgson, the Secretary of the Faith and Order movement, declared that Faith and Order had no wish to impose its own standard on the Council as a whole, but would be satisfied if its own work could be conducted on the basis which it had adopted from the beginning.

Many speakers favoured the adoption of the Faith and Order formula, since this had proved in practice an adequate basis for the meeting of the Christian Churches. The overwhelming majority were agreed that, if a World Council of Churches was to be formed, it should be made clear from the outset that the Churches were gathered together by the divine Lord of the Church. The Chairman could, therefore, sum up by saying that it was clearly desirable to use the Faith and Order basis, but that it was necessary to keep the door open for co-operation in some form with bodies which could not accept it.

The Basis adopted at Utrecht and confirmed at the first Assembly of the World Council of Churches is as follows: "The World Council of Churches is a fellowship of Churches which accept our Lord Jesus Christ as God and Saviour."

Another problem discussed very fully was the method of appointment of the Central Committee. The proposals before the Conference were based on a system of regional representation, but a strong plea was made by some delegates for a system of confessional representation. The regional principle was finally adopted, but the advocates of the confessional principle reserved the right to come back to this question later.[1]

The Utrecht Conference had also to make provision for the interim period till a General Assembly could be convened. A Provisional Committee was created, consisting of the members of the Committee of Fourteen and their alternates and some other members appointed by Life and Work and Faith and Order. This Provisional Committee held its first meeting in Utrecht on 13 May. It elected the Archbishop of York (Temple) as Chairman, and Dr John R. Mott, Archbishop Germanos, and Dr Marc Boegner as Vice-Chairmen. An Administrative Committee was appointed with Dr Marc Boegner as Chairman. Dr W. A. Visser 't Hooft was invited to become General Secretary, and Dr William Paton and Dr Henry Smith Leiper to become Associate General Secretaries.

The Administrative Committee of Life and Work had transferred its responsibilities to this Provisional Committee, so that the latter body became directly responsible for the activities of Life and Work, as for all new projects initiated during the interim period. The Faith and Order Continuation Committee continued to be responsible for Faith and Order activities. The result was that Faith and Order retained separate identity, whereas the former tasks of Life and Work were merged with the new tasks which the Provisional Committee undertook.

According to the decision of the Edinburgh Conference, the completed plan had to be submitted to the Continuation Committee of Faith and Order. This was done at a meeting at Clarens (Switzerland), 29 August to 1 September 1938. The Committee proposed some minor modifications, but decided that "the constitution of the World Council, as presented and amended, conforms to the requirements made at Edinburgh". The plan could now be submitted to the

[1] See p. 703.

Churches, and in autumn 1938 the Constitution of the proposed World Council of Churches, together with an Explanatory Memorandum drawn up by Archbishop Temple and a letter of invitation to join the Council signed by the members of the Committee of Fourteen, was sent to all the Churches which had been invited to the Oxford and Edinburgh Conferences.

Although several officers of the I.M.C. had been among the most active participants in drawing up the plan for the World Council, the question of the relationship between the I.M.C. and the World Council had not yet been faced. This question was important to both movements, for the World Council stood in need of the experience and evangelistic zeal of the missionary movement, while the latter needed to be in touch with the ecumenical conversations and planning of the Churches. A real difficulty was the difference in the structure of the two bodies, for while the I.M.C. was a Council made up of National Conferences of Missionary Societies and National Christian Councils, the World Council of Churches was a Council in which the Churches had direct membership. The Meeting of the I.M.C. at Tambaram (Madras) at the end of 1938 provided an opportunity for thorough discussion. Dr William Paton spoke strongly in favour of close relations with the World Council, which he described as "a symbol of the Church within the churches, an acknowledgment of the existence of a universal fellowship of Christians really living and active in spite of our ecclesiastical divisions".[1] The main argument in favour of drawing close to the World Council was, he said, "that the International Missionary Council has no meaning except in so far as it is a constant reminder of the Christian obligation to the evangelisation of the world" and that it had therefore "something of priceless value to bring into the whole Christian ecumenical movement, something without which that movement could hardly live".[2]

The Conference accepted the finding of its section on Co-operation and Unity, that "we have heard with interest of the proposed formation of the World Council of Churches", but added the cautionary note that "in welcoming the appearance of this Council we consider that the distinctive service and organization of the International Missionary Council should be maintained. It is of particular importance that nothing should be done to undermine the confidence in the International Missionary Council that has been built up during so many years".[3]

A little later the Council itself affirmed that it was responsive to the desire that mutually helpful relationships should be established, and authorized its committee to carry forward negotiations to this end.[4] It further proposed that a Joint Committee be set up to study matters of common concern, and formally agreed that Dr Willam Paton, one of the I.M.C.'s Secretaries, should give part-time service to the World Council—a decision of considerable significance for the future relations of the two bodies.

One of the major concerns of the I.M.C. was that full advantage should be taken by the ecumenical movement of the spiritual gifts which the younger Churches were now in a position to offer. In the first Faith and Order and Life and Work Conferences the representation of the younger Churches had been wholly inadequate. In 1934 it had been decided, on the motion of Dr Paton, that the National Christian Councils in Asia and Africa should be accepted as doing the work of the "fifth section" of Life and Work.[5] At the 1937 Conferences

[1] *Tambaram, Madras, Series*, VII, p. 122.   [2] Ibid., p. 123.   [3] Ibid., IV, p. 375.
[4] *I.M.C. Minutes, Madras 1938*, pp. 46–60.   [5] See Chap. xii, pp. 553 f.

younger Church leaders had made outstanding contributions. But there was still a widespread feeling that the ecumenical movement continued to be far too exclusively Western. For this reason the Tambaram Meeting put itself on record to the effect that "we look forward with confidence to the part which the younger churches will play in the future work of the Council. We trust that in the application of the constitution care will be taken to insure that the membership of the Council is genuinely representative of indigenous leadership."[1]

A few weeks later, in January 1939, the second full meeting of the Provisional Committee of the World Council was held at St Germain. In spite of the political tension and the menace of war, the meeting looked to the future. It was decided provisionally to fix August 1941 as the date for the first Assembly. The action of the Tambaram Meeting of the I.M.C. was welcomed and steps were taken to set up a Joint Committee of the I.M.C. and the W.C.C. It was decided that a letter be sent to the Vatican, giving information about the formation of the World Council.[2]

During this period the officers of the Provisional Committee followed the increasingly serious development of the Church conflict in Germany with intense concern. In so doing they maintained the policy of their Life and Work predecessors in giving spiritual support to the Confessing Church, which was felt to represent the whole Church of Christ in its battle for the purity and truth of the Christian message. When eleven German Church leaders (mostly belonging to the so-called German Christian party) issued a declaration which condemned "every supranational or international Church structure, whether in the form of Roman Catholicism or of World Protestantism, as a political distortion of Christianity" (it also contained anti-Semitic pronouncements), the officers of the Provisional Committee issued a declaration expressing their belief in the spiritual unity of all those who are in Christ, irrespective of race, nation, or sex.

An important conference on the international situation under the auspices of the Council and the World Alliance met in July 1939 at Geneva. It was a small but representative group of specialists on international questions and Church leaders. Among them were Mr John Foster Dulles (U.S.A.), Professor Max Huber (Switzerland), M. Charles Rist (France), Professor van Asbeck (Holland), and Dr von der Gablentz (Germany). Meeting as it did in the poisoned international atmosphere of the last weeks before the outbreak of war, the conference had many dramatic moments, but there was substantial agreement on crucial points. Its report stated:

> "We believe that no decision secured by force of arms will be just and that out of the evil forces thereby set in motion, more evil is bound to come. We believe that decision by negotiation, conference, and methods of conciliation should always be an available alternative method. We believe that such procedures should be adopted free of the menace of force."

The report was submitted to the Administrative Committee at its meeting in Zeist (Holland) later in July. The Committee decided to send the report to the Churches, again calling special attention to the section on the tasks of the Church in time of war—true Christian prayer and preaching centred on the righteousness of the Kingdom; maintenance of brotherly relations between the Churches

---

[1] *Tambaram, Madras, Series*, IV, p. 375.   [2] See Chap. xv, p. 686.

in spite of propaganda; preparation of a just and lasting peace; counteracting hatred; ministry to prisoners of war and refugees. A cynic might well have asked if there were any chance that in case of total war the Churches would remember these good intentions. But it can and must be said that, when total war came, the great majority of Church leaders did not forget their obligation to the Lord of the Church and their obligation to their fellow Christians. A comparison of the attitude of the Churches in the first world war with their message in the second shows that ecumenical intercourse had made a real difference.

The Provisional Committee took a considerable share in the World Conference of Christian Youth held at Amsterdam, 24 July to 2 August 1939, under the auspices of all Christian ecumenical bodies concerned with youth. The Christian young people of seventy-one nations were represented. It was an opportunity to share the results of years of intensive ecumenical work with young people from all over the world. In the providence of God it was much more—a lighthouse which threw its rays into the darkness of the following years. In its Message the Amsterdam Conference declared: "The nations and peoples of the world are drifting apart, the Churches are coming together. There is a growing conviction of the essential togetherness of all Christians." These words were confirmed by the events of the years to come. For many young men and women the message of *Christus Victor* remained a firm anchor in the chaos of destruction.

Within four weeks of the closing of the Youth Conference the second world war had broken out.

2. THE YEARS OF WAR, 1939–1945

The war years were the testing time of the World Council. The first issue to be faced was the definition of the specific duty of the Council in time of war. This was fully discussed at the meeting of the Administrative Committee near Apeldoorn, Holland, in January 1940.[1] The Committee found itself confronted with a complex problem. On the initiative of Bishop Berggrav of Oslo, leaders of the Scandinavian Churches had declared themselves in favour of mediation between the hostile powers, and Bishop Berggrav had visited statesmen in Berlin and London for this purpose. The Scandinavian representatives who had come to Holland wished therefore to discuss further steps towards mediation which might be taken by the Churches concerned. Such discussion took place outside the Administrative Committee; the result was a statement drawn up by Archbishop Temple and signed by the four British participants concerning the conditions under which, in their opinion, negotiations could be opened. This statement was later published in the British Press.

When the Administrative Committee itself came to discuss the question of the attitude of the World Council, there was considerable difference of opinion. Several believed that the one urgent task of the Church was to work for mediation, and that a pronouncement concerning the basic issues at stake in the conflict would jeopardize action for peace. Others believed that a definite statement should be made condemning aggression and the suppression of freedom. It

[1] The story of the meeting near Apeldoorn is told more fully in Margaret Sinclair, *William Paton*, pp. 234–39. That account, however, gives the impression that the discussion concerning Bishop Berggrav's efforts at mediation took place in the meeting of the Administrative Committee. As a matter of fact, two separate meetings were held at Apeldoorn. One meeting was concerned with peace negotiations; the other was a regular meeting of the Administrative Committee.

proved impossible to issue a common statement; all drafts submitted to the Committee were rejected. It was decided to continue the discussion by correspondence. In April the General Secretary submitted a new proposal for a common pronouncement. But, before answers had come in from the members, in May 1940 the "real war" had broken out and a wholly different situation had arisen.

From 1940 to 1945 the Council was unable to act normally through its responsible committees. It seemed at first that the war would not merely slow up the process of the formation of the Council, but might well lead to its complete disintegration. The staff became smaller and smaller. Many plans—first and foremost the plan to hold the Assembly in 1941—had to be cancelled. The provisional structure of the Council, which had not yet been authorized by the Churches, seemed altogether too shaky to stand the strain. It appeared for a time as though hardly any contacts could be maintained with the Churches.

But in the midst of the war years the tide turned. Instead of a period of stagnation the war proved to be a time of deepening and intensifying ecumenical fellowship. In 1945 Bishop Berggrav could say: "In these last years we have lived more intimately with each other than in times when we could communicate with each other. We prayed together more, we listened together more to the Word of God, our hearts were together more." The struggle to be the Church—essentially one and the same struggle in many countries—the common defence against the ideological attack on the Church Universal, the common suffering, the opportunity to serve prisoners of war and refugees from other nations—these proved more powerful factors in building ecumenical conviction than conferences, committees, or journeys.

Churches and individual churchmen proved willing to pay a heavy price for their membership in the *Una Sancta*. The Churches which openly declared their faith in the Holy Catholic Church over against pagan or semi-pagan nationalistic distortions of Christianity; the men and women who shared the life of the refugees and fought to save them from death; the men and women of many nationalities and positions who as officers, as civilians, or as "illegal" couriers kept the Churches in touch with one another, were in those years the real builders of the ecumenical fellowship.

It was the privilege of the World Council headquarters in Geneva to become one of the main centres of this creative movement. It proved possible to maintain relationships in various unusual ways with most of the Churches of Europe and with those of the United States. Geneva was a city in which servants of the philanthropic societies, diplomats, resistance-leaders, refugees, and Church leaders of many nations met and helped each other to keep the lines of communication open. In some cases documents crossed the frontiers in diplomatic bags; in other cases through the courier-service which the illegal press of the resistance movements had established between the various countries. Much of the material came in the form of tiny microfilms which might be hidden in a piece of shaving-soap or a fountain-pen. In this way information constantly streamed through the World Council office and was passed on to the Churches through the Ecumenical Press Service or in less official ways. Much of this information found its way into the illegal press. The story of the spiritual resistance of the Churches in one country encouraged and strengthened those of other countries. It made all the difference to men in the dangerous or lonely sections of the Church's battlefront to know that they were surrounded by the whole company of the faithful. A special tribute is due to Dr H. Schönfeld, whose untiring and perilous labours opened up lines of communication with many who otherwise could never have been reached.

Constant contact was maintained with Christian leaders in both camps, and thus in a quiet but very real way the words of the Message of the Oxford Conference came true:

> "If war breaks out, then pre-eminently the Church must manifestly be the Church, still united as the one body of Christ, though the nations wherein it is planted fight each other."

Specially significant were the visits of Dietrich Bonhoeffer of Germany to Geneva and Stockholm, as occasions for thorough discussions concerning the specific responsibility of the Church for the future international order. In spite of instructions given by the National Socialist authorities to watch the World Council and its emissaries, its relationships with the Confessing Church in Germany were never interrupted. A secret Gestapo document, published after the war,[1] states that the influence of the ecumenical movement on German church life is very considerable, and gives the order that an agent must be placed in the ecumenical bodies in Geneva. It is probable that this order was never carried out.

Contacts with Britain and the United States were relatively frequent until the end of 1942, when the whole of France was occupied by the Germans. It was fortunate indeed that in the spring of 1942 Dr Visser 't Hooft was able to visit Britain, and that, just before the passage across France was blocked, Dr Cavert could come from America to Geneva. Since it proved impossible to hold fully representative meetings, the Provisional Committee met and continued to meet in three groups—one in Geneva under the leadership of Dr Boegner (later of Dr Koechlin), one in Britain under Archbishop Temple, and one in New York under Dr John R. Mott. From these meetings a number of messages were sent to all the Churches which could be reached. The fact that the World Council had offices in New York, London, and Geneva proved a blessing, for each office had its area of contacts with Churches which the others could not reach. The solidarity of the Churches in different parts of the world was demonstrated in a remarkable way as (largely owing to the untiring efforts of Dr Leiper and Dr Paton) American and British Churches, as well as the Churches in neutral countries, continued to raise considerable funds for the various war-time activities of the Council.

During the war years both friends and critics often asked why the World Council as a whole did not speak out concerning the great issues which were at stake. Attempts to arrive at agreed statements were made more than once, but the prevailing opinion was that during its period of formation the World Council was not competent to speak in the name of the Churches. There was a further consideration which Archbishop Temple formulated in a letter to the General Secretary (20 May 1940) as follows:

> "If we speak corporately we may find that we have erected fresh barriers to the reconstruction of the fellowship. Christians from one country can meet Christians from another country with which they have been fighting in an organization which has not corporately taken sides; it will be difficult,

---

[1] The relevant sections of these instructions are published in Heinrich Schmied, *Apokalyptisches Wetterleuchten* Munich, 1947, p. 208.

almost impossible, to do this in an organization which has officially condemned, directly or by implication, their own country. . . . I want us all to prophesy individually and to do this in contact with one another through your office: so the same message will be given ecumenically though with a variety of emphases."

This was precisely what happened during the critical years. Church leaders in different countries spoke individually, but sought to remember that they spoke as members of a supranational fellowship.

It was, moreover, during the war years that the Council began to concern itself with spiritual and material aid to the needy. Refugees and prisoners of war in their isolation rejoiced to find that the ministry of their own Churches was being temporarily taken over by the ecumenical bodies. Many lonely men and women discovered in their camps what it means to belong to the world-wide fellowship in Christ which seeks its children wherever they are. For the World Council, which had so far moved too exclusively in the sphere of conferences, reports, and documents, it was a searching and salutary experience to enter into immediate contact with the stark needs of human beings.

Work for refugees, begun before the war, grew rapidly as thousands of non-Aryans sought to escape from Germany or occupied areas or were deported to various countries. The World Council, with the help of funds from the United States, Sweden, and Switzerland, was able to make the existence of the refugees in their miserable circumstances more bearable. It could give support to those Christian workers in the countries most concerned, such as Pastor Grüber in Germany and the leaders of the "Cimade"[1] in France, who took great personal risks in seeking to save non-Aryans from almost certain death. It was a joy to work with that gallant band of men and women who brought the refugees across mountains and rivers to places of safety.

Work for prisoners of war grew even more rapidly. It began in 1940 in a small way. Its purpose was to help prisoners of war in the creation of active Christian congregations in the camps and to give them as much spiritual encouragement as possible. The first Easter booklet went out in French in 3,000 copies. But the Christmas booklet for 1944 was circulated in 68,000 copies and in six languages. During the whole period of service more than five million copies of books, pamphlets, tracts, and periodicals were published for prisoners of war. With the support of the American Bible Society, large quantities of Scriptures were also printed and distributed—twenty-four editions in eleven languages. At the same time a ministry of visitation and correspondence was carried on amongst prisoners in many countries.[2] In this work there was close co-operation with the Y.M.C.A., the Y.W.C.A.,[3] and the Red Cross. Christians of all Churches and nations collaborated in the most whole-hearted manner. The Emergency Committee of Christian Organizations, already formed in Geneva in the first months of the war, and later also in other places, provided an indispensable clearing-house and channel of mutual help.

In 1942, on the occasion of Dr Cavert's visit to Geneva, plans were made for post-war reconstruction and inter-Church aid. The extent of the need and the extent of the co-operation which had developed between the Churches made it

[1] See Chap. xiii, p. 605.
[2] The story of the "Churches in Captivity" is given in *Églises de la Captivité*, Geneva, 1942.
[3] See Chap. xiii, pp. 604 f.

clear that post-war reconstruction could and should be conceived in such a way that "all Churches which can help should come to the rescue of all Churches which need help". The World Council was the natural clearing-house for such a process of mutual help, and could build on the traditions of the European Central Bureau for Inter-Church Aid, of which Professor Adolph Keller was the Director.[1] Thanks to the fact that the preparations had begun so early in Geneva, in Britain (on Dr Paton's initiative), and in America (on the initiative of Dr Ralph Diffendorfer; Dr Warnshuis' visit to the Continent in 1944 also helped greatly in this respect), the Department of Reconstruction and Inter-Church Aid was able to begin its work in western Europe from the moment at which any territory was liberated.

Much time and energy were devoted to the problems of the post-war settlement. Since the Geneva headquarters was almost the only place in constant touch with supporters of the ecumenical movement in both camps, it was natural that discussion concerning the character of the future peace should be developed with great intensity. Specific discussions could be carried on only by small groups and without publicity; but such discussions resulted from time to time in suggestions and proposals which were passed on to responsible statesmen. The most important of these were proposals made by German resistance leaders and transmitted to London in April 1942 through World Council leaders who had talked with them in Geneva; and those which arrived a little later as the fruit of similar ecumenical contacts in Stockholm in May of the same year.[2]

In the meantime the Study Department promoted a more general discussion concerning post-war international order between several groups on the Continent, the Just and Durable Peace Commission of the Federal Council, and the Peace Aims Group in Britain. All these groups were eager to discover the convictions of Christians in other lands, to remove misunderstandings, and to prepare the way for that fraternal and constructive meeting of minds which took place immediately after the war. Many of the plans developed in the war years could not be carried out. In the light of later developments much now seems strangely idealistic. But it remains a significant fact that in the midst of a total war it proved possible to pursue this fraternal and constructive planning for the future.

Thus the war years, which might so easily have brought about the total disruption and destruction of the ecumenical movement as it had grown up in the 1920's and 1930's, had in fact given it more substance. Paradoxically, it was in those years that the movement learned to stand on its own feet, and live from day to day in the conviction that the Lord would continue to gather his children together. The report of the General Secretary early in 1946 affirmed that:

> "For those who have had the privilege to be associated with the Council in war-time, these years will always stand out as the time when the ecumenical task was spiritually easy and simple, because in spite of the enormous technical difficulties, the marching orders were so very clear and the basic unity of the defenders of the faith was so deeply felt."

Many leaders were taken away during the war years.

The loss of Archbishop William Temple, to whom the whole movement

[1] See Chap. xii, p. 558.
[2] The story of the discussions in Stockholm is told by the Bishop of Chichester (Bell) in his *The Church and Humanity*, London, 1946, pp. 165–76.

looked as its God-given leader, was the severest of all. Sir John Maud has recorded that the Archbishop once said of a young friend who was killed: "He will not do on earth the work that we had hoped. So we must do it for him. We shall not do it so well." It is impossible to feel otherwise about William Temple himself.

For William Temple had an unique place in the ecumenical movement. He belonged to all parts of it. Since the Lausanne Conference he had been closely identified with Faith and Order, of which he later became Chairman. Since the Jerusalem Conference (he wrote the greater part of its Message) he had participated in the life of the I.M.C. The Message of Oxford 1937 was largely his work. When the Provisional Committee of the World Council of Churches was formed, there was not the slightest doubt that he was the right man to preside over it. He was equally in the closest touch with the younger generation and in constant demand for national and international student and youth conferences.

Temple's strength as an ecumenical leader consisted in the rare combination of a clear theological and ecclesiastical position and a penetrating insight into other positions. His was a mind which did not need to become a closed mind in order to take a firm stand, and which ever remained open to new aspects of the truth. He could lead his readers or hearers to the deep places, as in his *Readings in St John's Gospel* or in his sermons on the Christocentric nature of true ecumenical unity. But he could also show amazing breadth as he sought to summarize complicated discussions in which the most divergent viewpoints had been put forward, and as he sought to remain in touch with new movements of thought in the younger generation. In his own country he has been called "everybody's Archbishop", because he was considered to be a leader of all and a spokesman for all. His position in the ecumenical movement was similar, in that all parts of it and all Churches looked upon him as its leader.

Of equal gravity was the loss of William Paton, one of the true architects of the Council, who would have been one of its most trusted leaders in the difficult postwar years and would have helped powerfully in establishing close relationships with the I.M.C. and the younger Churches. Paton was first and foremost a missionary, and his primary concern was for the world-wide missionary outreach of the Church as it found embodiment in the I.M.C. But it was precisely because of his strong conviction about the missionary obligation of the Church that he came to take a deep interest in Faith and Order, in Life and Work, and later on in the formation of the World Council of Churches. The one theme which came to pervade all his speaking and writing was that of the emergence of a world Christian community as the great fact, but also as the great challenge, for our generation. He was a man of strong opinions and of single purpose. There was in him a rock-like quality which made him a leader to be relied upon, and his death seemed an almost irreparable loss to the ecumenical movement at a critical stage of its life.

Another grievous loss was the death in January 1945 of Bishop V. S. Azariah of Dornakal, the great champion of ecumenism amongst the younger Churches. We had also to mourn William Adams Brown, pioneer for closer collaboration between Faith and Order and Life and Work; Dr J. Ross Stevenson, who had so wisely chaired the committee on the World Council at Edinburgh 1937; Dr A. E. Garvie, a leader in both Faith and Order and Life and Work; and Bishop George Craig Stewart of the Protestant Episcopal Church. Pastor Dietrich Bonhoeffer was killed in a concentration camp just before the end of the war. He was the ecumenical theologian and ambassador of the Confessing Church who risked his life in order to maintain the links between the Church in Germany and the World Council. Among younger men a severe loss was Theodore Carswell Hume, first American representative on the staff of the World Council. The aircraft in which he was travelling to Stockholm in 1943 was shot down.

3. THE POST-WAR YEARS, 1945–1948

The post-war years were a time of great expansion of the opportunities and tasks of the World Council. The needs which had to be met by inter-Church collaboration, the desire for renewal of ecumenical fellowship, the deeper understanding in the Churches of their ecumenical privileges and obligations, were powerful factors forcing the Provisional Committee to accept much larger responsibilities than it had originally intended to assume during the period of the Council's formation. It did so believing that the work undertaken was in line with the intentions of the Oxford, Edinburgh, and Utrecht Conferences, and that the whole question of the nature and scope of World Council activities would be reviewed at the first Assembly.

During the weeks just before and after the end of hostilities in Europe, groups of members of the Provisional Committee held important meetings in London and New York in which the foundation was laid for the work of the post-war period. The New York meetings were attended by a European delegation— Pastor Boegner, the Bishop of Chichester, and the General Secretary. It was an immense help that the Federal Council of Churches were able to lend the services of Dr Cavert for some months to the headquarters in Geneva.

After the Armistice in Europe the World Council staff grew by leaps and bounds. This was mainly due to the fact that the Reconstruction Department was faced with an almost overwhelming task, and had to build up almost overnight an adequate organization to meet the immediate needs of the Churches in Europe. The response of the Churches, notably of those of the United States, Great Britain, Switzerland, and Sweden, partly by making workers available and especially in the provision of funds, was most encouraging. Thus, under Dr J. Hutchison Cockburn's leadership, the Department was able to help, and to help quickly, in the many places where without outside aid the work of the Church could not be carried on. Soon it became clear that conditions in many parts of Europe were such that it was indispensable to add direct material relief in the form of food and clothing, and a special section of the Department under the direction of Dr S. C. Michelfelder was set up to meet this need. There can be no question that this work of reconstruction became one of the most powerful factors in arousing in the Churches, both giving and receiving, a new sense of ecumenical solidarity across confessional as well as national boundaries.

In its Message the New York meeting of May 1945 had said:

> "We hope that means may be found in the near future for frank and intimate discussions among churchmen of both sides of the war who have put the service of their Lord above every other consideration. . . . It is the heart of the Gospel that through men's reconciliation with God by the Cross, their reconciliation with one another is possible."

But would it really be possible to arrive at a restoration of confidence not merely between the very small group of those who had kept more or less in touch with each other but between the Churches, including those who had suffered so deeply? Would the Churches follow their leaders? Or would the movement be condemned to go through that same interminable and painful process of sterile discussions concerning war guilt which had hung like a heavy cloud over the ecumenical movement after the first world war?

It was with such questions in mind that a World Council delegation, composed of American, British, Dutch, French, and Swiss churchmen went to Stuttgart in October 1945 in order to meet with the new Council of the Evangelical Church in Germany. Their uncertainty was quickly dispelled, for at the very beginning of the meeting the members of the new Council expressed in the clearest terms their consciousness of implication in the guilt of the German people, their determination to make a new beginning in the life of their Church, and their desire to participate fully in the ecumenical fellowship. The World Council delegates could therefore declare with conviction that a new foundation for the building up of fraternal relationships had been laid, and that they would do whatever was in their power to support the German Church spiritually and materially in its new period of life.

The "Stuttgart Declaration" was received with joy by many Churches, and several responded to it in messages expressing gratitude for the restoration of fellowship. In Germany itself the Declaration found both strong supporters and violent critics. The latter feared that it would be exploited for political purposes. In actual fact, the main result of the Stuttgart meeting was that the German Church leaders were the first Germans to take their place in international life on terms of equality, and the World Council and its member Churches were able to make the reconstruction of church life in Germany one of their major concerns.

The Stuttgart meeting helped greatly to create that spirit of understanding and mutual responsibility which characterized ecumenical meetings and activities in years to come. After the first world war the question of war guilt poisoned inter-Church relations for more than a decade. After the second, it provided an opportunity for the creation of deeper mutual confidence.

This confidence was specially evident in the first post-war meeting of the Provisional Committee held at Geneva in February 1946. As Bishop Berggrav put it in his sermon at the impressive ecumenical service in the Cathedral of St Pierre, the surprise of that meeting was that it was no surprise to find the sense of fellowship so real among those who had but lately been political and military enemies. The fact that even during the war years, despite all uncertainties about the future, no less than fifty Churches had decided to join the fifty member Churches already in the Council was a demonstration of these unbroken relationships. It was clear that the time was ripe for the decision to hold the first Assembly of the World Council. The date was fixed for the summer of 1948 and Amsterdam was chosen as the place.

At the same meeting, the creation of the Ecumenical Institute, made possible by the generous gift of Mr John D. Rockefeller, Jr, was approved. Much progress was made in relationships with the I.M.C., which held its meeting in Geneva just before the Provisional Committee, and thus brought the Committee into direct contact with leaders of the younger Churches. Important resolutions were adopted about the plight of the refugees and deported populations in Central Europe. A message was issued which pleaded with all peoples for a turning from the old ways of reliance upon mere might towards a new beginning in relations between the nations, and called upon the Churches to fulfil their ministry of reconciliation and solidarity. Five Presidents were chosen: the Archbishop of Canterbury (Fisher), the Archbishop of Uppsala (Eidem), Archbishop Germanos of Thyateira, Pastor Marc Boegner, and Dr John R. Mott.

The main new development in the summer of 1946 was the setting up of the Commission of the Churches on International Affairs. This was effected at a conference at Cambridge prepared with the help of the Federal Council (and notably of Dr Walter Van Kirk), and meeting under the joint auspices of the I.M.C. and the World Council. The new Commission was conceived as an organ for study and witness in the field of international relationships. Mr (later Sir) Kenneth Grubb (London) was appointed Director, and Dr O. F. Nolde (New York) Associate Director.

In September 1946 the Ecumenical Institute was officially opened at the Château de Bossey, twelve miles from Geneva. Its purpose was defined as the formation of an apostolic type of leadership "which not only aims at changing the life of individuals, but also seeks to achieve a peaceful penetration into the various sections of the community and the various areas of life". The theme of the opening address of the Director, Professor Hendrik Kraemer, was that "the orb is still at the foot of the cross". The first courses brought together young laymen and women from many countries who had learned the hard lessons of the war years and were eager to take their part in the rebuilding of their Church and nation.

The usefulness and significance of the Institute was greatly increased in these early post-war years by the spontaneous and simultaneous growth of movements and centres of lay activity in many Churches. The Institute was able to act as a centre of co-ordination for all these movements, and thus to aid them in working out a new approach to lay people, directed towards enabling them not merely to fulfil their duties within the Church, but also to serve in their secular occupations as ambassadors of the Church to the world.

At its meeting in February 1946, the Provisional Committee had instructed its officers to make a special approach to the Orthodox Churches, in the hope that these Churches would be able to take their full and rightful place in the Council. The officers decided, therefore, to propose to the Church of Russia that a meeting of delegations from that Church and from the World Council should be held. The proposed meeting with representatives of the Moscow Patriarchate never took place. Agreement was reached about the time and place of the meeting; but a later message from Moscow requested a postponement, and in spite of repeated inquiries on the part of the World Council no new proposals for a suitable date were made. It was, however, made clear to the Moscow Patriarchate that the World Council remained desirous to establish direct contact, and full information concerning the nature and activities of the Council was sent to the Patriarchate.

The Conference of Heads and Representatives of Orthodox Churches held in Moscow in July 1948, to which many, but by no means all, Orthodox Churches had sent representatives, gave considerable time to discussion of the ecumenical movement. Among the reports on the ecumenical movement submitted to that Conference there were some which showed a very real understanding of its life and purpose. But others, and particularly the report of Archpriest

Razoumovsky,[1] which seems to have dominated the discussions, were written by men who had to admit that, since no representative of the Orthodox Church of Russia had ever had personal contact with the ecumenical movement, they were not well acquainted with it.[2] It was owing to this lack of information and to misinterpretations of the available material that the Conference arrived at the conclusion that the World Council's purpose was to create an "Ecumenical Church" which would become a centre of political power, and that it was not really concerned with Christian unity. The voices raised in defence of the World Council were too few to influence the final decision, namely, that the Churches represented at the Conference felt obliged "to refuse the invitation to participate in the ecumenical movement in its present form". The last words seemed to indicate that there was at least a possibility that at some time in the future the conversation might be resumed. And it was encouraging to find that, in several of the Churches which had been represented at Moscow, there were leaders who continued to show deep interest in, and attachment to, the World Council.[3]

The officers of the World Council had decided to send a delegation to the Orthodox Churches and the other Eastern Churches of the Mediterranean area. In February 1947 a delegation of the Council, consisting of Bishop Brilioth of Växjö, the Bishop of Worcester (Cash), the Rev. Edward R. Hardy of the Protestant Episcopal Church in America, and the Rev. Oliver Tomkins, visited Athens, Constantinople, Cyprus, Antioch, Alexandria, and Cairo. On their return, the delegation gave an encouraging report:

> "It is with humility and gratitude that representatives of this very new 'Ecumenical Movement' record their warm and loving reception by representatives of churches which first gave to Christendom the meaning of the word 'Ecumenical'. . . . We submit the report which follows in the confidence that the Provisional Committee can count upon the reaffirmed co-operation of the churches which we visited and their full participation in the Assembly of 1948."[4]

An important forward step was taken in 1947 in relationships with the International Missionary Council. Acting on the recommendations of the Joint Committee of the I.M.C. and the W.C.C. under the chairmanship of Dr John R. Mott, the Provisional Committee decided to propose to the Assembly that the World Council and the International Missionary Council should be known as being "in association with" each other, and that this association should find expression in their titles. This decision was by no means a mere matter of nomenclature. It was the expression of a conviction which had been growing ever since the matter was discussed at the Tambaram Conference of 1938 and which had its historical basis in the story of the inter-relationship between missions and ecumenism.[5] The Joint Committee expressed this conviction in the following terms:

> "We deem it necessary that the International Missionary Council and the World Council of Churches shall make clear to all their identity of purpose

[1] *The Ecumenical Movement and the Russian Church*, published by the Patriarchate of Moscow.
[2] *Actes de la Conférence des Églises Autocéphales Orthodoxes*, II, p. 108; cf. *Ecumenical Review*, Vol. I, No. 2, pp. 188–97.
[3] See Chap. xiv, pp. 666 f.
[4] See full report in *Minutes . . . Provisional Committee, Buck Hill Falls 1947*, pp. 104–17.
[5] See Chap. vii, pp. 310 f.; and Chap. viii, pp. 353 ff., and *passim*.

and concern for the evangelisation of the world, shall co-operate in every possible way, and shall draw progressively closer together in all their undertakings for Christian fellowship, witness and service."[1]

The Joint Committee also drew up an additional list of Churches in Asia, Africa, Latin America, and the Pacific Islands which might be invited to membership in the Council. Five leaders of younger Churches were co-opted as members of the Provisional Committee.

As a result of these discussions, in 1947 an East Asia Commission was set up under the auspices of both organizations, to lay plans for an East Asia Conference, and to consult the Churches and the Councils in East Asia concerning the possibility of establishing a joint secretariat of the I.M.C. and the World Council in East Asia. This Commission met in Manila (Philippines) in February 1948. Bishop Stephen Neill represented the World Council. It was decided to hold an East Asia Conference. (This Conference was held at Bangkok in February 1949, and considered and approved the plan for the formation by the W.C.C. and the I.M.C. of a Joint Secretariat for East Asia.) Following Bishop Neill's visit to many countries in Asia, a considerable number of Asian Churches decided to join the World Council.[2]

Amsterdam in 1939 had been the scene of the last great ecumenical meeting before the second world war—the World Conference of Christian Youth. Oslo in 1947 saw the first great post-war ecumenical gathering—again of Christian Youth. In both cases the four initiating organizations were the World's Alliance of Y.M.C.A.s, the World's Y.W.C.A., the W.S.C.F., and the World Council of Churches. The Rev. Francis House, Secretary of the World Council's Youth Department, was the Executive Secretary of the Conference. Oslo 1947 was remarkable for the very considerable share taken by the more than two hundred delegates from Asia, Africa, and Latin America, and for the joyous rediscovery of a fellowship in common obedience to Jesus Christ as Lord which bound the delegates together in spite of strong tensions and disagreements on political questions.

During the last two and a half years before the Assembly the Provisional Committee and its staff had to concentrate all their efforts on preparations for the Assembly. For it was realized that the significance of the meeting would largely depend on the thoroughness of these preparations, and the time was short. A committee of arrangements under Dr Cavert supervised the planning. The theme chosen was "Man's Disorder and God's Design", for, as the memorandum of the Study Department put it, the peculiar function of the Church is "to place the efforts at world reconstruction in a totally different perspective by announcing the stupendous fact that God Himself is at work rebuilding His own order amid the disorder of man". This theme was subdivided into four sectional themes, each of which was to form the subject of discussion for one section of the Assembly. The first of these themes was chosen in the area of concern and study of Faith and Order, "The Universal Church in God's Design". The second, "The Church's Witness to God's Design", embraced the missionary and evangelistic task of the Churches and the field of study of the I.M.C. The third, "The Church and the Disorder of Society", was in line with the Life and Work

---

[1] *Minutes . . . Provisional Committee, Buck Hill Falls 1947*, p. 67.
[2] See Chap. viii, pp. 400 f.; and Stephen Neill, *The Cross over Asia*, London, 1948.

tradition. The fourth, "The Church and International Disorder", was a continuation of the work done in this field by Life and Work and by the World Alliance, but in the new form given to it by the C.C.I.A.

The Study Department and the officers of the preparatory commissions had the almost impossible task of preparing an international symposium on each theme and of getting these into the hands of the delegates before the Assembly, each in three languages. They succeeded, but it is doubtful whether the delegates had sufficient time to study the volumes.

One year before the Assembly the Provisional Committee issued its Call to the Churches concerning the Assembly.[1] The Call reminded the Churches that "through the trials and persecutions of these last years, a new consciousness of fellowship has been awakened" but that "the Churches of Christ have failed in preventing man's disorder", and that therefore "our first and deepest need is not new organisation, but the renewal, or rather the rebirth, of the actual churches". What, then, was the task of the new Council? "It aspires after an expression of unity in which Christians and Christian churches, joyously aware of their oneness in Jesus Christ their Lord, and pursuing an ever fuller realisation of union, shall in time of need give help and comfort to one another, and at all times inspire and exhort one another to live worthily of their common membership in the Body of Christ."

4. THE FIRST ASSEMBLY OF THE WORLD COUNCIL OF CHURCHES

The opening service of the Assembly took place in the Nieuwe Kerk at Amsterdam on Sunday, 22 August 1948. 147 Churches in forty-four countries were represented by 351 official delegates. With these were hundreds of alternates, consultants, accredited visitors, youth delegates, and representatives of the Press. It was encouraging that the Churches of Asia had sent strong delegations. Africa, with fewer autonomous Churches, was also represented. The very ancient Lesser Eastern Churches, and the Protestant Churches of Eastern Europe and the Levant, were present. But the Orthodox Church of Russia and the Orthodox Churches which followed its lead had not sent delegates. Thus it came about that the representatives of the Orthodox Churches of Constantinople, of Greece, and of the emigration, a relatively small group, had to bear the heavy burden of keeping continuously before the mind of the Assembly the great and varied traditions of the whole Orthodox world. No Roman Catholics were present, since the few unofficial observers who had been invited had not received the necessary permission to accept the invitation.[2]

Few of those who held leading positions in the Assembly had taken part in the ecumenical movement during its earliest phases. But Dr John R. Mott, Ruth Rouse, and Dr J. H. Oldham provided the link with that year of ecumenical beginnings, Edinburgh 1910. Archbishop Germanos, Professor Hamilcar Alivisatos, Bishop Yngve Brilioth, Professor Adolph Keller, and Dr Friedrich Siegmund-Schultze had been in the movement since the Geneva meetings of 1920. The Bishop of Chichester (Bell) and Dr Alphons Koechlin had been leaders at Stockholm in 1925, and Bishop Dibelius and Dr G. W. Richards had taken active part in the Lausanne Conference of 1927. The writer of this chapter had been at Stockholm in 1925—the youngest delegate present in that great gather-

[1] Minutes ... Provisional Committee, Buck Hill Falls 1947, pp. 84 ff.
[2] See Chap. xv, pp. 689 f.

ing. Among the consultants there were many who had ecumenical experience. But for very many of the official delegates the Assembly had the freshness of a new, unexpected discovery.

On the morning of Monday, 23 August 1948 the World Council of Churches came into existence. The resolution "that the formation of the World Council of Churches be declared to be and is hereby completed" was presented by Dr Marc Boegner, one of the Presidents of the Provisional Committee and Chairman of its Administrative Committee. The Chairman of the session, the Archbishop of Canterbury (Fisher), announced that the resolution had been adopted *nem. con.* There followed a moment of silent prayer, after which the Archbishop led in spoken prayer:

> "Almighty God, here we offer unto Thee our thanksgiving and praise, that Thou hast brought us to this hour and this act in the faith of Christ and by the power of the Holy Spirit. As Thou hast prospered those into whose labours we enter, so, we pray Thee, prosper us in this our undertaking by Thy most gracious favour, that in all our works begun, continued and ended in Thee we may set forth Thy glory for the well-being of Thy Holy Church and the salvation of all Thy people."

For many this was the central moment in the Assembly. The process of formation which, contrary to all expectations, had taken eleven years, had come to an end. The Council was in existence. The Churches had actually come together and entered into a new relationship with each other. The true significance of the event found expression at a later moment when the Message of the Assembly was adopted. For in that Message there were some simple sentences which found a strong echo in the Assembly and indeed far beyond it. These words are: "Christ has made us His own, and He is not divided. In seeking Him we find one another. Here at Amsterdam we have committed ourselves afresh to Him, and have covenanted with one another in constituting this World Council of Churches. We intend to stay together."

Several committees worked hard on questions of constitution and organization. The Constitution which was adopted did not differ greatly from the draft constitution worked out at Utrecht, except on two points: the procedure concerning admission to membership, and the application of the confessional as well as the geographical principle of representation in the composition of the Central Committee and the Assembly.

With regard to the Basis, the decision of 1938 was confirmed. Since some Churches had asked for clarification or amplification, it was decided that Churches could present their desires in writing to the Central Committee, and that the Central Committee should study any proposals received, but that it should keep its study within the limits set by the Christological principle included in the original Basis.

The main proposals of the Provisional Committee concerning the structure of the Council and concerning its association with the I.M.C. were also approved.

The four sections held lively meetings in which the points of difference as well as the points of agreement were clearly brought out. Thus the first section, which discussed the nature of the Church, found a given unity which is God's creation and not our achievement, but it faced in that light "our deepest difference", and particularly the division between a "Protestant" emphasis on the initiative of the Word of God and the response of faith, and a "Catholic" emphasis on the visible continuity of the Church. And the fourth section dealing with the problem of peace and war had to register once again divergent positions on the Christian attitude to war, but arrived at a clear word of guidance concerning the rule of international law and the fundamental human rights and freedoms.

The statements of the four sections were discussed in plenary session and, after the necessary amendments had been made, were received by the Assembly and commended to the Churches for their serious consideration and appropriate action. In the light of all that is involved in getting the delegates of 150 Churches, which are just beginning to work together, to agree on anything at all in relation to difficult and controversial questions, it is remarkable that these statements give evidence of such deep and extensive agreement.

But it should not be imagined that there were no tensions at Amsterdam. It was inevitable that the deep political division in the world should be reflected in the addresses, particularly when Professor J. L. Hromadka of Prague and Mr John Foster Dulles gave their several views on the international situation, and in the discussions. It was, however, recognized that it belonged to the very essence of the ecumenical relationship that such divergences, however real, should not be allowed to become an obstacle to Christian fellowship. In this connection it was of the highest importance that the report of the third section made it clear that in matters concerning society the Church of Christ cannot be the spokesman or advocate of one particular system over against others, but that in complete independence it must raise its voice against injustices in any and every system.

What is the place of the Assembly in the history of the ecumenical movement? In view of the fact that it had taken nearly thirty years to reach the point at which the Churches themselves accepted responsibility for a permanent ecumenical body, there would seem to be strong reasons for presenting the Assembly as a point of arrival and as the happy solution of an old problem. But that would represent neither the objective situation nor the attitude of the Assembly itself. For it became very clear to all at Amsterdam that the formation of the World Council represented only a stage in a process which was far from having reached its end, and that it had created a whole series of new problems.

What, then, was the true significance of this date in ecumenical history? It was that the Churches themselves accepted the responsibility for the ecumenical movement and, conversely, that the ecumenical movement received a firm foundation in the continuous life of the Churches. There are those to whom this ecclesiastical character of the movement seems a danger rather than an advantage. On this two remarks must be made. First, it must be noted that the World Council, as it took shape at Amsterdam, does not stand for a static unity between the Churches as they are. The report of the first section put this clearly:

"We pray for the churches' renewal as we pray for their unity. As Christ purifies us by His Spirit we shall find that we are drawn together and that there is no gain in unity unless it is unity in truth and holiness. . . . We embark upon our work in the World Council of Churches in penitence for what we are, in hope for what we shall be."[1]

[1] *The First Assembly of the World Council of Churches*, pp. 56 f.

Secondly, it is evident that the battle for the unity of the Church must be fought where the real issues arise, that is in the life of the existing Churches. The problem of the ecumenical movement is that the Churches are as yet too little concerned with the Biblical promises and commandments about the oneness of the People of God, and the special task of the ecumenical movement is therefore to permeate the life of the Churches themselves with the ecumenical vision.

It should be added that the World Council of Churches does not claim to monopolize the ecumenical movement, and that it recognizes in its Constitution and its policy the existence of "other ecumenical organizations", several of which are not officially linked to the Churches.[1] In other words, the creation of the World Council means that an important part of the ecumenical movement becomes rooted in the life of the Churches, but that much ecumenical activity will go on through other channels, and in Churches which are not members of the World Council.

At Amsterdam, and in the years since Amsterdam, it became clear that the creation of the Council was the beginning of a new common pilgrimage, and that the Churches could only go forward in the faith of Abraham, not knowing whither they went, "to goals which we but dimly discern".[2] But there were certain immediate tasks to which the Council had to address itself. The most important are the following:

To clarify the nature of the Council. The Assembly had said relatively little on the new relationship into which the Churches had entered. It had been clearly stated that the Council was not to be considered as an end in itself and did not intend to set up a "Super-Church". But the implications of the existence of the Council needed to be worked out more clearly. An important further step was taken at the meeting of the Central Committee in Toronto in 1950 when the Committee received a statement on "The Church, the Churches, and the World Council of Churches", and sent this to the Churches as a basis for further study and discussion.[3]

In this document many misunderstandings about the Council were resolved. It was clearly stated that the Council is not based upon any one particular conception of the Church, or of the unity of the Church, for it exists in order that the Churches may face their differences and that the various conceptions of unity may enter into dynamic relations with each other. And it was affirmed that the main convictions underlying the World Council are that Christ is the Divine Head of the Body, that the Church of Christ is one, and that each Church should do its utmost for the manifestation of the Church in its oneness. The rôle of the Council itself is merely instrumental. It must decrease in order that the *Una Sancta* may increase.

To find the right relation between confessional and ecumenical loyalties. The Assembly had said: "It is not always easy to reconcile our confessional and ecumenical loyalties. . . . We bring these, and all other difficulties between us, into the World Council of Churches in order that we steadily may face them together."[4] In the years after the Assembly this became a very real issue, for the strong ecumenical affirmations of the Assembly contributed to the strengthening of the confessional consciousness in many Churches and in several confessional alliances. In the perspective of ecumenical history this development is not surprising. The great question for the future is, however, whether the new

---

[1] See Chap. xiii, pp. 599, 610. [2] *The First Assembly*, p. 56.
[3] *Ecumenical Review*, Vol. III, No. 1, pp. 47 ff. [4] *The First Assembly*, p. 56.

confessional emphasis will lead to a deadlock in the ecumenical discussions between the Churches, or whether it will lead to an encounter on a deeper and therefore more fruitful level.

To manifest that the Council is truly a World Council. Although the old Churches of Eastern Europe and the Near East and the young Churches of Asia and Africa and Latin America made a real contribution to the Assembly, it cannot be said that the Council has yet sufficiently demonstrated that it is a World Council and not a Council of Western Christendom.

This problem has two aspects. The first is that of relations with Eastern Orthodoxy and with the Lesser Eastern Churches. A new attempt will have to be made to arrive at a much deeper understanding between these ancient Churches and the other Churches in the Council, and the goal that all the great Orthodox Churches should participate in the Council must be kept clearly in mind.

The second is that of the place of the younger Churches in the World Council. This question is so closely connected with the crucial issue of the relation between the Church's concern for missions and the Church's concern for unity that it can only be answered by the younger Churches themselves, together with the World Council and the I.M.C. A promising beginning was made at the Bangkok Conference of the Churches of East Asia, held under the joint auspices of the two world-wide organizations in 1949.[1] But much thinking needs to be done in order to bring the movements for unity and for missionary expansion, both of which are pillars of the ecumenical movement, as closely together as they ought to be. It is now very widely understood that the two movements are spiritually interdependent.

To learn to bear together concrete witness to the modern world. Through the Stockholm, Oxford, and Amsterdam Conferences the Churches have begun to bear a common witness concerning the problems of modern society and of international relations. But to speak out together once in five or more years is hardly sufficient. Now the Central Committee can also speak, and the Commission of the Churches on International Affairs has increasingly become a competent and efficient organ of continuous action. But these bodies can only be a true "voice" of the Churches in the Council if the Churches themselves take seriously their "prophetic" task in the world, and express their convictions concerning the crucial issues of social and international life. We have learned much since Archbishop Söderblom called the Churches together in 1925 for this purpose. But we have to learn a great deal more in order to be able to serve the world adequately through the Church's prophetic ministry and the concrete proclamation of God's judgement and mercy.

To maintain the unity and independence of the ecumenical movement. It is one of the greatest facts in the history of the ecumenical movement that it has in general succeeded in maintaining relations of fellowship and confidence between Churches and individuals separated by political divergences or even by international conflict and war. But owing to the depth of the gulf which has come to divide the world, this task of maintaining unity is increasingly hard to fulfil. Moreover, the fundamental spiritual independence which the World Council must maintain if it is to be true to its mission is constantly being challenged. The Council has sought to make it clear that it believes in the Lordship

---

[1] See *The Christian Prospect in Eastern Asia: Papers and Minutes of the Eastern Asia Christian Conference, Bangkok, December 3–11, 1949*, New York, 1950.

of Christ over all realms of life, that it must therefore speak out when great questions of principle are at stake, but that it cannot identify itself with any ideology or group of nations. The great question in this respect will be whether the member Churches are ready to stand by this policy and to help the Council in avoiding both irrelevance and partisanship. At this point much ecumenical education is still needed. The road along which the Council must travel in the world of our time is a narrow road. It can only praise God for the foretaste of the unity of his people which he has given to it, and continue hopefully to serve the Churches as they prepare to meet their Lord, who knows only one flock.

EPILOGUE

by

STEPHEN CHARLES NEILL

(with the help of an Editorial Group)

Almost from the beginning division has been present in the Christian Church, but division has never been finally acquiesced in as the normal condition of that Church. The vision of perfect unity, sometimes faint and elusive, has always been before the eyes of Christians, and in every Church and age some have been found ready to pursue that vision. The ideal of a Christian community in which all Christians shall be united in the confession of a common faith, bound together by an all-embracing charity and nourished by the same Word and Sacraments, and shall bear witness to the world through a fellowship transcending every difference of race and colour and civilization, has never lost its power to attract, and endless failure to realize the ideal has not availed to dull the ardour of those who have been inspired by the vision. If there is one thing more than another to which the preceding pages bear irrefutable testimony, it is this.

In Christendom, there is hardly any Christian body which has remained untouched by aspirations after Christian unity and by efforts to promote it. All the great historic Protestant confessions—Lutheran, Reformed, and others—have been involved, some of them for centuries, in ecumenical concerns. The same is true of most of the large Protestant bodies of more recent origin, such as the Methodists and the Disciples of Christ. Anglicans and Old Catholics have taken the lead in many ecumenical enterprises. Historical and political circumstances have to a large extent kept the Orthodox and other Eastern Churches in separation from their brethren in the West; but this History shows that the participation of some among these Churches in the contemporary ecumenical movement is the renewal of a unitive tendency which has found expression at intervals throughout their history. The exclusive claims of the Church of Rome limit the possibilities of its direct participation in any ecumenical movement; but many chapters of this History contain the names of Roman Catholics who in perfect sincerity have desired and sought oneness with their separated fellow-believers. In those Protestant communions also which for one reason or another have felt it impossible to join as such in unitive movements, there have always been individuals and movements devoted to the cause of Christian unity, and pursuing their ideal of it with high-minded and devoted ardour.

Ecumenical activity is not a monopoly of any part or region of the world. The younger Churches which have come into existence in the last two centuries as a result of the expansion or the missionary activities of the West sometimes show greater zeal and less hesitation than the older Churches from which they are sprung. The smaller the Church the greater the enthusiasm it seems to show for incorporation into a world-wide movement to promote the unity of all Christians. New Zealand, a small country remote from most of the great Christian centres of the world, has an exemplary record of ecumenical spirit and action.

In the course of the centuries, an astonishing variety of methods for promoting unity has been evolved—coercion, theological discussion, agreement to differ, the production of irenic formulas, the harmonization of confessions, concentration on fundamental articles, abandonment of all confessional statements other than the New Testament. Countless schemes have been devised, and most of them have been tried—toleration, co-existence without assimilation, absorption, organic union, federation, co-operation, and the rest. And still the human mind is fertile; still new schemes are tried, still new methods evolved, often with little realization that they are only old and familiar methods under a different name.

A flower cannot be dissected and analysed until it is dead or dying. Similarly, no definitive history of a movement can be written until the movement is exhausted and no longer moves. Since this History is concerned with a movement which lives and daily grows, it is impossible to end this volume with a neat classification of lessons to be learned, or of causes of success and failure drawn up in trim categories. Such a conclusion would be false, since, however accurate in detail, the static impression it would leave would not correspond to the realities and the complexities of a living object. Yet out of this long survey of four centuries, certain principles seem to become evident and to recur, not by artificial construction, but by the inner necessity of constantly recurring situations.

On a broad survey, it is possible to distinguish three main types of ecumenical endeavour, which may be identified roughly as the search for unity in doctrine and Church order, the search for unity in the essentials of Christian belief, and the search for unity as the expression of a common Christian experience. In the first tradition, there has always been insistence on the necessity of full and detailed doctrinal agreement as a preliminary to Church fellowship, and in particular to common participation in the Holy Communion. The second, recognizing the many human elements in all the Churches as they historically exist, has desired to eliminate the peculiarities of the confessions by a return, in one form or another, to unity in what is regarded by its supporters as the essence of New Testament truth. The third, starting from the undeniable experience of fellowship and unity that comes to separated Christians when they pray and work together, has desired to find the way to full Christian unity by deepening and extending this experience of the unity that already exists. The three are not altogether mutually exclusive. The most ardent enthusiast for doctrinal purity must recognize that Christianity is a life as well as an intellectual belief; the advocate of unity through experience cannot become indifferent to truth, or his enterprise is likely to end in mere sentimentality. In point of fact, most ecumenical enterprises have been marked by a combination of two or more of these three types, and at no period has any one of the three succeeded in entirely dominating the ecumenical movement.

The study of ecumenical history leads inescapably to the question why so little positive achievement has followed on so much devoted effort. One reason certainly is that periods of advance through comparative disregard of dogmatic difficulties have been followed by periods marked by a resurgence of confessional precision. Doctrinal rigidity has intervened to check movements towards union which, from the point of view of confessional correctness, would involve lax and timid compromises at the expense of truth. Later, the experience of Christian fellowship across confessional boundaries, especially in times of hardship or persecution, again tends to modify the purely confessional position, and to open the door for a further irenical approach. This movement back and forth of conviction still continues, and lends variety to the ecumenical scene, though it sometimes also spells frustration for those who are discontented at that slow pace, which to others seems already precipitately fast.

Until the end of the 19th century, it is difficult to speak otherwise than proleptically of an ecumenical "movement". Almost all the earlier efforts were the work of individuals or groups, fired with a passion and a special sense of mission which they were able only in a very small degree to communicate to their Churches. From the vantage-ground of history, these efforts, though often noble and full of lessons by which posterity may well profit, appear discontinuous, spasmodic, and in many cases frustrated by the death of their promoters. Such successes as there were before the beginning of the 19th century were due rather to the pressure exercised by rulers—actuated at least as much by political as by religious motives—than to the expression of the inmost convictions of the Churches themselves. During the 19th century, considerable progress was effected through the work of voluntary societies and in what was then called "the mission-field". The new lessons of the 20th century are that continuous and permanent progress cannot be hoped for, unless the Churches learn to act on a basis of faith and conviction and of nothing else, and unless the Churches as such come officially to be engaged in the ecumenical movement.

The immense change which came about as the 20th century advanced was that for the first time a large number of Churches as such did begin to be concerned about the ecumenical movement, and pledged themselves to a continuing search for unity in faith, in life, in worship, and in common action.

If it appears that the Churches were extremely slow to commit themselves to the movement, it must be remembered that this was in part because the problem of Christian unity had come to present itself in a new form, largely because of a subtle but remarkable change in the meaning attached to the word "Church". In common speech in many languages to-day the word "Church" is frequently used in the sense of "denomination", a usage almost wholly unknown in earlier centuries. The ideal of the unity of the Church survived the Reformation; the one Church might manifest itself in different forms in different places, but in each city, in each area, it could only be one. The idea of rival, or even friendly, groups of Christians in one city, worshipping God in separation and according to different rites, seemed to many Christians monstrous, and was by many contended against with passion. The possibility of the co-existence of denominations was not fully accepted in England till 1689. The permission granted in 1707 for the formation of a Lutheran congregation in Geneva was regarded as a remarkable concession to the ecumenical spirit. Equality of privilege for the separate denominations was achieved in some countries during the 19th century, but even in the 20th is still far from having been completely achieved or assured.

The Churches were slow to adapt themselves to a changed situation and to new ideas. This in part explains why in the 19th century ecumenical progress was to such a large extent in the hands of the voluntary agencies. But in the 20th century the Churches as such were once more ready, slowly and hesitantly at first, but with increasing conviction, to take up the ecumenical concern. The first great manifestation of the change was the World Missionary Conference held at Edinburgh in 1910; it is for this reason that that Conference is given so central a place in this History. It was not yet a Conference of the Churches, but many of the delegates came not as interested individuals but as the officially accredited delegates of their Churches or Mission Boards.

It is the official engagement of the Churches in the ecumenical movement that has made possible the formation of the World Council of Churches, in which more than a hundred and fifty Church bodies have formally pledged themselves to loyalty to one another and have affirmed in the face of the world that they intend to stay together. The ecumenical movement to-day is not to be identified with the World Council of Churches. Many older movements, such as the voluntary Christian lay movements, continue their separate existence, and make their fruitful contribution along their own lines. Some Churches which are not members of the World Council have also a sense of ecumenical vocation and in their own way work for unity. Yet, when all this has been said, it is still unquestionably true that, in the course of this century, a new thing has happened in the history of the Church; a new movement has come into being, the full potentialities of which can be revealed only by a far longer period of history than that which has been recorded in these pages.

Even if the World Council of Churches is accepted as representing the central stream of the ecumenical movement, attention must be directed to the limits within which that stream still flows. The Roman Catholic Church has nothing officially to do with it; it follows with minute attention the course of the movement, and friendly gestures, some with official backing, are from time to time to be observed. But there is a deep incompatibility between Roman Catholic ideals of unity and those professed by all the other Churches. Orthodox participation has been increasingly valuable; but, largely for non-ecclesiastical reasons, more Orthodox Churches, including some of the largest, are outside the movement than are within it; and even those that are within make plain the reservations on which the continuance of their membership depends. Some large Protestant Churches, such as the Southern Baptist Convention in the United States, for one reason or another withhold their support.

A second limitation is the isolation from one another in which Churches and individual Christians pass their lives. Much has been done by way of mutual education; yet the strangest misconceptions and prejudices still persist, and ignorance of other Churches is still one of the strongest obstacles in the way of self-commitment to the ecumenical cause.

Yet, even when these limitations are recognized, a new fellowship has come into being. Never in history have so many Churches, representing so wide a confessional range, come together in a fellowship in which freedom and mutual responsibility are so nicely balanced. The World Council provides a permanent forum for frank and friendly discussion, in which charity endures without offence the utmost boldness of speech. It provides a continuing service of information, through which Churches which make use of it can come to know one another as never before. It makes possible corporate charitable action on a scale never previously considered possible, and unsurpassed as a means of creating genuine Christian fellowship. It has taken the first steps in corporate witness to the whole body of the Churches and to the world.

The World Council does not concern itself directly with projects for the union of the Churches. But it is perhaps no accident that the years which have led up to the formation of the World Council have been more fruitful than any others in the achievement of actual unions between separated Churches. In the past, such unions have generally led to no more than the restoration of the breaches which time had wrought in the fabric of one or another of the great confessions. This century has been marked by the achievement of trans-confessional unions of a kind never seen before. These unions, though their history is short, give every promise of stability. The existence of such Churches in Canada, in South India, and elsewhere, has already presented a stern challenge to the denominational organization to which over the centuries the Churches had become almost unquestioningly accustomed. These Churches fit into no existing pattern; they demand that older Churches should look at themselves and at least face the question whether much that they had regarded as permanent is in reality more than temporary and transitional.

Many schemes of Church union are under discussion. Not all of them will lead to the formation of united Churches, but it may be expected that progress along this line will continue. In this connection, however, the word "progress" has to be used with caution; the challenge of these new Churches to confessional traditions and convictions has been so sharp that some in all the Churches regard them as betrayals rather than as achievements, and as hindrances rather than helps to that full ecumenical unity which is desired by all. This is not the place to attempt a judgement on a controversial issue. That a new ferment has been set up can hardly be questioned; and the ecumenical movement can live only through willingness to reconsider much that in the past has been accepted as sacrosanct.

Apart from the limitations of which we have already spoken, certain weaknesses in the ecumenical movement, as it has recently taken shape, are readily observable.

It has yet far to go before it becomes genuinely universal. The increasing participation of the younger Churches, both through membership as Churches and through the positive contributions of their leaders and scholars, is encouraging. Yet almost all ecumenical programmes are still weighted on the Western side, and tend to be related to Western categories of thought. For the time being this may be necessary; but the representatives of the younger Churches are never tired of reminding their brethren that, though their Churches are small, in a sense they are the Christian expression of the needs and hopes, and prophetically of the Christian contribution, of more than half the human race.

The movement cannot escape involvement in the political strains and tensions of the world in which it lives. The World Council has again and again disclaimed any idea of being associated with any power bloc or with any one form of political order. It is free in relation to all. The last thing it would desire would be the imposition of any kind of a spiritual Iron Curtain between groups of Churches. Yet it remains the fact that in one part of the world Church leaders can meet freely and without difficulty, and welcome visitors from countries under a different political régime; in another part of the world Church leaders, even of contiguous countries, have the utmost difficulty in meeting, and some countries are hermetically sealed against the entry of Christians from elsewhere. Inevitably this produces an appearance, and to some extent a reality, of separation wholly contrary to the ecumenical spirit.

So far the movement has been too urban. It reflects the preoccupations and the problems of that urban civilization which is the characteristic product of the West, and tends to overlook the fact that more than half the people in the world still live in villages. This is, perhaps, inevitable, since ideas have always tended to be born amid the more intense life of the city, and to spread slowly outwards to the countryside; yet the urban civilization cannot exist without the development of the rural, and an exclusive preoccupation with one at the expense of the other upsets the true ecumenical balance of concern.

The movement is still too much an affair of leaders in the Church, of ministers rather than of lay folk, and of those who can afford time to go to conferences rather than of those who must stay at home. This again is doubtless inevitable at the start; ideas begin with the few, and a long time must be allowed for the dissemination of those ideas in the mass. In point of fact, what is remarkable is not so much that many in the Churches have remained unaffected as that the ecumenical idea has penetrated so deeply into the lay world. The space given to ecumenical affairs in the secular Press of the world is a fair indication of the interest of the average man; and the reaction of the lay Christian to the ecumenical idea, when presented to him, is usually that the Churches are at last beginning to do what they ought to have done long ago. Nothing in ecumenical concerns is more encouraging than the renewed emphasis on the responsibility of lay folk and the evidence in many Churches of a response on the part of the laity to this new challenge.

One of the chief problems of the ecumenical movement in the mid-20th century is that occasioned by the separation between its two essential components. This History has shown at point after point the intimate connection between the missionary work of the Church and the ecumenical ideal. Throughout, the word "ecumenical" has been used to designate the efforts of Christians to seek and promote unity; but it should by now be plain to the reader that these efforts are not an end in themselves: the aim of Christian union is *that the world may believe*. The world includes the non-Christian world as well as Christendom. Evangelism, missionary work, the proclamation of the Gospel to earth's remotest end, are not extras or fringes on the ecumenical movement; they are essentials without which its true nature cannot be grasped. Unhappily, in the thought of the Churches the two aspects have not always been held together. One expression of this separation is the co-existence of the World Council of Churches and the International Missionary Council. That each officially describes itself as being "in association with" the other is far more than a conveniently diplomatic phrase: the expression indicates close identity of aim, constant personal co-operation, and progress towards ever closer mutual understanding. Yet it is hardly possible that this measure of co-operation can be other than a halting-place on the way to some form of yet more complete integration. But the manner in which this more perfect integration should be brought about and the form which it should take have not yet become evident even to those who most desire it.

At this point history breaks off, and what is further written must be of the nature of prophecy. And who would wish to prophesy in 1954? In the mid-20th century the flow of ecumenical movements seems to be in a certain direction. But a glance backward shows how little of the present state of affairs could have been foreseen even in the recent past. If we take our stand in the year 1900 and look forward, what has happened in these fifty years must needs seem astonishing. In that year no one was prophesying any one of the things that has actually happened. No one foresaw the rapidity of the growth and extension of the Churches, or the speed with which the younger Churches would become independent and adult. Missionary co-operation was only in its beginnings. No one then imagined that an international missionary council could become a permanent part of the furniture of the Church. This is easily forgotten by those who come after. Things which are taken for granted to-day were certainly not taken for granted a generation ago. To achieve them meant faith, patience, and a spirit of adventure. Why it should have been so hard to convince societies and Churches of the necessity of an international missionary council, it is difficult for us to see; but just this difficulty is a warning that things which to-day seem incredible or impossible will seem plain and obvious to our children, and that the strains and sacrifices of our time will by them be wholly forgotten.

What is true of one great ecumenical adventure is true in one form or another of all the rest. It seems obvious to-day that Churches should meet in fellowship to discuss their problems in every area of the Church's life. We stand amazed at the record of the delays and hesitations of the early period both of Faith and Order and of Life and Work; we find it hard to believe that there really were such mountains of prejudice and doubt to be overcome; we underestimate the faith and persistence of the ecumenical leaders of those days. And yet, after all, their faith did triumph and did hand on to their successors a legacy which is sometimes more lightly prized than it should be.

These things are an encouragement. It is not certain that the ecumenical movement will go forward on the path which now seems indicated for it and add success to success. The story of the Christian Church is marked by as many failures as successes. The Church is more bitterly assaulted than it has been for a thousand years, and is facing dangers as grave as any that it has survived in the past. What will be the outcome of these crises and perils no man can even dimly foresee. Yet the final word of this History must be one of quiet hope. The unity of all Christian people is the will of God. Never in history have so many people been so deeply concerned about that unity. Never before has so short a period seen such rapid progress in thought and action. We may venture to hope that if, in fifty years' time, a further volume of this History comes to be written, those who undertake it, looking back over the second half of the 20th century, will find no less cause than we to rejoice, and to glorify God for what he has wrought.

APPENDICES

APPENDIX I

By Willem Adolf Visser 't Hooft

The Word "Ecumenical"—its History and Use

The title of this work, *A History of the Ecumenical Movement*, appears to demand some preliminary justification. For, although "ecumenical", in the sense of "that which concerns the unity and the world-wide mission of the Church of Jesus Christ", is widely used and now generally understood, that is not the meaning traditionally assigned to the word. Yet this new usage seems to have established itself, with a good prospect of permanence, in at least ten European languages, and even in ecclesiastical Latin.

A full lexical study of the word has not yet been made; but sufficient material is available to put before the reader of the History succinctly some evidence both as to the traditional uses of the word, and as to the subtle processes by which it has gradually come to be accepted in "ecumenical" circles with its present connotations.

In the course of history we can distinguish seven meanings of the word "ecumenical":

(*a*) pertaining to or representing the whole (inhabited) earth;
(*b*) pertaining to or representing the whole of the (Roman) Empire;
(*c*) pertaining to or representing the whole of the Church;
(*d*) that which has universal ecclesiastical validity;
(*e*) pertaining to the world-wide missionary outreach of the Church;
(*f*) pertaining to the relations between and unity of two or more Churches (or of Christians of various confessions);
(*g*) that quality or attitude which expresses the consciousness of and desire for Christian unity.

The first two meanings are found in the Greco-Roman world generally and also in the New Testament. The third and fourth meanings arise gradually in the life of the Church of the early centuries. The fifth, sixth, and seventh meanings are modern developments.

The word *oikoumene* occurs fifteen times in the New Testament. The Septuagint had used *oikoumene* quite often to translate various Hebrew words meaning world, earth, or land. But in the Hellenistic world *oikoumene* was used in several other ways. It could mean the whole inhabited world, but also the civilized world, the realm of Greco-Latin culture. And it could also be used as a synonym for "empire". As the Roman Empire grows in power and extent, the world is simply the empire and the empire is the world.

In a number of New Testament texts *oikoumene* simply means "the whole world", without any specific cultural or political connotation, e.g. Acts 17.31; Matt. 24.14. But there are other texts where *oikoumene* is used in the sense of the one great political unit, the Empire, e.g. Luke 2.1, where the census mentioned is a census decreed by the Emperor; probably also Acts 17.6: the Christians are accused of acting against the decrees of Caesar and they are thereby disturbing the *oikoumene*, that is the Empire. Elsewhere *oikoumene* may mean either "world" or "empire" (Acts 11.28; 19.27).

The view that the New Testament use of *oikoumene* contains an element of polemic directed against the Empire does not seem to rest on sufficient evidence; but there are at least hints that the political *oikoumene* is a passing phenomenon, and that the true *oikoumene* is that of the Kingdom of Christ. This interpretation finds confirmation in the expression *oikoumene mellousa*, the coming *oikoumene*, in Hebrews 2.5. For that expression stresses the transitory character of the present *oikoumene* and includes the tremendous affirmation that there will be a new and transformed *oikoumene* under the direct rule of Jesus Christ.

In Christian writings of the first centuries, *oikoumene* is sometimes used in the sense of "world" (1 Clement 60.1) and sometimes in the sense of "empire". It is first linked with the Church in the *Martyrdom of Polycarp* (2nd century). The author refers three times to the "catholic Church throughout the *oikoumene*".

Origen uses the word not infrequently in a variety of senses. The most illuminating, perhaps, is in the passage where, commenting on Psalm 32.8, "all they that inhabit the *oikoumene*" (LXX), he explains the phrase as referring to those "who dwell in the *oikoumene* of the Church of God". Carrying the same line of thought still farther, Basil the Great, in his commentary on Psalm 48, interprets "the nations" (*ethnē*) as those who are strangers to the Faith, and "those who inhabit the *oikoumene*" as those who are already in the Church. He adds that "the inhabitants of the *oikoumene* should receive with love those who are strangers to the Covenant"—an interesting early example of the conviction that "ecumenical concern is sterile without evangelistic concern".

The word enters into official ecclesiastical usage when in the year 381 the Council of Constantinople speaks of the Council of Nicea as an "ecumenical synod". It is taken for granted that an Ecumenical Council is convened by the Emperor and meets under his authority. On the other hand, since the Ecumenical Council is the highest organ of the Church and its decisions possess general authority and validity in the life of the Church, the word "ecumenical" acquires the special connotation of that which is accepted as authoritative and valid throughout the whole Church.

In ecclesiastical usage a council is ecumenical when it is accepted as speaking on behalf of the Church as a whole. The conditions which must be fulfilled in order to make a council truly ecumenical are defined in various ways. Roman Catholics affirm that a council is only ecumenical if its decisions have been confirmed by the Pope. In the view of most Orthodox theologians the whole Church must have accepted its decisions. Thus the Orthodox Churches speak of seven Ecumenical Councils, because only seven are accepted by the Church in both East and West as characterized by orthodox doctrine.

In the 6th century the use of the word "ecumenical" played a considerable rôle in the conflict between Rome and Constantinople. The title "ecumenical" had been used sporadically as an honorific title of several patriarchs and of the Pope, but began to be used by the Patriarch John the Faster as a title exclusively attached to the Patriarchate of Constantinople. Pope Gregory the Great protested against this in the most energetic terms, since he understood the term "ecumenical" in the sense of *universalis*. It is more than probable, however, that this conflict was at least in part based upon a misunderstanding. The title was meant as recognition of the fact that the Patriarch of Constantinople, whose see is also the capital of the Empire, the *oikoumene*, has a special place and function in that *oikoumene*. Once again the Empire and the "habitable world" are identified.

A more ecclesiastical use of the word "ecumenical" is the designation of three great theologians of the Church as "ecumenical doctors". These three are Basil the Great, Gregory Nazianzen, and John Chrysostom. Their "ecumenical" authority is based on the truth of their teaching, which is accepted as serving as a norm and standard for the whole Church.

When the Byzantine Empire collapsed, the word ceased to have political overtones, and there remained only the ecclesiastical meaning. The battle between the secular and the Christian meaning which had begun in the New Testament had finally been decided. The *oikoumene* is the Church Universal. But the full consequences of this change in significance were destined to appear only at a much later date.

In the 16th century a new ecclesiastical use of the word is found—the three most widely used Creeds (the Apostles', the Nicene, and the Athanasian Creeds) are designated "ecumenical". In the Latin edition of the Formula of Concord[1] the three Creeds appear under the title: "*Tria symbola catholica et oecumenica.*"

It is interesting to note that John Eliot, the first missionary to New England Indians, proposed in 1665 the setting up of an "Oecumenical Council" which would sit permanently in Jerusalem. But he was using the word simply in its traditional ecclesiastical sense. In the 17th and 18th centuries the term is used only in relation to the Councils, the Creeds, and the Patriarchate of Constantinople. Other words—catholic, irenical, accommodation, toleration—were at that time used to describe actions and attitudes which in a later age would be called "ecumenical".[2]

Throughout the 19th century and after, the word continued to be used traditionally in its geographical and ecclesiastical sense.

In 1900 the Ecumenical Missionary Conference was held in New York.[3] Here the use of the word was purely geographical; it was chosen not because the Conference was to represent the whole Church or every branch of it, but "because the plan . . . which it proposes covers the whole area of the inhabited globe".[4] A parallel, though denominational, use was that of the Methodists, who in 1881 held the first Ecumenical Methodist Conference, to represent the interests and discuss the affairs of world-wide Methodism.[5]

The sense of the word as denoting the whole world-wide Church in all its branches was never entirely forgotten. In the early stages of its preparation, the Edinburgh Missionary Conference of 1910 was regularly known as the Third Ecumenical Missionary Conference 1910; in 1908 this title was dropped, perhaps under Anglican influence, it being felt that the word "ecumenical" was hardly applicable to a Conference at which neither the Roman Catholic nor the Orthodox Churches would be represented, and that, associated as it was "with conciliar and legislative action, it was . . . inappropriate for a strictly deliberative conference".[6]

From a considerably earlier period, however, there were circles in which the

---

[1] See Chap. i, p. 47.
[2] The remarkably comprehensive bibliography of books concerning the conception of the Church published in the 16th, 17th, 18th, and 19th centuries, which covers twenty-five pages in Thils, *Les Notes de l'Église*, 1937, does not contain a single title in which the word "ecumenical" occurs.
[3] See Chap. viii, pp. 354, 357.   [4] Hogg, *Ecumenical Foundations*, p. 45.
[5] See Chap. vi, p. 267.   [6] Hogg, *Ecumenical Foundations*, p. 109.

word "ecumenical" was coming back into currency as a living term, and in part with new and unprecedented connotations.

Some of the earliest instances are in connection with the foundation of the Evangelical Alliance in 1846, and with the efforts, which preceded it, of Dean Kniewel of Danzig to secure support for his plans for an "evangelical œcumenical universal Council". At the constitutive Conference of the Alliance, held in London in 1846, several speakers used the word "ecumenical" quite readily. At the close of the Conference, the French Reformed Pastor Adolphe Monod thanked his British brethren for the "fervour of their piety" and their "*esprit vraiment oecuménique*"; this seems to be the first instance on record of the use of the word to indicate an attitude rather than a fact—the sense of already belonging to a world-wide unity of the Church of Christ, which transcends national and confessional differences.

Several striking instances of the new departure are to be found in the letters of Henri Dunant, who was not only the founder of the Red Cross, but also a pioneer of the Y.M.C.A. and Secretary of the Geneva branch of the Evangelical Alliance. In the correspondence which he carried on on behalf of the Geneva Y.M.C.A. with Y.M.C.A.s in other countries[1] he emphasizes again and again that the Y.M.C.A. must be "ecumenical". He writes of the "attempt to propagate that ecumenical spirit which transcends nationality and language, denominations and ecclesiastical questions, class and profession"; and elsewhere defines his use of the term "ecumenical" as follows: "that Christians of different denominations can and must unite in love, associate with each other, and work together in charity for the glory of God, while maintaining their individual liberty and even their right to defend, if necessary, but with tolerance and charity, their personal points of view and their particular religious convictions". This quotation shows that the word "ecumenical" has acquired a new meaning. To speak of a small local group of Christians of differing denominations as "ecumenical", to speak of the "ecumenical spirit", is a use of language which would have seemed incomprehensible in earlier periods.

At the Evangelical Alliance Conference in Basle in 1879 Dr Hermann Plitt, a leader of the Moravians in Germany, speaking of the unity of the Spirit as witnessed to by the Moravians and the Alliance, calls that witness an "ecumenical" witness.[2] And it is clear from the context that he refers to the *content* of the witness. "Ecumenical" is here used with reference to a consciousness of the Church Universal and to the essential unity of its various branches, and not merely to the objective fact of extension in space or of validity accepted by the whole Church. Similarly, Archbishop Söderblom spoke in 1912 of the "ecumenical attitude" of Gustavus Adolphus.[3]

But this use was by no means general. Up to the first world war the word was not frequently used, and, when used, it was generally in the purely geographical or in the traditionally ecclesiastical sense. A change begins to be seen with the development of the Faith and Order and Life and Work movements, to which we now turn.

In its early days Faith and Order did not generally describe its work as "ecumenical". Nevertheless, in 1916 Bishop Anderson of Chicago said in his

---

[1] See Clarence Shedd, "Henri Dunant et les Y.M.C.A.", in *Bulletin, Société d'Histoire et d'Archéologie de Genève*, 1949, especially p. 231.
[2] *Basel Conference Report*, p. 915.　　　　[3] *Die Eiche*, 1932, p. 205.

introductory address at the Garden City Conference :[1] "It [the proposed World Conference] is not to be, if its plans carry, a pan-Protestant conference, nor a pan-Catholic conference. It is to be pan-Christian. It is neither sectional nor partisan in its conception. It seeks to be truly representative of all Christendom, thoroughly ecumenical in its reach. . . ."[2] In presenting the invitation to the Patriarchate of Constantinople, the delegation from the Protestant Episcopal Church in the United States said in April 1919: "It [the Conference] is not, of course, to be an Ecumenical Council, but it does aim to be ecumenical in its wide representative character and in its far-reaching influence."[3]

A new phase in the history of the word "ecumenical" began when, during the first world war, Archbishop Söderblom began to plan for international Christian conferences dealing with the problem of peace and social justice. In 1917 the three Scandinavian Primates issued an invitation to an international meeting to be held in April 1918 which they describe as an "ecumenical conference". The word is definitely used in the sense of "concerning the life of the Church as a whole".[4]

In 1919 at Oud Wassenaar, the Archbishop proposed to the World Alliance for Promoting International Friendship through the Churches the creation of a permanent "Ecumenical Council of the Churches". His proposal as such was not accepted, but the word became attached to the plan to call a general conference of the Churches to consider their urgent practical tasks in society. The decision of the 1919 meeting speaks of an "ecumenical conference", and a Committee on Ecumenical Conference was set up.[5] The Federal Council of the Churches of Christ in America used the same terminology, and its Committee on Ecumenical Conference planned and called the preliminary Conference in Geneva in 1920. It was therefore natural that at that meeting the title for the world conference as it was proposed by the American delegates included "ecumenical". But that title was not generally acceptable, and it was finally decided that in English the word "universal" rather than "ecumenical" should be used. The remark was added in the Minutes: "It is hoped that this conference will become ecumenical."[6] This refers to the problem of Roman Catholic participation in the meeting. There had been some resistance against inviting the Church of Rome, and it had been answered that an "ecumenical" conference of Protestant Churches was a *contradictio in adjecto*. Thus in 1920 the original sense of "ecumenical" as "representing the *whole* Church of Christ" was still strongly felt.

But the word "ecumenical" had now become too closely attached to the new movement to be dropped altogether. It was retained in both the Latin and Greek titles of Stockholm 1925. And though this was not the official name, in Germany the Conference was generally referred to as *die ökumenische Konferenz*. But it was in Sweden that the word entered most fully into common usage. At the time of the Stockholm Conference the words *ekumenik* (ecumenicity) and *ekumen* (a person actively concerned with the ecumenical movement) were widely used in that country.[7]

It was also in the early 1920's that the word became current in the French

---

[1] See Chap. ix, p. 414.   [2] *F. and O. Pamphlet No. 30*, pp. 23 f.
[3] *F. and O. Pamphlet No. 32*, p. 26.
[4] N. Karlström, *Kristna Samförståndsstravanden*, p. 651.
[5] C. S. Macfarland, *Christian Unity in the Making*, p. 166.
[6] *Records of the preliminary meeting*, pp. 5, 8, 28.
[7] See Söderblom in *Die Eiche*, 1928, pp. 137, 140.

Student Christian Movement in connection with contacts between Protestant and Roman Catholic, and between Protestant and Orthodox students.

In 1929 at Eisenach[1] the German and French, but not the English, titles of the Universal Christian Council for Life and Work were changed and the word "ecumenical" was adopted as the official designation in these languages. From that time onwards the word became widely known on the continent of Europe. It was, however, not so readily adopted in the English-speaking world. This is reflected in the fact that in the titles proposed in 1937 for the new World Council of Churches the word "ecumenical" was used in French and German but not in English.[2]

The Oxford Conference of 1937 did much to give the word wider currency and to establish its wider and more substantial meaning. It declared: "The term ecumenical refers to the expression within history of the given unity of the Church. The thought and action of the Church are ecumenical, in so far as they attempt to realize the *Una Sancta*, the fellowship of Christians, who acknowledge the one Lord."[3] From that time on the term has been used in both the traditional sense of "concerning the Church as a whole", and in the modern senses of "concerning the relationship of different Churches" and "expressing the consciousness of the wholeness of the Church".

During and after the second world war the word became very widely used. In several theological seminaries "ecumenism" or "ecumenics" appeared in the curriculum. And the number of associations, periodicals, and books which use the word in their titles has grown to such an extent that there is some danger of an ecumenical inflation.

The following reasons seem to account for the widespread adoption of the word:

(1) It had a venerable history.

(2) It was "available", since it had not been appropriated by any one confession.

(3) It could express the nature of the modern movement for co-operation and unity which seeks to manifest the fundamental unity and universality of the Church of Christ.[4]

---

[1] See Chap. xii, p. 571.

[2] In the English tradition, the association of the word with the Ecumenical Councils was so strong as to make difficult the acceptance of its use with a different significance.

[3] *The Churches Survey Their Task*, pp. 168 f.

[4] See the much fuller presentation of the evidence in W. A. Visser 't Hooft, *The Meaning of Ecumenical* (The Burge Memorial Lecture, 1953), London, 1953.

APPENDIX II

By Stephen Charles Neill

INTERCOMMUNION

The problem of intercommunion has presented itself in different forms in successive periods of the Church's life, each being closely related to the changing external situation of the Church and to varying views as to its nature.

Before the Reformation, it was mainly a question of orthodoxy and heresy. Churches, patriarchates, or dioceses which regarded one another, or one another's bishops, as heretical, naturally had no communion with one another. In certain cases the separation was only temporary, and after a longer or shorter interval communion was restored. In other cases, such as that of the Lesser Eastern and the Orthodox Churches, the separation has continued almost unchanged from the 5th century till the present day.[1]

After the Reformation, a new situation was created by the recognition of the territorial principle. A number of Churches which had passed through the Reformation were territorially organized in Germany, Sweden, England, the Swiss Republics, and elsewhere, all with a certain common feeling, and the majority more or less convinced of one another's orthodoxy. Could such Churches accord to one another such recognition as would make intercommunion possible? As a result of the adoption of the territorial principle, the question arose mainly in connection with envoys, exiles, and occasional common synods and discussions on the subject of Church unity.

As far as the Lutherans and the Reformed were concerned, the question was in the main settled by the failure of the German and Swiss Reformers to agree at Marburg in 1529.[2] Though the French Synod of Charenton in 1631[3] recommended intercommunion, this initiative was not followed up, and, with exceptions varying in frequency from century to century and from area to area, the 16th-century situation has persisted until the present day. Some Anglicans took the view that, where general agreement on the principles of the Faith existed, the loss of episcopacy by the Continental Churches, which it was hoped would be only temporary, need not stand in the way of fellowship, and intercommunion was fairly widely practised, though without synodical authorization. The Laudian school, however, took a stricter view, and in general resisted intercommunion. This inconsistency in Anglican views and practice has persisted until the present day.[4]

A further major change was brought about through the co-existence in one territory of a number of separate Churches. The principle that only one form of the Christian Church could exist in the territory of one ruler—*cuius regio eius religio*—long survived the Reformation. It was upheld as firmly by the Republic of Geneva as by the King of Spain. The idea of co-existence was not clearly accepted in England until after the Revolution of 1688. It gained ground slowly,

---

[1] See Introduction, pp. 12 ff.   [2] See Chap. i, p. 44.
[3] See Chap. i, p. 66.
[4] See Chap. iii, pp. 128 ff.; Chap. vii, p. 337.

e.g. in Sweden, where religious inequality was finally removed only in 1952. Even in the United States, where religious liberty developed more rapidly and completely than elsewhere, it was not fully accepted until the end of the 18th century.[1]

Yet even where a number of Churches existed in freedom side by side, on the whole they lived their lives so much in separation that intercommunion was not a burning question. Undoubtedly greater freedom was exercised in missionary territories and on the frontiers of the Church, where such exceptional arrangements existed as the appointment by the Anglican S.P.C.K. of missionaries in Lutheran Orders to full charge of mission stations and chaplaincies.[2] But it was only with the rise of a new ecumenical spirit in the 19th century, and in particular in relation to the many international and interdenominational conferences to which it gave rise,[3] that the problem presented itself to the Christian conscience as urgent. The varying positions taken up at such conferences and by the Churches concerned in them are indicated in the relevant connections in this History.

Approaches to the question by the Churches may be listed under six heads:

(1) Refusal of all intercommunion on any basis other than that of total unification (the Roman Catholic Church).[4]

(2) "Economy"—refusal of all intercommunion, subject to *ad hoc* modification in particular circumstances (generally dictated by Christian charity or circumstances of pastoral urgency) of a rule which is nevertheless accepted as generally binding (the Orthodox Churches).[5]

(3) Full intercommunion, without fusion of organization and administration (the Anglican and Old Catholic Churches).[6]

(4) Limited intercommunion, involving mutual recognition but generally confined to exceptional circumstances (the Churches of England and Sweden; the Mar Thoma Syrian Church and the Church of India, Pakistan, Burma, and Ceylon).[7]

(5) Occasional hospitality to *bona fide* communicants temporarily separated from the ministrations of their own Church, or in other exceptional circumstances (most Anglican and some Lutheran Churches).

(6) "Open Communion"—the reception to the Lord's Table of all who desire to participate, without regard to the particular denomination to which they belong (many churches of the Reformed, Baptist, Methodist, and Congregational traditions).

The problem is felt with special acuteness in relation to gatherings at which Christians of many communions are present. There would be general agreement that "a body like the World Council of Churches or the World's Student Christian Federation must not, as such, hold its own Communion Services, because

---

[1] See Chap. v, pp. 224 f., 232. [2] See Chap. iii, pp. 160 f.
[3] See Chap. vii, p. 337. [4] See Chap. xv, *passim.*
[5] See Chap. iv, p. 212; Chap. x, p. 487.
[6] See Chap. vi, p. 294; Chap. x, pp. 469 ff.
[7] See Chap. x, pp. 471 ff., and Table of Plans of Union and Reunion (39), p. 499.

such a body is not a Church. And yet the life of such a body, met in conference for a period, cannot be complete without Holy Communion".[1] The World Council has always acted on this principle. To meet the difficulties of the situation, various solutions, none of them giving universal satisfaction, have been adopted or proposed:

(1) That during such gatherings there should be no celebration of the Holy Communion, such fasting from the Sacrament being accepted by all as a sign of penitence for the sin of division.

(2) That one Celebration should be arranged by a Church which according to its own principles is able to invite the baptized communicant members of other communions to partake of the Lord's Supper, and that all who are conscientiously able to do so should be encouraged to receive Communion at this service.

(3) That a number of Celebrations should be arranged by the individual Churches, so that all members of the gathering may be able to receive Communion at one or other of these services, and that all may have the opportunity of participating spiritually in the Liturgy of communions other than their own, even where they cannot physically receive the Sacrament.

This third practice, which was followed at Amsterdam in 1948 and elsewhere, has revealed a divergence of practice on the part of the different communions:

(1) Some, such as the Orthodox Churches, permit no intercommunion in either direction.

(2) Some, such as in most cases the Anglican Churches, have rules making it possible, in such exceptional circumstances as are presented by an ecumenical conference, e.g. Oxford 1937,[2] to invite the faithful of other communions to receive the Sacrament with them; but not all such Churches have felt it right to encourage their faithful to receive the Sacrament at the Communion services of non-episcopal Churches.

(3) Yet others, such as the Dutch Reformed Church at Amsterdam in 1948, and the Church of Sweden at Lund in 1952, have been willing to invite all baptized communicant members of other communions to receive the Sacrament at the service arranged by them, whilst respecting the principles of those who are unable, through personal conviction or because of the rules of their Church, to accept the invitation.

All such invitations are addressed to individuals attending the conference, and are not intended to prejudge or to force any issues as regards the relationship of the Churches as such to one another.

It has to be recognized that individuals often claim for themselves a liberty greater than that which is recognized by the rules of the communion to which they belong. This has been true of individuals of all communions. In the majority of cases, such individual assertions of liberty remain unknown to the authorities concerned, or are not visited with any disciplinary action.

It remains to mention one further deep division of opinion among Christians on the subject of intercommunion. Some hold that intercommunion should be the final expression of an agreement on faith and order between two Churches. They consider that individual acts of intercommunion, even though they may have received some sanction from Church authorities, do not promote the cause of Christian union, and may even hinder it, through obscuring the real sources of division which exist as between the Churches, and making people content with

[1] *Intercommunion: Faith and Order Commission Papers No. 5*, p. 23.
[2] See Chap. ix, p. 424, and Chap. xii, p. 589.

something much less than full organic union. Others hold equally strongly that participation together in the Lord's Supper, even while the Churches remain in separation, is the best possible means of promoting the spirit of unity, expressing the spiritual unity which already exists, and helping forward the movement towards the outward expression of that inward unity in corporate union.

A full discussion of these issues would be out of place in a History; and is the less necessary since extensive studies on the question have been made by the Faith and Order section of the World Council of Churches. For further information, the student is directed to the *Report of the Third World Conference on Faith and Order, Lund, Sweden, August 15–28, 1952*, pp. 36–45, to the volume *Intercommunion*, prepared by a theological commission of Faith and Order for the same Conference, and to the Report of the Commission, *Intercommunion: Faith and Order Commission Papers No. 5.*

BIBLIOGRAPHY

The bibliography of the first edition has been carefully checked, corrected, and augmented by approximately two hundred titles of important old and new books dealing with ecumenical history up to 1948. No attempt has been made to compile a complete bibliography of ecumenical history, which would require a separate volume. The bibliography remains essentially a selective, and not a comprehensive, list of works. It is arranged to correspond with the chapters of the book, the reader being referred first to the primary sources which are basic for his research, and frequently to other sources where more detailed bibliographical information may be found.

Many of the books mentioned in this list also contain bibliographies which deal with specific aspects of the ecumenical movement.

GENERAL BIBLIOGRAPHY

I. Ecumenical Libraries and Archives

The Library of the World Council of Churches (150 Route de Ferney, Geneva, Switzerland), including a steadily increasing collection of unprinted ecumenical archives.

The Library of Union Theological Seminary (Broadway at 120th Street, New York 27, N.Y., U.S.A.) (*a*) The William Adams Brown Ecumenical Library. (*b*) The Missionary Research Library.

The Day Historical Library of Foreign Missions in Yale University (New Haven, Conn., U.S.A.).

The Söderblom Archives (Uppsala, Sweden).

Archives of the World Conference on Faith and Order (General Theological Seminary, Chelsea Square, New York 11, N.Y., U.S.A.).

Archives of the World Alliance for Promoting International Friendship through the Churches ((*a*) 37 Quai Wilson, Geneva, Switzerland. (*b*) The University Library, Uppsala, Sweden).

II. Ecumenical Bibliographies

Brandreth, Henry R. T.: *Unity and Reunion: a Bibliography*; 2nd ed. with supplement, London, 1948.

Crow, Paul A., jr.: *The Ecumenical Movement in Bibliographical Outline*, New York, 1965.

Douglass, H. P.: *A Preliminary Working Bibliography of Christian Unity from the American Standpoint*, New York, 1938.

Hall, F. J.: *A Bibliography of Topics relating to Church Unity*, Boston, 1913.

International Missionary Bibliography: a monthly supplement to *The International Review of Missions*.

Lilienfeld, A. de: *Pour l'union: documents et bibliographie*, Amay-sur-Meuse, 1927.

Macy, Paul Griswold: *An ecumenical Bibliography*, New York, 1946.

Senaud, Auguste: *Christian Unity: a Bibliography*, Geneva, 1937.

III. General Histories of Ecumenical and Unitive Effort

Bell, G. K. A. (ed.), *Documents on Christian Unity, First Series, 1920–4*, London, 1924; *Second Series*, London, 1930; *Third Series, 1930–48*, London, 1948; *Fourth Series, 1948–57*, London, 1958.

Cavert, Samuel McCrea: *The Ecumenical Movement: Retrospect and Prospect*, New York, 1959

Conord, P.: *Brève histoire de l'oecuménisme*, Paris, 1958.

Estep, William R., jr.: *A historical Study of the Ecumenical Movement*, Southwestern Baptist, 1951.

Garrison, James H.: *Christian Union: a historical Study*, St Louis, 1906.

Hering, Carl Wilh.: *Geschichte der kirchlichen Unionsversuche seit der Reformation bis auf unsere Zeit*, 2 vols., Leipzig, 1836.

Hornig, Ernst: *Der Weg der Weltchristenheit: eine Einführung in die ökumenische Bewegung, ihre Geschichte, und Probleme*; 2nd ed., Stuttgart, 1958.

Joss, Gottlieb: *Die Vereinigung der christlichen Kirchen*, Leiden, 1877.

Paul, André: *L'unité chrétienne: schismes et rapprochements*, Paris, 1930.

Rabaut, le jeune, M.: *Détails historiques et receuil de pièces sur les divers projets de réunion de toutes les communions chrétiennes*, Paris, 1806.

Slosser, Gaius Jackson: *Christian Unity: its history and Challenge in all Communions, in all Lands*, New York, 1929.

Tabaraud, M.: *Histoire critique des projets formés depuis trois cents ans pour la réunion des communions chrétiennes*, Paris, 1808; 2nd ed., 1824.

Tavard, Georges: *Petite histoire du mouvement oecuménique*, Paris, 1960.

Two Centuries of Ecumenism, Notre Dame, 1960.

IV. Histories of Organizations with a Special Ecumenical Concern

Basle Missionary Society

Schlatter, Wilhelm: *Geschichte der Basler Mission, 1815–1915*, 3 vols., Basle, 1916.

Bible Societies

American Bible Society: *Annual report: together with a list of auxiliary and cooperating societies, their officers and other data*, New York, Vol. I, 1816 [?].

Canton, W.: *History of the British and Foreign Bible Society*, 5 vols., London, 1904–10.

Douen, O.: *Histoire de la Société biblique protestante de Paris, 1818 à 1868*. Avec des notices biographiques par F. Schickler, Paris, 1868.

Dwight, Henry Otis: *Centennial History of the American Bible Society*, New York, 1916.

Owen, John: *The History of the Origin and first ten Years of the British and Foreign Bible Society*, 3 vols., London, 1816–20.

Church Missionary Society

Stock, Eugene: *The History of the Church Missionary Society, its Environment, its Men, and its Work*, 4 vols., London, 1899–1916.

International Missionary Council

Hogg, William Richey: *Ecumenical Foundations: a History of the International Missionary Council and its nineteenth-century Background*, New York, 1952.

Society for the Propagation of the Gospel in Foreign Parts

Pascoe, C. F.: *Two hundred Years of the S.P.G., 1701–1900*, 2 vols., London, 1901.

Thompson, H. P.: *Into All Lands: the History of the Society for the Propagation of the Gospel in Foreign Parts, 1701–1950*, London, 1951.

Society for Promoting Christian Knowledge

Allen, W. O. B., and McClure, Edmund: *Two Hundred Years: the History of the Society for Promoting Christian Knowledge, 1698–1898*, London, 1898.

WORLD'S EVANGELICAL ALLIANCE

Ewing, J. W.: *Goodly Fellowship: a Centenary Tribute to the Life and Work of the World's Evangelical Alliance, 1846–1946*, London, 1946.

Massie, J. W.: *The Evangelical Alliance; its Origin and Development*, London, 1847.

Newman, Ernst: *Evangeliska Alliansen: en studie i protestantisk enhets-och frihetssträvan*, Lund, 1937.

WORLD'S STUDENT CHRISTIAN FEDERATION, AND STUDENT CHRISTIAN MOVEMENTS

Diétrich, Suzanne de: *Cinquante ans d'histoire: la Fédération universelle des Associations chrétiennes d'Étudiants, 1895–1945*, Paris, 1948.

Mott, John R.: *The World's Student Christian Federation: Origin, Achievements, Forecast*, New York, 1920.

The World's Student Christian Federation, New York, 1947.

Rouse, Ruth: *The World's Student Christian Federation: a History of the first thirty Years*, London, 1948.

Shedd, Clarence P.: *Two Centuries of Student Christian Movements*, New York, 1934.

Tatlow, Tissington: *The Story of the Student Christian Movement of Great Britain and Ireland*, London, 1933.

WORLD'S ALLIANCE OF YOUNG MEN'S CHRISTIAN ASSOCIATIONS

Doggett, L. L., *History of the Young Men's Christian Association*, Vol. I, *The Founding of the Association, 1844–1855*, New York, 1896.

Hopkins, C. Howard: *History of the Y.M.C.A. in North America*, New York, 1951.

Shedd, Clarence Prouty: *History of the World's Alliance of Young Men's Christian Associations*, London, 1955.

WORLD'S YOUNG WOMEN'S CHRISTIAN ASSOCIATION

Rice, Anna V.: *A History of the World's Young Women's Christian Association*, New York, 1947.

V. THE GREAT CONFERENCES

EDINBURGH 1910

World Missionary Conference 1910, 9 vols., Edinburgh and London, n.d.

Appenzeller, Karl: *Das Problem der Bodenständigkeit von Christentum und Kirche auf dem Missionsfeld in den Verhandlungen der Weltmissionskonferenz zu Edinburgh* (1910), Würzburg, 1940.

Gairdner, W. H. T.: *"Edinburgh 1910": an Account and Interpretation of the World Missionary Conference*, Edinburgh and London, 1910.

Mott, John R.: *The Decisive Hour of Christian Missions*, New York, 1910.

Schreiber, A. W.: *Die Edinburger Welt-Missions-Konferenz. Bilder und Berichte von Vertretern deutscher Missionsgesellschaften*, Basle, 1910.

STOCKHOLM 1925

Bell, G. K. A. (ed.): *The Stockholm Conference 1925: Official Report of the Universal Christian Conference on Life and Work held in Stockholm, 19–30 August 1925*, London, 1926.

Deissmann, Adolf (ed.): *Die Stockholmer Weltkirchenkonferenz: Vorge-schichte, Dienst, und Arbeit der Weltkonferenz für praktisches Christentum 19–30 August 1925*, Berlin, 1926.

La Conférence universelle du christianisme pratiqué, tenue à Stockholm, 19–29 août 1925 in *Christianisme social* (Oct.–Nov. 1925), Paris, 1925, pp. 851–1182.

LAUSANNE 1927

Bate, H. N. (ed.): *Faith and Order: Proceedings of the World Conference, Lausanne, August 3–21, 1927*, London, 1927.

Church Assembly: *Report of the Committee appointed by the Archbishops of Canterbury and York to consider the findings of the Lausanne Conference on Faith and Order, 1928–30*, London, 1930.

La Conférence de Lausanne: Conférence universelle pour la Foi et la Consti-tution de l'Église in *Christianisme social* (Nov.–Dec. 1927), Paris, 1927, pp. 1005–87.

Hodgson, Leonard (ed.): *Convictions: a Selection from the Responses of the Churches to . . . Lausanne in 1927*, London, 1934.

Sasse, Hermann (ed.): *Die Weltkonferenz für Glauben und Kirchenverfassung*, Berlin, 1929.

Woods, E. S.: *Lausanne 1927: an Interpretation of the World Conference on Faith and Order . . .* , London, 1927.

JERUSALEM 1928

Report of the Jerusalem Meeting of the International Missionary Council, March 24th–April 8th, 1928 (The Jerusalem Series), 8 vols., London, 1928.

Christianity and the Growth of Industrialism in Asia, Africa, and South America: Report of the Jerusalem Meeting, Oxford, 1928.

Mathews, Basil: *Roads to the City of God: a World Outlook from Jerusalem*, London, 1928.

Schlunk, M. (ed.), *Von den Höhen des Ölberges: Bericht der deutschen Abord-nung über die Missionstagung in Jerusalem*, Basle and Stuttgart, 1928.

OXFORD 1937

The Churches survey their Task: the Report of the Conference at Oxford, July 1937, on Church, Community, and State, London, 1937.

The Church, Community, and State Series, 7 vols., London, 1937–38.

Ehrenström, Nils: *Christian Faith and the modern state; an ecumenical approach*. Tr. by Denzil Patrick and Olive Wyon. Preface by J. H. Oldham, London, 1937.

Fenn, Eric: *That they go forward: an Impression of the Oxford Conference on Church, Community, and State*, London, 1938.

OXFORD 1937 and EDINBURGH 1937

Keller, Adolf: *Five Minutes to Twelve: a Spiritual Interpretation of the Oxford and Edinburgh Conferences*, Nashville, 1938.

Leiper, Henry Smith: *Christ's Way and the World's in Church, State, and Society*, New York, 1936.

World Chaos or World Christianity: a Popular Interpretation of Oxford and Edinburgh 1937, Chicago and New York, 1937.

EDINBURGH 1937

Douglass, H. Paul: *A Decade of objective Progress in Church Unity, 1927–1936, Report No. 4. Prepared by the Commission on the Church's Unity in Life and Worship . . . for the World Conference on Faith and Order, Edinburgh, 1937,* New York, 1937.

Hodgson, Leonard (ed.): *The Second World Conference on Faith and Order held at Edinburgh, August 3–18, 1937,* London, 1938.

Martin, Hugh: *Edinburgh 1937: the Story of the Second World Conference on Faith and Order,* London, 1937.

TAMBARAM–MADRAS 1938

The Church faces the World: a Joint Statement prepared for the Madras Conference of the International Missionary Council, New York, 1939.

International Missionary Council Meeting at Tambaram, Madras, December 12th to 29th, 1938 (Tambaram–Madras Series), 7 vols., Oxford, 1939.

The World Mission of the Church: Findings and Recommendations of the Meeting of the International Missionary Council, Tambaram, Madras, India, Dec. 12–29, 1938, London and New York, 1939.

Hartenstein, Karl: *Die Weltmissionskonferenz Tambaram 1938,* Stuttgart and Basle, 2nd ed., n.d.

Schlunk, M. (ed.): *Das Wunder der Kirche unter den Völkern der Erde: Bericht über die Weltmissionskonferenz in Tambaram (Südindien) 1938,* Stuttgart, 1938.

AMSTERDAM 1939

Patrick, Denzil G. M. (ed.): *Christus Victor: Report of the World Conference of Christian Youth, Amsterdam, Holland, July 24 to August 2, 1939,* Geneva, 1939.

OSLO 1947

Macy, Paul G. (ed.): *The Report of the Second World Conference of Christian Youth, Oslo, Norway, July 22–31, 1947,* Geneva, 1947.

WHITBY 1947

Latourette, Kenneth Scott, and Hogg, William Richey: *Tomorrow is here: a Survey of the world-wide Mission and Work of the Christian Church,* London, 1948; a slightly different ed., New York, 1948.

Ranson, C. W. (ed.): *Renewal and Advance: Christian Witness in a revolutionary World,* London, 1948.

AMSTERDAM 1948

Man's Disorder and God's Design, Amsterdam Assembly Series, 5 vols.. London, 1948. (Esp. Vol. 5, *The First Assembly of the World Council of Churches . . . Amsterdam, August 22nd to September 4th, 1948;* ed. W. A. Visser 't Hooft.)

Menn, Wilhelm (ed.): *Die Ordnung Gottes und die Unordnung der Welt: Deutsche Beiträge zum Amsterdamer ökumenischen Gespräch 1948,* Stuttgart, 1948.

Kennedy, James W.: *Venture of faith: the birth of the World Council of Churches.* Foreword by Henry Smith Leiper. New York, 1948.

WILLINGEN 1952

Minutes of the Enlarged Meeting and the Committee of the International Missionary Council, Willingen, Germany, July 5th to 21st, 1952, London and New York, 1952.

The Missionary Obligation of the Church, Willingen, Germany, July 5–17, 1952, London, 1953.

Battie, J. A. T.: *The Mission of the Church: a Report on the Willingen Conference of the International Missionary Council*, Port Harcourt, 1953.

Freytag, W., and others (eds.): *Mission zwischen gestern und morgen: vom Gestaltenwandel der Weltmission der Christenheit im Lichte der Konferenz des Internationalen Missionsrates in Willingen*, Stuttgart, 1952.

Goodall, Norman (ed.): *Missions under the Cross: Addresses . . . at Willingen . . . with Statements issued by the Meeting*, London, 1953.

Northcott, Cecil: *Christian World Mission*, London, 1952.

LUND 1952

Report of the Third World Conference on Faith and Order, Lund, Sweden, August 15–28, 1952, London, 1952.

Responses of the Churches to the Report of the Third World Conference on Faith and Order, Lund 1952, Geneva, 1957.

Robertson, E. H.: *Lund 1952*, London, 1952.

Tomkins, Oliver S. (ed.): *The Third World Conference on Faith and Order held at Lund, August 15th to 28th, 1952*, London, 1953.

Preparatory Volumes:

Intercommunion: Report of the Theological Commission. Ed. Donald Baillie and John Marsh, London, 1952.

The Nature of the Church: Papers presented to the Theological Commission . . . of . . . Faith and Order. Ed. R. Newton Flew, London, 1952.

Ways of Worship: Report of a Theological Commission of Faith and Order. Ed. Pehr Edwall, Eric Hayman, William D. Maxwell, London, 1951.

VI. PERIODICAL LITERATURE

Only those periodicals are included which can be described as definitely ecumenical in aim, or which contain ecumenical material of special value.

Bulletin du Monde chrétien, écho de l'Alliance évangélique, Paris, 1848–70.

Christendom. Quarterly. Chicago and New York, 1935–48.

(Continuation of *Christian Union Quarterly* and continued by *The Ecumenical Review, q.v.*)

Christian East, The (Organ of the Anglican and Eastern Churches Association). Quarterly. London, 1920–.

Christian Union Quarterly, Baltimore, 1911–35.

(Continued by *Christendom, q.v.*)

Christianisme social, Le. Monthly. Saint-Étienne, Ganges, and Paris, 1887–.

Church Union News and Views (Organ of the Continuation Committee of the South India Joint Committee on Union). Quarterly. Madras, 1930–47.

Churches in Action. News Letters of the Universal Christian Council on Life and Work and the World Alliance for International Friendship through the Churches. Quarterly. Geneva, 1931–38.

Constructive Quarterly, The. A Journal of the Faith, Work, and Thought of Christendom, New York, 1913–28.

Eastern Churches Quarterly, London, 1936–64.

(Continued by *One in Christ, q.v.*)

Ecumenical Courier, The, New York, Vol. 1, No. 1, June, 1941.

Ecumenical Press Service (Mimeographed in English, German, and French). Geneva, 1949–.

(Continuation of *International Christian Press and Information Service, q.v.*)

Ecumenical Review, The (The official review of the World Council of Churches). Quarterly. Geneva, 1948–.

Eiche, Die. Quarterly. Gotha, 1913–33.

(Continued by *Eine Heilige Kirche, q.v.*)

Eine Heilige Kirche, Munich, 1933–39, 1953–58.

(Continuation of *Die Eiche, Die Hochkirche,* and *Religiöse Besinnung, q.v.*)

Eirene (Official organ of the Anglican and Eastern Churches Union. In English and Greek). Annual. London, 1908–13.

Ekklesia (modern Greek, published in Athens).

Evangelical Alliance Quarterly, The. London, Nos. 1–22, July 1899–Oct. 1904. New Series: Jan.–Oct. 1905.

Evangelical Christendom (Official organ of the Evangelical Alliance). Issued monthly, bi-monthly, or quarterly since 1847. Quarterly since 1941. London, 1847–.

Evangelischer Wochenbrief (Ed. A. Deissmann). Berlin, 1914–21.

Friends of Reunion Bulletin. Occasional. London, 1933–63.

(Continued by *Reunion Record*, which later (Winter 1964) joined with *Frontier*.)

Goodwill. A Review of International Christian Friendship (Publ. by the British Council of the World Alliance for International Friendship through the Churches). Quarterly. London, 1915–38.

Herder Korrespondenz, Orbis catholicus. Monthly. Vol. 1. 1946/47. Freiburg i. Br. English ed., *Herder Correspondence*. Monthly. Vol. 1, London, 1964–.

Hochkirche, Die. Monthly. Munich, 1919–33.

(Continued by *Eine Heilige Kirche, q.v.*)

International Christendom (Orgaan van de Nederlandsche Afdeeling van de Wereldbond voor Internationaale Vriendschap door de Kerken). Utrecht, 1915–39/40.

International Christian Press and Information Service, Geneva, 1933–48.

(Continued by *Ecumenical Press Service, q.v.*)

International Review of Missions (The official organ of the International Missionary Council, later (1962), of the Division on World Mission and Evangelism of the World Council of Churches. Invaluable bibliographies, and annual survey of missionary developments). Quarterly. London, 1912–.

Internationale Kirchliche Zeitschrift (As *Die Internationale Theologische Zeitschrift*, 1893–94; then as *La Revue internationale de Théologie*, 1895–1909; published by the Old Catholic Churches; specially valuable material on the Orthodox Churches). Quarterly. Berne, 1910–.

Irénikon (Roman Catholic; published by the Benedictines of Chevetogne). Bi-monthly. Chevetogne, 1926–.

Kristen Gemenskap (The common ecumenical journal of the Scandinavian countries). Quarterly. Uppsala, 1928–.

Kyrios. Vierteljahrschrift für Kirchen- und Geistes-geschichte Osteuropas. Königsberg, 1936–43, 1960/61–.

Life and Work. Bulletin of the International Social Institute. Occasional. Geneva, 1927–30.

One in Christ. Quarterly. London, 1965–.
(Continuation of *Eastern Churches Quarterly, q.v.*)

Orientalia Christiana Periodica. Quarterly. Rome, 1935–.

Put ("The Way", Russian, published in Paris).

Religiöse Besinnung. Quarterly. Stuttgart, 1928–33.
(Continuation of *Una Sancta: Ein Ruf an die Christenheit* and continued by *EineHeilige Kirche, q.v.*)

Reunion. Quarterly. Banstead, 1934, etc.

Review of the Churches, The. A Constructive Quarterly. Ed. Sir Henry Lunn. Monthly. London, 1891–95; Quarterly. London, 1895–96, 1924–30.

Revue anglo-romaine. Weekly. Paris, 1895–96.

Roma e l'Oriente: Rivista criptoferratense per l'Unione delle Chiese. Monthly. Badia di Grottaferrata, 1910–28.

Sobornost: The Journal of the Fellowship of S. Alban and S. Sergius (mimeographed under title *The Journal*, etc., 1928–33; printed under title *The Journal*, etc., 1934). Quarterly. London, 1935–.

Stockholm. International Review for the Social Action Activities of the Churches. (Trilingual) Quarterly. Göttingen, 1928–31.

Student World, The (Published by the World's Student Christian Federation). Quarterly. Geneva, 1895–.

Una Sancta: Ein Ruf an die Christenheit. Quarterly. Stuttgart, 1925–27.
(Continued by *Religiöse Besinnung, q.v.*)

Union chrétienne, L' (Orthodox; published by Wladimir Guetteé). Weekly, later monthly. Paris, 1859–92.

Union of the Churches, The (Greek and English). Fortnightly, London, Nos. 1–61, 1903–5.

Union Review, The. A magazine of Catholic literature and art (Organ of the Association for the Promotion of the Unity of Christendom), London, 1863–74.

Unitas (Published by the Association *Unitas*; English, French, Italian, and Spanish editions). Bi-monthly. Rome, 1946–.

Vers l'Unité chrétienne. Bulletin catholique d'Information (mimeographed; later printed; issued by the Dominicans of the Institute Istina, Boulogne-sur-Seine, France). Bi-monthly. Paris, 1948–.

VII. Ecumenical Memoirs

In this section are included biographies and memoirs only of leaders part at least of whose activity extended into the 20th century and covered several fields of ecumenical interest. Biographies of earlier leaders, and those with a more limited range, will be found in the special bibliographies to the various chapters.

Ainslie: Idleman, Finis S.: *Peter Ainslie, Ambassador of Goodwill*, Chicago, 1941.

Azariah: Graham, Carol: *Azariah of Dornakal*, London, 1946.

Brent: Zabriskie, Alexander C.: *Bishop Brent, Crusader for Christian Unity*, Philadelphia, 1948.

Brown: Brown, William Adams: *A Teacher and his Times: a Story of two Worlds*, New York, 1940.

Davidson: Bell, G. K. A.: *Randall Davidson, Archbishop of Canterbury*; 3rd ed., 2 vols., London, 1952.

Garvie: Garvie, Alfred E.: *Memories and Meanings of my Life*, London, 1938.

Keller: Keller, Adolf: *Von Geist und Liebe: ein Bilderbuch aus dem Leben*, Gotha, 1933.

Lang: Lockhart, J. G.: *Cosmo Gordon Lang*, London, 1949.

Lunn: Lunn, Henry S.: *Chapters from my Life, with special Reference to Reunion*, London, 1918.

Macfarland: Macfarland, Charles S.: *Across the Years*, New York, 1936.

Monod: Monod, Wilfred: *Après la journée, 1867–1937: souvenirs et visions*, Paris, 1938.

Mott: Fisher, Galen M.: *John R. Mott, Architect of Co-operation and Unity*, New York, 1952.

Mathews, Basil: *John R. Mott, World Citizen*, New York and London, 1934.

Rouse, Ruth: *John R. Mott: an Appreciation*, Geneva, 1930.

Paton: Sinclair, Margaret: *William Paton*, London, 1945.

Söderblom: Andrae, Tor: *Nathan Söderblom*; 2nd ed., Berlin, 1957.

Hoffmann, Jean G. H.: *Nathan Soederblom, prophète de l'oecuménisme*, Geneva, 1948.

N. Karlström (ed.): *Nathan Söderblom: in Memoriam*, Stockholm, 1931.

Temple: Iremonger, F. A.: *William Temple, Archbishop of Canterbury: his Life and Letters*, Oxford, 1948.

CHAPTER 1

In addition to the collected works of the Reformers and others, and to special studies on particular points, for which indications are given in the footnotes, the following works are valuable for closer study of the period:

Cardauns, L.: *Zur Geschichte der kirchlichen Unions- und Reformbestrebungen von 1538–1542*, Rome, 1910.

Delius, Walter: *Antonio Possevino, und Ivan Groznyj: ein Beitrag zur Geschichte der kirchlichen Union und der Gegenreformation des 16. Jahrhunderts*. Beiheft zum Jahrbuch "Kirche im Osten", Vol. III. Stuttgart, 1962.

Denis, Ernest: *Les Origines de l'Unité des Frères bohèmes*, Angers, 1885.

Félice, F. de: *Histoire des synodes nationaux des Églises réformées de France*, Paris, 1864.

Gindely, Anton: *Geschichte der böhmischen Brüder*. 2 vols. Prague, 1856; 2nd ed., Prague, 1861–68.

Goll, Jaroslav: *Quellen und Untersuchungen zur Geschichte der böhmischen Brüder*, 2 vols., Prague, 1878, 1882.

Herminjard, A. L.: *Correspondance des réformateurs dans les pays de langue française*, 9 vols., Geneva, 1866–97.

Jörgensen, K. E. J.: *Ökumenische Bestrebungen unter den polnischen Protestanten bis zum Jahre 1645*, Copenhagen, 1942.

Kantzenbach, Friedrich W.: *Das Ringen um die Einheit der Kirche im Jahrhundert der Reformation: Vertreter, Quellen, und Motive des "ökumenischen" Gedankens von Erasmus von Rotterdam bis Georg Calixt*, Stuttgart, 1957.

Kattenbusch, Ferd.: *Lehrbuch der vergleichenden Confessionskunde*, 3 vols., Freiburg i. Br., 1890–92.

Koehler, Walther: *Zwingli und Luther: Ihr Streit über das Abendmahl nach seinen politischen und religiösen Beziehungen*, Vols. 1, 2, Gütersloh, 1924, 1953.

McNeill, John Thomas: *Unitive Protestantism: a Study in our religious Resources*, New York, 1930; rev. ed., *Unitive Protestantism: the ecumenical Spirit and its persistent Expression*, Richmond, Va., 1964.

Martin, Alfred von (ed.): *Luther in oekumenischer Sicht: von evangelischen und katholischen Mitarbeitern*, Stuttgart, 1929.

Niemeyer, H. A.: *Collectio confessionum in ecclesiis reformatis publicatarum*, Leipzig, 1840.

Pastor, L.: *Die kirchlichen Reunionsbestrebungen während der Regierung Karls V.*, 1879.

Schaff, P.: *The Creeds of Christendom*, 3 vols., New York, 1919.

Schweinitz, Edmund: *The History of the Church known as the Unitas Fratrum or the Unity of Brethren*, Bethlehem, 1885, 1901.

Stupperich, R.: *Der Humanismus und die Wiedervereinigung der Konfessionen*, Leipzig, 1936.

The contributions made by individuals can well be studied in their biographies, of which the following is a short selection:

Beza

Baum, Joh. Wilh.: *Theodor Beza*, 2 vols., Leipzig, 1843–52.

Geisendorf, P. F.: *Théodore de Bèze*, Geneva, 1949.

Bucer

Anrich, Gustave: *Martin Bucer*, Strasbourg, 1914.

Courvoisier, Jacques: *La notion de l'Église chez Bucer dans son développement historique*, Paris, 1933.

Eells, Hastings: *Martin Bucer*, New Haven, 1931.

Hopf, Constantin: *Martin Bucer and the English Reformation*, Oxford, 1946.

Bullinger

Bouvier, A.: *Henri Bullinger, réformateur et conseiller oecuménique, le successeur de Zwingli*, Neuchâtel and Paris, 1940.

Calvin

Doumergue, E.: *Jean Calvin: les hommes et les choses de son temps*, 7 vols., Lausanne, 1899–1927.

Holl, Karl: *Johannes Calvin*, Tübingen, 1909; also in Gesammelte Aufsätze zur Kirchengeschichte, Vol. 3, Tübingen, 1928.

Reichel, Gerh.: *Calvin als Unionsmann*, Tübingen, 1909.

Cranmer

Pollard, A. F.: *Thomas Cranmer and the English Reformation*, 1489–1556, London, 1904; new ed., 1926.

Smyth, Charles: *Cranmer and the Reformation under Edward VI*, Cambridge, 1926.

Erasmus

Allen, Percy Stafford: *Erasmus: Lectures and wayfaring Sketches* (Esp. ch. IV), Oxford, 1934.

à Lasco

Dalton, Hermann: *Johannes à Lasco: Beitrag zur Reformationsgeschichte Polens, Deutschlands, und Englands*, Gotha, 1881.

Luther

Bainton, Roland H.: *Here I Stand: a Life of Martin Luther*, New York, 1950.
Holl, Karl, *Luther*. Gesammelte Aufsätze zur Kirchengeschichte, Vol. 1. 6th ed., Tübingen, 1932.
MacKinnon, James: *Luther and the Reformation*, 4 vols., London, 1925–30.

Melanchthon

Engelland, Hans: *Melanchthon: Glauben und Handeln*, Munich, 1931.
Richard, J. W.: *Philip Melanchthon, the Protestant Preceptor of Germany, 1497–1560*, New York, 1898.
Hildebrandt, F.: *Melanchthon, Alien or Ally?*, Cambridge, 1946.

Parker

Strype, John: *The Life and Acts of Matthew Parker, Archbishop of Canterbury*, 3 vols., Oxford, 1821.

Witzel

Schmidt, G. L.: *Georg Witzel, ein Altkatholik des XVI Jahrhunderts*, Vienna, 1876.
Trusen, Winfred: *Um die Reform und Einheit der Kirche: zum Leben und Werk Georg Witzels*, Münster, 1957.

Zwingli

Koehler, Walther: *Huldrych Zwingli*, Leipzig, 1943.

CHAPTER 2

Good articles on many of the persons named in this chapter, with further bibliographical indications, are to be found in:

Hauck-Herzog: *Realenzyklopädie für protestantische Theologie und Kirche*, 3rd ed., 24 vols., Leipzig, 1896–1913.
The New Schaff-Herzog Encyclopedia of Religious Knowledge, 13 vols., Grand Rapids, 1950–51.
Die Religion in Geschichte und Gegenwart, 3rd ed., Tübingen, Mohr, 6 vols., 1957–62.
Dictionnaire de théologie catholique, 15 vols., Paris, 1935–.

I. ECUMENICAL WRITINGS OF THE 17TH AND 18TH CENTURIES

Acontius, Jakob: *Stratagemata Satanae* (1564). Ed. Gualtherus Koehler, The Hague, 1927.
Amyraut, Moïse (Amyraldus): *De secessione ab ecclesia romana et de ratione pacis inter evangelicos constituendae disputatio*, Saumur, 1647.
Arnd, Johann: *Wahres Christentum*, 4 vols., 1609–10.
Betke, Joachim: *Sacerdotium, hoc est Neu-Testamentliches Königliches Proester-thumb*, Amsterdam, 1640.

Blondel, David: *Actes authentiques des Églises réformées de France, Germanie, Grande Bretaigne, Pologne, Hongrie, Pays Bas . . . touchant la paix et charité fraternelle, que tous les serviteurs de Dieu doivent sainctement entretenir avec les Protestants . . .*, Amsterdam, 1655.

Boehme, Jakob: *Aurora, oder die Morgenröte im Aufgang*, 1613; new ed., Berlin, 1780.

　Der Weg zu Christo, 1624. Eng. tr., *The Way to Christ*, by John Joseph Stoudt. Foreword by Rufus M. Jones, New York and London, 1947.

Bourignon, Antoinette: *La lumière née en ténèbres*, Antwerp, 1669; 2nd ed., Amsterdam, 1684.

　L'Antéchrist découvert, Amsterdam, 1681.

Bythner, Bartholomäus: *Fraterna exhortatio*, 1607/1618: *eine Denkschrift der reformierten Kirche in Polen zur Einigung der evangelischen Kirchen Europas*. Ed. Arnold Starke, Poznan, 1935.

Calixtus, George: *Disputationes de praecipuis religionis christianae capitibus*, 1613. [s.l.]

Casaubon, Isaac: *De rebus sacris et ecclesiasticis exercitationes XVI ad Cardinalis Baronii . . . annales*, London, 1614.

Comenius, John Amos: *Haggaeus Redivivus* (1632) in *Veškeré Spisy*, 17, pp. 157–260, Brno, 1912.

　De rerum humanarum emendatione consultatio Catholica (1656), Halle, 1702.

　De bono unitatis, 1660. Eng. tr., *An Exhortation of the Churches of Bohemia to the Church of England wherein is set forth the good of unity . . . and obedience*, London, 1661.

　The Labyrinth of the World and the Paradise of the Heart. Eng. tr. by Matthew Spinka, Chicago, 1942.

Daillé, Jean: *Traité de l'employ des Saints Pères pour le jugement des différences qui sont aujourd'huy en la religion*, Geneva, 1632.

Dippel, Johann Konrad: *Ein Hirt und eine Heerde oder ohnfehlbare Methode alle Secten und Religionen zu einer wahren Kirche und Religion zu vereinigen* (1705) in Bauer, Edgar, ed.: *Bibl. der dt. Aufklärer des 18. Jahrhunderts*, Vol. 5, 1846–47, pp. 175–251.

Francke, August Hermann: *Nicodemus, oder Tractätlein von der Menschen-Furcht*, Halle, 1701. Eng. tr., *Nicodemus, or a Treatise against the Fear of Man*, London, 1706.

　Segensvolle Fusstapfen des noch lebenden und waltenden, liebreichen, und getreuen Gottes, Halle, 1701. Eng. tr., *Pietas Hallensis*, 1709.

Gichtel, Johann Georg: *Theosophia Practica*, Leiden, 1722.

Grotius, Hugo: *Via ad pacem ecclesiasticam*, Amsterdam, 1642.

Guyon, Mme de la Mothe: *Moyen court et facile pour l'oraison, que tous peuvent pratiquer très aisément, et arriver par là en peu à une haute perfection*, 1688; 2nd ed., 1690.

Hoburg, Christian: *Unbekannter Christus*, Hamburg [?], 1727.

Hoornbeck, Johann: *Dissertatio de consociatione evangelica Reformatorum et Augustanae confessionis, sive de colloquio Casselano*, Amsterdam, 1663.

Junius, Franciscus: *Eirenicum in Opera Theologica*, cols. 677–762, Geneva, 1608.

Jurieu, Pierre: *De pace inter Protestantes ineunda consultatio*, Utrecht, 1688.

　Traité de l'unité de l'Église et des points fondamentaux contre Monsieur Nicole, Rotterdam, 1688.

Köpke, Balthasar: *Dialogus de templo Salomonis sive de tribus sanctorum gradibus*, Amsterdam, 1698.

Leade (or Lead), Jane: *The Heavenly Cloud now Breaking—The Lord Christ's Ascension-Ladder sent down*, 1681.

A Fountain of Gardens watered by the Rivers of Divine Pleasure, and springing up into all the Variety of Spiritual Plants . . . 3 vols., 1696–1701.

Leibniz, Gottfried Wilhelm von: *Sämtliche Schriften und Briefe*: IV Reihe, *Politische Schriften*, 1931; VI Reihe, *Philosophische Schriften*, 1930. (Ausgabe der Preussischen Akademie der Wissenschaften.)

Meiderlin, Peter, *Paraenesis votiva pro pace ecclesiastica*, 1626.

"Menander": *Neues und sonderbares Friedens-Project auff was Art zwischen allen drey Hauptreligionen* . . . *das heilsame Band des Friedens glücklich ersetzet werden könne*, Friedens-Burg, 1704. (This date, given on the title-page, appears to be an error, since this is certainly the earlier of the two tracts. Cf. Chap. ii, pp. 104 f.)

Neues unvorgreifliches Friedens-Project auf was Art zwischen beyden Protestirenden Religionen das heilsame Band des Friedens glücklich ersetzet werden könne, Friedensburg, 1703.

Mentzer, Balthasar: *Collatio Augustanae Confessionis cum doctrina Zwinglii, Calvini, Bezae, et sociorum*, Giessen, 1606.

Molanus, Gerhard Walther: *Correspondence with Bossuet* in Migne's ed. of Bossuet, Vol. IX, cols. 809–1070, Paris, 1856.

La nécessité d'une ligue protestante et catholique pour le maintien de la liberté commune, Cologne, 1702.

Pareus, David: *Irenicum, sive de unione et synodo evangelicorum concilianda liber votivus Pace Ecclesiae, et desideriis pacificorum dicatus*, Heidelberg, 1615.

Spener, Philipp Jakob: *Pia Desideria, oder herzliches Verlangen nach gottgefälliger Besserung der wahren evang. Kirchen samt einigen dahin abzweckenden Christl. Vorschlagen*, 1675; ed. K. Aland; 2nd ed., Berlin, 1955.

Consilia et judicia theologica latina, Frankfurt a.M., 1709.

Theologische Bedenken, 4 vols., Halle, 1712–15.

Turrettini, Jean Alphonse: *Nubes testium pro moderato et pacifico de rebus theologicis judicio et instituenda inter Protestantes concordia*, Geneva, 1719.

Oratio octava de componendis Protestantium dissidiis in *Orationes academicae*, Geneva, 1737, pp. 213–40.

Weltz, Justinian, Freiherr von: *Kurzer Bericht, wie eine neue Gesellschaft unter den rechtgläubigen Christen Augsburgischer Konfession aufgerichtet werden könne*, 1633.

Wiederholte treuherzige und ernsthafte Vermahnung die Bekehrung ungläubiger Völker vorzunehmen, 1664.

Werenfels, Samuel: *Cogitationes generales de ratione uniendi Ecclesias Protestantes, quae vulgo Lutheranarum et Reformatarum nominibus distingui solent* in *Opuscula theologica, philosophica et philologica*, Vol. II, Basle, 1782, pp. 61–80.

Dissertatio de Ratione Uniendi Ecclesias Protestantes in *Opuscula theologica, philosophica, et philologica*, Vol. II, Basle, 1782, pp. 83–120.

Zinzendorf, Nicolaus Ludwig von: περὶ ἑαυτοῦ *Naturelle Reflexionen*, Ebersdorf, 1746.

Zwicker, Daniel: *Irenicum Irenicorum, seu reconciliatoris christianorum norma triplex*, Amsterdam, 1658.

II. General Works, covering the Whole Period, or several Parts of the Subject

Benz, Ernst: *Ecclesia Spiritualis: Kirchenidee und Geschichts-theologie der franziskanischen Reformation*, Stuttgart, 1934.

Drummond, Andrew Landale: *German Protestantism since Luther*, London, 1951.

Geiger, Max: *Die Basler Kirche und Theologie im Zeitalter der Hochorthodoxie*, Zürich, 1952.

Hazard, Paul: *La crise de la conscience européenne, 1680–1715*, 2 vols. and 1 vol., notes and references, Paris, 1935.

Hutton, J. E.: *A History of the Moravian Church*, London, 1909.

Kvačala, Jan: *Irenische Bestrebungen zur Zeit des dreissigjährigen Krieges*, 1894 (Universitas Jurievensis).

Leube, Hans: *Die Reformideen in der deutschen lutherischen Kirche zur Zeit der Orthodoxie*, Leipzig, 1924.

Kalvinismus und Luthertum, Vol. I, *Der Kampf um die Herrschaft im protestantischen Deutschland*, Leipzig, 1928.

Nuttall, Geoffrey F., and Chadwick, Owen (eds.): *From Uniformity to Unity, 1662–1962*, London, 1962.

Ritschl, Albrecht: *Geschichte des Pietismus*, 3 vols., Bonn, 1880–86.

Ritschl, Otto: *Dogmengeschichte des Protestantismus*, Vol. IV, *Orthodoxie und Synkretismus in der altprotestantischen Theologie*, Göttingen, 1927.

Schreyer, P.: *Valentin Ernst Löscher und die Unionsversuche seiner Zeit*, Schwabach, 1938.

Seeberg, Erich: *Gottfried Arnold, die Wissenschaft und die Mystik seiner Zeit*, Meerane, 1923.

Stephan, Horst, and Leube Hans: *Handbuch der Kirchengeschichte*, Vol. IV, *Die Neuzeit*; 2nd ed., Tübingen, 1931.

Weber, Hans Emil: *Reformation, Orthodoxie, und Rationalismus*, 2 vols., Gütersloh, 1951.

Wernle, Paul: *Der schweizerische Protestantismus im 18. Jahrhundert*, 3 vols., 1923–25.

III. Special Studies, Mainly Biographical

Acontius

Cantimori, Delio: *Italienische Häretiker der Spätrenaissance*. German tr. (from the Italian), by Werner Kaegi, Basle, 1949.

Hassinger, Erich: *Studien zu Jacobus Acontius*, Berlin, 1934.

Annoni

Riggenbach, Christoph Johannes: *Hieronymus Annoni: ein Abriss seines Lebens . . .* , Basle, 1870.

Boehme

Benz, Ernst: *Der vollkommene Mensch nach Jakob Böhme*, Stuttgart, 1937.

Bornkamm, Heinrich: *Luther und Böhme*, Bonn, 1925.

Bossuet

Crousle, L.: *Bossuet et le protestantisme: étude historique*, Paris, 1901.

Julien, E.: *Bossuet et les protestants*, Paris, 1910.

Casaubon

Nazelle, L. J.: *Isaac Casaubon, sa vie et son temps, 1559–1614*, Paris, 1897.
Pattison, Mark: *Isaac Casaubon, 1559–1614*, London, 1875.

Calixtus

Dowding, W. C.: *The Life and Correspondence of George Calixtus*, Oxford and London, 1863.
Friedrich, Hans: *Georg Calixtus, der Unionsmann des 17. Jahrhunderts*, Anklam, 1891.
Henke, Ernst Ludwig Theodor: *Georg Calixtus und seine Zeit*, 2 vols., Halle, 1853–60.
Schussler, Hermann: *Georg Calixt: Theologie und Kirchenpolitik*, Wiesbaden, 1961.

Comenius

Criegern, Hermann Ferdinand von: *Johann Amos Comenius als Theolog*, Leipzig and Heidelberg, 1881.
Heyberger, Anna: *Jean Amos Comenius (Komenský), sa vie et son oeuvre d'éducateur*, Paris, 1928.
Laurie, S. S.: *John Amos Comenius, Bishop of the Moravians: his Life and educational Work*, Boston, 1885.
Odložilik, O.: "Comenius and Christian Unity", *Slavonic Review*, Vol. 9, 1930.
Pusch, C.: *Comenius und seine Beziehungen zum Neuhumanismus*, Dresden, 1911.
Spinka, Matthew: *John Amos Comenius, that incomparable Moravian*, Chicago, 1943.

Dury

Batten, J. Minton: *John Dury, Advocate of Christian Reunion*, Chicago, 1944.
Brauer, Karl: *Die Unionstätigkeit John Duries unter dem Protektorat Cromwells*, Marburg, 1907.
Turnbull, G. H.: *Hartlib, Dury, and Comenius: Gleanings from Hartlib's Papers*, London, 1947.
Westin, Gunnar: *John Durie in Sweden, 1636–1638: Documents and Letters*, Uppsala, 1934–36.
Negotiations about Church Unity, 1628–1634: John Durie, Gustavus Adolphus, Axel Oxenstierna. Uppsala Universitets Årsskrift 1932, Teologi 3, Uppsala, 1932.

Francke and the Pietism of Halle

Benz, Ernst: "August Hermann Francke und die deutschen evangelischen Gemeinden in Russland", *Jahrbuch Auslanddeutschtum und evangelische Kirche*, pp. 143–191, 1936.
Beyreuther, E.: *August Hermann Francke*, Marburg, 1957.
A. H. Francke und die Anfänge der oekumenischen Bewegung, 1958.
Kammel, Richard: *August Hermann Franckes Tätigkeit für die Diaspora des Ostens*, 1939; also in *Die evangelische Diaspora*, 20, 1938, pp. 312–51.
Kramer, Gust.: *August Hermann Francke*, 2 vols., 1880–82.
Salomies, Ilmari: *Der Hallesche Pietismus in Russland zur Zeit Peters des Grossen.* Annales Academiae scientiarum Fennicae, Ser. B. 31, 2, Helsingfors, 1936.

Schmidt, Martin: "Das Hallesche Waisenhaus und England im 18. Jahrhundert", *Theologische Zeitschrift*, Jg. 7, 1951, pp. 38–55.

Grotius

Blanke, Fritz: "Pax Ecclesiae: Hugo Grotius und die Einigung der christlichen Kirchen", *Reformatio*, 1963, pp. 595–609.
Haentjens, A. H.: *Hugo de Groot als godsdienstig denker*, Amsterdam, 1946.
Schlüter, Joachim: *Die Theologie des Hugo Grotius*, Göttingen, 1919.

Hochmann von Hochenau

Renkewitz, Heinz: *Hochmann von Hochenau*, Breslau, 1935.

Jablonski

Dalton, Hermann: *Daniel Ernst Jablonski*, Berlin, 1903.
Sykes, Norman: *Daniel Ernst Jablonski and the Church of England: a Study of an Essay towards Protestant Union*, London, 1950.

Labadie

Goeters, Wilhelm: *Die Vorbereitung des Pietismus in der reformierten Kirche der Niederlande bis zur labadistischen Krisis 1670*, Leipzig, 1911.
Queckbörner, M.: *Ph. J. Speners Reformtätigkeit in Frankfurt/M. unter besonderer Berücksichtigung seines Verhältnisses zu Jean de Labadie*, Mainz, 1960.

Jane Leade

Thune, Nils: *The Behmenists and the Philadelphians: a Contribution to the Study of English Mysticism in the 17th and 18th Centuries*, Uppsala, 1948.

Leibniz

Baruzi, Jean: *Leibniz et l'organisation religieuse de la terre*, Paris, 1907.
Benz, Ernst: *Leibniz und Peter der Grosse*, Berlin, 1947.
Hefele, C. J.: *Die Unionsverhandlungen am Ende des 17. Jahrhunderts und Leibnitzens Teilnahme an Denselben*, Tübingen, 1864.
Hildebrandt, Philipp: *Die kirchlichen Religionsverhandlungen in der zweiten Hälfte des 17. Jahrhunderts*, 1922.
Jordan, George J.: *The Reunion of the Churches: a Study of G. W. Leibnitz and his great Attempt*, London, 1927.
Kiefl, Franz Xavier: *Der Friedensplan des Leibniz z. Wiedervereinigung d. getrennten christl. Kirche . . .* , Paderborn, 1908; 2nd ed., *Leibniz und die religiöse Wiedervereinigung Deutschlands. Seine Verhandlungen mit Bossuet und europ. Fürstenhöfen über d. Versöhnung d. christl. Konfessionen*, Regensburg, 1925.

Meiderlin

Bauer, Ludwig: *M. Peter Meiderlin, Ephorus des Kollegiums bei St Anna*, Augsburg, 1906.

Molanus

Weidemann, Heinz: *Gerard Wolter Molanus*, 2 vols., Göttingen, 1925–29.

Spener

Aland, K.: *Spener Studien*. Arbeiten zur Kirchengeschichte, 28.
Grünberg, Paul: *Philip Jakob Spener*, 3 vols., 1893–1906.

Weltz

Grössel, Paul: *Der Missionsweckruf des Barons Justinian von Weltz* (1664, *facs.*), Leipzig, 1890.

Laubach, F.: *Justinian Freiherr von Weltz und sein Plan einer Missionsgesellschaft*, Tübingen, 1955. (Cf. *Theologische Literaturzeitung*, 81, 1956, 567 f.)

Zinzendorf

Becker, Bernard: *Zinzendorf und sein Christentum im Verhältnis zum kirchlichen und religiösen Leben seiner Zeit*; 2nd ed., Leipzig, 1900.

Blanke, Fritz: *Zinzendorf und die Einheit der Kinder Gottes*, Basle, 1950.

Motel, Heinz: *Zinzendorf als ökumenischer Theologe*, Basle, 1941.

Reichel, Gerhard: *Der "Senfkornorden" Zinzendorfs*, 2 vols., Herrnhut, 1914.

CHAPTER 3

The starting-point of study must be:

Sykes, Norman: *The Church of England and Non-episcopal Churches in the Sixteenth and Seventeenth Centuries: an Essay towards an Historical Interpretation of the Anglican Tradition from Whitgift to Wake*. "Theology" Occasional Papers, No. 11, London, 1948.

and the numerous footnote references there given.

I. COLLECTED WORKS OF CONTEMPORARY DIVINES

(Almost all these collections include a Life of the Author)

Andrewes, Lancelot (Bishop of Winchester): *Works*, 11 vols., Oxford, 1841–54.

Baxter, Richard: *The Practical Works of the late Reverend and Pious Mr Richard Baxter*, 23 vols., London, 1830.

Bingham, Joseph: *Works*, 10 vols. Ed. R. Bingham, Oxford, 1821–29.

Bramhall, John (Archbishop of Armagh): *Works*, 5 vols., Oxford, 1842–45.

Cosin, John (Bishop of Durham): *Works*, 5 vols., Oxford, 1843–55.

Hall, Joseph (Bishop of Norwich): *Works*, 12 vols., Oxford, 1837–39.

Hooker, Richard: *Works*, arranged by John Keble (1874); 3rd ed., 3 vols., Oxford, 1955.

Laud, William (Archbishop of Canterbury): *Works*, 7 vols., Oxford, 1847–60.

Patrick, Simon (Bishop of Chichester, and later of Ely): *Works*, 9 vols., Oxford, 1838.

Secker, Thomas (Archbishop of Canterbury): *Works* (1811); new ed., 6 vols., London, 1825.

Taylor, Jeremy (Bishop of Down): *Whole Works*, 10 vols., London, 1847–54.

Thorndike, Herbert: *Theological Works*, 6 vols., Oxford, 1844–56.

Ussher, James (Archbishop of Armagh): *Works*. Ed. C. R. Elrington and J. H. Todd, 17 vols., Dublin and London, 1847–64.

Whitgift, John (Archbishop of Canterbury): *Works*, 3 vols., Cambridge, 1851–53.

II. CONTEMPORARY IRENICAL WORKS

Davenant, John (Bishop of Salisbury): *Exhortation to Brotherly Communion betwixt the Protestant Churches* (1640); new ed., London, 1841.

Dury, John: *De Pacis Ecclesiasticae Rationibus inter Evangelicos usurpandis* . . . , 1634.

A *Briefe relation of that which hath been lately attempted to procure Ecclesiastical Peace amongst Protestants*, London, 1641.

A *Summary Discourse concerning the work of Peace Ecclesiasticall* . . . , Cambridge, 1641.

A *Peacemaker without Partiality and Hypocrisy* . . . , London, 1648.

An Earnest Plea for Gospel Communion in the Way of Godliness. London, 1654.

Johannis Duraei Irenicorum Tractatuum Prodromus . . . , Amsterdam, 1662.

Hartlib, Samuel: *The Necessity of some nearer Conjunction and Correspondency amongst Evangelicall Protestants* . . . , London, 1644.

Oxenham, H. N. (ed.): *An Eirenicon of the eighteenth century*, London, 1879.

Saywell, William: *Evangelical and Catholic Unity maintained in the Church of England . . . Also the . . . Bishop of Ely's vindication*, London, 1682.

III. General Works

Abbey, C. J., and Overton, J. H.: *The English Church in the eighteenth century*, 2 vols., London, 1878.

Burnet, Gilbert: *History of my own Time*. Ed. O. Airy, 2 vols., Oxford, 1897–1900.

Cardwell, E.: *Documentary Annals of the Reformed Church of England*, 2 vols., Oxford, 1844.

Collier, Jeremy: *An Ecclesiastical History of Great Britain* . . . , 2 vols., London, 1708.

Frere, W. H.: *The English Church in the reigns of Elizabeth and James I, 1558–1625*, London, 1904.

Fuller, Thomas: *The Church History of Britain* (1655); new ed. by J. S. Brewer, 6 vols., London, 1845.

Gee, Henry, and Hardy, W. J. (eds.): *Documents Illustrative of English Church History*, London, 1896.

Hunt, J.: *Religious Thought in England from the Reformation to the End of the last century*, 3 vols., London, 1870–73.

Hutton, W. H.: *The English Church from the Accession of Charles I to the Death of Anne, 1625–1714*, London, 1903.

Jordan, W. K.: *The Development of Religious Toleration in England*, 4 vols., London, 1930–40.

Montague, Richard: *De Originibus Ecclesiasticis Commentationum*, Vol. I (two parts in one), London, 1636–40.

Neal, Daniel: *History of the Puritans or Protestant Non-conformists from* . . . *1517 to* . . . *1688*. Ed. J. Toulmin, 5 vols., London, 1822.

Overton, J. H., and Relton, F.: *The English Church from the Accession of George I to the End of the eighteenth century, 1714–1800*, London, 1906.

Shaw, W. A.: *A History of the English Church, 1640–1660*, 2 vols., London, 1900.

Stoughton, John: *A History of Religion in England from the Opening of the Long Parliament to 1850*; 4th ed., 8 vols., London, 1901. (Esp. Vols. III and IV.)

Symonds, H. E.: *The Council of Trent and the Anglican Formularies*, Oxford, 1933.

Wood, A. Harold: *Church Unity without Uniformity; a Study of seventeenth-century English Church Movements and Richard Baxter's Proposals for a Comprehensive Church*, London, 1963.

IV. BIOGRAPHIES

Basire: Darnell, W. N.: *The Correspondence of Isaac Basire . . . with a memoir of his life*, London, 1830.

Baxter: Baxter, Richard: *Reliquiae Baxterianae, or Mr Richard Baxter's Narrative of the most memorable Passages of his Life and Times*. Ed. M. Sylvester, London, 1696.

　Brown, Earl Kent: *Richard Baxter's Contribution to the Comprehension Controversy: a Study in projected Church Union*, Boston, 1956.

Calamy: Calamy, Edmund: *A Historical Account of my own Life with some Reflections on the Times I have lived in, 1671–1731*, 2 vols., London, 1829.

Doddridge: The Correspondence and Diary of Philip Doddridge. Ed. J. D. Humphreys, 4 vols., London, 1829.

　Stanford, C.: *Philip Doddridge*, London, 1880.

Dury: Batten, J. Minton: *John Dury, Advocate of Christian Reunion*, Chicago, 1944.

Hartlib: Dircks, H.: *A biographical Memoir of Samuel Hartlib*, London, 1865.

　Turnbull, G. H.: *Samuel Hartlib; a Sketch of his Life and his Relation to J. A. Comenius*, Oxford, 1920.

Howe: Calamy, Edmund: *Memoirs of the Life of the late Revd John Howe*, 1724; Library of Christian Biography, Vol. 11, London, 1839.

　Horton, Robert Forman: *John Howe*, London, 1895.

Laud: Heylyn, Peter: *Cyprianus Anglicus*, London, 1668.

Patrick: Patrick, Simon: *Autobiography*, London, 1839.

Sancroft: D'Oyly, George: *Life of William Sancroft*, 2 vols., London, 1821.

Secker: Porteus, Beilby: *A Review of the Life and Character of Archbishop Secker*, in Secker, *Works*, London, 1775.

Sharp: Sharp, Thomas: *Life of John Sharp*, 2 vols., London, 1825.

　Hart, A. Tindale: *The Life and Times of John Sharp, Archbishop of York*, London, 1949.

Tenison: Carpenter, Edward: *Thomas Tenison, Archbishop of Canterbury: his Life and Times*, London, 1948.

Thorndike: Lacey T. A.: *Herbert Thorndike, 1598–1672*, London, 1929.

Tillotson: Birch, Thomas: *Life of the Most Reverend Dr John Tillotson*, London, 1753.

Ussher: Carr, J. A.: *The Life and Times of James Ussher, Archbishop of Armagh*, London, 1895.

　Parr, R.: *The Life of . . . James Usher*, 1686.

Wesley: Tyerman, L.: *Life of John Wesley*, 3 vols., London, 1870–71.

Whitgift: Strype, J.: *Life and Acts of John Whitgift*, 3 vols., Oxford, 1822.

V. SOME SPECIAL STUDIES

Bosher, Robert S.: *The Making of the Restoration Settlement: the Influence of the Laudians 1649–1662*, London, 1951.

Calamy, Edmund (1671–1732), *An abridgement of Mr Baxter's History of his life and times: with an account of the Ministers, etc who were ejected after the restauration, of King Charles II . . . and the continuation of their history to the passing of the Bible against occasional conformity, in 1711*; 2nd ed., London, 1713.

A continuation of the Account of the ministers, lecturers, masters and fellows of colleges, and schoolmasters, who were ejected or silenced after the restauration in 1660, by or before the Act of Uniformity. To which is added, *The Church and dissenters compar'd as to persecution, in some remarks on Dr Walker's Attempt to recover the names and sufferings of the clergy that were sequestered, etc., between 1640 and 1660.* And also *Some free remarks on the twenty-eighth chapter of Dr Bennet's Essay on the 39 articles of religion . . .*, London, 1727.

Davies, Horton: *The English Free Churches*, London, 1952.

The Worship of the English Puritans, London, 1948.

Kirk, K. E.: *The Apostolic Ministry: essays on the History and the Doctrine of Episcopacy*, 1946.

Lupton, J. H.: *Archbishop Wake and the Project of Union (1717–20) between the Gallican and Anglican Churches*, London, 1896.

Manning, Bernard: *The Protestant Dissenting Deputies.* Ed. O. Greenwood, Cambridge, 1952.

Mason, A. J.: *The Church of England and Episcopacy*, Cambridge, 1914.

Matthews, A. G.: *Calamy Revised*, Oxford, 1934.

Walker Revised, Oxford, 1948.

Nédoncelle, Maurice: *Trois aspects du problème anglo-catholique* [i.e., Anglican and Roman Catholic] *au XVIIème siècle: avec une analyse des 39 articles d'après Chr. Davenport et J. H. Newman*, Paris, 1951.

Payne, Ernest Alexander: *The Free Church Tradition in the Life of England*; 3rd ed., London, 1951.

Préclin, E.: *L'union des Églises gallicane et anglicane: une tentative au temps de Louis XV: P.-F. le Courayer (de 1681 à 1732) et Guillaume Wake*, Paris, 1928.

Rigg, J. H.: *The Relations of John Wesley and of Wesleyan Methodism to the Church of England investigated and determined*, London, 1868.

Smyth, Charles: *Simeon and Church Order*, Cambridge, 1940.

Sykes, Norman: *Church and State in England in the eighteenth century*, Cambridge, 1934.

Daniel Ernst Jablonski and the Church of England: a Study of an Essay towards Protestant Union, London, 1950.

Turnbull, G. H.: *Hartlib, Dury, and Comenius: Gleanings from Hartlib's Papers*, London, 1947.

Walker, J.: *Sufferings of the Clergy of the Church of England*, London, 1714; abridged ed. by R. Whittaker, London, 1863.

Williams, Colin W.: *Methodism and the Ecumenical Movement*, Drew, 1958.

CHAPTER 4

Most of the authorities are in modern Greek and the Slavonic languages. As far as possible, those books are listed here which are available in languages more widely known in Western Europe and America.

Much information, not otherwise accessible, is to be found in the periodical: *Kyrios: Vierteljahrschrift für Kirchen- und Geistesgeschichte Osteuropas.* Quarterly. Königsberg, 1936–.

Later Orthodox ecumenical discussions can be followed from year to year in the files of:

Internationale Theologische Zeitschrift.
Revue Internationale de Théologie.
Internationale Kirchliche Zeitschrift.

A number of valuable articles, especially on Orthodox leaders, are to be found in *Dictionnaire de théologie catholique.*

I. General Works

No single book covers the whole field. For a general survey of the subject, the following may be recommended:

Benz, Ernst: *Die Ostkirche im Lichte der protestantischen Geschichtsschreibung von der Reformation bis zur Gegenwart*, Freiburg i. Br. and Munich, 1952.

Bischofsamt und apostolische Sukzession im deutschen Protestantismus, Stuttgart, 1953.

Blackmore, R.: *The Doctrine of the Orthodox Church*, Aberdeen, 1844.

Bubnoff, N. von, and Ehrenberg, Hans (eds.): *Östliches Christentum: Dokumente*, 2 vols., Munich, 1923–25.

Jugie, M.: *Theologia dogmatica christianorum orientalium ab ecclesia catholica dissidentium*, 5 vols., Paris, 1926–35.

Karmiris, John: 'Ορθοδοξία καὶ Προτεσταντισμός, Vol. 1, Athens, 1937. (In modern Greek only, with specially valuable bibliographies.)

Τὰ δογματικὰ καὶ συμβολικὰ μνημεῖα τῆς 'Ορθοδόξου Καθολικῆς 'Εκκλησίας, 2 vols., Athens, 1952–53.

Lossky, Vladimir: *Essai sur la théologie mystique de l'Église d'orient*, Paris, 1944.

Müller, Ludolf: *Die Kritik des Protestantismus in der russischen Theologie vom 16. bis zum 18. Jahrhundert*, Mainz, 1951.

Russischer Geist und Evangelisches Christentum, Witten-Ruhr, 1951.

Neale, John Mason: *A History of the Holy Eastern Church*, 4 vols., London, 1847–50 (still valuable for background).

Pierling, P.: *La Russie et le Saint Siège*, 3 vols., Paris, 1896–1901.

Plank, P. Bernhard: *Katholizität und Sobornost: Ein Beitrag zum Verständnis der Katholizität der Kirche bei den russischen Theologen in der zweiten Hälfte des vorigen Jahrhunderts*, Würzburg, 1960.

Romanoff, H. C.: *Rites and Customs of the Greco-Russian Church*, London, 1868.

Schmemann, Alexander: *The Historical Road of Eastern Orthodoxy*, New York, 1963.

Scott, S. H.: *The Eastern Churches and the Papacy*, London, 1928.

Tyciak, Julius: *Wege östlicher Theologie*, Bonn, 1946.

II. Special Studies

16th-Century Lutherans and Constantinople

Benz, Ernst: *Wittenberg und Byzanz: zur Begegnung und Auseinandersetzung der Reformation und der östlich-orthodoxen Kirche*, Marburg, 1949.

Chytraeus, David: *Oratio de statu Ecclesiae hoc tempore in Graecia, Asia, Bohemia*, etc., Frankfurt, 1583.

Florovsky, Georges: "An Early Ecumenical Correspondence" (Patriarch Jeremiah II and the Lutheran Divines), *World Lutheranism of Today* . . . Stockholm, 1950, pp. 98–111.

Gerlach, M. Samuel: *Stefan Gerlachs des Älteren Türckisches Tagebuch*, Frankfurt a.M., 1674.

Hefele, C. J.: "Versuche zur Protestantisierung der griechischen Kirche", *Beiträge zur Kirchengeschichte, Archaeologie, und Liturgik, 1*, Tübingen, 1864 pp. 444–90.

Jeremias II, patriarch of Constantinople: *Acta et scripta theologorum Wirtembergensium et Patriarchae Constantinopolitani D. Hieremiae quae utrique ab anno MDLXXVI usque ad annum MDLXXXI de Augustana Confessione inter se miserunt* (In Greek and Latin), Wittenberg, 1584.

Renaudin, P.: *Luthériens et Grecs orthodoxes*, Paris, 1903.

Poland and Eastern Europe

Amman, Albert M.: *Abriss der ostslavischen Kirchengeschichte*, Vienna, 1950.

Friese, Chr.: *Beiträge zu der Reformationsgeschichte in Polen und Litthauen besonders*. Kirchengeschichte des Königreichs Polen, Vol. II/1, Breslau, 1786.

Krasinski, B.: *Geschichte des Ursprungs, Fortschritts, und Verfalls der Reformation in Polen*, Leipzig, 1841.

Likowski, E.: *Die ruthenisch-römische Kirchenvereinigung genannt Union zu Brest*. German tr. (from the Polish), by P. Jedzink, Freiburg i. Br., 1904.

Cyril Loukaris

Germanos, Metropolitan of Thyateira: *Kyrillos Loukaris, 1572–1638*, London, 1951.

Mettetal, A.: *Études historiques sur le patriarche Cyrille Lucar*, Strasbourg, 1869.

Pichler, Aloys: *Geschichte des Protestantismus in der orientalischen Kirche im 17. Jahrhundert, oder Der Patriarch Cyrillus Lucaris und seine Zeit*, Munich, 1862.

Schlier, Richard: *Der Patriarch Kyrill Lukaris von Konstantinopel: sein Leben und Glaubensbekenntnis*, Marburg, 1927.

Smith, Thomas: *Narratio de vita, studiis, gestis, et martyrio D. Cyrilli Lucaris Patriarchae Constantinopolitani*, London, 1707.

Mogila, Dositheos, Prokopovich

Goloubiev, C.: *Peter Mogila, Metropolitan of Kiev* (in Russian), 2 vols., Kiev, 1883–98.

Jugie, M.: "Pierre Moghila", *D.Th.C.* Vol. X, cols. 2063–81.

Palmieri, Aurelio: *Dositeo Patriarca greco di Gerusalemme. Contributo alla storia della teologia Greco-ortodossa nel seculo XVII*, Firenze, 1909.

Buddeus, Johann Franz: *Ecclesia Romana cum Ruthenica irreconciliabilis*, Jena, 1719.

Koch, Hans: *Die russische Orthodoxie im Petrinischen Zeitalter*, Breslau, 1929.

Kohl, Johann Peter: *Ecclesia graeca lutheranizans; sive exercitatio de consensu et dissensu orientalis graecae, speciatim russicae, et occidentalis lutheranae ecclesiae in dogmatibus*, Lübeck, 1723.

Confessions

Michalcescu, J.: *Die Bekenntnisse und die wichtigsten Glaubens-zeugnisse der griechisch-orientalischen Kirche*, Leipzig, 1904.

Non-jurors and Orthodox

Williams, George: *The Orthodox Church of the East in the eighteenth century, being the Correspondence between the Eastern Patriarchs and the Nonjuring Bishops. With an Introduction on various Projects of Reunion between the Eastern Church and the Anglican Communion*, London, 1868.

Bible Society in Russia, etc.

Benz, Ernst: *Die abendländische Sendung der östlich-orthodoxen Kirche: die russische Kirche und das abendländische Christentum im Zeitalter der Heiligen Allianz*, Mainz, 1950.

Grellet, Stephen: *Memoirs of the Life and Gospel Labours of Stephen Grellet.* Ed. Benjamin Seebohm, 2 vols., Philadelphia, 1860.

Henderson, Ebenezer: *Biblical Researches and Travels in Russia*, London, 1826.

Paterson, J., *The Book for every Land: Reminiscences of Labour and Adventure in the Work for Bible Circulation in the North of Europe and in Russia.* Ed. W. L. Alexander, London, 1858.

Metropolitan Philaret, etc.

Philaret, Wasilij Michailovitsch Drozdow: *Select Sermons of the late Metropolitan of Moscow.* Eng. tr. (from the Russian), by E. T. Tytcheff, London, 1873.

Choix de sermons et discours de S. Em. Mgr. Philarète. French tr. (from the Russian), by A. Serpinet, Paris, 1866.

Exposition of the Differences between the Eastern and Western Churches. Eng. tr. (from the Russian) in Pinkerton, Robert: *Russia, or Miscellaneous Observations* . . . London, 1833, pp. 39–54.

Stourdza, Alexandre de: *Considérations sur la doctrine et l'esprit de l'Église orthodoxe*, Stuttgart, 1816.

Moehler, Johann Adam

Bolshakoff, Serge: *The Doctrine of the Unity of the Church in the Works of Khomyakov and Moehler*, London, 1946.

Chaillet, P. (ed.): *L'Église est Une: Hommage à Moehler*, Paris, 1939.

Eschweiler, K.: *Joh. Adam Möhlers Kirchenbegriff*, Braunsberg, 1930.

Geiselmann, Josef Rupert: *J. A. Möhler: die Einheit der Kirche und die Wiedervereinigung der Konfessionen*, Vienna, 1940.

Moehler, Johann Adam: *Die Einheit in der Kirche, oder das Prinzip des Katholizismus.* New ed. by Josef Rupert Geiselmann, Darmstadt, 1957.

Tuechle, H. (ed.): *Die eine Kirche: zum Gedenken J. A. Möhlers, 1838–1938*, Paderborn, 1939.

Baader, Franz von

Baader, Franz von: *Der morgenländische und der abendländische Katholizismus mehr in seinem Innern wesentlichen als in seinem äussern Verhältnisse dargestellt*, Stuttgart, 1841.

Lettres inédites de Franz von Baader. Ed. Eugène Susini, Vol. 1, Paris, 1942; Vols. 2 and 3, Vienna, 1951.

Palmer, William

Birkbeck, W. J. (ed.): *Russia and the English Church during the last fifty Years . . . Correspondence between . . . Palmer and . . . Khomiakov, 1844–1854*, London, 1895.

Palmer, William: *Dissertations on Subjects Relating to the "Orthodox" or "Eastern-Catholic" Communion*, London, 1853.

The Patriarch [i.e., Nikon VI of Moscow] *and the Tsar*, 6 vols., London, 1871–76.

Notes on a Visit to the Russian Church in the Years 1840–41. Ed. J. H. Newman, London, 1882.

Shaw, P. E.: *The early Tractarians and the Eastern Church*, Milwaukee and London, 1930.

Khomiakov, Alexis Stepanovitch

Baron, P.: *Un théologien laïc orthodoxe russe au XIX siècle, Alexis Stépanovitch Khomiakov (1804–1860). Son ecclésiologie: exposé et critique.* Orientalia Christiana Analecta 127, Rome, 1940.

Bolshakoff, Serge: *The Doctrine of the Unity of the Church in the works of Khomiakov*, 1946.

Gratieux, A.: *A. S. Khomiakov et le mouvement slavophile*, 2 vols., Paris, 1939.

Khomiakov, A. S.: *L'Église latine et le protestantisme au point de vue de l'Église d'orient*, Lausanne, 1872.

The Church is One, London, 1948.

Guettée, Wladimir

Guettée, Wladimir: *Souvenirs d'un prêtre romain devenu prêtre orthodoxe*, Paris, 1889.

Overbeck, J. J.

Overbeck, J. J.: *Catholic Orthodoxy and Anglo-Catholicism: a word about intercommunion between the English and the Orthodox Churches*, London, 1866.

Die providentielle Stellung des Orthodoxen Russland und sein Beruf zur Wiederherstellung der Rechtgläubigen katholischen Kirche des Abendlandes, Halle, 1869.

Libellus invitatorius ad clerum laicosque romano-catholicos . . . , Halle, 1870.

Die Wiedervereinigung der morgen- und abendländischen Kirche, Halle, 1873.

Orthodox and Old Catholics

Janyschew, J., *Über das Verhältnis der Altkatholiken zur Orthodoxie*, Wiesbaden, 1891.

Kiréeff, A.: *Le général Alexandre Kiréeff et l'ancien-catholicisme* (receuil des articles d'A. Kiréeff parus dans la *Revue internationale de Théologie*, publié par Olga Novikoff); 2nd ed., Berne, 1893–1910.

Quelques lettres du général Alexandre Kiréeff au professeur Michaud sur l'ancien-catholicisme. (Publiées par Olga Novikoff) Paris and Neuchâtel, 1913.

Osinin, I. T.: *An Eastern View of the two Conferences at Bonn*. Eng. tr., 1876.
Overbeck, J. J.: *Die Bonner Unionskonferenz, oder Altkatholizismus und Anglikanismus in ihrem Verhältnis zur Orthodoxie*, Halle, 1876.

Anglicans and Orthodox

Androutsos, Chrestos; *The Validity of English Ordinations from an Orthodox Catholic point of view* (in Greek), 1905. Eng. tr. by F. W. Groves Campbell, London, 1909.
Beaven, J.: *On Intercourse between the Church of England and the Churches of the East, and on ecclesiastical Condition of the English abroad*, London, 1840.
Biggs, C. R. D.: *Russia and Reunion*, London, 1908.
Bulgakov, Athanasy Ivanovich: *The Question of Anglican Orders in Respect to a "Vindication" of the Papal Decision* . . . . Eng. tr. by W. J. Birkbeck, London, 1899.
Chitty, D.: *Orthodoxy and the Conversion of England*, St Albans, 1947.
Covel, John: *Some Accounts of the Present Greek Church with Reflections on their present Doctrines and Disciplines*, Cambridge, 1722.
Douglas, J. A.: *The Relations of the Anglican Churches with the Eastern Orthodox, especially in regard to Anglican Orders*, London, 1921.
Germanos, Metropolitan of Thyateira: *The Relations between the Anglican and the Orthodox Churches*, Cardiff, 1942.
Hardy, E. R., jr. (ed.): *Orthodox Statements on Anglican Orders*, New York, 1946.
Leeming, B.: *A Note on the Report of the Doctrinal Commission between the Anglican and the Eastern Orthodox Churches*, Rome, 1933.
Papadopoulos, Chrysostom, *The Validity of Anglican Ordinations* (in Greek), 1925. Eng. tr. by J. A. Douglas, London, 1931.
Ramsey, Michael: *The Church of England and the Eastern Orthodox Church: why their Unity is Important*, London, 1946.
Report of the Joint Doctrinal Commission appointed by the Ecumenical Patriarch and the Archbishop of Canterbury for Consultation on the Points of Agreement and Difference between the Anglican and the Eastern Orthodox Churches, London, 1932.
Report of the Proceedings of the Reunion Conference held at Bonn . . . *September* . . . , *1874*, London, 1875.
Report of the Reunion Conference held at Bonn between the 10th and 16th of August, 1875, London, 1876.
Riley, Athelstan (ed.): *Birkbeck and the Russian Church. Essays and Articles* . . . *written in the years 1888–1915*, London, 1917.

Soloviev, Vladimir

Birkbeck, W. J. (ed.): *Russia and the English Church during the last fifty Years* . . . *Correspondence between* . . . *Palmer and* . . . *Khomiakov, 1844–1854*, London, 1895.
Herbigny, Michel d': *Un Newman russe, Vladimir Soloviev, 1853–1900*; 6th ed., Paris, 1934.
Müller, Ludolf: *Solovjev und der Protestantismus*, Freiburg i. Br., 1951.
Soloviev, Vladimir: *Deutsche Gesamtausgabe der Werke*. Ed. Wladimir Szylkarski, Freiburg i. Br., 1954.
Drei Gespräche. German tr. (from the Russian), by E. Müller-Kamp, Bonn, 1954.

La Russie et l'Église universelle, Paris, 1889. Eng. tr., *Russia and the Universal Church*, London, 1948.
Die Erzählung vom Antichrist, Lucerne, 1946.
Stremooukhoff, D.: *Vladimir Soloviev et son oeuvre messianique*, Paris, 1935.
Tilloy, A.: *Les Églises orientales dissidentes et l'Église romaine: réponse à neuf questions de M. Soloviev*, Paris, 1899.

CHAPTER 5

Biographical articles on a number of the ecumenical leaders referred to in this chapter are to be found in *The Dictionary of American Biography*, 21 vols., Oxford, 1928–44; Supplement up to 1940, New York, 1958.

I. ORIGINAL ECUMENICAL WRITINGS

Ainslie, Peter: *The Message of the Disciples for the Union of the Church, including their Origin and History*, New York, etc., 1913.
Towards Church Unity, Baltimore, 1918.
If not a united Church—what? New York, 1920.
Ashworth, Robert A.: *The Union of Christian Forces in America*, Philadelphia, 1915.
Baird, Robert: *Religion in America, or an Account of the Origin, Progress, Relation to the State, and present Condition of the Evangelical Churches in the United States. With Notes of the unevangelical Denominations*, New York, 1844.
Briggs, Charles Augustus: *Church Unity: Studies of its most important Problems*, New York, 1909.
Brown, William M.: *The Level Plan for Church Union*, New York, 1910.
Campbell, Alexander: *Christianity Restored*, Bethany, Va., 1835; 2nd ed., *The Christian System, in Reference to the Union of Christians . . .* , Pittsburg, 1839.
Campbell, Thomas: *Declaration and Address* (1809) in Young, Charles Alexander (ed.): *Historical Documents advocating Christian Union*, Chicago, 1904, pp. 71–209.
Edwards, Jonathan: *A Humble Attempt to Promote Explicit Agreement and Visible Union of God's People in Extraordinary Prayer, For the Revival of Religion and the Advancement of Christ's Kingdom on Earth, Pursuant to Scripture Promises and Prophecies Concerning the Last Time* (1748) in *The Works of President Edwards*, New York, 1843, Vol. 3, pp. 427–508.
Eliot, John: *Communion of churches, or The divine management of gospel-churches by the ordinance of councils, constituted in order according to the Scriptures. As also, the way of bringing all Christian parishes to be particular Reforming Congregational Churches: humbly proposed, As a Way which hath so much Light from the Scriptures of truth, as that it may lawfully be submitted unto by all; and may, by the blessing of the Lord, be a means of uniting those two holy and eminent parties, the Presbyterians and the Congregationals. As also to prepare for the hoped-for resurrection of the churches; and to propose a way to bring all Christian nations into a unity of the faith and order of the gospel*, Cambridge, Mass., 1665.

Huntingdon, William Reed: *The Church Idea: an Essay towards Unity*, 1870; 3rd ed., New York, 1884.

A National Church. The Bedell Lectures for 1897, New York, 1898.

Kennedy, William S.: *The Plan of Union, or a History of the Presbyterian and Congregational Churches of the Western Reserve; with biographical Sketches of the early Missionaries*, Hudson, Ohio, 1856.

Lewis, William H.: *Christian Union and the Protestant Episcopal Church in its Relations to Church Unity*, New York, 1858.

Muhlenberg, William Augustus: *Evangelical Catholic Papers; a Collection of Essays, Letters and Tractates*, Ed. Anne Ayres, 2 vols., New York, 1875.

Schaff, Philip: *The Principle of Protestantism,* Chambersburg, Pa., 1845; *facs.* Philadelphia, 1964.

Harmony of the reformed Confessions, New York, 1877.

The Reunion of Christendom: a paper prepared for the Parliament of religions and the National conference of the Evangelical Alliance, Chicago, 1893, New York, 1893.

Schmucker, Samuel S.: *Fraternal Appeal to the American Churches: with a Plan for Catholic Union on apostolic Principles*, New York, 1839.

The true Unity of Christ's Church: being a renewed Appeal to the Friends of the Redeemer, on Primitive Christian Union, and the history of its Corruption, including a modified Plan for the Re-Union of all Evangelical Churches; 3rd ed., New York, 1838.

Overture on Christian Union, New York, 1846.

The Church of the Redeemer as developed within the General Synod of the Lutheran Church in America (including the *Fraternal Appeal*), Baltimore, 1865, 2nd ed., 1868.

Shields, Charles Woodruff: *The United Church of the United States*, New York, 1895.

Strong, Josiah: *Our Country, its possible Future and its present Crisis*, New York, 1885.

The new Era or the Coming Kingdom, New York, 1893.

Vail, Thomas H.: *The Comprehensive Church: or Christian Unity and Ecclesiastical Union in the Protestant Episcopal Church*, Hartford, Conn., 1841; 2nd ed., 1879; 3rd ed., 1883.

II. BIOGRAPHICAL MATERIAL

Ainslie: Idleman, Finis S.: *Peter Ainslie, Ambassador of Good Will*, Chicago and New York, 1941.

Campbell, Alexander: Richardson, Robert: *Memoirs of Alexander Campbell, embracing a View of the Origin, Progress, and Principles of the religious Reformation which he advocated*, 2 vols., Cincinnati, 1872.

Campbell, Thomas: Campbell, Alexander: *Memoirs of Elder Thomas Campbell*, Cincinnati, 1861.

Eliot: Mather, Cotton: *The Life and Death of John Eliot*, in *Magnalia*, London, 1702; new ed., London, 1820.

Huntington: Suter, John Wallace: *Life and Letters of William Reed Huntington, a Champion of Unity*, New York and London, 1925.

Muhlenberg, H. M.: Muhlenberg, H. M.: *The Journals of Henry Melchior Muhlenberg.* Eng. tr. by Theodore G. Tappert and John W. Doberstein, 3 vols., Philadelphia, 1942–45[?].

Muhlenberg, W. A.: Ayres, Anne: *The Life and Work of William Augustus Muhlenberg,* New York, 1880.

Nevin: Appel, Theodore: *The Life and Work of John Williamson Nevin . . . ,* Philadelphia, 1889.

O'Kelly: MacClenny, Wilbur E.: *The Life of Rev. James O'Kelly and the early History of the Christian Church in the South,* Raleigh, N.C., 1910.

Schaff: Schaff, David S.: *The Life of Philip Schaff: in part autobiographical,* New York, 1897.

Schmucker: Anstadt, P.: *Life and Times of Rev. S. S. Schmucker, D.D.,* York, Pa., 1896.

Stone: Rogers, John: *The Biography of Eld. Barton Warren Stone, written by himself with additions and reflections,* Cincinnati, 1847.

  Ware, C. C.: *Barton Warren Stone, pathfinder of Christian Union: a story of his life and times,* St Louis, 1932.

III. MODERN WORKS OF ECUMENICAL INTEREST

Addison, James Thayer: *The Episcopal Church in the United States, 1789–1931,* New York, 1951.

Addison, W. G.: *The Renewed Church of the United Brethren, 1722–1930,* London, 1932.

Arends, Robert Lowell: *Early American Methodism and the Church of England,* New Haven, 1948.

Atkins, Gaius Glenn: *Religion in our Times,* New York, 1932.

Binkley, Luther John: *The Mercersburg Theology,* Cambridge, Mass., 1950.

Blanke, Fritz: *Zinzendorf und die Einheit der Kinder Gottes,* Basle, 1950.

Cavert, Samuel McCrea, and Van Dusen, Henry Pitney (eds.): *The Church Through Half a Century: Essays in Honor of William Adams Brown . . . ,* New York, 1936.

Clark, Elmer Talmage: *The Small Sects in America;* rev. ed., New York, 1949.

Cole, Stewart G.: *The History of Fundamentalism,* New York, 1931.

Douglass, H. Paul: *Church Unity Movements in the United States,* New York, 1934.

Ferm, Vergilius: *The Crisis in American Lutheran Theology: a Study of the Issue between American Lutheranism and Old Lutheranism,* New York, 1927.

Garrison, Winfred Ernest: *The March of Faith: the Story of Religion in America since 1865,* New York, 1933.

Good, James I.: *History of the Reformed Church in the U.S. in the nineteenth century,* New York, 1911.

Hutchison, John A.: *We are not divided: a critical and historical Study of the Federal Council of the Churches of Christ in America,* New York, 1941.

Lynch, F.: *The Christian Unity Movement in America,* London, 1922.

Macfarland, Charles S.: *The Churches of the Federal Council; their History, Organization, and distinctive Characteristics, and a Statement of the Development of the Federal Council,* New York, 1916.

  The Progress of Church Federation, New York, 1917.

  Christian Unity in Practice and Prophecy, New York, 1933.

Christian Unity in the making; the first twenty-five Years of the Federal Council of Churches of Christ in America, 1905–1930, New York, 1948.

Christian Unity at Work: the Federal Council of the Churches of Christ in America, in Quadrennial Session at Chicago, Ill., 1912, New York, 1913.

Mode, Peter G.: *The Frontier Spirit in American Christianity*, New York, 1923.

Niebuhr, H. Richard: *The Social Sources of Denominationalism*, New York, 1929.

Richards, George Warren: *The Historical Significance of Denominationalism*, Philadelphia, 1919.

History of the Theological Seminary of the Reformed Church in the United States, 1825–1934, Evangelical and Reformed Church, 1934–1952, Lancaster, Pa., 1952.

Robinson, W.: *The shattered Cross: the Many Churches and the one Church*, Birmingham, 1945.

Rowe, Henry Kalloch: *The History of Religion in the United States*, New York, 1924.

Sanford, Elias B.: *The Origin and History of the Federal Council of Churches of Christ in America*, Hartford, Conn., 1916.

(ed.): *Church Federation. First Annual Report of the Executive Committee of the Inter-Church Conference on Federation, 1906*, New York, 1906.

(ed.): *The Federal Council of Churches of Christ in America. Report of the First Meeting of the Federal Council, Philadelphia, 1908*, New York, 1909.

Shaw, P. E.: *American Contacts with the Eastern Churches, 1820–1870*, Chicago, 1937.

Sperry, Willard L.: *Religion in America*, Cambridge, 1945.

Sweet, William Warren: *The Story of Religion in America*, New York and London, 1939.

Religion in colonial America, New York, 1943.

Religion on the American Frontier, 1783–1840, 4 vols., Chicago, 1931–46.

Religion in the Development of American Culture, 1765–1840, New York, 1952.

Revivalism in America: its Origin, Growth, and Decline, New York, 1945.

Tietjen, J. H.: *The Principles of Church Union expressed in the nineteenth century Attempts to unite the Lutheran Churches in America*, New York, 1959.

CHAPTER 6

I. Original Ecumenical Works

Appleyard, E. S.: *The Claims of the Church of Rome considered with a View to Unity*, London, 1848.

Arnold, Thomas: *Principles of Church Reform*, London, 1833; new ed. with an Introductory Essay by M. J. Jackson and J. Rogan, London, 1962.

Balmes, Jacques: *Le protestantisme comparé au catholicisme dans ses rapports avec la civilisation européenne*. Rev. and enlarged. ed. with introduction by A. de Blanche-Raffin, 3 vols., Paris, 1875.

Barrington, Shute: *Charges to the Clergy of Durham*, London, 1813.

Bennet, W. J. E.: *Foreign Churches in relation to the Anglican: an Essay towards Reunion*, London, 1882.

Cooper, James: *Reunion: a Voice from Scotland*, London, 1918.

Crawford, Alexander William Lindsay, Earl of: *Ecumenicity in Relation to the Church of England*, London, 1870.

De Lisle, Ambrose Lisle March Phillipps: *On the Future Unity of Christendom*, London, 1836.

Döllinger, Ignaz von: *Lectures on the Reunion of the Churches*. Tr. and with Preface by Henry Nutcombe Oxenham, London, 1872; German ed., *Die Wiedervereinigung der christlichen Kirchen*, Munich, 1888.

Earle, W.: *The Reunion of Christendom in Apostolic Succession for the Evangelisation of the World*, London, 1895.

Essays on Christian Union, London, 1845. (By leaders in the Scottish Churches.)

Forrester, H.: *Christian Unity and the historic Episcopate*, New York, 1889.

Grueber, C. S.: *An Eirenicon, or Appeal to the Archbishops and Bishops of the Church of England in behalf of due and lawful Means of promoting Union*, London, 1873.

Halifax, Charles Lindley Wood, Viscount: *The Reunion of Christendom*, London, 1895.

Catholic Unity and the Relation of National Churches to the Church Universal, London, 1902.

Call to Reunion, arising out of Discussions with Cardinal Mercier, London, 1922.

(ed.): *The Conversations at Malines, 1921–25: original Documents*, London, 1930.

Harper, T.: *Peace through the Truth: Essays connected with Dr Pusey's Eirenicon*, 2 vols., London, 1866–74.

Headlam, A. C.: *The Doctrine of the Church and Christian Reunion*, London, 1920.

Heiler, Friedrich: *Im Ringen um die Kirche: Gesammelte Aufsätze und Vorträge*, Munich, 1931.

Kettlewell, S.: *An Inquiry into the Basis of true Christian Unity*, 2 vols., London, 1888–89.

Krüger, Gustav: *Die neueren Bestrebungen um Wiedervereinigung der christlichen Kirchen*, 1897.

Lacey, T. A.: *Unity and Schism. The Bishop Paddock Lectures for 1917*, London, 1917.

Lee, F. G. (ed.): *Sermons on the Re-Union of Christendom by Members of the Roman Catholic, Oriental, and Anglican Communions*, 2 vols., London, 1964–65.

Essays on the Re-union of Christendom. By members of the Roman Catholic, Oriental, and Anglican Communities, London, 1867.

Manning, H. E.: *The Unity of the Church*, London, 1842.

The Reunion of Christendom: a Pastoral Letter, London, 1866.

Maurice, Frederick Denison: *The Kingdom of Christ, or Hints on the principles, Ordinances and Constitution of the Catholic Church in Letters to a Member of the Society of Friends. By a Clergyman of the Church of England*, London, 1837–38, 3 vols. (Also Everyman Edition, 2 vols.)

Meyrick, F. (ed.): *Correspondence between Members of the Anglo-Continental Society and (1) Old Catholics and (2) Oriental Churchmen*, London, 1874.

Möhler, Johann Adam: *Neue Untersuchungen der Lehrgegensätze zwischen den*

Katholiken und Protestanten: eine Verteidigung meiner Symbolik gegen die Kritik des Herrn Professors Dr Baur in Tübingen; 2nd ed., Mainz and Vienna, 1835.

Nelson, Horatio, Earl, *Home Reunion: Reflections on the present position of Nonconformists and an appeal for a better mutual understanding*, London, 1905.

Newman, J. H.: *A Letter to the Rev. E. B. Pusey, D.D., on his recent Eirenicon*, London, 1866.

Letters and Correspondence of J. H. Newman during his Life in the English Church. Ed. Anne Mozley, 2 vols., London, 1891.

Noel, Baptist Wrothesby: *The Unity of the Church, another Tract for the Times, addressed especially to the Members of the Establishment*, London, 1836.

Oxenham, H. N.: *Dr Pusey's Eirenicon considered in Relation to Catholic Unity: a Letter to the Rev. Father Lockhart of the Institute of Charity*, London, 1866.

Pusey, Edward Bouverie: *The Church of England a Portion of Christ's One Holy Catholic Church, and a Means of Restoring Visible Unity: an Eirenicon, in a Letter to the Author of "The Christian Year"*, London, 1865.

First Letter to the Very Rev. J. H. Newman, D.D., In Explanation chiefly in Regard to the Reverential Love due to the Ever-blessed Theotokos, and the Doctrine of her Immaculate Conception. Eirenicon, Part II, London, 1869.

Is Healthful Reunion Impossible? A second letter to the . . . Rev. J. H. Newman, Oxford and London, 1870.

Reynolds, Henry Roberts (ed.): *Ecclesia: Church Problems considered in a Series of Essays*, London, 1870; new ed., 2 vols., London, 1872–74.

Schleiermacher, Friedrich: *Zwei unvorgreifliche Gutachten in Sachen des protestantischen Kirchenwesens*, 1804.

Ueber die für die protestantische Kirche des preussischen Staats einzurichtende Synodalverfassung, Berlin, 1817.

Kurze Darstellung des theologischen Studiums, Leipzig, 1910.

Wordsworth, Charles: *Public Appeals on Behalf of Christian Unity*. 12 pamphlets in 2 vols. with special reference to the condition of the Church in Scotland, Edinburgh, 1886.

II. Biographies

Arnold: Stanley, A. P.: *The Life and Correspondence of Thomas Arnold, D.D.*; 4th ed., London, 1891.

Birkbeck: Birkbeck, R. K.: *Life and Letters of W. J. Birkbeck*, by his wife, London, 1922.

Cooper: Wotherspoon, H. J.: *James Cooper: a Memoir*, London, 1926.

De Lisle: Purcell, Edmund Sheridan: *The Life and Letters of Ambrose Phillipps de Lisle*, 2 vols., London, 1900.

Forbes: Perry, William: *Alexander Penrose Forbes, Bishop of Brechin, the Scottish Pusey*, London, 1939.

Gobat: Gobat, Samuel: *Samuel Gobat, Bishop of Jerusalem, his Life and Work: a biographical Sketch drawn chiefly from his own Journals*, London, 1884.

Halifax: Gratieux, A.: *L'amitié au service de l'union: Lord Halifax et l'abbé Portal*, Paris, 1951.

Lockhart, J. G.: *Charles Lindley, Viscount Halifax*, 2 vols., London, 1935–36.

Hope-Scott: Hope-Scott, James Robert, *Memoirs of James Robert Hope-Scott.* Ed. Robert Ornsby, 2 vols., London, 1884.

Hort: Hort, Arthur Fenton: *Life and Letters of Fenton John Anthony Hort,* 2 vols., London, 1896.

Hughes: Hughes, Dorothea Price: *The Life of Hugh Price Hughes,* by his daughter, London, 1907.

Maurice: Maurice, Frederick: *The Life of Frederick Denison Maurice, chiefly told in his own Letters,* by his son, 2 vols., London, 1884; 4th ed., London, 1885.

Kingsley: Kingsley, Charles: *Charles Kingsley, his Letters and Memories of his Life,* Ed. by his wife, 2 vols., London, 1877; 2nd ed. in 1 vol., 1883; 1895.

Newman: Bouyer, L.: *Newman, sa vie, sa spiritualité,* Paris, 1952.

Ward, W.: *The Life of J. H. Newman,* 2 vols., London, 1912.

Portal: Hemmer, H.: *Fernand Portal, 1855–1926, Apostle of Unity.* Tr. from the French, *Monsieur Portal, prêtre de la mission,* and ed. by Arthur T. Macmillan, London, 1961; American ed., New York, 1961.

Pusey: Liddon, Henry Parry: *Life of Edward Bouverie Pusey,* 4 vols., London, 1893–97.

Stanley: Prothero, Rowland E.: *Life and Letters of Dean Stanley;* new ed., London, 1909.

Stoughton: Lewis, G. K.: *John Stoughton, D.D.; a short Record of a long Life,* by his daughter, London, 1898.

Vaughan: Snead-Cox, J. G.: *Life of Cardinal Vaughan,* 2 vols., London, 1910.

Wordsworth: Wordsworth, John: *The Episcopate of Charles Wordsworth, 1853–1892,* London, 1899.

III. Studies of Particular Subjects

Adam, Alfred: *Die Nassauische Union von 1817,* Darmstadt, 1949.

Bennet, W. J. E.: *The Church's Broken Unity,* 5 vols., London, 1867.

Benz, Ernst: *Bischofsamt und apostolische Sukzession im deutschen Protestantismus,* Stuttgart, 1953.

Birkbeck, W. J. (ed.): *Russia and the English Church during the last fifty Years . . . Correspondence between . . . Palmer and . . . Khomiakov, 1844–1854,* London, 1895.

Bivort de la Saudée, Jacques de: *Anglicans et catholiques: le problème de l'union anglo-romaine, 1833–1933,* Paris, 1949.

(ed.): *Documents sur le problème de l'union anglo-romaine, 1921–1927: anglicans et catholiques,* Paris, 1949.

Brandreth, Henry R. T.: *The oecumenical Ideals of the Oxford Movement,* London, 1947.

Brownlow, W. R.: *The Reunion of England and Rome,* London, 1896.

Call for Christian Unity: a Volume of Essays contributed at the Request of the Anglican Evangelical Group Movement, London, 1930.

Calvet, J.: *Rome and Reunion,* London, 1928.

Carson, W. R.: *Reunion Essays,* London, 1903.

Chandler, A.: *The English Church and Reunion,* London, 1916.

Church, R. W.: *The Oxford Movement, 1833–45,* 1891.

Cross, F. L.: *The Tractarians and Roman Catholicism,* London, 1933.

Dieux, M. A.: *Croisade pour l'unité du monde chrétien,* Paris, 1926.

Drummond, Andrew Landale: *German Protestantism since Luther*, London, 1951.

Fleming, J. R.: *The Story of Church Union in Scotland, its Origins and Progress, 1560–1929*, London, 1929.

Foerster, Erich: *Die Entstehung der Preussischen Landeskirche unter der Regierung König Friedrich Wilhelms des Dritten*, 2 vols., Tübingen, 1905–07.

Geppert, Walter: *Das Wesen der preussischen Union: eine kirchen-geschichtliche und konfessionskundliche Untersuchung*, Berlin, 1939.

Gondon, J.: *Du mouvement religieux en Angleterre, ou le progrès du catholicisme et le rétour de l'Église anglicane à l'unité*, Paris, 1844.
De la Réunion de l'Église d'Angleterre protestante à l'Église catholique, Paris, 1867.

Gratieux, A., and Guitton, J.: *Trois serviteurs de l'unité chrétienne* [Charles, Viscount Halifax: Cardinal Mercier: M. l'abbé Portal], Paris, 1937.

Halifax, Charles Lindley Wood, Viscount: *Leo XIII and Anglican Orders*, London, 1912.
(ed.): *The Conversations at Malines, 1921–25: original Documents*, London, 1930.

Harrison, A. W., and others: *The Methodist Church: its Origin, Divisions, and Reunion*, London, 1932.

Haselmayer, L. A.: *Lambeth and Unity*, New York and London, 1948.

Hauck, Albert: *Deutschland und England in ihren kirchlichen Beziehungen: acht Vorlesungen im Oktober 1916 an der Universität Upsala gehalten*, Leipzig, 1917.

Hechler, W. H.: *The Jerusalem Bishopric*, London, 1883.

Hunkin, J. W.: *Episcopal Ordination and Confirmation in Relation to Intercommunion and Reunion*, Cambridge, 1929.

Hunter, A.: *England's Awakening: a few Words on the History of Anglo-Catholicism, and the Attitude towards the Prospect of a future Reunion*, London, 1923.

Jones, Spencer: *England and the Holy See: an Essay towards Reunion*, London, 1902. (Not to be confused with *L'Église d'Angleterre et le Saint Siège: propos sur la réunion*, 1941, by the same author, which was written specially for French readers.)

Lacey, T. A.: *The Unity of the Church as treated by the English Theologians*, London, 1898.
A Roman Diary, and other Documents relating to the Papal Inquiry into English Ordinations, London, 1910.
The Universal Church: a Study in the Lambeth Call to Union, London, 1921.

McCrie, C. G.: *The Church of Scotland: her Divisions and her Re-unions*, Edinburgh, 1901.

Mackenzie, K. D.: *The Confusion of the Churches*, London, 1925.

Moss, C. B.: *The Old Catholic Movement: its Origins and History*, London, 1948; 2nd ed., London, 1964.

Müller, J.: *Die evangelische Union: ihr Wesen und göttliches Recht*, Berlin, 1854.

Noir, Louis: *L'union des Églises protestantes en Prusse sous Frédéric-Guillaume III*, Lausanne, 1906.

Ollard, S. L.: *Reunion*, London, 1919. [A history of efforts at reunion on the part of the Church of England.]

Riley, Athelstan (ed.): *Birkbeck and the Russian Church. Essays and Articles ... written in the years 1888–1915*, London, 1917.

Rivington, L.: *Anglican Fallacies, or Lord Halifax on Reunion*, London, 1895.

Scheibel, J. G.: *Antwort auf das offene Sendschreiben eines Verborgenen; die Unionsgeschichte betreffend nebst einem Zusatz über die neuesten Gegenschriften gegen die lutherische Kirche überhaupt*, Nuremberg, 1834.

Schiffers, N.: *Die Einheit der Kirche nach John Henry Newman*, Düsseldorf, 1956.

Schubert, E.: *Die deutsch- evangelischen Einheitsbestrebungen vom Beginn des 19. Jahrhunderts bis zur Gegenwart*, 1919.

Shaw, P. E.: *The early Tractarians and the Eastern Church*, Milwaukee and London, 1930.

Silcox, Claris Edwin: *Church Union in Canada: its Causes and Consequences*, New York, 1933.

Smyth, N.: *A Story of Church Unity, including the Lambeth Conference of Anglican Bishops and the Congregational-Episcopal Approaches*, New Haven, 1923.

Swinstead, J. Howard: *The Swedish Church and ours*, London, 1921.

Thureau-Dangin, P.: *La renaissance catholique en Angleterre au XIXe siècle*, Paris, 3 vols., 1899–1906.

Tondini da Quarenghi, C.: *Anglicanism, Old Catholicism, and the Union of the Christian Episcopal Churches*, London, 1875.

Townsend, W. J.: *The Story of Methodist Union*, London, n.d.

Wangemann, Hermann Theodor: *Die preussische Union in ihrem Verhältnis zur Una Sancta*, Berlin, 1884.

Williams, Gershom Mott: *The Church of Sweden and the Anglican Communion*, Milwaukee, 1910. (Reprint from *The Living Church*, 1910.)

Williams, N. P., and Harris, C. (eds.): *Northern Catholicism: Centenary Studies in the Oxford and parallel Movements*, London, 1933.

Wilson, H. A.: *Episcopacy and Unity: a Historical Inquiry into the Relations between the Church of England and the non-Episcopal Churches at home and abroad, from the Reformation to the Repeal of the Occasional Conformity Act*, London, 1912.

Wordsworth, John: *The National Church of Sweden*, London, 1911.

CHAPTER 7

A complete or systematic bibliography cannot be given, since the material has been gathered from countless memoranda, pamphlets, minutes of committees, etc. The following hints may be useful to the student:

I. HISTORIES OF MOVEMENTS AND ASSOCIATIONS

Of those listed in the General Bibliography, consult especially Ewing, Massie, Newman, Rice, Rouse, Tatlow, Shedd.

II. HISTORIES OF MISSIONARY SOCIETIES

More important than any other is:
Stock, Eugene: *The History of the Church Missionary Society*, 4 vols., London, 1899–1916.

But reference to the Histories of the following will also be found rewarding:
The Baptist Missionary Society (London).
The Basle Missionary Socicty (Basle).
The London Missionary Society (London).
The Methodist Missionary Society (London).
The British and Foreign Bible Society (London).

III. Periodicals

Of the periodicals listed in the General Bibliography, those which have special importance for this chapter are:
The Review of the Churches. Ed. Sir Henry Lunn.
Evangelical Christendom.

IV. Evangelical Alliance

Aldis, J.: *Six Lectures on the Importance and Practicability of Christian Union, chiefly in relation to the Movement of the Evangelical Alliance*, London, 1846.

Bonnet, L.: *L'unité de l'Esprit par le lien de la paix: lettres sur l'Alliance evangélique*, Paris, 1847.

Evangelical Alliance: Report of the Proceedings of the Conference, held at Freemasons' hall, London, from August 19th to September 2nd inclusive, 1846, London, 1847.

Monod, Jean: *Conférence de l'Alliance évangélique à Londres 1851*, Paris, 1852.

Monod, Guillaume (ed.): *Conférence de chrétiens évangéliques de toute nation à Paris 1855*. Paris, 1856.

Reineck, Karl Eduard (ed.): *Verhandlungen der Versammlung evangelischer Christen Deutschlands und anderer Länder vom 9. bis 17. September 1857 in Berlin*, Authorized ed., Berlin, 1857.

Tissot, D.: *Les Conférences de Genève 1861. Rapport et discours publiés au nom du Comité de l'Alliance évangélique*, Geneva and Paris [186–?].

Cohen Stuart, M.: *Evangelische Alliantie: verslag van de vijfde algemeene vergadering, gehouden te Amsterdam, 18–27 Augustus 1867*, Rotterdam 1868.

Schaff, Philip (ed.): *History, Essays, Orations and other documents of the Sixth General Conference of the Evangelical Alliance, held in New York, October 2–12, 1873*, New York, 1874.

Riggenbach, Christoph Johannes: *Siebente Hauptversammlung der Evangelischen Allianz gehalten in Basel 31. August bis 7. September 1879, Berichte und Reden*, Basle, 1879/1880.

Redford, R. A. (ed.): *Christendom from the standpoint of Italy. Proceedings of the Ninth General Conference of the Evangelical Alliance held in Florence, 1891*, London, 1891.

Maintaining the Unity. Proceedings of the 11th International Conference and Diamond Jubilee Celebration of the Evangelical Alliance held in London, July 1907, London, 1907.

The Problem of Unity (Papers read at the 63rd Annual Conference of the Evangelical Alliance), London, 1911.

Nagel, G. F. (ed.): *Eine heilige christliche Kirche: Mitteilungen aus der Geschichte der Evangelischen Allianz*, Bad Blankenburg, 1931.

V. Student Christian Movement

Fenn, Eric: *Learning Wisdom: Fifty years of the Student Christian Movement*, London, 1939.

Mott, John R.: *Strategic Points in the World's Conquest*, Westwood, N.J., 1897.

Rouse, Ruth: *Rebuilding Europe: the student Chapter in post-war Reconstruction*, London, 1925.

Wilson, Elizabeth: *Fifty Years of Association Work amongst Young Women, 1866–1916: a History of the Y.W.C.A. in the U.S.A.*, New York, 1916.

Wishard, Luther D.: *A New Programme of Missions: A Movement to make the Colleges in all Lands Centres of Evangelization*, Westwood, N.J., 1895.

VI. Biographies

A short selection may be given of biographies specially useful for one or more sections of the chapter:

Buchanan: Pearson, Hugh: *Memoirs of the Life and Writings of the Rev. Claudius Buchanan*, 2 vols., London, 1817.

Carey: Carey, S. Pearce: *William Carey*, London, 1924.

 Smith, George: *The Life of William Carey, shoemaker and missionary*, London, 1885; new ed., 1909.

Chalmers: Hanna, William: *Memoirs of the Life and Writings of Thomas Chalmers*, 4 vols., Edinburgh, 1849–52; 2 vol. ed., Edinburgh and London, 1878.

Couturier: À la mémoire de l'abbé Paul Couturier ... apôtre de l'unité chrétienne, 1881–1953, Paris, 1954.

 Allchin, D.: *L'abbé Paul Couturier* (in English), London, 1959.

 Curtis, Geoffrey: *Paul Couturier and unity in Christ*, London, 1964.

Drummond: Smith, George Adam: *The Life of Henry Drummond*, New York, 1898.

Fallot: Boegner, Marc: *La vie et la pensée de T. Fallot*, 2 vols., Paris, 1914–26.

Finney, Bushnell, and Gladden: Grover, Norman Lamotte: *The Church and Social Action in the Thought of Finney, Bushnell, and Gladden*, Vanderbilt, 1956.

Martyn: Sargent, John: *Life and Letters of the Rev. H. Martyn*; 10th ed., London, 1885.

 Smith, George: *Henry Martyn, saint and scholar, first missionary to the Mohammedans, 1781–1812*, London, 1892.

Monod: Monod, Adolphe: *Souvenirs de sa vie*, Paris, 1885–1902.

Moody: Moody, R. W.: *The Life of Dwight L. Moody*, London, n.d.

Mott: Mathews, B.: *John R. Mott*, New York and London, 1934.

Naville: Naville, Hélène: *Ernest Naville, sa vie et sa pensée*, 2 vols., Geneva, 1913–17.

Oberlin: Leenhardt, Camille: *La vie de J.-F. Oberlin 1740–1826*, de D.-E. Stoeber, refondue ... complétée et augmentée ... , Paris and Nancy, 1911.

Stanley: Prothero, Rowland E.: *Life and Letters of Dean Stanley*; new ed., London, 1909.

Stewart: Stewart, David Dale: *Memoir of the life of the Rev. James Haldane Stewart 1776–1854*, London, 1857.

Wattson: Cranny, Titus: *Father Paul and Christian unity; an Anthology on Christian Reunion prepared from the Writings, Sermons, and Addresses of*

Father Paul James Francis [Wattson], *S.A., 1863–1940*, New York, 1963.
Gannon, David: *Father Paul of Graymoor*, New York, 1951.
Westcott: Westcott, Arthur: *Life and Letters of Brooke Foss Westcott, sometime Bishop of Durham*, 2 vols., New York, 1903.
Wichern: Oldenberg, Friedrich: *Johann Hinrich Wichern, sein Leben und Wirken*, 2 vols., Hamburg, 1884–87.
Wilberforce: Coupland, R.: *William Wilberforce*, Oxford, 1923.
　　Maury, L.: *Le réveil religieux dans l'Église réformée à Genève et en France, 1810–1850*, Paris, 1892.
Wilder: Braisted, Ruth Wilder: *In this Generation: the Story of Robert P. Wilder*, New York, 1944.
Wishard: Ober, C. K.: *Luther D. Wishard, Projector of World Movements*, New York, 1927.
Patten, John A.: *These Remarkable Men; the Beginnings of a World Enterprise*, London, 1945. (Short biographies of leading early Evangelicals specially connected with the Bible Society.)

VII. Prayer for Unity

Brenner, S. F.: *The Way of Worship: a Study in ecumenical Recovery*, New York, 1944.
Church Unity and Intercession, London, 1912. (Essays by members of the World's Evangelical Alliance.)
Couturier, P.: *Pour l'unité des Chrétiens*, Paris, 1935. Eng. tr. (from the French), *The Universal Prayer of Christians for Christian Unity*, London and Oxford, 1938.
Faith and Order Conference, Lausanne: *A Manual of Prayer for Unity* (in preparation), Gardiner, 1915.
Suggestions for an Octave of Prayer for Unity, Gardiner, 1922.
Fleming, D. J.: *The World at One in Prayer*, New York, 1942.
Jugie, M.: *La prière pour l'unité chrétienne*, Paris, 1919.

CHAPTER 8

I. Reports of Conferences, Minutes of Committees, etc.

Johnston, James (ed.): *Report of the Centenary Conference on the Protestant Missions of the World . . . London, 1888*, 2 vols., London, 1889.
Ecumenical Missionary Conference, New York, 1900, 2 vols., New York, 1900.
World Missionary Conference, 1910, 9 vols., Edinburgh and London, n.d.
Conference on Missions held in 1860 at Liverpool, London, 1860.
The Continuation Committee Conferences in Asia, 1912–1913, New York, 1913.
Minute [sic] *of International Missionary Meeting, held at Crans, near Geneva, June 22–28, 1920*.
Minutes of the International Missionary Council, Lake Mohonk, N.Y., U.S.A., October 1–6, 1921.
Minutes of the International Missionary Council (including *Minutes of the Committee of the Council* and *Minutes of the Ad Interim Committee*) from 1921 onwards.

Report of the Jerusalem Meeting of the International Missionary Council, March 24th–April 8th, 1928 (The Jerusalem Series), 8 vols., London, 1928.

The World Mission of the Church. Findings and Recommendations of the Meeting of the International Missionary Council, Tambaram, Madras, India, Dec. 12–29, 1938 (The Madras Series), London and New York, 1939.

Questions for the International Missionary Council at Madras, India. Dec. 13–30, 1938, London, 1938.

Minutes of the Enlarged Meeting of the International Missionary Council and of the Committee of the Council, Whitby, Ontario, July 5–24, 1947, London and New York, 1947.

Minutes of the Meeting of the Joint Commission on East Asia of the International Missionary Council and the World Council of Churches, Manila, Philippine Republic, February 4, 6 and 7, 1948, n.p., n.d.

Hocking, William Ernest (ed.): *Re-thinking Missions: a Layman's Inquiry after one Hundred Years*, by the Commission of Appraisal, New York and London, 1932.

Laymen's Foreign Missions Inquiry: Fact-Finders' Reports, 6 vols., New York, 1933.

Committee on the War and the Religious Outlook: *Christian Unity: its Principles and Possibilities*, New York, 1921.

Handy, Robert T.: *We witness together: a History of cooperative Home Missions*, New York, 1956.

China Centenary Missionary Conference Record: Report of the Great Conference held at Shanghai, April 5th [read 25th] *to May 8th, 1907*, New York, 1907.

Christian Education in China: a Study by an Educational Commission representing the Mission Boards and Societies conducting Work in China, New York, 1922.

Education for Service in the Christian Church in China: the Report of a Survey Commission, Shanghai, 1935.

The Christian Movement in Japan, Tokyo, 1903–06.

The Japan Mission Year Book, Tokyo, 1927–31.

The Japan Christian Year Book, Tokyo, 1932–40. (Continuation of the Japan Mission Yearbook.)

The Missionary Conference: South India and Ceylon, 1879, 2 vols., Madras, 1880.

The Christian Prospect in Eastern Asia: Papers and Minutes of the Eastern Asia Christian Conference, Bangkok, Dec. 3–11, 1949, New York, 1950.

Christ the Hope of Asia: Papers and Minutes of the Ecumenical Study Conference for East Asia, Lucknow, India, Dec. 27–30, 1952, Madras, 1953.

Fraser, A. G. (ed.): *Village Education in India: the Report of a Commission of Inquiry*, London, 1920.

The Christian College in India: the Report of the Commission on Higher Education in India, Oxford, 1931.

Christian Work in Latin America: Congress on Christian Work in Latin America, Panama, February 1916, 3 vols., New York, 1917.

Regional Conferences in Latin America: the Reports of a Series of Seven Conferences Following the Panama Congress in 1916, New York, 1917.

Congress on Christian work in South America, Montevideo, 1925: Official Report, 2 vols., New York and Chicago, 1925.

The Evangelical Handbook of Latin America, New York, 1939.

Foreign Missions Conference of North America: Reports, New York, 1893 onwards. (Esp. 1920, 1921, 1923.)

II. GENERAL WORKS

Hogg, William Richey: *Ecumenical Foundations: a History of the International Missionary Council and its nineteenth century Background*, New York, 1952. (With magnificent bibliography, covering almost the whole field of this chapter.)

Latourette, Kenneth Scott: *Christianity in a revolutionary Age: a History of Christianity in the nineteenth and twentieth centuries*, Vols. III and V, London, 1961, 1962.

A History of the Expansion of Christianity, 7 vols., London and New York, 1937–45. (Esp. Vols. VI and VII.)

Mott: John R.: *Addresses and Papers*, 6 vols., New York, 1946–47. (Esp. Vol. V.)

III. BOOKS ON PARTICULAR ASPECTS OF THE SUBJECT

For books dealing with the great missionary conferences, and for ecumenical biographies, see General Bibliography.

Ashby, Philip Harrison: *Christian Missions and their Approach to contemporary primitive cultures*, Chicago, 1951.

Barth, K.: "Die Theologie und die Mission in der Gegenwart", *Zwischen den Zeiten*, X, Koblenz, 1932, pp. 189–215.

Braga, Erasmo, and Grubb, K. G.: *The Republic of Brazil: a Survey of the Religious Situation*, London, 1932.

Broomfield, G. W.: *Revelation and Reunion: a Response to Tambaram*, London, 1942.

Butterfield, Kenyon L.: *The Christian Mission in Rural India*, New York and London, 1930.

The Rural Mission of the Church in Eastern Asia, with a Foreword by John R. Mott, New York, 1931.

Capon, M. G.: *Towards Unity in Kenya: the Story of Cooperation between Missions and Churches in Kenya, 1913–1947*, Nairobi, 1962.

Cash, W. W.: *The Missionary Church: a Study in the Contribution of modern Missions to oecumenical Christianity*, London, 1939.

Clayton, A. C.: *Christian Literature in India and Ceylon: an Account of the Christian Literature published in the Vernacular Languages and in English by Protestant Missions*, Madras, 1920.

Davis, J. Merle: *Modern Industry and the African*, London, 1933.

New Buildings on Old Foundations: a Handbook on Stabilizing the Younger Churches in their Environment, New York, 1945.

(ed.): *The Economic and Social Environment of the Younger Churches*, London, 1939.

Fahs, Charles Harvey, and Davis, Helen E.: *Conspectus of Cooperative Missionary Enterprises*, New York, 1935.

Groves, Charles P.: *The Planting of Christianity in Africa*, 4 vols., London, 1948–1958.

Hartenstein, K.: *Die Mission als theologisches Problem: Beiträge zum grund-sätzlichen Verständnis der Mission*, Berlin, 1933.

Heggoy, Willy Normann: *Fifty Years of Evangelical Missionary Movement in North Africa, 1881–1931*, Hartford, Conn., 1960.

Kraemer, Hendrik: *The Christian Message in a non-Christian World*, New York and London, 1938: reprinted 1947.

Latourette, Kenneth Scott: *A History of Christian Missions in China*, New York, 1929.

Latourette, Kenneth Scott, and Hogg, William Richey: *World Christian Community in Action: the Story of World War II and Orphaned Missions*, New York and London, 1949.

Maclennan, Kenneth: *Twenty Years of Missionary Co-operation*, London, 1927.

Neill, Stephen: *Christian Partnership*, London, 1952.

  Christ, his Church, and his World, London, 1948.

  Evangelism: the primary Responsibility of all the Churches, New York, 1948.

Niles, D. T.: *That they may have Life*, New York, 1951.

Oldham, J. H.: *The new Christian adventure: a statement made to the International Missionary Council . . . July 1929*, London, 1929.

O'Neill, S. W.: *Christian Unity: Thoughts of an Indian Missionary on the Controversies of the Day*, London, 1879.

Paik, L. George: *The History of Protestant Missions in Korea, 1832–1910*, Pyong Yang, 1929.

Parker, Joseph I. (ed.): *Directory of World Missions*, New York and London, 1938.

Ranson, C. W.: *The Christian Minister in India, his Vocation and his Training*, Madras, 1945; 2nd ed., London, 1946.

Rauws, J., and others: *The Netherlands Indies*, London, 1935.

Ritson, J. H.: *Christian Literature in the Mission Field*, London, 1915.

Smith, Edwin W.: *The Christian Mission in Africa*, London, 1926.

Warren, M. A. C.: *The Christian Mission*, London, 1951; 2nd ed., 1953.

Wrong, Margaret: *Africa and the Making of Books, being a survey of Africa's need of literature*, New York and London, 1934.

CHAPTER 9

Bate, H. N.: *A Bibliography of Literature dealing with the Subjects, with which the Faith and Order Movement is concerned*, Ipswich, 1931.

Anderson, C. P.: *The Manifestation of Unity*, Boston, 1913.

Baillie, Donald (ed.): *Intercommunion: the report of the theological commission appointed by the continuation committee of the World Conference on Faith and Order together with a selection from the material presented to the commission*, London, 1952.

Can the Church unite? A Symposium, New York and London, 1927.

Dunkerley, R., and Headlam, A. C. (eds.): *The Ministry and the Sacraments: Report of the Theological Commission under the Chairmanship of the Right Rev. A. C. Headlam, C.H., D.D., Bishop of Gloucester*, London, 1937.

Flew, R. Newton (ed.): *The Nature of the Church; papers presented to the theological commission appointed by the continuation committee of the World Conference on Faith and Order*, London, 1952.

De Groot, Alfred T.: *Check List, Faith and Order Commission, Official, Numbered Publications:* (S 1, 1910–1948; S 2, 1948–1962), Fort Worth, Texas, 1958; Geneva, 1963.

Gore, C.: *Orders and Unity*, London, 1909.

Goudge, H. L.: *The Church of England and Reunion*, London, 1938.

Hodgson, Leonard (ed.): *Convictions: a Selection from the Responses of the Churches to the Report of the World Conference on Faith and Order held at Lausanne in 1927*, London, 1934.

The Ecumenical Movement: three Lectures, Sewanee, Tenn., 1951.

Kennedy, James W.: *He that gathereth; a first hand Account of the Third World Conference on Faith and Order, held in Lund, Sweden, Aug. 15–28, 1952*, New York, 1952.

McBee, Silas: *An eirenic Itinerary: Impressions of our Tour . . .*, London, 1911.

Nelson, J. Robert: *The Realm of Redemption: Studies in the Doctrine of the Nature of the Church in contemporary Protestant Theology*, University of Zürich, 1951; London, 1951.

Siegmund-Schultze, F.: *Die Weltkirchenkonferenz von Lausanne vom 3. bis 21 August 1927*, Berlin-Steglitz, 1927.

Skoglund, J. E., and Nelson, J. R.: *Fifty Years of Faith and Order; an interpretation of the Faith and Order Movement*, St Louis, 1964.

Söderblom, Nathan: "Randbemerkungen zu Lausanne", *Zeitschrift für systematische Theologie*, pp. 538–98, Gütersloh, 1928.

"Pater Max Pribilla und die ökumenische Bewegung", *Kyrkohistorisk Årsskrift*, 1931, Uppsala, 1931.

Soper, Edmund D.: *Lausanne: the Will to Understand*, New York, 1928.

Steady, Leo J.: *Intercommunion in the Faith and Order Movement 1927–1952*, Ottawa, 1964.

Tomkins, Oliver S.: *The Wholeness of the Church*, London, 1949.

The Church in the Purpose of God. Faith and Order Commission Papers, No. 3, London, 1950, and New York, 1951.

Vischer, Lukas (ed.): *A documentary history of the Faith and Order Movement 1927–1963*, St Louis, 1963.

Woods, E. S.: *Moving towards Unity*, London, 1936. (A brief history of the Faith and Order Movement.)

CHAPTER 10

I. GENERAL WORKS

The Lambeth Conferences 1867–1948, London, 1948: 1920, pp. 119–41; 1930, pp. 214–44; Appendix (1867–98), pp. 296–303; 1948, pp. 41–80. *Lambeth Conference 1958*, London, 1958, pp. 66 and 171.

Bell, G. K. A.: *Documents on Christian Unity, First Series, 1920–4*, London, 1924; *Second Series*, London, 1930; *Third Series, 1930–48*, London, 1948; *Fourth Series, 1948–57*, London, 1958.

Douglass, H. Paul: *A Decade of objective Progress in Church Unity, 1927–1936*, New York and London, 1937.

Hooker, Elizabeth R.: *United Churches*, New York, 1926.

Neill, Stephen: *Towards Church Union, 1937–1952*, London, 1952.

II. On Individual Schemes of Union

The ebb and flow of Church Union discussions can be followed only in pamphlets and periodicals, far too numerous to mention. *Christendom* and *Die internationale Kirchliche Zeitschrift* will be found invaluable, except when very detailed information is required.

Australia

Australia and Reunion, Sydney, 1922. (Contains full reports of the conferences and discussions to date.)

Batty, F. de Witt: *The Australian Proposals for Intercommunion*, London, 1948.

Canada

Chown, S. D.: *The Story of Church Union in Canada*, Toronto, 1930.

Dow, John: *This is our faith: an exposition of the statement of faith of the United Church of Canada*, Toronto, 1943.

File, Edgar F.: *A sociological Analysis of Church Union in Canada*, Boston, 1962.

Morrow, E. Ll.: *Church Union in Canada*, Toronto, 1923.

Pidgeon, George C.: *The United Church of Canada: the Story of the Union*, Toronto, 1950.

Schwarz, Edward Richard: *Samuel Dwight Chown: an Architect of Canadian Church Union*, Boston, 1961.

Scott, E.: *Church Union and the Presbyterian Church in Canada*, Toronto, n.d.

Silcox, Claris Edwin: *Church Union in Canada: its Causes and Consequences*, New York, 1933.

China

The China Mission Yearbook, Shanghai, 1910–1925, and *The China Christian Yearbook*, Shanghai, 1926–1939.

Let us unite: The Church of Christ in China: Church Unity in China and Church Mission Cooperation, Shanghai, 1938.

Japan

Baker, Richard Terrill: *Darkness of the Sun: the Story of Christianity in the Japanese Empire*, Nashville, 1947.

Church Assembly: *The Church in post-war Japan: Report of the Anglican Commission to Nippon Sei Ko kwai* (Anglican Church in Japan), London, 1947.

Iglehart, Charles W.: *A Century of Protestant Christianity in Japan*, Ruthland, Vermont, and Tokyo, 1959.

The Japan Christian Year Book 1951, Tokyo, 1951.

Significant Documents of the United Church of Christ in Japan, Indianapolis, 1956.

North India

The Plan of Church Union in North India and Pakistan, prepared by the Negotiating Committee for Church Union in North India and Pakistan, Madras, 1951; 2nd ed., 1953; 3rd ed., 1957.

South India

Proposed Scheme of Union including Draft Basis . . . , *prepared by the Joint Committee of the Church of India, Burma and Ceylon, the South India United Church, and the South India Provincial Synod of the Methodist Church*; 7th ed., Madras, 1943.

Arangaden, A. J.: *Church Union in South India: its Progress and Consummation*; 2nd ed., Mangalore, 1947.

Haselmayer, Louis A.: *The Church of South India: its Relationship to the Anglican Communion*, New York, 1948.

Hodgson, Leonard: *Anglicanism and South India*, Cambridge, 1943.

Horsley, Cecil Douglas: *Some Problems connected with the proposed Scheme of Church Union in South India*, London, 1942.

Jalland, T. G.: *The Bible, the Church, and South India*, London, 1944.

Neill, Stephen: *Towards a United Church, 1913–1947*, London, 1947.

Christian Partnership, London, 1952.

Newbigin, J. E. Lesslie: *The Reunion of the Church: a Defence of the South India Scheme*, London, 1948; 2nd rev. ed., London, 1960.

Noble, Walter James: *Christian Union in South India: an Adventure in Fellowship*, London, 1936.

Paul, Rajaiah D.: *The first Decade: an Account of the Church of South India*, Madras, 1958.

Rawlinson, A. E. J.: *The Church of South India*, London, 1951.

Sundkler, Bengt: *Church of South India: the Movement towards Union 1900–1947*, London, 1954.

Waller, E. H. M.: *Church Union in South India: the Story of the Negotiations*, London, 1929.

Willis, J. J., Arthur, J. W., Neill, Stephen, and others: *Towards a United Church 1913–1949*, London, 1947.

Ceylon

Proposed Scheme of Church Union in Ceylon prepared by the Negotiating Committee for Church Union in Ceylon . . . , Madras and Colombo, 1949; 2nd rev. ed., Madras and Colombo, 1953; 3rd rev. ed., Madras, 1955.

The Scheme for Church Union in Ceylon: being the Report of a Committee of Theologians appointed by the Archbishop of Canterbury, London, 1951.

Niles, D. T.: *The Temple of Christ in Ceylon, being an Exposition of the Ceylon Scheme of Church Union*, London, 1948.

England

The Lambeth Conferences 1867–1948, London, 1948; see p. 787 of this book.

The Lambeth Conference 1958, London, 1958, pp. 66 and 171.

Outline of a Reunion Scheme for the Church of England and the Evangelical Free Churches of England, London, 1938.

Church Relations in England: being the Report of Conversations between Representatives of the Archbishop of Canterbury and Representatives of the Evangelical Free Churches in England, London, 1950.

Bell, G. K. A.: *Christian Unity: the Anglican Position*, London, 1948.

Documents on Christian Unity, First Series, 1920–4, London, 1924; *Second Series*, London, 1930; *Third Series, 1930–48*, London, 1948; *Fourth Series, 1948–57*, London, 1958.

Gorton, Neville: *The Anglican Church and Christian Unity*, New York, 1948.
Nelson, Horatio, Earl: *Home Reunion*, London, 1905.
Talbot, N. S.: *Thoughts on Unity*, London, 1920.
Turberville, A. C.: *Steps towards Christian Unity*, London, 1902.
Wordsworth, Charles: *A United Church of England, Scotland and Ireland Advocated: a Discourse on the Scottish Reformation to which are added Proofs and Illustrations, designed to form a Manual of Reformation Facts and Principles*, Edinburgh, 1861.

Scotland

Reports of the Joint Committee on Church Union in Scotland, Edinburgh, 1909–29.

The Church of Scotland and Presbyterian Reunion: Report of the General Assembly's Committee together with Memorandum and the Speech of the Moderator in presenting the Report to the General Assembly, 27th May, 1913, Edinburgh, 1913.

Fleming, J. R.: *The Story of the Church Union in Scotland: its Origins and Progress, 1560–1929*, London, 1929.

Macgregor, J.: *Reunion of the Scottish Churches on the Lines of the Reformation*, Edinburgh, 1891.

Martin, A.: *Church Union in Scotland: the first Phase*, Edinburgh, 1923.

Warr, Charles L.: *The Presbyterian Tradition: a Scottish layman's handbook*, London, 1933.

France

Actes de l'Assemblée constituante de l'Église Réformée de France, tenue à Lyon du 25 au 29 avril 1938, Paris, 1938.

Germany

Hermelink, Heinrich: *Kirche im Kampf: Dokumente des Widerstands und des Aufbaus in der Evangelischen Kirche Deutschlands, von 1933 bis 1945*, Tübingen and Stuttgart, 1950.

Herman, Stewart: *The Rebirth of the German Church*, London and New York, 1946.

Kirchliches Jahrbuch, 1933–1944, Gütersloh, 1948–50.

Kirchliches Jahrbuch, 1945–1948, Gütersloh, 1950.

Northern Europe

The Relations of the Church of England and the Church of Finland: the Resolutions of the Convocations of the Church of England in 1935 and of the official Reply of the Archbishop of Finland to the Archbishop of Canterbury in 1936 (English, Finnish, and Swedish texts), Turku, 1948.

Williams, G. M.: *The Church of Sweden and the Anglican Communion*, Milwaukee, 1911.

Wordsworth, John: *The National Church of Sweden*, London, 1911.

United States of America (Congregational Christian and Evangelical and Reformed)

The Basis of Union of the Congregational Christian Churches and the Evangelical and Reformed Church, 1947; with *The Interpretations* added, 1949.

Christy, Wayne H.: *The United Presbyterian Church and Church Union*, Pittsburgh, 1947.

Douglass, H. P.: *Protestant Cooperation in American Cities*, New York, 1930.

Kenyon, Helen: *Cadman Memorial Congregational Society of Brooklyn and the Cadman Memorial Church suing* . . ., [*as*] *plaintiffs-respondents, against Helen Kenyon, as Moderator of the General Council of the Congregational Christian Churches of the U.S., defendant-appellant: Case on appeal*, New York, 1949.

United States of America (*Methodist*)

Garber, Paul Neff: *The Methodists are one People*, Nashville, 1939.

McElreath, Walter; *Methodist Union in the Courts*, Nashville, 1946.

Moore, John M.: *The long Road to Methodist Union*, New York, 1943.

Mott, John R.: *Methodists united for Action*, Nashville, 1939.

Sweet, William Warren: *Methodist Unification*, in *American Culture and Religion*, Dallas, 1951.

The Old Catholic Churches

Die Altkatholische Kirche in *Ekklesia*, Vol. III. 11. Gotha, 1935. p. 151.

Andrews, Theodore: *The Polish National Catholic Church in America and Poland*, London, 1953.

Gauthier, Léon: "Pour le 25e anniversaire de l'intercommunion anglicane et vieille-catholique", *Internationale Kirchliche Zeitschrift*, Berne, 1956.

Lagerwey, E.: *De Oudkatholieke Kerk van Nederland: haar leer en leven*, Amsterdam, 1951.

Moss, C. B.: *The Old Catholic Movement, its Origins and History*, London, 1948; 2nd ed., London, 1964.

Schmidt, Kurt Dietrich: *Die Bekenntnisse und grundsätzlichen Äusserungen zur Kirchenfrage*, 3 vols., Göttingen, 1933–36.

Orthodox Churches

Actes de la conférences des chefs et des représentants des Églises orthodoxes autocéphales . . . Mouscou, 8–18 juillet 1948, 2 vols., Moscow, 1950–52.

Bratsiotis, P.: 'Ορθόδοξοι καὶ 'Αγγλικανοί, *1918–1930*, Athens, 1931.

Hardy, E. R., jr. (ed.): *Orthodox Statements on Anglican Orders*, New York and London, 1946.

Conclusion

Report of the Third World Conference on Faith and Order, Lund, Sweden, August 15–28, 1952, London, 1952.

Tomkins, Oliver S. (ed.): *The Third World Conference on Faith and Order held at Lund, August 15th to 28th, 1952*, London, 1953.

CHAPTERS 11 AND 12

I. PERIODICALS

See in General Bibliography especially *Le Christianisme Social: Die Eiche, Kristen Gemenskap*, and *Stockholm*; and add

The Churches in Action: News Letter of the Universal Christian Council for Life and Work and the World Alliance for International Friendship through the Churches. Quarterly. Geneva, 1931–38. (Also French and German edd.)

Life and Work: Bulletin of the International Social Institute. Occasional. Geneva, 1927–30. (Also French and German edd.)

II. PUBLICATIONS OF LIFE AND WORK

(in chronological order)

The Universal Council for Life and Work: Minutes and Reports, 1920–1938.

Keller, Adolf: *Die Kirche und die soziale Arbeit,* Zürich, 1927.

Temple, William: *Christianity and the State,* London, 1928.

Bell, G. K. A., and Deissmann, Adolf (ed.): *Mysterium Christi: Christologische Studien britischer und deutscher Theologen;* Eng. tr., *Mysterium Christi: Christological Studies by British and German Theologians,* London, 1930.

The Churches and Present-day Economic Problems, Conference of Christian social workers, London, 1930.

Kirche, Bekenntnis, und Sozialethos; die sozialethische Grundhaltung des Urchristentums, der orthodoxen Kirche, des Altkatholizismus, des Luthertums, des Calvinismus, und des Anglikanismus. Geneva, 1934.

Die Kirche und das Staatsproblem in der Gegenwart, 2nd enlarged ed., Geneva, 1935.

Kirche, Staat, und Mensch: Russisch-orthodoxe Studien, Geneva, 1937.

Totaler Staat und christlicher Freiheit (a symposium), Geneva, 1937.

III. PUBLICATIONS OF THE WORLD ALLIANCE

(in chronological order)

World Alliance for Promoting International Friendship through the Churches: Minutes and Reports, 1914–1946.

World Alliance for Promoting International Friendship throughout the Churches: Handbooks, 1916–46.

Felce, W.: *The War of Freedom and the Unity of Christendom,* London, 1915.

Gulick, Sidney L., and Macfarland, Charles S. (ed.): *The Church and International Relations: Report of the Commission on Peace and Arbitration, I–IV,* New York, 1917.

Siegmund Schultze, F. (ed.): *Die Weltkirchenkonferenz von Prag: Gesamtbericht des Kongresses für Frieden und Freundschaft, gehalten vom 24. bis 30. August 1928,* Berlin-Steglitz, 1928.

White, John: *Reunion and international Friendship,* Oxford, 1930.

IV. C.O.P.E.C. PUBLICATIONS

C.O.P.E.C. Commission Reports (Conference on Christian Politics, Economics and Citizenship, at Birmingham, April 5–12, 1924), 12 vols., London, 1924–25.

Shillito, Edward: *Christian Citizenship: the Story and the Meaning of C.O.P.E.C.,* London, 1924.

Wood, H. G. (ed.): *C.O.P.E.C. Conference Handbook, Birmingham, 1924,* Birmingham, 1924.

V. Stockholm 1925 and its Echoes

In addition to General Bibliography, see:

Brent, Charles Henry: *Understanding: being an Interpretation of the Universal Christian Conference on Life and Work, held in Stockholm, August 15–30 1925*, London, 1926.

Deissmann, Adolf: *Die Stockholmer Bewegung: die Weltkirchenkonferenzen zu Stockholm 1925 und Bern 1926 von innen betrachtet*, Berlin, 1927.

Journet, Charles: *L'Union des Églises et le Christianisme pratiqué*, Paris, 1926.

Koechlin, Alphons: *Die Weltkonferenz für praktisches Christentum in Stockholm, 19. bis 30. August, 1925*, Basle, 1925.

Sandegren, Paul: *Life and Work: the Universal Christian Conference on Life and Work, held in Stockholm, 1925*, London, 1926.

Shillito, Edward: *Life and Work: the Universal Christian Conference on Life and Work held in Stockholm, 1925*, London, 1926.

Siegmund-Schultze, F.: *Die Weltkirchenkonferenz in Stockholm: Gesamt-Bericht über die Allgemeine Konferenz der Kirche Christi für praktisches Christentum*, Berlin, 1925.

Grundfragen zur Einigung der Kirche Christi: Deutsche Beiträge zur Allgemeinen Konferenz der Kirche Christi für Praktisches Christentum, by A. Schlatter, and others, Munich, 1925.

Söderblom, Nathan, *Christian Fellowship or The United Life and Work of Christendom*, New York, 1923.

Kristenhetens möte i Stockholm Augusti Nittonhundratjugufem: Historik, aktstycken, grundtankar, personligheter, eftermäle, Stockholm, 1926.

Christliche Einheit!, Berlin, 1928.

Wallau, René Heinrich: *Die Einigung der Kirche vom evangelischen Glaube aus*, Berlin, 1925.

VI. Oxford 1937 and its Echoes

In addition to General Bibliography, see:

Böhm, Hans (ed.): *Kirche, Volk und Staat: Bericht des ökumenischen Ausschusses der Vorläufigen Leitung der Deutschen Evangelischen Kirche*, Stuttgart, 1948.

Gerstenmaier, E. (ed.) *Kirche, Volk und Staat: Stimmen aus der deutschen evangelischen Kirche zu Oxforder Weltkirchenkonferenz*, Berlin, 1937.

Les grandes conférences oecuméniques d'Oxford et d'Édimbourg, in *Christianisme social*, Sept.–Dec., 1937.

Iseland, Otto (ed.): *Die Kirche Christi: Grundfragen der Menschenbildung und Weltgestaltung*, Einsiedeln and Cologne, n.d.

Monnier, Henri: *Vers l'union des Églises: la conférence universelle de Stockholm*, Paris, 1926.

VII. Biographies

In addition to those listed in General Bibliography, see:

Ammundsen: *In Memoriam Bishop Valdemar Ammundsen, 1875–1936*, Geneva, 1937.

Baker: Baker, Elizabeth B., and Baker, J. P. Noel: *J. Allen Baker, M.P.: a Memoir*, London, 1927.

Söderblom: Brilioth, Yngve: *A biographical Introduction*, in Nathan Söderblom, *The Living God*, Oxford, 1933.

Nystedt, Olle: *Nathan Söderblom: ein Lebensbild*, Berlin, 1932.
Temple: MacConomy, Edward N.: *The Political Thought of William Temple*, Michigan, 1962.

VIII. STUDIES OF PARTICULAR SUBJECTS

Abrams, Ray H.: *Preachers present Arms: a study of the war-time Attitudes and Activities of the Churches and the Clergy in the United States, 1914–18*, Philadelphia, 1933.
Brown, William Adams: *Church and State in Contemporary America*, New York, 1936.
Toward a United Church: three Decades of Ecumenical Christianity, New York, 1946.
Cole, Patricia Ann: *The Function of the Church as Critic of Society exemplified in the Area of United States International Policy*, Boston, 1963. (Includes an extensive discussion of ecumenical materials.)
Cavert, Samuel McCrea, and Van Dusen, Henry Pitney (eds.): *The Church through Half a Century: Essays in Honor of William Adams Brown*, New York, 1936.
Committee on the War and Religious Outlook: *Christian Unity: its Principles and Possibilities*, New York, 1921.
Deissmann, Adolf: *Una Sancta: zum Geleit in das ökumenische Jahr 1937*, Gütersloh, 1936.
Douglass, H. P.: *A Study of Cooperative Church Extension in American Cities*, Garden City, 1929.
Horton, Walter Marshall: *Toward a Reborn Church: a Review and Forecast of the Ecumenical Movement*, New York, 1949.
Hutchison, John A.: *We are not divided: a Critical and Historical Study of the Federal Council of Churches of Christ in America*, New York, 1941.
Karlström, Nils: *Kristna samförståndssträvanden under världskriget 1914–1918, mer särskild hänsyn till Nathan Söderbloms insats*, Stockholm, 1947.
Keller, Adolf: *Dynamis: Formen und Kräfte des amerikanischen Protestantismus*, Tübingen, 1922.
Zur Lage des europäischen Protestantismus: Übersicht über Notstände und Hilfswerke im Gebiet der europäischen evangelischen Kirchen, Zürich, 1922.
Die Kirchen und der Friede mit besonderer Berücksichtigung ihrer Stellung zum Völkerbund, Zürich, 1927.
Karl Barth and Christian Unity: the Influence of the Barthian Movement upon the Churches of the World, London, n.d. Eng. tr. from, *Der Weg der dialektischen Theologie durch die kirchliche Welt*, Munich, 1931.
Church and State on the European Continent, London, 1936.
Keller, Adolf, and Stewart, George: *Protestant Europe: its Crisis and Outlook*, London, 1927.
Kelly, H. H.: *The Church and Religious Unity*, London, 1913.
Latourette, Kenneth Scott (ed.): *The Gospel, the Church, and the World*, New York, 1946.
Lee, Robert: *Social Sources of Ecumenicity: an Interpretation of the Social History of the Church Unity Movement in American Protestantism*, New York, 1958.

Macfarland, Charles S.: *International Christian Movements*, New York and Chicago, 1924.

Christian Unity in Practice and Prophecy, New York, 1933.

Steps toward the World Council: origins of the Ecumenical Movement as Expressed in the Universal Christian Council for Life and Work, New York, 1938.

Pioneers for Peace through Religion, based on the Records of the Church Peace Union, 1914–1945, New York, 1946.

En marche vers l'unité chrétienne: aperçu de l'histoire, des principes et des expériences actuelles du mouvement oecuménique, in *Christianisme social*, Jan.–Feb., 1937.

Martin, H.: *Christian Reunion: a Plea for Action*, London, 1941.

Miller, Randolph C.: *The Church and organized Movements*, New York, 1946.

The Significance of the Barmen Declaration for the Oecumenical Church, "Theology" Occasional Papers, New Series, No. 59, London, 1943.

Temple, William: *Christianity and the social order*, Harmondsworth, 1942; 3rd ed., London, 1950.

Van Kirk, Walter William: *Religion renounces War*, Chicago, 1934.

CHAPTER 13

Much of the material of this chapter has been gathered from periodicals, minutes of committees, and specially written memoranda. As many different subjects are covered in this chapter, no attempt has been made to compile a bibliography.

The student is recommended to pay special attention to the Histories and periodicals of such bodies as the W.S.C.F., the Y.M.C.A. and the Y.W.C.A.; and to consult further the General Bibliography which refers to some of the appropriate sources of information.

CHAPTER 14

I. PERIODICALS

Much of the material for further study must be sought in periodicals, especially:

Ekklesia (modern Greek, published in Athens).

Put ("The Way", Russian, published in Paris).

Those who do not know these languages are recommended to study especially:

Christian East, The.

Eastern Churches Quarterly, The.

Ecumenical Review, The.

Irénikon.

Internationale Kirchliche Zeitschrift, Die.

Sobornost.

(For details, see General Bibliography, p. 752.)

II. THE GREAT CONFERENCES

Orthodox contributions of great value are to be found in the Reports and the preparatory volumes for most of these Conferences. (Details in General

Bibliography.) See especially the three preparatory volumes for Lund 1952: *Intercommunion. The Report of the Theological Commission.* Ed. Donald Baillie and John Marsh, London, 1952.

The Nature of the Church. Papers Presented to the Theological Commission . . . of . . . Faith and Order. Ed. R. Newton Flew, London, 1952.

Ways of Worship. Report of a Theological Commission of Faith and Order. Ed. Pehr Edwall, Eric Hayman, William D. Maxwell, London, 1951.

Gregg, John A. F.: "One, Holy, Catholic, Apostolic Church", in *The Universal Church in God's Design*, Amsterdam Assembly Series, Vol. 1, London, 1948, pp. 59–66.

III. SOURCE-BOOKS

Two basic and authoritative source-books are:

Actes de la conférence des chefs et des représentants des Églises orthodoxes autocéphales . . . Mouscou 8–18 juillet 1948, 2 vols., Moscow, 1950–52.

Major Portions of the Proceedings of the Conference of Heads and Representatives of the Autocephalous Orthodox Churches, Moscow, 8–18 July 1948, Paris, 1952.

Procès-verbaux du premier congrès de théologie orthodoxe à Athènes, 29 nov.–6 déc. 1936, Athens, 1939.

Tyciak, Julius: *Die Union mit den Ostkirchen; Bericht über die Wiener Unionstagung . . . 1926*, Leipzig, 1928.

IV. SPECIAL STUDIES OF ORTHODOXY AND ECUMENISM

Albert, Frank J.: *A Study of the Eastern Orthodox Church in the Ecumenical Movement*, Cambridge, Mass., 1964.

Arrighini, P. A.: *Ai nostri Fratelli separati*, Turin, 1937.

Arseniev, N.: *La sainte Moscou*, Paris, 1948.

Behr-Sigel, E.: *Prière et sainteté dans l'Église russe*, Paris, 1950.

Bousquet, J.: *L'unité de l'Église et le schisme grec*, Paris, 1913.

Benz, Ernst: *Die Ostkirche im Lichte der protestantischen Geschichtsschreibung von der Reformation bis zur Gegenwart*, Freiburg i. Br. and Munich, 1952.

(ed.): *Die Ostkirche und die russische Christenheit*, Tübingen, 1949.

Benz, Ernst, and Zander, L. A. (eds.): *Evangelisches und Orthodoxes Christentum in Begegnung und Auseinandersetzung*, Hamburg, 1952.

Bulgakov, Sergius: *The Orthodox Church*, London, 1935.

Crivelli, C.: *Protestanti e cristiani orientali*, Rome, 1944.

Fedotov, G.: *The Russian Religious Mind*, Cambridge, Mass., 1946.

Fortescue, A.: *The Uniate Eastern Churches*, London, 1923.

French, R.: *The Eastern Orthodox Church*, London, 1951.

Glubokovsky, N., and others: *Den ortodoxa kristenheten och kyrkans enhet*, Stockholm, 1921.

Gulovich, Stephan: *Windows Westward; Rome, Russia, Reunion*, New York, 1947.

Heiler, Friedrich: *Urkirche und Ostkirche: die katholische Kirche des Ostens und des Westens*, Vol. 1, Munich, 1937.

Herbigny, Michel d': *L'anglicanisme et l'orthodoxie gréco-slave*, Paris, 1922.

Karmiris, J.: *The Orthodox Catholic Church and her Relations with the other Churches and with the World Council of Churches*, Geneva, 1949.

Makrakis, A.: *Orthodox-Protestant Debate*, Chicago, 1949.

Malatakis, M.: *Réponse à la Lettre patriarcale et synodale de l'Église de Constantinople sur les divergences qui divisent le deux Églises*, Constantinople, 1896.

Mascall, E. L. (ed.): *The Church of God: an Anglo-Russian Symposium*, London, 1934.

Michel, P.: *L'Orient et Rome: Étude sur l'Union*, Saint-Amand, 1895.

Neander, Hermann: *Orientens kyrkor och den ekumeniska tanken*, Stockholm, 1926.

Prezdziecki, H.: *L'oeuvre de l'union en Pologne*, Warsaw, n.d.

Quénet, Ch.: *L'unité de l'Église. Les Églises séparées d'orient et la réunion des Églises*, Paris, 1923.

Seraphim, Metropolitan: *Die Ostkirche*, Stuttgart, 1950.

Swietlinski, C.: *La conception sociologique de l'oecuménisme dans la pensée religieuse russe contemporaine*, Paris, 1939.

Tondini da Quarenghi, C.: *La Russie et l'Union des Églises*, Paris, 1897.

Tournebize, F.: *L'Église greque orthodoxe et l'union*, Paris, 1901.

Visser 't Hooft, W. A.: *Anglo-Catholicism and Orthodoxy: a Protestant View*, London, 1933.

Zander, L. A.: *The Essence of the Ecumenical Movement*, Geneva, 1937.

Vision and Action. Eng. tr. (from the Russian), London, 1952.

Zankow, Stefan: *Das orthodoxe Christentum des Ostens, sein Wesen, und seine gegenwärtige Gestalt*, Berlin, 1928.

Die orthodoxe Kirche des Osten in ökumenischer Sicht, Zürich, 1946.

Zernov, Nicolas: *The Church of the Eastern Christians*, London, 1942.

The Reintegration of the Church: a Study in Intercommunion, London, 1952.

The Christian East: the Eastern Orthodox Church and Indian Christianity, Delhi, 1956.

Eastern Christendom: a Study of the Origin and Development of the Eastern Orthodox Church, London, 1961.

Orthodox Encounter: the Christian East and the Ecumenical Movement, London, 1961.

The Russian Religious Renaissance of the twentieth century, London, 1963.

CHAPTER 15

In the General Bibliography, see especially:

Bell, G. K. A.: *Documents on Christian Unity*, 2nd and 3rd Series, and under periodicals:

Eastern Churches Quarterly.

Herder Korrespondenz.

Irénikon.

Unitas.

Vers l'Unité chrétienne.

I. Official Documents

Ecclesia Catholica: an Instruction to local Ordinaries on the Ecumenical Movement, 20 Dec. 1949 in *Osservatore Romano*, 28 Feb. 1950. Eng. tr., *The Tablet*, 2 Sept. 1950.

Humani Generis: Encyciical of Pope Pius XII, 12 Aug. 1950. Eng. tr., *The Tablet,* 2 Sept. 1950.

Mortalium Animos: Encyclical of Pope Pius XI, 6 Jan. 1928. Eng. tr. with introduction by Cardinal Bourne, London, Catholic Truth Society, 1928.

Mystici Corporis Christi: Encyclical of Pope Pius XII, 29 June 1943. Eng. tr., London, Catholic Truth Society, 1943.

Orientalis Ecclesiae: Encyclical of Pope Pius XII, 9 April 1944. Eng. tr., London, Catholic Truth Society, 1944.

II. SERIES OF ECUMENICAL WRITINGS

"Chrétiens devant l'oecuménisme", *Catholicité,* fasc. 8–10, juillet 1947, Lille, 1947.

Bivort de la Saudée, Jacques de: *Anglicans et catholiques,* 2 vols., Paris, 1949.

Ronds-Points (Paris and Lyons):
    Le Christ, réconciliateur des chrétiens, 1950.
    Dialogue sur la Vierge (by Roman Catholic and Protestant writers), 1950.

III. INDIVIDUAL WORKS

Adam, K.: *Vers l'unité chrétienne du point de vue catholique,* Paris, 1946.
    One and Holy, New York, 1951. (An approach to Lutheran-Catholic accord in Germany.)

Algermissen, Konrad: *Christian Denominations,* St Louis, 1945.

Attwater, Donald: *The Christian Churches of the East:* Vol. I, *Churches in communion with Rome,* and Vol. II, *Churches not in communion with Rome,* Milwaukee, 1961–62.

Aubert, R.: *Le Saint Siège et l'union des Églises,* Brussels, 1947.

Bain, John A.: *The New Reformation: recent Evangelical Movements in the Roman Catholic Church,* Edinburgh, 1906.

Baronchelli, Dom Manfredo: *Ecumenismo cattolico: Commento all'ottava per l'unità,* Bergamo, 1947.

Bauhofer, Oskar: *Einheit im Glauben: von göttlicher Ordnung und menschlicher Not,* Einsiedeln, 1935.

Baum, Gregory: *That they may be one: a Study of papal doctrine (Leo XIII– Pius XII),* London, 1958.

Berkouwer, Gerrit C.: *Conflict met Rome,* Kampen, 1948. Eng. tr. (from the Dutch), *The Conflict with Rome,* Philadelphia, 1958.

Boyer, Charles: *Unus Pastor,* Rome, 1948. Eng. tr. (from the French), *One Shepherd: the Problem of Christian Reunion,* New York, 1952.

Casper, J.: *Um die Einheit der Kirche,* Vienna, 1940.

Congar, Yves M. J.: *Chrétiens désunis,* Paris, 1937. Eng. tr., *Divided Christendom: a Catholic Study of the Problem of Reunion,* London, 1939.
    Vraie et fausse réforme dans l'Église, Paris, 1950.
    1054–1954: L'Église et les Églises, neuf siècles de douloureuse séparation entre l'orient et l'occident; études et travaux sur l'unité chrétienne offerts à Dom Lambert Beauduin, 2 vols., Paris, 1954. Eng. tr., *After Nine Hundred Years,* Fordham, N.Y., 1959.
    Chrétiens en dialogue: Contributions catholiques à l'oecuménisme, Paris, 1964.

Crivelli, C.: *Protestanti e cristiani orientali,* Rome, 1944.

Duggan, J.: *Steps towards Reunion,* London, 1937.

Dumont, C.-J.: *Les voies de l'unité chrétienne*, Paris, 1954.

Griffin, Bernard W.: *The Catholic Church and Reunion*, London, 1950.

Hanahoe, Edward F.: *Catholic Ecumenism: the Reunion of Christendom in contemporary papal Pronouncements*, Washington, 1953.

Jones, Spencer: *L'Église d'Angleterre et le Saint Siège: propos sur la réunion*, Grenoble, 1941. (Written specially for French readers and not to be confused with *England and the Holy See: an Essay towards Reunion*, 1902, by the same author.)

Journet, Charles: *L'union des Églises et le christianisme pratiqué*, Paris, 1927.

Koncevicius, J. B.: *Russia's Attitude towards Union with Rome (9th–16th centuries)*, Washington, 1927.

Krczmar, K.: *Rom und der Ruf zur Einheit*, Vienna, 1929.

Krebs, E.: *Die Protestanten und wir : Einigendes und Trennendes*, Munich, 1922.

Lambinet, Ludwig: *Das Wesen des katholisch-protestantischen Gegensatzes*, Einsiedeln and Cologne, 1946.

Leiper, Henry Smith: *Relations between the Ecumenical Movement and the Vatican in the twentieth century*. (Mimeographed) New York, n.d.

Leenhardt, Franz J.: *L'Église et le royaume de Dieu: réflexions sur l'unité de l'Église et sur le salut des non-Catholiques*, Geneva, 1942.

Linde, H. van der: *Rome en de Una Sancta: het oecumenisch Vraagstuk en de Arbeid van Rome voor de Hereniging der Kerken*, Nijkerk, 1947; 2nd ed., 1948.

Lortz, J.: *Die Reformation als religiöses Anliegen heute: vier Vorträge im Dienste der Una Sancta*, Trier, 1948.

Messenger, E. C. (ed.): *Rome and Reunion: a Collection of papal Pronouncements*, London, 1934.

Ohlemüller, G. (ed.): *Amtliche römisch-katholische Kundgebungen zur Einigungsfrage der christlichen Kirchen*, Berlin, 1928.

Kritische Stimmen zum päpstlichen Rundschreiben über die Einigungsfrage der Kirchen, Berlin, 1928.

Pfeilschifter, G.: *Die kirchlichen Wiedervereinigungsbetrebungen der Nachkriegszeit*, Munich, 1923.

Pol, W. H. van de: *Het christelijk Dilemma*. Eng. tr. (from the Dutch), *The Christian Dilemma: Catholic Church—Reformation*, London, 1952.

Pribilla, Max: *Um die Wiedervereinigung im Glauben*, Freiburg i. Br., 1926.

Um kirchliche Einheit: Stockholm—Lausanne—Rom. Geschichtlich-theologische Darstellung der neueren Einigungsbetrebungen, Freiburg i. Br., 1929.

Rademacher, A.: *Der religiöse Sinn unserer Zeit und der ökumenische Gedanke*, Bonn, 1939.

Die innere Einheit des Glaubens: ein theologisches Prolegomenon zur Frage der Kirchenunion, Bonn, 1937.

Die Wiedervereinigung christlichen Kirchen, Bonn, 1937.

Ramsey, Michael: *The Gospel and the Catholic Church*, London, 1936; 2nd ed., 1956.

Reinkens, J. H.: *Über die Einheit der katholischen Kirche*, Würzburg, 1877.

St John, Henry: *Essays in Christian Unity, 1928–1954*, London, 1955.

Sartory, Thomas: *Die ökumenische Bewegung und die Einheit der Kirche: ein Beitrag im Dienste einer ökumenischen Ekklesiologie*, Meitlingen, 1955.

Simon, Paul: *Wiedervereinigung im Glauben*, Paderborn, 1925.

Zum Gespräch zwischen den Konfessionen, Munich, n.d.

Skydsgaard, Kristen-Ejnar: "The Roman Catholic Church and the Ecumenical Movement", with "Comments by a Roman Catholic Writer", in *The Universal Church in God's Design*, Amsterdam Assembly Series, Vol. 1, London, 1948.

Smit, Jan Olav: *Roma e l'Oriente cristiano: l'azione dei Papi per l'unità della Chiesa*, Rome, 1944.

Tavard, Georges: *À la rencontre du protestantisme*, Paris, 1951.

Thils, G.: *Histoire doctrinale du mouvement oecuménique*, Louvain, 1955.

Todd, John: *Catholicism and the Ecumenical Movement*, London, 1956.

Tromp, S.: *Corpus Christi quod est ecclesia*, Rome, 1946.

Tuechle, H. (ed.): *Die eine Kirche: zum Gedenken J. A. Möhlers, 1838–1938*, Paderborn, 1939.

Valeske, Ulrich: *Votum ecclesiae*. Part I: *Das Ringen um die Kirche in der neueren römisch-katholischen Theologie. Dargestellt auf dem Hintergrund der evangelischen und ökumenischen Parallelentwicklung*. Part II: *Interkonfessionelle ekklesiologische Bibliographie*, Munich, 1962.

Villain, Maurice: *L'abbé Paul Couturier, apôtre de l'unité chrétienne: souvenirs et documents*. Preface by A. Latreille; 3rd ed., Tournai and Paris, 1959.

Introduction à l'Oecuménisme; 3rd ed., Tournai, 1961. Eng. tr., *Unity: a History and some reflexions*, London, 1963; Baltimore, 1963.

Villain, M., and Clémence, J.: *Pour l'unité chrétienne*, 2 vols., Grenoble, 1943.

CHAPTER 16

Full records of the first Assembly of the World Council of Churches, and of the processes of preparation which led up to it, are preserved at the library of the World Council, 150 Route de Ferney, Geneva, and are available for study.

Much of the history must be sought in periodicals, of which the most valuable for the purpose are:

Christendom.

Ecumenical Press Service, The.

and, for the latest period,

Ecumenical Review, The.

In addition to the official reports, biographies, and other books, listed in the General Bibliography, the following are essential, or specially valuable, aids to further study:

I. OFFICIAL PUBLICATIONS

Visser 't Hooft, W. A. (ed.): *The First Assembly of the World Council of Churches held at Amsterdam, August 22nd to September 4th 1948*, Amsterdam Assembly Series, Vol. 5, London, 1948.

The Ten Formative Years, 1938–1948: Report on the Activities of the World Council of Churches during its Period of Formation, Geneva, 1948.

The Provisional Committee of the World Council of Churches: *The World Council of Churches, its Process of Formation: Minutes and Reports . . . Geneva from February 21st to 23rd, 1946 . . .*, ed. W. A. Visser 't Hooft, Geneva, 1946.

World Council of Churches. Minutes and Reports of the Meeting of the Provisional Committee . . . Buck Hill Falls, Penn., April 1947, Geneva, n.d.
The Central Committee of the World Council of Churches:
Minutes and Reports of the Second Meeting . . . Chichester (England), July 9–15, 1949, Geneva, n.d.
Minutes and Reports of the Third Meeting . . . Toronto (Canada), July 9–15, 1950, Geneva, n.d.
Minutes and Reports of the Fourth Meeting . . . Rolle (Switzerland), August 4–11, 1951, Geneva, n.d.
Minutes and Reports of the Fifth Meeting. . . . Lucknow (India), December 31, 1952–January 8, 1953, Geneva, n.d.

II. OTHER WORKS

Barth, Karl, Daniélou, J., and Niebuhr, R.: *Amsterdamer Fragen und Antworten*, Munich, 1949.
Beard, O. J.: *On the Road to Amsterdam*, London, 1948.
Bell, G. K. A.: *Christianity and World Order*, Harmondsworth, 1940.
The Kingship of Christ: the Story of the World Council of Churches, Harmondsworth 1954.
Boegner, Marc: *Le problème de l'unité chrétienne*, Paris, 1946.
Böhme, Kurt: *Die Weltkirchenkonferenz in Amsterdam*, Hamburg, 1948.
Brash, Alan A.: *Amsterdam 1948*, Christchurch, N.Z., n.d.
Brown, William Adams: *Toward a United Church*, New York, 1946.
Craig, C. T.: *The One Church in the Light of the New Testament*, New York, 1951.
Fueter, Karl: *Die Oekumene, gestern, heute, und morgen*, Zürich, 1947.
Goodall, Norman: *The Ecumenical Movement; what it is and what it does*, New York, 1964.
Herklots, H. G. G., and Leiper, Henry Smith: *Pilgrimage to Amsterdam*, New York, 1947.
Iremonger, F. A.: *William Temple, Archbishop of Canterbury: his Life and Letters*, London, 1948. (Esp. ch. XXIV, *The Oecumenical Movement*.)
Leiper, Henry Smith (ed.): *Christianity Today: a Survey of the State of the Churches*, New York, 1947.
Linde, H. van der: *De eerste steen gelegd. De eerste Assemblée van de Wereldraad van Kerken te Amsterdam*, Amsterdam, 1949.
Mascall, E. L.: *The Recovery of Unity: a theological Approach*, London, 1959.
Menn, Wilhelm: *Die ökumenische Bewegung, 1932–1948*, Gütersloh, 1949.
(ed.): *Die Ordnung Gottes und die Unordnung der Welt: Deutsche Beiträge zum Amsterdamer ökumenischen Gespräch 1948*, Tübingen, 1948.
Mönnich, C. W.: *Jezus Christus, God en Heiland. Proeve ener vrijzinnige beschouwing over de basis-formule van de Wereldraad der Kerken*, Utrecht, 1948.
Van Dusen, Henry Pitney: *What is the Church Doing?* London, 1943.
Walker, Alan: *World Encounter: to Amsterdam and beyond*, London, 1949.
Winterhanger, Jürgen W.: *Der Weltrat der Kirchen: sein Ziel und sein Problematik dargestellt an den Vorgängen und Folgen von Amsterdam*, Berlin, 1949.

GLOSSARY AND EXPLANATORY NOTES

Bishop (Episcopos). Most scholars would agree that in the New Testament no distinction can be made out between the words *episcopos* and *presbyteros*. But, from a period not later than the middle of the 2nd century, the term was restricted to the single head of a diocese; and from at latest the 4th century it became the custom that a new bishop should be consecrated by not less than three bishops, no one but a bishop having the power or authority to consecrate a bishop. But at the Reformation a number of regional Churches departed from this tradition, some among them (e.g. Denmark) retaining the title "bishop" for Church leaders, who had not been consecrated by bishops. This History simply follows the usage of each Church, without committing itself as to the greater or less legitimacy of the various uses. (See also Presbyter, Episcopacy.)

Bishops' War. The war between England and Scotland in 1639, precipitated by the desire of Charles I to enforce Anglican observances in Scotland, and by the determination of the Scots to abolish episcopacy.

Black Rubric. The Rubric (liturgical instruction), at the end of the Anglican Order of Holy Communion, on the nature of the presence of Christ in the Eucharist. This was inserted in the Prayer Book of 1552 by the King's Council, without consultation with the Church, and is not strictly part of the Prayer Book. For this reason, it was printed in black letters, to distinguish it from the Church rubrics, which were printed in red.

Calixtines. The name given to the more conservative among the followers of John Hus (d. 1415), in contrast to the more extreme section, known as the Taborites. The word *calix* (from which their name is derived) = chalice; and their main emphasis was on the right of the laity to receive the Holy Communion in both kinds (*sub utraque*, whence the name Utraquists, by which they were also known).

Catholic—catholic. The word originally meant "universal", and when so used in this History is usually spelt with a small initial letter. From the 3rd century onwards, however, the word came to be used rather with the significance of "orthodox, holding the full truth of the Christian faith"; this sense is here generally indicated by the use of a capital initial letter. Some writers use the word incorrectly as the antithesis of "Protestant"; this use is as far as possible avoided in this History. Others use it to denote those Churches which identify Faith and Order, and regard the hierarchical order of the Church as part of the revelation given by God himself; in this sense, the word is, in this History, generally printed in inverted commas. In a few contexts, generally in quotations from Roman Catholic writers, the word is used as equivalent to Roman Catholic.

Catholicos. A title used in some Lesser Eastern Churches, e.g. in the Armenian Church, for the head of a regional or national Church. In the Syrian Orthodox Church of South India, the Catholicos is the locally elected head; the refusal of the Patriarch of Antioch to approve this election was one of the causes which led to long-continued division within the Church.

Chrismation. A term used in the Orthodox Churches for the rite which in the West is generally known as Confirmation; since in the East this is administered not by the laying on of hands by the bishop, but by anointing with Chrism (holy oil specially consecrated at certain seasons by the Patriarch or other high ecclesiastical dignitary to whose office this responsibility attaches), a rite performed by a priest and not necessarily by a bishop.

Church—church.   In this History, the word "Church" is spelt with a capital (1) when it refers to the one Church of Jesus Christ, (2) when it refers to a Christian Communion which describes itself as a Church, (3) when it refers to a regional Church, such as the Church of Sweden. It is spelt with a small initial letter (1) when it refers to a church building, (2) when it refers to a local church body or congregation (*Gemeinde*), (3) usually when the word is used as an adjective; but we have retained the capital in some phrases, e.g. "Church union", since this is really a compendious expression for "union *between Churches*", and does not signify simply "ecclesiastical union".

Classic, classical.   The form of Church Organization in Classes (groups of Presbyteries) modelled on that of the Church of Geneva, which the Puritans in England in the reign of Queen Elizabeth I and King James I desired to introduce in the Church of England.

Coloured.   This term is used in the United States as equivalent to "Negro"; thus one of the Negro Churches is known as the Coloured Methodist Episcopal Church.
   In the Union of South Africa and some other areas, "Coloured" is used exclusively of those of mixed parentage, part European or Oriental, and part African.

Communion.   When referring to the Holy Communion, the word is generally printed with a capital; but with a small initial letter when referring to Church fellowship in the Sacrament between several Churches, or to fellowship in a more general Christian sense. The word is also used sometimes as equivalent to Church, group of Churches, or Confession; in these cases, it is printed with a small initial letter, except when it refers to one specific group of Churches—e.g. the Anglican Communion.

Communion, Occasional (Conformity, Occasional).   At a time when, in England, office under the Crown was open only to communicants of the Established Church, some non-conformists adopted the practice of receiving Holy Communion in the Church of England occasionally, and with a view to qualifying themselves for office. Others (see Chap. iii, pp. 150 f.) maintained the practice as a sign of spiritual fellowship with a Church which they respected, though their consciences would not permit them to become full members of it. In 1711, under Anglican High Church influences, the Occasional Conformity Act was passed in order to make the practice impossible; it was not, however, entirely brought to an end.

Conciliarist.   A supporter of that movement in the 15th century which desired to reform the Church through the operation of Councils, and by establishing the principle of the authority of a lawfully assembled Council of the whole Church as superior to that of the Pope.

Confessing Church.   The usual English translation for *Die bekennende Kirche*—the group within the German Evangelical Churches which, under the Hitler régime, from 1934 onwards, carried on the conflict against the attempts of the régime and the German Christian party to subvert the Churches by the introduction of ideas and practices contrary to the teaching of the New Testament, and of the Confessions on which those Churches were based.

Confession.   This word is not infrequently used as synonymous with "communion" to denote a Church, or a group of Churches, organized on the basis of the common profession of some one form of the Christian Faith. But it is also used of certain statements of the contents of the Christian Faith, officially accepted by some among the Churches. When the reference is to a specific Confession, e.g. the Augsburg Confession of 1530, the word is printed with a capital letter.

Consensus Quinquesaecularis. "The agreement of the five centuries"—the view, specially associated with the name of George Calixtus, that those doctrines and practices on which the Churches of the first five centuries were agreed might be taken as the basis for the reunion of the Churches in the post-Reformation period.

Covenants. A characteristic feature of Scottish Church life. The first was that of 1537: "to establish the most blessed word of God and his congregation", and to "forsake and renounce the congregation of Satan". This was renewed in 1581, and later in 1638, as an affirmation of the national will to continue in the Protestant profession, and to defend it against errors and corruptions. The most famous covenant was that of 1643, the Solemn League and Covenant, "to endeavour to bring the Church of God in the three kingdoms to the nearest possible uniformity and conjunction, and to aim at the extirpation of popery and prelacy, superstition, heresy, schism and profaneness". This Covenant was accepted by the Westminster Assembly of Divines on 25 September 1643.

Creeds, Ecumenical. The only strictly ecumenical Creed (in the sense of being used both liturgically and as a standard of doctrine by Orthodox, Roman Catholic, Old Catholic, Lesser Eastern, Anglican, and Protestant Churches) is the Nicene-Constantinopolitan Creed, commonly called the Nicene Creed. But since the Reformation, the three Creeds most widely used in the West—those commonly called the Apostles', the Nicene, and the Athanasian Creeds—have been known as the Ecumenical Creeds, and have sometimes been referred to as such in official documents of the Churches.

Crypto-Calvinists. The followers of Philip Melanchthon, also known as Philippists, who, in the period of acute Lutheran controversy in the second half of the 16th century, were accused of holding secretly Calvinistic views, especially on the Lord's Supper. At one time highly influential, they rapidly lost ground after the acceptance by many regional Churches of the Formula of Concord of 1577.

Cuius Regio Eius Religio (literally "Whose realm his religion"). The principle, first established by the Peace of Augsburg in 1555, according to which it was part of the prerogative of a sovereign ruler to lay down that within his territories his subjects might profess and practise only that form of the Christian faith which he himself professed and practised. There were comparatively few territories in which the principle was put into effect in full rigidity (for instance, the existence of the Jews was tolerated by many rulers); but vestiges of it have survived even into the 20th century.

Deacon. In all the Churches which have preserved unaltered the ancient Orders of bishops, priests, and deacons, the deacon is an ordained person, ranking next in dignity to the priest, and directly under the authority of the bishop. The great majority of deacons pass on to the priesthood, though in the Orthodox and Lesser Eastern Churches the permanent diaconate is a regular feature of Church life. In the Reformed Churches and some other Protestant Churches, the deacons are lay persons, set apart with greater or less solemnity to assist the ordained minister in the performance of some of the functions of his office. In this History, the context will show in every case which of these two meanings is to be assigned to the word.

Decretals; Decretals, False. A Decretal is a decree or official pronouncement of the Pope. The first Decretal generally accepted as genuine is that issued by Pope Siricius on 11 February 385. In the West, papal Decretals are recognized as among the sources of Canon Law; in the East, they have never been accepted as authoritative.

The False Decretals are a large collection, in which genuine and spurious documents are intermingled. It was produced somewhere in France during the 9th century, and was widely used throughout the Middle Ages in support of the papal claims. Its unauthentic character was conclusively demonstrated in the 15th century; this demonstration helped to shake confidence in the validity of the papal claims.

de fide. In the Roman Catholic Church, those doctrines which have been defined as belonging to the essential content of the Faith, and therefore necessary to be believed for eternal salvation; as contrasted with "pious opinion"—those areas in which, because no authoritative definition has been given, difference of opinion among theologians is permitted. The latest doctrine to be declared *de fide* was that of the corporal Assumption of the Blessed Virgin Mary (1951).

Diaspora. The Greek word means simply "that which is scattered". Used over a long period of the scattered groups of Jews living outside Palestine among non-Jewish populations, it has more recently come to be used of any ethnic or religious group living in isolation from the main body to which originally it belonged. The displacement of populations after the second world war has immensely increased the number of groups and areas to which the word can be not incorrectly applied.

Dissent, Dissenter. The classical term in English for those Protestants who do not adhere to the doctrine and discipline of the Church of England. In recent times, the old term has tended to be superseded by "Free Church, Free Churchman", which are felt to be less invidious terms. (See also Nonconformist.)

Ecclesiola in Ecclesia. "The little Church within the Church"—a typical expression of the Pietists, who had no wish to separate themselves from the Church to which they belonged or to form new sects; but believed that the way to the renewal of the Church was the gathering together within the Church of such kindred spirits as were prepared to seek a higher level of devotion and Christian holiness on the Pietist pattern.

Ecclesiology. English dictionaries define this word as "the science of churches, esp. of church building and decoration". In recent years, under the influence of the German *Ekklesiologie*, it has come to be used not infrequently in the sense of "that part of dogmatic theology which deals with the nature and existence of the Church"; or even more generally in the sense of "the doctrine of the Church". It seems likely that this use will come to establish itself in good English.

Economy. In the Orthodox Churches, dispensations from the strict requirements of Canonical order and practice are sometimes given, usually in situations where Christian charity or pastoral urgency recommend a deviation from the strict rule. These are made in accordance with the principle of Economy (Greek *oeconomia*: administration). But in no case does such action based on Economy affect the validity of the Canon or rule, which is still regarded as being fully in force, except for the particular modification provided for in the specific instance. A theological doctrine of Economy has never been worked out. For some of the principles involved, see Hamilcar S. Alivisatos in *Dispensation in Practice and Theory*, London, 1944, pp. 27–44.

Enthusiasm. The term "enthusiasm" was frequently used in 18th-century English to denote what would now be more generally termed "fanaticism"—the unrestrained indulgence in religious feeling, allegedly under the direct control of the Holy Spirit, and the disordered actions which sometimes follow upon such indulgence.

"Enthusiast", "Enthusiasm" are perhaps the best English equivalents for *Schwärmer* and *Schwärmerei*, words frequently used by Luther and others to designate the sectaries of the extreme left wing of the Protestant Reformation.

Episcopacy, Episcopal. Traditionally the words "Episcopacy" and "Episcopal" have been used only of those Churches whose bishops claim to be in the unbroken historic succession from the apostles; and in general this use is followed in this History. But since the Reformation many Christian communions (notably the Methodist Church in America) have had officers called bishops, though they make no claim to any historic connection with the episcopacy of the undivided Church. In almost every instance in this History, the term "Episcopal Churches" refers only to those Churches which claim to stand within the historic succession; the context will usually make it plain, where a wider reference is intended.

Erastianism. Commonly used as a general term for all views and doctrines which tend to uphold the supremacy of the State over the Church, or the right of the State to control or to direct the Church. From Erastus (1524–83), a Swiss theologian, who wrote in 1568 what became a famous tract, upholding the view that to punish the sins of professing Christians is the responsibility of magistrates, and not of pastors or elders.

Evangelical. The word means simply "belonging to the Gospel", "connected with the Gospel", or "conformable to the Gospel". But three quasi-technical uses will be found in this History: (1) On the Continent of Europe, the word is often used as exactly equivalent to Protestant in the sense of non-Roman Catholic. (2) In America it is sometimes used in the sense of orthodox, as contrasted with Unitarian. (3) In the Church of England, it is the name of that party which in some respects carries on the tradition of the old Low Church party. See Note on Party Terminology in the Church of England, p. 306. In many contexts, these special uses are distinguished by the use of an initial capital letter.

Evangelism, Evangelistic. The term now generally used to denote efforts to bring home the Gospel, or to make it real, to those who are unfamiliar with it. At an earlier date, the word "evangelical" was not infrequently used in this sense, especially in Scotland. But this use has been avoided in this History, because of the possibility of confusion with other uses of the word "evangelical" set out in the note above. (See Evangelical.)

Federation (Church), Federal Union. In ecclesiastical affairs, a federation of Churches is a co-operative organization for limited and particular objectives, in which each constituent Church retains its full independence and liberty of action. Such federation involves the setting-up of a special central organization, but does not involve the fusion of the existing organizations of the separate bodies.

Filioque. The phrase "proceeding from the Father *and the Son*" in the Nicene-Constantinopolitan Creed as recited in the Western Church. The phrase seems first to be found in the Acts of the Council of Toledo in 589; was officially approved by Charlemagne in 809; but seems not to have entered into universal use in the West till the 11th century. This is one of the perpetually recurring points of controversy between the East and the West. Some Eastern authorities condemn the addition as heretical; even those which do not so condemn it affirm that one part of the Church has no right to make an addition to a Creed which has behind it the authority of an Ecumenical Council.

Formula of Concord. A confessional document, drawn up by a group of Lutheran theologians and presented to the Elector of Saxony on 28 May 1577. Its aim was to exclude what were judged to be the errors of the later teaching of Melanchthon, with its tendencies towards Calvinism, and of Flacius Illyricus and the Gnesio-Lutherans. It was widely, though not universally, accepted by the German Lutheran Churches, and was rejected by, amongst others, the Church of Denmark. The *Book of Concord*, of which the "Formula" is the concluding section, was published on 25 June 1580.

Free Church, Free Churchman. A Free Church is one which has no connection with the State. In Germany, *die Freikirchen* are those Protestant bodies not incorporated in the official regional Churches or in the 'Evangelical Church in Germany. In Britain, with the increasing sense of the Church in what were formerly known as the nonconformist or dissenting bodies, the term "Free Churches" came into increasing currency towards the end of the 19th century. In the United States the term "Free Church" is sometimes used of those bodies, Congregationalist and others, which have never had, or have not kept, the strict ecclesiastical and liturgical order which Episcopalians, Lutherans, and some Presbyterians brought with them from Europe, and have retained.

Fundamental Articles. The idea of a distinction between fundamental (or essential) and secondary articles of the Faith goes back to the theologians Cassander and Calixtus in the 16th and 17th centuries, and reappears periodically in ecumenical discussions. No permanent and authoritative list of Fundamental Articles has ever been drawn up; each theologian (or each Church) drew up an individual list of those articles on which agreement was deemed indispensable, if Church union was to be secured. Non-fundamental articles are those on which it was judged that disagreement need not necessarily be a bar to communion between the Churches.

Fundamentalism, Fundamentalist. Early in the 20th century, when Biblical criticism and the "Social Gospel" were beginning to penetrate the American Churches, a series of small books *The Fundamentals*, setting forth a conservative position in Biblical and theological matters, was produced and very widely distributed. From this, the term "Fundamentalist" came to be generally used in America of those Churches and groups which hold to the verbal inerrancy of Holy Scripture, and in other respects maintain a rigidly conservative theological position. From America, the usage gradually spread across the Atlantic; the term "Fundamentalist" is perhaps more often used by those who disapprove of this theological position than by those who hold it.

Gorham Case. An ecclesiastical case at law, which agitated the Church of England from 1847 to 1851. The Bishop of Exeter (Phillpotts) refused to institute the Rev. G. C. Gorham to a living in his diocese, on the ground that he held heretical views concerning baptismal regeneration. Gorham took the matter to court; in the end the judicial committee of the Privy Council decided in Gorham's favour, and he was instituted to his living. Many High Churchmen felt that the decision by a secular court of an ecclesiastical case involving matters of faith was intolerable; some of them, including H. E. (later Cardinal) Manning, in consequence left the Church of England and joined the Church of Rome.

High Church. See Note on Party Terminology in the Church of England, p. 306.

Home Missions. In Britain, this term is generally used of evangelistic enterprise among groups which, though of Christian origin, have become temporarily or permanently estranged from the regular ministrations of the Churches. In the United States, the term is used rather more widely, to include such enterprises as missions to American Indians, to immigrants, to migrants, and to other groups not reached by the ordinary activities of the Churches. (See also *Innere Mission*.)

In Commendam. The technical term for the holding of one ecclesiastical dignity in plurality with another, with the right to draw the revenues deriving from such dignity, but in many cases without the obligation to carry out in person the spiritual responsibilities attaching to it.

Independency, Independents. The 17th-century term for those Christian groups which insisted on the total independence of the local "gathered" Church, as having within it the plenitude of the life of the Church, and denied that the ordained minister possessed any special "character" distinguishing him from his lay brother. The successors of the Independents were generally known in later times as Congregationalists; but the Baptists and the Disciples of Christ also have a strongly "independent" tradition.

Index. The shortened form, in common use, of the term *Index Expurgatorius*, or *Index Librorum Prohibitorum*, the list, published officially at Rome from time to time, of books condemned by the authority of the Roman Catholic Church, which Roman Catholics are not permitted to read, unless special permission to do so has been accorded to them by their ecclesiastical superiors.

Innere Mission. This term, which is much wider in its scope than the term "Home Missions" in Britain or America, is used of a most characteristic activity of the German Churches. It covers an immense range of evangelistic, educational, practical and charitable activities, its purpose, as defined by its founder, J. H. Wichern, being "the spiritual reformation of the whole land". (See also Home Missions.)

Interdenominational, Interconfessional. The term used to designate those joint enterprises in which several Christian communions join, as denominations but without infringement of their denominational independence and authority. All National Christian Councils are, in the strict sense of the term, interdenominational or interconfessional. They are not "undenominational", since the denominational character of their constituent members is recognized and safeguarded. (See also Undenominational.)

Jacobite. 1. The name by which a number of Monophysite Churches, including the Syrian Orthodox Church of South India, are commonly known. The name derives from Jacob Baradaeus, Bishop of Edessa (541–78), who rescued the Monophysite community from the extinction with which it was threatened through imperial persecution.
2. The name by which, after the expulsion of King James II of England in 1688, supporters faithful to his cause, and to that of his son and grandson, were known in England and particularly in Scotland.

Liberal. In theological connections, the word "liberal" is correctly used only of the attitude which demands that the Scriptures, Church dogma, and tradition should not be regarded as exempt from critical study and evaluation, that the Church must be open to new light and knowledge, and that it must be prepared to restate its faith in relation to the changing human situation. It is also, however, incorrectly used as equivalent to "unorthodox", and in some circles to "Unitarian". It is not unknown as a term of abuse. In general, the word will be found in this History only in its proper sense.

Liturgy, Liturgical. Any form of Christian worship which depends in part on set forms, and not on the immediate inspiration of the minister or the participants, is so far liturgical. In practice, the term "liturgy" is often used of the officially received service books of a Christian communion; it is also found in a more restricted application to the order of service of the Holy Communion. In this History, the context generally makes clear whether the word is to be taken in the wider, or in the more restricted, sense.

Low Church. See Note on Party Terminology in the Church of England, p. 306.

Marian Exiles. English Protestants, who had fled before the religious persecution instituted by Queen Mary (1553–58) and found refuge in Continental cities, notably

Geneva, Strasburg and Zurich. Many of them, after their return to England, took the lead in the attempt to impose a Presbyterian form of government on the Church of England.

Mason and Dixon Line. The line of the southern boundary of Pennsylvania, U.S.A., continued westwards along the course of the Ohio River, which came to be the boundary between those States in which slavery was permitted and those in which it had been abolished, or had never existed.

Mason and Dixon were the two English surveyors who ran the line in 1763.

Metropolitan. "The bishop of the mother city." In the Orthodox Churches, all bishops are, and are referred to as, Metropolitans. In the Anglican Churches, all Archbishops are Metropolitans; but the title is in common use only with reference to the Bishop of Calcutta, on whom this title, but not that of Archbishop, was conferred by Parliament in 1835.

Mozarabic Rite. The ancient liturgical rite of the Churches of Spain and Portugal. Gradually superseded by the Roman rite, and now surviving only in a few churches, mainly in the diocese of Toledo.

Nocent Ceremonies. Ceremonies, such as the sign of the Cross in baptism, objected to by the English Puritans, especially in the 17th century, as having no certain warrant in Holy Scripture, and being therefore "nocent", i.e. harmful, or unlawful in the practice of the Church.

Nonconformist. One who does not conform to the doctrine and discipline of the Established Church of England. In practice limited to *Protestant* dissenters, Roman Catholics ("Recusants") not being included under the term. Sometimes used more generally of members of non-episcopal Churches. Occasionally in this History still more generally of protesters against the dominant order or religion of their time, and in such cases usually spelt "non-conformist."

Ordinal, The. "The Form and Manner of Making, Ordaining and Consecrating Bishops, Priests, and Deacons according to the Order of the Church of England", almost always bound up with the Book of Common Prayer, though technically it does not form part of it.

Orthodox, Orthodoxy—orthodox, orthodoxy. The original meaning in Greek of this group of words is simply "right belief or opinion". In this History, Orthodox and Orthodoxy with capitals are used exclusively of those Eastern Churches which themselves use the word as part of their official title, and of their members. When used with a more general reference to "adherence to the traditional Faith of the Church, as expressed in the Bible, the Creeds, and other confessional statements of the Churches", the words are printed with a small initial letter.

Patriarch. In the early Church, three Sees only—Antioch, Alexandria, Rome—carried the patriarchal title. The occupants of these Sees had great eminence in the Church, and a wide though undefined authority. In the 5th century, Byzantium and Jerusalem were added to the three earlier patriarchal Sees. In modern times, the heads of several autocephalous Orthodox Churches—Russia, Yugoslavia, Rumania, etc., have acquired the patriarchal title. In the Roman Catholic Church, the heads of certain Uniate Churches (e.g. Greek Catholic in Alexandria) and certain Archbishops (e.g. Venice, Goa) also have the title Patriarch.

Per Saltum. A technical term for the omission of one or more of the (traditional) lower grades of the ministry in progress towards the higher. Used in reference to the consecration of Scottish Presbyterian ministers to the episcopate, without previous ordination to the Anglican priesthood, in 1610; and, by some, of the consecration of Free Church ministers to the episcopate of the Church of South India in 1947 and later.

Priest, Presbyter. In origin these two words are identical, being simply variant forms of the Greek *presbyteros*, elder. In practice, however, there are wide differences in the usages of the several Christian communions. In the Roman Catholic and Orthodox Churches, the English word "priest" is regularly used as a translation of the Greek *hiereus* and the Latin *sacerdos*, and is understood to imply the indelible character received at his ordination by the individual minister, which enables him to carry out functions (especially the offering of the Eucharistic sacrifice) in which he cannot be replaced by any layman. In some Lutheran Churches (e.g. Norway) the word "priest" is regularly used, but without any "sacerdotal" connotation. In the Anglican Churches the forms "presbyter" and "priest" are both found in official documents. In many communions, especially those of the "Free Church" type, in which special stress is laid on the "universal priesthood of believers", the term "priest" is not used of the individual minister, though in some of them the term "presbyter" is in regular use.

Proselytism. In this History the term is used exclusively of the attempt to persuade an adherent of one Christian body to change his religious allegiance and to adhere to some other Christian body. The word generally has the connotation of the use of undesirable methods—unfair pressure, or the appeal to unworthy motives. One of the unsolved problems of the ecumenical movement.

Protosynkellos. A senior monk, generally an Archimandrite, who lives with a bishop of the Orthodox Church, acts as his chaplain, and carries out important administrative work on his behalf.

Reformed—reformed. In ordinary English usage, any Church can be referred to as "reformed" which passed through a reformation in the 16th century, the two universally distinguishing marks of such Churches being the acceptance of the supremacy of Scripture, and the use in public worship of a language generally understood by the people. In Continental usage, the term "Reformed" is generally used only of those Churches which have sprung from the Reformation in Switzerland and are mainly either Calvinist or Zwinglian in character. In this History, when the first sense is intended, the word is printed with a small initial letter, the second sense being indicated by an initial capital.

Reunion. The term generally used for the recovery of the unity of the Churches by those who hold that such recovery can never be more than the restoration of an originally given unity. It is objected to by some who maintain that, since in many parts of the world, e.g. America, one single Church has never existed, the word "Union" should be used, to indicate that what is sought is a unity which in such areas has never previously existed. In this History, some variety may be noted in the usage of the several authors.

Symbol, Symbolic Books. From very early times the word "Symbol" (in Greek = token, watchword) has been used of the Creed, especially in connection with its use as a baptismal confession of faith. The term "Symbolic Books" seems to have been first used by J. B. Carpzov in 1665, and since then has passed into general currency, to denote those documents which are accepted by the several Confessions as setting forth authoritatively the faith and doctrine by which they live.

(This theological use is quite distinct from the more common use of "symbol" in the sense of representing something "by possession of analogous qualities or by association in fact or thought".)

Symbolo-Fideist. The movement in French Protestant theology, chiefly represented by A. Sabatier and F. Ménégoz, which, neither rationalistic nor orthodox, desired to retain the full spiritual values of the Faith, while at the same time affirming that all the intellectual forms in which the Faith expresses itself are time- and situation-conditioned.

Syncretism. This word is used in two senses: (1) in old, and especially 16th-century, documents, it is used in the sense of that fellowship and union between the Churches which it was the aim of the irenical writers to bring about; (2) in modern writers it is generally used in the sense of a superficial amalgamation of religious ideas and traditions which are in reality incompatible with one another.

Syrian (in India). Members of the large body of Christians in South-west India, belonging to the various divisions of the ancient Church believed to have been founded by St Thomas, are commonly called "Syrians" by themselves and by the Hindus among whom they live. The term arose as a result of the very ancient connection of this Church with Mesopotamia; and one section of it, the Malankara Church, is bound by ties of ecclesiastical dependence to the Patriarch of the Syrian Orthodox (Monophysite) Church in Syria. But the Church in India is now purely Indian; and the term "Syrian" approximates so closely to a caste-title that members of other Hindu communities who have later become Christians are not known as Syrians.

Tropenidee. The view of denominations within the Christian Church characteristic of Zinzendorf and his successors among the Moravian Brethren. This involves a positive attitude towards denominations regarded as entities which divine providence has permitted to exist; every denomination, as long as it exists, should regard its particular tradition as a treasure held in trust for the benefit of the whole Body of Christ, and as a gift through which the members of the several denominations can be enriched, when they meet together in fellowship.

Tulchan Bishops. Titular bishops, without spiritual jurisdiction, introduced in Scotland after the Reformation, in order that lay barons might in their names draw the revenues of the Scottish bishoprics. A "tulchan" was a calf's skin stuffed with straw and placed beside a cow to encourage her to give milk.

Ubiquity of Christ's Body. The doctrine of ubiquity is an element in Luther's doctrine of the Lord's Supper, through which he endeavours both to hold fast to the reality of the presence of Christ in the Eucharist and to deny the Roman doctrine of transubstantiation. His doctrine may be briefly summarized in the following syllogistic form: "The body of Christ is at the right hand of God; the right hand of God is everywhere; therefore the body of Christ is in the bread of the Eucharist."

Una Sancta. The one holy Catholic Church of Christ. The term has come to be used not infrequently to connote that unity of all Christ's people, which persists unbroken in spite of the many divisions existing among those who call themselves Christians—a unity which is striving to come to visible expression through the ecumenical activities of the World Council of Churches and other Christian bodies.

Undenominational. Under this term are included common efforts of Christians, in which the sharing of a common Christian Faith or of certain emphases within the Christian Faith is felt to be so important that the question of the denomination to which particular supporters of the common cause belong is either not raised, or is not felt to be significant. A good example is the Keswick (England) Convention for the deepening of spiritual life. (See also Interdominational.)

INDEX

THE
ECUMENICAL ADVANCE

A HISTORY OF
THE ECUMENICAL MOVEMENT
VOLUME 2
1948-1968

THE
ECUMENICAL ADVANCE

A HISTORY OF
THE ECUMENICAL MOVEMENT
VOLUME 2
1948–1968

EDITED BY

HAROLD E. FEY

Third edition
with updated bibliography

WORLD COUNCIL OF CHURCHES
GENEVA

First published in 1970 by SPCK, London,
and The Westminster Press, Philadelphia
Second edition, 1986
Third edition, 1993

ISBN 2-8254-1110-8

Cover design: Rob Lucas

CONTENTS

ABBREVIATIONS

AAS	*Acta Apostolicae Sedis*
A.A C.C.	All Africa Conference of Churches
A.C.T.S.	Advisory Committee for Technical Services
A.F.P.R.O.	Action for Food Production
Amsterdam	*The First Assembly of the World Council of Churches*, ed. W. A. Visser 't Hooft. London, S.C.M. Press, 1949
A.P.I.D.E.P.	Association Protestante Internationale des Prêts (International Protestant Loan Association)
B.B.C.	British Broadcasting Corporation
B.W.A.	Baptist World Alliance
C.A.S.A.	Christian Agency for Social Action (National Christian Council of India)
C.B.M.S.	Conference of British Missionary Societies
C.C.I.A.	The Commission of the Churches on International Affairs
C.C.L.A.	Committee on Co-operation in Latin America
C.C.S.A.	Christian Committee for Service in Algeria
C.E.C.	Conference of European Churches
C.E.L.A.M.	The Latin American Episcopal Council (Roman Catholic)
C.E.L.A.D.E.C.	The Latin American Commission on Christian Education (Protestant)
C.I.M.A.D.E.	Comité Inter-mouvements auprès des Evacués
C.J.D.P.	The Commission on a Just and Durable Peace
C.O.R.A.G.S.	Committee on Relief and Gift Supplies (National Christian Council of India)
C.U.P.S.A.	Casa Unida de Publicaciones, S.A. (Mexico D.F.)
C.R.O.P.	Christian Rural Organization Programme
C.W.M.E.	Council on World Missions and Evangelism
C.W.S.	Church World Service
D.F.M.	Division of Foreign Missions
D.I.C.A.R.W.S.	Division of Inter-Church Aid, Refugee, and World Service

D.I.C.A.S.R.	Department of Inter-Church Aid and Service to Refugees
D.W.M.E.	Division of World Mission and Evangelism
E.A.C.C.	East Asia Christian Conference
E.C.L.O.F.	The Ecumenical Church Loan Fund
ECOSOC	Economic and Social Council of the U.N.
Edinburgh	*The Second World Conference on Faith and Order*, ed. Leonard Hodgson. New York, The Macmillan Company, 1938
E.P.E.A.A.	Ecumenical Programme for Emergency Action in Africa
Evanston	*The Evanston Report: The Second Assembly of the World Council of Churches, 1954*, ed. W. A. Visser 't Hooft. New York, Harper and Brothers Publishers, 1955
Faith and Order	Commission on Faith and Order of the World Council of Churches
F.A.O.	Food and Agriculture Organization of the United Nations, Rome
FO No.	Refers to Faith and Order Numbered Paper, New Series
F.W.C.C.	Society of Friends World Committee for Consultation
H.E.K.D.	Hilfswerk der Evangelischen Kirchen in Deutschland (Relief Work of the Protestant Churches in Germany)
H.E.K.S.	Hilfswerk der Evangelischen Kirchen der Schweiz (The Swiss Protestant Churches Relief Agency)
I.C.C.	International Congregational Council
I.C.C.C.	International Council of Christian Churches
I.C.E.M.	Intergovernmental Committee for European Migration
I.L.O.	International Labour Organization, Geneva
I.M.C.	International Missionary Council
IRM	*International Review of Missions*
I.R.O.	International Refugee Organization
I.S.A.L.	Iglesia y Sociedad en America Latina (Church and Society in Latin America)
Lausanne	*Faith and Order: Proceedings of the World Conference, Lausanne, 3–21 August 1927*, ed. H. N. Bate. London, S.C.M. Press, 1927
Life and Work	The Universal Christian Council on Life and Work; first meeting, Stockholm 1925
Lund	*The Third World Conference on Faith and Order*, ed. Oliver S. Tomkins. London, S.C.M. Press, 1953
L.W.F.	Lutheran World Federation, Geneva

Montreal	*The Fourth World Conference on Faith and Order*, ed. P. C. Rodger and Lukas Vischer. London, S.C.M. Press, 1964
MRCC	Refers to the Minutes and Reports of the Central Committee of the year in question
M.R.I.	Mutual Responsibility and Interdependence in the Body of Christ
N.C.C.C.U.S.A.	National Council of Churches of Christ of the United States of America
N.E.C.C.	Near East Christian Council
New Delhi	*The New Delhi Report: The Third Assembly of the World Council of Churches, 1961*, ed. W. A. Visser 't Hooft. New York, Association Press, 1962
N.S.C.F.	National Student Christian Federation
Oxford	Conference on Church, Community, and State, Oxford, England, 1937
P.C.C.	Pacific Conference of Churches
R.A.V.E.M.C.O.	Radio, Visual Education, and Mass Communication of the Division of Foreign Missions of N.C.C.C.U.S.A.
S.C.M.	Student Christian Movement
S.A.S.P.	Committee on Specialized Assistance to Social Projects
S.P.C.K.	Society for Promoting Christian Knowledge
S.V.M.	Student Volunteer Movement
U.L.A.J.E.	Union of Latin American Evangelical Youth
U.C.M.	University Christian Movement
U.N.	United Nations Organization
U.N.E.L.A.M.	The Provisional Committee on Christian Unity in Latin America
U.N.E.S.C.O.	United Nations Educational, Scientific, and Cultural Organization
U.N.C.T.A.D.	United Nations Conference on Trade and Development
U.N.H.C.R.	United Nations High Commission for Refugees
U.N.I.C.E.F.	United Nations Children's Fund
U.N.R.R.A.	United Nations Relief and Rehabilitation Agency
U.N.R.W.A.	United Nations Relief and Works Agency
Uppsala	*The Uppsala Report 1968: Official Report of the Fourth Assembly of the World Council of Churches, Uppsala 4–20 July 1968*
U.S.C.L.	United Society for Christian Literature
U.S.E.P.	United States Escapee Programme

W.A.R.C.	World Alliance of Reformed Churches
W.C.C.	World Council of Churches
W.C.C.E.	World Council of Christian Education
W.M.C.	World Methodist Council
World Alliance	World Alliance of Reformed Churches
W.S.C.F.	World Student Christian Federation
Y.M.C.A.	Young Men's Christian Association
Y.W.C.A.	Young Women's Christian Association

CONTRIBUTORS TO THIS VOLUME

PAUL R. ABRECHT is Executive Secretary of the Department on Church and Society of the World Council of Churches. A Baptist minister, he is an honours graduate in economics of the University of California and holds a divinity degree from Union Theological Seminary, New York. He is the author of *The Churches and Rapid Social Change* (1961) and other studies. He was also editor of the important series of four books which were published in 1966 in connection with the world conference on "Christians in the Technical and Social Revolutions of Our Time", of which conference he was the secretary responsible for organization.

EUGENE CARSON BLAKE became the second General Secretary of the World Council of Churches in 1966. For the previous fifteen years he was Stated Clerk of the United Presbyterian Church in the U.S.A. Under his leadership the United Presbyterian Church became active in the civil rights movement. He was active in the preparation of the first new American Presbyterian confession of faith since 1648 and initiated the Consultation on Church Union, in which nine denominations are now seeking to form a Church "truly catholic, truly evangelical, and truly reformed". Dr Blake has long been actively engaged in the ecumenical movement. He was President of the National Council of Churches in the U.S.A. and continued on its General Board until he went to Geneva. In the W.C.C. he was a member of the policy-making Central Committee and of its Executive Committee, was Chairman of the Division of Inter-Church Aid and Chairman of the Finance Committee. He studied at Princeton and Edinburgh and once taught at Forman Christian College, Lahore, India. He served pastorates in New York and California, has received honorary degrees from eighteen colleges and universities, and is the author of four books.

DAVID LAWRENCE EDWARDS, a priest of the Church of England, has been Dean of King's College, Cambridge, since 1966. Born in 1929, he was formerly a Fellow of All Souls College, Oxford, and Editor of the Student Christian Movement Press, London. He lectures in modern church history in Cambridge University and is the author of eight books.

HAROLD E. FEY was Editor of the *Christian Century*, Chicago, from 1956 until he retired in 1964. Later he served for four years as Visiting Professor of Christian Social Ethics in Christian Theological Seminary, Indianapolis. He received his theological degree from Yale Divinity School, served as pastor of congregations of the Christian Church, Disciples of Christ, taught as a missionary in Union Theological Seminary, Manila, Philippine Islands, was Editor of *World Call*, a Christian Church monthly magazine, and was U.S. Secretary for the Fellowship of Reconciliation. He is a member of the Executive Committee of the Council on Christian Unity of the Christian Church, Disciples of Christ and represents his Church on some committees of the National Council of Churches. He joined the editorial staff of the *Christian Century* in 1940 and is the author of several books. His home is in Indianapolis.

MEREDITH B. HANDSPICKER is a native of Malden, Massachusetts and a professor in Andover-Newton Theological Seminary near Boston. He graduated from Bates College, Maine, *summa cum laude* in Philosophy. He received the B.D. degree from Yale Divinity School *magna cum laude* and later received the M.A. and the Ph.D. at Yale. He was Secretary of the Faith and Order Department of the W.C.C. from 1963 to 1967. He is a minister of the United Church of Christ.

VASIL T. ISTAVRIDIS is a lay theologian of the Greek Orthodox Church. He graduated from the Theological School of Halki, Istanbul, where he is teaching modern church history, including the history of the ecumenical movement. He also studied at Andover-Newton Theological Seminary and at Boston University, receiving the Th.D. degree from the latter institution. He is the author of pamphlets and books on inter-Church relations, including the theological dialogue between Orthodox and Anglicans, on the history of the ecumenical movement, and on great ecumenists. He is a member of the World Council Central Committee. He has participated in many ecumenical gatherings.

HANFRIED KRÜGER first studied law, then turned to theology and comparative religion, receiving his Ph.D. in 1937. His thesis which he wrote under Professor Friedrich Heiler in Marburg, was on "Verständnis und Wertung der Mystik im neueren Protestantismus". He served as an assistant minister from 1938 to 1940 in Hannover and Loccum in the Evangelical Church of Hannover and from 1941 to 1943 in Hannover and from 1943 to 1951 in Lauenstein, Hannover. From 1951 to 1953 he worked in church administration in Hannover. In 1953 he became Secretary for Ecumenical Affairs in the Foreign Relations Office of the E.K.D. in Frankfurt/Main. As head of the Ökumenische Centrale and chief editor of the quarterly journal *Ökumenische Rundschau* since 1956, he was appointed Secretary of the Deutscher Ökumenischer Studienausshuss from 1956 to 1967 and also Secretary of the Arbeitsgemeinschaft Christlicher Kirchen in Deutschland since 1963.

HANS JOCHEN MARGULL has since 1967 been Professor of Missions at the University of Hamburg, Germany, from which university he received the Th.D. degree in 1958. He was a missionary of the United Presbyterian Church (U.S.A.) to the United Church in Japan from 1965 to 1967. Earlier he headed the Department on Studies in Evangelism of the World Council of Churches and earlier still was a student minister in Germany. A Lutheran, he studied at Griefswald Halle, Mainz, and New York Theological Seminary. He is the author of three books, one of which was published in Japanese.

GEOFFREY MURRAY is information officer of the Division of Inter-Church Aid, Refugee, and World Service of the World Council of Churches. Before joining the staff of the W.C.C. early in 1961 he spent thirty-two years as a newspaper reporter on the *Daily Express, Daily Mirror, Daily Dispatch,* and *News Chronicle* of London, broken only by four years' service with the Royal Air Force during the Second World War. He is now Geneva correspondent of the *Christian Century*. He is the author of six books and has attended and reported many ecumenical meetings.

J. E. LESSLIE NEWBIGIN is Bishop of the diocese of Madura and Ramnad of the Church of South India. He was and continues to be an ordained minister of the Church of Scotland. He was present at the founding of the World Council of Churches in 1948 and served as Chairman of the commission which wrote the statement on the theme of the Second W.C.C. Assembly in 1954. He was Secretary of the International Missionary Council from 1959 to 1961 and Director of the W.C.C. Division of World Mission and Evangelism from 1961 to 1965, when he was elected bishop. He was a Secretary of the Student Christian Movement for two years after he received the M.A. degree from Cambridge University. He is the author of nine published books.

O. FREDERICK NOLDE of New York City was Director of the World Council of Churches Commission of the Churches on International Affairs from 1946 to 1968 and since 1948 an Associate General Secretary of the World Council. He is unofficially recognized to be the chief architect of the article on freedom of thought, conscience, and religion in the Universal Declaration of Human Rights, proclaimed by the United Nations in 1948. For more than two decades he has been a spokesman for the W.C.C. and the C.C.I.A. before the United Nations and intergovernmental conferences in New York, Geneva, Paris, Berlin, Seoul, and elsewhere. His representations have sought, among other objectives, the cessation of nuclear weapons testing, disarmament, and the peaceful settlement of international disputes. Dr Nolde holds degrees from Muhlenberg College, the Lutheran Theological Seminary at Philadelphia, and the University of Pennsylvania. He served as pastor, as professor, and later as dean of the graduate school at Lutheran Theological Seminary. He has several honorary degrees.

FRANK SHORT, now minister of the Sherborne Congregational Church in England, was from 1953 to 1965 Asia Secretary and General Secretary of the Conference of Missionary Societies in Great Britain and Ireland. From 1926 to 1953 he was a missionary in China of the London Missionary Society, serving in the last four years of that period as Secretary of the China Council of the L.M.S. and as representative of the L.M.S. in South Asia. From 1961 to 1965 he was a member of the Committee on National Council of Churches relationships of the Division of World Mission and Evangelism of the World Council of Churches.

LUKAS VISCHER, an ordained minister of the Swiss Reformed Church, is the Director of the Secretariat on Faith and Order of the World Council of Churches. He has been associated with the W.C.C. since 1961. He served as one of the World Council's observers at all four sessions of the Second Vatican Council. A native of Basle, he studied at the Universities of Basle, Strasbourg, Göttingen, and Oxford. His Th.D. degree in early church history came from the University of Basle. Before joining the World Council staff, he was for eight years pastor in Herblingen, Switzerland. He has written several books and articles dealing with the ecumenical movement.

W. A. VISSER 'T HOOFT was General Secretary of the World Council of Churches from 1948 to 1966 and was made Honorary President in 1968 by the Fourth Assembly of the W.C.C. He is an ordained minister of the Netherlands Reformed Church and of the Protestant Church of Geneva. His doctoral thesis at the University of Leyden on "The Background of the Social Gospel in America" became the first of the dozen books he wrote. Beginning with the Stockholm Conference on Life and Work in 1925 and work with the International Y.M.C.A. and the World's Student Christian Federation, his ecumenical interest and service has been lifelong. In 1938 he became General Secretary of the Provisional Committee of the World Council of Churches and ten years later General Secretary of the World Council of Churches. He received honorary degrees from many of the world's leading universities, was honoured by the Ecumenical Patriarch of Constantinople and the Orthodox Church of Russia, and received high honours from the governments of The Netherlands, France, and Germany. During his administration the World Council of Churches moved from tentative and provisional beginnings to becoming the acknowledged chief instrument and channel of the ecumenical movement.

HANS-RUEDI WEBER is Associate Director of the Ecumenical Institute of the World Council of Churches at Chateau de Bossey near Geneva. He was appointed to this post in 1961. A Swiss Reformed pastor, he was Executive Secretary of the World Council's Department of the Laity from 1955 to 1961. Earlier he was a missionary to Central Celebes and Java in Indonesia and Secretary of the Student Christian Movement in Switzerland. Dr Weber received the Bachelor of Theology degree from the University of Berne, a diploma from the W.C.C.'s Graduate School, and a doctorate in Theology from the University of Geneva. Dr Weber is the author of books published in English, French, and German.

INTRODUCTION

The present volume is a sequel to *A History of the Ecumenical Movement 1517–1948*, edited by Ruth Rouse and Stephen C. Neill, which was published in 1954. It differs from that volume in that this book covers only the twenty-year period from 1948 to 1968, whereas the former volume covered more than four centuries (1517–1948). This book is smaller in size and is intended to be of interest to the much wider public which is now following the development of the ecumenical movement.

It may be thought that, if history is written so close to the event, the authors will have difficulty in seeing actions in their proper perspective. Each of the distinguished authors who have contributed to the present volume is aware of this difficulty and is prepared to leave historians who write in the future to place events in a different light from that in which they now appear. But we believe that our contributors are rendering a service of genuine importance in running the risks involved in evaluating developments so close to their happening. The last two decades have been rich in important events and, as this record shows, full of promise for the decade which we are now entering. This is sufficient justification for what is here attempted.

Here it should be emphasized that the ecumenical movement must not be regarded as identical with the World Council of Churches, nor has the latter ever claimed to be its only expression. Nevertheless, it is universally recognized that the World Council occupies in it a place of special responsibility, being at present the most strongly organized inter-Church body for promoting the aims of the movement. This explains why so many of the following pages are devoted to the developments of the World Council and to what it has been able to accomplish in promoting the cause of ecumenism during the first years of its existence.

The development of the World Council during the last twenty years has had three main aspects. In the first place, its membership has greatly increased. The Churches whose delegates met at Amsterdam in 1948 and on 23 August sealed this pact of fraternity, were 147 in number, Protestant, Anglican, Orthodox, and Old Catholic. Today the member Churches are 235. The increase is mainly due to the fact that several of the great Orthodox Churches entered into membership in 1961, and equally a large number of young Churches in Asia, Africa, Latin America, and Oceania, which had recently become independent. Orthodoxy, which for too long had been a minority in the ecumenical movement, has thus been able to exercise increasing influence and to make its full contribution. On the other hand, the increased number of Churches from the Third World has given the World Council a more universal character. Thus the centre of gravity has shifted considerably in two ways: confessionally the Reformation Churches are less prominent, regionally the Western Churches are less dominant.

Secondly, ecumenism is interpreted today in a wider sense than it was in 1948. It has been increasingly realized that unity is not an end in itself and should not be sought for its own sake but rather to accomplish more effectively God's purpose for all mankind. In 1951 the Central Committee proclaimed that unity and mission are inseparable realities. The vital link between them was forged in 1961 when the International Missionary Council was integrated into the World Council of Churches. Mission is no longer regarded as a form of "one way traffic" from "Christian" Europe and America to the "pagan" continents, but the task of the whole Church in the world as a whole. Moreover, this concept was broadened at the Fourth Assembly of the W.C.C. at Uppsala in its discussion of catholicity to say that the mission is to the whole person in the whole society, with all its principalities and powers, in every country.

This leads to the third aspect of development which is visible not only within the World Council but within the entire ecumenical movement: the increasing concern for the world and its problems. The World Council has constantly reminded its members that the Church does not live for itself and that its vocation is to serve mankind. For that reason it has drawn them into more and more extensive programmes of inter-Church aid and relief, service to refugees, and help in regions of rapid social change. Simultaneously the World Council organized regular studies of all kinds on social and international problems to inspire and guide the Churches' action. So doing it has been faithful to the heritage of the "Life and Work Movement" founded in 1925 at the Stockholm Conference. Finally, the World Conference on "Church and Society" held in Geneva in 1966 and the Uppsala Assembly have, as will be seen in these pages, plunged the Churches into the heart of the human crisis.

All these developments are direct continuations of ecumenical efforts of the past whose vitality is expressed in the deepening and expanding process described here. But near the end of the period reviewed in this volume an event of great significance occurred which marks a turning-point in the history of the ecumenical movement, namely the Second Vatican Council (1962–5). While the Roman Catholic Church had previously maintained an attitude of extreme reserve with regard to the ecumenical movement, it now decided to associate itself with it and to participate actively in the dialogue which the World Council has encouraged for many years. A significant change has taken place in the atmosphere of the relations between the Roman Catholic Church and non-Roman Christendom, and this has opened the way to an era of trust and co-operation in many fields.

The above comments suffice to show that "movement" is the right word to associate with ecumenical. This movement is assuming new forms to meet new conditions. It is impossible to foresee what shapes will emerge in the future, since the world and the Churches are passing through a deep crisis. The younger generation is judging all existing institutions. The World Council of Churches is not exempt from their scrutiny. Within the Church, young Christians do not conceal the fact that their conception of Christian unity and action differs from that of the older generation. But the ecumenical movement has clearly been guided by God in the past, and this is sufficient guarantee for its future.

The committee which assumes responsibility for the publication of this volume on the History of the Ecumenical Movement 1948–68 has been fortunate to secure as editor Dr Harold E. Fey, whose great experience in such matters particularly qualifies him for this delicate task. We wish to express our gratitude for the distinguished manner in which he has accomplished this task.

In closing, the Committee wishes to express its deep appreciation to the Christian Church, Disciples of Christ, to its Council on Christian Unity and to its "Week of Compassion" for generously providing funds which made possible the writing, editing, and publication of this continuation of the History of the Ecumenical Movement, as they did for the previous volume, *A History of the Ecumenical Movement 1517–1948.*

HENRI D'ESPINE

Chairman of the Committee
on Ecumenical History.

PREFACE TO THE THIRD EDITION

The two titles included in this volume — *A History of the Ecumenical Movement 1517-1948* and *The Ecumenical Advance 1948-1968* — were originally published jointly by SPCK and Westminster Press and reprinted in 1986 by WCC Publications. Although there are other histories of the ecumenical movement, they still represent the only "official" literature on the subject.

The World Council of Churches itself was involved in the choice of writers and editors and in the final production of the titles. The aim was to present a detailed and impartial account of the many ecumenical impulses, initiatives and activities during these centuries, and to make a systematic survey of the ecumenical history of the churches.

Taking the Reformation as its starting point, the first title covers four centuries of varied endeavours towards church unity in Europe and North America. In particular it deals with the Faith and Order, World Mission and Evangelism, and Life and Work movements in the twentieth century, which led to the formation of the World Council of Churches.

The second title is mainly concerned with developments within the World Council, its programmes and activities, from 1948 through the Fourth Assembly at Uppsala in 1968. It also includes chapters on the Orthodox and Roman Catholic involvement in the ecumenical movement, on the origin and growth of national and regional councils of churches, and on the part played by confessional families in the ecumenical movement from 1948 onwards.

It has often been pointed out that as the ecumenical pioneers of the twentieth century pass from the scene, we suffer from a loss of "ecumenical memory". Even those committed to the ecumenical cause often work with only limited knowledge of past ecumenical efforts and of the continuity in the programmes, concerns and activities of the World Council of Churches and other ecumenical bodies since 1948. These volumes continue to refresh our memory and can broaden our perspective. For, when the past is forgotten, the present loses perspective and the future lacks direction. More recent trends and developments, which have become increasingly complex and controversial, can be recorded and evaluated only if the challenge, the vision and the enthusiasm of earlier decades are newly experienced.

These two titles have been out of print for some time. It is our hope that their re-publication now, in one volume, will be of help to both individuals and institutions.

Konrad Raiser
General Secretary
World Council of Churches

Geneva

xix

1
The General
Ecumenical Development
since 1948

W. A. VISSER 'T HOOFT

The Third Generation

By 1948 the ecumenical movement could look back on two important periods of its life.

The first had been the period of the pioneers. A small group of men had begun to plant the ecumenical idea in the minds of church leaders. The initiatives they took were due to their own conviction and imagination rather than to any widespread movement in the Churches. So they met with a good deal of resistance and scepticism. But they had that patient tenacity which comes from devotion to a great spiritual cause. Two laymen, John R. Mott and J. H. Oldham, succeeded in 1910 in bringing the missionary forces together. A missionary bishop and a lawyer, Charles Brent and Robert Gardiner, created "Faith and Order" and prepared the Lausanne Conference of 1927. An archbishop, Nathan Söderblom, was able to organize almost singlehandedly the first conference on "Life and Work" in Stockholm in 1925. Another layman, Sir Willoughby Dickinson, with the support of a German professor, Friedrich Siegmund-Schultze, built the World Alliance for Friendship through the Churches. In the meantime another spontaneous initiative had been taken in Constantinople by Archbishop Germanos, who was also largely responsible for bringing the Greek Orthodox Churches into the ecumenical bodies.

This period is therefore characterized by numerous energetic initiatives which led to the formation of a variety of ecumenical bodies, each of which had its loyal adherents in the Churches, but none of which was considered by the Churches as their own instrument for ecumenical action.

The second period was that of the architects who sought to give a more clearly defined shape to the ecumenical movement. The outstanding names are William Temple, J. H. Oldham, William Adams Brown, Archbishop Germanos (Thyateira), George Bell (Chichester), Marc Boegner, Alphons Koechlin, William Paton. Theirs was a threefold task: to arrive at an integration of the ecumenical bodies, to relate these bodies more directly to the Churches, and to work out a specific programme of common action. By 1937, at the time of the Oxford and Edinburgh conferences, a specific plan could be submitted. It was proposed to bring Faith and Order and Life and Work together in a single organization. Close relationship would be established between the new body and the International Missionary Council. A year later in Utrecht a representative conference of the Churches elaborated the Constitution of the World Council of Churches. But this second period had to last longer than was expected. The Second World War came and the first Assembly which was to have been held in 1941 could not meet until 1948. This proved to be to the advantage of the movement, for in the war years the ecumenical convictions were tested and deepened.

The year 1948 marked the beginning of the third period. A new generation took over. We can call it the generation of the builders. Among the leaders in this new period there were only a few who had known the period of the pioneers—George Bell (died 1958), Alphons Koechlin (died 1965), Yngve Brilioth (died 1959), Otto Dibelius (died 1967), Hamilcar Alivisatos. The task

3

was now to ensure that the ecumenical movement should really become ecumenical, that it should become the ecumenical movement of the Churches, and that it should develop adequate structures.

At the time of the first Assembly in 1948, the World Council was still far from representing all of Christendom. It is true that through the International Missionary Council, through confessional alliances, through the Y.M.C.A., Y.W.C.A., and the World Student Christian Federation, Christian leaders in Asia, Africa, and Latin America were in contact with Christians in other countries. But the Churches of these continents were not yet in regular communication with the Churches in other parts of the world and had no independent centres of initiative. At the Amsterdam Assembly of 1948 the number of representatives of the younger Churches was so limited that they "were swamped in a sea of delegates from older churches" and that "their opinion on many issues was not clearly heard".[1]

At the same time Eastern Orthodoxy was in those days only represented by the Greek-speaking Orthodox Churches. The other Orthodox Churches which had taken part in the Moscow Church Conference of 1948 had decided against participation in the World Council of Churches.

In the Roman Catholic Church a small group of theologians had begun to show their deep interest in ecumenism, but the Church as such stood aloof and did not give permission to such Roman Catholic observers as had been invited to attend the Amsterdam Assembly.

Thus the ecumenical movement of 1948 had its geographical and confessional limitations. The story of the years since 1948 is essentially the story of the process through which the ecumenical movement became universalized. It is a story of ecumenical mobilization of practically all Christian Churches.

The Historical Context of the Ecumenical Mobilization

The fast development of the ecumenical movement from a relatively esoteric concern of individual Christians with a great vision in some of the Churches to a widespread movement of thought and life affecting all the Churches in one way or another obliges us to inquire why this new factor in church history appeared at this particular time. What was the historical context in which this rediscovery of the universal dimension of the Christian faith took place?

We can only note the most essential features of the changed situation of the Church. These can be summarized as follows:

Precisely at the time when the world is being unified and a world civilization begins to take shape, the world position of Christianity is undermined and the process of estrangement between Church and world becomes increasingly acute and manifest.

These three related developments are so well known that they need little comment. Powerful forces make the many separate worlds of yesterday into one world. The unity of mankind is no longer a pious dream; it becomes a practical necessity as the interdependence of the nations grows and all are confronted with the same opportunities and the same dangers. A world

[1] Chandran Devanesan in *Ecumenical Review*, vol. i (January 1949), p. 143.

civilization comes into being, but it takes the form of a Great Society based on the dynamic forces of technology and economic development in which Christian values play a minor role. At the same time the world position of Christianity, which had been a position of privilege in the period when governments of traditionally Christian countries were in direct or indirect control of most of the world, is severely shaken when in many of the newly independent nations the national revival leads also to a resurgence of the indigenous religions. And a very large part of the world, including Russia with its ancient Christian tradition and China, a country which had often been considered one of the most promising mission fields, came under the domination of an ideology which sought to replace Christianity.

The third development is the most complex. The estrangement between the Church and the world has in it an element of emancipation, of a natural affirmation of the autonomy of culture over against a Church which had too often sought to keep the world under its tutelage. On the other hand, secularism can take an aggressively anti-Christian form and develop ideologies which become practically pseudo-religions. But there is another element in the estrangement between Church and world. It is the new sense of the integrity of the Church and the refusal on the part of Christians to accept a coexistence with the world in which Christianity loses its identity. The estrangement is not only due to Karl Marx or to Auguste Comte and Friedrich Nietzsche. It is also due to Kierkegaard, Karl Barth, Nicolai Berdyaev, and the men of the confessing Church in Germany and other countries. There had to be a 'No' to a wrong relation between Church and world before there could again be a 'Yes' and a new turning to the world on the basis of a clearer conception of Church and world.

Does this context then explain the emergence of the ecumenical movement? Sociologists will be inclined to answer this question affirmatively and to interpret the ecumenical movement as the response of the Churches to external challenges, threats, and pressures. Theologians will be inclined to deny such sociological conditioning and point out that the movement is fundamentally a rediscovery and reaffirmation of a dimension of truth which is inherent in the very nature of the Church from the beginning. It would seem that there is more truth in the sociological interpretation than most theologians are willing to admit and more truth in the theological understanding than the sociologists accept.

That the theologians have a strong point can be shown by the fact that the ecumenical movement has not followed what may be called the line of least cultural resistance. If the movement had been essentially a response to an external threat, it would surely have organized itself as a movement to defend traditional Western civilization against its enemies inside and outside the camp. But this has not happened. On the contrary the ecumenical movement has been a critical element in Western culture and sought to find new answers to the problems of relations between the ideological West and the ideological East, or between the traditionally Christian countries and those dominated by other religions, answers which grew out of Christian convictions rather than out of traditional cultural attitudes. It must also be remembered that the ecumenical movement has shown that it is not dependent upon the ups and downs of internationalism and that during the Second World War and again during the post-war tensions it has shown that it can transcend the socio-political forces which drive men apart.

On the other hand, the sociologists are surely right if they maintain that the development of the ecumenical movement has been helped and intensified by the historical situation in which the Churches find themselves in this period of their history. The recall to the universal dimension of the faith has found a wider echo in our time because the Church cannot perform its calling in the "one world" if it remains divided and provincial in its outlook. Roger Mehl puts the matter clearly: "To say that the ecumenical movement was born in a given sociological context, to say that its birth and its development have been favoured, influenced and orientated by a certain number of sociological facts, does not mean at all to pronounce a judgment on the significance of the movement."[1] For that significance lies ultimately on the common recapturing of the simple biblical truth that the Church as the people of God and the body of Christ must exemplify in this world how God gathers men together from the ends of the earth in order to live as a new humanity.

Return to the Source

Already during the 1930s and 1940s the *Biblical Renewal*[2] had been a powerful factor in bringing Christians of different traditions together. This had been shown in the life of the Christian youth movements and particularly at the World Conference of Christian Youth in Amsterdam, 1939. In the post-war years it was increasingly realized that the Word of God was "the true bond of ecumenical unity". At a World Council meeting in Oxford 1949, biblical scholars from many confessions issued a statement concerning "guiding principles for the interpretation of the Bible" and said: "We have found a measure of agreement that surprised us all .... It is an actual experience within the ecumenical movement that, when we meet together, with pre-suppositions of which we may be largely unconscious, and bring these suppositions to the judgement of Scripture, some of the very difficulties are removed which prevent the Gospel from being heard."[3]

This insight that the Bible provided the true meeting ground led to increased emphasis on Bible study in ecumenical meetings, including the W.C.C. Assemblies. It led also to the insertion in the basis of the W.C.C. of the words "according to the Scriptures". The addition of these words was a recognition of the place which the Bible had in fact occupied in the development of the ecumenical movement. Without the common biblical theology the ecumenical movement would have had no backbone. The deepest motive for the seeking of unity was the biblical conception of the gathering into one of the people of God by the Lord Jesus Christ.

[1] *Traité de Sociologie du Protestantisme*, pp. 185–6.
[2] Title of a book by Suzanne de Diétrich (1945) in the Series "Ecclesia Militans" under the auspices of the W.C.C.
[3] *Biblical Authority for Today*. London 1951.

But the return to the source did not only affect the member Churches of the World Council. In the Roman Catholic Church there had been a most remarkable revival of Bible study and of concern for the use of the Bible by the faithful. Thus, as Cardinal Bea has said, the desire to go back to the pure sources of our faith is today a common characteristic of all of Christendom.[1] For the first time Bible translations were being prepared by scholars of all confessions together. And the first results of this common translation work show a surprising consensus, not only concerning the best rendering of the original into modern languages, but also concerning the meaning of the text.

This common return to the source could not fail to have a decisive influence on the ecumenical dialogue. This became visible in the formulations concerning the relation between Scripture and tradition which have been given on the one hand by the Montreal Conference on Faith and Order and on the other hand by the Second Vatican Council. For these formulations show that in this crucial matter the various confessional positions are not as far apart as earlier generations have thought. There are still real divergences to be overcome; but it is already the case that in biblical research and biblical theology all the Churches have now the opportunity and the duty to learn from each other and to enrich each other. This is a great promise for the healthy development of the ecumenical movement.

The Churches Accept Responsibility

In the period before the creation of the World Council of Churches the relationship of the Churches to the ecumenical bodies remained undefined. The Churches were asked to send delegates to world conferences, but these world conferences set up their own continuation committees which were responsible for ongoing work. When the plan to form the World Council was launched, all Churches had to consider whether they would accept responsibility for, and a commitment to, an ongoing organization which would be the expression of their will "to stay together" and which would be controlled by them. Thus from 1948 onwards a new ecumenical situation was created. Ecumenism had no longer that informal character which it had had so far. The largest, most conspicuous, and comprehensive part of the ecumenical movement had become an instrument of the Churches.

There were those who were unhappy about this development. They feared that the movement would lose its spontaneous character and that the voice of the prophets would no longer be heard. On the other hand, most of the men who had played such a large role in the creation of the early ecumenical movement were convinced that the time had come to give the movement firm rootage in the life of the Churches. It was not that suddenly the movement was captured by church administrators. It was rather that laymen such as Oldham and Mott and church leaders who were of a prophetic rather than of a bureaucratic type such as William Temple, George Bell, and William Adams Brown saw clearly that in order to make the ecumenical movement

[1] *Gedanken zum Theologischen Wörterbuch zum Neuen Testament.* Juli 1964.

relevant to the actual life of the Churches the Churches should be asked to accept a specific responsibility for its life. It was not intended that the World Council would in any way seek to have a monopoly or a hegemony. It was realized that the independent movements which had paved the way would continue to make their own specific contribution to the ecumenical cause.

During the following years the advantages of the new situation became clear. For in this way ecumenism penetrated far more deeply into the life of the Churches than it could have done if the Council had not been a Council of Churches. And it can be said that most member Churches have at least shown in the financial assistance given to the W.C.C., in sending their delegates to meetings, and in many other ways that they took their membership seriously. It is true that there was another side to the picture. Far too often W.C.C. initiatives did not meet with any considerable response in the member Churches. Too few of the Churches had set up an adequate structure to deal with ecumenical matters. Too many letters remained unanswered. Too few of the decisions of Assemblies or Central Committee have been seriously considered and ratified by member Churches. But this was not so much due to any unwillingness of the Churches to play their part as to the fact that they were unprepared for quick and sometimes stormy ecumenical developments.

The men who had worked out the W.C.C. plan, and very especially Dr J. H. Oldham, had had in mind that the W.C.C. would use for its work not only the service of the official church leaders, but also "lay people holding posts of responsibility and influence in the secular world", for such men would be needed if the Church would give a relevant witness in the modern world.[1] This principle has been observed in many aspects of the work of the World Council, more especially in its work on social and international problems. Many laymen, who do not regard themselves as official representatives of their Churches, have played a very considerable part in the conferences and in the study and work of the World Council. This is illustrated by the fact that the important World Conference on Church and Society in 1966 was largely composed of such laymen, whose names had been approved by the Churches concerned. It was therefore considered to be a conference speaking to the Churches and the World Council rather than speaking on behalf of the Churches and the World Council. In this and other ways laymen, and also theologians invited as experts rather than as official church leaders, have made a very great contribution to the ecumenical movement. But this is not an adequate solution of the problem of the place of laymen in the responsible leadership of the World Council.

It is true that a number of laymen have served on the official organs of the W.C.C. But the original intention that they should have a very considerable voice in the leadership has not been fulfilled. The Constitution of the W.C.C. as adopted at Utrecht and Amsterdam instructed the Central Committee to urge the Churches to ensure that approximately one third of the Assembly should consist of lay persons, men and women. But this goal has not been attained. Too few Churches are willing to carry out in practice what the whole

---

[1] Report of the "Committee of Thirty-Five" to the Oxford and Edinburgh Conferences in 1937.

ecumenical family has so often said about the place of the laity, both men and women, in the life of the Church.

The Search for Renewal

The call to the Churches concerning the first Assembly of the World Council of Churches had said: "Our first and deepest need is not new organization, but the renewal, or rather the rebirth, of the actual churches." And both in the preparatory volumes for the Assembly and at the Assembly itself there had been strong emphasis on the relation between unity and renewal. "We pray for the churches' renewal as we pray for their unity. As Christ purifies us by His Spirit we shall find that we are drawn together and that there is no gain in unity unless it is unity in truth and holiness."[1]

Thus from the outset the World Council realized that unity could come only through shared renewal. During the war years and those immediately following, many movements of renewal had sprung up in the Churches and the World Council sought to make whatever inspiration and new ideas were found in each place available for the whole fellowship. The Ecumenical Institute which began to operate in 1947 and the first director of which was a prophet of church renewal (Dr Hendrik Kraemer) stood for "the reawakening of the Church through the spiritual mobilization of the laity". Before long a secretariat and later a department for the laity were organized with the same purpose. And in many other aspects of the Council's life the theme of church renewal became a dominating theme.

These first years after the Assembly were years of great hopes concerning the renewal of the Churches. Many Churches had found new life as they had been confronted with modern forms of paganism and had begun to transform their obsolete institutional structures. There was a new realization that not only in the so-called mission field but in all parts of the world the Churches were called to a comprehensive evangelistic and missionary approach. New forms of the Christian ministry were being worked out. And even more important, it was widely understood that, as the Evanston Assembly put it, "An immense opportunity is open to the churches in the world through their laity not to be seized for ecclesiastical domination, but for Christian witness."

It cannot be denied that the movement for church renewal has produced results and that these results are to a considerable extent due to the mutual stimulation and inspiration which could take place only because there was an ecumenical movement. Many Churches have a new conception of their mission in and to the world and created new structures to fulfil that mission. Evangelical academies and similar institutions in many countries have been "energizing centres". The "Kirchentag", of which Dr Reinhold von Thadden was the pioneer, has not only in Germany but also in other places injected fertile ideas into the life of the Churches. The youth movements, both those under church auspices and those which have an independent existence, notably the World's Student Christian Federation with its studies and conferences on "The Life and Mission of the Church", have made their contribu-

[1] Report of the first section of the Amsterdam Assembly.

tion through sharp, but also constructive, criticism of the ecclesiastical established order. But it is also true that the renewal of the life in the Churches has not been as deep and as widespread as had been hoped in the early years of the Council's life. Many, especially among the younger generation, felt a sense of deep disappointment. Why had the renewal movement not transformed church life more thoroughly? Was it due to a lack of spiritual depth and dynamic or to the institutional immobilism of the ecclesiastical structure or to both? The ecumenical movement itself made the issue of institutionalism a main subject of study.[1] But it cannot be said that adequate answers have been given to the basic issue.

As the Second Vatican Council became a council of *aggiornamento* and in Roman Catholic theology the theme of "reform—an essential element in the Church" (as Cardinal Döpfner formulated it) came to the fore, all open-minded Christians became confronted in a new way with the great theme of renewal. Once again the struggle for renewal in one Church stimulated and challenged the other Churches. In this field especially there is every reason to apply the principle dear to the ecumenical pioneer, Abbé Couturier, that the true ecumenical way is the way of "spiritual emulation". The greatest contribution to unity will be made by the Church which is most ready to let itself be thoroughly renewed by the Holy Spirit.

The Common Calling to Mission

The first effective initiatives leading to ecumenical co-operation had been taken by the missionary movement and had inspired the pioneers of co-operation between the Churches. But the missionary movement had created its own strong organization under the dynamic leadership of such men as John R. Mott, J. H. Oldham, William Paton. This International Missionary Council, based on the national councils and missionary councils, was in the 1920s and 1930s much ahead of all other ecumenical bodies in clarity of purpose and efficacy. On the other hand, the men of the I.M.C. became increasingly involved in the other ecumenical movements. By the time of the Madras Conference of 1938 it was clear that some link would have to be established between the I.M.C. and the World Council of Churches. It was therefore decided at the first Assembly of the W.C.C. in Amsterdam that the two bodies should be known as being "in association with" each other.

This arrangement proved to be useful, but, as co-operation became more intensive, the question as to the maintaining of two separate organizations became increasingly insistent. The strongest demand for full integration came from the Churches in Asia and Africa. They desired to be in full partnership with the Churches in Europe and America and to participate in the ecumenical movement of the Churches, and they found it difficult to have to deal with two different world organizations. In the countries of the older Churches the problem was, however, that the responsibility for missions was often in the hands of missionary societies which had grown up because the Churches had

---

[1] *Institutionalism and Church Unity* (a study prepared under the auspices of Faith and Order). New York 1963.

not waked up to their missionary calling. Would an integration of I.M.C. and W.C.C. not lead to a weakening rather than to a deepening of concern for the evangelization of the world? Were the Churches ready to accept their responsibility for the world-wide apostolate?

In the ten years between 1948 and 1958 these questions were discussed with great intensity. It was found that owing to the new realization of the position of the Church in a "non-Christian world" and owing to the rediscovery of the missionary nature of the Church itself many Churches were now eager to take their full share in the common missionary task. Thus by 1958 it was possible for both I.M.C. and W.C.C. to decide that they would work towards a full integration of the two bodies. The integration took place at the New Delhi Assembly in 1961.

Fears which had been expressed in some quarters that a considerable part of the constituency of the International Missionary Council would not desire to co-operate with the integrated council, did not materialize, for only very few members of the I.M.C. remained outside the new Division of World Mission and Evangelism. Even a short time after the date of integration it was truthfully said that it seemed that the two bodies had been together for many years.

Although Churches and missionary bodies in each country remained free to follow or not to follow the international pattern, the integration of I.M.C. and W.C.C. led to similar action in a good many national situations. Thus the Churches have accepted more direct and definite responsibility for missionary activity and the missionary societies have related themselves more closely to the Churches. This was all the more necessary since not only outside, but also within the Churches, radical questions were raised with regard to missions. These had not only to do with missionary policies, but with the very *raison d'être* of missions. The modern mood of relativism and of syncretism made its influence felt. The true *raison d'être* of missions as a constraint put on the Church by its Lord, which had nothing to do with cultural imperialism, needed to be clarified by the whole ecumenical fellowship. And it had to be shown that there was no difference in principle between the evangelistic task in continents of Christian tradition and that in continents where other religions dominated. In all six continents the Church was called to mission. This was the theme worked out in the World Council Assemblies and in the Mexico meeting of the Commission of World Mission and Evangelism. At the same time the Evangelism Department of the W.C.C. concentrated on the study of "the missionary structure of the congregation". This study met with stronger response than any other study undertaken by the W.C.C. in recent years.

Coming to grips with the World

The Oxford Conference on Life and Work in 1937 had helped many Churches to realize that the Church had a prophetic mission towards society. And the experience of the war years made it very clear that one of the principal tasks of the Church was to perform the "office of the watchman". Thus many Churches which had taken for granted that the civilization in which they lived was and would remain a Christianized civilization realized suddenly that the very foundations of their society were shaking and began to rediscover the social dimension of their calling. Churches which had been silent about the great human issues of our time and had lived a self-centred existence began to speak out. They found that, while their voice was no longer a dominant voice, they could nevertheless help their members to steer a Christian course in their daily life and exert a not inconsiderable amount of influence on public opinion.

But they found at the same time that with regard to the basic issues of our time their witness would have to be a common witness. In this respect especially the statement of the Stockholm Conference was applicable: "The world is too strong for a divided Church." Thus the task to formulate common Christian convictions concerning those social and international problems which were of world-wide dimensions was to a large extent entrusted to the organs of the ecumenical movement.

A passage from the consultation on the future of the Commission of the Churches on International Affairs (C.C.I.A.), held in 1967 in Scheveningen, shows clearly that this concern belongs to the nature of the ecumenical movement. It said:

> We draw attention to the providential reality . . . that precisely at the time when the unity of mankind is becoming an inescapable fact, the privilege of ecumenical fellowship is being progressively realized by the churches. The discovery of their unity, transcending without destroying the ecclesiastical traditions and national loyalties of Christians throughout the world, gives churches a new perspective from which they may come to more objective judgment of the conflicts of our time.[1]

It was also increasingly understood that neither the world nor the church membership would listen to a mere repetition of statements concerning general Christian principles. On the other hand, the Churches had no right to express a conviction about specific world problems unless they could do so on the basis of a thorough study of the issues undertaken by men whose competence would be respected. That is why the Commission of the Churches on International Affairs was formed as a body of church people who had experience in the field of international affairs and who were served by a permanent staff of men in daily contact with international developments. That is why in the realm of Church and Society very concrete studies were undertaken on the implications of "rapid social change" for the Churches in many parts of the world. And that is why the World Conference on Church and Society in 1966 concentrated on such concrete human issues as the problems of development and the relations between the affluent nations and the nations engaged in a desperate struggle against poverty.

It is a remarkable fact that in spite of the extreme variety of national, political, and theological background it has so often been possible to arrive at a common mind about difficult and controversial problems. There were, of course, also a number of questions, some of them crucial, on which no such *communis opinio* was reached and it became clear that the ecumenical

---

[1] *Ecumenical Review*, vol. xix (July 1967), p. 317.

movement can never "rest on its laurels" and that every new generation has to go through its own struggle to find a common basis for witness and action. Towards the end of our period new possibilities of consultation and co-operation in the field of social and international issues between the W.C.C. and the Roman Catholic Church began to materialize. When one compares what the World Conference on Church and Society said about the issues of world economic justice and development with the recommendations made in the papal encyclical *Populorum progressio* one finds that a substantial consensus in this crucial subject is developing.

The Impact of Asia, Africa, and Latin America

At the beginning of our 1958–68 period, the status of the younger Churches in the ecumenical movement was still ambiguous and uncertain. Only twenty-four of these Churches had joined the World Council. So they represented a small minority. And within their different regions they had little contact with each other. Most younger Churches knew a great deal more about the Churches in the country from which their missionaries had come than about the Churches in their own part of the world. But in the years since 1948 very many younger Churches became members of the Council. This meant that "they were recognized as equals of the older churches" and "this enabled them to gain a new sense of their own destiny in the economy of God in the world".[1] But they would not be able to fulfil their ecumenical calling unless they could come together on a regional or continental level in order to learn from each other, to undertake common tasks, and to bring their specific contribution to the whole movement.

The Asians led the way. In a series of meetings from 1949 onwards, plans were defined and the East Asia Christian Conference came into being. Africa, ·Latin America, and the Pacific Islands followed a few years later.

This development of a regional ecumenism was in no way a withdrawal from the world-wide movement. On the contrary. It was an effort to formulate more clearly what were the specific concerns of each region and what contribution it could make to the whole. At the same time it was realized that the great question how to bring the Christian message to the peoples of Asia or Africa in a manner truly comprehensible in the indigenous cultural situations, but with full loyalty to the essential content of the gospel, was a question which could best be answered by the Churches together, continent by continent.

Thus a whole new dimension was added to the ecumenical movement. This became increasingly clear at the meetings of the Central Committee and of the Assemblies of the World Council. The issues being discussed were no longer only those which were of greater concern to Europe and North America. The Central Committee meetings in Lucknow 1952 and Enugu 1965 and the Assembly at New Delhi were opportunities for confrontation with the realities of the Asian and African situation. And the World Conference on Church and Society in Geneva 1966 was in fact a dialogue between the

[1] V. E. Devadutt in *Lessons for Tomorrow's Mission* (W.S.C.F. 1960), p. 213.

"North" and the "South" in which the voices of Asians, Africans, and Latin Americans were heard as never before in the ecumenical movement.

The impact of the Churches of these continents on the ecumenical movement can be summarized in the following points:

1. They have helped the other Churches to realize that the position of Christianity in the world is that of a minority the future of which depends on its missionary energy.

2. They contribute to the creation of a different sense of proportion in doctrinal and theological matters. For the issues which are crucial for them are not the traditional interconfessional issues, but rather the issues of a right interpretation of basic Christian truth in terms of cultures dominated by other religions.

3. They help the other Churches to face the problem of world poverty hunger, and underdevelopment as the number one problem for humanity and as an inescapable challenge to all Christians.

The ecumenical movement is still not fully ecumenical in so far as in its concerns, in its leadership, in the composition of many of its meetings, older Churches hold a dominating position. But progress in the direction of a truly effective participation of the total Christian family has been made.

The Impact of Eastern Orthodoxy

One of the earliest initiatives to arrive at the creation of a fellowship of Churches had been taken in 1920 by the Ecumenical Patriarchate of Constantinople, and a number of Orthodox Churches had taken part in the ecumenical meetings of the 1920s and 1930s. But by the time of the Amsterdam Assembly of 1948 only a few had accepted membership in the W.C.C. and only two (the Ecumenical Patriarchate and the Church of Greece) had been able to send delegations to Amsterdam. Attempts made to arrive at a fraternal discussion with the Moscow Patriarchate had failed. The situation was similar in other ecumenical organizations. That large part of Eastern Orthodoxy which lived in the countries under a communist regime was for the time being unable to maintain contacts with other Churches. It is true that Orthodox leaders in Western Europe and the U.S.A. continued to make a valuable contribution, but the general situation remained, nevertheless, that during a considerable period the Orthodox Churches were not present on the ecumenical scene in such numbers and with such weight that they could make their voice sufficiently heard.

The situation began to change after the Evanston Assembly of 1954. After a period of correspondence delegations of the Orthodox Church of Russia and of the W.C.C. met in Utrecht 1958 and found a basis for closer relations. Visits of W.C.C. leaders and staff-members to Russia and of Russian Church leaders to Geneva were arranged. Many questions were clarified.

In 1961 the Orthodox Churches of Russia, Rumania, Bulgaria, and Poland became members of the W.C.C. They were followed by other Orthodox

Churches and also by other Eastern Churches, notably the Armenian Church, so that by 1964 practically all large Churches of Eastern tradition were actively participating in the movement. The persistent policy of co-operation with, and support of, the W.C.C. maintained by Patriarch Athenagoras of Constantinople was an important element in this development.

In the meantime the Orthodox Churches had also to consider what should be their attitude to the Second Vatican Council to which they were asked to send observers. This led to a series of meetings of Orthodox Church leaders at which decisions were taken concerning the policy of the Orthodox Churches in the new ecumenical situation. Unprecedented personal contacts were established when Pope Paul VI and Patriarch Athenagoras of Constantinople met in Jerusalem, later in Constantinople and in Rome, and when dignitaries of several Orthodox Churches visited Rome.

This was therefore the period in which Eastern Christianity began to make its impact felt in the ecumenical movement. The Montreal Faith and Order Report 1963 said: "For the first time in the Faith and Order dialogue, the Eastern Orthodox and other Eastern Churches have been strongly represented in our meetings. A new dimension of Faith and Order has opened up and we can only begin to see its future possibilities."[1] These last words deserve emphasis. The active participation of the Eastern Churches, not only in Faith and Order meetings, but in the conferences on Church and Society, on international affairs and many others has made a real difference to the ecumenical movement. They have raised questions about the place of worship among the concerns of the ecumenical movement. They have added new dimensions to the discussion on ecclesiology by maintaining at the same time a high doctrine of the Church and a strong emphasis on the autonomy of each national Church. On the other hand, the ecumenical movement has made it necessary for them to face anew the issue of the Church's responsibility in the field of social ethics. But it must also be said that after so many centuries of separation between East and West and at a time when many of the Orthodox Churches are living under great external pressures, it is still exceedingly difficult to arrive at a full sharing between the Christian East and the Christian West. Neither in the West nor in the East has enough been done to find and prepare men for the task of ecumenical interpretation and cross-fertilization between two main parts of Christendom which have been separated for ten centuries.

The Roman Catholic Church
Enters upon the Ecumenical Scene

Individual Roman Catholics had shown deep interest in the ecumenical movement since its beginning and in the 1930s small groups of Roman Catholics, Protestants, and Orthodox had come together quietly to explore the possibilities of a dialogue. The World's Student Christian Federation was a pioneer in this field. The attendance was largely from some of the countries of western Europe. During the Second World War many new contacts were established.

[1] Montreal, p. 56.

B

Not only in the countries where Roman Catholics and Protestants were both in conflict with national socialism, but also in Great Britain, there were conversations at the level of the hierarchy, and in some cases common declarations were issued. It was therefore hoped that a number of individually invited Roman Catholic observers would be allowed to attend the first World Council Assembly, but this hope was not fulfilled. In 1949 the Vatican defined its attitude to the ecumenical movement (*De motione ecumenica*) and recognized the significance of the ecumenical movement. It was also stated that no Roman Catholics should attend international ecumenical meetings unless they had permission to do so from the Vatican. When the Second Assembly took place in 1954, the Roman Catholic Archbishop of Chicago forbade any Roman Catholics to attend the meeting in Evanston, a suburb of Chicago.

In the meantime the informal theological contacts had been intensified. Roman Catholic ecumenists made increasingly helpful contributions to the ecumenical discussion. The questions they raised about the nature and policies of the World Council stimulated the Council to clarify its position. Thus the important Toronto declaration of 1950 on "The Church, the Churches and the World Council of Churches" was at least in part an answer to questions which Roman Catholic theologians had raised.

A new situation was created in 1960 when Pope John XXIII created the Secretariat for the Promotion of Unity among Christians. Up to that moment the W.C.C. or other ecumenical organizations had no "address" in the Roman Catholic Church to which they could turn to discuss specific problems of relationships or of common concern. From that moment onwards there was regular consultation. Cardinal Bea, who headed the new secretariat, went out of his way to facilitate personal contacts with leaders of the W.C.C. and of the different Churches. Thus it became possible to have at the Third Assembly a group of Roman Catholic observers designated by the Roman Catholic Church, and thus it came about that observers from many confessional bodies, from the W.C.C. and from some Churches, attended the Second Vatican Council. Their role at the Council went far beyond observing and really led to a real dialogue about the great themes on the agenda of the Council. The Decree on Ecumenism which the Council adopted opened new doors for ecumenical contacts. Its definition of ecumenism had a good deal in common with that underlying the life of the W.C.C.; but the difference between the two conceptions was that the Vatican Council thinks in terms of a bringing of the other Churches to a renewed and more truly catholic Roman Catholic Church, whereas the ecumenism of the W.C.C. considers the question of the ultimate form of unity as an open question the answer to which will have to be found during the common ecumenical pilgrimage.

An important result of the new situation was the creation of a Joint Working Group between the Roman Catholic Church and the W.C.C. During the short time of its existence this group has already shown its usefulness as a platform for the discussion of common concerns. Its reports have been well received by the Central Committee of the W.C.C. and by the Vatican authorities.

The ecumenical mobilization of the Roman Catholics has modified the ecumenical situation very profoundly. Both at the international and at the national level there has been a tremendous increase in opportunities for contact, for serious conversation, and for practical co-operation. It was inevitable that these new and unexpected possibilities came to occupy the centre of the ecumenical stage. It seemed for a time as if the one and only important ecumenical problem was that of the relations between the Roman Catholic Church and other Churches. And there was a good deal of naive optimism about the removal of age-old divisions in the very near future. Some people declared that the centre of the ecumenical movement had shifted and that the ecumenical initiative had passed to the Roman Catholic Church. But they forget that ecumenism is not a game of football. There is no place in the ecumenical movement for a form of competition which seeks to eliminate other participants. For that would be to deny the very principle of gathering and the creation of true fellowship.

There is a place in the ecumenical movement for what the Abbé Couturier called "spiritual emulation", that is, for mutual stimulation to deeper and better Christian obedience and discipleship. Now the ecumenical movement as it had taken shape in the W.C.C. had been a stimulus for the Roman Catholic Church. Similarly, the entrance of the Roman Catholic Church upon the ecumenical scene has stimulated and will continue to stimulate the W.C.C. and its member Churches. It has not only led many Churches to rethink their attitude to the Roman Catholic Church, but it has led them to ask again whether they themselves were sufficiently active in the cause of church unity. Thus it is shown again that the cause of ecumenism is indivisible, that, as the Decree on Ecumenism of the Second Vatican Council said, there is one ecumenical movement, and that the spiritual gift of the active desire for unity, as all spiritual gifts, is given for the common good of the whole People of God.

Confessional Consciousness

Most confessions or denominations had developed their own federations, alliances, or organs of consultation before the ecumenical movement took shape. But in the period after the Second World War most of them re-organized themselves and became more active than they had been before, and some developed a strong secretariat and undertook a wide variety of tasks.

This development was partly due to the specific needs of their member Churches, but it was also due to the emergence of the ecumenical movement. The new unprecedented ecumenical situation obliged each confession to consider anew what position it should take with regard to the issues of church unity, and this led naturally to a new reflection on the significance of the common confessional heritage. All has to ask: What can our confessional family contribute to the wider ecumenical family? What is the basic truth for which it must stand at all cost?

It was equally inevitable that the growth of the confessional bodies would create problems of relationship between these bodies and the W.C.C. There were the practical problems such as the demands in time, in energy, in finance which the W.C.C. and the confessional bodies were making on the same Churches. There was the fundamental issue of the relative claims of confessional unity and of unity on the national scale. Fortunately most of these bodies were willing and eager to co-operate with the World Council and the World Council itself understood that the support of these bodies was essential for its own development. Thus regular means of consultation were developed and it proved possible to remove a number of misunderstandings.

In recent years several of the confessional families have found a very important role in paving the way for church unity by entering in dialogue with other confessions. In this respect the invitation issued by the Roman Catholic Church to all confessional bodies to send observers to the Second Vatican Council has had important consequences. As the confessional families reflected on their attitude to the Roman Catholic Church and in many cases agreed to enter into conversation with the Roman Catholic Church, they realized that more could and should be done on a world level about conversations with the other confessions. The more specific discussions on reunion will have to a very large extent to take place on a national level, but discussions on the world level can prepare the way. Thus we find in recent years that a whole network of interconfessional dialogue is developing.

Evangelical Critique of Ecumenism

During the period concerned the growing influence of the ecumenical movement also led to growing criticism on the part of Christians who mistrusted the basic motives of the movement. The wilder form of opposition, expressing itself in accusations that the movement was infiltrated by communists or that it was scheming to gather all the Churches under the authority of the Pope, created a certain amount of confusion among ignorant people, but never had enough backing of responsible churchmen to become a real problem. But the criticism that came from responsible conservative Evangelical circles had to do with real issues which had to be faced. For these issues were important in themselves, and failure to answer them could lead to increasing estrangement between the ecumenism of the W.C.C. and the ecumenism of evangelical bodies, some of which had a considerable following in member Churches of the W.C.C.

The main issue was ecclesiological in character. Is the unity of which the New Testament speaks to be conceived exclusively as a "spiritual" and "invisible" unity or as a unity which must also find concrete structural expression in the life of the Church? The W.C.C. made it clear, very particularly in its New Delhi statement on unity, that, while it could not choose for any particular form of unity, it stood for unity which would express itself in tangible form. This stand was not taken because of a desire for the concentration of ecclesiastical power, or in order to increase the influence of the Church in the world, but rather because, according to the Scriptures, it is an essential part of the calling and witness of the Church to manifest the oneness of the people of God.

It was stressed again and again that the W.C.C. Churches did not conceive such concrete unity as the centralized unity of a super-Church, that real unity did not mean uniformity, and that it was out of the question that any of these Churches would give up the spiritual independence which they cherished so greatly. The suspicion that there was an ecumenical conspiracy to create a vast and powerful ecclesiastical machinery of world-wide dimensions has not yet been removed. But, as the Central Committee of the W.C.C. noted in 1966, "In those Evangelical circles where ecumenism has been suspect hitherto, there are now increasing signs of concern about Christian unity."[1] There were other points of criticism. Many Evangelicals feared that the ecumenical movement would lead to theological relativism or even syncretism. This fear is not wholly unfounded since there are a certain number of people in several of the member Churches of the W.C.C. whose "ecumenism" takes the form of a theological indifferentism or of a general embracing of all religions. The W.C.C. has, however, been able to answer that the main thrust of its theological studies and pronouncements has been clearly biblical and christocentric and that the basic principle of its ecumenism has always been that unity at the expense of truth is not unity at all.

Perhaps the most relevant question raised by the conservative Evangelicals has been whether the ecumenical movement has concentrated its energies too much on social and international problems and neglected the primary task of mission and evangelism. The question is all the more relevant since a comparison between the W.C.C. Churches and the evangelical bodies shows that the latter are spending a much greater proportion of their resources of men and money on evangelism and foreign missions. But the great question arises: What is evangelism? Is the Church evangelistic only if it preaches the gospel to individuals? Or is it also evangelistic if it throws the light of the gospel on the great human problems of our time? The debate continues and both partners in the conversation have to learn from each other. For, as the Central Committee of the W.C.C. said in 1965: "The member churches of the World Council, which have already experienced something of the mutual correction and edification which is made possible by our common membership in the Council, need also the contribution of these evangelical churches. . . ."

Churchly Ecumenism Challenged

We have noted that during the 1930s and 1940s there had been a "rediscovery of the Church".[2] This had been partly due to the convergent development in biblical theology, so that it was possible to speak of a "new consensus" of scholars from differing confessions concerning the decisive place of the Church in the New Testament. But it was also the consequence drawn from the church conflicts first in Germany, then in the occupied countries, in which it had been shown that the Christian cause could be defended only by confessing Churches deeply conscious of their God-given mission. Moreover, the witness which had to be given to society, national or international, at a time

---

[1] MRCC (Geneva 1966), p. 72.

[2] See *A History of the Ecumenical Movement 1517–1948*, ed. Rouse and Neill, pp. 574 and 700.

of the shaking of the foundations could be effective only if it was given by Churches who could speak on behalf of a coherent community of the faithful. The fact that with the creation of the World Council of Churches the ecumenical movement became more definitely "churchly" in character was therefore widely accepted as a necessary development.

But not many years later the question was raised whether this emphasis on the Church was really justified. Had the movement not lost some of its spontaneity and of its revolutionary character by linking itself so closely to the Churches? Was there not a danger that the World Council, which had begun its life with a very small staff working in a chalet and in wooden barracks and which within twenty years had become a considerable organization housed in impressive buildings, was itself becoming the victim of the iron law of institutional development? Some began to use the word "ecumenical bureaucracy".

And there was an even deeper issue. Was it right to be so strongly concerned about the formation of an *oikoumene* of the Churches? Should not the original meaning of *oikoumene*, namely "the whole inhabited world", become the true focus of the movement, so that it should be really concerned with the world rather than with the Church?

These ideas met with considerable response among young people who were deeply disappointed by the lack of effective renewal in the Churches and by the slowness of advance toward church unity. They received further encouragement from the more general anti-institutional wave which became a characteristic of the life of the younger generation in the 1960s. The result has been the growth of various forms of spontaneous ecumenism, outside or in very undefined relation with the ecumenical movement of the Churches. In so far as these forms of ecumenism are completely unrelated to the life of the Churches and combat not only institutionalism but also the very existence of institutions, they are not likely to have a lasting effect. For no spiritual movement can make any real impression on the course of church history or world history unless it becomes incarnate in some tangible (and that means some institutional) form. It was precisely the concern for relevance to the new world situation which led the men of 1937 to the conclusion that the ecumenical movement should have a more definite shape. But in so far as these new movements seek to act as pioneers for the Churches, to challenge bureaucratic and immobile structures, and to make imaginative experiments, they may render a service similar to that which was rendered by the Christian youth movements in the early days of the ecumenical movement.

The fact that the ecumenical movement has continued to grow is not in itself a cause for alarm, but for gratitude. For that growth has been a response to a great need in the life of the Church. And the churchly *oikoumene* can only serve the world *oikoumene* if it develops adequate instruments for the fulfilment of its task. Moreover, whether a movement becomes institutionalist and bureaucratic is far more a problem of quality than of quantity. The best answer to institutionalism is therefore to ensure that within the given institutions it is the calling rather than the organization, the goal rather than the means, which dominate.

Theological Tensions

The 1930s and 1940s were a period of remarkable convergence in theological thought. The ecumenical movement had helped to overcome divisions and was in turn greatly strengthened by the common turning to a biblical theology with strong emphasis on the calling of the Church in the world. By the time of the Oxford Conference 1937, the tension between the "activist" and the "otherworldly" theologies had lost a good deal of its sharpness because the world situation had forced the "activists" to revise their optimistic view of history and had forced the "otherworldly" to take the task of the Church in society more seriously. There remained enough important theological problems, such as those between the "Catholic" and the "Protestant" conceptions of the Church, but in 1941 a Dominican, Father F. M. Braun, could write that "a new consensus"[1] was emerging in this respect. And the Amsterdam Assembly 1948, while stressing the very real difference between the "Catholic" and "Protestant" conceptions, found a substantial consensus on "the Universal Church in God's design". It said: "Beneath these disagreements we find an agreement in a unity which drew us together and will not let us go."[2]

During the years of preparation for the Second Assembly with its main theme "Christ the Hope of the World", there was again a lively discussion concerning the meaning and relevance of eschatology. The Advisory Committee on the main theme, composed of Christian thinkers of extremely varied background, had a hard time arriving at a common document and the Assembly did not accept it as its own word. But the Assembly admitted that the report "exhibits a substantial ecumenical consensus" and that "it indicates the direction in which we must all move".[3] And there can be no doubt that the report exerted a wide influence in the following years. The revision of the Basis of the W.C.C. 1961, so that it included a definite reference to the authority of the holy Scriptures and an explicit statement concerning the Trinity was also a sign of growing consensus. And the most impressive aspect of the theological development was that Roman Catholic, Orthodox, and Protestant were not only learning from each other, but that they discovered large areas of agreement about theological issues which had kept them apart for many centuries.

But the story of theology, as the story of human thought generally, is a story of ever new beginnings. And so during the period many of the results of the theological work of earlier generations were again called in question. There is practically no Church which escapes this theological shaking of the foundations. The Roman Catholic theologian Karl Rahner speaks of a sense of "historical dizziness". Now it is inevitable that in a time of intensive inter-Church contacts, new movements of thought cross the frontiers of the confessions. And so the new divergence of convictions concerning demythologization and *Heilsgeschichte*, concerning the "end of religion" and the meaning of secularism, concerning existentialism and the "death of God", is

---

[1] F. M. Braun. *Aspects nouveaux du problème de l'Église* (Fribourg 1941), chapter 3.
[2] Amsterdam, p. 55. [3] Evanston, p. 70.

not one between the different confessions, but a subject of debate within each confession and within the ecumenical movement as a whole.

This "transconfessional" character of the great theological debates of recent years is bound to have considerable effect on the relations between the Churches. Already the representatives of the new theological currents in the different Churches have a stronger bond among themselves across confessional frontiers than they have with many of their fellow-churchmen who do not accept the new ideas. This brings an element of confusion into the inter-Church situation, but it may also help to show that many of the old lines of division and demarcation are no longer the truly important ones. The Commission on Faith and Order is deeply aware of this new situation and has therefore decided that it must not only be concerned with the "controversies which have their origin in the past", but also with the "new threats to unity" and that in its future work priority should be given to the great controversies of today.

For the ecumenical movement as a whole the question arises whether out of the present theological tensions a new consensus will emerge which can serve as a foundation for the common witness and the common task. There is no reason to deplore the fact that new situations require the reformulation of the truth, but there is every reason to be watchful that the basic insights which have created the ecumenical movement and kept it alive will not be lost in the process of rethinking.

Non-Theological Tensions

The hope which many had expressed that after the Second World War the ecumenical ship could sail on less troubled waters was not fulfilled. The post-war period became a period of acute political tensions and conflicts and these had considerable repercussions on inter-Church relations. The ecumenical movement could have taken one of two lines of least resistance. It could have identified itself uncritically with one particular power-constellation or one ideology. The temptation to do this was all the greater, since in the first years after the Amsterdam Assembly only very few Churches in communist countries could participate in the life of the movement. Voices were not wanting which urged the World Council to enter into alliance with the Western powers and to defend their policies without reserve. But the ecumenical movement had learned the important lesson that its strength could consist only in its integrity and independence as a movement exclusively motivated by Christian convictions and constantly concerned about the maintenance of fellowship between Christians in all parts of the world and living under the most diverse political regimes.

The other line of least resistance would have been to decide that, in view of the repercussions which statements on controversial issues might have for the cohesion of the movement, the World Council should remain silent concerning such issues. Many times the W.C.C. has been warned that if it continued to speak out on the burning issues of international relations it would surely endanger its own life. But the ecumenical movement had precisely become relevant when it had become a fellowship of common convictions and for common witness and sought to throw the light of the gospel upon the grave issues facing mankind. An ecumenical movement which would proclaim only vague generalities could hardly expect to be taken seriously by the Churches and by the world.

The dilemma created by the duty to witness to justice and peace and the duty to maintain fellowship led to a number of greater and smaller crises. At the time of the war in Korea, during the Hungarian crisis and the Suez War, at the moment of the Cuba conflict, and on a number of other occasions the responsible committees of the Council or its officers made specific declarations. In doing so they sought to take their stand on principles which had been adopted by the Assemblies. More frequently the officers of the Commission of the Churches on International Affairs expressed their mind concerning possible solutions of international problems. In many cases these statements were well received. In some cases they led to a good deal of controversy within the movement. It is, however, remarkable that in no case did they lead to a real break in the ecumenical fellowship. The decision of three Dutch Reformed Churches in South Africa to leave the Council is no exception, since their decision was mainly based on the rejection of the report of the Cottesloe Conference[1] which had been approved overwhelmingly by their own chosen delegates.

When, by the time of the Third Assembly in New Delhi 1961, the Churches of Russia, Rumania, Bulgaria as well as a large number of Churches from Asia and Africa had joined, the W.C.C. became a body in which nearly all the international tensions of our time were at least potentially reflected. And at each meeting of the Central or Executive Committees or of the C.C.I.A. some of these tensions had to be dealt with and if possible overcome. It cannot be said that the attempt was always successful. But it can be said that on the whole the struggle to arrive at a common mind has often strengthened rather than weakened the sense of common sharing in a fellowship which transcends all political divisions. Thus at the World Conference on Church and Society hard words were said by the representatives of the poorer nations to those of the rich nations and vice versa, but it was precisely on the basis of this frankness that it became possible to reach a common mind on many important problems.

The experience of these years shows how difficult it is for all Churches to rise above the necessarily limited viewpoint of their national and social environment, but it has also shown that it is precisely through the ecumenical encounter that the necessary mutual correction can take place so that the Churches can arrive at a more objective judgement concerning the road to true peace and real justice.

The W.C.C. was, however, by no means the only Christian body to deal with international problems and non-theological tensions between Christians. During the period under discussion there was a considerable improvement

[1] The Cottesloe Conference was a meeting of delegates of the W.C.C. member Churches in South Africa together with a small delegation of the W.C.C. It dealt with the Christian attitude to race relations in South Africa.

in the relations between the Roman Catholic Church and the Churches in communist countries and even an improvement in its relations with some of the governments of these countries. The great exception remained China. Contacts with Christians in China became fewer and fewer in spite of all attempts to restore fellowship. This was even true in the case of the Prague Peace Conference which in the beginning had had participants from the Chinese Churches. That Peace Conference played an important role in bringing Christian leaders from eastern Europe together and in promoting a dialogue between them and Christians from countries in the West, in Asia, Africa, and Latin America. It is not organized as a body representing all the Churches in an official way and considers its task as complementary to the work of the W.C.C. From time to time discussions have taken place between the W.C.C. and the Prague Peace Conference in order to clarify the position of each body in relation to the other.

The Growing Ecumenical Network

International ecumenism had received much of its original inspiration from national bodies, very especially from the Federal Council of Churches in the U.S.A. But the emergence of the ecumenical movement on the world level led to the formation of national councils in many countries in which such councils did not yet exist. Where these councils were well organized and co-operated with the World Council, or where they were member councils of the International Missionary Council and became members of the new Division of Missions and Evangelism of the W.C.C., they helped greatly in relating the programme of the world bodies to the Churches. It was in the realm of inter-Church aid, relief work, and service to refugees that the most effective system of continuous co-operation was elaborated. For the first time in church history the Churches possessed an instrument of service through which they could act speedily and efficiently whenever a great human need had to be met in any part of the world.

It must be added that in many places there has been a considerable development of ecumenical activity on the local level. There are still cities and villages where local congregations belonging to church bodies which are active in the ecumenical movement have little contact with each other. But the number of local councils which understand that ecumenism begins at home is growing, and it is increasingly understood that local councils should not only be concerned with common practical problems, but also with a real spiritual sharing between the Churches.

The regional (continental) councils have been created in the period since the Amsterdam Assembly. They are of varying strength, but several of them have already become indispensable instruments for ecumenical action and it is largely due to their work that each continent can now make its voice heard in the world-wide dialogue.

With regard to ecumenical education there was also considerable progress. Ecumenism became under a variety of names a recognized subject of study in many theological faculties and colleges. Ecumenical Institutes were formed in many places. It can be said that the number of people who give full time to the service of the ecumenical cause on the international, national, and local level has increased beyond anything which the most optimistic supporters of the ecumenical movement had conceived possible in 1948.

The more specialized movements, which are organizationally independent, but collaborate in many ways with the W.C.C. and with the Churches, remained as indispensable for the ecumenical movement as a whole as they had been before the formation of the World Council of Churches, for they performed tasks which could not, at least not in the same way, be performed by the Churches or the W.C.C. All of them had to face new problems and discovered new opportunities as the ecumenical movement advanced. Thus the United Bible Societies entered in consultation with the authorities of the Roman Catholic Church about common translations of the Scriptures. And the Y.M.C.A., Y.W.C.A., and the W.S.C.F. also developed their relations with Roman Catholic youth organizations.

What was Achieved and What was Not Achieved?

The strength and weakness of the ecumenical movement as it developed during the last twenty years can be summarized in the following seven points—five of them dealing with points of strength and two of them dealing with points of weakness.

The points of strength would seem to be the following:

1. All Churches have been obliged to respond to the fundamental question which the ecumenical movement puts before them, the question of their relation to other Churches, the question of their obedience to the original mandate to gather with the Lord of the Church the dispersed children of God into one. Every Church must make up its mind about this new fact in the history of the Church, that the Churches after centuries in isolation and self-centredness are again turning towards each other and seeking to manifest that the bond of common faith in Jesus Christ must lead to a common life and a common witness.

2. The Churches live again as members of a family, a family in which there is still a great deal of friction and misunderstanding, but a family which cannot fail to realize that it has a common history and a common destiny, that it has its own identity and its own ethos and that its members need to support each other and to share their spiritual and material gifts. The times when Churches could live as self-contained entities is irrevocably gone. Theology can no longer be carried on in the form of confessional monologue.

3. The existence of the ecumenical movement has given encouragement to Churches which are under the pressure of a hostile environment or live a very isolated existence. For them the sense of belonging to a world-wide fellowship has an existential significance which it can hardly have in the same way in Churches living in more favourable external conditions.

4. The ecumenical movement has enabled the Churches to render a common

witness at the world level. In a time in which the grave human issues are issues of global dimensions the Churches can hardly make their voice heard if they do not speak together and if they do not speak in terms of the total world situation. The ecumenical movement has shown that their common faith enables the Churches to arrive at common convictions concerning the tensions and conflicts of our time and so to help in breaking through the deadlock situations which are characteristic of international life in our time.

5. The ecumenical movement has enabled the Churches to practise solidarity in their relations with each other and to become an effective instrument for the meeting of human need in all parts of the world.

The points of weakness would seem to be the following:

1. The ecumenical movement cannot yet claim that very significant results have been reached with regard to church unity. The word "unity" is here taken in the wider sense, for the ecumenical movement must not be judged exclusively by the number of organizational unions, but also by the other ways in which growing fellowship expresses itself, such as intercommunion. With regard to actual unions it can be said that a considerable number of Churches have become united with each other. While in most cases these Churches belonged to the same or closely related confessional families, the trend toward interconfessional unions is increasing. It is also true that a very large number of Churches are at present in negotiation with each other about unity. But few of these schemes are as yet approaching the moment of completion and realization.

With regard to full intercommunion there has been some progress. But in many circles, notably among the young, there is a sense of disappointment that after several decades of living together the Churches have not solved this distressing problem.

Thus the ecumenical movement has now reached a critical stage. Will it be content with that by no means inconsiderable, but nevertheless very incomplete, form of unity which it has already achieved? Or will it press on to that full unity which alone is worthy of the Church of Christ and which is the deepest *raison d'être* of the movement itself.

2. The ecumenical movement is not sufficiently rooted in the life of the local congregations. In spite of all attempts made to educate church members for participation in the ecumenical enterprise the movement is still too much an army with many generals and officers, but with too few soldiers. It would seem that not enough has been done to show that the ecumenical concern is not to be conceived as one of the many concerns in which a local congregation may take interest, but as a concern which arises out of the very nature of the Church. It is clear that real advance towards full unity will be made only if in the coming years local congregations and their members discover that to follow Christ means to follow him in his work of the building on the one Body, his Body.

2
The Life and Activities
of the World Council of Churches

H. KRÜGER

Defining the Nature and Function of the World Council of Churches, from the Toronto Statement (1950) to the Ecumenical Way (1966)

It is a noteworthy fact that the World Council "in process of formation" had to solve extremely far-reaching and important problems during the formative years between 1938 and 1948, before it had been officially constituted. It is also noteworthy that it existed for several years before it rendered an account of its own nature. At Amsterdam the Assembly adopted a statement from the Provisional Committee on the "Nature of the Council".[1] It is quite natural that in those first years many misunderstandings arose, especially from the Orthodox side, about the nature and purpose of the W.C.C. because a body of this kind had never existed before. Until then ecumenical relationships had been comparatively loose and non-committal. Through the formation of the W.C.C. they were now raised to an official level, and the member Churches were compelled to understand clearly their own status in this new fellowship. The comments and reflections were summed up in a draft entitled "The Ecclesiological Significance of the World Council of Churches" which was submitted to the Central Committee at Toronto in 1950. This formed the basis for the famous "Toronto statement" which clearly defined the relation of the member Churches to one another.[2]

The Toronto statement declares: "The World Council of Churches is not and must never become a Super-Church" (III. 1). Its competence does not even cover union negotiations; its purpose is "to bring the churches into living contact with each other" (III. 2). The W.C.C. has no ecclesiology of its own (III. 3), therefore no Church is obliged to change its own ecclesiology (III. 4) nor to accept "a specific doctrine concerning the nature of Church unity" (III. 5). The basis for fellowship in the W.C.C. is merely "the common recognition that Christ is the Divine Head of the body" (IV. 1). Admittedly the Churches belonging to the W.C.C. recognize "that the membership of the Church of Christ is more inclusive than the membership of their own Church body" (IV. 3); but this does imply "that each Church must regard the other member churches as churches in the true and full sense of the word". But "they recognize one another as serving the One Lord" (IV. 4) and "recognize in other churches elements of the true Church" (IV. 5). It is on this basis that they seek "a common witness before the world" (IV. 6), "render assistance to each other in case of need, and refrain from such actions as are incompatible with brotherly relationships" (IV. 7). "The member churches enter into spiritual relationships through which they seek to learn from each other and to give help to each other in order that the body of Christ may be built up and that the life of the churches may be renewed" (IV. 8).

All this sounds very cautious and reserved. Clearly it was intended more to describe the existing situation than to point towards a future goal, in order that all the member Churches might participate and co-operate. (This

---

[1] Amsterdam, pp. 127–8.   [2] *The First Six Years, 1948–1954*, pp. 113–19.

reticence applied not only to the Orthodox Churches but also to many Reformation Churches.) It is only with extreme caution that reference is made in the last paragraph to "a very real unity" which has repeatedly "been discovered in ecumenical meetings". "It exists and we receive it again and again as an unmerited gift from the Lord. We praise God for this foretaste of the unity of His People and continue hopefully with the work to which He has called us together. For the Council exists to serve the churches as they prepare to meet their Lord Who knows only *one* flock."

At the Third Assembly of the W.C.C. at New Delhi (1961) the Toronto statement was confirmed (see report of the section on "Unity", paras. 4, 49, and 50), because it "still best expresses our understanding of the Council's nature" (para. 48). However, the developments of the last ten years force us "to seek further clarification". "Mere insistence upon deeper study will not guarantee fresh insight. We are learning what the Council is by *living* together within it." "Nevertheless, the need for careful reflection on the theological meaning of our new life in the Council continues to be unfulfilled" (para. 48). "At least we are able to say that the World Council is not something wholly other than the member churches. It is the churches in continuing council" (para. 49).

Following the reconsideration in New Delhi, the question was taken up again at the Fourth World Conference on Faith and Order held at Montreal (1963), at which the theme "The Church and the World Council of Churches" was one of the questions dealt with by a subcommittee of the Section on "The Church in the Purpose of God" (para. 48). Certain tendencies to concede that the World Council of Churches bears certain marks which are marks of the Church of Christ were energetically opposed, especially by the Orthodox, because this would change the nature and basic assumptions of the W.C.C. The crucial sentence in the final report is the following: "The Council is not the Church; it is not seeking to be a Church or *the* Church", but it "offers itself as a servant of the churches and of the Church".[1] On the other hand, this statement was also made:

> The Council gratefully acknowledges that in sustained fellowship it has received something new, an enrichment of our Christian existence and a new vision of our Christian task in the world . . . . We do not concur in the precise definition of this experience, but we are agreed that it is a new dimension in the Council. We therefore express the ardent wish that this new experience should grow and increase steadily through God's help and guidance, leading us to final unity.

At Montreal the hope had been expressed that the Central Committee would devote further attention to this matter. At the Central Committee held at Rochester, U.S.A., in the same year the General Secretary, Dr Visser 't Hooft, therefore spoke on the subject "What can we say together about the meaning of membership in the World Council of Churches?"[2] While conceding that the Toronto statement had "rendered very good service", Dr Visser 't Hooft said:

[1] Montreal, pp. 48–9.   [2] MRCC (Rochester, U.S.A. 1963), pp. 134–8.

[It had been] criticized because its concept of the World Council of Churches was static rather than dynamic. . . . The Toronto statement and other documents of the council had not ascribed ecclesiological quality (in the strict sense of the word) to the W.C.C. But had the churches in the Council not learned something as they had lived together? Was there a growth in fellowship which should express itself in a deeper and richer self-understanding of the Council and did that experience not force us to admit that the nature of the Council should be described in ecclesiological categories? Several theologians have answered this question in the affirmative and speak of the W.C.C. as *une réalité ecclésiale*.

Dr Visser 't Hooft then drew attention to three issues important for future discussion of the meaning of membership in the W.C.C.

1. The Churches had not yet developed the categories of thought which can adequately describe the "ecumenical experience", which is a completely new experience in church history. Remarkably enough, the various confessional world bodies had also left the problem of their own ecclesiological character largely unsolved. "We try to define ecumenical realities in the thought-forms of a pre-ecumenical age." An additional difficulty is that Churches employ different terminologies in approaching the questions.

2. Another question that must be raised was whether the ecumenical experience can be described in terms "which are wholly or partly institutional".

3. The W.C.C. did not want to become a "Super-Church", and must not do so; but could one describe it in ecclesiological terms "without erroneously implying that the World Council is after all in some sense the Church and that membership in it adds something to the ecclesiological reality of its member churches"?

What were the implications of the above questions? (said Dr Visser 't Hooft):

> We should find a way to express what God has given to the churches in and through their fellowship in the Council, but we must ensure that we express it in such a way that the very provisional nature of the Council is clearly understood and that there cannot arise any confusion between that provisional unity and the unity which belongs to the Church Universal. Also: As churches live, speak, act together *a new reality* begins to emerge. . . . We cannot possibly call it the *Una Sancta*. . . . What we can say is that we receive together spiritual gifts which are signs of that oneness which was at the beginning when "the company of those who believed were of one heart and soul" (Acts 4. 32) and a first fruit of that oneness which will come into existence when all who bear the name of Christ will have been fully gathered together by the Lord of the Church.

Dr Visser 't Hooft insisted that "we must carefully distinguish between the World Council of Churches and this new ecumenical reality", because the ecumenical movement was wider than the World Council of Churches, and if the description of the emerging ecumenical reality were transferred to the World Council this would be "to confuse the instrument with the product". In conclusion Dr Visser 't Hooft proposed that the member Churches be requested to give further attention to this question. But he wisely added, "It is better to live with a reality which transcends definition than to live with a definition which claims more substance than exists in reality."

The anticipated critical response came in the ensuing discussion. The fact was stressed again from the Orthodox side that "the Orthodox Church could never regard the World Council as a Church". But also with respect to the conservative Evangelicals Dr Hendrikus Berkhof, among others, pointed out: "We can live beyond Toronto, but we cannot formulate beyond Toronto."[1]

Similar reserve was shown by the member Churches to whom the document was sent, in the name of the Central Committee, for study and comment. It was evident that the overwhelming majority of the member Churches had not reached the point in their own thinking which would enable them to formulate in precise terms their understanding and the nature of their membership in the World Council. In some cases, however, this reserve may have been motivated by the fear that they would have to draw practical conclusions from recognizing the theological significance of the W.C.C., that is, to concede to it greater power and authority.

This experience paved the way for another document entitled *The Ecumenical Way* which was discussed by the Central Committee in Geneva in 1966.[2] This document was not concerned with describing the nature of the W.C.C. or its self-understanding; it was rather an attempt to take stock of the situation and to agree upon the policy of the World Council. The document was also sent to the national and regional Christian Councils and to the confessional organizations. It was also intended as a basis for discussion in local congregations and at inter-Church conferences; it stressed the work done by the W.C.C., on which emphasis had already been laid at New Delhi ("All in each place") and at Montreal. This document also says something about the W.C.C. (IV. paras. 12 and 13); it stresses the need for flexibility in the institutions of the W.C.C., for spiritual inspiration and renewal, and its responsibility for the world.

The response to this document was astonishingly meagre. On the one hand, the lack of balance in its thinking and formulation was more strongly criticized than usual. On the other hand (as Lukas Vischer stated in 1967 to the Central Committee at Heraklion), some of the comments made one feel "something of a hope and an expectation that the World Council will give pastoral help to the churches, and especially to the local churches".[3] Vischer comes to the sober conclusion:

> Both the document itself and especially the answers show that the discussion on the meaning of the World Council has come to a dead end. No helpful suggestions have been made from any quarter. The discussion is confined to agreement, or more often disagreement, with the Toronto statement of 1950, and when one has finished reading the replies one has the feeling that one has been turning round in circles to no purpose. When a discussion comes to a dead

[1] MRCC (Rochester, U.S.A. 1963), pp. 17–21.
[2] MRCC (Geneva 1966), pp. 89–92 (original form) and pp. 70–5 (final form).
[3] MRCC (Heraklion 1967), pp. 130–1.

end, the wisest thing is to leave it alone for a time. The great questions raised by the present situation cannot be directly included in a discussion on the nature of the World Council.

However, the document has helped to strengthen the forward movement. The views expressed require courageous action on the part of the W.C.C., and this is perhaps the most promising aspect of the whole question.

This confirms the statement made by Dr Visser 't Hooft that the self-understanding of the World Council of Churches, and the importance which its member Churches attach to their membership in it, must be built up step by step through living and working together, before they can be defined in words. Surely it should be emphasized that two decades is much too short a time for there to be any consensus among the member Churches on the ecclesiological significance of the W.C.C. However, despite all the sober conclusions, one should not disregard the dynamism which is at work within the growing fellowship of Churches, which was described by Edmund Schlink in his address at the Lund Conference in the following manner:

> Let us therefore hurry forward on this way and not stand still. Let us look forward. Let not our eyes be held to the present, but let us tear our eyes away from the visible divisions which we have not yet overcome, and let us look firmly to the One Lord towards whom we are moving. In the view ahead, in the expectation of the Coming Judge of the World and the Redeemer, we shall recognize the temporary character and the lack of finality of many things which divide us now.[1]

The Basis of the W.C.C. Clarified[2]

In Article I of its Constitution the World Council defined its "Basis" as follows: "The World Council of Churches is a fellowship of churches which accept our Lord Jesus Christ as God and Saviour."[3] Already at Amsterdam, however, the desire was expressed "for clarification or amplification of the affirmation of the Christian faith set forth in the Basis of the Council". Although the Assembly held the view "that the Basis set forth in the Constitution is adequate for the present purposes of the World Council of Churches", those Churches which desired the Basis to be changed were requested to present their desires in writing to the Central Committee for study, and the Central Committee was instructed to keep its study of possible changes within the christological principle set forth in the present Basis.[4]

At the meeting of the Central Committee in Toronto (1950) Dr Visser 't Hooft reported for the first time that one member Church had proposed an amendment (Remonstrant Church of Holland), but action on the request was postponed until the next meeting of the Central Committee.[5] Later on the Society of Friends of Philadelphia and Vicinity, and then the Presbyterian Church of Australia, sent in proposals for amending the Basis. At Rolle in 1951 a subcommittee was appointed (consisting of Douglas Horton, Georges

---

[1] *Ecumenical Review*, vol. v (October 1952), p. 36.
[2] See Wolfdieter Theurer, *Die trinitarische Basis des ORK*. Frankfurt-am-Main 1967.
[3] Amsterdam, p. 197.   [4] Ibid., pp. 115 ff.   [5] MRCC (Toronto 1950), p. 53.

Florovsky, and Anders Nygren) to which Dr Visser 't Hooft presented a memorandum dated 1 October 1951.[1] At the next meeting of the Central Committee in Lucknow the subcommittee reported that it had received a great deal of material to work on.[2] It was not considered necessary to change the Basis, but the Assembly should explain that the incarnation and the Trinity were implicit in the Amsterdam Basis. The Assembly should also define the meaning of the Basis, and for this the subcommittee presented a draft.

Shortly before the Second Assembly of the W.C.C. at Evanston (1954) the Church of Norway came forward with the suggestion that the words "in accordance with Holy Scripture" be added to the Basis,[3] but the proposal was received too late to be considered by the Second Assembly. At Evanston a "Statement on the purpose and function of the Basis" was accepted,[4] saying that the Basis performs three functions: it indicates the nature of the ecumenical fellowship, provides the orientation point for the work which the World Council undertakes, and indicates the range of the fellowship which the member Churches seek to establish. It stated that "while the Basis is less than a confession, it is much more than a mere formula or agreement".

At Evanston the new Central Committee appointed a new subcomittee, under the chairmanship of Dr E. A. Payne, to examine the Norwegian proposal and other requests for amendments relating to the Trinity.[5] In the negotiations which followed the desire soon became apparent for the Basis to be extended on biblical and trinitarian lines. In October 1956 Dr Payne and Dr Visser 't Hooft sent a memorandum to a number of theologians and church leaders asking for their personal comments; these would be submitted to the subcommittee at its meeting before the Central Committee in New Haven in 1957. The answers received showed that a change in the formulation of the Basis was considered inadvisable at that time, although the arguments in favour of doing so were in many cases admitted. At New Haven the subcommittee then submitted a full report to the Central Committee; this contained not only the changes proposed by Churches and individuals, but also the draft of a new formulation.[6]

> The World Council of Churches is a fellowship of Churches which, in accord-ance with Holy Scripture, confess our Lord Jesus Christ as the Son of God who was made man for our salvation, in whom the Father was revealed, and to whom the Holy Spirit bears witness guiding us into all the truth.

After a long discussion[7] it was decided to defer decision until 1958, and in the meantime to ask the members of the Central Committee to reflect on the matter and to consult with members of their Churches. At the Central Committee held in 1958 at Nyborg there was no time to examine this question, so that it had to be deferred until the following year. Dr Payne also

---

[1] MRCC (Rolle 1951), pp. 20ff.
[2] MRCC (Lucknow 1952–3), pp. 35f and Appendix VIII, pp. 95f.
[3] Evanston, p. 215.   [4] Ibid., pp. 306f.   [5] MRCC (Evanston 1954), p. 13.
[6] MRCC (New Haven 1957), Appendix XXII, pp. 132–5.
[7] MRCC (New Haven 1957), pp. 67–9.

stated that the number of comments received had been disappointingly small.[1]

For the Central Committee in Rhodes in 1959 the subcommittee submitted an expansion of the existing Basis[2], which was adopted by the Central Committee. The Faith and Order Commission was requested to make a study of the declaration suggested at New Haven and also the real nature and function of the Basis of the W.C.C. If the Faith and Order Commission undertook this task, the fact would be reported by the Central Committee to the member Churches and to the Third Assembly, together with an account of the study and discussion of the matter since the Evanston Assembly in 1954. At the same time it would be made clear that the Central Committee was in no way opposed to the suggested additional affirmations, believing them to be in accord with the beliefs of the member Churches.

Things then developed so rapidly, to a large extent owing to the stimulus of Dr Visser 't Hooft, that the Faith and Order Commission did not need to undertake this task. Prompted by Orthodox recommendations, in January 1960 Dr Visser 't Hooft proposed the following formulation:

> The World Council of Churches is a fellowship of churches which believe in Jesus Christ and which under the guidance of the Holy Spirit seek to fulfil together their common calling to manifest their unity as children of one heavenly Father.[3]

The following month the Executive Committee, meeting in Buenos Aires, agreed to another proposal, which read as follows:

> The World Council of Churches is a fellowship of churches which, under the guidance of the Holy Spirit and according to the Scriptures, confess the Lord Jesus Christ as God and Saviour and therefore seek to fulfil together their common calling to the glory of God the Father.[4]

The Executive Committee decided to pass on this proposal to the sub-committee on the Basis and, if it agreed, to take all the steps required to prepare for the acceptance of this new formulation of the Basis at the Third Assembly. Dr Payne reported to the Central Committee, which met at St Andrews in August 1960, about the latest developments. At the suggestion of Policy Reference Committee III, the Central Committee then decided on the existing form of the Basis to be submitted to the Third Assembly:

> The World Council of Churches is a fellowship of churches which confess the Lord Jesus Christ as God the Saviour according to the Scriptures and therefore seek to fulfil together their common calling to the glory of the one God, Father, Son and Holy Spirit.

In this connection the Central Committee again stressed the fact that the Basis had never been intended to be a creed nor as a full statement of the Christian faith, but merely "to say what holds us together in the World

---

[1] MRCC (Nyborg 1958), p. 66.   [2] MRCC (Rhodes 1959), pp. 201f.

[3] Letter from Visser't Hooft dated 4 January 1960 to Fry, Payne, Bridston. Copy in W.C.C. archive "The Basis After Evanston".

[4] See minutes of meeting of Executive Committee, 8–12 February 1960, W.C.C. archive "The Basis after Evanston".

Council, what is the starting-point of our conversation and the foundation of our collaboration". The proposed new formulation was merely an expansion of what was already contained in the existing Basis. It was important to mention this, in order to avoid misunderstandings, and to fulfil widespread wishes. Four specific changes had been requested:

   (i) the substitution of the word "confess" for "accept";
   (ii) the use of "the" instead of "our" before "Lord Jesus Christ";
   (iii) the addition of the phrase "according to the Scriptures"; this goes back to the earliest Christian confessions of faith and stresses the authority of Scripture for all Christians;
   (iv) the trinitarian character of the Basis is in line with the statement adopted at Evanston. The end and object of our fellowship together is acknowledged by adding the phrase "and therefore seek to fulfil together their common calling to the Glory of God".[1]

The concluding sentence brings out the missionary element which became a strong influence on the ecumenical fellowship through the integration with the International Missionary Council at New Delhi.

   Admittedly the discussions at New Delhi did not run as smoothly as those at St Andrews. Objections were raised by some Baptists, Mennonites, Remonstrants, and Quakers mainly to the words "God and Saviour", which existed already in the old version of the Basis. However, the result of the ballot showed a majority of far more than the two-thirds required: 383 in favour, thirty-six against, and seven abstentions.[2] After years of discussion, the acceptance of the new Basis sharpened the self-understanding of the W.C.C. and served to strengthen its inner coherence.

The Significance of the Three Assemblies

In order to evaluate rightly the importance of the Assemblies, it is essential to take as the norm the constitutional functions and powers of the W.C.C., of which the Assembly is "the principal authority" (Constitution, V. (i)). Paragraph III of the Constitution lists the functions of the W.C.C. as defined at New Delhi, including its missionary task and its relations with national and regional Christian Councils:

   (i) To carry on the work of the world movements for Faith and Order and Life and Work and of the International Missionary Council.
   (ii) To facilitate common action by the churches.
   (iii) To promote co-operation in study.
   (iv) To promote the growth of ecumenical and missionary consciousness in the members of all churches.
   (v) To support the churches in their world-wide missionary and evangelistic task.
   (vi) To establish and maintain relations with national and regional councils, world confessional bodies, and other ecumenical organizations.
   (vii) To call world conferences on specific subjects as occasion may require, such conferences being empowered to publish their own findings.[3]

[1] MRCC (St Andrews 1960), pp. 211f.   [2] New Delhi, pp. 152–9.
[3] Ibid., pp. 426–7.

In paragraph IV of the Constitution the Authority, which provides a framework for the above functions, is defined:

> The World Council shall offer counsel and provide opportunity of united action in matters of common interest.
>
> It may take action on behalf of constituent churches in such matters as one or more of them may commit to it.
>
> It shall have authority to call regional and world conferences on specific subjects as occasion may require.
>
> The World Council shall not legislate for the churches; nor shall it act for them in any manner except as indicated above or as may hereafter be specified by the constituent churches.

From these aspects and in accordance with these norms, how are the first three Assemblies to be evaluated? How did they fulfil their mandate and what were their particular characteristics?

Amsterdam

The first Assembly held at Amsterdam, 22 August–4 September 1948, and attended by 351 delegates representing 145 Churches from forty-four countries, can be regarded as the point at which the nascent W.C.C. gathered the ecumenical community to take stock of the Churches' position, and tried to point out the responsibility of world Christendom in face of the upheavals caused by the Second World War. Here on 23 August the World Council was unanimously declared to be constituted, at a plenary session chaired by the Archbishop of Canterbury, Dr Geoffrey Fisher. The resolution was submitted by Pastor Marc Boegner in the name of the Committee of Fourteen and the Provisional Committee. The great moment had come when "the churches themselves assumed responsibility for the ecumenical movement and conversely the ecumenical movement won a secure foundation in the life of the churches".[1] The Message of the Assembly expressed this fact as follows:

> Christ has made us His own, and He is not divided. In seeking Him we can find one another. Here at Amsterdam we have committed ourselves afresh to Him, and have covenanted with one another in constituting this World Council of Churches. We intend to stay together.

The "nature of the Council" was more closely defined in a separate statement.[2] It was clearly stated that the churches had decided to make common cause in accordance with the will of the Lord of the Church. Where this common way would lead them was unforeseeable. But, to quote the Report of Section I, "We acknowledge that He is powerfully at work amongst us to lead us further to goals which we but dimly discern."[3]

To what extent did the First Assembly take account of these aims and follow them up? This question cannot be answered by generalizations or by impressions based on feelings; it can only be answered by listening intently

---

[1] Visser 't Hooft. See *A History of the Ecumenical Movement, 1517–1948*, p. 720.
[2] Amsterdam, pp. 9 and 127f.   [3] Ibid., p. 56.

to the trends and the achievements of the separate Sections and Commissions. The general theme of the Assembly was "Man's Disorder and God's Design".

The themes of the four Sections were derived from it:

1. The Universal Church in God's Design.
2. The Church's Witness to God's Design.
3. The Church and the Disorder of Society.
4. The Church and the International Disorder.

Against the background of the widely differing political situations and church traditions it was, of course, impossible to expect the Sections to come to homogeneous findings. However, they manifested their common readiness and their conviction that they should bear witness of God's design as a factor bringing order into a disordered and disrupted world.

The theological groundwork (Section I), in which Karl Barth and Michael Ramsey participated, expressed the indissoluble connection between unity and inner renewal: "We pray for the churches' renewal as we pray for their unity. As Christ purifies us by His Spirit we shall find that we are drawn together and that there is no gain in unity unless it is unity in truth and holiness."[1] At the same time the Report of Section I speaks of the basis of the fellowship within the W.C.C.: "The World Council of Churches has come into existence because we have already recognized a responsibility to one another's churches in our Lord Jesus Christ."[2] This basic undertone continues as a strong influence right up to the document on Proselytism in 1960. The simplified distinction drawn in this Section between a "Protestant" and a "Catholic" type of Church, as being the deepest of all our differences, later seemed to be inadequate.

In Section II it was strongly realized for the first time that evangelism is the common task of all the Churches, and that "the present day is the beginning of a new epoch of missionary enterprise".[3] No distinction is drawn any longer between mission and evangelism, because it must be recognized that the traditional distinction between the "Christian" and "non-Christian" countries no longer exists.[4] Above all, however, a strong appeal was addressed to "the laity": "This is the day of opportunity for the lay membership of the Church."[5] The question of the training of the laity was examined by a special committee, which took as its starting-point the experience of the Ecumenical Institute at Bossey.[6] The report of the committee on "The Life and Work of Women in the Church" was on the same lines.[7] Recognition of the importance of the laity in the Church was one of the outstanding features of the Amsterdam Assembly. It found strong expression also in the reports of Sections III and IV in which the lay delegates to the Assembly played a decisive role.

It is to Section III that the ecumenical discussion during the years that followed owes the concept of "the responsible society" as an alternative to capitalism on the one hand and communism on the other. In order "to prevent an undue centralization of power in modern technically organized

[1] Amsterdam, p. 56. [2] Ibid., p. 57. [3] Ibid., p. 66. [4] Ibid., p. 66.
[5] Ibid., p. 68. [6] Ibid., pp. 153–6. [7] Ibid., pp. 146–8.

communities" it was suggested that society should have "a rich variety of smaller forms of community",[1] which would ensure scope for personal responsibility.

The fact that Section IV included such divergent attitudes as those of Professor J. Hromadka and John Foster Dulles and was able to support them shows the strength of a fellowship like that of the newly formed W.C.C., and put it to the test for the first time. Two points which arose in Section IV deserve special mention owing to their significance for the Assembly as a whole and for the future of the W.C.C.: (*a*) the rejection of war in principle ("war is contrary to the will of God") but also the inability to accept this attitude unanimously as Christians;[2] (*b*) the clear political statement that "Christianity cannot be equated with any" political system.[3] Every kind of tyranny and imperialism was a call for struggle, and for efforts to secure human rights and basic liberties, especially religious liberty.

If one tries to evaluate the Amsterdam Assembly as a whole one can say that it was no longer marked by the enthusiasm and optimism which had dominated some earlier conferences. It was too close to the Second World War for that. On the other hand, the First Assembly gave evidence of the Churches' sense of common responsibility in service to the world, as required by "God's design" in Christ. It was taken far more seriously than during the first decade of the ecumenical movement. Joint action by the Churches of this kind could spring only from their unity in Christ, which was maintained in inner renewal and in responsibility for one another.

Evanston

The work of Amsterdam was continued by the Second Assembly of the W.C.C. held at Evanston, U.S.A., 15–31 August 1954 and attended by 502 delegates from 161 member Churches. Especially important was the fact that the Second Assembly was held in the U.S.A. and gave the strongest member Churches an opportunity to acquaint themselves directly and immediately with the W.C.C.

At Amsterdam the Churches had announced their intention "to stay together". At Evanston they expressed their desire "to grow together" with certain reservations: "We dedicate ourselves to God anew, that He may enable us to grow together."[4] It was this deep sense of belonging together and of the responsibility which it implied that enabled the Assembly to tackle the main theme "Christ—the Hope of the World", theologically an extremely difficult one. Compared with Amsterdam this theme clearly represented a turning towards the centre which linked together all the Churches belonging to the World Council. However, this theme now gave rise to differing opinions. The concept of the Christian hope held by the European Churches tended to be eschatological, whereas the concept of the American Churches was more optimistic and more concerned with the Christian's hope in this world here and now. The statement on the report of the Advisory Commission on the Main Theme, in which body eminent theologians had co-

---

[1] Amsterdam, p. 77.   [2] Ibid., p. 89.   [3] Ibid., p. 91.   [4] Evanston, p. 91.

operated for years, said that "sharp differences in theological viewpoint were expressed" in the discussion. "The note of joyous affirmation and radiant expectancy which should mark a statement of the Christian hope does not sufficiently illuminate the report." The statement draws attention to certain important omissions: "The present work of the Holy Spirit in the Church and the world; specific reference to 'signs of hope'; adequate treatment of the theme of creation and cosmic redemption."

"We are not agreed on the relationship between the Christian's hope here and now, and his ultimate hope", said the Second Assembly. However, the report was submitted to the Churches with the desire "that all who read it will be moved to give utterance to the Christian hope in their own words and with the additions which their thought and prayer discover".[1] A discordant note was introduced by the reference to the hope of Israel (Rom. 9—11) which was finally omitted after a heated debate. However, repercussions of the debate were felt for a long time, and the disagreement of the outvoted minority had to be recorded at the plenary session. The vote showed first that many did not recognize that the Jewish people occupy a special place in the history of salvation, and second that some delegates were motivated by political considerations.

The connection between the Sections and the Main Theme was a very loose one, if it existed at all (to quote Walter Freytag). The Sections continued the trends stressed at Amsterdam (and Section I also continued the work of the Third Conference of Faith and Order held at Lund in 1952). This time there were six Sections:

1. Our Oneness in Christ and our Disunity as Churches.
2. The Mission of the Church to those outside her Life.
3. The Responsible Society in a World Perspective.
4. Christians in the Struggle for World Community.
5. The Churches amid Racial and Ethnic Tensions.
6. The Laity: the Christian in his Vocation.

The so-called "Younger Churches", except those in China, were much more strongly represented than at Amsterdam, and their presence was felt in many ways (especially when discussing the unity of the Church) in the form of an impatient urge for concrete action. Moreover, the missionary dimension, which had been so characteristic of Amsterdam, was missing at Evanston, for instance in the Report of Section I. However, to quote Walter Freytag again: "Yet it must be stated that the report on Evanston offers the most biblical testimony yet given by any ecumenical world gathering."[2] It showed that the W.C.C. was penetrating more deeply into holy Scripture, which was helping it to become clearer theologically in every sphere, and helping the Churches to discover their common convictions.

In continuation of the ideas worked out at Amsterdam, the missionary task of the laity was also strongly stressed (Section II). Section VI combined it with important considerations about "the Christian concept of work" in order to "bridge the gulf between the Church and the world".

[1] Evanston, pp. 70f.   [2] *Ecumenical Review*, vol. vii (*October 1954*), p. 12.

The Amsterdam phrase "the responsible society" was more clearly defined at Evanston; it was made clear that it did not indicate "an alternative social or political system" but "a criterion by which we judge all existing social orders and at the same time a standard to guide us in the specific choices we have to make" (Section III. I.7). The simplified distinction between two opposing economic systems which dominated the discussions at Amsterdam was superseded at Evanston by more careful differentiations. Priority was given especially to the social and economic "problems in the economically underdeveloped regions" (Section III), a question to which the W.C.C. paid increasing attention. In Sections IV and V the Second Assembly again affirmed its responsibility for international peace and justice and issued an appeal to governments urging the prohibition of all weapons of mass destruction, and abstention from aggression. The Assembly also issued statements on religious liberty and on "inter-group relations" (insisting on racial equality). Both themes had been introduced at Amsterdam (see Amsterdam Report, Section VI). As a result of the Assembly's report on "The Churches amid Racial and Ethnic Tensions" a department for racial and ethnic relations was set up within the W.C.C. This was followed in 1958 by the setting up of a secretariat on questions concerning religious liberty.

New Delhi

The years between the Assembly at Evanston and that at New Delhi (1954–61) were crucial for the development of the W.C.C. both internally and externally. The Third Assembly was held at New Delhi, 19 November– 5 December 1961. It was attended by 577 delegates from just under 200 member Churches, as well as by a large number of advisers, youth delegates, fraternal delegates, observers, and visitors. The main theme "Jesus Christ— the Light of the World" continued the Christocentric line of the W.C.C., extending it now into the sphere of the non-Christian religions. It was liable to misinterpretation in view of the fact that light is one of the symbols that appear in the Asian religions. In order to avoid being misunderstood as syncretism, the theme therefore had to be worked out with great care on its biblical basis. This time the main theme was not given great precedence, as had been the case at Evanston; it was merely regarded as a guiding principle. The deliberations were to spring from the ongoing work of the W.C.C., and not be forced into the formula of a dominating main theme. On the other hand, an effort was made to ensure that the main theme permeated the sections and influenced them more than it had done at Evanston.

The Third Assembly may be summed up from two aspects: its external extension and its internal strengthening.

1. At New Delhi twenty-three more Churches were admitted to membership of the W.C.C., bringing the number of member Churches up to 198. The new member Churches included three groups:

(*a*) The Orthodox Churches of eastern Europe, whose adhesion was rightly regarded as extremely important by the General Secretary. Dr Visser 't Hooft said: "In this way a tremendous opportunity is offered to us, the opportunity to ensure that a real spiritual dialogue shall take place between the Eastern Churches and the churches which have their origin in the West. If we accept this opportunity our ecumenical task will not become easier, but we shall surely be greatly enriched."[1]

(b) Younger Churches joined in sufficient strength to make their influence felt. Of the twenty-three new member Churches, eleven were in Africa, five in Asia, and two in South America. Only five were from Europe or North America. Altogether eighteen of the twenty-three new member Churches belonged to the "Third World".

(c) The two Pentecostal Churches from Chile formed a bridge to the Evangelical Churches, most of which dissociated themselves from the W.C.C. and still do so. The application of these Churches for membership was equally important theologically, because it brought out the pneumatological aspect of the theological discussion in the ecumenical movement.

The World Council was also very considerably extended externally through its integration with the International Missionary Council at the Third Assembly.

2. The tremendous variety of ecumenical work was summed up at New Delhi under three points, so as to concentrate the discussion and in order to relate the three aspects to one another. They were: Witness, Service, and Unity. The internal norm for this was the new Basis, the external point of reference was "the local Church" which (to quote Dr Visser 't Hooft in his report) must be made "ready for unity" in accordance with the statement "All in each place". As compared with the assemblies at Amsterdam and Evanston, therefore, the emphasis had clearly shifted from the individual to the local congregation.

The main theme "Jesus Christ—the Light of the World" had testified to the uniqueness of Christ. On the other hand, in the section on "Witness" a theological problem arose which has continued to preoccupy the W.C.C. ever since: the influence of Christ in other religions, i.e. to what extent God's action in the non-Christian religions is in accordance with the Christian faith, and what possibilities might arise from it, for instance in connection with the Asian form of Christianity. This logical conclusion from the universal implications of the Lordship of God and of the salvation of Christ as well as consideration of the changes in the other religions led the section on "Witness" to make pronouncements like the following:

> The Church is sent, knowing that God has not left himself without witness even among men who do not yet know Christ, and knowing also that the reconciliation wrought through Christ embraces all creation and the whole of mankind. . . . In the churches, we have but little understanding of the wisdom, love and power which God has given to men of other faiths and of no faith, or of the changes wrought in other faiths by their long encounter with Christianity. We must take up the conversations about Christ with them,

[1] *Ecumenical Review*, vol. xiv (January 1962), p. 222.

knowing that Christ addresses them through us and us through them" (Report of Section on "Witness", III. 7).[1]

"In solidarity with all men" new structures and new forms of witness were sought, in which the "laity" must occupy a definite status. (This met with some objections, not only from the Orthodox, because it seemed to devalue the status of the traditional ministry. This difference is constantly coming up in many spheres of the ecumenical conversation.)

The same concept of "solidarity" was also taken up by the Section on "Service" as a link with the call "to participate in service in all these areas of the contemporary world" (para. 4).[2] But by relating it clearly to God's love for men, a distinction was drawn between Christian service and mere philanthrophy (para. 1). The Section on "Service" already revealed a characteristic which became even more apparent at the World Conference on Church and Society in Geneva in 1966: it lacked a substantial, valid theological foundation, and among so many different kinds of Churches it was almost impossible to achieve one. The primary aim of the section was to face the problems of political, economic, and social change, and thus to help the "younger Churches" in their situation. Christians were therefore warned against all forms of conformity with past or present social systems. As at Amsterdam, the section refused to identify itself with any economic, social, or political system, and stressed the importance of human dignity. The absolute Lordship of Jesus Christ over history is the main concept running through the whole report, for he makes it "possible for a Christian to live (or die) with integrity under any political system; it is possible for the Church to obey its Lord in all kinds of external circumstances" (Report of Section on Service, para. 34).[3]

The Section on "Unity" centred around the so-called "unity formula of New Delhi", which had been worked out at the meeting of the Faith and Order Commission at St Andrews in 1960. Here at the highest level of the Assembly the section endeavoured to define the aim of unity which had given rise to the W.C.C. and which inspired it:

> We believe that the unity which is both God's will and his gift to his Church is being made visible as all in each place who are baptized into Jesus Christ and confess him as Lord and Saviour are brought by the Holy Spirit into one fully committed fellowship, holding the one apostolic faith, preaching the one Gospel, breaking the one bread, joining in common prayer, and having a corporate life reaching out in witness and service to all and who at the same time are united with the whole Christian fellowship in all places and all ages in such wise that ministry and members are accepted by all, and that all can act and speak together as occasion requires for the tasks to which God calls his people. It is for such unity that we believe we must pray and work (Report of Section on Unity, para. 2).[4]

Realizing the inadequacy of what had previously been said, the above was an attempt to describe the common task without giving a "definition of

[1] New Delhi, pp. 81–2.   [2] Ibid., p. 94.   [3] Ibid., p. 100.   [4] Ibid., p. 116.

the Church", so as to emerge at last from an "ecclesiological docetism" (Edmund Schlink). Admittedly the separate formulas and concepts needed to be implemented, and this urgent task was not tackled seriously enough by the member Churches during the years that followed. But at New Delhi the aim was to arrive at concrete conclusions, as is shown by the "implications" which the section tried to draw for the life of the local Churches, the confessions, and the ecumenical movement. It even recommended taking "responsible risk" (para. 30). The W.C.C. was urged to extend its "educative function" (para. 42d) and to play a more active part in negotiations for union (para. 45g).[1]

Altogether the tendency at New Delhi was to strengthen the position of the W.C.C. Thus the Policy Reference Committee recommended "that the Council should give its member churches spiritual and practical guidance in a Christian approach to the actual questions and problems of our day, such as materialism, secularism, peace and war, and social justice. The W.C.C. should certainly not wait to be pushed into critical situations, but should always take the lead and initiative in asking. What is the command of our Lord in the present time? At the same time, the churches themselves should be encouraged to bring their requests in this regard before the W.C.C."[2]

Thus between the First and Third Assemblies, the World Council, as "the ecumenical conscience of the churches", became more and more the mouthpiece of the member Churches. This was shown at New Delhi in a renewed stand on religious liberty, a resolution on anti-semitism, a stand on international crises, a message to the Christians in South Africa, and an "Appeal to all Governments and Peoples".[3] At the same time the W.C.C. assumed increasing responsibility for relief to people in distress, refugees and victims of natural catastrophes all over the world. After three assemblies the ecumenical fellowship had stood the test. The Churches' desire to stay together (Amsterdam) and to grow together (Evanston) had developed into joint progress in assuming new tasks (New Delhi). This tremendous task of ecumenical unity, renewal, and co-operation was re-examined at Uppsala in 1968 in the light of the promise of the Lord when he shall return, "Behold I make all things new!"

The Work of the Central Committee and the Executive Committee

The Constitution of the W.C.C. (para. V (ii)) defined the powers of the Central Committee. The Central Committee originally consisted of ninety members; at New Delhi the number was raised to 100, at Uppsala to 120. The definition follows: "It shall, between meetings of the Assembly, carry out the Assembly's instructions and exercise its functions, except that of amending the Constitution, or modifying the allocation of its own members."[4] The Central Committee shall meet normally once every calendar year, and shall have power to appoint its own executive committee. The Executive Committee (originally consisting of twelve members, since New Delhi fourteen

---

[1] New Delhi, p. 130.   [2] Ibid., p. 145   [3] Ibid., p. 280.   [4] Ibid., p. 428.

members, and since Uppsala sixteen members) shall meet twice a year. It shall carry out the decisions of the Central Committee, just as the latter carries out the decisions of the Assembly (Rules of the W.C.C., VI (2)).[1]

It is a noteworthy fact that during the course of time the importance of the Executive Committee has increased, and it has become more independent of the Central Committee, so that it often gave the impression of controlling the Central Committee instead of carrying out the latter's instructions. To a considerable extent this is due to the fact that during the time between the assemblies the membership of the Executive Committee has remained almost unchanged, in spite of re-elections every year; this has given it a great deal of stability. This trend has also been encouraged by the two chairmen of the Central Committee (or/and Executive Committee): the Bishop of Chichester, Dr Bell (1948–54) whose cordial, friendly character did so much to establish friendly contacts between others, and Dr Franklin Clark Fry of the Lutheran Church of America (1954–68) whose gift of leadership was respected by all, and who carried out his duties as chairman combining authority with humour. He was ably assisted by Dr Ernest Payne and, after 1966, by Dr Russell Chandran.

Both the Central Committee and the Executive Committee have met in different places nearly every time, so as to get to know all the member Churches and to strengthen their sense of solidarity with the World Council. During the years between the Amsterdam and Evanston Assemblies the Central Committee met in Holland, England, Canada, Switzerland, and India. During the time between the Evanston and New Delhi Assemblies it met in Switzerland, Hungary, the U.S.A., Denmark, Greece, and Scotland. During the years between the New Delhi and Uppsala Assemblies it met in France, the U.S.A., Nigeria, Switzerland, and Greece. In addition, both the Central and Executive Committees held meeting in connection with each of the assemblies. As well as meeting at the same time as the Central Committee, the Executive Committee also held separate meetings, for instance in Germany (1954), Australia (1956), Latin America (1960), and the U.S.S.R. (1964).

The Central Committee and also the Executive Committee might easily have confined themselves exclusively to the organizational tasks entrusted to them by the Assembly, or which arose in course of time. The danger that they would do this was increased owing to the shortness of their meetings. However, both the Central and Executive Committees resisted these temptations and kept their attention fixed on the basic themes which needed consideration both for the development of the ecumenical fellowship within the World Council and for the fulfilment of its responsibilities outside. In addition to the Toronto statement (already mentioned) *The Church, the Churches, and the World Council of Churches* (1950) and the statement entitled *The Ecumenical Way* (1966), these included the statement of the Central Committee at Rolle (1951) "The Calling of the Church to Mission and to Unity",[2] and the report on "Christian Witness, Proselytism and Religious Liberty in the setting of the World Council of Churches", drawn up by a committee under the chairmanship of Bishop Angus Dun and approved first at the

[1] New Delhi, p. 435.   [2] *The First Six Years*, p. 124.

Central Committee in Galyatetö in 1956, and then in its final form at St Andrews in 1960, which defined the relation of the member Churches to each other;[1] it was accepted by the Assembly at New Delhi and commended to the Churches.

In relation to the secular sphere a number of statements were made (mainly drafted by the Commission of the Churches on International Affairs) on Religious Liberty and Freedom of Conscience, on the menace of nuclear warfare, on the problems of disarmament, and on special political danger spots such as Korea (1950). (The resolution on Korea aroused considerable tensions and differences within the W.C.C., which led to the resignation of one of its Presidents, Dr T. C. Chao of China.) Statements were also made on the war in Vietnam and on the conflict between Israel and Egypt. The question may be asked: What purposes are served by making all these statements concerning events in the world? The booklet *New Delhi to Uppsala* draws attention to their threefold purpose: "First, to serve as a crystalization point for world Christian opinion; second, to help the member churches in deciding what stand they should take; third, to give World Council spokesmen, particularly the Commission of the Churches on International Affairs, a firm foundation for the approaches which they make to international governmental bodies and individual governments" (English edn, p. 10).

There is therefore no question of making normative statements which would be binding upon the member Churches, or which would oblige them to take certain steps. None of the resolutions passed by the World Council of Churches does so. They become binding only if they are accepted by the member Churches. The W.C.C. wants only to be the "instrument" of the Churches; it offers itself as a help in guiding them in their further reflections and practical conclusions. It cannot and must not depart from this principle if it is to remain meaningful as the point of intersection and the co-ordinating centre of all the Christian traditions and systems of thought.

But even when the deliberations did not result in any special pronouncements, recommendations, or resolutions, the Central Committee has always been ready to learn about current problems which concern the whole ecumenical movement, and has discussed them, so as not to become drowned under the weight of routine business, but to remain constantly on the alert and ready to assume responsibility for its task. The socio-ethical issues ranged from "responsible parenthood and the problem of population" to the fundamental questions of Christian unity, evangelism, and joint responsibility for inter-Church aid and relief projects. In addition the Central Committee is responsible for a third category of spiritual leadership and guidance: the tremendous number of study projects started by the Central Committee either on its own account or through the competent divisions and departments.

Among these studies mention should be made of the following: "The Lordship of Christ over the World and the Church" (1955–9),[2] "Christians and the Prevention of War in an Atomic Age—a theological discussion" (also started in 1955), the extensive studies on "Rapid Social Change"

---

[1] *Evanston to New Delhi*, Appendix VIII, paras. 239–45.
[2] Ibid., paras. 34, 35.

(1955–60), and the study projects decided upon at New Delhi: "The Finality of Christ in the Age of Universal History"[1] and "The Missionary Structure of the Congregation".[2]

All this demands a great deal of time and energy from the members of the Central Committee and Executive Committee, for in addition to the actual meetings nearly all the members are engaged in work in committees and study groups whose purpose is to promote the development of the whole work of the W.C.C. In his report of the Assembly at New Delhi, Dr Fry said: "Practically nothing occurs in the Council's life between Assemblies that lies outside the portfolio of the Central Committee."[3] The Central Committee has therefore become the real power-field and radiation-centre of the W.C.C., not only in regard to the organization for which it is responsible, but also in its influence upon the Churches, many of which do not yet possess the necessary channels to carry out what has already been approved at the highest level.

Structure, Staff, and Headquarters

1. *Structure* The structures assumed by an organization are not to be regarded as unimportant. Its effectiveness will always depend on whether it finds suitable forms for its work. In this respect the W.C.C. has always shown flexibility, but without falling into arbitrary experimentation or improvization. *Life and Work* and *Faith and Order* already had decades of organizational experience behind them, which they contributed to the World Council. The rapid growth in the membership of the W.C.C. and the increased demands made upon it caused the Central Committee three years after Amsterdam to set up a "Committee on Structure and Functioning" to examine the organization and working of the W.C.C.; this committee presented a long report to the Central Committee at Lucknow in 1953,[4] which was followed by an equally long debate. The proposals were re-examined and thoroughly discussed at the Evanston Assembly.[5] The sub-division into divisions and departments formed the structural basis for the years that followed and "has given much greater coherence to the work of the Council".[6] There were to be three main divisions concerned with Studies, Inter-Church Aid, and Ecumenical Action. The heads of these three divisions are at the same time Associate General Secretaries. Discussion continued, however, about this pattern of organization and whether it was permanently suited to the work of the Council or should be changed.

One important change made at Evanston was the decision that the Presidents could no longer be re-elected. This caused some misgivings, because the Anglicans (for instance) were anxious that the Archbishop of Canterbury should always be one of the Presidents of the W.C.C. It was felt, however, that by electing new presidents at each Assembly more Churches and countries could be involved in the work of the Council.

[1] New Delhi, p. 165. [2] Ibid., p. 195. [3] Ibid., p. 338.
[4] MRCC (Lucknow 1953). [5] Evanston, pp. 174–214.
[6] *Evanston to New Delhi*, para. 26.

C

After Evanston the plans for the integration of the International Missionary Council with the World Council of Churches (see Section 6 below) made it necessary to consider further changes of structure. These were studied by the Committee on Programme and Finance, of which the Chairman was Dr Eugene Carson Blake. The findings of this committee concerning the organization of the W.C.C. are contained in its report to the Assembly at New Delhi.[1] In the view of the committee, it was too soon to make basic changes. However, attention may be drawn to some points in the report because they reflect certain tendencies. For instance, it was proposed to appoint a "Committee on National Council Relationships" to give "continuous attention to the development of relationships of mutual helpfulness between the W.C.C. and national and regional councils of churches and Christian councils". The position of Faith and Order was also strengthened; it was not promoted to the status of a division, but it was given scope to have more influence on the ecumenical work as a whole and its staff was increased. The staff of the General Secretariat was also increased. Lastly, it was proposed that there be a "Staff Co-ordinating and Advisory Committee on Studies" to co-ordinate the study work of the different divisions; this was made urgently necessary by the organizational extension of the W.C.C. The Assembly passed the report, instructing the Central Committee to take the necessary steps to examine the organizational structure within two years.[2]

In accordance with the instructions of the New Delhi Assembly, the Central Committee at Rochester (1963) appointed a committee to examine the structure of the W.C.C. with Norman Goodall as chairman. This committee was to study and consider how the separate aspects of the work of the W.C.C. could best be co-ordinated, in the light of the suggestions already made. This committee presented its first report at Enugu.[3] Among other things, Faith and Order was given the status of an autonomous secretariat of the Faith and Order Commission. lodged within the Division of Studies and having representation in the Staff Executive Group; but the nomination of Assistant General Secretaries was still postponed.

The committee presented another report in 1967 at the meeting of the Central Committee in Crete.[4] The Central Committee approved the committee's view that no change should be made yet in the structure of the divisions. It was decided to reconstitute the committee with Bishop James K. Matthews as chairman and to ask it to present a report to the Central Committee immediately before Uppsala. The Assembly at Uppsala appointed a new committee on structure, which undertook to examine the existing structures within three years, taking due account of new factors such as regional developments, relations to non-member Churches, and to the Roman Catholic Church. This presents a broad field to the W.C.C. in which it will need greater dynamism through more intensive concentration and more rational application of its strength.

2. *Staff* However, what use would the most perfect structures be without

[1] New Delhi, pp. 351–7. [2] Ibid., pp. 351–7. [3] MRCC (Enugu 1965), pp. 102–16.
[4] MRCC (Heraklion 1967), pp. 122–6.

the men and women who fill them with life and spirit? During the twenty years since it was formed the W.C.C. has been blessed with persons who devoted their whole energies to the W.C.C. The problem of suitable staff is particularly difficult in the W.C.C. because account has to be taken not only of personal abilities but also of the person's confessional and geographical background. The Geneva staff must reflect the membership of the Churches which belong to it.

Continuity was maintained with the earlier stages of the ecumenical movement thanks to the outstanding personality of Dr Visser 't Hooft, who was General Secretary for eighteen years (1948–66). In him great theological, linguistic, and spiritual gifts were combined with a capacity for organization and leadership which made him the real inspiration and architect of the W.C.C. When Dr Visser 't Hooft made it known at the age of sixty-five (in 1965) that he wished to retire in order to devote himself to writing and other scholarly work, the Central Committee was confronted by an extremely important task—that of choosing a new General Secretary. At Rochester in 1963 the Executive Committee (through the Central Committee) proposed the appointment of a nominations committee. However, the Central Committee took up a suggestion, made by the Bishop of Winchester, that the Executive Committee should act as a nominations committee. At Tutzing (1964) the Executive Committee decided to propose to the Central Committee the Reverend Patrick C. Rodger (from the Episcopal Church of Scotland), Executive Secretary of the Department of Faith and Order, as Dr Visser 't Hooft's successor. At the same time Dr Visser 't Hooft was asked to continue in his position until 1966. Before this nomination was presented to the Central Committee, the news was given to the press by the Executive Committee and some of the member Churches expressed negative reactions, not against the person nominated, but against the procedure whereby the Central Committee found itself confronted with a *fait accompli*.

At the meeting of the Central Committee at Enugu (1965) the Executive Committee still maintained its nomination of the Reverend Patrick C. Rodger, but the Central Committee could not agree about the nomination. It wanted to have more scope for choice between several candidates, especially in view of the different concepts held about the office of General Secretary. Owing to the personality of Dr Visser 't Hooft this position had never been defined; he had been General Secretary for nearly two decades and had carried out his functions in a way that no one else could hope to emulate. At the Central Committee meeting in Geneva (1966) the only name presented for consideration by the new nominations committee (appointed at Enugu) was that of Dr Eugene Carson Blake, who since 1951 had been Stated Clerk of the United Presbyterian Church in the U.S.A. He was elected almost unanimously. Dr Visser 't Hooft still remained available in an advisory capacity.

If one were to mention other members of the Geneva staff, this would imply that others who were not mentioned were less important. However, a few names must be noted among those who helped to build up the W.C.C. both organizationally and inwardly. During the first years of the W.C.C.'s existence Oliver S. Tomkins and Stephen Neill were working in the General

Secretariat. The ever-growing tasks of the Division of Inter-Church Aid, Refugee and World Service were directed first by Dr Robert Mackie, then by Dr Leslie Cooke. The work of the Commission of the Churches for International Affairs is indissolubly bound up with the names of Sir Kenneth Grubb and Dr O. Frederick Nolde, who showed themselves prudent advisers in difficult situations for the W.C.C. and its member Churches, and who also acted as the mouthpiece of the W.C.C. in relations with governments and international organizations.

Madeleine Barot of France untiringly reminded the W.C.C. of the concerns of women in the Churches. The Division of Studies was first under the direction of Nils Ehrenström (1948–54) and then of Robert Bilheimer (1954–63). A large number of study projects were undertaken. Father Paul Verghese contributed immensely to the Division of Ecumenical Action as its Director from 1962–7. The work of the Ecumenical Institute at Bossey, set going by Hendrik Kraemer in co-operation with Suzanne de Diétrich, continued from 1955–66 under Professor H. H. Wolf and since then under Professor N. A. Nissiotis. The burden of responsibility for financial affairs was borne by Frank Northam. The Information Department was first under John Garrett, then under Philippe Maury until his death in 1967. The question of religious liberty benefited greatly from the expert knowledge of Dr Carillo de Albornoz. The W.C.C. office in New York was run for many years by H. S. Leiper, S. McCrea Cavert, and Roswell P. Barnes; now Dr Eugene Smith succeeds them. The late Z. K. Matthews served as the first Area Secretary for Africa within D.I.C.A.R.W.S. Many many more names could be mentioned.

Nor should the many secretaries and staff members be forgotten who carried out different functions at the W.C.C. for longer or shorter periods. Without their help and knowledge the W.C.C. could never have carried out its world-wide tasks.

The Assembly at Amsterdam had given its approval to a staff of thirty-six executive secretaries. However, owing to the initial difficulties (for instance the Information Department had not yet been set up) this number was not reached. In 1968 the staff is made up as follows: executive, ninety-seven; administrative, secretarial, and clerical staff, 130; mail, telephone, cyclostyle, and other ancillary services, twenty-four; total 251. People outside are often astonished that the W.C.C. is able to cope with such tremendous tasks with such a comparatively small staff.

3. *Headquarters* As the staff increased, the premises at No. 17 route de Malagnou, Geneva, became more and more inadequate. Already soon after the Evanston Assembly the Executive Committee had appointed a "Head-quarters Committee" to examine the question of office accommodation. At the Central Committee at Davos in 1955 permission was given to work out plans to build on the same site, but owing to lack of space the plan had to be abandoned. After long negotiations with the authorities of the City and Canton of Geneva, the W.C.C. exchanged the site in the route de Malagnou for a site four times the size in Grand-Saconnex, an area of Geneva devoted

to international organizations. The new address is 150 Route de Ferney, 1211 Geneva 20.

In order to cover the cost of building, the Central Committee appointed a committee whose chairman was Bishop Henry Knox Sherrill, one of the Presidents of the W.C.C. at that time. Thanks to generous financial aid from many of the member Churches, from individuals, and from foundations the new building was erected and was occupied in April 1964. It was officially consecrated in July 1965 on the occasion of the meeting of the Executive Committee. It contains an adequate number of offices, which were extended in 1968 by adding two more floors to one of the wings, so that it can now accommodate ten world confessional bodies and ecumenical organizations. It also has several spacious meeting-rooms, which enabled the Central Committee to be held there in 1966, and also the World Conference on Church and Society in the same year. The chapel is open to all the member Churches for worship, and is used by the staff for services and intercession. The library and archives have been greatly extended and occupy a separate building, so that the new headquarters is becoming an "ecumenical centre" to which people come to work and to visit from all over the world.[1]

Integration of the I.M.C. and the W.C.C.[2]

One of the most decisive events in the life of the W.C.C. was the integration of the International Missionary Council with the World Council of Churches. It was the outcome of an inner necessity based on the basic ecumenical approach that unity and mission are both essential aspects of the Churches; that it is the Church's mission which has revealed the necessity of its unity, and that mission has been one of the main roots of the ecumenical movement. This conviction carried even more weight than organizational considerations and practical demands. At Amsterdam John A. Mackay had said: "The Ecumenical Church is a child of the missionary movement" for "the Christian Church, to be truly the Church, must be a missionary as well as a worshipping Church".[3]

The relations between the I.M.C. and the W.C.C. had grown constantly closer since 1938.[4] The Joint Committee set up in 1939 became the basis for joint projects such as the Commission of the Churches for International Affairs founded in 1946, the East Asia Secretariat (1949) which was developed in 1957 into the East Asian Christian Conference, the Ecumenical Press Service (started in 1948), and (in accordance with a decision by the Evanston Assembly in 1954) the Study Division of the W.C.C. In addition the two organizations co-operated closely in inter-Church aid projects. After the Amsterdam Assembly both organizations officially added the words "in association with" the other one to their own title.

Dr Mackay presented a report to the Central Committee at Lucknow in

---

[1] Cf. *Evanston to New Delhi*, pp. 21f; New Delhi, p. 75; *New Delhi to Uppsala*, p. 17.
[2] Cf. *Why Integration?* by Ernest A. Payne and David G. Moses. London 1957.
[3] Amsterdam, p. 26.
[4] *A History of the Ecumenical Movement, 1517–1948*, pp. 398–400, 414–16.

1953 in which he said that the Joint Committee of the I.M.C. and the W.C.C. (at its meeting in London in 1952) had come to the conclusion: "It is clear that we are approaching the time when we must look to some corporate form of the two organizations."[1] However, in the report made by the Joint Committee at Evanston the question of full integration was still left open.[2]

At the meeting of the Central Committee at Davos the following year, the Joint Committee (which had Henry P. Van Dusen as its chairman and Norman Goodall as its secretary) stated that more than half the work of the W.C.C. was already being done jointly with the I.M.C.: "There was general agreement that the committee should not immediately concentrate on the question of the possible integration of the W.C.C. and the I.M.C. While the consideration of this issue is the direct responsibility of the committee, its solution is likely to be reached more effectively if time is taken to develop co-operation further."[3]

In its report to the Central Committee at Galyatetö in 1956 the Joint Committee affirmed its conviction that the time had come "when the W.C.C· and I.M.C. should consider afresh the possibility of an integration of the two councils. The committee regards it as imperative that any such integration should be in a form which ensures that missions belong to the heart of the ecumenical movement." Three reasons were given for the new development: the deepening missionary consciousness of the Churches, the ever closer working relationships necessitating processes which go beyond "association", and the increasing overlap in membership. The Central Committee instructed the Joint Committee "to undertake the formulation—in the fullest possible consultation with all concerned—of a draft Plan of Integration for presentation to the W.C.C. Central Committee in 1957 and to the I.M.C. Assembly at the Gold Coast in December–January 1957-8".[4]

The membership of the Joint Committee was increased from twelve to twenty, and it then presented its report to the Central Committee at New Haven in 1957. It made provision for the creation of a Commission on World Mission and Evangelism (similar to the Commission on Faith and Order) which would carry out its work through a "Division on World Mission and Evangelism" (an additional division of the W.C.C.). Care must also be taken to ensure that missionary concerns were adequately represented on the Executive and Central Committees and in the other divisions of the W.C.C.[5]

Although the draft had been kept very flexible and allowed scope for modifications, the tremendous difficulties presented by integration had to be faced. In the first place, the W.C.C. was composed of Churches, whereas the I.M.C. members were national and regional Christian Councils which often included in their membership missionary organizations or Church-bodies which did not want to be associated with the W.C.C., for example, certain fundamentalist groups. Should the I.M.C. break off its connection with these groups for the sake of integration with the W.C.C.? Misgivings on this score

---

[1] MRCC (Lucknow 1953), p. 46.   [2] Evanston, p. 322.
[3] MRCC (Davos 1955), p. 121.   [4] MRCC (Galyatetö 1956), pp 110f.
[5] MRCC (New Haven 1957), pp. 44f, 116–22.

were expressed at the meetings of the Central Committee at New Haven and the following year at Nyborg by representatives of Norway and France.

Furthermore, anxiety was felt that the I.M.C. (if it became a commission within the W.C.C.) might become neutralized and restricted in its action in the same way as the Faith and Order movement seemed to some people to have been. Similar views were expressed at the World Mission Conference in Ghana (28 December 1957–8 January 1958). At that conference the proposed integration was approved by fifty-eight votes to seven; at the same time strong sympathy was expressed for the misgivings of some missionary councils (especially in Africa, Latin America, and Scandinavia) and assurance was given that the plan for integration would be re-examined accordingly. A request was made at Ghana that the next Assembly of the W.C.C. be postponed from 1960 to 1961, so as to enable all the questions raised to be clarified; this proposal was also approved by the Central Committee of the W.C.C. in 1958.

However, some of the member Churches of the W.C.C. expressed strong reserve toward the proposed integration. In this case it was the Orthodox who were afraid that the character of the W.C.C. as a Council of Churches would be menaced by the merger with the I.M.C. They also feared that a "mammoth organization" would be produced, which would present dangers, and that the project was not yet ripe because the nature and tasks of the W.C.C. had not yet found sufficient understanding in the local Churches. Moreover, as most of the mission work was run by Protestant missions, the W.C.C. would (they maintained) become more and more "pan-Protestant" in its policy. Criticisms of this kind were voiced at the Central Committees at New Haven, Nyborg, and Rhodes.

Under such circumstances the idea of integration was slow in gaining ground on both sides. Until the Central Committee met at Rhodes in 1959 only forty-six of the 171 member Churches had expressed their opinion about integration with the I.M.C.; of these, forty-four were in agreement. By the same date twenty-two of the thirty-eight councils belonging to the I.M.C. had expressed themselves in favour of the merger, and three had declared themselves opposed (Norway, Belgium, and Brazil). One council had left the I.M.C. (the Belgian Congo). The tensions did not by any means die down at the Central Committee meeting at St Andrews in 1960. There was still a real fear that the question of integration might create a breach within the W.C.C. and within the I.M.C., because of the disagreement of the Orthodox and fundamentalist Churches.

But by the time of the meeting at St Andrews the difference with the Orthodox Churches had largely been resolved. The Orthodox Churches had avoided adopting any official attitude towards integration, and some of the Orthodox members of the Central Committee exercised "fraternal abstention" when the final vote was taken, while others (including the delegates from the Church of Greece) actually voted in favour. This may have been partly due to the plan to modify the Basis and to draw up the document concerning Proselytism. Many Orthodox may have been influenced by the fact that through integrating the W.C.C. and I.M.C. it would be easier to keep control over tendencies to proselytize. At the final vote there was an overwhelming majority in favour of integration. There was only one vote against it (by the Old Catholic representative) and three abstentions (including the Church of Norway, where the situation is particularly complicated).

Thus it was assured beforehand that integration would be accepted at New Delhi. At the last meeting of the I.M.C. immediately before the Assembly it gave its official approval to integration, and the plan was then accepted as it stood by the Assembly with all the changes which it involved in the constitution and the rules of the W.C.C. without a single dissenting vote. The chairman at that meeting, Archbishop Iakovos, then solemnly declared that "these two Councils are now united in one body with the name of the World Council of Churches".[1]

At the opening session of the Assembly, Bishop Lesslie Newbigin, then General Secretary of the I.M.C., had spoken on the theme "The Missionary Dimension of the Ecumenical Movement". He strongly advocated integration. He stressed the fact that no movement has the right to call itself ecumenical unless it does its utmost to bring the gospel to the whole world. "For the churches which constitute the World Council this means the acknowledgement that the missionary task is no less central to the life of the Church than the pursuit of renewal and unity."[2]

It was the positive conclusion of decades of development; but at the same time the Churches belonging to the World Council had confirmed their responsibility for their united mission to the world.

Growth of W.C.C. Membership[3]

In the rules of the W.C.C., the following criteria for membership are laid down, in addition to the primary requirement of the constitution that Churches eligible for consideration for membership shall be those "which express their agreement with the Basis" (Rules of the W.C.C., I. (3)):

(a) *Autonomy* An autonomous Church is one which, while recognizing the essential interdependence of the churches, particularly those of the same confession, is responsible to no other Church for the conduct of its own life.

(b) *Stability* A Church should not be admitted unless it has given sufficient evidence of stability in life and organization to become recognized as a Church by its sister churches.

(c) *Size*

(d) *Relationship with other Churches*

(The last two criteria are not defined in the Rules.)

Furthermore, "Before churches which are recognized as full members of one of the confessional or denominational world alliances with which the Council co-operates are admitted, the advice of these world alliances shall be sought" (I(4)). The same applies to Churches which belong to a Council

[1] New Delhi, p. 60.　　[2] Ibid., p. 4.　　[3] Ibid., p. 430.

associated with the W.C.C. or affiliated to the Commission on World Mission and Evangelism (I (5)). The application for membership must be approved by a majority of two-thirds at the Assembly or between assemblies in the Central Committee. The Central Committee shall then inform all the member Churches, "and unless objection is received from more than one-third of the member churches within six months the applicants shall be declared elected" (Constitution, II).[1]

The report entitled *The First Six Years, 1948–1954* (p. 9) states that "all churches which by the time of the Amsterdam Assembly had taken official action to join the World Council have remained members." The only withdrawal was the Baptist Union of Wales and Monmouthshire which did so "in view of the fact that many of its local churches had also membership in the Baptist Union of Great Britain and Ireland". Since 1948 nine Churches had been admitted into membership, bringing the total membership (immediately before the Evanston Assembly) to 161 Churches. The report said that the membership was still weak in Africa and Latin America. In Africa "the situation is slowly improving as mission churches become autonomous churches and apply for membership. In Latin America special efforts will have to be made to interpret the true character of the World Council." The hesitant attitude of the Orthodox Churches was not mentioned. At Amsterdam the only Orthodox Churches represented were the Church of Greece, the Ecumenical Patriarchate of Constantinople, the small national Eastern Orthodox Churches, the Russian Orthodox Church in Exile, and the Rumanian Orthodox Episcopate in America. However, the old Patriarchates of Alexandria, Antioch, and Jerusalem soon associated themselves.

The report *Evanston to New Delhi, 1954–1961* stated that during those seven years nineteen more churches had joined, including eight from Africa and five from Asia. Geographically the smallest number of member Churches was in Latin America. No reference was made either to the fact that no other Orthodox Churches had applied for membership. However, after 1957 negotiations opened with the Russian Orthodox Church, which were soon to alter the situation.

The largest expansion in membership took place at New Delhi when twenty-three new Churches joined the W.C.C. (see New Delhi, p. 9). This brought the number of member Churches up to 198. Although the Protestant Churches of Czechoslovakia, Hungary, and Poland had been represented in the W.C.C. from the beginning, relations with eastern Europe were greatly strengthened by the accession of the Orthodox Churches of Russia, Bulgaria, Rumania, and Poland. During the years which followed other Churches from eastern Europe (both Orthodox and non-Orthodox) also joined the W.C.C., so that it could now claim to be a fairly complete representation of non-Roman Catholic Christendom. The number of member Churches in Asia and especially in Africa also increased. The report *From New Delhi to Uppsala, 1961–1968* (p. 10) stated that if the Churches which joined at the New Delhi Assembly are added to those which joined since that date, twenty-one African Churches and seven Churches of the Eastern Orthodox

[1] New Delhi, p. 426.

tradition had been added to the membership up to 1966. The report also stated that two Pentecostalist Churches from Chile were accepted into membership, thus forming the first bridge to church bodies of a specially Evangelical character. However, the attitude of these groups to the W.C.C. is still marked by reservations, for different reasons. In order to enable smaller Churches with fewer than 10,000 members to co-operate in the W.C.C. (this being the minimum number fixed for membership of the W.C.C.) the New Delhi Assembly created the category of "associated Churches". This was in recognition of the fact that, if a large number of very small Churches became actual members, it would be almost impossible to allocate places at the Assembly. On the other hand, the W.C.C. wanted to strengthen the fellowship between itself and these small Churches, which were often living in a non-Christian environment, if they fulfilled all the other conditions for membership. Since New Delhi twelve Churches became "associated" with the W.C.C. They can send observers to the Assembly.

Before Uppsala the total number of member Churches was 232. Attention must, however, be drawn to the fact that the actual figures do not always reflect the size of the W.C.C. membership. For instance, some Churches which have merged in a union count in future only as one single Church, and do not need to apply for membership again.

The rapid growth of the W.C.C. has admittedly been offset by some painful setbacks. Because of the Korean crisis in 1951 the four member Churches in China withdrew from co-operation in the W.C.C., although they did not formally cancel their membership. Nevertheless, Bishop K. H. Ting of China attended the Central Committee meeting of Galyatetö in 1956. In 1955 the Baptist Union of Scotland withdrew from the W.C.C. In 1961 the three Dutch Reformed Churches in South Africa (the two Synods of the Transvaal and the Cape of the main Dutch Reformed Church, and the small Dutch Reformed Church of Africa) left the W.C.C. owing to basic differences of opinion on the policy of apartheid (which the W.C.C. had tried in vain to overcome). In 1963 the Union of Baptist Churches in the Netherlands decided to cancel their membership in the W.C.C. and in future merely to send observers to its conferences, because the W.C.C. (they alleged) was marked by "the imperialism of the national churches, *rapprochement* with the Catholic Church, the danger of Marxist infiltration, ecumenical impatience and a theology of relativism". In the latter case some misunderstandings may have crept in.

Relations with Regional Bodies

From the very outset the W.C.C. has fostered relations with National Councils of Churches and National Christian Councils, and later with regional organizations, and sought their co-operation in solving ecumenical tasks on the regional level. These efforts are described in Chapters 3 and 4 of this volume, and so will not be discussed here.

Relations with Confessional Bodies

The relations between the W.C.C. and the confessional and denominational bodies promoting ecumenism on the regional level presented comparatively few problems. The difficulties were far greater in the relations between the W.C.C. and the confessional world organizations, which vary widely in character and structure. Here it had to deal with definitely confessional bodies on a world level—confessional bodies which felt obliged to foster their own particular church tradition or confessional consciousness, and to make it clear. From the outset the W.C.C. has endeavoured to transform the differences into creative tensions. Of course, a basic attitude which is definitely confessional is always in danger of leading to isolation from other confessions and to theological rigidity (or even theological self-righteousness). The leaders of the W.C.C. have therefore never been afraid to point out the dangers of such trends. On the other hand, they have constantly stressed the fact that clear knowledge of one's own theological standpoint and of one's own church tradition are indispensable for a fruitful ecumenical conversation. For this reason, from the very outset the W.C.C. has sought contact with the confessional world bodies and other ecumenical organizations. This is laid down in the Constitution of the W.C.C., in Articles III and VII, where it is stated that "such world confessional associations and such ecumenical organizations as may be designated by the Central Committee may be invited to send representatives to the sessions of the Assembly and of the Central Committee in a consultative capacity".

It is noteworthy that simultaneously with the extension and strengthening of the W.C.C., the confessional world bodies were also growing larger and stronger. The Report *The First Six Years, 1948–1954* says: "It would seem that this development is due partly to the increased sense of solidarity and the desire to help churches which belong to the same confessional family, and partly to the desire to clarify the specific position of a particular confession in the wider ecumenical conversation" (p. 16). The problems which arise are evident: overlapping in the practical work, divided loyalties, and the anxious question "how the growth of a strong confessional consciousness will affect the ecumenical situation".[1] In its reports the W.C.C. was able to state again and again that the co-operation with the world confessional bodies (especially in the field of Inter-Church Aid) was making good progress, and that many of these world confessional bodies had clearly expressed their desire "to take their part in the ecumenical movement and to support the World Council of Churches".[2]

(The relation between confessional families and the ecumenical movement is discussed at greater length in Chapter 5 of this volume.)

Criticisms, Misunderstandings, and Opposition

It is absolutely inevitable that a phenomenon as significant as the World Council of Churches in its impact on church history and world history should

[1] *The First Six Years, 1948–1954*, p. 16.   [2] *Evanston to New Delhi, 1954–1961*, para. 16.

encounter criticism from outside. Criticism acts as a healthy corrective. In addition the Council must constantly re-examine its own form and its own action. The W.C.C. has from the outset always tried to exercise self-criticism of this kind. It is not necessary to repeat here what Dr Visser 't Hooft has stated in the first chapter of this book. I will merely complement and underline certain points. The W.C.C. has always been prepared to remember that primarily it is not an organization but a movement, and that it must remain so. Some of the pioneers of the 1920s and 1930s were filled with misgivings when the dynamic ecumenical movement (marked by the personalities of great leaders) developed in 1948 into "a fellowship of Churches". They were afraid that the *élan* of the first decades might become smothered by a fixed form of organization. It was not primarily the younger generation which protested against the institutionalization and bureaucratization of the ecumenical movement. Among the middle generation and the older generation also there have always been men who realized the gulf between "movement" and "institution". In this connection mention should be made of the book *Unity in Mid-Career*, edited by Keith R. Bridston and Walter D. Wagoner (New York 1963).

When the question arose of building a new headquarters for the W.C.C. in Geneva, *The British Weekly* brought out an anxious article entitled "Movement or Monument?" Similar examples could be quoted indefinitely. Every movement (whether secular or church) sooner or later reaches the critical phase between the uncontrolled dynamic of its birth and the time when it has to become institutionalized and to have fixed working forms. It must be admitted, however, that the W.C.C. has always remained aware of this tension. It has never claimed that the whole ecumenical movement is contained within its own divisions, committees, and conferences, nor has the W.C.C. any desire to channel the ecumenical movement in this way. Again and again it has been affirmed that the ecumenical movement is something far more extensive than the World Council. Again and again the World Council has accepted suggestions from ecumenical groups and associations outside its own organization, and has tried to establish contacts with them.

It is not surprising that a fellowship as heterogeneous as the W.C.C. has difficulty in arriving at joint statements on theology, or even on political and social questions. Western and Eastern traditions, loyalty to Scripture alone and loyalty to tradition, free parish structure and sacramental liturgical structures, loyalty to the confessional tradition and strong insistence on unity, widely differing political views (from east and west and from the Third World)—all these coexist within the W.C.C. and rub along together day in day out. But they do so on their common Basis in which they "confess the Lord Jesus Christ as God and Saviour according to the Scriptures and therefore seek to fulfil together their common calling to the glory of the one God, Father, Son, and Holy Spirit".

The divergences which arise, therefore, are not "criticisms"; they are inherent in the nature of the ecumenical fellowship and of the ecumenical dialogue. The contribution which the Roman Catholic Church has to make in its dialogue with the W.C.C. also belongs to a different category.

On the other hand, the W.C.C. does receive criticism from many Evangelical groups as represented, for example, in the World Evangelical Fellowship, which even misunderstand and misinterpret it. These criticisms range from theological questions to political suspicions. Again and again the W.C.C. is attacked because it tolerates within its own fellowship Churches which embrace in their membership both active, committed Christians and Christians whose relation to the Church is more nominal than real. The critics overlook the fact that the fellowship of Churches belonging to the W.C.C. have made it their aim to help one another (through the power of the gospel) to undertake inner renewal and to educate their members to become real, conscious Christians. Instead of holding aloof, those Christian groups whose first concern is the genuine conversion of their own members to Christ would fulfil their particular task far better if they tried to express their concept of what it means to be a Christian within the framework of the other Churches.

The same applies to the criticism (often made by the Evangelical groups) that the W.C.C.'s contacts with the Orthodox Churches and with the Roman Catholic Church during the last few years have assumed undue importance. As a result of several Orthodox Churches having joined the W.C.C. in the early 1960s, and of the Second Vatican Council, certain tendencies towards "over-compensation" can be discerned in the work of the W.C.C., some of which may be described as "the need to make up for lost time"—because intensive official conversations with the above-mentioned Churches had been difficult or impossible for several decades. Now they are open.

However, the W.C.C. has always made it absolutely clear that the dialogue with the Roman Catholic Church must be carried on within the framework of the whole concept of ecumenism, in such a way that it promotes the formation and extension of relations to other Churches: "It is important to ensure that new relationships are developed in such a way that existing relationships are deepened and strengthened, and that freedom is retained for the fuller development of fellowship among all Christians."[1] In the same connection stress was laid on the fact that the contribution of the so-called "Evangelical Churches" is indispensable for the W.C.C., and the importance of seizing opportunities for mutual discussion and co-operation with them. Those member Churches which had "Evangelical" trends and groups within their own congregations were requested to "seek ways by which this witness may be more adequately represented in the life of the World Council" in view of the fact that their "theological convictions, spiritual experience, and missionary zeal might well find more vital expression in the life of the Council".[2] The W.C.C. has repeatedly made similar statements urging the Churches not only to listen to the criticisms and warnings of the conservative Evangelicals, but also to learn something from the Christian life that they practise and from their exemplary efforts for mission and evangelism. Since no official connection could be established with the conservative Evangelicals, the W.C.C. has tried to make contacts with them unofficially through

[1] MRCC (Enugu 1965), p. 38.   [2] MRCC (Enugu 1965), p. 40.

consultations. In many cases this has helped to clear up misunderstandings and has furthered mutual understanding.

During the last few years the appearance of so-called "modern theology" has aroused considerable misgivings among conservative Evangelicals. They have criticized the W.C.C. for allowing exponents of this "modern theology" to speak at ecumenical conferences and to contribute to ecumenical statements, thus endangering the unchangeable bases of the biblical message. However, through authorized spokesmen, the W.C.C. has more than once unmistakably made it clear that it takes its stand on the whole biblical message of salvation centred in Christ in its trinitarian interpretation.[1] On the other hand, the W.C.C. cannot and must not close its eyes to the new trends in theology nor to their disturbing effect on its own member Churches.

The W.C.C. certainly does not support these extremist trends which have strayed away from the centre of the Christian faith, and this is what the conservative Evangelicals fail to understand. But the W.C.C. cannot shirk facing the challenge of the modern theology, which has caused a great deal of confusion within its member Churches. Just because of its responsibility for those Churches, the W.C.C. must try to clarify these modern trends. In doing so the W.C.C. must carefully avoid giving the impression of being a doctrinal authority of any kind. That would help to justify the criticism that it wants to set itself up as a super-Church.[2]

In the cases described above there may be some ground for criticism or for misunderstanding. But the "International Council of Christian Churches" is an entirely different matter. This is a definite countermovement to the W.C.C. led by Dr Carl McIntire; the fundamentalist groups belonging to it are small, but extremely active.

This association, which was founded in 1948 parallel with the Amsterdam Assembly, accuses the W.C.C. of modernism and relativism in relation to the basic truths of the Bible, of fraternizing with the Roman Catholic Church, of compromising with communism, and of promoting pacificism. It is not an over-simplification to say that the I.C.C.C. is an isolated group and that its assertions are absurd. Misconceptions and suspicions of the same kind extend deep down into the member Churches belonging to the W.C.C., and the latter will have to strive continually to convince the Churches, and secular public opinion also, by clarity in its attitude and precision in its statements concerning its policy and its aims.

Where the W.C.C. has Succeeded and Where it has Failed

In this swiftly moving age the tendency is rather to register failures or inadequacies than to recognize progress and success resulting from the efforts of many generations. This applies also to the ecumenical movement. It is only the oldest people living today who can remember the complete lack of connection which formerly existed between the Churches, the divisions

---

[1] MRCC (Heraklion 1967), pp. 100–4 (Report of the General Secretary, Dr Blake).
[2] See W. A. Visser 't Hooft, "The Super Church and the Ecumenical Movement", in *Ecumenical Review* vol. x (July 1958), pp. 365–85.

and conflicts which had continued for centuries and were taken for granted and passed on, and the consequent prejudice against other Churches or religious groups and condemnation of them. The far-reaching changes in the relations between the Churches, thanks to the ecumenical movement, are simply taken for granted today. Many people fail to realize how much work and effort had to be made for decades by men and women in all Churches before the present state of ecumenical fellowship was attained. In all its statements the W.C.C. has constantly made it clear that this fellowship cannot be understood in the sense of an easy-going ignoring of existing differences.

The sole aim of the W.C.C. was to bring the Churches out of their isolation and to draw them into consultation with one another; in this the W.C.C. merely wanted to be an instrument and to provide a basis. After twenty years' experience the W.C.C. has definitely shown that it has achieved this aim in all essentials. In the W.C.C. and through it the Churches have not only learned to know and understand each other better; they have also realized afresh their responsibility for each other and for service to the world. Smaller Churches, or Churches which were persecuted and which were obliged to live in isolation, have experienced the strengthening fellowship of world Christendom through their membership of the W.C.C. Their mutual support in emergencies through world-wide relief projects has created a sense of belonging to one single family, which is felt even in the local congregations. Most important of all, the Churches which belong to the W.C.C. are compelled all the time to examine themselves and to strive for renewal, by listening together to the Word of God and by learning from one another.

Against this background of achievement certain weaknesses do admittedly still exist, and also certain dangers of wrong development. Have the member Churches fully recognized all the obligations which spring from their membership in the World Council? When the World Council sends out questionnaires or asks the Churches to pronounce their opinion, it finds again and again that the response from the member Churches is extremely small. In some cases this may be due to the lack, in some Churches, of organs to deal with such tasks. On the other hand, the W.C.C. cannot fulfil its many different tasks unless its thought and action is adequately supported by its member Churches. Otherwise the balance would shift from the life of the member Churches to the Geneva headquarters, which would conjure up the spectre of "secretariocracy".

Is it not possible that this lack of response is due to the fact that the delegates who attend the assemblies and who sit on the executive committees of the W.C.C. have too little contact with their own Churches, and that they do too little to relate their work in the W.C.C. to the life of their home-Churches and carry it out there? It is an old complaint that is constantly heard in the local congregations that the W.C.C. is an affair for theologians and church leaders; and hitherto the W.C.C. has not succeeded in proving this criticism groundless.

This brings us to the most painful gap in the whole network of ecumenical work: the fact that it is inadequately rooted in the local Churches. It would be over-simple to generalize about this. The reasons for it differ widely. They range from lack of attention to the ecumenical movement during the theological training to the indifferent introversion of the local Churches. Admittedly, during the past decades a great improvement has taken place in this respect and grass-roots co-operation between congregations is growing, even when their Churches or denominations remain apart. But ultimately the future of the ecumenical movement will depend on whether it succeeds in uniting "all in each place" in joint witness and service. The separation and the opposition between the Christian Churches on the local level was the starting-point of the ecumenical movement; it is therefore only on the local level that it can come to fulfilment.

This certainly does not mean that (as many people fear) the question of truth should be regarded as relative, and that priority should be given to a pragmatic solution for unity on the local level. But the W.C.C. and its member Churches must constantly face the question how the ecumenical agreements and resolutions are being carried out in practice. Eminent theologians such as Professor Edmund Schlink have often remarked resignedly that in W.C.C. commissions agreements about important theological questions have been reached without the member Churches afterwards hearing anything about them, not to mention doing anything to put the agreements into practice. Furthermore, in the 1950s Professor Walter Freytag once expressed his concern about the fact that even within ecumenical commissions the members themselves often did not remember, and consequently did not apply, what had been said and done on the same question years before, or even decades before. This also involves a structural problem at ecumenical conferences. Up to the present the W.C.C. has not succeeded in developing conference-procedure which will ensure that the participants are not overwhelmed with material, and which will also ensure that adequate time is available for examining and dealing with questions. It is evident that the W.C.C. might lag fatally behind the Roman Catholic Church's precise doctrinal statements because its own statements are not sufficiently mature or not adequately formulated. Only by concentration of emphasis, continuity and tenacious dynamism can the fellowship of Churches belonging to the W.C.C. be obedient to the call which has gathered them together under their one Lord and has placed them on the path of discipleship.

3

Out of
All Continents and Nations

A REVIEW OF REGIONAL DEVELOPMENTS
IN THE ECUMENICAL MOVEMENT

HANS-RUEDI WEBER

When on 23 August 1948 the World Council of Churches was solemnly inaugurated, the non-Western delegates had mixed feelings. On the one hand, they rejoiced in the fact that now as younger Churches they could meet with the older Churches on an equal level, as sisters rather than as daughters. On the other hand, however, they had serious apprehensions.

Beyond Western Parochialism

The major apprehension concerned the question whether the newly created body would not have a one-sided Western character. The two movements which merged—"Life and Work" and "Faith and Order"—had in their history shown little awareness of the pioneering ecumenical work being done outside eastern and western Europe and North America. "Faith and Order" conferences had several times been shocked out of their Western parochialism by people such as Bishop Azariah from South India; but these incidents had little consequence. For "Faith and Order" the "East" remained the Orthodox Churches, and only at Lund in 1952 did this movement begin to grow aware of the challenging significance of the existence of younger Churches in the non-Western world. No wonder that the Amsterdam statements about unity disappointed in particular the Indians, who less than eleven months earlier had seen the inauguration of the Church of South India. D. T. Niles expressed their feelings in a telling image: "The older churches were discussing the reasons and circumstances which had led to their earlier divorce: the younger churches were only just getting married and did not wish to be asked their opinion on the subjects which had led to the quarrels between the older churches."[1]

In the "Life and Work" movement Western parochialism reigned no less. Indeed, it was not until the W.C.C. study on "Our common Christian responsibility towards areas of rapid social change" (1955–61) that the "Life and Work" stream of the ecumenical movement became aware of the challenges of revolutionary Asia, Africa, and Latin America for Christian social thinking and action. At the first W.C.C. assembly, however, the treatment of the East–West conflict still gave the impression that the East ended with the Bosporus, as C. Devanesen observed.[2]

Such Western parochialism had been gradually overcome in the ecumenical youth movements and—with a delay of about one generation—in the International Missionary Council. They were not among the founding organizations of the W.C.C., but in all continents they had formed many of the actual and potential W.C.C. leaders, who immediately struggled for breaking through the traditional Western parochialism and worked hard for the manifestation of true universality. In 1947 W. A. Visser 't Hooft said in his report to the Provisional Committee of the W.C.C.: "It is . . . important that the younger churches should participate very fully in the setting up of the Council in order that they may make their full contribution to it and consider it from the start

[1] Amsterdam Series, 1948, vol. v, p. 62.
[2] "Post Amsterdam Thought from a Younger Churchman", in the *Ecumenical Review*, vol. i (January 1949), p. 143.

as their own instrument of ecumenical fellowship and action."[1] In the same year Stephen C. Neill was sent as an ecumenical ambassador to Asia and early in 1948 a special Far Eastern Commission was set up in Manila. Moreover, since its first meeting in 1946 the Joint Committee of the I.M.C. and the W.C.C. played an important role in letting the voice of the younger Churches be heard. As a result of all these initiatives, among the 351 official delegates at the Amsterdam Assembly there sat twenty-six nationals from Asia, six nationals from Africa, three Latin Americans, one from the Near East, but none yet from the Pacific.

Despite these efforts to make the W.C.C. an instrument of and for the Churches in all continents, P. D. Devanandan later confessed:

> Some of us from the so-called younger churches left Amsterdam with a heavy heart, because we could not help feeling that somehow we did not belong. The entire trend of discussion veered round problems of life and thought which primarily concerned the older churches. Moreover, we gained the impression, rightly or wrongly, that we were being made to think and act in accordance with the ideas, doctrinal and political, which are current in the older churches.[2]

This *malaise* came partly from a strong emphasis on the confessional loyalty in the early W.C.C., revealed by a significant change in the rules about the principles of representation. In the earliest draft of the W.C.C. constitution (1938) the membership in the Assembly and Central Committee was to be chosen according to a regional principle.[3] At Amsterdam this rule was changed and the accepted constitution says that seats must be allocated "due regard being given to such factors as numerical size, adequate confessional representation and adequate geographic distribution".[4] The confessional and the proportionate numerical representation were therefore set beside or even before the regional representation. Many delegates from the younger Churches who were involved in union negotiations had hoped that the W.C.C. would give a clear priority to the regional over the confessional loyalty. This did not happen and younger churchmen ever since have raised the question whether the W.C.C. does not foster an inter-confessional ecumenism at the expense of the equally important, perhaps even more important, inter-regional aspect of the ecumenical movement. "To us of the younger churches it is the international nature of our faith that strikes the imagination; . . . to us it is vital that ecumenical Christianity be both international and missionary."[5]

The insistence on the region does not therefore spring from an isolationist

---

[1] W.C.C. Buck Hill Falls Meeting, 1947, MRCC, p. 54. He did not tire of insisting on this point; cf. his reports to the W.C.C. Central Committee in Amsterdam 1948, MRCC, p. 30; in Chichester 1949, MRCC, pp. 65ff.

[2] *Ecumenical Review* vol. iv (January 1952), p. 163.

[3] G. K. A. Bell, ed., *Documents on Christian Unity* (Third Series, London 1948), pp. 294ff. This was in accordance with the proposal of the Committee of Thirty-Five in 1937; cf. *Oxford Series* (1937), vol. viii, p. 280.

[4] Amsterdam Series 1948, vol. v, p. 199. Cf. also the article by O. S. Tomkins on "Regional and confessional loyalties in the Universal Church", in Amsterdam Series 1948, vol. i, pp. 135–46.

[5] P. D. Devanandan, "The ecumenical movement and the younger churches", Amsterdam Series 1948, vol. i, pp. 152ff.

regionalism with the aim to counterbalance the factual Western parochialism of most ecumenical organizations by creating an Asian, African, or Latin American parochialism. The deepest motive is the concern that the Church become truly catholic (out of all the nations of the earth) and truly missionary (sent to all the nations of the earth). Ecumenical regionalism is an act of obedience. This was clearly expressed in the solemn declaration which inaugurated in 1959 the first regional ecumenical body: "Believing that the purpose of God for the churches in East Asia is life together in a common obedience to Him for the doing of His will in the world, the East Asia Christian Conference is hereby constituted."[1]

It is interesting to note that a similar movement from one-sided Western and inter-confessional ecumenism to regional developments and an emphasis on inter-continental ecumenism is present within the Roman Catholic Church. The Second Vatican Council defined the ecumenical movement as "those activities and enterprises which, according to various needs of the Church and opportune occasions, are started and organized for the fostering of unity among Christians".[2] Unity is seen here exclusively as unity with "the separated brethren", with the Churches and ecclesial communions separated from the Roman Apostolic See. Only the interconfessional aspect of the ecumenical movement is emphasized which reflects the concern of the Western Roman Catholic ecumenists. The Second Vatican Council, however, has also brought to the fore the intercontinental aspect of the ecumenical movement, although this happened not so much through the influence of the ecumenists and under the subject of ecumenism, but through the influence of the bishops from Africa, Asia, and Latin America and under the subjects of catholicity and mission. The Church is seen as the sacrament of the salvation of the world and of the unity of mankind. In this connection the necessary regional development is strongly emphasized. In order that the Church become truly catholic, particular Churches in the different regions and nations must retain their own traditions and thus contribute through their special gifts to the good of the other parts and of the whole of the Church.[3] This catholic nature of the Church makes her missionary and leads to the establishment of particular Churches in the different regions of the world.[4] It is a pity that in the documents of Vatican II this necessity of regional developments within the Church in order that she may be truly catholic and missionary has not been recognized as a primary *ecumenical* concern.

The Asian Region

When in 1921 the Far Eastern Olympic Games were held in Shanghai, the Chinese Y.M.C.A. took the initiative of organizing what was probably the first Asian Christian meeting. Asian Christians had, of course, met earlier at

[1] E.A.C.C. Inaugural Assembly at Kuala Lumpur, 1959, *Report*, p. 10.
[2] *Decree on Ecumenism*, no. 4.
[3] *Dogmatic Constitution on the Church*, no. 13.
[4] *Decree on the Missionary Activity of the Church*, nos. 1, 19–22.

world meetings. The world conference of the World's Student Christian Federation in Tokyo in 1907 was an especially important step in this Asian Christian self-discovery. Yet until 1921 no special initiative was taken to gather Asian Christians together. The experiment must have been convincing because only one year later, in 1922, at the World Student Christian Federation (W.S.C.F.) world conference in Peking, it was recommended "that an international conference in the Far East be continued regularly as a means to promote co-operation between the Eastern Movements and to make them know and understand one another better".[1] However, the birth pangs of the Asian revolution prevented early fulfilment of such plans for regular co-operation.

The uniting force still came from outside Asia, especially in the dynamic person of John R. Mott. His travels through Asia—first in 1895-7, then in 1907, in 1912-13, and many times later—set the ecumenical movement in motion in that continent. Many of its leaders were discovered and given confidence and training by him. He organized the visiting of Asian Christians among themselves, for instance the important visit of T. Z. Koo from China to the students in India in 1922. Most Asian National Christian Councils are the fruit of J. R. Mott's initiative. It was therefore a proper expression of gratitude when one of the first actions taken by the E.A.C.C. at its inaugural assembly was the inauguration of the "John R. Mott Lectures".

The above-mentioned Peking resolution was first implemented at Tjiteureup on Java in September 1933. The young Student Christian Movement of Java had invited its sister student movements from Asia and Australasia for a meeting which in a remarkable way foreshadowed the discussions of the I.M.C. assembly in Tambaram, India in December 1938 and of the later E.A.C.C. meetings. Because the living Christ, his uniqueness and finality, was put in the centre of the common study, it became possible to discuss in a very frank way such delicate subjects as colonialism and nationalism, the relationship between the Asian Church and Western missionary societies, the attitude of Christian faith to the syncretism and the religions of Asia.

These were subjects taken up five years later at Tambaram. There for the first time nationals of the lands of younger Churches formed a small majority of official delegates in a Christian world assembly, and among them were almost all the future leaders of the E.A.C.C. A deep solidarity in faith between Asian Christians had become a reality. This was forcefully demonstrated by the fellowship between the Chinese and Japanese delegations, even though their countries were at war with one another. "Wherever we looked we saw Chinese and Japanese together", wrote an African delegate.[2] This already existing fellowship in Christ had now also to receive a visible, organizational expression.

Communications from the Chinese and Japanese National Christian Councils about the desirability of a far eastern office of the I.M.C. were considered at Tambaram, and one year later A. L. Warnshuis was appointed

---

[1] W.S.C.F. General Committee (Peking 1922), *Minutes*, p. 27. Cf. also H.-R. Weber, *Asia and the Ecumenical Movement 1895–1961* (London 1966), pp. 277–92.

[2] M. T. Soga, quoted in R. I. Seabury, *Daughter of Africa* (Boston 1945), p. 75.

secretary of this office. But war intervened. The Geneva meeting of the I.M.C. committee in 1945 had again to decide on this matter, this time on the basis of a proposal sent by the Chinese and the Indian National Councils of Churches. This proposal set out the following long-term objectives for the planned East Asia Regional Committee:

(i) To promote and give expression to the spirit of Christian unity among the churches of East Asia. (ii) To promote fellowship and mutual helpfulness among Christians in East Asia through conference, exchange of delegations and such other measures as may be agreed upon. (iii) To promote a sense of the responsibility of the churches in East Asia for the Christian witness and for the building up of the churches in this area. (iv) To deepen the unity of the churches in East Asia with the world Church. (v) To bring to the life of the world Church the distinctive contribution of the churches in East Asia.[1]

The memorandum states clearly the purpose of an Asian regional body within and for the ecumenical movement. It was interesting, however, how differently this aim was interpreted in action by the existing Western ecumenical organizations and by the Asian Christians. The Joint Committee of the I.M.C. and W.C.C. thought in terms of an *office* and in 1947 approved such an ecumenical organizational structure. Yet in a special consultative session held in July 1947 during the I.M.C. meeting in Whitby, Asians showed little enthusiasm for such an office. What they wanted was an opportunity for consulting together, as R. D. Manikam reported in their name:

Prior to the establishment of an East Asia office . . . preliminary steps should be taken immediately to plan for an East Asia conference, whereby representatives of the churches can share their experience and concern, join in meditation and prayer and make common plans for participating more fully in the life of the ecumenical Church.[2]

The first East Asian Christian Conference met at Bangkok in December 1949. Although organized by a Chinese (S. C. Leung), China was absent for the first time. Having surveyed the contemporary situation in the Asian Churches and discussed their common task, the conference decided to appoint an Asian as their "ambassadorial representative". One year later R. B. Manikam from India began to fulfil this function. Especially in the years 1952-3 Asia became the scene of perhaps too many ecumenical gatherings organized by the W.C.C. and other agencies. Probably the most important was the study conference for East Asia at Lucknow, India, where Asian Christians prepared their contribution to the W.C.C. assembly in Evanston.

In July 1955 the Asia Council on Ecumenical Mission held its first meeting in Hong Kong. This organization was created mainly by Presbyterian and United Church mission boards and their daughter Churches in East Asia in order to stimulate inter-Church aid and exchange of personnel. The creation of this body accelerated the plans for establishing a more representative regional church conference. When in March 1957 the Second East Asian Christian Conference met therefore in the thoroughly Asian atmosphere of

[1] I.M.C. Committee (Geneva 1946), *Minutes*, p. 46.
[2] I.M.C. Committee (Whitby 1947), *Minutes*, p. 32.

the small fishing village, Prapat, in revolutionary Indonesia, firm proposals were drawn up for creating the E.A.C.C. The core of the mobile E.A.C.C. staff team began to work, each secretary based in his home country and working from there: D. T. Niles from Ceylon, U Kyaw Than from Burma, and Alan Brash from New Zealand.

This last name indicates an important development. Many had feared that the meeting in Prapat might become a mere ecclesiastical replica of the Asian–African Bandung conference in 1955, where a political power bloc formed itself over against the western nations. But true ecumenical regionalism has nothing to do with the forming of continental or racial power blocs. One of the first acts of the chairman at Prapat was therefore to move the delegates from Australia and New Zealand from the observers section into the full membership section. Ever since the Churches in Australia and New Zealand have played an important role in the E.A.C.C.

The E.A.C.C. assembly has so far met three times: for its inaugural assembly in Kuala Lumpur, Malaya in May 1959, and twice in Bangkok, Thailand, in February–March 1964 and January–February 1968. Typical, especially for the first of these, were the outstanding contributions which Asian laymen made to its deliberations. The assemblies have authorized a series of important consultations. In India, Japan, the Philippines, Korea, and Indonesia the consultations on "New Patterns of Christian Service" (1960–2) showed the present Asian Christian thinking about the relationship between social service and social action as well as the trend from separate Christian service institutions to the involvement of Christians in state and secular service programmes. The "situation conferences" in India, Japan, and Singapore tried to discern what joint action for mission means today in the three major areas of East Asia. A meeting in Hong Kong in 1966 and one in Seoul in 1967 summed up present Asian thinking and convictions about Faith and Order and Church and Society matters respectively. This is only a very selective list of meetings, by-passing many consultations organized by E.A.C.C. committees and excluding those organized by the various Asian study centres and by the W.C.C.; and not least the third assembly of the W.C.C. at New Delhi in 1961.

The E.A.C.C. assemblies also authorized and surveyed a growing number of inter-Church aid and missionary projects. Deeply involved with the questions of the home and family life, the E.A.C.C. has stimulated much concern in the Asian Churches about planned parenthood. The exchange of fraternal workers within Asia and the sending of Asian missionaries—over two hundred are now listed—were fostered. Asian churches remain thus no longer merely receiving Churches. This is also true financially. Between fifteen and twenty thousand U.S. dollars a year are given by Asian Christians in response to W.C.C. emergency appeals for aid somewhere in the world. Especially significant was the establishment of the Asian Christian Service in Vietnam where through the costly service of the E.A.C.C. area personnel Asian Churches fulfil together their ministry of reconciliation. This short and incomplete list shows that the E.A.C.C. is not only a ferment of ideas—although this aspect of regional developments is emphasized in the description of this chapter—but also a programme of common witness and service.

What is the purpose of all these projects and meetings? D. T. Niles, the retiring E.A.C.C. general secretary, said in his ten-years report: "The complex of ideas and principles within which our churches in East Asia usually functioned was within the context of world denominations and confessions. The E.A.C.C. helped to provide the other eye with which the churches could look at their work and witness." Thus it helped to build up "within the life of each church and country a group of men and women, both older and younger, who are willing to probe the frontiers of the Christian enterprise" and "to give to these frontiersmen a sense of solidarity, encouragement and sharpened insight". "All we have sought to do is to inject into situations ideas which we felt were right at this time, to get key individuals in every country committed to these ideas, and then to put pressure behind these ideas so as to make costly any attempt to disregard them."[1] If this is a fair description of the E.A.C.C.'s work, then it is essential to examine which ideas were studied in order to understand the main thrust of the Asian regional body. The earlier mentioned John R. Mott Lectures are a helpful guide for such an examination.

The first John R. Mott lecture series (1959) stood under the theme, "A decisive hour for the Christian mission".[2] First, some Western friends were asked to situate the Asian churches within the ecumenical movement. This led up to the much noted lecture by D. T. Niles on "A Church and Its 'Selfhood' " which became a programme because it expressed in a prophetic way what had to be said at that time and place. Just as a child suddenly says "I" and his self thus ceases to be a mere object, so Asian Churches have become conscious of their self-hood. This happened in their worship, in their mission to a given place and in their secular engagement, i.e. Christian involvement in the political, economic, and social affairs. However, this self-hood can grow only in relationship with other "selves". For a long time relationships have existed between Churches and their missionary agencies in the West with the Churches in Asia, but the relationships do not yet sufficiently take account of the newly acquired selfhood of Asian Churches. D. T. Niles therefore spelled out what changes are overdue in these missionary relationships. There are also growing relationships of conversation, belonging, and oneness among the Asian Churches themselves. Now "the E.A.C.C. is one more expression of this growth of the churches in Asia into selfhood. It is the instrument of our resolve to be churches together here in Asia. It is to be the means by which we enter into a meaningful participation in the missionary task of the Church."

The second John R. Mott lecture series (1961) dealt with the subject "Christ's Ministry and Ours",[3] emphasizing the ministry of the laity. The main speaker, Masao Takenaka from Japan, pointed especially to the New Testament image of the Church as the community of the first fruits of the new humanity.

It somehow transcends the notion of a majority or minority situation. It gives a real qualitative representation rather than one determined by quantitative

[1] D. T. Niles, "Ideas and Services", unpublished manuscript.
[2] *A Decisive Hour for the Christian Mission* (London 1960), p. 96.
[3] Published in *The South East Asia Journal of Theology*, III. 3 (January 1962), p. 18.

number. A Christian layman in industrial society, no matter how insignificant he appears to be, is a first fruit in that particular and concrete place. He is a pledge of the Holy Spirit that the great harvest is to come. I believe this concept of the first fruits gives real strength and support to Christian presence and involvement in a concrete place of work and living in our Asian setting.

Takenaka and the other lecturers then spelled out what such a qualitative representation means for the everyday life of ordinary Christians and for the ministries and structures of Asian church life.

Under the title "Grace and Apostleship"[1] the third series of the John R. Mott lectures (1964) continued the reflection on the themes of the first two series, but the main accent lay now on the understanding of the tides of history. M. M. Thomas showed that ever since the Bangkok meeting in 1949 the E.A.C.C. has overcome the traditional pietistic indifference to the tides of history. At the inaugural assembly at Kuala Lumpur in 1959 it was even stated that "the Church must endeavour to discern how Christ is at work in the revolutions of contemporary Asia; releasing new creative forces, judging idolatry and false gods, leading people to a decision for or against him and gathering to himself those who respond in faith to him, in order to send them back into the world to be witnesses to his Kingship".

It was a sign of healthy realism that in his 1964 lecture M. M. Thomas concentrated on the forces which tend to betray the promises of God in the revolutionary tides of Asia. He thus showed how the tide of nationalism brings for Asia the danger to pass from the traditional conformist collectivism to the modern technical mass society without having discovered the human person and the personal community. Similarly the true humanity which Christ reveals can be endangered by the negative aspects of the tides of growing group consciousness, or by the tide of growing economic tension between the rich nations of the North and the poor nations of the South.

Having reflected on the necessary selfhood which the Asian Churches need for fulfilling their task in new Asia, having rediscovered the ministry of the laity, their vocation to be the first fruits of the new humanity, and having now also made a realistic appraisal of the Asian scene, the time was ripe to think about the theme "Confessing the Faith in Asia Today".[2] This was the subject of the fourth series of the John R. Mott lectures (1966). The fact that among the seven lecturers only two were Asian nationals shows the awareness of the E.A.C.C. that while Christ has to be confessed in the concrete region of Asia today, this confession must happen in full communion with the Church universal. This, however, does not mean that the Churches in Asia can simply take over the confessions of the Western Churches. C. H. Hwang said:

> The sad thing is that, before becoming first a confessing Church in the missionary situation, the younger churches were prematurely projected into a "confessional" situation which was not their own, that is, before they knew and became a Community of Christ they were told to become a Presbyterian, Lutheran,

---

[1] Published in *The South East Asia Journal of Theology*, v. 4 (April 1964).

[2] *The South East Asia Journal of Theology*, viii. 3 (January 1967). C. H. Hwang's lecture in the same journal, viii. 1–2, pp. 77f.

Methodist or Anglican Church. They were divided without even being able to know why. I believe that the way to recover the unity of the Church on the road is to return to the confessing church first, and only secondly to become a confessional church, and hold steadfastly the second within the context of the first. Finally, I believe that God has once again put not only the younger churches but also the older churches and the ancient churches in a new missionary situation—not only in Asia today but also in the world today—so that we may learn our way back to the unity of the *confessio viatorum.*

Such a *confessio viatorum* is not in the first place the affair of theologians but of the pilgrim people. It was therefore right and according to the best tradition of the E.A.C.C. that also an Asian layman, T. B. Simatupang, was asked to speak on this theme.

The African Region

Within the cataclysms of modern African history the Church can survive only if it struggles with the following tasks: Will it be able to build up a Christian family life for Africa without becoming legalistic and disregarding the African social heritage? Will Christians overcome the fear of sorcery and witchcraft which survives even among many sophisticated African believers and nevertheless have a sympathetic approach to the old African world view? Will the Church be able to stem the growing proliferation of separatist sects without losing the positive search for community and indigenization which finds expression in these movements? To this list of C. P. Groves, the foremost historian of the Church in Africa,[1] new challenges must be added today: What is the role of the Church in the midst of the clash of cultures? What contribution can Christians make for abolishing the economic exploitation of the African peoples and for nation-building?

In the predominantly autobiographical novels of contemporary African writers such questions appear again and again. How do Christians in Africa answer these challenges? What insights have they gained to contribute to the Church universal? An important beginning of the answer to these questions is the way in which African Christians and Churches increasingly learn to face the above-mentioned challenges together, to consult with one another and support one another in their discipleship.

Unfortunately, William Carey's "pleasing dream" of 1806—to hold from 1810 onwards decennial world missionary conferences at the Cape of Good Hope—was never realized, otherwise Africa's ecumenical history might have begun already at the beginning of the nineteenth century. In actual fact the earliest interdenominational missionary conference met only in 1904 in Johannesburg. At that time South Africa was already active in the World Student Christian Federation, because only one year after the foundation of the Federation at Vadstena in 1895 one of its founder members, Luther Wishard, had helped to establish the mostly Dutch South African Student Christian Association. In 1906 John R. Mott visited South Africa for the first

---

[1] C. P. Groves, *The Planting of Christianity in Africa*, vol. iv (London 1958), pp. 315–56.

time. It was not until the 1920s, however, that Africa was discovered in ecumenical history.

This discovery happened in Asia. At the World Student Christian Federation meeting at Peking in 1922, for the first time a son of Africa was asked to speak at a world conference—the American Negro Willis King, who was later the Methodist bishop in Liberia. He made a deep impression, and the important policy decisions made in Peking concerning race relations and the building up of ecumenical student work in Africa was to a great extent due to him. One and a half decades later it was again in Asia, at the I.M.C. assembly in Tambaram, that for the first time Africa was well represented in a world gathering and experienced the dynamic of the ecumenical movement. "My journey out of Africa turned me from a South African into an African. Madras made me a world Christian", wrote Mina T. Soga.[1] The First Asio-African Conference in Bandung, Indonesia in 1955, strengthened the African political leaders in their quest for a free Africa, and this movement in turn influenced the African Churches' quest for selfhood.

Meanwhile James E. K. Aggrey from the Gold Coast had been fighting relentlessly for understanding and sympathy for Africa and its people among the Christians in North America and Great Britain. In 1921 he attended the first meeting of the I.M.C. at Lake Mohonk, New York and was appointed a member of the Council. One year later he appealed to the Foreign Missions Conference of North America:

> Give us a full-rounded chance. The sea of difference between you and us should be no more. The sea of our failure to bring any contribution to the Kingdom of God shall be no more. You white folks may bring your gold, your great banks and your big buildings, your sanitation and other marvellous achievements to the manger, but that will not be enough. Let the Chinese and the Japanese and the Indians bring their frankincense of ceremony, but that will not be enough. We black people must step in with our myrrh of child-like faith. . . . If you take our child-likeness, our love for God, our belief in humanity, our belief in God, and our love for you, whether you hate us or not, then the gifts will be complete. . . . God grant that you who have heard . . . this plea from Africa will trust us, will come and educate us, and will give us a chance to make that contribution to the world which is in the design of God.[2]

"Come and educate us!" This call was heard by Europe and North America. During the next decades the Christian commitment for education in Africa became a first attempt to see Africa as a whole. In 1920–1 an educational survey commission was sent by the U.S.A. Foreign Missions Conference and the Phelps-Stokes Fund to Central, West, and South Africa, and in 1923–4 a second commission, mainly British, surveyed East Africa. Both were led by Jesse Jones and in both Aggrey collaborated. Meanwhile, one of the greatest ecumenical pioneers, the I.M.C. secretary J. H. Oldham, became almost totally absorbed in African affairs. He was the prime mover for the first international conference on the Christian Mission in Africa.

[1] R. I. Seabury, op.cit., p. 77.
[2] Edwin W. Smith, *Aggrey in Africa* (London 1929), pp. 188f.

It met in September 1926, not in Africa but in Le Zoute, Belgium.[1] In the same year the Institute of African Languages and Culture was launched in London, and in 1929 the I.M.C. created its International Committee on Christian Literature for Africa. Five years later John R. Mott became instrumental in getting Christian Councils started in Southern and Central Africa.

After the inquiries made in the 1920s in the field of general and religious education, the Tambaram assembly of the I.M.C. decided in 1938 that a comprehensive inquiry be made concerning the present condition of theological education. Especially in Africa the great lack of adequately trained ministers had become a major obstacle to the growth of the Church. "It is impossible to exaggerate the importance of the work of those who teach theology and train ministers of the African Churches." This first conclusion of the inquiry led immediately to the second one, namely the obligation for co-operation in theological training.

> The judgement of the succeeding generation may well be that the fateful issue of our own time for the advance or the decline of Protestant Christianity in Africa was the achievement or refusal of Christian co-operation; and that the issue was basically determined in the type, spirit, and quality of the schools for pastors.[2]

In the post-war years some experiments in joint theological training appeared (Limuru in Kenya, Trinity College in Kumasi, the Yaounde theological faculty, etc.). A meeting of representatives of Protestant missions and Churches was held at Leopoldville, and by 1955 there were Christian Councils in fourteen African territories, although only three of these—Belgian Congo, Sierra Leone, and South Africa—were affiliated to the I.M.C.

In the new Africa where in the period between 1958 and 1961 eighteen nations reached independence, intercontinental co-operation was indeed needed. But were the Western missionary organizations and the African Churches ready for it? "The tendency was unmistakably for the extension of confessional organizations rather than for the fostering of inter-confessional unions."[3] The clearest sign of this trend is the fact that the first (Church or secular) All Africa Conference which met in Africa itself was organized by the Lutheran World Federation. In 1955 it called together the memorable All AfricaLutheran Conference on the slopes of Mount Kilimanjaro at Marangu, Tanganyika. The stated purpose of that meeting was to bring all the Lutheran Churches and mission fields in Africa out of isolation in order that they might begin to think as an African Lutheran Church and see the vision of the Christian Church throughout the whole continent of Africa.

The enthusiastic reports of delegates and visitors—out of a total of 168 participants 116 were Africans—show that this purpose was achieved despite the great difficulties of communication. Undoubtedly a real community has

---

[1] The special Africa issue of *IRM* (July 1926), with the preparatory papers for the Le Zoute Conference, gives an excellent survey of Africa in the 1920s and the task which the Church faced then in that continent.

[2] *Survey of the Training of the Ministry in Africa*, Part iii, p. 61 and Part ii, p. 95.

[3] C. P. Groves, op.cit., vol. iv (London 1958), p. 305; cf. pp. 304–7.

grown among Lutherans in Africa. Yet for the African delegates the discovery was not so much Lutheranism as the Church in Africa. This appeared especially in the discussions on faith and confession. The call for a *confessio Africana* was strong and the Marangu report recommends that "a comprehensive confessional statement—*confessio Africana*—may be worked out, not necessarily replacing the old confessions, but amplifying the Lutheran teaching in terms and in a language which will be understood by the modern African".[1]

Unfortunately, the two following All Africa Lutheran Conferences did not go very far in implementing this recommendation. At Antsirabé in 1960 the accent lay on "the faith of our fathers", and at Addis Ababa in 1965 only Josiah Kibira came back to the Marangu recommendation in his courageous keynote address where he said:

> Theologically, there is a lack of freedom of mind. With the exception of a few cases, we can hardly think independently. We depend mostly on advisers from Europe and America. Our theological boards are very inadequate as long as they reflect American, Swedish or German Lutheran theologies rather than African theologies. . . . And yet we must stress the universality of Christ's Church. We must guard ourselves against an African church and against what we mean by a *confessio Africana*. Yet the question is this: how long must we depend on the European churches to do our thinking in the very things we wish to do?[2]

Kibira struggled here with the basic issue of true regionalism in the ecumenical movement. Regionalism does not aim at a Church and confession which is more Asian or African than Christian. It wants to maintain the universality of Christ's Church. But, at the same time, it wants to counterbalance the existing strong European and American character of the present manifestation of Christ's Church. Churches and theologians of the West had taken Aggrey's words about the African child-like faith too literally. Dr Akanu (formerly Sir Francis) Ibiam once said that to many white missionaries "Africa must stay where she is—the baby of the world—not only in political affairs, or in economic matters, or sociologically, but even in church life and Christian emancipation".[3] In order to grow out of this tutelage ecumenical regionalism aims at creating structures in which there is freedom of mind for Christians in a given region to think, confess, and act according to God's will for this region. Kibira's problem was that a Lutheran or any other confessional all Africa conference is not the best possible structure for such a freedom of mind. Meanwhile, a better structure had been created, although it still has many growing-pains: the All Africa Conference of Churches (A.A.C.C.).

Over New Year 1957-8 an ecumenical body, the I.M.C., held for the first time a world assembly in Africa, at Accra in Ghana. This provided a good occasion for organizing the first representative All Africa Church Conference which met at Ibadan, Nigeria in January 1958. The conference was held under

---

[1] Marangu Report (Geneva 1956), p. 48.
[2] Addis Ababa Report (Geneva 1966), p. 19.
[3] *Witnesses Together*, E.A.C.C. Kuala Lumpur Report, p. 146.

the auspices of the Christian Council of Nigeria although the initiative had mainly come from the I.M.C. A largely African committee had worked out the programme which under the general theme "The Church in Changing Africa" included lectures and discussion groups on (i) the Church, youth and the family, (ii) the Church and economic life, (iii) the Church and citizenship, (iv) the Church and culture, and (v) the growing Church. Among the 195 people who actually attended, ninety-six represented the Churches in twenty-five African countries and territories. An open and flexible programme, together with the corporate Bible studies, ensured that the purpose of the meeting was achieved: the African Christian self-discovery and a first grasp of the task ahead.

The discovery was sometimes painful, not only because there exists no *lingua franca* for Africa, but because Africa is culturally, racially, politically, and ecclesiastically such a diverse and torn-apart continent. Alan Paton from South Africa, for instance, introduced himself to the conference as "a native of Africa, though a white one as you can see". The delegates were impressed both by the planned church union in Nigeria and by the reports about the Prapat conference and its resolve to create the E.A.C.C. Despite all tensions and difficulties, they opted for a visible organizational expression of the unity which they had already found and whose strengthening they felt to be imperative. A provisional committee was named and Ibadan 1958 became for the A.A.C.C. what Bangkok 1955 and Prapat 1957 had been for the E.A.C.C.

Youth pressed forward. With the help of the ecumenical world youth organizations they expressed strongly their aspirations in the All Africa Christian Youth Assembly at Nairobi in December 1962. Meanwhile Donald M'Timkulu from South Africa had been appointed to organize the inaugural assembly of the A.A.C.C. It met at Kampala, Uganda in April 1963 bringing together representatives from some 100 Churches and forty-two countries in Africa. The presence of three official observers from the Roman Catholic Church was a sign of the changing climate. In Uganda Anglicans and Catholics fought and killed one another in 1892. Now, since January 1964, the two Churches are together in Uganda's Christian Council.

At the opening of the assembly the delegates voted unanimously for the establishment of the A.A.C.C., an act which after a solemn silence was loudly heralded by the beating of African drums. The constitution—with almost the same preamble as that of the E.A.C.C.—and the future work commissions of the A.A.C.C. were shaped and accepted. The commissions are: (i) the life of the Church, dealing with the forms of worship, evangelization, and the training of ministers and the laity; (ii) social, national, and international responsibility of the Church, including especially the search for a true Christian family life in Africa; (iii) youth, to continue the work begun at Nairobi; (iv) education, with the subdivisions of formal education and Christian education; (v) literature and mass communication. In the course of the next years an A.A.C.C. secretariat was built up, stationed first at the Mindolo Ecumenical Centre at Kitwe, Zambia and since 1965 in Nairobi. The growing A.A.C.C. staff now helps the A.A.C.C. commissions to fulfil their task. Only a few examples can be mentioned which show that African Christians begin to face the earlier-mentioned questions which are decisive for the Church's mission to modern Africa.

The emergency situations created by civil wars, race discrimination, refugees, and hunger, become a severe test for the community of Churches which develops in the A.A.C.C. A continent-wide survey of the needs in Africa was made for the W.C.C. by the late Z. K. Matthews and Sir Hugh Foot. An ecumenical emergency fund for Africa was created, which makes it possible to operate service and training projects all over the continent.

True Christian family life and, related to it, the question of church discipline, remain burning issues. Ever since the first work group at the Ibadan conference discussed that subject, the A.A.C.C. and W.C.C. have jointly sponsored mobile teams and meetings for consulting and advising the African Churches in this field. Immediately before the Kampala Assembly, a two-month seminar on the Christian home and family life worked out recommendations on such controversial questions as bride price, polygamy, family planning, and prostitution. No less urgent remains the question of the Christian participation in nation-building and economic development. The results of the W.C.C. study on rapid social change in Africa were therefore summarized in a preparatory volume for the Kampala Assembly. In January 1965 a remarkable group of African laymen and church leaders met at Enugu, Nigeria for discerning "The Christian Response to the African Revolution". Having thus both in study and action been involved as Christians in the African revolution the Africans were well prepared for contributing to the World Conference on Church and Society at Geneva in 1966, and their interventions often astonished, irritated, and enlightened participants from the West.

The basic theological question which must be studied in the African context is the relationship between "Biblical Revelation and African Beliefs". This was the subject of the first consultation of African theologians which met in January 1966 at Ibadan. Unless this relationship is studied and the gospel preached in its context, fear of sorcery and witchcraft will remain smouldering under the surface of Christian belief. This study also emphasizes elements of the biblical message which have been neglected by Western Christians, for example, the importance of sacrifice and Christ's victory over the powers and principalities. Many other initiatives were taken by the A.A.C.C., usually in collaboration with ecumenical world organizations: the conference on Christian Education in a Changing Africa over New Year 1962–3 at Salisbury, work in the field of race relations, contact with African separatist movements, evangelism in urban Africa, the survey and consultation on the evangelization of West Africa, leadership training courses for the laity and ministers, seminars for African writers, artists, and specialists in mass media, work in collaboration with the World Council of Christian Education which held its fourth world institute at Nairobi in July 1967.

Africa is no longer "the baby of the world" but is coming of age. Helped by the A.A.C.C., the Churches in Africa began to face together their costly vocation of which the inaugural assembly's message said:

Here in Kampala at the tombs of the first Baganda martyrs, we have been reminded of all the saints who died for His cause on this continent. We share the burden of all on this continent who suffer persecution, oppression and injustice in any form and from whomsoever. We have been made conscious that the faithful proclamation of Christ as the only Saviour of the world may, even in our day, have to be tried out by a Cross and martyrdom.[1]

Other Regional Developments

Space does not allow as extensive a description of the origin and development of other regional bodies as that which we have given to the Asian and African scene. In any case the E.A.C.C. and the A.A.C.C. have pioneered on this way of ecumenical regionalism and they have gone furthest so far. The reasons for establishing regional conferences or councils of Churches are essentially the same in all continents, although the special characteristics of the Churches and the society in each region mark both the specific form and tempo of each regional development.

Near East

In between Asia and Africa lies the geographically ill-defined region of the Near (or Middle) East. It is the cradle of Judaism, Christianity, and Islam. The characteristics of this immensely diverse region, from Morocco to Iran and from Turkey to central Sudan, are the dominance of Islam, the Arab–Israeli tension, political instability, oil, and poverty. Christians form a small minority, deeply divided among various ancient Eastern Churches, Roman Catholics, and numerous Protestant bodies. The wounds of the Crusades are still open. Proselytism by Protestants and Roman Catholics among the ancient Eastern Christians and, more recently, political divisions and the unresolved refugee problem have created an atmosphere of mistrust in which co-operation and common worship, study, and action are extremely difficult.

The first stimulus for a common Christian approach in this area came from an I.M.C. conference on missions to Moslems at Lucknow in 1911. Later, from February to April 1924, John R. Mott conducted a series of "Moslem conferences" in Algeria, Egypt, Lebanon, and Iraq, leading up to a general conference in Jerusalem in April 1924. In its findings the first proposal for an area council is made. Together with a Christian Literature Committee for Moslems—also an outcome of the Jerusalem conference—the planned area council was constituted in 1927 (since 1929 called the Near East Christian Council (N.E.C.C.). Unlike the E.A.C.C. and the A.A.C.C., it is not based on the prior foundation of National Christian Councils in the area, and stands thus half way between a national and a regional body. The work of the N.E.C.C. was from its beginning very much hampered by the fact that its leadership came mainly from foreign missionaries and that it remained almost exclusively Protestant in an area where the ancient Orthodox Churches form the majority.

[1] *Drumbeats from Kampala*, p. 16.

D

The Christian approach to Islam remains a major concern for the N.E.C.C. From 1957 to 1962, for instance, the exemplary study pamphlet series *Operation Reach* was published in order to prepare Christians in the Near East for their missionary encounter with Moslems. Each study contains the exposition of a salient theme in Islamics and a meditation on the truth of the gospel in an Islamic context. One of these meditations deals with an art which not only Christians in the Near East but in all continents must learn, namely "the art of being a minority".[1] Annual summer schools helping missionaries and church leaders to understand Moslems and to witness to Christ in a Moslem world are organized in Jerusalem and Isfahan.

Much of this work was focused in a study conference held in April 1959 at Asmara in Eritrea. The conference message expressed a distinctive new spirit in the Christian approach to Moslems:

> We have been conscious of the failure of the Church, both in the past and now, to live and act according to the measure . . . of God's seeking, suffering, re-deeming love, demonstrated in Christ and His Cross. With penitence and humility we confess our need for cleansing and a new spirit of respect and friendship for Moslems, through which the barriers of suspicion and fear will disappear. . . . We wish to relate the Christian message constructively to Islamic thought and experience and to enter as fully as we may into areas of mutural practical concern.[2]

The missionary aspect of the N.E.C.C. continues equally in its work of co-ordinating Christian literature. The Council sponsored in 1960 a three weeks Christian writers institute in Alexandria. In 1961 it reorganized and expanded its literature department. In the same year it also began its partner-ship with "The Radio Voice of the Gospel", the Lutheran radio station in Addis Ababa, Ethiopia.

One of the most important results of the Asmara Conference was the participation of delegates from the ancient Orthodox Churches. The Ethiopian Church delegation gradually progressed, for instance, from complaint about Protestant mission efforts proselytizing among Orthodox to an awakening interest in the task of the whole Church to bear witness to Christ among Moslems and people of other faiths. This beginning of an understanding between Protestant and Orthodox was partly a result of the growing Protest-ant–Orthodox community in the W.C.C. Moreover, vigorous Orthodox youth movements had sprung up in the Near East which were no longer content with the merely Protestant character of the N.E.C.C. In ecumenical work camps held in the Near East young Orthodox and Protestants had discovered one another. After Easter 1955 an ecumenical youth leaders con-sultation was held in Beirut. Jointly sponsored by the World Student Christian Federation and the W.C.C. youth department, Gabi Habib began work in the whole Near East region from 1964 onwards. In July 1964 a Middle East Youth and Student Assembly was held in Broumana, Lebanon.

[1] K. Cragg, "The Art of Being a Minority", in *Operation Reach* (Beirut March-April 1959), pp. 6–18.
[2] *The Christian Faith and the Contemporary Middle Eastern World: Report of the Asmara study conference.* New York 1959.

Another strong stimulus for making the N.E.C.C. confessionally more representative is mentioned by its long-time secretary, Harry Dorman:

> The plan of integration of the W.C.C. and the I.M.C. has accentuated the special problems and opportunities which confront the ecumenical movement in the Near East. . . . Here the great majority of Christians belong to the ancient eastern churches, many of which have been unsympathetic with the modern missionary movement from the West. . . . What does integration imply for this situation?[1]

The first implication had to be a change in the N.E.C.C. itself. In 1964 the N.E.C.C. changed its name to become "The Near East Council of Churches". The crucial paragraph of the revised N.E.C.C. constitution now reads:

> The aims of the N.E.C.C. are to aid the Church in the Near East in her proclamation to all men of the gospel of salvation through Jesus Christ; to give expression to the unity of churches in this task; and to relate the gospel to the many problems which confront men and nations in the Near East.

The first step in doing this is seen in the promotion of "fellowship among churches working in the area so that all may bring into the common treasury the riches of their own traditions and spiritual experience".[2] In 1964 still only one Orthodox Church, the Syrian Orthodox Patriarchate, sent delegates to the N.E.C.C. This situation has not changed substantially, although since 1965 for the first time a national, Albert Isteero from the Coptic Evangelical Church in Egypt, has been general secretary of the N.E.C.C.

The strongest impetus for a much greater fellowship among Christians in the Near East is undoubtedly the emergency situation created by the Arab–Israeli wars and the seemingly insoluble refugee problem. In the service to refugees, Orthodox, Protestant, and Roman Catholic Christians have met. Whether this service be done under the auspices of the N.E.C.C., the W.C.C., or any other religious or secular agency, here is a common task. In May 1951 the I.M.C. and W.C.C. held therefore a conference on refugees in Beirut, in order to begin to co-ordinate the work done by many Protestants and the N.E.C.C. Committee for Refugee Work with both state and intergovernmental agencies and the ancient Orthodox communities. A second conference was held at the same place and under the same auspices in May 1956. The full participation of several outstanding Orthodox leaders in this second Beirut conference helped much to foster a community of service among Protestants and Orthodox in the area.

Despite this beginning of co-operation, the time seems not yet ripe for Christians in the Near East to face their greatest theological issue, namely the dialogue between the sons of Abraham—Jews, Christians, and Moslems. "In a Near Eastern setting it is impossible today to deal with the problem posed by Romans 9—11 and with the related problem of the use of the Old Testament in Christian worship."[3] Yet exactly this encounter of Jewish, Christian, and

[1] Harry Dorman, "Churches and Missions in the Near East", in *IRM* (1962), p. 42.

[2] *The Constitutions of the Near East Council of Churches*, as revised at the Fourteenth Plenary Meeting of the Council at Cairo, 14–17 April 1964.

[3] Horace M. McMullen, "Spiritual aspects of the plight of Arab refugees: a report from the second Beirut Conference", in *IRM* (1957), p. 57.

Moslem faiths and what Christians can learn from it and contribute to it will be the major theological task of the N.E.C.C.

Europe and North America

The ecumenical history of Europe and North America and the general ecumenical history are so intimately intermingled that it is difficult to distinguish between the two. General ecumenical history has still a strongly Western character in its thought-forms and procedures, its committee membership and staff, its meeting-places and languages. The headquarters of almost all ecumenical organizations are now in Geneva and—last but not least—the Vatican is in Rome. The staff of all world organizations has therefore functioned for the ecumenical movement in the whole world but simultaneously and especially in Europe and North America.

North America remains the only continent which has no distinct regional body. This is mainly due to the fact that especially in the U.S.A. a strong National Council has been built up which, together with the Canadian Council of Churches, almost covers the whole continent.[1] Whenever necessary these two councils consult and collaborate together. The New York office of the W.C.C. links the U.S.A. member Churches with the Geneva headquarters, and it organizes yearly a conference of these member Churches which make up about thirty per cent of the W.C.C. constituency and upon whom the W.C.C. largely depends financially. The absence of a regional body has not excluded North American regional initiatives. The laymen's conference held at Buffalo in 1952 on "The Christian in his Daily Work", the North American Youth Assembly at Ann Arbor in 1961, and, more important still, the excellently prepared North American Faith and Order conference at Oberlin in 1957, show what can be done regionally even without an established regional organization.

In 1939 Europe once again became the battlefield of the world. Contrary to experience in the 1914–18 war, however, in the Second World War the fellowship of Christians never ceased, and the W.C.C. in process of formation played no small role in maintaining contacts. The story of the church struggles in Europe, of the various church renewal movements which sprang from it, and the remarkable story of inter-Church aid in post-war Europe belongs to the general ecumenical history. The largest operation of the W.C.C., the Division of Inter-Church Aid and Service to Refugees, worked almost exclusively for Europe until 1955, after which concrete plans were made to develop its work outside Europe. This giving and receiving of aid created a bond among European Churches which was not broken even when political divisions made contacts between eastern and western European countries difficult or impossible. The friendship which had grown in the courses of the Ecumenical Institute at Bossey near Geneva, in the European rest house "Casa Locarno" in southern Switzerland, in the German "Kirchentag", and in other meeting-places or movements, survived the years of separation

[1] Cf. *The History of the Ecumenical Movement, 1517–1948*, pp. 256–9, 518f, 621–4, the chapter on National Councils in this volume, and the definitive book by S. McCrea Cavert, *The American Churches in the Ecumenical Movement: 1900–1968* (New York 1968).

between the East and the West. Gradually this newly discovered solidarity of Christians in Europe had to find organizational expression.

In April 1947 the Ecumenical Institute called together the leaders of the lay training centres and vocational groups which sprang up simultaneously in many European countries just after the war. This group continued to meet and in 1957 it constituted itself as the Directors Association of Laymen's Colleges in Europe with annual meetings and a full-time secretariat. From 1947 onwards national church youth secretaries in Europe met annually to review and plan their work together. At the Amsterdam assembly of the W.C.C. the organization of regional laymen's conferences was proposed and the first of these met in July 1951 at Bad Boll in Germany. One of the leaders of this meeting wrote later:

> The conference in Bad Boll noted that anyone on the Continent desiring to say something of sound value concerning political, social or cultural problems needs to examine those problems in an overall European perspective, and thence to extend the lines of that perspective out into the world as a whole. Any attempt to renounce large-scale co-operation would be turning our backs on reality.[1]

A few months earlier the Europeans present at the W.C.C. Central Committee at Rolle began to discuss plans for a conference of Churches in Europe, and these discussions were continued in 1952 at the Faith and Order Conference at Lund. So the "Prapat" for Europe was planned.

At Brussels in 1955 a German and a Dutch church leader, Ernst Wilm and Egbert Emmen, were asked to investigate the possibility of calling an unofficial conference of European Churches. This conference met in May 1957 at Liselund in Denmark. Because the initiative came mainly from Reformed and United Churches, many large Lutheran Churches were cautious about committing themselves. Also the Anglican and the Orthodox were not yet represented except by a delegate of the ecumenical patriarchate. But delegates came from both the East and West of Europe. Especially for the participants of the small Protestant minority Churches in the U.S.S.R., Poland, Czechoslovakia, Hungary, Yugoslavia, and Greece as well as for those of the Latin countries of Europe, this meeting proved to be a great event.

Much work had still to be done in order to gather a more representative European conference. Nevertheless, this minor miracle happened in January 1959 at Nyborg in Denmark. This time a number of the larger Lutheran, Anglican, and Orthodox Churches were represented. Organizationally things remained open, but the "Conference of European Churches" (C.E.C.) had become a fact. The series of "Nyborgs" in the now famous hotel at Nyborg-strand in Denmark had begun. Nyborg II met in October 1960. Two years later Nyborg III decided to give C.E.C. a more definite structure. The inaugural C.E.C. assembly, Nyborg IV, revived the old Christian symbol of the Church as a ship, because it met in October 1964 on board M.S. "Bornholm". Participants from the German Democratic Republic had *visa* diffi-

---

[1] "The European Laymen's Conference", in *Laymen's Work* (Geneva), no. 2 (November 1951), p. 19.

culties. The organizers therefore decided to charter a Danish ship and to take the East German delegation on board at sea, on the international line between Denmark and Sweden, off Malmö.

This seafaring assembly adopted the constitution of the C.E.C., but did not yet give the European regional body adequate means for work. But three years later, at Nyborg V, meeting at Pörtschach in Austria, the budget of C.E.C. was increased fourfold. G. G. Williams from Wales was appointed as a full-time secretary and he took up office in 1968. Meanwhile the presidency of C.E.C. had also been enlarged in order to have an adequate representation of the Orthodox and the Anglican Churches at the highest level. This is the organizational history of C.E.C. What are its major concerns, visions, and worries?

The meetings of C.E.C. give European church leaders the opportunity to reflect together periodically about the Church's task in divided Europe and the changing world. The subjects which were presented in the Nyborg lectures, discussed in preparatory committees and in the conference study groups give, therefore, an interesting survey of what is "in the air" on the European continent. At Liselund (1957) the proclamation of the one gospel in a divided Europe and the responsibility for one another among the Churches in the East and the West were the themes considered. The phenomenon of secularization in the modern technical society, where the Constantinian era has come to its end, was at the centre of deliberations at Nyborg I (1959) which also asked whether indeed a common heritage and a common task exist for the Churches in Europe.

Nyborg II (1960) studied this common task: the service which the Churches render to one another and which they have to render to a European society which is dechristianized and threatened by war. This led Nyborg III (1962) to consider the Churches of Europe and the crisis of modern man. Under this general theme an evaluation of European humanism was made and man's encounter with Christ and the renewal of the Church for a new service were studied. Perhaps the two most urgent tasks in this new service were then discussed at Nyborg IV (1964): the living together of continents and thus the commitment of European Churches to other continents and the living together as generations in the present tension between the generations. Nyborg V (1967) finally looked at some special new emphases in the European Churches' task to serve and reconcile, for example, in the new situations created by specialization and man's isolation in society and by the increased leisure time.

Some of the most outstanding Protestant and Orthodox thinkers in East and West Europe were found to introduce these subjects. The Nyborg Reports, in which these lectures are printed, remain thus most valuable documents. Why is it then that C.E.C. still does not seem to have come into its own? Why this persistent feeling of crisis in the European regional body? At least three reasons can be given:

The C.E.C. participants lists reveal impressive European church representation. The Russian Orthodox Church, for instance, sent delegates to the Nyborg conferences before it became a member of the W.C.C. There are eighteen European Churches at present members of the C.E.C. which are not members of the W.C.C. Yet the same lists reveal that despite the increasing lay participation the C.E.C. is still basically an assembly of bishops, church presidents, and pastors. The first impetus for collaboration among Christians in Europe had come from the laity. Yet most of the vision and vigour of these European youth and lay movements seem to have gone into the life of the W.C.C. rather than of the C.E.C. An example is the first European ecumenical youth assembly which met in July 1960 at Lausanne. Little of its impatience, for instance with regard to intercommunion and the renewal of the local Church, seems to have spilled over into C.E.C.

There are too many other groups, events, and movements in European church life which go alongside the work of C.E.C. and partly overlap with it. These include the Conference of the Protestant Churches in Latin countries of Europe, the work done in Europe by confessional world bodies, the Committee on Christian Responsibility for European Co-operation, the ecumenical work done by the Taizé Community and other Christian organizations. Moreover, in the same period when the Nyborg conferences began, the Prague Peace Conference was convened. Although this is not a regional, but is intentionally at least a world organization, it gathers the same or a similar group of people and discusses similar subjects as C.E.C.

The greatest handicap for a European regional church body, however, is Europe itself, its division of languages, cultures, and political barriers. The fact that Nyborg IV had to meet on the high sea is but one illustration. German, French, Russian, and English are used as conference languages and nevertheless many delegates have to speak in a language other than their own. When the linguistic problem is solved, the deeper problems of understanding begin, those between Protestant and Orthodox, between church leaders from the East and from the West. Yet exactly this unsettled mosaic of Europe calls for the reconciling community of those who preach the *one* gospel in a divided continent.

Latin America[1]

The ecumenical pioneer in Latin America was the Committee on Co-operation in Latin America (C.C.L.A.), originating in North America. Its history goes back to a controversial decision of the world missionary conference at Edinburgh in 1910. The planning committee had decided in 1908 that only societies sending missionaries "among non-Christian peoples" would be eligible for membership in the conference. The interpretation of this clause aroused hot discussions in the further preparation and at the conference itself, creating for J. H. Oldham his "gravest issue" as the conference secretary. In particular the Europeans who disliked the work of American evangelists among Catholics in Latin countries of Europe kept strictly to the principle of the planning committee, excluding thus from consideration at Edinburgh also missions to Latin America, except those to the non-Christian Indians. Under the leadership of Robert E. Speer, many North Americans who had a better knowledge of the actual situation in Latin America pleaded for the inclusion

[1] Some of the following information has been provided by Louis Odell from Uruguay who kindly wrote a memorandum about regional developments in Latin America.

of missions in that continent. They lost their cause but organized at Edinburgh itself two informal meetings on Latin America.

The controversial exclusion of Latin America drew much attention to that continent. As an outcome of the discussions at Edinburgh, the U.S.A. Foreign Missions Conference appointed in March 1913 a tentative committee on co-operation in Latin America. Thus the hispanic and traditionally Roman Catholic continent of Latin America became increasingly a "mission-field" for Anglo-Saxon, North American missionary societies. Among these the conservative evangelical faith missions, which do not collaborate with ecumenical world bodies, and more recently the rapidly growing Pentecostal movements, form the large majority.

With John R. Mott as secretary of the above-mentioned committee, the first Congress on Christian Work in Latin America became a notable ecumenical event. It met in February 1916 at Panama. Its programme was a near replica of the Edinburgh conference, and with regard to participants it did even better: of the 230 official delegates twenty-one were Latin Americans. Roman Catholics had been invited but did not attend. The congress unanimously asked the organizing committee to be its continuing organization and the C.C.L.A. was thus constituted. In the following two months deputations of congress members visited Peru, Chile, Argentina, Brazil, Colombia, Cuba, and Puerto Rico and held follow-up conferences in these countries.

In April 1925 a second congress was held in Montevideo, Uruguay, this time not for the whole of Latin America, but for South America only. With Spanish as the congress language, Latin American Protestantism showed its vigour and leadership capacity. While at Panama effective evangelization had been stressed, the Montevideo congress emphasized also strongly the Churches' social responsibility. Organized and led completely by Spanish speaking Evangelicals, the Evangelical Congress for Mexico, Central America, and the Caribbean area at Havana in June 1929 had an even more clearly Latin American character. "Latinization" was the key word and W. R. Hogg writes that "probably never before in any 'missionary conference' had the missionary voice been so silent—that of the indigenous church so pronounced".[1] At this congress the establishment of a Latin American Evangelical Federation was recommended for the first time.

Almost twenty years after the Havana congress investigations were made whether the Caribbean area should not have its own regional ecumenical body. Staff visits were made, especially by the late E. J. Bingle,[2] and a consultation was held in May 1957 at San German, Puerto Rico. Regional work in the realms of Christian education and of Christian marriage and family life were initiated, but so far little progress was made in establishing a Caribbean conference of Churches.

The above-mentioned congresses and the continuing work of C.C.L.A. were instrumental in creating a series of National Christian Councils. That of Puerto Rico was founded as early as in 1905, followed by those of Mexico

[1] W. R. Hogg, *Ecumenical Foundations* (New York 1952), p. 268.
[2] Cf. E. J. Bingle, *Cuba to Surinam: Report of a Journey in the Caribbean* (I.M.C., London, 1954).

in 1928, Brazil in 1934, the River Plate (Argentina, Uruguay, and Paraguay) and Jamaica in 1939, Peru in 1940, Chile and Cuba in 1941. These councils worked in a fruitful way together with the C.C.L.A. It must not be overlooked, however, that the co-operative ventures raised more interest in the "historical" Churches. At the Montevideo meeting the new anti-ecumenical Christian Missionary Alliance and the Evangelical Union of South America participated. But this was not going to last. In the tremendous growth of Evangelicals in Latin America—from about 12,500 in 1900 to about 9,000,000 in 1961—the mostly anti-ecumenical faith missions and later the Pentecostal movement became much stronger than the "historical" Churches. This new situation and the growing Latin American consciousness called for a reconsideration of the co-ordinating structures, all the more so when after the war the C.C.L.A. became an area committee of the Division of Foreign Mission, in the National Council of Churches of the U.S.A.

Upon the initiative of the National Christian Councils in Mexico and the River Plate, Latin American leaders organized what they called the First Latin American Evangelical Conference. It met in July 1949 in Buenos Aires. This small study conference considered the background of Protestantism in Latin America, its message and the strategies and priorities of its mission. The report laid great emphasis on the study of the Bible so that every member can become an evangelist. "For the Evangelical Christian, evangelism is a matter of life or death. Every Evangelical Christian should be aflame for the redemption of his neighbours who do not know the depth of the grace of our Lord."[1]

Due to the lack of a continuation committee, almost twelve years passed before the Second Latin American Evangelical Conference met in July/August 1961, in Lima, Peru. The 220 delegates and visitors represented thirty-four denominations in all Latin American countries with the exception of Panama and Nicaragua. Reading the reports of Buenos Aires and Lima one is struck by the great difference of emphasis. In Lima all the speakers were Latin Americans and a new generation of leaders became vocal and set the pattern. This change of atmosphere is perhaps clearest in the different ways the two meetings spoke about the role of laymen. "In the first conference, we find the traditional emphasis on the work of laymen as helpers to pastors, as instruments for securing individual conversions and the growth of the congregations. The means of evangelism are focused on the same purpose. The second conference took seriously the structures of society and the need to change these structures through the presence within them of the Christian laity."[2]

How did this change happen? Through the services of C.C.L.A. and several ecumenical world bodies such as the World Council of Christian Education and the ecumenical youth organizations an increasing number of young Latin American Evangelicals had come into contact with the ecumenical movement. Already in 1941 at a meeting in Lima the Union of Latin American

---

[1] B. Foster Stockwell, "Latin American Evangelical Conference", in *IRM* (1950), p. 80.

[2] A. E. Fernandez Arlt, "The Laity in the Latin American Evangelical Churches", in Stephen C. Neill and H. R. Weber, ed., *The Layman in Christian History* (London 1963), p. 372.

Evangelical Youth (U.L.A.J.E.) had been formed which held several continent-wide congresses and leadership training seminars. The 1956 congress in
Baranquilla, Columbia had, for instance, the following courageous and
confident theme for a revolutionary continent: "Religious liberty and social
justice: Good news to the poor. To the captives, liberty". From 1951 the
World Student Christian Federation had greatly intensified its work in Latin
America, and Valdo Galland was appointed as its travelling secretary for that
continent. From November 1956 to February 1957 an ecumenical youth
team extensively visited Latin America.

Even more important was the impact of the W.C.C.'s Church and Society
department's study on rapid social change. National consultations on the
Christian responsibility in society were held in Brazil (1955, 1957, 1960) and
in the River Plate area (1957, 1959). Other areas were visited by staff. In 1959
a bulletin on Church and Society was spontaneously started in Uruguay, as a
local initiative. This bulletin later became the magazine *Christianismo y
Sociedad*, the official organ of Iglesia y Sociedad en América Latina (I.S.A.L.).
The response that the rapid social change study had in Brazil and the River
Plate area led to the convocation prior to the Lima conference of the First
Latin American Consultation on Church and Society. It was held in Huam-
pani, near Lima, in July 1961. As a result of this consultation the Latin
American Commission on Church and Society (I.S.A.L.) was constituted in
February, 1962 and has been active ever since. Parallel to the Huampani
consultation another one was held to deal with problems of Christian educa-
tion which again in 1962 led to the formal constitution of the Latin American
Commission on Christian Education (C.E.L.A.D.E.C.). U.L.A.J.E. held
further congresses in 1961 and 1966. Through the work of the Theological
Education Fund the collaboration between theological colleges is growing.

All these developments call for a Latin American regional body. Yet the
Lima conference had established a continuation committee with only a
rotating secretaryship from one National Christian Council to the other. As
many expected, this did not work. A new step forward came when on the
occasion of the first I.S.A.L. consultation on Christian social action and
service the presidents of several National Christian Councils met and strongly
emphasized the need for a continental confederation of Evangelicals in the
"Declaration of Corcovado" (Brazil), in September 1963. One year later, in a
meeting at Montevideo, Uruguay, the formal decision was adopted to create
the long-expected regional body, the Provisional Committee on Christian
Unity in Latin America (U.N.E.L.A.M.) and Emilio Castro was appointed
its part-time secretary. This committee is now co-ordinating and fostering the
ecumenical forces in the midst of the very precarious ecumenical situation of
Latin America.

Nowhere else is there more mistrust of, and mal-information concerning,
the ecumenical movement than in Latin America. In particular those groups
in which the leadership is still in the hands of the conservative evangelical
missionaries are against a common worship, service, and witness. Nowhere
else does the present *aggiornamento* of the Roman Catholic Church affect
Evangelicals more than in Latin America. During these last years many young

Evangelicals have found much more understanding and support in their social and political commitment from progressive Roman Catholic priests and bishops than from their own church leaders. I.S.A.L. and other progressive evangelical groups work increasingly together with Roman Catholics and the already existing Roman Catholic regional body (C.E.L.A.M.—the Latin American Episcopal Council). An anti-Catholic evangelical regional body will therefore not find much enthusiasm among younger Latin American Evangelicals.

Added to mistrust from the faith missions and the changing relationships with the Roman Catholics is a great theological uncertainty among the ecumenically minded Evangelicals themselves.

> We are going to and fro between two heresies: the fundamentalistic, which tends to ignore the fact that Christ reconciled the world unto himself and the other that insinuates and forgets at the same time the call to faith, conversion, decision as well as to biblical eschatology; the former denies the fact that faith creates a necessary change, the latter speaks about identification and incarnation irresponsibly in an "impressionistic" manner, without seeking for the biblical affirmations.[1]

How is it possible to combine a strong concern for social action with the great heritage of Latin American evangelical commitment to evangelism? What is the specific task of Latin American Evangelicals in a continent where a strong minority of the leadership in the Roman Catholic Church is involved in a far-reaching *aggiornamento*? How to maintain and deepen the fellowship with conservative evangelical faith missions and the Pentecostal movement and at the same time grow in communion with the Catholic, Orthodox, and historic Protestant streams of Christianity? These are some of the questions with which Latin American Evangelicals must struggle and where they have to make their contribution to the ecumenical movement.

The Pacific

In no region of the world was a regional development pastorally more needed than in the Pacific. Although jet aeroplanes now criss-cross that immense area between the Americas and Asia, life behind the reefs of the Pacific islands still remains very isolated, self-sufficient, and, to the problem-ridden Western visitor, strangely harmonious. On some islands there exists an intact *corpus Christianum*, while in some mountain valleys of New Guinea the first contacts between the Church and only recently discovered tribes are just beginning. The consecutive invasions of soldiers during the war and of tourists after the war, the threat of atomic fall-out through the testing of bombs, the ferment of new ideas and expectations in the minds of young people who are no longer at ease in a patriarchal and static society and Church—all these factors of change have forced Christians in the Pacific to face their common plight and their common task.

In February 1959 a number of Churches and missions in the Pacific area asked the I.M.C. to organize a regional conference. A small advisory group

[1] *America Hoy—Iglesia y Sociedad en America Latina* (Montevideo 1966), p. 54.

met in Suva, Fiji in March 1960 and planned the conference and its preparatory work. Five topics were chosen to be considered in lectures and study
groups: (1) the ministry; (2) the unfinished evangelistic task; (3) the relevance
of the gospel to the changing conditions of life in the Pacific; (4) the place of
young people in the life of the Church; and (5) the Christian family. Behind
these topics, which could have been chosen in almost every region of the
world, lies a deeper one. It shows the great discernment of the advisory group
meeting at Suva that it so clearly recognized this fact and wrote to the
Churches:

> In the days before the coming of the Gospel, men's lives were ruled largely by
> fear. The coming of Christianity wrought a marvellous change in the life of
> our peoples. But we have to ask, "Did the coming of Christianity mean that
> fear was replaced by love, or did it mean that men transferred their fear to a
> new object and began to fear God with a pagan fear?" . . . Our churches often
> seem to be more governed by fear than by love, more concerned to enforce
> conformity to certain laws of behaviour than to show their love to God by
> loving and forgiving others. It sometimes seems that our churches are places
> where certain standards are demanded, rather than places where God gives
> sinners forgiveness and victory over sin.[1]

The deepest aim of this first conference of Churches and missions in the
Pacific was thus nothing less than a reformation. With a view to this the
Churches were asked to pray for the conference and to make a self-examination
concerning the themes proposed in the light of the message of Paul's letter to
the Galatians.

Probably no ecumenical event in the post-war ecumenical history has been
so fervently prepared in local groups of a whole region and has been carried
so intensely by the prayer of ordinary Christians as this first Pacific conference
which met at Malua on the island of Samoa in April–May 1961. It became
much more than a planning conference for establishing a new regional body
within the ecumenical movement, although it fulfilled this function according
to the now well-known pattern of appointing a continuation-committee,
authorizing the work of a regional secretary, and preparing the way for a later
inaugural assembly. This conference became in fact a reformation event, and
in the conference Bible studies Paul's letter to the Galatians spoke in a disturbing and renewing way to the basic topic which the advisory group had so
clearly outlined. The daily "news-sessions" also helped much to break the
isolation of life behind the reefs, so that the conference report was rightly
called "Beyond the Reef".

The continuation committee immediately began its work, planning the
continued study of the five conference subjects and appointing Vavae Toma
from Samoa as the regional secretary. He became a pastoral visitor to the
isolated Churches on the Pacific islands. Immediately after the Samoa Conference the Theological Education Fund convened a consultation at Suva in
Fiji and it was here that plans for a united Pacific theological college were
discussed. After difficult negotiations this college became a reality in April

---

[1] *Beyond the Reef: Records of the Conference of Churches and Missions in the Pacific*
(London 1961), pp. 7f.

1966, at Suva. It now plays an important role in helping the coming leadership of the Pacific Churches to discern together God's will for the Pacific region.

At the meeting of the continuation committee at Tonga in 1965 the plans were finalized for the inaugural assembly of the Pacific Conference of Churches (P.C.C.). It was held in May–June 1966 at Chapanehe on the island of Lifou in the Loyalty Islands. The topics chosen for discussion were education, marriage, custom, stewardship, and citizenship. Simultaneously with the P.C.C. a number of National Christian Councils came into being. Such councils were founded in the New Hebrides and Fiji Islands, then the Melanesian Council of Churches was formed, one of whose first tasks is to cooperate with the Roman Catholics in establishing a joint Christian centre at the University planned for Port Moresby. Other councils are now planned in the Solomon Islands and the Samoan group.

Due to the work of the continuation committee, its study commissions and the visits of Vavae Toma—since 1967 succeeded by Setareki Tuilovoni from Fiji—the Churches had come to know one another better. At the Lifou assembly the accent lay therefore no longer in the first place on the meeting and hearing from one another, but on the planning for doing things together. The Second Vatican Council begins to bear fruit and in Samoa and Tonga Protestants and Roman Catholics are now working together on a common vernacular version of the Bible. As in other areas, so also in the Pacific the regional body which was only just created is already too narrow for the widening scope of the ecumenical movement.

This quick journey through the *oikoumene* has shown that virtually in all continents regional ecumenical bodies now exist. This is a new fact in ecumenical history. It must be taken seriously by National Christian Councils and its member Churches. This new fact must also influence the central operations, emphases, and structures of the W.C.C. and other world ecumenical bodies. A beginning has been made for the executives of the various regional bodies to consult together (meetings in Geneva in 1965 and 1967), and the Uppsala Assembly of the W.C.C. has authorized the appointment of a new associate general secretary for relationships with national and regional councils.

Regional ecumenical bodies have their particular dangers.[1] They could easily become either continental ecclesiastical power blocs or mere administrative outposts of ecumenical world organizations. In both cases they would hinder rather than foster the full participation of local Churches in the ecumenical movement. The foregoing description of the beginning of these regional bodies shows, however, that such dangers are clearly faced. Regional

---

[1] For an analysis of the promises and dangers of regional ecumenical bodies see, for example, W. A. Visser 't Hooft, "Die Bedeutung der Regionalen Kirchlichen Zusammenarbeit für die Oekumeniche Bewegung", in *Die europäische Christenheit in der heutigen sakularisierten Welt* (Zurich 1960), pp. 118–23; U Kyaw Than, "East of New Delhi: Regionalism or Centralism?" in K. R. Bridston and W. D. Wagoner, ed., *Unity in Mid-Career* (New York 1963), pp. 57–67; Heinrich Meyer, "Regionalismus and Konfessionalismus", *Oekumenische Rundschau* (1961), pp. 197–208.

ecumenism must not be overstressed. In many central ecumenical issues the real divisions go now not only across confessional families but also right across continental boundaries. Nevertheless, the future may show that the intercontinental character of the ecumenical movement is equally, or perhaps even more, important than its interconfessional character. God's liberating Word is witnessed to all nations and continents. Out of all nations and continents the Church is called to be the first fruits of a new humanity.

4

National Councils of Churches

FRANK SHORT

INTRODUCTION

Dr J. H. Oldham, as far back as 1922, wrote of the proposed formation of National Christian Councils as "New Spiritual Adventures in the Mission Field".[1] They were to be the visible organs through which units and common purpose would find expression. Richey Hogg, in *Ecumenical Foundations*, refers to Dr Mott's judgement, "My first and my greatest contribution to the International Missionary Council was to bring about the formation of the National Christian Councils" (p. 156). Hogg also links the International Missionary Council, the National Christian Councils, and the younger Churches, in his statement, "For years no other body existed to knit the younger Churches, through the National Christian Councils, into the organized fabric of world Christianity" (p. 283).

K. S. Latourette, in the summary to his chapter on "Ecumenical Bearings of the Missionary Movement and the International Missionary Council" in *A History of the Ecumenical Movement 1517–1948* (pp. 401–2), notes that the younger Churches had a mounting share in the ecumenical movement and that their most numerous forms of ecumenical experiment were co-operative ventures undertaken by national and regional units, which had been drawn into a global structure through the International Missionary Council. These comments indicate the significance of Christian Councils for the ecumenical movement, and the importance of the contribution they were then making to its development. The question may well be asked if the National Christian Councils have fulfilled the expectation and promise of these earlier years.

The Growth of the National Christian Councils

In 1910 there were only two National Christian Councils through which limited co-operation was possible. By 1928, at the time of the Jerusalem Meeting of the International Missionary Council, there were twenty-three; by 1938, the year of the Madras Conference, there were twenty-six, and a decade later there were thirty.

It is instructive to look at the list of the thirty councils which were members of the International Missionary Council at the end of 1948. (The list appears at the end of the January 1949 issue of *International Review of Missions*.)

Australia National Missionary Council of Australia.
Belgium Conseil missionaire Protestant de Belgique.
Brazil Confederacao Evangelica do Brasil.
Ceylon National Christian Council.
China National Christian Council.
Congo Conseil Protestant du Congo.
Denmark Dansk Missionsraad.
Finland Suomen Lahetysneuvosto.
France Société des Missions Évangéliques de Paris.
Germany Deutscher Evangelischer Missionsrat.
Great Britain Conference of Missionary Societies in Great Britain and Ireland.

[1] *International Review of Missions*, vol. ii, no. 44, pp. 526–50.

India and Pakistan   National Christian Council of India, Pakistan, and Burma.
Japan   National Christian Council.
Korea   National Christian Council.
Latin America   Committee on Co-operation.
Malaya   Christian Council.
Mexico   Concilio Nacional Evangelico de Mexico.
Near East   Near East Christian Council for Missionary Co-operation.
Netherlands   Nederlandsche Zendings-Raad.
Netherlands Indies   Zendings Consulaat.
New Zealand   National Missionary Council of New Zealand.
Norway   Norsk Misjonsrad.
Philippine Islands   Philippine Federation of Evangelical Churches.
Puerto Rico   Association of Evangelical Churches.
River Plate   Confederacion de Iglesias Evangelicas del Rico de la Plate
   (Argentina, Paraguay, Uruguay).
Siam   National Christian Council of Siam.
South Africa   Christian Council of South Africa.
Sweden   Svenska Missionsradet.
Switzerland   Schweizerischer Evangelischer Missionsrat. Conseil Suisse des
   Missions Evangeliques.
United States and Canada   Foreign Missions Conference of North America.

Richey Hogg had commented (p. 253) that in 1928 the National Christian
Councils encircled the globe and could spread and implement the decisions of
the Jerusalem Conference. The progressive growth in the number of such
Councils incorporated still further areas of the world, and brought them
increasingly within the area of impact of the subsequent gatherings of the
International Missionary Council.

These Councils of Churches and missionary societies, and the national or
regional missionary agencies, now existed in every continent. Those in the
"sending" countries, lands of the missionary agencies, included two Councils
or comparable bodies in Australia and New Zealand, ten in Europe, and one
in North America. In the "receiving" countries, lands of the younger Churches, there were five in Latin America, nine in Asia, and three in Africa and
the Near East.

Nor was that all. In addition to these member bodies of the International
Missionary Council there were, in 1948, twenty-two other co-operative
organizations, of one kind or another, in different parts of the world, with
which the International Missionary Council was in touch. They are listed in
the January 1949 issue of International Review of Missions. Thirteen of them
were in African territories, one was in Asia, four were in the West Indies, and
four were in Latin America. They varied from Evangelical Alliances, Social
Welfare Councils, Councils of Churches, to Inter-Mission Councils or other
forms of missionary co-operation. Ten of them subsequently became
members of the International Missionary Council.

When it is remembered that the functions of the International Missionary
Council had been defined, in part, in its Constitution as:

To stimulate thinking and investigation on questions related to the mission
and expansion of Christianity in all the world. . . . To help to co-ordinate the

activities of the national missionary organizations and Christian Councils of the different countries, and to bring about united action where necessary in missionary matters . . .

it is not difficult to see the measure of the possible contribution of this network of Christian councils to the furtherance of ecumenical idea and action in the field of mission. Moreover, a study of the reports of the meetings of the International Missionary Council at Jerusalem, Madras, Whitby, Willingen, and Ghana, reveals how wide were the interests and concerns in which the member councils were involved. There was not much that had its place in the growth of the Church, in its witness and its service, which was absent from international consideration, and from challenge to these national organs of co-operation.

CHANGE AND DEVELOPMENT
IN NATIONAL CHRISTIAN COUNCILS

1

A study of the 1948 membership of the International Missionary Council reveals already some of the changes and developments which would occur more frequently in the next two decades. The changes in the political structure of nations in Asia and Africa which would arise from the ending of the colonial era were already foreshadowed. The National Christian Council of India, Burma, and Ceylon had become the National Christian Council of India, Pakistan, and Burma. Ceylon had already become a separate member council. Within a few years Burma, Pakistan, and India would each have separate National Christian Councils. The Christian Council of Malaya became the Council of Churches in Malaysia and Singapore reflecting the separate independence of both Malaya and Singapore. The Zendings Consulaat of the Netherlands Indies would cease to be a member council, and in 1952 its place would be taken by the National Council of Churches in Indonesia.

Comparable changes were to take place, somewhat later, in Africa—though for the most part in councils which were not then members of the International Missionary Council. New nations were established, some with names which replaced those of earlier colonial days. Ghana (Gold Coast), Madagascar, Rhodesia, Sierra Leone, and Zambia (Northern Rhodesia) became member councils between the years 1954 and 1961. New names which occur in the 1968 list of non-member councils include Uganda, Burundi, Rwanda, Malawi (Nyasaland), Tanzania (Tanganyika). In a word, existing councils adjusted themselves to their changed political situation, and they together with newly formed councils sought to respond to the challenges of the new era.

Changes occurred also in Latin America. The Committee on Co-operation in Latin America withdrew from separate membership of the International Missionary Council on the ground that it was strictly a committee of the division of foreign missions of the National Council of Churches in the U.S.A. (N.C.C.C.U.S.A.). The River Plate Federation of Evangelical Churches withdrew in 1963, when Federations of Evangelical Churches in Argentina and Uruguay and the Evangelical Council of Chile became separate affiliated councils of the Commission on World Mission and Evangelism of the World Council of Churches. In 1952 the Cuban Council of Evangelical Churches became a member council of the International Missionary Council, as did the Jamaica Christian Council in 1954, and in 1967 the Christian Council of Trinidad and Tobago became an Affiliated Council of the Commission on World Mission and Evangelism.

2

The process by which missionary councils developed into Christian Councils, and then, even if not always in name, into Councils of Churches, was already far advanced by 1948. In the following period it was to be carried further, and that in a variety of ways.

(a) In Asia and in Africa it was realized increasingly that it was inappropriate, and that for many reasons, for missionary agencies as such to have membership in a National Christian Council. While their financial contribution was useful, and even necessary, their membership both obscured the nature of the council, and diminished its effective relationship to government and community. The National Christian Council of India is a typical example of this development. Under its constitution the Council was a Council of Churches and Missions. Between the years 1950 and 1956 there was considerable discussion on the desirability of the Council becoming a Council of Churches only.

The Asia Secretary of the Conference of British Missionary Societies visited India in the autumn of 1955, and conferred with the National Christian Council. He was made aware of the importance which was attached to the closest relationship of the Council with the Churches of India, and of the desire that the consequent amendment of the Constitution should not endanger the financial support given by the co-operating missionary agencies. The Conference accepted the recommendation which he made in his report

> That the National Christian Council of India be informed that British missionary societies represented in the Conference no longer desire direct representation on the Council, and that they suggest the constitution of the Council should be reviewed in the light of this action with a view to securing the maximum responsible relationship with the Churches of India.[1]

In the revised constitution of 1956 it was determined that "only organized Church bodies are entitled to direct representation in the Council". Missions still not integrated in a Church in India could become associate members. Missionaries might still serve on the Council as the elected representatives of the Church with which they were associated. Thereafter, and not only in India, the Christian Councils became increasingly Councils of Churches.

(b) There has been notable development in the Near East. In 1948 the Council was the Near East Christian Council for Missionary Co-operation. It later became the Near East Christian Council, and more recently still the Near East Council of Churches. Contemporary ecumenical developments, the

[1] C.B.M.S., A/5/56.

political struggles and tensions of the area, the vast and continuing problem of the Arab refugees, have combined to bring the Churches of the region into new and closer ecumenical relationship.

(c) Developments have also taken place in the missionary councils of the West. Member bodies of the International Missionary Council in 1948 included the National Missionary Councils of Australia and New Zealand, the Conference of Missionary Societies of Great Britain and Ireland, and the Foreign Missions Conference of North America (the U.S.A. and Canada). The first has now become the Division of Mission of the Australian Council of Churches. The second member body is now the National Council of Churches of New Zealand—which is of interest in that it has a "Commission on Overseas Mission and Inter-Church Aid" thus following the pattern set by the East Asia Christian Conference. The Conference of British Missionary Societies alone remains unchanged in its status of "In association with the British Council of Churches", though the pattern of future relationship has recently been under discussion.

Developments in North America have been far-reaching. The Foreign Missions Conference of North America, which had begun its notable history as far back as 1893, in 1950 became the Division of Foreign Missions of the National Council of the Churches of Christ in the United States of America. That organization, so well known by its initials N.C.C.C.U.S.A., was the long-considered development of the Federal Council of the Churches of Christ in America, which had been founded in 1908. Professor K. S. Latourette, in the Rouse–Neill volume (p. 374), gives a vivid description of "the ever widening scope of co-operation" in and through the Foreign Missions Conference which had been achieved by 1948. In a later chapter of the same book (pp. 623f) Miss Rouse records the birth of the National Council, and the "euthanasia" of the old Federal Council, involving the union, towards the end of 1950, of eight separate national councils, which included, in addition to the Federal Council and the Foreign Missions Conference, Councils for Home Missions, Religious Education, Higher Education, Missionary Education, Stewardship, and the Council of Church Women. Miss Rouse's last word on this transformed Council is that it "united practically all organized aspects of the Churches' common life in an ecclesiastically-constituted organ of common action. This is a long step towards a practically united Church in the United States. It is the longest step, short of organic union, as yet taken in any country towards union among the Churches" (p. 624).

The Council was still not satisfied with its structure, and discussion continued for some years on the future pattern of organization. The completion of the massive and impressive Inter-Church Center at 475 Riverside Drive, New York, and its official opening on 29 May 1960 brought many member units into the one building, and so facilitated closer relationship between the member Churches and also with the various organs of co-operative activity. In the later reorganization the Division of Foreign Missions became the Division of Overseas Ministries—in part a recognition of the ambiguity and misunderstanding generally associated with the words "foreign" and "missions".

A detailed account of the N.C.C.C.U.S.A. is included in a book by Dr Samuel McCrea Cavert on "American Churches in the Ecumenical Movement", published in 1968 by Association Press, New York.

The discussions which led to the formation of the N.C.C.C.U.S.A. were paralleled by discussions in Canada which in 1944 resulted in the formation of the Canadian Council of Churches. In 1946 a separate Canadian Overseas Mission Council came into being, which in 1952 became the Department of Overseas Missions of the Canadian Council of Churches. The Constitution of the Council of Churches provided for the maintenance of close relationship with, *inter alia*, the Council of the Churches in the U.S.A., and the Department of Overseas Mission entered into a new fraternal relationship with the Division of Foreign Missions of the N.C.C.C.U.S.A. While it is the N.C.C.C. U.S.A. which is now affiliated to the Commission on World Mission of the World Council of Churches, where Canada is concerned it is the Department of Overseas Missions which is so affiliated.

The Relation of the National Christian Councils to the Ecumenical Movement

Many National Christian Councils, particularly in the lands of the so-called younger Churches, owed their origin to the initiative of the International Missionary Council, and for much of the period up to 1948, through their membership in that Council, they were an important and integral part of the ecumenical movement.

But in the period covered by the present volume their place in, and their relationship to, the ecumenical movement has been subject to considerable development. The changes which took place in the years 1948–68 affected their relationship to the World Council of Churches, to the International Missionary Council, and to the regional ecumenical organizations which came into existence in the second half of the period.

The main story of these developments will be told in other chapters of this history, but no account of the National Christian Councils would be complete without reference to these far-reaching changes in their relationships and in their activities.

Relationship of National Christian Councils to the World Council of Churches

While it has been emphasized repeatedly that the World Council of Churches is essentially and necessarily a Council of Churches, and the International Missionary Council was basically and creatively a Council of Councils, the World Council of Churches from a very early date realized the potential importance of National Christian Councils for the furtherance of its own work and influence, and the International Missionary Council always needed close and intimate touch with the churches related to its member councils.

It is, therefore, not surprising that as early as September 1948 the Central Committee of the World Council of Churches decided that some constituent councils of the International Missionary Council in "younger Church areas" should be invited to assist the World Council of Churches in the promotion of its activities. Such Councils would have an opportunity to send representatives to meetings of the Assembly and of the Central Committee. On the other hand, the World Council, in the promotion of its departmental activities, would work normally through the offices of the National Christian Councils with which it had this relationship. At the same time provision was made for working relationships with a number of "nation-wide councils" in lands of the "older Churches".

The Second W.C.C. Assembly at Evanston made provision for a more formal working relationship of National Christian Councils with the World Council by creating a category of "associated councils". By the time of the Third Assembly at New Delhi, eighteen councils had accepted the invitation to become thus associated. These included councils in Asia, Australasia, Europe, and North America.

The importance of this development for the understanding of the nature and significance of the contribution made by the National Christian Councils to the ecumenical movement is indicated by the extent to which these councils had become the normal channel for the interpretation, support, and implementation of World Council activities. The meetings of National Christian Councils provided opportunity for the discussion of World Council proposals in the context of local situations. Some councils reproduced in their own structures some parts of the departmental organization in the World Council of Churches. This development not only recognized the growing commitment of the National Christian Councils to the life and work of the ecumenical movement, but progressively increased their involvement in that movement, both in the work of the World Council of Churches itself, and in ecumenical activities in their several areas.

In September 1967 there were twenty-three of these Associated Councils of the World Council of Churches. Only two of them are in Africa (Rhodesia and South Africa), seven are in Asia (Burma, Ceylon, India, Indonesia, Japan, Malaysia, Philippines), two are in Australasia (Australia and New Zealand), ten are in Europe (Austria, Czechoslovakia, Denmark, Finland, Germany, Hungary, Netherlands, Poland, Sweden, and Great Britain), and two are in North America (Canada and the U.S.A.).

While there are gaps in the territories so represented, notably in Africa and in Latin America, it is obvious that the contribution which the twenty-three associated councils can make to the ecumenical movement is considerable, and indeed is necessary if the ecumenical is to become rooted in the local situation.

The Relationship of National Christian Councils to the International Missionary Council

The history of the relationship of National Christian Councils to the International Missionary Council has been spelled out in detail in the two volumes, *A History of the Ecumenical Movement* and *Ecumenical Foundations*. But the end of 1961 was to see the conclusion of the story of the International Missionary Council as such, and its integration in the World Council of Churches as its Division and Commission on World Mission and Evangelism. The member councils of the International Missionary Council became affiliated councils of the C.W.M.E., and so entered into a new and direct relationship with the World Council of Churches.

There was an inevitability about this development. As far back as 1946 the joint committee of the W.C.C. and the I.M.C. had called attention to the common origin and the common calling and purpose of the two bodies, and had seen the necessity of steps being taken which would "quicken the mission-consciousness of the churches and the Church-consciousness of missions". Something more than being "in association with each other" was necessary if the theological insights of the relation of Church and mission, and of mission and unity, were to govern the relationship of the W.C.C. and the I.M.C. within the ecumenical movement.

The member councils of the I.M.C. did not accept readily the proposals for the integration of the two bodies, and it speaks volumes for the patient wisdom of the joint committee and of its two parent bodies that the Third Assembly at New Delhi was able to carry through the impressive act of integration.

The mind of the member councils had been made plain at the Ghana Assembly of the International Missionary Council in December 1957–January 1958.[1] The debate revealed that, while there was strong support for integration from some councils, and a favourable attitude to it in others, serious reservations existed in parts of Latin America and Africa and by certain councils in northern Europe.

To some extent these reservations derived from misunderstanding concerning the World Council of Churches. Delegates could not be unaware of prevalent propaganda which charged the World Council with intent to become a "super-Church", with having an inadequate doctrinal basis, and with lacking real evangelistic concern.

To some extent these reservations derived from a fear that integration would result in the creation of a mammoth and bureaucratic organization in which missionary vision and thrust would be lost. To a much larger extent reservation and misgiving arose from the fear that integration would have a divisive effect within the constituent councils of the International Missionary Council, and would endanger the maintenance of existing co-operation between member bodies who were in sympathy with the ecumenical movement, and those who, for varying reasons, were not.

The long resolution which the Ghana Assembly passed accepted in principle the integration of the two bodies and adjudged the draft plan prepared by the joint committee of both organizations to be a "generally suitable instrument for integration". It recognized the sincere and deep concern of those who feared that integration might result in the relinquishment of the

[1] See *Report*, pp. 156–700.

purposes for which the International Missionary Council had been founded, and instructed its Secretariat to give special attention to ways in which mis-understanding of the World Council of Churches and ignorance about the existing relations between that body and the International Missionary Council could be removed.

The Assembly commended the draft plan to its member organizations for further study, but realized that it would be impossible for its consideration, and consequent action upon it, to be completed in time for the Assembly of the World Council of Churches which it was proposed to hold in 1960. The World Council was therefore invited to postpone its Assembly until 1961.

The additional year gave an opportunity for detailed study of the plan by member councils of the International Missionary Council, and for consulta-tion with its secretaries. It was possible for many misgivings to be removed, and for some councils to make provision within their constitutions for the continued participation of member societies who were unable to give approval to the proposed integration with the World Council of Churches.

The draft plan had wisely provided that all constituent councils of the International Missionary Council at the time of integration would auto-matically become "affiliated" members of the Commission on World Mission and Evangelism of the World Council of Churches. When the final Assembly of the International Missionary Council was held in New Delhi in November 1961, it was able to confirm the approval given by its administrative commit-tee to the plan for integration with the knowledge that only two member Councils had withdrawn from membership—the Congo Protestant Council and the Norway Missionary Council.

The action of the Congo Protestant Council had been taken at an early stage in the discussion on integration. It arose from a desire to maintain the unity of the council, when faced with pressure exerted by related missionary agencies with headquarters in the United States which strenuously opposed any association with the World Council of Churches. The action of the Nor-way Missionary Council sprang in part from the nature of its relationship with the Churches of Norway, in part from theological fears concerning the World Council itself, and in part from the fear that integration would result in a weakening of concern for the missionary task of the Church.

It is probably worth while to record that the membership of the Commis-sion is comprised of eighty representatives of affiliated councils, and thirty-five who are nominated by the Central Committee of the World Council of Churches. This act in itself betokens the way in which the Churches and the missionary agencies, now integrated in the World Council of Churches, are both involved in the task of world missionary service and evangelism.

The Constitution of the World Council of Churches makes it clear that the old member councils of the International Missionary Council, now either "affiliated" to the Commission on World Mission, or "associated" with the World Council as a whole, or having both these relationships, can rightly feel that the mission-consciousness of the Churches and the church-consciousness of missions has been "quickened", and the purpose which had so long governed the I.M.C.: "To deepen the sense of missionary obligation in the churches throughout the world and to further the effective proclamation to all men of the Gospel of Jesus Christ, as Lord and Saviour" has been more than safeguarded.

For the functions of the World Council of Churches now include: "to promote the growth of ecumenical and missionary consciousness in the members of all churches; to support the Churches in their world-wide missionary and evangelistic task". And the aim of the Commission on World Missions and Evangelism is defined as: "to further the proclamation to the whole world of the Gospel of Jesus Christ, to the end that all men may believe in Him and be saved".

Moreover, it is of importance to the affiliated and associated councils that the missionary task of the Church now has relevance for each and all of the departments and divisions within the World Council structure. And it could be that the advantages of the location of the Commission and Division within the Ecumenical Centre in Geneva more than outweigh the disadvantages which some feared might arise from the concentration of the whole of the integrated structure in that city.

National Councils in association with the World Council of Churches

Australian Council of Churches
Ökumenischer Rat der Kirchen in Österreich
Burma Christian Council
Canadian Council of Churches
National Christian Council of Ceylon
Ecumenical Council of Churches in Czechoslovakia
Ecumenical Council in Denmark
Ecumenical Council of Finland
Arbeitsgeneinschaft Christlicher Kirchen in Deutschland
Ecumenical Council of Churches in Hungary
National Christian Council of India
Council of Churches in Indonesia
National Christian Council of Japan
Council of Churches in Malaysia and Singapore
Ecumenical Council of Churches in the Netherlands
National Council of Churches in New Zealand
National Council of Churches in the Philippines
Polish Ecumenical Council
The Christian Council of Rhodesia
South African Council of Churches
Swedish Ecumenical Council
The British Council of Churches
National Council of the Churches of Christ in the U.S.A.
Ecumenical Council of Churches in Yugoslavia

Regional Ecumenical Developments and National Christian Councils

This history and significance of the regional ecumenical developments which have taken place in the decades covered by this volume are dealt with in another chapter. It is necessary, however, to refer briefly in this chapter to the effect of this development on the life and work of National Christian Councils. The East Asia Christian Conference, which in many ways pioneered regional developments, illustrates what is probably common, in varying degree, to all such developments.

There was a concern for a regional area as such, and a recognition of common problems and tasks within that area, which it was felt should be shared by all Churches and councils within that area. Immediately a new relatedness was created within the region which brought councils and Churches into a fellowship of knowledge and service. In the case of East Asia it encompasses those Churches and councils in lands stretching from India and Pakistan to Japan, and down to Australia and New Zealand. And it has to be remembered that it brought together representative Christians who otherwise would never have met. And the same process of making the remote near has taken place in Africa with the organization of the All Africa Conference of Churches.

Secondly, in the same way as Latourette states that the "compelling motive" of the various forms of co-operation which he had been describing[1] was evangelism, so again the compelling motive behind the Asian regional development was a passion for mission. It had been evidenced by the earlier Asia Council on Ecumenical Mission. It was evidenced by the passionate words of Bishop Enrique Sobrepena of the Philippines at Prapat, when he spoke of the Asian Churches being "haunted by a sense of mission". It was evidenced by the themes of successive assemblies. At Prapat in 1957 it was "The Common Evangelistic Task". At Kuala Lumpur in 1959 it was "Witnesses Together". And at Kuala Lumpur there began a consciousness of the extent and significance of Asian participation in missionary service. Nor has evangelism been absent from the concerns of African regional development. It is impossible to overestimate the importance of this missionary emphasis for the work of the associated National Christian Councils and Churches. At a time when the missionary emphasis was diminishing in Christian Councils this concern for mission was both an inspiration and a challenge.

Thirdly, there has been manifested a concern for the political, economic, industrial, and social issues of the region, and for the relation of the Christian gospel to those issues. In illustration it is enough to recall that the theme arising from the Bangkok Assembly of the E.A.C.C. (1964) was "The Christian Community within the Human Community", and to point to the work of the Bangalore Christian Institute for the Study of Religion and Society, and its relationship to the National Christian Council of India. The activities of the All Africa Conference of Churches amply provide evidence of a like

---

[1] *A History of the Ecumenical Movement, 1517–1948*, p. 402.

development. Again, the agenda of Christian Councils has had to find place for this range of issues, as well as for the other concerns which arise from regional ecumenicity.

In brief, this regional development has added another dimension to the task of National Christian Councils. Over and above national responsibilities and world ecumenical commitment there is now the pressure of regional concerns and activities.

The continental area of Latin America, which lacks organized expression of regional development comparable to that in Asia, Africa, or the Pacific, has experienced similarly the pressure of this regional dimension through the involvement of National Christian Councils in co-operative activities on a continental basis. Latin American Evangelical Conferences have been held in Argentina in 1949, and in Peru in 1961. and a third conference is being planned to meet in Brazil in February 1969. This co-operative relationship has been expressed in other fields of common concern such as literature, youth work, education, audio-visual aids, and radio evangelism. Regional organization is following in the wake of these developments. In 1961 two Latin American Commissions were formed—one on Christian Education and the other on Church and Society. There have also been developments leading towards a permanent organization for Evangelical co-operation in Latin America. In this connection a "Provisional Committee for Evangelical Unity" was formed at a consultation held in Uruguay in December 1964.

The Committee on National Council Relationships

The draft plan for the integration of the World Council of Churches and the International Missionary Council asked the Central Committee of the World Council of Churches to consider the appointment of a Standing Committee on National Council Relationships so that continuous attention might be given to relationships of mutual helpfulness with all national and regional councils.

Enough has already been written in this chapter to indicate the complexity of national council relationships within the structure of the ecumenical movement. Affiliated councils share in the policy making of the Commission on World Mission, while associated councils, of which the affiliated council may be a part, may be invited to send representatives to meetings of the Central Committee, but without vote. Similarly the importance of these councils for the furtherance of the ecumenical movement and activity has been duly noted.

In 1961 the Third Assembly, meeting at New Delhi, the Assembly of integration, did appoint such a committee within the General Secretariat, and gave to it a mandate which included:

> The functions of the committee shall be:
> i to develop patterns of relationship and co-operation whereby the World Council of Churches and national councils of churches and other Christian councils can strengthen each other and best serve the needs of their constituencies;

   ii to assist such councils in utilizing the resources of the World Council of Churches and to assist the divisions of the World Council to relate their programmes to the needs of such councils;

  iii to keep before all the divisions and departments of the World Council and its member churches the significance of such councils in the fulfilment of the purposes of the ecumenical movement; and

  iv to recommend to the Central Committee ways in which such councils can participate most effectively in the life of the World Council.

The committee had its first meeting in Paris in 1962. It met again in Rochester, New York, in 1963, and again in Enugu, Nigeria, in 1965.

From its inception the committee became aware of two difficulties. Meetings of the committee were necessarily held around the time of meetings of other World Council committees. Many of the members were also involved in some of these meetings, and so found it difficult to attend throughout the sessions of the Committee on National Council Relationships. Further, the committee quickly realized that its work would make greater demands on the time of its secretary than his total commitments would permit.

The Paris meeting was important because it both indicated the range of questions and issues which came properly within the terms of its mandate, and also outlined matters of major importance which would continue to engage the committee in its subsequent meetings. The committee was impressed with the number and range of contacts which were being maintained between Christian Councils and the World Council of Churches. It was said that the various divisions of the World Council were in regular co-operation with nearly thirty councils which were neither "associated" nor "affiliated". The committee was conscious also of the wide diversities between councils. They differed in basis of membership, aim, function, structure, and resources. It was thought that a thorough study needed to be made of the nature and scale of the services a council might properly undertake, of the financial support of councils, of the role of councils within the ecumenical movement, and of the constitutional position of councils in the World Council of Churches.

The committee found reason to emphasize the need for constant co-ordination between the divisions and departments of the World Council in their dealings with Christian Councils. It believed that, as the interdependence of the World Council and other Christian Councils grew, it would be important to keep under review the formal relationships between them.

The subject of the nature of Christian Councils in relation to their financial support was considered again at the Rochester meeting of the committee. The following statement was adopted:

A Christian Council is primarily a representative body for the churches within its own area. Its effective witness to the wider significance of the ecumenical movement depends on this basic requirement, and if this representative character is weak or ambiguous all its work suffers, no matter what resources it may have at its disposal from outside its area. In particular, a Christian council should be able to act in relation to the government of its country, and be recognized by the people, as the responsible voice of the churches in that country. Otherwise its integrity is challenged.

The meeting at Enugu carried the discussion on the financial support of Christian Councils still further, and decided to explore the possibility of establishing a mutual assistance fund for National Christian Councils which needed financial aid beyond the resources which they received from their member organizations.

This continuing discussion revealed the perplexities and complexities, which over several decades had troubled the International Missionary Council in its consideration of the support of Christian Councils in days of increasing national sensitivity. And it was still found impossible to assemble factual data about financial support being received susceptible of accurate analysis and interpretation.

The inherent difficulty of reaching conclusions on a problem which involved a wide diversity of circumstances and need, and which might hold promise of assisting Christian Councils in their growth and service within and beyond their own land, and that without endangering their self-hood and integrity, pointed inexorably to the need of an officer within the World Council structure who would be able to devote the whole of his time to the fulfilment of the mandate given to the Committee on National Council Relationships. Such an appointment was approved at the Fourth Assembly of the W.C.C., meeting at Uppsala, Sweden in 1968.

The Contribution of the Ecumenical Movement to National Christian Councils

National Christian Councils, in their varied manifestations, regional councils and conferences, and the integrated World Council of Churches itself, are all expressions of the ever-widening involvement of the "parts" of the Christian family with its "whole", and with the totality of the Christian task and witness inherent in the Lordship of Jesus Christ. Through it the individual Christian in his local congregation has his place and responsibility in the ecumenical movement.

It is not that all Churches and missionary agencies are equally committed everywhere to, or associated with, this inclusive ecumenical relationship. There are exceptions in every land. In some cases the reason rests in theological belief. In others, the desire of even a majority of members on a Christian Council to retain in its local fellowship a minority of members for whom an association with the World Council of Churches is not possible inhibits any formal relationship with the World Council or with its Commission on World Mission and Evangelism. In some cases, particularly in Latin America and parts of Africa, interest in the ecumenical movement is hindered and limited by the pressure of related missions whose headquarters are opposed to any association with the ecumenical structure, and to any involvement in ecumenical activity. In still other cases the political situation in a country may limit the free association of council and Church with the wider relationships of ecumenical organization and responsibility. Even so, it is frequently and increasingly true that there are avenues of communication and of service which are able to link the ecumenical movement with councils which, while seeking to further co-operation and unity in their own lands, are unable to be responsibly related to the ecumenical movement beyond their borders.

The provision in the constitution of the World Council of Churches for relationship with national and regional councils states that "the purpose of such working relationships shall be to help national councils in their work". It would be possible to write exhaustively of the actual help which is given by or through the World Council of Churches to national Christian Councils in almost every aspect of their work.

At a relatively low level, and even if it be true that almost insoluble problems have been involved, it remains a fact that the financial aid which has been given to councils, first through the International Missionary Council and its agencies, latterly through affiliated councils of the C.W.M.E., and increasingly through the Division of Inter-Church Aid, Refugee, and World Service, has not only over the years amounted to very considerable sums of money, but has enabled those councils to undertake a range of work and service on behalf of their member Churches and of the communities in which they are set which otherwise it would have been impossible to fulfil.

Further, in almost every one of the activities pursued by Christian Councils, there is within the World Council structure continuing creative thought and experiment and potential assistance which can be made available to the national councils for their challenge, inspiration, and help. Through the divisions of the World Council, such as World Mission and Evangelism, Studies, Ecumenical Action, and Inter-Church Aid, through the Commission of the Churches on International Affairs, and, above all, through the personal visitation by members of the World Council staff, the National Councils are encouraged and helped in the varied tasks they attempt to perform on behalf of their member bodies.

In a memorandum written by Mr Louis Odell on "The relationship of the National Christian Councils of Latin America to the Ecumenical Movement", acknowledgement is made of the important part played by the Division of Inter-Church Aid, Refugee, and World Service in creating a better climate of relationship between the National Christian Councils and the ecumenical movement. He says: "As a result of the creation of the Secretariat for Latin America within the Division of Inter-Church Aid, Refugee, and World Service, ecumenical relationships are improving, and are gaining noticeable importance. Regular visits to Latin America, the formulation of projects, the search for ecumenical support, the conduct of studies, and the exchange of information, have meant a more complete understanding of the nature of the World Council of Churches, and of its role vis-à-vis the Churches, the will of God, and Christian unity. As a result, a better and more creative association with the World Council of Churches has been established, and relationship has become possible with Churches and councils which were traditionally opposed to the ecumenical movement, and, consequently, fresh avenues of communication and mutual collaboration have been opened.

Of even greater importance and significance is the help derived by national councils from their involvement in the ecumenical movement. In it they not only have a vision of the "whole" in the realm of the life and witness of the Church, but through their relationship with it they are involved in participation in it, in both study and action, in fellowship with the representatives of other Christian councils, and to the enrichment of their service for the Kingdom of God in their own lands. To be engaged with Christians of other continents, from other confessions, and from differing background and circumstance, in the consideration of any of the varied ecumenical activities in which the World Council of Churches is engaged, is to be immeasurably enriched in the understanding of the world task of the Church, and uplifted by the consciousness of having some part in that task in the sometimes lonely and difficult situation in which Christian councils may at times be placed.

The Contribution of National Christian Councils to the Ecumenical Movement

The provision in the Constitution of the World Council of Churches for relationship with national councils also states that "the purpose of such working relationships shall be ... to encourage them to help the World Council of Churches in the promotion of ecumenical activities in the area concerned ...". There has been ample recognition that, in the same way as the International Missionary Council depended upon its member councils for the furtherance of its work and policies, so the World Council has needed the co-operation and participation of national and other councils.

Documents of the Joint Committee of the World Council of Churches and the International Missionary Council contain such statements as:

> In the day to day work of the W.C.C. there is a growing dependence on the service of national councils.[1]

> The W.C.C. has always recognized the vital role national and other Christian councils occupy in the ecumenical movement. The W.C.C. has also acknowledged its dependence on the co-operation of Christian councils in the furtherance of its own policy and programmes. While the primary point of reference from the W.C.C. is to its member churches, divisions and departments habitually correspond with Christian councils, engage their interest and activity in studies and projects, work through them to a growing extent, and often respond to initiatives taken by the councils.[2]

In a document on the "Relationship of the Division of Inter-Church Aid and Service to Refugees and National Councils of Churches and National Christian Councils" it is stated: "The programme of the Division is commended to the member churches mainly through departments of National Councils of Churches, and resources for the programme are collected mainly through the same channels."

The nature of the services rendered by Christian Councils to the ecumenical movement naturally will differ according to the variations in their own

[1] Joint Committee 10/8.   [2] Joint Committee, September 1961.

structure, resources, and function. Some have been able to assist considerably with service connected with arrangements for meetings of Assemblies and committees of the W.C.C., and in other ways are able to assist in the promotion and furtherance of its programmes and policies. Inevitably the requests made for assistance are greater in the case of some councils than others. But the Christian Council, whatever its structure and function, makes a contribution by its very existence. It is part of the structure of co-operation and unity which links Church with Church and other Christian agencies in the area, and therefore has a necessary place in the structures of co-operation which link the Churches of a given area with those of other lands and continents. It is part of a complete chain of co-operation and communication which stretches from the individual Christian to the W.C.C., and which reaches back from the W.C.C. to the local congregation and its individual members. As Dr Oldham argued in his article on "New Spiritual Adventures in the Mission Field", "If our unity is real, and we have a common purpose, these must express themselves through some visible organ."[1] And such organs of co-operation are necessary for the fulfilment of the tasks of the World Council of Churches, and of the ecumenical movement as a whole.

Probably the greatest contribution made by the National Christian Councils and regional organizations to the ecumenical movement has been in the outstanding leadership which has been made available for the service of that movement. It has come from every continent, and has continued from 1910 until the present day. It would be invidious, and maybe tedious, to begin to name them. But a study of reports of assemblies, commissions, and the like, over the years would provide frequent evidence of the contribution in vision and outlook of those who have had much of their training in and through their service to National Christian Councils. This contribution has involved equally valuable participation in the work of the committees of the various departments and activities of the World Council—representing a costly contribution by the national councils themselves in the time and service of their secretaries released for ecumenical service. Admittedly, in the process, the national councils have gained from the added experience of their officers which flowed back into the life and work of the councils to which they belonged.

Nor is it possible to measure the influence of Christian Councils, particularly in the lands of the younger Churches, in their insistence on facing the realities of the ecumenical challenge in the context of their own situation, in which traditional confessional pressures have sometimes become entrenched.

It is not without meaning and challenge for the ecumenical movement as a whole that the National Council of Churches in Indonesia, founded in 1950, defines its aims and functions as:

> Establish one Christian Church in Indonesia, promote and execute co-operation according to agreements among Churches: establish relations with mission and ecumenical bodies at home and abroad: seek to enlarge and deepen present ecumenical relations: represent Churches in dealing with government in matters of common interest.

[1] *IRM*, no. 44 (1922), p. 547.

E

The Ecclesiological Significance of Christian Councils

Towards the end of the period covered by this history there has been considerable interest concerning the ecclesiological significance of Christian Councils—the World Council of Churches itself as well as the National Christian Councils. A document produced by the joint committee of the World Council of Churches and the International Missionary Council in July 1960 raises the issue in this way:

> The increasing importance of national and regional councils, not only as useful adjuncts to the World Council of Churches and valuable aids to ecumenical experience, but as a fundamental part of the structure of the ecumenical movement gives importance to the insistent question—What is the ecclesiological significance of councils?

In reporting to the Central Committee, after its first meeting in Paris in August 1962, the Committee on National Council Relationships "noted with appreciation that in the forthcoming World Conference on Faith and Order provision is being made for consideration of what has been termed 'the ecclesiological significance of Christian Councils'."

The Fourth World Conference on Faith and Order (Montreal 1963) did give some consideration to the issue, and took note of the report of the National Council of Churches in the U.S.A. of "the Ecclesiological Significance of Councils of Churches", and an essay by the Reverend Kenneth Slack of the British Council of Churches. The section report on "The Church and the World Council of Churches", apart from commenting on the ambiguity involved in the English expression "councils of churches", is chiefly concerned with the World Council of Churches, and that without "presuming to give a definite answer".

An article by Dr Lukas Vischer entitled "Christian Councils—their Future as Instruments of the Ecumenical Movement"[1] does, however, attempt to deal precisely with the question: What is the ecclesiological significance of Christian Councils? It merits close study, and should occasion considerable debate. He is aware that the character, structure, and powers of Christian Councils vary so greatly that any ecclesiological formula is bound to be inadequate. But, he says,

> However great the difficulties may be, the question of the ecclesiological significance of Christian councils needs to be kept in view. The very inability to state what they ecclesiologically are shows at least one thing with unmistakable clarity; they are in fact an ecclesiological anomaly which ought not to continue indefinitely in its present form.

Dr Vischer's conclusion is that Christian Councils can fulfil their function only if they are understood as transitional institutions which overcome the ecclesiological anomaly of division, and make increasingly visible the unity which binds the Churches together. He shares the belief that a conciliar structure belongs to the very essence of the Church, and believes that in the

[1] *Study Encounter*, June 1968.

new period in the history of Christian Councils which is now beginning, the structure of Councils should be modified to meet the challenges represented by the increasing number of Churches seeking union with each other, and by the willingness of Roman Catholic local Churches, in some places, to join Christian Councils as full members.

The next volume of ecumenical history will reveal the extent to which National Christian Councils themselves have found the answers to questions as to their nature and ecclesiological significance, and the extent to which they have been led to modify their structures and functions.

5

Confessional Families
and the Ecumenical Movement

HAROLD E. FEY

During the two decades covered by this history, relations between confessional families and the ecumenical movement assumed new importance and complexity. Attempts to deal with these relations required sharper definitions. Definitions of confessionalism were not easy to make because no two denominational groupings found the same meaning in the word or in the reality it signified. So clarification efforts became adventures in self-examination. In 1967, after other names had been discarded as unsatisfactory, the secretaries of the world confessional groups adopted the term "world confessional families". They said the families consist of "the various Christian traditions taken as a whole. Each world confessional family consists of Churches belonging to the same tradition and held together by this common heritage; they are conscious of living in the same universal fellowship and give to this consciousness at least some structured visible expression."[1]

Beginnings of Confessional Organizations

The forms of these "structured visible expressions" vary greatly. One confessional family has a thousand employees and annual budgets in the millions. Several have small but highly competent staffs and moderate budgets. Others are served by part-time secretaries without assistance who earn their living at other tasks. Some had origins which preceded the modern ecumenical movement by many decades. Others were formed or assumed their present level of activities since the World Council of Churches was officially launched in 1948. Anglicans deny that theirs is a confessional grouping and they did not in fact develop a continuing organization until after 1958. But the first Lambeth Conference, which began the process of consultation, was held in 1867. The "Alliance of Reformed Churches Throughout the World holding the Presbyterian System" was the first formally organized confessional family. It was launched in 1875 and held its first meeting in 1877. The Methodists started holding "World Ecumenical Conferences" in 1881 but did not organize their World Methodist Council until 1951. The Lutherans did not begin the process of consultation until 1923, when the Lutheran World Conference began to meet, and did not launch the Lutheran World Federation until 1947. Today it is the largest of all.

Nevertheless, difficult as they are to define and varied as they are in their "structured visible expressions", the world confessional families are very much alive and must be taken into account in their relationship with the ecumenical movement. In their beginnings they were in fact the principal existing forms of the ecumenical movement, giving the members of their Churches a new consciousness of universality through the discovery of the world-wide dimensions of their own fellowships. Many of their leaders participated in the formation of the World Council of Churches and today have positions of leadership in it.

In the last two decades confessional groupings have increased in strength and in scope of work. At the same time their status has paradoxically been limited by the growth of the ecumenical movement. While today some church-

[1] Report of Secretaries of World Confessional Families. Geneva 1967.

117

men within these groupings and more outside of them consider that they have become a hindrance to the ecumenical movement, confessional organizations continue. Shorn of any claim to absolutism that may ever have been attributed to them, they seek and generally find constructive roles as they examine their reasons for separate existence and their unquestionably expanding and deepening relations with other confessional families.

While the World Council of Churches is not the ecumenical movement, its emergence and development has been and is a prominent factor in that movement. The issue of confessionalism has been a matter that has had to be considered since the earliest meetings for planning of the W.C.C. The first meeting for definitive projection of the W.C.C. was held in Utrecht, Holland in 1938. Here Lutherans argued that membership in the W.C.C. should consist of Churches and that seats in its Assembly and Central Committee should be allocated on a confessional basis. According to church historian Abdel Ross Wentz, the Lutheran representative said:

> It is our conviction that the World Council itself will move more quickly and more certainly towards a united testimony before the world if the churches themselves associated in confessional groups are permitted to speak frankly with one another in friendly comparison of views—far more quickly and certainly than if Christians speak with one another as national or geographical groups. The way to a united Christian testimony before the world of today would be rendered more difficult by sectionalism than by sectarianism.

His argument for membership by Churches prevailed; but the attempt to associate Churches in confessional blocs within the structure of the W.C.C. did not prevail.

After the Second World War, when the committee on arrangements for the Amsterdam Assembly met in England, the same argument was put forward. In reply the committee held that invitations had already been issued and that the basis of membership in the World Council would have to be settled when the First Assembly met. Following this meeting but before Amsterdam, Henry Pitney Van Dusen, President of Union Theological Seminary, New York, wrote that the confessional issue would be "much the most explosive issue and one which is most likely to erupt with some sharpness on the floor of the Assembly". He said that tension was between regionalism and nationalism on the one hand and denominationalism or confessionalism on the other. "The interests of confessionalism are being urged by some Orthodox and Anglican churchmen, by a few Reformed or Presbyterian leaders, but most convincedly and insistently by certain spokesmen for American Lutheranism."[1]

Confessionalism and the W.C.C.

When the Lutheran World Federation was formed in 1947 at Lund, Sweden, Bishop Anders Nygren and others continued to advocate a confessional basis for the W.C.C. The General Secretary of the W.C.C. provisional committee

---

[1] *Christianity and Crisis*, vol. viii, no. 7.

appeared before the Lund conference and appealed for support in the following carefully chosen words:

> The World Council is deeply aware of the fact that the ecumenical task can only be performed if the main confessional federations and alliances perform their task of bringing the churches of their confessional family together in close fellowship and so prepare the way for the even greater and more difficult task of establishing the wider ecumenical Christian brotherhood.

The breadth of vision which turned an either–or into a both–and approach finally won the day.

The issue was resolved when the Amsterdam Assembly adopted the formula proposed by the provisional committee: "Seats in the Assembly shall be allocated to the member churches by the Central Committee, due regard being given to such factors as numerical size, adequate confessional representation and adequate geographical distribution." This was a compromise. The formula recognized the existence of confessional groups; but the basis of membership was still Churches, not confessional groups.[1]

The Amsterdam Assembly also approved the following additional action:

> The Constitution of the Council authorizes the Council to establish consultative relationships with denominational federations to send representatives to the Assembly and the Central Committee in a consultative capacity. The provisional Committee recommends that these bodies should be especially consulted with regard to membership of Churches of their confession. In so far as they enter into the field of inter-church aid and reconstruction they should, furthermore, be invited to relate their activities as closely as possible to the Council's reconstruction department. It is inevitable that in their manifold approaches to the churches the activities of the Council and of the confessional federations overlap to some extent. It is therefore most desirable that regular contacts be maintained between the executive officers concerned. And the most appropriate solutions would be that as many of the federations as possible should follow the example of those which have set up offices in Geneva or sent special representatives to Geneva.

This compromise did not lay to rest all the concerns which were inherent in the situation, particularly as confessional groups developed a new vigour following the formation of the World Council of Churches. So Charles Ranson spoke for others as well as for himself when he addressed the board of directors of the London Missionary Society on 19 September 1951. He said:

> The growth of the World Council of Churches and the ecumenical idea has stimulated a revival of organized confessionalism. There are two aspects of this development. One is tremendously important and potentially creative. This is the concern which has quite properly developed within the churches that they shall understand deeply their own heritage and thus be able to talk with meaning and realism with other churches with whom they are in ecumenical conversation.

[1] See Abdel Ross Wentz, *The Lutheran Churches and the Ecumenical Movement* in *World Lutheranism Today: A Tribute to Anders Nygren* (Oxford: Rock Island, Illinois 1950).

The other aspect, which gives real cause for concern to those of us whose interest lies largely in the life of the younger churches, is the way this is expressing itself organizationally in world-wide confessional bodies. These tend to project themselves across the world and to fasten upon the younger churches those leading strings from which we have been trying to free them for many years. The real growing points of ecumenicity today are in the life of the younger churches. The real driving force in this organized confessionalism which is in danger of hardening into ecumenical sectarianism lies in the older Christendom, often among people who have no conception of the implications of what they are doing for the life of the younger churches.[1]

The emphasis in this statement was prophetic, for in the years since Dr Ranson spoke, the most searching questions concerning the effect of confessional activities have come from the East Asia Christian Council.

Co-operation in Compassion

In the first decade following the Second World War major ecumenical energies were absorbed by work to relieve suffering humanity and to repair war damage to church structures and relationships. Inter-Church aid and help for refugees, first within Europe and then in widening circles throughout the world, became a major preoccupation of confessional and ecumenical organizations alike. Many Churches co-ordinated their efforts under the World Council, whose substantial humanitarian efforts are described in Chapter 8 of this book. Others channeled some resources of man-power and materials through the W.C.C. and with them carried on denominational enterprises for their own most afflicted people.

Because vastly more Lutherans were uprooted and more Lutheran Churches were disrupted by reason of the struggle in Europe than were members or Churches of other Protestant groups, the Lutheran World Federation organized its own massive programme of assistance to refugees and aid to Churches. The achievements of the L.W.F. in relief, resettlement, and reconstruction constitute an heroic chapter in church history. Abroad, work that began during the war as service to "orphaned missions" expanded in various directions, one of which was resettlement of European and other refugees. It is important to recognize that while this work was done under the auspices of the L.W.F., a confessional organization, the L.W.F. also assisted the efforts of other ecumenical organizations and was assisted by them as resources permitted. While the L.W.F. still carries on a large programme, the trend is towards more co-operation rather than towards more competition.

By 1957 the immediate urgencies of the post-war crisis were tapering off and the Churches could once more turn to examining their relationships with one another. The Second World Assembly, held in 1954 at Evanston, Illinois, had invited observers from non-member Churches, but had not otherwise disturbed the balance of ecumenical/confessional relationships. Because confessional organizations were growing in strength, the impression spread that they might be heading towards a collision course with ecumenical institutions,

[1] Quoted by Michael Hollis in *Mission, Unity and Truth* (London 1967), p. 10.

which were also gaining acceptance. Even those who did not hold this view recognized that consultation was required to take into account changes in relationships and attitudes. The increase in the number of Churches which were uniting with other Churches or were engaged in negotiations looking toward union was also a factor. So the time was ripe for representatives of confessional organizations to meet to discuss their relationships with each other and with the W.C.C. This began in 1957.

Since 1957 the officers of fourteen world confessional families have met in Geneva, generally annually, for conversations among themselves and with members of the staff of the World Council of Churches. Not all are represented at every meeting. The families whose representatives have met are the Anglican Communion, the Baptist World Alliance, the Ecumenical Patriarchate (Constantinople), the Friends World Committee for Consultation, the International Congregational Council, the Lutheran World Federation, the Mennonite World Conference, the Old Catholic Church, the Pentecostal World Conference, the Patriarchate of Moscow, the Salvation Army, the World Convention of Churches of Christ, the Methodist World Council, and the World Alliance of Reformed Churches. The Standing Committee of Oriental Orthodox Churches joined the conversations in 1967.

Annual Meeting of Confessional Representatives

How did the meetings of confessional bodies begin? It is significant that the initiative was taken by one of them. At the 1956 meeting of the executive committee of the World Alliance of Reformed Churches in Prague, President John A. Mackay of the W.A.R.C. spoke of the rebirth of churchmanship and of the importance of the ecumenical movement. He then described "the resurgence of confessionalism" as a positive factor. The new confessionalism differed from the old, he said, in that there was now no disposition to "absolutize their several confessional structures or loyalties. No single confession believes that it represents the one and only Church of Christ, the Una Sancta." But each seeks to make its specific contribution to the "ecumenical treasure house of Christian faith and life".

Since confessional movements and the ecumenical movement are growing side by side, he said, they could either collide or co-operate. Dr Mackay thought that, if co-operation is to result, "the confessional movement must be taken seriously by the World Council of Churches". He therefore proposed that "confessional leaders come together for the exchange of information and the discussion of policies in an atmosphere of Christian confidence". He had talked with W.C.C. leaders and said they favoured confessional leaders conferring on an autonomous basis. Later that morning the executive committee of the W.A.R.C. voted to sponsor an invitation to confessional leaders to meet informally to explore prospects of co-operation.

The informal gathering was held at New Haven when the Central Committee of the W.C.C. met during the following summer, 1957. Leaders of seven confessional groups got together and approved the idea of a larger meeting of presidents and secretaries of confessional groups. This larger meeting was held at the W.C.C. in the autumn of the same year. The W.A.R.C. suggestions for the agenda were comprehensive. As they were stated by the W.A.R.C. executive group in 1957 they included:

> . . . frank and friendly discussion of the place of confessionalism in the ecumenical movement; the contribution which a resurgent confessionalism can make to the enrichment of that movement; the points at which, if any, confessionalism becomes a threat to that growing oneness in Christ which ecumenical movement seeks; the ways in which the commitment of the churches to the ecumenical movement presupposes some restraint on the consciousness and practice of mission on the part of confessional groups with reference to each other.

In some sense these points have constituted the agenda of each meeting of confessional leaders since 1957.[1]

While the conferences have always been held under the auspices of the confessional groups themselves, meetings have been held at the World Council of Churches headquarters and staff members of that organization have been welcome contributors to the discussions. As a matter of fact, the initiation of this series of annual conferences of leaders of confessional organizations was most welcome to W.C.C. leaders. The issue of ecumenical/confessional relationships was recognized to require discussion. Here was a way that discussion could begin. The struggle of confessional groups to define their own character has been helped, even if it is not solved, by sharing with others having like problems. Relationships between confessional families and the ecumenical movement have benefited from open confrontation of issues. Again, issues have not been finally resolved, but they have been clarified and put on the way to resolution because, as Dr Mackay said, the tendency to absolutize confessional structures or loyalties is a thing of the past.

The point of view from which these conversations proceeded was that taken by Henry Carter, a British Methodist, who wrote:

> The ecumenical movement has taken two forms, inter- and intra-confessional, and Methodism as a world-wide confession is explicitly related to both. It might seem that a major and divisive issue confronts us here. To pursue the line of confessional activity with only intermittent regard for the call of the Universal Church would mean intensification of denominational feelings and policy, with heightening of barriers against unity. To respond to the Universal Church with scant concern for confessional loyalty and duty, as though the ecumenical movement could here and now dissolve that elemental bond, would scatter, not conserve, the spiritual treasure which the confession holds in trust. Yet the bare statement of the issue in this way points to the true line of action. The recognition that inter- and intra-confessional movements have progressed side by side and stage by stage points to an unfolding purpose, to which churches of many confessions and in all parts of the world have become sensitive and responsive. We can thankfully acknowledge the continuing guidance of Divine Spirit on the way that leads to the true unity and wholeness of Christ's Church, the Una Sancta.[2]

[1] From the minutes of the executive committee of the World Alliance of Reformed Churches, 1956, at Prague, and 1957, at Stoney Point, New York.

[2] *The Methodist Heritage* (London 1951), p. 218.

The early years of the conferences of representatives of confessional families were not notably productive. But the passage of time and the proddings of providence working through events finally combined to break down reticence and to open the minds of confessional leaders to one another. At first each was so preoccupied with the practicalities of confessional ministries that serious theological conversation was difficult. The result was that it was easier to make ecumenical affirmations than it was to study and work together. It was, after all, the Churches which commanded the major resources of men and money. These made it possible for church leaders to launch enterprises which they considered to be ecumenical in spirit yet which were confessional in personnel, orientation, and result. Lack of patience with theological discussion on the nature of the one Church under its one Lord encouraged unilateral action and short-circuited possible ecumenical achievements. This was not changed until voices began to be raised, especially by the youth of the Churches, which questioned the seriousness of ecumenical commitments which expressed themselves verbally in terms of identity with the ecumenical movement, but structurally, financially, and empirically in pre-ecumenical terms.

Ecumenical Evangelism

Another factor which was at work was what might be called ecumenical evangelism. It found expression at the crucial time when the ecumenical movement had to move past its initial stage or die in its infancy. One example of many that might be cited was heard at the service which was held in Oslo Cathedral during the 1961 meeting of the World Methodist Council: W. A. Visser 't Hooft preached from the text in Romans 15 which was adapted for his closing words. He declared that, while some people consider that the very existence of the denominations constitutes a difficulty for the ecumenical movement, there are many "extremely positive elements" in the denominational heritage. He hoped that the time would never come when Methodists would not express their gratitude for John Wesley. He urged them to share their spiritual heritage. But there is a denominationalism, he said, which expresses itself in "spiritual laziness, in withdrawing, in refusing to face the consequences of a real confrontation with other denominations" for fear of the sacrifices which might be demanded. This kind of denominationalism, he said, was bad. So also is the ecclesiastical power politics which uses confessional words and forms as levers to achieve its ends. Then he came to the point:

> But there is one more thing [said Dr Visser 't Hooft]. Do we always remember that denominations by their nature are provisional in character, or do we sometimes think and speak about them as if they were final embodiments of Christian truth? Now Martin Luther and John Calvin and John Wesley have all made it abundantly clear that they did not think of the church formation which they saw growing up in their lifetime as the last word. On the contrary, they all thought in terms of the Church Catholic and prayed for the restoration of the full catholicity and unity of the church. And should we be more

confessional than our confessional leaders? More confessional than Luther or Calvin, or more than Wesley? Surely not! . . . What we need most of all from you is precisely that desire which is also at the heart of Methodism, which was surely in the heart of John Wesley, that desire to render a more obedient, a more convincing witness than the world has seen for many centuries to the unity, to the universality of the people of God and the Body of Christ. May the God of steadfastness and encouragement grant you to live in such harmony with one another—yes, with one another as Methodists, but also with all who call upon the name of the Lord Jesus Christ, in accord with Jesus Christ, that together you may with one voice glorify the God and Father of our Lord Jesus Christ.[1]

A major factor in raising the confessional question in inescapable form was the action of a new regional ecumenical organization—the East Asia Christian Conference. Meeting at Bangalore, India in 1961, the E.A.C.C. declared that "the very vitality of these confessional loyalties often create serious obstacles in the life of the younger churches". This touched upon the sensitive issue which had set the ecumenical movement on its way at the world mission conference in Edinburgh in 1910, namely that of churchly divisions throwing a road block in the way of the world mission which had been entrusted to the Church by its Lord. The timing of the E.A.C.C. was perfect, since the Third Assembly of the World Council of Churches was about to be held in New Delhi. It could hardly afford to ignore the challenge.

The Asian Challenge to Confessionalism

New Delhi did not ignore the question, but also it did not face it squarely. In the report of the section on Church Unity, which made the famous "all in each place" statement, the Assembly noted that most of the confessional organizations existed many years before the founding of the World Council. This was an interesting but not a relevant point. It affirmed that "their purpose is not only to clarify and strengthen confessional understanding and loyalty but to serve responsibly in the wider ecumenical movement. But opinion is divided today over the effects of their existence and work upon the participation of their churches in the movement for unity and upon the course they ought to take in the future."

The New Delhi Assembly observed that some believe that a deeper understanding of the various confessions is necessary if the quest for unity in the truth is at length to be successful, and that it is the duty of the confessional organizations to advance that deeper understanding. On the other hand, the Churches have in their membership leaders who see world confessional bodies as a threat to wider unity, particularly in Asia and Africa. The New Delhi Assembly had already agreed to its famous statement concerning "the centrality of unity of all Christians in each place which must of course always seek to be a 'unity of the truth'". It therefore concluded that, if the leaders of confessional bodies believe this, "they will not consider the union of one of

[1] *Proceedings of the Tenth World Methodist Conference, Oslo, Norway, 1961* (London: Nashville 1961), p. 280.

their churches as a loss, but as a gain for the whole Church. And a service can be rendered to such churches if the confessional bodies assist them in the responsible study of all issues which are involved in the proposed union."

This observation represented a legitimate hope but it did not attempt to resolve the questions involved in the simultaneous rise of the ecumenical movement and increase in the strength of the confessional bodies. Some of these questions appeared in the *Ecumenical Review* for October 1964. They had been raised by the East Asia Christian Conference Assembly which met in Bangkok in February of that year. The E.A.C.C. Assembly recommended that the E.A.C.C. executive group bring together representatives of confessional bodies and of the younger Churches in a "major consultation". The question the Assembly raised for discussion suggests the nature of the continuing dialogue over confessionalism in so far as it concerns the mission of the Church.

Affirming their belief that "the Church is One Body, the Body of Christ", the Asian Churches pointed out that they are moving toward autonomy, not merely to achieve organizational independence, but also so that each Church will "find its own selfhood, being able under God to make its own response to its Lord in the specific situation it has been called to mission". Therefore, "on such a matter as church union, a church must make up its own mind and accept the consequences of its own obedience". Since the parent churches are involved, "they too must decide how best to help in the process of decision-making without violating their own integrity or that of the younger churches". The Bangkok Assembly called on confessional bodies to give help to Churches of the same family "within the framework of the total ecumenical operation". Moreover, the Assembly summoned confessional organizations to make plans which "strengthen and do not weaken the movements toward larger co-operation, closer co-ordination [and] joint action for mission and unity".

The East Asia churchmen asked confessional organizations to work within the ecumenical movement to help people within their respective families to understand how the Asian Churches see and are trying to interpret the Christian faith. An informational role which each confessional body should undertake ought also to be carried out concerning the experiences of Christians in other confessional families "so that they can take courage and pray intelligently for each other". Before these organizations carry out these essentially theological functions, their Asian colleagues asked them to face three hard questions:

1. Do the world confessional organizations rest on a theological principle or do they simply gather together Churches because of a common history and tradition?

2. Even where world confessional organizations are seeking to preserve for the universal Church some fundamental insight into an aspect of Christian truth, is this best done by an organization built around that truth?

3. Are the confessions and doctrines which are the historical basis of these world confessional organizations living realities among the people in these confessional families?

E.A.C.C. approach to "Big Three"

Finally, these Asian Churchmen ventured to doubt the relevance and usefulness of world meetings which had been proposed by various confessional bodies. Instead, the E.A.C.C. churchmen asked them "to support the ecumenical programmes that are now developing for the handling of these issues". They then addressed directly the World Methodist Council, the Anglican Communion, and the Lutheran World Federation. To the Methodists, who were reported to be rethinking their organizational structure, Bangkok asked that the World Council of Churches and the regional conferences of Asia and Africa be consulted about plans. Asian churchmen also warned that, while Methodist Churches of the United States, Great Britain, and Europe face similar problems and so might profitably confer on them, they should not assume that this was true of the Churches of Asia. There, "the issues lie between the churches together and the world", they said.

Turning then to the Anglican Communion, the Bangkok Assembly noted that, since Anglican officers are being appointed to serve in regions of Asia, these officers and the metropolitans in the area should meet with the working committee of the East Asia Christian Conference to deal with problems of inter-Church aid, joint action for mission, and "the growing together of the churches in each local area". The E.A.C.C. also sought information on the sponsorship and powers of the Anglican regional officers, and asked that this new initiative should "not isolate the Anglican churches from other churches and from giving aid to and receiving from them".

The Bangkok Assembly finally appealed to the Lutheran World Federation "to make it entirely clear that Lutheran Churches in Asia, which are involved in discussion of proposals for church union, will have full encouragement and help from other Lutheran Churches in the world in seeking a basis of union which is in conformity with holy Scripture. Only so will it be clear that the Lutheran World Federation is not a step towards a World Lutheran Church." It also asked if the L.W.F. "could consider making its present inter-Church aid operation one more closely integrated with the work of" the division of Inter-Church Aid of the World Council of Churches and also with that of the E.A.C.C. Later the L.W.F. did vote to assure Lutheran Churches which might enter into unions that they would not suffer loss of funds or man-power by such action.

Bangkok appealed to all confessional organizations to recognize that, as the Churches of a region unite, it will be increasingly important that such regional ecumenical organizations be strengthened.

> There are always risks involved when the churches reflect a common ethnic origin or common nationality or a common economic status. These risks can be provided against only by strengthening conciliar structures that cross all national and ethnic dividing lines. The ultimate aim must be the restoration of the one Holy Church, to the end that the united church in any one area will have an organic place in the Church Universal.

Immediate results from these appeals were not expected and did not appear.

World conferences or conventions of world confessional bodies continued to meet. But in East Asia a series of "situation conferences" were held by the E.A.C.C. Out of these came a positive proposal for "Joint Action in Mission". The idea was that in the great areas of responsibility in which the missions held a common mandate united efforts could still go forward unhindered by confessional differences. The idea was excellent; performance on it was slow in starting. But the request of the E.A.C.C. for an enlarged meeting of the world confessional bodies was not forgotten, and soon plans for it entered the active stage.

Confessional Representatives' Response

The enlarged meeting was held in Geneva, on 12 and 13 October 1965. Thirty-three representatives of nine world confessional bodies gathered. With them were three staff members from the Lutheran World Federation, three from the World Presbyterian Alliance, and ten persons from the staff of the World Council of Churches. The representation was: Anglican four, Baptist World Alliance five, Friends World Committee for Consultation three, International Congregational Council two, Lutheran World Federation four, Salvation Army three, World Convention of Churches of Christ three, World Methodist Council six, and World Presbyterian Alliance three.

World confessional groups which did not send representatives to this meeting were the Old Catholic Church, the Mennonite World Conference, whose executive cannot remember receiving any correspondence about it, the Pentecostal World Conference, the Ecumenical Patriarchate (Istanbul), and the Patriarchate of Moscow. Notably missing from the conference also were representatives of the younger Churches of Asia, Africa, and Latin America. With the exception of one staff member of the World Council and one executive of a mission board, all of the participants were North Americans or Europeans.

The 1965 conference accepted without changes the working definitions of "confessional bodies" which had been adopted in 1962, although by this time questions were being raised concerning its adequacy. After two days of discussion the conference adopted a set of findings which represented its consensus. Originally they were largely the work of W. A. Visser 't Hooft, the general secretary of the World Council of Churches, but were accepted as a fair statement of the level of agreement which had been reached.

As published in the *Ecumenical Review* (vol. xviii, 1966, pp. 91ff) under the title "Statement of a Joint Consultation Concerning Confessional Movements and Mission and Unity", the statement said that during recent years officers of the world confessional bodies had been meeting regularly "for conversations among themselves about matters of common interest. Since 1962 much of the discussion has centred upon the role of the confessional bodies in the ecumenical movement." The statement then outlined the purpose of the present meeting between "representatives of the mission agencies of the churches to discuss the significance of the confessional movement for the task of the churches in mission and unity". It said that it was hoped that the consultation would result in a much wider discussion and continuing conversation. It repeated the 1962 definition of confessional bodies and then said:

> We believe that to think and act as if the historic confessional church families represent the only spiritual reality to be taken seriously is to live in the "pre-ecumenical" age. In that sense the statement of a Lutheran theologian that the confessional era is at an end is true. On the other hand, we believe that to think and act as if the fully ecumenical age had been reached, in which confessional disagreements have been overcome and in which it is possible to think only in terms of an integrated world-wide Christian community is premature and therefore also unrealistic. It is characteristic of the present period of church history that the Church lives "between the times" when the confessions remain the main expressions of its life but in which these confessions have all to answer the ecumenical questions: "What is the relevance of the faith that all the confessions hold in common for their relationships to each other and for the unity and mission of the Church of Christ today?" and "How can they express in common witness and new ecclesiastical structure" the unity in Christ which exists already and for which they are responsible to our Lord for the sake of the world?

The Geneva conference then posed a set of questions of principle and another set of questions of function which it had been led to confront and which it believed the Churches must face. The first question of principle was: "How does the Church confess Christ in a true and contemporary way both in its witness and its structure?" While historic confessions of the faith had arisen from an endeavour to state what it meant in specific situations to be faithful to the word of God, what should happen now that the situations have changed? So also with ecclesiastical structures; they had been formed to meet specific challenges, but now other challenges are raised.

> Within their four walls the separate churches tend to speak at times as though their specific confessional traditions were the only criteria of truth. Yet in the arena of ecumenical encounter and partnership in mission they find themselves compelled to think of their confessions and structures in a new perspective and therefore open to development and reconciliation.

So ecumenical experience leads to a new appraisal of traditions and structures. How then "define theologically the relationship between the One Faith in which all are baptized and the 'confessions' which certain churches or groups of churches feel called in obedience to the Gospel to make separately?"

What Answer to Youth?

The second question of principle asked how the Churches can deal with their young people who take seriously the "ecumenical imperatives"? Often the result is that young people revolt when church leaders proclaim their determination to work for renewal through unity and mission, yet cling tenaciously to the *status quo*. This intensifies the conflict between generations within the Church. The effects of this revolt on students who are subjected to confessionally oriented theological education is particularly serious for them and for the Church. The third question of principle arises within Churches whose confessional stand or form of ecclesiastical structure has become the subject of tension or division within the church body. While leaders give "the appearance of solidarity" on confessional or ecclesiastical matters, they and the world often know that the appearance does not always correspond with the reality. To a greater or lesser extent this is the case in every denomination. Obviously this is "a matter for the most serious consideration".

The question of function raised by the 1965 conference of confessional bodies dealt with such matters as what is or should be the relation of the confessional movements to the "conciliar ecumenical movement and the future of the total mission of the Church"? National Christian Councils provide forums for discussion of important issues and provide facilities for common action in missionary and evangelistic tasks of the Churches, such as "Joint Action for Mission". This is an important and urgent issue. Also the Churches must ask: "What relation has the confessional and ecumenical understanding of the Churches to their processes of decision-making in respect of their upbuilding of the Church and their mission to the world?" The answer involves pastoral care, education, church extension, and missionary activities which in turn affect the Churches' use of money and personnel.

A noticeable discrepancy between ecumenical affirmation in one direction and expenditure of money in other directions, said the conference, does the Church no good. So the Churches must ask themselves: "How can we establish the criteria of responsible partnership between the affluent and the needy on the one hand, and between confessional bodies and National Councils on the other?" This is also applied both to decision-making and to the allocation of funds. For example, what happens when a Church or church agency is asked to help other Churches "with which they are not in theological agreement or in full communion?" Some agreed criteria for responsible partnership are called for.

Finally the 1965 conference asked: What should be the relationship of the united Churches to the confessional bodies of which the uniting Churches were members? And what priority should be given to regional ecumenical organizations in the development by a Church of its missionary strategy? The statement ended with recognition that the answer to these questions would not easily be found, since the consequences of whatever decision is reached on them will be far-reaching. But "we have formulated these questions in the hope that God may be pleased to use the discussions which they will provoke to further his purpose of unity for his people".

So the questions which came into the open at Bangalore and had echoed through the discussions at New Delhi and in other conferences were further emphasized and deepened at Geneva. They were more readily asked than answered; but there was no doubt that they had deeply penetrated the consciousness of leaders of the confessional bodies. In respect of the original impetus for asking the questions, Geneva left something to be desired, for the younger Churches were not represented by their own people. But confessionalism had arisen in the West, and so it was necessary that it be considered by Western Christians. They may be sure that Christians in other parts of the world are not indifferent to it. Westerners were more intimately concerned with its origins and could conceivably do most to reconcile confessionalism and ecumenism. The discussion might have profited if the younger Churches had been represented; but they had raised the question in such a way that henceforth it could not be ignored, whether or not they were present.

Comment which followed the Geneva conference varied. One participant noted that "the spirit of caution" was pronounced. He cited as evidence the fact that a spokesman for the International Congregational Council had received no support when he proposed as a question to be included in the concluding statement of the meeting: "Under what circumstances can we feel that the confessional bodies have fulfilled their function and can disappear as such?" The I.C.C. representative received no encouragement and the question was not included. The conference had the opportunity to advance "Joint Action for Mission" which had been launched in the Situation Conference in Asia and had subsequently been endorsed by the W.C.C. Division of World Mission and Evangelism at its meeting in Mexico City. But the idea of Joint Action for Mission received inadequate attention at Geneva and was "only slowly, very slowly, being implemented" anywhere.

Another line of comment noted that the prevailing definition of "confessional bodies" was such that Orthodox, Anglican, and Roman Catholic Churches would have difficulty in recognizing themselves in it. Does the fellowship between confessional bodies consist solely in the fact that each has specific convictions of a doctrinal or ecclesiological character to support, as Lukas Vischer asked in an article written in August 1966? This is, as he noted, clearly a "pre-ecumencial" definition, an "ecumenical formalism which does not do justice to reality". The deeper question, which must be faced in an ecumenical context, arises between Churches, such as the Orthodox and the Roman Catholic on the one hand and the Western confessional bodies on the other, concerning whether church structures must be fashioned on the historical model of the first centuries or may follow synodical principles which evolved much later and influenced not only ecclesiastical but parliamentary institutions.

Merging of Confessional Organizations

Denominational forms of Christian association are provisional, argued W. A. Visser 't Hooft before the Methodists at Oslo. Now it begins to appear that organizations of confessional families, which have evolved in relatively recent times, may also be regarded as provisional. The World Alliance of Reformed Churches and the International Congregational Council have taken decisive steps towards merging in 1970. The merger of two confessional organizations is, so far as we are aware, without precedent in modern times. This one is therefore a matter of exceptional interest.

"Over ten years of prayerful and harmonious discussions between the International Congregational Council and the World Alliance of Reformed

Churches", wrote General Secretary Marcel Pradervand of the W.A.R.C., "have taken place on the questions of closer relations between the two world families of churches". Conversations were officially approved on both sides by repeated actions as the discussions moved forward step by step towards merger. Official visitors or fraternal delegates were present at meetings of both organizations since 1958. Staff and officers have also kept in regular contact. A joint committee was formed in 1964 to prepare and present principles and proposals concerning relations between the two bodies.

A factor which contributed substantially towards union between the World Alliance and the I.C.C. was the fact that four of the twenty-one members of the I.C.C. are also members of the W.A.R.C. These are the United Churches of Canada, Jamaica and Grand Cayman, the United States, and Zambia. The I.C.C. is also "in fellowship" with four other United Churches which are members of the alliance. They are the Church of Christ in China, the United Church of North India, the United Church in Japan, and the United Church of Christ in the Philippines. In addition, Congregational and Presbyterian Churches are looking forward to union between themselves in Australia, New Zealand, and Great Britain, Union negotiations have begun in South Africa, Scotland and the Netherlands. The I.C.C. has member Churches in Argentina, Brazil, Czechoslovakia, Finland, Guyana, Madagascar, Samoa, South Africa, and Sweden. In many of these places ties exist or are being created with one or another of the 101 member Churches of the Alliance, which has twenty-eight members in Africa, twenty in Asia, three in Australia, twenty-eight in Europe, twelve in Latin America, and ten in North America.

A statement of "Principles", from which the factual data above has been taken, was circulated among I.C.C. and W.A.R.C. members. It also says:

> Both organizations have consistently gone on record in recognition and support of United Churches. Nearly all of their members are presently engaged in some form of church union negotiation or exploration which are in position to do so, in many instances involving the relations with churches belonging to traditions not normally associated with the names Congregational, Presbyterian or Reformed. In each case the intention has been to enter into a fuller relation with other Christian brethren, within one church, Catholic and Reformed. Accordingly, in principle the name "Reformed" by which these churches express their desire to be "continually reformed according to the Word of God" is applicable to any church which holds that same desire. Likewise, the name "Catholic" they would also claim for themselves, as representing their acknowledgement of Christ's presence even among the diverse fragments of a divided church, their identification with all the struggles of the Church and with its whole sanctified life throughout human history, and their will to live under and to pray for that fullness of community which Christ alone can bring, by the Witness of the Gospel and the power of the Holy Spirit.

Another ground for union is found in the fact that sixty-one of the Alliance's 101 members and seventeen of the I.C.C.'s twenty-one members are members of the World Council of Churches. The Principles express the desire of both families of Churches "to do nothing separately which can be done in co-operation and to enter as fully as facilities allow into its (the W.C.C.'s) programme, especially in the area of studies. We do not wish to administer Inter-Church Aid or other similar funds, but prefer to support aid programmes of the World Council of Churches, providing special counsel on the situation of minority churches." The Principles and proposals for union were adopted by the executive committees of the two organizations in 1966.

The draft constitution which is proposed for adoption in 1970 states that "the Church is founded solely upon Jesus Christ as Lord and . . . is one Body in the communion of the Holy Spirit under the headship of the one Lord, Jesus Christ". After outlining the histories of the two organizations, the constitution declares that they are joined into one organization under the name "The World Alliance of Reformed Churches (Presbyterian and Congregational)" and in shorter form: "The World Alliance of Reformed Churches".

It is significant that the W.A.R.C./I.C.C. merger will be open-ended, assuming that the constitution is adopted as proposed. Article II on membership, says that

> Any church which accepts Jesus Christ as Lord and Saviour, which holds the Scriptures of the Old and New Testaments to be the supreme authority in matters of faith and life; acknowledges the need for the continuing reformation of the Church catholic; whose position in faith and evangelism is in general agreement with that of the historic Reformed confessions, recognizing that the Reformed tradition is a biblical, evangelical and doctrinal ethos, rather than a narrow and exclusive definition of faith and order, shall be eligible for admission to the Alliance.

Article II concludes:

> United Churches which share this understanding of the nature and calling of the Church shall be eligible for admission. Membership in the Alliance does not restrict the relationship of any Church with other Churches or with other inter-Church bodies.

The ecumenical purpose which is exemplified in the merger and is implicit in the histories of the merged confessional bodies will be continued under the new World Alliance of Reformed Churches. Article III, section 9 of the proposed constitution states that a purpose of the Alliance shall be

> to facilitate the contribution to the ecumenical movement of the experiences and insights which the churches within the Reformed family have been given in their history, and to share with churches of other traditions within that movement, and particularly in the World Council of Churches, in the discovery of forms of church life and practice which will enable the people of God more fully to understand and express together God's will for his people.

The Alliance is to meet in General Council ordinarily once in five years. In the interval an executive committee serves in its stead, having full powers to speak and act for the Alliance in conformity with its constitution.

Member bodies of the W.A.R.C. and I.C.C. were asked to report their actions, favourable or unfavourable, on the proposals for merger by 30 June 1968. Officials of both families of Churches met at Uppsala at the time of the

Fourth Assembly of the World Council of Churches to receive the actions of the Churches, to summarize them, and to announce the result. Since the result is favourable, the Twentieth General Council of the World Alliance of Reformed Churches will become the Uniting Council.

Self-Evaluation of Confessional Families

After ten years of annual meetings, the secretaries of world confessional families produced a document at their 1967 meeting which will probably stand for some time as a statement of "the Place of World Confessional Families in the Ecumenical Movement". We quoted their definition for the term at the beginning of this chapter. Their statement explained that members of some families have a strong consciousness of belonging together as a universal fellowship, but others are hardly aware of any such bond. Some made the visible structure of their universal fellowship a part of their ecclesiology, while others think of structure as a "mere organizational convenience". Differences are explained in part by historical origins, in part by teachings about the nature of the Church, in part by relations with other Churches. Even the term confessional is misleading, says the statement, for not all families are bound together mainly by their "confession of faith". Not all depend upon organization to furnish the bond between Churches. "World Communion" is acceptable to some "because it points to the Eucharist as a bond of unity and even families which have not yet realized full communion are earnestly seeking to establish it as soon as possible". So families, which maintain unity in spite of diversity, seems to be the best term.

The 1967 statement recognized that world families are an historical fact and are "at present a necessity". Each Church has to give some expression to its universal character; but on the world scale this still adds up to division. So there is a necessary connection between world families and the World Council of Churches. Both are elements in the ecumenical movement. The W.C.C. reminds the world families of their limits and roles in the ecumenical movement. It gives them a place "to meet and co-operate" and thus to realize a fuller universality than any single world family will ever be able to realize. The world families remind the W.C.C. "that there is a true universality only if it is rooted in truth". Hence the W.C.C. and the families are interdependent.

Recognition of this interdependence, says the 1967 statement, leads to four conclusions. One is the need for contacts between the W.C.C. and the families and between the families themselves; if the ecumenical movement is to be furthered, these contacts should be co-ordinated. Second, there is need for greater exchange of information and co-ordination of studies. W.C.C. studies are mainly directed towards furthering the ecumenical task; world family studies "aim at clarifying the contribution to the ecumenical movement of churches within one tradition". The two kinds of studies should be related, for both are concerned with the theological problem of the catholicity of the Church and its practical results. The world families therefore welcome the invitation of the Secretariat of Faith and Order to appoint liaison officers for this purpose.

Third, more use should be made of the possibilities for practical co-operation between world families. These include the field of inter-Church aid, where W.C.C./L.W.F. co-operation is already widespread, and joint consultation and action for mission. Also in the Church's witness in international affairs an extension of the co-operation which already exists would be practical and much more effective. The revised constitution of the C.C.I.A. makes this possible. Finally, the multiplying problems of religious liberty in many countries invite closer W.C.C./World Families co-operation and co-ordination.

The statement ended with a paragraph which shows as clearly as anything that has been said by an ecumenical body in the direction in which the Churches are being moved:

> The number of churches engaged in union negotiations is rising. World Families whose member churches are committed to union require further conversations about the problems arising from this commitment. Everything possible should be done by the Confessional Families together, and by the Confessional Families and the World Council of Churches to encourage the realization of further unity among the churches.

Confessional Family Organizations

Brief descriptions of eleven of the world confessional family organizations follow. Each of these is entitled to appoint advisers to the Central Committee and to the Assemblies of the World Council of Churches. Each is invited to send representatives of the annual meetings of World Confessional families at Geneva and usually does so. In addition, the Ecumenical Patriarchate of Constantinople, the Patriarchate of Moscow, the Standing Committee of the Oriental Orthodox Churches, and the Pentecostal World Conference are entitled to appoint W.C.C. advisers and to be represented at annual meetings of the Confessional families at Geneva. Descriptions of the Orthodox Churches appear in Chapter 11 of this book.

The Anglican Communion

The Anglican communion consists of nineteen independent, autonomous, national, and regional churches, having a total membership of forty million. (See World Christian Handbook.) Its central office in London, established as recently as 1963, is directed in 1968 by Bishop Ralph Stanley Dean, who is secretary of "the Advisory Council on Missionary Strategy". The name Anglican does not appear in the title, although Bishop Dean is in fact also executive officer of the Anglican Communion and secretary to the Lambeth Conference, which meets each decade. All but one of the nineteen Churches are members of the World Council of Churches. In pointing out that "the Anglican is not a confessional body in the ordinary sense of the term" and that Anglican Churches are independent and autonomous, Bishop Dean notes:

> They are bound together chiefly by the fact that each is in communion with the See of Canterbury and with each other. There is no specifically Anglican Confession of Faith; there is no central authoritative structure; there is no

longer even one book of Common Prayer, for at least eight different rites now obtain, though all partake of a common shape of the liturgy. The Anglican Communion holds to the Holy Scriptures, the Catholic creeds of the undivided church, the Dominical Sacraments and the threefold order of bishops, priests and deacons.

The Advisory Council on Missionary Strategy operates under the terms of a document called *Mutual Responsibility and Interdependence in the Body of Christ*. While it was criticized at first as a step toward pan-Anglicanism, criticisms have abated as it is seen to be a channel of communication within the Anglican Communion and with the Church of Christ as a whole. In the last twenty years, the five new indigenous national Churches which have emerged within the Anglican Communion have all become constituent members of the World Council of Churches. Since Anglican provinces and dioceses in many parts of the world are included in plans for united Churches in their area, the Advisory Council on Missionary Strategy recommends that where such a scheme for church unity is approved by the province concerned, "the contribution brought to it by Anglicans should be in every way as whole-hearted and complete as possible". The council says these contributions should include capital and development funds and that financial or personal support from outside the area "should not be lessened because of the participation of the church in unity Schemes". Unity conversations and negotiations in various stages and in many countries now include the Consultation on Church Union in America, dialogues with Orthodox and Roman Catholics, official visits between the Archbishop of Canterbury and their highest officials, and in some cases official commissions for continuing study.

The Baptist World Alliance

The Baptist World Alliance is a voluntary association between Baptists in seventy-eight unions or conventions of Churches having a total membership in 1968 of 25,914,000. An additional three million Baptists belong to Churches which are not members of the Alliance. The Alliance has headquarters in London and in Washington. It holds congresses every five years and publishes a monthly journal, "The Baptist World". Dr Josef Nordenhaug, its executive secretary, lives in Washington. Eleven of the seventy-eight member denominations are members of the World Council of Churches. The B.W.A. exists to increase fellowship and co-operation between Baptist Churches. It is specifically enjoined against interfering with the independence of member Churches or the administrative functions of existing organizations.

A 144-person executive committee governs the B.W.A. between Congresses. Each member body elects at least one representative. About two-thirds of the budget of the Baptist World Alliance comes from the ten-million member Southern Baptist Convention (U.S.A.) whose only official ecumenical relationship on a membership basis is with the B.W.A. The B.W.A. was not represented by observers at the Second Vatican Council, but did authorize its general secretary to send observers to the meeting in Rome on the Lay Apostolate in 1967. The B.W.A. has a relief department; but several of its member Churches contribute to human need through the Inter-Church Aid department of the W.C.C. and through Church World Service in the U.S.A. Regional sub-organizations of the B.W.A. exist in North America, where nine-tenths of all Baptists live, and in Europe. The B.W.A. has study commissions working on Baptist doctrine, mission and evangelism, religious liberty and human rights, Christian teaching and training, and co-operative Christianity. The last of these commissions was authorized in 1967.

Friends World Committee for Consultation

Forty-six "Yearly Meetings" of the Society of Friends form the Friends World Committee for Consultation, which has an office in Birmingham, England. It was created in 1937, at a world conference in the U.S.A. The first such world conference was held in London in 1920. A few Yearly Meetings are not represented in F.W.C.C., being mainly those in the Evangelical Friends Alliance. About 200,000 persons form the membership of the Society of Friends.

The F.W.C.C. is not in any sense a controlling body. It seeks to encourage consultation and help Friends understand the world-wide character of the Society, to strengthen the spiritual life within the Society, to keep under review the Quaker contribution in world affairs, and "to promote understanding between Friends of all countries and members of other branches of the Christian Church and with members of other religious faiths". The World Committee sent observers to the Second Vatican Council, to the Prague Christian Peace Conference, and it sends representatives to participate in the International Association for Liberal Christianity and Religious Freedom.

The Friends United Meeting and the Friends General Conference, both of the U.S.A., were among the 147 Churches which constituted the World Council of Churches in 1948. They include over half the total membership of the Society of Friends in the world. Yearly Meetings hold membership in the National Councils of Churches in the United States, Canada, the Netherlands, Ireland, Australia, New Zealand, Madagascar, Pemba, and Rhodesia. Mrs Blanche Shaffer is general secretary of the F.W.C.C.

The International Congregational Council

The International Congregational Council was founded in London in 1891 as an *ad hoc* gathering without permanent organization. It was reorganized in 1949 as a constitutional body with staff. It holds assemblies every four or five years. It does not regard itself as a confessional body and plans to merge with the World Alliance of Reformed Churches in 1970. Its head offices are in London. Dr Ralph R. G. Calder is its executive secretary.

In 1966, when it held its tenth assembly, representatives of seventeen constituent member Churches met at Swansea, United Kingdom. The largest Congregational Church, having about 1,250,000 members, entered the United Church of Christ, U.S.A. in 1957, but this did not invalidate its tie to the I.C.C., which has several United Churches in its membership. In fact, about seventy-five per cent of members of Churches in the I.C.C. belong to United Churches. Other Churches are considering mergers.

From its earliest meeting the I.C.C. had an ecumenical purpose, inviting discussion on Congregationalism's relationship with the "Church Catholic". The 1966 Assembly "agreed without dissent" to approve the proposed merger of the I.C.C. with the World Alliance of Reformed Churches. "At the same time", Dr Calder wrote, "there remains a strong conviction among many that certain Congregational (though not denominational) convictions as to the liberty of the Christian man, and as to the dangers of ecclesiastical uniformity and rigidity and particularly as to the essential wrongness of clericalism, call for some form of continued witness, whether it calls itself Congregational or not."

The Lutheran World Federation

The largest and one of the most distinctively "Confessional" bodies is the Lutheran World Federation, which has in its membership a large share of the 72,500,000 Lutherans in the world. It is about a year older than the World Council of Churches, with which it shares the Ecumenical Centre in Geneva. Its total number of employees is around 1,000. In Geneva it has a staff of over sixty persons, of whom twenty-one are executives. The L.W.F. general secretary is Mr Andre Appel. The Federation was constituted in 1947; it succeeded a more loosely knit consultative organization called the Lutheran World Convention, which held its first world meeting in 1923. The *Lutheran World*, which the L.W.F. publishes quarterly, has a circulation of 4,000. It takes a leading part in the discussion of relations between confessionalism and the ecumenical movement. Lutheran world assemblies are held at six-year intervals.

The Lutheran World Federation is a "free association of Lutheran churches". According to its constitution,

> It shall not exercise churchly functions on its own authority, nor shall it have power to legislate for the churches belonging to it or to limit the autonomy of any member church.

Its functions are:

> to further a united witness before the world to the gospel of Jesus Christ as the power of God for salvation; cultivate unity of faith and confession among the Lutheran Churches of the world; develop fellowship and co-operation in study among Lutherans; foster Lutheran interest in, concern for, and participation in, ecumenical movements; support Lutheran Churches and groups as they endeavour to meet the spiritual needs of other Lutheran Churches and groups to help meet physical needs.

It can take action on behalf of one or more member Churches in such matters as they commit to it.

The L.W.F. service for refugees has since 1947 provided new homelands for over 100,000 refugees. The World Service division of L.W.F. handles relief commodities and assistance to the value of $10 million per year; its other budgets total around $3 million. In its earliest years most of its money came from the United States; now gifts from Germany and Sweden exceed those from the U.S.A. The L.W.F. owns and operates the Radio Voice of the Gospel, a powerful station costing $1.5 million located in Ethiopia, which makes half of its broadcast time available to Churches affiliated with the W.C.C. The L.W.F. also established the Lutheran Foundation for Inter-Confessional Research at Strasbourg, France, which carries on study in basic theological problems, currently those concerned with Roman Catholic/ Protestant questions.

Its world missions department grew out of the needs of "orphaned missions" during the Second World War and now serves Churches and missions in Asia and Africa. A final area of work is the L.W.F. Community Development Liaison and Validation service. It serves as a link between Lutheran Churches and operating projects of general welfare or economic development and fund-raising agencies with resources to put into such activities. Co-operation between the W.C.C. and the L.W.F. is continuous and many-sided. Carl H. Mau, Jr, associate general secretary of the L.W.F., says of the two organizations: "Their continued close coexistence to the present day has undoubtedly contributed greatly to the influence that each has had on the other and to the mutual understanding of their respective purposes that exists between them, particularly on the staff level."

The late Franklin Clark Fry, then President of the L.W.F., said at the opening of its Fourth Assembly:

> We in Helsinki are here consciously as a part of the Church of God. We make no pretence to be the whole of it. We would do violence both to our fathers and to ourselves, and of course also to the truth, if we were to do so, for our fathers designed the noble expositions of the Word of God to which we hold, not as partisan documents, but as ecumenical confessions. As their sons we are prepared in spirit to reach out to brethren everywhere in a search for the fuller oneness of all who call Christ Lord in the midst of a hostile world, on the basis of a common adherence to him who is and who teaches the truth.[1]

Old Catholic Churches

Old Catholic Churches of Austria, Germany, the Netherlands, Switzerland, the Polish-Catholic Church in Poland, and the Polish National Catholic Church in America are members of the World Council of Churches. The Old Catholic Churches in Czechoslovakia and Yugoslavia are not yet members. Old Catholic Churches are self-governing national Churches but one in the faith, deriving their origins from Latin Christendom. The International Conferences of the Old Catholic Bishops, founded in 1889 as the Union of Utrecht, expressed their unity. The first originated in Holland in 1723, when the Chapter of Utrecht maintained its ancient right to elect the Archbishop of Utrecht, against the opposition of Rome. The term "Old Catholic" was adopted to mean original Catholicism. The Old Catholic Churches of Germany, Switzerland, and Austria were formed in 1870 in consequence of their protest against the dogmas of the First Vatican Council concerning papal supremacy and papal infallibility. The Polish National Catholic Church in America was constituted between 1897 and 1907; the Churches in Czechoslovakia, Poland, and Yugoslavia after the First World War. Old

---

[1] *Proceedings of the Fourth Assembly of the Lutheran World Federation* (Helsinki, 30 July to 11 August 1963), p. 37. Published by the Lutheran World Federation, Geneva.

Catholic Churches are found in eight countries and have a total of around 500,000 members. They have missions in France and Italy.

On 7 November 1966 Cardinal Alfrink of the Roman Catholic Church, at a public ceremony in the Old Catholic cathedral in Utrecht, announced that the Roman Catholic Church renounced the requirement that the Old Catholic Church accept papal condemnations of the Old Catholic Church concerning Jansenism, especially the papal statements issued in 1665 and 1713. Since Cardinal Alfrink's pronouncement at Utrecht, official dialogues between the Old Catholic Churches and the Roman Catholic Church have begun in Holland, Germany, Austria, and Switzerland. Consistent with their inter-communion with the Anglican Communion, the Old Catholic Churches support an Anglican mission in South Africa. They are studying the union discussions between the Anglican and Methodist Churches. Also, the dialogue between Old Catholic and Orthodox Churches has taken on new vigour. In Switzerland they shared in the preparation of a document on mixed marriages, published by the Federation of Swiss Protestant Churches and the Roman Catholic Bishop's Conference. In 1965 the Old Catholic Churches extended their intercommunion with the Anglicans to the Episcopal Reformed Church of Spain, the Lusitanian Church (Portugal), and the Independent Church of the Philippines.

The Salvation Army

So far as the ecumenical movement is concerned, the Salvation Army is regarded as a Church, so it is represented in meetings of the World Confessional Bodies. It works in seventy countries and has 18,563 officers (or ministers) who preach the gospel in 146 languages through 16,190 preaching stations. It publishes 129 periodicals with a circulation of over two million. The Army conducts social service programmes through 2,000 social centres, sixty-nine hospitals, and over 800 day schools. Its primary aim is "to proclaim the Gospel of the Lord Jesus Christ to men, women and young people untouched or uninfluenced by the Gospel and to develop its membership into a fighting force of God".[1]

The headquarters of the Salvation Army is in London, where its work began in 1865. The General of the Army is elected by a high council consisting of Salvation Army leaders from all over the world. World leaders meet at agreed intervals to review work and to plan further advance. Relationships between the Army and the historic Churches are marked by free and friendly co-operation. It is a long-established rule with the Army not to proselytize and not to criticize the doctrine, worship, or organization of Churches. The Salvation Army is a full member of the World Council of Churches and has been since its beginning. Commissioner F. A. Evans says:

> There has been no change in the relationship of the Salvation Army with the W.C.C. during the last twenty years except a growing awareness of the usefulness of the W.C.C. and a greater desire to enter into fraternal relationship with all members.

[1] Figures from *The Salvation Army Year Book, 1967*. Published by Salvation Publishing and Supplies Ltd, London W.C.1.

Mennonite World Conference

Organized in 1925, the Mennonite World Conference is generally represented in the meeting of confessional organizations in Geneva. The Mennonites of the Netherlands are members of the World Council of Churches. Several North American Mennonite Conferences are members of the National Association of Evangelicals. The number of Mennonites in the world is estimated to be 400,000.

In the forty-two years between the first and the eighth world conferences, the Mennonites set up a General Council, which normally meets annually. Its executive secretary, Cornelius J. Dyck, is a full-time faculty member of the Mennonite Biblical Seminary. The office of the council is now located in Elkhart, Indiana, but is "passed around as the brotherhood sees fit". In addition, there is a Mennonite Central Committee, which was organized in 1920 as a relief and service agency. Its headquarters are in Akron, Ohio. It carries on humanitarian work in Vietnam, India, Africa, Latin America, and elsewhere. Co-operation in relief and humanitarian work has allayed Mennonite fear of "entangling alliances", so that Professor Dyck says:

> There seems to have emerged a new readiness on the part of Mennonites to dialogue with any and all who are willing and to leave the fruit of such encounter to future developments.

World Alliance of Reformed Churches

The oldest of the organized confessional families came into existence in 1875 as the "Alliance of Reformed Churches Throughout the World Holding the Presbyterian System". Its first assembly was held in Edinburgh in 1877. Present were delegates representing forty-one Churches in fourteen countries. Now the Alliance serves 109 churches of the Reformed Church Family in seventy countries, having a total membership of around 55 million. Renamed the World Alliance of Reformed Churches, its budget is less than $100,000. Its staff numbers seven. Its offices were moved from Edinburgh to Geneva in 1948 and are now in the Ecumenical Centre. Its general secretary is Marcel Pradervand.

The Alliance holds a world meeting every five or six years. An area council meets in Europe about as often; the North American area council meets annually. Fully ninety-five per cent of all Reformed and Presbyterian Churches hold membership in the Alliance, and sixty-two of the 109 member Churches of the W.A.R.C. are also members of the World Council of Churches. They have furnished a considerable share of the W.C.C. leadership. In 1951 the W.A.R.C. executive committee declared:

> The Reformed tradition in post-Reformation Christianity is thus by nature ecumenical, that is to say, it is committed to the pursuit of Christian unity upon the basis of loyal commitment to the essential verities in the Christian faith.

In its meeting held in 1949, the Executive Committee of the Alliance set forth its programme as (*a*) support for Inter-Church Aid as administered by the World Council of Churches, (*b*) development of contacts between

Churches and ecumenical organizations, and (c) engagement in common study. In 1954 the General Council of the Alliance reaffirmed the position previously taken concerning Inter-Church Aid, saying that the Alliance "is not organized for the administration of inter-church aid and does not propose so to organize because of the conviction of many of our churches that the giving and receiving of aid has implications beyond our Reformed family". It was through the initiative of the Alliance that representatives of confessional families first began to hold meetings in 1957. The Alliance persistently tries to act as an intermediary between the ecumenical movement and those Reformed Churches which remain outside it. The World Alliance and the International Congregational Council plan to merge in 1970.

World Convention of the Churches of Christ (Disciples)

The World Convention of the Churches of Christ (Disciples) was begun in 1930 in the United States, where about nine-tenths of the two million members of Churches belonging to the Convention live. Its office is in New York, although the denominational offices are in Indianapolis. The Reverend L. V. Kirkpatrick is its executive secretary. Its principal activity is to hold a world convention at five-year intervals. Each convention elects an executive committee to which the executive secretary is responsible. In the intervals between conventions work is carried on through four committees: study, finance, programme, and inter-faith relations.

The preamble to the constitution of the World Convention says: "The World Convention of Churches of Christ (Disciples) exists in order to show more fully the essential oneness of the churches in the Lord Jesus Christ". Other purposes named are to "impart inspiration", to "cultivate fellowship", and to "promote unity". The executive says that "the World Convention considers its ecumenical responsibilities include helping to maintain ecumenical dialogue within the world family of Churches of Christ and Disciples of Christ itself". This is not easy, as the following paragraph will suggest:

The Christian Church, Disciples of Christ, is by far the largest denomination of this "confessional family", assuming that this term applies. It is a member of the World and National Councils of Churches and of the Consultation on Church Union. Since 1961 conversations looking toward church union have been carried on under the auspices of the Consultation. Considerable progress has been made. So the preoccupations of "co-operative" Disciples with union and the confessional preoccupations of Churches which think ecumenically only in denominational terms tend to diverge. These divergencies widen as the movements for and against union grow. What will be the role of the World Convention in the event its largest constituent denomination enters into a United Church does not yet appear.

The World Methodist Council

Twenty Methodist denominations having Churches in eighty-six countries make up the association known as the World Methodist Council. It has offices in London and Lake Junaluska, North Carolina and has voted to set up an office in Geneva. The Handbook of Information of the World Methodist Council says that there are in the world 18,824,352 Methodists, of whom over 14 million are in North America.[1]

The World Methodist Council was formed in 1951. It succeeded a series of Methodist ecumenical conferences, held at intervals beginning in 1881. When the W.M.C. was formed, the launching conference adopted a message to the Methodists of the world which said, *inter alia,*

> We wish to affirm explicitly that, far from being in rivalry with the World Council of Churches, or wishing to isolate ourselves from the movement toward the reunion of the churches, our purpose in promoting the closer unity of Methodism is that this may make a stronger contribution to the larger unity of Christ's Church throughout the world.

The W.M.C. holds conferences at intervals of several years, the last being held in London in 1966. The 1961 revision of its constitution set as the first purpose "to deepen the fellowship of the Methodist people . . .". The second was "to foster Methodist participation in the ecumenical movement and to promote the unity of Methodist witness and service in that movement". The third was "to advance unity of theological and moral standards in the Methodist churches of the world". The principal activity under this head is the Oxford Theological Institute, held for ten days every two or three years, in which around 100 Methodists participate. The W.M.C. also has a committee which studies all union proposals which involve Methodists and offers advice when requested. The organization also arranges the exchange of preachers.

The Methodist Church in the United States (which became the United Methodist Church in 1968) has included in its organization congregations, conferences, and episcopal areas in many countries. The 1968 general conference, in which the Methodist and the Evangelical United Brethren Churches became the United Methodist Church, granted twenty-eight annual conferences in fourteen countries permission to become autonomous bodies or to merge with other Churches. Since the United Methodist Church itself is a member of the Consultation on Church Union in the U.S.A. and the Methodist Church in Great Britain is considering reunion with the Church of England, it is safe to predict that the World Methodist Structure Congress, which is to be held before or during 1972, will not suffer for lack of business to discuss. Where the World Methodist Council will emerge from this discussion it is impossible to predict.

Since many confessional families confront similar problems, it seems likely that discussions between world confessional families will sharply increase in vigour and relevance in the near future.

---

[1] *World Methodist Council Handbook of Information, 1966–1971.* Published by the secretariat, W.M.C., Lake Junaluska, N.C., U.S.A.).

6
Faith and Order 1948–1968

MEREDITH B. HANDSPICKER

F

Introduction

> St Paul strikes sectarianism of all ages between the eyes by calling divisions "carnal" ... Division in the eyes of this intense man is fatal to the life of the church.[1]

Bishop Charles Brent was also "an intense man". Deeply moved by the great World Missionary Conference in Edinburgh in 1910, he was instrumental in having his Church, the Protestant Episcopal Church in the U.S.A., issue a call later that year which invited "all Christian bodies throughout the world which accept our Lord Jesus Christ as God and Saviour" to send delegates to a world conference to discuss questions "pertaining to the Faith and Order of the Church of Christ".[2] Divisions and divisiveness mark the life of the Church of Christ. Such division mars the effectiveness of the Church, and strikes at the very nature of the Church, its unity. "God calls man to unity—his ideal. Man calls to God for unity—his need."[3] Divided, the Church gets in its own way.

"The Faith and Order movement at its best is solely concerned with the truth."[4] Tissington Tatlow closes his history of Faith and Order up to 1948 with these words. The unity which the movement seeks is not obtained through ecclesiastical joinery, nor by compromise in matters of faith. Woven together in the complex motivation which gives life to the movement are a number of convictions: first, that the Church is intended by its Lord to be one; second, that only a truly united Church can function effectively in fulfilling its mission; third, that only in a Church which is one can the fullness of Christian truth be discerned.

In Lausanne Bishop Brent took as his text John 17. 20–3: "That they may be one ... that the world may believe". This has been a favourite text in the ecumenical movement; but the conviction that unity is of the essence of the Church rests not on this one text, but on the whole tenor of the apostolic writings.

In the British Faith and Order Conference in 1964, the theme of the meeting was "One Church, Renewed for Mission". The then chairman of the Faith and Order Working Committee, Dr Oliver Tomkins, the Bishop of Bristol, presided. In his remarks to the conference Bishop Tomkins noted that the missionary orientation of Faith and Order sought to insure that in coming into union we do not merely continue to follow old patterns, but discern the shape of the Church God demands of us today.

The concern for truth is manifest in the commission given to negotiators in Australia from the Congregational, Methodist, and Presbyterian Churches: to discover not "how we can reduce the different traditions to a common

---

[1] Bishop Charles Brent, "The Call to Unity", Lausanne, p. 6.

[2] Ibid., p. vii. For the history of Faith and Order prior to 1948 the reader is referred to the proceedings of both the Lausanne Conference and the Edinburgh Conference, the numbered papers in the "Old Series", Rouse and Neill, *A History of the Ecumenical Movement*, pp. 405ff, and relevant sections of Vischer, *A Documentary History of the Faith and Order Movement*.

[3] Ibid., p. 7.   [4] Rouse and Neill, op. cit., p. 441.

factor", but rather to seek the fullness of "what we must confess together today as the Faith of the Church".[1]

How have these motivations led to action? In what ways has the Faith and Order movement sought to bring about the unity of the Church, its more effective missionary thrust, and its growth into the fullness of Christian truth? Its work has been guided by two principles, first articulated in the constitution accepted in 1948: to draw the Churches out of isolation into conference, and to leave to the Churches all initiatives towards reunion with one another.[2]

As a Commission of the World Council, Faith and Order has kept its traditional function of "calling the churches out of isolation into conference". Membership in the Commission is not tied to membership in the World Council, nor is invitation to World Conferences on Faith and Order. Thus at the theological heart of the Council is a Commission now having among its membership not only representatives of conservative Protestant Churches and Pentecostal groups who do not feel able to join the Council, but Roman Catholic representatives as well. This *can* insure that the Council does not itself develop a provincial outlook which becomes that of just one more ecclesiastical in-group. Later in this chapter we shall examine in detail the kinds of study and activities by which Faith and Order has sought to deepen understanding among the Churches and open up possibilities for greater unity.

But while Faith and Order exists to serve church unity, the second principle in its constitution states that only the Churches themselves are competent to initiate actual negotiations for unity. Such initiatives have been going on for a long while, and the results have been recorded in surveys of union negotiations.[3] While initiative continues to remain with the Churches, we shall see how Faith and Order has become more and more involved in the movement towards union.

One way to examine the growth of a movement would be to trace its development chronologically: What did it do from one important conference to another? Those who wish to trace the history of Faith and Order in this manner can be aided by the summary histories prepared for each Assembly of the World Council.[4] Such a study can well supplement the approach taken in this chapter, which will be to examine the various studies undertaken by the Faith and Order Commission in order to discover what development has occurred, and what consensus has been reached, in each area of concern. This will provide a record of how Faith and Order has sought to be true to its vocation to seek the truth.

But truth is never sought abstractly. The search is both pragmatic and

---

[1] *Ecumenical Review*, vol. xviii, (July 1966), p. 362.

[2] FO, no. 1, p. 68. Compare FO, no. 50, p. 169 for the current wording.

[3] The first such was published by H. Paul Dougless, *A Decade of Objective Progress in Church Unity: 1927–1936.* New York 1937. It was followed by a survey made by Stephen Neill, *Towards Church Union: 1937–1952.* London 1952. Since then biennial surveys have been prepared by the Faith and Order Secretariat and published in the *Ecumenical Review*, April 1954, October 1955, April 1957, January 1960, April 1962, July 1964, and July 1966.

[4] *The First Six Years: 1948–1954.* Geneva 1964. *Evanston to New Delhi: 1954–1961.* Geneva 1961. *New Delhi to Uppsala: 1961–1968.* Geneva 1968.

personal. In this case the search is for the sake of church unity; we shall therefore turn after a survey of the studies to an examination of Faith and Order in relation to the movement for church union. The search is carried out by persons; we shall in closing discuss the people of Faith and Order, those individuals and their organizational means of co-operation whereby the work of Faith and Order has been carried forward.

Faith and Order Studies

The Nature of Unity

Competing claims and counter-claims compound confusion. The missionary task of the Church and its claim to preach the truth are impeded by disunity and divisiveness. But in our search together for unity, what is the nature of the goal which we are seeking? At the beginning of Faith and Order work, there was but a listing of differing viewpoints concerning the nature of unity.[1] By 1937 the delegates to Edinburgh had a somewhat clearer vision of the goal, which is to "realize the idea of the Church as one living body, worshipping and serving God in Christ".[2] This would involve both an inner spiritual unity and that outward unity "which expresses itself in mutual recognition, co-operative action, and corporate or institutional unity".[3]

At Amsterdam the basis for the search for outward unity was articulated: "God has *given* to His people in Jesus Christ a unity which is His creation and not our achievement".[4] The authors of this statement, coming from the section on "The Universal Church in God's Design", included some of the outstanding theological figures of the day: Karl Barth, Edmund Schlink, K. E. Skydsgaard, George Florovsky, and Douglas Horton—the latter four all to be exceptionally active in subsequent Faith and Order work. They wrought well, for this notion of the givenness of our unity undergirded all subsequent Faith and Order discussion of the nature of the unity we seek. Broad lines were indicated concerning the latter by the Amsterdam section on "The Church's Witness to God's Design"; the Churches were called to "move forward, as God guides them, to further unity in faith, in fellowship, at the table of the Lord, and in united proclamation of the word of life".[5]

The theme of "outward" unity which was introduced at Edinburgh was further developed at the Third World Conference in Lund, 1952. "We are agreed that there are not two churches, one visible and the other invisible, but one Church which must find visible expression on earth."[6] While the delegates differed on whether certain doctrinal, sacramental, and ministerial forms are of the essence of the Church, they looked forward to a time when all Christians could have unrestricted communion in sacrament and fellowship with each other.

Insistence on the visibility of unity was at variance with another World Council document on "The Church, the Churches and the World Council of Churches", adopted by the Central Committee at Toronto in 1950. There it

---

[1] Lausanne, pp. 465ff.   [2] Edinburgh, p. 250.   [3] Ibid., p. 259.
[4] Amsterdam, p. 51 (italics inserted).   [5] Ibid., p. 69.   [6] Lund, p. 33.

was clearly stated that "membership in the World Council does not imply the acceptance of a specific doctrine concerning the nature of church unity".[1] Among the various options listed in the statement was one which "held that visible unity is inessential or even undesirable."[2] The main point of this earlier statement was the insistence that no doctrine concerning church unity was a prerequisite for membership in the Council. But to insist that for this reason no growth in consensus among the members could be achieved would be to cut at the very heart of the ecumenical movement and to rest satisfied with the *status quo*. Lund was one more step in moving away from the *status quo*. It indicated a growing agreement on the "notes of unity"—one of these was to be "visibility".

At the Evanston Assembly in 1954 the givenness of our unity was assumed, as was our task to manifest it "not for the sake of the Church as an historical society, but for the sake of the world". "The being and unity of the Church belong to Christ and therefore to His mission."[3] The Assembly also underscored the dynamic inherent in the ecumenical movement—its opposition to the *status quo*. Reaffirming the Amsterdam covenant to "stay together", the Assembly stated, "But beyond that, as the Holy Spirit may guide us, we intend to unite."[4] If this were to be the intention, a still clearer vision of the goal was necessary.

Such a situation challenged Faith and Order to rethink its own role in the ecumenical movement. In 1957 a committee, chaired by Dr Oliver Tomkins, was constituted to study "The Future of Faith and Order",[5] and it brought in its interim report the next year. While it agreed that no one definition of unity can be demanded as a condition of membership in the Council, it nevertheless underscored the task of Faith and Order "to stand for the unity of the Church as the will of God, and for a ceaseless effort to know what obedience to that will means concretely."[6] In that same year, 1958, Bishop Lesslie Newbigin, a member of the committee, published a book in which he developed his own vision of unity. In part he said,

> For myself I do not believe that we can be content with anything less than a form of unity which enables all who confess Christ as Lord to be recognizably one family in each place and all places, united in the visible bonds of word, sacrament, ministry and congregational fellowship, and in the invisible bond which the Spirit Himself creates through these means, one family offering to all men everywhere the secret of reconciliation with God the Father.[7]

In 1959 Bishop Newbigin presented the Working Committee with a paper detailing his views of the nature of "churchly unity".[8] After revision this was added to the beginning of the report on the Future of Faith and Order which was then submitted to the Central Committee of the World Council meeting in Rhodes that year, further revised by the Commission in 1960, and this introductory section sent on for consideration by the section on Unity at the

---

[1] Vischer, op. cit., p. 171.   [2] Loc. cit.   [3] Evanston, p. 85.
[4] Ibid., p. 90.   [5] FO, no. 25, p. 28.   [6] FO, no. 26, p. 47.
[7] Lesslie Newbigin, *One Body, One Gospel, One World* (London 1958), p. 56.
[8] FO, no. 27, p. 2.

Assembly in New Delhi, 1961.[1] This led to the now-famous New Delhi Statement on Unity, which the Assembly voted to approve and commend to the Churches "for study and appropriate action". The key paragraph, a sentence of Pauline complexity, indicates the growth in consensus on unity since Lausanne.

> We believe that the unity which is both God's will and his gift to his Church is being made visible as all in each place who are baptized into Jesus Christ and confess him as Lord and Saviour are brought by the Holy Spirit into one fully committed fellowship, holding the one apostolic faith, preaching the one Gospel, breaking the one bread, joining in common prayer, and having a corporate life reaching out in witness and service to all and who at the same time are united with the whole Christian fellowship in all places and all ages in such wise that ministry and members are accepted by all, and that all can act and speak together as occasion requires for the tasks to which God calls his people.
>
> It is for such unity that we believe we must pray and work.[2]

While there was a dearth of official church reaction, the phrase "all in each place" caught the imagination of churchmen all over the world. The power of the phrase is evident in the response it evoked from the British Faith and Order Conference in 1964. There the section on "All in Each Place" issued a call to the British Council of Churches to covenant to reach union by an agreed date, hopefully not later than 1980.[3] Perhaps one reason for the warm reception of the statement was its concreteness. Lund had agreed that the quest of the ecumenical movement is for visible unity; in the New Delhi Statement the marks of such unity were spelled out and the implications made clear for the Church "in each place". This brought abstract theorizing down to earth, and the implications of church union for the "grassroots" were specific. Faith and Order was at last beginning to fill in the picture of the kind of unity we are seeking together. Men and women could see what this would mean for them in the places where they lived out their lives.

Criticisms came in, however. While the goal was stated, the way to it was not. While the unity of all in each place was spelled out, the relationship of those in one "place" to those in other "places" was not. The catholicity of the Church was indicated ("united with the whole Christian fellowship in all places and all ages"), but its "marks" were not given.

Further impetus was given to consider catholicity by the calling of the Second Vatican Council in 1962. A number of Faith and Order Commission members were observers at the Council, and Professor K. E. Skydsgaard of Denmark and the then Research Secretary of the Commission, Dr Lukas Vischer, were at all its sessions. This increase in communication was furthered by the presence of Roman Catholic observers at the Fourth World Conference on Faith and Order in Montreal in 1963. There one evening session was devoted

[1] See MRCC (1959), pp. 175ff; FO, no. 31, pp. 113ff.

[2] New Delhi, p. 116. A collection of reactions to the statement compiled from press reports, articles, and official church actions, was prepared by Mr Mark Santer and is in the Faith and Order archives.

[3] *Unity Begins at Home* (London 1964), p. 77.

to a consideration of catholicity;[1] an address on "Protestant Catholicity" was delivered at an ecumenical rally during the conference; and the sections themselves grappled with the question.

Both Section I on "The Church in the Purpose of God" and V on "All in Each Place" discussed catholicity in terms of its "qualitative" character. It was discerned in terms of the participation of each Church or congregation in Christ, and therefore related to Churches of other times and places. The whole Catholic Church is present in every local congregation gathered for the hearing of the Word and the celebration of the Lord's Supper.[2] Granted that this is the heart of catholicity, what does it mean for the organized life of the Churches?

At its meeting in Aarhus in 1964 the Working Committee appointed some of its number, together with consultants, to pursue the study of unity. Their report was presented to the Commission in Bristol in 1967 and accepted as the basis for discussion in Section I of the Assembly in Uppsala in 1968.[3] Entitled "The Holy Spirit and the Catholicity of the Church", this document seeks to supplement the christological definition of catholicity adumbrated at Montreal, to root it clearly in the trinitarian faith, and to pursue further the meaning of the phrase in the New Delhi Statement: "are brought together by the Holy Spirit into one fully committed fellowship". The kernel of this document is found in two questions: "When will God's gift of unity in the Spirit lead us to a visible union of all Christians? How can we find one common life in which it is not necessary to press forms and ways into a single mould?"[4]

Unlike the New Delhi Statement, this latest attempt to articulate the nature of the unity we seek does not have one compendious paragraph summarizing its conclusions. It is perhaps too early for that. But it expresses a clear hope that the Churches of the world will be able to speak and act together, perhaps through a universal council "which will speak of the faith which all confess and the obedience to which all are called". In its[5] concluding sentence the commentary on the statement specifies the ultimate aim of the unity we seek, for it is more than just the unity of the Church. "Christians work in the certainty that the unity and destiny of the human race depends upon the faithfulness of God."[6]

One can discern clearly a growing consensus among the member Churches of the World Council since 1948. In Amsterdam they "intended to stay together"; at Lund unity was sought by focusing on the common centre, Christ; in New Delhi they affirmed the oneness of "all in each place"; at Montreal they sought for catholicity amongst the diversity of theologies; at Bristol they began to take steps to indicate what catholicity implies. The twenty years have been difficult ones. Often the goal has not seemed clear

[1] Addresses were given by Archpriest Vitaly Borovoy of the Russian Orthodox Church, and Professor Claude Welch of the Methodist Church, U.S.A. For the full texts see the *Ecumenical Review* (October 1963), pp. 26–42.

[2] See Montreal, pp. 45f (para. 24) and pp. 80ff.

[3] For the full text see *Drafts for Sections* (Geneva 1968), pp. 7–27.

[4] Ibid., p. 11.   [5] Ibid., p. 18.   [6] Ibid., p. 27.

when the exigencies of immediate problems clouded one's vision. Yet seen in short compass the progress towards clarifying the kind of unity sought by the ecumenical movement has been steady and cumulative. Only the future actions of Churches and Christians all over the globe will demonstrate what real authority this growth in consensus exercises. But this consensus concerning church unity is not without roots. It has been supported by a sub-structure of other Faith and Order studies.

Ecclesiology

We have so far examined one aspect of this topic, namely the nature of church unity. To deal in full with Faith and Order's work on the doctrine of the Church over the past twenty years would be impossible in the scope of this chapter. The reader is therefore referred to the documents cited in the course of this section; not only would a wealth of material have to be covered, scores of theologians and churchmen would have to be mentioned as well. What we shall be examining is the result of hundreds of man-hours, miles of travel, and scholarly dedication. This is true of all Faith and Order work, for at bottom it is a highly personal affair.

In order to grasp what has happened in the course of the last twenty years, we shall try to see whether any overall pattern has emerged. The best way to begin is to see the state of affairs shortly after 1948. The Edinburgh Conference had laid plans for international theological commissions. Between 1948 and the Lund Conference in 1952 these commissions were drawing the results of their work together. The preparatory volume for Lund entitled "The Nature of the Church" is an excellent indication of where Faith and Order had come in ecclesiology. It is, in effect, a monument to what has been termed "comparative ecclesiology". Its essays describe different Churches and communions in terms of their "distinctives". It is also the end of a road. In "A Word to the Churches" the Lund Conference reported:

> We have seen clearly that we can make no real advance towards unity if we only compare our several conceptions of the nature of the Church and the traditions in which they are embodied.[1]

To get beyond this impasse, the Conference recommended that in the future, Faith and Order treat the doctrine of the Church "in close relation both to the doctrine of Christ and to the doctrine of the Holy Spirit".[2] Rather than to compare positions, people from all Churches were asked to study together the relationship between God and his Church. The full trinitarian thrust was made clear in a recommendation from the next World Conference, held at Montreal in 1963. There the section on "The Church in the Purpose of God" requested further study of "the proper relation of creation and redemption".[3]

It would appear in retrospect that the study of the doctrine of the Church over the past twenty years has in fact been carried on at least implicitly with reference to a trinitarian understanding of God. This becomes clearer as we

---

[1] Lund, p. 15.   [2] Ibid., p. 22.   [3] Montreal, p. 43n.

look at the various studies and see from what perspective they view the Church.

A need was felt as far back as 1937 to study the Church as a part of the created order. An American group had been working on "the non-theological factors in the making and unmaking of church union". More accurately these factors can be termed those aspects of the Church which characterize it as an organization among other organizations. A letter by Professor C. H. Dodd, read at the Commission meeting in 1949, spoke of "unavowed motives in ecumenical discussions". These concerns were then discussed in more detail just prior to Lund at the Ecumenical Institute in Bossey. The group concluded: "Such factors have acquired enormous power over us. They are not incidental: they are compounded of the very stuff of earthly history and human sin."[1] As Dr Ernest Payne later observed, if a thorough study in the area of the so-called "non-theological "factors were pursued it would have finally to deal with the Christian doctrine of creation and history.[2]

Many factors could be studied. The Commission decided in 1955 to isolate "institutionalism" for examination and constituted a study commission for the purpose. In its interim report published in 1961 the study commission put the problem clearly:

> Granted that institutions are an integral aspect of the divine–human nature of the Church, the question inevitably arises: On what basis is it possible to distinguish between constitutive and permanent and, on the other hand, derivative and historically variable features?[3]

Sociological analysis and case studies were pursued to seek further clarification of the problem. The study brought to awareness the intransigent quality of "organizational inertia" whereby the Church, along with other institutions, has a built-in resistance to change.[4] In its pursuit of sociological analysis the study has enabled the theological questions to be posed more precisely and pointedly.

Further work along these lines was recommended by the Commission in Aarhus in 1964 when it initiated a study entitled "Spirit, Order and Organization". Careful empirical study was to be continued; but the aim would be to analyse the process of change, rather than the resistance to change, in the Church. In such a way it was hoped that the relationship between the Holy Spirit and the Church would be clarified. Yet here too the Church itself would be studied empirically, namely as a part of the created order.[5]

For the most part the study of institutionalism had proceeded only partially aware of its theological rootage. However, at Montreal the desire for an

[1] C. H. Dodd, G. R. Cragg, Jacques Ellul, *Social and Cultural Factors in Church Divisions*, FO, no. 10, p. 32.
[2] FO, no. 17, p. 37.
[3] *The Old and the New in the Church* (London 1961), FO, no. 34, p. 78.
[4] The final report of the Commission is published in *Faith and Order Findings*, ed. Paul S. Minear (London 1963). Numerous essays and case-studies written in the course of study can be found in *Institutionalism and Church Unity*, ed. Nils Ehrenstrom and Walter G. Muelder (New York 1963).
[5] See FO, no. 44, pp. 58ff.; FO, no. 50, p. 156.

explicit examination of the Church in relation to creation was forcefully made. Because of the recommendations from that conference the Commission instituted a study in 1964 entitled "Creation, New Creation and the Unity of the Church". This took Faith and Order into the realm of more general theological study. But this was necessary both because the Church is rooted in the world, and because of increasing controversy over the proper relationship between Church and world, redemption and creation.

The first stage in this study was completed with the presentation of the report "God in Nature and History" to the Commission meeting in Bristol in 1967. It was largely drafted by Professor Hendrikus Berkhof of the Netherlands, and many people had had a part in the work. Historians, natural scientists, and behavioural scientists, as well as theologians, had entered into the discussion. After examining the various ways in which one can speak of the relationship between God and the world, the document points to the ambiguities involved in judgements concerning this relationship, and draws some consequences for our understanding of the Church.

The Christian has to know for himself where he sees the forces of the Spirit at work, so that he can support them, and where he sees the forces of darkness at work, so that he can resist them. But while we need to interpret history, there is no clear authority. Our various interpretations call for "confirmation, amendment or rejection by the common body of Christ".[1] For this reason the widest possible participation is desired and the need for the ecumenical movement itself is emphasized. Not only individuals but Churches must "wrestle to find a common interpretation of the contemporary situation, as the basis for their common endeavour".[2]

After accepting the document on "God in Nature and History" as the first stage of this new work, the Commission authorized as a second stage a study of "Man in Nature and History". In part this study is seen as "preventive medicine"—attempting to avoid new and different schisms over theological differences. As Tissington Tatlow had observed in his history of Faith and Order, today on no major theological question "do the dividing lines exactly correspond with denominational allegiance". He noted that this fluidity might betoken "the dawn of a much wider unity or of a different pattern of schism".[3] After noting the difficulties of the "generation gap" in the ecumenical movement, and the desire especially of the younger generation for involvement "in the world", the Bishop of Bristol, Dr Oliver Tomkins, spoke in his closing remarks at the Commission meeting in 1967 of this "new dimension" in Faith and Order work. This new study on "Man in Nature and History" is important, for "it is the task of Faith and Order to discern the New Man in Christ: to discern what is the form of a true humanity. To see the answer to that question is to understand afresh the form of the Church. The New Man cannot be a schizophrenic. A divided Church obscures from humanity the form of its own destiny."[4]

[1] *New Directions in Faith and Order*, FO, no. 50, p. 30.
[2] Loc. cit.
[3] Rouse and Neill, op. cit., p. 441.
[4] FO, no. 50, p. 164.

The institutionalism study, and those which followed it, had studied the Church as a created organization, part and parcel of the area open to socio-logical inquiry. In these new studies, however, the focus was on the manner in which the Church could respond to the work of God in the created order. In both cases we discover more about the Church in its relation to creation.

Major ecclesiological study between Lund and Montreal was carried out by the Theological Commission on Christ and the Church. Its interim report "One Lord, One Baptism" had as its subtitle "The Divine Trinity and the Unity of the Church."[1] The task was considered to involve an acknowledge-ment of the unity which exists already among the Churches, a unity in Christ and in the Spirit, and a drawing of the consequences for the actual life of the Churches in their search for outward unity. Among the salient points of the report were its insistence upon the inextricable relation of the Church to creation; its integral relationship to the Israel of God called prior to Christ; the distinct life of the Church based on the life, death, and resurrection of Christ; and the basis of the Church's unity in the perfect unity of the triune God.[2]

The study was primarily preoccupied with the redemptive function of the Church. In the accompanying paper on baptism emphasis is placed on baptism based upon the "efficacy of Christ's saving act". Starting from this point we can think of all other rites of the Church "as dependent upon and in various ways renewing or more specifically expressing the fulness of baptism itself".[3]

"Christ and the Church", the final report of the theological commission, was received by Section I on "The Church in the Purpose of God" at Mont-real. It was in two parts, one from a North American section and one from a European section.[4] While both worked along different lines, the stress, as is indicated by the title, was on "Christ and the Church". The Church was seen as "grounded in the eternal purpose of the Father to send his Son Jesus Christ into the world".[5] Yet neither document was truly accepted as a basis for work. The make-up of the section membership can help explain this. Prominent in the discussion were Professors Ernst Käsemann and Eduard Schweitzer; both brought the tools of post-Bultmannian scholarship to bear in criticism of the documents. But articulate Orthodox members resisted their emphasis on *theologia crucis* at the expense of *theologia gloriae*. Reformed and Lutheran members split over the question of the relationship of the Church to creation and redemption. Further creative complications arose from hearty participation in the discussion by observers from the Roman Catholic Church, the Lutheran Church–Missouri Synod, and the Southern Baptist Convention.

While the Lund method of focusing on the relation between God and the Church had been used in the preparation of the two documents, discussion in the section made it clear that "comparative ecclesiology" is still a necessary

---

[1] *One Lord, One Baptism* (London 1960), FO, no. 29.
[2] Ibid., pp. 13f.   [3] Ibid., p. 70.
[4] See *Faith and Order Findings*, ed. Paul S. Minear. London 1963.
[5] Ibid., p. 38 of FO, no. 38.

ecumenical tool. The report itself indicated this when it pointed to "elements of tension which we neither minimize nor disguise". It went on to indicate that these differences reflect the present ecumenical situation, and that "the growth of the World Council of Churches has enlarged the areas of possible disagreement".[1] At New Delhi in 1961 many Orthodox Churches had been admitted into membership in the Council, as well as two Pentecostal Churches. Added to this was increased Roman Catholic participation. This led Montreal to be described as a "promising chaos": a chaos, because the growth in membership meant that achieved consensus needed to be rethought and achieved again; promising, because of the much wider constituency which was now involved in ecumenical discussion.[2]

While the report of the Montreal section did not contain much that was an "advance" over previous work, it led, through the very disagreements which were revealed in the discussion, to new avenues of Faith and Order study. We have already mentioned the study on "Creation, New Creation and the Unity of the Church". But additional studies were also approved by the Commission in 1964. A study on "The Church and the Jewish People" was initiated, which helped the self-understanding of the Church through an examination of its relationship with biblical Israel, and tried to clarify Christian–Jewish relationships today.[3]

Other studies indicate the desire to examine more carefully the relationship between the Church and the Holy Spirit. We have seen above how this gave new direction to the study of the empirical nature of the Church with the study of "Spirit, Order and Organization". Further concentration on the work of the Holy Spirit was evoked by the Montreal section's insistence that the nature of conciliarity, both in ecclesiology proper and in evaluating the role of "councils of churches", needed thorough study. [4] In discussing "Christ, the Church and the Churches", the section placed great emphasis on the Church as "both present in, and one with, the local congregation gathered for the hearing of the Word and the celebration of the Lord's Supper".[5] This reinforced the work of Section IV on "Worship and the Oneness of Christ's Church" and led to the institution of a study on "The Eucharist: a Sacrament of Unity".[6] These latter two studies received impetus from other quarters as well. Their results will be reported below.

At Lund an era of study in comparative ecclesiology ended. A new method was begun with promise in the work of the theological commissions, especially that on "Church and the Church". But with the growth of the World Council, and wider participation even by non-member Churches in its deliberations, some retrenchment had to be made. Yet after the "promising chaos" of Montreal new studies were conceived, quickly initiated, and interim reports were ready in a scant three years. When one views the study programme from 1948 to 1968 one discovers that, viewed as a whole, discussion of ecclesiology in fact was carried on in a trinitarian context. In diverse ways the nature of the

---

[1] Montreal, p. 41 (paras. 8 and 9).
[2] Ibid., p. 7.
[3] See Montreal, p. 44, no. 1; FO, no. 44, p. 42; FO, no. 50, pp. 69–82.
[4] Montreal, pp. 48ff.   [5] Ibid., pp. 45f.   [6] FO, no. 44, p. 54.

Church was studied in relation to creation, redemption, and the ongoing life of the Church as the fellowship of the Holy Spirit.

Most important, in the process of study scholars and churchmen of the Roman Catholic and Protestant West and of the Orthodox East, from the developed countries of North America and Europe and the developing countries of Asia, Latin America, and Africa, have worked together. What remains, and it is a large task indeed, is to see the fruits of their common labour communicated to the vast memberships of their Churches across the globe.

Worship

Study of worship has had a continuing role in Faith and Order. As important, however, has been the corporate worship which always has characterized meetings of the Commission and World Conferences. Here direct knowledge of other traditions was possible, and this informed the study process.

In the early stages comparative studies played an important role. In preparation for the Lund Conference a volume entitled *Ways of Worship* was prepared to provide information on worship in the various traditions.[1] It was basically a comparative study. The subsequent work of the section on worship at Lund made clear that consensus in this area was still not possible. The "unsolved problems" listed were too many to recount. Differences existed between "low" and "high" Church; there was much disagreement in the discussion of the Eucharist and concerning the relation between Word and Sacrament. Clearly much work remained to be done.

Also under discussion at Lund was the preparatory volume on *Intercommunion*.[2] It contained both historical studies on the problem in different ages and a section on comparative attitudes and practices. In discussing the preparatory volume, the Conference noted that the urgent desire for fellowship in the Eucharist "is very widely felt in all parts of the world". But ultimately, it noted, the urgency "comes from our Lord's call to us".[3] While not making notable progress toward solving problems, the Conference did make recommendations concerning communion services at ecumenical gatherings.[4]

Subsequent to Lund study in worship was carried on by an international theological commission with three sections, each with a different mandate. One was based in East Asia, one in Europe, and one in North America.[5] Reports from each group were presented to the Montreal Conference in 1963.[6]

Whereas at Lund a good deal of consensus was reached concerning Christ and the Church, and at Montreal deeper disagreements were revealed, with

---

[1] *Ways of Worship*, edited by Pehr Edwall, Eric Hayman, and Wm. D. Maxwell London 1951.

[2] *Intercommunion*, ed. Donald Baillie and John Marsh. London 1952.

[3] Ibid., pp. 49f.

[4] Ibid., p. 58. Note the revisions in these recommendations made at the Montreal Conference in 1963: Montreal, pp. 79f.

[5] FO, no. 17, pp. 25ff.

[6] *Faith and Order Findings*, ed. Paul S. Minear. London 1936. FO, no. 39.

regard to worship the process was reversed. A large measure of agreement was in fact registered by the section on "Worship and the Oneness of Christ's Church" in 1963. For instance, the section could state that despite many disagreements regarding Holy Communion, they could agree that the Eucharist is "a sacrament of the presence of the crucified and glorified Christ until he come, and a means whereby the sacrifice of the cross, which we proclaim, is operative within the Church".[1] Growth together in the ecumenical movement had made all Churches more deeply committed to sacramental worship and liturgical renewal. Agreement on the "presence" of Christ in the Eucharist, and on its sacrificial character, were significant advances over the disagreements at Lund.

The consensus which was evident at Montreal was no abstract agreement among liturgiologists; it was a consensus deeply rooted in common commitment to the celebrative, educative, and missionary character of the worship of Christ's Church. The growing liturgical sensitivity was not an attempt to revive traditional forms, for when a man has a living faith in God he should be encouraged to express it "in spontaneous praise and thanksgiving".[2] A growing agreement on the sacramental character of the Church's worship was evident in the work of the section; but this agreement was focused on the contemporaneity of the traditional and the spontaneity of the orderly.

After Montreal the Commission decided to centre study on the Eucharist and authorized a study in 1964 entitled "The Eucharist: A Sacrament of Unity". To aid the study Professor J. J. von Allmen of Switzerland was commissioned to write an essay as an aid to discussion, and this was published in 1967 after it had been discussed and revised by an international theological commission.[3] This provided further basis for discussion by the theological commission, whose work was presented to the Commission at its meeting in Bristol in 1967.

In this report major emphasis was placed on an analysis of the Eucharist in terms of its "anamnetic and epikletic" character, namely in terms of the way it functions as representation and anticipation, and the way in which it necessarily includes the invocation of the Holy Spirit. Further, the report speaks of the catholic character of the Eucharist, and carries on the emphasis made in Montreal on the local eucharistic fellowship as having "the fulness of catholicity".[4] Therefore, lack of local unity is a challenge to "Christians in that place": "A mockery is made of the Eucharist when walls of separation destroyed by Christ on his cross are allowed to persist: those between races, nationalities, tongues, classes, congregations, confessions, etc."[5]

One can see even in this cursory review that the work of studies such as this one feeds into our general understanding of the nature of the Church. This emphasis on the "qualitative catholicity" of the local eucharistic fellowship helps one understand better the nature of the Church, the kind of unity sought "in each place", and the way in which Churches in one place are related to those in other places and times.

[1] Montreal, p. 93 (para. 117).   [2] Ibid., p. 76.
[3] J. J. von Allmen, *The Lord's Supper*. London 1969.
[4] FO, no. 50, pp. 61–3.   [5] Ibid., p. 63.

In plans for further study the Commission in 1967 picked up the other theme in the Montreal report on worship, and in the interim report on "Christ and the Church". It proposed that further study in worship might "find its focus in the relation of Baptism and the Eucharist".[1] This theme, plus further work on the knotty problem of intercommunion, continues the work of Faith and Order in the area of worship.

Ministry

Questions of "order" are among the thorniest which face Churches in union negotiations or discussions of full eucharistic fellowship. It is therefore surprising that in recent years study in this area has not evoked more interest from the Churches. It was not always so.

At Lausanne in 1927 delegates focused on what appeared to them to be three major forms of church order: episcopal, presbyteral, and congregational. In their report they maintained that "these several elements must all, under conditions which require further study, have an appropriate place in the order of life of a reunited Church".[2] In surveys of present plans of union one discovers that in most cases provision is made to weave these three elements together, a healthy legacy from the early days of Faith and Order. Edinburgh in 1937 continued study in this area under the title "Ministry and Sacraments". For the most part the section's report merely listed various positions.[3] Little progress was made at Lund. Discussion centred on what constitutes a "valid" ministry.[4]

Direct study of the ministry ceased, really, between Edinburgh in 1937 and Montreal in 1963, at the very time when church union negotiations were increasing. At Montreal, since no special material had been prepared, the section on "The Redemptive Work of Christ and the Ministry of His Church" used some material from the report on "Christ and the Church", a bulletin (no. 15) prepared by the Laity Department, and documents from the Division of World Mission and Evangelism.

At Montreal discussion centred not on types of order, nor on the "validity" of orders, but on the ordained ministry as such. Beginning with an affirmation of "the recovery of the biblical teaching about the royal priesthood of the whole people of God", the report then goes on rather wryly to acknowledge that the Church "has always had and (so far as we know) always must have what we may call a 'special ministry' ".[5] The emphasis is on the ministry of the whole body; the ordained ministry is seen as one among "the differing gifts bestowed by the Spirit".[6] All in the section agreed that orderly transmission of authority is normally "an essential part of the means by which the Church is kept from generation to generation in the apostolic faith". But then the traditional differences emerged, ranging from the Orthodox insistence upon "unbroken succession of episcopal ordination from the apostles" to Quaker insistence that there is not sufficient New Testament authority to warrant

[1] FO, no. 50, p. 156.   [2] Lausanne, p. 469.   [3] Edinburgh, pp. 245-9.
[4] Lund, pp. 255 and 266.   [5] Montreal, p. 62 (paras. 77 and 80).
[6] Ibid., p. 65 (para. 92).

ordination.[1] Increasing consensus on the theological bases of ministry has not yet led to greater agreement on matters of order.

After Montreal the Commission authorized, at its meeting in 1964, a study on "Christ, the Holy Spirit and the Ministry". Yet this study itself suffered from "a relative lack of support".[2] No findings were available to be presented to the Commission at its meeting in 1967. At that time, however, the decision was made to tackle the central problem head on. The study would focus on ordination. Use could be made of the not insignificant materials already collected; growing consensus in other areas of ecclesiology might provide new insights. Such a study, with the growth of union negotiations over the face of the earth, is both necessary and long overdue.

One can only speculate on the reasons why such a central question of church order has received such scant attention and evoked little support from churchmen. It is at least possible that part of the "hidden agenda" in discussions concerning order is the institutional identity of church bodies, and, for that matter, the self-identity of churchmen and ministers as well. The very fact that for many Churches order provides the main thread of continuity, at least in their own self-understanding, means that reaction to change in this order will be strong. "Organizational inertia" mounts to a well-nigh immovable force where organizational identity is in question. Continued probing of what had been termed "non-theological factors" may be necessary in conjunction with study of the specifically theological aspects of order.

Tradition and traditions

Early discussion in this area centred on "Scripture and tradition", the proper relation between the two, and the use of creeds.[3] It was mainly an intra-Western discussion between those of Catholic and Protestant persuasions. Orthodoxy's influence was felt more strongly at Edinburgh, and the definition of tradition offered by that conference in 1937, "the living stream of the Church's life", opened the vistas of discussion.[4] It prompted one Western Free-Church theologian to observe that theologians of Churches other than Orthodox need now "to look again at their own understanding of tradition".[5]

Lund did not deal specifically with this area of study; but concern with the question ran through many areas of its work. The very next year, in 1953, the Working Committee of the commission discussed the topic,[6] and in 1954 the Faith and Order Commission authorized a Theologian Commission on Tradition and Traditions.[7] Its two sections, European and North American, published interim reports in 1961.[8] They approached their task differently, the European group centring on the dogmatic issue of Scripture and tradition, while the North American group took a more historical perspective, attempting to discover whether "it is intelligible to speak of the identity and continuity of the Christian *reality* in historical terms".[9]

---

[1] Montreal, pp. 65f (para. 95).   [2] FO, no. 50, p. 144.   [3] Lausanne, pp. 466f.
[4] Edinburgh, p. 229.
[5] Daniel Jenkins, *Tradition, Freedom and the Spirit* (Philadelphia 1951), p. 16.
[6] FO, no. 17, pp. 33f.   [7] FO, no. 21, p. 28.
[8] *The Old and the New in the Church*. London 1961. FO, no. 34.   [9] Ibid., p. 14.

With diverse approaches, the final reports nevertheless showed a large measure of agreement, especially in the use of terms. Slight differences in usage were resolved in the final report of the Montreal Conference itself in 1963:

> By *the Tradition* is meant the Gospel itself, transmitted from generation to generation in and by the Church, Christ himself present in the life of the Church. By tradition is meant the traditionary process. The term *traditions* is used in two senses, to indicate both the diversity of forms of expression and also what we call confessional traditions, for instance the Lutheran tradition or the Reformed tradition.[1]

This is a working out of the implications of the Edinburgh definition of tradition as the "ongoing life of the Church". With such an understanding, what is transmitted in tradition is "the Christian faith, not only as a sum of tenets, but as a living reality transmitted through the operation of the Holy Spirit".[2]

A common awareness of *the Tradition*, and an affirmation that it is one indication of the unity which is given in Christ to the Church, led to questions about the ways in which "the traditionary process" operates in our Churches, especially in Christian education. The New Delhi Assembly had already asked the Youth Department to engage in a study of catechetical materials; the Montreal Conference recommended a similar course of action to the Faith and Order Secretariat.[3] Collaboration between these two departments and the World Council on Christian Education began soon afterwards and the Commission approved the study in 1964.[4] A consultation in 1965 produced an interim report[5] which was widely circulated for comment, and an international drafting committee prepared the final report which was approved by all three groups for publication in 1967.[6] Its recommendations include common preparation of educational materials and ecumenical Christian education in local centres. The purpose of the report was to indicate to our Churches how they can bring their educational programmes in line with the ecumenical commitments they have made, and to grow in both.

Highly technical scholarly work was necessary in the area of Tradition and traditions as well. The first study of this type was a patristics study group. It met in Paris in 1962 in response to the request made at New Delhi that the Commission "establish a programme of joint study of theological problems by Orthodox and non-Orthodox theologians".[7] The group examined St Basil's treatise on the Holy Spirit in order (1) to clarify the authority and significance of the Fathers of the early centuries, and (2) to establish some hermeneutical principles for work in patristics. Its conclusions were reported to the Commission meeting in 1967.[8]

---

[1] Montreal, p. 50 (para. 39).   [2] Ibid., p. 52 (para. 46).

[3] New Delhi, pp. 221f; Montreal, pp. 60f (paras. 74–6).

[4] FO, no. 44, pp. 36 and 42.   [5] *Risk*. January 1966.

[6] *World Christian Education*. January 1968. Reprints are available under the title *Ecumenical Commitment and Christian Education*. Geneva 1968.

[7] FO, no. 50, p. 120; FO, no. 48, p. 12.

[8] FO, no. 50, pp. 41–8.

Two other studies in this general area of Tradition and traditions were also requested at New Delhi: one on the function of Councils throughout the history of the Church, and the other on the problem of theological discourse, including the problem of hermeneutics.[1] The first of these, like the study of patristics, was made up of an equal number of Orthodox and non-Orthodox scholars. It studied the conciliar process in the ancient Church. Among its conclusions were the following: conciliarity belongs necessarily to the life of the Church; conciliar processes continue in the separated Churches. But because of separation we have not had a genuine ecumenical council since the early centuries. This is desirable still, and the ecumenical movement, and the World Council of Churches "can be seen as a tool for the preparation of a true Ecumenical Council".[2] The work of this group will be combined with that of the patristic study group and centre on the Council of Chalcedon and its reception by the Churches.[3]

An examination of "Biblical Hermeneutics and its Significance for the Ecumenical Movement" started in 1964, jointly sponsored by the Division of Studies. An interim report was presented to the Commission in 1964,[4] and five regional groups in Europe and North America were formed to carry the work further. The final report, prepared by an international consultation in 1967, indicated that a consensus was gained on the use of literary and historical methods and on the process of interpretation in general. In addition it made some observations about the present stage of ecumenical discussion on the Bible.[5] Its report was received by the Commission in 1967, and further study was authorized on the topic "The Authority of the Bible".[6]

Throughout these studies in Tradition and traditions, whether of Christian education or of patristics, run themes which are crucial for the everyday life of Christians and therefore for the unity of the Church. Basically one can say that they deal with authority for Christian living. They deal with the passing on of the gospel, and with its appropriation in understanding. All these studies indicate that it is only as the gospel itself is continually re-appropriated that it is effective in guiding the Church's worship, witness, and service in the world.

Summary

Of necessity this summary has been cursory, yet it is clear what a wide range of studies underlies Faith and Order's attempt to discern (1) the nature of the unity we seek, and (2) the path to take towards that goal. Clearly the beginning of the path lies in understanding one another. The task of "comparative ecclesiology" is a continuing one. But then comes the arduous task of attempting to discern the shape of a common life in the future for Churches which are now separated. Then comes the even more difficult task of creating that

---

[1] New Delhi, pp. 174 and 173.   [2] FO, no. 50, pp. 57f.   [3] Ibid., p. 58.
[4] FO, no. 44, pp. 61ff.   [5] FO, no. 50, pp. 32–41.
[6] FO, no. 50, p. 156. Compare the results of this study with those reached at an Ecumenical Study Conference sponsored by the Study Department on the World Council at Oxford in 1949. *Biblical Authority for Today*, ed. Alan Richardson and Wolfgang Schweitzer (Philadelphia 1951), pp. 270–6.

life together in united Churches. This is what the movement toward church union is all about, and to it we now turn.

Faith and Order and Church Union

Stephen Neill surveyed with remarkable completeness the development of "Plans of Union and Reunion: 1910–1948" in the previous volume of this series.[1] Since that time, as we have mentioned above, there have been regular surveys published, and for the reader wishing detailed analysis these are indispensable.[2] Within the confines of this chapter we can but examine the general relationship of Faith and Order to the movement towards church union.

The church union movement

Movement for the unification of Churches has been an aspect of the ecumenical movement which proceeded quite independently of its varied organizational forms. In brief, there can be little causal connection drawn, say, between Life and Work, Faith and Order, or the World Council on the one hand and the unions which have been achieved. There has been parallel growth and an increasing rate of growth.

Between 1925, the year of the first Conference on Life and Work, and 1948, the founding of the World Council, nineteen united Churches were formed, including fifty-seven Churches in fifteen countries. Between 1948 and 1966 (the last year for which figures are available as I write) twenty-three more united Churches were formed, including seventy-four more Churches. That this movement is world-wide is indicated by the fact that these unions took place on all six continents and included a total of twenty-one countries.[3]

The movement continues, for in 1966 there were 121 different Churches involved in forty-six negotiations, again on all six continents. More significantly, these new figures indicate an increase in negotiations which seek to transcend confessional or polity barriers. Of the unions since 1925, about one-third transcended such barriers, while of negotiations now under way two-thirds seek to overcome these significant differences.[4]

Issues in church union

Among most of the Churches which have already joined, or are about to join, doctrinal issues seem to be least important. The main exception to this is in highly confessional Churches such as the Lutheran Church of Australia or between such Churches as the Reformed Presbyterian Church and the Orthodox Presbyterian Church in the United States. This is not to say that doctrine is unimportant for these churches, but that it is not primarily a divisive issue. For example, the proposed uniting Church in Australia has as the first fruit of negotiations a forty-four page pamphlet on "The Faith of the Church".

[1] Rouse and Neill, op. cit., pp. 445–508.   [2] See above, p. 146, n. 3.
[3] M. B. Handspicker, "Church Union" in *World Christian Handbook* (1968), ed. H. Wakelin Coxill and Sir Kenneth Grubb. London 1968.
[4] Ibid.

Where doctrinal differences do exist among churchmen negotiating for union such differences do not follow denominational lines. They are differences which exist within all the Churches.

From the beginning the issue which was most difficult to overcome was church order or polity. Since 1925 only one negotiation, that which led to the Church of South India, has succeeded in uniting a Church with bishops in the apostolic succession with non-episcopally ordered Churches. Only a few negotiations succeeded across Congregational–Presbyterian polity lines before 1948, although now difficulties here have lessened—to the extent that the International Congregational Council and the World Alliance of Reformed Churches propose to merge in 1970. But in some unions of this type dissident groups have broken away from or refused to enter the united Church. This is most notable in the United Church of Canada, with the continuation of the Presbyterian Church, and in the United Church of Christ in the United States, with a continuing association of Congregational Churches.

The inclusion of the historic episcopate in the Chicago–Lambeth Quadrilateral of the Anglican Communion as a "non-negotiable" item has meant that episcopacy is an issue in any negotiation where Anglicans are involved.[1] At present they are working towards union in sixteen negotiations. In the course of time, however, consensus has been developing that the historic episcopate, usually in a modified form, is a desirable element in the ordering of church life.[2] Certainly the early agreement at Lausanne that both Congregational, Presbyterian, and Episcopal elements were desirable had some influence in developing this consensus. More recently the decision by the negotiating committee of the Presbyterian, Methodist, and Congregational Churches in Australia to have a church order with bishops in the historic episcopate has been evidence that choice of such an order is not merely an expedient to enable episcopal and non-episcopal Churches to unite, since none of these Churches is at present episcopally ordered.[3]

The major issue at present takes a twofold form: the unification of ministries and the order of the united Church. The first is seen in discussions such as those in Great Britain between Anglicans and Methodists where the proposed "Service of Reconciliation" between ministries and memberships has caused much discussion.[4] At the moment one live option seems to be that used in forming the Church of South India, where all ministers of the uniting Churches were accepted into the ministry of the united Church, with all subsequent ministers receiving episcopal ordination. The other was devised in the course of discussions in North India and Ceylon; here bishops of the united Church will receive into their jurisdiction ministers of the uniting Churches with the laying on of hands and prayer.[5] At issue in this latter is

---

[1] See Rouse and Neill, op. cit., pp. 264ff.   [2] See FO, no. 43, p. 4.

[3] See *The Church: Its Nature, Function and Ordering* (Melbourne 1963).

[4] *Conversations between the Church of England and the Methodist Church.* London 1963. *Relations between The Church of England and the Methodist Church.* London 1965. *Towards Reconciliation.* London 1967. *Anglican–Methodist Union in Wales.* Penarth 1965.

[5] See, for example *Scheme of Church Union in Ceylon.* Third rev. ed., 1955, as amended in 1963 (Colombo 1964, pp. 10–27). Other similar schemes, each with some differences, are found in the North India plan, and those for union in Ghana and Nigeria.

whether it truly recognizes the validity of all the ministries being united, a question also raised about Anglican–Methodist plans in Great Britain. In attempting to interpret the first plan for scrupulous Anglicans an increasing number of theologians are contending that acceptance by a bishop in the historic episcopate, and acceptance of that bishop's jurisdiction, constitutes a "valid" ministry.

Such discussion about the ministry of a united Church, and the uniting of ministries, led the Very Reverend Patrick C. Rodger, when he was a member of the Faith and Order Secretariat, to observe that in the eyes of many laymen "church union negotiations seem to be mainly ministers discussing the ministry". The fact that this does seem to be one of the major issues makes all the more regrettable the lack of attention paid to the ministry in Faith and Order studies of the past few decades. The problems in this area are both helped and hindered by an increasing focus on the ministry of the whole people of God— both in ecumenical discussion and in church union plans as well. All the more reason, therefore, for thorough and swift study by Faith and Order of the ministry of the Church and its ordering.

Another sub-issue in the discussion of ministry seems an impending obstacle to church union in some parts of the world. Negotiations in Asia, Australasia, the United Kingdom, and North America are under way between Churches which have ordained women presbyters and those who refuse ordination to women. While an increasing number of theologians, including Roman Catholics, see no theological issue here, the sociological and psychological issues are by no means insignificant. Faith and Order has begun work in this area, most recently with its publication of a study entitled *Concerning the Ordination of Women*,[1] More thorough work is still needed, especially since, while the practice of ordaining women differs between Churches, differing attitudes towards their ordination obtain within almost all Churches.

This discussion of issues has been limited to two areas: polity and ministry. This is not because these are the only issues in church union, but because they are the most widespread. Stephen Neill, in his earlier survey, noted that "only a full-scale survey could give an idea of the range of problems that have had to be faced, the variety and ingenuity of the solutions that have been tried".[2] These issues vary not only with the denominations involved, but according to the places and times negotiations are carried on. Issues which were once church-divisive, such as the relation between Scripture and tradition, sacramental theology, and even church discipline, are still divisive in some contexts. But increasingly these are becoming issues more of church unity than of church union. In other words, these are differences within the various Churches. Already we have mentioned the issue of the relationship between Church and world as having the incipient power of schism—across denominational and confessional lines. In these various areas the future function of Faith and Order may increasingly come to be prevention of schism or of "ecclesiastical drop-outs".

[1] Geneva 1965.   [2] Rouse and Neill, op, cit., p. 448.

Faith and Order in Church Union

While the role of Faith and Order with regard to particular initiatives for union is still strictly circumscribed, in recent years it has been able to participate with more direct effectiveness in furthering initiatives already taken. The surveys of negotiations help to provide a network of communications among the negotiating committees. The Secretariat has now been asked to use this network to channel information about successes in one area to others facing similar problems, and to communicate information about World Council studies which may aid negotiating committees.[1] This will help remedy the real deficiency to date in communicating the results of ecumenical study to the places where it can help to effect change.

Another area where Faith and Order could have been of help for a long time was that of providing consultants for negotiators. This would provide expertise garnered from other negotiations, or from study, for committees requesting it. As far back as 1955 the Working Committee suggested that church union committees, where possible, should invite the Faith and Order secretary to "sit with the negotiating committee as an observer or consultant".[2] Some felt that this was exceeding Faith and Order's mandate. Strenuous discussion occurred on the topic at the Central Committee meeting in 1959.[3] The first visit of Faith and Order consultants occurred that year, but since then these visits have not only increased in number, but are understood to be a regular part of the work of the Secretariat.

Finally, one can only say that while there may be little direct relationship between the work of Faith and Order and the movements toward unity, it is clear that its study and discussion have helped to create an ethos conducive to union. Further, many individuals intimately involved in negotiating are themselves in part formed by their work in Faith and Order. Informal and *ad hoc* though they may be, the links between Faith and Order and union negotiations are strong.

One way in which these have been strengthened is through consultation among negotiators from various parts of the world. At first only unofficial consultations were held at times when large numbers of people were gathered at an Assembly. Such were held after Lund, and the Evanston and New Delhi Assemblies.[4] In 1964 the Commission authorized the calling of a large consultation, and this was held at the Ecumenical Institute in Bossey, Switzerland in April 1967.[5] Recommendations were submitted by the consultation to the Faith and Order Commission, and among them was a request that the Secretariat continue to organize such meetings.[6] Representatives from union committees and united Churches had discovered that such direct consultation provided clarity of communication unavailable in any other way.

---

[1] FO, no. 50, p. 148.   [2] FO, no. 22, p. 17.
[3] MRCC (1959), pp. 33ff, 175ff.   [4] FO, no. 22, p. 17.
[5] FO, no. 44, p. 34. See *Midstream*, vol. vi, no. 3, for texts of the meeting.
[6] FO, no. 50, p. 149.

Summary

Faith and Order provides a favourable climate for union, and its studies undergird the movement so far as they are known and used. In addition, the work of the Secretariat serves to communicate information, and to bring knowledgeable people together. But at this point a suggestion may be made. It is time that a volume similar to those prepared by H. Paul Douglass and Stephen Neill was published. The biennial surveys keep those who are interested up to date. But periodic reviews and assessments of longer periods of time are a continuing need in this area.

The People and Organization of Faith and Order

People give Faith and Order its life and its style. The very beginnings are inconceivable without the fire of Bishop Charles Brent and the dogged devotion of Robert Gardiner. This has continued to be the case since its merger into the World Council of Churches in 1948. One important change took place at that time: Faith and Order was to have a full-time secretary in the person of the Reverend Oliver Tomkins, although he would have offices in both London and Geneva. Dr Leonard Hodgson would continue as theological secretary, and the indefatigable archivist of Faith and Order, Dr Floyd Tomkins held the title of associate secretary in America. These men, together with the Chairman of the Commission, Bishop Yngve Brilioth of Sweden and the Vice-Chairman, Principal R. Newton Flew, oversaw the work of the theological commissions as they prepared for the Lund Conference.

Yet the real work of Faith and Order is carried out by numberless persons whose names would take pages to list. Here we can but indicate officers and staff. But the international theological commissions of the earlier days of Faith and Order, and the numerous committees and study groups which have characterized its work since 1964, are the backbone of Faith and Order study. For the days between 1948 and 1963, the names of those to be mentioned are clear. The officers of the theological and study commissions are those who bore the brunt of preparation. Prior to Lund there were three such. For the Commission on the Church Dr R. Newton Flew was Chairman, Professor K. E. Skysgaard, Vice-Chairman, Dean C. T. Craig, Chairman of the American group, and the Reverend Kenneth Riches, Secretary. The group working on "Ways of Worship" was chaired by Professor G. van der Leeuw, with Dr H. Asmussen as Vice-Chairman, Professor W. J. Kooiman as Secretary and Mr W. Vos as Co-Secretary. That working on "Intercommunion" had as Chairman Professor Donald M. Baillie, with Professor H. S. Alivisatos as Vice-Chairman and Professor John Marsh as Secretary.

The list lengthens after Lund, when Faith and Order was preparing for Montreal in 1963. That stepchild of Faith and Order study, the Study Commission on Institutionalism, was chaired by Dean Walter Meulder and had as Secretary Professor Nils Ehrenstrom—probably the only commission officered completely by men from the same theological faculty. The North American section on Christ and the Church was chaired consecutively by Professors Robert Calhoun and W. Norman Pittenger, with Professors

G. R. Cragg and Claude Welch as Secretaries. In Europe this theological commission had as officers Bishop Anders Nygren and Professor G. W. H. Lampe.

A variety of style of work is indicated by the varied ways in which the sections of the Commission on Worship were organized. In North America Professor Joseph Sittler served as Chairman. In Europe the officers included Professor Regin Prenter as Chairman and Principal A. Raymond George as Secretary. But in Asia, where the distances to be travelled were considerable, officers multiplied: Principal J. Russel Chandran was Chairman, with Bishop Lakdasa de Mel and President C. Kishi as Vice-Chairmen and Dr J. R. Fleming as Secretary.

Finally, the Commission on Tradition and Traditions, composed of two sections, had as North American officers, Professor Albert C. Outler as Chairman, Father Georges Florovsky as Vice-Chairman, and Professor David Hay as Secretary. In Europe the section was chaired by Professor K. E. Skydsgaard with Professor S. L. Greenslade as Vice-Chairman.

This listing of names is only to indicate the spread of responsibility in any Faith and Order study. It is possible within a short compass to give names only for the work done prior to 1964. Since its meeting in Aarhus the Commission has adopted a varied method of study which involves many more *ad hoc* committees in addition to study commissions. An indication of what this means can be found in the list of participants in Faith and Order studies included in *New Directions in Faith and Order*.[1] In contrast to the three groups working prior to Lund, and the four prior to Montreal, the report lists eleven separate studies, two of them with five sub-groups each.

Recent proliferation of studies has been made possible because of changes in the organization of Faith and Order. This too can be traced through the succession of persons involved in the work of the Commission. After Lund 1952, Bishop Brilioth's work as Chairman was complemented by the work of Dr Oliver Tomkins as Chairman of the Working Committee—an organizational differentiation to enhance the work of Faith and Order. When Dr Tomkins left as Secretary he was replaced by Dr J. Robert Nelson, who continued through 1957. That year leadership changed in two ways, with Dr Keith Bridston coming to Faith and Order as Secretary, and Dean Douglas Horton replacing Bishop Brilioth as Chairman.

From 1957 onward "The Future of Faith and Order" was a continuing subject of discussion. Drafts of a report on the topic were submitted to the Central Committee in the years 1957, 1959, and 1960.[2] A number of important changes in Faith and Order's functioning were rendered possible through the action of the Central Committee of the World Council in 1960: (1) the secretariat would report to the Central Committee each year on issues in the realm of unity; (2) time at assemblies would continue to be allotted for discussion of unity; (3) provisions would be made from time to time for

---

[1] FO, no. 50, pp. 174–8.

[2] FO, no. 26, pp. 47ff; 27, pp. 23ff; 31, pp. 113ff. For one man's view of what was at stake, see Keith Bridston, "Domesticating the Revolution", *Unity in Mid-Career*, ed. Keith Bridston and Walter D. Wagoner (New York 1963), pp. 30–46.

World Conferences; (4) the staff of Faith and Order would be increased to three, and the director of the secretariat would be a member of the Staff Executive Group, the staff policy-making body in Geneva.

In 1961 the staff changed again, this time increasing in numbers. Professor Paul Minear became Director, the Reverend Patrick C. Rodger, Executive Secretary, and Dr Lukas Vischer, Research Secretary. This was the staff which took care of the final organization of the Montreal World Conference on Faith and Order in 1963. Since that time the secretariat has been maintained at full strength, with Dr M. B. Handspicker coming on the staff as Assistant Secretary in 1963 when Professor Minear returned to his teaching and became Chairman of the Commission, and Archpriest Vitaly Borovoy becoming Associate Director when, in 1966, Patrick Rodger left the staff and Dr Vischer became Director. The secretariat's work has also been augmented by assistant secretaries seconded from member Churches, the Reverend Reinhard Groscurth coming in 1966 and Dr John Zizioulas in 1968.

Faith and Order's future in 1967 was placed in the hands of new chairmen of both the Commission, Professor H. H. Harms, and the Working Committee, Professor J. Robert Nelson. The resignation of Dr Minear saw a former Director and Chairman of the Commission cease his official connection with the Commission. That of Dr Oliver Tomkins, the Bishop of Bristol, ended a relationship which had begun in 1948 with his election as Secretary, and which was continued from 1952 to 1968 by a sixteen-year tenure as Chairman of the Working Committee.

For a full history of the "people of Faith and Order", in distinction from this history of a commission, a department, and a secretariat, many more pages would be needed. Faith and Order work has, thankfully, spread wider and wider—both in terms of the people involved and the organizational means whereby they are involved. National Faith and Order conferences have been held in Australia and New Zealand, in North America, the British Isles, and East Asia. Regional conferences have taken place within numerous countries, including those in the British Isles, North America, India, and others. Lay groups have become involved, especially through the series of "Living Room Dialogues" in the United States, and study groups sponsored by the ecumenical secretariat of the Evangelical Church in Germany. Faith and Order secretaries, and even multiple-staffed secretariats, have been constituted by national and regional councils of Churches.

Here is where we see the continuing character of Faith and Order as a movement. In the World Council of Churches, Faith and Order has become a secretariat within an institution, a needed ecumenical institution. But this institutional position enables it to encourage and support further work outside its specific oversight. The spirit which encouraged and inflamed Bishop Brent still finds ways to continue, and the institutional and organizational forms, while continually having to be reviewed, can aid and abet this spirit.

Church union committees, theological commissions, *ad hoc* study groups, laymen talking in living rooms or academies, conferences at retreat centres or universities, working committees, the Commission, the Secretariat—each and every one of these groups is part of that movement which is seeking the union of Christ's Church according to his will, and in his own time.

Conclusion

In the early 1930s Abbé Paul Couturier of Lyons sought a formula of prayer in which all could unite to pray for the unity of the Church. He advocated that we pray that "our Lord would grant to His Church on earth that peace and unity which were in His mind and purpose, when, on the eve of His Passion, He prayed that all might be one".[1] In 1941, in large part as a result of this change in intention, Faith and Order changed its week of prayer (which had been started in 1920) to coincide with the Week of Prayer for Christian Unity, celebrated annually in most parts of the world from 18 to 25 January. This "spiritual ecumenism" has been important to the Faith and Order movement from the outset, and the now widespread observance of the Week testifies to a growing response on the part of all Christians to the appeal for their participation.

Prayer for unity is an act in which all Christians, from whatever station in life or part of the world, can participate. It can involve a change of heart and a new breadth of vision for those who engage in it. It is essential if the work of Faith and Order is to take root in the vast constituencies of our Churches.

Faith and Order began as a movement among people deeply interested in the unity of the Church for the sake of its mission. Through the years both the scope of its work and its organization and methods developed slowly but surely.

With the formation of the World Council in 1948 the ecumenical movement became increasingly institutionalized. This had to be the case if the movement was to effect change in the institutions we call Churches. During the life of the Council it is not surprising to find growing concern for the "future of Faith and Order". The movement, if it were to continue as a movement, had to have adequate organizational form, determined by its own missionary and theological dynamic.

As the future breaks before us, it is clear that further growth and change in the work of Faith and Order is mandatory. Broader participation by the membership of all of our Churches has to come if unity is to be achieved—or received. Prayer and study are ways in which many can become involved. The so-called "grassroots" are increasingly leaping over the boundaries set by church discipline. A growing "anonymous ecumenical movement" threatens subtle schism if organizational intertia continues to block movements toward union.

The goal of the movement is "One Church Renewed for Mission". Bishop Tomkins, when still Secretary of the Department, observed that the function of the ecumenical movement can best be understood by analogy to the work of the physician.

> As the physician pursues the treatment in his relentless mercy, the patient's early hopes of cure and sense of greater strength may well have to be followed

[1] Rouse and Neill, op. cit., p. 348.

by a phase in which knowledge of unsuspected depths in his disease, the discovery of vitiation in organs he thought were healthy, must be the prelude to more lasting cure. Today we dare not speak of the unity of the Church without also speaking of its *renewal*.[1]

This is eminently still the case; renewal is the necessary prelude to true unity. But in addition we must grapple with issues which, while they have not yet divided the Church, promise division, alienation, or growing apathy. Whether one speaks of the "anonymous ecumenical movement" or the "underground church", one points to a reality of increasing power. There is the threat of a "horizontal schism" threatening all our Churches. The reasons for this are many, but perhaps a key one is seen in differing attitudes towards the world. Many Christians are now discerning the activity of the Spirit in the emergence of free nations, in international groupings, and in projects where Christians and non-Christians seek together for peace and justice in the new social structures created by the technological revolution overtaking all societies.

Other Christians see the Church as the ark of salvation, as a means to escape from the ambiguities and negativities of the world in which they live. It is a means of disengagement rather than a source of power and inspiration for engagement. The former group often finds little to inspire them in the internal life of organized Churches, and disparages worship and organized communal life. The latter group sees engagement and action in the world as a threat to the *status quo*, including that of the Churches.

In the midst of this increasing polarization, the work of Faith and Order is pastoral as well as theological. It needs to seek the roots of reconciliation between these two poles, and there are the resources within the Churches to accomplish this. Many of our churchmen, clergy as well as laymen, unite within themselves a deep spiritual life with a lively engagement with the problems of the contemporary world. The tragedy is that many of these folk, including large numbers of our younger churchmen, find neither spiritual resources nor the mutual support of a loving community within the organized life of our Churches.

The Bishop of Bristol's remarks are still germane. Renewal is the prerequisite of unity if we are not to unite organizations and programmes which are engaged in doing what need not be done, or even what ought not to be done. In its recent forays into more general theological issues, such as "God in Nature and History" and "Man in Nature and History", Faith and Order promises to regain its function as the theological *avant garde* of the ecumenical movement. Continuing, persistent, and courageous effort is necessary if Faith and Order is to fulfil its contemporary function of preserving unity, as well as its historical function of furthering reunion.

[1] ΓΟ, no. 2, p. 16.

7
Mission to Six Continents

LESSLIE NEWBIGIN

The Context

The two decades with which this history deals were a period in which the foreign missionary movement of the non-Roman Catholic Churches faced the most profound crisis of its history. Six factors combined to create this crisis of missions.

1. The Dismantling of the Colonial Empires

The opinion that missions were simply the spiritual and cultural aspect of western colonialism has been so often expressed as to risk being accepted as part of the unexamined mythology of our time. Careful historical study (for example in *Colonialism and Christian Missions*, by S. C. Neill) shows that the facts are far more complex than this simple statement allows. Nevertheless, it is a fact that the colonial systems of the western powers provided for the most part the political and cultural framework within which missions operated in most parts of what is now called the "third world" during the century and a half prior to 1947. That year, in which the Indian sub-continent became independent of British rule, may be taken as the starting-point of the process of decolonization which has been almost completed within less than twenty years. A change so profound and so rapid, which removed within a few years the framework within which missions had been operating for two centuries, could not fail to shake profoundly the whole missionary movement, even though the discerning missionary leaders had been for many years advocating and preparing for the liberation of the dependent peoples, and even though the work of missions was itself one of the most powerful forces preparing for that liberation.

2. The End of Missions in China

The most massive effort of Protestant missions during the century preceding the period of this survey had been directed to China. At the World Missionary Conference at Tambaram in 1938, the Chinese delegation had been outstanding in quality. The Chinese Church, though small, seemed full of immense promise. Yet, within a few years of the establishment of communist rule in China, missions had been completely eliminated from the country and much of the fruit of their century of work had apparently been destroyed. This shattering event led to much searching of heart among those responsible for leadership in the foreign missionary movement. It helped to produce a sense of crisis, though it is to be doubted whether the rethinking was sufficiently profound. Perhaps the most searching questions arise from the fact—generally accepted—that the communist government in China has been able to accomplish many of the reforms for which missions were the early advocates but which they were not strong enough to complete. The end of missions in China has therefore raised very profound questions regarding the relation of the Christian world mission to the whole world-wide process of secularization, and to the exercise of political power.

173

3. The Growth of a Sense of Global Human Interdependence

One of the most important spiritual facts of this twenty-year period is the growth, among ordinary men and women in all continents, of the feeling that the human race is a single entity bound together for better for worse, facing common problems, threatened by common dangers, and seeking common goals. It is true that the colossal exception to this was China; indeed one can say that the Chinese people, constituting one quarter of the human race, were completely absent from the developing ecumenical story which this chapter records. Moreover, towards the end of the twenty-year period there were many evidences that a movement of separatism, leading to the break-up of nations or to acute conflicts within them, was gathering force. Nevertheless, it remains true that, during the period of our survey, and for the people involved in the story, the growth of a sense of global interdependence was one of the most important elements in the spiritual climate.

Much of the power of missions had come from their appeal to the sense of what is beyond the frontiers of normal experience. The appeal to go "to the ends of the earth", evoked not only echoes of the "Great Commission", but also led to a deep response from that in every man which wants to press beyond the known to the unknown. Livingstone's vision of "the smoke of a thousand villages which have never yet heard the Gospel" spoke not only to the believer in every Christian, but also to the explorer in every man. In the decades under review, missions have had to come to terms with the fact that the "frontier" in that sense no longer exists. The world has become one parish, in a sense different from that which was in John Wesley's mind. Everything is part of one world. The question arises whether "foreign missions", as distinct from the general duty of witness which rests upon every Christian everywhere, have any distinctive *raison d'être*.

4. The Growth of the Concept of "Development"

A few years before the period under review began, the British Parliament had voted a small sum for "development" in the colonies. In the course of the subsequent years the conviction that it was the duty of the "developed" nations to aid the others towards a higher standard of life became one of the dominating ideas of international life. This was partly rooted in the expansion of the idea of the welfare state, partly no doubt in the sense of moral obligation towards peoples who had formerly been in subjection to the great powers, partly in economic self-interest, and partly in the growing conviction that mankind has the technical resources to banish poverty and create decent living conditions for all. As the sense of a single global community grew stronger, so also did the sense that an obligation rested upon the wealthy nations to help the poorer to raise their standards of living. This conviction found expression in many ways—from voluntary movements among students to "miss a meal" in order to help some development scheme in India, to massive programmes under the U.N. "Development Decade". On the other hand, this movement had an interesting effect upon the relations between missions and governments: as the governments of the western powers began to interest themselves in development they discovered that missions sent from their own countries had been engaged in development (though innocent of the word) for many decades, and found it convenient to use the help of missions for their programmes. On the other hand, many former supporters of missions began to feel that "development aid" was the modern equivalent for the missionary activities of the past. The acceptable ideal was no longer the man who went across the frontier to unknown lands to preach the gospel; it was rather the man who went as a teacher, a technician, a health worker, to help needy brethren in the one human family. The great programmes of Inter-Church Aid seemed to some to offer a more acceptable way of helping one's neighbour than the kind of missionary work which was felt to carry too much of the old arrogance of the colonial era. Even Christian congregations would offer resources for work abroad on the condition that they should not be used for anything connected with missions.

5. The Crisis of Faith in the West

This is something which it is difficult to describe, because both writer and readers are in the midst of it. Nevertheless, it must be referred to as one of the potent factors shaping missionary thinking and action during the period of our study. There is, firstly, the long-term questioning of the very foundations of faith which may be said to have been an essential element of Protestantism ever since the eighteenth century and which from time to time produces a spiritual situation out of which foreign missions simply cannot come. Secondly, and more exactly to our present point, there is the dissolution of the "Christendom" situation in the western world, which results in an increasingly sharp separation between missions on the one hand and the general cultural and political influence of the western nations on the other. And finally, there is the very marked change in the years following 1947 which may be characterized in two ways. On the one hand, a chronic bad conscience has seized the western white man in his relations with the rest of the world so that he fears above everything else the charge of arrogance. On the other hand, a profound crisis of faith within the Western Churches has led to a loss of conviction that there is anything in the Christian faith which is so vital that without it men will perish.

In so far as the overwhelming preponderance of missionary activity in the past two centuries has been from the Western Churches, this crisis of faith, allied to the wider factors to which reference has been made, has created a situation for missions which shakes them to their foundations. Perhaps the impact of this crisis upon the work of foreign missions was delayed by the fact that those concerned were thinking more about the meeting of the gospel with the traditional non-Christian religions than about the meeting of the gospel with the anti-traditional secularized societies of the West. As the movement towards a "six-continent approach" developed, it became clear that there was a gulf between the language used in discussions of "the theology of missions" and the language which the normal western Christian used about his own belief. By the end of the period under survey the gulf had become apparent, and the resultant spiritual problem had become inescapable.

G

6. The Growth of the Ecumenical Movement

The fruit of the work of missions has been the creation of a world-wide family of Churches. But the very existence of these Churches calls for a profound re-examination of the nature of the missionary movement itself. Is the work of missions done when the Church has been planted in every nation? Does the task not now rest upon the Church in each nation, rather than upon the foreign missionary? What, then, is the further need for the mission? These questions were present in missionary discussions long before the period we are now reviewing, but they could not be pressed with their full force while the "younger Churches" were isolated from one another and dependent for contact with the rest of the Christian world solely upon their parent missions. The development of the International Missionary Council brought able representatives of the younger Churches together periodically on a world level, and helped to bring pressure on missions to face this question. But it was when the World Council of Churches became fully organized, and brought together as equal members the young Churches of Asia, Africa, and Latin America and the older Churches from which the missions had been sent, that this question became inescapable.

Within the growing fellowship of the World Council an increasingly rich exchange of thought, experience, personnel, and resources began to develop. The younger Churches found themselves related to, and stimulated by, the other Churches in all kinds of new ways. In the growing programmes of inter-Church aid they found themselves sharing in help from older Churches quite outside the old missionary channels. To an increasing number of people it seemed that this pattern of interdependence within one world-wide Church represented the true pattern for the future, and that the type of organization developed by foreign missions should be completely discarded. The intimate association, leading in 1961 to complete integration, between the International Missionary Council and the World Council of Churches, ensured that the debate was conducted within one fellowship. Nevertheless, the questions put from the side of the World Council of Churches, and the issues raised by the W.C.C.'s programme of inter-Church aid, were among the factors which compelled a radical rethinking of the nature of the missionary task in an era of global interdependence.

Whitby to Amsterdam

The World Missionary Conference which met at Tambaram, India in 1938 dramatized for a very great number of people the fact that the Christian Church had become a truly world-wide company. The place of meeting had been shifted from China because of the outbreak of war there. The shadow of a demonic totalitarianism lay over the world. Tambaram, with the excellent work done in making it widely known, shone as a beacon of hope to Christians in many lands. The darkness of the world made its light shine brighter. The famous words spoken by William Temple at his enthronement as Archbishop of Canterbury during the darkest days of the war had as their background the vivid realization which Tambaram had given of the existence of a world-wide Christian family as the "great new fact of our time".

As soon as possible after the war, the International Missionary Council convened a world consultation at Whitby, Ontario. The title of the volume which embodies the record of this meeting—"Renewal and Advance"—well indicates its dominant mood. Even during the terrible period of war, the International Missionary Council had been able to maintain to a remarkable degree the fabric of co-operation, especially through the vast programme of support for "orphaned missions". Now in 1947 the world-wide family which had met at Tambaram could meet again. There was joy and confidence in planning for the future. It had not yet become clear how drastic were the changes which the world had undergone as the result of the convulsions of the war years. The complete extinction of the colonial pattern, most dramatically in China, but also throughout the rest of Asia and Africa, was still in the future. The extent of the spiritual damage which the old Christendom had suffered could not yet be assessed. The call was to go forward with renewed courage, and in the confidence that the world was eager to hear the gospel. "Expectant Evangelism" was one of the two distinctive slogans of the meeting. The other was "Partnership in Obedience", and to this phrase we have to give some attention.

The problem of the relation between missionary bodies in the West and the "younger Churches" which were the fruit of their labour in the East and South, had been already for several decades the dominating problem for missions. In the prevailing atmosphere of the colonial era it was not easy for missions to develop a satisfactory relation with the Churches which they still regarded as their children. The various programmes for devolution of responsibility from mission to Church did not have smooth sailing. At the Whitby meeting, the representatives of the older and younger Churches met separately to discuss this matter. The findings of the two groups showed such a remarkable measure of agreement that the conference was able to come with great unanimity to a common statement. The key phrase was "partnership in obedience". Older and younger Churches were equally called to accept the responsibility of mission, and they were to work in an equal partnership, each contributing the gifts that God had given.

The context of this partnership was still the missionary task in the "non-Christian world". Attention was focused, as was natural in a gathering sponsored by the International Missionary Council, upon the task in the traditional "mission lands". The fact that the "younger Churches" are also partners with the older in the evangelization of Europe and North America had not yet become clear.

In the following year (1948) the World Council of Churches was constituted at the Amsterdam Assembly. The International Missionary Council was to be in a relation of "association" with the new body, and very many of those who had been leaders at the Whitby meeting were prominent in the discussions at Amsterdam. One of the four sections into which the Assembly divided was concerned with the missionary and evangelistic task of the Church. Nevertheless, there were very marked differences between the Amsterdam discussions and those of Whitby. At Amsterdam those who were involved in what were traditionally called "foreign missions", whether as missionaries or as "younger churchmen", were a minority. The context was certainly fully ecumenical. It was concerned with all the six continents. But the point of view was that of the Christian dealing with his non-Christian neighbour. The particular problems which haunt every discussion held under the rubric "to the ends of the earth" were absent. The discussion reflected the growing uncertainty within Christendom about the whole matter of evangelism. Significantly the closing chapter of the volume dealing with this section is headed: "Is there a problem of evangelism?" One could say that this discussion was about evangelism in six continents, rather than about mission to six continents. The question had not yet been raised which would dominate the discussion ten years later: "Is there a specifically missionary task which is, on the one hand, more than the evangelism of one's neighbours, and is, on the other, valid even when the geographical division of the world into "Christian" and "Mission" lands is no longer valid?"

Willingen

Five years after Whitby, in 1952, the International Missionary Council convened a major meeting at Willingen in Germany. This meeting was widely thought at the time to have failed in its major task. But subsequent history has shown that it was in fact one of the most significant in the series of world missionary conferences.

The primary purpose for which the meeting was called was a profound rethinking of the nature of the missionary obligation of the Church. In a phrase which was frequently used in the course of the preparatory work, there was felt to be urgent need for a "theology of missions". The very foundations of the whole missionary movement were in need of re-examination; and the changes in the world were so revolutionary as to raise the question whether missions in the traditional sense were not already a thing of the past. When Canon Max Warren told the conference: "We have to be ready to see the day of missions, as we have known them, as having already come to an end", he was expressing the central questioning which had led to the calling of the conference. When the conference documents were assembled in one volume, they were given the title: "Mission under the Cross", for, in the words of Dr Norman Goodall, the editor: "The moments at which the whole gathering felt itself most surely under the leading of God . . . were those in which the Cross and its 'hiddenness' were the focus of worship and the theme of exposition."

Two issues dominated the discussions of the section which was charged with the preparation of a statement on the missionary obligation of the Church. On the one hand, a sharp attack was launched, primarily by J. C. Hoekendijk of the Netherlands, against the Church-centric view of missions which was implied by the title of the study, and which had been dominant in the thinking of the I.M.C. since the Tambaram conference. On the other hand, and closely related to the first, there was a strong effort made, especially by the North American study group which had prepared for the conference, to relate the missionary task to the signs of Christ's present sovereignty in the secular world. In the time available at the conference the group could not produce a statement which commanded the assent of the whole gathering. A substitute document was prepared which, without really coming to grips with these two issues, nevertheless gave a clear affirmation of the basis of the missionary calling of the Church in the being of the Triune God himself.

While the Willingen meeting could not reach an acceptable reconciliation of these theological tensions, its work has proved fruitful in the subsequent years. The affirmation that the mission is the *Missio Dei*, and that mission belongs to the very being of the Church itself, has been determinative of much later thinking. The statement of Willingen that "there is no participation in Christ without participation in His mission to the world" has reverberated down the subsequent years. At the same time those who struggled unsuccessfully at Willingen to develop a doctrine of mission which takes more account of what God is doing in the world outside the Church have been justified by subsequent developments in thought. It has become plain that a completely "Churchcentric" theology of mission is inadequate. The mission of God is more than Church extension. The question of the relation of Church to mission is a matter of continuing debate, but there is no doubt that Willingen gave the debate much of its direction and its power.

Beside the theological question which was the main reason for meeting, Willingen was the starting-point of a number of lines of thought and experiment which have been important in subsequent ecumenical history.

New forms of ministry

Tambaram had given much attention to the need for a more adequately trained professional ministry. Willingen asked whether a full-time paid ministry is "fundamental to the nature of the Christian ministry, or is it an uncritical transplantation to another soil of what was appropriate to a different environment?" The call to examine this question was repeated at the Ghana Assembly of the I.M.C. in 1957 and has led to the widespread ecumenical study of forms of the ministry which is still going on.

The role of the layman abroad in the mission of the Church

One of the most important words spoken at the Willingen Assembly was the call of Canon Max Warren for "an entirely new type of missionary activity to be developed alongside the traditional modes".

> We need [he said] to envisage men and women of scientific training who will be ready to give their service in development schemes, going to their work as ordinary salaried officials and bringing their expert knowledge to bear on some local situation. But they will go, not merely as those whose Christian convictions are marginal to their work . . . Rather they will go with a vocation consciously and deliberately to seek to work out a distinctive and purified technology in the light of Christian insights.

The Assembly drew attention to the fact that while there were 300 Swiss missionaries serving abroad, there were 65,000 Swiss serving abroad in secular occupations, and to the plans developed by the Swiss Missions Council for the training of Christians going abroad in such service. The birth of the movement of "development" which was to become so prominent in the 1960s, constituted a challenge to the Churches to a new kind of missionary action. Though Willingen called for action to follow up the call of Canon Warren, it must be admitted that the response came only slowly. It was not until 1960 that the I.M.C. appointed a Secretary (Dr Paul Löffler) for this specific purpose.

The Creation of Regional Study Centres

During a visit to India prior to the Willingen meeting, H. Kraemer had expressed the opinion that the Church there lacked the means of coming into direct contact at a deep level with the thought of the country. There was need for the creation of some sort of centre at which men with adequate specialist training could devote time to study, research, and promotion of dialogue with representatives of living movements of thought outside the Church. This conviction was shared with others, at an informal meeting at Willingen convened by Glora M. Wysner, and a recommendation was made to the I.M.C. favouring "the establishment of regional centres for study and research on questions related to the work of the Christian mission and the growth of the Church, affording opportunity to individuals and groups for study, writing, training and conference, and also undertaking the publication of relevant studies and research". This recommendation was taken up vigorously by the I.M.C. Dr Wysner undertook a journey in the Near East and Asia as the result of which plans were developed for study centres in Jerusalem and Bangalore and other places. With steady encouragement this programme has developed greatly during the subsequent years, and the chain of study centres in Asia, Africa, and Latin America is now playing an important role in the mission of the Church.

Missionary Mobility

During the debates at Willingen there was a sharp attack upon the immobility of missions. "It was roundly declared that the greater part of the contribution of the Western Churches towards the world mission of the Church, in service and money, was no longer employed on the frontier between Church and the world; it was absorbed in the support of a relatively static, long-established Christian enterprise."[1] In response to this challenge separate sessions of the delegates of younger and older Churches were held at which the question was asked: How can the Church recover its missionary initiative and achieve greater mobility? No very clear directives emerged from these discussions; but the conviction was registered that new patterns of partnership were needed if mobility was to be recovered. This conviction was to bear fruit later in the concept of "Joint Action for Mission". At the same time the Assembly

---

[1] N. Goodall, ed., *Missions under the Cross* (London 1953), pp. 18–19.

devoted a considerable amount of time to the place of institutions in the mission of the Church, and drew up a series of criteria which were to be widely influential during the subsequent decade.

Mission and Unity

The Assembly also adopted a statement on "The Calling of the Church to Mission and Unity", which echoed much of what had been said in the preceding year in a document prepared by the Central Committee of the World Council of Churches at Rolle, Switzerland. The statement urged member councils to seek fresh ways of relating themselves to the work of the Commission on Faith and Order of the W.C.C. At the same time the Administrative Committee of the I.M.C. had before it a formal letter from the Joint Committee of the I.M.C./W.C.C. which asked it to consider seriously the implications for practical life of the statement made at Rolle:

> It is clear in the New Testament that the Church is called at the same time to proclaim the Gospel to the whole world and to manifest in and to that world the fellowship and unity which is in Christ. These two aspects of the calling of the Church are interdependent ... Can we articulate clearly how these two are related to each other; and can we express in the life of our congregations, our churches and our ecumenical movements this fundamental unity?[1]

In response to this call, the I.M.C. made a series of practical recommendations for further co-operation, especially in the fields of Faith and Order and Inter-Church Aid. This latter area of co-operation was soon to dominate the further discussion of relationships between the two world bodies.

Towards Integration from Evanston

The next major world gathering was the Second Assembly of the World Council of Churches at Evanston in 1954. The attention which was directed to Christian eschatology, especially in the preparatory studies on the main theme, powerfully influenced the thinking of the Churches about their missionary task—for a true theology of missions must be intimately related to eschatology. The Assembly did not, however, produce any explicit new thinking on missionary questions. The section on evangelism did not feel itself called to discuss the specific problems which arise for foreign missions from the fact that their "home base" has become world-wide. The Assembly did, however, take important practical steps leading further towards the integration of the I.M.C. and the World Council. It had before it both the Rolle statement and the correspondence arising therefrom, and also the report of the East Asian Study Consultation at Lucknow (December 1952) which had called for more serious consideration of the relation between the two world bodies. The Assembly decided to reconstitute the Joint Committee with a full-time secretariat, and also to constitute a joint Division of Studies to serve both Councils. It also took note of the experience gained through the appointment of R. B. Manikam as joint Secretary for the two bodies in East Asia, and recommended that the I.M.C., on behalf of both bodies, should

[1] MRCC (Willingen 1952), pp. 34–5.

take the initiative in exploring the possibility of further co-operative action in Africa. The Joint Committee, with Norman Goodall as its full-time Secretary and Henry P. Van Dusen as its Chairman, began a vigorous new phase of its existence.

Its first meeting following Evanston took place in July 1955. It had before it the findings of the recent meeting organized by the Division of Inter-Church Aid at Les Rasses, Switzerland on world needs and strategy. The pressure of human needs and the growing obligation of "development" were compelling Christians to think in much more far-reaching terms about the world and about the service of the Churches. The joint committee noted that in responding to the call to a wider, more far-reaching, and more positive service by all the Churches to one another, and by all the Churches together to human needs throughout the world, further questions are bound to arise calling for joint consideration by W.C.C. and I.M.C. The Division of Inter-Church Aid now felt itself called to enter with massive programmes of aid into the areas in which the missionary societies had long been at work. These societies had been for many decades seeking to lead the Churches to financial self-support and had therefore been reducing the level of aid for on-going work. There was anxiety lest the coming in of large new resources from organizations which were interested in service rather than in mission might both hinder the development of self-support and also deflect the younger Churches from their missionary task. Many years were to be spent in seeking to define the relations between inter-Church aid and mission in such a way as to do justice to both. In the meantime, however, the joint committee recorded its opinion that it "should not immediately concentrate on the question of the possible 'integration' of the World Council of Churches and of the International Missionary Council. While the consideration of this issue is the direct responsibility of the committee, its solution is likely to be reached more effectively if time is taken to develop co-operation together."

A year later, the perspective had changed. The joint committee in 1956 found itself compelled "to recommend to the parent bodies that in the opinion of the joint committee the time has come when consideration should be given to the possibility of full integration between the World Council of Churches and the International Missionary Council, subject to an adequate safeguarding in any plan of integration of the distinctive expression of the mission of the Church as this has been embodied in the International Missionary Council".

The last phrase in this minute voices the anxiety expressed by some missionary leaders that the integration of the two bodies might lead to the pushing of missionary concern to the periphery. Much of the missionary thrust of the preceding century had come from bodies organized independently of the great Churches, and often against their opposition. Was it possible now to trust the Churches with the responsibility for world mission? In answer to this it was pointed out that the strong theological movements of the time were rediscovering, from one angle or another, the missionary nature of the Church. From the point of view of the W.C.C. it was a matter of its spiritual health whether it could go on saying that mission belongs to the very nature of the Church without becoming involved in the life of missions. The question, to quote Dr Visser 't Hooft at the 1956 meeting, was not one of "churchifying mission but of mobilizing the Church for its mission".

At the same meeting (Herrenalb 1956) the joint committee approved of a "list of categories of need for which Inter-Church Aid might seek the support of the churches" for aid to Churches in Asia, Africa, and Latin America. These included, in addition to emergency needs, projects designed to strengthen the Churches' witness or service which went beyond their existing resources. The way was thus opened up for a massive contribution from wealthier Churches through channels other than the traditional missionary channels.

As the result of the 1956 decision on integration, a meeting was held at Lambeth Palace in April 1957, which drafted a plan of integration between the two world bodies for submission to the joint committee. This plan came before the joint committee in July of the same year and after very full discussions an amendment was adopted for presentation to the two bodies. The discussion clearly revealed both the reasons which led many in both councils to seek integration and also the strength of the resistance which could be expected from both sides. On the one hand, the World Council had in its membership Orthodox Churches whose direct experience of Protestant missions had been gained through the work of bodies which had built up Churches mainly composed of converts from among their members. On the other hand, the member councils of the I.M.C., especially in Europe, included many vigorous and effective missionary societies which were organizationally independent of the Churches and which did not desire close administrative connection with them.

It was of great importance that the powerful voice of Dr Walter Freytag, speaking out of the German context in which missions were organized independently of the Churches, was raised in a definite affirmation of the need for integration. Delaying decision, he said, would be a refusal to grow. If mission is the heart of the Church, the heart cannot be separated from the rest of the Church's life. We are approaching a situation in which the Churches are becoming convinced about the missionary obligation, but are continuing to delegate responsibility for the universal aspect of mission to the missionary societies. There is a very grave spiritual danger in this both for the Churches and for the societies. The Churches' understanding of their mission becomes limited and the societies come to have too narrow an understanding of their work.

The Central Committee of the World Council at its meeting the same summer spent much time on the plan of integration and agreed to commend the plan to its member Churches for study, asking them to answer the following two questions:

(a) Are you in principle in favour of integration provided that a satisfactory plan is evolved?

(b) What comment have you to offer on the details of the proposed plan?

In sending the plan to member Churches the committee tried to allay the fear that integration would alter the character of the W.C.C. as a council of *Churches*. It pointed out to those who were afraid of proselytization by evangelical bodies that the I.M.C. had always worked towards co-operation and unity in mission. It drew attention to the document on "Christian Witness, Proselytism and Religious Liberty in the Setting of the World Council" which had been already commended to the Churches, and argued that the problems of proselytism could be better dealt with in an integrated council than by two separate bodies.

Ghana and the Theological Education Fund

At the end of the same year the I.M.C. held a major international assembly at University College, Accra, Ghana. The consideration of the plan of integration was one of the chief matters on the agenda. Several of the member councils had indicated serious reservations about the plan and many had not yet considered it. It was recognized that a very great deal of further discussion was needed. However, the Assembly decided to "accept in principle" the integration of the two councils and recorded its opinion that the draft plan was a "generally suitable instrument" for this purpose. The plan was sent to the member councils for their study and comment.

During the ensuing four years a vigorous discussion took place among the member Churches and member councils of the two world bodies. These culminated in the integration of the two bodies which was accepted by the Assemblies of both of them held in New Delhi at the end of 1961. Two member councils of the I.M.C. declined to accept the integration. They were the Norwegian Missionary Council and the Congo Protestant Council. It must be noted, however, that the relations between the Congo Council and the World Council of Churches after integration became in practice much more intimate than had been its earlier relationships with the I.M.C.

The accomplishment of administrative integration was an exceedingly important moment in the evolution of missionary thinking in an ecumenical context. However, it is important to recognize that the fundamental debates were continuing both before and after integration on the same basic issues. These issues were vividly expressed by Dr Freytag at the Ghana Assembly. He spoke of the "lost directness" of missions. At an earlier stage missions had understood their task as the sending of the gospel to the nations which had not heard it. In the new situation, where there were Churches in all countries bound together in an ecumenical fellowship, missions could not be conceived in the same terms. The new way to conceive them had not yet been clearly seen. The main thing was to see missions as part of the mission of God. The essential task is being sent to proclaim the gospel outside the Church. It is necessary "to remind every church that it cannot be the Church, in limiting itself within its own area, that it is called to take part in the responsibility of God's outgoing into the whole world, that it has the Gospel because it is meant for the nations of the earth, and that the Church has its life towards that end, the goal of God in the coming again of Christ".[1]

[1] The Ghana Assembly of the I.M.C., p. 146.

Following the lines of Dr Freytag, the Ghana Assembly accepted a statement on "the Christian mission at this hour", which took as its starting-point the phrase "the Christian world mission is Christ's, not ours". The statement affirmed that the distinction between older and younger Churches was no longer valid or helpful because it obscured the fact that every Church, because it is a Church, is equally called to a missionary task. "If they *are* churches, they are all alike called to mission."

The same assembly was the occasion of the launching of a very significant new form of ecumenical missionary action. During the years following the Tambaram Assembly the I.M.C. had given much attention to the training of the ministry in the younger Churches. It had sponsored surveys in several parts of the world, and particularly a series of surveys covering the whole of Africa and Madagascar. These had shown the terrible weakness of the Churches' theological training programmes, and the urgent need for more co-operation. As the result of initiatives taken by Charles Ranson, General Secretary of the I.M.C., John D. Rockefeller, Jr had made an offer of two million dollars to be matched by an equal amount from the mission boards in order to create a fund for the strengthening of theological education in the younger Churches. It was proposed that the fund should "select for individual institutional support those seminaries which on the basis of their strategic location, the excellence of their present work, and their plans for development, offer the greatest possibilities for qualitative growth in the future. It would pursue a policy of concentration by limiting its institutional grants to approximately twenty seminaries throughout the younger church areas, thereby endeavouring to build on strength rather than weakness." The Assembly learned that nine North American mission boards had pledged a total of two million dollars to match the offer of Mr Rockefeller. It was therefore resolved to establish the "Theological Education Fund" with Dr Charles Ranson as its first director. The creation of this fund constituted a new form of co-operative action. The resources of the fund, and in particular the services of its staff, were so wisely deployed over the ensuing years as to bring about a radical change in the quality and strength of the theological education in the younger Churches. The example of "TEF" was later followed by the creation in 1964 of a similar fund for Christian literature.

Kuala Lumpur and Joint Action

The Ghana Assembly had spoken of the missionary obligation resting upon every Church however young or small. While this statement was theologically impeccable it was difficult to make its meaning vivid. Missions still had the appearance of a one-way traffic from the Churches of Europe and North America. On the other hand, the World Council of Churches was creating a network of relationships among Churches in which all felt that they could both give and receive. Such a network corresponded much more closely to the contemporary sense of global unity than did the picture presented by missions. Moreover, the growing work of inter-Church aid in Asia, Africa, and Latin America, especially since the adoption of the "Herrenalb categories", gave increasing vividness to the new picture of ecumenical fellowship. There were some for whom it seemed obvious that such inter-Church aid was the modern equivalent of missions. Since the Church existed in almost every country it could be said that the missionary task in the traditional sense had been completed. The idea that a *foreign* missionary task, as envisaged by Dr Freytag, could still be valid in an age of ecumenical fellowship was difficult to grasp.

It was at this point that the development of regional co-operation in East Asia became important for the whole ecumenical discussion. In December 1949, the I.M.C. and the W.C.C. had jointly sponsored an East Asia Christian Conference at Bangkok, Thailand. Following this Dr R. B. Manikam had been appointed by the two bodies as their joint East Asia Secretary. In July 1955, some of the Churches in the eastern part of the region, with encouragement from the Board of World Mission of the Presbyterian Church in the U.S.A., had come together in Hong Kong to set up the "Asia Council on Ecumenical Mission". In the following year the two world bodies called a consultation in Bangkok to consider the future form of regional development in East Asia, and in March 1957 a representative conference was held at Prapat, Sumatra, which planned the creation of a permanent regional organization.

The East Asia Christian Conference was duly constituted at Kuala Lumpur, in May 1959, forty-eight churches committing themselves to its fellowship. The Kuala Lumpur meeting made plain the fact that the acceptance of missionary responsibility by the younger Churches had passed beyond the stage of theological affirmation to that of practical implementation. A survey embodied in the report of the conference showed that there was already a large number of foreign missionaries sent out by the Asian Churches and serving in countries overseas. The Assembly established machinery for the strengthening of this missionary outreach. It adopted an important statement on "the missionary obligation of the Asian churches" which dealt both with the receiving of missionaries from abroad and with the selection and sending of missionaries from the Asian Churches. In the context of the ecumenical discussion of missions it was a matter of the greatest importance that Kuala Lumpur could demonstrate that the foreign missionary task belongs to younger Churches equally with older and retains its validity in the new context of global ecumenical fellowship.

In another direction also, the Kuala Lumpur Assembly broke new ground. The Willingen Assembly had faced the fact that too much of the strength of missions was absorbed in the support of relatively static younger Churches. The need for a more effective and dynamic partnership between missions and the related younger Churches had been seen. The Kuala Lumpur Assembly saw that, in order to achieve this, the first step was to broaden the relations between them. The umbilical cord which had united young Churches to their parent missions in the earliest days should not remain for ever. The aim should be not simple severance leading to total independence, but rather the development of open and adult relations between all the Churches and missions working in a given area with a view to the accomplishment of their task together. The Kuala Lumpur meeting resolved:

That E.A.C.C. initiate ways of helping Asian churches and mission boards and agencies through national Christian councils and missionary councils to face together their total task with a view to deploying the total resources available in the most strategic way for the fulfilment of the mission. This may involve an increasing shift from the present bilateral relationships to a more ecumenical pattern of relationships.

The staff of the I.M.C. had been struggling to develop some coherent thinking along these lines. The Whitby and Willingen Conferences had seen the need for "internationalizing missions", and the I.M.C. staff had tried to develop this idea. The pamphlet *Out of Every Nation* by R. K. Orchard (1959) sought to give more precise expression to it, and in the staff paper *One Body, One Gospel, One World* (1961) the same idea was put forward under the title of "multi-lateral relationships". Encouraged by the proposals of the E.A.C.C., the I.M.C. staff devoted further time to the development of the idea and, at the next annual staff conference, produced a document entitled *Joint Action for Mission*. These proposals came before the Assembly at New Delhi and were welcomed. The Assembly adopted the following statement on the subject:

It believes that missionary advance in many parts of the world requires a redeployment of the resources available in specific geographical areas. A first necessary step towards this is that churches and related missionary bodies in a given area should together survey the needs and opportunities confronting them and the total resources available to meet them. This process of survey should be followed by a consultation of the churches and mission bodies in that area, aimed at securing real and effective redeployment of resources in the light of the agreed goals. This kind of common action will be impossible unless there is a fresh penitence, reconciliation and commitment on the part of all the bodies concerned. It will also raise in many cases searching issues in the realm of faith and churchmanship. The facing of these issues, both spiritual and confessional, will be a necessary precondition of missionary advance. The committee therefore hopes that the Commission and Division will seek to implement these proposals in consultation with churches, related mission agencies, and national and regional councils, taking due account of the confessional issues which may be involved, and making use of the best material available on questions of missionary strategy.[1]

In view of the fact that the Ghana Assembly had accepted in principle the integration of the two world bodies, and that this integration was likely to take place, the I.M.C. convened a consultation in Oxford in September 1958 which sought to make a restatement of the nature of the missionary task in the new ecumenical context. It was now clear that "foreign missions" could no longer be geographically defined. Europe was as much a mission field as Asia, and the "home base" was in Africa as well as in America. The *differentia of* missions could no longer be stated in geographical terms. Nevertheless, one should not draw from this the conclusion that the whole concept of missions and missionaries should be abandoned in favour of such terms as "inter-Church aid" and "fraternal workers". To abandon the concept of mission would be to abandon the New Testament. There remains a distinctively

[1] New Delhi, pp. 251–2.

missionary task, but it is to be defined essentially in terms of "the crossing of the frontier between faith in Christ as Lord and unbelief". To make clear, and to keep clear, this, the distinctive meaning of the word "missionary", is one of the most important requirements of the present discussion. "He who is sent to make Christ known and obeyed as Lord among those who do not know Him is a missionary whether his journey be long or short. The missionary frontier runs through every land where there are communities living without the knowledge of Christ as Lord."[1] But, the statement continued, it belongs to the essence of the gospel that it concerns the ends of the earth, and therefore it follows that "it is the duty and privilege of every part of the Church everywhere to be involved not only in the missionary task at its own door, but also in some other part of the world-wide task . . . To say that the 'home base' is everywhere is not the obliteration of 'foreign missions' but the universalizing of them."[2]

It has been seen that this thinking was already finding practical expression in East Asia. It also had immediate consequence in the formulation of the tasks of the new Commission on World Mission and Evangelism which was to be created within the integrated World Council of Churches. These tasks were outlined in a paper which was presented to, and accepted by, the Assembly in New Delhi. The first task was formulated as follows:

> To assist churches, missions and other Christian bodies to recognize and draw the practical conclusions from the fact that:
> (i) The Christian mission is one throughout the world, for the Gospel is the same and the need of salvation is the same for all men.
> (ii) This world mission has a base which is world-wide and is not confined to the areas once regarded as constituting "Western Christendom".
> (iii) The mission implies a reaching out both to one's own neighbourhood and to the ends of the earth.

In its statement accepting this task the committee of the Assembly at New Delhi wrote as follows:

> The programme of the new Division is not here fully described. It will provide a new frontier, a new dimension of the World Council. We have made a general outline of its task. We cannot now define all its deeper meanings nor the extent of its activities. Only the experience of living and working together can teach us these. Our temptation will be to think of the Division simply as the continuation of the interests of the International Missionary Council with emphasis on Asia, Africa and South America. We must resist this temptation. This is the Division of the World Mission and Evangelism of the World Council of Churches. We are concerned not with three continents but six.

Integration Achieved at New Delhi

The International Missionary Council and the World Council of Churches became one body at the Assembly in New Delhi in November 1961. The

---

[1] *One Body, One World*, p. 29.   [2] *Op. cit.*, p. 31.

integrated Council had immediately to accept a wide range of responsibilities in the field of missionary study, experiment, and joint action.

1. The Department of Missionary Studies inherited and carried forward work in the four main areas.

(a) The study of the theological basis of missions, begun in connection with the Willingen meeting, had not been completed. In a fresh effort to bring together fundamental thinking and ordinary missionary practice, groups around the world were invited to study a book written for the purpose by Johannes Blauw of the Netherlands on "The Missionary Nature of the Church". The results of these world-wide discussions were reflected on in a book by D. T. Niles entitled *Upon the Earth* (1962).

(b) The study of the Christian encounter with other faiths was the major concern of the Centres for the Study of Non-Christian Religions,[1] and the Department sought to stimulate and co-ordinate their work through contact with, and periodical meetings of, the directors of these centres. An important stage in the whole discussion was reached at the meeting of the directors and others held at Kandy, Ceylon, in 1967 on "Christians in Dialogue with Men of Other Faiths". In the preceding year the Department had also organized, at Brummana, Lebanon, a world consultation on "Christian–Muslim Relations".

(c) One of the biggest and most far-reaching of the projects of the Department of Missionary Studies has been a series of studies in depth of the growth of younger Churches in different selected situations. Originally entitled "Studies in the Life and Growth of Younger Churches", it was later replanned on a "six-continent" basis and renamed "World Studies of Churches in Missions". At the time of writing eight volumes have been published dealing with Churches in Uganda, Zambia, Togo, India, the South Pacific, England, Japan, and Congo-Brazzaville. These studies will in turn provide data for further research on the factors which bear upon the growth of the Church and its witness in its environment.

In addition to these major studies, each of which involved not less than a year of field-work by one or more scholars, there have been other consultations on church growth and related issues. At Mindolo, Zambia, a meeting of leaders of African independent Churches, or scholars who had studied the life of these Churches, and of leaders in several National Christian Councils in Africa was held in 1962 which both opened up valuable contacts between the two groups of Churches and also helped to bring out the lessons to be learned from the experience of the independent Churches. A consultation held at Iberville, Canada, in 1963 dealt with general principles of church growth. And in 1964 a meeting at Yaounde in the Cameroons gathered together the results of a survey conducted by a team during the preceding year on the growth, or absence of growth, of Churches in different parts of West Africa.

[1] See p. 180 above.

(*d*) The Department also continued and added to the series of research pamphlets on a variety of missionary topics which had been begun by the International Missionary Council.

2. The relations between the Divisions of World Mission and Inter-Church Aid had yet to be worked out in detail. The problems which had arisen in relating these two concerns in their day-to-day working had been among the factors leading to the decision to unite the two world bodies. After New Delhi the two concerns were administered within one structure, which meant that there were much better facilities for mutual consultation both on general policy and on specific projects. The basic problems had not been solved, but a structure had been created in which they could be solved. As a first step the New Delhi Assembly accepted the following statement of the relation:

> The integration of the two world bodies will make for greater co-operation of the two Divisions in their common purpose to express the ecumenical solidarity of the churches through mutual aid in order to strengthen them in their life and mission. Within this common purpose the Division of Inter-Church Aid and Service to Refugees is especially concerned to help the churches to serve the world around them, while the Division of World Mission and Evangelism is especially concerned to further the proclamation to the whole world of the Gospel of Jesus Christ to the end that all men may believe in Him and be saved.

The two Divisions would thus be working within a common field, but each would have a distinct focus of concern. This distinction was of real value in helping the new Division to sharpen its specifically missionary intent, but it left open for discussion very large administrative questions, and these were to be the subject of continuing discussion during the ensuing years.

3. The necessity to work out a new relationship with the Division of Inter-Church Aid forced the new Division constantly to face the following question: Does the conviction that "the home base of mission is everywhere" imply that new ecumenical missionary structures have to be created? Specifically, should the new Division initiate and manage missionary projects of an international and ecumenical character? Or should it concentrate upon stimulating joint action in local situations? There were strong convictions on both sides of this matter. Some feared the creation of a large centralized and expensive bureaucracy and pointed out that it was precisely the fear of this which had led some in the missionary councils to oppose integration with the World Council of Churches. Others urged that the missionary movement could only measure up to the demands of the new age by embarking upon such international and ecumenical action. The New Delhi Assembly approved a statement which authorized the Division to experiment in both directions. It authorized on the one hand: "Study, survey, consultation and the establishment of contacts designed to secure a more effective deployment of resources, more co-ordination of effort, the encouragement of more experiments in "multilateral' action, and more joint action where appropriate, special attention being given to the discovery of, and planning for, those geographical areas where there is no continuing Christian witness" and on the other hand "projects of an

international and interdenominational character initiated by the Commission to meet specific needs".[1]

At the time when these words were written, the Theological Education Fund was the most impressive example of such ecumenical projects. The I.M.C. had, however, also initiated other actions on a smaller scale. These included the Centres for the Study of Non-Christian Religions (to which reference has already been made), the publications of "World Christian Books", the programmes of study and training on the Christian Home and Family Life, and the "Islam in Africa Project". This latter was a particularly significant attempt to strengthen the witness of the Church in those areas of Africa where Islam is advancing by providing specialists, literature, and training courses. The Administrative Committee of the I.M.C. had, in 1959, given careful consideration to the proposal for "an International Fund for Mission". As a result of this, and after much discussion, it was decided to constitute a "Projects Fund" to be financed apart from the administrative budget of the Council, and to support such programmes as those just described, as well as the Department of Missionary Studies, the strengthening of national and regional councils, and the exchange of personnel between Councils and Churches. From a modest beginning this project fund has developed during the years following integration. As a result of continuing discussion with the Division of Inter-Church Aid it was agreed that matters which could properly be described as "projects" should be the responsibility of the latter Division, and that the undertakings sponsored by the Division of World Mission and Evangelism be characterized as "programmes". Among the international and ecumenical missionary programmes which have thus been supported the following may be mentioned in addition to those already referred to:

(a) In implementation of the call originally given at Willingen for a new type of non-professional lay missionary the Division collaborated with the Division of Inter-Church Aid in the establishment of a "Secretariat for Laymen Abroad". This did much to stimulate both missions and Churches to provide the means by which laymen going abroad in secular service could play their part in the mission of the Church.

(b) In order to complete the series of surveys on the training of the ministry, which the I.M.C. had undertaken, the new Division arranged for comprehensive surveys of the training of the ministry in Latin America and the Caribbean, under the leadership of Wilfred Scopes.

(c) In the year 1960 the attention of the I.M.C. had been directed to the need for helping the African Churches to meet the challenge of rapid industrialization. Following the general pattern of the "Islam in Africa" project, the administrative committee, at its meeting in St Andrews in 1960, authorized an "Urban Africa Project" under which provision was made for specialist assistance, travel, and conferences. Following the New Delhi Assembly, and collaboration with the E.A.C.C., the Division sponsored the visit of an international team of specialists to a large number of developing industrial centres

---

[1] *New Delhi Work Book*, p. 144.

in India. It became plain that there was here an area which called for co-operative international action and, at its meeting in 1964, the executive committee of the Division authorized a programme designed "to involve the total Church in all continents in the ecumenical task of urban industrial evangelism and so to promote greater co-operation and a common understanding of its goals".

(d) From the time of the Edinburgh Conference of 1910 the training of professional missionaries had been an important item on the agenda of ecumenical missionary meetings. The Willingen Conference had given much attention to it, but disappointingly little had been done to implement its findings. The Division sponsored a programme of study and consultation, which was focused in a meeting held in Toronto in August 1963. The implementation of the findings of this conference has been among the continuing tasks of the Division.

(e) There were certain kinds of work in which the responsibility for ecumenical action had been carried for many years by one or two national agencies, especially the specialized agencies of the (then) Division of Foreign Missions of the National Council of Churches in the U.S.A. One of these was Christian literature. The D.F.M.'s Department of Literature and Literacy, together with the Christian Literature Council of the Conference of Missionary Societies in Great Britain, had long carried the burden of literature work in many parts of the world. There was, however, no ecumenical agency dealing with Christian literature from a world base. The New Delhi Assembly recommended that the Division should undertake world-wide consultations with a view to a more effective ecumenical co-ordination of the production of Christian literature. As a result of these consultations, the 1963 Mexico meeting of the Commission authorized the creation of a Christian Literature Fund, analogous in its organization to the Theological Education Fund, with a capital of $3,000,000.

(f) In the field of radio and audio-visual aids the agency of the D.F.M., universally known as R.A.V.E.M.C.O., had for long been serving Churches all over the world. There was also an association of Christian broadcasters, which had its main strength in Europe and owed its beginning largely to the initiative of the B.B.C. The need was felt for the creation of a more effective agency in this field, and in 1962 the Division collaborated with the department of information in sponsoring the appointment of a secretary in the field of radio communication. In this way it proved possible to assist in the creation of an effective World Association of Christian Broadcasters. The Division also took the initiative in organizing a co-ordinating committee for inter-continental broadcasting under the leadership of Dr George W. Carpenter, in order to stimulate and co-ordinate ecumenical support for, and use of, the powerful station "Radio Voice of the Gospel" established by the Lutheran World Federation in Addis Ababa, Ethiopia.

(g) The healing ministry has been from the beginning an integral part of the Church's mission, but the rapid changes characteristic of the post-colonial era, and especially the development of welfare states in the former colonial territories, posed very grave problems for the medical missions. The question had to be asked whether, in a modern secular welfare state, there is any longer justification for the great expense involved in the maintenance of hospitals under Christian auspices. At the request of the Department of World Mission of the Lutheran World Federation, and with their collaboration, the Division organized a consultation in Tubingen, Germany, in 1964. This was intended merely to explore methods of further work, but it issued a brief statement concerning the specifically Christian understanding of the nature of healing which evoked a remarkable response throughout the world, not least in the lands of the older Churches. It became apparent that there was need for ecumenical action to assist the Churches in implementing the new insights given to them regarding the healing ministry in the mission of the Church. As a consequence, the Central Committee at its meeting in Crete 1967 authorized the creation of a Christian Medical Commission related to the Divisions of World Mission and Evangelism and of Inter-Church Aid, Refugee, and World Service.

(*h*) In addition to these major items, the Programme Fund also includes a small amount available at the discretion of the staff for giving immediate assistance to promising missionary projects of ecumenical significance. The existence of this fund has made possible the initiation and growth of many promising ventures in different parts of the world.

Mexico and Mission to Six Continents

The Division has accepted as a basis of its work the conviction that "the home base of the world mission" is world-wide, and that the "mission field" is also world-wide. The problem has always been to make these abstract statements credible through concrete examples. It has been seen that the development of a vigorous foreign missionary movement by the Asian Churches did much to put substance into the doctrine that the "home base" is indeed not confined to the old "Christendom". It was equally necessary to give substance to the other half of the basic conviction. This could happen only when those who were actively engaged in missionary tasks in Europe and North America could be intimately involved in the work of the Division. The achievement of the meeting of the commission in Mexico City (December 1963) was that this happened on a substantial scale for the first time. By general consent the most significant discussions at the Mexico meeting took place in Sections II and III which dealt respectively with "The Christian Witness to Men in the Secular World" and "The Witness of the Congregation in its Neighbourhood". These discussions, held within the context of a world missionary meeting, made vivid for all the participants the fact that the mission field is indeed in all six continents.

It would, of course, be absurd to suggest that concern with the missionary task in the lands of the "older Churches" was something entirely new in the thinking of the foreign missionary movement. The Jerusalem Conference of

1928 had concerned itself with the rise of secularism as a world-wide movement. Dr J. H. Oldham had become convinced, at least during the early
1930s, that if the missionary movement did not concern itself with the situation in the old "Christendom" it would soon be left in a backwater, and it
was with the cordial approval of his colleagues that he was set free to devote
his immense powers to the issues which led up to, and followed from, the
Oxford Conference on Church, Community and State (1937). But the Mexico
meeting broke new ground in the fact that, for the first time at a world missionary gathering, expert attention was given to the specific problems of
mission in Europe and North America. Men and women engaged in "home
missions" were present in a strength sufficient to ensure that this concern was
at no point overshadowed by that of "foreign missions".

The Mexico meeting gathered together and concentrated the thinking which
had been developed through a variety of study programmes. Reference has
already been made to the continued studies on the theological basis of missions by the Department of Missionary Studies. The Department on Studies
in Evangelism, following the New Delhi Assembly, launched a world-wide
study on "The Missionary Structure of the Congregation", which raised
radical questions concerning the nature of the Church and of evangelism.
And the work of Asian theologians, reflecting on the meaning of events in
that continent, had brought into the main stream of missionary thinking the
conviction that God is somehow at work in the secular events of our time,
beyond the bounds of the Church. These and other streams of thought flowed
together at the Mexico meeting to produce a very vigorous process of thinking
about mission in the context of six continents. If the Tambaram meeting had
placed the Christian mission firmly in a churchly context, and if Willingen
had struggled unsuccessfully to break out of this, Mexico must be regarded
as especially significant for the fact that it conceived the missionary task in the
context of what God is doing in the secular events of our time. "The Pattern
of Christian mission in the secular world", said the report of Section II, "must
therefore be one of constant encounter with the real needs of our age. Its
form must be that of dialogue, using contemporary language and modes of
thought, learning from the scientific and sociological categories, and meeting
people in their own situations."[1] Plainly such language is equally relevant in
Boston or Tokyo. The mission field is everywhere.

The section at Mexico which dealt with the Christian witness to men of
other faiths failed to achieve any significant fresh insights. The study launched
by the (combined) Division of Studies in 1956 on "The Word of God and the
Living Faiths of Men" was still in process. It had been seen to be necessary
that responsibility for this study should be lodged with the study centres
which were actually working in the midst of these living faiths. But there was
little sign at Mexico of the emergence of a clear consensus on this matter.
This is no doubt partly an aspect of the profound crisis of faith in the Western
Churches to which reference was made at the beginning of this chapter. It is
also perhaps a symptom of the fact that the discussion of relations between
the gospel and other religions has not yet taken sufficient account of the

[1] MRCC (Mexico City 1963), p. 121.

insights which are being developed in the encounter of the gospel with the secular world.

The fourth section of the Mexico meeting dealt with "The Witness of the Church across National and Confessional Boundaries". In spite of the hesitations of some members, the section advocated advance in the direction of more international and ecumenical action in the field of mission. Its report was a mandate to the Division to move faster than had yet been thought possible in the direction of joint action both on a world scale and in local situations. The missionary agencies have shown their willingness to move in this direction by putting larger resources at the disposal of the programme fund of the Division, and by underwriting the new funds for Christian literature and for the ministry of healing.

The Church and the Jewish People

Among the programmes for which the International Missionary Conference had at an early stage decided to take responsibility was the work of assisting the Churches in their mission to the Jewish people. A Committee on the Christian Approach to the Jews was formed in 1930 as a sponsored agency of the I.M.C., and it developed a full programme of training consultation and conference. At the Amsterdam Assembly it sponsored a declaration on anti-semitism which was taken up by many of the member Churches. At the New Delhi Assembly, when the two world councils were integrated, the committee was reconstituted as the W.C.C.'s Committee on the Church and the Jewish People. The New Delhi Assembly also issued a statement on anti-semitism which was followed up by a number of member Churches and was warmly welcomed in Jewish circles. Encouraged by this welcome the Committee arranged an international consultation between Christian and Jewish leaders at Bossey in August 1965. The difficulties of the meeting were summed up by one of the Jewish leaders as follows: "Most Christians are unable to engage in dialogue about faith and most Jews are unwilling to do so." The comment aptly indicates the difficulty which the Committee faces. Its purpose has always been both to foster relations of mutual understanding and charity between Christians and Jews and also to help the Churches in their mission to the Jewish people to whom, as to all mankind, the Christian is under an obligation to make known the saving truth of the gospel. It is inevitable that there should be a certain tension between these two elements in the responsibility of the Church towards the Jewish people, and to seek the resolution of it has been the main concern of this committee during the past decade. It is of some significance that whereas in the Roman Catholic Church the concern for relations with the Jewish people is lodged in the Secretariat for Unity, the corresponding concern in the World Council of Churches is expressed through the missionary arm of the Council.

Catholic, Evangelical, and Orthodox

In this, as in other matters, the period under review has seen a radical transformation in the relations between the World Council and the Roman
Catholic Church. While the scheme *De missionibus* was still under discussion at the Second Vatican Council, an informal meeting was arranged in
Switzerland in May 1965 between representatives of the World Council and
the Roman Catholic Church to discuss missionary questions. During a week
of very frank and intimate discussion many agreements were registered
between the two groups. There was a strong conviction that it is not enough
for the Churches to collaborate in service to society since, if collaboration
stops short with this, the witness which the Churches give to the world is
distorted. Collaboration must, above all, serve to glorify Christ; and therefore,
granted the great difficulties involved, every effort must be made to avoid the
scandal caused by mutual rivalry and hostility in missionary work. The
consultation opened up many lines of study concerning both the substance of the gospel we proclaim and the manner in which it is to be
proclaimed. It had some effect upon the final shape of the Vatican
Decree *Ad gentes*, and it has laid the foundations for further consultation
and collaboration.

It is unfortunately not possible to record similar progress in respect of
contact with the missionary work of the Conservative Evangelical agencies.
It is well known that these agencies maintain a larger number of foreign
missionaries than do the agencies connected with the World Council of
Churches. While the Churches with which they are related constitute a very
much smaller body than the membership of the World Council, the vigour
and volume of their missionary witness constitute a standing challenge to the
Churches which collaborate in the ecumenical movement. During the period
under review there have been some opportunities for mutually fruitful consultation. It remains true, however, that the Division has not yet been able
to do much to fulfil that section of its mandate which requires it "to establish
contact with evangelistic groups and movements which are still unrelated to
the ecumenical movement". It is to be hoped that the growing strength and
maturity of these movements will in due time encourage them to enter more
fully into the kind of dialogue with other missionary agencies which can
mutually enrich both partners.

During the period when the question of integration was under discussion
in the two world councils, there was some anxiety among the Orthodox
member Churches of the W.C.C. about the possible consequences of this
step. Since the integration took place, Orthodox Churchmen have participated
in the work of the Commission and Division of World Mission and Evangelism. The staff have had fruitful contacts with the Greek missionary movement *Porefthendes*, and have been able to render some small assistance to that
vigorous movement. There has been a consultation in Aarhus in 1964 with
Orthodox theologians on theological questions connected with the
missionary task of the Church. The International Review of Missions
has also carried valuable articles on the missionary work of the Orthodox

Churches. Much more remains to be done to integrate the missionary witness of the Orthodox Churches more fully in the life of the World Council of Churches.

Urgent New Questions

The questions which were most strenuously discussed during the period of history which we have briefly reviewed were questions concerning the form and structure of missions. The shift from the "three-continent" to the "six-continent" perspective was a matter of structure. The problems posed for missions by the rise of the younger Churches, the end of colonialism, and the development of inter-Church aid on a massive scale were questions about the forms and patterns of missionary action. It would certainly be untrue to say that these problems have been solved; but it can be said that, as a result of the decisions made during this period, a structure has been created within which missions can operate in an ecumenical context. It has been shown that it is not necessary to abandon missionary calling, the calling to take the gospel across the frontier to those who do not have it, in order to be part of the modern ecumenical reality. If one compares the present situation with that at the time of the Ghana Conference, one can perhaps say that the beginnings of an answer have been given by Dr Freytag's question about the "lost directness".

The questions which face the ecumenical movement now are different ones. They are questions about the substance of the gospel itself. The World Council of Churches has a Division whose aim is "to further the proclamation to the whole world of the Gospel of Jesus Christ, to the end that all men believe in Him and be saved". The questions that have now to be answered concern the content of that proclamation itself. What is the relation of this proclamation to the action of God in the secular world, to the service rendered by Christians to their fellow men, and to the life of the Church? There is a crisis of faith in the Church, and upon its outcome will depend the possibility of faithful proclamation. During the years in which drastic changes of structure were being made, those involved largely took the content of the gospel for granted. Today that can no longer be done. The course of the next stage in the world-wide mission of the Church will depend upon the recovery by the Church of clarity regarding the gospel which it has to proclaim.

8
Joint Service
as an Instrument of Renewal

GEOFFREY MURRAY

Introduction

In the epilogue to *A History of the Ecumenical Movement 1517–1948*, Bishop Stephen C. Neill wrote:

> It, [the World Council of Churches] makes possible corporate charitable action on a scale never previously considered possible, and unsurpassed as a means of creating genuine Christian fellowship. It has taken the first steps in corporate witness to the whole body of the churches and to the world (p. 728).

Even in the short time since that judgement was written there have been changes of attitude and outlook. Today those associated with the W.C.C.'s Division of Inter-Church Aid, Refugee, and World Service would shrink from referring to the work in which they are engaged as "charity". Rather, they now speak of the work they do as an endeavour to facilitate the sharing of resources—spiritual, personal, material, and financial—by the ecumenical fellowship to help meet needs on behalf of humanity, and without distinction of creed, caste, race, nationality, or politics. During the 1960s the Churches began to take part in those governmental and intergovernmental programmes known as Development Aid. The role which many Churches played, and are continuing to play in the United Nations' Freedom from Hunger Campaign, World Food Programme, and the Development Decade goes far beyond the accepted limits of "charity".

Nevertheless, Bishop Neill's general statement is still true. Action has been, and is being, taken "on a scale never previously considered possible, and unsurpassed as a means of creating genuine Christian fellowship". This action is what is known as Inter-Church Aid. The first measures tentatively sketched in the Rouse and Neill *History* have gathered an astonishing dynamism and momentum during the past quarter of a century.

They began with one man and a secretary working in a small office in Geneva in the spring of 1945 and gradually evolved to become the largest single Division of the World Council of Churches. In round figures, one person in every four on the headquarters staff of the World Council of Churches in Geneva at the beginning of 1968 was working in the Division of Inter-Church Aid, Refugee, and World Service, and some 200 more were employed by it around the world. Again, the Division raised its own budget and this was, in the mid-1960s, roughly fifty per cent more than the entire general budget of the World Council.

With this money the Division paid its staff, administrative costs, and over-head expenses. It also helped to support other divisions and departments of the World Council, to strengthen various national and regional councils of Churches. It financed certain programmes of its own, such as the Scholarships Programme, the Health Programme, the Literature Programme, and part of the budget of Casa Locarno, the ecumenical rest centre for pastors and church workers and their wives, which it maintained jointly with the Swiss Protestant Churches.

In addition, the Division circulated to the member Churches and their service agencies an annual project list which detailed some 600 projects in about sixty countries which requested support totalling about $20,000,000 a year. In response to these requests, and to emergency appeals which the Division put out from time to time after natural or man-made disasters, roughly $13,000,000 flowed through the Division every year, and these sums were passed on without any deduction whatsoever to the designated recipients.

Two inferences are usually drawn from the figures given in the last paragraph. The first is that the Churches find it easier to act together in relieving human suffering than to act together in any other cause. The second inference is that this joint action creates, as Bishop Neill said in the passage quoted, genuine Christian fellowship. This solidarity of Christian compassion in the face of want and deprivation has taken many forms. Among them are services to tens of thousands of refugees and displaced persons, the provision of theological books, the offering of surgical and medical treatments that could not otherwise be obtained, the means to build churches and parish houses. Also skilled persons are sent to carry out technical services that the Churches have called for. The augmenting of pastors' stipends, funds for the defence of religious liberty and civil rights, the provision of trade training schools, the building of houses for the homeless, the provision of well-boring rigs, the stocking of farms with seeds, animals, and tools, the equipping of hospitals, and a thousand other acts of mercy are regularly undertaken. All this has combined to remove doubts and hesitations about the reality of the Christian fellowship. A not unimportant by-product is that it has persuaded many Churches to enlist in the ecumenical movement.

An attempt will be made in the present chapter to narrate how Inter-Church Aid has grown. But before embarking on the story it is necessary to define what is meant, within the World Council, by "Inter-Church Aid". The present chapter is emphatically not a history of "charity", however conceived, since 1948. The writer is acutely aware of what is being done by denominations, world confessional bodies, mission societies, Roman Catholics, Jews, the Red Cross, inter-governmental and U.N. special agencies, and others. But he has had necessarily to confine himself to the joint service undertaken by the member Churches of the World Council through its Division of Inter-Church Aid, Refugee, and World Service (D.I.C.A.R.W.S.).

Inter-Church Aid Defined

From the beginning the Church has been, or has tried to be, obedient to the command of Jesus to succour those in distress. An early instance of this is cited in Acts 11. 29-30: "Then the disciples, every man according to his ability, determined to send relief unto the brethren which dwelt in Judaea: Which also they did, and sent it to the elders by the hands of Barnabas and Saul." This illustration could be multiplied endlessly. The outcome has been a ministry of service that has spread throughout the world.

But, as the work grew, it was generally marked until recent times by the concern of the Churches for their own people. Church activities of this kind continue and are often international or supranational. Help given by a "mother" Church to a "daughter" Church—by, for example, Methodists in the U.S.A. to Methodists in Ghana, or by Baptists in Britain to Baptists in Pakistan—is right and proper. But this is not Inter-Church Aid as its practitioners have come to understand it. Within the World Council, Inter-Church Aid is interpreted as joint action in service that crosses ecclesiastical and geographical boundaries. In other words, Inter-Church Aid, thus understood, is given when a Church in one part of the world is helped by a Church or Churches of different Christian traditions located elsewhere to carry out the efforts it is making to meet the needs of its neighbours whoever they may be. Inter-Church Aid strives through service to promote the renewal of the Churches.

The core of the work done by the W.C.C.'s Division of Inter-Church Aid, Refugee, and World Service is the co-ordination of inter-Church aid programmes and projects. At the beginning there were those who thought that the way to achieve this was by a pooling of funds. Others believed that inter-Church aid should be effected as a Church-to-Church operation. The genius of the World Council has been to make a circle around the whole network of "service" relationships and in this way give expression to Christian solidarity in helping to meet church, social, and economic needs of almost every kind. A new understanding has emerged that the place where Christ himself is to be served is in the persons of those in need wherever they are and whoever they may be. By serving the whole of mankind in all its diversity, inter-Church aid witnesses both to Christians and others to the oneness of the human family under God.

Inter-Church Aid, in the special ecumenical sense here given to it, has thus established within a relatively few years an entirely new pattern of Christian stewardship and for the dispensing of resources often contributed by those outside the Churches. In one way it has enormously widened ecclesiastical horizons. In another it has dovetailed into a firmly jointed whole a great variety of means for showing the solidarity of Christian compassion in the face of adversity. The conception of "giving" and "receiving" Churches which sometimes carries with it in the "Third World" implications of neo-colonialism and dependence is being phased out by the ecumenical practice. All are together as equals in a common enterprise of service in which they give and share from their own free choice according to their talents, their means, and their opportunities.

Thus, the National Council of the Churches of Christ in the U.S.A. can seek support for its Mississippi Delta Ministry which is helping Negroes and white sympathizers to change the structure of society, in a way that will afford social justice for all. The Mississippi Delta Ministry has attracted workers from overseas as well as contributions from Churches in Africa, Asia, and Europe. Inter-Church Aid includes those who plan, serve, and administer in National and Regional Councils of Churches, and in certain self-governing bodies such as Japan Church World Service, those who give money and material aid, and, no less, those who pray and lend spiritual and moral support. All become partners in a world-wide ministry of mercy.

The role of the Division of Inter-Church Aid, Refugee, and World Service is to foster the renewal of the Churches through service in unity. The Division is charged to ensure that no project admitted to its list for support by members of the World Council is calculated to entice adherents from one Church and enroll them in another.

In reaching this interpretation of Inter-Church Aid, the ecumenical fellowship is indebted incalculably to the late Adolf Keller. The term "Inter-Church Aid" can probably be ascribed to him. It appears in the title of the European Central Bureau for Inter-Church Aid, the body which he was largely instrumental in founding in 1922 and carried on until it was merged in the provisional World Council of Churches in 1944 as an integral part of the Department of Reconstruction and Inter-Church Aid. Dr J. Hutchinson Cockburn, a former Moderator of the Church of Scotland, accepted the post of Senior Secretary of the Department in December 1944. It is at this point that this chapter resumes the history of ecumenical service, begun in the Rouse and Neill book, which is now conceived as the responsibility of a world fellowship of Churches.

The W.C.C. Department of Reconstruction and Inter-Church Aid[1]

Dr Cockburn did not reach Geneva until March 1945, and then only after hammering daily for many weeks on the door of the French authorities in London for permission to travel. The journey from Britain to Switzerland then involved five changes of trains, for bridges and tunnels along the line between Paris and Geneva had been damaged. Flying from Britain to Switzerland appears not to have been possible at that time. These facts serve to indicate something of the conditions of chaos in which the department was to go to work.

In Geneva, Dr Cockburn was installed in an office at the top of a small house in the Champel district which then constituted the headquarters of the World Council. His staff was a shorthand typist who was adept at languages. While the war in Europe dragged on for another two months, Dr Cockburn learned his job, chiefly from various memoranda about countries and their Churches that were put in his hands. One of these memoranda was the mandate for the department. It had been drawn up by W. A. Visser 't Hooft and approved by the Provisional Committee of the World Council of Churches in 1943. It said:

> The paramount principle is that which is implied in the very existence of the World Council, namely, that the task of reconstruction is to be conceived as an ecumenical task in which all the churches participate to the limit of their ability, and that the common objective is to rebuild the whole life of the fellowship of churches which finds expression in the World Council. If this ecumenical principle is taken seriously, this will mean that the churches will agree to co-ordinate their policies and activities in order to make certain that all needy churches receive adequate help, that the churches will not confine

[1] For the following section, the writer has drawn extensively from a Memorandum written by Dr Cockburn and given to the late Dr Leslie E. Cooke, who would have been the author of the present chapter had he not died in February 1967.

their help exclusively to the churches belonging to the same denomination or confession, and that the autonomy and desires of the receiving churches are taken into full consideration.[1]

Cockburn began energetically to recruit staff to carry out the immense task that he saw required to be done. Tremendous though the work before him was, he regarded it as no more than to meet a temporary emergency and looked to its completion within three years, when the First Assembly was to meet in Amsterdam. The first and most urgent need that was seen was to dispense food and clothing. To manage this service of direct material aid a division was created within the Department of Reconstruction and Inter-Church Aid under the direction of S. C. Michelfelder, a Lutheran from the U.S.A.[2] Dr Michelfelder had been sent to Geneva as a special commissioner of the American section of the Lutheran World Convention. He was invited by the World Council of Churches to serve as its material aid secretary in addition to his other responsibilities. The agreement for him to serve in this dual capacity was one of the earliest forms of co-operation between the W.C.C. and what is now the Lutheran World Federation.

A World Council Secretariat for non-Aryan Refugees had been formed as early as February 1939, under the Reverend Adolf Freudenberg, who now became Cockburn's associate. Freudenberg, along with Oliver Béguin, had been giving attention for some time to reconstruction activities. Cockburn soon had a department with eleven divisions. These divisions were: (1) General Support of Churches and Pastors' Salaries; (2) Material Aid; (3) Bibles and Literature; (4) Theological Education and Scholarships; (5) Wooden Churches and Halls; (6) Youth Movements; (7) Refugees; (8) German Churches; (9) German Literature; (10) Finance; and (11) Publicity.

It was accepted in 1945 that each secretary of a departmental division would deal with the matters committed to him in all countries, but it was thought that it would be "valuable" if each made himself an authority on the church life of one country or group of countries. Cockburn therefore made the following allocations. He himself took responsibility for Italy and Greece. Others were allocated for Germany; Scandinavian countries; Rumania, Bulgaria, Yugoslavia, Austria, and Hungary; Holland, Czechoslovakia, Spain, and Portugal; France and Belgium; and Finland and Poland. He began in Europe, for this was the area of greatest immediate damage. Additional expert advice and knowledge were available, when required, from other members of the World Council staff.

Cockburn recruited his divisional secretaries in the U.S.A., Britain, Switzerland and other countries. Among them were those who represented individual Churches, federations of Churches, or National Councils of Churches. Some members of the department were recruited because of their special talents or experience. One was invited to come from the Allied Military

---

[1] Quoted by Bishop George Bell, *The Kingship of Christ*, p. 38.

[2] The knowledgeable may think this is a reversal of W.C.C. terminology, for its Departments are either autonomous or embraced by "Divisions", but this nomenclature was not adopted until the Second Assembly at Evanston 1954; until then there were divisions within "Departments".

Control in Germany; another was called from a foreign congregation in London. Some persons were appointed to give their energies to a particular country whose language they spoke and wrote. By 1948 Cockburn had built up an organization of sixty-seven persons, including attachés or seconded staff. About twenty had executive status.

The dislocation that prevailed in Europe when the department began added urgency. At that moment there were an estimated 12,500,000 refugees, displaced persons, and uprooted persons in western Europe. There were 10,000 damaged or destroyed church buildings throughout the Continent. More than 3,200 church buildings had been completely demolished. An additional 2,000 pastors' houses, parish halls, and other Church-owned premises had been severely battered by warfare. Many more churches in Britain had been destroyed, in addition to the above. Germany alone had 6,400 ravaged churches. Apart from the spiritual hunger that came from the disruption of church life in so many parishes, physical hunger was also endemic. Food in vast quantities was urgently required for distribution among the starving, as well as an enormous tonnage of clothing, blankets, medicines, beds, and other goods. Telegrams were continually being received that pleaded for the replacement of hospital equipment lost in the bombing, for blankets needed to cover patients in danger of freezing, and of beds, blankets, and mattresses for tuberculous children.

Moreover, it must be stressed that the physical devastation, with its ruined towns, wrecked railways, and shattered factories, and all the chronic shortages of food, clothing, shelter, work, and man-power which accompanied it, was only an outward sign of an inner trauma. There was in Germany the psychological disturbance that came with the realization of defeat and the occupation of the country by the Allies and their soldiers. In France, Denmark, and the Netherlands there was the reverse experience of being "occupied" one day and free the next. Throughout the war years it had been honourable to kill, to lie, to be engaged in sabotage and hate; but after the cease-fire such actions were held once more to be sinful. The tremendous task of renewing the life of the Churches so that they might proclaim the Christian gospel was an "inside" affair. They needed love and friendship.

The Department of Reconstruction and Inter-Church Aid attacked this situation along two lines. First it set up, or, if they already existed, it adopted, corresponding bodies, representative councils or committees in those countries which were able and ready to help the Churches in countries devastated by war. Supporting agencies of this kind were active at first in the U.S.A., Britain, Switzerland, Denmark and Sweden; later in Canada, New Zealand, and Australia. Second, it wrote to, and, where possible, its representatives visited, non-Catholic Churches in European countries and asked them to appoint representatives to meet together, in common council, to discuss their needs. (The Roman Catholic Church was not approached because it had its own plans and organizations.)

The response was most encouraging. Committees of the kind suggested were set up in France, Belgium, Holland, Norway, Germany, Poland, Austria, Czechoslovakia, and Hungary. It was found that in some countries the leaders of a number of Churches had never met for discussion of common needs and purposes. Either at a first meeting or later Cockburn or another member of his staff spent some days in discussion with the committees. Then a report was presented to the department for it to communicate to the supporting agencies so that whatever help was available could be co-ordinated and shipped. Thus was the classic pattern of Inter-Church Aid set and developed.

Assistance was at first tentative, but it quickly mounted as the department was able to gather and validate the needs of the Churches in the war-ruined countries. As early as 15 May 1945 the Central Office for Inter-Church Aid in New York had intimated that it would place $100,000 at the department's disposal. Within a few months the total had grown to $600,000 contributed by Churches in the U.S.A. This was available to buy supplies. Considerable quantities of goods were offered by Churches in Switzerland and Sweden, as well as by others in the U.S.A.

By February 1946 the Provisional Committee of the World Council of Churches had been informed that the World Council Services Committee in the U.S.A. was hoping to raise $9,000,000 over a four-year period. This would be passed to the department or sent directly to needy Churches. The Swiss Reconstruction Committee had raised and spent its first million francs ($233,640) and was appealing for its second million. The British Committee for Reconstruction in Europe also had substantial funds and would spend these as allowed by the regulations controlling the transfer of sterling. In the upshot, the British Committee raised a "Million Pound Fund" (then worth about $4,000,000) at a time when Britain was still enduring severe food rationing and was itself rebuilding war damaged buildings and factories. The Swedish Committee was helping generously its sister Churches in Norway and Finland, and had sent help to Holland and Germany.

The aid given included medicines, food, clothing, footwear, blankets, equipment of various kinds, Bibles, books, libraries in many languages, cattle, seeds, and some thousands of tons of cellulose to enable paper mills to restart and publications to begin. At one point Cockburn telephoned to New York and said that he needed $500,000 in three days for relief work; he got it, and $60,000 in addition. Bishop Berggrav of Norway asked for help to adapt a large fishing boat, with its fish hold made into a church, so that a pastor could sail up the coast beyond the North Cape to offer services of worship, marriage, and baptism to villagers whose churches had been destroyed during the German retreat. Cockburn backed the plan and found supporters in Britain to help pay for it.

Church life had been disrupted and had to be restarted. The "Wooden Churches" division began with a programme to buy 138 barrack huts from the Swiss and Swedish armies and to convert these huts into places of worship, parsonages, and parish centres for those who lacked them. These wooden churches, costing more than $700,000, were allotted to congregations in areas of greatest need: Germany was given forty-four, France forty, Holland thirty-seven, Austria eleven. Two each were sent to Belgium, Hungary, and Poland. They were the direct gift of American Christians, co-operating through Church World Service and Lutheran World Federation, and of British,

H

Canadian, Danish, New Zealand, Swedish, and Swiss church people. Contributions were also received from the Lutheran Church–Missouri Synod which was outside the World Council fellowship.

The department was at pains to encourage and find support for self-help programmes. In Germany, H.E.K.D. (*Hilfswerk der Evangelischen Kirche in Deutschland*—Relief Work of the Protestant Churches in Germany), under the leadership of Dr Eugen Gerstenmaier, quickly became the largest voluntary relief agency in that war-torn country. It channelled the distribution of supplies from abroad and collected goods and money within Germany. Ninety thousand laymen were recruited to administer its programme. Between 1945 and 1950 H.E.K.D. distributed 66,000 tons of goods, clothing, shoes, medicines, raw materials, and books that had been sent to Germany by Churches in twenty-four countries.

In the introduction to a booklet[1] published in 1960, the late Bishop Dr Otto Dibelius, then the Bishop of Berlin and Chairman of the Evangelical Churches in Germany, wrote:

> Every German knows the generosity with which America has assisted the German people to rebuild a new life out of destruction. Our gratitude will never cease, and nowhere is this gratitude felt more strongly than in the Evangelical Churches of Germany. Much aid has come through free-giving in your congregations, but you have also made strong efforts to ensure that the surplus commodities of the U.S.A. did not pass by church institutions. Your giving has been an example of brotherly and personal concern and care . . . thus establishing a fraternal relationship which until now was unknown between the churches of different countries. This ecumenical fellowship will bear fruit.

Nor were the Orthodox Churches and countries of eastern Europe overlooked. These were the concern, as they continue to be, of the Department. They were helped to restore their church life where this had been disrupted by war. Scholarships were provided for their students. Their priests were helped. Books and periodicals were shipped to their seminaries and theological faculties. Medical treatment was offered to church workers and their families who were sick. In all this, the Orthodox and non-Orthodox were served as equals in the ecumenical fellowship. This loving concern gradually convinced those Orthodox Churches that had refrained from joining the World Council that theological and ecclesiastical hesitations should not keep them out of the ecumenical fellowship, and by 1968 virtually all the Orthodox Churches were members.

Over the years, Orthodox Churchmen have commented on the help given to their people by denominations in other countries and often of radically different Christian tradition from their own. Thus, in 1950, during the meeting of the Central Committee of the W.C.C. at Toronto, Archbishop Strinopoulos Germanos, Metropolitan of Thyateira and at that time one of the Presidents of the World Council, expressed appreciation for the work of the Inter-Church

---

[1] *Dank für Hilfe durch das Amerikanische Volk 1945–1960.* This was published only in German, so that the quotation which follows is an English translation from the original German.

Aid Department among Orthodox clergy and laity in Germany and Greece. Such help, he said, had not been confined to money, but had included essentials needed by chaplains in the camps, down to candles and oil for services. He added that he had been asked by the Ecumenical Patriarch of Constantinople to convey his gratitude to the W.C.C. and Inter-Church Aid. The following year, during the Central Committee meeting at Rolle, Switzerland, Professor H. S. Alivisatos expressed heartiest thanks on behalf of the Greek Churches for allocations to poor clergy, for food and clothing for refugees and the poor, for scholarships, for help with church and religious publications, for a new educational centre for the Church, and for a new printing press. Many others, including Metropolitan James, expressed similar views.

As a footnote to this section, the story of E.C.L.O.F. (The Ecumenical Church Loan Fund) should be remembered. It was established in 1946 to be a supplementary source of funds for Churches wishing to find money to complete their building projects or to buy necessary equipment. In the 1920s, Gustav Hentsch, a Genevan banker, led in founding A.P.I.D.E.P. (*Association Protestante Internationale des Prêts*—International Protestant Loan Association). Hentsch believed that the situation after the Second World War called for a loan organization more broadly based and more flexible than A.P.I.D.E.P. He therefore created E.C.L.O.F. with its central board which allocates capital to national E.C.L.O.F. committees in Europe, Asia, Africa, and Latin America. Money repaid to a national committee stays in that country where it continues to "revolve". The interest charged is nominal. E.C.L.O.F. is an independent body, but the Division, under its various names, is closely associated with it and seeks additions to its capital. A.P.I.D.E.P. and E.C.L.O.F. continued as separate organizations until 1963, when they were brought together in a centralized administration. The capital currently exceeds $700,000 and more than 1,000 loans have been made without any Church defaulting.

Refugee Programme

Arrangements to transfer ecumenical responsibility for refugees and displaced persons to the Department of Reconstruction had been made in July 1945. The mandate of the Refugee Secretariat was:

1. To seek and distribute knowledge on the situation of refugees.
2. To co-ordinate and promote church efforts on their behalf, to help Churches in disaster areas, to help refugees where no Christian organization was available, to minister to their spiritual needs, and to represent the World Council of Churches before intergovernmental and governmental groups interested in refugees.

A Refugee Committee was constituted and had for its chairman the Reverend Henry Carter, a distinguished British Methodist who was honoured by the King of England for his work with refugees.

Broadly, the mandate set out above has continued to govern the work of the World Council of Churches for refugees and displaced persons. Technically, a "refugee" is someone who has fled from his homeland and has no prospect of being readmitted to it; a "displaced person" is someone who has been forced to move to another area but may be repatriated. In popular usage, the two terms are often employed synonymously, but, in fact, they refer to two distinct categories of people. A third category, of whom little was heard outside Western Germany, were those known as "expellees". They included ten million Germans from former German territories that had come under Russian or Polish administration. These people were forced to move and could not be repatriated because they were considered to be Germans moving into another part of Germany. "Expellees" were not "refugees" unless they fled across the right border.

Immediately after the Second World War, U.N.R.R.A. (the United Nations' Relief and Rehabilitation Agency) was charged to meet human need, to foster reconstruction, and to assist governments throughout eastern and western Europe following the devastation caused by the conflict. U.N.R.R.A., which had no mandate to care for the repatriated and displaced persons, was succeeded in 1948 by the I.R.O. (International Refugee Organization), another specialized agency of the United Nations. This, as its name makes clear, had responsibility for refugees. I.R.O. was replaced in 1951 by the United Nations' High Commissioner for Refugees (U.N.H.C.R.) and, for Palestine Arab refugees, by U.N.R.W.A. (United Nations Relief and Works Agency). The U.N.H.C.R. is concerned to provide legal protection for refugees and to assist governments and voluntary agencies to find permanent solutions for refugee problems. Another organization, I.C.E.M. (Intergovernmental Committee for European Migration) is composed of representatives of twenty-seven governments, and serves to facilitate the movement out of Europe of migrants and refugees who would not otherwise be moved. A kindred body was the United States Escapee Programme (U.S.E.P.). This was part of the U.S. State Department and operated among those refugees who had fled from eastern Europe.

The W.C.C. Refugee Programme did not distinguish between refugees, displaced persons, or "escapees" but took "need" as its criterion. It had working relationships with the U.N.H.C.R., U.N.R.R.A., U.S.E.P., and I.C.E.M., and had liaison in Geneva with the National Catholic Welfare Conference, the Lutheran World Federation, and the League of Red Cross Societies, as well as with other bodies that cared for refugees and displaced persons. So far as was practicable, National and Regional Councils of Churches have been encouraged to care for refugees and to integrate them into local communities. But it has always been recognized that to befriend refugees by advising them and trying to find the best solution of their particular problem calls for a great deal of specialized knowledge, especially when the solution is to move them from "countries of first asylum" to countries of resettlement, sometimes halfway around the world.

Legal requirements and intricate knowledge of sources where specialized help can be found, and familiarity with the mandates of intergovernmental, international, governmental, and voluntary agencies all call for unusual attainments and technical skill that National Councils of Churches cannot usually be expected to command. In post-war Europe, staff of the Service to Refugees helped the local Churches to solve refugee problems so vast and complex that they felt they needed help from outside to tackle them. It was not so much that the local Churches lacked skill and knowledge but that they seriously lacked funds and personnel to do all that had to be done if lives were to be saved. Consequently, a centralized service, now known as the Refugee Programme, was set up by the World Council, and this programme has also been, with the full approval of the Churches, an operational one, in the sense of itself carrying out projects for the social integration of refugees unable, for one reason or another, to emigrate from a country of asylum to one of re-settlement. But whenever circumstances have required that services to refugees be operational, the aim has always been to hand over as soon as possible the project to a local Church or ecumenical agency for its mainten-ance. In the operational side of its work, the Division collaborates with organizations engaged in similar activities, including Jewish agencies.

An important step towards the fulfilment of one aspect of the original mandate of the Refugee Secretariat was an agreement entered into in May 1946, with U.N.R.R.A. It was agreed that the Department should operate at first in Germany, Austria, and Italy, and, as developments showed to be desirable and practicable, in Poland, Czechoslovakia, and Hungary. It was expressly stated that the Department's work in Central Europe would not be primarily among Lutheran Displaced Persons of the Latvian and Estonian Churches, who would be the responsibility of Lutheran organizations, but would include Orthodox from eastern countries and Protestants of various denominations from Poland and Czechoslovakia. This apportioning of responsibilities was never regarded as rigid.

The services to be offered by the Department for the rehabilitation of refugees would include the supply and distribution of food, clothing, and medicines, and the provision of facilities and equipment for work among young people, such as the formation of youth clubs associated with Churches; also craft equipment, and supplies and equipment necessary for the main-tenance of divine worship. The Department would draw supplies consigned to it by National Councils or Councils of Churches. U.N.R.R.A. for its part agreed to assist wherever possible in the shipment of supplies to the Depart-ment's field workers. All costs, including those of sea transport, would be borne by the voluntary agencies sending supplies. In the upshot, the Depart-ment recruited many volunteers from all over the world and there was much interchanging of personnel with U.N.R.R.A.

When Cockburn set up the Department of Reconstruction, various church agencies from many countries were working among refugees in Europe. Among these was Church World Service, which was created in 1946 out of various committees to be the service arm of the Federal Council of Churches in the U.S.A. One of the first concerns of Church World Service was the resettlement of the mass of Europe's displaced persons in association with the International Refugee Organization and the United Nations' Relief and Rehabilitation Agency (U.N.R.R.A.). Church World Service soon set up its own displaced persons department, which provided services in Europe in co-operation with the World Council of Churches.

During 1947 the American Christian Committee for Refugees turned over its commitments for assisting refugees and displaced persons to Church World Service, and for the first time there was a joint agency offering refugee and resettlement services on behalf of Protestant and Orthodox Churches in the United States.

Harold E. Fey has noted:

> When Church World Service was launched in 1946, it assumed responsibility for eight material aid centres or warehouses in the United States belonging to the Church Committee on Overseas Relief and Reconstruction. A ninth centre, opened by the Southern Baptists in New Orleans, was also used as a collection point. In 1946, the churches gave through Church World Service 11,069,068 pounds of clothing, medical supplies, food and books, valued at $4.8 million. Church World Service shipped forty-eight car loads of food and 4,000,000 pounds of clothing. This was 88 per cent of all the relief material shipped during the year (although, of course, the armed services supplied relief assistance).[1]

Within a few months of coming into existence, Church World Service had resettled 1,488 refugees in thirty-two cities and 124 communities in the United States. In Europe, it helped the department to serve displaced persons in the camps, and assisted the Y.M.C.A. and Y.W.C.A. to work with war prisoners and to set up summer camps where 41,000 undernourished children were fed.

When Church World Service was reorganized in 1950, it transferred its refugee resettlement field operations to the Department, which by then had been renamed that of Inter-Church Aid and Service to Refugees. When this transfer took place, Church World Service had resettled 51,299 displaced persons, 221 orphans and 7,151 *Volksdeutsche* (ethnic Germans who had been uprooted and were numbered among the "expellees" mentioned previously). The handing over did not mean that Church World Service severed its connection with refugee work. On the contrary, it continued this activity through the W.C.C. and in particular maintained an enormous programme for the reception and integration of refugees in the U.S.A. By 1966 Church World Service had resettled in America 147,000 refugees. What is especially significant about the W.C.C.'s Refugee Service in the early post-war period is the way in which it helped in common with the Division of Inter-Church Aid as a whole to renew the life of the Churches in countries that had been at war or had been occupied. A spiritual as well as physical renewal began to reanimate the Churches.

Amsterdam to Evanston

When the World Council of Churches was formally constituted at Amsterdam in 1948, the Department of Reconstruction and Inter-Church Aid had a sizeable operation to report to the First Assembly. Its heaviest expenditure, financed by member Churches in the U.S.A., Britain, Switzerland, Canada,

---

[1] *Co-operation in Compassion* (New York 1966), p. 36.

New Zealand, and Sweden, was $1,088,300 for temporary churches and $900,000 for the salaries of pastors and clergy of different denominations. The balance of its three-year budget of $3,905,500 had gone to the rebuilding of Christian orphanages, hospitals, schools, and homes for the aged.

> All the countries occupied during the war were recipients, without discrimination [Bishop George Bell of Chichester commented], but perhaps the most remarkable example of the "love of the brethren" developed by the World Council was the widespread and generous help given to Germany by the churches, in the U.S.A. most of all, but also by those in Britain and other countries. Those who visited Germany, as I did, in the very early post-war years could not fail to observe both the liberality of the giving and the quality of the personal approach.[1]

The Assembly received the report from its Committee on Christian Reconstruction and Inter-Church Aid. It was recognized that the work in hand could no longer be thought of as temporary. The Assembly authorized the extension of the Department's concern into new regions, particularly the Middle East, where there were 660,000 Arab refugees from Palestine. The task of redesigning the Department was passed to its committee and a cut-back in staff was called for. The proposal was that the general budget of the World Council should be fixed at $756,350, but this was pruned to $300,000. Separately the Department of Reconstruction expected to receive from its supporters for administrative expenses $176,660, out of which it had agreed to contribute $8,000 to the budget of the W.C.C. publicity department. By way of comparison, the general budget of the World Council for 1967 was around $1,000,000, and the separately raised budget—known as the Service Programme—of the Division of Inter-Church Aid, Refugee, and World Service around $1,500,000—almost ten times the figure for 1949.

Dr J. Hutchinson Cockburn came to the end of his term of office at Amsterdam and Dr Robert Mackie, an ecumenical veteran and minister of the Church of Scotland, was appointed to succeed him. Dr Mackie directed this department until the summer of 1955, when be became Chairman of the Administrative Committee on Inter-Church Aid. Dr Elfan Rees, who had been in charge of the Refugee Division of the Department since 1947, continued to direct the refugee work until 1949, when he transferred to the Commission of the Churches on International Affairs, with responsibility for refugee matters. His place as Director of the Refugee Division was taken by Dr Edgar Chandler, from the U.S.A.

In the reorganization of the Department's work that took place after Amsterdam, the main desks became those for refugees; German, Latin, and Orthodox countries; scholarships; health; literature; and publicity. To carry out one directive given at Amsterdam, the welfare of the refugees in the Middle East became a concern of the Department, which responded by calling conferences to make known the needs of Palestinian refugees, and by the channelling of funds to a regional committee that was formed to provide for the welfare of stateless persons in the area.

When the Central Committee of the W.C.C. met at Chichester, England,

[1] *The Kingship of Christ*, p. 110.

in July 1949, the Department was given a new name—that of Inter-Church Aid and Service to Refugees (D.I.C.A.S.R. for short)—to express awareness of a new era that was beginning in its work. The Central Committee reminded the member Churches, in one of the resolutions passed at Chichester, that Inter-Church Aid is a permanent obligation of a World Council of Churches which seeks to be true to its name; that many of the Churches in Europe were desperately in need of assistance; that millions of stateless refugees in Europe had a pressing and incontrovertible claim upon the help of the Churches; and therefore that a fresh approach must be made to their members by the Churches which were able to help for renewed and generous giving on behalf of their fellow-Christians in Europe.

This resolution for the first time recognized inter-Church aid as a "permanent obligation". Reconstruction is a task which is undertaken for a period and comes to an end when it has been accomplished. Inter-Church aid, it was now seen, was a responsibility of the ecumenical life of the Churches. Also, inter-Church aid was related to the permanent spiritual tasks of the Church. The real transition was between a time when an effort was made in a spirit of compassion to restore what had been destroyed to a time of striving to make the Church more effective for the task laid upon it. Chichester recognized that the refugees themselves were in large measure members of Churches and, further, that some of the most acute difficulties of European Churches were occasioned because great numbers of their members were stateless persons, so for an added reason they must be helped.

The report of the Department for 1950 records that 50,206 people, chiefly Orthodox and non-Lutheran displaced persons, had been helped to emigrate to new lands of opportunity. Of this total, 26,791 had gone to the U.S.A. and another 5,000 to South America, Australia, and Canada. The Lutheran World Federation had assisted another 35,000 refugees to migrate. Along with such aid, the Churches maintained a spiritual ministry for members of refugee Churches.

In 1950 also, Congregational–Christian Churches in the U.S.A. had carried out a programme which had led 748 young Christians of thirty-three nationalities to a dozen ecumenical work camps closely related to reconstruction projects and experiments in lay witness and evangelism in several European countries. The camps had been supported by Congregational–Christian, Evangelical and Reformed, Presbyterian and Protestant Episcopal funds totalling $42,200; other camps had been conducted by Brethren, Lutheran, Mennonite, and Quaker bodies. Ecumenical Work Camps developed into an important programme of the W.C.C.'s youth department, and were supported year by year by the member Churches through D.I.C.A.S.R.'s service programme budget.

That same year, 127 theological students from thirteen countries were given scholarships to study for one year in the U.S.A., Britain, Sweden, Switzerland, France, or Germany, through the Department's scholarships programme. Other students were assisted by the Lutheran World Federation and the Swiss Churches. Opportunities to study were arranged directly by British and

German Churches. Also, 132 pastors and church workers had been brought to Casa Locarno in Switzerland for six-week recuperation periods. Another thirty-five church leaders suffering from tuberculosis had been invited to sanatoria in Switzerland for treatment. Medicines otherwise unobtainable had been sent to sick pastors and church leaders in eastern Europe. This had often been the sole means whereby contacts had been possible. Packages of penicillin, insulin, and rare drugs became symbols of Christian solidarity. The scholarships and health programmes cost $80,062 in 1950. This amount was supplemented by other funds provided by church committees in Britain, Scandinavia, Switzerland, and the U.S.A. D.I.C.A.S.R.'s year-end report records that the Inter-Church Aid programme had included ecumenical agencies in Australia, Canada, Denmark, Great Britain, the Netherlands, New Zealand, South Africa, Sweden, Switzerland, and the U.S.A., as well as the Baptist World Alliance and the Lutheran World Federation.

"The first period of Christian reconstruction in Europe is over"—so Dr Mackie[1] began an article in the *Ecumenical Review* in the winter of 1950.[1] This did not mean that the Churches had been able to restore all that had been destroyed by war nor that the physical distress of such countries as Greece and eastern Europe could be passed by, but now minds must reach out into the future. Six months later, in another article headed "A Strategy for Inter-Church Aid in Europe for 1951"[2] Mackie wrote:

> Without an ecumenical perspective it becomes impossible for any church to know how to be wise and fair in assistance. Without an ecumenical pattern of sharing some segment of the total work of the Church, some isolated forgotten community of Christians will not receive the assistance required, and the total life of the Church will thus be weakened. Further, we have to think on a large scale if we are going to secure the loyalty of individual Christians and churches to the task of Inter-Church Aid . . . Flexibility [he concluded] is required if changing needs and fresh opportunities are not to be overlooked.

The need for flexibility, and for immediate access to funds to meet emergencies, was dramatically underscored before the year was out. In December news was received by the International Refugee Organization in Geneva that a camp for 5,500 Russian refugees who had fled from China to the Philippines had been wrecked by a typhoon and that it was necessary to remove the survivors immediately. The situation was made unusually difficult because the disaster came at a moment when the I.R.O. was passing out of existence and it was not known what its successor was to be. Help was therefore sought from the Department. Within forty-eight hours, Edgar Chandler had left by air for the Philippines to make detailed arrangements for the transfer of survivors from the wrecked island and to consult with the Philippines government. The outcome of his flight was that the department was given grants of money to provide immediate emergency aid for all and successfully resettled even 130 "hard-core" refugees on a long-term basis in Church-supported institutions of a dozen countries around the world. The immense skill which Edgar Chandler showed was widely acknowledged. Since then the channelling

---

[1] Vol. ii, no. 2.   [2] *Ecumenical Review*, vol. iii (January 1951).

of ecumenical aid to victims of earthquakes, fires, hurricanes, volcanic eruptions, droughts, floods, and man-made upheavals, has become part of the accustomed responsibilities of Inter-Church Aid.

The year 1951 also marked an important stage in the growing involvement of the Department with Arab refugees in the Middle East. This was the outcome of a conference arranged in Beirut by the Department jointly with the International Missionary Council. Before that time, giving had been generous for Arab refugees, especially from the United States. After the meeting, the flow of gifts increased notably, the sources were enlarged, and regional cooperation was firmly established. In 1952, $40,000 in new grants for this work were received from Australia, Britain, Canada, Germany, New Zealand, and the U.S.A., and these increased the total programme, costing $218,000, of relief and social services sustained by American Churches. By 1954, $2.5 million in cash and kind had been contributed by the Churches for continued succour to Arab refugees, who then numbered some 900,000. A second "Beirut Conference" took place in 1956 and was similarly influential. Both meetings were arranged by Dr Elfan Rees.

By 1952, when the International Refugee Organization closed, to be succeeded by other specialized agencies of the United Nations, two million refugees had been enabled to emigrate, ninety per cent of them to the New World. Four-fifths of these refugee immigrants had been received by Protestant, Roman Catholic, Orthodox, and Jewish bodies that had sponsored them, not all through the W.C.C.

In May 1953, by agreement between the International Missionary Council and the World Council of Churches, the Department became responsible for co-ordinating and commending to the Churches a programme of Emergency Inter-Church Aid and Relief in all countries. Plans were made for adding to the assistance from North American Churches through Church World Service for Korea, Indonesia, India, Pakistan, and Hong Kong by contributions from Australia, Britain, Denmark, Germany, New Zealand, Sweden, and Switzerland.

The conclusion of the truce in Korea in July 1953, which halted the war which had been going on for four years in that country, brought a new challenge to the Churches to send aid to the tens of thousands of war victims and refugees there. Church World Service was already at work. The W.C.C. negotiated an official relationship between D.I.C.A.S.R. and the relief committee of the Korean National Christian Council. An ecumenical staff was recruited to serve in Korea. The department sought support from the member Churches for projects to aid those who had lost limbs, the tubercular, widows, orphans, and others who had suffered in the war. When the executive committee of the W.C.C. met at Bossey, Switzerland, in August 1953, it urged the member Churches to press their governments to participate fully in all intergovernmental relief measures and themselves to support through Christian liberality the relief committee of the National Christian Council of Korea in the work of national reconstruction.

Also in 1953, relief was channelled to flood victims in Britain, Holland, Italy, and Japan, to those who had suffered from earthquakes in Greece and

Cyprus, to those who hungered in India and Pakistan, and to those bereft by fire disasters in Hong Kong and Korea. Thus, when the Second Assembly of the World Council met at Evanston, Illinois, in 1954, the Department, as the ecumenical channel of Inter-Church Aid, was already reaching out far beyond Europe, where it had begun its work.

Evanston to New Delhi

The Second Assembly recognized the Department's ever widening horizons and authorized it to be world-wide in its scope. Robert Mackie was coming to the end of his term as director of this work, and Leslie E. Cooke was appointed to succeed him. Dr Cooke, at the time of his appointment, was general secretary of the Congregational Union of England and Wales. He had been a delegate to the First and Second Assemblies of the World Council and a member of its central and executive committees.

One of the earliest duties of the new director of what became the Division of Inter-Church Aid and Service to Refugees was to work out with the International Missionary Council a clear line of distinction between the projects for which the Division should seek support and those which were the concern of the I.M.C. This demarcation was worked out at two conferences between the Division and the I.M.C., held at Les Rasses in Switzerland and Herrenalb in Germany. Criteria were established which became known as the "Herrenalb categories"[1] and operations continued under them for a decade.

As soon as this had been done, attention was given to building up the Division's annual project list. This list was designed to give details of undertakings for which Churches, Councils of Churches, and ecumenical bodies around the world were seeking support. It was circulated to the members of the World Council and their agencies. It has become an important instrument for communicating needs and for finding funds to meet them. The validating of projects for the list according to agreed ecumenical criteria and the finding of funds to meet these projects were made major concerns of the Division. The first project list was circulated in 1956. It contained 150 projects in forty-five countries and the askings totalled just short of $3,000,000. Today some 600 projects from about eighty countries are listed for the ensuing year, and the askings amount all told to around $25,000,000.

---

[1] Under the Herrenalb agreement, it was laid down that projects from Asia, Africa, and Latin America, submitted through the Division, should be confined to:

1. Needs arising from situations which were strictly of an emergency character created by natural disasters, economic crises, political and social upheavals, and the like.
2. The needs of refugees and displaced persons.
3. The needs of Churches not in regular relation with any missionary society and therefore not normally receiving help from this source.
4. Urgent inter-Church and ecumenical projects, whether designed to strengthen the Churches or the service of the community, in so far as such projects could not be adequately supported either from local sources or through mission boards.
5. Social service or relief projects clearly demanded by the local situation but beyond the resources of the local Churches or the missionary societies co-operating with them.
6. Experiments aimed at ensuring the self-respect of the Church or Christian community where these experiments had been adequately examined and duly commended.

The Herrenalb categories were replaced in 1966 by a new agreement by which the Division of World Mission and Evangelism, the successor to the International Missionary Council, became responsible for long-term programmes and the Division of Inter-Church Aid for projects usually expected to become self-supporting within five years. This agreement opened the way for missionary projects to be included in the Division's project list. The 1967 project list was published by the Division "in collaboration with the Division of World Mission and Evangelism"—an innovation. The project list has been widened to include refugee projects and those world youth projects which are compiled jointly by the World Council's Youth Department and the World Council for Christian Education.

Attention was also given to the development and support of the Division's basic budget, the service programme. Through this, the Division was able to nourish, on behalf of the member Churches, many National and Regional Councils of Churches. It supported various departments and divisions of the World Council in some work not covered by the World Council's general budget. The service programme budget includes the salaries of the Division's staff, administrative and overhead expenses, and the cost of meetings and consultations. Finally, the service programme finds the money to carry on certain programmes which the Churches have decided should be centrally administered. These include health, literature, Casa Locarno, and scholarships.

The change that was coming over inter-Church aid was given considerable impetus by a study of conditions in Asia that was made jointly by Reginald H. Helfferich of Church World Service and Ulrich van Beyma from the Netherlands. Dr van Beyma had joined the Division in November 1954, as secretary for "non-European areas". At about the same time, Church World Service released temporarily Dr Helfferich to be an ambassador of the World Council of Churches to Asia and Africa, with special reference to the U.S.A.'s surplus commodities programme. The survey that Helfferich and van Beyma carried out together in East Asia early in 1955 resulted in Church World Service acting as the agent of the Division for massive feeding programmes that began in Asia and were later extended to Africa, eastern Europe, and Latin America. The Helfferich–van Beyma survey was a key factor in the developing strategy of inter-Church aid. Besides their study, Dr Helfferich and Dr van Beyma created the confidence necessary for Asian projects to be added to the project list.

The most severe demand that had thus far been made on the Service to Refugees came in the autumn of 1956 with the uprising in Hungary. The uprising led to the precipitate flight of about 180,000 new refugees, principally into Austria. At the first news of a threatened emergency, Edgar Chandler, then Director of the Refugee Service, flew to Vienna. After he had consulted with officials of the Austrian Churches and of various international organizations, Chandler began to plan a W.C.C. relief operation with the Director of the Service to Refugees in Austria. On 31 October, the first convoy of two trucks, laden with food, blankets, and medical supplies, went to Hungary. They were received by Lutheran and Reformed parishes in the city of Györ.

All inter-Church aid committees were informed by cable from Geneva that Church supplies were being sent to Hungary, that blankets, clothes, and medicines should be sent direct to *Hilfswerk* in Austria, and that considerable funds would be needed for emergency needs. Five thousand blankets bought in Germany by *Hilfswerk* reached Vienna on 1 November, and funds were pledged by British, United States, and other sources. Next day, Church World Service flew in $16,743 worth of medicines, vitamins, concentrated food, and blankets. Simultaneously, a convoy of nine vehicles, carrying twenty tons of supplies, left Vienna for Hungary. The convoy was stopped at one point by Russian military tanks, but eventually it reached Györ.

By the end of November, 85,000 new refugees had entered Austria and others continued to arrive at the rate of 5,000 a day. The stream continued unabated for many weeks. The Division organized a comprehensive relief, counselling, and welfare service. The Service to Refugees engaged in a massive emigration programme for the Hungarian refugees. For those who could not emigrate, integration projects of many kinds were carried out. Three appeals were made by the Division to the member Churches of the World Council. The first was for $200,000 to cover a unified service by the Division to the Hungarian refugees. The second was for $25,000 as the W.C.C. contribution to the supplies shipped to Hungary by the International Red Cross. The third was for $150,000 as the W.C.C.'s response to the needs of the Hungarian Churches and their social and educational institutions. Ultimately, the response to the Division's appeals reached $734,532.

This total included $249,013 from the U.S.A., $187,000 from Canada, $143,000 from Britain, and contributions from twenty-nine other countries or territories, one of which was the Cook Islands. More than 2,500 pastors and other church workers received emergency outfit allowances valued at the equivalent of one month's salary, and 2,430 retired church workers were given emergency grants amounting to two months' pension. A score of church institutions for the handicapped were enabled to replace damaged equipment. Wrecked church buildings were restored. Rest homes and conference centres were given grants. Raw cotton was shipped and processed for bedding and underclothing for thousands. Paper was provided for 200,000 hymn books and 100,000 Bibles. And more than 26,000 refugees were helped by the Division to emigrate to the U.S.A., Britain, Canada, France, Switzerland, Australia, Germany, and elsewhere.[1]

Through the effort known as World Refugee Year, 1959–60, in which eighty international voluntary agencies joined, the Division received funds that enabled many important projects to be undertaken for the permanent rehabilitation of thousands of people that would not have otherwise been possible. More than $1,780,000 was given by the Churches out of World Refugee Year collections to help the Division and National Councils of Churches to extend their work for refugees. An outline of some of the things accomplished in this way is given in a W.C.C. pamphlet *A Time of Compassion*.

[1] W.C.C. pamphlet: *Hungary—Special Report* and the Division's annual report for 1957. For additional information about this ecumenical operation, see Chandler, *The High Tower of Refuge* (London 1959).

An unusual project carried through at this time in partnership with the United Nations' High Commissioner for Refugees was the establishment of Old Believers, a Russian sect which had defied authority since Peter the Great (1672–1725), as a colony in Brazil.

At the time of the Russian Revolution of 1917, some Old Believers fled to China, where they established themselves as self-contained, self-supporting units. But when China became communist after the Second World War, the future of the Old Believers again became precarious. The Division sought for them a country where they could resettle and live in freedom according to their tenets. Brazil was willing to receive them, and so, with the co-operation and assistance of the United Nations' High Commissioner for Refugees, more than one thousand of these Old Believers were sent by ship half-way across the world. They were also provided with materials, seeds, livestock, and tools with which to build and furnish their own villages. At the end of two years, the Old Believers had become self-supporting and they have continued to thrive in Brazil while adhering as firmly as ever to their faith. The success of the venture led to other colonies being established for them in Argentina. A substantial number of Old Believers from China have also been helped to emigrate, as individuals or families, to Australia and New Zealand.

To fulfil the directive given it at Evanston to go out into all the world the Division's "area desks" were increased in number. Already in existence were desks for Europe, for the Orthodox and the Near East, and for "countries outside Europe". By early 1961, new desks had been named for Asia, for Latin America, and for the "study and survey of areas of acute human need". The geographical spread was completed in 1962 when the Africa desk was inaugurated.

Earlier, a Secretary for Migration had been appointed to study the situation occasioned by waves, millions strong, of migratory workers in many part of the world. Out of expert knowledge the secretary has been able to provide the Churches with advice about the spiritual, social, and physical needs of these people and to stimulate measures for their welfare. The first fruits of the work of the Secretary for Migration was the calling of a world conference which met at Leysin, Switzerland, in 1961. There the relationship between the Churches and migrant workers, who included Roman Catholics, Orthodox, Muslims, and others, was more clearly seen.

The Bengal Refugee Service was also set up in 1961 under the direction of Dean Johannes Krohn of Denmark. It was the outcome of a thoroughgoing survey made for Church World Service by a team whose leader was Dean Herbert Stroup of Brooklyn College, New York. The aim was to provide a co-ordinated programme for thousands of displaced persons, including students, from East Pakistan. By the time that the Bengal Refugee Service was wound up in 1965, it had cleared Sealdah Railway Station of 8,000 men, women, and children who had been living in the precincts for more than a decade as squatters, and had established them in three villages, which they had largely built themselves, some twenty miles to the north of Calcutta. Medical services for displaced persons had also been provided and a number of small cottage industries had been launched. The role of the Division in all this was that of seeking funds amounting to roughly $1,000,000 to finance the work from the member Churches of the World Council.

At the final assessment, it was agreed that the Bengal Refugee Service had not fully realized the high hopes with which it had begun, and this was in part attributed to inexperience in setting up such a body. Yet from this partial failure much was learned that was soon to be turned to profit. The willingness of the Anglican, Methodist, Mennonite, and Presbyterian Churches in Calcutta to continue the work begun by the Bengal Refugee Service, with some financial support from outside, meant the growth of inter-Church aid through the active participation of local congregations.

New Delhi and Afterwards

A radical change had thus taken place in the Division when the Third Assembly met at New Delhi towards the end of 1961. Once more, the Assembly changed the name of the Division, this time to Division of Inter-Church Aid, Refugee, and World Service (D.I.C.A.R.W.S., as it became known for short) and furnished it with a new mandate. This said:

> The aim of the division shall be to express the ecumenical solidarity of the churches through mutual aid in order to strengthen them in their life and mission and especially in their service to the world around them (*diakonia*), and to provide facilities by which the churches may serve men and women in acute human need everywhere, especially orphaned peoples, including refugees of all categories.

To this was added:

> The basic approach of the division to the churches and peoples will be on the basis of areas. The area secretaries will have primary responsibility for the relations of the division with churches and councils in their areas and for relationships with such ecumenical regional organizations as are or may be established . . .

Functional secretaries were to be responsible for refugees, material aid, scholarships, fraternal workers, health, E.C.L.O.F. (the Ecumenical Church Loan Fund), migration, areas of acute human need, and information.

Authority was thus given for the creation of two new "desks" for material aid and fraternal workers. The desk for material aid was not staffed until early in 1967. However, the desk for fraternal workers, to which was added certain responsibilites for teams and personnel, was manned soon after the Third Assembly. It kept the Churches informed of needs and opportunities for personal service abroad.

With its new mandate, "to express the solidarity of the churches . . . especially in their service to the world around them", the Division began to encourage Churches to take social action with a new emphasis, that of engaging in "nation-building" projects and to submit these for inclusion in the yearly project list. This led to requests for support for projects of increased size and complexity and brought problems of its own. Where was the competence to be found that qualified men to advise upon the wisdom and feasibility of such proposals? But need had arisen and ways to meet it were sought. The Rapid Social Change Studies made by the W.C.C. between Evanston and New Delhi helped, and at the Third Assembly authority was given to the Division to take such action as seemed appropriate.

The outcome was that the Central Committee agreed in 1962 to set up a new body, to be known as the Committee of Specialized Assistance to Social Projects (S.A.S.P.). It was to serve, if called upon to do so, the whole World Council and the member Churches and their agencies. Miss Janet Lacey, the Division's Vice-Chairman, was appointed Chairman of S.A.S.P., which set about its work by establishing panels of specialists on press and periodicals, health and medical work, agriculture and rural development, economic development, and urban social work and community development. The duty of these panels was to look at projects which W.C.C. staff had found to present unusual difficulties, and to advise the S.A.S.P. Committee about these. The committee also had power to initiate pilot programmes. A secretariat for S.A.S.P. was provided within the Division which was also responsible for seeking its budget. It was found that the need for such an expert, advisory body was so great that at its first meeting no fewer than eighty projects of unusual difficulty were brought before it! At the Fourth Assembly of the W.C.C. in Uppsala in 1968, S.A.S.P. was dissolved and reconstituted as the Advisory Committee on Technical Services (A.C.T.S.) with a new mandate, staff, and constitution. A.C.T.S. continues to serve the whole World Council, but is administratively located within D.I.C.A.R.W.S.

The end of the seven years' war that had raged in Algeria brought a new challenge in 1962. How best could the Churches help the people of that newly independent, devastated Muslim country. The peace settlement was followed by a mass exodus to France of some 800,000 civil servants, teachers, doctors, accountants, farmers, engineers, pastors, and others with skilled and professional training. The relatively few Churches in Algeria were denuded of their congregations. Even for those Christians who remained in the country it was difficult to provide pastors. The Division met the emergency by calling a conference of interested Churches and agencies, including the Lutheran World Federation, the Mennonites, C.I.M.A.D.E. (*Comité Inter-Mouvements auprès des Evacués*—the ecumenical relief agency of the French Churches), and the Y.M.C.A.s and Y.W.C.A.s.

Because of the impossibility of looking to the weakened indigenous Churches to provide an organization for the carrying out of an inter-Church aid relief programme, it was agreed to create a special agency, the Christian Committee for Service in Algeria (C.C.S.A.). The work which C.I.M.A.D.E. had done throughout the war with courage, persistence, and devotion had given that body an entrée to the new Algerian government. C.I.M.A.D.E. was eager to continue its services to the people of Algeria, and the other Churches and church agencies were equally desirous of supplementing its efforts. The activities of C.I.M.A.D.E.'s teams in Algeria were therefore built into the new organization. Particular responsibilities were allotted to other church bodies, such as the Mennonite Central Committee for a demonstration farm, within the C.C.S.A.'s structure. This structure was rapidly and most imaginatively devised by Heinrich Hellstern, of Swiss H.E.K.S. (*Hilfswerk der Evangelische Kirchen der Schweitz*—the Swiss Protestant Churches' Relief Agency), who was asked to inaugurate the programme. Dr Hellstern served as director of the C.C.S.A. for six months; he then handed over to Pastor Hans Aurbakken, an American Methodist of Norwegian background, who continued as director until the summer of 1966.

Pastor Aurbakken was succeeded by Jacques Blanc, a French pastor, who had been associated with the C.C.S.A. from the beginning. The Division provided a secretariat in Geneva for the C.C.S.A., and sought funds, which reached a total of around $3,000,000 to finance the programme. Church World Service furnished some of C.C.S.A.'s key personnel in the field, much cash, and enormous quantities of food and clothing for the relief service. Other major supporters were Germany, whose contributions from "Bread for the World" were the largest of all, the Christian Aid department of the British Council of Churches, and Inter-Church Aid Committees in Denmark, the Netherlands, Switzerland, and other countries.

From the beginning, the Christian Committee for Service in Algeria determined to ensure that its programme would help the people of Algeria to get on their feet again in the shortest possible time. In the early days, when an emergency situation prevailed, the Algerian government invited the C.C.S.A., the Roman Catholic agencies, and the Red Cross each to take a third of the country for immediate relief work. Operating large-scale school-feeding and milk distribution programmes, distributing blankets and clothing, providing a medical service, and giving help to orphanages and young people, the care of the C.C.S.A. operation soon became a vast reafforestation enterprise. Hundreds of men, teenagers, and even war widows were trained in skills fitting them to earn their own livelinood. At the height of this activity, 90,000 persons were employed. This was made possible by using agricultural commodities from the U.S.A., given by Church World Service on a food-for-work offer. By the time that the reafforestation work was handed over to a government agency in 1965, 22,600,000 fruit and timber trees had been planted and a further 50,000,000 seedlings were being raised in the C.C.S.A.'s nurseries. To some observers the Christian Committee for Service in Algeria seemed to offer a new pattern of ecumenical action. Since 1967, when the five-year programme for which it was set up was phased out, C.C.S.A. has continued to function but with a radically new emphasis in its work. It is still an autonomous body supported by the Churches through D.I.C.A.R.W.S.

The decision to gear the reafforestation activities of the Christian Committee for Service in Algeria to a food-for-work programme was the outcome of lessons learned by experience in many lands. To emergencies created by war, earthquake, famine, and pestilence, the compassionate respond with food, clothing, medicine, and shelter as soon as possible. Here speed saves lives. Repeatedly ecumenical service has temporarily carried out massive feeding programmes for those who were starving. But then what? Endemic need, it is now believed, calls for more than the permanent soup-kitchen and the inexhaustible giving of hand-outs. Indeed, such practices can be shameful and corrupting. This was the lesson taught in Taiwan, where Presbyterians,

Lutherans, and Roman Catholics engaged for a time in the free distribution of food, but turned the responsibility over to the government when abuses crept in which the Churches were powerless to prevent. Similar conclusions were reached in Korea and elsewhere.

The outcome was that alternative methods were sought, and one of these was to invite people to work for the food they were given. In this way, self-respect could be engendered and the possibility of corruption reduced. Similarly, church service agencies in a number of countries began to turn away during the 1960s from the practice of collecting used clothing and shipping it overseas for free distribution to the poor. Old clothes, if given indiscriminately, destroy human dignity. It became clear that Christian compassion to clothe the naked, if it were to be true to itself, must provide people with the means of making new clothes that would enable them to hold their heads high. Not only should whole cloth be provided, but also tailoring, dressmaking, and knitting classes should be formed, equipped, and staffed with competent instructors. All this is indicative of the change in ideas which began to animate Inter-Church Aid during the 1960s.

Yet another instrument for expressing Christian solidarity was found in 1963 when, in response to an offer from the Lutheran World Federation, the Division invited that body to become the agent of the World Council of Churches in administering the Tanganyika Christian Refugee Service. The initiative came from the Lutheran World Federation which made the proposal to the divisional committee of D.I.C.A.R.W.S. The divisional committee sought and obtained the authority of the World Council's Executive Committee for this pioneering venture. The Lutheran World Federation most generously undertook to finance the work which called for a budget by 1967 of $427,800—a sum that was entirely covered by the L.W.F., except for a gift of $14,000 from Britain. The L.W.F. reported regularly to the Divisional Committee on Inter-Church Aid, Refugee and World Service concerning the progress of the operation in Tanzania.

A crucial dilemma that confronted the Division and some of its supporting agencies was resolved by the Central Committee of the World Council when it met at Rochester, New York, in 1963. It must be explained that in the U.S.A. most of the major denominations have their own long-established fund-raising agencies and co-ordinate much of this work in the central department of Church World Service. In other countries, the Churches have organized their inter-Church aid work through national bodies, usually as departments of the National Church Councils. The British Council of Churches has its department of Christian Aid, which stems from work begun in 1942. The Canadian Churches have built up relief and inter-Church aid organizations of their own, and have co-ordinated the work of these in their National Council without creating a distinct national operating agency. The Swiss Protestant Churches are served by H.E.K.S. Similarly, Lutheran Churches have created the Lutheran World Federation/World Service and, in the U.S.A., Lutheran World Relief.

By 1967, L.W.F./World Service had recommended some 200 projects, with requests amounting to about $21,000,000 to potential donor agencies, so that the younger Churches in Africa, Asia, and Latin America could be strengthened in their community welfare service in the fields of medicine, education, and agriculture. Also, the world-wide Anglican Communion launched in 1963 its programme of Mutual Responsibility and Interdependence in the Body of Christ (M.R.I.), and a number of these projects were listed in the D.I.C.A.R.W.S./D.W.M.E. project list and were supported by Churches outside the Anglican Communion. After the Second World War, the German Churches formed the *Hilfswerk* (Relief) organization, which later merged with the older traditional body known as *Innere Mission*, and then went on to create the *Brot für die Welt* (Bread for the World) annual fund-raising campaign of Churches and mission societies which had extraordinary success.

The German experience was, indeed, altogether exceptional, because up to 1960 the German Churches, although to a yearly diminishing degree, had received outside support, as earlier passages in this chapter have shown. But after 1960 the Churches of Germany rapidly became one of the most active participants in, and generous supporters of, ecumenical service. Since 1957 they have been raising money in *Kirchen helfen Kirchen* (Churches help Churches) a programme of "classical" inter-Church aid, that gave about $25,000 a year to projects of this nature on the D.I.C.A.R.W.S./D.W.M.E. Project List, and to the Division's service programme budget. They had also programmes for scholarships, migration, and integration, and service overseas. Through "Bread for the World" they were giving about $5,000,000 a year, from Churches in both Western and Eastern Germany, to church projects in developing countries of feeding, emergency relief, and material aid. Others were connected with self-help, health, vocational training, community development, and nation-building, the service of laymen abroad, or structural research, planning, and preparation for special undertakings. Nor must it be forgotten that besides these large contributions from Churches in affluent countries, there is a continual stream of small gifts, no less significant, for emergencies and projects from congregations in Asia, Africa, and the Pacific.

By the early 1960s, the West German Government in Bonn was inviting the Churches in Germany to accept funds for them to carry out or to support projects overseas. This was part of a pattern that had already been set by the United States Government with its surplus commodities programme, by Swiss Aid to Europe and its successor, and by funds made available by the Swedish and other governments. These States had gone ahead on their own. But before the German Churches entered into an agreement with their government to accept state money for use in church projects overseas, they consulted the World Council. This brought into the open the question whether such funds could properly be accepted when the needs to be met were so grave and extensive. Ought monies from Church and State to be kept separate, even if this meant depriving the needy of aid?

The stand taken by the Division contained four points. It believed that the use by Churches of funds from governments should be subject to the following considerations:

1. Projects which fall within its (the Division's) categories and conform to its criteria, or to those of the Committee on Specialized Assistance to Social Projects (S.A.S.P.), might properly use such money.

2. Government aid should not be sought for the normal work of the Churches, for example, in church-building, maintenance of the ministry, and church and mission administration.

3. Government aid should be sought for capital expenditure for projects which will be completed within a specific period of years or which will eventually be self-supporting, or within the resources of the initiating Church or Council to maintain.

4. Government aid should preferably be sought for projects of a pioneering or pilot nature, especially in the fields of social service, leadership training, technical assistance, community and agricultural development, and the permanent rehabilitation or integration of orphaned people.

Before publishing these recommendations, however, the Division turned to the Executive and Central Committee of the W.C.C. for advice. After a long and probing debate, the Central Committee adopted a resolution, of which the following is the substantive part:

> Agreed that the Central Committee instructs the staff to continue the study of this matter, and authorize the Divisional Committee of the Division of Inter-Church Aid, Refugee, and World Service and of the Division of World Mission and Evangelism to deal in the light of this discussion with specific cases on their merits in consultation with the National Christian Council of the country concerned and with the East Asia Christian Conference and All Africa Conference of Churches.[1]

This resolution enabled the German Churches to establish a special bureau, *Evangelische Zentralstelle für Entwicklungshilfe* (Protestant Central Agency for Development Aid), through which funds from the West German government were channelled. Many Churches and Councils of Churches have received generous allocations from the *Zentralstelle* for projects on the Division's project list. The Division's practice has continued to be in line with the Central Committee's resolution. After funds became available from the West Germany government for church projects abroad, a similar source was offered by the Netherlands government. The Fourth Assembly of the W.C.C., held in Sweden in 1968, gave a resounding call to the Churches to become involved in aid to the developing countries of the "Third World". The role of the World Council in general and of D.I.C.A.R.W.S. in particular was still under urgent discussion in the summer of 1969 and had still to be determined. But as this chapter tries to show, inter-Church aid frequently grows into "development aid" and for the time being at least it remained the responsibility of D.I.C.A.R.W.S.

In 1964, the National Council of the Churches of Christ in the U.S.A. requested the Churches of the world, through the World Council, to show

[1] MRCC (Rochester, New York).

ecumenical solidarity with the Churches of America by joining with them in support of the Mississippi Delta Ministry which was designed to serve in an area of grave racial turbulence. The call was for cash and for persons who had experience in areas of tension to take part in the relief, rehabilitation, and reconciliation projects that were being devised by the Mississippi Delta Ministry. The aim was to help to bring about a transformation of society that would ensure social justice for all. This was the first time that the N.C.C.C.U.S.A. had ever turned for support to the other members of the World Council, and it did so because it wished the Church as a whole to share in this ministry. The Division, strongly backed by the Executive Committee of the World Council, responded at once by circulating an emergency appeal to the member Churches, and arranged for the Mississippi Delta Ministry to be included in its project list. The outcome was donations amounting to more than $150,000 from Churches outside the U.S.A. and the finding of a number of persons to work in the project. The Mississippi Delta Ministry has continued to be listed for support year by year by D.I.C.A.R.W.S. At the time of Martin Luther King's assassination in 1968, a collection made by the Division raised some $100,000 additional to the normal response for this project as a memorial to the Negro leader.

That year 1964 also saw the launching of the Ecumenical Programme for Emergency Action in Africa (E.P.E.A.A.). It called for $10,000,000 over five years to finance a programme of urgent nation-building projects and the relief and rehabilitation of refugees throughout the continent. The following year, the All Africa Conference of Churches agreed to be responsible for the general direction and administration of E.P.E.A.A. and created a special agency to do this. This special agency soon had an executive staff comprising the director, the refugee officer, the information officer, and two administrative secretaries.

Of the many emergency appeals after natural disasters that the Division sent to the member Churches and their agencies since New Delhi, three deserve mention. Earthquakes in Iran, 1962, Yugoslavia, 1963, and Turkey, 1966, brought Christian aid for the permanent rehabilitation of people who had suffered grievously in these disasters. The response to the first of these appeals enabled the Christian Council of Iran to rebuild a Muslim village, Esmatabad, that had been wrecked in the catastrophe. Here, 306 houses were put up as well as such community amenities as public baths, an administrative centre, and a water tower. The Armenian Archbishop of Teheran, whose Church is not a member of the Christian Council of Iran, was also enabled to build houses for those of his people who had fled from the earthquakes and resettled in Teheran. After they were housed, a new church was built on a site adjoining their homes. Some restoration work was also done in other villages in the earthquake zone for Muslims and Christians alike, and this included considerable repairs to a mosque.

After the earthquake at Skopje, Yugoslavia, through funds transmitted by Churches through the Division, 125 prefabricated houses were bought and erected in a new suburb. These houses, to each of which the *oikoumene* symbol was attached, have become known as the "Churches' Sector". This work was supervised for the Division by Harald H. Lund, the Church World Service/Lutheran World Relief representative in Yugoslavia. The Serbian Orthodox Church was also enabled to repair churches that had been damaged in the disaster.

For those who had lost their homes in the earthquake in Eastern Anatolia, Turkey, winter shelters were built for about one hundred families as well as two permanent technical schools in the towns of Hinis and Varto. No churches were affected. For each of these emergency appeals the response was more than $700,000.

In the new climate of ecumenism that followed the Second Vatican Council it was suggested that working relations between Roman Catholic agencies and the Division could be extended. Accordingly, an official working party was set up by the Vatican and the World Council and met in Geneva in 1966 and in Rome in 1967. Other meetings were to follow. At the first meeting the news came of the grave threat of impending famine in India. The meeting recommended that synchronized appeals should be made by the Vatican and the Division at the same time as an appeal was put out by the United Nations. This was done. The Division's appeal was for $3,000,000 over a period of three years, to support a co-ordinated programme designed to strike at the causes of hunger in India. Following these appeals, a meeting took place in New Delhi at which it was agreed to set up a new body, Action for Food Production (A.F.P.R.O.), that would co-ordinate the programmes to be carried out by the Roman Catholics and the National Christian Council of India, and would speak with one voice in approaches to government departments. Funds subscribed in response to the Division's appeal were channelled to the experienced Committee on Relief and Gift Supplies (C.O.R.A.G.S.) of the National Christian Council of India. It was later renamed Christian Agency for Social Action (C.A.S.A.).

During 1966, the Service to Refugees, renamed the Refugee Programme, was radically restructured to bring it into still closer accord with emerging needs. A social service officer and a programme officer were appointed to help the assistant director in his work. Negotiations were begun with several National Councils for them to take over refugee responsibilities. In December 1966 Miss Margaret Jaboor retired. She had been with the service to refugees for fifteen years and as director for the last four. When the divisional committee said farewell to her, it was stated that through her work she had directed the resettlement of 300,000 refugees—an "illustrious chapter", it was said, in the story of ecumenical service. But this one figure of 300,000 refugees resettled in other countries indicates only a part of the work done by the refugee programme over the years.

To fill in the picture, mention must also be made of the aged and handicapped, numbering more than 5,000, who were given lifetime security in Old People's Homes, thanks to the funds provided by Churches, governments, and intergovernmental organizations. Again, integration projects were devised for thousands of individuals in many countries. These projects, also financed at the beginning by Churches, governments, and intergovernmental organizations, enabled the refugees who benefited to become self-supporting.

And behind all these activities has lain the pastoral, education, material, and welfare services of all kinds given by the staff of the refugee programme to tens of thousands of bewildered, friendless, and despairing people in many places.

During 1966, two conferences took place which affected the development of inter-Church aid. The first of these had for its theme "Inter-Church Aid in the Next Ten Years". This world conference was held at Swanwick, England. It was immediately followed by the Church and Society World Conference in Geneva. At both of these the Churches were urged to align themselves more closely to governmental and intergovernmental programmes of development aid. For some years this had been one of the main concerns of the Division's secretariat for the study and survey of areas of acute human need. But to extend this work, expressed largely in the Churches' involvement with the Freedom from Hunger Campaign and the World Food Programme, it was decided to establish an additional, new desk—that for development education.

For ten years, considerable thought had been given to the concept of *diakonia* (service). The report of the W.C.C. Conference on Church and Society at Thessalonica, 1959, said: "God loves not only the Christians but the whole world; and all the revolutions of this world take place in some fashion under God's providence to serve the final goals of the divine will of love." A World Council of Churches' pamphlet[1] comments:

> In a sense, the challenge of the contemporary revolution to the churches' *diakonia* today is to develop new policies, new concepts, new forms of action which will, on the one hand, continue to meet individual, family and wider social needs, and, on the other, to promote social justice on a community or national and ecumenical world basis rather than on a strictly personal one.

The Thessalonica Conference was followed by three consultations arranged by the Division. The first of these was held in Geneva in 1961, and had as its theme "The Role of Institutional Christian Service in Modern Society". The second, which was limited to representatives of Churches in North America and Europe, took place at Mülheim, Germany, in 1962, and was concerned with "The Role of the Churches in Social Service". The third consultation met in Geneva in August 1965, and was called in response to a request of the divisional committee of D.I.C.A.R.W.S. that the staff should prepare a contribution to the World Conference on Church and Society 1966 with regard to the role of the *diakonia* in contemporary society and its future forms of service. Leslie E. Cooke, at that time the Director of the Division, said that the fact that the World Council numbered more than two hundred Churches implied a wholly new relationship between the Churches themselves. Within the World Council, those Churches had equal status; requests for aid and offers of aid had taken on a wholly different connotation. There was no room for paternalistic charity, only for partnership and sharing. Moreover, there was ground for a new solidarity in meeting human need. Ecumenical *diakonia* had thus gained significance.

Other aspects of the new thinking about inter-Church aid were mentioned

[1] *The Role of the Diakonia of the Church in Contemporary Society* (1966), p 34.

by Leslie Cooke in the concluding address he gave to the Swanwick Consultation 1966.

> There will be many [Dr Cooke said] who have been generous in their giving for relief who will become hesitant, if not resistant, when they realize that our aim is to change the *status quo*. They will think that the Church has gone leftist, or socialist, or communist . . . There will be those among the rising generation, and in the churches of the developing countries, who are radical, who will say: "At last the churches are with us—they have espoused our cause, they have joined the revolution." Then there will come a moment when to the word "revolution" we will have to add the word "reconciliation", and these heralds of the new dawn will be disappointed and disillusioned as they see that the Church cannot deploy into the long lines to face the enemies of change for violent battle. We shall face grave misunderstanding.
>
> . . . That we are now caught up to go beyond aid to challenge the structures of churches and society, even by aid we give and the purposes to which we give it, is beyond doubt. That there is a price to be paid is also beyond doubt. The only two uncertainties are what the cost will be and whether we are prepared to pay it.
>
> We have to press on beyond co-operation to community . . . The overwhelming compulsion to move from co-operation to community derives from the fact that it is clear that many of the problems which face mankind can be solved only by the building of a world community. Perhaps the most significant contribution the churches can make is in manifesting that they are a world community, that they in fact share a common life in the body of Christ.

Over the years such ecumenical bodies as the East Asia Christian Conference, the All Africa Conference of Churches, and the Near East Council of Churches have been responsible, in one way or another, for inter-Church aid in their region. The East Asia Christian Conference sponsors the Asian Christian Service in Vietnam for which support is sought through the Division. In co-operation with the Asian Churchwomen's Conference, the E.A.C.C. also allocates funds received from the "Fellowship of the Least Coin"; these funds total year by year around $50,000. In January 1965 the All Africa Conference of Churches accepted responsibility for the administering of the Ecumenical Programme for Emergency Action in Africa (E.P.E.A.A.) for which the Division set itself to raise outside Africa $10,000,000 over a five-year period. The All Africa Conference of Churches has set up its own special agency to carry out the E.P.E.A.A.

I.S.A.L. (Church and Society in Latin America) formulated projects which were included in the annual project list of the World Council's Divisions of Inter-Church Aid, Refugee, and World Service and of World Mission and Evangelism. Again, the National Christian Council of India's Christian Agency for Social Action (C.A.S.A.) had its own relief and rehabilitation programmes and also worked out ways in which ecumenical support could be channelled through it to A.F.P.R.O. (Action for Food Production). The Near East Council of Churches had likewise a long-standing programme of Christian service in its area. Many other examples of inter-Church aid in developing areas could be cited.

Somewhat paradoxically, inter-Church aid activities in Europe, where the work had been born, had never been the responsibility of a regional European ecumenical organization, but had been left to the European desk of a division of the World Council of Churches. Should such a regional body be created for some forms of inter-Church aid in Europe? The question became pressing when the World Council of Churches' Divisional Committee on Inter-Church Aid, Refugee, and World Service decided to call a meeting on Inter-Church Aid and appointed a preparatory commission to prepare the agenda. When the preparatory commission met in Geneva in February 1967, it sent an official message to the Presidium of the Conference of European Churches, saying that it regarded the question of a European inter-Church aid organization as a cardinal one, and asked that the Presidium should give careful consideration to it and distinguish between those matters which could and should be carried out by such a body and those better left to the World Council.

During this meeting of the preparatory commission, the news was received of the death in New York of Dr Leslie Cooke, the Director of the Division, and with his passing the story of Inter-Church Aid since the Second World War may appropriately be broken off. Leslie Cooke was a man of unusual vision who was also a man of practical affairs. He coloured indelibly the work of the Division, not only in its structure but also in the quality of its performance. He never forgot, in all the administrative detail with which he was involved, the human touch. Cooke excelled in the interpretation of the inner meaning of Inter-Church Aid, and this had great effect on those churchmen whose commitment to mission might have led them to misunderstand service. His prophetic vision enabled him to seize upon changing needs and situations and to adapt Inter-Church Aid to meet these.

Inevitably, in the years to come Inter-Church Aid will change, since change is a law of life. But whatever the transformations that come about, it is certain that Inter-Church Aid will remain what the smiths who forged it intended—a sharing by Churches and between Churches brought together in the service of their Master, who by his example and commands has charged them to heal, feed, clothe, house, and comfort the distressed and to wash the painful feet of tired men limping along the highways of this troubled world.

9

The Development of
Ecumenical Social Thought
and Action

PAUL ABRECHT

Introduction

A large part of the energy of the ecumenical movement has been directed to the search for a common Christian witness to the problems of modern society. Indeed, for laymen, most of the attraction of the ecumenical movement is in its creativity and vitality in facing social issues and in the challenge they have posed to Churches, too much identified with the political and social system of a particular region or country. The importance of the ecumenical witness on social questions was recognized by most of the early leaders of the World Council of Churches, in particular by Bishop George K. A. Bell of Chichester, Archbishop William Temple, Dr J. H. Oldham, and above all by the first General Secretary, Dr W. A. Visser 't Hooft, who in numerous articles and addresses constantly emphasized the prophetic and reconciling function of the ecumenical movement in relation to social problems. All were keenly aware that the ecumenical movement would have a vital role in the dialogue between the Church and the world, especially where the Churches had allowed themselves to become separated and divided by national and regional interests.

In the beginning, co-operation was hampered by the lack of substantial agreement concerning the theological foundations of Christian action in society and also by disagreements about the method by which Christian thought should proceed in determining the Christian's role in society. It has been well said that, in the first ecumenical discussions of social questions,

> there was no common body of social thought, no common experience in dealing with these issues, not even any agreement as to which issues were of primary importance. There was only a common concern about the urgency of the world's need for social reconstruction ... and a common conviction that Christians and the Christian churches were called to play a part in that reconstruction.[1]

The search for a common strategy has, moreover, obliged the Churches to make new evaluations of the discoveries of the social and behavioural sciences. As a result, there has developed a new dialectic between theology and Christian doctrine on the one side, and ideology, social experience, and social science on the other. It is this dialectic which has given ecumenical social ethics its particular dynamic. It has also ensured that laymen would find an important role in ecumenical social thinking.

The discovery of the constantly changing interplay between Christian and secular thought has been fundamental to the development of ecumenical social thinking. It accounts for the double-sided character of that thought: on the one hand, the attempt to define the ends and purposes of social institutions and the criteria for judging these; on the other, the investigation of the way in which Christians or Churches in specific situations have met their responsibilities and the analysis they have made of their social problems. The second concern has meant increasing emphasis on the importance of thorough and systematic study of various social problems.

[1] *Statements of the World Council of Churches on Social Questions* (2nd edn, Geneva 1956), p. 6.

Surprisingly there have been only a few substantial studies of the development of World Council social thought.[1] Most of these were written shortly after the Second Assembly in 1954. Since then there has been a great widening of interests and concerns and some of the issues which preoccupied Christian thought up to the 1954 Assembly have receded in importance, while others, particularly the issues of rapid social change in Africa, Asia, and Latin America, have become central themes in ecumenical study and action. In more recent years all the problems of dynamic/affluent and ailing/under-developed societies have been thrust upon the Christian conscience and preoccupy the Churches.

The Social and Theological Dynamics
of the First Ecumenical Discussions

It is almost fifty years since Archbishop Nathan Söderblom launched his idea of an Ecumenical Council of Churches "which should be able to speak on behalf of Christendom on the religious, moral and social concerns of men". To Söderblom and to those other international church leaders who collaborated with him in the meeting in Geneva, 2–12 August 1920, to prepare for the Universal Christian Conference on Life and Work in Stockholm, in 1925, the task was an urgent one. They saw the First World War as a great catastrophe for mankind and for Christianity. How otherwise explain the situation of Christian nations which had entered into such a terrible struggle against each other, costing so many millions of lives and the destruction of so many lands? The post-war situation seemed scarcely more promising, as the spirit of vengeance and nationalism prevented co-operation in the rebuilding of destroyed societies and the establishment of world peace. It was apparent also that capitalism had not solved the problems of unemployment, and that industrial disputes and strife would wrack the post-war world even more deeply than the pre-war one.

Despite the sense of ugency and the serious preliminary studies, the great hopes for a bold new Christian programme for world order and social reconstruction were disappointed at Stockholm. Indeed, it is often said that the first efforts (1919–25) to develop a new social teaching in the non-Roman Churches are interesting only because they provided the starting-point for what was later to become a theologically more profound and socially more perceptive movement. The conference showed that the Churches had to do much more serious thinking about both the nature of the problems and the Christian approach to them.

Yet it would be wrong to overlook or underestimate some fundamental achievements of this first effort. Like Roman Catholic social movements in the latter half of the nineteenth century, Protestant, Anglican, and Orthodox

---

[1] Edward Duff, s.j., *The Social Thought of the World Council of Churches*. London and New York 1956. Also H. ten Dornkaat, *Die ökumenischen Arbeiten zur sozialen Frage*. Zürich 1954. Professor H. D. Wendland also treats some of the systematic theological problems in the development of ecumenical social ethics in his *Die Kirche in der modernen Gesellschaft* (2nd edn, Hamburg 1958).

leaders had committed themselves to a new involvement in the world in the interest of social justice. They perceived that the spirit of pious individualism which predominated at that time was no answer to the problems of industrial revolution and world conflict. They sought to construct a new ecumenical concern based upon the inspiration of various Christian social movements of the day. These were prophetic movements, movements of outrage and protest against social evils, movements of reform and action. It is useful to recall in summary form their basic presuppositions:

1. The rejection of the prevailing static conception of human nature and society, and the refusal to interpret the Christian doctrine of sin and the fall of man as an argument against working for social betterment.

2. The insistence that God is at work in the protest movements within society, and that man must co-operate with him in realizing his will to establish his Kingdom.

3. The rejection of all atomistic and mechanistic conceptions of society such as were dominant in the hey-day of *laissez-faire* capitalism.

4. The insistence that men are largely shaped by their social environment, and the conviction that social structures can be altered in order to promote better conditions of human life.

5. The emphasis on the role of the State and the community in regulating various aspects of social life and in developing new and more just patterns of society.

6. The concern for the solidarity of men and for equality of opportunity as a vital element in the Christian understanding of social reform and social change.

It has been said that the Stockholm Conference of 1925, by endorsing these ideas, gave an ecumenical blessing to the social gospel movements which has already gained momentum in the United States, Great Britain, and many countries of Europe. It would perhaps be more true to say that the Churches incorporated certain insights of these movements into their thinking, while remaining critical of some of the conclusions which the movements themselves drew from these insights.

In later years it has also been said that this was the beginning of an Anglo-Saxon theological domination of ecumenical social ethics, but this overlooks the deep interest in Christian social thought in many European countries at that time (especially Germany, Switzerland, France, and Scandinavia), and the efforts to develop a social ethics combining Christian thought with the insights of the social protest movements and the ideals of socialism. The attraction for Europeans of the American social gospel movement was precisely that it seemed to offer the possibility of a new Christian social concern. A European Christian student leader, writing his doctoral thesis in 1928 on the American social gospel, observed: "In America this ethic constitutes the one most important attempt made to transcend the individualistic notions of the last centuries and arrive at a solidaristic conception of social life."[1]

The appreciation of socialism's contribution to Christian social thought was recognized by European Christian thinkers also. Adolf Harnack, in his classic study of *The Mission and Expansion of Christianity* (London 1908), describing the social expression of Christianity in the first three centuries, concluded:

> The gospel, it has been truly said, is at bottom both individualistic and socialistic. Its tendency towards mutual association, so far from being an accidental phenomenon in its history, is inherent in its character. It spiritualizes the irresistible impulse which draws one man to another, and raises the social connection of human beings from the sphere of a convention to that of a moral obligation. In this way it serves to heighten the worth of man, and essays to recast contemporary society, to transform the socialism which involves a conflict of interests into the socialism which rests upon the consciousness of spiritual unity and a common goal.

The great work of Troeltsch on *The Social Teaching of the Christian Churches* (London 1911) had also opened world Christian thinking to a new concern for society by showing the ethical and sociological pattern of various forms of Christianity and their appeal to particular social classes and groups.

It would be instructive at this point to compare these developments with Roman Catholic social thinking as it developed in the great social encyclicals from *Rerum novarum* (1891) to *Quadragesimo anno* (1931). It might be argued that whereas in later years Roman Catholicism had to overcome an uncompromising rejection of socialism and Marxism, non-Roman social thinkers were obliged to rid themselves of some illusions about man and society which an idealist socialist reading of the Bible had fostered. The economic depression in the western capitalist countries and the rise of the totalitarian political systems in Europe showed the inadequacy of some of the theological and ethical ideas with which the Church was working. A deeper theological basis was needed. This was to be one of the chief contributions of the second major international conference on social questions organized by the Churches—the Conference on Church, Community and State, which met at Oxford in 1937.

New Conceptions of Christian Social Witness
The Oxford Conference of 1937

The 1937 Conference on Church, Community and State was called and prepared for by the Continuation Committee on Life and Work, set up after Stockholm. Like the Stockholm Conference, the Conference of Oxford can be understood only against the background of the economic and political situation and the changing attitudes within the Church regarding its task in society.

[1] W. A. Visser 't Hooft, *The Background of the Social Gospel in America*. New York, 1928.

The world economic and social situation had steadily worsened during the 1930s. The effects of the economic depression in the great industrial nations had spread around the whole world, and the social tensions they produced convulsed practically every society. New ideologies offering new solutions to economic order and social justice competed for power, and the battle for supremacy shook the foundations of all the western nations. The trade union movement struggled to gain new power for the workers, and the Churches were called upon to declare where they stood in the midst of industrial strife. The Oxford Conference is noteworthy particularly for what it said about the economic situation and the problem of inequality in the distribution of wealth and income.

It also brought into the open the debate about the theological and biblical basis of Christian social ethics which had been simmering since the 1925 Conference in Stockholm. J. H. Oldham, the chief architect of the Oxford Conference, summarized thus the three theological perspectives presented to the Conference:

1. A Christian ethics based on principles derived from New Testament teaching, especially the Sermon on the Mount, representing the position of Stockholm.

2. A personal ethics of salvation—suspicious of "Christian social programmes" —was held by several continental theologians who maintained that the Christian ethic could not be identified with that of the Sermon on the Mount. Thus Professor Emil Brunner of Zurich argued that "The Christian Church has no right to lay down a social programme, because it is not its business to establish any kind of system. It is doubtful whether we ought to speak of a Christian ethic at all, since an ethic means something which has an independent existence and which once for all lays down rules for the various relations of life."

3. A Christian ethics of justice derived from the love commandment. This view emphasized the prophetic mission of the Church in relation to the family, the nation, the state, economics and culture. In contrast to the first position, it stressed the reality of evil and the difficulty of direct applications of the love commandment.[1]

There is no evidence that the Oxford Conference formally adopted any one of these interpretations; but it is clear that the third position greatly influenced the conference reports and Christian social thinking in the following years.[2]

The optimism inherent in the view that social and political reform would solve all human ills, or that new social systems would totally eradicate social evils had persisted after the First World War, but it came under challenge in the Oxford Conference, and practically disappeared with the Second World War.

The theological corrective which the Oxford Conference applied to the

---

[1] The Oxford Conference (1937), Official Report, pp. 27–32.

[2] John C. Bennett wrote the preliminary draft for the section on Economic Life in co-operation with J. H. Oldham. The influence of Reinhold Niebuhr is also apparent in the formulation of the theological passages. The book by Archbishop William Temple, *Christianity and Social Order* (London 1942), is one example of writing based on the theological ideas of Oxford.

I

thinking of the 1925 Stockholm Conference is well illustrated in the report on economic life. It is argued that a Christian social ethic cannot be developed directly from the love commandment or the Kingdom of God, since these, because of human sinfulness, are in contradiction with the world. Therefore, "in so far as the Kingdom of God is in conflict with the world and is therefore still to come, the Christian finds himself under the necessity of discovering the best available means of checking human sinfulness and of increasing the possibilities and opportunities of love within a sinful world." The task of the Christian is to make use of the "principle of justice, as the relative expression of the commandment of love in any critique of economic, political and social institutions".

In opposition to some interpretations of Lutheran social ethics, the report emphasized that:

> The laws of justice are not purely negative. They are not merely "dykes against sin". The political and economic structure of society is also the mechanical skeleton which carries the organic element of society. Forms of production and methods of co-operation may serve the cause of human brotherhood by serving and extending the principle of love beyond the sphere of purely personal relations.

The Oxford Report illustrated this by indicating four ways in which the economic order of that day challenged the Christian understanding of man and society:

1. by its enhancement of acquisitiveness;
2. by its inequalities;
3. by the irresponsible possession of economic power;
4. by the frustration of the sense of Christian vocation.

Concerning these problems the report set forth a body of "Christian teaching" representing the "kind of guidance which it is possible to receive from the Christian faith for economic life". What followed constituted the most comprehensive and systematic review ever made by a group of Protestant, Anglican, and Orthodox Churches of the problems of economic life. It was specifically noted that the teaching would apply for about a decade. As matters turned out, the Second World War shortened that period considerably, bringing with it a new concern for social justice and order which was to lead to great economic changes and the rapid development of the modern welfare society and state.

The need for a larger authority for the State in ordering economic life did not lead the participants in the 1937 Conference to overlook the dangers of growing state power. The rise of Nazism and totalitarian communism posed this problem very acutely, and forced participants to a new examination of the power of the State: "Since we believe in the holy God as the source of justice, we do not consider the state as the ultimate source of law but as its guarantor. It is not the lord but the servant of justice. There can be for the Christian no ultimate authority but very God."

The report also declared that, in the present situation, "the widespread tendency of the state to control the totality of human life in all its individual and social aspects, combined with the tendency to attribute absolute value to the state itself", forced the Church to reconsider its relation to the State. The Conference agreed that there are areas where the social activities of Church and State overlap; tensions are therefore unavoidable and solutions will vary in different historical circumstances. The report emphasized that the Church as a Christian community has a responsibility to help its members to interpret their responsibility in relation to the State.

Developments after the Second World War
The Responsible Society

Ecumenical discussion of social questions was interrupted by the Second World War, but Churches in various regions struggled to prepare themselves for the post-war period by their discussions of the conditions of peace and post-war reconstruction. Their debates now focused on the issues of state planning and the welfare society, as alternatives to capitalism and communism, and this came to be the main social issue in the discussions of the First Assembly which constituted the World Council of Churches in Amsterdam in 1948.

In the Assembly report on "The Church and the Disorder of Society", the Churches refused to accept either complete state planning or unqualified freedom in economic affairs. "Coherent and purposeful ordering of society has now become a major necessity. Here governments have responsibilities which they must not shirk. But centres of initiative in economic life must be so encouraged as to avoid placing too great a burden upon centralized judgment and decision." The Assembly stressed that Christians should reject the extreme ideologies of both communism and *laissez-faire* capitalism, and "should seek to draw men away from the false assumption that these extremes are the only alternatives". It could not "resolve the debate between those who feel that the primary solution is to socialize the means of production, and those who fear that such a course will merely lead to new and inordinate combinations of political power, culminating finally in an omnicompetent state".

Before the Amsterdam Assembly, J. H. Oldham, W. A. Visser 't Hooft, Reinhold Niebuhr, and M. M. Thomas discussed the best term for identifying the responsibility of the Church in society. Various phrases had been considered: "the open society", "the free society", and "the free and responsible society". Finally "responsible society" was adopted, and it proved to be the key phrase in over a decade of ecumenical social thought. (The term was held to include freedom, responsibility being impossible without freedom to exercise it.)

The definition of the responsible society set forth at Amsterdam is as follows:

> Man is created and called to be a free being, responsible to God and his neighbour. Any tendencies in state and society depriving man of the possibility of acting responsibly are a denial of God's intention for man and his work of

salvation. A responsible society is one where freedom is the freedom of men who acknowledge responsibility to justice and public order, and where those who hold political authority or economic power are responsible for its exercise to God and the people whose welfare is affected by it . . . For a society to be responsible under modern conditions it is required that the people have freedom to control, to criticize, and to change their governments, that power be made responsible by law and tradition, and be distributed as widely as possible through the whole community. It is required that economic justice and provision of equality of opportunity be established for all the members of society.

At the Second Assembly of the World Council of Churches in 1954 the term was broadened and its meaning as a guide for action clarified:

> Responsible society is not an alternative social political system, but a criterion by which we judge all existing social orders and at the same time a standard to guide us in the specific choices we have to make. Christians are called to live responsibly, to live in response to God's act of redemption in Christ, in any society, even within the most unfavourable social structures.

In contrast with the earlier Assembly, the Second Assembly (1954) pointed to the great changes in economic and social policy which had come about in many countries in the post-war years:

> These developments suggest that disputes about "capitalism" and "socialism" disguise the more important issues in the field of economic and social policy. Each word is applied to many different social forms and economic systems. It is not the case that we have merely a choice between two easily distinguishable types of economic organization . . . . The concrete issues in all countries concern the newly evolving forms of economic organization, and the relative roles of the state, organized groups and private enterprises.

The concept of responsible society helped many Churches in the West in their debates about economic and social policy, especially those in danger of being caught up in the sterile and self-righteous anti-communist crusade which obsessed many western countries in the 1950s. But it found little acceptance among Christians in the Third World who felt the need for concepts which related more closely to the dynamic social conditions in which they lived.

Enlarging the Ecumenical Dialogue

With the formation of the World Council of Churches in 1948 it was possible to launch more continuous systematic study on social questions. Within the Study Department, supervised by Dr Nils Ehrenström of Sweden, an inquiry on "Christian Action in Society" was started, and in August 1949 Paul Abrecht from the U.S.A. was invited to direct this programme.

The organization of an ecumenical programme on this large theme was a challenge. Considering the limited resources of staff and finances available, what should be the structure and the method of such work? What were the critical issues for the Churches, and with what sense of priority should they be considered? Those were real and difficult questions! Attention gradually focused on three issues: (a) the witness of the Church in communist societies;

(*b*) the role of the Church in working for a responsible society; and (*c*) the meaning of work in a technical age.[1]

By 1952 new Christian thinkers were appearing in the ecumenical discussion of these questions. Charles West of the U.S.A. contributed greatly to the discussion of Christianity and Marxism from his experience in China during the triumph of communism, and later from his work in Berlin.[2] Denys Munby, then a young reader in economics at the University of Aberdeen, became known for his writing on economic issues. In 1956 he published *Christianity and Economic Problems*, the first systematic treatise since A. D. Lindsay's *Christianity and Economics*, and the most important book yet written on this theme. Among the theologians, H. D. Wendland of Germany, a veteran of the Oxford Conference, returned to the ecumenical discussion with his contributions on the relation of eschatology and ethics.

A western European group of laymen and theologians, formed in 1951 to reflect from a Christian perspective on the movement for European economic and political integration, became a source of new insights on the meaning of responsible society in Europe. Here European socialists, liberals, and conservatives debated the Christian responsibility for the future of Europe. Members of the group included such laymen as the late John Edwards, Labour M.P. from the United Kingdom, later to become president of the Council of Europe; André Philip, Professor of Economics at the Sorbonne and one of the leaders of the European movement; Max Kohnstamm of Holland, the first secretary of the High Authority for the European Coal and Steel Community; and from Germany, Hermann Ehlers, *Oberkirchenrat* and President of the German *Bundestag*, and Gustav Heinemann, then a strong advocate of a neutral and united Germany, now minister of the interior in the present (1968) German government. The motor of this group was Dr C. L. Patijn of Holland, a leading official of the Dutch Foreign Office, and Chairman of Section III at Amsterdam and Evanston. Other active participants were Jean Rey of Belgium, later to become President of the European Common Market, and Mario Rollier of the Socialist Party of Italy, member of the Milan City Council and nuclear physicist. This lay group opened its discussions to church leaders and theologians from both eastern and western Europe. In 1953 there was a debate in Paris with Bishop Albert Berecsky, and Bishop Janos Peter of Hungary who became foreign minister of Hungary after the uprisings of 1956, participating.

In 1949 and 1952 there were study conferences on social issues in east Asia which opened the door to a new and larger vision of the ecumenical responsibility.

The method of work during these years was non-institutionalized and decentralized, depending much on local initiative. The purpose was to draw in laymen and theologians interested in applying ecumenical criteria to the

---

[1] An inquiry into this last topic started with the publication of a report on the *Work in Modern Society* by J. H. Oldham in 1949, but the resources were lacking to pursue it.

[2] His writings and those of others on this theme appeared in *Background Information on Church and Society*, a mimeographed publication of the Study Department which was started in 1951.

problems of society in particular areas. In this way the staff gained experience and tested the capacity of the ecumenical movement to encourage the new and creative thinking asked for by the First Assembly.

The new structure for the World Council adopted in 1954 provided for a Department on Church and Society within a new Division of Studies. The new Director of the Division, Dr Robert Bilheimer, strongly encouraged the ecumenical study programme on social questions and gave much time to it until he left the World Council staff in 1963. Above all the new department provided the organizational basis and the liberty of action needed for the expansion which began in 1955.

The Ecumenical Witness Against Racism

The Evanston Assembly of 1954 gave its attention primarily to social problems which had preoccupied the ecumenical discussion in the period after the Amsterdam Assembly: the trend towards the "mixed" social planning–private enterprise economies in the West; the function of the Church in relation to communist/non-communist tension; and the problems of the economically underdeveloped regions; but it also attacked the issue of racism.

Many of the Churches affiliated to the World Council of Churches had expressed their opposition to racial and ethnic segregation and discrimination, and the Oxford Conference had made a clear ecumenical critique of racism, but this was the first occasion when the issue was thoroughly debated within the Council. The report received by the Assembly and commended to the Churches for their study and action was unequivocal:

> Racial and ethnic fears, hates and prejudices are more than social problems with whose existence we must reckon; they are sins against God and His commandments that the Gospel alone can cure. To the Church has been committed the preaching of the Gospel. To proclaim the "healing of the nations" through Christ is verily her task . . . As part of its task of challenging the conscience of society, it is the duty of the Church to protest against any law or arrangement that is unjust to any human being or which would make Christian fellowship impossible, or would prevent the Christian from practising his vocation. Some of its members may feel bound to disobey such a law. The Church does not contemplate lightly any breaking of the law, but it recognizes the duty of a Christian to do so when he feels that he has reached that point where the honour and glory of God command him to obey God rather than man. In so doing, the Church must point out the possible consequent necessity for spiritual discipline according to the Gospel.

The Assembly report added:

> The Church of Christ cannot approve of any law which discriminates on grounds of race, which restricts the opportunity of any person to acquire education to prepare himself for his vocation, to procure or to practise employment in his vocation, or in any other way curtails his exercise of the full rights and responsibilities of citizenship and of sharing in the responsibilities and duties of government.[1]

[1] Intergroup Relations—the Church Amid Racial and Ethnic Tensions", *Ecumenical Statements on Race Relations* (Geneva 1965), pp. 17–22.

In a resolution the Second Assembly also declared its conviction that

> any form of segregation based on race, colour, or ethnic origin is contrary to the Gospel, and is incompatible with the Christian doctrine of man and with the nature of the Church of Christ. The Assembly urges the churches within its membership to renounce all forms of segregation, of discrimination, and to work for their abolition within their own life and within society.

These declarations strengthened the position of those struggling against the evils of racism, though they did not move many Churches immediately to bold new action against racism in their own fellowship. So great was the confidence in the prophetic word that the World Council itself acted only relatively slowly to implement a further resolution of the Assembly recommending "that the Central Committee, in consultation with the International Missionary Council, make structural provision for an organisation, preferably a department, giving assistance to the constituent Churches in their efforts to bring the gospel to bear more effectively upon relations between racial and ethnic groups". But increasing racial conflict showed the need for a more active ecumenical role.

The killing of Africans in Sharpeville in South Africa in March 1960, and a request of the Archbishop of Cape Town, led to a meeting on "Church and Apartheid" in South Africa in December 1960. It was attended by a delegation of six leaders from the World Council of Churches. At Cottesloe (near Johannesburg) they met ten representatives from each of the eight Churches in South Africa to consider the Christian witness for racial justice in view of the apartheid policy of that country. The report of the meeting affirmed that no Christian could be excluded from any Church on grounds of race and colour, and it called attention to the injustices and hardships suffered by the African because of the system of communal separation and the restrictions on his participation in the economic and political life of South Africa.[1] The report, though approved by eighty per cent of the participants, was later repudiated by the three Dutch Reformed Churches of South Africa, which also withdrew from the World Council of Churches.[2]

In 1960 the World Council also established a Secretariat on Racial and Ethnic Relations within the Department on Church and Society to strengthen the ecumenical witness in situations of racial and ethnic tensions and to offer assistance to those Churches which were seeking new and creative answers. As the anger and violence created by racism increased, especially in the U.S.A. and Southern Africa, this secretariat endeavoured to arouse greater awareness of the enormous task confronting the Churches. A series of field visits and consultations was organized in many different regions of the world, perhaps the most remarkable being the Ecumenical Consultation on Chris-

---

[1] *Cottesloe Consultation—The Report of the Consultation Among South African Member Churches of the World Council of Churches, 7–14 December, 1960, Cottesloe, Johannesburg*. Johannesburg 1961. The Consultation was prepared by Dr Robert Bilheimer, who made several visits to South Africa to meet church leaders and to reach agreement on the agenda for the meeting.

[2] See "Message to Christians in South Africa", *The New Delhi Report: Third Assembly of the World Council of Churches, 1961*, p. 322.

tians and Race Relations in Southern Africa, held in Kitwe, Zambia, 25 May–2 June 1964, under the auspices of the Mindolo Ecumenical Foundation, the South African Institute of Race Relations, and the World Council of Churches. The Conference was chaired by Dr Daisuke Kitagawa of the U.S.A., who had previously (1960–3) directed the World Council Secretariat on Race Relations, and was attended by sixty church leaders and laymen from the countries of Southern Africa. The finding that "the unjust patterns of race relations now prevailing in most of Southern Africa must be changed" was detailed in a report of thirty-seven pages.[1] The report provoked new intense discussion, especially in South Africa where it became one of the principal issues in a celebrated civil law suit between two Christian leaders who supported the ecumenical position on racism, and a theologian who opposed it.[2] (The court made its judgement in favour of the two plaintiffs in the suit for libel.)

The Kitwe Conference emphasized that the problem of racial justice cannot be solved without great changes in economic and political structures, and this was reiterated in the 1966 Conference on Church and Society which pressed the Churches to become more deeply involved in the world-wide struggle against racism. The issue was brought to the forefront of the Conference by the sermon of Dr Martin Luther King, who, though prevented from coming by race riots in Chicago, was seen and heard by millions of viewers on European television, and by the inability of Bishop Alpheus Zulu of South Africa, one of the presidents of the Conference, to participate, as he had been denied a passport by the South African government.

In the Fourth Assembly at Uppsala (1968) the ecumenical consideration of racism reached a new and sharper focus, reflecting no doubt the increasing violence of race conflict and the determination of the coloured people, especially black Americans, to attain full equality of political and social rights with whites. Two addresses on the theme, "White Racism or World Community?", by Mr James Baldwin, the distinguished American writer, and Lord Caradon, delegate of the United Kingdom to the United Nations, showed the increasing impatience with Christian tolerance or support of white racism. Mr Baldwin's address expressed this in unmistakable terms:

> At this moment in the world's history it becomes necessary for me, for my own survival, not to listen to what you say but to watch very carefully what you do, not to read your pronouncements, but to go back to the source and to check it out for myself. And if that is so, then it may very well mean that the revolution which was begun two thousand years ago by a disreputable Hebrew criminal may now have to be begun again by people equally disreputable and equally improbable. It has to be admitted that if you are born under the circumstances in which most black people in the West are born, that means really black people over the entire world, . . . and having attained something resembling adulthood, it is perfectly true that one can see that the destruction of the Christian

---

[1] *Christians and Race Relations in Southern Africa.* Geneva 1964.

[2] See "Summary of Judgement in the Supreme Court of South Africa" between Professor A. S. Geyser, C. F. B. Naudé (plaintiffs) and Professor A. D. Pont (defendant), 1 August 1967. Published by the Christian Institute, Johannesburg, 1967.

Church as it is presently constituted may not only be desirable but may be necessary.

A "black caucus" at work in the Fourth Assembly put new force behind the familiar ecumenical declarations of good intentions concerning racism. In every area of ecumenical witness white racism was challenged; and in the election of the new Central Committee a new militant group of black ministers and laymen from the U.S.A. was selected, so insuring that black participation in the World Council would be more than a formality. It is noteworthy that the first decision of the new Central Committee was to endorse the recommendation of the Uppsala Assembly in favour of a World Council programme of study and action on the elimination of racism and to authorize its preparation. It is this new dynamic concern for racial justice together with the urgent demand for Christian involvement in the struggle for freedom and justice in the Third World which more than any other factor accounts for the revolutionary spirit arising within the ecumenical movement in recent years.

The Christian Responsibility for Rapid Social Change in the New Nations

It is a sobering thought that the ecumenical movement discovered the urgent problems of the nations of Africa, Asia, Latin America, and the Middle East only after the process of radical decolonization was well under way. There are institutional reasons which help to explain that fact. The World Council of Churches had very few member Churches from these countries in 1948 and most of the Christian concern for social and political welfare in these lands was expressed through western missionary societies identified with the International Missionary Council until that body merged with the W.C.C. in 1961. Despite the real interest of western Christians, they could not be expected to see the need for revolutionary change as clearly as Christians in the emerging nations.

Nevertheless, as early as 1949 the Churches of Asia had called attention to the confrontation between Christianity and revolutionary social change shaping up there. The Eastern Asia Christian Conference, held in Bangkok in December 1949, the first regional meeting of its kind to be held in Asia, emphasized the challenge to the Church in the social and political life: "The struggle for, and the attainment of, political freedom has awakened the hitherto submerged peoples of East Asia to a new sense of dignity and historical mission. Those are basic elements in the revolutionary ferment which are at work in the contemporary revolts and power-conflicts in Asia."

In 1952 the Study Department of the World Council, taking advantage of the first meeting of the Central Committee of the World Council to be held in Asia, organized in Lucknow an Ecumenical Study Conference for East Asia. The Conference was divided into three sections: Section II dealt with The Responsible Society in East Asia in the light of the World Situation, and Section III, Racial, Class, and Caste Tensions. One of the papers for this meeting was prepared by Professor Egbert de Vries. It was the beginning of the enormous contribution which this renowned specialist on the economics of development was to make to the social thinking of the World Council.[1]

As seen by the Asian Churches the task was to maintain a positive attitude to the social revolution taking place in East Asia as the best answer to the dynamic challenge of communism. The opening paragraphs of the Lucknow report put the issue in this perspective:

> We are concerned with social justice, that is to say with the development of social conditions in which human dignity and freedom can find their expression as befits the nature and destiny of man as a child of God. Communism has awakened and challenged our conscience to see the need for action. It is not, however, primarily the fear of communism but our concern for our brothers for whom Christ died, that should impel us to fulfil our social obligations. But a positive programme for social justice will help to meet the challenge of Communism.

The positive programme proposed by the Lucknow Conference included radical reform of land tenure systems, planned economic development, support of the struggle for freedom and self-determination in East Asia, and new policies by western nations in support of political and economic change in Asia.

The Lucknow meeting had a great influence on the further consideration of Christian action in Asia and on the subsequent decision of the World Council to develop a comprehensive programme in support of Churches facing issues of rapid social change in Africa, Asia, and Latin America. The decision to launch such a programme was taken in July 1955 at the first meeting of the new working committee for the Department on Church and Society, in Davos, Switzerland. It was approved by the Central Committee immediately after.[2]

A strong team of officers and staff was assembled to provide leadership for this inquiry which had as its theme "The Common Christian Responsibility Toward Areas of Rapid Social Change".[3] Professor E. de Vries, as chairman of the working committee, gave constant help, and the staff, now enlarged, included Paul Abrecht and Daisuke Kitagawa with M. M. Thomas as staff consultant for Asia and Dr John Karefa Smart as staff consultant for Africa (1956–7). Over the next five years this group was constantly on the move in Africa, Asia, Latin America, and the Middle East, contacting church and mission leaders, searching for new talent among theologians and laymen, organizing consultations and projects, and pressing the Churches to take up the themes of the rapid social change study. Churches and missions that had previously scarcely heard of the World Council suddenly found themselves plunged into a strenuous ecumenical debate. Sometimes the intrusion of these questions was vigorously opposed in both Church and mission; but

[1] Egbert de Vries, "The Churches and the Problems of Social and Economic Development in South and Southeast Asia", *Ecumenical Review*, vol. v (April 1953), pp. 233–43.

[2] See MRCC (Davos 1955).

[3] Two official statements were published on the goals of the programme: *The Common Christian Responsibility Toward Areas of Rapid Social Change* (Geneva 1955) and *Second Statement on the Issues in the Study of Rapid Social Change* (Geneva 1956).

the growing interest in the discovery of new lines of action for the Church in fast-changing societies gradually overcame the hesitations and fears. For many of these Churches the study provided the first opportunity to analyse the role of the Church in their society, and for the World Council it was to lead to a remarkable broadening of social perspective and concern, and a significantly new stage in the development of a truly universal Christian social ethic.

The programme was so constructed that an international series of conferences and publications supported the national and regional programme and vice versa. Over $200,000 was raised to finance this six-year programme (1955–61). Roughly half of this sum was for projects in the new nations and the other half for the international dimension of the inquiry. The results are catalogued in a number of study booklets and pamphlets and in two volumes which summarize the findings of the study.[1]

The development of the World Council's concern for social change seemed at first to require no new theological–ethical categories. But inevitably it became necessary to think in terms of theological perspectives for radical change, and to find a Christian interpretation of the emancipation of the new nations and of their efforts at nation-building.

In contrast with the familiar ecumenical emphasis on gradual social change and reform, the inquiries in the new nations pointed to the rapid breakdown of old social systems and traditions and the need for political and economic systems supporting rapid development. In contrast with western Christian thought which despite all its preoccupation with secularization was based on assumptions of a society still greatly influenced by Christian values and institutions, Christian social thinking in the new nations tended to emphasize the Christian contribution to a pluralistic social ethic which would promote human values in a national perspective. In contrast with the extremely critical attitude manifested toward nationalism in many of the Western Churches, the "younger Churches" stressed the creative role of the new nation-states in the work of development and in creating a new sense of dignity and self-respect. In opposition to the Western Churches, which still placed great confidence in the traditional structures of world political and economic relations, Christians from the new nations pointed to their inherent biases, and challenged the assumption of an "international law" developed by the western powers and imposed on the rest of the world.

This challenge to traditional ecumenical social thinking is well illustrated in the report of the International Ecumenical Study Conference on Social Change, held in Thessalonica, Greece, in July 1959, on the theme "Christian Action in Rapid Social Change; Dilemmas and Opportunities".

> In the earlier years of the ecumenical movement, and particularly at the Oxford Conference of 1937, the subject of nationalism was fully discussed. But in view of the circumstances at that time, attention was concentrated almost exclusively on the nationalist movement in western countries. The specific task in the light of the present situation is to concentrate on a different kind of nationalism in a

[1] Egbert de Vries, *Man in Rapid Social Change* and Paul Abrecht, *The Churches and Rapid Social Change*. New York 1961.

different phase of history in the areas of rapid social change, especially Asia and Africa . . . .

The nationalism of hitherto subject peoples and races gives tangible form to their awakening to a sense of human dignity and their struggle to discover and express their corporate selfhood. This nationalism finds the focus of its unity in the sense of common fate and common fight, that is, in the common determination of peoples to free themselves from alien political domination and racial discrimination.[1]

Similarly in the area of economic development the Thessalonica Conference pointed to the need for a new understanding of world economic justice and welfare.

Our ultimate aim should be a situation where there is no unnecessary poverty among nations, and where each nation by the use of its resources and abilities attacks its own conditions of poverty and contributes to the wellbeing of the whole . . . . Those with greater resources and abilities have the greater obligations. This applies between countries as much as within countries . . . . There is an enormous amount that can and should be done . . . . These responsibilities include not only technical aid and financial help (perhaps as a given proportion of national income), but also a recognition and correction of the ill effects on the poorer countries of western policies on immigration, tariffs and subsidies in foreign trade, stabilization of commodity prices, defence policies, use of surpluses (such as wheat, coal and shipping), and the whole trend of industrial development towards more or less self-sufficiency. Above all, the rich countries need to be aware of the impact of what they do on others. In many cases their contribution to economic development in Africa, Asia and Latin America is totally inadequate . . . .[2]

By 1961, the Churches realized that their social thinking, looked at in the world perspective of social and political change, was in need of a major re-examination, in view of the new problems arising and new ideas about the task of the Church in society. However, the Third Assembly of the World Council of Churches (New Delhi 1961), was unprepared to cope with this new situation. It could only recognize the problem and suggest the need for further ecumenical analysis and consultation, utilizing the insights of Churches and Christians from every continent. It was in recognition of the scope and the urgency of this task that the proposal for a World Conference on Church and Society arose.

The Geneva Conference of 1966

Why was it necessary to wait nearly thirty years after the Oxford Conference for a new World Conference on Church and Society? The answer is that with the formation of the World Council of Churches in 1948, it had been assumed that the Assemblies, meeting at regular intervals of six or seven years would provide the needed opportunity for official World Council action on social

[1] *Dilemmas and Opportunities: Christian Action in Rapid Social Change.* Report of an International Ecumenical Study Conference (Thessalonica 25 July–2 August 1959). Geneva 1959.

[2] Ibid., p. 74.

questions. Indeed the Assemblies of Amsterdam (1948) and Evanston (1954) had contributed significantly to ecumenical reflection. But New Delhi revealed that the amount of time which an Assembly could give to serious consideration of social questions was diminishing; and that the participation of laymen in the discussion of social question was hampered by the predominantly ecclesiastical character and structure of an Assembly. Moreover, the "official" nature of an Assembly inhibited adventurous social thinking; it could only put the seal of World Council approval on ideas already accepted by the Churches, rather than risk new ideas which the Churches had yet to grasp. The search for a way around these obstacles led to the proposal of the staff in 1962 to convene a World Conference on Church and Society, and this was submitted to the Working Committee meeting in 1962.

The Working Committee for Church and Society now included many new faces: M. M. Thomas of India, active in ecumenical social study since 1947, became Chairman, Bishop J. Brooke Mosley of the U.S.A., Vice-Chairman. Other members included Dr Margaret Mead, the noted anthropologist, Professor Mikio Sumiya, an economist from Japan; Bishop Pitirim, the first member from the U.S.S.R.; and Professor Jan M. Lochman of Czechoslovakia. This group, meeting in Paris in July 1962, put forward a plan for a "World Conference on God, Man and Contemporary Society", and their recommendation was approved by the Central Committee a few weeks later.[1]

In structure and organization the World Conference on Church and Society held in Geneva in July 1966 differed from previous world Christian conferences on social questions in two fundamental respects: the majority of the participants were laymen rather than clergy or church officials, and of the 420 participants roughly equal numbers came from the countries of the "third world", from North America, and from western Europe, making it the first large ecumenical conference in which the participants from the western countries were not in a majority. These two features explain the great impact of the Geneva Conference on ecumenical social thought and action.

The Geneva Conference was undoubtedly the most serious attempt on the part of the World Council of Churches to understand the revolutionary realities which shape the modern world. Preparations continued over three years involving the publication of four volumes of essays on the issues of world-wide social change.[2]

The Central Committee further agreed that the Conference should be empowered to speak *to* rather than *for* the Churches and the World Council, thus giving it freedom to explore issues and suggest new approaches. A

---

[1] Subsequently at its meeting in Enugu (1965), the Central Committee reviewed the aims of the Conference and resolved that it should be described as a "World Conference on Church and Society: Christian Response to the Technical and Social Revolutions of our Time". This theme was later abbreviated to "Christians in the Technical and Social Revolutions of our Time".

[2] *Christian Social Ethics in a Changing World*, ed. John C. Bennett. New York 1966.
Responsible Government in a Revolutionary Age, ed. Z. K. Matthews. New York 1966.
Economic Growth in World Perspective, ed. Denys Munby. New York 1966.
Man in Community, ed. Egbert de Vries. New York 1966.

process of selecting participants was devised to correspond with the emphasis on the need for lay experts from the various fields of social life.[1]

The basic work of the Conference was done in four sections on:

I Economic Development in a World Perspective.
II The Nature and Function of the State in a Revolutionary Age.
III Structures of International Co-operation—Living Together in Peace in a Pluralistic World Society.
IV Man and Community in Changing Societies.

In addition there were three Conference working groups on three issues which cut across the concerns of the sections:

1. Theological Issues in Social Ethics.
2. Potentialities of the Contemporary Technological and Scientific Revolution.
3. The Church's Action in Society.

The official report of 162 pages and the conference addresses have been widely studied and discussed. The impact not only on Christian social ethics but on every aspect of the ecumenical movement, whether mission, service, unity, or ministry, has been far-reaching. The Conference has, moreover, produced a chain reaction of follow-up consultations in which Churches and Christian groups around the world have been stimulated to new reflection and consideration on contemporary issues of Church and Society.[2] The theological and intellectual ferment thus created very substantially influenced the thinking of the Fourth Assembly of the World Council meeting at Uppsala in July 1968.

Out of this process of ecumenical inquiry and debate have come many new insights and concerns, radically changing the scope of Christian social thought and action. The resulting debate in the Churches on three concerns of the Geneva Conference deserves special attention because they provide important clues to the future of the ecumenical social thinking.

1. *The Christian Responsibility for World Economic and Social Development*

The 1966 Conference made the issue of world economic development a major concern of the Churches. The conference report on this theme set before them a new comprehensive understanding of the hopes and concerns of the developing countries, the contributions needed from the "richer" nations, and the changes in world economic and political structures required if world economic growth was to be achieved. The report also recommended a number of practical steps which would involve new commitments on the part of the Churches to world economic and social justice.

The papal encyclical *Populorum progressio*, published early in 1967,

---

[1] World Conference on Church and Society (Geneva 1966), Official Report, pp. 8–9.

[2] For a list of these consultations and an account of the reactions to the World Conference, see *Report to the Uppsala Assembly on the 1966 World Conference on Church and Society and the Subsequent Discussion in the Churches*, by Paul Abrecht (Geneva 1968).

supported similar goals of world development and opened the door to new common Christian action. As a result, a joint Roman Catholic–World Council Exploratory Committee on Society, Development, and Peace was formed. Also a conference on World Co-operation for Development, sponsored by the Pontifical Commission on Justice and Peace and the World Council of Churches, was held in Beirut in April 1968. This was the first major international Christian conference to be so jointly sponsored, organized, and financed.[1] This meeting proposed a larger ecumenical action in favour of world economic co-operation and their proposals were endorsed by the Fourth Assembly at Uppsala.

Stimulated by the challenge of the Geneva Conference and the Beirut meeting, the Uppsala Assembly focused major attention on the issues of development. It is noteworthy that the Assembly's report urges the Churches to go beyond the charitable understanding of "rich" nations helping "poor" nations; it emphasizes the need for fundamental social changes based on a new urgent concern for social justice in a world perspective.

> Effective world development requires radical changes in institutions and structures at three levels: within developing countries, within developed countries, and in the international economy. Precisely because such structural changes have not been promoted, we find that as a community of nations we are unable to do the good we would and efforts for international co-operation tend to be paralysed. At all three levels it is necessary to instil social and economic processes with a new dynamic of human solidarity and justice.[2]

This statement of the Assembly perhaps reflected the address of Professor S. L. Parmar of India who, in speaking to the Assembly on this issue, declared:

> Rightly understood, development is disorder because it changes existing social and economic relationships, breaks up old institutions to create new ones, brings about radical alterations in the values and structures of society. If we engage in development through international co-operation, we must recognize that basic changes become necessary in developing and developed nations as also in the international economy. "Development is the new name for peace." But development is disorder, it is revolution. Can we attempt to understand this apparently paradoxical situation which would imply that disorder and revolution are the new name for peace?[3]

Thus, the Christian discussion of world development, formerly treated almost exclusively in terms of new and expanding forms of aid and trade, has tended more and more to merge with the discussion of revolutionary social

---

[1] *World Development—Challenge to the Churches—Official Report of the Beirut Conference*, edited by Father George Dunne. Geneva 1968.
Several other World Council projects contributed notably to ecumenical thinking on development prior to the Assembly. The work of the Committee on Specialized Assistance to Social Projects (S.A.S.P.) should be mentioned. See especially, *Line and Plummet, The Churches and Development. A report to S.A.S.P.*, by Richard Dickinson (Geneva 1968).

[2] Uppsala Assembly: Report of Section III, on "World Economic and Social Development" (Geneva 1968).

[3] Uppsala Assembly: Professor S. L. Parmar, Statement to the Plenary on the Work of Section III.

change. This is due, no doubt, to the great disappointment with the results of previous efforts of world economic development and the recognition that the familiar patterns of world aid and technical assistance have often increased rather than diminished many of the social problems of the developing nations. There is a widespread desire for new ideas, new techniques, and new initiatives.

The Churches working within the ecumenical movement can make an important contribution in this area—especially in the search for new understanding and new ideas as the basis for new and effective action. It remains to be seen whether, having exposed themselves to a new understanding of human aspirations in the movement for world-wide development, they will discover the imagination, the resources, and the ingenuity to contribute to dynamic action in this field, and give practical expression to their concern for world economic justice. This is perhaps the greatest challenge facing them in the future, and one which will, undoubtedly, test profoundly their ecumenical loyalty and solidarity.

2. *The Revolutionary Transformation of Society*

It is precisely because the call to development is a call to accept and even to initiate revolutionary change that many Christians have become suspicious or even hostile concerning the direction of ecumenical social thought today. Certainly, of all the issues raised by the 1966 Conference none has created more controversy and debate than that on the Church and revolution. The much discussed addresses on this topic by three theologians, Professor H. D. Wendland of Germany, Professor Richard Shaull of the U.S.A., and Archpriest Vitaly Borovoy of the U.S.S.R., brought this issue sharply before the World Conference. Both the message and the report of the Conference reflect one fundamental point of agreement, that the Church must recognize the need for revolutionary change in social and political structures. This view is stated as follows in the conference message:

> As Christians, we are committed to working for the transformation of society. In the past we have usually done this through quiet efforts at social renewal, working in and through the established institutions, according to their rules. Today, a significant number of those who are dedicated to the service of Christ and their neighbour assume a more radical or revolutionary position. They do not deny the value of tradition nor of social order, but they are searching for a new strategy by which to bring about basic changes in society without too much delay. It is possible that the tension between these two positions will have an important place in the life of the Christian community for some time to come. At the present moment, it is important for us to recognize that this radical position has a solid foundation in Christian tradition and should have its rightful place in the life of the Church and in the ongoing discussion of social responsibility.[1]

Around such declarations have arisen demands for a "theology of revolution", now being very widely debated by theologians in many countries.[2]

[1] Official Report, Message of the Conference, para. 6, p. 49.

[2] See for example Arthur Rich, in *Kirchenblatt für die Reformierte Schweiz*, no. 17 (25 August 1966). Also Trutz Rendtorff and H. E. Tödt, *Theologie der Revolution* (Frankfurt 1968).

Some commentators have pointed to the ambiguity of the term "revolution", and the different meanings it has for Westerners, who refer to the profound and silent transformation of the structures of industrial society, and for the representatives of the Third World, who mean by it the violent transformations which characterize the post-colonial and pre-industrial period. Professor Roger Mehl of France has observed that what the latter

> asked from the Church was to give them a theology and an ethic which could help them to live in that revolutionary period and to assume often frightening responsibilities in it. They would have liked theologians to start elaborating a theology of revolution—a legitimate claim if one remembers that for centuries theologians have taught nothing but a theology of order and have had a vision of an entirely static human universe. Dangerous claim also if care is not taken ... not to recognize in each of these often ambiguous revolutions the very dynamic of God's Kingdom.[1]

The post-conference discussion on this issue has sought to clarify the meaning of revolutionary change and to provide ethical guide-lines for Christians involved in contemporary revolutionary ferment. An ecumenical consultation of theologians and laymen convened by the Department on Church and Society and the Commission of Faith and Order, 17–23 March 1968 (in Zagorsk, U.S.S.R.), offered its "Reflections on Theology and Revolution" which carry the debate a considerable step further. These may be summarized as follows:

Christian theology warns against sacralizing either the *status quo* or the revolution and should guard against the temptations of false messianism and the fury of self-righteousness. At the same time, theology should free Christians and the Churches for interpretations of creation, providence, and law which have generally exaggerated the importance of order relative to justice, in order to make possible a more dynamic relation between order and justice.

Christians in a revolutionary situation have a moral duty to do all in their power to exercise a ministry of reconciliation to enable the revolutionary change to take place non-violently or, if this is not possible, with a minimum of violence.

Christian theology cannot remove the ambiguity of political ethics in a revolutionary situation. Nevertheless, it should relate the universality of the Church, which includes political opponents, to the Christian's special responsibility as a matter of vocation.

The ecumenical idea of a responsible society still has relevance to the new structures established after the revolutionary overthrow of old ones, when it becomes necessary to make power and technology responsible and to allow for a permanent renewal of structures without the disruption of order.

As already noted, the Uppsala Assembly recognized the need for revolutionary alteration of social and political structures to create the essential conditions of development. In its declaration on the issue of revolution, the Assembly very largely confirmed the conclusions of the Geneva Conference in its own declaration on this problem:

[1] Roger Mehl, article in *Le Monde*, 27 July 1966.

Revolution is not to be identified with violence .... In countries where the ruling groups are oppressive or indifferent to the aspirations of the people, are often supported by foreign interests, and seek to resist all changes by the use of coercive or violent measures, including the "law and order" which may itself be a form of violence, the revolutionary change may take a violent form. Such changes are morally ambiguous. The churches have a special contribution towards the development of effective non-violent strategies of revolution and social change. Nevertheless we are called to participate creatively in the building of political institutions to implement the social changes that are desperately needed.[1]

Undoubtedly many new problems will arise in the future as Christians endeavour to give expression to such concerns, and the Churches will have much further thinking to do on the Christian responsibility in particular revolutionary situations.

3. Co-operation with the Roman Catholic Church in Christian Thought and Action

One of the important discoveries made during the preparation for the World Conference on Church and Society was the convergence at certain points of Roman Catholic and World Council social thinking. The Second Vatican Council had begun its discussion of the Church and human needs at almost the same moment that the Central Committee of the World Council decided to convene the Church and Society Conference. The social encyclicals of Pope John XXIII, *Mater et magistra* (1961) and *Pacem in terris* (1963), showed a new trend in Roman Catholic social thinking which was carried further by the adoption by the Vatican Council of the *Pastoral Constitution on the Church in the Modern World* (1965). Two ecumenical consultations of Roman Catholic and World Council theologians and scholars, in March 1965 and February 1966, revealed wide areas of agreement and encouraged the making of plans for joint programmes of study on theological and practical questions. As the second consultation reported:

> Having considered recent W.C.C. and Roman Catholic documents within the general field of Church and Society, this consultation is firmly convinced that there is no sufficient reason why further work on this theme should be carried on in isolation, but rather that there ought to be consultation (or, as far as their ways of working will allow, collaboration) between the W.C.C. and the Roman Catholic Church . . .[2]

Eight Roman Catholic observers attended the 1966 World Conference on Church and Society.[3] Each observer was a well-known leader in Roman Catholic thinking on social questions. Their participation contributed greatly to the desire on both sides to explore ways of working together. Such co-operation became reality a year later with the establishment in early 1967

[1] Report of Section III to the Uppsala Assembly, para. 15.
[2] "Theology and Social Ethics" in *Study Encounter*, vol. ii, no. 2 (1966) p. 98.
[3] Over a score of Roman Catholic priests and laymen attended as guests or as press representatives.

of the Pontifical Commission on Justice and Peace, with Monsignor Joseph Gremillion as secretary.

By June 1967 a joint R.C./W.C.C. Exploratory Committee was formed to search for ways relating the work of the Pontifical Commission and the World Council activities in this area of common concern. This has since become the Exploratory Committee on Society, Development, and Peace, with Monsignor Gremillion and Mr Max Kohnstamm, a layman active in World Council studies on social and international affairs, as co-chairman. In January 1968, the two sides agreed to name as joint secretary to this Exploratory Committee, Father George Dunne, s.j., the first man to serve the Churches in such a larger ecumenical enterprise. The Conference on Development in Beirut (1968) was the first project of the Exploratory Committee, and a major test of the reality of this new co-operative effort. Its success provided a strong indication that this joint work could expand substantially during the coming years. Such wider ecumenical collaboration is likely to influence greatly the shape and direction of ecumenical social thinking in the period ahead.

The Assembly at Uppsala welcomed this collaboration and emphasized "the importance of co-operating at every level with the Roman Catholic Church . . . and indeed with men of good will everywhere". The publication of the latest papal encyclical, *Humanae vitae* shows, however, that fundamental disagreements on certain social issues remain, and it would be wrong to expect that some of these will be quickly or easily overcome. Indeed, it is likely that at many points the Roman Catholic Church, working within long-established structures, will have an uneasy part in the ecumenical dialogue, based as it is on the principles of renewal and self-criticism. Obviously it is not alone in this difficulty.

The Question of Theological Basis

Those who are sceptical about ecumenical social thinking ask: How is it that theologians and laymen are able to come to a relatively large measure of agreement on practical Christian social action in spite of their inability to resolve certain fundamental theological issues of faith and order? This has raised the further question, debated repeatedly in ecumenical circles: How much of a common theological or ecclesiological rationale is necessary before an authentic ecumenical word on social questions can be spoken?

The failure to achieve prior agreement on basic theological or biblical perspectives appears as a serious weakness (and even deception) to those who believe that it is hazardous, if not impossible, to make common Christian declarations on social issues before the theological assumptions underlying them are made explicit. But opposed to that point of view is another which maintains that ecumenical agreement on social questions does not and cannot proceed always from basic theological principles to agreement on practical issues. This viewpoint recognizes that there will probably never be complete agreement on theological debate to be constantly enlivened by new questions. The fact that Churches with different theological outlooks have been able to agree on attitudes or actions in society can be a recognition of a common experience or even of some common theological assumptions which go deeper than the theological differences.

In recent years, the debate about inductive versus deductive social ethics or an ethics of principles versus a contextual ethic has shown how difficult it is to follow one line of reasoning. The World Council has constantly struggled to see the validity of these two perspectives, recognizing, on the one hand, the importance of exploratory work on fundamental theological issues relating to Church and society and at the same time launching inquiries on specific practical concerns. It can easily be demonstrated that ecumenical social thinking has been illuminated by both approaches. Thus, during the years 1948-52, the World Council Study on "The Bible and the Church's Message to the World", directed by the German biblical scholar, Dr Wolfgang Schweitzer, helped to relate biblical exegesis and interpretation to social ethics. And from 1951-4 a substantial study of the main theme of the Second Assembly, "Christ the Hope of the World", involving extensive discussions among thirty-five of the world's foremost theologians, gave much attention to the nature of the Church's witness in society. More recent studies on "The Lordship of Christ over the World and the Church" (concluded in 1958) and on "The Finality of Jesus Christ in an Age of Universal History" (1961-8) provided considerable theological background for the practical work of the World Council in the area of Church and Society.

It is true that there was, often, very little integration or cross-fertilization between these theological studies and the practical inquiries carried on simultaneously. It is also true that laymen have been looking for a more dynamic dialectical relation between the theological reflection and the concrete ethical problems facing them in society than was provided by the theological inquiries.

All these questions were examined at length in the Consultation of theologians and laymen meeting in Russia in March 1968, called to make a theological evaluation of the 1966 Conference. The consultation reviewed the theological method as well as the ecclesiological rationale for ecumenical work on social questions. It observed that various denominations often proceed functionally along similar lines in thinking about the role of the Church in society. It acknowledged that this has made possible the formation of groups or movements within and between the Churches which can engage in social action and study and which in turn have led to the discovery of provisional agreements, bridging differences between Christians and showing the possibility of a larger corporate witness.[1] It urged also that there be more systematic theological study of the ethical issues arising from the practical ecumenical work and welcomed the fact that this particular consultation had been jointly sponsored by the Faith and Order Commission and the Department on Church and Society.

---

[1] See "Ecclesiology and Social Ethics", Section 4 of the report of the Zagorsk Consultation, *Study Encounter* (1968).

Conclusion

Despite the achievements in recent years, ecumenical social thinking remains a precarious enterprise. A substantial number of Christians in our Churches are probably still very much opposed to the directions it takes or would criticize the World Council and other ecumenical bodies for giving too much attention to social issues. Moreover, as the pressures for rapid change in society increase, the polarization of opinion in our Churches on basic social questions will undoubtedly become greater rather than diminish. The continuing division of the Churches on basic issues of theology and ecclesiology also weakens the possibility of a more substantial Christian social witness.

Up to the present, the ecumenical consensus on Christian social responsibility has been limited, experimental, and provisional, and with relatively slight impact on the action of the Churches in society. And no doubt the ecumenical witness will become more difficult in the future. But wherever Christians struggle to maintain the transcendence of the faith to their fellow men, combining the desire for justice with the spirit of compassion, the search for the ecumenical community of ideas and witness will proceed. Possibly the most significant achievement of the ecumenical movement has been its ability to encourage and nourish that dialectic of obedience and unity even in situations where opposing points of view seemed to make real encounter impossible. We can hope for no more and should aspire to no less in the future.

10

Ecumenical Action
in International Affairs

O. FREDERICK NOLDE

The responsibility of the churches to promote international good will is inescapable. Progressive recognition of their imperative involvement in the affairs of nations has sprung from no new or strange faith. The Churches' primary contribution to peace with justice and freedom lies in the steadfast proclamation of the gospel at home and to the uttermost parts of the earth and in the growing solidarity of a Christian fellowship which transcends race, class, and national frontiers. Christian witness to the world of nations is an inevitable projection of Christian faith and experience.[1]

Backgrounds and Origins

At the close of the Second World War—the second within less than half a century and with peace still not secured—Christian leaders felt impelled to look for a new and more direct way to play their responsible part in international affairs. While the particular instrumentality which they conceived had no precedent, the emerging ecumenical movement over a period of some thirty years had been building a solid foundation. Specific Christian concern for peace and justice had been expressed by the Stockholm Conference of 1925, the Oxford Conference of 1937 under the Universal Christian Council for Life and Work, and by the Madras Conference of the International Missionary Council in 1938. These conferences had delineated areas of concern for the Christian witness, but had provided no specialized structure or secretariat for continuing work.

Direct impetus for a new venture came from a war-time agency of the Churches in the United States and Canada—the Commission on a Just and Durable Peace (C.J.D.P.) of the Federal Council of the Churches of Christ in America. It was reinforced by the British Commission on Christian Social Responsibility, led by Archbishop William Temple. Especially in the former, remote from the scene of actual military conflict, were resources available for concentration on post-war planning. The International Round Table at Princeton, N.J., convened in July 1943, by the C.J.D.P., brought together sixty-one Christian leaders from twelve countries in North America, Europe, Asia, and from Australia and New Zealand. One of its purposes was to formulate, in so far as possible, a consensus on the problems of order in the post-war world. The Round Table stimulated an international Christian impact upon the deliberations of the Conference on International Organization at San Francisco in 1945, where the Charter of the United Nations was drafted. It also gave impetus to an organized ecumenical approach to problems of peace, justice, and freedom.

The Commission of the Churches on International Affairs was founded in 1946 at a conference of church leaders in Cambridge, England. The background and intent of the conference were set forth in an explanation signed by Dr Marc Boegner of France, Chairman of the Administrative Committee of the World Council of Churches (in process of formation), and by Bishop

[1] While this chapter appears over my name, all my colleagues in the Commission of the Churches on International Affairs have in varying degrees contributed to it. I acknowledge particularly my indebtedness to Dr Richard M. Fagley because, in preparing this review, I have borrowed heavily from his study entitled *The First Twenty Years.—O.F.N.*

James C. Baker of the United States, Chairman of the International Missionary Council:

> As a result of actions taken at Geneva, Switzerland, at the February 1946 meetings of the *ad interim* Committee of the International Missionary Council and the Provisional Committee of the World Council of Churches, the Commision on a Just and Durable Peace of the Federal Council of the Churches of Christ in America was asked to arrange a conference of church leaders to consider the problems of peace and war.

> This was generously undertaken by the officers of the latter Commission. Mr John Foster Dulles and Dr Walter W. Van Kirk, chairman and secretary respectively, made the preparations which resulted in the gathering at Girton College, Cambridge, August 4–7 (1946) of 60 persons coming from 15 countries. The gathering was held under the joint sponsorship of the International Missionary Council and the World Council of Churches and on mandate from those bodies undertook to collaborate with a joint committee of the two in setting up a joint permanent Commission of the Churches on International Affairs to carry forward the type of work to which God's design and man's disorder call the churches.

The composition of the Cambridge Conference appears strange today, but at the time it seemed to be and quite probably was a realistic reflection of the existing situation. Over half the sixty participants were from Anglo-Saxon countries. The conference chairman, the chairman of the drafting committee, and one of the two secretaries were American. Travel difficulties reduced the East European representation to two, the participants from the "younger Churches" to one, and the Orthodox representation to one. These difficulties exaggerated a preponderance which was present even in planning. However, the conference would have been in the circumstances overwhelmingly West European and North American in any case.

Similarly the orientation of the Cambridge Conference was such as would have been expected in the immediate post-war period. There seemed to be no advantage in stating in detail the theological presuppositions; in fact, participants were aware that undue emphasis upon precise theological formulations could rob action of the very considerable unanimity by which it was supported. The difficulties lay rather in ascertaining the hard facts of international life and the responses the Churches were called upon to make to them. There was acute consciousness of the havoc created by war, the new atomic insecurity, and the dangerous signs of tensions among the major powers. Nevertheless, there was a good deal of confidence in regard to the struggle for world order. The issue was the practical one of blocking out the areas for major attention and getting the new organization under way. The emphasis was on action.

The heart of the work of the Cambridge Conference was the "Charter", since called "Aims of the C.C.I.A.", in which the Conference outlined nine functions for the new organization in serving its parent bodies. These aims of the Commission of the Churches on International Affairs stood the test of intervening years. They were only slightly modified at the Third Assembly of the World Council of Churches in New Delhi where the integration of the

International Missionary Council and the World Council took place and again in the new constitution adopted at the Fourth Assembly in 1968. The officers, supported by the Commission, viewed the nine points as a broad definition of areas into which C.C.I.A. was encouraged to move when resources of personnel and budget were available. Their position was that it was better to perform some of the functions reasonably well than to stretch the available resources too thinly.

The first two aims dealt with education and action at the national and denominational level. They reflected the convictions stated in the conclusion of the Cambridge Report, that "witness that is truly ecumenical must spring from local conviction and determination". The C.C.I.A. was encouraged to aid in the formation of national and denominational commissions on international affairs, and to gather, appraise, and disseminate the best available materials on the relations of the Churches to public affairs. Particularly in the early years, the principal officers visited church leaders in a number of countries to stimulate the formation or reorganization of national committees. While only three active national commissions existed when the C.C.I.A. was founded, twenty years later twenty-five national or regional interdenominational agencies were co-operating with it with varying degrees of competence and effectiveness. While efforts were made to stimulate education in Christian responsibility for international affairs, the C.C.I.A. because of lack of resources attempted no general clearing house function, but was forced to rely upon the action of national and regional groups.

The next three aims dealt with the study function of "selected problems of international justice and world order including economic and social questions". While the C.C.I.A. did not pursue study in the formal sense, by the very nature of its work it was forced to rely upon a variety of study procedures. It was involved in the symposium on international affairs for the First Assembly of the World Council of Churches, as well as in the preparatory work for the Second and Third Assemblies. It conducted various surveys on the requirements of religious liberty leading to the World Council of Churches–International Missionary Council "Declaration on Religious Liberty" of 1948 which was recognized to have played a significant role in the formulation of provisions for religious liberty in the Universal Declaration of Human Rights and in the Covenant of Civil and Political Rights. In 1955 it analysed the status of religious liberty in the face of "dominant forces". It prepared the symposium for its tenth anniversary in 1956 as well as for its twentieth in 1966. Each filled an entire volume of the *Ecumenical Review*. Individual studies produced in books or in articles dealt with the plight of refugees, development strategy, the population problem, power politics, and human rights. One longer range study on the question of an international ethos did not fare very well for a variety of reasons, but it did serve the Commission in its representative work.

The C.C.I.A. was also required to do a very considerable amount of direct study of the background of issues in preparing the representations on the international issues with which it dealt. In many instances these issues were submitted to the W.C.C. Executive and Central Committees for action. This helped to establish in at least some Christian minds that comprehension of the hard political realities was a starting-place for discovering Christian obedience. Experience showed that, while there was need for longer-range study through whatever agency was assigned the task, it would never be met by sacrificing that form of study which is the immediate handmaiden of action.

The next three points in the aims dealt with the realm of action. These provided the main general guide-lines for the C.C.I.A. in the first two decades of its life. The C.C.I.A. was to call attention to urgent international problems and to suggest effective Christian action. It was to advise its parent bodies or speak in its own name on "Christian principles", indicating their bearing on immediate issues. It also represented the parent bodies in relations with international organizations such as the United Nations and its related agencies.

The final point of the aims empowered the Commission to "concert from time to time with other organizations holding similar objectives in the advancement of particular ends". Behind this point, not otherwise reflected in the Cambridge Report, was a considerable discussion of the question of possible collaboration with agencies and leaders of the Roman Catholic Church—a twenty-year forecast of the development of contemporary relationships. In the end, however, it was agreed not to refer specifically to the possibilities of collaboration with the Roman Catholics, taking into account such obstacles as differing stances toward communist societies, matters of religious freedom, and the patterns and forms of Vatican diplomacy.

Operation and Relationships in an Ecumenical Setting

The first battle-line of the World Council of Churches in its offensive against war and injustice is drawn in its far-flung programmes of witness, study, and service, rooted in the faith and commitment of its constituent members. It is against this background that the Commission of the Churches on International Affairs functions as a specialized agency to relate the common ecumenical witness to specific international problems.

The operation of the C.C.I.A. can be most simply described in terms of a two-way line of communication. This involved, on the one hand, contact with Churches and church leaders around the world and, on the other, contacts with intergovernmental bodies.

To serve as a "source of stimulus and knowledge" the C.C.I.A. sought to develop closer relations with Christian groups within the ecumenical fellowship through its commissioners, through national commissions on international affairs, through the constituent Churches and Christian councils, and through special correspondents, as well as through the officially designated representatives of member Churches in World Council Assemblies and meetings of the Central and Executive Committees.

The commissioners, who numbered about fifty, were elected by the parent bodies after careful consultation with church leaders to ensure stature in international affairs and acceptability to Churches at the national level. The large majority were laymen, although place, all too limited, was given to women. Selection was made on the basis of competence in the political and diplomatic fields. Wherever possible commissioners were sought who, in addition to other qualifications, could act as a door into the "corridors of power" and thus facilitate direct representation at highest levels. The continuity of the Commission was relatively high, fourteen of the current commissioners were among the original group. However, the benefits of continuity were diluted by the fact that only a handful were able to attend meetings regularly. Continuity also exacted a price in the age composition of the Commission.

The eminence of the commissioners helped to assure C.C.I.A. access to important information and to expert counsel. But the question remains whether the combined talents of this able group were sufficiently engaged in the formation of policy and whether there was enough dialogue between the officers' groups and the commissioners. In the early years, there was considerable consultation by correspondence. Later, as the officers became more experienced and self-reliant and the commissioners gained greater confidence in their judgement, there was, with a few exceptions, a slackening in the give and take. While there was no doubt that, if commissioners had taken strong exception to positions taken by the officers, they would have been heard from, tacit support, no matter how genuine, was a far cry from the kind of active involvement desirable for such a body.

The importance of ecumenical work at the national level was a constant theme of C.C.I.A. in view of the fact that primary decisions in international affairs are made at that level and most of the Churches are organized along national lines. The arrangement of relationships with regional and national church commissions, however, was a rather curious one in that, while they co-operated on an informal basis with the international C.C.I.A., they remained formal agents of Regional or National Councils. It may well be that the experience of two decades will lead to new forms of collaboration without losing the advantages of that arrangement.

One of the most effective ways in which the Commission maintained roots in the World Council constituency was in meetings of the Council's major organs. It was in assemblies and meetings of the Executive and Central Committees, as well as in meetings of the C.C.I.A. itself or of its Executive Committee, that problems were most sharply seen and positions developed. Contacts in the Churches were also maintained through various mailings to some four hundred churchmen. These included the memoranda prepared by the New York office on selected issues coming before each U.N. General Assembly, and an occasional bulletin of background information and analysis of some current issue prepared by the London office under the title of *C.C.I.A. Brief.* Memoranda also were circulated periodically to solicit information from commissioners and national commissions and to inform them of actions taken.

In an operation of this kind, officers and staff played no small part and no historical sketch would be complete without reference to them. Since the Commission in 1946 had perforce to start on a very modest financial basis—the initial appropriation being $4,000 a year with some additional funds secured from outside sources, it secured the part-time services of two participants in the Cambridge Conference. These were Kenneth Grubb (now Sir Kenneth Grubb), formerly of the Ministry of Information of the United Kingdom and active in Anglican and Latin American affairs, and myself, at that time Dean of the Graduate School of the Lutheran Theological Seminary in Philadelphia and a member of the Commission on a Just and Durable Peace. (I had also served as a consultant at the San Francisco Conference on United Nations Organization.) We were initially designated as director and associate director, but the manner in which the work developed soon led to the titles of chairman and director—Sir Kenneth giving general oversight to organizational matters and I to substantive work, particularly at the United Nations. Professor Frederick van Asbeck of the Netherlands, wise veteran in international relations, had earlier been named president. He served until the W.C.C.'s Second Assembly. Since then the post has remained unfulfilled.

The staffing arrangements were modest for an international agency of the scope proposed in the aims. Starting with secretaries in London and New York, the executive staff, in addition to the two principal officers, grew to four a decade ago and remained at that level, despite explorations seeking additional personnel, particularly from developing countries. The turnover in the staff was small; the average service of the present staff, apart from the chairman and director, has been twelve years. Dr Richard Fagley has been executive secretary, working out of the New York office, since 1951; Dr Elfan Rees has served as representative in Europe since 1952 and earlier was a consultant to the C.C.I.A.; the Reverend A. Dominique Micheli was appointed as secretary in New York in 1955 and now serves as secretary in Geneva; the Reverend Alan Booth served as secretary in London since 1957. The cumulative experience of the officers made possible a continued development of the work.

The founding fathers granted the new agency considerable flexibility and autonomy, subject to prior consultation and subsequent review by the parent bodies. Because of the infrequent stated meetings of the W.C.C. and the I.M.C., the C.C.I.A. and its officers were given the right to speak in their own name so that they might cope with the time-table of events and take advantage of a wider variety of possible resources. This responsibility placed no small burden upon C.C.I.A. officers and staff. It required not only that they ascertain the views predominantly held in the World Council constituency, but that they possess the specialized and technical competence needed to command the respect of the governmental and intergovernmental agencies to whom they communicated the views of the Churches.

There thus developed an "international civil service" of the Churches with a system of staff specialization which gave to each member a major responsibility. The chairman, in the main, was responsible for general administration; the director, in the early years, for work for human rights and later for disarmament and tension points. Rees worked on behalf of refugees; Micheli for human rights; Booth for African problems; Fagley on development and population problems. Other concerns were distributed on an *ad hoc* basis, and each member of the staff played his part in a system of checks and balances for the entire programme. The director's task of co-ordination increased with the expansion of activities. Additional technical and specialized resources of the kind not readily available in ecclesiastical circles were accessible in institutes and foundations. These included the Institute of Strategic Studies, the Institute of Race Relations, and the Overseas Development Institute in London and Carnegie Endowment for International Peace in New York and Geneva. With these the several officers were associated in their personal capacities.

Considerable efforts were made to enlarge the staff to use the potential offered by the regional Christian agencies in Asia and Africa—the East Asia Christian Council and the All African Conference of Churches. Officers met a number of times with agencies of the two bodies to explore the possibilities of establishing regular and significant co-operation. As a result the consultative services were secured of U. Kyaw Than for E.A.C.C. and of Mr Samuel Amissah on behalf of A.A.C.C. In view of the increasing significance of intergovernmental regional associations and programmes, it is important that contacts with regional Christian agencies be strengthened in this field.

C.C.I.A. officers also gave considerable attention to regional manifestations of world problems such as a divided Germany, the tensions of the "cold war", and refugees and migration. Several C.C.I.A. officers participated as members in the discussions of the Committee for Christian Responsibility for European Co-operation and also had contacts with the Christian Peace Conference of Prague. But they did not find it feasible to devote a large portion of staff resources to European developments on the ground that other regions would have to be given attention, and that the limited resources of the C.C.I.A. were more appropriately employed when focused on global problems and institutions. The emergence of a more effective European Council of Churches may open new avenues for co-operation.

A distinctive aspect of C.C.I.A. work in its first twenty years was the attention devoted to relationships with the intergovernmental institutions in the United Nations family of agencies. Several of these came to birth near the time of the Cambridge Conference and the first part of the First General Assembly of the United Nations was held in London just six months before the C.C.I.A.'s founding meeting. The new agencies represented possibilities in the making, a future still malleable and opportunity still bright. They were global in character and offered a chance for concentrated and extended contacts at a minimum of effort with a wide variety of national delegations on issues of ecumenical concern.

The United Nations Charter provided for a consultative relationship with non-governmental organizations and each of the specialized agencies formulated its own plan for observation or representation. The infant C.C.I.A. promptly established such a relationship—formally with ECOSOC, but much broader in practice to include other organs, particularly the General Assembly, and subsequently with F.A.O., U.N.E.S.C.O., the I.L.O., and U.N.I.C.E.F. These relationships provided an important arena for C.C.I.A.

action although in no sense was the total programme operated within the structural limits of inter-governmental organs.

In approaching the substantive issues which have commanded C.C.I.A. attention, one cannot ignore the frequently raised question about the effectiveness of such a Christian witness. The commission and its officers adopted an approach which does not lend itself to a clear-cut answer. They recognized that many forces play upon an international problem or issue and that normally only where a coincidence of interests is achieved can progress towards a solution be advanced. The witness animated by Christian faith and experience must be made without the sure prospect of success. In concert with other constructive forces it may prove effective—whether its effectiveness be identifiable or obscured in history's course. The event and the outcome are in God's hand.

The programme of activities as they evolved came to comprise six major concerns. The following brief account of them should be read with the understanding that the ecumenical constituency is ever enlarging. This was true first within the World Council of Churches whose membership during this period expanded to include Churches in communist countries, particularly Russia, as well as in many developing countries. Secondly, there was growing co-operation with the Roman Catholic Church. In this world Christian setting, now more accurately reflective of the world political scene, action to reconcile peoples and nations had to reckon with the recurring danger of compromising justice in the interest of peace and witness in the interest of unity.

Human Rights—Religious Liberty

When the officers of the newly formed Commission looked about them to ascertain a good place to begin, the answer seemed clearly to lie in the field of human rights in general and the exercise of religious freedom in particular. This was obviously an area in which Christians were vitally concerned, not only for themselves but equally for all men, and in which they could be expected to have special competence.

There was ample precedent for such concern. The Oxford Conference of 1937 and the Madras Conference of 1938 had put forward a number of elements of religious and missionary freedom. The United States National Study Conference early in 1945, supported by joint committees on religious liberty in the United States and Britain, had made the inclusion in the United Nations Charter of a provision for a Commission on Human Rights to devise international standards for basic human rights a main plank in its propositions for improvement of the Dumbarton Oaks proposals. (In fact, it fell to my lot to serve as spokesman for forty-two non-governmental organizations at the 1945 San Francisco Conference on United Nations organization in pressing for this inclusion.) The C.C.I.A.'s founding conference had listed among the six objectives for work by the new body the maintenance of contacts with international agencies, particularly with the United Nations, for the "encouragement of respect for, and observance of, human rights and fundamental freedoms, special attention being given to the problem of religious liberty".

To an extent unprecedented in history, the opportunities seemed to be at hand to move toward a recognition of international responsibility for the protection of human rights, either by agencies such as the Commission on Human Rights or by international instruments such as Declarations, Covenants, and Conventions. Aware that any formulation accepted would stand little chance of modification or improvement for many decades to come, the C.C.I.A. adopted as a first point in its strategy the objective of seeing to it that the international standards which were being set were acceptable in the light of the Christian conception of man and society. As an initial step, C.C.I.A. officers sent inquiries to commissioners and other church leaders in many countries asking their assistance in identifying the essential elements in religious freedom and the potential support for them in the ecumenical constituency. The immediate result of these inquiries was the adoption in 1948 by the World Council of Churches and by the International Missionary Council of a *Declaration of Religious Liberty*, a document which remains a landmark in the field to this day. Thirteen years later the Third Assembly of the World Council of Churches adopted a second basic instrument, a *Statement on Religious Liberty*. While emphasis in both these documents was laid on religious freedom, concern for related rights and in fact for all fundamental freedoms is clearly expressed.

An immediate practical application of the position expressed in the World Council Declaration came the same year, 1948, at the Paris session of the United Nations General Assembly. There the draft United Nations Declaration on Human Rights, prepared by its Human Rights Commission, came up for consideration and adoption. During the preparatory period C.C.I.A. officers had submitted to the United Nations a "Memorandum on Provisions for Religious Liberty in an International Bill of Rights" and made supporting oral interventions. C.C.I.A. staff followed the detailed work of drafting virtually every minute of the deliberations. The article on religious freedom, as finally adopted in face of strong initial opposition, incorporated the essential points for which the C.C.I.A. had been pressing, namely, freedom to change one's religion or belief, and freedom, either alone or in community with others, and in public or in private, to manifest one's religion or belief in worship, teaching, practice, and observance.

As work continued on the two covenants on human rights—the Covenant on Civil and Political Rights and the Covenant on Economic, Social, and Cultural Rights—C.C.I.A. representation headed by Micheli met periodic challenges to recognition of freedom to change one's religion or belief and to oppose efforts to reduce freedom of manifestation to worship. The current effort to achieve an international Convention on the Elimination of All Forms of Religious Intolerance is highly significant because for the first time in history the four manifestations contained in the Universal Declaration are being elaborated in the form of an internationally binding treaty. In this connection, the Director's statement before the meeting of the W.C.C. Executive Committee at Odessa, U.S.S.R., in 1964, recognizing the right of

K

atheists to be atheists but defending the equal right of all to propagate their faith, underscored the concept of human rights without discrimination. Unhappily, there has not as yet developed a common ethos throughout the world sufficient to sustain, on an inclusive basis, legally binding instruments and the machinery to enforce them. The progress being made on a regional scale in the European Convention on Human Rights is significant in pointing the way.

A further element in the C.C.I.A. human rights strategy involved the efforts to promote the advancement of dependent peoples to independence and to help to bring national constitutions, laws, court decisions, and domestic practice into conformity with emerging international standards. These involved visits to new countries in process of preparing constitutions and laws, and the preparation of detailed information for use by their statesmen and church leaders. Emphasis was placed on education with the clear understanding that laws, whether international or national, are effective only when supported by predominant public opinion. Major and minor violations and curtailments of human rights commanded attention. This included the problems faced by Evangelicals in Spain, Italy, and Colombia to which the Chairman gave particular attention, as well as those faced by Buddhists in Tibet and South Vietnam. It also dealt with difficulties in the Southern Sudan, Indonesia, Greece, Mozambique, Nigeria, Yugoslavia, Israel, Angola, Turkey, Nepal, Rumania, Mexico, Ghana, the U.S.S.R., South Africa, South West Africa, India (the Nagas), and other places. These situations called for a variety of responses ranging from quiet inquiry to public statement and protest. Some of the situations have been frustratingly protracted while in other cases good results came quickly.

In the area of racial and ethnic tensions, the C.C.I.A. responsibility dealt particularly with the international aspects of efforts seeking achievement of human rights without discrimination. The fuller story of action by the W.C.C. is dealt with in the chapter on "The Development of Social Thought and Action". At every point the C.C.I.A. made available to United Nations committees dealing with apartheid and other racial problems, the positions formally taken by World Council organs and conferences held under their auspices. It served in a liaison capacity to enable the W.C.C. to co-operate with the United Nations Trust Fund in the distribution of resources in its humanitarian programme for victims of apartheid. It also supported consideration of South African policies and practices by the International Court of Justice and protested against the procedures for the trials of South West African prisoners.

International Peace and Security

By the time of the W.C.C. First Assembly, and the official establishment of the C.C.I.A., it was clear that political and military issues would form a principal preoccupation of the new agency for a long time to come. The test between the power blocs in the Berlin blockade and airlift formed the backdrop for the Amsterdam Assembly. The following year saw the formation of N.A.T.O., the proclamation of the People's Republic of China, and the end of the United States atomic monopoly. In 1950 the atomic arms race began in earnest. It was a sombre infancy for the new venture.

Most of the C.C.I.A. responses to the international crisis of the early Cold War period were made in relation to particular crises, a programmatic approach which characterized the first two decades of its life. But effort also was made to analyse and speak to the broader aspects of the ideological and power conflict. In 1949 C.C.I.A. sponsored a consultation on "The Ideological Conflict and the International Tensions Involved in It". In 1951 the C.C.I.A. Executive Committee issued a widely quoted summary statement entitled "Christians Stand for Peace", partly to distinguish the C.C.I.A. approach from lines taken by secular agencies serving ideological purposes. The statement stressed both peace and justice, declaring that, "we must neither purchase peace at the price of tyranny nor in the name of justice look on war as a way to justice or as a ground of hope".

In 1949 the Netherlands–Indonesia dispute provided a major challenge. In addition to supporting international efforts to help to resolve the dispute, C.C.I.A. officers secured memoranda on the situation which had been prepared by Christian leaders on either side and arranged for their exchange. When these leaders later met at The Hague Round Table, it was evident that the exchange had contributed to the mutual understanding required for peaceful settlement. The action was a good illustration of the kind of useful approach across lines of division which may be possible when there are strong Christian groups on both sides.

In 1950 the outbreak of the Korean war again launched the world into crisis. Acting on the advice of the C.C.I.A. Executive Committee, the World Council of Churches issued a statement which stressed that it was an on-the-spot United Nations Commission which had identified the aggressor. It supported the United Nations for authorizing a "police measure" and emphasized action for a "just settlement by negotiation and conciliation". This statement received both support and criticism, particularly as the fighting became more intense and protracted. When the conflict was enlarged in November, 1950, representations were made at high levels in the United States and United Kingdom on behalf of policies of moderation and restraint.

Three initiatives of a practical character, advanced by the C.C.I.A. Director, emerged from the efforts to grapple with the issues of the Korean war. The first was the idea of the formation of a United Nations corps of international peace observers to be available for sending to areas of tension to discourage aggression by their presence or to identify the aggressor if aggression occurs. The basic idea was unanimously supported in the establishment of the Peace Observation Commission by the 1950 United Nations General Assembly, and, while the machinery has been used only once (in the Balkan pressures on Greece), it remains a tool of peace available to the United Nations and stands as a precursor of diversified peace-keeping efforts.

The second initiative was a "Plan for Deferred Action on Prisoners of War in Korea". Designed to facilitate a truce without forcible detention or repatriation of prisoners, it was an important contribution to the overcoming of a thorny obstacle in the armistice negotiations.

The third initiative came when misunderstandings between the R.O.K. (South Korea) Government and the United Nations High Command threatened prospects for a truce. Then the C.C.I.A. made its good offices available when the Director flew to Pusan and Seoul for consultations with church leaders and to serve as an intermediary between contending parties within the United Nations forces. This venture was formally recognized by the United States Government, representing the United Nations High Command as "a factor in creating an atmosphere conducive to peace".

The protracted crisis over a divided Germany was the subject of repeated examinations in meetings of the C.C.I.A. Executive and of the Committee on Christian Responsibility for European Co-operation. A more active phase began in 1958 with the tightening of restrictions on religious freedom in East Germany. In 1961 the worsening of the situation by the erection of the Berlin wall prompted the first of a continuing series of C.C.I.A. visits with churchmen and government officials in West and East Berlin. These visits sought both to express concern with the human aspects of the situation, such as the separation of families, and to foster better understanding between church leaders in West and East Germany as a means of contributing indirectly to progress towards a political solution.

In most instances the consultative process between the W.C.C. and C.C.I.A. officers in political crises worked well, enabling responses to be made promptly at both church and political levels. The alert and informed interest of Dr W. A. Visser 't Hooft, General Secretary, and the late Dr Franklin Clark Fry, Chairman of the Central Committee of the World Council of Churches, did much to make this co-operation effective. The sudden "eyeball to eyeball" confrontation between the U.S.A. and the U.S.S.R. over military bases in Cuba in 1962 was initially in this regard an exception due to a somewhat different reading of the portents. As a consequence the statement issued by the officers of the World Council was at variance with the position prepared by the C.C.I.A. for submission to the United Nations Security Council, although the two were eventually reconciled. This crisis of the super-powers, in which the United Nations could play only a limited though useful role, was also a reminder of the need to keep in realistic perspective the United Nations and the realities of the power situation.

The requirements of brevity permit only reference by title to some of the critical situations in which C.C.I.A. officers attempted to make timely and relevant representations. They included: the 1954 Indo-China situation, the conflict and tensions in the Formosa Straits in 1955 and again in 1958, Suez and Hungary in 1956, the 1958 crisis in Lebanon, the tragic events in Tibet the same year, the critical situation in the Congo beginning in 1960, U.S.A.-U.S.S.R. involvement in Cuba, the conflict in Laos as of 1961, the continuing conflict in Algeria, the problems of Angola and Mozambique, and the tensions between the United States and Panama in 1964. Also included were the tensions and conflict in Cyprus that flared in 1964, the "confrontation" of Malaysia by Indonesia, the mounting conflict in Vietnam and various subsequent measures of escalation, United States intervention in the Dominican Republic in 1965, and the fighting between Pakistan and India in 1965 against the background of the long-standing dispute over Kashmir.

In a number of these situations the lack of a strong constituency related to the W.C.C. on one or both sides was a limiting factor both in regard to the securing of balanced information and the taking of effective action. Many problems have not yielded to solution and men have been forced to live with them. World Council and C.C.I.A. concern about Vietnam, expressed at the time of the Geneva Conference in 1954, deepened with the escalation of the conflict after 1962. The W.C.C. Central and Executive Committees and the C.C.I.A. Executive Committee found in the actions of the National Council of Churches in the U.S.A. and of the East Asia Christian Conference strong support for efforts to move the parties in conflict from the battlefield to the conference table. When the official consultations opened at Paris in May 1968, C.C.I.A. officers personally delivered to the chief delegates of the United States and the People's Republic of North Vietnam letters of encouragement to seek a negotiated settlement.

The situation in Nigeria, where Biafra had declared its independence, involved related problems of material help, pastoral care, and political accommodation. While church and mission leaders of D.I.C.A.R.W.S. and A.A.C.C. were active in many ways, C.C.I.A. efforts were directed under the leadership of Alan Booth, whose church and political contacts and attention to preliminary talks in London were followed by further negotiations at Kampala. The approach to the Nigerian conflict was notable for being the first occasion in which the Roman Catholic Church and the World Council issued a joint statement calling for a peaceful settlement.

The representations, with variations adapted to the circumstances, have stressed fundamental themes: the avoidance of unilateral intervention; the avoidance or cessation of violence and recourse to procedures of negotiation and/or mediation; policies of moderation and restraint; the value of a United Nations presence in some form for keeping the peace and United Nations action on behalf of peaceful settlement.

Disarmament

Hand in hand with efforts to bring a moderating influence on specific conflicts and disputes went a very considerable amount of work on the problems of disarmament. No international body, apart from the United Nations General Assembly, received as much C.C.I.A. attention as the committees and conferences on disarmament meeting in Geneva. Following a suggestion made at New Delhi in 1961, two special consultations brought together Christian leaders from communist and non-communist countries to confer with delegates to the disarmament conference from the U.K., U.S.S.R., and the U.S.A., as well as with delegates from several of the non-aligned countries. These discussions contributed to an understanding among Christians from both sides and provided an incentive to government representatives.

It is not possible here to summarize adequately the positions taken in regard to disarmament. An early statement (1949) called for international control of the hydrogen bomb. In succeeding years, emphasis was placed on the political and moral factors affecting a disarmament agreement. The Section on International Affairs at the W.C.C.'s Second Assembly in 1954 stressed the obligation of nations to refrain from the threat or use of weapons of mass destruction against civilians in open cities and underlined the positive uses of atomic power. One of the major C.C.I.A. statements in this field was adopted by its Executive Committee at its 1955 meeting in Davos and subsequently by the Central Committee. It was a pioneer analysis of the relationship between measures to advance peaceful change and settlement and the furtherance of a significant disarmament agreement. *Christians and the Prevention of War in an Atomic Age*, a study completed in 1958, emphasized the restraints which governments must accept and essential positive steps in avoiding the holocaust of nuclear destruction.

Another key statement was adopted by the 1957 C.C.I.A. Executive Committee. This set forth a programme on disarmament, which featured a ban on atomic tests as the first step but related it to a longer-range strategy. Three related principles were emphasized:

1. The main concern must always be the prevention of war itself, for the evil of war is an offence to the spiritual nature of man.

2. The objectives of a strategy to combat the menace of atomic war are interrelated and interdependent, such as ceasing tests, halting production, reducing existing armaments with provision for warning against surprise attacks, the peaceful uses of atomic energy, peaceful settlement, and peaceful change.

3. If persistent efforts bring no sufficient agreements on any of the interrelated objectives, partial agreements should be seriously explored and, if need be, reasonable risks should be taken to advance the objectives which must continue to stand as interdependent.

A decade later this statement continued to provide a framework for various action on the disarmament question. A series of memoranda informed church leaders about scientific data regarding the health hazards of atomic radiation, emphasizing that many peoples, not party to atomic tests, would have to bear the consequences. Convinced that rivalries on earth were too dangerous to project into outer space, C.C.I.A. vigorously supported moves towards its international control. The W.C.C. New Delhi Assembly's Appeal supporting a theme familiar in C.C.I.A. representations, called upon nations to run reasonable risks for peace, in order to break the vicious circle of suspicion. The resumption of tests by the U.S.S.R. in 1961 was regretted, as was the undertaking of tests by France. The W.C.C. and the C.C.I.A. continued to press for the cessation of testing and the former's Executive Committee in a statement at Buenos Aires in 1960 virtually forecast the details of the 1963 Moscow Treaty to ban tests in outer space, in the atmosphere, and under water. The Moscow–Washington agreement on a "hotline" was welcomed. The importance of agreements to halt the proliferation of nuclear arsenals was repeatedly emphasized.

Disarmament is obviously an area where the criterion of Christian witness is patient obedience rather than worldly success. A good excuse can be made for the time and effort devoted to the Geneva negotiations in the hope that a slight nudge in the right direction at the right moment might tip the balance in favour of a step forward.

Refugees and Migrants

The millions of human beings uprooted by the Second World War and its consequences—the refugees and expellees, the stateless and the homeless— challenged the World Council to supplement the work of intergovernmental agencies and to provide a united Christian witness in service to the suffering. The main response was through the service programmes now correlated by the Division of Inter-Church Aid, Refugee, and World Service, but C.C.I.A. was involved at a fairly early stage in issues at intergovernmental levels. While representations to strengthen and extend the international agencies, to broaden their mandate, and to secure more adequate financial support played a considerable part in this work, an even larger role was played by the day-to-day consultations seeking to facilitate co-operation between agencies of the World Council and the United Nations at the field level.

It quickly became clear that the refugee problem was not confined to Europe and that a broad definition of the term was required to cover the human needs involved. In 1949, in response to a Central Committee request to continue its work in this field, C.C.I.A. officers urged the United Nations General Assembly to consider the need for an inclusive definition of the refugee problem and the need for more adequate financial support. They also expressed concern for the Palestine refugee problem. To the Central Committee they reported the need for a "comprehensive plan of action" by the international community both for the stateless refugees and for those who were homeless but not stateless.

The establishment of the Office of the United Nations High Commissioner for Refugees in Geneva at the beginning of 1951 marked a new phase of this consultative work. C.C.I.A. officers supported the formation of a voluntary International Assistance Fund, which in turn made it possible for agencies like the W.C.C. and Inter-Church Aid Division and Lutheran World Relief to extend their humanitarian services. Effective relations with the High Commissioner for Refugees were maintained through three administrations and continue in the fourth as well as with I.C.E.M. and the Council of Europe's Sub-Committee on Refugees.

Improvement in the European situation was accompanied by new refugee problems, in the Near East, and later in Asia and Africa. In 1949 and 1961 C.C.I.A. issued statements of concern for the plight of the Palestinian refugees. C.C.I.A. officers worked with the parent bodies in convening the first Beirut Conference on Palestine Refugees in 1957, This conference asked the C.C.I.A. to seek adequate provision for relief until a permanent solution could be found; stressed, while recognizing the justice of repatriation, the need of funds for resettlement; emphasized the necessity of unfreezing assets and a speedy decision on compensation; and spoke of the need for international guarantees of frontiers and for a reorganization of United Nations agencies in Palestine. A second Beirut Conference in 1956 renewed and reinforced this mandate.

In 1954, after tens of thousands of new homeless from the Korean war had swollen the world's refugee population to an estimated forty million persons, the Commission called for the reunion in freedom of all arbitrarily divided nations, and the repatriation of refugees desiring it. In connection with World Refugee Year (1959–60) Rees, who from the start headed C.C.I.A. work in this field, was elected Chairman of the Executive Committee of the International Committee for the year. He also prepared the special report, *We Strangers and Afraid*, published that year. In more recent years, attention was given to other refugee needs, as in Hong Kong and Rwanda Burundi. The survey on the problems of the 650,000 African refugees, made in 1965 by Sir Hugh Foot (now Lord Caradon) and the late Professor Z. K. Matthews (Ambassador of Botswana to the United Nations and the U.S.A.) focused the attention of the United Nations delegates upon the serious needs to be met there. Support was also given for the extension and broadening of the mandate of the High Commissioner for Refugees, and close contact was maintained in regard to relief projects.

The growth of migration within Europe and outside led to increased attention to this separate but related area. In 1957 a joint study on "The Role of the Churches in Migration" by the C.C.I.A. and the Division of Inter-Church Aid prepared the way for the Conference on Migration held at Leysin, Switzerland in 1961. This was followed by the establishment of the Secretariat on Migration within D.I.C.A.R.W.S.

The work in the field of human rights, like the work on refugee and related problems, was an effort to champion the dignity and worth of the human person. It asserted that Christians have an international interest and obligation, as well as an ecumenical duty in helping to care for human beings uprooted by tyranny, war, or natural calamity. While refugee problems on the whole grew more rapidly than their solution during the two decades, attention in meeting elemental human needs was increasingly centred on anticipatory action as distinct from emergency relief. Prospective food shortages in poor countries stimulated international efforts to secure more adequate food supplies and better nutrition, through F.A.O. and the Freedom from Hunger Campaign.

The Advancement of Dependent Peoples

The most quoted of the C.C.I.A. aims was that which directed it to assist in "acceptance by all nations of the obligation to promote to the utmost the well-being of dependent peoples including their advance toward self-government and the development of their political institutions". One reason this point was cited so frequently was that the constituency of the W.C.C. like that of the United Nations, was divided as to the proper tempo and scope of the decolonization process. Some churchmen, particularly those from Europe, stressed the careful preparation of dependent peoples for self-government or independence. Others, particularly those from the "Younger Churches", chafed with growing impatience against the slow pace of decolonization. However, despite the difference as to application, there was support for the broad Charter principles underlying the Trusteeship Council and the Declaration on Non-Self-Governing Territories.

The result was a rather cautious, quite possibly an over-cautious approach to most of the colonial issues. C.C.I.A. officers informed interested church leaders from time to time of possible contacts with visiting missions of the Trusteeship Council, and called attention to reports on economic, social, and educational conditions in non-self-governing territories. They alerted commissions in countries administering territories to concern expressed in some of the United Nations debates. At one point (1955) certain Central American delegations were persuaded to withdraw a proposal on reports by non-governmental organizations that might have jeopardized the essentially non-political work of the Churches and missions. The welcome increase in progress towards emancipation was tempered by doubts whether there was in a number of cases sufficient preparations to keep them viable. The 1960 United Nations Declaration on Colonialism, which expresses the central convictions of the burgeoning anti-colonial bloc, played an important role in advancing moves towards independence. The W.C.C. and C.C.I.A. officers symbolized their support of this development by formal participation in a number of independence celebrations.

The tendency to make an absolute of self-determination apart from the other considerations which must figure in the responsible society complicated the situation. A frustrating problem, for the C.C.I.A. as well as for the world at large, was to establish a sound view of self-determination. The report of Section IV of the W.C.C.'s Second Assembly had stated that the "legitimate right of the self-determination of peoples must be recognized". But it did not give a clue as to the relationship of this right to other rights, nor to its application to national majorities and national minorities in multi-national societies. A sizeable body of data and considerations, showing the various aspects and complexities of the issues, was brought together, under the title "Notes on Self-Determination", for discussion at the 1956 C.C.I.A. Executive Committee. The discussion tended to recognize that the principle became a concrete right only when certain conditions were present, but it did not go very far in pinning down the conditions.

On certain specific issues the record is clearer. The C.C.I.A. Executive Committee in 1949 supported the reference of the legal status of South West Africa to the International Court. At its 1954 meeting in Chicago, the Commission agreed on "the right and fitness of the people of Cyprus to determine for themselves their future status". The Chairman's and Director's subsequent visit to Cyprus and to the countries most involved, and the interventions to secure on the one hand formal acknowledgment of the right of self-determination, and on the other acceptance of a certain transitional period of self-government, constituted an important chapter in the effort to distinguish between the principle and the right of self-determination. Later actions and interventions supported and encouraged by various W.C.C. bodies were concerned with Angola, Mozambique, Southern Rhodesia, and South West Africa.

In historical perspective, the transition of formerly dependent peoples to independence appears to have been both rapid and relatively peaceful. Nearly one-third of mankind live in countries which have achieved sovereignty within the last twenty years; but the process has raised a host of new problems in regard to economic and social, as well as to political, developments. The 1960 C.C.I.A. Executive Committee recognized that "newly liberated man has many needs, material and spiritual". The result was a correspondingly greater emphasis in C.C.I.A. work beginning in the early 1950s on the sector called "economic and social development".

Economic and Social Development

The undertaking by the United Nations of an expanded programme of technical assistance, and similar enterprises of a bilateral character, convinced the officers that specialized attention should be given to this area. While some effort was made to keep abreast of the more significant trends and events in bilateral and regional programmes, most of the detailed attention was concentrated on the United Nations programmes and those of certain specialized agencies: F.A.O., U.N.E.S.C.O., I.L.O., and U.N.I.C.E.F. As the various interests of the W.C.C. in this field grew, especially those of D.I.C.A.R.W.S., with its projects in areas of acute human need and its Specialized Assistance for Social Projects (S.A.S.P.), the requirements upon C.C.I.A. to facilitate useful contacts were increased.

In addition to the particular issues handled by the officers in their representational work, the Commission and its Executives approved a series of guide-lines on broader policy issues, which sought to make ecumenical concerns relevant without being too specific on the technical aspect which lay outside their competence. In general, these guide-lines stayed ahead of events, possibly though by no means necessarily having some modest influence on them.

The first of these policy guide-lines was a "Statement on Technical Assistant Programmes" approved by the 1951 C.C.I.A. Executive Committee. It put forward seven requirements for effective international development assistance, and some observations on the potential contributions of Christians and Christian agencies. Starting in 1952, the statements approved by the Executive Committee began to develop a major theme of C.C.I.A. representation in this area. They stressed the need for an overall strategy of development, with the United Nations playing a leading role in a longer-range evaluation of programmes, both multilateral and bilateral; consideration of the different sectors of development in their interrelationships; identification of unmet needs and priorities; and provision for more rational assurance for winning this basic war against the ancient enemies of mankind. Elaborated in various ways, this theme was a central testimony in this field.

A statement approved in 1952 provided guide-lines for the relationship to the Food and Agricultural Organization. It stressed requirements for the right use and conservation of both human and natural resources, and offered guidance in regard to such projects as the Freedom from Hunger Campaign and the World Food Programme. The next year the Executive Committee approved certain directions to help to improve the United Nations assistance programme, such as the development of country programming, the resident representatives system, and sustained financial support for a growing United Nations programme.

By 1956 there was obvious need for more ecumenical attention to the population problem and the related question of family planning. It was becoming evident that the impact of successful public health programmes on death rates was not being matched by comparable educational and medical effect on birth rates. C.C.I.A. advanced the position that Christian neglect of the population problem was a contributory factor to neglect at the international level, with possibly fateful consequencies for the development struggle. With the support of his colleagues Richard Fagley began to give specialized attention to the population–parenthood complex of issues and to helping to alert church leaders to the dangers. This led to a number of articles, speeches, and background memoranda, an ecumenical study group on population and responsible parenthood convened at Mansfield College in 1959, a book by Fagley on *The Population Explosion and Christian Responsibility*, a preliminary debate at the 1960 Central Committee, conversations with Roman Catholic scholars, an E.A.C.C. consultation on the Asian Churches and Responsible Parenthood at Bangkok in 1964, and a study on the doctrines and attitudes of major religions for the Second World Population Conference at Belgrade in 1965. During this period a number of communions and councils took a more forthright position on the question of responsible parenthood, a development which had a partial counterpart at the Vatican Council in 1965. The specialized attention given to this set of issues had not been planned or foreseen; but the procedures of C.C.I.A. proved flexible enough to take advantage of the opportunities presented even though at some cost to other concerns, and its work was widely recognized as having been a major factor in the dramatic "break-through" which focused world attention on the problem.

In a 1956 statement approved by the C.C.I.A. Executive Committee, another major theme made its appearance—the concern for strengthening the basis for greater participation by developing countries in international trade as a long-term mainstay for securing the goods and services needed to modernize their economies. A summary entitled "Elements of a Strategy of Development" was given general approval by the Commission at its Bangalore meeting in 1961. Three of its eleven points dealt with the need for positive measures to expand the exports of developing countries, for action to lessen or offset harmful price fluctuations in primary commodities, and for greater trade within the underdeveloped world to promote employment, to meet consumer needs, and to make more effective use of foreign exchange reserves. These points were further developed in a statement on "Trade for Development" which was approved by the 1965 C.C.I.A. Executive Committee to provide guidance for contacts with the new United Nations trade agency—United Nations Conference on Trade and Development (U.N.C.T.A.D.).

Earlier, at Nyborg, Denmark in 1958, officers of C.C.I.A. and the Department on Church and Society had collaborated in advising the Central Committee on a summary statement of development needs. This statement held that the picture would be brighter if countries would contribute at least one per cent of national income to international development. The idea was subsequently incorporated in a unanimous resolution by the United Nations General Assembly, and later by U.N.C.T.A.D. The 1961 Bangalore C.C.I.A. statement, however, had warned that the minimum "one per cent" target might soon become too small, for the costs of a successful struggle would rise with delay in mounting a more adequate international effort.

While C.C.I.A. work in this field remained a rather modest undertaking, concentrated at intergovernmental level in the hope of stimulating a more dynamic and coherent approach to the challenge, there was a gratifying growth of ecumenical concern in the great struggle against world poverty. It received ever-increasing attention in the work of Inter-Church Aid. It was a major topic in the W.C.C. Conference on Church and Society. Possibilities of co-operation with a proposed Vatican agency on world justice and development beckoned. There was also new activity at the national level. The British Council of Churches issued a report on "World Poverty and British Responsibility". Similarly the United States National Council of Churches pressed for a recognition of need and action. Thus voices grew in support of greater efforts than the halfway and half-hearted measures which had characterized the struggle in the past. Stimulated by the C.C.I.A., the W.C.C. Executive and the Central Committees in 1967 called for realistic action to face the growing food gap. But the scope of the challenge, and the threat of catastrophe, continued to mount in Asia, Africa, and Latin America.

The transcendent importance of the war against world poverty fully occupied the very limited resources of C.C.I.A. in the economic field. The idea of enlisting an advisory group of lay experts on problems of international economic co-operation was discussed more than once, but limited resources did not permit action. Consequently, large areas of this concern were touched upon only lightly and in quite general or superficial terms, as for example, the problems of economic collaboration within the western world, the Common Market, and others), and the possibilities of increasing mutual interest and confidence in a divided world through increased trade between the free market economies and the centrally planned economies.

International Law and Institutions

While work on specific issues before the United Nations constituted the largest segment of C.C.I.A. activity during the first two decades, comparatively little attention could be devoted to the longer-range or theoretical aspects of international organizations and their foundations. Even in regard to the question of the development and codification of international law, the officers had to follow evolutions at second hand through commissioners involved in this area.

Attention, however, was devoted to one basic long-range issue. This was the question of an international ethos, needed to undergird international law· and institutions. C.C.I.A. was a co-sponsor of a Conference on the Foundations of International Law in 1950, which attempted to clarify some of the duties and stressed the fact that there was hardly any common ethos binding the large power blocs together. Following the Evanston Assembly, where the International Affairs Section emphasized the need for greater attention to the question of common moral foundations, the C.C.I.A. Executive Committee authorized a study on a Christian Approach to an International Ethos. An able but predominantly European group was enlisted, and some stimulating papers were contributed. The study, however, did not develop beyond the initial phase. The plan was probably over-ambitious with insufficiently clear objectives, and adequate staff and budgetary resources were lacking. The challenge remains to dig more deeply into this basic subject.

Evaluation of the United Nations as a world institution, in addition to what had been said at the Amsterdam, Evanston, and New Delhi Assemblies was attempted on two occasions. The first was the statement *Christians Look at the United Nations*, approved by the 1953 C.C.I.A. Executive Committee. The second was a new statement approved in 1965. Both attempted, in summary fashion, to take stock of the United Nations' values and weaknesses, and emphasized the importance of the practical development of the potentials in the world organization. On the whole, C.C.I.A. has tended to be critical of world government schemes as unrealistic, finding no viable alternative to improvement and reinforcement of the existing body, the United Nations.

Conclusion

Reflecting on the developments over some twenty years one may say that the C.C.I.A. programme was marked by five characteristics:

1. Since international issues are highly complex, the process of relating Christian truth to them requires technical skill and extensive study as well as reliable information. Oversimplification is dangerous. Shibboleths, slogans, and vague peace generalizations often do more harm than good. The agency of the Churches which is assigned responsibility in the field of international affairs should be composed of persons who are not only motivated by Christian faith but who also have the competence to ensure that any proposal advanced will command the respectful consideration of government and intergovernmental officials.

2. Periodic conferences are valuable in shaping policy and in arousing public sentiment; but an effective contribution to peace requires a programme which can function virtually every day of the year. Issues of war and peace do not readily accommodate themselves to the schedule of church conferences and councils.

3. Resolutions or pronouncements indicate the direction which should be followed and may take on general educational value. If they are to become politically influential, they must be explained and registered at the time and place of international political decision. Moreover, they must be kept relevant to the level of immediate negotiation and thus will require adjustment in face of the particular obstacles encountered at any given moment. It is not enough, for example, to say that "nuclear testing should cease". Many a government official would reply, "I agree, but how can we do it?" It is necessary for the representatives of the Churches to get down into the arena where the struggle for peace in any particular form is being waged and to help to break an impasse there or to advance the cause on that front until a new battle line for peace is drawn.

4. While formal responsibility for representation in international affairs perforce rests upon a limited number of technically trained officials, the work of an organization for peace must rely upon the prayers and support of an informed constituency. While some progress in this respect has been made over the last fifteen years, much remains to be done to build a system which can move swiftly as demanded by international events, but will also in fact constitute a witness evangelical in its motivation and democratic in its procedure.

5. The fifth characteristic is barely discernible in formal fashion and is only beginning to emerge—especially from the standpoint of the World Council of Churches and the Roman Catholic Church. The ninth aim in the C.C.I.A. Charter reads: "To concert from time to time with other organizations holding similar objectives in the advancement of particular ends". The adoption and promulgation of the decree *De oecumenismo* by the Roman Catholic Church opened the way for fuller co-operation. The Central Committee of the World Council of Churches formally proposed at Enugu, Nigeria, in January 1965, after prior consultation with the Vatican, that a joint working group be established. It listed among subjects to be considered "practical consideration in the fields of philanthropy, social and international affairs". Cardinal Bea, during his visit to World Council headquarters in February, 1965, formally announced the Vatican's acquiescence in this proposal. A joint working party was established. The World Council of Churches and the Pontifical Commission on Justice and Peace are now formally consulting and acting together. The way is thus being opened to the co-operation of two great Christian communities and, perhaps eventually, to co-operation with all men of good will, whether they profess another faith or a faith other than Christian.

The affirmation contained in the Evanston report on "Christians in the Struggle for World Community" can serve as a continued stimulus to effort and a source of strength in action:

> This troubled world, disfigured and distorted as it is, is God's world. He rules and overrules its tangled history. In praying "Thy will be done on earth as it is

in heaven" we commit ourselves to seek earthly justice, freedom and peace for all men. Here as everywhere Christ is our hope. Our confidence lies not in our own reason or strength, but in the power that comes from God. Impelled by this faith, all our actions will be but humble, grateful, and obedient acknowledgment that He has redeemed the world. The fruit of our efforts rests in His hands. We can therefore live and work as those who know that God reigns, undaunted by all the arrogant pretensions of evil, ready to face situations that seem hopeless and yet to act in them as men whose hope is indestructible.

11

The Orthodox Churches
in the Ecumenical Movement
1948-1968

VASIL T. ISTAVRIDIS

Introduction

Eastern Europe and the Middle East are the geographical areas where Christian Churches known as Orthodox, Greek Orthodox, Eastern Orthodox, or Orthodox Catholic are found. Sometimes they are known by nationality, such as Russian Orthodox. Fifteen of these Churches are described as "autocephalous", meaning self-governing, Churches. Ranking first in honour are the ancient Patriarchates: Constantinople, Alexandria, Antioch, and Jerusalem in that order. The members adhering directly to these patriarchates total fewer than three million. The Russian Orthodox Church has an estimated 50 million members; the Rumanian, 14 million; the Serbian, 8 million; the Greek, 7.5 million; the Bulgarian, 6 million; the Georgian, 1.2 million; the Cyprian, 400,000; the Czecholsovakian, 350,000; the Polish, 350,000; the Albanian, 200,000. Finally, there is the autonomous church or monastery on Mount Sinai, having fewer than 100 members. Churches in Finland, China, Japan, and Macedonia, having a few thousand members each, are termed "autonomous" but not "autocephalous". Three autonomous church administrations are found among the Russians outside Russia. Orthodoxy maintains ecclesiastical provinces in Europe, North and South America, and Australia. These are related to one of the autocephalous Churches or to a Russian jurisdiction in emigration. The above Churches, which constitute what is generally known as Orthodoxy, probably have between eighty and 100 million members.

In addition, Churches which refer to themselves as Oriental Orthodox Churches have histories which go back to the Nestorian and Monophysite controversies over the one or two natures of Christ of the fourth and fifth centuries. The "ancient non-Greek" Orthodox are the Coptic and Ethiopic, the Syrian or Jacobite, the Nestorian, the Armenian Churches of Cilicia and Russia, the Syrian Orthodox of India, and the Maronite of Lebanon. These Churches, which have a total of around 20 million members, are not in communion with the Eastern Orthodox but are generally held to belong to the family of Eastern Churches. They are also referred to as Ancient Oriental, Lesser Eastern, and Pre- or Ante-Chalcedonian Churches. Among the latter the Ethiopian is the only established or state Church.

Developments within the Orthodox Churches between 1948 and 1968 were greatly affected by the Second World War. Dr N. Zernov enumerates the effects of the struggle under five heads, each of which had important consequences which still continue:

1. The re-emergence of the Orthodox Church in Russia and its appearance as an organized and articulate body on the scene of ecumenical relations.

2. The setting up of Communist rule in Rumania, Bulgaria, Yugoslavia, Albania, Poland, and Czechoslovakia.

3. The disappearance of the autonomous Churches of Latvia, Lithuania. and Estonia.

4. The healing in 1945 of the schism between the Bulgarians and the Church of Constantinople which dated from 1872.

5. The coming to the West of a large new contingent of refugees from eastern and central Europe, among whom were many Eastern Christians.

Inter-Church and Inter-Christian Relations

Orthodoxy is not an outsider to the ecumenical movement. In the ecumenical age in which we live, the Eastern Churches, like those in the West, participate in many different forms of relations with other Churches. Some of them are new and others go back to before the present century. Ecclesiastical and theological conversations between Orthodox and Anglicans and between Orthodox and Old Catholics helped the Orthodox to formulate a method of holding conversations with other Churches. They also revealed to the Orthodox their own inner unity and encouraged them to take it more seriously.

The Orthodox Church claims to be the one, holy, Catholic, and Apostolic Church of the Nicene Creed, going back through an unbroken continuity to the years of Jesus Christ and the Apostles. Well known is the ecclesiological principle of Orthodoxy, according to which no communion in the sacraments can be achieved before a full dogmatic union with the other Churches. These positions have not made ecumenical relations impossible; but the understanding between the two cultural and ecclesiastical worlds of East and West has been difficult. In addition, the principle of autocephalicity is often not easy for Western Christians to grasp. It means the independence of each patriarchate or autocephalous Church. This independence, added to the obstacles raised by the conditions under which these Churches live, does not help to promote their sincere wishes for *rapprochement* with other Churches. Nevertheless, some progress has been made towards understanding among the Orthodox Churches themselves and between them and the wider Christian world.

Inter-Orthodox Relations

Eastern Orthodox. The Orthodox Church does not have an external centre of authority, like the office of Pope within the Roman Catholic Church. The Ecumenical Patriarch (Constantinople) is accepted by all Orthodox Churches as *primus inter pares* which gives him the right of initiative in calling pan-Orthodox conferences and in some matters affecting relations with other Churches. In 1948 Athenagoras, the Greek Orthodox Archbishop of America, became the Ecumenical Patriarch. He has been pursuing a policy of closer co-operation within and without Orthodoxy ever since. A special concern of the Ecumenical Patriarch is the problem of the Orthodox Diaspora, which is being gradually solved through the co-operation of ecclesiastical leaders and through the Standing Conference of Canonical Orthodox Bishops in America, founded in 1960, and a similar grouping in France, founded in 1967.

In the year when the present Ecumenical Patriarch was enthroned, when there was great tension between the communist and the capitalist worlds, a celebration was staged in Moscow of the five hundredth anniversary of the autocephalicity of the Orthodox Church of Russia. Officials of the Orthodox Churches which were behind the Iron Curtain were present. The Conference did not claim the authority of a Church Council. Its resolutions criticized the Vatican, the Anglican Church, and the ecumenical movement as represented by the World Council of Churches. The arguments which were used seemed to be influenced by the Russian foreign policy of the Stalin era. It condemned the Roman Catholic and the Anglican Churches, denounced the World Council as "an instrument of American imperialism", and denied any intention to co-operate with these bodies. Nevertheless a great change was imminent.

The difference which can be made by dedicated leadership and the passage of time is indicated by the difference between these actions of 1948 and what happened at the First Pan-Orthodox Conference, called by Patriarch Athenagoras to meet in Rhodes in 1961. The greatest achievement of this conference was the presence in Rhodes of representatives from all Orthodox Churches except the Church of Albania. Other pan-Orthodox conferences followed in Rhodes in 1963 and 1964. The agenda for a future pan-Orthodox pro-Synod was agreed upon and decisions were taken on dialogue with the Churches of Rome, the Anglicans, and the Old Catholics. The attitude towards the ecumenical movement was affirmative and hopeful.

Several festivals or celebrations had brought Orthodox leaders together in the interval. An extended series of visits between Orthodox leaders had helped the ecumenical spirit to grow. An international organization of Orthodox youth movements called Syndesmos, founded in Paris in 1953, had repeatedly convened general assemblies. The constitution of Syndesmos states that its aim is to establish living contact between youth movements and groups, to encourage co-operation, to develop Orthodox unity and mutual aid, and "to assist Orthodox youth in its relations with the non-Orthodox".

Oriental Orthodox Churches   "In the summer of 1948 at Amsterdam at the first Assembly of the World Council of Churches, perhaps for the first time in about a thousand years, a few members of the scattered 'Monophysite' denominations got together", wrote Fr K. M. Simon of the Syrian Orthodox Church in 1951. This took place at a dinner given by his Grace Abuna Theophilos of the Ethiopian Orthodox Church.

> In this meeting, to our great surprise, we discovered that although we were in communion with each other and held the same doctrine, we knew almost next to nothing about each other or even about our common heritage. In our discussions we realized that, while others have progressed in every field, we have been mostly static. This we were convinced was chiefly due to our lack of unity and co-ordination.

Fr Simon then visited Churches of his tradition in Syria, Egypt, and Ethiopia and learned that there was a general willingness to co-operate. So he purposed the holding of a World Conference of the Oriental Orthodox Churches.

The World Conference was held in January 1965 in Addis Ababa upon the invitation of the Emperor Haile Selassie I. Attending were the heads of the Coptic Orthodox, the Syrian Orthodox of Antioch, the Armenian Orthodox of Cilicia, the Syrian Orthodox of India, and the Ethiopian Orthodox Churches. Catholicos Vazken of the Armenian Orthodox Church of Etchmiadzin was present, but did not take part officially. The Conference set up a standing committee of the Oriental Orthodox Churches which met in Addis Ababa later in 1965, in Cairo in 1966, and in Antelias, Lebanon in 1967. It also organized co-operation at the theological education level, with the result that an Armenian theologian and three theologians from the Syrian Orthodox Church of India were appointed to the faculty of the Theological College of the Holy Trinity in Addis Ababa. The Churches represented in the Conference agreed to co-operate in evangelism and in determining their relations with other Churches. The meeting ended with a statement on peace and justice in the world and with a resolution declaring Emperor Haile Selassie as the "Defender of the Faith" because of his work for the unity of these Churches.

In the twenty years following Amsterdam (1948) the growth of ecumenical concern had wrought important changes within the Oriental Orthodox Churches. A division which had sundered the Syrian Orthodox Church in India in 1910 was healed in 1958. The Church in Ethiopia acquired patriarchal status in 1959 from the mother Church in Egypt. The tension between the two Armenian catholicossates—Etchmiadzin in Armenia, U.S.S.R. and Cilicia in Antelias, Lebanon—abated. Primacy of honour has always been recognized by Cilicia as belonging to Etchmiadzin. Vasken I, the Catholicos of Etchmiadzin, visited the World Council of Churches in 1967. He had also visited the Middle East in 1956 and Jerusalem and India in 1963. Emperor Haile Selassie and dignitaries of the Coptic and Ethiopian Churches visited the Syrian Orthodox Church in India at the time of the Third World Assembly of Churches in India in 1961.

Eastern Orthodox Oriental–Orthodox Relations The First Pan-Orthodox Conference, held in Rhodes in 1961, discussed the relations between the two branches of Orthodoxy. It urged the establishment of brotherly attitudes in order to re-establish the union between them. It encouraged visits of professors, students, and church leaders, the study of the history, faith, worship, and organization of Churches on both sides, and collaboration in meetings of an ecumenical character. This work was already under way. Delegates from the different Oriental Orthodox Churches participated in the one thousand nine hundredth anniversary of the coming of St Paul to Greece in 1951 and in the celebrations marking the milennium of Mount Athos in 1963. In 1953 and 1954 theological discussions were held between representatives of the Russian Orthodox Church and the Syrian Orthodox Church of India.

The World Council of Churches helped the representatives of the Eastern Orthodox and the Oriental Orthodox Churches to come together. Because of W.C.C. meetings a small unofficial group from both sides living in Geneva brought together a meeting at Aarhus, Denmark, 11–15 August 1964. After several papers and many conversations, the Conference adjourned with a joint statement which said: "We recognize in each other the one Orthodox faith of the Church. Fifteen centuries of alienation have not led us astray from the faith of our fathers . . . We see the need to move forward together." A similar meeting was held in connection with the Faith and Order meeting held in Bristol, England 25–9 July 1967. So there is growing a belief that the theological differences between these Churches today do not appear to be of such a nature that they cannot be overcome by patient study and the growth of mutual understanding.

The Ecumenical Patriarchate proposed to the Eastern Orthodox Churches in 1965 the establishment of an Inter-Orthodox, Inter-Oriental Orthodox Theological Commission to prepare for an eventual dogmatic union. Earlier the Ecumenical Patriarch had visited the patriarchs of the Syrian Orthodox and the Coptic Orthodox. Other visitors among Orthodox prelates included Iakovos of Melita, now Archbishop of America, to Malabar and Ethiopia; various Orthodox delegates to the Third World Assembly visiting the Syrian Orthodox Church of India; the Catholicos of Etchmiadzin, who made numerous trips outside of Russia and visited almost all Orthodox Patriarchates; the Rumanian Patriarch to Armenia; the Syrian Orthodox Patriarch to the Ecumenical Patriarch; and the Catholicos of Cilicia to Greece. Meanwhile students from the Coptic, the Ethiopian, and the Syrian Churches study theology at schools in Athens, Thessalonika, Halki, Bucharest, and Addis Ababa.

Orthodoxy and Roman Catholicism   In the last two decades the relations between the Orthodox and the Roman Catholic Churches have undergone a great change for the better. Popes John XXIII and Paul VI and Ecumenical Patriarch Athenagoras were major factors in the changing climate. The fact that the Patriarchate of Moscow was represented by observers from the first session of the Second Vatican Council onwards was also important. Tragic events taking place during the Second World War among the Orthodox Churches of the Balkans and Russia unfavourably dominated relations at the beginning of the period. The first major move toward improvement was the 1958 Christmas message of the late Pope John to Patriarch Athenagoras, who responded immediately and affirmatively by sending a New Year's greeting at the beginning of 1959. Relations suffered a temporary setback in 1959 because of a misunderstanding which arose in connection with a meeting of the Central Committee of the World Council of Churches in Rhodes. The misunderstanding arose because of misleading publicity given to an unofficial meeting there between Orthodox delegates and Roman Catholic observers or press representatives. It caused Archbishop Iakovos to declare that the Orthodox had no intention of establishing direct contacts with Rome if the Protestant Churches and the World Council of Churches were not invited to participate. But the matter was cleared up without permanent damage.

The pan-Orthodox Conferences of 1961, 1963, and 1964 discussed the relations of Orthodoxy and the Catholic Church. On the question whether observers should be sent to the Second Vatican Council it was decided that each Orthodox Church should make its own decision. Not all Orthodox responded favourably in the beginning to the invitation of Rome to send observers. At the first and second sessions (1962, 1963) only the Churches of Russia and Georgia sent observers. To the third session observers from Constantinople and Alexandria were added, and in the final session the patriarchates of Serbia and Bulgaria also sent observers. The Secretariat for the Promotion of Christian Unity, established by Pope John and headed by Cardinal Bea, helped immensely to facilitate good relations.

Pope Paul VI continued the efforts of his predecessor. On his visit to Jerusalem in 1964 the meetings between him and the Ecumenical Patriarch and the Patriarch of Jerusalem made history. The mutual lifting in 1965 of the anathemas between Rome and Constantinople, which had stood since 1054, was followed by the visit by Pope Paul to the Ecumenical Patriarchate in Istanbul and the return visit to Rome by Athenagoras in 1967. Roman Catholics were officially invited to come as observers to the Pan-Orthodox Conference in Rhodes, to the Mount Athos celebration of its first thousand years in 1964, and to a commemoration in Thessalonika in 1966 of the work of Cyril and Methodius, apostles to the Slavs. The return from the Western Church of the relics of several saints to churches in Jerusalem, Patras, Crete, and Chios added another evidence of good will. Theologians from the Catholic and Orthodox Churches are meeting in the United States under the auspices of their respective Churches. So the change for the better continues to grow better.

Orthodox–Old Catholic Relations Orthodoxy had friendly relations with the Old Catholic Church since its formation as an independent Church after 1870. In 1931 a meeting of a Joint Doctrinal Commission of Orthodox and Old Catholics was held in Bonn. A substantial degree of agreement was found to exist. Since the Second World War efforts have been made to revive the work of the Joint Commission. This was discussed at the First Pan-Orthodox Conference at Rhodes, where Old Catholics were present as official observers. Theologians belonging to the Patriarchates of Constantinople, Russia, and Greece have held unofficial conversations with Old Catholic theologians. When Andreas Rinkel, Archbishop of Utrecht, visited the Ecumenical Patriarchate in 1962, it was decided to recreate the Joint Commission. The Archbishop later visited the Church of Russia. The pan-Orthodox commission on the dialogue with Old Catholics met at Belgrade in 1966.

Orthodox–Anglican Relations In the last two decades work for reunion between these two communions, which began long ago, has been strongly revived. Present relations between the two Churches continue the Orthodox–Anglican discussions held at the 1930 Lambeth Conference and the Joint Doctrinal Commission which met in London a year later. The negative decision on Anglican orders which was taken at the 1948 Moscow Conference, joined in by the Russian, Rumanian, and the Alexandrine delegates, constitute a temporary reversal. But an Anglo-Russian theological conference held in Moscow in 1956 brought the Russian Church to the same level which other Orthodox Churches had reached with reference to the Anglicans.

The visit of Michael Ramsey, Archbishop of Canterbury, to Moscow in 1962 and the return visit to London of Patriarch Alexii in 1964 confirmed these improved relations. Dr Ramsey visited the Ecumenical Patriarch and the Churches of Greece in 1962, Rumania in 1965, and Jerusalem and Belgrade in 1966. He was host to the Patriarch of Rumania in the same year. Anglican observers have been present on invitation at various pan-Orthodox meetings. In the U.S.A. an officially appointed Orthodox Theological Commission meets with a similar group from the Protestant Episcopal Church.

Orthodox–Protestant Relations   Between 1948 and 1968 Orthodoxy has met the Protestant world mainly through the ecumenical movement. Formerly tension developed because some Evangelical communities developed missionary work in Orthodox areas, but more recently proselyting seems to have stopped and good will and co-operation are the rule. This has led to better understanding. Greek Orthodoxy was not prepared for the problems which arose when thousands of Greeks spread over Protestant and Catholic areas of Europe in search of work. Generally Protestant and Catholic Churches have adopted a co-operative attitude which has helped workers meet differences in tradition, religion, ethics, and style of living.

In Germany several consultations have been held between Protestant and Orthodox theologians. Theologians of the Orthodox Church of Russia and of the Evangelical Church of Germany met in Arnoldshain, West Germany in 1959; in Zagorsk, Moscow in 1963 and in Hocst, Odenwald, West Germany in 1967. But the Orthodox–Protestant encounter is not limited to theologians. Most of the professors of the Orthodox theological faculties in Athens and Salonika finished their advanced studies in Germany. Since 1946 Orthodox theologians have lectured before German Protestant faculties. Protestant students have studied the Orthodox liturgy at the Ecumenical Institute at Chateau Bossey, Switzerland and at the Orthodox St Serge Institute in Paris. The latter has, with the Russian Student Christian Movement, carried out broad ecumenical activity. There have been many excursions of Protestant and Orthodox students into Egypt, Syria, and Ethiopia and many Orthodox–Protestant youth and student conferences in Germany, France, Belgium, England, Scotland, Greece, and Finland. Professor Leo Zander, Secretary of the Orthodox Student Christian Movement, carried out indefatigable lifelong activity dedicated to the ecumenical approach of the Orthodox Church to the Western Churches.

Ecumenical periodicals render an important service in informing Western Christianity about the Eastern Orthodox Churches. *Irenikon*, published by the Benedictine monks in Chevetogne in Belgium, *Istina*, published by the Dominican order in Paris, *Kyrios*, edited by Professor Meinhood in Kiel, and the *Ostkirchliche Studien*, edited by Professor Stupperich in Münster, give scholarly theological and historical information about Orthodox Churches and their ecumenical relations. They review books and articles and give news about the ecumenical life of the Orthodox Churches.

The W.C.C. department of Faith and Order has brought together Orthodox and Protestant theologians twice: at Athens in 1959 and at Montreal in 1963. The Standing Conference of Orthodox Canonical Bishops in America, which met early in 1967, approved participation in a Orthodox–Lutheran colloquy later that year. The meeting took place in New York, discovered a "basic understanding" on Scripture and tradition, and concluded that "the enormously illuminating and constructive" conversation would "ultimately produce a valuable contribution to ecumenical progress on the American scene". The Bishops' Conference[1] also accepted in "in principle" an invitation to start a similar dialogue with the Presbyterians, but declined because of shortage of Orthodox personnel in the U.S.A. to start an Orthodox–Methodist discussion, even "in principle".

Oriental Orthodox and Western Churches   Contacts have begun to multiply between the Oriental Orthodox Churches and those of the West. At the invitation of Pope Paul VI, the Catholicos of the Syrian Orthodox Church of India attended the Eucharistic Congress held in Bombay in 1964 and met the Pope. Pope Paul exchanged visits with the Armenian Patriarch of Istanbul during his visit in 1967. The Armenian Catholicos Khoren I of Cilicia paid an official visit to Pope Paul in Rome in the same year. In 1965 the Addis Ababa Conference of the Oriental Orthodox Churches noted with approval "the new awareness which the Roman Catholic Church has begun to show" of other Churches, and offered to enter into conversations designed to improve mutual understanding.

Concerning other member Churches of the W.C.C., the conference statement expressed appreciation of the cordial relations with other Churches which the W.C.C. made possible and prayed "that God would open the way for our mutual understanding wherever possible". The statement expressed special interest in dialogue with Anglican and Old Catholic Churches. It asked both Protestants and Catholics to refrain from proselyting "among members of our Churches" and expressed faith "that God who has brought our Churches and the other member Churches of the World Council of Churches together into friendly relation through that Council will help us to grow in fellowship with one another and restore us all into fullness of unity in his own time and in the manner He ordains".

Conclusion   Inter-Orthodox relations have improved immensely, especially during the 1958–68 decade. This has been the work of God. Eastern Orthodoxy has been accused by some of not being able to move fast enough. Admittedly, it does not have a permanent standing office or instrument of pan-Orthodox character, except Syndesmos, the youth organization, which has the blessing of the Ecumenical Patriarchate. On the other hand, the Oriental Orthodox Churches have established "the Standing Committee of the Oriental Orthodox Churches" which does act on their behalf. Since Eastern Orthodoxy maintains old, and has started new, relations or theological contacts with other Churches, and since developments of an ecumenical character are multiplying, the question arises whether Orthodoxy is adequately prepared or has sufficient trained personnel to cope with the demands being made upon it. Without

[1] L.W.F. Press Release, no. 44/67.

criticizing the sincerity of Orthodox intentions, it is obvious that it will take a longer time for their Churches to participate effectively and meet all the demands than the movement of events would make desirable.

Orthodoxy and Wider Ecumenical Manifestations

Introduction

The ecumenical movement, which includes the World Council of Churches, is a wider and richer stream than any council. Movements parallel with, and complementary to, the W.C.C. often originated before 1948 but need to be taken into account. These wider ecumenical manifestations help Orthodox laity, youth, clergy, monks, and others who participate in them to experience and learn about one phase or another of the ecumenical movement. One of the most important of these is missions.

Missions

In modern times, it has been too easy to forget that in times past Orthodox missionaries carried the gospel of Jesus Christ to people in vast areas of what we now know as Christendom. Missionary awareness is not dead within the Eastern Churches, although it has been dormant for too long. Political and other reasons mainly account for this state of affairs, but ecclesiastical reasons also play their part. Protestant missionary expansion within lands to which the gospel was first brought by missionaries of Orthodoxy was viewed by Orthodox leaders as disruptive. In the early years of the ecumenical movement, Orthodox representatives did not fail to protest against proselytism. This led to the formation of a special commission of the W.C.C. Its report, entitled "Christian Witness, Proselytism, and Religious Liberty", was presented to the Third World Assembly of Churches in New Dehli in 1961. This document, in which proselytism is called a corruption of Christian witness, was well accepted by Eastern Orthodox Churches.

New Dehli was also the Assembly at which the International Missionary Council and the World Council of Churches were merged. Orthodoxy's experiences as a result of some Protestant missionary activity had made them miss the very important studies and work done in the field of evangelism by the I.M.C. They concentrated on expressing doubts and concern about the rightness of the proposed merger. When a mandate was given to a joint committee to study the integration of the two councils, the Ecumenical Patriarchate prepared and sent a memorandum to the sister Orthodox Churches. Archbishop Michael of America expressed to the 1957 meeting of the Central Committee of the W.C.C. the reservations which Orthodoxy had on the proposed integration. Later Metropolitan, now Archbishop, Iakovos, presented these reservations at a meeting of the I.M.C. in Ghana, where he was present as an observer. Objections by these and other Orthodox caused the dropping of the theological preamble to the statement of integration and the way for them to participate in its adoption was cleared by the adoption of the statement against proselytizing. The former International Missionary Council became the Commission on World Mission and Evangelism of the World Council of Churches, with a divisional structure within the W.C.C. Participation by the Orthodox in this Commission will hopefully reawaken their missionary zeal.

Oriental Orthodox Churches conducting missionary work include the Church at Malabar, through the Missionary Association of the Servants of the Cross (1924), the Evangelistic Associations of the East (1925), and the Christu Sishya Ashram (1933). The Church of Ethiopia conducts missionary work through its department of mission and some religious associations. The Addis Ababa Conference encouraged member Churches to "examine the experience of the various missionary organizations . . . and see what can be done to co-ordinate our missionary efforts".

In East Africa an African Greek Orthodox Church has developed. It has an estimated membership of 10,000 to 30,000. It represents a merger of Christian groups which originated separately around 1930. The background of these groups was respectively Anglican, Scottish Presbyterian, Pentecostal, and the Society of Friends. Leaders established contact first with the Syrian Orthodox and later with the Greek Orthodox Church. Out of these contacts came the African Greek Orthodox Church. In 1959 the Patriarch of Alexandria appointed a metropolitan to administer the Church.[1]

Within the Orthodox Church of Greece and the Greek Orthodox archdiocese of America there are some projects to help the missionary Churches of Korea as well as these in Uganda. The Fourth General Assembly of Syndesmos (1958) established an international missionary society with headquarters in Athens. Three years later the Fifth Assembly transformed this headquarters into a pan-Orthodox missionary centre with the title *Porefthentes* (Go Ye). Through this centre, through a bulletin with the same title published in Greek and English, through material help to missionary Churches, and by meetings and correspondence, Syndesmos has become a major centre of influence for mission.

Laity

In the Orthodox Church laymen play active roles in church organization, in worship, in service as artists and writers, in philanthropy, in education, including theological education, as monks, and in the mission of the Church. Each baptized member has a special call to verify the genuine church conscience. While one cannot generalize, generally it is true that ecumenical education lags among laity. In villages laymen obtain their information about the ecumenical movement from the priests, the majority of whom take a defensive and rather negative stand. Others are apathetic, but a small minority show a hopeful attitude toward ecumenism. Because of the rising standards of education and Europeanization, "time is working with the ecumenical spirit" in Greece and other Orthodox countries. Since Orthodox monasticism is predominantly of a lay character, the attitude of monks is important. According to Mario Rinvolucri, "with a very few individual exceptions, the

[1] Article by D. E. Wentink, *Ecumenical Review*, vol. xx (January 1968).

monks are emotionally the most anti-ecumenically disposed group in Greek society". The Orthodox Patriarchal Centre at Taizé, France as well as the Orthodox working in the Ecumenical Centre in Geneva may be expected to make the development of good relations between Orthodox monasticism and ecumenism a matter of concern.

The lay element is predominant in the religious movements known as Zoe, Soter, and the movements of Fr Nissiotis (Union of Orthodox Youth) and Fr (now Metropolitan) Kandiotis. So far these movements have not shown a noticeable willingness to co-operate among themselves or with the official Church. Zoe shows signs of developing a more favourable attitude toward ecumenical affairs. It wields considerable influence among the dominant bourgeoisie. The Soter Brotherhood is much more conservative and un-ecumenical. The most ecumenically minded religious movement in Greece is probably that of Fr Nissiotis. Lay professors of theology in the theological schools greatly influence ecumenical education among the Orthodox by their knowledge, their writings, and their teachings. The department of the laity of the World Council of Churches held a consultation on the laity at Beirut, Lebanon in 1967. In such meetings and in other ways the department is of help to the laity of the Eastern Churches.

Youth

The development of associations through which Orthodox youth could work has been an important aspect of ecumenical growth between 1948 and 1968. We have already referred to Syndesmos, the pan-Orthodox youth organiza-tion. Some youth organizations of Protestant origin, such as the Young Men's and the Young Women's Christian Associations, have also contributed. In connection with the World Assemblies of Churches in 1948, 1954, 1961, and 1968 three youth conferences have been held, two in Lebanon and one in Switzerland. The 1955 Consultation in Beirut brought together for the first time leaders responsible for youth work among the Eastern Orthodox, the Oriental Orthodox, the Anglicans, and the Evangelicals. It was the first time in modern centuries for Christians of this whole area to come together and feel their oneness in Christ. Eastern Orthodox were in the majority.

The Assembly of European Youth which was held in Lausanne in 1960 had the support of Syndesmos. The sixty-five page preparatory book of the Assembly was translated into several languages, including Greek and Finnish. Over 100 persons, including forty Greeks, represented Eastern Orthodoxy. Observers included Russians, Yugolavs, Bulgarians, and three Ethiopians. In 1964 a broad range of Middle Eastern countries was again represented in another youth conference in Lebanon. The youth department of the World Council of Churches and the World Student Christian Federation joined resources and appointed Gaby Habib, an Orthodox, to be youth secretary for the Churches of the Middle East. He successfully organized this conference, of which a participant said: "It was the first meeting of its kind to take such a broad range of Middle Eastern countries and to penetrate to the heart of the Christian youth organizations of the region."[1] Strong youth delegations,

[1] Editorial of *The Student World* (1965), quoting Bishop Ignatius Hazim.

Protestant and Orthodox, also took part in the programme celebrating the one thousand nine hundredth anniversary of the arrival of St Paul in Greece. The needs of youth were discussed at the First Pan-Orthodox Conference held in Rhodes in 1961 and in the Conference of Oriental Orthodox Churches held in Addis Ababa in 1965. Orthodox youth often appear earlier in the ecumenical movement than do their elders and sometimes venture beyond the areas of official church co-operation.

Orthodox Religious Education and Bible Societies

From the Protestant world, Eastern Orthodox and Oriental Orthodox Churches have taken the modern idea of the Sunday school. With modifications they have adapted its methods and teaching manuals. In Greece the *Apostolike Diakonia* (Home Missions) of the Church of Greece has finally, after some delay, taken over Sunday school materials and development. The movement has problems in Greece, as it has elsewhere.

The Standing Conference of Canonical Bishops in America has a committee and a programme for united pan-Orthodox action in religious education in America. The Oriental Churches at their Addis Ababa Conference launched a committee of experts to outline a curriculum for Christian education to be used by the Churches. The committee met in 1967 in Antelias for a week and produced the outline for a joint curriculum.

Because proselytism by Protestants was identified with dissemination of the Bible, the Orthodox Churches were at first reluctant to deal with Bible Societies. This reluctance seems to be fading. Eastern Orthodox scholars have participated in translating and editing parts or the whole of the Bible on a regional level. Now members of these Churches buy and distribute scriptures or materials connected with the Bible produced by these societies in local languages. The Rumanian Patriarchate works through a missionary institute and the Serbian Patriarchate is especially active in catechization. A committee of Orthodox biblical scholars, under instructions from the Standing Conference of Orthodox Bishops of America, began planning in 1967 to produce an "American Orthodox" Bible. This will be based on the Revised Standard Version, with some alterations to conform with distinctive Orthodox understandings. The special importance attached to the Septuagint by the Orthodox Church may present the major problems in this enterprise.

Theological Education in the Orthodox Churches

The ecumenical movement is being accepted as the most important feature of ecclesiastical life in the twentieth century, so Orthodox theological schools have taken this into account. Some have added a course on ecumenical significance for theology and church life. The Orthodox Theological Institute of St Sergius is one of the collaborating theological schools in the Roman Catholic Superior Institute of Ecumenical Studies in Paris which was formed in 1967.

Orthodox professors of theology regularly give courses in the Ecumenical Institute at Chateau Bossey in Switzerland. Dr Nikos Nissiotis of the Church of Greece is now director of this institute, which is connected with the World Council of Churches. He was an observer for the W.C.C. at the Second Vatican Council. Orthodox theologians are well represented also in the Ecumenical Institute on Soteriological Studies in Jerusalem. They play significant roles in the Secretariat on Faith and Order of the W.C.C. and in the four-year World Council Study on Patterns of Ministry and Theological Education. They help to advise the administrators of the Theological Education Fund, which is interested in theological schools generally and particularly in some Orthodox theological schools in the Near East and India. Through this fund consultations have been held on church history (1956-9), on ecumenical theology (1960), hermeneutics (1963), patristic studies and practical theology (1967).

The last pan-Orthodox congress on theology was held in Athens in 1936. The 1965 Oriental Orthodox Conference at Addis Ababa urged that a "Common Centre for Advanced Studies and Research" be established, that the writing of theological books and the exchange of students and professors be encouraged. Mixed groups for theological discussions exist in Athens and at the University of Thessalonika. In Great Britain some of the work done by the Anglican and Eastern Churches Association and by the Fellowship of St Alban and St Sergius could be included. The latter group maintain St Basil's House, London, which has a good library, publishes the excellent magazine *Sobornost*, holds conferences, and has Chapters in Britain, Canada, and Australia.

Press, Radio, Television

The Orthodox Churches do not now have a paper exclusively dedicated to the ecumenical movement. Between 1956 and 1962 the liaison office of the Ecumenical Patriarchate at the headquarters of the World Council of Churches published such a paper in Greek each month. The weekly paper *Apostolos Andreas* of the Ecumenical Patriarchate, which continued from 1951 to 1964, published a rich variety of material on the ecumenical movement. A monthly entitled *Orthodoxy* is issued by the autonomous Russian Orthodox Church of America. Other Orthodox periodicals carry ecumenical news and opinions. Some are published by church officials, others by theological schools. The Greek Archbishopric of Crete has its own radio station. The Syrian Orthodox Church is a member of the Near East Council of Churches, which helps to sponsor the radio station at Addis Ababa. In general it must be said that participation in the ministry of communication by the Orthodox Church is in its early stages.

Orthodox Worship

Fr Alexander Schmemann in an article on "Worship and the Ecumenical Encounter" starts with the assertion that the ecumenical encounter of Churches takes place in and through worship.[1] For some, the ecumenical movement moves towards unity through intercommunion by those who

[1] *The Student World*, 51 (1958), pp. 34-5.

accept it as a way towards fuller unity. For the Orthodox, who on ecclesiological grounds reject intercommunion, accepting their Church as the *Una Sancta*, this way is closed. So the most liturgical of all Christian bodies, for which the liturgy is the full and unique expression of Christian fellowship, has to oppose the "liturgical encounter" and to withdraw from all attempt at intercommunion. This tragedy is keenly felt, for nowhere do we realize more what it means to be divided than at the altar, at the table of the Lord.

This does not mean that the Eastern Orthodox do not pray together with their brother Christians. They welcome the presence of fellow-Christians in their worship services, and at the end of each liturgy the *antidoron*, the blessed bread, is given. In Orthodox lands during ecumenical meetings, such as the Central Committee of the W.C.C. at Crete in 1967, non-Orthodox are allowed to preach the sermon and to recite together the Lord's Prayer.

In ecumenical services, Orthodox clergy lead prayers or participate in services in the presence of members of other Churches. Participation in the Week of Prayer for the Unity of the Church is growing from year to year. The Council of Churches of Alexandria, including the Roman Catholic Church, has held every year since 1959 a special service of intercession. What does this mean for co-operation with ecumenical bodies? The Ecumenical Patriarchate issued an encyclical in 1952 on the World Council of Churches. It included the following words, among others:

> (c) It is meet that Orthodox clerics who are delegates [of their Church] should be as careful as possible about services of worship in which they join with the heterodox, as these are contrary to the sacred canons and make less acute the confessional sensitiveness of the Orthodox. They should aim at celebrating, if possible, purely Orthodox liturgical services and rites, that they may thereby manifest, before the eyes of the heterodox, the splendour and majesty of Orthodox adoration.

Again in 1967 an encyclical was sent from the same source to the hierarchs saying: "Intercommunion between the Orthodox Church and other churches does not as yet exist."

Professor Nikos Nissiotis adds an additional illuminating comment.

> From the doctrinal point of view intercommunion is not possible in the Orthodox Church. However some local Orthodox Churches of different jurisdictions do not even have communion with one another if their canonical relationship is broken and if full love and spiritual communion are lacking in either of them. On this basis I would like to modify somewhat the harsh statement that where there is no doctrinal agreement about the Church, its ministry and the significance of the Eucharist there cannot be intercommunion. Instead I would say that, for the Orthodox, love and spiritual communion are equally important when we participate in the same chalice. The Orthodox cannot say that intercommunion is simply the crowning event of a pre-existing, detailed doctrinal agreement (which never existed in a full sense between East and West even before the schism, when intercommunion was nevertheless practised). It is also the God-given means of maintaining unity and of healing divisions, if this unity is at stake or if the appropriate conditions for restoring it exist.
>
> It might be that the developments in ecumenical relationships and especially

the recognition of the positive signs of the growing fellowship between separated churches could create the basis for the Orthodox to make an exception. However, this exception can only be made by means of the *dispensation* (*kat' oikonomian*) which is already practised in many other cases, particularly as far as the recognition of baptism is concerned. The *dispensatio* can override the decisions of Canon Law in cases where pastoral care should have priority over the letter of the law. I have concluded by these observations on this crucial problem because again and again the Eastern Church has shown the *kat' oikonomian* to be the expression of the fundamental ecclesiological principle of its own belief and thoughts. It is the love which results from the "unity of the spirit in the bond of peace" for all those who want to keep the unity of the spirit. It manifests the creative spirit of love which breaks through all barriers raised by human failure and shortcomings which divide that which cannot exist as divided, namely communion in the one family of God.[1]

Confessional Bodies, Organic Church Unions, Regional and National Councils

Confessional Bodies Orthodoxy does not regard herself as one of the confessions, but as the true Church, the *Una Sancta* of the Symbol of Faith, and so it is out of place to speak of the efforts spent and the results achieved in the domain of inter-Orthodox relations. However, Orthodoxy is represented at annual meetings in Geneva of representatives of confessional bodies, with representatives of the W.C.C.

Organic Church Unions The relations of the Orthodox Churches to other Churches are almost in their beginnings. A solid step forward is the formation of joint doctrinal commissions of the Orthodox with Anglican, Old Catholic, and Oriental Orthodox Churches.

Regional and National Councils Eastern and Oriental Orthodox Churches participate in these councils. Orthodox Churches and jurisdictions are members of the National Christian Councils of Poland, Czechoslovakia, the United Arab Republic, Great Britain, the United States of America, Canada, and Australia. The Syrian Orthodox Church is a member of the Regional Council of Churches in the Middle East. Orthodox Churches are members of the All-Africa Conference of Churches, of the East Asia Christian Council, and of the European Conference of Churches.

Orthodoxy and the World Council of Churches

Eastern Orthodoxy, without compromising her ecclesiological claims of being the one and true Church of Christ, takes part almost unanimously in the ecumenical movement. Today the following Orthodox Patriarchates, autocephalous or autonomous Churches, are members of the World Council of Churches: (1) Constantinople (2) Alexandria (3) Antioch (4) Jerusalem (5) Russia (6) Serbia (7) Rumania (8) Bulgaria (9) Cyprus (10) Greece (11) Poland

[1] N. A. Nissiotis. "Kirche und Welt in Orthodoxer Sicht", *Evangelisches Verlagswerk* Stuttgart 1968.

L

(12) Iberia (Georgia) (13) Czechoslovakia (14) Russian Orthodox of America (15) Archbishopric of the Patriarchate of Antioch in America (16) Rumanian Orthodox Episcopate in America. With the exception of the Orthodox Church of Albania the whole of Eastern Orthodoxy holds membership in the World Council of Churches.

Official co-operation with the ecumenical movement started as long ago as 1920 when the Ecumenical Patriarch, then the Metropolitan of Thyateira, Germanos, sent delegates to the preliminary meeting on Faith and Order which was held in Geneva. Until the year 1937, when it was decided to unite the two movements of Life and Work and Faith and Order in one organiza-tion, the World Council of Churches, participation of Orthodox Churches was unanimous, with the exception of the Russian Orthodox Church, which could not get into touch with the ecumenical movement because of political persecution until later. After 1937 co-operation continued with Life and Work, but the Orthodox stand within Faith and Order was not the same.

While the ecumenical movement appeared to be understood and practised only by a handful of clerics and professors of theology, with little impact on the wider membership of the Church, professors of religious philosophy and theology, including the Russians Berdyaev, Bulgakow, Ilmin, and Frank, through their writings had a broad influence on Western Christianity and broadened the understanding of Orthodox thought and literature.

When the World Council of Churches came formally into existence in 1948, it confronted the Orthodox Churches with new problems. The Russian Orthodox Church, which was unable to have contact with the ecumenical movement until after the Second World War, was not prepared for the new event. Consequently the Conference of Orthodox Churches called in Moscow in July of 1948 decided "to decline participation in the ecumenical movement, in its present form". In addition to the Moscow Patriarchate, the Orthodox Churches of Serbia, Rumania, Poland, Albania, Bulgaria, Czechoslovakia, and of Alexandria and Antioch, joined in rejecting membership. Their statement showed lack of knowledge of the nature and work of the World Council of Churches. They accused the W.C.C. of intending to form "an ecumenical church", of projecting social and political activity "which was a diversion of the church's labours towards the taking of human souls . . .", of "losing faith too soon in the possibility of union in one Holy, Catholic and Apostolic Church", and of reducing its statement of purpose "to the simple recognition of Christ as our Lord" which "lowers the Christian faith to such a degree as to be accessible even to the devils". These misunderstandings were cleared up and the position changed radically by 1961 when the Russian Orthodox Church and others entered the World Council of Churches.

The Ecumenical Patriarchate, as we have seen earlier, took a more co-operative attitude in its 1952 encyclical, which approved as "necessary" the participation by the Orthodox Churches in the W.C.C. The practical co-operation as envisaged by the W.C.C. was seen as a "task pleasing to God as an attempt and a manifestation of a noble desire that the churches of Christ should face together the great problems of humanity". It enabled the Orthodox Church "to make known and to impart to the heterodox the riches of her faith, worship and order and her religious and ascetic experience". It would also help Orthodox Churches to learn about new methods and conceptions of church life and activity which would be of great benefit to them. But the Orthodox must avoid discussion of dogmas in the Commission on Faith and Order, must study and act together on problems raised in the W.C.C., and must adopt a reserved attitude towards the worship of the non-Orthodox and celebrate their own worship services.

But the restriction concerning Faith and Order has also been softened. Now delegates of the Ecumenical Patriarchate and the other Orthodox Churches have taken and are taking part in the work of the W.C.C. secretariat of Faith and Order. The way to implement the suggested policy in relation to Faith and Order has been left to the personal discretion of each delegate.

A sign of the change of feelings and the improved relations is seen in the letter of Patriarch Alexii of Moscow to W. A. Visser 't Hooft, the General Secretary of the World Council of Churches, under date of 1 April 1961. It said in part:

> We declare our agreement with the Basis of the World Council of Churches as expressed in paragraph one of its Constitution . . . The Russian Orthodox Church has always attached the utmost importance to the problems of mutual *rapprochement* between all Christians, the deepening of mutual understanding among committed Christians and the strengthening of universal brotherhood, love and peace among the nations on the basis of the Gospel.

The letter said that the Russian Orthodox Church counted on the W.C.C. to strengthen the spirit of ecumenical brotherhood and that that Church

> . . . is fully determined to make her contribution to the great task of Christian unity on the lines of the previous movements of "Faith and Order", "Life and Work" and "International Friendship through the Churches" which now find their common expression in the different forms and aspects of the activities of the World Council of Churches.

When the Russian Orthodox Church entered into membership of the W.C.C. at New Dehli in the same year, the Orthodox Churches of Rumania, Bulgaria, and Poland were also received into membership. The Patriarchate of Jerusalem, whose name appeared in the official documents of the W.C.C. as one of its members, also sent delegates. Following these the Orthodox Churches of Iberia (Georgia), Serbia, and Czechoslovakia came in 1962, 1965, and 1966 respectively into the membership of the W.C.C. To the Second World Assembly of Churches, which was held in the U.S.A. in 1954, came the Orthodox Churches of Constantinople, Antioch, Cyprus, Greece, the autonomous Russian Orthodox Church in America, the Rumanian Episcopate in America, and the Archbishopric of the Church of Antioch in America.

Many factors helped to bring about the remarkable change which took place in the relations of the Russian Orthodox Church and the W.C.C. between 1948 and 1961. One of these was the act of the W.C.C. secretariat in sending to the Moscow Patriarchate all of the publications relating to the Second Assembly of the World Council of Churches in 1954. This opened a correspondence which had constructive results. At Utrecht, Holland in 1958 there was a meeting between the W.C.C. and Russian Orthodox representatives at which many questions were asked and answered. Meetings of the Central Committee of the W.C.C. were opened to observers of the Russian Church, as to others. Finally, an official W.C.C. delegation went in December 1959 to visit the Moscow Patriarchate.

Co-operation between the Eastern Orthodox and the World Council of Churches is indicated by figures showing participation by Orthodox in World Assemblies of Churches. In the First Assembly at Amsterdam, eighty-five seats out of a total of 351 official delegates were assigned to Orthodox but only thirteen seats were filled by participating delegates. A few other Orthodox were present in various capacities. At the Second Assembly (Evanston 1954), out of 502 delegates, thirty Orthodox were present as delegates. At the Third Assembly (New Dehli 1961) out of 600 delegates there were sixty-four Orthodox, but with the admission of the Russian and other Churches the number rose to close on 100. In the Fourth Assembly (Uppsala 1968) the Orthodox had 160 seats assigned out of a total of 800 delegates. While not all were able to attend, the Orthodox delegation was one of the largest in the Assembly. The steady growth in numbers has a psychological effect on the Orthodox, helping them to throw off the inferiority complex implicit in a small representation amidst large delegations of Western Christians. For the first time, at Uppsala, Orthodox participation in a World Council Assembly was numerous, wholehearted, and contributed greatly to the value of the Assembly at all levels.

In the World Council of Churches, the Orthodox delegates seem to have been able to present a common line in dogmatic–ecclesiological matters, with some differences among them on external and social questions. They continue to meet together and to follow a common line in the discussions. Since the New Delhi Assembly, however, the Orthodox have refrained from presenting to the Assembly as a whole separate declarations on points of major difference. Previously on a number of occasions such declarations were· made. Now Orthodox delegates are content to make the voice of Orthodoxy heard in discussions within the separate sections, resulting in some influence on the official reports. Orthodox serve as officers in the General Assemblies and give their share of the major addresses. A strong effort is now made by Orthodox leaders to make sure that their delegates are well prepared to participate in the discussions. One of the six Presidents of the W.C.C. at Uppsala was Archbishop Iakovos, Primate of America. Before him Orthodox who had served as presidents were Germanos of Thyateira (1948–51), Athenagoras of Thyateria (1951–4), and Michael of America (1954–8). At Uppsala, the Serbian Orthodox Patriarch was elected to the presidency.

Several developments at New Delhi were the result of the efforts of Orthodox, among others, to influence the World Council of Churches. Perhaps the most important of these was the change in the first article of "Basis" of the constitution of the World Council of Churches. As voted at New Delhi, the "Basis" now includes the trinitarian formula: "The World Council of Churches is a fellowship of churches which confess the Lord

Jesus as God and Saviour according to the Scriptures and therefore seek to fulfil together their common calling to the glory of the one God, Father, Son and Holy Spirit".

Other changes which particularly pleased the Orthodox were the approval of the document opposing proselytism and the New Delhi statement on the unity of the Church, emphasizing unity among "all in each place". Finally, the Orthodox approved the enactment of integration of the International Missionary Council and the World Council of Churches. The vote was taken in a plenary session chaired by Archbishop Iakovos, after several modifications were made in the draft document to meet criticisms, including those of the Orthodox.

In 1955 the Ecumenical Patriarchate established its office for liaison at the headquarters of the World Council of Churches in Geneva. Its first Director was the Bishop of Melita, now Archbishop of America, Iakovos, who grew into one of the leading ecumenicists. His successor since 1959 is Metropolitan Emilianos of Calabria. The office is another sign of continuous interest and co-operation on the part of the Ecumenical Patriarchate. Of similar interest and purpose was the establishment in 1962 of an office of the same nature at W.C.C. headquarters by the Church of Russia, with Proto-Presbyter Vitali Borovoy as its Director. He presently serves also as an Associate Director of the Faith and Order Commission. Other Orthodox officers at the World Council include Fr George Tsetsis, Co-Secretary of the Orthodox Churches in the Division of Inter-Church Aid, Refugee, and World Service, and Professor Nikos Nissiotis, Director of the Ecumenical Institute and Associate General Secretary of the W.C.C.

The holding of ecumenical meetings and conferences in Orthodox territories has aided the growth of knowledge and co-operation. Central Committee meetings of the W.C.C. met in Rhodes in 1959 and in Crete in 1967. Members and staff of this annual meeting total around 200 people. The W.C.C. Executive Committee met at the invitation of the Orthodox Church of Russia in Odessa in 1964; the Working Committee of the Secretariat of Faith and Order met at Zagorsk near Moscow in 1966. We have already mentioned that conferences of youth and laity met in Lebanon in 1955, 1964, and 1967.

It is also important that when the World Council holds meetings and conferences the Orthodox are given opportunities to meet among themselves. Meetings of Eastern Orthodox at such times take place with the representatives of Oriental Orthodox, the Anglican and the Old Catholic Churches. Also the Secretariat on Faith and Order has called unofficial meetings for theological discussion between Orthodox and Protestant (in Greece in 1959 and in Montreal in 1963), and of Eastern Orthodox with Oriental Orthodox (in Denmark 1964 and in England in 1967). All of these contribute to better understanding.

Oriental Orthodox Churches and the W.C.C.

The Church of Ethiopia and the Syrian Orthodox Church of India have been members of the World Council of Churches since its beginning. At the

Second World Assembly the Coptic and the Assyrian Churches entered the Council. At the Third Assembly delegates of the Syrian Orthodox Church of Syria were present. In 1962 at the Central Committee meeting in Paris the Armenian Catholicossates of Etchmiadzin and Cilicia joined the Council.

Notable personalities from the Syrian Orthodox Church of India who work or have worked at the W.C.C. headquarters in Geneva include Fr Paul Verghese, Associate General Secretary 1961–7; C. I. Itty, Associate Executive Secretary in the department of the laity since 1961; and the Reverend J. C. Joseph, Secretary for Scholarships from 1967. Among leaders of these Churches who are well known for their ecumenical work are Bishop Samuel of the Coptic Church, Bishop Karekin Sarkissian of the Armenian Catholicossate of Cilicia, and Bishop K. Philiposa of the Syrian Orthodox Church of India.

Before the 1965 Conference of Addis Ababa closed, it adopted a statement which deserves to be remembered as a keynote to the future. On relations with other member Churches of the W.C.C., it said:

> With the non-Orthodox member churches of the World Council of Churches we have cordial relations through it and we hope and pray that God will open the way for our mutual understanding and co-operation wherever possible . . . We believe that God who has brought our churches and the other member churches of the World Council of Churches together into friendly relations through that council will help us to grow in fellowship with one another and restore us all into fullness of unity in his own time and in the manner he ordains.

On the ecumenical movement, the statement said:

> Before we conclude, we would like to express a genuine appreciation of the whole ecumenical movement such as that made manifest through the World Council of Churches. The new spirit of fellowship, mutual understanding and co-operation fostered by the ecumenical movement has had beneficial effects in the life of all the churches involved. We hope and pray that God will strengthen every effort made for the progress of the ecumenical movement to enable the churches to fulfil their mission through common and concerted efforts in ever greater faithfulness to our common Lord, Jesus Christ.

Evaluation

The ecumenical movement will acquire its full ecumenical form with the eventual and complete participation of the Roman Catholic Church. Meanwhile, the presence of Eastern and Oriental Orthodox Churches within that movement gives it a pan-Christian and not solely a Protestant character, although many of its structures, forms of thought, publications, and officers still belong mainly to the Protestant world. In the ecumenical movement, East and West are finding a common ground and a common language.

Orthodox participation in the W.C.C. has on some occasions been thought of as lacking in balance, in consistency, continuity, and wholeness. To some extent, this is true in comparison with Western Churches. This was probably because of the divided line of action taken by the Orthodox, the unpreparedness of some Orthodox delegates, and their inability to follow the discussions, due to language deficiencies.

The negative attitude against ecumenism taken by conservative Orthodox circles has not helped. The number of well-prepared Orthodox ecumenists, participating in the activities of the Council and working in the ecumenical movement at various levels, is much too small. Since Orthodoxy is now a full partner in the movement, there is a great need to have as many as possible able and well-prepared persons to deal adequately with ecumenical affairs, to work in them and to fill the existing gaps. Orthodox theology should work consistently to prepare these persons.

Participation in the ecumenical movement presents challenges to Orthodoxy. Fr Bobrinskoy says:

> In its confrontation with the churches of Rome and of the Reformation, contemporary Orthodoxy, forced out of its many centuries of isolation, is rediscovering its universal dimensions and is compelled to answer in new terms the question: What is the message of Orthodoxy? It is in terms of plenitude, of experience of trinitarian life, of the divine life radiant in Christians through eucharistic communion that this answer must be built up.

He concludes by saying that the substance of the message of Orthodoxy is inseparable from an attitude of humility and penitence.

My own conclusion is that a process of give and take is in existence between those Churches which participate in the ecumenical movement.

The Orthodox are prepared to learn from others simplicity in personal life, schemes of piety, and Christian life, methods of work, progress in the art of preaching and in the whole field of the expression of Christianity to the world. The Orthodox, meeting the non-Orthodox, are conscious of the enormous progress made by them in theology and especially in some branches of it, such as the comparative study of religions, social Christianity, pastoral psychology, biblical studies, and they try to profit from the work of scholarship carried out by other Churches. The Orthodox know well to what extent others have helped them on the practical level through the many-sided assistance rendered by inter-Church aid, in which Christian love is so abundantly operating.

The presence of Orthodoxy in the ecumenical movement is a witness of Orthodox faith and worship made available for others. She presents to the western world the dimensions and experiences of a Christianity which goes back through an historic continuity and a living tradition to the beginnings of the Faith. The western world has shown a keen interest in the concept of dogma, the liturgical life, the patristic spirit, the religious, mystical, and ascetic concepts of Christian experience, and the work of scholarship to be found in Orthodoxy.

The future lies in the hands of God.

12

The Ecumenical Movement
and the Roman Catholic Church

LUKAS VISCHER

Introduction

The Roman Catholic Church underwent great changes in the years dealt with in this volume. The ecumenical movement unexpectedly gained ground. Whereas at the time when the World Council of Churches was founded at Amsterdam the ecumenical movement and the Roman Catholic Church could with some justification be set in contrast, after the pontificate of John XXIII and the Second Vatican Council such a contrast no longer accorded with the facts. The Roman Catholic Church became increasingly influenced by the movement and is now playing an ever more active role within it.

It is obviously impossible to tell the story of this change in a few pages with any adequacy. Twenty years ago it was a simpler story. The Roman Catholic Church stood aside; the official pronouncements and decisions documenting this attitude took little time to summarize. The essentials could be presented by listing the efforts of scattered individual pioneers and small groups overshadowed by this official attitude. Today, however, the subject proves much harder to survey. The ecumenical movement influences the Roman Catholic Church in so many ways that a true picture can be given only by taking account of the entire life of the Church in all its forms. It is no longer possible to limit the theme. Once genuine relationships with the other Churches had been established, everything assumed importance for the Churches' relationships with one another. At the same time the Second Vatican Council shattered the uniformity of the Roman Catholic Church. Many things became fluid. The variety which had indeed always been characteristic of the Roman Catholic Church became more patent, and so our account must cover the new developments in particular sections of the Church.

But the complications do not end there. We are still so close to the events that an objective survey is hardly possible. Many of the cross-connections are not yet clear. All the sources are not yet accessible. How often has the historical pattern been transformed by the discovery of some original documents or letters which put a completely different complexion on certain events! Temporal proximity to events has the advantage of ensuring freshness of recollection, but its drawback is a greater degree of distortion in the picture as a result of personal experience and interests. Most of the accounts appearing today, therefore, present only part of the story. Certain factors are overstressed, others omitted. Everyone tends to give pride of place to what seems to him impressive and significant for the future.

The greatest difficulty, however, is that the change to be described here is still in process. In what direction will the Roman Catholic Church be led? What will the upheaval of recent years mean for the Churches generally? Are they already beginning to absorb the shock? Or is the Second Vatican Council only one of a continuing series of shocks? Will the Council finally go down in history as the beginning of a great renewal or will the future historian see it as the beginning of a decline? Again, what form will the future relationship of the Churches to one another take? Will the Churches successfully develop a viable fellowship? Or will they simply continue their coexistence? These are all still open questions today and the factors affecting

313

future developments are so imponderable that it is impossible to predict the answer to them. Again, our picture of the past will itself inevitably change in accordance with future developments. What has happened will all at once acquire fresh meaning. Every representation of the recent past is fraught with this uncertainty and every interpretation will prove to have been influenced by personal hopes and expectations. The account which follows will be no exception.

From the End of the Second World War to the Death of Pius XII (1945–58)

If we consult the official documents of these years we get the impression, at least at first glance, that the ecumenical movement presented no real problem at all to the Roman Catholic Church of that period. Its response seemed to be settled in advance and the concept of unity underlying its pronouncements so clear and unambiguous that dialogue or even any kind of discussion seemed pointless. This impression is, however, misleading. In reality, the history of those years was marked by considerable tensions. Although official documents and obviously many theologians as well[1] call to mind the concept of unity influenced by the Counter-Reformation and the First Vatican Council, a growing number of theologians were seeking to investigate the questions raised by the ecumenical movement and to offer new answers. In Roman Catholic circles there was a deepening interest in the work of the ecumenical movement and the discussion was marked by increased personal involvement. The official statements of the Magisterium indirectly demonstrate the vigour of this trend. Warnings were felt to be necessary because the Church's official position was in fact being questioned.

The years immediately following the Second World War were notable for an extraordinary movement towards unity. The confessional walls had become transparent as never before. On the non-Roman side the movement led to the founding of the World Council of Churches and, although this was the implementation of an old plan, the energy and enthusiasm with which this was done can be explained only by the mood of those years. Something of this movement to unity was also at work in the Roman Catholic Church. War-time experiences as well as present tasks demanded a coming together of divided Christians. Representatives of different confessions had shared persecution, made common cause on behalf of the Jews, met in concentration camps and in the resistance movement against National Socialism. They had suddenly found themsleves in an unexpected solidarity of contemporary witness to the truth.[2]

---

[1] Cf., for example, E. F. Hanahoe, *Catholic Ecumenism* (Washington 1953); an extremely naive presentation of the ecumenical problem. "All elements are clearly in evidence: the point of departure, the goal to be sought, and the way towards its realisation" (p. 43).

[2] It was certainly no accident that the ecumenical idea gained most ground wherever these experiences had been most deeply felt. When later, at the Second Vatican Council, Dutch, French, and German bishops in particular supported the ecumenical movement of the Church, the comment was made with some justice that the "hand of Hitler" could be seen here.

In these situations many abiding friendships were formed. These friendships ought surely to be maintained. The war had brought with it the transplantation of whole peoples. Even where the war had had no direct influence, the increasing mobility of society led to an ever greater intermingling of the confessions. The number of mixed marriages grew. It was surely essential to establish a new relationship between the confessions. Above all, the Churches were involved in the upheavals which the war brought in its wake not merely in Europe and America but throughout the world. They found themselves faced with gigantic new tasks. Not surprisingly the view gained ground that past confessional conflicts could no longer automatically be regarded as present problems and that by persisting in these conflicts the Churches might be neglecting their proper tasks. All these factors called in question the traditional confessional structure. Although they were not enough to produce a new attitude in the Roman Catholic Church, they did lead to many meetings and to the formation of mixed groups and similar activities in the early postwar years.

But the impetus did not come only from external factors; the development of Roman Catholic theology also played its part. The liturgical movement, stressing what is original and primitive and also pastoral responsibility towards modern man, gave worship a new character and laid the foundation for deeper understanding between the confessions. The new concern for holy Scripture brought into prominence the common authority to which all the divided Churches owed obedience. The outstanding work of Roman Catholics in the field of biblical scholarship almost inevitably made it imperative to re-examine the long-standing controversial question of the relation between Scripture and tradition, an investigation which, at the same time and quite independently, was also being undertaken in the non-Roman Churches.[1]

The greatest stimulus, however, came from the increasingly significant discussion of the nature of the Church. What is the Church? What is the task which Christ has entrusted to the Church? How is the Church to fulfil this task through all its members, both clerical and lay? In both theology and practice these questions began to come to the fore. As the traditional ecclesiology was deepened, so the problem of unity was also seen in a new light. Since ecclesiology had as a result of the ecumenical movement become a major theme in the non-Roman Churches as well, a host of new points of contact resulted. True, the special ecclesiological convictions of the Roman Catholic Church made it a difficult encounter, but the very difficulty forced non-Roman theologians to fresh thinking. Here it proved a happy chance that

---

[1]It was also no accident that the Faith and Order Commission decided after the Third World Conference at Lund (1952) to indicate a study of the problem of tradition. The theme was an obvious choice. A survey of the most important works of both Roman Catholic and other writers in the period 1930–62 may be found in *Schrift und Tradition*, ed. K. E. Skydsgaard and Lukas Vischer (Zürich 1963). Among Roman Catholic theologians particular mention should be made of J. R. Geiselmann, *Lebendiger Glaube aus geheiligter Überlieferung* (Mainz 1942) and *Jesus der Christus* (Stuttgart 1951); later G. H. Tavard, *Holy Writ or Holy Church, The Crisis of Protestant Reformation* (London 1959); and Yves Congar, *La tradition et les traditions* (Paris 1960).

the First Vatican Council had not reached the point of defining a full ecclesiology. Roman Catholic theologians were thus able to deal with this theme more freely and to establish new standpoints.[1]

The decisions of the Magisterium certainly appeared soon to call a halt to this development and, although at first it may still have been reasonable to hope that the Roman Church might play an active part in the ecumenical movement, any such hope seemed in the years that followed doomed to extinction.

The attitude of the Holy See continued to be determined by the conviction that, as the one body of Christ, the Roman Catholic Church could and should fulfil the task committed to that body by its Lord. There can be no denying the achievements accomplished on the basis of this conviction. The pontificate of Pius XII undoubtedly helped to strengthen respect for the Roman Catholic Church and to extend its influence. The Pope's speeches and allocutions contain many proofs of an astonishing awareness of contemporary problems.[2] But this view of Roman Catholic responsibility excluded any genuine understanding of the ecumenical movement and its problems.

Many Roman Catholic theologians had hoped that their Church would be represented at the First Assembly at Amsterdam at least by a few observers. A list of ten possible participants had been drawn up in private conversations. Since at that time it was still possible to assume that the national hierarchies were competent in the matter, it was submitted to Cardinal de Jong of Utrecht. In a *Monitum* of 5 June 1948, however, the Vatican issued a reminder that only the Holy Office could give permission to participate in an international gathering, and it soon afterwards became clear that no official permission would be forthcoming for such participation. Only a few Roman Catholic theologians were able to follow the Assembly's proceedings, unobtrusively (eg. Father C. Boyer). A year and half later the *Instructio Ecclesia catholica* was issued (20 December 1949; published 1 March 1950). Although this text recognized that the movement towards unity was the work of the Holy Spirit in men's hearts, its main thrust was that of warning. References to the encyclicals *Mortalium animos* and *Mystici corporis* recalled the Roman Catholic understanding of unity. The danger of all irenic attitudes was stressed. Roman Catholic teaching had to be presented as a whole and without a watering down of any of its parts.

---

[1] Cf., for example, Yves Congar, "Notes sur les mots 'Confession', 'Eglise', et 'Communion'", *Irenikon* xxii (1950), pp. 3ff; H. de Lubac, *Méditations sur l'Eglise* (Paris 1953); K. Rahner, *Die Frieheit in der Kirche, Lebendiges Zeugnis* (1953), pp. 21ff; M. Villain and J. Baciocchi, *La vocation de l'Eglise* (Paris 1953); detailed bibliography in Ulrich Valeske, *Votum ecclesiae* (Munich 1962). It is significant that Roman Catholic ecumenists relatively seldom dealt with the problem of mission. The divisions of the Church in its missionary outreach had been, for the non-Roman Churches, a primary impetus in the formation of the ecumenical movement, and the call for common witness was one of the major themes from the Edinburgh Missionary Conference onwards. Roman Catholic Christians obviously felt this urgency less; they started rather from the view that the Church by its very nature had to be one.

[2] Cf. *Discorsi e radiomessagi di Sua Santità Pio XII*. 20 vols. Città del Vaticano 1941–59.

Opinons which had been put forward by Roman Catholic ecumenists were condemned as an abandonment of Roman Catholic convictions. Permission from the hierarchy was required for participation in meetings to further the unity of all Christians and precise instructions were given about the authority competent to grant such permission.[1]

More important than this *Instructio* was the encyclical *Humani generis*, which was issued a few months later (12 August 1950).[2] This document was more wide-ranging. It was concerned that the purity of doctrine might be endangered. Even its opening sentences refer to mistaken views which call in question the fundamentals of Catholic doctrine. It was not only outside the Church that these views were to be found but even among Catholic theologians. "Some . . . desirous of novelty and fearing to be considered ignorant of recent scientific findings, tend to withdraw themselves from the Sacred Teaching authority" (para. 11). The encyclical vigorously attacked this tendency. Particular errors were enumerated. They included the idea that dogma is subject to development and has to be constantly reformulated; the relativizing of the concept as distinct from the truth as such; scepticism about the inspiration of Scripture, with a particular reference to Genesis 1–11; and distinguishing between the mystical body of Christ and the Roman Catholic Church. All these views were branded as dangerous and there was an emphatic reminder of the obligatory norms of Catholic doctrine.

This text makes a rather strange impression on anyone re-reading it now, twenty years later. Is it not precisely the ideas which were then rejected which later were to play a decisive role at the Second Vatican Council? Has not almost everything which the encyclical then mentioned only to condemn now been favourably received by the Council? The encyclical was not successful in uprooting and destroying the ideas which it regarded as emerging dangers. In one sense, *Humani generis* already contained the themes of the Second Vatican Council.

In the very same year—the Holy Year—the doctrine of the bodily assumption of Mary was solemnly promulgated (1 November 1950).[3] When the intention of making this definition was announced, many Roman Catholics and non-Roman Catholics advised against it. Their advice went unheeded. The doctrine of the Assumption was defined as binding upon the whole Church. Whereas in previous texts only warnings had been involved, this new step created a new concrete obstacle. For the first time since the First Vatican Council a pope had clearly spoken *ex cathedra*. Quite apart from the fact that a belief had thereby been proclaimed which the vast majority of non-Roman Churches did not share and which even in the view of most Roman Catholic theologians could not be established from holy Scripture and certainly not from Scripture alone, it seemed clear from this act that the Roman Catholic Church was unwilling to take account of the fellowship

[1] For the reaction of the W.C.C., see MRCC (Toronto 1950), p. 62.

[2] *Acta Apostolicae Sedis* (*AAS*) (1950), pp. 561–77.

[3] *Munificentissimus Deus*, *AAS* xlii (1950), pp. 753–71.

which had come into being as the result of the ecumenical movement. The disappointment this caused was such that in many places initially promising contacts were broken off. Reactions were frank and explicit[1] and many non-Roman Catholics saw their picture of Rome confirmed.[2] Criticisms now made contained a new element, however. They latched not merely on to doctrinal error but also on to the lack of ecumenical spirit. Increasingly the Roman Catholic Church found itself charged with lacking any interest at all in unity.

The Orthodox Churches also joined in this criticism, indeed they often expressed themselves much more forcibly. Although on the Roman Catholic side the special and substantial relationship to Orthodoxy was stressed with increasing frequency, the estrangement between the Churches was no less great. The Pope's utterances about the Churches of the East could serve only to widen the gulf. For example, the encyclical *Sempiternus rex*, which was addressed to the Eastern Churches on 8 September 1951 on the occasion of the commemoration of Chalcedon, was expressed in terms which could not but wound the Orthodox reader, as had also been the case with the earlier *Orientalis ecclesiae decus* (9 April 1944). "Let those who, because of the iniquity of the times, especially in Eastern lands, are separated from the bosom and unity of the Church, follow the teaching and example of their forefathers and not hesitate to render duly reverent homage to the Primacy of the Roman Pontiff . . . ".[3]

The Roman Catholic Church's attitude to the ecumenical movement placed the World Council of Churches in a particularly difficult position. What was its reaction to be? Was not the ecumenical movement bound to continue to direct itself to the whole of Christendom? All who confessed Jesus Christ as God and Saviour must be led together into one fellowship. Must not everything be done, therefore, to further relationships? There were indeed many who at heart, usually silently but sometimes openly, were glad that the Roman Church stood aside. Many member Churches would have been embarrassed by active co-operation. But the movement had to remain in principle open and to keep the Roman Catholic Church in view. Many leaders of the ecumenical movement openly expressed the hope that

---

[1] One of the most thorough and detailed commentaries was that produced by professors of the Theological Faculty of Heidelberg, *Evangelisches Gutachten zur Dogmatisierung der leiblichen Himmelfahrt Mariens* (Munich 1950).

[2] The Mariological encyclicals of the following years, *Fulgens corona gloriae* (8 September 1953) and *Ad caeli reginam* (11 October 1954), showed that Rome intended to continue steadily along the road once taken.

[3] *Sempiternus rex*, para. 4. On all the papal utterances concerning the Eastern Churches in the years 1850–1950, see P. E. Hermann in the periodical *Periodica de re morali et liturgica* (Rome 1950–1). Relations with the Slav Orthodox Churches were further complicated by the attitude which the Roman Catholic Church adopted towards communism. Many papal statements deal with the persecutions in the East; but the Orthodox Christians are hardly mentioned (cf. encyclical *Orientales Ecclesias* (15 December 1952). The dissolution of the Uniate Churches in the Ukraine (1946) and in Rumania (1948) created a special problem still unresolved to this day. Cf. encyclical *Orientales omnes* (1945), and a text of 17 July 1948.

ultimately even fellowship with the Roman Church might become possible.[1] The rejection was, indeed, so categorical that the World Council of Churches could develop, at least at first, only as a fellowship of non-Roman Churches. If practical co-operation of any kind was to be achieved between Churches, the attitude of the Roman Catholic Church could not be constantly taken into consideration. The essential inconsistencies of this situation frequently showed themselves, in a particularly blatant way at the Amsterdam Assembly,[2] but also on subsequent occasions. In general the World Council adopted a waiting attitude and avoided controversy as well as any special cultivation of contacts with the Roman Catholic Church.

Official statements about the ecumenical movement and negative reactions to signs of renewal in theology were clearly only the outward expression of the spirit which dominated in Rome. Theologians participating in the ecumenical movement found themselves increasingly in trouble. The Holy Office intensified its surveillance and, especially from 1950 onwards, many of them were proceeded against. During these years many of the theologians who had made a decisive contribution to the advance of ecumenical thought were warned, forbidden to publish their works, or forced to give up their work as teachers. To mention only a few who were affected in one or the other way: Yves Congar,[3] Henri de Lubac, Karl Rahner, John Courtney Murray, M. D. Chenu, Pierre Yves Féres. A period of mistrust and suspicion began. In some instances it lasted even into the pontificate of John XXIII. As late as 1962, immediately prior to the opening of the Council, two professors of the Papal Biblical Institute in Rome were temporarily suspended from their chairs.

Although these measures undoubtedly caused much suffering in the lives of many people, they could not halt the ecumenical movement. Even if ecumenical activity had to keep the limits imposed, it nevertheless still continued. A variety of levels must be mentioned here. Firstly, even in these years co-operation in theological study and scholarship was intensified. Existing societies of an academic nature continued their work and others were founded.[4] Of particular significance was the exchange in biblical and patristic studies. But even contacts of an academic nature established between particular Churches were maintained. One important example of this was the *Evangelisch–katholische ökumenische Arbeitskreis* which had been founded in Germany in 1945 with the express approval of the church authorities. Presided over by Bishop Wilhelm Stählin and Archbishop Lorenz Jaeger,

---

[1] Archbishop William Temple said, for example, in his sermon at the opening of the Second World Conference on Faith and Order: "We deeply lament the absence from this collaboration of the great Church of Rome, the Church which more than any other has known how to speak to the nations so that the nations hear" (*Second World Conference on Faith and Order*, ed. Leonard Hodgson (London 1938), p. 20).

[2] Cf. Karl Barth's comments and the ensuing controversy with Jean Daniélou in "Amsterdamer Fragen und Antworten", *Theologische Existenz Heute*, no. 15 (Munich 1949).

[3] Cf. Yves Congar, *Chrétiens en dialogue* (Paris 1964), pp. xlv–lvii.

[4] Societas Veteris Testamenti, 1950; Societas Novi Testamenti; International Patristic Conference, 1952.

it met annually to discuss some important controversial theological subject.[1]

In these years a special part was played by a number of fraternities (for example the *Michaelsbruderschaft*), by certain Anglican orders, and above all by the monastic community at Taizé. Because of their own spiritual interests and aims, these communities had natural points of contact with the Roman Catholic Church and, since they did not represent the Church as such, they enjoyed much more freedom of movement.[2] The Taizé brothers in particular helped to prepare many Roman Catholics and Protestants for the ecumenical discussion. On the Roman Catholic side, special mention must be made of the Istina Centre, directed by Father Christophe Dumont, o.s.p., and the Benedictine Monasteries at Chevetogne and Niederaltaich.

Relations with the World Council were not severed either. Roman Catholic theologians followed its work with the greatest interest. It has often been said that the findings of the World Council were far more carefully studied, analysed, and interpreted on the Roman Catholic side than they were in many member Churches. This work of interpretation did not pass unheeded in the World Council and it is no exaggeration to say that in this quiet and unobtrusive way Roman Catholic theology was a continuing partner in the discussions in the World Council. Except for the Roman Catholic contribution many questions would have been posed differently. In particular, Roman Catholic theologians joined in the discussion of the ecclesiological significance of the World Council of Churches and when the World Council in 1950 was drawing up its statement *The Church, the Churches and the World Council of Churches*, the so-called Toronto statement, a discussion took place in Paris at the Istina Centre with Roman Catholic theologians. This exchange had considerable influence on the drafting of the document.[3]

An important step taken in 1952 was the founding of the *Conférence catholique pour les questions oecuméniques*, the purpose of which was to bring together Roman Catholic ecumenists for regular discussions. The initiative came from the two Dutch priests, Frans Thijssen and Jan Willebrands; the latter became its secretary. The very first theme for discussion obviously bore upon the World Council, namely, the Roman Catholic view of the *vestigia ecclesiae*, a term which had been employed in the Toronto statement. At the end of 1953, Father Willebrands established direct contact with the World Council and from then on the work of the *Conférence* was focused even more closely on the studies being pursued by the World Council. Preparations for the Second Assembly of the World Council of Churches in Evanston (1954) provided an appropriate occasion for a Roman Catholic statement. The *Conférence* produced a detailed study of the Evanston theme, "Christ—the Hope of the World". Father Yves Congar with others played

---

[1] A selection of the addresses given has been collected into a special volume; cf. *Pro Veritate, ein theologischer Dialog* (Münster-Kassel 1963), ed. Edmund Schlink and Hermann Volk.

[2] This freedom led occasionally to serious tensions with the Church to which the community was most closely related.

[3] Among the participants was Father Jérôme Hamer, o.p. He has since then frequently written on the questions raised by the Toronto statement.

a large part in drafting this document. Since it was rather late in arriving, it could only be duplicated and distributed at Evanston, otherwise it would certainly have left an even deeper mark on the discussion and reports.

Contacts with the *Conférence* from the World Council side were primarily in the hands of Pastor Hans-Heinrich Harms who at that time was working in the Division of Studies of the World Council. On several occasions he visited Rome to meet with Roman Catholic theologians. The Evanston Assembly had decided that the central theme for the World Council's study programme should be "The Lordship of Christ over the World and the Church". In 1956 the *Conférence* adopted this theme and after much correspondence it was arranged to hold a joint meeting in Assisi. The meeting was to have been held in 1960 and might well have been the open culmination of a more or less secret dialogue. But the proposed meeting had in the end to be abandoned through a serious deterioration of relations caused by an incident at the Central Committee's meeting in Rhodes, 1959.[1]

The deepening of relationships was the fruit, above all, of the contacts made in connection with the Week of Prayer for Christian Unity. These annual weeks provided an opportunity for representatives of different confessions to meet together in a frank and natural way, to pray together and to reflect upon the significance of the ecumenical movement. Many received the first stimulus towards their "ecumenical conversion" during these Weeks of Prayer.

Prayer for unity still faced one great difficulty at that time. On the Roman Catholic side there was no agreement about the way unity should be prayed for. The formula suggested by Abbé Paul Couturier: "to pray for the unity of the Church of Jesus Christ as He wills and when He wills", was not universally accepted. Indeed, it was vigorously opposed by many who regarded it as a dilution of fundamental convictions and above all, as a source of misunderstandings. Those who opposed it demanded that the specifically Roman Catholic understanding of unity should be clearly stated during these Weeks of Prayer. The chief exponents of this position were the Friars of the Atonement in the United States. Each year they produced material for the Week of Prayer from this standpoint and their literature was widely distributed in many countries. Their line was supported by Father Charles Boyer and the Unitas Centre in Rome which he directed. In numerous articles in his journal *Unitas*, Father Boyer urged the need to insist quite clearly on the principles of unity.[2]

The work done by Abbé Couturier in Lyons, and after his death in 1956 by Father Pierre Michalon, won increasing support in ever widening circles of the Roman Catholic Church. With every year the numbers of those prepared for joint prayer in this sense grew. Abbé Paul Couturier for this reason deserves a special place in the history of the ecumenical movement.[3] It was not surprising that the ceremonies in Lyons following his death

---

[1] See below, p. 326.

[2] Cf., for example, Father C. Boyer, "Le intenzioni della settimana dell'unità", *Unitas* (1960), pp. 97f.

[3] Cf. Maurice Villain, *L'Abbé Paul Couturier* (Louvain 1959)[3].

assumed the proportions of a moving demonstration of the growing ecumenical fellowship.

In the following years co-operation with the World Council continued to develop. As early as 1942 the Faith and Order movement had decided to change the timing of the Week of Prayer, which had remained unchanged since 1920, in order to facilitate joint prayer with Roman Catholics. From 1958 onwards the preparation of material for the Week was co-ordinated and from 1960 onwards was discussed together in detail.[1]

The problem of conflicting intentions in such prayer for unity was explicitly and finally resolved after the Second Vatican Council. In 1966 complete agreement was reached between the Roman Catholic Church and the World Council of Churches concerning preparations for the Week of Prayer,[2] and since then the introductory leaflets for the Week of Prayer have been prepared by a mixed group.

All these pointers show how the ecumenical movement, despite all the difficulties, made further progress in the Roman Catholic Church beneath the surface. When John XXIII was elected Pope and shortly afterwards announced the calling of a Roman Catholic Council, the forces were already at hand to give shape to genuine ecumenical intentions, and the voices of theologians who had stood firm for their convictions and who had experienced hard times, now had the more weight just because of this spiritual trial.[3] Many of them played an important part at the Second Vatican Council and were shown marks of esteem which contrasted strangely with their earlier experiences.

The Pontificate of John XXIII and the Beginning of the Second Vatican Council

Pope Pius XII died in October 1958 and at the end of that month Cardinal Angelo Guiseppe Roncalli was elected to succeed him. Within a few months it became clear that this election would mark the beginning of a new era not only for the Roman Catholic Church but also for the ecumenical movement. On 25 January 1959 Pope John XXIII announced, to the surprise of the entire world and even of the circles closest to him, the calling of an "Ecumenical Council". The Pope himself declared that the decision had been a sudden inspiration "like the spontaneous flower of an unexpected springtime".[4] The idea had in fact suggested itself to some of his predecessors.

[1] Among these developments must be mentioned, for example, the setting up of the Conference to Promote Prayer for Unity in the United Kingdom. The suggestion of mutual collections, originally made by Oscar Cullmann in 1958, has played in important part in many places; cf. Oscar Cullmann, *Catholics and Protestants, A Proposal for Realizing Christian Solidarity* (London 1960).

[2] Cf. *Prayer for Unity:* The report of the consultation on "The Future of the Week of Prayer for Christian Unity" (Geneva, October 1966) in *One in Christ* (1967), pp. 251ff.

[3] "At the very moment when the Holy See emerged from its semi-absenteeism in ecumenical matters, it found the ground already turned over and sown, covered with a sturdy and already considerable crop."—Yves Congar, *Chrétiens en dialogue* (1964), p. liii.

[4] *Acta et documenta Concilio Oecumenica Vaticano II apparando* (Rome 1960), p. 45.

Pius XI[1] as well as Pius XII had seriously considered calling a Council. Pius XII reflected on the idea in the years 1949 to 1951 and a Commission appointed by him had explored the possibility in detail.[2] One may well wonder what would have emerged from a Council convened at such a time! Historically there is not much point in asking this question, however, because at that time the decision to hold a Council could hardly be taken; the Commission had to come to the conclusion that such an undertaking would involve too many risks.

What distinguished John XXIII's plan from earlier ones was the fact that he made his decision and announced it before giving commissions the task of weighing the pros and cons in detail and of establishing the procedure. This fact was of the greatest significance for the Council's course. The very absence of precise terms of reference at the beginning stirred the imagination and secured the attention of a far greater public. In a sense the charismatic decision was itself an appeal to the charismatic forces in the Church. Theologians and lay people began to speak of the renewal of the Church; the Roman Catholic Church began to live "in outline".

This new attitude was important for the ecumenical movement as well. The announcement did at first give rise to misunderstandings. Because the meaning attached to the term "ecumenical" in official Roman Catholic usage was not widely known, many thought that what was proposed was an inter-confessional assembly or that the real aim of the proposed Council was the reunion of Christendom. This assumption seemed to be justified by many utterances in the early days.[3] It was, however, quickly made clear that what was intended was an assembly of all the Roman Catholic bishops and that the main purpose was the renewal of the Roman Catholic Church. Only indirectly would the work of the Council promote the unity of all Christians. The Pope's own understanding of unity did not greatly differ from the traditional view. Like his predecessors he often spoke of return as the only way to unity.

> May this marvellous spectacle of unity which distinguishes the Catholic Church and which is a luminous example for all, together with her entreaties and prayers by which she implores of God the same unity for all, serve as an incitement to your mind and move it in a salutary manner. We say "your", for we are speaking to those who are separated from this Holy See . . . Note, we beg of you, that when we lovingly invite you to the unity of the Church we are inviting you not to the home of a stranger but to your own, to the Father's house which belongs to all . . .[4]

Although these papal utterances seemed to herald no decisive changes, the

---

[1] "Giovanni Caprile, Pio XI e la ripresa del Concilio Vaticano", *Civiltà Cattolica* (1966), qu. 2785, pp. 27–39.

[2] "Giovanni Caprile, Pio XII e un nuovo progetto di Concilio Ecumenico", *Civiltà Cattolica* (1966), qu. 2787–8, pp. 209–28.

[3] John XXIII declared, for example, on 30 January 1959, with reference to the Churches of the East: "We have no wish to conduct a trial of history. We have no wish to try to show who was right and who was wrong. Responsibility is shared. We simply wish to say: "Let us come together and make an end of divisions."

[4] Encyclical *Ad Petri cathedram* (29 June 1959), *AAS* LI, pp. 498ff.

opening announcement nevertheless continued to exercise great influence. Ideas which hitherto had been considered in relatively limited ecumenical circles were all at once thrown into the public discussion. The dam erected by *Humani generis* began to collapse. The chorus of voices urging that the way to unity should be seen not as a return but rather as the common renewal of all the Churches grew stronger. The Council should open the doors to this process. Polemics should give way to dialogue and the Roman Catholic Church should begin to learn from other Churches in the dialogue and adopt whatever might promote her own renewal. Although the validity of earlier statements was not in doubt, there was a great deal which might be glossed, interpreted, or restated for the sake of truth and for the sake of unity with the separated Churches. Deeper reflection on the tradition could prove important in this connection. Above all, ecclesiology was in need of renewal and enrichment. The Council would be able to contribute much to unity indirectly, by stressing the spiritual and sacramental rather than the juridical and institutional character of the Church, by making room for greater variety in the Church, by reducing in some measure the excessive centralism of recent decades, by redefining the relationship between the hierarchy and the people of God, making much clearer the Church's character as a fellowship, by a deeper understanding of the relationship between the one Church and divided Christendom, and by laying the foundation for serious recognition of the non-Roman Churches as Churches.[1]

Soon the preparations for the Council began to take shape. On 17 May 1959 the Pope nominated a *Commissio antepraeparatoria*, with the task of sounding the views of the bishops, and on 5 June 1960 the Preparatory Commissions were appointed. The same *Motu proprio Superno Dei nutu* also provided for the establishment of a Secretariat for Promoting Christian

---

[1] Countless names would have to be listed in this connection. Obviously we must mention once again men like Yves Congar, Christophe Dumont, and Oliver Rousseau, the pioneers who had for years supported the ecumenical movement. Gustav Weigel, s.j. did great service in the cause of spreading ecumenical thought in the Roman Catholic Church in the United States; cf. *A Catholic Primer on the Ecumenical Movement* (Woodstock Papers I, 1957), but, above all, *Catholic Theology in Dialogue* (New York 1961). George H. Tavard published a new history of the ecumenical movement which enjoyed wide circulation —*Two Centuries of Ecumenism* (London 1960). Karl Rahner wrote on a whole series of problems which were later to assume importance at the Council; cf., for example, Karl Rahner and Joseph Ratzinger, *The Episcopate and the Primacy* (New York 1963). Beside the older generation, however, a younger generation now claimed a hearing. The publication which aroused most interest and was quickly translated into many languages was Hans Küng's *Konzil und Wiedervereinigung, Erneuerung als Ruf zur Einheit*, 1960 (*The Council and Reunion*, London/New York 1961)—a book which, building on ideas long common to the ecumenical movement, outlined a new view of the ecumenical problem. He was one among many. It is only possible here to mention several. Gregory Baum, *That All May Be One* (1958), had even earlier attempted to interpret the view of unity in the papal documents in such a way as to enable the views of Roman Catholic ecumenists to claim the protection of the Church authority. Bernard Lambert, *Le problème oecuménique*, 1962 (*Ecumenism: Theology and History*, London 1966) provided one of the first extensive analyses of the whole ecumenical problem, an attempt which contained a host of new starting-points. Otto B. Roegele, *Was erwarten wir vom Konzil?* (1960), wrote from the standpoint of a layman. On the other hand, of course, there was no lack of conservative presentations.

Unity.[1] Cardinal Augustin Bea was named as its first President and Monsignor Jan Willebrands as its Secretary. The Commission, which was to be responsible for the activity of the Secretariat, was composed of seventeen voting members and nineteen consultants. This was a significant step forward. Although the Secretariat had originally been created simply in order to prepare for the Council, the function it fulfilled went far beyond this, and it later became clear that it not only had an important role to play in the Council itself but would also become a permanent organ even when the Council was over. If the Roman Catholic Church wished to communicate with other Churches officially, a special organ for this purpose was required and the other Churches needed to be clear to whom they should direct their communications. To a limited extent such a channel already existed for the Orthodox Churches. But the Congregation for the Eastern Churches was primarily responsible for the Uniate Churches and was, therefore, not in an advantageous position to encourage any other relationships.

The Secretariat for Christian Unity soon set to work. Its first full meeting took place in November 1960. Its immediate task was to inform non-Roman Catholics about the Council and to make possible their participation in a limited way. The idea soon gained ground that the non-Roman Churches should be invited to be represented at the Council by observers. But the Secretariat also had a role to play in the actual preparation of the Council itself. It had to draw the attention of Commissions to views which were of importance to the ecumenical movement and it produced a number of preparatory texts (on the ecumenical movement, on religious freedom, on prayer, on the Jewish people), and on others.

With the announcement of the Council and the creation of the Secretariat for Unity, there was a gradual change in the attitude of the Roman Catholic Church towards the World Council of Churches. The World Council's own attitude was at first cautious. The Executive Committee, meeting in Geneva in February 1959, shortly after the announcement of the Council, considered the new situation in detail. A brief communiqué summarized the most important results of the discussion. It drew attention firstly to the fact that much depended on the way in which "the Council will be called" and in what spirit "the question of unity will be approached". "The question is: How ecumenical will the Council be in composition and in spirit?" The communiqué next expressed the conviction that real progress on the way to unity could be made "when churches meet together on the basis of mutual respect and with a full commitment on the part of each church to the truth of the Gospel". It added finally that it would be of great gain to the ecumenical movement if "all the churches would join in securing full religious liberty for all people in all lands", a point which was to be frequently repeated in the days to come.

This first comment by the World Council is also significant as the first in a long series. Repeatedly from that time attitudes were articulated towards the developments in the Roman Catholic Church, and anyone reading through these statements will sense a steadily growing World Council involvement in

[1] *AAS* LII (1960), p. 433.

what was occurring. They show that this inner connection was intensified from sheer necessity.

There was a temporary setback in relationships because of an unfortunate incident at the meeting of the Central Committee in Rhodes (August 1959). Roman Catholic theologians, attending the meeting as journalists, met with Orthodox delegates and discussed with them the possibility of bilateral theological discussions. This action was felt on the World Council side to have been a breach of hospitality, especially since a little later a news item broadcast by Vatican Radio left the impression that high authorities in the Vatican had authorized this contact. It took a little time for misunderstandings to be dispelled and for confidence to be restored.

The situation then changed rapidly. The World Council invited the Roman Catholic Church to send observers to the meetings of the Faith and Order Commission and of the Central Committee at St Andrews (August 1960). The invitation was accepted. Father I. Beaupère, Father J. Hamer, and Father B. Leeming attended the meeting of the Faith and Order Commission and Mgr Willebrands and Father Leeming that of the Central Committee. Cardinal Bea attached great importance to putting the World Council in the picture from the very beginning about the creation and work of the Secretariat. Mgr Willebrands visited Geneva a few days after the Pope's decision and on 22 September, i.e., before the first full session of the Secretariat, Cardinal Bea and Dr W. A. Visser't Hooft met in Milan.[1] This meeting provided an opportunity to discuss many points. On the one hand, the sending of Roman Catholic observers to the Third Assembly in New Delhi was discussed, on the other, the way in which non-Roman Catholics might participate in the Vatican Council was considered. The idea of observers was examined, and it was agreed that the Secretariat should draft more detailed proposals. At the same time, plans were made for unofficial meetings about "Renewal of the Church" and "Religious Freedom as an inter-Church problem". These informal meetings would provide an indirect contribution to the preparations for the Council.[2]

Already in these first contacts a problem emerged which would frequently reappear in the years ahead. Was it possible for the World Council as a "fellowship of churches" to enter into a direct relationship with the Roman Catholic Church? Was it qualified to conduct conversations about the sending of observers? Could it agree to being itself represented by observers? Could it adopt a position on what was happening in the Roman Catholic Church? Could it establish a Joint Working Group and initiate a whole programme of joint work? Did it not have to leave all these steps to the individual member Churches? The World Council has no authority over the member Churches. It cannot speak or act for them. Above all, in the matter of achieving church unity they alone are competent to act. On the

---

[1] Cf. Augustin Kardinal Bea—Willem A. Visser't Hooft, *Friede zwischen Christen* Herder-Bücheri 269, 1966), pp. 14f.

[2] Only the second of these two conferences took place (1–12 May 1961). It was organized by the *Conférence catholique pour les questions oecuméniques* and the World Council of Churches.

other hand, however, could the World Council remain aloof? The Churches had come together and found each other within the Council and had committed themselves to ever greater unity in a provisional fellowship; was the Council not then bound to act in their name within the limits set and to seize the opportunities which presented themselves of developing the ecumenical movement?

This dilemma finds particularly clear expression in the statement issued at the Central Committee's meeting at St Andrews (1960). The statement recalled the limited powers of the World Council, but it also stressed the need to seize the opportunities now offered:

(a) The fact that a dialogue with the Roman Catholic Church becomes possible is to be welcomed.

(b) It is to be hoped, however, that this new development will not mean that the informal discussions which have been going on between Roman Catholic theologians and those of other churches will henceforth be entirely superseded by more official discussions, for at the present stage it is precisely the informal discussions which can best contribute to the removal of misunderstanding.

(c) No church should fear that the W.C.C. will in any way seek to act or speak for its member churches in matters concerning church union. The W.C.C. is, according to its constitution, not authorized to act for the churches in such matters. In these matters each church takes its own decisions in full freedom. This is for us an obvious point. But it must be made because the question is sometimes raised whether the W.C.C. will enter into formal or informal conversations with the Roman Catholic Church about church union. The answer is that this is quite out of the question because of the character of our movement.

(d) The W.C.C. may, however, use such opportunities as may present themselves to make known to the new Secretariat certain basic convictions which have been expressed by the Assembly or Central Committee (e.g. issues of religious liberty, of Christian social action, etc.).

(e) It should be remembered that the creation of the Secretariat does not mean that any of the fundamental differences which exist between the Roman Catholic Church and the churches in the W.C.C. have been solved. The change is a change in procedure and climate. The opportunity for dialogue is to be grasped, but it means that the real problems will come to the fore. Our task in that dialogue will be to represent the insights which God has given us together in the fifty years since our movement was started.[1]

Subsequent statements were progressively less reserved. The need for direct contacts with the Roman Catholic Church was ever more widely recognized. The tension evident in the St Andrews statement, however, continued to accompany the extension of relationships and has not been completely overcome even today.

Relationships were strengthened by the sending of five Roman Catholic observers to the Assembly at New Delhi. No Roman Catholic observers had been present at the Second Assembly at Evanston, any more than at the First Assembly at Amsterdam; indeed, on the very eve of the Evanston Assembly

[1] MRCC (St Andrews 16–24 August 1960), p. 105.

the Archbishop of Chicago, Cardinal Stritch, had issued a clear warning against the ecumenical movement in a pastoral letter.[1] Since then the situation had changed. Even so the appointment of the Roman Catholic observers still proved difficult. The Holy Office claimed the right to settle the question and decided that no observers should be sent. The Secretariat for Unity appealed to the Pope and succeeded in having this decision reversed. It was forced, however, to abandon its original list of nominees and to choose theologians who were not among the Secretariat's consultants. The outcome of this dispute made plain the Secretariat's determination to carry out the functions entrusted to it.

The Assembly repeatedly expressed its joy at the presence of the Roman Catholic observers and at the developments in the Roman Catholic Church generally. With regard to the Second Vatican Council, the words which made the deepest impression summed the matter up in this way: "It would undoubtedly mean much for Christendom and the world if it became clear . . . that these councils do not meet against each other and that each does not seek its own advantage but seeks only to serve the Lord Jesus Christ."[2]

Soon after the Assembly, preparations for the Second Vatican Council entered a new phase. On 25 December, 1961 the Pope announced that the Council would meet the following year. The Secretariat, meanwhile, had already prepared a statute dealing with the observers who were to be invited. Negotiations with the Churches could begin. The Secretariat made direct contact with the Patriarch of Constantinople and the other ancient Patriarchs. The invitation was delivered to the Ecumenical Patriarch and, since Athenagoras I had often expressed his interest in the Council, it was generally expected that Orthodoxy would be represented there by observers. But, in fact, after sounding out the views of other Orthodox Churches, the Ecumenical Patriarch felt unable for the present to accept the invitation. Many of the Orthodox were of the opinion that it demeaned Orthodoxy to send mere observers who could have no real part in the proceedings.

The Patriarch of Moscow, to everyone's surprise, finally decided to accept the invitation. Just before the opening of the Council, two observers, Archpriest Vitaly Borovoy and Vladimir Katliarov, arrived in Rome. Evidently misunderstandings had arisen. The Moscow Patriarchate had assumed that Constantinople had already decided in favour of accepting the invitation. The resultant imbalance did not last long. The number of Orthodox observers increased at later sessions. The other Eastern Churches and the Anglican Communion were invited in like manner. Mgr Jan Willebrands paid personal visits to the Patriarchs and to the Archbishop of Canterbury.

Inviting the other Churches presented special problems. As a result of many discussions it had been concluded that it would be better to approach the confessional families rather than the Churches of each country, and the Secretariat set to work on this basis. The positive response of certain Churches was already assured. Contacts with the Lutheran World Federation, for example, had been favourable. On 3 April 1962 Mgr Willebrands was able,

[1] Cf. *Ecumenical Review*, vol. vii (January 1955), p. 169.
[2] Edmund Schlink in *New Delhi Report*, ed. W. A. Visser't Hooft, p. 6.

through the good offices of the World Council of Churches, to outline the plans for the forthcoming Vatican Council to the executive secretaries of the World Confessional Organizations then meeting in Geneva. He asked them to inform him whether they were willing to accept an invitation to send observers. With the exception of the Baptist World Alliance, the Churches accepted this offer. The only individual Churches to receive an invitation to send observers were the Evangelical Church in Germany and, later, the Kyodan (Japan) and the Church of South India. Shortly before the opening of the Council, the number of observers was further increased by several personally invited guests, including in particular Oscar Cullmann and two Taizé brothers.[1]

The invitation to the World Council of Churches was dealt with at the Central Committee at its meeting in Paris (August 1962). Although the invitation was accepted without lengthy discussion, the choice of the observers presented difficulties. It had originally been intended to send two observers, one representing the Eastern tradition and the other the Western. An Orthodox bishop was proposed, but Orthodox delegates raised objections to the World Council's being represented by a bishop. In the end it was decided to appoint only one observer. At subsequent sessions the World Council was able to fill the two to three places offered to it.

These conversations and negotiations could not have produced the results they did had not the preparations for the Council been followed in the Churches with growing interest. The announcement of the Council had aroused the theological and spiritual interest not only of the Roman Catholic Church but of the other Churches as well, particularly the Churches of the West. The General Secretary of the World Council expressed something of the mood of that time when, in his report to the Central Committee in Paris (1962), he raised the serious question as to whether there was to be a genuine dialogue, on the one hand, and on the other hand strongly emphasized the fact that the Vatican Council was the concern of all the Churches: *Nostra res agitur.*[2] The growing interest was initially expressed in a great flood of publications. Many non-Roman Catholic theologians published their views on the forthcoming Council on the Roman Catholic Church and its relationship to other Churches, or on particular aspects of doctrine and practice where more thorough discussion could lead to greater unity. The announcement of the Council gave a fresh stimulus to ecumenical discussion and, to some extent, even provided new themes.[3] The Churches themselves also began to take a more active interest in what was happening. In December 1960 the Archbishop of Canterbury, Dr G. Fisher, visited the Pope; his successor, sometime later, appointed a permanent representative in Rome. The

---

[1] In all there were about 150 observers who attended the Council for longer or shorter periods or were present at one or other of its sessions. Only a few followed the entire proceedings: cf. *Observateurs-délégués et hôtes du Secrétariat pour l'Unité des Chrétiens au Deuxième Concile du Vatican* (Vatican 1965).

[2] General Secretary's Report, MRCC (Paris 1962), p. 79.

[3] Particularly striking is the number of publications dealing with the history and nature of Councils; cf., for example, *The Councils of the Church, History and Analysis*, ed. H. J. Margull (1966).

Lutheran World Federation gave a group of theologians the task of preparing a volume containing not only detailed information about the Council but also comments on the developments in the Roman Catholic Church.[1] In 1962 Professor Edmund Schlink spent some time in Rome making contacts and keeping the Evangelical Church in Germany fully informed about the work being prepared. Examples of this kind could easily be multiplied.

As relationships continued to improve, preparations for the Council had also advanced. The commissions and secretariats had produced a great many documents. Friends of the ecumenical movement with knowledge of these documents were far from satisfied with their contents. The traditional attitude seemed to have gained the ascendancy despite all the changes. They began to issue warnings against exaggerated hopes, and right up to the opening of the Council remained completely unsure what its outcome would be. The turning-point was the address given by Pope John XXIII at the opening of the Council on 12 October 1962, an event in many respects comparable with the first announcement of the Council. Instead of presenting the assembled bishops with a detailed programme, the Pope limited himself to indicating a few general guide-lines: the Council would be primarily pastoral in character, it would be an expression of love and would, therefore, pronounce no anathemas. He also took the opportunity of asserting that one should distinguish between the *depositum fidei* and its formulation, a hint whose importance can hardly be exaggerated. Was this not the opening of a door? Did it not prevent the Council from merely repeating unaltered the old formulas? Was it not now free, with a freedom hitherto abjured, to seek the formulation demanded by the present age? The whole address, but this hint especially, made clear the Pope's wish that the Council should develop a "personality" of its own. It should not be content merely to safeguard and transmit the received heritage but, as an assembly of this age, was to speak to this age.

It would exceed the purpose and the proportions of this chapter to relate the course of the Council in detail. Even if we restricted our narration to the most important events, it would take us too far.[2] All we can do here is to recall certain steps of decisive importance for the development of the ecumenical movement. This rapid survey will also bring out the unresolved difficulties inherent in the present ecumenical situation.

The First Session made it clear that the Roman Catholic Church's attitude towards the other Churches would change in a far-reaching way. It had been obvious from the outset that the Council would deal with the question of relations with other Churches. The theme of unity had been from the be-

---

[1] K. E. Skydsgaard, ed., *The Papal Council and the Gospel: Protestant Theologians Evaluate the coming Vatican Council* (Minneapolis 1961); cf. also the later volumes, G. A. Lindbeck, ed., *Dialogue on the Way: Protestants report from Rome on the Vatican Council* (Minneapolis 1964); W. A. Quanbeck ed., *Challenge and Response: Protestant Perspective of the Vatican Council* (Minneapolis 1966).

[2] A great many accounts have appeared, for example:
Antoine Wenger, *Vatican II*, 4 vols. Paris 1962–6.
Robert Rouquette, s.j., *La fin d'une chrétienté*, Chroniques, 2 vols. Paris 1968.
Bernard Lambert, *De Rome à Jérusalem*. Paris 1964.
René Laurentin, *Bilan du Concile*. Paris 1966.

ginning so much to the fore that it was bound to be discussed. What was still quite uncertain was how this would be done. Which view of unity would carry the day? Would the views and proposals of those who had been involved in the ecumenical movement have decisive influence, or would the old traditional view be repeated in different terms? Would the Council deal with the question in a way that would invite controversy and produce upheaval? Or would it adopt some formula easy to accept and therefore of no great consequence?

The debates of the First Session made it clear that the majority of the bishops were not only eager to pose the problem but also ready to tread new paths. The desire to arrive at a new understanding of the separated brethren, the desire for encounter and dialogue was more and more widely shared. True, many were able to express this desire only in inadequate ways. Many started from a view of unity and of the ecumenical movement from which it was difficult to see the need for encounter, dialogue, and joint witness. For many this First Session was an unexpected revelation and experience to assimilate which took time. But at least the proceedings of the First Session soon made it clear that the Council would not be satisfied with a hasty solution.

The way the texts presented to the bishops for discussion were dealt with indicated that this was the case. Two *schemata* on unity had been distributed during the First Session. One was the work of the Theological Commission, the other of the Commission for the Eastern Churches. Neither document was much more than a fresh summary of traditional views. The one spoke of the one Church in such a way that there could hardly be any question of other Churches. The other explained how those Christians separated from Rome, particularly those of the Eastern tradition, could restore unity. A third document, prepared by the Secretariat for Unity, was not brought to the notice of the bishops at all. The Council found itself unable to accept either of the texts and they were referred back. A mixed commission was entrusted with the drafting of a new text. The Secretariat for Unity, which at the very beginning of the Session had been given equal status with the other conciliar Commissions, would play the decisive role in this mixed Commission.

Other texts experienced similar treatment, especially the *schema* on the Sources of Revelation. This text was of great importance for the further course of the Council, since here the question of the relation of Scripture and tradition would be decided. Would the final text be one in which scripturally oriented theological thinking played a greater role? Or would it simply reaffirm the Tridentine position? The first draft did not seem very promising in this respect, but, in a memorable vote on 20 November 1962, it was referred back by the Council by a large majority. Although the requisite two-thirds majority was not obtained, the Pope nevertheless decided that a new *schema* should be drafted.

These decisions were much more important than their description suggests. By rejecting these draft texts the Council had already in principle decided in favour of real relationships with other Churches. True, a great variety of motives played their part in these decisions and the Council was very far from a common mind. While many simply clung to traditional ideas, others believed that the goal might be reached without really radical changes. Only a minority was clear what participation in the ecumenical movement would mean. The future course of the Council could still produce stubborn resistance and disappointing reactions. Yet something like a breakthrough had been achieved. A change had become imperative in the Roman Catholic Church and, consequent on this, in the other Churches as well. *Heil uns, weh uns, der Tauwind weht!*(Nietzsche), as someone exclaimed after the first reports of the First Session.

The presence of the observers had not been without influence on the course so far. The observers had, of course, no possibility of taking any active part in the proceedings. Many of them were instructed by their Churches to exercise the greatest reserve.[1] Yet their very presence had the profound effect of continually pointing to the ecumenical problem. Over and above this, they were able each week to talk informally with members of the Secretariat about the texts being discussed, and many of their comments were passed on to the appropriate commissions. The longer the Council went on, the greater became their freedom of action. Some individual observers produced actual commentaries, and it is possible in some cases to discover traces of these in the conciliar documents. Perhaps even more important were the personal conversations and the meetings in small groups.

The First Session ended without having produced any tangible results. But, in a way far removed from what was originally intended, the Council had become a "spectacle" which drew the attention of the whole world. The very differences which had appeared put the Roman Catholic Church in a new light. The picture which the Roman Catholic Church had presented to non-Roman Catholic Christians began to change and for the first time large numbers began to follow with impartial interest what was happening in the Roman Catholic Church. This change is reflected in the almost unlimited and unqualified sympathy evoked by Pope John XXIII on all sides. The encyclical *Pacem in terris*, although hardly any more remarkable than earlier documents apart from its universal aims, met with a response never given to any papal document. This sympathy deepened still more during the Pope's last illness. John XXIII had become a symbol of agreement, peace, dialogue, and friendship among men. When he died, shortly after Pentecost 1963, he was universally mourned.

The change that had taken place soon made itself felt in the ecumenical movement. An increasing number of Roman Catholics participated in ecumenical meetings. The character of the ecumenical movement began to change. Whereas before at best only a section of the different separated Churches had taken part, now increasingly all traditions were represented. The first example of this on a wider scale was the Fourth World Conference on Faith and Order, held in Montreal (July 1963). Even here, to be sure, the Roman Catholic Church was represented only by observers. But their participation in fact went much further. The themes to be discussed at the Conference had been previously discussed at a special meeting with Roman

[1] Cf., for example, MRCC (Paris 1962), p. 26.

Catholic theologians (18–23 March 1963) at the Ecumenical Institute in Bossey. Papers by Roman Catholic theologians had been distributed to the members of the Conference. As well as the official observers, many guests and journalists attended and took so active a part in the proceedings that the Roman Catholic position was as fully presented as that of any other Church. One of the chief speakers at the conference was a Roman Catholic, Father Raymond Brown. The spirit of fellowship found visible expression in a great public gathering held in the Catholic University of Montreal, with Cardinal Léger of Montreal taking part along with leaders of the Conference.

The work of the Conference produced some remarkable and to some extent unexpected agreements. In particular, the report on the problem of Tradition revealed an important consensus. The report which was agreed upon would have some influence on later discussions at the Second Vatican Council and on the drafting of the Constitution *De divina revelatione*. Certainly the Conference also proved how little the new situation had even then been exhausted either spiritually or intellectually. The President of the Conference, Bishop Oliver S. Tomkins, spoke of "promising chaos",[1] and, while this phrase does not quite do justice to the positive results of the Conference, it surely characterized accurately something of the mood which prevailed in it, as well as that of the whole period between the First and Second Sessions[2] of the Vatican Council.

The comment also sprang from something else which the Conference experienced. Whereas previously the dominant theme of the Faith and Order movement had been ecclesiology in the strict sense, the Montreal delegates suddenly saw this theme in a new light. Was not the search for church unity basically only a secondary question? Should not attention be concentrated mainly on the Church's proving itself to be the Church in the modern world? At least the connection between the concern for unity and this self-authentication of the Church in the world must be demonstrated. And did this not mean tackling new theological themes? The Conference posed this question with great urgency and, while not reaching any firm conclusions, the discussions revealed a whole complex of problems which, in the coming years, and in connection with the Second Vatican Council, would become inescapable.

Shortly after the Faith and Order Conference, the Central Committee held its annual meeting (Rochester, New York, August 1963). After receiving the report on the First Session of the Second Vatican Council, it issued a short statement. This statement first expressed gratitude for what had happened in the Council. It next recalled that Christ was the basis of all genuine ecumenical dialogue, and stressed that the mutual recognition of the divided Churches as Churches was of great importance for the development of the dialogue. Whereas previously it had always been critical problems which had been mentioned (problems hampering relationships, such as, for example, religious

---

[1] Cf. *The Fourth World Conference on Faith and Order* (Montreal 1963), p. 7.

[2] At the Fourth Assembly of the Lutheran World Federation in Helsinki (Summer 1963) and at the Meeting of the Division of World Mission and Evangelism (December 1963) Roman Catholic observers took an active part in the proceedings.

freedom and mixed marriages), now for the first time it spoke also of the need to reach the maximum of agreement in the missionary activity of the Church.[1]

Continuation of the Second Vatican Council under the Pontificate of Paul VI

On 21 June, 1963, after a relatively short conclave, Cardinal Giovanni Battista Montini, Archbishop of Milan, was chosen to succeed Pope John XXIII. A few days later he was enthroned as Pope Paul VI. He at once declared that he intended to continue the Council in the spirit of his predecessor, and it soon became clear that he was determined to introduce reforms. Shortly after his entry to office, addressing the members of the Curia, he announced a thorough reorganization of the central structures. This caused a sensation and had an encouraging effect on the forces seeking a renewal of the Church.[2]

The beginning of his pontificate came, of course, at a time when the character of the Council was bound to change, apart from any change in the supreme leadership of the Church. In its First Session the Council had made its own the widespread demand for renewal, openness, and dialogue. On this basis it had rejected many draft texts. Now it had to work out in detail what it proposed to say affirmatively. Anything radically new was out of the question. Although Pope John XXIII had introduced the distinction between the *depositum fidei* and its formulation and thereby made many new developments possible, this distinction nevertheless rested on the conviction that the Church had at all times preserved the *depositum fidei*, and it followed, therefore, that all the Council's statements had to be shown to be in some way an organic continuation of earlier statements. When the drafting of the texts began, discussion was, therefore, inevitably dominated to a much greater extent by a consideration of the past. Much of the momentum characteristic of the First Session was in consequence lost and many deplored this change. One African bishop, for example, declared after a few weeks of the Second Session that he suddenly found himself, after the invigorating heights of the First Session, back once more in the undergrowth of European history. But this development was undoubtedly inevitable.

In his opening address at the Second Session, Pope Paul VI announced that ecclesiology would be the central theme of the whole Council.[3] This decision had been in the air from the beginning. Already towards the end of the First Session, Cardinal Suenens had pointed out in a widely noted speech that this theme was fundamental to almost all the *schemata* with which the Council would be dealing. This choice of theme in fact was almost inevitable. The First Vatican Council had intended to clarify the doctrine of the Church and a text had even been prepared. Only the premature ending of that Council had prevented its discussion. Was it not essential to

---

[1] MRCC (Rochester 1963), pp. 32ff.
[2] 21 September 1963; cf. *AAS* LV (1963), pp. 793ff.
[3] *AAS* LV (1963), pp. 841ff.

complete what had been begun? In any event this theme was central to the theological and practical interests of the Roman Catholic Church. Countless questions towards which the Council would have to adopt a position if it was not to disappoint expectations were rooted in ecclesiological assumptions (such as renewal of worship, mission of the laity, missionary activity of the Church). It was, therefore, in this area that the theological orientation had to be found.

At the same time, the Pope's address undoubtedly provided a glimpse of the problems facing the Second Vatican Council. Ecclesiology was not a theme where discussion could move with complete freedom. There were the statements of the First Vatican Council to reckon with and the question arose how those statements were to be related to the new insights into the Church's nature and task in the world today. The discussions of the First Session had projected a new picture of the Church. Three distortions of its nature—legalism, hierarchism, triumphalism—had again and again been condemned. The Church was to be seen, much more than it had ever been seen before, as a fellowship of the Spirit, as the people of God, and as a servant. But what did this "much more" mean? Was it a matter of expanding and developing the statements of the First Vatican Council by these new emphases? Or was a thorough revision absolutely essential? The sharpest debates of the Council centred around this question. Nobody questioned the binding force of the First Vatican Council's doctrinal statements for the Church, but opinion was divided as to how those statements were to be interpreted today. Even the texts finally agreed upon are not fully clear on this point. Old and new stand side by side, often unconnected, and leave unanswered the question whether the new is to be interpreted in terms of the old or vice versa.

There were also obvious ecumenical reasons pressing this theme to the fore. If genuine relationships with other Churches were to be established, was not fresh clarification needed as to the nature of the Church and especially as to the nature of its unity? Hitherto the Roman Catholic Church had stood aside from the ecumenical movement mainly for ecclesiological reasons. Was it not incumbent on her now to explain why participation in that movement was not only possible but even mandatory today? But even here discussion was bound to produce a discordant result. She could not simply abandon the reasons which had held her back from the ecumenical movement, and, since her ecclesiology was developed on the basis of Roman Catholic presuppositions, even the convictions which divided the Roman Catholic Church from other Churches had to be given a fresh lease of life. Therefore the texts finally promulgated have a double tendency. On the one hand, they make it plain that the differences which had in the past prevented agreement, particularly the doctrine of the primacy and universal jurisdiction of the Pope, have not been left behind. On the other hand, they show that today there are far more points of contact between the Churches.

Insights into the nature of the Church, the fruit of the biblical, liturgical, and ecumenical movements of recent decades, have increasingly become the common possession of all Churches. What is the relationship between these

M

two tendencies? What view of the ecumenical movement follows from the tension between them? Is it to be mere openness towards the "separated brethren" or the joint witness of all Christians? Emphasis on the uniqueness and centrality of the Roman Catholic Churches or the fellowship of all Churches? Non-Roman Christians too were thereby presented with a difficult problem. Ought they to heed the warnings of those who were urging that in principle nothing had changed? Or should they take seriously the evidence of change, the new emphases and, above all, the steady spiritual impetus, and cultivate the fellowship? Even today the tension between these various possibilities still exists. Since the Second Vatican Council this is one of the problems with which the ecumenical movement has to live and for which a solution will be found only as it lives with it.

What was the new Pope's role in these debates? Perhaps his position may best be described by saying that on the one hand he seeks to preserve the Church's tradition in all its range and on the other hand is convinced of the need for the Church to break out of its isolation and to present an effective witness in the modern world. This twofold attitude has most clearly emerged in the way he has understood and exercised his office. He brought with him a high view of the papal office. As Archbishop of Milan he had already on occasion spoken vigorously of the significance of the Roman See.[1] He had spent a good deal of his life working in the Vatican in the Secretariat of State. He was well acquainted with the problems of the Curia. He had always been profoundly convinced of Rome's high mission. When, during the Council's proceedings, he saw the papal authority endangered, he frequently and some-times a little anxiously issued reminders that this authority was not to be diminished. At the same time he sought to give his office a new significance. Whereas earlier popes had represented the Church's centre in a static way, he sought to secure it a hearing in a dynamic way.

Symbolic of the Pope's conception of his office are the journeys which he has undertaken. To the surprise of the bishops, he announced at the close of the Second Session his intention to undertake a pilgrimage to Jerusalem to the sources of the gospel. The unusual character of this proposal exercised a great fascination, and the journey was followed with great interest and sympathy by the entire world. Shortly thereafter he made a second "mission-ary" journey, this time to India. The occasion was the Eucharistic Congress in Bombay (Autumn 1964). Perhaps even more significant was his visit to the United Nations Organization in New York during the Fourth Session (4 October 1965). Here the mission of the Holy See was fulfilled in a dramatic way: the Pope as the messenger of peace before the nations of the world. His

---

[1] For example, in a pastoral letter to the archdiocese of Milan (Easter 1962) he said: " . . . Rome is the city of the Church; a Council is a phase of the Church's fullness. Rome is the city of Christ; a Council is a period when Christ's mystic presence operates in his Church and in the world. So it seems to us that the Council will give Rome a period of sublime splendour greater than it has ever enjoyed before . . . a charism of prophecy will animate Rome and the human city will be transmuted into a city of God. Rome will become Jerusalem . . ." (*The Mind of Paul VI*, ed. James Walsh, s.j., introduction by Cardinal Bea (London 1964), p. 225; cf. also pp. 223ff, 250).

numerous later efforts to further the peace of the world should also be mentioned in this context.[1]

In August 1964, a little more than a year after entering on his pontificate, Paul VI published his first encyclical *Ecclesiam suam*, a document of programmatic character, which decisively influenced the further course of the Council.[2] In this the Pope expounded his view of the Church and its task in the world. He adopted the concept of dialogue and sketched a picture of the Church turning responsibly with understanding and in service towards the near and the far. The document elicited a mixed response. On the one hand, the Pope's stand in favour of openness and renewal and his consequent encouragement of the best elements in the Vatican Council were welcomed; on the other hand, doubts were raised. On the basis of such a view could there be any real encounter between the Churches? Did it not place the Roman Catholic Church too much in the centre, and around it, in ever descending concentric circles, other Christians, Jews, non-Christian religions, and other men, whether of good will or bad? Was not dialogue here, therefore, a unilateral affair rather than the encounter of equal partners willing to learn from each other?

At the end of the Third Session, three conciliar texts were approved which are particularly important for the ecumenical movement: the Dogmatic Constitution of the Church, the Decree on Ecumenism, and the Decree on the Eastern Catholic Churches. In these texts the Council expressed the essence of its understanding of the ecumenical movement. The texts had been several times discussed and frequently revised during the Second and Third Sessions. The Council had been able to formulate in these documents a series of agreed statements which hardly anyone would have thought possible at the beginning of the Council or even after the Second Session. Taken as a whole, the Decree on Ecumenism presents an understanding of the ecumenical movement which makes encounter with other Churches possible in a way which is convincing. The new attitude can be illustrated by a change which was adopted in the course of the debates. An earlier version of the Decree still spoke of presenting the principles of Roman Catholic ecumenism whereas the final text reads "Roman Catholic principles of ecumenism". This change expresses in the shortest possible way that the Roman Catholic Church does not wish to rival the ecumenical movement but to align itself with it.

Even in the final text it is still possible to discern the different tendencies represented in the Council. Many questions are left open, many expressions can be variously interpreted. Different conclusions may be drawn from it according to the hermeneutical criteria employed. This was indeed the reason why the debates on the Decree continued right to the very last

---

[1] The series of journeys was continued after the Council. When Florence was overwhelmed by floods in 1966, the Pope visited the city and celebrated the Christmas Mass there. The journey to Fatima in May 1967 aroused mixed feelings because of its political connotations. Shortly afterwards came the visit to the Ecumenical Patriarch in Constantinople (July 1967) and in the following year the visit to Colombia for the Eucharistic Congress being celebrated there.

[2] *AAS* LVI (1964), pp. 609ff.

moment. The opposition tried to secure modifications in the text in the closing days of the session, and even to postpone the promulgation. The Pope himself intervened in this dispute. When the text seemed to have been finalized, he himself presented a list of emendations designed to remove certain obscurities. Some of these restricted the openness of the text. Two other facts cast a certain shadow over the promulgation. Simultaneously with the Decree another text, dealing with the Eastern Catholic Churches in communion with Rome, was also approved. The document as such presented no special difficulties—why should the Roman Catholic Church not express its mind on this important internal problem? But the document also included references to relations with the Orthodox Churches and the question was inevitably raised why these comments were made in this context. Even more distressing was the fact that the Declaration on Religious Freedom should by rights also have been promulgated; but the opposition succeeded in delaying the vote and demanding further revision. Although these events of the final weeks caused considerable sensation, the fact remained that with the promulgation of the Decree the Roman Catholic Church had explicitly and irrevocably committed itself to the ecumenical movement. Compared with this fact, the qualifications and disappointments of the final weeks carried little weight.

The Council's proceedings were, of course, followed closely in the World Council of Churches, and, as the work advanced, the question presented itself with growing urgency: What form would relations between the Roman Catholic Church and the World Council take in the future? Would there be any relations at all? Was not the interest of the Roman Catholic Church directed more to the individual Churches than to the World Council? Was she not more interested in constructing her own network of relationships than in aligning herself with an existing fellowship of Churches? Isolated voices even went so far as to predict the end of the World Council in its present form. The former Archbishop of Canterbury, Dr G. Fisher, proposed, for example, that the Council should be transformed into an organization for inter-Church aid, an organization loose enough to present the Roman Catholic Church with no difficulties in joining its membership. Future development depended, of course, largely on how the Vatican Council would define the ecumenical task of the Roman Catholic Church. If it went no further than an ecumenism centred on the Roman Catholic Church, no genuine relationship with the World Council seemed likely to be possible. But if there were some stress on dialogue, co-operation, and joint witness of all Churches, then such a relationship was almost inevitable.

The drafts of the Constitution *De ecclesia* and the Decree *De oecumenismo* which had been discussed and revised at the Second Session gave rise to fears that a narrow view of ecumenism might win the day at the Council. There was a danger of real tensions emerging. At its meeting in Osades (10–14 February 1964), the Executive Committee of the World Council discussed this situation at length. The brief statement on "Christian Unity", issued as a result of this discussion, betrays something of the anxiety which dominated the meeting. "The real crux of the ecumenical problem remains that of the relationships between the churches. The question is how separated Churches may meet each other in dialogue and co-operation. . . . All are equally bound to confess the truth revealed in Christ. How can they meet together and work towards that full unity which they . . . should manifest?" In answer to this question certain basic principles were recalled which had made the fellowship of the World Council possible and which, in the opinion of the Executive Committee, must also continue to be determinative in the future. Even before the meeting in Odessa, a memorandum had been sent to Cardinal Bea in the name of the Presidents of the World Council containing detailed suggestions for improving the Decree on Ecumenism. This memorandum had later been taken into consideration in the revision of the text.

A few weeks later Cardinal Bea proposed an unofficial meeting between representatives of the Secretariat for Unity and of the World Council. This meeting was held on 15 April 1964 in Milan. The number of participants was limited. Present on the Roman Catholic side, apart from Cardinal Bea, were Bishop Jan Willebrands, Father Jérôme Hamer, and Father Pierre Duprey; and on the World Council side the General Secretary and the two permanent observers at the Vatican Council. The talks cleared the air. The Roman Catholic delegation stressed the importance they attached to good relationships with the World Council. The Roman Catholic Church, though not a member of the World Council and unable in the foreseeable future to become a member, bore a joint responsibility for its life and future development. The idea of appointing permanent representatives in Rome and Geneva was discussed but rejected for the present. Instead it was agreed to remain in close contact by means of regular visits. For the first time the possibility of setting up joint working parties was considered. At that time three different work groups were envisaged, one to consider the principles of future co-operation, the second to study theological questions, and the third to deal with practical matters. But it was agreed that any such step needed careful preparation on both sides and could not be taken before the promulgation of the Decree on Ecumenism.

Discussions were continued in the World Council in the following months. In order to obtain a clearer picture of the attitude of the member Churches, a wider group of leading personalities and a number of observers who had represented their Churches at sessions of the Council were invited to a meeting held at Rummelsberg near Nuremberg on 24-7 July 1964. After a discussion on the general significance of the Council, the results of the Milan talks were reported. The idea of joint working parties found general acceptance, although some doubts were voiced. The Executive Committee, meeting immediately afterwards in the Evangelical Academy at Tutzing near Munich, reached agreement on this plan. The General Secretary was authorized to work out details in further talks. This was done during the Third Session of the Council. The World Council's observers met twice with Bishop Willebrands and other representatives of the Secretariat for Unity. The plan was also presented personally to the Pope.

After the close of the Third Session and the promulgation of the Decree on Ecumenism, the time seemed ripe to implement the plan. The events of the closing weeks of the session had indeed again raised doubts as to whether the establishment of closer relationships should yet be undertaken. It was nevertheless decided to present to the Central Committee at its meeting in Enugu, Nigeria (12–21 January 1965) a more modest plan for discussion. After only brief discussion, it was almost unanimously agreed to propose to the Roman Catholic Church the establishment of a Joint Working Group. This proposal was assured of acceptance in advance. The text presented to the Central Committee had previously been discussed with Bishop Willebrands and he had secured agreement in principle from the highest authorities. The Working Group would have fourteen members—six from the Roman Catholic side and eight from the World Council of Churches. Their task would be to clarify the principles and practical problems of future collaboration.[1] Compared with the original idea this plan had the advantage of leaving open to a far greater degree the future developments; all further co-operation would have to grow from the discussions of the Joint Working Group. A few weeks after the Enugu meeting Cardinal Bea visited the Secretariat of the World Council of Churches in Geneva and conveyed the official answer of the Holy See. The importance of this step was emphasized during a small ceremony in The Ecumenical Centre. Pastor Marc Boegner, a former President of the World Council of Churches, replied to Cardinal Bea.[2] The relationships between Roman Catholic Christendom and the World Council thereby entered at last on a new stage. By the establishment of the Joint Working Group both sides had publicly affirmed their readiness to remain in permanent contact and to deepen the ecumenical fellowship as much as possible. Work could now begin on a more complete manifestation of the ecumenical movement than had hitherto been possible.

This whole development would not have been possible without the simultaneous establishment of contacts at many other levels. The first announcement and still more the impetus of the First Session had already been fruitful in this connection. The longer the Council went on, the more numerous and intensive the contacts became. The message of dialogue had spread so widely that many members of the Roman Catholic Church did not wait for the promulgation of the Decree on Ecumenism but had anticipated the results of the Council by establishing relationships. In many places the hitherto closed confessional borders were being opened up in an astonishing way and the non-Roman Churches found themselves suddenly confronted with a partner they had previously reckoned with at a distance.

Official steps also helped to change the climate. The most important event in this respect was perhaps the meeting between the Ecumenical Patriarch Athenagoras I and Pope Paul VI in Jerusalem (January 1964). After the Pope had announced his intention of visiting Jerusalem, the Ecumenical Patriarch suddenly announced that he too would go to the Holy City. As a result of this meeting, the "journey to the sources" took on a distinctively ecumenical character. The Vatican also showed the importance it attached

[1] MRCC (Geneva 1965), pp. 36ff.
[2] For the text of the speeches see *Rencontre oecuménique à Genève* (Geneva 1965).

to reconcilation with the Eastern Churches in the following years, particularly by such gestures as the return of relics which for one reason or another had been brought from the East to the West (the head of Andrew to Patras 1964, the relics of St Sabas to Jerusalem 1965). Official contacts were also discussed with other Churches; for example, simultaneously with the discussions between the Secretariat and the World Council, discussions were also taking place about the establishment of a mixed commission with the Lutheran World Federation.

At the time of the formation of the Joint Working Group, the Vatican Council had still not ended. Many texts were still not yet at hand, and in many respects it was still not clear what their final form would be. After the postponement of the vote at the end of the Third Session, further developments were awaited with some anxiety. The decision in this matter was especially important for the World Council of Churches. Having indicated in numerous statements how important a clear recognition of the principle of religious liberty was for the co-operation and joint witness of the Churches, a great deal depended on the Council's statement on this matter for the collaboration envisaged between the Roman Catholic Church and the World Council. The Declaration finally adopted rests, especially in its theoretical section, on specifically Roman Catholic premises and cannot in this respect be wholly endorsed by other Churches. But the practical requirements coincide very closely with those found in the statements made by the World Council of Churches, and in this respect it can be said that a common basis has been arrived at. The work of the World Council, and especially the tireless efforts of Dr A. F. Carrillo de Albornoz, doubtless had some share in bringing about this result.[1]

The other texts still to be dealt with had at first glance less to do with the ecumenical movement. They concerned internal problems of renewal and witness in the world. But they were none the less important for future co-operation. For they raised the question of how these texts approached the idea of co-operation and joint witness. Did the Council regard its task as ended with the promulgation of the Decree on Ecumenism? Or did the other texts take the insights of the Decree into account explicitly and carry them further? Was ecumenism only a special self-contained theme? Or would it permeate the life of the Roman Catholic Church in all its forms? The question was not settled with complete clarity during the Fourth Session. Several texts, especially the Decree on the Church's Missionary Activity, and the Pastoral Constitution on the Church in the Modern World, contain explicit references to the need for co-operation with other Christians. Others make no mention of this, and one occasionally has the impression that the Roman Catholic Church is once again preoccupied with its own problems. The general framework established by the Council certainly ensured that all the texts of the Council were increasingly read and interpreted in the light of the ecumenical movement.

[1] Cf., for example, *Le Catholicisme et la liberté religieuse* (Paris 1961); on the Council's Declaration, cf. "The Ecumenical and World Significance of the Vatican Declaration on Religious Liberty, *Ecumenical Review*, vol. XVIII (1966), pp. 58ff.

The Pastoral Constitution on the Church in the Modern World deserves special mention. In this the Council declared its mind on the great problems of the present time. This text was the only one for which there was no draft in existence prior to the opening of the Council. It was drawn up by various groups during the Council proceedings and this process was doubtless the result of the growing realization that the Church could not remain pre-occupied with itself but had to face up to the problems of our time. Just for this reason, the Constitution was an important contribution to the ecumenical movement. For was this not the point where the divided Churches could most easily co-operate together? Was it not here that the weight of our differences was least in evidence? And might it not be that, when the Churches faced together the questions of the time, they might also be shown even new ways to greater unity? This had again and again been the experience of the ecumenical movement. The Constitution could, therefore, pave the way to a collaboration which might be of the greatest significance for the ecumenical movement. The first thrusts in this direction were already made during the Fourth Session.

Once the Joint Working Group had been established between the Roman Catholic Church and the World Council of Churches, much more intensive relationships would be cultivated. Various questions relative to the Council were discussed at the first sessions of the Joint Working Group. Two special consultations were organized to deal with particular themes. One of these brought together a number of specialists on missionary problems (April 1965). The results of the discussion[1] were in many ways encouraging and the meeting undoubtedly helped indirectly to give the conciliar Decree on the Church's Missionary Activity the strongly ecumenical flavour which characterizes it. The other consultation was concerned with questions of "Church and Society" (March 1965) and provided an opportunity for discussion of the work on the Pastoral Constitution *Gaudium et spes*. The contacts with the various groups responsible for the drafting of the text had been especially close from the beginning. The fact that the World Council had worked in almost all the areas which the Constitution was to deal with made it seem advisable to seek discussion with it. The World Council's observers were given many opportunities to comment on the various draft texts of the document. The consultation in Geneva placed these contacts on a broader footing.[2]

On 8 December 1965 the Council was brought impressively to its close. The final days were marked by two events which were of great consequence for the ecumenical movement. On 4 December the non-Roman Catholic observers were invited to join with the Pope in a service in *San Paolo fuori le mura*. Some of the observers were asked to read the lessons and the prayers. The Pope had thereby given his personal example of common worship. On the last day but one of the Council, an event took place which was of significance especially for relations between the Roman Catholic Church and the Orthodox Church. It was the joint decision to strike from memory the

---

[1] Text obtainable only in duplicated form, W.C.C.
[2] Cf. *Study Encounter*, vol. ii (1966), pp. 75ff.

mutual excommunication of 1054, a step reinforced by solemn ceremonies both in Rome and in Constantinople. While this decision strictly speaking concerned only the relation between the Roman Catholic Church and the Church of Constantinople, it nevertheless had far wider significance. An important step in reconciliation had been taken.[1]

Although the question of the Church's unity had once more dominated the final days, it played hardly any part in the magnificent closing ceremony in St Peter's Square. The ceremony was very much a symbolic presentation of the Roman Catholic Church turning towards the world. The ceremonial, impressive in itself, once again awakened in one's mind with special urgency the question which every observer of the Council could not but ask, especially in these last days. Where had the Council really led? Had it after all been only a matter of renewing the Roman Catholic Church and its witness? Or was it in fact the fellowship and the common witness of all Churches which were the beneficiaries?

From the Second Vatican Council to Uppsala

The end of the Council did not mean the end of the conciliar event. What had been discussed and proposed, formulated and decided, continued to have its effect and had now to pass into the life of the Church. This process of "reception" could lead to extremely varied results. Certainly the texts which had been promulgated contained many formulations and guide-lines. But just because the Council had been concerned not "to close any doors", these texts were in many respects open and could be interpreted in various ways. However, the texts were perhaps not really the most important thing. Much more depended on the way in which the atmosphere of the Council would continue to influence the Roman Catholic Church. After the shocks brought by the Council, would it be possible to restore an order comparable with that of the pre-conciliar period? Or would the questioning and seeking which had marked the sessions of the Council henceforth be a feature of the life of the Church as a whole?

The Council had given rise to a new image of the Church. The very fact that for several years vital questions had been discussed openly before the whole Church, indeed before the whole world, had clearly demonstrated that the Church is most alive when it is moving forward, when it proclaims the gospel while at the same time asking itself questions about the gospel. Had not the Council itself planned with this movement in mind? Had it not continually stressed the Church's readiness for dialogue with the world? The final ceremony on St Peter's Square provided a particularly striking illustration of this aim. On the day after the last texts had been promulgated, the Council briefly addressed various sections and groups (workers, intellectuals, women, etc.) and assured them that the Church recognized its solidarity with them and shared their problems.[2] One by one, representatives of the different sections of the human community received the text of the Declaration. This symbolic action was in one sense a summing up of the Council's

[1] *AAS* LVIII (1966), pp. 40f.   [2] *AAS* LVIII (1966), pp. 5ff.

dominant concern. But could the Church face the problems of the modern world without also continuing its questioning and seeking?

The ferment produced by the Council put the Magisterium in a difficult situation. On the one hand, the Pope had the duty of carrying out the intentions of the Council; on the other hand, included in these intentions was the wish that none of its decisions should hamper a genuine confrontation with the contemporary world. A new exercise of the papal office was needed. The Pope had to become the exponent and symbol of movement. The need for this change was all the greater because of the crisis concerning authority in the Church brought on by the Council. The authority which had been accepted without question before was now being questioned in many quarters, especially among young people. The Pope could no longer count on the unqualified assent of the faithful. To a far greater extent than any of his predecessors he had to appeal to conscience.

The difficulty confronting the Pope is illustrated by the manner in which the decisions of the Council were carried out. On the one hand, Pope Paul arranged for the issue of directives dealing with the implementation of the constitutions and decrees.[1] The Council for the Reform of the Liturgy in particular performed a tremendous task, and the proposals for reshaping the liturgy soon began to be put into operation in most parts of the Church. The Pope also supervised the creation of the new structures demanded by the Council. Even while the Council was still in session, on his own initiative he established two new secretariats—one for relations with other religions and the other for dialogue with atheism. Some time after the close of the Council, the establishment of a Laity Council and a Pontifical Commission for Justice and Peace was announced (6 January 1967).[2] The Council on the Laity was to provide a focus for the work of the laity. The Commission for Justice and Peace was to deal with the questions of development. A few months later came the long-awaited reform of the Curia (18 August 1967),[3] and, although many had hoped for more radical changes, a series of measures was taken which made possible a more effective co-operation within the Curia, a modernizing of its work, its internationalizing and increased mobility.

But it was not only the central government which was reorganized; many of the religious orders also began to make changes. The Pope was above all concerned, however, to continue along the line which had been intimated during the Council through his visit to the United Nations. He repeatedly made new efforts to help to secure peace in the world; his pontificate is so dominated by this concern that some refer to him as the "Pope of Peace". In this connection one of the most important utterances is the encyclical *Populorum progressio* (26 March 1967),[4] in which he summoned the Roman Catholic Church to greater responsibility in the face of the widening gap between rich and poor nations. "Peace, today, means development."

[1] Cf. *Motu proprio Finis concilio*, *AAS* LVIII (1966), pp. 37ff.
[2] *Motu proprio Catholicam Christi Ecclesiam*, *AAS* LIX (1967), pp. 25ff.
[3] Apostolic Constitution *Regimini Ecclesiae*, *AAS* LIX (1967), pp. 885ff.
[4] *AAS* LIX (1967), pp. 257ff.

But, on the other hand, the pontificate of Paul VI is marked by a concern lest the movement initiated by the Council should go too far and the Magisterium lose control over it. Again and again he has insisted that the received tradition must be preserved intact. The Council had spoken on particular questions only and it was not in accord with its spirit to want to call everything in question. He frequently appealed for obedience to the Magisterium.[1] Many decisions were obviously affected by this concern. Here must be mentioned, above all, those questions which, although raised by the Council, had been left expressly for the Pope to decide. Almost without exception they have been decided in a conservative sense.

The Apostolic Constitution *Indulgentiarum doctrina* (1 January 1967) repeated with only slight modifications the traditional doctrine of indulgence.[2] Hardly any heed was paid to the views expressed by many speakers at the Council which went much further. The detailed encyclical *Coelibatus sacerdotalis* (24 June 1967), while certainly recognizing the serious pastoral problems arising in connection with celibacy, rejected any change in the existing rules;[3] only new rules regarding the diaconate were conceded. However, the most widespread discussion was provoked by the encyclical *Humanae vitae* on birth-control (25 July 1968).[4] To the surprise of many, it confirmed the utterances which had been made by Pope Pius XII. Dealing as it did with a question which entered deeply into personal life, this encyclical raised in especially wide circles the question of the Pope's authority in the Church.

The tensions found in the Roman Catholic Church after the Council were vividly illustrated in the autumn of 1967 when the Episcopal Synod and the Laity Congress held their meetings simultaneously in Rome. The Pope had already announced during the Council that he would from time to time summon a synod of bishops. The Synod would enable the consultations initiated by the Council to be continued, at least in some measure. The Synod would, to be sure, have only an advisory function. Final decision was to be in the hands of the Pope. In the first session of the Synod, which took place from 29 September to 29 October, the bishops were asked to advise on a number of clearly defined matters (liturgy, canon law, crisis of faith, mixed marriages, seminaries). An opportunity was at hand to examine the state of the Church and carefully to weigh the pros and cons of certain reforms. Some important steps were taken, especially in the field of liturgical renewal. But the Synod was not able to become a focus of the post-conciliar spirit.

At the same time a large congress of lay people met in Rome (11–18 October 1967). There had been similar congresses before. But this congress was in many respects something quite new; it was here that it was made quite clear that the laity were determined to play a vocal and active part in the life of the Church. For the great majority the Council was obviously

---

[1] General Audience, 12 January 1966; General Audience, 15 December 1965; General Audience, 7 September 1966; Address to Theologians' Congress members, Rome 1 October 1966; General Audience, 5 October 1966.

[2] *AAS* LIX (1967), pp. 5ff.   [3] *AAS* LIX (1967), pp. 657ff.   [4] *AAS* LX (1968), p. 481.

not an end; it was a beginning, and the Congress called for the speedier introduction of many reforms. Since a great many representatives of other Churches were present, the discussions acquired a distinctively ecumenical character.[1] It is perhaps significant that the Pope should have chosen the occasion of his speech to this Congress to recall in urgent terms the place of authority in the Church.[2]

Roman Catholic Participation in the Ecumenical Movement

Similar tensions are also found in the Roman Catholic participation in the ecumenical movement. The impetus given by the Council continued to have great influence. Once the Decree on Ecumenism had been promulgated, meetings, dialogue, and co-operation no longer needed to be confined to special circles. Ecumenism had become the task of the Church as a whole. After the Council, therefore, participation became increasingly the rule. There were, indeed, considerable differences from place to place. In some countries the picture changed rapidly; in others the change was small. Many factors were at work here: the historical circumstances, the attitude of the bishop, the political background, and, finally, the manner in which the non-Roman Churches themselves approached the new possibility of encounter and co-operation. The impetus of the Council, however, also produced results in many places which went beyond what had been formulated in the Decree on Ecumenism. Had not the Council spoken of real encounter? Must not real spiritual fellowship increase? Must not steps be taken to realize these aims without delay? Many individual Christians, many small groups, posed such questions and began to work along these lines. A spontaneous movement began which often found itself in opposition to the explicit instructions of church authorities, by whom it was usually simply tolerated. Joint experiments were undertaken and, with increasing frequency, particular groups were found joining together in communion services.

The Pope himself often acknowledged that the whole Church was committed to the ecumenical movement. For example, in a speech to the members of the Secretariat for Unity: "The ecumenical problem has been raised by Rome in all its urgency, in all its magnitude, and in all its doctrinal and practical aspects. It is not just glanced at occasionally or incidentally. On the contrary! It has become the object of continuing concern, systematic study, and unlimited love. It has become a line which from now on is part of the programme of our apostolic office."[3] Shortly after the end of the Council the Pope announced that the Secretariat for Unity, which had originally been created only for the duration of the Council, was to continue in existence. Its activity had already developed during the Council; subsequently it increased year by year.

One of its most important initial tasks was to draft a document containing directives for the application of the Decree on Ecumenism. Work on this *directorium de re oecumenica* had already begun during the Fourth Session

---

[1] Cf. Report of Congress, *God's People on Man's Journey* (Rome 1968).
[2] *AAS* LIX (1967), pp. 1040ff.   [3] 28 April 1967, *AAS* LIX (1967), pp. 494f.

and the text was eventually published at Pentecost 1967.[1] Among the selected themes it covered were these: it recommended the setting up of ecumenical commissions in each country; directives were issued concerning the recognition of baptisms administered in other Churches; the spirit of ecumenism (*oecumenismus spiritualis*) and, above all, the Week of Prayer for Unity and especially the problems of common worship (*communicatio in spiritualibus*) were discussed. Other questions were to be dealt with in a further document. This *directorium* showed, in the first place, that the Roman Catholic Church was to be introduced to the ecumenical movement in a serious way. The establishment of ecumenical commissions was a particularly significant step and the Secretariat sought to enhance their importance by beginning to hold regular meetings of their secretaries in Rome. At the same time the *directorium* was unquestionably a reminder of the limits which had to be set to participation in the ecumenical movement, limits which had already been and were still being exceeded in certain quarters.

The issue of mixed marriages, though it had an immediate bearing on the ecumenical movement and was considered by many to be the ecumenical issue *par excellence*, was not within the sole competence of the Secretariat for Unity. Towards the end of its Third Session the Council had discussed a proposed revision of the existing regulations, but no decision had been made. The proposals had been passed on to the Pope along with the views of the bishops; the decision was held in abeyance. Opposition to any change in existing rules was obviously strong in many countries, and many bishops warned against any radical departure from the traditional practice. The Holy Office finally published an *Instructio matrimonii sacramentum* (18 March 1966),[2] which, in the case of the recognition of mixed marriages performed in non-Roman Churches, did not even go as far as the original proposals. This was not to say that the matter was now closed. The *instructio* stressed that the new directives had force only *ad experimentum*. Further discussion was, therefore, possible. The problem was discussed with representatives of other Churches on several occasions, in particular at a meeting with the World Council (1–4 March 1967). The Episcopal Synod reconsidered the matter in the autumn of 1967 and, although it was not prepared to make far-reaching changes, further developments are not ruled out.

The Secretariat for Unity was not only in charge of working out directives for ecumenical work; it also had the main responsibility for developing relations with other Churches. In a relatively short time it succeeded in constructing a whole network of new contacts. Special care was devoted to relations with the Orthodox Churches. These had always played a special role in Roman Catholic ecumenical thought and, not surprisingly therefore, especially after the impressive gesture at the close of the Council, reconciliation between East and West was given priority. The Pope himself travelled in July 1967 to Istanbul on a short visit to the Ecumenical Patriarch,[3] and Athenagoras I returned this visit in October of the same year. Both journeys provided an opportunity of emphasizing the common heritage.

[1] *AAS* LIX (1967), pp. 574ff.   [2] *AAS* LVIII (1966), pp. 235ff.
[3] Cf. *AAS* LIX (1967), p. 833

The Joint Rome Declaration (28 October 1967) is especially important. Among other things, this Declaration affirms the common conviction that the true dialogue of love, the essential basis of all relationships between them and their Churches, must be rooted in complete obedience to the one Lord and in mutual respect for each other's traditions.[1] Although these gestures in many respects improved the atmosphere between the Churches, no real discussions yet took place. Two pan-Orthodox meetings had some time previously discussed this possibility (Rhodes 1964 and 1965), but had not arrived at any unanimous agreement since the final decision had to be postponed. Even the pan-Orthodox meeting in Geneva (June 1968) produced no essentially different result.[2] The difficulty of actually engaging in the dialogue so frequently proposed is a fresh sign of the West's constant tendency to underestimate the gravity of the difference which divides it from the East.

Initial discussions with the Lutheran World Federation had already been started between the Third and Fourth Sessions of the Council. After two preparatory conferences (August 1965 and April 1966) a mixed group was set up in July 1966. Their main task was to deal with theological questions, particularly with that of "the Gospel and the Church". This group has already held several meetings. Similar contacts have also been established in certain areas. Remarkable results have come in particular from discussions in the United States on the Creed, Baptism, and the Eucharist.[3]

A dialogue with the Anglican Communion was officially announced in March 1966. The Archbishop of Canterbury's meeting with the Pope in Rome (23–4 March 1966) provided the occasion. The joint statement declared that a serious dialogue should be initiated which, based on the Gospel and the ancient common tradition, should lead to the unity for which Christ prayed.[4] A mixed commission was set up to examine the steps to be taken. After three meetings (January 1967, September 1967, and January 1968), it proposed that a permanent commission should be created to deal with all questions of a general character. Special commissions should deal with the most difficult theological problems which divide the two Churches from each other (Church and ministry; authority, its nature, exercise, and implications). This proposal was agreed upon. Closer contacts with the World Methodist Council were established in 1967. A mixed commission was formed and held its first meeting in October 1967. Further contacts of this kind are not impossible in the future.

All these conversations constitute a new element in the ecumenical movement. Encounters at the level of the confessional families had previously been the exception. The World Council of Churches had not been founded as a fellowship of confessional families but primarily as a fellowship of the

---

[1] Cf. *AAS* LIX (1967), p. 1054; quotation on p. 1055.

[2] Discussions on social questions with Russian Orthodox theologians took place in Leningrad in December 1967.

[3] Cf. *The Status of the Nicene Creed as Dogma of the Church* (1965); *One Baptism for the Remission of Sins* (1966); *The Eucharist as Sacrifice* (1967). The results of a Roman Catholic–Reformed dialogue have been published under the title, *Reconsiderations* (New York 1967).

[4] *AAS* LVIII (1966), p. 286.

Churches of the individual countries. The entry of the Roman Catholic Church into the ecumenical movement changed this situation. Being itself a universal fellowship, it saw the confessional families as its natural partners. Although the confessional families were for other reasons becoming more important in the ecumenical movement, this did much to secure increased attention for them. This development was clearly felt at the Fourth Assembly of the World Council of Churches at Uppsala.[1]

Relations with the World Council of Churches

But what of the contacts which had already been established earlier with the World Council? Bilateral relations with the individual confessions were in many respects more in accord with Roman Catholic thinking than co-operation with, or even membership in, a fellowship of Churches. It is not surprising, therefore, that the Roman Catholic Church, and the Pope especially, at first attached more importance to these relationships. Even at the national level, contacts were often sought primarily with the individual Churches. There were sound reasons for this. If the Churches wished to draw nearer together, they had to face and overcome in direct conversations the barriers dividing them, and the various bilateral discussions had in fact already led to notable steps towards reconciliation. But must not encounter and co-operation still be sought at another level? Must not all Churches, even though they are still divided, form a provisional fellowship with one another? The goal of the ecumenical movement is the unity and common witness of the whole people of God. Is not this goal most likely to be reached if all the Churches remain in permanent contact, if they live together and, anticipating the ultimate fellowship as far as possible, bear common witness? Relationships with the World Council were, therefore, of the greatest importance, and, to the extent that co-operation developed at all levels, the question regarding the co-operation of the Roman Catholic Church in the National Christian Councils naturally also arose.

The Joint Working Group of the Roman Catholic Church and the World Council of Churches (established in 1965; see above, p. 340), from its inception held two meetings every year, each meeting lasting several days. So far it has twice presented a report to the Holy See and to the Central Committee of the W.C.C., together with proposals and recommendations concerning the form of the relationship and of co-operation (February 1966 and August 1967).[2] Both reports were approved.

The task of the group was first to clarify general questions. How did each side understand the ecumenical movement? Had the Vatican Council expressed a view which differed from that of the Churches bound together in the World Council of Churches—which would inevitably entail a different form of ecumenical work? Or could the Roman Catholic Church declare its fundamental agreement with the view of the World Council of Churches?

[1] *The Uppsala Report*, p. 225.
[2] The first report has been published in *Ecumenical Review*, vol. xviii (1966), pp. 243ff (see also MRCC (Geneva 1966), pp. 47ff). The second report has been published in MRCC (Heraklion 1967), pp. 140ff (cf. also pp. 53ff).

The question soon became even more pointed. Was it conceivable that the Roman Catholic Church might become a member of the World Council? The Joint Working Group has not yet ended its discussions on this matter. So far it has reached only a number of provisional conclusions. Its second report stresses that at all events there can be only one ecumenical movement and that both the Roman Catholic Church and the World Council of Churches are committed to serve this one movement. Membership of the World Council of Churches is, therefore, not excluded in principle. The report expressly emphasizes that the present structures cannot be regarded as final. However, obstacles which stand in the way of a more complete manifestation of the one ecumenical movement may not be underestimated either. They can be overcome only gradually. Indeed, it is possible, since the relationships are still so new, that they have not yet been seen in their full extent. The Joint Working Group, therefore, recommends that the common work should proceed step by step.[1]

The conversations are not confined to such general questions, however. The Joint Working Group has been no less concerned with tasks which even now can be undertaken together. The range and importance of these tasks increases with each meeting. Its first report consisted for the most part of a list of the areas in which contacts should be sought. Many of these plans were translated into action in the months which followed. New groups came onto being to deal with particular aspects of co-operation. The second repor if the Joint Working Group contained a survey of these groups; six different areas were mentioned. There are the theological and liturgical questions. A special commission examined the problem of the "Catholicity and Apostolicity" of the Church. Conversations about joint services at ecumenical gatherings,[2] and above all about the joint planning of the Week of Prayer were held; contacts were made with the Consilium for the Reform of the Liturgy. Co-operation over missionary problems was only slowly developed, despite the fact that the Conciliar Decree had stressed the ecumenical task; even today it is still embryonic. Far more advanced are the contacts in matters concerning the service and task of the laity in the Church. Various meetings in this regard have taken place;[3] the Laity Congress in Rome, in particular, afforded an opportunity for a fruitful exchange.

Furthest developed, however, is co-operation in the field of social ethics. The World Conference on Church and Society in Geneva (1966) was not only a powerful stimulus to the member Churches of the World Council but also to the development of relationships with the Roman Catholic Church. Roman Catholic theologians played an important part in the Conference. The creation of the Pontifical Commission for Justice and Peace the following year provided the opportunity to extend co-operation. A joint Secretariat was set up in Geneva and in the spring of 1968 a large joint conference on the

---

[1] On this discussion cf. *Ecumenist*, vol. iv. 3 (1966); *Ecumenical Review*, vol. xx (1968), pp. 205–44.

[2] *Ecumenical Review*, vol. xviii (1966), pp. 252ff.

[3] Cf. *Laity Formation*, Proceedings of the Ecumenical Consultation Gazzada (Rome 1966); Report of the Women's International Ecumenical Conference (Taizé 1967).

Church's responsibility in the problems of development was held at Beirut.[1] The Assembly in Uppsala attached great importance to this co-operation.

Useful contacts were also established in the field of inter-church aid. A number of consultations led to closer collaboration between Roman Catholic aid organizations, Caritas in particular, and the World Council of Churches. In February 1966 the World Council and the Roman Catholic Church made a joint appeal in view of the threatened famine in India. It proved far more difficult to reach a common witness in international affairs. In this sphere the traditions and structures of the Roman Catholic Church are least favourable to co-operation. Nevertheless, in the spring of 1968, a joint declaration on the increasingly critical situation in Nigeria was issued. Last to be mentioned is the fact that the Joint Working Group continued—either itself or through special groups—to study problems which constitute special hindrances to the ecumenical movement, such as mixed marriages and proselytism.

Developing Roman Catholic relations with other international Christian organizations must also be referred to in this context. Of particular importance is the co-operation with the United Bible Societies. This arose naturally out of the Vatican Council. The fresh emphasis on the importance of the Bible in the life of the Church, and, above all, the decision to give more place to the vernacular in the liturgy, made it necessary to increase the production of biblical translations and the number of its editions. The Constitution on Revelation had, in this connection, expressly encouraged "co-operation with the separated brethren" in producing such translations (para. 22). This co-operation grew rapidly. Following extended discussions full agreement was reached on the principles of translation and editing. Joint translations and editions of the Bible are already in preparation in many countries.

The 1968 Uppsala Assembly of the W.C.C. signified another important step forward in the development of relationships. The question of mutual relationships was, as it had already been at the meetings of the Central Committee, one of the dominant themes of the Fourth Assembly. The Roman Catholic Church sent fourteen observers, and in addition several guests and consultants attended. A great number of Catholic journalists followed the proceedings. The Pope as well as Cardinal Bea sent official messages. Two speakers—Father Roberto Tucci and Lady Barbara Jackson —addressed the Assembly. Shortly before the Assembly opened, the Vatican had given permission for Roman Catholic theologians to become full members of the Faith and Order Commission. The Assembly made use of this opportunity by appointing nine Roman Catholics to the Commission. The Roman Catholic Church is, therefore, like the member Churches of the World Council, now represented in the Faith and Order movement.

On many occasions the hope was voiced that relations might develop in other directions too, and the question of membership was again and again raised, especially in private discussions. Father Roberto Tucci had explicitly taken it up in his address to the Assembly and, though not concealing the

[1] *World Development, Challenge to the Churches.* Geneva 1968.

difficulties, he had made it quite clear that Roman Catholic ecclesiology did not make membership impossible. The Assembly itself spoke vigorously on the subject. Not only did it approve the previous work of the Joint Working Group, but it also made it absolutely clear that from the side of the World Council of Churches there was, in principle, no obstacle to the membership of the Roman Catholic Church in the Council. The Assembly also, for the first time, expressed the desire that a complete manifestation of the one ecumenical movement might actually be realized. The realization of this desire may still take a long time, but at least the task has now been made explicit.[1]

Increasingly, of course, the question arises: What significance is to be attributed to the expansion of relations between the Churches? How do all the bilateral relationships contribute to the renewal of the people of God? How would this renewal be furthered, supposing we were successful in creating a fellowship of the majority of the now divided Churches? The decisive question is whether Christianity can stand the test in the present world. The urgency of this question becomes increasingly obvious, and more and more people are asking with a certain uneasiness whether ecumenical relationships are at bottom simply a new form of the Church's self-pre-occupation. This doubt surfaced at the Fourth World Conference on Faith and Order and, in a more reticent way, at the Second Vatican Council. It was posed, above all, at the World Conference on Church and Society, emphatically and unequivocally. The future of the ecumenical movement lies, therefore, not—or, at least, not exclusively—in the further development of relationships but in the places where the Church authenticates itself.

[1] Cf. *The Uppsala Report*, p. 178.

13

The Ecumenical Movement
in the Churches and at
the Parish Level

HANS JOCHEN MARGULL

The One People of God in Each Place

In the ordinary daily life of the Churches and local parishes the ecumenical movement has only just begun. Apart from a few and important exceptions, ecumenicity on the denominational and local level lags far behind the bold and lofty thrusts of the world ecumenical conferences. Sometimes one even gets the impression that the waves that rushed forward at the conferences set up a backwash at the local level. At any rate it is noticeable that on the whole the ecumenical movement in the Churches and parishes advances much more slowly and ponderously than at the great world-wide or regional gatherings. It is easier to adopt certain principles than to carry them out. However, no one would underestimate what has been accomplished, especially during the last few years.

The Churches have not only become aware of one another; they have also drawn closer to each other. This is clearly shown by the exchange of visits between church representatives, by the intercession, the mutual help, by some very promising consultations to prepare the way for church unions and some actual mergers, by the growing number of theological conversations, the agreements about many joint projects, the exchange of statements and information, and by many of the events described in the preceding pages. Even in cases where, owing to the formation and development of the World Council of Churches and to the break-through of ecumenism in the Roman Catholic Church, the tendency is rather to wait, or even to start anti-ecumenical campaigns or attempts to divide Churches (as in Korea), the question of the One Lord of the world and the Church cannot be ignored for very long, as the consequence of the question of the One Church in the world.

The word "ecumenical", which was hardly known a generation ago, is no longer strange; it has become more and more meaningful. One can see how the names of the places where the Assemblies of the World Council of Churches have been held have become as familiar in sermons and in Christian education as the work of the Second Vatican Council. One frequently hears people speak of the situation "before Amsterdam", or about the main theme at "Evanston", or about the basis of the World Council "since New Delhi", or about the emphases of "Uppsala". Sometimes one can even notice how in theological thinking there is a tendency to divide newer church history and the history of theology into periods marked by the Assemblies of the W.C.C. and the Second Vatican Council. In the Churches and at the parish level, therefore, we really have moved forward since 1948.

The gap between the ecumenical movement at its conferences and in the places where it has to be lived out day by day may be considerable; but it cannot be so large that there is no longer any connection between a world conference and a local Church. On the one hand, the insights and challenges of the conferences are dependent on what is alive to a certain extent in the Churches and at the parish level. On the other hand, ever since the ecumenical movement started, it has been realized that "the universal must be local to be real".[1] At its conferences, therefore, attention was constantly drawn to

[1] Montreal, p. 81.

355

the importance of the local Church for the witness, service, and unity of the Church nevertheless. A growing ecumenical questioning both in and of the local Churches, especially during the last few years, was needed before a World Conference on Faith and Order like the one at Montreal could decide to have a whole section on the ecumenical importance of the local congregation.

This section had as its theme "All in each place: the process of growing together". The unity formula of New Delhi was taken up and used in the formulation of this theme. This formula has an interesting history, which it is not without importance to mention here. The formula goes back to Lesslie Newbigin, Bishop in the Church of South India, formerly in Madurai, now in Madras. Its *Sitz im Leben* arises from situations on which the Bishop reported in 1958 and 1959. When he visited local Churches in South India the Hindus and Muslims in the place used to crowd around out of curiosity when the local congregation gathered in front of the church building to welcome their bishop. He then felt that it was incumbent upon him to say something to these people who surrounded the Christian congregation. And it became clear to him that what he said would be understood if the local congregation surrounded by non-Christians was a genuine Church of Jesus Christ.

In 1958 Bishop Newbigin became General Secretary of the International Missionary Council. In the same year, in preparation for the integration of the World Council of Churches and the International Missionary Council, he published a book entitled *One Body, One Gospel, One World*, from which we quote:

> For myself, I do not believe that we can be content with anything less than a form of unity which enables *all who confess Christ as Lord to be recognizably one family in each place and in all places*, united in the visible bonds of word, sacrament, ministry and congregational fellowship, and in the invisible bond which the Spirit Himself creates through these means, one family offering to all men everywhere the secret of reconciliation with God the Father. I believe that missionary obedience in our day requires of us that we should treat the issue of such visible churchly unit as an issue not for tomorrow but for today.[1]

Thus the expression concerning the unity of all Christians "in each place" was coined. The Faith and Order Commission took it up at its meeting at St Andrews, Scotland, in 1960, and passed it on to the discussion at the World Council's Assembly at New Delhi. Here it was explained that as God's will and God's gift unity must become visible among "all in each place".[2] The place, the local stage for separated Christians and Churches was thus indicated as the platform for the gift and the task of unity. Consequently the local congregation gained high attention in the ecumenical discussion. In the conclusions of the report of Section V at Montreal we read:

> We acknowledge that many of God's gifts to his whole Church cannot be shared by us in our local churches until we recognize ourselves as the one people

---

[1] Lesslie Newbigin, op. cit., pp. 55–6.
[2] *New Delhi Report*, ed. W. A. Visser 't Hooft (London 1962), p. 116.

of God in each place, and are prepared to embody this fact in new and bold ventures of living faith today.[1]

We now turn our attention to ecumenical events which took place at the level of the Churches (denominations) and local parishes after 1948. These events are so numerous that only a few examples of them can be mentioned in this limited space; and they are of so many different kinds that a selection is justifiable only if attention is also drawn to the references to the subject in the other chapters of this book.

Meetings

There were meetings and visits not only between Pope Paul VI and the Ecumenical Patriarch of Constantinople, Athenagoras, whose historic meeting in the Holy Land in 1964 and in Istanbul and Rome in 1967 have attracted world-wide attention and aroused strong ecumenial hopes within Christendom. Important visits were paid not only to the Holy See, for instance by Bishop Otto Dibelius of Berlin, by the Very Reverend Dr A. C. Craig in his capacity as Moderator of the Church of Scotland, by the Archbishop of Canterbury, and by Metropolitan Nikodim of the Russian Orthodox Church. Equally important for the ecumenical movement were the contacts between representatives of individual Churches and local congregations, which aroused much less attention, but the number of which has meanwhile become too numerous to count or to estimate.

Many visits take place on the occasion of the conferences of the World Council of Churches. A large number of the delegates to its Assemblies, its Central Committee meetings, and its Commission meetings, pay visits to other Churches in the country or area where the meeting takes place, also stopping on their journeys to visit local congregations, church conferences, and theological seminaries. And as there are few areas where the World Council of Churches has not held any conferences, or which were not accessible on the way to its conferences, there are now very few Churches which have not received visits from representatives of another Church that plays an active part in the ecumenical movement. Every such visit has been a manifestation of the ecumenical movement, has helped to broaden the horizon of the Churches, and has often also deepened the problem of divided church traditions. Each has thereby raised the question of direct co-operation, and has strengthened the hope of unity in the mission and life of the Churches. Not infrequently permanent contacts have been formed. Even more often further visits have been arranged between Churches and churchmen of different countries and continents.

One outcome of such visits is, for instance, a passage which has been inserted into the Deed of Appointment of pastors belonging to the Evangelical Church in Germany when they serve abroad:

We expect you to maintain the link between your Church and the Evangelical

---

[1] *Fourth World Conference on Faith and Order*, p. 90 (para. 190).

Church in Germany and *to support and promote the contacts with the Christian Churches belonging to the World Council of Churches.*[1]

Visits take place not only between Christians living in fairly close proximity to each other but also over great geographical distances. Since 1948 not a single summer has passed in which groups of church people from North America (beginning with students, then extended to include older people) have not visited Europe, Latin America, and finally even Asia, Africa, and Australia. Some times they came for short visits, sometimes they stayed longer. In a large number of cases they met together with congregations or church groups for conferences. In quite a number of cases these visits were returned. The United Church of Christ in Japan had to appoint a full-time person to look after the visitors, who came mainly from North America and Australia. In the summer time a group of about twenty pastors came regularly from North America to assist Japanese pastors in the evangelism of remote districts in the North of Japan. Within Europe, since the beginning of the 1950s a great deal of inter-Church visiting has been going on. Many theological seminaries sent their students for one or two weeks to seminaries abroad. The exchange started within western Europe, but it soon extended so as to include eastern Europe.

A similar movement goes on between the different Lay Institutes. So many ecumenical guests attended the German Protestant Kirchentag that it was obliged to make arrangements for a programme in English. Characteristic of the nature of these contacts was a visit paid by sixty members of the Anglican Church of St Helen's, Kensington (London) in 1965 to attend the consecration of the Lutheran Church of St Andreas at Hildesheim (Germany). The church at Hildesheim, which was nearly 600 years old, was destroyed in 1945 by British bombs. Twenty years later it was rebuilt, and the church leaders of the Kensington church and of the Hildesheim church entered the new building together. The liturgy was celebrated partly in English and partly in German. The sermons were preached by the local Bishop and by the Provost of the Anglican Cathedral of Coventry. The presence of the Provost illustrated the contact made with Coventry in the previous years, when young Christians from Germany helped to rebuild Coventry Cathedral. Like Coventry Cathedral, the old church at Hildesheim was to be a place of reconciliation.

Equally characteristic of the new ecumenical movement was the presence of Protestant and Roman Catholic clergy at the consecration of the first Russian Orthodox Cathedral in the traditionally Lutheran city of Hamburg that same year. In fact, since the formation of the World Council of Churches and still more since the Second Vatican Council, it has become customary for clergy from Churches of different traditions to attend consecration services of Churches and of priests, ordinations, and induction services. The enthronement of the Anglican Archbishop of Sydney in 1966 was attended

---

[1] This phrase was included in the Deed of Appointment read at the introduction of the Pastor of the German-speaking Protestant Church in Tokyo-Yokohama on 24 October 1965.

not only by representatives of the Methodist, Presbyterian, Congregationalist, Baptist, and Greek Orthodox Churches, and of the Salvation Army, but also by the Roman Catholic Archbishop of Sydney; the two Archbishops sat facing each other in the chancel of the Cathedral. Furthermore the sermon of the Archbishop who was being enthroned was concerned with the responsibility of the Australian Church for the people in Asia and the Pacific. Even in Columbia (South America) where in the 1950s the small Protestant groups were often suppressed by force, in 1965 a Roman Catholic priest representing the archdiocese of Bogota was able to attend the ordination of the first native Anglican clergyman. This was an exceptional case then; such events increase in number every year.

Particularly important were the meetings of Protestant and Anglican Church leaders and theologians with representatives of the Orthodox Church and (somewhat later) of the Lutheran Churches and of the Union of the Evangelical Christian Baptists of U.S.S.R. Equally important were the return visits in western Europe and North America. After the Russian Revolution the Church of England continued to maintain contact with the Moscow Patriarchate. In September 1943 the Patriarchate was legalized by the Soviet Government, and in the same month the Archbishop of York went to Moscow. As soon as the war was over, Patriarch Alexis sent Metropolitan Nikolai to London as his representative. In 1952 Pastor Martin Niemöller, who was then President of one of the "Landeskirchen" in Western Germany and a member of the Executive Committee of the W.C.C., visited Moscow. More church delegations followed between 1950 and 1955.

In 1956 a delegation from the National Council of Churches of Christ in the U.S.A., led by Dr Eugene Carson Blake, who was then its President, paid a visit to Moscow which was to have far-reaching consequences. One of the members of this delegation was the late Dr Franklin Clark Fry of New York, then Chairman of the W.C.C. Central Committee. A delegation from the Moscow Patriarchate and other Russian Churches paid a return visit to the United States. In 1958 conversations were opened between the Moscow Patriarchate and the World Council of Churches which led in 1961 to the Russian Orthodox Church becoming a member of the W.C.C. This event opened the way for a large number of visits from the Western Churches to Russia during the next few years. Hardly ever had any ecumenical event been followed with such close attention as the reports on the meeting with the Churches in the Soviet Union. It evoked such keen interest that during the last few years whole groups of church members from the West have been to Russia to visit the Churches there.

At these meetings theological conversations played an important role. The Russo-American meetings were concerned mainly with situation analyses and the question of the Church's task in the world today. The communiqué after the mutual visits between Moscow and New York summed up the conversations as follows: "In the first centuries when the relations between the peoples were just as confused as they are today, it was said that the Christians held the world together. God grant that we may play the same role!"[1] Questions relating to the history of dogma, church order, and liturgical problems, were on the agendas of the different Anglican–Orthodox conferences.

Fundamental problems which divide the Russian Orthodox Church from the Reformation Churches were discussed at the conference of theologians of the Moscow Patriarchate and of the Evangelical Church in Germany. The first of these conferences was held in 1959 at Arnoldshain, near Frankfurt; the second in 1963 at Zagorsk Monastery, near Moscow; and the third in 1967 at Höchst, near Darmstadt. For the first and most important conversation the Orthodox theologians had prepared a questionnaire, containing questions about the Lutheran concept of Scripture and tradition, faith and works (both the traditional concept and the concept held today). As a result the problem of tradition and the question of justification by faith became central in the conversations. Like many of the theological meetings held during recent years between representatives of different church traditions in all kinds of places, the outcome of this meeting was surprising.

The outcome was the possibility of a free and promising theological conversation between Lutherans and Orthodox, and in this case between Germans and Russians. In the discussion itself joint statements were reached like the following:

> In the theology of both churches, tradition is extremely important; consequently the contrast between the Orthodox principle of "Scripture and Tradition" and the Protestant principle of "Scripture alone" is not apposite. We receive justification through grace in faith in the redemption through our Lord Jesus Christ. There is no justification on the basis of good works. This excludes the misconception that in Orthodox theology good works are a necessary prerequisite for justification, or that Protestant theology rejects the New Testament's teaching about judging men by their works. The Reformation experience of justification by faith has its counterpart, to a large extent, in Orthodox liturgy and ascetism.[2]

Conversations like these revealed the new possibility and readiness for dialogue also in many other places, such as the many recent interconfessional conversations in America.

In this connection mention must be made of one result of many years of contact in France, which were not without tension. During the Week of Prayer for Christian Unity in 1966, for the first time a joint version of the Lord's Prayer was used, which had been worked out by a commission of Lutheran, Reformed, Roman Catholic, and Orthodox theologians. It has received the approval of the Pope also for the French-speaking Catholics in Belgium, Switzerland, Canada, and the African countries. Since Easter 1966 this approved version has been compulsory for use at Catholic Mass.

The exchange of students between different countries, Churches, and

---

[1] *News* from the National Council of the Churches of Christ in the U.S.A., New York (13 June 1956); also *Journal of the Moscow Patriarchate*, No. 8 (1956), pp. 24ff.

[2] The conversation between Protestants and Orthodox at Arnoldshain (*Ökumenische Rundschau* 9 (1960), pp. 26ff); see "Tradition und Glaubensgerechtigkeit", *Arnoldshain Conversation 1959* (Witten/Ruhr 1961).

continents, especially since the Second World War, has borne rich ecumenical fruit. In many cases this exchange was arranged through the scholarship programme of the World Council of Churches; in many other cases it was due to the private initiative of theological seminaries, Churches, and congregations. As a result thousands of theological students received the opportunity of getting to know other Churches and their history, other situations and their problems, and of obtaining theological knowledge which was beyond their reach in their own countries. Many of the men who later on took part in theological conversations between representatives of different Churches, or who have been entrusted by their own Church with responsibility for ecumenical contacts and for promoting the ecumenical cause in the local Churches, or who have translated important literature or even founded ecumenical centres, or who became leaders of local, regional, or world-wide Christian movements and Councils, were once holders of ecumenical scholarships.

The Student Christian Movement, which in many cases has been the historic source of the ecumenial movement, has done a great deal also since 1948 to promote meetings between Christians and Churches. Only two facts can be mentioned here. They were extraordinary, but their exceptional character is an indication of developments which have been going on during the last few years in the life of all the Student Christian Movements. In 1965 a joint Student Conference was held in Göttingen, Germany, for Protestant and Catholic students, critically followed by the Churches. It was expected of this meeting that Protestant and Catholic students would deliberate together about one of their joint problems, namely the rapidly increasing specialization in university studies. It was also expected that in the discussion on this problem the common Christian life of Protestants and Catholics would find its expression. Both these expectations were fulfilled. Finally, it became an actual fact, experienced and confirmed, that the groups of Protestant and Catholic students at the universities have the task of learning to think together and for one another.

On the other side of the Atlantic in the U.S.A., the University Christian Movement was founded in 1966 by the ecumenical union of groups of Protestant, Anglican, Roman Catholic, and Orthodox student associations which had hitherto been separate. This merger on the national level is so far unique. It brought hope of a more intensive encounter and co-operation between Christian students on the local level everywhere.

Different in kind were the encounters in ecumenical work camps and meetings between campers and Christians in the places where the camps were held. It is usually not realized that the history of ecumenical work camps goes back to an experiment made by the International Fellowship of Reconciliation in 1920. In that year young people of different nationalities came together on the site of the German and French battle of Verdun in order to overcome their estrangement and to promote reconciliation and peace. In 1947 the Congregational Christian Service Committee in the U.S.A. arranged a work camp for a group of young American and French Christians at Le-Chambon-sur-Lignon in France. The concept of reconciliation was now joined by another concept: that of service. A year later six camps of this kind were held in western Europe. In 1949 sixteen were held in Europe and Asia, including three camps in Japan, two in Korea, and two in the Philippines. A camp at Nagasaki undertook the task of rebuilding a Christian school destroyed by the atom bomb. A camp in Quezon City (Philippines) helped with an anti-malarial campaign.

In 1950 work camps (which had arisen as a result of free ecumenical contacts) were taken into the programme of the Youth Department of the World Council of Churches. The financial responsibility for them, which existed in spite of the considerable amounts paid by the campers themselves for their travel and living expenses, was assumed by the Division of Inter-Church Aid, Refugee, and World Service of the W.C.C. The number of camps increased. In 1954 there were thirty-four; in 1957 there were forty; in 1961 there were fifty-three. Since 1950 ecumenical work camps have been held in no fewer than fifty-one countries in Asia, Africa, the Middle East, North America, South America, and Europe, and every year not less than 1,000 young people from over fifty different countries and from many different Churches belonging to the World Council have attended these camps. It should be borne in mind that these figures refer only to camps organized in connection with the Youth Department of the World Council. They do not include the large number of camps organized locally, nationally, or denomi-nationally by church associations and Y.M.C.A.s and Y.W.C.A.s for youth or by national Youth Councils.

Most of the camps were attended by an average of twenty young Christians from different countries and different Churches. They usually lasted three to four weeks for building churches, kindergartens, youth centres, hospitals, homes, schools, camps for refugees, or for rebuilding houses destroyed by war or catastrophe. Since 1962, however, the Youth Department of the W.C.C. has also organized camps of longer duration, which provide an opportunity for young people (especially from America and Europe) to give a year's service in co-operation with young Christians of the same age in Asia and Africa. In 1962–3 a camp helped to remove the damage done by the flooding of the River Tana in Kenya. In 1963–4 an ecumenical work camp of this kind was held at Chiengmai, Thailand, which helped to build a conference centre for the young people there. In 1964–5 a group of twenty-two volunteers co-operated in a development programme of Indonesian Inter-Church Aid on the island of Bali. In 1965–6 one camp built an orphanage and an agricultural training centre in Korea.

At these camps, and also at the shorter camps, the campers worked six hours a day simply doing physical work, and then had three or four hours for worship, Bible study, and discussion. "A project of this kind", said the appeal to this ecumenical commitment, "offers everyone a unity of living, working, worship, and fellowship, which has become rare in modern society." The gain for the ecumenical movement was tremendous. At these camps most of the participants for the first time encountered people from other congregations and Churches. They sang hymns that they had never heard. They attended services with which they were not familiar. They worked, talked, slept, ate, and prayed together with people of whose existence they had previously had no conception (or a most inadequate one). Religious, national, and racial prejudices were broken down. It no longer mattered what colour a person was, nor what kind of passport he carried. Superficial differences between Churches became obsolete.

Admittedly, now and again there was a dangerous tendency to ignore important differences. But the faith shared by all was expressed in the hymn, "In Christ there is no East nor West", which was sung with enthusiasm again and again. As a result the local Churches discovered that the Christian Church is far wider than they had hitherto experienced. They often came together for the first time with other local Churches, either in preparing for the camp or through the contacts made by the campers. The campers themselves took back reports to their own countries, the most striking point being the change in the personality of the campers themselves as a result of their experiences of an ecumenical work camp. The ecumenical movement found important expression in the camps, which proved to be a permanent instrument for the renewal of the Churches and for promoting their efforts for unity.

Churches for Others

The ecumenical movement was also going on in the Lay Institutes, a considerable number of which (like the Ecumenical Foundation at Mindolo, Zambia) had been founded as ecumenical projects. It is probable that they have promoted ecumenical contacts more than almost any other organizations. They arranged meetings between people from all over the world, and they opened their doors to Christians who had no opportunity to attend theological conferences, for example, or theological discussion groups, people who could not take part in ecumenical work camps or similar projects. They were opened in many parts of the world, and during the last few years an increasing number of them have been created for people who usually represent the local congregation, although this does not imply that pastors and young people have no share in their work. Here, as in the ecumenical work camps, the encounter did not take place merely for the sake of encounter, but in order to answer the question what it means to be a Christian in a world which has become both larger and smaller, more united and at the same time more divided, more mature and at the same time more dangerous. The Lay Institutes, rightly called "centres of renewal", place themselves at the service of Christians from different Churches, so as to encourage them to undertake service both inside and outside their own local congregations. The lay movement also grew stronger and spread more widely in the ecumenical movement.

What was happening in many places and at countless meetings, which usually discussed very concrete questions of daily life, found expression in a statement made by the Department on the Laity in 1956 to the Central Committee of the World Council of Churches. Speaking of the new insights that had been gained, the statement said "that the whole Church shares Christ's ministry in the world and that the effective exercise of this ministry must largely be by Church members when they are dispersed in the life of the world".[1]

The ecumenical question involved on the one hand the concept of the Church itself, on the other hand the relevance of church traditions outside the walls of the Church. The statement continues:

As was said in Evanston: "The real battles of faith today are being fought in factories, shops, offices and farms, in political parties and government agencies, in countless homes, in the press, radio and television, in the relationship of nations. Very often it is said that the Church should 'go into these spheres', but the fact is that the Church *is* already in these spheres in the persons of its laity." There is nothing new in this conception, for our Lord said, "Ye are the salt of the earth . . .", but it is a truth which has been obscured over many periods of the Church's life.[2]

It was a joint ecumenical task to bring this truth to light in the Lay Institutes. How seriously this task was taken is shown by the following sentences in the statement:

None of us fully understands, in our complex modern world, what this ministry of the laity really is. God reveals it to those who listen; every situation in His world can speak to us. But it is becoming clear that one of the main tasks of the Church, when it assembles its scattered members, is to listen to them speaking of their trials and difficulties, hopes and fears, opportunities and needs, and even simply about the facts of life in the world. The assembled Church cannot become a teaching Church until it listens. We urgently need a Church that will teach out of the experience of listening.

It is sentences like these which have given rise to the question (which has come to the fore in the ecumenical movement especially during the last few years) whether the Church is not called to live for others, namely for people which do not yet belong to it, or no longer belong to it; the question whether, by courageously shouldering this task, the Church may be able to achieve unity in a way that is not possible merely by discussing doctrinal matters. We describe below the attempts made to formulate this question; its importance was shown by the fact that for years the publications concerning the question of the laity, and that of the Church in the world today, were the most widely read of any of the periodical literature published in Geneva. The efforts within the World Council to stimulate the broad mass of church members to think in ecumenical dimensions proved more successful here than anywhere else.

A great many lay movements have sprung up transcending the boundaries of local Churches. They were a response to the increasing need to break down parochial barriers in an increasingly homogeneous world. But they arose also from the increasing recognition of the fact that it is hardly ever possible for a single Church, or a single congregation, to deal single-handedly with the situations that arise today. Lastly, they were an attempt to express as far as possible the unity given in the One Lord Jesus Christ.

[1] MRCC (Galyatető, Hungary, 1956), p. 26.
[2] Quoted from *The Evanston Report*, p. 168.

One striking example of these lay movements is the "Fellowship of the Least Coin", an association of Christian women, located mainly in East Asia. Founded in 1956 by Mrs Shanti R. Solomon, a modest member of the United Church of North India, it became the most striking expression of the wide and deep ecumenical concern found among Christian women in many Churches. Speaking at a meeting of the Asian Church Women's Conference, which spontaneously and wholeheartedly followed her example, she said: "We Asians always want to interpret spiritual feelings through concrete actions, to connect prayer with action. Every woman can put a least coin aside as a token that she has prayed for specific concerns". In a few years an association had grown up which spread far beyond Asia, and which she herself defined as follows: "It joins together women and many denominations and nations through the common acts of prayer and of giving the least coins of their countries to a common fund for special missions projects."

During the ten years since the association was founded its members have collected 223,775 dollars. The amazing thing was that this money did not remain entirely in Asia. It has been used to support ninety-one projects in all six continents. Thus the women of Asia helped with the Child Care Programme of the East Harlem Protestant Parish in New York, with youth conferences in Asia, with a hospital for Indians in Argentina, with evangelism in Spain. Their money was spent on medicines and treatment for sufferers from tuberculosis in India, to support the Protestant Medical Centre at Kimpese (in the Congo), and finally they sent a cheque to people in a place called Strike City in Mississippi where racial tensions are very strong. The oppressed congregations in this poor little town sent a reply. At the third Asian Church Women's Conference in Tokyo in 1966, a carved wooden Nativity scene was on view; it was a gift from Strike City thousands of miles away, and a token of its gratitude.

The help to the people in Strike City was sent through the so-called "Delta Ministry" of the National Council of the Churches of Christ in the United States of America. The name of this ministry was derived from the fifteen counties in the Delta of the Mississippi. The ministry itself was an attempt to improve the situation of the coloured people in this region. It would have been reasonable to expect that the appeal to support this ministry would have been sent only to rich American Churches. However, the request for co-operation was sent out through the member Churches of the National Council of Churches (U.S.A.) to all the Churches belonging to the World Council of Churches. The racial struggle in the 1950s and 1960s, which in the U.S.A. itself had become an ecumenical concern of the Churches, was thus through this request brought to the attention of the Churches all over the world. In 1966, 480,000 dollars were allocated to the Delta Ministry; of this sum 384,000 dollars were to be contributed by America itself and 96,000 dollars were expected from non-American sources. Thus for the first time in the history of Inter-Church Aid, funds flowed into the U.S.A., whose Churches had always been "giving" Churches since the Second World War, financially never "receiving" Churches.

In this connection mention must at least be made of the fact that in the

Churches and local congregations the ecumenical movement has found its most direct, obvious, and perhaps also its most lasting expression both in the giving Churches and in the receiving Churches, in the many forms of help, both large and small, that have been given by one Church to another, by one local congregation to another, by individuals to individuals, more and more transcending the barriers of denomination, confession, nation, and race.

The aims of the Delta Ministry revealed the tasks which confront the Churches everywhere today, where they seek to give service to men. This ministry began by giving direct help to people who could not help themselves, and who needed to be helped in a way that would enable them to help themselves. Its first concern was for reconciliation between the white and the coloured congregations, and for the promotion of human dignity among the members of both groups. Its ultimate aim was to develop a peaceful community of people co-operating in a region in which fate had brought them together, These aims were rooted in the Christian gospel of love for one's neighbour and the forgiveness of sins. At the same time, however, it became clear that the gospel was being preached in normal sermons and in all forms of proclamation, and thus the being of the Church as the Church of the loving, forgiving Lord, had to be lived out in pursuance of these aims.

The ecumenical fellowship between the Churches in the U.S.A., and especially the readiness of many local congregations to participate in such fellowship, had to pass the hard test of the racial struggle. At the same time this highly complex and often extremely confusing struggle brought a deeper experience and understanding of the ecumenical relationship between the Churches and congregations in many places. A new feature of the ecumenical movement in America found expression in the demonstration marches for which Dr Martin Luther King, Jr had set the example. His martyrdom in 1968 only intensified the struggle. These marches brought together people from South and North, from widely differing church traditions, not only Christians but also Jews and humanists, and pointed the way to co-operation in faith and action between Protestants and Catholics which sometimes far transcended the achievements arrived at hitherto by the ecumenical movement. Just as it was in the concentration camps during the Second World War, so now it was, especially in the prisons, that people who had not really taken one another seriously as Christians, and had often mistrusted each other, were reminded of the one baptism into the death and resurrection of the one Lord of the world and of the Church.

Events in many coloured congregations revealed perspectives about the Church in the past and in the future, which were of deep ecumenical importance. The racial struggle in America revealed with fresh clarity that in emergency situations those separated Churches are brought together which are open to that which is human. The decision to take action in face of the racial challenge raised the question whether it was possible for Churches with different traditions to co-operate. The response to this question then deepened the fellowship between the Churches, even if that response could not be unconditional. Thereby it was discovered that emergency situations can be tackled by Churches and local congregations only in an ecumenical way.

The meetings, ecumenical and public, which were held as part of the struggle led to a kind of liturgy both new and appropriate to the situation. Hymns in the form of the traditional spirituals were sung about the recent events. Equally spontaneous were the prayers for the freedom movement and for its enemies. The sermon was followed by discussion on future action and the recruitment of persons prepared to undertake it. The collection was devoted to the current tasks of the congregation (a congregation composed for the first time of many Churches). A report on this says that furthermore "it is really non-essential whether the leadership is in the hands of an ordained minister or of a non-ordained person". The determination to find a solution for the situation, and the confidence that the right solution would be found, produced new charismatic leaders. And the action itself gave rise to the faith that one was called to co-operate in God's work in order to let the world be reconciled with him, by forcing the world out of its bastions into the open where it could receive the freedom and justice ordained by him.

This faith gave rise to a renewed sense of social responsibility due to the belief that the Church is the people of God. The new ecumenical fellowship made Christians realize that they have a task for the world, which is God's own world. In some important places in the South of the U.S.A. one idea was thoroughly understood. It was an idea that was born among Christian students in Eastern Germany in relation to the question whether coexistence is possible between the Church and an atheist–socialist social order, or with the world at all. The idea was given the name "pro-existence". Through the ecumenical discussion it reached Christians engaged in the racial struggle in America. They then began to see and to say that a Church of Jesus Christ cannot be anything but a fellowship for pro-existence, following the pattern of Jesus Christ who lived and died for all men. Having arrived at this understanding of what the Church is, and having stood up for their convictions courageously again and again, these Christians then appealed to the Church all over the world to take a stand against all forms of injustice, and especially racial injustice, and urged it to repent wherever it accepted or even promoted any kind of discrimination. The ecumenical intention inherent in this appeal found simultaneous expression in the request to make intercession, to give help, to be prepared to suffer with others. This appeal did not fall on deaf ears, as is shown by the response to it all over the world, including that of the Fellowship of the Least Coin.

The above, very provisional summary of the ecumenical importance of church action in the racial struggle in America was based on a paper drafted under the leadership of the Reverend Andrew Young, a colleague of Martin Luther King, in connection with the study on Structures for Missionary Congregations.[1] The theme of this study arose from the intensive ecumenical discussion about evangelism since Amsterdam (1948) which produced both many insights due to fresh encounters with the world and the realization

[1] "Missionary Presence in the Racial Revolution", in *Planning for Mission*, ed. Thomas Wieser (N.C.C.U.S.A., New York 1966), pp. 164ff.

N

that in many cases the local Churches, owing to their introspective structure, are incapable of carrying out the evangelism that is required today. By raising the question what form a local Church ought to assume, this discussion again brought up some of the problems and findings of the discussion on the role of the laity in a rapidly changing world. The study was launched at the Third Assembly of the World Council of Churches in 1961, at the time of the integration of the World Council and the International Missionary Council, that is, just at the moment when Churches and local congregations had to face the question of how the Church and the missions should come together in the daily life of a local parish.

The response to this study was amazing. An unprecedented number of study groups for this and related questions was discovered. They showed the strength of the view, held especially by young pastors and committed lay Christians, that the local Church cannot become related again to its environment unless it transforms its own self-concept, and its own form. Also the study was in accordance with the conviction of many people that ultimately the problems both of the renewal of the Church and of evangelism can be solved only through ecumenical co-operation. But the discussion raised the question whether there can be any attempt at unity without new efforts to evangelize and to renew the Church beginning with drastic changes at the local level.

Working groups had been formed in many parts of the world to undertake this study. Their wide exploration of immediate and long-range needs for new forms and structures of Churches, particularly in their localities, eventually led them both to identify and to interpret what already was happening with certain groups of Christians, certain congregations, and certain church associations. Basically, then, all they were required to do was, in certain prominent parts of recent church history, to describe the way in which pioneers were walking already and to which the Churches would be led, each in its own place all over the world, when the time came. Side by side with some local Churches which took up the racial struggle in America, with the Industrial Missions in Great Britain or in India and Japan, and with many achievements of the Lay Institutes, special attention was drawn to the Port Harcourt project in Biafra, East Nigeria and to the Church of the Saviour in Washington, U.S.A.

In Port Harcourt the Church had to discover how to serve in a large town which had sprung up like a mushroom during the last few years in the marshland at the delta of the River Niger.[1] The attempt to carry out this task clearly showed that local Churches, in a place of this kind which is undergoing rapid industrialization and urbanization, cannot venture to evangelize unless their evangelism forms the kernel of a far-reaching concern for man living in an unfamiliar environment which presents many new dangers, and unless the whole effort is ecumenical from the outset. The need to promote ecumenical co-operation was evident owing to the fact that, as already pointed out in 1925 at the Stockholm Conference, the world is too strong for a divided Church. It was also evident that the people converted to the one Christ were

[1] The Port Harcourt Project (*Monthly Letter about Evangelism*, Geneva April–May 1965).

not destined to be just members of a large number of different separate Churches. So the work was begun by an ecumenical team, consisting mainly of members of Churches which were negotiating about a united Church of Nigeria. Church union on the local level was to be promoted. The team consisted of pastors and laymen, missionaries and social workers. It worked on the pattern of the Group Ministry in the East Harlem Protestant Parish, New York. The work undertaken in the young city aimed at showing the local Churches, whose people only a short time previously had been living in little towns and villages how they must meet the new situation in the light of witness, service, and unity. As in many other places, the team and some local Churches in Port Harcourt learned that witness has to be made within and in the face of the social tensions of our time. They realized that service must take many different forms in the actual local situation. They understood that unity must be envisaged as a form of Church highly differentiated, yet coherent.

When the Church of the Saviour was founded in Washington in 1946, it boldly announced that it was an ecumenical Church. The formulation was as follows:

> An ecumenical Church is one whose heart is heavy because of a divided Christendom. It will pray and work for the healing of its divisions. Its only weapon is love. It will at all times consciously feel itself a part of the World Church and give its first loyalty to the world Christian fellowship. It will be openminded and sympathetic. This is different from tolerance. This spirit is born, not of indifference, but of deep conviction. An ecumenical church gives unqualified corporate allegiance to Jesus Christ.[1]

The importance of this Church, however, lay in the strict commitment of its members, in the elimination of the traditional distinction between pastors and laity, and in a unique form of Christian service which led especially in the U.S.A. and in Australia to the coffee-house movement. Assuming as a matter of course that a local Church exists to serve people, and that this is the only way of convincingly presenting the message, this Washington Church with great personal sacrifice bought a shop in a busy street in Washington and turned it into a café, so as to provide people with a place where they could meet, ask questions, air their grievances, have conversation, and receive help. Groups of church members waited at the tables in the evenings. This service was itself a witness and led to witness. It also became a witness to many local Churches of different denominations which sent their people to Washington from all over the United States in order to see and to ask advice, so that they could do the same. Many Christian coffee houses were then opened in other places, run by different local Churches or by Christians from different denominations together. The ecumenical character of this work attracted wide notice. But it has not yet received ecclesiological recognition; the question whether this kind of coffee house is a new type of Church has still to be answered.

---

[1] E. O'Connor, *Call to Commitment*. New York 1963.

Ecumenical Pioneers

In 1966 and 1967 an unexpectedly large number of people in Indonesia made inquiries about the Christian faith. Churches and congregations reacted not only by increasing evangelism; they sought, wherever possible, a wide ecumenical evangelism. So, in the market place at Bandung, in Java, great services were held daily, led by evangelists and pastors of different Protestant Churches. Joint campaigns of this kind are no longer unusual in many parts of the world. Regional and local Christian Councils (and also well-known evangelists) usually succeed in bringing Churches together for joint evangelism campaigns. The great ecumenical step towards joint baptism, however, hardly occurred. It became possible in Karobatakland, North Sumatra, a remote, ethnically homogenous area where different forms of denominations were still unknown. Here, on 19 June 1966 in a village called Tigalinga, nearly 2,000 people were baptized by fifteen pastors belonging to six different denominations. The baptized people were then integrated into one single Church called the Karobatak Church. The pastors came from the Batak Church, the Simalungun Church, the Niass Church (which are Lutheran in trend), from the Protestant Church in western Indonesia (which is Reformed in tendency), from the Methodist Church in Sumatra, and from the small Karobatak Church itself. These Churches had previously conducted a joint mission campaign lasting several months, on the lines of the Joint Action for Mission programme advocated by the Division of World Mission and Evangelism of the W.C.C. since 1962. Without being particularly well known there, this programme attained its goal in the baptism at Tigalinga.

The rise of new towns has opened the way to further ecumenical action in some cases, even if only on a small scale. For instance, in 1965 in the new industrial town of Churchill, in Victoria, Australia, the Anglican, Presbyterian, and Methodist Churches and the Church of Christ started joint parish work, with the aim of setting up a single Church in the town. In 1966 in the new town of Livingston, near Edinburgh, Scotland, a pastor of the Church of Scotland and a priest of the Scottish Episcopal Church were ordained together for their work in that town. Later a Congregational clergyman joined their team. They co-operate in the work among youth, men, and women and in the Church's relations with the town. The church building of the Church of Scotland, which was still unfinished, was placed at the disposal of the Episcopal congregation, and the hope was expressed that an ecumenical centre will be built, which can be used also by other Churches. Similar decisions were taken in view of the future work and life of Churches in some inner cities where the rapid social change is recognized by many Churches.

In the inner city situations, the East Harlem Protestant Parish in New York became the pattern for the union of local Churches with similar traditions. This parish was created in 1948 in recognition of the irrelevance of maintaining traditional Sunday congregations in an extreme inner city situation. It was a union of four congregations, and adopted new, comprehensive working methods based on the group ministry. In a few years it had become an ecumenically integrated congregation. Similar parishes exist in Chicago and elsewhere.

Following this example, a Presbyterian Church and a Methodist Church in the centre of Sydney have decided to merge, thus providing a starting-point for a larger "United Church of the City of Sydney". Even in the prosperous suburbs of the American towns where after the Second World War a very large number of new churches of widely differing denominations were built, perhaps too many in the view of an ecumenical observer, and therefore had to be filled with people, mergers have been effected between two or three denominations, especially during recent years. At least in some places, for instance in Trenton, a suburb of Detroit, the United Presbyterian Church and the United Church of Christ united in 1966. More important than this, however, was a joint project undertaken by the Lutheran Church in America, the Methodist Church, the Reformed Church in America, the United Church of Christ, and the United Presbyterian Church, to undertake service to the people living in a new residential area in Orange County, north of the city f New York, in the hope that it would develop into a single Church. Here he tradition of the federated Churches and the "community" Churches is ollowed with a new ecumenical consciousness.

In many places for many years local Churches have placed their church remises at the disposal of other denominations. Many Protestant Churches n Germany offered hospitality to Roman Catholic congregations which, owing to the stream of refugees after the war, found themselves in places where no Roman Catholic church existed. Similar hospitality was extended to Orthodox congregations in many towns in western Europe, the last example being in Birmingham, England in 1965. In 1965 a Roman Catholic Church in Saxony, a traditionally Lutheran area of Eastern Germany, offered hospitality to the Lutheran congregation of Deutzen, when their old church building was pulled down owing to the extension of the coal-mining industry. In Islamabad, the new capital of Pakistan, when a site was made available for building a church, the Protestants and Roman Catholics agreed in 1967 to co-operate in building one single church with two separate chapels underground for Sunday services, the main church however being available for use on festival occasions by all the Christians in the country. In 1967 a permanent arrangement was made between the Protestants and Catholics in the industrial centre of Hoogvliet near Rotterdam to share their church buildings. In this case, as a Roman Catholic church could not be built for financial reasons, the Reformed Church invited the Catholic congregation to use its premises, which made it unnecessary for the Catholics to build a church of their own.

Nevertheless, ecumenical co-operation of this kind is still very unusual. This is shown by an appeal made by the Dutch Ecumenical Council to the Churches of Holland, to regard themselves in future wherever possible as "churches in the process of becoming united", and to act accordingly. The Churches in one place should regard themselves (and each other) as the Church of that place, and thus gradually develop a common life. As had been recognized in the ecumenical movement at all levels, this is the first step, and certainly an extremely important one, towards ecumenism on the local level. To quote a phrase of W. A. Visser 't Hooft, if this step were taken the Churches would go a long way towards being "unitable".[1] In order to take it hundreds of thousands of local Churches all over the world must show greater readiness to live in the light of the promise that there shall be one Church and one World, through faith in the future of him who came.

At its meeting in Geneva in February 1966 the Central Committee of the W.C.C. issued a statement "On the Ecumenical Way" which read as follows:

Walking in the ecumenical way requires of local congregations:
(a) That Church members be now prepared for a wider and deeper unity with Christians of other Communions;
(b) That both in public and in private, specific intercessions be offered for other churches, and not only general prayers for unity;
(c) That religious education be given an ecumenical dimension both in experience and in word;
(d) That the reading of the Scriptures be faithfully practised by Church members, as the necessary inspiration of the ecumenical way;
(e) That in preaching, the scriptural vision of the one people of God united under the cross of Christ should be insistently proclaimed;
(f) That congregations and their members bear a costly part in the mission of the Church and be given a vision of the significance of the churches' task as "mission in six continents";
(g) That a generous response be made to the claims of human need in a world in which men are hungry both for bread and for knowledge;
(h) That Christian citizens actively seek to secure human dignity and rights for all men and that they diligently exercise a responsible citizenship wherever they may live.[2]

The draft had contained another sentence, which was not included in the statement:

We welcome the obedience in which local groups of Christians are led to make ecumenical experiments both towards each other and in common action to the community. Such obedience helps to make clear the ecumenical way and to revitalize the movement.[3]

[1] W. A. Visser 't Hooft, "The Una Sancta and the Local Church", *Ecumenical Review*, vol. 13 (October 1960), p. 12.
[2] "On the Ecumenical Way", *Ecumenical Review*, vol. 18 (1966), p. 228.
[3] MRCC (Geneva 1966), pp. 91f.

14
Signs of Radicalism
in the Ecumenical Movement

DAVID L. EDWARDS

Introduction

Some Christians have been convinced that desirable changes in the Churches would come from listening to the swiftly changing world and from serving it, in order to hear and serve the revolutionary God revealed in Jesus Christ. This conviction holds that mankind matters more than the institutional Church, and the future more than the past; and it constitutes radicalism in the ecumenical movement. *Oikoumene* meant in Greek "the inhabited earth"; "ecumenical" means more than "inter-Church".

The pioneers of the modern ecumenical movement, properly subordinating ecclesiastical questions to the Kingdom of God, believed that the Churches could be united by their work in the world, by their commitment to evangelism, or by working out a "social gospel" based on a liberal theology, through hospitals, colleges, schools, clubs for the unemployed, and organizations for peace and temperance. When the dismantling of the colonial empires destroyed the old simplicity in the missionary enterprise, and when the social gospel seemed powerless to heal the deep tragedies of the nations, the Churches began to acknowledge that the ecumenical movement must be more costly. If the Christian mission was to be discharged in the world, if the gospel was to be proclaimed meaningfully and practised relevantly, if the Church was to be a model for society, there must be changes in the Churches. To Churches as to individuals the word had been spoken: they must die before rising. Christians began to pay this cost of discipleship afresh under Hitler, and it was in the prayer of discipleship that the World Council of Churches was constituted.[1]

Since 1948, however, the extent of the changes required has been seen more clearly. It is the task of this chapter to describe some experiments through which some Christians have risen to this challenge. These Christians have shown a new courage and a new flexibility, and they have glimpsed, beyond their continuing divisions and problems, a new hope and a new unity for the Church serving the Kingdom.

The word "radical" when transferred from left-wing politics to religion is, however, ambiguous. Many "radicals" have responded to the challenge of the modern world by abandoning belief in any God distinguishable from man and the universe. Their faith has been in the actual or potential lordship of man, who stands on his own. Some such radicals have called themselves Christians. To them the death of Jesus without any miracle to save him has been a specially effective demonstration of the fact that there is no God, but they have been greatly moved by the personal freedom and the outgoing love which they have seen in Jesus. A religious emotion based on the "death of God" was expounded in the United States during the later 1960s by some radicals who wished to say that Christian theologians could and should be atheists.

We may agree that this "death of God" theology has been a valuable reminder that the liberal theologians of a past era addressed themselves to some important questions. How could minds shaped by an age of science

[1] W. A. Visser 't Hooft, *The Renewal of the Church*. London 1956.

375

get into any relationship with dogmas inherited from a vanished age of faith? How could a "natural" theology based on a contemplation of nature and history, including mankind's religious experience, get into any relationship with the specifically Christian commitment and obedience to the transcendent God as Lord and Father? These questions were not answered by orthodox or neo-orthodox theologians such as Karl Barth who gloried in the discontinuity between science and faith, between the God of nature and the God of revelation; and it was inevitable that the questions should be raised again when the historical circumstances favouring a conservative theology (the Churches' resistance to Hitler, etc.) had passed. Many competent Christian theologians have wrestled with these questions since 1948, and no lack of sympathy with their struggles is implied if we exclude the "death of God" from the scope of this chapter.[1]

Many Christians who have maintained a faith which others could recognize as faith in God through Jesus Christ have been unwilling to go regularly to any local Church. Already before 1948 this attitude was very common, for example among the millions who had lapsed from attendance at public worship while preserving nominal connections with the national Churches in Europe. Something of the same attitude was also found among many in Asia who respected the teachings of Jesus Christ, but refused to be baptized because they had been born into a non-Christian national religion. Since 1948 the total number of such churchless Christians has probably not varied greatly, but their attitude has been voiced more freely.

Since 1948 belief in a Christianity outside the historic denominations has indeed been expressed with a vigour which has earned the use of the term "radical". A phrase of Dietrich Bonhoeffer's has been used, and often misused, in this context: the phrase translated as "religionless Christianity". However, many of these churchless Christians have developed in such a way as to place them outside the ecumenical movement, for they have abandoned the vision and the struggle of the whole Church taking the whole gospel to the whole world. Religious broadcasts, and perhaps some fairly haphazard religious readings, have been their only contacts with articulate belief. Their warnings against the complacency of the Churches have grown less urgent as they have themselves become more completely absorbed in their own jobs and homes.

The only Christians who come within the scope of this chapter are, therefore, those believers in God through Christ who have seriously sought and persistently supported the emergence of new forms of Christian fellowship, or the renewal of the old forms, for the sake of the service of God in the world. Ecclesiastical traditions have been attacked or ignored when they seemed to be irrelevant to the life and work of Christians in an age of swift change. On the other hand, some movement or group has been valued, for these rebels have been sure that they have needed a fellowship if they were to be Christians at all, and they have hoped that this fellowship would deepen the authenticity of their faith. Such convictions have connected this kind of

[1] I offered discussions of theological radicalism in Chapter 1 of *The Honest to God Debate* which I edited (London 1963) and in *Religion and Change* (London 1969).

protest with the ecumenical movement, in previous periods as in our own. For example, the Mukyokai (no-Church) movement in Japan, consisting largely of Bible study groups and independent students of the Bible, has been continuous since the work of the independent evangelist Kanzo Uchimura at the beginning of the century. Without full-time organizers, this movement has been given some cohesion by occasional rallies and by literature. It is believed to include some twenty to fifty thousand Japanese, many of whom are also members of normal congregations.[1]

The form of Christian radicalism which has been most useful to ecumenical progress has, however, been the form taken by protest when it has worked within the Churches out of love for the Church. Such radicals have been convinced that, under the power of the Holy Spirit, the denominations as they naturally were should and could be loved into renewal. Dietrich Bonhoeffer, for one, never separated himself from the devotion and discipleship of the Church, the Communion of Saints about which he wrote profoundly as a young man.

Radically minded churchmen of this breed have, of course, not found it easy to remain loyal to the Churches. When American sociologists analysed mercilessly the sentimental and escapist shallowness of the piety of the suburban Churches, when a Canadian journalist hit at those who slumbered in comfortable pews instead of addressing themselves to the great challenges of the twentieth century, when British paperbacks or German broadcasts discussed at length what was wrong with the remnants of European Christendom, when Marxists declared that the religion of the Churches was opium administered to the workers by capitalists and landowners, when Afro-Asian nationalists denounced the "white man's religion" controlled by missionaries, these Christians have recognized the force and the justice in such attacks. They, too, have known how tragically often the Churches have backed a sinful *status quo* and how tragically often the renewal of the Church has degenerated into tricks to fill unchanged churches.

If these churchmen have not yielded to despair about the Church, it has been because of inspiration drawn from unusual movements or groups or prophets. But they have cared about their fellow-Christians in those comfortable pews, and any insights which they have gained have been related to the question of the future of the Church. Thus they have not abandoned the rediscovery of the missionary urgency of the gospel of God, or the rediscovery of the People of God, made in earlier periods of ecumenism. Nor have they forgotten that the most testing challenge to Christian radicalism comes from the new age announced in the Bible, not from the new events announced in the newspapers. "We have no intention of becoming a sect or a para-church", wrote one industrial chaplain. "Neither are we concerned to find a theology for industry, but rather to relate Christian theology to the community in which we live."[2] Such radicals have carried the misery of the Church, "God's frozen people", in their minds and hearts because they have

---

[1] Emil Brunner paid a tribute to the Mukyokai in *Religion and Culture: Essays in Honour of Paul Tillich* (New York 1958), pp. 287–90.

[2] Leonard Dryden in *Theology* (London December 1966), p. 531.

been convinced that the People of God is not dead, that the Church's real grandeur is hidden in the invincible purpose of God for all men.[1]

The Sign of Taizé: Religious Communities

The cry of these radicals in the ecumenical movement has been for action. The pace of the official inter-Church encounters has seemed too slow for a revolutionary world, and for a revolutionary God. But the most useful of these radicals have not forgotten the true nature of Christian action. Their small actions have been contributed as prophetic signs, pointing to the character of the activity of God. They opened the Bible, they found there the great Sign of Jesus Christ, and they prayed. They asked for strength from the one source beyond human resources; and when their actions ended in failure they knew that the God on whom they relied could still show his power as King, if necessary by the resurrection of the dead.

It seems right to mention first the prophetic sign of Taizé.[2] When Roger Schutz, a Reformed theologian, came to this half-abandoned French village in August 1940, he found an empty house and a plea from the old peasant woman who gave him a meal: "Buy this house, stay here, we are so lonely, so isolated." In that house Schutz cared for refugees. Then he had to take refuge himself, back in the Switzerland where he had been born; but when he returned to Taizé it was with the nucleus of a community in which seven brothers took life vows at Easter 1948. The brethren were under a rule modelled on the monastic (or coenobetic) tradition of the Catholic Church. More than four centuries after Luther's attack on monastic vows, the first Taizé brothers said their regular "offices" together in the cathedral of St Peter in Geneva, where Calvin (who also condemned the monastic life) had preached.

Back in France, the community has continued to be a sign of Christian care for the world's needs. It has raised the efficiency of farming in its district, and has founded a co-operative instead of growing rich. The brothers have given the skills learned in their former professions to help their neighbours in Burgundy, and have been sent to industrial France and to other nations. Notably since 1958 they have gone to Latin America, in "Operation Hope" which has concentrated on agricultural co-operatives and the distribution of the New Testament in a translation approved by the Catholic hierarchy. Taizé has also welcomed many thousands of students and other young people.

The brothers' life of prayer, sustaining this service to others, has not been a mere imitation of the ancient monastic centres such as Cluny and Cîteaux, although both historic sites lie near Taizé in Burgundy. When the *Office de Taizé* was published in 1962, its careful balance of old and new aroused the attention of many who were concerned for the renewal of Christian worship around the world. Nor has the life of Taizé been the product of a mere

---

[1] Mark Gibbs and T. Ralph Morton have written two popular books: *God's Frozen People* (London 1964) and *God's Lively People* (London 1969). Collin Williams has summed up "new directions" in thinking about *The Church* (New York 1969).

[2] For this section, see Bibliography, p. 449 below.

enthusiasm. The writings of Roger Schutz have been valued widely as the writings of a master of the spiritual life, while another able theologian in the community, Max Thurian, has made a fresh approach to some of the most difficult problems in the Catholic–Protestant dialogue from a biblical basis: celibacy, confession, confirmation, inter-Communion, the Eucharist, and devotion to the Blessed Virgin Mary. Taizé has maintained the theological review *Verbum Caro*, and has included an Orthodox centre as a witness to the relevance of the Eastern tradition.

This establishment by Protestants of a community both charitable and liturgical has challenged both Protestants and Catholics to reconsider their past rejection of each other. Here a comparison may be made between Taizé and older communities which have lived under a religious rule within Churches of the Reformation. Almost exactly a century before the arrival of Roger Schutz in Taizé, Marion Hughes took her religious vows for life in Oxford, and since then many monastic communities for men and women have been founded in the Anglican Communion. These communities have been centres of prayer for Christian unity, and the humble French Catholic priest, Paul Couturier, who was the founder of the Week of Prayer for Unity in its contemporary form, found a quick understanding among the religious of the Church of England during his visits to that island. Anglican monks and nuns have had a special interest in developing contacts with the Roman Catholics to whose examples they have been indebted in the life of the spirit, and they have done other ecumenical work.

Among Lutherans also, there has been a revival of *Life Together* (the title of a little book by the young Dietrich Bonhoeffer). Communities of deaconesses in Germany began in 1836 and have combined a life of common prayer with their charitable and pastoral work in the parishes; by 1968 there were about 40,000 deaconesses based on almost 120 houses. The Sisterhood of Mary at Darmstadt, founded by Mother Basilea (Klara Schlink) in 1947, has concentrated on a deep prayer life. This community has reached out to the Jews in penitence for the recent past, emphasizing that Israel has its own place in the hope of the coming of the Kingdom of God. Deaconesses and some small communities of women vowed to the life of prayer have also arisen in the Churches of Sweden and Denmark.

If the question is asked why Taizé has developed its extraordinary influence on the ecumenical movement, one answer is that its roots in Calvin's Geneva have made its closeness to Rome interesting and even astonishing. Its only precedents were women's communities. A community of deaconesses was founded in Reuilly near Paris in 1841, and others followed. In 1923 a community of Veilleurs (Watchmen) was founded by the French pastor Wilfred Monod, modelled on the Franciscan third order but with no mother house. At the retreat house at Pomeyrol in the South of France, in 1950 four sisters pledged themselves for life in poverty, chastity, and obedience. Another house of prayer was founded in 1936 at Grandchamp near Neuchâtel in Switzerland, and the sisters in it formed a community with life vows under Geneviève Micheli in 1952; next year they adopted the rule of Taizé. But the brothers of Taizé were more consciously ecumenical than those women aspired to be; for it was no accident that the new community of men who were Swiss and Reformed was placed in the middle of a Catholic (or ex-Catholic) France. Couturier had spoken of an "invisible monastery" in the ecumenism of prayer; Schutz founded a community which was to be inter-national and interdenominational because it was to be a visible sign of unity.

At Taizé the opportunities for extensive fellowship with Catholics did not come quickly, although the community was allowed to use the parish church for some of its worship; and many Protestants were suspicious of a compro-mise with a Catholicism which seemed superstitious and reactionary. The change came when Roger Schutz was received in audience by Pope John XXIII in 1958. After that meeting it was "spring" at Taizé as part of the "spring" of the Catholic Church (as the Pope himself said), and the com-munity was asked to send its own observers to the Second Vatican Council. Members of Catholic religious orders have shared in the life and work of Taizé and have used it for their own conferences.

The first large-scale meeting of Catholic and Protestant leaders in France took place at Taizé, four hundred years after the disastrous Colloquies of Poissy. In 1962 Christian young people from Germany built the large Church of Reconciliation in order to welcome the mainly Catholic crowds. Catholic and Orthodox chapels were built in the crypt. A large conference centre also became necessary. In the twenty-fifth year after Schutz's arrival in the village, 200,000 people came to see the sign at Taizé. The radical courage of one Protestant theologian, and of the brothers who had joined him, had come at the right time.

What of the future? Taizé stresses that its experiments have all been "provisional". Although Protestants from many nations have admired this community, and have even contributed recruits to it, at present it seems likely that less traditional forms of community life will appeal more. The Taizé brothers take the traditional vows of lifelong poverty, chastity, and obedience (slightly modified in that some use of personal possessions is allowed, and obedience is to the community rather than to the Prior alone). Some modern communities have shown that these vows have not been necessary to their purposes.

A number of ashrams in India and Ceylon have adapted Hindu models for a life of devout simplicity and they have found that this life speaks to their neighbours.[1] Perhaps the most notable example has been Joytiniketan, founded by Murray Rogers. St Julian's Community in Sussex, founded by Florence Allshorn, has adapted the model of the English country house. It grew from a concern for the spiritual refreshment of missionaries on furlough, and has been remarkable for its courage in getting away from the retreat house atmosphere in its hospitality to many guests. It now has a daughter house in Kenya.[2]

The Iona Community in Scotland, founded in 1938, has completed the

---

[1]Bishop A. J. Appasamy described twenty-five ashrams founded after 1921 (when an experiment was begun at Tiruppattur near Madras) in *Frontier* (London, Winter 1961), pp. 281–5.

[2] Margaret Potts, *St Julian's*. London, 1968.

buildings on the hallowed island of Iona where its worship and conferences are maintained each summer. It has also expanded the work of its members in Glasgow, in the "church-extension charges" of the new housing areas, and in other parishes. This fellowship of ministers and laymen lives under a simple discipline covering prayer and expenditure, and this has been an indispensable element in its contribution to the renewal of the (Presbyterian) Church of Scotland. But the inspiration of its founder, George (now Lord) MacLeod, has made the community evangelistic and political rather than "Catholicizing" and theological as Taizé is.[1]

Whether or not the traditional monastic vows will be regarded as essential, the sign of Taizé seems likely to remind many Christians that the spirit of discipline founded on worship is essential if Christians are to live in what the Taizé brothers call "the joy, simplicity and pity of the Gospel". To give two examples: it is through this spirit that Christian laymen serving abroad can be envoys of the Church in its ecumenical mission, and Christian laymen staying at home can be stewards responsible to God for the faithful use of their time, talents, and money.[2]

Even in its narrower sense of inter-Church relations, the ecumenical movement seems bound to involve a radical courage in the life of the spirit if it is to involve more than theological conversations and paper schemes. Specialist agents of this movement such as the staffs of Councils of Churches will be seen to resemble the members of a religious order more closely than the members of a civil service. Missionaries sent from one Church to the assistance of another will be understood mainly as ecumenical workers, and in their training and support it will not be forgotten that when Count Zinzendorf in 1732 launched the modern Protestant missionary movement into the world (with a strong emphasis on Christian reunion), it was from the base of the Moravian religious community at Herrnhut.

The Sign of Pentecostalism

There seems to be no connection between the "Calvinist monks" of Taizé and a movement which has rejected Catholic forms of prayer and belief and which has criticized the ecumenical movement for including non-fundamentalist theologians. However, a connection exists, for both the Taizé brothers and the Pentecostals have combined a conservative theology with radical experiments in fellowship.[3]

When the Pentecostal movement began in the U.S.A. and Wales as this century began, it was a movement within a number of denominations for a

---

[1] George F. MacLeod, *Only One Way Left* (Glasgow 1956) and T. Ralph Morton, *The Iona Community Story* (London 1957).

[2] The concern of the ecumenical movement in these areas is reflected in the reports on *Laymen Abroad* in the *International Review of Missions* (October 1967), pp. 444–58, and on *Christian Stewardship and Ecumenical Confrontation* (New York 1961).

[3] In this section I am indebted to Dr W. J. Hollenweger, whose *Enthusiastisches Christentum* (Zürich 1969) is now the standard work. An English translation is in preparation. See also his article on "The Pentecostal Movement and the World Council of Churches" in the *Ecumenical Review* (July 1966), pp. 310–20.

revival of the simplicity and fervour of the Acts of the Apostles; it was in that sense ecumenical. Today Pentecostalism has largely, although not entirely, become a family of new denominations, and its greatest strength lies in the warmth of its worship. Its lay members communicate spontaneously among themselves and with their pastor on the basis of the Bible; it is in that sense a liturgical movement. Pentecostalism, like the Taizé community, longs to see all Christians united in a more joyous and courageous fellowship of the Spirit. While Pentecostalism may seem to be an emotionalism appealing to the ignorant, in fact the nearest secular parallel is the jam session of a jazz band. Here, too, there is an underlying pattern which may be varied by the members of the band according to their own understanding of it. Here, too, we find the expression of a disinherited subculture which is now being accepted by more sophisticated people as a valuable way of making music. And here, too, there is a communal vitality which many need in the modern world.

The growth of Pentecostalism in this period has been phenomenal. Its best-known manifestations, "speaking in tongues" (*glossolalia*), "divine healing", and prophecy, are parts of a charismatic revival which has affected many in the traditional Churches in the U.S.A. and Europe. In Italy Pentecostals outnumber all other Protestants, and their small communities survive and spread in Russia and China. In Africa and Latin America Pentecostals form a "new tribe" which often has a quicker appeal than any other form of the Christian mission. In Brazil and Chile, it is estimated that Pentecostals constitute a fifth of the voters. Here is "soul-saving", but here also is one expression of a whole people in crisis, one factor highly relevant to social change.

Although suspicion has been dominant on both sides, consultations have taken place between leaders of Pentecostalism and of the official ecumenical movement, recognizing that "whereas Catholicism and Protestantism have laid immense stress upon what is given and unalterable, the type of Christian faith which I have called Pentecostal has laid its stress on that which is to be known and recognized in present experience, the power of the ever living Spirit of God".[1] Small Pentecostal Churches have joined the World Council of Churches, and some of its leaders have taken part in its meetings.

Some attempts have also begun to bring into the ecumenical dialogue the Africans, estimated to number around seven millions, who have expressed their Christian faith enthusiastically through "independent" or "prophetic" Churches. These religious movements, using African, not European, forms of worship, and charismatic, not bureaucratic, forms of fellowship, are similar to the Pentecostals in their warmth and simplicity. There were about six thousand of them in Africa by 1968, and it was an open question whether the older Churches in that continent—Churches which had doubled in size every ten years—would absorb such a ferment of enthusiasm.[2]

---

[1] Lesslie Newbigin, *The Household of God* (London 1953), p. 98.

[2] Victor Hayward, *African Independent Church Movements* (London 1963), and David B. Barrett, *Schism and Renewal in Africa* (Nairobi 1968).

Bad Boll and Bangalore: Lay Institutes and Study Centres

In the centres of Christian renewal which are to be mentioned now, the work has been formed not around the traditional order of common prayer, and not around the free worship of Spirit-filled groups of believers, but around the contemporary disorder of life in the world.[1] The laymen who have gone to the Evangelical Academies in Germany—about 40,000 a year—have gone in order to discuss their own problems freely with each other and with theologians whose thought is relevant to these problems, so that, when they return to their jobs and their homes, they may live with a fresh insight into their secular responsibilities. In these Evangelical Academies the laity come together, but only in order that they may scatter.

The Evangelical Academies were born as a result of the ruin of Germany in the 1940s. Until Hitler fell, the ruin was moral: too many Germans allowed themselves to be corrupted by Nazism. In 1945 almost all the institutions of the country were, like many of its physical assets, destroyed or despised. The universities, for example, which had always been isolated from the life of ordinary men, had compromised themselves by subordinating their liberal values to the ideology of Nazi power. Amid the ruins of a nation the Churches were left standing, if not completely in either a physical or a moral sense, at least enough to be spiritual centres of the national reconstruction. Two Protestant theologians, Helmut Thielicke and Eberhard Müller, supported by Bishop Wurm, therefore invited lawyers and industrialists to talk freely about their problems in this tragic crisis. In September 1945, 150 came to a hotel in the health resort of Bad Boll. Other groups were invited to later conferences, until twenty-three years later the Evangelical Academy at Bad Boll had enough work to keep a permanent staff of 130 (not including domestic help) busy with from 350 to 400 conferences a year, on a budget equivalent to almost one and a half million United States dollars.

Bad Boll has remained the largest, but other academies have sprung up in Germany, analysing and meeting people's spiritual and intellectual needs. Both the authorities of the Federal (Western) Republic and the Churches have been willing to support them despite their high cost in man-power and money. The Federal Republic has subsidized the discussions as part of its drive for adult education, and employers have encouraged people to attend in working time. The Churches have benefited from the arrangement by which the State collects a "church tax" from all citizens except the minority which has deliberately opted out of all church connections. So far the Churches have been willing to use part of these resources in equipping the academies, although probably most people who use them have not been, and have never become, active members of a parish congregation. In December 1945, Bad Boll convened a conference of industrial workers by relying on recommendations from parish Churches. The group did not represent the workers, and this method of invitation was not repeated. Worship in the chapels is voluntary and often poorly attended, but the conference day usually includes corporate study of the Bible. The Christian theologians and sociologists on

[1] See Bibliography, p. 449 below.

the staff contribute to each course, and they are listened to because of their knowledge of the subject under discussion and because they are familiar with the techniques of free group work.

The academies have varied in emphasis and method. Those at Arnoldshain and Loccum owe their foundations more clearly than Bad Boll to the initiatives of the Churches in their areas. Loccum, with its staff of forty, runs in addition to conferences retreats for church people and week-long courses for workers under twenty-five. The approach of Bad Boll to a group through problems arising in that group's common job has been adopted by other academies with various modifications. The Tutzing Academy by its lake specializes in cultural themes, while the Friedewald Academy in its castle specializes in courses for politicians and trade unionists. For years the Hamburg Academy owned no house, but sponsored many study groups.

Both the "pastoral" desire to serve the visible Churches and the "frontier" desire to serve laymen who are probably alienated from these Churches are present in the German academy movement. Some confusion of aim has been inevitable. However, all the academies are convinced that the Church's traditional pattern of work through parish Churches is not sufficient by itself, for "the world has become different".[1] It would not be enough to minister to people on a residential basis, even if there were enough ministers. Laymen must be helped to relate the Christian faith to their places of work and to the political and other questions which dominate modern life. This idea has made the academy movement a sign to Christians, although not a panacea to solve all the problems of the Churches.

The idea was in the air, apart from the particular circumstances which produced the first Bad Boll conference in 1945. As long back as 1915 Manfred Bjorkquist began the foundation of Sigtuna above Lake Mälar in Sweden. That foundation enabled students and industrialists to meet industrial workers at a time when social divisions went deep; and the discussions of life's problems in a free and open, basically Christian context at Sigtuna have been continuous since 1918. Sigtuna now includes a boarding school, a people's college for adult education, a large library, the Cultural Institute of the Church of Sweden, and the Scandinavian Ecumenical Institute; and it is famous for its encouragement of drama and experimental worship. There are other lay training centres in the Swedish dioceses.[2]

In England, another country with an established Church but a largely unchurched population, no Bad Boll or Sigtuna has happened. But J. H. Oldham took the lead in the Christian Frontier Council, a body of thirty to forty prominent laymen in London with its organ the *Christian Newsletter* (latterly called *Frontier*). Under Anglican auspices St George's College, Windsor, has run short courses for lay leaders and clergy, and William Temple College, Rugby, has specialized in lectures to (and discussions by) industrialists and trade unionists, and in theological training for men and women in one or two-year courses. At Dunblane in Scotland an ecumenical centre for lay training (Scottish Churches' House) was opened in 1961.

[1] Eberhard Müller, *Die Welt ist anders geworden.* Hamburg 1953.
[2] Olov Hartman, *The Sigtuna Foundation.* London 1955

In the Netherlands the involvement of the Church in the world has been studied more systematically, partly, it would seem, because of many Dutchmen's continuing zeal in theology, but also because this country went through the experience of occupation in the war. At the world-famous Kerk en Wereld Institute (on the estate known as De Horst at Driebergen near Utrecht) the programme has included courses of three or four years for training lay workers for the parishes and schools, as well as short conferences. At Oud Poelgeest near Leiden the laymen's conferences last for a week or a week-end, with special emphasis on international meetings and cultural activities. The Catholic Church has established a centre at De Dreef, where the emphasis is on adjusting rural Catholics to urbanization, and other centres have been thrown up by the ferment of the 1960s in Dutch Catholicism.

The most influential Dutch Reformed pioneer was Hendrik Kraemer, who like Dietrich Bonhoeffer saw in a Nazi prison that the Church must change radically if it was to take part in the life of the post-war world. Kraemer was called to be the first Director of the Ecumenical Institute founded by the World Council of Churches (thanks to the generosity of John D. Rockefeller, Jr) in the Château de Bossey near Geneva in 1946. Also on the staff was Suzanne de Diétrich, the French leader in study groups for biblical theology.

Under that great leadership, and under the next two directors, H. H. Wolf and Nikos Nissiotis, the institute at Bossey has held many international meetings for different professions and around different concerns of the contemporary world. In the winters it has also arranged a Graduate School where theological students could acquaint themselves with the work and thinking of the World Council of Churches and the wider ecumenical movement, and go back to their Churches enlightened and disturbed. Despite the difficulties which are inevitable when busy men have to organize internationally and when participants face many problems of language and idiom, Bossey has been a home of creative dialogue and study. Being stimulated by lay pressures, some of its thinking has been radical.

Although mention must be made of the beautiful centre at Boldern on the lake near Zürich, and of one of the French centres in an industrial area at Glay, the lay institutes of Europe have now become too numerous to list.

Lay institutes have spread outside Europe. Academies have been founded with German support in Japan, at Oiso near Tokyo and at Kyoto, and in Korea at Seoul. The Ecumenical Christian Centre at Bangalore and the Ecumenical Institute at Calcutta were conceived as Indian versions of Bossey, while the Ecumenical Centre at Sukabumi serves Indonesia. The Mindolo Foundation in Zambia, including the Dag Hammarskjöld Memorial Library as a Swedish gift, and the Limuru Conference Centre in Kenya were the first in a growing number of institutes where Christian participation in the new African nations could be studied and served. In South Africa, Wilgerspuit and other centres have battled for interracial co-operation and other forms of Christian action. Sometimes a council has been supplied with the resources to sponsor such lay training, as the Christian Council of Kenya did between the Mau Mau emergency and the first years of independence, publishing a brave journal of political and social comment, *Rock*. At other times a Council of Churches has given autonomy to a lay fellowship which could include many non-churchmen in its concern for special problems. A successful example has been "Australian Frontier", under the leadership of Sir James Darling and of Peter Mathews (formerly Director at Mindolo).

Such academies or training programmes have needed to be supplemented by more systematic investigations of the social and spiritual conditions of an era in close collaboration with non-Christians, leading to small consultations and to publications. Since many areas have not been too well served by Christian scholars in the universities, a world-wide chain of "study centres" has been forged since 1957. Eighteen such centres could be counted in 1968, and more were planned (such as an Institute for the Study of Man and Society in Canberra, Australia). Major contributions to research and reflection have been made in India by the Christian Institute for the Study of Religion and Society at Bangalore under the outstanding leadership of Paul Devanandan and M. M. Thomas, and in Latin America by the River Plate Christian Study Centre which has sponsored research in Montevideo under Julio de Santa Ana and in Buenos Aires under Leopoldo Niilus.

Other centres have studied the religion and culture of the Muslims (at Algiers and at the Henry Martyn Institute which has recently moved to Lucknow in India), the Buddhists (at Colombo), the Sikhs (at Batala), the Chinese (at Tao Fong Shan near Hong Kong), the Japanese (at Kyoto), the animists (at Manila), and a new socialist society (at Havana in Cuba). Other study programmes have been conducted, notably the studies of Islam directed by Kenneth Cragg for the Near East Christian Council; and the Councils of Churches in the western countries have also sponsored "working parties"— notably in London and New York—which have produced some expert reports on current political problems.

But an estimate of the world-wide influence of the academy movement must partly depend on a judgement about the willingness of North American Christians to renew their vast "lay training" programmes, stressing the techniques used and the insights gained in Germany. One of the problems here is that so many elements have been combined in the network of lay institutes and study centres. In 1948 the American Committee for the World Council of Churches published a brochure in which Walter M. Horton urged that many more centres of "re-Christianization" should be formed in America as in Europe. He included five elements in his plea:

(*a*) a sociological institute to make a national or regional survey;

(*b*) a study circle, to think out the cultural problems revealed by the survey, in the light of the affirmations of Christian faith and the principles of Christian ethics (these first two elements demand the services of a university faculty);

(*c*) a community of some sort, with a permanent leader and at least semi-permanent fraternal members, where new patterns of Christian culture can actually be tried out and launched (this and the following elements demand a rural retreat);

(*d*) an adult education programme (conferences, courses, laymen's training schools) which conveys the inspiration of the community to the nation or region, by personal contact and free persuasion;

(*e*) an ecumenical bureau.[1]

Since then, a number of books have tried to sort out the elements in such a plea which are most relevant to the American scene, and in each case they have concentrated on Horton's element (*d*)—on the idea of an academy. However, American Protestantism through twenty years seems to have agreed that academies are not for import. Instead, the lay movement which Professor Horton advocated has spread in a less organized way.

Mainly it has spread through small groups in the local Churches and projects sponsored by the national, state, or area Councils of Churches, but there have been symbolic centres. The United Church of Canada has developed four lay leadership centres. In the United States, where conference centres for youth work have a long history, many experiments have been made, although few have secured wide or long-term influence. The best-known new centres have been Pendle Hill near Philadelphia (Quaker), Kirkridge in Pennsylvania under John Oliver Nelson, and Packard Manse in Massachusetts under Paul Chapman. Such centres have conducted seminars on a very wide variety of subjects in lay people's minds, and the relevance of a renewed Christianity to the secular world has emerged through this "problem-centred" free discussion.

Paris and Sheffield: Industrial Mission

Some of these lay institutes have considered carefully problems of life in industry, and other centres, including some local Churches, have been placed in the industrial world in more than a geographical sense.[2] Examples in England are the Luton Industrial College under the Methodist Bill Gowland and the new Anglican Cathedral at Coventry which has an Industrial Chaplain on its staff and a large programme to train youth in civic responsibility. In France the Mission Populaire Evangelique (founded in 1871 as a piece of inter-Church aid by an Englishman, Robert McAll) has developed centres where agnostics can meet Christians in order to talk and work together on the problems of the industrial neighbourhood and the world.

Perhaps the most influential example has been given by the Gossner Haus at Mainz-Kostel in West Germany, under Horst Symanowski. There the Christian witness is thoroughly adjusted to the surrounding factories. Symanowski invites agnostic workers to help his sermon preparation, and has run courses for young pastors about industry; but first he himself worked for six months of each of five years as a labourer in a cement factory.

It is, however, futile to expect workers to visit such buildings unless

[1] Walter M. Horton, *Centres of New Life in European Christendom* (New York 1948), pp. 21–2.

[2] In this section I am indebted to the Reverend Richard Taylor. See Bibliography, p. 506 below.

Christians witness within industry. Since the Church and the proletariat have been divorced for a long time, some bold experiments have had to struggle to express a quiet Christian presence.

The two most famous of these experiments both had their origins during the war of 1939–45. Many Catholics then discovered France as a "missionary country" (*pays de mission*). They saw that the mission to the dechristianized countryside demanded new work by new teams (*équipes*) of priests with a new training in the Mission de France. And they saw that the industrial areas presented an even worse problem. Some priests, therefore, entered the lives of the anti-clerical (and often Communist) workers by doing full-time manual jobs in their midst, by joining their trade unions, and by living anonymously in the style of the proletariat. By the mid-1950s this courageous mission included about a hundred "worker priests". They knew no precedent except the priests who during the war had gone to Germany among the deported labourers.

In England, on the other hand, the complete identification of the priest with the worker has not seemed necessary, although there have been some worker priests in the Church of England. Because anti-clericalism has been less fierce in England, it has been possible to ask management and workers to receive full-time industrial chaplains, and by the mid-1960s there were about seventy of these. During the war some munition factories had appointed chaplains. Among these was E. R. Wickham, who later began the Sheffield Industrial Mission in the steel works in 1944.

Such missions on the shop floor were daring departures from the normal work of a clergyman, and the priests both in France and in England have known agonizing problems. In Paris worker priests felt obliged in conscience to identify themselves with the left-wing politics of the working class. Some of them took part in strikes and anti-N.A.T.O. riots. Many of them grew increasingly estranged from the devotional and other habits of the normal bourgeois clergy. A best-seller was written about them: *Les Saints vont en enfer* (*The Saints Go to Hell*), by Georges Cesbron. Punishment came in 1954 when the Vatican, after various warnings, ended the permission to priests to do full-time industrial work. Some of the worker priests loyally submitted to this tragedy, and eventually permission came from Rome for the Mission Ouvrière to be resumed under new conditions designed to preserve the worker priests' devotional life and to shield them from publicity. Others, however, left the priesthood rather than leave the class whose sufferings and dreams they had come to share.

In Sheffield "Ted" Wickham showed that an industrial chaplain could become a useful friend and an acceptable critic with a bold analysis, both theological and sociological. This required not only pastoral skill but also an ability to speak a rough, everyday language and a dialetical method based on an understanding of the real issues which men faced at their work. Although many small groups met for discussion with the chaplains, the chief aim was not to "win souls" or to "build congregations" in the old sense. In 1965–6, after Wickham's departure to be Bishop of Middleton, most of the clergy in the Sheffield Industrial Mission resigned because they believed that the policy of continuous experiment, and of service to industry, had been abandoned in favour of a more traditional view of evangelism. Many laymen also protested that the basis had been changed. However, the mission continued in Sheffield, and elsewhere in England Wickham's ideas had won such influence that this crisis was not a disastrous blow.

Such problems remind us of the debt owed to the church leaders who originally conceived these visions, Cardinal Suhard of Paris and Bishop Hunter of Sheffield. While experience has been gained at great human cost, tensions and dilemmas are bound to continue. A great gap continues to divide the urban, industrial masses from the traditional parishes. Another gap exists within industry, between the managers and the men (and women) who contribute their labour, but who feel alienated because they do not participate responsibly either in the work or in the surrounding society. Christians who enter these gaps must meet the cross. Quick campaigns are worse than useless. Hymns in canteens would be impertinent. Long-term commitment is essential; but the industrial mission has to be at least as flexible as the changes taking place in the community.

Since its beginning in 1956, the Detroit Industrial Mission has inspired many other industrial and urban missions in North America. Detroit has shown how an experiment which breaks loose from the conventional patterns of church life can change gear every few years. At first the ministers involved were learners. Slowly they acquired the knowledge which equipped them as counsellors, slowly they gathered groups for discussion, and slowly these groups discussed the social goals of an industrial society. By 1968 the thrust had become an emphasis on the participation of all workers in their work. The mission now spoke of the need for a fourth industrial revolution, where the focus would be on people, not on the methods of the previous three revolutions: manufacturing by hired "hands", assembly line production, and cybernetic control mechanisms.[1]

A conference in 1966 at Kyoto, Japan, brought together experienced industrial missioners from the advanced industrial countries of Japan and Australia and from nations where centuries-old traditions were being eroded (India, Korea, the Philippines, Taiwan, Thailand). The involvement of the Churches included community service among workers and their families, educational courses for labour unions, study programmes for executives, and, in Australia, visitation by chaplains.[2]

In Asia, as in Europe, by 1968 denominational differences were seen as obstacles to a Christian presence among the machines, and all over the world there was a search by Christians and others for a goal better than the old forms of capitalism and communism. Pioneering missionaries such as the ecumenical teams at Nairobi in Kenya or at Port Harcourt in Nigeria had in many places helped to urge the Churches to relate to urban life; but everything done was inadequate now that the same questions were being pressed in Africa as in the North American "secular city".

[1] See *Church in Metropolis*, (New York 1968), pp. 11–14. The story of *The Detroit Industrial Mission* (New York 1969) has been told by one of its leaders, Scott Paradise.
[2] *God's People in Asian Industrial Society*. Kyoto 1967.

Signs of Political Mission

Radically minded Christians have responded to the political drama of this period in two ways. First, they have attempted to rescue some of the miserable people who have been its victims. Second, they have attempted to influence the actual process of change, so that change may be for the sake of greater justice in society. Among all the groups which have worked in either or both of these directions, only a few, all coming from continental Europe, can be discussed here. There is not space enough even for movements as active as Christian Action in London or the Oxford Committee for Famine Relief, both of which had their origins in co-operation between Anglicans and Roman Catholics during the 1940s.[1]

C.I.M.A.D.E. (*Comité Inter-Mouvements auprès des Evacués*) began in 1939 when young French Protestants responded to the needs of refugees from Alsace. During the war it helped Jews and others to escape from an occupied France. Afterwards it met urgent needs in a ruined France, but also sent "teams" to work among refugees and young people in Germany.[2] The end of the 1940s did not, however, bring an end to the calls on C.I.M.A.D.E.'s compassion. Within France, old people, the chronic unemployed, discharged prisoners, foreign students, and migrant workers have been among the up-rooted people to whom C.I.M.A.D.E.'s workers have given friendship and some security. Through the long agony of the French defeat in North Africa teams from C.I.M.A.D.E. won the confidence of Muslims by their relief and educational work, so that an independent Algeria has continued to welcome their many activities.

C.I.M.A.D.E. describes itself as "the Church on the spot, a presence in new and difficult situations needing rapid relief or new ways of Christian witness". Mainly Protestant, it has collaborated closely with Roman Catholics and has included Orthodox colleagues. Two-thirds French, it has drawn many volunteers and also financial help from Christians in other countries. Its teams have been committed to put themselves at the service of those who suffer, regardless of religion, race, nationality, or politics. But after twenty-five years one of its leaders said:

> We must not come to the wrong conclusion that C.I.M.A.D.E. is powerful, important, admirable. The daily struggle for, and with, people in a labyrinth of problems . . . weakness, doubts and defeats, slow maturing of ideas, patient plodding . . . this is C.I.M.A.D.E.; but all this takes on a new meaning through the joy that springs from the commitment of a Christian in the fellowship of the Church.[3]

The Sjaloom movement in the Netherlands has been even more radically ecumenical than C.I.M.A.D.E. in France, although much smaller. For years Catholic and Protestant young people, laity and clergy, had been co-operating

---

[1] The founder of Christian Action has told his own story: L. John Collins, *Faith under Fire* (London 1966). "Oxfam" is not exclusively Christian.

[2] Jeanne Merle d'Aubigné, *Les Clandestins de Dieu*. Paris 1968.

[3] Pierre Buogener, address distributed by C.I.M.A.D.E., 1965.

in projects related to the renewal of the Church ("the small *oikoumene*") and the peace and development of the world ("the large *oikoumene*"). In 1963 most of the members of the group which had planned an Ecumenical Youth Congress on the needs of the world, with the theme "Five Loaves and Two Fishes", resolved to stay together in a movement to which they gave the Hebrew name for a healthy, prosperous peace based on justice.

This Sjaloom movement was soon criticized because it expressed its unity in *agape* meals (with bread and wine) which ignored the Catholic–Protestant divisions, but it has concentrated on social and political questions. Its members have, for example, taxed themselves voluntarily in order to protest against the inadequacy of government aid for the underdeveloped countries. Within five years the nucleus consisted of about thirty people, at work in almost as many professions, but a far wider circle had been touched by the monthly magazine *Sjaloom*, by other publications, and by local discussions.[1]

Agape is the name of a centre built in North Italy after the war by international youth teams in order to provide a meeting place for young people concerned for the renewal of the Church or the world (or preferably both). Its leader, the Waldensian pastor Tullio Vinay, then moved with a team to the Sicilian village of Riesi, in order that the presence of a team of Christians might bring hope and help in a scene of poverty and apathy. In Riesi, as at Agape, the work around Tullio Vinay has aroused the interest and respect of Christians and non-Christians in many nations, as a sign of a new desire in the Churches in western Europe to identify themselves with the young and the poor in their own nations and in the world.[2]

The Christian Peace Conference held its first Assembly in Prague in 1958. It originated in the desire of Protestant Christians in eastern Europe to find in the conditions of their socialist countries a way in which Christians might address themselves to public world affairs as Christians and not merely as loyal citizens of their countries.[3] The theme of "peace", already familiar for political reasons, provided an acceptable basis, and the support of the Russian Church provided financial help for an international operation. But in securing participation from other parts of the world, the Conference had the assets that its full-time secretariat was largely Czech, and its moving spirit Professor Josef Hromadka of the Comenius Theological Faculty.

Although most of the leaders steadily maintained that they sought western colleagues in their movement, although the integrity of Dr Hromadka and many of his associates was recognized in the West, and although the representative quality of western participation steadily improved, the West was never present at Prague in the person of churchmen who could match in rank the eastern leaders. Moreover, although western and especially American and N.A.T.O. policies have been rigorously and even stridently criticized, criticism

[1] For the story of Sjaloom, see *De Tafel van één* (Utrecht 1967) and *Shalom* (London 1969).

[2] Two books by Tullio Vinay are: *Agape: ein Wagnis der Hoffnuag für unsere Zeit* (Wuppertal-Barmen 1960) and *Reisi: Geschichte eines Christlichen Abenteuers* (Stuttgart 1964).

[3] In this section I am indebted to Canon David Paton.

of eastern and especially Russian policies has been expressed, if at all, in very subdued tones. None the less, there has been steady progress, and the third All-Christian Peace Assembly in March–April 1968 was marked by a much stronger and more representative western participation among the 500 delegates, by much more genuine dialogue, by a considerable decrease in crudely political speeches, and by a more open attitude all round.

The 1968 Assembly met in Prague a few months before the intervention by the Red Army in Czechoslovakia's liberalization. But it was preoccupied with the issue of international economic justice between the rich North and the poor South, rather than with the East–West "cold war". Chinese Christians were last present in 1961 when they spoke bitterly of the *pax Russo-Americana*. The Asians, Africans, and Latin Americans later took up this theme in a less polemical way. A feature of 1968 was the lack of interest of the Third World in the German question, and their tendency, notably in the Indian delegation, to call in question the decisiveness of the distinction between capitalist and socialist.

The Prague movement, as the Conference has aptly been called, had thus become a world movement within ten years, and from one point of view it could be regarded as the eastern European form of the ecumenical movement —that part where the discussion was conducted according to socialist rules, as in the East Asia Christian Conference the rules were Asian. At the same time, Prague must be affected by arguments between Communists and by developments in the eastern European countries. By 1968 some of those who started it were felt by impatient younger people to have accepted too many assumptions of the Stalinist period, and there were reminders that the anti-official "underground" churches (in Russia specially) were worthy of respect in working out the harsh problems of twentieth-century Christianity.[1]

If it could survive the political tensions, it might turn out that the Prague movement was essential to the healthy functioning of the World Council of Churches not only because of its eastern European character, but also because it focused the revolutionary thrust of the 1966 Church and Society Conference at Geneva. In 1968 Professor Hromadka recalled that "ten years ago, we met in order to tackle a simple programme to work for disarmament, to call for the destruction of atomic and hydrogen weapons, and to deliberate about peaceful coexistence between the so-called West and the so-called East". And he added that although the "cold war" had diminished in Europe, the contradiction between the socialist and capitalist systems, illustrated by the Vietnam war, had deepened until "we are confronted by a much more dangerous international crisis than has occurred since the end of the Second World War".[2] Yet we may conclude that the Prague movement has remained a sign of hope, for by 1968 there was some prospect not only of socialist criticisms of capitalism but also of radical criticisms within an acceptance of Communist-led revolutions.

The more basic themes of dialogue between Christians and Marxists also

[1] Michael Bordeaux has done his best to report from outside the Soviet Union on *Opium of the People* (London 1965) and *Religious Ferment in Russia* (London 1968).
[2] J. L. Hromadka, *Save Man: Peace is Possible* (Prague 1968), pp. 1, 4.

began to emerge during the 1960s—and not only in Prague. Outside China and Russia, official Communist pressure against the Churches has slackened off. Some Marxists such as Togliatti in Italy, Machovec in Czechoslovakia, and Garaudy in France have been saying that, if the future cannot be built without the Communists, neither can it be built without the Christians. Some scientific students of socialist societies have observed, and have respected, the strong survival of religious feelings after any revolution so far achieved. On the Marxist side, therefore, there has been some willingness to accept, and even to invite, the collaboration of religious believers in the struggles for "justice and peace" and (more rarely) some willingness to listen to the theologians' own explanations of religious belief.

On the Christian side of this dialogue, there has also been a much more active sympathy with the Communists. Pastors such as Dr Hromadka himself, Johannes Hamel in East Germany, and Bishop K. H. Ting in China have urged their fellow-churchmen to stay and accept the Communist regimes established in their countries, without forsaking belief in God as the ultimate transcendence and in Christ as the deepest liberator. Only after that acceptance could there be a gospel for atheists. Outside the Communist countries, Protestant theologians such as Helmut Gollwitzer and Georges Casalis have urged that, in a world where oppression is often a reality and religion an illusion, Karl Marx must be acknowledged as a prophet of Israel. A theology of the "just revolution" has been attempted by analogy with the "just war" approved by Augustine and Aquinas.

Although a decree from Rome in 1949 had excommunicated all Communists and had warned all those co-operating with Communists, some gestures by Pope John and the Second Vatican Council have been interpreted as softening this condemnation without changing the doctrinal attitude to Marxist atheism. Bishops have spoken up for the workers and the peasants, and have authorised some gestures such as the sale of church lands at a loss or a reduction in expensive buildings. Numbers of Roman Catholics have identified themselves with the exploited in less official, and even rebellious, ways which Communists could applaud. The best known among these was Camilo Torres, the former priest and university lecturer who was killed among the guerillas fighting the government of Colombia in 1966. Thus collaboration and dialogue with Marxists have been made possible, where before there were only anathemas.[1]

The Sign of the Kirchentag: Lay Movements

Although these lay institutes and industrial and political missions have exercised an influence, sometimes intense, on those who have taken part in their work, a radical ecumenism could not be content with the awakening of a fraction of the laity. If it is true that all Christians should contribute to the renewal of the Church and to the betterment of human life in society, means

[1] The Christian–Marxist dialogue was summarized in *Study Encounter*, vol. iv, no. 1 (Geneva 1968). See also Roger Garaudy, *De L'Anathème au Dialogue* (Paris 1965), translated as *From Anathema to Dialogue* (New York 1966).

must be found to bring their responsibilities and opportunities home to the millions.

In Germany the Bad Boll Academy has recognized the problem of linking its conferences with the whole of society, and has had the resources to prepare and carry out not only courses for parish ministers but also courses in the areas where lay people live and work, thus making an impact on a total community. But the chief instrument of the wider lay awakening has been the Kirchentag. The enterprise which now brings together some 40,000 Germans and about a thousand international visitors for four days of intensive education and argument after extensive preparation has owed its existence to the courage of one man, Reinold von Thadden-Trieglaff. This German aristocrat was a leader among Christian students and in the Confessing Church in Germany.[1] While close to death as a result of his treatment as a prisoner in Russia, he kept the vision of a popular lay movement which would bring a Christian understanding into the life of Germany. He drew some of his inspiration from (comparatively smaller) pre-war rallies of Protestants and Catholics, but the post-war difficulties and the suspicions of many church leaders were so great that he often wondered whether anyone would listen.

In the event, more than 25,000 people attended the whole programme of lectures and study circles, recitals and plays, exhibitions and sectional gatherings, in the first Kirchentag which was held at Essen, the centre of the Ruhr industrial belt, in August 1950; and about 200,000 came to the closing assembly. The Kirchentag crossed the political barriers dividing Germany at Berlin next year, and again at Leipzig in 1954, when over 600,000 were at the closing assembly. Combining Bible study with current problems of secular life, it has been in some sense a Protestant parliament, but it has been more also. The small groups into which it has been divided, and the regional and local meetings which have prepared for its great rallies, have given many lay people some experience of a personal participation in Christian thinking, and have encouraged them to speak their own minds. Collaboration with Catholics has also grown.

The massive efficiency and success of the Kirchentag have attracted many ecumenical visitors. Dr von Thadden-Trieglaff stressed from the first that it was to be more than a German affair. The Kirchentag has also inspired some modest imitations: the Kerk Dagen in regions of the Netherlands, the Rassemblement Protestant in France, and Kirk Week in Scotland. Nor should it be forgotten that the Maraman Conventions of the Mar Thoma Church in South India, which have continued to attract and educate great numbers, were already flourishing long before 1950. However, experience has suggested that outside Germany only occasional Catholic congresses and conservative Evangelical crusades are likely to bring great numbers together at a central rally.

The outstanding success in mass evangelism has been scored by the crusades of Billy Graham. These crusades resemble the Kirchentag in some ways. They are organized and financed on an independent basis, and they show that

---

[1] Werner Hühne, *Thadden-Trieglaff, Ein Ceben unter uns* (Stuttgart 1959), translated as *A Man to be Reckoned With*, with additional material by Mark Gibbs (London 1962).

dramatically big events still appeal, but they rely heavily on the good will of the local Churches and they make no attempt to found a new denomination (indeed, Dr Graham has often demonstrated his support of the World Council of Churches). There has been some strong teaching on specific moral issues: Dr Graham often denounces sexual laxity, warns against the danger of nuclear war, and refuses to hold racially segregated meetings. However, these Evangelical crusades have avoided the practical, controversial discussion of contemporary problems—the discussion which has been the hallmark of the Kirchentag.

The main answer to the problem of the diffusion of the radical emphasis in the ecumenical movement must, it would seem, lie in the books, periodicals, and broadcasts which supplement and influence the normal lay training of programmes of the Churches. The emphasis on ecumenism and the emphasis on radicalism, and the emphasis on the two together, have been strong at many levels of Christian writings, from the academic to the popular, during 1948–68. Journals such as *The Christian Century* in Chicago, *Christianity and Crisis* in New York, *New Christian* in London, *Réforme* in Paris, the German *Evangelische Kommentare*, and the Roman Catholic *Herder Correspondence* and *Concilium*, would provide a wealth of material, and a list of other relevant publications would seem endless. The present volume which the reader holds is only a drop in the ocean of literature which has collected the fresh experience and thoughts of Christians around the world, and the present chapter is only a brief, quiet reference to the storm of criticism which has been unleashed by writers against conventional churchgoers.

Many have purchased such books and periodicals. Less thoughtful, but even more widely read, has been the increasing volume of reportage in the newspapers and magazines with a mass circulation. But it has been through broadcasting that most have been reached.

The Sign of Addis Ababa: Broadcasting

The rapid development of means of communication during the period under review has, indeed, left the Churches stunned and exhilarated.[1] Scientific forecast has outstripped science fiction, so that Marshall McLuhan's "global village" seems about to become a reality. With satellite communication direct to the remotest corner of the world, everyone will be forced to know everyone else's business. The Churches find themselves like blundering amateurs in a highly technical world, with budgets inadequate to match the astronomical figures which only governments and vast monopolies can supply. At the same time they are exhilarated by the thought that for the first time in history it is possible to take literally the commission recorded in Matthew 28.19: "Go therefore and make disciples of all nations". This challenge has called for new structures, and because these have arisen at a time when denominationalism has been under fire, they are structures which do not depend upon the old denominational structures—apart from a few exceptions such as Vatican Radio.

[1] In this section I am indebted to the Reverend E. H. Robertson.

The advent of radio had already set a pattern for these new structures; for the pioneers of missionary radio, almost entirely from the U.S.A. and operating principally in Latin America, were from various denominations. This whole world of missionary radio, including now a TV station, has grown enormously since the Second World War, with radio stations in every Latin American country and studios in Africa, Asia, and Latin America. The transmitters have increased in strength and now pour out programmes from Quito, Manila, Monte Carlo, Monrovia, the Maldive Islands, and soon the Seychelles, to mention only the international transmitters. They all have vast follow-through operations and seek to build up the Churches overseas. They help the governments in their educational projects; but the intention is to preach the gospel, and on this basis they raise their money from Evangelical bodies, usually such as are not associated with the World Council of Churches.

Meanwhile, other structures have developed, more closely associated with the Churches of the ecumenical movement and arising partly from secular organizations. In Britain the B.B.C., largely under the direction of its first Director General, John (now Lord) Reith, evolved a Religious Broadcasting Department as part of a public corporation. That department, made up mostly of ordained ministers of various denominations including Roman Catholics and Protestants, now numbers more than thirty executives. They are responsible to the B.B.C., which pays them, and not directly to the Churches. This pattern of a religious broadcasting department within a public corporation (or a commercial radio or TV system) has become the accepted pattern in most of Europe and the Commonwealth.[1]

There are, however, other patterns. The Netherlands has developed a "pillar system" of its own. While operating like the other public corporations by means of licence fees, this has given the public an opportunity to choose its own corporation and has allowed for the ownership of programme companies by church groups. But the greater alternative was that pioneered by the U.S.A., which began with denominational structures and eventually led to co-operative ventures. Although the separate denominations still produce programmes and provide much of the money, local Councils of Churches advise local radio stations about their religious content, and the Churches' relation to the major networks is partially co-ordinated by a Broadcasting and Films Commission of the National Council of Churches. In overseas work the American Churches have also co-operated in this and related fields through R.A.V.E.M.C.O.

The Lutheran World Federation has also taken a considerable share in the use of radio for missionary work. The building of the international transmitter at Addis Ababa, "Radio Voice of the Gospel" (R.V.O.G.), was on Lutheran initiative. It has become ecumenical through co-operation with the N.E.C.C., E.A.C.C., A.A.C.C., and the Division of World Mission and

---

[1] For the reflections of the head of religious broadcasting at the B.B.C., 1955–63, see Roy McKay, *Take Care of the Sense* (London 1964). Arrangements for religious broadcasting were surveyed in the European Broadcasting Union's *Review* for December 1966 (E.B.U., Geneva).

Evangelism of the W.C.C. A similar transmitter has more recently been erected in Manila. The principle behind these transmitters has been that programmes should be produced in the countries for which they are intended and the transmitter used to send them back. By producing a balanced and responsible programme, including news and music, the aim has been to set an example of responsible broadcasting for the building up, rather than the exploiting, of the nations. The partner to the Lutheran World Federation in this work has been the Co-ordinating Committee for Christian Broadcasting. In 1968 this body united with the World Association for Christian Broadcasting, another product of the period under review, to form the World Association for Christian Communication.

The Churches thus find themselves within a communications revolution. They can try to build their own radio stations and thereby have a share in the world of broadcasting, bidding on the open market but in danger of confining their influence to a ghetto of religious people. They can recognize that they are at present privileged because they are invited to take a share in secular radio and TV, and they can take up this opportunity within whichever structure their country provides. The Churches can also encourage their members within broadcasting organizations, not in order to make it easy for a Church to gain time on the air, but in order to influence effectively the policy of those organizations as they affect the lives of the people. The only choice not left open to the Churches is evasion. The Churches are within the broadcasting industry, whether they like it or not, and they have responsibilities within it which they dare not neglect. Those responsibilities seem to be:

1. *A pastoral ministry to those engaged full-time in the industry*
   whether as producers of religious or of secular programmes

The conscience of the programme director needs the nurture of the Christian Church. The loneliness of men in the great industries of radio and television, making decisions which influence the lives of millions, must be recognized as clearly as that of political leaders.

2. *A prophetic ministry to the mass media*
   in relation to what they are doing to people

When due allowance is made for the dangers of uniformed protests, there remains an abiding need to study the effect of the mass media upon our culture and to see that as prophets the Churches warn the centres of power about the consequences of certain decisions and attitudes taken.

3. *A teaching ministry which includes the gospel*
   in the things that are being taught

If broadcasting develops, as seems most likely, there will be a greater freedom of choice among different programmes. The Churches must see to it that it is possible to choose the gospel.

4. *A recognized place in the world*

At a time when the structures of the Churches are under radical reappraisal, the broadcasting media must make the disarray evident. Already televised discussions of theological problems have brought distress to many conservative believers and stimulus to many confused seekers; already broadcasts of worship in the patterns of many denominational traditions have constituted an ecumenical movement in themselves; and already many people have found their faith sustained through TV and radio, not through local Churches. It is therefore essential that Christians should decide what really constitutes the essence without which there is no Church, if they are to be exposed in the open communications of a global village.[1]

The Sign of Strasbourg: Students

In our "global village" students and other young people have, of course sensed most quickly the revolutionary drama of our time. This changing mood can be seen in the World Student Christian Federation. The W.S.C.F. has grown to unite Student Christian Movements in about eighty countries, and obviously so many students have not all moved at one pace. But the intellectual vitality of the W.S.C.F., expressed through conferences and the journal *Student World*, has been impressive, and its leadership has been small enough to make its story coherent. And during this period the W.S.C.F. has handled more and more money, mainly in its "Ecumenical Assistance Programme", has sponsored "Frontier Study and Service Projects" for young graduates to work among the world's students, and has arranged much leadership training. Such things have made its life more than a succession of meetings.

The story begins with a task which was "not so much one of reconstruction as a struggle against threatening chaos".[2] These were grim days; but in the late 1940s the Federation struggled with a confidence born in the Bible study which had been filled with fresh meaning and excitement for many groups in the European Resistance. The struggle was to build on this biblical basis a stronger and more comprehensive understanding of *The Task of the Christian in the University*, the title of a W.S.C.F. "Grey Book" by John Coleman.

Co-operation among Christians in the universities and colleges was one clear aim in this period. In the United States, the United Student Christian Council, formed in 1944, encouraged contacts and co-operative projects although the bulk of "religious activity" on the campus was organized by the now flourishing Churches. In Germany the student parishes (*studentengemeinde*) gathered Evangelical students in fellowships under pastors appointed by the Churches. In Asia the S.C.M.s were the main representatives of Protestant Christianity among students, and the task was to train their leadership. The W.S.C.F. itself provided this training and acted as a channel for the generosity of American and other Christians towards the students in

---

[1] A good beginning to the necessary discussion about these responsibilities was made in the document on "The Church and the Media of Mass Communication" presented by the W.C.C. communications department to the Uppsala Assembly of the W.C.C.

[2] *Unto a Lively Hope*, a report on the W.S.C.F. 1946–9 (Geneva 1949), p. 12.

physical or mental need, first in war-destroyed Europe, and then in Asia, Africa, and Latin America.

But what was to be the aim of the work? It took some time for the S.C.M. to see what could replace, or supplement, the old call to missionary work overseas. This answer was already clear to some leaders in 1949:

> We must see the significance of vocation not so much in mere personal, social and even ecclesiastical terms, but first of all in terms of God's work of bringing history to its consummation and of the re-creation of the whole universe. This divine plan is the only movement or process in the universe to which every individual must say his Yes or No.[1]

In such words may be read the basic theology of a radical ecumenism. However, in the 1950s, while the post-war reconstruction slowly proceeded, problems of personal life seemed to most students more urgent than the large and probably insoluble problems of the world; and Christian students shared this attitude. "The prevailing temper of our S.C.M. has become more conservative", the Canadians reported in 1952, adding: "There is a danger of a superficial orthodoxy which is simply not interested in asking questions."[2] In the U.S.A. it became customary for their more public-spirited elders to lament the "silent generation" then at college, interested only in "fraternities, football, and fornication". The Churches built centres for recreation and pastoral care on the edge of the campus, and welcomed considerable numbers of students to worship services which contributed to the peace and pleasure of the weekend.

This safe period in student Christianity ended towards 1960—partly as a consequence of the spread of S.C.M.s in the 1950s. The first W.S.C.F. secretary was appointed for Latin America (Valdo Galland, later General Secretary). African activity grew in higher education as well as in the schools, and the work in Asia was expanded. Because it was more global than ever before, the Federation listened more and more attentively to the post-colonial world's angry and eager talk, even when western Europe and North America had grown bored with politics. In 1952 M. M. Thomas of India collaborated with Davis McCaughey to write a W.S.C.F. "Grey Book" on *The Christian in the World Struggle*. It was a call to Christians to take part in the social revolution, sometimes with a No but often with a Yes and always with a conviction that God's purposes for his world (not merely for the Church) could be discerned and obeyed.[3]

In 1956 the General Committee of the Federation, meeting in the Evangelical Academy at Tutzing with strong delegations from the younger S.C.M.s, took two decisions which together summed up one period and inaugurated another. First, the Federation's aims were revised. The new words declared the intention to lead students to live as disciples of Jesus

---

[1] *Unto a Lively Hope*, p. 67.

[2] *Witnessing in the University Communities*, a report on the W.S.C.F. 1949–52 (Geneva 1952), p. 4.

[3] *Witnessing to Jesus Christ the Reconciler*, a report on the W.S.C.F. 1953–6 (Geneva 1956) and Philippe Maury, *Politics and Evangelism* (New York 1959).

o

Christ "within the life and mission of the Church". Second, a new programme of conferences and publications was inaugurated on "the Life and Mission of the Church". The leaders of the Federation at this juncture (notably D. T. Niles, the Chairman from Ceylon, and Philippe Maury, the General Secretary from France) believed that an "ecumenical consensus" had emerged about the revealed nature of the gospel and the missionary nature of the Church. The programme was designed in order to educate students in this theological consensus, and in order to train them for the mission to the world. But as the project developed, the cries of a revolutionary world almost drowned the dynamic simplicity of this original massege, and the ecumenism which had emerged in the Federation countless words later was no longer neo-orthodox: it was radical.

At Strasbourg in 1960 the Federation held a world "teaching conference". Some of the Church's ablest speakers—Barth, Niles, Visser 't Hooft, and Newbigin were four of the galaxy—did their best to pass on the vision. But at Christmas 1958 a preparatory conference in Rangoon had already indicated another trend; for young Asians, afire with the promise of a new world, had their own sharp questions for the missionary Church. As Davis McCaughey wrote, "Rangoon marked an important step away from high biblicism or high churchmanship into a high view of God's dealings with the world: high worldmanship."[1] So at Strasbourg the eloquent theologians might have some radical ideas to propound, but the audience was restless. There seemed to be too much speaking about the life of the Church; what students wanted was action in their world. And there seemed to be too much mission; what students wanted was a welcome to this world.

Subsequent conferences attempted to see what the right actions would be within a setting of acceptance. How could Christian students serve the revolution in Asia, Africa, and Latin America? How could they serve in a western world which was being united by an economic progress which brought secularization? The building of new nations seemed to these students a cause more sacred than the expansion of the more narrowly Christian work which the missionaries had led. The new secular city in Europe or America seemed a place of life and hope while the Christian denominations argued about the past. A European conference at Graz in Austria in 1962 took as its theme "Who is Man? The Presence of Jesus Christ in our World". The basic thought was that Europe was bored with religion (and perhaps North America also, although the churchgoing there made this conclusion less plausible), so Christianity must be shown as a humanism, as "proexistence", and one of Christianity's few permanent assets was the example of the humanity of the Son of Man. It was by meeting the revolution in the world that a new generation would meet Jesus Christ.

When the General Committee of the Federation met in Argentina in 1964, at Embalse Rio Tercero, it approved a statement on "The Christian Community in the Academic World". The statement recognized the diversity both in higher education and in Christian theology around the world, but it

[1] *Students and the Life and Mission of the Church*, a report on the W.S.C.F. 1956–64 (Geneva 1964), p. 6.

clarified some basic convictions about the style of approach which was right for Christian students. It was a humble approach.

> Presence for us means engagement, involvement in the concrete structures of our society. . . . First we have to be there before we can see our task clearly. . . . We have no Christian philosophy of education and no ideology about the academic world. We are partners in the ongoing discussion about them.

But it was also an approach of Christian hope.

> For us, to be present in the name of Christ spells death to the *status quo*, both in society and in the Christian community: we will not tire of pleading and working for the restoration of normal manhood as we see it in Jesus. . . . From what happened to the Lord, we know what resistance and opposition to expect. And as for our weak faith, our poverty of understanding of what we believe, we trust that while present we will be given new words or an authentic silence.

Some characteristics of the Christian community in the university were listed by the 1964 document: openness to persons and groups, diversity, experimentation, unity among Christian students, and an understanding with the Churches. The Federation then called for many consultations about an "ecumenical strategy" in the academic world, but it emphasized a new meaning of ecumenism. "By this we mean the discovery which the churches participating in the ecumenical adventures are beginning to make: that the basic ecumenical concern is the relationship between the Church and the world."[1]

It was in the United States that the new emphasis on Christian presence within the secular world came to its sharpest focus. There, students had the opportunity not only to discuss the world but also to transform a significant part of it, and Christian students had a cause which they could serve with enthusiasm. In 1959 the United Student Christian Council became the National Student Christian Federation, a body with a greater identity. The N.S.C.F. encouraged a new generation in American religion, tougher and outward-looking, and the movement to assert the civil rights of America's own coloured people gave a cutting edge to it. There was a cause both worldly and humanitarian, which had Negro ministers already prominent in the leadership and which could arouse many consciences in the white Churches. There was a cause which was momentous in itself and which connected with the response of Christians to the whole Afro-Asian revolt. There was a cause which demanded political action and physical risk in demonstrations, but which also asked individuals to co-operate as friends, "black and white together", and to think strenuously; and here was a cause which, if served worthily, would overcome.

More than 3,500 students went to a conference at Athens, Ohio, in December 1959, many of them after preparation in study groups which were international, interdenominational, and interracial. There they discussed the Christian world mission, and in the new year many of them were involved in civil rights demonstrations which included "sit-ins" (when Negro and white

[1] See also Martin Conway, *The Undivided Vision: Students Explore a Worldly Christianity* (London 1966).

students would sit until they were served in segregated restaurants—or thrown out). When James Lawson was expelled from Vanderbilt Divinity School for his part in these demonstrations, the right to take part in civil disobedience and passive resistance in order to uphold God's law of human equality was affirmed in a statement issued rapidly by the N.S.C.F. As the civil rights movement gathered strength, more and more Christian students took part in its protests. The activism of the Student Non-Violent Co-ordinating Committee spilled over into international work camps and into the Peace Corps as part of the idealism of John Kennedy's presidency.

Those Kennedy years ended in blood; but as the United States got more deeply involved in the horror and futility of the Vietnam war and in the riots of the cities at home, the non-violent philosophy learned in the civil rights struggle combined with the new wave of sympathy with coloured mankind's grievances to feed an anti-war and anti-poverty campaign led passionately and effectively by students and their teachers and by clergymen. In 1966 such pressure transformed the N.S.C.F. into the more integrated University Christian Movement, including many Roman Catholics. Organizational difficulties soon seemed to be frustrating that particular adventure, but it was clear that many Christian students were still radical in politics and religion. When Martin Luther King was murdered in 1968, he became the triumphant martyr of a "Freedom Movement" which had begun in civil rights, but which would not now rest content until peace and justice had come nearer to the whole world. Here, as students struggled for the future of the world, was a working embodiment of the "secular" gospel of which the theologians were speaking. The world was now so powerful that it had "come of age"; but those who would serve God in it must accept both the action and the suffering to which Christians had been called by one who was now the most influential theologian of them all: Dietrich Bonhoeffer, martyred twenty-three years before Martin Luther King.[1]

Outside the United States the involvement of Christian students in the political life of the world has been on a smaller scale, but in almost every country during the 1960s student protests made the headlines and attracted the (often influential) participation of young Christians. The Uniao Christa de Estudiantes do Brasil, for example, adopted in 1961 the position that "the contemporaneity of Christianity is on the Left", and since then it has been strengthened in its revolutionary work by a covenant with the New England S.C.M. Already in the late 1950s the Federation Française des Associations Chrétiennes des Etudiants had declared its solidarity with all Frenchmen who refused to take part in the war in Algeria, and in the winter of 1960-1 its Executive Committee condemned "conscious or unconscious apoliticism as a sin in the light of the Incarnation", asking all members if the time had not come to join the ranks of the Communists or the Socialists. Both in Brazil and in France these militant students cheerfully defied the caution of the church leaders, and did it before "protest" became the student posture.

Other radically political moves involving young Christians included the

---

[1] See the lively magazine of the U.C.M., *Motive*, founded by the Methodists but dominated by a radical ecumenism treating secular subjects.

efforts of Australian students to question the "white Australia" immigration laws; the 1968 student riots which attacked the conservatism of West Germany and France; the anti-militarization demonstrations in Japan; and the anti-apartheid demonstrations throughout the western world. In 1964 the Student Christian Association of South Africa, arguing that the W.S.C.F. had become a political organization, left the world body, only to find, a few months later, that it must split up itself on the racial issue.[1]

The Sign of Lausanne: Youth

The World Student Christian Federation has become a political organization (if not in the sense alleged from South Africa) partly because the students in its membership have *not* been really typical of young Christians. The circles organized by chaplains appointed by the Churches, or the Christian or Scripture Unions which are linked in the International Fellowship of Evangelical Students, have probably been more typical of students with an interest in Christianity (a minority of all students), while of course most young people have not been in higher education. By 1968 over half of mankind was under twenty years of age. So we have to look beyond the colleges in order to ask: Do new ideas about Christianity appeal to the new generation?

> Our experience at Martin Luther King's talk was very good [was one entry in a diary kept by three young Roman Catholics and three young Lutherans as part of a small project of ecumenical education in Chicago in 1966]. Here is an issue we can confront together and not piddle around with or get bogged down with doctrine. That's what I want to see the Church do—face the problems of the world together.

Another of these young people wrote:

> My Church is two churches. One is the surface; the other is the depth. The depth is coming to the fore as people realize that God, man, love, life, Christ cannot be defined. The truth can only be plumbed when he realizes that the important questions are mysteries. But most of us want to define God!

An adult summed up their experience:

> The young people involved in this project discovered that to have new life in Christ and to be open to his new creation requires death . . . perhaps the death of one's own traditions and one's own identification as a Lutheran or Roman Catholic. . . . Is not this the meaning of reformation?[2]

It is impossible to say how widespread are the concerns and convictions indicated by those three excerpts from one experiment in Chicago. However, the Youth Department of the World Council of Churches has often pointed to these as the themes which are vital to the new generation.[3] Apart from its sponsorship of ecumenical work camps, the Youth Department has made no

---

[1] *Reflections on Protest*, ed. Bruce Douglass (Richmond, Virginia 1967).

[2] *Wine in Separate Cups* (Chicago 1967), pp. 62. 87, 120.

[3] As in its document on "Youth in God's World" for the Uppsala Assembly of the W.C.C. See also *The New Creation and the New Generation*, ed. Albert H. van den Heuvel (New York 1965).

attempt to be an executive body with an ambitious budget; but its staff and publications (especially the imaginative magazine *Risk*) have probably encouraged many leaders of young people's groups. These leaders would recognize the words from Chicago as echoes of the thoughts of their own more sensitive and articulate young friends. Enough confidence may have been gained in this period to justify a great multiplication of ecumenical educational projects and of ecumenical teams of young people in longer-term social service over the next twenty years.

The work of the Y.M.C.A. and Y.W.C.A. has indeed already given some indication of what a truly ecumenical programme for youth might look like. These bodies were pioneers in what the *History of the Ecumenical Movement, 1517–1948*, rather unhappily called "diffused ecumenicity". In the last twenty years their work has grown in two main directions. By providing clubs and hostels for the social, cultural, and physical development of young people in every nation where they were allowed to do so, and by arranging some colleges and courses to train young people as workers and citizens, the Ys have quietly practised the gospel which the more sophisticated W.S.C.F. began to preach in the 1960s: the gospel of "cohumanity" with a humble serving "presence" among those unrelated to the active life of the Churches. Non-Christians have therefore trusted the Ys as they have trusted few other Christian organizations.[1] And by earning the good will of many churchmen for this practical service to young people, the Ys have secured an important basis for the participation of Christians in common prayer, Bible study, and work.

At the Centennial World Conference in Paris in 1955 there was a growing awareness of the need to pay fresh attention to the Christian basis and ecumenical opportunities of the Ys as lay movements, and a world-wide discussion began.[2] A consultation at St Cergue in Switzerland in 1962, with both Orthodox and Roman Catholic participation, affirmed about the Ys: "As world movements they are not organically related to any Church or confession." Locally "each Association must be challenged to scrutinize its own practices and programme to see whether unconsciously it may be treating persons of another confession as guests rather than full members".[3] This ecumenical policy of both movements received a clear emphasis in statements by their World Councils in the years 1963–5.

The work in predominantly Orthodox communities has always been conducted in harmony with the principles of the Orthodox Church, since the days of John R. Mott;[4] and the World Conference of Young Adults at Beirut in 1964, for example, showed this policy in action. An international meeting of Y leaders of the Roman Catholic confession was held in Geneva in 1961. Bishops in Canada and the U.S.A. approved the full participation of Roman Catholics in the Ys where appropriate conditions obtained locally. In other

---

[1] *An Open Door*, a report on a consultation at Kandy on the talk of the Ys in countries where dominant faith is non-Christian (Geneva 1967).

[2] *The Y.M.C.A., the Church and Christian Unity* (Geneva 1957) supplements the *History of the World Alliance of Y.M.C.A.'s* by C. P. Shedd and others (London 1955).

[3] *Report of the Consultation on Ecumenical Policy and Practice for Lay Christian Movements* (Geneva 1962), pp. 28–9.

[4] See Paul B. Anderson, *Orthodoxy and the Y.M.C.A.* (Geneva 1963).

areas such as Latin America and the Philippines, where large numbers of
Roman Catholics had already availed themselves of the facilities and fellowship of the Ys, this participation has begun to be blessed by the ecclesiastical
authorities. Such developments show how much has changed since 1920,
when the Holy Office in Rome denounced the Y.M.C.A.

A detailed commentary on the problems of the Churches has, however, not
been forthcoming from the Ys, either from their local units, which have been
mostly absorbed in their own social work, or at the world level, where a
certain suspicion of theology has been natural (although the work of the
world conference centre at Castle Mainau has been an exception). The 1952
World Conference of Christian Youth at Travancore, India, was also quiet
in its criticisms. In order to provide a forum for plainer speaking, an Ecumenical Youth Assembly for Europe was sponsored by the World Council
of Churches at Lausanne in Switzerland in July 1960.

Some 1,700 young people and their leaders, delegated and prepared by their
Churches, came to Lausanne from almost every country in Europe. Their
enthusiasm was a tonic to those grown weary in the service of the ecumenical
movement. It was also a rebuke; for these young Europeans were hurt and
angry to discover that they knew so little about other Churches and nations,
that they were unable to agree about so many ecclesiastical, political, and
personal questions, and that they were forbidden to receive Holy Communion
together.

Most of the young people did share in an open Communion outside the
conference programme. All of them accepted some radical findings which
urgently pleaded for a movement of "aid and reparation" from Europe to the
poorer continents, and a movement of Christian renewal and reunion within
Europe. This message stated:

> The ecumenical movement is not a liberation from the bounds of the local
> Church, but a calling to a more conscious participation in the life of the Church.
> We are agreed that we are more than ever committed to our local Church.
> But we belong to them now as people who know that in our local Church the
> whole Church is supposed to be there for the whole world in its need. We
> belong to our local churches henceforth as restless and impatient members
> called to critical participation. . . . We are going home as Christians who have
> experienced what it means not to be able to become one at the Lord's Table,
> and who do not want to shrug off this pain and no longer want to conceal this
> guilt from themselves.

Although several Churches have made progress towards intercommunion
and reunion since 1960, the radical attacks on outworn conventions which
stimulated the Lausanne Assembly would not have been entirely answered
even if all barriers at the Lord's Table were to come down. For the Christian
mission was seen at Lausanne to demand new methods.

These young Europeans said:

> We go home with the knowledge that mission is not advertisement but service,
> a real entering into the need of other people, and the struggle with their need in
> practical help, prayer, and witness in daily life. We go home with the know-

ledge that mission of this kind is perhaps more a concern of lay people than of pastors, because they are closer to the everyday life of their fellow men; and that the fulfilment of mission is thus our concern, particularly in regard to our contemporaries. We go home with the urgent question as to whether the mission of the local Church is not best fulfilled by small, flexible, closely-knit communities of people living or working together, communities which by their presence in the everyday world of today, by the manner of their life together, and by the fact of their being unconditionally at the disposal of their fellow men, create trust and bear witness to the reality of Christ's presence.

In other words, the Lausanne Youth Assembly, like the simultaneous Strasbourg Conference of the W.S.C.F., saw the beginnings of a radical re-interpretation of the ecumenical task. More than thirty years after the First World Conference on Faith and Order (Lausanne 1927), a new generation in the Christian Church responded to speakers such as the Dutch theologian, J. C. Hoekendijk, who asked:

> Are there no revolutionaries here? People who do not want to improve or to modify the structures and institutions of our Christian life but who are ready to break out of these prisons. . . .? Is there any chance for you to avoid one of the major ecumenical sins, that is to be churchy?[1]

Other continental Youth Assemblies (for North America at Ann Arbor in 1961, for Africa at Nairobi in 1962, and for Asia at Damaguete City at the turn of 1964–5) saw further beginnings. Asian youth, for example, stirred to the protest of T. B. Simatupang, the lay Chairman of the National Council of Churches in Indonesia:

> What is going on often gives the impression as being not much more than just a repetition of the endless dialogues between the different denominations among the Western churches. Sometimes I wonder whether what we need in facing the call to unity, service and witness now is not a kind of revolution. . . .[2]

And this would certainly be thought an understatement by the ardent revolutionaries in movements such as the Union Latinoamerican de Juventudes Evangelicas.

The Radical Renewal of the Church

What would this revolution for the sake of mission bring to the Churches of Europe or Asia or anywhere? The World Council of Churches has produced many exhortations and hints at its meetings, and the European and North American working groups set up by the Council to study "the missionary structure of the congregation" produced in 1967 reports which excited a widespread discussion. These reports virtually confessed that the problem of the renewal of the local Church in its parish had proved too big.

Readers who noted how few parish ministers had served in these high-powered groups could not be surprised by this failure. Readers in Asia and Africa, where habits of communal worship have often survived, and Christians

[1] A report of the Assembly was in *Youth* (W.C.C., Geneva) for October 1960.
[2] *Christ the Life* (Colombo 1965), p. 71.

under communism, who are usually allowed *only* their communal worship, have been disappointed by the apparent irrelevance of the reports to their situations. The academic flavour was pronounced: "to speak of God's action in the contemporary world is to raise the problem of *Christus extra muros ecclesiae* . . ." So too was the bureaucratic style: "The world provides the agenda . . ."

But what emerged from the reports, despite these limitations, was an emphasis on new congregations, meeting around the needs of particular parts of the secular world. These new "zones" were the natural units of working or social life, and often they were unrelated to the parochial boundaries which divided residential neighbourhoods. The para-parochial congregations related to the new "zones" would find their validity from that participation in the divine purpose which the reports insisted on Latinizing as *missio Dei*. And they would soon learn that "in *Mission* every denominational difference is irrelevant".[1]

The European group pleaded that some "theological competence" was now needed by all and spent most of its energy working towards a new theology of the mission, but it hinted at the practical implications. It could point to several of the "signs" mentioned in this chapter together with the *Aktion Sühnezeichen* (Action Reconciliation) movement of young Christians in Germany (contributing labour to new buildings at Taizé, Coventry Cathedral, and elsewhere)[2] and the world-wide movement of Telephone Samaritans founded by a London priest to help those tempted to despair or suicide.[3] The North American group decided to get at the theory through the practice, and gave most of its energy to evaluations of its members' participation in "task forces". The projects described included involvement in the Freedom Movement and in new fellowships for artists, scientists, and young adults in San Francisco, in concern for the schools of Vermont and the gaols of Los Angeles, work for the underprivileged of Chicago and San Francisco, the study and action of the Metropolitan Association of Philadelphia, and experiments in training ministers.

The reports thus indicated a new energy among Christians who turned to the world in order to serve it as the students and young people in Strasbourg and Lausanne had recommended. Another sign of the times was a survey by the W.C.C. of the development of the ordained ministry in western Europe. Of the 52,400 ordained ministers of the member-Churches of the World Council in this area, 6,800 were in specialist ministries, such as education, evangelism, administration, hospitals, armed forces, retreat houses, and religious communities. Most of these specialists were carrying on work long recognized by the Churches; the chaplain was a familiar enough figure. But observing the 1960s one could say that some notice had been taken of the fact that the greater diversification of modern urban life demanded more chaplaincies if the church structures were to be relevant. The possibility had been faced that many more ordained ministers would work mainly in secular employment and only part-time as professional clergymen; and, whether or

---

[1] *The Church for Others* (Geneva 1967), pp. 11, 20, 35.
[2] Ansgar Skriver, *Aktion Sühnezeichen*. Stuttgart 1962.
[3] Chad Varah, *The Samaritans*. London 1965.

not many non-parochial congregations were on the horizon, more emphasis had been placed on the life and work of the laity as 99.9 per cent of Christian witness and service. It had been agreed, even if the agreement had not been worked out in practice, that the Church must scatter to do its work in the world, but also that somehow it must continue to be the Church in the world, for many pressures in the world were liable to destroy Christian faith and life.

By 1968 many hopes of a radical renewal in the parishes in order that the laity might be equipped for this daily task had been disappointed. Many of the Bible study groups and house churches and many of the experiments in youth work which had been inspired in the war-time or post-war atmosphere had been ended. Albert van den Heuvel complained in 1963:

> When we look back at the period since 1945, we see the renewal movement imprisoned in carefully defined and tentative experiments which were never allowed to become a strategy. We see courageous new initiatives domesticated, and others stopped because they were dangerous; some were institutionalized, and only a handful are still swimming against the stream of easy restoration. . . . The result is an ever increasing and ever continuing exodus of our best laymen and pastors, and the growing sense of conservatism among many who despair of total renewal. There is a terrific frustration among those who stayed and who still feel God is in the structure of the Church.[1]

But, as the previous chapter in this volume shows and as Albert van den Heuvel has urged with equal eloquence elsewhere, despair would not do justice to the whole picture. By 1968 there were some signs that some of the themes of "renewal" were stirring the parishes. It was clear that, if renewal came, it would be through congregations meeting their Lord in worship which would offer the common life of the Body of Christ; meeting themselves in discussions which might replace many sermons, and in house churches; and meeting their neighbours in action teams, in open groups, in humble service, in new church buildings which would not be used only for worship, in worship which would have meaning for modern men.[2] It was no accident that some of the Churches' most effective in work for a neighbourhood sprang out of the commitment of a team of ordained and lay Christians to that neighbourhood and to each other. So the Christian community bred a larger community, when the inner team of Christians had a radically ecumenical concern for the world.

The dramatic and unexpected changes in Roman Catholicism during this period suggested that a radical renewal might not be an impossibility within official structures and traditional patterns. For Roman Catholic ecumenism has not been confined to the new spirit of prayer, courtesy, and co-operation with other Christians at the official level. As Roman Catholics have questioned traditional customs and teachings for the sake of a more effective mission in the modern world, there has been an ecumenism of *aggiornamento* (updating). The priesthood and the religious orders have been examined afresh. The liturgy has been reformed and put into the local language in order to make it

---

[1] Albert H. van den Heuvel, *The Humiliation of the Church* (Philadelphia 1966), pp. 52–3.

[2] J. G. Davies, *Worship and Mission*. London 1966,

more clearly the offering of the people. A new emphasis has been placed on the layman's responsibility and initiative, especially in Roman Catholic movements of students and young people. Within the Eastern Orthodox tradition also, especially among more than three million Orthodox in the U.S.A., some similar stirrings and changes have begun. [1]

No one in our period was able to say definitely exactly what changes would finally result in the Churches. Exciting words such as "radicalism", "renewal", "revolution", and "reformation" have been used without agreement as to their content, despite many attempts at definitions. In a period which future generations might regard as the eve of a new reformation, all that had been gained was a vision; and the "signs" would have to multiply if the Churches were to be changed and if the world was to be served in the name of Christ. But precisely here, in the 1960s, lay the challenge. Hoekendijk at Lausanne told the young people about some of the groups formed in Europe's new missionary era. He added:

> When we try to define the character of these groups we can combine the key words of the Iona Community, *commitment*, and of Taizé, *disponibilité* (being disposable). There is no mystery at all in starting these groups. Each one of us could do it. Just find one other partner and try to explore what life in *commitment* and *disponibilité* actually means. Before long you will have a house Church around you, I can assure you. . . . When do you begin to think of the partner with whom to start this group?

[1] Some Christian groups in revolt against normal church life, but given a sense of direction by political protest, have arisen informally in the United States and are described in *The Underground Church*, ed. Malcolm Boyd (New York 1969).

15
Uppsala and Afterwards

EUGENE CARSON BLAKE

INTRODUCTION

The Fourth Assembly of the World Council of Churches opened with worship of God in the Cathedral of Uppsala, Sweden, on 4 July 1968. The year 1968 had been marked by "the excitement of new scientific discoveries, the protest of student revolts, the shock of assassinations, the clash of wars".[1] It will not be possible to assess the accomplishments of the Assembly, its limitations, or its implications for the future, without careful attention to what was going on in the world in 1968 as the delegates of the Churches gathered in Uppsala.

Every report received, document approved, and programme envisaged was affected by the state of the world even more than by the state of the Church. Technology had caught up with and passed the vision and programme of the ecumenical movement. The members of the Assembly knew that the world had become one technologically. The world, for better or for worse, was now a neighbourhood, made so by instant communication, rapid mobility, economic interdependence, and mutual political involvement. But these world neighbours were clearly not yet a community. Men's attitudes towards each other in 1968 remained limited by the old and familiar smaller unities of race, nation, confession, ideology, class, and even of tribe and family. Whether consciously or not, each member of the Assembly knew in his depths that radical change, creative and destructive, was the mark of the times forcing all to re-examine the foundations, to dream new dreams, to build new structures in order to be relevant to the ultimate fears and hopes of man.

The question faced by the Assembly, a question too great to find a cosy place on the docket, was whether the world community demanded by the world's new technological interdependence could and would be established in time to prevent that nuclear self-destruction imminent since Hiroshima. And a secondary question was faced by the Assembly. Did the faith in God revealed in Jesus Christ which had drawn the Churches together in the World Council of Churches have power enough to contribute to the human necessity of 1968?

The conservatism of the Uppsala Assembly was marked by its worship of a God still believed to be very much alive, and by its continued dependence upon the Scriptures. These two convictions were summed up in its biblical theme "Behold, I make all things new" (Rev. 21. 5). This theme of the Uppsala Assembly was more than a motto. Its meaning was seriously expounded in the opening sermon, and exegetically examined in the main theme address. But even more than this, the present activity of the living God in anticipation of his plan of cosmic salvation for his world was assumed and acted upon by most of the delegates to the Fourth Assembly. This was not an easy faith to hold to in 1968. There in the pulpit at the opening service was a substitute preacher because Martin Luther King, who had been invited to preach because he was reckoned to be the Christian leader most "with it" in 1968, had fallen to an assassin's bullet.

[1] This statement was part of the concluding message of the Fourth Assembly; see Uppsala, p. 5.

One could have asked whether God's design was still relevant after this kind of disorder in 1968. One could have lost nerve in a revolutionary, reactionary, divided, and materialistic world wondering whether Jesus Christ still signified either hope or light. Yet despite world-wide fear, despair, and cynicism, the Uppsala Assembly revealed that the gospel of Jesus Christ is still revolutionary when it is heeded, still powerful to convert men and nations, and is still the only reason that the Church and the Churches are important.

But the Uppsala Assembly was not conservative in the bad sense which many "progressive" critics predicted it would be. It did not reject the findings of the 1966 Church and Society Conference. On the contrary, it approved a message which read in part:

> All men have become neighbours to one another. Torn by our diversities and tensions, we do not yet know how to live together. *But God makes new.* Christ wants his Church to foreshadow a renewed human community. Therefore, we Christians will manifest our unity in Christ by entering into full fellowship with those of other races, classes, age, religious and political convictions, in the place where we live.

The Fourth Assembly did not limit its radical newness to the approval of messages and resolutions, but responded positively and enthusiastically to the several new programmes of action, described below, which had been proposed to it by the staff with the approval of the retiring Central Committee.

Again, the Uppsala Assembly did not bog down or retreat, as had been widely predicted, because of the presence in its membership of many more representatives of the Orthodox Churches than had been present in any previous Assembly. The Orthodox members of the Assembly did not in fact become a bloc either politically or theologically any more than, for example, were the Anglican members or the representatives of the American Churches. It was to be expected that Orthodoxy would have its own theological traditions and convictions. The Orthodox members were there to reflect and express them. The fact that so many Protestant progressives feared the influence of the greater numbers of Orthodox is an indication of how important Orthodox–Protestant dialogue has become. Such dialogue must be mutually corrective as the concluding message put it: "We reaffirm our covenant to support and correct one another." This covenant was honoured at Uppsala. For the first time in a major ecumenical meeting fully attended by the Eastern Churches, their representatives at no place found themselves forced by conscience or theological conviction to make a separate Orthodox statement on the subject at issue. This was a tribute not only to the members and leadership of the Assembly itself but also to the preparations for the Assembly which had provided for full Orthodox participation from the very beginning. The Uppsala Assembly was clearly the most ecumenical assembly of the World Council of Churches because of this large and effective Orthodox presence.

Nor did the Fourth Assembly waver or hesitate to approve dynamic new relationships with the Roman Catholic Church which since New Delhi had affected the World Council of Churches in almost every part of its life and programme. It had been widely predicted that sharp criticisms would be voiced or deep hesitations expressed about this new intimate collaboration with Rome especially from minority Protestant Churches in the Latin countries and from some of the Orthodox Churches in eastern Europe. This did not occur either in the Policy Reference Committee or in plenary session of the Assembly.

This fact should not be cited to prove that no such concern is felt by these or other Churches. We know that the effects of nine centuries of polemics, East and West, do not disappear in five years. We know that the vexing problems of Uniate Churches have hardly begun to be discussed in the new post-Vatican Council II atmosphere. Nor is it to be expected that nearly five hundred years of ecclesiastical war in the West, hot and cold, can be forgotten especially in areas where there has been as yet little change in attitude or practice arising out of the ecumenical movement. But the point is that very important reports of the Joint Working Group were received and approved[1] anew, programmes of collaboration were recommended, and even the ultimate question of Roman Catholic membership was not shirked.[2]

Thus a rather strong case for the success of the Uppsala Assembly can be made on a purely negative basis. What the prophets of gloom predicted did not happen.

The Fourth Assembly of the World Council of Churches was the largest and most complete gathering of representatives of Christian Churches in over nine hundred years. And due to the missionary expansion of the nineteenth century, it may be said that this Assembly was the most widely representative world gathering of Christian Churches ever held.

Note who were there: 704 delegates from 235 member Churches. Delegated observers (a new category established for the first time at Uppsala) from 29 non-member Churches including 14 from the Roman Catholic Church, 4 from the Lutheran Church Missouri Synod, and 3 from the Seventh Day Adventist Church. There were also delegated observers from 7 associate member Churches, too small to be included in full World Council membership. Add to these 12 fraternal delegates from Christian Councils and from world Christian organizations. Also there were present 15 observers from 14 non-member Churches even though they were not officially delegated by them. Guests, advisers and youth participants, all invited by the Executive Committee, increased the total. 330 of staff, regular and co-opted, were included in the official Assembly roster. Of the 750 press representatives it must be admitted that several hundred were there for personal interest as much as for the stories they contracted to write, this despite strenuous efforts to limit press applicants to those who were bona fide press men and women. Add to all these several hundreds of visitors who had no official status in the Assembly but came to Uppsala anyway. The accomplishments of the Assembly must be assessed, therefore, in the light of who were there. Only

---

[1] See Uppsala, pp. 177–9   [2] See ibid., p. 178.

those who had illusions about what could happen at such an Assembly came
away disillusioned.

No assembly which was representative of any "establishment" could
expect to meet in 1968 without criticisms and demonstrations by youth and
student groups. Youth was visibly present and clearly critical of what went
on at the Uppsala Assembly. Around 150 youth participants had been
invited to the Assembly by the Executive Committee according to a plan
approved by the Central Committee which provided for their nomination by
youth bodies in the various nations and regions, and 127 arrived. Considerable
subsidy for their travel and entertainment had been provided in the Assembly
budget. In addition to these official participants youth was present in the
persons of 345 stewards (mostly from Sweden) who provided domestic and
technical services for the delegates and staff and at the same time entered
fully into youth discussions of the ecumenical issues in the late night hours.
Furthermore, the Swedish Student Christian Movement under the title
Club '68 brought many other students to Uppsala and provided the best
place for dialogue between youth and establishment. The Swedish students
from the beginning with their march from Stockholm to Uppsala made it
clear, however, that they were marching in support of the World Council of
Churches.

The official youth participants met in a special pre-Assembly conference
of their own arranged for them by the World Council Youth Department.
The general distrust of "establishment", including their own, made hard
going of the first day of their own meeting. They insisted on voting about
their own programme. Some were not sure that they wanted to hear the
distinguished leaders who were available to address them. A small minority,
chiefly continental European, apparently came with the intention of disruption. The whole group were clearly dissatisfied with their place in the
Assembly itself. They did not like it that they had no votes in the Assembly
even though it was clearly explained to them that they had been invited, as
were the advisers (who had no votes), because the Central Committee felt
that their corrective and creative presence was needed.

Youth participants made it clear that constitutional requirements for
limiting votes to those who were appointed as delegates by the Churches was
not and would not be satisfactory to them so long as the Churches failed to
appoint a higher percentage of young delegates. On the other hand, the
great majority of the youth participants decided against any revolutionary
policity of disruption of the Assembly in favour of participating in sections,
committees, and plenary sessions. Their presence and applause at the plenary
sessions did make a contribution to the whole atmosphere of the Assembly,
a contribution welcomed by some of the delegates. It was less happily
received by others. It was reported that there was good and useful participation by many of the youth participants in many sections, sub-sections, and
committees although the excellence of youth participation varied as did that
of the delegates themselves. The final resolutions of the youth participants
were heard by the Assembly in plenary session on the last day. They were
received with thanks but were not discussed. Generally speaking the concrete

proposals of the youth participants on the subjects before the Assembly were neither better not more "radical" than the proposals officially before the Assembly backed by the authority of the central and other "establishment" departmental and divisional committees. One method of youth participation that had some effect was provided through "Hot News", an every-other-day publication highly critical of all that went on, although some older participants noted that "Hot News" avoided any sharp criticism or even discussion of unresolved differences or even questionable activities of the youth themselves.

The final effort of youth, which centred in a twenty-four hour vigil in the cathedral beginning on the last night before the closing service, resulted in their unplanned participation in that service. These young people insisted upon this participation even though permission was asked only a few hours before the service was due to begin. The closing service itself was simple and impressive; a real part of its excellence was provided by the solemn marching of the young people carrying placards upon which were quotations from some of the most important actions taken by the Assembly and calling for the personal dedication of the worshippers to carry them out by costly self-dedication. This visible participation was briefly but eloquently underlined by a youth leader who was invited to make the only address at the closing service.

The Uppsala Assembly marked an end to an era of the ecumenical movement. It also marked a new beginning.

The name of Archbishop Nathan Söderblom was often referred to by speakers. His continuing influence as the founder of the "Life and Work" movement, which held an influential conference in Stockholm, Sweden in 1925, in part determined the emphasis on Christian service to humanity which will likely be what is most remembered as characteristic of the Uppsala Assembly. The reports of Uppsala Sections III and IV particularly, along with major programmes which were approved, were in the "Life and Work" tradition. Nevertheless, it would be wrong to say that Faith and Order contribution or the missionary tradition of the former International Missionary Council were eclipsed by this emphasis. Sections V and VI provided a new emphasis upon renewal in worship and in personal commitment. The emphases in Sections I and II on unity and mission respectively revealed that the World Council of Churches enters its new era with the same creative tensions between Unity, Mission, and Renewal that have marked and characterized its life from the beginning.

Although it must be said, therefore, that all of the past continues to make its contribution to the new era which began with Uppsala and that there was no radical break with that past, nevertheless it is evident that it is indeed a new era which began at Uppsala. The Structure Committee report which will be discussed below provides for a thorough examination and reorganization of the function and structure of the World Council of Churches, including the structure and function of the Fifth Assembly. There will never be another assembly in the pattern of the first four assemblies.

Furthermore, the elections at Uppsala put into responsible leadership for the next period a new generation of leadership. By 1968 the founding veterans of 1948 had mostly given place to a younger generation of ecclesiastical leaders. The elections at Uppsala hastened this process by choosing a Central Committee which in turn elected officers and an Executive Committee which have a very small carry-over of persons who have had previous experience in the central life of the World Council. Even the six presidents, who have always been the father figures in the organization, contain only four real veterans, W. A. Visser 't Hooft, Honorary President, Bishop Hanns Lilje, Ernest Payne, and D. T. Niles. With the exception of John Coventry Smith, the others have never served before, even on the Central Committee.

The new Executive Committee, which includes the Presidents, is more representative of Asia and Africa than formerly. It consists of an entirely new membership with the exception of Juan Faune of the Philippines and Metropolitan Nikodim of the Russian Orthodox Church. One of the new Vice-Chairmen, Miss Pauline Webb, has not served before on the Central Committee. The other Vice-Chairman, Metropolitan Meliton, has not been a member until now of the Executive Committee.

After each assembly, it has taken a little time for the new committees to become acquainted and to become effective groups. After the Fourth Assembly, it is clear that, however influential the experienced members may be, the new leadership elected at Uppsala will be responsible for a new and exciting and more ecumenical era in the life of the Council.

THE SECTION REPORTS

The Uppsala Assembly was divided into six sections. Approximately half of its sixteen days was spent in the Sections, discussing, amending, and rewriting draft statements on major ecumenical concerns which had been prepared by representative committees of ecclesiastics and experts assisted by the staff. Each draft was approximately 2,500 words in length. They had been put into print and widely distributed for study months before the Assembly. Each Section was asked to consider the draft, to amend or rewrite it if desired, and if possible to indicate how its concerns could best be related to the Churches. It was suggested that the maximum length of the final report of a Section should be 3,500 words.

As usual, there was a great deal of complaint about the procedure of attempting to do such important work in such large and varied groups in so short a time. In Uppsala this was aggravated by the fact that the overall time of the Assembly had been shortened by twenty-four hours due to date problems of the university on the one hand and the Lambeth Conference on the other. While the procedures of work of the Sections at Uppsala were sharply criticized by most of the delegates, it is not clear that the alternative suggestions which were offered for future assemblies would in fact work out any better. Some of these suggestions had been tried before. Others had been examined and rejected for what appeared to be good reasons. When the structure of the next assembly has been determined, careful attention must be given to finding a way to retain the value of generalized intellectual and spiritual discussion in an assembly, not allowing it to become simply an administrative and programme body, nor asking it to do more than it reasonably can be expected to accomplish, nor changing it into an educational training school for church representatives by self-styled experts.

The Section documents are not supposed to be authoritative dogma for the Church. They were not even offered to the Assembly for its adoption on behalf of the World Council of Churches as if it were a Church or the Church. "The substance of each of the Section reports, which are discussed below, was approved and commended to the churches for study and appropriate action."

This does not, however, lessen their importance for the future of the ecumenical movement. In general they reveal how much consensus has been reached on the most important areas of life and thought confronting all the Churches. They indicate directions for further study and action. Some contain seed thoughts or new insights that may determine the shape that the renewal and obedience of the Churches must take.

Section I: The Holy Spirit and the Catholicity of the Church

Perhaps the best way to assess the value of the report of Section I at the Fourth Assembly is to note first the issues that stand out in theoretical and practical discussion of church unity in 1968 and then to examine the document to see what light, if any, it throws upon each of them.

Is there an irreconcilable difference between evangelical Protestant understanding of Faith and Church and Catholic understanding whether Orthodox, Anglican, or Roman?

This is obviously the most fundamental question that faces the ecumenical movement in the whole area of church unity. At the Amsterdam Assembly in 1948 it was stated:

> Yet from among these shades of meaning, we would draw special attention to a difference to which, by many paths, we are constantly brought back. Historically it has been loosely described as the difference between "Catholic" and "Protestant",[1] although we have learned to mistrust any over-simple formula to describe it. The essence of our situation is that, from each side of the division, we see the Christian faith and life as a self-consistent whole, but our two conceptions of the whole are inconsistent with each other.[2]

Does this Amsterdam comment still hold true, twenty years later, after the massive entrance of the Oriental Churches into the life of the World Council, after Vatican Council II, and after two decades of faith and order work, highlighted at Lund (1952) and Montreal (1963)?

Section I at Uppsala tackles this basic question, first of all by its title and second by the general structure of the whole report. To put together in the title the Holy Spirit on the one hand and Catholicity of the Church on the

---

[1] Clearly "Catholic" is not used here to mean Roman Catholic, and "Protestant" in most of Europe is better rendered "Evangelical".

[2] Amsterdam, p. 52.

other is itself to come to grips with this central question. The ethos of evangelical Christianity has always depended upon a belief that God the Holy Spirit was not confined in his action to the visible structures of the established Catholic Church. Martin Luther could not have taken his stand without the confidence that the Holy Spirit was his guide to the understanding of the Word contained in the Scriptures. John Calvin developed his ecclesiology and his sacramental theology on a high doctrine of the Holy Spirit. And the farther to the left you go in Protestant theology, the more is ecclesiastical authority directly understood to be dependent upon whether or not the Holy Spirit is actively present with Christ's people guiding and inspiring. The Pentecostal Churches with whom the World Council is seeking closer relations and better understanding are clearly at this theological pole.

The very word Catholic, however carefully you define it, has for nearly 500 years caught up connotations which contradict this evangelical understanding of the Holy Spirit at almost every crucial point. For example, to the average Evangelical the Catholic position on the efficacy of the sacraments seems to be a precise attack upon their understanding of God's activity in the Church and in the world.

That this is still a central issue in the ecumenical movement became evident during the preparations for Section I at the Central Committee meeting in Crete in 1967. There was a considerable group of Evangelicals who did not want to use the word Catholic or Catholicity even in the title of the Section, not because of what the word denoted, but because of the connotations of the 500 years' ecclesiastical cold war in the West.

Despite these reservations, it was decided not only to keep Catholic in the title but also to draft the document itself in such a way that the issue could not be dodged. Paragraphs 14 and 15 of the draft document that was submitted to the Section on Uppsala[1] and which do not appear in the final Uppsala document, recognize the depth of the theological disagreement in terms little advanced beyond Amsterdam. For example, in paragraph 15, we read: "While some of us consider it both possible and necessary for the divided churches to come together at the same table, as the direct implication of God's reconciliation in Christ, to others such a step is both impermissible and dangerous."

This division is nowhere spelled out so clearly in the final document except perhaps by implication from its description of the remaining task. "We must continue to seek the union of all Christians in a common profession of faith in the observance of Baptism and the Eucharist, and in recognition of a ministry for the whole Church."[2]

It must be admitted that the strength of the final draft of Section I is not in a startling new insight or conclusion about how evangelical and Catholic can be truly united, but rather in its spelling out of the commonly accepted assumptions of the gospel which demand that Holy Spirit and Catholic must no longer be used in opposition to each other.

---

[1] *Drafts for Sections* (Uppsala 1968), p. 11.
[2] Uppsala, p. 17, para. I, 17.

Does the gospel permit Christians to concern
themselves with questions of ecclesiastical unity
when it is the unity and reconciliation of mankind
which is alone relevant in 1968?

It was to answer this question fully that the Uppsala document was chiefly changed from that which the Section received from the preparatory committee and the Faith and Order Commission. Although the draft document did begin in its preface with an attempt to set ecclesiastical unity in the world of 1968 by making such statements as: "Within the Church we long for unity in faith, order and common life. Within human society we seek for all men the realization of justice and integrity, freedom and joy",[1] and "How can that universal community express the wholeness of the life and truth of Christ, the Lord of *all* men?"[2]

The Church and Society Conference of 1966 is referred to in paragraph 4 and in paragraph 5 of the preparatory document. An attempt was made to break out of the ecclesiastical ghetto by including these sentences:

> The oneness of the *world* is an inescapable fact; the oneness of *humanity* is an essential aspiration. As the Spirit of God has drawn the churches towards a stronger fellowship with each other, the belief is also awakening that God in his inscrutable ways is working out His purposes in contemporary history.[3]

The final report of Section I at Uppsala did not find God's ways quite so inscrutable, as is illustrated by these quotations. It said:

> . . . we are confronted with the fact that the basis of our endeavour for unity [clearly in the context, church unity] is being widely questioned. It seems to many, inside and outside the Church, that the struggle for Christian unity in its present form is irrelevant to the immediate crisis of our times. The Church, they say, should seek its unity through solidarity with those forces in modern life, such as the struggle for social equality, and should give up its concern with patching up its own internal disputes.[4]

In response to this challenge, the report reads:

> In the agonising arena of contemporary history—and very often among the members of the Churches—we see the work of demonic forces that battle against the rights and liberties of man, but we also see the activity of the life-giving Spirit of God. We have come to view this world of men as the place where God is already at work to make all things new, and where he summons us to work with him.[5]

The unity and Catholicity of the Church is thus squarely set in God's activity in history.

> The purpose of Christ is to bring people of all times, of all races, of all places, of all conditions, into an organic and living unity in Christ by the Holy Spirit under the universal fatherhood of God.[6]

[1] *Drafts for Sections* (Uppsala 1968), p. 7, para. 1.
[2] Ibid., pp. 7–8, para. 3 (italics added).
[3] Ibid., p. 8, para 5 (italics added).
[4] Uppsala, p. 12, para. 3.   [5] Ibid., p. 12, para. 4.   [6] Ibid., p. 13, para. 6.

In a list of "confusions" caused by Christians misusing their freedom under the Spirit, there are included examples,

> ... wherever Christian communities allow their membership to be determined by discrimination based on race, wealth, social class or education; ... [and] allow cultural, ethnic, or political allegiances to prevent the organic union of churches which confess the same faith in the same region; ... [or] permit loyalty to their own nation to hinder or destroy their desire for mutual fellowship with Christians of another nation.[1]

This kind of statement is not unusual in ecumenical documents, but it is unusual in a document on the unity of the Church. Faith and Order is by this report pushed or drawn into the arena of Church and Society and International Affairs. Furthermore, as was indicated above, these theologians do not think that God's ways in history are inscrutable. They call racial discrimination demonic, and civil rights movements a part of the Spirit's activity in the world. If church unity is sought in this new context, no one ought to fault the continuing effort by the World Council of Churches in this area of ecclesiastical activity.

Is there an irreconcilable conflict between continuity of the Church with the past and its renewal for the present and the future?

The answer of the report of Section I to this question is a resounding "No". The report recognized both as necessities.

> The Church is faced by the twin demands of continuity in the one Holy Spirit, and of renewal in response to the call of the Spirit amid the changes of human history.[2]

The Holy Spirit is not to be thought of, as so often we have done, as being confined on the one hand to new insight or changed understandings or practices; on the other hand, his action is not to be discussed only in the vitalization of ancient traditions and practices. Both renewal and continuity are functions of the Holy Spirit in the Church and in the world.

This double action of the Holy Spirit is outlined in four statements which emphasize a unity and continuity broader and deeper than dogmatic formulation or organizational arrangements or programmatic functions.

> The Church is revealed as one body of Christ, the one people of God in every age, and so its continuity is made *actual* in the "faith once given to the saints" embodied in the Scriptures, confessed in the Church and proclaimed to the world; in the liturgical life of the Church, its worship and sacraments; in the continuous succession of apostolic ministry of Word and Sacrament; in constantly preparing the people of God to go into the world and meet human needs; in the unbroken witness of the lives of prophets, martyrs and saints.[3]

This refusal to tear apart tradition and renewal is perhaps the greatest contribution of the report and gives a sure foundation for the ongoing dialogue and active collaboration within the ecumenical movement.

[1] Uppsala, pp. 14–15, para. 10.   [2] Ibid., p. 16, para. 15.
[3] Ibid., p. 16, para. 14 (italics added).

At the world level, to what may we look forward
or for what should we work?

This has been a question that has haunted ecumenists from the beginning and has grown sharper since the New Delhi statement, which envisioned the unity of "all in each place", and since Vatican Council II, which revealed that the Holy Spirit was beginning to move the Roman Catholic Church to an alternative conception of unity to that of return. Perhaps the most startling sentences of this report, and hardly noticed, read:

> The ecumenical movement helps to enlarge this experience of universality, and its regional councils and its World Council may be regarded as a transitional opportunity for eventually actualizing a truly universal, ecumenical, conciliar form of common life and witness. The members of the World Council of Churches, committed to each other, should work for the time when a genuinely universal council may once more speak for all Christians, and lead the way into the future.[1]

Here the next stage, "a genuinely universal council", is for the first time seriously articulated by the official representatives of the Churches in an Assembly. Note the points: (i) No final structure of universal unity is envisioned. (ii) But the World Council is seen as an instrument of transition to the next stage of world unity—a central and crucial instrument for that transition. (iii) The next stage is flatly stated to be a truly universal council able to speak for all Christians. Here is a pattern that clearly implies a universal council with the kind of authority of the seven ancient ecumenical Councils of the Church.

If this vision finds approval in the Churches, it will become the most important guiding action for the future of the ecumenical movement. Here is not the place to discuss the relationships between present world confessional families and the World Council of Churches; but it does definitely project the guide-lines for ecumenical work in the next period.

In conclusion one can say that the report of Section I at Uppsala may, through its influence on the Churches, the regional and confessional bodies, and upon the World Council of Churches, contribute greatly to the unity of the one pilgrim people of God. A position has been taken which cannot be ignored in the future; it must be adopted or amended.

Section II: Renewal in Mission

The preparation for the section work of the Uppsala Assembly included a wide circulation of the Section drafts for study and response in the Churches before the Assembly. This had never been done before. Of the six drafts, that on "Renewal in Mission" stirred up more controversy than any other and revealed deeper issues of understanding and conviction as well. In Scandinavia the original draft was so badly received that an entirely new draft was prepared and proposed as a substitute starting-point for the discussion in Section II. Parties and blocs began to form even before the

[1] Uppsala, p. 17, para. 19.

Assembly convened, and there were moments in its sessions when communication, let alone agreement, seemed impossible.

In view of the fundamental importance of the subject matter and the ecclesiastical–political implications of the controversy, it is surprising that the Section was able in its limited time to put together a report that was generally acceptable to its members and to the Assembly. An analysis of the issues which tended to divide the Section and the Assembly into partisan blocs reveals that there is a great deal of creative work based upon mutual communication still to be done.

Perhaps the chief underlying reason for the controversy was that sociologists do not write like theologians, and theologians do not write like sociologists. Since the 1961 integration of the International Missionary Council and the World Council of Churches, one of the most important developments has been the gradual development of "mission on six continents" as the ethos of the W.C.C. Division of World Mission and Evangelism. This has brought together in the World Council mission administrators whose work is oriented sociologically to mission in what once was "Christendom" and others whose whole work has been in the areas of the younger mission-founded Churches. This is the reason that the study on the missionary structure of the congregation found such wide acceptance. Former "foreign" mission people and "home" mission people thoroughly agreed that a new acceptance of mission was required in the parish-congregations of the Churches everywhere. The representatives of the "younger" Churches, third or fourth generation Christians, found themselves facing the same problems. How can an organized parish be (not merely support) a missionary movement?

Most serious home mission administrators had sought and found help from sociologists and sociological thinkers as they had been struggling with evangelism in the increasingly secular societies from which converts must come if there were to be any conversions. The first draft of Section II seemed to many "foreign" missionary society leaders as a capitulation to a secular, if not secularized, description of the mission of the Church and even a betrayal of the gospel. Anyone who knew the people responsible for the draft knew that they were not betrayers of the gospel even though their language seemed strange and new. On the other hand, those responsible for the draft felt that the theological language insisted upon by some of the missions people was in effect obscurantist to anyone not already inside the Church.

In addition to this, however, it should be noted that real theological differences among the membership of the Churches, still unresolved, found their focus here. "Pietists" understand conversion and evangelism in highly individualistic terms and expect that the resultant Christians will be obviously "not of the world". Many other Christians see conversion in the context of "this world" conforming much more to the ways of the world in an external sense, but, on the other hand, attacking society's structures and values much more radically than does the average pietist. All Churches have within their membership both kinds of members. Their styles of life[1] are different and each remains sharply critical of the other.

[1] See Section VI below.

Another sharp contrast among twentieth-century Christians (as old, however, as the New Testament) is between those who see salvation in other-worldly terms primarily, and those who believe that other-worldliness is an escape. Furthermore, there are some Christians who believe that "proclamation" of the gospel is usually triumphalist and self-defeating, while there are others who believe that "dialogue" with non-Christians is engaged in only by Christians who have already lost their faith. Clearly these attitudes towards other Christians and their ideas are unfair to the other Christians, but it is also clear that these "parties" do represent real theological differences that could not be resolved in this report.

With this analysis as a background, it is encouraging to see how many important things about the mission of the Church the Uppsala Assembly was able to say. First, it was agreed that there must be an ethical and social content to conversion.

> Our part in evangelism might be described as bringing about the occasions for men's reponse to Jesus Christ. Often the turning point does not appear as a religious choice at all. Yet it is a new birth. . . . For we have to be torn out of the restricted and perverted life of "the old man"! We have to "put on the new man" and this change is always embodied in some actual change of attitude and relationship. For there is no turning to God which does not bring a man face to face with his fellow men in a new way. The new life frees men for community, enabling them to break through racial, national, religious and other barriers that divide the unity of mankind.[1]

Again the report states the first criterion for priorities of missionary programmes as a positive reply to this question: "Do they place the Church alongside the poor, the defenceless, the abused, the forgotten, the bored?"[2]

Second, it is agreed in the report that all the structures of the Church from local to world level must be examined to see whether they enable the Church and its members to be a mission, or obstruct them from it. The question is not "Have we the right structures for mission?" but "Are we totally structured for mission?"[3] The call is made for a total restructuring of the Church at all levels aimed at its renewal for the function of mission.

Third, despite a great deal of dispute as to whether mission is properly aimed at baptisms and new church members on the one hand, or at "new men" who might very well not make any open "religious" shift on the other hand, the report was able to say:

> Mission bears fruit as people find their true life in the Body of Christ, in the Church's life of Word and Sacrament, fellowship in the Spirit and existence for others. There the signs of the new humanity are experienced and the People of God reach out in solidarity with the whole of mankind in service and witness. The growth of the Church, therefore, both inward and outward, is of urgent importance.[4]

Here as elsewhere the report was able to escape the horns of a dilemma by stating concretely and positively that the mission of Jesus Christ includes both purposes and that you dare not choose between them.

[1] Uppsala, p. 28, para. I, 4.   [2] Ibid., p. 32, para. II, 3.
[3] See ibid., p. 33, para. III, 1.   [4] Ibid., p. 29, para. I, 5.

Fourthly, the report eloquently states the dependence of mission upon a biblical foundation. Missionary education "needs to be rooted in a Biblical understanding of mission, so that people share the encouragement and insights which Bible study can give. If a congregation is engaged in mission, it needs Biblical nurture; if it is opposed or persecuted, it needs Biblical encouragement; if it fails in missionary calling, it needs Biblical vision."[2] The distinction sometimes made between Bible-believing Christians and ecumenical Christians is given no encouragement in this report.

Finally, the report makes it clear that truly ecumenical mission is a necessity.

> There is but one mission on all six continents. This makes it now imperative that Christians engage effectively in joint planning and action in both local and international situations. Only ecumenical co-operation can be adequate for the immensity of our task. . . . Present structures obviously do not provide adequate vehicles for developing joint strategy. We must determine to find ways in which joint action can become operative . . . we find it impossible to envisage any situation where it would not be more effective to act together across all frontiers rather than going it alone.[1]

The report of Section II of the Uppsala Assembly must be seen as an interim report. Until theological divergence is bridged, until mutual confidence is increased, until resources are redeployed, until societies and Churches seriously build ecumenical structures through which to do their work, until the Church recaptures her nerve and is able to proclaim her faith in terms that are understandable and persuasive to outsiders, mission will remain the most controversial area of the Churches' life. More dialogue with the world and more effective proclamation of the good news are equally needed.

Section III: World Economic and Social Development

It was widely predicted before the Uppsala Assembly that the delegates of the Churches would reject, or at least emasculate the findings of the 1966 Church and Society Conference. This did not happen for two reasons: first, the 1966 report was subjected to widespread study and criticism; before Uppsala clarifications and amendments were made carefully and after mature consultation and consideration. Second, the representatives of the Churches in the Assembly were clearly conscious of the bankruptcy of the status quo in 1968, and were therefore ready to support the concrete programmes proposed in the area of the development and to approve their theoretical and theological foundations.

> If our false security in the old and our fear of revolutionary change tempt us to defend the status quo or to patch it up with half-hearted measures, we may all perish. The death of the old may cause pain to some, but failure to build up a new world community may bring death to all.[2]

It is difficult to summarize the most important insights in this report since it is a closely written document which needs to be read in full for full

---

[1] Uppsala, pp. 35–6, para. III, 3.   [2] Ibid., p. 45, para. 4.

understanding. Here it may be valuable to emphasize the theoretical points made in this report as a background for the later description of the practical programmes also approved in the area of development by the Uppsala Assembly.[1]

(a) Christians in the twentieth century must learn to recognize the moral issues in the economic life of the world as they came to see those issues in the nineteenth century in the life of individual nations.[2]

(b) Neo-isolationism is gaining ground in both developed and developing nations because they earlier supposed that world development could be accomplished without "radical changes in institutions and structures at three levels: within developing countries, within developed countries, and in the international economy".[3] These changes will not come without a new instillation of a morality which includes total human solidarity and world-wide justice.[4]

(c) Although development has usually been chiefly thought of in economic terms, not only must new morality be introduced into the world's thought,[5] but also new political insights must become a part of man's concern. These political insights must include at least two recognitions of reality: (i) "The new technological possibilities turn what were dreams into realities."[6] This is to say that modern technology is a new fact. (ii) But there is another fact, not so new, which must equally be reckoned with: " . . . the creation of *political* instruments of development becomes important. Since mankind is politically organized in nation-states, these instruments have to be related to the politics of sovereign nations."[7] In a world which is becoming unified technically at an amazing pace, the political instrumentalities to cope with that new fact must be developed, and Churches must be concerned even politically (in this sense) or they will be irrelevant to the real solutions of the development problems. "No structures—ecclesiastical, industrial, governmental or international—lie outside the scope of the churches' task . . . "[8]

(d) Public opinion must be persuaded to support changes in both developed and developing nations. Not only must the Churches work at this programme of education, but "students and the intelligentsia can play a crucial role in the shaping of public opinion". "Powerful political lobbies are essential to create the necessary conditions" of commitment to development.[9]

(e) "The central issue in development is the criteria of the human. We reject a definition of development which makes man the object of the operation of mechanical forces . . . "[10] The humanization of modern technological life must be a chief concern of the Churches in both developed and developing nations. It must not be taken for granted that modernization, as such, is good for men. A variety of cultures, a distribution of power, non-

[1] See below, p. 457.   [2] See Uppsala, p. 45, para. 3.   [3] Ibid., p. 46, para. 11.
[4] See ibid., p. 47, para. 12.   [5] See above, p. 414.   [6] Uppsala, p. 45, para. 1.
[7] Ibid., p. 47, para. 14 (italics added).   [8] Ibid., p. 52, para. 35.
[9] Ibid., p. 49, para. 19.   [10] Ibid., p. 49, para. 20.

discrimination with respect to colour or age or sex, must be included in the Churches' concerns.[1]

(f) The production and distribution of food must in these next years be a technical preoccupation of all who are interested in development. The population explosion lays impossible burdens upon nations which are attempting to develop technologically. Means of population control must be sought and implemented even though Christians are divided on the question of what are the moral means for family planning.[2]

The Uppsala Assembly will likely be remembered longest for its emphasis on development. Progress was made both in the theoretical understanding of the problems and Christians' responsibility to work at their solutions. The report of Section III will remain for many years as the charter of the newest task of all the Churches and of the ecumenical movement itself.

Section IV: Towards Justice and Peace in International Affairs

A study of the drafts for the Sections and the reports for Committees of the Assembly revealed, some months before the representatives of the Churches arrived in Uppsala, a remarkable theological convergence of many of these documents. They all pointed towards a new emphasis at this time on the human, whether they concerned Christology or education, development or international affairs. As will be noted later, the study programme of the World Council for the next years has been built upon this convergence of theological emphasis and direction.

Few people would, however, have expected that one of the important theological statements of the Assembly would be found in Section IV, since many people have taken it for granted that in the area of international affairs the ecumenical movement was more skilful diplomatically than theologically. Nevertheless, the theological base for this Section's report was important not only because of its inherent worth, but also because of its crucial relevance to the main question facing man today, namely, whether he can survive.

The report begins by stating succinctly the faith in God's promise contained in the theme of the Assembly "Behold, I make [am making] all things new." "This word includes the certainty that in Christ the new reconciled creation has already dawned. The Church lives in this certainty and presses on towards this hope."[3]

The effect in political affairs of this basic certainty is to substitute a Christian hope for worldly uncertainty and a Christian sober humility for worldly romanticism and utopianism. "We are directed away from anxiety, resignation, self-assertion and oppression by guilt towards openness and solidarity with all men, towards the venture of trust and the readiness to sacrifice for constructive solutions."[4] Since "the aim of our political thinking and acting is to benefit and to help men"[5] we are led to co-operate with non-Christians who have the same aim of human service. " . . . our particular

---

[1] Uppsala, pp. 49–50, paras. 20–3.   [2] See ibid., p. 50, paras. 24 and 25.
[3] Ibid., p. 60, para. 1.   [4] Ibid., pp. 60–1, para. 2.   [5] Ibid., p. 61, para. 2.

contribution will be made not only in the sober realization that all we do remains inadequate and limited, but also in our unshakable hope..."[1]

Specific Christian witness and work in international affairs depends upon insights which come from the Word of God. They are listed as follows: (a) The unity of creation and the unity of all men in Christ. (b) Because of Christ's own sacrifice, Christians are challenged not only to ask sacrifices of others, but to make them ourselves. (c) Christians must always identify themselves with the poor and oppressed in their struggle for justice. (d) We must seek change and not resist it. (e) Christian peace is built upon love of enemies. (f) Reconcilation is based upon the reconciling work of God in the world.[2]

The Church must make a costly witness:

> It must speak out where no one else dares to, or where truth is not respected, where human lives or human dignity are endangered, and where opportunities for a better future are neglected. . . . The ecumenical fellowship can help them [the Churches] to stand by their convictions and not simply to reflect the predominant opinions in their own country.[3]

With this as a theological basis, the report proceeds to analyse the major tasks in international affairs.

The first of these is the prevention of disastrous wars, large or small. The points made are that the prevention of nuclear war is the first duty of all governments. This must be done by moving "away from the balance of terror towards disarmament".[4] There are three aspects of this problem. The relationships between the nuclear powers, primarily the U.S.A. and the U.S.S.R., but including China, Great Britain, and France, the relationships to the non-nuclear powers and their relationship to each other to make for peace, and finally, methods of change without increasing the threat of nuclear destruction.[5] "Since smaller nations are expected to accept the discipline of nuclear abstinence, the nuclear powers should accept the discipline of phased disarmament in all categories of weapons."[6] Christian pacifists and non-pacifists must work together to control the use of weapons of any sort. "Wars by proxy through the competitive delivery of armaments" create "an international scandal which governments must no longer tolerate or permit."[7]

The next major task of the Churches is the protection of individuals and groups. Human rights must be supported everywhere, both by encouraging regional and national protection of fundamental liberties, and also by strengthening the efforts of the United Nations in winning universal sanction for these liberties. Protection of conscience and religious liberty, freedom of expression—all aiming at human dignity is the work of the Churches.[8]

In this effort, the Churches must recognize that minorities of all kinds must be protected from the tyranny of the majority and that the majority must not be prevented from governing by unreasonable demands of

---

[1] Uppsala, p. 61, para. 3.   [2] Ibid., p. 61, paras. 4–9.   [3] Ibid., p. 62, para. 10.
[4] Ibid., p. 62, para. 11.   [5] Ibid., p. 62, para. I, 12.   [6] Ibid., p. 63, para. I, 13.
[7] Ibid., p. 63, para. I, 15.   [8] Ibid., pp. 63–4, para. II. A.

minorities.[1] Racism is recognized as an underlying danger to peace and justice and deserves constant attention to its root causes to avoid widespread violence or war. Racism is particularly dangerous because it is linked with economic exploitation; it is based upon false myths, generalizations, and stereotypes, and it produces counter-racism.[2]

Other minority groups that require the continued attention of the Churches are refugees, displaced persons, and migrants. The long-term effort must be to eliminate the conditions that create these tragic groups of men. In the meantime, they must remain in the special care of the Churches.[3]

In addition to a briefer treatment of the relationship of economic justice to world order and peace,[4] more fully treated in Section II of the Assembly, the report of Section IV includes a requirement that Christians give full support to the importance of international and multilateral structures if they are to contribute to world peace. Nationalism must give way to regionalism since nations are too small to survive in complete independence from each other. But regions must also be comprehended in world community if political arrangements are to keep pace with the growing technological unity of the planet. The United Nations, the rule of law both to restrain disorder and to create new order must be supported by the Churches.[5]

It is finally noted that the growth of the ecumenical movement gives new possibilities for "concerted contributions to international relations".[6] Such Christian co-operation should, however, include "more serious efforts at dialogue with the adherents of other religions and all men of good-will".[7]

In a world which is threatened with ultimate disaster through nuclear war, the report of Section IV was remarkably strong both in its overall Christian basis, in its analysis of the concrete issues, and in its suggestions of programmes and positions that Christians must take on the basis of their faith and hope.

Section V: Worship

At Uppsala for the first time in a World Council Assembly, a Section was devoted to the study of Worship. This does not mean that there had been no previous attention given to the subject by the World Council of Churches, or by other instrumentalities of the ecumenical movement. Faith and Order had produced a useful volume called "Ways of Worship" in preparation for its conference in Lund in 1952. Liturgical scholars from many Churches had found themselves often in more ecumenical agreement about worship than the actual practices of their Churches would have led anyone to expect. But the fact is that World Council Assemblies had not before studied worship together and there was much hope that this section would mark a new beginning in mutual understanding and mutual help in the renewal of worship in the Churches. It may be that the beginning made in the work of

---

[1] Uppsala, p. 65, para. II. B.   [2] Ibid., pp. 65–6, para. II. C.
[3] Ibid., pp. 66–7, para. II. D, 29.   [4] Ibid., pp. 67–9, paras. III, 30–3.
[5] Ibid., pp. 69–70, paras. IV. B, 37–41.   [6] Ibid., p. 70, para. V, 42.
[7] Ibid., p. 71, para. V, 42.

Section V and the increased and fruitful attention of the Assembly to its own worship, already referred to, will be one of the most memorable contributions of Uppsala.

The practice of worship in the various families of Churches in the membership of the World Council of Churches indicates more concretely than anything else the wide divergence of ethos of these divided Churches. One thing all of them have in common is that their people resist change in their accustomed form of worship, especially if it appears that the suggested change comes out of the other traditions. Although, as noted above, liturgical scholars have found much in common in their basic criticism of all the actual practices of worship, the practices themselves do not change easily except by accretion or elimination.

Accepting this as the ecclesiastical background for the work of Section V, the problem is complicated by today's process of secularization which affects the worship of all the Churches. More and more it appears that modern man feels himself to be in a strange and alien atmosphere when he enters any church from his familiar world of office, factory, laboratory, theatre, home, or athletic stadium. Unless he has strong childhood memories which the worship recalls, he is apt to find Christian worship meaningless and boring, no matter whether it be that of Salvation Army, Pentecostal, Methodist, Anglicans, Lutheran, Orthodox, or Roman Catholic. Section V had to develop its report, then, against the two strong realities of 1968: great diversity of practice in worship among the Churches and the alienation of modern man from all worship.

The report begins by recognizing two attitudes towards worship among its own members: some who find joy in the old forms of worship and others "who do not find the old forms helpful and who are glad that there is now a radical questioning of all traditions".[1] A further complication was also recognized at the outset, that members of the so-called younger Churches in Asia and Africa feel frustrated at the alien cultural forms (especially music and art) in which Christian worship has been brought to them and their Churches, along with the gospel itself.

Again it is noted that part of the anxiety about formal worship in the Churches arises out of a breakdown of personal and private prayer discipline which in turn arises from the crisis of faith. Without argument the Section rejected the radical suggestion of many progressives who are saying that God is praised only when he is served in the person of the neighbour in the world.[2] While rejecting this radical position, the report recognizes the need for "a study of fundamental Christian faith in order to deal more profoundly with the crisis of worship".[3]

With all of these complications and difficulties it is interesting to see how much it was possible to say together and to note how basic are the agreements.

"Worship needs no more justification than does love." So the report begins. The mystery of human life and being is accepted by all as the pro-

[1] Uppsala, p. 78, para. 1. [2] Ibid., p. 78, para. 3. [3] Ibid., p. 78, para. 3.

P

found basis for worship. Those who believe in the being of God believe that he gathers his people for worship and elicits their response.[1]

Christian worship is centred in Jesus Christ. Its form is not as important as that Jesus be there enabling the worshipper to "share in the joy, the peace, and the love of God". "Worship is a privilege more than a problem."[2]

Because of its christocentric nature, Christian worship is ethical and social in nature and can never be true worship unless it is oriented towards the social injustices and divisions of mankind. Arrogant sectarianism, narrow nationalism, racism, war or oppression, poverty or wealth are the demonic forces to which Christian worship is opposed in a battle in which Jesus Christ has already won the final victory.[3] Here the report lays its foundation for the embarrassing questions which it asks the representatives of all Churches and traditions to ask themselves.

> We are bound to ask the churches; whether there should not be changes in language, music, vestments, ceremonies, to make worship more intelligible; whether fresh categories of people (industrial workers, students, scientists, journalists, etc.) should not find a place in the churches' prayers; whether lay people should not be encouraged to take a greater share in public worship; whether our forms of worship should not avoid unnecessary repetition, and leave room for silence; whether biblical and liturgical texts should not be so chosen that people are helped to worship with understanding; whether meetings of Christians for prayer in the Eucharist (Holy Communion, the Lord's Supper) should be confined to church buildings or to traditional hours?[4]

The form of these questions implies a positive answer. And it should be noted that the questions are aimed at the several traditions of worship, evangelical and catholic.

But the Section was able to do more together than to ask questions. It was agreed that "proclamation of the Word is essential".[5] This is not understood, however, as an unqualified support of the sermon as traditionally prepared and preached.[6] New forms are suggested for experiment in proclamation.

Because of the basic theological agreement as to the significance of baptism (considered as a part of worship), the Section was able to urge on all the Churches "their mutual recognition of the one baptism", and their continued effort to establish agreement as to the liturgical elements to be included by all so that the mutual recognition would be easier for all. The report further urges that baptism take place normatively in the presence of a worshipping congregation, and that Churches should be more careful as to those for whom they authorize baptism in order to avoid allowing baptism to be a social custom only.[7]

Again, the report accepts as fact that the Eucharist including Communion is at the heart of Christian worship.[8] On this basis the report urges:

[1] Uppsala, pp. 78–9, para. 5   [2] Ibid., pp. 78–9, para. 5.   [3] Ibid., p. 79, para. 7.
[4] Ibid., p. 81, para. 24.   [5] Ibid., p. 81, para. 26.   [6] See ibid., p. 81, para. 27
[7] See ibid., p. 82, para. 30.   [8] See ibid., p. 82, para. 31

(a) that all churches consider seriously the desirability of adopting the early Christian tradition of celebrating the Eucharist every Sunday; (b) that they consider the desirability of new styles of celebration of the Eucharist; (c) that all Christians present at the Eucharistic service should normally take part in holy communion; and (d) that every church should examine its reasons for its present disciplines about participation in holy communion, remembering Christ's prayer for unity and his command to be reconciled.[1]

Again it should be noted that these urgings upon the Churches are directed to all the Churches and that some are more difficult for Orthodox or Catholic Churches and others more difficult for Evangelicals.

The final section of the report is aimed at the practical task of helping people to worship God. It makes four points: (a) worship is dependent upon symbols that are cognitively and emotionally understood. There is need, therefore, to examine our use of symbols to see whether they continue to perform this function; (b) all Christians should be open to learn from the practices of worship of other Christians—uniformity and freedom, the universal and the local, continuity and change are all valuable; (c) segregation by race or class must be rejected in Christian worship; and (d) God, through the Holy Spirit, is the one who alone can quicken our worship and make it alive. We need to pray to be enabled to pray.[2]

If the Churches take seriously the questions, suggestions, and exhortations of this report, their unity and renewal will be furthered at the most fundamental levels of their life; a good beginning has been made by the Assembly.

Section VI: Towards New Styles of Living

There had been two hopes often expressed in the preparation time for the Assembly with regard to the task of Section VI. One of these was that this Section might make a practical ethical contribution in the area of dispute between contextual ethics and moral principles. The other hope was that the Section would help Christians everywhere to make a sharp distinction between ethics of the gospel on the one hand, and cultural mores blessed by the varied Christian communities on the other.

It must be admitted that the Section failed in its report to solve these important problems, or to give clear direction as to their solution. Perhaps this was too much to expect. On the positive side it can be said that there is little phariseeism in the report and many creative hints and suggestions which, if followed, would renew the life of individual Christians and of communities of Christians.

The report begins well with a call to Christians "to leave familiar territory and venture out towards unknown horizons".[3] The basis of this challenge is history's reminder that Christians have at different times and in different places been a conserving force or a renewing force. In our time of radical change the position is clearly taken that Christians today ought to choose the latter role.

[1] Uppsala, p. 82, para. 32.   [2] See ibid., pp. 82-3, paras. 33-9.
[3] Ibid., p. 87, para. 1.

The rest of the opening section does not adequately follow up the beginning. In these "theological passages" there is too great a preoccupation with trying to say the "right" thing biblically and theologically. Furthermore, there is a tendency to avoid the hard questions posed by an examination of what Christian communities really are in favour of a discussion of subjective attitudes about them both positive and negative. The positive descriptions breathe a sense of unreality, as, for example, the sentence "As we wait upon God, day after day, praying and reflecting upon his revelation in Jesus Christ, and actively involved in the secular world, we can be . . . examples of that love for one another by which men recognize disciples of Christ".[1] No one can fault the vision here of the Church as it ought to be or even might become. But there is introduced a sense of unreality when the report continues: "As we share our possessions and break together the bread of Holy Communion, our life becomes an offering to God."[2] The fact is that we are not sharing our goods like those of the way described in the Book of Acts and we are scandalously divided at the communion table.

The report[3] then describes in sharp and accurate terms the typical view of the Church held by those outside the Church, but the effect is to cancel out the ideal of the Church described in the preceding paragraph. Nor does the last paragraph of the introduction successfully resolve the issue; its only contribution is to remind us that the novel or new is not always God's action and that the Christian must feel himself part of the whole Church and of all of humanity.[4]

With this disappointing introduction, the report goes on to say some very important things about various aspects of the new styles of Christian life as they are made concrete by the major issues before man in 1968—namely, the attitude of and towards youth, the issue of the rich and poor, and finally, the issues of sexual relations.

In general the report comes out in favour of earlier and more active participation of youth in our whole society and particularly in the Church. The ground for this is laid in a fact of 1968 that, due to longer life, three or four generations of men are living at the same time in large numbers. The problem is that the old are often retired from most areas of life before they are ready to quit, the young are kept from full participation in the decisions that affect them until they are no longer young, and the middle-aged are overburdened by caring for too many human beings who really should not be "cared for", but should be fully involved in the caring process.[5]

The problem of the old is analysed, but no solution is offered.[6] The concrete suggestion[7] is that the Church as community should be a locus of communication and reconciliation. The Churches themselves and the World Council of Churches must be sure to include youth in their decisive assemblies. The old are already there in positions of power and authority.

The problem of rich and poor is examined next, and very fruitfully, because the consideration begins with the question of power concentrated

---

[1] Uppsala, pp. 87–8, para. 2.   [2] Ibid., p. 88, para. 2.   [3] See ibid., p. 88, para. 3.
[4] See ibid., p. 88, para. 4.   [5] Ibid., pp. 88–9, paras. 5–7, 9.
[6] See ibid., p. 89, para. 8.   [7] See ibid., p. 89, para. 9.

in the hands of the few rather than with money as such. Money, as the saying goes, is important only for what it can buy. That buying power may be directed by the governments of wealthy nations towards armaments, roads, schools, theatres, or factories. Rich men can also choose what they will buy. Those who are poor have no choice but to buy food, clothes, and shelter. It is recognized that money may bring as much boredom as it does happiness, as leisure time is increased collectively or individually.[1]

Power in our world is largely in the hands of "middle class people" whether in socialist or other countries. Middle class people tend to be conservative and to devote themselves to the preservation of the *status quo* with only such slight changes as the power of the two-thirds of mankind who are poor makes necessary.[2]

The divisions of the world are seen along three lines chiefly: colour, wealth, and knowledge.[3] Lack of education or being black makes it hard to shift from poor to rich; but if one is rich one can make a life transcending colour and one can buy education.

The positive conclusion of the report is that any Christian style of life must be fully involved in the suffering of all who are deprived and must be fully dedicated to equity and justice.[4]

Concrete suggestions are made for life patterns of Christian behaviour whether the Christian is one of the privileged or the underprivileged. These include political, protest, and career actions which should all be the vocation of the new styles of Christian life.[5]

The report looks at the moral issues of sex in terms of creative partnership between men and women. It welcomes the process by which women in many societies are no longer merely the agents of man's creativity, but are becoming collaborators.[6] Sex is seen not simply as a natural physical relationship but as a creative component adding to the zest for human community and activity. Women must have full rights as persons if life is to be full.

The positive values of chastity and celibacy are asserted, although the report says flatly: "There is an essential link between healthy sexuality and personal fulfilment."[7]

Responsible parenthood and family planning are supported in general terms which would imply the use of adequate techniques of birth control so long as such programmes do not become substitutes for a positive attack on the increase of economic development, especially in the areas of food production.[6]

The fact that traditional patterns of family life are under pressure in all societies due to urbanization and modern industrial practices is recognized. No solution is offered, but a request for study of such a wide variety of problems as "polygamy, marriage and celibacy, birth control, divorce, abortion and also of homosexuality".[9]

In conclusion, the report grapples in general terms with the crucial problem

[1] See Uppsala, p. 90, para. 11.   [2] See ibid., p. 90, paras. 11 and 12.
[3] See ibid., pp. 89–90, para. 10.   [4] See ibid., pp. 90–1, paras. 14–15.
[5] See ibid., p. 91, para. 16.   [6] See ibid., p. 92, para. 18.
[7] Ibid., p. 92, para. 19   [8] Ibid., p. 92, para. 20.   [9] Ibid., p. 93, para. 22.

of how does a Christian truly make his ethical decisions. The report makes it clear that social and cultural differences make a single style of Christian life impossible and even wrong. But are there rules or standards or principles? In answer, the report does not choose an antinomian contextualism, but it does emphasize that morals are attached to varied mores which are produced by people in various environments.[1] But how do we hear the command of God?

> The command of God is holy, just and good. Human rules, which grasp and express this command, can guide us in discerning the will of God and in making our decisions. But when rules become detached from the Spirit they can make us blind to the recklessness of the Gospel and to those signs of the times by which God is speaking to us.[2]

Having refused finally to choose between contextualism and "rules", the report concludes by pressing eloquently for the position that individual moral choices can be made only in community. We all need each other. We all can help each other as we can all drag each other down. This becomes a strong argument for true Christian communities held together by biblical insight and the communion table.[3] The report concludes with a plea for personal commitment which produces new styles of life which cannot be produced by documents.[4]

DECISIONS FOR THE FUTURE

Some friends of the ecumenical movement had decided even before Uppsala that the great days of the World Council of Churches were in its past. They believed that the increasing size of the organization of the World Council and the transition of its leadership from Student Christian Movement types to ecclesiastical "leaders of Churches" types must inevitably produce a kind of Council unable to keep pace with, let alone lead, the ecumenical movement. I shall not attempt here to make a judgement as to whether they are right or wrong. That judgement will have to be made in some future volume of ecumenical history.

The programme actions taken at the Uppsala Assembly were, however, new and radical enough to indicate that the committees and staff who had prepared these recommendations were envisioning a World Council which, both in the short and long range, would continue to press forward with the ecumenical movement rather than to settle down into organizational ease. It will be impossible within the length of this chapter to comment upon all the programmes and organizational decisions taken at Uppsala. A selection of these will be made below on the basis of their relevance to the major question just posed: "Can the World Council move fast enough to retain its central place in the ecumenical movement?" Obviously, final judgement must be reserved until it is seen how effectively the committees and staff carry out the Uppsala decisions.

In the twenty years since the founding of the World Council of Churches

[1] See Uppsala, p. 93, para. 24.   [2] Ibid., p. 93, para. 25.   [3] Ibid., p. 94, para. 27.
[4] See ibid., p. 94, para. 28.

the most fundamental structural decisions were made at the Evanston Assembly in 1954. Amsterdam in 1948 provided for essential ecumenical functions to continue under the auspices of the newly established Council. The present basic structure of the World Council of Churches was approved at Evanston. The Programme and Finance Committee that reported to the New Delhi (Third) Assembly decided that it would be better to delay any major changes in World Council structure until after integration with the International Missionary Council had taken place. Some at the New Delhi Assembly were disappointed at this decision and pressed for a new structure committee immediately to work out the implications of integration in the period between New Delhi and Uppsala. This did not happen.

The first years were full of necessary adjustments on the basis of the simply enlarged Evanston structure. These years were also taken up with the reception into membership of the last of the Orthodox Churches and with watching with increasing interest the implications for the World Council of Vatican Council II. Add to this the retirement of the first General Secretary in 1966, his pre-occupation with the matters referred to above, and the fact that he had intended to retire at least a year earlier than he did, and the reluctance of the new General Secretary to allow basic structural changes to be decided upon before he had the opportunity to be fully involved in the discussions, and it is easy to see why the report of the Structure Committee, authorized at New Delhi in 1961, established at Enugu in 1965, was a transitional document leaving the most important decisions about the basic structure and functioning of the World Council until after Uppsala. The above analysis is intended as a criticism of no one, least of all of the members of the Structure Committee itself or its distinguished chairmen.

The report of the Structure Committee approved at Uppsala consisted of three parts. The first part recorded what had happened since New Delhi and the minor structural changes that had been made by the Central Committee during the seven-year period. Part two consisted of recommendations for immediate actions to be put into effect at Uppsala for the three-year period during which there would be a basic study of changes now needed in the structure of the World Council as recommended in part three. The new Central Committee was authorized and instructed to undertake a comprehensive structure study during the three years 1969-71, and to implement its decisions beginning 1 January 1972 in so far as the Constitution would permit the Central Committee so to act.[1]

New Programmes Approved

A cursory examination of Section II of the Structure Committee report plus the implementing actions taken in various committees for the immediate future will reveal that there is no tendency upon the part of the World Council of Churches to mark time during the next three years. Despite real financial restrictions under the general budget, the following new programmes, to start at once, were approved by the Assembly:

[1] See Uppsala, p. 183, para. 4(d).

(*a*) The appointment of a new Associate General Secretary to be responsible for relations with National and Regional Christian Councils of Churches. The Reverend Victor Hayward is already appointed to study these relationships full-time and to prepare for a consultation within a three-year period looking towards closer and more satisfactory mutual relationships among the councils. The expectation that this office will be partly supported by a number of the National Councils symbolizes the conception that this new Associate General Secretary will represent the National and Regional Councils to the World Council, as well as represent the World Council to them.[1] This appointment is new and arose from the conviction that these council relationships are central to world-wide ecumenical progress. Despite much good work done in the General Secretariat from New Delhi onwards, experience had revealed that adequate progress would not be made without the full-time attention of a staff member at the highest level in the General Secretariat.

(*b*) Arising out of the three-year study on education, jointly conducted by the Division of Ecumenical Action and the World Council of Christian Education, there was approved a new programme consisting of at least three executive staff within the Division of Ecumenical Action, designed to serve not only that division but also the other divisions and departments. This will for the first time put the World Council squarely into the technical problems of education. Until Uppsala the World Council had stayed out of the field partly because of the existence of the World Council of Christian Education. The work together during the three years preceding the Fourth Assembly had indicated from both sides the real possibility of merging the W.C.C.E. into the World Council of Churches. It was thought, necessary however, to create a new educational staff in the World Council itself in order that such a uniting of the two world bodies would not be a mere take-over by the W.C.C. of the present ethos and functions of the World Council of Christian Education. This new department is expected to secure persons competent in general education, Christian nurture, and theological education (broadly interpreted as education for ministry, both ordained and lay). This programme was approved at Uppsala to begin when financial support could be secured from new educational sources within the member Churches. Investigation of these financial possibilities was already well begun before the Assembly and considerable interest has been shown by Churches in the U.S.A., Canada, Britain, and the continent to establish the programme, looking forward to the possible merger referred to above. The new Structure Committee will conduct or co-ordinate such merger discussions which are scheduled to begin in 1968.

(*c*) A new post of Senior Press Officer was established, the decision becoming operative on 1 October 1968, in order to make viable the enlarged Department of Communication which had been created by the Central Committee in 1967. This new central department includes the former departments of Information, Publication, and Translation. In view of the increasing im-

[1] See Uppsala, p. 181, para. C. (c) 2.

portance to the ecumenical movement of communication, this new staff post is significant as a pledge of better and increased communication by the World Council of Churches.

(*d*) Due to the financial stringency affecting the general budget, a race relations secretariat had not been proposed to the Assembly at Uppsala. Events in 1968 and the obvious long-range importance of racial equality and justice to the whole programme of the Council, persuaded the Assembly to direct the Central Committee to act positively in the field of race relations. The newly elected Central Committee took action even at Uppsala to carry out this directive. It is expected that a programme on race, administratively located within the Department of Church and Society, but also related directly to the General Secretariat, will be under way early in 1969.

(*e*) A further growth made possible by the Uppsala Assembly was an enlarged and renewed Commission of the Churches on International Affairs (C.C.I.A.). An examination of this Commission had begun with actions taken by the Central Committee at Enugu in 1965, and at Geneva in 1966. A consultation on the C.C.I.A. with world-wide representation had been held at The Hague in April 1967. The General Secretary-elect began to work on this before he took office. The concrete result of the Hague consultation was a new constitution for the C.C.I.A., which came to the Assembly from the Central Committee (Heraklion and Uppsala) through the Structure Committee. This instrument makes it possible to envisage a larger and more representative staff, closer relations with world confessional families and with national and regional councils, and more intimacy of relationship with the other units of the World Council itself. A new Director, who it is hoped may begin work by 1 July 1969, will have the opportunity and responsibility to lead the newly elected Commission to develop the new possibilities provided for in the revised constitution approved by the Assembly. Although there have been inevitably sharp criticisms of the C.C.I.A., careful examination of the record revealed how well the ecumenical movement had been served for over twenty years under the leadership of the Chairman and Director, Sir Kenneth Grubb and Dr O. Frederick Nolde, respectively.

Studies in the World Council of Churches

Considerable unrest had been developing in the constituency of the Council, especially in Europe, at the long delay in filling the post of Director of the Division of Studies since the resignation of Dr Robert Bilheimer in 1963. This unrest increased with the election of the new General Secretary in 1966, who was relatively unknown to the continental constituency and without the personal competence in academic theology of his predecessor. In part the unrest was not justified under either regime. All of the study of the World Council of Churches had never been within the Division of Studies. The Ecumenical Institute and the Division of World Misson and Evangelism had been carrying on studies at a very high level since New Delhi. And despite the lack of a permanent director in the Division of Studies, the work of Faith and Order, Church and Society, and the Department of Missionary Studies had expanded and deepened during these years.

Nevertheless, the unrest about "study" and the fear that the World Council would become more activist and less intellectual increased during 1966 and 1967. The climax came when, due to financial limitations, the Executive Committee meeting at Windsor in February 1967 decided that the two vacancies, then foreseen, of the Directors of the Division of Ecumenical Action and of the Division of Studies could not both be filled before Uppsala. This was even more alarming to some when, in January 1968, it was the Director of the Division of Ecumenical Action, the Reverend Ernst Lange, who was appointed, and the post of the Director of the Division of Studies remained in the hands of an acting director. Mr Lange was asked to replace Mr Hayward, who had been acting director of studies, because Mr Hayward was overburdened with Assembly preparations of which he had been in charge from the beginning.

A most creative series of events and actions, under Professor Lange's staff leadership, made it possible to bring to the Uppsala Assembly a recommendation on World Council study that had the approval of staff, Executive Committee, and Central Committee. The Assembly warmly approved the actions taken and the recommendations made for the study work of the Council for the three-year period during which the new Structure Committee will examine and determine how the World Council should be organized more permanently to perform its study functions along with its other functions and responsibilities.

This interim programme for World Council study includes:

(a) The appointment of "a highly qualified full-time co-ordinator for a minimum period of three years to act as a research consultant or study adviser".[1] It is understood that this three-year project must be supported outside the budget and that its programme will be integrated into the new structure of the Council when it is effected in 1972.

(b) There will be "an *ad hoc* consultative committee to advise the co-ordinator for the studies on man". The concept of "studies on man" referred to in this action had grown out of careful examination of the Work Book prepared for the Assembly. This examination had revealed that in the various departmental recommendations for study there was a remarkable convergence on this theme. The Study on Man as approved at Uppsala is not a separate unified study project in addition to the studies approved for the various units of the Council, but rather a plan to unify and accent the whole study programme of the Council.

(c) In view of the above, the Division of Studies will be suspended for the three-year period, the Director of Church and Society being added to the staff executive group in which the Director of Faith and Order had already been sitting. The Department of Missionary Studies is temporarily attached administratively to the Division of World Mission and Evangelism.

[1] Uppsala, p. 203, para. B. (c).

(*d*) The new Structure Committee is instructed "to give careful attention to the future development of ecumenical study".

In view of the unrest referred to above, and the shortness of time available to create the plan for study, the ecumenical movement is greatly in debt to Ernst Lange for his inspiring and inspired leadership in the first six months of his service to the World Council of Churches.

The Other Major Divisions

A careful study of the Assembly actions bearing upon the work of the Divisions of Ecumenical Action, World Mission and Evangelism, and Inter-Church Aid will reveal that in each of these divisions under the distinguished new Directors (Mr Philip Potter, Mrs Browne-Mayers, and Mr Lange) thorough internal reorganization is already under way in looking to creative new programmes and co-ordinated activities. Due to space limitations these cannot be discussed in this chapter.[1]

Roman Catholic Relationships

Between 1961 and 1968, as has been recounted in this volume, ecumenical developments in the Roman Catholic Church in connection with Vatican Council II had completely transformed the relationships of that Church, not only with the member Churches and the world confessional bodies but also with the World Council of Churches which remains their overall ecumenical instrument. The Uppsala Assembly approved the two official reports of the Joint Working Group of the World Council of Churches and the Roman Catholic Church.

The story revealed in these two reports, now approved by the highest authority of both the Roman Catholic Church and the World Council of Churches, is one of almost unbelievable progress and development in a very short time. Consultation and co-operation has rapidly developed in all the major areas of work of the World Council: mission, service, international affairs, youth activity, faith and order, and development activity. The ecumenical story revealed in these two reports is not finished; it has hardly begun. The recognition and approval of "more dynamic" relationships between the World Council of Churches and the Roman Catholic Church suggests that the next five years will be as excitingly new as the last. This is not to conceal or cover up the ever present difficulties of learning to work together, or to say that no setbacks will take place. The reports assume that there is only one ecumenical movement and that it is the common task of all Churches and Councils to co-operate in that one movement. This is a revolution which we have witnessed in our time.

The question of membership of the Roman Catholic Church in the World Council of Churches could not be avoided, although the question has so many theoretical and practical problems connected with it that the official

[1]See Uppsala, pp. 228–66.

reports made it clear that concentration on membership at this time would be premature.

In approving the official reports of the Joint Working Group, however, the Uppsala Assembly took action which expresses succinctly the World Council's attitude towards such membership in terms which have been well received by Roman Catholic ecumenists. The report of Reference Committee 1 as approved by the Assembly states:

> The Assembly encourages the Joint Working Group to continue to give attention to the question of the membership of the Roman Catholic Church in the World Council of Churches. Membership depends upon the initiative of individual churches willing to accept the basis. The World Council reaffirms its eagerness to extend its membership to include all those Christian Churches at present outside its fellowship.[1]

In the same report there is an additional statement which emphasizes the adherence of the Assembly to the ecumenical stance of the World Council of Churches within the one ecumenical movement. "In the World Council of Churches, separate churches have been drawn into a Koinonia by common acceptance of its Basis and by a covenant to fulfil their common calling together. The Assembly affirms its belief that this Koinonia is essential to the one ecumenical movement and that it must be more fully manifested."[2] It should be remembered that the discussion of "membership" has been equally of interest to Roman Catholic ecumenists and officials. It is clear that this will continue to be discussed while we shall continue to collaborate more and more dynamically. The fact that Roman Catholic members were elected to the Faith and Order Commission, with the approval of their Church, makes it clear that the new relationships are truly dynamic.

The area of collaboration and joint activity most rapidly developing between the Roman Catholic Church and the World Council of Churches is in the area of the programme in Church and Society, Development and Peace. This collaboration is with the Pontifical Commission on Justice and Peace appointed by Pope Paul VI in January 1967. The new commission, determined to be ecumenical from the beginning, is now fully committed to working with the World Council on a joint programme *ad experimentum* for the years 1969–71. In January 1968 a first staff member was employed jointly for six months to mount a world consultation on economic strategy for peace which was held in Beirut in April of the same year. Father George Dunne, s.j. was appointed by Cardinal Roy, Chairman of the Pontifical Commission, and by the General Secretary of the World Council of Churches under the authority of the Executive Committee. His office is in the Ecumenical Centre in Geneva. The Uppsala Assembly approved the continuance and development of this joint project.[3] In September 1968 the announcement was made by Cardinal Roy and the W.C.C. General Secretary that Father Dunne's appointment was continued for three years.

The joint project is planned to be an all-out educational campaign among

---

[1] Uppsala, p. 178, para. I. (iii).   [2] Ibid., p. 179, para. I. (viii).
[3] See ibid., p. 179, para. II. (ii).

the constituencies of all the Churches to change the minds of their ordinary members as to their Christian responsibility for world development in the broadest sense. Based generally upon the common thinking in the report of the World Council's 1966 Church and Society Conference and in the papal encyclical *Populorum progressio*, economic, political, spiritual, and moral considerations will be combined to mobilize Christians everywhere to help overcome the growing gap between the rich and the poor nations. This increase of justice is understood to be the only adequate basis for the long-range establishment of world peace.

In the exploratory period in the spring of 1968 the Beirut Conference was held. During the same period plans were formed for a political and theological process of world consultation on the same high level. In the meantime a programme of education of the Churches has been projected to spend over a million and a half dollars during the three years. It is expected that resources for this programme will be provided by several foundations and some individuals. Enough of this support had already been promised to enable Father Dunne's staff to be expanded in the autumn of 1968 so that the programme will be fully under way early in 1969. The joint effort will be supervised by a strengthened joint committee under the co-chairmanship of Mr Max Kohnstamm for the World Council of Churches and Mgr Joseph Gremillion for the Pontifical Commission for Justice and Peace.

Long before the Uppsala Assembly it had been hoped that the Fourth Assembly would make its greatest contribution in the area of development. No one could have believed that, in addition to the ideas conceived and the purposes approved, it would be possible to plan so important a concrete effort ready to be implemented so quickly. And no one would have supposed that such a programme could be mounted jointly with the Roman Catholic Church. Yet within two years of the date of its appointment the Pontifical Commission was able not only to organize itself to do its task but also to join to create the first common world-wide programme with the World Council of Churches. The World Council of Churches proved its own flexibility by making its full contribution to the exploration and planning. The future of wide ecumenical co-operation will depend heavily upon the success of this first great effort together.

Next Steps

What of the future? This is a book of history rather than one of prophecy. It is best therefore to point towards the future by examining part III of the report of the Structure Committee referred to above[1] in which the Uppsala Assembly directed the Central Committee to restructure the World Council in the light of the functions that the ecumenical movement now requires of it. It is important to note that the new Committee on Structure, which began its work in December 1968, was not asked merely to tinker with organizational procedures in order to produce organizational efficiency even though that is doubtless useful and necessary. The report begins: "After twenty years of

[1] See p. 437 above.

life together the member churches need to review their understanding of the significance of the World Council of Churches and the meaning of their membership in it."[1] The report then goes on to suggest the major considerations that should be in mind for the future. These are:

1. The effect of the World Council's growth away from the North Atlantic region which gave it birth "towards the Third World".
2. The fact that Orthodox Churches now play a larger role in its life.
3. The ramifying partnership with the Roman Catholic Church since Vatican Council II and with other non-member Churches.[2]

Furthermore, the new Structure Committee is reminded that

> They need to consider what are the specific ways in which the World Council functions; how its life can be renewed from fresh springs of life in the churches and in the world; how the influence of official leaders of the churches (who are mostly clerical) can best be balanced with men and women, especially younger men and women, whose primary field of Christian service is in the world.[3]

The new Committee is warned against supposing that all programmes and functions must necessarily be continued, and it is directed to attempt to see "how the World Council of Churches can be both faithful and flexible in its response to the calling of God".[4]

It is recognized further that it will not be easy for a structure committee to "grapple with questions of worship and spiritual life or with our differing assumptions about the way in which Christians live together in the Church".

> Nevertheless, it should ask itself whether, in the life of the Council, its Assembly, its committees and its headquarters, there are unexamined ways of doing things or leaving them undone, which render the Council a place in which Orthodox Christians, Christians from the people's democracies, and Christians from the third world of Asia and Africa, Latin America and the Pacific, do not easily feel at home, and whether there are implications in this for the structure of the World Council.[5]

The Committee is further instructed to take into its consideration the implications of the regional Councils of Churches on the one hand and of the existence of the world confessional families on the other. A warning is noted about the cost and complexities that can arise out of Roman Catholic co-operation and the cultivation of new relationships with other non-member Churches.[6]

An examination of the Assembly and of all the committee structure is also called for. The two most important questions that need to be considered are

> (a) The relations between church representation and legislative authority and responsibility and between ecclesiastical control and lay professional expertise and insight. . . . (e) . . . how the committees needed can in practice secure an attendance more fully representative geographically and confessionally and also of the varied energies and enthusiasms, with experience and insight, within the churches.[7]

[1] Uppsala, p. 376, para. 58.   [2] See ibid., p. 376, para. 59.
[3] Ibid., p. 376, para. 60.   [4] Ibid., p. 376, para. 61.
[5] Ibid., p. 377, para. 63.   [6] Ibid., p. 377, paras. 64, 65.   [7] Ibid., p. 378, para. 67.

Conclusion

If a study of the structure of the World Council of Churches, conceived of in such terms as the above, can be completed and implemented in the next three years, it is likely to be the best hope and promise for the future of the ecumenical movement at least as far as the World Council can serve the movement. Effective programmes carried on by viable structures built upon a discernment of the right functions and priorities which in turn arise out of the enduring truth of the Christian faith are the essence of the World Council. New and younger leadership is now established in the Central and Executive Committees. Since January 1967 new directors are in charge or are soon coming to take charge of almost all the major programmes and service units of the Council. It is a new era.

The attitude of the world towards the World Council of Churches remains as ambivalent as its attitude toward the Churches themselves. Hope and fear, criticism and appreciation, longing for faith and a retreat towards nihilism— all are compounded to make up this attitude.

Positive and effective action, in identification with the poor and the exploited, based upon strong intellectual and spiritual insights from the Christian faith can alone answer the widespread criticism of Christianity. The World Council of Churches is in a position to provide the ecumenical leadership that the years ahead demand. Some will pray fervently that the promises of the Uppsala Assembly will be fulfilled.

Bibliography

ANS J. VAN DER BENT

The bibliography of this book has been compiled in a way similar to the bibliography of the first volume of the *History of the Ecumenical Movement*. It is a selective bibliography referring the reader only to major documentary sources and important ecumenical books and pamphlets published during the last twenty years.

Purposely no attempt has been made to compile a comprehensive and systematic bibliography covering all ecumenical literature since the Amsterdam Assembly, 1948. Such a bibliography would make up a thick volume of several hundred pages and would still not be complete. Fortunately, a number of useful ecumenical bibliographies have been published and are still relatively up to date. The following bibliographies can be consulted by those readers who wish to refer to more detailed bibliographical information:

Paul A. Crow, *The Ecumenical Movement in Bibliographical Outline*. New York, U.S.A., 1965.

J. F. Lescrauwaet, M.S.C., *Critical Bibliography of Ecumenical Literature*. Nymegen, Bestel Centrale V.S.K.B., 1965.

International Ecumenical Bibliography. Mainz, Matthias—Grünewald-Verlag; München, Chr. Kaiser Verlag, vol. i, 1962-3, published in 1967.
A second volume covering the years 1964-5 will be issued in the course of the year 1969. Thereafter annual volumes are planned.

Some bibliographies dealing with special subjects should be mentioned also:

Ulrich Valeske, *Votum Ecclesiae*. München, Claudius Verlag, 1962.
Part II represents an extensive interconfessional ecclesiological bibliography.

Laici in Ecclesia: An ecumenical bibliography on the role of the laity in the life and mission of the church. Geneva, Department of the Laity of the World Council of Churches, 1961.

An excellent service is rendered by the Missionary Research Library, New York, Broadway at 120th Street 10027, U.S.A., which publishes regularly selected lists of books and detailed bibliographies in some special fields of missions.

Finally, the reader might want to consult the *International Review of Missions* and the *Ecumenical Review*, both published by W.C.C. in Geneva, which carry in each number a well-selected bibliography of current publications. Also the catalogues of the Publication Department of the World Council of Churches, 150 Route de Ferney, 1211 Geneva 20, should be consulted; these give a complete list of books and pamphlets still for sale.

All these and other bibliographical sources together provide the student with a more or less complete view of the ecumenical literature over the last twenty years. This bibliography, therefore, contains no general bibliography, no lists of ecumenical periodicals, *Festschriften*, doctoral dissertations, or ecumenical memoirs and biographies. Each chapter is documented only by a choice of the most significant works on the subject and a selection of the most important official World Council of Churches documents. For the chapter on the *Roman Catholic Church and the Ecumenical Movement* only a few major Catholic evaluations and Protestant, Anglican, and Orthodox re-actions to Vatican II are indicated. No official sources are listed.

In case an English work has been translated into French or German, the title of the French or German translation has been added to the bibliographi-cal description of the book in English. When a book was written originally in French or German, the English version has been given first with the indication that the work was translated from the French or German. Only in an exceptional case has a book not written in either English, French, or German been added to the bibliography.

Finally, the reader should bear in mind that numerous World Council of Churches and other ecumenical publications exist only in type-written or mimeographed form. All these papers, minutes, reports, etc. can be consulted in the Archives of the Library of the World Council of Churches in Geneva. This Ecumenical Library now also houses the complete records of the International Missionary Council from 1910 to 1961 and continues to collect extensively materials prepared by national and regional Councils of Churches and other ecumenical organizations in six continents.

ANS J. VAN DER BENT
Librarian, World Council of Churches

CHAPTER 1

The General Ecumenical Development since 1948

GENERAL SURVEYS

ALTHAUS, Hans-Ludwig, *Oekumenische Dokumente, Quellenstücke über die Einheit der Kirche.* 251pp. Göttingen, Vandenhoeck & Ruprecht, 1962.

BELL, G. K. A., ed., *Documents on Christian Unity.* 4 vols. London, Oxford University Press, 1920–57.

BENZ, Ernst, *Kirchengeschichte in ökumenischer Sicht.* 147pp. (Oekumenische Studien, 3. Leiden, Brill, 1961.

BILHEIMER, Robert S., *The Quest for Christian Unity.* 181pp. New York, Association Press, 1952.

BOYER, Charles, *Christian Unity and the Ecumenical Movement.* 131pp. (Faith and fact books, 138). London, Burns & Oates, 1962. Translated from the Italian *Unità cristiana e movimento ecumenico.*

CONORD, Paul, *Brève histoire de l'oecuménisme.* 233pp. Paris, Collection "Les Bergers et les Mages", 1958.

GOLTERMAN, W. F., *Eenheid in de chaos der Kerken.* 207pp. (Volksuniversiteits Bibliotheek, 68.) Haarlem, De Erven F. Bohn, 1962.

GOODALL, Norman, *The Ecumenical Movement: What it is and what it does.* 2nd edn. 257pp. London, New York, Oxford University Press, 1964.

HOPE, Norman V., *One Christ, One World, One Church: A short introduction to the ecumenical movement.* 96pp. Philadelphia, The Church Historical Society, 1953.

HORNIG, Ernst, *Der Weg der Weltchristenheit. Eine Einführung in die ökumenische Bewegung, ihre Geschichte und Probleme.* 2. Aufl. 338pp. Stuttgart, Evangelisches Verlagswerk, 1958.

KINDER, Ernst, *Die ökumenische Bewegung, 1948–1961.* 135pp. (Kirchengeschichtliche Quellenhefte, 12/13.) Gladbeck, Schriftenmissions-Verlag, 1963.

MCNEILL, John T., *Unitive Protestantism; The ecumenical spirit and its persistent expression.* 352pp. Richmond, Virginia, John Knox Press, 1964.

MICHALON, Pierre, *L'Unité des chrétiens.* 127pp. Paris, Arthème Fayard, 1965. German translation *Der Sinn für den anderen. Auf dem Weg zur Einheit der Christen.*

NELSON, John Robert, *Overcoming Christian Divisions.* Rev. edn. 126pp. (1958 edn. entitled: *One Lord, One Church.*) New York, Association Press, 1962. German translation *Die Einheit der Kirche in Welt und Gemeinde.*

NUTTALL, Geoffrey F., and CHADWICK, Owen, ed., *From Uniformity to Unity, 1662–1962.* 423pp. London, S.P.C.K., 1962.

O'BRIEN, John A., *Steps to Christian Unity.* 321pp. Garden City, New York, Doubleday & Company, 1964.

RENKEWITZ, Heinz, *Die Kirchen auf dem Wege zur Einheit.* 189pp. (Evang. Enzyklopädie.) Gütersloh, Gütersloher Verlagshaus Gerd Mohn, 1964.

ROUSE, Ruth, and NEILL, Stephen C., ed., *A History of the Ecumenical Movement, 1517–1948.* 2nd edn. with revised bibliography. 838pp. London, S.P.C.K., 1967. German translation *Geschichte der ökumenischen Bewegung, 1517–1948.* 2 vols.

SLACK, Kenneth, *The Ecumenical Movement.* 44pp. London, Edinburgh House Press, 1960.

Weltkirchen-Lexicon. Handbuch der Oekumene; im Auftrag des Deutschen Evangelischen Kirchentages, hrsg. von F. H. Littell und H. H. Walz. 1756pp. Stuttgart, Kreuz Verlag, 1960.

WINTERHAGER, Jürgen Wilhelm, *Kirchen-Unionen des zwanzigsten Jahrhunderts*. 253pp. Zürich, Gotthelf-Verlag, 1961.

INTERPRETATIVE INTRODUCTIONS

BAROT, Madeleine, *Le mouvement oecuménique*. 128pp. (Que sais-je?, 841.) Paris, Presses Universitaires de France, 1967.

BLAKEMORE, W. B., ed., *The Challenge of Christian Unity*. 144pp. St Louis, Bethany Press, 1963.

BOEGNER, Marc, *L'exigence oecuménique. Souvenirs et perspectives*. 366pp. Paris, Ed. Albin Michel, 1968.

BRADSHAW, Marion J., *Free Churches and Christian Unity: Critical view of the ecumenical movement and the World Council of Churches*. 225pp. Boston, Beacon Press, 1954.

BRIDSTON, Keith R., and WAGONER, Walter D., *Unity in mid-career, an ecumenical critique*. 211pp. New York, London, Macmillan, 1963.

BROMILEY, G. W., *The Unity and Disunity of the Church*. 104pp. Grand Rapids, Mich., Eerdmans, 1958.

BRUCE, Michael, *Barriers to Unity*. 112pp. London, Faith Press, 1959.

CAVERT, Samuel McCrea, *On the Road to Christian Unity: An appraisal of the ecumenical movement*. 192pp. New York, Harper, 1961.

FLETCHER, Grace N., *The Whole World's in his Hand*. 219pp. New York, Dutton, 1962.

HENDERSON, Ian, *Power without Glory: A study in ecumenical politics*. 184pp. London, Hutchinson, 1967.

HORTON, Walter M., *Christian Theology: An ecumenical approach*. Rev. edn. 320pp. New York, Harper, 1958.

JENTSCH, Werner, *Vielfalt und Einfalt. Eine ökumenische Besinnung*. 222pp. Kassel, Eichenkreuzverlag, 1966.

KEAN, Charles D., *The Road to Reunion*. 145pp. Greenwich, Conn., Seabury Press, 1958.

LAMBERT, Bernard, *Ecumenism: Theology and history*. 533pp. London, Burns and Oates, 1966. Translated from the French *Le problème oecuménique*. German translation *Das ökumenische Problem*.

LAWRENCE, John, *The Hard Facts of Unity*. 127pp. London, S.C.M. Press, 1961.

MACKAY, John A., *Ecumenics: The Science of the Church Universal*. 294pp. Englewoods Cliff, N.J., Prentice-Hall, 1964.

MARXSEN, Willi, *Einheit der Kirche?* 148pp. Ringvorlesungen der Evang.-Theologischen Fakultät der Westfälischen Wilhelms-Universität Münster. In Verbindung mit Kurt Aland, Wilhelm Anz, Ernst Kinder, Helmut Kittel, Heinz-Dietrich Wendland und Siegfried Hebart. Witten, Luther Verlag, 1964.

MASCALL, Eric L., *The Recovery of Unity: A theological approach*. 242pp. New York, Longmans, Green, 1958.

MEINHOLD, Peter, *Die Kirchen auf neuen Wegen. Wie sie heute aufeinander blicken*. 172pp. Freiburg, Herder, 1964.

MEINHOLD, Peter, *Oekumenische Kirchenkunde*. 652pp. Stuttgart, Kreuz-Verlag 1962.

MICHAEL, J. P., *Christen glauben eine Kirche.* 239pp. Recklinghausen, Paulus Verlag, 1962.

MUDGE, Lewis S., *One Church: Catholic and Reformed.* 96pp. Philadelphia, Westminster, 1963.

NEWBIGIN, Bp J. E. Lesslie, *The Reunion of the Church: A defense of the South India scheme.* Rev. edn. 192pp. London, S.C.M. Press, 1960.

NEILL, Stephen, *The Church and Christian Union.* 423pp. (The Bampton Lectures, 1964.) London, Oxford University Press, 1968.

NEUMANN, Johannes, *Auf Hoffnung hin; eine Sammlung ökumenischer Gedanken.* 284pp. Meitingen bei Augsburg, Kyrios-Verlag, 1964.

NICHOLLS, William, *Ecumenism and catholicity.* 159pp. London, S.C.M. Press, 1952.

Un nouvel age oecuménique. Etude du Centre international d'information et de documentation sur l'Eglise conciliaire. 394pp. (L'Eglise en son temps—études, 10.) Paris, Editions du Centurion, 1966.

OUTLER, Albert C., *The Christian Tradition and the Unity we Seek. Given as Richard Lectures at the University of Virginia in Charlottesville.* 165pp. New York, Oxford University Press, 1957.

PIPER, Otto A., *Protestantism in an Ecumenical Age: Its root, its task.* 254pp. Philadelphia, Fortress Press, 1965.

RISTON, Helmut, and BURGERT, Helmuth, ed., *Konfession und Oekumene. Aspekte—Probleme—Aufgaben.* 588pp. Berlin, Evang. Verlagsanstalt, 1965.

ROBINSON, William, *The Shattered Cross: The many churches and the one church.* 92pp. Birmingham, Berean Press, 1955.

SARTORY, Thomas, *Ecumenical Movement and the Unity of the Church.* 290pp. Oxford, Blackwell, 1963. Translated from the German *Die ökumenische Bewegung und die Einheit der Kirche: ein Beitrag im Dienste einer ökumenischen Ekklesiologie.*

SCHLINK, Edmund, *The Coming Christ and the Coming Church.* 333pp. Edinburgh, Oliver & Boyd, 1967. Translated from the German *Der kommende Christus und die kirchlichen Traditionen.*

SCHUTZ, Roger, *Unity: Man's tomorrow.* 94pp. London, Faith Press, 1962. Translated from the French *L'unité, espérance de vie.* German translation *Einheit und Zukunft. Die Christenheit im technischen Zeitalter.*

SPINKA, Matthew, *The Quest for Church Unity.* 85pp. New York, Macmillan, 1960.

TAVARD, George, *Two centuries of ecumenism.* 239pp. Notre Dame, Fides, 1960. Translated from the French *Petite histoire du mouvement oecuménique.* German translation *Geschichte der ökumenischen Bewegung.*

THILS, Gustave, *Histoire doctrinale du mouvement oecuménique.* Nouvelle édition. 340pp. Louvain, E. Warny, 1962.

THURIAN, Max: *Visible Unity and Tradition.* 137pp. London, Darton, Longman and Todd, 1964. Translated from the French *L'unité visible des chrétiens et la tradition.* German translation *Sichtbare Einheit.*

TOMKINS, Oliver, *A Time for Unity.* 127pp. London, S.C.M. Press, 1964.

TORRANCE, T. F., *Conflict and agreement in the Church.* 2 vols. 331pp. and 213pp. London, Lutterworth Press, 1959–60.

VILLAIN, Maurice, *Unity: A history and some reflections.* 3rd rev. and augmented edn. 381pp. London, Harvill, 1963. Translated from the French *Introduction à l'oecuménisme.*

VISSER 'T HOOFT, W. A., *The meaning of ecumenical.* 28pp. London, S.C.M. Press, 1953.

VISSER 'T HOOFT, W. A., *Hauptschriften.* 2 vols.—1. *Die ganze Kirche für die ganze Welt;* 2. *Oekumenischer Aufbruch.* Berling, Kreuz Verlag, 1967.

VISSER 'T HOOFT, Willem A., *Oekumenische Bilanz*. Reden und Aufsätze aus zwei Jahrzehnten. Mit Vorwort von Hanfried Krüger. 168pp. Stuttgart, Evang. Missionsverlag, 1966.

VISSER 'T HOOFT, W. A., *The Pressure of our Common Calling*. 90pp. Garden City, New York, Doubleday, 1959. French translation *Les exigences de notre vocation commune*. German translation *Unter dem einen Ruf*.

CHAPTER 2

The Life and Activities of the World Council of Churches

ASSEMBLIES

First Assembly: Amsterdam 1948

The First Assembly of the World Council of Churches, 1948. 271pp. Ed. W. A. Visser 't Hooft. London, S.C.M. Press, 1949.

KENNEDY, James W., *Venture of Faith: The birth of the World Council of Churches*. 120pp. New York, Morehouse-Gorham Co., 1948.

Man's Disorder and God's Design. The Amsterdam Assembly series. 4 vols.—1. *The Universal Church in God's Design*. 217pp.; 2. *The Church's Witness to God's Design*. 226 pp.; 3. *The Church and the Disorder of Society*. 205pp.; 4. *The Church and the International Disorder*. 232pp. New York, Harper, 1949.

Second Assembly: Evanston 1954

Assembly work book. Prepared for the Second Assembly of the World Council of Churches at Evanston, *1954*. 108pp. Geneva, W.C.C., 1954.

The Christian Hope and the Task of the Church. Six ecumenical surveys and the report of the assembly prepared by the Advisory Commission on the main theme. 405pp. New York, Harper, 1954.

"Evanston Main Theme" in *Ecumenical Review*, vol. vi, no. 4, pp. 431–65. Geneva, W.C.C., July 1954.

The Evanston Report: The Second Assembly of the World Council of Churches, 1954. 360pp. London, S.C.M. Press, 1955.

Evanston Speaks: Reports from the Second Assembly of the World Council of Churches, 1954. 71pp. Geneva, W.C.C., 1954.

The First Six Years 1948–1954. A report of the Central Committee of the World Council of Churches on the activities of the departments and secretariats of the Council. 149pp. Geneva, W.C.C., 1954. French translation *Les six premières années 1948–1954*. German translation *Die ersten sechs Jahre 1948–1954*.

HERKLOTS, Hugh G. G., *Looking at Evanston*. A study of the Second Assembly of the World Council of Churches. Evanston, 1954. 114pp. London, S.C.M. Press, 1954.

KENNEDY, James W., *Evanston Scrapbook*. An account of the Second Assembly of the World Council of Churches, held in Evanston, *1954*. 124pp. Lebanon, Pa., Sowers Printing Co., 1954.

MARSH, John, *The Significance of Evanston*. 72pp. London, Independent Press, 1954.

NICHOLS, James H., *Evanston: An interpretation*. 155pp. New York, Harper, 1954.

Response to Evanston. A survey of the comments sent in by the member Churches on the report of the Second Assembly of the World Council of Churches at Evanston, 1954. 87pp. Geneva, W.C.C., 1957.

Third Assembly: New Delhi 1961

Constitution and Rules of the World Council of Churches. As adopted by the Assembly at Amsterdam, 1948, amended at Evanston, 1954 and further amended at New Delhi, 1961. 20pp. Geneva, W.C.C., 1961.

Evanston to New Delhi, 1954–1961. Report of the Central Committee to the Third Assembly of the World Council of Churches. 288pp. Geneva, W.C.C., 1961.

Jesus Christ, the Light of the World. World Council of Churches. Third Assembly, New Delhi, 1961. 76pp. Geneva, W.C.C., 1961.

KENNEDY, James W., *No Darkness At All*. 122pp. St Louis, Bethany Press, 1962.

The New Delhi Report: The Third Assembly of the World Council of Churches, 1961. 448pp. London, S.C.M. Press, 1962.

New Delhi Speaks: About christian witness, service and unity. The message, appeal, and section reports of the Third Assembly in New Delhi, 1961, ed. W. A. Visser 't Hooft. 124pp. New York, Association Press, 1962.

SLACK, Kenneth, *Despatch from New Delhi*. 111pp. London, S.C.M. Press, 1962.

The Work Book for the Assembly Committee. Prepared for the Third Assembly of the World Council of Churches. 188pp. Geneva, W.C.C., 1961.

Fourth Assembly: Uppsala 1968

All things new. Fourth Assembly Uppsala 1968. 48pp. Geneva, W.C.C., 1967.

Drafts for sections prepared for the Fourth Assembly of the World Council of Churches, Uppsala, 1968. 136pp. Geneva, W.C.C., 1968.

FEY, Harold E., *Life: new style. How the hope for a new style of life for humanity was advanced by the Fourth Assembly of the World Council of Churches meeting in Uppsala, Sweden, July 4 to 20, 1968.* 128pp. Cincinnati, Forward Movement Publications, 1968.

FRIELING, Reinhard, *Uppsala 1968: Erneuerung der Welt?* 105pp. Göttingen, Vandenhoeck and Ruprecht, 1968.

New Delhi to Uppsala, 1961–1968. Report of the Central Committee to the Fourth Assembly of the World Council of Churches. 220pp. Geneva, W.C.C., 1968.

PERCHENET, Annie, *Chrétiens ensemble. Journal d'Upsal, juillet 1968.* 206pp. Paris, Desclée, 1968.

SCHELZ, Sepp, *Weltkirche in Aktion. Ein Bericht über die Weltkirchenkonferenz in Uppsala 1968.* 157pp. München, Siebenstern Taschenbuch Verlag, 1968.

SLACK, Kenneth, *Uppsala Report. The story of the World Council of Churches Fourth Assembly, Uppsala, Sweden, 4–19 July 1968.* 88pp. London, S.C.M. Press, 1968.

Unity of mankind. Speeches from the Fourth Assembly of the World Council of Churches, Uppsala 1968, ed. Albert H. van den Heuvel. 142pp. Geneva, W.C.C., 1969.

The Uppsala Report 1968, Official report of the Fourth Assembly of the World Council of Churches, Uppsala July 4–20, 1968, ed. Norman Goodall. 513pp. Geneva, W.C.C., 1968. German version *Bericht aus Uppsala 68*. French version *Rapport d'Upsal 68*.

WENGER, Antoine, *Upsal, le défi du siècle aux Eglises*. 384pp. Paris, Editions du Centurion, 1968.

Workbook for the Assembly Committees. Prepared for the Fourth Assembly of the World Council of Churches, Uppsala, 1968. 200pp. Geneva, W.C.C., 1968.

Central Committees

Minutes and Reports of the .... *Meeting of the Central Committee of the World Council of Churches* .... Geneva, W.C.C., 1949–67.

1949	2nd	Meeting	Chichester	127pp.
1950	3rd	„	Toronto	133pp.
1951	4th	„	Rolle	138pp.
1952/53	5th	„	Lucknow	140pp.
1954	6th	„	Chicago	56pp.
1954	7th	„	Evanston	37pp.
1955	8th	„	Davos	146pp.
1956	9th	„	Galyatetö	128pp.
1957	10th	„	New Haven	136pp.
1958	11th	„	Nyborg Strand	133pp.
1959	12th	„	Rhodes	208pp.
1960	13th	„	St Andrews	218pp.
1961	14th and 15th	„	New Delhi	59pp.
1962	16th	„	Paris	153pp.
1963	17th	„	Rochester	142pp.
1965	18th	„	Enugu	167pp.
1966	19th	„	Geneva	151pp.
1967	20th	„	Heraklion	270pp.

Executive Committees

Minutes of meetings of the Executive Committee of the World Council of Churches (mimeographed, in Archives of W.C.C. Library).

1949, Feb.	Bossey	1959, Feb.	Geneva
1949, July	Chichester	1959, Aug.	Kifissia
1950, Feb.	Bossey	1960, Feb.	Buenos Aires
1950, July	Toronto	1960, Aug.	St Andrews
1951, Jan.	Bièvres	1961, Feb.	Geneva
1951, Aug.	Rolle	1961, June	Bossey
1952, Feb.	London	1961, Nov.	New Delhi
1952, Aug.	Nykøbing	1961, Dec.	New Delhi
1952, Dec.–		1962, March	Geneva
1953, Jan.	Lucknow	1962, Aug.	Paris
1953, Aug.	Bossey	1963, Feb.	Geneva
1954, Feb.	Königstein im Taunus	1963, Aug.	Rochester
1954, Aug.	Chicago	1964, Feb.	Odessa
1955, Feb.	Geneva	1964, July	Tutzing
1955, July/Aug.	Davos	1965, Jan.	Enugu
1956, Feb.	Gilbulla	1965, July	Geneva
1956, July	Vienna	1966, Aug.	Geneva
1957, Feb.	Geneva	1966, Feb.	Geneva
1957, July	Greenwich	1967, Feb.	Windsor
1958, Feb.	London	1967, Aug.	Heraklion
1958, Aug.	Nyborg Strand	1968, Feb.	Geneva

BOOKS ABOUT THE WORLD COUNCIL OF CHURCHES

BELL, George Kennedy Allen, *The Kingship of Christ. The story of the World Council of Churches*. 183pp. Harmondsworth, Penguin Books, 1954. German translation *Die Königsherrschaft Jesu Christi; Die Geschichte des Oekumenischen Rates der Kirchen.*

DUFF, Edward, S.J., *The Social Thought of the World Council of Churches*. 339pp. New York, Association Press, 1956.

GAINES, David P., *The World Council of Churches: A study of its background and history*. 1302 pp. Peterborough, Richard R. Smith, 1966.

GOODALL, Norman, *The Ecumenical Movement: What it is and what it does*. 2nd edn. 257pp. London, New York, Oxford University Press, 1964.

GRANT, John Webster, *The Ship under the Cross*. 106pp. Toronto, The Ryerson Press, 1960.

Index to Ecumenical Statements and World Council of Churches Official Reports. 119pp. Trilingual. Geneva, W.C.C., 1968.

KRÜGER, Hanfried, *Oekumenische Bewegung, 1955–1958* (Sonderdruck aus *Kirchliches Jahrbuch für die evangelische Kirche in Deutschland*. 1958. Gütersloh, Gerd Mohn), pp. 310–78. Also surveys for the years 1959, 1960–1, 1962, 1963–4.

MACY, Paul Griswold, *If it be of God: The story of the World Council of Churches*. 192pp. St Louis, Mo., Bethany Press, 1960.

NEILL, Stephen C., *Men of Unity*. 192pp. London, S.C.M. Press, 1960. (American edn. with title: *Brothers of Faith*. Nashville, Abingdon Press, 1960.) German translation *Männer der Einheit; ökumenische Bewegung von Edinburgh bis Neu-Delhi.*

THEURER, Wolfdieter, *Die trinitarische Basis des ORK*. 285pp. Frankfurt/M., Verlag Gerhard Kaffke, 1967.

CHAPTER 3

Out of All Continents and Nations
A review of regional developments in the ecumenical movement

ASIA

ASSEMBLIES

With the exception of Asia and North America no specific studies have been made concerning regional developments in other continents. The sources for the study of ecumenical regionalism remain the reports and minutes of various assemblies and committees of regional ecumenical organizations as well as some articles published in their periodicals.

Bangkok 1949

The Christian Prospect in Eastern Asia. Papers and minutes of the E.A.C.C. Bangkok, December 3–11 1949. 156pp. New York, published for the International Missionary Council and the World Council of Churches by Friendship Press, 1950.

Prapat 1957

The Common Evangelistic Task of the Churches in East Asia. Papers and minutes of the E.A.C.C. Prapat, Indonesia, March 17–26, 1957. 167pp.

Kuala Lumpur 1959

Witnesses Together, being the Official Report of the Inaugural Assembly of the E.A.C.C., held at Kuala Lumpur, Malaya, May 14–24, 1959. 179pp. Ed. by U Kyaw Than. Rangoon, E.A.C.C., 1959.

Bangkok 1964

The Christian Community within the Human Community. Containing statements from the Bangkok Assembly of the E.A.C.C., Feb. 25–March 5, 1964. 84pp. Bangalore, India 1964.

Bangkok 1968

In Christ All Things Hold Together. Statements and findings of the Fourth Assembly of the E.A.C.C. 60pp. Bangkok 1968.

OTHER CONFERENCES

The Asian Churches and Responsible Parenthood. Bangkok, Thailand, E.A.C.C. Consultation 1964. 100pp. E.A.C.C. 1964.

Christ—the Hope of Asia. Papers and minutes of the ecumenical study conference for East Asia, Lucknow, India, December 27–30, 1952. 102pp. Madras, The Christian Literature Society, 1953.

Church's Witness in relation to religion, society, international affairs and religious liberty. Programme for 1964–68. 129pp. Bangkok, E.A.C.C., 1964.

Confessing the Faith in Asia Today. The First Faith and Order meeting in Hongkong, 1966. 116pp. Redfern, Epworth Press, 1967.

Consultation Digest. First Asian Consultation on Inter-Church Aid held under the joint auspices of D.I.C.A.R.W.S.–E.A.C.C. at Hongkong, Oct. 17–23, 1963. 118pp. Geneva, W.C.C., 1964.

Consultation on the Place of Education in the Mission of the Church. Singapore, E.A.C.C., April 4–8, 1961. 59pp. Wellawatte, Wesley Press, 1961.

Consultations on New Patterns of Christian Service, 1960–62:

New Forms of Christian Service and Participation. Nasrapur, October 1960 (Kottayam 1960).

New Forms of Christian Service in the Philippines. Quezon City, 1–4 April 1961 (Manila 1961).

Towards the New Form of Service in Japan. Atami, Japan, 29–31 March 1961 (Tokyo 1961).

New Forms of Christian Service and Participation in Korea. Onyang, Korea (Bangalore 1961).

Christian Service in the Revolution. Sukabumi, Indonesia, 14–18 November 1962. (Bangalore 1963).

East Asia Christian Conference. Minutes of the meeting of the enlarged Continuation Committee of the E.A.C.C., held at Bangalore, India, 7–12 November 1961. 135pp. Jaffna, St Joseph's Catholic Press, 1962.

East Asia Christian Conference. Report of Situation Conferences, convened by the E.A.C.C., February–March 1963. 56pp. Bangkok, E.A.C.C., 1963.

East Asia Christian Conference. Summary Reports of E.A.C.C. Committees (1959–64). 55pp. Bangkok, Rajadaromp Printery and Typefoundry, 1964.

East Asia Christian Literature Conference, Minutes of the . . . Tomlinson Hall, Singapore, December 7–11 1951. Sponsored by the International Missionary Council and the World Council of Churches. 48pp. Mysore City, Wesley Press, 1952.

God's People in Asian Industrial Society. The report of the E.A.C.C. on Christians in industry and lay training, ed. Robert M. Fukada. 198pp. Kyoto, Doshisha University School of Theology, 1967.

Men and Women in Home, Church and Community in Asia. Papers and statements of an Asian consultation on "The Christian home in a changing society". 114pp. Rangoon, Burma, 1963.

The Mission of the Church and the Cultural Minorities. Sagada, Philippines, Oct. 26 to Nov. 4, 1963. 27pp. E.A.C.C., Committee on Church and Society, 1964.

ROSE, Douglas A., *Seed of the Lotus: A diary of the Asian Christian Youth Assembly 1964/1965.* 68pp.

Structures for a Missionary Congregation. The shape of the Christian community in Asia today. 124pp. Singapore, E.A.C.C., 1964.

Towards Kuala Lumpur, 1959. Papers prepared for the Inaugural Assembly of the East Asia Christian Conference, ed. U Kyaw Than. Rangoon, E.A.C.C., 1959.

The Witness of the Churches in the midst of Social Change: A survey of ecumenical social thought. Papers for preparatory reading for the assembly of the East Asia Christian Conference, Port Dickson, Malaya, May 14–24 1959. 146pp. Rangoon, E.A.C.C., 1959.

Church and Society, 1960—. Official periodical of the East Asia Christian Conference.

A Decisive Hour for the Christian Mission. The East Asia Christian Conference and the John R. Mott memorial lectures. Norman Goodall, James Edward Lesslie Newbigin, Willem Adolf Visser 't Hooft, Daniel Thambirajah Niles. 96pp. London, S.C.M. Press, 1960.

MANIKAM, Rajah B., ed., *Christianity and the Asian Revolution.* 293pp. Madras, Joint East Asia Secretariat of the I.M.C. and W.C.C., 1954.

South East Asia Journal of Theology, 1959—. Contains several official papers published by E.A.C.C.

WEBER, Hans-Ruedi: *Asia and the Ecumenical Movement 1895–1961.* 319pp. London, S.C.M. Press, 1966.

AFRICA

ASSEMBLIES

Ibadan 1958

The Church in Changing Africa. Report of the All Africa Church Conference, held at Ibadan, Nigeria, January 10–19, 1958. 106pp. New York, I.M.C., 1958. French translation *Ibadan, Conférence des Eglises d'Afrique, 1958.*

Kampala 1963

Drumbeats from Kampala. Report of the First Assembly of the All Africa Conference of Churches held at Kampala, April 20 to April 30, 1963. 77pp. London, U.S.C.L., Lutterworth Press, 1963. French translation La Conférence de Kampala.

OTHER CONFERENCES

Africa in Transition: The Challenge and the Christian Response. 95pp. Published by All Africa Churches Conferences in collaboration with the Dept on Church and Society, Division of Studies, World Council of Churches, Geneva, W.C.C., 1962. French translation L'Afrique en devenir.

Africa Seminar on the Christian Home and Family Life, held at Mindolo Ecumenical Centre, Kitwe, N. Rhodesia, 17 Feb. to 10 April, 1963. Sponsored by the A.A.C.C. in collaboration with the W.C.C. 72pp. Geneva, W.C.C., 1963. French translation Séminaire panafricain sur le foyer chrétien et la vie de famille.

Approved programme. Ecumenical programme for emergency action in Africa. 78pp. Geneva, W.C.C., D.I.C.A.R.W.S., 1965.

Christian Education in Africa. Report of a conference held at Salisbury, Southern Rhodesia, 29 December 1962 to 10 January 1963. 120pp. London, Oxford University Press, 1963. French translation L'Education chrétienne en Afrique.

Christian Women of Africa Share in Responsibility. Report of the Consultation on the Responsibility of Christian Women in Africa today, held at Makerere University, Kampala, Uganda, April 11–19th, 1963. 45pp. Geneva, W.C.C. and the Department on Co-operation of Men and Women in Church, Family, and Society, 1963. French translation Les femmes chrétiennes d'Afrique assument leur part de responsabilité.

Consultation Digest. A summary of reports and addresses. A.A.C.C. Inter-Church Aid Consultation. Sponsored jointly by the A.A.C.C., D.I.C.A.R.W.S., and C.C.I.A. 116pp. Geneva, W.C.C., 1965.

The Urban Africa Consultation, held in Nairobi, Kenya, March 1961. Sponsored by the A.A.C.C. in conjunction with the I.M.C. 55pp. New York, Commission on World Mission and Evangelism, 1962.

A.A.C.C. Bulletin, 1963–1967. English and French editions.

BEETHAM, T. A., Christianity and the New Africa. 206pp. London, Pall Mall Press, 1967.

L'oecuménisme en Afrique. Ecumenism in Africa. 169pp. Roma, C.I.P.A., 1966

LATIN AMERICA

CONGRESSES AND ASSEMBLIES

Congress on Christian Work in Latin America, Panama, 1916. 3 vols. New York, Missionary Education Movement, C.C.L.A., 1917.

Christian Work in South America. Report of the Montevideo Congress, 1925. Robert E. Speer and other editors. 2 vols. New York, C.C.L.A., 1925.

Hacia la renovacion religiosa en Hispano-América. Report of the Congreso Evangélico Hispano-americano, Havana, 1929. 213pp. Mexico, C.U.P.S.A., 1930.

El cristianismo en la América Latina. Report of the First Latin American Evangelical Conference in Buenos Aires, 1949. 103pp. Buenos Aires, La Awrora, 1949.

Cristo la Esperanza para América Latina. Segunda Conferencia Evangelica Latino-america. 176pp. Lima, 1961.

OTHER CONFERENCES AND LITERATURE

America hoy; accion de Dios y responsabilidad del hombre: II consulta latinoamericana de Iglesia y Sociedad. 132pp. Montevideo, I.S.A.L., 1966.

Christians and Social Change in Latin America. Findings of the first Latin American Evangelical Consultation on Church and Society, 23rd to 27th July 1961. 22pp. Huampani, Peru. Geneva, W.C.C., 1961. Translated from the Spanish *Encuentro y desafio.*

CONSIDINE, John J., ed., *The Church in the New Latin America.* 240pp. Notre Dame, Fides Publishers, 1964.

Cristianismo y sociedad, 1963—. Montevideo, I.S.A.L. The Official Latin American Church and Society journal.

The Listening Isles. Records of the Caribbean Consultation, San German, Puerto Rico, May 17–24, 1957. New York, I.M.C., 1958.

MACKAY, John A., *The Latin American Churches and the Ecumenical Movement.* 34pp. New York, N.C.C.C.U.S.A., the Committee on Co-operation in Latin America, Division of Foreign Missions, 1963.

N.C.C.C.U.S.A. Committee on Co-operation in Latin America. Study Conferences, Buck Hill Falls, 10–12 November 1957, 6–8 November 1958, 12–14 November 1959, 20–2 November 1960, 5–7 November 1961. Each Conference issued several short reports.

OBERMÜLLER, Rudolf., *Evangelism in Latin America: An ecumenical survey.* 32pp. (World evangelism today, 2). Published for the W.C.C. by U.S.C.L., London, Lutterworth Press, 1957.

Raise a Signal: God's Action and the Church's Task in Latin America Today. A Symposium compiled by Hyla S. Converse. 126pp. New York, Friendship Press, 1961.

SINCLAIR, John H., *Protestantism in Latin America: A bibliographical guide.* 213pp. Austin, Texas, Hispanic American Institute, 1967.

PACIFIC

Beyond the reef. Records of the Conference of Churches and Missions in the Pacific. Malua Theological College, Western Samoa, April 22–May 4, 1961. 114pp. London, I.M.C., 1961. French translation *La route du soleil.*

EUROPE

Konferenz Europäischer Kirchen. Ein Bericht über die Tagung in Liselund, Dänemark vom 27–31 Mai 1957. Den Haag, Konferenz Europäischer Kirchen, 1957.

Nyborg I

Die europäische Christenheit in der heutigen säkularisierten Welt. Konferenz europäischer Kirchen, Nyborg-Dänemark, 6–9 Januar 1959. 141pp. Vorträge und Berichte. Zürich, Frankfurt/M., Gotthelf-Verlag, 1960.

Nyborg II

Der Dienst der Kirche in einer sich veränderten Welt. Konferenz europäischer Kirchen, 3–8 Okt. 1960. 114pp. Zürich, Gotthelf-Verlag, 1961.

Nyborg III

Die Kirche in Europa und die Krise des modernen Menschen. Konferenz Europäischer Kirchen, 1–5 Okt. 1962. 160pp. Zürich, Gotthelf-Verlag, 1963.

Nyborg IV

Zusammen leben als Kontinente und Generationen. Konferenz Europäischer Kirchen vom 5–9 Okt. 1964. 224pp. Zürich, Gotthelf-Verlag, 1965.

Nyborg V

To serve and to reconcile. The task of the European Churches today. Preparatory document for the "Nyborg V" Assembly of the C.E.C., 1967. 38pp.

DE-LA-NOY, Michael, *A Task for the Churches in Europe: To serve and reconcile. A report of the "Nyborg V" Assembly in Pförtschach, 1967.* 48pp. Geneva, C.E.C., 1968. German report by Schulz, Otmar. *Die Aufgabe der europäischen Kirchen: Dienen und Versöhnen.* More complete than English edn.

NEAR EAST

The Christian Faith in the Contemporary Middle Eastern World. Asmara Study Conference, April 1–9, 1959. New York, 1959.

N.E.C.C. Study Programme in Islam. Operation reach. 1st–5th series, 1957/58–1961/62. Beirut, 1957–1962. 24 fasc.

News Bulletin of the N.E.C.C. Beirut, 1945—.

Survey of the Training of the Ministry in the Middle East. Report of a survey of theological education in Iran, the Arabian-Persian Gulf, Jordan, Lebanon, Syria, and Egypt, undertaken in September to November, 1961 by Douglas Webster and K. L. Nasir. 63pp. Geneva, Commission on World Mission and Evangelism, 1962.

CHAPTER 4

National Councils of Churches

The basic sources for studying the history of national developments within the ecumenical movement remain the minutes of committees and reports of conferences and consultations of the various national councils, which frequently exist only in mimeographed form. The W.C.C. Library has a special collection of these stenciled documents.

GENERAL WORKS

Directory of Christian Councils. 1959. 214pp. Mimeographed. London, Joint Committee of the W.C.C. and I.M.C. Supplement 1960.

MACCRACKEN, James, *Church World Service Support of National Christian Councils.* 81pp. Mimeographed. 1968.

De oecumenische situatie in de verschillende landen. J. Hamer, T. F. Stransky, L. G. M. Alting van Geusau (and others). 184pp. Hilversum, Antwerpen, Paul Brand, 1965.

La situation oecuménique dans le monde. Etudes du Centre international d'Information et de documentation sur l'Eglise conciliare. 254pp. Paris, Editions du Centurion, 1967.

NATIONAL COUNCIL OF THE CHURCHES OF CHRIST IN THE U.S.A.

CAVERT, Samuel McCrea, *The American Churches in the Ecumenical Movement, 1900–1968.* 288pp. New York, Association Press, 1968.

Christian Faith in Action. Commemorative volume; the founding of the National Council of Churches of Christ in the U.S.A. 272pp. New York, N.C.C.C.U.S.A., 1951.

The Churches Working Together for a Christian America. 32pp. New York, N.C.C.C.U.S.A., 1962.

The Ecclesiological Significance of Councils of Churches. 26pp. New York, N.C.C.C. U.S.A., 1963.

KNAPP, Forrest L., *Church Co-operation; Deadend street or highway to unity?* 249pp. New York, Doubleday, 1966.

MACFARLAND, Charles S., *Christian Unity in the Making. The first twenty-five years of the Federal Council of the Churches of Christ in America, 1905–1930.* 376pp. New York, Federal Council of the Churches of Christ, 1948.

National Council of the Churches of Christ in the U.S.A. *Biennial and Triennial Reports. Annual Division Reports.* New York, National Council of Churches, 1952—.

ROSS, Roy G., *The Ecumenical Movement and the Local Church. A statement of imperative and suggested plans, as approved by the General Board, March 2, 1962.* 16pp. New York, N.C.C.C.U.S.A., 1962.

RYCROFT, W. Stanley, *The Ecumenical Witness of the United Presbyterian Church in the U.S.A.* 332pp. Published by the Board of Christian Education of the United Presbyterian Church in the U.S.A., 1968.

SANDERSON, Ross W., *Church Co-operation in the United States. The nation-wide backgrounds and ecumenical significance of state and local Councils of Churches in their historical perspective.* 272pp. Hartford, Conn., Association of Council Secretaries, 1960.

CANADIAN COUNCIL OF CHURCHES

Canadian Council of Churches. *Record of proceedings, 13th, St Catharines, Ontario* Nov. 3–7, 1960. Also later biennial assemblies.

GALLAGHER, W. J., *The Canadian Council of Churches.* Mimeographed, n.d.

GRANT, John Webster, *The Canadian Experience of Church Union,* 106pp. (Ecumenical Studies in History, 8). London, Lutterworth Press, 1967.

GRANT, John Webster, *The Churches and the Canadian Experience; A Faith and Order study of the Christian tradition.* Foreword by David W. Hay. 161pp. Toronto, Ryerson, 1963.

WILSON, Douglas J., *The Church Grows in Canada.* 224pp. Published by the Committee on Missionary Education, Canadian Council of Churches. Toronto, New York, Friendship Press, 1966.

Q

BRITISH COUNCIL OF CHURCHES

CAIRD, George B., *Making it Visible.* 29pp. (The unity we seek, 2). London, B.C.C., 1964.

DAVIES, Rupert E., *In All Places and All Ages.* 37pp. (The unity we seek, 5). London, B.C.C., 1964.

First Ecumenical Work-Book. Programme suggestions for local councils of churches, united Christian youth groups, ecumenical fellowships and parishes and congregations. 34pp. London, B.C.C., 1960.

SLACK, Kenneth, *Growing Together Locally. Some suggestions as to how the ecumenical movement can be made a reality wherever Christians of different traditions are found together.* 40pp. London, B.C.C., 1958.

Unity Begins at Home. A report from the First British Conference on Faith and Order, Nottingham, 1964. 95pp. London, S.C.M. Press, 1964.

NATIONAL CHRISTIAN COUNCIL OF INDIA

BAAGO, K., *A History of the National Christian Council of India, 1914–1964.* 89pp. Nagpur, The National Christian Council. Christian Council Lodge, 1965.

Ecumenical Development among Christian Youth in India. Work of the Central Youth Committee. 12pp. National Christian Council of India, 1963.

KELLOCK, James, *Breakthrough for Church Union in North India and Pakistan.* 146pp. Madras, Christian Literature Society, 1965.

National Christian Council of India. *Worship and the Church's Mission and Unity. A report of the third Indian Conference on Worship held under the auspices of the National Christian Council of India and the East Asia Theological Commission of the World Council of Churches at Bangalore, May 26–30, 1960.* 65pp.

SADIQ, John W., *Adventure in Christian Fellowship. The story of the Life and Work of the National Christian Council of India.* 46pp. Delhi, I.S.P.C.K., 1966.

NATIONAL COUNCIL OF CHURCHES IN NEW ZEALAND

One Lord, one World. Being the official report of the Third New Zealand Ecumenical Youth Conference, held at Lower Hutt, December 27, 1960–January 4, 1961. 64pp. Christchurch, H. F. Cross, 1961.

Towards the One Church. Questions and answers by the Churches. 49pp. Christchurch, National Council of Churches in New Zealand, 1954.

WATSON, Nigel M., *A report of the Third New Zealand Faith and Order Conference, held at Massey University College of the Manawan, February 4–11, 1964.* 68pp. Christchurch, National Council of Churches in New Zealand, 1964.

OTHER COUNTRIES

BROWN, Basil H. M., ed., *The New Dimensions of Mission for South Africa Today. Reports and addresses of a National Conference held in Johannesburg, May 1964.* 89pp. Cape Town, Christian Council of South Africa, 1964.

BRUNOTTE, Heinz, *Die Evangelische Kirche in Deutschland. Geschichte, Organisation und Gestalt der EKD.* 208pp. Gütersloh, Gütersloher Verlagshaus Gerd Mohn, 1964.

The Burma Directory of Christian Service. Agencies affiliated to or in co-operation with, the Burma Christian Council (1956–1957). 84pp. Rangoon, St Gabriel's Church, 1958.

The Church and the Problems of the Town. Tanganyika rapid social change study, commission "C", sponsored by the Christian Council of Tanganyika and the East Africa Urban Consultation, 14–21 May 1964. 109pp. Dar-es-Salaam, Tanganyika, 1964.

Die Evangelische Kirche im ökumenischen Spannungsfeld. Synode der Evangelischen Kirche in Deutschland, Berlin Spandau/Potsdam-Babelsberg, 1966. Herausgegeben von Wilhelm Gundert. 79pp. Witten, Luther-Verlag, 1966.

DUYVENDAK, J. H., *Memorandum on the History of the Ecumenical Movement in the Netherlands.* 68pp. Geneva, W.C.C., 1950.

Fellowship of Service. Life and work of Protestant Churches in Czechoslovakia. 120pp. Prague, Ecumenical Council of Churches in Czechoslovakia, 1961.

GOWING, Peter C., *Islands under the Cross. The story of the Church in the Philippines.* 286pp. Manila, National Council of Churches in the Philippines, 1967.

Où en est l'oecuménisme? Suède, Espagne, Belgique. 56pp. Lyou, "Unite Chrétienne", 1961.

PORKSEN, Martin, *Uebermorgen; die Hoffnung der indonesischen Christenheit.* 167pp. Wuppertal-Barmen, Verlag der Rheinischen Mission, 1965.

Projects in Church Unity. Studies prepared for Australian Churches with suggestions for group discussion and action. 32pp. Sydney, Australian Council of Churches, n.d.

SOBREPENA, Enrique S., *That They may be One. A brief account of the United Church Movement in the Philippines.* 177pp. Manila, United Church of Christ in the Philippines, 1964.

TIPPETT, A. R., *Solomon Islands Christianity Obstruction.* 407pp. (World studies of churches in mission). London, Lutterworth Press, 1967.

Towards a Better Life. An appraisal of Christian rural work, undertaken by a conference held at the Conference Centre of the Institute of Administration, Zaria, Nigeria, 1966, with a view to determining more clearly the role of the Church in rural development. 65pp. Ibadan, Christian Council of Nigeria, Daystar Press, 1966.

Unser Weg. Vom Leben der Mitgliedskirchen des Polnischen Oekumenischen Rates. 223pp. Warsau, der Polnische Oekumenische Rat, 1966.

VISCHER, Lukas, *Der Schweizerische Evangelische Kirchenbund, Bund oder Kirche?* 58pp. Zürich, EVZ-Verlag, 1962. French translation *La Fédération des Eglises protestantes de la Suisse, Fédération ou église?*

We Were Brought Together. Report of the National Conference of Australian Churches held at Melbourne University, 1960, ed. David M. Taylor. 181pp. Sydney, Australian Council for the World Council of Churches, 1960.

WELCH, F. G., *Towards an African Church.* 128pp. Nairobi, Christian Council of Kenya, 1962.

CHAPTER 5

Confessional Families and the Ecumenical Movement

GENERAL WORKS ABOUT CONFESSIONALISM, CREEDS AND HISTORY OF DENOMINATIONS

Creeds of the Churches. Ed. J. H. Leith. 589pp. New York, Doubleday, 1963.

The Faith of Christendom. A source-book of creeds and confessions. Selected, edited, and introduced by B. A. Gerrish. 371pp. New York, World Publishing Co., 1963.

GRUNDER, J., *Lexikon der christlichen Kirchen und Sekten; unter Berücksichtigung der Missionsgesellschaftlichen und zwischenkirchlichen Organisationen.* 2 vols. Wien, Herder, 1961.

Die Kirchen der Welt. Hrsg. von F. Sigg, H. H. Harms und H. H. Wolf. Reihe A: Selbstdarstellungen der Kirchen. Reihe B: Ergänzungsbände. Stuttgart, Evangelisches Verlagswerk, 1959.

MEAD, Frank S., *Handbook of Denominations in the United States.* 2nd. rev. edn. 272pp. New York, Abingdon, 1961.

MEINHOLD, P., *Oekumenische Kirchenkunde. Lebensformen der Christenheit heute.* 652pp. Stuttgart, Kreuz Verlag, 1962.

"Und ihr Netz zerriss"; die Grosskirchen in Selbstdarstellungen. Hrsg. von H. Lamparter. 456pp. Stuttgart, Quell-Verlag der Evang. Gesellschaft, 1957.

Weltkirchen-Lexikon. Handbuch der Oekumene; im Auftrag des Deutschen Evangelischen Kirchentages. Hrsg. von F. H. Littell und H. H. Walz. 1756pp. Stuttgart, Kreuz Verlag, 1960.

World Christian Handbook. 5th edn. 1968. 378pp. Ed. H. W. Coxill and K. Grubb. London, Lutterworth Press, 1967.

WORKS ON THE HISTORY AND THEOLOGY OF VARIOUS DENOMINATIONS

ARMSTRONG, A., *Rediscovering Eastern Christendom. Essays in commemoration oj Dom Bede Winslow.* Ed. A. H. Armstrong and E. F. B. Fry. 166pp. London, Darton, Longman & Todd, 1963.

ATIYA, Aziz S., *A History of Eastern Christianity.* 468pp. London, Methuen, 1968.

ATTWATER, Donald, *The Christian Churches of the East.* 2 vols. London, Chapman, 1961.

BAYNE, Stephen F., *An Anglican Turning Point; Documents and intepretations.* 317pp. Austin, Texas, Church Historical Society, 1964.

Bekenntnisschriften und Kirchenordnungen der nach Gottes Wort reformierten Kirche; 3. Aufl. Hrsg. von W. Niesel. 358pp. Zürich, EVZ-Verlag, 1958.

BENZ, Ernst, *The Eastern Orthodox Church: Its thought and life.* 230pp. New York, Doubleday, 1963. Translated from the German *Geist und Leben der Ostkirche.*

The Book of Concord: The confessions of the Evangelical Lutheran Church. Ed. Th. G. Tappert. 717pp. Philadelphia, Mühlenberg Press, 1959.

CASTLE, E. B., *Approach to Quakerism.* 178pp. London, Bannisdale Press, 1961.

DAVIES, H., *The English Free Churches.* 2nd edn. 216pp. London, Oxford University Press, 1963.

DAVIES, Rupert E., *Methodism.* 224pp. Harmondsworth, Penguin Books, 1963.

EMPIE, Paul C., and McCORD, James I., ed., *Marburg revisited: A re-examination of Lutheran and Reformed traditions*. 193pp. Minneapolis, Augsburg Publishing House, 1966.

GRUNDMANN, Siegfried: *Der Lutherische Weltbund. Grundfragen—Herkunft—Aufbau*. 586pp. Köln, Böhlau, 1957.

HARMON, Nolan B., *Understanding the Methodist Church*. 191pp. Nashville, Methodist Publishing House, 1955.

The History of American Methodism, ed. Emory S. Bucke. 3 vols. New York, Abingdon, 1964.

HORTON, Douglas, *The United Church of Christ; Its origins, organization and role in the world today*. 287pp. Edinburgh, New York, Thomas Nelson, 1962.

LORD, F. Townley, *Baptist World Fellowship: A short history of the Baptist World Alliance*. 185pp. London, Carey Kingsgate Press, 1955.

LOUKES, Harold, *The Quaker Contribution*. 528pp. London, S.C.M. Press, 1965.

LUCCOCK, Halford E., and HUTCHINSON, Paul, *The Story of Methodism*. 528pp. New York, Abingdon, 1949.

The Lutheran Churches of the World, ed. Abdel Ross Wentz. 443pp. Geneva, L.W.F., 1952.

Lutheran Directory, 1963. Part I: *Lutheran Churches of the World*. Part II: *Lutheran World Federation*. Berlin, Lutherisches Verlagshaus, 1963. Supplement 1968. Also German translation.

MEYENDORFF, Jean, *The Orthodox Church: Its past and its role in the world today*. 244pp. New York, Pantheon, 1962. Translated from the French *L'Eglise orthodoxe hier et aujourd'hui*. German translation *Die orthodoxe Kirche gestern und heute*.

MEYENDORFF, Jean, *Orthodoxy and Catholicity*. 180pp. New York, Sheed and Ward, 1966. Translated from the French *Orthodoxie et catholicité*.

Moss, C. B., *The Old Catholic Movement: Its origins and history*. 2nd edn. 362pp. London, S.P.C.K., 1964.

"The Nature of the L.W.F. Documents", in *Lutheran World* (Geneva), vol. ii, no. 2 (April 1964), pp. 161–215.

NEILL, Stephen C., *Anglicanism. An explanation, in the light of history and theology, of the nature and working of the Anglican Communion, its relationship with other Christian groups and its part in the movement for Christian unity*. 466pp. London, Penguin, 1958.

NIESEL, Wilhelm, *Reformed symbolics*. 400pp. Edinburgh, Oliver and Boyd, 1964. Translated from the German.

PAYNE, Ernest A., *The Baptist Union; A short history*. 317pp. London, Carey Kingsgate Press, 1959.

RACK, Henry D., *The Future of John Wesley's Methodism*. 80pp. (Ecumenical studies in history, 2). London, Lutterworth Press, 1965.

ROBINSON, William, *What Churches of Christ stand for*. 4th edn. 112pp. Birmingham, Berean Press, 1959.

ROUTLEY, Erik, *The Story of Congregationalism*. 177pp. London, Independent Press, 1961.

SANDALL, Robert, and WIGGINS, Arch, *The History of the Salvation Army*. 4 vols. London, Thomas Nelson, 1964.

SCHLINK, E., *Theology of the Lutheran Confessions*. 353pp. Philadelphia, Muhlenberg Press, 1961. Translated from the German *Theologie der lutherischen Bekenntnisschriften*.

SMITH, C. Henry, *The Story of the Mennonites*. 4th edn. revised and enlarged by Cornelis Krahn. 856pp. Newton, Kansas, 1957.

TORBET, Robert G., *A History of the Baptists*. 540pp. Philadelphia, Judson Press, 1955.

TRUEBLOOD, David E., *The People Called Quakers*. 298pp. New York, Harper, 1966.

VAJTA, Vilmos, ed., *Church in Fellowship: Pulpit and altar fellowship among Lutherans*. 279pp. Minneapolis, Augsburg Press, 1963. Translated from the German *Kirche und Abendmahl*.

VAJTA, Vilmos and WEISSGERBER, Hans, ed., *The Church and the Confessions. The role of the confessions in the life and doctrine of the Lutheran Churches*. 218pp. Philadelphia, Fortress Press, 1963. Translated from the German *Das Bekenntnis im Leben der Kirche*.

WARE, Timothy, *The Orthodox Church*. 352pp. Harmondsworth, Penguin Books, 1963.

We believe. A digest of Salvationist doctrine. 39pp. London, Salvationist Publishing and Supplies, 1963.

WENGER, J. C., *The Mennonite Church in America*. 384pp. Scottdale, Herald Press, 1966.

The World Alliance of Reformed Churches. 104pp. Geneva, World Presbyterian Alliance, 1964.

World Lutheranism Today (Welt-Luthertum von heute). A tribute to Anders Nygren. 438pp. Oxford, Blackwell; Rock Island, Ill., Augustana Book Concern, 1950.

WORKS ON THE APPROACH OF DENOMINATIONS AND OF CONFESSIONAL BODIES TO THE ECUMENICAL MOVEMENT AND TO PROBLEMS OF CHURCH UNION

Anglican Initiatives in Christian Unity: Lectures delivered in Lambeth Palace Library, ed. E. G. W. Bill. 168pp. London, S.P.C.K., 1967.

Baptists and Unity. 60pp. London, Baptist Union of Great Britain and Ireland, 1967.

Baptists for Unity. 34pp. Coventry, Reynolds Press. 1968.

The Church for Others and the Church for the World: A quest for structures for missionary congregations. Final report of the Western European Working Group and North American Working Group of the Department on Studies in Evangelism. 135pp. Geneva, W.C.C., 1967.

"Confessional loyalty at all costs?" *Risk*, vol. ii, no. 4, 1966. 102pp. Geneva, W.C.C.

"Consultation on Church Union Negotiations. Bossey, April 9–15, 1967", *Midstream*, vol. vi, no. 3, Spring 1968. Indianapolis, Council on Christian Unity.

DAMMERS, A. H., *A.D. 1980: A study in Christian unity, mission and renewal*. 125pp. London, Lutterworth Press, 1966.

ESTEP, William R., *Baptists and Christian Unity*. 200pp. Nashville, Broadman Press, 1967.

FORSYTH, P. T., *Congregationalism and Reunion*. 78pp. London, Independent Press, 1952.

GARRISON, Winfred E., *Christian Unity and Disciples of Christ*. 286pp. St Louis, Bethany Press, 1955.

GASSMANN, Gunther, *Das historische Bischofsamt und die Einheit der Kirche in der neueren anglikanischen Theologie*. 283pp. Göttingen, Vandenhoeck und Ruprecht, 1964.

HOLLIS, Michael, *Mission, Unity and Truth: A study of confessional families and the churches in Asia*. 138pp. London, Lutterworth, 1967.

JOHN, Glynmor, *Congregationalism in an Ecumenical Era*. 23pp. London, Independent Press, 1967.

KIK, J. Marcellus, *Ecumenism and the Evangelical*. 152pp. Philadelphia, Presbyterian and Reformed Publishing Co., 1958.

LAMPE, G. W. H., *An Anglican Approach to Intercommunication and Reunion*. 20pp. London, S.P.C.K., 1962.

PACKER, J. I., *All in Each Place; Towards reunion in England. Ten Anglican essays with some Free Church comments*. 237pp. Appleford, Abingdon, Berks., Marcham Manor Press, 1965.

PATON, David, *Anglicans and Unity*. 115pp. (Starbooks on reunion, 2). London, Mowbray, 1962.

PERCHENET, A., *Renouveau communautaire et unité chrétienne: Regards sur les communautés anglicanes et protestantes*. 480pp. Paris, Mame, 1967.

ROBERTS-THOMSON, E., *With Hands Outstretched. Baptists and the ecumenical movement*. 128pp. London, Marshall Morgan and Scott, 1967.

ROUTLEY, Erik, *Congregationalists and Unity*. 94pp. London, Mowbray, 1962.

RYCROFT, W. Stanley, *The Ecumenical Witness of the United Presbyterian Church in the U.S.A.* 332pp. Published for the Commission on Ecumenical Missions and Relations by the Board of Christian Education of the United Presbyterian Church in the U.S.A., 1968.

SANSBURY, Kenneth, *Truth, Unity and Concord: Anglican faith in ecumenical setting*. 262pp. London, Mowbray, 1967.

SHORT, Howard E., *Christian Unity is Our Business: Disciples of Christ within the ecumenical fellowship*. 59pp. St Louis, Bethany Press, 1953.

"World Confessionalism and the Ecumenical Movement", *Lutheran World* (January 1963), vol. x, no. 1. 4 articles.

YODER, John H., *The Ecumenical Movement and the Faithful Church*. 44pp. Scottdale, Mennonite Publishing House, 1958.

Minutes of the Meetings of Representatives of World Confessional Groups, held in Geneva, 1957— (mimeographed, in Archives of W.C.C. Library).

International Meetings of World Confessional Bodies

Anglican Congresses

Minneapolis 1957
Toronto 1962
Lambeth Conferences 1948, 1958, 1968

Assembly of the International Congregational Council

7th, St Andrews, Scotland 1953
8th, Hartford, Conn. 1958
9th, Rotterdam 1962
10th, Swansea, Wales 1966

Assembly of the Lutheran World Federation

2nd, Hanover, Germany 1952
3rd, Minneapolis, Minn. 1957
4th, Helsinki 1963

Baptist World Congress

8th, Cleveland, Ohio 1950
9th, London 1955
10th, Rio de Janeiro 1960
11th, Miami Beach, Florida 1965

General Council of the Alliance of the Reformed Churches Holding the Presbyterian Order

17th, Princeton, N.J. 1954
18th, Sao Paulo, Brazil 1959
19th, Frankfurt/Main 1964

World Conference of Friends

3rd, Oxford, England 1952
4th, Greensboro, North Carolina 1967

World Methodist Conference

8th, Oxford 1951
9th, Lake Junaluska, North Carolina 1956
10th, Oslo 1961
11th, London 1966

World Convention of the Disciples of Christ

1955 Toronto
1960 Edinburgh
1965 San Juan, Puerto Rico

CHAPTER 6

Faith and Order 1948—1968

GENERAL WORKS

DEGROOT, Alfred T., ed., *Check list Faith and Order Commission official, numbered publications, series I, 1910–1948; series II, 1948 to date 1962.* Ed. A. T. D. with the special assistance of the Reverend Dr Floyd W. Tomkins. Geneva, W.C.C., 1963.

SKOGLUND, John E., *Fifty Years of Faith and Order. An interpretation of the Faith and Order Movement.* 159pp. St Louis, Bethany Press, 1964.

VISCHER, Lukas, ed., *A Documentary History of the Faith and Order Movement.* 246pp. St Louis, Bethany Press, 1963. German edition *Die Einheit der Kirche.* French edition *Foi et constitution.*

LUND 1952

BAILLIE, Donald, ed., *Intercommuntion: The report of the theological commission.* 406pp. London, S.C.M. Press, 1952.

FLEW, R. Newton, ed., *The Nature of the Church. Papers presented to the theological commission.* 347pp. London, S.C.M. Press, 1952.

KENNEDY, James W., *He that Gathereth. A first-hand account of the third world conference on Faith and Order, held at Lund, Sweden, August 15–28, 1952.* 112pp. New York, W.C.C., 1952.

TOMKINS, Oliver Stratford, *The Church in the purpose of God. An introduction to the work of the commission on Faith and Order of the World Council of Churches, in preparation for the third world conference on Faith and Order to be held at Lund, Sweden, in 1952.* 118pp. (Faith and Order papers, 3). London, S.C.M. Press, 1950.

TOMKINS, Oliver Stratford, ed., *The Third World Conference on Faith and Order held at Lund, August 15th to 28th, 1952.* 380pp. London, S.C.M. Press, 1953. French translation *Rapport de la troisième conférence mondiale de "Foi et Constitution".* German translation *Lund; dritte Weltkonferenz der Kirchen für Glauben und Kirchenverfassung.*

Ways of worship. The report of a theological commission on Faith and Order. 362pp. Ed. Pehr Edwall, Eric Hayman, William D. Maxwell. London, S.C.M. Press, 1951.

MONTREAL 1963

MINEAR, Paul S., ed., *Faith and Order findings. The final report of the theological commissions to the fourth world conference on Faith and Order, Montreal 1963.* 31pp., 62pp., 63pp., 64pp. (Faith and Order papers, 37–40: Institutionalism; Christ and the Church; Worship; Tradition and traditions, printed in one volume.) London, S.C.M. Press, 1963.

The Old and the New in the Church. Report on tradition and traditions, report on institutionalism and unity presented to the commission 1961. 96pp. (Faith and Order papers, 34). London, S.C.M. Press, 1961.

One Lord, One Baptism: Report on the Divine Trinity and the unity of the Church and report on the meaning of Baptism, by the theological commission on Christ and the Church. 79pp. (Faith and Order papers, 29). London, S.C.M. Press, 1960. French translation *Un seul Seigneur, un seul baptême.*

RODGER, Patrick C., and VISCHER, Lukas, ed., *The Fourth World Conference on Faith and Order, Montreal, 1963.* 126pp. (Faith and Order papers, 42). London, S.C.M. Press, 1964. French translation *4e Conférence mondiale de Foi et Constitution.* German translation *Montreal 1963. Bericht.*

OTHER CONFERENCES

Confessing the Faith in Asia Today. Statement issued by the consultation convened by the East Asia Christian Conference and held in Hongkong, October 26–November 3, 1966. 116pp. Redfern, Epworth Press, 1967. And in *South East Asia Journal of Theology.* October 1966–January 1967.

MINEAR, Paul S., ed., *The Nature of the Unity we Seek. Official report of the North American Conference on Faith and Order, September 3–10, 1957, Oberlin, Ohio.* 304pp. St Louis, Bethany Press, 1958.

472   BIBLIOGRAPHY

Minutes of the meetings of the Faith and Order Commission and Working Committee held at the University of Aarhus, Denmark, 15–27 August 1964. 104pp. (Faith and Order papers, 44). Geneva, W.C.C., 1965.

NELSON, J. Robert., ed., *Christian unity in North America: A symposium.* 208pp. St Louis, Bethany Press, 1958.

New directions in Faith and Order, Bristol, 1967: Reports, minutes, documents. 183pp. (Faith and Order papers, 50). Geneva, W.C.C., 1968. German translation *Bristol 1967.* French translation *Nouveauté dans l'oecuménisme.*

Unity Begins at Home: A report from the first British Conference on Faith and Order, Nottingham, 1964. 95pp. (S.C.M. Press Broadsheet). London, S.C.M. Press, 1964.

WATSON, Nigel M., *Massey 1964. A report on the third New Zealand Faith and Order Conference, 1964.* 68pp. Christchurch, National Council of Churches in New Zealand, 1964.

SECRETARIAT ON FAITH AND ORDER

Concerning the Ordination of Women. 72pp. (World Council Studies, 1). Department on Faith and Order. Geneva, W.C.C., 1964. French translation *De l'ordination des femmes.* German translation *Zur Frage der Ordination der Frau.*

The Deaconess. 86pp. (World Council Studies, 4). Geneva, W.C.C., 1966. French translation *La diaconesse.* German translation *Die Diakonisse.*

An Ecumenical Exercise. The Southern Baptist Convention, the Seventh-Day Adventist Church, the Kimbanquist Church in the Congo, the Pentecostal Movement in Europe, ed. M. B. Handspicker and Lukas Vischer. 46pp. (Faith and Order papers, 49). Geneva, W.C.C., 1967.

The Ministry of Deacons. 86pp. (World Council Studies, 2). Geneva, W.C.C., 1965. French translation *Le ministère des diacres.* German translation *Das Amt der Diakone.*

ECUMENICAL THEOLOGY

Biblical Authority for Today. A World Council of Churches symposium on "the biblical authority for the churches social and political message today". Ed. Alan Richardson and W. Schweitzer. 347pp. London, S.C.M. Press, 1951.

EHRENSTROM, Nils, and MUELDER, Walter G., ed., *Institutionalism and Church Unity. Symposium prepared by the Study Commission on Institutionalism, Commission on Faith and Order, World Council of Churches.* 378pp. London, S.C.M. Press, 1963.

JENKINS, Daniel, *Tradition, Freedom, and the Spirit.* 195pp. Philadelphia, Westminster Press, 1951.

LASH, Nicholas, ed., *Doctrinal Development and Christian Unity.* 223pp. London, Sheed and Ward, 1967.

SCHLINK, Edmund, *The Coming Christ and the Coming Church.* 33pp. Edinburgh, Oliver and Boyd, 1967. Translated from the German *Der kommende Christus und die kirchlichen Traditionen.*

SWIDLER, Leonard J., ed., *Scripture and Ecumenism: Protestant, Catholic, Orthodox, and Jewish.* 197 pp. Pittsburgh, Pa., Duquesne University Press, 1965.

THURIAN, Max, *Visible Unity and Tradition.* 137pp. Baltimore, Helicon Press, 1962. Translated from *L'Unité visible des chrétiens et la tradition.* German translation *Sichtbare Einheit.*

TOMKINS, Oliver Stratford, *A Time for Unity*. 127pp. London, S.C.M. Press, 1964.
VISSER 'T HOOFT, Willem Adolf, *The Pressure of our Common Calling*. 192pp.
London, S.C.M. Press, 1959. French translation *Les exigences de notre vocation
commune*. German translation *Unter dem einen Ruf*.

PRAYER FOR CHRISTIAN UNITY

AUBERT, Roger, *Unité; la semaine de prière pour l'unité chrétienne*. Edition remaniée.
94pp. Bruxelles, Editions Pro Apostolis, 1959.
Christen beten gemeinsam. Herausgegeben vom Arbeitskreis "Gemeinsames Beten".
163pp. Bonn, Witten, Luther-Verlag, 1968.
HURLEY, Michael, *Praying for Christian Unity. A handbook of studies, meditations
and prayer*. Foreword by the Bishop of Down and Connor. 240pp. Dublin, The
Furrow Trust Gill and Son, 1963.
"Prayer for Unity. The report of the Consultation on the future of the week of
prayer for Christian Unity, Geneva, 16–20 October 1966." Published in *One in
Christ*, vol. iii, no. 3, 1967. pp. 251–304.

ECUMENICAL ECCLESIOLOGY

BERKHOF, Hendrik, *Die Katholizität der Kirche*. 112pp. Zürich, EVZ-Verlag, 1964.
Translated from the Dutch *De Katholiciteit der Kerk*.
*The Church, the Churches and the World Council of Churches. The Ecclesiological
significance of the World Council of Churches*. 16pp. New York, W.C.C., 1950.
HAMER, Jerome, *The Church is a Communion*. 240pp. London, Geoffrey Chapman,
1964. Translated from the French *L'Eglise est une communion*.
MINEAR, Paul, *Images of the Church in the New Testament*. 294pp. London, Lutterworth, 1961.
NEWBIGIN, Lesslie, *The Household of God. Lectures on the nature of the Church*.
160pp. London, S.C.M. Press, 1964. French translation *L'Eglise, peuple des
croyants, corps du Christ, temple de l'Esprit*. German translation *Von der Spaltung
zur Einheit*.
NEWBIGIN, Lesslie, *One Body, One Gospel, One World: The Christian mission today*.
56pp. London, I.M.C., 1958.
WEISSGERBER, Hans, *Die Frage nach der wahren Kirche. Einer Untersuchung zu den
ekklesiologischen Problemen der ökumenischen Bewegung*. 391pp. Essen, Ludgerus-
Verlag Hubert Wingen, 1963.

SACRAMENTS AND INTERCOMMUNION

ALLMEN, Jean-Jacques von, *Essai sur le repas du Seigneur*. 124pp. (Cahiers théolo-
giques, 55). Neuchâtel, Delachaux et Niestlé, 1966.
BLENKIN, Hugh, *Immortal Sacrifice. A study, in the cause of Christian unity of the
relation between the Sacrifice of Christ and the Holy Communion Service*. 101pp.
London, Darton, Longman & Todd, 1964.
GILMORE, A., *Baptism and Christian Unity*. 108pp. London, Lutterworth Press, 1966.
HURLEY, Michael, *Church and Eucharist*. 298pp. Dublin and Melbourne, Gill and
Son, 1966.
*Intercommunion Today, being the report of the Archbishops' Commission on Inter-
communion*. 174pp. London, Church Information Office, 1968.

LAUBENTHAL, Allan R., *The Eucharist as Sacrifice in the Faith and Order Movement. Dissertation*. 93pp. Roma, Pontificia Studiorum Universitas A. S. Thoma Aq. in Urbe, 1968.

McDONNELL, Kilian, *John Calvin, the Church, and the Eucharist*. 410pp. Princeton, New Jersey, Princeton University Press, 1967.

MARSHALL, Romey P., *Liturgy and Christian Unity*. 186pp. Englewood Cliffs, N.J. Prentice-Hall, 1965.

The Sacraments, an Ecumenical Dilemma. 178pp. (Concilium, 24). New York, Paulist Press, 1967.

SIMPSON, E. P. Y., *Ordination and Christian Unity*. 184pp. Valley Forge, The Judson Press, 1966.

STEADY, Leo J., *Intercommunion in the Faith and Order Movement 1927–1952. A dissertation submitted to the Faculty of Theology of the University of Ottawa in partial fulfilment of the requirements for the degree of Doctor of Theology*. 367pp. Ottawa 1964.

SWIDLER, Leonard, ed., *Ecumenism, the Spirit and worship*. 258pp. Louvain, Ed. E. Nauwelaerts, 1967.

THURIAN, Max, *The Eucharistic Memorial*. 2 vols. (Ecumenical studies in worship, 7–8). London, Lutterworth Press, 1960–1961. Translated from the French *L'Eucharistie*. German translation *Eucharistie*.

VISCHER, Lukas, "Questions on the Eucharist, its past and future celebration", in *Studia Liturgica* (Rotterdam), vol. v, no. 2. Summer 1966. pp. 65–86.

CHURCH UNION

Anglican Initiatives in Christian Unity: Lectures delivered in Lambeth Palace Library. ed. E. G. W. Bill. 168pp. London, S.P.C.K., 1967.

Auf dem Weg. Lutherisch-reformierte Kirchengemeinschaft. Berichte und Texte zusammengestellt und herausgegeben vom Sekretariat für Glauben und Kirchenverfassung. 124pp. (Polis, 33). Zürich, EVZ-Verlag, 1967.

Autorität und geistliche Vollmacht; Bericht über eine theologische Konferenz zwischen Vertretern der Kirche von England und der Evangelischen Kirche in Deutschland. Herausgegeben von Wolfgang Schweitzer und Claus Kemper. 81pp. Stuttgart, Evang. Missionsverlag, 1965. (Beihefte zur Ökumenischen Rundschau, 1). English edn *Authority and the Church*, ed. R. R. Williams. 92pp. London, S.P.C.K., 1965.

BECKWITH, R. T., *Priesthood and Sacraments. A study in the Anglican-Methodist report*. 128pp. (Latimer Monographs, 1). Appleford, Marcham Manor Press, 1964.

BLAKE, Eugene Carson, *A Proposal toward the Reunion of Christ's Church*. 16pp. Philadelphia, General Assembly Office of the United Presbyterian Church in the U.S.A., 1961.

BROWN, Robert McAfee, *The Challenge to Reunion. The Blake proposal under scrutiny*. 292pp. New York, McGraw-Hill Co., 1963.

BURBIDGE, John, *One in Hope and Doctrine: A study in the theology of church union*. 101pp. Toronto, The Ryerson Press, 1968.

COCU, *The official reports of the first four meetings of the consultation*. 96pp. Cincinnati, Forward Movement Publications, 1966.

Consultation on Church Union. Principles of Church Union; guidelines for structure, and study guide. 144pp. Cincinnati, Forward Movement Publications, 1967.

Conversations between the Church of England and the Methodist Church. A report to the Archbishops of Canterbury and York and the Conference of the Methodist Church. 63pp. Church Information Office and Epworth Press, 1963.

CROW, Paul A., *A Bibliography of the Consultation on Church Union.* 23pp. mimeographed. Lexington, Kentucky, Consultation on Church Union, 1967.

Digest of the Proceedings of the Consultation on Church Union for 1962 and 1963, 1964, 1965, 1966, 1967. 5 vols. Fanwood, New Jersey, C.O.C.U., 1963-7.

GRANT, J. Webster, *The Canadian Experience of Church Union.* 106pp. (Ecumenical studies in History, 8). London, Lutterworth Press, 1967.

KEMP, Eric W., *The Anglican-Methodist Conversations: A comment from within.* 45pp. London, New York, Oxford University Press, 1964.

NEILL, Stephen, *The Church and Christian Union. The Bampton lectures 1964.* 448pp. London, Oxford University Press, 1967.

NEILL, Stephen, *Towards Church Union, 1937–1952. A Survey of approaches to closer union among the churches.* 96pp. (Faith and Order Papers, 11). Published on behalf of the Faith and Order Commission of the W.C.C. London, S.C.M. Press, 1952.

FISHER, Geoffrey Francis, *The Anglican-Methodist Conversations and Problems of Church Unity. Some personal reflections.* 44pp. London, Oxford University Press, 1964.

HUNT, George L., and CROW, Paul A., *Where we are in Church Union.* 126pp. New York, Association Press, 1965.

LEE, Robert, *The Social Sources of Church Unity. An interpretation of unitive movements in American protestantism.* 238pp. New York, Abingdon, 1960.

NELSON, Robert J., *Church Union in Focus.* 87pp. Boston, Philadelphia, United Church Press, 1968.

PACKER, J. I., *The Church of England and the Methodist Church. A consideration of the report; conversations between the Church of England and the Methodist Church; ten essays.* 63pp. Appleford, Marcham Manor Press, 1963.

Principles of Church Union, adopted by the consultation at its meeting in Dallas, 1966. 96pp. Cincinnati, Forward Movement Publications, 1966.

Survey of Church Union Negotiations. 18pp. (Faith and Order papers, 11b). Geneva, W.C.C., 1955.

Survey of Church Union Negotiations, 1957–1959. 32pp. (Faith and Order papers, 28). Geneva, W.C.C., 1960.

Survey of Church Union Negotiations, 1959–1961, Lukas Vischer. 31pp. (Faith and Order papers, 35). Geneva, W.C.C., 1962.

Survey of Church Union Negotiations, 1961–1963, Meredith B. Handspicker. 40pp. (Faith and Order papers, 43). Geneva, W.C.C., 1964.

Survey of Church Union Negotiations, 1963–1965, Meredith B. Handspicker. 43pp. (Faith and Order papers, 47). Geneva, W.C.C., 1966.

Survey of Church Union Negotiations, 1965–1967, Gerald F. Moede. 32pp. (Faith and Order papers, 52). Geneva, W.C.C., 1968.

"Unofficial consultation between theologians of Eastern Orthodox and Oriental Orthodox Churches, August 11–15, 1964. Papers and minutes", ed. John S. Romanides, Paul Verghese, N. A. Nissiotis, *The Greek Orthodox Theological Review,* vol. x, no. 2, Winter 1964–5. 168pp.

Versöhnung. Das deutsch-russische Gespräch über das christliche Verständnis der Versöhnung zwischen Vertretern der Evangelischen Kirche in Deutschland und der Russischen Orthodoxen Kirche. Hrsg. vom Aussenamt der Evang. Kirche in Deutschland. 197pp. Witten, Luther Verlag, 1967.

WINTERHAGER, Jürgen Wilhelm, *Kirchen-Unionen des zwanzigsten Jahrhunderts.* 253pp. Zürich, Gotthelf-Verlag, 1961.

Wort und Abendmahl. Bericht über die zweite Konferenz zwischen Vertretern der

Kirche von England und der Evangelischen Kirche in Deutschland. Herausgegeben von Ronald R. Williams. 110pp. (Beihefte zur Ökumenischen Rundschau, 5). Stuttgart, Evang. Missionsverlag, 1967.

CHURCH OF SOUTH INDIA

Church of South India. *Commission on Integration and Joint Action. 1963 renewal and advance*. 209pp. Madras, published for the Synod of the Church of South-India by the Christian Literature Society, 1963.

The Constitution of the Church of South India. With amendments up to 31 December 1951 together with the Basis of Union as adopted by the Governing Bodies of the Uniting Churches in India and elsewhere. 97pp. Madras, Christian Literature Society for India, 1952.

The C.S.I.–Lutheran Theological Conversations 1948–1959. A selection of the papers read together with the Agreed Statements. 196pp. Madras, Christian Literature Society, 1964.

Empty Shoes: A study of the Church of South India. 153pp. New York, The National Council Protestant Episcopal Church, 1956.

GIBBARD, Mark, *Unity is not enough: Reflections after a visit to the Church of South India*. 145pp. London, Mowbray, 1965.

GRAMBERG, Th. B. W. G., *Oecume in India en Ceylon; op weg naar Gods ene kerk*. 366pp. 's-Gravenhage, Boekencentrum, 1962.

HOLLIS, Michael, *Paternalism and the Church: A study of South India Church history*. 144pp. London, Oxford University Press, 1962.

HOLLIS, Michael, *The Significance of South India*. 82pp. (Ecumenical Studies in History, 5). London, Lutterworth Press, 1966.

The Holy Spirit and the Life in Christ. Papers submitted to the joint theological commission of the Church of South India and the Lutheran Churches, July 1953. 52pp. Madras, Christian Literature Society, 1953.

LA CROCE, Jacobus F., *The Catholicity of the Church of South India. A comparison of its formularies with those of the Anglican Church on the doctrines of the Church and the Ministry. Exerpta ex dissertatione ad Lauream in Facultate Theologica Pontificiae Universitatis Gregorianae*. 110pp. Roma 1965.

NEWBIGIN, James Edwards Lesslie, *The Reunion of the Church. A defence of the South Indian Scheme*. Revised edn. 192pp. London, S.C.M. Press, 1960.

NEWBIGIN, James Edwards Lesslie, *A South India Diary*. 125pp. London, S.C.M. Press, 1951. French translation *Journées indiennes*. German translation *Südindisches Tagebuch*.

RAWLINSON, A. E. J., *The Church of South India*. 128pp. London, Hodder and Stoughton, 1951.

Report on South India. Being the report of the delegation to the Church of South India with certain recommendations and theological comments. 84pp. New York, Joint Commission on Ecumenical Relations, 1957.

The Sacraments. The meeting of the Joint Theological Commission of the Church of South India and the Federation of Evangelical Lutheran Churches in India, March 1955. 166pp. Madras, Christian Literature Society, 1956.

Unity in Faith and Life. The Joint Theological Commission of the Church of South India and the Federation of Evangelical Lutheran Churches in India, Bangalore 1954. 105pp. Madras, Christian Literature Society, 1955.

WAGNER, Herwig, *Erstgestalten einer einheimischen Theologie in Südindien; ein Kapitel indischer Theologiegeschichte als kritischer Beitrag zur Definition von "einheimischer Theologie"*. 306pp. München, Chr. Kaiser, 1963.

NORTH INDIA AND PAKISTAN

KELLOCK, James, *Breakthrough for Church Union in North India and Pakistan*. 146pp. Madras, Christian Literature Society, 1965.

Plan of Church Union in North India and Pakistan. Prepared by the Negotiating Committee for Church Union in North India and Pakistan, as revised in April 1957. 3rd edn. 64pp. Madras, Christian Literature Society, 1957.

CEYLON

BOISVERT, Robert G., *The Scheme of Church Union in Ceylon and the Problem it Presents to the Anglican Communion*. Pars dissertationis. 160pp. Rome, Catholic Book Agency, 1964.

GRAMBERG, Th. B., *Oecumene in India en Ceylon; op weg naar Gods ene kerk*. 366pp. 's Gravenhage, Boekencentrum, 1962.

Proposed Scheme of Church Union in Ceylon. Prepared by the Negotiating Committee for Church Union in Ceylon, June 1955. 3rd edn. 111pp. Madras, Christian Literature Society, 1955.

CHAPTER 7

Mission in Six Continents

GENERAL WORKS

The Encyclopedia of modern christian missions. The agencies. A publication of the Faculty of Gordon Divinity School. Ed. Rurton L. Goddard. 743pp. Camden, New Jersey, Thomas Nelson and Sons, 1967.

HOGG, William Richey, *Ecumenical Foundations. A history of the International Missionary Council and its nineteenth-century background*. 466pp. New York, Harper, 1952. German translation *Mission und Oekumene*.

Index to International Review of Missions, 1912–1966. 82pp. Geneva, W.C.C., 1968.

LATOURETTE, Kenneth Scott, *Christianity in a Revolutionary Age. A history of Christianity in the nineteenth and twentieth centuries*. vols. iii and v. New York, Harper and Row, 1961–2.

Zur Sendung der Kirche. Material der ökumenischen Bewegung. Hrsg. von H. J. Margull. 378pp. München, Kaiser Verlag, 1963.

INTERNATIONAL MISSIONARY COUNCIL

Minutes of the Committee of the I.M.C. London, I.M.C. 1948–58:
1948 Oegstgeest
1950 Whitby
1952 Willingen
1954 New York
1958 Ghana

Willingen 1952

GOODALL, Norman, ed., *Missions under the cross. Addresses delivered at the enlarged meeting of the Committee of the International Missionary Council at Willingen, in Germany, 1952, with statements issued by the meeting.* 264pp. London, I.M.C., 1953.

Ghana 1957–8

ORCHARD, Ronald Kenneth, *The Ghana Assembly of the International Missionary Council, 28 December 1957–8 January 1958.* Selected papers, with an essay on the role of the I.M.C. 240pp. London, Edinburgh House Press, 1958.

INTEGRATION I.M.C.–W.C.C. NEW DELHI, 1961

Minutes of the Assembly of the I.M.C., November 17–18, 1961 and of the first meeting of the Commission on World Mission and Evangelism of the W.C.C., December 7–8, 1961 at New Delhi. 93pp. Geneva, W.C.C., 1962.

PAYNE, Ernest A., and MOSES, David G., *Why integration? An explanation of the proposal before the World Council of Churches and the International Missionary Council.* 80pp. London, Edinburgh House Press, 1957.

Report to the final Assembly of the I.M.C. and the third Assembly of the W.C.C., New Delhi 1961. 48pp. Lausanne, Impr. La Concorde, 1961. French translation *Conseil international des missions. Rapport présenté . . .* German translation *Internationaler Missionsrat. Bericht an die . . .*

MEXICO CITY 1963

LATHAM, Robert O., *God for All Men. The meeting of the Commission on World Mission and Evangelism of the W.C.C. at Mexico City, December 8th to 19th, 1963.* 84pp. London, Edinburgh House Press, 1964.

Minutes of the second meeting of the Commission on World Mission and Evangelism, Mexico City, December 8th–19th, 1963. 135pp. Geneva, W.C.C., 1964.

NEWBIGIN, Lesslie, *Gottes Mission und unsere Aufgabe. Treffpunkt 1963 Mexiko.* 31pp. (Weltmission heute, 23). Stuttgart, Evang. Missionsverlag, 1963.

ORCHARD, Ronald Kenneth, *Witness in Six Continents. Records of the meeting of the Commission on World Mission and Evangelism of the World Council of Churches, held in Mexico City, December 8th to 19th, 1963.* 200pp. London, Edinburgh House Press, 1964.

D.W.M.E.

The Christian Ministry in Latin America and the Caribbean. Report of a survey of theological education in the Evangelical Churches undertaken February–May 1961 on behalf of the I.M.C., now the Commission on World Mission and Evangelism of the W.C.C. by Bp Foster Stockwell . . ., ed. Wilfred Scopes. 264pp. Geneva, D.W.M.E., 1962.

HAYWARD, Victor E. W., ed., *African Independent Church Movements.* 94pp. (C.W.M.E. Research pamphlets, 11). Published for the W.C.C. Commission on World Mission and Evangelism. London, Edinburgh House Press, 1963.

The Healing Church. The Tübingen consultation 1964. 55pp. (World Council Studies

3). Geneva, W.C.C., 1965. Franch translation *Eglise et guérison*. German translation *Auftrag zu heilen*.

LOEFFLER, Paul, ed., *Secular man and Christian Mission. A discussion through correspondence*. 48pp. (C.W.M.E. Study pamphlets, 3). Geneva, W.C.C., Commission on World Mission and Evangelism. New York, Friendship Press, 1968.

PATON, David M., ed., *New Forms of Ministry*. 102pp. London, published for the W.C.C. Commission on World Mission and Evangelism by Edinburgh House Press, 1965.

EVANGELISM

The Church for Others and the Church for the World. A quest for structures for missionary congregations. Final report of the Western European Working Group and North American Working Group of the Department on Studies in Evangelism. 135pp. Geneva, W.C.C., 1967. German translation *Die Kirche für andere.*

Planning for Mission. Working papers on the new quest for missionary communities. 230pp. New York, U.S. Conference for the W.C.C., 1966. French adaptation *Vers une Eglise pour les autres.* German adaptation *Mission als Strukturprinzip.*

ECUMENICAL ASPECTS OF MISSIONS

ANDERSON, Gerald H., ed., *The Theology of the Christian Mission*. 341pp. New York, McGraw-Hill, 1961.

BATES, M. Searle, and PAUCK, Wilhelm, *The Prospects of Christianity throughout the World*. 286pp. New York, Charles Scribner's Sons, 1964.

BEAVER, R. Perce, *Ecumenical Beginnings in Protestant World Mission*. 366pp. New York, T. Nelson, 1962.

BECKMANN, Joachim, *Mission und Diakonie in ökumenischer Verantwortung. Synode der Evangelischen Kirche in Deutschland, Bethel, 1963*. Herausgegeben im Auftrag der Synode von Joachim Beckmann. 77pp. Witten, Luther-Verlag, 1963.

BLAUW, Johannes, *The Missionary Nature of the Church. A survey of the biblical theology of mission.* 182pp. New York, McGraw-Hill, 1962.

BRENNECKE, Gerhard, *Weltmission in ökumenischer Zeit*. Herausgegeben von G.B. und 28 Mitarbeitern. 336pp. Stuttgart, Evang. Missionsverlag, 1961.

BRIDSTON, Keith, *Mission, Myth and Reality*. 128pp. New York, Friendship Press, 1965.

CATE, William B., *The Ecumenical Scandal on Main Street*. 126pp. New York, Association Press, 1965.

HANDY, Robert T., *We Witness Together: A history of co-operative home missions.* 273pp. New York, Friendship Press, 1956.

History's Lessons for Tomorrow's Mission. 300pp. Geneva, W.S.C.F., 1960.

HOGG, William Richey, *One World, One Mission*. 165pp. New York, Friendship Press, 1960.

KARLSTRÖM, Nils, *Oekumene in Mission und Kirche. Entwicklungslinien der heutigen ökumenischen Bewegung*. 280pp. München, Claudius Verlag, 1962. Translated from *Mission och ekumenik*.

KLAPPERT, Erich, *Dialog mit Rom. Zusammenarbeit und Zukunft der Mission auf ökumenischer Basis, 450 Jahre nach Luther*. 280pp. Wuppertal, Aussaat Verlag, 1967.

LEE, Robert, *Stranger in the Land. A Study of the Church in Japan*. 216pp. (World Studies of Churches in mission). London, Lutterworth Press, 1967.

LE GUILLOU, M-J., *Mission et unité. Les exigences de la communion*. 2 vols. (Unam Santcam, 33–34). Paris, Editions du Cerf, 1960.

MARGULL, H. J., *Hope in Action: the Church's Task in the World*. 298pp. Philadelphia, Muhlenberg Press, 1962. Translated from *Theologie der missionarischen Verkündigung*.

MEYER, Heinrich, *Mission in ökumenischer Verantwortung; Referat auf der Synode der Evangelischen Kirche in Deutschland, im März 1963 in Bethel*. 24pp. (Christus und die Welt, 15). Bad Salzuflen, MBK-Verlag, Verlag für Missions- und Biblekunde, 1963.

NEILL, Stephen Charles, *The Unfinished Task*. 228pp. London, Edinburgh House Press, 1957. German translation *Mission zwischen Kolonialismus und Oekumene*.

NEWBIGIN, Lesslie, *One Body, one Gospel, one World. The Christian Mission today*. 58pp. London, International Missionary Council, 1958.

NEWBIGIN, Lesslie, *The Relevance of Trinitarian Doctrine*. 78pp. Published for the World Council of Churches, Commission on World Mission and Evangelism. London, Edinburgh House Press, 1963.

NILES, Daniel Thambyrajah, *Upon the Earth: the mission of God and the Missionary enterprise of the churches*. 270pp. London, Lutterworth Press, 1962. French translation *Sur la terre*. German translation *Feuer auf Erden*.

ORCHARD, Ronald K., *Out of every nation. A discussion of the internationalizing of missions*. 78pp. (I.M.C. Research Pamphlets, 7). London, S.C.M. Press, 1959.

PORTMANN, John R., *The Concepts of Mission and Unity in the World Council of Churches. A study of the official documents of the Central Committee from its inception to the New Delhi Assembly, 1961*. 134pp. Pars dissentationis ad lauream in Facultate S. Theologiae apud Pontificiam Universitatem S. Thomae de Urbe, Rome. Catholic Book Agency, 1966.

SUNDKLER, Bengt, *The World of Mission*. 318pp. London, Lutterworth Press, 1965.

TIPPETT, A. R., *Solomon Islands Christianity. A study in growth and obstruction*. 407pp. (World Studies of Churches in Mission). London, Lutterworth Press, 1967.

VAN DUSEN, Henry P., *One Great Ground of Hope. Christian missions and Christian unity*. 206pp. Philadelphia, Westminster Press, 1961.

VICEDOM, Georg, *Mission im ökumenischen Zeitalter*. 208pp. (Evangelische Enzyklopädie, 17/18). Gütersloh, Gütersloher Verlagshaus Gerd Mohn, 1967.

WARREN, Max, *The Missionary Movement from Britain in Modern History*. 192pp. London, S.C.M. Press, 1965.

CHAPTER 8

Joint Service as an Instrument of Renewal

D.I.C.A.R.W.S.—OFFICIAL REPORTS

Division of Inter-Church Aid, Refugee and World Service. Consultation Digest. Geneva, W.C.C., 1956–67.
Les Rasses 1956
Eastbourne 1957
Evian 1958
Berlin 1960
Nyborg 1962

Hong Kong 1963

Consultation Digest. A summary of reports and addresses. First Asian consultation on Inter-Church Aid, held under the joint auspices of D.I.C.A.R.W.S.–E.A.C.C., at Hong Kong, October 17–23, 1963. 117pp. mimeographed. Geneva, W.C.C., 1964.

Enugu 1965

Consultation Digest. A summary of reports and addresses. All Africa Conference of Churches, Inter-Church Aid Consultation, Enugu, Eastern Nigeria, January 4–9, 1965. 116pp. Geneva, W.C.C., 1965. French translation *Consultation en abrégé.*

Swanwick 1966

Digest of the 1966 World Consultation on Inter-Church Aid, at Swanwick, Great Britain. 136pp. Geneva, W.C.C., D.I.C.A.R.W.S., 1966. French translation *Colloque de Swanwick.* German translation *Swanwick Konsultation.*

Belgrade 1967

Digest of the European consultation on Inter-Church Aid, at Belgrade, Yugoslavia, December 4–9, 1967. 99pp. mimeographed. Geneva, W.C.C.–D.I.C.A.R.W.S., 1968.

Inter-Church Aid. Year and Report. Geneva, W.C.C.–D.I.C.A.R.W.S., 1953. 1953: (*a*) *Year and Report 1953;* (*b*) Statistical Summaries; (*c*) The Service to Refugees; (*d*) Greece, 1953. 1954: *Year and Report 1954.* 1955: *Pain and Promise.* 1956: *Inter-Church Aid in 1956.* 1957: *Inter-Church Aid 1957.* 1958: *Inter-Church Aid 1958.* 1959: *Inter-Church Aid 1959.* 1960: *Across My Desk.* 1961: *Inter-Church Aid in 1961.* 1962: *Many Churches, One Service.* 1963: *Service in Unity.* 1964: *Rooted in Love.* 1965: *To Live in Hope.* 1966: *A World of Difference* (also in German). 1967: *From One to Another* (also in French and German).
Service Programme and List of Projects. 8 vols. Geneva, W.C.C.–D.I.C.A.R.W.S., 1961–8.

FIRST PERIOD OF INTER-CHURCH AID

RYBERG, James A., ed., *Church-aided Projects. A visitor's guide to Church-aided projects in Europe.* 40pp. Geneva, W.C.C., Department of Inter-Church Aid, 1950.
RYBERG, James A., ed., *Europe's Homeless. The plight of refugees—Europe's homeless—an international problem.* 48pp. Geneva, W.C.C., Department of Inter-Church Aid, 1951.
RYBERG, James A., ed., *Fellowship in christian sharing. The story of Inter-Church Aid.* 40pp. Geneva, W.C.C., Department of Inter-Church Aid, 1951.
VISSER 'T HOOFT, Willem Adolf, *La reconstruction des Eglises en Europe.* 13pp. Lausanne, Impr. La Concorde, 1944.

D.I.C.A.R.W.S.

COOKE, Leslie E., *The Church is There.* 59pp. Greenwich, Conn., The Seabury Press, 1957.

COOKE, Leslie, *Entwicklungshilfe der Mitgliedskirchen des Oekumenischen Rates der Kirchen*. 44pp. Stuttgart, Kreuz-Verlag; Mainz, Matthias-Grünewald, 1966. (Sonderdruck aus Entwicklungspolitik; Handbuch und Lexicon, pp. 879–922).

COOKE, Leslie E., *The World Council of Churches and the Division of Inter-Church Aid, Refugee, and World Service. An address given by L.E.C. at the opening session of the Asian Consultation on Inter-Church Aid, Hong Kong, October 17–23, 1963*. 16pp. (Extr. from *Ecumenical Review*, vol. 16, no. 2, January 1964). Geneva, W.C.C., 1964.

D.I.C.A.R.W.S. in Action and Study. The report of the Division on Inter-Church Aid, Refugee, and World Service to the Central Committee of the World Council of Churches at its meeting in Geneva, Switzerland, February 1966. 12pp. Geneva, W.C.C.–D.I.C.A.R.W.S. 1966. French translation *Action et étude*. German translation *Studium und Aktion*.

In the service of mankind. A manual of inter-church aid. Geneva, W.C.C.–D.I.C.A.R.W.S., 1963.

Inter-Church Aid Directory. 48pp. Geneva, W.C.C., 1965.

MACKIE, Robert C., *Inter-Church Aid and Service to Refugees Today. The director's report—Division of Inter-Church Aid and Service to Refugees*. 16pp. Geneva, W.C.C., 1955.

MATTHEWS, Z. K., *Africa Survey Report. Together with "Ferment in Africa", an article by Sir Hugh Foot; an account of a visit to Africa by Sir Hugh Foot and Dr Z. K. Matthews on behalf of the Division of Inter-Church Aid, Refugee, and World Service*. 96pp. Geneva, W.C.C.–D.I.C.A.R.W.S., 1964.

MATTHEWS, Z. K., *Africa Surveys I and II. Survey I: Report by Z. K. Matthews together with "Ferment in Africa", an article by Sir Hugh Foot. Survey II: Report by Jean Fisher, Frank Hutchison, James Lawson*. 119pp. Geneva, W.C.C.–D.I.C.A.R.W.S., 1964–5.

MURRAY, Geoffrey, *Number one, Sophocles Street*. 40pp. Geneva, W.C.C.–D.I.C.A.R.W.S., 1963. German translation: *Das Haus in der Sophokles-Strasse*.

The Role of the Churches in Social Service: An international perspective. Reporting a consultation held at Mülheim, Germany, July 16–20, 1962. 106pp. Auspices: W.C.C. and D.I.C.A.R.W.S. New York, National Council of Churches, 1963.

The Role of the diakonia of the Church in Contemporary Society. Report to the World Conference on Church and Society 1966: Christians in the Technical and Social Revolution of our time. 63pp. Geneva, W.C.C., 1966. French translation *L'Eglise dans son rôle diaconal*. German translation *Die Diakonie der Kirche in der gegenwärtigen Gesellschaft*.

A Statement of the Aim, Functions, Facilities and Procedures of its Programme and Project Listening. 18pp. Geneva, W.C.C.–D.I.C.A.R.W.S., 1964.

THOMPSON, Betty, *Turning world*. 128pp. New York, Friendship Press, 1960.

World Council of Churches and All Africa Conference of Churches. Approved programme. Ecumenical programme for emergency action in Africa. 78pp. Geneva, W.C.C.–D.I.C.A.R.W.S., 1965.

REFUGEES

Report from Hamburg. A survey of the German refugee problem in 1949. 32pp. Geneva, World Council of Churches, Refugee Division, 1949. German translation *Hamburger Bericht*.

Report from Salzburg. Conference in Salzburg on Austria's refugee problems. January 17–19, 1950. 42pp. Geneva, World Council of Churches, Service to Refugees, 1950. German translation: *Salzburger Bericht*.

Hungary, special report. 30pp. Geneva, W.C.C., 1957.

Report from Beirut. A report of a conference on Arab refugee problems, Beirut, Lebanon, May 4–8, 1951. Jointly convened by I.M.C. and the Department of Inter-Church Aid and Service to Refugees of the W.C.C. 56pp. Geneva, W.C.C., 1951.

Second report from Beirut. Report of a conference on the problem of Arab refugees from Palestine, held at Beirut, Lebanon, May 21–25, 1956. 61pp. Geneva, W.C.C., 1956.

A Time of Compassion. A report on the Churches' contribution to world refugee year. 34pp. Geneva, W.C.C., 1961.

MIGRATION

In a Strange Land. A report of a world conference on problems of international migration and the responsibility of the Churches, held at Leysin, Switzerland, June 11–16, 1961. 96pp. Geneva, W.C.C.–D.I.C.A.R.W.S., 1961.

Migrant workers: a test case of human relationship. Consultation on migrant workers in Western Europe. Bossey, May 29–June 4, 1965. Ecumenical Institute of Bossey, Churches Committee on Migrant Workers in Western Europe. 55pp. Geneva, Churches Committee on Migrant Workers in Western Europe, 1965. French translation *Les migrations de travailleurs.* German translation *Ausländische Arbeitnehmer.*

Within Thy Gates. A report of the conference on migrant workers in Western Europe, held at Arnoldshain, Western Germany, June 10–15, 1963. 96pp. Geneva, W.C.C. Secretariat for Migration, 1964. French translation *L'Etranger qui est dans tes portes.* German translation *Fremde unter uns.*

CHURCH WORLD SERVICE

CHAKERIAN, Charles G., *From Rescue to Child Welfare.* 92pp. New York, Church World Service, 1968.

Community compassion. The story of C.R.O.P. 32pp. Elkhart, Indiana, C.R.O.P., 1967.

FEY, Harold E., *Co-operation in compassion. The story of Church World Service.* 175pp. New York, Friendship Press, 1966.

GOODALL, Norman, *Christian Ambassador. A life of A. Livingstone Warnshuis.* 174pp. (Pertinent as a biography of a founder of Church World Service). New York, Channel Press; London, Edinburgh House Press, 1963.

GRODKA, Sonia, and HENNES, Gerhard, *Homeless No More. A discussion on integration between sponsor and refugee.* 126pp. New York, Church World Service, 1960.

HACKSHAW, James, *Social and Economic Planning in the Leeward and Windward Islands.* 36pp. New York, Church World Service, 1967.

LANDIS, Benson Y., and Jacquet, Constant H. Jr, *Immigration Programs and Policies of Churches of the United States.* 71pp. New York, N.C.C.C.U.S.A., 1957.

MacCRACKEN, James, *Church World Service support of National Christian Councils.* 81pp. mimeographed. 1968.

MOOMAW, I. W., *Crusade against Hunger.* 199pp. (esp. C.W.S. ref. on page 197). New York, Harper and Row, 1966.

MOOMAW, I. W., *The Challenge of Hunger.* 222pp. (esp. C.W.S. ref. on pages 51, 54 and 133). New York and London, Frederick A. Praeger, 1966.

MYERS, Melvin B., and ABBOTT, John W., *Resource Guide on World Hunger*. 207pp. New York, Church World Service, 1968.

STANLEY, Frances, *The New World Refugee: The Cuban exodus*. 64pp. New York, Church World Service, 1967.

STEVENSON, Russell, *A More Excellent Way*. 16pp. New York, Church World Service, 1959.

The Wanted Child. Report of 1967 family planning survey of five islands in the Caribbean. 58pp. New York, Church World Service, 1967.

Witness for Immigration. Report of the consultation on immigration policy in the U.S. Washington, D.C., 13–14 April 1961. 112pp. New York, National Council of Churches, 1961.

CHAPTER 9

The Development of Ecumenical Social Thought and Action

DEPARTMENT ON CHURCH AND SOCIETY

Africa in Transition: The challenge and the Christian response. 95pp. Published by All Africa Churches Conference in collaboration with the Department on Church and Society, Division of Studies, World Council of Churches. Geneva, W.C.C., 1965. French translation *L'Afrique en devenir*.

Christian Action in Society: An ecumenical inquiry. 19pp. Geneva, W.C.C. Study Department, 1949. French translation *L'Action chrétienne dans la vie sociale*.

Main Ecumenical Statements on Principles concerning Religious Freedom. 47pp. mimeographed. Geneva, W.C.C., Secretariat on Religious Liberty, 1965.

The Meaning of Work. 20pp. (Christian action in society, 2). Geneva, W.C.C., Study Department, 1950.

Statements of the World Council of Churches on Social Questions. With a preface on the development of ecumenical social thinking. 2nd edn. 72pp. Geneva, W.C.C., Department on Church and Society, 1956.

TURNBULL, John W., *Ecumenical Documents on Church and Society, 1925–1953*. 172pp. Geneva, W.C.C., 1954.

RAPID SOCIAL CHANGE

ABRECHT, Paul, *The Churches and Rapid Social Change*. 216pp. New York, Doubleday, 1961.

The Common Christian Responsibility toward Areas of Rapid Social Change. 2nd statement. 39pp. Geneva, W.C.C., Department on Church and Society, 1956. French translation *La responsabilité commune des chrétiens à l'égard des sociétés en pleine évolution*. German translation *Die gemeinsame christliche Verantwortung gegenüber Gebieten raschen sozialen Umbruchs*.

Dilemmas and Opportunities; Christian action in rapid social change. Report of an international ecumenical study conference, Thessalonica, Greece, July 25–August 2, 1959. 104pp. Geneva, World Council of Churches, 1959. French translation *Dilemmes et possibilités*. German translation *Aufgaben und Möglichkeiten*.

SCHWEITZER, Wolfgang, *Christians in Changing Societies*. 80pp. (World christian books, 58). London, Lutterworth Press, 1967. Translated from the German *Christen im raschen sozialen Umbruch heute*.

VRIES, Egbert de, *Man In Rapid Social Change*. 240pp. Garden City, New York, Doubleday, 1961.

RESPONSIBLE SOCIETY

The Arnoldshain report 1956. A regional conference on the responsible society in national and international affairs. 30pp. Geneva, W.C.C., Division of Studies, 1956. German translation *Der Arnoldshain Bericht 1956*.

MUELDER, Walter G., *The Idea of the Responsible Society*. 26pp. Boston, Boston University Press, 1955.

The Responsible Society. 24pp. (Christian Action in Society, 1). Geneva, W.C.C., Study Department, 1949.

Social Questions—the Responsible Society in a World Perspective. An ecumenical survey prepared under the auspices of the World Council of Churches. 68pp. (Evanston surveys, 3). London, S.C.M. Press, 1954. French translation *Questions sociales*. German translation *Soziale Fragen*.

WORLD CONFERENCE ON CHURCH AND SOCIETY, GENEVA, 1966

Christian Social Ethics in a Changing World: An ecumenical theological inquiry, ed. John C. Bennett. 381pp. (Church and Society, 1). London, S.C.M. Press, New York, Association Press, 1966. French translation *L'éthique sociale chrétienne dans un monde en transformation*.

Responsible Government in a Revolutionary Age, ed. Z. K. Matthews. 381pp. (Church and Society, 2). New York, Association Press: London, S.C.M. Press, 1966. French translation *La responsabilité des gouvernements à une époque révolutionnaire*.

Economic Growth in World Perspective, ed. Denys Munby. 380pp. (Church and Society, 3). New York, Association Press: London, S.C.M. Press, 1966. French translation *Le développement économique dans une perspective mondiale*.

Man in Community: Christian concern for the human in changing society, ed. Egbert de Vries. 382pp. (Church and Society, 4). New York, Association Press: London, S.C.M. Press, 1966. French translation *L'individu et le groupe*. German translation of the Church and Society series *Kirche als Faktor einer kommenden Weltgemeinschaft*.

EDWARDS, David L., *Christian in a New World*. 77pp. London, S.C.M. Press, 1966.

Kirche und Gesellschaft. Berichte und Vorträge nach der Konferenz, A. Lavanchy, A. Rich, H. Rieben, W. A. Visser 't Hooft. 70pp. (Polis, 29). Zürich, EVZ Verlag, 1967.

MOSLEY, J. Brooke, *Christians in the Technical and Social Revolutions of Our Time. Suggestions for study and action*. 141pp. (A Forward Movement miniature book). Cincinnati, Ohio, Forward Movement Publications, 1956. German translation *Christen leben in der technischen und gesellschaftlichen Revolution unserer Zeit*.

RAMSEY, Paul, *Who Speaks for the Church? A critique of the 1966 conference on Church and Society*. 189pp. Nashville, Tenn., Abingdon Press, 1967.

RENDTORFF, Trutz, und TÖDT, Heinz E., *Theologie der Revolution: Analysen und Materialen*. 165pp. Frankfurt am Main, Suhrkamp Verlag, 1968.

TÖDT, Heinz Eduard, "Bedeutung und Mängel der Genfer Weltkirchenkonferenz", in *Zeitschrift für evangelische Ethik*, Jg. 11, 1967: 1, pp. 2–19.

TÖDT, Heinz Eduard, "Theologie der Revolution". "Revolution als sozialethisches Konzept und seine theologischen Grenzen", in *Oekumenische Rundschau*, Jg. 17, 1968: 1, pp. 1–22.

World Conference on Church and Society, Geneva, July 12–26, 1966. Christians in the Technical and Social Revolutions of Our Time. The official report with a description of the conference by M. M. Thomas and Paul Abrecht. 232pp. Geneva, W.C.C., 1967. French translation *Conférence mondiale Eglise et Société, 1966.* German translation *Appell an die Kirchen der Welt.*

CHURCH AND SOCIETY IN LATIN AMERICA

America hoy; accion de Dios y responsabilidad del hombre. II consulta latinoamericana de Iglesia y Sociedad. 132pp. Montevideo, "Iglesia y Sociedad en América Latina", 1966.

Christians and Social Change in Latin America. Findings of the first Latin American Evangelical Consultation on Church and Society, 23rd to 27th July, 1961 at Huampani, Peru. 22pp. Geneva, W.C.C., 1961. Translated from the Spanish *Encuentro y desafio.*

Hombre, ideologia y revolucion en america latina. 133pp. Montevideo, "Iglesia y Sociedad en América Latina", 1965.

La responsabilidad social del cristiano. Guia de Estudios. 140pp. Montevideo, "Iglesia y Sociedad en América Latina", 1964.

RACE PROBLEMS

BECKMANN, Klaus-Martin, ed., *Die Kirche und die Rassenfrage.* Beiträge von E. C. Blake, W. A. Visser 't Hooft and others. 147pp. ("Kirche im Volk", 34). Berlin, Kreuz-Verlag, 1967.

Christians and Race Relations in Southern Africa: Report on an ecumenical consultation on Christian practice and desirable action in social change and race relations in Southern Africa, held at Kitwe, Zambia, May 25–June 2, 1964. 37pp. Geneva, W.C.C., Department on Church and Society, 1964.

Ecumenical Statements on Race Relations: Development of ecumenical thought on race relations 1937–1964. 47pp. Geneva, W.C.C., 1965.

Intergroup Relations: The Church amid racial and ethic tensions. An ecumenical survey prepared under the auspices of the World Council of Churches. 54pp. (Evanston surveys, 5). London, S.C.M. Press, 1954. French translation *Relations entre groupes humains.* German translation *Gemeinschaftsprobleme.*

Mission in South Africa, April–December 1960. Prepared by the W.C.C. delegation to the consultation in December 1960, F. C. Fry, W. A. Visser 't Hooft, R. S. Bilheimer, etc. 36pp. Geneva, W.C.C., 1961. French translation *Mission en Afrique du Sud.* German translation *Der Auftrag in Südafrika.*

VISSER 'T HOOFT, Willem Adolf, *The Ecumenical Movement and the Racial Problem.* 70pp. (The race question and modern thought). Paris, U.N.E.S.C.O., 1954. French translation *Le mouvement oecuménique et la question raciale.*

SOCIOLOGICAL ASPECTS OF THE ECUMENICAL MOVEMENT

BARNES, Roswell P., *Under Orders: The Churches and public affairs*. 138pp. Garden City, N.Y., Doubleday, 1961.

COLE, Patricia Ann, *The Function of the Church as Critic of Society Exemplified in the Area of United States International Policy*. Boston 1963.

DICKINSON, Richard, *Line and Plummet: The Churches and development*. 112pp. Geneva, W.C.C., 1968. French translation *La règle et le niveau*. German translation *Richtschnur und Waage*.

DOORNKAAT, Hans ten, *Die oekumenischen Arbeiten zur sozialen Frage*. 274pp. Zürich, Gotthelf-Verlag, 1954.

DUFF, Edward, *The Social Thought of the World Council of Churches*. 339pp. London, Longmans, Green and Co., 1956.

GREET, Kenneth, and REARDON, Martin, *Social questions*. 58pp. (Star books on reunion). London, Mowbray, 1964.

HASE, Hans Christoph von, *Diakonie als ökumenische Aufgabe*. 2 vols. Berlin, Christlicher Zeitschriftenverlag, 1961–3.

MEHL, Roger, *Traité de sociologie du protestantisme*. 283pp. (Bibliothèque théologique). Neuchâtel, Delachaux et Niestlé, 1965.

Methodism and society. 4 vols. New York, Nashville, Abingdon Press, 1960–2.

MOBERG, David O., *The Church as a Social Institution. The sociology of American religion*. 569pp. Englewood Cliffs, N.J. Prentice-Hall, 1964.

NELSON, Claud D., *Religion and Society: The ecumenical impact*. 181pp. New York, Sheed and Ward, 1966.

ROSE, Stephen C., ed., "The development apocalypse" or "Will internationa injustice kill the ecumenical movement". *Risk*, vol. iii, nos. 1 and 2, 1967. 152pp

CHRISTIAN SOCIAL THEOLOGY

BARRY, F. R., *Christian ethics and secular society*. 287pp. London, Hodder and Stoughton, 1966.

Cox, Harvey, *The secular city; secularization and urbanization in theological perspective*. 276pp. London, S.C.M. Press, 1965. German translation *Stadt ohne Gott?*

DUNNE, George H., ed., *Poverty in plenty*. New York, P. J. Kennedy and Sons, 1964.

Evangelisches Soziallexikon. Im Auftrag des Deutschen Evangelischen Kirchentages. Hrsg. von Friedrich Karrenberg. 1400pp. Berlin, Kreuz-Verlag, 1965.

FAGLEY, Richard M., *The Population Explosion and Christian Responsibility*. 260pp. New York, Oxford University Press, 1960. German translation *Zu viel Menschen*.

SCHALLER, Lyle E., *The Churches' War on Poverty*. 160pp. Nashville, Tenn., Abingdon Press, 1967.

WALTHER, Christian, *Theologie und Gesellschaft. Ortsbestimmung der evangelischen Sozialethik*. 204pp. Zürich, Zwingli Verlag, 1967.

WENDLAND, Heinz-Dietrich, *Einführung in die Sozialethik*. 144pp. (Sammlung Göschen, 1203). Berlin, Walter de Gruyter, 1963.

WENDLAND, Heinz-Dietrich, *Die Kirche in der revolutionären Gesellschaft. Sozialethische Aufsätze und Reden*. 259pp. Gütersloh, Gütersloher Verlagshaus Gerd Mohn, 1967.

WENDLAND, Heinz-Dietrich, *Person und Gesellschaft in evangelischer Sicht*. 219pp. Köln, J. P. Bachem, 1965.

R.C. CHURCH AND SOCIAL QUESTIONS

BIGO, Pierre, *La doctrine sociale de l'église. Recherche et dialogue.* 548pp. Paris, P.U.F., 1966.

CALVEZ, Jean Yves, and PERRIN, Jacques, *The Church and Social Justice. The social teaching of the popes from Leo XIII to Pius XII (1878–1958).* 466pp. London, Burns and Oates, 1961. Translated from *Eglise et société économique.* German translation *Kirche und Wirtschafts-Gesellschaft.*

The documents of Vatican II. Edited by Walter M. Abbott. 794pp. London, Dublin, G. Chapman, 1966. (See mainly the pastoral constitution on the church in the modern world, *Gaudium et spes,* pp. 199–308).

John XXIII, Encyclical letter of His Holiness John XXIII . . . on establishing universal peace in truth, justice, charity and liberty. Pacem in terris. 47pp. Vatican, Vatican Polyglot Press, 1963.

John XXIII, Encyclical letter of His Holiness John XXIII . . . on recent developments of the social question in the light of christian teaching. Mater et magistra. 61pp. Vaticano, Tipografia poliglotta vaticana, 1961.

Paul VI, Encyclical letter of His Holiness Paul VI . . ., on the development of peoples Populorum progressio. 62pp. Vatican Polyglot Press, 1967.

EXPLORATORY COMMITTEE ON SOCIETY, DEVELOPMENT AND PEACE

World Development: The challenge to the Churches. The Conference on World Co-operation for development, Beirut, Lebanon, April 21–27, 1968. Sponsored by the Exploratory Committee on Society, Development and Peace. The Official report . . . 65pp., Geneva, W.C.C., 1968. French translation *Les Eglises face au problème du développement.* German translation *Weltentwicklung.*

CHAPTER 10

Ecumenical Action in International Affairs

The most important documents of the C.C.I.A. are printed in the Minutes of the Central Committee and Executive Committee meetings and in the volumes of W.C.C. Assemblies. For more information see Chapter 2. See also the Minutes of I.M.C. meetings in Chapter 7.

C.C.I.A. Brief. London. Commission of the Churches on International Affairs. 1959—. Irregular.

Commission of the Churches on International Affairs. Memorandum. C.C.I.A. and the session of the general assembly (UNO). New York, C.C.I.A., 1952–66.

Commission of the Churches on International Affairs. Memorandum on Selected Actions. United Nations General Assembly. Session. New York, C.C.I.A., 1952–67.

Commission of the Churches on International Affairs. Report. Annual. Geneva, W.C.C., 1946–67.

For the tenth anniversary of the C.C.I.A. *Ecumenical Review,* July 1956. Entire number.

For the twentieth anniversary of the C.C.I.A. *Ecumenical Review*, April 1967. Entire number.

THOMPSON, Betty, *Commission of the Churches on International Affairs, 1946-1956. A joint agency of the World Council of Churches and the International Missionary Council.* Prepared by the Information Department of the W.C.C., Geneva, W.C.C., 1956.

RELIGIOUS LIBERTY AND HUMAN RIGHTS

CARRILLO DE ALBORNOZ, A. F., *Religious Liberty*. 209pp. New York, Sheed and Ward, 1967. Translated from the Spanish *La libertad religiosa y el Concilio Vaticano II.* French translation *Le Concile et la liberté religieuse.*

CARRILLO DE ALBORNOZ, A. F., *Religious Liberty in the World: A general review of the world situation in 1965.* 42pp. Geneva, W.C.C., Secretariat on Religious Liberty, 1966.

Ecumenical Statements on Race Relations, 1937-1964. 47pp. Geneva, W.C.C., 1965.

KELSEY, George D., *Racism and the christian understanding of man.* 178pp. New York, Charles Scribner's Sons, 1965.

La liberté religieuse: exigence spirituelle et problème politique, E. Schillebeeckx, A. F. Carrillo de Albornoz, etc. En annexe: Documents du Conseil oecuménique des Eglises. 224pp. (L'Eglise en son temps). Paris, Editions du Centurion, 1965.

Main Ecumenical Statements on Principles concerning Religious Freedom. 47pp. mimeographed. Geneva, Secretariat on Religious Liberty, 1965.

MURRAY, John Courtney, ed., *Religious Liberty: An end and a beginning. The declaration on religious freedom: an ecumenical discussion.* 192pp. New York, The Macmillan Company, 1966.

NOLDE, O. Frederick, *Free and Equal: Human rights in ecumenical perspective.* With reflections on the origin of the Universal Declaration of Human Rights by Charles H. Malik. 88pp. Geneva, W.C.C., 1968.

WEIL, Gordon L., *The European Convention on Human Rights. Background, development and prospects.* 260pp. Leyden, Sythoff, 1963.

WOGAMAN, Philip, *Protestant Faith and Religious Liberty.* 254pp. Nashville, Abingdon Press, 1967.

INTERNATIONAL PEACE AND SECURITY

BAINTON, Roland Herbert, *Christian Attitudes towards War and Peace; A historical survey and critical re-evaluation.* 299pp. London, Hodder and Stoughton, 1961.

BOOTH, Alan R., *Not only Peace: Christian realism and the conflicts of the twentieth century.* 141pp. London, S.C.M. Press, 1967.

The Christian Faith and War in the Nuclear Age. 108pp. New York, Nashville, Abingdon Press, 1963.

Christians and the Prevention of War in an Atomic Age. A theological discussion. A provisional study document on... Mimeographed. Geneva, W.C.C., Division of Studies, 1958. French translation *Les chrétiens et la prévention de la guerre au siècle de l'atôme.* German translation *Christen und die Verhütung des Krieges im Atomzeitalter.*

COMBLIN, Joseph, *Théologie de la paix.* 2 vols. (Encyclopédie universitaire). Paris, Editions Universitaires, 1960.

DIRKS, Walter, ed., *Friede im Atomzeitalter.* 94pp. Mainz, Matthias-Grünewald-Verlag, 1967. Translated from the Dutch *Met Pacem in terris onder weg.*

FLANNERY, Harry W., ed., *Pattern for Peace: Catholic statements on international order*. 411pp. Westminster, Maryland, Newman Press, 1962.

HORMANN, Karl, *Peace and Modern War in the Judgment of the Church*. 162pp. Westminster, Newman Press, 1966. Translated from the German *Friede und moderner Krieg im Urteil der Kirche*.

MILFORD, T. R., *The Valley of Decision: The Christian dilemma in the nuclear age*. 50pp. London, B.C.C., 1961.?

REGAMEY, P., *Non-violence and the Christian Conscience*. 172pp. London, Darton, Longman and Todd, 1966. Translated from the French *Non-violence et conscience chrétienne*.

TAYLOR, Thomas M., and BILHEIMER, Robert S., ed., *Christians and the Prevention of War in an Atomic Age: A theological discussion*. 46pp. London, S.C.M. Press, 1961.

MIGRATION AND REFUGEES
see also chapter 8 (I.C.A.)

BOUSCAREN, Anthony T., *International Migrations since 1945*. 176pp. New York, F. A. Praeger, 1963.

REES, Elfan, *We Strangers and Afraid: The Refugee story today*. 72pp. New York, Carnegie Endowment for International Peace, 1959.

THOMAS, Brinley, *International Migration and Economic Development*. A trend report and bibliography. 85pp. Paris, U.N.E.S.C.O., 1961.

ADVANCEMENT OF DEPENDENT PEOPLES

BIRMINGHAM, Walter, and FORD, A. G., ed., *Planning and Growth in Rich and Poor Countries*. 267pp. London, Allen and Unwin, 1966.

Dictionnaire des sciences économiques. 2 vols. Paris, P.U.F., 1958.

Entwicklungspolitik. Handbuch und Lexikon. Im Auftrag von Bernhard Haussler und Hans Hermann Walz. Hrsg. von H. Besters und Ernst E. Boesch. 1770pp., parallel columns. Berlin, Kreuz-Verlag, 1966.

FAGLEY, Richard M., *The Population Explosion and Christian Responsibility*. 260pp. New York, Oxford University Press, 1960. German translation *Zu viel Menschen*.

International Encyclopedia of the Social Sciences. 17 vols. London, Collier-Macmillan Ltd, 1957.

LACY, Creighton, ed., *Christianity amid Rising Men and Nations*. 192pp. New York, Association Press, 1965.

LEBRET, L. J., *Dynamique concrète du développement*. 550pp. (Développement et civilisations). Publié avec le concours du C.N.R.S. Paris, Les Editions ouvrières, 1961.

MOOMAW, I. W., *Crusade against Hunger. The dramatic story of the world-wide antipoverty crusades of the churches*. 199pp. New York, Harper and Row, 1966.

Le Tiers-monde, l'occident et l'Église, B. Atangana, G. de Bernis, etc. 325pp. (Parole et mission, 13). Paris, Les Editions du Cerf, 1967.

TURIN, Laurent, *Combat pour le développement*. 311pp. (Développement et civilisations). Paris, les Editions ouvrières, 1965.

WARD, Barbara, *The Rich Nations and the Poor Nations*. 159pp. New York, W. W. Norton and Co, 1962: London, Hamish Hamilton, 1962.

WARD, Barbara, *Spaceship Earth*. 152pp. New York, Columbia University Press, 1966: London, Hamish Hamilton, 1966.

WARD, Richard J., ed., *The Challenge of Development. Theory and practice.* 500pp. Chicago, Adling Publishing Co., 1967.

Weltarmut. Eine kirkliche Denkschrift. Herausgegeben, einegeleitet und kommentiert von Klaus-Martin Beckmann und Klaus Lefringhausen. 95pp. Stuttgart, Kreuz Verlag, 1967.

World Poverty and British Responsibility. 80pp. Published for the British Council of Churches. London, S.C.M. Press, 1966.

INTERNATIONAL LAW

BENNETT, John C., *Christians and the State.* 302pp. New York, Charles Scribner's Sons, 1958.

BENNETT, John C., *Foreign Policy in Christian Persepctive.* 160pp. New York, Charles Scribner's Sons, 1966.

Christians in the Struggle for World Community. Report of the section on international affairs received by the second assembly of the W.C.C., Evanston, 1954, remitted to delegates to the ninth general assembly of the United Nations by the Presidents during the second assembly. 16pp. New York, W.C.C., 1954.

DEWART, Leslie, *Christianity and Revolution: The lesson of Cuba.* 320pp. New York, Herder and Herder, 1963.

ELERT, Werner, *Law and Gospel.* 53pp. (Facet books. Social ethics series, 16). Philadelphia, Fortress Press, 1967.

Evangelisches Staatslexikon. Hrsg. von H. Kunst und S. Grundmann in Verbindung mit W. Schneemelcher und R. Herzog. 2688pp., parallel columns. Berlin, Kreuz-Verlag, 1966.

HUEGLI, Albert G., ed., *Church and State under God.* 516pp. St Louis, Missouri, Concordia Publishing House, 1964.

International Affairs: Christians in the struggle for world community. An ecumenical survey prepared under the auspices of the W.C.C. 54pp. (Evanston surveys, 4). London, S.C.M. Press, 1954. French translation *Affaires internationales.* German translation *Internationale Angelegenheiten.*

JAMES, Walter, *The Christian in Politics.* 217pp. London, Oxford University Press, 1962.

KRAMER, Leonard J., *Man amid Change in World Affairs.* 175pp. New York, Friendship Press, 1964.

McDONAGH, Edna, *The Declaration on Religious Freedom of Vatican Council II. The text with commentary in the context of the church–state discussion.* 155pp. London, Darton, Longman and Todd, 1967.

SANDERS, Thomas G., *Protestant Concepts of Church and State: Historical background and approaches for the future.* 388pp. (Anchor book). New York, Doubleday, 1964.

SCHREY, Heinz-Horst, and HERMANN, Hans, and WHITEHOUSE, W. A., *The Biblical Doctrine of Justice and Law.* 208pp. (Ecumenical biblical studies, 3). London, S.C.M. Press, 1955. Translated from the German *Gerechtigkeit in biblischer Sicht.*

SMITH, Elwyn, *Church–State Relations in Ecumenical Perspective.* 280pp. (Duquesne ecumenical books). Pittsburgh, Pa., Duquesne University Press, 1966.

The Treysa Conference on "the biblical doctrine of law and justice". Report of a conference arranged by the Study Department of the World Council of Churches, held at Treysa, Germany, August 2nd to 7th, 1950. 60pp. Geneva, W.C.C., 1951. Translated from the German *Die Treysa-Konferenz 1950.*

CHAPTER 11

The Orthodox Churches in the Ecumenical Movement

ORTHODOXY IN DIALOGUE WITH OTHER DENOMINATIONS

The Dialogue of East and West in Christendom. Lectures delivered at a conference arranged by the Fellowship of St Alban and St Sergius in Oxford, March 10, 1962. Foreword by A. M. Allchin. 47pp. London, published for the Fellowship of St Alban and St Sergius by the Faith Press, 1963.

EVERY, George, *Misunderstandings between East and West*. 70pp. (Ecumenical Studies in History, 4). Richmond, Va., John Knox Press, 1966.

GILL, Joseph, and FLOOD, Edmund, *The Orthodox: Their relations with Rome*. 58pp. (Where we stand). London, Darton, Longman and Todd, 1964.

GILL, Joseph, *The Orthodox and the Ecumenical Movements*. London, The Mouth, 1962.

ISTAVRIDIS, Vasil T., *The Ecumenical Patriarchate and the World Council of Churches*. 18pp. Brookline, Mass., 1963. In *The Greek-Orthodox Theological Review*, vol. 9, no. 1, Summer 1963, pp. 9–28.

ISTAVRIDIS, Vasil T., *Die griechisch-orthodoxe Bibliographie zur ökumenischen Bewegung*. Würzburg, Augustinus Verlag, 1961.

ISTAVRIDIS, Vasil T., "The Orthodox World", in *The Layman in Christian History*, ed. S. C. Neill and H. R. Weber, pp. 276–97. London, S.C.M. Press, 1963.

ISTAVRIDIS, Vasil T., *Orthodoxy and Anglicanism*. 185pp. Translated from the Greek. London, S.P.C.K., 1966.

Major Portions of the Proceedings of the Conference of Heads and Representatives of the Autocephalous Orthodox Churches, Moscow, 8–18 July 1948. 250pp. Paris, Y.M.C.A. Press, 1952.

MAXIMOS IV, Patriarch of Antioch, Alexandria and Jerusalem: *The Eastern Churches and Catholic Unity*. 236pp. Edinburgh/London, Nelson, 1963.

Die Moskauer Konferenz vom Juli 1948. Herausgegeben vom Kirchlichen Aussenamt der E.K.D. 79pp. Witten, Luther-Verlag, 1949? (Dokumente der orthodoxen Kirchen zur ökumenischen Frage, 1).

Orthodoxy. A Faith and Order Dialogue. 80pp. (Faith and Order papers, 30). Geneva, W.C.C., 1960.

SAVRAMIS, Demosthenes, *Oekumenische Probleme in der neugriechischen Theologie*. 118pp. (Oekumenische Studien, 6). Leiden/Köln, Brill, 1964.

SLENCZKA, Reinhard, *Ostkirche und Oekumene. Die Einheit der Kirche als dogmatisches Problem in der neueren ostkirchlichen Theologie*. 316pp. (Forschungen zur systematischen und ökumenischen Theologie, Bd. 9). Göttingen, Vandenhoeck & Ruprecht, 1962.

STAWROWSKY, Alexis, *Essai de théologie irénique: L'Orthodoxie et le Catholicisme*. 266pp. Paris, Sedim, 1966.

STUPPERICH, Robert, *Die Russische Orthodoxe Kirche in Lehre und Leben*. 312pp. (Studienausschuss der EKU für Fragen der Orthodoxen Kirche, Schriftenreihe, 2). Witten, Luther-Verlag, 1966.

Toward a Protestant understanding of Orthodoxy. 23pp. (Resources for ecumenical encounter, 2). New York, Commission on ecumenical mission and relations, 1966.

Versöhnung. Das deutsch-russische Gespräch über das christliche Verständnis der Versöhnung zwischen Vertretern der Evangelischen Kirche in Deutschland und der

Russischen Orthodoxen Kirche. Hrsg. vom Aussenamt der Evangelische Kirche in Deutschland. 197pp. Witten, Luther Verlag, 1967.

VRIES, Wilhelm de, *Orthodoxie et catholicisme.* 183pp. Paris, Desclée, 1967. Translated from the German *Orthodoxie und Katholizismus.*

WADDAMS, Herbert, *Meeting the Orthodox Churches.* 128pp. London, S.C.M. Press, 1964.

ZERNOV, Nicolas, *Orthodox Encounter: The Christian East and the ecumenical movement.* 200pp. London, J. Clarke, 1961.

STUDIES ON ORTHODOXY

ATIYA, Aziz S., *A History of Eastern Christianity.* 486pp. London, Methuen, 1968.

ATTWATER, D., *The Christian Churches of the East.* 3rd rev. edn. 2 vols. London, Chapman, 1961.

BARSOTTI, Divo, *Christianisme russe.* Traduit de l'italien par Ch. Roux de Bézieux et Y. Mourbarac. 196pp. Tournai, Paris, Casterman, 1963.

BENZ, Ernst, *The Eastern Orthodox Church: Its thought and life.* 230pp. New York, Doubleday, 1963. Translated from the German *Geist und Leben der Ostkirche.*

BENZ, Ernst, *Die russische Kirche und das abendländische Christentum.* 186pp. München, Nymphenburger Verlagshandlung, 1966. Chapter II, pp. 39–73: "Die gegenwärtige Stellung der östlich-orthodoxen Kirche in der Oekumene".

BOGOLEPOV, Alexander A., *Toward an American Orthodox Church. The establishment of an Autocephalous Orthodox Church.* 124pp. New York, Morehouse-Barlow, 1963.

BRATSIOTIS, Panagiotis, *Von der griechischen Orthodoxie.* 156pp. Würzburg, Echter-Verlag, 1966.

CLEMENT, Olivier, *L'Eglise orthodoxe.* 128pp. (Que sais-je? 949). Paris, P.U.F., 1961.

CONSTANTELOS, Demetrios J., *The Greek Orthodox Church: Faith, history and practice.* 127pp. New York, The Seabury Press, 1967.

DALMAIS, Irénée-Henri, *The Eastern Liturgies.* 144pp. London, Burns and Oates, 1960. Translated from the French *Les liturgies d'Orient.* German translation *Die Liturgie der Ostkirchen.*

ETTELDORF, Raymond, *The Soul of Greece.* 235pp. Westminster, Maryland, Newman Press, 1963.

EVDOKIMOV, Paul, *L'Orthodoxie; la foi et la vie des Eglises d'Orient.* 352pp. (Bibliothèque théologique). Neuchâtel, Delachaux et Niestlé, 1959.

LE GUILLOU, M.-J., *L'esprit de l'orthodoxie grecque et russe.* Préface par R. P. Dumont. 127pp. (Encyclopédie du catholique au XXe siècle "Je sais—je crois", 13e partie: Frères séparés). Paris, A. Fayard, 1961.

LOSSKY, Vladimir, *A l'image et à la ressemblance de Dieu.* 225pp. Paris, Aubier-Montaigne, 1967.

LOSSKY, Vladimir, *The Vision of God.* 139pp. Westminster, Faith Press, 1963. French translation *Vision de Dieu.* German translation *Schau Gottes.*

MEYENDORFF, Jean, *The Orthodox Church: Its past and its role in the world today.* Translated from the French by John Caphin with additions made by the author for this new English edition. 245pp. London, Darton, Longman & Todd, 1963. Translated from the original *L'Eglise orthodoxe; hier et aujourd-hui.* German translation *Die Orthodoxe Kirche gestern und heute.*

MEYENDORFF, Jean, *Orthodoxy and Catholicity.* 180pp. New York, Sheed and Ward, 1966. Translated from the French *Orthodoxie et catholicité.*

ONASCH, Konrad, *Einführung in die Konfessionskunde der orthodoxen Kirchen.* 291pp. (Sammlung Göschen, 1197/1197a). Berlin, Walter de Gruyter, 1962.

Orthodoxy 1964: a pan-orthodox symposium, Athens. 444pp. The Brotherhood of theologians "Zoe", 1964.

PHILIPPOU, A. J., *The Orthodox Ethos. Essays in honour of the centenary of the Greek Orthodox Archdiocese of North and South America.* 288pp. Oxford, England, Holywell Press, 1964.

POSPISCHIL, Viktor, *Der Patriarch in der Serbisch-orthodoxen Kirche.* 271pp. Wien, Herder Verlag, 1966.

La primauté de Pierre dans l'Eglise orthodoxe, N. Afanassieff, N. Koulomzine, J. Meyendorff, A. Schmemann. 152pp. Neuchâtel, Paris, Editions Delachaux & Niestlé, 1960. German translation *Der Primat des Petrus in der orthodoxen Kirche.* Zürich, EVZ, 1961.

RINVOLUCRI, Mario, *Anatomy of a Church: Greek orthodoxy today.* 192pp. London, Burns & Oates, 1966.

SARTORIUS, Bernard, *L'Eglise orthodoxe.* 350pp. (Les Grandes religions du monde, 10). Genève, le Cercle du Bibliophile, 1968.

SCHMEMANN, Alexander, *The Historical Road of Eastern Orthodoxy.* Translated by Lydia W. Kesich. 359pp. London, Harvill Press, 1963.

SCHMEMANN, Alexander, *Sacraments and Orthodoxy.* 124pp. New York, Herder and Herder, 1965.

ZANANIRI, Gaston, *Catholicisme oriental.* 266pp. Paris, Editions SPES, 1966.

ZANANIRI, Gaston, *Pape et patriarches.* Préface du T. R. P. Dumont. 221pp. Paris, Nouvelle Editions Latines, 1961.

ZERNOV, Nicolas, *Eastern Christendom. A study of the origin and development of the Eastern Orthodox Church.* 326pp. (The Weidenfeld and Nicolson History of Religion). London, Weidenfeld & Nicolson, 1961.

ORIENTAL ORTHODOX CHURCHES

CHAKMAKJIAN, Hagop A., *Armenian Christology and Evangelization of Islam.* 146pp. Leiden, E. J. Brill, 1965.

HANNA, Shenouda, *What are the Copts.* 110pp. Cairo, C. Tsoumas, 1958.

KAWERAV, Peter, *Die jakobitische Kirche im Zeitalter der syrischen Renaissance.* 153pp. Berlin, Akademie-Verlag, 1960.

LEPISA, Titus, *The Cult of Saints in the Ethiopian Church.* 55pp. Roma, Universitas gregoriana, 1963.

MATHEW, C.-P., and THOMAS, M. M., *The Indian Churches of Saint Thomas.* 168pp. Delhi, I.S.P.C.K., 1967.

SARKISSIAN, Karekin, *The Council of Chalcedon and the Armenian Church.* 264pp. London, S.P.C.K., 1965.

"Unofficial consultation between theologians of Eastern Orthodox and Oriental Orthodox Churches, August 11–15, 1964. Papers and minutes", ed. John S. Romanides, Paul Verghese, Nikos A. Nissiotis, *The Greek Orthodox Theological Review,* vol. x, no. 2, Winter 1964–5, 168pp.

CHAPTER 12

The Ecumenical Movement and the Roman Catholic Church

ROMAN CATHOLIC APPROACHES TO THE ECUMENICAL MOVEMENT

At-one-ment: Studies on Christian unity. Washington, D.C., Friars of the Atonement, 1959—. Annual volumes.

BAUM, Gregory, *The Quest for Christian Unity.* 285pp. London, Sheed and Ward, 1963.

BEA, Augustinus, Cardinal, *The Unity of Christians,* ed. Bernard Leeming. Introduction by Gerald P. O'Hara. 231pp. London, Chapman, 1963. Translated from Italian *L'Unione dei Cristiani; problemi e principi, ostacli e mezzi, realizzazioni e prospettive.* French translation *Pour l'unité des chrétiens; problèmes et principes, obstacles et moyens, réalisations et perspectives.* German translation *Die Einheit der Christen. Probleme und Prinzipien, Hindernisse und Mittel, Verwirklichungen und Aussichten.*

BEA, Augustinus, *The Way to Unity after the Council.* 256pp. London, Geoffrey Chapman, 1967. Translated from the Italian *Il cammino all'unione dopo il Concilio.* French translation *Le chemin de l'unité.* German translation *Der Weg zur Einheit nach dem Konzil.*

BIOT, François, *De la polémique au dialogue.* 2 vols. Paris, Editions du Cerf, 1963. Contents: vol. 1: *L'église face aux chrétiens séparés.* 140pp. vol. 2: *Les chrétiens séparés face à l'église.* 135 pp.

BOELENS, Wim L., *Die Arnoldshainer Abendmahlsthesen. Die Suche nach einem Abendmahlskonsens in der Evangelischen Kirche in Deutschland 1947–1957 und eine Würdigung aus katholischer Sicht.* 393pp. Assen, Van Gorcum, 1964.

BOILLAT, Fernand, *L'oecuménisme catholique.* 83pp. St Maurice, Editions St Augustin, 1964.

BOYER, Charles, *Christian unity.* 131pp. (Twentieth century Encyclopedia of Catholicism, v. 138). New York, Hawthorn, 1962.

CRANNY, Titus, ed., *The Episcopate and Christian Unity. A symposium conducted by the Graymoor Friars Saint Pius X Seminary, September 1–4, 1964.* 158pp. Garrison, N.Y., Chair of Unity Apostolate Graymoor, 1965.

HAMER, Jerome, *The Church is a Communion.* 240pp. London, Geoffrey Chapman, 1964. Translated from the French *L'Eglise est une communion.*

HASTINGS, Adrian, *One and Apostolic.* 200pp. London, Darton, Longman & Todd, 1963.

HEUFELDER, Emmanuel Maria, *In the Hope of his Coming. Studies in christian unity.* 261pp. Indiana, Fides, 1964.

IOANNIS XXIII, *Pope John and christian unity.* Compiled and edited by Titus Cranny. 95pp. Graymoore, Garrison, Chair of Unity Apostolate, 1962.

LAMARQUE, Alfred, *Vers l'unité? Catholiques et protestants.* 335pp. Paris, Editions du Cerf, 1963.

LAMBERT, Bernard, *Ecumenism: Theology and history.* 533pp. London, Burns and Oates, 1966. Translated from the French *Le problème oecuménique.* German translation *Das ökumenische Problem.*

R

LEEMING, Bernard, *The Church and the Churches; A study of ecumenism.* 340pp. London, Darton, Longman and Todd, 1960.

LEFEBVRE, Georges, *L'Unité mystère de vie.* 107pp. Paris, Bruges, Desclée de Brouwer, 1964.

MARSHALL, Romey P., *Liturgy and Christian Unity.* 186pp. Englewood Cliffs, N.J., Prentice-Hall, 1965.

MOOY, Suitberto, *Problemas ecumenicos; na igreja e nas igrejas.* 255pp. Sao Paulo. Editora Herder, 1963.

O'BRIEN, John A., *Steps to Christian Unity.* 321pp. Garden City, New York, Doubleday, 1964.

Problems before Unity, J. G. M. Willebrands, Shawn G. Sheehan, Paul Mailleux. Foreword by Augustine Cardinal Bea. 149pp. Dublin, Helicon, 1962.

ST JOHN, Henry, *Essays in Christian Unity 1928–1954.* 144pp. London, Blackfriars, 1955.

SARTORY, Thomas, *The Oecumenical Movement and the Unity of the Church,* tr. Hilda C. Graef. 290pp. Oxford, Blackwell, 1963. Translated from the German *Die ökumenische Bewegung und die Einheit der Kirche; ein Beitrag im Dienste einer ökumenischen Ekklesiologie.*

SCHÜTTE, Heinz, *Um die Wiedervereinigung im Glauben. Vierte, wieder stark erweiterte Auflage, 1961.* 228pp. Essen, Fredebeul & Koenen, 1961.

SWIDLER, Leonard, *Ecumenism; The Spirit and Worship.* 258pp. Louvain, ed. E. Nauwelaerts, Duquesne University Press, 1967.

TAVARD, George, *The Church Tomorrow.* 190pp. London, Darton, Longman & Todd, 1965.

TAYLOR, Michael J., *The Protestant Liturgical Renewal; A catholic viewpoint.* 336pp. Westminster, Maryland, Newman Press, 1963.

VALESKE, Ulrich, *Votum Ecclesiae. I. Teil: Das Ringen um die Kirche in der neuen röm. kath. Theologie. Dargestellt auf dem Hintergrund der evangelischen und ökumenischen parallell Entwicklung. II. Teil: Interkonfessionelle ekklesiologische Bibliographie.* 210pp. München, Claudius, 1962.

VILLAIN, Maurice, *Unity: A history and some reflections.* Translated by J. R. Foster from the third revised and augmented edition. 381pp. London, Harvill, 1963. Translated from the French *Introduction à l'oecuménisme.*

WACKER, Paulus, *Theologie als ökumenischer Dialog. Herman Schell und die ökumenische Situation der Gegenwart.* 571pp. München, Wien, Verlag Ferdinand Schöningh, 1964.

WILLEBRANDS, J. G. ed., *Problems before Unity.* 149pp. Baltimore, Helicon Press, 1962.

ROMAN CATHOLIC—PROTESTANT, ANGLICAN, ORTHODOX DIALOGUE

ASMUSSEN, Hans, and STÄHLIN, Wilhelm, ed., *Die Katholizität der Kirche. Beiträge zum Gespräch zwischen der evangelischen und der römisch-katholischen Kirche.* 390pp. Stuttgart, Evang. Verlagswerk, 1957.

ASMUSSEN, Hans, and SARTORY, Thomas, *Lutheran–Catholic dialogue.* Baltimore, Helicon Press, 1960.

BEVAN, R. J. W., ed., *The Churches and Christian Unity.* 263pp. London, Oxford University Press, 1963.

BOSC, Jean, *Geeint durch das, was trennt. Ein katholisch-protestantisches Gespräch.* Mit einem Geleitwort von Albert Brandenburg. 163pp. Graz-Wien, Köln, Styria, 1963.

BROWN, Robert M., and WEIGEL, Gustave, *An American Dialogue. A Protestant looks at catholicism and a Catholic looks at protestantism.* Foreword by Willy Herberg. 216pp. Garden City, New York, Doubleday, 1960.

BRUNE, Friedrich, *Die Begegnung der evangelischen und katholischen Gemeinden im Alltag.* 68pp. Witten, Luther-Verlag, 1962.

CALLAHAN, Daniel, ed., *Christianity Divided; Protestant and Roman Catholic theological issues.* 335pp. New York, Sheed and Ward, 1961.

The Catholic Protestant Dialogue, Jean Bosc, Jean Guitton, Jean Daniélou. 138pp. Baltimore, Helicon Press, 1960. Translated from the French *Le dialogue catholique-protestant.*

CONGAR, Yves Marie Joseph, *Dialogue between Christians: Catholic contribution to ecumenism.* 472pp. Westminster, Maryland. Newman Press, 1966. Translated from the French *Chrétiens en dialogue; contributions catholiques à l'oecuménisme.*

CULLMANN, Oscar, *Message to Catholics and Protestants.* 57pp. Grand Rapids, Eerdmans, 1959. Translated from the German *Katholiken und Protestanten. Ein Vorschlag zur Verwirklichung christlicher Solidarität.*

Do we know the others? Ecumenical theology. 180pp. New York, Paulist Press, 1966.

Ecumenical dialogue in Europe. The ecumenical conversations at Les Dombes (1937–1955) inspired by the Abbé Couturier. Introduced by Patrick C. Rodger. 83pp. London, Lutterworth Press, 1966.

EMPIE, Paul, and BAUM, William W., ed., *Lutherans and Catholics in dialogue.* II: *One Baptism for the Remission of Sins.* 87pp. New York, National Committee of the Lutheran World Federation, Bishop's Commission for Ecumenical Affairs, 1966.

GARRETT, James Leo, *Baptists and Roman Catholicism.* 45pp. Nashville, Tennessee, Broadway Press, 1965.

GRANT, Frederick C., *Rome and Reunion.* 196pp. New York, Oxford University Press, 1965.

GREENSPUN, William B., and NORGREN, William A., *Living room dialogues.* 255pp. N.C.C.C.U.S.A., Glen Rock, Paulist Press, 1965.

L'infaillibilité de l'église: journées oecuméniques de Chevetogne, 25–29 Septembre 1961, O. Rousseau, J. J. von Allmen, B.-D. Dupuy, etc. 268pp. Chevetogne, Editions de Chevetogne, 1963.

KING, Betty, and JULIANA, Lorraine, *The wall between us. A Protestant–Catholic dialogue.* 173pp. Milwaukee, The Bruce Publishing Co., 1964.

KLEIN, Laurentius, und MEINHOLD, Peter, *Ueber Wesen und Gestalt der Kirche; ein katholisch-evangelischer Briefwechsel.* 124pp. Freiburg, Basel und Wien, Herder-Bücherei, 1963.

MILLER, Samuel H., and WRIGHT, Ernest G., *Ecumenical Dialogue at Harvard: The Roman Catholic–Protestant colloquium.* 385pp. Cambridge, Mass., Belknap Press of Harvard University Press, 1964.

PELIKAN, Jaroslav J., *Obedient Rebels; Catholic substance and Protestant principle in Luther's reformation.* 212pp. New York, Harper, 1964.

Reconsiderations. Roman Catholic–Presbyterian and Reformed conversation of the Bishop's Committee for Ecumenical and Inter-religious Affairs and the North American Area of the World Alliance of Reformed Churches. 158pp. New York, World Horizons, 1967.

Rencontre oecuménique à Genève. 124pp. Genève Editions Labor et Fides. Paris, Librairie Protestante, 1965.

SWIDLER, Leonard, ed., *Dialogue for Reunion: The Catholic premises.* 88pp. New York, Herder and Herder, 1962.

TAVARD, George, *La poursuite de la catholicité; étude sur la pensée anglicane.* 247pp. Paris, Editions du Cerf, 1965.

WEIGEL, Gustave, *Catholic theology in Dialogue*. 126pp. New York, Harper, 1961.

ZANANIRI, Gaston, *Catholicisme oriental*. 266pp. Paris, Editions SPES, 1966.

ZANDER, Leo A., *Einheit ohne Vereinigung; ökumenische Betrachtungen eines russischen Orthodoxen. Aus dem Russischen von Reinhard Slenczka*. Mit einem Geleitwort von E. Schlink. Stuttgart, Evangelisches Verlagswerk, 1959.

ROMAN CATHOLIC REACTIONS TO VATICAN II

BAUMANN, Richard, *Vom Konzil zur Einheit*. 2 vols. Vol. 1 *Auch wir sind Kirche*. 211pp. Vol. 2 *Hoffnung aus Sankt Paul*. 292pp. Essen, Verlag Hans Driewer, 1965.

HÄRING, Bernhard, *The Johannine Council: Witness to unity*. 155pp. New York, Herder and Herder, 1964.

JAEGER, Lorenz, *The Ecumenical Council, the Church and Christendom*. 194pp. London, Geoffrey Chapman, 1961. Translation from the German *Das ökumenische Konzil, die Kirche und die Christenheit*.

KÜNG, Hans, *The Council and Reunion*. Translated by Cecil Hastings. 307pp. (Stagbooks). London, New York, Sheed and Ward, 1961. Translated from the German *Konzil und Wiedervereinigung: Erneuerung als Ruf in die Einheit*. French translation *Concile et retour à l'unité; se renouveler pour susciter l'unité*.

KÜNG, Hans, *The Living Church: Reflections on the Second Vatican Council*. Translated by Cecily Hastings and N. D. Smith. 421pp. London, New York, Sheed and Ward, 1963. Translated from the German *Strukturen der Kirche*. French translation *Structures de l'Église*.

VILLAIN, Maurice, *Vatican II et le dialogue oecuménique*. 236pp. Tournai, Casterman, 1966.

PROTESTANT, ANGLICAN AND ORTHODOX REACTIONS TO VATICAN II

Die Autorität der Freiheit. Gegenwart des Konzils und Zukunft der Kirche im ökumenischen Disput. 3 vols. Herausgegeben von Johann Christoph Hampe. München, Kösel-Verlag, 1967.

BARTH, Karl, *Ad Limina Apostolorum*. 66pp. Zürich, EVZ-Verlag, 1967.

BERKOUWER, G. C., *The Second Vatican Council and the New Catholicism*. 264pp. Translated by Lewis B. Smedes. Grand Rapids, Michigan, Eerdmans, 1965. Translated from the Dutch *Vatikaans concilie en nieuwe theologie*.

Challenge . . . and Response: A protestant perspective of the Vatican Council, ed. Warren A. Quanbeck in consultation with Friedrich Wilhelm Kantzenbach and Vilmos Vajta. 226pp. Minneapolis, Augsburg Publishing House, 1952.

HAMPE, Johann Christoph, *Ende der Gegenreformation? Das Konzil Dokumente und Deutung*. 445pp. Stuttgart u. Berlin, Kreuz-Verlag, 1964; Mainz, Matthias-Grünewald-Verlag, 1964.

HORTON, Douglas, *Toward an undivided Church*. 96pp. New York, Association Press, 1967.

HORTON, Douglas, *Vatican Diary. A Protestant observes the third session of Vatican Council II*. 4 vols. Philadelphia, Boston, United Church Press, 1966.

KARRER, Otto, *Das Zweite Vatikanische Konzil. Reflexionen zu seiner geschichtlichen und geistlichen Wirklichkeit*. 275pp. München, Kösel-Verlag, 1966.

LINDBECK, George A., *Dialogue on the way; Protestants report from Rome on the Vatican Council*. 270pp. Minneapolis, Augsburg Publishing House, 1965. French translation *Le dialogue est ouvert. Le Concile vu par les observateurs luthériens. Les trois première sessions du Concile Vatican II.* German translation *Dialog unterwegs; eine evangelische Bestandesaufnahme zum Konzil.*

MEINHOLD, Peter, *Die Kirchen auf neuen Wegen. Wie sie heute aufeinander blicken.* 172pp. Freiburg, Herder, 1964.

MILLER, John H., *Vatican II an interfaith appraisal. International theological conference, 1966.* 656pp. Notre Dame and London, University of Notre Dame, 1966.

NEUMANN, Johannes, *Auf Hoffnung hin; eine Sammlung oekumenischer Gedanken.* 284pp. Meitingen bei Augsburg, Kyrios-Verlag, 1964.

OUTLER, Albert C., *Methodist Observer at Vatican II.* 189pp. New York, Newman Press, 1967.

The Papal Council and the Gospel. Protestant theologians evaluate the coming Vatican Council, ed. K. E. Skydsgaard. 213pp. Minneapolis, Augsburg Publishing House, 1961. German translation *Konzil und Evangelism.*

PAWLEY, Bernard C., *The Second Vatican Council: Studies by eight Anglican observers.* 262pp. London, Oxford University Press, 1967.

Points de vue de théologiens protestants: Etudes sur les décrets du Concile Vatican II, J. Bosc, G. Casalis, H. Roux. 269pp. Paris, Editions du Cerf, 1967.

ROUX, Hébert, *Détresse et promesse de Vatican II: Réflexions et expériences d'un observateur au concile.* 205pp. Paris, Editions du Seuil, 1967.

SCHLINK, Edmund, *After the Council: The meaning of Vatican II for protestantism and the ecumenical dialogue.* Philadelphia, Fortress Press, 1968. Translated from the German *Nach dem Konzil.*

STUBER, Stanley, and NELSON, Claude D., *Implementing Vatican II in your community. Dialogue and action manual based on the sixteen documents of the Second Vatican Council.* 239pp. New York, Association Press.

SUBILLA, Vittorio, *La nuova cattolicità del Cattolicesimo. Una valutazione protestante del Concilio Vaticano II.* 309pp. Torino, Editrice Claudiana, 1967.

SUBILIA, Vittorio, *The Problem of Catholicism.* 190pp. London, S.C.M. Press, 1964. Translated from the Italian *Il problema del cattolicesimo.*

VINAY, Valdo, *Rom und die anderen. Das Verhältnis der römischen Kirche zur nichtrömischen Christenheit an Hand der Konstitution "De Ecclesia" und des Dekrets "De Oecumenismo".* 41pp. Göttingen, Vandenhoeck & Ruprecht, 1965.

VISCHER, Lukas, *Ueberlegungen nach dem Vatikanischen Konzil.* 79pp. Zürich, EVZ-Verlag, 1966.

JOINT WORKING GROUP BETWEEN THE ROMAN CATHOLIC CHURCH AND THE WORLD COUNCIL OF CHURCHES

"First Official Report", in *Ecumenical Review,* vol. xviii, no. 2, April 1966, pp. 243–55. See also *Minutes of the Central Committee, Geneva, February 1966,* pp. 47–51.

"Second Official Report", in *Ecumenical Review,* vol. xix, no. 4, October 1967, pp. 461–9. See also *Minutes of the Central Committee, Heraklion, August 1967,* pp. 53–5.

"On the Ecumenical Dialogue. A Working Paper", in *Ecumenical Review,* vol. xix, no. 4, October 1967, pp. 469–73.

CHAPTER 13

The Ecumenical Movement in the Churches and at the Parish Level

ECUMENISM AT LOCAL LEVEL

Agenda for the Churches. A report on the "People Next Door" programme, Kenneth Sansbury, Robert Latham, Pauline Webb. With appendixes by Vere Ducker. 71pp. London, S.C.M. Press, 1968.

BENIGNUS, Emma, *All in Each Place: A guide to local ecumenism*. 127pp. Cincinnati, a Forward Movement Publication, 1966.

BLAKEMORE, William Barnett, *The Challenge of Christian Unity*. 144pp. (The William Henry Hoover Lectures on Christian unity, 1963). St Louis, Missouri, Bethany Press, 1963.

BRENNECKE, Ursula, *Gelebte Verantwortung: Ein ökumenischer Rundblick in die Frauenarbeit der Kirchen*. 239pp. Berlin, Evangelische Verlagsanstalt, 1966.

BRUNE, Friedrich, *Die Begegnung der evangelischen und katholischen Gemeinden im Alltag*. 68pp. Witten, Luther-Verlag, 1962.

DAVIES, Rupert E., *In All Places and All Ages*. 37pp. (The unity we seek, 5). London, B.C.C., 1964.

First ecumenical workbook. Programme suggestions for local Councils of Churches, united Christian youth groups, ecumenical fellowships, and parishes and congregations. London, B.C.C., 1960.

FRANZMANN, Martin H., and LUEKING, F. D., *Grace under Pressure: The way of weakness in ecumenical relations*. 105pp. St Louis, Concordia Publishing House, 1966.

GOODALL, Norman, *The Local Church: Its resources and responsibilities*. 63pp. London, Hodder and Stoughton, 1966.

GREENSPOON, William B., and NORGREN, William A., ed., *Living Room Dialogues*. 255pp. Glen Rock, Paulist Press, 1965.

GREENSPOON, William B., and WEDEL, Cynthia C., *Second Living Room Dialogues*. 270pp. Glen Rock, Paulist Press, 1967.

HORNIG, Ernst, *Die Bedeutung der ökumenischen Bewegung für die Ortsgmeinde. Herrn Generalsekretär Dr W. A. Visser 't Hooft zum 65. Geburtstag*. 24pp. Sonderdruck aus Pastoralblätter 5/6 1965 im Kreuz-Verlag, Berlin.

HOSKINS, Fred, *Servants of the Eternal Christ; Local ecumenicity. A study book for local Churches. In preparation for the 1963 General Assembly of the National Council of Churches*. 48pp. New York, The Office of publication and distribution, National Council of Churches, 1962.

Interim Guidelines for Ecumenical Activities in the Archdiocese of Boston. 24pp. Boston, Archdiocesan Ecumenical Commission, 1967.

KEABLE, Gladys, *Squares in Circles; Reshaping the local church*. 135pp. London, Darton, Longman and Todd, 1965.

LEE, Robert, *Church Co-operation of the Local Level through Comity*. With a foreword by Meryl Ruoss. 15pp. New York, Protestant Council of the City of New York, Department of Church Planning and Research, 1954.

Oekumene am Ort; Gedanken, Berichte und Vorschläge zur ökumenischen Arbeit in den Ortsgemeinden. Zusammengestellt von Ludwig Rott mit Beiträgen von

Nevill B. Cryer, Walter Fritz, etc. 44pp. (Oekumenische Arbeitshefte, 5). Kassel, Werkbrüder-Verlag, 1963.

PRICE, Hetley, and WAKEFIELD, Gordon S., *Unity at the Local Level*. 58pp. (Star books on reunion). Oxford, Mowbray, 1964.

ROSS, Roy G., *The Ecumenical Movement and the Local Church. A statement of imperative and suggested plans, as approved by the General Board, March 2, 1962*. 16pp. New York, N.C.C.C.U.S.A., 1962.

SANDERSON, ROSS W., *Church Co-operation in the United States. The nation-wide backgrounds and ecumenical significance of state and local Councils of Churches in their historical perspectives*. 272pp. New York, Association of Council Secretaries, 1960.

SILLS, Horace S., ed., *Grassroots ecumenicity: Case studies in local Church consolidation*. 140pp. Philadelphia, United Church Press, 1967.

SLACK, Kenneth, *Growing Together Locally. Some suggestions as to how the ecumenical movement can be made a reality wherever Christians of different traditions are found together*. 40pp. London, B.C.C., 1958.

SLUSSER, Gerald H., *The Local Church in Transition; Theology, education, and ministry*. 204pp. Philadelphia, Westminster, 1964.

WIESER, Thomas, "A new ecumenical discussion on the congregation", in *Ecumenical Review*, vol. xvi (1963–4), no. 2, pp. 153–7.

WILLIAMS, Colin W., *For the World: A study book for local Churches. In preparation for the 1966 general assembly*. 64pp. New York, The National Council of Churches, 1965.

LAITY

BLISS, Kathleen, *We the People: A book about laity*. 139pp. London, S.C.M. Press, 1963.

CHENU, M. D., *Peuple de Dieu dans le monde*. 159pp. (Foi vivante, 35). Paris, Editions du Cerf, 1966.

CONGAR, Yves M. J., *Lay People in the Church: A study for a theology of laity*. 447pp. London, Bloomsbury Publishing Co., 1957. Translated from the French *Jalons pour une théologie du laicat*. German translation *Der Laie*.

GIBBS, Mark, and MORTON, T. Ralph, *God's Frozen People; A book for and about ordinary Christians*. 190pp. London, Collins, 1965.

God's People in Asian Industrial Society. The report of the East Asia Christian Conference on Christians in Industry and Lay Training. 198pp. Kyoto, Doshisha University School of Theology, 1967.

GRIMES, Howard, *The Rebirth of the Laity*. New York, Abingdon, 1962.

GRUPP, Kenneth G., *A Layman looks at the Church*. 190pp. London, Hodder and Stoughton, 1964.

KRAEMER, Hendrik, *A Theology of the Laity*. 192pp. London, Lutterworth, 1958.

Laici in Ecclesia. An ecumenical bibliography on the role of the laity in the life and mission of the Church. 107pp. Geneva, W.C.C., Department on the Laity, 1961.

The Laity: The Christian in his Vocation. An ecumenical survey prepared under the auspices of the W.C.C. 58pp. (Evanston surveys, 6). London, S.C.M. Press, 1954. French translation *Les laïcs*. German translation *Laienarbeit*.

Laity formation. Proceedings of the Ecumenical Consultation Gazzada (Italy), September 7–10, 1965; jointly sponsored by the Department on the Laity of the W.C.C. and the Permanent Committee for International Congresses of the Lay Apostolate. 94pp. Rome, Arti Grafiche Scalia, 1966.

Layman's Church, J. A. T. Robinson and others. 99pp. London, Lutterworth Press, 1963.

LÖFFLER, Paul, *The layman abroad in the mission of the church. A decade of discussion and experiment.* 96pp. (C.W.M.E., research pamphlets, no. 10). London, Edinburgh House Press, published for the W.C.C. Committee on World Mission and Evangelism, 1962.

ROLLET, Henri, *Les laïcs d'après le Concile.* 304pp. Paris, Editions de Gigord, 1965.

THURIAN, Max, *Consecration of the Layman; New approaches to the sacrament of confirmation.* 118pp. Baltimore, Dublin, Helicon Press, 1963. Translated from the French *La confirmation.*

WEBER, Hans-Ruedi, *The Militant Ministry: People and pastors of the early Church and today.* 108pp. Philadelphia, Board of Publication of the Lutheran Church in America, 1963.

WENTZ, Frederick K., *The Layman's Role Today.* 229pp. Garden City, N.Y., Doubleday, 1963.

STRUCTURES FOR MISSIONARY CONGREGATIONS

BRIDSTON, Keith, *Mission, Myth and Reality.* 128pp. New York, Friendship Press, 1965.

The Church for Others and the Church for the World: A quest for structures for missionary congregations. Final report of the Western European Working Group of the Department on Studies in Evangelism. 35pp. Geneva, W.C.C., 1967. German translation *Die Kirche für andere.*

GARDNER, E. Clinton, *The Church as a Prophetic Community.* 254pp. Philadelphia, The Westminster Press, 1967.

HILLMAN, Eugene, *The Church as Mission.* 144pp. London, Sheed and Ward, 1966.

MARGULL, Hans Jochen, *Mission als Strukturprinzip; ein Arbeitsbuch zur Frage missionarischer Gemeinden.* 246pp. Genf, Ö.R.K., 1965.

METZ, Donald L., *New congregations: Security and mission in conflict.* 170pp. Philadelphia, Westminster Press, 1967.

O'CONNOR, Elisabeth, *Call to Commitment.* 205pp. New York, Harper, 1963.

Structures for a Missionary Congregation. 123pp. Singapore, E.A.C.C., 1964.

WEBBER, George W., *The Congregation in Mission; Emerging structures for the Church in an urban society.* 208pp. New York, Abingdon Press, 1964.

WIESER, Thomas, ed., *Planning for Mission: Working papers on the new quest for missionary communities.* 230pp. New York, U.S. Conference for the W.C.C. 1966.

WILLIAMS, Colin W., *What in the World?* 105pp. New York, N.C.C.C.U.S.A., 1964.

WILLIAMS, Colin W., *Where in the World? Changing form of the church's witness.* 116pp. New York, N.C.C.C.U.S.A., 1963. German translation *Gemeinden für andere.*

HOUSE CHURCHES

"The Church in the House", in *Laity* (W.C.C.), no. 3, April 1957.

Die Gemeinde im Haus; Berichte über eine wiederentdeckte Lebensform der Kirche; mit Beiträgen von W. D. Cattanach, A. Klamer, Hilda Lehotsky, etc. 40pp. (Oekumenische Arbeitshefte, 3). Frankfurt a.M., Arbeitsgemeinschaft christlicher Kirchen in Deutschland, Ökumenische Zentrale, 1961.

HIRATA, Satoshi, "House Churches in Osaka", in *Laity* (W.C.C.), no. 18, 1964, pp. 45–8.

KLESSMANN, Ernst, *Die Hausgemeinde*. 56pp. (Handbücherei für Gemeindearbeit, 8). Gütersloher Verlagshaus Gerd Mohn, 1960.

MORTON, T. Ralph, "The House Church in Scotland", in *Frontier* (London, vol. 5, Spring 1962), pp. 342–4.

ORR, David C., *The House Church. An Iona Community Pamphlet*. Glasgow, Iona Community Publishing Department.

PERRY, John D., *The Coffee House Ministry*. 127pp. Richmond, Va., John Knox Press, 1966.

SOUTHCOTT, Ernest W., *The House Church*. 14pp. (Evangelism Broad Sheets, no. 1). London, B.C.C., n.d.

THOMAS, Donald F., *Manual for the Church in the Home. Procedures for the creation of small groups as outposts of the gathered Church*. 39pp. Valley Forge, Pa., American Baptist Home Mission Societies, Division of Evangelism. 1961.

TEAM MINISTRIES

BEESON, Trevor, ed., *Partnership in Ministry*. 148pp. London, A. R. Mowbray, 1964.

BUSIA, K. A., *Urban Churches in Britain: A question of relevance*. 173pp. (World studies of churches in mission). London, Lutterworth Press, 1966.

HUGHES, Robert, *Team Ministry*. For the team at St Mary's, Woolwich, Nicolas Stacey, Robert Hughes, and others. 16pp. Copies may be obtained from Mitre House, 177 Regent Street, London W.1.

JUDY, Marvin T., *The Co-operative Parish in Non-metropolitan Areas*. 208pp. Nashville, Abingdon Press, 1967.

JUDY, Marvin T., *The Larger Parish and Group Ministry*. Nashville, Abingdon Press, 1959.

KENRICK, Bruce, *Come Out the Wilderness*. 254pp. London, Collins, 1963.

O'CONNOR, Elisabeth, *Journey Inward, Journey Outward*. 175pp. New York, Harper, 1968.

Partners in Ministry. Being the report of the commission on the development and payment of the clergy. 112pp. Westminster, Church Information Office, 1967.

PAUL, Leslie, *The Deployment and Payment of the Clergy*. 311pp. Westminster, Church Information Office, 1964.

SMITH, Arthur C., *Team and Group Ministry*. 111pp. Westminster, Church Information Office, 1965.

VINAY, Tullio, *Agape: ein Wagnis der Hoffnung für unsere Zeit*. 64pp. Wuppertal-Barmen, John. Kiefel Verlag, 1966.

VINAY, Tullio, und VINAY, Gio, *Riesi; Geschichte eines christlichen Abenteuers*. Herausgegeben und bearbeitet von Reinhard W. Schmidt. 221pp. Stuttgart, Kreuz-Verlag, 1964.

CHAPTER 14

Signs of Radicalism in the Ecumenical Movement

CRITICISM OF THE ESTABLISHED CHURCH AND OF TRADITIONAL CHRISTIAN THEOLOGY

ADOLFS, Robert, *The Grave of God: Has the Church a future?* 157pp. New York Harper, 1967. Translated from the Dutch *Het graf van God.*

BERGER, Peter L., *The Noise of Solemn Assemblies.* 189pp. Garden City, Doubleday, 1961.

BERTON, Pierre, *The Comfortable Pew: A critical look at Christianity and the religious establishment in the new age.* 158pp. Toronto, McClelland and Stewart, 1965.

BROCKWAY, Allan R., *The Secular Saint.* 238pp. Garden City, New York, Doubleday, 1968.

CALLAHAN, Daniel, *Honesty in the Church.* 188pp. London, Constable, 1965.

COX, Harvey, *The Secular City: Secularization and urbanization in theological perspective.* 276pp. London, S.C.M. Press, 1965.

EAGLETON, Terence, *The New Left Church.* 180pp. London, Sheed and Ward, 1966.

EDWARDS, David L., ed., *The Honest to God Debate.* 287pp. London, S.C.M. Press, 1963.

FOSTER, John, *Requiem for a Parish: An inquiry into customary practices and procedures in the contemporary parish.* 155pp. Westminster, Maryland, Newman Press, 1962.

GILKEY, Langdon, *How the Church Can Minister to the World without Losing Itself.* 151pp. New York, Harper, 1964.

HOEKENDIJK, J. C., *The Church Inside Out.* 212pp. Philadelphia, Westminster Press, 1966. Translated from the Dutch *De Kerk binnenste buiten.*

KEABLE, Gladys, *Squares in Circles: Reshaping the local Church.* 135pp. London, Darton, Longman and Todd, 1965.

LOHSE, Jens M., *Kirche ohne Kontakte? Beziehungsformen in einem Industrieraum.* 212pp. Stuttgart, Kreuz Verlag, 1967.

MARTY, Martin E., ed., *Death and Birth of the Parish.* Martin E. Marty, editor and author with Paul R. Biegner, Roy Blumhorst and Kenneth R. Young. 163pp. St Louis, Concordia, 1964.

MARTY, Martin E., *The New Shape of American Religion.* 180pp. New York, Harper, 1959.

MATTHES, Joachim, *Die Emigration der Kirche aus der Gesellschaft.* 113pp. Hamburg, Furche-Verlag, 1964.

METZ, Donald L., *New Congregations: Security and mission in conflict.* 170pp. Philadelphia, Westminster, 1967.

PIKE, James A., *If This be Heresy.* 205pp. New York, Harper, 1967.

ROBINSON, John A. T., *Honest to God.* 143pp. London, S.C.M. Press, 1963.

ROBINSON, John A. T., *The New Reformation?* 142pp. London, S.C.M. Press, 1965.

ROSE, Stephen C., *The Grassroots Church: A manifesto for Protestant renewal.* Introduction by Harvey Cox. 174pp. New York, Holt, Rinehart and Winston, 1966.

SCHULTZ, Hans Juergen, ed., *Kritik an der Kirche.* 335pp. Stuttgart, Kreuz Verlag, 1960.

STAMMLER, Eberhard, *Churchless Protestants*. 223pp. Philadelphia, Westminster, 1964. Translated from the German *Protestanten ohne Kirche*.

THIELICKE, Helmut, *The Trouble with the Church: A call for renewal*, translated and edited by John W. Doberstein. 136pp. New York, Harper, 1965. Translated from the German *Leiden an der Kirche*.

Who's Killing the Church? ed. Stephen C. Rose. 141pp. Chicago, Renewal Magazine, 1966.

WINTER, Gibson, *The new creation as metropolis*. 152pp. New York, London, Macmillan, 1963.

WINTER, Gibson, *The suburban captivity of the churches: An analysis of Protestant responsibility in the expanding metropolis*. 216pp. New York, Doubleday, 1961.

WORLD STUDENT CHRISTIAN FEDERATION

Students and the Life and Mission of the Church. A report on the World Student Christian Federation, 1956–1964. 108pp. Geneva, W.S.C.F., 1965.

Unto a Lively Hope. A report on the life of the World's Student Christian Federation and related National Student Christian Movements during the years 1946–1949. 127pp. Geneva, W.S.C.F., 1950.

Witnessing in the University Communities. A report of the World's Student Christian Federation and related National Student Christian Movements during the years 1949 to 1952. 88pp. Geneva, W.S.C.F., 1953.

Witnessing to Jesus Christ the Reconciler. A report on the life of the W.S.C.F. and related national S.C.M.s during the years 1953–1956. 142pp. Geneva, W.S.C.F., 1957.

WORLD ALLIANCE OF Y.M.C.A.s AND WORLD Y.W.C.A.

ANDERSON, Paul B., *A Study of Orthodoxy and the Y.M.C.A*. Geneva, World Alliance of Y.M.C.A.s, 1963.

And Now—Tomorrow. Report of the World Y.M.C.A. Conferences, Paris, France, August 1955. Geneva, World Alliance of Y.M.C.A.s, 1955.

Basic Issues in Y.M.C.A. Ecumenical Policy and Practice. Geneva, World Alliance of Y.M.C.A.s, 1962.

Called to New Things: Report of the 3rd meeting of the World Council of Y.M.C.A.s, Geneva, Switzerland, July 1961. Geneva, World Alliance of Y.M.C.A.s, 1961.

History of the World's Alliance of Y.M.C.A.s, C. P. Shedd and other contributors. London, S.P.C.K., 1955.

Into All the World. Report of the 2nd meeting of the World Council of Y.M.C.A.s, Kassell, Germany, July 1957. Geneva, World Alliance of Y.M.C.A.s, 1957.

Meeting of Y.M.C.A. Leaders of Roman Catholic Confession, Geneva, July 1961. Geneva, World Alliance of Y.M.C.A.s, 1961.

Report of the Consultation on Ecumenical Policy and Practice for Lay Christian Movements, St Cergue, Switzerland, July 1962. Geneva, World Alliance of Y.M.C.A.s and World Y.W.C.A., 1962.

Varieties of Service but the Same Lord. Report of 4th meeting of the World Council of Y.M.C.A.s, Tozanso, Japan, August 1965. Geneva, World Alliance of Y.M.C.A.s, 1965.

WORLD COUNCIL OF CHURCHES YOUTH DEPARTMENT AND ECUMENICAL YOUTH CONFERENCES

Christ the Life. The report of the Asian Christian Youth Assembly, ed. Soritua A. E. Nabadan. 130pp. Silliman University, Dumaguete City, 1965.

Ecumenical Youth Assembly in Europe, Lausanne, 1960, ed. Rod French. 91pp. (Youth no. 2, October 1960). Geneva, W.C.C., Youth Department, 1960.

Footprints in Travancore. Report of the Third World Conference of Christian Youth, December 11–26, 1952. 95pp. Coonoor, Nilgiris, India Sunday School Union, 1953.

HEUVEL, Albert H. van den, ed., *The New Creation and the New Generation: A forum for youth workers*. 128pp. New York, Friendship Press, 1965.

North American Youth Assembly, Ann Arbor, 1961, ed. Rod French. 50pp. (Youth no. 4, November 1961). Geneva, W.C.C., Youth Department, 1961.

Risk. Published by the Youth Department of the World Council of Churches, vol. 1, 1965—.

INDUSTRIAL MISSION

EDWARDS, David L., ed., *Priests and Workers: An Anglo-French Discussion*. 160pp. London, S.C.M. Press, 1961.

Priest and worker. The Autobiography of Henry Perrin. 247pp. London, Macmillan, 1965. Translated from the French *Itinéraire de Henri Perrin*.

ROWE, John, *Priests and Workers: A refounder*. 78pp. London, Darton, Longman and Todd, 1965.

SIEFER, Gregor, *The Church and Industrial Society*. 355pp. London, Darton, Longman and Todd, 1964. Translated from the German *Die Mission der Arbeiterpriester*.

SYMANOWSKI, Horst, *The Christian Witness in an Industrial Society*. 160pp. Philadelphia, Westminster Press, 1964. Translated from the German *Gegen die Weltfremdheit*.

TAYLOR, Richard, *Christians in an Industrial Society*. 128pp. London, S.C.M. Press, 1961.

VELTEN, Georges, *Mission in Industrial France*. London, S.C.M. Press, 1968.

WICKHAM, E. R., *Church and People in an Industrial City*. 292pp. London, Lutterworth Press, 1957.

WINTER, Gibson, *The New Creation as Metropolis*. 152pp. New York, Macmillan, 1963.

EVANGELICAL ACADEMIES AND LAY TRAINING CENTRES

Centres of Renewal for Study and Lay Training. 64pp. Geneva, W.C.C., Dept. on the Laity, 1964.

Directory of Lay Training Centres. 2 vols. Geneva, W.C.C., Dept. on the Laity, 1962–3.

DOEHRING, Johannes, ed., *Die Gemeinde in der modernen Gesellschaft*. Loccum, Evangelical Academy Loccum, 1960.

Evangelical Academies in the German Federal Republic. 77pp. Published by the Directors' Association of the Evangelical Academies in Germany, Inc., 1966. Translated from the German *Evangelische Akademien in der Bundersrepublik Deutschland*.

FRAKES, Margaret, *Bridges to Understanding: The "Academy Movement" in Europe and North America.* 134pp. Philadelphia, Muhlenberg Press, 1960.

GABLE, Lee J., *Church and World Encounter: The Evangelical Academies in Germany and their meaning for the ecumenical Church.* 111pp. Philadelphia, United Church Press, 1964.

HARTMAN, Olov, *The Sigtuna Foundation.* 54pp. London, S.C.M. Press, 1955.

KOLLER, Martin, ed., *A New Road in Germany: Evangelical academy.* Hamburg, Furche Verlag, 1956.

Signs of Renewal: The life of the lay institute in Europe, ed. Hans-Ruedi Weber. 63pp. Geneva, W.C.C., Dept. on the Laity, 1956. German translation *Zeichen des Aufbruchs.*

WEBER, Hans-Ruedi, *Salty Christians: A handbook for leaders of lay training courses.* 43pp. Geneva, W.C.C., Dept. on the Laity, 1962.

IONA COMMUNITY

MACLEOD, George F., *Only One Way Left.* Glasgow, Iona Community, 1956.

MORTON, T. Ralph, *The Community of Faith.* U.S. edn. with added chapters by Alexander Miller and John O. Nelson. New York, Association Press, 1954. English edn. *The Household of Faith* (1951).

MORTON, T. Ralph, *The Iona Community Story.* 96pp. London, Lutterworth Press, 1957.

ORDERS

BRUMMET, Jacob, *Die Kirche ist immer jung.* München, J. Pfeiffer, 1960.

Frauen entdecken ihren Auftrag. Weibliche Diakonie im Wandel eines Jahrhunderts. Dargestellt von Hermann Schauer. 252 pp. Göttingen, Vandenhoeck und Ruprecht, 1960.

PERCHENET,. Annie, *Renouveau communautaire et unité chrétienne. Regards sur les communautés anglicanes et protestantes.* 479pp. Paris, Mame, 1967.

PRÄGER, Lydia, *Frei für Gott und die Menschen. Evangelische Bruder- und Schwesternschaften der Gegenwart in Selbstdarstellungen.* 591pp. Stuttgart, Quell-Verlag der Evang. Gesellschaft, 1964.

WYON, Olive, *Living springs: New religious movements in Western Europe,* 28pp. London, S.C.M. Press, 1963.

TAIZÉ

The Eucharistic liturgy of Taizé. With an introductory essay by Max Thurian. 85pp. London, Faith Press, 1962. Translated from the French *Eucharistie à Taizé.*

HEIJKE, John, *An Ecumenical Light on the Renewal of Religious Community Life, Taizé.* 203pp. Pittsburgh, Pa., Duquesne University Press, 1967.

PAUPERT, Jean-Marie, *Taizé et l'Église de demain.* 268pp. (Le Signe, grandes études oecuméniques). Paris, Fayard, 1967.

The Rule of Taizé in French and English. 78pp. Taizé, Presses de Taizé, 1961.

"Taizé, 25 ans de communauté, 25 ans d'oecuménisme", in *Fêtes et saisons,* no. 191. January 1965. 28pp.

GRANDCHAMP

Communauté de Grandchamp. 16pp. Lausanne, Imprimerie Centrale, 1959.

SJALOOM MOVEMENT

De tafel van één. Leren rekennen met een nieuwe wereld. Een documentaire van de sjaloomgroep. 204pp. Utrecht, Ambo, 1967.
Sjaloom (Den Haag), vol. 1, 1964—.

AKTION SÜHNEZEICHEN

SKRIVER, Ansgar, *Aktion Sühnezeichen. Brücken über Blut und Asche.* 150pp. Stuttgart, Kreuz-Verlag, 1962.

ALL CHRISTIAN PEACE ASSEMBLY

Prague 1–4 June 1958
Task and Witness. Christian Peace Conference. 87pp. Prague, Ecumenical Institute of the Comenius Faculty, 1958.

Prague 1960
The Only Future. Documents of the Third Session of the Christian Peace Conference 134pp. Prague, 1960.

Prague 13–18 June 1961
... And on earth peace. Documents of the First All Christian Peace Assembly, Prague, 1962. 190pp.

Prague 28 June–3 July 1964
Documents and Informations from the Second All Christian Peace Assembly. Prague. International Secretariat of the Christian Peace Conference, 1965. 147pp. 48pp.

Christian Peace Conference. Published by the International Secretariat of the Christian Peace Conference. Praha 1, Jungmannova 9. Bi-monthly.
HUDAK, Adalbert, *Die Prager Friedenskonferenz; Kirche und kommunistischer Totalstaat in der Begegnung.* 47pp. München, Bergstadt-Verlag Wilh. Gottl. Korn, 1964.

Bibliography of the Ecumenical Movement and the World Council of Churches 1968-1985

This is an updated bibliography, and includes the major publications on ecumenical developments since 1968, dealing with the life and activities of the World Council of Churches, regional developments in the ecumenical movement, and current concerns of the Orthodox Churches and the Roman Catholic Church in the area of ecumenism.

But the bibliography, like the previous bibliography covering the years 1948-68, is necessarily selective. There are a great many books and pamphlets — not to mention articles in periodicals — and a wealth of stencilled and off-set literature and archival material not included here. Nor does it list translations of the reports of assemblies and major conferences and other official publications.

For more detailed bibliographical information readers should consult the *Classified Catalogue of the Ecumenical Movement*, 1972, 2 volumes; 1981 First Supplement (Boston: G.K. Hall and Co.); *The International Ecumenical Bibliography*, 1962-77 (München: Chr. Kaiser Verlag; Mainz: Matthias-Grünewald-Verlag); the *Répertoire Bibliographique des Institutions Chrétiennes*, 1968- (Strasbourg: CERDIC-Publications). These reference works also contain extensive bibliographical information on other ecumenical subjects and concerns not covered in this bibliography.

Geneva, July 1986   Ans J. van der Bent

General Surveys

THE GENERAL ECUMENICAL DEVELOPMENT SINCE 1968

Bloch-Hoell, Nils E. *Okumenikk. Fakta og Meniger*. Oslo: Gyldendal Norsk Forlag, 1976. 167pp.

Congar, Yves. *Essais oecuméniques: Le mouvement, les hommes, les problèmes*. Paris: Le Centurion, 1984. 316pp.

Crow, Paul A. *Christian Unity: Matrix for Mission*. New York: Friendship Press, 1982. 119pp.

Davies, Rupert E. *The Church in Our Times*. An Ecumenical History from a British Perspective. London: Epworth, 1979. 132pp.

Desseaux, Jacques Elisée. *Vingt siècles d'histoire œcuménique*. Paris: Ed. du Cerf, 1983. 110pp.

Dias, Patrick V. *Vielfalt der Kirche in der Vielfalt der Jünger, Zeugen und Diener*. Freiburg: Herder, 1968. 407pp. (Ökumenische Forschungen, Ekklesiologische Abteilung, 2).

Ecumene. By Cesare Vasoli, Hans Küng, Carlo Molari and others. Roma: Jouvence, 1983. 112pp. (La Nuova Critica, XVII Serie).

Ecumenical Methodology. Documentation and Report. Ed. by Peder Hoejen. Geneva: LWF, 1978. 129pp.

Ecumenismo anni '80. Verona: Il Segno Editrice, 1984. 420pp.

Ecumenismo oggi. Bilancio e prospettive. Asti: Ed. L.D.C., 1976. 416pp.

Fahlbusch, Erwin. *Kirchenkunde der Gegenwart.* Stuttgart: Kohlhammer, 1979. 288pp.

Fiolet, Herman A. *De Kerk op de kruispunten van de geschiedenis: Onmacht en Uitdaging.* Baarn: Ten Have, 1982. 142pp. (Oekumene, 3).

Fox, Helmut. *Ökumene, Hoffnung oder Illusion?* Eine Katholische Bilanz. Trier: Spee-Verlag, 1974. 168pp.

Frost, Francis. *Œcuménisme.* Paris: Letouzey et Ané, 1984. 99pp.

Für Willem A. Visser 't Hooft zum 80. Geburtstag. Mit Beiträgen von Nikos A. Nissiotis, Lukas Vischer, Heinrich Stirnimann, Vitali Borovoy and others. In: Reformatio, 1980. 106pp.

Gleixner, Christine. *Ökumene heute.* Eine Orientierungshilfe. Wien: Verlag Herold, 1980. 232pp.

Goodall, Norman. *Ecumenical Progress. A Decade of Change in the Ecumenical Movement, 1961-1971.* London: Oxford University Press, 1972. 173pp.

Heel de kerk. Een oekumenisch werkboek. Door A Houtepen, P. van Leeuwen, J. Roes, J. Roos, A van de Weijer. Ingeleid door N.K. van den Akker. Hilversum: Gooi en Sticht, 1977. 208pp.

Huelin, Gordon. *The Church and the Churches.* London: Sheldon Press, 1970. 87pp.

Une introduction à l'œcuménisme. Paris: Secrétariat national pour l'unité des chrétiens, 1982. 43pp.

Die Kirche im Gespräch der Kirchen. Ökumenische Themen, ausgewählt und eingeleitet vom Ökumenischen Institut Berlin. Berlin: Evangelische Verlagsanstalt, 1975. 286pp.

Kirchen auf gemeinsamen Wegen. Ed. by Johannes J. Degenhardt, Heinrich Tenhumberg, Hans Thimme. Bielefeld: Luther Verlag, 1977, 200pp.

Krüger, Hanfried. *Ökumenische Bewegung 1965-1968.* Stuttgart: Evang. Missionverlag, 1970. 172pp. (Ökumenische Rundschau, Beihefte, 12-13)

Krüger, Hanfried. *Ökumenische Bewegung 1969-1972.* Stuttgart: Evang. Missionverlag, 1973. 193pp. (Ökumenische Rundschau, Beihefte, 28).

Krüger, Hanfried. *Ökumenische Bewegung 1973-1974.* Stuttgart: Evang. Missionsverlag, 1975. (Ökumenische Rundschau, Beihefte, 29).

Lehmann, Wolfgang. *Kirche im Schmelzprozess. Berichte über zehn Frankfurter Gespräche.* Wuppertal: Verlag R. Brockhaus, 1969. 151pp.

Macquarrie, John. *Christian Unity and Christian Diversity.* London: SCM Press, 1975. 118pp.

Minus, Paul M. *The Catholic Rediscovery of Protestantism. A History of Roman Catholic Ecumenical Pioneering.* New York: Paulist Press, 1976. 261pp.

Müller-Römheld, Walter. *Zueinander — Miteinander. Kirchliche Zusammenarbeit im 20. Jahrhundert.* Frankfurt am Main: Lembeck Verlag, 1971. 196pp.

Neill, Stephen. *The Church and Christian Union.* London: Oxford University Press, 1968. 423pp.

Neuner, Peter. *Kleines Handbuch der Ökumene.* Düsseldorf: Patmos Verlag, 1984. 184pp.

Oecumene. Utrecht: Ambo, 1968. 144pp.

L'œcuménisme. Ambilly: Le Monde religieux, 1975. 276pp.

L'œcuménisme. Pierre Struve, René Beaupère, Maurice Ferrier-Welti. Tours: Mame, 1968. 166pp. (Eglises en dialogue, 7).

L'œcuménisme. Unité chrétienne et identité confessionnelle. Paris: Beauchesne, 1985. 123pp.

Ökumenische Gestalten. Brückenbauer der Einen Kirche. Hrsg. von Günther Gloede. Berlin: Evangelische Verlagsanstalt, 1974. 373pp.

Ökumenische Spannungen. Philip Potter, Konrad Raiser, Ian M. Fraser and others. Göttingen: Vandenhoeck & Ruprecht, 1974. 80pp. (Wissenschaft und Praxis in Kirche und Gesellschaft, Heft 4, April 1974).

Orientierung Ökumene. Ein Handbuch. Im Auftrag der Theologischen Studienabteilung beim Bund der Evangelischen Kirchen in der DDR, hrsg. von Hans-Martin Moderow und Matthias Sens. Berlin: Evangelische Verlagsanstalt, 1979. 342pp.

Our Common History as Christians. Essays in Honour of Albert C. Outler. Ed. by John Deschner, Leroy T. Howe, and Klaus Penzel. New York: Oxford University Press, 1975. 298pp.

Powers, Edward A. *In Essentials, Unity*. An Ecumenical Sampler. New York: Friendship Press, 1982. 119pp.

Rusch, William G. *Ecumenism — A Movement Toward Church Unity*. Philadelphia: Fortress Press, 1985. 133pp.

Schütte, Heinz. *Ziel-Kirchengemeinschaft: Zur ökumenischen Orientierung*. Paderborn: Verlag Bonifatius, 1985. 207pp.

Theologie in Entstehen. Beiträge zum ökumenischen Gespräch im Spannungsfeld kirchlicher Situationen. Hrsg. von Lukas Vischer. München: Kaiser, 1976. 144pp.

Theologischer Konsens und Kirchenspaltung. Hrsg. von Peter Lengsfeld und Heinz-Günther Stobbe. Stuttgart: Kohlhammer, 1981. 174pp.

Torrance, Thomas F. *Theology in Reconciliation*. Essays Towards Evangelical and Catholic Unity in East and West. Grand Rapids: Wm. B. Eerdmans, 1976. 302pp.

Towards Christian Unity. A Symposium. Ed. by Bernhard Leeming. London: Geoffrey Chapman, 1968. 167pp.

Unity: The Next Step? Ed. by Peter Morgan. With contributions by David L. Edwards, Michael Turnbull and others. London: SPCK, 1972. 91pp.

Vismann, Dieter. *Ökumene*. Hannover: Lutherhaus Verlag, 1980. 140pp.

Voies vers l'unité. Colloque organisé à l'occasion de l'éméritat de Mgr Gustave Thils. Louvain-la-Neuve, 27-28 avril 1979. Louvain-la-Neuve: Faculté de Théologie, 1981. 102pp.

Wainwright, Geoffrey. *The Ecumenical Movement. Crisis and Opportunity for the Church*. Grand Rapids: Wm. B. Eerdmans, 1983. 263pp.

Weinberg, Karl. *Ende der Konfessionen. Eins in Christus*. München: Profil Verlag, 1985. 110pp.

Welche Ökumene meinen wir? Eine Bilanz der Ökumene seit Nairobi. Mit Beiträgen von Richard Boeckler, Johannes Brosseder, Reinhard Frieling, Peter Lengsfeld, Harding Meyer, Otmar Schultz and others. Frankfurt am Main: Lembeck Verlag, 1978. 120pp. (Ökumenische Rundschau, Beihefte, 32).

Whale, J.S. *Christian Reunion. Historic Divisions Reconsidered*. London: Lutterworth Press, 1971. 141pp.

What Unity Implies. Six Essays after Uppsala. Ed. by Reinhard Groscurth. Geneva. WCC, 1969. 135pp. (World Council of Churches Studies, 7).

INTERPRETATIVE INTRODUCTIONS

Against the World for the World. The Hartford Appeal and the Future of American Religion. Ed. by Peter L. Berger and Richard J. Neuhaus. New York: Seabury Press, 1976. 164pp.

Beaupère René. *La trame de l'œcuménisme*. Paris: Editions œcuméniques, 1970. 5 vols.

Begegnung. Beiträge zu einer Hermeneutik des theologischen Gesprächs. Festschrift für Heinrich Fries. Hrsg. von Max Seckler, Otto Pesch, Johannes Brosseder, Wolfhart Pannenberg. Wien: Verlag Styria, 1972. 839pp.

Bent, Ans J. van der. *God So Loves the World. The Immaturity of World Christianity*. Maryknoll: Orbis Books, 1979. 150pp.

Bent, Ans J. van der. *Incarnation and New Creation. The Ecumenical Movement at the Crossroads*. Madras: Christian Literature Society, 1985. 171pp.

Bent, Ans J. van der. *Major Studies and Themes in the Ecumenical Movement*. Geneva: WCC, 1980.

Bent, Ans J. van der. *Theology — Miserable and Wonderful*. Some Personal Reflections in European and Asian Contexts. Madras: Christian Literature Society, 1982. 170pp.

Bent, Ans J. van der. *Vital Ecumenical Concerns. A Collection of Sixteen Historical, Analytical and Documentary Surveys*. Geneva: WCC, 1986, 333pp.

Biehler, Ekkehard. *Der Umbruch theologischen Denkens in der Ökumene zwischen New-Delhi und Uppsala*. Berlin: Kirchliche Hochschule, 1974. 201pp.

Boegner, Marc. *The Long Road to Unity*. Memories and Anticipations. London: Collins, 1970. 416pp.

Boss, Gerhard. *Ökumene — Fragen und Antworten*. Anregungen zum ökumenischen Gespräch. Düsseldorf: Verlag Haus Altenberg, 1970. 179pp.

Boyd, Robin. *Ecumenism, Threat or Promise?* Dublin: Irish School of Ecumenics, 1981. 15pp.

Brown, Robert McAfee. *Frontiers for the Church Today*. New York: Oxford University Press, 1973. 149pp.

Brunner, Peter. *Bemühungen um die einigende Wahrheit*. Aufsätze. Göttingen: Vandenhoeck und Ruprecht, 1977. 292pp.

Chenu, Bruno; Neusch, Marcel. *Au pays de la théologie. A la découverte des hommes et des courants*. Paris: Le Centurion, 1979. 199pp.

Congar, Yves. *Une passion: l'unité*. Réflections et souvenirs, 1929-1973. Paris: Ed. du Cerf, 1974. 117pp.

Contemporary Christian Trends. Perspectives on the Present. Ed. By William M. Pinson. Waco: Texas Word Books, 1972. 217pp.

Coventry, John. *Reconciling*. London: SCM Press, 1985. 136pp.

Desseaux, Jacques Elisée. *Dialogues théologiques et accords œcuméniques*. Paris: Ed. du Cerf, 1982. 199pp.

Directions. Theology in a Changing Church. Dublin: APCK, 1970. 255pp.

Duchrow, Ulrich. *Conflict over the Ecumenical Movement. Confessing Christ Today in the Universal Church*. Geneva: WCC, 1981. 443pp.

Fiolet, Herman A. *Ecumenical Breakthrough. An Integration of the Catholic and the Reformed Faith*. Pittsburgh, PA: Duquesne University Press, 1969. 475pp.

Fries, Heinrich. *Ökumene statt Konfessionen? Das Ringen der Kirche um Einheit*. Frankfurt am Main: J. Knecht, 1977. 168pp.

The Future of Ecumenism. Ed. by Hans Küng. New York: Paulist Press, 1969. (Concilium, 44)

Göllner, Reinhard. *Der Beitrag des Romanwerks Gertrud von le Forts zum ökumenischen Gespräch*. Paderborn: Verlag Bonifatius, 1973. 154pp.

Goodall, Norman. *Second Fiddle. Recollections and Reflections*. London: SPCK, 1979. 168pp.

Herbst, Karl. *Jenseits aller Ansprüche. Neue ökumenische Perspektiven*. Mit Nachworten von Anton Antweiler und Norbert Greinacher. München: J. Pfeiffer, 1972. 232pp.

Huber, Wolfgang. *Der Streit um die Wahrheit und die Fähigkeit zum Frieden*. Vier Kapitel ökumenischer Theologie. München: Kaiser, 1980. 147pp.

Jungclaussen, Emmanuel. *Die grössere Ökumene. Gespräch um Friedrich Heiler*. Regensburg: Verlag Friedrich Pustet, 1970. 101pp.

Krüger, Hanfried. *Ökumenischer Katechismus*. Eine kurze Einführung in Wesen, Werden und Wirken der Ökumeme. Frankfurt: Evangelisches Verlagswerk, 1985. 92pp.

May, John. *Sprache der Ökumene — Sprache der Einheit*. Die Einheit der Menschheit: zukünftige Grundlage der theologischen Ethik der Katholischen Kirche und des Oekumenischen Rates der Kirchen. Bonn: Linguistica Biblica, 1976. 521pp.

Metz, Johann Baptist. *Reform und Gegenreformation heute. Zwei Thesen zur ökumenischen Situation der Kirchen*. Mainz: Matthias-Grünewald Verlag, 1969. 44pp.

Newbigin, Lesslie. *The Other Side of 1984*. Questions for the Churches. Geneva: WCC, 1983. 75pp. (Risk Book Series, No. 18).

Newbigin, Leslie. *Unfinished Agenda. An Autobiography*. London: SPCK, 1985. 263pp.

No Man is Alien. Essays on the Unity of Mankind in Honour of Willem Adolf Visser 't Hooft. Ed. by J. Robert Nelson. Leiden: Brill, 1971. 334pp.

Oecumenica. An Annual Symposium of Ecumenical Research. Ed. by Friedrich Wilhelm Kantzenbach and Vilmos Vajta. Neuchâtel: Delachaux et Niestlé, 1968, 1970, 1971, 1972.

Ökumene: Möglichkeiten und Grenzen heute. Oscar Cullmann zum achtzigsten Geburtstag, 1982. Hrsg. von Karlfried Froehlich. Tübingen: Mohr, 1982. 173pp.

Oekumene verändert die Kirchen. Beiträge von Helmut Hild, Christian Hübener und André Appel. Göttingen: Vandenhoeck und Ruprecht, 1976. 50pp.

Ökumenische Theologie. Ein Arbeitsbuch. Hrsg. von Peter Lengsfeld. Stuttgart: Kohlhammer, 1980. 508pp.

Pluralisme et œcuménisme en recherches théologiques. Mélanges offerts au R.P. Dockx, O.P. par Y. Congar, N. Zernov et al. Gembloux: Duculot, 1976. 314pp.

Post-Ecumenical Christianity. Ed. by Hans Küng. New York: Herder and Herder, 1970. 160pp. (Concilium, 54).

Potter, Philip A. *Life in All its Fulness*. Geneva: WCC, 1981. 173pp.

Richter, Hans-Friedemann. *Die Kommende Ökumene. Theologische Untersuchungen*. Zum 25.jährigen Bestehen des Ökumenischen Seminars an der Kirchlichen Hochschule Berlin. Festschrift für Jürgen W. Winterhager. Wuppertal: Verlag Rolf Brockhaus, 1972. 288pp.

Roux, Hébert. *De la désunion vers la communion*. Un itinéraire pastoral et œcuménique. Paris: Le Centurion, 1978. 311pp.

Scheele, Paul-Werner. *Alle eins: Theologische Beiträge II*. Paderborn: Verlag Bonifatius, 1979. 269pp.

Schmidt-Clausen, Kurt. *Reformation als ökumenisches Ereignis*. Reden und Aufsätze zu
Themen der ökumenischen Bewegung. Berlin: Lutherisches Verlagshaus, 1970.
331pp.

Schrey, Heinz-Horst. *Christliche Daseinsgestaltung. Ökumenische Stellungnahmen zu
Fragen der Gegenwart*. Bremen: C. Schünemann, 1971. 617pp.

Stobbe, Heinz Günther. *Hermeneutik — ein ökumenisches Problem*. Eine Kritik der
katholischen Gadamer-Rezeption. Zürich: Benziger, 1981. 178pp.

Till, Barry. *The Churches Search for Unity*. Harmondsworth, Middlesex: Penguin
Books, 1972. 556pp.

Unterwegs zur Einheit. Festschrift für Heinrich Stirnimann. Hrsg. von Johannes
Brantschen und Pietro Selvatico. Freiburg: Universitätsverlag, 1980. 942pp.

Until He Comes. A Study in the Progress Toward Christian Unity. Ed. by Nicolas Lash.
Dayton, Ohio: Pflaum Press, 1968. 223pp.

Vischer, Lukas. *Ökumenische Skizzen*. Zwölf Beiträge. Frankfurt am Main: Lembeck
Verlag, 1972. 246pp.

Visser 't Hooft, Willem Adolf. *Has the Ecumenical Movement a Future?* Belfast:
Christian Journals Limited, 1974. 97pp.

Visser 't Hooft, Willem Adolf. *Memoirs*. London: SCM press, 1973. 379pp.

Voices of Unity. Essays in Honour of Willem Adolf Visser 't Hooft on the Occasion of
His 80th Birthday. Ed. by Ans J. van der Bent. Geneva: WCC, 1981. 101pp.

Zukunft der Ökumene. Drei Vorträge von Heinrich Stirnimann, Willem Adolf Visser 't
Hooft, Hans Jochen Margull. Freiburg: Universitätsverlag, 1974. 42pp.
(Ökumenische Beihefte, 7).

Die Zukunft des Ökumenismus. Mit Beiträgen von Per Lonning, Georges Casalis,
Bernhard Hering und einer Einleitung von Günther Gassmann. Frankfurt am Main:
Otto Lembeck, 1972. 109pp. (Ökumenische Perspektiven, 1).

Books about the World Council of Churches

Bent, Ans J. van der. *Six Hundred Ecumenical Consultations, 1948-1982*. Geneva:
WCC, 1983. 246pp.

Bent, Ans J. van der. *The Utopia of World Community. An Interpretation of the World
Council of Churches for Outsiders*. London: SCM Press, 1973. 150pp.

Bent, Ans J. van der. *What in the World is the World Council of Churches?* With an
Interview with Philip Potter. Geneva: WCC, 1978. 4th printing, 1983. 90pp.

Bock, Paul. *In Search of a Responsible World Society. The Social Teachings of the
World Council of Churches*. Philadelphia: Westminster Press, 1974. 251pp.

Bouman, Johan. *Der Glaube an das Menschenmögliche. Der Ökumenische Rat der
Kirchen und der Friede*. Giessen: Brunnen Verlag, 1984. 69pp.

Brash, Alan A. *The World Council of Churches*. Geneva: WCC, 1978. 34pp.

Chappuis, Jean-Marc. *Divisions des chrétiens ou service de l'unité? Jalons pour
interpréter l'action du Conseil œcuménique des Eglises*. Genève: Labor et Fides,
1979. 57pp.

Chenu, Bruno. *La signification ecclésiologique du Conseil œcuménique des Eglises,
1945-1963*. Thèse de doctorat en théologie. Paris: Beauchesne, 1972. 418pp.

Constitution and Rules of the World Council of Churches as Approved by the Vth Assembly at Nairobi and Amended by the Central Committee at Geneva, 28 July to 6 August 1977. Geneva: WCC, 1977. 32pp.

Faith and Faithfulness. Essays on Contemporary Ecumenical Themes. A Tribute to Philip A. Potter. Ed. by Pauline Webb. Geneva: WCC, 1984. 128pp.

Fuerth, Patrick W. *The Concept of Catholicity in the Documents of the World Council of Churches 1948-1968.* A Historical Study with Systematic-Theological Reflections. Roma: Editrice Anselmiana, 1973. 291pp.

García Hernando, Julián. *El Consejo Ecuménico de las Iglesias. Ante la Asamblea de Vancouver 1983.* Madrid: Centro Ecuménico "Misionarias de la Unidad", 1982. 64pp.

Handbook of Member Churches of the World Council of Churches. Ed. by Ans J. van der Bent. Geneva: WCC, 1982. 1985 (revised edition). 281pp.

Howell, Leon. *Acting in Faith. The World Council of Churches since 1975.* Geneva, WCC, 1982. 120pp.

The Human Face of the World Council of Churches. London: The Methodist Church Overseas Division, 1981. 32pp.

Payne, Ernest A. *The World Council of Churches, 1948-1969.* London: The Baptist Union of Great Britain and Ireland, 1970. 20pp.

Rowe, Richard C. *Bible Study in the World Council of Churches.* Geneva: WCC, 1969. 81pp. (CWME Research Pamphlets, 16).

Runia, K. *De Wereldraad in Discussie.* Met reacties van E. Flesseman-van Leer, H. Berkhof, A.H. van den Heuvel. Kampen: J.H. Kok, 1978. 184pp.

Schrotenboer, Paul G. *The Social Teaching of the World Council of Churches.* Grand Rapids: Reformed Ecumenical Synod, 1978. 31pp.

Visser 't Hooft, Willem Adolf. *The Genesis and Formation of the World Council of Churches.* Geneva: WCC, 1982. 130pp.

Wegener-Feuter, Hildburg. *Kirche und Ökumene.* Das Kirchenbild des Ökumenischen Rates der Kirchen nach den Vollversammlungsdokumenten von 1948-1968. Göttingen: Vandenhoek und Ruprecht, 1979. 306pp.

The World Council of Churches and the Churches. By Anna Marie Aagaard, Johannes M. Aagaard and others. Aarhus: IDOC, 1969. 94pp.

The Life and Activities of the World Council of Churches

Fifth Assembly: Nairobi 1975

Breaking Barriers, Nairobi 1975. The Official Report of the Fifth Assembly of the World Council of Churches, Nairobi, 23 November-10 December 1975. Ed. by David M. Paton. London: SPCK; Grand Rapids: Wm. B. Eerdmans, 1976. 411pp.

Dat was Nairobi. H.A.M. Fiolet, Hendrik Greven, A.H. van den Heuvel, H.M. de Lange, D.C. Mulder. 's-Gravenhage: Boekencentrum, 1976. 112pp.

Eenheid door bevrijding: Jesus Christus bevrijdt en verenigt. A.H. van den Heuvel, H. Berkhof, H.A. Fiolet and others. Kampen: Kok, 1975. 109pp.

Jesus Christ Frees and Unites. World Council of Churches, Fifth Assembly Jakarta, 1975. New York: Friendship Press, 1974. 48pp.

Jesus Christ Frees and Unites. Bible Studies Prepared for the Fifth Assembly of the World Council of Churches, Nairobi 1975. 37pp.

Jesus Christ Frees and Unites. Dossiers. 5th Assembly World Council of Churches, Nairobi 1975. Geneva: WCC, 1974. 6 vols.

Leitourgia. A Worship Book for the Fifth Assembly of the World Council of Churches. Geneva: WCC, 1975 (Risk, Vol. 11, No. 2-3, 1975). 96pp.

Ökumene im Spiegel von Nairobi '75. Hrsg. von Peter Beyerhaus und Ulrich Betz. Bad Liebenzell: Verlag der Liebenzeller Mission, 1976. 376pp.

Orthodox Contributions to Nairobi. Papers Compiled and Presented by the Orthodox Task Force of the WCC. Geneva: WCC, 1975. 35pp.

Runia, K. *Nairobi in Perspektief.* Kampen: Kok, 1976. 106pp.

Scheele, Paul-Werner. *Nairobi, Genf, Rom.* Die Weltchristenheit vor und nach der 5. Vollversammlung des Ökumenischen Rates der Kirchen. Paderborn: Verlag-Bonifacius, 1976. 198pp.

Slack, Kenneth. *Nairobi Narrative.* The Story of the Fifth Assembly of the World Council of Churches 1975. London: SCM Press, 1976. 90pp.

Uppsala to Nairobi 1968-1975. Report of the Central Committee to the Fifth Assembly of the World Council of Churches. Ed. by David E. Johnson. London: SPCK, 1975. 256pp.

Vischer, Lukas. *Veränderung der Welt — Bekehrung der Kirchen.* Denkanstösse der Fünften Vollversammlung des Ökumenischen Rates der Kirchen in Nairobi. Frankfurt: Lembeck, 1976. 111pp.

Welche Ökumene meinen wir? Eine Bilanz der Ökumene seit Nairobi. Mit Beiträgen von Richard Boeckler, Johannes Brosseder, Reinhard Frieling, Peter Lengsfeld, Harding Meyer, Otmar Schultz, and others. Frankfurt: Lembeck, 1978 (Ökumenische Rundschau, Beihefte, 32). 120pp.

Workbook for the Fifth Assembly of the World Council of Churches. Nairobi, Kenya, 23 November-10 December 1975. Geneva: WCC, 1975. 176pp.

Sixth Assembly: Vancouver 1983

An African Call for Life. Contribution to the World Council of Churches Sixth Assembly Theme "Jesus Christ — the Life of the World". Ed. by Masamba ma Mpolo, Reginald Stober, Evelyn V. Appiah. Geneva: WCC, 1983, 152pp.

Assembly Assembling. Towards the Sixth Assembly of the World Council of Churches, Vancouver 1983. Geneva: WCC, 1981. 15pp.

Assembly Directory. Sixth Assembly of the World Council of Churches, Vancouver 1983. Vancouver: WCC Assembly, 1983. 28pp.

Booth, Rodney M. *The Winds of God.* The Canadian Church faces the 1980s. Geneva: WCC, 1982. 128pp. (Risk Book Series, No. 16).

Christians for Peace and Justice. Contribution of the Christian Peace Conference to the Sixth Assembly of the World Council of Churches in Vancouver. Prague: CPC, 1983. 45pp.

Conway, Martin. *Look – Listen – Care.* London: British Council of Churches, 1983. 62pp.

Driemaal de basis, en eenmaal de top. Over het thema van Vancouver. Amsterdam: Allerwegen, 1983. 52pp.

The Feast of Life. The Eucharist at the Sixth Assembly of the World Council of Churches, Vancouver 1983. La fête de la vie... Das Fest des Lebens... Geneva: WCC, 1983. 40pp.

Fiolet, Herman A.M. *Vanuit Vancouver*. Impressies en rapporten van de zesde assemblee van de Wereldraad van Kerken, gehouden te Vancouver in de periode 24 juli-10 augustus 1983. Amersfoort: De Horstink, 1983. 139pp.

García Hernando, Julián. *El Consejo Ecuménico de las Iglesias*. Ante la Asamblea de Vancouver 1983. Madrid: Centro Ecuménico "Misioneras de la Unidad", 1982. 64pp.

Gathered for Life. Official Report, Sixth Assembly of the World Council of Churches, Vancouver, Canada, 24 July-10 August 1983. Ed. by David Gill. Geneva: WCC; Grand Rapids: Eerdmans, 1983. 355pp.

Gerechtigheid, eenheid en vrede. De oecumenische agenda van de Wereldraadbijeenkomst te Vancouver 1983. Een bundel studies onder redactie van Anton Houtepen. Amersfoort: De Horstink, 1982. 150pp.

Images of Life. An Invitation to Bible Study. Geneva: WCC, 1982. Pagination varies.

Issues. Discussion Papers on Issues Arising Out of the Life and Work of the World Council of Churches in Preparation for its Sixth Assembly, Vancouver, Canada, 24 July-10 August 1983. Geneva: WCC, 1982. Pagination varies.

Jesus Christ — the Life of the World. An Orthodox Contribution to the Vancouver Theme. Ed. by Ion Bria. Geneva: WCC, 1982. 121pp.

Jesus Christ — the Life of the World. Jésus-Christ, vie du monde. Jesus Christus, das Leben der Welt. Jesucristo, vida del mundo. A Worship Book for the Sixth Assembly... Geneva: WCC, 1983. 166pp.

Jesus Christ With People in Asia. Report of the Asian Consultation in Singapore, 5-11 July, 1982 on the Theme "Jesus Christ — the Life of the World". Singapore: Asia Task Force of the WCC Office, 1983. 73pp.

Long, Charles Henry. *Vancouver Voices*. The Sixth Assembly of the World Council of Churches. A Personal Report. Cincinnati: Forward Movement Publications, 1983. 119pp.

The Lord of Life. Theological Explorations of the Theme "Jesus Christ — the Life of the World". Ed. by William H. Lazareth. Geneva: WCC, 1983. 164pp.

Lorenz Günter. *Vancouver — erlebt und notiert*. Eindrücke von der sechsten Weltkirchenkonferenz. Berlin: Evangelische Verlagsanstalt, 1984. 135pp.

The Meaning of Life. A Multifaith Consultation in Preparation for the Sixth Assembly of the World Council of Churches. Mauritius, 25 January-3 February 1983. Geneva: WCC, 1983. 20pp.

Nairobi to Vancouver, 1975-83. Report of the Central Committee to the Sixth Assembly of the World Council of Churches. Geneva: WCC, 1983. 238pp.

No Longer Strangers. A Resource of Women and Worship. Ed. by Iben Gjerding and Katherine Kinnamon. Geneva: WCC, 1983. 80pp.

Ökumenische Impressionen Vancouver 1983. Mit Beiträgen von Gerhard E. Stoll, Dieter Trautwein and others. Hrsg. von Konrad Raiser. Frankfurt: Lembeck, 1983. 134pp.

Poulton John. *The Feast of Life*. A Theological Reflection on the Theme "Jesus Christ — the Life of the World". Geneva: WCC, 1982. 78pp. (Risk Book Series, 14).

Struggle Against Death. WCC Vancouver Assembly 1983. Co-Ordinators of the Study Programme: Paulos Gregorios, M.J. Joseph, K.M. George. Kottayam: The Editorial Board for the Study Programme, 1982. 167pp.

Who's Who. Revised Edition November 1983. Geneva: WCC, 1983. No pagination.

Work Book Vancouver 83. Work Book for the Sixth Assembly of the World Council of Churches, Vancouver, Canada, 24 July-10 August 1983. 119pp.

Central Committees

Minutes and Reports of the ... meeting of the Central Committee of the World Council of Churches, Geneva, WCC, 1968-85:

1968	21st meeting	Uppsala, Sweden	22pp.
1968	22nd meeting	Uppsala, Sweden	13pp.
1969	23rd meeting	Canterbury, Great Britain	296pp.
1971	24th meeting	Addis Abeba, Ethiopia	313pp.
1972	25th meeting	Utrecht, The Netherlands	274pp.
1973	26th meeting	Geneva, Switzerland	260pp.
1974	27th meeting	Berlin (West)	87pp.
1975	28th meeting	Nairobi, Kenya	35pp.
1976	29th meeting	Geneva, Switzerland	114pp.
1977	30th meeting	Geneva, Switzerland	123pp.
1979	31st meeting	Kingston, Jamaica	171pp.
1980	32nd meeting	Geneva, Switzerland	175pp.
1981	33rd meeting	Dresden, German Democratic Republic	163pp.
1982	34th meeting	Geneva, Switzerland	153pp.
1983	35th meeting	Vancouver, Canada	42pp.
1984	36th meeting	Geneva, Switzerland	195pp.
1985	37th meeting	Buenos Aires, Argentina	128pp.

Executive Committees

Minutes of meetings of the Executive Committee of the World Council of Churches (mimeographed, in archives of WCC library), 1969-86.

1969, Jan.	Tulsa, OK, USA
1969, Aug.	Canterbury, England
1970, Febr.	Geneva, Switzerland
1970, Aug./Sept.	Arnoldshain, Federal Republic of Germany
1971, Jan.	Addis Abeba, Ethiopia
1971, Sept.	Sofia, Bulgaria
1972, Febr.	Auckland, New Zealand
1972, Aug.	Utrecht, The Netherlands
1973, Jan.	Bangalore, India
1973, Aug.	Geneva, Switzerland
1974, Febr.	Bad Saarow, German Democratic Republic
1974, Aug.	Berlin (West)
1975, Apr.	Geneva, Switzerland
1975, Nov.	Nairobi, Kenya
1976, Mar.	Geneva, Switzerland
1976, Aug.	Geneva, Switzerland
1977, Febr.	Geneva, Switzerland
1977, July	Geneva, Switzerland
1978, Febr.	Zurich, Switzerland
1978, Sept.	Helsinki, Finland
1978, Dec.	Kingston, Jamaica
1979, Sept.	Bossey, Switzerland

1980, Febr.	Liebfrauenberg, Woerth, France
1980, Aug.	Geneva, Switzerland
1981, Febr.	Geneva, Switzerland
1981, Aug.	Dresden, German Democratic Republic
1982, Febr.	Geneva, Switzerland
1982, July	Geneva, Switzerland
1983, Febr./Mar.	Geneva, Switzerland
1983, July	Vancouver, BC, Canada
1984, Febr.	Geneva, Switzerland
1984, July	Geneva, Switzerland
1985, Febr.	Geneva, Switzerland
1985, July	Buenos Aires, Argentina

Conferences and Official Publications
of the Sub-Units of the World Council of Churches

UNIT I

Faith and Order

Faith and Order. Louvain 1971. Study Reports and Documents. Geneva: WCC, 1971. 264pp. (Faith and Order Paper, No. 59).

Uniting in Hope. Reports and Documents from the Meeting of the Faith and Order Commission. 23 July-5 August 1974, University of Ghana, Legon. Geneva: WCC, 1975. 144pp. (Faith and Order Paper, No. 72).

Sharing in One Hope. Reports and Documents from the Meeting of the Faith and Order Commission, 15-30 August 1978, Bangalore, India. Geneva: WCC, 1978. 290pp. (Faith and Order Paper, No. 92).

Towards Visible Unity. Commission on Faith and Order, Lima 1982. Vol. I: Minutes and Addresses; Vol. II: Study Papers and Reports. Ed. by Michael Kinnamon. Geneva: WCC, 1982. 2 vols. (Faith and Order Paper, Nos. 112 and 113).

Faith and Renewal. Reports and Documents of the Commission on Faith and Order, Stavanger, Norway, 13-25 August 1985. Ed. by Thomas F. Best. Geneva: WCC, 1986. 256pp. (Faith and Order Paper, No. 131).

And Do Not Hinder Them. An Ecumenical Plea for the Admission of Children to the Eucharist. Ed. by Geiko Müller-Fahrenholz. Geneva: WCC, 1982. 81pp. (Faith and Order Paper, No. 109).

Apostolic Faith Today. A Handbook for Study. Ed. by Hans-Georg Link. Geneva: WCC, 1985. 280pp. (Faith and Order Paper, No. 124).

Baptism and Eucharist. Ecumenical Conversion in Celebration. Ed. by Max Thurian and Geoffrey Wainwright. Geneva: WCC; Grand Rapids: Eerdmans, 1983. 258pp. (Faith and Order Paper, No. 117).

Baptism, Eucharist and Ministry. Geneva: WCC, 1982. 33pp. (Faith and Order Paper, No. 111).

The Bible: Its Authority and Interpretation in the Ecumenical Movement. Ed. by Ellen Flesseman-van-Leer. Geneva: WCC, 1980. 79pp. (Faith and Order Paper, No. 99).

Called to be One in Christ. United Churches and the Ecumenical Movement. Ed. by Michael Kinnamon and Thomas F. Best. Geneva: WCC, 1985. 77pp. (Faith and Order Paper, No. 127).

Church and State. Opening a New Ecumenical Discussion. A Colloquium Held at the Ecumenical Institute Bossey, 19-25 August 1976. Geneva: WCC, 1976. 181pp. (Faith and Order Paper, No. 85).

Churches Respond to BEM. Official Responses to the "Baptism, Eucharist and Ministry" Text, Vol 1. Ed. by Max Thurian. Geneva: WCC, 1986. 129pp. (Faith and Order Paper, No. 129).

Confessing our Faith Around the World, I. With a Foreword by C.S. Song. Geneva: WCC, 1980. 84pp. (Faith and Order Paper, No. 104).

Confessing Our Faith Around the World, II. Ed. by Hans-Georg Link. Geneva: WCC, 1983. 100pp. (Faith and Order Paper, No. 120).

Confessing Our Faith Around the World, III. The Caribbean and Central America. Ed. by Hans-George Link. Geneva: WCC, 1984. 110pp. (Faith and Order Paper, No. 123).

Confessing Our Faith Around the World, IV. South America. Ed. by Hans-Georg Link. Geneva: WCC, 1985. 111pp. (Faith and Order Paper, No. 126).

Councils, Conciliarity and a Genuinely Universal Council. Geneva: WCC, 1974. 24pp. (Faith and Order Paper, No. 70).

Ecumenical Exercise II. The Church of God, the Russian Old Ritualists, the Church of the Nazarene. Ed. by Gerald F. Moede. Geneva: WCC, 1971. 50pp. (Faith and Order Paper, No. 58).

Ecumenical Exercise III. The Church of the Lord, the Assemblies of the Brethren, the African Brotherhood Church. Ed. by Gerald F. Moede. Geneva: WCC, 1972. 41pp. (Faith and Order Paper, No. 61).

Ecumenical Exercise IV. The Wesleyan Church. The Christ Apostolic Church. Mennonites. Ed. by Robert Welsh. Geneva: WCC, 1976. 32pp. (Faith and Order Paper, No. 79).

Ecumenical Exercise V. The Presbyterian Church in Mizoram. The Gypsy Evangelical Church. The Churches of Christ. Ed. by Stephen Cranford. Geneva: WCC, 1979. 24pp. (Faith and Order Paper, No. 94).

Ecumenical Perspectives on Baptism, Eucharist and Ministry. Ed. by Max Thurian. Geneva: WCC, 1983. 246pp. (Faith and Order Paper, No. 116).

Ehrenström, Nils and Gassmann, Günther. *Confessions in Dialogue*. A Survey of Bilateral Conversations Among World Confessional Families 1962-1971. Geneva: WCC, 1972. 166pp. (Faith and Order Paper, No. 63).

Ehrenström, Nils and Gassmann, Günther. *Confessions in Dialogue*. A Survey of Bilateral Conversations Among World Confessional Families 1959-1974. Geneva: WCC, 1975. 266pp. (Faith and Order Paper, No. 74).

Ehrenström, Nils. *Mutual Recognition of Baptism in Inter-Church Agreements*. Geneva: WCC, 1978. (Faith and Order Paper, No. 90).

Episkopé and Episcopate in Ecumenical Perspective. Geneva: WCC, 1980. 59pp. (Faith and Order Paper, No. 102).

Fourth Forum on Bilateral Conversations. Report. Geneva: WCC, 1985. 20pp. (Faith and Order Paper, No. 125).

Giving Account of the Hope Today. Geneva: WCC, 1976. 54pp. (Faith and Order Paper, No. 81).

Giving Account of the Hope Together. Geneva: WCC, 1978. 135pp. (Faith and Order Paper, No. 86).

Growing Towards Consensus and Commitment. Report of the Fourth International Consultation of United and Uniting Churches, Colombo, Sri Lanka, 1980. Geneva: WCC, 1981. 82pp. (Faith and Order Paper, No. 110).

Growth in Agreement. Reports and Agreed Statements of Ecumenical Conversations on a World Level. Ed. by Harding Meyer and Lukas Vischer. Geneva: WCC, 1984. 514pp. (Faith and Order Paper, No. 108).

How Can Unity be Achieved?. Ecumenical Case Studies: Ghana, Korea, Rumania, Switzerland, Uruguay. Ed. by Robert Welsh. Geneva: WCC, 1975. 35pp. (Faith and Order Paper, No. 75).

How Does the Church Teach Authoritatively Today? Geneva: WCC, 17pp. (Faith and Order Paper, No. 91).

Lausanne 77. Fifty Years of Faith and Order. Geneva: WCC, 1977. 82pp. (Faith and Order Paper, No. 82).

Lazareth, William H. *Growing Together in Baptism, Eucharist and Ministry.* A Study Guide. Geneva: WCC, 1982. 107pp. (Faith and Order Paper, No. 114).

Louisville: Consultation on Baptism. Geneva: WCC, 1980. 108pp. (Faith and Order Paper, No. 97).

Müller-Fahrenholz, Geiko. *Partners in Life. The Handicapped and the Church.* Geneva: WCC, 1979. 184pp. (Faith and Order Paper, No. 89).

Müller-Fahrenholz, Geiko. *Unity in Today's World.* The Faith and Order Studies on: "Unity of the Church — Unity of Humankind". Geneva: WCC, 1978. 240pp. (Faith and Order Paper, No. 88).

One Baptism, one Eucharist and a Mutually Recognized Ministry. Three Agreed Statements. Geneva: WCC, 1975. 65pp. (Faith and Order Paper, No. 73).

Ordination of Women in Ecumenical Perspective. Workbook for the Church's Future. Ed. by Constance F. Parvey. Geneva: WCC, 1980. 96pp. (Faith and Order Paper, No. 105).

The Orthodox Church and the Churches of the Reformation. A Survey of Orthodox-Protestant Dialogues. Geneva: WCC, 1975. 101pp. (Faith and Order Paper, No. 76).

Orthodox Perspectives on Baptism, Eucharist, and Ministry. Ed. by Gennadios Limouris and Nomikos M. Vaporis. Brookline, Mass.: Holy Cross Orthodox Press, 1985. 168pp. (Faith and Order Paper, No. 128).

The Roots of Our Common Faith. Faith in Scriptures and in the Early Church. Ed. by Hans-Georg Link. Geneva: WCC, 1984. 135pp. (Faith and Order Paper, No. 119).

Spirit of God, Spirit of Christ. Ecumenical Reflections on the Filioque Controversy. Ed. by Lukas Vischer. Geneva: WCC, 1981. 186pp. (Faith and Order Paper, No. 103).

Survey of Church Union Negotiations 1967-1969. Geneva: WCC, 1970. 34pp. (Faith and Order Paper, No. 56).

Survey of Church Union Negotiations 1969-1971. Geneva: WCC, 1972. 20pp. (Faith and Order Paper, No. 64).

Survey of Church Union Negotiations 1971-1973. Geneva: WCC, 1974. 22pp. (Faith and Order Paper, No. 68).

Survey of Church Union Negotiations 1973-1975. Geneva: WCC, 1976. 42pp. (Faith and Order Paper, No. 78).

Survey of Church Union Negotiations 1975-1977. Geneva: WCC, 1978. 30pp. (Faith and Order Paper, No. 87).

Survey of Church Union Negotiations 1977-1979. Ed. by A.H. Harry Oussoren. Geneva: WCC, 1980. 30pp. (Faith and Order Paper, No. 101).

Survey of Church Union Negotiations 1979-1981. Ed. by Michael Kinnamon. Geneva: WCC, 1982. 32pp. (Faith and Order Paper, No. 115).

Survey of Church Union Negotiations 1981-1982. Ed. by Thomas F. Best. Geneva: WCC, 1984. 16pp. (Faith and Order Paper, No. 122).

The Three Reports of the Forum on Bilateral Conversations. Geneva: WCC, 1981. 52pp. (Faith and Order Paper, No. 107).

Towards a Confession of the Common Faith. Geneva: WCC, 1980. 13pp. (Faith and Order Paper, No. 100).

Towards an Ecumenical Consensus on Baptism, the Eucharist and the Ministry. Geneva: WCC, 1977. 31pp. (Faith and Order Paper, No. 84).

Unity In Each Place — In All Places. United Churches and the Christian World Communions. Ed. by Michael Kinnamon. Geneva: WCC, 1983. 135pp. (Faith and Order Paper, No. 118).

Vischer, Lukas. *Intercession*. Geneva: WCC, 1980. 66pp. (Faith and Order Paper, No. 95).

What kind of Unity? Geneva: WCC, 1974. 131pp. (Faith and Order Paper, No. 69).

What Unity Requires. Papers and Report on the Unity of the Church. Geneva: WCC, 1976. 74pp. (Faith and Order Paper, No. 77).

World Mission and Evangelism

Salvation Today and Contemporary Experience. A Collection of Texts for Critical Study and Reflection. Geneva: WCC, 1972. 110pp.

Bangkok Assembly 1973. Minutes and Reports of the Assembly of the Commission on World Mission and Evangelism, 31 December, 1972 and 9-12 January 1973. Geneva: WCC, 1973. 118pp.

Beyerhaus, Peter. *Bangkok 1973. The Beginning or End of the World Mission?* Grand Rapids: Zondervan, 1973. 192pp.

The Evangelical Response to Bangkok. Ed. by Ralph Winter. South Pasadena, CA: William Carey, 1973. 153pp.

From Mexico City to Bangkok. Report of the Commission on World Mission and Evangelism 1963-1972. Geneva: WCC, 1973. 94pp.

Sovik, Arne. *Salvation Today*. Minneapolis, Minnesota: Augsburg Publishing House, 1973. 112pp.

Webb, Pauline. *Salvation Today*. London: SCM Press, 1974. 117pp.

Gort, Jerald D. *World Missionary Conference Melbourne, May 1980*. An Historical and Missiological Interpretation. Amsterdam: Free University, Department of Missiology, 1980. 30pp.

Newbigin, Lesslie. *Sign of the Kingdom* Grand Rapids: Eerdmans, 1980. 70pp.

Your Kingdom Come. Mission Perspectives. Report of the World Conference on Mission and Evangelism at Melbourne, Australia, 12-25 May 1980. Geneva: WCC, 1980. 283pp.

Witnessing to the Kingdom. Melbourne and Beyond. Ed. by Gerald H. Anderson. Maryknoll, NY: Orbis Books, 1982. 170pp.

Banana, Canaan. *The Gospel According to the Ghetto*. Salisbury: Mambo Press, 1980. 88pp.

Can Churches be Compared? Reflections on Fifteen Study Projects. Ed. by Steven G. Mackie. Geneva: WCC, 1970. 101pp. (CWME Research Pamphlets, No. 17).

Castro, Emilio. *Freedom in Mission. The Perspective of the Kingdom of God*. An Ecumenical Inquiry. Geneva: WCC, 1985. 348pp.

Castro, Emilio. *Sent Free. Mission and Unity in the Perspective of the Kingdom*. Geneva: WCC, 1985. 102pp. (Risk Book Series, No. 23).

The Christian Community in Mission — in a Near and Global Context. A European Seminar on Education for Mission, Aarhus, Denmark, May 1977. Geneva: WCC, 1978. 40pp.

Crossing Boundaries. Stories from the Frontier Intership in Mission Programme. Compiled by Kathleen Todd. Geneva: WCC, 1985. 108pp. (WCC Mission Series, No. 5).

Directory of Study Centres. Geneva: WCC, 1982. 83pp.

Edinburgh to Melbourne. Geneva: WCC, 1978. In: *International Review of Mission*, Vol. 67, No. 27, pp.249-396.

Eve of the Storm, The Great Debate in Mission. Ed. by Donald McGavran. Waco, Texas: World Books, 1972. 299pp.

Go Forth in Peace A Pastoral and Missionary Guidebook. Reports and Documents from the Orthodox Missionary Consultations 1974-1980. Ed. by Ion Bria. Geneva: WCC, 1982. 54pp.

Hallencreutz, Carl F. *New Approaches to Men of Other Faiths, 1938-1968*. A Theological Discussion. Geneva: WCC, 1970. 95pp. (Research Pamphlet, No. 18).

Howell, Leon. *People are the Subject*. Stories of Urban Rural Mission. Geneva: WCC, 1980. 80pp.

McGavran, Donald. *The Conciliar-Evangelical Debate*. The Crucial Documents, 1964-1976. South Pasadena, CA: William Carey, 1977. 397pp.

Martyria — Mission. The Witness of the Orthodox Churches Today. Ed. by Ion Bria. Geneva: WCC, 1980. 255pp.

Mission and Evangelism. An Ecumenical Affirmation. Geneva: WCC, 1982. 24pp.

Mission and Evangelism. An Ecumenical Affirmation. A Study Guide Compiled by Jean Stromberg. Geneva: WCC, 1983. 84pp.

Mission and Justice. Urban and Industrial Mission at Work. Geneva: WCC, 1977. 70pp.

Orthodox Consultation on Confessing Christ Through Liturgical Life of the Church Today. Report of the Orthodox Consultation at Etchmiadzine, Armenia, 16-21 September 1975. Geneva: WCC, 1975. 31pp.

The Role of the Study Centres. Consultation Report, Singapore, 2-8 December 1980. Geneva: WCC, 1981. 25pp.

Sharing One Bread, Sharing One Mission. The Eucharist as Missionary Event. Ed. by Jean Stromberg. Geneva: WCC, 1983. 79pp. (WCC Mission Series, No. 3).

Struggle to be Human. Stories of Urban-Industrial Mission. Ed. by Bobbi Wells Hargleroad. Geneva: WCC, 1972. 78pp.

Urban Rural Mission. Africa Urban Rural Mission Consultation, Nairobi, Kenya, 3-8 October 1979. Geneva: WCC, 1979. 69pp.

The Witness of St Methodius. Orthodox Mission in the 9th century. Ed. by Ion Bria. Geneva: WCC, 1985. 43pp.

What is CWME? A Brief History of the Commission on World Mission and Evangelism. Geneva: WCC, 1984. 25pp.

Church and Society

From Here to Where? Technology, Faith and the Future of Man. Report on an Exploratory Conference, Geneva, 28 June-4 July 1970. Ed. by David Gill. Geneva: WCC, 1970. 111pp.

Report of an Ecumenical Consultation on Global Environment, Economic Growth and Social Justice. Cardiff, 3-8 September 1972. Geneva: WCC, 1972. 34pp. *Anticipation*, No. 13.

Report of an Ecumenical Conference on the Scientific, Technological and Social Revolutions in Asian Perspective. Kuala Lumpur, Malaysia, 19-23 April 1973. Geneva: WCC, 1973. 36pp. *Anticipation*, No. 14.

The Technological Future of the Industrialized Nations and the Quality of Life. Report from a North American — European Conference, Pont-à-Mousson, France, 27 May-2 June 1973. Geneva: WCC, 1973. 49pp. *Anticipation*, No. 15.

Science and Technology for Human Development. The Ambiguous Future and the Christian Hope. Selected Preparatory Papers for the 1974 World Conference in Bucharest, Romania. Geneva: WCC, 1974. 61pp. *Anticipation*, No. 17.

Science and Technology for Human Development. The Ambiguous Future and the Christian Hope. Report of the 1974 World Conference in Bucharest, Romania. Geneva: WCC, 1974. 43pp. *Anticipation*, No. 19.

Faith, Science and the Future. Preparatory Readings for a World Conference, Cambridge, Mass., 12-24 July 1979. Ed. by Paul Abrecht, Charles Birch, John Francis. Geneva: WCC, 1978. 236pp.

Faith and Science in an Unjust World. Report of the WCC Conference on Faith, Science and the Future, Cambridge, Mass., 12-24 July 1979. Vol. 1: Plenary Presentations. Ed. by Roger L. Shinn. Geneva: WCC, 1980. 392pp.

Faith and Science in an Unjust World. Report of the WCC Conference on Faith, Science and the Future, Cambridge, Mass., 12-24 July 1979. Vol. 2: Reports and Recommendations. Ed. by Paul Abrecht. Geneva: WCC, 1980. 214pp.

Burning Issues. Papers from the Consultation in Cambridge, 20-26 1977. Papers from the Consultation in Zürich, 11-16 July 1977. Geneva: WCC, 1979. 79pp. *Anticipation*, No. 25.

Burning Issues. The New International Economic Order, Transnational Corporations and World Disarmament. Ed. by Paulos Gregorios. Kottayam: Sophia Centre Publications, 1977. 98pp.

Church and Society. Ecumenical Perspectives. Essays in Honour of Paul Abrecht. Geneva: WCC, 1985. 163pp.

Church and Society. Three Reports of the Working Committee on Church and Society in Nemi, Italy 20-26 June, 1971. Geneva: WCC, 1971. 24pp.

The Churches and the Nuclear Debate. Geneva: WCC, 1977. 50pp. *Anticipation*, No. 24.

Energy for My Neighbour. An Action Programme of the WCC. Geneva: WCC, 1978. 32pp.

Energy for My Neighbour. Perspectives from Asia. Towards More Just and More Sustainable Policies of Energy Development. Ed. by Janos Pasztor. Geneva: WCC, 1981. 158pp.

Energy for My Neighbour. Report of the Latin American Regional Consultation, Held in Lima, Peru 26-31 October, 1981. Geneva: WCC, 1982. 52pp.

Facing up to Nuclear Power. Geneva: WCC, 1975. 43pp. *Anticipation*, No. 20.

Facing up to Nuclear Power. A Contribution to the Debate on the Risks and Potentialities of the Large-Scale Use of Nuclear Energy. Ed. by John Francis and Paul Abrecht. Edinburgh: Saint Andrew Press, 1976. 244pp.

Genetics and the Quality of Life. Ed. by Charles Birch and Paul Abrecht. Elmsford: Pergamon Press, 1975. 232pp.

MacClure, Michael F. *The Contribution of the World Council of Churches to an Ethic and a Just, Participatory and Sustainable Society*. Banyo, Australia: The Pius XII Provincial Seminary, 1982. 278pp.

Manipulating Life. Ethical Issues in Genetic Engineering. Geneva: WCC, 1982. 36pp.

Paulos Gregorios. *The Human Presence*. An Orthodox View of Nature. Geneva: WCC, 1978. 104pp.

Report on Nuclear Energy. Geneva: WCC, 1975. 47pp. *Anticipation*, No. 21.

Science and Our Future. Ed. by Paulos Gregorios. Madras: Christian Literature Society, 1978. 131pp.

Science Education and Ethical Values. Introducing Ethics and Religion into the Science Classroom and Laboratory. Ed. by Bert Musschenga and David Gosling. Geneva: WCC, 1985. 115pp.

Thomas, M.M. *Religion and the Revolt of the Oppressed*. Delhi: ISPCK, 1981. 69pp.

Dialogue with People of Living Faiths and Ideologies

Dialogue Between Men of Living Faiths. The Ajaltoun Memorandum. Geneva: WCC, 1970. 10pp.

Dialogue between Men of Living Faiths. Papers Presented at a Consultation Held at Ajaltoun, Lebanon, March 1970. Ed. by Stanley J. Samartha. Geneva: WCC, 1971. 127pp.

Christian-Muslim Dialogue. Papers Presented at the Broumana Consultation 12-18 July 1972. Ed. by S.J. Samartha and J.B. Taylor. Geneva: WCC, 1973. 167pp.

Towards World Community. Resources and Responsibilities for Living Together. Memorandum, Multi-Lateral Dialogue, Colombo, 17-26 April 1974. Geneva: WCC, 1974. 23pp.

Primal World Views. Christian Dialogue with Traditional Thought Forms. Ed. by J.B. Taylor. Ibadan: Daystar Press, 1976. 131pp.

Faith in the Midst of Faiths. Reflections on Dialogue in Community. Consultation at Chiang Mai, 1977. Geneva: WCC, 1977. 198pp.

Inside Out, a Style for Dialogue Where We Have Come From (Chiang Mai, 1977). Geneva: WCC, 1977. 77pp.

Religious Experience in Humanity's Relation with Nature. A Consultation, Yaoundé, Cameroon, 1978. Geneva: WCC, 1979. 37pp.

Christian Presence and Witness in Relation to Muslim Neighbours. A Conference, Mombasa, Kenya, 1979. Geneva: WCC, 1981. 88pp.

Ariarajah, S. Wesley. *The Bible and People of Other Faiths*. Geneva: WCC, 1985. 71pp. (Risk Book Series, No. 26).

Christian-Jewish Relations in Ecumenical Perspective with Special Emphasis on Africa. Ed. by F. von Hammerstein. Geneva: WCC, 1978. 146pp.

Christians Meeting Muslims. WCC Papers on Ten Years of Christian-Muslim Dialogue. Geneva: WCC, 1977. 155pp.

Churches Among Ideologies. Report of a Consultation and Recommendations to Fellow Christians, 15-22 December 1981, Grand Saconnex, Switzerland. Geneva: WCC, 1982. 60pp.

Cracknell, Kenneth. *Why Dialogue?* A First British Comment on the WCC Guidelines. London: British Council of Churches, 1982. 80pp.

Dialogue in Community. Essays in Honour of Stanley J. Samartha. Ed. by Constantine D. Jathanna. Balmatta, Bangalore, India: Karnataka Theological Research Institute, 1982. 259pp.

Ecumenical Considerations on Jewish-Christian Dialogue. Geneva: WCC, 1983. 11pp.

Faith and Ideologies. An Ecumenical Discussion. Cartigny, Geneva, May 1975. Geneva: WCC, 1975. 13pp.

Guidelines on Dialogue with People of Living Faiths and Ideologies. Geneva: WCC, 1979. 23pp.

Hallencreutz, Carl F. *Dialogue and Community*. Ecumenical Issues in Inter-Religious Relationships. Geneva: WCC, 1977. 109pp.

Jewish-Christian Dialogue. Six Years of Christian-Jewish Consultations. The Quest for World Community. Geneva: WCC, 1975. 72pp.

Living Faiths and the Ecumenical Movement. Ed. by Stanley J. Samartha. Geneva: WCC, 1971. 183pp.

Living Faiths and Ultimate Goals. A Continuing Dialogue. Ed. by Stanley J. Samartha. Geneva: WCC, 1974. 120pp.

Man in Nature: Guest or Engineer? A Preliminary Enquiry by Christians and Buddhists into the Religious Dimensions in Humanity's Relation to Nature. Ed. by Stanley J. Samartha and Lynn de Silva. Colombo: Ecumenical Institute for Study and Dialogue, 1979. 106pp.

The Meaning of Life. A Multifaith Consultation in Preparation for the Sixth Assembly of the WCC at Vancouver 1983; Mauritius, 15 January-3 February 1983. Geneva: WCC, 1983. 20pp.

Mulder, D.C. *Ontmoeting van gelovigen*. Over de dialoog tussen aanhangers van verschillende religies. Baarn: Bosch en Keuning, 1977. 100pp.

Religious Resources for a Just Society. A Hindu — Christian Dialogue at Rajpur, North India, 30 May-6 June 1981. Geneva: WCC, 1981. 22pp.

Samartha, Stanley J. *Courage for Dialogue*. Ecumenical Issues in Inter-Religious Relationships. Geneva: WCC, 1981. 157pp.

Towards World Community. The Colombo Papers. Ed. by Stanley J. Samartha. Geneva: WCC, 1975. 165pp.

UNIT II

Commission on the Churches' Participation in Development

Building a Fellowship of Commitment. Report of the CCPD Network Meeting, Crete, 1980. Ed. by Wolfgang Schmidt. Geneva: WCC, 1980. 126pp.

Caribbean Ecumenical Consultation for Development, Chaguaramas, Trinidad, November 1971. *Called To Be*. Official Report. Bridgetown: CADEC, 1971. 80pp.

Churches and the Transnational Corporations: an Ecumenical Programme. Geneva: WCC, 1983. 145pp.

Comprehensiveness in the Churches' Participation in Development: the Challenge of the Eighties. Report of a CCPD Consultation, Crêt-Bérard, Switzerland, 28-31 January 1981. Geneva: WCC, 1981 67pp.

Creative Commitment: the Response of the Churches in Indonesia to the Development Challenge. Ed. by Wolfgang Schmidt. Geneva: WCC, 1979. 137pp.

Dejung, Karl-Heinz. *Die ökumenische Bewegung im Entwicklungskonflikt 1910-1968.* Stuttgart: Ernst Klett, 1973. 494pp.

Dickinson, Richard D.N. *Poor, Yet Making Many Rich: the Poor as Agents of Creative Justice.* Geneva: WCC, 1983. 219pp.

Dickinson, Richard D.N. *To Set at Liberty the Oppressed.* Towards an Understanding of Christian Responsibilities of Development/Liberation. Geneva: WCC, 1975. 193pp.

Ecumenical Development Cooperative Society. *A Model for Action in Development Cooperation.* Comp. and ed. by Fred Bronkema. New York: EDCS, 1979. 16pp.

Ecumenical Perspectives on Political Ethics. The Report of a Consultation, Cyprus, 18-25 October 1981. Geneva: WCC, 28pp.

Elliott, Charles. *Patterns of Poverty in the Third World.* A Study of Social and Economic Stratification. Assisted by Françoise de Morsier. London: Praeger, 1975. 416pp.

Gallis, Marion. *Trade for Justice: Myth or Mandate?* Geneva: WCC, 1972. 146pp.

Gruber, Pamela H. *Fetters of Injustice.* Report of an Ecumenical Consultation on Ecumenical Assistance to Development Projects, Montreux, 26-31 January 1970. Geneva: WCC, 1970. 164pp.

Hürni, Bettina S. *Development Work of the World Council of Churches.* Geneva: Médecine et hygiène, 1974. 318pp.

The International Financial System: an Ecumenical Critique. Report of the Meeting of the Advisory Group on Economic Matters, Geneva, 1-4 November 1984. Ed. by Reginald Green. Geneva: WCC, 1985. 88pp.

Just Development for Fullness of Life: a Responsible Christian Participation. Orthodox Consultation in Kiev, 22-30 June 1982. Geneva: WCC, 1983. 138pp.

Justice and Development. Asia Forum on: CCA-WCC-CCPD, Singapore, 26-30 November 1984. Ed. by Yong-Bock Kim. Seoul: Yang Seo Press, 1985. 333pp.

Learning in the Struggle. The Report of an Interregional Consultation on Education for Development: Action for Justice, Cuba, 4-16 November 1979. Ed. by Reinhild Traitler. Geneva. WCC, 1980. 75pp.

Millwood, David. *The Poverty Makers.* Geneva: WCC, 1977. 69pp.

Minutes of the First Exploratory Consultation on Transnational Corporations, Cartigny, 26-28 January 1977. Geneva: WCC, 1977. Pagination varies.

Perspectives on Political Ethics: an Ecumenical Enquiry. Ed. by Koson Srisang. Geneva: WCC, 1983. 193pp.

Pury, Pascal de. *People's Technologies and People's Participation.* Geneva: WCC, 1983. 164pp.

Report of the Commission on the Churches' Participation in Development 1970-1976. Geneva: WCC, 1977. 70pp.

Rudersdorf, Karl Heinrich. *Das Entwicklungskonzept des Weltkirchenrates.* Entstehung und Entwicklung des Konzepts der Entwicklungsforderung im Weltrat der Kirchen. Saarbrücken: Verlag der SSIP-Schriften, 1975. 355pp.

Santa Ana, Julio de. *Good News to the Poor.* The Challenge of the Poor in the History of the Church. Geneva: WCC, 1977. 124pp.

Separation Without Hope? Essays on the Relation Between the Church and the Poor During the Industrial Revolution and the Western Colonial Expansion. Ed. by Julio de Santa Ana. Maryknoll: Orbis Books, 1980. 192pp.

Towards a Church of the Poor. The Work of an Ecumenical Group on the Church and the Poor. Geneva: WCC, 1979. 210pp.

Sartorius, Peter. *Churches in Rural Development.* Guidelines for Action. Geneva: WCC, 1975. 157pp.

Signs of Hope and Justice. Ed. by Jether Pereira Ramalho. Geneva: WCC, 1980. 134pp.

To Break the Chains of Oppression. Results of an Ecumenical Study Process on Domination and Dependence. Geneva: WCC, 1975. 113pp.

Towards a Church in Solidarity with the Poor. Ed. by IDOC International. Rome: IDOC, 1980. 99p.

Traitler, Reinhild. *Leaping Over the Wall.* An Assessment of Ten Years' Development Education. Geneva: WCC, 1982. 83pp.

World Hunger, a Christian Reappraisal. Report of the Fourth Meeting of the Advisory Group on Economic Matters, Held in Washington, 5-8 October 1981. Ed. by Diogo de Gaspar, Caesar Espiritu and Reginald Green. Geneva: WCC, 1982. 63pp.

Numerous numbers of *CCPD Documents* deal with specific concerns and problems

Churches in International Affairs

Barnaby, Frank. *Nuclear Proliferation and the South African Threat.* Geneva: WCC, 1977. 22pp.

Before It's Too Late: the Challenge of Nuclear Disarmament. The Complete Record of the Public Hearing on Nuclear Weapons and Disarmament, Amsterdam, 1981. Ed. by Paul Abrecht and Ninan Koshy. Geneva: WCC, 1983. 391pp.

Churches as Peacemakers? An Analysis of Recent Church Statements on Peace, Disarmament and War. By Friedhelm Sölms and Marc Reuver. Rome: IDOC, 1985. 85pp.

The Churches in International Affairs. Reports, 1970-1973, 1974-1978, 1979-1982. Geneva: CCIA, 1974, 1979, 1983.

Derr, Thomas Sieger. *The Political Thought of the Ecumenical Movement, 1900-1939.* Ann Arbor, Michigan: University Microfilms, 1972. 758pp.

Evans, Archibald A. *Workers' Rights Are Human Rights.* A Guide on International Labour Standards. Rome: IDOC, 1981. 112pp.

Fonseca, Glenda Da. *How to File Complaints of Human Rights Violations.* A Practical Guide to Intergovernmental Procedures. Geneva: WCC, 1975. 152pp.

Grubb, Kenneth. *Crypts of Power: an Autobiography.* London: Hodder & Stoughton, 1971. 253pp.

Hamelink, Cees. Towards a New International Information Order. *CCIA Background Information,* 1978, No. 7.

Hudson, Darril. *The World Council of Churches in International Affairs.* Leighton Buzzard: Faith Press, 1977. 336pp.

Hudson, Darril. *The Ecumenical Movement in World Affairs.* London: Weidenfeld & Nicolson, 1969. 286pp.

Human Rights: a Challenge to Theology. Ed. by Marc Reuver. Rome: IDOC; Geneva: WCC, 1983. 174pp.

Human Rights and Christian Responsibility. Report of the Consultation in St Pölten, Austria, 21-26 October 1974. Geneva: WCC, 1974. 68pp.

Militarism and Human Rights. Reports and Papers of a Workshop at Glion, Switzerland, 10-14 November 1981. *CCIA Background Information*, 1982, No. 3.

Nolde, O. Frederick. *The Churches and the Nations.* Philadelphia: Fortress Press, 1970, 184pp.

Peace and Disarmament. Documents of the WCC presented by the Commission of the Churches on International Affairs, and of the Roman Catholic Church Presented by the Pontifical Commission Iustitia et Pax. Geneva: WCC, 1982. 254pp.

Regehr, Ernie. *Militarism and the World Military Order.* A Study Guide for Churches. Geneva: WCC, 1980. 69pp.

Religious Freedom. Main Statements by the World Council of Churches, 1948-1975. Geneva: WCC, 1976. 75pp.

Report of the Conference on Disarmament, Glion, Switzerland, 9-15 April 1978. Geneva: WCC, 1978. *CCIA Background Information*, 1978, No. 4. 29pp.

Report of the Consultation on Militarism, Glion, Switzerland, 13-18 November 1977. Geneva: WCC, 1977. *CCIA Background Information*, 1977, No. 2. 22pp.

Report of the Hague Consultation on the CCIA, 12-17 April 1967. Geneva: WCC, 1967. 46pp.

The Security Trap: Arms Race, Militarism and Disarmament. A Concern for Christians. Ed. by José-Antonio Viera Gallo. Rome: IDOC, 1979. 291pp. Revised ed. 1982, 291pp.

Violence, Nonviolence and Civil Conflict. Geneva: WCC, 1983. 32pp.

WCC Statements on Nuclear Weapons and Disarmament, 1948-1981. Prepared for the Public Hearing at Amsterdam, 23-27 November 1981. Geneva: WCC, 1981. 56pp.

Weingärtner, Erich. Human Rights on the Ecumenical Agenda. Report and Assessment. *CCIA Background Information*, 1983, No. 3.

Zalaquett, Jose. The Human Rights Issue and the Human Rights Movement: Characterization, Evaluation, Propositions. *CCIA Background Information*, 1981, No. 3.

Many numbers of *CCIA Background Information* (1975-) deal with specific concerns in various countries and regions.

Programme to Combat Racism

Aboriginal Issues. Racism in Australia. Geneva: WCC, 1971. 29pp.

Adler, Elisabeth. *A Small Beginning.* An Assessment of the First Five Years of the Programme To Combat Racism. Geneva: WCC, 1974. 102pp.

Austin, George. *World Council of Churches' Programme to Combat Racism.* London: Institute for the Study of Conflict, 1979. 30pp. (Conflict Studies, No. 105).

Bank Loans to South Africa Mid-1982 to End 1984. Prepared by Eva Militz. Geneva: WCC, 1985. 124pp.

Bassarak, Gerhard; Günter Wirth. *Herausforderung des Gewissens.* Über den Ökumenischen Beitrag zum Kampf gegen den Rassismus. Berlin: Union Verlag, 1977. 77pp.

Breaking Down the Walls. World Council of Churches Statements and Actions on Racism 1948-1985. Ed. by Ans J. van der Bent. Geneva: WCC, 1986. 107pp.

Challenge to the Churches. Official Report of the Joint AACC/PCR — WCC Consultation on the Church and the Liberation of South Africa. Nairobi: AACC, 1976. 61pp.

Christian Response to Race and Minority Issues in Asia. Proceedings and Findings of a Regional Consultation, 24-29 March 1980, New Delhi. Hong Kong: CCA-URM, 1980. 124pp.

Church Investments Corporations and Southern Africa. New York: Friendship Press, 1973. 242pp.

The Churches' Involvement in Southern Africa. Geneva: WCC, 1982. 76pp.

Churches Responding to Racism in the 1980s. Noordwijkerhout, Netherlands, 16-21 June 1980. Geneva: WCC, 1980. 88pp. (PCR Information, No. 9).

Cunene Dam Scheme and the Struggle for the Liberation of Southern Africa. Geneva: WCC, 1971. 47pp.

Downing, John. *Now You Do Know.* An Independent Report on Racial Oppression in Britain. London: WOW Campaigns, 1980. 80pp.

Ecumenical Involvement in Southern Africa. Geneva: CETIM, 1975. 173pp.

Fuchs, Erika. *Antirassismus-Programm 1969-1979.* Eine Dokumentation. Hrsg. von Peter Karner. Wien: Evangelischer Oberkirchenrat H.B., 1979. 260pp. (Aktuelle Reihe, N. 16).

Fuelling Apartheid. Shell and the Military. Geneva: WCC, 1984. Pagination varies.

Heuvel, Albert van den. *Shalom and Combat.* A Personal Struggle Against Racism. Geneva: WCC, 1979. 53pp. (Risk Book Series, No. 5).

Justice for Aboriginal Australians. Report of the WCC Team Visit to the Aborigines, 15 June-3 July 1981. Sydney: Australian Council of Churches, 1981. 91pp.

Die Kirchen im Kampf gegen den Rassismus. Eine Materialsammlung, zusammengestellt vom Kirchlichen Aussenamt der EKD. Verantwortlich Lothar Coenen. Frankfurt: Lembeck, 1980. 104pp.

Luckhardt, Ken. *Working for Freedom.* Black Trade Union Development in South Africa Throughout the 1970s. Geneva: WCC, 1981. 118pp.

Meyers-Herwartz, Christel. *Die Rezeption des Antirassismus-programms in der EKD.* Stuttgart: Kohlhammer, 1979. 378pp.

Muntendam, J.W. Th. *De bestrijding van het racisme en de oecumene.* Utrecht: Interuniversiteit Instituut voor Missiologie en Oecumenica, 1973. 76pp.

Payne, Ernest A.. *Violence, Non-Violence and Human Rights.* London: The Baptist Union of Great Britain and Ireland, 1971. 15pp. (Living Issues, No. 15).

Racism in Children's and School Textbooks. A Report. Evangelische Akademie Arnoldshain, 13-18 Oktober 1978. Geneva: WCC, 1979, 28pp.

Racism in Theology and Theology Against Racism. Geneva: WCC, 1975. 21pp.

Richardson, Neville. *The World Council of Churches and Race Relations: 1960 to 1969.* Bern: H. Lang, 1977. 78pp. (Studien zur interkulturellen Geschichte des Christentums, N. 9).

Rogers, Barbara. *Race: No Peace Without Justice.* Churches Confront the Mounting Racism of the 1980s. Geneva: WCC, 1980. 132pp.

Sansbury, Kenneth. *Combating Racism.* London: British Council of Churches, 1975. 78pp.

Schmidt, Robert Frederick. *The Legitimacy of Revolution.* The World Council of Churches' Grants to Liberation Movements in Southern Africa, 1983. 347pp.

Sjollema, Baldwin. *Isolating Apartheid.* Western Collaboration with Southern Africa. Geneva: WCC, 1982. 136pp.

The Slant of the Pen. Racism in Children's Books. Ed. by Roy Preiswerk. Geneva: WCC, 1980. 151pp.

Time to Withdraw. Investments in Southern Africa. Geneva: WCC, 1972. 27pp.

Verkuyl, J. *Bestrijding van het racisme en de kerken in Nederland.* Kampen: Kok, 1972. 72pp.

Vincent, John J. *The Race Race*. London: Notting Hill, 1969. London: SCM Press, 1970. 116pp.

Walther, Christian. *Rassismus*. Berlin: Lutherisches Verlagshaus, 1971. 101pp. (Kirchliche Aspekte Heute, Nr. 6).

Weisse, Wolfram. *Südafrika und das Antirassismusprogramm*. Kirchen im Spannungsfeld einer Rassengesellschaft. Bern: H. Lang. Frankfurt: lang, 1975. 465pp. (Studien zur interkulturellen Geschichte des Christentums, 1).

Wie lange noch? Apartheid als Herausforderung für Südafrikas Christen und Kirchen: Dokumente 1970 bis 1980. Hrsg. und eingeleitet von Elisabeth Adler. Berlin: Union Verlag, 1982. 255pp.

Williamson, Roger. *Alternative Strategies?* Reactions in the Two Germanies to the World Council of Churches' Programme to Combat Racism, 1969-75. Dissertation, Birminghham, 1980. 250pp.

The World Council of Churches and Bank Loans to Apartheid. Geneva: WCC, 1977. 95pp.

Many numbers of *PCR Information* deal with specific concerns, problems and conflicts.

Commission on Inter-Church Aid, Refugee and World Service

Asia Country Papers. Geneva: WCC, 1975. 112pp.

Bouman, Pieter. *Tears and Rejoicing*. The Story of European Inter-Church Aid 1922-1956. 1983. 473pp.

Bouwen, Frans. *An Ecumenical Concern*. The Participation of Refugees. Geneva: WCC, 1982. 79pp.

The Churches and the World Refugee Crisis. Geneva: WCC, 1981. 18pp.

The Churches in Eastern Europe and the Ecumenical Sharing of Resources. Report of the Consultation on the Ecumenical Sharing of Resources with the Churches in Eastern Europe, Sofia, 24-26 May, 1982. Geneva: WCC, 1983. 56pp.

Contemporary Understandings of Diakonia. Report of a Consultation. Geneva, Switzerland, 22-26 November 1982. Geneva: WCC, 1983. 67pp.

Cooke, Leslie E. *Bread and Laughter*. Geneva: WCC, 1968. 280pp.

Early, Tracy. *Simply Sharing*. A Personal Survey of How Well the Ecumenical Movement Shares its Resources. Geneva: WCC, 1980. 84pp. (Risk Book Series, No. 8).

Ecumenical Church Loan Fund. *Consultations of National ECLOF Committee Chairmen, September 1979*. Geneva: WCC, 1979. 68pp.

Ecumenical Church Loan Fund. *Lending a Hand*. Geneva: WCC, 1983. 16pp.

Empty Hands. An Agenda for the Churches: a Study Guide on the Ecumenical Sharing of Resources for Use by Churches, Local Congregations and Other Groups. Geneva: WCC, 1980. 60pp.

Fryer, Jonathan. *Food for Thought*. The Use and Abuse of Food Aid in the Fight Against World Hunger. Geneva: WCC, 1982. 54pp.

Government Funding. Report of the Consultation Held at Aurora Conference Centre. Toronto, Canada, 8-10 February 1983. Geneva: WCC, 1983. 68pp.

Hennes, Gerhard G. *Alone, You Get Nowhere*. An Attempt at Assessing the Involvement of Personnel in the Sudan Relief and Rehabilitation Programme 1972-75. Geneva: WCC, 1977. 114pp.

King, Michael Christopher. *The Palestinians and the Churches* Geneva: WCC, 1981.

Newby, Donald O. *Toward a New Process for Mission and Service*. A Report on the Project List Review for the Commission on Interchurch Aid, Refugee and World

Service, New Windsor, Maryland, 24-28 April 1979, and the Commission on World
Mission and Evangelism, Wuppertal, 14-22 May, 1979. Geneva: WCC, 1979. 48pp.

The Orthodox Approach to Diaconia. Consultation on Church and Service: Orthodox
Academy of Crete, 20-25 November, 1978. Geneva: WCC, 1980. 64pp.

Palestine Refugees-Aid with Justice. The Report of the Consultation on the Palestine
Refugee Problem. Geneva: WCC, 1970. 100pp.

Partners. A World Council of Churches' Contribution for the International Year of
Disabled Persons, 1981. Geneva: WCC, 1981. 20pp.

Partners in the Family of God. The Church Includes Persons with Disabilities. Geneva:
WCC, 1981. 92pp.

Programme Unit on Justice and Service. Ecumenical Consultation on Indochina: Hong
Kong, 17-21 April 1978. Geneva: WCC, 1978. 79pp.

Refugees, a Global Concern. Geneva: WCC, 1977. 92pp.

Report of a Consultation with Agencies for Service and Development and Mission
Boards on the Resource Sharing System, Geneva, 10-11 October 1983. Geneva:
WCC, 1984. 26pp.

Report of the Middle East Consultation on Inter-Church Aid, Salamis, Cyprus, 12-14
November 1972. Geneva: WCC, 1972. 95pp.

Resource Sharing System. Progress Reports, Decisions and Recommendations. Geneva:
WCC, 1983. 49pp.

Reuschle, Helmut. *Material Resources in Asia.* A Survey Report. Geneva: WCC, 1978,
219pp.

Schot, Willem J. *Do We Project Ourselves in Projects?* An Examination of the Project
System in Relation to Service, Mission and Development. Geneva: WCC, 1979.
28pp.

Towards a New System for Sharing. Report of the Consultation Held at Glion,
Switzerland on 3-6 February, Geneva: WCC, 1983. 40pp.

Towards an Ecumenical Commitment for Resource Sharing. Geneva: WCC, 1984. 16pp.

Unity in Service with the Palestinians. Consultation on Service to Palestine Refugees.
Beirut: MECC, 1980. 116pp.

Christian Medical Commission

Caribbean Regional Conference on the Churches' Role in Health and Wholeness. Port of
Spain, Trinidad, 12-16 March 1979. Geneva: WCC, 1979. 51p.

Cottingham, Jane. *Bottle Babies.* A Guide to the Baby Foods Issue. Geneva: WCC,
1976. 47pp.

The Future Role of the Church in Health Care Programmes in Ghana. Proceedings of a
Workshop. The Ghana Institute of Public Administration, Greenhill, Ghana, 17-23
August 1975. Compiled from notes supplied by Mary Zosso. 1975. 38pp.

Genetics and the Quality of Life. Ed. by Charles Birch and Paul Abrecht. Rushcutters
Bay, N.S.W.: Pergamon Press, 1975. 232pp.

Genetics and the Quality of Life. Report of a Consultation of Church and Society/
Christian Medical Commission, Zürich June 1973. Geneva: WCC, 1975. 26pp.

Health, the Human Factor. Readings in Health, Development and Community Participation. Guest ed. Susan B. Rifkin. Geneva: WCC, 1980. 124p.

Hellberg, J.H. *Community, Health and the Church.* Geneva: WCC, 1971. 74pp.

Kingma, Stuart J. *Survey of Church and Mission Health Programmes in Sierra Leone
and Workshop, 6-31 May 1975.* Geneva: WCC, 1975. 35pp.

MacGilvray, James C. *The Quest for Health and Wholeness*. Tübingen: German Institute for Medical Missions, 1981. 118pp.

Pacific Regional Consultation on the Christian Understanding of Health, Healing and Wholeness. Madang, Papua New Guinea, 23-29 October 1981. Geneva: WCC, 1982. 80pp.

The Principles and Practice of Primary Health Care. Geneva: WCC, 1979. 112pp.

The Search for a Christian Understanding of Health, Healing and Wholeness. A Summary Report on the Study Programme of the Christian Medical Commission of the World Council of Churches 1976-1982. Geneva: WCC, 1982. 41pp.

Seminar on the Healing Ministry of the Church. Ecumenical Institute Bossey, 25 June-7 July 1979. Geneva: WCC, 1979. 74pp.

The Third Conference for Coordinators of Church-Related Health Work in Africa. Mombasa, Kenya, 18-21 February 1975. Geneva: WCC, 1975. 29pp.

UNIT III

Education

Christians and Education in a Multi-Faith World. Considerations on Christian Participation in Education in a Multi-Faith Environment. Geneva: WCC, 1982. 43pp.

Encuentro. New Perspectives for Christian Education. Geneva: WCC, 1971. 183pp.

Freire, Paulo. *Pedagogy in Process*. The Letters to Guinea-Bissau. New York, Seabury Press, 1978. 178pp.

Freire, Paulo. *Education for Critical Consciousness*. New York, Seabury Press, 1973. 164pp.

Seeing Education Whole. Geneva: WCC, 1970. 126pp.

Tradition and Renewal in Orthodox Education. Report of the Consultation on "Tradition and Renewal in Orthodox Education" held in the Neamt Monastery, Romania, 6-12 September 1976. Ed. by Maurice Assad, 1977. 130pp.

World Council of Churches. *Ecumenical Scholarship Programme*. Geneva: WCC, 1980. 23pp.

World Council of Churches. Office of Education. *Learning Community*. A Consultation on Evaluating the Sunday School Contribution to Church Education in Europe Today, Glion-sur-Montreux, Switzerland, 24-28 September 1973. Geneva: WCC, 1973. 129pp.

When I'm Grown Up I'm Going to Change Things. Children at the 6th Assembly, World Council of Churches, Vancouver 1983. Geneva: WCC, 1985. 41pp.

Women in Church and Society

Bam, Brigalia, ed. *New Perspectives for Third World Women*. Madras: The Christian Literature Society, 1979. 42pp.

Bam, Brigalia. *What is Ordination Coming To?* Report of a Consultation on the Ordination of Women Held in Cartigny, Geneva, Switzerland, 21-26 September 1970. Geneva: WCC, 1971. 86pp.

By Our Lives. Stories of Women — Today and in the Bible. Geneva: WCC, 1985. 57pp.

A Caring Community. A Consultation of the World Council of Churches, Sao Paulo, Brazil, 23-29 November 1981. Geneva: WCC, 1982. 8pp.

Choose Life — Work for Peace. Report of an International Workshop, the Sub-Unit on Women in Church and Society, 27 November-7 December 1981, Nassau, Bahamas. Geneva: WCC, 1982. 40pp.

The Church and the Aging in a Changing World. Geneva: WCC, 1983. 198pp.

The Community of Women and Men in the Church. Report of the Asian Consultation Held at the United Theological College, Bangalore, 11-15 August 1978. Geneva: WCC, 1978. 105pp.

Community of Women and Men in the Church. New York, National Council of Churches, Commission on Faith and Order, 1981. 27pp.

Consultation of European Christian Women. Brussels, 19 January-4 February 1978. Geneva: WCC, 1978. 63pp.

Davies, Margaret and Davies, Rupert. *Circles of Community.* A Study Guide. Towards a Renewed Community of Women and Men in Church and Society, Based on a World Council of Churches Consultation, Sheffield, 1981. London, British Council of Churches, 1982. 15pp.

Family Power. A Report on a Consultation of an International Ad Hoc Advisory Committee of the Office of Family Ministries, Assembled at Salina Bay, Malta, 25 April-3 May 1973. Geneva: WCC, 1973. 57pp.

Family Profiles. Stories of Families in Transition. Ed. by Masamba Ma Mpolo. Geneva: WCC, 1984. 96pp.

Half the World's People. A Report of the Consultation of Church Women Executives. Glion, Switzerland, January 1977. Geneva: WCC, 1978. 64pp.

Hahn, Elisabeth. *Partnership.* Geneva: WCC, 1954. 72pp.

Herzel, Susannah. *A Voice for Women.* The Women's Department of the World Council of Churches. Geneva: WCC, 1981. 197pp.

In God's Image. Reflections on Identity, Human Wholeness and the Authority of Scripture. Ed. by Janet Crawford and Michael Kinnamon. Geneva: WCC, 1983. 108pp.

Middle East Council of Churches Consultation. *The Community of Women and Men in the Church.* Beirut, Lebanon, 22-26 January 1980. Geneva: WCC, 1981. 87pp.

Orthodox Women, the Role and Participation in the Orthodox Church. Report on the Consultation of Orthodox Women, 11-17 September 1976. Agapia, Romania. Geneva: WCC, 1977. 55pp.

Report of Conference on Women, Human Rights and Mission. Venice, Italy, 24-30 June 1979. Geneva: WCC, 1979. 64pp.

Report of the Fourth Seminar on Marriage and Family Life. New Caledonia, 18 January-8 February 1975. Geneva: WCC, 1975. 40pp.

Report on the Consultation "Pastoral Care and Those Confronted With Abortion". Monbachtal, Federal Republic of Germany, 6-11 October 1974. Geneva: WCC. 1974. Pagination varies.

Sexism in the 1970s. Discrimination Against Women. A Report of a World Council of Churches Consultation West Berlin 1974. Geneva: WCC, 1975. 150pp.

Study on the Community of Women and Men in the Church. Geneva: WCC, 1979. 39pp.

Thompson, Betty. *A Chance to Change.* Women and Men in the Church. Geneva: WCC, 1982. 121pp.

Towards Self-Reliance I. A Handbook on Rural Development. Geneva: WCC, 1980. 54pp.

Towards Self-Reliance II. A Handbook on Rural Development. Report of Asian Regional Workshop for Rural Women, 28 April-8 May 1980. Tagaytay City, Philippines. Geneva: WCC, 1981. 54pp.

Ujamaa Safari. An Impression of the World Assembly on the Family, Familia 74, Tanzania, June 1974. Geneva: WCC, 1974. 49pp. (Risk. Vol. 10, No. 4, 1974).

We Listened Long, Before We Spoke. Women Theological Students. A Consultation of the Sub-unit on Women in Church and Society of the World Council of Churches. Geneva: WCC, 1979. 56pp.

WCC, Community of Women and Men in the Church. *A Space to Grow In*. European Regional Consultation, Bad Segeberg, FRG, 20-24 June 1980. Geneva: WCC, 1981. 32pp.

WCC, Community of Women and Men in the Church. *Theological Anthropology, Towards a Theology of Human Wholeness*. The Benedictine Abbey at Niederaltaich, FRG, September 1980. Geneva: WCC, 1981. 53pp.

WCC, The Office of Family Education. *The Multicultural Context of Family Education, Challenges of the Eighties*. Report of Advisory Group Meeting, Alexandria, Egypt, 10-16 November 1980. Geneva: WCC, 1981. 177pp.

WCC, The Office of Family Education. *Marriage and Family Education in Theological Perspective*. Pastoral and Practical Implications. Report of a Consultation, Milan, Italy, 2-7 November 1979. Geneva: WCC, 1980. 109pp.

WCC, Office of Family Education. *Oaxtepec, Mexico, January 1980*. Geneva: WCC, 1980. 151pp.

WCC, Office of Family Education. *The Pan African Ecumenical Consultation on Christian Family and Family Life Education*. Yaounde, 17-23 April 1983. Geneva: WCC, 1983. 93pp.

WCC, Office of Family Education. *Participation in Change*. A Group Process of Action, Reflection in Family Education. Geneva. WCC, 1981. 65pp.

WCC, Office of Family Education. *Report of a Consultation on Humanity and Wholeness of Persons with Disabilities*. São Paulo, Brazil, 23-30 November 1981. Geneva: WCC, 1982. 142pp.

Renewal and Congregational Life

The Church is Charismatic. Ed. by Arnold Bittlinger. Geneva: WCC, 1981. 241pp.

Lange, Ernst. *Leben im Wandel*. Überlegungen zu einer zeitgemässen Moral. Gelnhausen, Burckhardthaus-Verlag, 1971. 111pp.

A Spirituality for Our Times. Report of a Consultation, Annecy, France, 3-8 December 1984. Geneva: WCC, 1985. 23pp.

Vision '83. Geneva: WCC, 1983. 24pp.

Voices of Solidarity. A Story of Christian Lay Centres, Academies and Movements for Social Concerns. Geneva: WCC, 1981. 56pp.

Youth

Bent, Ans J. van der. *From Generation to Generation*. The Story of Youth in the World Council of Churches. Geneva: WCC, 1986. 136pp.

Christian Youth in a Troubled Society. Ayia Napa, Cyprus, 13-20 July 1978. Geneva: WCC, 1978. 75pp.

First Interregional Ecumenical Youth Encounter. Human Rights, Peoples' Rights, Panama, August 1980. Berlin: Ecumenical Youth Council in Europe, 1981. 92pp.

Macbay, Joanne. *Youth Participation in the World Council of Churches Assemblies*. 1982. 47pp.

Pacific Conference of Churches. *The Dancing Convention. Youths of the 80s.* Suva: Lotu
   Pasifika Productions, 1980. 45pp.

Programme on Theological Education
Directory. Theological Schools in Africa, Asia, the Caribbean, Latin America and the
   South Pacific, June 1970. Bromley, Kent: TEF, 1970. 58pp.
Directory. Theological Schools and Related Institutions in Africa, Asia, the Caribbean,
   Latin America and the South Pacific. Bromley, Kent: TEF, 1974. 227pp.
*Ecumenical Responses to Theological Education in Africa, Asia, Near East, the South
   Pacific, Latin America and the Caribbean.* London, 1976. 64pp.
Fleming, Bruce C.E. *Contextualization of Theology.* An Evangelical Assessment.
   Pasadena: William Carey Library, 1980. 147pp.
Fleming, Bruce. *Global Solidarity in Theological Education.* Report of the US-Canadian
   Consultation Held at Trinity College, University of Toronto, 12-15 July 1981.
   Geneva: WCC, 1981. 140pp.
Kinsler, F. Ross. *The Extension Movement in Theological Education.* A Call to the
   Renewal of the Ministry. Pasadena: William Carey Library, 1981. 294pp.
Lienemann-Perrin, Christian. *Training for a Relevant Ministry.* Madras: The Christian
   Literature Society and Geneva: WCC, 1981. 252pp.
Learning in Context. The Search for Innovative Patterns in Theological Education.
   Bromley: New Life Press, 1973. 195pp.
Ministerial Formation. Report, Tagaytay City, Manila, Philippines, 7-10 July 1979.
   Geneva: WCC, 1979. 109pp.
Ministry by the People. Theological Education by Extension. Geneva: WCC, 1983,
   332pp.
Ministry in Context. The Third Mandate Programme of the Theological Education Fund,
   1970-77. Ed. by the TEF Staff. Bromley, Kent, 1972. 108pp.
Ministry with the Poor. Geneva: WCC, 1977. 80pp.
Orthodox Theological Education for the Life and Witness of the Church. Report on the
   Consultation at Basel, Switzerland, 4-8 July, 1978. Geneva: WCC, 1978. 117pp.
Theological Education in Europe. Report of the Consultation Held in Herrnhut, GDR, 8-
   14 October 1980. Geneva: WCC, 1981. 129pp.
Zorn, Herbert M. *Viability in Context.* A Study of the Financial Viability of Theological
   Education in the Third World, Seedbed or Sheltered Garden? Bromley, Kent, 1975.
   108pp.

Biblical Studies
Communicating Across Cultural Barriers. A Dynamic Equivalent Approach to the Use
   of Radio and Other Media in Biblical Evangelism. Ed. by Charles T. Hein. Nairobi:
   1977. 139pp.
Schrotenboer, Paul G. *The Bible in the World Council of Churches.* 1977. 20pp.
Weber, Hans-Ruedi. *Experiments with Bible Study.* Geneva: WCC, 1981. 319pp.
Weber, Hans-Ruedi. *Immanuel: The coming of Jesus in Art and the Bible.* Geneva:
   WCC, 1984. 122pp.
Weber, Hans-Ruedi. *Jesus and the Children.* Biblical Resources for Study and Preach-
   ing. Geneva: WCC, 1979. 95pp.
Weber, Hans-Ruedi. *The Cross.* Tradition and Interpretation. London: 1979. 162pp.
Weber, Hans-Ruedi. *On a Friday Noon.* Meditations under the Cross. Geneva: WCC,
   1979. 94pp.

Regional Ecumenical Developments

AFRICA

All Africa Conference of Churches. *Directory of AACC Member Churches.* Kenya: 1981. 224pp.

All Africa Conference of Churches. *Fourth General Assembly.* Nairobi, Kenya, 2-12 August 1981. Nairobi: AACC, 1981. 20pp.

All Africa Conference of Churches. Lusaka 1974. *The Struggle Continues.* Nairobi: AACC, 1974. 20pp.

All Africa Conference of Churches. *The Hard Road to Peace.* A Report of the Churches in Their Part in the Reconciliation in the Sudan and an Appeal. Nairobi: AACC, 1972. 28pp.

All Africa Conference of Churches. *Follow Me — Feed my Lambs.* Fourth Assembly, Nairobi, Kenya, 2-12 August 1981. Nairobi: AACC, 1982. 124pp.

Challenge to the Churches. WCC Consultation of the Church and the Liberation of South Africa. Nairobi: AACC, 1976. 61pp.

Drumbeats from Kampala. Report of the First Assembly of the All Africa Conference of Churches Held at Kampala, 20-30 April 1963. London, United Society for Christian Literature. Lutterworth Press, 1963. 77pp.

M'Passou, Denis. *Mindolo, a Story of the Eumenical Movement in Africa.* To Mark the 25th Anniversary of Mindolo Ecumenical Foundation. Kabulong Lusaka: Multimedia Publications, 1983. 118pp.

Mugambi, Jesse. *Ecumenical Initiatives in Eastern Africa.* Final Report of the Joint Research Project of the All African Conference of Churches and the Association of Member Episcopal Conferences of Eastern Africa 1976-1981. Co-authored by Jesse Murgambi and others and ed. by Brian Hearne. Nairobi: AACC, 1982. 188pp.

The Nuclear Conspiracy. Nairobi, AACC, 1977. 116pp.

Rafransoa, Maxime. *Eglise d'Afrique, qui es-tu?* Lausanne: Editions du Soc, 1983. 77pp.

Report of a Consultation for Directors of Lay Centres in Africa. Sponsored by All African Conference of Churches and the Mindolo Ecumenical Foundation, 19-23 May 1970. 97pp.

Report of Regional Consultation on Community of Men and Women in the Church Study. Nairobi: AACC, 1981. Pagination varies.

Salvation — Development — Liberation. Nairobi: AACC, 1972. 41pp.

The Struggle Continues. Official Report Third Assembly All Africa Conference of Churches Lusaka-Zambia, 12-24 May 1974. Nairobi: AACC, 1975. 132pp.

Together in One Place. The Story of PACLA (Pan African Christian Leadership Assembly), 9-19 December 1976. Ed. by Michael Cassidy and Gottfried Osei-Mensah. Nairobi: Evangelical Publishing House, 1978. 301pp.

Vers l'autonomie. CETA 1975-78. Nairobi: La conférence des Eglises de toute l'Afrique, 1975. 33pp.

ASIA

Achutegui, Pedro S. de, ed. *Towards a "Dialogue of Life".* Ecumenism in the Asian Context. First Asian Congress of Jesuit Ecumenists, Manila 18-23 June 1975. Manila: Loyola School of Theology, 1976. 337pp.

Asia Youth Assembly, Delhi 1984. *Out of Control.* Official Report. Ed. by Chris Tremewan. Singapore: CCA, 1985. 208pp.

Asian Christian Leaders in China. Impressions and Reflections of a Visit to China, 1-14 June 1983. Singapore: CCA, 1983. 72pp.

Asian Christian Peace Conference, 9-14 January 1975. Kottayam, India. 84pp.

The Asian Christian Peace Conference. Theological Consultation on the Theological Basis for Cooperation with the Living Faiths for Peace with Justice. Colombo, Sri Lanka, 23-26 October 1980. Christian Peace Conference, 1980. 54pp.

Asian Realities and Christian Response: the Search for a New Community. Record and Proceedings, Asia Regional Consultation, 11-20 November 1979. Dhyana Pura, Bali, Indonesia. Sponsored by the CCA and the WCC, 1980. 106pp.

Asian Theological Reflections on Suffering and Hope. Ed. by Yap Kim Hao. Singapore: CCA, 1977. 80pp.

Asians and Blacks. Bangkok, Thailand: EACC, 1973. 81pp.

Asian's Struggle for Full Humanity: Towards a Relevant Theology. Papers from the Asian Theological Conference, 7-20 January 1979, Wennappuwa, Sri Lanka. Ed. by Virginia Fabella. Maryknoll, Orbis Books, 1980. 202pp.

Breaking Through Oppressions. An Asian Minority Women's Consultation Report. Race and Minority Women's Consultation Osaka, Japan, 13-18 October 1983. Hong Kong: CCA, 1983. 67pp.

Captives on the Land. Report of a Consultation on Land, Colombo, February 1976. Tokyo: CCA, 1977. 69pp.

CCA Consultation with Church Leaders from China. Hong Kong, 23-26 March 1981. Singapore: CCA, 1981. 80pp.

Christian Action in the Asian Struggle. Ed. by M.M. Thomas, Emilio Castro, Willem Adolf Visser 't Hooft and others. Singapore: CCA, 1973. 100pp.

Christian Conference of Asia. The First Christian Conference of Asia Urban Rural Mission Committee Meeting, Hong Kong, 30 August-5 September 1974. 74pp.

Christian Conference of Asia. Fifth Assembly, 6-12 June 1973. Singapore: CCA, 1973. 112pp.

Christian Conference of Asia. *Minutes,* Sixth Assembly, 31 May-9 June 1977. Penang, Singapore: CCA, 1977. 149pp.

Christian Conference of Asia. *Sixth Assembly,* 31 May-9 June 1977. Singapore: CCA, 1977. 75pp.

Christian Conference of Asia. *A Call to Vulnerable Discipleship.* CCA Seventh Assembly, 1981. Singapore: CCA, 1982. 114pp.

Christian Conference of Asia. *From Penang to Bangalore.* A Programme Report of the Work of the Christian Conference of Asia for the Years 1977 to 1981, Written as Preparation for the Seventh Assembly, Bangalore, India, May 1981. Singapore: CCA, 1981. 84pp.

Christian Conference of Asia. *Seventh Assembly,* Bangalore, India, 18-28 May 1981. Singapore: CCA, 1981. 124pp.

Christian Conference of Asia. *From Bangalore to Seoul*. Eighth Assembly. A Programme Report of the Work of the CCA for the Years 1981-85. Singapore: CCA, 1985. 142pp.

Christian Conference of Asia. *Minutes*. Eighth Assembly, Seoul, 26 June-2 July 1985. Singapore: CCA, 1985. 144pp.

Christian Conference of Asia. *Communicators Consultation*, 23-29 June 1975. Singapore: CCA, 1975. 66pp.

Christian Conference of Asia. *Minutes*, National Reports, Biblical Reflections, Twelfth Committee Meeting, Singapore, 7-9 September 1981. Singapore: CCA, 1981. 123pp.

Christian Conference of Asia. *Spirituality for Combat*. Published by the CCA Urban Rural Mission. Hongkong: CCA, 1983. 63pp.

Christian Response to Race and Minority Issues in Asia. Proceedings and Findings of a Regional Consultation Organized by the Christian Conference of Asia in Cooperation with the World Council of Churches, 24-29 March 1980. Hong Kong: CCA, 124pp.

Christianity in Asia. Ed. by T.K. Thomas. Singapore: CCA, 1979. 112pp.

The Church and Education in Asia. Ed. by Rob Evans, Tosh Arai. Singapore: CCA, 1980. 113pp.

Daniel, Kiran and Jin, Lee Soo, eds. *Asian Women Confront, Challenge, Change*. Singapore: CCA, 1977. 66pp.

East Asia Christian Conference. *Fifth Assembly*, Singapore, 6-12 June 1973. Singapore, CCA, 1973. 46pp.

East Asian Christian Conference. *1971 Reports of Urban Industrial Mission Projects in the East Asia Christian Conference Area*. Tokyo: EACC, 1972. 83pp.

Ecumenical Communication in Asia. Ed. by T.K. Thomas. Singapore: CCA, 1981. 71pp.

An Ecounter with Education for Liberation and Community. Ed. by John C. England. Singapore: CCA, 1975. 101pp.

Escape from Domination. A Consultation Report on the Patterns of Domination and People's Movements in Asia. Tokyo: CCA, 1980. 110pp.

Glimpses of Asian Youth in Life, Strife and Developments. Singapore: CCA, 1973. 74pp.

Guidelines for Development. Ed. by Harvey L. Perkins. Singapore: CCA, 1980. 95pp.

Handbook of the Association for Theological Education in South East Asia and the South East Asia Graduate School of Theology. Singapore: CCA, 1982. 65pp.

Health in the Development of Nations. Asian Ecumenical Conference on the Role of Health in the Development of Nations, 7-13 December 1972. Bangkok: 1973. 91pp.

Heiwa, Life for the People. Report of the Asia Heiwa Conference, Okinawa, Japan 19-23 February 1985. Kowloon: CCA, 1985. 172pp.

The Human and the Holy. Asian Perspectives in Christian Theology. Ed. by Emerito P. Nacpil and Douglas J. Elwood. Maryknoll, Orbis Books, 1980. 367pp.

In Clenched Fists of Struggle. Report of the Workshop on the Impact of TNCs in Asia. Hong Kong: CCA, 1981. 172pp.

Inheritors of the Earth. Report of the People's Forum on People, Land and Justice. Ed. by Alison O'Grady. Hong Kong: CCA, 1981. 114pp.

Islam's Challenge for Asian Churches. Papers from a Consultation on "The Challenge of Islam for Asian Churches". Ed. by Yap Kim Hao. Singapore: CCA, 1980. 50pp.

Jesus Christ with People in Asia. Report of the Asian Consultation in Singapore, 5-11 July 1982. Singapore: Asia Task Force of the WCC Office, 1983. 73pp.

Judiciary under Siege. Report of the Consultation on Asian Lawyers for Justice and Human Rights. Hong Kong: CCA, 1984. 136pp.

Justice and Development. Singapore, 26-30 November 1984. Ed. by Yong-Bock Kim. Seoul, Yang Seo Press, 1985. 333pp.

Living in Faith. Report of Asia Youth Resource Conference I, Kabanjahe, North Sumatra, Indonesia, 26 November-10 December 1979. Singapore: CCA, 1980. 115pp.

Minangkabau. Story of the People vs TNCs in Asia. Hong Kong: CCA, 1981. 154pp.

Minjung Theology: People as the Subjects of History. Ed. by Kim Yong Bock. Singapore: CCA, 1981. 196pp.

Mission in Asia Today. Papers from Hong Kong, 1975. Singapore: CCA, 1976. 103pp.

Models of Christian Education in Asia. Singapore: CCA, 1977. 55pp.

No Place in the Inn. Voices of Minority Peoples in Asia. Tokyo: CCA, 1979. 130pp.

O'Grady, Ron. *Christian Art in Asia.* Report of a Consultation Held at Dhyana Pura, Bali, Indonesia, 24-30 August 1978. Singapore: CCA, 1979. 47pp.

O'Grady, Ron. *Singapore to Penang.* The Christian Conference of Asia from 1973 to 1977. Singapore: CCA, 1977. 62pp.

People Against Domination. A Consultation Report on People's Movements and Structures of Domination in Asia, Kuala Lumpur, Malaysia, 24-28 February 1981. Tokyo: CCA, 1981. 197pp.

People Toiling under Pharaoh. Report of the Action-Research Process on Economic Justice in Asia. Ed. by Kim Yong Bock and Pharis J. Harvey. Tokyo: CCA, 1976. 282pp.

Proclaiming Christ in Solidarity with the Poor. Hong Kong: CCA, 1983. 83pp.

Profit at Gunpoint. Militarization and Economic Domination, a Christian Response. Fourth Asia Youth Resource Conference, Mindanao, Philippines, 15-30 Maz, 1983. Singapore: CCA, 1984. 186pp.

Race and Minority Women's Consultation, Korean Christian Centre, Osaka, Japan, 13-18 October, 1983. 67pp.

Rajendra, Cecil. *Refugees and Other Despairs.* Singapore: Choice Books, 1980. 91pp.

Religion and Asian Politics. An Islamic Perspective. Report of the Consultation on Religion and Asian Politics. Hong Kong, 19-22 November 1984. Kowloon: CCA, 1985. 138pp.

Report of an Asian Ecumenical Consultation on Development. Priorities and Guidelines. Singapore: CCA, 1974. 97pp.

Rifkin, Susan B. *Community Health in Asia.* Report on Two Workshops. Singapore: CCA, 1977. 149pp.

Rural Youth in Asia. Report of the Christian Conference of Asia Rural Youth Study Group, Sibu, Malaysia, 1976. Singapore: CCA, 1977. 51pp.

Set Free to Struggle for Freedom. Ed. by Barbara Weatherspoon. Hong Kong: CCA, 1985. 115pp.

Struggle With People is Living in Christ. Ed. by George Mathew. Hong Kong: CCA, 1981. 157pp

Tarakwon '83: Asian Ecumenical Youth Leaders' Seminar and Minutes of the Third Meeting of the Christian Conference of Asia Youth Programme Committee, Tarakwon, Korea, 19-26 April 1983. Singapore: CCA, 1984. 130pp.

Theology and Ideology in Asian People's Struggle. Ed. by George Ninan. Hong Kong: CCA, 1985. 82pp.

There Is No End. Check list of EACC-CCA Publications and Other Related Asian
   Ecumenical Documents 1948-1981. Comp. by Dorothy M. Harvey. Singapore:
   CCA, 1982. 104pp.
Thomas, T.K. ed. *Testimony Amid Asian Suffering.* Singapore: CCA, 1977. 102pp.
Towards an Asian Sense of Science and Technology. Papers of a Consultation on "the
   Future — Science, Faith and Justice in Asia", Manila, Philippines, 18-22 December
   1983. Ed. by Lourdino A. Yuzon. Singapore: CCA, 1984. 197pp.
Towards the Sovereignty of the People. A Search for an Alternative Form of Democratic
   Politics in Asia. A Christian Discussion. Singapore: CCA, 1983. 193pp.
Varieties of Witness. Ed. by Preman Niles and T.K. Thomas. Singapore: CCA, 1980.
   139pp.
Witnessing to the Kingdom. Ed. by Preman Niles and T.K. Thomas. Singapore: CCA,
   1979. 76pp.
Women in Asia: Status and Image. Ed. by Mary John Mananzan. Singapore: CCA, 1979.
   51pp.

CARIBBEAN

Caribbean Christian Challenge. The Report of the Ecumenical Team from the Caribbean
   who Visited Britain in the Autumn of 1981. London: BCC, 1981. 71pp.
Caribbean Conference of Churches. *CCC-CADEC: Report of the Third Biennial Local-
   isation Meeting,* Grenada, May 1981: "Towards More Effective Management".
   Barbados: CADEC, 1981. 68pp.
Caribbean Conference of Churches. *The CCC Communications Cluster.* The Second
   Assembly, Georgetown, Guyana, 16-23 November 1977. Kingston: CCC, 1977.
   40pp.
Caribbean Conference of Churches. *Common Ground.* Some Discussion Notes for the
   Second General Assembly, Georgetown, Guyana, 16-23 November 1977. Kingston:
   CCC, 1977. 56pp.
Caribbean Conference of Churches *Report.* Continuation Committee Held in Port-au-
   Prince, Haiti, 5-11 June 1974. Trinidad: CCC, 1974. 33pp.
Caribbean Conference of Churches. *Report of the Caribbean Ecumenical Programme.*
   Consultation on Personnel in Mission, Trinidad, 15-18 December 1981. Ed. by M.
   Ramcharan. Trinidad: CCC, 1981. 37pp.
Caribbean Conference of Churches. *Report* of the Inaugural Assembly Held in Kingston,
   Jamaica, 13-16 November 1973. Kingston: CCC, 1973. 143pp.
Caribbean Conference of Churches. *The Right Hand of God.* Inaugural Assembly, 1973.
   CCC Assembly. Kingston: CCC, 1976. 24pp.
Caribbean Conference of Churches. *Workers Together With Christ.* Report of the Second
   General Assembly, Georgetown, Guyana, 16-23 November 1977. Georgetown:
   CCC, 1978. 102pp.
Caribbean Ecumenical Consultation for Development. Chaguaramas, Trinidad,
   November 1971. *Called to be.* Official Report of the Consultation. Bridgetown,
   Barbados, West India: CADEC, 1971. 80pp.
Caribbean Ecumenical Consultation for Development. Chaguaramas, Trinidad,
   November 1971. *Called to be.* Second Version. 1973, 59pp.

Caribbean Regional Conference on the Churches' Role in Health and Wholeness. Port of Spain, Trinidad, 12-16 March 1979. Geneva: WCC, 1979. 51pp.

Caribbean Women in Communication for Development. Report of Workshop, Mona Campus, Jamaica, 13-15 June 1975. Ed. by Marlene Cuthbert. Barbados: Cedar Press, 1975. 61pp.

Consultation on Church-Communications-Development. Held at Codrington College, Barbados, 3-8 January 1972. Geneva: SODEPAX, 1972. 59pp.

Davis, Kortright. *Mission for Caribbean Change.* Caribbean Development as Theological Enterprise. Frankfurt: Lang, 1982. 259pp. (Studien zur interkulturellen Geschichte des Christentums, Nr. 28).

The First Ten Years. CCC/CADEC/ARC. A Synopsis of the Movement 1967-77. Specially Prepared to Commemorate the Second General Assembly of the CCC, Held in Georgetown, Guyana, 16-23 November 1977. Barbados: CADEC, CCC, 1977. 18pp.

Handbook of Churches in the Caribbean. Specially Prepared for the Inaugural Assembly of the Caribbean Conference of Churches, 13-16 November 1973. Ed. by Joan A. Brathwaite, Bridgetown: Barbados, CADEC, 1973. 234pp.

Handbook of Churches in the Caribbean. Comp. by Lisa Bessil-Watson. Bridgetown: CEDAR Press, 1982. 134pp.

In Search of Partnership. Report of the First CCC Consortium Held at Mt St Benedict, Trinidad, 24-26 February 1977. Bridgetown, Barbados: CADEC, 1977.

Troubling of the Waters. A Collection of Papers and Responses Presented at Two Conferences on Creative Theological Reflection Held in Jamaica on 3-4 May and in Trinidad on 28-30 May 1973. Ed. by Idris Hadrid. San Fernando, Trinidad, Rahaman, 1973. 207pp.

Out of the Depths. A Collection of Papers Presented at Four Missiology Conferences Held in Antigua, Guyana, Jamaica and Trinidad in 1975. Ed. by Idris Hamid. San Fernando, Trinidad: St Andrew's Theological College, 1977. 261pp.

With Eyes Wide Open. A Collection of Papers by Caribbean Scholars on Caribbean Christian Concerns. Ed. by David I. Mitchell. Published by CADEC to Commemorate the Inaugural Assembly of the CCC, Jamaica, November 1973. Bridgetown, Barbados: CADEC, 1973. 202pp.

EUROPE

Alive to the World in the Power of the Holy Spirit. Theological Preparatory Document for Conference of European Churches, Eighth Assembly in Crete, 25-28 October 1979. Geneva: CEC, 1979. 90pp.

Christen und Europa. Der Beitrag der christlichen Kirchen zur europäischen Integration. Andernach: Pontes 1977. 99pp.

The Churches and Islam in Europe (II). Geneva: CEC, 1982. 76pp.

Churches in Conciliar Fellowship? A Discussion Amongst European Churches on Unity and Cooperation. Report of a Consultation at Sofia-Bulgaria, 3-8 October 1977. Geneva: CEC, 1978. 116pp. (CEC, Occasional Paper, No. 10).

The Churches of Europe and the Churches of Other Continents. Report of a Consultation Held at Basle, Switzerland, 27-30 November 1976. Geneva: CEC, 1968. 90pp.

The Common Christian Roots of the European Nations. An International Colloquium in the Vatican (Rome, 1981). Florence: Le Monnier, 1982. 300pp.

The Communion of the Holy Spirit Today: Trinity, Church, Creation. Report of the Study Consultation of the Conference of European Churches, 24-28 March 1981, Cardiff, Great Britain. Geneva: CEC, 1981. 90pp.

Conference of European Churches. *Directory of Theological Training Institutions in Europe (non-Roman Catholic).* Annuaire des établissements d'enseignement théologique en Europe (non catholiques romains). Verzeichnis theologischer Ausbildungsstätten in Europa. (nichtrömisch-katholisch). Geneva: CEC, 1970. 57pp.

Conference of European Churches. *Dossier On Danger.* European Churches React to International Tension. Geneva: CEC, 1980. 108pp.

Conference of European Churches. *This Happened at Nyborg VI.* The Report of the Sixth Assembly of the Conference of European Churches, 26 April-3 May 1971. Geneva: CEC, 1971. 268pp.

Conference of European Churches. *To Be One "That the World May Believe".* Report of the European Ecumenical Encounter CCEE-CEC, Chantilly, France, 10-13 April 1978. Conference of European Churches and Consilium Conferentiarum Episcopalium Europae. Geneva: CEC, 1978. 111pp.

Conference of European Churches. *Why is it? What is it? Who is it?* Geneva: CEC, 1971. Pagination varies.

Conference of European Churches. Assembly *Nyborg VI to Nyborg VII,* reports to the Assembly: Nyborg VII Assembly, 16-23 September 1974, Engelberg, Switzerland. Geneva: CEC, 1974. 63pp.

Conference of European Churches. *From Engelberg to Crete, Reports to the Assembly.* Eighth Assembly, 18-25 October 1979, Crete, Greece. Geneva: CEC, 1980. 119pp.

Conference of European Churches. *Unity in the Spirit, Diversity in the Churches.* The Report of the Conference of European Churches' Assembly VIII, 18-25 October 1979. Crete. Geneva: CEC, 1980. 337pp.

The Conference on Security and Cooperation in Europe and the Churches. Study Material for Use in Churches and Congregations. Report of a Consultation at Buckow, GDR, 27-31 October 1975. Conference of European Churches. Geneva: CEC, 1976. 70pp. (CEC, Occasional Paper No. 7).

Europe After Helsinki and the Developing Regions. Spiritual, Moral and Practical Responsibilities of our Churches. Study Material for Use in Churches and Congregations. Report of a Consultation, 7-11 March 1977, Gallneukirchen near Linz. Geneva: CEC, 1977. 100pp. (CEC, Occassional Paper, No. 9).

European Security and the Churches. Report of a Consultation Held at Gwatt (Lake Thun), Switzerland, 25-28 November 1969. Geneva: CEC, 1970. 44pp. (CEC, Occasional Paper, No. 3).

European Theology Challenged by the Worldwide Church. Study Material for Use in Churches and Theological Faculties, Seminaries and Congregations. Report of a Consultation at Geneva, 29 March-2 April 1976. Geneva: Conference of European Churches, 1976. 145pp. (CEC, Occasional Paper, No. 8).

The Groaning of Creation, European Christians in Quest of Their Responsibility Today. Report of the Study Consultation of the CEC, 22-26 March 1982, Bucharest, Romania. Geneva: CEC, 1982. 102pp. (CEC, Occasional Paper, No. 14).

Holmes, Ann. *Church, Property and People.* A Study of the Attitudes of Churches to Their Property in Three Multi-Racial, Multi-Faith Areas, Bradford, Derby and Lambeth. London: British Council of Churches, 1973. 57pp.

Jesus Christ: Contemporary Europe. A Reflection on Some Church Activities. Report of a Consultation at Götzis, Austria, 4-9 March 1973. Geneva: CEC, 1973. 73pp. (CEC, Occasional Paper, No. 5).

Milligan, W.J. *The New Nomads: Challenge Facing Christians in Western Europe.* Geneva: WCC, 1984. 130pp. (The Risk Book Series, No. 21).

Pastoral Care for the Traveller. Report of a Consultation Held at Glion sur Montreux, Switzerland, 19-24 January 1970. Geneva: CEC, 1970. 60pp. (CEC, Occasional Paper, No. 4).

Peace in Europe — the Churches' Role. Report of a Consultation Held at Engelberg, Switzerland, 28 May-1 June 1973. Geneva: CEC, 1973. 109pp. (CEC, Occasional Paper, No. 6).

Relations Between Western Europe Countries and Southern Africa. The Responsibility of Churches in the Struggle for Justice and Liberation. Rotterdam: Ecumenical Research Exchange, 1975. 73pp.

Security, Disarmament and Economics. Socio-Ethical Challenges for European Churches and Christians after Helsinki and Belgrade. Report of the Third Post-Helsinki/Belgrade Consultation of the Conference of European Churches, 26-29 September 1978, Siofok, Hungary. Geneva: CEC, 1979. 126pp. (CEC, Occasional Paper, No. 11).

A Short Bibliography on Muslim-Christian Relations. Consultative Committee on Islam in Europe of the Conference of European Churches. Compiled by Jan Slomp. Leusden: Committee on Islam in Europe of the CEC, 1982. 17pp.

Tschuy, Theo. *An Ecumenical Experiment in Human Rights.* Geneva: The Churches' Human Rights Programme, 1985. 47pp.

Will, James E. *Must Walls Divide?* The Creative Witness of the Churches in Europe. New York: Friendship Press, 1981.

Witness to God in Secular Europe. Report of a Consultation Held in St. Pölten, Austria, 5-10 March 1984. Geneva: CEC, 1985. 75pp.

LATIN AMERICA

¿Cómo enfrentar el racismo en la década del 80? Consulta de Iglesias Latinoamericanas. Lima: Celadec, 1980. 77pp.

La condición social de los jóvenes. Lima: ULAJE, 1979. 52pp. (Documentos ULAJE, No. 2).

Consejo Latinoamericano de Iglesias. *Comprometidos con el Reino.* Recopilación de declaraciones, resoluciones y cartas del CLAI, 1978-1982. Lima: CLAI, 1982. 110pp.

Consejo Latinoamericano de Iglesias. *Jesus Cristo — vocação comprometida com o reino.* São Paulo: CLAI, 1982. 126pp.

Consejo Latinoamericano de Iglesias. En Formación. *Oaxtepec 1978.* Unidad y misión en América Latina. San José: CLAI, 1980. 228pp.

Consejo Latinoamericano de Iglesias. *Semilla de comunión.* Carlos A. Valle editor. Buenos Aires: La Aurora, 1983. 164pp.

Consejo Latinoamericano de Iglesias. *Semente de comunhão, 11-18 de novembro de 1982.* Assembléia Constitutiva do CLAI, Lima. São Paulo: CLAI, 1983. 188pp.

De Panamá a Oaxtepec. El protestantismo latinoamericano en busca de unidad. San José: Centro Evangélico Latinoamericano de Estudios Pastorales, 1978. 172pp.

Declaración de los derechos del niño. Fundamentación bíblica. Buenos Aires: CLAI, 1984. 32pp.

Elementos de pastoral ecuménica. Guía y léxico, sección de ecumenismo. Buenos Aires: CLAI, 1982. 162pp.

En defensa de los pueblos indígenas. Lima: Comisión Evangélica Latinoamericana de Educación Cristiana, 1980. 190pp.

Encuentro Evangélico Latinoamericano de Juventudes. Lima, 21-27 de Febrero de 1982. CLAI, 1982. Pagination varies.

La esperanza en el presente de América Latina. Ponencias presentadas al II Encuentro de Científicos Sociales y Teólogos sobre el tema "El discernimiento de las utopias", Costa Rica, 11-16 de julio de 1983. Raúl Vidales y Luis Rivera Pagán editores. San José: DEI, 1983. 479pp.

Evaluación crítica de la práctica ecuménica latinoamericana. Reflexiones sobre el desarrollo y las perspectivas de las relaciones ecuménicas en el ámbito latinoamericano. Buenos Aires: Tierra Nueva, 1979. 38pp.

Evangelization and Politics. Addresses and Related papers. Matanzas, Cuba, 25 February-2 March 1979. Editors: Sergio Arce Martínez, Oden Marichal Rodríguez. New York: New York Circus, 1982. 224pp.

El futuro del ecumenismo en América Latina. By Julio Barreiro, Oscar Bolioli and Jorge E. Monterroso. Buenos Aires: Tierra Nueva, 1977. 55pp.

International Ecumenical Congress of Theology. *The Challenge of Basic Christian Communities.* Papers from the International Ecumenical Congress of Theology, 20-February-2 March 1980, Sao Paulo. Ed. by Sergio Torres and John Eagleson. Maryknoll: Orbis Books, 1981. 283pp.

Jesus Cristo a vida do mundo. São Paulo: Centro Ecumênico de Documentação e Informação, 1984. 128pp.

Porque de ellos es la tierra. El derecho a la tierra de los pueblos aborígenes. Lima: CLAI, 1983. 144pp.

Míguez Bonino, José. *Integración humana y unidad cristiana.* Publicado por: Seminario Evangélico de Puerto Rico. Puerto Rico: La Reforma, 1969, 102pp. (Conferencias Ecuménicas, No 1).

Premazzi, Javier. *Reflexiones sobre el ecumenismo en América Latina.* Geneva: 1982. 188pp.

El proceso de urbanización en América Latina. Resultados de un encuentro interdisciplinario. Montevideo: ISAL, 1970. 217pp.

Putting Theology to Work. Papers of the Latin America-UK Theological Consultation at Fircroft, May 1980. Ed. by Derek Winter. London: British Council of Churches, 1980. 93pp.

Tamez, Elsa. *La Hora de la Vida.* Lecturas bíblicas. San José: DEI, 1980. 125pp.

Teología desde el Tercer Mundo. Documentos finales de los cinco congresos internacionales de la Asociación Ecuménica de Teólogos del Tercer Mundo. San José: Departamento Ecuménico de Investigaciones, 1982. 99pp.

A Transnacionalização da América Latina e a Missão das Igrejas. Itaici, São Paulo, Outubro de 1980. Rio de Janeiro: Centro Ecumênico de Documentação e Informação, 1983. 52pp.

MIDDLE EAST

Christian Youth in a Troubled Society. Ayia Napa, Cyprus, 13-20 July 1978. Geneva: WCC, Middle East Council of Churches Youth Programme, 1978. 75pp.

The Ecumenical Popular Education Project (EPEP). WSCF Middle East: 1979. 18pp.

Horner, Norman A. *Rediscovering Christianity Where it Began.* A Survey of Contemporary Churches in the Middle East and Ethiopia. Lebanon: Heidelberg Press, 1974. 110pp.

Horner, Norman A. *A Statistical Survey of Christian Communities in Cyprus, Egypt, Ethiopia, Iran, Iraq, Jordan, Lebanon, Sudan, Syria, Turkey, Beirut, 1972.* 37pp.

Middle East Council of Churches. Documentation Office. *Directory on Christian Communication in the Middle East 1985.* Beirut: MECC, 1985. 76pp.

Middle East Council of Churches. *Minutes of the Inaugural Assembly,* Nicosia, Cyprus, 28-30 May 1974. MECC: 1974, 24pp.

Middle East Council of Churches. General Assembly. *Your Kingdom Come.* Third General Assembly of the Middle East Council of Churches, Nicosia, Cyprus, 28 November-4 December 1980. Beirut: MECC, 1980, 283pp.

Middle East Council of Churches. *A Handbook for the MECC Fourth General Assembly,* 13-19 February 1985, Nicosia, Cyprus. Beirut: MECC, 1985. 99pp.

Middle East Council of Churches. Inaugural Assembly. *Our Common Christian Message Today.* Nicosia, Cyprus, 28-30 May 1974. Nicosia, Cyprus: MECC, 1974. 40pp.

Middle East Council of Churches. *Report of the Activities of the Youth Programme 1983.* Beirut: MECC, 1983. 32pp.

Middle East Council of Churches Consultation. *The Community of Women and Men in the Church.* Beirut, Lebanon, 22-26 January 1980. Geneva: WCC, Community of Women and Men in the Church Study, 1981. 87pp.

Our Service for the Life of the World. Kiev, The Soviet Union, 14-27 September 1983. Beirut: Middle East Churches Youth Programme, 1983. 32pp.

Towards Development and Justice with Palestinians. 1982 Larnaca Consultation. MECC, Department on Service to Palestine Refugees, 1982, 136pp.

Unity in Service with the Palestinians. Consultation on Service to Palestine Refugees: Called by the Middle East Council of Churches in Cooperation with the Commission on Inter-Church Aid, Refugee and World Service of the World Council of Churches, Nicosia, Cyprus, 4-8 November 1979. Beirut: MECC, 1980. 116pp.

NORTH AMERICA

3aptism Confirmation. Implications for the Younger Generation. New York: NCCC, Department of Youth Ministry, 1979. 73pp.

Against the World for the World. The Hartford Appeal and the Future of American Religion. Ed. by Peter L. Berger and Richard John Neuhaus. New York: Seabury Press, 1976. 164pp.

U.S. Catholic Ecumenism — Ten Years Later. Ed. by David J. Bowman. Washington: US Catholic Conference, 1975. 90pp.

Cavert, Samuel McCrea. *The American Churches in the Ecumenical Movement, 1900-1968.* New York: Association Press, 1968. 288pp.

Cavert, Samuel McCrea. *Church Cooperation and Unity in America. A Historical Review, 1900-1970.* New York: Association Press, 1970. 400pp.

The Church and Southern Africa. Report on a Consultation Convened by the National Council of Churches of Christ in the USA and the US Catholic Conference, 7-11 March 1977, Marcy, New York. New York: NCC, 1977. 80pp.

Church Investments Corporations and Southern Africa. New York: Friendship Press, 1973. 242pp.

Conciliar Fellowship. A Study of the Commission on Faith and Order of the National Council of Churches of Christ in the USA. Indianapolis: COCU, 1982. 26pp.

Curry Lerond. *Protestant-Catholic Relations in America. World War I Through Vatican II.* Lexington: University Press of Kentucky, 1972. 124pp.

An Ecumenical Encounter. A Discussion Between the National Council of Churches of Christ in the USA and the NCC in India. Ed. by R.L. Turnipseed and Mathai Zachariah. Delhi: ISPCK, 1984. 97pp.

Emerging Models of Christian Mission. A Special Consultation, Ventnor, N.J. 11-14 May. Co-sponsored by the Future of the Missionary Enterprise Project of IDOC, International, Maryknoll Mission Institute and Overseas Ministries Study Centre. Ventnor: OMSC, 1976. 159pp.

Energy Ethics, a Christian Response. Outgrowth of a Seminar of the Energy-Study Panel of the National Council of Churches in the USA Held at Abiquiu, Summer 1978. Ed. by Dieter T. Hessel. New York: Friendship Press, 1979. 170pp.

Holton, Margaret L., ed. *Spirit of Toronto 1834-1984.* Toronto: Image Publishing, 1983. 336pp.

Hoyer, H. Conrad. *Ecumenopolis USA.* The Church in Mission in Community. Minneapolis, Min.: Augsburg Publishing House, 1971. 159pp.

Life Amid Death in Central America. Conversations Between Church Leaders of North and Central America, Summer 1983. New York: NCCC, 1983. 37pp.

Listening to Lay People. Report of the All Lay National Committee of the Listening-to-Lay-People Project of the NCCC in the USA. New York: Council Press, 1971. 73pp.

Modras, Ronald E. *Paths to Unity.* American Religion Today and Tomorrow. New York: Sheed and Ward, 1968. 309pp.

Muelder, Walter G. *A Comparative Study of Twenty-One North American Churches on Church Unity.* A Report of the Work Group on Education for Ecumenism of the US Conference for the WCC. US Conference of the WCC, 1978. 65pp.

National Council of the Churches of Christ in the USA. *A Guide to the NCC Archives 1950-1972.* Ed. by Donald L. Haggerty and Alan Thomson. Philadelphia: Presbyterian Historical Society, 1984. 2 vols.

Report on Possible Roman Catholic Membership in the National Council of Churches by the Study Committee on the Relationship of the NCC and the RCC in the USA. Washington: United States Conference, 1972. 47pp.

Restructure of the National Council of Churches. A Proposal by the General Board to the Ninth General Assembly, 3-7 December 1972. New York: NCCC, 1972. 47pp.

Solomonow, Allan. *Where We Stand.* Official Statements of American Churches on the Middle East Conflict. New York: The Middle East Consultation Group, 1977. 32pp.

Speight, R. Marston. *Christian-Muslim Relations.* An Introduction for Christians in the USA. Hartford: NCCC in the USA, Task Force on Christian-Muslim Relations, 1983. 85pp.

Stowe, David M. *Ecumenicity and Evangelism.* Grand Rapids, Michigan: Eerdmans, 1970. 94pp.

To Love or to Perish. The Technological Crisis and the Churches. A Report of the USA Task Force on the Future of Mankind in a World of Science-Based Technology, Co-sponsored by the NCCC and Union Theological Seminary of New York. Ed. by J. Edward Carothers, Margaret Mead and others. New York: Friendship Press, 1972. 153pp.

Vanderwerf, Nathan H. *The Times Were Very Full*. A Perspective on the First 25 Years of the National Council of the Churches of Christ in the USA, 1950-1975. New York: NCCC, 1975. 128pp.

Whalen, William J. *Separated Brethren*. A survey of Protestant, Anglican, Eastern Orthodox and Other Denominations in the USA. Huntington: Our Sunday Visitor, 1979. 252pp.

PACIFIC

Biddlecomb, Cynthia Z. *Pacific Tourism*. Contrasts in Values and Expectations. Suva: PCC, 1981. 61pp.

Christen, Philippe, comp. *A Bibliography on the Pacific*. A List of Resources Concerning the Pacific Region Available in the WCC Library. Ed. by Pierre Beffa. Geneva: WCC, 1985. 17pp.

Church and Church Membership: Adult Studies. Ed. by Joyce Trudinger, Inoke Nabulivou and P.N. Wellock. Suva: Pacific Islands Christian Education Council, 1969. 41pp.

Garrett, John. *To Live Among the Stars*. Christian Origins in Oceania. Geneva: WCC, Suva: Institute of Pacific Studies, 1982. 412pp.

Garrett, John and Mavor, John. *Worship the Pacific Way*. Suva, Fiji: Lotu Pasifika Productions, 1973. 76pp.

Hezel, Francis X. *Yesterday's Myths, Today's Realities*. A Second Look at Development Strategies in Micronesia. Port Vila, Vanuatu: Pacific Churches Research Centre, 1980. 10pp.

Mission, Churches, and Sects in Oceania. Ed. by James A. Boutilier, Daniel T. Hughes, Sharon W. Tiffany. London: University Press of America, 1978. 500pp.

Pacific Conference of Churches. *Report of the Third Assembly*, Port Moresby. Fiji: PCC; 1976. 110pp.

Pacific Conference of Churches. *The Fourth World Meets*. Suva: PCC, 1972. 110pp.

Pacific Conference of Churches. *Report of the Fourth Assembly, 3-15 May 1981*, Nuku'alofa, Tonga. Suva: PCC, 1981. 298pp.

Pacific Conference of Churches. *The Dancing Convention*. Youths of the 80s. Suva: Lotu Pasifika Productions, 1980. 45pp.

Pacific Regional Consultation on the Christian Understanding of Health, Healing and Wholeness. Papua New Guinea, 23-29 October 1981. Geneva: WCC, Christian Medical Commission, 1982, 80pp.

Richards, Charles G. *Christian Communication in the South-West Pacific*. Report of Consultation Held at Nobonob, Madang, New Guinea, August 1969. Dodoma, Tanzania: Central Tanganika Press, 1970, 173pp.

Siwatibau, Suliana and Williams, David. *A Call to a New Exodus: An Anti-Nuclear Primer for Pacific People*. Suva: Lotu Pasifika Production, 1982., 96pp.

Tides of Change. Pacific Christians Review their Problems and Hopes. Ed. by Vaughan Hinton. Melbourne: The Commission for World Mission of the Uniting Church in Australia, 1981, 127pp.

What Happened at Waitangi in 1983? A Report to the New Zealand Churches Concerning the Treaty of Waitangi, its Observance, and its Ceremonial Commemoration. Auckland: National Council of Churches in New Zealand, 1983, 108pp.

Winkler, James E. *Losing Control.* Towards an Understanding of Transnational Corporations in the Pacific Islands Context. Suva: PCC, 1981, 82pp.

Women Speak Out. A Report of the Pacific Women's Conference Suva, 27 October-2 November 1975. Ed. and Comp. by Vanessa Griffen. Suva: Pacific Women's Conference, 1976, 141pp.

Wright, Cliff. *New Hebridean Culture and Christian Faith.* Report of Education Workshop, Aulua, New Hebrides, 19 April-3 May 1979. Vila, New Hebrides: Pacific Churches Research Centre, 1980, 35pp.

Wright, Cliff. *Seeds of the World.* Tongan Cultures and Christian Faith. Report of Tonga Workshop, 20 June-3 July 1970. Vila, New Hebrides: Pacific Churches Research Centre, 1980. 43pp.

Orthodox Churches in the Ecumenical Movement

Baker, Derek. *The Orthodox Churches and the West.* Papers Read at the Fourteenth Summer Meeting and the Fifteenth Winter Meeting of the Ecclesiastical History Society. Oxford: Blackwell, 1976, 336pp.

Christian Unity and Ecumenism. Encyclical Letter of the Synod of Bishops of the Orthodox Church in America. 1973, 16pp.

Congrès de théologie orthodoxe. Procès-verbaux du deuxième congrès de théologie orthodoxe à Athènes, 19-29 août 1976. Ed. by Savas Chr. Agouridès. Athènes, 1978, 585pp.

Declaration of the Ecumenical Patriarchate on the Occasion of the 25th Anniversary of the World Council of Churches. Déclaration du patriarcat... Erklärung des Patriarchates... Istanbul: Patriarchal Institute for Patristic Studies, 1973, 64pp.

Hebly, J.A. *The Russians and the World Council of Churches.* Documentary Survey of the Accession of the Russian Orthodox Church to the WCC, with Commentary. Belfast: Christian Journals, 1978, 181pp.

Istavridis, Vasil T. *The Ecumenicity of Orthodoxy.* Geneva: WCC, 1977, 13pp. In: Ecumenical Review, vol. 29, 1977. pp.182-195.

Jesus Christ — the Life of the World. An Orthodox Contribution to the Vancouver Theme. Ed. by Ion Bria. Geneva: WCC, 1982, 121pp.

Meyendorff, John. *Catholicity and the Church.* Crestwood, NY: St Vladimir's Seminary Press, 1983, 160pp.

The New Valamo Consultation. *The Ecumenical Nature of the Orthodox Witness.* New Valamo, Finland, 24-30 September 1977. Geneva: WCC, 1978, 86pp.

Nissiotis, Nikos A. *Interpreting Orthodoxy.* Minneapolis: Light and Live Publishing Co., 48pp.

Orthodox Contributions to Nairobi. Papers Compiled and Presented by the Orthodox Task Force of the WCC. Geneva: WCC, 1975, 35pp.

Orthodox Thought. Reports of Orthodox Consultations Organized by the World Council of Churches, 1975-1982. Ed. by Georges Tsetsis. Geneva: WCC, Orthodox Task Force, 1983, 96pp.

Patelos, Constantin G. *The Orthodox Church in the Ecumenical Movement*. Documents and Statements 1902-1975. Geneva: WCC, 1978, 360pp.

Romita, Angelo. *La Tradizione e le tradizioni nella vita della Chiesa*. Storia di un dialogo ecumenico fra teologi orientali e occidentali. Leumann: Elle di Ci, 1983, 240pp.

The Sofia Consultation: Orthodox Involvement in the World Council of Churches. Ed. by Todor Sabev. Geneva: WCC, Orthodox Task Force, 1982, 129pp.

Stephanopoulos, Robert G. *Guidelines of Orthodox Christians in Ecumenical Relations*. Published by the Standing Conference of Canonical Orthodox Bishops in America and Commended to the Clergy for Guidance. New York: Standing Conference of Canonical Orthodox Bishops in America, 1973, 66pp.

The Roman Catholic Church in the Ecumenical Movement

Achutegui, Pedro S. de, ed. *The Dublin Papers on Ecumenism*. Fourth Congress of Jesuit Ecumenists. Manila: Loyola School of Theology, Ateneo Manila University, 1972, 211pp.

Achutegui, Pedro S. de, ed. *Ecumenism and Vatican II; Select Perspectives*. Manila: Loyola House of Studies, 1972, 198pp.

Aspekte der Ökumene. Anregungen für Theorie und Praxis/mit Beiträgen von Ambrosius Backhaus, Johannes Brosseder, Damaskinos Papandreou and others. Hamburg: Katholische Akademie, 1984, 120pp.

Bea, Augustine. *Ecumenism in Focus*. London: G. Chapman, 1969, 311pp.

Bekes, Gerard and Vajta, Vilmos, eds. *Unitatis redintegratio, 1964-1974*. The Impact of the Decree on Ecumenism. With Contributions by Nikos Nissiotis, Yves Congar, Lukas Vischer, and others. Roma, Ed. Anselmiana, 1977, 176pp.

Bowman, David J., ed. *US Catholic Ecumenism — Ten Years Later*. Foreword by Archbishop William W. Baum. Washington: Publications Office United States Catholic Conference, 1975, 90pp.

Boyer, Charles. *Le mouvement œcuménique, les faits — le dialogue*. Rome: Presses de l'Université grégorienne, 1976, 262pp.

Brunello, Aristide. *Vivere l'ecumenismo*. Roma: Edizioni Paoline, 1971, 95pp.

Butler, B.C. *The Church and Unity*. An Essay. London: Chapman 1979, 271pp.

Catholicisme ouvert par un groupe de spécialistes. Yves Congar, Christophe J. Dumont, Jérôme Hamer, Bernard Lambert, Emmanuel Lanne, Pierre Michalon, Charles Moeller, Jean Willebrands and others. Paris: Apostolat des Editions, 1971, 416pp.

Congar, Yves. *Essais œcuméniques. Le mouvement, les hommes, les problèmes*. Paris: Le Centurion, 1984, 316pp.

Congar, Yves. *Une passion: l'unité.* Réflections et souvenirs 1929-1973. Paris, Editions du Cerf, 1974, 117pp.

Desseaux, Jacques Elisée. *Twenty Centuries of Ecumenism.* New York: Paulist Press, 1985, 103pp.

Dulles, Avery. *Church Membership as a Catholic and Ecumenical Problem.* Milwaukee: Marquette University, Theology Department, 1974, 114pp.

Fiolet, Herman A. *Ecumenical Breakthrough.* An Integration of the Catholic and the Reformational Faith. Pittsburgh, Pa.: Duquesne University Press, 1969, 475pp.

Fouilloux, Etienne. *Les catholiques et l'unité chrétienne du XIXe au XXe siècle.* Itinéraires européens d'expression française. Paris: Le Centurion, 1982, 1007pp.

Fox, Helmut. *Ökumene Hoffnung oder Illusion?* Eine katholische Bilanz. Trier: Spee-Verlag, 1974, 168pp.

Fries, Heinrich and Rahner, Karl, eds. *Unity of the Churches: An Actual Possibility.* Philadelphia: Fortress Press, 1985, 146pp.

Girault, René. *L'œcuménisme, où vont les Eglises?* Paris: Le Centurion, 1983, 239pp.

Gleixner, Christine. *Ökumene heute: Eine Orientierungshilfe.* Wien: Verlag Herold, 1980, 232pp.

Hoppenot, Marguerite Ph. *Pleins pouvoirs à l'Esprit Saint.* Paris: Le Centurion, 1975, 181pp.

Horgan, Thaddeus and Gouthro, Arthur. *Parish Ecumenism.* Garrison: Graymoor Ecumenical Institute, 1977, 77pp.

Iung, Nicolas. *Bilan de l'œcuménisme contemporain.* Les Eglises chrétiennes non romaines à la recherche de l'unité, l'action œcuménique de l'Eglise catholique, points de divergence et d'accord. Paris: Mame, 1971, 336pp.

Jaeger, Lorenz. *Einheit und Gemeinschaft.* Stellungnahmen zu Fragen der christlichen Einheit. Hg. vom Johann-Adam-Möhler-Institut. Paderborn: Bonifacius 1972, 427pp.

Joannes Paulus II. *Addresses and Homilies on Ecumenism: 1978-1980.* Ed. by John B. Sheerin and John F. Hotchkin. Washington: US Catholic Conference, 1980, 172pp.

Lescrauwaet, J.F. *Die Einheit der Ökumene.* Perspektiven nach dem Zweiten Vatikanischen Konzil. Stein a.Rhein: Christiania Verlag, 1969, 153pp.

Margerie, Bertrand de, ed. *Vers la plénitude de la communion.* Paris: Tequi, 1980, 184pp.

Neuner, Peter. *Kleines Handbuch der Ökumene.* Düsseldorf: Patmos Verlag, 1984, 184pp.

L'œcuménisme: Unité chrétienne et identité confessionnelle. Paris: Beauchesne, 1985, 123pp.

Rodriguez, Pedro. *Iglesia y ecumenismo.* Madrid: Ediciones Rialp, 1979, 418pp.

Ryan, Thomas. *Tales of Christian Unity: The Adventures of an Ecumenical Pilgrim.* New York: Paulist Press, 1983, 281pp.

Schütte, Heinz. *Ziel — Kirchengemeinschaft: Zur ökumenischen Orientierung.* Paderborn: Verlag Bonifatius-Druckerei, 1985, 207pp.

Secretariat for Promoting Christian Unity. *Ecumenical Collaboration at the Regional National and Local Levels.* London: Catholic Truth Society, 1975, 32pp.

Toinet, Paul. *L'œcuménisme entre vie et mort: l'heure du discernement.* Chambray: C.L.D., 1981, 223pp.

Vaquero, José Sanchez. *Ecumenismo.* Manual de formación ecuménica. Salamanca: Centro Ecuménico Juan XXIII, 1971, 635pp.

Villain, Maurice. *La prière œcuménique*. Paris: Editions Paulines, 1970, 135pp.
Wacker, Paulus Gerhard. *Ökumene provokativ*. Zur Versöhnung der Christenheit. Paderborn: Ferdinand Schöningh, 1973, 199pp.
Willebrands, J. *Œcuménisme et problèmes actuels*. Paris: Les Editions du Cerf, 1969, 212pp.
Yarnold, Edward. *They Are in Earnest*. Christian Unity in the Statements of Paul VI, John Paul I, John Paul II. Middlegreen-Slough: St Paul Publications, 1982, 257pp.

The Joint Working Group between the Roman Catholic Church and the World Council of Churches

First Official Report. In: *Ecumenical Review*, Vol. 18, No. 2, 1966. pp.243-255.
Second Official Report. In: *Ecumenical Review*, Vol. 19, No. 4, 1967. pp.461-467.
Third Official Report. In: *Ecumenical Review*, Vol. 23, No. 1, 1971, pp.44-69.
Fourth Official Report. In: *Ecumenical Review*, Vol. 28, No. 1, 1976. pp.87-96.
Fifth Official Report. In: *Ecumenical Review*, Vol. 35, No. 2, 1983. pp.198-218.
Catholicity and Apostolicity. In: *One in Christ*, Vol. 6, No. 3, 1970. pp.452-483.
Common Witness. A Study Document. Geneva: WCC, 1981, 54pp. (CWME Series, 1).
Patterns of Relationships between the Roman Catholic Church and the World Council of Churches. In: *Ecumenical Review*, Vol. 24, No. 3, 1972. pp.247-288.
Towards a Confession of the Common Faith. Geneva: WCC, 1980, 13pp. (Faith and Order Paper, No. 100).
Vischer, Lukas. *Die Eine ökumenische Bewegung*. Die gemeiname Arbeitsgruppe zurischen der Römisch-katholischen Kirche und dem Ökumenischen Rat der Kirchen. Bericht und Dokumente 1965-1969. Zürich: EVZ Verlag, 1969, 129pp. (Polis, 40).

The Committee on Society, Development and Peace

Asian Ecumenical Conference for Development. Tokyo, July 1970. Geneva: SODEPAX, 1970, 69pp.
Caribbean Ecumenical Consultation for Development, Chaguaramas, Trinidad, November, 1971. Bridgetown: Barbados, 1971, 80pp.
The Challenges of Development. A Sequel to the Beirut Conference of 21-27 April 1968 at Montreal, 9-12 May 1969. Geneva: SODEPAX, 1969, 37pp.
Church Communication Development. Papers from a SODEPAX Consultation. Driebergen, 12-16 March 1970. Geneva: WCC, 1970, 111pp.
Dunne, George H. *The Right to Development*. New York: Paulist Press, 1974, 141pp.
In Search of a Theology of Development. Papers from a Consultation Held in Cartigny, Switzerland, November, 1969. Geneva: SODEPAX, 1970, 221pp.

Millwood, David. *Help or Hindrance?* Aid, Trade and the Rich Nations' Responsibility to the Third World. Geneva: SODEPAX, 1971, 42pp.

Money in a Village World. Papers from a Colloquium on the Interests of the Developing Countries and International Monetary Reform. Geneva: SODEPAX, 1970, 84pp.

Partnership or Privilege? An Ecumenical Reaction to the Second Development Decade. Geneva: WCC, 1970, 118pp.

Peace — the Desperate Imperative. The Consultation on Christian Concern for Peace. Baden, Austria, 3-9 April 1970. Sponsored by SODEPAX. Geneva: WCC, 1970, 83pp.

Picking Up the Pieces. A Report of a SODEPAX Conference on the Churches in Development Planning and Action, Limuru, Kenya, January 1971. Geneva: WCC, 1971, 77pp.

Towards a Theology of Development. An Annotated Bibliography Compiled by Gerhard Bauer for SODEPAX. Geneva: WCC, 1970, 201pp.

World Development: Challenge to the Churches. The Official Report of the Conference on Society, Development and Peace Held, at Beirut, 21-27 April 1968. Washington: Corpus Books, 1969, 208pp.

INDEXES

GENERAL INDEX

The items which are printed in bold italics are fixed topics raised in official discussion.

INDEX OF AUTHORS IN THE
BIBLIOGRAPHY

THE COMMITTEE ON ECUMENICAL HISTORY
RESPONSIBLE FOR THE
PUBLICATION OF THIS VOLUME

The Reverend A. J. van der Bent (*Secretary*)

Dr Eugene Carson Blake

Archpriest Vitaly Borovoy

Professor H. D'Espine (*Chairman*)

Curé L. Gauthier

Dr J. Handspicker

The Reverend V. Hayward

The Reverend P. Hoffman

Dr W. Müller-Römheld

The Reverend P. Rodger

Metropolitan Emilianos Timiadis

Dr W. A. Visser 't Hooft

Dr Hans-Ruedi Weber

Professor H. H. Wolf